KU-471-404

Contents

Scrabble Consultants
Darryl Francis
Allan Simmons
David Sutton

Editors
Robert Groves
Helen Newstead
Mary O'Neill

Computing Support
Thomas Callan
Claire Dimeo

For the Publisher
Gerry Breslin
Kerry Ferguson

EAST RIDING OF

LIBRARY AND

Collins

OFFICIAL
SCRABBLE
BRAND Crossword Game
WORDS

902825846 9

Published by Collins
An imprint of HarperCollins Publishers
Westerhill Road
Bishopbriggs
Glasgow G64 2QT

Fourth Edition 2016

10 9 8 7 6 5 4 3 2

© HarperCollins Publishers 2004, 2005, 2006, 2007, 2011, 2016

ISBN 978-0-00-758908-1

Collins® is a registered trademark of HarperCollins Publishers Limited

SCRABBLE™ and associated trademarks and trade dress are owned by, and used under licence from, J. W. Spear & Sons Limited, a subsidiary of Mattel, Inc. © 2016 Mattel, Inc. All Rights Reserved.

www.collinsdictionary.com
www.harpercollins.co.uk/scrabble

Typeset by Davidson Publishing Solutions, Glasgow

Printed in Great Britain by CPI Group (UK) Ltd, Croydon CR0 4YY

All rights reserved. No part of this book may be reproduced, stored in a retrieval system, or transmitted in any form or by any means, electronic, mechanical, photocopying, recording or otherwise, without the prior permission in writing of the Publisher. This book is sold subject to the conditions that it shall not, by way of trade or otherwise, be lent, re-sold, hired out or otherwise circulated without the Publisher's prior consent in any form of binding or cover other than that in which it is published and without a similar condition including this condition being imposed on the subsequent purchaser.

Entered words that we have reason to believe constitute trademarks have been designated as such. However, neither the presence nor absence of such designation should be regarded as affecting the legal status of any trademark.

The contents of this publication are believed correct at the time of printing. Nevertheless the Publisher can accept no responsibility for errors or omissions, changes in the detail given or for any expense or loss thereby caused.

HarperCollins does not warrant that any website mentioned in this title will be provided uninterrupted, that any website will be error free, that defects will be corrected, or that the website or the server that makes it available are free of viruses or bugs. For full terms and conditions please refer to the site terms provided on the website.

A catalogue record for this book is available from the British Library.

If you would like to comment on any aspect of this book, please contact us at the given address or online.
E-mail: puzzles@harpercollins.co.uk
 facebook.com/collinsdictionary
 @collinsdict

MIX
Paper from
responsible sources
FSC C007454
www.fsc.org

FSC™ is a non-profit international organisation established to promote the responsible management of the world's forests. Products carrying the FSC label are independently certified to assure consumers that they come from forests that are managed to meet the social, economic and ecological needs of present and future generations, and other controlled sources.

Find out more about HarperCollins and the environment at
www.harpercollins.co.uk/green

Foreword

The new edition of *Collins Official Scrabble Words* adds more than 6,000 new words to the existing quarter of a million available to the Scrabble player. *Thanx* are due to Allan Simmons and Darryl Francis of the WESPA Dictionary Committee plus their numerous helpers. There was evidently a *heckuva* lot of work for all of them to do. Whether you play Scrabble in tournaments, online or with friends and family, you'll find it hugely helpful to use for adjudication and to learn new words.

The primary purpose of revising *Collins Official Scrabble Words* is, of course, to allow for new words that have come into the language to be playable across the board. Now we can use *blinged*, *chillax*, *ezine*, *facetime*, *netbook* and *frack* when playing our favourite game with our *besties* and *clubmates*. When we get those elusive 7 or 8-letter words we can say that we *bonused* or *bingoed* without guiltily knowing that we're using words in everyday speech that aren't allowed in Scrabble. That sort of thing is important to Scrabble players, we're proud of our *geekery*! At last we can wear our *cozzie* or *onesie*, use a *satnav*, take a *selfie* and *twerk* to our heart's content with a clear conscience. To quote will.i.am, 'It's the *dopest*'.

There are plenty of great new 7-letter words to help increase our scores. I particularly like *adrates*, *aeradio*, *goaties*, *orature*, *senitis* and *taenite*. If there's a floating letter then *anodiser*, *ollieing*, *rainsuit* and *steerier* will undoubtedly come in useful, helping take your score *outasite* of your opponent's.

If you're not playing bonuses then you should look to score well with the high scoring letters – J, Q, X and Z. Your ammunition now includes *griz*, *lolz*, *eques*, *ixnay*, *oxic*, *xed* and *soju*.

One of the problems for regular players is that occasionally you will play a word that you believe to be everyday only to find that for several valid reasons it isn't allowable. In the past, I've played *conman*, *tangoes*, *pianola* and *ensuite* only to have to take the letters back and forfeit my turn. At least I won't be making those particular mistakes again, but there are so many traps for the unwary in Scrabble that I expect I will find other ways of losing a turn. A particularly thorny issue is what can be pluralised and there are several new additions here which will help, including *inkjets*, *jeons*, *keyrings* and *probings*.

In my foreword to the last edition, I lamented the loss of the word *tanaiste* – mainly because I claim to be one of the few people who can pronounce it correctly. I'm sure this had no effect on the editors; they are people of impeccable integrity. However, I'm delighted to report that it is back alongside some other unusual favourites like *aerobus* and *wasm*. We even say hello again to *addios*.

I can't imagine playing Scrabble without *Collins Official Scrabble Words*. If you haven't bought it before, welcome to the club. Have a look at page 8 for further Scrabble resources. I know you'll enjoy using *Collins Official Scrabble Words* as much as I do.

Philip Nelkon
www.tripleword.co.uk

Introduction

This new edition of *Collins Official Scrabble Words* marks the completion of an epic amount of work carried out by the World English-Language Scrabble Players Association (WESPA) Dictionary Committee, comprising Darryl Francis, Chairman, with Allan Simmons and David Sutton, and others, working in tandem with Collins lexicographers. The team at Collins had just completed work on the largest single-volume English dictionary in print, *Collins English Dictionary*, and presented the WESPA Dictionary Committee with a huge selection task to identify the candidates for inclusion according to the rules that apply to the Scrabble wordlist, which now boasts 276,663 word forms and will be officially adopted for use in WESPA tournaments by 1st September 2015.

Rules for the Scrabble wordlist

- Only includes words of between 2 and 15 letters in length
- Does not include proper nouns, place names, and words with an initial capital letter, unless such words can also be spelt with a lowercase initial letter
- Does not include abbreviations, prefixes, suffixes, words requiring apostrophes or hyphens
- Includes foreign words that are considered to have been absorbed into the English language
- Includes inflected forms, such as plurals and verbs forms, eg plumb, plumbs, plumbed, plumbing
- Includes words that are old, obsolete, dialectal, historical and/or literary
- Includes World English, including spelling and variants from the US, South Africa, Australia, New Zealand, etc
- Includes words that are denoted contractions, short forms and slang
- Includes words which may be deemed rude or offensive

Disclaimer

The words in this list are published in accordance with the rules of the WESPA Dictionary Committee and based on the strict criteria above. They are valid for use in Scrabble games under the aegis of WESPA, and no word is excluded on the grounds of religion, gender, race, or for any reason other than that it is an invalid word form for the game of Scrabble. The presence or exclusion of any word does not in any way represent the views of WESPA or the Publisher, HarperCollins.

The Collins Editorial Team and WESPA

Other Scrabble resources

Associations

World English-Language Scrabble Players Association (WESPA) –
www.wespa.org

The WESPA website also provides access to an Initiation Kit,
highlighting major differences between the 2011 third edition of
Collins Official Scrabble Words and the 2015 fourth edition.

Association of British Scrabble Players (ABSP) – www.absp.org.uk

The ABSP website includes details of UK Scrabble clubs and UK tournaments
Schools Scrabble contact – youthscrabble@absp.org.uk

Mindsports Academy – www.mindsportsacademy.com

Facebook

Scrabble Facebook Fan Page – www.facebook.com/scrabble

Play Online Scrabble on Facebook – search for Scrabble Worldwide

Interactive Scrabble games

Internet Scrabble Club (ISC) – www.isc.ro

Mobile phone – Real Networks

Sky Interactive – Sky TV platform

iTouch / iPhone / Android / iPad – Electronic Arts (EA)

Scrabble App

Download *Collins Official Scrabble Checker and Solver* app from the iTunes Store

two to nine letter words

A

AA	ABAMPS	ABATORS	ABDOMEN	ABERRATES
AAH	ABAND	ABATTIS	ABDOMENS	ABERS
AAHED	ABANDED	ABATTISES	ABDOMINA	ABESSIVE
AAHING	ABANDING	ABATTOIR	ABDOMINAL	ABESSIVES
AAHS	ABANDON	ABATTOIRS	ABDUCE	ABET
AAL	ABANDONED	ABATTU	ABDUCED	ABETMENT
AALII	ABANDONEE	ABATURE	ABDUCENS	ABETMENTS
AALIIS	ABANDONER	ABATURES	ABDUCENT	ABETS
AALS	ABANDONS	ABAXIAL	ABDUCES	ABETTAL
AARDVARK	ABANDS	ABAXILE	ABDUCING	ABETTALS
AARDVARKS	ABAPICAL	ABAYA	ABDUCT	ABETTED
AARDWOLF	ABAS	ABAYAS	ABDUCTED	ABETTER
AARGH	ABASE	ABB	ABDUCTEE	ABETTERS
AARRGH	ABASED	ABBA	ABDUCTEES	ABETTING
AARRGHH	ABASEDLY	ABBACIES	ABDUCTING	ABETTOR
AARTI	ABASEMENT	ABBACY	ABDUCTION	ABETTORS
AARTIS	ABASER	ABBAS	ABDUCTOR	ABEYANCE
AAS	ABASERS	ABBATIAL	ABDUCTORS	ABEYANCES
AASVOGEL	ABASES	ABBE	ABDUCTS	ABEYANCY
AASVOGELS	ABASH	ABBED	ABEAM	ABEYANT
AB	ABASHED	ABBES	ABEAR	ABFARAD
ABA	ABASHEDLY	ABBESS	ABEARING	ABFARADS
ABAC	ABASHES	ABBESSES	ABEARS	ABHENRIES
ABACA	ABASHING	ABBEY	ABED	ABHENRY
ABACAS	ABASHLESS	ABBEYS	ABEGGING	ABHENRYS
ABACI	ABASHMENT	ABBOT	ABEIGH	ABHOR
ABACK	ABASIA	ABBOTCIES	ABELE	ABHORRED
ABACS	ABASIAS	ABBOTCY	ABELES	ABHORRENT
ABACTINAL	ABASING	ABBOTS	ABELIA	ABHORRER
ABACTOR	ABASK	ABBOTSHIP	ABELIAN	ABHORRERS
ABACTORS	ABATABLE	ABBS	ABELIAS	ABHORRING
ABACUS	ABATE	ABCEE	ABELMOSK	ABHORS
ABACUSES	ABATED	ABCEES	ABELMOSKS	ABID
ABAFT	ABATEMENT	ABCOULOMB	ABER	ABIDANCE
ABAKA	ABATER	ABDABS	ABERNETHY	ABIDANCES
ABAKAS	ABATERS	ABDICABLE	ABERRANCE	ABIDDEN
ABALONE	ABATES	ABDICANT	ABERRANCY	ABIDE
ABALONES	ABATING	ABDICATE	ABERRANT	ABIDED
ABAMP	ABATIS	ABDICATED	ABERRANTS	ABIDER
ABAMPERE	ABATISES	ABDICATES	ABERRATE	ABIDERS
ABAMPERES	ABATOR	ABDICATOR	ABERRATED	ABIDES

ABIDING	ABLEGATES	ABOITEAUX	ABOS	ABREGE
ABIDINGLY	ABLEISM	ABOLISH	ABOUGHT	ABREGES
ABIDINGS	ABLEISMS	ABOLISHED	ABOULIA	ABRI
ABIES	ABLEIST	ABOLISHER	ABOULIAS	ABRICOCK
ABIETIC	ABLEISTS	ABOLISHES	ABOULIC	ABRICOCKS
ABIGAIL	ABLER	ABOLITION	ABOUND	ABRIDGE
ABIGAILS	ABLES	ABOLLA	ABOUNDED	ABRIDGED
ABILITIES	ABLEST	ABOLLAE	ABOUNDING	ABRIDGER
ABILITY	ABLET	ABOLLAS	ABOUNDS	ABRIDGERS
ABIOGENIC	ABLETS	ABOMA	ABOUT	ABRIDGES
ABIOSES	ABLING	ABOMAS	ABOUTS	ABRIDGING
ABIOSIS	ABLINGS	ABOMASA	ABOVE	ABRIM
ABIOTIC	ABLINS	ABOMASAL	ABOVES	ABRIN
ABITUR	ABLOOM	ABOMASI	ABRACHIA	ABRINS
ABITURS	ABLOW	ABOMASUM	ABRACHIAS	ABRIS
ABJECT	ABLUENT	ABOMASUS	ABRADABLE	ABROACH
ABJECTED	ABLUENTS	ABOMINATE	ABRADANT	ABROAD
ABJECTING	ABLUSH	ABONDANCE	ABRADANTS	ABROADS
ABJECTION	ABLUTED	ABOON	ABRADE	ABROGABLE
ABJECTLY	ABLUTION	ABORAL	ABRADED	ABROGATE
ABJECTS	ABLUTIONS	ABORALLY	ABRADER	ABROGATED
ABJOINT	ABLY	ABORD	ABRADERS	ABROGATES
ABJOINTED	ABMHO	ABORDED	ABRADES	ABROGATOR
ABJOINTS	ABMHOS	ABORDING	ABRADING	ABROOKE
ABJURE	ABNEGATE	ABORDS	ABRAID	ABROOKED
ABJURED	ABNEGATED	ABORE	ABRAIDED	ABROOKES
ABJURER	ABNEGATES	ABORIGEN	ABRAIDING	ABROOKING
ABJURERS	ABNEGATOR	ABORIGENS	ABRAIDS	ABROSIA
ABJURES	ABNORMAL	ABORIGIN	ABRAM	ABROSIAS
ABJURING	ABNORMALS	ABORIGINE	ABRASAX	ABRUPT
ABLATE	ABNORMITY	ABORIGINS	ABRASAXES	ABRUPTER
ABLATED	ABNORMOUS	ABORNE	ABRASION	ABRUPTEST
ABLATES	ABO	ABORNING	ABRASIONS	ABRUPTION
ABLATING	ABOARD	ABORT	ABRASIVE	ABRUPTLY
ABLATION	ABODE	ABORTED	ABRASIVES	ABRUPTS
ABLATIONS	ABODED	ABORTEE	ABRAXAS	ABS
ABLATIVAL	ABODEMENT	ABORTEES	ABRAXASES	ABSCESS
ABLATIVE	ABODES	ABORTER	ABRAY	ABSCESSED
ABLATIVES	ABODING	ABORTERS	ABRAYED	ABSCESSES
ABLATOR	ABOHM	ABORTING	ABRAYING	ABSCIND
ABLATORS	ABOHMS	ABORTION	ABRAYS	ABSCINDED
ABLAUT	ABOIDEAU	ABORTIONS	ABRAZO	ABSCINDS
ABLAUTS	ABOIDEAUS	ABORTIVE	ABRAZOS	ABSCISE
ABLAZE	ABOIDEAUX	ABORTS	ABREACT	ABSCISED
ABLE	ABOIL	ABORTUARY	ABREACTED	ABSCISES
ABLED	ABOITEAU	ABORTUS	ABREACTS	ABSCISIC
ABLEGATE	ABOITEAUS	ABORTUSES	ABREAST	ABSCISIN

ABSCISING
ABSCISINS
ABSCISS
ABSCISSA
ABSCISSAE
ABSCISSAS
ABSCISSE
ABSCISSES
ABSCISSIN
ABSCOND
ABSCONDED
ABSCONDER
ABSCONDS
ABSEIL
ABSEILED
ABSEILER
ABSEILERS
ABSEILING
ABSEILS
ABSENCE
ABSENCES
ABSENT
ABSENTED
ABSENTEE
ABSENTEES
ABSENTER
ABSENTERS
ABSENTING
ABSENTLY
ABSENTS
ABSEY
ABSEYS
ABSINTH
ABSINTHE
ABSINTHES
ABSINTHS
ABSIT
ABSITS
ABSOLUTE
ABSOLUTER
ABSOLUTES
ABSOLVE
ABSOLVED
ABSOLVENT
ABSOLVER
ABSOLVERS
ABSOLVES

ABSOLVING
ABSONANT
ABSORB
ABSORBANT
ABSORBATE
ABSORBED
ABSORBENT
ABSORBER
ABSORBERS
ABSORBING
ABSORBS
ABSTAIN
ABSTAINED
ABSTAINER
ABSTAINS
ABSTERGE
ABSTERGED
ABSTERGES
ABSTINENT
ABSTRACT
ABSTRACTS
ABSTRICT
ABSTRICTS
ABSTRUSE
ABSTRUSER
ABSURD
ABSURDER
ABSURDEST
ABSURDISM
ABSURDIST
ABSURDITY
ABSURDLY
ABSURDS
ABTHANE
ABTHANES
ABUBBLE
ABUILDING
ABULIA
ABULIAS
ABULIC
ABUNA
ABUNAS
ABUNDANCE
ABUNDANCY
ABUNDANT
ABUNE
ABURST

ABUSABLE
ABUSAGE
ABUSAGES
ABUSE
ABUSED
ABUSER
ABUSERS
ABUSES
ABUSING
ABUSION
ABUSIONS
ABUSIVE
ABUSIVELY
ABUT
ABUTILON
ABUTILONS
ABUTMENT
ABUTMENTS
ABUTS
ABUTTAL
ABUTTALS
ABUTTED
ABUTTER
ABUTTERS
ABUTTING
ABUZZ
ABVOLT
ABVOLTS
ABWATT
ABWATTS
ABY
ABYE
ABYEING
ABYES
ABYING
ABYS
ABYSM
ABYSMAL
ABYSMALLY
ABYSMS
ABYSS
ABYSSAL
ABYSSES
ACACIA
ACACIAS
ACADEME
ACADEMES

ACADEMIA
ACADEMIAS
ACADEMIC
ACADEMICS
ACADEMIES
ACADEMISM
ACADEMIST
ACADEMY
ACAI
ACAIS
ACAJOU
ACAJOUS
ACALCULIA
ACALEPH
ACALEPHAE
ACALEPHAN
ACALEPHE
ACALEPHES
ACALEPHS
ACANTH
ACANTHA
ACANTHAE
ACANTHAS
ACANTHI
ACANTHIN
ACANTHINE
ACANTHINS
ACANTHOID
ACANTHOUS
ACANTHS
ACANTHUS
ACAPNIA
ACAPNIAS
ACARBOSE
ACARBOSES
ACARI
ACARIAN
ACARIASES
ACARIASIS
ACARICIDE
ACARID
ACARIDAN
ACARIDANS
ACARIDEAN
ACARIDIAN
ACARIDS
ACARINE

ACARINES
ACAROID
ACAROLOGY
ACARPOUS
ACARUS
ACATER
ACATERS
ACATES
ACATHISIA
ACATOUR
ACATOURS
ACAUDAL
ACAUDATE
ACAULINE
ACAULOSE
ACAULOUS
ACCA
ACCABLE
ACCAS
ACCEDE
ACCEDED
ACCEDENCE
ACCEDER
ACCEDERS
ACCEDES
ACCEDING
ACCEND
ACCENDED
ACCENDING
ACCENDS
ACCENSION
ACCENT
ACCENTED
ACCENTING
ACCENTOR
ACCENTORS
ACCENTS
ACCENTUAL
ACCEPT
ACCEPTANT
ACCEPTED
ACCEPTEE
ACCEPTEES
ACCEPTER
ACCEPTERS
ACCEPTING
ACCEPTIVE

A

ACCEPTOR	ACCOMPT	ACCROIDES	ACERBATED	ACETYLIC
ACCEPTORS	ACCOMPTED	ACCRUABLE	ACERBATES	ACETYLIDE
ACCEPTS	ACCOMPTS	ACCRUAL	ACERBER	ACETYLS
ACCESS	ACCORAGE	ACCRUALS	ACERBEST	ACH
ACCESSARY	ACCORAGED	ACCRUE	ACERBIC	ACHAENIA
ACCESSED	ACCORAGES	ACCRUED	ACERBITY	ACHAENIUM
ACCESSES	ACCORD	ACCRUES	ACEROLA	ACHAGE
ACCESSING	ACCORDANT	ACCRUING	ACEROLAS	ACHAGES
ACCESSION	ACCORDED	ACCUMBENT	ACEROSE	ACHALASIA
ACCESSORY	ACCORDER	ACCURACY	ACEROUS	ACHAR
ACCIDENCE	ACCORDERS	ACCURATE	ACERS	ACHARNE
ACCIDENT	ACCORDING	ACCURSE	ACERVATE	ACHARS
ACCIDENTS	ACCORDION	ACCURSED	ACERVULI	ACHARYA
ACCIDIA	ACCORDS	ACCURSES	ACERVULUS	ACHARYAS
ACCIDIAS	ACCOST	ACCURSING	ACES	ACHATES
ACCIDIE	ACCOSTED	ACCURST	ACESCENCE	ACHE
ACCIDIES	ACCOSTING	ACCUSABLE	ACESCENCY	ACHED
ACCINGE	ACCOSTS	ACCUSABLY	ACESCENT	ACHENE
ACCINGED	ACCOUNT	ACCUSAL	ACESCENTS	ACHENES
ACCINGES	ACCOUNTED	ACCUSALS	ACETA	ACHENIA
ACCINGING	ACCOUNTS	ACCUSANT	ACETABULA	ACHENIAL
ACCIPITER	ACCOURAGE	ACCUSANTS	ACETAL	ACHENIUM
ACCITE	ACCOURT	ACCUSE	ACETALS	ACHENIUMS
ACCITED	ACCOURTED	ACCUSED	ACETAMID	ACHES
ACCITES	ACCOURTS	ACCUSER	ACETAMIDE	ACHIER
ACCITING	ACCOUTER	ACCUSERS	ACETAMIDS	ACHIEST
ACCLAIM	ACCOUTERS	ACCUSES	ACETATE	ACHIEVE
ACCLAIMED	ACCOUTRE	ACCUSING	ACETATED	ACHIEVED
ACCLAIMER	ACCOUTRED	ACCUSTOM	ACETATES	ACHIEVER
ACCLAIMS	ACCOUTRES	ACCUSTOMS	ACETIC	ACHIEVERS
ACCLIMATE	ACCOY	ACE	ACETIFIED	ACHIEVES
ACCLIVITY	ACCOYED	ACED	ACETIFIER	ACHIEVING
ACCLIVOUS	ACCOYING	ACEDIA	ACETIFIES	ACHILLEA
ACCLOY	ACCOYLD	ACEDIAS	ACETIFY	ACHILLEAS
ACCLOYED	ACCOYS	ACELDAMA	ACETIN	ACHIMENES
ACCLOYING	ACCREDIT	ACELDAMAS	ACETINS	ACHINESS
ACCLOYS	ACCREDITS	ACELLULAR	ACETONE	ACHING
ACCOAST	ACCRETE	ACENTRIC	ACETONES	ACHINGLY
ACCOASTED	ACCRETED	ACENTRICS	ACETONIC	ACHINGS
ACCOASTS	ACCRETES	ACEPHALIC	ACETOSE	ACHIOTE
ACCOIED	ACCRETING	ACEQUIA	ACETOUS	ACHIOTES
ACCOIL	ACCRETION	ACEQUIAS	ACETOXYL	ACHIRAL
ACCOILS	ACCRETIVE	ACER	ACETOXYLS	ACHKAN
ACCOLADE	ACCREW	ACERATE	ACETUM	ACHKANS
ACCOLADED	ACCREWED	ACERATED	ACETYL	ACHOLIA
ACCOLADES	ACCREWING	ACERB	ACETYLATE	ACHOLIAS
ACCOMPANY	ACCREWS	ACERBATE	ACETYLENE	ACHOO

ACHOOS
ACHROMAT
ACHROMATS
ACHROMIC
ACHROMOUS
ACHY
ACICLOVIR
ACICULA
ACICULAE
ACICULAR
ACICULAS
ACICULATE
ACICULUM
ACICULUMS
ACID
ACIDEMIA
ACIDEMIAS
ACIDER
ACIDEST
ACIDHEAD
ACIDHEADS
ACIDIC
ACIDIER
ACIDIEST
ACIDIFIED
ACIDIFIER
ACIDIFIES
ACIDIFY
ACIDITIES
ACIDITY
ACIDLY
ACIDNESS
ACIDOPHIL
ACIDOSES
ACIDOSIS
ACIDOTIC
ACIDS
ACIDULATE
ACIDULENT
ACIDULOUS
ACIDURIA
ACIDURIAS
ACIDY
ACIERAGE
ACIERAGES
ACIERATE
ACIERATED

ACIERATES
ACIFORM
ACINAR
ACING
ACINI
ACINIC
ACINIFORM
ACINOSE
ACINOUS
ACINUS
ACKEE
ACKEES
ACKER
ACKERS
ACKNEW
ACKNOW
ACKNOWING
ACKNOWN
ACKNOWNE
ACKNOWS
ACLINIC
ACMATIC
ACME
ACMES
ACMIC
ACMITE
ACMITES
ACNE
ACNED
ACNES
ACNODAL
ACNODE
ACNODES
ACOCK
ACOELOUS
ACOEMETI
ACOLD
ACOLUTHIC
ACOLYTE
ACOLYTES
ACOLYTH
ACOLYTHS
ACONITE
ACONITES
ACONITIC
ACONITINE
ACONITUM

ACONITUMS
ACORN
ACORNED
ACORNS
ACOSMISM
ACOSMISMS
ACOSMIST
ACOSMISTS
ACOUCHI
ACOUCHIES
ACOUCHIS
ACOUCHY
ACOUSTIC
ACOUSTICS
ACQUAINT
ACQUAINTS
ACQUEST
ACQUESTS
ACQUIESCE
ACQUIGHT
ACQUIGHTS
ACQUIRAL
ACQUIRALS
ACQUIRE
ACQUIRED
ACQUIREE
ACQUIREES
ACQUIRER
ACQUIRERS
ACQUIRES
ACQUIRING
ACQUIS
ACQUIST
ACQUISTS
ACQUIT
ACQUITE
ACQUITES
ACQUITING
ACQUITS
ACQUITTAL
ACQUITTED
ACQUITTER
ACRASIA
ACRASIAS
ACRASIN
ACRASINS
ACRATIC

ACRAWL
ACRE
ACREAGE
ACREAGES
ACRED
ACRES
ACRID
ACRIDER
ACRIDEST
ACRIDIN
ACRIDINE
ACRIDINES
ACRIDINS
ACRIDITY
ACRIDLY
ACRIDNESS
ACRIMONY
ACRITARCH
ACRITICAL
ACRO
ACROBAT
ACROBATIC
ACROBATS
ACRODONT
ACRODONTS
ACRODROME
ACROGEN
ACROGENIC
ACROGENS
ACROLECT
ACROLECTS
ACROLEIN
ACROLEINS
ACROLITH
ACROLITHS
ACROMIA
ACROMIAL
ACROMION
ACRONIC
ACRONICAL
ACRONYCAL
ACRONYM
ACRONYMIC
ACRONYMS
ACROPETAL
ACROPHOBE
ACROPHONY

ACROPOLIS
ACROS
ACROSOMAL
ACROSOME
ACROSOMES
ACROSPIRE
ACROSS
ACROSTIC
ACROSTICS
ACROTER
ACROTERIA
ACROTERS
ACROTIC
ACROTISM
ACROTISMS
ACRYLATE
ACRYLATES
ACRYLIC
ACRYLICS
ACRYLYL
ACRYLYLS
ACT
ACTA
ACTABLE
ACTANT
ACTANTS
ACTED
ACTIN
ACTINAL
ACTINALLY
ACTING
ACTINGS
ACTINIA
ACTINIAE
ACTINIAN
ACTINIANS
ACTINIAS
ACTINIC
ACTINIDE
ACTINIDES
ACTINISM
ACTINISMS
ACTINIUM
ACTINIUMS
ACTINOID
ACTINOIDS
ACTINON

ACTINONS	ACTUARIES	ACYLOINS	ADDEEMS	ADDUCENT
ACTINOPOD	ACTUARY	ACYLS	ADDEND	ADDUCER
ACTINS	ACTUATE	AD	ADDENDA	ADDUCERS
ACTION	ACTUATED	ADAGE	ADDENDS	ADDUCES
ACTIONED	ACTUATES	ADAGES	ADDENDUM	ADDUCIBLE
ACTIONER	ACTUATING	ADAGIAL	ADDENDUMS	ADDUCING
ACTIONERS	ACTUATION	ADAGIO	ADDER	ADDUCT
ACTIONING	ACTUATOR	ADAGIOS	ADDERBEAD	ADDUCTED
ACTIONIST	ACTUATORS	ADAMANCE	ADDERS	ADDUCTING
ACTIONS	ACTURE	ADAMANCES	ADDERWORT	ADDUCTION
ACTIVATE	ACTURES	ADAMANCY	ADDIBLE	ADDUCTIVE
ACTIVATED	ACUATE	ADAMANT	ADDICT	ADDUCTOR
ACTIVATES	ACUATED	ADAMANTLY	ADDICTED	ADDUCTORS
ACTIVATOR	ACUATES	ADAMANTS	ADDICTING	ADDUCTS
ACTIVE	ACUATING	ADAMSITE	ADDICTION	ADDY
ACTIVELY	ACUITIES	ADAMSITES	ADDICTIVE	ADEEM
ACTIVES	ACUITY	ADAPT	ADDICTS	ADEEMED
ACTIVISE	ACULEATE	ADAPTABLE	ADDIES	ADEEMING
ACTIVISED	ACULEATED	ADAPTED	ADDING	ADEEMS
ACTIVISES	ACULEATES	ADAPTER	ADDINGS	ADELGID
ACTIVISM	ACULEI	ADAPTERS	ADDIO	ADELGIDS
ACTIVISMS	ACULEUS	ADAPTING	ADDIOS	ADEMPTION
ACTIVIST	ACUMEN	ADAPTION	ADDITION	ADENINE
ACTIVISTS	ACUMENS	ADAPTIONS	ADDITIONS	ADENINES
ACTIVITY	ACUMINATE	ADAPTIVE	ADDITIVE	ADENITIS
ACTIVIZE	ACUMINOUS	ADAPTOGEN	ADDITIVES	ADENOID
ACTIVIZED	ACUPOINT	ADAPTOR	ADDITORY	ADENOIDAL
ACTIVIZES	ACUPOINTS	ADAPTORS	ADDLE	ADENOIDS
ACTON	ACUSHLA	ADAPTS	ADDLED	ADENOMA
ACTONS	ACUSHLAS	ADAW	ADDLEMENT	ADENOMAS
ACTOR	ACUTANCE	ADAWED	ADDLES	ADENOMATA
ACTORISH	ACUTANCES	ADAWING	ADDLING	ADENOSES
ACTORLY	ACUTE	ADAWS	ADDOOM	ADENOSINE
ACTORS	ACUTELY	ADAXIAL	ADDOOMED	ADENOSIS
ACTRESS	ACUTENESS	ADAYS	ADDOOMING	ADENYL
ACTRESSES	ACUTER	ADBOT	ADDOOMS	ADENYLIC
ACTRESSY	ACUTES	ADBOTS	ADDORSED	ADENYLS
ACTS	ACUTEST	ADD	ADDRESS	ADEPT
ACTUAL	ACYCLIC	ADDABLE	ADDRESSED	ADEPTER
ACTUALISE	ACYCLOVIR	ADDAX	ADDRESSEE	ADEPTEST
ACTUALIST	ACYL	ADDAXES	ADDRESSER	ADEPTLY
ACTUALITE	ACYLATE	ADDEBTED	ADDRESSES	ADEPTNESS
ACTUALITY	ACYLATED	ADDED	ADDRESSOR	ADEPTS
ACTUALIZE	ACYLATES	ADDEDLY	ADDREST	ADEQUACY
ACTUALLY	ACYLATING	ADDEEM	ADDS	ADEQUATE
ACTUALS	ACYLATION	ADDEEMED	ADDUCE	ADERMIN
ACTUARIAL	ACYLOIN	ADDEEMING	ADDUCED	ADERMINS

ADESPOTA	ADJACENCY	ADLAND	ADNOUN	ADORNMENT
ADESSIVE	ADJACENT	ADLANDS	ADNOUNS	ADORNS
ADESSIVES	ADJACENTS	ADMAN	ADO	ADOS
ADHAN	ADJECTIVE	ADMASS	ADOBE	ADOWN
ADHANS	ADJIGO	ADMASSES	ADOBELIKE	ADOZE
ADHARMA	ADJIGOS	ADMEASURE	ADOBES	ADPRESS
ADHARMAS	ADJOIN	ADMEN	ADOBO	ADPRESSED
ADHERABLE	ADJOINED	ADMIN	ADOBOS	ADPRESSES
ADHERE	ADJOINING	ADMINICLE	ADONIS	ADRAD
ADHERED	ADJOINS	ADMINS	ADONISE	ADRATE
ADHERENCE	ADJOINT	ADMIRABLE	ADONISED	ADRATES
ADHEREND	ADJOINTS	ADMIRABLY	ADONISES	ADREAD
ADHERENDS	ADJOURN	ADMIRAL	ADONISING	ADREADED
ADHERENT	ADJOURNED	ADMIRALS	ADONIZE	ADREADING
ADHERENTS	ADJOURNS	ADMIRALTY	ADONIZED	ADREADS
ADHERER	ADJUDGE	ADMIRANCE	ADONIZES	ADRED
ADHERERS	ADJUDGED	ADMIRE	ADONIZING	ADRENAL
ADHERES	ADJUDGES	ADMIRED	ADOORS	ADRENALIN
ADHERING	ADJUDGING	ADMIRER	ADOPT	ADRENALLY
ADHESION	ADJUNCT	ADMIRERS	ADOPTABLE	ADRENALS
ADHESIONS	ADJUNCTLY	ADMIRES	ADOPTED	ADRIFT
ADHESIVE	ADJUNCTS	ADMIRING	ADOPTEE	ADROIT
ADHESIVES	ADJURE	ADMISSION	ADOPTEES	ADROITER
ADHIBIT	ADJURED	ADMISSIVE	ADOPTER	ADROITEST
ADHIBITED	ADJURER	ADMIT	ADOPTERS	ADROITLY
ADHIBITS	ADJURERS	ADMITS	ADOPTING	ADRY
ADHOCRACY	ADJURES	ADMITTED	ADOPTION	ADS
ADIABATIC	ADJURING	ADMITTEE	ADOPTIONS	ADSCRIPT
ADIAPHORA	ADJUROR	ADMITTEES	ADOPTIOUS	ADSCRIPTS
ADIEU	ADJURORS	ADMITTER	ADOPTIVE	ADSORB
ADIEUS	ADJUST	ADMITTERS	ADOPTS	ADSORBATE
ADIEUX	ADJUSTED	ADMITTING	ADORABLE	ADSORBED
ADIOS	ADJUSTER	ADMIX	ADORABLY	ADSORBENT
ADIOSES	ADJUSTERS	ADMIXED	ADORATION	ADSORBER
ADIPIC	ADJUSTING	ADMIXES	ADORE	ADSORBERS
ADIPOCERE	ADJUSTIVE	ADMIXING	ADORED	ADSORBING
ADIPOCYTE	ADJUSTOR	ADMIXT	ADORER	ADSORBS
ADIPOSE	ADJUSTORS	ADMIXTURE	ADORERS	ADSPEAK
ADIPOSES	ADJUSTS	ADMONISH	ADORES	ADSPEAKS
ADIPOSIS	ADJUTAGE	ADMONITOR	ADORING	ADSUKI
ADIPOSITY	ADJUTAGES	ADNASCENT	ADORINGLY	ADSUKIS
ADIPOUS	ADJUTANCY	ADNATE	ADORKABLE	ADSUM
ADIPSIA	ADJUTANT	ADNATION	ADORN	ADUKI
ADIPSIAS	ADJUTANTS	ADNATIONS	ADORNED	ADUKIS
ADIT	ADJUVANCY	ADNEXA	ADORNER	ADULARIA
ADITS	ADJUVANT	ADNEXAL	ADORNERS	ADULARIAS
ADJACENCE	ADJUVANTS	ADNOMINAL	ADORNING	ADULATE

ADULATED	ADVENTURE	ADVOUTRY	AEGROTATS	AEROBATS
ADULATES	ADVERB	ADVOWSON	AEMULE	AEROBE
ADULATING	ADVERBIAL	ADVOWSONS	AEMULED	AEROBES
ADULATION	ADVERBS	ADWARD	AEMULES	AEROBIA
ADULATOR	ADVERSARY	ADWARDED	AEMULING	AEROBIC
ADULATORS	ADVERSE	ADWARDING	AENEOUS	AEROBICS
ADULATORY	ADVERSELY	ADWARDS	AENEUS	AEROBIONT
ADULT	ADVERSER	ADWARE	AENEUSES	AEROBIUM
ADULTERER	ADVERSEST	ADWARES	AEOLIAN	AEROBOMB
ADULTERY	ADVERSITY	ADWOMAN	AEOLIPILE	AEROBOMBS
ADULTHOOD	ADVERT	ADWOMEN	AEOLIPYLE	AEROBOT
ADULTLIKE	ADVERTED	ADYNAMIA	AEON	AEROBOTS
ADULTLY	ADVERTENT	ADYNAMIAS	AEONIAN	AEROBRAKE
ADULTNESS	ADVERTING	ADYNAMIC	AEONIC	AEROBUS
ADULTRESS	ADVERTISE	ADYTA	AEONS	AEROBUSES
ADULTS	ADVERTIZE	ADYTUM	AEPYORNIS	AERODART
ADUMBRAL	ADVERTS	ADZ	AEQUORIN	AERODARTS
ADUMBRATE	ADVEW	ADZE	AEQUORINS	AERODROME
ADUNC	ADVEWED	ADZED	AERADIO	AERODUCT
ADUNCATE	ADVEWING	ADZES	AERADIOS	AERODUCTS
ADUNCATED	ADVEWS	ADZING	AERATE	AERODYNE
ADUNCITY	ADVICE	ADZUKI	AERATED	AERODYNES
ADUNCOUS	ADVICEFUL	ADZUKIS	AERATES	AEROFOIL
ADUST	ADVICES	AE	AERATING	AEROFOILS
ADUSTED	ADVISABLE	AECIA	AERATION	AEROGEL
ADUSTING	ADVISABLY	AECIAL	AERATIONS	AEROGELS
ADUSTS	ADVISE	AECIDIA	AERATOR	AEROGRAM
ADVANCE	ADVISED	AECIDIAL	AERATORS	AEROGRAMS
ADVANCED	ADVISEDLY	AECIDIUM	AERIAL	AEROGRAPH
ADVANCER	ADVISEE	AECIUM	AERIALIST	AEROLITE
ADVANCERS	ADVISEES	AEDES	AERIALITY	AEROLITES
ADVANCES	ADVISER	AEDICULE	AERIALLY	AEROLITH
ADVANCING	ADVISERS	AEDICULES	AERIALS	AEROLITHS
ADVANTAGE	ADVISES	AEDILE	AERIE	AEROLITIC
ADVECT	ADVISING	AEDILES	AERIED	AEROLOGIC
ADVECTED	ADVISINGS	AEDINE	AERIER	AEROLOGY
ADVECTING	ADVISOR	AEFALD	AERIES	AEROMANCY
ADVECTION	ADVISORS	AEFAULD	AERIEST	AEROMETER
ADVECTIVE	ADVISORY	AEGIRINE	AERIFIED	AEROMETRY
ADVECTS	ADVOCAAT	AEGIRINES	AERIFIES	AEROMOTOR
ADVENE	ADVOCAATS	AEGIRITE	AERIFORM	AERONAUT
ADVENED	ADVOCACY	AEGIRITES	AERIFY	AERONAUTS
ADVENES	ADVOCATE	AEGIS	AERIFYING	AERONOMER
ADVENING	ADVOCATED	AEGISES	AERILY	AERONOMIC
ADVENT	ADVOCATES	AEGLOGUE	AERO	AERONOMY
ADVENTIVE	ADVOCATOR	AEGLOGUES	AEROBAT	AEROPAUSE
ADVENTS	ADVOUTRER	AEGROTAT	AEROBATIC	AEROPHAGY

AEROPHOBE	AFARAS	AFFILIATE	AFFORCES	AFOREHAND
AEROPHONE	AFARS	AFFINAL	AFFORCING	AFORESAID
AEROPHORE	AFAWLD	AFFINE	AFFORD	AFORETIME
AEROPHYTE	AFEAR	AFFINED	AFFORDED	AFOUL
AEROPLANE	AFEARD	AFFINELY	AFFORDING	AFRAID
AEROPULSE	AFEARED	AFFINES	AFFORDS	AFREET
AEROS	AFEARING	AFFINITY	AFFOREST	AFREETS
AEROSAT	AFEARS	AFFIRM	AFFORESTS	AFRESH
AEROSATS	AFEBRILE	AFFIRMANT	AFFRAP	AFRIT
AEROSCOPE	AFF	AFFIRMED	AFFRAPPED	AFRITS
AEROSHELL	AFFABLE	AFFIRMER	AFFRAPS	AFRO
AEROSOL	AFFABLY	AFFIRMERS	AFFRAY	AFRONT
AEROSOLS	AFFAIR	AFFIRMING	AFFRAYED	AFROS
AEROSPACE	AFFAIRE	AFFIRMS	AFFRAYER	AFT
AEROSPIKE	AFFAIRES	AFFIX	AFFRAYERS	AFTER
AEROSTAT	AFFAIRS	AFFIXABLE	AFFRAYING	AFTERBODY
AEROSTATS	AFFEAR	AFFIXAL	AFFRAYS	AFTERCARE
AEROTAXES	AFFEARD	AFFIXED	AFFRENDED	AFTERCLAP
AEROTAXIS	AFFEARE	AFFIXER	AFFRET	AFTERDAMP
AEROTONE	AFFEARED	AFFIXERS	AFFRETS	AFTERDECK
AEROTONES	AFFEARES	AFFIXES	AFFRICATE	AFTEREYE
AEROTRAIN	AFFEARING	AFFIXIAL	AFFRIGHT	AFTEREYED
AERUGO	AFFEARS	AFFIXING	AFFRIGHTS	AFTEREYES
AERUGOS	AFFECT	AFFIXMENT	AFFRONT	AFTERGAME
AERY	AFFECTED	AFFIXTURE	AFFRONTE	AFTERGLOW
AESC	AFFECTER	AFFLATED	AFFRONTED	AFTERHEAT
AESCES	AFFECTERS	AFFLATION	AFFRONTEE	AFTERINGS
AESCULIN	AFFECTING	AFFLATUS	AFFRONTS	AFTERLIFE
AESCULINS	AFFECTION	AFFLICT	AFFUSION	AFTERMATH
AESIR	AFFECTIVE	AFFLICTED	AFFUSIONS	AFTERMOST
AESTHESES	AFFECTS	AFFLICTER	AFFY	AFTERNOON
AESTHESIA	AFFEER	AFFLICTS	AFFYDE	AFTERPAIN
AESTHESIS	AFFEERED	AFFLUENCE	AFFYING	AFTERPEAK
AESTHETE	AFFEERING	AFFLUENCY	AFGHAN	AFTERS
AESTHETES	AFFEERS	AFFLUENT	AFGHANI	AFTERSHOW
AESTHETIC	AFFERENT	AFFLUENTS	AFGHANIS	AFTERSUN
AESTIVAL	AFFERENTS	AFFLUENZA	AFGHANS	AFTERSUNS
AESTIVATE	AFFIANCE	AFFLUX	AFIELD	AFTERTAX
AETATIS	AFFIANCED	AFFLUXES	AFIRE	AFTERTIME
AETHER	AFFIANCES	AFFLUXION	AFLAJ	AFTERWARD
AETHEREAL	AFFIANT	AFFOGATO	AFLAME	AFTERWORD
AETHERIC	AFFIANTS	AFFOGATOS	AFLATOXIN	AFTMOST
AETHERS	AFFICHE	AFFOORD	AFLOAT	AFTOSA
AETIOLOGY	AFFICHES	AFFOORDED	AFLUTTER	AFTOSAS
AFALD	AFFIDAVIT	AFFOORDS	AFOCAL	AG
AFAR	AFFIED	AFFORCE	AFOOT	AGA
AFARA	AFFIES	AFFORCED	AFORE	AGACANT

AGACANTE	AGATISED	AGENISES	AGGRATING	AGITABLE
AGACERIE	AGATISES	AGENISING	AGGRAVATE	AGITANS
AGACERIES	AGATISING	AGENIZE	AGGREGATE	AGITAS
AGAIN	AGATIZE	AGENIZED	AGGRESS	AGITATE
AGAINST	AGATIZED	AGENIZES	AGGRESSED	AGITATED
AGALACTIA	AGATIZES	AGENIZING	AGGRESSES	AGITATES
AGALLOCH	AGATIZING	AGENT	AGGRESSOR	AGITATING
AGALLOCHS	AGATOID	AGENTED	AGGRI	AGITATION
AGALWOOD	AGAVE	AGENTIAL	AGGRIEVE	AGITATIVE
AGALWOODS	AGAVES	AGENTING	AGGRIEVED	AGITATO
AGAMA	AGAZE	AGENTINGS	AGGRIEVES	AGITATOR
AGAMAS	AGAZED	AGENTIVAL	AGGRO	AGITATORS
AGAMETE	AGE	AGENTIVE	AGGROS	AGITPOP
AGAMETES	AGED	AGENTIVES	AGGRY	AGITPOPS
AGAMI	AGEDLY	AGENTRIES	AGHA	AGITPROP
AGAMIC	AGEDNESS	AGENTRY	AGHAS	AGITPROPS
AGAMID	AGEE	AGENTS	AGHAST	AGLARE
AGAMIDS	AGEING	AGER	AGILA	AGLEAM
AGAMIS	AGEINGS	AGERATUM	AGILAS	AGLEE
AGAMOGONY	AGEISM	AGERATUMS	AGILE	AGLET
AGAMOID	AGEISMS	AGERS	AGILELY	AGLETS
AGAMOIDS	AGEIST	AGES	AGILENESS	AGLEY
AGAMONT	AGEISTS	AGEUSIA	AGILER	AGLIMMER
AGAMONTS	AGELAST	AGEUSIAS	AGILEST	AGLITTER
AGAMOUS	AGELASTIC	AGFLATION	AGILITIES	AGLOO
AGAPAE	AGELASTS	AGGADA	AGILITY	AGLOOS
AGAPAI	AGELESS	AGGADAH	AGIN	AGLOSSAL
AGAPE	AGELESSLY	AGGADAHS	AGING	AGLOSSATE
AGAPEIC	AGELONG	AGGADAS	AGINGS	AGLOSSIA
AGAPES	AGEMATE	AGGADIC	AGINNER	AGLOSSIAS
AGAR	AGEMATES	AGGADOT	AGINNERS	AGLOW
AGARIC	AGEN	AGGADOTH	AGIO	AGLU
AGARICS	AGENCIES	AGGER	AGIOS	AGLUS
AGAROSE	AGENCY	AGGERS	AGIOTAGE	AGLY
AGAROSES	AGENDA	AGGIE	AGIOTAGES	AGLYCON
AGARS	AGENDAS	AGGIES	AGISM	AGLYCONE
AGARWOOD	AGENDUM	AGGRACE	AGISMS	AGLYCONES
AGARWOODS	AGENDUMS	AGGRACED	AGIST	AGLYCONS
AGAS	AGENE	AGGRACES	AGISTED	AGMA
AGAST	AGENES	AGGRACING	AGISTER	AGMAS
AGASTED	AGENESES	AGGRADE	AGISTERS	AGMINATE
AGASTING	AGENESIA	AGGRADED	AGISTING	AGNAIL
AGASTS	AGENESIAS	AGGRADES	AGISTMENT	AGNAILS
AGATE	AGENESIS	AGGRADING	AGISTOR	AGNAME
AGATES	AGENETIC	AGGRATE	AGISTORS	AGNAMED
AGATEWARE	AGENISE	AGGRATED	AGISTS	AGNAMES
AGATISE	AGENISED	AGGRATES	AGITA	AGNATE

AGNATES	AGONISTIC	AGRESTIC	AGUIZES	AIDANTS
AGNATHAN	AGONISTS	AGRIA	AGUIZING	AIDAS
AGNATHANS	AGONIZE	AGRIAS	AGUNA	AIDE
AGNATHOUS	AGONIZED	AGRIMONY	AGUNAH	AIDED
AGNATIC	AGONIZES	AGRIN	AGUNOT	AIDER
AGNATICAL	AGONIZING	AGRINS	AGUNOTH	AIDERS
AGNATION	AGONS	AGRIOLOGY	AGUTI	AIDES
AGNATIONS	AGONY	AGRISE	AGUTIS	AIDFUL
AGNISE	AGOOD	AGRISED	AH	AIDING
AGNISED	AGORA	AGRISES	AHA	AIDLESS
AGNISES	AGORAE	AGRISING	AHCHOO	AIDMAN
AGNISING	AGORAS	AGRIZE	AHEAD	AIDMEN
AGNIZE	AGOROT	AGRIZED	AHEAP	AIDOI
AGNIZED	AGOROTH	AGRIZES	AHED	AIDOS
AGNIZES	AGOUTA	AGRIZING	AHEIGHT	AIDS
AGNIZING	AGOUTAS	AGRO	AHEM	AIERIES
AGNOLOTTI	AGOUTI	AGRODOLCE	AHEMERAL	AIERY
AGNOMEN	AGOUTIES	AGROLOGIC	AHENT	AIGA
AGNOMENS	AGOUTIS	AGROLOGY	AHI	AIGAS
AGNOMINA	AGOUTY	AGRONOMIC	AHIGH	AIGHT
AGNOMINAL	AGRAFE	AGRONOMY	AHIMSA	AIGLET
AGNOSIA	AGRAFES	AGROS	AHIMSAS	AIGLETS
AGNOSIAS	AGRAFFE	AGROUND	AHIND	AIGRET
AGNOSIC	AGRAFFES	AGRYPNIA	AHING	AIGRETS
AGNOSTIC	AGRAPHA	AGRYPNIAS	AHINT	AIGRETTE
AGNOSTICS	AGRAPHIA	AGRYZE	AHIS	AIGRETTES
AGO	AGRAPHIAS	AGRYZED	AHISTORIC	AIGUILLE
AGOG	AGRAPHIC	AGRYZES	AHOLD	AIGUILLES
AGOGE	AGRAPHON	AGRYZING	AHOLDS	AIKIDO
AGOGES	AGRARIAN	AGS	AHORSE	AIKIDOS
AGOGIC	AGRARIANS	AGTERSKOT	AHOY	AIKONA
AGOGICS	AGRASTE	AGUACATE	AHS	AIL
AGOING	AGRAVIC	AGUACATES	AHULL	AILANTHIC
AGON	AGREE	AGUE	AHUNGERED	AILANTHUS
AGONAL	AGREEABLE	AGUED	AHUNGRY	AILANTO
AGONE	AGREEABLY	AGUELIKE	AHURU	AILANTOS
AGONES	AGREED	AGUES	AHURUHURU	AILED
AGONIC	AGREEING	AGUEWEED	AHURUS	AILERON
AGONIES	AGREEMENT	AGUEWEEDS	AI	AILERONS
AGONISE	AGREES	AGUISE	AIA	AILETTE
AGONISED	AGREGE	AGUISED	AIAS	AILETTES
AGONISES	AGREGES	AGUISES	AIBLINS	AILING
AGONISING	AGREMENS	AGUISH	AID	AILMENT
AGONISM	AGREMENT	AGUISHLY	AIDA	AILMENTS
AGONISMS	AGREMENTS	AGUISING	AIDANCE	AILS
AGONIST	AGRESTAL	AGUIZE	AIDANCES	AIM
AGONISTES	AGRESTIAL	AGUIZED	AIDANT	AIMED

AIMER	AIRDATE	AIRLINERS	AIRSIDES	AIT
AIMERS	AIRDATES	AIRLINES	AIRSOME	AITCH
AIMFUL	AIRDRAWN	AIRLOCK	AIRSPACE	AITCHBONE
AIMFULLY	AIRDROME	AIRLOCKS	AIRSPACES	AITCHES
AIMING	AIRDROMES	AIRMAIL	AIRSPEED	AITS
AIMLESS	AIRDROP	AIRMAILED	AIRSPEEDS	AITU
AIMLESSLY	AIRDROPS	AIRMAILS	AIRSTOP	AITUS
AIMS	AIRED	AIRMAN	AIRSTOPS	AIVER
AIN	AIRER	AIRMEN	AIRSTREAM	AIVERS
AINE	AIRERS	AIRMOBILE	AIRSTRIKE	AIYEE
AINEE	AIREST	AIRN	AIRSTRIP	AIZLE
AINGA	AIRFARE	AIRNED	AIRSTRIPS	AIZLES
AINGAS	AIRFARES	AIRNING	AIRT	AJAR
AINS	AIRFIELD	AIRNS	AIRTED	AJEE
AINSELL	AIRFIELDS	AIRPARK	AIRTH	AJI
AINSELLS	AIRFLOW	AIRPARKS	AIRTHED	AJIS
AIOLI	AIRFLOWS	AIRPLANE	AIRTHING	AJIVA
AIOLIS	AIRFOIL	AIRPLANES	AIRTHS	AJIVAS
AIR	AIRFOILS	AIRPLAY	AIRTIGHT	AJOWAN
AIRBAG	AIRFRAME	AIRPLAYS	AIRTIME	AJOWANS
AIRBAGS	AIRFRAMES	AIRPORT	AIRTIMES	AJUGA
AIRBALL	AIRGAP	AIRPORTS	AIRTING	AJUGAS
AIRBALLS	AIRGAPS	AIRPOST	AIRTRAM	AJUTAGE
AIRBASE	AIRGLOW	AIRPOSTS	AIRTRAMS	AJUTAGES
AIRBASES	AIRGLOWS	AIRPOWER	AIRTS	AJWAN
AIRBOARD	AIRGRAPH	AIRPOWERS	AIRVAC	AJWANS
AIRBOARDS	AIRGRAPHS	AIRPROOF	AIRVACS	AKA
AIRBOAT	AIRGUN	AIRPROOFS	AIRWARD	AKARYOTE
AIRBOATS	AIRGUNS	AIRPROX	AIRWARDS	AKARYOTES
AIRBORNE	AIRHEAD	AIRPROXES	AIRWAVE	AKARYOTIC
AIRBOUND	AIRHEADED	AIRS	AIRWAVES	AKAS
AIRBRICK	AIRHEADS	AIRSCAPE	AIRWAY	AKATEA
AIRBRICKS	AIRHOLE	AIRSCAPES	AIRWAYS	AKATEAS
AIRBRUSH	AIRHOLES	AIRSCREW	AIRWISE	AKATHISIA
AIRBURST	AIRIER	AIRSCREWS	AIRWOMAN	AKE
AIRBURSTS	AIRIEST	AIRSHAFT	AIRWOMEN	AKEAKE
AIRBUS	AIRILY	AIRSHAFTS	AIRWORTHY	AKEAKES
AIRBUSES	AIRINESS	AIRSHED	AIRY	AKEBIA
AIRBUSSES	AIRING	AIRSHEDS	AIS	AKEBIAS
AIRCHECK	AIRINGS	AIRSHIP	AISLE	AKED
AIRCHECKS	AIRLESS	AIRSHIPS	AISLED	AKEDAH
AIRCOACH	AIRLIFT	AIRSHOT	AISLELESS	AKEDAHS
AIRCON	AIRLIFTED	AIRSHOTS	AISLES	AKEE
AIRCONS	AIRLIFTS	AIRSHOW	AISLEWAY	AKEES
AIRCRAFT	AIRLIKE	AIRSHOWS	AISLEWAYS	AKELA
AIRCREW	AIRLINE	AIRSICK	AISLING	AKELAS
AIRCREWS	AIRLINER	AIRSIDE	AISLINGS	AKENE

AKENES	ALAMORT	ALATED	ALBITISE	ALCHEMY
AKENIAL	ALAMOS	ALATES	ALBITISED	ALCHERA
AKES	ALAN	ALATION	ALBITISES	ALCHERAS
AKHARA	ALAND	ALATIONS	ALBITIZE	ALCHYMIES
AKHARAS	ALANDS	ALAY	ALBITIZED	ALCHYMY
AKIMBO	ALANE	ALAYED	ALBITIZES	ALCID
AKIN	ALANG	ALAYING	ALBIZIA	ALCIDINE
AKINESES	ALANGS	ALAYS	ALBIZIAS	ALCIDS
AKINESIA	ALANIN	ALB	ALBIZZIA	ALCO
AKINESIAS	ALANINE	ALBA	ALBIZZIAS	ALCOHOL
AKINESIS	ALANINES	ALBACORE	ALBRICIAS	ALCOHOLIC
AKINETIC	ALANINS	ALBACORES	ALBS	ALCOHOLS
AKING	ALANNAH	ALBARELLI	ALBUGO	ALCOLOCK
AKIRAHO	ALANNAHS	ALBARELLO	ALBUGOS	ALCOLOCKS
AKIRAHOS	ALANS	ALBAS	ALBUM	ALCOOL
AKITA	ALANT	ALBATA	ALBUMEN	ALCOOLS
AKITAS	ALANTS	ALBATAS	ALBUMENS	ALCOPOP
AKKAS	ALANYL	ALBATROSS	ALBUMIN	ALCOPOPS
AKOLUTHOS	ALANYLS	ALBE	ALBUMINS	ALCORZA
AKRASIA	ALAP	ALBEDO	ALBUMOSE	ALCORZAS
AKRASIAS	ALAPA	ALBEDOES	ALBUMOSES	ALCOS
AKRATIC	ALAPAS	ALBEDOS	ALBUMS	ALCOVE
AKVAVIT	ALAPS	ALBEE	ALBURNOUS	ALCOVED
AKVAVITS	ALAR	ALBEIT	ALBURNUM	ALCOVES
AL	ALARM	ALBERGHI	ALBURNUMS	ALDEA
ALA	ALARMABLE	ALBERGO	ALBUTEROL	ALDEAS
ALAAP	ALARMED	ALBERT	ALCADE	ALDEHYDE
ALAAPS	ALARMEDLY	ALBERTITE	ALCADES	ALDEHYDES
ALABAMINE	ALARMING	ALBERTS	ALCAHEST	ALDEHYDIC
ALABASTER	ALARMISM	ALBESCENT	ALCAHESTS	ALDER
ALACHLOR	ALARMISMS	ALBESPINE	ALCAIC	ALDERFLY
ALACHLORS	ALARMIST	ALBESPYNE	ALCAICS	ALDERMAN
ALACK	ALARMISTS	ALBICORE	ALCAIDE	ALDERMEN
ALACKADAY	ALARMS	ALBICORES	ALCAIDES	ALDERN
ALACRITY	ALARUM	ALBINAL	ALCALDE	ALDERS
ALAE	ALARUMED	ALBINESS	ALCALDES	ALDICARB
ALAIMENT	ALARUMING	ALBINIC	ALCARRAZA	ALDICARBS
ALAIMENTS	ALARUMS	ALBINISM	ALCATRAS	ALDOL
ALALAGMOI	ALARY	ALBINISMS	ALCAYDE	ALDOLASE
ALALAGMOS	ALAS	ALBINO	ALCAYDES	ALDOLASES
ALALIA	ALASKA	ALBINOISM	ALCAZAR	ALDOLS
ALALIAS	ALASKAS	ALBINOS	ALCAZARS	ALDOSE
ALAMEDA	ALASTOR	ALBINOTIC	ALCHEMIC	ALDOSES
ALAMEDAS	ALASTORS	ALBITE	ALCHEMIES	ALDOXIME
ALAMO	ALASTRIM	ALBITES	ALCHEMISE	ALDOXIMES
ALAMODE	ALASTRIMS	ALBITIC	ALCHEMIST	ALDRIN
ALAMODES	ALATE	ALBITICAL	ALCHEMIZE	ALDRINS

ALE	ALETHIC	ALGAE	ALIAS	ALIGHTED
ALEATORIC	ALEURON	ALGAECIDE	ALIASED	ALIGHTING
ALEATORY	ALEURONE	ALGAL	ALIASES	ALIGHTS
ALEBENCH	ALEURONES	ALGAROBA	ALIASING	ALIGN
ALEC	ALEURONIC	ALGAROBAS	ALIASINGS	ALIGNED
ALECITHAL	ALEURONS	ALGARROBA	ALIBI	ALIGNER
ALECK	ALEVIN	ALGARROBO	ALIBIED	ALIGNERS
ALECKS	ALEVINS	ALGAS	ALIBIES	ALIGNING
ALECOST	ALEW	ALGATE	ALIBIING	ALIGNMENT
ALECOSTS	ALEWASHED	ALGATES	ALIBIS	ALIGNS
ALECS	ALEWIFE	ALGEBRA	ALIBLE	ALIKE
ALECTRYON	ALEWIVES	ALGEBRAIC	ALICANT	ALIKENESS
ALEE	ALEWS	ALGEBRAS	ALICANTS	ALIMENT
ALEF	ALEXANDER	ALGERINE	ALICYCLIC	ALIMENTAL
ALEFS	ALEXIA	ALGERINES	ALIDAD	ALIMENTED
ALEFT	ALEXIAS	ALGESES	ALIDADE	ALIMENTS
ALEGAR	ALEXIC	ALGESIA	ALIDADES	ALIMONIED
ALEGARS	ALEXIN	ALGESIAS	ALIDADS	ALIMONIES
ALEGGE	ALEXINE	ALGESIC	ALIEN	ALIMONY
ALEGGED	ALEXINES	ALGESIS	ALIENABLE	ALINE
ALEGGES	ALEXINIC	ALGETIC	ALIENAGE	ALINED
ALEGGING	ALEXINS	ALGICIDAL	ALIENAGES	ALINEMENT
ALEHOUSE	ALEYE	ALGICIDE	ALIENATE	ALINER
ALEHOUSES	ALEYED	ALGICIDES	ALIENATED	ALINERS
ALEMBIC	ALEYES	ALGID	ALIENATES	ALINES
ALEMBICS	ALEYING	ALGIDITY	ALIENATOR	ALINING
ALEMBROTH	ALF	ALGIDNESS	ALIENED	ALIPED
ALENCON	ALFA	ALGIN	ALIENEE	ALIPEDS
ALENCONS	ALFAKI	ALGINATE	ALIENEES	ALIPHATIC
ALENGTH	ALFAKIS	ALGINATES	ALIENER	ALIQUANT
ALEPH	ALFALFA	ALGINIC	ALIENERS	ALIQUOT
ALEPHS	ALFALFAS	ALGINS	ALIENING	ALIQUOTS
ALEPINE	ALFAQUI	ALGOID	ALIENISM	ALISMA
ALEPINES	ALFAQUIN	ALGOLOGY	ALIENISMS	ALISMAS
ALERCE	ALFAQUINS	ALGOMETER	ALIENIST	ALISON
ALERCES	ALFAQUIS	ALGOMETRY	ALIENISTS	ALISONS
ALERION	ALFAS	ALGOR	ALIENLY	ALIST
ALERIONS	ALFERECES	ALGORISM	ALIENNESS	ALIT
ALERT	ALFEREZ	ALGORISMS	ALIENOR	ALITERACY
ALERTED	ALFILARIA	ALGORITHM	ALIENORS	ALITERATE
ALERTER	ALFILERIA	ALGORS	ALIENS	ALIUNDE
ALERTEST	ALFORJA	ALGUACIL	ALIF	ALIVE
ALERTING	ALFORJAS	ALGUACILS	ALIFORM	ALIVENESS
ALERTLY	ALFREDO	ALGUAZIL	ALIFS	ALIYA
ALERTNESS	ALFRESCO	ALGUAZILS	ALIGARTA	ALIYAH
ALERTS	ALFS	ALGUM	ALIGARTAS	ALIYAHS
ALES	ALGA	ALGUMS	ALIGHT	ALIYAS

A

ALIYOS	ALKY	ALLEGORIC	ALLICIN	ALLOPATH
ALIYOT	ALKYD	ALLEGORY	ALLICINS	ALLOPATHS
ALIYOTH	ALKYDS	ALLEGRO	ALLIED	ALLOPATHY
ALIZARI	ALKYL	ALLEGROS	ALLIES	ALLOPATRY
ALIZARIN	ALKYLATE	ALLEL	ALLIGARTA	ALLOPHANE
ALIZARINE	ALKYLATED	ALLELE	ALLIGATE	ALLOPHONE
ALIZARINS	ALKYLATES	ALLELES	ALLIGATED	ALLOPLASM
ALIZARIS	ALKYLIC	ALLELIC	ALLIGATES	ALLOSAUR
ALKAHEST	ALKYLS	ALLELISM	ALLIGATOR	ALLOSAURS
ALKAHESTS	ALKYNE	ALLELISMS	ALLIS	ALLOSTERY
ALKALI	ALKYNES	ALLELS	ALLISES	ALLOT
ALKALIC	ALL	ALLELUIA	ALLIUM	ALLOTMENT
ALKALIES	ALLANITE	ALLELUIAH	ALLIUMS	ALLOTROPE
ALKALIFY	ALLANITES	ALLELUIAS	ALLNESS	ALLOTROPY
ALKALIN	ALLANTOIC	ALLEMANDE	ALLNESSES	ALLOTS
ALKALINE	ALLANTOID	ALLENARLY	ALLNIGHT	ALLOTTED
ALKALIS	ALLANTOIN	ALLERGEN	ALLOBAR	ALLOTTEE
ALKALISE	ALLANTOIS	ALLERGENS	ALLOBARS	ALLOTTEES
ALKALISED	ALLATIVE	ALLERGIC	ALLOCABLE	ALLOTTER
ALKALISER	ALLATIVES	ALLERGICS	ALLOCARPY	ALLOTTERS
ALKALISES	ALLAY	ALLERGIES	ALLOCATE	ALLOTTERY
ALKALIZE	ALLAYED	ALLERGIN	ALLOCATED	ALLOTTING
ALKALIZED	ALLAYER	ALLERGINS	ALLOCATES	ALLOTYPE
ALKALIZER	ALLAYERS	ALLERGIST	ALLOCATOR	ALLOTYPES
ALKALIZES	ALLAYING	ALLERGY	ALLOD	ALLOTYPIC
ALKALOID	ALLAYINGS	ALLERION	ALLODIA	ALLOTYPY
ALKALOIDS	ALLAYMENT	ALLERIONS	ALLODIAL	ALLOVER
ALKALOSES	ALLAYS	ALLETHRIN	ALLODIUM	ALLOVERS
ALKALOSIS	ALLCOMERS	ALLEVIANT	ALLODIUMS	ALLOW
ALKALOTIC	ALLEDGE	ALLEVIATE	ALLODS	ALLOWABLE
ALKANE	ALLEDGED	ALLEY	ALLODYNIA	ALLOWABLY
ALKANES	ALLEDGES	ALLEYCAT	ALLOGAMY	ALLOWANCE
ALKANET	ALLEDGING	ALLEYCATS	ALLOGENIC	ALLOWED
ALKANETS	ALLEE	ALLEYED	ALLOGRAFT	ALLOWEDLY
ALKANNIN	ALLEES	ALLEYS	ALLOGRAPH	ALLOWING
ALKANNINS	ALLEGE	ALLEYWAY	ALLOMERIC	ALLOWS
ALKENE	ALLEGED	ALLEYWAYS	ALLOMETRY	ALLOXAN
ALKENES	ALLEGEDLY	ALLHEAL	ALLOMONE	ALLOXANS
ALKIE	ALLEGER	ALLHEALS	ALLOMONES	ALLOY
ALKIES	ALLEGERS	ALLIABLE	ALLOMORPH	ALLOYED
ALKINE	ALLEGES	ALLIAK	ALLONGE	ALLOYING
ALKINES	ALLEGGE	ALLIAKS	ALLONGED	ALLOYS
ALKO	ALLEGGED	ALLIANCE	ALLONGES	ALLOZYME
ALKOS	ALLEGGES	ALLIANCES	ALLONGING	ALLOZYMES
ALKOXIDE	ALLEGGING	ALLICE	ALLONS	ALLS
ALKOXIDES	ALLEGIANT	ALLICES	ALLONYM	ALLSEED
ALKOXY .	ALLEGING	ALLICHOLY	ALLONYMS	ALLSEEDS

ALLSORTS	ALMEMARS	ALODIUMS	ALPHAS	ALTERNES
ALLSPICE	ALMERIES	ALODS	ALPHASORT	ALTERS
ALLSPICES	ALMERY	ALOE	ALPHATEST	ALTESSE
ALLUDE	ALMES	ALOED	ALPHORN	ALTESSES
ALLUDED	ALMIGHTY	ALOES	ALPHORNS	ALTEZA
ALLUDES	ALMIRAH	ALOESWOOD	ALPHOSIS	ALTEZAS
ALLUDING	ALMIRAHS	ALOETIC	ALPHYL	ALTEZZA
ALLURE	ALMNER	ALOETICS	ALPHYLS	ALTEZZAS
ALLURED	ALMNERS	ALOFT	ALPINE	ALTHAEA
ALLURER	ALMOND	ALOGIA	ALPINELY	ALTHAEAS
ALLURERS	ALMONDIER	ALOGIAS	ALPINES	ALTHEA
ALLURES	ALMONDITE	ALOGICAL	ALPINISM	ALTHEAS
ALLURING	ALMONDS	ALOHA	ALPINISMS	ALTHO
ALLUSION	ALMONDY	ALOHAS	ALPINIST	ALTHORN
ALLUSIONS	ALMONER	ALOIN	ALPINISTS	ALTHORNS
ALLUSIVE	ALMONERS	ALOINS	ALPS	ALTHOUGH
ALLUVIA	ALMONRIES	ALONE	ALREADY	ALTIGRAPH
ALLUVIAL	ALMONRY	ALONELY	ALRIGHT	ALTIMETER
ALLUVIALS	ALMOST	ALONENESS	ALS	ALTIMETRY
ALLUVION	ALMOUS	ALONG	ALSIKE	ALTIPLANO
ALLUVIONS	ALMS	ALONGSIDE	ALSIKES	ALTISSIMO
ALLUVIUM	ALMSGIVER	ALONGST	ALSO	ALTITUDE
ALLUVIUMS	ALMSHOUSE	ALOO	ALSOON	ALTITUDES
ALLY	ALMSMAN	ALOOF	ALSOONE	ALTO
ALLYING	ALMSMEN	ALOOFLY	ALT	ALTOIST
ALLYL	ALMSWOMAN	ALOOFNESS	ALTAR	ALTOISTS
ALLYLIC	ALMSWOMEN	ALOOS	ALTARAGE	ALTOS
ALLYLS	ALMUCE	ALOPECIA	ALTARAGES	ALTRICES
ALLYOU	ALMUCES	ALOPECIAS	ALTARS	ALTRICIAL
ALMA	ALMUD	ALOPECIC	ALTARWISE	ALTRUISM
ALMAGEST	ALMUDE	ALOPECOID	ALTER	ALTRUISMS
ALMAGESTS	ALMUDES	ALOUD	ALTERABLE	ALTRUIST
ALMAH	ALMUDS	ALOW	ALTERABLY	ALTRUISTS
ALMAHS	ALMUG	ALOWE	ALTERANT	ALTS
ALMAIN	ALMUGS	ALP	ALTERANTS	ALU
ALMAINS	ALNAGE	ALPACA	ALTERCATE	ALUDEL
ALMANAC	ALNAGER	ALPACAS	ALTERED	ALUDELS
ALMANACK	ALNAGERS	ALPACCA	ALTERER	ALULA
ALMANACKS	ALNAGES	ALPACCAS	ALTERERS	ALULAE
ALMANACS	ALNICO	ALPARGATA	ALTERING	ALULAR
ALMANDINE	ALNICOS	ALPEEN	ALTERITY	ALULAS
ALMANDITE	ALOCASIA	ALPEENS	ALTERN	ALUM
ALMAS	ALOCASIAS	ALPENGLOW	ALTERNANT	ALUMIN
ALME	ALOD	ALPENHORN	ALTERNAT	ALUMINA
ALMEH	ALODIA	ALPHA	ALTERNATE	ALUMINAS
ALMEHS	ALODIAL	ALPHABET	ALTERNATS	ALUMINATE
ALMEMAR	ALODIUM	ALPHABETS	ALTERNE	ALUMINE

ALUMINES	AMADODA	AMATING	AMBEERS	AMBOYNAS
ALUMINIC	AMADOU	AMATION	AMBER	AMBRIES
ALUMINISE	AMADOUS	AMATIONS	AMBERED	AMBROID
ALUMINIUM	AMAH	AMATIVE	AMBERGRIS	AMBROIDS
ALUMINIZE	AMAHS	AMATIVELY	AMBERIES	AMBROSIA
ALUMINOUS	AMAIN	AMATOL	AMBERINA	AMBROSIAL
ALUMINS	AMAKOSI	AMATOLS	AMBERINAS	AMBROSIAN
ALUMINUM	AMALGAM	AMATORIAL	AMBERITE	AMBROSIAS
ALUMINUMS	AMALGAMS	AMATORIAN	AMBERITES	AMBROTYPE
ALUMISH	AMANDINE	AMATORY	AMBERJACK	AMBRY
ALUMIUM	AMANDINES	AMAUROSES	AMBEROID	AMBSACE
ALUMIUMS	AMANDLA	AMAUROSIS	AMBEROIDS	AMBSACES
ALUMNA	AMANDLAS	AMAUROTIC	AMBEROUS	AMBULACRA
ALUMNAE	AMANITA	AMAUT	AMBERS	AMBULANCE
ALUMNI	AMANITAS	AMAUTI	AMBERY	AMBULANT
ALUMNUS	AMANITIN	AMAUTIK	AMBIANCE	AMBULANTS
ALUMROOT	AMANITINS	AMAUTIKS	AMBIANCES	AMBULATE
ALUMROOTS	AMARACUS	AMAUTIS	AMBIENCE	AMBULATED
ALUMS	AMARANT	AMAUTS	AMBIENCES	AMBULATES
ALUMSTONE	AMARANTH	AMAZE	AMBIENT	AMBULATOR
ALUNITE	AMARANTHS	AMAZED	AMBIENTS	AMBULETTE
ALUNITES	AMARANTIN	AMAZEDLY	AMBIGUITY	AMBUSCADE
ALURE	AMARANTS	AMAZEMENT	AMBIGUOUS	AMBUSCADO
ALURES	AMARELLE	AMAZES	AMBIPOLAR	AMBUSH
ALUS	AMARELLES	AMAZING	AMBIT	AMBUSHED
ALVAR	AMARETTI	AMAZINGLY	AMBITION	AMBUSHER
ALVARS	AMARETTO	AMAZON	AMBITIONS	AMBUSHERS
ALVEARIES	AMARETTOS	AMAZONIAN	AMBITIOUS	AMBUSHES
ALVEARY	AMARNA	AMAZONITE	AMBITS	AMBUSHING
ALVEATED	AMARONE	AMAZONS	AMBITTY	AME
ALVEOLAR	AMARONES	AMBACH	AMBIVERT	AMEARST
ALVEOLARS	AMARYLLID	AMBACHES	AMBIVERTS	AMEBA
ALVEOLATE	AMARYLLIS	AMBAGE	AMBLE	AMEBAE
ALVEOLE	AMAS	AMBAGES	AMBLED	AMEBAN
ALVEOLES	AMASS	AMBAGIOUS	AMBLER	AMEBAS
ALVEOLI	AMASSABLE	AMBAN	AMBLERS	AMEBEAN
ALVEOLUS	AMASSED	AMBANS	AMBLES	AMEBIASES
ALVINE	AMASSER	AMBARI	AMBLING	AMEBIASIS
ALWAY	AMASSERS	AMBARIES	AMBLINGS	AMEBIC
ALWAYS	AMASSES	AMBARIS	AMBLYOPIA	AMEBOCYTE
ALYSSUM	AMASSING	AMBARY	AMBLYOPIC	AMEBOID
ALYSSUMS	AMASSMENT	AMBASSAGE	AMBO	AMEER
AM	AMATE	AMBASSIES	AMBOINA	AMEERATE
AMA	AMATED	AMBASSY	AMBOINAS	AMEERATES
AMABILE	AMATES	AMBATCH	AMBONES	AMEERS
AMADAVAT	AMATEUR	AMBATCHES	AMBOS	AMEIOSES
AMADAVATS	AMATEURS	AMBEER	AMBOYNA	AMEIOSIS

AMELCORN	AMETROPIA	AMINES	AMMONIAC	AMOKS
AMELCORNS	AMETROPIC	AMINIC	AMMONIACS	AMOKURA
AMELIA	AMI	AMINITIES	AMMONIAS	AMOKURAS
AMELIAS	AMIA	AMINITY	AMMONIATE	AMOLE
AMEN	AMIABLE	AMINO	AMMONIC	AMOLES
AMENABLE	AMIABLY	AMINOS	AMMONICAL	AMOMUM
AMENABLY	AMIANTHUS	AMINS	AMMONIFY	AMOMUMS
AMENAGE	AMIANTUS	AMIR	AMMONITE	AMONG
AMENAGED	AMIAS	AMIRATE	AMMONITES	AMONGST
AMENAGES	AMICABLE	AMIRATES	AMMONITIC	AMOOVE
AMENAGING	AMICABLY	AMIRS	AMMONIUM	AMOOVED
AMENAUNCE	AMICE	AMIS	AMMONIUMS	AMOOVES
AMEND	AMICES	AMISES	AMMONO	AMOOVING
AMENDABLE	AMICI	AMISS	AMMONOID	AMORAL
AMENDE	AMICUS	AMISSES	AMMONOIDS	AMORALISM
AMENDED	AMID	AMISSIBLE	AMMONS	AMORALIST
AMENDER	AMIDASE	AMISSING	AMMOS	AMORALITY
AMENDERS	AMIDASES	AMITIES	AMNESIA	AMORALLY
AMENDES	AMIDE	AMITOSES	AMNESIAC	AMORANCE
AMENDING	AMIDES	AMITOSIS	AMNESIACS	AMORANCES
AMENDMENT	AMIDIC	AMITOTIC	AMNESIAS	AMORANT
AMENDS	AMIDIN	AMITROLE	AMNESIC	AMORCE
AMENE	AMIDINE	AMITROLES	AMNESICS	AMORCES
AMENED	AMIDINES	AMITY	AMNESTIC	AMORET
AMENING	AMIDINS	AMLA	AMNESTIED	AMORETS
AMENITIES	AMIDMOST	AMLAS	AMNESTIES	AMORETTI
AMENITY	AMIDO	AMMAN	AMNESTY	AMORETTO
AMENS	AMIDOGEN	AMMANS	AMNIA	AMORETTOS
AMENT	AMIDOGENS	AMMETER	AMNIC	AMORINI
AMENTA	AMIDOL	AMMETERS	AMNIO	AMORINO
AMENTAL	AMIDOLS	AMMINE	AMNION	AMORISM
AMENTIA	AMIDONE	AMMINES	AMNIONIC	AMORISMS
AMENTIAS	AMIDONES	AMMINO	AMNIONS	AMORIST
AMENTS	AMIDS	AMMIRAL	AMNIOS	AMORISTIC
AMENTUM	AMIDSHIP	AMMIRALS	AMNIOTE	AMORISTS
AMERCE	AMIDSHIPS	AMMO	AMNIOTES	AMORNINGS
AMERCED	AMIDST	AMMOCETE	AMNIOTIC	AMOROSA
AMERCER	AMIE	AMMOCETES	AMNIOTOMY	AMOROSAS
AMERCERS	AMIES	AMMOCOETE	AMOEBA	AMOROSITY
AMERCES	AMIGA	AMMOLITE	AMOEBAE	AMOROSO
AMERCING	AMIGAS	AMMOLITES	AMOEBAEAN	AMOROSOS
AMERICIUM	AMIGO	AMMON	AMOEBAN	AMOROUS
AMES	AMIGOS	AMMONAL	AMOEBAS	AMOROUSLY
AMESACE	AMILDAR	AMMONALS	AMOEBEAN	AMORPHISM
AMESACES	AMILDARS	AMMONATE	AMOEBIC	AMORPHOUS
AMETHYST	AMIN	AMMONATES	AMOEBOID	AMORT
AMETHYSTS	AMINE	AMMONIA	AMOK	AMORTISE

AMORTISED	AMPHORIC	AMU	AMYLS	ANAGOGIES
AMORTISES	AMPING	AMUCK	AMYLUM	ANAGOGY
AMORTIZE	AMPLE	AMUCKS	AMYLUMS	ANAGRAM
AMORTIZED	AMPLENESS	AMULET	AMYOTONIA	ANAGRAMS
AMORTIZES	AMPLER	AMULETIC	AMYTAL	ANAL
AMOSITE	AMPLEST	AMULETS	AMYTALS	ANALCIME
AMOSITES	AMPLEXUS	AMUS	AN	ANALCIMES
AMOTION	AMPLIDYNE	AMUSABLE	ANA	ANALCIMIC
AMOTIONS	AMPLIFIED	AMUSE	ANABAENA	ANALCITE
AMOUNT	AMPLIFIER	AMUSEABLE	ANABAENAS	ANALCITES
AMOUNTED	AMPLIFIES	AMUSED	ANABANTID	ANALECTA
AMOUNTING	AMPLIFY	AMUSEDLY	ANABAS	ANALECTIC
AMOUNTS	AMPLITUDE	AMUSEMENT	ANABASES	ANALECTS
AMOUR	AMPLOSOME	AMUSER	ANABASIS	ANALEMMA
AMOURETTE	AMPLY	AMUSERS	ANABATIC	ANALEMMAS
AMOURS	AMPOULE	AMUSES	ANABIOSES	ANALEPTIC
AMOVE	AMPOULES	AMUSETTE	ANABIOSIS	ANALGESIA
AMOVED	AMPS	AMUSETTES	ANABIOTIC	ANALGESIC
AMOVES	AMPUL	AMUSIA	ANABLEPS	ANALGETIC
AMOVING	AMPULE	AMUSIAS	ANABOLIC	ANALGIA
AMOWT	AMPULES	AMUSIC	ANABOLISM	ANALGIAS
AMOWTS	AMPULLA	AMUSING	ANABOLITE	ANALITIES
AMP	AMPULLAE	AMUSINGLY	ANABRANCH	ANALITY
AMPASSIES	AMPULLAR	AMUSIVE	ANACHARIS	ANALLY
AMPASSY	AMPULLARY	AMYGDAL	ANACLINAL	ANALOG
AMPED	AMPULS	AMYGDALA	ANACLISES	ANALOGA
AMPERAGE	AMPUTATE	AMYGDALAE	ANACLISIS	ANALOGIC
AMPERAGES	AMPUTATED	AMYGDALE	ANACLITIC	ANALOGIES
AMPERE	AMPUTATES	AMYGDALES	ANACONDA	ANALOGISE
AMPERES	AMPUTATOR	AMYGDALIN	ANACONDAS	ANALOGISM
AMPERSAND	AMPUTEE	AMYGDALS	ANACRUSES	ANALOGIST
AMPERZAND	AMPUTEES	AMYGDULE	ANACRUSIS	ANALOGIZE
AMPHIBIA	AMREETA	AMYGDULES	ANADEM	ANALOGON
AMPHIBIAN	AMREETAS	AMYL	ANADEMS	ANALOGONS
AMPHIBOLE	AMRIT	AMYLASE	ANAEMIA	ANALOGOUS
AMPHIBOLY	AMRITA	AMYLASES	ANAEMIAS	ANALOGS
AMPHIGORY	AMRITAS	AMYLENE	ANAEMIC	ANALOGUE
AMPHIOXI	AMRITS	AMYLENES	ANAEROBE	ANALOGUES
AMPHIOXUS	AMSINCKIA	AMYLIC	ANAEROBES	ANALOGY
AMPHIPATH	AMTMAN	AMYLOGEN	ANAEROBIA	ANALYSAND
AMPHIPOD	AMTMANS	AMYLOGENS	ANAEROBIC	ANALYSE
AMPHIPODS	AMTRAC	AMYLOID	ANAGLYPH	ANALYSED
AMPHOLYTE	AMTRACK	AMYLOIDAL	ANAGLYPHS	ANALYSER
AMPHORA	AMTRACKS	AMYLOIDS	ANAGLYPHY	ANALYSERS
AMPHORAE	AMTRACS	AMYLOPSIN	ANAGOGE	ANALYSES
AMPHORAL	AMTRAK	AMYLOSE	ANAGOGES	ANALYSING
AMPHORAS	AMTRAKS	AMYLOSES	ANAGOGIC	ANALYSIS

ANALYST	ANARCHIES	ANCHOR	ANDANTES	ANELES
ANALYSTS	ANARCHISE	ANCHORAGE	ANDANTINI	ANELING
ANALYTE	ANARCHISM	ANCHORED	ANDANTINO	ANELLI
ANALYTES	ANARCHIST	ANCHORESS	ANDESINE	ANEMIA
ANALYTIC	ANARCHIZE	ANCHORET	ANDESINES	ANEMIAS
ANALYTICS	ANARCHS	ANCHORETS	ANDESITE	ANEMIC
ANALYZE	ANARCHY	ANCHORING	ANDESITES	ANEMOGRAM
ANALYZED	ANARTHRIA	ANCHORITE	ANDESITIC	ANEMOLOGY
ANALYZER	ANARTHRIC	ANCHORMAN	ANDESYTE	ANEMONE
ANALYZERS	ANAS	ANCHORMEN	ANDESYTES	ANEMONES
ANALYZES	ANASARCA	ANCHORS	ANDIRON	ANEMOSES
ANALYZING	ANASARCAS	ANCHOS	ANDIRONS	ANEMOSIS
ANAMNESES	ANASTASES	ANCHOVETA	ANDOUILLE	ANENST
ANAMNESIS	ANASTASIS	ANCHOVIES	ANDRADITE	ANENT
ANAMNIOTE	ANASTATIC	ANCHOVY	ANDRO	ANERGIA
ANAN	ANATA	ANCHUSA	ANDROECIA	ANERGIAS
ANANA	ANATAS	ANCHUSAS	ANDROGEN	ANERGIC
ANANAS	ANATASE	ANCHUSIN	ANDROGENS	ANERGIES
ANANASES	ANATASES	ANCHUSINS	ANDROGYNE	ANERGY
ANANDA	ANATEXES	ANCHYLOSE	ANDROGYNY	ANERLY
ANANDAS	ANATEXIS	ANCIENT	ANDROID	ANEROID
ANANDROUS	ANATHEMA	ANCIENTER	ANDROIDS	ANEROIDS
ANANKE	ANATHEMAS	ANCIENTLY	ANDROLOGY	ANES
ANANKES	ANATMAN	ANCIENTRY	ANDROMEDA	ANESTRA
ANANTHOUS	ANATMANS	ANCIENTS	ANDROS	ANESTRI
ANAPAEST	ANATOMIC	ANCILE	ANDS	ANESTROUS
ANAPAESTS	ANATOMIES	ANCILIA	ANDVILE	ANESTRUM
ANAPEST	ANATOMISE	ANCILLA	ANDVILES	ANESTRUS
ANAPESTIC	ANATOMIST	ANCILLAE	ANE	ANETHOL
ANAPESTS	ANATOMIZE	ANCILLARY	ANEAR	ANETHOLE
ANAPHASE	ANATOMY	ANCILLAS	ANEARED	ANETHOLES
ANAPHASES	ANATOXIN	ANCIPITAL	ANEARING	ANETHOLS
ANAPHASIC	ANATOXINS	ANCLE	ANEARS	ANETIC
ANAPHOR	ANATROPY	ANCLES	ANEATH	ANEUPLOID
ANAPHORA	ANATTA	ANCOME	ANECDOTA	ANEURIN
ANAPHORAL	ANATTAS	ANCOMES	ANECDOTAL	ANEURINS
ANAPHORAS	ANATTO	ANCON	ANECDOTE	ANEURISM
ANAPHORIC	ANATTOS	ANCONAL	ANECDOTES	ANEURISMS
ANAPHORS	ANAXIAL	ANCONE	ANECDOTIC	ANEURYSM
ANAPLASIA	ANBURIES	ANCONEAL	ANECDYSES	ANEURYSMS
ANAPLASTY	ANBURY	ANCONES	ANECDYSIS	ANEW
ANAPTYXES	ANCE	ANCONOID	ANECHOIC	ANGA
ANAPTYXIS	ANCESTOR	ANCORA	ANELACE	ANGAKOK
ANARCH	ANCESTORS	ANCRESS	ANELACES	ANGAKOKS
ANARCHAL	ANCESTRAL	ANCRESSES	ANELASTIC	ANGARIA
ANARCHIAL	ANCESTRY	AND	ANELE	ANGARIAS
ANARCHIC	ANCHO	ANDANTE	ANELED	ANGARIES

ANGARY	ANGLES	ANGULATE	ANIMALIST	ANISETTES
ANGAS	ANGLESITE	ANGULATED	ANIMALITY	ANISIC
ANGASHORE	ANGLEWISE	ANGULATES	ANIMALIZE	ANISOGAMY
ANGEKKOK	ANGLEWORM	ANGULOSE	ANIMALLY	ANISOLE
ANGEKKOKS	ANGLICE	ANGULOUS	ANIMALS	ANISOLES
ANGEKOK	ANGLICISE	ANHEDONIA	ANIMAS	ANKER
ANGEKOKS	ANGLICISM	ANHEDONIC	ANIMATE	ANKERITE
ANGEL	ANGLICIST	ANHEDRAL	ANIMATED	ANKERITES
ANGELED	ANGLICIZE	ANHEDRALS	ANIMATELY	ANKERS
ANGELFISH	ANGLIFIED	ANHINGA	ANIMATER	ANKH
ANGELHOOD	ANGLIFIES	ANHINGAS	ANIMATERS	ANKHS
ANGELIC	ANGLIFY	ANHUNGRED	ANIMATES	ANKLE
ANGELICA	ANGLING	ANHYDRASE	ANIMATI	ANKLEBONE
ANGELICAL	ANGLINGS	ANHYDRIDE	ANIMATIC	ANKLED
ANGELICAS	ANGLIST	ANHYDRITE	ANIMATICS	ANKLES
ANGELING	ANGLISTS	ANHYDROUS	ANIMATING	ANKLET
ANGELS	ANGLO	ANI	ANIMATION	ANKLETS
ANGELUS	ANGLOPHIL	ANICCA	ANIMATISM	ANKLING
ANGELUSES	ANGLOS	ANICCAS	ANIMATIST	ANKLONG
ANGER	ANGOLA	ANICONIC	ANIMATO	ANKLONGS
ANGERED	ANGOPHORA	ANICONISM	ANIMATOR	ANKLUNG
ANGERING	ANGORA	ANICONIST	ANIMATORS	ANKLUNGS
ANGERLESS	ANGORAS	ANICUT	ANIMATOS	ANKUS
ANGERLY	ANGOSTURA	ANICUTS	ANIME	ANKUSES
ANGERS	ANGRIER	ANIDROSES	ANIMES	ANKUSH
ANGICO	ANGRIES	ANIDROSIS	ANIMI	ANKUSHES
ANGICOS	ANGRIEST	ANIGH	ANIMIS	ANKYLOSE
ANGINA	ANGRILY	ANIGHT	ANIMISM	ANKYLOSED
ANGINAL	ANGRINESS	ANIL	ANIMISMS	ANKYLOSES
ANGINAS	ANGRY	ANILE	ANIMIST	ANKYLOSIS
ANGINOSE	ANGST	ANILIN	ANIMISTIC	ANKYLOTIC
ANGINOUS	ANGSTIER	ANILINE	ANIMISTS	ANLACE
ANGIOGRAM	ANGSTIEST	ANILINES	ANIMOSITY	ANLACES
ANGIOLOGY	ANGSTROM	ANILINGUS	ANIMUS	ANLAGE
ANGIOMA	ANGSTROMS	ANILINS	ANIMUSES	ANLAGEN
ANGIOMAS	ANGSTS	ANILITIES	ANION	ANLAGES
ANGIOMATA	ANGSTY	ANILITY	ANIONIC	ANLAS
ANGKLUNG	ANGUIFORM	ANILS	ANIONS	ANLASES
ANGKLUNGS	ANGUINE	ANIMA	ANIRIDIA	ANN
ANGLE	ANGUIPED	ANIMACIES	ANIRIDIAS	ANNA
ANGLED	ANGUIPEDE	ANIMACY	ANIRIDIC	ANNAL
ANGLEDUG	ANGUIPEDS	ANIMAL	ANIS	ANNALISE
ANGLEDUGS	ANGUISH	ANIMALIAN	ANISE	ANNALISED
ANGLEPOD	ANGUISHED	ANIMALIC	ANISEED	ANNALISES
ANGLEPODS	ANGUISHES	ANIMALIER	ANISEEDS	ANNALIST
ANGLER	ANGULAR	ANIMALISE	ANISES	ANNALISTS
ANGLERS	ANGULARLY	ANIMALISM	ANISETTE	ANNALIZE

ANNALIZED	ANNOYED	ANODIZED	ANOPSIA	ANSWERING
ANNALIZES	ANNOYER	ANODIZER	ANOPSIAS	ANSWERS
ANNALS	ANNOYERS	ANODIZERS	ANORAK	ANT
ANNAS	ANNOYING	ANODIZES	ANORAKS	ANTA
ANNAT	ANNOYS	ANODIZING	ANORECTAL	ANTACID
ANNATES	ANNS	ANODONTIA	ANORECTIC	ANTACIDS
ANNATS	ANNUAL	ANODYNE	ANORETIC	ANTAE
ANNATTA	ANNUALISE	ANODYNES	ANORETICS	ANTALGIC
ANNATTAS	ANNUALIZE	ANODYNIC	ANOREXIA	ANTALGICS
ANNATTO	ANNUALLY	ANOESES	ANOREXIAS	ANTALKALI
ANNATTOS	ANNUALS	ANOESIS	ANOREXIC	ANTAR
ANNEAL	ANNUITANT	ANOESTRA	ANOREXICS	ANTARA
ANNEALED	ANNUITIES	ANOESTRI	ANOREXIES	ANTARAS
ANNEALER	ANNUITY	ANOESTRUM	ANOREXY	ANTARCTIC
ANNEALERS	ANNUL	ANOESTRUS	ANORTHIC	ANTARS
ANNEALING	ANNULAR	ANOETIC	ANORTHITE	ANTAS
ANNEALS	ANNULARLY	ANOINT	ANOSMATIC	ANTBEAR
ANNECTENT	ANNULARS	ANOINTED	ANOSMIA	ANTBEARS
ANNELID	ANNULATE	ANOINTER	ANOSMIAS	ANTBIRD
ANNELIDAN	ANNULATED	ANOINTERS	ANOSMIC	ANTBIRDS
ANNELIDS	ANNULATES	ANOINTING	ANOTHER	ANTE
ANNEX	ANNULET	ANOINTS	ANOUGH	ANTEATER
ANNEXABLE	ANNULETS	ANOLE	ANOUROUS	ANTEATERS
ANNEXE	ANNULI	ANOLES	ANOVULANT	ANTECEDE
ANNEXED	ANNULLED	ANOLYTE	ANOVULAR	ANTECEDED
ANNEXES	ANNULLING	ANOLYTES	ANOW	ANTECEDES
ANNEXING	ANNULMENT	ANOMALIES	ANOXAEMIA	ANTECHOIR
ANNEXION	ANNULOSE	ANOMALOUS	ANOXAEMIC	ANTED
ANNEXIONS	ANNULS	ANOMALY	ANOXEMIA	ANTEDATE
ANNEXMENT	ANNULUS	ANOMIC	ANOXEMIAS	ANTEDATED
ANNEXURE	ANNULUSES	ANOMIE	ANOXEMIC	ANTEDATES
ANNEXURES	ANOA	ANOMIES	ANOXIA	ANTEED
ANNICUT	ANOAS	ANOMY	ANOXIAS	ANTEFIX
ANNICUTS	ANOBIID	ANON	ANOXIC	ANTEFIXA
ANNO	ANOBIIDS	ANONYM	ANS	ANTEFIXAE
ANNONA	ANODAL	ANONYMA	ANSA	ANTEFIXAL
ANNONAS	ANODALLY	ANONYMAS	ANSAE	ANTEFIXES
ANNOTATE	ANODE	ANONYMISE	ANSAPHONE	ANTEING
ANNOTATED	ANODES	ANONYMITY	ANSATE	ANTELOPE
ANNOTATES	ANODIC	ANONYMIZE	ANSATED	ANTELOPES
ANNOTATOR	ANODISE	ANONYMOUS	ANSERINE	ANTELUCAN
ANNOUNCE	ANODISED	ANONYMS	ANSERINES	ANTENATAL
ANNOUNCED	ANODISER	ANOOPSIA	ANSEROUS	ANTENATI
ANNOUNCER	ANODISERS	ANOOPSIAS	ANSWER	ANTENNA
ANNOUNCES	ANODISES	ANOPHELES	ANSWERED	ANTENNAE
ANNOY	ANODISING	ANOPIA	ANSWERER	ANTENNAL
ANNOYANCE	ANODIZE	ANOPIAS	ANSWERERS	ANTENNARY

ANTENNAS	ANTHROS	ANTICRACK	ANTILOG	ANTIPOLE
ANTENNULE	ANTHURIUM	ANTICRIME	ANTILOGS	ANTIPOLES
ANTEPAST	ANTI	ANTICS	ANTILOGY	ANTIPOPE
ANTEPASTS	ANTIABUSE	ANTICULT	ANTIMACHO	ANTIPOPES
ANTERIOR	ANTIACNE	ANTICULTS	ANTIMALE	ANTIPORN
ANTEROOM	ANTIAGING	ANTIDORA	ANTIMAN	ANTIPOT
ANTEROOMS	ANTIAIR	ANTIDORON	ANTIMASK	ANTIPRESS
ANTES	ANTIALIEN	ANTIDOTAL	ANTIMASKS	ANTIPYIC
ANTETYPE	ANTIAR	ANTIDOTE	ANTIMEN	ANTIPYICS
ANTETYPES	ANTIARIN	ANTIDOTED	ANTIMERE	ANTIQUARK
ANTEVERT	ANTIARINS	ANTIDOTES	ANTIMERES	ANTIQUARY
ANTEVERTS	ANTIARMOR	ANTIDRAFT	ANTIMERIC	ANTIQUATE
ANTHELIA	ANTIARS	ANTIDRUG	ANTIMINE	ANTIQUE
ANTHELION	ANTIATOM	ANTIDUNE	ANTIMONIC	ANTIQUED
ANTHELIX	ANTIATOMS	ANTIDUNES	ANTIMONY	ANTIQUELY
ANTHEM	ANTIAUXIN	ANTIELITE	ANTIMONYL	ANTIQUER
ANTHEMED	ANTIBIAS	ANTIENT	ANTIMUON	ANTIQUERS
ANTHEMIA	ANTIBLACK	ANTIENTS	ANTIMUONS	ANTIQUES
ANTHEMIC	ANTIBODY	ANTIFAT	ANTIMUSIC	ANTIQUEY
ANTHEMING	ANTIBOSS	ANTIFLU	ANTIMYCIN	ANTIQUING
ANTHEMION	ANTIBUG	ANTIFOAM	ANTING	ANTIQUITY
ANTHEMIS	ANTIBUSER	ANTIFOG	ANTINGS	ANTIRADAR
ANTHEMS	ANTIC	ANTIFRAUD	ANTINODAL	ANTIRAPE
ANTHER	ANTICAL	ANTIFUR	ANTINODE	ANTIRED
ANTHERAL	ANTICALLY	ANTIGANG	ANTINODES	ANTIRIOT
ANTHERID	ANTICAR	ANTIGAY	ANTINOISE	ANTIROCK
ANTHERIDS	ANTICHLOR	ANTIGEN	ANTINOME	ANTIROLL
ANTHERS	ANTICISE	ANTIGENE	ANTINOMES	ANTIROYAL
ANTHESES	ANTICISED	ANTIGENES	ANTINOMIC	ANTIRUST
ANTHESIS	ANTICISES	ANTIGENIC	ANTINOMY	ANTIRUSTS
ANTHILL	ANTICITY	ANTIGENS	ANTINOVEL	ANTIS
ANTHILLS	ANTICIVIC	ANTIGLARE	ANTINUKE	ANTISAG
ANTHOCARP	ANTICIZE	ANTIGRAFT	ANTINUKER	ANTISCIAN
ANTHOCYAN	ANTICIZED	ANTIGUN	ANTINUKES	ANTISENSE
ANTHODIA	ANTICIZES	ANTIHELIX	ANTIPAPAL	ANTISERA
ANTHODIUM	ANTICK	ANTIHERO	ANTIPARTY	ANTISERUM
ANTHOID	ANTICKE	ANTIHUMAN	ANTIPASTI	ANTISEX
ANTHOLOGY	ANTICKED	ANTIJAM	ANTIPASTO	ANTISHAKE
ANTHOTAXY	ANTICKES	ANTIKING	ANTIPATHY	ANTISHARK
ANTHOZOAN	ANTICKING	ANTIKINGS	ANTIPHON	ANTISHIP
ANTHOZOIC	ANTICKS	ANTIKNOCK	ANTIPHONS	ANTISHOCK
ANTHRACES	ANTICLINE	ANTILABOR	ANTIPHONY	ANTISKID
ANTHRACIC	ANTICLING	ANTILEAK	ANTIPILL	ANTISLEEP
ANTHRAX	ANTICLY	ANTILEFT	ANTIPODAL	ANTISLIP
ANTHRAXES	ANTICODON	ANTILIFE	ANTIPODE	ANTISMOG
ANTHRO	ANTICOLD	ANTILIFER	ANTIPODES	ANTISMOKE
ANTHROPIC	ANTICOUS	ANTILOCK	ANTIPOLAR	ANTISMUT

ANTISNOB	ANTLIONS	ANYBODIES	APARTHEID	APERY
ANTISNOBS	ANTONYM	ANYBODY	APARTMENT	APES
ANTISOLAR	ANTONYMIC	ANYHOW	APARTNESS	APESHIT
ANTISPAM	ANTONYMS	ANYMORE	APATETIC	APETALIES
ANTISPAST	ANTONYMY	ANYON	APATHATON	APETALOUS
ANTISTAT	ANTPITTA	ANYONE	APATHETIC	APETALY
ANTISTATE	ANTPITTAS	ANYONES	APATHIES	APEX
ANTISTATS	ANTRA	ANYONS	APATHY	APEXES
ANTISTICK	ANTRAL	ANYPLACE	APATITE	APGAR
ANTISTORY	ANTRE	ANYROAD	APATITES	APHAGIA
ANTISTYLE	ANTRES	ANYTHING	APATOSAUR	APHAGIAS
ANTITANK	ANTRORSE	ANYTHINGS	APAY	APHAKIA
ANTITAX	ANTRUM	ANYTIME	APAYD	APHAKIAS
ANTITHEFT	ANTRUMS	ANYWAY	APAYING	APHANITE
ANTITHET	ANTS	ANYWAYS	APAYS	APHANITES
ANTITHETS	ANTSIER	ANYWHEN	APE	APHANITIC
ANTITOXIC	ANTSIEST	ANYWHERE	APEAK	APHASIA
ANTITOXIN	ANTSINESS	ANYWHERES	APED	APHASIAC
ANTITRADE	ANTSY	ANYWISE	APEDOM	APHASIACS
ANTITRAGI	ANTWACKIE	ANZIANI	APEDOMS	APHASIAS
ANTITRUST	ANUCLEATE	AORIST	APEEK	APHASIC
ANTITUMOR	ANURA	AORISTIC	APEHOOD	APHASICS
ANTITYPAL	ANURAL	AORISTS	APEHOODS	APHELIA
ANTITYPE	ANURAN	AORTA	APELIKE	APHELIAN
ANTITYPES	ANURANS	AORTAE	APEMAN	APHELION
ANTITYPIC	ANURESES	AORTAL	APEMEN	APHELIONS
ANTIULCER	ANURESIS	AORTAS	APEPSIA	APHERESES
ANTIUNION	ANURETIC	AORTIC	APEPSIAS	APHERESIS
ANTIURBAN	ANURIA	AORTITIS	APEPSIES	APHERETIC
ANTIVENIN	ANURIAS	AOUDAD	APEPSY	APHESES
ANTIVENOM	ANURIC	AOUDADS	APER	APHESIS
ANTIVIRAL	ANUROUS	APACE	APERCU	APHETIC
ANTIVIRUS	ANUS	APACHE	APERCUS	APHETISE
ANTIWAR	ANUSES	APACHES	APERIENT	APHETISED
ANTIWEAR	ANVIL	APADANA	APERIENTS	APHETISES
ANTIWEED	ANVILED	APADANAS	APERIES	APHETIZE
ANTIWHITE	ANVILING	APAGE	APERIODIC	APHETIZED
ANTIWOMAN	ANVILLED	APAGOGE	APERITIF	APHETIZES
ANTIWORLD	ANVILLING	APAGOGES	APERITIFS	APHICIDE
ANTLER	ANVILS	APAGOGIC	APERITIVE	APHICIDES
ANTLERED	ANVILTOP	APAID	APERS	APHID
ANTLERS	ANVILTOPS	APANAGE	APERT	APHIDES
ANTLIA	ANXIETIES	APANAGED	APERTNESS	APHIDIAN
ANTLIAE	ANXIETY	APANAGES	APERTURAL	APHIDIANS
ANTLIATE	ANXIOUS	APAREJO	APERTURE	APHIDIOUS
ANTLIKE	ANXIOUSLY	APAREJOS	APERTURED	APHIDS
ANTLION	ANY	APART	APERTURES	APHIS

APHOLATE	APIMANIA	APOCOPIC	APOOP	APOZEMS
APHOLATES	APIMANIAS	APOCRINE	APOPHASES	APP
APHONIA	APING	APOCRYPHA	APOPHASIS	APPAID
APHONIAS	APIOL	APOD	APOPHATIC	APPAIR
APHONIC	APIOLOGY	APODAL	APOPHONY	APPAIRED
APHONICS	APIOLS	APODE	APOPHYGE	APPAIRING
APHONIES	APISH	APODES	APOPHYGES	APPAIRS
APHONOUS	APISHLY	APODICTIC	APOPHYSES	APPAL
APHONY	APISHNESS	APODOSES	APOPHYSIS	APPALL
APHORISE	APISM	APODOSIS	APOPLAST	APPALLED
APHORISED	APISMS	APODOUS	APOPLASTS	APPALLING
APHORISER	APIVOROUS	APODS	APOPLEX	APPALLS
APHORISES	APLANAT	APOENZYME	APOPLEXED	APPALOOSA
APHORISM	APLANATIC	APOGAEIC	APOPLEXES	APPALS
APHORISMS	APLANATS	APOGAMIC	APOPLEXY	APPALTI
APHORIST	APLANETIC	APOGAMIES	APOPTOSES	APPALTO
APHORISTS	APLASIA	APOGAMOUS	APOPTOSIS	APPANAGE
APHORIZE	APLASIAS	APOGAMY	APOPTOTIC	APPANAGED
APHORIZED	APLASTIC	APOGEAL	APORETIC	APPANAGES
APHORIZER	APLENTY	APOGEAN	APORIA	APPARAT
APHORIZES	APLITE	APOGEE	APORIAS	APPARATS
APHOTIC	APLITES	APOGEES	APORT	APPARATUS
APHRODITE	APLITIC	APOGEIC	APOS	APPAREL
APHTHA	APLOMB	APOGRAPH	APOSITIA	APPARELED
APHTHAE	APLOMBS	APOGRAPHS	APOSITIAS	APPARELS
APHTHOUS	APLUSTRE	APOLLO	APOSITIC	APPARENCY
APHYLLIES	APLUSTRES	APOLLOS	APOSPORIC	APPARENT
APHYLLOUS	APNEA	APOLOG	APOSPORY	APPARENTS
APHYLLY	APNEAL	APOLOGAL	APOSTACY	APPARITOR
APIACEOUS	APNEAS	APOLOGIA	APOSTASY	APPAY
APIAN	APNEIC	APOLOGIAE	APOSTATE	APPAYD
APIARIAN	APNEUSES	APOLOGIAS	APOSTATES	APPAYING
APIARIANS	APNEUSIS	APOLOGIES	APOSTATIC	APPAYS
APIARIES	APNEUSTIC	APOLOGISE	APOSTIL	APPEACH
APIARIST	APNOEA	APOLOGIST	APOSTILLE	APPEACHED
APIARISTS	APNOEAL	APOLOGIZE	APOSTILS	APPEACHES
APIARY	APNOEAS	APOLOGS	APOSTLE	APPEAL
APICAL	APNOEIC	APOLOGUE	APOSTLES	APPEALED
APICALLY	APO	APOLOGUES	APOSTOLIC	APPEALER
APICALS	APOAPSES	APOLOGY	APOTHECE	APPEALERS
APICES	APOAPSIS	APOLUNE	APOTHECES	APPEALING
APICIAN	APOCARP	APOLUNES	APOTHECIA	APPEALS
APICULATE	APOCARPS	APOMICT	APOTHEGM	APPEAR
APICULI	APOCARPY	APOMICTIC	APOTHEGMS	APPEARED
APICULUS	APOCOPATE	APOMICTS	APOTHEM	APPEARER
APIECE	APOCOPE	APOMIXES	APOTHEMS	APPEARERS
APIEZON	APOCOPES	APOMIXIS	APOZEM	APPEARING

APPEARS	APPLAUDS	APPRAISES	APRICATE	APTNESS
APPEASE	APPLAUSE	APPREHEND	APRICATED	APTNESSES
APPEASED	APPLAUSES	APPRESS	APRICATES	APTOTE
APPEASER	APPLE	APPRESSED	APRICOCK	APTOTES
APPEASERS	APPLECART	APPRESSES	APRICOCKS	APTOTIC
APPEASES	APPLEJACK	APPRISE	APRICOT	APTS
APPEASING	APPLES	APPRISED	APRICOTS	APYRASE
APPEL	APPLET	APPRISER	APRIORISM	APYRASES
APPELLANT	APPLETINI	APPRISERS	APRIORIST	APYRETIC
APPELLATE	APPLETS	APPRISES	APRIORITY	APYREXIA
APPELLEE	APPLEY	APPRISING	APRON	APYREXIAS
APPELLEES	APPLIABLE	APPRIZE	APRONED	AQUA
APPELLOR	APPLIANCE	APPRIZED	APRONFUL	AQUABATIC
APPELLORS	APPLICANT	APPRIZER	APRONFULS	AQUABOARD
APPELS	APPLICATE	APPRIZERS	APRONING	AQUACADE
APPEND	APPLIED	APPRIZES	APRONLIKE	AQUACADES
APPENDAGE	APPLIER	APPRIZING	APRONS	AQUADROME
APPENDANT	APPLIERS	APPRO	APROPOS	AQUAE
APPENDED	APPLIES	APPROACH	APROTIC	AQUAFARM
APPENDENT	APPLIEST	APPROBATE	APSARAS	AQUAFARMS
APPENDING	APPLIQUE	APPROOF	APSARASES	AQUAFER
APPENDIX	APPLIQUED	APPROOFS	APSE	AQUAFERS
APPENDS	APPLIQUES	APPROS	APSES	AQUAFIT
APPERIL	APPLY	APPROVAL	APSIDAL	AQUAFITS
APPERILL	APPLYING	APPROVALS	APSIDES	AQUALUNG
APPERILLS	APPOINT	APPROVE	APSIDIOLE	AQUALUNGS
APPERILS	APPOINTED	APPROVED	APSIS	AQUANAUT
APPERTAIN	APPOINTEE	APPROVER	APSO	AQUANAUTS
APPESTAT	APPOINTER	APPROVERS	APSOS	AQUAPHOBE
APPESTATS	APPOINTOR	APPROVES	APT	AQUAPLANE
APPETENCE	APPOINTS	APPROVING	APTAMER	AQUAPORIN
APPETENCY	APPORT	APPS	APTAMERS	AQUARELLE
APPETENT	APPORTION	APPUI	APTED	AQUARIA
APPETIBLE	APPORTS	APPUIED	APTER	AQUARIAL
APPETISE	APPOSABLE	APPUIS	APTERAL	AQUARIAN
APPETISED	APPOSE	APPULSE	APTERIA	AQUARIANS
APPETISER	APPOSED	APPULSES	APTERISM	AQUARIIST
APPETISES	APPOSER	APPULSIVE	APTERISMS	AQUARIST
APPETITE	APPOSERS	APPUY	APTERIUM	AQUARISTS
APPETITES	APPOSES	APPUYED	APTEROUS	AQUARIUM
APPETIZE	APPOSING	APPUYING	APTERYX	AQUARIUMS
APPETIZED	APPOSITE	APPUYS	APTERYXES	AQUAROBIC
APPETIZER	APPRAISAL	APRACTIC	APTEST	AQUAS
APPETIZES	APPRAISE	APRAXIA	APTING	AQUASCAPE
APPLAUD	APPRAISED	APRAXIAS	APTITUDE	AQUASHOW
APPLAUDED	APPRAISEE	APRAXIC	APTITUDES	AQUASHOWS
APPLAUDER	APPRAISER	APRES	APTLY	AQUATIC

AQUATICS	ARACEOUS	ARBITER	ARCADED	ARCHDUKES
AQUATINT	ARACHIS	ARBITERS	ARCADES	ARCHEAN
AQUATINTA	ARACHISES	ARBITRAGE	ARCADIA	ARCHED
AQUATINTS	ARACHNID	ARBITRAL	ARCADIAN	ARCHEI
AQUATONE	ARACHNIDS	ARBITRARY	ARCADIANS	ARCHENEMY
AQUATONES	ARACHNOID	ARBITRATE	ARCADIAS	ARCHER
AQUAVIT	ARAGONITE	ARBITRESS	ARCADING	ARCHERESS
AQUAVITS	ARAISE	ARBITRIUM	ARCADINGS	ARCHERIES
AQUEDUCT	ARAISED	ARBLAST	ARCANA	ARCHERS
AQUEDUCTS	ARAISES	ARBLASTER	ARCANAS	ARCHERY
AQUEOUS	ARAISING	ARBLASTS	ARCANE	ARCHES
AQUEOUSLY	ARAK	ARBOR	ARCANELY	ARCHEST
AQUIFER	ARAKS	ARBOREAL	ARCANIST	ARCHETYPE
AQUIFERS	ARALIA	ARBORED	ARCANISTS	ARCHEUS
AQUILEGIA	ARALIAS	ARBOREOUS	ARCANUM	ARCHFIEND
AQUILINE	ARAME	ARBORES	ARCANUMS	ARCHFOE
AQUILON	ARAMES	ARBORET	ARCATURE	ARCHFOES
AQUILONS	ARAMID	ARBORETA	ARCATURES	ARCHI
AQUIVER	ARAMIDS	ARBORETS	ARCCOSINE	ARCHICARP
AR	ARANEID	ARBORETUM	ARCED	ARCHIL
ARAARA	ARANEIDAN	ARBORIO	ARCH	ARCHILOWE
ARAARAS	ARANEIDS	ARBORIOS	ARCHAEA	ARCHILS
ARABA	ARANEOUS	ARBORISE	ARCHAEAL	ARCHIMAGE
ARABAS	ARAPAIMA	ARBORISED	ARCHAEAN	ARCHINE
ARABESK	ARAPAIMAS	ARBORISES	ARCHAEANS	ARCHINES
ARABESKS	ARAPONGA	ARBORIST	ARCHAEI	ARCHING
ARABESQUE	ARAPONGAS	ARBORISTS	ARCHAEON	ARCHINGS
ARABIC	ARAPUNGA	ARBORIZE	ARCHAEUS	ARCHITECT
ARABICA	ARAPUNGAS	ARBORIZED	ARCHAIC	ARCHITYPE
ARABICAS	ARAR	ARBORIZES	ARCHAICAL	ARCHIVAL
ARABICISE	ARAROBA	ARBOROUS	ARCHAISE	ARCHIVE
ARABICIZE	ARAROBAS	ARBORS	ARCHAISED	ARCHIVED
ARABILITY	ARARS	ARBOUR	ARCHAISER	ARCHIVES
ARABIN	ARAUCARIA	ARBOURED	ARCHAISES	ARCHIVING
ARABINOSE	ARAYSE	ARBOURS	ARCHAISM	ARCHIVIST
ARABINS	ARAYSED	ARBOVIRAL	ARCHAISMS	ARCHIVOLT
ARABIS	ARAYSES	ARBOVIRUS	ARCHAIST	ARCHLET
ARABISE	ARAYSING	ARBS	ARCHAISTS	ARCHLETS
ARABISED	ARB	ARBUSCLE	ARCHAIZE	ARCHLUTE
ARABISES	ARBA	ARBUSCLES	ARCHAIZED	ARCHLUTES
ARABISING	ARBALEST	ARBUTE	ARCHAIZER	ARCHLY
ARABIZE	ARBALESTS	ARBUTEAN	ARCHAIZES	ARCHNESS
ARABIZED	ARBALIST	ARBUTES	ARCHANGEL	ARCHOLOGY
ARABIZES	ARBALISTS	ARBUTUS	ARCHDRUID	ARCHON
ARABIZING	ARBAS	ARBUTUSES	ARCHDUCAL	ARCHONS
ARABLE	ARBELEST	ARC	ARCHDUCHY	ARCHONTIC
ARABLES	ARBELESTS	ARCADE	ARCHDUKE	ARCHOSAUR

ARCHRIVAL	ARDRI	ARENOUS	ARGENTOUS	ARGUMENT
ARCHSTONE	ARDRIGH	AREOLA	ARGENTS	ARGUMENTA
ARCHWAY	ARDRIGHS	AREOLAE	ARGENTUM	ARGUMENTS
ARCHWAYS	ARDRIS	AREOLAR	ARGENTUMS	ARGUS
ARCHWISE	ARDS	AREOLAS	ARGH	ARGUSES
ARCIFORM	ARDUOUS	AREOLATE	ARGHAN	ARGUTE
ARCING	ARDUOUSLY	AREOLATED	ARGHANS	ARGUTELY
ARCINGS	ARE	AREOLE	ARGIL	ARGYLE
ARCKED	AREA	AREOLES	ARGILLITE	ARGYLES
ARCKING	AREACH	AREOLOGY	ARGILS	ARGYLL
ARCKINGS	AREACHED	AREOMETER	ARGINASE	ARGYLLS
ARCMIN	AREACHES	AREOMETRY	ARGINASES	ARGYRIA
ARCMINS	AREACHING	AREOSTYLE	ARGININE	ARGYRIAS
ARCMINUTE	AREAD	AREPA	ARGININES	ARGYRITE
ARCO	AREADING	AREPAS	ARGLE	ARGYRITES
ARCOGRAPH	AREADS	ARERE	ARGLED	ARHAT
ARCOLOGY	AREAE	ARES	ARGLES	ARHATS
ARCOS	AREAL	ARET	ARGLING	ARHATSHIP
ARCS	AREALLY	ARETE	ARGOL	ARHYTHMIA
ARCSEC	AREAR	ARETES	ARGOLS	ARHYTHMIC
ARCSECOND	AREARS	ARETHUSA	ARGON	ARIA
ARCSECS	AREAS	ARETHUSAS	ARGONAUT	ARIARIES
ARCSINE	AREAWAY	ARETS	ARGONAUTS	ARIARY
ARCSINES	AREAWAYS	ARETT	ARGONON	ARIAS
ARCTIC	ARECA	ARETTED	ARGONONS	ARID
ARCTICS	ARECAS	ARETTING	ARGONS	ARIDER
ARCTIID	ARECOLINE	ARETTS	ARGOSIES	ARIDEST
ARCTIIDS	ARED	AREW	ARGOSY	ARIDITIES
ARCTOID	AREDD	ARF	ARGOT	ARIDITY
ARCTOPHIL	AREDE	ARFS	ARGOTIC	ARIDLY
ARCUATE	AREDES	ARGAL	ARGOTS	ARIDNESS
ARCUATED	AREDING	ARGALA	ARGUABLE	ARIEL
ARCUATELY	AREFIED	ARGALAS	ARGUABLY	ARIELS
ARCUATION	AREFIES	ARGALI	ARGUE	ARIETTA
ARCUS	AREFY	ARGALIS	ARGUED	ARIETTAS
ARCUSES	AREFYING	ARGALS	ARGUER	ARIETTE
ARD	AREG	ARGAN	ARGUERS	ARIETTES
ARDEB	AREIC	ARGAND	ARGUES	ARIGHT
ARDEBS	ARENA	ARGANDS	ARGUFIED	ARIKI
ARDENCIES	ARENAS	ARGANS	ARGUFIER	ARIKIS
ARDENCY	ARENATION	ARGEMONE	ARGUFIERS	ARIL
ARDENT	ARENE	ARGEMONES	ARGUFIES	ARILED
ARDENTLY	ARENES	ARGENT	ARGUFY	ARILLARY
ARDOR	ARENITE	ARGENTAL	ARGUFYING	ARILLATE
ARDORS	ARENITES	ARGENTIC	ARGUING	ARILLATED
ARDOUR	ARENITIC	ARGENTINE	ARGULI	ARILLI
ARDOURS	ARENOSE	ARGENTITE	ARGULUS	ARILLODE

ARILLODES	ARMATURES	ARMOR	AROBAS	ARRAH
ARILLOID	ARMBAND	ARMORED	AROHA	ARRAIGN
ARILLUS	ARMBANDS	ARMORER	AROHAS	ARRAIGNED
ARILS	ARMCHAIR	ARMORERS	AROID	ARRAIGNER
ARIOSE	ARMCHAIRS	ARMORIAL	AROIDS	ARRAIGNS
ARIOSI	ARMED	ARMORIALS	AROINT	ARRANGE
ARIOSO	ARMER	ARMORIES	AROINTED	ARRANGED
ARIOSOS	ARMERIA	ARMORING	AROINTING	ARRANGER
ARIOT	ARMERIAS	ARMORIST	AROINTS	ARRANGERS
ARIPPLE	ARMERS	ARMORISTS	AROLLA	ARRANGES
ARIS	ARMET	ARMORLESS	AROLLAS	ARRANGING
ARISE	ARMETS	ARMORS	AROMA	ARRANT
ARISEN	ARMFUL	ARMORY	AROMAS	ARRANTLY
ARISES	ARMFULS	ARMOUR	AROMATASE	ARRAS
ARISH	ARMGAUNT	ARMOURED	AROMATIC	ARRASED
ARISHES	ARMGUARD	ARMOURER	AROMATICS	ARRASENE
ARISING	ARMGUARDS	ARMOURERS	AROMATISE	ARRASENES
ARISTA	ARMHOLE	ARMOURIES	AROMATIZE	ARRASES
ARISTAE	ARMHOLES	ARMOURING	AROSE	ARRAUGHT
ARISTAS	ARMIES	ARMOURS	AROUND	ARRAY
ARISTATE	ARMIGER	ARMOURY	AROUSABLE	ARRAYAL
ARISTO	ARMIGERAL	ARMOZEEN	AROUSAL	ARRAYALS
ARISTOS	ARMIGERO	ARMOZEENS	AROUSALS	ARRAYED
ARISTOTLE	ARMIGEROS	ARMOZINE	AROUSE	ARRAYER
ARK	ARMIGERS	ARMOZINES	AROUSED	ARRAYERS
ARKED	ARMIL	ARMPIT	AROUSER	ARRAYING
ARKING	ARMILLA	ARMPITS	AROUSERS	ARRAYMENT
ARKITE	ARMILLAE	ARMREST	AROUSES	ARRAYS
ARKITES	ARMILLARY	ARMRESTS	AROUSING	ARREAR
ARKOSE	ARMILLAS	ARMS	AROW	ARREARAGE
ARKOSES	ARMILS	ARMSFUL	AROYNT	ARREARS
ARKOSIC	ARMING	ARMURE	AROYNTED	ARRECT
ARKS	ARMINGS	ARMURES	AROYNTING	ARREEDE
ARLE	ARMISTICE	ARMY	AROYNTS	ARREEDES
ARLED	ARMLESS	ARMYWORM	ARPA	ARREEDING
ARLES	ARMLET	ARMYWORMS	ARPAS	ARREST
ARLING	ARMLETS	ARNA	ARPEGGIO	ARRESTANT
ARM	ARMLIKE	ARNAS	ARPEGGIOS	ARRESTED
ARMADA	ARMLOAD	ARNATTO	ARPEN	ARRESTEE
ARMADAS	ARMLOADS	ARNATTOS	ARPENS	ARRESTEES
ARMADILLO	ARMLOCK	ARNICA	ARPENT	ARRESTER
ARMAGNAC	ARMLOCKED	ARNICAS	ARPENTS	ARRESTERS
ARMAGNACS	ARMLOCKS	ARNOTTO	ARPILLERA	ARRESTING
ARMAMENT	ARMOIRE	ARNOTTOS	ARQUEBUS	ARRESTIVE
ARMAMENTS	ARMOIRES	ARNUT	ARRACACHA	ARRESTOR
ARMATURE	ARMONICA	ARNUTS	ARRACK	ARRESTORS
ARMATURED	ARMONICAS	AROBA	ARRACKS	ARRESTS

ARRET	ARROWWOOD	ARSONITES	ARTILLERY	ARYBALLOS
ARRETS	ARROWWORM	ARSONOUS	ARTILY	ARYL
ARRHIZAL	ARROWY	ARSONS	ARTINESS	ARYLS
ARRIAGE	ARROYO	ARSY	ARTIS	ARYTENOID
ARRIAGES	ARROYOS	ART	ARTISAN	ARYTHMIA
ARRIBA	ARROZ	ARTAL	ARTISANAL	ARYTHMIAS
ARRIDE	ARROZES	ARTEFACT	ARTISANS	ARYTHMIC
ARRIDED	ARS	ARTEFACTS	ARTIST	AS
ARRIDES	ARSE	ARTEL	ARTISTE	ASAFETIDA
ARRIDING	ARSED	ARTELS	ARTISTES	ASANA
ARRIERE	ARSEHOLE	ARTEMISIA	ARTISTIC	ASANAS
ARRIERO	ARSEHOLED	ARTERIAL	ARTISTRY	ASAR
ARRIEROS	ARSEHOLES	ARTERIALS	ARTISTS	ASARUM
ARRIS	ARSENAL	ARTERIES	ARTLESS	ASARUMS
ARRISES	ARSENALS	ARTERIOLE	ARTLESSLY	ASBESTIC
ARRISH	ARSENATE	ARTERITIS	ARTMAKER	ASBESTINE
ARRISHES	ARSENATES	ARTERY	ARTMAKERS	ASBESTOS
ARRIVAL	ARSENIATE	ARTESIAN	ARTS	ASBESTOUS
ARRIVALS	ARSENIC	ARTFUL	ARTSIE	ASBESTUS
ARRIVANCE	ARSENICAL	ARTFULLY	ARTSIER	ASCARED
ARRIVANCY	ARSENICS	ARTHOUSE	ARTSIES	ASCARID
ARRIVE	ARSENIDE	ARTHOUSES	ARTSIEST	ASCARIDES
ARRIVED	ARSENIDES	ARTHRITIC	ARTSINESS	ASCARIDS
ARRIVER	ARSENIOUS	ARTHRITIS	ARTSMAN	ASCARIS
ARRIVERS	ARSENITE	ARTHRODIA	ARTSMEN	ASCARISES
ARRIVES	ARSENITES	ARTHROPOD	ARTSY	ASCAUNT
ARRIVING	ARSENO	ARTHROSES	ARTWORK	ASCEND
ARRIVISME	ARSENOUS	ARTHROSIS	ARTWORKS	ASCENDANT
ARRIVISTE	ARSES	ARTI	ARTY	ASCENDED
ARROBA	ARSEY	ARTIC	ARUGOLA	ASCENDENT
ARROBAS	ARSHEEN	ARTICHOKE	ARUGOLAS	ASCENDER
ARROCES	ARSHEENS	ARTICLE	ARUGULA	ASCENDERS
ARROGANCE	ARSHIN	ARTICLED	ARUGULAS	ASCENDEUR
ARROGANCY	ARSHINE	ARTICLES	ARUHE	ASCENDING
ARROGANT	ARSHINES	ARTICLING	ARUHES	ASCENDS
ARROGATE	ARSHINS	ARTICS	ARUM	ASCENSION
ARROGATED	ARSIER	ARTICULAR	ARUMS	ASCENSIVE
ARROGATES	ARSIEST	ARTIER	ARUSPEX	ASCENT
ARROGATOR	ARSINE	ARTIES	ARUSPICES	ASCENTS
ARROW	ARSINES	ARTIEST	ARVAL	ASCERTAIN
ARROWED	ARSING	ARTIFACT	ARVEE	ASCESES
ARROWHEAD	ARSINO	ARTIFACTS	ARVEES	ASCESIS
ARROWING	ARSIS	ARTIFICE	ARVICOLE	ASCETIC
ARROWLESS	ARSON	ARTIFICER	ARVICOLES	ASCETICAL
ARROWLIKE	ARSONIST	ARTIFICES	ARVO	ASCETICS
ARROWROOT	ARSONISTS	ARTIGI	ARVOS	ASCI
ARROWS	ARSONITE	ARTIGIS	ARY	ASCIAN

ASCIANS	ASHAMEDLY	ASHTANGAS	ASOCIAL	ASPHALTS
ASCIDIA	ASHAMES	ASHTRAY	ASOCIALS	ASPHALTUM
ASCIDIAN	ASHAMING	ASHTRAYS	ASP	ASPHERIC
ASCIDIANS	ASHCAKE	ASHY	ASPARAGUS	ASPHERICS
ASCIDIATE	ASHCAKES	ASIAGO	ASPARKLE	ASPHODEL
ASCIDIUM	ASHCAN	ASIAGOS	ASPARTAME	ASPHODELS
ASCITES	ASHCANS	ASIDE	ASPARTATE	ASPHYXIA
ASCITIC	ASHED	ASIDES	ASPARTIC	ASPHYXIAL
ASCITICAL	ASHEN	ASINICO	ASPECT	ASPHYXIAS
ASCLEPIAD	ASHERIES	ASINICOS	ASPECTED	ASPHYXIES
ASCLEPIAS	ASHERY	ASININE	ASPECTING	ASPHYXY
ASCOCARP	ASHES	ASININELY	ASPECTS	ASPIC
ASCOCARPS	ASHET	ASININITY	ASPECTUAL	ASPICK
ASCOGONIA	ASHETS	ASK	ASPEN	ASPICKS
ASCON	ASHFALL	ASKANCE	ASPENS	ASPICS
ASCONCE	ASHFALLS	ASKANCED	ASPER	ASPIDIA
ASCONOID	ASHIER	ASKANCES	ASPERATE	ASPIDIOID
ASCONS	ASHIEST	ASKANCING	ASPERATED	ASPIDIUM
ASCORBATE	ASHINE	ASKANT	ASPERATES	ASPINE
ASCORBIC	ASHINESS	ASKANTED	ASPERGE	ASPINES
ASCOSPORE	ASHING	ASKANTING	ASPERGED	ASPIRANT
ASCOT	ASHIVER	ASKANTS	ASPERGER	ASPIRANTS
ASCOTS	ASHKEY	ASKARI	ASPERGERS	ASPIRATA
ASCRIBE	ASHKEYS	ASKARIS	ASPERGES	ASPIRATAE
ASCRIBED	ASHLAR	ASKED	ASPERGILL	ASPIRATE
ASCRIBES	ASHLARED	ASKER	ASPERGING	ASPIRATED
ASCRIBING	ASHLARING	ASKERS	ASPERITY	ASPIRATES
ASCUS	ASHLARS	ASKESES	ASPERMIA	ASPIRATOR
ASDIC	ASHLER	ASKESIS	ASPERMIAS	ASPIRE
ASDICS	ASHLERED	ASKEW	ASPEROUS	ASPIRED
ASEA	ASHLERING	ASKEWNESS	ASPERS	ASPIRER
ASEISMIC	ASHLERS	ASKING	ASPERSE	ASPIRERS
ASEITIES	ASHLESS	ASKINGS	ASPERSED	ASPIRES
ASEITY	ASHMAN	ASKLENT	ASPERSER	ASPIRIN
ASEMANTIC	ASHMEN	ASKOI	ASPERSERS	ASPIRING
ASEPALOUS	ASHORE	ASKOS	ASPERSES	ASPIRINS
ASEPSES	ASHPAN	ASKS	ASPERSING	ASPIS
ASEPSIS	ASHPANS	ASLAKE	ASPERSION	ASPISES
ASEPTATE	ASHPLANT	ASLAKED	ASPERSIVE	ASPISH
ASEPTIC	ASHPLANTS	ASLAKES	ASPERSOIR	ASPLENIUM
ASEPTICS	ASHRAF	ASLAKING	ASPERSOR	ASPORT
ASEXUAL	ASHRAM	ASLANT	ASPERSORS	ASPORTED
ASEXUALLY	ASHRAMA	ASLEEP	ASPERSORY	ASPORTING
ASH	ASHRAMAS	ASLOPE	ASPHALT	ASPORTS
ASHAKE	ASHRAMITE	ASLOSH	ASPHALTED	ASPOUT
ASHAME	ASHRAMS	ASMEAR	ASPHALTER	ASPRAWL
ASHAMED	ASHTANGA	ASMOULDER	ASPHALTIC	ASPREAD

ASPRO	ASSEMBLED	ASSIENTOS	ASSORTIVE	ASTANGAS
ASPROS	ASSEMBLER	ASSIGN	ASSORTS	ASTARE
ASPROUT	ASSEMBLES	ASSIGNAT	ASSOT	ASTART
ASPS	ASSEMBLY	ASSIGNATS	ASSOTS	ASTARTED
ASQUAT	ASSENT	ASSIGNED	ASSOTT	ASTARTING
ASQUINT	ASSENTED	ASSIGNEE	ASSOTTED	ASTARTS
ASRAMA	ASSENTER	ASSIGNEES	ASSOTTING	ASTASIA
ASRAMAS	ASSENTERS	ASSIGNER	ASSUAGE	ASTASIAS
ASS	ASSENTING	ASSIGNERS	ASSUAGED	ASTATIC
ASSAGAI	ASSENTIVE	ASSIGNING	ASSUAGER	ASTATIDE
ASSAGAIED	ASSENTOR	ASSIGNOR	ASSUAGERS	ASTATIDES
ASSAGAIS	ASSENTORS	ASSIGNORS	ASSUAGES	ASTATINE
ASSAI	ASSENTS	ASSIGNS	ASSUAGING	ASTATINES
ASSAIL	ASSERT	ASSIST	ASSUASIVE	ASTATKI
ASSAILANT	ASSERTED	ASSISTANT	ASSUETUDE	ASTATKIS
ASSAILED	ASSERTER	ASSISTED	ASSUMABLE	ASTEISM
ASSAILER	ASSERTERS	ASSISTER	ASSUMABLY	ASTEISMS
ASSAILERS	ASSERTING	ASSISTERS	ASSUME	ASTELIC
ASSAILING	ASSERTION	ASSISTING	ASSUMED	ASTELIES
ASSAILS	ASSERTIVE	ASSISTIVE	ASSUMEDLY	ASTELY
ASSAIS	ASSERTOR	ASSISTOR	ASSUMER	ASTER
ASSAM	ASSERTORS	ASSISTORS	ASSUMERS	ASTERIA
ASSAMS	ASSERTORY	ASSISTS	ASSUMES	ASTERIAS
ASSART	ASSERTS	ASSIZE	ASSUMING	ASTERID
ASSARTED	ASSES	ASSIZED	ASSUMINGS	ASTERIDS
ASSARTING	ASSESS	ASSIZER	ASSUMPSIT	ASTERISK
ASSARTS	ASSESSED	ASSIZERS	ASSURABLE	ASTERISKS
ASSASSIN	ASSESSES	ASSIZES	ASSURANCE	ASTERISM
ASSASSINS	ASSESSING	ASSIZING	ASSURE	ASTERISMS
ASSAULT	ASSESSOR	ASSLIKE	ASSURED	ASTERN
ASSAULTED	ASSESSORS	ASSOCIATE	ASSUREDLY	ASTERNAL
ASSAULTER	ASSET	ASSOIL	ASSUREDS	ASTEROID
ASSAULTS	ASSETLESS	ASSOILED	ASSURER	ASTEROIDS
ASSAY	ASSETS	ASSOILING	ASSURERS	ASTERS
ASSAYABLE	ASSEVER	ASSOILS	ASSURES	ASTERT
ASSAYED	ASSEVERED	ASSOILZIE	ASSURGENT	ASTERTED
ASSAYER	ASSEVERS	ASSONANCE	ASSURING	ASTERTING
ASSAYERS	ASSEZ	ASSONANT	ASSUROR	ASTERTS
ASSAYING	ASSHOLE	ASSONANTS	ASSURORS	ASTHANGA
ASSAYINGS	ASSHOLES	ASSONATE	ASSWAGE	ASTHANGAS
ASSAYS	ASSIDUITY	ASSONATED	ASSWAGED	ASTHENIA
ASSEGAAI	ASSIDUOUS	ASSONATES	ASSWAGES	ASTHENIAS
ASSEGAAIS	ASSIEGE	ASSORT	ASSWAGING	ASTHENIC
ASSEGAI	ASSIEGED	ASSORTED	ASSWIPE	ASTHENICS
ASSEGAIED	ASSIEGES	ASSORTER	ASSWIPES	ASTHENIES
ASSEGAIS	ASSIEGING	ASSORTERS	ASTABLE	ASTHENY
ASSEMBLE	ASSIENTO	ASSORTING	ASTANGA	ASTHMA

ASTHMAS	ASTROFELL	ASYSTOLIC	ATCHIEVES	ATHETISE
ASTHMATIC	ASTROID	AT	ATE	ATHETISED
ASTHORE	ASTROIDS	ATAATA	ATEBRIN	ATHETISES
ASTHORES	ASTROLABE	ATAATAS	ATEBRINS	ATHETIZE
ASTICHOUS	ASTROLOGY	ATABAL	ATECHNIC	ATHETIZED
ASTIGMIA	ASTRONAUT	ATABALS	ATECHNICS	ATHETIZES
ASTIGMIAS	ASTRONOMY	ATABEG	ATELIC	ATHETOID
ASTILBE	ASTROPHEL	ATABEGS	ATELIER	ATHETOSES
ASTILBES	ASTRUT	ATABEK	ATELIERS	ATHETOSIC
ASTIR	ASTUCIOUS	ATABEKS	ATEMOYA	ATHETOSIS
ASTOMATAL	ASTUCITY	ATABRIN	ATEMOYAS	ATHETOTIC
ASTOMOUS	ASTUN	ATABRINE	ATEMPORAL	ATHIRST
ASTONE	ASTUNNED	ATABRINES	ATENOLOL	ATHLETA
ASTONED	ASTUNNING	ATABRINS	ATENOLOLS	ATHLETAS
ASTONES	ASTUNS	ATACAMITE	ATES	ATHLETE
ASTONIED	ASTUTE	ATACTIC	ATHAME	ATHLETES
ASTONIES	ASTUTELY	ATAGHAN	ATHAMES	ATHLETIC
ASTONING	ASTUTER	ATAGHANS	ATHANASY	ATHLETICS
ASTONISH	ASTUTEST	ATALAYA	ATHANOR	ATHODYD
ASTONY	ASTYLAR	ATALAYAS	ATHANORS	ATHODYDS
ASTONYING	ASUDDEN	ATAMAN	ATHEISE	ATHRILL
ASTOOP	ASUNDER	ATAMANS	ATHEISED	ATHROB
ASTOUND	ASURA	ATAMASCO	ATHEISES	ATHROCYTE
ASTOUNDED	ASURAS	ATAMASCOS	ATHEISING	ATHWART
ASTOUNDS	ASWARM	ATAP	ATHEISM	ATIGI
ASTRACHAN	ASWAY	ATAPS	ATHEISMS	ATIGIS
ASTRADDLE	ASWIM	ATARACTIC	ATHEIST	ATILT
ASTRAGAL	ASWING	ATARAXIA	ATHEISTIC	ATIMIES
ASTRAGALI	ASWIRL	ATARAXIAS	ATHEISTS	ATIMY
ASTRAGALS	ASWOON	ATARAXIC	ATHEIZE	ATINGLE
ASTRAKHAN	ASYLA	ATARAXICS	ATHEIZED	ATISHOO
ASTRAL	ASYLEE	ATARAXIES	ATHEIZES	ATISHOOS
ASTRALLY	ASYLEES	ATARAXY	ATHEIZING	ATLANTES
ASTRALS	ASYLLABIC	ATAVIC	ATHELING	ATLAS
ASTRAND	ASYLUM	ATAVISM	ATHELINGS	ATLASES
ASTRANTIA	ASYLUMS	ATAVISMS	ATHEMATIC	ATLATL
ASTRAY	ASYMMETRY	ATAVIST	ATHENAEUM	ATLATLS
ASTRICT	ASYMPTOTE	ATAVISTIC	ATHENEUM	ATMA
ASTRICTED	ASYNAPSES	ATAVISTS	ATHENEUMS	ATMAN
ASTRICTS	ASYNAPSIS	ATAXIA	ATHEOLOGY	ATMANS
ASTRIDE	ASYNDETA	ATAXIAS	ATHEOUS	ATMAS
ASTRINGE	ASYNDETIC	ATAXIC	ATHERINE	ATMOLOGY
ASTRINGED	ASYNDETON	ATAXICS	ATHERINES	ATMOLYSE
ASTRINGER	ASYNERGIA	ATAXIES	ATHEROMA	ATMOLYSED
ASTRINGES	ASYNERGY	ATAXY	ATHEROMAS	ATMOLYSES
ASTROCYTE	ASYSTOLE	ATCHIEVE	ATHETESES	ATMOLYSIS
ASTRODOME	ASYSTOLES	ATCHIEVED	ATHETESIS	ATMOLYZE

ATMOLYZED	ATONALITY	ATROPINE	ATTEMPT	ATTIRING
ATMOLYZES	ATONALLY	ATROPINES	ATTEMPTED	ATTIRINGS
ATMOMETER	ATONE	ATROPINS	ATTEMPTER	ATTITUDE
ATMOMETRY	ATONEABLE	ATROPISM	ATTEMPTS	ATTITUDES
ATMOS	ATONED	ATROPISMS	ATTEND	ATTOLASER
ATMOSES	ATONEMENT	ATROPOUS	ATTENDANT	ATTOLLENS
ATOC	ATONER	ATS	ATTENDED	ATTOLLENT
ATOCIA	ATONERS	ATT	ATTENDEE	ATTONCE
ATOCIAS	ATONES	ATTABOY	ATTENDEES	ATTONE
ATOCS	ATONIA	ATTABOYS	ATTENDER	ATTONED
ATOK	ATONIAS	ATTACH	ATTENDERS	ATTONES
ATOKAL	ATONIC	ATTACHE	ATTENDING	ATTONING
ATOKE	ATONICITY	ATTACHED	ATTENDS	ATTORN
ATOKES	ATONICS	ATTACHER	ATTENT	ATTORNED
ATOKOUS	ATONIES	ATTACHERS	ATTENTAT	ATTORNEY
ATOKS	ATONING	ATTACHES	ATTENTATS	ATTORNEYS
ATOLL	ATONINGLY	ATTACHING	ATTENTION	ATTORNING
ATOLLS	ATONY	ATTACK	ATTENTIVE	ATTORNS
ATOM	ATOP	ATTACKED	ATTENTS	ATTRACT
ATOMIC	ATOPIC	ATTACKER	ATTENUANT	ATTRACTED
ATOMICAL	ATOPIES	ATTACKERS	ATTENUATE	ATTRACTER
ATOMICITY	ATOPY	ATTACKING	ATTERCOP	ATTRACTOR
ATOMICS	ATRAMENT	ATTACKMAN	ATTERCOPS	ATTRACTS
ATOMIES	ATRAMENTS	ATTACKMEN	ATTEST	ATTRAHENS
ATOMISE	ATRAZINE	ATTACKS	ATTESTANT	ATTRAHENT
ATOMISED	ATRAZINES	ATTAGIRL	ATTESTED	ATTRAP
ATOMISER	ATREMBLE	ATTAIN	ATTESTER	ATTRAPPED
ATOMISERS	ATRESIA	ATTAINDER	ATTESTERS	ATTRAPS
ATOMISES	ATRESIAS	ATTAINED	ATTESTING	ATTRIBUTE
ATOMISING	ATRESIC	ATTAINER	ATTESTOR	ATTRIST
ATOMISM	ATRETIC	ATTAINERS	ATTESTORS	ATTRISTED
ATOMISMS	ATRIA	ATTAINING	ATTESTS	ATTRISTS
ATOMIST	ATRIAL	ATTAINS	ATTIC	ATTRIT
ATOMISTIC	ATRIP	ATTAINT	ATTICISE	ATTRITE
ATOMISTS	ATRIUM	ATTAINTED	ATTICISED	ATTRITED
ATOMIZE	ATRIUMS	ATTAINTS	ATTICISES	ATTRITES
ATOMIZED	ATROCIOUS	ATTAP	ATTICISM	ATTRITING
ATOMIZER	ATROCITY	ATTAPS	ATTICISMS	ATTRITION
ATOMIZERS	ATROPHIA	ATTAR	ATTICIST	ATTRITIVE
ATOMIZES	ATROPHIAS	ATTARS	ATTICISTS	ATTRITS
ATOMIZING	ATROPHIC	ATTASK	ATTICIZE	ATTRITTED
ATOMS	ATROPHIED	ATTASKED	ATTICIZED	ATTUENT
ATOMY	ATROPHIES	ATTASKING	ATTICIZES	ATTUITE
ATONABLE	ATROPHY	ATTASKS	ATTICS	ATTUITED
ATONAL	ATROPIA	ATTASKT	ATTIRE	ATTUITES
ATONALISM	ATROPIAS	ATTEMPER	ATTIRED	ATTUITING
ATONALIST	ATROPIN	ATTEMPERS	ATTIRES	ATTUITION

ATTUITIVE	AUDIENCES	AUGITIC	AUMIL	AURICLED
ATTUNE	AUDIENCIA	AUGMENT	AUMILS	AURICLES
ATTUNED	AUDIENT	AUGMENTED	AUNE	AURICULA
ATTUNES	AUDIENTS	AUGMENTER	AUNES	AURICULAE
ATTUNING	AUDILE	AUGMENTOR	AUNT	AURICULAR
ATUA	AUDILES	AUGMENTS	AUNTER	AURICULAS
ATUAS	AUDING	AUGUR	AUNTERS	AURIFIED
ATWAIN	AUDINGS	AUGURAL	AUNTHOOD	AURIFIES
ATWEEL	AUDIO	AUGURED	AUNTHOODS	AURIFORM
ATWEEN	AUDIOBOOK	AUGURER	AUNTIE	AURIFY
ATWITTER	AUDIOGRAM	AUGURERS	AUNTIES	AURIFYING
ATWIXT	AUDIOLOGY	AUGURIES	AUNTLIER	AURIS
ATYPIC	AUDIOPHIL	AUGURING	AUNTLIEST	AURISCOPE
ATYPICAL	AUDIOS	AUGURS	AUNTLIKE	AURIST
AUA	AUDIOTAPE	AUGURSHIP	AUNTLY	AURISTS
AUAS	AUDIPHONE	AUGURY	AUNTS	AUROCHS
AUBADE	AUDIT	AUGUST	AUNTY	AUROCHSES
AUBADES	AUDITABLE	AUGUSTE	AURA	AURORA
AUBERGE	AUDITED	AUGUSTER	AURAE	AURORAE
AUBERGES	AUDITEE	AUGUSTES	AURAL	AURORAL
AUBERGINE	AUDITEES	AUGUSTEST	AURALITY	AURORALLY
AUBRETIA	AUDITING	AUGUSTLY	AURALLY	AURORAS
AUBRETIAS	AUDITINGS	AUGUSTS	AURAR	AUROREAN
AUBRIETA	AUDITION	AUK	AURAS	AUROUS
AUBRIETAS	AUDITIONS	AUKLET	AURATE	AURUM
AUBRIETIA	AUDITIVE	AUKLETS	AURATED	AURUMS
AUBURN	AUDITIVES	AUKS	AURATES	AUSFORM
AUBURNS	AUDITOR	AULA	AUREATE	AUSFORMED
AUCEPS	AUDITORIA	AULARIAN	AUREATELY	AUSFORMS
AUCEPSES	AUDITORS	AULARIANS	AUREI	AUSLANDER
AUCTION	AUDITORY	AULAS	AUREITIES	AUSPEX
AUCTIONED	AUDITRESS	AULD	AUREITY	AUSPICATE
AUCTIONS	AUDITS	AULDER	AURELIA	AUSPICE
AUCTORIAL	AUE	AULDEST	AURELIAN	AUSPICES
AUCUBA	AUF	AULIC	AURELIANS	AUSTENITE
AUCUBAS	AUFGABE	AULNAGE	AURELIAS	AUSTERE
AUDACIOUS	AUFGABES	AULNAGER	AUREOLA	AUSTERELY
AUDACITY	AUFS	AULNAGERS	AUREOLAE	AUSTERER
AUDAD	AUGEND	AULNAGES	AUREOLAS	AUSTEREST
AUDADS	AUGENDS	AULOI	AUREOLE	AUSTERITY
AUDIAL	AUGER	AULOS	AUREOLED	AUSTRAL
AUDIBLE	AUGERS	AUMAIL	AUREOLES	AUSTRALES
AUDIBLED	AUGH	AUMAILED	AUREOLING	AUSTRALIS
AUDIBLES	AUGHT	AUMAILING	AURES	AUSTRALS
AUDIBLING	AUGHTS	AUMAILS	AUREUS	AUSUBO
AUDIBLY	AUGITE	AUMBRIES	AURIC	AUSUBOS
AUDIENCE	AUGITES	AUMBRY	AURICLE	AUTACOID

AUTACOIDS	AUTOCARS	AUTOLYSIS	AUTOSCOPY	AVADAVATS
AUTARCH	AUTOCIDAL	AUTOLYTIC	AUTOSOMAL	AVAIL
AUTARCHIC	AUTOCLAVE	AUTOLYZE	AUTOSOME	AVAILABLE
AUTARCHS	AUTOCOID	AUTOLYZED	AUTOSOMES	AVAILABLY
AUTARCHY	AUTOCOIDS	AUTOLYZES	AUTOSPORE	AVAILE
AUTARKIC	AUTOCRACY	AUTOMAGIC	AUTOTELIC	AVAILED
AUTARKIES	AUTOCRAT	AUTOMAKER	AUTOTEST	AVAILES
AUTARKIST	AUTOCRATS	AUTOMAN	AUTOTESTS	AVAILFUL
AUTARKY	AUTOCRIME	AUTOMAT	AUTOTIMER	AVAILING
AUTECIOUS	AUTOCRINE	AUTOMATA	AUTOTOMIC	AVAILS
AUTECISM	AUTOCROSS	AUTOMATE	AUTOTOMY	AVAL
AUTECISMS	AUTOCUE	AUTOMATED	AUTOTOXIC	AVALANCHE
AUTEUR	AUTOCUES	AUTOMATES	AUTOTOXIN	AVALE
AUTEURISM	AUTOCUTIE	AUTOMATIC	AUTOTROPH	AVALED
AUTEURIST	AUTOCYCLE	AUTOMATON	AUTOTUNE	AVALEMENT
AUTEURS	AUTODIAL	AUTOMATS	AUTOTUNES	AVALES
AUTHENTIC	AUTODIALS	AUTOMEN	AUTOTYPE	AVALING
AUTHOR	AUTODROME	AUTOMETER	AUTOTYPED	AVANT
AUTHORED	AUTODYNE	AUTONOMIC	AUTOTYPES	AVANTI
AUTHORESS	AUTODYNES	AUTONOMY	AUTOTYPIC	AVANTIST
AUTHORIAL	AUTOECISM	AUTONYM	AUTOTYPY	AVANTISTS
AUTHORING	AUTOED	AUTONYMS	AUTOVAC	AVARICE
AUTHORISE	AUTOFLARE	AUTOPEN	AUTOVACS	AVARICES
AUTHORISH	AUTOFOCUS	AUTOPENS	AUTUMN	AVAS
AUTHORISM	AUTOGAMIC	AUTOPHAGY	AUTUMNAL	AVASCULAR
AUTHORITY	AUTOGAMY	AUTOPHOBY	AUTUMNS	AVAST
AUTHORIZE	AUTOGENIC	AUTOPHONY	AUTUMNY	AVATAR
AUTHORS	AUTOGENY	AUTOPHYTE	AUTUNITE	AVATARS
AUTISM	AUTOGIRO	AUTOPILOT	AUTUNITES	AVAUNT
AUTISMS	AUTOGIROS	AUTOPISTA	AUXESES	AVAUNTED
AUTIST	AUTOGRAFT	AUTOPOINT	AUXESIS	AVAUNTING
AUTISTIC	AUTOGRAPH	AUTOPSIA	AUXETIC	AVAUNTS
AUTISTICS	AUTOGUIDE	AUTOPSIAS	AUXETICS	AVE
AUTISTS	AUTOGYRO	AUTOPSIC	AUXILIAR	AVEL
AUTO	AUTOGYROS	AUTOPSIED	AUXILIARS	AVELLAN
AUTOBAHN	AUTOHARP	AUTOPSIES	AUXILIARY	AVELLANE
AUTOBAHNS	AUTOHARPS	AUTOPSIST	AUXIN	AVELS
AUTOBANK	AUTOICOUS	AUTOPSY	AUXINIC	AVENGE
AUTOBANKS	AUTOING	AUTOPTIC	AUXINS	AVENGED
AUTOBODY	AUTOLATRY	AUTOPUT	AUXOCYTE	AVENGEFUL
AUTOBUS	AUTOLOAD	AUTOPUTS	AUXOCYTES	AVENGER
AUTOBUSES	AUTOLOADS	AUTOREPLY	AUXOMETER	AVENGERS
AUTOCADE	AUTOLOGY	AUTOROUTE	AUXOSPORE	AVENGES
AUTOCADES	AUTOLYSE	AUTOS	AUXOTONIC	AVENGING
AUTOCAR	AUTOLYSED	AUTOSAVE	AUXOTROPH	AVENIR
AUTOCARP	AUTOLYSES	AUTOSAVED	AVA	AVENIRS
AUTOCARPS	AUTOLYSIN	AUTOSAVES	AVADAVAT	AVENS

AVENSES	AVIANISE	AVIRULENT	AVOURE	AWAKENER
AVENTAIL	AVIANISED	AVISANDUM	AVOURES	AWAKENERS
AVENTAILE	AVIANISES	AVISE	AVOUTERER	AWAKENING
AVENTAILS	AVIANIZE	AVISED	AVOUTRER	AWAKENS
AVENTRE	AVIANIZED	AVISEMENT	AVOUTRERS	AWAKES
AVENTRED	AVIANIZES	AVISES	AVOUTRIES	AWAKING
AVENTRES	AVIANS	AVISING	AVOUTRY	AWAKINGS
AVENTRING	AVIARIES	AVISO	AVOW	AWANTING
AVENTURE	AVIARIST	AVISOS	AVOWABLE	AWARD
AVENTURES	AVIARISTS	AVITAL	AVOWABLY	AWARDABLE
AVENTURIN	AVIARY	AVIZANDUM	AVOWAL	AWARDED
AVENUE	AVIATE	AVIZE	AVOWALS	AWARDEE
AVENUES	AVIATED	AVIZED	AVOWED	AWARDEES
AVER	AVIATES	AVIZEFULL	AVOWEDLY	AWARDER
AVERAGE	AVIATIC	AVIZES	AVOWER	AWARDERS
AVERAGED	AVIATING	AVIZING	AVOWERS	AWARDING
AVERAGELY	AVIATION	AVO	AVOWING	AWARDS
AVERAGER	AVIATIONS	AVOCADO	AVOWRIES	AWARE
AVERAGERS	AVIATOR	AVOCADOES	AVOWRY	AWARENESS
AVERAGES	AVIATORS	AVOCADOS	AVOWS	AWARER
AVERAGING	AVIATRESS	AVOCATION	AVOYER	AWAREST
AVERMENT	AVIATRICE	AVOCET	AVOYERS	AWARN
AVERMENTS	AVIATRIX	AVOCETS	AVRUGA	AWARNED
AVERRABLE	AVICULAR	AVODIRE	AVRUGAS	AWARNING
AVERRED	AVID	AVODIRES	AVULSE	AWARNS
AVERRING	AVIDER	AVOID	AVULSED	AWASH
AVERS	AVIDEST	AVOIDABLE	AVULSES	AWATCH
AVERSE	AVIDIN	AVOIDABLY	AVULSING	AWATO
AVERSELY	AVIDINS	AVOIDANCE	AVULSION	AWATOS
AVERSION	AVIDITIES	AVOIDANT	AVULSIONS	AWAVE
AVERSIONS	AVIDITY	AVOIDED	AVUNCULAR	AWAY
AVERSIVE	AVIDLY	AVOIDER	AVYZE	AWAYDAY
AVERSIVES	AVIDNESS	AVOIDERS	AVYZED	AWAYDAYS
AVERT	AVIETTE	AVOIDING	AVYZES	AWAYES
AVERTABLE	AVIETTES	AVOIDS	AVYZING	AWAYNESS
AVERTED	AVIFAUNA	AVOISION	AW	AWAYS
AVERTEDLY	AVIFAUNAE	AVOISIONS	AWA	AWDL
AVERTER	AVIFAUNAL	AVOPARCIN	AWAIT	AWDLS
AVERTERS	AVIFAUNAS	AVOS	AWAITED	AWE
AVERTIBLE	AVIFORM	AVOSET	AWAITER	AWEARIED
AVERTING	AVIGATOR	AVOSETS	AWAITERS	AWEARY
AVERTS	AVIGATORS	AVOUCH	AWAITING	AWEATHER
AVES	AVINE	AVOUCHED	AWAITS	AWED
AVGAS	AVION	AVOUCHER	AWAKE	AWEE
AVGASES	AVIONIC	AVOUCHERS	AWAKED	AWEEL
AVGASSES	AVIONICS	AVOUCHES	AWAKEN	AWEIGH
AVIAN	AVIONS	AVOUCHING	AWAKENED	AWEING

AWELESS	AWNIEST	AXIOMATIC	AYES	AZOTAEMIC
AWES	AWNING	AXIOMS	AYGRE	AZOTE
AWESOME	AWNINGED	AXION	AYIN	AZOTED
AWESOMELY	AWNINGS	AXIONS	AYINS	AZOTEMIA
AWESTRIKE	AWNLESS	AXIS	AYONT	AZOTEMIAS
AWESTRUCK	AWNS	AXISED	AYRE	AZOTEMIC
AWETO	AWNY	AXISES	AYRES	AZOTES
AWETOS	AWOKE	AXITE	AYRIE	AZOTH
AWFUL	AWOKEN	AXITES	AYRIES	AZOTHS
AWFULLER	AWOL	AXLE	AYS	AZOTIC
AWFULLEST	AWOLS	AXLED	AYU	AZOTISE
AWFULLY	AWORK	AXLES	AYURVEDA	AZOTISED
AWFULNESS	AWRACK	AXLETREE	AYURVEDAS	AZOTISES
AWFY	AWRONG	AXLETREES	AYURVEDIC	AZOTISING
AWHAPE	AWRY	AXLIKE	AYUS	AZOTIZE
AWHAPED	AWSOME	AXMAN	AYWORD	AZOTIZED
AWHAPES	AX	AXMEN	AYWORDS	AZOTIZES
AWHAPING	AXAL	AXOID	AZALEA	AZOTIZING
AWHATO	AXE	AXOIDS	AZALEAS	AZOTOUS
AWHATOS	AXEBIRD	AXOLEMMA	AZAN	AZOTURIA
AWHEEL	AXEBIRDS	AXOLEMMAS	AZANS	AZOTURIAS
AWHEELS	AXED	AXOLOTL	AZEDARACH	AZUKI
AWHETO	AXEL	AXOLOTLS	AZEOTROPE	AZUKIS
AWHETOS	AXELIKE	AXON	AZEOTROPY	AZULEJO
AWHILE	AXELS	AXONAL	AZERTY	AZULEJOS
AWHIRL	AXEMAN	AXONE	AZIDE	AZURE
AWING	AXEMEN	AXONEMAL	AZIDES	AZUREAN
AWK	AXENIC	AXONEME	AZIDO	AZURES
AWKS	AXES	AXONEMES	AZIMUTH	AZURIES
AWKWARD	AXIAL	AXONES	AZIMUTHAL	AZURINE
AWKWARDER	AXIALITY	AXONIC	AZIMUTHS	AZURINES
AWKWARDLY	AXIALLY	AXONS	AZINE	AZURITE
AWL	AXIL	AXOPLASM	AZINES	AZURITES
AWLBIRD	AXILE	AXOPLASMS	AZIONE	AZURN
AWLBIRDS	AXILEMMA	AXSEED	AZIONES	AZURY
AWLESS	AXILEMMAS	AXSEEDS	AZLON	AZYGIES
AWLS	AXILLA	AY	AZLONS	AZYGOS
AWLWORT	AXILLAE	AYAH	AZO	AZYGOSES
AWLWORTS	AXILLAR	AYAHS	AZOIC	AZYGOUS
AWMOUS	AXILLARS	AYAHUASCA	AZOLE	AZYGOUSLY
AWMRIE	AXILLARY	AYAHUASCO	AZOLES	AZYGY
AWMRIES	AXILLAS	AYATOLLAH	AZOLLA	AZYM
AWMRY	AXILS	AYAYA	AZOLLAS	AZYME
AWN	AXING	AYAYAS	AZON	AZYMES
AWNED	AXINITE	AYE	AZONAL	AZYMITE
AWNER	AXINITES	AYELP	AZONIC	AZYMITES
AWNERS	AXIOLOGY	AYENBITE	AZONS	AZYMOUS
AWNIER	AXIOM	AYENBITES	AZOTAEMIA	AZYMS

B

BA	BABBLIEST	BABUCHE	BACCARATS	BACKACTER
BAA	BABBLING	BABUCHES	BACCARE	BACKARE
BAAED	BABBLINGS	BABUDOM	BACCAS	BACKBAND
BAAING	BABBLY	BABUDOMS	BACCATE	BACKBANDS
BAAINGS	BABE	BABUISM	BACCATED	BACKBAR
BAAL	BABEL	BABUISMS	BACCHANAL	BACKBARS
BAALEBOS	BABELDOM	BABUL	BACCHANT	BACKBEAT
BAALIM	BABELDOMS	BABULS	BACCHANTE	BACKBEATS
BAALISM	BABELISH	BABUS	BACCHANTS	BACKBENCH
BAALISMS	BABELISM	BABUSHKA	BACCHIAC	BACKBEND
BAALS	BABELISMS	BABUSHKAS	BACCHIAN	BACKBENDS
BAAS	BABELS	BABY	BACCHIC	BACKBIT
BAASES	BABES	BABYCCINO	BACCHII	BACKBITE
BAASKAAP	BABESIA	BABYCINO	BACCHIUS	BACKBITER
BAASKAAPS	BABESIAS	BABYCINOS	BACCIES	BACKBITES
BAASKAP	BABICHE	BABYDOLL	BACCIFORM	BACKBLOCK
BAASKAPS	BABICHES	BABYDOLLS	BACCO	BACKBOARD
BAASSKAP	BABIED	BABYFOOD	BACCOES	BACKBOND
BAASSKAPS	BABIER	BABYFOODS	BACCOS	BACKBONDS
BABA	BABIES	BABYHOOD	BACCY	BACKBONE
BABACO	BABIEST	BABYHOODS	BACH	BACKBONED
BABACOOTE	BABIRUSA	BABYING	BACHA	BACKBONES
BABACOS	BABIRUSAS	BABYISH	BACHARACH	BACKBURN
BABACU	BABIRUSSA	BABYISHLY	BACHAS	BACKBURNS
BABACUS	BABKA	BABYLIKE	BACHATA	BACKCAST
BABALAS	BABKAS	BABYPROOF	BACHATAS	BACKCASTS
BABAS	BABLAH	BABYSAT	BACHCHA	BACKCHAT
BABASSU	BABLAHS	BABYSIT	BACHCHAS	BACKCHATS
BABASSUS	BABOO	BABYSITS	BACHED	BACKCHECK
BABBELAS	BABOOL	BAC	BACHELOR	BACKCLOTH
BABBITRY	BABOOLS	BACALAO	BACHELORS	BACKCOMB
BABBITT	BABOON	BACALAOS	BACHES	BACKCOMBS
BABBITTED	BABOONERY	BACALHAU	BACHING	BACKCOURT
BABBITTRY	BABOONISH	BACALHAUS	BACHS	BACKCROSS
BABBITTS	BABOONS	BACCA	BACILLAR	BACKDATE
BABBLE	BABOOS	BACCAE	BACILLARY	BACKDATED
BABBLED	BABOOSH	BACCALA	BACILLI	BACKDATES
BABBLER	BABOOSHES	BACCALAS	BACILLUS	BACKDOOR
BABBLERS	BABOUCHE	BACCARA	BACK	BACKDOWN
BABBLES	BABOUCHES	BACCARAS	BACKACHE	BACKDOWNS
BABBLIER	BABU	BACCARAT	BACKACHES	BACKDRAFT

BACKDROP	BACKLINES	BACKSPEIR	BACONS	BADLAND
BACKDROPS	BACKLIST	BACKSPIN	BACRONYM	BADLANDS
BACKDROPT	BACKLISTS	BACKSPINS	BACRONYMS	BADLY
BACKED	BACKLIT	BACKSTAB	BACS	BADMAN
BACKER	BACKLOAD	BACKSTABS	BACTERIA	BADMASH
BACKERS	BACKLOADS	BACKSTAGE	BACTERIAL	BADMASHES
BACKET	BACKLOG	BACKSTAIR	BACTERIAN	BADMEN
BACKETS	BACKLOGS	BACKSTALL	BACTERIAS	BADMINTON
BACKFALL	BACKLOT	BACKSTAMP	BACTERIC	BADMOUTH
BACKFALLS	BACKLOTS	BACKSTAY	BACTERIN	BADMOUTHS
BACKFAT	BACKMOST	BACKSTAYS	BACTERINS	BADNESS
BACKFATS	BACKOUT	BACKSTOP	BACTERISE	BADNESSES
BACKFIELD	BACKOUTS	BACKSTOPS	BACTERIUM	BADS
BACKFILE	BACKPACK	BACKSTORY	BACTERIZE	BADWARE
BACKFILES	BACKPACKS	BACKSWEPT	BACTEROID	BADWARES
BACKFILL	BACKPEDAL	BACKSWING	BACULA	BAEL
BACKFILLS	BACKPIECE	BACKSWORD	BACULINE	BAELS
BACKFIRE	BACKPLATE	BACKTALK	BACULITE	BAETYL
BACKFIRED	BACKRA	BACKTALKS	BACULITES	BAETYLS
BACKFIRES	BACKRAS	BACKTRACK	BACULUM	BAFF
BACKFISCH	BACKREST	BACKUP	BACULUMS	BAFFED
BACKFIT	BACKRESTS	BACKUPS	BAD	BAFFIES
BACKFITS	BACKRONYM	BACKVELD	BADASS	BAFFING
BACKFLIP	BACKROOM	BACKVELDS	BADASSED	BAFFLE
BACKFLIPS	BACKROOMS	BACKWARD	BADASSES	BAFFLED
BACKFLOW	BACKRUSH	BACKWARDS	BADDER	BAFFLEGAB
BACKFLOWS	BACKS	BACKWASH	BADDEST	BAFFLER
BACKHAND	BACKSAW	BACKWATER	BADDIE	BAFFLERS
BACKHANDS	BACKSAWS	BACKWIND	BADDIES	BAFFLES
BACKHAUL	BACKSEAT	BACKWINDS	BADDISH	BAFFLING
BACKHAULS	BACKSEATS	BACKWOOD	BADDY	BAFFS
BACKHOE	BACKSET	BACKWOODS	BADE	BAFFY
BACKHOED	BACKSETS	BACKWORD	BADGE	BAFT
BACKHOES	BACKSEY	BACKWORDS	BADGED	BAFTS
BACKHOUSE	BACKSEYS	BACKWORK	BADGELESS	BAG
BACKIE	BACKSHISH	BACKWORKS	BADGER	BAGARRE
BACKIES	BACKSHORE	BACKWRAP	BADGERED	BAGARRES
BACKING	BACKSIDE	BACKWRAPS	BADGERING	BAGASS
BACKINGS	BACKSIDES	BACKYARD	BADGERLY	BAGASSE
BACKLAND	BACKSIGHT	BACKYARDS	BADGERS	BAGASSES
BACKLANDS	BACKSLAP	BACLAVA	BADGES	BAGATELLE
BACKLASH	BACKSLAPS	BACLAVAS	BADGING	BAGEL
BACKLESS	BACKSLASH	BACLOFEN	BADINAGE	BAGELED
BACKLIFT	BACKSLID	BACLOFENS	BADINAGED	BAGELING
BACKLIFTS	BACKSLIDE	BACON	BADINAGES	BAGELLED
BACKLIGHT	BACKSPACE	BACONER	BADINERIE	BAGELLING
BACKLINE	BACKSPEER	BACONERS	BADIOUS	BAGELS

BAGFUL	BAGWASHES	BAILMENTS	BAJU	BALANCE
BAGFULS	BAGWIG	BAILOR	BAJUS	BALANCED
BAGGAGE	BAGWIGS	BAILORS	BAKE	BALANCER
BAGGAGES	BAGWORM	BAILOUT	BAKEAPPLE	BALANCERS
BAGGED	BAGWORMS	BAILOUTS	BAKEBOARD	BALANCES
BAGGER	BAH	BAILS	BAKED	BALANCING
BAGGERS	BAHADA	BAILSMAN	BAKEHOUSE	BALANITIS
BAGGIE	BAHADAS	BAILSMEN	BAKELITE	BALAS
BAGGIER	BAHADUR	BAININ	BAKELITES	BALASES
BAGGIES	BAHADURS	BAININS	BAKEMEAT	BALATA
BAGGIEST	BAHOOKIE	BAINITE	BAKEMEATS	BALATAS
BAGGILY	BAHOOKIES	BAINITES	BAKEN	BALAYAGE
BAGGINESS	BAHT	BAIRN	BAKEOFF	BALAYAGED
BAGGING	BAHTS	BAIRNISH	BAKEOFFS	BALAYAGES
BAGGINGS	BAHU	BAIRNLIER	BAKER	BALBOA
BAGGIT	BAHUS	BAIRNLIKE	BAKERIES	BALBOAS
BAGGITS	BAHUT	BAIRNLY	BAKERS	BALCONET
BAGGY	BAHUTS	BAIRNS	BAKERY	BALCONETS
BAGH	BAHUVRIHI	BAISA	BAKES	BALCONIED
BAGHOUSE	BAIDAR	BAISAS	BAKESHOP	BALCONIES
BAGHOUSES	BAIDARKA	BAISEMAIN	BAKESHOPS	BALCONY
BAGHS	BAIDARKAS	BAIT	BAKESTONE	BALD
BAGIE	BAIDARS	BAITED	BAKEWARE	BALDACHIN
BAGIES	BAIGNOIRE	BAITER	BAKEWARES	BALDAQUIN
BAGLESS	BAIL	BAITERS	BAKGAT	BALDED
BAGLIKE	BAILABLE	BAITFISH	BAKHSHISH	BALDER
BAGMAN	BAILBOND	BAITH	BAKING	BALDEST
BAGMEN	BAILBONDS	BAITING	BAKINGS	BALDFACED
BAGNETTE	BAILED	BAITINGS	BAKKIE	BALDHEAD
BAGNETTES	BAILEE	BAITS	BAKKIES	BALDHEADS
BAGNIO	BAILEES	BAIZA	BAKLAVA	BALDICOOT
BAGNIOS	BAILER	BAIZAS	BAKLAVAS	BALDIE
BAGPIPE	BAILERS	BAIZE	BAKLAWA	BALDIER
BAGPIPED	BAILEY	BAIZED	BAKLAWAS	BALDIES
BAGPIPER	BAILEYS	BAIZES	BAKRA	BALDIEST
BAGPIPERS	BAILIE	BAIZING	BAKRAS	BALDING
BAGPIPES	BAILIES	BAJADA	BAKSHEESH	BALDISH
BAGPIPING	BAILIFF	BAJADAS	BAKSHISH	BALDLY
BAGS	BAILIFFS	BAJAN	BAL	BALDMONEY
BAGSFUL	BAILING	BAJANS	BALACLAVA	BALDNESS
BAGUET	BAILIWICK	BAJILLION	BALADIN	BALDPATE
BAGUETS	BAILLI	BAJRA	BALADINE	BALDPATED
BAGUETTE	BAILLIAGE	BAJRAS	BALADINES	BALDPATES
BAGUETTES	BAILLIE	BAJREE	BALADINS	BALDRIC
BAGUIO	BAILLIES	BAJREES	BALAFON	BALDRICK
BAGUIOS	BAILLIS	BAJRI	BALAFONS	BALDRICKS
BAGWASH	BAILMENT	BAJRIS	BALALAIKA	BALDRICS

B

BALDS	BALLADES	BALLING	BALLYARD	BAM
BALDY	BALLADIC	BALLINGS	BALLYARDS	BAMBI
BALE	BALLADIN	BALLISTA	BALLYHOO	BAMBINI
BALECTION	BALLADINE	BALLISTAE	BALLYHOOS	BAMBINO
BALED	BALLADING	BALLISTAS	BALLYRAG	BAMBINOS
BALEEN	BALLADINS	BALLISTIC	BALLYRAGS	BAMBIS
BALEENS	BALLADIST	BALLIUM	BALM	BAMBOO
BALEFIRE	BALLADRY	BALLIUMS	BALMACAAN	BAMBOOS
BALEFIRES	BALLADS	BALLOCKS	BALMED	BAMBOOZLE
BALEFUL	BALLAN	BALLON	BALMIER	BAMMED
BALEFULLY	BALLANS	BALLONET	BALMIEST	BAMMER
BALER	BALLANT	BALLONETS	BALMILY	BAMMERS
BALERS	BALLANTED	BALLONNE	BALMINESS	BAMMING
BALES	BALLANTS	BALLONNES	BALMING	BAMPOT
BALING	BALLAST	BALLONS	BALMLIKE	BAMPOTS
BALINGS	BALLASTED	BALLOON	BALMORAL	BAMS
BALISAUR	BALLASTER	BALLOONED	BALMORALS	BAN
BALISAURS	BALLASTS	BALLOONS	BALMS	BANAK
BALISE	BALLAT	BALLOT	BALMY	BANAKS
BALISES	BALLATED	BALLOTED	BALNEAL	BANAL
BALISTA	BALLATING	BALLOTEE	BALNEARY	BANALER
BALISTAE	BALLATS	BALLOTEES	BALONEY	BANALEST
BALISTAS	BALLBOY	BALLOTER	BALONEYS	BANALISE
BALK	BALLBOYS	BALLOTERS	BALOO	BANALISED
BALKANISE	BALLCLAY	BALLOTING	BALOOS	BANALISES
BALKANIZE	BALLCLAYS	BALLOTINI	BALS	BANALITY
BALKED	BALLCOCK	BALLOTS	BALSA	BANALIZE
BALKER	BALLCOCKS	BALLOW	BALSAM	BANALIZED
BALKERS	BALLED	BALLOWS	BALSAMED	BANALIZES
BALKIER	BALLER	BALLPARK	BALSAMIC	BANALLY
BALKIEST	BALLERINA	BALLPARKS	BALSAMING	BANANA
BALKILY	BALLERINE	BALLPEEN	BALSAMS	BANANAS
BALKINESS	BALLERS	BALLPOINT	BALSAMY	BANAUSIAN
BALKING	BALLET	BALLROOM	BALSAS	BANAUSIC
BALKINGLY	BALLETED	BALLROOMS	BALSAWOOD	BANC
BALKINGS	BALLETIC	BALLS	BALTHASAR	BANCO
BALKLINE	BALLETING	BALLSED	BALTHAZAR	BANCOS
BALKLINES	BALLETS	BALLSES	BALTI	BANCS
BALKS	BALLGAME	BALLSIER	BALTIC	BAND
BALKY	BALLGAMES	BALLSIEST	BALTIS	BANDA
BALL	BALLGIRL	BALLSING	BALU	BANDAGE
BALLABILE	BALLGIRLS	BALLSY	BALUN	BANDAGED
BALLABILI	BALLGOWN	BALLUP	BALUNS	BANDAGER
BALLAD	BALLGOWNS	BALLUPS	BALUS	BANDAGERS
BALLADE	BALLHAWK	BALLUTE	BALUSTER	BANDAGES
BALLADED	BALLHAWKS	BALLUTES	BALUSTERS	BANDAGING
BALLADEER	BALLIES	BALLY	BALZARINE	BANDAID

BANDALORE
BANDANA
BANDANAS
BANDANNA
BANDANNAS
BANDAR
BANDARI
BANDARIS
BANDARS
BANDAS
BANDBOX
BANDBOXES
BANDBRAKE
BANDEAU
BANDEAUS
BANDEAUX
BANDED
BANDEIRA
BANDEIRAS
BANDELET
BANDELETS
BANDELIER
BANDER
BANDEROL
BANDEROLE
BANDEROLS
BANDERS
BANDFISH
BANDH
BANDHS
BANDICOOT
BANDIED
BANDIER
BANDIES
BANDIEST
BANDINESS
BANDING
BANDINGS
BANDIT
BANDITO
BANDITOS
BANDITRY
BANDITS
BANDITTI
BANDITTIS
BANDMATE
BANDMATES

BANDOBAST
BANDOBUST
BANDOG
BANDOGS
BANDOLEER
BANDOLEON
BANDOLERO
BANDOLIER
BANDOLINE
BANDONEON
BANDONION
BANDOOK
BANDOOKS
BANDORA
BANDORAS
BANDORE
BANDORES
BANDPASS
BANDROL
BANDROLS
BANDS
BANDSAW
BANDSAWS
BANDSHELL
BANDSMAN
BANDSMEN
BANDSTAND
BANDSTER
BANDSTERS
BANDURA
BANDURAS
BANDWAGON
BANDWIDTH
BANDY
BANDYING
BANDYINGS
BANDYMAN
BANDYMEN
BANE
BANEBERRY
BANED
BANEFUL
BANEFULLY
BANES
BANG
BANGALAY
BANGALAYS

BANGALORE
BANGALOW
BANGALOWS
BANGED
BANGER
BANGERS
BANGING
BANGKOK
BANGKOKS
BANGLE
BANGLED
BANGLES
BANGS
BANGSRING
BANGSTER
BANGSTERS
BANGTAIL
BANGTAILS
BANI
BANIA
BANIAN
BANIANS
BANIAS
BANING
BANISH
BANISHED
BANISHER
BANISHERS
BANISHES
BANISHING
BANISTER
BANISTERS
BANJAX
BANJAXED
BANJAXES
BANJAXING
BANJO
BANJOES
BANJOIST
BANJOISTS
BANJOLELE
BANJOS
BANJULELE
BANK
BANKABLE
BANKBOOK
BANKBOOKS

BANKCARD
BANKCARDS
BANKED
BANKER
BANKERLY
BANKERS
BANKET
BANKETS
BANKING
BANKINGS
BANKIT
BANKITS
BANKNOTE
BANKNOTES
BANKROLL
BANKROLLS
BANKRUPT
BANKRUPTS
BANKS
BANKSIA
BANKSIAS
BANKSIDE
BANKSIDES
BANKSMAN
BANKSMEN
BANKSTER
BANKSTERS
BANLIEUE
BANLIEUES
BANNABLE
BANNED
BANNER
BANNERALL
BANNERED
BANNERET
BANNERETS
BANNERING
BANNEROL
BANNEROLS
BANNERS
BANNET
BANNETS
BANNING
BANNINGS
BANNISTER
BANNOCK
BANNOCKS

BANNS
BANOFFEE
BANOFFEES
BANOFFI
BANOFFIS
BANQUET
BANQUETED
BANQUETER
BANQUETS
BANQUETTE
BANS
BANSELA
BANSELAS
BANSHEE
BANSHEES
BANSHIE
BANSHIES
BANT
BANTAM
BANTAMS
BANTED
BANTENG
BANTENGS
BANTER
BANTERED
BANTERER
BANTERERS
BANTERING
BANTERS
BANTIES
BANTING
BANTINGS
BANTLING
BANTLINGS
BANTS
BANTU
BANTUS
BANTY
BANXRING
BANXRINGS
BANYA
BANYAN
BANYANS
BANYAS
BANZAI
BANZAIS
BAOBAB

BAOBABS
BAP
BAPS
BAPTISE
BAPTISED
BAPTISER
BAPTISERS
BAPTISES
BAPTISIA
BAPTISIAS
BAPTISING
BAPTISM
BAPTISMAL
BAPTISMS
BAPTIST
BAPTISTRY
BAPTISTS
BAPTIZE
BAPTIZED
BAPTIZER
BAPTIZERS
BAPTIZES
BAPTIZING
BAPU
BAPUS
BAR
BARACAN
BARACANS
BARACHOIS
BARAGOUIN
BARASINGA
BARATHEA
BARATHEAS
BARATHRUM
BARAZA
BARAZAS
BARB
BARBAL
BARBARIAN
BARBARIC
BARBARISE
BARBARISM
BARBARITY
BARBARIZE
BARBAROUS
BARBASCO
BARBASCOS

BARBASTEL
BARBATE
BARBATED
BARBE
BARBECUE
BARBECUED
BARBECUER
BARBECUES
BARBED
BARBEL
BARBELL
BARBELLS
BARBELS
BARBEQUE
BARBEQUED
BARBEQUES
BARBER
BARBERED
BARBERING
BARBERRY
BARBERS
BARBES
BARBET
BARBETS
BARBETTE
BARBETTES
BARBICAN
BARBICANS
BARBICEL
BARBICELS
BARBIE
BARBIES
BARBING
BARBITAL
BARBITALS
BARBITONE
BARBLESS
BARBOLA
BARBOLAS
BARBOT
BARBOTINE
BARBOTS
BARBOTTE
BARBOTTES
BARBS
BARBULE
BARBULES

BARBUT
BARBUTS
BARBWIRE
BARBWIRES
BARBY
BARCA
BARCAROLE
BARCAS
BARCHAN
BARCHANE
BARCHANES
BARCHANS
BARCODE
BARCODED
BARCODES
BARD
BARDASH
BARDASHES
BARDE
BARDED
BARDES
BARDIC
BARDIE
BARDIER
BARDIES
BARDIEST
BARDING
BARDISM
BARDISMS
BARDLING
BARDLINGS
BARDO
BARDOS
BARDS
BARDSHIP
BARDSHIPS
BARDY
BARE
BAREBACK
BAREBACKS
BAREBOAT
BAREBOATS
BAREBONE
BAREBONED
BAREBONES
BARED
BAREFACED

BAREFIT
BAREFOOT
BAREGE
BAREGES
BAREGINE
BAREGINES
BAREHAND
BAREHANDS
BAREHEAD
BARELAND
BARELY
BARENESS
BARER
BARES
BARESARK
BARESARKS
BAREST
BARF
BARFED
BARFI
BARFING
BARFIS
BARFLIES
BARFLY
BARFS
BARFUL
BARGAIN
BARGAINED
BARGAINER
BARGAINS
BARGANDER
BARGE
BARGED
BARGEE
BARGEES
BARGEESE
BARGELLO
BARGELLOS
BARGEMAN
BARGEMEN
BARGEPOLE
BARGES
BARGEST
BARGESTS
BARGHEST
BARGHESTS
BARGING

BARGOON
BARGOONS
BARGOOSE
BARGUEST
BARGUESTS
BARHOP
BARHOPPED
BARHOPS
BARIATRIC
BARIC
BARILLA
BARILLAS
BARING
BARISH
BARISTA
BARISTAS
BARITE
BARITES
BARITONAL
BARITONE
BARITONES
BARIUM
BARIUMS
BARK
BARKAN
BARKANS
BARKED
BARKEEP
BARKEEPER
BARKEEPS
BARKEN
BARKENED
BARKENING
BARKENS
BARKER
BARKERS
BARKHAN
BARKHANS
BARKIER
BARKIEST
BARKING
BARKLESS
BARKS
BARKY
BARLEDUC
BARLEDUCS
BARLESS

BARLEY	BAROCKS	BARRACES	BARRETS	BARTIZANS
BARLEYS	BAROGRAM	BARRACK	BARRETTE	BARTON
BARLOW	BAROGRAMS	BARRACKED	BARRETTER	BARTONS
BARLOWS	BAROGRAPH	BARRACKER	BARRETTES	BARTSIA
BARM	BAROLO	BARRACKS	BARRICADE	BARTSIAS
BARMAID	BAROLOS	BARRACOON	BARRICADO	BARWARE
BARMAIDS	BAROMETER	BARRACUDA	BARRICO	BARWARES
BARMAN	BAROMETRY	BARRAGE	BARRICOES	BARWOOD
BARMBRACK	BAROMETZ	BARRAGED	BARRICOS	BARWOODS
BARMEN	BARON	BARRAGES	BARRIE	BARYE
BARMIE	BARONAGE	BARRAGING	BARRIER	BARYES
BARMIER	BARONAGES	BARRANCA	BARRIERED	BARYON
BARMIEST	BARONESS	BARRANCAS	BARRIERS	BARYONIC
BARMILY	BARONET	BARRANCO	BARRIES	BARYONS
BARMINESS	BARONETCY	BARRANCOS	BARRIEST	BARYTA
BARMKIN	BARONETS	BARRAS	BARRING	BARYTAS
BARMKINS	BARONG	BARRAT	BARRINGS	BARYTE
BARMPOT	BARONGS	BARRATED	BARRIO	BARYTES
BARMPOTS	BARONIAL	BARRATER	BARRIOS	BARYTIC
BARMS	BARONIES	BARRATERS	BARRIQUE	BARYTON
BARMY	BARONNE	BARRATING	BARRIQUES	BARYTONE
BARN	BARONNES	BARRATOR	BARRISTER	BARYTONES
BARNACLE	BARONS	BARRATORS	BARRO	BARYTONS
BARNACLED	BARONY	BARRATRY	BARROOM	BAS
BARNACLES	BAROPHILE	BARRATS	BARROOMS	BASAL
BARNBRACK	BAROQUE	BARRE	BARROW	BASALLY
BARNED	BAROQUELY	BARRED	BARROWFUL	BASALT
BARNET	BAROQUES	BARREED	BARROWS	BASALTES
BARNETS	BAROSAUR	BARREFULL	BARRULET	BASALTIC
BARNEY	BAROSAURS	BARREING	BARRULETS	BASALTINE
BARNEYED	BAROSCOPE	BARREL	BARRY	BASALTS
BARNEYING	BAROSTAT	BARRELAGE	BARS	BASAN
BARNEYS	BAROSTATS	BARRELED	BARSTOOL	BASANITE
BARNIER	BAROTITIS	BARRELFUL	BARSTOOLS	BASANITES
BARNIEST	BAROUCHE	BARRELING	BARTEND	BASANS
BARNING	BAROUCHES	BARRELLED	BARTENDED	BASANT
BARNLIKE	BARP	BARRELS	BARTENDER	BASANTS
BARNS	BARPERSON	BARREN	BARTENDS	BASCINET
BARNSTORM	BARPS	BARRENER	BARTER	BASCINETS
BARNWOOD	BARQUE	BARRENEST	BARTERED	BASCULE
BARNWOODS	BARQUES	BARRENLY	BARTERER	BASCULES
BARNY	BARQUETTE	BARRENS	BARTERERS	BASE
BARNYARD	BARRA	BARRES	BARTERING	BASEBALL
BARNYARDS	BARRABLE	BARRET	BARTERS	BASEBALLS
BAROCCO	BARRACAN	BARRETOR	BARTISAN	BASEBAND
BAROCCOS	BARRACANS	BARRETORS	BARTISANS	BASEBANDS
BAROCK	BARRACE	BARRETRY	BARTIZAN	BASEBOARD

BASEBORN	BASHO	BASIS	BASSLINE	BATARD
BASED	BASHTAG	BASK	BASSLINES	BATARDS
BASEEJ	BASHTAGS	BASKED	BASSLY	BATATA
BASEHEAD	BASIC	BASKET	BASSNESS	BATATAS
BASEHEADS	BASICALLY	BASKETFUL	BASSO	BATAVIA
BASELARD	BASICITY	BASKETRY	BASSOON	BATAVIAS
BASELARDS	BASICS	BASKETS	BASSOONS	BATBOY
BASELESS	BASIDIA	BASKING	BASSOS	BATBOYS
BASELINE	BASIDIAL	BASKS	BASSWOOD	BATCH
BASELINER	BASIDIUM	BASMATI	BASSWOODS	BATCHED
BASELINES	BASIFIED	BASMATIS	BASSY	BATCHER
BASELOAD	BASIFIER	BASNET	BAST	BATCHERS
BASELOADS	BASIFIERS	BASNETS	BASTA	BATCHES
BASELY	BASIFIES	BASOCHE	BASTARD	BATCHING
BASEMAN	BASIFIXED	BASOCHES	BASTARDLY	BATCHINGS
BASEMEN	BASIFUGAL	BASON	BASTARDRY	BATE
BASEMENT	BASIFY	BASONS	BASTARDS	BATEAU
BASEMENTS	BASIFYING	BASOPHIL	BASTARDY	BATEAUX
BASEN	BASIJ	BASOPHILE	BASTE	BATED
BASENESS	BASIL	BASOPHILS	BASTED	BATELESS
BASENJI	BASILAR	BASQUE	BASTER	BATELEUR
BASENJIS	BASILARY	BASQUED	BASTERS	BATELEURS
BASEPATH	BASILECT	BASQUES	BASTES	BATEMENT
BASEPATHS	BASILECTS	BASQUINE	BASTI	BATEMENTS
BASEPLATE	BASILIC	BASQUINES	BASTIDE	BATES
BASER	BASILICA	BASS	BASTIDES	BATFISH
BASES	BASILICAE	BASSE	BASTILE	BATFISHES
BASEST	BASILICAL	BASSED	BASTILES	BATFOWL
BASH	BASILICAN	BASSER	BASTILLE	BATFOWLED
BASHAW	BASILICAS	BASSERS	BASTILLES	BATFOWLER
BASHAWISM	BASILICON	BASSES	BASTINADE	BATFOWLS
BASHAWS	BASILISK	BASSEST	BASTINADO	BATGIRL
BASHED	BASILISKS	BASSET	BASTING	BATGIRLS
BASHER	BASILS	BASSETED	BASTINGS	BATH
BASHERS	BASIN	BASSETING	BASTION	BATHCUBE
BASHES	BASINAL	BASSETS	BASTIONED	BATHCUBES
BASHFUL	BASINED	BASSETT	BASTIONS	BATHE
BASHFULLY	BASINET	BASSETTED	BASTIS	BATHED
BASHING	BASINETS	BASSETTS	BASTLE	BATHER
BASHINGS	BASINFUL	BASSI	BASTLES	BATHERS
BASHLESS	BASINFULS	BASSIER	BASTO	BATHES
BASHLIK	BASING	BASSIEST	BASTOS	BATHETIC
BASHLIKS	BASINLIKE	BASSINET	BASTS	BATHHOUSE
BASHLYK	BASINS	BASSINETS	BASUCO	BATHING
BASHLYKS	BASION	BASSING	BASUCOS	BATHINGS
BASHMENT	BASIONS	BASSIST	BAT	BATHLESS
BASHMENTS	BASIPETAL	BASSISTS	BATABLE	BATHMAT

BATHMATS	BATSHIT	BATTILLS	BAUERAS	BAWDRY
BATHMIC	BATSMAN	BATTILY	BAUHINIA	BAWDS
BATHMISM	BATSMEN	BATTINESS	BAUHINIAS	BAWDY
BATHMISMS	BATSWING	BATTING	BAUK	BAWK
BATHOLITE	BATSWOMAN	BATTINGS	BAUKED	BAWKS
BATHOLITH	BATSWOMEN	BATTLE	BAUKING	BAWL
BATHORSE	BATT	BATTLEAX	BAUKS	BAWLED
BATHORSES	BATTA	BATTLEAXE	BAULK	BAWLER
BATHOS	BATTALIA	BATTLEBUS	BAULKED	BAWLERS
BATHOSES	BATTALIAS	BATTLED	BAULKER	BAWLEY
BATHROBE	BATTALION	BATTLER	BAULKERS	BAWLEYS
BATHROBES	BATTAS	BATTLERS	BAULKIER	BAWLING
BATHROOM	BATTEAU	BATTLES	BAULKIEST	BAWLINGS
BATHROOMS	BATTEAUX	BATTLING	BAULKILY	BAWLS
BATHS	BATTED	BATTOLOGY	BAULKING	BAWN
BATHTUB	BATTEL	BATTS	BAULKLINE	BAWNEEN
BATHTUBS	BATTELED	BATTU	BAULKS	BAWNEENS
BATHWATER	BATTELER	BATTUE	BAULKY	BAWNS
BATHYAL	BATTELERS	BATTUES	BAUR	BAWR
BATHYBIUS	BATTELING	BATTUTA	BAURS	BAWRS
BATHYLITE	BATTELLED	BATTUTAS	BAUSOND	BAWSUNT
BATHYLITH	BATTELS	BATTUTO	BAUXITE	BAWTIE
BATIK	BATTEMENT	BATTUTOS	BAUXITES	BAWTIES
BATIKED	BATTEN	BATTY	BAUXITIC	BAWTY
BATIKING	BATTENED	BATWING	BAVARDAGE	BAXTER
BATIKS	BATTENER	BATWOMAN	BAVAROIS	BAXTERS
BATING	BATTENERS	BATWOMEN	BAVIN	BAY
BATISTE	BATTENING	BAUBEE	BAVINED	BAYADEER
BATISTES	BATTENS	BAUBEES	BAVINING	BAYADEERS
BATLER	BATTER	BAUBLE	BAVINS	BAYADERE
BATLERS	BATTERED	BAUBLES	BAWBEE	BAYADERES
BATLET	BATTERER	BAUBLING	BAWBEES	BAYAMO
BATLETS	BATTERERS	BAUCHLE	BAWBLE	BAYAMOS
BATLIKE	BATTERIE	BAUCHLED	BAWBLES	BAYARD
BATMAN	BATTERIES	BAUCHLES	BAWCOCK	BAYARDS
BATMEN	BATTERING	BAUCHLING	BAWCOCKS	BAYBERRY
BATOLOGY	BATTERO	BAUD	BAWD	BAYE
BATON	BATTEROS	BAUDEKIN	BAWDIER	BAYED
BATONED	BATTERS	BAUDEKINS	BAWDIES	BAYES
BATONING	BATTERY	BAUDRIC	BAWDIEST	BAYFRONT
BATONS	BATTIER	BAUDRICK	BAWDILY	BAYFRONTS
BATOON	BATTIES	BAUDRICKE	BAWDINESS	BAYING
BATOONED	BATTIEST	BAUDRICKS	BAWDKIN	BAYLE
BATOONING	BATTIK	BAUDRICS	BAWDKINS	BAYLES
BATOONS	BATTIKS	BAUDRONS	BAWDRIC	BAYMAN
BATRACHIA	BATTILL	BAUDS	BAWDRICS	BAYMEN
BATS	BATTILLED	BAUERA	BAWDRIES	BAYNODDY

BAYONET
BAYONETED
BAYONETS
BAYOU
BAYOUS
BAYS
BAYSIDE
BAYSIDES
BAYT
BAYTED
BAYTING
BAYTS
BAYWOOD
BAYWOODS
BAYWOP
BAYWOPS
BAYYAN
BAYYANS
BAZAAR
BAZAARS
BAZAR
BAZARS
BAZAZZ
BAZAZZES
BAZILLION
BAZOO
BAZOOKA
BAZOOKAS
BAZOOM
BAZOOMS
BAZOOS
BAZOUKI
BAZOUKIS
BAZZ
BAZZAZZ
BAZZAZZES
BAZZED
BAZZES
BAZZING
BDELLIUM
BDELLIUMS
BE
BEACH
BEACHBALL
BEACHBOY
BEACHBOYS
BEACHCOMB

BEACHED
BEACHES
BEACHGOER
BEACHHEAD
BEACHIER
BEACHIEST
BEACHING
BEACHSIDE
BEACHWEAR
BEACHY
BEACON
BEACONED
BEACONING
BEACONS
BEAD
BEADBLAST
BEADED
BEADER
BEADERS
BEADHOUSE
BEADIER
BEADIEST
BEADILY
BEADINESS
BEADING
BEADINGS
BEADLE
BEADLEDOM
BEADLES
BEADLIKE
BEADMAN
BEADMEN
BEADROLL
BEADROLLS
BEADS
BEADSMAN
BEADSMEN
BEADWORK
BEADWORKS
BEADY
BEAGLE
BEAGLED
BEAGLER
BEAGLERS
BEAGLES
BEAGLING
BEAGLINGS

BEAK
BEAKED
BEAKER
BEAKERFUL
BEAKERS
BEAKIER
BEAKIEST
BEAKLESS
BEAKLIKE
BEAKS
BEAKY
BEAL
BEALING
BEALINGS
BEALS
BEAM
BEAMED
BEAMER
BEAMERS
BEAMIER
BEAMIEST
BEAMILY
BEAMINESS
BEAMING
BEAMINGLY
BEAMINGS
BEAMISH
BEAMISHLY
BEAMLESS
BEAMLET
BEAMLETS
BEAMLIKE
BEAMS
BEAMY
BEAN
BEANBAG
BEANBAGS
BEANBALL
BEANBALLS
BEANED
BEANERIES
BEANERY
BEANFEAST
BEANIE
BEANIES
BEANING
BEANLIKE

BEANO
BEANOS
BEANPOLE
BEANPOLES
BEANS
BEANSTALK
BEANY
BEAR
BEARABLE
BEARABLY
BEARBERRY
BEARBINE
BEARBINES
BEARCAT
BEARCATS
BEARD
BEARDED
BEARDIE
BEARDIER
BEARDIES
BEARDIEST
BEARDING
BEARDLESS
BEARDS
BEARDY
BEARE
BEARED
BEARER
BEARERS
BEARES
BEARGRASS
BEARHUG
BEARHUGS
BEARING
BEARINGS
BEARISH
BEARISHLY
BEARLIKE
BEARNAISE
BEARPAW
BEARPAWS
BEARS
BEARSKIN
BEARSKINS
BEARWARD
BEARWARDS
BEARWOOD

BEARWOODS
BEAST
BEASTED
BEASTHOOD
BEASTIE
BEASTIES
BEASTILY
BEASTING
BEASTINGS
BEASTLIER
BEASTLIKE
BEASTLY
BEASTS
BEAT
BEATABLE
BEATBOX
BEATBOXED
BEATBOXER
BEATBOXES
BEATEN
BEATER
BEATERS
BEATH
BEATHED
BEATHING
BEATHS
BEATIER
BEATIEST
BEATIFIC
BEATIFIED
BEATIFIES
BEATIFY
BEATING
BEATINGS
BEATITUDE
BEATLESS
BEATNIK
BEATNIKS
BEATS
BEATY
BEAU
BEAUCOUP
BEAUCOUPS
BEAUFET
BEAUFETS
BEAUFFET
BEAUFFETS

BEAUFIN	BECAP	BECLOGS	BEDAGGLED	BEDECKS
BEAUFINS	BECAPPED	BECLOTHE	BEDAGGLES	BEDEGUAR
BEAUISH	BECAPPING	BECLOTHED	BEDAMN	BEDEGUARS
BEAUS	BECAPS	BECLOTHES	BEDAMNED	BEDEHOUSE
BEAUT	BECARPET	BECLOUD	BEDAMNING	BEDEL
BEAUTEOUS	BECARPETS	BECLOUDED	BEDAMNS	BEDELL
BEAUTER	BECASSE	BECLOUDS	BEDARKEN	BEDELLS
BEAUTEST	BECASSES	BECLOWN	BEDARKENS	BEDELS
BEAUTIED	BECAUSE	BECLOWNED	BEDASH	BEDELSHIP
BEAUTIES	BECCACCIA	BECLOWNS	BEDASHED	BEDEMAN
BEAUTIFUL	BECCAFICO	BECOME	BEDASHES	BEDEMEN
BEAUTIFY	BECHALK	BECOMES	BEDASHING	BEDERAL
BEAUTS	BECHALKED	BECOMING	BEDAUB	BEDERALS
BEAUTY	BECHALKS	BECOMINGS	BEDAUBED	BEDES
BEAUTYING	BECHAMEL	BECOWARD	BEDAUBING	BEDESMAN
BEAUX	BECHAMELS	BECOWARDS	BEDAUBS	BEDESMEN
BEAUXITE	BECHANCE	BECQUEREL	BEDAWIN	BEDEVIL
BEAUXITES	BECHANCED	BECRAWL	BEDAWINS	BEDEVILED
BEAVER	BECHANCES	BECRAWLED	BEDAZE	BEDEVILS
BEAVERED	BECHARM	BECRAWLS	BEDAZED	BEDEW
BEAVERIES	BECHARMED	BECRIME	BEDAZES	BEDEWED
BEAVERING	BECHARMS	BECRIMED	BEDAZING	BEDEWING
BEAVERS	BECK	BECRIMES	BEDAZZLE	BEDEWS
BEAVERY	BECKE	BECRIMING	BEDAZZLED	BEDFAST
BEBEERINE	BECKED	BECROWD	BEDAZZLES	BEDFELLOW
BEBEERU	BECKES	BECROWDED	BEDBATH	BEDFRAME
BEBEERUS	BECKET	BECROWDS	BEDBATHS	BEDFRAMES
BEBLOOD	BECKETS	BECRUST	BEDBOARD	BEDGOWN
BEBLOODED	BECKING	BECRUSTED	BEDBOARDS	BEDGOWNS
BEBLOODS	BECKON	BECRUSTS	BEDBUG	BEDHEAD
BEBOP	BECKONED	BECUDGEL	BEDBUGS	BEDHEADS
BEBOPPED	BECKONER	BECUDGELS	BEDCHAIR	BEDIAPER
BEBOPPER	BECKONERS	BECURL	BEDCHAIRS	BEDIAPERS
BEBOPPERS	BECKONING	BECURLED	BEDCOVER	BEDIDE
BEBOPPING	BECKONS	BECURLING	BEDCOVERS	BEDIGHT
BEBOPS	BECKS	BECURLS	BEDDABLE	BEDIGHTED
BEBUNG	BECLAMOR	BECURSE	BEDDED	BEDIGHTS
BEBUNGS	BECLAMORS	BECURSED	BEDDER	BEDIM
BECALL	BECLAMOUR	BECURSES	BEDDERS	BEDIMMED
BECALLED	BECLASP	BECURSING	BEDDING	BEDIMMING
BECALLING	BECLASPED	BECURST	BEDDINGS	BEDIMPLE
BECALLS	BECLASPS	BED	BEDE	BEDIMPLED
BECALM	BECLOAK	BEDABBLE	BEDEAFEN	BEDIMPLES
BECALMED	BECLOAKED	BEDABBLED	BEDEAFENS	BEDIMS
BECALMING	BECLOAKS	BEDABBLES	BEDECK	BEDIRTIED
BECALMS	BECLOG	BEDAD	BEDECKED	BEDIRTIES
BECAME	BECLOGGED	BEDAGGLE	BEDECKING	BEDIRTY

BEDIZEN	BEDRITES	BEDUCKED	BEECHY	BEERAGES
BEDIZENED	BEDRIVEL	BEDUCKING	BEEDI	BEERFEST
BEDIZENS	BEDRIVELS	BEDUCKS	BEEDIE	BEERFESTS
BEDLAM	BEDROCK	BEDUIN	BEEDIES	BEERHALL
BEDLAMER	BEDROCKS	BEDUINS	BEEF	BEERHALLS
BEDLAMERS	BEDROLL	BEDUMB	BEEFALO	BEERIER
BEDLAMISM	BEDROLLS	BEDUMBED	BEEFALOES	BEERIEST
BEDLAMITE	BEDROOM	BEDUMBING	BEEFALOS	BEERILY
BEDLAMP	BEDROOMED	BEDUMBS	BEEFCAKE	BEERINESS
BEDLAMPS	BEDROOMS	BEDUNCE	BEEFCAKES	BEERMAT
BEDLAMS	BEDROP	BEDUNCED	BEEFEATER	BEERMATS
BEDLESS	BEDROPPED	BEDUNCES	BEEFED	BEERNUT
BEDLIKE	BEDROPS	BEDUNCING	BEEFIER	BEERNUTS
BEDLINER	BEDROPT	BEDUNG	BEEFIEST	BEERS
BEDLINERS	BEDRUG	BEDUNGED	BEEFILY	BEERSIES
BEDMAKER	BEDRUGGED	BEDUNGING	BEEFINESS	BEERY
BEDMAKERS	BEDRUGS	BEDUNGS	BEEFING	BEES
BEDMATE	BEDS	BEDUST	BEEFLESS	BEESOME
BEDMATES	BEDSHEET	BEDUSTED	BEEFS	BEESTING
BEDOTTED	BEDSHEETS	BEDUSTING	BEEFSTEAK	BEESTINGS
BEDOUIN	BEDSIDE	BEDUSTS	BEEFWOOD	BEESTUNG
BEDOUINS	BEDSIDES	BEDWARD	BEEFWOODS	BEESWAX
BEDPAN	BEDSIT	BEDWARDS	BEEFY	BEESWAXED
BEDPANS	BEDSITS	BEDWARF	BEEGAH	BEESWAXES
BEDPLATE	BEDSITTER	BEDWARFED	BEEGAHS	BEESWING
BEDPLATES	BEDSKIRT	BEDWARFS	BEEHIVE	BEESWINGS
BEDPOST	BEDSKIRTS	BEDWARMER	BEEHIVED	BEET
BEDPOSTS	BEDSOCK	BEDWETTER	BEEHIVES	BEETED
BEDQUILT	BEDSOCKS	BEDYDE	BEEKEEPER	BEETFLIES
BEDQUILTS	BEDSONIA	BEDYE	BEELIKE	BEETFLY
BEDRAGGLE	BEDSONIAS	BEDYED	BEELINE	BEETING
BEDRAIL	BEDSORE	BEDYEING	BEELINED	BEETLE
BEDRAILS	BEDSORES	BEDYES	BEELINES	BEETLED
BEDRAL	BEDSPREAD	BEE	BEELINING	BEETLER
BEDRALS	BEDSPRING	BEEBEE	BEEN	BEETLERS
BEDRAPE	BEDSTAND	BEEBEES	BEENAH	BEETLES
BEDRAPED	BEDSTANDS	BEEBREAD	BEENAHS	BEETLING
BEDRAPES	BEDSTEAD	BEEBREADS	BEENTO	BEETROOT
BEDRAPING	BEDSTEADS	BEECH	BEENTOS	BEETROOTS
BEDRENCH	BEDSTRAW	BEECHEN	BEEP	BEETS
BEDREST	BEDSTRAWS	BEECHES	BEEPED	BEEVES
BEDRESTS	BEDTICK	BEECHIER	BEEPER	BEEYARD
BEDRID	BEDTICKS	BEECHIEST	BEEPERS	BEEYARDS
BEDRIDDEN	BEDTIME	BEECHMAST	BEEPING	BEEZER
BEDRIGHT	BEDTIMES	BEECHNUT	BEEPS	BEEZERS
BEDRIGHTS	BEDU	BEECHNUTS	BEER	BEFALL
BEDRITE	BEDUCK	BEECHWOOD	BEERAGE	BEFALLEN

BEFALLING	BEFOULERS	BEGGINGLY	BEGONIA	BEHAPPEN
BEFALLS	BEFOULING	BEGGINGS	BEGONIAS	BEHAPPENS
BEFANA	BEFOULS	BEGHARD	BEGORAH	BEHATTED
BEFANAS	BEFRET	BEGHARDS	BEGORED	BEHAVE
BEFELD	BEFRETS	BEGIFT	BEGORRA	BEHAVED
BEFELL	BEFRETTED	BEGIFTED	BEGORRAH	BEHAVER
BEFFANA	BEFRIEND	BEGIFTING	BEGOT	BEHAVERS
BEFFANAS	BEFRIENDS	BEGIFTS	BEGOTTEN	BEHAVES
BEFINGER	BEFRINGE	BEGILD	BEGRIM	BEHAVING
BEFINGERS	BEFRINGED	BEGILDED	BEGRIME	BEHAVIOR
BEFINNED	BEFRINGES	BEGILDING	BEGRIMED	BEHAVIORS
BEFIT	BEFUDDLE	BEGILDS	BEGRIMES	BEHAVIOUR
BEFITS	BEFUDDLED	BEGILT	BEGRIMING	BEHEAD
BEFITTED	BEFUDDLES	BEGIN	BEGRIMMED	BEHEADAL
BEFITTING	BEG	BEGINNE	BEGRIMS	BEHEADALS
BEFLAG	BEGAD	BEGINNER	BEGROAN	BEHEADED
BEFLAGGED	BEGALL	BEGINNERS	BEGROANED	BEHEADER
BEFLAGS	BEGALLED	BEGINNES	BEGROANS	BEHEADERS
BEFLEA	BEGALLING	BEGINNING	BEGRUDGE	BEHEADING
BEFLEAED	BEGALLS	BEGINS	BEGRUDGED	BEHEADS
BEFLEAING	BEGAN	BEGIRD	BEGRUDGER	BEHELD
BEFLEAS	BEGAR	BEGIRDED	BEGRUDGES	BEHEMOTH
BEFLECK	BEGARS	BEGIRDING	BEGS	BEHEMOTHS
BEFLECKED	BEGAT	BEGIRDLE	BEGUILE	BEHEST
BEFLECKS	BEGAZE	BEGIRDLED	BEGUILED	BEHESTS
BEFLOWER	BEGAZED	BEGIRDLES	BEGUILER	BEHIGHT
BEFLOWERS	BEGAZES	BEGIRDS	BEGUILERS	BEHIGHTS
BEFLUM	BEGAZING	BEGIRT	BEGUILES	BEHIND
BEFLUMMED	BEGEM	BEGLAD	BEGUILING	BEHINDS
BEFLUMS	BEGEMMED	BEGLADDED	BEGUIN	BEHOLD
BEFOAM	BEGEMMING	BEGLADS	BEGUINAGE	BEHOLDEN
BEFOAMED	BEGEMS	BEGLAMOR	BEGUINE	BEHOLDER
BEFOAMING	BEGET	BEGLAMORS	BEGUINES	BEHOLDERS
BEFOAMS	BEGETS	BEGLAMOUR	BEGUINS	BEHOLDING
BEFOG	BEGETTER	BEGLERBEG	BEGULF	BEHOLDS
BEFOGGED	BEGETTERS	BEGLOOM	BEGULFED	BEHOOF
BEFOGGING	BEGETTING	BEGLOOMED	BEGULFING	BEHOOFS
BEFOGS	BEGGAR	BEGLOOMS	BEGULFS	BEHOOVE
BEFOOL	BEGGARDOM	BEGNAW	BEGUM	BEHOOVED
BEFOOLED	BEGGARED	BEGNAWED	BEGUMS	BEHOOVES
BEFOOLING	BEGGARIES	BEGNAWING	BEGUN	BEHOOVING
BEFOOLS	BEGGARING	BEGNAWS	BEGUNK	BEHOTE
BEFORE	BEGGARLY	BEGO	BEGUNKED	BEHOTES
BEFORTUNE	BEGGARS	BEGOES	BEGUNKING	BEHOTING
BEFOUL	BEGGARY	BEGOGGLED	BEGUNKS	BEHOVE
BEFOULED	BEGGED	BEGOING	BEHALF	BEHOVED
BEFOULER	BEGGING	BEGONE	BEHALVES	BEHOVEFUL

BEHOVELY
BEHOVES
BEHOVING
BEHOWL
BEHOWLED
BEHOWLING
BEHOWLS
BEIGE
BEIGEL
BEIGELS
BEIGER
BEIGES
BEIGEST
BEIGIER
BEIGIEST
BEIGNE
BEIGNES
BEIGNET
BEIGNETS
BEIGY
BEIN
BEINED
BEING
BEINGLESS
BEINGNESS
BEINGS
BEINING
BEINKED
BEINNESS
BEINS
BEJABBERS
BEJABERS
BEJADE
BEJADED
BEJADES
BEJADING
BEJANT
BEJANTS
BEJASUS
BEJASUSES
BEJEEBERS
BEJEEZUS
BEJESUIT
BEJESUITS
BEJESUS
BEJESUSES
BEJEWEL

BEJEWELED
BEJEWELS
BEJUMBLE
BEJUMBLED
BEJUMBLES
BEKAH
BEKAHS
BEKISS
BEKISSED
BEKISSES
BEKISSING
BEKNAVE
BEKNAVED
BEKNAVES
BEKNAVING
BEKNIGHT
BEKNIGHTS
BEKNOT
BEKNOTS
BEKNOTTED
BEKNOWN
BEL
BELABOR
BELABORED
BELABORS
BELABOUR
BELABOURS
BELACE
BELACED
BELACES
BELACING
BELADIED
BELADIES
BELADY
BELADYING
BELAH
BELAHS
BELAMIES
BELAMOUR
BELAMOURE
BELAMOURS
BELAMY
BELAR
BELARS
BELATE
BELATED
BELATEDLY

BELATES
BELATING
BELAUD
BELAUDED
BELAUDING
BELAUDS
BELAY
BELAYED
BELAYER
BELAYERS
BELAYING
BELAYS
BELCH
BELCHED
BELCHER
BELCHERS
BELCHES
BELCHING
BELDAM
BELDAME
BELDAMES
BELDAMS
BELEAGUER
BELEAP
BELEAPED
BELEAPING
BELEAPS
BELEAPT
BELEE
BELEED
BELEEING
BELEES
BELEMNITE
BELEMNOID
BELFRIED
BELFRIES
BELFRY
BELGA
BELGARD
BELGARDS
BELGAS
BELGICISM
BELIE
BELIED
BELIEF
BELIEFS
BELIER

BELIERS
BELIES
BELIEVE
BELIEVED
BELIEVER
BELIEVERS
BELIEVES
BELIEVING
BELIKE
BELIQUOR
BELIQUORS
BELITTLE
BELITTLED
BELITTLER
BELITTLES
BELIVE
BELL
BELLBIND
BELLBINDS
BELLBIRD
BELLBIRDS
BELLBOY
BELLBOYS
BELLBUOY
BELLBUOYS
BELLCAST
BELLCOTE
BELLCOTES
BELLE
BELLED
BELLEEK
BELLEEKS
BELLES
BELLETER
BELLETERS
BELLHOP
BELLHOPS
BELLIBONE
BELLICOSE
BELLIED
BELLIES
BELLING
BELLINGS
BELLINI
BELLINIS
BELLMAN
BELLMEN

BELLOCK
BELLOCKED
BELLOCKS
BELLOW
BELLOWED
BELLOWER
BELLOWERS
BELLOWING
BELLOWS
BELLPULL
BELLPULLS
BELLS
BELLWORT
BELLWORTS
BELLY
BELLYACHE
BELLYBAND
BELLYFUL
BELLYFULS
BELLYING
BELLYINGS
BELLYLIKE
BELOMANCY
BELON
BELONG
BELONGED
BELONGER
BELONGERS
BELONGING
BELONGS
BELONS
BELOVE
BELOVED
BELOVEDS
BELOVES
BELOVING
BELOW
BELOWS
BELS
BELT
BELTED
BELTER
BELTERS
BELTING
BELTINGS
BELTLESS
BELTLINE

BELTLINES	BEMIRED	BEMUZZLE	BENE	BENJAMIN
BELTMAN	BEMIRES	BEMUZZLED	BENEATH	BENJAMINS
BELTMEN	BEMIRING	BEMUZZLES	BENEDICK	BENJES
BELTS	BEMIST	BEN	BENEDICKS	BENNE
BELTWAY	BEMISTED	BENADRYL	BENEDICT	BENNES
BELTWAYS	BEMISTING	BENADRYLS	BENEDICTS	BENNET
BELUGA	BEMISTS	BENAME	BENEDIGHT	BENNETS
BELUGAS	BEMIX	BENAMED	BENEFACT	BENNI
BELVEDERE	BEMIXED	BENAMES	BENEFACTS	BENNIES
BELYING	BEMIXES	BENAMING	BENEFIC	BENNIS
BEMA	BEMIXING	BENCH	BENEFICE	BENNY
BEMAD	BEMIXT	BENCHED	BENEFICED	BENOMYL
BEMADAM	BEMOAN	BENCHER	BENEFICES	BENOMYLS
BEMADAMED	BEMOANED	BENCHERS	BENEFIT	BENS
BEMADAMS	BEMOANER	BENCHES	BENEFITED	BENT
BEMADDED	BEMOANERS	BENCHIER	BENEFITER	BENTGRASS
BEMADDEN	BEMOANING	BENCHIEST	BENEFITS	BENTHAL
BEMADDENS	BEMOANS	BENCHING	BENEMPT	BENTHIC
BEMADDING	BEMOCK	BENCHLAND	BENEMPTED	BENTHOAL
BEMADS	BEMOCKED	BENCHLESS	BENES	BENTHON
BEMAS	BEMOCKING	BENCHMARK	BENET	BENTHONIC
BEMATA	BEMOCKS	BENCHTOP	BENETS	BENTHONS
BEMAUL	BEMOIL	BENCHTOPS	BENETTED	BENTHOS
BEMAULED	BEMOILED	BENCHY	BENETTING	BENTHOSES
BEMAULING	BEMOILING	BEND	BENGA	BENTIER
BEMAULS	BEMOILS	BENDABLE	BENGALINE	BENTIEST
BEMAZED	BEMONSTER	BENDAY	BENGAS	BENTO
BEMBEX	BEMOUTH	BENDAYED	BENI	BENTONITE
BEMBEXES	BEMOUTHED	BENDAYING	BENIGHT	BENTOS
BEMBIX	BEMOUTHS	BENDAYS	BENIGHTED	BENTS
BEMBIXES	BEMUD	BENDED	BENIGHTEN	BENTWOOD
BEMEAN	BEMUDDED	BENDEE	BENIGHTER	BENTWOODS
BEMEANED	BEMUDDING	BENDEES	BENIGHTS	BENTY
BEMEANING	BEMUDDLE	BENDER	BENIGN	BENUMB
BEMEANS	BEMUDDLED	BENDERS	BENIGNANT	BENUMBED
BEMEANT	BEMUDDLES	BENDIER	BENIGNER	BENUMBING
BEMEDAL	BEMUDS	BENDIEST	BENIGNEST	BENUMBS
BEMEDALED	BEMUFFLE	BENDING	BENIGNITY	BENZAL
BEMEDALS	BEMUFFLED	BENDINGLY	BENIGNLY	BENZALS
BEMETE	BEMUFFLES	BENDINGS	BENIS	BENZENE
BEMETED	BEMURMUR	BENDLET	BENISEED	BENZENES
BEMETES	BEMURMURS	BENDLETS	BENISEEDS	BENZENOID
BEMETING	BEMUSE	BENDS	BENISON	BENZIDIN
BEMINGLE	BEMUSED	BENDWAYS	BENISONS	BENZIDINE
BEMINGLED	BEMUSEDLY	BENDWISE	BENITIER	BENZIDINS
BEMINGLES	BEMUSES	BENDY	BENITIERS	BENZIL
BEMIRE	BEMUSING	BENDYS	BENJ	BENZILS

B

BENZIN
BENZINE
BENZINES
BENZINS
BENZOATE
BENZOATES
BENZOIC
BENZOIN
BENZOINS
BENZOL
BENZOLE
BENZOLES
BENZOLINE
BENZOLS
BENZOYL
BENZOYLS
BENZYL
BENZYLIC
BENZYLS
BEPAINT
BEPAINTED
BEPAINTS
BEPAT
BEPATCHED
BEPATS
BEPATTED
BEPATTING
BEPEARL
BEPEARLED
BEPEARLS
BEPELT
BEPELTED
BEPELTING
BEPELTS
BEPEPPER
BEPEPPERS
BEPESTER
BEPESTERS
BEPIMPLE
BEPIMPLED
BEPIMPLES
BEPITIED
BEPITIES
BEPITY
BEPITYING
BEPLASTER
BEPLUMED

BEPOMMEL
BEPOMMELS
BEPOWDER
BEPOWDERS
BEPRAISE
BEPRAISED
BEPRAISES
BEPROSE
BEPROSED
BEPROSES
BEPROSING
BEPUFF
BEPUFFED
BEPUFFING
BEPUFFS
BEQUEATH
BEQUEATHS
BEQUEST
BEQUESTS
BERAKE
BERAKED
BERAKES
BERAKING
BERASCAL
BERASCALS
BERATE
BERATED
BERATES
BERATING
BERAY
BERAYED
BERAYING
BERAYS
BERBER
BERBERE
BERBERES
BERBERIN
BERBERINE
BERBERINS
BERBERIS
BERBERS
BERBICE
BERCEAU
BERCEAUX
BERCEUSE
BERCEUSES
BERDACHE

BERDACHES
BERDASH
BERDASHES
BERE
BEREAVE
BEREAVED
BEREAVEN
BEREAVER
BEREAVERS
BEREAVES
BEREAVING
BEREFT
BERES
BERET
BERETS
BERETTA
BERETTAS
BERG
BERGALI
BERGALIS
BERGAMA
BERGAMAS
BERGAMASK
BERGAMOT
BERGAMOTS
BERGANDER
BERGEN
BERGENIA
BERGENIAS
BERGENS
BERGERE
BERGERES
BERGFALL
BERGFALLS
BERGHAAN
BERGHAANS
BERGMEHL
BERGMEHLS
BERGOMASK
BERGS
BERGYLT
BERGYLTS
BERHYME
BERHYMED
BERHYMES
BERHYMING
BERIBERI

BERIBERIS
BERIMBAU
BERIMBAUS
BERIME
BERIMED
BERIMES
BERIMING
BERINGED
BERK
BERKELIUM
BERKO
BERKS
BERLEY
BERLEYED
BERLEYING
BERLEYS
BERLIN
BERLINE
BERLINES
BERLINS
BERM
BERME
BERMED
BERMES
BERMING
BERMS
BERMUDAS
BERNICLE
BERNICLES
BEROB
BEROBBED
BEROBBING
BEROBED
BEROBS
BEROUGED
BERRET
BERRETS
BERRETTA
BERRETTAS
BERRIED
BERRIES
BERRIGAN
BERRIGANS
BERRY
BERRYING
BERRYINGS
BERRYLESS

BERRYLIKE
BERSEEM
BERSEEMS
BERSERK
BERSERKER
BERSERKLY
BERSERKS
BERTH
BERTHA
BERTHAGE
BERTHAGES
BERTHAS
BERTHE
BERTHED
BERTHES
BERTHING
BERTHINGS
BERTHS
BERYL
BERYLINE
BERYLLIA
BERYLLIAS
BERYLLIUM
BERYLS
BES
BESAINT
BESAINTED
BESAINTS
BESANG
BESAT
BESAW
BESCATTER
BESCORCH
BESCOUR
BESCOURED
BESCOURS
BESCRAWL
BESCRAWLS
BESCREEN
BESCREENS
BESEE
BESEECH
BESEECHED
BESEECHER
BESEECHES
BESEEING
BESEEKE

BESEEKES	BESIGHS	BESOIN	BESPOUSED	BESTOWING
BESEEKING	BESING	BESOINS	BESPOUSES	BESTOWS
BESEEM	BESINGING	BESOM	BESPOUT	BESTREAK
BESEEMED	BESINGS	BESOMED	BESPOUTED	BESTREAKS
BESEEMING	BESIT	BESOMING	BESPOUTS	BESTREW
BESEEMLY	BESITS	BESOMS	BESPREAD	BESTREWED
BESEEMS	BESITTING	BESONIAN	BESPREADS	BESTREWN
BESEEN	BESLAVE	BESONIANS	BESPRENT	BESTREWS
BESEES	BESLAVED	BESOOTHE	BEST	BESTRID
BESES	BESLAVER	BESOOTHED	BESTAD	BESTRIDE
BESET	BESLAVERS	BESOOTHES	BESTADDE	BESTRIDES
BESETMENT	BESLAVES	BESORT	BESTAIN	BESTRODE
BESETS	BESLAVING	BESORTED	BESTAINED	BESTROW
BESETTER	BESLIME	BESORTING	BESTAINS	BESTROWED
BESETTERS	BESLIMED	BESORTS	BESTAR	BESTROWN
BESETTING	BESLIMES	BESOT	BESTARRED	BESTROWS
BESHADOW	BESLIMING	BESOTS	BESTARS	BESTS
BESHADOWS	BESLOBBER	BESOTTED	BESTEAD	BESTUCK
BESHAME	BESLUBBER	BESOTTING	BESTEADED	BESTUD
BESHAMED	BESMEAR	BESOUGHT	BESTEADS	BESTUDDED
BESHAMES	BESMEARED	BESOULED	BESTED	BESTUDS
BESHAMING	BESMEARER	BESPAKE	BESTI	BESUITED
BESHINE	BESMEARS	BESPANGLE	BESTIAL	BESUNG
BESHINES	BESMILE	BESPAT	BESTIALLY	BESWARM
BESHINING	BESMILED	BESPATE	BESTIALS	BESWARMED
BESHIVER	BESMILES	BESPATTER	BESTIARY	BESWARMS
BESHIVERS	BESMILING	BESPEAK	BESTICK	BET
BESHONE	BESMIRCH	BESPEAKS	BESTICKS	BETA
BESHOUT	BESMOKE	BESPECKLE	BESTIE	BETACISM
BESHOUTED	BESMOKED	BESPED	BESTIES	BETACISMS
BESHOUTS	BESMOKES	BESPEED	BESTILL	BETAINE
BESHREW	BESMOKING	BESPEEDS	BESTILLED	BETAINES
BESHREWED	BESMOOTH	BESPICE	BESTILLS	BETAKE
BESHREWS	BESMOOTHS	BESPICED	BESTING	BETAKEN
BESHROUD	BESMUDGE	BESPICES	BESTIR	BETAKES
BESHROUDS	BESMUDGED	BESPICING	BESTIRRED	BETAKING
BESIDE	BESMUDGES	BESPIT	BESTIRS	BETAS
BESIDES	BESMUT	BESPITS	BESTIS	BETATOPIC
BESIEGE	BESMUTCH	BESPOKE	BESTORM	BETATRON
BESIEGED	BESMUTS	BESPOKEN	BESTORMED	BETATRONS
BESIEGER	BESMUTTED	BESPORT	BESTORMS	BETATTER
BESIEGERS	BESNOW	BESPORTED	BESTOW	BETATTERS
BESIEGES	BESNOWED	BESPORTS	BESTOWAL	BETAXED
BESIEGING	BESNOWING	BESPOT	BESTOWALS	BETCHA
BESIGH	BESNOWS	BESPOTS	BESTOWED	BETE
BESIGHED	BESOGNIO	BESPOTTED	BESTOWER	BETED
BESIGHING	BESOGNIOS	BESPOUSE	BESTOWERS	BETEEM

BETEEME	BETISE	BETTERING	BEVVYING	BEWRAPPED
BETEEMED	BETISES	BETTERS	BEVY	BEWRAPS
BETEEMES	BETITLE	BETTIES	BEWAIL	BEWRAPT
BETEEMING	BETITLED	BETTING	BEWAILED	BEWRAY
BETEEMS	BETITLES	BETTINGS	BEWAILER	BEWRAYED
BETEL	BETITLING	BETTONG	BEWAILERS	BEWRAYER
BETELNUT	BETOIL	BETTONGS	BEWAILING	BEWRAYERS
BETELNUTS	BETOILED	BETTOR	BEWAILS	BEWRAYING
BETELS	BETOILING	BETTORS	BEWARE	BEWRAYS
BETES	BETOILS	BETTY	BEWARED	BEY
BETH	BETOKEN	BETUMBLED	BEWARES	BEYLIC
BETHANK	BETOKENED	BETWEEN	BEWARING	BEYLICS
BETHANKED	BETOKENS	BETWEENS	BEWEARIED	BEYLIK
BETHANKIT	BETON	BETWIXT	BEWEARIES	BEYLIKS
BETHANKS	BETONIES	BEUNCLED	BEWEARY	BEYOND
BETHEL	BETONS	BEURRE	BEWEEP	BEYONDS
BETHELS	BETONY	BEURRES	BEWEEPING	BEYS
BETHESDA	BETOOK	BEVATRON	BEWEEPS	BEZ
BETHESDAS	BETOSS	BEVATRONS	BEWENT	BEZANT
BETHINK	BETOSSED	BEVEL	BEWEPT	BEZANTS
BETHINKS	BETOSSES	BEVELED	BEWET	BEZAZZ
BETHORN	BETOSSING	BEVELER	BEWETS	BEZAZZES
BETHORNED	BETRAY	BEVELERS	BEWETTED	BEZEL
BETHORNS	BETRAYAL	BEVELING	BEWETTING	BEZELS
BETHOUGHT	BETRAYALS	BEVELLED	BEWHORE	BEZES
BETHRALL	BETRAYED	BEVELLER	BEWHORED	BEZIL
BETHRALLS	BETRAYER	BEVELLERS	BEWHORES	BEZILS
BETHS	BETRAYERS	BEVELLING	BEWHORING	BEZIQUE
BETHUMB	BETRAYING	BEVELMENT	BEWIG	BEZIQUES
BETHUMBED	BETRAYS	BEVELS	BEWIGGED	BEZOAR
BETHUMBS	BETREAD	BEVER	BEWIGGING	BEZOARDIC
BETHUMP	BETREADS	BEVERAGE	BEWIGS	BEZOARS
BETHUMPED	BETRIM	BEVERAGES	BEWILDER	BEZONIAN
BETHUMPS	BETRIMMED	BEVERED	BEWILDERS	BEZONIANS
BETHWACK	BETRIMS	BEVERING	BEWINGED	BEZZANT
BETHWACKS	BETROD	BEVERS	BEWITCH	BEZZANTS
BETID	BETRODDEN	BEVIES	BEWITCHED	BEZZAZZ
BETIDE	BETROTH	BEVOMIT	BEWITCHER	BEZZAZZES
BETIDED	BETROTHAL	BEVOMITED	BEWITCHES	BEZZIE
BETIDES	BETROTHED	BEVOMITS	BEWORM	BEZZIES
BETIDING	BETROTHS	BEVOR	BEWORMED	BEZZLE
BETIGHT	BETS	BEVORS	BEWORMING	BEZZLED
BETIME	BETTA	BEVUE	BEWORMS	BEZZLES
BETIMED	BETTAS	BEVUES	BEWORRIED	BEZZLING
BETIMES	BETTED	BEVVIED	BEWORRIES	BEZZY
BETIMING	BETTER	BEVVIES	BEWORRY	BHAGEE
BETING	BETTERED	BEVVY	BEWRAP	BHAGEES

B

BHAI	BHOOTS	BIBBING	BICKERS	BIDENTATE
BHAIS	BHUNA	BIBBINGS	BICKIE	BIDENTS
BHAJAN	BHUNAS	BIBBLE	BICKIES	BIDER
BHAJANS	BHUT	BIBBLES	BICOASTAL	BIDERS
BHAJEE	BHUTS	BIBBS	BICOLOR	BIDES
BHAJEES	BI	BIBCOCK	BICOLORED	BIDET
BHAJI	BIACETYL	BIBCOCKS	BICOLORS	BIDETS
BHAJIA	BIACETYLS	BIBE	BICOLOUR	BIDI
BHAJIS	BIACH	BIBELOT	BICOLOURS	BIDING
BHAKTA	BIACHES	BIBELOTS	BICONCAVE	BIDINGS
BHAKTAS	BIALI	BIBES	BICONVEX	BIDIS
BHAKTI	BIALIES	BIBFUL	BICORN	BIDON
BHAKTIS	BIALIS	BIBFULS	BICORNATE	BIDONS
BHANG	BIALY	BIBLE	BICORNE	BIDS
BHANGRA	BIALYS	BIBLES	BICORNES	BIELD
BHANGRAS	BIANNUAL	BIBLESS	BICORNS	BIELDED
BHANGS	BIANNUALS	BIBLICAL	BICRON	BIELDIER
BHARAL	BIAS	BIBLICISM	BICRONS	BIELDIEST
BHARALS	BIASED	BIBLICIST	BICUSPID	BIELDING
BHAT	BIASEDLY	BIBLIKE	BICUSPIDS	BIELDS
BHAVAN	BIASES	BIBLIOTIC	BICYCLE	BIELDY
BHAVANS	BIASING	BIBLIST	BICYCLED	BIEN
BHAWAN	BIASINGS	BIBLISTS	BICYCLER	BIENNALE
BHAWANS	BIASNESS	BIBS	BICYCLERS	BIENNALES
BHEESTIE	BIASSED	BIBULOUS	BICYCLES	BIENNIA
BHEESTIES	BIASSEDLY	BICAMERAL	BICYCLIC	BIENNIAL
BHEESTY	BIASSES	BICARB	BICYCLING	BIENNIALS
BHEL	BIASSING	BICARBS	BICYCLIST	BIENNIUM
BHELPURI	BIATCH	BICAUDAL	BID	BIENNIUMS
BHELPURIS	BIATCHES	BICCIES	BIDARKA	BIER
BHELS	BIATHLETE	BICCY	BIDARKAS	BIERS
BHIKHU	BIATHLON	BICE	BIDARKEE	BIESTINGS
BHIKHUS	BIATHLONS	BICENTRIC	BIDARKEES	BIFACE
BHIKKHUNI	BIAXAL	BICEP	BIDDABLE	BIFACES
BHINDI	BIAXIAL	BICEPS	BIDDABLY	BIFACIAL
BHINDIS	BIAXIALLY	BICEPSES	BIDDEN	BIFARIOUS
BHISHTI	BIB	BICES	BIDDER	BIFF
BHISHTIS	BIBACIOUS	BICHIR	BIDDERS	BIFFED
BHISTEE	BIBASIC	BICHIRS	BIDDIES	BIFFER
BHISTEES	BIBATION	BICHORD	BIDDING	BIFFERS
BHISTI	BIBATIONS	BICHROME	BIDDINGS	BIFFIES
BHISTIE	BIBB	BICIPITAL	BIDDY	BIFFIN
BHISTIES	BIBBED	BICKER	BIDE	BIFFING
BHISTIS	BIBBER	BICKERED	BIDED	BIFFINS
BHOONA	BIBBERIES	BICKERER	BIDENT	BIFFO
BHOONAS	BIBBERS	BICKERERS	BIDENTAL	BIFFOS
BHOOT	BIBBERY	BICKERING	BIDENTALS	BIFFS

BIFFY	BIGFEET	BIGOTS	BILBOA	BILLBUGS
BIFID	BIGFOOT	BIGS	BILBOAS	BILLED
BIFIDA	BIGFOOTED	BIGSTICK	BILBOES	BILLER
BIFIDITY	BIGFOOTS	BIGTIME	BILBOS	BILLERS
BIFIDLY	BIGG	BIGUANIDE	BILBY	BILLET
BIFIDUM	BIGGED	BIGUINE	BILE	BILLETED
BIFIDUMS	BIGGER	BIGUINES	BILECTION	BILLETEE
BIFIDUS	BIGGEST	BIGWIG	BILED	BILLETEES
BIFIDUSES	BIGGETY	BIGWIGS	BILES	BILLETER
BIFILAR	BIGGIE	BIHOURLY	BILESTONE	BILLETERS
BIFILARLY	BIGGIES	BIJECTION	BILEVEL	BILLETING
BIFLEX	BIGGIN	BIJECTIVE	BILEVELS	BILLETS
BIFOCAL	BIGGING	BIJOU	BILGE	BILLFISH
BIFOCALED	BIGGINGS	BIJOUS	BILGED	BILLFOLD
BIFOCALS	BIGGINS	BIJOUX	BILGES	BILLFOLDS
BIFOLD	BIGGISH	BIJUGATE	BILGIER	BILLHEAD
BIFOLDS	BIGGITIER	BIJUGOUS	BILGIEST	BILLHEADS
BIFOLIATE	BIGGITY	BIJURAL	BILGING	BILLHOOK
BIFORATE	BIGGON	BIJWONER	BILGY	BILLHOOKS
BIFORKED	BIGGONS	BIJWONERS	BILHARZIA	BILLIARD
BIFORM	BIGGS	BIKE	BILIAN	BILLIARDS
BIFORMED	BIGGY	BIKED	BILIANS	BILLIE
BIFTAH	BIGHA	BIKER	BILIARIES	BILLIES
BIFTAHS	BIGHAS	BIKERS	BILIARY	BILLING
BIFTER	BIGHEAD	BIKES	BILIMBI	BILLINGS
BIFTERS	BIGHEADED	BIKEWAY	BILIMBING	BILLION
BIFURCATE	BIGHEADS	BIKEWAYS	BILIMBIS	BILLIONS
BIG	BIGHORN	BIKIE	BILINEAR	BILLIONTH
BIGA	BIGHORNS	BIKIES	BILING	BILLMAN
BIGAE	BIGHT	BIKING	BILINGUAL	BILLMEN
BIGAMIES	BIGHTED	BIKINGS	BILIOUS	BILLON
BIGAMIST	BIGHTING	BIKINI	BILIOUSLY	BILLONS
BIGAMISTS	BIGHTS	BIKINIED	BILIRUBIN	BILLOW
BIGAMOUS	BIGLY	BIKINIS	BILITERAL	BILLOWED
BIGAMY	BIGMOUTH	BIKKIE	BILK	BILLOWIER
BIGARADE	BIGMOUTHS	BIKKIES	BILKED	BILLOWING
BIGARADES	BIGNESS	BILABIAL	BILKER	BILLOWS
BIGAROON	BIGNESSES	BILABIALS	BILKERS	BILLOWY
BIGAROONS	BIGNONIA	BILABIATE	BILKING	BILLS
BIGARREAU	BIGNONIAS	BILANDER	BILKS	BILLY
BIGEMINAL	BIGOS	BILANDERS	BILL	BILLYBOY
BIGEMINY	BIGOSES	BILATERAL	BILLABLE	BILLYBOYS
BIGENER	BIGOT	BILAYER	BILLABONG	BILLYCAN
BIGENERIC	BIGOTED	BILAYERS	BILLBOARD	BILLYCANS
BIGENERS	BIGOTEDLY	BILBERRY	BILLBOOK	BILLYCOCK
BIGEYE	BIGOTRIES	BILBIES	BILLBOOKS	BILLYO
BIGEYES	BIGOTRY	BILBO	BILLBUG	BILLYOH

BILLYOHS
BILLYOS
BILOBAR
BILOBATE
BILOBATED
BILOBED
BILOBULAR
BILOCULAR
BILSTED
BILSTEDS
BILTONG
BILTONGS
BIMA
BIMAH
BIMAHS
BIMANAL
BIMANOUS
BIMANUAL
BIMAS
BIMBASHI
BIMBASHIS
BIMBETTE
BIMBETTES
BIMBLE
BIMBO
BIMBOES
BIMBOS
BIMENSAL
BIMESTER
BIMESTERS
BIMETAL
BIMETALS
BIMETHYL
BIMETHYLS
BIMINI
BIMINIS
BIMODAL
BIMONTHLY
BIMORPH
BIMORPHS
BIN
BINAL
BINARIES
BINARISM
BINARISMS
BINARY
BINATE

BINATELY
BINAURAL
BIND
BINDABLE
BINDER
BINDERIES
BINDERS
BINDERY
BINDHI
BINDHIS
BINDI
BINDING
BINDINGLY
BINDINGS
BINDIS
BINDLE
BINDLES
BINDS
BINDWEED
BINDWEEDS
BINE
BINER
BINERS
BINERVATE
BINES
BING
BINGE
BINGED
BINGEING
BINGEINGS
BINGER
BINGERS
BINGES
BINGHI
BINGHIS
BINGIES
BINGING
BINGINGS
BINGLE
BINGLED
BINGLES
BINGLING
BINGO
BINGOED
BINGOES
BINGOING
BINGOS

BINGS
BINGY
BINIOU
BINIOUS
BINIT
BINITS
BINK
BINKS
BINMAN
BINMEN
BINNACLE
BINNACLES
BINNED
BINNING
BINOCLE
BINOCLES
BINOCS
BINOCULAR
BINOMIAL
BINOMIALS
BINOMINAL
BINOVULAR
BINS
BINT
BINTS
BINTURONG
BINUCLEAR
BIO
BIOACTIVE
BIOASSAY
BIOASSAYS
BIOBANK
BIOBANKS
BIOBLAST
BIOBLASTS
BIOCENOSE
BIOCHEMIC
BIOCHIP
BIOCHIPS
BIOCIDAL
BIOCIDE
BIOCIDES
BIOCLEAN
BIOCYCLE
BIOCYCLES
BIODATA
BIODIESEL

BIODOT
BIODOTS
BIOENERGY
BIOETHIC
BIOETHICS
BIOFACT
BIOFACTS
BIOFIBERS
BIOFIBRES
BIOFILM
BIOFILMS
BIOFOULER
BIOFUEL
BIOFUELED
BIOFUELS
BIOG
BIOGAS
BIOGASES
BIOGASSES
BIOGEN
BIOGENIC
BIOGENIES
BIOGENOUS
BIOGENS
BIOGENY
BIOGRAPH
BIOGRAPHS
BIOGRAPHY
BIOGS
BIOHAZARD
BIOHERM
BIOHERMS
BIOLOGIC
BIOLOGICS
BIOLOGIES
BIOLOGISM
BIOLOGIST
BIOLOGY
BIOLYSES
BIOLYSIS
BIOLYTIC
BIOMARKER
BIOMASS
BIOMASSES
BIOME
BIOMES
BIOMETER

BIOMETERS
BIOMETRIC
BIOMETRY
BIOMINING
BIOMORPH
BIOMORPHS
BIONIC
BIONICS
BIONOMIC
BIONOMICS
BIONOMIES
BIONOMIST
BIONOMY
BIONT
BIONTIC
BIONTS
BIOPARENT
BIOPHILIA
BIOPHOR
BIOPHORE
BIOPHORES
BIOPHORS
BIOPIC
BIOPICS
BIOPIRACY
BIOPIRATE
BIOPLASM
BIOPLASMS
BIOPLAST
BIOPLASTS
BIOPLAY
BIOPLAYS
BIOPSIC
BIOPSIED
BIOPSIES
BIOPSY
BIOPSYING
BIOPTIC
BIOREGION
BIORHYTHM
BIOS
BIOSAFETY
BIOSCOPE
BIOSCOPES
BIOSCOPY
BIOSENSOR
BIOSOCIAL

BIOSOLID	BIPHENYLS	BIRDINGS	BIRLINN	BISCUIT
BIOSOLIDS	BIPINNATE	BIRDLIFE	BIRLINNS	BISCUITS
BIOSPHERE	BIPLANE	BIRDLIFES	BIRLS	BISCUITY
BIOSTABLE	BIPLANES	BIRDLIKE	BIRO	BISE
BIOSTATIC	BIPOD	BIRDLIME	BIROS	BISECT
BIOSTROME	BIPODS	BIRDLIMED	BIRR	BISECTED
BIOTA	BIPOLAR	BIRDLIMES	BIRRED	BISECTING
BIOTAS	BIPRISM	BIRDMAN	BIRRETTA	BISECTION
BIOTECH	BIPRISMS	BIRDMEN	BIRRETTAS	BISECTOR
BIOTECHS	BIPYRAMID	BIRDS	BIRRING	BISECTORS
BIOTERROR	BIRACIAL	BIRDSEED	BIRROTCH	BISECTRIX
BIOTIC	BIRADIAL	BIRDSEEDS	BIRRS	BISECTS
BIOTICAL	BIRADICAL	BIRDSEYE	BIRSE	BISERIAL
BIOTICS	BIRAMOSE	BIRDSEYES	BIRSED	BISERIATE
BIOTIN	BIRAMOUS	BIRDSFOOT	BIRSES	BISERRATE
BIOTINS	BIRCH	BIRDSHOT	BIRSIER	BISES
BIOTITE	BIRCHBARK	BIRDSHOTS	BIRSIEST	BISEXUAL
BIOTITES	BIRCHED	BIRDSONG	BIRSING	BISEXUALS
BIOTITIC	BIRCHEN	BIRDSONGS	BIRSLE	BISH
BIOTOPE	BIRCHES	BIRDWATCH	BIRSLED	BISHES
BIOTOPES	BIRCHING	BIRDWING	BIRSLES	BISHOP
BIOTOXIN	BIRCHINGS	BIRDWINGS	BIRSLING	BISHOPDOM
BIOTOXINS	BIRCHIR	BIREME	BIRSY	BISHOPED
BIOTRON	BIRCHIRS	BIREMES	BIRTH	BISHOPESS
BIOTRONS	BIRD	BIRETTA	BIRTHDATE	BISHOPING
BIOTROPH	BIRDBATH	BIRETTAS	BIRTHDAY	BISHOPRIC
BIOTROPHS	BIRDBATHS	BIRIANI	BIRTHDAYS	BISHOPS
BIOTURBED	BIRDBRAIN	BIRIANIS	BIRTHDOM	BISK
BIOTYPE	BIRDCAGE	BIRIYANI	BIRTHDOMS	BISKS
BIOTYPES	BIRDCAGES	BIRIYANIS	BIRTHED	BISMAR
BIOTYPIC	BIRDCALL	BIRK	BIRTHER	BISMARCK
BIOVULAR	BIRDCALLS	BIRKEN	BIRTHERS	BISMARCKS
BIOWASTE	BIRDDOG	BIRKIE	BIRTHING	BISMARS
BIOWASTES	BIRDDOGS	BIRKIER	BIRTHINGS	BISMILLAH
BIOWEAPON	BIRDED	BIRKIES	BIRTHMARK	BISMUTH
BIPACK	BIRDER	BIRKIEST	BIRTHNAME	BISMUTHAL
BIPACKS	BIRDERS	BIRKS	BIRTHRATE	BISMUTHIC
BIPAROUS	BIRDFARM	BIRL	BIRTHROOT	BISMUTHS
BIPARTED	BIRDFARMS	BIRLE	BIRTHS	BISNAGA
BIPARTITE	BIRDFEED	BIRLED	BIRTHWORT	BISNAGAS
BIPARTY	BIRDFEEDS	BIRLER	BIRYANI	BISOM
BIPED	BIRDHOUSE	BIRLERS	BIRYANIS	BISOMS
BIPEDAL	BIRDIE	BIRLES	BIS	BISON
BIPEDALLY	BIRDIED	BIRLIEMAN	BISCACHA	BISONS
BIPEDS	BIRDIEING	BIRLIEMEN	BISCACHAS	BISONTINE
BIPHASIC	BIRDIES	BIRLING	BISCOTTI	BISPHENOL
BIPHENYL	BIRDING	BIRLINGS	BISCOTTO	BISQUE

BISQUES
BISSON
BISSONED
BISSONING
BISSONS
BIST
BISTABLE
BISTABLES
BISTATE
BISTER
BISTERED
BISTERS
BISTORT
BISTORTS
BISTOURY
BISTRE
BISTRED
BISTRES
BISTRO
BISTROIC
BISTROS
BISULCATE
BISULFATE
BISULFIDE
BISULFITE
BIT
BITABLE
BITCH
BITCHED
BITCHEN
BITCHERY
BITCHES
BITCHFEST
BITCHIER
BITCHIEST
BITCHILY
BITCHING
BITCHY
BITCOIN
BITCOINS
BITE
BITEABLE
BITEPLATE
BITER
BITERS
BITES
BITESIZE

BITEWING
BITEWINGS
BITING
BITINGLY
BITINGS
BITLESS
BITMAP
BITMAPPED
BITMAPS
BITO
BITONAL
BITOS
BITOU
BITS
BITSER
BITSERS
BITSIER
BITSIEST
BITSTOCK
BITSTOCKS
BITSTREAM
BITSY
BITT
BITTACLE
BITTACLES
BITTE
BITTED
BITTEN
BITTER
BITTERED
BITTERER
BITTEREST
BITTERING
BITTERISH
BITTERLY
BITTERN
BITTERNS
BITTERNUT
BITTERS
BITTIE
BITTIER
BITTIES
BITTIEST
BITTILY
BITTINESS
BITTING
BITTINGS

BITTOCK
BITTOCKS
BITTOR
BITTORS
BITTOUR
BITTOURS
BITTS
BITTUR
BITTURS
BITTY
BITUMED
BITUMEN
BITUMENS
BITWISE
BIUNIQUE
BIVALENCE
BIVALENCY
BIVALENT
BIVALENTS
BIVALVATE
BIVALVE
BIVALVED
BIVALVES
BIVARIANT
BIVARIATE
BIVIA
BIVINYL
BIVINYLS
BIVIOUS
BIVIUM
BIVOUAC
BIVOUACKS
BIVOUACS
BIVVIED
BIVVIES
BIVVY
BIVVYING
BIWEEKLY
BIYEARLY
BIZ
BIZARRE
BIZARRELY
BIZARRES
BIZARRO
BIZARROS
BIZAZZ
BIZAZZES

BIZCACHA
BIZCACHAS
BIZE
BIZES
BIZNAGA
BIZNAGAS
BIZONAL
BIZONE
BIZONES
BIZZES
BIZZIES
BIZZO
BIZZOS
BIZZY
BLAB
BLABBED
BLABBER
BLABBERED
BLABBERS
BLABBIER
BLABBIEST
BLABBING
BLABBINGS
BLABBY
BLABS
BLACK
BLACKBALL
BLACKBAND
BLACKBIRD
BLACKBODY
BLACKBOY
BLACKBOYS
BLACKBUCK
BLACKBUTT
BLACKCAP
BLACKCAPS
BLACKCOCK
BLACKDAMP
BLACKED
BLACKEN
BLACKENED
BLACKENER
BLACKENS
BLACKER
BLACKEST
BLACKFACE
BLACKFIN

BLACKFINS
BLACKFISH
BLACKFLY
BLACKGAME
BLACKGUM
BLACKGUMS
BLACKHEAD
BLACKING
BLACKINGS
BLACKISH
BLACKJACK
BLACKLAND
BLACKLEAD
BLACKLEG
BLACKLEGS
BLACKLIST
BLACKLY
BLACKMAIL
BLACKNESS
BLACKOUT
BLACKOUTS
BLACKPOLL
BLACKS
BLACKSPOT
BLACKTAIL
BLACKTOP
BLACKTOPS
BLACKWASH
BLACKWOOD
BLAD
BLADDED
BLADDER
BLADDERED
BLADDERS
BLADDERY
BLADDING
BLADE
BLADED
BLADELESS
BLADELIKE
BLADER
BLADERS
BLADES
BLADEWORK
BLADIER
BLADIEST
BLADING

BLADINGS	BLAMING	BLARNEYS	BLATE	BLAZONERS
BLADS	BLAMMED	BLART	BLATED	BLAZONING
BLADY	BLAMMING	BLARTED	BLATER	BLAZONRY
BLAE	BLAMS	BLARTING	BLATES	BLAZONS
BLAEBERRY	BLANCH	BLARTS	BLATEST	BLEACH
BLAER	BLANCHED	BLASE	BLATHER	BLEACHED
BLAES	BLANCHER	BLASH	BLATHERED	BLEACHER
BLAEST	BLANCHERS	BLASHED	BLATHERER	BLEACHERS
BLAFF	BLANCHES	BLASHES	BLATHERS	BLEACHERY
BLAFFED	BLANCHING	BLASHIER	BLATING	BLEACHES
BLAFFING	BLANCO	BLASHIEST	BLATS	BLEACHING
BLAFFS	BLANCOED	BLASHING	BLATT	BLEAK
BLAG	BLANCOING	BLASHY	BLATTANT	BLEAKER
BLAGGED	BLANCOS	BLASPHEME	BLATTED	BLEAKEST
BLAGGER	BLAND	BLASPHEMY	BLATTER	BLEAKISH
BLAGGERS	BLANDED	BLAST	BLATTERED	BLEAKLY
BLAGGING	BLANDER	BLASTED	BLATTERS	BLEAKNESS
BLAGGINGS	BLANDEST	BLASTEMA	BLATTING	BLEAKS
BLAGS	BLANDING	BLASTEMAL	BLATTS	BLEAKY
BLAGUE	BLANDISH	BLASTEMAS	BLAUBOK	BLEAR
BLAGUER	BLANDLY	BLASTEMIC	BLAUBOKS	BLEARED
BLAGUERS	BLANDNESS	BLASTER	BLAUD	BLEARER
BLAGUES	BLANDS	BLASTERS	BLAUDED	BLEAREST
BLAGUEUR	BLANK	BLASTIE	BLAUDING	BLEAREYED
BLAGUEURS	BLANKED	BLASTIER	BLAUDS	BLEARIER
BLAH	BLANKER	BLASTIES	BLAW	BLEARIEST
BLAHED	BLANKEST	BLASTIEST	BLAWED	BLEARILY
BLAHER	BLANKET	BLASTING	BLAWING	BLEARING
BLAHEST	BLANKETED	BLASTINGS	BLAWN	BLEARS
BLAHING	BLANKETS	BLASTMENT	BLAWORT	BLEARY
BLAHS	BLANKETY	BLASTOFF	BLAWORTS	BLEAT
BLAIN	BLANKIE	BLASTOFFS	BLAWS	BLEATED
BLAINS	BLANKIES	BLASTOID	BLAY	BLEATER
BLAISE	BLANKING	BLASTOIDS	BLAYS	BLEATERS
BLAIZE	BLANKINGS	BLASTOMA	BLAZAR	BLEATING
BLAM	BLANKLY	BLASTOMAS	BLAZARS	BLEATINGS
BLAMABLE	BLANKNESS	BLASTOPOR	BLAZE	BLEATS
BLAMABLY	BLANKS	BLASTS	BLAZED	BLEB
BLAME	BLANKY	BLASTULA	BLAZER	BLEBBIER
BLAMEABLE	BLANQUET	BLASTULAE	BLAZERED	BLEBBIEST
BLAMEABLY	BLANQUETS	BLASTULAR	BLAZERS	BLEBBING
BLAMED	BLARE	BLASTULAS	BLAZES	BLEBBINGS
BLAMEFUL	BLARED	BLASTY	BLAZING	BLEBBY
BLAMELESS	BLARES	BLAT	BLAZINGLY	BLEBS
BLAMER	BLARING	BLATANCY	BLAZON	BLECH
BLAMERS	BLARNEY	BLATANT	BLAZONED	BLED
BLAMES	BLARNEYED	BLATANTLY	BLAZONER	BLEE

BLEED	BLESSEDER	BLINDAGES	BLIPPING	BLOATWARE
BLEEDER	BLESSEDLY	BLINDED	BLIPS	BLOB
BLEEDERS	BLESSER	BLINDER	BLIPVERT	BLOBBED
BLEEDING	BLESSERS	BLINDERS	BLIPVERTS	BLOBBIER
BLEEDINGS	BLESSES	BLINDEST	BLISS	BLOBBIEST
BLEEDS	BLESSING	BLINDFISH	BLISSED	BLOBBING
BLEEP	BLESSINGS	BLINDFOLD	BLISSES	BLOBBY
BLEEPED	BLEST	BLINDGUT	BLISSFUL	BLOBS
BLEEPER	BLET	BLINDGUTS	BLISSING	BLOC
BLEEPERS	BLETHER	BLINDING	BLISSLESS	BLOCK
BLEEPING	BLETHERED	BLINDINGS	BLIST	BLOCKABLE
BLEEPS	BLETHERER	BLINDLESS	BLISTER	BLOCKADE
BLEES	BLETHERS	BLINDLY	BLISTERED	BLOCKADED
BLELLUM	BLETS	BLINDNESS	BLISTERS	BLOCKADER
BLELLUMS	BLETTED	BLINDS	BLISTERY	BLOCKADES
BLEMISH	BLETTING	BLINDSIDE	BLIT	BLOCKAGE
BLEMISHED	BLEUATRE	BLINDWORM	BLITE	BLOCKAGES
BLEMISHER	BLEW	BLING	BLITES	BLOCKBUST
BLEMISHES	BLEWART	BLINGED	BLITHE	BLOCKED
BLENCH	BLEWARTS	BLINGER	BLITHEFUL	BLOCKER
BLENCHED	BLEWIT	BLINGEST	BLITHELY	BLOCKERS
BLENCHER	BLEWITS	BLINGIER	BLITHER	BLOCKHEAD
BLENCHERS	BLEWITSES	BLINGIEST	BLITHERED	BLOCKHOLE
BLENCHES	BLEY	BLINGING	BLITHERS	BLOCKIE
BLENCHING	BLEYS	BLINGLISH	BLITHEST	BLOCKIER
BLEND	BLIGHT	BLINGS	BLITS	BLOCKIES
BLENDE	BLIGHTED	BLINGY	BLITTED	BLOCKIEST
BLENDED	BLIGHTER	BLINI	BLITTER	BLOCKING
BLENDER	BLIGHTERS	BLINIS	BLITTERS	BLOCKINGS
BLENDERS	BLIGHTIES	BLINK	BLITTING	BLOCKISH
BLENDES	BLIGHTING	BLINKARD	BLITZ	BLOCKS
BLENDING	BLIGHTS	BLINKARDS	BLITZED	BLOCKSHIP
BLENDINGS	BLIGHTY	BLINKED	BLITZER	BLOCKWORK
BLENDS	BLIKSEM	BLINKER	BLITZERS	BLOCKY
BLENNIES	BLIMBING	BLINKERED	BLITZES	BLOCS
BLENNIOID	BLIMBINGS	BLINKERS	BLITZING	BLOG
BLENNY	BLIMEY	BLINKING	BLIVE	BLOGGABLE
BLENT	BLIMP	BLINKS	BLIZZARD	BLOGGED
BLEOMYCIN	BLIMPED	BLINNED	BLIZZARDS	BLOGGER
BLERT	BLIMPERY	BLINNING	BLIZZARDY	BLOGGERS
BLERTS	BLIMPING	BLINS	BLOAT	BLOGGING
BLESBOK	BLIMPISH	BLINTZ	BLOATED	BLOGGINGS
BLESBOKS	BLIMPS	BLINTZE	BLOATER	BLOGPOST
BLESBUCK	BLIMY	BLINTZES	BLOATERS	BLOGPOSTS
BLESBUCKS	BLIN	BLINY	BLOATING	BLOGRING
BLESS	BLIND	BLIP	BLOATINGS	BLOGRINGS
BLESSED	BLINDAGE	BLIPPED	BLOATS	BLOGROLL

BLOGROLLS	BLOODSHOT	BLOTCHIER	BLOWGUN	BLUB
BLOGS	BLOODWOOD	BLOTCHILY	BLOWGUNS	BLUBBED
BLOKART	BLOODWORM	BLOTCHING	BLOWHARD	BLUBBER
BLOKARTS	BLOODWORT	BLOTCHY	BLOWHARDS	BLUBBERED
BLOKE	BLOODY	BLOTLESS	BLOWHOLE	BLUBBERER
BLOKEDOM	BLOODYING	BLOTS	BLOWHOLES	BLUBBERS
BLOKEDOMS	BLOOEY	BLOTTED	BLOWIE	BLUBBERY
BLOKEISH	BLOOIE	BLOTTER	BLOWIER	BLUBBING
BLOKES	BLOOK	BLOTTERS	BLOWIES	BLUBS
BLOKEY	BLOOKS	BLOTTIER	BLOWIEST	BLUCHER
BLOKIER	BLOOM	BLOTTIEST	BLOWINESS	BLUCHERS
BLOKIEST	BLOOMED	BLOTTING	BLOWING	BLUDE
BLOKISH	BLOOMER	BLOTTINGS	BLOWINGS	BLUDES
BLONCKET	BLOOMERS	BLOTTO	BLOWJOB	BLUDGE
BLOND	BLOOMERY	BLOTTY	BLOWJOBS	BLUDGED
BLONDE	BLOOMIER	BLOUBOK	BLOWKART	BLUDGEON
BLONDER	BLOOMIEST	BLOUBOKS	BLOWKARTS	BLUDGEONS
BLONDES	BLOOMING	BLOUSE	BLOWLAMP	BLUDGER
BLONDEST	BLOOMINGS	BLOUSED	BLOWLAMPS	BLUDGERS
BLONDINE	BLOOMLESS	BLOUSES	BLOWN	BLUDGES
BLONDINED	BLOOMS	BLOUSIER	BLOWOFF	BLUDGING
BLONDINES	BLOOMY	BLOUSIEST	BLOWOFFS	BLUDIE
BLONDING	BLOOP	BLOUSILY	BLOWOUT	BLUDIER
BLONDINGS	BLOOPED	BLOUSING	BLOWOUTS	BLUDIEST
BLONDISH	BLOOPER	BLOUSON	BLOWPIPE	BLUDY
BLONDNESS	BLOOPERS	BLOUSONS	BLOWPIPES	BLUE
BLONDS	BLOOPIER	BLOUSY	BLOWS	BLUEBACK
BLOOD	BLOOPIEST	BLOVIATE	BLOWSE	BLUEBACKS
BLOODBATH	BLOOPING	BLOVIATED	BLOWSED	BLUEBALL
BLOODED	BLOOPS	BLOVIATES	BLOWSES	BLUEBALLS
BLOODFIN	BLOOPY	BLOW	BLOWSIER	BLUEBEARD
BLOODFINS	BLOOSME	BLOWBACK	BLOWSIEST	BLUEBEAT
BLOODIED	BLOOSMED	BLOWBACKS	BLOWSILY	BLUEBEATS
BLOODIER	BLOOSMES	BLOWBALL	BLOWSY	BLUEBELL
BLOODIES	BLOOSMING	BLOWBALLS	BLOWTORCH	BLUEBELLS
BLOODIEST	BLOOTERED	BLOWBY	BLOWTUBE	BLUEBERRY
BLOODILY	BLOQUISTE	BLOWBYS	BLOWTUBES	BLUEBILL
BLOODING	BLORE	BLOWDART	BLOWUP	BLUEBILLS
BLOODINGS	BLORES	BLOWDARTS	BLOWUPS	BLUEBIRD
BLOODLESS	BLOSSOM	BLOWDOWN	BLOWY	BLUEBIRDS
BLOODLIKE	BLOSSOMED	BLOWDOWNS	BLOWZE	BLUEBLOOD
BLOODLINE	BLOSSOMS	BLOWED	BLOWZED	BLUEBOOK
BLOODLUST	BLOSSOMY	BLOWER	BLOWZES	BLUEBOOKS
BLOODRED	BLOT	BLOWERS	BLOWZIER	BLUEBUCK
BLOODROOT	BLOTCH	BLOWFISH	BLOWZIEST	BLUEBUCKS
BLOODS	BLOTCHED	BLOWFLIES	BLOWZILY	BLUEBUSH
BLOODSHED	BLOTCHES	BLOWFLY	BLOWZY	BLUECAP

BLUECAPS	BLUESY	BLUNDERS	BLUSHER	BOAS
BLUECOAT	BLUET	BLUNGE	BLUSHERS	BOAST
BLUECOATS	BLUETICK	BLUNGED	BLUSHES	BOASTED
BLUECURLS	BLUETICKS	BLUNGER	BLUSHET	BOASTER
BLUED	BLUETIT	BLUNGERS	BLUSHETS	BOASTERS
BLUEFIN	BLUETITS	BLUNGES	BLUSHFUL	BOASTFUL
BLUEFINS	BLUETS	BLUNGING	BLUSHING	BOASTING
BLUEFISH	BLUETTE	BLUNK	BLUSHINGS	BOASTINGS
BLUEGILL	BLUETTES	BLUNKED	BLUSHLESS	BOASTLESS
BLUEGILLS	BLUEWEED	BLUNKER	BLUSTER	BOASTS
BLUEGOWN	BLUEWEEDS	BLUNKERS	BLUSTERED	BOAT
BLUEGOWNS	BLUEWING	BLUNKING	BLUSTERER	BOATABLE
BLUEGRASS	BLUEWINGS	BLUNKS	BLUSTERS	BOATBILL
BLUEGUM	BLUEWOOD	BLUNT	BLUSTERY	BOATBILLS
BLUEGUMS	BLUEWOODS	BLUNTED	BLUSTROUS	BOATED
BLUEHEAD	BLUEY	BLUNTER	BLUTWURST	BOATEL
BLUEHEADS	BLUEYS	BLUNTEST	BLYPE	BOATELS
BLUEING	BLUFF	BLUNTHEAD	BLYPES	BOATER
BLUEINGS	BLUFFABLE	BLUNTING	BO	BOATERS
BLUEISH	BLUFFED	BLUNTISH	BOA	BOATFUL
BLUEJACK	BLUFFER	BLUNTLY	BOAB	BOATFULS
BLUEJACKS	BLUFFERS	BLUNTNESS	BOABS	BOATHOOK
BLUEJAY	BLUFFEST	BLUNTS	BOAK	BOATHOOKS
BLUEJAYS	BLUFFING	BLUR	BOAKED	BOATHOUSE
BLUEJEANS	BLUFFLY	BLURB	BOAKING	BOATIE
BLUELINE	BLUFFNESS	BLURBED	BOAKS	BOATIES
BLUELINER	BLUFFS	BLURBING	BOAR	BOATING
BLUELINES	BLUGGIER	BLURBIST	BOARD	BOATINGS
BLUELY	BLUGGIEST	BLURBISTS	BOARDABLE	BOATLIFT
BLUEMOUTH	BLUGGY	BLURBS	BOARDED	BOATLIFTS
BLUENESS	BLUID	BLURRED	BOARDER	BOATLIKE
BLUENOSE	BLUIDIER	BLURREDLY	BOARDERS	BOATLOAD
BLUENOSED	BLUIDIEST	BLURRIER	BOARDING	BOATLOADS
BLUENOSES	BLUIDS	BLURRIEST	BOARDINGS	BOATMAN
BLUEPOINT	BLUIDY	BLURRILY	BOARDLIKE	BOATMEN
BLUEPRINT	BLUIER	BLURRING	BOARDMAN	BOATNECK
BLUER	BLUIEST	BLURRY	BOARDMEN	BOATNECKS
BLUES	BLUING	BLURS	BOARDROOM	BOATPORT
BLUESHIFT	BLUINGS	BLURT	BOARDS	BOATPORTS
BLUESIER	BLUISH	BLURTED	BOARDWALK	BOATS
BLUESIEST	BLUME	BLURTER	BOARFISH	BOATSMAN
BLUESMAN	BLUMED	BLURTERS	BOARHOUND	BOATSMEN
BLUESMEN	BLUMES	BLURTING	BOARISH	BOATSWAIN
BLUEST	BLUMING	BLURTINGS	BOARISHLY	BOATTAIL
BLUESTEM	BLUNDER	BLURTS	BOARS	BOATTAILS
BLUESTEMS	BLUNDERED	BLUSH	BOART	BOATYARD
BLUESTONE	BLUNDERER	BLUSHED	BOARTS	BOATYARDS

BOB	BOBOLS	BODACH	BODYCHECK	BOGARTED
BOBA	BOBOS	BODACHS	BODYGUARD	BOGARTING
BOBAC	BOBOTIE	BODACIOUS	BODYING	BOGARTS
BOBACS	BOBOTIES	BODDLE	BODYLINE	BOGBEAN
BOBAK	BOBOWLER	BODDLES	BODYLINES	BOGBEANS
BOBAKS	BOBOWLERS	BODE	BODYMAN	BOGEY
BOBAS	BOBS	BODED	BODYMEN	BOGEYED
BOBBED	BOBSKATE	BODEFUL	BODYSHELL	BOGEYING
BOBBEJAAN	BOBSKATES	BODEGA	BODYSIDE	BOGEYISM
BOBBER	BOBSLED	BODEGAS	BODYSIDES	BOGEYISMS
BOBBERIES	BOBSLEDS	BODEGUERO	BODYSUIT	BOGEYMAN
BOBBERS	BOBSLEIGH	BODEMENT	BODYSUITS	BOGEYMEN
BOBBERY	BOBSTAY	BODEMENTS	BODYSURF	BOGEYS
BOBBIES	BOBSTAYS	BODES	BODYSURFS	BOGGARD
BOBBIN	BOBTAIL	BODGE	BODYWASH	BOGGARDS
BOBBINET	BOBTAILED	BODGED	BODYWORK	BOGGART
BOBBINETS	BOBTAILS	BODGER	BODYWORKS	BOGGARTS
BOBBING	BOBWEIGHT	BODGERS	BOEHMITE	BOGGED
BOBBINS	BOBWHEEL	BODGES	BOEHMITES	BOGGER
BOBBISH	BOBWHEELS	BODGIE	BOEP	BOGGERS
BOBBITT	BOBWHITE	BODGIER	BOEPS	BOGGIER
BOBBITTED	BOBWHITES	BODGIES	BOERBUL	BOGGIEST
BOBBITTS	BOBWIG	BODGIEST	BOERBULL	BOGGINESS
BOBBLE	BOBWIGS	BODGING	BOERBULLS	BOGGING
BOBBLED	BOCACCIO	BODHI	BOERBULS	BOGGISH
BOBBLES	BOCACCIOS	BODHRAN	BOEREWORS	BOGGLE
BOBBLIER	BOCAGE	BODHRANS	BOERTJIE	BOGGLED
BOBBLIEST	BOCAGES	BODICE	BOERTJIES	BOGGLER
BOBBLING	BOCCA	BODICES	BOET	BOGGLERS
BOBBLY	BOCCAS	BODIED	BOETS	BOGGLES
BOBBY	BOCCE	BODIES	BOEUF	BOGGLING
BOBBYSOCK	BOCCES	BODIKIN	BOEUFS	BOGGY
BOBBYSOX	BOCCI	BODIKINS	BOFF	BOGHEAD
BOBCAT	BOCCIA	BODILESS	BOFFED	BOGHOLE
BOBCATS	BOCCIAS	BODILY	BOFFIN	BOGHOLES
BOBECHE	BOCCIE	BODING	BOFFING	BOGIE
BOBECHES	BOCCIES	BODINGLY	BOFFINS	BOGIED
BOBFLOAT	BOCCIS	BODINGS	BOFFINY	BOGIEING
BOBFLOATS	BOCHE	BODKIN	BOFFO	BOGIES
BOBLET	BOCHES	BODKINS	BOFFOLA	BOGLAND
BOBLETS	BOCK	BODLE	BOFFOLAS	BOGLANDS
BOBO	BOCKED	BODLES	BOFFOS	BOGLE
BOBOL	BOCKEDY	BODRAG	BOFFS	BOGLED
BOBOLINK	BOCKING	BODRAGS	BOG	BOGLES
BOBOLINKS	BOCKS	BODS	BOGAN	BOGLING
BOBOLLED	BOCONCINI	BODY	BOGANS	BOGMAN
BOBOLLING	BOD	BODYBOARD	BOGART	BOGMEN

B

BOGOAK	BOILOVERS	BOLEROS	BOLOMETER	BOMBASINE
BOGOAKS	BOILS	BOLES	BOLOMETRY	BOMBAST
BOGONG	BOING	BOLETE	BOLONEY	BOMBASTED
BOGONGS	BOINGED	BOLETES	BOLONEYS	BOMBASTER
BOGS	BOINGING	BOLETI	BOLOS	BOMBASTIC
BOGUE	BOINGS	BOLETUS	BOLSHEVIK	BOMBASTS
BOGUES	BOINK	BOLETUSES	BOLSHIE	BOMBAX
BOGUS	BOINKED	BOLIDE	BOLSHIER	BOMBAXES
BOGUSLY	BOINKING	BOLIDES	BOLSHIES	BOMBAZINE
BOGUSNESS	BOINKS	BOLINE	BOLSHIEST	BOMBE
BOGWOOD	BOIS	BOLINES	BOLSHY	BOMBED
BOGWOODS	BOISERIE	BOLIVAR	BOLSON	BOMBER
BOGY	BOISERIES	BOLIVARES	BOLSONS	BOMBERS
BOGYISM	BOITE	BOLIVARS	BOLSTER	BOMBES
BOGYISMS	BOITES	BOLIVIA	BOLSTERED	BOMBESIN
BOGYMAN	BOK	BOLIVIANO	BOLSTERER	BOMBESINS
BOGYMEN	BOKE	BOLIVIAS	BOLSTERS	BOMBILATE
BOH	BOKED	BOLIX	BOLT	BOMBINATE
BOHEA	BOKES	BOLIXED	BOLTED	BOMBING
BOHEAS	BOKING	BOLIXES	BOLTER	BOMBINGS
BOHEMIA	BOKKEN	BOLIXING	BOLTERS	BOMBLET
BOHEMIAN	BOKKENS	BOLL	BOLTHEAD	BOMBLETS
BOHEMIANS	BOKO	BOLLARD	BOLTHEADS	BOMBLOAD
BOHEMIAS	BOKOS	BOLLARDS	BOLTHOLE	BOMBLOADS
BOHO	BOKS	BOLLED	BOLTHOLES	BOMBO
BOHOS	BOLA	BOLLEN	BOLTING	BOMBORA
BOHRIUM	BOLAR	BOLLETRIE	BOLTINGS	BOMBORAS
BOHRIUMS	BOLAS	BOLLING	BOLTLESS	BOMBOS
BOHS	BOLASES	BOLLIX	BOLTLIKE	BOMBPROOF
BOHUNK	BOLD	BOLLIXED	BOLTONIA	BOMBS
BOHUNKS	BOLDED	BOLLIXES	BOLTONIAS	BOMBSHELL
BOI	BOLDEN	BOLLIXING	BOLTROPE	BOMBSIGHT
BOIL	BOLDENED	BOLLOCK	BOLTROPES	BOMBSITE
BOILABLE	BOLDENING	BOLLOCKED	BOLTS	BOMBSITES
BOILED	BOLDENS	BOLLOCKS	BOLUS	BOMBYCID
BOILER	BOLDER	BOLLOX	BOLUSES	BOMBYCIDS
BOILERIES	BOLDEST	BOLLOXED	BOMA	BOMBYCOID
BOILERMAN	BOLDFACE	BOLLOXES	BOMAS	BOMBYX
BOILERMEN	BOLDFACED	BOLLOXING	BOMB	BOMBYXES
BOILERS	BOLDFACES	BOLLS	BOMBABLE	BOMMIE
BOILERY	BOLDING	BOLLWORM	BOMBARD	BOMMIES
BOILING	BOLDLY	BOLLWORMS	BOMBARDE	BON
BOILINGLY	BOLDNESS	BOLO	BOMBARDED	BONA
BOILINGS	BOLDS	BOLOGNA	BOMBARDER	BONACI
BOILOFF	BOLE	BOLOGNAS	BOMBARDES	BONACIS
BOILOFFS	BOLECTION	BOLOGNESE	BOMBARDON	BONAMANI
BOILOVER	BOLERO	BOLOGRAPH	BOMBARDS	BONAMANO

BONAMIA	BONERS	BONITAS	BONUSINGS	BOODLING
BONAMIAS	BONES	BONITO	BONUSSED	BOODY
BONANZA	BONESET	BONITOES	BONUSSES	BOODYING
BONANZAS	BONESETS	BONITOS	BONUSSING	BOOED
BONASSUS	BONETIRED	BONJOUR	BONXIE	BOOFHEAD
BONASUS	BONEY	BONK	BONXIES	BOOFHEADS
BONASUSES	BONEYARD	BONKED	BONY	BOOFIER
BONBON	BONEYARDS	BONKERS	BONZA	BOOFIEST
BONBONS	BONEYER	BONKING	BONZE	BOOFY
BONCE	BONEYEST	BONKINGS	BONZER	BOOGALOO
BONCES	BONFIRE	BONKS	BONZES	BOOGALOOS
BOND	BONFIRES	BONNE	BOO	BOOGER
BONDABLE	BONG	BONNES	BOOAI	BOOGERMAN
BONDAGE	BONGED	BONNET	BOOAIS	BOOGERMEN
BONDAGER	BONGING	BONNETED	BOOAY	BOOGERS
BONDAGERS	BONGO	BONNETING	BOOAYS	BOOGEY
BONDAGES	BONGOES	BONNETS	BOOB	BOOGEYED
BONDED	BONGOIST	BONNIBELL	BOOBED	BOOGEYING
BONDER	BONGOISTS	BONNIE	BOOBHEAD	BOOGEYMAN
BONDERS	BONGOS	BONNIER	BOOBHEADS	BOOGEYMEN
BONDING	BONGRACE	BONNIES	BOOBIALLA	BOOGEYS
BONDINGS	BONGRACES	BONNIEST	BOOBIE	BOOGIE
BONDLESS	BONGS	BONNILY	BOOBIES	BOOGIED
BONDMAID	BONHAM	BONNINESS	BOOBING	BOOGIEING
BONDMAIDS	BONHAMS	BONNOCK	BOOBIRD	BOOGIEMAN
BONDMAN	BONHOMIE	BONNOCKS	BOOBIRDS	BOOGIEMEN
BONDMEN	BONHOMIES	BONNY	BOOBISH	BOOGIES
BONDS	BONHOMMIE	BONOBO	BOOBOISIE	BOOGY
BONDSMAN	BONHOMOUS	BONOBOS	BOOBOO	BOOGYING
BONDSMEN	BONIATO	BONSAI	BOOBOOS	BOOGYMAN
BONDSTONE	BONIATOS	BONSELA	BOOBOOK	BOOGYMEN
BONDUC	BONIBELL	BONSELAS	BOOBOOKS	BOOH
BONDUCS	BONIBELLS	BONSELLA	BOOBOOS	BOOHAI
BONDWOMAN	BONIE	BONSELLAS	BOOBS	BOOHAIS
BONDWOMEN	BONIER	BONSOIR	BOOBY	BOOHED
BONE	BONIEST	BONSPELL	BOOBYISH	BOOHING
BONEBED	BONIFACE	BONSPELLS	BOOBYISM	BOOHOO
BONEBEDS	BONIFACES	BONSPIEL	BOOBYISMS	BOOHOOED
BONEBLACK	BONILASSE	BONSPIELS	BOOCOO	BOOHOOING
BONED	BONINESS	BONTBOK	BOOCOOS	BOOHOOS
BONEFISH	BONING	BONTBOKS	BOODIE	BOOHS
BONEHEAD	BONINGS	BONTEBOK	BOODIED	BOOING
BONEHEADS	BONISM	BONTEBOKS	BOODIES	BOOINGS
BONELESS	BONISMS	BONUS	BOODLE	BOOJUM
BONEMEAL	BONIST	BONUSED	BOODLED	BOOJUMS
BONEMEALS	BONISTS	BONUSES	BOODLER	BOOK
BONER	BONITA	BONUSING	BOODLERS	BOOKABLE
			BOODLES	

BOOKBAG
BOOKBAGS
BOOKCASE
BOOKCASES
BOOKED
BOOKEND
BOOKENDED
BOOKENDS
BOOKER
BOOKERS
BOOKFUL
BOOKFULS
BOOKIE
BOOKIER
BOOKIES
BOOKIEST
BOOKING
BOOKINGS
BOOKISH
BOOKISHLY
BOOKLAND
BOOKLANDS
BOOKLESS
BOOKLET
BOOKLETS
BOOKLICE
BOOKLIGHT
BOOKLORE
BOOKLORES
BOOKLOUSE
BOOKMAKER
BOOKMAN
BOOKMARK
BOOKMARKS
BOOKMEN
BOOKOO
BOOKOOS
BOOKPLATE
BOOKRACK
BOOKRACKS
BOOKREST
BOOKRESTS
BOOKS
BOOKSHELF
BOOKSHOP
BOOKSHOPS
BOOKSIE

BOOKSIER
BOOKSIEST
BOOKSTALL
BOOKSTAND
BOOKSTORE
BOOKSY
BOOKWORK
BOOKWORKS
BOOKWORM
BOOKWORMS
BOOKY
BOOL
BOOLED
BOOLING
BOOLS
BOOM
BOOMBOX
BOOMBOXES
BOOMBURB
BOOMBURBS
BOOMED
BOOMER
BOOMERANG
BOOMERS
BOOMIER
BOOMIEST
BOOMING
BOOMINGLY
BOOMINGS
BOOMKIN
BOOMKINS
BOOMLET
BOOMLETS
BOOMS
BOOMSLANG
BOOMTOWN
BOOMTOWNS
BOOMY
BOON
BOONDOCK
BOONDOCKS
BOONER
BOONERS
BOONG
BOONGA
BOONGARY
BOONGAS

BOONGS
BOONIES
BOONLESS
BOONS
BOOR
BOORD
BOORDE
BOORDES
BOORDS
BOORISH
BOORISHLY
BOORKA
BOORKAS
BOORS
BOORTREE
BOORTREES
BOOS
BOOSE
BOOSED
BOOSES
BOOSHIT
BOOSING
BOOST
BOOSTED
BOOSTER
BOOSTERS
BOOSTING
BOOSTS
BOOT
BOOTABLE
BOOTBLACK
BOOTCUT
BOOTED
BOOTEE
BOOTEES
BOOTERIES
BOOTERY
BOOTH
BOOTHOSE
BOOTHS
BOOTIE
BOOTIES
BOOTIKIN
BOOTIKINS
BOOTING
BOOTJACK
BOOTJACKS

BOOTLACE
BOOTLACES
BOOTLAST
BOOTLASTS
BOOTLEG
BOOTLEGS
BOOTLESS
BOOTLICK
BOOTLICKS
BOOTMAKER
BOOTS
BOOTSTRAP
BOOTY
BOOZE
BOOZED
BOOZER
BOOZERS
BOOZES
BOOZEY
BOOZIER
BOOZIEST
BOOZILY
BOOZINESS
BOOZING
BOOZINGS
BOOZY
BOP
BOPEEP
BOPEEPS
BOPPED
BOPPER
BOPPERS
BOPPIER
BOPPIEST
BOPPING
BOPPISH
BOPPY
BOPS
BOR
BORA
BORACES
BORACHIO
BORACHIOS
BORACIC
BORACITE
BORACITES
BORAGE

BORAGES
BORAK
BORAKS
BORAL
BORALS
BORANE
BORANES
BORAS
BORATE
BORATED
BORATES
BORATING
BORAX
BORAXES
BORAZON
BORAZONS
BORD
BORDAR
BORDARS
BORDE
BORDEAUX
BORDEL
BORDELLO
BORDELLOS
BORDELS
BORDER
BORDEREAU
BORDERED
BORDERER
BORDERERS
BORDERING
BORDERS
BORDES
BORDS
BORDURE
BORDURES
BORE
BOREAL
BOREALIS
BOREAS
BOREASES
BORECOLE
BORECOLES
BORED
BOREDOM
BOREDOMS
BOREE

BOREEN	BOROUGHS	BOSCHVARK	BOSSETS	BOTCHER
BOREENS	BORREL	BOSCHVELD	BOSSIER	BOTCHERS
BOREES	BORRELIA	BOSH	BOSSIES	BOTCHERY
BOREHOLE	BORRELIAS	BOSHBOK	BOSSIEST	BOTCHES
BOREHOLES	BORRELL	BOSHBOKS	BOSSILY	BOTCHIER
BOREL	BORROW	BOSHES	BOSSINESS	BOTCHIEST
BORELS	BORROWED	BOSHTA	BOSSING	BOTCHILY
BORER	BORROWER	BOSHTER	BOSSINGS	BOTCHING
BORERS	BORROWERS	BOSHVARK	BOSSISM	BOTCHINGS
BORES	BORROWING	BOSHVARKS	BOSSISMS	BOTCHY
BORESCOPE	BORROWS	BOSIE	BOSSY	BOTE
BORESOME	BORS	BOSIES	BOSTANGI	BOTEL
BORGHETTO	BORSCH	BOSK	BOSTANGIS	BOTELS
BORGO	BORSCHES	BOSKAGE	BOSTHOON	BOTES
BORGOS	BORSCHT	BOSKAGES	BOSTHOONS	BOTFLIES
BORIC	BORSCHTS	BOSKER	BOSTON	BOTFLY
BORIDE	BORSHCH	BOSKET	BOSTONS	BOTH
BORIDES	BORSHCHES	BOSKETS	BOSTRYX	BOTHAN
BORING	BORSHT	BOSKIER	BOSTRYXES	BOTHANS
BORINGLY	BORSHTS	BOSKIEST	BOSUN	BOTHER
BORINGS	BORSIC	BOSKINESS	BOSUNS	BOTHERED
BORK	BORSICS	BOSKS	BOT	BOTHERING
BORKED	BORSTAL	BOSKY	BOTA	BOTHERS
BORKING	BORSTALL	BOSOM	BOTANIC	BOTHIE
BORKINGS	BORSTALLS	BOSOMED	BOTANICA	BOTHIES
BORKS	BORSTALS	BOSOMIER	BOTANICAL	BOTHOLE
BORLOTTI	BORT	BOSOMIEST	BOTANICAS	BOTHOLES
BORM	BORTIER	BOSOMING	BOTANICS	BOTHRIA
BORMED	BORTIEST	BOSOMS	BOTANIES	BOTHRIUM
BORMING	BORTS	BOSOMY	BOTANISE	BOTHRIUMS
BORMS	BORTSCH	BOSON	BOTANISED	BOTHY
BORN	BORTSCHES	BOSONIC	BOTANISER	BOTHYMAN
BORNA	BORTY	BOSONS	BOTANISES	BOTHYMEN
BORNE	BORTZ	BOSQUE	BOTANIST	BOTNET
BORNEOL	BORTZES	BOSQUES	BOTANISTS	BOTNETS
BORNEOLS	BORZOI	BOSQUET	BOTANIZE	BOTONE
BORNITE	BORZOIS	BOSQUETS	BOTANIZED	BOTONEE
BORNITES	BOS	BOSS	BOTANIZER	BOTONNEE
BORNITIC	BOSBERAAD	BOSSBOY	BOTANIZES	BOTOXED
BORNYL	BOSBOK	BOSSBOYS	BOTANY	BOTRYOID
BORNYLS	BOSBOKS	BOSSDOM	BOTARGO	BOTRYOSE
BORON	BOSCAGE	BOSSDOMS	BOTARGOES	BOTRYTIS
BORONIA	BOSCAGES	BOSSED	BOTARGOS	BOTS
BORONIAS	BOSCHBOK	BOSSER	BOTAS	BOTT
BORONIC	BOSCHBOKS	BOSSES	BOTCH	BOTTARGA
BORONS	BOSCHE	BOSSEST	BOTCHED	BOTTARGAS
BOROUGH	BOSCHES	BOSSET	BOTCHEDLY	BOTTE

BOTTED
BOTTEGA
BOTTEGAS
BOTTES
BOTTIES
BOTTINE
BOTTINES
BOTTING
BOTTLE
BOTTLED
BOTTLEFUL
BOTTLER
BOTTLERS
BOTTLES
BOTTLING
BOTTLINGS
BOTTOM
BOTTOMED
BOTTOMER
BOTTOMERS
BOTTOMING
BOTTOMRY
BOTTOMS
BOTTOMSET
BOTTONY
BOTTS
BOTTY
BOTULIN
BOTULINAL
BOTULINS
BOTULINUM
BOTULINUS
BOTULISM
BOTULISMS
BOUBOU
BOUBOUS
BOUCHE
BOUCHEE
BOUCHEES
BOUCHES
BOUCLE
BOUCLEE
BOUCLEES
BOUCLES
BOUDERIE
BOUDERIES
BOUDIN

BOUDINS
BOUDOIR
BOUDOIRS
BOUFFANT
BOUFFANTS
BOUFFE
BOUFFES
BOUGE
BOUGED
BOUGES
BOUGET
BOUGETS
BOUGH
BOUGHED
BOUGHLESS
BOUGHPOT
BOUGHPOTS
BOUGHS
BOUGHT
BOUGHTEN
BOUGHTS
BOUGIE
BOUGIES
BOUGING
BOUILLI
BOUILLIS
BOUILLON
BOUILLONS
BOUK
BOUKS
BOULDER
BOULDERED
BOULDERER
BOULDERS
BOULDERY
BOULE
BOULES
BOULEVARD
BOULLE
BOULLES
BOULT
BOULTED
BOULTER
BOULTERS
BOULTING
BOULTINGS
BOULTS

BOUN
BOUNCE
BOUNCED
BOUNCER
BOUNCERS
BOUNCES
BOUNCIER
BOUNCIEST
BOUNCILY
BOUNCING
BOUNCY
BOUND
BOUNDABLE
BOUNDARY
BOUNDED
BOUNDEN
BOUNDER
BOUNDERS
BOUNDING
BOUNDLESS
BOUNDNESS
BOUNDS
BOUNED
BOUNING
BOUNS
BOUNTEOUS
BOUNTIED
BOUNTIES
BOUNTIFUL
BOUNTREE
BOUNTREES
BOUNTY
BOUNTYHED
BOUQUET
BOUQUETS
BOURASQUE
BOURBON
BOURBONS
BOURD
BOURDED
BOURDER
BOURDERS
BOURDING
BOURDON
BOURDONS
BOURDS
BOURG

BOURGEOIS
BOURGEON
BOURGEONS
BOURGS
BOURKHA
BOURKHAS
BOURLAW
BOURLAWS
BOURN
BOURNE
BOURNES
BOURNS
BOURREE
BOURREES
BOURRIDE
BOURRIDES
BOURSE
BOURSES
BOURSIER
BOURSIERS
BOURSIN
BOURSINS
BOURTREE
BOURTREES
BOUSE
BOUSED
BOUSES
BOUSIER
BOUSIEST
BOUSING
BOUSOUKI
BOUSOUKIA
BOUSOUKIS
BOUSY
BOUT
BOUTADE
BOUTADES
BOUTIQUE
BOUTIQUES
BOUTIQUEY
BOUTON
BOUTONNE
BOUTONNEE
BOUTONS
BOUTS
BOUVARDIA
BOUVIER

BOUVIERS
BOUZOUKI
BOUZOUKIA
BOUZOUKIS
BOVATE
BOVATES
BOVID
BOVIDS
BOVINE
BOVINELY
BOVINES
BOVINITY
BOVVER
BOVVERS
BOW
BOWAT
BOWATS
BOWBENT
BOWED
BOWEL
BOWELED
BOWELING
BOWELLED
BOWELLESS
BOWELLING
BOWELS
BOWER
BOWERBIRD
BOWERED
BOWERIES
BOWERING
BOWERS
BOWERY
BOWES
BOWET
BOWETS
BOWFIN
BOWFINS
BOWFRONT
BOWGET
BOWGETS
BOWHEAD
BOWHEADS
BOWHUNT
BOWHUNTED
BOWHUNTER
BOWHUNTS

BOWIE	BOWSIE	BOXLA	BOYO	BRACHIUM
BOWING	BOWSIES	BOXLAS	BOYOS	BRACHIUMS
BOWINGLY	BOWSING	BOXLIKE	BOYS	BRACHOT
BOWINGS	BOWSMAN	BOXPLOT	BOYSHORTS	BRACHS
BOWKNOT	BOWSMEN	BOXPLOTS	BOYSIER	BRACING
BOWKNOTS	BOWSPRIT	BOXROOM	BOYSIEST	BRACINGLY
BOWL	BOWSPRITS	BOXROOMS	BOYSY	BRACINGS
BOWLDER	BOWSTRING	BOXTHORN	BOZO	BRACIOLA
BOWLDERS	BOWSTRUNG	BOXTHORNS	BOZOS	BRACIOLAS
BOWLED	BOWWOOD	BOXTIES	BOZZETTI	BRACIOLE
BOWLEG	BOWWOODS	BOXTY	BOZZETTO	BRACIOLES
BOWLEGGED	BOWWOW	BOXWALLAH	BRA	BRACK
BOWLEGS	BOWWOWED	BOXWOOD	BRAAI	BRACKEN
BOWLER	BOWWOWING	BOXWOODS	BRAAIED	BRACKENS
BOWLERS	BOWWOWS	BOXY	BRAAIING	BRACKET
BOWLESS	BOWYANG	BOY	BRAAIS	BRACKETED
BOWLFUL	BOWYANGS	BOYAR	BRAATA	BRACKETS
BOWLFULS	BOWYER	BOYARD	BRAATAS	BRACKISH
BOWLIKE	BOWYERS	BOYARDS	BRAATASES	BRACKS
BOWLINE	BOX	BOYARISM	BRABBLE	BRACONID
BOWLINES	BOXBALL	BOYARISMS	BRABBLED	BRACONIDS
BOWLING	BOXBALLS	BOYARS	BRABBLER	BRACT
BOWLINGS	BOXBERRY	BOYAU	BRABBLERS	BRACTEAL
BOWLLIKE	BOXBOARD	BOYAUX	BRABBLES	BRACTEATE
BOWLS	BOXBOARDS	BOYCHICK	BRABBLING	BRACTED
BOWMAN	BOXCAR	BOYCHICKS	BRACCATE	BRACTEOLE
BOWMEN	BOXCARS	BOYCHIK	BRACCIA	BRACTLESS
BOWNE	BOXED	BOYCHIKS	BRACCIO	BRACTLET
BOWNED	BOXEN	BOYCOTT	BRACE	BRACTLETS
BOWNES	BOXER	BOYCOTTED	BRACED	BRACTS
BOWNING	BOXERCISE	BOYCOTTER	BRACELET	BRAD
BOWPOT	BOXERS	BOYCOTTS	BRACELETS	BRADAWL
BOWPOTS	BOXES	BOYED	BRACER	BRADAWLS
BOWR	BOXFISH	BOYF	BRACERO	BRADDED
BOWRS	BOXFISHES	BOYFRIEND	BRACEROS	BRADDING
BOWS	BOXFUL	BOYFS	BRACERS	BRADOON
BOWSAW	BOXFULS	BOYG	BRACES	BRADOONS
BOWSAWS	BOXHAUL	BOYGS	BRACH	BRADS
BOWSE	BOXHAULED	BOYHOOD	BRACHAH	BRAE
BOWSED	BOXHAULS	BOYHOODS	BRACHAHS	BRAEHEID
BOWSER	BOXIER	BOYING	BRACHES	BRAEHEIDS
BOWSERS	BOXIEST	BOYISH	BRACHET	BRAES
BOWSES	BOXILY	BOYISHLY	BRACHETS	BRAG
BOWSEY	BOXINESS	BOYKIE	BRACHIA	BRAGGART
BOWSEYS	BOXING	BOYKIES	BRACHIAL	BRAGGARTS
BOWSHOT	BOXINGS	BOYLA	BRACHIALS	BRAGGED
BOWSHOTS	BOXKEEPER	BOYLAS	BRACHIATE	BRAGGER

BRAGGERS
BRAGGEST
BRAGGIER
BRAGGIEST
BRAGGING
BRAGGINGS
BRAGGY
BRAGLY
BRAGS
BRAHMA
BRAHMAN
BRAHMANI
BRAHMANIS
BRAHMANS
BRAHMAS
BRAHMIN
BRAHMINS
BRAID
BRAIDE
BRAIDED
BRAIDER
BRAIDERS
BRAIDEST
BRAIDING
BRAIDINGS
BRAIDS
BRAIL
BRAILED
BRAILING
BRAILLE
BRAILLED
BRAILLER
BRAILLERS
BRAILLES
BRAILLING
BRAILLIST
BRAILS
BRAIN
BRAINBOX
BRAINCASE
BRAINDEAD
BRAINED
BRAINFART
BRAINFOOD
BRAINIAC
BRAINIACS
BRAINIER

BRAINIEST
BRAINILY
BRAINING
BRAINISH
BRAINLESS
BRAINPAN
BRAINPANS
BRAINS
BRAINSICK
BRAINSTEM
BRAINWASH
BRAINWAVE
BRAINWORK
BRAINY
BRAIRD
BRAIRDED
BRAIRDING
BRAIRDS
BRAISE
BRAISED
BRAISES
BRAISING
BRAIZE
BRAIZES
BRAK
BRAKE
BRAKEAGE
BRAKEAGES
BRAKED
BRAKELESS
BRAKEMAN
BRAKEMEN
BRAKES
BRAKESMAN
BRAKESMEN
BRAKIER
BRAKIEST
BRAKING
BRAKINGS
BRAKS
BRAKY
BRALESS
BRAMBLE
BRAMBLED
BRAMBLES
BRAMBLIER
BRAMBLING

BRAMBLY
BRAME
BRAMES
BRAN
BRANCARD
BRANCARDS
BRANCH
BRANCHED
BRANCHER
BRANCHERS
BRANCHERY
BRANCHES
BRANCHIA
BRANCHIAE
BRANCHIAL
BRANCHIER
BRANCHING
BRANCHLET
BRANCHY
BRAND
BRANDADE
BRANDADES
BRANDED
BRANDER
BRANDERED
BRANDERS
BRANDIED
BRANDIES
BRANDING
BRANDINGS
BRANDISE
BRANDISES
BRANDISH
BRANDLESS
BRANDLING
BRANDRETH
BRANDS
BRANDY
BRANDYING
BRANE
BRANES
BRANGLE
BRANGLED
BRANGLES
BRANGLING
BRANK
BRANKED

BRANKIER
BRANKIEST
BRANKING
BRANKS
BRANKY
BRANLE
BRANLES
BRANNED
BRANNER
BRANNERS
BRANNIER
BRANNIEST
BRANNIGAN
BRANNING
BRANNY
BRANS
BRANSLE
BRANSLES
BRANT
BRANTAIL
BRANTAILS
BRANTLE
BRANTLES
BRANTS
BRAP
BRAS
BRASCO
BRASCOS
BRASERO
BRASEROS
BRASES
BRASH
BRASHED
BRASHER
BRASHES
BRASHEST
BRASHIER
BRASHIEST
BRASHING
BRASHLY
BRASHNESS
BRASHY
BRASIER
BRASIERS
BRASIL
BRASILEIN
BRASILIN

BRASILINS
BRASILS
BRASS
BRASSAGE
BRASSAGES
BRASSARD
BRASSARDS
BRASSART
BRASSARTS
BRASSED
BRASSERIE
BRASSES
BRASSET
BRASSETS
BRASSICA
BRASSICAS
BRASSIE
BRASSIER
BRASSIERE
BRASSIES
BRASSIEST
BRASSILY
BRASSING
BRASSISH
BRASSWARE
BRASSY
BRAST
BRASTING
BRASTS
BRAT
BRATCHET
BRATCHETS
BRATLING
BRATLINGS
BRATPACK
BRATPACKS
BRATS
BRATTICE
BRATTICED
BRATTICES
BRATTIER
BRATTIEST
BRATTISH
BRATTLE
BRATTLED
BRATTLES
BRATTLING

BRATTY
BRATWURST
BRAUNCH
BRAUNCHED
BRAUNCHES
BRAUNITE
BRAUNITES
BRAVA
BRAVADO
BRAVADOED
BRAVADOES
BRAVADOS
BRAVAS
BRAVE
BRAVED
BRAVELY
BRAVENESS
BRAVER
BRAVERIES
BRAVERS
BRAVERY
BRAVES
BRAVEST
BRAVI
BRAVING
BRAVO
BRAVOED
BRAVOES
BRAVOING
BRAVOS
BRAVURA
BRAVURAS
BRAVURE
BRAW
BRAWER
BRAWEST
BRAWL
BRAWLED
BRAWLER
BRAWLERS
BRAWLIE
BRAWLIER
BRAWLIEST
BRAWLING
BRAWLINGS
BRAWLS
BRAWLY

BRAWN
BRAWNED
BRAWNIER
BRAWNIEST
BRAWNILY
BRAWNS
BRAWNY
BRAWS
BRAXIES
BRAXY
BRAY
BRAYED
BRAYER
BRAYERS
BRAYING
BRAYS
BRAZA
BRAZAS
BRAZE
BRAZED
BRAZELESS
BRAZEN
BRAZENED
BRAZENING
BRAZENLY
BRAZENRY
BRAZENS
BRAZER
BRAZERS
BRAZES
BRAZIER
BRAZIERS
BRAZIERY
BRAZIL
BRAZILEIN
BRAZILIN
BRAZILINS
BRAZILS
BRAZING
BREACH
BREACHED
BREACHER
BREACHERS
BREACHES
BREACHING
BREAD
BREADBIN

BREADBINS
BREADBOX
BREADED
BREADHEAD
BREADIER
BREADIEST
BREADING
BREADLESS
BREADLINE
BREADNUT
BREADNUTS
BREADROOM
BREADROOT
BREADS
BREADTH
BREADTHS
BREADY
BREAK
BREAKABLE
BREAKAGE
BREAKAGES
BREAKAWAY
BREAKBACK
BREAKBEAT
BREAKBONE
BREAKDOWN
BREAKER
BREAKERS
BREAKEVEN
BREAKFAST
BREAKING
BREAKINGS
BREAKNECK
BREAKOFF
BREAKOFFS
BREAKOUT
BREAKOUTS
BREAKS
BREAKTIME
BREAKUP
BREAKUPS
BREAKWALL
BREAM
BREAMED
BREAMING
BREAMS
BREARE

BREARES
BREASKIT
BREASKITS
BREAST
BREASTED
BREASTFED
BREASTING
BREASTPIN
BREASTS
BREATH
BREATHE
BREATHED
BREATHER
BREATHERS
BREATHES
BREATHFUL
BREATHIER
BREATHILY
BREATHING
BREATHS
BREATHY
BRECCIA
BRECCIAL
BRECCIAS
BRECCIATE
BRECHAM
BRECHAMS
BRECHAN
BRECHANS
BRED
BREDE
BREDED
BREDES
BREDIE
BREDIES
BREDING
BREDREN
BREDRENS
BREDRIN
BREDRINS
BREDS
BREE
BREECH
BREECHED
BREECHES
BREECHING
BREED

BREEDER
BREEDERS
BREEDING
BREEDINGS
BREEDS
BREEKS
BREEM
BREENGE
BREENGED
BREENGES
BREENGING
BREER
BREERED
BREERING
BREERS
BREES
BREESE
BREESES
BREEST
BREESTS
BREEZE
BREEZED
BREEZES
BREEZEWAY
BREEZIER
BREEZIEST
BREEZILY
BREEZING
BREEZY
BREGMA
BREGMAS
BREGMATA
BREGMATE
BREGMATIC
BREHON
BREHONS
BREI
BREID
BREIDS
BREIING
BREINGE
BREINGED
BREINGES
BREINGING
BREIS
BREIST
BREISTS

BREKKIE	BREVITY	BRIBING	BRIDGING	BRIGHT
BREKKIES	BREW	BRICABRAC	BRIDGINGS	BRIGHTEN
BREKKY	BREWAGE	BRICHT	BRIDIE	BRIGHTENS
BRELOQUE	BREWAGES	BRICHTER	BRIDIES	BRIGHTER
BRELOQUES	BREWED	BRICHTEST	BRIDING	BRIGHTEST
BREME	BREWER	BRICK	BRIDLE	BRIGHTISH
BREN	BREWERIES	BRICKBAT	BRIDLED	BRIGHTLY
BRENNE	BREWERS	BRICKBATS	BRIDLER	BRIGHTS
BRENNES	BREWERY	BRICKCLAY	BRIDLERS	BRIGS
BRENNING	BREWHOUSE	BRICKED	BRIDLES	BRIGUE
BRENS	BREWING	BRICKEN	BRIDLEWAY	BRIGUED
BRENT	BREWINGS	BRICKIE	BRIDLING	BRIGUES
BRENTER	BREWIS	BRICKIER	BRIDOON	BRIGUING
BRENTEST	BREWISES	BRICKIES	BRIDOONS	BRIGUINGS
BRENTS	BREWPUB	BRICKIEST	BRIE	BRIK
BRER	BREWPUBS	BRICKING	BRIEF	BRIKI
BRERE	BREWS	BRICKINGS	BRIEFCASE	BRIKIS
BRERES	BREWSKI	BRICKKILN	BRIEFED	BRIKS
BRERS	BREWSKIES	BRICKLE	BRIEFER	BRILL
BRESAOLA	BREWSKIS	BRICKLES	BRIEFERS	BRILLER
BRESAOLAS	BREWSTER	BRICKLIKE	BRIEFEST	BRILLEST
BRETASCHE	BREWSTERS	BRICKS	BRIEFING	BRILLIANT
BRETESSE	BREY	BRICKWALL	BRIEFINGS	BRILLO
BRETESSES	BREYED	BRICKWORK	BRIEFLESS	BRILLOS
BRETHREN	BREYING	BRICKY	BRIEFLY	BRILLS
BRETON	BREYS	BRICKYARD	BRIEFNESS	BRIM
BRETONS	BRIAR	BRICOLAGE	BRIEFS	BRIMFUL
BRETTICE	BRIARD	BRICOLE	BRIER	BRIMFULL
BRETTICED	BRIARDS	BRICOLES	BRIERED	BRIMFULLY
BRETTICES	BRIARED	BRICOLEUR	BRIERIER	BRIMING
BREVE	BRIARIER	BRIDAL	BRIERIEST	BRIMINGS
BREVES	BRIARIEST	BRIDALLY	BRIERROOT	BRIMLESS
BREVET	BRIARROOT	BRIDALS	BRIERS	BRIMMED
BREVETCY	BRIARS	BRIDE	BRIERWOOD	BRIMMER
BREVETE	BRIARWOOD	BRIDECAKE	BRIERY	BRIMMERS
BREVETED	BRIARY	BRIDED	BRIES	BRIMMING
BREVETING	BRIBABLE	BRIDEMAID	BRIG	BRIMS
BREVETS	BRIBE	BRIDEMAN	BRIGADE	BRIMSTONE
BREVETTED	BRIBEABLE	BRIDEMEN	BRIGADED	BRIMSTONY
BREVIARY	BRIBED	BRIDES	BRIGADES	BRIN
BREVIATE	BRIBEE	BRIDESMAN	BRIGADIER	BRINDED
BREVIATES	BRIBEES	BRIDESMEN	BRIGADING	BRINDISI
BREVIER	BRIBER	BRIDEWELL	BRIGALOW	BRINDISIS
BREVIERS	BRIBERIES	BRIDGABLE	BRIGALOWS	BRINDLE
BREVIS	BRIBERS	BRIDGE	BRIGAND	BRINDLED
BREVISES	BRIBERY	BRIDGED	BRIGANDRY	BRINDLES
BREVITIES	BRIBES	BRIDGES	BRIGANDS	BRINE

BRINED	BRISKEN	BRITTLY	BROCADED	BRODS
BRINELESS	BRISKENED	BRITTS	BROCADES	BROEKIES
BRINER	BRISKENS	BRITZKA	BROCADING	BROG
BRINERS	BRISKER	BRITZKAS	BROCAGE	BROGAN
BRINES	BRISKEST	BRITZSKA	BROCAGES	BROGANS
BRING	BRISKET	BRITZSKAS	BROCARD	BROGGED
BRINGDOWN	BRISKETS	BRIZE	BROCARDS	BROGGING
BRINGER	BRISKIER	BRIZES	BROCATEL	BROGH
BRINGERS	BRISKIEST	BRO	BROCATELS	BROGHS
BRINGING	BRISKING	BROACH	BROCCOLI	BROGS
BRINGINGS	BRISKISH	BROACHED	BROCCOLIS	BROGUE
BRINGS	BRISKLY	BROACHER	BROCH	BROGUEISH
BRINIER	BRISKNESS	BROACHERS	BROCHAN	BROGUERY
BRINIES	BRISKS	BROACHES	BROCHANS	BROGUES
BRINIEST	BRISKY	BROACHING	BROCHE	BROGUISH
BRININESS	BRISLING	BROAD	BROCHED	BROIDER
BRINING	BRISLINGS	BROADAX	BROCHES	BROIDERED
BRINISH	BRISS	BROADAXE	BROCHETTE	BROIDERER
BRINJAL	BRISSES	BROADAXES	BROCHING	BROIDERS
BRINJALS	BRISTLE	BROADBAND	BROCHO	BROIDERY
BRINJARRY	BRISTLED	BROADBEAN	BROCHOS	BROIL
BRINK	BRISTLES	BROADBILL	BROCHS	BROILED
BRINKMAN	BRISTLIER	BROADBRIM	BROCHURE	BROILER
BRINKMEN	BRISTLING	BROADCAST	BROCHURES	BROILERS
BRINKS	BRISTLY	BROADEN	BROCK	BROILING
BRINNIES	BRISTOL	BROADENED	BROCKAGE	BROILS
BRINNY	BRISTOLS	BROADENER	BROCKAGES	BROKAGE
BRINS	BRISURE	BROADENS	BROCKED	BROKAGES
BRINY	BRISURES	BROADER	BROCKET	BROKE
BRIO	BRIT	BROADEST	BROCKETS	BROKED
BRIOCHE	BRITANNIA	BROADISH	BROCKIT	BROKEN
BRIOCHES	BRITCHES	BROADLEAF	BROCKRAM	BROKENLY
BRIOLETTE	BRITH	BROADLINE	BROCKRAMS	BROKER
BRIONIES	BRITHS	BROADLOOM	BROCKS	BROKERAGE
BRIONY	BRITS	BROADLY	BROCOLI	BROKERED
BRIOS	BRITSCHKA	BROADNESS	BROCOLIS	BROKERIES
BRIQUET	BRITSKA	BROADS	BROD	BROKERING
BRIQUETS	BRITSKAS	BROADSIDE	BRODDED	BROKERS
BRIQUETTE	BRITT	BROADTAIL	BRODDING	BROKERY
BRIS	BRITTANIA	BROADWAY	BRODDLE	BROKES
BRISANCE	BRITTLE	BROADWAYS	BRODDLED	BROKING
BRISANCES	BRITTLED	BROADWISE	BRODDLES	BROKINGS
BRISANT	BRITTLELY	BROAST	BRODDLING	BROLGA
BRISE	BRITTLER	BROASTED	BRODEKIN	BROLGAS
BRISES	BRITTLES	BROASTING	BRODEKINS	BROLLIES
BRISK	BRITTLEST	BROASTS	BRODKIN	BROLLY
BRISKED	BRITTLING	BROCADE	BRODKINS	BROMAL

BROMALS	BRONCHIAL	BROOKIES	BROUGHS	BROWSING
BROMANCE	BRONCHIUM	BROOKING	BROUGHT	BROWSINGS
BROMANCES	BRONCHO	BROOKITE	BROUGHTA	BROWST
BROMANTIC	BRONCHOS	BROOKITES	BROUGHTAS	BROWSTS
BROMATE	BRONCHUS	BROOKLET	BROUHAHA	BROWSY
BROMATED	BRONCO	BROOKLETS	BROUHAHAS	BRR
BROMATES	BRONCOS	BROOKLIKE	BROUZE	BRRR
BROMATING	BRONCS	BROOKLIME	BROUZES	BRU
BROME	BROND	BROOKS	BROW	BRUCELLA
BROMELAIN	BRONDS	BROOKWEED	BROWALLIA	BRUCELLAE
BROMELIA	BRONDYRON	BROOL	BROWBAND	BRUCELLAS
BROMELIAD	BRONZE	BROOLS	BROWBANDS	BRUCHID
BROMELIAS	BRONZED	BROOM	BROWBEAT	BRUCHIDS
BROMELIN	BRONZEN	BROOMBALL	BROWBEATS	BRUCIN
BROMELINS	BRONZER	BROOMCORN	BROWBONE	BRUCINE
BROMEOSIN	BRONZERS	BROOMED	BROWBONES	BRUCINES
BROMES	BRONZES	BROOMIER	BROWED	BRUCINS
BROMIC	BRONZIER	BROOMIEST	BROWLESS	BRUCITE
BROMID	BRONZIEST	BROOMING	BROWN	BRUCITES
BROMIDE	BRONZIFY	BROOMRAPE	BROWNED	BRUCKLE
BROMIDES	BRONZING	BROOMS	BROWNER	BRUGH
BROMIDIC	BRONZINGS	BROOMY	BROWNERS	BRUGHS
BROMIDS	BRONZITE	BROOS	BROWNEST	BRUHAHA
BROMIN	BRONZITES	BROOSE	BROWNIE	BRUHAHAS
BROMINATE	BRONZY	BROOSES	BROWNIER	BRUILZIE
BROMINE	BROO	BROS	BROWNIES	BRUILZIES
BROMINES	BROOCH	BROSE	BROWNIEST	BRUIN
BROMINISM	BROOCHED	BROSES	BROWNING	BRUINS
BROMINS	BROOCHES	BROSIER	BROWNINGS	BRUISE
BROMISE	BROOCHING	BROSIEST	BROWNISH	BRUISED
BROMISED	BROOD	BROSY	BROWNNESS	BRUISER
BROMISES	BROODED	BROTH	BROWNNOSE	BRUISERS
BROMISING	BROODER	BROTHA	BROWNOUT	BRUISES
BROMISM	BROODERS	BROTHAS	BROWNOUTS	BRUISING
BROMISMS	BROODIER	BROTHEL	BROWNS	BRUISINGS
BROMIZE	BROODIEST	BROTHELS	BROWNTAIL	BRUIT
BROMIZED	BROODILY	BROTHER	BROWNY	BRUITED
BROMIZES	BROODING	BROTHERED	BROWRIDGE	BRUITER
BROMIZING	BROODINGS	BROTHERLY	BROWS	BRUITERS
BROMMER	BROODLESS	BROTHERS	BROWSABLE	BRUITING
BROMMERS	BROODMARE	BROTHIER	BROWSE	BRUITS
BROMO	BROODS	BROTHIEST	BROWSED	BRULE
BROMOFORM	BROODY	BROTHS	BROWSER	BRULES
BROMOS	BROOK	BROTHY	BROWSERS	BRULOT
BRONC	BROOKABLE	BROUGH	BROWSES	BRULOTS
BRONCHI	BROOKED	BROUGHAM	BROWSIER	BRULYIE
BRONCHIA	BROOKIE	BROUGHAMS	BROWSIEST	BRULYIES

BRULZIE
BRULZIES
BRUMAL
BRUMBIES
BRUMBY
BRUME
BRUMES
BRUMMAGEM
BRUMMER
BRUMMERS
BRUMOUS
BRUNCH
BRUNCHED
BRUNCHER
BRUNCHERS
BRUNCHES
BRUNCHING
BRUNET
BRUNETS
BRUNETTE
BRUNETTES
BRUNG
BRUNIZEM
BRUNIZEMS
BRUNT
BRUNTED
BRUNTING
BRUNTS
BRUS
BRUSH
BRUSHBACK
BRUSHED
BRUSHER
BRUSHERS
BRUSHES
BRUSHFIRE
BRUSHIER
BRUSHIEST
BRUSHING
BRUSHINGS
BRUSHLAND
BRUSHLESS
BRUSHLIKE
BRUSHMARK
BRUSHOFF
BRUSHOFFS
BRUSHUP

BRUSHUPS
BRUSHWOOD
BRUSHWORK
BRUSHY
BRUSK
BRUSKER
BRUSKEST
BRUSQUE
BRUSQUELY
BRUSQUER
BRUSQUEST
BRUSSELS
BRUSSEN
BRUST
BRUSTING
BRUSTS
BRUT
BRUTAL
BRUTALISE
BRUTALISM
BRUTALIST
BRUTALITY
BRUTALIZE
BRUTALLY
BRUTE
BRUTED
BRUTELIKE
BRUTELY
BRUTENESS
BRUTER
BRUTERS
BRUTES
BRUTEST
BRUTIFIED
BRUTIFIES
BRUTIFY
BRUTING
BRUTINGS
BRUTISH
BRUTISHLY
BRUTISM
BRUTISMS
BRUTS
BRUX
BRUXED
BRUXES
BRUXING

BRUXISM
BRUXISMS
BRYOLOGY
BRYONIES
BRYONY
BRYOPHYTE
BRYOZOAN
BRYOZOANS
BUAT
BUATS
BUAZE
BUAZES
BUB
BUBA
BUBAL
BUBALE
BUBALES
BUBALINE
BUBALIS
BUBALISES
BUBALS
BUBAS
BUBBA
BUBBAS
BUBBE
BUBBES
BUBBIE
BUBBIES
BUBBLE
BUBBLED
BUBBLEGUM
BUBBLER
BUBBLERS
BUBBLES
BUBBLIER
BUBBLIES
BUBBLIEST
BUBBLING
BUBBLY
BUBBY
BUBINGA
BUBINGAS
BUBKES
BUBKIS
BUBO
BUBOED
BUBOES

BUBONIC
BUBS
BUBU
BUBUKLE
BUBUKLES
BUBUS
BUCARDO
BUCARDOS
BUCATINI
BUCCAL
BUCCALLY
BUCCANEER
BUCCANIER
BUCCINA
BUCCINAS
BUCELLAS
BUCENTAUR
BUCHU
BUCHUS
BUCK
BUCKAROO
BUCKAROOS
BUCKAYRO
BUCKAYROS
BUCKBEAN
BUCKBEANS
BUCKBOARD
BUCKBRUSH
BUCKED
BUCKEEN
BUCKEENS
BUCKER
BUCKEROO
BUCKEROOS
BUCKERS
BUCKET
BUCKETED
BUCKETFUL
BUCKETING
BUCKETS
BUCKEYE
BUCKEYES
BUCKHORN
BUCKHORNS
BUCKHOUND
BUCKIE
BUCKIES

BUCKING
BUCKINGS
BUCKISH
BUCKISHLY
BUCKLE
BUCKLED
BUCKLER
BUCKLERED
BUCKLERS
BUCKLES
BUCKLING
BUCKLINGS
BUCKO
BUCKOES
BUCKOS
BUCKRA
BUCKRAKE
BUCKRAKES
BUCKRAM
BUCKRAMED
BUCKRAMS
BUCKRAS
BUCKS
BUCKSAW
BUCKSAWS
BUCKSHEE
BUCKSHEES
BUCKSHISH
BUCKSHOT
BUCKSHOTS
BUCKSKIN
BUCKSKINS
BUCKSOM
BUCKTAIL
BUCKTAILS
BUCKTEETH
BUCKTHORN
BUCKTOOTH
BUCKU
BUCKUS
BUCKWHEAT
BUCKYBALL
BUCKYTUBE
BUCOLIC
BUCOLICAL
BUCOLICS
BUD

BUDA	BUDMASHES	BUGABOO	BUGSEEDS	BULBAR
BUDAS	BUDO	BUGABOOS	BUGSHA	BULBED
BUDDED	BUDOS	BUGBANE	BUGSHAS	BULBEL
BUDDER	BUDS	BUGBANES	BUGWORT	BULBELS
BUDDERS	BUDWOOD	BUGBEAR	BUGWORTS	BULBIL
BUDDHA	BUDWOODS	BUGBEARS	BUHL	BULBILS
BUDDHAS	BUDWORM	BUGEYE	BUHLS	BULBING
BUDDIED	BUDWORMS	BUGEYES	BUHLWORK	BULBLET
BUDDIER	BUFF	BUGGAN	BUHLWORKS	BULBLETS
BUDDIES	BUFFA	BUGGANE	BUHR	BULBOSITY
BUDDIEST	BUFFABLE	BUGGANES	BUHRS	BULBOUS
BUDDING	BUFFALO	BUGGANS	BUHRSTONE	BULBOUSLY
BUDDINGS	BUFFALOED	BUGGED	BUHUND	BULBS
BUDDLE	BUFFALOES	BUGGER	BUHUNDS	BULBUL
BUDDLED	BUFFALOS	BUGGERED	BUIBUI	BULBULS
BUDDLEIA	BUFFE	BUGGERIES	BUIBUIS	BULGAR
BUDDLEIAS	BUFFED	BUGGERING	BUIK	BULGARS
BUDDLES	BUFFEL	BUGGERS	BUIKS	BULGE
BUDDLING	BUFFER	BUGGERY	BUILD	BULGED
BUDDY	BUFFERED	BUGGIER	BUILDABLE	BULGER
BUDDYING	BUFFERING	BUGGIES	BUILDDOWN	BULGERS
BUDGE	BUFFERS	BUGGIEST	BUILDED	BULGES
BUDGED	BUFFEST	BUGGIN	BUILDER	BULGHUR
BUDGER	BUFFET	BUGGINESS	BUILDERS	BULGHURS
BUDGEREE	BUFFETED	BUGGING	BUILDING	BULGIER
BUDGERO	BUFFETER	BUGGINGS	BUILDINGS	BULGIEST
BUDGEROS	BUFFETERS	BUGGINS	BUILDOUT	BULGINE
BUDGEROW	BUFFETING	BUGGY	BUILDOUTS	BULGINES
BUDGEROWS	BUFFETS	BUGHOUSE	BUILDS	BULGINESS
BUDGERS	BUFFI	BUGHOUSES	BUILDUP	BULGING
BUDGES	BUFFIER	BUGLE	BUILDUPS	BULGINGLY
BUDGET	BUFFIEST	BUGLED	BUILT	BULGUR
BUDGETARY	BUFFING	BUGLER	BUIRDLIER	BULGURS
BUDGETED	BUFFINGS	BUGLERS	BUIRDLY	BULGY
BUDGETEER	BUFFO	BUGLES	BUIST	BULIMIA
BUDGETER	BUFFOON	BUGLET	BUISTED	BULIMIAC
BUDGETERS	BUFFOONS	BUGLETS	BUISTING	BULIMIAS
BUDGETING	BUFFOS	BUGLEWEED	BUISTS	BULIMIC
BUDGETS	BUFFS	BUGLING	BUKE	BULIMICS
BUDGIE	BUFFY	BUGLOSS	BUKES	BULIMIES
BUDGIES	BUFO	BUGLOSSES	BUKKAKE	BULIMUS
BUDGING	BUFOS	BUGONG	BUKKAKES	BULIMUSES
BUDI	BUFOTALIN	BUGONGS	BUKSHEE	BULIMY
BUDIS	BUFTIE	BUGOUT	BUKSHEES	BULK
BUDLESS	BUFTIES	BUGOUTS	BUKSHI	BULKAGE
BUDLIKE	BUFTY	BUGS	BUKSHIS	BULKAGES
BUDMASH	BUG	BUGSEED	BULB	BULKED

BULKER	BULLETINS	BULLSHIT	BUMBLERS	BUMPIER
BULKERS	BULLETRIE	BULLSHITS	BUMBLES	BUMPIEST
BULKHEAD	BULLETS	BULLSHOT	BUMBLING	BUMPILY
BULKHEADS	BULLEY	BULLSHOTS	BUMBLINGS	BUMPINESS
BULKIER	BULLEYS	BULLSNAKE	BUMBO	BUMPING
BULKIEST	BULLFIGHT	BULLWADDY	BUMBOAT	BUMPINGS
BULKILY	BULLFINCH	BULLWEED	BUMBOATS	BUMPKIN
BULKINESS	BULLFROG	BULLWEEDS	BUMBOS	BUMPKINLY
BULKING	BULLFROGS	BULLWHACK	BUMBOY	BUMPKINS
BULKINGS	BULLGINE	BULLWHIP	BUMBOYS	BUMPOLOGY
BULKS	BULLGINES	BULLWHIPS	BUMELIA	BUMPS
BULKY	BULLHEAD	BULLY	BUMELIAS	BUMPTIOUS
BULL	BULLHEADS	BULLYBOY	BUMF	BUMPY
BULLA	BULLHORN	BULLYBOYS	BUMFLUFF	BUMS
BULLACE	BULLHORNS	BULLYCIDE	BUMFLUFFS	BUMSTER
BULLACES	BULLIED	BULLYING	BUMFS	BUMSTERS
BULLAE	BULLIER	BULLYISM	BUMFUCK	BUMSUCKER
BULLARIES	BULLIES	BULLYISMS	BUMFUCKS	BUMWAD
BULLARY	BULLIEST	BULLYRAG	BUMFUZZLE	BUMWADS
BULLATE	BULLING	BULLYRAGS	BUMKIN	BUN
BULLBARS	BULLINGS	BULNBULN	BUMKINS	BUNA
BULLBAT	BULLION	BULNBULNS	BUMMALO	BUNAS
BULLBATS	BULLIONS	BULRUSH	BUMMALOS	BUNBURIED
BULLBRIER	BULLISH	BULRUSHES	BUMMALOTI	BUNBURIES
BULLCOOK	BULLISHLY	BULRUSHY	BUMMAREE	BUNBURY
BULLCOOKS	BULLNECK	BULSE	BUMMAREES	BUNCE
BULLDIKE	BULLNECKS	BULSES	BUMMED	BUNCED
BULLDIKES	BULLNOSE	BULWADDEE	BUMMEL	BUNCES
BULLDOG	BULLNOSED	BULWADDY	BUMMELS	BUNCH
BULLDOGS	BULLNOSES	BULWARK	BUMMER	BUNCHED
BULLDOZE	BULLOCK	BULWARKED	BUMMERS	BUNCHER
BULLDOZED	BULLOCKED	BULWARKS	BUMMEST	BUNCHERS
BULLDOZER	BULLOCKS	BUM	BUMMING	BUNCHES
BULLDOZES	BULLOCKY	BUMALO	BUMMLE	BUNCHIER
BULLDUST	BULLOSA	BUMALOTI	BUMMLED	BUNCHIEST
BULLDUSTS	BULLOUS	BUMALOTIS	BUMMLES	BUNCHILY
BULLDYKE	BULLPEN	BUMBAG	BUMMLING	BUNCHING
BULLDYKES	BULLPENS	BUMBAGS	BUMMOCK	BUNCHINGS
BULLED	BULLPOUT	BUMBAZE	BUMMOCKS	BUNCHY
BULLER	BULLPOUTS	BUMBAZED	BUMP	BUNCING
BULLERED	BULLRING	BUMBAZES	BUMPED	BUNCO
BULLERING	BULLRINGS	BUMBAZING	BUMPER	BUNCOED
BULLERS	BULLRUSH	BUMBLE	BUMPERED	BUNCOES
BULLET	BULLS	BUMBLEBEE	BUMPERING	BUNCOING
BULLETED	BULLSEYE	BUMBLED	BUMPERS	BUNCOMBE
BULLETIN	BULLSEYES	BUMBLEDOM	BUMPH	BUNCOMBES
BULLETING	BULLSHAT	BUMBLER	BUMPHS	BUNCOS

BUND	BUNGLE	BUNNIAS	BUPRESTID	BURFI
BUNDE	BUNGLED	BUNNIES	BUPROPION	BURFIS
BUNDED	BUNGLER	BUNNS	BUQSHA	BURG
BUNDH	BUNGLERS	BUNNY	BUQSHAS	BURGAGE
BUNDHS	BUNGLES	BUNODONT	BUR	BURGAGES
BUNDIED	BUNGLING	BUNRAKU	BURA	BURGANET
BUNDIES	BUNGLINGS	BUNRAKUS	BURAN	BURGANETS
BUNDING	BUNGS	BUNS	BURANS	BURGEE
BUNDIST	BUNGWALL	BUNSEN	BURAS	BURGEES
BUNDISTS	BUNGWALLS	BUNSENS	BURB	BURGEON
BUNDLE	BUNGY	BUNT	BURBLE	BURGEONED
BUNDLED	BUNHEAD	BUNTAL	BURBLED	BURGEONS
BUNDLER	BUNHEADS	BUNTALS	BURBLER	BURGER
BUNDLERS	BUNIA	BUNTED	BURBLERS	BURGERS
BUNDLES	BUNIAS	BUNTER	BURBLES	BURGESS
BUNDLING	BUNION	BUNTERS	BURBLIER	BURGESSES
BUNDLINGS	BUNIONS	BUNTIER	BURBLIEST	BURGH
BUNDOBUST	BUNJE	BUNTIEST	BURBLING	BURGHAL
BUNDOOK	BUNJEE	BUNTING	BURBLINGS	BURGHER
BUNDOOKS	BUNJEES	BUNTINGS	BURBLY	BURGHERS
BUNDS	BUNJES	BUNTLINE	BURBOT	BURGHS
BUNDT	BUNJIE	BUNTLINES	BURBOTS	BURGHUL
BUNDTS	BUNJIES	BUNTS	BURBS	BURGHULS
BUNDU	BUNJY	BUNTY	BURD	BURGLAR
BUNDUS	BUNK	BUNYA	BURDASH	BURGLARED
BUNDWALL	BUNKED	BUNYAS	BURDASHES	BURGLARS
BUNDWALLS	BUNKER	BUNYIP	BURDEN	BURGLARY
BUNDY	BUNKERED	BUNYIPS	BURDENED	BURGLE
BUNDYING	BUNKERING	BUOY	BURDENER	BURGLED
BUNFIGHT	BUNKERS	BUOYAGE	BURDENERS	BURGLES
BUNFIGHTS	BUNKHOUSE	BUOYAGES	BURDENING	BURGLING
BUNG	BUNKIE	BUOYANCE	BURDENOUS	BURGONET
BUNGALOID	BUNKIES	BUOYANCES	BURDENS	BURGONETS
BUNGALOW	BUNKING	BUOYANCY	BURDIE	BURGOO
BUNGALOWS	BUNKMATE	BUOYANT	BURDIES	BURGOOS
BUNGED	BUNKMATES	BUOYANTLY	BURDIZZO	BURGOUT
BUNGEE	BUNKO	BUOYED	BURDIZZOS	BURGOUTS
BUNGEES	BUNKOED	BUOYING	BURDOCK	BURGRAVE
BUNGER	BUNKOING	BUOYS	BURDOCKS	BURGRAVES
BUNGERS	BUNKOS	BUPKES	BURDS	BURGS
BUNGEY	BUNKS	BUPKIS	BUREAU	BURGUNDY
BUNGEYS	BUNKUM	BUPKUS	BUREAUS	BURHEL
BUNGHOLE	BUNKUMS	BUPLEVER	BUREAUX	BURHELS
BUNGHOLES	BUNN	BUPLEVERS	BURET	BURIAL
BUNGIE	BUNNET	BUPPIE	BURETS	BURIALS
BUNGIES	BUNNETS	BUPPIES	BURETTE	BURIED
BUNGING	BUNNIA	BUPPY	BURETTES	BURIER

BURIERS	BURLY	BURREL	BURSTEN	BUSHELS
BURIES	BURN	BURRELL	BURSTER	BUSHER
BURIN	BURNABLE	BURRELLS	BURSTERS	BUSHERS
BURINIST	BURNABLES	BURRELS	BURSTIER	BUSHES
BURINISTS	BURNED	BURRER	BURSTIEST	BUSHFIRE
BURINS	BURNER	BURRERS	BURSTING	BUSHFIRES
BURITI	BURNERS	BURRFISH	BURSTONE	BUSHFLIES
BURITIS	BURNET	BURRHEL	BURSTONES	BUSHFLY
BURK	BURNETS	BURRHELS	BURSTS	BUSHGOAT
BURKA	BURNIE	BURRIER	BURSTY	BUSHGOATS
BURKAS	BURNIES	BURRIEST	BURTHEN	BUSHIDO
BURKE	BURNING	BURRING	BURTHENED	BUSHIDOS
BURKED	BURNINGLY	BURRITO	BURTHENS	BUSHIE
BURKER	BURNINGS	BURRITOS	BURTON	BUSHIER
BURKERS	BURNISH	BURRO	BURTONS	BUSHIES
BURKES	BURNISHED	BURROS	BURWEED	BUSHIEST
BURKHA	BURNISHER	BURROW	BURWEEDS	BUSHILY
BURKHAS	BURNISHES	BURROWED	BURY	BUSHINESS
BURKING	BURNOOSE	BURROWER	BURYING	BUSHING
BURKINI	BURNOOSED	BURROWERS	BUS	BUSHINGS
BURKINIS	BURNOOSES	BURROWING	BUSBAR	BUSHLAND
BURKITE	BURNOUS	BURROWS	BUSBARS	BUSHLANDS
BURKITES	BURNOUSE	BURRS	BUSBIES	BUSHLESS
BURKS	BURNOUSED	BURRSTONE	BUSBOY	BUSHLIKE
BURL	BURNOUSES	BURRY	BUSBOYS	BUSHLOT
BURLADERO	BURNOUT	BURS	BUSBY	BUSHLOTS
BURLAP	BURNOUTS	BURSA	BUSED	BUSHMAN
BURLAPS	BURNS	BURSAE	BUSERA	BUSHMEAT
BURLED	BURNSIDE	BURSAL	BUSERAS	BUSHMEATS
BURLER	BURNSIDES	BURSAR	BUSES	BUSHMEN
BURLERS	BURNT	BURSARIAL	BUSGIRL	BUSHPIG
BURLESK	BUROO	BURSARIES	BUSGIRLS	BUSHPIGS
BURLESKS	BUROOS	BURSARS	BUSH	BUSHTIT
BURLESQUE	BURP	BURSARY	BUSHBABY	BUSHTITS
BURLETTA	BURPED	BURSAS	BUSHBUCK	BUSHVELD
BURLETTAS	BURPEE	BURSATE	BUSHBUCKS	BUSHVELDS
BURLEY	BURPEES	BURSE	BUSHCRAFT	BUSHWA
BURLEYCUE	BURPING	BURSEED	BUSHED	BUSHWAH
BURLEYED	BURPS	BURSEEDS	BUSHEL	BUSHWAHS
BURLEYING	BURQA	BURSERA	BUSHELED	BUSHWALK
BURLEYS	BURQAS	BURSES	BUSHELER	BUSHWALKS
BURLIER	BURR	BURSICON	BUSHELERS	BUSHWAS
BURLIEST	BURRAMYS	BURSICONS	BUSHELING	BUSHWHACK
BURLILY	BURRATA	BURSIFORM	BUSHELLED	BUSHWOMAN
BURLINESS	BURRATAS	BURSITIS	BUSHELLER	BUSHWOMEN
BURLING	BURRAWANG	BURST	BUSHELMAN	BUSHY
BURLS	BURRED	BURSTED	BUSHELMEN	BUSIED

BUSIER
BUSIES
BUSIEST
BUSILY
BUSINESS
BUSINESSY
BUSING
BUSINGS
BUSK
BUSKED
BUSKER
BUSKERS
BUSKET
BUSKETS
BUSKIN
BUSKINED
BUSKING
BUSKINGS
BUSKINS
BUSKS
BUSKY
BUSLOAD
BUSLOADS
BUSMAN
BUSMEN
BUSS
BUSSED
BUSSES
BUSSING
BUSSINGS
BUSSU
BUSSUS
BUST
BUSTARD
BUSTARDS
BUSTED
BUSTEE
BUSTEES
BUSTER
BUSTERS
BUSTI
BUSTIC
BUSTICATE
BUSTICS
BUSTIER
BUSTIERS
BUSTIEST

BUSTINESS
BUSTING
BUSTINGS
BUSTIS
BUSTLE
BUSTLED
BUSTLER
BUSTLERS
BUSTLES
BUSTLINE
BUSTLINES
BUSTLING
BUSTS
BUSTY
BUSULFAN
BUSULFANS
BUSUUTI
BUSUUTIS
BUSY
BUSYBODY
BUSYING
BUSYNESS
BUSYWORK
BUSYWORKS
BUT
BUTADIENE
BUTANE
BUTANES
BUTANOIC
BUTANOL
BUTANOLS
BUTANONE
BUTANONES
BUTCH
BUTCHER
BUTCHERED
BUTCHERER
BUTCHERLY
BUTCHERS
BUTCHERY
BUTCHES
BUTCHEST
BUTCHING
BUTCHINGS
BUTCHNESS
BUTE
BUTENE

BUTENES
BUTEO
BUTEONINE
BUTEOS
BUTES
BUTLE
BUTLED
BUTLER
BUTLERAGE
BUTLERED
BUTLERIES
BUTLERING
BUTLERS
BUTLERY
BUTLES
BUTLING
BUTMENT
BUTMENTS
BUTOH
BUTOHS
BUTS
BUTSUDAN
BUTSUDANS
BUTT
BUTTALS
BUTTE
BUTTED
BUTTER
BUTTERBUR
BUTTERCUP
BUTTERED
BUTTERFAT
BUTTERFLY
BUTTERIER
BUTTERIES
BUTTERINE
BUTTERING
BUTTERNUT
BUTTERS
BUTTERY
BUTTES
BUTTHEAD
BUTTHEADS
BUTTIES
BUTTING
BUTTINSKI
BUTTINSKY

BUTTLE
BUTTLED
BUTTLES
BUTTLING
BUTTOCK
BUTTOCKED
BUTTOCKS
BUTTON
BUTTONED
BUTTONER
BUTTONERS
BUTTONING
BUTTONS
BUTTONY
BUTTRESS
BUTTS
BUTTSTOCK
BUTTY
BUTTYMAN
BUTTYMEN
BUTUT
BUTUTS
BUTYL
BUTYLATE
BUTYLATED
BUTYLATES
BUTYLENE
BUTYLENES
BUTYLS
BUTYRAL
BUTYRALS
BUTYRATE
BUTYRATES
BUTYRIC
BUTYRIN
BUTYRINS
BUTYROUS
BUTYRYL
BUTYRYLS
BUVETTE
BUVETTES
BUXOM
BUXOMER
BUXOMEST
BUXOMLY
BUXOMNESS
BUY

BUYABLE
BUYABLES
BUYBACK
BUYBACKS
BUYER
BUYERS
BUYING
BUYINGS
BUYOFF
BUYOFFS
BUYOUT
BUYOUTS
BUYS
BUZKASHI
BUZKASHIS
BUZUKI
BUZUKIA
BUZUKIS
BUZZ
BUZZARD
BUZZARDS
BUZZBAIT
BUZZBAITS
BUZZCUT
BUZZCUTS
BUZZED
BUZZER
BUZZERS
BUZZES
BUZZIER
BUZZIEST
BUZZING
BUZZINGLY
BUZZINGS
BUZZKILL
BUZZKILLS
BUZZSAW
BUZZSAWS
BUZZWIG
BUZZWIGS
BUZZWORD
BUZZWORDS
BUZZY
BWANA
BWANAS
BWAZI
BWAZIS

B

BY
BYCATCH
BYCATCHES
BYCOKET
BYCOKETS
BYDE
BYDED
BYDES
BYDING
BYE
BYELAW
BYELAWS
BYES
BYGONE
BYGONES
BYKE
BYKED
BYKES
BYKING

BYLANDER
BYLANDERS
BYLANE
BYLANES
BYLAW
BYLAWS
BYLINE
BYLINED
BYLINER
BYLINERS
BYLINES
BYLINING
BYLIVE
BYNAME
BYNAMES
BYNEMPT
BYPASS
BYPASSED
BYPASSES

BYPASSING
BYPAST
BYPATH
BYPATHS
BYPLACE
BYPLACES
BYPLAY
BYPLAYS
BYPRODUCT
BYRE
BYREMAN
BYREMEN
BYRES
BYREWOMAN
BYREWOMEN
BYRL
BYRLADY
BYRLAKIN
BYRLAW

BYRLAWS
BYRLED
BYRLING
BYRLS
BYRNIE
BYRNIES
BYROAD
BYROADS
BYROOM
BYROOMS
BYS
BYSSAL
BYSSI
BYSSINE
BYSSOID
BYSSUS
BYSSUSES
BYSTANDER
BYSTREET

BYSTREETS
BYTALK
BYTALKS
BYTE
BYTES
BYTOWNITE
BYWAY
BYWAYS
BYWONER
BYWONERS
BYWORD
BYWORDS
BYWORK
BYWORKS
BYZANT
BYZANTINE
BYZANTS

C

CAA
CAAED
CAAING
CAAS
CAATINGA
CAATINGAS
CAB
CABA
CABAL
CABALA
CABALAS
CABALETTA
CABALETTE
CABALISM
CABALISMS
CABALIST
CABALISTS
CABALLED
CABALLER
CABALLERO
CABALLERS
CABALLINE
CABALLING
CABALS
CABANA
CABANAS
CABARET
CABARETS
CABAS
CABBAGE
CABBAGED
CABBAGES
CABBAGEY
CABBAGING
CABBAGY
CABBALA
CABBALAH
CABBALAHS
CABBALAS
CABBALISM
CABBALIST

CABBED
CABBIE
CABBIES
CABBING
CABBY
CABDRIVER
CABER
CABERNET
CABERNETS
CABERS
CABESTRO
CABESTROS
CABEZON
CABEZONE
CABEZONES
CABEZONS
CABILDO
CABILDOS
CABIN
CABINED
CABINET
CABINETRY
CABINETS
CABINING
CABINMATE
CABINS
CABLE
CABLECAST
CABLED
CABLEGRAM
CABLER
CABLERS
CABLES
CABLET
CABLETS
CABLEWAY
CABLEWAYS
CABLING
CABLINGS
CABMAN
CABMEN

CABOB
CABOBBED
CABOBBING
CABOBS
CABOC
CABOCEER
CABOCEERS
CABOCHED
CABOCHON
CABOCHONS
CABOCS
CABOMBA
CABOMBAS
CABOODLE
CABOODLES
CABOOSE
CABOOSES
CABOSHED
CABOTAGE
CABOTAGES
CABOVER
CABOVERS
CABRE
CABRESTA
CABRESTAS
CABRESTO
CABRESTOS
CABRETTA
CABRETTAS
CABRIE
CABRIES
CABRILLA
CABRILLAS
CABRIO
CABRIOLE
CABRIOLES
CABRIOLET
CABRIOS
CABRIT
CABRITS
CABS

CABSTAND
CABSTANDS
CACA
CACAFOGO
CACAFOGOS
CACAFUEGO
CACAO
CACAOS
CACAS
CACHACA
CACHACAS
CACHAEMIA
CACHAEMIC
CACHALOT
CACHALOTS
CACHE
CACHECTIC
CACHED
CACHEPOT
CACHEPOTS
CACHES
CACHET
CACHETED
CACHETING
CACHETS
CACHEXIA
CACHEXIAS
CACHEXIC
CACHEXIES
CACHEXY
CACHING
CACHOLONG
CACHOLOT
CACHOLOTS
CACHOU
CACHOUS
CACHUCHA
CACHUCHAS
CACIQUE
CACIQUES
CACIQUISM

CACK
CACKED
CACKIER
CACKIEST
CACKING
CACKLE
CACKLED
CACKLER
CACKLERS
CACKLES
CACKLING
CACKS
CACKY
CACODEMON
CACODOXY
CACODYL
CACODYLIC
CACODYLS
CACOEPIES
CACOEPY
CACOETHES
CACOETHIC
CACOGENIC
CACOLET
CACOLETS
CACOLOGY
CACOMIXL
CACOMIXLE
CACOMIXLS
CACONYM
CACONYMS
CACONYMY
CACOON
CACOONS
CACOPHONY
CACOTOPIA
CACTI
CACTIFORM
CACTOID
CACTUS
CACTUSES

CACUMEN	CADENZA	CAESARISM	CAGELINGS	CAIN
CACUMENS	CADENZAS	CAESARS	CAGER	CAINS
CACUMINA	CADES	CAESE	CAGERS	CAIQUE
CACUMINAL	CADET	CAESIOUS	CAGES	CAIQUES
CAD	CADETS	CAESIUM	CAGEWORK	CAIRD
CADAGA	CADETSHIP	CAESIUMS	CAGEWORKS	CAIRDS
CADAGAS	CADGE	CAESTUS	CAGEY	CAIRN
CADAGI	CADGED	CAESTUSES	CAGEYNESS	CAIRNED
CADAGIS	CADGER	CAESURA	CAGIER	CAIRNGORM
CADASTER	CADGERS	CAESURAE	CAGIEST	CAIRNIER
CADASTERS	CADGES	CAESURAL	CAGILY	CAIRNIEST
CADASTRAL	CADGIER	CAESURAS	CAGINESS	CAIRNS
CADASTRE	CADGIEST	CAESURIC	CAGING	CAIRNY
CADASTRES	CADGING	CAF	CAGMAG	CAISSON
CADAVER	CADGY	CAFARD	CAGMAGGED	CAISSONS
CADAVERIC	CADI	CAFARDS	CAGMAGS	CAITIFF
CADAVERS	CADIE	CAFE	CAGOT	CAITIFFS
CADDICE	CADIES	CAFES	CAGOTS	CAITIVE
CADDICES	CADIS	CAFETERIA	CAGOUL	CAITIVES
CADDIE	CADMIC	CAFETIERE	CAGOULE	CAJAPUT
CADDIED	CADMIUM	CAFETORIA	CAGOULES	CAJAPUTS
CADDIES	CADMIUMS	CAFF	CAGOULS	CAJEPUT
CADDIS	CADRANS	CAFFEIN	CAGS	CAJEPUTS
CADDISED	CADRANSES	CAFFEINE	CAGY	CAJOLE
CADDISES	CADRE	CAFFEINES	CAGYNESS	CAJOLED
CADDISFLY	CADRES	CAFFEINIC	CAHIER	CAJOLER
CADDISH	CADS	CAFFEINS	CAHIERS	CAJOLERS
CADDISHLY	CADUAC	CAFFEISM	CAHOOT	CAJOLERY
CADDY	CADUACS	CAFFEISMS	CAHOOTS	CAJOLES
CADDYING	CADUCEAN	CAFFILA	CAHOUN	CAJOLING
CADDYSS	CADUCEI	CAFFILAS	CAHOUNS	CAJON
CADDYSSES	CADUCEUS	CAFFS	CAHOW	CAJONES
CADE	CADUCITY	CAFILA	CAHOWS	CAJUN
CADEAU	CADUCOUS	CAFILAS	CAID	CAJUPUT
CADEAUX	CAECA	CAFS	CAIDS	CAJUPUTS
CADEE	CAECAL	CAFTAN	CAILLACH	CAKE
CADEES	CAECALLY	CAFTANED	CAILLACHS	CAKEAGE
CADELLE	CAECILIAN	CAFTANS	CAILLE	CAKEAGES
CADELLES	CAECITIS	CAG	CAILLEACH	CAKEBOX
CADENCE	CAECUM	CAGANER	CAILLES	CAKEBOXES
CADENCED	CAEOMA	CAGANERS	CAILLIACH	CAKED
CADENCES	CAEOMAS	CAGE	CAIMAC	CAKEHOLE
CADENCIES	CAERULE	CAGED	CAIMACAM	CAKEHOLES
CADENCING	CAERULEAN	CAGEFUL	CAIMACAMS	CAKES
CADENCY	CAESAR	CAGEFULS	CAIMACS	CAKEWALK
CADENT	CAESAREAN	CAGELIKE	CAIMAN	CAKEWALKS
CADENTIAL	CAESARIAN	CAGELING	CAIMANS	CAKEY

CAKIER	CALATHOS	CALCULATE	CALIBRATE	CALKERS
CAKIEST	CALATHUS	CALCULI	CALIBRE	CALKIN
CAKINESS	CALAVANCE	CALCULOSE	CALIBRED	CALKING
CAKING	CALCANEA	CALCULOUS	CALIBRES	CALKINGS
CAKINGS	CALCANEAL	CALCULUS	CALICES	CALKINS
CAKY	CALCANEAN	CALDARIA	CALICHE	CALKS
CAL	CALCANEI	CALDARIUM	CALICHES	CALL
CALABASH	CALCANEUM	CALDERA	CALICLE	CALLA
CALABAZA	CALCANEUS	CALDERAS	CALICLES	CALLABLE
CALABAZAS	CALCAR	CALDRON	CALICO	CALLAIDES
CALABOGUS	CALCARATE	CALDRONS	CALICOES	CALLAIS
CALABOOSE	CALCARIA	CALECHE	CALICOS	CALLALOO
CALABRESE	CALCARINE	CALECHES	CALICULAR	CALLALOOS
CALADIUM	CALCARS	CALEFIED	CALID	CALLALOU
CALADIUMS	CALCEATE	CALEFIES	CALIDITY	CALLALOUS
CALALOO	CALCEATED	CALEFY	CALIF	CALLAN
CALALOOS	CALCEATES	CALEFYING	CALIFATE	CALLANS
CALALU	CALCED	CALEMBOUR	CALIFATES	CALLANT
CALALUS	CALCEDONY	CALENDAL	CALIFONT	CALLANTS
CALAMANCO	CALCES	CALENDAR	CALIFONTS	CALLAS
CALAMAR	CALCIC	CALENDARS	CALIFS	CALLBACK
CALAMARI	CALCICOLE	CALENDER	CALIGO	CALLBACKS
CALAMARIS	CALCIFIC	CALENDERS	CALIGOES	CALLBOARD
CALAMARS	CALCIFIED	CALENDRER	CALIGOS	CALLBOY
CALAMARY	CALCIFIES	CALENDRIC	CALIMA	CALLBOYS
CALAMATA	CALCIFUGE	CALENDRY	CALIMAS	CALLED
CALAMATAS	CALCIFY	CALENDS	CALIMOCHO	CALLEE
CALAMI	CALCIMINE	CALENDULA	CALIOLOGY	CALLEES
CALAMINE	CALCINE	CALENTURE	CALIPASH	CALLER
CALAMINED	CALCINED	CALESA	CALIPEE	CALLERS
CALAMINES	CALCINES	CALESAS	CALIPEES	CALLET
CALAMINT	CALCINING	CALESCENT	CALIPER	CALLETS
CALAMINTS	CALCITE	CALF	CALIPERED	CALLID
CALAMITE	CALCITES	CALFDOZER	CALIPERS	CALLIDITY
CALAMITES	CALCITIC	CALFHOOD	CALIPH	CALLIGRAM
CALAMITY	CALCIUM	CALFHOODS	CALIPHAL	CALLING
CALAMUS	CALCIUMS	CALFLESS	CALIPHATE	CALLINGS
CALAMUSES	CALCRETE	CALFLICK	CALIPHS	CALLIOPE
CALANDO	CALCRETES	CALFLICKS	CALISAYA	CALLIOPES
CALANDRIA	CALCSPAR	CALFLIKE	CALISAYAS	CALLIPASH
CALANTHE	CALCSPARS	CALFS	CALIVER	CALLIPEE
CALANTHES	CALCTUFA	CALFSKIN	CALIVERS	CALLIPEES
CALASH	CALCTUFAS	CALFSKINS	CALIX	CALLIPER
CALASHES	CALCTUFF	CALIATOUR	CALIXES	CALLIPERS
CALATHEA	CALCTUFFS	CALIBER	CALK	CALLOP
CALATHEAS	CALCULAR	CALIBERED	CALKED	CALLOPS
CALATHI	CALCULARY	CALIBERS	CALKER	CALLOSE

CALLOSES
CALLOSITY
CALLOUS
CALLOUSED
CALLOUSES
CALLOUSLY
CALLOUT
CALLOUTS
CALLOW
CALLOWER
CALLOWEST
CALLOWLY
CALLOWS
CALLS
CALLTIME
CALLTIMES
CALLUNA
CALLUNAS
CALLUS
CALLUSED
CALLUSES
CALLUSING
CALM
CALMANT
CALMANTS
CALMATIVE
CALMED
CALMER
CALMEST
CALMIER
CALMIEST
CALMING
CALMINGLY
CALMINGS
CALMLY
CALMNESS
CALMS
CALMSTANE
CALMSTONE
CALMY
CALO
CALOMEL
CALOMELS
CALORIC
CALORICS
CALORIE
CALORIES

CALORIFIC
CALORISE
CALORISED
CALORISES
CALORIST
CALORISTS
CALORIZE
CALORIZED
CALORIZES
CALORY
CALOS
CALOTTE
CALOTTES
CALOTYPE
CALOTYPES
CALOYER
CALOYERS
CALP
CALPA
CALPAC
CALPACK
CALPACKS
CALPACS
CALPAIN
CALPAINS
CALPAS
CALPS
CALQUE
CALQUED
CALQUES
CALQUING
CALTHA
CALTHAS
CALTHROP
CALTHROPS
CALTRAP
CALTRAPS
CALTROP
CALTROPS
CALUMBA
CALUMBAS
CALUMET
CALUMETS
CALUMNIED
CALUMNIES
CALUMNY
CALUTRON

CALUTRONS
CALVADOS
CALVARIA
CALVARIAL
CALVARIAN
CALVARIAS
CALVARIES
CALVARIUM
CALVARY
CALVE
CALVED
CALVER
CALVERED
CALVERING
CALVERS
CALVES
CALVING
CALVITIES
CALX
CALXES
CALYCATE
CALYCEAL
CALYCES
CALYCINAL
CALYCINE
CALYCLE
CALYCLED
CALYCLES
CALYCOID
CALYCULAR
CALYCULE
CALYCULES
CALYCULI
CALYCULUS
CALYPSO
CALYPSOES
CALYPSOS
CALYPTER
CALYPTERA
CALYPTERS
CALYPTRA
CALYPTRAS
CALYX
CALYXES
CALZONE
CALZONES
CALZONI

CAM
CAMA
CAMAIEU
CAMAIEUX
CAMAIL
CAMAILED
CAMAILS
CAMAN
CAMANACHD
CAMANS
CAMARILLA
CAMARON
CAMARONS
CAMAS
CAMASES
CAMASH
CAMASHES
CAMASS
CAMASSES
CAMBER
CAMBERED
CAMBERING
CAMBERS
CAMBIA
CAMBIAL
CAMBIFORM
CAMBISM
CAMBISMS
CAMBIST
CAMBISTRY
CAMBISTS
CAMBIUM
CAMBIUMS
CAMBOGE
CAMBOGES
CAMBOGIA
CAMBOGIAS
CAMBOOSE
CAMBOOSES
CAMBREL
CAMBRELS
CAMBRIC
CAMBRICS
CAMCORD
CAMCORDED
CAMCORDER
CAMCORDS

CAME
CAMEL
CAMELBACK
CAMELEER
CAMELEERS
CAMELEON
CAMELEONS
CAMELHAIR
CAMELIA
CAMELIAS
CAMELID
CAMELIDS
CAMELINE
CAMELINES
CAMELISH
CAMELLIA
CAMELLIAS
CAMELLIKE
CAMELOID
CAMELOIDS
CAMELOT
CAMELOTS
CAMELRIES
CAMELRY
CAMELS
CAMEO
CAMEOED
CAMEOING
CAMEOS
CAMERA
CAMERAE
CAMERAL
CAMERAMAN
CAMERAMEN
CAMERAS
CAMERATED
CAMES
CAMESE
CAMESES
CAMI
CAMION
CAMIONS
CAMIS
CAMISA
CAMISADE
CAMISADES
CAMISADO

CAMISADOS	CAMPERS	CAMPSITE	CANALLERS	CANDIDAL
CAMISAS	CAMPERY	CAMPSITES	CANALLING	CANDIDAS
CAMISE	CAMPESINO	CAMPSTOOL	CANALS	CANDIDATE
CAMISES	CAMPEST	CAMPUS	CANAPE	CANDIDER
CAMISIA	CAMPFIRE	CAMPUSED	CANAPES	CANDIDEST
CAMISIAS	CAMPFIRES	CAMPUSES	CANARD	CANDIDLY
CAMISOLE	CAMPHANE	CAMPUSING	CANARDS	CANDIDS
CAMISOLES	CAMPHANES	CAMPY	CANARIED	CANDIE
CAMLET	CAMPHENE	CAMS	CANARIES	CANDIED
CAMLETS	CAMPHENES	CAMSHAFT	CANARY	CANDIES
CAMMED	CAMPHINE	CAMSHAFTS	CANARYING	CANDIRU
CAMMIE	CAMPHINES	CAMSHO	CANASTA	CANDIRUS
CAMMIES	CAMPHIRE	CAMSHOCH	CANASTAS	CANDLE
CAMMING	CAMPHIRES	CAMSTAIRY	CANASTER	CANDLED
CAMO	CAMPHOL	CAMSTANE	CANASTERS	CANDLELIT
CAMOGIE	CAMPHOLS	CAMSTANES	CANBANK	CANDLENUT
CAMOGIES	CAMPHONE	CAMSTEARY	CANBANKS	CANDLEPIN
CAMOMILE	CAMPHONES	CAMSTONE	CANCAN	CANDLER
CAMOMILES	CAMPHOR	CAMSTONES	CANCANS	CANDLERS
CAMOODI	CAMPHORIC	CAMUS	CANCEL	CANDLES
CAMOODIS	CAMPHORS	CAMUSES	CANCELBOT	CANDLING
CAMORRA	CAMPI	CAMWHORE	CANCELED	CANDOCK
CAMORRAS	CAMPIER	CAMWHORED	CANCELEER	CANDOCKS
CAMORRIST	CAMPIEST	CAMWHORES	CANCELER	CANDOR
CAMOS	CAMPILY	CAMWOOD	CANCELERS	CANDORS
CAMOTE	CAMPINESS	CAMWOODS	CANCELIER	CANDOUR
CAMOTES	CAMPING	CAN	CANCELING	CANDOURS
CAMOUFLET	CAMPINGS	CANADA	CANCELLED	CANDY
CAMP	CAMPION	CANADAS	CANCELLER	CANDYGRAM
CAMPAGNA	CAMPIONS	CANAIGRE	CANCELLI	CANDYING
CAMPAGNAS	CAMPLE	CANAIGRES	CANCELS	CANDYMAN
CAMPAGNE	CAMPLED	CANAILLE	CANCER	CANDYMEN
CAMPAIGN	CAMPLES	CANAILLES	CANCERATE	CANDYTUFT
CAMPAIGNS	CAMPLING	CANAKIN	CANCERED	CANE
CAMPANA	CAMPLY	CANAKINS	CANCEROUS	CANEBRAKE
CAMPANAS	CAMPNESS	CANAL	CANCERS	CANED
CAMPANERO	CAMPO	CANALBOAT	CANCHA	CANEFRUIT
CAMPANILE	CAMPODEID	CANALED	CANCHAS	CANEGRUB
CAMPANILI	CAMPONG	CANALING	CANCRINE	CANEGRUBS
CAMPANIST	CAMPONGS	CANALISE	CANCROID	CANEH
CAMPANULA	CAMPOREE	CANALISED	CANCROIDS	CANEHS
CAMPCRAFT	CAMPOREES	CANALISES	CANDELA	CANELLA
CAMPEACHY	CAMPOS	CANALIZE	CANDELAS	CANELLAS
CAMPEADOR	CAMPOUT	CANALIZED	CANDENT	CANELLINI
CAMPED	CAMPOUTS	CANALIZES	CANDID	CANEPHOR
CAMPER	CAMPS	CANALLED	CANDIDA	CANEPHORA
CAMPERIES	CAMPSHIRT	CANALLER	CANDIDACY	CANEPHORE

CANEPHORS	CANNABIN	CANNY	CANST	CANTICUMS
CANER	CANNABINS	CANOE	CANSTICK	CANTIER
CANERS	CANNABIS	CANOEABLE	CANSTICKS	CANTIEST
CANES	CANNACH	CANOED	CANT	CANTILENA
CANESCENT	CANNACHS	CANOEING	CANTABANK	CANTILY
CANEWARE	CANNAE	CANOEINGS	CANTABILE	CANTINA
CANEWARES	CANNAS	CANOEIST	CANTAL	CANTINAS
CANFIELD	CANNED	CANOEISTS	CANTALA	CANTINESS
CANFIELDS	CANNEL	CANOEMAN	CANTALAS	CANTING
CANFUL	CANNELON	CANOEMEN	CANTALOUP	CANTINGLY
CANFULS	CANNELONI	CANOER	CANTALS	CANTINGS
CANG	CANNELONS	CANOERS	CANTAR	CANTION
CANGLE	CANNELS	CANOES	CANTARS	CANTIONS
CANGLED	CANNELURE	CANOEWOOD	CANTATA	CANTLE
CANGLES	CANNER	CANOLA	CANTATAS	CANTLED
CANGLING	CANNERIES	CANOLAS	CANTATE	CANTLES
CANGS	CANNERS	CANON	CANTATES	CANTLET
CANGUE	CANNERY	CANONESS	CANTDOG	CANTLETS
CANGUES	CANNIBAL	CANONIC	CANTDOGS	CANTLING
CANICULAR	CANNIBALS	CANONICAL	CANTED	CANTO
CANID	CANNIE	CANONISE	CANTEEN	CANTON
CANIDS	CANNIER	CANONISED	CANTEENS	CANTONAL
CANIER	CANNIEST	CANONISER	CANTER	CANTONED
CANIEST	CANNIKIN	CANONISES	CANTERED	CANTONING
CANIKIN	CANNIKINS	CANONIST	CANTERING	CANTONISE
CANIKINS	CANNILY	CANONISTS	CANTERS	CANTONIZE
CANINE	CANNINESS	CANONIZE	CANTEST	CANTONS
CANINES	CANNING	CANONIZED	CANTHAL	CANTOR
CANING	CANNINGS	CANONIZER	CANTHARI	CANTORIAL
CANINGS	CANNISTER	CANONIZES	CANTHARID	CANTORIS
CANINITY	CANNOLI	CANONRIES	CANTHARIS	CANTORS
CANISTEL	CANNOLIS	CANONRY	CANTHARUS	CANTOS
CANISTELS	CANNON	CANONS	CANTHI	CANTRAIP
CANISTER	CANNONADE	CANOODLE	CANTHIC	CANTRAIPS
CANISTERS	CANNONED	CANOODLED	CANTHITIS	CANTRAP
CANITIES	CANNONEER	CANOODLER	CANTHOOK	CANTRAPS
CANKER	CANNONIER	CANOODLES	CANTHOOKS	CANTRED
CANKERED	CANNONING	CANOPIC	CANTHUS	CANTREDS
CANKERING	CANNONRY	CANOPIED	CANTIC	CANTREF
CANKEROUS	CANNONS	CANOPIES	CANTICLE	CANTREFS
CANKERS	CANNOT	CANOPY	CANTICLES	CANTRIP
CANKERY	CANNS	CANOPYING	CANTICO	CANTRIPS
CANKLE	CANNULA	CANOROUS	CANTICOED	CANTS
CANKLES	CANNULAE	CANS	CANTICOS	CANTUS
CANN	CANNULAR	CANSFUL	CANTICOY	CANTUSES
CANNA	CANNULAS	CANSO	CANTICOYS	CANTY
CANNABIC	CANNULATE	CANSOS	CANTICUM	CANULA

CANULAE	CAPELINE	CAPITULA	CAPPINGS	CAPSIZING
CANULAR	CAPELINES	CAPITULAR	CAPRATE	CAPSOMER
CANULAS	CAPELINS	CAPITULUM	CAPRATES	CAPSOMERE
CANULATE	CAPELLET	CAPIZ	CAPRESE	CAPSOMERS
CANULATED	CAPELLETS	CAPIZES	CAPRESES	CAPSTAN
CANULATES	CAPELLINE	CAPLE	CAPRI	CAPSTANS
CANVAS	CAPELLINI	CAPLES	CAPRIC	CAPSTONE
CANVASED	CAPER	CAPLESS	CAPRICCI	CAPSTONES
CANVASER	CAPERED	CAPLET	CAPRICCIO	CAPSULAR
CANVASERS	CAPERER	CAPLETS	CAPRICE	CAPSULARY
CANVASES	CAPERERS	CAPLIN	CAPRICES	CAPSULATE
CANVASING	CAPERING	CAPLINS	CAPRID	CAPSULE
CANVASS	CAPERS	CAPMAKER	CAPRIDS	CAPSULED
CANVASSED	CAPES	CAPMAKERS	CAPRIFIED	CAPSULES
CANVASSER	CAPESKIN	CAPO	CAPRIFIES	CAPSULING
CANVASSES	CAPESKINS	CAPOCCHIA	CAPRIFIG	CAPSULISE
CANY	CAPEWORK	CAPOEIRA	CAPRIFIGS	CAPSULIZE
CANYON	CAPEWORKS	CAPOEIRAS	CAPRIFOIL	CAPTAIN
CANYONEER	CAPEX	CAPON	CAPRIFOLE	CAPTAINCY
CANYONING	CAPEXES	CAPONATA	CAPRIFORM	CAPTAINED
CANYONS	CAPFUL	CAPONATAS	CAPRIFY	CAPTAINRY
CANZONA	CAPFULS	CAPONIER	CAPRINE	CAPTAINS
CANZONAS	CAPH	CAPONIERE	CAPRIOLE	CAPTAN
CANZONE	CAPHS	CAPONIERS	CAPRIOLED	CAPTANS
CANZONES	CAPI	CAPONISE	CAPRIOLES	CAPTCHA
CANZONET	CAPIAS	CAPONISED	CAPRIS	CAPTCHAS
CANZONETS	CAPIASES	CAPONISES	CAPROATE	CAPTION
CANZONI	CAPILLARY	CAPONIZE	CAPROATES	CAPTIONED
CAP	CAPING	CAPONIZED	CAPROCK	CAPTIONS
CAPA	CAPISCE	CAPONIZES	CAPROCKS	CAPTIOUS
CAPABLE	CAPITA	CAPONS	CAPROIC	CAPTIVATE
CAPABLER	CAPITAL	CAPORAL	CAPRYLATE	CAPTIVE
CAPABLEST	CAPITALLY	CAPORALS	CAPRYLIC	CAPTIVED
CAPABLY	CAPITALS	CAPOS	CAPS	CAPTIVES
CAPACIOUS	CAPITAN	CAPOT	CAPSAICIN	CAPTIVING
CAPACITOR	CAPITANI	CAPOTASTO	CAPSICIN	CAPTIVITY
CAPACITY	CAPITANO	CAPOTE	CAPSICINS	CAPTOPRIL
CAPARISON	CAPITANOS	CAPOTES	CAPSICUM	CAPTOR
CAPAS	CAPITANS	CAPOTS	CAPSICUMS	CAPTORS
CAPE	CAPITATE	CAPOTTED	CAPSID	CAPTURE
CAPED	CAPITATED	CAPOTTING	CAPSIDAL	CAPTURED
CAPEESH	CAPITATES	CAPOUCH	CAPSIDS	CAPTURER
CAPELAN	CAPITAYN	CAPOUCHES	CAPSIZAL	CAPTURERS
CAPELANS	CAPITAYNS	CAPPED	CAPSIZALS	CAPTURES
CAPELET	CAPITELLA	CAPPER	CAPSIZE	CAPTURING
CAPELETS	CAPITOL	CAPPERS	CAPSIZED	CAPUCCIO
CAPELIN	CAPITOLS	CAPPING	CAPSIZES	CAPUCCIOS

CAPUCHE	CARAMEL	CARBEEN	CARBY	CARDIES
CAPUCHED	CARAMELS	CARBEENS	CARCAJOU	CARDIGAN
CAPUCHES	CARANGID	CARBENE	CARCAJOUS	CARDIGANS
CAPUCHIN	CARANGIDS	CARBENES	CARCAKE	CARDINAL
CAPUCHINS	CARANGOID	CARBIDE	CARCAKES	CARDINALS
CAPUERA	CARANNA	CARBIDES	CARCANET	CARDING
CAPUERAS	CARANNAS	CARBIES	CARCANETS	CARDINGS
CAPUL	CARAP	CARBINE	CARCASE	CARDIO
CAPULS	CARAPACE	CARBINEER	CARCASED	CARDIOID
CAPUT	CARAPACED	CARBINES	CARCASES	CARDIOIDS
CAPYBARA	CARAPACES	CARBINIER	CARCASING	CARDIOS
CAPYBARAS	CARAPAX	CARBINOL	CARCASS	CARDIS
CAR	CARAPAXES	CARBINOLS	CARCASSED	CARDITIC
CARABAO	CARAPS	CARBO	CARCASSES	CARDITIS
CARABAOS	CARASSOW	CARBOLIC	CARCEL	CARDON
CARABID	CARASSOWS	CARBOLICS	CARCELS	CARDONS
CARABIDS	CARAT	CARBOLISE	CARCERAL	CARDOON
CARABIN	CARATE	CARBOLIZE	CARCINOID	CARDOONS
CARABINE	CARATES	CARBON	CARCINOMA	CARDPHONE
CARABINER	CARATS	CARBONADE	CARD	CARDPUNCH
CARABINES	CARAUNA	CARBONADO	CARDAMINE	CARDS
CARABINS	CARAUNAS	CARBONARA	CARDAMOM	CARDSHARP
CARACAL	CARAVAN	CARBONATE	CARDAMOMS	CARDUUS
CARACALS	CARAVANCE	CARBONIC	CARDAMON	CARDUUSES
CARACARA	CARAVANED	CARBONISE	CARDAMONS	CARDY
CARACARAS	CARAVANER	CARBONIUM	CARDAMUM	CARE
CARACK	CARAVANS	CARBONIZE	CARDAMUMS	CARED
CARACKS	CARAVEL	CARBONOUS	CARDAN	CAREEN
CARACOL	CARAVELLE	CARBONS	CARDBOARD	CAREENAGE
CARACOLE	CARAVELS	CARBONYL	CARDCASE	CAREENED
CARACOLED	CARAWAY	CARBONYLS	CARDCASES	CAREENER
CARACOLER	CARAWAYS	CARBORA	CARDECU	CAREENERS
CARACOLES	CARB	CARBORAS	CARDECUE	CAREENING
CARACOLS	CARBACHOL	CARBORNE	CARDECUES	CAREENS
CARACT	CARBAMATE	CARBOS	CARDECUS	CAREER
CARACTS	CARBAMIC	CARBOXYL	CARDED	CAREERED
CARACUL	CARBAMIDE	CARBOXYLS	CARDER	CAREERER
CARACULS	CARBAMINO	CARBOY	CARDERS	CAREERERS
CARAFE	CARBAMOYL	CARBOYED	CARDI	CAREERING
CARAFES	CARBAMYL	CARBOYS	CARDIA	CAREERISM
CARAGANA	CARBAMYLS	CARBS	CARDIAC	CAREERIST
CARAGANAS	CARBANION	CARBUNCLE	CARDIACAL	CAREERS
CARAGEEN	CARBARN	CARBURATE	CARDIACS	CAREFREE
CARAGEENS	CARBARNS	CARBURET	CARDIAE	CAREFUL
CARAMBA	CARBARYL	CARBURETS	CARDIALGY	CAREFULLY
CARAMBOLA	CARBARYLS	CARBURISE	CARDIAS	CAREGIVER
CARAMBOLE	CARBAZOLE	CARBURIZE	CARDIE	CARELESS

CARELINE
CARELINES
CAREME
CAREMES
CARER
CARERS
CARES
CARESS
CARESSED
CARESSER
CARESSERS
CARESSES
CARESSING
CARESSIVE
CARET
CARETAKE
CARETAKEN
CARETAKER
CARETAKES
CARETOOK
CARETS
CAREWARE
CAREWARES
CAREWORN
CAREX
CARFARE
CARFARES
CARFAX
CARFAXES
CARFOX
CARFOXES
CARFUFFLE
CARFUL
CARFULS
CARGEESE
CARGO
CARGOED
CARGOES
CARGOING
CARGOOSE
CARGOS
CARHOP
CARHOPPED
CARHOPS
CARIACOU
CARIACOUS
CARIAMA

CARIAMAS
CARIBE
CARIBES
CARIBOO
CARIBOOS
CARIBOU
CARIBOUS
CARICES
CARIED
CARIERE
CARIERES
CARIES
CARILLON
CARILLONS
CARINA
CARINAE
CARINAL
CARINAS
CARINATE
CARINATED
CARING
CARINGLY
CARINGS
CARIOCA
CARIOCAS
CARIOLE
CARIOLES
CARIOSE
CARIOSITY
CARIOUS
CARITAS
CARITASES
CARITATES
CARJACK
CARJACKED
CARJACKER
CARJACKS
CARJACOU
CARJACOUS
CARK
CARKED
CARKING
CARKS
CARL
CARLE
CARLES
CARLESS

CARLIN
CARLINE
CARLINES
CARLING
CARLINGS
CARLINS
CARLISH
CARLOAD
CARLOADS
CARLOCK
CARLOCKS
CARLOT
CARLOTS
CARLS
CARMAKER
CARMAKERS
CARMAN
CARMELITE
CARMEN
CARMINE
CARMINES
CARN
CARNAGE
CARNAGES
CARNAHUBA
CARNAL
CARNALISE
CARNALISM
CARNALIST
CARNALITY
CARNALIZE
CARNALLED
CARNALLY
CARNALS
CARNAROLI
CARNATION
CARNAUBA
CARNAUBAS
CARNELIAN
CARNEOUS
CARNET
CARNETS
CARNEY
CARNEYED
CARNEYING
CARNEYS
CARNIE

CARNIED
CARNIER
CARNIES
CARNIEST
CARNIFEX
CARNIFIED
CARNIFIES
CARNIFY
CARNITINE
CARNIVAL
CARNIVALS
CARNIVORA
CARNIVORE
CARNIVORY
CARNOSAUR
CARNOSE
CARNOSITY
CARNOTITE
CARNS
CARNY
CARNYING
CARNYX
CARNYXES
CAROACH
CAROACHES
CAROB
CAROBS
CAROCH
CAROCHE
CAROCHES
CAROL
CAROLED
CAROLER
CAROLERS
CAROLI
CAROLING
CAROLINGS
CAROLLED
CAROLLER
CAROLLERS
CAROLLING
CAROLS
CAROLUS
CAROLUSES
CAROM
CAROMED
CAROMEL

CAROMELS
CAROMING
CAROMS
CARON
CARONS
CAROTENE
CAROTENES
CAROTID
CAROTIDAL
CAROTIDS
CAROTIN
CAROTINS
CAROUSAL
CAROUSALS
CAROUSE
CAROUSED
CAROUSEL
CAROUSELS
CAROUSER
CAROUSERS
CAROUSES
CAROUSING
CARP
CARPACCIO
CARPAL
CARPALE
CARPALES
CARPALIA
CARPALS
CARPED
CARPEL
CARPELS
CARPENTER
CARPENTRY
CARPER
CARPERS
CARPET
CARPETBAG
CARPETED
CARPETING
CARPETS
CARPHONE
CARPHONES
CARPI
CARPING
CARPINGLY
CARPINGS

CARPOLOGY	CARROTIER	CARTERS	CARVERY	CASEBOOKS
CARPOOL	CARROTIN	CARTES	CARVES	CASEBOUND
CARPOOLED	CARROTINS	CARTFUL	CARVIES	CASED
CARPOOLER	CARROTS	CARTFULS	CARVING	CASEFIED
CARPOOLS	CARROTTOP	CARTHORSE	CARVINGS	CASEFIES
CARPORT	CARROTY	CARTILAGE	CARVY	CASEFY
CARPORTS	CARROUSEL	CARTING	CARWASH	CASEFYING
CARPS	CARRS	CARTLOAD	CARWASHES	CASEIC
CARPUS	CARRY	CARTLOADS	CARYATIC	CASEIN
CARR	CARRYALL	CARTOGRAM	CARYATID	CASEINATE
CARRACK	CARRYALLS	CARTOLOGY	CARYATIDS	CASEINS
CARRACKS	CARRYBACK	CARTON	CARYOPSES	CASELAW
CARRACT	CARRYCOT	CARTONAGE	CARYOPSIS	CASELAWS
CARRACTS	CARRYCOTS	CARTONED	CARYOTIN	CASELOAD
CARRAGEEN	CARRYING	CARTONING	CARYOTINS	CASELOADS
CARRAT	CARRYON	CARTONS	CASA	CASEMAKER
CARRATS	CARRYONS	CARTOON	CASABA	CASEMAN
CARRAWAY	CARRYOUT	CARTOONED	CASABAS	CASEMATE
CARRAWAYS	CARRYOUTS	CARTOONS	CASAS	CASEMATED
CARRECT	CARRYOVER	CARTOONY	CASAVA	CASEMATES
CARRECTS	CARRYTALE	CARTOP	CASAVAS	CASEMEN
CARREFOUR	CARS	CARTOPPER	CASBAH	CASEMENT
CARREL	CARSE	CARTOUCH	CASBAHS	CASEMENTS
CARRELL	CARSES	CARTOUCHE	CASCABEL	CASEMIX
CARRELLS	CARSEY	CARTRIDGE	CASCABELS	CASEMIXES
CARRELS	CARSEYS	CARTROAD	CASCABLE	CASEOSE
CARRIAGE	CARSHARE	CARTROADS	CASCABLES	CASEOSES
CARRIAGES	CARSHARED	CARTS	CASCADE	CASEOUS
CARRICK	CARSHARES	CARTULARY	CASCADED	CASERN
CARRIED	CARSICK	CARTWAY	CASCADES	CASERNE
CARRIER	CARSPIEL	CARTWAYS	CASCADING	CASERNES
CARRIERS	CARSPIELS	CARTWHEEL	CASCADURA	CASERNS
CARRIES	CART	CARUCAGE	CASCARA	CASES
CARRIOLE	CARTA	CARUCAGES	CASCARAS	CASETTE
CARRIOLES	CARTABLE	CARUCATE	CASCHROM	CASETTES
CARRION	CARTAGE	CARUCATES	CASCHROMS	CASEVAC
CARRIONS	CARTAGES	CARUNCLE	CASCO	CASEVACED
CARRITCH	CARTAS	CARUNCLES	CASCOS	CASEVACS
CARROCH	CARTE	CARVACROL	CASE	CASEWORK
CARROCHES	CARTED	CARVE	CASEASE	CASEWORKS
CARROM	CARTEL	CARVED	CASEASES	CASEWORM
CARROMED	CARTELISE	CARVEL	CASEATE	CASEWORMS
CARROMING	CARTELISM	CARVELS	CASEATED	CASH
CARROMS	CARTELIST	CARVEN	CASEATES	CASHABLE
CARRON	CARTELIZE	CARVER	CASEATING	CASHAW
CARRONADE	CARTELS	CARVERIES	CASEATION	CASHAWS
CARROT	CARTER	CARVERS	CASEBOOK	CASHBACK

CASHBACKS	CASQUES	CASTAWAYS	CASUARINA	CATAMITE
CASHBOOK	CASSABA	CASTE	CASUIST	CATAMITES
CASHBOOKS	CASSABAS	CASTED	CASUISTIC	CATAMOUNT
CASHBOX	CASSAREEP	CASTEISM	CASUISTRY	CATAPAN
CASHBOXES	CASSATA	CASTEISMS	CASUISTS	CATAPANS
CASHED	CASSATAS	CASTELESS	CASUS	CATAPHOR
CASHES	CASSATION	CASTELLA	CAT	CATAPHORA
CASHEW	CASSAVA	CASTELLAN	CATABASES	CATAPHORS
CASHEWS	CASSAVAS	CASTELLUM	CATABASIS	CATAPHYLL
CASHIER	CASSENA	CASTER	CATABATIC	CATAPLASM
CASHIERED	CASSENAS	CASTERED	CATABOLIC	CATAPLEXY
CASHIERER	CASSENE	CASTERS	CATACLASM	CATAPULT
CASHIERS	CASSENES	CASTES	CATACLYSM	CATAPULTS
CASHING	CASSEROLE	CASTIGATE	CATACOMB	CATARACT
CASHLESS	CASSETTE	CASTING	CATACOMBS	CATARACTS
CASHMERE	CASSETTES	CASTINGS	CATAFALCO	CATARHINE
CASHMERES	CASSIA	CASTLE	CATALASE	CATARRH
CASHOO	CASSIAS	CASTLED	CATALASES	CATARRHAL
CASHOOS	CASSIE	CASTLES	CATALATIC	CATARRHS
CASHPOINT	CASSIES	CASTLING	CATALEPSY	CATASTA
CASIMERE	CASSIMERE	CASTLINGS	CATALEXES	CATASTAS
CASIMERES	CASSINA	CASTOCK	CATALEXIS	CATATONIA
CASIMIRE	CASSINAS	CASTOCKS	CATALO	CATATONIC
CASIMIRES	CASSINE	CASTOFF	CATALOES	CATATONY
CASING	CASSINES	CASTOFFS	CATALOG	CATAWBA
CASINGS	CASSINGLE	CASTOR	CATALOGED	CATAWBAS
CASINI	CASSINO	CASTOREUM	CATALOGER	CATBIRD
CASINO	CASSINOS	CASTORIES	CATALOGIC	CATBIRDS
CASINOS	CASSIOPE	CASTORS	CATALOGS	CATBOAT
CASITA	CASSIOPES	CASTORY	CATALOGUE	CATBOATS
CASITAS	CASSIS	CASTRAL	CATALOS	CATBRIAR
CASK	CASSISES	CASTRATE	CATALPA	CATBRIARS
CASKED	CASSOCK	CASTRATED	CATALPAS	CATBRIER
CASKET	CASSOCKED	CASTRATER	CATALYSE	CATBRIERS
CASKETED	CASSOCKS	CASTRATES	CATALYSED	CATCALL
CASKETING	CASSONADE	CASTRATI	CATALYSER	CATCALLED
CASKETS	CASSONE	CASTRATO	CATALYSES	CATCALLER
CASKIER	CASSONES	CASTRATOR	CATALYSIS	CATCALLS
CASKIEST	CASSOULET	CASTRATOS	CATALYST	CATCH
CASKING	CASSOWARY	CASTS	CATALYSTS	CATCHABLE
CASKS	CASSPIR	CASUAL	CATALYTIC	CATCHALL
CASKSTAND	CASSPIRS	CASUALISE	CATALYZE	CATCHALLS
CASKY	CAST	CASUALISM	CATALYZED	CATCHCRY
CASPASE	CASTABLE	CASUALIZE	CATALYZER	CATCHED
CASPASES	CASTANET	CASUALLY	CATALYZES	CATCHEN
CASQUE	CASTANETS	CASUALS	CATAMARAN	CATCHER
CASQUED	CASTAWAY	CASUALTY	CATAMENIA	CATCHERS

CATCHES	CATER	CATHEXES	CATS	CAUDAD
CATCHFLY	CATERAN	CATHEXIS	CATSKIN	CAUDAE
CATCHIER	CATERANS	CATHINONE	CATSKINS	CAUDAL
CATCHIEST	CATERED	CATHISMA	CATSPAW	CAUDALLY
CATCHILY	CATERER	CATHISMAS	CATSPAWS	CAUDATE
CATCHING	CATERERS	CATHODAL	CATSUIT	CAUDATED
CATCHINGS	CATERESS	CATHODE	CATSUITS	CAUDATES
CATCHLINE	CATERING	CATHODES	CATSUP	CAUDATION
CATCHMENT	CATERINGS	CATHODIC	CATSUPS	CAUDEX
CATCHPOLE	CATERS	CATHOLE	CATTABU	CAUDEXES
CATCHPOLL	CATERWAUL	CATHOLES	CATTABUS	CAUDICES
CATCHT	CATES	CATHOLIC	CATTAIL	CAUDICLE
CATCHUP	CATFACE	CATHOLICS	CATTAILS	CAUDICLES
CATCHUPS	CATFACES	CATHOLYTE	CATTALO	CAUDILLO
CATCHWEED	CATFACING	CATHOOD	CATTALOES	CAUDILLOS
CATCHWORD	CATFALL	CATHOODS	CATTALOS	CAUDLE
CATCHY	CATFALLS	CATHOUSE	CATTED	CAUDLED
CATCLAW	CATFIGHT	CATHOUSES	CATTERIES	CAUDLES
CATCLAWS	CATFIGHTS	CATION	CATTERY	CAUDLING
CATCON	CATFISH	CATIONIC	CATTIE	CAUDRON
CATCONS	CATFISHES	CATIONS	CATTIER	CAUDRONS
CATE	CATFLAP	CATJANG	CATTIES	CAUF
CATECHIN	CATFLAPS	CATJANGS	CATTIEST	CAUGHT
CATECHINS	CATFOOD	CATKIN	CATTILY	CAUK
CATECHISE	CATFOODS	CATKINATE	CATTINESS	CAUKER
CATECHISM	CATGUT	CATKINS	CATTING	CAUKERS
CATECHIST	CATGUTS	CATLIKE	CATTISH	CAUKS
CATECHIZE	CATHARISE	CATLIN	CATTISHLY	CAUL
CATECHOL	CATHARIZE	CATLING	CATTLE	CAULD
CATECHOLS	CATHARSES	CATLINGS	CATTLEMAN	CAULDER
CATECHU	CATHARSIS	CATLINS	CATTLEMEN	CAULDEST
CATECHUS	CATHARTIC	CATMINT	CATTLEYA	CAULDRIFE
CATEGORIC	CATHEAD	CATMINTS	CATTLEYAS	CAULDRON
CATEGORY	CATHEADS	CATNAP	CATTY	CAULDRONS
CATELOG	CATHECT	CATNAPER	CATWALK	CAULDS
CATELOGS	CATHECTED	CATNAPERS	CATWALKS	CAULES
CATENA	CATHECTIC	CATNAPPED	CATWORKS	CAULICLE
CATENAE	CATHECTS	CATNAPPER	CATWORM	CAULICLES
CATENANE	CATHEDRA	CATNAPS	CATWORMS	CAULICULI
CATENANES	CATHEDRAE	CATNEP	CAUCHEMAR	CAULIFORM
CATENARY	CATHEDRAL	CATNEPS	CAUCUS	CAULINARY
CATENAS	CATHEDRAS	CATNIP	CAUCUSED	CAULINE
CATENATE	CATHEPSIN	CATNIPS	CAUCUSES	CAULIS
CATENATED	CATHEPTIC	CATOLYTE	CAUCUSING	CAULK
CATENATES	CATHETER	CATOLYTES	CAUCUSSED	CAULKED
CATENOID	CATHETERS	CATOPTRIC	CAUCUSSES	CAULKER
CATENOIDS	CATHETUS	CATRIGGED	CAUDA	CAULKERS

CAULKING	CAUTELS	CAVEMAN	CAVORT	CEBOID
CAULKINGS	CAUTER	CAVEMEN	CAVORTED	CEBOIDS
CAULKS	CAUTERANT	CAVENDISH	CAVORTER	CECA
CAULOME	CAUTERIES	CAVER	CAVORTERS	CECAL
CAULOMES	CAUTERISE	CAVERN	CAVORTING	CECALLY
CAULS	CAUTERISM	CAVERNED	CAVORTS	CECILS
CAUM	CAUTERIZE	CAVERNING	CAVY	CECITIES
CAUMED	CAUTERS	CAVERNOUS	CAW	CECITIS
CAUMING	CAUTERY	CAVERNS	CAWED	CECITISES
CAUMS	CAUTION	CAVERS	CAWING	CECITY
CAUMSTANE	CAUTIONED	CAVES	CAWINGS	CECROPIA
CAUMSTONE	CAUTIONER	CAVESSON	CAWK	CECROPIAS
CAUP	CAUTIONRY	CAVESSONS	CAWKER	CECROPIN
CAUPS	CAUTIONS	CAVETTI	CAWKERS	CECROPINS
CAURI	CAUTIOUS	CAVETTO	CAWKS	CECUM
CAURIS	CAUVES	CAVETTOS	CAWS	CEDAR
CAUSA	CAVA	CAVIAR	CAXON	CEDARBIRD
CAUSABLE	CAVALCADE	CAVIARE	CAXONS	CEDARED
CAUSAE	CAVALERO	CAVIARES	CAY	CEDARN
CAUSAL	CAVALEROS	CAVIARIE	CAYENNE	CEDARS
CAUSALGIA	CAVALETTI	CAVIARIES	CAYENNED	CEDARWOOD
CAUSALGIC	CAVALIER	CAVIARS	CAYENNES	CEDARY
CAUSALITY	CAVALIERS	CAVICORN	CAYMAN	CEDE
CAUSALLY	CAVALLA	CAVICORNS	CAYMANS	CEDED
CAUSALS	CAVALLAS	CAVIE	CAYS	CEDER
CAUSATION	CAVALLIES	CAVIER	CAYUSE	CEDERS
CAUSATIVE	CAVALLY	CAVIERS	CAYUSES	CEDES
CAUSE	CAVALRIES	CAVIES	CAZ	CEDI
CAUSED	CAVALRY	CAVIL	CAZH	CEDILLA
CAUSELESS	CAVAS	CAVILED	CAZIQUE	CEDILLAS
CAUSEN	CAVASS	CAVILER	CAZIQUES	CEDING
CAUSER	CAVASSES	CAVILERS	CEANOTHUS	CEDIS
CAUSERIE	CAVATINA	CAVILING	CEAS	CEDRATE
CAUSERIES	CAVATINAS	CAVILLED	CEASE	CEDRATES
CAUSERS	CAVATINE	CAVILLER	CEASED	CEDRINE
CAUSES	CAVE	CAVILLERS	CEASEFIRE	CEDULA
CAUSEWAY	CAVEAT	CAVILLING	CEASELESS	CEDULAS
CAUSEWAYS	CAVEATED	CAVILS	CEASES	CEE
CAUSEY	CAVEATING	CAVING	CEASING	CEES
CAUSEYED	CAVEATOR	CAVINGS	CEASINGS	CEIBA
CAUSEYS	CAVEATORS	CAVITARY	CEAZE	CEIBAS
CAUSING	CAVEATS	CAVITATE	CEAZED	CEIL
CAUSTIC	CAVED	CAVITATED	CEAZES	CEILED
CAUSTICAL	CAVEFISH	CAVITATES	CEAZING	CEILER
CAUSTICS	CAVEL	CAVITIED	CEBADILLA	CEILERS
CAUTEL	CAVELIKE	CAVITIES	CEBID	CEILI
CAUTELOUS	CAVELS	CAVITY	CEBIDS	CEILIDH

CEILIDHS	CELLARIST	CEMBRA	CENSUSED	CENTONATE
CEILING	CELLARMAN	CEMBRAS	CENSUSES	CENTONEL
CEILINGED	CELLARMEN	CEMENT	CENSUSING	CENTONELL
CEILINGS	CELLAROUS	CEMENTA	CENT	CENTONELLS
CEILIS	CELLARS	CEMENTED	CENTAGE	CENTONES
CEILS	CELLARWAY	CEMENTER	CENTAGES	CENTONIST
CEINTURE	CELLBLOCK	CEMENTERS	CENTAI	CENTOS
CEINTURES	CELLED	CEMENTING	CENTAL	CENTRA
CEL	CELLI	CEMENTITE	CENTALS	CENTRAL
CELADON	CELLING	CEMENTS	CENTARE	CENTRALER
CELADONS	CELLINGS	CEMENTUM	CENTARES	CENTRALLY
CELANDINE	CELLIST	CEMENTUMS	CENTAS	CENTRALS
CELEB	CELLISTS	CEMETERY	CENTAUR	CENTRE
CELEBRANT	CELLMATE	CEMITARE	CENTAUREA	CENTRED
CELEBRATE	CELLMATES	CEMITARES	CENTAURIC	CENTREING
CELEBRITY	CELLO	CENACLE	CENTAURS	CENTRES
CELEBS	CELLOIDIN	CENACLES	CENTAURY	CENTRIC
CELECOXIB	CELLOS	CENDRE	CENTAVO	CENTRICAL
CELERIAC	CELLOSE	CENOBITE	CENTAVOS	CENTRIES
CELERIACS	CELLOSES	CENOBITES	CENTENARY	CENTRING
CELERIES	CELLPHONE	CENOBITIC	CENTENIER	CENTRINGS
CELERITY	CELLS	CENOTAPH	CENTER	CENTRIOLE
CELERY	CELLULAR	CENOTAPHS	CENTERED	CENTRISM
CELESTA	CELLULARS	CENOTE	CENTERING	CENTRISMS
CELESTAS	CELLULASE	CENOTES	CENTERS	CENTRIST
CELESTE	CELLULE	CENOZOIC	CENTESES	CENTRISTS
CELESTES	CELLULES	CENS	CENTESIMI	CENTRODE
CELESTIAL	CELLULITE	CENSE	CENTESIMO	CENTRODES
CELESTINE	CELLULOID	CENSED	CENTESIS	CENTROID
CELESTITE	CELLULOSE	CENSER	CENTIARE	CENTROIDS
CELIAC	CELLULOUS	CENSERS	CENTIARES	CENTRUM
CELIACS	CELOM	CENSES	CENTIGRAM	CENTRUMS
CELIBACY	CELOMATA	CENSING	CENTILE	CENTRY
CELIBATE	CELOMIC	CENSOR	CENTILES	CENTS
CELIBATES	CELOMS	CENSORED	CENTIME	CENTU
CELIBATIC	CELOSIA	CENSORIAL	CENTIMES	CENTUM
CELL	CELOSIAS	CENSORIAN	CENTIMO	CENTUMS
CELLA	CELOTEX	CENSORING	CENTIMOS	CENTUMVIR
CELLAE	CELOTEXES	CENSORS	CENTINEL	CENTUPLE
CELLAR	CELS	CENSUAL	CENTINELL	CENTUPLED
CELLARAGE	CELSITUDE	CENSURE	CENTINELS	CENTUPLES
CELLARED	CELT	CENSURED	CENTIPEDE	CENTURIAL
CELLARER	CELTS	CENSURER	CENTNER	CENTURIES
CELLARERS	CEMBALI	CENSURERS	CENTNERS	CENTURION
CELLARET	CEMBALIST	CENSURES	CENTO	CENTURY
CELLARETS	CEMBALO	CENSURING	CENTOIST	CEORL
CELLARING	CEMBALOS	CENSUS	CENTOISTS	CEORLISH

CEORLS	CERCIS	CERMET	CERUSITES	CESTOS
CEP	CERCISES	CERMETS	CERUSSITE	CESTOSES
CEPACEOUS	CERCLAGE	CERNE	CERVELAS	CESTUI
CEPAGE	CERCLAGES	CERNED	CERVELAT	CESTUIS
CEPAGES	CERCOPID	CERNES	CERVELATS	CESTUS
CEPE	CERCOPIDS	CERNING	CERVEZA	CESTUSES
CEPES	CERCUS	CERNUOUS	CERVEZAS	CESURA
CEPHALAD	CERE	CERO	CERVICAL	CESURAE
CEPHALATE	CEREAL	CEROGRAPH	CERVICES	CESURAL
CEPHALIC	CEREALIST	CEROMANCY	CERVICUM	CESURAS
CEPHALICS	CEREALS	CEROON	CERVICUMS	CESURE
CEPHALIN	CEREBELLA	CEROONS	CERVID	CESURES
CEPHALINS	CEREBRA	CEROS	CERVIDS	CETACEAN
CEPHALOUS	CEREBRAL	CEROTIC	CERVINE	CETACEANS
CEPHEID	CEREBRALS	CEROTYPE	CERVIX	CETACEOUS
CEPHEIDS	CEREBRATE	CEROTYPES	CERVIXES	CETANE
CEPS	CEREBRIC	CEROUS	CESAREAN	CETANES
CERACEOUS	CEREBROID	CERRADO	CESAREANS	CETE
CERAMAL	CEREBRUM	CERRADOS	CESAREVNA	CETERACH
CERAMALS	CEREBRUMS	CERRIAL	CESARIAN	CETERACHS
CERAMIC	CERECLOTH	CERRIS	CESARIANS	CETES
CERAMICS	CERED	CERRISES	CESIOUS	CETOLOGY
CERAMIDE	CEREMENT	CERT	CESIUM	CETRIMIDE
CERAMIDES	CEREMENTS	CERTAIN	CESIUMS	CETUXIMAB
CERAMIST	CEREMONY	CERTAINER	CESPITOSE	CETYL
CERAMISTS	CEREOUS	CERTAINLY	CESS	CETYLS
CERASIN	CERES	CERTAINTY	CESSATION	CETYWALL
CERASINS	CERESIN	CERTES	CESSE	CETYWALLS
CERASTES	CERESINE	CERTIE	CESSED	CEVADILLA
CERASTIUM	CERESINES	CERTIFIED	CESSER	CEVAPCICI
CERATE	CERESINS	CERTIFIER	CESSERS	CEVICHE
CERATED	CEREUS	CERTIFIES	CESSES	CEVICHES
CERATES	CEREUSES	CERTIFY	CESSING	CEVITAMIC
CERATIN	CERGE	CERTITUDE	CESSION	CEYLANITE
CERATINS	CERGES	CERTS	CESSIONS	CEYLONITE
CERATITIS	CERIA	CERTY	CESSPIT	CEZVE
CERATODUS	CERIAS	CERULE	CESSPITS	CEZVES
CERATOID	CERIC	CERULEAN	CESSPOOL	CH
CERBEREAN	CERING	CERULEANS	CESSPOOLS	CHA
CERBERIAN	CERIPH	CERULEIN	CESTA	CHABAZITE
CERCAL	CERIPHS	CERULEINS	CESTAS	CHABLIS
CERCARIA	CERISE	CERULEOUS	CESTI	CHABOUK
CERCARIAE	CERISES	CERUMEN	CESTODE	CHABOUKS
CERCARIAL	CERITE	CERUMENS	CESTODES	CHABUK
CERCARIAN	CERITES	CERUSE	CESTOI	CHABUKS
CERCARIAS	CERIUM	CERUSES	CESTOID	CHACE
CERCI	CERIUMS	CERUSITE	CESTOIDS	CHACED

CHACES
CHACHKA
CHACHKAS
CHACING
CHACK
CHACKED
CHACKING
CHACKS
CHACMA
CHACMAS
CHACO
CHACOES
CHACONINE
CHACONNE
CHACONNES
CHACOS
CHAD
CHADAR
CHADARIM
CHADARS
CHADDAR
CHADDARS
CHADDOR
CHADDORS
CHADLESS
CHADO
CHADOR
CHADORS
CHADOS
CHADRI
CHADS
CHAEBOL
CHAEBOLS
CHAETA
CHAETAE
CHAETAL
CHAETODON
CHAETOPOD
CHAFE
CHAFED
CHAFER
CHAFERS
CHAFES
CHAFF
CHAFFED
CHAFFER
CHAFFERED

CHAFFERER
CHAFFERS
CHAFFERY
CHAFFIER
CHAFFIEST
CHAFFINCH
CHAFFING
CHAFFINGS
CHAFFRON
CHAFFRONS
CHAFFS
CHAFFY
CHAFING
CHAFT
CHAFTS
CHAGAN
CHAGANS
CHAGRIN
CHAGRINED
CHAGRINS
CHAI
CHAIN
CHAINE
CHAINED
CHAINER
CHAINERS
CHAINES
CHAINFALL
CHAINING
CHAINLESS
CHAINLET
CHAINLETS
CHAINMAN
CHAINMEN
CHAINS
CHAINSAW
CHAINSAWS
CHAINSHOT
CHAINWORK
CHAIR
CHAIRBACK
CHAIRDAYS
CHAIRED
CHAIRING
CHAIRLIFT
CHAIRMAN
CHAIRMANS

CHAIRMEN
CHAIRS
CHAIS
CHAISE
CHAISES
CHAKALAKA
CHAKRA
CHAKRAS
CHAL
CHALAH
CHALAHS
CHALAN
CHALANED
CHALANING
CHALANNED
CHALANS
CHALAZA
CHALAZAE
CHALAZAL
CHALAZAS
CHALAZIA
CHALAZION
CHALCID
CHALCIDS
CHALCOGEN
CHALDER
CHALDERS
CHALDRON
CHALDRONS
CHALEH
CHALEHS
CHALET
CHALETS
CHALICE
CHALICED
CHALICES
CHALK
CHALKED
CHALKFACE
CHALKIER
CHALKIEST
CHALKING
CHALKLIKE
CHALKMARK
CHALKPIT
CHALKPITS
CHALKS

CHALKY
CHALLA
CHALLAH
CHALLAHS
CHALLAN
CHALLANS
CHALLAS
CHALLENGE
CHALLIE
CHALLIES
CHALLIS
CHALLISES
CHALLOT
CHALLOTH
CHALLY
CHALONE
CHALONES
CHALONIC
CHALOT
CHALOTH
CHALS
CHALUMEAU
CHALUPA
CHALUPAS
CHALUTZ
CHALUTZES
CHALUTZIM
CHALYBEAN
CHALYBITE
CHAM
CHAMADE
CHAMADES
CHAMBER
CHAMBERED
CHAMBERER
CHAMBERS
CHAMBRAY
CHAMBRAYS
CHAMBRE
CHAMELEON
CHAMELOT
CHAMELOTS
CHAMETZ
CHAMETZES
CHAMFER
CHAMFERED
CHAMFERER

CHAMFERS
CHAMFRAIN
CHAMFRON
CHAMFRONS
CHAMISA
CHAMISAL
CHAMISALS
CHAMISAS
CHAMISE
CHAMISES
CHAMISO
CHAMISOS
CHAMLET
CHAMLETS
CHAMMIED
CHAMMIES
CHAMMY
CHAMMYING
CHAMOIS
CHAMOISED
CHAMOISES
CHAMOIX
CHAMOMILE
CHAMP
CHAMPAC
CHAMPACA
CHAMPACAS
CHAMPACS
CHAMPAGNE
CHAMPAIGN
CHAMPAK
CHAMPAKS
CHAMPART
CHAMPARTS
CHAMPED
CHAMPER
CHAMPERS
CHAMPERTY
CHAMPIER
CHAMPIEST
CHAMPING
CHAMPION
CHAMPIONS
CHAMPLEVE
CHAMPS
CHAMPY
CHAMS

CHANA	CHANOYO	CHAPEAUX	CHAR	CHARIOT
CHANAS	CHANOYOS	CHAPEL	CHARA	CHARIOTED
CHANCE	CHANOYU	CHAPELESS	CHARABANC	CHARIOTS
CHANCED	CHANOYUS	CHAPELRY	CHARACID	CHARISM
CHANCEFUL	CHANSON	CHAPELS	CHARACIDS	CHARISMA
CHANCEL	CHANSONS	CHAPERON	CHARACIN	CHARISMAS
CHANCELS	CHANT	CHAPERONE	CHARACINS	CHARISMS
CHANCER	CHANTABLE	CHAPERONS	CHARACT	CHARITIES
CHANCERS	CHANTAGE	CHAPES	CHARACTER	CHARITY
CHANCERY	CHANTAGES	CHAPESS	CHARACTS	CHARIVARI
CHANCES	CHANTED	CHAPESSES	CHARADE	CHARK
CHANCEY	CHANTER	CHAPITER	CHARADES	CHARKA
CHANCIER	CHANTERS	CHAPITERS	CHARANGA	CHARKAS
CHANCIEST	CHANTEUSE	CHAPKA	CHARANGAS	CHARKED
CHANCILY	CHANTEY	CHAPKAS	CHARANGO	CHARKHA
CHANCING	CHANTEYS	CHAPLAIN	CHARANGOS	CHARKHAS
CHANCRE	CHANTIE	CHAPLAINS	CHARAS	CHARKING
CHANCRES	CHANTIES	CHAPLESS	CHARASES	CHARKS
CHANCROID	CHANTILLY	CHAPLET	CHARBROIL	CHARLADY
CHANCROUS	CHANTING	CHAPLETED	CHARCOAL	CHARLATAN
CHANCY	CHANTINGS	CHAPLETS	CHARCOALS	CHARLEY
CHANDELLE	CHANTOR	CHAPMAN	CHARCOALY	CHARLEYS
CHANDLER	CHANTORS	CHAPMEN	CHARD	CHARLIE
CHANDLERS	CHANTRESS	CHAPPAL	CHARDS	CHARLIER
CHANDLERY	CHANTRIES	CHAPPALS	CHARE	CHARLIES
CHANFRON	CHANTRY	CHAPPATI	CHARED	CHARLOCK
CHANFRONS	CHANTS	CHAPPATIS	CHARES	CHARLOCKS
CHANG	CHANTY	CHAPPED	CHARET	CHARLOTTE
CHANGA	CHANUKIAH	CHAPPESS	CHARETS	CHARM
CHANGE	CHAO	CHAPPIE	CHARETTE	CHARMED
CHANGED	CHAOLOGY	CHAPPIER	CHARETTES	CHARMER
CHANGEFUL	CHAORDIC	CHAPPIES	CHARGE	CHARMERS
CHANGER	CHAOS	CHAPPIEST	CHARGED	CHARMEUSE
CHANGERS	CHAOSES	CHAPPING	CHARGEFUL	CHARMFUL
CHANGES	CHAOTIC	CHAPPY	CHARGER	CHARMING
CHANGEUP	CHAP	CHAPRASSI	CHARGERS	CHARMLESS
CHANGEUPS	CHAPARRAL	CHAPS	CHARGES	CHARMONIA
CHANGING	CHAPATI	CHAPSTICK	CHARGING	CHARMS
CHANGS	CHAPATIES	CHAPT	CHARGINGS	CHARNECO
CHANK	CHAPATIS	CHAPTER	CHARGRILL	CHARNECOS
CHANKS	CHAPATTI	CHAPTERAL	CHARIDEE	CHARNEL
CHANNEL	CHAPATTIS	CHAPTERED	CHARIDEES	CHARNELS
CHANNELED	CHAPBOOK	CHAPTERS	CHARIER	CHAROSET
CHANNELER	CHAPBOOKS	CHAPTREL	CHARIEST	CHAROSETH
CHANNELS	CHAPE	CHAPTRELS	CHARILY	CHAROSETS
CHANNER	CHAPEAU	CHAQUETA	CHARINESS	CHARPAI
CHANNERS	CHAPEAUS	CHAQUETAS	CHARING	CHARPAIS

CHARPIE	CHASING	CHATON	CHAUNT	CHAZZENIM
CHARPIES	CHASINGS	CHATONS	CHAUNTED	CHAZZENS
CHARPOY	CHASM	CHATOYANT	CHAUNTER	CHE
CHARPOYS	CHASMAL	CHATROOM	CHAUNTERS	CHEAP
CHARQUI	CHASMED	CHATROOMS	CHAUNTING	CHEAPED
CHARQUID	CHASMIC	CHATS	CHAUNTRY	CHEAPEN
CHARQUIS	CHASMIER	CHATTA	CHAUNTS	CHEAPENED
CHARR	CHASMIEST	CHATTAS	CHAUSSES	CHEAPENER
CHARREADA	CHASMS	CHATTED	CHAUSSURE	CHEAPENS
CHARRED	CHASMY	CHATTEL	CHAUVIN	CHEAPER
CHARRIER	CHASSE	CHATTELS	CHAUVINS	CHEAPEST
CHARRIEST	CHASSED	CHATTER	CHAV	CHEAPIE
CHARRING	CHASSEED	CHATTERED	CHAVE	CHEAPIES
CHARRO	CHASSEING	CHATTERER	CHAVENDER	CHEAPING
CHARROS	CHASSEPOT	CHATTERS	CHAVETTE	CHEAPISH
CHARRS	CHASSES	CHATTERY	CHAVETTES	CHEAPJACK
CHARRY	CHASSEUR	CHATTI	CHAVISH	CHEAPLY
CHARS	CHASSEURS	CHATTIER	CHAVS	CHEAPNESS
CHART	CHASSIS	CHATTIES	CHAVVIER	CHEAPO
CHARTA	CHASTE	CHATTIEST	CHAVVIEST	CHEAPOS
CHARTABLE	CHASTELY	CHATTILY	CHAVVY	CHEAPS
CHARTAS	CHASTEN	CHATTING	CHAW	CHEAPSHOT
CHARTED	CHASTENED	CHATTIS	CHAWBACON	CHEAPY
CHARTER	CHASTENER	CHATTY	CHAWDRON	CHEAT
CHARTERED	CHASTENS	CHAUFE	CHAWDRONS	CHEATABLE
CHARTERER	CHASTER	CHAUFED	CHAWED	CHEATED
CHARTERS	CHASTEST	CHAUFER	CHAWER	CHEATER
CHARTING	CHASTISE	CHAUFERS	CHAWERS	CHEATERS
CHARTISM	CHASTISED	CHAUFES	CHAWING	CHEATERY
CHARTISMS	CHASTISER	CHAUFF	CHAWK	CHEATING
CHARTIST	CHASTISES	CHAUFFED	CHAWKS	CHEATINGS
CHARTISTS	CHASTITY	CHAUFFER	CHAWS	CHEATS
CHARTLESS	CHASUBLE	CHAUFFERS	CHAY	CHEBEC
CHARTS	CHASUBLES	CHAUFFEUR	CHAYA	CHEBECS
CHARVER	CHAT	CHAUFFING	CHAYAS	CHECHAKO
CHARVERS	CHATBOT	CHAUFFS	CHAYOTE	CHECHAKOS
CHARWOMAN	CHATBOTS	CHAUFING	CHAYOTES	CHECHAQUO
CHARWOMEN	CHATCHKA	CHAUMER	CHAYROOT	CHECHIA
CHARY	CHATCHKAS	CHAUMERS	CHAYROOTS	CHECHIAS
CHAS	CHATCHKE	CHAUNCE	CHAYS	CHECK
CHASE	CHATCHKES	CHAUNCED	CHAZAN	CHECKABLE
CHASEABLE	CHATEAU	CHAUNCES	CHAZANIM	CHECKBOOK
CHASED	CHATEAUS	CHAUNCING	CHAZANS	CHECKBOX
CHASEPORT	CHATEAUX	CHAUNGE	CHAZZAN	CHECKED
CHASER	CHATELAIN	CHAUNGED	CHAZZANIM	CHECKER
CHASERS	CHATLINE	CHAUNGES	CHAZZANS	CHECKERED
CHASES	CHATLINES	CHAUNGING	CHAZZEN	CHECKERS

CHECKIER	CHEEPED	CHEFING	CHEMIST	CHEROOT
CHECKIEST	CHEEPER	CHEFS	CHEMISTRY	CHEROOTS
CHECKING	CHEEPERS	CHEGOE	CHEMISTS	CHERRIED
CHECKINGS	CHEEPING	CHEGOES	CHEMITYPE	CHERRIER
CHECKLESS	CHEEPS	CHEILITIS	CHEMITYPY	CHERRIES
CHECKLIST	CHEER	CHEKA	CHEMMIES	CHERRIEST
CHECKMARK	CHEERED	CHEKAS	CHEMMY	CHERRY
CHECKMATE	CHEERER	CHEKIST	CHEMO	CHERRYING
CHECKOFF	CHEERERS	CHEKISTS	CHEMOKINE	CHERT
CHECKOFFS	CHEERFUL	CHELA	CHEMOS	CHERTIER
CHECKOUT	CHEERIER	CHELAE	CHEMOSORB	CHERTIEST
CHECKOUTS	CHEERIEST	CHELAS	CHEMOSTAT	CHERTS
CHECKRAIL	CHEERILY	CHELASHIP	CHEMPADUK	CHERTY
CHECKREIN	CHEERING	CHELATE	CHEMS	CHERUB
CHECKROOM	CHEERINGS	CHELATED	CHEMTRAIL	CHERUBIC
CHECKROW	CHEERIO	CHELATES	CHEMURGIC	CHERUBIM
CHECKROWS	CHEERIOS	CHELATING	CHEMURGY	CHERUBIMS
CHECKS	CHEERLEAD	CHELATION	CHENAR	CHERUBIN
CHECKSUM	CHEERLED	CHELATOR	CHENARS	CHERUBINS
CHECKSUMS	CHEERLESS	CHELATORS	CHENET	CHERUBS
CHECKUP	CHEERLY	CHELICERA	CHENETS	CHERUP
CHECKUPS	CHEERO	CHELIFORM	CHENILLE	CHERUPED
CHECKY	CHEEROS	CHELIPED	CHENILLES	CHERUPING
CHEDARIM	CHEERS	CHELIPEDS	CHENIX	CHERUPS
CHEDDAR	CHEERY	CHELLUP	CHENIXES	CHERVIL
CHEDDARS	CHEESE	CHELLUPS	CHENOPOD	CHERVILS
CHEDDARY	CHEESED	CHELOID	CHENOPODS	CHESHIRE
CHEDDITE	CHEESES	CHELOIDAL	CHEONGSAM	CHESHIRES
CHEDDITES	CHEESEVAT	CHELOIDS	CHEQUE	CHESIL
CHEDER	CHEESIER	CHELONE	CHEQUER	CHESILS
CHEDERS	CHEESIEST	CHELONES	CHEQUERED	CHESNUT
CHEDITE	CHEESILY	CHELONIAN	CHEQUERS	CHESNUTS
CHEDITES	CHEESING	CHELP	CHEQUES	CHESS
CHEECHAKO	CHEESY	CHELPED	CHEQUIER	CHESSEL
CHEEK	CHEETAH	CHELPING	CHEQUIEST	CHESSELS
CHEEKBONE	CHEETAHS	CHELPS	CHEQUING	CHESSES
CHEEKED	CHEEWINK	CHEM	CHEQUY	CHESSMAN
CHEEKFUL	CHEEWINKS	CHEMIC	CHER	CHESSMEN
CHEEKFULS	CHEF	CHEMICAL	CHERALITE	CHEST
CHEEKIER	CHEFDOM	CHEMICALS	CHERE	CHESTED
CHEEKIEST	CHEFDOMS	CHEMICKED	CHERIMOYA	CHESTFUL
CHEEKILY	CHEFED	CHEMICS	CHERISH	CHESTFULS
CHEEKING	CHEFFED	CHEMISE	CHERISHED	CHESTIER
CHEEKLESS	CHEFFIER	CHEMISES	CHERISHER	CHESTIEST
CHEEKS	CHEFFIEST	CHEMISM	CHERISHES	CHESTILY
CHEEKY	CHEFFING	CHEMISMS	CHERMOULA	CHESTING
CHEEP	CHEFFY	CHEMISORB	CHERNOZEM	CHESTNUT

CHESTNUTS
CHESTS
CHESTY
CHETAH
CHETAHS
CHETH
CHETHS
CHETNIK
CHETNIKS
CHETRUM
CHETRUMS
CHEVAL
CHEVALET
CHEVALETS
CHEVALIER
CHEVELURE
CHEVEN
CHEVENS
CHEVEREL
CHEVERELS
CHEVERIL
CHEVERILS
CHEVERON
CHEVERONS
CHEVERYE
CHEVERYES
CHEVET
CHEVETS
CHEVIED
CHEVIES
CHEVILLE
CHEVILLES
CHEVIN
CHEVINS
CHEVIOT
CHEVIOTS
CHEVRE
CHEVRES
CHEVRET
CHEVRETS
CHEVRETTE
CHEVRON
CHEVRONED
CHEVRONS
CHEVRONY
CHEVY
CHEVYING

CHEW
CHEWABLE
CHEWED
CHEWER
CHEWERS
CHEWET
CHEWETS
CHEWIE
CHEWIER
CHEWIES
CHEWIEST
CHEWINESS
CHEWING
CHEWINK
CHEWINKS
CHEWS
CHEWY
CHEZ
CHI
CHIA
CHIACK
CHIACKED
CHIACKING
CHIACKS
CHIANTI
CHIANTIS
CHIAO
CHIAREZZA
CHIAREZZE
CHIAS
CHIASM
CHIASMA
CHIASMAL
CHIASMAS
CHIASMATA
CHIASMI
CHIASMIC
CHIASMS
CHIASMUS
CHIASTIC
CHIAUS
CHIAUSED
CHIAUSES
CHIAUSING
CHIB
CHIBBED
CHIBBING

CHIBOL
CHIBOLS
CHIBOUK
CHIBOUKS
CHIBOUQUE
CHIBS
CHIC
CHICA
CHICALOTE
CHICANA
CHICANAS
CHICANE
CHICANED
CHICANER
CHICANERS
CHICANERY
CHICANES
CHICANING
CHICANO
CHICANOS
CHICAS
CHICCORY
CHICER
CHICEST
CHICH
CHICHA
CHICHAS
CHICHES
CHICHI
CHICHIER
CHICHIEST
CHICHIS
CHICK
CHICKADEE
CHICKAREE
CHICKEE
CHICKEES
CHICKEN
CHICKENED
CHICKENS
CHICKLING
CHICKORY
CHICKPEA
CHICKPEAS
CHICKS
CHICKWEED
CHICLE

CHICLES
CHICLY
CHICNESS
CHICO
CHICON
CHICONS
CHICORIES
CHICORY
CHICOS
CHICOT
CHICOTS
CHICS
CHID
CHIDDEN
CHIDE
CHIDED
CHIDER
CHIDERS
CHIDES
CHIDING
CHIDINGLY
CHIDINGS
CHIDLINGS
CHIEF
CHIEFDOM
CHIEFDOMS
CHIEFER
CHIEFERY
CHIEFESS
CHIEFEST
CHIEFLESS
CHIEFLING
CHIEFLY
CHIEFRIES
CHIEFRY
CHIEFS
CHIEFSHIP
CHIEFTAIN
CHIEL
CHIELD
CHIELDS
CHIELS
CHIFFON
CHIFFONS
CHIFFONY
CHIGETAI
CHIGETAIS

CHIGGA
CHIGGAS
CHIGGER
CHIGGERS
CHIGNON
CHIGNONED
CHIGNONS
CHIGOE
CHIGOES
CHIGRE
CHIGRES
CHIHUAHUA
CHIK
CHIKARA
CHIKARAS
CHIKHOR
CHIKHORS
CHIKOR
CHIKORS
CHIKS
CHILBLAIN
CHILD
CHILDBED
CHILDBEDS
CHILDCARE
CHILDE
CHILDED
CHILDER
CHILDES
CHILDHOOD
CHILDING
CHILDISH
CHILDLESS
CHILDLIER
CHILDLIKE
CHILDLY
CHILDNESS
CHILDREN
CHILDS
CHILE
CHILES
CHILI
CHILIAD
CHILIADAL
CHILIADIC
CHILIADS
CHILIAGON

CHILIARCH	CHIMED	CHINCOUGH	CHINWAGS	CHIROLOGY
CHILIASM	CHIMENEA	CHINDIT	CHIP	CHIRONOMY
CHILIASMS	CHIMENEAS	CHINDITS	CHIPBOARD	CHIROPODY
CHILIAST	CHIMER	CHINE	CHIPMUCK	CHIROPTER
CHILIASTS	CHIMERA	CHINED	CHIPMUCKS	CHIROS
CHILIDOG	CHIMERAS	CHINES	CHIPMUNK	CHIRP
CHILIDOGS	CHIMERE	CHINESE	CHIPMUNKS	CHIRPED
CHILIES	CHIMERES	CHING	CHIPOCHIA	CHIRPER
CHILIS	CHIMERIC	CHINGS	CHIPOLATA	CHIRPERS
CHILL	CHIMERID	CHINING	CHIPOTLE	CHIRPIER
CHILLADA	CHIMERIDS	CHINK	CHIPOTLES	CHIRPIEST
CHILLADAS	CHIMERISM	CHINKAPIN	CHIPPABLE	CHIRPILY
CHILLAX	CHIMERS	CHINKARA	CHIPPED	CHIRPING
CHILLAXED	CHIMES	CHINKARAS	CHIPPER	CHIRPINGS
CHILLAXES	CHIMINEA	CHINKED	CHIPPERED	CHIRPS
CHILLED	CHIMINEAS	CHINKIE	CHIPPERS	CHIRPY
CHILLER	CHIMING	CHINKIER	CHIPPIE	CHIRR
CHILLERS	CHIMLA	CHINKIES	CHIPPIER	CHIRRE
CHILLEST	CHIMLAS	CHINKIEST	CHIPPIES	CHIRRED
CHILLI	CHIMLEY	CHINKING	CHIPPIEST	CHIRREN
CHILLIER	CHIMLEYS	CHINKS	CHIPPING	CHIRRES
CHILLIES	CHIMNEY	CHINKY	CHIPPINGS	CHIRRING
CHILLIEST	CHIMNEYED	CHINLESS	CHIPPY	CHIRRS
CHILLILY	CHIMNEYS	CHINNED	CHIPS	CHIRRUP
CHILLING	CHIMO	CHINNING	CHIPSET	CHIRRUPED
CHILLINGS	CHIMP	CHINO	CHIPSETS	CHIRRUPER
CHILLIS	CHIMPS	CHINOIS	CHIRAGRA	CHIRRUPS
CHILLNESS	CHIN	CHINOISES	CHIRAGRAS	CHIRRUPY
CHILLS	CHINA	CHINONE	CHIRAGRIC	CHIRT
CHILLUM	CHINAMAN	CHINONES	CHIRAL	CHIRTED
CHILLUMS	CHINAMEN	CHINOOK	CHIRALITY	CHIRTING
CHILLY	CHINAMPA	CHINOOKS	CHIRIMOYA	CHIRTS
CHILOPOD	CHINAMPAS	CHINOS	CHIRK	CHIRU
CHILOPODS	CHINAR	CHINOVNIK	CHIRKED	CHIRUS
CHILTEPIN	CHINAROOT	CHINS	CHIRKER	CHIS
CHIMAERA	CHINARS	CHINSE	CHIRKEST	CHISEL
CHIMAERAS	CHINAS	CHINSED	CHIRKING	CHISELED
CHIMAERIC	CHINAWARE	CHINSES	CHIRKS	CHISELER
CHIMAR	CHINBONE	CHINSING	CHIRL	CHISELERS
CHIMARS	CHINBONES	CHINSTRAP	CHIRLED	CHISELING
CHIMB	CHINCAPIN	CHINTS	CHIRLING	CHISELLED
CHIMBLEY	CHINCH	CHINTSES	CHIRLS	CHISELLER
CHIMBLEYS	CHINCHED	CHINTZ	CHIRM	CHISELS
CHIMBLIES	CHINCHES	CHINTZES	CHIRMED	CHIT
CHIMBLY	CHINCHIER	CHINTZIER	CHIRMING	CHITAL
CHIMBS	CHINCHING	CHINTZY	CHIRMS	CHITALS
CHIME	CHINCHY	CHINWAG	CHIRO	CHITCHAT

CHITCHATS	CHIYOGAMI	CHOCHO	CHOKEHOLD	CHOLLAS
CHITIN	CHIZ	CHOCHOS	CHOKER	CHOLLERS
CHITINOID	CHIZZ	CHOCK	CHOKERS	CHOLO
CHITINOUS	CHIZZED	CHOCKED	CHOKES	CHOLOS
CHITINS	CHIZZES	CHOCKER	CHOKEY	CHOLTRIES
CHITLIN	CHIZZING	CHOCKFUL	CHOKEYS	CHOLTRY
CHITLING	CHLAMYDES	CHOCKFULL	CHOKIDAR	CHOMETZ
CHITLINGS	CHLAMYDIA	CHOCKING	CHOKIDARS	CHOMETZES
CHITLINS	CHLAMYS	CHOCKO	CHOKIER	CHOMMIE
CHITON	CHLAMYSES	CHOCKOS	CHOKIES	CHOMMIES
CHITONS	CHLOASMA	CHOCKS	CHOKIEST	CHOMP
CHITOSAN	CHLOASMAS	CHOCO	CHOKING	CHOMPED
CHITOSANS	CHLORACNE	CHOCOLATE	CHOKINGLY	CHOMPER
CHITS	CHLORAL	CHOCOLATY	CHOKO	CHOMPERS
CHITTED	CHLORALS	CHOCOS	CHOKOS	CHOMPING
CHITTER	CHLORATE	CHOCS	CHOKRA	CHOMPS
CHITTERED	CHLORATES	CHOCTAW	CHOKRAS	CHON
CHITTERS	CHLORDAN	CHOCTAWS	CHOKRI	CHONDRAL
CHITTIER	CHLORDANE	CHODE	CHOKRIS	CHONDRE
CHITTIES	CHLORDANS	CHOENIX	CHOKY	CHONDRES
CHITTIEST	CHLORELLA	CHOENIXES	CHOLA	CHONDRI
CHITTING	CHLORIC	CHOG	CHOLAEMIA	CHONDRIFY
CHITTY	CHLORID	CHOGS	CHOLAEMIC	CHONDRIN
CHIV	CHLORIDE	CHOICE	CHOLAS	CHONDRINS
CHIVALRIC	CHLORIDES	CHOICEFUL	CHOLATE	CHONDRITE
CHIVALRY	CHLORIDIC	CHOICELY	CHOLATES	CHONDROID
CHIVAREE	CHLORIDS	CHOICER	CHOLECYST	CHONDROMA
CHIVAREED	CHLORIN	CHOICES	CHOLELITH	CHONDRULE
CHIVAREES	CHLORINE	CHOICEST	CHOLEMIA	CHONDRUS
CHIVARI	CHLORINES	CHOIL	CHOLEMIAS	CHONS
CHIVARIED	CHLORINS	CHOILS	CHOLENT	CHOOF
CHIVARIES	CHLORITE	CHOIR	CHOLENTS	CHOOFED
CHIVE	CHLORITES	CHOIRBOY	CHOLER	CHOOFING
CHIVED	CHLORITIC	CHOIRBOYS	CHOLERA	CHOOFS
CHIVES	CHLOROSES	CHOIRED	CHOLERAIC	CHOOK
CHIVIED	CHLOROSIS	CHOIRGIRL	CHOLERAS	CHOOKED
CHIVIES	CHLOROTIC	CHOIRING	CHOLERIC	CHOOKIE
CHIVING	CHLOROUS	CHOIRLIKE	CHOLEROID	CHOOKIES
CHIVS	CHOANA	CHOIRMAN	CHOLERS	CHOOKING
CHIVVED	CHOANAE	CHOIRMEN	CHOLI	CHOOKS
CHIVVIED	CHOBDAR	CHOIRS	CHOLIAMB	CHOOM
CHIVVIES	CHOBDARS	CHOKE	CHOLIAMBS	CHOOMS
CHIVVING	CHOC	CHOKEABLE	CHOLIC	CHOON
CHIVVY	CHOCCIER	CHOKEBORE	CHOLINE	CHOONS
CHIVVYING	CHOCCIES	CHOKECOIL	CHOLINES	CHOOSE
CHIVY	CHOCCIEST	CHOKED	CHOLIS	CHOOSER
CHIVYING	CHOCCY	CHOKEDAMP	CHOLLA	CHOOSERS

CHOOSES	CHORDS	CHOROIDAL	CHOWDERS	CHROME
CHOOSEY	CHORDWISE	CHOROIDS	CHOWDOWN	CHROMED
CHOOSIER	CHORE	CHOROLOGY	CHOWDOWNS	CHROMEL
CHOOSIEST	CHOREA	CHORRIE	CHOWED	CHROMELS
CHOOSILY	CHOREAL	CHORRIES	CHOWHOUND	CHROMENE
CHOOSING	CHOREAS	CHORTEN	CHOWING	CHROMENES
CHOOSY	CHOREATIC	CHORTENS	CHOWK	CHROMES
CHOP	CHOREBOY	CHORTLE	CHOWKIDAR	CHROMIC
CHOPHOUSE	CHOREBOYS	CHORTLED	CHOWKS	CHROMIDE
CHOPIN	CHORED	CHORTLER	CHOWRI	CHROMIDES
CHOPINE	CHOREE	CHORTLERS	CHOWRIES	CHROMIDIA
CHOPINES	CHOREES	CHORTLES	CHOWRIS	CHROMIER
CHOPINS	CHOREGI	CHORTLING	CHOWRY	CHROMIEST
CHOPLOGIC	CHOREGIC	CHORUS	CHOWS	CHROMING
CHOPPED	CHOREGUS	CHORUSED	CHOWSE	CHROMINGS
CHOPPER	CHOREIC	CHORUSES	CHOWSED	CHROMISE
CHOPPERED	CHOREMAN	CHORUSING	CHOWSES	CHROMISED
CHOPPERS	CHOREMEN	CHORUSSED	CHOWSING	CHROMISES
CHOPPIER	CHOREOID	CHORUSSES	CHOWTIME	CHROMITE
CHOPPIEST	CHORES	CHOSE	CHOWTIMES	CHROMITES
CHOPPILY	CHOREUS	CHOSEN	CHRESARD	CHROMIUM
CHOPPING	CHOREUSES	CHOSES	CHRESARDS	CHROMIUMS
CHOPPINGS	CHORIA	CHOTA	CHRISM	CHROMIZE
CHOPPY	CHORIAL	CHOTT	CHRISMA	CHROMIZED
CHOPS	CHORIAMB	CHOTTS	CHRISMAL	CHROMIZES
CHOPSOCKY	CHORIAMBI	CHOU	CHRISMALS	CHROMO
CHOPSTICK	CHORIAMBS	CHOUGH	CHRISMON	CHROMOGEN
CHORAGI	CHORIC	CHOUGHS	CHRISMONS	CHROMOLY
CHORAGIC	CHORINE	CHOULTRY	CHRISMS	CHROMOS
CHORAGUS	CHORINES	CHOUNTER	CHRISOM	CHROMOUS
CHORAL	CHORING	CHOUNTERS	CHRISOMS	CHROMY
CHORALE	CHORIOID	CHOUSE	CHRISTEN	CHROMYL
CHORALES	CHORIOIDS	CHOUSED	CHRISTENS	CHROMYLS
CHORALIST	CHORION	CHOUSER	CHRISTIAN	CHRONAXIE
CHORALLY	CHORIONIC	CHOUSERS	CHRISTIE	CHRONAXY
CHORALS	CHORIONS	CHOUSES	CHRISTIES	CHRONIC
CHORD	CHORISES	CHOUSH	CHRISTOM	CHRONICAL
CHORDA	CHORISIS	CHOUSHES	CHRISTOMS	CHRONICLE
CHORDAE	CHORISM	CHOUSING	CHRISTY	CHRONICS
CHORDAL	CHORISMS	CHOUT	CHROMA	CHRONON
CHORDATE	CHORIST	CHOUTS	CHROMAKEY	CHRONONS
CHORDATES	CHORISTER	CHOUX	CHROMAS	CHRYSALID
CHORDED	CHORISTS	CHOW	CHROMATE	CHRYSALIS
CHORDEE	CHORIZO	CHOWCHOW	CHROMATES	CHRYSANTH
CHORDEES	CHORIZONT	CHOWCHOWS	CHROMATIC	CHTHONIAN
CHORDING	CHORIZOS	CHOWDER	CHROMATID	CHTHONIC
CHORDINGS	CHOROID	CHOWDERED	CHROMATIN	CHUB

CHUBASCO
CHUBASCOS
CHUBBIER
CHUBBIEST
CHUBBILY
CHUBBY
CHUBS
CHUCK
CHUCKED
CHUCKER
CHUCKERS
CHUCKHOLE
CHUCKIE
CHUCKIES
CHUCKING
CHUCKLE
CHUCKLED
CHUCKLER
CHUCKLERS
CHUCKLES
CHUCKLING
CHUCKS
CHUCKY
CHUDDAH
CHUDDAHS
CHUDDAR
CHUDDARS
CHUDDER
CHUDDERS
CHUDDIES
CHUDDY
CHUFA
CHUFAS
CHUFF
CHUFFED
CHUFFER
CHUFFEST
CHUFFIER
CHUFFIEST
CHUFFING
CHUFFS
CHUFFY
CHUG
CHUGALUG
CHUGALUGS
CHUGGED
CHUGGER

CHUGGERS
CHUGGING
CHUGS
CHUKAR
CHUKARS
CHUKKA
CHUKKAR
CHUKKARS
CHUKKAS
CHUKKER
CHUKKERS
CHUKOR
CHUKORS
CHUM
CHUMASH
CHUMASHES
CHUMASHIM
CHUMLEY
CHUMLEYS
CHUMMAGE
CHUMMAGES
CHUMMED
CHUMMIER
CHUMMIES
CHUMMIEST
CHUMMILY
CHUMMING
CHUMMY
CHUMP
CHUMPED
CHUMPING
CHUMPINGS
CHUMPS
CHUMS
CHUMSHIP
CHUMSHIPS
CHUNDER
CHUNDERED
CHUNDERS
CHUNK
CHUNKED
CHUNKIER
CHUNKIEST
CHUNKILY
CHUNKING
CHUNKINGS
CHUNKS

CHUNKY
CHUNNEL
CHUNNELS
CHUNNER
CHUNNERED
CHUNNERS
CHUNTER
CHUNTERED
CHUNTERS
CHUPATI
CHUPATIS
CHUPATTI
CHUPATTIS
CHUPATTY
CHUPPA
CHUPPAH
CHUPPAHS
CHUPPAS
CHUPPOT
CHUPPOTH
CHUPRASSY
CHUR
CHURCH
CHURCHED
CHURCHES
CHURCHIER
CHURCHING
CHURCHISM
CHURCHLY
CHURCHMAN
CHURCHMEN
CHURCHWAY
CHURCHY
CHURIDAR
CHURIDARS
CHURINGA
CHURINGAS
CHURL
CHURLISH
CHURLS
CHURN
CHURNED
CHURNER
CHURNERS
CHURNING
CHURNINGS
CHURNMILK

CHURNS
CHURR
CHURRED
CHURRING
CHURRO
CHURROS
CHURRS
CHURRUS
CHURRUSES
CHUSE
CHUSED
CHUSES
CHUSING
CHUT
CHUTE
CHUTED
CHUTES
CHUTING
CHUTIST
CHUTISTS
CHUTNEE
CHUTNEES
CHUTNEY
CHUTNEYS
CHUTS
CHUTZPA
CHUTZPAH
CHUTZPAHS
CHUTZPAS
CHYACK
CHYACKED
CHYACKING
CHYACKS
CHYLDE
CHYLE
CHYLES
CHYLIFIED
CHYLIFIES
CHYLIFY
CHYLOUS
CHYLURIA
CHYLURIAS
CHYME
CHYMES
CHYMIC
CHYMICS
CHYMIFIED

CHYMIFIES
CHYMIFY
CHYMIST
CHYMISTRY
CHYMISTS
CHYMOSIN
CHYMOSINS
CHYMOUS
CHYND
CHYPRE
CHYPRES
CHYTRID
CHYTRIDS
CIABATTA
CIABATTAS
CIABATTE
CIAO
CIBATION
CIBATIONS
CIBOL
CIBOLS
CIBORIA
CIBORIUM
CIBOULE
CIBOULES
CICADA
CICADAE
CICADAS
CICALA
CICALAS
CICALE
CICATRICE
CICATRISE
CICATRIX
CICATRIZE
CICELIES
CICELY
CICERO
CICERONE
CICERONED
CICERONES
CICERONI
CICEROS
CICHLID
CICHLIDAE
CICHLIDS
CICHLOID

CICINNUS	CILANTROS	CINDERY	CIOPPINOS	CIRE
CICISBEI	CILIA	CINE	CIPAILLE	CIRES
CICISBEO	CILIARY	CINEAST	CIPAILLES	CIRL
CICISBEOS	CILIATE	CINEASTE	CIPHER	CIRLS
CICLATON	CILIATED	CINEASTES	CIPHERED	CIRQUE
CICLATONS	CILIATELY	CINEASTS	CIPHERER	CIRQUES
CICLATOUN	CILIATES	CINEMA	CIPHERERS	CIRRATE
CICOREE	CILIATION	CINEMAS	CIPHERING	CIRRHOSED
CICOREES	CILICE	CINEMATIC	CIPHERS	CIRRHOSES
CICUTA	CILICES	CINEOL	CIPHONIES	CIRRHOSIS
CICUTAS	CILICIOUS	CINEOLE	CIPHONY	CIRRHOTIC
CICUTINE	CILIOLATE	CINEOLES	CIPOLIN	CIRRI
CICUTINES	CILIUM	CINEOLS	CIPOLINS	CIRRIFORM
CID	CILL	CINEPHILE	CIPOLLINO	CIRRIPED
CIDARIS	CILLS	CINEPLEX	CIPPI	CIRRIPEDE
CIDARISES	CIMAR	CINERAMIC	CIPPUS	CIRRIPEDS
CIDE	CIMARS	CINERARIA	CIRCA	CIRROSE
CIDED	CIMBALOM	CINERARY	CIRCADIAN	CIRROUS
CIDER	CIMBALOMS	CINERATOR	CIRCAR	CIRRUS
CIDERKIN	CIMELIA	CINEREA	CIRCARS	CIRRUSES
CIDERKINS	CIMEX	CINEREAL	CIRCINATE	CIRSOID
CIDERS	CIMICES	CINEREAS	CIRCITER	CIS
CIDERY	CIMIER	CINEREOUS	CIRCLE	CISALPINE
CIDES	CIMIERS	CINERIN	CIRCLED	CISCO
CIDING	CIMINITE	CINERINS	CIRCLER	CISCOES
CIDS	CIMINITES	CINES	CIRCLERS	CISCOS
CIEL	CIMMERIAN	CINGULA	CIRCLES	CISELEUR
CIELED	CIMOLITE	CINGULAR	CIRCLET	CISELEURS
CIELING	CIMOLITES	CINGULATE	CIRCLETS	CISELURE
CIELINGS	CINCH	CINGULUM	CIRCLING	CISELURES
CIELS	CINCHED	CINNABAR	CIRCLINGS	CISLUNAR
CIERGE	CINCHES	CINNABARS	CIRCLIP	CISPADANE
CIERGES	CINCHING	CINNAMIC	CIRCLIPS	CISPLATIN
CIG	CINCHINGS	CINNAMON	CIRCS	CISSIER
CIGAR	CINCHONA	CINNAMONS	CIRCUIT	CISSIES
CIGARET	CINCHONAS	CINNAMONY	CIRCUITAL	CISSIEST
CIGARETS	CINCHONIC	CINNAMYL	CIRCUITED	CISSIFIED
CIGARETTE	CINCINNUS	CINNAMYLS	CIRCUITRY	CISSING
CIGARILLO	CINCT	CINQ	CIRCUITS	CISSINGS
CIGARLIKE	CINCTURE	CINQS	CIRCUITY	CISSOID
CIGARS	CINCTURED	CINQUAIN	CIRCULAR	CISSOIDS
CIGGIE	CINCTURES	CINQUAINS	CIRCULARS	CISSUS
CIGGIES	CINDER	CINQUE	CIRCULATE	CISSUSES
CIGGY	CINDERED	CINQUES	CIRCUS	CISSY
CIGS	CINDERING	CION	CIRCUSES	CIST
CIGUATERA	CINDEROUS	CIONS	CIRCUSSY	CISTED
CILANTRO	CINDERS	CIOPPINO	CIRCUSY	CISTERN

CISTERNA	CITIGRADE	CIVETLIKE	CLACKING	CLAMBAKE
CISTERNAE	CITING	CIVETS	CLACKS	CLAMBAKES
CISTERNAL	CITIZEN	CIVIC	CLAD	CLAMBE
CISTERNS	CITIZENLY	CIVICALLY	CLADDAGH	CLAMBER
CISTIC	CITIZENRY	CIVICISM	CLADDAGHS	CLAMBERED
CISTRON	CITIZENS	CIVICISMS	CLADDED	CLAMBERER
CISTRONIC	CITO	CIVICS	CLADDER	CLAMBERS
CISTRONS	CITOLA	CIVIE	CLADDERS	CLAME
CISTS	CITOLAS	CIVIES	CLADDIE	CLAMES
CISTUS	CITOLE	CIVIL	CLADDIES	CLAMLIKE
CISTUSES	CITOLES	CIVILIAN	CLADDING	CLAMMED
CISTVAEN	CITRAL	CIVILIANS	CLADDINGS	CLAMMER
CISTVAENS	CITRALS	CIVILISE	CLADE	CLAMMERS
CIT	CITRANGE	CIVILISED	CLADES	CLAMMIER
CITABLE	CITRANGES	CIVILISER	CLADISM	CLAMMIEST
CITADEL	CITRATE	CIVILISES	CLADISMS	CLAMMILY
CITADELS	CITRATED	CIVILIST	CLADIST	CLAMMING
CITAL	CITRATES	CIVILISTS	CLADISTIC	CLAMMY
CITALS	CITREOUS	CIVILITY	CLADISTS	CLAMOR
CITATION	CITRIC	CIVILIZE	CLADODE	CLAMORED
CITATIONS	CITRIN	CIVILIZED	CLADODES	CLAMORER
CITATOR	CITRINE	CIVILIZER	CLADODIAL	CLAMORERS
CITATORS	CITRINES	CIVILIZES	CLADOGRAM	CLAMORING
CITATORY	CITRININ	CIVILLY	CLADS	CLAMOROUS
CITE	CITRININS	CIVILNESS	CLAES	CLAMORS
CITEABLE	CITRINS	CIVILS	CLAFOUTI	CLAMOUR
CITED	CITRON	CIVISM	CLAFOUTIS	CLAMOURED
CITER	CITRONS	CIVISMS	CLAG	CLAMOURER
CITERS	CITROUS	CIVVIES	CLAGGED	CLAMOURS
CITES	CITRUS	CIVVY	CLAGGIER	CLAMP
CITESS	CITRUSES	CIZERS	CLAGGIEST	CLAMPDOWN
CITESSES	CITRUSSY	CLABBER	CLAGGING	CLAMPED
CITHARA	CITRUSY	CLABBERED	CLAGGY	CLAMPER
CITHARAS	CITS	CLABBERS	CLAGS	CLAMPERED
CITHARIST	CITTERN	CLACH	CLAIM	CLAMPERS
CITHER	CITTERNS	CLACHAN	CLAIMABLE	CLAMPING
CITHERN	CITY	CLACHANS	CLAIMANT	CLAMPINGS
CITHERNS	CITYFIED	CLACHED	CLAIMANTS	CLAMPS
CITHERS	CITYFIES	CLACHES	CLAIMED	CLAMS
CITHREN	CITYFY	CLACHING	CLAIMER	CLAMSHELL
CITHRENS	CITYFYING	CLACHS	CLAIMERS	CLAMWORM
CITIED	CITYSCAPE	CLACK	CLAIMING	CLAMWORMS
CITIES	CITYWARD	CLACKBOX	CLAIMS	CLAN
CITIFIED	CITYWIDE	CLACKDISH	CLAM	CLANG
CITIFIES	CIVE	CLACKED	CLAMANCY	CLANGBOX
CITIFY	CIVES	CLACKER	CLAMANT	CLANGED
CITIFYING	CIVET	CLACKERS	CLAMANTLY	CLANGER

CLANGERS	CLARENCE	CLASPED	CLATCHING	CLAVIER
CLANGING	CLARENCES	CLASPER	CLATHRATE	CLAVIERS
CLANGINGS	CLARENDON	CLASPERS	CLATS	CLAVIES
CLANGOR	CLARET	CLASPING	CLATTED	CLAVIFORM
CLANGORED	CLARETED	CLASPINGS	CLATTER	CLAVIGER
CLANGORS	CLARETING	CLASPS	CLATTERED	CLAVIGERS
CLANGOUR	CLARETS	CLASPT	CLATTERER	CLAVIS
CLANGOURS	CLARIES	CLASS	CLATTERS	CLAVULATE
CLANGS	CLARIFIED	CLASSABLE	CLATTERY	CLAVUS
CLANK	CLARIFIER	CLASSED	CLATTING	CLAW
CLANKED	CLARIFIES	CLASSER	CLAUCHT	CLAWBACK
CLANKIER	CLARIFY	CLASSERS	CLAUCHTED	CLAWBACKS
CLANKIEST	CLARINET	CLASSES	CLAUCHTS	CLAWED
CLANKING	CLARINETS	CLASSIBLE	CLAUGHT	CLAWER
CLANKINGS	CLARINI	CLASSIC	CLAUGHTED	CLAWERS
CLANKS	CLARINO	CLASSICAL	CLAUGHTS	CLAWING
CLANKY	CLARINOS	CLASSICO	CLAUSAL	CLAWLESS
CLANNISH	CLARION	CLASSICS	CLAUSE	CLAWLIKE
CLANS	CLARIONED	CLASSIER	CLAUSES	CLAWS
CLANSHIP	CLARIONET	CLASSIEST	CLAUSTRA	CLAXON
CLANSHIPS	CLARIONS	CLASSIFIC	CLAUSTRAL	CLAXONS
CLANSMAN	CLARITIES	CLASSIFY	CLAUSTRUM	CLAY
CLANSMEN	CLARITY	CLASSILY	CLAUSULA	CLAYBANK
CLAP	CLARKIA	CLASSING	CLAUSULAE	CLAYBANKS
CLAPBOARD	CLARKIAS	CLASSINGS	CLAUSULAR	CLAYED
CLAPBREAD	CLARO	CLASSIS	CLAUT	CLAYEY
CLAPDISH	CLAROES	CLASSISM	CLAUTED	CLAYIER
CLAPNET	CLAROS	CLASSISMS	CLAUTING	CLAYIEST
CLAPNETS	CLARSACH	CLASSIST	CLAUTS	CLAYING
CLAPPED	CLARSACHS	CLASSISTS	CLAVATE	CLAYISH
CLAPPER	CLART	CLASSLESS	CLAVATED	CLAYLIKE
CLAPPERED	CLARTED	CLASSMAN	CLAVATELY	CLAYMORE
CLAPPERS	CLARTHEAD	CLASSMATE	CLAVATION	CLAYMORES
CLAPPING	CLARTIER	CLASSMEN	CLAVE	CLAYPAN
CLAPPINGS	CLARTIEST	CLASSON	CLAVECIN	CLAYPANS
CLAPS	CLARTING	CLASSONS	CLAVECINS	CLAYS
CLAPT	CLARTS	CLASSROOM	CLAVER	CLAYSTONE
CLAPTRAP	CLARTY	CLASSWORK	CLAVERED	CLAYTONIA
CLAPTRAPS	CLARY	CLASSY	CLAVERING	CLAYWARE
CLAQUE	CLASH	CLAST	CLAVERS	CLAYWARES
CLAQUER	CLASHED	CLASTIC	CLAVES	CLEAN
CLAQUERS	CLASHER	CLASTICS	CLAVI	CLEANABLE
CLAQUES	CLASHERS	CLASTS	CLAVICLE	CLEANED
CLAQUEUR	CLASHES	CLAT	CLAVICLES	CLEANER
CLAQUEURS	CLASHING	CLATCH	CLAVICORN	CLEANERS
CLARAIN	CLASHINGS	CLATCHED	CLAVICULA	CLEANEST
CLARAINS	CLASP	CLATCHES	CLAVIE	CLEANING

CLEANINGS	CLEAVABLE	CLEMMED	CLERUCH	CLIENTS
CLEANISH	CLEAVAGE	CLEMMING	CLERUCHIA	CLIES
CLEANLIER	CLEAVAGES	CLEMS	CLERUCHS	CLIFF
CLEANLILY	CLEAVE	CLENCH	CLERUCHY	CLIFFED
CLEANLY	CLEAVED	CLENCHED	CLEUCH	CLIFFHANG
CLEANNESS	CLEAVER	CLENCHER	CLEUCHS	CLIFFHUNG
CLEANOUT	CLEAVERS	CLENCHERS	CLEUGH	CLIFFIER
CLEANOUTS	CLEAVES	CLENCHES	CLEUGHS	CLIFFIEST
CLEANS	CLEAVING	CLENCHING	CLEVE	CLIFFLIKE
CLEANSE	CLEAVINGS	CLEOME	CLEVEITE	CLIFFS
CLEANSED	CLECHE	CLEOMES	CLEVEITES	CLIFFSIDE
CLEANSER	CLECK	CLEOPATRA	CLEVER	CLIFFTOP
CLEANSERS	CLECKED	CLEPE	CLEVERER	CLIFFTOPS
CLEANSES	CLECKIER	CLEPED	CLEVEREST	CLIFFY
CLEANSING	CLECKIEST	CLEPES	CLEVERISH	CLIFT
CLEANSKIN	CLECKING	CLEPING	CLEVERLY	CLIFTED
CLEANUP	CLECKINGS	CLEPSYDRA	CLEVES	CLIFTIER
CLEANUPS	CLECKS	CLEPT	CLEVIS	CLIFTIEST
CLEAR	CLECKY	CLERGIES	CLEVISES	CLIFTS
CLEARABLE	CLEEK	CLERGY	CLEW	CLIFTY
CLEARAGE	CLEEKED	CLERGYMAN	CLEWED	CLIMACTIC
CLEARAGES	CLEEKING	CLERGYMEN	CLEWING	CLIMATAL
CLEARANCE	CLEEKIT	CLERIC	CLEWS	CLIMATE
CLEARCOLE	CLEEKS	CLERICAL	CLIANTHUS	CLIMATED
CLEARCUT	CLEEP	CLERICALS	CLICHE	CLIMATES
CLEARCUTS	CLEEPED	CLERICATE	CLICHED	CLIMATIC
CLEARED	CLEEPING	CLERICITY	CLICHEED	CLIMATING
CLEARER	CLEEPS	CLERICS	CLICHES	CLIMATISE
CLEARERS	CLEEVE	CLERID	CLICK	CLIMATIZE
CLEAREST	CLEEVES	CLERIDS	CLICKABLE	CLIMATURE
CLEAREYED	CLEF	CLERIHEW	CLICKBAIT	CLIMAX
CLEARING	CLEFS	CLERIHEWS	CLICKED	CLIMAXED
CLEARINGS	CLEFT	CLERISIES	CLICKER	CLIMAXES
CLEARLY	CLEFTED	CLERISY	CLICKERS	CLIMAXING
CLEARNESS	CLEFTING	CLERK	CLICKET	CLIMB
CLEAROUT	CLEFTS	CLERKDOM	CLICKETED	CLIMBABLE
CLEAROUTS	CLEG	CLERKDOMS	CLICKETS	CLIMBDOWN
CLEARS	CLEGS	CLERKED	CLICKING	CLIMBED
CLEARSKIN	CLEIDOIC	CLERKESS	CLICKINGS	CLIMBER
CLEARWAY	CLEIK	CLERKING	CLICKLESS	CLIMBERS
CLEARWAYS	CLEIKS	CLERKISH	CLICKS	CLIMBING
CLEARWEED	CLEITHRAL	CLERKLIER	CLICKWRAP	CLIMBINGS
CLEARWING	CLEM	CLERKLIKE	CLIED	CLIMBS
CLEAT	CLEMATIS	CLERKLING	CLIENT	CLIME
CLEATED	CLEMENCY	CLERKLY	CLIENTAGE	CLIMES
CLEATING	CLEMENT	CLERKS	CLIENTAL	CLINAL
CLEATS	CLEMENTLY	CLERKSHIP	CLIENTELE	CLINALLY

CLINAMEN	CLIPED	CLOACAL	CLOGDANCE	CLONKY
CLINAMENS	CLIPES	CLOACAS	CLOGGED	CLONS
CLINCH	CLIPING	CLOACINAL	CLOGGER	CLONUS
CLINCHED	CLIPPABLE	CLOACITIS	CLOGGERS	CLONUSES
CLINCHER	CLIPPED	CLOAK	CLOGGIER	CLOOP
CLINCHERS	CLIPPER	CLOAKED	CLOGGIEST	CLOOPS
CLINCHES	CLIPPERS	CLOAKING	CLOGGILY	CLOOT
CLINCHING	CLIPPIE	CLOAKROOM	CLOGGING	CLOOTIE
CLINE	CLIPPIES	CLOAKS	CLOGGINGS	CLOOTS
CLINES	CLIPPING	CLOAM	CLOGGY	CLOP
CLING	CLIPPINGS	CLOAMS	CLOGS	CLOPPED
CLINGED	CLIPS	CLOBBER	CLOISON	CLOPPING
CLINGER	CLIPSHEAR	CLOBBERED	CLOISONNE	CLOPS
CLINGERS	CLIPSHEET	CLOBBERS	CLOISONS	CLOQUE
CLINGFILM	CLIPT	CLOCHARD	CLOISTER	CLOQUES
CLINGFISH	CLIQUE	CLOCHARDS	CLOISTERS	CLOSABLE
CLINGIER	CLIQUED	CLOCHE	CLOISTRAL	CLOSE
CLINGIEST	CLIQUES	CLOCHES	CLOKE	CLOSEABLE
CLINGING	CLIQUEY	CLOCK	CLOKED	CLOSED
CLINGS	CLIQUIER	CLOCKED	CLOKES	CLOSEDOWN
CLINGWRAP	CLIQUIEST	CLOCKER	CLOKING	CLOSEHEAD
CLINGY	CLIQUING	CLOCKERS	CLOMB	CLOSELY
CLINIC	CLIQUISH	CLOCKING	CLOMP	CLOSENESS
CLINICAL	CLIQUISM	CLOCKINGS	CLOMPED	CLOSEOUT
CLINICIAN	CLIQUISMS	CLOCKLIKE	CLOMPING	CLOSEOUTS
CLINICS	CLIQUY	CLOCKS	CLOMPS	CLOSER
CLINIQUE	CLIT	CLOCKWISE	CLON	CLOSERS
CLINIQUES	CLITELLA	CLOCKWORK	CLONAL	CLOSES
CLINK	CLITELLAR	CLOD	CLONALLY	CLOSEST
CLINKED	CLITELLUM	CLODDED	CLONE	CLOSET
CLINKER	CLITHRAL	CLODDIER	CLONED	CLOSETED
CLINKERED	CLITIC	CLODDIEST	CLONER	CLOSETFUL
CLINKERS	CLITICISE	CLODDING	CLONERS	CLOSETING
CLINKING	CLITICIZE	CLODDISH	CLONES	CLOSETS
CLINKS	CLITICS	CLODDY	CLONIC	CLOSEUP
CLINOAXES	CLITORAL	CLODLY	CLONICITY	CLOSEUPS
CLINOAXIS	CLITORIC	CLODPATE	CLONIDINE	CLOSING
CLINOSTAT	CLITORIS	CLODPATED	CLONING	CLOSINGS
CLINQUANT	CLITS	CLODPATES	CLONINGS	CLOSURE
CLINT	CLITTER	CLODPOLE	CLONISM	CLOSURED
CLINTONIA	CLITTERED	CLODPOLES	CLONISMS	CLOSURES
CLINTS	CLITTERS	CLODPOLL	CLONK	CLOSURING
CLIP	CLIVERS	CLODPOLLS	CLONKED	CLOT
CLIPART	CLIVIA	CLODS	CLONKIER	CLOTBUR
CLIPARTS	CLIVIAS	CLOFF	CLONKIEST	CLOTBURS
CLIPBOARD	CLOACA	CLOFFS	CLONKING	CLOTE
CLIPE	CLOACAE	CLOG	CLONKS	CLOTES

CLOTH	CLOUR	CLOZES	CLUCKERS	CLUNKY
CLOTHE	CLOURED	CLUB	CLUCKIER	CLUPEID
CLOTHED	CLOURING	CLUBABLE	CLUCKIEST	CLUPEIDS
CLOTHES	CLOURS	CLUBBABLE	CLUCKING	CLUPEOID
CLOTHIER	CLOUS	CLUBBED	CLUCKS	CLUPEOIDS
CLOTHIERS	CLOUT	CLUBBER	CLUCKY	CLUSIA
CLOTHING	CLOUTED	CLUBBERS	CLUDGIE	CLUSIAS
CLOTHINGS	CLOUTER	CLUBBIER	CLUDGIES	CLUSTER
CLOTHLIKE	CLOUTERLY	CLUBBIEST	CLUE	CLUSTERED
CLOTHS	CLOUTERS	CLUBBILY	CLUED	CLUSTERS
CLOTPOLL	CLOUTING	CLUBBING	CLUEING	CLUSTERY
CLOTPOLLS	CLOUTS	CLUBBINGS	CLUELESS	CLUTCH
CLOTS	CLOVE	CLUBBISH	CLUES	CLUTCHED
CLOTTED	CLOVEN	CLUBBISM	CLUEY	CLUTCHES
CLOTTER	CLOVER	CLUBBISMS	CLUIER	CLUTCHIER
CLOTTERED	CLOVERED	CLUBBIST	CLUIEST	CLUTCHING
CLOTTERS	CLOVERS	CLUBBISTS	CLUING	CLUTCHY
CLOTTIER	CLOVERY	CLUBBY	CLUMBER	CLUTTER
CLOTTIEST	CLOVES	CLUBFACE	CLUMBERS	CLUTTERED
CLOTTING	CLOVIS	CLUBFACES	CLUMP	CLUTTERS
CLOTTINGS	CLOW	CLUBFEET	CLUMPED	CLUTTERY
CLOTTISH	CLOWDER	CLUBFOOT	CLUMPER	CLY
CLOTTY	CLOWDERS	CLUBHAND	CLUMPERS	CLYING
CLOTURE	CLOWED	CLUBHANDS	CLUMPET	CLYPE
CLOTURED	CLOWING	CLUBHAUL	CLUMPETS	CLYPEAL
CLOTURES	CLOWN	CLUBHAULS	CLUMPIER	CLYPEATE
CLOTURING	CLOWNED	CLUBHEAD	CLUMPIEST	CLYPED
CLOU	CLOWNERY	CLUBHEADS	CLUMPING	CLYPEI
CLOUD	CLOWNFISH	CLUBHOUSE	CLUMPISH	CLYPES
CLOUDAGE	CLOWNING	CLUBLAND	CLUMPLIKE	CLYPEUS
CLOUDAGES	CLOWNINGS	CLUBLANDS	CLUMPS	CLYPING
CLOUDED	CLOWNISH	CLUBMAN	CLUMPY	CLYSTER
CLOUDIER	CLOWNS	CLUBMATE	CLUMSIER	CLYSTERS
CLOUDIEST	CLOWS	CLUBMATES	CLUMSIEST	CNEMIAL
CLOUDILY	CLOY	CLUBMEN	CLUMSILY	CNEMIDES
CLOUDING	CLOYE	CLUBMOSS	CLUMSY	CNEMIS
CLOUDINGS	CLOYED	CLUBROOM	CLUNCH	CNIDA
CLOUDLAND	CLOYES	CLUBROOMS	CLUNCHES	CNIDAE
CLOUDLESS	CLOYING	CLUBROOT	CLUNG	CNIDARIAN
CLOUDLET	CLOYINGLY	CLUBROOTS	CLUNK	COACH
CLOUDLETS	CLOYLESS	CLUBRUSH	CLUNKED	COACHABLE
CLOUDLIKE	CLOYMENT	CLUBS	CLUNKER	COACHDOG
CLOUDS	CLOYMENTS	CLUBWOMAN	CLUNKERS	COACHDOGS
CLOUDTOWN	CLOYS	CLUBWOMEN	CLUNKIER	COACHED
CLOUDY	CLOYSOME	CLUCK	CLUNKIEST	COACHEE
CLOUGH	CLOZAPINE	CLUCKED	CLUNKING	COACHEES
CLOUGHS	CLOZE	CLUCKER	CLUNKS	COACHER

COACHERS	COAL	COALS	COASTS	COBALTIC
COACHES	COALA	COALSACK	COASTWARD	COBALTINE
COACHIER	COALAS	COALSACKS	COASTWISE	COBALTITE
COACHIES	COALBALL	COALSHED	COAT	COBALTOUS
COACHIEST	COALBALLS	COALSHEDS	COATDRESS	COBALTS
COACHING	COALBIN	COALY	COATE	COBB
COACHINGS	COALBINS	COALYARD	COATED	COBBED
COACHLINE	COALBOX	COALYARDS	COATEE	COBBER
COACHLOAD	COALBOXES	COAMING	COATEES	COBBERS
COACHMAN	COALDUST	COAMINGS	COATER	COBBIER
COACHMEN	COALDUSTS	COANCHOR	COATERS	COBBIEST
COACHWHIP	COALED	COANCHORS	COATES	COBBING
COACHWOOD	COALER	COANNEX	COATI	COBBLE
COACHWORK	COALERS	COANNEXED	COATING	COBBLED
COACHY	COALESCE	COANNEXES	COATINGS	COBBLER
COACT	COALESCED	COAPPEAR	COATIS	COBBLERS
COACTED	COALESCES	COAPPEARS	COATLESS	COBBLERY
COACTING	COALFACE	COAPT	COATRACK	COBBLES
COACTION	COALFACES	COAPTED	COATRACKS	COBBLING
COACTIONS	COALFIELD	COAPTING	COATROOM	COBBLINGS
COACTIVE	COALFISH	COAPTS	COATROOMS	COBBS
COACTOR	COALHOLE	COARB	COATS	COBBY
COACTORS	COALHOLES	COARBS	COATSTAND	COBIA
COACTS	COALHOUSE	COARCTATE	COATTAIL	COBIAS
COADAPTED	COALIER	COARSE	COATTAILS	COBLE
COADIES	COALIEST	COARSELY	COATTEND	COBLES
COADJUTOR	COALIFIED	COARSEN	COATTENDS	COBLOAF
COADMIRE	COALIFIES	COARSENED	COATTEST	COBLOAVES
COADMIRED	COALIFY	COARSENS	COATTESTS	COBNUT
COADMIRES	COALING	COARSER	COAUTHOR	COBNUTS
COADMIT	COALISE	COARSEST	COAUTHORS	COBRA
COADMITS	COALISED	COARSISH	COAX	COBRAS
COADUNATE	COALISES	COASSIST	COAXAL	COBRIC
COADY	COALISING	COASSISTS	COAXED	COBRIFORM
COAEVAL	COALITION	COASSUME	COAXER	COBS
COAEVALS	COALIZE	COASSUMED	COAXERS	COBURG
COAGENCY	COALIZED	COASSUMES	COAXES	COBURGS
COAGENT	COALIZES	COAST	COAXIAL	COBWEB
COAGENTS	COALIZING	COASTAL	COAXIALLY	COBWEBBED
COAGULA	COALLESS	COASTALLY	COAXING	COBWEBBY
COAGULANT	COALMAN	COASTED	COAXINGLY	COBWEBS
COAGULASE	COALMEN	COASTER	COAXINGS	COBZA
COAGULATE	COALMINE	COASTERS	COB	COBZAS
COAGULUM	COALMINER	COASTING	COBAEA	COCA
COAGULUMS	COALMINES	COASTINGS	COBAEAS	COCAIN
COAITA	COALPIT	COASTLAND	COBALAMIN	COCAINE
COAITAS	COALPITS	COASTLINE	COBALT	COCAINES

COCAINISE
COCAINISM
COCAINIST
COCAINIZE
COCAINS
COCAPTAIN
COCAS
COCCAL
COCCI
COCCIC
COCCID
COCCIDIA
COCCIDIUM
COCCIDS
COCCO
COCCOID
COCCOIDAL
COCCOIDS
COCCOLITE
COCCOLITH
COCCOS
COCCOUS
COCCUS
COCCYGEAL
COCCYGES
COCCYGIAN
COCCYX
COCCYXES
COCH
COCHAIR
COCHAIRED
COCHAIRS
COCHES
COCHIN
COCHINEAL
COCHINS
COCHLEA
COCHLEAE
COCHLEAR
COCHLEARE
COCHLEARS
COCHLEAS
COCHLEATE
COCINERA
COCINERAS
COCK
COCKADE

COCKADED
COCKADES
COCKAMAMY
COCKAPOO
COCKAPOOS
COCKATEEL
COCKATIEL
COCKATOO
COCKATOOS
COCKBILL
COCKBILLS
COCKBIRD
COCKBIRDS
COCKBOAT
COCKBOATS
COCKCROW
COCKCROWS
COCKED
COCKER
COCKERED
COCKEREL
COCKERELS
COCKERING
COCKERS
COCKET
COCKETS
COCKEYE
COCKEYED
COCKEYES
COCKFIGHT
COCKHORSE
COCKIER
COCKIES
COCKIEST
COCKILY
COCKINESS
COCKING
COCKISH
COCKLE
COCKLEBUR
COCKLED
COCKLEERT
COCKLEMAN
COCKLEMEN
COCKLER
COCKLERS
COCKLES

COCKLIKE
COCKLING
COCKLINGS
COCKLOFT
COCKLOFTS
COCKMATCH
COCKNEY
COCKNEYFY
COCKNEYS
COCKNIFY
COCKPIT
COCKPITS
COCKROACH
COCKS
COCKSCOMB
COCKSFOOT
COCKSHIES
COCKSHOT
COCKSHOTS
COCKSHUT
COCKSHUTS
COCKSHY
COCKSIER
COCKSIEST
COCKSMAN
COCKSMEN
COCKSPUR
COCKSPURS
COCKSURE
COCKSWAIN
COCKSY
COCKTAIL
COCKTAILS
COCKUP
COCKUPS
COCKY
COCO
COCOA
COCOANUT
COCOANUTS
COCOAS
COCOBOLA
COCOBOLAS
COCOBOLO
COCOBOLOS
COCOMAT
COCOMATS

COCONUT
COCONUTS
COCOON
COCOONED
COCOONER
COCOONERS
COCOONERY
COCOONING
COCOONS
COCOPAN
COCOPANS
COCOPLUM
COCOPLUMS
COCOS
COCOTTE
COCOTTES
COCOUNSEL
COCOYAM
COCOYAMS
COCOZELLE
COCREATE
COCREATED
COCREATES
COCREATOR
COCTILE
COCTION
COCTIONS
COCULTURE
COCURATOR
COCUSWOOD
COD
CODA
CODABLE
CODAS
CODDED
CODDER
CODDERS
CODDING
CODDLE
CODDLED
CODDLER
CODDLERS
CODDLES
CODDLING
CODE
CODEBOOK
CODEBOOKS

CODEBTOR
CODEBTORS
CODEC
CODECS
CODED
CODEIA
CODEIAS
CODEIN
CODEINA
CODEINAS
CODEINE
CODEINES
CODEINS
CODELESS
CODEN
CODENAME
CODENAMES
CODENS
CODER
CODERIVE
CODERIVED
CODERIVES
CODERS
CODES
CODESIGN
CODESIGNS
CODETTA
CODETTAS
CODEVELOP
CODEWORD
CODEWORDS
CODEX
CODEXES
CODFISH
CODFISHES
CODGER
CODGERS
CODICES
CODICIL
CODICILS
CODIFIED
CODIFIER
CODIFIERS
CODIFIES
CODIFY
CODIFYING
CODILLA

CODILLAS	COELOMIC	COERCION	COFFRET	COGNATES
CODILLE	COELOMS	COERCIONS	COFFRETS	COGNATION
CODILLES	COELOSTAT	COERCIVE	COFFS	COGNISANT
CODING	COEMBODY	COERECT	COFINANCE	COGNISE
CODINGS	COEMPLOY	COERECTED	COFIRING	COGNISED
CODIRECT	COEMPLOYS	COERECTS	COFIRINGS	COGNISER
CODIRECTS	COEMPT	COESITE	COFOUND	COGNISERS
CODIST	COEMPTED	COESITES	COFOUNDED	COGNISES
CODISTS	COEMPTING	COETERNAL	COFOUNDER	COGNISING
CODLIN	COEMPTION	COEVAL	COFOUNDS	COGNITION
CODLING	COEMPTS	COEVALITY	COFT	COGNITIVE
CODLINGS	COENACLE	COEVALLY	COG	COGNIZANT
CODLINS	COENACLES	COEVALS	COGENCE	COGNIZE
CODOLOGY	COENACT	COEVOLVE	COGENCES	COGNIZED
CODOMAIN	COENACTED	COEVOLVED	COGENCIES	COGNIZER
CODOMAINS	COENACTS	COEVOLVES	COGENCY	COGNIZERS
CODON	COENAMOR	COEXERT	COGENER	COGNIZES
CODONS	COENAMORS	COEXERTED	COGENERS	COGNIZING
CODPIECE	COENAMOUR	COEXERTS	COGENT	COGNOMEN
CODPIECES	COENDURE	COEXIST	COGENTLY	COGNOMENS
CODRIVE	COENDURED	COEXISTED	COGGED	COGNOMINA
CODRIVEN	COENDURES	COEXISTS	COGGER	COGNOSCE
CODRIVER	COENOBIA	COEXTEND	COGGERS	COGNOSCED
CODRIVERS	COENOBITE	COEXTENDS	COGGIE	COGNOSCES
CODRIVES	COENOBIUM	COFACTOR	COGGIES	COGNOVIT
CODRIVING	COENOCYTE	COFACTORS	COGGING	COGNOVITS
CODROVE	COENOSARC	COFEATURE	COGGINGS	COGON
CODS	COENURE	COFF	COGGLE	COGONS
COED	COENURES	COFFED	COGGLED	COGS
COEDIT	COENURI	COFFEE	COGGLES	COGUE
COEDITED	COENURUS	COFFEEPOT	COGGLIER	COGUES
COEDITING	COENZYME	COFFEES	COGGLIEST	COGWAY
COEDITOR	COENZYMES	COFFER	COGGLING	COGWAYS
COEDITORS	COEQUAL	COFFERDAM	COGGLY	COGWHEEL
COEDITS	COEQUALLY	COFFERED	COGIE	COGWHEELS
COEDS	COEQUALS	COFFERING	COGIES	COHAB
COEFFECT	COEQUATE	COFFERS	COGITABLE	COHABIT
COEFFECTS	COEQUATED	COFFIN	COGITATE	COHABITED
COEHORN	COEQUATES	COFFINED	COGITATED	COHABITEE
COEHORNS	COERCE	COFFING	COGITATES	COHABITER
COELIAC	COERCED	COFFINING	COGITATOR	COHABITOR
COELIACS	COERCER	COFFINITE	COGITO	COHABITS
COELOM	COERCERS	COFFINS	COGITOS	COHABS
COELOMATA	COERCES	COFFLE	COGNAC	COHEAD
COELOMATE	COERCIBLE	COFFLED	COGNACS	COHEADED
COELOME	COERCIBLY	COFFLES	COGNATE	COHEADING
COELOMES	COERCING	COFFLING	COGNATELY	COHEADS

COHEIR	COHYPONYM	COINMATES	COL	COLEWORT
COHEIRESS	COIF	COINOP	COLA	COLEWORTS
COHEIRS	COIFED	COINS	COLANDER	COLEY
COHEN	COIFFE	COINSURE	COLANDERS	COLEYS
COHENS	COIFFED	COINSURED	COLAS	COLIBRI
COHERE	COIFFES	COINSURER	COLBIES	COLIBRIS
COHERED	COIFFEUR	COINSURES	COLBY	COLIC
COHERENCE	COIFFEURS	COINTER	COLBYS	COLICIN
COHERENCY	COIFFEUSE	COINTERS	COLCANNON	COLICINE
COHERENT	COIFFING	COINTREAU	COLCHICA	COLICINES
COHERER	COIFFURE	COINVENT	COLCHICUM	COLICINS
COHERERS	COIFFURED	COINVENTS	COLCOTHAR	COLICKIER
COHERES	COIFFURES	COIR	COLD	COLICKY
COHERING	COIFING	COIRS	COLDBLOOD	COLICROOT
COHERITOR	COIFS	COISTREL	COLDCOCK	COLICS
COHESIBLE	COIGN	COISTRELS	COLDCOCKS	COLICWEED
COHESION	COIGNE	COISTRIL	COLDER	COLIES
COHESIONS	COIGNED	COISTRILS	COLDEST	COLIFORM
COHESIVE	COIGNES	COIT	COLDHOUSE	COLIFORMS
COHIBIT	COIGNING	COITAL	COLDIE	COLIN
COHIBITED	COIGNS	COITALLY	COLDIES	COLINEAR
COHIBITS	COIL	COITION	COLDISH	COLINS
COHO	COILED	COITIONAL	COLDLY	COLIPHAGE
COHOBATE	COILER	COITIONS	COLDNESS	COLISEUM
COHOBATED	COILERS	COITS	COLDS	COLISEUMS
COHOBATES	COILING	COITUS	COLE	COLISTIN
COHOE	COILS	COITUSES	COLEAD	COLISTINS
COHOES	COIN	COJOIN	COLEADER	COLITIC
COHOG	COINABLE	COJOINED	COLEADERS	COLITIS
COHOGS	COINAGE	COJOINING	COLEADING	COLITISES
COHOLDER	COINAGES	COJOINS	COLEADS	COLL
COHOLDERS	COINCIDE	COJONES	COLECTOMY	COLLAGE
COHORN	COINCIDED	COKE	COLED	COLLAGED
COHORNS	COINCIDES	COKED	COLEOPTER	COLLAGEN
COHORT	COINED	COKEHEAD	COLES	COLLAGENS
COHORTS	COINER	COKEHEADS	COLESEED	COLLAGES
COHOS	COINERS	COKELIKE	COLESEEDS	COLLAGING
COHOSH	COINFECT	COKERNUT	COLESLAW	COLLAGIST
COHOSHES	COINFECTS	COKERNUTS	COLESLAWS	COLLAPSAR
COHOST	COINFER	COKES	COLESSEE	COLLAPSE
COHOSTED	COINFERS	COKESES	COLESSEES	COLLAPSED
COHOSTESS	COINHERE	COKIER	COLESSOR	COLLAPSES
COHOSTING	COINHERED	COKIEST	COLESSORS	COLLAR
COHOSTS	COINHERES	COKING	COLETIT	COLLARD
COHOUSING	COINING	COKINGS	COLETITS	COLLARDS
COHUNE	COININGS	COKULORIS	COLEUS	COLLARED
COHUNES	COINMATE	COKY	COLEUSES	COLLARET

COLLARETS	COLLING	COLOCATE	COLORCAST	COLOURISE
COLLARING	COLLINGS	COLOCATED	COLORED	COLOURISM
COLLARS	COLLINS	COLOCATES	COLOREDS	COLOURIST
COLLATE	COLLINSES	COLOCYNTH	COLORER	COLOURIZE
COLLATED	COLLINSIA	COLOG	COLORERS	COLOURMAN
COLLATES	COLLISION	COLOGNE	COLORFAST	COLOURMEN
COLLATING	COLLOCATE	COLOGNED	COLORFUL	COLOURS
COLLATION	COLLODION	COLOGNES	COLORIFIC	COLOURWAY
COLLATIVE	COLLODIUM	COLOGS	COLORING	COLOURY
COLLATOR	COLLOGUE	COLOMBARD	COLORINGS	COLPITIS
COLLATORS	COLLOGUED	COLON	COLORISE	COLPOTOMY
COLLEAGUE	COLLOGUES	COLONE	COLORISED	COLS
COLLECT	COLLOID	COLONEL	COLORISER	COLT
COLLECTED	COLLOIDAL	COLONELCY	COLORISES	COLTAN
COLLECTOR	COLLOIDS	COLONELS	COLORISM	COLTANS
COLLECTS	COLLOP	COLONES	COLORISMS	COLTED
COLLED	COLLOPS	COLONI	COLORIST	COLTER
COLLEEN	COLLOQUE	COLONIAL	COLORISTS	COLTERS
COLLEENS	COLLOQUED	COLONIALS	COLORIZE	COLTHOOD
COLLEGE	COLLOQUES	COLONIC	COLORIZED	COLTHOODS
COLLEGER	COLLOQUIA	COLONICS	COLORIZER	COLTING
COLLEGERS	COLLOQUY	COLONIES	COLORIZES	COLTISH
COLLEGES	COLLOTYPE	COLONISE	COLORLESS	COLTISHLY
COLLEGIA	COLLOTYPY	COLONISED	COLORMAN	COLTS
COLLEGIAL	COLLS	COLONISER	COLORMEN	COLTSFOOT
COLLEGIAN	COLLUDE	COLONISES	COLORS	COLTWOOD
COLLEGIUM	COLLUDED	COLONIST	COLORWASH	COLTWOODS
COLLET	COLLUDER	COLONISTS	COLORWAY	COLUBRIAD
COLLETED	COLLUDERS	COLONITIS	COLORWAYS	COLUBRID
COLLETING	COLLUDES	COLONIZE	COLORY	COLUBRIDS
COLLETS	COLLUDING	COLONIZED	COLOSSAL	COLUBRINE
COLLICULI	COLLUSION	COLONIZER	COLOSSEUM	COLUGO
COLLIDE	COLLUSIVE	COLONIZES	COLOSSI	COLUGOS
COLLIDED	COLLUVIA	COLONNADE	COLOSSUS	COLUMBARY
COLLIDER	COLLUVIAL	COLONS	COLOSTOMY	COLUMBATE
COLLIDERS	COLLUVIES	COLONUS	COLOSTRAL	COLUMBIC
COLLIDES	COLLUVIUM	COLONY	COLOSTRIC	COLUMBINE
COLLIDING	COLLY	COLOPHON	COLOSTRUM	COLUMBITE
COLLIE	COLLYING	COLOPHONS	COLOTOMY	COLUMBIUM
COLLIED	COLLYRIA	COLOPHONY	COLOUR	COLUMBOUS
COLLIER	COLLYRIUM	COLOR	COLOURANT	COLUMEL
COLLIERS	COLOBI	COLORABLE	COLOURED	COLUMELLA
COLLIERY	COLOBID	COLORABLY	COLOUREDS	COLUMELS
COLLIES	COLOBOMA	COLORADO	COLOURER	COLUMN
COLLIGATE	COLOBOMAS	COLORANT	COLOURERS	COLUMNAL
COLLIMATE	COLOBUS	COLORANTS	COLOURFUL	COLUMNAR
COLLINEAR	COLOBUSES	COLORBRED	COLOURING	COLUMNEA

COLUMNEAS	COMBED	COMEDO	COMINGLES	COMMERS
COLUMNED	COMBER	COMEDONES	COMINGS	COMMIE
COLUMNIST	COMBERS	COMEDOS	COMIQUE	COMMIES
COLUMNS	COMBES	COMEDOWN	COMIQUES	COMMINATE
COLURE	COMBI	COMEDOWNS	COMITADJI	COMMINGLE
COLURES	COMBIER	COMEDY	COMITAL	COMMINUTE
COLY	COMBIES	COMELIER	COMITATUS	COMMIS
COLZA	COMBIEST	COMELIEST	COMITIA	COMMISH
COLZAS	COMBINATE	COMELILY	COMITIAL	COMMISHES
COMA	COMBINE	COMELY	COMITIAS	COMMISSAR
COMADE	COMBINED	COMEMBER	COMITIES	COMMIT
COMAE	COMBINEDS	COMEMBERS	COMITY	COMMITS
COMAKE	COMBINER	COMEOVER	COMIX	COMMITTAL
COMAKER	COMBINERS	COMEOVERS	COMM	COMMITTED
COMAKERS	COMBINES	COMER	COMMA	COMMITTEE
COMAKES	COMBING	COMERS	COMMAND	COMMITTER
COMAKING	COMBINGS	COMES	COMMANDED	COMMIX
COMAL	COMBINING	COMET	COMMANDER	COMMIXED
COMANAGE	COMBIS	COMETARY	COMMANDO	COMMIXES
COMANAGED	COMBLE	COMETH	COMMANDOS	COMMIXING
COMANAGER	COMBLES	COMETHER	COMMANDS	COMMIXT
COMANAGES	COMBLESS	COMETHERS	COMMAS	COMMO
COMARB	COMBLIKE	COMETIC	COMMATA	COMMODE
COMARBS	COMBO	COMETS	COMMENCE	COMMODES
COMART	COMBOS	COMFIER	COMMENCED	COMMODIFY
COMARTS	COMBOVER	COMFIEST	COMMENCER	COMMODITY
COMAS	COMBOVERS	COMFILY	COMMENCES	COMMODO
COMATE	COMBRETUM	COMFINESS	COMMEND	COMMODORE
COMATES	COMBS	COMFIT	COMMENDAM	COMMON
COMATIC	COMBUST	COMFITS	COMMENDED	COMMONAGE
COMATIK	COMBUSTED	COMFITURE	COMMENDER	COMMONED
COMATIKS	COMBUSTOR	COMFORT	COMMENDS	COMMONER
COMATOSE	COMBUSTS	COMFORTED	COMMENSAL	COMMONERS
COMATULA	COMBWISE	COMFORTER	COMMENT	COMMONEST
COMATULAE	COMBY	COMFORTS	COMMENTED	COMMONEY
COMATULID	COME	COMFREY	COMMENTER	COMMONEYS
COMB	COMEBACK	COMFREYS	COMMENTOR	COMMONING
COMBAT	COMEBACKS	COMFY	COMMENTS	COMMONLY
COMBATANT	COMEDDLE	COMIC	COMMER	COMMONS
COMBATED	COMEDDLED	COMICAL	COMMERCE	COMMORANT
COMBATER	COMEDDLES	COMICALLY	COMMERCED	COMMOS
COMBATERS	COMEDIAN	COMICE	COMMERCES	COMMOT
COMBATING	COMEDIANS	COMICES	COMMERE	COMMOTE
COMBATIVE	COMEDIC	COMICS	COMMERES	COMMOTES
COMBATS	COMEDIES	COMING	COMMERGE	COMMOTION
COMBATTED	COMEDIST	COMINGLE	COMMERGED	COMMOTS
COMBE	COMEDISTS	COMINGLED	COMMERGES	COMMOVE

COMMOVED	COMPANDS	COMPETING	COMPONENT	COMPULSED
COMMOVES	COMPANIED	COMPILE	COMPONY	COMPULSES
COMMOVING	COMPANIES	COMPILED	COMPORT	COMPUTANT
COMMS	COMPANING	COMPILER	COMPORTED	COMPUTE
COMMUNAL	COMPANION	COMPILERS	COMPORTS	COMPUTED
COMMUNARD	COMPANY	COMPILES	COMPOS	COMPUTER
COMMUNE	COMPARE	COMPILING	COMPOSE	COMPUTERS
COMMUNED	COMPARED	COMPING	COMPOSED	COMPUTES
COMMUNER	COMPARER	COMPINGS	COMPOSER	COMPUTING
COMMUNERS	COMPARERS	COMPITAL	COMPOSERS	COMPUTIST
COMMUNES	COMPARES	COMPLAIN	COMPOSES	COMRADE
COMMUNING	COMPARING	COMPLAINS	COMPOSING	COMRADELY
COMMUNION	COMPART	COMPLAINT	COMPOSITE	COMRADERY
COMMUNISE	COMPARTED	COMPLEAT	COMPOST	COMRADES
COMMUNISM	COMPARTS	COMPLEATS	COMPOSTED	COMS
COMMUNIST	COMPAS	COMPLECT	COMPOSTER	COMSAT
COMMUNITY	COMPASS	COMPLECTS	COMPOSTS	COMSATS
COMMUNIZE	COMPASSED	COMPLETE	COMPOSURE	COMSYMP
COMMUTATE	COMPASSES	COMPLETED	COMPOT	COMSYMPS
COMMUTE	COMPAST	COMPLETER	COMPOTE	COMTE
COMMUTED	COMPEAR	COMPLETES	COMPOTES	COMTES
COMMUTER	COMPEARED	COMPLEX	COMPOTIER	COMUS
COMMUTERS	COMPEARS	COMPLEXED	COMPOTS	COMUSES
COMMUTES	COMPED	COMPLEXER	COMPOUND	CON
COMMUTING	COMPEER	COMPLEXES	COMPOUNDS	CONACRE
COMMUTUAL	COMPEERED	COMPLEXLY	COMPRADOR	CONACRED
COMMY	COMPEERS	COMPLEXUS	COMPRESS	CONACRES
COMODO	COMPEL	COMPLIANT	COMPRINT	CONACRING
COMONOMER	COMPELLED	COMPLICE	COMPRINTS	CONARIA
COMORBID	COMPELLER	COMPLICES	COMPRISAL	CONARIAL
COMOSE	COMPELS	COMPLICIT	COMPRISE	CONARIUM
COMOUS	COMPEND	COMPLIED	COMPRISED	CONATION
COMP	COMPENDIA	COMPLIER	COMPRISES	CONATIONS
COMPACT	COMPENDS	COMPLIERS	COMPRIZE	CONATIVE
COMPACTED	COMPER	COMPLIES	COMPRIZED	CONATUS
COMPACTER	COMPERE	COMPLIN	COMPRIZES	CONCAUSE
COMPACTLY	COMPERED	COMPLINE	COMPS	CONCAUSES
COMPACTOR	COMPERES	COMPLINES	COMPT	CONCAVE
COMPACTS	COMPERING	COMPLINS	COMPTABLE	CONCAVED
COMPADRE	COMPERS	COMPLISH	COMPTED	CONCAVELY
COMPADRES	COMPESCE	COMPLOT	COMPTER	CONCAVES
COMPAGE	COMPESCED	COMPLOTS	COMPTERS	CONCAVING
COMPAGES	COMPESCES	COMPLUVIA	COMPTIBLE	CONCAVITY
COMPAND	COMPETE	COMPLY	COMPTING	CONCEAL
COMPANDED	COMPETED	COMPLYING	COMPTROLL	CONCEALED
COMPANDER	COMPETENT	COMPO	COMPTS	CONCEALER
COMPANDOR	COMPETES	COMPONE	COMPULSE	CONCEALS

CONCEDE	CONCHITIS	CONCURRED	CONDUCED	CONFERVA
CONCEDED	CONCHO	CONCURS	CONDUCER	CONFERVAE
CONCEDER	CONCHOID	CONCUSS	CONDUCERS	CONFERVAL
CONCEDERS	CONCHOIDS	CONCUSSED	CONDUCES	CONFERVAS
CONCEDES	CONCHOS	CONCUSSES	CONDUCING	CONFESS
CONCEDING	CONCHS	CONCYCLIC	CONDUCIVE	CONFESSED
CONCEDO	CONCHY	COND	CONDUCT	CONFESSES
CONCEIT	CONCIERGE	CONDEMN	CONDUCTED	CONFESSOR
CONCEITED	CONCILIAR	CONDEMNED	CONDUCTI	CONFEST
CONCEITS	CONCISE	CONDEMNER	CONDUCTOR	CONFESTLY
CONCEITY	CONCISED	CONDEMNOR	CONDUCTS	CONFETTI
CONCEIVE	CONCISELY	CONDEMNS	CONDUCTUS	CONFETTO
CONCEIVED	CONCISER	CONDENSE	CONDUIT	CONFIDANT
CONCEIVER	CONCISES	CONDENSED	CONDUITS	CONFIDE
CONCEIVES	CONCISEST	CONDENSER	CONDYLAR	CONFIDED
CONCENT	CONCISING	CONDENSES	CONDYLE	CONFIDENT
CONCENTER	CONCISION	CONDER	CONDYLES	CONFIDER
CONCENTRE	CONCLAVE	CONDERS	CONDYLOID	CONFIDERS
CONCENTS	CONCLAVES	CONDIDDLE	CONDYLOMA	CONFIDES
CONCENTUS	CONCLUDE	CONDIE	CONE	CONFIDING
CONCEPT	CONCLUDED	CONDIES	CONED	CONFIGURE
CONCEPTI	CONCLUDER	CONDIGN	CONELRAD	CONFINE
CONCEPTS	CONCLUDES	CONDIGNLY	CONELRADS	CONFINED
CONCEPTUS	CONCOCT	CONDIMENT	CONENOSE	CONFINER
CONCERN	CONCOCTED	CONDITION	CONENOSES	CONFINERS
CONCERNED	CONCOCTER	CONDO	CONEPATE	CONFINES
CONCERNS	CONCOCTOR	CONDOES	CONEPATES	CONFINING
CONCERT	CONCOCTS	CONDOLE	CONEPATL	CONFIRM
CONCERTED	CONCOLOR	CONDOLED	CONEPATLS	CONFIRMED
CONCERTI	CONCORD	CONDOLENT	CONES	CONFIRMEE
CONCERTO	CONCORDAL	CONDOLER	CONEY	CONFIRMER
CONCERTOS	CONCORDAT	CONDOLERS	CONEYS	CONFIRMOR
CONCERTS	CONCORDED	CONDOLES	CONF	CONFIRMS
CONCETTI	CONCORDS	CONDOLING	CONFAB	CONFISEUR
CONCETTO	CONCOURS	CONDOM	CONFABBED	CONFIT
CONCH	CONCOURSE	CONDOMS	CONFABS	CONFITEOR
CONCHA	CONCREATE	CONDONE	CONFECT	CONFITS
CONCHAE	CONCRETE	CONDONED	CONFECTED	CONFITURE
CONCHAL	CONCRETED	CONDONER	CONFECTS	CONFIX
CONCHAS	CONCRETES	CONDONERS	CONFER	CONFIXED
CONCHATE	CONCREW	CONDONES	CONFEREE	CONFIXES
CONCHE	CONCREWED	CONDONING	CONFEREES	CONFIXING
CONCHED	CONCREWS	CONDOR	CONFERRAL	CONFLATE
CONCHES	CONCUBINE	CONDORES	CONFERRED	CONFLATED
CONCHIE	CONCUPIES	CONDORS	CONFERREE	CONFLATES
CONCHIES	CONCUPY	CONDOS	CONFERRER	CONFLICT
CONCHING	CONCUR	CONDUCE	CONFERS	CONFLICTS

CONFLUENT	CONGENIC	CONIES	CONK	CONNOTES
CONFLUX	CONGER	CONIFER	CONKED	CONNOTING
CONFLUXES	CONGERIES	CONIFERS	CONKER	CONNOTIVE
CONFOCAL	CONGERS	CONIFORM	CONKERS	CONNS
CONFORM	CONGES	CONIINE	CONKIER	CONNUBIAL
CONFORMAL	CONGEST	CONIINES	CONKIEST	CONODONT
CONFORMED	CONGESTED	CONIMA	CONKING	CONODONTS
CONFORMER	CONGESTS	CONIMAS	CONKOUT	CONOID
CONFORMS	CONGIARY	CONIN	CONKOUTS	CONOIDAL
CONFOUND	CONGII	CONINE	CONKS	CONOIDIC
CONFOUNDS	CONGIUS	CONINES	CONKY	CONOIDS
CONFRERE	CONGLOBE	CONING	CONMAN	CONOMINEE
CONFRERES	CONGLOBED	CONINS	CONMEN	CONQUER
CONFRERIE	CONGLOBES	CONIOLOGY	CONN	CONQUERED
CONFRONT	CONGO	CONIOSES	CONNATE	CONQUERER
CONFRONTE	CONGOES	CONIOSIS	CONNATELY	CONQUEROR
CONFRONTS	CONGOS	CONIUM	CONNATION	CONQUERS
CONFS	CONGOU	CONIUMS	CONNATURE	CONQUEST
CONFUSE	CONGOUS	CONJECT	CONNE	CONQUESTS
CONFUSED	CONGRATS	CONJECTED	CONNECT	CONQUIAN
CONFUSES	CONGREE	CONJECTS	CONNECTED	CONQUIANS
CONFUSING	CONGREED	CONJEE	CONNECTER	CONS
CONFUSION	CONGREES	CONJEED	CONNECTOR	CONSCIENT
CONFUTE	CONGREET	CONJEEING	CONNECTS	CONSCIOUS
CONFUTED	CONGREETS	CONJEES	CONNED	CONSCRIBE
CONFUTER	CONGRESS	CONJOIN	CONNER	CONSCRIPT
CONFUTERS	CONGRUE	CONJOINED	CONNERS	CONSEIL
CONFUTES	CONGRUED	CONJOINER	CONNES	CONSEILS
CONFUTING	CONGRUENT	CONJOINS	CONNEXION	CONSENSUS
CONGA	CONGRUES	CONJOINT	CONNEXIVE	CONSENT
CONGAED	CONGRUING	CONJUGAL	CONNIE	CONSENTED
CONGAING	CONGRUITY	CONJUGANT	CONNIES	CONSENTER
CONGAS	CONGRUOUS	CONJUGATE	CONNING	CONSENTS
CONGE	CONI	CONJUNCT	CONNINGS	CONSERVE
CONGEAL	CONIA	CONJUNCTS	CONNIVE	CONSERVED
CONGEALED	CONIAS	CONJUNTO	CONNIVED	CONSERVER
CONGEALER	CONIC	CONJUNTOS	CONNIVENT	CONSERVES
CONGEALS	CONICAL	CONJURE	CONNIVER	CONSIDER
CONGED	CONICALLY	CONJURED	CONNIVERS	CONSIDERS
CONGEE	CONICINE	CONJURER	CONNIVERY	CONSIGN
CONGEED	CONICINES	CONJURERS	CONNIVES	CONSIGNED
CONGEEING	CONICITY	CONJURES	CONNIVING	CONSIGNEE
CONGEES	CONICS	CONJURIES	CONNOR	CONSIGNER
CONGEING	CONIDIA	CONJURING	CONNORS	CONSIGNOR
CONGENER	CONIDIAL	CONJUROR	CONNOTATE	CONSIGNS
CONGENERS	CONIDIAN	CONJURORS	CONNOTE	CONSIST
CONGENIAL	CONIDIUM	CONJURY	CONNOTED	CONSISTED

CONSISTS	CONSUL	CONTEMNS	CONTRACT	CONVECTOR
CONSOCIES	CONSULAGE	CONTEMPER	CONTRACTS	CONVECTS
CONSOL	CONSULAR	CONTEMPO	CONTRAIL	CONVENE
CONSOLATE	CONSULARS	CONTEMPT	CONTRAILS	CONVENED
CONSOLE	CONSULATE	CONTEMPTS	CONTRAIR	CONVENER
CONSOLED	CONSULS	CONTEND	CONTRALTI	CONVENERS
CONSOLER	CONSULT	CONTENDED	CONTRALTO	CONVENES
CONSOLERS	CONSULTA	CONTENDER	CONTRARY	CONVENING
CONSOLES	CONSULTAS	CONTENDS	CONTRAS	CONVENOR
CONSOLING	CONSULTED	CONTENT	CONTRAST	CONVENORS
CONSOLS	CONSULTEE	CONTENTED	CONTRASTS	CONVENT
CONSOLUTE	CONSULTER	CONTENTLY	CONTRASTY	CONVENTED
CONSOMME	CONSULTOR	CONTENTS	CONTRAT	CONVENTS
CONSOMMES	CONSULTS	CONTES	CONTRATE	CONVERGE
CONSONANT	CONSUME	CONTESSA	CONTRATS	CONVERGED
CONSONOUS	CONSUMED	CONTESSAS	CONTRIST	CONVERGES
CONSORT	CONSUMER	CONTEST	CONTRISTS	CONVERSE
CONSORTED	CONSUMERS	CONTESTED	CONTRITE	CONVERSED
CONSORTER	CONSUMES	CONTESTER	CONTRIVE	CONVERSER
CONSORTIA	CONSUMING	CONTESTS	CONTRIVED	CONVERSES
CONSORTS	CONSUMPT	CONTEXT	CONTRIVER	CONVERSO
CONSPIRE	CONSUMPTS	CONTEXTS	CONTRIVES	CONVERSOS
CONSPIRED	CONTACT	CONTICENT	CONTROL	CONVERT
CONSPIRER	CONTACTED	CONTINENT	CONTROLE	CONVERTED
CONSPIRES	CONTACTEE	CONTINUA	CONTROLS	CONVERTER
CONSPUE	CONTACTOR	CONTINUAL	CONTROUL	CONVERTOR
CONSPUED	CONTACTS	CONTINUE	CONTROULS	CONVERTS
CONSPUES	CONTADINA	CONTINUED	CONTUMACY	CONVEX
CONSPUING	CONTADINE	CONTINUER	CONTUMELY	CONVEXED
CONSTABLE	CONTADINI	CONTINUES	CONTUND	CONVEXES
CONSTANCY	CONTADINO	CONTINUO	CONTUNDED	CONVEXING
CONSTANT	CONTAGIA	CONTINUOS	CONTUNDS	CONVEXITY
CONSTANTS	CONTAGION	CONTINUUM	CONTUSE	CONVEXLY
CONSTATE	CONTAGIUM	CONTLINE	CONTUSED	CONVEY
CONSTATED	CONTAIN	CONTLINES	CONTUSES	CONVEYAL
CONSTATES	CONTAINED	CONTO	CONTUSING	CONVEYALS
CONSTER	CONTAINER	CONTORNI	CONTUSION	CONVEYED
CONSTERED	CONTAINS	CONTORNO	CONTUSIVE	CONVEYER
CONSTERS	CONTANGO	CONTORNOS	CONUNDRUM	CONVEYERS
CONSTRAIN	CONTANGOS	CONTORT	CONURBAN	CONVEYING
CONSTRICT	CONTE	CONTORTED	CONURBIA	CONVEYOR
CONSTRUAL	CONTECK	CONTORTS	CONURBIAS	CONVEYORS
CONSTRUCT	CONTECKS	CONTOS	CONURE	CONVEYS
CONSTRUE	CONTEMN	CONTOUR	CONURES	CONVICT
CONSTRUED	CONTEMNED	CONTOURED	CONUS	CONVICTED
CONSTRUER	CONTEMNER	CONTOURS	CONVECT	CONVICTS
CONSTRUES	CONTEMNOR	CONTRA	CONVECTED	CONVINCE

CONVINCED	COOFS	COOLDOWN	COONTIE	COOTIKIN
CONVINCER	COOING	COOLDOWNS	COONTIES	COOTIKINS
CONVINCES	COOINGLY	COOLED	COONTY	COOTS
CONVIVE	COOINGS	COOLER	COOP	COOZE
CONVIVED	COOK	COOLERS	COOPED	COOZES
CONVIVES	COOKABLE	COOLEST	COOPER	COP
CONVIVIAL	COOKABLES	COOLHOUSE	COOPERAGE	COPACETIC
CONVIVING	COOKBOOK	COOLIBAH	COOPERATE	COPAIBA
CONVO	COOKBOOKS	COOLIBAHS	COOPERED	COPAIBAS
CONVOCATE	COOKED	COOLIBAR	COOPERIES	COPAIVA
CONVOKE	COOKER	COOLIBARS	COOPERING	COPAIVAS
CONVOKED	COOKERIES	COOLIE	COOPERS	COPAL
CONVOKER	COOKERS	COOLIES	COOPERY	COPALM
CONVOKERS	COOKERY	COOLING	COOPING	COPALMS
CONVOKES	COOKEY	COOLINGLY	COOPS	COPALS
CONVOKING	COOKEYS	COOLINGS	COOPT	COPARCENY
CONVOLUTE	COOKHOUSE	COOLISH	COOPTED	COPARENT
CONVOLVE	COOKIE	COOLIST	COOPTING	COPARENTS
CONVOLVED	COOKIES	COOLISTS	COOPTION	COPARTNER
CONVOLVES	COOKING	COOLLY	COOPTIONS	COPASETIC
CONVOS	COOKINGS	COOLNESS	COOPTS	COPASTOR
CONVOY	COOKLESS	COOLS	COORDINAL	COPASTORS
CONVOYED	COOKMAID	COOLTH	COORIE	COPATAINE
CONVOYING	COOKMAIDS	COOLTHS	COORIED	COPATRIOT
CONVOYS	COOKOFF	COOLY	COORIEING	COPATRON
CONVULSE	COOKOFFS	COOM	COORIES	COPATRONS
CONVULSED	COOKOUT	COOMB	COOS	COPAY
CONVULSES	COOKOUTS	COOMBE	COOSEN	COPAYMENT
CONWOMAN	COOKROOM	COOMBES	COOSENED	COPAYS
CONWOMEN	COOKROOMS	COOMBS	COOSENING	COPE
CONY	COOKS	COOMED	COOSENS	COPECK
COO	COOKSHACK	COOMIER	COOSER	COPECKS
COOCH	COOKSHOP	COOMIEST	COOSERS	COPED
COOCHES	COOKSHOPS	COOMING	COOSIN	COPEMATE
COOCOO	COOKSTOVE	COOMS	COOSINED	COPEMATES
COOED	COOKTOP	COOMY	COOSINING	COPEN
COOEE	COOKTOPS	COON	COOSINS	COPENS
COOEED	COOKWARE	COONCAN	COOST	COPEPOD
COOEEING	COOKWARES	COONCANS	COOT	COPEPODS
COOEES	COOKY	COONDOG	COOTCH	COPER
COOER	COOL	COONDOGS	COOTCHED	COPERED
COOERS	COOLABAH	COONHOUND	COOTCHES	COPERING
COOEY	COOLABAHS	COONS	COOTCHING	COPERS
COOEYED	COOLAMON	COONSHIT	COOTER	COPES
COOEYING	COOLAMONS	COONSHITS	COOTERS	COPESETIC
COOEYS	COOLANT	COONSKIN	COOTIE	COPESTONE
COOF	COOLANTS	COONSKINS	COOTIES	COPIABLE

COPIED	COPRAEMIC	COPYCATS	CORALLINE	CORDERS
COPIER	COPRAH	COPYDESK	CORALLITE	CORDGRASS
COPIERS	COPRAHS	COPYDESKS	CORALLOID	CORDIAL
COPIES	COPRAS	COPYEDIT	CORALLUM	CORDIALLY
COPIHUE	COPREMIA	COPYEDITS	CORALROOT	CORDIALS
COPIHUES	COPREMIAS	COPYFIGHT	CORALS	CORDIFORM
COPILOT	COPREMIC	COPYGIRL	CORALWORT	CORDINER
COPILOTED	COPRESENT	COPYGIRLS	CORAM	CORDINERS
COPILOTS	COPRINCE	COPYGRAPH	CORAMINE	CORDING
COPING	COPRINCES	COPYHOLD	CORAMINES	CORDINGS
COPINGS	COPRODUCE	COPYHOLDS	CORANACH	CORDITE
COPIOUS	COPRODUCT	COPYING	CORANACHS	CORDITES
COPIOUSLY	COPROLITE	COPYINGS	CORANTO	CORDLESS
COPITA	COPROLITH	COPYISM	CORANTOES	CORDLIKE
COPITAS	COPROLOGY	COPYISMS	CORANTOS	CORDOBA
COPLANAR	COPROSMA	COPYIST	CORBAN	CORDOBAS
COPLOT	COPROSMAS	COPYISTS	CORBANS	CORDON
COPLOTS	COPROZOIC	COPYLEFT	CORBE	CORDONED
COPLOTTED	COPS	COPYLEFTS	CORBEAU	CORDONING
COPOLYMER	COPSE	COPYREAD	CORBEAUS	CORDONNET
COPOUT	COPSED	COPYREADS	CORBEIL	CORDONS
COPOUTS	COPSES	COPYRIGHT	CORBEILLE	CORDOTOMY
COPPED	COPSEWOOD	COPYTAKER	CORBEILS	CORDOVAN
COPPER	COPSHOP	COQUET	CORBEL	CORDOVANS
COPPERAH	COPSHOPS	COQUETRY	CORBELED	CORDS
COPPERAHS	COPSIER	COQUETS	CORBELING	CORDUROY
COPPERAS	COPSIEST	COQUETTE	CORBELLED	CORDUROYS
COPPERED	COPSING	COQUETTED	CORBELS	CORDWAIN
COPPERING	COPSY	COQUETTES	CORBES	CORDWAINS
COPPERISH	COPTER	COQUI	CORBICULA	CORDWOOD
COPPERS	COPTERS	COQUILLA	CORBIE	CORDWOODS
COPPERY	COPUBLISH	COQUILLAS	CORBIES	CORDYLINE
COPPICE	COPULA	COQUILLE	CORBINA	CORE
COPPICED	COPULAE	COQUILLES	CORBINAS	CORED
COPPICES	COPULAR	COQUINA	CORBY	COREDEEM
COPPICING	COPULAS	COQUINAS	CORCASS	COREDEEMS
COPPIES	COPULATE	COQUIS	CORCASSES	COREGENT
COPPIN	COPULATED	COQUITO	CORD	COREGENTS
COPPING	COPULATES	COQUITOS	CORDAGE	COREIGN
COPPINS	COPURIFY	COR	CORDAGES	COREIGNS
COPPLE	COPY	CORACLE	CORDATE	CORELATE
COPPLES	COPYABLE	CORACLES	CORDATELY	CORELATED
COPPRA	COPYBOOK	CORACOID	CORDED	CORELATES
COPPRAS	COPYBOOKS	CORACOIDS	CORDELLE	CORELESS
COPPY	COPYBOY	CORAGGIO	CORDELLED	CORELLA
COPRA	COPYBOYS	CORAL	CORDELLES	CORELLAS
COPRAEMIA	COPYCAT	CORALLA	CORDER	COREMIA

COREMIUM	CORM	CORNERMEN	CORNLOFTS	COROLLINE
COREOPSIS	CORMEL	CORNERS	CORNMEAL	CORONA
CORER	CORMELS	CORNET	CORNMEALS	CORONACH
CORERS	CORMIDIA	CORNETCY	CORNMILL	CORONACHS
CORES	CORMIDIUM	CORNETIST	CORNMILLS	CORONAE
COREY	CORMLET	CORNETS	CORNMOTH	CORONAL
COREYS	CORMLETS	CORNETT	CORNMOTHS	CORONALLY
CORF	CORMLIKE	CORNETTI	CORNO	CORONALS
CORFHOUSE	CORMOID	CORNETTO	CORNOPEAN	CORONARY
CORGI	CORMORANT	CORNETTOS	CORNPIPE	CORONAS
CORGIS	CORMOUS	CORNETTS	CORNPIPES	CORONATE
CORIA	CORMS	CORNFED	CORNPONE	CORONATED
CORIANDER	CORMUS	CORNFIELD	CORNPONES	CORONATES
CORIES	CORMUSES	CORNFLAG	CORNRENT	CORONEL
CORING	CORN	CORNFLAGS	CORNRENTS	CORONELS
CORIOUS	CORNACRE	CORNFLAKE	CORNROW	CORONER
CORIUM	CORNACRES	CORNFLIES	CORNROWED	CORONERS
CORIUMS	CORNAGE	CORNFLOUR	CORNROWS	CORONET
CORIVAL	CORNAGES	CORNFLY	CORNS	CORONETED
CORIVALRY	CORNBALL	CORNHUSK	CORNSILK	CORONETS
CORIVALS	CORNBALLS	CORNHUSKS	CORNSILKS	CORONIAL
CORIXID	CORNBORER	CORNI	CORNSTALK	CORONIS
CORIXIDS	CORNBRAID	CORNICE	CORNSTONE	CORONISES
CORK	CORNBRASH	CORNICED	CORNU	CORONIUM
CORKAGE	CORNBREAD	CORNICES	CORNUA	CORONIUMS
CORKAGES	CORNCAKE	CORNICHE	CORNUAL	CORONOID
CORKBOARD	CORNCAKES	CORNICHES	CORNUS	COROTATE
CORKBORER	CORNCOB	CORNICHON	CORNUSES	COROTATED
CORKED	CORNCOBS	CORNICING	CORNUTE	COROTATES
CORKER	CORNCRAKE	CORNICLE	CORNUTED	COROZO
CORKERS	CORNCRIB	CORNICLES	CORNUTES	COROZOS
CORKIER	CORNCRIBS	CORNICULA	CORNUTING	CORPORA
CORKIEST	CORNEA	CORNIER	CORNUTO	CORPORAL
CORKINESS	CORNEAE	CORNIEST	CORNUTOS	CORPORALE
CORKING	CORNEAL	CORNIFIC	CORNWORM	CORPORALS
CORKIR	CORNEAS	CORNIFIED	CORNWORMS	CORPORAS
CORKIRS	CORNED	CORNIFIES	CORNY	CORPORATE
CORKLIKE	CORNEITIS	CORNIFORM	COROCORE	CORPOREAL
CORKS	CORNEL	CORNIFY	COROCORES	CORPORIFY
CORKSCREW	CORNELIAN	CORNILY	COROCORO	CORPOSANT
CORKTREE	CORNELS	CORNINESS	COROCOROS	CORPS
CORKTREES	CORNEMUSE	CORNING	CORODIES	CORPSE
CORKWING	CORNEOUS	CORNIST	CORODY	CORPSED
CORKWINGS	CORNER	CORNISTS	COROLLA	CORPSES
CORKWOOD	CORNERED	CORNLAND	COROLLARY	CORPSING
CORKWOODS	CORNERING	CORNLANDS	COROLLAS	CORPSMAN
CORKY	CORNERMAN	CORNLOFT	COROLLATE	CORPSMEN

CORPULENT	CORRUPTED	CORTINA	CORYZAL	COSINESS
CORPUS	CORRUPTER	CORTINAS	CORYZAS	COSING
CORPUSCLE	CORRUPTLY	CORTINS	COS	COSMEA
CORPUSES	CORRUPTOR	CORTISOL	COSCRIPT	COSMEAS
CORRADE	CORRUPTS	CORTISOLS	COSCRIPTS	COSMESES
CORRADED	CORS	CORTISONE	COSE	COSMESIS
CORRADES	CORSAC	CORULER	COSEC	COSMETIC
CORRADING	CORSACS	CORULERS	COSECANT	COSMETICS
CORRAL	CORSAGE	CORUNDUM	COSECANTS	COSMIC
CORRALLED	CORSAGES	CORUNDUMS	COSECH	COSMICAL
CORRALS	CORSAIR	CORUSCANT	COSECHS	COSMID
CORRASION	CORSAIRS	CORUSCATE	COSECS	COSMIDS
CORRASIVE	CORSE	CORVEE	COSED	COSMIN
CORREA	CORSELET	CORVEES	COSEISMAL	COSMINE
CORREAS	CORSELETS	CORVES	COSEISMIC	COSMINES
CORRECT	CORSES	CORVET	COSES	COSMINS
CORRECTED	CORSET	CORVETED	COSET	COSMISM
CORRECTER	CORSETED	CORVETING	COSETS	COSMISMS
CORRECTLY	CORSETIER	CORVETS	COSEY	COSMIST
CORRECTOR	CORSETING	CORVETTE	COSEYS	COSMISTS
CORRECTS	CORSETRY	CORVETTED	COSH	COSMOCRAT
CORRELATE	CORSETS	CORVETTES	COSHED	COSMOGENY
CORRETTO	CORSEY	CORVID	COSHER	COSMOGONY
CORRETTOS	CORSEYS	CORVIDS	COSHERED	COSMOID
CORRIDA	CORSITE	CORVINA	COSHERER	COSMOLINE
CORRIDAS	CORSITES	CORVINAS	COSHERERS	COSMOLOGY
CORRIDOR	CORSIVE	CORVINE	COSHERIES	COSMONAUT
CORRIDORS	CORSIVES	CORVUS	COSHERING	COSMORAMA
CORRIE	CORSLET	CORVUSES	COSHERS	COSMOS
CORRIES	CORSLETED	CORY	COSHERY	COSMOSES
CORRIGENT	CORSLETS	CORYBANT	COSHES	COSMOTRON
CORRIVAL	CORSNED	CORYBANTS	COSHING	COSPHERED
CORRIVALS	CORSNEDS	CORYDALIS	COSIE	COSPLAY
CORRODANT	CORSO	CORYLUS	COSIED	COSPLAYS
CORRODE	CORSOS	CORYLUSES	COSIER	COSPONSOR
CORRODED	CORTEGE	CORYMB	COSIERS	COSS
CORRODENT	CORTEGES	CORYMBED	COSIES	COSSACK
CORRODER	CORTEX	CORYMBOSE	COSIEST	COSSACKS
CORRODERS	CORTEXES	CORYMBOUS	COSIGN	COSSES
CORRODES	CORTICAL	CORYMBS	COSIGNED	COSSET
CORRODIES	CORTICATE	CORYPHAEI	COSIGNER	COSSETED
CORRODING	CORTICES	CORYPHE	COSIGNERS	COSSETING
CORRODY	CORTICOID	CORYPHEE	COSIGNING	COSSETS
CORROSION	CORTICOSE	CORYPHEES	COSIGNS	COSSETTED
CORROSIVE	CORTILE	CORYPHENE	COSILY	COSSIE
CORRUGATE	CORTILI	CORYPHES	COSINE	COSSIES
CORRUPT	CORTIN	CORYZA	COSINES	COST

COSTA	COT	COTTABUS	COTYPE	COUMARIC
COSTAE	COTAN	COTTAE	COTYPES	COUMARIN
COSTAL	COTANGENT	COTTAGE	COUCAL	COUMARINS
COSTALGIA	COTANS	COTTAGED	COUCALS	COUMARONE
COSTALLY	COTE	COTTAGER	COUCH	COUMAROU
COSTALS	COTEAU	COTTAGERS	COUCHANT	COUMAROUS
COSTAR	COTEAUS	COTTAGES	COUCHE	COUNCIL
COSTARD	COTEAUX	COTTAGEY	COUCHED	COUNCILOR
COSTARDS	COTED	COTTAGING	COUCHEE	COUNCILS
COSTARRED	COTELETTE	COTTAR	COUCHEES	COUNSEL
COSTARS	COTELINE	COTTARS	COUCHER	COUNSELED
COSTATE	COTELINES	COTTAS	COUCHERS	COUNSELEE
COSTATED	COTENANCY	COTTED	COUCHES	COUNSELOR
COSTE	COTENANT	COTTER	COUCHETTE	COUNSELS
COSTEAN	COTENANTS	COTTERED	COUCHING	COUNT
COSTEANED	COTERIE	COTTERING	COUCHINGS	COUNTABLE
COSTEANS	COTERIES	COTTERS	COUDE	COUNTABLY
COSTED	COTES	COTTID	COUDES	COUNTBACK
COSTER	COTH	COTTIDS	COUGAN	COUNTDOWN
COSTERS	COTHS	COTTIER	COUGANS	COUNTED
COSTES	COTHURN	COTTIERS	COUGAR	COUNTER
COSTING	COTHURNAL	COTTING	COUGARS	COUNTERED
COSTINGS	COTHURNI	COTTISE	COUGH	COUNTERS
COSTIVE	COTHURNS	COTTISED	COUGHED	COUNTESS
COSTIVELY	COTHURNUS	COTTISES	COUGHER	COUNTIAN
COSTLESS	COTICULAR	COTTISING	COUGHERS	COUNTIANS
COSTLIER	COTIDAL	COTTOID	COUGHING	COUNTIES
COSTLIEST	COTILLION	COTTON	COUGHINGS	COUNTING
COSTLY	COTILLON	COTTONADE	COUGHS	COUNTLESS
COSTMARY	COTILLONS	COTTONED	COUGUAR	COUNTLINE
COSTOTOMY	COTING	COTTONING	COUGUARS	COUNTRIES
COSTREL	COTINGA	COTTONS	COULD	COUNTROL
COSTRELS	COTINGAS	COTTONY	COULDEST	COUNTROLS
COSTS	COTININE	COTTOWN	COULDST	COUNTRY
COSTUME	COTININES	COTTOWNS	COULEE	COUNTS
COSTUMED	COTISE	COTTS	COULEES	COUNTSHIP
COSTUMER	COTISED	COTTUS	COULIBIAC	COUNTY
COSTUMERS	COTISES	COTTUSES	COULIS	COUP
COSTUMERY	COTISING	COTURNIX	COULISSE	COUPE
COSTUMES	COTLAND	COTWAL	COULISSES	COUPED
COSTUMEY	COTLANDS	COTWALS	COULOIR	COUPEE
COSTUMIER	COTQUEAN	COTYLAE	COULOIRS	COUPEES
COSTUMING	COTQUEANS	COTYLE	COULOMB	COUPER
COSTUS	COTRUSTEE	COTYLEDON	COULOMBIC	COUPERS
COSTUSES	COTS	COTYLES	COULOMBS	COUPES
COSY	COTT	COTYLOID	COULTER	COUPING
COSYING	COTTA	COTYLOIDS	COULTERS	COUPLE

COUPLED	COURSED	COUTHS	COVERLESS	COWARDING
COUPLEDOM	COURSER	COUTHY	COVERLET	COWARDLY
COUPLER	COURSERS	COUTIL	COVERLETS	COWARDRY
COUPLERS	COURSES	COUTILLE	COVERLID	COWARDS
COUPLES	COURSING	COUTILLES	COVERLIDS	COWBANE
COUPLET	COURSINGS	COUTILS	COVERS	COWBANES
COUPLING	COURT	COUTURE	COVERSED	COWBELL
COUPLINGS	COURTED	COUTURES	COVERSINE	COWBELLS
COUPON	COURTEOUS	COUTURIER	COVERSLIP	COWBERRY
COUPONING	COURTER	COUVADE	COVERT	COWBIND
COUPONS	COURTERS	COUVADES	COVERTLY	COWBINDS
COUPS	COURTESAN	COUVERT	COVERTS	COWBIRD
COUPURE	COURTESY	COUVERTS	COVERTURE	COWBIRDS
COUPURES	COURTEZAN	COUZIN	COVERUP	COWBOY
COUR	COURTIER	COUZINS	COVERUPS	COWBOYED
COURAGE	COURTIERS	COVALENCE	COVES	COWBOYING
COURAGES	COURTING	COVALENCY	COVET	COWBOYS
COURANT	COURTINGS	COVALENT	COVETABLE	COWED
COURANTE	COURTLET	COVARIANT	COVETED	COWEDLY
COURANTES	COURTLETS	COVARIATE	COVETER	COWER
COURANTO	COURTLIER	COVARIED	COVETERS	COWERED
COURANTOS	COURTLIKE	COVARIES	COVETING	COWERING
COURANTS	COURTLING	COVARY	COVETISE	COWERS
COURB	COURTLY	COVARYING	COVETISES	COWFEEDER
COURBARIL	COURTROOM	COVE	COVETOUS	COWFISH
COURBED	COURTS	COVED	COVETS	COWFISHES
COURBETTE	COURTSHIP	COVELET	COVEY	COWFLAP
COURBING	COURTSIDE	COVELETS	COVEYS	COWFLAPS
COURBS	COURTYARD	COVELLINE	COVIN	COWFLOP
COURD	COUSCOUS	COVELLITE	COVINE	COWFLOPS
COURE	COUSIN	COVEN	COVINES	COWGIRL
COURED	COUSINAGE	COVENANT	COVING	COWGIRLS
COURES	COUSINLY	COVENANTS	COVINGS	COWGRASS
COURGETTE	COUSINRY	COVENS	COVINOUS	COWHAGE
COURIE	COUSINS	COVENT	COVINS	COWHAGES
COURIED	COUTA	COVENTS	COVYNE	COWHAND
COURIEING	COUTAS	COVER	COVYNES	COWHANDS
COURIER	COUTEAU	COVERABLE	COW	COWHEARD
COURIERED	COUTEAUX	COVERAGE	COWAGE	COWHEARDS
COURIERS	COUTER	COVERAGES	COWAGES	COWHEEL
COURIES	COUTERS	COVERALL	COWAL	COWHEELS
COURING	COUTH	COVERALLS	COWALS	COWHERB
COURLAN	COUTHER	COVERED	COWAN	COWHERBS
COURLANS	COUTHEST	COVERER	COWANS	COWHERD
COURS	COUTHIE	COVERERS	COWARD	COWHERDS
COURSE	COUTHIER	COVERING	COWARDED	COWHIDE
	COUTHIEST	COVERINGS	COWARDICE	COWHIDED

COWHIDES	COWPUNKS	COXSWAIN	COZIES	CRACKHEAD
COWHIDING	COWRIE	COXSWAINS	COZIEST	CRACKIE
COWHOUSE	COWRIES	COXY	COZILY	CRACKIER
COWHOUSES	COWRITE	COY	COZINESS	CRACKIES
COWIER	COWRITER	COYAU	COZING	CRACKIEST
COWIEST	COWRITERS	COYAUS	COZY	CRACKING
COWING	COWRITES	COYDOG	COZYING	CRACKINGS
COWINNER	COWRITING	COYDOGS	COZZES	CRACKJAW
COWINNERS	COWRITTEN	COYED	COZZIE	CRACKJAWS
COWISH	COWROTE	COYER	COZZIES	CRACKLE
COWISHES	COWRY	COYEST	CRAAL	CRACKLED
COWITCH	COWS	COYING	CRAALED	CRACKLES
COWITCHES	COWSHED	COYISH	CRAALING	CRACKLIER
COWK	COWSHEDS	COYISHLY	CRAALS	CRACKLING
COWKED	COWSKIN	COYLY	CRAB	CRACKLY
COWKING	COWSKINS	COYNESS	CRABAPPLE	CRACKNEL
COWKS	COWSLIP	COYNESSES	CRABBED	CRACKNELS
COWL	COWSLIPS	COYOTE	CRABBEDLY	CRACKPOT
COWLED	COWTOWN	COYOTES	CRABBER	CRACKPOTS
COWLICK	COWTOWNS	COYOTILLO	CRABBERS	CRACKS
COWLICKS	COWTREE	COYPOU	CRABBIER	CRACKSMAN
COWLIKE	COWTREES	COYPOUS	CRABBIEST	CRACKSMEN
COWLING	COWY	COYPU	CRABBILY	CRACKUP
COWLINGS	COX	COYPUS	CRABBING	CRACKUPS
COWLS	COXA	COYS	CRABBIT	CRACKY
COWLSTAFF	COXAE	COYSTREL	CRABBY	CRACOWE
COWMAN	COXAL	COYSTRELS	CRABEATER	CRACOWES
COWMEN	COXALGIA	COYSTRIL	CRABGRASS	CRADLE
COWORKER	COXALGIAS	COYSTRILS	CRABLIKE	CRADLED
COWORKERS	COXALGIC	COZ	CRABMEAT	CRADLER
COWP	COXALGIES	COZE	CRABMEATS	CRADLERS
COWPAT	COXALGY	COZED	CRABS	CRADLES
COWPATS	COXCOMB	COZEN	CRABSTICK	CRADLING
COWPEA	COXCOMBIC	COZENAGE	CRABWISE	CRADLINGS
COWPEAS	COXCOMBRY	COZENAGES	CRABWOOD	CRAFT
COWPED	COXCOMBS	COZENED	CRABWOODS	CRAFTED
COWPIE	COXED	COZENER	CRACHACH	CRAFTER
COWPIES	COXES	COZENERS	CRACK	CRAFTERS
COWPING	COXIB	COZENING	CRACKA	CRAFTIER
COWPLOP	COXIBS	COZENS	CRACKAS	CRAFTIEST
COWPLOPS	COXIER	COZES	CRACKBACK	CRAFTILY
COWPOKE	COXIEST	COZEY	CRACKDOWN	CRAFTING
COWPOKES	COXINESS	COZEYS	CRACKED	CRAFTLESS
COWPOX	COXING	COZIE	CRACKER	CRAFTS
COWPOXES	COXITIDES	COZIED	CRACKERS	CRAFTSMAN
COWPS	COXITIS	COZIER	CRACKET	CRAFTSMEN
COWPUNK	COXLESS	COZIERS	CRACKETS	CRAFTWORK

C

CRAFTY	CRAMPFISH	CRANKLES	CRAPULOUS	CRAVATS
CRAG	CRAMPIER	CRANKLING	CRAPY	CRAVATTED
CRAGFAST	CRAMPIEST	CRANKLY	CRARE	CRAVE
CRAGGED	CRAMPING	CRANKNESS	CRARES	CRAVED
CRAGGER	CRAMPIT	CRANKOUS	CRASES	CRAVEN
CRAGGERS	CRAMPITS	CRANKPIN	CRASH	CRAVENED
CRAGGIER	CRAMPON	CRANKPINS	CRASHED	CRAVENING
CRAGGIEST	CRAMPONED	CRANKS	CRASHER	CRAVENLY
CRAGGILY	CRAMPONS	CRANKY	CRASHERS	CRAVENS
CRAGGY	CRAMPOON	CRANNIED	CRASHES	CRAVER
CRAGS	CRAMPOONS	CRANNIES	CRASHING	CRAVERS
CRAGSMAN	CRAMPS	CRANNOG	CRASHPAD	CRAVES
CRAGSMEN	CRAMPY	CRANNOGE	CRASHPADS	CRAVING
CRAIC	CRAMS	CRANNOGES	CRASIS	CRAVINGS
CRAICS	CRAN	CRANNOGS	CRASS	CRAW
CRAIG	CRANACHAN	CRANNY	CRASSER	CRAWDAD
CRAIGS	CRANAGE	CRANNYING	CRASSEST	CRAWDADDY
CRAKE	CRANAGES	CRANREUCH	CRASSLY	CRAWDADS
CRAKED	CRANBERRY	CRANS	CRASSNESS	CRAWFISH
CRAKES	CRANCH	CRANTS	CRATCH	CRAWL
CRAKING	CRANCHED	CRANTSES	CRATCHES	CRAWLED
CRAM	CRANCHES	CRAP	CRATE	CRAWLER
CRAMBE	CRANCHING	CRAPAUD	CRATED	CRAWLERS
CRAMBES	CRANE	CRAPAUDS	CRATEFUL	CRAWLIER
CRAMBO	CRANED	CRAPE	CRATEFULS	CRAWLIEST
CRAMBOES	CRANEFLY	CRAPED	CRATER	CRAWLING
CRAMBOS	CRANES	CRAPELIKE	CRATERED	CRAWLINGS
CRAME	CRANIA	CRAPES	CRATERING	CRAWLS
CRAMES	CRANIAL	CRAPIER	CRATERLET	CRAWLWAY
CRAMESIES	CRANIALLY	CRAPIEST	CRATEROUS	CRAWLWAYS
CRAMESY	CRANIATE	CRAPING	CRATERS	CRAWLY
CRAMFULL	CRANIATES	CRAPLE	CRATES	CRAWS
CRAMMABLE	CRANING	CRAPLES	CRATHUR	CRAY
CRAMMED	CRANIUM	CRAPOLA	CRATHURS	CRAYER
CRAMMER	CRANIUMS	CRAPOLAS	CRATING	CRAYERS
CRAMMERS	CRANK	CRAPPED	CRATON	CRAYFISH
CRAMMING	CRANKCASE	CRAPPER	CRATONIC	CRAYON
CRAMMINGS	CRANKED	CRAPPERS	CRATONS	CRAYONED
CRAMOISIE	CRANKER	CRAPPIE	CRATUR	CRAYONER
CRAMOISY	CRANKEST	CRAPPIER	CRATURS	CRAYONERS
CRAMP	CRANKIER	CRAPPIES	CRAUNCH	CRAYONING
CRAMPBARK	CRANKIEST	CRAPPIEST	CRAUNCHED	CRAYONIST
CRAMPED	CRANKILY	CRAPPING	CRAUNCHES	CRAYONS
CRAMPER	CRANKING	CRAPPY	CRAUNCHY	CRAYS
CRAMPERS	CRANKISH	CRAPS	CRAVAT	CRAYTHUR
CRAMPET	CRANKLE	CRAPSHOOT	CRAVATE	CRAYTHURS
CRAMPETS	CRANKLED	CRAPULENT	CRAVATES	CRAZE

CRAZED	CREASES	CREDITS	CREESING	CREOLE
CRAZES	CREASIER	CREDO	CREM	CREOLES
CRAZIER	CREASIEST	CREDOS	CREMAINS	CREOLIAN
CRAZIES	CREASING	CREDS	CREMANT	CREOLIANS
CRAZIEST	CREASOTE	CREDULITY	CREMASTER	CREOLISE
CRAZILY	CREASOTED	CREDULOUS	CREMATE	CREOLISED
CRAZINESS	CREASOTES	CREE	CREMATED	CREOLISES
CRAZING	CREASY	CREED	CREMATES	CREOLIST
CRAZINGS	CREATABLE	CREEDAL	CREMATING	CREOLISTS
CRAZY	CREATE	CREEDS	CREMATION	CREOLIZE
CRAZYWEED	CREATED	CREEING	CREMATOR	CREOLIZED
CREACH	CREATES	CREEK	CREMATORS	CREOLIZES
CREACHS	CREATIC	CREEKIER	CREMATORY	CREOPHAGY
CREAGH	CREATIN	CREEKIEST	CREME	CREOSOL
CREAGHS	CREATINE	CREEKS	CREMES	CREOSOLS
CREAK	CREATINES	CREEKSIDE	CREMINI	CREOSOTE
CREAKED	CREATING	CREEKY	CREMINIS	CREOSOTED
CREAKIER	CREATINS	CREEL	CREMOCARP	CREOSOTES
CREAKIEST	CREATION	CREELED	CREMONA	CREOSOTIC
CREAKILY	CREATIONS	CREELING	CREMONAS	CREPANCE
CREAKING	CREATIVE	CREELS	CREMOR	CREPANCES
CREAKS	CREATIVES	CREEP	CREMORNE	CREPE
CREAKY	CREATOR	CREEPAGE	CREMORNES	CREPED
CREAM	CREATORS	CREEPAGES	CREMORS	CREPERIE
CREAMCUPS	CREATRESS	CREEPED	CREMOSIN	CREPERIES
CREAMED	CREATRIX	CREEPER	CREMS	CREPES
CREAMER	CREATURAL	CREEPERED	CREMSIN	CREPEY
CREAMERS	CREATURE	CREEPERS	CRENA	CREPIER
CREAMERY	CREATURES	CREEPIE	CRENAS	CREPIEST
CREAMIER	CRECHE	CREEPIER	CRENATE	CREPINESS
CREAMIEST	CRECHES	CREEPIES	CRENATED	CREPING
CREAMILY	CRED	CREEPIEST	CRENATELY	CREPITANT
CREAMING	CREDAL	CREEPILY	CRENATION	CREPITATE
CREAMLAID	CREDENCE	CREEPING	CRENATURE	CREPITUS
CREAMLIKE	CREDENCES	CREEPMICE	CRENEL	CREPOLINE
CREAMPUFF	CREDENDA	CREEPS	CRENELATE	CREPON
CREAMS	CREDENDUM	CREEPY	CRENELED	CREPONS
CREAMWARE	CREDENT	CREES	CRENELING	CREPS
CREAMWOVE	CREDENZA	CREESE	CRENELLE	CREPT
CREAMY	CREDENZAS	CREESED	CRENELLED	CREPUSCLE
CREANCE	CREDIBLE	CREESES	CRENELLES	CREPY
CREANCES	CREDIBLY	CREESH	CRENELS	CRESCENDI
CREANT	CREDIT	CREESHED	CRENSHAW	CRESCENDO
CREASE	CREDITED	CREESHES	CRENSHAWS	CRESCENT
CREASED	CREDITING	CREESHIER	CRENULATE	CRESCENTS
CREASER	CREDITOR	CREESHING	CREODONT	CRESCIVE
CREASERS	CREDITORS	CREESHY	CREODONTS	CRESOL

CRESOLS	CREVICES	CRICK	CRIMPLING	CRIPPLED
CRESS	CREW	CRICKED	CRIMPS	CRIPPLER
CRESSES	CREWCUT	CRICKET	CRIMPY	CRIPPLERS
CRESSET	CREWCUTS	CRICKETED	CRIMS	CRIPPLES
CRESSETS	CREWE	CRICKETER	CRIMSON	CRIPPLING
CRESSIER	CREWED	CRICKETS	CRIMSONED	CRIPS
CRESSIEST	CREWEL	CRICKEY	CRIMSONS	CRIS
CRESSY	CREWELIST	CRICKING	CRINAL	CRISE
CREST	CREWELLED	CRICKS	CRINATE	CRISES
CRESTA	CREWELS	CRICKY	CRINATED	CRISIC
CRESTAL	CREWES	CRICOID	CRINE	CRISIS
CRESTALS	CREWING	CRICOIDS	CRINED	CRISP
CRESTED	CREWLESS	CRIED	CRINES	CRISPATE
CRESTING	CREWMAN	CRIER	CRINGE	CRISPATED
CRESTINGS	CREWMATE	CRIERS	CRINGED	CRISPED
CRESTLESS	CREWMATES	CRIES	CRINGER	CRISPEN
CRESTON	CREWMEN	CRIKEY	CRINGERS	CRISPENED
CRESTONS	CREWNECK	CRIM	CRINGES	CRISPENS
CRESTS	CREWNECKS	CRIME	CRINGING	CRISPER
CRESYL	CREWS	CRIMED	CRINGINGS	CRISPERS
CRESYLIC	CRIA	CRIMEFUL	CRINGLE	CRISPEST
CRESYLS	CRIANT	CRIMELESS	CRINGLES	CRISPHEAD
CRETIC	CRIAS	CRIMEN	CRINING	CRISPIER
CRETICS	CRIB	CRIMES	CRINITE	CRISPIES
CRETIN	CRIBBAGE	CRIMEWAVE	CRINITES	CRISPIEST
CRETINISE	CRIBBAGES	CRIMINA	CRINKLE	CRISPILY
CRETINISM	CRIBBED	CRIMINAL	CRINKLED	CRISPIN
CRETINIZE	CRIBBER	CRIMINALS	CRINKLES	CRISPING
CRETINOID	CRIBBERS	CRIMINATE	CRINKLIER	CRISPINS
CRETINOUS	CRIBBING	CRIMINE	CRINKLIES	CRISPLY
CRETINS	CRIBBINGS	CRIMING	CRINKLING	CRISPNESS
CRETISM	CRIBBLE	CRIMINI	CRINKLY	CRISPS
CRETISMS	CRIBBLED	CRIMINIS	CRINOID	CRISPY
CRETONNE	CRIBBLES	CRIMINOUS	CRINOIDAL	CRISSA
CRETONNES	CRIBBLING	CRIMINY	CRINOIDS	CRISSAL
CRETONS	CRIBELLA	CRIMMER	CRINOLINE	CRISSUM
CREUTZER	CRIBELLAR	CRIMMERS	CRINOSE	CRISTA
CREUTZERS	CRIBELLUM	CRIMP	CRINUM	CRISTAE
CREVALLE	CRIBLE	CRIMPED	CRINUMS	CRISTATE
CREVALLES	CRIBRATE	CRIMPER	CRIOLLO	CRISTATED
CREVASSE	CRIBROSE	CRIMPERS	CRIOLLOS	CRIT
CREVASSED	CRIBROUS	CRIMPIER	CRIOS	CRITERIA
CREVASSES	CRIBS	CRIMPIEST	CRIOSES	CRITERIAL
CREVETTE	CRIBWORK	CRIMPING	CRIP	CRITERION
CREVETTES	CRIBWORKS	CRIMPLE	CRIPE	CRITERIUM
CREVICE	CRICETID	CRIMPLED	CRIPES	CRITH
CREVICED	CRICETIDS	CRIMPLES	CRIPPLE	CRITHS

CRITIC	CROCKETS	CRON	CROPFUL	CROSSED
CRITICAL	CROCKING	CRONE	CROPFULL	CROSSER
CRITICISE	CROCKPOT	CRONES	CROPFULLS	CROSSERS
CRITICISM	CROCKPOTS	CRONET	CROPFULS	CROSSES
CRITICIZE	CROCKS	CRONETS	CROPLAND	CROSSEST
CRITICS	CROCODILE	CRONIES	CROPLANDS	CROSSETTE
CRITIQUE	CROCOITE	CRONISH	CROPLESS	CROSSFALL
CRITIQUED	CROCOITES	CRONK	CROPPED	CROSSFIRE
CRITIQUES	CROCOSMIA	CRONKER	CROPPER	CROSSFISH
CRITS	CROCS	CRONKEST	CROPPERS	CROSSHAIR
CRITTER	CROCUS	CRONS	CROPPIE	CROSSHEAD
CRITTERS	CROCUSES	CRONY	CROPPIES	CROSSING
CRITTUR	CROFT	CRONYISM	CROPPING	CROSSINGS
CRITTURS	CROFTED	CRONYISMS	CROPPINGS	CROSSISH
CRIVENS	CROFTER	CROODLE	CROPPY	CROSSJACK
CRIVVENS	CROFTERS	CROODLED	CROPS	CROSSLET
CROAK	CROFTING	CROODLES	CROPSICK	CROSSLETS
CROAKED	CROFTINGS	CROODLING	CROQUANTE	CROSSLY
CROAKER	CROFTS	CROOK	CROQUET	CROSSNESS
CROAKERS	CROG	CROOKBACK	CROQUETED	CROSSOVER
CROAKIER	CROGGED	CROOKED	CROQUETS	CROSSPLY
CROAKIEST	CROGGIES	CROOKEDER	CROQUETTE	CROSSROAD
CROAKILY	CROGGING	CROOKEDLY	CROQUIS	CROSSRUFF
CROAKING	CROGGY	CROOKER	CRORE	CROSSTALK
CROAKINGS	CROGS	CROOKERY	CROREPATI	CROSSTIE
CROAKS	CROISSANT	CROOKEST	CRORES	CROSSTIED
CROAKY	CROJIK	CROOKING	CROSIER	CROSSTIES
CROC	CROJIKS	CROOKNECK	CROSIERED	CROSSTOWN
CROCEATE	CROKINOLE	CROOKS	CROSIERS	CROSSTREE
CROCEIN	CROMACK	CROOL	CROSS	CROSSWALK
CROCEINE	CROMACKS	CROOLED	CROSSABLE	CROSSWAY
CROCEINES	CROMB	CROOLING	CROSSARM	CROSSWAYS
CROCEINS	CROMBEC	CROOLS	CROSSARMS	CROSSWIND
CROCEOUS	CROMBECS	CROON	CROSSBAND	CROSSWIRE
CROCHE	CROMBED	CROONED	CROSSBAR	CROSSWISE
CROCHES	CROMBING	CROONER	CROSSBARS	CROSSWORD
CROCHET	CROMBS	CROONERS	CROSSBEAM	CROSSWORT
CROCHETED	CROME	CROONIER	CROSSBILL	CROST
CROCHETER	CROMED	CROONIEST	CROSSBIT	CROSTATA
CROCHETS	CROMES	CROONING	CROSSBITE	CROSTATAS
CROCI	CROMING	CROONINGS	CROSSBOW	CROSTINI
CROCINE	CROMLECH	CROONS	CROSSBOWS	CROSTINIS
CROCK	CROMLECHS	CROONY	CROSSBRED	CROSTINO
CROCKED	CROMORNA	CROOVE	CROSSBUCK	CROTAL
CROCKERY	CROMORNAS	CROOVES	CROSSCUT	CROTALA
CROCKET	CROMORNE	CROP	CROSSCUTS	CROTALE
CROCKETED	CROMORNES	CROPBOUND	CROSSE	CROTALES

CROTALINE	CROW	CROWSTEP	CRUDIER	CRUMBED
CROTALISM	CROWBAIT	CROWSTEPS	CRUDIEST	CRUMBER
CROTALS	CROWBAITS	CROZE	CRUDITES	CRUMBERS
CROTALUM	CROWBAR	CROZER	CRUDITIES	CRUMBIER
CROTCH	CROWBARS	CROZERS	CRUDITY	CRUMBIEST
CROTCHED	CROWBERRY	CROZES	CRUDO	CRUMBING
CROTCHES	CROWBOOT	CROZIER	CRUDOS	CRUMBLE
CROTCHET	CROWBOOTS	CROZIERS	CRUDS	CRUMBLED
CROTCHETS	CROWD	CROZZLED	CRUDY	CRUMBLES
CROTCHETY	CROWDED	CRU	CRUE	CRUMBLIER
CROTON	CROWDEDLY	CRUBEEN	CRUEL	CRUMBLIES
CROTONBUG	CROWDER	CRUBEENS	CRUELER	CRUMBLING
CROTONIC	CROWDERS	CRUCES	CRUELEST	CRUMBLY
CROTONS	CROWDFUND	CRUCIAL	CRUELLER	CRUMBS
CROTTLE	CROWDIE	CRUCIALLY	CRUELLEST	CRUMBUM
CROTTLES	CROWDIES	CRUCIAN	CRUELLS	CRUMBUMS
CROUCH	CROWDING	CRUCIANS	CRUELLY	CRUMBY
CROUCHED	CROWDS	CRUCIATE	CRUELNESS	CRUMEN
CROUCHES	CROWDY	CRUCIATES	CRUELS	CRUMENAL
CROUCHING	CROWEA	CRUCIBLE	CRUELTIES	CRUMENALS
CROUP	CROWEAS	CRUCIBLES	CRUELTY	CRUMENS
CROUPADE	CROWED	CRUCIFER	CRUES	CRUMHORN
CROUPADES	CROWER	CRUCIFERS	CRUET	CRUMHORNS
CROUPE	CROWERS	CRUCIFIED	CRUETS	CRUMMACK
CROUPED	CROWFEET	CRUCIFIER	CRUFT	CRUMMACKS
CROUPER	CROWFOOT	CRUCIFIES	CRUFTS	CRUMMIE
CROUPERS	CROWFOOTS	CRUCIFIX	CRUISE	CRUMMIER
CROUPES	CROWING	CRUCIFORM	CRUISED	CRUMMIES
CROUPIER	CROWINGLY	CRUCIFY	CRUISER	CRUMMIEST
CROUPIERS	CROWINGS	CRUCK	CRUISERS	CRUMMILY
CROUPIEST	CROWN	CRUCKS	CRUISES	CRUMMOCK
CROUPILY	CROWNED	CRUD	CRUISEWAY	CRUMMOCKS
CROUPING	CROWNER	CRUDDED	CRUISEY	CRUMMY
CROUPON	CROWNERS	CRUDDIER	CRUISIE	CRUMP
CROUPONS	CROWNET	CRUDDIEST	CRUISIER	CRUMPED
CROUPOUS	CROWNETS	CRUDDING	CRUISIES	CRUMPER
CROUPS	CROWNING	CRUDDLE	CRUISIEST	CRUMPEST
CROUPY	CROWNINGS	CRUDDLED	CRUISING	CRUMPET
CROUSE	CROWNLAND	CRUDDLES	CRUISINGS	CRUMPETS
CROUSELY	CROWNLESS	CRUDDLING	CRUISY	CRUMPIER
CROUSTADE	CROWNLET	CRUDDY	CRUIVE	CRUMPIEST
CROUT	CROWNLETS	CRUDE	CRUIVES	CRUMPING
CROUTE	CROWNS	CRUDELY	CRUIZIE	CRUMPLE
CROUTES	CROWNWORK	CRUDENESS	CRUIZIES	CRUMPLED
CROUTON	CROWS	CRUDER	CRULLER	CRUMPLES
CROUTONS	CROWSFEET	CRUDES	CRULLERS	CRUMPLIER
CROUTS	CROWSFOOT	CRUDEST	CRUMB	CRUMPLING

CRUMPLY	CRUSHED	CRYBABIES	CTENIDIUM	CUBISM
CRUMPS	CRUSHER	CRYBABY	CTENIFORM	CUBISMS
CRUMPY	CRUSHERS	CRYER	CTENOID	CUBIST
CRUNCH	CRUSHES	CRYERS	CUADRILLA	CUBISTIC
CRUNCHED	CRUSHING	CRYING	CUATRO	CUBISTS
CRUNCHER	CRUSIAN	CRYINGLY	CUATROS	CUBIT
CRUNCHERS	CRUSIANS	CRYINGS	CUB	CUBITAL
CRUNCHES	CRUSIE	CRYOBANK	CUBAGE	CUBITI
CRUNCHIE	CRUSIES	CRYOBANKS	CUBAGES	CUBITS
CRUNCHIER	CRUSILY	CRYOCABLE	CUBANE	CUBITUS
CRUNCHIES	CRUST	CRYOGEN	CUBANELLE	CUBITUSES
CRUNCHILY	CRUSTA	CRYOGENIC	CUBANES	CUBLESS
CRUNCHING	CRUSTACEA	CRYOGENS	CUBATURE	CUBOID
CRUNCHY	CRUSTAE	CRYOGENY	CUBATURES	CUBOIDAL
CRUNK	CRUSTAL	CRYOLITE	CUBBED	CUBOIDS
CRUNKED	CRUSTAS	CRYOLITES	CUBBIER	CUBS
CRUNKLE	CRUSTATE	CRYOMETER	CUBBIES	CUCKING
CRUNKLED	CRUSTATED	CRYOMETRY	CUBBIEST	CUCKOLD
CRUNKLES	CRUSTED	CRYONIC	CUBBING	CUCKOLDED
CRUNKLING	CRUSTIER	CRYONICS	CUBBINGS	CUCKOLDLY
CRUNKS	CRUSTIES	CRYOPHYTE	CUBBISH	CUCKOLDOM
CRUNODAL	CRUSTIEST	CRYOPROBE	CUBBISHLY	CUCKOLDRY
CRUNODE	CRUSTILY	CRYOSCOPE	CUBBY	CUCKOLDS
CRUNODES	CRUSTING	CRYOSCOPY	CUBBYHOLE	CUCKOO
CRUOR	CRUSTLESS	CRYOSTAT	CUBE	CUCKOOED
CRUORES	CRUSTOSE	CRYOSTATS	CUBEB	CUCKOOING
CRUORS	CRUSTS	CRYOTRON	CUBEBS	CUCKOOS
CRUPPER	CRUSTY	CRYOTRONS	CUBED	CUCULLATE
CRUPPERS	CRUSY	CRYPT	CUBER	CUCUMBER
CRURA	CRUTCH	CRYPTADIA	CUBERS	CUCUMBERS
CRURAL	CRUTCHED	CRYPTAL	CUBES	CUCURBIT
CRUS	CRUTCHES	CRYPTIC	CUBHOOD	CUCURBITS
CRUSADE	CRUTCHING	CRYPTICAL	CUBHOODS	CUD
CRUSADED	CRUVE	CRYPTO	CUBIC	CUDBEAR
CRUSADER	CRUVES	CRYPTOGAM	CUBICA	CUDBEARS
CRUSADERS	CRUX	CRYPTON	CUBICAL	CUDDEN
CRUSADES	CRUXES	CRYPTONS	CUBICALLY	CUDDENS
CRUSADING	CRUZADO	CRYPTONYM	CUBICAS	CUDDIE
CRUSADO	CRUZADOES	CRYPTOS	CUBICITY	CUDDIES
CRUSADOES	CRUZADOS	CRYPTS	CUBICLE	CUDDIN
CRUSADOS	CRUZEIRO	CRYSTAL	CUBICLES	CUDDINS
CRUSE	CRUZEIROS	CRYSTALS	CUBICLY	CUDDLE
CRUSES	CRUZIE	CSARDAS	CUBICS	CUDDLED
CRUSET	CRUZIES	CSARDASES	CUBICULA	CUDDLER
CRUSETS	CRWTH	CTENE	CUBICULUM	CUDDLERS
CRUSH	CRWTHS	CTENES	CUBIFORM	CUDDLES
CRUSHABLE	CRY	CTENIDIA	CUBING	CUDDLIER

CUDDLIEST	CUIRASSES	CULLERS	CULTIGEN	CUMBIA
CUDDLING	CUISH	CULLET	CULTIGENS	CUMBIAS
CUDDLY	CUISHES	CULLETS	CULTISH	CUMBRANCE
CUDDY	CUISINART	CULLIED	CULTISHLY	CUMBROUS
CUDGEL	CUISINE	CULLIES	CULTISM	CUMBUNGI
CUDGELED	CUISINES	CULLING	CULTISMS	CUMBUNGIS
CUDGELER	CUISINIER	CULLINGS	CULTIST	CUMEC
CUDGELERS	CUISSE	CULLION	CULTISTS	CUMECS
CUDGELING	CUISSER	CULLIONLY	CULTIVAR	CUMIN
CUDGELLED	CUISSERS	CULLIONS	CULTIVARS	CUMINS
CUDGELLER	CUISSES	CULLIS	CULTIVATE	CUMMED
CUDGELS	CUIT	CULLISES	CULTLIKE	CUMMER
CUDGERIE	CUITER	CULLS	CULTRATE	CUMMERS
CUDGERIES	CUITERED	CULLY	CULTRATED	CUMMIN
CUDS	CUITERING	CULLYING	CULTS	CUMMING
CUDWEED	CUITERS	CULLYISM	CULTURAL	CUMMINS
CUDWEEDS	CUITIKIN	CULLYISMS	CULTURATI	CUMQUAT
CUE	CUITIKINS	CULM	CULTURE	CUMQUATS
CUED	CUITS	CULMED	CULTURED	CUMS
CUEING	CUITTLE	CULMEN	CULTURES	CUMSHAW
CUEINGS	CUITTLED	CULMINA	CULTURING	CUMSHAWS
CUEIST	CUITTLES	CULMINANT	CULTURIST	CUMULATE
CUEISTS	CUITTLING	CULMINATE	CULTUS	CUMULATED
CUES	CUKE	CULMING	CULTUSES	CUMULATES
CUESTA	CUKES	CULMS	CULTY	CUMULET
CUESTAS	CULCH	CULOTTE	CULVER	CUMULETS
CUFF	CULCHES	CULOTTES	CULVERIN	CUMULI
CUFFABLE	CULCHIE	CULPA	CULVERINS	CUMULOSE
CUFFED	CULCHIER	CULPABLE	CULVERS	CUMULOUS
CUFFIN	CULCHIES	CULPABLY	CULVERT	CUMULUS
CUFFING	CULCHIEST	CULPAE	CULVERTED	CUMULUSES
CUFFINS	CULET	CULPATORY	CULVERTS	CUNABULA
CUFFLE	CULETS	CULPRIT	CUM	CUNCTATOR
CUFFLED	CULEX	CULPRITS	CUMACEAN	CUNDIES
CUFFLES	CULEXES	CULSHIE	CUMACEANS	CUNDUM
CUFFLESS	CULICES	CULSHIER	CUMARIC	CUNDUMS
CUFFLING	CULICID	CULSHIES	CUMARIN	CUNDY
CUFFLINK	CULICIDS	CULSHIEST	CUMARINS	CUNEAL
CUFFLINKS	CULICINE	CULT	CUMARONE	CUNEATE
CUFFO	CULICINES	CULTCH	CUMARONES	CUNEATED
CUFFS	CULINARY	CULTCHES	CUMBENT	CUNEATELY
CUFFUFFLE	CULL	CULTER	CUMBER	CUNEATIC
CUIF	CULLAY	CULTERS	CUMBERED	CUNEI
CUIFS	CULLAYS	CULTI	CUMBERER	CUNEIFORM
CUING	CULLED	CULTIC	CUMBERERS	CUNETTE
CUIRASS	CULLENDER	CULTIER	CUMBERING	CUNETTES
CUIRASSED	CULLER	CULTIEST	CUMBERS	CUNEUS

CUNIFORM	CUPOLAS	CURARINES	CURD	CURIOSITY
CUNIFORMS	CUPOLATED	CURARIS	CURDED	CURIOUS
CUNIT	CUPPA	CURARISE	CURDIER	CURIOUSER
CUNITS	CUPPAS	CURARISED	CURDIEST	CURIOUSLY
CUNJEVOI	CUPPED	CURARISES	CURDINESS	CURITE
CUNJEVOIS	CUPPER	CURARIZE	CURDING	CURITES
CUNNER	CUPPERS	CURARIZED	CURDLE	CURIUM
CUNNERS	CUPPIER	CURARIZES	CURDLED	CURIUMS
CUNNING	CUPPIEST	CURASSOW	CURDLER	CURL
CUNNINGER	CUPPING	CURASSOWS	CURDLERS	CURLED
CUNNINGLY	CUPPINGS	CURAT	CURDLES	CURLER
CUNNINGS	CUPPY	CURATE	CURDLING	CURLERS
CUNT	CUPREOUS	CURATED	CURDS	CURLEW
CUNTS	CUPRESSUS	CURATES	CURDY	CURLEWS
CUP	CUPRIC	CURATING	CURE	CURLI
CUPBEARER	CUPRITE	CURATION	CURED	CURLICUE
CUPBOARD	CUPRITES	CURATIONS	CURELESS	CURLICUED
CUPBOARDS	CUPROUS	CURATIVE	CURER	CURLICUES
CUPCAKE	CUPRUM	CURATIVES	CURERS	CURLIER
CUPCAKES	CUPRUMS	CURATOR	CURES	CURLIES
CUPEL	CUPS	CURATORS	CURET	CURLIEST
CUPELED	CUPSFUL	CURATORY	CURETS	CURLILY
CUPELER	CUPULA	CURATRIX	CURETTAGE	CURLINESS
CUPELERS	CUPULAE	CURATS	CURETTE	CURLING
CUPELING	CUPULAR	CURB	CURETTED	CURLINGS
CUPELLED	CUPULATE	CURBABLE	CURETTES	CURLPAPER
CUPELLER	CUPULE	CURBED	CURETTING	CURLS
CUPELLERS	CUPULES	CURBER	CURF	CURLY
CUPELLING	CUR	CURBERS	CURFEW	CURLYCUE
CUPELS	CURABLE	CURBING	CURFEWS	CURLYCUES
CUPFERRON	CURABLY	CURBINGS	CURFS	CURN
CUPFUL	CURACAO	CURBLESS	CURFUFFLE	CURNEY
CUPFULS	CURACAOS	CURBS	CURIA	CURNIER
CUPGALL	CURACIES	CURBSIDE	CURIAE	CURNIEST
CUPGALLS	CURACOA	CURBSIDES	CURIAL	CURNS
CUPHEAD	CURACOAS	CURBSTONE	CURIALISM	CURNY
CUPHEADS	CURACY	CURCH	CURIALIST	CURPEL
CUPID	CURAGH	CURCHEF	CURIAS	CURPELS
CUPIDITY	CURAGHS	CURCHEFS	CURIE	CURR
CUPIDS	CURANDERA	CURCHES	CURIES	CURRACH
CUPLIKE	CURANDERO	CURCULIO	CURIET	CURRACHS
CUPMAN	CURARA	CURCULIOS	CURIETS	CURRAGH
CUPMEN	CURARAS	CURCUMA	CURING	CURRAGHS
CUPOLA	CURARE	CURCUMAS	CURINGS	CURRAJONG
CUPOLAED	CURARES	CURCUMIN	CURIO	CURRAN
CUPOLAING	CURARI	CURCUMINE	CURIOS	CURRANS
CUPOLAR	CURARINE	CURCUMINS	CURIOSA	CURRANT

CURRANTS	CURSIVELY	CURVATION	CUSK	CUSTOMERS
CURRANTY	CURSIVES	CURVATIVE	CUSKS	CUSTOMISE
CURRAWONG	CURSOR	CURVATURE	CUSP	CUSTOMIZE
CURRED	CURSORARY	CURVE	CUSPAL	CUSTOMS
CURREJONG	CURSORES	CURVEBALL	CUSPATE	CUSTOS
CURRENCY	CURSORIAL	CURVED	CUSPATED	CUSTREL
CURRENT	CURSORILY	CURVEDLY	CUSPED	CUSTRELS
CURRENTLY	CURSORS	CURVES	CUSPID	CUSTUMAL
CURRENTS	CURSORY	CURVESOME	CUSPIDAL	CUSTUMALS
CURRICLE	CURST	CURVET	CUSPIDATE	CUSTUMARY
CURRICLES	CURSTNESS	CURVETED	CUSPIDES	CUSUM
CURRICULA	CURSUS	CURVETING	CUSPIDOR	CUSUMS
CURRIE	CURT	CURVETS	CUSPIDORE	CUT
CURRIED	CURTAIL	CURVETTED	CUSPIDORS	CUTANEOUS
CURRIER	CURTAILED	CURVEY	CUSPIDS	CUTAWAY
CURRIERS	CURTAILER	CURVIER	CUSPIER	CUTAWAYS
CURRIERY	CURTAILS	CURVIEST	CUSPIEST	CUTBACK
CURRIES	CURTAIN	CURVIFORM	CUSPIS	CUTBACKS
CURRIJONG	CURTAINED	CURVINESS	CUSPS	CUTBANK
CURRING	CURTAINS	CURVING	CUSPY	CUTBANKS
CURRISH	CURTAL	CURVITAL	CUSS	CUTBLOCK
CURRISHLY	CURTALAX	CURVITIES	CUSSED	CUTBLOCKS
CURRS	CURTALAXE	CURVITY	CUSSEDLY	CUTCH
CURRY	CURTALS	CURVY	CUSSER	CUTCHA
CURRYCOMB	CURTANA	CUSCUS	CUSSERS	CUTCHERRY
CURRYING	CURTANAS	CUSCUSES	CUSSES	CUTCHERY
CURRYINGS	CURTATE	CUSEC	CUSSING	CUTCHES
CURS	CURTATION	CUSECS	CUSSO	CUTDOWN
CURSAL	CURTAXE	CUSH	CUSSOS	CUTDOWNS
CURSE	CURTAXES	CUSHAT	CUSSWORD	CUTE
CURSED	CURTER	CUSHATS	CUSSWORDS	CUTELY
CURSEDER	CURTESIES	CUSHAW	CUSTARD	CUTENESS
CURSEDEST	CURTEST	CUSHAWS	CUSTARDS	CUTER
CURSEDLY	CURTESY	CUSHES	CUSTARDY	CUTES
CURSENARY	CURTILAGE	CUSHIE	CUSTOCK	CUTESIE
CURSER	CURTLY	CUSHIER	CUSTOCKS	CUTESIER
CURSERS	CURTNESS	CUSHIES	CUSTODE	CUTESIEST
CURSES	CURTSEY	CUSHIEST	CUSTODES	CUTEST
CURSI	CURTSEYED	CUSHILY	CUSTODIAL	CUTESY
CURSILLO	CURTSEYS	CUSHINESS	CUSTODIAN	CUTEY
CURSILLOS	CURTSIED	CUSHION	CUSTODIER	CUTEYS
CURSING	CURTSIES	CUSHIONED	CUSTODIES	CUTGLASS
CURSINGS	CURTSY	CUSHIONET	CUSTODY	CUTGRASS
CURSITOR	CURTSYING	CUSHIONS	CUSTOM	CUTICLE
CURSITORS	CURULE	CUSHIONY	CUSTOMARY	CUTICLES
CURSITORY	CURVATE	CUSHTY	CUSTOMED	CUTICULA
CURSIVE	CURVATED	CUSHY	CUSTOMER	CUTICULAE

CUTICULAR	CUTTIES	CYANIDING	CYBORGS	CYCLIZED
CUTIE	CUTTIEST	CYANIDS	CYBRARIAN	CYCLIZES
CUTIES	CUTTING	CYANIN	CYBRID	CYCLIZINE
CUTIKIN	CUTTINGLY	CYANINE	CYBRIDS	CYCLIZING
CUTIKINS	CUTTINGS	CYANINES	CYCAD	CYCLO
CUTIN	CUTTLE	CYANINS	CYCADEOID	CYCLOGIRO
CUTINISE	CUTTLED	CYANISE	CYCADS	CYCLOID
CUTINISED	CUTTLES	CYANISED	CYCAS	CYCLOIDAL
CUTINISES	CUTTLING	CYANISES	CYCASES	CYCLOIDS
CUTINIZE	CUTTO	CYANISING	CYCASIN	CYCLOLITH
CUTINIZED	CUTTOE	CYANITE	CYCASINS	CYCLONAL
CUTINIZES	CUTTOES	CYANITES	CYCLAMATE	CYCLONE
CUTINS	CUTTY	CYANITIC	CYCLAMEN	CYCLONES
CUTIS	CUTUP	CYANIZE	CYCLAMENS	CYCLONIC
CUTISES	CUTUPS	CYANIZED	CYCLASE	CYCLONITE
CUTLAS	CUTWATER	CYANIZES	CYCLASES	CYCLOPEAN
CUTLASES	CUTWATERS	CYANIZING	CYCLE	CYCLOPES
CUTLASS	CUTWORK	CYANO	CYCLECAR	CYCLOPIAN
CUTLASSES	CUTWORKS	CYANOGEN	CYCLECARS	CYCLOPIC
CUTLER	CUTWORM	CYANOGENS	CYCLED	CYCLOPS
CUTLERIES	CUTWORMS	CYANOSE	CYCLEPATH	CYCLORAMA
CUTLERS	CUVEE	CYANOSED	CYCLER	CYCLOS
CUTLERY	CUVEES	CYANOSES	CYCLERIES	CYCLOSES
CUTLET	CUVETTE	CYANOSIS	CYCLERS	CYCLOSIS
CUTLETS	CUVETTES	CYANOTIC	CYCLERY	CYCLOTRON
CUTLETTE	CUZ	CYANOTYPE	CYCLES	CYCLUS
CUTLETTES	CUZES	CYANS	CYCLEWAY	CYCLUSES
CUTLINE	CUZZES	CYANURATE	CYCLEWAYS	CYDER
CUTLINES	CUZZIE	CYANURET	CYCLIC	CYDERS
CUTOFF	CUZZIES	CYANURETS	CYCLICAL	CYESES
CUTOFFS	CWM	CYATHI	CYCLICALS	CYESIS
CUTOUT	CWMS	CYATHIA	CYCLICISM	CYGNET
CUTOUTS	CWTCH	CYATHIUM	CYCLICITY	CYGNETS
CUTOVER	CWTCHED	CYATHUS	CYCLICLY	CYLICES
CUTOVERS	CWTCHES	CYBER	CYCLIN	CYLIKES
CUTPURSE	CWTCHING	CYBERCAFE	CYCLING	CYLINDER
CUTPURSES	CYAN	CYBERCAST	CYCLINGS	CYLINDERS
CUTS	CYANAMID	CYBERNATE	CYCLINS	CYLINDRIC
CUTSCENE	CYANAMIDE	CYBERNAUT	CYCLISE	CYLIX
CUTSCENES	CYANAMIDS	CYBERPET	CYCLISED	CYMA
CUTTABLE	CYANATE	CYBERPETS	CYCLISES	CYMAE
CUTTAGE	CYANATES	CYBERPORN	CYCLISING	CYMAGRAPH
CUTTAGES	CYANIC	CYBERPUNK	CYCLIST	CYMAR
CUTTER	CYANID	CYBERSEX	CYCLISTS	CYMARS
CUTTERS	CYANIDE	CYBERWAR	CYCLITOL	CYMAS
CUTTHROAT	CYANIDED	CYBERWARS	CYCLITOLS	CYMATIA
CUTTIER	CYANIDES	CYBORG	CYCLIZE	CYMATICS

CYMATIUM	CYMOSE	CYPRINES	CYTASTER	CYTOSINE
CYMBAL	CYMOSELY	CYPRINID	CYTASTERS	CYTOSINES
CYMBALEER	CYMOUS	CYPRINIDS	CYTE	CYTOSOL
CYMBALER	CYNANCHE	CYPRINOID	CYTES	CYTOSOLIC
CYMBALERS	CYNANCHES	CYPRIS	CYTIDINE	CYTOSOLS
CYMBALIST	CYNEGETIC	CYPRUS	CYTIDINES	CYTOSOME
CYMBALO	CYNIC	CYPRUSES	CYTIDYLIC	CYTOSOMES
CYMBALOES	CYNICAL	CYPSELA	CYTISI	CYTOTAXES
CYMBALOM	CYNICALLY	CYPSELAE	CYTISINE	CYTOTAXIS
CYMBALOMS	CYNICISM	CYST	CYTISINES	CYTOTOXIC
CYMBALOS	CYNICISMS	CYSTEIN	CYTISUS	CYTOTOXIN
CYMBALS	CYNICS	CYSTEINE	CYTODE	CZAPKA
CYMBIDIA	CYNODONT	CYSTEINES	CYTODES	CZAPKAS
CYMBIDIUM	CYNODONTS	CYSTEINIC	CYTOGENY	CZAR
CYMBIFORM	CYNOMOLGI	CYSTEINS	CYTOID	CZARDAS
CYMBLING	CYNOSURAL	CYSTIC	CYTOKINE	CZARDASES
CYMBLINGS	CYNOSURE	CYSTID	CYTOKINES	CZARDOM
CYME	CYNOSURES	CYSTIDEAN	CYTOKININ	CZARDOMS
CYMENE	CYPHER	CYSTIDS	CYTOLOGIC	CZAREVICH
CYMENES	CYPHERED	CYSTIFORM	CYTOLOGY	CZAREVNA
CYMES	CYPHERING	CYSTINE	CYTOLYSES	CZAREVNAS
CYMLIN	CYPHERS	CYSTINES	CYTOLYSIN	CZARINA
CYMLING	CYPRES	CYSTITIS	CYTOLYSIS	CZARINAS
CYMLINGS	CYPRESES	CYSTOCARP	CYTOLYTIC	CZARISM
CYMLINS	CYPRESS	CYSTOCELE	CYTOMETER	CZARISMS
CYMOGENE	CYPRESSES	CYSTOID	CYTOMETRY	CZARIST
CYMOGENES	CYPRIAN	CYSTOIDS	CYTON	CZARISTS
CYMOGRAPH	CYPRIANS	CYSTOLITH	CYTONS	CZARITSA
CYMOID	CYPRID	CYSTOTOMY	CYTOPATHY	CZARITSAS
CYMOL	CYPRIDES	CYSTS	CYTOPENIA	CZARITZA
CYMOLS	CYPRIDS	CYTASE	CYTOPLASM	CZARITZAS
CYMOPHANE	CYPRINE	CYTASES	CYTOPLAST	CZARS

D

DA
DAAL
DAALS
DAB
DABBA
DABBAS
DABBED
DABBER
DABBERS
DABBING
DABBITIES
DABBITY
DABBLE
DABBLED
DABBLER
DABBLERS
DABBLES
DABBLING
DABBLINGS
DABCHICK
DABCHICKS
DABS
DABSTER
DABSTERS
DACE
DACES
DACHA
DACHAS
DACHSHUND
DACITE
DACITES
DACK
DACKED
DACKER
DACKERED
DACKERING
DACKERS
DACKING
DACKS
DACOIT
DACOITAGE

DACOITIES
DACOITS
DACOITY
DACQUOISE
DACRON
DACRONS
DACTYL
DACTYLAR
DACTYLI
DACTYLIC
DACTYLICS
DACTYLIST
DACTYLS
DACTYLUS
DAD
DADA
DADAH
DADAHS
DADAISM
DADAISMS
DADAIST
DADAISTIC
DADAISTS
DADAS
DADCHELOR
DADDED
DADDIES
DADDING
DADDLE
DADDLED
DADDLES
DADDLING
DADDOCK
DADDOCKS
DADDY
DADGUM
DADO
DADOED
DADOES
DADOING
DADOS

DADS
DAE
DAEDAL
DAEDALEAN
DAEDALIAN
DAEDALIC
DAEING
DAEMON
DAEMONES
DAEMONIC
DAEMONS
DAES
DAFF
DAFFED
DAFFIER
DAFFIES
DAFFIEST
DAFFILY
DAFFINESS
DAFFING
DAFFINGS
DAFFODIL
DAFFODILS
DAFFS
DAFFY
DAFT
DAFTAR
DAFTARS
DAFTER
DAFTEST
DAFTIE
DAFTIES
DAFTLY
DAFTNESS
DAG
DAGABA
DAGABAS
DAGGA
DAGGAS
DAGGED
DAGGER

DAGGERED
DAGGERING
DAGGERS
DAGGIER
DAGGIEST
DAGGING
DAGGINGS
DAGGLE
DAGGLED
DAGGLES
DAGGLING
DAGGY
DAGLOCK
DAGLOCKS
DAGO
DAGOBA
DAGOBAS
DAGOES
DAGOS
DAGS
DAGWOOD
DAGWOODS
DAH
DAHABEAH
DAHABEAHS
DAHABEEAH
DAHABIAH
DAHABIAHS
DAHABIEH
DAHABIEHS
DAHABIYA
DAHABIYAH
DAHABIYAS
DAHABIYEH
DAHL
DAHLIA
DAHLIAS
DAHLS
DAHOON
DAHOONS
DAHS

DAIDLE
DAIDLED
DAIDLES
DAIDLING
DAIDZEIN
DAIDZEINS
DAIKER
DAIKERED
DAIKERING
DAIKERS
DAIKO
DAIKON
DAIKONS
DAIKOS
DAILIES
DAILINESS
DAILY
DAILYNESS
DAIMEN
DAIMIO
DAIMIOS
DAIMOKU
DAIMOKUS
DAIMON
DAIMONES
DAIMONIC
DAIMONS
DAIMYO
DAIMYOS
DAINE
DAINED
DAINES
DAINING
DAINT
DAINTIER
DAINTIES
DAINTIEST
DAINTILY
DAINTS
DAINTY
DAIQUIRI

DAIQUIRIS	DALIS	DAMBOARD	DAMPED	DANDELION
DAIRIES	DALLE	DAMBOARDS	DAMPEN	DANDER
DAIRY	DALLES	DAMBROD	DAMPENED	DANDERED
DAIRYING	DALLIANCE	DAMBRODS	DAMPENER	DANDERING
DAIRYINGS	DALLIED	DAME	DAMPENERS	DANDERS
DAIRYMAID	DALLIER	DAMES	DAMPENING	DANDIACAL
DAIRYMAN	DALLIERS	DAMEWORT	DAMPENS	DANDIER
DAIRYMEN	DALLIES	DAMEWORTS	DAMPER	DANDIES
DAIS	DALLOP	DAMFOOL	DAMPERS	DANDIEST
DAISES	DALLOPS	DAMFOOLS	DAMPEST	DANDIFIED
DAISHIKI	DALLY	DAMIANA	DAMPIER	DANDIFIES
DAISHIKIS	DALLYING	DAMIANAS	DAMPIEST	DANDIFY
DAISIED	DALMAHOY	DAMMAR	DAMPING	DANDILY
DAISIES	DALMAHOYS	DAMMARS	DAMPINGS	DANDIPRAT
DAISY	DALMATIAN	DAMME	DAMPISH	DANDLE
DAK	DALMATIC	DAMMED	DAMPLY	DANDLED
DAKER	DALMATICS	DAMMER	DAMPNESS	DANDLER
DAKERED	DALS	DAMMERS	DAMPS	DANDLERS
DAKERHEN	DALT	DAMMING	DAMPY	DANDLES
DAKERHENS	DALTON	DAMMIT	DAMS	DANDLING
DAKERING	DALTONIAN	DAMN	DAMSEL	DANDRIFF
DAKERS	DALTONIC	DAMNABLE	DAMSELFLY	DANDRIFFS
DAKOIT	DALTONISM	DAMNABLY	DAMSELS	DANDRUFF
DAKOITI	DALTONS	DAMNATION	DAMSON	DANDRUFFS
DAKOITIES	DALTS	DAMNATORY	DAMSONS	DANDRUFFY
DAKOITIS	DAM	DAMNDEST	DAN	DANDY
DAKOITS	DAMAGE	DAMNDESTS	DANAZOL	DANDYFUNK
DAKOITY	DAMAGED	DAMNED	DANAZOLS	DANDYISH
DAKS	DAMAGER	DAMNEDER	DANCE	DANDYISM
DAL	DAMAGERS	DAMNEDEST	DANCEABLE	DANDYISMS
DALAPON	DAMAGES	DAMNER	DANCED	DANDYPRAT
DALAPONS	DAMAGING	DAMNERS	DANCEHALL	DANEGELD
DALASI	DAMAN	DAMNEST	DANCER	DANEGELDS
DALASIS	DAMANS	DAMNESTS	DANCERS	DANEGELT
DALE	DAMAR	DAMNIFIED	DANCES	DANEGELTS
DALED	DAMARS	DAMNIFIES	DANCETTE	DANELAGH
DALEDH	DAMASCENE	DAMNIFY	DANCETTEE	DANELAGHS
DALEDHS	DAMASK	DAMNING	DANCETTES	DANELAW
DALEDS	DAMASKED	DAMNINGLY	DANCETTY	DANELAWS
DALES	DAMASKEEN	DAMNS	DANCEY	DANEWEED
DALESMAN	DAMASKIN	DAMOISEL	DANCICAL	DANEWEEDS
DALESMEN	DAMASKING	DAMOISELS	DANCICALS	DANEWORT
DALETH	DAMASKINS	DAMOSEL	DANCIER	DANEWORTS
DALETHS	DAMASKS	DAMOSELS	DANCIEST	DANG
DALGYTE	DAMASQUIN	DAMOZEL	DANCING	DANGED
DALGYTES	DAMASSIN	DAMOZELS	DANCINGS	DANGER
DALI	DAMASSINS	DAMP	DANCY	DANGERED

DANGERING	DAPHNES	DARI	DARNATION	DARTRES
DANGEROUS	DAPHNIA	DARIC	DARNDEST	DARTROUS
DANGERS	DAPHNIAS	DARICS	DARNDESTS	DARTS
DANGING	DAPHNID	DARING	DARNED	DARZI
DANGLE	DAPHNIDS	DARINGLY	DARNEDER	DARZIS
DANGLED	DAPPED	DARINGS	DARNEDEST	DAS
DANGLER	DAPPER	DARIOLE	DARNEL	DASH
DANGLERS	DAPPERER	DARIOLES	DARNELS	DASHBOARD
DANGLES	DAPPEREST	DARIS	DARNER	DASHED
DANGLIER	DAPPERLY	DARK	DARNERS	DASHEEN
DANGLIEST	DAPPERS	DARKED	DARNEST	DASHEENS
DANGLING	DAPPING	DARKEN	DARNESTS	DASHEKI
DANGLINGS	DAPPLE	DARKENED	DARNING	DASHEKIS
DANGLY	DAPPLED	DARKENER	DARNINGS	DASHER
DANGS	DAPPLES	DARKENERS	DARNS	DASHERS
DANIO	DAPPLING	DARKENING	DAROGHA	DASHES
DANIOS	DAPS	DARKENS	DAROGHAS	DASHI
DANISH	DAPSONE	DARKER	DARRAIGN	DASHIER
DANISHES	DAPSONES	DARKEST	DARRAIGNE	DASHIEST
DANK	DAQUIRI	DARKEY	DARRAIGNS	DASHIKI
DANKER	DAQUIRIS	DARKEYS	DARRAIN	DASHIKIS
DANKEST	DARAF	DARKFIELD	DARRAINE	DASHING
DANKISH	DARAFS	DARKIE	DARRAINED	DASHINGLY
DANKLY	DARB	DARKIES	DARRAINES	DASHIS
DANKNESS	DARBAR	DARKING	DARRAINS	DASHLIGHT
DANKS	DARBARS	DARKISH	DARRAYN	DASHPOT
DANNEBROG	DARBIES	DARKLE	DARRAYNED	DASHPOTS
DANNIES	DARBS	DARKLED	DARRAYNS	DASHY
DANNY	DARCIES	DARKLES	DARRE	DASSIE
DANS	DARCY	DARKLIER	DARRED	DASSIES
DANSAK	DARCYS	DARKLIEST	DARRES	DASTARD
DANSAKS	DARE	DARKLING	DARRING	DASTARDLY
DANSEUR	DARED	DARKLINGS	DARSHAN	DASTARDS
DANSEURS	DAREDEVIL	DARKLY	DARSHANS	DASTARDY
DANSEUSE	DAREFUL	DARKMANS	DART	DASYMETER
DANSEUSES	DARER	DARKNESS	DARTBOARD	DASYPOD
DANT	DARERS	DARKNET	DARTED	DASYPODS
DANTED	DARES	DARKNETS	DARTER	DASYURE
DANTHONIA	DARESAY	DARKROOM	DARTERS	DASYURES
DANTING	DARG	DARKROOMS	DARTING	DATA
DANTON	DARGA	DARKS	DARTINGLY	DATABANK
DANTONED	DARGAH	DARKSOME	DARTITIS	DATABANKS
DANTONING	DARGAHS	DARKY	DARTLE	DATABASE
DANTONS	DARGAS	DARLING	DARTLED	DATABASED
DANTS	DARGLE	DARLINGLY	DARTLES	DATABASES
DAP	DARGLES	DARLINGS	DARTLING	DATABLE
DAPHNE	DARGS	DARN	DARTRE	DATABUS

DATABUSES	DATURAS	DAUPHINE	DAWK	DAYFLIES
DATACARD	DATURIC	DAUPHINES	DAWKS	DAYFLOWER
DATACARDS	DATURINE	DAUPHINS	DAWN	DAYFLY
DATACOMMS	DATURINES	DAUR	DAWNED	DAYGIRL
DATAFLOW	DAUB	DAURED	DAWNER	DAYGIRLS
DATAGLOVE	DAUBE	DAURING	DAWNERED	DAYGLO
DATAGRAM	DAUBED	DAURS	DAWNERING	DAYGLOW
DATAGRAMS	DAUBER	DAUT	DAWNERS	DAYGLOWS
DATAL	DAUBERIES	DAUTED	DAWNEY	DAYLIGHT
DATALLER	DAUBERS	DAUTIE	DAWNING	DAYLIGHTS
DATALLERS	DAUBERY	DAUTIES	DAWNINGS	DAYLILIES
DATALS	DAUBES	DAUTING	DAWNLIKE	DAYLILY
DATARIA	DAUBIER	DAUTS	DAWNS	DAYLIT
DATARIAS	DAUBIEST	DAVEN	DAWS	DAYLONG
DATARIES	DAUBING	DAVENED	DAWSONITE	DAYMARE
DATARY	DAUBINGLY	DAVENING	DAWT	DAYMARES
DATCHA	DAUBINGS	DAVENPORT	DAWTED	DAYMARK
DATCHAS	DAUBRIES	DAVENS	DAWTIE	DAYMARKS
DATE	DAUBRY	DAVIDIA	DAWTIES	DAYNT
DATEABLE	DAUBS	DAVIDIAS	DAWTING	DAYNTS
DATEBOOK	DAUBY	DAVIES	DAWTS	DAYPACK
DATEBOOKS	DAUD	DAVIT	DAY	DAYPACKS
DATED	DAUDED	DAVITS	DAYAN	DAYROOM
DATEDLY	DAUDING	DAVY	DAYANIM	DAYROOMS
DATEDNESS	DAUDS	DAW	DAYANS	DAYS
DATELESS	DAUGHTER	DAWAH	DAYBED	DAYSACK
DATELINE	DAUGHTERS	DAWAHS	DAYBEDS	DAYSACKS
DATELINED	DAULT	DAWBAKE	DAYBOAT	DAYSAIL
DATELINES	DAULTS	DAWBAKES	DAYBOATS	DAYSAILED
DATER	DAUNDER	DAWBRIES	DAYBOOK	DAYSAILER
DATERS	DAUNDERED	DAWBRY	DAYBOOKS	DAYSAILOR
DATES	DAUNDERS	DAWCOCK	DAYBOY	DAYSAILS
DATING	DAUNER	DAWCOCKS	DAYBOYS	DAYSHELL
DATINGS	DAUNERED	DAWD	DAYBREAK	DAYSHELLS
DATIVAL	DAUNERING	DAWDED	DAYBREAKS	DAYSIDE
DATIVE	DAUNERS	DAWDING	DAYCARE	DAYSIDES
DATIVELY	DAUNT	DAWDLE	DAYCARES	DAYSMAN
DATIVES	DAUNTED	DAWDLED	DAYCATION	DAYSMEN
DATO	DAUNTER	DAWDLER	DAYCENTRE	DAYSPRING
DATOLITE	DAUNTERS	DAWDLERS	DAYCH	DAYSTAR
DATOLITES	DAUNTING	DAWDLES	DAYCHED	DAYSTARS
DATOS	DAUNTLESS	DAWDLING	DAYCHES	DAYTALE
DATTO	DAUNTON	DAWDS	DAYCHING	DAYTALER
DATTOS	DAUNTONED	DAWED	DAYDREAM	DAYTALERS
DATUM	DAUNTONS	DAWEN	DAYDREAMS	DAYTALES
DATUMS	DAUNTS	DAWING	DAYDREAMT	DAYTIME
DATURA	DAUPHIN	DAWISH	DAYDREAMY	DAYTIMES

DAYWEAR
DAYWEARS
DAYWORK
DAYWORKER
DAYWORKS
DAZE
DAZED
DAZEDLY
DAZEDNESS
DAZER
DAZERS
DAZES
DAZING
DAZZLE
DAZZLED
DAZZLER
DAZZLERS
DAZZLES
DAZZLING
DAZZLINGS
DE
DEACIDIFY
DEACON
DEACONED
DEACONESS
DEACONING
DEACONRY
DEACONS
DEAD
DEADBEAT
DEADBEATS
DEADBOLT
DEADBOLTS
DEADBOY
DEADBOYS
DEADED
DEADEN
DEADENED
DEADENER
DEADENERS
DEADENING
DEADENS
DEADER
DEADERS
DEADEST
DEADEYE
DEADEYES

DEADFALL
DEADFALLS
DEADHEAD
DEADHEADS
DEADHOUSE
DEADING
DEADLIER
DEADLIEST
DEADLIFT
DEADLIFTS
DEADLIGHT
DEADLINE
DEADLINED
DEADLINES
DEADLOCK
DEADLOCKS
DEADLY
DEADMAN
DEADMEN
DEADNESS
DEADPAN
DEADPANS
DEADS
DEADSTOCK
DEADWOOD
DEADWOODS
DEAERATE
DEAERATED
DEAERATES
DEAERATOR
DEAF
DEAFBLIND
DEAFEN
DEAFENED
DEAFENING
DEAFENS
DEAFER
DEAFEST
DEAFISH
DEAFLY
DEAFNESS
DEAIR
DEAIRED
DEAIRING
DEAIRS
DEAL
DEALATE

DEALATED
DEALATES
DEALATION
DEALBATE
DEALER
DEALERS
DEALFISH
DEALIGN
DEALIGNED
DEALIGNS
DEALING
DEALINGS
DEALMAKER
DEALS
DEALT
DEAMINASE
DEAMINATE
DEAMINISE
DEAMINIZE
DEAN
DEANED
DEANER
DEANERIES
DEANERS
DEANERY
DEANING
DEANS
DEANSHIP
DEANSHIPS
DEAR
DEARE
DEARED
DEARER
DEARES
DEAREST
DEARESTS
DEARIE
DEARIES
DEARING
DEARLING
DEARLINGS
DEARLY
DEARN
DEARNED
DEARNESS
DEARNFUL
DEARNING

DEARNLY
DEARNS
DEARS
DEARTH
DEARTHS
DEARY
DEASH
DEASHED
DEASHES
DEASHING
DEASIL
DEASILS
DEASIUL
DEASIULS
DEASOIL
DEASOILS
DEATH
DEATHBED
DEATHBEDS
DEATHBLOW
DEATHCARE
DEATHCUP
DEATHCUPS
DEATHFUL
DEATHIER
DEATHIEST
DEATHLESS
DEATHLIER
DEATHLIKE
DEATHLY
DEATHS
DEATHSMAN
DEATHSMEN
DEATHTRAP
DEATHWARD
DEATHY
DEAVE
DEAVED
DEAVES
DEAVING
DEAW
DEAWED
DEAWIE
DEAWING
DEAWS
DEAWY
DEB

DEBACLE
DEBACLES
DEBAG
DEBAGGED
DEBAGGING
DEBAGS
DEBAR
DEBARK
DEBARKED
DEBARKER
DEBARKERS
DEBARKING
DEBARKS
DEBARMENT
DEBARRASS
DEBARRED
DEBARRING
DEBARS
DEBASE
DEBASED
DEBASER
DEBASERS
DEBASES
DEBASING
DEBATABLE
DEBATABLY
DEBATE
DEBATED
DEBATEFUL
DEBATER
DEBATERS
DEBATES
DEBATING
DEBATINGS
DEBAUCH
DEBAUCHED
DEBAUCHEE
DEBAUCHER
DEBAUCHES
DEBBIER
DEBBIES
DEBBIEST
DEBBY
DEBE
DEBEAK
DEBEAKED
DEBEAKING

D

DEBEAKS	DEBRUISE	DEBUTS	DECANOIC	DECEIVERS
DEBEARD	DEBRUISED	DEBYE	DECANS	DECEIVES
DEBEARDED	DEBRUISES	DEBYES	DECANT	DECEIVING
DEBEARDS	DEBS	DECACHORD	DECANTATE	DECELERON
DEBEL	DEBT	DECAD	DECANTED	DECEMVIR
DEBELLED	DEBTED	DECADAL	DECANTER	DECEMVIRI
DEBELLING	DEBTEE	DECADE	DECANTERS	DECEMVIRS
DEBELS	DEBTEES	DECADENCE	DECANTING	DECENARY
DEBENTURE	DEBTLESS	DECADENCY	DECANTS	DECENCIES
DEBES	DEBTOR	DECADENT	DECAPOD	DECENCY
DEBILE	DEBTORS	DECADENTS	DECAPODAL	DECENNARY
DEBILITY	DEBTS	DECADES	DECAPODAN	DECENNIA
DEBIT	DEBUD	DECADS	DECAPODS	DECENNIAL
DEBITED	DEBUDDED	DECAF	DECARB	DECENNIUM
DEBITING	DEBUDDING	DECAFF	DECARBED	DECENT
DEBITOR	DEBUDS	DECAFFS	DECARBING	DECENTER
DEBITORS	DEBUG	DECAFS	DECARBS	DECENTERS
DEBITS	DEBUGGED	DECAGON	DECARE	DECENTEST
DEBONAIR	DEBUGGER	DECAGONAL	DECARES	DECENTLY
DEBONAIRE	DEBUGGERS	DECAGONS	DECASTERE	DECENTRE
DEBONE	DEBUGGING	DECAGRAM	DECASTICH	DECENTRED
DEBONED	DEBUGS	DECAGRAMS	DECASTYLE	DECENTRES
DEBONER	DEBUNK	DECAHEDRA	DECATHLON	DECEPTION
DEBONERS	DEBUNKED	DECAL	DECAUDATE	DECEPTIVE
DEBONES	DEBUNKER	DECALCIFY	DECAY	DECEPTORY
DEBONING	DEBUNKERS	DECALED	DECAYABLE	DECERN
DEBOSH	DEBUNKING	DECALING	DECAYED	DECERNED
DEBOSHED	DEBUNKS	DECALITER	DECAYER	DECERNING
DEBOSHES	DEBUR	DECALITRE	DECAYERS	DECERNS
DEBOSHING	DEBURR	DECALLED	DECAYING	DECERTIFY
DEBOSS	DEBURRED	DECALLING	DECAYLESS	DECESSION
DEBOSSED	DEBURRING	DECALOG	DECAYS	DECHEANCE
DEBOSSES	DEBURRS	DECALOGS	DECCIE	DECIARE
DEBOSSING	DEBURS	DECALOGUE	DECCIES	DECIARES
DEBOUCH	DEBUS	DECALS	DECEASE	DECIBEL
DEBOUCHE	DEBUSED	DECAMETER	DECEASED	DECIBELS
DEBOUCHED	DEBUSES	DECAMETRE	DECEASEDS	DECIDABLE
DEBOUCHES	DEBUSING	DECAMP	DECEASES	DECIDE
DEBRIDE	DEBUSSED	DECAMPED	DECEASING	DECIDED
DEBRIDED	DEBUSSES	DECAMPING	DECEDENT	DECIDEDLY
DEBRIDES	DEBUSSING	DECAMPS	DECEDENTS	DECIDER
DEBRIDING	DEBUT	DECAN	DECEIT	DECIDERS
DEBRIEF	DEBUTANT	DECANAL	DECEITFUL	DECIDES
DEBRIEFED	DEBUTANTE	DECANALLY	DECEITS	DECIDING
DEBRIEFER	DEBUTANTS	DECANE	DECEIVE	DECIDUA
DEBRIEFS	DEBUTED	DECANES	DECEIVED	DECIDUAE
DEBRIS	DEBUTING	DECANI	DECEIVER	DECIDUAL

DECIDUAS
DECIDUATE
DECIDUOUS
DECIGRAM
DECIGRAMS
DECILE
DECILES
DECILITER
DECILITRE
DECILLION
DECIMAL
DECIMALLY
DECIMALS
DECIMATE
DECIMATED
DECIMATES
DECIMATOR
DECIME
DECIMES
DECIMETER
DECIMETRE
DECIPHER
DECIPHERS
DECISION
DECISIONS
DECISIVE
DECISORY
DECISTERE
DECK
DECKCHAIR
DECKED
DECKEL
DECKELS
DECKER
DECKERS
DECKHAND
DECKHANDS
DECKHOUSE
DECKING
DECKINGS
DECKLE
DECKLED
DECKLES
DECKLESS
DECKO
DECKOED
DECKOING

DECKOS
DECKS
DECLAIM
DECLAIMED
DECLAIMER
DECLAIMS
DECLARANT
DECLARE
DECLARED
DECLARER
DECLARERS
DECLARES
DECLARING
DECLASS
DECLASSE
DECLASSED
DECLASSEE
DECLASSES
DECLAW
DECLAWED
DECLAWING
DECLAWS
DECLINAL
DECLINALS
DECLINANT
DECLINATE
DECLINE
DECLINED
DECLINER
DECLINERS
DECLINES
DECLINING
DECLINIST
DECLIVITY
DECLIVOUS
DECLUTCH
DECLUTTER
DECO
DECOCT
DECOCTED
DECOCTING
DECOCTION
DECOCTIVE
DECOCTS
DECOCTURE
DECODE
DECODED

DECODER
DECODERS
DECODES
DECODING
DECODINGS
DECOHERER
DECOKE
DECOKED
DECOKES
DECOKING
DECOLLATE
DECOLLETE
DECOLOR
DECOLORED
DECOLORS
DECOLOUR
DECOLOURS
DECOMMIT
DECOMMITS
DECOMPLEX
DECOMPOSE
DECONGEST
DECONTROL
DECOR
DECORATE
DECORATED
DECORATES
DECORATOR
DECOROUS
DECORS
DECORUM
DECORUMS
DECOS
DECOUPAGE
DECOUPLE
DECOUPLED
DECOUPLER
DECOUPLES
DECOY
DECOYED
DECOYER
DECOYERS
DECOYING
DECOYS
DECREASE
DECREASED
DECREASES

DECREE
DECREED
DECREEING
DECREER
DECREERS
DECREES
DECREET
DECREETS
DECREMENT
DECREPIT
DECRETAL
DECRETALS
DECRETIST
DECRETIVE
DECRETORY
DECREW
DECREWED
DECREWING
DECREWS
DECRIAL
DECRIALS
DECRIED
DECRIER
DECRIERS
DECRIES
DECROWN
DECROWNED
DECROWNS
DECRY
DECRYING
DECRYPT
DECRYPTED
DECRYPTS
DECTET
DECTETS
DECUBITAL
DECUBITI
DECUBITUS
DECUMAN
DECUMANS
DECUMBENT
DECUPLE
DECUPLED
DECUPLES
DECUPLING
DECURIA
DECURIAS

DECURIES
DECURION
DECURIONS
DECURRENT
DECURSION
DECURSIVE
DECURVE
DECURVED
DECURVES
DECURVING
DECURY
DECUSSATE
DEDAL
DEDALIAN
DEDANS
DEDENDA
DEDENDUM
DEDENDUMS
DEDICANT
DEDICANTS
DEDICATE
DEDICATED
DEDICATEE
DEDICATES
DEDICATOR
DEDIMUS
DEDIMUSES
DEDUCE
DEDUCED
DEDUCES
DEDUCIBLE
DEDUCIBLY
DEDUCING
DEDUCT
DEDUCTED
DEDUCTING
DEDUCTION
DEDUCTIVE
DEDUCTS
DEE
DEED
DEEDED
DEEDER
DEEDEST
DEEDFUL
DEEDIER
DEEDIEST

D

DEEDILY	DEERHOUND	DEFATTING	DEFERMENT	DEFLATER
DEEDING	DEERLET	DEFAULT	DEFERRAL	DEFLATERS
DEEDLESS	DEERLETS	DEFAULTED	DEFERRALS	DEFLATES
DEEDS	DEERLIKE	DEFAULTER	DEFERRED	DEFLATING
DEEDY	DEERS	DEFAULTS	DEFERRER	DEFLATION
DEEING	DEERSKIN	DEFEAT	DEFERRERS	DEFLATOR
DEEJAY	DEERSKINS	DEFEATED	DEFERRING	DEFLATORS
DEEJAYED	DEERWEED	DEFEATER	DEFERS	DEFLEA
DEEJAYING	DEERWEEDS	DEFEATERS	DEFFER	DEFLEAED
DEEJAYS	DEERYARD	DEFEATING	DEFFEST	DEFLEAING
DEEK	DEERYARDS	DEFEATISM	DEFFLY	DEFLEAS
DEELY	DEES	DEFEATIST	DEFFO	DEFLECT
DEEM	DEET	DEFEATS	DEFI	DEFLECTED
DEEMED	DEETS	DEFEATURE	DEFIANCE	DEFLECTOR
DEEMING	DEEV	DEFECATE	DEFIANCES	DEFLECTS
DEEMS	DEEVE	DEFECATED	DEFIANT	DEFLEX
DEEMSTER	DEEVED	DEFECATES	DEFIANTLY	DEFLEXED
DEEMSTERS	DEEVES	DEFECATOR	DEFICIENT	DEFLEXES
DEEN	DEEVING	DEFECT	DEFICIT	DEFLEXING
DEENS	DEEVS	DEFECTED	DEFICITS	DEFLEXION
DEEP	DEEWAN	DEFECTING	DEFIED	DEFLEXURE
DEEPEN	DEEWANS	DEFECTION	DEFIER	DEFLORATE
DEEPENED	DEF	DEFECTIVE	DEFIERS	DEFLOWER
DEEPENER	DEFACE	DEFECTOR	DEFIES	DEFLOWERS
DEEPENERS	DEFACED	DEFECTORS	DEFILADE	DEFLUENT
DEEPENING	DEFACER	DEFECTS	DEFILADED	DEFLUXION
DEEPENS	DEFACERS	DEFENCE	DEFILADES	DEFO
DEEPER	DEFACES	DEFENCED	DEFILE	DEFOAM
DEEPEST	DEFACING	DEFENCES	DEFILED	DEFOAMED
DEEPFELT	DEFAECATE	DEFENCING	DEFILER	DEFOAMER
DEEPFROZE	DEFALCATE	DEFEND	DEFILERS	DEFOAMERS
DEEPIE	DEFAME	DEFENDANT	DEFILES	DEFOAMING
DEEPIES	DEFAMED	DEFENDED	DEFILING	DEFOAMS
DEEPLY	DEFAMER	DEFENDER	DEFINABLE	DEFOCUS
DEEPMOST	DEFAMERS	DEFENDERS	DEFINABLY	DEFOCUSED
DEEPNESS	DEFAMES	DEFENDING	DEFINE	DEFOCUSES
DEEPS	DEFAMING	DEFENDS	DEFINED	DEFOG
DEEPWATER	DEFAMINGS	DEFENSE	DEFINER	DEFOGGED
DEER	DEFANG	DEFENSED	DEFINERS	DEFOGGER
DEERBERRY	DEFANGED	DEFENSES	DEFINES	DEFOGGERS
DEERE	DEFANGING	DEFENSING	DEFINIENS	DEFOGGING
DEERES	DEFANGS	DEFENSIVE	DEFINING	DEFOGS
DEERFLIES	DEFAST	DEFER	DEFINITE	DEFOLIANT
DEERFLY	DEFASTE	DEFERABLE	DEFINITES	DEFOLIATE
DEERGRASS	DEFAT	DEFERENCE	DEFIS	DEFORCE
DEERHORN	DEFATS	DEFERENT	DEFLATE	DEFORCED
DEERHORNS	DEFATTED	DEFERENTS	DEFLATED	DEFORCER

D

DEFORCERS	DEFTEST	DEGERM	DEHISCES	DEIGNS
DEFORCES	DEFTLY	DEGERMED	DEHISCING	DEIL
DEFORCING	DEFTNESS	DEGERMING	DEHORN	DEILS
DEFOREST	DEFUEL	DEGERMS	DEHORNED	DEINDEX
DEFORESTS	DEFUELED	DEGGED	DEHORNER	DEINDEXED
DEFORM	DEFUELING	DEGGING	DEHORNERS	DEINDEXES
DEFORMED	DEFUELLED	DEGLAZE	DEHORNING	DEINOSAUR
DEFORMER	DEFUELS	DEGLAZED	DEHORNS	DEIONISE
DEFORMERS	DEFUNCT	DEGLAZES	DEHORS	DEIONISED
DEFORMING	DEFUNCTS	DEGLAZING	DEHORT	DEIONISER
DEFORMITY	DEFUND	DEGOUT	DEHORTED	DEIONISES
DEFORMS	DEFUNDED	DEGOUTED	DEHORTER	DEIONIZE
DEFOUL	DEFUNDING	DEGOUTING	DEHORTERS	DEIONIZED
DEFOULED	DEFUNDS	DEGOUTS	DEHORTING	DEIONIZER
DEFOULING	DEFUSE	DEGRADE	DEHORTS	DEIONIZES
DEFOULS	DEFUSED	DEGRADED	DEHYDRATE	DEIPAROUS
DEFRAG	DEFUSER	DEGRADER	DEI	DEISEAL
DEFRAGGED	DEFUSERS	DEGRADERS	DEICE	DEISEALS
DEFRAGGER	DEFUSES	DEGRADES	DEICED	DEISHEAL
DEFRAGS	DEFUSING	DEGRADING	DEICER	DEISHEALS
DEFRAUD	DEFUZE	DEGRAS	DEICERS	DEISM
DEFRAUDED	DEFUZED	DEGREASE	DEICES	DEISMS
DEFRAUDER	DEFUZES	DEGREASED	DEICIDAL	DEIST
DEFRAUDS	DEFUZING	DEGREASER	DEICIDE	DEISTIC
DEFRAY	DEFY	DEGREASES	DEICIDES	DEISTICAL
DEFRAYAL	DEFYING	DEGREE	DEICING	DEISTS
DEFRAYALS	DEG	DEGREED	DEICTIC	DEITIES
DEFRAYED	DEGAGE	DEGREES	DEICTICS	DEITY
DEFRAYER	DEGAME	DEGS	DEID	DEIXES
DEFRAYERS	DEGAMES	DEGU	DEIDER	DEIXIS
DEFRAYING	DEGAMI	DEGUM	DEIDEST	DEIXISES
DEFRAYS	DEGAMIS	DEGUMMED	DEIDS	DEJECT
DEFREEZE	DEGARNISH	DEGUMMING	DEIF	DEJECTA
DEFREEZES	DEGAS	DEGUMS	DEIFER	DEJECTED
DEFRIEND	DEGASES	DEGUS	DEIFEST	DEJECTING
DEFRIENDS	DEGASSED	DEGUST	DEIFIC	DEJECTION
DEFROCK	DEGASSER	DEGUSTATE	DEIFICAL	DEJECTORY
DEFROCKED	DEGASSERS	DEGUSTED	DEIFIED	DEJECTS
DEFROCKS	DEGASSES	DEGUSTING	DEIFIER	DEJEUNE
DEFROST	DEGASSING	DEGUSTS	DEIFIERS	DEJEUNER
DEFROSTED	DEGAUSS	DEHAIR	DEIFIES	DEJEUNERS
DEFROSTER	DEGAUSSED	DEHAIRED	DEIFORM	DEJEUNES
DEFROSTS	DEGAUSSER	DEHAIRING	DEIFY	DEKAGRAM
DEFROZE	DEGAUSSES	DEHAIRS	DEIFYING	DEKAGRAMS
DEFROZEN	DEGEARING	DEHISCE	DEIGN	DEKALITER
DEFT	DEGENDER	DEHISCED	DEIGNED	DEKALITRE
DEFTER	DEGENDERS	DEHISCENT	DEIGNING	DEKALOGY

DEKAMETER	DELED	DELIMITED	DELPHINIA	DEMAGOGUE
DEKAMETRE	DELEGABLE	DELIMITER	DELPHINS	DEMAGOGY
DEKARE	DELEGACY	DELIMITS	DELPHS	DEMAIN
DEKARES	DELEGATE	DELINEATE	DELS	DEMAINE
DEKE	DELEGATED	DELINK	DELT	DEMAINES
DEKED	DELEGATEE	DELINKED	DELTA	DEMAINS
DEKEING	DELEGATES	DELINKING	DELTAIC	DEMAN
DEKES	DELEGATOR	DELINKS	DELTAS	DEMAND
DEKING	DELEING	DELIQUIUM	DELTIC	DEMANDANT
DEKKO	DELENDA	DELIRIA	DELTOID	DEMANDED
DEKKOED	DELES	DELIRIANT	DELTOIDEI	DEMANDER
DEKKOING	DELETABLE	DELIRIOUS	DELTOIDS	DEMANDERS
DEKKOS	DELETE	DELIRIUM	DELTS	DEMANDING
DEL	DELETED	DELIRIUMS	DELUBRUM	DEMANDS
DELAINE	DELETES	DELIS	DELUBRUMS	DEMANNED
DELAINES	DELETING	DELISH	DELUDABLE	DEMANNING
DELAPSE	DELETION	DELIST	DELUDE	DEMANS
DELAPSED	DELETIONS	DELISTED	DELUDED	DEMANTOID
DELAPSES	DELETIVE	DELISTING	DELUDER	DEMARCATE
DELAPSING	DELETORY	DELISTS	DELUDERS	DEMARCHE
DELAPSION	DELF	DELIVER	DELUDES	DEMARCHES
DELATE	DELFS	DELIVERED	DELUDING	DEMARK
DELATED	DELFT	DELIVERER	DELUGE	DEMARKED
DELATES	DELFTS	DELIVERLY	DELUGED	DEMARKET
DELATING	DELFTWARE	DELIVERS	DELUGES	DEMARKETS
DELATION	DELI	DELIVERY	DELUGING	DEMARKING
DELATIONS	DELIBATE	DELL	DELUNDUNG	DEMARKS
DELATOR	DELIBATED	DELLIER	DELUSION	DEMAST
DELATORS	DELIBATES	DELLIES	DELUSIONS	DEMASTED
DELAY	DELIBLE	DELLIEST	DELUSIVE	DEMASTING
DELAYABLE	DELICACY	DELLS	DELUSORY	DEMASTS
DELAYED	DELICATE	DELLY	DELUSTER	DEMAYNE
DELAYER	DELICATES	DELO	DELUSTERS	DEMAYNES
DELAYERS	DELICE	DELOPE	DELUSTRE	DEME
DELAYING	DELICES	DELOPED	DELUSTRED	DEMEAN
DELAYS	DELICIOUS	DELOPES	DELUSTRES	DEMEANE
DELE	DELICT	DELOPING	DELUXE	DEMEANED
DELEAD	DELICTS	DELOS	DELVE	DEMEANES
DELEADED	DELIGHT	DELOUSE	DELVED	DEMEANING
DELEADING	DELIGHTED	DELOUSED	DELVER	DEMEANOR
DELEADS	DELIGHTER	DELOUSER	DELVERS	DEMEANORS
DELEAVE	DELIGHTS	DELOUSERS	DELVES	DEMEANOUR
DELEAVED	DELIME	DELOUSES	DELVING	DEMEANS
DELEAVES	DELIMED	DELOUSING	DEMAGOG	DEMENT
DELEAVING	DELIMES	DELPH	DEMAGOGED	DEMENTATE
DELEBLE	DELIMING	DELPHIC	DEMAGOGIC	DEMENTED
DELECTATE	DELIMIT	DELPHIN	DEMAGOGS	DEMENTI

DEMENTIA	DEMISED	DEMONIACS	DEMURRAL	DENIABLE
DEMENTIAL	DEMISES	DEMONIAN	DEMURRALS	DENIABLY
DEMENTIAS	DEMISING	DEMONIC	DEMURRED	DENIAL
DEMENTING	DEMISS	DEMONICAL	DEMURRER	DENIALIST
DEMENTIS	DEMISSION	DEMONISE	DEMURRERS	DENIALS
DEMENTS	DEMISSIVE	DEMONISED	DEMURRING	DENIED
DEMERARA	DEMISSLY	DEMONISES	DEMURS	DENIER
DEMERARAN	DEMIST	DEMONISM	DEMY	DENIERS
DEMERARAS	DEMISTED	DEMONISMS	DEMYSHIP	DENIES
DEMERGE	DEMISTER	DEMONIST	DEMYSHIPS	DENIGRATE
DEMERGED	DEMISTERS	DEMONISTS	DEMYSTIFY	DENIM
DEMERGER	DEMISTING	DEMONIZE	DEMYTHIFY	DENIMED
DEMERGERS	DEMISTS	DEMONIZED	DEN	DENIMS
DEMERGES	DEMIT	DEMONIZES	DENAR	DENIS
DEMERGING	DEMITASSE	DEMONRIES	DENARI	DENITRATE
DEMERIT	DEMITS	DEMONRY	DENARIES	DENITRIFY
DEMERITED	DEMITTED	DEMONS	DENARII	DENIZEN
DEMERITS	DEMITTING	DEMOS	DENARIUS	DENIZENED
DEMERSAL	DEMIURGE	DEMOSCENE	DENARS	DENIZENS
DEMERSE	DEMIURGES	DEMOSES	DENARY	DENNED
DEMERSED	DEMIURGIC	DEMOTE	DENATURE	DENNET
DEMERSES	DEMIURGUS	DEMOTED	DENATURED	DENNETS
DEMERSING	DEMIVEG	DEMOTES	DENATURES	DENNING
DEMERSION	DEMIVEGES	DEMOTIC	DENAY	DENOMINAL
DEMES	DEMIVOLT	DEMOTICS	DENAYED	DENOTABLE
DEMESNE	DEMIVOLTE	DEMOTING	DENAYING	DENOTATE
DEMESNES	DEMIVOLTS	DEMOTION	DENAYS	DENOTATED
DEMETON	DEMIWORLD	DEMOTIONS	DENAZIFY	DENOTATES
DEMETONS	DEMO	DEMOTIST	DENCH	DENOTE
DEMIC	DEMOB	DEMOTISTS	DENDRIMER	DENOTED
DEMIES	DEMOBBED	DEMOUNT	DENDRITE	DENOTES
DEMIGOD	DEMOBBING	DEMOUNTED	DENDRITES	DENOTING
DEMIGODS	DEMOBS	DEMOUNTS	DENDRITIC	DENOTIVE
DEMIJOHN	DEMOCRACY	DEMPSTER	DENDROID	DENOUNCE
DEMIJOHNS	DEMOCRAT	DEMPSTERS	DENDROIDS	DENOUNCED
DEMILUNE	DEMOCRATS	DEMPT	DENDRON	DENOUNCER
DEMILUNES	DEMOCRATY	DEMULCENT	DENDRONS	DENOUNCES
DEMIMONDE	DEMODE	DEMULSIFY	DENE	DENS
DEMINER	DEMODED	DEMUR	DENERVATE	DENSE
DEMINERS	DEMOED	DEMURE	DENES	DENSELY
DEMINING	DEMOI	DEMURED	DENET	DENSENESS
DEMININGS	DEMOING	DEMURELY	DENETS	DENSER
DEMIPIQUE	DEMOLISH	DEMURER	DENETTED	DENSEST
DEMIREP	DEMOLOGY	DEMURES	DENETTING	DENSIFIED
DEMIREPS	DEMON	DEMUREST	DENGUE	DENSIFIER
DEMISABLE	DEMONESS	DEMURING	DENGUES	DENSIFIES
DEMISE	DEMONIAC	DEMURRAGE	DENI	DENSIFY

DENSITIES	DENUDATE	DEPASTURE	DEPLETION	DEPOT
DENSITY	DENUDATED	DEPECHE	DEPLETIVE	DEPOTS
DENT	DENUDATES	DEPECHED	DEPLETORY	DEPRAVE
DENTAL	DENUDE	DEPECHES	DEPLORE	DEPRAVED
DENTALIA	DENUDED	DEPECHING	DEPLORED	DEPRAVER
DENTALITY	DENUDER	DEPEINCT	DEPLORER	DEPRAVERS
DENTALIUM	DENUDERS	DEPEINCTS	DEPLORERS	DEPRAVES
DENTALLY	DENUDES	DEPEND	DEPLORES	DEPRAVING
DENTALS	DENUDING	DEPENDANT	DEPLORING	DEPRAVITY
DENTARIA	DENY	DEPENDED	DEPLOY	DEPRECATE
DENTARIAS	DENYING	DEPENDENT	DEPLOYED	DEPREDATE
DENTARIES	DENYINGLY	DEPENDING	DEPLOYER	DEPREHEND
DENTARY	DEODAND	DEPENDS	DEPLOYERS	DEPRENYL
DENTATE	DEODANDS	DEPEOPLE	DEPLOYING	DEPRENYLS
DENTATED	DEODAR	DEPEOPLED	DEPLOYS	DEPRESS
DENTATELY	DEODARA	DEPEOPLES	DEPLUME	DEPRESSED
DENTATION	DEODARAS	DEPERM	DEPLUMED	DEPRESSES
DENTED	DEODARS	DEPERMED	DEPLUMES	DEPRESSOR
DENTEL	DEODATE	DEPERMING	DEPLUMING	DEPRIVAL
DENTELLE	DEODATES	DEPERMS	DEPOLISH	DEPRIVALS
DENTELLES	DEODORANT	DEPICT	DEPONE	DEPRIVE
DENTELS	DEODORISE	DEPICTED	DEPONED	DEPRIVED
DENTEX	DEODORIZE	DEPICTER	DEPONENT	DEPRIVER
DENTEXES	DEONTIC	DEPICTERS	DEPONENTS	DEPRIVERS
DENTICLE	DEONTICS	DEPICTING	DEPONES	DEPRIVES
DENTICLES	DEORBIT	DEPICTION	DEPONING	DEPRIVING
DENTIFORM	DEORBITED	DEPICTIVE	DEPORT	DEPROGRAM
DENTIL	DEORBITS	DEPICTOR	DEPORTED	DEPS
DENTILED	DEOXIDATE	DEPICTORS	DEPORTEE	DEPSIDE
DENTILS	DEOXIDISE	DEPICTS	DEPORTEES	DEPSIDES
DENTIN	DEOXIDIZE	DEPICTURE	DEPORTER	DEPTH
DENTINAL	DEOXY	DEPIGMENT	DEPORTERS	DEPTHLESS
DENTINE	DEP	DEPILATE	DEPORTING	DEPTHS
DENTINES	DEPAINT	DEPILATED	DEPORTS	DEPURANT
DENTING	DEPAINTED	DEPILATES	DEPOSABLE	DEPURANTS
DENTINS	DEPAINTS	DEPILATOR	DEPOSAL	DEPURATE
DENTIST	DEPANNEUR	DEPLANE	DEPOSALS	DEPURATED
DENTISTRY	DEPART	DEPLANED	DEPOSE	DEPURATES
DENTISTS	DEPARTED	DEPLANES	DEPOSED	DEPURATOR
DENTITION	DEPARTEDS	DEPLANING	DEPOSER	DEPUTABLE
DENTOID	DEPARTEE	DEPLENISH	DEPOSERS	DEPUTE
DENTS	DEPARTEES	DEPLETE	DEPOSES	DEPUTED
DENTULOUS	DEPARTER	DEPLETED	DEPOSING	DEPUTES
DENTURAL	DEPARTERS	DEPLETER	DEPOSIT	DEPUTIES
DENTURE	DEPARTING	DEPLETERS	DEPOSITED	DEPUTING
DENTURES	DEPARTS	DEPLETES	DEPOSITOR	DEPUTISE
DENTURIST	DEPARTURE	DEPLETING	DEPOSITS	DEPUTISED

DEPUTISES	DERELICT	DERMOIDS	DESCALING	DESERVERS
DEPUTIZE	DERELICTS	DERMS	DESCANT	DESERVES
DEPUTIZED	DEREPRESS	DERN	DESCANTED	DESERVING
DEPUTIZES	DERES	DERNED	DESCANTER	DESEX
DEPUTY	DERHAM	DERNFUL	DESCANTS	DESEXED
DEQUEUE	DERHAMS	DERNIER	DESCEND	DESEXES
DEQUEUED	DERIDE	DERNING	DESCENDED	DESEXING
DEQUEUES	DERIDED	DERNLY	DESCENDER	DESHI
DEQUEUING	DERIDER	DERNS	DESCENDS	DESHIS
DERACINE	DERIDERS	DERO	DESCENT	DESI
DERACINES	DERIDES	DEROGATE	DESCENTS	DESICCANT
DERAIGN	DERIDING	DEROGATED	DESCHOOL	DESICCATE
DERAIGNED	DERIG	DEROGATES	DESCHOOLS	DESIGN
DERAIGNS	DERIGGED	DEROS	DESCRIBE	DESIGNATE
DERAIL	DERIGGING	DERRICK	DESCRIBED	DESIGNED
DERAILED	DERIGS	DERRICKED	DESCRIBER	DESIGNEE
DERAILER	DERING	DERRICKS	DESCRIBES	DESIGNEES
DERAILERS	DERINGER	DERRIERE	DESCRIED	DESIGNER
DERAILING	DERINGERS	DERRIERES	DESCRIER	DESIGNERS
DERAILS	DERISIBLE	DERRIES	DESCRIERS	DESIGNFUL
DERANGE	DERISION	DERRINGER	DESCRIES	DESIGNING
DERANGED	DERISIONS	DERRIS	DESCRIVE	DESIGNS
DERANGER	DERISIVE	DERRISES	DESCRIVED	DESILVER
DERANGERS	DERISORY	DERRO	DESCRIVES	DESILVERS
DERANGES	DERIVABLE	DERROS	DESCRY	DESINE
DERANGING	DERIVABLY	DERRY	DESCRYING	DESINED
DERAT	DERIVATE	DERTH	DESECRATE	DESINENCE
DERATE	DERIVATED	DERTHS	DESEED	DESINENT
DERATED	DERIVATES	DERV	DESEEDED	DESINES
DERATES	DERIVE	DERVISH	DESEEDER	DESINING
DERATING	DERIVED	DERVISHES	DESEEDERS	DESIPIENT
DERATINGS	DERIVER	DERVS	DESEEDING	DESIRABLE
DERATION	DERIVERS	DESALT	DESEEDS	DESIRABLY
DERATIONS	DERIVES	DESALTED	DESELECT	DESIRE
DERATS	DERIVING	DESALTER	DESELECTS	DESIRED
DERATTED	DERM	DESALTERS	DESERT	DESIRER
DERATTING	DERMA	DESALTING	DESERTED	DESIRERS
DERAY	DERMAL	DESALTS	DESERTER	DESIRES
DERAYED	DERMAS	DESAND	DESERTERS	DESIRING
DERAYING	DERMATIC	DESANDED	DESERTIC	DESIROUS
DERAYS	DERMATOID	DESANDING	DESERTIFY	DESIS
DERBIES	DERMATOME	DESANDS	DESERTING	DESIST
DERBY	DERMESTID	DESCALE	DESERTION	DESISTED
DERE	DERMIC	DESCALED	DESERTS	DESISTING
DERECHO	DERMIS	DESCALER	DESERVE	DESISTS
DERECHOS	DERMISES	DESCALERS	DESERVED	DESK
DERED	DERMOID	DESCALES	DESERVER	DESKBOUND

DESKFAST	DESPERATE	DESTOCK	DETAINING	DETESTED
DESKFASTS	DESPIGHT	DESTOCKED	DETAINS	DETESTER
DESKILL	DESPIGHTS	DESTOCKS	DETANGLE	DETESTERS
DESKILLED	DESPISAL	DESTREAM	DETANGLED	DETESTING
DESKILLS	DESPISALS	DESTREAMS	DETANGLER	DETESTS
DESKING	DESPISE	DESTRESS	DETANGLES	DETHATCH
DESKINGS	DESPISED	DESTRIER	DETASSEL	DETHRONE
DESKMAN	DESPISER	DESTRIERS	DETASSELS	DETHRONED
DESKMEN	DESPISERS	DESTROY	DETECT	DETHRONER
DESKNOTE	DESPISES	DESTROYED	DETECTED	DETHRONES
DESKNOTES	DESPISING	DESTROYER	DETECTER	DETICK
DESKS	DESPITE	DESTROYS	DETECTERS	DETICKED
DESKTOP	DESPITED	DESTRUCT	DETECTING	DETICKER
DESKTOPS	DESPITES	DESTRUCTO	DETECTION	DETICKERS
DESMAN	DESPITING	DESTRUCTS	DETECTIVE	DETICKING
DESMANS	DESPOIL	DESUETUDE	DETECTOR	DETICKS
DESMID	DESPOILED	DESUGAR	DETECTORS	DETINUE
DESMIDIAN	DESPOILER	DESUGARED	DETECTS	DETINUES
DESMIDS	DESPOILS	DESUGARS	DETENT	DETONABLE
DESMINE	DESPOND	DESULFUR	DETENTE	DETONATE
DESMINES	DESPONDED	DESULFURS	DETENTES	DETONATED
DESMODIUM	DESPONDS	DESULPHUR	DETENTION	DETONATES
DESMOID	DESPOT	DESULTORY	DETENTIST	DETONATOR
DESMOIDS	DESPOTAT	DESYATIN	DETENTS	DETORSION
DESMOSOME	DESPOTATE	DESYATINS	DETENU	DETORT
DESNOOD	DESPOTATS	DESYNE	DETENUE	DETORTED
DESNOODED	DESPOTIC	DESYNED	DETENUES	DETORTING
DESNOODS	DESPOTISM	DESYNES	DETENUS	DETORTION
DESOEUVRE	DESPOTS	DESYNING	DETER	DETORTS
DESOLATE	DESPUMATE	DETACH	DETERGE	DETOUR
DESOLATED	DESSE	DETACHED	DETERGED	DETOURED
DESOLATER	DESSERT	DETACHER	DETERGENT	DETOURING
DESOLATES	DESSERTS	DETACHERS	DETERGER	DETOURS
DESOLATOR	DESSES	DETACHES	DETERGERS	DETOX
DESORB	DESSYATIN	DETACHING	DETERGES	DETOXED
DESORBED	DESTAIN	DETAIL	DETERGING	DETOXES
DESORBER	DESTAINED	DETAILED	DETERMENT	DETOXIFY
DESORBERS	DESTAINS	DETAILER	DETERMINE	DETOXING
DESORBING	DESTEMPER	DETAILERS	DETERRED	DETRACT
DESORBS	DESTINATE	DETAILING	DETERRENT	DETRACTED
DESOXY	DESTINE	DETAILS	DETERRER	DETRACTOR
DESPAIR	DESTINED	DETAIN	DETERRERS	DETRACTS
DESPAIRED	DESTINES	DETAINED	DETERRING	DETRAIN
DESPAIRER	DESTINIES	DETAINEE	DETERS	DETRAINED
DESPAIRS	DESTINING	DETAINEES	DETERSION	DETRAINS
DESPATCH	DESTINY	DETAINER	DETERSIVE	DETRAQUE
DESPERADO	DESTITUTE	DETAINERS	DETEST	DETRAQUEE

DETRAQUES	DEVEIN	DEVILETS	DEVOLVES	DEWAX
DETRIMENT	DEVEINED	DEVILFISH	DEVOLVING	DEWAXED
DETRITAL	DEVEINING	DEVILING	DEVON	DEWAXES
DETRITION	DEVEINS	DEVILINGS	DEVONIAN	DEWAXING
DETRITUS	DEVEL	DEVILISH	DEVONPORT	DEWBERRY
DETRUDE	DEVELED	DEVILISM	DEVONS	DEWCLAW
DETRUDED	DEVELING	DEVILISMS	DEVORE	DEWCLAWED
DETRUDES	DEVELLED	DEVILKIN	DEVORES	DEWCLAWS
DETRUDING	DEVELLING	DEVILKINS	DEVOS	DEWDROP
DETRUSION	DEVELOP	DEVILLED	DEVOT	DEWDROPS
DETRUSOR	DEVELOPE	DEVILLING	DEVOTE	DEWED
DETRUSORS	DEVELOPED	DEVILMENT	DEVOTED	DEWFALL
DETUNE	DEVELOPER	DEVILRIES	DEVOTEDLY	DEWFALLS
DETUNED	DEVELOPES	DEVILRY	DEVOTEE	DEWFULL
DETUNES	DEVELOPPE	DEVILS	DEVOTEES	DEWIER
DETUNING	DEVELOPS	DEVILSHIP	DEVOTES	DEWIEST
DEUCE	DEVELS	DEVILTRY	DEVOTING	DEWILY
DEUCED	DEVERBAL	DEVILWOOD	DEVOTION	DEWINESS
DEUCEDLY	DEVERBALS	DEVIOUS	DEVOTIONS	DEWING
DEUCES	DEVEST	DEVIOUSLY	DEVOTS	DEWITT
DEUCING	DEVESTED	DEVIS	DEVOUR	DEWITTED
DEUDDARN	DEVESTING	DEVISABLE	DEVOURED	DEWITTING
DEUDDARNS	DEVESTS	DEVISAL	DEVOURER	DEWITTS
DEUS	DEVI	DEVISALS	DEVOURERS	DEWLAP
DEUTERATE	DEVIANCE	DEVISE	DEVOURING	DEWLAPPED
DEUTERIC	DEVIANCES	DEVISED	DEVOURS	DEWLAPS
DEUTERIDE	DEVIANCY	DEVISEE	DEVOUT	DEWLAPT
DEUTERIUM	DEVIANT	DEVISEES	DEVOUTER	DEWLESS
DEUTERON	DEVIANTS	DEVISER	DEVOUTEST	DEWOOL
DEUTERONS	DEVIATE	DEVISERS	DEVOUTLY	DEWOOLED
DEUTON	DEVIATED	DEVISES	DEVS	DEWOOLING
DEUTONS	DEVIATES	DEVISING	DEVVEL	DEWOOLS
DEUTZIA	DEVIATING	DEVISOR	DEVVELLED	DEWORM
DEUTZIAS	DEVIATION	DEVISORS	DEVVELS	DEWORMED
DEV	DEVIATIVE	DEVITRIFY	DEW	DEWORMER
DEVA	DEVIATOR	DEVLING	DEWAN	DEWORMERS
DEVALL	DEVIATORS	DEVLINGS	DEWANI	DEWORMING
DEVALLED	DEVIATORY	DEVO	DEWANIS	DEWORMS
DEVALLING	DEVICE	DEVOICE	DEWANNIES	DEWPOINT
DEVALLS	DEVICEFUL	DEVOICED	DEWANNY	DEWPOINTS
DEVALUATE	DEVICES	DEVOICES	DEWANS	DEWS
DEVALUE	DEVIL	DEVOICING	DEWAR	DEWY
DEVALUED	DEVILDOM	DEVOID	DEWARS	DEX
DEVALUES	DEVILDOMS	DEVOIR	DEWATER	DEXES
DEVALUING	DEVILED	DEVOIRS	DEWATERED	DEXIE
DEVAS	DEVILESS	DEVOLVE	DEWATERER	DEXIES
DEVASTATE	DEVILET	DEVOLVED	DEWATERS	DEXTER

DEXTERITY	DHOLAKS	DIABOLOGY	DIAL	DIALYSING
DEXTEROUS	DHOLE	DIABOLOS	DIALECT	DIALYSIS
DEXTERS	DHOLES	DIACETYL	DIALECTAL	DIALYTIC
DEXTRAL	DHOLL	DIACETYLS	DIALECTIC	DIALYZATE
DEXTRALLY	DHOLLS	DIACHRONY	DIALECTS	DIALYZE
DEXTRALS	DHOLS	DIACHYLON	DIALED	DIALYZED
DEXTRAN	DHOOLIES	DIACHYLUM	DIALER	DIALYZER
DEXTRANS	DHOOLY	DIACID	DIALERS	DIALYZERS
DEXTRIN	DHOORA	DIACIDIC	DIALING	DIALYZES
DEXTRINE	DHOORAS	DIACIDS	DIALINGS	DIALYZING
DEXTRINES	DHOOTI	DIACODION	DIALIST	DIAMAGNET
DEXTRINS	DHOOTIE	DIACODIUM	DIALISTS	DIAMANTE
DEXTRO	DHOOTIES	DIACONAL	DIALLAGE	DIAMANTES
DEXTRORSE	DHOOTIS	DIACONATE	DIALLAGES	DIAMETER
DEXTROSE	DHOTI	DIACRITIC	DIALLAGIC	DIAMETERS
DEXTROSES	DHOTIS	DIACT	DIALLED	DIAMETRAL
DEXTROUS	DHOURRA	DIACTINAL	DIALLEL	DIAMETRIC
DEXY	DHOURRAS	DIACTINE	DIALLELS	DIAMIDE
DEY	DHOW	DIACTINES	DIALLER	DIAMIDES
DEYS	DHOWS	DIACTINIC	DIALLERS	DIAMIN
DEZINC	DHURNA	DIACTS	DIALLING	DIAMINE
DEZINCED	DHURNAS	DIADEM	DIALLINGS	DIAMINES
DEZINCING	DHURRA	DIADEMED	DIALLIST	DIAMINS
DEZINCKED	DHURRAS	DIADEMING	DIALLISTS	DIAMOND
DEZINCS	DHURRIE	DIADEMS	DIALOG	DIAMONDED
DHAK	DHUTI	DIADOCHI	DIALOGED	DIAMONDS
DHAKS	DHUTIS	DIADOCHY	DIALOGER	DIAMYL
DHAL	DHYANA	DIADROM	DIALOGERS	DIANDRIES
DHALS	DHYANAS	DIADROMS	DIALOGIC	DIANDROUS
DHAMMA	DI	DIAERESES	DIALOGING	DIANDRY
DHAMMAS	DIABASE	DIAERESIS	DIALOGISE	DIANE
DHANSAK	DIABASES	DIAERETIC	DIALOGISM	DIANODAL
DHANSAKS	DIABASIC	DIAGLYPH	DIALOGIST	DIANOETIC
DHARMA	DIABETES	DIAGLYPHS	DIALOGITE	DIANOIA
DHARMAS	DIABETIC	DIAGNOSE	DIALOGIZE	DIANOIAS
DHARMIC	DIABETICS	DIAGNOSED	DIALOGS	DIANTHUS
DHARMSALA	DIABLE	DIAGNOSES	DIALOGUE	DIAPASE
DHARNA	DIABLERIE	DIAGNOSIS	DIALOGUED	DIAPASES
DHARNAS	DIABLERY	DIAGONAL	DIALOGUER	DIAPASON
DHIKR	DIABLES	DIAGONALS	DIALOGUES	DIAPASONS
DHIKRS	DIABOLIC	DIAGRAM	DIALS	DIAPAUSE
DHIMMI	DIABOLISE	DIAGRAMED	DIALYSATE	DIAPAUSED
DHIMMIS	DIABOLISM	DIAGRAMS	DIALYSE	DIAPAUSES
DHOBI	DIABOLIST	DIAGRAPH	DIALYSED	DIAPENTE
DHOBIS	DIABOLIZE	DIAGRAPHS	DIALYSER	DIAPENTES
DHOL	DIABOLO	DIAGRID	DIALYSERS	DIAPER
DHOLAK		DIAGRIDS	DIALYSES	DIAPERED

D

DIAPERING	DIASPORA	DIAZIN	DICENTRIC	DICKING
DIAPERS	DIASPORAS	DIAZINE	DICER	DICKINGS
DIAPHONE	DIASPORE	DIAZINES	DICERS	DICKS
DIAPHONES	DIASPORES	DIAZINON	DICES	DICKTIER
DIAPHONIC	DIASPORIC	DIAZINONS	DICEY	DICKTIEST
DIAPHONY	DIASTASE	DIAZINS	DICH	DICKTY
DIAPHRAGM	DIASTASES	DIAZO	DICHASIA	DICKY
DIAPHYSES	DIASTASIC	DIAZOES	DICHASIAL	DICKYBIRD
DIAPHYSIS	DIASTASIS	DIAZOLE	DICHASIUM	DICLINIES
DIAPIR	DIASTATIC	DIAZOLES	DICHOGAMY	DICLINISM
DIAPIRIC	DIASTEM	DIAZONIUM	DICHONDRA	DICLINOUS
DIAPIRISM	DIASTEMA	DIAZOS	DICHOPTIC	DICLINY
DIAPIRS	DIASTEMAS	DIAZOTISE	DICHORD	DICOT
DIAPSID	DIASTEMS	DIAZOTIZE	DICHORDS	DICOTS
DIAPSIDS	DIASTER	DIB	DICHOTIC	DICOTYL
DIAPYESES	DIASTERS	DIBASIC	DICHOTOMY	DICOTYLS
DIAPYESIS	DIASTOLE	DIBBED	DICHROIC	DICROTAL
DIAPYETIC	DIASTOLES	DIBBER	DICHROISM	DICROTIC
DIARCH	DIASTOLIC	DIBBERS	DICHROITE	DICROTISM
DIARCHAL	DIASTRAL	DIBBING	DICHROMAT	DICROTOUS
DIARCHIC	DIASTYLE	DIBBLE	DICHROMIC	DICT
DIARCHIES	DIASTYLES	DIBBLED	DICHT	DICTA
DIARCHY	DIATHERMY	DIBBLER	DICHTED	DICTATE
DIARIAL	DIATHESES	DIBBLERS	DICHTING	DICTATED
DIARIAN	DIATHESIS	DIBBLES	DICHTS	DICTATES
DIARIES	DIATHETIC	DIBBLING	DICIER	DICTATING
DIARISE	DIATOM	DIBBS	DICIEST	DICTATION
DIARISED	DIATOMIC	DIBBUK	DICING	DICTATOR
DIARISES	DIATOMIST	DIBBUKIM	DICINGS	DICTATORS
DIARISING	DIATOMITE	DIBBUKKIM	DICK	DICTATORY
DIARIST	DIATOMS	DIBBUKS	DICKED	DICTATRIX
DIARISTIC	DIATONIC	DIBROMIDE	DICKENS	DICTATURE
DIARISTS	DIATREME	DIBS	DICKENSES	DICTED
DIARIZE	DIATREMES	DIBUTYL	DICKER	DICTIER
DIARIZED	DIATRETA	DICACIOUS	DICKERED	DICTIEST
DIARIZES	DIATRETUM	DICACITY	DICKERER	DICTING
DIARIZING	DIATRIBE	DICACODYL	DICKERERS	DICTION
DIARRHEA	DIATRIBES	DICAMBA	DICKERING	DICTIONAL
DIARRHEAL	DIATRON	DICAMBAS	DICKERS	DICTIONS
DIARRHEAS	DIATRONS	DICAST	DICKEY	DICTS
DIARRHEIC	DIATROPIC	DICASTERY	DICKEYS	DICTUM
DIARRHOEA	DIAXON	DICASTIC	DICKHEAD	DICTUMS
DIARY	DIAXONS	DICASTS	DICKHEADS	DICTY
DIASCIA	DIAZEPAM	DICE	DICKIE	DICTYOGEN
DIASCIAS	DIAZEPAMS	DICED	DICKIER	DICUMAROL
DIASCOPE	DIAZEUXES	DICENTRA	DICKIES	DICYCLIC
DIASCOPES	DIAZEUXIS	DICENTRAS	DICKIEST	DICYCLIES

DICYCLY	DIDRACHM	DIESELS	DIFFRACT	DIGHT
DID	DIDRACHMA	DIESES	DIFFRACTS	DIGHTED
DIDACT	DIDRACHMS	DIESINKER	DIFFS	DIGHTING
DIDACTIC	DIDST	DIESIS	DIFFUSE	DIGHTS
DIDACTICS	DIDY	DIESTER	DIFFUSED	DIGICAM
DIDACTS	DIDYMIUM	DIESTERS	DIFFUSELY	DIGICAMS
DIDACTYL	DIDYMIUMS	DIESTOCK	DIFFUSER	DIGIPACK
DIDACTYLS	DIDYMOUS	DIESTOCKS	DIFFUSERS	DIGIPACKS
DIDAKAI	DIDYNAMY	DIESTROUS	DIFFUSES	DIGIT
DIDAKAIS	DIE	DIESTRUM	DIFFUSING	DIGITAL
DIDAKEI	DIEB	DIESTRUMS	DIFFUSION	DIGITALIN
DIDAKEIS	DIEBACK	DIESTRUS	DIFFUSIVE	DIGITALIS
DIDAPPER	DIEBACKS	DIET	DIFFUSOR	DIGITALLY
DIDAPPERS	DIEBS	DIETARIAN	DIFFUSORS	DIGITALS
DIDDER	DIECIOUS	DIETARIES	DIFS	DIGITATE
DIDDERED	DIED	DIETARILY	DIG	DIGITATED
DIDDERING	DIEDRAL	DIETARY	DIGAMIES	DIGITISE
DIDDERS	DIEDRALS	DIETED	DIGAMIST	DIGITISED
DIDDICOY	DIEDRE	DIETER	DIGAMISTS	DIGITISER
DIDDICOYS	DIEDRES	DIETERS	DIGAMMA	DIGITISES
DIDDIER	DIEGESES	DIETETIC	DIGAMMAS	DIGITIZE
DIDDIES	DIEGESIS	DIETETICS	DIGAMOUS	DIGITIZED
DIDDIEST	DIEGETIC	DIETHER	DIGAMY	DIGITIZER
DIDDLE	DIEHARD	DIETHERS	DIGASTRIC	DIGITIZES
DIDDLED	DIEHARDS	DIETHYL	DIGENESES	DIGITONIN
DIDDLER	DIEING	DIETHYLS	DIGENESIS	DIGITOXIN
DIDDLERS	DIEL	DIETICIAN	DIGENETIC	DIGITRON
DIDDLES	DIELDRIN	DIETINE	DIGERATI	DIGITRONS
DIDDLEY	DIELDRINS	DIETINES	DIGEST	DIGITS
DIDDLEYS	DIELS	DIETING	DIGESTANT	DIGITULE
DIDDLIES	DIELYTRA	DIETINGS	DIGESTED	DIGITULES
DIDDLING	DIELYTRAS	DIETIST	DIGESTER	DIGLOSSIA
DIDDLY	DIEMAKER	DIETISTS	DIGESTERS	DIGLOSSIC
DIDDUMS	DIEMAKERS	DIETITIAN	DIGESTIF	DIGLOT
DIDDY	DIENE	DIETS	DIGESTIFS	DIGLOTS
DIDELPHIC	DIENES	DIF	DIGESTING	DIGLOTTIC
DIDELPHID	DIEOFF	DIFF	DIGESTION	DIGLYPH
DIDICOI	DIEOFFS	DIFFER	DIGESTIVE	DIGLYPHS
DIDICOIS	DIERESES	DIFFERED	DIGESTOR	DIGNIFIED
DIDICOY	DIERESIS	DIFFERENT	DIGESTORS	DIGNIFIES
DIDICOYS	DIERETIC	DIFFERING	DIGESTS	DIGNIFY
DIDIE	DIES	DIFFERS	DIGGABLE	DIGNITARY
DIDIES	DIESEL	DIFFICILE	DIGGED	DIGNITIES
DIDJERIDU	DIESELED	DIFFICULT	DIGGER	DIGNITY
DIDO	DIESELING	DIFFIDENT	DIGGERS	DIGONAL
DIDOES	DIESELISE	DIFFLUENT	DIGGING	DIGOXIN
DIDOS	DIESELIZE	DIFFORM	DIGGINGS	DIGOXINS

DIGRAPH	DILATED	DILUTION	DIMMERS	DINFUL
DIGRAPHIC	DILATER	DILUTIONS	DIMMEST	DING
DIGRAPHS	DILATERS	DILUTIVE	DIMMING	DINGBAT
DIGRESS	DILATES	DILUTOR	DIMMINGS	DINGBATS
DIGRESSED	DILATING	DILUTORS	DIMMISH	DINGDONG
DIGRESSER	DILATION	DILUVIA	DIMNESS	DINGDONGS
DIGRESSES	DILATIONS	DILUVIAL	DIMNESSES	DINGE
DIGS	DILATIVE	DILUVIAN	DIMORPH	DINGED
DIGYNIAN	DILATOR	DILUVION	DIMORPHIC	DINGER
DIGYNOUS	DILATORS	DILUVIONS	DIMORPHS	DINGERS
DIHEDRA	DILATORY	DILUVIUM	DIMOUT	DINGES
DIHEDRAL	DILDO	DILUVIUMS	DIMOUTS	DINGESES
DIHEDRALS	DILDOE	DIM	DIMP	DINGEY
DIHEDRON	DILDOES	DIMBLE	DIMPLE	DINGEYS
DIHEDRONS	DILDOS	DIMBLES	DIMPLED	DINGHIES
DIHYBRID	DILEMMA	DIMBO	DIMPLES	DINGHY
DIHYBRIDS	DILEMMAS	DIMBOES	DIMPLIER	DINGIED
DIHYDRIC	DILEMMIC	DIMBOS	DIMPLIEST	DINGIER
DIKA	DILIGENCE	DIME	DIMPLING	DINGIES
DIKAS	DILIGENT	DIMENSION	DIMPLY	DINGIEST
DIKAST	DILL	DIMER	DIMPS	DINGILY
DIKASTS	DILLED	DIMERIC	DIMPSIES	DINGINESS
DIKDIK	DILLI	DIMERISE	DIMPSY	DINGING
DIKDIKS	DILLIER	DIMERISED	DIMS	DINGLE
DIKE	DILLIES	DIMERISES	DIMWIT	DINGLES
DIKED	DILLIEST	DIMERISM	DIMWITS	DINGO
DIKER	DILLING	DIMERISMS	DIMWITTED	DINGOED
DIKERS	DILLINGS	DIMERIZE	DIMYARIAN	DINGOES
DIKES	DILLIS	DIMERIZED	DIMYARY	DINGOING
DIKETONE	DILLS	DIMERIZES	DIN	DINGOS
DIKETONES	DILLWEED	DIMEROUS	DINAR	DINGS
DIKEY	DILLWEEDS	DIMERS	DINARCHY	DINGUS
DIKIER	DILLY	DIMES	DINARS	DINGUSES
DIKIEST	DILSCOOP	DIMETER	DINDLE	DINGY
DIKING	DILSCOOPS	DIMETERS	DINDLED	DINGYING
DIKKOP	DILTIAZEM	DIMETHYL	DINDLES	DINIC
DIKKOPS	DILUENT	DIMETHYLS	DINDLING	DINICS
DIKTAT	DILUENTS	DIMETRIC	DINE	DINING
DIKTATS	DILUTABLE	DIMIDIATE	DINED	DININGS
DILATABLE	DILUTE	DIMINISH	DINER	DINITRO
DILATABLY	DILUTED	DIMISSORY	DINERIC	DINK
DILATANCY	DILUTEE	DIMITIES	DINERO	DINKED
DILATANT	DILUTEES	DIMITY	DINEROS	DINKER
DILATANTS	DILUTER	DIMLY	DINERS	DINKEST
DILATATE	DILUTERS	DIMMABLE	DINES	DINKEY
DILATATOR	DILUTES	DIMMED	DINETTE	DINKEYS
DILATE	DILUTING	DIMMER	DINETTES	DINKIE

DINKIER	DIODES	DIOXIN	DIPLOPODS	DIPTERIST
DINKIES	DIOECIES	DIOXINS	DIPLOSES	DIPTEROI
DINKIEST	DIOECIOUS	DIP	DIPLOSIS	DIPTERON
DINKING	DIOECISM	DIPCHICK	DIPLOTENE	DIPTERONS
DINKLIER	DIOECISMS	DIPCHICKS	DIPLOZOA	DIPTEROS
DINKLIEST	DIOECY	DIPEPTIDE	DIPLOZOIC	DIPTEROUS
DINKLY	DIOESTRUS	DIPHASE	DIPLOZOON	DIPTYCA
DINKS	DIOICOUS	DIPHASIC	DIPNET	DIPTYCAS
DINKUM	DIOL	DIPHENYL	DIPNETS	DIPTYCH
DINKUMS	DIOLEFIN	DIPHENYLS	DIPNETTED	DIPTYCHS
DINKY	DIOLEFINS	DIPHONE	DIPNOAN	DIQUARK
DINMONT	DIOLS	DIPHONES	DIPNOANS	DIQUARKS
DINMONTS	DIONYSIAC	DIPHTHONG	DIPNOOUS	DIQUAT
DINNA	DIONYSIAN	DIPHYSITE	DIPODIC	DIQUATS
DINNAE	DIOPSIDE	DIPLEGIA	DIPODIES	DIRAM
DINNED	DIOPSIDES	DIPLEGIAS	DIPODY	DIRAMS
DINNER	DIOPSIDIC	DIPLEGIC	DIPOLAR	DIRDAM
DINNERED	DIOPTASE	DIPLEX	DIPOLE	DIRDAMS
DINNERING	DIOPTASES	DIPLEXER	DIPOLES	DIRDUM
DINNERS	DIOPTER	DIPLEXERS	DIPPABLE	DIRDUMS
DINNING	DIOPTERS	DIPLOE	DIPPED	DIRE
DINNLE	DIOPTRAL	DIPLOES	DIPPER	DIRECT
DINNLED	DIOPTRATE	DIPLOGEN	DIPPERFUL	DIRECTED
DINNLES	DIOPTRE	DIPLOGENS	DIPPERS	DIRECTER
DINNLING	DIOPTRES	DIPLOIC	DIPPIER	DIRECTEST
DINO	DIOPTRIC	DIPLOID	DIPPIEST	DIRECTING
DINOCERAS	DIOPTRICS	DIPLOIDIC	DIPPINESS	DIRECTION
DINOMANIA	DIORAMA	DIPLOIDS	DIPPING	DIRECTIVE
DINOS	DIORAMAS	DIPLOIDY	DIPPINGS	DIRECTLY
DINOSAUR	DIORAMIC	DIPLOMA	DIPPY	DIRECTOR
DINOSAURS	DIORISM	DIPLOMACY	DIPROTIC	DIRECTORS
DINOTHERE	DIORISMS	DIPLOMAED	DIPS	DIRECTORY
DINS	DIORISTIC	DIPLOMAS	DIPSADES	DIRECTRIX
DINT	DIORITE	DIPLOMAT	DIPSAS	DIRECTS
DINTED	DIORITES	DIPLOMATA	DIPSHIT	DIREFUL
DINTING	DIORITIC	DIPLOMATE	DIPSHITS	DIREFULLY
DINTLESS	DIOSGENIN	DIPLOMATS	DIPSO	DIRELY
DINTS	DIOTA	DIPLON	DIPSOS	DIREMPT
DIOBOL	DIOTAS	DIPLONEMA	DIPSTICK	DIREMPTED
DIOBOLON	DIOXAN	DIPLONS	DIPSTICKS	DIREMPTS
DIOBOLONS	DIOXANE	DIPLONT	DIPSWITCH	DIRENESS
DIOBOLS	DIOXANES	DIPLONTIC	DIPT	DIRER
DIOCESAN	DIOXANS	DIPLONTS	DIPTERA	DIREST
DIOCESANS	DIOXID	DIPLOPIA	DIPTERAL	DIRGE
DIOCESE	DIOXIDE	DIPLOPIAS	DIPTERAN	DIRGEFUL
DIOCESES	DIOXIDES	DIPLOPIC	DIPTERANS	DIRGELIKE
DIODE	DIOXIDS	DIPLOPOD	DIPTERAS	DIRGES

DIRHAM	DISABLES	DISBAND	DISCASING	DISCOLORS
DIRHAMS	DISABLING	DISBANDED	DISCED	DISCOLOUR
DIRHEM	DISABLISM	DISBANDS	DISCEPT	DISCOMFIT
DIRHEMS	DISABLIST	DISBAR	DISCEPTED	DISCOMMON
DIRIGE	DISABUSAL	DISBARK	DISCEPTS	DISCORD
DIRIGENT	DISABUSE	DISBARKED	DISCERN	DISCORDED
DIRIGES	DISABUSED	DISBARKS	DISCERNED	DISCORDS
DIRIGIBLE	DISABUSES	DISBARRED	DISCERNER	DISCOS
DIRIGISM	DISACCORD	DISBARS	DISCERNS	DISCOUNT
DIRIGISME	DISADORN	DISBELIEF	DISCERP	DISCOUNTS
DIRIGISMS	DISADORNS	DISBENCH	DISCERPED	DISCOURE
DIRIGISTE	DISAFFECT	DISBODIED	DISCERPS	DISCOURED
DIRIMENT	DISAFFIRM	DISBOSOM	DISCHARGE	DISCOURES
DIRK	DISAGREE	DISBOSOMS	DISCHURCH	DISCOURSE
DIRKE	DISAGREED	DISBOUND	DISCI	DISCOVER
DIRKED	DISAGREES	DISBOWEL	DISCIDE	DISCOVERS
DIRKES	DISALLIED	DISBOWELS	DISCIDED	DISCOVERT
DIRKING	DISALLIES	DISBRANCH	DISCIDES	DISCOVERY
DIRKS	DISALLOW	DISBUD	DISCIDING	DISCREDIT
DIRL	DISALLOWS	DISBUDDED	DISCIFORM	DISCREET
DIRLED	DISALLY	DISBUDS	DISCINCT	DISCRETE
DIRLING	DISANCHOR	DISBURDEN	DISCING	DISCRETER
DIRLS	DISANNEX	DISBURSAL	DISCIPLE	DISCROWN
DIRNDL	DISANNUL	DISBURSE	DISCIPLED	DISCROWNS
DIRNDLS	DISANNULS	DISBURSED	DISCIPLES	DISCS
DIRT	DISANOINT	DISBURSER	DISCLAIM	DISCUMBER
DIRTBAG	DISAPPEAR	DISBURSES	DISCLAIMS	DISCURE
DIRTBAGS	DISAPPLY	DISC	DISCLESS	DISCURED
DIRTBALL	DISARM	DISCAGE	DISCLIKE	DISCURES
DIRTBALLS	DISARMED	DISCAGED	DISCLIMAX	DISCURING
DIRTED	DISARMER	DISCAGES	DISCLOSE	DISCURSUS
DIRTIED	DISARMERS	DISCAGING	DISCLOSED	DISCUS
DIRTIER	DISARMING	DISCAL	DISCLOSER	DISCUSES
DIRTIES	DISARMS	DISCALCED	DISCLOSES	DISCUSS
DIRTIEST	DISARRAY	DISCANDIE	DISCLOST	DISCUSSED
DIRTILY	DISARRAYS	DISCANDY	DISCO	DISCUSSER
DIRTINESS	DISAS	DISCANT	DISCOBOLI	DISCUSSES
DIRTING	DISASTER	DISCANTED	DISCOED	DISDAIN
DIRTS	DISASTERS	DISCANTER	DISCOER	DISDAINED
DIRTY	DISATTIRE	DISCANTS	DISCOERS	DISDAINS
DIRTYING	DISATTUNE	DISCARD	DISCOES	DISEASE
DIS	DISAVOUCH	DISCARDED	DISCOID	DISEASED
DISA	DISAVOW	DISCARDER	DISCOIDAL	DISEASES
DISABLE	DISAVOWAL	DISCARDS	DISCOIDS	DISEASING
DISABLED	DISAVOWED	DISCASE	DISCOING	DISEDGE
DISABLER	DISAVOWER	DISCASED	DISCOLOGY	DISEDGED
DISABLERS	DISAVOWS	DISCASES	DISCOLOR	DISEDGES

DISEDGING	DISGRACED	DISHOMING	DISJUNCT	DISLOIGN
DISEMBARK	DISGRACER	DISHONEST	DISJUNCTS	DISLOIGNS
DISEMBODY	DISGRACES	DISHONOR	DISJUNE	DISLOYAL
DISEMPLOY	DISGRADE	DISHONORS	DISJUNED	DISLUSTRE
DISENABLE	DISGRADED	DISHONOUR	DISJUNES	DISMAL
DISENDOW	DISGRADES	DISHORN	DISJUNING	DISMALER
DISENDOWS	DISGUISE	DISHORNED	DISK	DISMALEST
DISENGAGE	DISGUISED	DISHORNS	DISKED	DISMALITY
DISENROL	DISGUISER	DISHORSE	DISKER	DISMALLER
DISENROLS	DISGUISES	DISHORSED	DISKERS	DISMALLY
DISENTAIL	DISGUST	DISHORSES	DISKETTE	DISMALS
DISENTOMB	DISGUSTED	DISHOUSE	DISKETTES	DISMAN
DISESTEEM	DISGUSTS	DISHOUSED	DISKING	DISMANNED
DISEUR	DISH	DISHOUSES	DISKLESS	DISMANS
DISEURS	DISHABIT	DISHPAN	DISKLIKE	DISMANTLE
DISEUSE	DISHABITS	DISHPANS	DISKS	DISMASK
DISEUSES	DISHABLE	DISHRAG	DISLEAF	DISMASKED
DISFAME	DISHABLED	DISHRAGS	DISLEAFED	DISMASKS
DISFAMED	DISHABLES	DISHTOWEL	DISLEAFS	DISMAST
DISFAMES	DISHALLOW	DISHUMOUR	DISLEAL	DISMASTED
DISFAMING	DISHCLOTH	DISHWARE	DISLEAVE	DISMASTS
DISFAVOR	DISHCLOUT	DISHWARES	DISLEAVED	DISMAY
DISFAVORS	DISHDASH	DISHWATER	DISLEAVES	DISMAYD
DISFAVOUR	DISHDASHA	DISHY	DISLIKE	DISMAYED
DISFIGURE	DISHED	DISILLUDE	DISLIKED	DISMAYFUL
DISFLESH	DISHELM	DISIMMURE	DISLIKEN	DISMAYING
DISFLUENT	DISHELMED	DISINFECT	DISLIKENS	DISMAYL
DISFOREST	DISHELMS	DISINFEST	DISLIKER	DISMAYLED
DISFORM	DISHERIT	DISINFORM	DISLIKERS	DISMAYLS
DISFORMED	DISHERITS	DISINHUME	DISLIKES	DISMAYS
DISFORMS	DISHES	DISINTER	DISLIKING	DISME
DISFROCK	DISHEVEL	DISINTERS	DISLIMB	DISMEMBER
DISFROCKS	DISHEVELS	DISINURE	DISLIMBED	DISMES
DISGAVEL	DISHFUL	DISINURED	DISLIMBS	DISMISS
DISGAVELS	DISHFULS	DISINURES	DISLIMN	DISMISSAL
DISGEST	DISHIER	DISINVENT	DISLIMNED	DISMISSED
DISGESTED	DISHIEST	DISINVEST	DISLIMNS	DISMISSES
DISGESTS	DISHING	DISINVITE	DISLINK	DISMODED
DISGODDED	DISHINGS	DISJASKIT	DISLINKED	DISMOUNT
DISGORGE	DISHLIKE	DISJECT	DISLINKS	DISMOUNTS
DISGORGED	DISHMOP	DISJECTED	DISLOAD	DISNATURE
DISGORGER	DISHMOPS	DISJECTS	DISLOADED	DISNEST
DISGORGES	DISHOARD	DISJOIN	DISLOADS	DISNESTED
DISGOWN	DISHOARDS	DISJOINED	DISLOCATE	DISNESTS
DISGOWNED	DISHOME	DISJOINS	DISLODGE	DISOBEY
DISGOWNS	DISHOMED	DISJOINT	DISLODGED	DISOBEYED
DISGRACE	DISHOMES	DISJOINTS	DISLODGES	DISOBEYER

DISOBEYS	DISPENSES	DISPOSE	DISRANKED	DISSEIZEE
DISOBLIGE	DISPEOPLE	DISPOSED	DISRANKS	DISSEIZES
DISODIUM	DISPERSAL	DISPOSER	DISRATE	DISSEIZIN
DISOMIC	DISPERSE	DISPOSERS	DISRATED	DISSEIZOR
DISOMIES	DISPERSED	DISPOSES	DISRATES	DISSEMBLE
DISOMY	DISPERSER	DISPOSING	DISRATING	DISSEMBLY
DISORBED	DISPERSES	DISPOST	DISREGARD	DISSENSUS
DISORDER	DISPIRIT	DISPOSTED	DISRELISH	DISSENT
DISORDERS	DISPIRITS	DISPOSTS	DISREPAIR	DISSENTED
DISORIENT	DISPLACE	DISPOSURE	DISREPUTE	DISSENTER
DISOWN	DISPLACED	DISPRAD	DISROBE	DISSENTS
DISOWNED	DISPLACER	DISPRAISE	DISROBED	DISSERT
DISOWNER	DISPLACES	DISPREAD	DISROBER	DISSERTED
DISOWNERS	DISPLANT	DISPREADS	DISROBERS	DISSERTS
DISOWNING	DISPLANTS	DISPRED	DISROBES	DISSERVE
DISOWNS	DISPLAY	DISPREDS	DISROBING	DISSERVED
DISPACE	DISPLAYED	DISPRISON	DISROOT	DISSERVES
DISPACED	DISPLAYER	DISPRIZE	DISROOTED	DISSES
DISPACES	DISPLAYS	DISPRIZED	DISROOTS	DISSEVER
DISPACING	DISPLE	DISPRIZES	DISRUPT	DISSEVERS
DISPARAGE	DISPLEASE	DISPROFIT	DISRUPTED	DISSHIVER
DISPARATE	DISPLED	DISPROOF	DISRUPTER	DISSIDENT
DISPARITY	DISPLES	DISPROOFS	DISRUPTOR	DISSIGHT
DISPARK	DISPLING	DISPROOVE	DISRUPTS	DISSIGHTS
DISPARKED	DISPLODE	DISPROVAL	DISS	DISSIMILE
DISPARKS	DISPLODED	DISPROVE	DISSAVE	DISSING
DISPART	DISPLODES	DISPROVED	DISSAVED	DISSIPATE
DISPARTED	DISPLUME	DISPROVEN	DISSAVER	DISSOCIAL
DISPARTS	DISPLUMED	DISPROVER	DISSAVERS	DISSOLUTE
DISPATCH	DISPLUMES	DISPROVES	DISSAVES	DISSOLVE
DISPATHY	DISPONDEE	DISPUNGE	DISSAVING	DISSOLVED
DISPAUPER	DISPONE	DISPUNGED	DISSEAT	DISSOLVER
DISPEACE	DISPONED	DISPUNGES	DISSEATED	DISSOLVES
DISPEACES	DISPONEE	DISPURSE	DISSEATS	DISSONANT
DISPEL	DISPONEES	DISPURSED	DISSECT	DISSUADE
DISPELLED	DISPONER	DISPURSES	DISSECTED	DISSUADED
DISPELLER	DISPONERS	DISPURVEY	DISSECTOR	DISSUADER
DISPELS	DISPONES	DISPUTANT	DISSECTS	DISSUADES
DISPENCE	DISPONGE	DISPUTE	DISSED	DISSUNDER
DISPENCED	DISPONGED	DISPUTED	DISSEISE	DISTAFF
DISPENCES	DISPONGES	DISPUTER	DISSEISED	DISTAFFS
DISPEND	DISPONING	DISPUTERS	DISSEISEE	DISTAIN
DISPENDED	DISPORT	DISPUTES	DISSEISES	DISTAINED
DISPENDS	DISPORTED	DISPUTING	DISSEISIN	DISTAINS
DISPENSE	DISPORTS	DISQUIET	DISSEISOR	DISTAL
DISPENSED	DISPOSAL	DISQUIETS	DISSEIZE	DISTALLY
DISPENSER	DISPOSALS	DISRANK	DISSEIZED	DISTANCE

DISTANCED	DISTRIX	DITCHERS	DITTIT	DIVERGING
DISTANCES	DISTRIXES	DITCHES	DITTO	DIVERS
DISTANT	DISTRUST	DITCHING	DITTOED	DIVERSE
DISTANTLY	DISTRUSTS	DITCHLESS	DITTOING	DIVERSED
DISTASTE	DISTUNE	DITE	DITTOLOGY	DIVERSELY
DISTASTED	DISTUNED	DITED	DITTOS	DIVERSES
DISTASTES	DISTUNES	DITES	DITTS	DIVERSIFY
DISTAVES	DISTUNING	DITHECAL	DITTY	DIVERSING
DISTEMPER	DISTURB	DITHECOUS	DITTYING	DIVERSION
DISTEND	DISTURBED	DITHEISM	DITZ	DIVERSITY
DISTENDED	DISTURBER	DITHEISMS	DITZES	DIVERSLY
DISTENDER	DISTURBS	DITHEIST	DITZIER	DIVERT
DISTENDS	DISTYLE	DITHEISTS	DITZIEST	DIVERTED
DISTENT	DISTYLES	DITHELETE	DITZINESS	DIVERTER
DISTENTS	DISULFATE	DITHELISM	DITZY	DIVERTERS
DISTHENE	DISULFID	DITHER	DIURESES	DIVERTING
DISTHENES	DISULFIDE	DITHERED	DIURESIS	DIVERTIVE
DISTHRONE	DISULFIDS	DITHERER	DIURETIC	DIVERTS
DISTICH	DISUNION	DITHERERS	DIURETICS	DIVES
DISTICHAL	DISUNIONS	DITHERIER	DIURNAL	DIVEST
DISTICHS	DISUNITE	DITHERING	DIURNALLY	DIVESTED
DISTIL	DISUNITED	DITHERS	DIURNALS	DIVESTING
DISTILL	DISUNITER	DITHERY	DIURON	DIVESTS
DISTILLED	DISUNITES	DITHIOL	DIURONS	DIVESTURE
DISTILLER	DISUNITY	DITHIOLS	DIUTURNAL	DIVI
DISTILLS	DISUSAGE	DITHIONIC	DIV	DIVIDABLE
DISTILS	DISUSAGES	DITHYRAMB	DIVA	DIVIDANT
DISTINCT	DISUSE	DITING	DIVAGATE	DIVIDE
DISTINGUE	DISUSED	DITOKOUS	DIVAGATED	DIVIDED
DISTOME	DISUSES	DITONE	DIVAGATES	DIVIDEDLY
DISTOMES	DISUSING	DITONES	DIVALENCE	DIVIDEND
DISTORT	DISVALUE	DITROCHEE	DIVALENCY	DIVIDENDS
DISTORTED	DISVALUED	DITS	DIVALENT	DIVIDER
DISTORTER	DISVALUES	DITSIER	DIVALENTS	DIVIDERS
DISTORTS	DISVOUCH	DITSIEST	DIVAN	DIVIDES
DISTRACT	DISYOKE	DITSINESS	DIVANS	DIVIDING
DISTRACTS	DISYOKED	DITSY	DIVAS	DIVIDINGS
DISTRAIL	DISYOKES	DITT	DIVE	DIVIDIVI
DISTRAILS	DISYOKING	DITTANDER	DIVEBOMB	DIVIDIVIS
DISTRAIN	DIT	DITTANIES	DIVEBOMBS	DIVIDUAL
DISTRAINS	DITA	DITTANY	DIVED	DIVIDUOUS
DISTRAINT	DITAL	DITTAY	DIVELLENT	DIVIED
DISTRAIT	DITALS	DITTAYS	DIVER	DIVINABLE
DISTRAITE	DITAS	DITTED	DIVERGE	DIVINATOR
DISTRESS	DITCH	DITTIED	DIVERGED	DIVINE
DISTRICT	DITCHED	DITTIES	DIVERGENT	DIVINED
DISTRICTS	DITCHER	DITTING	DIVERGES	DIVINELY

DIVINER	DIVULSED	DJEMBES	DOBRO	DOCKLANDS
DIVINERS	DIVULSES	DJIBBA	DOBROS	DOCKS
DIVINES	DIVULSING	DJIBBAH	DOBS	DOCKSIDE
DIVINEST	DIVULSION	DJIBBAHS	DOBSON	DOCKSIDES
DIVING	DIVULSIVE	DJIBBAS	DOBSONFLY	DOCKYARD
DIVINGS	DIVVIED	DJIN	DOBSONS	DOCKYARDS
DIVINIFY	DIVVIER	DJINN	DOBY	DOCO
DIVINING	DIVVIES	DJINNI	DOC	DOCOS
DIVINISE	DIVVIEST	DJINNS	DOCENT	DOCQUET
DIVINISED	DIVVY	DJINNY	DOCENTS	DOCQUETED
DIVINISES	DIVVYING	DJINS	DOCETIC	DOCQUETS
DIVINITY	DIVYING	DO	DOCHMIAC	DOCS
DIVINIZE	DIWAN	DOAB	DOCHMII	DOCTOR
DIVINIZED	DIWANS	DOABLE	DOCHMIUS	DOCTORAL
DIVINIZES	DIXI	DOABS	DOCHT	DOCTORAND
DIVIS	DIXIE	DOAT	DOCIBLE	DOCTORATE
DIVISIBLE	DIXIES	DOATED	DOCILE	DOCTORED
DIVISIBLY	DIXIT	DOATER	DOCILELY	DOCTORESS
DIVISIM	DIXITS	DOATERS	DOCILER	DOCTORIAL
DIVISION	DIXY	DOATING	DOCILEST	DOCTORING
DIVISIONS	DIYA	DOATINGS	DOCILITY	DOCTORLY
DIVISIVE	DIYAS	DOATS	DOCIMASY	DOCTORS
DIVISOR	DIZAIN	DOB	DOCK	DOCTRESS
DIVISORS	DIZAINS	DOBBED	DOCKAGE	DOCTRINAL
DIVNA	DIZEN	DOBBER	DOCKAGES	DOCTRINE
DIVO	DIZENED	DOBBERS	DOCKED	DOCTRINES
DIVORCE	DIZENING	DOBBIE	DOCKEN	DOCU
DIVORCED	DIZENMENT	DOBBIES	DOCKENS	DOCUDRAMA
DIVORCEE	DIZENS	DOBBIN	DOCKER	DOCUMENT
DIVORCEES	DIZYGOTIC	DOBBING	DOCKERS	DOCUMENTS
DIVORCER	DIZYGOUS	DOBBINS	DOCKET	DOCUS
DIVORCERS	DIZZARD	DOBBY	DOCKETED	DOCUSOAP
DIVORCES	DIZZARDS	DOBCHICK	DOCKETING	DOCUSOAPS
DIVORCING	DIZZIED	DOBCHICKS	DOCKETS	DOD
DIVORCIVE	DIZZIER	DOBE	DOCKHAND	DODDARD
DIVOS	DIZZIES	DOBES	DOCKHANDS	DODDARDS
DIVOT	DIZZIEST	DOBHASH	DOCKING	DODDED
DIVOTS	DIZZILY	DOBHASHES	DOCKINGS	DODDER
DIVS	DIZZINESS	DOBIE	DOCKISE	DODDERED
DIVULGATE	DIZZY	DOBIES	DOCKISED	DODDERER
DIVULGE	DIZZYING	DOBLA	DOCKISES	DODDERERS
DIVULGED	DJEBEL	DOBLAS	DOCKISING	DODDERIER
DIVULGER	DJEBELS	DOBLON	DOCKIZE	DODDERING
DIVULGERS	DJELLABA	DOBLONES	DOCKIZED	DODDERS
DIVULGES	DJELLABAH	DOBLONS	DOCKIZES	DODDERY
DIVULGING	DJELLABAS	DOBRA	DOCKIZING	DODDIER
DIVULSE	DJEMBE	DOBRAS	DOCKLAND	DODDIES

D

DODDIEST	DOFFED	DOGGEDEST	DOGMATICS	DOGWOODS
DODDING	DOFFER	DOGGEDLY	DOGMATISE	DOGY
DODDIPOLL	DOFFERS	DOGGER	DOGMATISM	DOH
DODDLE	DOFFING	DOGGEREL	DOGMATIST	DOHS
DODDLES	DOFFS	DOGGERELS	DOGMATIZE	DOHYO
DODDY	DOG	DOGGERIES	DOGMATORY	DOHYOS
DODDYPOLL	DOGAN	DOGGERMAN	DOGMEN	DOILED
DODECAGON	DOGANS	DOGGERMEN	DOGNAP	DOILIED
DODGE	DOGARESSA	DOGGERS	DOGNAPED	DOILIES
DODGEBALL	DOGATE	DOGGERY	DOGNAPER	DOILT
DODGED	DOGATES	DOGGESS	DOGNAPERS	DOILTER
DODGEM	DOGBANE	DOGGESSES	DOGNAPING	DOILTEST
DODGEMS	DOGBANES	DOGGIE	DOGNAPPED	DOILY
DODGER	DOGBERRY	DOGGIER	DOGNAPPER	DOING
DODGERIES	DOGBOLT	DOGGIES	DOGNAPS	DOINGS
DODGERS	DOGBOLTS	DOGGIEST	DOGPILE	DOIT
DODGERY	DOGCART	DOGGINESS	DOGPILES	DOITED
DODGES	DOGCARTS	DOGGING	DOGREL	DOITIT
DODGIER	DOGDOM	DOGGINGS	DOGRELS	DOITKIN
DODGIEST	DOGDOMS	DOGGISH	DOGROBBER	DOITKINS
DODGINESS	DOGE	DOGGISHLY	DOGS	DOITS
DODGING	DOGEAR	DOGGO	DOGSBODY	DOJO
DODGINGS	DOGEARED	DOGGONE	DOGSHIP	DOJOS
DODGY	DOGEARING	DOGGONED	DOGSHIPS	DOL
DODKIN	DOGEARS	DOGGONER	DOGSHORES	DOLABRATE
DODKINS	DOGEATE	DOGGONES	DOGSHOW	DOLCE
DODMAN	DOGEATES	DOGGONEST	DOGSHOWS	DOLCES
DODMANS	DOGEDOM	DOGGONING	DOGSKIN	DOLCETTO
DODO	DOGEDOMS	DOGGREL	DOGSKINS	DOLCETTOS
DODOES	DOGES	DOGGRELS	DOGSLED	DOLCI
DODOISM	DOGESHIP	DOGGY	DOGSLEDS	DOLDRUMS
DODOISMS	DOGESHIPS	DOGHANGED	DOGSLEEP	DOLE
DODOS	DOGEY	DOGHOLE	DOGSLEEPS	DOLED
DODS	DOGEYS	DOGHOLES	DOGSTAIL	DOLEFUL
DOE	DOGFACE	DOGHOUSE	DOGSTAILS	DOLEFULLY
DOEK	DOGFACES	DOGHOUSES	DOGTAIL	DOLENT
DOEKS	DOGFIGHT	DOGIE	DOGTAILS	DOLENTE
DOEN	DOGFIGHTS	DOGIES	DOGTEETH	DOLERITE
DOER	DOGFISH	DOGLEG	DOGTOOTH	DOLERITES
DOERS	DOGFISHES	DOGLEGGED	DOGTOWN	DOLERITIC
DOES	DOGFOOD	DOGLEGS	DOGTOWNS	DOLES
DOESKIN	DOGFOODS	DOGLIKE	DOGTROT	DOLESOME
DOESKINS	DOGFOUGHT	DOGMA	DOGTROTS	DOLIA
DOEST	DOGFOX	DOGMAN	DOGVANE	DOLICHOS
DOETH	DOGFOXES	DOGMAS	DOGVANES	DOLICHURI
DOF	DOGGED	DOGMATA	DOGWATCH	DOLINA
DOFF	DOGGEDER	DOGMATIC	DOGWOOD	DOLINAS

DOLINE
DOLINES
DOLING
DOLIUM
DOLL
DOLLAR
DOLLARED
DOLLARISE
DOLLARIZE
DOLLARS
DOLLDOM
DOLLDOMS
DOLLED
DOLLHOOD
DOLLHOODS
DOLLHOUSE
DOLLIED
DOLLIER
DOLLIERS
DOLLIES
DOLLINESS
DOLLING
DOLLISH
DOLLISHLY
DOLLOP
DOLLOPED
DOLLOPING
DOLLOPS
DOLLS
DOLLY
DOLLYBIRD
DOLLYING
DOLMA
DOLMADES
DOLMAN
DOLMANS
DOLMAS
DOLMEN
DOLMENIC
DOLMENS
DOLOMITE
DOLOMITES
DOLOMITIC
DOLOR
DOLORIFIC
DOLOROSO
DOLOROUS

DOLORS
DOLOS
DOLOSSE
DOLOSTONE
DOLOUR
DOLOURS
DOLPHIN
DOLPHINET
DOLPHINS
DOLS
DOLT
DOLTISH
DOLTISHLY
DOLTS
DOM
DOMAIN
DOMAINAL
DOMAINE
DOMAINES
DOMAINS
DOMAL
DOMANIAL
DOMATIA
DOMATIUM
DOME
DOMED
DOMELIKE
DOMES
DOMESDAY
DOMESDAYS
DOMESTIC
DOMESTICS
DOMETT
DOMETTS
DOMIC
DOMICAL
DOMICALLY
DOMICIL
DOMICILE
DOMICILED
DOMICILES
DOMICILS
DOMIER
DOMIEST
DOMINANCE
DOMINANCY
DOMINANT

DOMINANTS
DOMINATE
DOMINATED
DOMINATES
DOMINATOR
DOMINE
DOMINEE
DOMINEER
DOMINEERS
DOMINEES
DOMINES
DOMING
DOMINICAL
DOMINICK
DOMINICKS
DOMINIE
DOMINIES
DOMINION
DOMINIONS
DOMINIQUE
DOMINIUM
DOMINIUMS
DOMINO
DOMINOES
DOMINOS
DOMOIC
DOMS
DOMY
DON
DONA
DONAH
DONAHS
DONAIR
DONAIRS
DONARIES
DONARY
DONAS
DONATARY
DONATE
DONATED
DONATES
DONATING
DONATION
DONATIONS
DONATISM
DONATISMS
DONATIVE

DONATIVES
DONATOR
DONATORS
DONATORY
DONDER
DONDERED
DONDERING
DONDERS
DONE
DONEE
DONEES
DONEGAL
DONEGALS
DONENESS
DONEPEZIL
DONER
DONG
DONGA
DONGAS
DONGED
DONGING
DONGLE
DONGLES
DONGOLA
DONGOLAS
DONGS
DONING
DONINGS
DONJON
DONJONS
DONKEY
DONKEYS
DONKO
DONKOS
DONNA
DONNARD
DONNART
DONNAS
DONNAT
DONNATS
DONNE
DONNED
DONNEE
DONNEES
DONNERD
DONNERED
DONNERT

DONNES
DONNICKER
DONNIES
DONNIKER
DONNIKERS
DONNING
DONNISH
DONNISHLY
DONNISM
DONNISMS
DONNOT
DONNOTS
DONNY
DONOR
DONORS
DONORSHIP
DONS
DONSHIP
DONSHIPS
DONSIE
DONSIER
DONSIEST
DONSY
DONUT
DONUTS
DONUTTED
DONUTTING
DONZEL
DONZELS
DOO
DOOB
DOOBIE
DOOBIES
DOOBREY
DOOBREYS
DOOBRIE
DOOBRIES
DOOBRY
DOOBS
DOOCE
DOOCED
DOOCES
DOOCING
DOOCOT
DOOCOTS
DOODAD
DOODADS

DOODAH	DOOMSDAYS	DOORWOMAN	DOPPIE	DORLACHS
DOODAHS	DOOMSMAN	DOORWOMEN	DOPPIES	DORM
DOODIES	DOOMSMEN	DOORYARD	DOPPING	DORMANCY
DOODLE	DOOMSTER	DOORYARDS	DOPPINGS	DORMANT
DOODLEBUG	DOOMSTERS	DOOS	DOPPIO	DORMANTS
DOODLED	DOOMWATCH	DOOSRA	DOPPIOS	DORMER
DOODLER	DOOMY	DOOSRAS	DOPS	DORMERED
DOODLERS	DOON	DOOWOP	DOPY	DORMERS
DOODLES	DOONA	DOOWOPS	DOR	DORMICE
DOODLING	DOONAS	DOOZER	DORAD	DORMIE
DOODOO	DOOR	DOOZERS	DORADO	DORMIENT
DOODOOS	DOORBELL	DOOZIE	DORADOS	DORMIN
DOODY	DOORBELLS	DOOZIES	DORADS	DORMINS
DOOFER	DOORCASE	DOOZY	DORB	DORMITION
DOOFERS	DOORCASES	DOP	DORBA	DORMITIVE
DOOFUS	DOORED	DOPA	DORBAS	DORMITORY
DOOFUSES	DOORFRAME	DOPAMINE	DORBEETLE	DORMOUSE
DOOHICKEY	DOORJAMB	DOPAMINES	DORBS	DORMS
DOOK	DOORJAMBS	DOPANT	DORBUG	DORMY
DOOKED	DOORKNOB	DOPANTS	DORBUGS	DORNECK
DOOKET	DOORKNOBS	DOPAS	DORE	DORNECKS
DOOKETS	DOORKNOCK	DOPATTA	DOREE	DORNICK
DOOKING	DOORLESS	DOPATTAS	DOREES	DORNICKS
DOOKS	DOORMAN	DOPE	DORES	DORNOCK
DOOL	DOORMAT	DOPED	DORHAWK	DORNOCKS
DOOLALLY	DOORMATS	DOPEHEAD	DORHAWKS	DORONICUM
DOOLAN	DOORMEN	DOPEHEADS	DORIC	DORP
DOOLANS	DOORN	DOPER	DORIDOID	DORPER
DOOLE	DOORNAIL	DOPERS	DORIDOIDS	DORPERS
DOOLEE	DOORNAILS	DOPES	DORIES	DORPS
DOOLEES	DOORNBOOM	DOPESHEET	DORIS	DORR
DOOLES	DOORNS	DOPEST	DORISE	DORRED
DOOLIE	DOORPLATE	DOPESTER	DORISED	DORRING
DOOLIES	DOORPOST	DOPESTERS	DORISES	DORRS
DOOLS	DOORPOSTS	DOPEY	DORISING	DORS
DOOLY	DOORS	DOPEYNESS	DORIZE	DORSA
DOOM	DOORSILL	DOPIAZA	DORIZED	DORSAD
DOOMED	DOORSILLS	DOPIAZAS	DORIZES	DORSAL
DOOMFUL	DOORSMAN	DOPIER	DORIZING	DORSALLY
DOOMFULLY	DOORSMEN	DOPIEST	DORK	DORSALS
DOOMIER	DOORSTEP	DOPILY	DORKIER	DORSE
DOOMIEST	DOORSTEPS	DOPINESS	DORKIEST	DORSEL
DOOMILY	DOORSTONE	DOPING	DORKINESS	DORSELS
DOOMING	DOORSTOP	DOPINGS	DORKISH	DORSER
DOOMS	DOORSTOPS	DOPPED	DORKS	DORSERS
DOOMSAYER	DOORWAY	DOPPER	DORKY	DORSES
DOOMSDAY	DOORWAYS	DOPPERS	DORLACH	DORSIFLEX

DORSUM	DOSSERETS	DOTTINESS	DOUCENESS	DOUPIONI
DORT	DOSSERS	DOTTING	DOUCEPERE	DOUPIONIS
DORTED	DOSSES	DOTTLE	DOUCER	DOUPPIONI
DORTER	DOSSHOUSE	DOTTLED	DOUCEST	DOUPS
DORTERS	DOSSIER	DOTTLER	DOUCET	DOUR
DORTIER	DOSSIERS	DOTTLES	DOUCETS	DOURA
DORTIEST	DOSSIL	DOTTLEST	DOUCEUR	DOURAH
DORTINESS	DOSSILS	DOTTREL	DOUCEURS	DOURAHS
DORTING	DOSSING	DOTTRELS	DOUCHE	DOURAS
DORTOUR	DOST	DOTTY	DOUCHEBAG	DOURER
DORTOURS	DOT	DOTY	DOUCHED	DOUREST
DORTS	DOTAGE	DOUANE	DOUCHES	DOURINE
DORTY	DOTAGES	DOUANES	DOUCHING	DOURINES
DORY	DOTAL	DOUANIER	DOUCHINGS	DOURLY
DORYMAN	DOTANT	DOUANIERS	DOUCINE	DOURNESS
DORYMEN	DOTANTS	DOUAR	DOUCINES	DOUSE
DOS	DOTARD	DOUARS	DOUCS	DOUSED
DOSA	DOTARDLY	DOUBLE	DOUGH	DOUSER
DOSAGE	DOTARDS	DOUBLED	DOUGHBALL	DOUSERS
DOSAGES	DOTATION	DOUBLER	DOUGHBOY	DOUSES
DOSAI	DOTATIONS	DOUBLERS	DOUGHBOYS	DOUSING
DOSAS	DOTCOM	DOUBLES	DOUGHFACE	DOUT
DOSE	DOTCOMMER	DOUBLET	DOUGHIER	DOUTED
DOSED	DOTCOMS	DOUBLETON	DOUGHIEST	DOUTER
DOSEH	DOTE	DOUBLETS	DOUGHLIKE	DOUTERS
DOSEHS	DOTED	DOUBLING	DOUGHNUT	DOUTING
DOSEMETER	DOTER	DOUBLINGS	DOUGHNUTS	DOUTS
DOSER	DOTERS	DOUBLOON	DOUGHS	DOUX
DOSERS	DOTES	DOUBLOONS	DOUGHT	DOUZEPER
DOSES	DOTH	DOUBLURE	DOUGHTIER	DOUZEPERS
DOSH	DOTIER	DOUBLURES	DOUGHTILY	DOVE
DOSHA	DOTIEST	DOUBLY	DOUGHTY	DOVECOT
DOSHAS	DOTING	DOUBT	DOUGHY	DOVECOTE
DOSHES	DOTINGLY	DOUBTABLE	DOUK	DOVECOTES
DOSIMETER	DOTINGS	DOUBTABLY	DOUKED	DOVECOTS
DOSIMETRY	DOTISH	DOUBTED	DOUKING	DOVED
DOSING	DOTS	DOUBTER	DOUKS	DOVEISH
DOSIOLOGY	DOTTED	DOUBTERS	DOULA	DOVEKEY
DOSOLOGY	DOTTEL	DOUBTFUL	DOULAS	DOVEKEYS
DOSS	DOTTELS	DOUBTFULS	DOULEIA	DOVEKIE
DOSSAL	DOTTER	DOUBTING	DOULEIAS	DOVEKIES
DOSSALS	DOTTEREL	DOUBTINGS	DOUM	DOVELET
DOSSED	DOTTERELS	DOUBTLESS	DOUMA	DOVELETS
DOSSEL	DOTTERS	DOUBTS	DOUMAS	DOVELIKE
DOSSELS	DOTTIER	DOUC	DOUMS	DOVEN
DOSSER	DOTTIEST	DOUCE	DOUN	DOVENED
DOSSERET	DOTTILY	DOUCELY	DOUP	DOVENING

D

DOVENS	DOWIE	DOWNHILLS	DOWNSTAGE	DOXASTICS
DOVER	DOWIER	DOWNHOLE	DOWNSTAIR	DOXIE
DOVERED	DOWIEST	DOWNIER	DOWNSTATE	DOXIES
DOVERING	DOWING	DOWNIES	DOWNSWEPT	DOXOLOGY
DOVERS	DOWITCHER	DOWNIEST	DOWNSWING	DOXY
DOVES	DOWL	DOWNILY	DOWNTHROW	DOY
DOVETAIL	DOWLAS	DOWNINESS	DOWNTICK	DOYEN
DOVETAILS	DOWLASES	DOWNING	DOWNTICKS	DOYENNE
DOVIE	DOWLE	DOWNLAND	DOWNTIME	DOYENNES
DOVIER	DOWLES	DOWNLANDS	DOWNTIMES	DOYENS
DOVIEST	DOWLIER	DOWNLESS	DOWNTOWN	DOYLEY
DOVING	DOWLIEST	DOWNLIGHT	DOWNTOWNS	DOYLEYS
DOVISH	DOWLNE	DOWNLIKE	DOWNTREND	DOYLIES
DOW	DOWLNES	DOWNLINK	DOWNTROD	DOYLY
DOWABLE	DOWLNEY	DOWNLINKS	DOWNTURN	DOYS
DOWAGER	DOWLS	DOWNLOAD	DOWNTURNS	DOZE
DOWAGERS	DOWLY	DOWNLOADS	DOWNWARD	DOZED
DOWAR	DOWN	DOWNLOW	DOWNWARDS	DOZEN
DOWARS	DOWNA	DOWNLOWS	DOWNWARP	DOZENED
DOWD	DOWNBEAT	DOWNMOST	DOWNWARPS	DOZENING
DOWDIER	DOWNBEATS	DOWNPIPE	DOWNWASH	DOZENS
DOWDIES	DOWNBOW	DOWNPIPES	DOWNWIND	DOZENTH
DOWDIEST	DOWNBOWS	DOWNPLAY	DOWNY	DOZENTHS
DOWDILY	DOWNBURST	DOWNPLAYS	DOWNZONE	DOZER
DOWDINESS	DOWNCAST	DOWNPOUR	DOWNZONED	DOZERS
DOWDS	DOWNCASTS	DOWNPOURS	DOWNZONES	DOZES
DOWDY	DOWNCOME	DOWNRANGE	DOWP	DOZIER
DOWDYISH	DOWNCOMER	DOWNRATE	DOWPS	DOZIEST
DOWDYISM	DOWNCOMES	DOWNRATED	DOWRIES	DOZILY
DOWDYISMS	DOWNCOURT	DOWNRATES	DOWRY	DOZINESS
DOWED	DOWNCRIED	DOWNRIGHT	DOWS	DOZING
DOWEL	DOWNCRIES	DOWNRIVER	DOWSABEL	DOZINGS
DOWELED	DOWNCRY	DOWNRUSH	DOWSABELS	DOZY
DOWELING	DOWNDRAFT	DOWNS	DOWSE	DRAB
DOWELINGS	DOWNED	DOWNSCALE	DOWSED	DRABBED
DOWELLED	DOWNER	DOWNSHIFT	DOWSER	DRABBER
DOWELLING	DOWNERS	DOWNSIDE	DOWSERS	DRABBERS
DOWELS	DOWNFALL	DOWNSIDES	DOWSES	DRABBEST
DOWER	DOWNFALLS	DOWNSIZE	DOWSET	DRABBET
DOWERED	DOWNFIELD	DOWNSIZED	DOWSETS	DRABBETS
DOWERIES	DOWNFLOW	DOWNSIZER	DOWSING	DRABBIER
DOWERING	DOWNFLOWS	DOWNSIZES	DOWSINGS	DRABBIEST
DOWERLESS	DOWNFORCE	DOWNSLIDE	DOWT	DRABBING
DOWERS	DOWNGRADE	DOWNSLOPE	DOWTS	DRABBISH
DOWERY	DOWNHAUL	DOWNSPIN	DOXAPRAM	DRABBLE
DOWF	DOWNHAULS	DOWNSPINS	DOXAPRAMS	DRABBLED
DOWFNESS	DOWNHILL	DOWNSPOUT	DOXASTIC	DRABBLER

DRABBLERS	DRAFTING	DRAGSMEN	DRAMSHOPS	DRAUNTS
DRABBLES	DRAFTINGS	DRAGSTER	DRANGWAY	DRAVE
DRABBLING	DRAFTS	DRAGSTERS	DRANGWAYS	DRAW
DRABBY	DRAFTSMAN	DRAGSTRIP	DRANK	DRAWABLE
DRABETTE	DRAFTSMEN	DRAGWAY	DRANT	DRAWBACK
DRABETTES	DRAFTY	DRAGWAYS	DRANTED	DRAWBACKS
DRABLER	DRAG	DRAIL	DRANTING	DRAWBAR
DRABLERS	DRAGEE	DRAILED	DRANTS	DRAWBARS
DRABLY	DRAGEES	DRAILING	DRAP	DRAWBORE
DRABNESS	DRAGGED	DRAILS	DRAPABLE	DRAWBORES
DRABS	DRAGGER	DRAIN	DRAPE	DRAWCORD
DRAC	DRAGGERS	DRAINABLE	DRAPEABLE	DRAWCORDS
DRACAENA	DRAGGIER	DRAINAGE	DRAPED	DRAWDOWN
DRACAENAS	DRAGGIEST	DRAINAGES	DRAPER	DRAWDOWNS
DRACENA	DRAGGING	DRAINED	DRAPERIED	DRAWEE
DRACENAS	DRAGGINGS	DRAINER	DRAPERIES	DRAWEES
DRACHM	DRAGGLE	DRAINERS	DRAPERS	DRAWER
DRACHMA	DRAGGLED	DRAINING	DRAPERY	DRAWERFUL
DRACHMAE	DRAGGLES	DRAINPIPE	DRAPES	DRAWERS
DRACHMAI	DRAGGLING	DRAINS	DRAPET	DRAWING
DRACHMAS	DRAGGY	DRAISENE	DRAPETS	DRAWINGS
DRACHMS	DRAGHOUND	DRAISENES	DRAPEY	DRAWKNIFE
DRACK	DRAGLINE	DRAISINE	DRAPIER	DRAWL
DRACO	DRAGLINES	DRAISINES	DRAPIERS	DRAWLED
DRACONE	DRAGNET	DRAKE	DRAPIEST	DRAWLER
DRACONES	DRAGNETS	DRAKES	DRAPING	DRAWLERS
DRACONIAN	DRAGOMAN	DRAM	DRAPPED	DRAWLIER
DRACONIC	DRAGOMANS	DRAMA	DRAPPIE	DRAWLIEST
DRACONISM	DRAGOMEN	DRAMADIES	DRAPPIES	DRAWLING
DRACONTIC	DRAGON	DRAMADY	DRAPPING	DRAWLS
DRAD	DRAGONESS	DRAMAS	DRAPPY	DRAWLY
DRAFF	DRAGONET	DRAMATIC	DRAPS	DRAWN
DRAFFIER	DRAGONETS	DRAMATICS	DRASTIC	DRAWNWORK
DRAFFIEST	DRAGONFLY	DRAMATISE	DRASTICS	DRAWPLATE
DRAFFISH	DRAGONISE	DRAMATIST	DRAT	DRAWS
DRAFFS	DRAGONISH	DRAMATIZE	DRATCHELL	DRAWSHAVE
DRAFFY	DRAGONISM	DRAMATURG	DRATS	DRAWTUBE
DRAFT	DRAGONIZE	DRAMEDIES	DRATTED	DRAWTUBES
DRAFTABLE	DRAGONNE	DRAMEDY	DRATTING	DRAY
DRAFTED	DRAGONS	DRAMMACH	DRAUGHT	DRAYAGE
DRAFTEE	DRAGOON	DRAMMACHS	DRAUGHTED	DRAYAGES
DRAFTEES	DRAGOONED	DRAMMED	DRAUGHTER	DRAYED
DRAFTER	DRAGOONS	DRAMMING	DRAUGHTS	DRAYHORSE
DRAFTERS	DRAGROPE	DRAMMOCK	DRAUGHTY	DRAYING
DRAFTIER	DRAGROPES	DRAMMOCKS	DRAUNT	DRAYMAN
DRAFTIEST	DRAGS	DRAMS	DRAUNTED	DRAYMEN
DRAFTILY	DRAGSMAN	DRAMSHOP	DRAUNTING	DRAYS

DRAZEL	DRECK	DRENCHING	DRICE	DRIP
DRAZELS	DRECKIER	DRENT	DRICES	DRIPLESS
DREAD	DRECKIEST	DREPANID	DRICKSIE	DRIPPED
DREADED	DRECKISH	DREPANIDS	DRICKSIER	DRIPPER
DREADER	DRECKS	DREPANIUM	DRIED	DRIPPERS
DREADERS	DRECKSILL	DRERE	DRIEGH	DRIPPIER
DREADEST	DRECKY	DRERES	DRIER	DRIPPIEST
DREADFUL	DREDGE	DRERIHEAD	DRIERS	DRIPPILY
DREADFULS	DREDGED	DRESS	DRIES	DRIPPING
DREADING	DREDGER	DRESSAGE	DRIEST	DRIPPINGS
DREADLESS	DREDGERS	DRESSAGES	DRIFT	DRIPPY
DREADLOCK	DREDGES	DRESSED	DRIFTAGE	DRIPS
DREADLY	DREDGING	DRESSER	DRIFTAGES	DRIPSTONE
DREADS	DREDGINGS	DRESSERS	DRIFTED	DRIPT
DREAM	DREE	DRESSES	DRIFTER	DRISHEEN
DREAMBOAT	DREED	DRESSIER	DRIFTERS	DRISHEENS
DREAMED	DREEING	DRESSIEST	DRIFTIER	DRIVABLE
DREAMER	DREER	DRESSILY	DRIFTIEST	DRIVE
DREAMERS	DREES	DRESSING	DRIFTING	DRIVEABLE
DREAMERY	DREEST	DRESSINGS	DRIFTINGS	DRIVEL
DREAMFUL	DREG	DRESSMADE	DRIFTLESS	DRIVELED
DREAMHOLE	DREGGIER	DRESSMAKE	DRIFTNET	DRIVELER
DREAMIER	DREGGIEST	DRESSY	DRIFTNETS	DRIVELERS
DREAMIEST	DREGGISH	DREST	DRIFTPIN	DRIVELINE
DREAMILY	DREGGY	DREVILL	DRIFTPINS	DRIVELING
DREAMING	DREGS	DREVILLS	DRIFTS	DRIVELLED
DREAMINGS	DREICH	DREW	DRIFTWOOD	DRIVELLER
DREAMLAND	DREICHER	DREY	DRIFTY	DRIVELS
DREAMLESS	DREICHEST	DREYS	DRILL	DRIVEN
DREAMLIKE	DREIDEL	DRIB	DRILLABLE	DRIVER
DREAMS	DREIDELS	DRIBBED	DRILLED	DRIVERS
DREAMT	DREIDL	DRIBBER	DRILLER	DRIVES
DREAMTIME	DREIDLS	DRIBBERS	DRILLERS	DRIVEWAY
DREAMY	DREIGH	DRIBBING	DRILLHOLE	DRIVEWAYS
DREAR	DREIGHER	DRIBBLE	DRILLING	DRIVING
DREARE	DREIGHEST	DRIBBLED	DRILLINGS	DRIVINGLY
DREARER	DREK	DRIBBLER	DRILLS	DRIVINGS
DREARES	DREKKIER	DRIBBLERS	DRILLSHIP	DRIZZLE
DREAREST	DREKKIEST	DRIBBLES	DRILY	DRIZZLED
DREARIER	DREKKISH	DRIBBLET	DRINK	DRIZZLES
DREARIES	DREKKY	DRIBBLETS	DRINKABLE	DRIZZLIER
DREARIEST	DREKS	DRIBBLIER	DRINKABLY	DRIZZLING
DREARILY	DRENCH	DRIBBLING	DRINKER	DRIZZLY
DREARING	DRENCHED	DRIBBLY	DRINKERS	DROGER
DREARINGS	DRENCHER	DRIBLET	DRINKING	DROGERS
DREARS	DRENCHERS	DRIBLETS	DRINKINGS	DROGHER
DREARY	DRENCHES	DRIBS	DRINKS	DROGHERS

DROGUE	DRONER	DROPFORGE	DROSSY	DRUBBED
DROGUES	DRONERS	DROPHEAD	DROSTDIES	DRUBBER
DROGUET	DRONES	DROPHEADS	DROSTDY	DRUBBERS
DROGUETS	DRONGO	DROPKICK	DROSTDYS	DRUBBING
DROICH	DRONGOES	DROPKICKS	DROUGHT	DRUBBINGS
DROICHIER	DRONGOS	DROPLET	DROUGHTS	DRUBS
DROICHS	DRONIER	DROPLETS	DROUGHTY	DRUCKEN
DROICHY	DRONIEST	DROPLIGHT	DROUK	DRUDGE
DROID	DRONING	DROPLOCK	DROUKED	DRUDGED
DROIDS	DRONINGLY	DROPLOCKS	DROUKING	DRUDGER
DROIL	DRONISH	DROPOUT	DROUKINGS	DRUDGERS
DROILED	DRONISHLY	DROPOUTS	DROUKIT	DRUDGERY
DROILING	DRONKLAP	DROPPABLE	DROUKS	DRUDGES
DROILS	DRONKLAPS	DROPPED	DROUTH	DRUDGING
DROIT	DRONY	DROPPER	DROUTHIER	DRUDGISM
DROITS	DROOB	DROPPERS	DROUTHS	DRUDGISMS
DROKE	DROOBS	DROPPING	DROUTHY	DRUG
DROKES	DROOG	DROPPINGS	DROVE	DRUGGED
DROLE	DROOGISH	DROPPLE	DROVED	DRUGGER
DROLER	DROOGS	DROPPLES	DROVER	DRUGGERS
DROLES	DROOK	DROPS	DROVERS	DRUGGET
DROLEST	DROOKED	DROPSEED	DROVES	DRUGGETS
DROLL	DROOKING	DROPSEEDS	DROVING	DRUGGIE
DROLLED	DROOKINGS	DROPSHOT	DROVINGS	DRUGGIER
DROLLER	DROOKIT	DROPSHOTS	DROW	DRUGGIES
DROLLERY	DROOKS	DROPSICAL	DROWN	DRUGGIEST
DROLLEST	DROOL	DROPSIED	DROWND	DRUGGING
DROLLING	DROOLED	DROPSIES	DROWNDED	DRUGGIST
DROLLINGS	DROOLIER	DROPSONDE	DROWNDING	DRUGGISTS
DROLLISH	DROOLIEST	DROPSTONE	DROWNDS	DRUGGY
DROLLNESS	DROOLING	DROPSY	DROWNED	DRUGLESS
DROLLS	DROOLS	DROPT	DROWNER	DRUGLORD
DROLLY	DROOLY	DROPTOP	DROWNERS	DRUGLORDS
DROME	DROOME	DROPTOPS	DROWNING	DRUGMAKER
DROMEDARE	DROOMES	DROPWISE	DROWNINGS	DRUGS
DROMEDARY	DROOP	DROPWORT	DROWNS	DRUGSTER
DROMES	DROOPED	DROPWORTS	DROWS	DRUGSTERS
DROMIC	DROOPIER	DROSERA	DROWSE	DRUGSTORE
DROMICAL	DROOPIEST	DROSERAS	DROWSED	DRUID
DROMOI	DROOPILY	DROSHKIES	DROWSES	DRUIDESS
DROMON	DROOPING	DROSHKY	DROWSIER	DRUIDIC
DROMOND	DROOPS	DROSKIES	DROWSIEST	DRUIDICAL
DROMONDS	DROOPY	DROSKY	DROWSIHED	DRUIDISM
DROMONS	DROP	DROSS	DROWSILY	DRUIDISMS
DROMOS	DROPCLOTH	DROSSES	DROWSING	DRUIDRIES
DRONE	DROPFLIES	DROSSIER	DROWSY	DRUIDRY
DRONED	DROPFLY	DROSSIEST	DRUB	DRUIDS

DRUM	DRUSEN	DRYWELLS	DUBBINED	DUCKERS
DRUMBEAT	DRUSES	DSO	DUBBING	DUCKFOOT
DRUMBEATS	DRUSIER	DSOBO	DUBBINGS	DUCKIE
DRUMBLE	DRUSIEST	DSOBOS	DUBBINING	DUCKIER
DRUMBLED	DRUSY	DSOMO	DUBBINS	DUCKIES
DRUMBLES	DRUTHER	DSOMOS	DUBBO	DUCKIEST
DRUMBLING	DRUTHERS	DSOS	DUBBOS	DUCKING
DRUMFIRE	DRUXIER	DUAD	DUBIETIES	DUCKINGS
DRUMFIRES	DRUXIEST	DUADS	DUBIETY	DUCKISH
DRUMFISH	DRUXY	DUAL	DUBIOSITY	DUCKISHES
DRUMHEAD	DRY	DUALIN	DUBIOUS	DUCKLING
DRUMHEADS	DRYABLE	DUALINS	DUBIOUSLY	DUCKLINGS
DRUMLIER	DRYAD	DUALISE	DUBITABLE	DUCKMOLE
DRUMLIEST	DRYADES	DUALISED	DUBITABLY	DUCKMOLES
DRUMLIKE	DRYADIC	DUALISES	DUBITANCY	DUCKPIN
DRUMLIN	DRYADS	DUALISING	DUBITATE	DUCKPINS
DRUMLINS	DRYAS	DUALISM	DUBITATED	DUCKS
DRUMLY	DRYASDUST	DUALISMS	DUBITATES	DUCKSHOVE
DRUMMED	DRYBEAT	DUALIST	DUBNIUM	DUCKTAIL
DRUMMER	DRYBEATEN	DUALISTIC	DUBNIUMS	DUCKTAILS
DRUMMERS	DRYBEATS	DUALISTS	DUBONNET	DUCKWALK
DRUMMIES	DRYER	DUALITIES	DUBONNETS	DUCKWALKS
DRUMMING	DRYERS	DUALITY	DUBS	DUCKWEED
DRUMMINGS	DRYEST	DUALIZE	DUBSTEP	DUCKWEEDS
DRUMMOCK	DRYING	DUALIZED	DUBSTEPS	DUCKY
DRUMMOCKS	DRYINGS	DUALIZES	DUCAL	DUCT
DRUMMY	DRYISH	DUALIZING	DUCALLY	DUCTAL
DRUMROLL	DRYLAND	DUALLED	DUCAT	DUCTED
DRUMROLLS	DRYLANDS	DUALLIE	DUCATOON	DUCTILE
DRUMS	DRYLOT	DUALLIES	DUCATOONS	DUCTILELY
DRUMSTICK	DRYLOTS	DUALLING	DUCATS	DUCTILITY
DRUNK	DRYLY	DUALLY	DUCDAME	DUCTING
DRUNKARD	DRYMOUTH	DUALS	DUCE	DUCTINGS
DRUNKARDS	DRYMOUTHS	DUAN	DUCES	DUCTLESS
DRUNKEN	DRYNESS	DUANS	DUCHESS	DUCTS
DRUNKENLY	DRYNESSES	DUAR	DUCHESSE	DUCTULE
DRUNKER	DRYPOINT	DUARCHIES	DUCHESSED	DUCTULES
DRUNKEST	DRYPOINTS	DUARCHY	DUCHESSES	DUCTWORK
DRUNKISH	DRYS	DUARS	DUCHIES	DUCTWORKS
DRUNKS	DRYSALTER	DUATHLETE	DUCHY	DUD
DRUPE	DRYSTONE	DUATHLON	DUCI	DUDDER
DRUPEL	DRYSUIT	DUATHLONS	DUCK	DUDDERED
DRUPELET	DRYSUITS	DUB	DUCKBILL	DUDDERIES
DRUPELETS	DRYWALL	DUBBED	DUCKBILLS	DUDDERING
DRUPELS	DRYWALLED	DUBBER	DUCKBOARD	DUDDERS
DRUPES	DRYWALLS	DUBBERS	DUCKED	DUDDERY
DRUSE	DRYWELL	DUBBIN	DUCKER	DUDDIE

DUDDIER	DUENDE	DUHKHA	DULCITE	DUMBFOUND
DUDDIES	DUENDES	DUHKHAS	DULCITES	DUMBHEAD
DUDDIEST	DUENESS	DUI	DULCITOL	DUMBHEADS
DUDDY	DUENESSES	DUIKER	DULCITOLS	DUMBING
DUDE	DUENNA	DUIKERBOK	DULCITUDE	DUMBLY
DUDED	DUENNAS	DUIKERS	DULCOSE	DUMBNESS
DUDEEN	DUES	DUING	DULCOSES	DUMBO
DUDEENS	DUET	DUIT	DULE	DUMBOS
DUDENESS	DUETED	DUITS	DULES	DUMBS
DUDES	DUETING	DUKA	DULIA	DUMBSHIT
DUDETTE	DUETS	DUKAS	DULIAS	DUMBSHITS
DUDETTES	DUETT	DUKE	DULL	DUMBSHOW
DUDGEON	DUETTED	DUKED	DULLARD	DUMBSHOWS
DUDGEONS	DUETTI	DUKEDOM	DULLARDS	DUMBSIZE
DUDHEEN	DUETTING	DUKEDOMS	DULLED	DUMBSIZED
DUDHEENS	DUETTINO	DUKELING	DULLER	DUMBSIZES
DUDING	DUETTINOS	DUKELINGS	DULLEST	DUMDUM
DUDISH	DUETTIST	DUKERIES	DULLIER	DUMDUMS
DUDISHLY	DUETTISTS	DUKERY	DULLIEST	DUMELA
DUDISM	DUETTO	DUKES	DULLING	DUMFOUND
DUDISMS	DUETTOS	DUKESHIP	DULLISH	DUMFOUNDS
DUDS	DUETTS	DUKESHIPS	DULLISHLY	DUMKA
DUE	DUFF	DUKING	DULLNESS	DUMKAS
DUECENTO	DUFFED	DUKKA	DULLS	DUMKY
DUECENTOS	DUFFEL	DUKKAH	DULLY	DUMMERER
DUED	DUFFELS	DUKKAHS	DULNESS	DUMMERERS
DUEFUL	DUFFER	DUKKAS	DULNESSES	DUMMIED
DUEL	DUFFERDOM	DUKKHA	DULOCRACY	DUMMIER
DUELED	DUFFERISM	DUKKHAS	DULOSES	DUMMIES
DUELER	DUFFERS	DULCAMARA	DULOSIS	DUMMIEST
DUELERS	DUFFEST	DULCE	DULOTIC	DUMMINESS
DUELING	DUFFING	DULCES	DULSE	DUMMKOPF
DUELINGS	DUFFINGS	DULCET	DULSES	DUMMKOPFS
DUELIST	DUFFLE	DULCETLY	DULY	DUMMY
DUELISTS	DUFFLES	DULCETS	DUM	DUMMYING
DUELLED	DUFFS	DULCIAN	DUMA	DUMOSE
DUELLER	DUFUS	DULCIANA	DUMAIST	DUMOSITY
DUELLERS	DUFUSES	DULCIANAS	DUMAISTS	DUMOUS
DUELLI	DUG	DULCIANS	DUMAS	DUMP
DUELLING	DUGITE	DULCIFIED	DUMB	DUMPBIN
DUELLINGS	DUGITES	DULCIFIES	DUMBBELL	DUMPBINS
DUELLIST	DUGONG	DULCIFY	DUMBBELLS	DUMPCART
DUELLISTS	DUGONGS	DULCIMER	DUMBCANE	DUMPCARTS
DUELLO	DUGOUT	DULCIMERS	DUMBCANES	DUMPED
DUELLOS	DUGOUTS	DULCIMORE	DUMBED	DUMPEE
DUELS	DUGS	DULCINEA	DUMBER	DUMPEES
DUELSOME	DUH	DULCINEAS	DUMBEST	DUMPER

DUMPERS	DUNGAREE	DUNNING	DUPERS	DURATIVE
DUMPIER	DUNGAREED	DUNNINGS	DUPERY	DURATIVES
DUMPIES	DUNGAREES	DUNNISH	DUPES	DURBAR
DUMPIEST	DUNGED	DUNNITE	DUPING	DURBARS
DUMPILY	DUNGEON	DUNNITES	DUPINGS	DURDUM
DUMPINESS	DUNGEONED	DUNNO	DUPION	DURDUMS
DUMPING	DUNGEONER	DUNNOCK	DUPIONS	DURE
DUMPINGS	DUNGEONS	DUNNOCKS	DUPLE	DURED
DUMPISH	DUNGER	DUNNY	DUPLET	DUREFUL
DUMPISHLY	DUNGERS	DUNS	DUPLETS	DURES
DUMPLE	DUNGHEAP	DUNSH	DUPLEX	DURESS
DUMPLED	DUNGHEAPS	DUNSHED	DUPLEXED	DURESSE
DUMPLES	DUNGHILL	DUNSHES	DUPLEXER	DURESSES
DUMPLING	DUNGHILLS	DUNSHING	DUPLEXERS	DURGAH
DUMPLINGS	DUNGIER	DUNT	DUPLEXES	DURGAHS
DUMPS	DUNGIEST	DUNTED	DUPLEXING	DURGAN
DUMPSITE	DUNGING	DUNTING	DUPLEXITY	DURGANS
DUMPSITES	DUNGMERE	DUNTS	DUPLICAND	DURGIER
DUMPSTER	DUNGMERES	DUO	DUPLICATE	DURGIEST
DUMPSTERS	DUNGS	DUOBINARY	DUPLICITY	DURGY
DUMPTRUCK	DUNGY	DUODECIMO	DUPLIED	DURIAN
DUMPY	DUNITE	DUODENA	DUPLIES	DURIANS
DUN	DUNITES	DUODENAL	DUPLY	DURICRUST
DUNAM	DUNITIC	DUODENARY	DUPLYING	DURING
DUNAMS	DUNK	DUODENUM	DUPONDII	DURION
DUNCE	DUNKED	DUODENUMS	DUPONDIUS	DURIONS
DUNCEDOM	DUNKER	DUOLOG	DUPPED	DURMAST
DUNCEDOMS	DUNKERS	DUOLOGS	DUPPIES	DURMASTS
DUNCELIKE	DUNKING	DUOLOGUE	DUPPING	DURN
DUNCERIES	DUNKINGS	DUOLOGUES	DUPPY	DURNDEST
DUNCERY	DUNKS	DUOMI	DUPS	DURNED
DUNCES	DUNLIN	DUOMO	DURA	DURNEDER
DUNCH	DUNLINS	DUOMOS	DURABLE	DURNEDEST
DUNCHED	DUNNAGE	DUOPOLIES	DURABLES	DURNING
DUNCHES	DUNNAGES	DUOPOLY	DURABLY	DURNS
DUNCHING	DUNNAKIN	DUOPSONY	DURAL	DURO
DUNCICAL	DUNNAKINS	DUOS	DURALS	DUROC
DUNCISH	DUNNART	DUOTONE	DURALUMIN	DUROCS
DUNCISHLY	DUNNARTS	DUOTONES	DURAMEN	DUROMETER
DUNDER	DUNNED	DUP	DURAMENS	DUROS
DUNDERS	DUNNER	DUPABLE	DURANCE	DUROY
DUNE	DUNNESS	DUPATTA	DURANCES	DUROYS
DUNELAND	DUNNESSES	DUPATTAS	DURANT	DURR
DUNELANDS	DUNNEST	DUPE	DURANTS	DURRA
DUNELIKE	DUNNIER	DUPED	DURAS	DURRAS
DUNES	DUNNIES	DUPER	DURATION	DURRIE
DUNG	DUNNIEST	DUPERIES	DURATIONS	DURRIES

DURRS	DUSTHEAPS	DUVETYNS	DWELLED	DYEWOODS
DURRY	DUSTIER	DUX	DWELLER	DYEWORKS
DURST	DUSTIEST	DUXELLES	DWELLERS	DYING
DURUKULI	DUSTILY	DUXES	DWELLING	DYINGLY
DURUKULIS	DUSTINESS	DUYKER	DWELLINGS	DYINGNESS
DURUM	DUSTING	DUYKERS	DWELLS	DYINGS
DURUMS	DUSTINGS	DVANDVA	DWELT	DYKE
DURZI	DUSTLESS	DVANDVAS	DWILE	DYKED
DURZIS	DUSTLIKE	DVORNIK	DWILES	DYKES
DUSH	DUSTMAN	DVORNIKS	DWINDLE	DYKEY
DUSHED	DUSTMEN	DWAAL	DWINDLED	DYKIER
DUSHES	DUSTOFF	DWAALS	DWINDLES	DYKIEST
DUSHING	DUSTOFFS	DWALE	DWINDLING	DYKING
DUSK	DUSTPAN	DWALES	DWINE	DYKON
DUSKED	DUSTPANS	DWALM	DWINED	DYKONS
DUSKEN	DUSTPROOF	DWALMED	DWINES	DYNAMETER
DUSKENED	DUSTRAG	DWALMING	DWINING	DYNAMIC
DUSKENING	DUSTRAGS	DWALMS	DYABLE	DYNAMICAL
DUSKENS	DUSTS	DWAM	DYAD	DYNAMICS
DUSKER	DUSTSHEET	DWAMMED	DYADIC	DYNAMISE
DUSKEST	DUSTSTORM	DWAMMING	DYADICS	DYNAMISED
DUSKIER	DUSTUP	DWAMS	DYADS	DYNAMISES
DUSKIEST	DUSTUPS	DWANG	DYARCHAL	DYNAMISM
DUSKILY	DUSTY	DWANGS	DYARCHIC	DYNAMISMS
DUSKINESS	DUTCH	DWARF	DYARCHIES	DYNAMIST
DUSKING	DUTCHES	DWARFED	DYARCHY	DYNAMISTS
DUSKISH	DUTCHMAN	DWARFER	DYBBUK	DYNAMITE
DUSKISHLY	DUTCHMEN	DWARFEST	DYBBUKIM	DYNAMITED
DUSKLY	DUTEOUS	DWARFING	DYBBUKKIM	DYNAMITER
DUSKNESS	DUTEOUSLY	DWARFISH	DYBBUKS	DYNAMITES
DUSKS	DUTIABLE	DWARFISM	DYE	DYNAMITIC
DUSKY	DUTIED	DWARFISMS	DYEABLE	DYNAMIZE
DUST	DUTIES	DWARFLIKE	DYED	DYNAMIZED
DUSTBALL	DUTIFUL	DWARFNESS	DYEING	DYNAMIZES
DUSTBALLS	DUTIFULLY	DWARFS	DYEINGS	DYNAMO
DUSTBIN	DUTY	DWARVES	DYELINE	DYNAMOS
DUSTBINS	DUUMVIR	DWAUM	DYELINES	DYNAMOTOR
DUSTCART	DUUMVIRAL	DWAUMED	DYER	DYNAST
DUSTCARTS	DUUMVIRI	DWAUMING	DYERS	DYNASTIC
DUSTCLOTH	DUUMVIRS	DWAUMS	DYES	DYNASTIES
DUSTCOAT	DUVET	DWEEB	DYESTER	DYNASTS
DUSTCOATS	DUVETINE	DWEEBIER	DYESTERS	DYNASTY
DUSTCOVER	DUVETINES	DWEEBIEST	DYESTUFF	DYNATRON
DUSTED	DUVETS	DWEEBISH	DYESTUFFS	DYNATRONS
DUSTER	DUVETYN	DWEEBS	DYEWEED	DYNE
DUSTERS	DUVETYNE	DWEEBY	DYEWEEDS	DYNEIN
DUSTHEAP	DUVETYNES	DWELL	DYEWOOD	DYNEINS

DYNEL	DYSLEXIA	DYSPHAGIA	DYSPRAXIA	DYSTROPHY
DYNELS	DYSLEXIAS	DYSPHAGIC	DYSPRAXIC	DYSURIA
DYNES	DYSLEXIC	DYSPHAGY	DYSTAXIA	DYSURIAS
DYNODE	DYSLEXICS	DYSPHASIA	DYSTAXIAS	DYSURIC
DYNODES	DYSLOGIES	DYSPHASIC	DYSTAXIC	DYSURIES
DYNORPHIN	DYSLOGY	DYSPHONIA	DYSTECTIC	DYSURY
DYSBINDIN	DYSMELIA	DYSPHONIC	DYSTHESIA	DYTISCID
DYSCHROA	DYSMELIAS	DYSPHORIA	DYSTHETIC	DYTISCIDS
DYSCHROAS	DYSMELIC	DYSPHORIC	DYSTHYMIA	DYVOUR
DYSCHROIA	DYSODIL	DYSPLASIA	DYSTHYMIC	DYVOURIES
DYSCRASIA	DYSODILE	DYSPNEA	DYSTOCIA	DYVOURS
DYSCRASIC	DYSODILES	DYSPNEAL	DYSTOCIAL	DYVOURY
DYSCRATIC	DYSODILS	DYSPNEAS	DYSTOCIAS	DZEREN
DYSENTERY	DYSODYLE	DYSPNEIC	DYSTONIA	DZERENS
DYSGENIC	DYSODYLES	DYSPNOEA	DYSTONIAS	DZHO
DYSGENICS	DYSPATHY	DYSPNOEAL	DYSTONIC	DZHOS
DYSLALIA	DYSPEPSIA	DYSPNOEAS	DYSTOPIA	DZIGGETAI
DYSLALIAS	DYSPEPSY	DYSPNOEIC	DYSTOPIAN	DZO
DYSLECTIC	DYSPEPTIC	DYSPNOIC	DYSTOPIAS	DZOS

E

EA	EARBASHES	EARLSHIPS	EARTHFLAX	EASELED
EACH	EARBOB	EARLY	EARTHIER	EASELESS
EACHWHERE	EARBOBS	EARLYWOOD	EARTHIEST	EASELS
EADISH	EARBUD	EARMARK	EARTHILY	EASEMENT
EADISHES	EARBUDS	EARMARKED	EARTHING	EASEMENTS
EAGER	EARCON	EARMARKS	EARTHLIER	EASER
EAGERER	EARCONS	EARMUFF	EARTHLIES	EASERS
EAGEREST	EARD	EARMUFFS	EARTHLIKE	EASES
EAGERLY	EARDED	EARN	EARTHLING	EASIED
EAGERNESS	EARDING	EARNED	EARTHLY	EASIER
EAGERS	EARDROP	EARNER	EARTHMAN	EASIES
EAGLE	EARDROPS	EARNERS	EARTHMEN	EASIEST
EAGLED	EARDRUM	EARNEST	EARTHNUT	EASILY
EAGLEHAWK	EARDRUMS	EARNESTLY	EARTHNUTS	EASINESS
EAGLES	EARDS	EARNESTS	EARTHPEA	EASING
EAGLET	EARED	EARNING	EARTHPEAS	EASINGS
EAGLETS	EARFLAP	EARNINGS	EARTHRISE	EASLE
EAGLEWOOD	EARFLAPS	EARNS	EARTHS	EASLES
EAGLING	EARFUL	EARPHONE	EARTHSET	EASSEL
EAGRE	EARFULS	EARPHONES	EARTHSETS	EASSIL
EAGRES	EARHOLE	EARPICK	EARTHSTAR	EAST
EALDORMAN	EARHOLES	EARPICKS	EARTHWARD	EASTABOUT
EALDORMEN	EARING	EARPIECE	EARTHWAX	EASTBOUND
EALE	EARINGS	EARPIECES	EARTHWOLF	EASTED
EALED	EARL	EARPLUG	EARTHWORK	EASTER
EALES	EARLAP	EARPLUGS	EARTHWORM	EASTERLY
EALING	EARLAPS	EARRING	EARTHY	EASTERN
EAN	EARLDOM	EARRINGED	EARWAX	EASTERNER
EANED	EARLDOMS	EARRINGS	EARWAXES	EASTERS
EANING	EARLESS	EARS	EARWIG	EASTING
EANLING	EARLIER	EARSHOT	EARWIGGED	EASTINGS
EANLINGS	EARLIES	EARSHOTS	EARWIGGY	EASTLAND
EANS	EARLIEST	EARST	EARWIGS	EASTLANDS
EAR	EARLIKE	EARSTONE	EARWORM	EASTLIN
EARACHE	EARLINESS	EARSTONES	EARWORMS	EASTLING
EARACHES	EARLOBE	EARTH	EAS	EASTLINGS
EARBALL	EARLOBES	EARTHBORN	EASE	EASTLINS
EARBALLS	EARLOCK	EARTHED	EASED	EASTMOST
EARBASH	EARLOCKS	EARTHEN	EASEFUL	EASTS
EARBASHED	EARLS	EARTHFALL	EASEFULLY	EASTWARD
EARBASHER	EARLSHIP	EARTHFAST	EASEL	EASTWARDS

EASY	EBIONISE	ECBOLICS	ECHINI	ECLATS
EASYGOING	EBIONISED	ECCE	ECHINOID	ECLECTIC
EASYING	EBIONISES	ECCENTRIC	ECHINOIDS	ECLECTICS
EAT	EBIONISM	ECCLESIA	ECHINUS	ECLIPSE
EATABLE	EBIONISMS	ECCLESIAE	ECHINUSES	ECLIPSED
EATABLES	EBIONITIC	ECCLESIAL	ECHIUM	ECLIPSER
EATAGE	EBIONIZE	ECCO	ECHIUMS	ECLIPSERS
EATAGES	EBIONIZED	ECCRINE	ECHIURAN	ECLIPSES
EATCHE	EBIONIZES	ECCRISES	ECHIURANS	ECLIPSING
EATCHES	EBON	ECCRISIS	ECHIUROID	ECLIPSIS
EATEN	EBONICS	ECCRITIC	ECHO	ECLIPTIC
EATER	EBONIES	ECCRITICS	ECHOED	ECLIPTICS
EATERIE	EBONISE	ECDEMIC	ECHOER	ECLOGITE
EATERIES	EBONISED	ECDYSES	ECHOERS	ECLOGITES
EATERS	EBONISES	ECDYSIAL	ECHOES	ECLOGUE
EATERY	EBONISING	ECDYSIAST	ECHOEY	ECLOGUES
EATH	EBONIST	ECDYSIS	ECHOGRAM	ECLOSE
EATHE	EBONISTS	ECDYSISES	ECHOGRAMS	ECLOSED
EATHLY	EBONITE	ECDYSON	ECHOGRAPH	ECLOSES
EATING	EBONITES	ECDYSONE	ECHOIC	ECLOSING
EATINGS	EBONIZE	ECDYSONES	ECHOIER	ECLOSION
EATS	EBONIZED	ECDYSONS	ECHOIEST	ECLOSIONS
EAU	EBONIZES	ECESIC	ECHOING	ECO
EAUS	EBONIZING	ECESIS	ECHOISE	ECOCIDAL
EAUX	EBONS	ECESISES	ECHOISED	ECOCIDE
EAVE	EBONY	ECH	ECHOISES	ECOCIDES
EAVED	EBOOK	ECHAPPE	ECHOISING	ECOD
EAVES	EBOOKS	ECHAPPES	ECHOISM	ECOFREAK
EAVESDRIP	EBRIATE	ECHARD	ECHOISMS	ECOFREAKS
EAVESDROP	EBRIATED	ECHARDS	ECHOIST	ECOGIFT
EBAUCHE	EBRIETIES	ECHE	ECHOISTS	ECOGIFTS
EBAUCHES	EBRIETY	ECHED	ECHOIZE	ECOLODGE
EBAYER	EBRILLADE	ECHELLE	ECHOIZED	ECOLODGES
EBAYERS	EBRIOSE	ECHELLES	ECHOIZES	ECOLOGIC
EBAYING	EBRIOSITY	ECHELON	ECHOIZING	ECOLOGIES
EBAYINGS	EBULLIENT	ECHELONED	ECHOLALIA	ECOLOGIST
EBB	EBURNEAN	ECHELONS	ECHOLALIC	ECOLOGY
EBBED	EBURNEOUS	ECHES	ECHOLESS	ECOMAP
EBBET	ECAD	ECHEVERIA	ECHOS	ECOMAPS
EBBETS	ECADS	ECHIDNA	ECHOVIRUS	ECOMMERCE
EBBING	ECARINATE	ECHIDNAE	ECHT	ECONOBOX
EBBLESS	ECARTE	ECHIDNAS	ECLAIR	ECONOMIC
EBBS	ECARTES	ECHIDNINE	ECLAIRS	ECONOMICS
EBENEZER	ECAUDATE	ECHINACEA	ECLAMPSIA	ECONOMIES
EBENEZERS	ECBOLE	ECHINATE	ECLAMPSY	ECONOMISE
EBENISTE	ECBOLES	ECHINATED	ECLAMPTIC	ECONOMISM
EBENISTES	ECBOLIC	ECHING	ECLAT	ECONOMIST

ECONOMIZE	ECTASIA	ECUMENICS	EDGING	EDUCATIVE
ECONOMY	ECTASIAS	ECUMENISM	EDGINGS	EDUCATOR
ECONUT	ECTASIS	ECUMENIST	EDGY	EDUCATORS
ECONUTS	ECTATIC	ECURIE	EDH	EDUCATORY
ECOPHOBIA	ECTHYMA	ECURIES	EDHS	EDUCE
ECORCHE	ECTHYMAS	ECUS	EDIBILITY	EDUCED
ECORCHES	ECTHYMATA	ECZEMA	EDIBLE	EDUCEMENT
ECOREGION	ECTOBLAST	ECZEMAS	EDIBLES	EDUCES
ECOS	ECTOCRINE	ED	EDICT	EDUCIBLE
ECOSPHERE	ECTODERM	EDACIOUS	EDICTAL	EDUCING
ECOSSAISE	ECTODERMS	EDACITIES	EDICTALLY	EDUCT
ECOSTATE	ECTOGENE	EDACITY	EDICTS	EDUCTION
ECOSYSTEM	ECTOGENES	EDAMAME	EDIFICE	EDUCTIONS
ECOTAGE	ECTOGENIC	EDAMAMES	EDIFICES	EDUCTIVE
ECOTAGES	ECTOGENY	EDAPHIC	EDIFICIAL	EDUCTOR
ECOTARIAN	ECTOMERE	EDDIED	EDIFIED	EDUCTORS
ECOTONAL	ECTOMERES	EDDIES	EDIFIER	EDUCTS
ECOTONE	ECTOMERIC	EDDISH	EDIFIERS	EE
ECOTONES	ECTOMORPH	EDDISHES	EDIFIES	EECH
ECOTOPIA	ECTOPHYTE	EDDO	EDIFY	EECHED
ECOTOPIAS	ECTOPIA	EDDOES	EDIFYING	EECHES
ECOTOUR	ECTOPIAS	EDDY	EDILE	EECHING
ECOTOURED	ECTOPIC	EDDYING	EDILES	EEEW
ECOTOURS	ECTOPIES	EDELWEISS	EDIT	EEJIT
ECOTOXIC	ECTOPLASM	EDEMA	EDITABLE	EEJITS
ECOTYPE	ECTOPROCT	EDEMAS	EDITED	EEK
ECOTYPES	ECTOPY	EDEMATA	EDITING	EEL
ECOTYPIC	ECTOSARC	EDEMATOSE	EDITINGS	EELFARE
ECOZONE	ECTOSARCS	EDEMATOUS	EDITION	EELFARES
ECOZONES	ECTOTHERM	EDENIC	EDITIONED	EELGRASS
ECPHRASES	ECTOZOA	EDENTAL	EDITIONS	EELIER
ECPHRASIS	ECTOZOAN	EDENTATE	EDITOR	EELIEST
ECRASEUR	ECTOZOANS	EDENTATES	EDITORIAL	EELLIKE
ECRASEURS	ECTOZOIC	EDGE	EDITORS	EELPOUT
ECRITOIRE	ECTOZOON	EDGEBONE	EDITRESS	EELPOUTS
ECRU	ECTROPIC	EDGEBONES	EDITRICES	EELS
ECRUS	ECTROPION	EDGED	EDITRIX	EELWORM
ECSTASES	ECTROPIUM	EDGELESS	EDITRIXES	EELWORMS
ECSTASIED	ECTYPAL	EDGER	EDITS	EELWRACK
ECSTASIES	ECTYPE	EDGERS	EDS	EELWRACKS
ECSTASIS	ECTYPES	EDGES	EDUCABLE	EELY
ECSTASISE	ECU	EDGEWAYS	EDUCABLES	EEN
ECSTASIZE	ECUELLE	EDGEWISE	EDUCATE	EENSIER
ECSTASY	ECUELLES	EDGIER	EDUCATED	EENSIEST
ECSTATIC	ECUMENE	EDGIEST	EDUCATES	EENSY
ECSTATICS	ECUMENES	EDGILY	EDUCATING	EERIE
ECTASES	ECUMENIC	EDGINESS	EDUCATION	EERIER

EERIEST	EFFICIENT	EGAD	EGGMASS	EGOTISTIC
EERILY	EFFIERCE	EGADS	EGGMASSES	EGOTISTS
EERINESS	EFFIERCED	EGAL	EGGNOG	EGOTIZE
EERY	EFFIERCES	EGALITE	EGGNOGS	EGOTIZED
EEVEN	EFFIGIAL	EGALITES	EGGPLANT	EGOTIZES
EEVENS	EFFIGIES	EGALITIES	EGGPLANTS	EGOTIZING
EEVN	EFFIGY	EGALITY	EGGS	EGREGIOUS
EEVNING	EFFING	EGALLY	EGGSHELL	EGRESS
EEVNINGS	EFFINGS	EGAREMENT	EGGSHELLS	EGRESSED
EEVNS	EFFLUENCE	EGENCE	EGGWASH	EGRESSES
EEW	EFFLUENT	EGENCES	EGGWASHES	EGRESSING
EF	EFFLUENTS	EGENCIES	EGGWHISK	EGRESSION
EFF	EFFLUVIA	EGENCY	EGGWHISKS	EGRESSIVE
EFFABLE	EFFLUVIAL	EGER	EGGY	EGRET
EFFACE	EFFLUVIUM	EGERS	EGIS	EGRETS
EFFACED	EFFLUX	EGEST	EGISES	EGYPTIAN
EFFACER	EFFLUXES	EGESTA	EGLANTINE	EGYPTIANS
EFFACERS	EFFLUXION	EGESTED	EGLATERE	EH
EFFACES	EFFORCE	EGESTING	EGLATERES	EHED
EFFACING	EFFORCED	EGESTION	EGLOMISE	EHING
EFFECT	EFFORCES	EGESTIONS	EGLOMISES	EHS
EFFECTED	EFFORCING	EGESTIVE	EGMA	EIDE
EFFECTER	EFFORT	EGESTS	EGMAS	EIDENT
EFFECTERS	EFFORTFUL	EGG	EGO	EIDER
EFFECTING	EFFORTS	EGGAR	EGOISM	EIDERDOWN
EFFECTIVE	EFFRAIDE	EGGARS	EGOISMS	EIDERS
EFFECTOR	EFFRAY	EGGBEATER	EGOIST	EIDETIC
EFFECTORS	EFFRAYS	EGGCORN	EGOISTIC	EIDETICS
EFFECTS	EFFS	EGGCORNS	EGOISTS	EIDOGRAPH
EFFECTUAL	EFFULGE	EGGCUP	EGOITIES	EIDOLA
EFFED	EFFULGED	EGGCUPS	EGOITY	EIDOLIC
EFFEIR	EFFULGENT	EGGED	EGOLESS	EIDOLON
EFFEIRED	EFFULGES	EGGER	EGOMANIA	EIDOLONS
EFFEIRING	EFFULGING	EGGERIES	EGOMANIAC	EIDOS
EFFEIRS	EFFUSE	EGGERS	EGOMANIAS	EIGENMODE
EFFENDI	EFFUSED	EGGERY	EGOS	EIGENTONE
EFFENDIS	EFFUSES	EGGFRUIT	EGOSURF	EIGHT
EFFERE	EFFUSING	EGGFRUITS	EGOSURFED	EIGHTBALL
EFFERED	EFFUSION	EGGHEAD	EGOSURFS	EIGHTEEN
EFFERENCE	EFFUSIONS	EGGHEADED	EGOTHEISM	EIGHTEENS
EFFERENT	EFFUSIVE	EGGHEADS	EGOTISE	EIGHTFOIL
EFFERENTS	EFS	EGGIER	EGOTISED	EIGHTFOLD
EFFERES	EFT	EGGIEST	EGOTISES	EIGHTFOOT
EFFERING	EFTEST	EGGING	EGOTISING	EIGHTH
EFFETE	EFTS	EGGLER	EGOTISM	EIGHTHLY
EFFETELY	EFTSOON	EGGLERS	EGOTISMS	EIGHTHS
EFFICACY	EFTSOONS	EGGLESS	EGOTIST	EIGHTIES

EIGHTIETH	EJECTING	ELAPIDS	ELDERLY	ELEDOISIN
EIGHTS	EJECTION	ELAPINE	ELDERS	ELEGANCE
EIGHTSMAN	EJECTIONS	ELAPSE	ELDERSHIP	ELEGANCES
EIGHTSMEN	EJECTIVE	ELAPSED	ELDEST	ELEGANCY
EIGHTSOME	EJECTIVES	ELAPSES	ELDESTS	ELEGANT
EIGHTVO	EJECTMENT	ELAPSING	ELDIN	ELEGANTLY
EIGHTVOS	EJECTOR	ELASTANCE	ELDING	ELEGIAC
EIGHTY	EJECTORS	ELASTANE	ELDINGS	ELEGIACAL
EIGNE	EJECTS	ELASTANES	ELDINS	ELEGIACS
EIK	EJIDO	ELASTASE	ELDORADO	ELEGIAST
EIKED	EJIDOS	ELASTASES	ELDORADOS	ELEGIASTS
EIKING	EKE	ELASTIC	ELDRESS	ELEGIES
EIKON	EKED	ELASTICS	ELDRESSES	ELEGISE
EIKONES	EKES	ELASTIN	ELDRICH	ELEGISED
EIKONS	EKING	ELASTINS	ELDRITCH	ELEGISES
EIKS	EKISTIC	ELASTOMER	ELDS	ELEGISING
EILD	EKISTICAL	ELATE	ELECT	ELEGIST
EILDING	EKISTICS	ELATED	ELECTABLE	ELEGISTS
EILDINGS	EKKA	ELATEDLY	ELECTED	ELEGIT
EILDS	EKKAS	ELATER	ELECTEE	ELEGITS
EINA	EKLOGITE	ELATERID	ELECTEES	ELEGIZE
EINE	EKLOGITES	ELATERIDS	ELECTING	ELEGIZED
EINKORN	EKPHRASES	ELATERIN	ELECTION	ELEGIZES
EINKORNS	EKPHRASIS	ELATERINS	ELECTIONS	ELEGIZING
EINSTEIN	EKPWELE	ELATERITE	ELECTIVE	ELEGY
EINSTEINS	EKPWELES	ELATERIUM	ELECTIVES	ELEMENT
EIRACK	EKTEXINE	ELATERS	ELECTOR	ELEMENTAL
EIRACKS	EKTEXINES	ELATES	ELECTORAL	ELEMENTS
EIRENIC	EKUELE	ELATING	ELECTORS	ELEMI
EIRENICAL	EL	ELATION	ELECTRESS	ELEMIS
EIRENICON	ELABORATE	ELATIONS	ELECTRET	ELENCH
EIRENICS	ELAEOLITE	ELATIVE	ELECTRETS	ELENCHI
EISEGESES	ELAIN	ELATIVES	ELECTRIC	ELENCHIC
EISEGESIS	ELAINS	ELBOW	ELECTRICS	ELENCHS
EISEL	ELAIOSOME	ELBOWED	ELECTRIFY	ELENCHTIC
EISELL	ELAN	ELBOWING	ELECTRISE	ELENCHUS
EISELLS	ELANCE	ELBOWINGS	ELECTRIZE	ELENCTIC
EISELS	ELANCED	ELBOWROOM	ELECTRO	ELEOPTENE
EISH	ELANCES	ELBOWS	ELECTRODE	ELEPHANT
EISWEIN	ELANCING	ELCHEE	ELECTROED	ELEPHANTS
EISWEINS	ELAND	ELCHEES	ELECTRON	ELEUTHERI
EITHER	ELANDS	ELCHI	ELECTRONS	ELEVATE
EJACULATE	ELANET	ELCHIS	ELECTROS	ELEVATED
EJECT	ELANETS	ELD	ELECTRUM	ELEVATEDS
EJECTA	ELANS	ELDER	ELECTRUMS	ELEVATES
EJECTABLE	ELAPHINE	ELDERCARE	ELECTS	ELEVATING
EJECTED	ELAPID	ELDERLIES	ELECTUARY	ELEVATION

ELEVATOR
ELEVATORS
ELEVATORY
ELEVEN
ELEVENS
ELEVENSES
ELEVENTH
ELEVENTHS
ELEVON
ELEVONS
ELF
ELFED
ELFHOOD
ELFHOODS
ELFIN
ELFING
ELFINS
ELFISH
ELFISHLY
ELFLAND
ELFLANDS
ELFLIKE
ELFLOCK
ELFLOCKS
ELFS
ELHI
ELIAD
ELIADS
ELICHE
ELICHES
ELICIT
ELICITED
ELICITING
ELICITOR
ELICITORS
ELICITS
ELIDE
ELIDED
ELIDES
ELIDIBLE
ELIDING
ELIGIBLE
ELIGIBLES
ELIGIBLY
ELIMINANT
ELIMINATE
ELINT

ELINTS
ELISION
ELISIONS
ELITE
ELITES
ELITISM
ELITISMS
ELITIST
ELITISTS
ELIXIR
ELIXIRS
ELK
ELKHORN
ELKHOUND
ELKHOUNDS
ELKS
ELL
ELLAGIC
ELLIPSE
ELLIPSES
ELLIPSIS
ELLIPSOID
ELLIPTIC
ELLOPS
ELLOPSES
ELLS
ELLWAND
ELLWANDS
ELM
ELMEN
ELMIER
ELMIEST
ELMS
ELMWOOD
ELMWOODS
ELMY
ELOCUTE
ELOCUTED
ELOCUTES
ELOCUTING
ELOCUTION
ELOCUTORY
ELODEA
ELODEAS
ELOGE
ELOGES
ELOGIES

ELOGIST
ELOGISTS
ELOGIUM
ELOGIUMS
ELOGY
ELOIGN
ELOIGNED
ELOIGNER
ELOIGNERS
ELOIGNING
ELOIGNS
ELOIN
ELOINED
ELOINER
ELOINERS
ELOINING
ELOINMENT
ELOINS
ELONGATE
ELONGATED
ELONGATES
ELOPE
ELOPED
ELOPEMENT
ELOPER
ELOPERS
ELOPES
ELOPING
ELOPS
ELOPSES
ELOQUENCE
ELOQUENT
ELPEE
ELPEES
ELS
ELSE
ELSEWHERE
ELSEWISE
ELSHIN
ELSHINS
ELSIN
ELSINS
ELT
ELTCHI
ELTCHIS
ELTS
ELUANT

ELUANTS
ELUATE
ELUATES
ELUCIDATE
ELUDE
ELUDED
ELUDER
ELUDERS
ELUDES
ELUDIBLE
ELUDING
ELUENT
ELUENTS
ELUSION
ELUSIONS
ELUSIVE
ELUSIVELY
ELUSORY
ELUTE
ELUTED
ELUTES
ELUTING
ELUTION
ELUTIONS
ELUTOR
ELUTORS
ELUTRIATE
ELUVIA
ELUVIAL
ELUVIATE
ELUVIATED
ELUVIATES
ELUVIUM
ELUVIUMS
ELVAN
ELVANITE
ELVANITES
ELVANS
ELVEN
ELVER
ELVERS
ELVES
ELVISH
ELVISHLY
ELYSIAN
ELYTRA
ELYTRAL

ELYTROID
ELYTRON
ELYTROUS
ELYTRUM
EM
EMACIATE
EMACIATED
EMACIATES
EMACS
EMACSEN
EMAIL
EMAILED
EMAILER
EMAILERS
EMAILING
EMAILINGS
EMAILS
EMANANT
EMANATE
EMANATED
EMANATES
EMANATING
EMANATION
EMANATIST
EMANATIVE
EMANATOR
EMANATORS
EMANATORY
EMBACE
EMBACES
EMBACING
EMBAIL
EMBAILED
EMBAILING
EMBAILS
EMBALE
EMBALED
EMBALES
EMBALING
EMBALL
EMBALLED
EMBALLING
EMBALLS
EMBALM
EMBALMED
EMBALMER
EMBALMERS

EMBALMING
EMBALMS
EMBANK
EMBANKED
EMBANKER
EMBANKERS
EMBANKING
EMBANKS
EMBAR
EMBARGO
EMBARGOED
EMBARGOES
EMBARK
EMBARKED
EMBARKING
EMBARKS
EMBARRAS
EMBARRASS
EMBARRED
EMBARRING
EMBARS
EMBASE
EMBASED
EMBASES
EMBASING
EMBASSADE
EMBASSAGE
EMBASSIES
EMBASSY
EMBASTE
EMBATHE
EMBATHED
EMBATHES
EMBATHING
EMBATTLE
EMBATTLED
EMBATTLES
EMBAY
EMBAYED
EMBAYING
EMBAYLD
EMBAYMENT
EMBAYS
EMBED
EMBEDDED
EMBEDDING
EMBEDMENT

EMBEDS
EMBELLISH
EMBER
EMBERS
EMBEZZLE
EMBEZZLED
EMBEZZLER
EMBEZZLES
EMBITTER
EMBITTERS
EMBLAZE
EMBLAZED
EMBLAZER
EMBLAZERS
EMBLAZES
EMBLAZING
EMBLAZON
EMBLAZONS
EMBLEM
EMBLEMA
EMBLEMATA
EMBLEMED
EMBLEMING
EMBLEMISE
EMBLEMIZE
EMBLEMS
EMBLIC
EMBLICS
EMBLOOM
EMBLOOMED
EMBLOOMS
EMBLOSSOM
EMBODIED
EMBODIER
EMBODIERS
EMBODIES
EMBODY
EMBODYING
EMBOG
EMBOGGED
EMBOGGING
EMBOGS
EMBOGUE
EMBOGUED
EMBOGUES
EMBOGUING
EMBOIL

EMBOILED
EMBOILING
EMBOILS
EMBOLDEN
EMBOLDENS
EMBOLI
EMBOLIC
EMBOLIES
EMBOLISE
EMBOLISED
EMBOLISES
EMBOLISM
EMBOLISMS
EMBOLIZE
EMBOLIZED
EMBOLIZES
EMBOLUS
EMBOLUSES
EMBOLY
EMBORDER
EMBORDERS
EMBOSCATA
EMBOSK
EMBOSKED
EMBOSKING
EMBOSKS
EMBOSOM
EMBOSOMED
EMBOSOMS
EMBOSS
EMBOSSED
EMBOSSER
EMBOSSERS
EMBOSSES
EMBOSSING
EMBOST
EMBOUND
EMBOUNDED
EMBOUNDS
EMBOW
EMBOWED
EMBOWEL
EMBOWELED
EMBOWELS
EMBOWER
EMBOWERED
EMBOWERS

EMBOWING
EMBOWMENT
EMBOWS
EMBOX
EMBOXED
EMBOXES
EMBOXING
EMBRACE
EMBRACED
EMBRACEOR
EMBRACER
EMBRACERS
EMBRACERY
EMBRACES
EMBRACING
EMBRACIVE
EMBRAID
EMBRAIDED
EMBRAIDS
EMBRANGLE
EMBRASOR
EMBRASORS
EMBRASURE
EMBRAVE
EMBRAVED
EMBRAVES
EMBRAVING
EMBRAZURE
EMBREAD
EMBREADED
EMBREADS
EMBREATHE
EMBRITTLE
EMBROCATE
EMBROGLIO
EMBROIDER
EMBROIL
EMBROILED
EMBROILER
EMBROILS
EMBROWN
EMBROWNED
EMBROWNS
EMBRUE
EMBRUED
EMBRUES
EMBRUING

EMBRUTE
EMBRUTED
EMBRUTES
EMBRUTING
EMBRYO
EMBRYOID
EMBRYOIDS
EMBRYON
EMBRYONAL
EMBRYONIC
EMBRYONS
EMBRYOS
EMBRYOTIC
EMBUS
EMBUSED
EMBUSES
EMBUSIED
EMBUSIES
EMBUSING
EMBUSQUE
EMBUSQUES
EMBUSSED
EMBUSSES
EMBUSSING
EMBUSY
EMBUSYING
EMCEE
EMCEED
EMCEEING
EMCEES
EMDASH
EMDASHES
EME
EMEER
EMEERATE
EMEERATES
EMEERS
EMEND
EMENDABLE
EMENDALS
EMENDATE
EMENDATED
EMENDATES
EMENDATOR
EMENDED
EMENDER
EMENDERS

EMENDING	EMEUTES	EMMERS	EMOTIVITY	EMPAYRING
EMENDS	EMIC	EMMESH	EMOVE	EMPEACH
EMERALD	EMICANT	EMMESHED	EMOVED	EMPEACHED
EMERALDS	EMICATE	EMMESHES	EMOVES	EMPEACHES
EMERAUDE	EMICATED	EMMESHING	EMOVING	EMPENNAGE
EMERAUDES	EMICATES	EMMET	EMPACKET	EMPEOPLE
EMERG	EMICATING	EMMETROPE	EMPACKETS	EMPEOPLED
EMERGE	EMICATION	EMMETS	EMPAESTIC	EMPEOPLES
EMERGED	EMICS	EMMEW	EMPAIRE	EMPERCE
EMERGENCE	EMICTION	EMMEWED	EMPAIRED	EMPERCED
EMERGENCY	EMICTIONS	EMMEWING	EMPAIRES	EMPERCES
EMERGENT	EMICTORY	EMMEWS	EMPAIRING	EMPERCING
EMERGENTS	EMIGRANT	EMMOVE	EMPALE	EMPERIES
EMERGES	EMIGRANTS	EMMOVED	EMPALED	EMPERISE
EMERGING	EMIGRATE	EMMOVES	EMPALER	EMPERISED
EMERGS	EMIGRATED	EMMOVING	EMPALERS	EMPERISES
EMERIED	EMIGRATES	EMMY	EMPALES	EMPERISH
EMERIES	EMIGRE	EMMYS	EMPALING	EMPERIZE
EMERITA	EMIGRES	EMO	EMPANADA	EMPERIZED
EMERITAE	EMINENCE	EMOCORE	EMPANADAS	EMPERIZES
EMERITAS	EMINENCES	EMOCORES	EMPANEL	EMPEROR
EMERITI	EMINENCY	EMODIN	EMPANELED	EMPERORS
EMERITUS	EMINENT	EMODINS	EMPANELS	EMPERY
EMEROD	EMINENTLY	EMOJI	EMPANOPLY	EMPHASES
EMERODS	EMIR	EMOJIS	EMPARE	EMPHASIS
EMEROID	EMIRATE	EMOLLIATE	EMPARED	EMPHASISE
EMEROIDS	EMIRATES	EMOLLIENT	EMPARES	EMPHASIZE
EMERSE	EMIRS	EMOLUMENT	EMPARING	EMPHATIC
EMERSED	EMISSARY	EMONG	EMPARL	EMPHATICS
EMERSION	EMISSILE	EMONGES	EMPARLED	EMPHLYSES
EMERSIONS	EMISSION	EMONGEST	EMPARLING	EMPHLYSIS
EMERY	EMISSIONS	EMONGST	EMPARLS	EMPHYSEMA
EMERYING	EMISSIVE	EMOS	EMPART	EMPIERCE
EMES	EMIT	EMOTE	EMPARTED	EMPIERCED
EMESES	EMITS	EMOTED	EMPARTING	EMPIERCES
EMESIS	EMITTANCE	EMOTER	EMPARTS	EMPIGHT
EMESISES	EMITTED	EMOTERS	EMPATHIC	EMPIGHTED
EMETIC	EMITTER	EMOTES	EMPATHIES	EMPIGHTS
EMETICAL	EMITTERS	EMOTICON	EMPATHISE	EMPIRE
EMETICS	EMITTING	EMOTICONS	EMPATHIST	EMPIRES
EMETIN	EMLETS	EMOTING	EMPATHIZE	EMPIRIC
EMETINE	EMMA	EMOTION	EMPATHY	EMPIRICAL
EMETINES	EMMARBLE	EMOTIONAL	EMPATRON	EMPIRICS
EMETINS	EMMARBLED	EMOTIONS	EMPATRONS	EMPLACE
EMEU	EMMARBLES	EMOTIVE	EMPAYRE	EMPLACED
EMEUS	EMMAS	EMOTIVELY	EMPAYRED	EMPLACES
EMEUTE	EMMER	EMOTIVISM	EMPAYRES	EMPLACING

EMPLANE	EMPTIER	EMULES	ENACTING	ENATION
EMPLANED	EMPTIERS	EMULGE	ENACTION	ENATIONS
EMPLANES	EMPTIES	EMULGED	ENACTIONS	ENAUNTER
EMPLANING	EMPTIEST	EMULGENCE	ENACTIVE	ENCAENIA
EMPLASTER	EMPTILY	EMULGENT	ENACTMENT	ENCAENIAS
EMPLASTIC	EMPTINESS	EMULGES	ENACTOR	ENCAGE
EMPLEACH	EMPTING	EMULGING	ENACTORS	ENCAGED
EMPLECTON	EMPTINGS	EMULING	ENACTORY	ENCAGES
EMPLECTUM	EMPTINS	EMULOUS	ENACTS	ENCAGING
EMPLONGE	EMPTION	EMULOUSLY	ENACTURE	ENCALM
EMPLONGED	EMPTIONAL	EMULSIBLE	ENACTURES	ENCALMED
EMPLONGES	EMPTIONS	EMULSIFY	ENALAPRIL	ENCALMING
EMPLOY	EMPTS	EMULSIN	ENALLAGE	ENCALMS
EMPLOYE	EMPTY	EMULSINS	ENALLAGES	ENCAMP
EMPLOYED	EMPTYING	EMULSION	ENAMEL	ENCAMPED
EMPLOYEE	EMPTYINGS	EMULSIONS	ENAMELED	ENCAMPING
EMPLOYEES	EMPTYSES	EMULSIVE	ENAMELER	ENCAMPS
EMPLOYER	EMPTYSIS	EMULSOID	ENAMELERS	ENCANTHIS
EMPLOYERS	EMPURPLE	EMULSOIDS	ENAMELING	ENCAPSULE
EMPLOYES	EMPURPLED	EMULSOR	ENAMELIST	ENCARPUS
EMPLOYING	EMPURPLES	EMULSORS	ENAMELLED	ENCASE
EMPLOYS	EMPUSA	EMUNCTION	ENAMELLER	ENCASED
EMPLUME	EMPUSAS	EMUNCTORY	ENAMELS	ENCASES
EMPLUMED	EMPUSE	EMUNGE	ENAMINE	ENCASH
EMPLUMES	EMPUSES	EMUNGED	ENAMINES	ENCASHED
EMPLUMING	EMPYEMA	EMUNGES	ENAMOR	ENCASHES
EMPOISON	EMPYEMAS	EMUNGING	ENAMORADO	ENCASHING
EMPOISONS	EMPYEMATA	EMURE	ENAMORED	ENCASING
EMPOLDER	EMPYEMIC	EMURED	ENAMORING	ENCASTRE
EMPOLDERS	EMPYESES	EMURES	ENAMORS	ENCAUSTIC
EMPORIA	EMPYESIS	EMURING	ENAMOUR	ENCAVE
EMPORIUM	EMPYREAL	EMUS	ENAMOURED	ENCAVED
EMPORIUMS	EMPYREAN	EMYD	ENAMOURS	ENCAVES
EMPOWER	EMPYREANS	EMYDE	ENANTHEMA	ENCAVING
EMPOWERED	EMPYREUMA	EMYDES	ENARCH	ENCEINTE
EMPOWERS	EMS	EMYDS	ENARCHED	ENCEINTES
EMPRESS	EMU	EMYS	ENARCHES	ENCEPHALA
EMPRESSE	EMULATE	EN	ENARCHING	ENCHAFE
EMPRESSES	EMULATED	ENABLE	ENARGITE	ENCHAFED
EMPRISE	EMULATES	ENABLED	ENARGITES	ENCHAFES
EMPRISES	EMULATING	ENABLER	ENARM	ENCHAFING
EMPRIZE	EMULATION	ENABLERS	ENARMED	ENCHAIN
EMPRIZES	EMULATIVE	ENABLES	ENARMING	ENCHAINED
EMPT	EMULATOR	ENABLING	ENARMS	ENCHAINS
EMPTED	EMULATORS	ENACT	ENATE	ENCHANT
EMPTIABLE	EMULE	ENACTABLE	ENATES	ENCHANTED
EMPTIED	EMULED	ENACTED	ENATIC	ENCHANTER

ENCHANTS	ENCLOSURE	ENCRUSTED	ENDEIXES	ENDOCAST
ENCHARGE	ENCLOTHE	ENCRUSTS	ENDEIXIS	ENDOCASTS
ENCHARGED	ENCLOTHED	ENCRYPT	ENDEMIAL	ENDOCRINE
ENCHARGES	ENCLOTHES	ENCRYPTED	ENDEMIC	ENDOCYTIC
ENCHARM	ENCLOUD	ENCRYPTS	ENDEMICAL	ENDODERM
ENCHARMED	ENCLOUDED	ENCUMBER	ENDEMICS	ENDODERMS
ENCHARMS	ENCLOUDS	ENCUMBERS	ENDEMISM	ENDODYNE
ENCHASE	ENCODABLE	ENCURTAIN	ENDEMISMS	ENDOERGIC
ENCHASED	ENCODE	ENCYCLIC	ENDENIZEN	ENDOGAMIC
ENCHASER	ENCODED	ENCYCLICS	ENDER	ENDOGAMY
ENCHASERS	ENCODER	ENCYST	ENDERMIC	ENDOGEN
ENCHASES	ENCODERS	ENCYSTED	ENDERON	ENDOGENIC
ENCHASING	ENCODES	ENCYSTING	ENDERONS	ENDOGENS
ENCHEASON	ENCODING	ENCYSTS	ENDERS	ENDOGENY
ENCHEER	ENCODINGS	END	ENDEW	ENDOLYMPH
ENCHEERED	ENCOLOUR	ENDAMAGE	ENDEWED	ENDOMIXES
ENCHEERS	ENCOLOURS	ENDAMAGED	ENDEWING	ENDOMIXIS
ENCHILADA	ENCOLPION	ENDAMAGES	ENDEWS	ENDOMORPH
ENCHORIAL	ENCOLPIUM	ENDAMEBA	ENDEXINE	ENDOPHAGY
ENCHORIC	ENCOLURE	ENDAMEBAE	ENDEXINES	ENDOPHYTE
ENCIERRO	ENCOLURES	ENDAMEBAS	ENDGAME	ENDOPLASM
ENCIERROS	ENCOMIA	ENDAMEBIC	ENDGAMES	ENDOPOD
ENCINA	ENCOMIAST	ENDAMOEBA	ENDGATE	ENDOPODS
ENCINAL	ENCOMION	ENDANGER	ENDGATES	ENDOPROCT
ENCINAS	ENCOMIUM	ENDANGERS	ENDING	ENDORPHIN
ENCIPHER	ENCOMIUMS	ENDARCH	ENDINGS	ENDORSE
ENCIPHERS	ENCOMPASS	ENDARCHY	ENDIRON	ENDORSED
ENCIRCLE	ENCORE	ENDART	ENDIRONS	ENDORSEE
ENCIRCLED	ENCORED	ENDARTED	ENDITE	ENDORSEES
ENCIRCLES	ENCORES	ENDARTING	ENDITED	ENDORSER
ENCLASP	ENCORING	ENDARTS	ENDITES	ENDORSERS
ENCLASPED	ENCOUNTER	ENDASH	ENDITING	ENDORSES
ENCLASPS	ENCOURAGE	ENDASHES	ENDIVE	ENDORSING
ENCLAVE	ENCRADLE	ENDBRAIN	ENDIVES	ENDORSIVE
ENCLAVED	ENCRADLED	ENDBRAINS	ENDLANG	ENDORSOR
ENCLAVES	ENCRADLES	ENDCAP	ENDLEAF	ENDORSORS
ENCLAVING	ENCRATIES	ENDCAPS	ENDLEAFS	ENDOSARC
ENCLISES	ENCRATY	ENDEAR	ENDLEAVES	ENDOSARCS
ENCLISIS	ENCREASE	ENDEARED	ENDLESS	ENDOSCOPE
ENCLITIC	ENCREASED	ENDEARING	ENDLESSLY	ENDOSCOPY
ENCLITICS	ENCREASES	ENDEARS	ENDLONG	ENDOSMOS
ENCLOSE	ENCRIMSON	ENDEAVOR	ENDMOST	ENDOSMOSE
ENCLOSED	ENCRINAL	ENDEAVORS	ENDNOTE	ENDOSOME
ENCLOSER	ENCRINIC	ENDEAVOUR	ENDNOTES	ENDOSOMES
ENCLOSERS	ENCRINITE	ENDECAGON	ENDOBLAST	ENDOSPERM
ENCLOSES	ENCROACH	ENDED	ENDOCARP	ENDOSPORE
ENCLOSING	ENCRUST	ENDEICTIC	ENDOCARPS	ENDOSS

ENDOSSED	ENDURING	ENFANT	ENFOLDS	ENGILDS
ENDOSSES	ENDURO	ENFANTS	ENFORCE	ENGILT
ENDOSSING	ENDUROS	ENFEEBLE	ENFORCED	ENGINE
ENDOSTEA	ENDWAYS	ENFEEBLED	ENFORCER	ENGINED
ENDOSTEAL	ENDWISE	ENFEEBLER	ENFORCERS	ENGINEER
ENDOSTEUM	ENDYSES	ENFEEBLES	ENFORCES	ENGINEERS
ENDOSTYLE	ENDYSIS	ENFELON	ENFORCING	ENGINER
ENDOTHERM	ENDZONE	ENFELONED	ENFOREST	ENGINERS
ENDOTOXIC	ENDZONES	ENFELONS	ENFORESTS	ENGINERY
ENDOTOXIN	ENE	ENFEOFF	ENFORM	ENGINES
ENDOW	ENEMA	ENFEOFFED	ENFORMED	ENGINING
ENDOWED	ENEMAS	ENFEOFFS	ENFORMING	ENGINOUS
ENDOWER	ENEMATA	ENFESTED	ENFORMS	ENGIRD
ENDOWERS	ENEMIES	ENFETTER	ENFRAME	ENGIRDED
ENDOWING	ENEMY	ENFETTERS	ENFRAMED	ENGIRDING
ENDOWMENT	ENERGETIC	ENFEVER	ENFRAMES	ENGIRDLE
ENDOWS	ENERGIC	ENFEVERED	ENFRAMING	ENGIRDLED
ENDOZOA	ENERGID	ENFEVERS	ENFREE	ENGIRDLES
ENDOZOIC	ENERGIDS	ENFIERCE	ENFREED	ENGIRDS
ENDOZOON	ENERGIES	ENFIERCED	ENFREEDOM	ENGIRT
ENDPAPER	ENERGISE	ENFIERCES	ENFREEING	ENGLACIAL
ENDPAPERS	ENERGISED	ENFILADE	ENFREES	ENGLISH
ENDPLATE	ENERGISER	ENFILADED	ENFREEZE	ENGLISHED
ENDPLATES	ENERGISES	ENFILADES	ENFREEZES	ENGLISHES
ENDPLAY	ENERGIZE	ENFILED	ENFROSEN	ENGLOBE
ENDPLAYED	ENERGIZED	ENFIRE	ENFROZE	ENGLOBED
ENDPLAYS	ENERGIZER	ENFIRED	ENFROZEN	ENGLOBES
ENDPOINT	ENERGIZES	ENFIRES	ENG	ENGLOBING
ENDPOINTS	ENERGUMEN	ENFIRING	ENGAGE	ENGLOOM
ENDRIN	ENERGY	ENFIX	ENGAGED	ENGLOOMED
ENDRINS	ENERVATE	ENFIXED	ENGAGEDLY	ENGLOOMS
ENDS	ENERVATED	ENFIXES	ENGAGEE	ENGLUT
ENDSHIP	ENERVATES	ENFIXING	ENGAGER	ENGLUTS
ENDSHIPS	ENERVATOR	ENFLAME	ENGAGERS	ENGLUTTED
ENDUE	ENERVE	ENFLAMED	ENGAGES	ENGOBE
ENDUED	ENERVED	ENFLAMES	ENGAGING	ENGOBES
ENDUES	ENERVES	ENFLAMING	ENGAOL	ENGORE
ENDUING	ENERVING	ENFLESH	ENGAOLED	ENGORED
ENDUNGEON	ENES	ENFLESHED	ENGAOLING	ENGORES
ENDURABLE	ENEW	ENFLESHES	ENGAOLS	ENGORGE
ENDURABLY	ENEWED	ENFLOWER	ENGARLAND	ENGORGED
ENDURANCE	ENEWING	ENFLOWERS	ENGENDER	ENGORGES
ENDURE	ENEWS	ENFOLD	ENGENDERS	ENGORGING
ENDURED	ENFACE	ENFOLDED	ENGENDURE	ENGORING
ENDURER	ENFACED	ENFOLDER	ENGILD	ENGOULED
ENDURERS	ENFACES	ENFOLDERS	ENGILDED	ENGOUMENT
ENDURES	ENFACING	ENFOLDING	ENGILDING	ENGRACE

E

ENGRACED	ENGUARDED	ENJOINED	ENLISTEE	ENNOG
ENGRACES	ENGUARDS	ENJOINER	ENLISTEES	ENNOGS
ENGRACING	ENGULF	ENJOINERS	ENLISTER	ENNUI
ENGRAFF	ENGULFED	ENJOINING	ENLISTERS	ENNUIED
ENGRAFFED	ENGULFING	ENJOINS	ENLISTING	ENNUIS
ENGRAFFS	ENGULFS	ENJOY	ENLISTS	ENNUYE
ENGRAFT	ENGULPH	ENJOYABLE	ENLIT	ENNUYED
ENGRAFTED	ENGULPHED	ENJOYABLY	ENLIVEN	ENNUYEE
ENGRAFTS	ENGULPHS	ENJOYED	ENLIVENED	ENNUYING
ENGRAIL	ENGYSCOPE	ENJOYER	ENLIVENER	ENODAL
ENGRAILED	ENHALO	ENJOYERS	ENLIVENS	ENOKI
ENGRAILS	ENHALOED	ENJOYING	ENLOCK	ENOKIDAKE
ENGRAIN	ENHALOES	ENJOYMENT	ENLOCKED	ENOKIS
ENGRAINED	ENHALOING	ENJOYS	ENLOCKING	ENOKITAKE
ENGRAINER	ENHALOS	ENKERNEL	ENLOCKS	ENOL
ENGRAINS	ENHANCE	ENKERNELS	ENLUMINE	ENOLASE
ENGRAM	ENHANCED	ENKINDLE	ENLUMINED	ENOLASES
ENGRAMMA	ENHANCER	ENKINDLED	ENLUMINES	ENOLIC
ENGRAMMAS	ENHANCERS	ENKINDLER	ENMESH	ENOLOGIES
ENGRAMME	ENHANCES	ENKINDLES	ENMESHED	ENOLOGIST
ENGRAMMES	ENHANCING	ENLACE	ENMESHES	ENOLOGY
ENGRAMMIC	ENHANCIVE	ENLACED	ENMESHING	ENOLS
ENGRAMS	ENHEARSE	ENLACES	ENMEW	ENOMOTIES
ENGRASP	ENHEARSED	ENLACING	ENMEWED	ENOMOTY
ENGRASPED	ENHEARSES	ENLARD	ENMEWING	ENOPHILE
ENGRASPS	ENHEARTEN	ENLARDED	ENMEWS	ENOPHILES
ENGRAVE	ENHUNGER	ENLARDING	ENMITIES	ENORM
ENGRAVED	ENHUNGERS	ENLARDS	ENMITY	ENORMITY
ENGRAVEN	ENHYDRITE	ENLARGE	ENMOSSED	ENORMOUS
ENGRAVER	ENHYDROS	ENLARGED	ENMOVE	ENOSES
ENGRAVERS	ENHYDROUS	ENLARGEN	ENMOVED	ENOSIS
ENGRAVERY	ENIAC	ENLARGENS	ENMOVES	ENOSISES
ENGRAVES	ENIACS	ENLARGER	ENMOVING	ENOUGH
ENGRAVING	ENIGMA	ENLARGERS	ENNAGE	ENOUGHS
ENGRENAGE	ENIGMAS	ENLARGES	ENNAGES	ENOUNCE
ENGRIEVE	ENIGMATA	ENLARGING	ENNEAD	ENOUNCED
ENGRIEVED	ENIGMATIC	ENLEVE	ENNEADIC	ENOUNCES
ENGRIEVES	ENISLE	ENLIGHT	ENNEADS	ENOUNCING
ENGROOVE	ENISLED	ENLIGHTED	ENNEAGON	ENOW
ENGROOVED	ENISLES	ENLIGHTEN	ENNEAGONS	ENOWS
ENGROOVES	ENISLING	ENLIGHTS	ENNEAGRAM	ENPLANE
ENGROSS	ENJAMB	ENLINK	ENNOBLE	ENPLANED
ENGROSSED	ENJAMBED	ENLINKED	ENNOBLED	ENPLANES
ENGROSSER	ENJAMBING	ENLINKING	ENNOBLER	ENPLANING
ENGROSSES	ENJAMBS	ENLINKS	ENNOBLERS	ENPRINT
ENGS	ENJOIN	ENLIST	ENNOBLES	ENPRINTS
ENGUARD	ENJOINDER	ENLISTED	ENNOBLING	ENQUEUE

ENQUEUED
ENQUEUES
ENQUEUING
ENQUIRE
ENQUIRED
ENQUIRER
ENQUIRERS
ENQUIRES
ENQUIRIES
ENQUIRING
ENQUIRY
ENRACE
ENRACED
ENRACES
ENRACING
ENRAGE
ENRAGED
ENRAGEDLY
ENRAGES
ENRAGING
ENRANCKLE
ENRANGE
ENRANGED
ENRANGES
ENRANGING
ENRANK
ENRANKED
ENRANKING
ENRANKS
ENRAPT
ENRAPTURE
ENRAUNGE
ENRAUNGED
ENRAUNGES
ENRAVISH
ENRHEUM
ENRHEUMED
ENRHEUMS
ENRICH
ENRICHED
ENRICHER
ENRICHERS
ENRICHES
ENRICHING
ENRIDGED
ENRING
ENRINGED

ENRINGING
ENRINGS
ENRIVEN
ENROBE
ENROBED
ENROBER
ENROBERS
ENROBES
ENROBING
ENROL
ENROLL
ENROLLED
ENROLLEE
ENROLLEES
ENROLLER
ENROLLERS
ENROLLING
ENROLLS
ENROLMENT
ENROLS
ENROOT
ENROOTED
ENROOTING
ENROOTS
ENROUGH
ENROUGHED
ENROUGHS
ENROUND
ENROUNDED
ENROUNDS
ENS
ENSAMPLE
ENSAMPLED
ENSAMPLES
ENSATE
ENSCONCE
ENSCONCED
ENSCONCES
ENSCROLL
ENSCROLLS
ENSEAL
ENSEALED
ENSEALING
ENSEALS
ENSEAM
ENSEAMED
ENSEAMING

ENSEAMS
ENSEAR
ENSEARED
ENSEARING
ENSEARS
ENSEMBLE
ENSEMBLES
ENSERF
ENSERFED
ENSERFING
ENSERFS
ENSEW
ENSEWED
ENSEWING
ENSEWS
ENSHEATH
ENSHEATHE
ENSHEATHS
ENSHELL
ENSHELLED
ENSHELLS
ENSHELTER
ENSHIELD
ENSHIELDS
ENSHRINE
ENSHRINED
ENSHRINEE
ENSHRINES
ENSHROUD
ENSHROUDS
ENSIFORM
ENSIGN
ENSIGNCY
ENSIGNED
ENSIGNING
ENSIGNS
ENSILAGE
ENSILAGED
ENSILAGES
ENSILE
ENSILED
ENSILES
ENSILING
ENSKIED
ENSKIES
ENSKY
ENSKYED

ENSKYING
ENSLAVE
ENSLAVED
ENSLAVER
ENSLAVERS
ENSLAVES
ENSLAVING
ENSNARE
ENSNARED
ENSNARER
ENSNARERS
ENSNARES
ENSNARING
ENSNARL
ENSNARLED
ENSNARLS
ENSORCEL
ENSORCELL
ENSORCELS
ENSOUL
ENSOULED
ENSOULING
ENSOULS
ENSPHERE
ENSPHERED
ENSPHERES
ENSTAMP
ENSTAMPED
ENSTAMPS
ENSTATITE
ENSTEEP
ENSTEEPED
ENSTEEPS
ENSTYLE
ENSTYLED
ENSTYLES
ENSTYLING
ENSUE
ENSUED
ENSUES
ENSUING
ENSUITE
ENSUITES
ENSURE
ENSURED
ENSURER
ENSURERS

ENSURES
ENSURING
ENSWATHE
ENSWATHED
ENSWATHES
ENSWEEP
ENSWEEPS
ENSWEPT
ENTAIL
ENTAILED
ENTAILER
ENTAILERS
ENTAILING
ENTAILS
ENTAME
ENTAMEBA
ENTAMEBAE
ENTAMEBAS
ENTAMED
ENTAMES
ENTAMING
ENTAMOEBA
ENTANGLE
ENTANGLED
ENTANGLER
ENTANGLES
ENTASES
ENTASIA
ENTASIAS
ENTASIS
ENTASTIC
ENTAYLE
ENTAYLED
ENTAYLES
ENTAYLING
ENTELECHY
ENTELLUS
ENTENDER
ENTENDERS
ENTENTE
ENTENTES
ENTER
ENTERA
ENTERABLE
ENTERAL
ENTERALLY
ENTERATE

ENTERED	ENTITY	ENTREATS	ENURE	ENVISION
ENTERER	ENTOBLAST	ENTREATY	ENURED	ENVISIONS
ENTERERS	ENTODERM	ENTRECHAT	ENUREMENT	ENVOI
ENTERIC	ENTODERMS	ENTRECOTE	ENURES	ENVOIS
ENTERICS	ENTOIL	ENTREE	ENURESES	ENVOY
ENTERING	ENTOILED	ENTREES	ENURESIS	ENVOYS
ENTERINGS	ENTOILING	ENTREMES	ENURETIC	ENVOYSHIP
ENTERITIS	ENTOILS	ENTREMETS	ENURETICS	ENVY
ENTERON	ENTOMB	ENTRENCH	ENURING	ENVYING
ENTERONS	ENTOMBED	ENTREPOT	ENURN	ENVYINGLY
ENTERS	ENTOMBING	ENTREPOTS	ENURNED	ENVYINGS
ENTERTAIN	ENTOMBS	ENTRESOL	ENURNING	ENWALL
ENTERTAKE	ENTOMIC	ENTRESOLS	ENURNS	ENWALLED
ENTERTOOK	ENTOPHYTE	ENTREZ	ENVASSAL	ENWALLING
ENTETE	ENTOPIC	ENTRIES	ENVASSALS	ENWALLOW
ENTETEE	ENTOPROCT	ENTRISM	ENVAULT	ENWALLOWS
ENTHALPY	ENTOPTIC	ENTRISMS	ENVAULTED	ENWALLS
ENTHETIC	ENTOPTICS	ENTRIST	ENVAULTS	ENWHEEL
ENTHRAL	ENTOTIC	ENTRISTS	ENVEIGLE	ENWHEELED
ENTHRALL	ENTOURAGE	ENTROLD	ENVEIGLED	ENWHEELS
ENTHRALLS	ENTOZOA	ENTROPIC	ENVEIGLES	ENWIND
ENTHRALS	ENTOZOAL	ENTROPIES	ENVELOP	ENWINDING
ENTHRONE	ENTOZOAN	ENTROPION	ENVELOPE	ENWINDS
ENTHRONED	ENTOZOANS	ENTROPIUM	ENVELOPED	ENWOMB
ENTHRONES	ENTOZOIC	ENTROPY	ENVELOPER	ENWOMBED
ENTHUSE	ENTOZOON	ENTRUST	ENVELOPES	ENWOMBING
ENTHUSED	ENTRAIL	ENTRUSTED	ENVELOPS	ENWOMBS
ENTHUSES	ENTRAILED	ENTRUSTS	ENVENOM	ENWOUND
ENTHUSING	ENTRAILS	ENTRY	ENVENOMED	ENWRAP
ENTHYMEME	ENTRAIN	ENTRYISM	ENVENOMS	ENWRAPPED
ENTIA	ENTRAINED	ENTRYISMS	ENVERMEIL	ENWRAPS
ENTICE	ENTRAINER	ENTRYIST	ENVIABLE	ENWREATH
ENTICED	ENTRAINS	ENTRYISTS	ENVIABLY	ENWREATHE
ENTICER	ENTRALL	ENTRYWAY	ENVIED	ENWREATHS
ENTICERS	ENTRALLES	ENTRYWAYS	ENVIER	ENZIAN
ENTICES	ENTRAMMEL	ENTS	ENVIERS	ENZIANS
ENTICING	ENTRANCE	ENTWINE	ENVIES	ENZONE
ENTICINGS	ENTRANCED	ENTWINED	ENVIOUS	ENZONED
ENTIRE	ENTRANCES	ENTWINES	ENVIOUSLY	ENZONES
ENTIRELY	ENTRANT	ENTWINING	ENVIRO	ENZONING
ENTIRES	ENTRANTS	ENTWIST	ENVIRON	ENZOOTIC
ENTIRETY	ENTRAP	ENTWISTED	ENVIRONED	ENZOOTICS
ENTITIES	ENTRAPPED	ENTWISTS	ENVIRONS	ENZYM
ENTITLE	ENTRAPPER	ENUCLEATE	ENVIROS	ENZYMATIC
ENTITLED	ENTRAPS	ENUF	ENVISAGE	ENZYME
ENTITLES	ENTREAT	ENUMERATE	ENVISAGED	ENZYMES
ENTITLING	ENTREATED	ENUNCIATE	ENVISAGES	ENZYMIC

ENZYMS	EPATER	EPHELIDES	EPICENTRA	EPIGAEAL
EOAN	EPATERED	EPHELIS	EPICENTRE	EPIGAEAN
EOBIONT	EPATERING	EPHEMERA	EPICIER	EPIGAEOUS
EOBIONTS	EPATERS	EPHEMERAE	EPICIERS	EPIGAMIC
EOCENE	EPAULE	EPHEMERAL	EPICISM	EPIGEAL
EOHIPPUS	EPAULES	EPHEMERAS	EPICISMS	EPIGEAN
EOLIAN	EPAULET	EPHEMERID	EPICIST	EPIGEIC
EOLIENNE	EPAULETED	EPHEMERIS	EPICISTS	EPIGENE
EOLIENNES	EPAULETS	EPHEMERON	EPICLESES	EPIGENIC
EOLIPILE	EPAULETTE	EPHIALTES	EPICLESIS	EPIGENIST
EOLIPILES	EPAXIAL	EPHOD	EPICLIKE	EPIGENOUS
EOLITH	EPAZOTE	EPHODS	EPICORMIC	EPIGEOUS
EOLITHIC	EPAZOTES	EPHOR	EPICOTYL	EPIGON
EOLITHS	EPEDAPHIC	EPHORAL	EPICOTYLS	EPIGONE
EOLOPILE	EPEE	EPHORALTY	EPICRANIA	EPIGONES
EOLOPILES	EPEEIST	EPHORATE	EPICRISES	EPIGONI
EON	EPEEISTS	EPHORATES	EPICRISIS	EPIGONIC
EONIAN	EPEES	EPHORI	EPICRITIC	EPIGONISM
EONISM	EPEIRA	EPHORS	EPICS	EPIGONOUS
EONISMS	EPEIRAS	EPIBIOSES	EPICURE	EPIGONS
EONS	EPEIRIC	EPIBIOSIS	EPICUREAN	EPIGONUS
EORL	EPEIRID	EPIBIOTIC	EPICURES	EPIGRAM
EORLS	EPEIRIDS	EPIBLAST	EPICURISE	EPIGRAMS
EOSIN	EPENDYMA	EPIBLASTS	EPICURISM	EPIGRAPH
EOSINE	EPENDYMAL	EPIBLEM	EPICURIZE	EPIGRAPHS
EOSINES	EPENDYMAS	EPIBLEMS	EPICYCLE	EPIGRAPHY
EOSINIC	EPEOLATRY	EPIBOLIC	EPICYCLES	EPIGYNIES
EOSINS	EPERDU	EPIBOLIES	EPICYCLIC	EPIGYNOUS
EOTHEN	EPERDUE	EPIBOLY	EPIDEMIC	EPIGYNY
EPACRID	EPERGNE	EPIC	EPIDEMICS	EPILATE
EPACRIDS	EPERGNES	EPICAL	EPIDERM	EPILATED
EPACRIS	EPHA	EPICALLY	EPIDERMAL	EPILATES
EPACRISES	EPHAH	EPICALYX	EPIDERMIC	EPILATING
EPACT	EPHAHS	EPICANTHI	EPIDERMIS	EPILATION
EPACTS	EPHAS	EPICARDIA	EPIDERMS	EPILATOR
EPAENETIC	EPHEBE	EPICARP	EPIDICTIC	EPILATORS
EPAGOGE	EPHEBES	EPICARPS	EPIDOSITE	EPILEPSY
EPAGOGES	EPHEBI	EPICEDE	EPIDOTE	EPILEPTIC
EPAGOGIC	EPHEBIC	EPICEDES	EPIDOTES	EPILIMNIA
EPANODOS	EPHEBOI	EPICEDIA	EPIDOTIC	EPILITHIC
EPARCH	EPHEBOS	EPICEDIAL	EPIDURAL	EPILOBIUM
EPARCHATE	EPHEBUS	EPICEDIAN	EPIDURALS	EPILOG
EPARCHIAL	EPHEDRA	EPICEDIUM	EPIFAUNA	EPILOGIC
EPARCHIES	EPHEDRAS	EPICENE	EPIFAUNAE	EPILOGISE
EPARCHS	EPHEDRIN	EPICENES	EPIFAUNAL	EPILOGIST
EPARCHY	EPHEDRINE	EPICENISM	EPIFAUNAS	EPILOGIZE
EPATANT	EPHEDRINS	EPICENTER	EPIFOCAL	EPILOGS

EPILOGUE	EPISEMON	EPITAXY	EPONYM	EQUABLE
EPILOGUED	EPISEMONS	EPITHECA	EPONYMIC	EQUABLY
EPILOGUES	EPISODAL	EPITHECAE	EPONYMIES	EQUAL
EPIMER	EPISODE	EPITHELIA	EPONYMOUS	EQUALED
EPIMERASE	EPISODES	EPITHEM	EPONYMS	EQUALI
EPIMERE	EPISODIAL	EPITHEMA	EPONYMY	EQUALING
EPIMERES	EPISODIC	EPITHEMS	EPOPEE	EQUALISE
EPIMERIC	EPISOMAL	EPITHESES	EPOPEES	EQUALISED
EPIMERISE	EPISOME	EPITHESIS	EPOPOEIA	EQUALISER
EPIMERISM	EPISOMES	EPITHET	EPOPOEIAS	EQUALISES
EPIMERIZE	EPISPERM	EPITHETED	EPOPT	EQUALITY
EPIMERS	EPISPERMS	EPITHETIC	EPOPTS	EQUALIZE
EPIMYSIA	EPISPORE	EPITHETON	EPOS	EQUALIZED
EPIMYSIUM	EPISPORES	EPITHETS	EPOSES	EQUALIZER
EPINAOI	EPISTASES	EPITOME	EPOXIDE	EQUALIZES
EPINAOS	EPISTASIS	EPITOMES	EPOXIDES	EQUALLED
EPINASTIC	EPISTASY	EPITOMIC	EPOXIDISE	EQUALLING
EPINASTY	EPISTATIC	EPITOMISE	EPOXIDIZE	EQUALLY
EPINEURAL	EPISTAXES	EPITOMIST	EPOXIED	EQUALNESS
EPINEURIA	EPISTAXIS	EPITOMIZE	EPOXIES	EQUALS
EPINICIAN	EPISTEMIC	EPITONIC	EPOXY	EQUANT
EPINICION	EPISTERNA	EPITOPE	EPOXYED	EQUANTS
EPINIKIAN	EPISTLE	EPITOPES	EPOXYING	EQUATABLE
EPINIKION	EPISTLED	EPITRITE	EPRIS	EQUATE
EPINOSIC	EPISTLER	EPITRITES	EPRISE	EQUATED
EPIPHANIC	EPISTLERS	EPIZEUXES	EPSILON	EQUATES
EPIPHANY	EPISTLES	EPIZEUXIS	EPSILONIC	EQUATING
EPIPHRAGM	EPISTLING	EPIZOA	EPSILONS	EQUATION
EPIPHYSES	EPISTOLER	EPIZOAN	EPSOMITE	EQUATIONS
EPIPHYSIS	EPISTOLET	EPIZOANS	EPSOMITES	EQUATIVE
EPIPHYTAL	EPISTOLIC	EPIZOIC	EPUISE	EQUATOR
EPIPHYTE	EPISTOME	EPIZOISM	EPUISEE	EQUATORS
EPIPHYTES	EPISTOMES	EPIZOISMS	EPULARY	EQUERRIES
EPIPHYTIC	EPISTYLE	EPIZOITE	EPULATION	EQUERRY
EPIPLOIC	EPISTYLES	EPIZOITES	EPULIDES	EQUES
EPIPLOON	EPITAPH	EPIZOON	EPULIS	EQUID
EPIPLOONS	EPITAPHED	EPIZOOTIC	EPULISES	EQUIDS
EPIPOLIC	EPITAPHER	EPIZOOTY	EPULOTIC	EQUIFINAL
EPIPOLISM	EPITAPHIC	EPOCH	EPULOTICS	EQUIMOLAL
EPIROGENY	EPITAPHS	EPOCHA	EPURATE	EQUIMOLAR
EPIRRHEMA	EPITASES	EPOCHAL	EPURATED	EQUINAL
EPISCIA	EPITASIS	EPOCHALLY	EPURATES	EQUINE
EPISCIAS	EPITAXES	EPOCHAS	EPURATING	EQUINELY
EPISCOPAL	EPITAXIAL	EPOCHS	EPURATION	EQUINES
EPISCOPE	EPITAXIC	EPODE	EPYLLIA	EQUINIA
EPISCOPES	EPITAXIES	EPODES	EPYLLION	EQUINIAS
EPISCOPY	EPITAXIS	EPODIC	EPYLLIONS	EQUINITY

EQUINOX	ERASURE	ERF	ERIGERONS	EROSE
EQUINOXES	ERASURES	ERG	ERING	EROSELY
EQUIP	ERATHEM	ERGASTIC	ERINGO	EROSES
EQUIPAGE	ERATHEMS	ERGATANER	ERINGOES	EROSIBLE
EQUIPAGED	ERBIA	ERGATE	ERINGOS	EROSION
EQUIPAGES	ERBIAS	ERGATES	ERINITE	EROSIONAL
EQUIPE	ERBIUM	ERGATIVE	ERINITES	EROSIONS
EQUIPES	ERBIUMS	ERGATIVES	ERINUS	EROSIVE
EQUIPMENT	ERE	ERGATOID	ERINUSES	EROSIVITY
EQUIPOISE	ERECT	ERGATOIDS	ERIOMETER	EROSTRATE
EQUIPPED	ERECTABLE	ERGO	ERIONITE	EROTEMA
EQUIPPER	ERECTED	ERGODIC	ERIONITES	EROTEMAS
EQUIPPERS	ERECTER	ERGOGENIC	ERIOPHYID	EROTEME
EQUIPPING	ERECTERS	ERGOGRAM	ERISTIC	EROTEMES
EQUIPS	ERECTILE	ERGOGRAMS	ERISTICAL	EROTESES
EQUISETA	ERECTING	ERGOGRAPH	ERISTICS	EROTESIS
EQUISETIC	ERECTION	ERGOMANIA	ERK	EROTETIC
EQUISETUM	ERECTIONS	ERGOMETER	ERKS	EROTIC
EQUITABLE	ERECTIVE	ERGOMETRY	ERLANG	EROTICA
EQUITABLY	ERECTLY	ERGON	ERLANGS	EROTICAL
EQUITANT	ERECTNESS	ERGONOMIC	ERLKING	EROTICAS
EQUITES	ERECTOR	ERGONS	ERLKINGS	EROTICISE
EQUITIES	ERECTORS	ERGOS	ERM	EROTICISM
EQUITY	ERECTS	ERGOT	ERMELIN	EROTICIST
EQUIVALVE	ERED	ERGOTIC	ERMELINS	EROTICIZE
EQUIVOCAL	ERELONG	ERGOTISE	ERMINE	EROTICS
EQUIVOKE	EREMIC	ERGOTISED	ERMINED	EROTISE
EQUIVOKES	EREMITAL	ERGOTISES	ERMINES	EROTISED
EQUIVOQUE	EREMITE	ERGOTISM	ERN	EROTISES
ER	EREMITES	ERGOTISMS	ERNE	EROTISING
ERA	EREMITIC	ERGOTIZE	ERNED	EROTISM
ERADIATE	EREMITISH	ERGOTIZED	ERNES	EROTISMS
ERADIATED	EREMITISM	ERGOTIZES	ERNING	EROTIZE
ERADIATES	EREMURI	ERGOTS	ERNS	EROTIZED
ERADICANT	EREMURUS	ERGS	ERODABLE	EROTIZES
ERADICATE	ERENOW	ERHU	ERODE	EROTIZING
ERAS	EREPSIN	ERHUS	ERODED	EROTOLOGY
ERASABLE	EREPSINS	ERIACH	ERODENT	ERR
ERASE	ERES	ERIACHS	ERODENTS	ERRABLE
ERASED	ERETHIC	ERIC	ERODES	ERRANCIES
ERASEMENT	ERETHISM	ERICA	ERODIBLE	ERRANCY
ERASER	ERETHISMS	ERICAS	ERODING	ERRAND
ERASERS	ERETHITIC	ERICK	ERODIUM	ERRANDS
ERASES	EREV	ERICKS	ERODIUMS	ERRANT
ERASING	EREVS	ERICOID	EROGENIC	ERRANTLY
ERASION	EREWHILE	ERICS	EROGENOUS	ERRANTRY
ERASIONS	EREWHILES	ERIGERON	EROS	ERRANTS

ERRATA	ERUPTIVE	ESCAPADE	ESCORTAGE	ESLOYNE
ERRATAS	ERUPTIVES	ESCAPADES	ESCORTED	ESLOYNED
ERRATIC	ERUPTS	ESCAPADO	ESCORTING	ESLOYNES
ERRATICAL	ERUV	ESCAPADOS	ESCORTS	ESLOYNING
ERRATICS	ERUVIM	ESCAPE	ESCOT	ESNE
ERRATUM	ERUVIN	ESCAPED	ESCOTED	ESNECIES
ERRED	ERUVS	ESCAPEE	ESCOTING	ESNECY
ERRHINE	ERVALENTA	ESCAPEES	ESCOTS	ESNES
ERRHINES	ERVEN	ESCAPER	ESCOTTED	ESOPHAGI
ERRING	ERVIL	ESCAPERS	ESCOTTING	ESOPHAGUS
ERRINGLY	ERVILS	ESCAPES	ESCRIBANO	ESOTERIC
ERRINGS	ERYNGIUM	ESCAPING	ESCRIBE	ESOTERICA
ERRONEOUS	ERYNGIUMS	ESCAPISM	ESCRIBED	ESOTERIES
ERROR	ERYNGO	ESCAPISMS	ESCRIBES	ESOTERISM
ERRORIST	ERYNGOES	ESCAPIST	ESCRIBING	ESOTERY
ERRORISTS	ERYNGOS	ESCAPISTS	ESCROC	ESOTROPIA
ERRORLESS	ERYTHEMA	ESCAR	ESCROCS	ESOTROPIC
ERRORS	ERYTHEMAL	ESCARGOT	ESCROL	ESPADA
ERRS	ERYTHEMAS	ESCARGOTS	ESCROLL	ESPADAS
ERS	ERYTHEMIC	ESCAROLE	ESCROLLS	ESPAGNOLE
ERSATZ	ERYTHRINA	ESCAROLES	ESCROLS	ESPALIER
ERSATZES	ERYTHRISM	ESCARP	ESCROW	ESPALIERS
ERSES	ERYTHRITE	ESCARPED	ESCROWED	ESPANOL
ERST	ERYTHROID	ESCARPING	ESCROWING	ESPANOLES
ERSTWHILE	ERYTHRON	ESCARPS	ESCROWS	ESPARTO
ERUCIC	ERYTHRONS	ESCARS	ESCUAGE	ESPARTOS
ERUCIFORM	ES	ESCHALOT	ESCUAGES	ESPECIAL
ERUCT	ESCABECHE	ESCHALOTS	ESCUDO	ESPERANCE
ERUCTATE	ESCALADE	ESCHAR	ESCUDOS	ESPIAL
ERUCTATED	ESCALADED	ESCHARS	ESCULENT	ESPIALS
ERUCTATES	ESCALADER	ESCHEAT	ESCULENTS	ESPIED
ERUCTED	ESCALADES	ESCHEATED	ESEMPLASY	ESPIEGLE
ERUCTING	ESCALADO	ESCHEATOR	ESERINE	ESPIER
ERUCTS	ESCALATE	ESCHEATS	ESERINES	ESPIERS
ERUDITE	ESCALATED	ESCHEW	ESES	ESPIES
ERUDITELY	ESCALATES	ESCHEWAL	ESILE	ESPIONAGE
ERUDITES	ESCALATOR	ESCHEWALS	ESILES	ESPLANADE
ERUDITION	ESCALIER	ESCHEWED	ESKAR	ESPOIR
ERUGO	ESCALIERS	ESCHEWER	ESKARS	ESPOIRS
ERUGOS	ESCALLOP	ESCHEWERS	ESKER	ESPOUSAL
ERUMPENT	ESCALLOPS	ESCHEWING	ESKERS	ESPOUSALS
ERUPT	ESCALOP	ESCHEWS	ESKIES	ESPOUSE
ERUPTED	ESCALOPE	ESCLANDRE	ESKY	ESPOUSED
ERUPTIBLE	ESCALOPED	ESCOLAR	ESLOIN	ESPOUSER
ERUPTING	ESCALOPES	ESCOLARS	ESLOINED	ESPOUSERS
ERUPTION	ESCALOPS	ESCOPETTE	ESLOINING	ESPOUSES
ERUPTIONS	ESCAPABLE	ESCORT	ESLOINS	ESPOUSING

ESPRESSO	ESTAFETTE	ESTOVER	ESTUARIAN	ETCHINGS
ESPRESSOS	ESTAMINET	ESTOVERS	ESTUARIES	ETEN
ESPRIT	ESTANCIA	ESTRADE	ESTUARINE	ETENS
ESPRITS	ESTANCIAS	ESTRADES	ESTUARY	ETERNAL
ESPUMOSO	ESTATE	ESTRADIOL	ESURIENCE	ETERNALLY
ESPUMOSOS	ESTATED	ESTRAGON	ESURIENCY	ETERNALS
ESPY	ESTATES	ESTRAGONS	ESURIENT	ETERNE
ESPYING	ESTATING	ESTRAL	ET	ETERNISE
ESQUIRE	ESTEEM	ESTRANGE	ETA	ETERNISED
ESQUIRED	ESTEEMED	ESTRANGED	ETACISM	ETERNISES
ESQUIRES	ESTEEMING	ESTRANGER	ETACISMS	ETERNITY
ESQUIRESS	ESTEEMS	ESTRANGES	ETAERIO	ETERNIZE
ESQUIRING	ESTER	ESTRAPADE	ETAERIOS	ETERNIZED
ESQUISSE	ESTERASE	ESTRAY	ETAGE	ETERNIZES
ESQUISSES	ESTERASES	ESTRAYED	ETAGERE	ETESIAN
ESS	ESTERIFY	ESTRAYING	ETAGERES	ETESIANS
ESSAY	ESTERS	ESTRAYS	ETAGES	ETH
ESSAYED	ESTHESES	ESTREAT	ETALAGE	ETHAL
ESSAYER	ESTHESIA	ESTREATED	ETALAGES	ETHALS
ESSAYERS	ESTHESIAS	ESTREATS	ETALON	ETHANAL
ESSAYETTE	ESTHESIS	ESTREPE	ETALONS	ETHANALS
ESSAYING	ESTHETE	ESTREPED	ETAMIN	ETHANE
ESSAYISH	ESTHETES	ESTREPES	ETAMINE	ETHANES
ESSAYIST	ESTHETIC	ESTREPING	ETAMINES	ETHANOATE
ESSAYISTS	ESTHETICS	ESTRICH	ETAMINS	ETHANOIC
ESSAYS	ESTIMABLE	ESTRICHES	ETAPE	ETHANOL
ESSE	ESTIMABLY	ESTRIDGE	ETAPES	ETHANOLS
ESSENCE	ESTIMATE	ESTRIDGES	ETAS	ETHANOYL
ESSENCES	ESTIMATED	ESTRILDID	ETAT	ETHANOYLS
ESSENTIAL	ESTIMATES	ESTRIN	ETATISM	ETHE
ESSES	ESTIMATOR	ESTRINS	ETATISME	ETHENE
ESSIVE	ESTIVAL	ESTRIOL	ETATISMES	ETHENES
ESSIVES	ESTIVATE	ESTRIOLS	ETATISMS	ETHEPHON
ESSOIN	ESTIVATED	ESTRO	ETATIST	ETHEPHONS
ESSOINED	ESTIVATES	ESTROGEN	ETATISTE	ETHER
ESSOINER	ESTIVATOR	ESTROGENS	ETATISTES	ETHERCAP
ESSOINERS	ESTOC	ESTRONE	ETATS	ETHERCAPS
ESSOINING	ESTOCS	ESTRONES	ETCETERA	ETHEREAL
ESSOINS	ESTOILE	ESTROS	ETCETERAS	ETHEREOUS
ESSONITE	ESTOILES	ESTROUS	ETCH	ETHERIAL
ESSONITES	ESTOP	ESTRUAL	ETCHANT	ETHERIC
ESSOYNE	ESTOPPAGE	ESTRUM	ETCHANTS	ETHERICAL
ESSOYNES	ESTOPPED	ESTRUMS	ETCHED	ETHERIFY
EST	ESTOPPEL	ESTRUS	ETCHER	ETHERION
ESTABLISH	ESTOPPELS	ESTRUSES	ETCHERS	ETHERIONS
ESTACADE	ESTOPPING	ESTS	ETCHES	ETHERISE
ESTACADES	ESTOPS	ESTUARIAL	ETCHING	ETHERISED

ETHERISER	ETHNICS	ETNAS	EUCHARIS	EUGLENIDS
ETHERISES	ETHNOCIDE	ETOILE	EUCHLORIC	EUGLENOID
ETHERISH	ETHNOGENY	ETOILES	EUCHLORIN	EUK
ETHERISM	ETHNOLOGY	ETOUFFEE	EUCHOLOGY	EUKARYON
ETHERISMS	ETHNONYM	ETOUFFEES	EUCHRE	EUKARYONS
ETHERIST	ETHNONYMS	ETOURDI	EUCHRED	EUKARYOT
ETHERISTS	ETHNOS	ETOURDIE	EUCHRES	EUKARYOTE
ETHERIZE	ETHNOSES	ETRANGER	EUCHRING	EUKARYOTS
ETHERIZED	ETHOGRAM	ETRANGERE	EUCLASE	EUKED
ETHERIZER	ETHOGRAMS	ETRANGERS	EUCLASES	EUKING
ETHERIZES	ETHOLOGIC	ETRENNE	EUCLIDEAN	EUKS
ETHERS	ETHOLOGY	ETRENNES	EUCLIDIAN	EULACHAN
ETHIC	ETHONONE	ETRIER	EUCRITE	EULACHANS
ETHICAL	ETHONONES	ETRIERS	EUCRITES	EULACHON
ETHICALLY	ETHOS	ETTERCAP	EUCRITIC	EULACHONS
ETHICALS	ETHOSES	ETTERCAPS	EUCRYPHIA	EULOGIA
ETHICIAN	ETHOXIDE	ETTIN	EUCYCLIC	EULOGIAE
ETHICIANS	ETHOXIDES	ETTINS	EUDAEMON	EULOGIAS
ETHICISE	ETHOXIES	ETTLE	EUDAEMONS	EULOGIES
ETHICISED	ETHOXY	ETTLED	EUDAEMONY	EULOGISE
ETHICISES	ETHOXYL	ETTLES	EUDAIMON	EULOGISED
ETHICISM	ETHOXYLS	ETTLING	EUDAIMONS	EULOGISER
ETHICISMS	ETHS	ETUDE	EUDEMON	EULOGISES
ETHICIST	ETHYL	ETUDES	EUDEMONIA	EULOGIST
ETHICISTS	ETHYLATE	ETUI	EUDEMONIC	EULOGISTS
ETHICIZE	ETHYLATED	ETUIS	EUDEMONS	EULOGIUM
ETHICIZED	ETHYLATES	ETWEE	EUDIALYTE	EULOGIUMS
ETHICIZES	ETHYLENE	ETWEES	EUGARIE	EULOGIZE
ETHICS	ETHYLENES	ETYMA	EUGARIES	EULOGIZED
ETHINYL	ETHYLENIC	ETYMIC	EUGE	EULOGIZER
ETHINYLS	ETHYLIC	ETYMOLOGY	EUGENIA	EULOGIZES
ETHION	ETHYLS	ETYMON	EUGENIAS	EULOGY
ETHIONINE	ETHYNE	ETYMONS	EUGENIC	EUMELANIN
ETHIONS	ETHYNES	ETYPIC	EUGENICAL	EUMERISM
ETHIOPS	ETHYNYL	ETYPICAL	EUGENICS	EUMERISMS
ETHIOPSES	ETHYNYLS	EUCAIN	EUGENISM	EUMONG
ETHMOID	ETIC	EUCAINE	EUGENISMS	EUMONGS
ETHMOIDAL	ETICS	EUCAINES	EUGENIST	EUMUNG
ETHMOIDS	ETIOLATE	EUCAINS	EUGENISTS	EUMUNGS
ETHNARCH	ETIOLATED	EUCALYPT	EUGENOL	EUNUCH
ETHNARCHS	ETIOLATES	EUCALYPTI	EUGENOLS	EUNUCHISE
ETHNARCHY	ETIOLIN	EUCALYPTS	EUGH	EUNUCHISM
ETHNE	ETIOLINS	EUCARYON	EUGHEN	EUNUCHIZE
ETHNIC	ETIOLOGIC	EUCARYONS	EUGHS	EUNUCHOID
ETHNICAL	ETIOLOGY	EUCARYOT	EUGLENA	EUNUCHS
ETHNICISM	ETIQUETTE	EUCARYOTE	EUGLENAS	EUOI
ETHNICITY	ETNA	EUCARYOTS	EUGLENID	EUONYMIN

EUONYMINS	EUPHUISM	EURYOKOUS	EUTROPY	EVECTION
EUONYMUS	EUPHUISMS	EURYOKY	EUXENITE	EVECTIONS
EUOUAE	EUPHUIST	EURYTHERM	EUXENITES	EVEJAR
EUOUAES	EUPHUISTS	EURYTHMIC	EVACUANT	EVEJARS
EUPAD	EUPHUIZE	EURYTHMY	EVACUANTS	EVEN
EUPADS	EUPHUIZED	EURYTOPIC	EVACUATE	EVENED
EUPATRID	EUPHUIZES	EUSOCIAL	EVACUATED	EVENEMENT
EUPATRIDS	EUPLASTIC	EUSOL	EVACUATES	EVENER
EUPEPSIA	EUPLOID	EUSOLS	EVACUATOR	EVENERS
EUPEPSIAS	EUPLOIDS	EUSTACIES	EVACUEE	EVENEST
EUPEPSIES	EUPLOIDY	EUSTACY	EVACUEES	EVENFALL
EUPEPSY	EUPNEA	EUSTASIES	EVADABLE	EVENFALLS
EUPEPTIC	EUPNEAS	EUSTASY	EVADE	EVENING
EUPHAUSID	EUPNEIC	EUSTATIC	EVADED	EVENINGS
EUPHEMISE	EUPNOEA	EUSTELE	EVADER	EVENLY
EUPHEMISM	EUPNOEAS	EUSTELES	EVADERS	EVENNESS
EUPHEMIST	EUPNOEIC	EUSTYLE	EVADES	EVENS
EUPHEMIZE	EUREKA	EUSTYLES	EVADIBLE	EVENSONG
EUPHENIC	EUREKAS	EUTAXIA	EVADING	EVENSONGS
EUPHENICS	EURHYTHMY	EUTAXIAS	EVADINGLY	EVENT
EUPHOBIA	EURIPI	EUTAXIES	EVAGATION	EVENTED
EUPHOBIAS	EURIPUS	EUTAXITE	EVAGINATE	EVENTER
EUPHON	EURIPUSES	EUTAXITES	EVALUABLE	EVENTERS
EUPHONIA	EURO	EUTAXITIC	EVALUATE	EVENTFUL
EUPHONIAS	EUROBOND	EUTAXY	EVALUATED	EVENTIDE
EUPHONIC	EUROBONDS	EUTECTIC	EVALUATES	EVENTIDES
EUPHONIES	EUROCRAT	EUTECTICS	EVALUATOR	EVENTING
EUPHONISE	EUROCRATS	EUTECTOID	EVANESCE	EVENTINGS
EUPHONISM	EUROCREEP	EUTEXIA	EVANESCED	EVENTIVE
EUPHONIUM	EUROKIES	EUTEXIAS	EVANESCES	EVENTLESS
EUPHONIZE	EUROKOUS	EUTHANASE	EVANGEL	EVENTRATE
EUPHONS	EUROKY	EUTHANASY	EVANGELIC	EVENTS
EUPHONY	EUROLAND	EUTHANAZE	EVANGELS	EVENTUAL
EUPHORBIA	EUROLANDS	EUTHANISE	EVANGELY	EVENTUATE
EUPHORIA	EURONOTE	EUTHANIZE	EVANISH	EVER
EUPHORIAS	EURONOTES	EUTHENICS	EVANISHED	EVERGLADE
EUPHORIC	EUROPHILE	EUTHENIST	EVANISHES	EVERGREEN
EUPHORIES	EUROPIUM	EUTHERIAN	EVANITION	EVERMORE
EUPHORY	EUROPIUMS	EUTHYMIA	EVAPORATE	EVERNET
EUPHOTIC	EUROPOP	EUTHYMIAS	EVAPORITE	EVERNETS
EUPHRASIA	EUROPOPS	EUTHYROID	EVASIBLE	EVERSIBLE
EUPHRASY	EUROS	EUTRAPELY	EVASION	EVERSION
EUPHROE	EUROZONE	EUTROPHIC	EVASIONAL	EVERSIONS
EUPHROES	EUROZONES	EUTROPHY	EVASIONS	EVERT
EUPHUISE	EURYBATH	EUTROPIC	EVASIVE	EVERTED
EUPHUISED	EURYBATHS	EUTROPIES	EVASIVELY	EVERTING
EUPHUISES	EURYOKIES	EUTROPOUS	EVE	EVERTOR

EVERTORS	EVINCIBLE	EVOLVE	EXACTEST	EXARATE
EVERTS	EVINCIBLY	EVOLVED	EXACTING	EXARATION
EVERWHERE	EVINCING	EVOLVENT	EXACTION	EXARCH
EVERWHICH	EVINCIVE	EVOLVENTS	EXACTIONS	EXARCHAL
EVERY	EVIRATE	EVOLVER	EXACTLY	EXARCHATE
EVERYBODY	EVIRATED	EVOLVERS	EXACTMENT	EXARCHIES
EVERYDAY	EVIRATES	EVOLVES	EXACTNESS	EXARCHIST
EVERYDAYS	EVIRATING	EVOLVING	EXACTOR	EXARCHS
EVERYMAN	EVITABLE	EVONYMUS	EXACTORS	EXARCHY
EVERYMEN	EVITATE	EVOS	EXACTRESS	EXCAMB
EVERYONE	EVITATED	EVOVAE	EXACTS	EXCAMBED
EVERYWAY	EVITATES	EVOVAES	EXACUM	EXCAMBING
EVERYWHEN	EVITATING	EVULGATE	EXACUMS	EXCAMBION
EVES	EVITATION	EVULGATED	EXAHERTZ	EXCAMBIUM
EVET	EVITE	EVULGATES	EXALT	EXCAMBS
EVETS	EVITED	EVULSE	EXALTED	EXCARNATE
EVHOE	EVITERNAL	EVULSED	EXALTEDLY	EXCAUDATE
EVICT	EVITES	EVULSES	EXALTER	EXCAVATE
EVICTED	EVITING	EVULSING	EXALTERS	EXCAVATED
EVICTEE	EVO	EVULSION	EXALTING	EXCAVATES
EVICTEES	EVOCABLE	EVULSIONS	EXALTS	EXCAVATOR
EVICTING	EVOCATE	EVZONE	EXAM	EXCEED
EVICTION	EVOCATED	EVZONES	EXAMEN	EXCEEDED
EVICTIONS	EVOCATES	EWE	EXAMENS	EXCEEDER
EVICTOR	EVOCATING	EWER	EXAMINANT	EXCEEDERS
EVICTORS	EVOCATION	EWERS	EXAMINATE	EXCEEDING
EVICTS	EVOCATIVE	EWES	EXAMINE	EXCEEDS
EVIDENCE	EVOCATOR	EWEST	EXAMINED	EXCEL
EVIDENCED	EVOCATORS	EWFTES	EXAMINEE	EXCELLED
EVIDENCES	EVOCATORY	EWGHEN	EXAMINEES	EXCELLENT
EVIDENT	EVOE	EWHOW	EXAMINER	EXCELLING
EVIDENTLY	EVOHE	EWK	EXAMINERS	EXCELS
EVIDENTS	EVOKE	EWKED	EXAMINES	EXCELSIOR
EVIL	EVOKED	EWKING	EXAMINING	EXCENTRIC
EVILDOER	EVOKER	EWKS	EXAMPLAR	EXCEPT
EVILDOERS	EVOKERS	EWT	EXAMPLARS	EXCEPTANT
EVILDOING	EVOKES	EWTS	EXAMPLE	EXCEPTED
EVILER	EVOKING	EX	EXAMPLED	EXCEPTING
EVILEST	EVOLUE	EXABYTE	EXAMPLES	EXCEPTION
EVILLER	EVOLUES	EXABYTES	EXAMPLING	EXCEPTIVE
EVILLEST	EVOLUTE	EXACT	EXAMS	EXCEPTOR
EVILLY	EVOLUTED	EXACTA	EXANIMATE	EXCEPTORS
EVILNESS	EVOLUTES	EXACTABLE	EXANTHEM	EXCEPTS
EVILS	EVOLUTING	EXACTAS	EXANTHEMA	EXCERPT
EVINCE	EVOLUTION	EXACTED	EXANTHEMS	EXCERPTA
EVINCED	EVOLUTIVE	EXACTER	EXAPTED	EXCERPTED
EVINCES	EVOLVABLE	EXACTERS	EXAPTIVE	EXCERPTER

EXCERPTOR	EXCITONS	EXCUSAL	EXEGETICS	EXFILS
EXCERPTS	EXCITOR	EXCUSALS	EXEGETIST	EXFOLIANT
EXCERPTUM	EXCITORS	EXCUSE	EXEME	EXFOLIATE
EXCESS	EXCLAIM	EXCUSED	EXEMED	EXHALABLE
EXCESSED	EXCLAIMED	EXCUSER	EXEMES	EXHALANT
EXCESSES	EXCLAIMER	EXCUSERS	EXEMING	EXHALANTS
EXCESSING	EXCLAIMS	EXCUSES	EXEMPLA	EXHALE
EXCESSIVE	EXCLAVE	EXCUSING	EXEMPLAR	EXHALED
EXCHANGE	EXCLAVES	EXCUSIVE	EXEMPLARS	EXHALENT
EXCHANGED	EXCLOSURE	EXEAT	EXEMPLARY	EXHALENTS
EXCHANGER	EXCLUDE	EXEATS	EXEMPLE	EXHALES
EXCHANGES	EXCLUDED	EXEC	EXEMPLES	EXHALING
EXCHEAT	EXCLUDEE	EXECRABLE	EXEMPLIFY	EXHAUST
EXCHEATS	EXCLUDEES	EXECRABLY	EXEMPLUM	EXHAUSTED
EXCHEQUER	EXCLUDER	EXECRATE	EXEMPT	EXHAUSTER
EXCIDE	EXCLUDERS	EXECRATED	EXEMPTED	EXHAUSTS
EXCIDED	EXCLUDES	EXECRATES	EXEMPTING	EXHEDRA
EXCIDES	EXCLUDING	EXECRATOR	EXEMPTION	EXHEDRAE
EXCIDING	EXCLUSION	EXECS	EXEMPTIVE	EXHIBIT
EXCIMER	EXCLUSIVE	EXECUTANT	EXEMPTS	EXHIBITED
EXCIMERS	EXCLUSORY	EXECUTARY	EXEQUATUR	EXHIBITER
EXCIPIENT	EXCORIATE	EXECUTE	EXEQUIAL	EXHIBITOR
EXCIPLE	EXCREMENT	EXECUTED	EXEQUIES	EXHIBITS
EXCIPLES	EXCRETA	EXECUTER	EXEQUY	EXHORT
EXCISABLE	EXCRETAL	EXECUTERS	EXERCISE	EXHORTED
EXCISE	EXCRETE	EXECUTES	EXERCISED	EXHORTER
EXCISED	EXCRETED	EXECUTING	EXERCISER	EXHORTERS
EXCISEMAN	EXCRETER	EXECUTION	EXERCISES	EXHORTING
EXCISEMEN	EXCRETERS	EXECUTIVE	EXERCYCLE	EXHORTS
EXCISES	EXCRETES	EXECUTOR	EXERGIES	EXHUMATE
EXCISING	EXCRETING	EXECUTORS	EXERGONIC	EXHUMATED
EXCISION	EXCRETION	EXECUTORY	EXERGUAL	EXHUMATES
EXCISIONS	EXCRETIVE	EXECUTRIX	EXERGUE	EXHUME
EXCITABLE	EXCRETORY	EXECUTRY	EXERGUES	EXHUMED
EXCITABLY	EXCUBANT	EXED	EXERGY	EXHUMER
EXCITANCY	EXCUDIT	EXEDRA	EXERT	EXHUMERS
EXCITANT	EXCULPATE	EXEDRAE	EXERTED	EXHUMES
EXCITANTS	EXCURRENT	EXEDRAS	EXERTING	EXHUMING
EXCITE	EXCURSE	EXEEM	EXERTION	EXIES
EXCITED	EXCURSED	EXEEMED	EXERTIONS	EXIGEANT
EXCITEDLY	EXCURSES	EXEEMING	EXERTIVE	EXIGEANTE
EXCITER	EXCURSING	EXEEMS	EXERTS	EXIGENCE
EXCITERS	EXCURSION	EXEGESES	EXES	EXIGENCES
EXCITES	EXCURSIVE	EXEGESIS	EXEUNT	EXIGENCY
EXCITING	EXCURSUS	EXEGETE	EXFIL	EXIGENT
EXCITON	EXCUSABLE	EXEGETES	EXFILLED	EXIGENTLY
EXCITONIC	EXCUSABLY	EXEGETIC	EXFILLING	EXIGENTS

EXIGIBLE	EXODIC	EXORCIST	EXPANSILE	EXPERTS
EXIGUITY	EXODIST	EXORCISTS	EXPANSION	EXPIABLE
EXIGUOUS	EXODISTS	EXORCIZE	EXPANSIVE	EXPIATE
EXILABLE	EXODOI	EXORCIZED	EXPAT	EXPIATED
EXILE	EXODONTIA	EXORCIZER	EXPATIATE	EXPIATES
EXILED	EXODOS	EXORCIZES	EXPATS	EXPIATING
EXILEMENT	EXODUS	EXORDIA	EXPECT	EXPIATION
EXILER	EXODUSES	EXORDIAL	EXPECTANT	EXPIATOR
EXILERS	EXOENZYME	EXORDIUM	EXPECTED	EXPIATORS
EXILES	EXOERGIC	EXORDIUMS	EXPECTER	EXPIATORY
EXILIAN	EXOGAMIC	EXOSMIC	EXPECTERS	EXPIRABLE
EXILIC	EXOGAMIES	EXOSMOSE	EXPECTING	EXPIRANT
EXILING	EXOGAMOUS	EXOSMOSES	EXPECTS	EXPIRANTS
EXILITIES	EXOGAMY	EXOSMOSIS	EXPEDIENT	EXPIRE
EXILITY	EXOGEN	EXOSMOTIC	EXPEDITE	EXPIRED
EXIMIOUS	EXOGENIC	EXOSPHERE	EXPEDITED	EXPIRER
EXINE	EXOGENISM	EXOSPORAL	EXPEDITER	EXPIRERS
EXINES	EXOGENOUS	EXOSPORE	EXPEDITES	EXPIRES
EXING	EXOGENS	EXOSPORES	EXPEDITOR	EXPIRIES
EXIST	EXOMION	EXOSPORIA	EXPEL	EXPIRING
EXISTED	EXOMIONS	EXOSTOSES	EXPELLANT	EXPIRY
EXISTENCE	EXOMIS	EXOSTOSIS	EXPELLED	EXPISCATE
EXISTENT	EXOMISES	EXOTERIC	EXPELLEE	EXPLAIN
EXISTENTS	EXON	EXOTIC	EXPELLEES	EXPLAINED
EXISTING	EXONERATE	EXOTICA	EXPELLENT	EXPLAINER
EXISTS	EXONIC	EXOTICISE	EXPELLER	EXPLAINS
EXIT	EXONS	EXOTICISM	EXPELLERS	EXPLANT
EXITANCE	EXONUMIA	EXOTICIST	EXPELLING	EXPLANTED
EXITANCES	EXONUMIST	EXOTICIZE	EXPELS	EXPLANTS
EXITED	EXONYM	EXOTICS	EXPEND	EXPLETIVE
EXITING	EXONYMS	EXOTISM	EXPENDED	EXPLETORY
EXITLESS	EXOPHAGY	EXOTISMS	EXPENDER	EXPLICATE
EXITS	EXOPHORIC	EXOTOXIC	EXPENDERS	EXPLICIT
EXO	EXOPLANET	EXOTOXIN	EXPENDING	EXPLICITS
EXOCARP	EXOPLASM	EXOTOXINS	EXPENDS	EXPLODE
EXOCARPS	EXOPLASMS	EXOTROPIA	EXPENSE	EXPLODED
EXOCRINE	EXOPOD	EXOTROPIC	EXPENSED	EXPLODER
EXOCRINES	EXOPODITE	EXPAND	EXPENSES	EXPLODERS
EXOCYCLIC	EXOPODS	EXPANDED	EXPENSING	EXPLODES
EXOCYTIC	EXORABLE	EXPANDER	EXPENSIVE	EXPLODING
EXOCYTOSE	EXORATION	EXPANDERS	EXPERT	EXPLOIT
EXODE	EXORCISE	EXPANDING	EXPERTED	EXPLOITED
EXODERM	EXORCISED	EXPANDOR	EXPERTING	EXPLOITER
EXODERMAL	EXORCISER	EXPANDORS	EXPERTISE	EXPLOITS
EXODERMIS	EXORCISES	EXPANDS	EXPERTISM	EXPLORE
EXODERMS	EXORCISM	EXPANSE	EXPERTIZE	EXPLORED
EXODES	EXORCISMS	EXPANSES	EXPERTLY	EXPLORER

EXPLORERS	EXPUGNING	EXTEMPORE	EXTOLLS	EXTROPIES
EXPLORES	EXPUGNS	EXTEND	EXTOLMENT	EXTROPY
EXPLORING	EXPULSE	EXTENDANT	EXTOLS	EXTRORSAL
EXPLOSION	EXPULSED	EXTENDED	EXTORSIVE	EXTRORSE
EXPLOSIVE	EXPULSES	EXTENDER	EXTORT	EXTROVERT
EXPO	EXPULSING	EXTENDERS	EXTORTED	EXTRUDE
EXPONENT	EXPULSION	EXTENDING	EXTORTER	EXTRUDED
EXPONENTS	EXPULSIVE	EXTENDS	EXTORTERS	EXTRUDER
EXPONIBLE	EXPUNCT	EXTENSE	EXTORTING	EXTRUDERS
EXPORT	EXPUNCTED	EXTENSES	EXTORTION	EXTRUDES
EXPORTED	EXPUNCTS	EXTENSILE	EXTORTIVE	EXTRUDING
EXPORTER	EXPUNGE	EXTENSION	EXTORTS	EXTRUSILE
EXPORTERS	EXPUNGED	EXTENSITY	EXTRA	EXTRUSION
EXPORTING	EXPUNGER	EXTENSIVE	EXTRABOLD	EXTRUSIVE
EXPORTS	EXPUNGERS	EXTENSOR	EXTRACT	EXTRUSORY
EXPOS	EXPUNGES	EXTENSORS	EXTRACTED	EXTUBATE
EXPOSABLE	EXPUNGING	EXTENT	EXTRACTOR	EXTUBATED
EXPOSAL	EXPURGATE	EXTENTS	EXTRACTS	EXTUBATES
EXPOSALS	EXPURGE	EXTENUATE	EXTRADITE	EXUBERANT
EXPOSE	EXPURGED	EXTERIOR	EXTRADOS	EXUBERATE
EXPOSED	EXPURGES	EXTERIORS	EXTRAIT	EXUDATE
EXPOSER	EXPURGING	EXTERMINE	EXTRAITS	EXUDATES
EXPOSERS	EXQUISITE	EXTERN	EXTRALITY	EXUDATION
EXPOSES	EXSCIND	EXTERNAL	EXTRANET	EXUDATIVE
EXPOSING	EXSCINDED	EXTERNALS	EXTRANETS	EXUDE
EXPOSIT	EXSCINDS	EXTERNAT	EXTRAPOSE	EXUDED
EXPOSITED	EXSECANT	EXTERNATS	EXTRAS	EXUDES
EXPOSITOR	EXSECANTS	EXTERNE	EXTRAUGHT	EXUDING
EXPOSITS	EXSECT	EXTERNES	EXTRAVERT	EXUL
EXPOSOME	EXSECTED	EXTERNS	EXTREAT	EXULLED
EXPOSOMES	EXSECTING	EXTINCT	EXTREATED	EXULLING
EXPOSTURE	EXSECTION	EXTINCTED	EXTREATS	EXULS
EXPOSURE	EXSECTS	EXTINCTS	EXTREMA	EXULT
EXPOSURES	EXSERT	EXTINE	EXTREMAL	EXULTANCE
EXPOUND	EXSERTED	EXTINES	EXTREMALS	EXULTANCY
EXPOUNDED	EXSERTILE	EXTIRP	EXTREME	EXULTANT
EXPOUNDER	EXSERTING	EXTIRPATE	EXTREMELY	EXULTED
EXPOUNDS	EXSERTION	EXTIRPED	EXTREMER	EXULTING
EXPRESS	EXSERTS	EXTIRPING	EXTREMES	EXULTS
EXPRESSED	EXSICCANT	EXTIRPS	EXTREMEST	EXURB
EXPRESSER	EXSICCATE	EXTOL	EXTREMISM	EXURBAN
EXPRESSES	EXSTROPHY	EXTOLD	EXTREMIST	EXURBIA
EXPRESSLY	EXSUCCOUS	EXTOLL	EXTREMITY	EXURBIAS
EXPRESSO	EXTANT	EXTOLLED	EXTREMUM	EXURBS
EXPRESSOS	EXTASIES	EXTOLLER	EXTREMUMS	EXUVIA
EXPUGN	EXTASY	EXTOLLERS	EXTRICATE	EXUVIAE
EXPUGNED	EXTATIC	EXTOLLING	EXTRINSIC	EXUVIAL

EXUVIATE	EYEBLINK	EYELESS	EYER	EYEWASHES
EXUVIATED	EYEBLINKS	EYELET	EYERS	EYEWATER
EXUVIATES	EYEBOLT	EYELETED	EYES	EYEWATERS
EXUVIUM	EYEBOLTS	EYELETEER	EYESHADE	EYEWEAR
EYALET	EYEBRIGHT	EYELETING	EYESHADES	EYEWEARS
EYALETS	EYEBROW	EYELETS	EYESHADOW	EYEWINK
EYAS	EYEBROWED	EYELETTED	EYESHINE	EYEWINKS
EYASES	EYEBROWS	EYELEVEL	EYESHINES	EYING
EYASS	EYECUP	EYELIAD	EYESHOT	EYLIAD
EYASSES	EYECUPS	EYELIADS	EYESHOTS	EYLIADS
EYE	EYED	EYELID	EYESIGHT	EYNE
EYEABLE	EYEDNESS	EYELIDS	EYESIGHTS	EYOT
EYEBALL	EYEDROPS	EYELIFT	EYESOME	EYOTS
EYEBALLED	EYEFOLD	EYELIFTS	EYESORE	EYRA
EYEBALLS	EYEFOLDS	EYELIKE	EYESORES	EYRAS
EYEBANK	EYEFUL	EYELINER	EYESPOT	EYRE
EYEBANKS	EYEFULS	EYELINERS	EYESPOTS	EYRES
EYEBAR	EYEGLASS	EYEN	EYESTALK	EYRIE
EYEBARS	EYEHOLE	EYEOPENER	EYESTALKS	EYRIES
EYEBATH	EYEHOLES	EYEPATCH	EYESTONE	EYRIR
EYEBATHS	EYEHOOK	EYEPIECE	EYESTONES	EYRY
EYEBEAM	EYEHOOKS	EYEPIECES	EYESTRAIN	EZINE
EYEBEAMS	EYEING	EYEPOINT	EYETEETH	EZINES
EYEBLACK	EYELASH	EYEPOINTS	EYETOOTH	
EYEBLACKS	EYELASHES	EYEPOPPER	EYEWASH	

E

F

FA	FABULIST	FACETIME	FACTIVE	FADDIST
FAA	FABULISTS	FACETIMED	FACTOID	FADDISTS
FAAING	FABULIZE	FACETIMES	FACTOIDAL	FADDLE
FAAN	FABULIZED	FACETING	FACTOIDS	FADDLED
FAAS	FABULIZES	FACETINGS	FACTOR	FADDLES
FAB	FABULOUS	FACETIOUS	FACTORAGE	FADDLING
FABACEOUS	FABURDEN	FACETS	FACTORED	FADDY
FABBER	FABURDENS	FACETTED	FACTORIAL	FADE
FABBEST	FACADE	FACETTING	FACTORIES	FADEAWAY
FABBIER	FACADES	FACEUP	FACTORING	FADEAWAYS
FABBIEST	FACE	FACIA	FACTORISE	FADED
FABBY	FACEABLE	FACIAE	FACTORIZE	FADEDLY
FABLE	FACEBAR	FACIAL	FACTORS	FADEDNESS
FABLED	FACEBARS	FACIALIST	FACTORY	FADEIN
FABLER	FACEBOOK	FACIALLY	FACTOTUM	FADEINS
FABLERS	FACEBOOKS	FACIALS	FACTOTUMS	FADELESS
FABLES	FACECLOTH	FACIAS	FACTS	FADEOUT
FABLET	FACED	FACIEND	FACTSHEET	FADEOUTS
FABLETS	FACEDOWN	FACIENDS	FACTUAL	FADER
FABLIAU	FACEDOWNS	FACIES	FACTUALLY	FADERS
FABLIAUX	FACELESS	FACILE	FACTUM	FADES
FABLING	FACELIFT	FACILELY	FACTUMS	FADEUR
FABLINGS	FACELIFTS	FACILITY	FACTURE	FADEURS
FABRIC	FACEMAIL	FACING	FACTURES	FADGE
FABRICANT	FACEMAILS	FACINGS	FACULA	FADGED
FABRICATE	FACEMAN	FACONNE	FACULAE	FADGES
FABRICKED	FACEMASK	FACONNES	FACULAR	FADGING
FABRICS	FACEMASKS	FACSIMILE	FACULTIES	FADIER
FABRIQUE	FACEMEN	FACT	FACULTY	FADIEST
FABRIQUES	FACEOFF	FACTA	FACUNDITY	FADING
FABS	FACEOFFS	FACTFUL	FAD	FADINGS
FABULAR	FACEPLATE	FACTICE	FADABLE	FADLIKE
FABULATE	FACEPRINT	FACTICES	FADAISE	FADO
FABULATED	FACER	FACTICITY	FADAISES	FADOMETER
FABULATES	FACERS	FACTION	FADDIER	FADOS
FABULATOR	FACES	FACTIONAL	FADDIEST	FADS
FABULISE	FACET	FACTIONS	FADDINESS	FADY
FABULISED	FACETE	FACTIOUS	FADDISH	FAE
FABULISES	FACETED	FACTIS	FADDISHLY	FAECAL
FABULISM	FACETELY	FACTISES	FADDISM	FAECES
FABULISMS	FACETIAE	FACTITIVE	FADDISMS	FAENA

FAENAS	FAHLORES	FAINTING	FAITHLESS	FALCON
FAERIE	FAHS	FAINTINGS	FAITHS	FALCONER
FAERIES	FAIBLE	FAINTISH	FAITOR	FALCONERS
FAERY	FAIBLES	FAINTLY	FAITORS	FALCONET
FAFF	FAIENCE	FAINTNESS	FAITOUR	FALCONETS
FAFFED	FAIENCES	FAINTS	FAITOURS	FALCONINE
FAFFIER	FAIK	FAINTY	FAIX	FALCONOID
FAFFIEST	FAIKED	FAIR	FAJITA	FALCONRY
FAFFING	FAIKES	FAIRED	FAJITAS	FALCONS
FAFFS	FAIKING	FAIRER	FAKE	FALCULA
FAFFY	FAIKS	FAIREST	FAKED	FALCULAE
FAG	FAIL	FAIRFACED	FAKEER	FALCULAS
FAGACEOUS	FAILED	FAIRGOER	FAKEERS	FALCULATE
FAGGED	FAILING	FAIRGOERS	FAKEMENT	FALDAGE
FAGGERIES	FAILINGLY	FAIRIER	FAKEMENTS	FALDAGES
FAGGERY	FAILINGS	FAIRIES	FAKER	FALDERAL
FAGGIER	FAILLE	FAIRIEST	FAKERIES	FALDERALS
FAGGIEST	FAILLES	FAIRILY	FAKERS	FALDEROL
FAGGING	FAILOVER	FAIRING	FAKERY	FALDEROLS
FAGGINGS	FAILOVERS	FAIRINGS	FAKES	FALDETTA
FAGGOT	FAILS	FAIRISH	FAKEY	FALDETTAS
FAGGOTED	FAILURE	FAIRISHLY	FAKEYS	FALDSTOOL
FAGGOTING	FAILURES	FAIRLEAD	FAKIE	FALL
FAGGOTRY	FAIN	FAIRLEADS	FAKIER	FALLACIES
FAGGOTS	FAINE	FAIRLY	FAKIES	FALLACY
FAGGOTY	FAINEANCE	FAIRNESS	FAKIEST	FALLAL
FAGGY	FAINEANCY	FAIRS	FAKING	FALLALERY
FAGIN	FAINEANT	FAIRWAY	FAKIR	FALLALISH
FAGINS	FAINEANTS	FAIRWAYS	FAKIRISM	FALLALS
FAGOT	FAINED	FAIRY	FAKIRISMS	FALLAWAY
FAGOTED	FAINER	FAIRYDOM	FAKIRS	FALLAWAYS
FAGOTER	FAINES	FAIRYDOMS	FALAFEL	FALLBACK
FAGOTERS	FAINEST	FAIRYHOOD	FALAFELS	FALLBACKS
FAGOTING	FAINING	FAIRYISM	FALAJ	FALLBOARD
FAGOTINGS	FAINITES	FAIRYISMS	FALANGISM	FALLEN
FAGOTS	FAINLY	FAIRYLAND	FALANGIST	FALLER
FAGOTTI	FAINNE	FAIRYLIKE	FALBALA	FALLERS
FAGOTTIST	FAINNES	FAIRYTALE	FALBALAS	FALLFISH
FAGOTTO	FAINNESS	FAITH	FALCADE	FALLIBLE
FAGOTTOS	FAINS	FAITHCURE	FALCADES	FALLIBLY
FAGS	FAINT	FAITHED	FALCATE	FALLING
FAH	FAINTED	FAITHER	FALCATED	FALLINGS
FAHLBAND	FAINTER	FAITHERS	FALCATION	FALLOFF
FAHLBANDS	FAINTERS	FAITHFUL	FALCES	FALLOFFS
FAHLERZ	FAINTEST	FAITHFULS	FALCHION	FALLOUT
FAHLERZES	FAINTIER	FAITHING	FALCHIONS	FALLOUTS
FAHLORE	FAINTIEST	FAITHINGS	FALCIFORM	FALLOW

F

FALLOWED	FAMILIES	FAND	FANJETS	FANTASM
FALLOWER	FAMILISM	FANDANGLE	FANK	FANTASMAL
FALLOWEST	FAMILISMS	FANDANGO	FANKED	FANTASMIC
FALLOWING	FAMILIST	FANDANGOS	FANKING	FANTASMS
FALLOWS	FAMILLE	FANDED	FANKLE	FANTASQUE
FALLS	FAMILLES	FANDING	FANKLED	FANTAST
FALSE	FAMILY	FANDOM	FANKLES	FANTASTIC
FALSED	FAMINE	FANDOMS	FANKLING	FANTASTRY
FALSEFACE	FAMINES	FANDS	FANKS	FANTASTS
FALSEHOOD	FAMING	FANE	FANLIGHT	FANTASY
FALSELY	FAMISH	FANEGA	FANLIGHTS	FANTEEG
FALSENESS	FAMISHED	FANEGADA	FANLIKE	FANTEEGS
FALSER	FAMISHES	FANEGADAS	FANNED	FANTIGUE
FALSERS	FAMISHING	FANEGAS	FANNEL	FANTIGUES
FALSES	FAMOUS	FANES	FANNELL	FANTOD
FALSEST	FAMOUSED	FANFARADE	FANNELLS	FANTODS
FALSETTO	FAMOUSES	FANFARE	FANNELS	FANTOM
FALSETTOS	FAMOUSING	FANFARED	FANNER	FANTOMS
FALSEWORK	FAMOUSLY	FANFARES	FANNERS	FANTOOSH
FALSIE	FAMULI	FANFARING	FANNIED	FANUM
FALSIES	FAMULUS	FANFARON	FANNIES	FANUMS
FALSIFIED	FAN	FANFARONA	FANNING	FANWISE
FALSIFIER	FANAL	FANFARONS	FANNINGS	FANWORT
FALSIFIES	FANALS	FANFIC	FANNY	FANWORTS
FALSIFY	FANATIC	FANFICS	FANNYING	FANZINE
FALSING	FANATICAL	FANFOLD	FANO	FANZINES
FALSISH	FANATICS	FANFOLDED	FANON	FAP
FALSISM	FANBASE	FANFOLDS	FANONS	FAQIR
FALSISMS	FANBASES	FANG	FANOS	FAQIRS
FALSITIES	FANBOY	FANGA	FANS	FAQUIR
FALSITY	FANBOYS	FANGAS	FANSITE	FAQUIRS
FALTBOAT	FANCIABLE	FANGED	FANSITES	FAR
FALTBOATS	FANCIED	FANGING	FANSUB	FARAD
FALTER	FANCIER	FANGIRL	FANSUBS	FARADAIC
FALTERED	FANCIERS	FANGIRLS	FANTAD	FARADAY
FALTERER	FANCIES	FANGLE	FANTADS	FARADAYS
FALTERERS	FANCIEST	FANGLED	FANTAIL	FARADIC
FALTERING	FANCIFIED	FANGLES	FANTAILED	FARADISE
FALTERS	FANCIFIES	FANGLESS	FANTAILS	FARADISED
FALX	FANCIFUL	FANGLIKE	FANTASIA	FARADISER
FAME	FANCIFY	FANGLING	FANTASIAS	FARADISES
FAMED	FANCILESS	FANGO	FANTASIE	FARADISM
FAMELESS	FANCILY	FANGOS	FANTASIED	FARADISMS
FAMES	FANCINESS	FANGS	FANTASIES	FARADIZE
FAMILIAL	FANCY	FANION	FANTASISE	FARADIZED
FAMILIAR	FANCYING	FANIONS	FANTASIST	FARADIZER
FAMILIARS	FANCYWORK	FANJET	FANTASIZE	FARADIZES

FARADS	FAREWELL	FARNESSES	FASCIA	FASTBALLS
FARAND	FAREWELLS	FARO	FASCIAE	FASTED
FARANDINE	FARFAL	FAROLITO	FASCIAL	FASTEN
FARANDOLE	FARFALLE	FAROLITOS	FASCIAS	FASTENED
FARAWAY	FARFALLES	FAROS	FASCIATE	FASTENER
FARAWAYS	FARFALS	FAROUCHE	FASCIATED	FASTENERS
FARCE	FARFEL	FARRAGO	FASCICLE	FASTENING
FARCED	FARFELS	FARRAGOES	FASCICLED	FASTENS
FARCEMEAT	FARFET	FARRAGOS	FASCICLES	FASTER
FARCER	FARINA	FARRAND	FASCICULE	FASTERS
FARCERS	FARINAS	FARRANT	FASCICULI	FASTEST
FARCES	FARING	FARRED	FASCIITIS	FASTI
FARCEUR	FARINHA	FARREN	FASCINATE	FASTIE
FARCEURS	FARINHAS	FARRENS	FASCINE	FASTIES
FARCEUSE	FARINOSE	FARRIER	FASCINES	FASTIGIUM
FARCEUSES	FARL	FARRIERS	FASCIO	FASTING
FARCI	FARLE	FARRIERY	FASCIOLA	FASTINGS
FARCICAL	FARLES	FARRING	FASCIOLAS	FASTISH
FARCIE	FARLS	FARROW	FASCIOLE	FASTLY
FARCIED	FARM	FARROWED	FASCIOLES	FASTNESS
FARCIES	FARMABLE	FARROWING	FASCIS	FASTS
FARCIFIED	FARMED	FARROWS	FASCISM	FASTUOUS
FARCIFIES	FARMER	FARRUCA	FASCISMI	FAT
FARCIFY	FARMERESS	FARRUCAS	FASCISMO	FATAL
FARCIN	FARMERIES	FARS	FASCISMS	FATALISM
FARCING	FARMERS	FARSE	FASCIST	FATALISMS
FARCINGS	FARMERY	FARSED	FASCISTA	FATALIST
FARCINS	FARMHAND	FARSEEING	FASCISTI	FATALISTS
FARCY	FARMHANDS	FARSES	FASCISTIC	FATALITY
FARD	FARMHOUSE	FARSIDE	FASCISTS	FATALLY
FARDAGE	FARMING	FARSIDES	FASCITIS	FATALNESS
FARDAGES	FARMINGS	FARSING	FASH	FATBACK
FARDED	FARMLAND	FART	FASHED	FATBACKS
FARDEL	FARMLANDS	FARTED	FASHERIES	FATBIRD
FARDELS	FARMOST	FARTHEL	FASHERY	FATBIRDS
FARDEN	FARMS	FARTHELS	FASHES	FATE
FARDENS	FARMSTEAD	FARTHER	FASHING	FATED
FARDING	FARMWIFE	FARTHEST	FASHION	FATEFUL
FARDINGS	FARMWIVES	FARTHING	FASHIONED	FATEFULLY
FARDS	FARMWORK	FARTHINGS	FASHIONER	FATES
FARE	FARMWORKS	FARTING	FASHIONS	FATHEAD
FAREBOX	FARMYARD	FARTLEK	FASHIONY	FATHEADED
FAREBOXES	FARMYARDS	FARTLEKS	FASHIOUS	FATHEADS
FARED	FARNARKEL	FARTS	FAST	FATHER
FARER	FARNESOL	FAS	FASTBACK	FATHERED
FARERS	FARNESOLS	FASCES	FASTBACKS	FATHERING
FARES	FARNESS	FASCI	FASTBALL	FATHERLY

FATHERS	FATTINESS	FAULTLESS	FAVELAS	FAWNINGS
FATHOM	FATTING	FAULTLINE	FAVELL	FAWNLIKE
FATHOMED	FATTISH	FAULTS	FAVELLA	FAWNS
FATHOMER	FATTISM	FAULTY	FAVELLAS	FAWNY
FATHOMERS	FATTISMS	FAUN	FAVELS	FAWS
FATHOMING	FATTIST	FAUNA	FAVEOLATE	FAX
FATHOMS	FATTISTS	FAUNAE	FAVER	FAXABLE
FATIDIC	FATTRELS	FAUNAL	FAVES	FAXED
FATIDICAL	FATTY	FAUNALLY	FAVEST	FAXES
FATIGABLE	FATUITIES	FAUNAS	FAVICON	FAXING
FATIGATE	FATUITOUS	FAUNIST	FAVICONS	FAY
FATIGATED	FATUITY	FAUNISTIC	FAVISM	FAYALITE
FATIGATES	FATUOUS	FAUNISTS	FAVISMS	FAYALITES
FATIGUE	FATUOUSLY	FAUNLIKE	FAVONIAN	FAYED
FATIGUED	FATWA	FAUNS	FAVOR	FAYENCE
FATIGUES	FATWAH	FAUNULA	FAVORABLE	FAYENCES
FATIGUING	FATWAHED	FAUNULAE	FAVORABLY	FAYER
FATING	FATWAHING	FAUNULE	FAVORED	FAYEST
FATISCENT	FATWAHS	FAUNULES	FAVORER	FAYING
FATLESS	FATWAING	FAUR	FAVORERS	FAYNE
FATLIKE	FATWAS	FAURD	FAVORING	FAYNED
FATLING	FATWOOD	FAURER	FAVORITE	FAYNES
FATLINGS	FATWOODS	FAUREST	FAVORITES	FAYNING
FATLY	FAUBOURG	FAUSTIAN	FAVORLESS	FAYRE
FATNESS	FAUBOURGS	FAUT	FAVORS	FAYRES
FATNESSES	FAUCAL	FAUTED	FAVOSE	FAYS
FATS	FAUCALS	FAUTEUIL	FAVOUR	FAZE
FATSIA	FAUCES	FAUTEUILS	FAVOURED	FAZED
FATSIAS	FAUCET	FAUTING	FAVOURER	FAZENDA
FATSO	FAUCETRY	FAUTOR	FAVOURERS	FAZENDAS
FATSOES	FAUCETS	FAUTORS	FAVOURING	FAZES
FATSOS	FAUCHION	FAUTS	FAVOURITE	FAZING
FATSTOCK	FAUCHIONS	FAUVE	FAVOURS	FE
FATSTOCKS	FAUCHON	FAUVES	FAVOUS	FEAGUE
FATTED	FAUCHONS	FAUVETTE	FAVRILE	FEAGUED
FATTEN	FAUCIAL	FAUVETTES	FAVRILES	FEAGUES
FATTENED	FAUGH	FAUVISM	FAVUS	FEAGUING
FATTENER	FAULCHION	FAUVISMS	FAVUSES	FEAL
FATTENERS	FAULD	FAUVIST	FAW	FEALED
FATTENING	FAULDS	FAUVISTS	FAWN	FEALING
FATTENS	FAULT	FAUX	FAWNED	FEALS
FATTER	FAULTED	FAUXMANCE	FAWNER	FEALTIES
FATTEST	FAULTFUL	FAVA	FAWNERS	FEALTY
FATTIER	FAULTIER	FAVAS	FAWNIER	FEAR
FATTIES	FAULTIEST	FAVE	FAWNIEST	FEARE
FATTIEST	FAULTILY	FAVEL	FAWNING	FEARED
FATTILY	FAULTING	FAVELA	FAWNINGLY	FEARER

FEARERS	FEAZE	FEDERAL	FEEDSTOCK	FEHS
FEARES	FEAZED	FEDERALLY	FEEDSTUFF	FEIGN
FEARFUL	FEAZES	FEDERALS	FEEDWATER	FEIGNED
FEARFULLY	FEAZING	FEDERARIE	FEEDYARD	FEIGNEDLY
FEARING	FEBLESSE	FEDERARY	FEEDYARDS	FEIGNER
FEARLESS	FEBLESSES	FEDERATE	FEEING	FEIGNERS
FEARS	FEBRICITY	FEDERATED	FEEL	FEIGNING
FEARSOME	FEBRICULA	FEDERATES	FEELBAD	FEIGNINGS
FEART	FEBRICULE	FEDERATOR	FEELER	FEIGNS
FEASANCE	FEBRIFIC	FEDEX	FEELERS	FEIJOA
FEASANCES	FEBRIFUGE	FEDEXED	FEELESS	FEIJOADA
FEASE	FEBRILE	FEDEXES	FEELGOOD	FEIJOADAS
FEASED	FEBRILITY	FEDEXING	FEELING	FEIJOAS
FEASES	FECAL	FEDORA	FEELINGLY	FEINT
FEASIBLE	FECES	FEDORAS	FEELINGS	FEINTED
FEASIBLY	FECHT	FEDS	FEELS	FEINTER
FEASING	FECHTER	FEE	FEEN	FEINTEST
FEAST	FECHTERS	FEEB	FEENS	FEINTING
FEASTED	FECHTING	FEEBLE	FEER	FEINTS
FEASTER	FECHTS	FEEBLED	FEERED	FEIRIE
FEASTERS	FECIAL	FEEBLER	FEERIE	FEIRIER
FEASTFUL	FECIALS	FEEBLES	FEERIES	FEIRIEST
FEASTING	FECIT	FEEBLEST	FEERIN	FEIS
FEASTINGS	FECK	FEEBLING	FEERING	FEISEANNA
FEASTLESS	FECKED	FEEBLISH	FEERINGS	FEIST
FEASTS	FECKIN	FEEBLY	FEERINS	FEISTIER
FEAT	FECKING	FEEBS	FEERS	FEISTIEST
FEATED	FECKLESS	FEED	FEES	FEISTILY
FEATEOUS	FECKLY	FEEDABLE	FEESE	FEISTS
FEATER	FECKS	FEEDBACK	FEESED	FEISTY
FEATEST	FECULA	FEEDBACKS	FEESES	FELAFEL
FEATHER	FECULAE	FEEDBAG	FEESING	FELAFELS
FEATHERED	FECULAS	FEEDBAGS	FEET	FELCH
FEATHERS	FECULENCE	FEEDBOX	FEETFIRST	FELCHED
FEATHERY	FECULENCY	FEEDBOXES	FEETLESS	FELCHES
FEATING	FECULENT	FEEDER	FEEZE	FELCHING
FEATLIER	FECUND	FEEDERS	FEEZED	FELDGRAU
FEATLIEST	FECUNDATE	FEEDGRAIN	FEEZES	FELDGRAUS
FEATLY	FECUNDITY	FEEDHOLE	FEEZING	FELDSCHAR
FEATOUS	FED	FEEDHOLES	FEG	FELDSCHER
FEATS	FEDARIE	FEEDING	FEGARIES	FELDSHER
FEATUOUS	FEDARIES	FEEDINGS	FEGARY	FELDSHERS
FEATURE	FEDAYEE	FEEDLOT	FEGS	FELDSPAR
FEATURED	FEDAYEEN	FEEDLOTS	FEH	FELDSPARS
FEATURELY	FEDELINI	FEEDPIPE	FEHM	FELDSPATH
FEATURES	FEDELINIS	FEEDPIPES	FEHME	FELICIA
FEATURING	FEDERACY	FEEDS	FEHMIC	FELICIAS

FELICIFIC	FELONIES	FEMICIDES	FENCIBLE	FENURON
FELICITER	FELONIOUS	FEMINACY	FENCIBLES	FENURONS
FELICITY	FELONOUS	FEMINAL	FENCING	FEOD
FELID	FELONRIES	FEMINAZI	FENCINGS	FEODAL
FELIDS	FELONRY	FEMINAZIS	FEND	FEODARIES
FELINE	FELONS	FEMINEITY	FENDED	FEODARY
FELINELY	FELONY	FEMINIE	FENDER	FEODS
FELINES	FELSIC	FEMINIES	FENDERED	FEOFF
FELINITY	FELSITE	FEMININE	FENDERS	FEOFFED
FELL	FELSITES	FEMININES	FENDIER	FEOFFEE
FELLA	FELSITIC	FEMINISE	FENDIEST	FEOFFEES
FELLABLE	FELSPAR	FEMINISED	FENDING	FEOFFER
FELLAH	FELSPARS	FEMINISES	FENDS	FEOFFERS
FELLAHEEN	FELSTONE	FEMINISM	FENDY	FEOFFING
FELLAHIN	FELSTONES	FEMINISMS	FENESTRA	FEOFFMENT
FELLAHS	FELT	FEMINIST	FENESTRAE	FEOFFOR
FELLAS	FELTED	FEMINISTS	FENESTRAL	FEOFFORS
FELLATE	FELTER	FEMINITY	FENESTRAS	FEOFFS
FELLATED	FELTERED	FEMINIZE	FENI	FER
FELLATES	FELTERING	FEMINIZED	FENING	FERACIOUS
FELLATING	FELTERS	FEMINIZES	FENINGS	FERACITY
FELLATIO	FELTIER	FEMITER	FENIS	FERAL
FELLATION	FELTIEST	FEMITERS	FENITAR	FERALISED
FELLATIOS	FELTING	FEMME	FENITARS	FERALIZED
FELLATOR	FELTINGS	FEMMES	FENKS	FERALS
FELLATORS	FELTLIKE	FEMMIER	FENLAND	FERBAM
FELLATRIX	FELTS	FEMMIEST	FENLANDS	FERBAMS
FELLED	FELTY	FEMMY	FENMAN	FERE
FELLER	FELUCCA	FEMORA	FENMEN	FERER
FELLERS	FELUCCAS	FEMORAL	FENNEC	FERES
FELLEST	FELWORT	FEMS	FENNECS	FEREST
FELLIES	FELWORTS	FEMUR	FENNEL	FERETORY
FELLING	FEM	FEMURS	FENNELS	FERIA
FELLINGS	FEMAL	FEN	FENNIER	FERIAE
FELLNESS	FEMALE	FENAGLE	FENNIES	FERIAL
FELLOE	FEMALES	FENAGLED	FENNIEST	FERIAS
FELLOES	FEMALITY	FENAGLES	FENNING	FERINE
FELLOW	FEMALS	FENAGLING	FENNISH	FERITIES
FELLOWED	FEME	FENCE	FENNY	FERITY
FELLOWING	FEMERALL	FENCED	FENS	FERLIE
FELLOWLY	FEMERALLS	FENCELESS	FENT	FERLIED
FELLOWMAN	FEMERELL	FENCELIKE	FENTANYL	FERLIER
FELLOWMEN	FEMERELLS	FENCER	FENTANYLS	FERLIES
FELLOWS	FEMES	FENCEROW	FENTHION	FERLIEST
FELLS	FEMETARY	FENCEROWS	FENTHIONS	FERLY
FELLY	FEMICIDAL	FENCERS	FENTS	FERLYING
FELON	FEMICIDE	FENCES	FENUGREEK	FERM

FERMATA
FERMATAS
FERMATE
FERMENT
FERMENTED
FERMENTER
FERMENTOR
FERMENTS
FERMI
FERMION
FERMIONIC
FERMIONS
FERMIS
FERMIUM
FERMIUMS
FERMS
FERN
FERNALLY
FERNBIRD
FERNBIRDS
FERNERIES
FERNERY
FERNIER
FERNIEST
FERNING
FERNINGS
FERNINST
FERNLESS
FERNLIKE
FERNS
FERNSHAW
FERNSHAWS
FERNTICLE
FERNY
FEROCIOUS
FEROCITY
FERRATE
FERRATES
FERREL
FERRELED
FERRELING
FERRELLED
FERRELS
FERREOUS
FERRET
FERRETED
FERRETER

FERRETERS
FERRETING
FERRETS
FERRETY
FERRIAGE
FERRIAGES
FERRIC
FERRIED
FERRIES
FERRITE
FERRITES
FERRITIC
FERRITIN
FERRITINS
FERROCENE
FERROGRAM
FERROTYPE
FERROUS
FERRUGO
FERRUGOS
FERRULE
FERRULED
FERRULES
FERRULING
FERRUM
FERRUMS
FERRY
FERRYBOAT
FERRYING
FERRYMAN
FERRYMEN
FERTIGATE
FERTILE
FERTILELY
FERTILER
FERTILEST
FERTILISE
FERTILITY
FERTILIZE
FERULA
FERULAE
FERULAS
FERULE
FERULED
FERULES
FERULING
FERVENCY

FERVENT
FERVENTER
FERVENTLY
FERVID
FERVIDER
FERVIDEST
FERVIDITY
FERVIDLY
FERVOR
FERVOROUS
FERVORS
FERVOUR
FERVOURS
FES
FESCUE
FESCUES
FESS
FESSE
FESSED
FESSES
FESSING
FESSWISE
FEST
FESTA
FESTAL
FESTALLY
FESTALS
FESTAS
FESTER
FESTERED
FESTERING
FESTERS
FESTIER
FESTIEST
FESTILOGY
FESTINATE
FESTIVAL
FESTIVALS
FESTIVE
FESTIVELY
FESTIVITY
FESTIVOUS
FESTOLOGY
FESTOON
FESTOONED
FESTOONS
FESTS

FESTY
FET
FETA
FETAL
FETAS
FETATION
FETATIONS
FETCH
FETCHED
FETCHER
FETCHERS
FETCHES
FETCHING
FETE
FETED
FETERITA
FETERITAS
FETES
FETIAL
FETIALES
FETIALIS
FETIALS
FETICH
FETICHE
FETICHES
FETICHISE
FETICHISM
FETICHIST
FETICHIZE
FETICIDAL
FETICIDE
FETICIDES
FETID
FETIDER
FETIDEST
FETIDITY
FETIDLY
FETIDNESS
FETING
FETISH
FETISHES
FETISHISE
FETISHISM
FETISHIST
FETISHIZE
FETLOCK
FETLOCKED

FETLOCKS
FETOLOGY
FETOR
FETORS
FETOSCOPE
FETOSCOPY
FETS
FETT
FETTA
FETTAS
FETTED
FETTER
FETTERED
FETTERER
FETTERERS
FETTERING
FETTERS
FETTING
FETTLE
FETTLED
FETTLER
FETTLERS
FETTLES
FETTLING
FETTLINGS
FETTS
FETTUCINE
FETTUCINI
FETUS
FETUSES
FETWA
FETWAS
FEU
FEUAR
FEUARS
FEUD
FEUDAL
FEUDALISE
FEUDALISM
FEUDALIST
FEUDALITY
FEUDALIZE
FEUDALLY
FEUDARIES
FEUDARY
FEUDATORY
FEUDED

FEUDING	FEZ	FIBRED	FICES	FIDELISTA
FEUDINGS	FEZES	FIBREFILL	FICHE	FIDELITY
FEUDIST	FEZZED	FIBRELESS	FICHES	FIDES
FEUDISTS	FEZZES	FIBRELIKE	FICHU	FIDGE
FEUDS	FEZZY	FIBRES	FICHUS	FIDGED
FEUED	FIACRE	FIBRIFORM	FICIN	FIDGES
FEUILLETE	FIACRES	FIBRIL	FICINS	FIDGET
FEUING	FIANCE	FIBRILAR	FICKLE	FIDGETED
FEUS	FIANCEE	FIBRILLA	FICKLED	FIDGETER
FEUTRE	FIANCEES	FIBRILLAE	FICKLER	FIDGETERS
FEUTRED	FIANCES	FIBRILLAR	FICKLES	FIDGETIER
FEUTRES	FIAR	FIBRILLIN	FICKLEST	FIDGETING
FEUTRING	FIARS	FIBRILS	FICKLING	FIDGETS
FEVER	FIASCHI	FIBRIN	FICKLY	FIDGETY
FEVERED	FIASCO	FIBRINOID	FICO	FIDGING
FEVERFEW	FIASCOES	FIBRINOUS	FICOES	FIDIBUS
FEVERFEWS	FIASCOS	FIBRINS	FICOS	FIDIBUSES
FEVERING	FIAT	FIBRO	FICTILE	FIDO
FEVERISH	FIATED	FIBROCYTE	FICTION	FIDOS
FEVERLESS	FIATING	FIBROID	FICTIONAL	FIDS
FEVEROUS	FIATS	FIBROIDS	FICTIONS	FIDUCIAL
FEVERROOT	FIAUNT	FIBROIN	FICTIVE	FIDUCIARY
FEVERS	FIAUNTS	FIBROINS	FICTIVELY	FIE
FEVERWEED	FIB	FIBROLINE	FICTOR	FIEF
FEVERWORT	FIBBED	FIBROLITE	FICTORS	FIEFDOM
FEW	FIBBER	FIBROMA	FICUS	FIEFDOMS
FEWER	FIBBERIES	FIBROMAS	FICUSES	FIEFS
FEWEST	FIBBERS	FIBROMATA	FID	FIELD
FEWMET	FIBBERY	FIBROS	FIDDIOUS	FIELDBOOT
FEWMETS	FIBBING	FIBROSE	FIDDLE	FIELDED
FEWNESS	FIBER	FIBROSED	FIDDLED	FIELDER
FEWNESSES	FIBERED	FIBROSES	FIDDLER	FIELDERS
FEWS	FIBERFILL	FIBROSING	FIDDLERS	FIELDFARE
FEWTER	FIBERISE	FIBROSIS	FIDDLES	FIELDING
FEWTERED	FIBERISED	FIBROTIC	FIDDLEY	FIELDINGS
FEWTERING	FIBERISES	FIBROUS	FIDDLEYS	FIELDMICE
FEWTERS	FIBERIZE	FIBROUSLY	FIDDLIER	FIELDS
FEWTRILS	FIBERIZED	FIBS	FIDDLIEST	FIELDSMAN
FEY	FIBERIZES	FIBSTER	FIDDLING	FIELDSMEN
FEYED	FIBERLESS	FIBSTERS	FIDDLINGS	FIELDVOLE
FEYER	FIBERLIKE	FIBULA	FIDDLY	FIELDWARD
FEYEST	FIBERS	FIBULAE	FIDEISM	FIELDWORK
FEYING	FIBRANNE	FIBULAR	FIDEISMS	FIEND
FEYLY	FIBRANNES	FIBULAS	FIDEIST	FIENDISH
FEYNESS	FIBRATE	FICAIN	FIDEISTIC	FIENDLIKE
FEYNESSES	FIBRATES	FICAINS	FIDEISTS	FIENDS
FEYS	FIBRE	FICE	FIDELISMO	FIENT

F

FIENTS	FIGHTING	FILABEGS	FILENAME	FILLESTER
FIER	FIGHTINGS	FILACEOUS	FILENAMES	FILLET
FIERCE	FIGHTS	FILACER	FILER	FILLETED
FIERCELY	FIGJAM	FILACERS	FILERS	FILLETER
FIERCER	FIGJAMS	FILAGGRIN	FILES	FILLETERS
FIERCEST	FIGMENT	FILAGREE	FILET	FILLETING
FIERE	FIGMENTS	FILAGREED	FILETED	FILLETS
FIERES	FIGO	FILAGREES	FILETING	FILLIBEG
FIERIER	FIGOS	FILAMENT	FILETS	FILLIBEGS
FIERIEST	FIGS	FILAMENTS	FILFOT	FILLIES
FIERILY	FIGTREE	FILANDER	FILFOTS	FILLING
FIERINESS	FIGTREES	FILANDERS	FILIAL	FILLINGS
FIERS	FIGULINE	FILAR	FILIALLY	FILLIP
FIERY	FIGULINES	FILAREE	FILIATE	FILLIPED
FIEST	FIGURABLE	FILAREES	FILIATED	FILLIPEEN
FIESTA	FIGURAL	FILARIA	FILIATES	FILLIPING
FIESTAS	FIGURALLY	FILARIAE	FILIATING	FILLIPS
FIFE	FIGURANT	FILARIAL	FILIATION	FILLISTER
FIFED	FIGURANTE	FILARIAN	FILIBEG	FILLO
FIFER	FIGURANTS	FILARIID	FILIBEGS	FILLOS
FIFERS	FIGURATE	FILARIIDS	FILICIDAL	FILLS
FIFES	FIGURE	FILASSE	FILICIDE	FILLY
FIFING	FIGURED	FILASSES	FILICIDES	FILM
FIFTEEN	FIGUREDLY	FILATORY	FILIFORM	FILMABLE
FIFTEENER	FIGURER	FILATURE	FILIGRAIN	FILMCARD
FIFTEENS	FIGURERS	FILATURES	FILIGRANE	FILMCARDS
FIFTEENTH	FIGURES	FILAZER	FILIGREE	FILMDOM
FIFTH	FIGURINE	FILAZERS	FILIGREED	FILMDOMS
FIFTHLY	FIGURINES	FILBERD	FILIGREES	FILMED
FIFTHS	FIGURING	FILBERDS	FILII	FILMER
FIFTIES	FIGURIST	FILBERT	FILING	FILMERS
FIFTIETH	FIGURISTS	FILBERTS	FILINGS	FILMFEST
FIFTIETHS	FIGWORT	FILCH	FILIOQUE	FILMFESTS
FIFTY	FIGWORTS	FILCHED	FILIOQUES	FILMGOER
FIFTYISH	FIKE	FILCHER	FILISTER	FILMGOERS
FIG	FIKED	FILCHERS	FILISTERS	FILMGOING
FIGEATER	FIKERIES	FILCHES	FILIUS	FILMI
FIGEATERS	FIKERY	FILCHING	FILK	FILMIC
FIGGED	FIKES	FILCHINGS	FILKS	FILMIER
FIGGERIES	FIKIER	FILE	FILL	FILMIEST
FIGGERY	FIKIEST	FILEABLE	FILLABLE	FILMILY
FIGGING	FIKING	FILECARD	FILLAGREE	FILMINESS
FIGHT	FIKISH	FILECARDS	FILLE	FILMING
FIGHTABLE	FIKY	FILED	FILLED	FILMIS
FIGHTBACK	FIL	FILEFISH	FILLER	FILMISH
FIGHTER	FILA	FILEMOT	FILLERS	FILMLAND
FIGHTERS	FILABEG	FILEMOTS	FILLES	FILMLANDS

FILMLESS	FINAGLING	FINEERING	FININGS	FINNOCHIO
FILMLIKE	FINAL	FINEERS	FINIS	FINNOCK
FILMMAKER	FINALE	FINEISH	FINISES	FINNOCKS
FILMS	FINALES	FINELESS	FINISH	FINNSKO
FILMSET	FINALIS	FINELY	FINISHED	FINNY
FILMSETS	FINALISE	FINENESS	FINISHER	FINO
FILMSTRIP	FINALISED	FINER	FINISHERS	FINOCCHIO
FILMY	FINALISER	FINERIES	FINISHES	FINOCHIO
FILO	FINALISES	FINERS	FINISHING	FINOCHIOS
FILOPLUME	FINALISM	FINERY	FINITE	FINOS
FILOPODIA	FINALISMS	FINES	FINITELY	FINS
FILOS	FINALIST	FINESPUN	FINITES	FINSKO
FILOSE	FINALISTS	FINESSE	FINITISM	FIORATURA
FILOSELLE	FINALITY	FINESSED	FINITISMS	FIORD
FILOVIRUS	FINALIZE	FINESSER	FINITIST	FIORDS
FILS	FINALIZED	FINESSERS	FINITISTS	FIORIN
FILTER	FINALIZER	FINESSES	FINITO	FIORINS
FILTERED	FINALIZES	FINESSING	FINITUDE	FIORITURA
FILTERER	FINALLY	FINEST	FINITUDES	FIORITURE
FILTERERS	FINALS	FINESTS	FINJAN	FIPPENCE
FILTERING	FINANCE	FINFISH	FINJANS	FIPPENCES
FILTERS	FINANCED	FINFISHES	FINK	FIPPLE
FILTH	FINANCES	FINFOOT	FINKED	FIPPLES
FILTHIER	FINANCIAL	FINFOOTS	FINKING	FIQH
FILTHIEST	FINANCIER	FINGAN	FINKS	FIQHS
FILTHILY	FINANCING	FINGANS	FINLESS	FIQUE
FILTHS	FINBACK	FINGER	FINLIKE	FIQUES
FILTHY	FINBACKS	FINGERED	FINLIT	FIR
FILTRABLE	FINCA	FINGERER	FINLITS	FIRE
FILTRATE	FINCAS	FINGERERS	FINMARK	FIREABLE
FILTRATED	FINCH	FINGERING	FINMARKS	FIREARM
FILTRATES	FINCHED	FINGERS	FINNAC	FIREARMED
FILTRE	FINCHES	FINGERTIP	FINNACK	FIREARMS
FILUM	FIND	FINI	FINNACKS	FIREBACK
FIMBLE	FINDABLE	FINIAL	FINNACS	FIREBACKS
FIMBLES	FINDER	FINIALED	FINNAN	FIREBALL
FIMBRIA	FINDERS	FINIALS	FINNANS	FIREBALLS
FIMBRIAE	FINDING	FINICAL	FINNED	FIREBASE
FIMBRIAL	FINDINGS	FINICALLY	FINNER	FIREBASES
FIMBRIATE	FINDRAM	FINICKETY	FINNERS	FIREBIRD
FIN	FINDRAMS	FINICKIER	FINNESKO	FIREBIRDS
FINABLE	FINDS	FINICKIN	FINNICKY	FIREBOARD
FINAGLE	FINE	FINICKING	FINNIER	FIREBOAT
FINAGLED	FINEABLE	FINICKY	FINNIEST	FIREBOATS
FINAGLER	FINED	FINIKIN	FINNING	FIREBOMB
FINAGLERS	FINEER	FINIKING	FINNMARK	FIREBOMBS
FINAGLES	FINEERED	FINING	FINNMARKS	FIREBOX

FIREBOXES
FIREBRAND
FIREBRAT
FIREBRATS
FIREBREAK
FIREBRICK
FIREBUG
FIREBUGS
FIREBUSH
FIRECLAY
FIRECLAYS
FIRECREST
FIRED
FIREDAMP
FIREDAMPS
FIREDOG
FIREDOGS
FIREDRAKE
FIREFANG
FIREFANGS
FIREFIGHT
FIREFLIES
FIREFLOAT
FIREFLOOD
FIREFLY
FIREGUARD
FIREHALL
FIREHALLS
FIREHOSE
FIREHOSES
FIREHOUSE
FIRELESS
FIRELIGHT
FIRELIT
FIRELOCK
FIRELOCKS
FIREMAN
FIREMANIC
FIREMARK
FIREMARKS
FIREMEN
FIREPAN
FIREPANS
FIREPINK
FIREPINKS
FIREPIT
FIREPITS

FIREPLACE
FIREPLUG
FIREPLUGS
FIREPOT
FIREPOTS
FIREPOWER
FIREPROOF
FIRER
FIREREEL
FIREREELS
FIREROOM
FIREROOMS
FIRERS
FIRES
FIRESCAPE
FIRESHIP
FIRESHIPS
FIRESIDE
FIRESIDES
FIRESTONE
FIRESTORM
FIRETHORN
FIRETRAP
FIRETRAPS
FIRETRUCK
FIREWALL
FIREWALLS
FIREWATER
FIREWEED
FIREWEEDS
FIREWOMAN
FIREWOMEN
FIREWOOD
FIREWOODS
FIREWORK
FIREWORKS
FIREWORM
FIREWORMS
FIRIE
FIRIES
FIRING
FIRINGS
FIRK
FIRKED
FIRKIN
FIRKING
FIRKINS

FIRKS
FIRLOT
FIRLOTS
FIRM
FIRMAMENT
FIRMAN
FIRMANS
FIRMED
FIRMER
FIRMERS
FIRMEST
FIRMING
FIRMLESS
FIRMLY
FIRMNESS
FIRMS
FIRMWARE
FIRMWARES
FIRN
FIRNS
FIRRIER
FIRRIEST
FIRRING
FIRRINGS
FIRRY
FIRS
FIRST
FIRSTBORN
FIRSTHAND
FIRSTLING
FIRSTLY
FIRSTNESS
FIRSTS
FIRTH
FIRTHS
FIRWOOD
FIRWOODS
FISC
FISCAL
FISCALIST
FISCALLY
FISCALS
FISCS
FISGIG
FISGIGS
FISH
FISHABLE

FISHBALL
FISHBALLS
FISHBOAT
FISHBOATS
FISHBOLT
FISHBOLTS
FISHBONE
FISHBONES
FISHBOWL
FISHBOWLS
FISHCAKE
FISHCAKES
FISHED
FISHER
FISHERIES
FISHERMAN
FISHERMEN
FISHERS
FISHERY
FISHES
FISHEYE
FISHEYES
FISHFUL
FISHGIG
FISHGIGS
FISHHOOK
FISHHOOKS
FISHIER
FISHIEST
FISHIFIED
FISHIFIES
FISHIFY
FISHILY
FISHINESS
FISHING
FISHINGS
FISHKILL
FISHKILLS
FISHLESS
FISHLIKE
FISHLINE
FISHLINES
FISHMEAL
FISHMEALS
FISHNET
FISHNETS
FISHPLATE

FISHPOLE
FISHPOLES
FISHPOND
FISHPONDS
FISHSKIN
FISHSKINS
FISHTAIL
FISHTAILS
FISHWAY
FISHWAYS
FISHWIFE
FISHWIVES
FISHWORM
FISHWORMS
FISHY
FISHYBACK
FISK
FISKED
FISKING
FISKS
FISNOMIE
FISNOMIES
FISSATE
FISSILE
FISSILITY
FISSION
FISSIONAL
FISSIONED
FISSIONS
FISSIPED
FISSIPEDE
FISSIPEDS
FISSIVE
FISSLE
FISSLED
FISSLES
FISSLING
FISSURAL
FISSURE
FISSURED
FISSURES
FISSURING
FIST
FISTED
FISTFIGHT
FISTFUL
FISTFULS

FISTIANA	FITTER	FIXURE	FLACKERY	FLAILED
FISTIC	FITTERS	FIXURES	FLACKET	FLAILING
FISTICAL	FITTES	FIZ	FLACKETED	FLAILS
FISTICUFF	FITTEST	FIZGIG	FLACKETS	FLAIR
FISTIER	FITTING	FIZGIGGED	FLACKING	FLAIRS
FISTIEST	FITTINGLY	FIZGIGS	FLACKS	FLAK
FISTING	FITTINGS	FIZZ	FLACON	FLAKE
FISTINGS	FITTS	FIZZED	FLACONS	FLAKED
FISTMELE	FIVE	FIZZEN	FLAFF	FLAKER
FISTMELES	FIVEFOLD	FIZZENS	FLAFFED	FLAKERS
FISTNOTE	FIVEPENCE	FIZZER	FLAFFER	FLAKES
FISTNOTES	FIVEPENNY	FIZZERS	FLAFFERED	FLAKEY
FISTS	FIVEPIN	FIZZES	FLAFFERS	FLAKIER
FISTULA	FIVEPINS	FIZZGIG	FLAFFING	FLAKIES
FISTULAE	FIVER	FIZZGIGS	FLAFFS	FLAKIEST
FISTULAR	FIVERS	FIZZIER	FLAG	FLAKILY
FISTULAS	FIVES	FIZZIEST	FLAGELLA	FLAKINESS
FISTULATE	FIX	FIZZILY	FLAGELLAR	FLAKING
FISTULOSE	FIXABLE	FIZZINESS	FLAGELLIN	FLAKS
FISTULOUS	FIXATE	FIZZING	FLAGELLUM	FLAKY
FISTY	FIXATED	FIZZINGS	FLAGEOLET	FLAM
FIT	FIXATES	FIZZLE	FLAGGED	FLAMBE
FITCH	FIXATIF	FIZZLED	FLAGGER	FLAMBEAU
FITCHE	FIXATIFS	FIZZLES	FLAGGERS	FLAMBEAUS
FITCHEE	FIXATING	FIZZLING	FLAGGIER	FLAMBEAUX
FITCHES	FIXATION	FIZZY	FLAGGIEST	FLAMBEE
FITCHET	FIXATIONS	FJELD	FLAGGING	FLAMBEED
FITCHETS	FIXATIVE	FJELDS	FLAGGINGS	FLAMBEES
FITCHEW	FIXATIVES	FJORD	FLAGGY	FLAMBEING
FITCHEWS	FIXATURE	FJORDIC	FLAGITATE	FLAMBES
FITCHY	FIXATURES	FJORDS	FLAGLESS	FLAME
FITFUL	FIXED	FLAB	FLAGMAN	FLAMED
FITFULLY	FIXEDLY	FLABBIER	FLAGMEN	FLAMELESS
FITLIER	FIXEDNESS	FLABBIEST	FLAGON	FLAMELET
FITLIEST	FIXER	FLABBILY	FLAGONS	FLAMELETS
FITLY	FIXERS	FLABBY	FLAGPOLE	FLAMELIKE
FITMENT	FIXES	FLABELLA	FLAGPOLES	FLAMEN
FITMENTS	FIXING	FLABELLUM	FLAGRANCE	FLAMENCO
FITNA	FIXINGS	FLABS	FLAGRANCY	FLAMENCOS
FITNAS	FIXIT	FLACCID	FLAGRANT	FLAMENS
FITNESS	FIXITIES	FLACCIDER	FLAGS	FLAMEOUT
FITNESSES	FIXITS	FLACCIDLY	FLAGSHIP	FLAMEOUTS
FITS	FIXITY	FLACK	FLAGSHIPS	FLAMER
FITT	FIXIVE	FLACKED	FLAGSTAFF	FLAMERS
FITTABLE	FIXT	FLACKER	FLAGSTICK	FLAMES
FITTE	FIXTURE	FLACKERED	FLAGSTONE	FLAMFEW
FITTED	FIXTURES	FLACKERS	FLAIL	FLAMFEWS

FLAMIER	FLANNEL	FLASHED	FLATLETS	FLATWORK
FLAMIEST	FLANNELED	FLASHER	FLATLINE	FLATWORKS
FLAMINES	FLANNELET	FLASHERS	FLATLINED	FLATWORM
FLAMING	FLANNELLY	FLASHES	FLATLINER	FLATWORMS
FLAMINGLY	FLANNELS	FLASHEST	FLATLINES	FLAUGHT
FLAMINGO	FLANNEN	FLASHGUN	FLATLING	FLAUGHTED
FLAMINGOS	FLANNENS	FLASHGUNS	FLATLINGS	FLAUGHTER
FLAMM	FLANNIE	FLASHIER	FLATLONG	FLAUGHTS
FLAMMABLE	FLANNIES	FLASHIEST	FLATLY	FLAUNCH
FLAMMED	FLANNY	FLASHILY	FLATMATE	FLAUNCHED
FLAMMING	FLANS	FLASHING	FLATMATES	FLAUNCHES
FLAMMS	FLAP	FLASHINGS	FLATNESS	FLAUNE
FLAMMULE	FLAPERON	FLASHLAMP	FLATPACK	FLAUNES
FLAMMULES	FLAPERONS	FLASHOVER	FLATPACKS	FLAUNT
FLAMS	FLAPJACK	FLASHTUBE	FLATPICK	FLAUNTED
FLAMY	FLAPJACKS	FLASHY	FLATPICKS	FLAUNTER
FLAN	FLAPLESS	FLASK	FLATS	FLAUNTERS
FLANCARD	FLAPPABLE	FLASKET	FLATSHARE	FLAUNTIER
FLANCARDS	FLAPPED	FLASKETS	FLATSTICK	FLAUNTILY
FLANCH	FLAPPER	FLASKS	FLATTED	FLAUNTING
FLANCHED	FLAPPERS	FLAT	FLATTEN	FLAUNTS
FLANCHES	FLAPPIER	FLATBACK	FLATTENED	FLAUNTY
FLANCHING	FLAPPIEST	FLATBACKS	FLATTENER	FLAUTA
FLANE	FLAPPING	FLATBED	FLATTENS	FLAUTAS
FLANED	FLAPPINGS	FLATBEDS	FLATTER	FLAUTIST
FLANERIE	FLAPPY	FLATBOAT	FLATTERED	FLAUTISTS
FLANERIES	FLAPS	FLATBOATS	FLATTERER	FLAVA
FLANES	FLAPTRACK	FLATBREAD	FLATTERS	FLAVANOL
FLANEUR	FLARE	FLATCAP	FLATTERY	FLAVANOLS
FLANEURS	FLAREBACK	FLATCAPS	FLATTEST	FLAVANONE
FLANGE	FLARED	FLATCAR	FLATTIE	FLAVAS
FLANGED	FLARES	FLATCARS	FLATTIES	FLAVIN
FLANGER	FLAREUP	FLATETTE	FLATTING	FLAVINE
FLANGERS	FLAREUPS	FLATETTES	FLATTINGS	FLAVINES
FLANGES	FLARIER	FLATFEET	FLATTISH	FLAVINS
FLANGING	FLARIEST	FLATFISH	FLATTOP	FLAVONE
FLANGINGS	FLARING	FLATFOOT	FLATTOPS	FLAVONES
FLANING	FLARINGLY	FLATFOOTS	FLATTY	FLAVONOID
FLANK	FLARY	FLATFORM	FLATULENT	FLAVONOL
FLANKED	FLASER	FLATFORMS	FLATUOUS	FLAVONOLS
FLANKEN	FLASERS	FLATHEAD	FLATUS	FLAVOR
FLANKENS	FLASH	FLATHEADS	FLATUSES	FLAVORED
FLANKER	FLASHBACK	FLATIRON	FLATWARE	FLAVORER
FLANKERED	FLASHBANG	FLATIRONS	FLATWARES	FLAVORERS
FLANKERS	FLASHBULB	FLATLAND	FLATWASH	FLAVORFUL
FLANKING	FLASHCARD	FLATLANDS	FLATWAYS	FLAVORING
FLANKS	FLASHCUBE	FLATLET	FLATWISE	FLAVORIST

FLAVOROUS	FLEASOME	FLEERED	FLESHER	FLEXIONAL
FLAVORS	FLEAWORT	FLEERER	FLESHERS	FLEXIONS
FLAVORY	FLEAWORTS	FLEERERS	FLESHES	FLEXITIME
FLAVOUR	FLECHE	FLEERING	FLESHHOOD	FLEXO
FLAVOURED	FLECHES	FLEERINGS	FLESHIER	FLEXOR
FLAVOURER	FLECHETTE	FLEERS	FLESHIEST	FLEXORS
FLAVOURS	FLECK	FLEES	FLESHILY	FLEXOS
FLAVOURY	FLECKED	FLEET	FLESHING	FLEXTIME
FLAW	FLECKER	FLEETED	FLESHINGS	FLEXTIMER
FLAWED	FLECKERED	FLEETER	FLESHLESS	FLEXTIMES
FLAWIER	FLECKERS	FLEETEST	FLESHLIER	FLEXUOSE
FLAWIEST	FLECKIER	FLEETING	FLESHLING	FLEXUOUS
FLAWING	FLECKIEST	FLEETLY	FLESHLY	FLEXURAL
FLAWLESS	FLECKING	FLEETNESS	FLESHMENT	FLEXURE
FLAWN	FLECKLESS	FLEETS	FLESHPOT	FLEXURES
FLAWNS	FLECKS	FLEG	FLESHPOTS	FLEXWING
FLAWS	FLECKY	FLEGGED	FLESHWORM	FLEXWINGS
FLAWY	FLECTION	FLEGGING	FLESHY	FLEY
FLAX	FLECTIONS	FLEGS	FLETCH	FLEYED
FLAXEN	FLED	FLEHMEN	FLETCHED	FLEYING
FLAXES	FLEDGE	FLEHMENED	FLETCHER	FLEYS
FLAXIER	FLEDGED	FLEHMENS	FLETCHERS	FLIBBERT
FLAXIEST	FLEDGES	FLEISHIG	FLETCHES	FLIBBERTS
FLAXSEED	FLEDGIER	FLEISHIK	FLETCHING	FLIC
FLAXSEEDS	FLEDGIEST	FLEME	FLETTON	FLICHTER
FLAXY	FLEDGING	FLEMED	FLETTONS	FLICHTERS
FLAY	FLEDGLING	FLEMES	FLEUR	FLICK
FLAYED	FLEDGY	FLEMING	FLEURET	FLICKABLE
FLAYER	FLEE	FLEMISH	FLEURETS	FLICKED
FLAYERS	FLEECE	FLEMISHED	FLEURETTE	FLICKER
FLAYING	FLEECED	FLEMISHES	FLEURON	FLICKERED
FLAYS	FLEECER	FLEMIT	FLEURONS	FLICKERS
FLAYSOME	FLEECERS	FLENCH	FLEURS	FLICKERY
FLEA	FLEECES	FLENCHED	FLEURY	FLICKING
FLEABAG	FLEECH	FLENCHER	FLEW	FLICKS
FLEABAGS	FLEECHED	FLENCHERS	FLEWED	FLICS
FLEABANE	FLEECHES	FLENCHES	FLEWS	FLIED
FLEABANES	FLEECHING	FLENCHING	FLEX	FLIER
FLEABITE	FLEECIE	FLENSE	FLEXAGON	FLIERS
FLEABITES	FLEECIER	FLENSED	FLEXAGONS	FLIES
FLEADH	FLEECIES	FLENSER	FLEXED	FLIEST
FLEADHS	FLEECIEST	FLENSERS	FLEXES	FLIGHT
FLEAM	FLEECILY	FLENSES	FLEXIBLE	FLIGHTED
FLEAMS	FLEECING	FLENSING	FLEXIBLY	FLIGHTIER
FLEAPIT	FLEECY	FLEROVIUM	FLEXILE	FLIGHTILY
FLEAPITS	FLEEING	FLESH	FLEXING	FLIGHTING
FLEAS	FLEER	FLESHED	FLEXION	FLIGHTS

FLIGHTY	FLIPFLOP	FLITTED	FLOCCULI	FLOORAGES
FLIM	FLIPFLOPS	FLITTER	FLOCCULUS	FLOORED
FLIMFLAM	FLIPPANCY	FLITTERED	FLOCCUS	FLOORER
FLIMFLAMS	FLIPPANT	FLITTERN	FLOCK	FLOORERS
FLIMP	FLIPPED	FLITTERNS	FLOCKED	FLOORHEAD
FLIMPED	FLIPPER	FLITTERS	FLOCKIER	FLOORING
FLIMPING	FLIPPERS	FLITTING	FLOCKIEST	FLOORINGS
FLIMPS	FLIPPEST	FLITTINGS	FLOCKING	FLOORLESS
FLIMS	FLIPPIER	FLITTS	FLOCKINGS	FLOORPAN
FLIMSIER	FLIPPIEST	FLIVVER	FLOCKLESS	FLOORPANS
FLIMSIES	FLIPPING	FLIVVERS	FLOCKS	FLOORS
FLIMSIEST	FLIPPINGS	FLIX	FLOCKY	FLOORSHOW
FLIMSILY	FLIPPY	FLIXED	FLOCS	FLOOSIE
FLIMSY	FLIPS	FLIXES	FLOE	FLOOSIES
FLINCH	FLIPSIDE	FLIXING	FLOES	FLOOSY
FLINCHED	FLIPSIDES	FLIXWEED	FLOG	FLOOZIE
FLINCHER	FLIR	FLIXWEEDS	FLOGGABLE	FLOOZIES
FLINCHERS	FLIRS	FLOAT	FLOGGED	FLOOZY
FLINCHES	FLIRT	FLOATABLE	FLOGGER	FLOP
FLINCHING	FLIRTED	FLOATAGE	FLOGGERS	FLOPHOUSE
FLINDER	FLIRTER	FLOATAGES	FLOGGING	FLOPOVER
FLINDERED	FLIRTERS	FLOATANT	FLOGGINGS	FLOPOVERS
FLINDERS	FLIRTIER	FLOATANTS	FLOGS	FLOPPED
FLING	FLIRTIEST	FLOATCUT	FLOKATI	FLOPPER
FLINGER	FLIRTING	FLOATED	FLOKATIS	FLOPPERS
FLINGERS	FLIRTINGS	FLOATEL	FLONG	FLOPPIER
FLINGING	FLIRTISH	FLOATELS	FLONGS	FLOPPIES
FLINGS	FLIRTS	FLOATER	FLOOD	FLOPPIEST
FLINKITE	FLIRTY	FLOATERS	FLOODABLE	FLOPPILY
FLINKITES	FLISK	FLOATIER	FLOODED	FLOPPING
FLINT	FLISKED	FLOATIEST	FLOODER	FLOPPY
FLINTED	FLISKIER	FLOATING	FLOODERS	FLOPS
FLINTHEAD	FLISKIEST	FLOATINGS	FLOODGATE	FLOPTICAL
FLINTIER	FLISKING	FLOATS	FLOODING	FLOR
FLINTIEST	FLISKS	FLOATY	FLOODINGS	FLORA
FLINTIFY	FLISKY	FLOB	FLOODLESS	FLORAE
FLINTILY	FLIT	FLOBBED	FLOODLIT	FLORAL
FLINTING	FLITCH	FLOBBING	FLOODMARK	FLORALLY
FLINTLIKE	FLITCHED	FLOBS	FLOODS	FLORALS
FLINTLOCK	FLITCHES	FLOC	FLOODTIDE	FLORAS
FLINTS	FLITCHING	FLOCCED	FLOODWALL	FLOREANT
FLINTY	FLITE	FLOCCI	FLOODWAY	FLOREAT
FLIP	FLITED	FLOCCING	FLOODWAYS	FLOREATED
FLIPBOARD	FLITES	FLOCCOSE	FLOOEY	FLORENCE
FLIPBOOK	FLITING	FLOCCULAR	FLOOIE	FLORENCES
FLIPBOOKS	FLITS	FLOCCULE	FLOOR	FLORET
FLIPCHART	FLITT	FLOCCULES	FLOORAGE	FLORETS

FLORIATED
FLORICANE
FLORID
FLORIDEAN
FLORIDER
FLORIDEST
FLORIDITY
FLORIDLY
FLORIER
FLORIEST
FLORIFORM
FLORIGEN
FLORIGENS
FLORIN
FLORINS
FLORIST
FLORISTIC
FLORISTRY
FLORISTS
FLORS
FLORUIT
FLORUITS
FLORULA
FLORULAE
FLORULE
FLORULES
FLORY
FLOSCULAR
FLOSCULE
FLOSCULES
FLOSH
FLOSHES
FLOSS
FLOSSED
FLOSSER
FLOSSERS
FLOSSES
FLOSSIE
FLOSSIER
FLOSSIES
FLOSSIEST
FLOSSILY
FLOSSING
FLOSSINGS
FLOSSY
FLOTA
FLOTAGE

FLOTAGES
FLOTANT
FLOTAS
FLOTATION
FLOTE
FLOTED
FLOTEL
FLOTELS
FLOTES
FLOTILLA
FLOTILLAS
FLOTING
FLOTSAM
FLOTSAMS
FLOUNCE
FLOUNCED
FLOUNCES
FLOUNCIER
FLOUNCING
FLOUNCY
FLOUNDER
FLOUNDERS
FLOUR
FLOURED
FLOURIER
FLOURIEST
FLOURING
FLOURISH
FLOURISHY
FLOURLESS
FLOURS
FLOURY
FLOUSE
FLOUSED
FLOUSES
FLOUSH
FLOUSHED
FLOUSHES
FLOUSHING
FLOUSING
FLOUT
FLOUTED
FLOUTER
FLOUTERS
FLOUTING
FLOUTS
FLOW

FLOWABLE
FLOWAGE
FLOWAGES
FLOWCHART
FLOWED
FLOWER
FLOWERAGE
FLOWERBED
FLOWERED
FLOWERER
FLOWERERS
FLOWERET
FLOWERETS
FLOWERFUL
FLOWERIER
FLOWERILY
FLOWERING
FLOWERPOT
FLOWERS
FLOWERY
FLOWING
FLOWINGLY
FLOWMETER
FLOWN
FLOWS
FLOWSTONE
FLOX
FLU
FLUATE
FLUATES
FLUB
FLUBBED
FLUBBER
FLUBBERS
FLUBBING
FLUBDUB
FLUBDUBS
FLUBS
FLUCTUANT
FLUCTUATE
FLUE
FLUED
FLUELLEN
FLUELLENS
FLUELLIN
FLUELLINS
FLUENCE

FLUENCES
FLUENCIES
FLUENCY
FLUENT
FLUENTLY
FLUENTS
FLUERIC
FLUERICS
FLUES
FLUEWORK
FLUEWORKS
FLUEY
FLUFF
FLUFFED
FLUFFER
FLUFFERS
FLUFFIER
FLUFFIEST
FLUFFILY
FLUFFING
FLUFFS
FLUFFY
FLUGEL
FLUGELMAN
FLUGELMEN
FLUGELS
FLUID
FLUIDAL
FLUIDALLY
FLUIDIC
FLUIDICS
FLUIDIFY
FLUIDISE
FLUIDISED
FLUIDISER
FLUIDISES
FLUIDITY
FLUIDIZE
FLUIDIZED
FLUIDIZER
FLUIDIZES
FLUIDLIKE
FLUIDLY
FLUIDNESS
FLUIDRAM
FLUIDRAMS
FLUIDS

FLUIER
FLUIEST
FLUISH
FLUKE
FLUKED
FLUKES
FLUKEY
FLUKIER
FLUKIEST
FLUKILY
FLUKINESS
FLUKING
FLUKY
FLUME
FLUMED
FLUMES
FLUMING
FLUMMERY
FLUMMOX
FLUMMOXED
FLUMMOXES
FLUMP
FLUMPED
FLUMPING
FLUMPS
FLUNG
FLUNK
FLUNKED
FLUNKER
FLUNKERS
FLUNKEY
FLUNKEYS
FLUNKIE
FLUNKIES
FLUNKING
FLUNKS
FLUNKY
FLUNKYISM
FLUOR
FLUORENE
FLUORENES
FLUORESCE
FLUORIC
FLUORID
FLUORIDE
FLUORIDES
FLUORIDS

F

FLUORIN	FLUTEYEST	FLYBOOKS	FLYTE	FOCALIZE
FLUORINE	FLUTIER	FLYBOY	FLYTED	FOCALIZED
FLUORINES	FLUTIEST	FLYBOYS	FLYTES	FOCALIZES
FLUORINS	FLUTINA	FLYBRIDGE	FLYTIER	FOCALLY
FLUORITE	FLUTINAS	FLYBY	FLYTIERS	FOCI
FLUORITES	FLUTING	FLYBYS	FLYTING	FOCIMETER
FLUOROSES	FLUTINGS	FLYER	FLYTINGS	FOCOMETER
FLUOROSIS	FLUTIST	FLYERS	FLYTRAP	FOCUS
FLUOROTIC	FLUTISTS	FLYEST	FLYTRAPS	FOCUSABLE
FLUORS	FLUTTER	FLYHAND	FLYWAY	FOCUSED
FLUORSPAR	FLUTTERED	FLYHANDS	FLYWAYS	FOCUSER
FLURR	FLUTTERER	FLYING	FLYWEIGHT	FOCUSERS
FLURRED	FLUTTERS	FLYINGS	FLYWHEEL	FOCUSES
FLURRIED	FLUTTERY	FLYLEAF	FLYWHEELS	FOCUSING
FLURRIES	FLUTY	FLYLEAVES	FOAL	FOCUSINGS
FLURRING	FLUVIAL	FLYLESS	FOALED	FOCUSLESS
FLURRS	FLUVIATIC	FLYLINE	FOALFOOT	FOCUSSED
FLURRY	FLUX	FLYLINES	FOALFOOTS	FOCUSSES
FLURRYING	FLUXED	FLYMAKER	FOALING	FOCUSSING
FLUS	FLUXES	FLYMAKERS	FOALINGS	FODDER
FLUSH	FLUXGATE	FLYMAN	FOALS	FODDERED
FLUSHABLE	FLUXGATES	FLYMEN	FOAM	FODDERER
FLUSHED	FLUXING	FLYOFF	FOAMABLE	FODDERERS
FLUSHER	FLUXION	FLYOFFS	FOAMED	FODDERING
FLUSHERS	FLUXIONAL	FLYOVER	FOAMER	FODDERS
FLUSHES	FLUXIONS	FLYOVERS	FOAMERS	FODGEL
FLUSHEST	FLUXIVE	FLYPAPER	FOAMIER	FOE
FLUSHIER	FLUXMETER	FLYPAPERS	FOAMIEST	FOEDARIE
FLUSHIEST	FLUYT	FLYPAST	FOAMILY	FOEDARIES
FLUSHING	FLUYTS	FLYPASTS	FOAMINESS	FOEDERATI
FLUSHINGS	FLY	FLYPE	FOAMING	FOEFIE
FLUSHNESS	FLYABLE	FLYPED	FOAMINGLY	FOEHN
FLUSHWORK	FLYAWAY	FLYPES	FOAMINGS	FOEHNS
FLUSHY	FLYAWAYS	FLYPING	FOAMLESS	FOEMAN
FLUSTER	FLYBACK	FLYPITCH	FOAMLIKE	FOEMEN
FLUSTERED	FLYBACKS	FLYPOSTER	FOAMS	FOEN
FLUSTERS	FLYBANE	FLYRODDER	FOAMY	FOES
FLUSTERY	FLYBANES	FLYSCH	FOB	FOETAL
FLUSTRATE	FLYBELT	FLYSCHES	FOBBED	FOETATION
FLUTE	FLYBELTS	FLYSCREEN	FOBBING	FOETICIDE
FLUTED	FLYBLEW	FLYSHEET	FOBS	FOETID
FLUTELIKE	FLYBLOW	FLYSHEETS	FOCACCIA	FOETIDER
FLUTER	FLYBLOWN	FLYSPECK	FOCACCIAS	FOETIDEST
FLUTERS	FLYBLOWS	FLYSPECKS	FOCAL	FOETIDLY
FLUTES	FLYBOAT	FLYSPRAY	FOCALISE	FOETOR
FLUTEY	FLYBOATS	FLYSPRAYS	FOCALISED	FOETORS
FLUTEYER	FLYBOOK	FLYSTRIKE	FOCALISES	FOETUS

FOETUSES	FOGS	FOLDBACKS	FOLKIEST	FOMENTERS
FOG	FOGY	FOLDBOAT	FOLKISH	FOMENTING
FOGASH	FOGYDOM	FOLDBOATS	FOLKLAND	FOMENTS
FOGASHES	FOGYDOMS	FOLDED	FOLKLANDS	FOMES
FOGBOUND	FOGYISH	FOLDER	FOLKLIFE	FOMITE
FOGBOW	FOGYISM	FOLDEROL	FOLKLIKE	FOMITES
FOGBOWS	FOGYISMS	FOLDEROLS	FOLKLIVES	FON
FOGDOG	FOH	FOLDERS	FOLKLORE	FOND
FOGDOGS	FOHN	FOLDING	FOLKLORES	FONDA
FOGEY	FOHNS	FOLDINGS	FOLKLORIC	FONDANT
FOGEYDOM	FOIBLE	FOLDOUT	FOLKMOOT	FONDANTS
FOGEYDOMS	FOIBLES	FOLDOUTS	FOLKMOOTS	FONDAS
FOGEYISH	FOID	FOLDS	FOLKMOT	FONDED
FOGEYISM	FOIDS	FOLDUP	FOLKMOTE	FONDER
FOGEYISMS	FOIL	FOLDUPS	FOLKMOTES	FONDEST
FOGEYS	FOILABLE	FOLEY	FOLKMOTS	FONDING
FOGFRUIT	FOILBORNE	FOLEYS	FOLKS	FONDLE
FOGFRUITS	FOILED	FOLIA	FOLKSIER	FONDLED
FOGGAGE	FOILING	FOLIAGE	FOLKSIEST	FONDLER
FOGGAGES	FOILINGS	FOLIAGED	FOLKSILY	FONDLERS
FOGGED	FOILIST	FOLIAGES	FOLKSONG	FONDLES
FOGGER	FOILISTS	FOLIAR	FOLKSONGS	FONDLING
FOGGERS	FOILS	FOLIATE	FOLKSY	FONDLINGS
FOGGIER	FOILSMAN	FOLIATED	FOLKTALE	FONDLY
FOGGIEST	FOILSMEN	FOLIATES	FOLKTALES	FONDNESS
FOGGILY	FOIN	FOLIATING	FOLKWAY	FONDS
FOGGINESS	FOINED	FOLIATION	FOLKWAYS	FONDU
FOGGING	FOINING	FOLIATURE	FOLKY	FONDUE
FOGGINGS	FOININGLY	FOLIC	FOLLES	FONDUED
FOGGY	FOINS	FOLIE	FOLLICLE	FONDUEING
FOGHORN	FOISON	FOLIES	FOLLICLES	FONDUES
FOGHORNS	FOISONS	FOLIO	FOLLIED	FONDUING
FOGIE	FOIST	FOLIOED	FOLLIES	FONDUS
FOGIES	FOISTED	FOLIOING	FOLLIS	FONE
FOGLE	FOISTER	FOLIOLATE	FOLLOW	FONLY
FOGLES	FOISTERS	FOLIOLE	FOLLOWED	FONNED
FOGLESS	FOISTING	FOLIOLES	FOLLOWER	FONNING
FOGLIGHT	FOISTS	FOLIOLOSE	FOLLOWERS	FONS
FOGLIGHTS	FOLACIN	FOLIOS	FOLLOWING	FONT
FOGMAN	FOLACINS	FOLIOSE	FOLLOWS	FONTAL
FOGMEN	FOLATE	FOLIOUS	FOLLOWUP	FONTANEL
FOGOU	FOLATES	FOLIUM	FOLLOWUPS	FONTANELS
FOGOUS	FOLD	FOLIUMS	FOLLY	FONTANGE
FOGRAM	FOLDABLE	FOLK	FOLLYING	FONTANGES
FOGRAMITE	FOLDAWAY	FOLKIE	FOMENT	FONTICULI
FOGRAMITY	FOLDAWAYS	FOLKIER	FOMENTED	FONTINA
FOGRAMS	FOLDBACK	FOLKIES	FOMENTER	FONTINAS

FONTLET	FOOTAGE	FOOTLONG	FOOTSTEPS	FORAMINAL
FONTLETS	FOOTAGES	FOOTLONGS	FOOTSTOCK	FORAMS
FONTS	FOOTBAG	FOOTLOOSE	FOOTSTONE	FORANE
FOO	FOOTBAGS	FOOTMAN	FOOTSTOOL	FORASMUCH
FOOBAR	FOOTBALL	FOOTMARK	FOOTSY	FORAY
FOOD	FOOTBALLS	FOOTMARKS	FOOTWALL	FORAYED
FOODBANK	FOOTBAR	FOOTMEN	FOOTWALLS	FORAYER
FOODBANKS	FOOTBARS	FOOTMUFF	FOOTWAY	FORAYERS
FOODERIES	FOOTBATH	FOOTMUFFS	FOOTWAYS	FORAYING
FOODERY	FOOTBATHS	FOOTNOTE	FOOTWEAR	FORAYS
FOODFUL	FOOTBED	FOOTNOTED	FOOTWEARS	FORB
FOODIE	FOOTBEDS	FOOTNOTES	FOOTWEARY	FORBAD
FOODIES	FOOTBOARD	FOOTPACE	FOOTWELL	FORBADE
FOODISM	FOOTBOY	FOOTPACES	FOOTWELLS	FORBARE
FOODISMS	FOOTBOYS	FOOTPAD	FOOTWORK	FORBEAR
FOODLAND	FOOTBRAKE	FOOTPADS	FOOTWORKS	FORBEARER
FOODLANDS	FOOTCLOTH	FOOTPAGE	FOOTWORN	FORBEARS
FOODLESS	FOOTED	FOOTPAGES	FOOTY	FORBID
FOODOIR	FOOTER	FOOTPATH	FOOZLE	FORBIDAL
FOODOIRS	FOOTERED	FOOTPATHS	FOOZLED	FORBIDALS
FOODS	FOOTERING	FOOTPLATE	FOOZLER	FORBIDDAL
FOODSHED	FOOTERS	FOOTPOST	FOOZLERS	FORBIDDEN
FOODSHEDS	FOOTFALL	FOOTPOSTS	FOOZLES	FORBIDDER
FOODSTUFF	FOOTFALLS	FOOTPRINT	FOOZLING	FORBIDS
FOODWAYS	FOOTFAULT	FOOTPUMP	FOOZLINGS	FORBODE
FOODY	FOOTGEAR	FOOTPUMPS	FOP	FORBODED
FOOFARAW	FOOTGEARS	FOOTRA	FOPLING	FORBODES
FOOFARAWS	FOOTHILL	FOOTRACE	FOPLINGS	FORBODING
FOOL	FOOTHILLS	FOOTRACES	FOPPED	FORBORE
FOOLED	FOOTHOLD	FOOTRAS	FOPPERIES	FORBORNE
FOOLERIES	FOOTHOLDS	FOOTREST	FOPPERY	FORBS
FOOLERY	FOOTIE	FOOTRESTS	FOPPING	FORBY
FOOLFISH	FOOTIER	FOOTROPE	FOPPISH	FORBYE
FOOLHARDY	FOOTIES	FOOTROPES	FOPPISHLY	FORCAT
FOOLING	FOOTIEST	FOOTRULE	FOPS	FORCATS
FOOLINGS	FOOTING	FOOTRULES	FOR	FORCE
FOOLISH	FOOTINGS	FOOTS	FORA	FORCEABLE
FOOLISHER	FOOTLE	FOOTSAL	FORAGE	FORCED
FOOLISHLY	FOOTLED	FOOTSALS	FORAGED	FORCEDLY
FOOLPROOF	FOOTLER	FOOTSIE	FORAGER	FORCEFUL
FOOLS	FOOTLERS	FOOTSIES	FORAGERS	FORCELESS
FOOLSCAP	FOOTLES	FOOTSLOG	FORAGES	FORCEMEAT
FOOLSCAPS	FOOTLESS	FOOTSLOGS	FORAGING	FORCEOUT
FOOS	FOOTLIGHT	FOOTSORE	FORAM	FORCEOUTS
FOOSBALL	FOOTLIKE	FOOTSTALK	FORAMEN	FORCEPS
FOOSBALLS	FOOTLING	FOOTSTALL	FORAMENS	FORCEPSES
FOOT	FOOTLINGS	FOOTSTEP	FORAMINA	FORCER

FORCERS	FORECHECK	FOREIGNLY	FORENSIC	FORESIDES
FORCES	FORECLOSE	FOREJUDGE	FORENSICS	FORESIGHT
FORCIBLE	FORECLOTH	FOREKING	FOREPART	FORESKIN
FORCIBLY	FORECOURT	FOREKINGS	FOREPARTS	FORESKINS
FORCING	FOREDATE	FOREKNEW	FOREPAST	FORESKIRT
FORCINGLY	FOREDATED	FOREKNOW	FOREPAW	FORESLACK
FORCIPATE	FOREDATES	FOREKNOWN	FOREPAWS	FORESLOW
FORCIPES	FOREDECK	FOREKNOWS	FOREPEAK	FORESLOWS
FORD	FOREDECKS	FOREL	FOREPEAKS	FORESPAKE
FORDABLE	FOREDID	FORELADY	FOREPLAN	FORESPEAK
FORDED	FOREDO	FORELAID	FOREPLANS	FORESPEND
FORDID	FOREDOES	FORELAIN	FOREPLAY	FORESPENT
FORDING	FOREDOING	FORELAND	FOREPLAYS	FORESPOKE
FORDLESS	FOREDONE	FORELANDS	FOREPOINT	FOREST
FORDO	FOREDOOM	FORELAY	FORERAN	FORESTAGE
FORDOES	FOREDOOMS	FORELAYS	FORERANK	FORESTAIR
FORDOING	FOREFACE	FORELEG	FORERANKS	FORESTAL
FORDONE	FOREFACES	FORELEGS	FOREREACH	FORESTALL
FORDONNE	FOREFEEL	FORELEND	FOREREAD	FORESTAY
FORDS	FOREFEELS	FORELENDS	FOREREADS	FORESTAYS
FORE	FOREFEET	FORELENT	FORERUN	FORESTEAL
FOREANENT	FOREFELT	FORELIE	FORERUNS	FORESTED
FOREARM	FOREFEND	FORELIES	FORES	FORESTER
FOREARMED	FOREFENDS	FORELIFT	FORESAID	FORESTERS
FOREARMS	FOREFOOT	FORELIFTS	FORESAIL	FORESTIAL
FOREBAY	FOREFRONT	FORELIMB	FORESAILS	FORESTINE
FOREBAYS	FOREGLEAM	FORELIMBS	FORESAW	FORESTING
FOREBEAR	FOREGO	FORELOCK	FORESAY	FORESTRY
FOREBEARS	FOREGOER	FORELOCKS	FORESAYS	FORESTS
FOREBITT	FOREGOERS	FORELS	FORESEE	FORESWEAR
FOREBITTS	FOREGOES	FORELYING	FORESEEN	FORESWORE
FOREBODE	FOREGOING	FOREMAN	FORESEER	FORESWORN
FOREBODED	FOREGONE	FOREMAST	FORESEERS	FORETASTE
FOREBODER	FOREGUT	FOREMASTS	FORESEES	FORETEACH
FOREBODES	FOREGUTS	FOREMEAN	FORESHANK	FORETEETH
FOREBODY	FOREHAND	FOREMEANS	FORESHEET	FORETELL
FOREBOOM	FOREHANDS	FOREMEANT	FORESHEW	FORETELLS
FOREBOOMS	FOREHEAD	FOREMEN	FORESHEWN	FORETHINK
FOREBRAIN	FOREHEADS	FOREMILK	FORESHEWS	FORETIME
FOREBY	FOREHENT	FOREMILKS	FORESHIP	FORETIMES
FOREBYE	FOREHENTS	FOREMOST	FORESHIPS	FORETOKEN
FORECABIN	FOREHOCK	FORENAME	FORESHOCK	FORETOLD
FORECADDY	FOREHOCKS	FORENAMED	FORESHORE	FORETOOTH
FORECAR	FOREHOOF	FORENAMES	FORESHOW	FORETOP
FORECARS	FOREHOOFS	FORENIGHT	FORESHOWN	FORETOPS
FORECAST	FOREIGN	FORENOON	FORESHOWS	FOREVER
FORECASTS	FOREIGNER	FORENOONS	FORESIDE	FOREVERS

FOREWARD	FORGERS	FORJUDGES	FORMALIST	FORMULAS
FOREWARDS	FORGERY	FORK	FORMALITY	FORMULATE
FOREWARN	FORGES	FORKBALL	FORMALIZE	FORMULISE
FOREWARNS	FORGET	FORKBALLS	FORMALLY	FORMULISM
FOREWEIGH	FORGETFUL	FORKED	FORMALS	FORMULIST
FOREWENT	FORGETIVE	FORKEDLY	FORMAMIDE	FORMULIZE
FOREWIND	FORGETS	FORKER	FORMANT	FORMWORK
FOREWINDS	FORGETTER	FORKERS	FORMANTS	FORMWORKS
FOREWING	FORGING	FORKFUL	FORMAT	FORMYL
FOREWINGS	FORGINGS	FORKFULS	FORMATE	FORMYLS
FOREWOMAN	FORGIVE	FORKHEAD	FORMATED	FORNENST
FOREWOMEN	FORGIVEN	FORKHEADS	FORMATES	FORNENT
FOREWORD	FORGIVER	FORKIER	FORMATING	FORNICAL
FOREWORDS	FORGIVERS	FORKIEST	FORMATION	FORNICATE
FOREWORN	FORGIVES	FORKINESS	FORMATIVE	FORNICES
FOREX	FORGIVING	FORKING	FORMATS	FORNIX
FOREXES	FORGO	FORKLESS	FORMATTED	FORPET
FOREYARD	FORGOER	FORKLIFT	FORMATTER	FORPETS
FOREYARDS	FORGOERS	FORKLIFTS	FORME	FORPINE
FORFAIR	FORGOES	FORKLIKE	FORMED	FORPINED
FORFAIRED	FORGOING	FORKS	FORMEE	FORPINES
FORFAIRN	FORGONE	FORKSFUL	FORMEES	FORPINING
FORFAIRS	FORGOT	FORKTAIL	FORMER	FORPIT
FORFAITER	FORGOTTEN	FORKTAILS	FORMERLY	FORPITS
FORFAULT	FORHAILE	FORKY	FORMERS	FORRAD
FORFAULTS	FORHAILED	FORLANA	FORMES	FORRADER
FORFEIT	FORHAILES	FORLANAS	FORMFUL	FORRADS
FORFEITED	FORHENT	FORLEND	FORMIATE	FORRARDER
FORFEITER	FORHENTS	FORLENDS	FORMIATES	FORRAY
FORFEITS	FORHOO	FORLENT	FORMIC	FORRAYED
FORFEND	FORHOOED	FORLESE	FORMICA	FORRAYING
FORFENDED	FORHOOIE	FORLESES	FORMICANT	FORRAYS
FORFENDS	FORHOOIED	FORLESING	FORMICARY	FORREN
FORFEX	FORHOOIES	FORLORE	FORMICAS	FORRIT
FORFEXES	FORHOOING	FORLORN	FORMICATE	FORSAID
FORFICATE	FORHOOS	FORLORNER	FORMING	FORSAKE
FORFOCHEN	FORHOW	FORLORNLY	FORMINGS	FORSAKEN
FORGAT	FORHOWED	FORLORNS	FORMLESS	FORSAKER
FORGATHER	FORHOWING	FORM	FORMOL	FORSAKERS
FORGAVE	FORHOWS	FORMABLE	FORMOLS	FORSAKES
FORGE	FORINSEC	FORMABLY	FORMS	FORSAKING
FORGEABLE	FORINT	FORMAL	FORMULA	FORSAY
FORGED	FORINTS	FORMALIN	FORMULAE	FORSAYING
FORGEMAN	FORJASKIT	FORMALINE	FORMULAIC	FORSAYS
FORGEMEN	FORJESKIT	FORMALINS	FORMULAR	FORSLACK
FORGER	FORJUDGE	FORMALISE	FORMULARS	FORSLACKS
FORGERIES	FORJUDGED	FORMALISM	FORMULARY	FORSLOE

FORSLOED	FORTLET	FOSSE	FOUGASSES	FOURBALLS
FORSLOES	FORTLETS	FOSSED	FOUGHT	FOURCHEE
FORSLOW	FORTNIGHT	FOSSES	FOUGHTEN	FOURCHEES
FORSLOWED	FORTRESS	FOSSETTE	FOUGHTIER	FOUREYED
FORSLOWS	FORTS	FOSSETTES	FOUGHTY	FOURFOLD
FORSOOK	FORTUITY	FOSSICK	FOUL	FOURGON
FORSOOTH	FORTUNATE	FOSSICKED	FOULARD	FOURGONS
FORSPEAK	FORTUNE	FOSSICKER	FOULARDS	FOURPENCE
FORSPEAKS	FORTUNED	FOSSICKS	FOULBROOD	FOURPENNY
FORSPEND	FORTUNES	FOSSIL	FOULDER	FOURPLAY
FORSPENDS	FORTUNING	FOSSILISE	FOULDERED	FOURPLAYS
FORSPENT	FORTUNISE	FOSSILIZE	FOULDERS	FOURPLEX
FORSPOKE	FORTUNIZE	FOSSILS	FOULE	FOURS
FORSPOKEN	FORTY	FOSSOR	FOULED	FOURSCORE
FORSWATT	FORTYISH	FOSSORIAL	FOULER	FOURSES
FORSWEAR	FORUM	FOSSORS	FOULES	FOURSOME
FORSWEARS	FORUMS	FOSSULA	FOULEST	FOURSOMES
FORSWINK	FORWANDER	FOSSULAE	FOULIE	FOURTEEN
FORSWINKS	FORWARD	FOSSULATE	FOULIES	FOURTEENS
FORSWONCK	FORWARDED	FOSTER	FOULING	FOURTH
FORSWORE	FORWARDER	FOSTERAGE	FOULINGS	FOURTHLY
FORSWORN	FORWARDLY	FOSTERED	FOULLY	FOURTHS
FORSWUNK	FORWARDS	FOSTERER	FOULMART	FOUS
FORSYTHIA	FORWARN	FOSTERERS	FOULMARTS	FOUSSA
FORT	FORWARNED	FOSTERING	FOULNESS	FOUSSAS
FORTALICE	FORWARNS	FOSTERS	FOULS	FOUSTIER
FORTE	FORWASTE	FOSTRESS	FOUMART	FOUSTIEST
FORTED	FORWASTED	FOTHER	FOUMARTS	FOUSTY
FORTES	FORWASTES	FOTHERED	FOUND	FOUTER
FORTH	FORWEARY	FOTHERING	FOUNDED	FOUTERED
FORTHCAME	FORWENT	FOTHERS	FOUNDER	FOUTERING
FORTHCOME	FORWHY	FOU	FOUNDERED	FOUTERS
FORTHINK	FORWORN	FOUAT	FOUNDERS	FOUTH
FORTHINKS	FORZA	FOUATS	FOUNDING	FOUTHS
FORTHWITH	FORZANDI	FOUD	FOUNDINGS	FOUTRA
FORTHY	FORZANDO	FOUDRIE	FOUNDLING	FOUTRAS
FORTIES	FORZANDOS	FOUDRIES	FOUNDRESS	FOUTRE
FORTIETH	FORZATI	FOUDS	FOUNDRIES	FOUTRED
FORTIETHS	FORZATO	FOUER	FOUNDRY	FOUTRES
FORTIFIED	FORZATOS	FOUEST	FOUNDS	FOUTRING
FORTIFIER	FORZE	FOUET	FOUNT	FOVEA
FORTIFIES	FOSCARNET	FOUETS	FOUNTAIN	FOVEAE
FORTIFY	FOSS	FOUETTE	FOUNTAINS	FOVEAL
FORTILAGE	FOSSA	FOUETTES	FOUNTFUL	FOVEAS
FORTING	FOSSAE	FOUGADE	FOUNTS	FOVEATE
FORTIS	FOSSAS	FOUGADES	FOUR	FOVEATED
FORTITUDE	FOSSATE	FOUGASSE	FOURBALL	FOVEIFORM

FOVEOLA	FOXSHARK	FRACTALS	FRAILTIES	FRANKABLE
FOVEOLAE	FOXSHARKS	FRACTED	FRAILTY	FRANKED
FOVEOLAR	FOXSHIP	FRACTI	FRAIM	FRANKER
FOVEOLAS	FOXSHIPS	FRACTING	FRAIMS	FRANKERS
FOVEOLATE	FOXSKIN	FRACTION	FRAISE	FRANKEST
FOVEOLE	FOXSKINS	FRACTIONS	FRAISED	FRANKFORT
FOVEOLES	FOXTAIL	FRACTIOUS	FRAISES	FRANKFURT
FOVEOLET	FOXTAILS	FRACTS	FRAISING	FRANKING
FOVEOLETS	FOXTROT	FRACTUR	FRAKTUR	FRANKLIN
FOWL	FOXTROTS	FRACTURAL	FRAKTURS	FRANKLINS
FOWLED	FOXY	FRACTURE	FRAMABLE	FRANKLY
FOWLER	FOY	FRACTURED	FRAMBESIA	FRANKNESS
FOWLERS	FOYBOAT	FRACTURER	FRAMBOISE	FRANKS
FOWLING	FOYBOATS	FRACTURES	FRAME	FRANKUM
FOWLINGS	FOYER	FRACTURS	FRAMEABLE	FRANKUMS
FOWLPOX	FOYERS	FRACTUS	FRAMED	FRANSERIA
FOWLPOXES	FOYLE	FRAE	FRAMELESS	FRANTIC
FOWLS	FOYLED	FRAENA	FRAMER	FRANTICLY
FOWTH	FOYLES	FRAENUM	FRAMERS	FRANZIER
FOWTHS	FOYLING	FRAENUMS	FRAMES	FRANZIEST
FOX	FOYNE	FRAG	FRAMEWORK	FRANZY
FOXBERRY	FOYNED	FRAGGED	FRAMING	FRAP
FOXED	FOYNES	FRAGGING	FRAMINGS	FRAPE
FOXES	FOYNING	FRAGGINGS	FRAMPAL	FRAPEAGE
FOXFIRE	FOYS	FRAGILE	FRAMPLER	FRAPEAGES
FOXFIRES	FOZIER	FRAGILELY	FRAMPLERS	FRAPED
FOXFISH	FOZIEST	FRAGILER	FRAMPOLD	FRAPES
FOXFISHES	FOZINESS	FRAGILEST	FRANC	FRAPING
FOXGLOVE	FOZY	FRAGILITY	FRANCHISE	FRAPPANT
FOXGLOVES	FRA	FRAGMENT	FRANCISE	FRAPPE
FOXHOLE	FRAB	FRAGMENTS	FRANCISED	FRAPPED
FOXHOLES	FRABBED	FRAGOR	FRANCISES	FRAPPEE
FOXHOUND	FRABBING	FRAGORS	FRANCIUM	FRAPPES
FOXHOUNDS	FRABBIT	FRAGRANCE	FRANCIUMS	FRAPPING
FOXHUNT	FRABJOUS	FRAGRANCY	FRANCIZE	FRAPS
FOXHUNTED	FRABS	FRAGRANT	FRANCIZED	FRAS
FOXHUNTER	FRACAS	FRAGS	FRANCIZES	FRASCATI
FOXHUNTS	FRACASES	FRAICHEUR	FRANCO	FRASCATIS
FOXIE	FRACK	FRAIL	FRANCOLIN	FRASS
FOXIER	FRACKED	FRAILER	FRANCS	FRASSES
FOXIES	FRACKER	FRAILEST	FRANGER	FRAT
FOXIEST	FRACKERS	FRAILISH	FRANGERS	FRATCH
FOXILY	FRACKING	FRAILLY	FRANGIBLE	FRATCHES
FOXINESS	FRACKINGS	FRAILNESS	FRANGLAIS	FRATCHETY
FOXING	FRACKS	FRAILS	FRANION	FRATCHIER
FOXINGS	FRACT	FRAILTEE	FRANIONS	FRATCHING
FOXLIKE	FRACTAL	FRAILTEES	FRANK	FRATCHY

FRATE	FREAKILY	FREELY	FREITY	FRESCOS
FRATER	FREAKING	FREEMAN	FREMD	FRESH
FRATERIES	FREAKISH	FREEMASON	FREMDS	FRESHED
FRATERNAL	FREAKOUT	FREEMEN	FREMIT	FRESHEN
FRATERS	FREAKOUTS	FREENESS	FREMITS	FRESHENED
FRATERY	FREAKS	FREEPHONE	FREMITUS	FRESHENER
FRATI	FREAKY	FREER	FRENA	FRESHENS
FRATRIES	FRECKLE	FREERIDE	FRENCH	FRESHER
FRATRY	FRECKLED	FREERIDES	FRENCHED	FRESHERS
FRATS	FRECKLES	FREERS	FRENCHES	FRESHES
FRAU	FRECKLIER	FREES	FRENCHIFY	FRESHEST
FRAUD	FRECKLING	FREESHEET	FRENCHING	FRESHET
FRAUDFUL	FRECKLY	FREESIA	FRENEMIES	FRESHETS
FRAUDS	FREDAINE	FREESIAS	FRENEMY	FRESHIE
FRAUDSMAN	FREDAINES	FREEST	FRENETIC	FRESHIES
FRAUDSMEN	FREE	FREESTONE	FRENETICS	FRESHING
FRAUDSTER	FREEBASE	FREESTYLE	FRENNE	FRESHISH
FRAUGHAN	FREEBASED	FREET	FRENNES	FRESHLY
FRAUGHANS	FREEBASER	FREETIER	FRENULA	FRESHMAN
FRAUGHT	FREEBASES	FREETIEST	FRENULAR	FRESHMEN
FRAUGHTED	FREEBEE	FREETS	FRENULUM	FRESHNESS
FRAUGHTER	FREEBEES	FREETY	FRENULUMS	FRESNEL
FRAUGHTS	FREEBIE	FREEWARE	FRENUM	FRESNELS
FRAULEIN	FREEBIES	FREEWARES	FRENUMS	FRET
FRAULEINS	FREEBOARD	FREEWAY	FRENZICAL	FRETBOARD
FRAUS	FREEBOOT	FREEWAYS	FRENZIED	FRETFUL
FRAUTAGE	FREEBOOTS	FREEWHEEL	FRENZIES	FRETFULLY
FRAUTAGES	FREEBOOTY	FREEWILL	FRENZILY	FRETLESS
FRAWZEY	FREEBORN	FREEWOMAN	FRENZY	FRETS
FRAWZEYS	FREECYCLE	FREEWOMEN	FRENZYING	FRETSAW
FRAY	FREED	FREEWRITE	FREON	FRETSAWS
FRAYED	FREEDIVER	FREEWROTE	FREONS	FRETSOME
FRAYING	FREEDMAN	FREEZABLE	FREQUENCE	FRETTED
FRAYINGS	FREEDMEN	FREEZE	FREQUENCY	FRETTER
FRAYS	FREEDOM	FREEZER	FREQUENT	FRETTERS
FRAZIL	FREEDOMS	FREEZERS	FREQUENTS	FRETTIER
FRAZILS	FREEFALL	FREEZES	FRERE	FRETTIEST
FRAZZLE	FREEFORM	FREEZING	FRERES	FRETTING
FRAZZLED	FREEGAN	FREEZINGS	FRESCADE	FRETTINGS
FRAZZLES	FREEGANS	FREIGHT	FRESCADES	FRETTY
FRAZZLING	FREEHAND	FREIGHTED	FRESCO	FRETWORK
FREAK	FREEHOLD	FREIGHTER	FRESCOED	FRETWORKS
FREAKED	FREEHOLDS	FREIGHTS	FRESCOER	FRIABLE
FREAKERY	FREEING	FREIT	FRESCOERS	FRIAND
FREAKFUL	FREELANCE	FREITIER	FRESCOES	FRIANDE
FREAKIER	FREELOAD	FREITIEST	FRESCOING	FRIANDES
FREAKIEST	FREELOADS	FREITS	FRESCOIST	FRIANDS

FRIAR
FRIARBIRD
FRIARIES
FRIARLY
FRIARS
FRIARY
FRIB
FRIBBLE
FRIBBLED
FRIBBLER
FRIBBLERS
FRIBBLES
FRIBBLING
FRIBBLISH
FRIBS
FRICADEL
FRICADELS
FRICANDO
FRICASSEE
FRICATIVE
FRICHT
FRICHTED
FRICHTING
FRICHTS
FRICKING
FRICOT
FRICOTS
FRICTION
FRICTIONS
FRIDGE
FRIDGED
FRIDGES
FRIDGING
FRIED
FRIEDCAKE
FRIEND
FRIENDED
FRIENDING
FRIENDLY
FRIENDS
FRIER
FRIERS
FRIES
FRIEZE
FRIEZED
FRIEZES
FRIEZING

FRIG
FRIGATE
FRIGATES
FRIGATOON
FRIGES
FRIGGED
FRIGGER
FRIGGERS
FRIGGING
FRIGGINGS
FRIGHT
FRIGHTED
FRIGHTEN
FRIGHTENS
FRIGHTFUL
FRIGHTING
FRIGHTS
FRIGID
FRIGIDER
FRIGIDEST
FRIGIDITY
FRIGIDLY
FRIGOT
FRIGOTS
FRIGS
FRIJOL
FRIJOLE
FRIJOLES
FRIKKADEL
FRILL
FRILLED
FRILLER
FRILLERS
FRILLERY
FRILLIER
FRILLIES
FRILLIEST
FRILLING
FRILLINGS
FRILLS
FRILLY
FRINGE
FRINGED
FRINGES
FRINGIER
FRINGIEST
FRINGING

FRINGINGS
FRINGY
FRIPON
FRIPONS
FRIPPER
FRIPPERER
FRIPPERS
FRIPPERY
FRIPPET
FRIPPETS
FRIS
FRISBEE
FRISBEES
FRISE
FRISEE
FRISEES
FRISES
FRISETTE
FRISETTES
FRISEUR
FRISEURS
FRISK
FRISKA
FRISKAS
FRISKED
FRISKER
FRISKERS
FRISKET
FRISKETS
FRISKFUL
FRISKIER
FRISKIEST
FRISKILY
FRISKING
FRISKINGS
FRISKS
FRISKY
FRISSON
FRISSONS
FRIST
FRISTED
FRISTING
FRISTS
FRISURE
FRISURES
FRIT
FRITES

FRITFLIES
FRITFLY
FRITH
FRITHBORH
FRITHS
FRITS
FRITT
FRITTATA
FRITTATAS
FRITTED
FRITTER
FRITTERED
FRITTERER
FRITTERS
FRITTING
FRITTS
FRITURE
FRITURES
FRITZ
FRITZED
FRITZES
FRITZING
FRIULANO
FRIULANOS
FRIVOL
FRIVOLED
FRIVOLER
FRIVOLERS
FRIVOLING
FRIVOLITY
FRIVOLLED
FRIVOLLER
FRIVOLOUS
FRIVOLS
FRIZ
FRIZADO
FRIZADOS
FRIZE
FRIZED
FRIZER
FRIZERS
FRIZES
FRIZETTE
FRIZETTES
FRIZING
FRIZZ
FRIZZANTE

FRIZZED
FRIZZER
FRIZZERS
FRIZZES
FRIZZIER
FRIZZIES
FRIZZIEST
FRIZZILY
FRIZZING
FRIZZLE
FRIZZLED
FRIZZLER
FRIZZLERS
FRIZZLES
FRIZZLIER
FRIZZLING
FRIZZLY
FRIZZY
FRO
FROCK
FROCKED
FROCKING
FROCKINGS
FROCKLESS
FROCKS
FROE
FROES
FROG
FROGBIT
FROGBITS
FROGEYE
FROGEYED
FROGEYES
FROGFISH
FROGGED
FROGGERY
FROGGIER
FROGGIEST
FROGGING
FROGGINGS
FROGGY
FROGLET
FROGLETS
FROGLIKE
FROGLING
FROGLINGS
FROGMAN

FROGMARCH	FRONTING	FROTHERS	FROWSTS	FRUITION
FROGMEN	FRONTLESS	FROTHERY	FROWSTY	FRUITIONS
FROGMOUTH	FRONTLET	FROTHIER	FROWSY	FRUITIVE
FROGS	FRONTLETS	FROTHIEST	FROWY	FRUITLESS
FROGSPAWN	FRONTLINE	FROTHILY	FROWZIER	FRUITLET
FROIDEUR	FRONTLIST	FROTHING	FROWZIEST	FRUITLETS
FROIDEURS	FRONTMAN	FROTHINGS	FROWZILY	FRUITLIKE
FROING	FRONTMEN	FROTHLESS	FROWZY	FRUITS
FROINGS	FRONTON	FROTHS	FROZE	FRUITWOOD
FROISE	FRONTONS	FROTHY	FROZEN	FRUITY
FROISES	FRONTOON	FROTTAGE	FROZENLY	FRUMENTY
FROLIC	FRONTOONS	FROTTAGES	FRUCTAN	FRUMP
FROLICKED	FRONTPAGE	FROTTEUR	FRUCTANS	FRUMPED
FROLICKER	FRONTS	FROTTEURS	FRUCTED	FRUMPIER
FROLICKY	FRONTWARD	FROUFROU	FRUCTIFY	FRUMPIEST
FROLICS	FRONTWAYS	FROUFROUS	FRUCTIVE	FRUMPILY
FROM	FRONTWISE	FROUGHIER	FRUCTOSE	FRUMPING
FROMAGE	FRORE	FROUGHY	FRUCTOSES	FRUMPISH
FROMAGES	FROREN	FROUNCE	FRUCTUARY	FRUMPLE
FROMENTY	FRORN	FROUNCED	FRUCTUATE	FRUMPLED
FROND	FRORNE	FROUNCES	FRUCTUOUS	FRUMPLES
FRONDAGE	FRORY	FROUNCING	FRUG	FRUMPLING
FRONDAGES	FROS	FROUZIER	FRUGAL	FRUMPS
FRONDED	FROSH	FROUZIEST	FRUGALIST	FRUMPY
FRONDENT	FROSHES	FROUZY	FRUGALITY	FRUSEMIDE
FRONDEUR	FROST	FROW	FRUGALLY	FRUSH
FRONDEURS	FROSTBIT	FROWARD	FRUGGED	FRUSHED
FRONDLESS	FROSTBITE	FROWARDLY	FRUGGING	FRUSHES
FRONDOSE	FROSTED	FROWARDS	FRUGIVORE	FRUSHING
FRONDOUS	FROSTEDS	FROWIE	FRUGS	FRUST
FRONDS	FROSTFISH	FROWIER	FRUICT	FRUSTA
FRONS	FROSTIER	FROWIEST	FRUICTS	FRUSTRATE
FRONT	FROSTIEST	FROWN	FRUIT	FRUSTS
FRONTAGE	FROSTILY	FROWNED	FRUITAGE	FRUSTULE
FRONTAGER	FROSTING	FROWNER	FRUITAGES	FRUSTULES
FRONTAGES	FROSTINGS	FROWNERS	FRUITCAKE	FRUSTUM
FRONTAL	FROSTLESS	FROWNING	FRUITED	FRUSTUMS
FRONTALLY	FROSTLIKE	FROWNS	FRUITER	FRUTEX
FRONTALS	FROSTLINE	FROWS	FRUITERER	FRUTICES
FRONTED	FROSTNIP	FROWSIER	FRUITERS	FRUTICOSE
FRONTENIS	FROSTNIPS	FROWSIEST	FRUITERY	FRUTIFIED
FRONTER	FROSTS	FROWST	FRUITFUL	FRUTIFIES
FRONTERS	FROSTWORK	FROWSTED	FRUITIER	FRUTIFY
FRONTES	FROSTY	FROWSTER	FRUITIEST	FRY
FRONTEST	FROTH	FROWSTERS	FRUITILY	FRYABLE
FRONTIER	FROTHED	FROWSTIER	FRUITING	FRYBREAD
FRONTIERS	FROTHER	FROWSTING	FRUITINGS	FRYBREADS

FRYER	FUCOIDS	FUFFING	FUJIS	FULLEST
FRYERS	FUCOSE	FUFFS	FULCRA	FULLFACE
FRYING	FUCOSES	FUFFY	FULCRATE	FULLFACES
FRYINGS	FUCOUS	FUG	FULCRUM	FULLING
FRYPAN	FUCUS	FUGACIOUS	FULCRUMS	FULLISH
FRYPANS	FUCUSED	FUGACITY	FULFIL	FULLNESS
FUB	FUCUSES	FUGAL	FULFILL	FULLS
FUBAR	FUD	FUGALLY	FULFILLED	FULLY
FUBBED	FUDDIER	FUGATO	FULFILLER	FULMAR
FUBBERIES	FUDDIES	FUGATOS	FULFILLS	FULMARS
FUBBERY	FUDDIEST	FUGGED	FULFILS	FULMINANT
FUBBIER	FUDDLE	FUGGIER	FULGENCY	FULMINATE
FUBBIEST	FUDDLED	FUGGIEST	FULGENT	FULMINE
FUBBING	FUDDLER	FUGGILY	FULGENTLY	FULMINED
FUBBY	FUDDLERS	FUGGINESS	FULGID	FULMINES
FUBS	FUDDLES	FUGGING	FULGOR	FULMINIC
FUBSIER	FUDDLING	FUGGY	FULGOROUS	FULMINING
FUBSIEST	FUDDLINGS	FUGHETTA	FULGORS	FULMINOUS
FUBSY	FUDDY	FUGHETTAS	FULGOUR	FULNESS
FUCHSIA	FUDGE	FUGIE	FULGOURS	FULNESSES
FUCHSIAS	FUDGED	FUGIES	FULGURAL	FULSOME
FUCHSIN	FUDGES	FUGIO	FULGURANT	FULSOMELY
FUCHSINE	FUDGIER	FUGIOS	FULGURATE	FULSOMER
FUCHSINES	FUDGIEST	FUGITIVE	FULGURITE	FULSOMEST
FUCHSINS	FUDGING	FUGITIVES	FULGUROUS	FULVID
FUCHSITE	FUDGY	FUGLE	FULHAM	FULVOUS
FUCHSITES	FUDS	FUGLED	FULHAMS	FUM
FUCI	FUEHRER	FUGLEMAN	FULL	FUMADO
FUCK	FUEHRERS	FUGLEMEN	FULLAGE	FUMADOES
FUCKED	FUEL	FUGLES	FULLAGES	FUMADOS
FUCKER	FUELED	FUGLIER	FULLAM	FUMAGE
FUCKERS	FUELER	FUGLIEST	FULLAMS	FUMAGES
FUCKFACE	FUELERS	FUGLING	FULLAN	FUMARASE
FUCKFACES	FUELING	FUGLY	FULLANS	FUMARASES
FUCKHEAD	FUELLED	FUGS	FULLBACK	FUMARATE
FUCKHEADS	FUELLER	FUGU	FULLBACKS	FUMARATES
FUCKING	FUELLERS	FUGUE	FULLBLOOD	FUMARIC
FUCKINGS	FUELLING	FUGUED	FULLED	FUMAROLE
FUCKOFF	FUELS	FUGUELIKE	FULLER	FUMAROLES
FUCKOFFS	FUELWOOD	FUGUES	FULLERED	FUMAROLIC
FUCKS	FUELWOODS	FUGUING	FULLERENE	FUMATORIA
FUCKUP	FUERO	FUGUIST	FULLERIDE	FUMATORY
FUCKUPS	FUEROS	FUGUISTS	FULLERIES	FUMBLE
FUCKWIT	FUFF	FUGUS	FULLERING	FUMBLED
FUCKWITS	FUFFED	FUHRER	FULLERITE	FUMBLER
FUCOID	FUFFIER	FUHRERS	FULLERS	FUMBLERS
FUCOIDAL	FUFFIEST	FUJI	FULLERY	FUMBLES

FUMBLING	FUNDER	FUNGUS	FUNSTERS	FURFUROL
FUME	FUNDERS	FUNGUSES	FUR	FURFUROLE
FUMED	FUNDI	FUNHOUSE	FURACIOUS	FURFUROLS
FUMELESS	FUNDIC	FUNHOUSES	FURACITY	FURFUROUS
FUMELIKE	FUNDIE	FUNICLE	FURAL	FURFURS
FUMER	FUNDIES	FUNICLES	FURALS	FURIBUND
FUMEROLE	FUNDING	FUNICULAR	FURAN	FURIES
FUMEROLES	FUNDINGS	FUNICULI	FURANE	FURIOSITY
FUMERS	FUNDIS	FUNICULUS	FURANES	FURIOSO
FUMES	FUNDLESS	FUNK	FURANOSE	FURIOSOS
FUMET	FUNDRAISE	FUNKED	FURANOSES	FURIOUS
FUMETS	FUNDS	FUNKER	FURANS	FURIOUSLY
FUMETTE	FUNDUS	FUNKERS	FURBALL	FURKID
FUMETTES	FUNDY	FUNKHOLE	FURBALLS	FURKIDS
FUMETTI	FUNEBRAL	FUNKHOLES	FURBEARER	FURL
FUMETTO	FUNEBRE	FUNKIA	FURBELOW	FURLABLE
FUMETTOS	FUNEBRIAL	FUNKIAS	FURBELOWS	FURLANA
FUMIER	FUNERAL	FUNKIER	FURBISH	FURLANAS
FUMIEST	FUNERALS	FUNKIEST	FURBISHED	FURLED
FUMIGANT	FUNERARY	FUNKILY	FURBISHER	FURLER
FUMIGANTS	FUNEREAL	FUNKINESS	FURBISHES	FURLERS
FUMIGATE	FUNEST	FUNKING	FURCA	FURLESS
FUMIGATED	FUNFAIR	FUNKS	FURCAE	FURLING
FUMIGATES	FUNFAIRS	FUNKSTER	FURCAL	FURLONG
FUMIGATOR	FUNFEST	FUNKSTERS	FURCATE	FURLONGS
FUMING	FUNFESTS	FUNKY	FURCATED	FURLOUGH
FUMINGLY	FUNG	FUNNED	FURCATELY	FURLOUGHS
FUMITORY	FUNGAL	FUNNEL	FURCATES	FURLS
FUMOSITY	FUNGALS	FUNNELED	FURCATING	FURMENTY
FUMOUS	FUNGI	FUNNELING	FURCATION	FURMETIES
FUMS	FUNGIBLE	FUNNELLED	FURCRAEA	FURMETY
FUMULI	FUNGIBLES	FUNNELS	FURCRAEAS	FURMITIES
FUMULUS	FUNGIC	FUNNER	FURCULA	FURMITY
FUMY	FUNGICIDE	FUNNEST	FURCULAE	FURNACE
FUN	FUNGIFORM	FUNNIER	FURCULAR	FURNACED
FUNBOARD	FUNGISTAT	FUNNIES	FURCULUM	FURNACES
FUNBOARDS	FUNGO	FUNNIEST	FURDER	FURNACING
FUNCKIA	FUNGOED	FUNNILY	FUREUR	FURNIMENT
FUNCKIAS	FUNGOES	FUNNINESS	FUREURS	FURNISH
FUNCTION	FUNGOID	FUNNING	FURFAIR	FURNISHED
FUNCTIONS	FUNGOIDAL	FUNNY	FURFAIRS	FURNISHER
FUNCTOR	FUNGOIDS	FUNNYMAN	FURFUR	FURNISHES
FUNCTORS	FUNGOING	FUNNYMEN	FURFURAL	FURNITURE
FUND	FUNGOS	FUNPLEX	FURFURALS	FUROL
FUNDABLE	FUNGOSITY	FUNPLEXES	FURFURAN	FUROLE
FUNDAMENT	FUNGOUS	FUNS	FURFURANS	FUROLES
FUNDED	FUNGS	FUNSTER	FURFURES	FUROLS

FUROR	FURZES	FUSILS	FUSTOC	FUZELESS
FURORE	FURZIER	FUSING	FUSTOCS	FUZES
FURORES	FURZIEST	FUSION	FUSTS	FUZIL
FURORS	FURZY	FUSIONAL	FUSTY	FUZILS
FURPHIES	FUSAIN	FUSIONISM	FUSULINID	FUZING
FURPHY	FUSAINS	FUSIONIST	FUSUMA	FUZZ
FURPIECE	FUSARIA	FUSIONS	FUTCHEL	FUZZBALL
FURPIECES	FUSARIUM	FUSK	FUTCHELS	FUZZBALLS
FURR	FUSARIUMS	FUSKED	FUTHARC	FUZZBOX
FURRED	FUSAROL	FUSKER	FUTHARCS	FUZZBOXES
FURRIER	FUSAROLE	FUSKERS	FUTHARK	FUZZED
FURRIERS	FUSAROLES	FUSKING	FUTHARKS	FUZZES
FURRIERY	FUSAROLS	FUSKS	FUTHORC	FUZZIER
FURRIES	FUSBALL	FUSS	FUTHORCS	FUZZIEST
FURRIEST	FUSBALLS	FUSSBALL	FUTHORK	FUZZILY
FURRILY	FUSC	FUSSBALLS	FUTHORKS	FUZZINESS
FURRINER	FUSCOUS	FUSSED	FUTILE	FUZZING
FURRINERS	FUSE	FUSSER	FUTILELY	FUZZLE
FURRINESS	FUSED	FUSSERS	FUTILER	FUZZLED
FURRING	FUSEE	FUSSES	FUTILEST	FUZZLES
FURRINGS	FUSEES	FUSSIER	FUTILITY	FUZZLING
FURROW	FUSEL	FUSSIEST	FUTON	FUZZTONE
FURROWED	FUSELAGE	FUSSILY	FUTONS	FUZZTONES
FURROWER	FUSELAGES	FUSSINESS	FUTSAL	FUZZY
FURROWERS	FUSELESS	FUSSING	FUTSALS	FY
FURROWING	FUSELIKE	FUSSPOT	FUTTOCK	FYCE
FURROWS	FUSELS	FUSSPOTS	FUTTOCKS	FYCES
FURROWY	FUSES	FUSSY	FUTURAL	FYKE
FURRS	FUSHION	FUST	FUTURE	FYKED
FURRY	FUSHIONS	FUSTED	FUTURES	FYKES
FURS	FUSIBLE	FUSTET	FUTURISM	FYKING
FURTH	FUSIBLY	FUSTETS	FUTURISMS	FYLE
FURTHER	FUSIDIC	FUSTIAN	FUTURIST	FYLES
FURTHERED	FUSIFORM	FUSTIANS	FUTURISTS	FYLFOT
FURTHERER	FUSIL	FUSTIC	FUTURITY	FYLFOTS
FURTHERS	FUSILE	FUSTICS	FUTZ	FYNBOS
FURTHEST	FUSILEER	FUSTIER	FUTZED	FYNBOSES
FURTIVE	FUSILEERS	FUSTIEST	FUTZES	FYRD
FURTIVELY	FUSILIER	FUSTIGATE	FUTZING	FYRDS
FURUNCLE	FUSILIERS	FUSTILUGS	FUZE	FYTTE
FURUNCLES	FUSILLADE	FUSTILY	FUZED	FYTTES
FURY	FUSILLI	FUSTINESS	FUZEE	
FURZE	FUSILLIS	FUSTING	FUZEES	

G

GAB
GABARDINE
GABBA
GABBARD
GABBARDS
GABBART
GABBARTS
GABBAS
GABBED
GABBER
GABBERS
GABBIER
GABBIEST
GABBINESS
GABBING
GABBLE
GABBLED
GABBLER
GABBLERS
GABBLES
GABBLING
GABBLINGS
GABBRO
GABBROIC
GABBROID
GABBROS
GABBY
GABELLE
GABELLED
GABELLER
GABELLERS
GABELLES
GABERDINE
GABFEST
GABFESTS
GABIES
GABION
GABIONADE
GABIONAGE
GABIONED
GABIONS

GABLE
GABLED
GABLELIKE
GABLES
GABLET
GABLETS
GABLING
GABNASH
GABNASHES
GABOON
GABOONS
GABS
GABY
GACH
GACHED
GACHER
GACHERS
GACHES
GACHING
GAD
GADABOUT
GADABOUTS
GADARENE
GADDED
GADDER
GADDERS
GADDI
GADDING
GADDIS
GADE
GADES
GADFLIES
GADFLY
GADGE
GADGES
GADGET
GADGETEER
GADGETRY
GADGETS
GADGETY
GADGIE

GADGIES
GADI
GADID
GADIDS
GADIS
GADJE
GADJES
GADJO
GADJOS
GADLING
GADLINGS
GADMAN
GADMEN
GADOID
GADOIDS
GADOLINIC
GADROON
GADROONED
GADROONS
GADS
GADSMAN
GADSMEN
GADSO
GADWALL
GADWALLS
GADZOOKS
GAE
GAED
GAEING
GAELICISE
GAELICISM
GAELICIZE
GAEN
GAES
GAFF
GAFFE
GAFFED
GAFFER
GAFFERS
GAFFES
GAFFING

GAFFINGS
GAFFS
GAFFSAIL
GAFFSAILS
GAG
GAGA
GAGAKU
GAGAKUS
GAGE
GAGEABLE
GAGEABLY
GAGED
GAGER
GAGERS
GAGES
GAGGED
GAGGER
GAGGERIES
GAGGERS
GAGGERY
GAGGING
GAGGLE
GAGGLED
GAGGLES
GAGGLING
GAGGLINGS
GAGING
GAGMAN
GAGMEN
GAGS
GAGSTER
GAGSTERS
GAHNITE
GAHNITES
GAID
GAIDS
GAIETIES
GAIETY
GAIJIN
GAILLARD
GAILLARDE

GAILY
GAIN
GAINABLE
GAINED
GAINER
GAINERS
GAINEST
GAINFUL
GAINFULLY
GAINING
GAININGS
GAINLESS
GAINLIER
GAINLIEST
GAINLY
GAINS
GAINSAID
GAINSAY
GAINSAYER
GAINSAYS
GAINST
GAIR
GAIRFOWL
GAIRFOWLS
GAIRS
GAIT
GAITA
GAITAS
GAITED
GAITER
GAITERED
GAITERS
GAITING
GAITS
GAITT
GAITTS
GAJO
GAJOS
GAK
GAKS
GAL

GALA	GALEAS	GALLEASS	GALLISING	GALLYING
GALABEA	GALEATE	GALLED	GALLISISE	GALOCHE
GALABEAH	GALEATED	GALLEIN	GALLISIZE	GALOCHED
GALABEAHS	GALED	GALLEINS	GALLIUM	GALOCHES
GALABEAS	GALEIFORM	GALLEON	GALLIUMS	GALOCHING
GALABIA	GALENA	GALLEONS	GALLIVANT	GALOOT
GALABIAH	GALENAS	GALLERIA	GALLIVAT	GALOOTS
GALABIAHS	GALENGALE	GALLERIAS	GALLIVATS	GALOP
GALABIAS	GALENIC	GALLERIED	GALLIWASP	GALOPADE
GALABIEH	GALENICAL	GALLERIES	GALLIZE	GALOPADES
GALABIEHS	GALENITE	GALLERIST	GALLIZED	GALOPED
GALABIYA	GALENITES	GALLERY	GALLIZES	GALOPIN
GALABIYAH	GALENOID	GALLET	GALLIZING	GALOPING
GALABIYAS	GALERE	GALLETA	GALLNUT	GALOPINS
GALACTIC	GALERES	GALLETAS	GALLNUTS	GALOPPED
GALACTICO	GALES	GALLETED	GALLOCK	GALOPPING
GALACTOSE	GALETTE	GALLETING	GALLON	GALOPS
GALAGE	GALETTES	GALLETS	GALLONAGE	GALORE
GALAGES	GALILEE	GALLEY	GALLONS	GALORES
GALAGO	GALILEES	GALLEYS	GALLOON	GALOSH
GALAGOS	GALING	GALLFLIES	GALLOONED	GALOSHE
GALAH	GALINGALE	GALLFLY	GALLOONS	GALOSHED
GALAHS	GALIONGEE	GALLIARD	GALLOOT	GALOSHES
GALANGA	GALIOT	GALLIARDS	GALLOOTS	GALOSHING
GALANGAL	GALIOTS	GALLIASS	GALLOP	GALOWSES
GALANGALS	GALIPOT	GALLIC	GALLOPADE	GALRAVAGE
GALANGAS	GALIPOTS	GALLICA	GALLOPED	GALS
GALANT	GALIVANT	GALLICAN	GALLOPER	GALTONIA
GALANTINE	GALIVANTS	GALLICAS	GALLOPERS	GALTONIAS
GALANTY	GALL	GALLICISE	GALLOPING	GALUMPH
GALAPAGO	GALLABEA	GALLICISM	GALLOPS	GALUMPHED
GALAPAGOS	GALLABEAH	GALLICIZE	GALLOUS	GALUMPHER
GALAS	GALLABEAS	GALLIED	GALLOW	GALUMPHS
GALATEA	GALLABIA	GALLIER	GALLOWAY	GALUT
GALATEAS	GALLABIAH	GALLIES	GALLOWAYS	GALUTH
GALAVANT	GALLABIAS	GALLIEST	GALLOWED	GALUTHS
GALAVANTS	GALLABIEH	GALLINAZO	GALLOWING	GALUTS
GALAX	GALLABIYA	GALLING	GALLOWS	GALVANIC
GALAXES	GALLAMINE	GALLINGLY	GALLOWSES	GALVANISE
GALAXIES	GALLANT	GALLINULE	GALLS	GALVANISM
GALAXY	GALLANTED	GALLIOT	GALLSTONE	GALVANIST
GALBANUM	GALLANTER	GALLIOTS	GALLUMPH	GALVANIZE
GALBANUMS	GALLANTLY	GALLIPOT	GALLUMPHS	GALVO
GALDRAGON	GALLANTRY	GALLIPOTS	GALLUS	GALVOS
GALE	GALLANTS	GALLISE	GALLUSED	GALYAC
GALEA	GALLATE	GALLISED	GALLUSES	GALYACS
GALEAE	GALLATES	GALLISES	GALLY	GALYAK

GALYAKS	GAMBOES	GAMESY	GAMMONING	GANGLED
GAM	GAMBOGE	GAMETAL	GAMMONS	GANGLES
GAMA	GAMBOGES	GAMETE	GAMMY	GANGLIA
GAMAHUCHE	GAMBOGIAN	GAMETES	GAMODEME	GANGLIAL
GAMARUCHE	GAMBOGIC	GAMETIC	GAMODEMES	GANGLIAR
GAMAS	GAMBOL	GAMEY	GAMONE	GANGLIATE
GAMASH	GAMBOLED	GAMEYNESS	GAMONES	GANGLIER
GAMASHES	GAMBOLING	GAMGEE	GAMP	GANGLIEST
GAMAY	GAMBOLLED	GAMIC	GAMPISH	GANGLING
GAMAYS	GAMBOLS	GAMIER	GAMPS	GANGLION
GAMB	GAMBOS	GAMIEST	GAMS	GANGLIONS
GAMBA	GAMBREL	GAMIFIED	GAMUT	GANGLY
GAMBADE	GAMBRELS	GAMIFIES	GAMUTS	GANGPLANK
GAMBADES	GAMBROON	GAMIFY	GAMY	GANGPLOW
GAMBADO	GAMBROONS	GAMIFYING	GAMYNESS	GANGPLOWS
GAMBADOED	GAMBS	GAMILY	GAN	GANGREL
GAMBADOES	GAMBUSIA	GAMIN	GANACHE	GANGRELS
GAMBADOS	GAMBUSIAS	GAMINE	GANACHES	GANGRENE
GAMBAS	GAME	GAMINERIE	GANCH	GANGRENED
GAMBE	GAMEBAG	GAMINES	GANCHED	GANGRENES
GAMBES	GAMEBAGS	GAMINESS	GANCHES	GANGS
GAMBESON	GAMEBOOK	GAMING	GANCHING	GANGSHAG
GAMBESONS	GAMEBOOKS	GAMINGS	GANDER	GANGSHAGS
GAMBET	GAMECOCK	GAMINS	GANDERED	GANGSMAN
GAMBETS	GAMECOCKS	GAMMA	GANDERING	GANGSMEN
GAMBETTA	GAMED	GAMMADIA	GANDERISM	GANGSTA
GAMBETTAS	GAMEFISH	GAMMADION	GANDERS	GANGSTAS
GAMBIA	GAMEFOWL	GAMMAS	GANDY	GANGSTER
GAMBIAS	GAMEFOWLS	GAMMAT	GANE	GANGSTERS
GAMBIER	GAMELAN	GAMMATIA	GANEF	GANGUE
GAMBIERS	GAMELANS	GAMMATION	GANEFS	GANGUES
GAMBIR	GAMELIKE	GAMMATS	GANEV	GANGWAY
GAMBIRS	GAMELY	GAMME	GANEVS	GANGWAYS
GAMBIST	GAMENESS	GAMMED	GANG	GANISTER
GAMBISTS	GAMEPLAY	GAMMER	GANGBANG	GANISTERS
GAMBIT	GAMEPLAYS	GAMMERS	GANGBANGS	GANJA
GAMBITED	GAMER	GAMMES	GANGBO	GANJAH
GAMBITING	GAMERS	GAMMIER	GANGBOARD	GANJAHS
GAMBITS	GAMES	GAMMIEST	GANGBOS	GANJAS
GAMBLE	GAMESIER	GAMMING	GANGED	GANNED
GAMBLED	GAMESIEST	GAMMOCK	GANGER	GANNET
GAMBLER	GAMESMAN	GAMMOCKED	GANGERS	GANNETRY
GAMBLERS	GAMESMEN	GAMMOCKS	GANGING	GANNETS
GAMBLES	GAMESOME	GAMMON	GANGINGS	GANNING
GAMBLING	GAMEST	GAMMONED	GANGLAND	GANNISTER
GAMBLINGS	GAMESTER	GAMMONER	GANGLANDS	GANOF
GAMBO	GAMESTERS	GAMMONERS	GANGLE	GANOFS

G

GANOID	GAPEWORM	GARBLER	GARGARIZE	GARNISHED
GANOIDS	GAPEWORMS	GARBLERS	GARGET	GARNISHEE
GANOIN	GAPIER	GARBLES	GARGETS	GARNISHER
GANOINE	GAPIEST	GARBLESS	GARGETY	GARNISHES
GANOINES	GAPING	GARBLING	GARGLE	GARNISHOR
GANOINS	GAPINGLY	GARBLINGS	GARGLED	GARNISHRY
GANS	GAPINGS	GARBO	GARGLER	GARNITURE
GANSEY	GAPLESS	GARBOARD	GARGLERS	GAROTE
GANSEYS	GAPO	GARBOARDS	GARGLES	GAROTED
GANT	GAPOS	GARBOIL	GARGLING	GAROTES
GANTED	GAPOSIS	GARBOILS	GARGOYLE	GAROTING
GANTELOPE	GAPOSISES	GARBOLOGY	GARGOYLED	GAROTTE
GANTING	GAPPED	GARBOS	GARGOYLES	GAROTTED
GANTLET	GAPPER	GARBS	GARI	GAROTTER
GANTLETED	GAPPERS	GARBURE	GARIAL	GAROTTERS
GANTLETS	GAPPIER	GARBURES	GARIALS	GAROTTES
GANTLINE	GAPPIEST	GARCINIA	GARIBALDI	GAROTTING
GANTLINES	GAPPING	GARCINIAS	GARIGUE	GAROUPA
GANTLOPE	GAPPINGS	GARCON	GARIGUES	GAROUPAS
GANTLOPES	GAPPY	GARCONS	GARIS	GARPIKE
GANTRIES	GAPS	GARDA	GARISH	GARPIKES
GANTRY	GAPY	GARDAI	GARISHED	GARRAN
GANTS	GAR	GARDANT	GARISHES	GARRANS
GANYMEDE	GARAGE	GARDANTS	GARISHING	GARRE
GANYMEDES	GARAGED	GARDEN	GARISHLY	GARRED
GANZFELD	GARAGEMAN	GARDENED	GARJAN	GARRES
GANZFELDS	GARAGEMEN	GARDENER	GARJANS	GARRET
GAOL	GARAGES	GARDENERS	GARLAND	GARRETED
GAOLBIRD	GARAGEY	GARDENFUL	GARLANDED	GARRETEER
GAOLBIRDS	GARAGING	GARDENIA	GARLANDRY	GARRETS
GAOLBREAK	GARAGINGS	GARDENIAS	GARLANDS	GARRIGUE
GAOLBROKE	GARAGIST	GARDENING	GARLIC	GARRIGUES
GAOLED	GARAGISTE	GARDENS	GARLICKED	GARRING
GAOLER	GARAGISTS	GARDEROBE	GARLICKY	GARRISON
GAOLERESS	GARB	GARDYLOO	GARLICS	GARRISONS
GAOLERS	GARBAGE	GARDYLOOS	GARMENT	GARRON
GAOLING	GARBAGES	GARE	GARMENTED	GARRONS
GAOLLESS	GARBAGEY	GAREFOWL	GARMENTS	GARROT
GAOLS	GARBAGY	GAREFOWLS	GARMS	GARROTE
GAP	GARBANZO	GARES	GARNER	GARROTED
GAPE	GARBANZOS	GARFISH	GARNERED	GARROTER
GAPED	GARBE	GARFISHES	GARNERING	GARROTERS
GAPER	GARBED	GARGANEY	GARNERS	GARROTES
GAPERS	GARBES	GARGANEYS	GARNET	GARROTING
GAPES	GARBING	GARGANTUA	GARNETS	GARROTS
GAPESEED	GARBLE	GARGARISE	GARNI	GARROTTE
GAPESEEDS	GARBLED	GARGARISM	GARNISH	GARROTTED

GARROTTER	GASHER	GASPEREAU	GASTRULAE	GATS
GARROTTES	GASHES	GASPERS	GASTRULAR	GATVOL
GARRULITY	GASHEST	GASPIER	GASTRULAS	GAU
GARRULOUS	GASHFUL	GASPIEST	GASTS	GAUCH
GARRYA	GASHING	GASPINESS	GASWORKS	GAUCHE
GARRYAS	GASHLIER	GASPING	GAT	GAUCHED
GARRYOWEN	GASHLIEST	GASPINGLY	GATCH	GAUCHELY
GARS	GASHLY	GASPINGS	GATCHED	GAUCHER
GART	GASHOLDER	GASPS	GATCHER	GAUCHERIE
GARTER	GASHOUSE	GASPY	GATCHERS	GAUCHERS
GARTERED	GASHOUSES	GASSED	GATCHES	GAUCHES
GARTERING	GASIFIED	GASSER	GATCHING	GAUCHESCO
GARTERS	GASIFIER	GASSERS	GATE	GAUCHEST
GARTH	GASIFIERS	GASSES	GATEAU	GAUCHING
GARTHS	GASIFIES	GASSIER	GATEAUS	GAUCHO
GARUDA	GASIFORM	GASSIEST	GATEAUX	GAUCHOS
GARUDAS	GASIFY	GASSILY	GATECRASH	GAUCIE
GARUM	GASIFYING	GASSINESS	GATED	GAUCIER
GARUMS	GASKET	GASSING	GATEFOLD	GAUCIEST
GARVEY	GASKETED	GASSINGS	GATEFOLDS	GAUCY
GARVEYS	GASKETS	GASSY	GATEHOUSE	GAUD
GARVIE	GASKIN	GAST	GATELEG	GAUDEAMUS
GARVIES	GASKING	GASTED	GATELEGS	GAUDED
GARVOCK	GASKINGS	GASTER	GATELESS	GAUDERIES
GARVOCKS	GASKINS	GASTERED	GATELIKE	GAUDERY
GAS	GASLESS	GASTERING	GATEMAN	GAUDGIE
GASAHOL	GASLIGHT	GASTERS	GATEMEN	GAUDGIES
GASAHOLS	GASLIGHTS	GASTFULL	GATEPOST	GAUDIER
GASALIER	GASLIT	GASTHAUS	GATEPOSTS	GAUDIES
GASALIERS	GASMAN	GASTIGHT	GATER	GAUDIEST
GASBAG	GASMEN	GASTING	GATERS	GAUDILY
GASBAGGED	GASOGENE	GASTNESS	GATES	GAUDINESS
GASBAGS	GASOGENES	GASTNESSE	GATEWAY	GAUDING
GASCON	GASOHOL	GASTRAEA	GATEWAYS	GAUDS
GASCONADE	GASOHOLS	GASTRAEAS	GATH	GAUDY
GASCONISM	GASOLENE	GASTRAEUM	GATHER	GAUFER
GASCONS	GASOLENES	GASTRAL	GATHERED	GAUFERS
GASEITIES	GASOLIER	GASTREA	GATHERER	GAUFFER
GASEITY	GASOLIERS	GASTREAS	GATHERERS	GAUFFERED
GASELIER	GASOLINE	GASTRIC	GATHERING	GAUFFERS
GASELIERS	GASOLINES	GASTRIN	GATHERS	GAUFRE
GASEOUS	GASOLINIC	GASTRINS	GATHS	GAUFRES
GASES	GASOMETER	GASTRITIC	GATING	GAUGE
GASFIELD	GASOMETRY	GASTRITIS	GATINGS	GAUGEABLE
GASFIELDS	GASP	GASTROPOD	GATLING	GAUGEABLY
GASH	GASPED	GASTROPUB	GATOR	GAUGED
GASHED	GASPER	GASTRULA	GATORS	GAUGER

GAUGERS	GAURS	GAWKIES	GAZANGED	GAZUMPING
GAUGES	GAUS	GAWKIEST	GAZANGING	GAZUMPS
GAUGING	GAUSS	GAWKIHOOD	GAZANGS	GAZUNDER
GAUGINGS	GAUSSES	GAWKILY	GAZANIA	GAZUNDERS
GAUJE	GAUSSIAN	GAWKINESS	GAZANIAS	GAZY
GAUJES	GAUZE	GAWKING	GAZAR	GEAL
GAULEITER	GAUZELIKE	GAWKISH	GAZARS	GEALED
GAULT	GAUZES	GAWKISHLY	GAZE	GEALING
GAULTER	GAUZIER	GAWKS	GAZEBO	GEALOUS
GAULTERS	GAUZIEST	GAWKY	GAZEBOES	GEALOUSY
GAULTS	GAUZILY	GAWMOGE	GAZEBOS	GEALS
GAUM	GAUZINESS	GAWMOGES	GAZED	GEAN
GAUMED	GAUZY	GAWP	GAZEFUL	GEANS
GAUMIER	GAVAGE	GAWPED	GAZEHOUND	GEAR
GAUMIEST	GAVAGES	GAWPER	GAZELLE	GEARBOX
GAUMING	GAVE	GAWPERS	GAZELLES	GEARBOXES
GAUMLESS	GAVEL	GAWPING	GAZEMENT	GEARCASE
GAUMS	GAVELED	GAWPS	GAZEMENTS	GEARCASES
GAUMY	GAVELING	GAWPUS	GAZER	GEARE
GAUN	GAVELKIND	GAWPUSES	GAZERS	GEARED
GAUNCH	GAVELLED	GAWS	GAZES	GEARES
GAUNCHED	GAVELLING	GAWSIE	GAZETTE	GEARHEAD
GAUNCHES	GAVELMAN	GAWSIER	GAZETTED	GEARHEADS
GAUNCHING	GAVELMEN	GAWSIEST	GAZETTEER	GEARING
GAUNT	GAVELOCK	GAWSY	GAZETTES	GEARINGS
GAUNTED	GAVELOCKS	GAY	GAZETTING	GEARLESS
GAUNTER	GAVELS	GAYAL	GAZIER	GEARS
GAUNTEST	GAVIAL	GAYALS	GAZIEST	GEARSHIFT
GAUNTING	GAVIALOID	GAYCATION	GAZILLION	GEARSTICK
GAUNTLET	GAVIALS	GAYDAR	GAZING	GEARWHEEL
GAUNTLETS	GAVOT	GAYDARS	GAZINGS	GEASON
GAUNTLY	GAVOTS	GAYER	GAZOGENE	GEAT
GAUNTNESS	GAVOTTE	GAYEST	GAZOGENES	GEATS
GAUNTREE	GAVOTTED	GAYETIES	GAZON	GEBUR
GAUNTREES	GAVOTTES	GAYETY	GAZONS	GEBURS
GAUNTRIES	GAVOTTING	GAYLY	GAZOO	GECK
GAUNTRY	GAW	GAYNESS	GAZOOKA	GECKED
GAUNTS	GAWCIER	GAYNESSES	GAZOOKAS	GECKING
GAUP	GAWCIEST	GAYS	GAZOON	GECKO
GAUPED	GAWCY	GAYSOME	GAZOONS	GECKOES
GAUPER	GAWD	GAYWINGS	GAZOOS	GECKOS
GAUPERS	GAWDS	GAZABO	GAZPACHO	GECKS
GAUPING	GAWK	GAZABOES	GAZPACHOS	GED
GAUPS	GAWKED	GAZABOS	GAZUMP	GEDACT
GAUPUS	GAWKER	GAZAL	GAZUMPED	GEDACTS
GAUPUSES	GAWKERS	GAZALS	GAZUMPER	GEDDIT
GAUR	GAWKIER	GAZANG	GAZUMPERS	GEDECKT

GEDECKTS	GEFULLTE	GELID	GEMMATION	GENEALOGY
GEDS	GEGGIE	GELIDER	GEMMATIVE	GENERA
GEE	GEGGIES	GELIDEST	GEMMED	GENERABLE
GEEBAG	GEHLENITE	GELIDITY	GEMMEN	GENERAL
GEEBAGS	GEISHA	GELIDLY	GEMMEOUS	GENERALCY
GEEBUNG	GEISHAS	GELIDNESS	GEMMERIES	GENERALE
GEEBUNGS	GEIST	GELIGNITE	GEMMERY	GENERALIA
GEECHEE	GEISTS	GELLANT	GEMMIER	GENERALLY
GEECHEES	GEIT	GELLANTS	GEMMIEST	GENERALS
GEED	GEITED	GELLED	GEMMILY	GENERANT
GEEGAW	GEITING	GELLIES	GEMMINESS	GENERANTS
GEEGAWS	GEITS	GELLING	GEMMING	GENERATE
GEEING	GEL	GELLY	GEMMOLOGY	GENERATED
GEEK	GELABLE	GELOSIES	GEMMULE	GENERATES
GEEKDOM	GELADA	GELOSY	GEMMULES	GENERATOR
GEEKDOMS	GELADAS	GELS	GEMMY	GENERIC
GEEKED	GELANDE	GELSEMIA	GEMOLOGY	GENERICAL
GEEKERIES	GELANT	GELSEMINE	GEMONY	GENERICS
GEEKERY	GELANTS	GELSEMIUM	GEMOT	GENEROUS
GEEKIER	GELASTIC	GELT	GEMOTE	GENES
GEEKIEST	GELATE	GELTS	GEMOTES	GENESES
GEEKINESS	GELATED	GEM	GEMOTS	GENESIS
GEEKISH	GELATES	GEMATRIA	GEMS	GENET
GEEKISM	GELATI	GEMATRIAS	GEMSBOK	GENETIC
GEEKISMS	GELATIN	GEMCLIP	GEMSBOKS	GENETICAL
GEEKS	GELATINE	GEMCLIPS	GEMSBUCK	GENETICS
GEEKSPEAK	GELATINES	GEMEL	GEMSBUCKS	GENETRIX
GEEKY	GELATING	GEMELS	GEMSHORN	GENETS
GEELBEK	GELATINS	GEMFISH	GEMSHORNS	GENETTE
GEELBEKS	GELATION	GEMFISHES	GEMSTONE	GENETTES
GEEP	GELATIONS	GEMINAL	GEMSTONES	GENEVA
GEEPOUND	GELATIS	GEMINALLY	GEMUTLICH	GENEVAS
GEEPOUNDS	GELATO	GEMINATE	GEN	GENIAL
GEEPS	GELATOS	GEMINATED	GENA	GENIALISE
GEES	GELCAP	GEMINATES	GENAL	GENIALITY
GEESE	GELCAPS	GEMINI	GENAPPE	GENIALIZE
GEEST	GELCOAT	GEMINIES	GENAPPES	GENIALLY
GEESTS	GELCOATS	GEMINOUS	GENAS	GENIC
GEEZ	GELD	GEMINY	GENDARME	GENICALLY
GEEZAH	GELDED	GEMLIKE	GENDARMES	GENICULAR
GEEZAHS	GELDER	GEMMA	GENDER	GENIE
GEEZER	GELDERS	GEMMAE	GENDERED	GENIES
GEEZERS	GELDING	GEMMAN	GENDERING	GENII
GEFILTE	GELDINGS	GEMMATE	GENDERISE	GENIP
GEFUFFLE	GELDS	GEMMATED	GENDERIZE	GENIPAP
GEFUFFLED	GELEE	GEMMATES	GENDERS	GENIPAPO
GEFUFFLES	GELEES	GEMMATING	GENE	GENIPAPOS

GENIPAPS
GENIPS
GENISTA
GENISTAS
GENISTEIN
GENITAL
GENITALIA
GENITALIC
GENITALLY
GENITALS
GENITIVAL
GENITIVE
GENITIVES
GENITOR
GENITORS
GENITRIX
GENITURE
GENITURES
GENIUS
GENIUSES
GENIZAH
GENIZAHS
GENIZOT
GENIZOTH
GENLOCK
GENLOCKED
GENLOCKS
GENNAKER
GENNAKERS
GENNED
GENNEL
GENNELS
GENNET
GENNETS
GENNIES
GENNING
GENNY
GENOA
GENOAS
GENOCIDAL
GENOCIDE
GENOCIDES
GENOGRAM
GENOGRAMS
GENOISE
GENOISES
GENOM

GENOME
GENOMES
GENOMIC
GENOMICS
GENOMS
GENOTOXIC
GENOTYPE
GENOTYPES
GENOTYPIC
GENRE
GENRES
GENRO
GENROS
GENS
GENSENG
GENSENGS
GENT
GENTEEL
GENTEELER
GENTEELLY
GENTES
GENTIAN
GENTIANS
GENTIER
GENTIEST
GENTIL
GENTILE
GENTILES
GENTILIC
GENTILISE
GENTILISH
GENTILISM
GENTILITY
GENTILIZE
GENTLE
GENTLED
GENTLEMAN
GENTLEMEN
GENTLER
GENTLES
GENTLEST
GENTLING
GENTLY
GENTOO
GENTOOS
GENTRICE
GENTRICES

GENTRIES
GENTRIFY
GENTRY
GENTS
GENTY
GENU
GENUA
GENUFLECT
GENUINE
GENUINELY
GENUS
GENUSES
GEO
GEOBOTANY
GEOCACHE
GEOCACHED
GEOCACHER
GEOCACHES
GEOCARPIC
GEOCARPY
GEOCODE
GEOCODED
GEOCODES
GEOCODING
GEOCORONA
GEODATA
GEODE
GEODES
GEODESIC
GEODESICS
GEODESIES
GEODESIST
GEODESY
GEODETIC
GEODETICS
GEODIC
GEODUCK
GEODUCKS
GEOFACT
GEOFACTS
GEOGENIES
GEOGENY
GEOGNOSES
GEOGNOSIS
GEOGNOST
GEOGNOSTS
GEOGNOSY

GEOGONIC
GEOGONIES
GEOGONY
GEOGRAPHY
GEOID
GEOIDAL
GEOIDS
GEOLATRY
GEOLOGER
GEOLOGERS
GEOLOGIAN
GEOLOGIC
GEOLOGIES
GEOLOGISE
GEOLOGIST
GEOLOGIZE
GEOLOGY
GEOMANCER
GEOMANCY
GEOMANT
GEOMANTIC
GEOMANTS
GEOMATICS
GEOMETER
GEOMETERS
GEOMETRIC
GEOMETRID
GEOMETRY
GEOMYOID
GEONOMICS
GEOPHAGIA
GEOPHAGY
GEOPHILIC
GEOPHONE
GEOPHONES
GEOPHYTE
GEOPHYTES
GEOPHYTIC
GEOPONIC
GEOPONICS
GEOPROBE
GEOPROBES
GEORGETTE
GEORGIC
GEORGICAL
GEORGICS
GEOS

GEOSPHERE
GEOSTATIC
GEOTACTIC
GEOTAG
GEOTAGGED
GEOTAGS
GEOTAXES
GEOTAXIS
GEOTHERM
GEOTHERMS
GEOTROPIC
GER
GERAH
GERAHS
GERANIAL
GERANIALS
GERANIOL
GERANIOLS
GERANIUM
GERANIUMS
GERARDIA
GERARDIAS
GERBE
GERBERA
GERBERAS
GERBES
GERBIL
GERBILLE
GERBILLES
GERBILS
GERE
GERENT
GERENTS
GERENUK
GERENUKS
GERES
GERFALCON
GERIATRIC
GERLE
GERLES
GERM
GERMAIN
GERMAINE
GERMAINES
GERMAINS
GERMAN
GERMANDER

GERMANE
GERMANELY
GERMANIC
GERMANISE
GERMANITE
GERMANIUM
GERMANIZE
GERMANOUS
GERMANS
GERMED
GERMEN
GERMENS
GERMFREE
GERMICIDE
GERMIER
GERMIEST
GERMIN
GERMINA
GERMINAL
GERMINANT
GERMINATE
GERMINESS
GERMING
GERMINS
GERMLIKE
GERMPLASM
GERMPROOF
GERMS
GERMY
GERNE
GERNED
GERNES
GERNING
GERONIMO
GERONTIC
GEROPIGA
GEROPIGAS
GERS
GERT
GERTCHA
GERUND
GERUNDIAL
GERUNDIVE
GERUNDS
GESNERIA
GESNERIAD
GESNERIAS

GESSAMINE
GESSE
GESSED
GESSES
GESSING
GESSO
GESSOED
GESSOES
GEST
GESTALT
GESTALTEN
GESTALTS
GESTANT
GESTAPO
GESTAPOS
GESTATE
GESTATED
GESTATES
GESTATING
GESTATION
GESTATIVE
GESTATORY
GESTE
GESTES
GESTIC
GESTICAL
GESTS
GESTURAL
GESTURE
GESTURED
GESTURER
GESTURERS
GESTURES
GESTURING
GET
GETA
GETABLE
GETAS
GETATABLE
GETAWAY
GETAWAYS
GETOUT
GETOUTS
GETS
GETTABLE
GETTER
GETTERED

GETTERING
GETTERS
GETTING
GETTINGS
GETUP
GETUPS
GEUM
GEUMS
GEWGAW
GEWGAWED
GEWGAWS
GEY
GEYAN
GEYER
GEYEST
GEYSER
GEYSERED
GEYSERING
GEYSERITE
GEYSERS
GHARIAL
GHARIALS
GHARRI
GHARRIES
GHARRIS
GHARRY
GHAST
GHASTED
GHASTFUL
GHASTING
GHASTLIER
GHASTLY
GHASTNESS
GHASTS
GHAT
GHATS
GHAUT
GHAUTS
GHAZAL
GHAZALS
GHAZEL
GHAZELS
GHAZI
GHAZIES
GHAZIS
GHEE
GHEES

GHERAO
GHERAOED
GHERAOES
GHERAOING
GHERAOS
GHERKIN
GHERKINS
GHESSE
GHESSED
GHESSES
GHESSING
GHEST
GHETTO
GHETTOED
GHETTOES
GHETTOING
GHETTOISE
GHETTOIZE
GHETTOS
GHI
GHIBLI
GHIBLIS
GHILGAI
GHILGAIS
GHILLIE
GHILLIED
GHILLIES
GHILLYING
GHIS
GHOST
GHOSTED
GHOSTIER
GHOSTIEST
GHOSTING
GHOSTINGS
GHOSTLIER
GHOSTLIKE
GHOSTLY
GHOSTS
GHOSTY
GHOUL
GHOULIE
GHOULIES
GHOULISH
GHOULS
GHRELIN
GHRELINS

GHUBAR
GHYLL
GHYLLS
GI
GIAMBEUX
GIANT
GIANTESS
GIANTHOOD
GIANTISM
GIANTISMS
GIANTLIER
GIANTLIKE
GIANTLY
GIANTRIES
GIANTRY
GIANTS
GIANTSHIP
GIAOUR
GIAOURS
GIARDIA
GIARDIAS
GIB
GIBBED
GIBBER
GIBBERED
GIBBERING
GIBBERISH
GIBBERS
GIBBET
GIBBETED
GIBBETING
GIBBETS
GIBBETTED
GIBBING
GIBBON
GIBBONS
GIBBOSE
GIBBOSITY
GIBBOUS
GIBBOUSLY
GIBBSITE
GIBBSITES
GIBE
GIBED
GIBEL
GIBELS
GIBER

G

GIBERS	GIFTINGS	GIGLOTS	GILLING	GIMMICKY
GIBES	GIFTLESS	GIGMAN	GILLION	GIMMIE
GIBING	GIFTS	GIGMANITY	GILLIONS	GIMMIES
GIBINGLY	GIFTSHOP	GIGMEN	GILLNET	GIMMOR
GIBLET	GIFTSHOPS	GIGOLO	GILLNETS	GIMMORS
GIBLETS	GIFTWARE	GIGOLOS	GILLS	GIMP
GIBLI	GIFTWARES	GIGOT	GILLY	GIMPED
GIBLIS	GIFTWRAP	GIGOTS	GILLYING	GIMPIER
GIBS	GIFTWRAPS	GIGS	GILLYVOR	GIMPIEST
GIBSON	GIG	GIGUE	GILLYVORS	GIMPING
GIBSONS	GIGA	GIGUES	GILPEY	GIMPS
GIBUS	GIGABIT	GILA	GILPEYS	GIMPY
GIBUSES	GIGABITS	GILAS	GILPIES	GIN
GID	GIGABYTE	GILBERT	GILPY	GINCH
GIDDAP	GIGABYTES	GILBERTS	GILRAVAGE	GINCHES
GIDDAY	GIGACYCLE	GILCUP	GILSONITE	GING
GIDDIED	GIGAFLOP	GILCUPS	GILT	GINGAL
GIDDIER	GIGAFLOPS	GILD	GILTCUP	GINGALL
GIDDIES	GIGAHERTZ	GILDED	GILTCUPS	GINGALLS
GIDDIEST	GIGANTEAN	GILDEN	GILTHEAD	GINGALS
GIDDILY	GIGANTIC	GILDER	GILTHEADS	GINGE
GIDDINESS	GIGANTISM	GILDERS	GILTS	GINGELEY
GIDDUP	GIGAS	GILDHALL	GILTWOOD	GINGELEYS
GIDDY	GIGATON	GILDHALLS	GIMBAL	GINGELI
GIDDYAP	GIGATONS	GILDING	GIMBALED	GINGELIES
GIDDYING	GIGAWATT	GILDINGS	GIMBALING	GINGELIS
GIDDYUP	GIGAWATTS	GILDS	GIMBALLED	GINGELLI
GIDGEE	GIGGED	GILDSMAN	GIMBALLING	GINGELLIS
GIDGEES	GIGGING	GILDSMEN	GIMBALS	GINGELLY
GIDJEE	GIGGIT	GILET	GIMCRACK	GINGELY
GIDJEES	GIGGITED	GILETS	GIMCRACKS	GINGER
GIDS	GIGGITING	GILGAI	GIMEL	GINGERADE
GIE	GIGGITS	GILGAIS	GIMELS	GINGERED
GIED	GIGGLE	GILGIE	GIMLET	GINGERING
GIEING	GIGGLED	GILGIES	GIMLETED	GINGERLY
GIEN	GIGGLER	GILL	GIMLETING	GINGEROUS
GIES	GIGGLERS	GILLAROO	GIMLETS	GINGERS
GIF	GIGGLES	GILLAROOS	GIMMAL	GINGERY
GIFS	GIGGLIER	GILLED	GIMMALLED	GINGES
GIFT	GIGGLIEST	GILLER	GIMMALS	GINGHAM
GIFTABLE	GIGGLING	GILLERS	GIMME	GINGHAMS
GIFTABLES	GIGGLINGS	GILLET	GIMMER	GINGILI
GIFTED	GIGGLY	GILLETS	GIMMERS	GINGILIS
GIFTEDLY	GIGHE	GILLFLIRT	GIMMES	GINGILLI
GIFTEE	GIGLET	GILLIE	GIMMICK	GINGILLIS
GIFTEES	GIGLETS	GILLIED	GIMMICKED	GINGIVA
GIFTING	GIGLOT	GILLIES	GIMMICKS	GINGIVAE

G

GINGIVAL	GIPPIES	GIRKIN	GIRTING	GIVER
GINGKO	GIPPING	GIRKINS	GIRTLINE	GIVERS
GINGKOES	GIPPO	GIRL	GIRTLINES	GIVES
GINGKOS	GIPPOES	GIRLHOOD	GIRTS	GIVING
GINGLE	GIPPOS	GIRLHOODS	GIS	GIVINGS
GINGLES	GIPPY	GIRLIE	GISARME	GIZMO
GINGLYMI	GIPS	GIRLIER	GISARMES	GIZMOLOGY
GINGLYMUS	GIPSEN	GIRLIES	GISM	GIZMOS
GINGS	GIPSENS	GIRLIEST	GISMO	GIZZ
GINHOUSE	GIPSIED	GIRLISH	GISMOLOGY	GIZZARD
GINHOUSES	GIPSIES	GIRLISHLY	GISMOS	GIZZARDS
GINK	GIPSY	GIRLOND	GISMS	GIZZEN
GINKGO	GIPSYDOM	GIRLONDS	GIST	GIZZENED
GINKGOES	GIPSYDOMS	GIRLS	GISTS	GIZZENING
GINKGOS	GIPSYHOOD	GIRLY	GIT	GIZZENS
GINKS	GIPSYING	GIRN	GITANA	GIZZES
GINN	GIPSYISH	GIRNED	GITANAS	GJETOST
GINNED	GIPSYISM	GIRNEL	GITANO	GJETOSTS
GINNEL	GIPSYISMS	GIRNELS	GITANOS	GJU
GINNELS	GIPSYWORT	GIRNER	GITCH	GJUS
GINNER	GIRAFFE	GIRNERS	GITCHES	GLABELLA
GINNERIES	GIRAFFES	GIRNIE	GITE	GLABELLAE
GINNERS	GIRAFFID	GIRNIER	GITES	GLABELLAR
GINNERY	GIRAFFIDS	GIRNIEST	GITS	GLABRATE
GINNIER	GIRAFFINE	GIRNING	GITTARONE	GLABROUS
GINNIEST	GIRAFFISH	GIRNS	GITTED	GLACE
GINNING	GIRAFFOID	GIRO	GITTERN	GLACED
GINNINGS	GIRANDOLA	GIROLLE	GITTERNED	GLACEED
GINNY	GIRANDOLE	GIROLLES	GITTERNS	GLACEING
GINORMOUS	GIRASOL	GIRON	GITTIN	GLACES
GINS	GIRASOLE	GIRONIC	GITTING	GLACIAL
GINSENG	GIRASOLES	GIRONNY	GIUST	GLACIALLY
GINSENGS	GIRASOLS	GIRONS	GIUSTED	GLACIALS
GINSHOP	GIRD	GIROS	GIUSTING	GLACIATE
GINSHOPS	GIRDED	GIROSOL	GIUSTO	GLACIATED
GINZO	GIRDER	GIROSOLS	GIUSTS	GLACIATES
GINZOES	GIRDERS	GIRR	GIVABLE	GLACIER
GINZOS	GIRDING	GIRRS	GIVE	GLACIERED
GIO	GIRDINGLY	GIRSH	GIVEABLE	GLACIERS
GIOCOSO	GIRDINGS	GIRSHES	GIVEAWAY	GLACIS
GIOS	GIRDLE	GIRT	GIVEAWAYS	GLACISES
GIP	GIRDLED	GIRTED	GIVEBACK	GLAD
GIPON	GIRDLER	GIRTH	GIVEBACKS	GLADDED
GIPONS	GIRDLERS	GIRTHED	GIVED	GLADDEN
GIPPED	GIRDLES	GIRTHING	GIVEN	GLADDENED
GIPPER	GIRDLING	GIRTHLINE	GIVENNESS	GLADDENER
GIPPERS	GIRDS	GIRTHS	GIVENS	GLADDENS

GLADDER	GLAIRING	GLAREAL	GLAURS	GLEDE
GLADDEST	GLAIRINS	GLARED	GLAURY	GLEDES
GLADDIE	GLAIRS	GLARELESS	GLAZE	GLEDGE
GLADDIES	GLAIRY	GLAREOUS	GLAZED	GLEDGED
GLADDING	GLAIVE	GLARES	GLAZEN	GLEDGES
GLADDON	GLAIVED	GLARIER	GLAZER	GLEDGING
GLADDONS	GLAIVES	GLARIEST	GLAZERS	GLEDS
GLADE	GLAM	GLARINESS	GLAZES	GLEE
GLADELIKE	GLAMMED	GLARING	GLAZIER	GLEED
GLADES	GLAMMER	GLARINGLY	GLAZIERS	GLEEDS
GLADFUL	GLAMMEST	GLARY	GLAZIERY	GLEEFUL
GLADIATE	GLAMMIER	GLASNOST	GLAZIEST	GLEEFULLY
GLADIATOR	GLAMMIEST	GLASNOSTS	GLAZILY	GLEEING
GLADIER	GLAMMING	GLASS	GLAZINESS	GLEEK
GLADIEST	GLAMMY	GLASSED	GLAZING	GLEEKED
GLADIOLA	GLAMOR	GLASSEN	GLAZINGS	GLEEKING
GLADIOLAR	GLAMORED	GLASSES	GLAZY	GLEEKS
GLADIOLAS	GLAMORING	GLASSFUL	GLEAM	GLEEMAN
GLADIOLE	GLAMORISE	GLASSFULS	GLEAMED	GLEEMEN
GLADIOLES	GLAMORIZE	GLASSIE	GLEAMER	GLEENIE
GLADIOLI	GLAMOROUS	GLASSIER	GLEAMERS	GLEENIES
GLADIOLUS	GLAMORS	GLASSIES	GLEAMIER	GLEES
GLADIUS	GLAMOUR	GLASSIEST	GLEAMIEST	GLEESOME
GLADIUSES	GLAMOURED	GLASSIFY	GLEAMING	GLEET
GLADLIER	GLAMOURS	GLASSILY	GLEAMINGS	GLEETED
GLADLIEST	GLAMPING	GLASSINE	GLEAMS	GLEETIER
GLADLY	GLAMPINGS	GLASSINES	GLEAMY	GLEETIEST
GLADNESS	GLAMS	GLASSING	GLEAN	GLEETING
GLADS	GLANCE	GLASSLESS	GLEANABLE	GLEETS
GLADSOME	GLANCED	GLASSLIKE	GLEANED	GLEETY
GLADSOMER	GLANCER	GLASSMAN	GLEANER	GLEG
GLADSTONE	GLANCERS	GLASSMEN	GLEANERS	GLEGGER
GLADWRAP	GLANCES	GLASSWARE	GLEANING	GLEGGEST
GLADWRAPS	GLANCING	GLASSWORK	GLEANINGS	GLEGLY
GLADY	GLANCINGS	GLASSWORM	GLEANS	GLEGNESS
GLAIK	GLAND	GLASSWORT	GLEAVE	GLEI
GLAIKET	GLANDERED	GLASSY	GLEAVES	GLEIS
GLAIKIT	GLANDERS	GLAUCOMA	GLEBA	GLEN
GLAIKS	GLANDES	GLAUCOMAS	GLEBAE	GLENGARRY
GLAIR	GLANDLESS	GLAUCOUS	GLEBE	GLENLIKE
GLAIRE	GLANDLIKE	GLAUM	GLEBELESS	GLENOID
GLAIRED	GLANDS	GLAUMED	GLEBES	GLENOIDAL
GLAIREOUS	GLANDULAR	GLAUMING	GLEBIER	GLENOIDS
GLAIRES	GLANDULE	GLAUMS	GLEBIEST	GLENS
GLAIRIER	GLANDULES	GLAUR	GLEBOUS	GLENT
GLAIRIEST	GLANS	GLAURIER	GLEBY	GLENTED
GLAIRIN	GLARE	GLAURIEST	GLED	GLENTING

GLENTS	GLIMING	GLITTERED	GLOBOID	GLOOMS
GLEY	GLIMMER	GLITTERS	GLOBOIDS	GLOOMY
GLEYED	GLIMMERED	GLITTERY	GLOBOSE	GLOOP
GLEYING	GLIMMERS	GLITZ	GLOBOSELY	GLOOPED
GLEYINGS	GLIMMERY	GLITZED	GLOBOSITY	GLOOPIER
GLEYS	GLIMPSE	GLITZES	GLOBOUS	GLOOPIEST
GLIA	GLIMPSED	GLITZIER	GLOBS	GLOOPING
GLIADIN	GLIMPSER	GLITZIEST	GLOBULAR	GLOOPS
GLIADINE	GLIMPSERS	GLITZILY	GLOBULARS	GLOOPY
GLIADINES	GLIMPSES	GLITZING	GLOBULE	GLOP
GLIADINS	GLIMPSING	GLITZY	GLOBULES	GLOPPED
GLIAL	GLIMS	GLOAM	GLOBULET	GLOPPIER
GLIAS	GLINT	GLOAMING	GLOBULETS	GLOPPIEST
GLIB	GLINTED	GLOAMINGS	GLOBULIN	GLOPPING
GLIBBED	GLINTIER	GLOAMS	GLOBULINS	GLOPPY
GLIBBER	GLINTIEST	GLOAT	GLOBULITE	GLOPS
GLIBBERY	GLINTING	GLOATED	GLOBULOUS	GLORIA
GLIBBEST	GLINTS	GLOATER	GLOBUS	GLORIAS
GLIBBING	GLINTY	GLOATERS	GLOBY	GLORIED
GLIBLY	GLIOMA	GLOATING	GLOCHID	GLORIES
GLIBNESS	GLIOMAS	GLOATINGS	GLOCHIDIA	GLORIFIED
GLIBS	GLIOMATA	GLOATS	GLOCHIDS	GLORIFIER
GLID	GLIOSES	GLOB	GLODE	GLORIFIES
GLIDDER	GLIOSIS	GLOBAL	GLOGG	GLORIFY
GLIDDERY	GLISK	GLOBALISE	GLOGGS	GLORIOLE
GLIDDEST	GLISKS	GLOBALISM	GLOIRE	GLORIOLES
GLIDE	GLISSADE	GLOBALIST	GLOIRES	GLORIOSA
GLIDED	GLISSADED	GLOBALIZE	GLOM	GLORIOSAS
GLIDEPATH	GLISSADER	GLOBALLY	GLOMERA	GLORIOUS
GLIDER	GLISSADES	GLOBATE	GLOMERATE	GLORY
GLIDERS	GLISSANDI	GLOBATED	GLOMERULE	GLORYING
GLIDES	GLISSANDO	GLOBBIER	GLOMERULI	GLOSS
GLIDING	GLISSE	GLOBBIEST	GLOMMED	GLOSSA
GLIDINGLY	GLISSES	GLOBBY	GLOMMING	GLOSSAE
GLIDINGS	GLISTEN	GLOBE	GLOMS	GLOSSAL
GLIFF	GLISTENED	GLOBED	GLOMUS	GLOSSARY
GLIFFING	GLISTENS	GLOBEFISH	GLONOIN	GLOSSAS
GLIFFINGS	GLISTER	GLOBELIKE	GLONOINS	GLOSSATOR
GLIFFS	GLISTERED	GLOBES	GLOOM	GLOSSED
GLIFT	GLISTERS	GLOBESITY	GLOOMED	GLOSSEME
GLIFTS	GLIT	GLOBETROT	GLOOMFUL	GLOSSEMES
GLIKE	GLITCH	GLOBI	GLOOMIER	GLOSSER
GLIKES	GLITCHES	GLOBIER	GLOOMIEST	GLOSSERS
GLIM	GLITCHIER	GLOBIEST	GLOOMILY	GLOSSES
GLIME	GLITCHY	GLOBIN	GLOOMING	GLOSSIER
GLIMED	GLITS	GLOBING	GLOOMINGS	GLOSSIES
GLIMES	GLITTER	GLOBINS	GLOOMLESS	GLOSSIEST

GLOSSILY
GLOSSINA
GLOSSINAS
GLOSSING
GLOSSIST
GLOSSISTS
GLOSSITIC
GLOSSITIS
GLOSSLESS
GLOSSY
GLOST
GLOSTS
GLOTTAL
GLOTTIC
GLOTTIDES
GLOTTIS
GLOTTISES
GLOUT
GLOUTED
GLOUTING
GLOUTS
GLOVE
GLOVEBOX
GLOVED
GLOVELESS
GLOVER
GLOVERS
GLOVES
GLOVING
GLOVINGS
GLOW
GLOWED
GLOWER
GLOWERED
GLOWERING
GLOWERS
GLOWFLIES
GLOWFLY
GLOWING
GLOWINGLY
GLOWLAMP
GLOWLAMPS
GLOWS
GLOWSTICK
GLOWWORM
GLOWWORMS
GLOXINIA

GLOXINIAS
GLOZE
GLOZED
GLOZES
GLOZING
GLOZINGS
GLUCAGON
GLUCAGONS
GLUCAN
GLUCANS
GLUCINA
GLUCINAS
GLUCINIC
GLUCINIUM
GLUCINUM
GLUCINUMS
GLUCONATE
GLUCONIC
GLUCOSE
GLUCOSES
GLUCOSIC
GLUCOSIDE
GLUE
GLUEBALL
GLUEBALLS
GLUED
GLUEING
GLUEISH
GLUELIKE
GLUEPOT
GLUEPOTS
GLUER
GLUERS
GLUES
GLUEY
GLUEYNESS
GLUG
GLUGGABLE
GLUGGED
GLUGGING
GLUGS
GLUHWEIN
GLUHWEINS
GLUIER
GLUIEST
GLUILY
GLUINESS

GLUING
GLUISH
GLUM
GLUME
GLUMELIKE
GLUMELLA
GLUMELLAS
GLUMES
GLUMLY
GLUMMER
GLUMMEST
GLUMNESS
GLUMPIER
GLUMPIEST
GLUMPILY
GLUMPISH
GLUMPS
GLUMPY
GLUMS
GLUNCH
GLUNCHED
GLUNCHES
GLUNCHING
GLUON
GLUONS
GLURGE
GLURGES
GLUT
GLUTAEAL
GLUTAEI
GLUTAEUS
GLUTAMATE
GLUTAMIC
GLUTAMINE
GLUTCH
GLUTCHED
GLUTCHES
GLUTCHING
GLUTE
GLUTEAL
GLUTEI
GLUTELIN
GLUTELINS
GLUTEN
GLUTENIN
GLUTENINS
GLUTENOUS

GLUTENS
GLUTES
GLUTEUS
GLUTINOUS
GLUTS
GLUTTED
GLUTTING
GLUTTON
GLUTTONS
GLUTTONY
GLYCAEMIA
GLYCAEMIC
GLYCAN
GLYCANS
GLYCATION
GLYCEMIA
GLYCEMIAS
GLYCEMIC
GLYCERIA
GLYCERIAS
GLYCERIC
GLYCERIDE
GLYCERIN
GLYCERINE
GLYCERINS
GLYCEROL
GLYCEROLS
GLYCERYL
GLYCERYLS
GLYCIN
GLYCINE
GLYCINES
GLYCINS
GLYCOCOLL
GLYCOGEN
GLYCOGENS
GLYCOL
GLYCOLIC
GLYCOLLIC
GLYCOLS
GLYCONIC
GLYCONICS
GLYCOSE
GLYCOSES
GLYCOSIDE
GLYCOSYL
GLYCOSYLS

GLYCYL
GLYCYLS
GLYPH
GLYPHIC
GLYPHS
GLYPTAL
GLYPTALS
GLYPTIC
GLYPTICS
GMELINITE
GNAMMA
GNAR
GNARL
GNARLED
GNARLIER
GNARLIEST
GNARLING
GNARLS
GNARLY
GNARR
GNARRED
GNARRING
GNARRS
GNARS
GNASH
GNASHED
GNASHER
GNASHERS
GNASHES
GNASHING
GNASHINGS
GNAT
GNATHAL
GNATHIC
GNATHION
GNATHIONS
GNATHITE
GNATHITES
GNATHONIC
GNATLIKE
GNATLING
GNATLINGS
GNATS
GNATTIER
GNATTIEST
GNATTY
GNATWREN

GNATWRENS	GOADSMEN	GOBAN	GODDAMMED	GODSONS
GNAW	GOADSTER	GOBANG	GODDAMMIT	GODSPEED
GNAWABLE	GOADSTERS	GOBANGS	GODDAMN	GODSPEEDS
GNAWED	GOAF	GOBANS	GODDAMNED	GODSQUAD
GNAWER	GOAFS	GOBAR	GODDAMNS	GODSQUADS
GNAWERS	GOAL	GOBBED	GODDAMS	GODWARD
GNAWING	GOALBALL	GOBBELINE	GODDED	GODWARDS
GNAWINGLY	GOALBALLS	GOBBET	GODDEN	GODWIT
GNAWINGS	GOALED	GOBBETS	GODDENS	GODWITS
GNAWN	GOALIE	GOBBI	GODDESS	GOE
GNAWS	GOALIES	GOBBIER	GODDESSES	GOEL
GNEISS	GOALING	GOBBIEST	GODDING	GOELS
GNEISSES	GOALLESS	GOBBING	GODET	GOER
GNEISSIC	GOALMOUTH	GOBBLE	GODETIA	GOERS
GNEISSOID	GOALPOST	GOBBLED	GODETIAS	GOES
GNEISSOSE	GOALPOSTS	GOBBLER	GODETS	GOEST
GNOCCHI	GOALS	GOBBLERS	GODFATHER	GOETH
GNOMAE	GOALWARD	GOBBLES	GODHEAD	GOETHITE
GNOME	GOALWARDS	GOBBLING	GODHEADS	GOETHITES
GNOMELIKE	GOANNA	GOBBO	GODHOOD	GOETIC
GNOMES	GOANNAS	GOBBY	GODHOODS	GOETIES
GNOMIC	GOARY	GOBI	GODLESS	GOETY
GNOMICAL	GOAS	GOBIES	GODLESSLY	GOEY
GNOMISH	GOAT	GOBIID	GODLIER	GOFER
GNOMIST	GOATEE	GOBIIDS	GODLIEST	GOFERS
GNOMISTS	GOATEED	GOBIOID	GODLIKE	GOFF
GNOMON	GOATEES	GOBIOIDS	GODLILY	GOFFED
GNOMONIC	GOATFISH	GOBIS	GODLINESS	GOFFER
GNOMONICS	GOATHERD	GOBLET	GODLING	GOFFERED
GNOMONS	GOATHERDS	GOBLETS	GODLINGS	GOFFERING
GNOSES	GOATIER	GOBLIN	GODLY	GOFFERS
GNOSIS	GOATIES	GOBLINS	GODMOTHER	GOFFING
GNOSTIC	GOATIEST	GOBO	GODOWN	GOFFS
GNOSTICAL	GOATISH	GOBOES	GODOWNS	GOGGA
GNOSTICS	GOATISHLY	GOBONEE	GODPARENT	GOGGAS
GNOW	GOATLIKE	GOBONY	GODROON	GOGGLE
GNOWS	GOATLING	GOBOS	GODROONED	GOGGLEBOX
GNU	GOATLINGS	GOBS	GODROONS	GOGGLED
GNUS	GOATS	GOBSHITE	GODS	GOGGLER
GO	GOATSE	GOBSHITES	GODSEND	GOGGLERS
GOA	GOATSES	GOBURRA	GODSENDS	GOGGLES
GOAD	GOATSKIN	GOBURRAS	GODSHIP	GOGGLIER
GOADED	GOATSKINS	GOBY	GODSHIPS	GOGGLIEST
GOADING	GOATWEED	GOD	GODSLOT	GOGGLING
GOADLIKE	GOATWEEDS	GODAWFUL	GODSLOTS	GOGGLINGS
GOADS	GOATY	GODCHILD	GODSO	GOGGLY
GOADSMAN	GOB	GODDAM	GODSON	GOGLET

G

GOGLETS
GOGO
GOGOS
GOHONZON
GOHONZONS
GOIER
GOIEST
GOING
GOINGS
GOITER
GOITERED
GOITERS
GOITRE
GOITRED
GOITRES
GOITROGEN
GOITROUS
GOJI
GOJIS
GOLCONDA
GOLCONDAS
GOLD
GOLDARN
GOLDARNED
GOLDARNS
GOLDBRICK
GOLDBUG
GOLDBUGS
GOLDCREST
GOLDEN
GOLDENED
GOLDENER
GOLDENEST
GOLDENEYE
GOLDENING
GOLDENLY
GOLDENROD
GOLDENS
GOLDER
GOLDEST
GOLDEYE
GOLDEYES
GOLDFIELD
GOLDFINCH
GOLDFINNY
GOLDFISH
GOLDIER

GOLDIES
GOLDIEST
GOLDISH
GOLDLESS
GOLDMINER
GOLDS
GOLDSINNY
GOLDSIZE
GOLDSIZES
GOLDSMITH
GOLDSPINK
GOLDSTICK
GOLDSTONE
GOLDTAIL
GOLDTONE
GOLDTONES
GOLDURN
GOLDURNS
GOLDWORK
GOLDWORKS
GOLDY
GOLE
GOLEM
GOLEMS
GOLES
GOLF
GOLFED
GOLFER
GOLFERS
GOLFIANA
GOLFIANAS
GOLFING
GOLFINGS
GOLFS
GOLGOTHA
GOLGOTHAS
GOLIARD
GOLIARDIC
GOLIARDS
GOLIARDY
GOLIAS
GOLIASED
GOLIASES
GOLIASING
GOLIATH
GOLIATHS
GOLLAN

GOLLAND
GOLLANDS
GOLLANS
GOLLAR
GOLLARED
GOLLARING
GOLLARS
GOLLER
GOLLERED
GOLLERING
GOLLERS
GOLLIED
GOLLIES
GOLLIWOG
GOLLIWOGG
GOLLIWOGS
GOLLOP
GOLLOPED
GOLLOPER
GOLLOPERS
GOLLOPING
GOLLOPS
GOLLY
GOLLYING
GOLLYWOG
GOLLYWOGS
GOLOMYNKA
GOLOSH
GOLOSHE
GOLOSHED
GOLOSHES
GOLOSHING
GOLOSHOES
GOLP
GOLPE
GOLPES
GOLPS
GOMBEEN
GOMBEENS
GOMBO
GOMBOS
GOMBRO
GOMBROON
GOMBROONS
GOMBROS
GOMER
GOMERAL

GOMERALS
GOMEREL
GOMERELS
GOMERIL
GOMERILS
GOMERS
GOMOKU
GOMOKUS
GOMPA
GOMPAS
GOMPHOSES
GOMPHOSIS
GOMUTI
GOMUTIS
GOMUTO
GOMUTOS
GON
GONAD
GONADAL
GONADIAL
GONADIC
GONADS
GONCH
GONCHES
GONDELAY
GONDELAYS
GONDOLA
GONDOLAS
GONDOLIER
GONE
GONEF
GONEFS
GONENESS
GONER
GONERS
GONFALON
GONFALONS
GONFANON
GONFANONS
GONG
GONGED
GONGING
GONGLIKE
GONGS
GONGSTER
GONGSTERS
GONGYO

GONGYOS
GONIA
GONIATITE
GONIDIA
GONIDIAL
GONIDIC
GONIDIUM
GONIF
GONIFF
GONIFFS
GONIFS
GONION
GONIUM
GONK
GONKS
GONNA
GONOCOCCI
GONOCYTE
GONOCYTES
GONODUCT
GONODUCTS
GONOF
GONOFS
GONOPH
GONOPHORE
GONOPHS
GONOPOD
GONOPODS
GONOPORE
GONOPORES
GONORRHEA
GONOSOME
GONOSOMES
GONS
GONYS
GONYSES
GONZO
GONZOS
GOO
GOOBER
GOOBERS
GOOBIES
GOOBY
GOOD
GOODBY
GOODBYE
GOODBYES

GOODBYS	GOOGLING	GOOR	GORALS	GORIEST
GOODFACED	GOOGLY	GOORAL	GORAMIES	GORILLA
GOODFELLA	GOOGOL	GOORALS	GORAMY	GORILLAS
GOODIE	GOOGOLS	GOORIE	GORAS	GORILLIAN
GOODIER	GOOGS	GOORIES	GORBELLY	GORILLINE
GOODIES	GOOIER	GOOROO	GORBLIMEY	GORILLOID
GOODIEST	GOOIEST	GOOROOS	GORBLIMY	GORILY
GOODINESS	GOOILY	GOORS	GORCOCK	GORINESS
GOODISH	GOOINESS	GOORY	GORCOCKS	GORING
GOODLIER	GOOK	GOOS	GORCROW	GORINGS
GOODLIEST	GOOKIER	GOOSANDER	GORCROWS	GORIS
GOODLY	GOOKIEST	GOOSE	GORDITA	GORM
GOODMAN	GOOKS	GOOSED	GORDITAS	GORMAND
GOODMEN	GOOKY	GOOSEFISH	GORE	GORMANDS
GOODNESS	GOOL	GOOSEFOOT	GORED	GORMED
GOODNIGHT	GOOLD	GOOSEGOB	GOREFEST	GORMIER
GOODS	GOOLDS	GOOSEGOBS	GOREFESTS	GORMIEST
GOODSIRE	GOOLEY	GOOSEGOG	GOREHOUND	GORMING
GOODSIRES	GOOLEYS	GOOSEGOGS	GORES	GORMLESS
GOODTIME	GOOLIE	GOOSEHERD	GORGE	GORMS
GOODWIFE	GOOLIES	GOOSENECK	GORGEABLE	GORMY
GOODWILL	GOOLS	GOOSERIES	GORGED	GORP
GOODWILLS	GOOLY	GOOSERY	GORGEDLY	GORPED
GOODWIVES	GOOMBAH	GOOSES	GORGEOUS	GORPING
GOODY	GOOMBAHS	GOOSEY	GORGER	GORPS
GOODYEAR	GOOMBAY	GOOSEYS	GORGERIN	GORS
GOODYEARS	GOOMBAYS	GOOSIER	GORGERINS	GORSE
GOOEY	GOON	GOOSIES	GORGERS	GORSEDD
GOOEYNESS	GOONDA	GOOSIEST	GORGES	GORSEDDS
GOOF	GOONDAS	GOOSINESS	GORGET	GORSES
GOOFBALL	GOONERIES	GOOSING	GORGETED	GORSIER
GOOFBALLS	GOONERY	GOOSY	GORGETS	GORSIEST
GOOFED	GOONEY	GOPAK	GORGIA	GORSOON
GOOFIER	GOONEYS	GOPAKS	GORGIAS	GORSOONS
GOOFIEST	GOONIE	GOPHER	GORGING	GORSY
GOOFILY	GOONIER	GOPHERED	GORGIO	GORY
GOOFINESS	GOONIES	GOPHERING	GORGIOS	GOS
GOOFING	GOONIEST	GOPHERS	GORGON	GOSH
GOOFS	GOONS	GOPIK	GORGONEIA	GOSHAWK
GOOFUS	GOONY	GOPIKS	GORGONIAN	GOSHAWKS
GOOFUSES	GOOP	GOPURA	GORGONISE	GOSHT
GOOFY	GOOPED	GOPURAM	GORGONIZE	GOSHTS
GOOG	GOOPIER	GOPURAMS	GORGONS	GOSLARITE
GOOGLE	GOOPIEST	GOPURAS	GORHEN	GOSLET
GOOGLED	GOOPINESS	GOR	GORHENS	GOSLETS
GOOGLES	GOOPS	GORA	GORI	GOSLING
GOOGLIES	GOOPY	GORAL	GORIER	GOSLINGS

GOSPEL	GOTCH	GOURDES	GOWDEST	GRABBABLE
GOSPELER	GOTCHA	GOURDFUL	GOWDS	GRABBED
GOSPELERS	GOTCHAS	GOURDFULS	GOWDSPINK	GRABBER
GOSPELISE	GOTCHES	GOURDIER	GOWF	GRABBERS
GOSPELIZE	GOTCHIES	GOURDIEST	GOWFED	GRABBIER
GOSPELLED	GOTH	GOURDLIKE	GOWFER	GRABBIEST
GOSPELLER	GOTHIC	GOURDS	GOWFERS	GRABBING
GOSPELLY	GOTHICISE	GOURDY	GOWFING	GRABBLE
GOSPELS	GOTHICISM	GOURMAND	GOWFS	GRABBLED
GOSPODA	GOTHICIZE	GOURMANDS	GOWK	GRABBLER
GOSPODAR	GOTHICS	GOURMET	GOWKS	GRABBLERS
GOSPODARS	GOTHIER	GOURMETS	GOWL	GRABBLES
GOSPODIN	GOTHIEST	GOUSTIER	GOWLAN	GRABBLING
GOSPORT	GOTHITE	GOUSTIEST	GOWLAND	GRABBY
GOSPORTS	GOTHITES	GOUSTROUS	GOWLANDS	GRABEN
GOSS	GOTHS	GOUSTY	GOWLANS	GRABENS
GOSSAMER	GOTHY	GOUT	GOWLED	GRABS
GOSSAMERS	GOTTA	GOUTFLIES	GOWLING	GRACE
GOSSAMERY	GOTTEN	GOUTFLY	GOWLS	GRACED
GOSSAN	GOUACHE	GOUTIER	GOWN	GRACEFUL
GOSSANS	GOUACHES	GOUTIEST	GOWNBOY	GRACELESS
GOSSE	GOUCH	GOUTILY	GOWNBOYS	GRACES
GOSSED	GOUCHED	GOUTINESS	GOWNED	GRACILE
GOSSES	GOUCHES	GOUTS	GOWNING	GRACILES
GOSSIB	GOUCHING	GOUTTE	GOWNMAN	GRACILIS
GOSSIBS	GOUGE	GOUTTES	GOWNMEN	GRACILITY
GOSSING	GOUGED	GOUTWEED	GOWNS	GRACING
GOSSIP	GOUGER	GOUTWEEDS	GOWNSMAN	GRACIOSO
GOSSIPED	GOUGERE	GOUTWORT	GOWNSMEN	GRACIOSOS
GOSSIPER	GOUGERES	GOUTWORTS	GOWPEN	GRACIOUS
GOSSIPERS	GOUGERS	GOUTY	GOWPENFUL	GRACKLE
GOSSIPING	GOUGES	GOV	GOWPENS	GRACKLES
GOSSIPPED	GOUGING	GOVERN	GOX	GRAD
GOSSIPPER	GOUJEERS	GOVERNALL	GOXES	GRADABLE
GOSSIPRY	GOUJON	GOVERNED	GOY	GRADABLES
GOSSIPS	GOUJONS	GOVERNESS	GOYIM	GRADATE
GOSSIPY	GOUK	GOVERNING	GOYISCH	GRADATED
GOSSOON	GOUKS	GOVERNOR	GOYISH	GRADATES
GOSSOONS	GOULASH	GOVERNORS	GOYISHE	GRADATIM
GOSSYPINE	GOULASHES	GOVERNS	GOYLE	GRADATING
GOSSYPOL	GOURA	GOVS	GOYLES	GRADATION
GOSSYPOLS	GOURAMI	GOWAN	GOYS	GRADATORY
GOSTER	GOURAMIES	GOWANED	GOZZAN	GRADDAN
GOSTERED	GOURAMIS	GOWANS	GOZZANS	GRADDANED
GOSTERING	GOURAS	GOWANY	GRAAL	GRADDANS
GOSTERS	GOURD	GOWD	GRAALS	GRADE
GOT	GOURDE	GOWDER	GRAB	GRADED

GRADELESS	GRAFTING	GRAMMA	GRANDKID	GRANTABLE
GRADELIER	GRAFTINGS	GRAMMAGE	GRANDKIDS	GRANTED
GRADELY	GRAFTS	GRAMMAGES	GRANDLY	GRANTEE
GRADER	GRAHAM	GRAMMAR	GRANDMA	GRANTEES
GRADERS	GRAHAMS	GRAMMARS	GRANDMAMA	GRANTER
GRADES	GRAIL	GRAMMAS	GRANDMAS	GRANTERS
GRADIENT	GRAILE	GRAMMATIC	GRANDNESS	GRANTING
GRADIENTS	GRAILES	GRAMME	GRANDPA	GRANTOR
GRADIN	GRAILS	GRAMMES	GRANDPAPA	GRANTORS
GRADINE	GRAIN	GRAMOCHE	GRANDPAS	GRANTS
GRADINES	GRAINAGE	GRAMOCHES	GRANDS	GRANTSMAN
GRADING	GRAINAGES	GRAMP	GRANDSIR	GRANTSMEN
GRADINGS	GRAINE	GRAMPA	GRANDSIRE	GRANULAR
GRADINI	GRAINED	GRAMPAS	GRANDSIRS	GRANULARY
GRADINO	GRAINER	GRAMPIES	GRANDSON	GRANULATE
GRADINS	GRAINERS	GRAMPS	GRANDSONS	GRANULE
GRADS	GRAINES	GRAMPUS	GRANFER	GRANULES
GRADUAL	GRAINIER	GRAMPUSES	GRANFERS	GRANULITE
GRADUALLY	GRAINIEST	GRAMPY	GRANGE	GRANULOMA
GRADUALS	GRAINING	GRAMS	GRANGER	GRANULOSE
GRADUAND	GRAININGS	GRAN	GRANGERS	GRANULOUS
GRADUANDS	GRAINLESS	GRANA	GRANGES	GRANUM
GRADUATE	GRAINS	GRANARIES	GRANITA	GRAPE
GRADUATED	GRAINY	GRANARY	GRANITAS	GRAPED
GRADUATES	GRAIP	GRAND	GRANITE	GRAPELESS
GRADUATOR	GRAIPS	GRANDAD	GRANITES	GRAPELICE
GRADUS	GRAITH	GRANDADDY	GRANITIC	GRAPELIKE
GRADUSES	GRAITHED	GRANDADS	GRANITISE	GRAPERIES
GRAECISE	GRAITHING	GRANDAM	GRANITITE	GRAPERY
GRAECISED	GRAITHLY	GRANDAME	GRANITIZE	GRAPES
GRAECISES	GRAITHS	GRANDAMES	GRANITOID	GRAPESEED
GRAECIZE	GRAKLE	GRANDAMS	GRANIVORE	GRAPESHOT
GRAECIZED	GRAKLES	GRANDAUNT	GRANNAM	GRAPETREE
GRAECIZES	GRALLOCH	GRANDBABY	GRANNAMS	GRAPEVINE
GRAFF	GRALLOCHS	GRANDDAD	GRANNIE	GRAPEY
GRAFFED	GRAM	GRANDDADS	GRANNIED	GRAPH
GRAFFING	GRAMA	GRANDDAM	GRANNIES	GRAPHED
GRAFFITI	GRAMARIES	GRANDDAMS	GRANNOM	GRAPHEME
GRAFFITIS	GRAMARY	GRANDE	GRANNOMS	GRAPHEMES
GRAFFITO	GRAMARYE	GRANDEE	GRANNY	GRAPHEMIC
GRAFFS	GRAMARYES	GRANDEES	GRANNYING	GRAPHENE
GRAFT	GRAMAS	GRANDER	GRANNYISH	GRAPHENES
GRAFTAGE	GRAMASH	GRANDEST	GRANOLA	GRAPHIC
GRAFTAGES	GRAMASHES	GRANDEUR	GRANOLAS	GRAPHICAL
GRAFTED	GRAME	GRANDEURS	GRANOLITH	GRAPHICLY
GRAFTER	GRAMERCY	GRANDIOSE	GRANS	GRAPHICS
GRAFTERS	GRAMES	GRANDIOSO	GRANT	GRAPHING

GRAPHITE	GRASSLAND	GRAVADLAX	GRAVURE	GRAZIERS
GRAPHITES	GRASSLESS	GRAVAMEN	GRAVURES	GRAZING
GRAPHITIC	GRASSLIKE	GRAVAMENS	GRAVY	GRAZINGLY
GRAPHIUM	GRASSPLOT	GRAVAMINA	GRAY	GRAZINGS
GRAPHIUMS	GRASSQUIT	GRAVE	GRAYBACK	GRAZIOSO
GRAPHS	GRASSROOT	GRAVED	GRAYBACKS	GREASE
GRAPIER	GRASSUM	GRAVEL	GRAYBEARD	GREASED
GRAPIEST	GRASSUMS	GRAVELED	GRAYED	GREASER
GRAPINESS	GRASSY	GRAVELESS	GRAYER	GREASERS
GRAPING	GRASTE	GRAVELIKE	GRAYEST	GREASES
GRAPLE	GRAT	GRAVELING	GRAYFISH	GREASIER
GRAPLES	GRATE	GRAVELISH	GRAYFLIES	GREASIES
GRAPLIN	GRATED	GRAVELLED	GRAYFLY	GREASIEST
GRAPLINE	GRATEFUL	GRAVELLY	GRAYHEAD	GREASILY
GRAPLINES	GRATELESS	GRAVELS	GRAYHEADS	GREASING
GRAPLINS	GRATER	GRAVELY	GRAYHEN	GREASY
GRAPNEL	GRATERS	GRAVEN	GRAYHENS	GREAT
GRAPNELS	GRATES	GRAVENESS	GRAYHOUND	GREATCOAT
GRAPPA	GRATICULE	GRAVER	GRAYING	GREATEN
GRAPPAS	GRATIFIED	GRAVERS	GRAYISH	GREATENED
GRAPPLE	GRATIFIER	GRAVES	GRAYLAG	GREATENS
GRAPPLED	GRATIFIES	GRAVESIDE	GRAYLAGS	GREATER
GRAPPLER	GRATIFY	GRAVESITE	GRAYLE	GREATEST
GRAPPLERS	GRATIN	GRAVEST	GRAYLES	GREATESTS
GRAPPLES	GRATINATE	GRAVEWARD	GRAYLING	GREATLY
GRAPPLING	GRATINE	GRAVEYARD	GRAYLINGS	GREATNESS
GRAPY	GRATINEE	GRAVID	GRAYLIST	GREATS
GRASP	GRATINEED	GRAVIDA	GRAYLISTS	GREAVE
GRASPABLE	GRATINEES	GRAVIDAE	GRAYLY	GREAVED
GRASPED	GRATING	GRAVIDAS	GRAYMAIL	GREAVES
GRASPER	GRATINGLY	GRAVIDITY	GRAYMAILS	GREAVING
GRASPERS	GRATINGS	GRAVIDLY	GRAYNESS	GREBE
GRASPING	GRATINS	GRAVIES	GRAYOUT	GREBES
GRASPLESS	GRATIS	GRAVING	GRAYOUTS	GREBO
GRASPS	GRATITUDE	GRAVINGS	GRAYS	GREBOS
GRASS	GRATTOIR	GRAVIS	GRAYSCALE	GRECE
GRASSBIRD	GRATTOIRS	GRAVITAS	GRAYSTONE	GRECES
GRASSED	GRATUITY	GRAVITATE	GRAYWACKE	GRECIAN
GRASSER	GRATULANT	GRAVITIES	GRAYWATER	GRECIANS
GRASSERS	GRATULATE	GRAVITINO	GRAZABLE	GRECISE
GRASSES	GRAUNCH	GRAVITON	GRAZE	GRECISED
GRASSHOOK	GRAUNCHED	GRAVITONS	GRAZEABLE	GRECISES
GRASSIER	GRAUNCHER	GRAVITY	GRAZED	GRECISING
GRASSIEST	GRAUNCHES	GRAVLAKS	GRAZER	GRECIZE
GRASSILY	GRAUPEL	GRAVLAX	GRAZERS	GRECIZED
GRASSING	GRAUPELS	GRAVLAXES	GRAZES	GRECIZES
GRASSINGS	GRAV	GRAVS	GRAZIER	GRECIZING

GRECQUE
GRECQUES
GREE
GREEBO
GREEBOES
GREECE
GREECES
GREED
GREEDIER
GREEDIEST
GREEDILY
GREEDLESS
GREEDS
GREEDSOME
GREEDY
GREEGREE
GREEGREES
GREEING
GREEK
GREEKED
GREEKING
GREEKINGS
GREEN
GREENBACK
GREENBELT
GREENBONE
GREENBUG
GREENBUGS
GREENED
GREENER
GREENERS
GREENERY
GREENEST
GREENEYE
GREENEYES
GREENFLY
GREENGAGE
GREENHAND
GREENHEAD
GREENHORN
GREENIE
GREENIER
GREENIES
GREENIEST
GREENING
GREENINGS
GREENISH

GREENLET
GREENLETS
GREENLING
GREENLIT
GREENLY
GREENMAIL
GREENNESS
GREENROOM
GREENS
GREENSAND
GREENSICK
GREENSOME
GREENTH
GREENTHS
GREENWASH
GREENWAY
GREENWAYS
GREENWEED
GREENWING
GREENWOOD
GREENY
GREES
GREESE
GREESES
GREESING
GREESINGS
GREET
GREETE
GREETED
GREETER
GREETERS
GREETES
GREETING
GREETINGS
GREETS
GREFFIER
GREFFIERS
GREGALE
GREGALES
GREGARIAN
GREGARINE
GREGATIM
GREGE
GREGED
GREGES
GREGING
GREGO

GREGOS
GREIGE
GREIGES
GREIN
GREINED
GREINING
GREINS
GREISEN
GREISENS
GREISLY
GREMIAL
GREMIALS
GREMLIN
GREMLINS
GREMMIE
GREMMIES
GREMMY
GREMOLATA
GREN
GRENACHE
GRENACHES
GRENADE
GRENADES
GRENADIER
GRENADINE
GRENNED
GRENNING
GRENS
GRESE
GRESES
GRESSING
GRESSINGS
GREVE
GREVES
GREVILLEA
GREW
GREWED
GREWHOUND
GREWING
GREWS
GREWSOME
GREWSOMER
GREX
GREXES
GREY
GREYBACK
GREYBACKS

GREYBEARD
GREYED
GREYER
GREYEST
GREYHEAD
GREYHEADS
GREYHEN
GREYHENS
GREYHOUND
GREYING
GREYINGS
GREYISH
GREYLAG
GREYLAGS
GREYLIST
GREYLISTS
GREYLY
GREYNESS
GREYS
GREYSCALE
GREYSTONE
GREYWACKE
GRIBBLE
GRIBBLES
GRICE
GRICED
GRICER
GRICERS
GRICES
GRICING
GRICINGS
GRID
GRIDDED
GRIDDER
GRIDDERS
GRIDDING
GRIDDLE
GRIDDLED
GRIDDLES
GRIDDLING
GRIDE
GRIDED
GRIDELIN
GRIDELINS
GRIDES
GRIDING
GRIDIRON

GRIDIRONS
GRIDLOCK
GRIDLOCKS
GRIDS
GRIECE
GRIECED
GRIECES
GRIEF
GRIEFER
GRIEFERS
GRIEFFUL
GRIEFLESS
GRIEFS
GRIESIE
GRIESLY
GRIESY
GRIEVANCE
GRIEVANT
GRIEVANTS
GRIEVE
GRIEVED
GRIEVER
GRIEVERS
GRIEVES
GRIEVING
GRIEVINGS
GRIEVOUS
GRIFF
GRIFFE
GRIFFES
GRIFFIN
GRIFFINS
GRIFFON
GRIFFONS
GRIFFS
GRIFT
GRIFTED
GRIFTER
GRIFTERS
GRIFTING
GRIFTS
GRIG
GRIGGED
GRIGGING
GRIGRI
GRIGRIS
GRIGS

G

GRIKE	GRINCHES	GRIPPY	GRITTER	GROGGERY
GRIKES	GRIND	GRIPS	GRITTERS	GROGGIER
GRILL	GRINDED	GRIPSACK	GRITTEST	GROGGIEST
GRILLADE	GRINDELIA	GRIPSACKS	GRITTIER	GROGGILY
GRILLADES	GRINDER	GRIPT	GRITTIEST	GROGGING
GRILLAGE	GRINDERS	GRIPTAPE	GRITTILY	GROGGY
GRILLAGES	GRINDERY	GRIPTAPES	GRITTING	GROGRAM
GRILLE	GRINDING	GRIPY	GRITTINGS	GROGRAMS
GRILLED	GRINDINGS	GRIS	GRITTY	GROGS
GRILLER	GRINDS	GRISAILLE	GRIVATION	GROGSHOP
GRILLERS	GRINGA	GRISE	GRIVET	GROGSHOPS
GRILLERY	GRINGAS	GRISED	GRIVETS	GROIN
GRILLES	GRINGO	GRISELY	GRIZ	GROINED
GRILLING	GRINGOS	GRISEOUS	GRIZE	GROINING
GRILLINGS	GRINNED	GRISES	GRIZES	GROININGS
GRILLION	GRINNER	GRISETTE	GRIZZLE	GROINS
GRILLIONS	GRINNERS	GRISETTES	GRIZZLED	GROK
GRILLROOM	GRINNING	GRISGRIS	GRIZZLER	GROKED
GRILLS	GRINNINGS	GRISING	GRIZZLERS	GROKING
GRILLWORK	GRINS	GRISKIN	GRIZZLES	GROKKED
GRILSE	GRIOT	GRISKINS	GRIZZLIER	GROKKING
GRILSES	GRIOTS	GRISLED	GRIZZLIES	GROKS
GRIM	GRIP	GRISLIER	GRIZZLING	GROMA
GRIMACE	GRIPE	GRISLIES	GRIZZLY	GROMAS
GRIMACED	GRIPED	GRISLIEST	GROAN	GROMET
GRIMACER	GRIPER	GRISLY	GROANED	GROMETS
GRIMACERS	GRIPERS	GRISON	GROANER	GROMMET
GRIMACES	GRIPES	GRISONS	GROANERS	GROMMETED
GRIMACING	GRIPEY	GRISSINI	GROANFUL	GROMMETS
GRIMALKIN	GRIPIER	GRISSINO	GROANING	GROMWELL
GRIME	GRIPIEST	GRIST	GROANINGS	GROMWELLS
GRIMED	GRIPING	GRISTER	GROANS	GRONE
GRIMES	GRIPINGLY	GRISTERS	GROAT	GRONED
GRIMIER	GRIPINGS	GRISTLE	GROATS	GRONEFULL
GRIMIEST	GRIPLE	GRISTLES	GROCER	GRONES
GRIMILY	GRIPMAN	GRISTLIER	GROCERIES	GRONING
GRIMINESS	GRIPMEN	GRISTLY	GROCERS	GROOF
GRIMING	GRIPPE	GRISTMILL	GROCERY	GROOFS
GRIMLY	GRIPPED	GRISTS	GROCKED	GROOLIER
GRIMMER	GRIPPER	GRISY	GROCKING	GROOLIEST
GRIMMEST	GRIPPERS	GRIT	GROCKLE	GROOLY
GRIMNESS	GRIPPES	GRITH	GROCKLES	GROOM
GRIMOIRE	GRIPPIER	GRITHS	GRODIER	GROOMED
GRIMOIRES	GRIPPIEST	GRITLESS	GRODIEST	GROOMER
GRIMY	GRIPPING	GRITS	GRODY	GROOMERS
GRIN	GRIPPLE	GRITSTONE	GROG	GROOMING
GRINCH	GRIPPLES	GRITTED	GROGGED	GROOMINGS

GROOMS
GROOMSMAN
GROOMSMEN
GROOVE
GROOVED
GROOVER
GROOVERS
GROOVES
GROOVIER
GROOVIEST
GROOVILY
GROOVING
GROOVY
GROPE
GROPED
GROPER
GROPERS
GROPES
GROPING
GROPINGLY
GROSBEAK
GROSBEAKS
GROSCHEN
GROSCHENS
GROSER
GROSERS
GROSERT
GROSERTS
GROSET
GROSETS
GROSGRAIN
GROSS
GROSSART
GROSSARTS
GROSSED
GROSSER
GROSSERS
GROSSES
GROSSEST
GROSSING
GROSSLY
GROSSNESS
GROSSULAR
GROSZ
GROSZE
GROSZY
GROT

GROTESQUE
GROTS
GROTTIER
GROTTIEST
GROTTO
GROTTOED
GROTTOES
GROTTOS
GROTTY
GROUCH
GROUCHED
GROUCHES
GROUCHIER
GROUCHILY
GROUCHING
GROUCHY
GROUF
GROUFS
GROUGH
GROUGHS
GROUND
GROUNDAGE
GROUNDED
GROUNDEN
GROUNDER
GROUNDERS
GROUNDHOG
GROUNDING
GROUNDMAN
GROUNDMEN
GROUNDNUT
GROUNDOUT
GROUNDS
GROUNDSEL
GROUP
GROUPABLE
GROUPAGE
GROUPAGES
GROUPED
GROUPER
GROUPERS
GROUPIE
GROUPIES
GROUPING
GROUPINGS
GROUPIST
GROUPISTS

GROUPLET
GROUPLETS
GROUPOID
GROUPOIDS
GROUPS
GROUPWARE
GROUPWORK
GROUPY
GROUSE
GROUSED
GROUSER
GROUSERS
GROUSES
GROUSEST
GROUSING
GROUT
GROUTED
GROUTER
GROUTERS
GROUTIER
GROUTIEST
GROUTING
GROUTINGS
GROUTS
GROUTY
GROVE
GROVED
GROVEL
GROVELED
GROVELER
GROVELERS
GROVELESS
GROVELING
GROVELLED
GROVELLER
GROVELS
GROVES
GROVET
GROVETS
GROVIER
GROVIEST
GROVY
GROW
GROWABLE
GROWER
GROWERS
GROWING

GROWINGLY
GROWINGS
GROWL
GROWLED
GROWLER
GROWLERS
GROWLERY
GROWLIER
GROWLIEST
GROWLING
GROWLINGS
GROWLS
GROWLY
GROWN
GROWNUP
GROWNUPS
GROWS
GROWTH
GROWTHIER
GROWTHIST
GROWTHS
GROWTHY
GROYNE
GROYNES
GROZING
GRR
GRRL
GRRLS
GRRRL
GRRRLS
GRUB
GRUBBED
GRUBBER
GRUBBERS
GRUBBIER
GRUBBIEST
GRUBBILY
GRUBBING
GRUBBLE
GRUBBLED
GRUBBLES
GRUBBLING
GRUBBY
GRUBS
GRUBSTAKE
GRUBWORM
GRUBWORMS

GRUDGE
GRUDGED
GRUDGEFUL
GRUDGER
GRUDGERS
GRUDGES
GRUDGING
GRUDGINGS
GRUE
GRUED
GRUEING
GRUEL
GRUELED
GRUELER
GRUELERS
GRUELING
GRUELINGS
GRUELLED
GRUELLER
GRUELLERS
GRUELLING
GRUELS
GRUES
GRUESOME
GRUESOMER
GRUFE
GRUFES
GRUFF
GRUFFED
GRUFFER
GRUFFEST
GRUFFIER
GRUFFIEST
GRUFFILY
GRUFFING
GRUFFISH
GRUFFLY
GRUFFNESS
GRUFFS
GRUFFY
GRUFTED
GRUGRU
GRUGRUS
GRUIFORM
GRUING
GRUM
GRUMBLE

G

GRUMBLED	GRUNION	GUACO	GUARANIES	GUBS
GRUMBLER	GRUNIONS	GUACOS	GUARANIS	GUCK
GRUMBLERS	GRUNT	GUAIAC	GUARANTEE	GUCKIER
GRUMBLES	GRUNTED	GUAIACOL	GUARANTOR	GUCKIEST
GRUMBLIER	GRUNTER	GUAIACOLS	GUARANTY	GUCKS
GRUMBLING	GRUNTERS	GUAIACS	GUARD	GUCKY
GRUMBLY	GRUNTING	GUAIACUM	GUARDABLE	GUDDLE
GRUME	GRUNTINGS	GUAIACUMS	GUARDAGE	GUDDLED
GRUMES	GRUNTLE	GUAIOCUM	GUARDAGES	GUDDLES
GRUMLY	GRUNTLED	GUAIOCUMS	GUARDANT	GUDDLING
GRUMMER	GRUNTLES	GUAN	GUARDANTS	GUDE
GRUMMEST	GRUNTLING	GUANA	GUARDDOG	GUDEMAN
GRUMMET	GRUNTS	GUANABANA	GUARDDOGS	GUDEMEN
GRUMMETED	GRUPPETTI	GUANACO	GUARDED	GUDES
GRUMMETS	GRUPPETTO	GUANACOS	GUARDEDLY	GUDESIRE
GRUMNESS	GRUSHIE	GUANAS	GUARDEE	GUDESIRES
GRUMOSE	GRUTCH	GUANASE	GUARDEES	GUDEWIFE
GRUMOUS	GRUTCHED	GUANASES	GUARDER	GUDEWIVES
GRUMP	GRUTCHES	GUANAY	GUARDERS	GUDGEON
GRUMPED	GRUTCHING	GUANAYS	GUARDIAN	GUDGEONED
GRUMPH	GRUTTEN	GUANAZOLO	GUARDIANS	GUDGEONS
GRUMPHED	GRUYERE	GUANGO	GUARDING	GUE
GRUMPHIE	GRUYERES	GUANGOS	GUARDLESS	GUELDER
GRUMPHIES	GRYCE	GUANIDIN	GUARDLIKE	GUENON
GRUMPHING	GRYCES	GUANIDINE	GUARDRAIL	GUENONS
GRUMPHS	GRYDE	GUANIDINS	GUARDROOM	GUERDON
GRUMPHY	GRYDED	GUANIN	GUARDS	GUERDONED
GRUMPIER	GRYDES	GUANINE	GUARDSHIP	GUERDONER
GRUMPIES	GRYDING	GUANINES	GUARDSMAN	GUERDONS
GRUMPIEST	GRYESY	GUANINS	GUARDSMEN	GUEREZA
GRUMPILY	GRYFON	GUANO	GUARISH	GUEREZAS
GRUMPING	GRYFONS	GUANOS	GUARISHED	GUERIDON
GRUMPISH	GRYKE	GUANOSINE	GUARISHES	GUERIDONS
GRUMPS	GRYKES	GUANS	GUARS	GUERILLA
GRUMPY	GRYPE	GUANXI	GUAVA	GUERILLAS
GRUND	GRYPES	GUANXIS	GUAVAS	GUERITE
GRUNDIES	GRYPHON	GUANYLIC	GUAYABERA	GUERITES
GRUNDLE	GRYPHONS	GUAR	GUAYULE	GUERNSEY
GRUNDLES	GRYPT	GUARACHA	GUAYULES	GUERNSEYS
GRUNGE	GRYSBOK	GUARACHAS	GUB	GUERRILLA
GRUNGER	GRYSBOKS	GUARACHE	GUBBAH	GUES
GRUNGERS	GRYSELY	GUARACHES	GUBBAHS	GUESS
GRUNGES	GRYSIE	GUARACHI	GUBBED	GUESSABLE
GRUNGEY	GU	GUARACHIS	GUBBING	GUESSED
GRUNGIER	GUACAMOLE	GUARANA	GUBBINS	GUESSER
GRUNGIEST	GUACHARO	GUARANAS	GUBBINSES	GUESSERS
GRUNGY	GUACHAROS	GUARANI	GUBERNIYA	GUESSES

G

GUESSING
GUESSINGS
GUESSWORK
GUEST
GUESTBOOK
GUESTED
GUESTEN
GUESTENED
GUESTENS
GUESTING
GUESTS
GUESTWISE
GUFF
GUFFAW
GUFFAWED
GUFFAWING
GUFFAWS
GUFFIE
GUFFIES
GUFFS
GUGA
GUGAS
GUGGLE
GUGGLED
GUGGLES
GUGGLING
GUGLET
GUGLETS
GUICHET
GUICHETS
GUID
GUIDABLE
GUIDAGE
GUIDAGES
GUIDANCE
GUIDANCES
GUIDE
GUIDEBOOK
GUIDED
GUIDELESS
GUIDELINE
GUIDEPOST
GUIDER
GUIDERS
GUIDES
GUIDESHIP
GUIDEWAY

GUIDEWAYS
GUIDEWORD
GUIDING
GUIDINGS
GUIDON
GUIDONS
GUIDS
GUILD
GUILDER
GUILDERS
GUILDHALL
GUILDRIES
GUILDRY
GUILDS
GUILDSHIP
GUILDSMAN
GUILDSMEN
GUILE
GUILED
GUILEFUL
GUILELESS
GUILER
GUILERS
GUILES
GUILING
GUILLEMET
GUILLEMOT
GUILLOCHE
GUILT
GUILTED
GUILTIER
GUILTIEST
GUILTILY
GUILTING
GUILTLESS
GUILTS
GUILTY
GUIMBARD
GUIMBARDS
GUIMP
GUIMPE
GUIMPED
GUIMPES
GUIMPING
GUIMPS
GUINEA
GUINEAS

GUINEP
GUINEPS
GUIPURE
GUIPURES
GUIRO
GUIROS
GUISARD
GUISARDS
GUISE
GUISED
GUISER
GUISERS
GUISES
GUISING
GUISINGS
GUITAR
GUITARIST
GUITARS
GUITGUIT
GUITGUITS
GUIZER
GUIZERS
GUL
GULA
GULAG
GULAGS
GULAR
GULARS
GULAS
GULCH
GULCHED
GULCHES
GULCHING
GULDEN
GULDENS
GULE
GULES
GULET
GULETS
GULF
GULFED
GULFIER
GULFIEST
GULFING
GULFLIKE
GULFS
GULFWEED

GULFWEEDS
GULFY
GULL
GULLABLE
GULLABLY
GULLED
GULLER
GULLERIES
GULLERS
GULLERY
GULLET
GULLETS
GULLEY
GULLEYED
GULLEYING
GULLEYS
GULLIBLE
GULLIBLY
GULLIED
GULLIES
GULLING
GULLISH
GULLS
GULLWING
GULLY
GULLYING
GULOSITY
GULP
GULPED
GULPER
GULPERS
GULPH
GULPHS
GULPIER
GULPIEST
GULPING
GULPINGLY
GULPS
GULPY
GULS
GULY
GUM
GUMBALL
GUMBALLS
GUMBO
GUMBOIL
GUMBOILS

GUMBOOT
GUMBOOTS
GUMBOS
GUMBOTIL
GUMBOTILS
GUMDROP
GUMDROPS
GUMLANDS
GUMLESS
GUMLIKE
GUMLINE
GUMLINES
GUMMA
GUMMAS
GUMMATA
GUMMATOUS
GUMMED
GUMMER
GUMMERS
GUMMI
GUMMIER
GUMMIES
GUMMIEST
GUMMILY
GUMMINESS
GUMMING
GUMMINGS
GUMMIS
GUMMITE
GUMMITES
GUMMOSE
GUMMOSES
GUMMOSIS
GUMMOSITY
GUMMOUS
GUMMY
GUMNUT
GUMNUTS
GUMP
GUMPED
GUMPHION
GUMPHIONS
GUMPING
GUMPS
GUMPTION
GUMPTIONS
GUMPTIOUS

GUMS
GUMSHIELD
GUMSHOE
GUMSHOED
GUMSHOES
GUMSUCKER
GUMTREE
GUMTREES
GUMWEED
GUMWEEDS
GUMWOOD
GUMWOODS
GUN
GUNBOAT
GUNBOATS
GUNCOTTON
GUNDIES
GUNDOG
GUNDOGS
GUNDY
GUNFIGHT
GUNFIGHTS
GUNFIRE
GUNFIRES
GUNFLINT
GUNFLINTS
GUNFOUGHT
GUNG
GUNGE
GUNGED
GUNGES
GUNGIER
GUNGIEST
GUNGING
GUNGY
GUNHOUSE
GUNHOUSES
GUNITE
GUNITES
GUNK
GUNKED
GUNKHOLE
GUNKHOLED
GUNKHOLES
GUNKIER
GUNKIEST
GUNKING

GUNKS
GUNKY
GUNLAYER
GUNLAYERS
GUNLESS
GUNLOCK
GUNLOCKS
GUNMAKER
GUNMAKERS
GUNMAN
GUNMEN
GUNMETAL
GUNMETALS
GUNNAGE
GUNNAGES
GUNNED
GUNNEL
GUNNELS
GUNNEN
GUNNER
GUNNERA
GUNNERAS
GUNNERIES
GUNNERS
GUNNERY
GUNNIES
GUNNING
GUNNINGS
GUNNY
GUNNYBAG
GUNNYBAGS
GUNNYSACK
GUNPAPER
GUNPAPERS
GUNPLAY
GUNPLAYS
GUNPOINT
GUNPOINTS
GUNPORT
GUNPORTS
GUNPOWDER
GUNROOM
GUNROOMS
GUNRUNNER
GUNS
GUNSEL
GUNSELS

GUNSHIP
GUNSHIPS
GUNSHOT
GUNSHOTS
GUNSIGHT
GUNSIGHTS
GUNSMITH
GUNSMITHS
GUNSTICK
GUNSTICKS
GUNSTOCK
GUNSTOCKS
GUNSTONE
GUNSTONES
GUNTER
GUNTERS
GUNWALE
GUNWALES
GUNYAH
GUNYAHS
GUP
GUPPIES
GUPPY
GUPS
GUQIN
GUQINS
GUR
GURAMI
GURAMIS
GURDIES
GURDWARA
GURDWARAS
GURDY
GURGE
GURGED
GURGES
GURGING
GURGLE
GURGLED
GURGLES
GURGLET
GURGLETS
GURGLIER
GURGLIEST
GURGLING
GURGLY
GURGOYLE

GURGOYLES
GURJUN
GURJUNS
GURL
GURLED
GURLET
GURLETS
GURLIER
GURLIEST
GURLING
GURLS
GURLY
GURN
GURNARD
GURNARDS
GURNED
GURNET
GURNETS
GURNEY
GURNEYS
GURNING
GURNS
GURRAH
GURRAHS
GURRIER
GURRIERS
GURRIES
GURRY
GURS
GURSH
GURSHES
GURU
GURUDOM
GURUDOMS
GURUISM
GURUISMS
GURUS
GURUSHIP
GURUSHIPS
GUS
GUSH
GUSHED
GUSHER
GUSHERS
GUSHES
GUSHIER
GUSHIEST

GUSHILY
GUSHINESS
GUSHING
GUSHINGLY
GUSHY
GUSLA
GUSLAR
GUSLARS
GUSLAS
GUSLE
GUSLES
GUSLI
GUSLIS
GUSSET
GUSSETED
GUSSETING
GUSSETS
GUSSIE
GUSSIED
GUSSIES
GUSSY
GUSSYING
GUST
GUSTABLE
GUSTABLES
GUSTATION
GUSTATIVE
GUSTATORY
GUSTED
GUSTFUL
GUSTIE
GUSTIER
GUSTIEST
GUSTILY
GUSTINESS
GUSTING
GUSTLESS
GUSTO
GUSTOES
GUSTOS
GUSTS
GUSTY
GUT
GUTBUCKET
GUTCHER
GUTCHERS
GUTFUL

GUTFULS	GUV	GYMKHANAS	GYNOECIUM	GYRATION
GUTLESS	GUVS	GYMMAL	GYNOPHOBE	GYRATIONS
GUTLESSLY	GUY	GYMMALS	GYNOPHORE	GYRATOR
GUTLIKE	GUYED	GYMNASIA	GYNOS	GYRATORS
GUTROT	GUYING	GYMNASIAL	GYNY	GYRATORY
GUTROTS	GUYLE	GYMNASIC	GYOZA	GYRE
GUTS	GUYLED	GYMNASIEN	GYOZAS	GYRED
GUTSED	GUYLER	GYMNASIUM	GYP	GYRENE
GUTSER	GUYLERS	GYMNAST	GYPLURE	GYRENES
GUTSERS	GUYLES	GYMNASTIC	GYPLURES	GYRES
GUTSES	GUYLINE	GYMNASTS	GYPO	GYRFALCON
GUTSFUL	GUYLINER	GYMNIC	GYPOS	GYRI
GUTSFULS	GUYLINERS	GYMNOSOPH	GYPPED	GYRING
GUTSIER	GUYLINES	GYMP	GYPPER	GYRO
GUTSIEST	GUYLING	GYMPED	GYPPERS	GYROCAR
GUTSILY	GUYOT	GYMPIE	GYPPIE	GYROCARS
GUTSINESS	GUYOTS	GYMPIES	GYPPIES	GYRODYNE
GUTSING	GUYS	GYMPING	GYPPING	GYRODYNES
GUTSY	GUYSE	GYMPS	GYPPO	GYROIDAL
GUTTA	GUYSES	GYMS	GYPPOS	GYROLITE
GUTTAE	GUZZLE	GYMSLIP	GYPPY	GYROLITES
GUTTAS	GUZZLED	GYMSLIPS	GYPS	GYROMANCY
GUTTATE	GUZZLER	GYMSUIT	GYPSEIAN	GYRON
GUTTATED	GUZZLERS	GYMSUITS	GYPSEOUS	GYRONIC
GUTTATES	GUZZLES	GYNAE	GYPSIED	GYRONNY
GUTTATING	GUZZLING	GYNAECEA	GYPSIES	GYRONS
GUTTATION	GWEDUC	GYNAECEUM	GYPSTER	GYROPILOT
GUTTED	GWEDUCK	GYNAECIA	GYPSTERS	GYROPLANE
GUTTER	GWEDUCKS	GYNAECIUM	GYPSUM	GYROS
GUTTERED	GWEDUCS	GYNAECOID	GYPSUMS	GYROSCOPE
GUTTERING	GWINE	GYNAES	GYPSY	GYROSE
GUTTERS	GWINIAD	GYNANDRY	GYPSYDOM	GYROSTAT
GUTTERY	GWINIADS	GYNARCHIC	GYPSYDOMS	GYROSTATS
GUTTIER	GWYNIAD	GYNARCHY	GYPSYHOOD	GYROUS
GUTTIES	GWYNIADS	GYNECIA	GYPSYING	GYROVAGUE
GUTTIEST	GYAL	GYNECIC	GYPSYISH	GYRUS
GUTTING	GYALS	GYNECIUM	GYPSYISM	GYRUSES
GUTTLE	GYBE	GYNECOID	GYPSYISMS	GYTE
GUTTLED	GYBED	GYNIATRY	GYPSYWORT	GYTES
GUTTLER	GYBES	GYNIE	GYRAL	GYTRASH
GUTTLERS	GYBING	GYNIES	GYRALLY	GYTRASHES
GUTTLES	GYELD	GYNNEY	GYRANT	GYTTJA
GUTTLING	GYELDS	GYNNEYS	GYRASE	GYTTJAS
GUTTURAL	GYLDEN	GYNNIES	GYRASES	GYVE
GUTTURALS	GYM	GYNNY	GYRATE	GYVED
GUTTY	GYMBAL	GYNO	GYRATED	GYVES
GUTZER	GYMBALS	GYNOCRACY	GYRATES	GYVING
GUTZERS	GYMKHANA	GYNOECIA	GYRATING	

G

H

HA	HABOOB	HACKLETS	HADJI	HAERES
HAAF	HABOOBS	HACKLIER	HADJIS	HAES
HAAFS	HABU	HACKLIEST	HADROME	HAET
HAANEPOOT	HABUS	HACKLING	HADROMES	HAETS
HAAR	HACEK	HACKLY	HADRON	HAFF
HAARS	HACEKS	HACKMAN	HADRONIC	HAFFET
HABANERA	HACENDADO	HACKMEN	HADRONS	HAFFETS
HABANERAS	HACHIS	HACKNEY	HADROSAUR	HAFFIT
HABANERO	HACHURE	HACKNEYED	HADS	HAFFITS
HABANEROS	HACHURED	HACKNEYS	HADST	HAFFLIN
HABDABS	HACHURES	HACKS	HAE	HAFFLINS
HABDALAH	HACHURING	HACKSAW	HAECCEITY	HAFFS
HABDALAHS	HACIENDA	HACKSAWED	HAED	HAFIZ
HABENDUM	HACIENDAS	HACKSAWN	HAEING	HAFIZES
HABENDUMS	HACK	HACKSAWS	HAEM	HAFNIUM
HABERDINE	HACKABLE	HACKWORK	HAEMAL	HAFNIUMS
HABERGEON	HACKAMORE	HACKWORKS	HAEMATAL	HAFT
HABILABLE	HACKBERRY	HACQUETON	HAEMATEIN	HAFTARA
HABILE	HACKBOLT	HAD	HAEMATIC	HAFTARAH
HABIT	HACKBOLTS	HADAL	HAEMATICS	HAFTARAHS
HABITABLE	HACKBUT	HADARIM	HAEMATIN	HAFTARAS
HABITABLY	HACKBUTS	HADAWAY	HAEMATINS	HAFTAROS
HABITAN	HACKED	HADDEN	HAEMATITE	HAFTAROT
HABITANS	HACKEE	HADDEST	HAEMATOID	HAFTAROTH
HABITANT	HACKEES	HADDIE	HAEMATOMA	HAFTED
HABITANTS	HACKER	HADDIES	HAEMIC	HAFTER
HABITAT	HACKERIES	HADDING	HAEMIN	HAFTERS
HABITATS	HACKERS	HADDOCK	HAEMINS	HAFTING
HABITED	HACKERY	HADDOCKS	HAEMOCOEL	HAFTORAH
HABITING	HACKETTE	HADE	HAEMOCYTE	HAFTORAHS
HABITS	HACKETTES	HADED	HAEMOID	HAFTOROS
HABITUAL	HACKIE	HADEDAH	HAEMOLYSE	HAFTOROT
HABITUALS	HACKIES	HADEDAHS	HAEMOLYZE	HAFTOROTH
HABITUATE	HACKING	HADES	HAEMONIES	HAFTS
HABITUDE	HACKINGS	HADING	HAEMONY	HAG
HABITUDES	HACKLE	HADITH	HAEMOSTAT	HAGADIC
HABITUE	HACKLED	HADITHS	HAEMS	HAGADIST
HABITUES	HACKLER	HADJ	HAEN	HAGADISTS
HABITUS	HACKLERS	HADJEE	HAEREDES	HAGBERRY
HABITUSES	HACKLES	HADJEES	HAEREMAI	HAGBOLT
HABLE	HACKLET	HADJES	HAEREMAIS	HAGBOLTS

HAGBORN	HAGRIDE	HAINTS	HAIRSTYLE	HALAKHAH
HAGBUSH	HAGRIDER	HAIQUE	HAIRTAIL	HALAKHAHS
HAGBUSHES	HAGRIDERS	HAIQUES	HAIRTAILS	HALAKHAS
HAGBUT	HAGRIDES	HAIR	HAIRWING	HALAKHIC
HAGBUTEER	HAGRIDING	HAIRBALL	HAIRWINGS	HALAKHIST
HAGBUTS	HAGRODE	HAIRBALLS	HAIRWORK	HALAKHOT
HAGBUTTER	HAGS	HAIRBAND	HAIRWORKS	HALAKHOTH
HAGDEN	HAH	HAIRBANDS	HAIRWORM	HALAKIC
HAGDENS	HAHA	HAIRBELL	HAIRWORMS	HALAKIST
HAGDON	HAHAS	HAIRBELLS	HAIRY	HALAKISTS
HAGDONS	HAHNIUM	HAIRBRUSH	HAIRYBACK	HALAKOTH
HAGDOWN	HAHNIUMS	HAIRCAP	HAITH	HALAL
HAGDOWNS	HAHS	HAIRCAPS	HAJ	HALALA
HAGFISH	HAICK	HAIRCLOTH	HAJES	HALALAH
HAGFISHES	HAICKS	HAIRCUT	HAJI	HALALAHS
HAGG	HAIDUK	HAIRCUTS	HAJIS	HALALAS
HAGGADA	HAIDUKS	HAIRDO	HAJJ	HALALLED
HAGGADAH	HAIK	HAIRDOS	HAJJAH	HALALLING
HAGGADAHS	HAIKA	HAIRDRIER	HAJJAHS	HALALS
HAGGADAS	HAIKAI	HAIRDRYER	HAJJES	HALATION
HAGGADIC	HAIKS	HAIRED	HAJJI	HALATIONS
HAGGADIST	HAIKU	HAIRGRIP	HAJJIS	HALAVAH
HAGGADOT	HAIKUS	HAIRGRIPS	HAKA	HALAVAHS
HAGGADOTH	HAIL	HAIRIER	HAKAM	HALAZONE
HAGGARD	HAILED	HAIRIEST	HAKAMS	HALAZONES
HAGGARDLY	HAILER	HAIRIF	HAKARI	HALBERD
HAGGARDS	HAILERS	HAIRIFS	HAKARIS	HALBERDS
HAGGED	HAILIER	HAIRILY	HAKAS	HALBERT
HAGGING	HAILIEST	HAIRINESS	HAKE	HALBERTS
HAGGIS	HAILING	HAIRING	HAKEA	HALCYON
HAGGISES	HAILS	HAIRLESS	HAKEAS	HALCYONIC
HAGGISH	HAILSHOT	HAIRLIKE	HAKEEM	HALCYONS
HAGGISHLY	HAILSHOTS	HAIRLINE	HAKEEMS	HALE
HAGGLE	HAILSTONE	HAIRLINES	HAKES	HALED
HAGGLED	HAILSTORM	HAIRLOCK	HAKIM	HALENESS
HAGGLER	HAILY	HAIRLOCKS	HAKIMS	HALER
HAGGLERS	HAIMISH	HAIRNET	HAKU	HALERS
HAGGLES	HAIN	HAIRNETS	HAKUS	HALERU
HAGGLING	HAINCH	HAIRPIECE	HALACHA	HALES
HAGGLINGS	HAINCHED	HAIRPIN	HALACHAS	HALEST
HAGGS	HAINCHES	HAIRPINS	HALACHIC	HALF
HAGIARCHY	HAINCHING	HAIRS	HALACHIST	HALFA
HAGIOLOGY	HAINED	HAIRSPRAY	HALACHOT	HALFAS
HAGLET	HAINING	HAIRST	HALACHOTH	HALFBACK
HAGLETS	HAININGS	HAIRSTED	HALAKAH	HALFBACKS
HAGLIKE	HAINS	HAIRSTING	HALAKAHS	HALFBEAK
HAGRIDDEN	HAINT	HAIRSTS	HALAKHA	HALFBEAKS

HALFEN	HALITES	HALLOUMIS	HALSERS	HAMAUL
HALFLIFE	HALITOSES	HALLOW	HALSES	HAMAULS
HALFLIN	HALITOSIS	HALLOWED	HALSING	HAMBA
HALFLING	HALITOTIC	HALLOWER	HALT	HAMBLE
HALFLINGS	HALITOUS	HALLOWERS	HALTED	HAMBLED
HALFLINS	HALITUS	HALLOWING	HALTER	HAMBLES
HALFLIVES	HALITUSES	HALLOWS	HALTERE	HAMBLING
HALFNESS	HALL	HALLS	HALTERED	HAMBONE
HALFPACE	HALLAH	HALLSTAND	HALTERES	HAMBONED
HALFPACES	HALLAHS	HALLUCAL	HALTERING	HAMBONES
HALFPENCE	HALLAL	HALLUCES	HALTERS	HAMBONING
HALFPENNY	HALLALI	HALLUX	HALTING	HAMBURG
HALFPIPE	HALLALIS	HALLWAY	HALTINGLY	HAMBURGER
HALFPIPES	HALLALLED	HALLWAYS	HALTINGS	HAMBURGS
HALFS	HALLALOO	HALLYON	HALTLESS	HAME
HALFTIME	HALLALOOS	HALLYONS	HALTS	HAMED
HALFTIMES	HALLALS	HALM	HALUTZ	HAMES
HALFTONE	HALLAN	HALMA	HALUTZIM	HAMEWITH
HALFTONES	HALLANS	HALMAS	HALVA	HAMFAT
HALFTRACK	HALLEL	HALMS	HALVAH	HAMFATS
HALFWAY	HALLELS	HALO	HALVAHS	HAMFATTER
HALFWIT	HALLIAN	HALOBIONT	HALVAS	HAMING
HALFWITS	HALLIANS	HALOCLINE	HALVE	HAMLET
HALIBUT	HALLIARD	HALOED	HALVED	HAMLETS
HALIBUTS	HALLIARDS	HALOES	HALVER	HAMMADA
HALICORE	HALLING	HALOGEN	HALVERS	HAMMADAS
HALICORES	HALLINGS	HALOGENS	HALVES	HAMMAL
HALID	HALLION	HALOGETON	HALVING	HAMMALS
HALIDE	HALLIONS	HALOID	HALVINGS	HAMMAM
HALIDES	HALLMARK	HALOIDS	HALWA	HAMMAMS
HALIDOM	HALLMARKS	HALOING	HALWAS	HAMMED
HALIDOME	HALLO	HALOLIKE	HALYARD	HAMMER
HALIDOMES	HALLOA	HALON	HALYARDS	HAMMERED
HALIDOMS	HALLOAED	HALONS	HAM	HAMMERER
HALIDS	HALLOAING	HALOPHILE	HAMADA	HAMMERERS
HALIER	HALLOAS	HALOPHILY	HAMADAS	HAMMERING
HALIEROV	HALLOED	HALOPHOBE	HAMADRYAD	HAMMERKOP
HALIERS	HALLOES	HALOPHYTE	HAMADRYAS	HAMMERMAN
HALIEUTIC	HALLOING	HALOS	HAMAL	HAMMERMEN
HALIMOT	HALLOO	HALOSERE	HAMALS	HAMMERS
HALIMOTE	HALLOOED	HALOSERES	HAMAMELIS	HAMMERTOE
HALIMOTES	HALLOOING	HALOTHANE	HAMARTIA	HAMMIER
HALIMOTS	HALLOOS	HALOUMI	HAMARTIAS	HAMMIEST
HALING	HALLOS	HALOUMIS	HAMATE	HAMMILY
HALIOTES	HALLOT	HALSE	HAMATES	HAMMINESS
HALIOTIS	HALLOTH	HALSED	HAMATSA	HAMMING
HALITE	HALLOUMI	HALSER	HAMATSAS	HAMMOCK

HAMMOCKS	HANDBELLS	HANDJOB	HANDSET	HANGMEN
HAMMY	HANDBILL	HANDJOBS	HANDSETS	HANGNAIL
HAMOSE	HANDBILLS	HANDKNIT	HANDSEWN	HANGNAILS
HAMOUS	HANDBLOWN	HANDKNITS	HANDSFUL	HANGNEST
HAMPER	HANDBOOK	HANDLE	HANDSHAKE	HANGNESTS
HAMPERED	HANDBOOKS	HANDLEBAR	HANDSOME	HANGOUT
HAMPERER	HANDBRAKE	HANDLED	HANDSOMER	HANGOUTS
HAMPERERS	HANDCAR	HANDLER	HANDSOMES	HANGOVER
HAMPERING	HANDCARS	HANDLERS	HANDSPIKE	HANGOVERS
HAMPERS	HANDCART	HANDLES	HANDSTAFF	HANGRIER
HAMPSTER	HANDCARTS	HANDLESS	HANDSTAMP	HANGRIEST
HAMPSTERS	HANDCLAP	HANDLIKE	HANDSTAND	HANGRY
HAMS	HANDCLAPS	HANDLINE	HANDSTURN	HANGS
HAMSTER	HANDCLASP	HANDLINES	HANDTOWEL	HANGTAG
HAMSTERS	HANDCRAFT	HANDLING	HANDWHEEL	HANGTAGS
HAMSTRING	HANDCUFF	HANDLINGS	HANDWORK	HANGUL
HAMSTRUNG	HANDCUFFS	HANDLIST	HANDWORKS	HANGUP
HAMULAR	HANDED	HANDLISTS	HANDWOVEN	HANGUPS
HAMULATE	HANDER	HANDLOOM	HANDWRIT	HANIWA
HAMULI	HANDERS	HANDLOOMS	HANDWRITE	HANJAR
HAMULOSE	HANDFAST	HANDMADE	HANDWROTE	HANJARS
HAMULOUS	HANDFASTS	HANDMAID	HANDY	HANK
HAMULUS	HANDFED	HANDMAIDS	HANDYMAN	HANKED
HAMZA	HANDFEED	HANDOFF	HANDYMEN	HANKER
HAMZAH	HANDFEEDS	HANDOFFS	HANDYWORK	HANKERED
HAMZAHS	HANDFUL	HANDOUT	HANEPOOT	HANKERER
HAMZAS	HANDFULS	HANDOUTS	HANEPOOTS	HANKERERS
HAN	HANDGRIP	HANDOVER	HANG	HANKERING
HANAP	HANDGRIPS	HANDOVERS	HANGABLE	HANKERS
HANAPER	HANDGUN	HANDPASS	HANGAR	HANKIE
HANAPERS	HANDGUNS	HANDPHONE	HANGARED	HANKIES
HANAPS	HANDHELD	HANDPICK	HANGARING	HANKING
HANCE	HANDHELDS	HANDPICKS	HANGARS	HANKS
HANCES	HANDHOLD	HANDPLAY	HANGBIRD	HANKY
HANCH	HANDHOLDS	HANDPLAYS	HANGBIRDS	HANSA
HANCHED	HANDICAP	HANDPRESS	HANGDOG	HANSAS
HANCHES	HANDICAPS	HANDPRINT	HANGDOGS	HANSE
HANCHING	HANDIER	HANDRAIL	HANGED	HANSEATIC
HAND	HANDIEST	HANDRAILS	HANGER	HANSEL
HANDAX	HANDILY	HANDROLL	HANGERS	HANSELED
HANDAXE	HANDINESS	HANDROLLS	HANGFIRE	HANSELING
HANDAXES	HANDING	HANDS	HANGFIRES	HANSELLED
HANDBAG	HANDISM	HANDSAW	HANGI	HANSELS
HANDBAGS	HANDISMS	HANDSAWS	HANGING	HANSES
HANDBALL	HANDIWORK	HANDSEL	HANGINGS	HANSOM
HANDBALLS	HANDJAR	HANDSELED	HANGIS	HANSOMS
HANDBELL	HANDJARS	HANDSELS	HANGMAN	HANT

HANTED	HAPPENING	HARANGUE	HARDCOVER	HARDROCKS
HANTING	HAPPENS	HARANGUED	HARDEDGE	HARDS
HANTLE	HAPPI	HARANGUER	HARDEDGES	HARDSCAPE
HANTLES	HAPPIED	HARANGUES	HARDEN	HARDSET
HANTS	HAPPIER	HARASS	HARDENED	HARDSHELL
HANUKIAH	HAPPIES	HARASSED	HARDENER	HARDSHIP
HANUKIAHS	HAPPIEST	HARASSER	HARDENERS	HARDSHIPS
HANUMAN	HAPPILY	HARASSERS	HARDENING	HARDSTAND
HANUMANS	HAPPINESS	HARASSES	HARDENS	HARDTACK
HAO	HAPPING	HARASSING	HARDER	HARDTACKS
HAOLE	HAPPIS	HARBINGER	HARDEST	HARDTAIL
HAOLES	HAPPOSHU	HARBOR	HARDFACE	HARDTAILS
HAOMA	HAPPOSHUS	HARBORAGE	HARDFACES	HARDTOP
HAOMAS	HAPPY	HARBORED	HARDGOODS	HARDTOPS
HAOS	HAPPYING	HARBORER	HARDGRASS	HARDWARE
HAP	HAPS	HARBORERS	HARDHACK	HARDWARES
HAPAX	HAPTEN	HARBORFUL	HARDHACKS	HARDWIRE
HAPAXES	HAPTENE	HARBORING	HARDHAT	HARDWIRED
HAPHAZARD	HAPTENES	HARBOROUS	HARDHATS	HARDWIRES
HAPHTARA	HAPTENIC	HARBORS	HARDHEAD	HARDWOOD
HAPHTARAH	HAPTENS	HARBOUR	HARDHEADS	HARDWOODS
HAPHTARAS	HAPTERON	HARBOURED	HARDIER	HARDY
HAPHTAROT	HAPTERONS	HARBOURER	HARDIES	HARE
HAPKIDO	HAPTIC	HARBOURS	HARDIEST	HAREBELL
HAPKIDOS	HAPTICAL	HARD	HARDIHEAD	HAREBELLS
HAPLESS	HAPTICS	HARDASS	HARDIHOOD	HARED
HAPLESSLY	HAPU	HARDASSES	HARDILY	HAREEM
HAPLITE	HAPUKA	HARDBACK	HARDIMENT	HAREEMS
HAPLITES	HAPUKAS	HARDBACKS	HARDINESS	HARELD
HAPLITIC	HAPUKU	HARDBAG	HARDISH	HARELDS
HAPLOID	HAPUKUS	HARDBAGS	HARDLINE	HARELIKE
HAPLOIDIC	HAPUS	HARDBAKE	HARDLINER	HARELIP
HAPLOIDS	HAQUETON	HARDBAKES	HARDLY	HARELIPS
HAPLOIDY	HAQUETONS	HARDBALL	HARDMAN	HAREM
HAPLOLOGY	HARAAM	HARDBALLS	HARDMEN	HAREMS
HAPLONT	HARAKEKE	HARDBEAM	HARDNESS	HARES
HAPLONTIC	HARAKEKES	HARDBEAMS	HARDNOSE	HARESTAIL
HAPLONTS	HARAM	HARDBOARD	HARDNOSED	HAREWOOD
HAPLOPIA	HARAMBEE	HARDBODY	HARDNOSES	HAREWOODS
HAPLOPIAS	HARAMBEES	HARDBOOT	HARDOKE	HARIANA
HAPLOSES	HARAMDA	HARDBOOTS	HARDOKES	HARIANAS
HAPLOSIS	HARAMDAS	HARDBOUND	HARDPACK	HARICOT
HAPLOTYPE	HARAMDI	HARDCASE	HARDPACKS	HARICOTS
HAPLY	HARAMDIS	HARDCASES	HARDPAN	HARIGALDS
HAPPED	HARAMS	HARDCORE	HARDPANS	HARIGALS
HAPPEN	HARAMZADA	HARDCORES	HARDPARTS	HARIJAN
HAPPENED	HARAMZADI	HARDCOURT	HARDROCK	HARIJANS

HARIM	HARMINES	HARPYLIKE	HARUSPEX	HASSOCKS
HARIMS	HARMING	HARQUEBUS	HARUSPICY	HASSOCKY
HARING	HARMINS	HARRIDAN	HARVEST	HAST
HARIOLATE	HARMLESS	HARRIDANS	HARVESTED	HASTA
HARIRA	HARMONIC	HARRIED	HARVESTER	HASTATE
HARIRAS	HARMONICA	HARRIER	HARVESTS	HASTATED
HARISH	HARMONICS	HARRIERS	HAS	HASTATELY
HARISSA	HARMONIES	HARRIES	HASBIAN	HASTE
HARISSAS	HARMONISE	HARROW	HASBIANS	HASTED
HARK	HARMONIST	HARROWED	HASH	HASTEFUL
HARKED	HARMONIUM	HARROWER	HASHED	HASTEN
HARKEN	HARMONIZE	HARROWERS	HASHEESH	HASTENED
HARKENED	HARMONY	HARROWING	HASHES	HASTENER
HARKENER	HARMOST	HARROWS	HASHHEAD	HASTENERS
HARKENERS	HARMOSTS	HARRUMPH	HASHHEADS	HASTENING
HARKENING	HARMOSTY	HARRUMPHS	HASHIER	HASTENS
HARKENS	HARMOTOME	HARRY	HASHIEST	HASTES
HARKING	HARMS	HARRYING	HASHING	HASTIER
HARKS	HARN	HARSH	HASHINGS	HASTIEST
HARL	HARNESS	HARSHED	HASHISH	HASTILY
HARLED	HARNESSED	HARSHEN	HASHISHES	HASTINESS
HARLEQUIN	HARNESSER	HARSHENED	HASHMARK	HASTING
HARLING	HARNESSES	HARSHENS	HASHMARKS	HASTINGS
HARLINGS	HARNS	HARSHER	HASHTAG	HASTY
HARLOT	HARO	HARSHES	HASHTAGS	HAT
HARLOTRY	HAROS	HARSHEST	HASHY	HATABLE
HARLOTS	HAROSET	HARSHING	HASK	HATBAND
HARLS	HAROSETH	HARSHLY	HASKS	HATBANDS
HARM	HAROSETHS	HARSHNESS	HASLET	HATBOX
HARMALA	HAROSETS	HARSLET	HASLETS	HATBOXES
HARMALAS	HARP	HARSLETS	HASP	HATBRUSH
HARMALIN	HARPED	HART	HASPED	HATCH
HARMALINE	HARPER	HARTAL	HASPING	HATCHABLE
HARMALINS	HARPERS	HARTALS	HASPS	HATCHBACK
HARMAN	HARPIES	HARTBEES	HASS	HATCHECK
HARMANS	HARPIN	HARTBEEST	HASSAR	HATCHECKS
HARMATTAN	HARPING	HARTELY	HASSARS	HATCHED
HARMDOING	HARPINGS	HARTEN	HASSEL	HATCHEL
HARMED	HARPINS	HARTENED	HASSELS	HATCHELED
HARMEL	HARPIST	HARTENING	HASSES	HATCHELS
HARMELS	HARPISTS	HARTENS	HASSIUM	HATCHER
HARMER	HARPOON	HARTLESSE	HASSIUMS	HATCHERS
HARMERS	HARPOONED	HARTS	HASSLE	HATCHERY
HARMFUL	HARPOONER	HARTSHORN	HASSLED	HATCHES
HARMFULLY	HARPOONS	HARUMPH	HASSLES	HATCHET
HARMIN	HARPS	HARUMPHED	HASSLING	HATCHETS
HARMINE	HARPY	HARUMPHS	HASSOCK	HATCHETY

H

HATCHING	HATTERS	HAUNCHED	HAVENS	HAWKEY
HATCHINGS	HATTING	HAUNCHES	HAVEOUR	HAWKEYED
HATCHLING	HATTINGS	HAUNCHING	HAVEOURS	HAWKEYS
HATCHMENT	HATTOCK	HAUNS	HAVER	HAWKIE
HATCHWAY	HATTOCKS	HAUNT	HAVERED	HAWKIES
HATCHWAYS	HAUBERK	HAUNTED	HAVEREL	HAWKING
HATE	HAUBERKS	HAUNTER	HAVERELS	HAWKINGS
HATEABLE	HAUBOIS	HAUNTERS	HAVERING	HAWKISH
HATED	HAUD	HAUNTING	HAVERINGS	HAWKISHLY
HATEFUL	HAUDING	HAUNTINGS	HAVERS	HAWKIT
HATEFULLY	HAUDS	HAUNTS	HAVERSACK	HAWKLIKE
HATELESS	HAUF	HAURIANT	HAVERSINE	HAWKMOTH
HATER	HAUFS	HAURIENT	HAVES	HAWKMOTHS
HATERENT	HAUGH	HAUSE	HAVILDAR	HAWKNOSE
HATERENTS	HAUGHS	HAUSED	HAVILDARS	HAWKNOSES
HATERS	HAUGHT	HAUSEN	HAVING	HAWKS
HATES	HAUGHTIER	HAUSENS	HAVINGS	HAWKSBILL
HATFUL	HAUGHTILY	HAUSES	HAVIOR	HAWKSHAW
HATFULS	HAUGHTY	HAUSFRAU	HAVIORS	HAWKSHAWS
HATGUARD	HAUL	HAUSFRAUS	HAVIOUR	HAWKWEED
HATGUARDS	HAULAGE	HAUSING	HAVIOURS	HAWKWEEDS
HATH	HAULAGES	HAUSTELLA	HAVOC	HAWM
HATHA	HAULBACK	HAUSTORIA	HAVOCKED	HAWMED
HATINATOR	HAULBACKS	HAUT	HAVOCKER	HAWMING
HATING	HAULD	HAUTBOIS	HAVOCKERS	HAWMS
HATLESS	HAULDS	HAUTBOY	HAVOCKING	HAWS
HATLIKE	HAULED	HAUTBOYS	HAVOCS	HAWSE
HATMAKER	HAULER	HAUTE	HAW	HAWSED
HATMAKERS	HAULERS	HAUTER	HAWALA	HAWSEHOLE
HATPEG	HAULIER	HAUTEST	HAWALAS	HAWSEPIPE
HATPEGS	HAULIERS	HAUTEUR	HAWBUCK	HAWSER
HATPIN	HAULING	HAUTEURS	HAWBUCKS	HAWSERS
HATPINS	HAULINGS	HAUYNE	HAWEATER	HAWSES
HATRACK	HAULM	HAUYNES	HAWEATERS	HAWSING
HATRACKS	HAULMIER	HAVARTI	HAWED	HAWTHORN
HATRED	HAULMIEST	HAVARTIS	HAWFINCH	HAWTHORNS
HATREDS	HAULMS	HAVDALAH	HAWING	HAWTHORNY
HATS	HAULMY	HAVDALAHS	HAWK	HAY
HATSFUL	HAULOUT	HAVDOLOH	HAWKBELL	HAYBAND
HATSTAND	HAULOUTS	HAVDOLOHS	HAWKBELLS	HAYBANDS
HATSTANDS	HAULS	HAVE	HAWKBILL	HAYBOX
HATTED	HAULST	HAVELOCK	HAWKBILLS	HAYBOXES
HATTER	HAULT	HAVELOCKS	HAWKBIT	HAYCATION
HATTERED	HAULYARD	HAVEN	HAWKBITS	HAYCOCK
HATTERIA	HAULYARDS	HAVENED	HAWKED	HAYCOCKS
HATTERIAS	HAUN	HAVENING	HAWKER	HAYED
HATTERING	HAUNCH	HAVENLESS	HAWKERS	HAYER

HAYERS	HAZARDING	HEADCOUNT	HEADMEN	HEADWALL
HAYEY	HAZARDIZE	HEADDRESS	HEADMOST	HEADWALLS
HAYFIELD	HAZARDOUS	HEADED	HEADNOTE	HEADWARD
HAYFIELDS	HAZARDRY	HEADEND	HEADNOTES	HEADWARDS
HAYFORK	HAZARDS	HEADENDS	HEADPEACE	HEADWATER
HAYFORKS	HAZE	HEADER	HEADPHONE	HEADWAY
HAYIER	HAZED	HEADERS	HEADPIECE	HEADWAYS
HAYIEST	HAZEL	HEADFAST	HEADPIN	HEADWIND
HAYING	HAZELHEN	HEADFASTS	HEADPINS	HEADWINDS
HAYINGS	HAZELHENS	HEADFIRST	HEADPOND	HEADWORD
HAYLAGE	HAZELLY	HEADFISH	HEADPONDS	HEADWORDS
HAYLAGES	HAZELNUT	HEADFRAME	HEADRACE	HEADWORK
HAYLE	HAZELNUTS	HEADFUCK	HEADRACES	HEADWORKS
HAYLES	HAZELS	HEADFUCKS	HEADRAIL	HEADY
HAYLOFT	HAZELWOOD	HEADFUL	HEADRAILS	HEAL
HAYLOFTS	HAZER	HEADFULS	HEADREACH	HEALABLE
HAYMAKER	HAZERS	HEADGATE	HEADREST	HEALD
HAYMAKERS	HAZES	HEADGATES	HEADRESTS	HEALDED
HAYMAKING	HAZIER	HEADGEAR	HEADRIG	HEALDING
HAYMOW	HAZIEST	HEADGEARS	HEADRIGS	HEALDS
HAYMOWS	HAZILY	HEADGUARD	HEADRING	HEALED
HAYRACK	HAZINESS	HEADHUNT	HEADRINGS	HEALEE
HAYRACKS	HAZING	HEADHUNTS	HEADROOM	HEALEES
HAYRAKE	HAZINGS	HEADIER	HEADROOMS	HEALER
HAYRAKES	HAZMAT	HEADIEST	HEADROPE	HEALERS
HAYRICK	HAZMATS	HEADILY	HEADROPES	HEALING
HAYRICKS	HAZY	HEADINESS	HEADS	HEALINGLY
HAYRIDE	HAZZAN	HEADING	HEADSAIL	HEALINGS
HAYRIDES	HAZZANIM	HEADINGS	HEADSAILS	HEALS
HAYS	HAZZANS	HEADLAMP	HEADSCARF	HEALSOME
HAYSEED	HE	HEADLAMPS	HEADSET	HEALTH
HAYSEEDS	HEAD	HEADLAND	HEADSETS	HEALTHFUL
HAYSEL	HEADACHE	HEADLANDS	HEADSHAKE	HEALTHIER
HAYSELS	HEADACHES	HEADLEASE	HEADSHIP	HEALTHILY
HAYSTACK	HEADACHEY	HEADLESS	HEADSHIPS	HEALTHISM
HAYSTACKS	HEADACHY	HEADLIGHT	HEADSHOT	HEALTHS
HAYWARD	HEADAGE	HEADLIKE	HEADSHOTS	HEALTHY
HAYWARDS	HEADAGES	HEADLINE	HEADSMAN	HEAME
HAYWIRE	HEADBAND	HEADLINED	HEADSMEN	HEAP
HAYWIRES	HEADBANDS	HEADLINER	HEADSPACE	HEAPED
HAZAN	HEADBANG	HEADLINES	HEADSTALL	HEAPER
HAZANIM	HEADBANGS	HEADLOCK	HEADSTAND	HEAPERS
HAZANS	HEADBOARD	HEADLOCKS	HEADSTAY	HEAPIER
HAZARD	HEADCASE	HEADLONG	HEADSTAYS	HEAPIEST
HAZARDED	HEADCASES	HEADMAN	HEADSTICK	HEAPING
HAZARDER	HEADCHAIR	HEADMARK	HEADSTOCK	HEAPS
HAZARDERS	HEADCLOTH	HEADMARKS	HEADSTONE	HEAPSTEAD

H

HEAPY	HEARTLESS	HEATPROOF	HEBRAIZED	HEDGED
HEAR	HEARTLET	HEATS	HEBRAIZES	HEDGEHOG
HEARABLE	HEARTLETS	HEATSPOT	HECATOMB	HEDGEHOGS
HEARD	HEARTLING	HEATSPOTS	HECATOMBS	HEDGEHOP
HEARDS	HEARTLY	HEATWAVE	HECH	HEDGEHOPS
HEARE	HEARTPEA	HEATWAVES	HECHT	HEDGEPIG
HEARER	HEARTPEAS	HEAUME	HECHTING	HEDGEPIGS
HEARERS	HEARTS	HEAUMES	HECHTS	HEDGER
HEARES	HEARTSEED	HEAVE	HECK	HEDGEROW
HEARIE	HEARTSICK	HEAVED	HECKLE	HEDGEROWS
HEARING	HEARTSINK	HEAVEN	HECKLED	HEDGERS
HEARINGS	HEARTSOME	HEAVENLY	HECKLER	HEDGES
HEARKEN	HEARTSORE	HEAVENS	HECKLERS	HEDGIER
HEARKENED	HEARTWOOD	HEAVER	HECKLES	HEDGIEST
HEARKENER	HEARTWORM	HEAVERS	HECKLING	HEDGING
HEARKENS	HEARTY	HEAVES	HECKLINGS	HEDGINGLY
HEARS	HEAST	HEAVIER	HECKS	HEDGINGS
HEARSAY	HEASTE	HEAVIES	HECKUVA	HEDGY
HEARSAYS	HEASTES	HEAVIEST	HECOGENIN	HEDONIC
HEARSE	HEASTS	HEAVILY	HECTARE	HEDONICS
HEARSED	HEAT	HEAVINESS	HECTARES	HEDONISM
HEARSES	HEATABLE	HEAVING	HECTIC	HEDONISMS
HEARSIER	HEATED	HEAVINGS	HECTICAL	HEDONIST
HEARSIEST	HEATEDLY	HEAVY	HECTICLY	HEDONISTS
HEARSING	HEATER	HEAVYISH	HECTICS	HEDYPHANE
HEARSY	HEATERS	HEAVYSET	HECTOGRAM	HEED
HEART	HEATH	HEBDOMAD	HECTOR	HEEDED
HEARTACHE	HEATHBIRD	HEBDOMADS	HECTORED	HEEDER
HEARTBEAT	HEATHCOCK	HEBE	HECTORER	HEEDERS
HEARTBURN	HEATHEN	HEBEN	HECTORERS	HEEDFUL
HEARTED	HEATHENRY	HEBENON	HECTORING	HEEDFULLY
HEARTEN	HEATHENS	HEBENONS	HECTORISM	HEEDIER
HEARTENED	HEATHER	HEBENS	HECTORLY	HEEDIEST
HEARTENER	HEATHERED	HEBES	HECTORS	HEEDINESS
HEARTENS	HEATHERS	HEBETANT	HEDARIM	HEEDING
HEARTFELT	HEATHERY	HEBETATE	HEDDLE	HEEDLESS
HEARTFREE	HEATHFOWL	HEBETATED	HEDDLED	HEEDS
HEARTH	HEATHIER	HEBETATES	HEDDLES	HEEDY
HEARTHRUG	HEATHIEST	HEBETIC	HEDDLING	HEEHAW
HEARTHS	HEATHLAND	HEBETUDE	HEDER	HEEHAWED
HEARTIER	HEATHLESS	HEBETUDES	HEDERA	HEEHAWING
HEARTIES	HEATHLIKE	HEBONA	HEDERAL	HEEHAWS
HEARTIEST	HEATHS	HEBONAS	HEDERAS	HEEL
HEARTIKIN	HEATHY	HEBRAISE	HEDERATED	HEELBALL
HEARTILY	HEATING	HEBRAISED	HEDERS	HEELBALLS
HEARTING	HEATINGS	HEBRAISES	HEDGE	HEELBAR
HEARTLAND	HEATLESS	HEBRAIZE	HEDGEBILL	HEELBARS

HEELED	HEHS	HEJIRAS	HELIODORS	HELLFIRE
HEELER	HEID	HEJRA	HELIOGRAM	HELLFIRES
HEELERS	HEIDS	HEJRAS	HELIOLOGY	HELLHOLE
HEELING	HEIFER	HEKETARA	HELIOPSES	HELLHOLES
HEELINGS	HEIFERS	HEKETARAS	HELIOPSIS	HELLHOUND
HEELLESS	HEIGH	HEKTARE	HELIOS	HELLICAT
HEELPIECE	HEIGHT	HEKTARES	HELIOSES	HELLICATS
HEELPLATE	HEIGHTEN	HEKTOGRAM	HELIOSIS	HELLIER
HEELPOST	HEIGHTENS	HELCOID	HELIOSTAT	HELLIERS
HEELPOSTS	HEIGHTH	HELD	HELIOTYPE	HELLING
HEELS	HEIGHTHS	HELE	HELIOTYPY	HELLION
HEELTAP	HEIGHTISM	HELED	HELIOZOAN	HELLIONS
HEELTAPS	HEIGHTS	HELENIUM	HELIOZOIC	HELLISH
HEEZE	HEIL	HELENIUMS	HELIPAD	HELLISHLY
HEEZED	HEILED	HELES	HELIPADS	HELLKITE
HEEZES	HEILING	HELIAC	HELIPILOT	HELLKITES
HEEZIE	HEILS	HELIACAL	HELIPORT	HELLO
HEEZIES	HEIMISH	HELIAST	HELIPORTS	HELLOED
HEEZING	HEINIE	HELIASTS	HELISKI	HELLOES
HEFT	HEINIES	HELIBORNE	HELISKIED	HELLOING
HEFTE	HEINOUS	HELIBUS	HELISKIS	HELLOS
HEFTED	HEINOUSLY	HELIBUSES	HELISTOP	HELLOVA
HEFTER	HEIR	HELICAL	HELISTOPS	HELLS
HEFTERS	HEIRDOM	HELICALLY	HELITACK	HELLUVA
HEFTIER	HEIRDOMS	HELICASE	HELITACKS	HELLWARD
HEFTIEST	HEIRED	HELICASES	HELIUM	HELLWARDS
HEFTILY	HEIRESS	HELICES	HELIUMS	HELM
HEFTINESS	HEIRESSES	HELICITY	HELIX	HELMED
HEFTING	HEIRING	HELICLINE	HELIXES	HELMER
HEFTS	HEIRLESS	HELICOID	HELL	HELMERS
HEFTY	HEIRLOOM	HELICOIDS	HELLBENT	HELMET
HEGARI	HEIRLOOMS	HELICON	HELLBOX	HELMETED
HEGARIS	HEIRS	HELICONIA	HELLBOXES	HELMETING
HEGEMON	HEIRSHIP	HELICONS	HELLBROTH	HELMETS
HEGEMONIC	HEIRSHIPS	HELICOPT	HELLCAT	HELMING
HEGEMONS	HEISHI	HELICOPTS	HELLCATS	HELMINTH
HEGEMONY	HEIST	HELICTITE	HELLDIVER	HELMINTHS
HEGIRA	HEISTED	HELIDECK	HELLEBORE	HELMLESS
HEGIRAS	HEISTER	HELIDECKS	HELLED	HELMS
HEGUMEN	HEISTERS	HELIDROME	HELLENISE	HELMSMAN
HEGUMENE	HEISTING	HELILIFT	HELLENIZE	HELMSMEN
HEGUMENES	HEISTS	HELILIFTS	HELLER	HELO
HEGUMENOI	HEITIKI	HELIMAN	HELLERI	HELOPHYTE
HEGUMENOS	HEITIKIS	HELIMEN	HELLERIES	HELOS
HEGUMENS	HEJAB	HELING	HELLERIS	HELOT
HEGUMENY	HEJABS	HELIO	HELLERS	HELOTAGE
HEH	HEJIRA	HELIODOR	HELLERY	HELOTAGES

H

HELOTISM	HEMATOID	HEMMER	HENCOOP	HENS
HELOTISMS	HEMATOMA	HEMMERS	HENCOOPS	HENT
HELOTRIES	HEMATOMAS	HEMMING	HEND	HENTED
HELOTRY	HEMATOSES	HEMOCOEL	HENDED	HENTING
HELOTS	HEMATOSIS	HEMOCOELS	HENDIADYS	HENTS
HELP	HEMATOZOA	HEMOCONIA	HENDING	HEP
HELPABLE	HEMATURIA	HEMOCYTE	HENDS	HEPAR
HELPDESK	HEMATURIC	HEMOCYTES	HENEQUEN	HEPARIN
HELPDESKS	HEME	HEMOID	HENEQUENS	HEPARINS
HELPED	HEMELYTRA	HEMOLYMPH	HENEQUIN	HEPARS
HELPER	HEMES	HEMOLYSE	HENEQUINS	HEPATIC
HELPERS	HEMIALGIA	HEMOLYSED	HENGE	HEPATICA
HELPFUL	HEMIC	HEMOLYSES	HENGES	HEPATICAE
HELPFULLY	HEMICYCLE	HEMOLYSIN	HENHOUSE	HEPATICAL
HELPING	HEMIHEDRA	HEMOLYSIS	HENHOUSES	HEPATICAS
HELPINGS	HEMIHEDRY	HEMOLYTIC	HENIQUEN	HEPATICS
HELPLESS	HEMIN	HEMOLYZE	HENIQUENS	HEPATISE
HELPLINE	HEMINA	HEMOLYZED	HENIQUIN	HEPATISED
HELPLINES	HEMINAS	HEMOLYZES	HENIQUINS	HEPATISES
HELPMATE	HEMINS	HEMOPHILE	HENLEY	HEPATITE
HELPMATES	HEMIOLA	HEMOSTAT	HENLEYS	HEPATITES
HELPMEET	HEMIOLAS	HEMOSTATS	HENLIKE	HEPATITIS
HELPMEETS	HEMIOLIA	HEMOTOXIC	HENNA	HEPATIZE
HELPS	HEMIOLIAS	HEMOTOXIN	HENNAED	HEPATIZED
HELVE	HEMIOLIC	HEMP	HENNAING	HEPATIZES
HELVED	HEMIONE	HEMPEN	HENNAS	HEPATOMA
HELVES	HEMIONES	HEMPIE	HENNED	HEPATOMAS
HELVETIUM	HEMIONUS	HEMPIER	HENNER	HEPCAT
HELVING	HEMIOPIA	HEMPIES	HENNERIES	HEPCATS
HEM	HEMIOPIAS	HEMPIEST	HENNERS	HEPPER
HEMAGOG	HEMIOPIC	HEMPLIKE	HENNERY	HEPPEST
HEMAGOGS	HEMIOPSIA	HEMPS	HENNIER	HEPS
HEMAGOGUE	HEMIPOD	HEMPSEED	HENNIES	HEPSTER
HEMAL	HEMIPODE	HEMPSEEDS	HENNIEST	HEPSTERS
HEMATAL	HEMIPODES	HEMPWEED	HENNIN	HEPT
HEMATEIN	HEMIPODS	HEMPWEEDS	HENNING	HEPTAD
HEMATEINS	HEMIPTER	HEMPY	HENNINS	HEPTADS
HEMATIC	HEMIPTERS	HEMS	HENNISH	HEPTAGLOT
HEMATICS	HEMISPACE	HEMSTITCH	HENNISHLY	HEPTAGON
HEMATIN	HEMISTICH	HEN	HENNY	HEPTAGONS
HEMATINE	HEMITROPE	HENBANE	HENOTIC	HEPTANE
HEMATINES	HEMITROPY	HENBANES	HENPECK	HEPTANES
HEMATINIC	HEMLINE	HENBIT	HENPECKED	HEPTAPODY
HEMATINS	HEMLINES	HENBITS	HENPECKS	HEPTARCH
HEMATITE	HEMLOCK	HENCE	HENRIES	HEPTARCHS
HEMATITES	HEMLOCKS	HENCHMAN	HENRY	HEPTARCHY
HEMATITIC	HEMMED	HENCHMEN	HENRYS	HEPTOSE

H

HEPTOSES	HERBY	HERETICS	HERNIAE	HERPETICS
HER	HERCOGAMY	HERETO	HERNIAL	HERPETOID
HERALD	HERCULEAN	HERETRIX	HERNIAS	HERPTILE
HERALDED	HERCULES	HEREUNDER	HERNIATE	HERRIED
HERALDIC	HERCYNITE	HEREUNTO	HERNIATED	HERRIES
HERALDING	HERD	HEREUPON	HERNIATES	HERRIMENT
HERALDIST	HERDBOY	HEREWITH	HERNS	HERRING
HERALDRY	HERDBOYS	HERIED	HERNSHAW	HERRINGER
HERALDS	HERDED	HERIES	HERNSHAWS	HERRINGS
HERB	HERDEN	HERIOT	HERO	HERRY
HERBAGE	HERDENS	HERIOTS	HEROES	HERRYING
HERBAGED	HERDER	HERISSE	HEROIC	HERRYMENT
HERBAGES	HERDERS	HERISSON	HEROICAL	HERS
HERBAL	HERDESS	HERISSONS	HEROICISE	HERSALL
HERBALISM	HERDESSES	HERITABLE	HEROICIZE	HERSALLS
HERBALIST	HERDIC	HERITABLY	HEROICLY	HERSE
HERBALS	HERDICS	HERITAGE	HEROICS	HERSED
HERBAR	HERDING	HERITAGES	HEROIN	HERSELF
HERBARIA	HERDINGS	HERITOR	HEROINE	HERSES
HERBARIAL	HERDLIKE	HERITORS	HEROINES	HERSHIP
HERBARIAN	HERDMAN	HERITRESS	HEROINISM	HERSHIPS
HERBARIES	HERDMEN	HERITRIX	HEROINS	HERSTORY
HERBARIUM	HERDS	HERKOGAMY	HEROISE	HERTZ
HERBARS	HERDSMAN	HERL	HEROISED	HERTZES
HERBARY	HERDSMEN	HERLING	HEROISES	HERY
HERBED	HERDWICK	HERLINGS	HEROISING	HERYE
HERBELET	HERDWICKS	HERLS	HEROISM	HERYED
HERBELETS	HERE	HERM	HEROISMS	HERYES
HERBICIDE	HEREABOUT	HERMA	HEROIZE	HERYING
HERBIER	HEREAFTER	HERMAE	HEROIZED	HES
HERBIEST	HEREAT	HERMAEAN	HEROIZES	HESITANCE
HERBIST	HEREAWAY	HERMAI	HEROIZING	HESITANCY
HERBISTS	HEREAWAYS	HERMANDAD	HERON	HESITANT
HERBIVORA	HEREBY	HERMETIC	HERONRIES	HESITATE
HERBIVORE	HEREDES	HERMETICS	HERONRY	HESITATED
HERBIVORY	HEREDITY	HERMETISM	HERONS	HESITATER
HERBLESS	HEREFROM	HERMETIST	HERONSEW	HESITATES
HERBLET	HEREIN	HERMIT	HERONSEWS	HESITATOR
HERBLETS	HEREINTO	HERMITAGE	HERONSHAW	HESP
HERBLIKE	HERENESS	HERMITESS	HEROON	HESPED
HERBOLOGY	HEREOF	HERMITIC	HEROONS	HESPERID
HERBORISE	HEREON	HERMITISM	HEROS	HESPERIDS
HERBORIST	HERES	HERMITRY	HEROSHIP	HESPING
HERBORIZE	HERESIES	HERMITS	HEROSHIPS	HESPS
HERBOSE	HERESY	HERMS	HERPES	HESSIAN
HERBOUS	HERETIC	HERN	HERPESES	HESSIANS
HERBS	HERETICAL	HERNIA	HERPETIC	HESSITE

HESSITES
HESSONITE
HEST
HESTERNAL
HESTS
HET
HETAERA
HETAERAE
HETAERAS
HETAERIC
HETAERISM
HETAERIST
HETAIRA
HETAIRAI
HETAIRAS
HETAIRIA
HETAIRIAS
HETAIRIC
HETAIRISM
HETAIRIST
HETE
HETERO
HETERODOX
HETERONYM
HETEROPOD
HETEROS
HETEROSES
HETEROSIS
HETEROTIC
HETES
HETH
HETHER
HETHS
HETING
HETMAN
HETMANATE
HETMANS
HETMEN
HETS
HETTIE
HETTIES
HEUCH
HEUCHERA
HEUCHERAS
HEUCHS
HEUGH
HEUGHS

HEUREKA
HEUREKAS
HEURETIC
HEURETICS
HEURISM
HEURISMS
HEURISTIC
HEVEA
HEVEAS
HEW
HEWABLE
HEWED
HEWER
HEWERS
HEWGH
HEWING
HEWINGS
HEWN
HEWS
HEX
HEXACHORD
HEXACT
HEXACTS
HEXAD
HEXADE
HEXADES
HEXADIC
HEXADS
HEXAFOIL
HEXAFOILS
HEXAGLOT
HEXAGLOTS
HEXAGON
HEXAGONAL
HEXAGONS
HEXAGRAM
HEXAGRAMS
HEXAHEDRA
HEXAMERAL
HEXAMETER
HEXAMINE
HEXAMINES
HEXANE
HEXANES
HEXANOIC
HEXAPLA
HEXAPLAR

HEXAPLAS
HEXAPLOID
HEXAPOD
HEXAPODAL
HEXAPODIC
HEXAPODS
HEXAPODY
HEXARCH
HEXARCHY
HEXASTICH
HEXASTYLE
HEXATHLON
HEXED
HEXENE
HEXENES
HEXER
HEXEREI
HEXEREIS
HEXERS
HEXES
HEXING
HEXINGS
HEXONE
HEXONES
HEXOSAN
HEXOSANS
HEXOSE
HEXOSES
HEXYL
HEXYLENE
HEXYLENES
HEXYLIC
HEXYLS
HEY
HEYDAY
HEYDAYS
HEYDEY
HEYDEYS
HEYDUCK
HEYDUCKS
HEYED
HEYING
HEYS
HI
HIANT
HIATAL
HIATUS

HIATUSES
HIBACHI
HIBACHIS
HIBAKUSHA
HIBERNAL
HIBERNATE
HIBERNISE
HIBERNIZE
HIBISCUS
HIC
HICATEE
HICATEES
HICCATEE
HICCATEES
HICCOUGH
HICCOUGHS
HICCUP
HICCUPED
HICCUPING
HICCUPPED
HICCUPS
HICCUPY
HICK
HICKER
HICKEST
HICKEY
HICKEYS
HICKIE
HICKIES
HICKISH
HICKORIES
HICKORY
HICKS
HICKWALL
HICKWALLS
HICKYMAL
HICKYMALS
HID
HIDABLE
HIDAGE
HIDAGES
HIDALGA
HIDALGAS
HIDALGO
HIDALGOS
HIDDEN
HIDDENITE

HIDDENLY
HIDDER
HIDDERS
HIDE
HIDEAWAY
HIDEAWAYS
HIDEBOUND
HIDED
HIDELESS
HIDEOSITY
HIDEOUS
HIDEOUSLY
HIDEOUT
HIDEOUTS
HIDER
HIDERS
HIDES
HIDING
HIDINGS
HIDLING
HIDLINGS
HIDLINS
HIDROSES
HIDROSIS
HIDROTIC
HIDROTICS
HIE
HIED
HIEING
HIELAMAN
HIELAMANS
HIELAND
HIEMAL
HIEMS
HIERACIUM
HIERARCH
HIERARCHS
HIERARCHY
HIERATIC
HIERATICA
HIERATICS
HIEROCRAT
HIERODULE
HIEROGRAM
HIEROLOGY
HIERURGY
HIES

HIFALUTIN	HIGHSPOTS	HILD	HIMATIA	HINGERS
HIGGLE	HIGHT	HILDING	HIMATION	HINGES
HIGGLED	HIGHTAIL	HILDINGS	HIMATIONS	HINGING
HIGGLER	HIGHTAILS	HILI	HIMBO	HINGS
HIGGLERS	HIGHTED	HILL	HIMBOS	HINKIER
HIGGLES	HIGHTH	HILLBILLY	HIMS	HINKIEST
HIGGLING	HIGHTHS	HILLCREST	HIMSELF	HINKY
HIGGLINGS	HIGHTING	HILLED	HIN	HINNIE
HIGH	HIGHTINGS	HILLER	HINAHINA	HINNIED
HIGHBALL	HIGHTOP	HILLERS	HINAHINAS	HINNIES
HIGHBALLS	HIGHTOPS	HILLFOLK	HINAU	HINNY
HIGHBORN	HIGHTS	HILLFORT	HINAUS	HINNYING
HIGHBOY	HIGHVELD	HILLFORTS	HIND	HINS
HIGHBOYS	HIGHVELDS	HILLIER	HINDBERRY	HINT
HIGHBRED	HIGHWAY	HILLIEST	HINDBRAIN	HINTED
HIGHBROW	HIGHWAYS	HILLINESS	HINDCAST	HINTER
HIGHBROWS	HIJAB	HILLING	HINDCASTS	HINTERS
HIGHBUSH	HIJABS	HILLINGS	HINDER	HINTING
HIGHCHAIR	HIJACK	HILLMEN	HINDERED	HINTINGLY
HIGHED	HIJACKED	HILLO	HINDERER	HINTINGS
HIGHER	HIJACKER	HILLOA	HINDERERS	HINTS
HIGHERED	HIJACKERS	HILLOAED	HINDERING	HIOI
HIGHERING	HIJACKING	HILLOAING	HINDERS	HIOIS
HIGHERS	HIJACKS	HILLOAS	HINDFEET	HIP
HIGHEST	HIJINKS	HILLOCK	HINDFOOT	HIPBONE
HIGHFLIER	HIJRA	HILLOCKED	HINDGUT	HIPBONES
HIGHFLYER	HIJRAH	HILLOCKS	HINDGUTS	HIPHUGGER
HIGHING	HIJRAHS	HILLOCKY	HINDHEAD	HIPLESS
HIGHISH	HIJRAS	HILLOED	HINDHEADS	HIPLIKE
HIGHJACK	HIKE	HILLOES	HINDLEG	HIPLINE
HIGHJACKS	HIKED	HILLOING	HINDLEGS	HIPLINES
HIGHLAND	HIKER	HILLOS	HINDMILK	HIPLY
HIGHLANDS	HIKERS	HILLS	HINDMILKS	HIPNESS
HIGHLIFE	HIKES	HILLSIDE	HINDMOST	HIPNESSES
HIGHLIFES	HIKING	HILLSIDES	HINDRANCE	HIPPARCH
HIGHLIGHT	HIKOI	HILLSLOPE	HINDS	HIPPARCHS
HIGHLY	HIKOIED	HILLTOP	HINDSHANK	HIPPED
HIGHMAN	HIKOIING	HILLTOPS	HINDSIGHT	HIPPEN
HIGHMEN	HIKOIS	HILLY	HINDWARD	HIPPENS
HIGHMOST	HILA	HILT	HINDWING	HIPPER
HIGHNESS	HILAR	HILTED	HINDWINGS	HIPPEST
HIGHRISE	HILARIOUS	HILTING	HING	HIPPIATRY
HIGHRISES	HILARITY	HILTLESS	HINGE	HIPPIC
HIGHROAD	HILCH	HILTS	HINGED	HIPPIE
HIGHROADS	HILCHED	HILUM	HINGELESS	HIPPIEDOM
HIGHS	HILCHES	HILUS	HINGELIKE	HIPPIEISH
HIGHSPOT	HILCHING	HIM	HINGER	HIPPIER

H

HIPPIES	HIRLING	HISTAMINE	HITHES	HOARDING
HIPPIEST	HIRLINGS	HISTAMINS	HITLESS	HOARDINGS
HIPPIN	HIRPLE	HISTED	HITMAKER	HOARDS
HIPPINESS	HIRPLED	HISTIDIN	HITMAKERS	HOARED
HIPPING	HIRPLES	HISTIDINE	HITMAN	HOARFROST
HIPPINGS	HIRPLING	HISTIDINS	HITMEN	HOARHEAD
HIPPINS	HIRRIENT	HISTIE	HITS	HOARHEADS
HIPPISH	HIRRIENTS	HISTING	HITTABLE	HOARHOUND
HIPPO	HIRSEL	HISTIOID	HITTER	HOARIER
HIPPOCRAS	HIRSELED	HISTOGEN	HITTERS	HOARIEST
HIPPODAME	HIRSELING	HISTOGENS	HITTING	HOARILY
HIPPOLOGY	HIRSELLED	HISTOGENY	HIVE	HOARINESS
HIPPOS	HIRSELS	HISTOGRAM	HIVED	HOARING
HIPPURIC	HIRSLE	HISTOID	HIVELESS	HOARS
HIPPURITE	HIRSLED	HISTOLOGY	HIVELIKE	HOARSE
HIPPUS	HIRSLES	HISTONE	HIVER	HOARSELY
HIPPUSES	HIRSLING	HISTONES	HIVERS	HOARSEN
HIPPY	HIRSTIE	HISTORIAN	HIVES	HOARSENED
HIPPYDOM	HIRSUTE	HISTORIC	HIVEWARD	HOARSENS
HIPPYDOMS	HIRSUTISM	HISTORIED	HIVEWARDS	HOARSER
HIPPYISH	HIRUDIN	HISTORIES	HIVING	HOARSEST
HIPS	HIRUDINS	HISTORIFY	HIYA	HOARY
HIPSHOT	HIRUNDINE	HISTORISM	HIZEN	HOAS
HIPSTER	HIS	HISTORY	HIZENS	HOAST
HIPSTERS	HISH	HISTRIO	HIZZ	HOASTED
HIPT	HISHED	HISTRION	HIZZED	HOASTING
HIRABLE	HISHES	HISTRIONS	HIZZES	HOASTMAN
HIRAGANA	HISHING	HISTRIOS	HIZZING	HOASTMEN
HIRAGANAS	HISN	HISTS	HIZZONER	HOASTS
HIRAGE	HISPANISM	HIT	HIZZONERS	HOATCHING
HIRAGES	HISPID	HITCH	HM	HOATZIN
HIRCINE	HISPIDITY	HITCHED	HMM	HOATZINES
HIRCOSITY	HISS	HITCHER	HMMM	HOATZINS
HIRE	HISSED	HITCHERS	HO	HOAX
HIREABLE	HISSELF	HITCHES	HOA	HOAXED
HIREAGE	HISSER	HITCHHIKE	HOACTZIN	HOAXER
HIREAGES	HISSERS	HITCHIER	HOACTZINS	HOAXERS
HIRED	HISSES	HITCHIEST	HOAED	HOAXES
HIREE	HISSIER	HITCHILY	HOAGIE	HOAXING
HIREES	HISSIES	HITCHING	HOAGIES	HOB
HIRELING	HISSIEST	HITCHY	HOAGY	HOBBED
HIRELINGS	HISSING	HITHE	HOAING	HOBBER
HIRER	HISSINGLY	HITHER	HOAR	HOBBERS
HIRERS	HISSINGS	HITHERED	HOARD	HOBBIES
HIRES	HISSY	HITHERING	HOARDED	HOBBING
HIRING	HIST	HITHERS	HOARDER	HOBBISH
HIRINGS	HISTAMIN	HITHERTO	HOARDERS	HOBBIT

HOBBITRY	HOCKERS	HOED	HOGNOSES	HOISING
HOBBITS	HOCKEY	HOEDOWN	HOGNUT	HOISINS
HOBBLE	HOCKEYS	HOEDOWNS	HOGNUTS	HOIST
HOBBLED	HOCKING	HOEING	HOGS	HOISTED
HOBBLER	HOCKLE	HOELIKE	HOGSHEAD	HOISTER
HOBBLERS	HOCKLED	HOER	HOGSHEADS	HOISTERS
HOBBLES	HOCKLES	HOERS	HOGTIE	HOISTING
HOBBLING	HOCKLING	HOES	HOGTIED	HOISTINGS
HOBBLINGS	HOCKS	HOG	HOGTIEING	HOISTMAN
HOBBY	HOCKSHOP	HOGAN	HOGTIES	HOISTMEN
HOBBYISM	HOCKSHOPS	HOGANS	HOGTYING	HOISTS
HOBBYISMS	HOCUS	HOGBACK	HOGWARD	HOISTWAY
HOBBYIST	HOCUSED	HOGBACKS	HOGWARDS	HOISTWAYS
HOBBYISTS	HOCUSES	HOGEN	HOGWASH	HOKA
HOBBYLESS	HOCUSING	HOGENS	HOGWASHES	HOKAS
HOBDAY	HOCUSSED	HOGFISH	HOGWEED	HOKE
HOBDAYED	HOCUSSES	HOGFISHES	HOGWEEDS	HOKED
HOBDAYING	HOCUSSING	HOGG	HOH	HOKES
HOBDAYS	HOD	HOGGED	HOHA	HOKEY
HOBGOBLIN	HODAD	HOGGER	HOHED	HOKEYNESS
HOBJOB	HODADDIES	HOGGEREL	HOHING	HOKI
HOBJOBBED	HODADDY	HOGGERELS	HOHS	HOKIER
HOBJOBBER	HODADS	HOGGERIES	HOI	HOKIEST
HOBJOBS	HODDED	HOGGERS	HOICK	HOKILY
HOBLIKE	HODDEN	HOGGERY	HOICKED	HOKINESS
HOBNAIL	HODDENS	HOGGET	HOICKING	HOKING
HOBNAILED	HODDIN	HOGGETS	HOICKS	HOKIS
HOBNAILS	HODDING	HOGGIN	HOICKSED	HOKKU
HOBNOB	HODDINS	HOGGING	HOICKSES	HOKONUI
HOBNOBBED	HODDLE	HOGGINGS	HOICKSING	HOKONUIS
HOBNOBBER	HODDLED	HOGGINS	HOIDEN	HOKUM
HOBNOBBY	HODDLES	HOGGISH	HOIDENED	HOKUMS
HOBNOBS	HODDLING	HOGGISHLY	HOIDENING	HOKYPOKY
HOBO	HODIERNAL	HOGGS	HOIDENISH	HOLANDRIC
HOBODOM	HODJA	HOGH	HOIDENS	HOLARCHY
HOBODOMS	HODJAS	HOGHOOD	HOIED	HOLARD
HOBOED	HODMAN	HOGHOODS	HOIING	HOLARDS
HOBOES	HODMANDOD	HOGHS	HOIK	HOLD
HOBOING	HODMEN	HOGLIKE	HOIKED	HOLDABLE
HOBOISM	HODOGRAPH	HOGMANAY	HOIKING	HOLDALL
HOBOISMS	HODOMETER	HOGMANAYS	HOIKS	HOLDALLS
HOBOS	HODOMETRY	HOGMANE	HOING	HOLDBACK
HOBS	HODOSCOPE	HOGMANES	HOIS	HOLDBACKS
HOC	HODS	HOGMENAY	HOISE	HOLDDOWN
HOCK	HOE	HOGMENAYS	HOISED	HOLDDOWNS
HOCKED	HOECAKE	HOGNOSE	HOISES	HOLDEN
HOCKER	HOECAKES	HOGNOSED	HOISIN	HOLDER

HOLDERBAT	HOLLAND	HOLOGRAM	HOMALOIDS	HOMEPAGES
HOLDERS	HOLLANDS	HOLOGRAMS	HOMAS	HOMEPLACE
HOLDFAST	HOLLAS	HOLOGRAPH	HOMBRE	HOMEPORT
HOLDFASTS	HOLLER	HOLOGYNIC	HOMBRES	HOMEPORTS
HOLDING	HOLLERED	HOLOGYNY	HOMBURG	HOMER
HOLDINGS	HOLLERING	HOLOHEDRA	HOMBURGS	HOMERED
HOLDOUT	HOLLERS	HOLON	HOME	HOMERIC
HOLDOUTS	HOLLIDAM	HOLONIC	HOMEBIRD	HOMERING
HOLDOVER	HOLLIDAMS	HOLONS	HOMEBIRDS	HOMEROOM
HOLDOVERS	HOLLIES	HOLOPHOTE	HOMEBIRTH	HOMEROOMS
HOLDS	HOLLO	HOLOPHYTE	HOMEBODY	HOMERS
HOLDUP	HOLLOA	HOLOPTIC	HOMEBOUND	HOMES
HOLDUPS	HOLLOAED	HOLOS	HOMEBOY	HOMESICK
HOLE	HOLLOAING	HOLOTYPE	HOMEBOYS	HOMESITE
HOLED	HOLLOAS	HOLOTYPES	HOMEBRED	HOMESITES
HOLELESS	HOLLOED	HOLOTYPIC	HOMEBREDS	HOMESPUN
HOLES	HOLLOES	HOLOZOIC	HOMEBREW	HOMESPUNS
HOLESOM	HOLLOING	HOLP	HOMEBREWS	HOMESTALL
HOLESOME	HOLLOO	HOLPEN	HOMEBUILT	HOMESTAND
HOLEY	HOLLOOED	HOLS	HOMEBUYER	HOMESTAY
HOLEYER	HOLLOOING	HOLSTEIN	HOMECOMER	HOMESTAYS
HOLEYEST	HOLLOOS	HOLSTEINS	HOMECRAFT	HOMESTEAD
HOLIBUT	HOLLOS	HOLSTER	HOMED	HOMETOWN
HOLIBUTS	HOLLOW	HOLSTERED	HOMEFELT	HOMETOWNS
HOLIDAY	HOLLOWARE	HOLSTERS	HOMEGIRL	HOMEWARD
HOLIDAYED	HOLLOWED	HOLT	HOMEGIRLS	HOMEWARDS
HOLIDAYER	HOLLOWER	HOLTS	HOMEGROWN	HOMEWARE
HOLIDAYS	HOLLOWEST	HOLUBTSI	HOMELAND	HOMEWARES
HOLIER	HOLLOWING	HOLY	HOMELANDS	HOMEWORK
HOLIES	HOLLOWLY	HOLYDAM	HOMELESS	HOMEWORKS
HOLIEST	HOLLOWS	HOLYDAME	HOMELIER	HOMEY
HOLILY	HOLLY	HOLYDAMES	HOMELIEST	HOMEYNESS
HOLINESS	HOLLYHOCK	HOLYDAMS	HOMELIKE	HOMEYS
HOLING	HOLM	HOLYDAY	HOMELILY	HOMICIDAL
HOLINGS	HOLME	HOLYDAYS	HOMELY	HOMICIDE
HOLISM	HOLMES	HOLYSTONE	HOMELYN	HOMICIDES
HOLISMS	HOLMIA	HOLYTIDE	HOMELYNS	HOMIE
HOLIST	HOLMIAS	HOLYTIDES	HOMEMADE	HOMIER
HOLISTIC	HOLMIC	HOM	HOMEMAKER	HOMIES
HOLISTS	HOLMIUM	HOMA	HOMEOBOX	HOMIEST
HOLK	HOLMIUMS	HOMAGE	HOMEOMERY	HOMILETIC
HOLKED	HOLMS	HOMAGED	HOMEOPATH	HOMILIES
HOLKING	HOLO	HOMAGER	HOMEOSES	HOMILIST
HOLKS	HOLOCAUST	HOMAGERS	HOMEOSIS	HOMILISTS
HOLLA	HOLOCENE	HOMAGES	HOMEOTIC	HOMILY
HOLLAED	HOLOCRINE	HOMAGING	HOMEOWNER	HOMINES
HOLLAING	HOLOGAMY	HOMALOID	HOMEPAGE	HOMINESS

HOMING	HOMOMORPH	HONDLES	HONKER	HOODIEST
HOMINGS	HOMONYM	HONDLING	HONKERS	HOODING
HOMINIAN	HOMONYMIC	HONDS	HONKEY	HOODLESS
HOMINIANS	HOMONYMS	HONE	HONKEYS	HOODLIKE
HOMINID	HOMONYMY	HONED	HONKIE	HOODLUM
HOMINIDS	HOMOPHILE	HONER	HONKIES	HOODLUMS
HOMINIES	HOMOPHOBE	HONERS	HONKING	HOODMAN
HOMININ	HOMOPHONE	HONES	HONKS	HOODMEN
HOMININE	HOMOPHONY	HONEST	HONKY	HOODMOLD
HOMININS	HOMOPHYLY	HONESTER	HONOR	HOODMOLDS
HOMINISE	HOMOPLASY	HONESTEST	HONORABLE	HOODOO
HOMINISED	HOMOPOLAR	HONESTIES	HONORABLY	HOODOOED
HOMINISES	HOMOS	HONESTLY	HONORAND	HOODOOING
HOMINIZE	HOMOSEX	HONESTY	HONORANDS	HOODOOISM
HOMINIZED	HOMOSEXES	HONEWORT	HONORARIA	HOODOOS
HOMINIZES	HOMOSPORY	HONEWORTS	HONORARY	HOODS
HOMINOID	HOMOSTYLY	HONEY	HONORED	HOODWINK
HOMINOIDS	HOMOTAXES	HONEYBEE	HONOREE	HOODWINKS
HOMINY	HOMOTAXIC	HONEYBEES	HONOREES	HOODY
HOMME	HOMOTAXIS	HONEYBUN	HONORER	HOOEY
HOMMES	HOMOTONIC	HONEYBUNS	HONORERS	HOOEYS
HOMMOCK	HOMOTONY	HONEYCOMB	HONORIFIC	HOOF
HOMMOCKS	HOMOTYPAL	HONEYDEW	HONORING	HOOFBEAT
HOMMOS	HOMOTYPE	HONEYDEWS	HONORLESS	HOOFBEATS
HOMMOSES	HOMOTYPES	HONEYED	HONORS	HOOFBOUND
HOMO	HOMOTYPIC	HONEYEDLY	HONOUR	HOOFED
HOMOCERCY	HOMOTYPY	HONEYFUL	HONOURARY	HOOFER
HOMODONT	HOMOUSIAN	HONEYING	HONOURED	HOOFERS
HOMODYNE	HOMS	HONEYLESS	HONOUREE	HOOFING
HOMOEOBOX	HOMUNCLE	HONEYMOON	HONOUREES	HOOFLESS
HOMOEOSES	HOMUNCLES	HONEYPOT	HONOURER	HOOFLIKE
HOMOEOSIS	HOMUNCULE	HONEYPOTS	HONOURERS	HOOFPRINT
HOMOEOTIC	HOMUNCULI	HONEYS	HONOURING	HOOFROT
HOMOGAMIC	HOMY	HONEYTRAP	HONOURS	HOOFROTS
HOMOGAMY	HON	HONG	HONS	HOOFS
HOMOGENY	HONAN	HONGI	HOO	HOOK
HOMOGONY	HONANS	HONGIED	HOOCH	HOOKA
HOMOGRAFT	HONCHO	HONGIES	HOOCHES	HOOKAH
HOMOGRAPH	HONCHOED	HONGIING	HOOCHIE	HOOKAHS
HOMOLOG	HONCHOES	HONGING	HOOCHIES	HOOKAS
HOMOLOGIC	HONCHOING	HONGIS	HOOD	HOOKCHECK
HOMOLOGS	HONCHOS	HONGS	HOODED	HOOKED
HOMOLOGUE	HOND	HONIED	HOODIA	HOOKER
HOMOLOGY	HONDA	HONIEDLY	HOODIAS	HOOKERS
HOMOLYSES	HONDAS	HONING	HOODIE	HOOKEY
HOMOLYSIS	HONDLE	HONK	HOODIER	HOOKEYS
HOMOLYTIC	HONDLED	HONKED	HOODIES	HOOKIER

HOOKIES	HOOPOOS	HOP	HOPSCOTCH	HORNBEAK
HOOKIEST	HOOPS	HOPAK	HOPTOAD	HORNBEAKS
HOOKING	HOOPSKIRT	HOPAKS	HOPTOADS	HORNBEAM
HOOKINGS	HOOPSTER	HOPBIND	HORA	HORNBEAMS
HOOKLESS	HOOPSTERS	HOPBINDS	HORAH	HORNBILL
HOOKLET	HOOR	HOPBINE	HORAHS	HORNBILLS
HOOKLETS	HOORAH	HOPBINES	HORAL	HORNBOOK
HOOKLIKE	HOORAHED	HOPDOG	HORARY	HORNBOOKS
HOOKNOSE	HOORAHING	HOPDOGS	HORAS	HORNBUG
HOOKNOSED	HOORAHS	HOPE	HORDE	HORNBUGS
HOOKNOSES	HOORAY	HOPED	HORDED	HORNDOG
HOOKS	HOORAYED	HOPEFUL	HORDEIN	HORNDOGS
HOOKUP	HOORAYING	HOPEFULLY	HORDEINS	HORNED
HOOKUPS	HOORAYS	HOPEFULS	HORDEOLA	HORNER
HOOKWORM	HOORD	HOPELESS	HORDEOLUM	HORNERS
HOOKWORMS	HOORDS	HOPER	HORDES	HORNET
HOOKY	HOOROO	HOPERS	HORDING	HORNETS
HOOLACHAN	HOORS	HOPES	HORDOCK	HORNFELS
HOOLEY	HOOSEGOW	HOPFIELD	HORDOCKS	HORNFUL
HOOLEYS	HOOSEGOWS	HOPFIELDS	HORE	HORNFULS
HOOLICAN	HOOSGOW	HOPHEAD	HOREHOUND	HORNGELD
HOOLICANS	HOOSGOWS	HOPHEADS	HORI	HORNGELDS
HOOLIE	HOOSH	HOPING	HORIATIKI	HORNIER
HOOLIER	HOOSHED	HOPINGLY	HORIS	HORNIEST
HOOLIES	HOOSHES	HOPLITE	HORIZON	HORNILY
HOOLIEST	HOOSHING	HOPLITES	HORIZONAL	HORNINESS
HOOLIGAN	HOOT	HOPLITIC	HORIZONS	HORNING
HOOLIGANS	HOOTCH	HOPLOLOGY	HORK	HORNINGS
HOOLOCK	HOOTCHES	HOPPED	HORKED	HORNISH
HOOLOCKS	HOOTED	HOPPER	HORKEY	HORNIST
HOOLY	HOOTER	HOPPERCAR	HORKEYS	HORNISTS
HOON	HOOTERS	HOPPERS	HORKING	HORNITO
HOONED	HOOTIER	HOPPIER	HORKS	HORNITOS
HOONING	HOOTIEST	HOPPIEST	HORLICKS	HORNLESS
HOONS	HOOTING	HOPPING	HORME	HORNLET
HOOP	HOOTNANNY	HOPPINGS	HORMES	HORNLETS
HOOPED	HOOTS	HOPPLE	HORMESES	HORNLIKE
HOOPER	HOOTY	HOPPLED	HORMESIS	HORNPIPE
HOOPERS	HOOVE	HOPPLER	HORMETIC	HORNPIPES
HOOPING	HOOVED	HOPPLERS	HORMIC	HORNPOUT
HOOPLA	HOOVEN	HOPPLES	HORMONAL	HORNPOUTS
HOOPLAS	HOOVER	HOPPLING	HORMONE	HORNS
HOOPLESS	HOOVERED	HOPPUS	HORMONES	HORNSTONE
HOOPLIKE	HOOVERING	HOPPY	HORMONIC	HORNTAIL
HOOPOE	HOOVERS	HOPS	HORN	HORNTAILS
HOOPOES	HOOVES	HOPSACK	HORNBAG	HORNWORK
HOOPOO	HOOVING	HOPSACKS	HORNBAGS	HORNWORKS

HORNWORM	HORSEFLY	HOSE	HOSTELRY	HOTELIERS
HORNWORMS	HORSEHAIR	HOSED	HOSTELS	HOTELING
HORNWORT	HORSEHIDE	HOSEL	HOSTESS	HOTELINGS
HORNWORTS	HORSELESS	HOSELIKE	HOSTESSED	HOTELLING
HORNWRACK	HORSELIKE	HOSELS	HOSTESSES	HOTELMAN
HORNY	HORSEMAN	HOSEMAN	HOSTIE	HOTELMEN
HORNYHEAD	HORSEMEAT	HOSEMEN	HOSTIES	HOTELS
HORNYWINK	HORSEMEN	HOSEN	HOSTILE	HOTEN
HOROEKA	HORSEMINT	HOSEPIPE	HOSTILELY	HOTFOOT
HOROEKAS	HORSEPLAY	HOSEPIPES	HOSTILES	HOTFOOTED
HOROKAKA	HORSEPOND	HOSER	HOSTILITY	HOTFOOTS
HOROKAKAS	HORSEPOX	HOSERS	HOSTING	HOTHEAD
HOROLOGE	HORSERACE	HOSES	HOSTINGS	HOTHEADED
HOROLOGER	HORSES	HOSEY	HOSTLER	HOTHEADS
HOROLOGES	HORSESHIT	HOSEYED	HOSTLERS	HOTHOUSE
HOROLOGIA	HORSESHOD	HOSEYING	HOSTLESS	HOTHOUSED
HOROLOGIC	HORSESHOE	HOSEYS	HOSTLESSE	HOTHOUSES
HOROLOGY	HORSETAIL	HOSIER	HOSTLY	HOTLINE
HOROMETRY	HORSEWAY	HOSIERIES	HOSTRIES	HOTLINER
HOROPITO	HORSEWAYS	HOSIERS	HOSTRY	HOTLINERS
HOROPITOS	HORSEWEED	HOSIERY	HOSTS	HOTLINES
HOROPTER	HORSEWHIP	HOSING	HOT	HOTLINK
HOROPTERS	HORSEY	HOSPICE	HOTBED	HOTLINKS
HOROSCOPE	HORSIE	HOSPICES	HOTBEDS	HOTLY
HOROSCOPY	HORSIER	HOSPITAGE	HOTBLOOD	HOTNESS
HORRENT	HORSIES	HOSPITAL	HOTBLOODS	HOTNESSES
HORRIBLE	HORSIEST	HOSPITALE	HOTBOX	HOTPLATE
HORRIBLES	HORSILY	HOSPITALS	HOTBOXED	HOTPLATES
HORRIBLY	HORSINESS	HOSPITIA	HOTBOXES	HOTPOT
HORRID	HORSING	HOSPITIUM	HOTBOXING	HOTPOTS
HORRIDER	HORSINGS	HOSPODAR	HOTCAKE	HOTPRESS
HORRIDEST	HORSON	HOSPODARS	HOTCAKES	HOTROD
HORRIDLY	HORSONS	HOSS	HOTCH	HOTRODS
HORRIFIC	HORST	HOSSES	HOTCHED	HOTS
HORRIFIED	HORSTE	HOST	HOTCHES	HOTSHOT
HORRIFIES	HORSTES	HOSTA	HOTCHING	HOTSHOTS
HORRIFY	HORSTS	HOSTAGE	HOTCHPOT	HOTSPOT
HORROR	HORSY	HOSTAGES	HOTCHPOTS	HOTSPOTS
HORRORS	HORTATION	HOSTAS	HOTDOG	HOTSPUR
HORS	HORTATIVE	HOSTED	HOTDOGGED	HOTSPURS
HORSE	HORTATORY	HOSTEL	HOTDOGGER	HOTTED
HORSEBACK	HOS	HOSTELED	HOTDOGS	HOTTENTOT
HORSEBEAN	HOSANNA	HOSTELER	HOTE	HOTTER
HORSEBOX	HOSANNAED	HOSTELERS	HOTEL	HOTTERED
HORSECAR	HOSANNAH	HOSTELING	HOTELDOM	HOTTERING
HORSECARS	HOSANNAHS	HOSTELLED	HOTELDOMS	HOTTERS
HORSED	HOSANNAS	HOSTELLER	HOTELIER	HOTTEST

HOTTIE	HOURS	HOUTING	HOWITZER	HRYVNA
HOTTIES	HOUSE	HOUTINGS	HOWITZERS	HRYVNAS
HOTTING	HOUSEBOAT	HOUTS	HOWK	HRYVNIA
HOTTINGS	HOUSEBOY	HOVE	HOWKED	HRYVNIAS
HOTTISH	HOUSEBOYS	HOVEA	HOWKER	HRYVNYA
HOTTY	HOUSECARL	HOVEAS	HOWKERS	HRYVNYAS
HOUDAH	HOUSECOAT	HOVED	HOWKING	HUANACO
HOUDAHS	HOUSED	HOVEL	HOWKS	HUANACOS
HOUDAN	HOUSEFLY	HOVELED	HOWL	HUAQUERO
HOUDANS	HOUSEFUL	HOVELING	HOWLBACK	HUAQUEROS
HOUF	HOUSEFULS	HOVELLED	HOWLBACKS	HUARACHE
HOUFED	HOUSEHOLD	HOVELLER	HOWLED	HUARACHES
HOUFF	HOUSEKEEP	HOVELLERS	HOWLER	HUARACHO
HOUFFED	HOUSEKEPT	HOVELLING	HOWLERS	HUARACHOS
HOUFFING	HOUSEL	HOVELS	HOWLET	HUB
HOUFFS	HOUSELED	HOVEN	HOWLETS	HUBBIES
HOUFING	HOUSELEEK	HOVER	HOWLING	HUBBLIER
HOUFS	HOUSELESS	HOVERED	HOWLINGLY	HUBBLIEST
HOUGH	HOUSELINE	HOVERER	HOWLINGS	HUBBLY
HOUGHED	HOUSELING	HOVERERS	HOWLROUND	HUBBUB
HOUGHING	HOUSELLED	HOVERFLY	HOWLS	HUBBUBOO
HOUGHS	HOUSELS	HOVERING	HOWRE	HUBBUBOOS
HOUHERE	HOUSEMAID	HOVERPORT	HOWRES	HUBBUBS
HOUHERES	HOUSEMAN	HOVERS	HOWS	HUBBY
HOUMMOS	HOUSEMATE	HOVES	HOWSO	HUBCAP
HOUMMOSES	HOUSEMEN	HOVING	HOWSOEVER	HUBCAPS
HOUMOUS	HOUSER	HOW	HOWTOWDIE	HUBLESS
HOUMOUSES	HOUSEROOM	HOWBE	HOWZAT	HUBRIS
HOUMUS	HOUSERS	HOWBEIT	HOWZIT	HUBRISES
HOUMUSES	HOUSES	HOWDAH	HOX	HUBRISTIC
HOUND	HOUSESAT	HOWDAHS	HOXED	HUBS
HOUNDED	HOUSESIT	HOWDIE	HOXES	HUCK
HOUNDER	HOUSESITS	HOWDIED	HOXING	HUCKABACK
HOUNDERS	HOUSETOP	HOWDIES	HOY	HUCKED
HOUNDFISH	HOUSETOPS	HOWDY	HOYA	HUCKERY
HOUNDING	HOUSEWIFE	HOWDYING	HOYAS	HUCKING
HOUNDS	HOUSEWORK	HOWE	HOYDEN	HUCKLE
HOUNGAN	HOUSEY	HOWES	HOYDENED	HUCKLED
HOUNGANS	HOUSIER	HOWEVER	HOYDENING	HUCKLES
HOUR	HOUSIEST	HOWF	HOYDENISH	HUCKLING
HOURGLASS	HOUSING	HOWFED	HOYDENISM	HUCKS
HOURI	HOUSINGS	HOWFF	HOYDENS	HUCKSTER
HOURIS	HOUSLING	HOWFFED	HOYED	HUCKSTERS
HOURLIES	HOUSLINGS	HOWFFING	HOYING	HUCKSTERY
HOURLONG	HOUSTONIA	HOWFFS	HOYLE	HUDDEN
HOURLY	HOUT	HOWFING	HOYLES	HUDDLE
HOURPLATE	HOUTED	HOWFS	HOYS	HUDDLED

HUDDLER	HUGS	HULLOOING	HUMBUCKER	HUMIFIES
HUDDLERS	HUGY	HULLOOS	HUMBUG	HUMIFY
HUDDLES	HUH	HULLOS	HUMBUGGED	HUMIFYING
HUDDLING	HUHU	HULLS	HUMBUGGER	HUMILIANT
HUDDUP	HUHUS	HULLY	HUMBUGS	HUMILIATE
HUDNA	HUI	HUM	HUMBUZZ	HUMILITY
HUDNAS	HUIA	HUMA	HUMBUZZES	HUMINT
HUDUD	HUIAS	HUMAN	HUMDINGER	HUMINTS
HUDUDS	HUIC	HUMANE	HUMDRUM	HUMITE
HUE	HUIPIL	HUMANELY	HUMDRUMS	HUMITES
HUED	HUIPILES	HUMANER	HUMECT	HUMITURE
HUELESS	HUIPILS	HUMANEST	HUMECTANT	HUMITURES
HUER	HUIS	HUMANHOOD	HUMECTATE	HUMLIE
HUERS	HUISACHE	HUMANISE	HUMECTED	HUMLIES
HUES	HUISACHES	HUMANISED	HUMECTING	HUMMABLE
HUFF	HUISSIER	HUMANISER	HUMECTIVE	HUMMAUM
HUFFED	HUISSIERS	HUMANISES	HUMECTS	HUMMAUMS
HUFFER	HUITAIN	HUMANISM	HUMEFIED	HUMMED
HUFFERS	HUITAINS	HUMANISMS	HUMEFIES	HUMMEL
HUFFIER	HULA	HUMANIST	HUMEFY	HUMMELLED
HUFFIEST	HULAS	HUMANISTS	HUMEFYING	HUMMELLER
HUFFILY	HULE	HUMANITY	HUMERAL	HUMMELS
HUFFINESS	HULES	HUMANIZE	HUMERALS	HUMMER
HUFFING	HULK	HUMANIZED	HUMERI	HUMMERS
HUFFINGS	HULKED	HUMANIZER	HUMERUS	HUMMING
HUFFISH	HULKIER	HUMANIZES	HUMF	HUMMINGS
HUFFISHLY	HULKIEST	HUMANKIND	HUMFED	HUMMLE
HUFFKIN	HULKING	HUMANLIKE	HUMFING	HUMMOCK
HUFFKINS	HULKS	HUMANLY	HUMFS	HUMMOCKED
HUFFS	HULKY	HUMANNESS	HUMHUM	HUMMOCKS
HUFFY	HULL	HUMANOID	HUMHUMS	HUMMOCKY
HUG	HULLED	HUMANOIDS	HUMIC	HUMMUM
HUGE	HULLER	HUMANS	HUMICOLE	HUMMUMS
HUGELY	HULLERS	HUMAS	HUMICOLES	HUMMUS
HUGENESS	HULLIER	HUMATE	HUMID	HUMMUSES
HUGEOUS	HULLIEST	HUMATES	HUMIDER	HUMOGEN
HUGEOUSLY	HULLING	HUMBLE	HUMIDEST	HUMOGENS
HUGER	HULLO	HUMBLEBEE	HUMIDEX	HUMONGOUS
HUGEST	HULLOA	HUMBLED	HUMIDEXES	HUMOR
HUGGABLE	HULLOAED	HUMBLER	HUMIDICES	HUMORAL
HUGGED	HULLOAING	HUMBLERS	HUMIDIFY	HUMORALLY
HUGGER	HULLOAS	HUMBLES	HUMIDITY	HUMORED
HUGGERS	HULLOED	HUMBLESSE	HUMIDLY	HUMORESK
HUGGIER	HULLOES	HUMBLEST	HUMIDNESS	HUMORESKS
HUGGIEST	HULLOING	HUMBLING	HUMIDOR	HUMORFUL
HUGGING	HULLOO	HUMBLINGS	HUMIDORS	HUMORING
HUGGY	HULLOOED	HUMBLY	HUMIFIED	HUMORIST

HUMORISTS	HUNCHED	HUNTING	HURRAHS	HUSHERS
HUMORLESS	HUNCHES	HUNTINGS	HURRAING	HUSHES
HUMOROUS	HUNCHING	HUNTRESS	HURRAS	HUSHFUL
HUMORS	HUNDRED	HUNTS	HURRAY	HUSHIER
HUMORSOME	HUNDREDER	HUNTSMAN	HURRAYED	HUSHIEST
HUMOUR	HUNDREDOR	HUNTSMEN	HURRAYING	HUSHING
HUMOURED	HUNDREDS	HUP	HURRAYS	HUSHPUPPY
HUMOURFUL	HUNDREDTH	HUPIRO	HURRICANE	HUSHY
HUMOURING	HUNG	HUPIROS	HURRICANO	HUSK
HUMOURS	HUNGAN	HUPPAH	HURRIED	HUSKED
HUMOUS	HUNGANS	HUPPAHS	HURRIEDLY	HUSKER
HUMOUSES	HUNGER	HUPPED	HURRIER	HUSKERS
HUMP	HUNGERED	HUPPING	HURRIERS	HUSKIER
HUMPBACK	HUNGERFUL	HUPPOT	HURRIES	HUSKIES
HUMPBACKS	HUNGERING	HUPPOTH	HURRY	HUSKIEST
HUMPED	HUNGERLY	HUPS	HURRYING	HUSKILY
HUMPEN	HUNGERS	HURCHEON	HURRYINGS	HUSKINESS
HUMPENS	HUNGOVER	HURCHEONS	HURST	HUSKING
HUMPER	HUNGRIER	HURDEN	HURSTS	HUSKINGS
HUMPERS	HUNGRIEST	HURDENS	HURT	HUSKLIKE
HUMPH	HUNGRILY	HURDIES	HURTER	HUSKS
HUMPHED	HUNGRY	HURDLE	HURTERS	HUSKY
HUMPHING	HUNH	HURDLED	HURTFUL	HUSO
HUMPHS	HUNK	HURDLER	HURTFULLY	HUSOS
HUMPIER	HUNKER	HURDLERS	HURTING	HUSS
HUMPIES	HUNKERED	HURDLES	HURTLE	HUSSAR
HUMPIEST	HUNKERING	HURDLING	HURTLED	HUSSARS
HUMPINESS	HUNKERS	HURDLINGS	HURTLES	HUSSES
HUMPING	HUNKEY	HURDS	HURTLESS	HUSSIES
HUMPLESS	HUNKEYS	HURL	HURTLING	HUSSIF
HUMPLIKE	HUNKIE	HURLBAT	HURTS	HUSSIFS
HUMPS	HUNKIER	HURLBATS	HUSBAND	HUSSY
HUMPTIES	HUNKIES	HURLED	HUSBANDED	HUSTINGS
HUMPTY	HUNKIEST	HURLER	HUSBANDER	HUSTLE
HUMPY	HUNKS	HURLERS	HUSBANDLY	HUSTLED
HUMS	HUNKSES	HURLEY	HUSBANDRY	HUSTLER
HUMSTRUM	HUNKY	HURLEYS	HUSBANDS	HUSTLERS
HUMSTRUMS	HUNNISH	HURLIES	HUSH	HUSTLES
HUMUNGOUS	HUNS	HURLING	HUSHABIED	HUSTLING
HUMUS	HUNT	HURLINGS	HUSHABIES	HUSTLINGS
HUMUSES	HUNTABLE	HURLS	HUSHABY	HUSWIFE
HUMUSY	HUNTAWAY	HURLY	HUSHABYE	HUSWIFES
HUMVEE	HUNTAWAYS	HURRA	HUSHED	HUSWIVES
HUMVEES	HUNTED	HURRAED	HUSHEDLY	HUT
HUN	HUNTEDLY	HURRAH	HUSHER	HUTCH
HUNCH	HUNTER	HURRAHED	HUSHERED	HUTCHED
HUNCHBACK	HUNTERS	HURRAHING	HUSHERING	HUTCHES

HUTCHIE	HYALOGENS	HYDRAZOIC	HYDROSOL	HYING
HUTCHIES	HYALOID	HYDREMIA	HYDROSOLS	HYKE
HUTCHING	HYALOIDS	HYDREMIAS	HYDROSOMA	HYKES
HUTIA	HYALONEMA	HYDRIA	HYDROSOME	HYLA
HUTIAS	HYBRID	HYDRIAE	HYDROSTAT	HYLAS
HUTLIKE	HYBRIDISE	HYDRIC	HYDROUS	HYLDING
HUTMENT	HYBRIDISM	HYDRID	HYDROVANE	HYLDINGS
HUTMENTS	HYBRIDIST	HYDRIDE	HYDROXIDE	HYLE
HUTS	HYBRIDITY	HYDRIDES	HYDROXIUM	HYLEG
HUTTED	HYBRIDIZE	HYDRIDS	HYDROXY	HYLEGS
HUTTING	HYBRIDOMA	HYDRILLA	HYDROXYL	HYLES
HUTTINGS	HYBRIDOUS	HYDRILLAS	HYDROXYLS	HYLIC
HUTZPA	HYBRIDS	HYDRIODIC	HYDROZOA	HYLICISM
HUTZPAH	HYBRIS	HYDRO	HYDROZOAN	HYLICISMS
HUTZPAHS	HYBRISES	HYDROCAST	HYDROZOON	HYLICIST
HUTZPAS	HYBRISTIC	HYDROCELE	HYDYNE	HYLICISTS
HUZOOR	HYDANTOIN	HYDROFOIL	HYDYNES	HYLISM
HUZOORS	HYDATHODE	HYDROGEL	HYE	HYLISMS
HUZZA	HYDATID	HYDROGELS	HYED	HYLIST
HUZZAED	HYDATIDS	HYDROGEN	HYEING	HYLISTS
HUZZAH	HYDATOID	HYDROGENS	HYEN	HYLOBATE
HUZZAHED	HYDRA	HYDROID	HYENA	HYLOBATES
HUZZAHING	HYDRACID	HYDROIDS	HYENAS	HYLOIST
HUZZAHS	HYDRACIDS	HYDROLASE	HYENIC	HYLOISTS
HUZZAING	HYDRAE	HYDROLOGY	HYENINE	HYLOPHYTE
HUZZAS	HYDRAEMIA	HYDROLYSE	HYENOID	HYLOZOIC
HUZZIES	HYDRAGOG	HYDROLYTE	HYENS	HYLOZOISM
HUZZY	HYDRAGOGS	HYDROLYZE	HYES	HYLOZOIST
HWAN	HYDRANGEA	HYDROMA	HYETAL	HYMEN
HWYL	HYDRANT	HYDROMAS	HYETOLOGY	HYMENAEAL
HWYLS	HYDRANTH	HYDROMATA	HYGEIST	HYMENAEAN
HYACINE	HYDRANTHS	HYDROMEL	HYGEISTS	HYMENAL
HYACINES	HYDRANTS	HYDROMELS	HYGIEIST	HYMENEAL
HYACINTH	HYDRAS	HYDRONAUT	HYGIEISTS	HYMENEALS
HYACINTHS	HYDRASE	HYDRONIC	HYGIENE	HYMENEAN
HYAENA	HYDRASES	HYDRONIUM	HYGIENES	HYMENEANS
HYAENAS	HYDRASTIS	HYDROPATH	HYGIENIC	HYMENIA
HYAENIC	HYDRATE	HYDROPIC	HYGIENICS	HYMENIAL
HYALIN	HYDRATED	HYDROPS	HYGIENIST	HYMENIUM
HYALINE	HYDRATES	HYDROPSES	HYGRISTOR	HYMENIUMS
HYALINES	HYDRATING	HYDROPSY	HYGRODEIK	HYMENS
HYALINISE	HYDRATION	HYDROPTIC	HYGROLOGY	HYMN
HYALINIZE	HYDRATOR	HYDROPULT	HYGROMA	HYMNAL
HYALINS	HYDRATORS	HYDROS	HYGROMAS	HYMNALS
HYALITE	HYDRAULIC	HYDROSERE	HYGROMATA	HYMNARIES
HYALITES	HYDRAZIDE	HYDROSKI	HYGROPHIL	HYMNARY
HYALOGEN	HYDRAZINE	HYDROSKIS	HYGROSTAT	HYMNBOOK

H

HYMNBOOKS	HYPERGAMY	HYPHENS	HYPOCRITE	HYPOS
HYMNED	HYPERGOL	HYPHIES	HYPODERM	HYPOSTOME
HYMNIC	HYPERGOLS	HYPHY	HYPODERMA	HYPOSTYLE
HYMNING	HYPERICIN	HYPING	HYPODERMS	HYPOTAXES
HYMNIST	HYPERICUM	HYPINGS	HYPOED	HYPOTAXIS
HYMNISTS	HYPERLINK	HYPINOSES	HYPOGAEA	HYPOTHEC
HYMNLESS	HYPERMART	HYPINOSIS	HYPOGAEAL	HYPOTHECA
HYMNLIKE	HYPERNOVA	HYPNIC	HYPOGAEAN	HYPOTHECS
HYMNODIES	HYPERNYM	HYPNICS	HYPOGAEUM	HYPOTONIA
HYMNODIST	HYPERNYMS	HYPNOGENY	HYPOGEA	HYPOTONIC
HYMNODY	HYPERNYMY	HYPNOID	HYPOGEAL	HYPOXEMIA
HYMNOLOGY	HYPERON	HYPNOIDAL	HYPOGEAN	HYPOXEMIC
HYMNS	HYPERONS	HYPNOLOGY	HYPOGENE	HYPOXIA
HYNDE	HYPEROPE	HYPNONE	HYPOGENIC	HYPOXIAS
HYNDES	HYPEROPES	HYPNONES	HYPOGEOUS	HYPOXIC
HYOID	HYPEROPIA	HYPNOSES	HYPOGEUM	HYPPED
HYOIDAL	HYPEROPIC	HYPNOSIS	HYPOGYNY	HYPPING
HYOIDEAN	HYPERPNEA	HYPNOTEE	HYPOID	HYPS
HYOIDS	HYPERPURE	HYPNOTEES	HYPOIDS	HYPURAL
HYOSCINE	HYPERREAL	HYPNOTIC	HYPOING	HYRACES
HYOSCINES	HYPERS	HYPNOTICS	HYPOMANIA	HYRACOID
HYP	HYPERTEXT	HYPNOTISE	HYPOMANIC	HYRACOIDS
HYPALGIA	HYPES	HYPNOTISM	HYPOMORPH	HYRAX
HYPALGIAS	HYPESTER	HYPNOTIST	HYPONASTY	HYRAXES
HYPALLAGE	HYPESTERS	HYPNOTIZE	HYPONEA	HYSON
HYPANTHIA	HYPETHRAL	HYPNOTOID	HYPONEAS	HYSONS
HYPATE	HYPHA	HYPNUM	HYPONOIA	HYSSOP
HYPATES	HYPHAE	HYPNUMS	HYPONOIAS	HYSSOPS
HYPE	HYPHAL	HYPO	HYPONYM	HYSTERIA
HYPED	HYPHEMIA	HYPOACID	HYPONYMS	HYSTERIAS
HYPER	HYPHEMIAS	HYPOBARIC	HYPONYMY	HYSTERIC
HYPERACID	HYPHEN	HYPOBLAST	HYPOPHYGE	HYSTERICS
HYPERARID	HYPHENATE	HYPOBOLE	HYPOPLOID	HYSTEROID
HYPERBOLA	HYPHENED	HYPOBOLES	HYPOPNEA	HYTE
HYPERBOLE	HYPHENIC	HYPOCAUST	HYPOPNEAS	HYTHE
HYPERCUBE	HYPHENING	HYPOCIST	HYPOPNEIC	HYTHES
HYPEREMIA	HYPHENISE	HYPOCISTS	HYPOPNOEA	
HYPEREMIC	HYPHENISM	HYPOCOTYL	HYPOPYON	
HYPERFINE	HYPHENIZE	HYPOCRISY	HYPOPYONS	

I

IAMB	ICEBOXES	ICHNITE	ICONIFIES	IDEALISTS
IAMBI	ICECAP	ICHNITES	ICONIFY	IDEALITY
IAMBIC	ICECAPPED	ICHNOLITE	ICONISE	IDEALIZE
IAMBICS	ICECAPS	ICHNOLOGY	ICONISED	IDEALIZED
IAMBIST	ICED	ICHOR	ICONISES	IDEALIZER
IAMBISTS	ICEFALL	ICHOROUS	ICONISING	IDEALIZES
IAMBS	ICEFALLS	ICHORS	ICONIZE	IDEALLESS
IAMBUS	ICEFIELD	ICHS	ICONIZED	IDEALLY
IAMBUSES	ICEFIELDS	ICHTHIC	ICONIZES	IDEALNESS
IANTHINE	ICEFISH	ICHTHYIC	ICONIZING	IDEALOGUE
IATRIC	ICEFISHED	ICHTHYOID	ICONOLOGY	IDEALOGY
IATRICAL	ICEFISHES	ICHTHYS	ICONOSTAS	IDEALS
IATROGENY	ICEHOUSE	ICHTHYSES	ICONS	IDEAS
IBADAH	ICEHOUSES	ICICLE	ICTAL	IDEATA
IBADAT	ICEKHANA	ICICLED	ICTERIC	IDEATE
IBERIS	ICEKHANAS	ICICLES	ICTERICAL	IDEATED
IBERISES	ICELESS	ICIER	ICTERICS	IDEATES
IBEX	ICELIKE	ICIEST	ICTERID	IDEATING
IBEXES	ICEMAKER	ICILY	ICTERIDS	IDEATION
IBICES	ICEMAKERS	ICINESS	ICTERINE	IDEATIONS
IBIDEM	ICEMAN	ICINESSES	ICTERUS	IDEATIVE
IBIS	ICEMEN	ICING	ICTERUSES	IDEATUM
IBISES	ICEPACK	ICINGS	ICTIC	IDEE
IBOGAINE	ICEPACKS	ICK	ICTUS	IDEES
IBOGAINES	ICER	ICKER	ICTUSES	IDEM
IBRIK	ICERS	ICKERS	ICY	IDENT
IBRIKS	ICES	ICKIER	ID	IDENTIC
IBUPROFEN	ICESCAPE	ICKIEST	IDANT	IDENTICAL
ICE	ICESCAPES	ICKILY	IDANTS	IDENTIFY
ICEBALL	ICESTONE	ICKINESS	IDE	IDENTIKIT
ICEBALLS	ICESTONES	ICKLE	IDEA	IDENTITY
ICEBERG	ICEWINE	ICKLER	IDEAED	IDENTS
ICEBERGS	ICEWINES	ICKLEST	IDEAL	IDEOGRAM
ICEBLINK	ICEWORM	ICKS	IDEALESS	IDEOGRAMS
ICEBLINKS	ICEWORMS	ICKY	IDEALISE	IDEOGRAPH
ICEBOAT	ICH	ICON	IDEALISED	IDEOLOGIC
ICEBOATED	ICHABOD	ICONES	IDEALISER	IDEOLOGUE
ICEBOATER	ICHED	ICONIC	IDEALISES	IDEOLOGY
ICEBOATS	ICHES	ICONICAL	IDEALISM	IDEOMOTOR
ICEBOUND	ICHING	ICONICITY	IDEALISMS	IDEOPHONE
ICEBOX	ICHNEUMON	ICONIFIED	IDEALIST	IDEOPOLIS

IDES	IDOLATOR	IGAPOS	IGNORANT	ILIUM
IDIOBLAST	IDOLATORS	IGARAPE	IGNORANTS	ILK
IDIOCIES	IDOLATRY	IGARAPES	IGNORE	ILKA
IDIOCY	IDOLISE	IGG	IGNORED	ILKADAY
IDIOGRAM	IDOLISED	IGGED	IGNORER	ILKADAYS
IDIOGRAMS	IDOLISER	IGGING	IGNORERS	ILKS
IDIOGRAPH	IDOLISERS	IGGS	IGNORES	ILL
IDIOLECT	IDOLISES	IGLOO	IGNORING	ILLAPSE
IDIOLECTS	IDOLISING	IGLOOS	IGUANA	ILLAPSED
IDIOM	IDOLISM	IGLU	IGUANAS	ILLAPSES
IDIOMATIC	IDOLISMS	IGLUS	IGUANIAN	ILLAPSING
IDIOMS	IDOLIST	IGNARO	IGUANIANS	ILLATION
IDIOPATHY	IDOLISTS	IGNAROES	IGUANID	ILLATIONS
IDIOPHONE	IDOLIZE	IGNAROS	IGUANIDS	ILLATIVE
IDIOPLASM	IDOLIZED	IGNATIA	IGUANODON	ILLATIVES
IDIOT	IDOLIZER	IGNATIAS	IHRAM	ILLAWARRA
IDIOTCIES	IDOLIZERS	IGNEOUS	IHRAMS	ILLEGAL
IDIOTCY	IDOLIZES	IGNESCENT	IJTIHAD	ILLEGALLY
IDIOTIC	IDOLIZING	IGNIFIED	IJTIHADS	ILLEGALS
IDIOTICAL	IDOLON	IGNIFIES	IKAN	ILLEGIBLE
IDIOTICON	IDOLS	IGNIFY	IKANS	ILLEGIBLY
IDIOTISH	IDOLUM	IGNIFYING	IKAT	ILLER
IDIOTISM	IDONEITY	IGNITABLE	IKATS	ILLEST
IDIOTISMS	IDONEOUS	IGNITE	IKEBANA	ILLIAD
IDIOTS	IDS	IGNITED	IKEBANAS	ILLIADS
IDIOTYPE	IDYL	IGNITER	IKON	ILLIBERAL
IDIOTYPES	IDYLIST	IGNITERS	IKONS	ILLICIT
IDIOTYPIC	IDYLISTS	IGNITES	ILEA	ILLICITLY
IDLE	IDYLL	IGNITIBLE	ILEAC	ILLIMITED
IDLED	IDYLLIAN	IGNITING	ILEAL	ILLINIUM
IDLEHOOD	IDYLLIC	IGNITION	ILEITIDES	ILLINIUMS
IDLEHOODS	IDYLLIST	IGNITIONS	ILEITIS	ILLIPE
IDLENESS	IDYLLISTS	IGNITOR	ILEITISES	ILLIPES
IDLER	IDYLLS	IGNITORS	ILEOSTOMY	ILLIQUID
IDLERS	IDYLS	IGNITRON	ILEUM	ILLISION
IDLES	IF	IGNITRONS	ILEUS	ILLISIONS
IDLESSE	IFF	IGNOBLE	ILEUSES	ILLITE
IDLESSES	IFFIER	IGNOBLER	ILEX	ILLITES
IDLEST	IFFIEST	IGNOBLEST	ILEXES	ILLITIC
IDLING	IFFILY	IGNOBLY	ILIA	ILLNESS
IDLY	IFFINESS	IGNOMIES	ILIAC	ILLNESSES
IDOCRASE	IFFY	IGNOMINY	ILIACUS	ILLOGIC
IDOCRASES	IFS	IGNOMY	ILIACUSES	ILLOGICAL
IDOL	IFTAR	IGNORABLE	ILIAD	ILLOGICS
IDOLA	IFTARS	IGNORAMI	ILIADS	ILLS
IDOLATER	IGAD	IGNORAMUS	ILIAL	ILLTH
IDOLATERS	IGAPO	IGNORANCE	ILICES	ILLTHS

ILLUDE	IMAGISM	IMBEDS	IMBRUED	IMMANTLE
ILLUDED	IMAGISMS	IMBIBE	IMBRUES	IMMANTLED
ILLUDES	IMAGIST	IMBIBED	IMBRUING	IMMANTLES
ILLUDING	IMAGISTIC	IMBIBER	IMBRUTE	IMMASK
ILLUME	IMAGISTS	IMBIBERS	IMBRUTED	IMMASKED
ILLUMED	IMAGO	IMBIBES	IMBRUTES	IMMASKING
ILLUMES	IMAGOES	IMBIBING	IMBRUTING	IMMASKS
ILLUMINE	IMAGOS	IMBITTER	IMBUE	IMMATURE
ILLUMINED	IMAM	IMBITTERS	IMBUED	IMMATURES
ILLUMINER	IMAMATE	IMBIZO	IMBUEMENT	IMMEDIACY
ILLUMINES	IMAMATES	IMBIZOS	IMBUES	IMMEDIATE
ILLUMING	IMAMS	IMBLAZE	IMBUING	IMMENSE
ILLUPI	IMARET	IMBLAZED	IMBURSE	IMMENSELY
ILLUPIS	IMARETS	IMBLAZES	IMBURSED	IMMENSER
ILLUSION	IMARI	IMBLAZING	IMBURSES	IMMENSEST
ILLUSIONS	IMARIS	IMBODIED	IMBURSING	IMMENSITY
ILLUSIVE	IMAUM	IMBODIES	IMID	IMMERGE
ILLUSORY	IMAUMS	IMBODY	IMIDAZOLE	IMMERGED
ILLUVIA	IMBALANCE	IMBODYING	IMIDE	IMMERGES
ILLUVIAL	IMBALM	IMBOLDEN	IMIDES	IMMERGING
ILLUVIATE	IMBALMED	IMBOLDENS	IMIDIC	IMMERSE
ILLUVIUM	IMBALMER	IMBORDER	IMIDO	IMMERSED
ILLUVIUMS	IMBALMERS	IMBORDERS	IMIDS	IMMERSER
ILLY	IMBALMING	IMBOSK	IMINAZOLE	IMMERSERS
ILMENITE	IMBALMS	IMBOSKED	IMINE	IMMERSES
ILMENITES	IMBAR	IMBOSKING	IMINES	IMMERSING
IMAGE	IMBARK	IMBOSKS	IMINO	IMMERSION
IMAGEABLE	IMBARKED	IMBOSOM	IMINOUREA	IMMERSIVE
IMAGED	IMBARKING	IMBOSOMED	IMITABLE	IMMESH
IMAGELESS	IMBARKS	IMBOSOMS	IMITANCY	IMMESHED
IMAGER	IMBARRED	IMBOSS	IMITANT	IMMESHES
IMAGERIES	IMBARRING	IMBOSSED	IMITANTS	IMMESHING
IMAGERS	IMBARS	IMBOSSES	IMITATE	IMMEW
IMAGERY	IMBASE	IMBOSSING	IMITATED	IMMEWED
IMAGES	IMBASED	IMBOWER	IMITATES	IMMEWING
IMAGINAL	IMBASES	IMBOWERED	IMITATING	IMMEWS
IMAGINARY	IMBASING	IMBOWERS	IMITATION	IMMIES
IMAGINE	IMBATHE	IMBRANGLE	IMITATIVE	IMMIGRANT
IMAGINED	IMBATHED	IMBRAST	IMITATOR	IMMIGRATE
IMAGINEER	IMBATHES	IMBREX	IMITATORS	IMMINENCE
IMAGINER	IMBATHING	IMBRICATE	IMMANACLE	IMMINENCY
IMAGINERS	IMBECILE	IMBRICES	IMMANE	IMMINENT
IMAGINES	IMBECILES	IMBROGLIO	IMMANELY	IMMINGLE
IMAGING	IMBECILIC	IMBROWN	IMMANENCE	IMMINGLED
IMAGINGS	IMBED	IMBROWNED	IMMANENCY	IMMINGLES
IMAGINING	IMBEDDED	IMBROWNS	IMMANENT	IMMINUTE
IMAGINIST	IMBEDDING	IMBRUE	IMMANITY	IMMISSION

IMMIT	IMPACTER	IMPARTING	IMPELLERS	IMPISH
IMMITS	IMPACTERS	IMPARTS	IMPELLING	IMPISHLY
IMMITTED	IMPACTFUL	IMPASSE	IMPELLOR	IMPLANT
IMMITTING	IMPACTING	IMPASSES	IMPELLORS	IMPLANTED
IMMIX	IMPACTION	IMPASSION	IMPELS	IMPLANTER
IMMIXED	IMPACTITE	IMPASSIVE	IMPEND	IMPLANTS
IMMIXES	IMPACTIVE	IMPASTE	IMPENDED	IMPLATE
IMMIXING	IMPACTOR	IMPASTED	IMPENDENT	IMPLATED
IMMIXTURE	IMPACTORS	IMPASTES	IMPENDING	IMPLATES
IMMOBILE	IMPACTS	IMPASTING	IMPENDS	IMPLATING
IMMODEST	IMPAINT	IMPASTO	IMPENNATE	IMPLEACH
IMMODESTY	IMPAINTED	IMPASTOED	IMPERATOR	IMPLEAD
IMMOLATE	IMPAINTS	IMPASTOS	IMPERFECT	IMPLEADED
IMMOLATED	IMPAIR	IMPATIENS	IMPERIA	IMPLEADER
IMMOLATES	IMPAIRED	IMPATIENT	IMPERIAL	IMPLEADS
IMMOLATOR	IMPAIRER	IMPAVE	IMPERIALS	IMPLED
IMMOMENT	IMPAIRERS	IMPAVED	IMPERIL	IMPLEDGE
IMMORAL	IMPAIRING	IMPAVES	IMPERILED	IMPLEDGED
IMMORALLY	IMPAIRS	IMPAVID	IMPERILS	IMPLEDGES
IMMORTAL	IMPALA	IMPAVIDLY	IMPERIOUS	IMPLEMENT
IMMORTALS	IMPALAS	IMPAVING	IMPERIUM	IMPLETE
IMMOTILE	IMPALE	IMPAWN	IMPERIUMS	IMPLETED
IMMOVABLE	IMPALED	IMPAWNED	IMPETICOS	IMPLETES
IMMOVABLY	IMPALER	IMPAWNING	IMPETIGO	IMPLETING
IMMUNE	IMPALERS	IMPAWNS	IMPETIGOS	IMPLETION
IMMUNES	IMPALES	IMPEACH	IMPETRATE	IMPLEX
IMMUNISE	IMPALING	IMPEACHED	IMPETUOUS	IMPLEXES
IMMUNISED	IMPANATE	IMPEACHER	IMPETUS	IMPLEXION
IMMUNISER	IMPANEL	IMPEACHES	IMPETUSES	IMPLICATE
IMMUNISES	IMPANELED	IMPEARL	IMPHEE	IMPLICIT
IMMUNITY	IMPANELS	IMPEARLED	IMPHEES	IMPLICITY
IMMUNIZE	IMPANNEL	IMPEARLS	IMPI	IMPLIED
IMMUNIZED	IMPANNELS	IMPECCANT	IMPIES	IMPLIEDLY
IMMUNIZER	IMPARITY	IMPED	IMPIETIES	IMPLIES
IMMUNIZES	IMPARK	IMPEDANCE	IMPIETY	IMPLODE
IMMUNOGEN	IMPARKED	IMPEDE	IMPING	IMPLODED
IMMURE	IMPARKING	IMPEDED	IMPINGE	IMPLODENT
IMMURED	IMPARKS	IMPEDER	IMPINGED	IMPLODES
IMMURES	IMPARL	IMPEDERS	IMPINGENT	IMPLODING
IMMURING	IMPARLED	IMPEDES	IMPINGER	IMPLORE
IMMUTABLE	IMPARLING	IMPEDING	IMPINGERS	IMPLORED
IMMUTABLY	IMPARLS	IMPEDOR	IMPINGES	IMPLORER
IMMY	IMPART	IMPEDORS	IMPINGING	IMPLORERS
IMP	IMPARTED	IMPEL	IMPINGS	IMPLORES
IMPACABLE	IMPARTER	IMPELLED	IMPIOUS	IMPLORING
IMPACT	IMPARTERS	IMPELLENT	IMPIOUSLY	IMPLOSION
IMPACTED	IMPARTIAL	IMPELLER	IMPIS	IMPLOSIVE

IMPLUNGE	IMPOSTUME	IMPROVER	INACTIONS	INBOXES
IMPLUNGED	IMPOSTURE	IMPROVERS	INACTIVE	INBREAK
IMPLUNGES	IMPOT	IMPROVES	INAIDABLE	INBREAKS
IMPLUVIA	IMPOTENCE	IMPROVING	INAMORATA	INBREATHE
IMPLUVIUM	IMPOTENCY	IMPROVISE	INAMORATI	INBRED
IMPLY	IMPOTENT	IMPROVS	INAMORATO	INBREDS
IMPLYING	IMPOTENTS	IMPRUDENT	INANE	INBREED
IMPOCKET	IMPOTS	IMPS	INANELY	INBREEDER
IMPOCKETS	IMPOUND	IMPSONITE	INANENESS	INBREEDS
IMPOLDER	IMPOUNDED	IMPUDENCE	INANER	INBRING
IMPOLDERS	IMPOUNDER	IMPUDENCY	INANES	INBRINGS
IMPOLICY	IMPOUNDS	IMPUDENT	INANEST	INBROUGHT
IMPOLITE	IMPOWER	IMPUGN	INANGA	INBUILT
IMPOLITER	IMPOWERED	IMPUGNED	INANGAS	INBURNING
IMPOLITIC	IMPOWERS	IMPUGNER	INANIMATE	INBURST
IMPONE	IMPRECATE	IMPUGNERS	INANITIES	INBURSTS
IMPONED	IMPRECISE	IMPUGNING	INANITION	INBY
IMPONENT	IMPREGN	IMPUGNS	INANITY	INBYE
IMPONENTS	IMPREGNED	IMPULSE	INAPT	INCAGE
IMPONES	IMPREGNS	IMPULSED	INAPTLY	INCAGED
IMPONING	IMPRESA	IMPULSES	INAPTNESS	INCAGES
IMPOROUS	IMPRESARI	IMPULSING	INARABLE	INCAGING
IMPORT	IMPRESAS	IMPULSION	INARCH	INCANT
IMPORTANT	IMPRESE	IMPULSIVE	INARCHED	INCANTED
IMPORTED	IMPRESES	IMPUNDULU	INARCHES	INCANTING
IMPORTER	IMPRESS	IMPUNITY	INARCHING	INCANTS
IMPORTERS	IMPRESSE	IMPURE	INARM	INCAPABLE
IMPORTING	IMPRESSED	IMPURELY	INARMED	INCAPABLY
IMPORTS	IMPRESSER	IMPURER	INARMING	INCARNATE
IMPORTUNE	IMPRESSES	IMPUREST	INARMS	INCASE
IMPOSABLE	IMPREST	IMPURITY	INASMUCH	INCASED
IMPOSE	IMPRESTS	IMPURPLE	INAUDIBLE	INCASES
IMPOSED	IMPRIMIS	IMPURPLED	INAUDIBLY	INCASING
IMPOSER	IMPRINT	IMPURPLES	INAUGURAL	INCAUTION
IMPOSERS	IMPRINTED	IMPUTABLE	INAURATE	INCAVE
IMPOSES	IMPRINTER	IMPUTABLY	INAURATED	INCAVED
IMPOSEX	IMPRINTS	IMPUTE	INAURATES	INCAVES
IMPOSEXES	IMPRISON	IMPUTED	INBEING	INCAVI
IMPOSING	IMPRISONS	IMPUTER	INBEINGS	INCAVING
IMPOST	IMPRO	IMPUTERS	INBENT	INCAVO
IMPOSTED	IMPROBITY	IMPUTES	INBOARD	INCEDE
IMPOSTER	IMPROMPTU	IMPUTING	INBOARDS	INCEDED
IMPOSTERS	IMPROPER	IMSHI	INBORN	INCEDES
IMPOSTING	IMPROS	IMSHY	INBOUND	INCEDING
IMPOSTOR	IMPROV	IN	INBOUNDED	INCENSE
IMPOSTORS	IMPROVE	INABILITY	INBOUNDS	INCENSED
IMPOSTS	IMPROVED	INACTION	INBOX	INCENSER

INCENSERS	INCIDENCE	INCLOSE	INCROSSED	INDABAS
INCENSES	INCIDENT	INCLOSED	INCROSSES	INDAGATE
INCENSING	INCIDENTS	INCLOSER	INCRUST	INDAGATED
INCENSOR	INCIPIENT	INCLOSERS	INCRUSTED	INDAGATES
INCENSORS	INCIPIT	INCLOSES	INCRUSTS	INDAGATOR
INCENSORY	INCIPITS	INCLOSING	INCUBATE	INDAMIN
INCENT	INCISAL	INCLOSURE	INCUBATED	INDAMINE
INCENTED	INCISE	INCLUDE	INCUBATES	INDAMINES
INCENTER	INCISED	INCLUDED	INCUBATOR	INDAMINS
INCENTERS	INCISES	INCLUDES	INCUBI	INDART
INCENTING	INCISING	INCLUDING	INCUBOUS	INDARTED
INCENTIVE	INCISION	INCLUSION	INCUBUS	INDARTING
INCENTRE	INCISIONS	INCLUSIVE	INCUBUSES	INDARTS
INCENTRES	INCISIVE	INCOG	INCUDAL	INDEBTED
INCENTS	INCISOR	INCOGNITA	INCUDATE	INDECENCY
INCEPT	INCISORS	INCOGNITO	INCUDES	INDECENT
INCEPTED	INCISORY	INCOGS	INCULCATE	INDECORUM
INCEPTING	INCISURAL	INCOME	INCULPATE	INDEED
INCEPTION	INCISURE	INCOMER	INCULT	INDEEDY
INCEPTIVE	INCISURES	INCOMERS	INCUMBENT	INDELIBLE
INCEPTOR	INCITABLE	INCOMES	INCUMBER	INDELIBLY
INCEPTORS	INCITANT	INCOMING	INCUMBERS	INDEMNIFY
INCEPTS	INCITANTS	INCOMINGS	INCUNABLE	INDEMNITY
INCERTAIN	INCITE	INCOMMODE	INCUR	INDENE
INCESSANT	INCITED	INCOMPACT	INCURABLE	INDENES
INCEST	INCITER	INCONDITE	INCURABLY	INDENT
INCESTS	INCITERS	INCONIE	INCURIOUS	INDENTED
INCH	INCITES	INCONNU	INCURRED	INDENTER
INCHASE	INCITING	INCONNUE	INCURRENT	INDENTERS
INCHASED	INCIVIL	INCONNUES	INCURRING	INDENTING
INCHASES	INCIVISM	INCONNUS	INCURS	INDENTION
INCHASING	INCIVISMS	INCONY	INCURSION	INDENTOR
INCHED	INCLASP	INCORPSE	INCURSIVE	INDENTORS
INCHER	INCLASPED	INCORPSED	INCURVATE	INDENTS
INCHERS	INCLASPS	INCORPSES	INCURVE	INDENTURE
INCHES	INCLE	INCORRECT	INCURVED	INDEVOUT
INCHING	INCLEMENT	INCORRUPT	INCURVES	INDEW
INCHMEAL	INCLES	INCREASE	INCURVING	INDEWED
INCHOATE	INCLINE	INCREASED	INCURVITY	INDEWING
INCHOATED	INCLINED	INCREASER	INCUS	INDEWS
INCHOATES	INCLINER	INCREASES	INCUSE	INDEX
INCHPIN	INCLINERS	INCREATE	INCUSED	INDEXABLE
INCHPINS	INCLINES	INCREMATE	INCUSES	INDEXAL
INCHTAPE	INCLINING	INCREMENT	INCUSING	INDEXED
INCHTAPES	INCLIP	INCRETION	INCUT	INDEXER
INCHWORM	INCLIPPED	INCRETORY	INCUTS	INDEXERS
INCHWORMS	INCLIPS	INCROSS	INDABA	INDEXES

INDEXICAL	INDIGNLY	INDOXYLS	INDUNA	INERTEST
INDEXING	INDIGO	INDRAFT	INDUNAS	INERTIA
INDEXINGS	INDIGOES	INDRAFTS	INDURATE	INERTIAE
INDEXLESS	INDIGOID	INDRAUGHT	INDURATED	INERTIAL
INDIA	INDIGOIDS	INDRAWN	INDURATES	INERTIAS
INDIAS	INDIGOS	INDRENCH	INDUSIA	INERTLY
INDICAN	INDIGOTIC	INDRI	INDUSIAL	INERTNESS
INDICANS	INDIGOTIN	INDRIS	INDUSIATE	INERTS
INDICANT	INDINAVIR	INDRISES	INDUSIUM	INERUDITE
INDICANTS	INDIRECT	INDUBIOUS	INDUSTRY	INESSIVE
INDICATE	INDIRUBIN	INDUCE	INDUVIAE	INESSIVES
INDICATED	INDISPOSE	INDUCED	INDUVIAL	INEXACT
INDICATES	INDITE	INDUCER	INDUVIATE	INEXACTLY
INDICATOR	INDITED	INDUCERS	INDWELL	INEXPERT
INDICES	INDITER	INDUCES	INDWELLER	INEXPERTS
INDICIA	INDITERS	INDUCIAE	INDWELLS	INFALL
INDICIAL	INDITES	INDUCIBLE	INDWELT	INFALLING
INDICIAS	INDITING	INDUCING	INEARTH	INFALLS
INDICIUM	INDIUM	INDUCT	INEARTHED	INFAME
INDICIUMS	INDIUMS	INDUCTED	INEARTHS	INFAMED
INDICT	INDIVIDUA	INDUCTEE	INEBRIANT	INFAMES
INDICTED	INDOCIBLE	INDUCTEES	INEBRIATE	INFAMIES
INDICTEE	INDOCILE	INDUCTILE	INEBRIETY	INFAMING
INDICTEES	INDOL	INDUCTING	INEBRIOUS	INFAMISE
INDICTER	INDOLE	INDUCTION	INEDIBLE	INFAMISED
INDICTERS	INDOLENCE	INDUCTIVE	INEDIBLY	INFAMISES
INDICTING	INDOLENCY	INDUCTOR	INEDITA	INFAMIZE
INDICTION	INDOLENT	INDUCTORS	INEDITED	INFAMIZED
INDICTOR	INDOLES	INDUCTS	INEFFABLE	INFAMIZES
INDICTORS	INDOLS	INDUE	INEFFABLY	INFAMOUS
INDICTS	INDOOR	INDUED	INELASTIC	INFAMY
INDIE	INDOORS	INDUES	INELEGANT	INFANCIES
INDIES	INDORSE	INDUING	INEPT	INFANCY
INDIGEN	INDORSED	INDULGE	INEPTER	INFANT
INDIGENCE	INDORSEE	INDULGED	INEPTEST	INFANTA
INDIGENCY	INDORSEES	INDULGENT	INEPTLY	INFANTAS
INDIGENE	INDORSER	INDULGER	INEPTNESS	INFANTE
INDIGENES	INDORSERS	INDULGERS	INEQUABLE	INFANTEER
INDIGENS	INDORSES	INDULGES	INEQUITY	INFANTES
INDIGENT	INDORSING	INDULGING	INERM	INFANTILE
INDIGENTS	INDORSOR	INDULIN	INERMOUS	INFANTINE
INDIGEST	INDORSORS	INDULINE	INERRABLE	INFANTRY
INDIGESTS	INDOW	INDULINES	INERRABLY	INFANTS
INDIGN	INDOWED	INDULINS	INERRANCY	INFARCT
INDIGNANT	INDOWING	INDULT	INERRANT	INFARCTED
INDIGNIFY	INDOWS	INDULTS	INERT	INFARCTS
INDIGNITY	INDOXYL	INDUMENTA	INERTER	INFARE

INFARES	INFEST	INFLAMING	INFORCES	INGATES
INFATUATE	INFESTANT	INFLATE	INFORCING	INGATHER
INFAUNA	INFESTED	INFLATED	INFORM	INGATHERS
INFAUNAE	INFESTER	INFLATER	INFORMAL	INGENER
INFAUNAL	INFESTERS	INFLATERS	INFORMANT	INGENERS
INFAUNAS	INFESTING	INFLATES	INFORMED	INGENIOUS
INFAUST	INFESTS	INFLATING	INFORMER	INGENIUM
INFECT	INFICETE	INFLATION	INFORMERS	INGENIUMS
INFECTANT	INFIDEL	INFLATIVE	INFORMING	INGENU
INFECTED	INFIDELIC	INFLATOR	INFORMS	INGENUE
INFECTER	INFIDELS	INFLATORS	INFORTUNE	INGENUES
INFECTERS	INFIELD	INFLATUS	INFOS	INGENUITY
INFECTING	INFIELDER	INFLECT	INFOTECH	INGENUOUS
INFECTION	INFIELDS	INFLECTED	INFOTECHS	INGENUS
INFECTIVE	INFIGHT	INFLECTOR	INFOUGHT	INGEST
INFECTOR	INFIGHTER	INFLECTS	INFRA	INGESTA
INFECTORS	INFIGHTS	INFLEXED	INFRACT	INGESTED
INFECTS	INFILL	INFLEXION	INFRACTED	INGESTING
INFECUND	INFILLED	INFLEXURE	INFRACTOR	INGESTION
INFEED	INFILLING	INFLICT	INFRACTS	INGESTIVE
INFEEDS	INFILLS	INFLICTED	INFRARED	INGESTS
INFEFT	INFIMA	INFLICTER	INFRAREDS	INGINE
INFEFTED	INFIMUM	INFLICTOR	INFRINGE	INGINES
INFEFTING	INFIMUMS	INFLICTS	INFRINGED	INGLE
INFEFTS	INFINITE	INFLIGHT	INFRINGER	INGLENEUK
INFELT	INFINITES	INFLOW	INFRINGES	INGLENOOK
INFEOFF	INFINITY	INFLOWING	INFRUGAL	INGLES
INFEOFFED	INFIRM	INFLOWS	INFULA	INGLOBE
INFEOFFS	INFIRMARY	INFLUENCE	INFULAE	INGLOBED
INFER	INFIRMED	INFLUENT	INFURIATE	INGLOBES
INFERABLE	INFIRMER	INFLUENTS	INFUSCATE	INGLOBING
INFERABLY	INFIRMEST	INFLUENZA	INFUSE	INGLUVIAL
INFERE	INFIRMING	INFLUX	INFUSED	INGLUVIES
INFERENCE	INFIRMITY	INFLUXES	INFUSER	INGO
INFERIAE	INFIRMLY	INFLUXION	INFUSERS	INGOES
INFERIBLE	INFIRMS	INFO	INFUSES	INGOING
INFERIOR	INFIX	INFOBAHN	INFUSIBLE	INGOINGS
INFERIORS	INFIXED	INFOBAHNS	INFUSING	INGOT
INFERNAL	INFIXES	INFOLD	INFUSION	INGOTED
INFERNO	INFIXING	INFOLDED	INFUSIONS	INGOTING
INFERNOS	INFIXION	INFOLDER	INFUSIVE	INGOTS
INFERRED	INFIXIONS	INFOLDERS	INFUSORIA	INGRAFT
INFERRER	INFLAME	INFOLDING	INFUSORY	INGRAFTED
INFERRERS	INFLAMED	INFOLDS	ING	INGRAFTS
INFERRING	INFLAMER	INFOMANIA	INGAN	INGRAIN
INFERS	INFLAMERS	INFORCE	INGANS	INGRAINED
INFERTILE	INFLAMES	INFORCED	INGATE	INGRAINER

INGRAINS	INHALING	INHUMATED	INJURE	INKSTANDS
INGRAM	INHARMONY	INHUMATES	INJURED	INKSTONE
INGRAMS	INHAUL	INHUME	INJURER	INKSTONES
INGRATE	INHAULER	INHUMED	INJURERS	INKWELL
INGRATELY	INHAULERS	INHUMER	INJURES	INKWELLS
INGRATES	INHAULS	INHUMERS	INJURIES	INKWOOD
INGRESS	INHAUST	INHUMES	INJURING	INKWOODS
INGRESSES	INHAUSTED	INHUMING	INJURIOUS	INKY
INGROOVE	INHAUSTS	INIA	INJURY	INLACE
INGROOVED	INHEARSE	INIMICAL	INJUSTICE	INLACED
INGROOVES	INHEARSED	INION	INK	INLACES
INGROSS	INHEARSES	INIONS	INKBERRY	INLACING
INGROSSED	INHERCE	INIQUITY	INKBLOT	INLAID
INGROSSES	INHERCED	INISLE	INKBLOTS	INLAND
INGROUND	INHERCES	INISLED	INKED	INLANDER
INGROUNDS	INHERCING	INISLES	INKER	INLANDERS
INGROUP	INHERE	INISLING	INKERS	INLANDS
INGROUPS	INHERED	INITIAL	INKHOLDER	INLAY
INGROWING	INHERENCE	INITIALED	INKHORN	INLAYER
INGROWN	INHERENCY	INITIALER	INKHORNS	INLAYERS
INGROWTH	INHERENT	INITIALLY	INKHOSI	INLAYING
INGROWTHS	INHERES	INITIALS	INKHOSIS	INLAYINGS
INGRUM	INHERING	INITIATE	INKIER	INLAYS
INGRUMS	INHERIT	INITIATED	INKIEST	INLET
INGS	INHERITED	INITIATES	INKINESS	INLETS
INGUINAL	INHERITOR	INITIATOR	INKING	INLETTING
INGULF	INHERITS	INJECT	INKJET	INLIER
INGULFED	INHESION	INJECTANT	INKJETS	INLIERS
INGULFING	INHESIONS	INJECTED	INKLE	INLOCK
INGULFS	INHIBIN	INJECTING	INKLED	INLOCKED
INGULPH	INHIBINS	INJECTION	INKLES	INLOCKING
INGULPHED	INHIBIT	INJECTIVE	INKLESS	INLOCKS
INGULPHS	INHIBITED	INJECTOR	INKLIKE	INLY
INHABIT	INHIBITER	INJECTORS	INKLING	INLYING
INHABITED	INHIBITOR	INJECTS	INKLINGS	INMATE
INHABITER	INHIBITS	INJELLIED	INKOSI	INMATES
INHABITOR	INHOLDER	INJELLIES	INKOSIS	INMESH
INHABITS	INHOLDERS	INJELLY	INKPAD	INMESHED
INHALABLE	INHOLDING	INJERA	INKPADS	INMESHES
INHALANT	INHOOP	INJERAS	INKPOT	INMESHING
INHALANTS	INHOOPED	INJOINT	INKPOTS	INMIGRANT
INHALATOR	INHOOPING	INJOINTED	INKS	INMOST
INHALE	INHOOPS	INJOINTS	INKSPOT	INN
INHALED	INHUMAN	INJUNCT	INKSPOTS	INNAGE
INHALER	INHUMANE	INJUNCTED	INKSTAIN	INNAGES
INHALERS	INHUMANLY	INJUNCTS	INKSTAINS	INNARDS
INHALES	INHUMATE	INJURABLE	INKSTAND	INNATE

INNATELY	INORBS	INQUORATE	INSECURE	INSINEWED
INNATIVE	INORGANIC	INRO	INSEEM	INSINEWS
INNED	INORNATE	INROAD	INSEEMED	INSINUATE
INNER	INOSINE	INROADS	INSEEMING	INSIPID
INNERLY	INOSINES	INRUN	INSEEMS	INSIPIDLY
INNERMOST	INOSITE	INRUNS	INSELBERG	INSIPIENT
INNERNESS	INOSITES	INRUSH	INSENSATE	INSIST
INNERS	INOSITOL	INRUSHES	INSERT	INSISTED
INNERSOLE	INOSITOLS	INRUSHING	INSERTED	INSISTENT
INNERVATE	INOTROPE	INS	INSERTER	INSISTER
INNERVE	INOTROPES	INSANE	INSERTERS	INSISTERS
INNERVED	INOTROPIC	INSANELY	INSERTING	INSISTING
INNERVES	INPATIENT	INSANER	INSERTION	INSISTS
INNERVING	INPAYMENT	INSANEST	INSERTS	INSNARE
INNERWEAR	INPHASE	INSANIE	INSET	INSNARED
INNING	INPOUR	INSANIES	INSETS	INSNARER
INNINGS	INPOURED	INSANITY	INSETTED	INSNARERS
INNINGSES	INPOURING	INSATIATE	INSETTER	INSNARES
INNIT	INPOURS	INSATIETY	INSETTERS	INSNARING
INNKEEPER	INPUT	INSCAPE	INSETTING	INSOFAR
INNLESS	INPUTS	INSCAPES	INSHALLAH	INSOLATE
INNOCENCE	INPUTTED	INSCIENCE	INSHEATH	INSOLATED
INNOCENCY	INPUTTER	INSCIENT	INSHEATHE	INSOLATES
INNOCENT	INPUTTERS	INSCONCE	INSHEATHS	INSOLE
INNOCENTS	INPUTTING	INSCONCED	INSHELL	INSOLENCE
INNOCUITY	INQILAB	INSCONCES	INSHELLED	INSOLENT
INNOCUOUS	INQILABS	INSCRIBE	INSHELLS	INSOLENTS
INNOVATE	INQUERE	INSCRIBED	INSHELTER	INSOLES
INNOVATED	INQUERED	INSCRIBER	INSHIP	INSOLUBLE
INNOVATES	INQUERES	INSCRIBES	INSHIPPED	INSOLUBLY
INNOVATOR	INQUERING	INSCROLL	INSHIPS	INSOLVENT
INNOXIOUS	INQUEST	INSCROLLS	INSHORE	INSOMNIA
INNS	INQUESTS	INSCULP	INSHRINE	INSOMNIAC
INNUENDO	INQUIET	INSCULPED	INSHRINED	INSOMNIAS
INNUENDOS	INQUIETED	INSCULPS	INSHRINES	INSOMUCH
INNYARD	INQUIETLY	INSCULPT	INSIDE	INSOOTH
INNYARDS	INQUIETS	INSEAM	INSIDER	INSOUL
INOCULA	INQUILINE	INSEAMED	INSIDERS	INSOULED
INOCULANT	INQUINATE	INSEAMING	INSIDES	INSOULING
INOCULATE	INQUIRE	INSEAMS	INSIDIOUS	INSOULS
INOCULUM	INQUIRED	INSECT	INSIGHT	INSOURCE
INOCULUMS	INQUIRER	INSECTAN	INSIGHTS	INSOURCED
INODOROUS	INQUIRERS	INSECTARY	INSIGNE	INSOURCES
INOPINATE	INQUIRES	INSECTEAN	INSIGNIA	INSPAN
INORB	INQUIRIES	INSECTILE	INSIGNIAS	INSPANNED
INORBED	INQUIRING	INSECTION	INSINCERE	INSPANS
INORBING	INQUIRY	INSECTS	INSINEW	INSPECT

INSPECTED	INSTINCTS	INSWINGER	INTENTS	INTERLACE
INSPECTOR	INSTITUTE	INSWINGS	INTER	INTERLAID
INSPECTS	INSTRESS	INTACT	INTERACT	INTERLAP
INSPHERE	INSTROKE	INTACTLY	INTERACTS	INTERLAPS
INSPHERED	INSTROKES	INTAGLI	INTERAGE	INTERLARD
INSPHERES	INSTRUCT	INTAGLIO	INTERARCH	INTERLAY
INSPIRE	INSTRUCTS	INTAGLIOS	INTERBANK	INTERLAYS
INSPIRED	INSUCKEN	INTAKE	INTERBED	INTERLEAF
INSPIRER	INSULA	INTAKES	INTERBEDS	INTERLEND
INSPIRERS	INSULAE	INTARSIA	INTERBRED	INTERLENT
INSPIRES	INSULANT	INTARSIAS	INTERCEDE	INTERLINE
INSPIRING	INSULANTS	INTEGER	INTERCELL	INTERLINK
INSPIRIT	INSULAR	INTEGERS	INTERCEPT	INTERLOAN
INSPIRITS	INSULARLY	INTEGRAL	INTERCITY	INTERLOCK
INSTABLE	INSULARS	INTEGRALS	INTERCLAN	INTERLOOP
INSTAL	INSULATE	INTEGRAND	INTERCLUB	INTERLOPE
INSTALL	INSULATED	INTEGRANT	INTERCOM	INTERLUDE
INSTALLED	INSULATES	INTEGRATE	INTERCOMS	INTERMALE
INSTALLER	INSULATOR	INTEGRIN	INTERCROP	INTERMAT
INSTALLS	INSULIN	INTEGRINS	INTERCUT	INTERMATS
INSTALS	INSULINS	INTEGRITY	INTERCUTS	INTERMENT
INSTANCE	INSULSE	INTEL	INTERDASH	INTERMESH
INSTANCED	INSULSITY	INTELLECT	INTERDEAL	INTERMIT
INSTANCES	INSULT	INTELS	INTERDICT	INTERMITS
INSTANCY	INSULTANT	INTENABLE	INTERDINE	INTERMIX
INSTANT	INSULTED	INTEND	INTERESS	INTERMONT
INSTANTER	INSULTER	INTENDANT	INTERESSE	INTERMURE
INSTANTLY	INSULTERS	INTENDED	INTEREST	INTERN
INSTANTS	INSULTING	INTENDEDS	INTERESTS	INTERNAL
INSTAR	INSULTS	INTENDER	INTERFACE	INTERNALS
INSTARRED	INSURABLE	INTENDERS	INTERFERE	INTERNE
INSTARS	INSURANCE	INTENDING	INTERFILE	INTERNED
INSTATE	INSURANT	INTENDS	INTERFIRM	INTERNEE
INSTATED	INSURANTS	INTENIBLE	INTERFLOW	INTERNEES
INSTATES	INSURE	INTENSATE	INTERFOLD	INTERNES
INSTATING	INSURED	INTENSE	INTERFUSE	INTERNET
INSTEAD	INSUREDS	INTENSELY	INTERGANG	INTERNETS
INSTEP	INSURER	INTENSER	INTERGREW	INTERNING
INSTEPS	INSURERS	INTENSEST	INTERGROW	INTERNIST
INSTIGATE	INSURES	INTENSIFY	INTERIM	INTERNODE
INSTIL	INSURGENT	INTENSION	INTERIMS	INTERNS
INSTILL	INSURING	INTENSITY	INTERIOR	INTERPAGE
INSTILLED	INSWATHE	INTENSIVE	INTERIORS	INTERPLAY
INSTILLER	INSWATHED	INTENT	INTERJECT	INTERPLED
INSTILLS	INSWATHES	INTENTION	INTERJOIN	INTERPONE
INSTILS	INSWEPT	INTENTIVE	INTERKNIT	INTERPOSE
INSTINCT	INSWING	INTENTLY	INTERKNOT	INTERPRET

INTERRACE	INTIMACY	INTORTED	INTROVERT	INUNCTION
INTERRAIL	INTIMAE	INTORTING	INTRUDE	INUNDANT
INTERRED	INTIMAL	INTORTION	INTRUDED	INUNDATE
INTERREX	INTIMAS	INTORTS	INTRUDER	INUNDATED
INTERRING	INTIMATE	INTOWN	INTRUDERS	INUNDATES
INTERROW	INTIMATED	INTRA	INTRUDES	INUNDATOR
INTERRUPT	INTIMATER	INTRACITY	INTRUDING	INURBANE
INTERS	INTIMATES	INTRADA	INTRUSION	INURE
INTERSECT	INTIME	INTRADAS	INTRUSIVE	INURED
INTERSERT	INTIMISM	INTRADAY	INTRUST	INUREMENT
INTERSEX	INTIMISMS	INTRADOS	INTRUSTED	INURES
INTERTERM	INTIMIST	INTRANET	INTRUSTS	INURING
INTERTEXT	INTIMISTE	INTRANETS	INTUBATE	INURN
INTERTIE	INTIMISTS	INTRANT	INTUBATED	INURNED
INTERTIES	INTIMITY	INTRANTS	INTUBATES	INURNING
INTERTILL	INTINE	INTREAT	INTUIT	INURNMENT
INTERUNIT	INTINES	INTREATED	INTUITED	INURNS
INTERVAL	INTIRE	INTREATS	INTUITING	INUSITATE
INTERVALE	INTIS	INTRENCH	INTUITION	INUST
INTERVALS	INTITLE	INTREPID	INTUITIVE	INUSTION
INTERVEIN	INTITLED	INTRICACY	INTUITS	INUSTIONS
INTERVENE	INTITLES	INTRICATE	INTUMESCE	INUTILE
INTERVIEW	INTITLING	INTRIGANT	INTURN	INUTILELY
INTERWAR	INTITULE	INTRIGUE	INTURNED	INUTILITY
INTERWEB	INTITULED	INTRIGUED	INTURNS	INVADABLE
INTERWEBS	INTITULES	INTRIGUER	INTUSE	INVADE
INTERWIND	INTO	INTRIGUES	INTUSES	INVADED
INTERWORK	INTOED	INTRINCE	INTWINE	INVADER
INTERWOVE	INTOMB	INTRINSIC	INTWINED	INVADERS
INTERZONE	INTOMBED	INTRO	INTWINES	INVADES
INTESTACY	INTOMBING	INTRODUCE	INTWINING	INVADING
INTESTATE	INTOMBS	INTROFIED	INTWIST	INVALID
INTESTINE	INTONACO	INTROFIES	INTWISTED	INVALIDED
INTHRAL	INTONACOS	INTROFY	INTWISTS	INVALIDLY
INTHRALL	INTONATE	INTROIT	INUKSHUIT	INVALIDS
INTHRALLS	INTONATED	INTROITAL	INUKSHUK	INVAR
INTHRALS	INTONATES	INTROITS	INUKSHUKS	INVARIANT
INTHRONE	INTONATOR	INTROITUS	INUKSUIT	INVARS
INTHRONED	INTONE	INTROJECT	INUKSUK	INVASION
INTHRONES	INTONED	INTROLD	INUKSUKS	INVASIONS
INTI	INTONER	INTROMIT	INULA	INVASIVE
INTIFADA	INTONERS	INTROMITS	INULAS	INVEAGLE
INTIFADAH	INTONES	INTRON	INULASE	INVEAGLED
INTIFADAS	INTONING	INTRONIC	INULASES	INVEAGLES
INTIFADEH	INTONINGS	INTRONS	INULIN	INVECKED
INTIL	INTORSION	INTRORSE	INULINS	INVECTED
INTIMA	INTORT	INTROS	INUMBRATE	INVECTIVE

INVEIGH	INVIABLE	INWALL	IODIDS	IONISING
INVEIGHED	INVIABLY	INWALLED	IODIN	IONIUM
INVEIGHER	INVIDIOUS	INWALLING	IODINATE	IONIUMS
INVEIGHS	INVIOLACY	INWALLS	IODINATED	IONIZABLE
INVEIGLE	INVIOLATE	INWARD	IODINATES	IONIZE
INVEIGLED	INVIOUS	INWARDLY	IODINE	IONIZED
INVEIGLER	INVIRILE	INWARDS	IODINES	IONIZER
INVEIGLES	INVISCID	INWEAVE	IODINS	IONIZERS
INVENIT	INVISIBLE	INWEAVED	IODISE	IONIZES
INVENT	INVISIBLY	INWEAVES	IODISED	IONIZING
INVENTED	INVITAL	INWEAVING	IODISER	IONOGEN
INVENTER	INVITE	INWICK	IODISERS	IONOGENIC
INVENTERS	INVITED	INWICKED	IODISES	IONOGENS
INVENTING	INVITEE	INWICKING	IODISING	IONOMER
INVENTION	INVITEES	INWICKS	IODISM	IONOMERS
INVENTIVE	INVITER	INWIND	IODISMS	IONONE
INVENTOR	INVITERS	INWINDING	IODIZE	IONONES
INVENTORS	INVITES	INWINDS	IODIZED	IONOPAUSE
INVENTORY	INVITING	INWIT	IODIZER	IONOPHORE
INVENTS	INVITINGS	INWITH	IODIZERS	IONOSONDE
INVERITY	INVOCABLE	INWITS	IODIZES	IONOTROPY
INVERNESS	INVOCATE	INWORK	IODIZING	IONS
INVERSE	INVOCATED	INWORKED	IODOFORM	IOPANOIC
INVERSED	INVOCATES	INWORKING	IODOFORMS	IOS
INVERSELY	INVOCATOR	INWORKS	IODOMETRY	IOTA
INVERSES	INVOICE	INWORN	IODOPHILE	IOTACISM
INVERSING	INVOICED	INWOUND	IODOPHOR	IOTACISMS
INVERSION	INVOICES	INWOVE	IODOPHORS	IOTAS
INVERSIVE	INVOICING	INWOVEN	IODOPSIN	IPECAC
INVERT	INVOKE	INWRAP	IODOPSINS	IPECACS
INVERTASE	INVOKED	INWRAPPED	IODOUS	IPOMOEA
INVERTED	INVOKER	INWRAPS	IODURET	IPOMOEAS
INVERTER	INVOKERS	INWREATHE	IODURETS	IPPON
INVERTERS	INVOKES	INWROUGHT	IODYRITE	IPPONS
INVERTIN	INVOKING	INYALA	IODYRITES	IPRINDOLE
INVERTING	INVOLUCEL	INYALAS	IOLITE	IRACUND
INVERTINS	INVOLUCRA	IO	IOLITES	IRADE
INVERTOR	INVOLUCRE	IODATE	ION	IRADES
INVERTORS	INVOLUTE	IODATED	IONIC	IRASCIBLE
INVERTS	INVOLUTED	IODATES	IONICITY	IRASCIBLY
INVEST	INVOLUTES	IODATING	IONICS	IRATE
INVESTED	INVOLVE	IODATION	IONISABLE	IRATELY
INVESTING	INVOLVED	IODATIONS	IONISE	IRATENESS
INVESTOR	INVOLVER	IODIC	IONISED	IRATER
INVESTORS	INVOLVERS	IODID	IONISER	IRATEST
INVESTS	INVOLVES	IODIDE	IONISERS	IRE
INVEXED	INVOLVING	IODIDES	IONISES	IRED

IREFUL	IRK	IRONWARES	ISABELLAS	ISLESMAN
IREFULLY	IRKED	IRONWEED	ISABELS	ISLESMEN
IRELESS	IRKING	IRONWEEDS	ISAGOGE	ISLET
IRENIC	IRKS	IRONWOMAN	ISAGOGES	ISLETED
IRENICAL	IRKSOME	IRONWOMEN	ISAGOGIC	ISLETS
IRENICISM	IRKSOMELY	IRONWOOD	ISAGOGICS	ISLING
IRENICON	IROKO	IRONWOODS	ISALLOBAR	ISLOMANIA
IRENICONS	IROKOS	IRONWORK	ISARITHM	ISM
IRENICS	IRON	IRONWORKS	ISARITHMS	ISMATIC
IRENOLOGY	IRONBARK	IRONY	ISATIN	ISMATICAL
IRES	IRONBARKS	IRRADIANT	ISATINE	ISMS
IRID	IRONBOUND	IRRADIATE	ISATINES	ISNA
IRIDAL	IRONCLAD	IRREAL	ISATINIC	ISNAE
IRIDEAL	IRONCLADS	IRREALITY	ISATINS	ISO
IRIDES	IRONE	IRREDENTA	ISBA	ISOAMYL
IRIDIAL	IRONED	IRREGULAR	ISBAS	ISOAMYLS
IRIDIAN	IRONER	IRRELATED	ISCHAEMIA	ISOBAR
IRIDIC	IRONERS	IRRIDENTA	ISCHAEMIC	ISOBARE
IRIDISE	IRONES	IRRIGABLE	ISCHEMIA	ISOBARES
IRIDISED	IRONIC	IRRIGABLY	ISCHEMIAS	ISOBARIC
IRIDISES	IRONICAL	IRRIGATE	ISCHEMIC	ISOBARISM
IRIDISING	IRONIER	IRRIGATED	ISCHIA	ISOBARS
IRIDIUM	IRONIES	IRRIGATES	ISCHIADIC	ISOBASE
IRIDIUMS	IRONIEST	IRRIGATOR	ISCHIAL	ISOBASES
IRIDIZE	IRONING	IRRIGUOUS	ISCHIATIC	ISOBATH
IRIDIZED	IRONINGS	IRRISION	ISCHIUM	ISOBATHIC
IRIDIZES	IRONISE	IRRISIONS	ISCHURIA	ISOBATHS
IRIDIZING	IRONISED	IRRISORY	ISCHURIAS	ISOBRONT
IRIDOCYTE	IRONISES	IRRITABLE	ISEIKONIA	ISOBRONTS
IRIDOLOGY	IRONISING	IRRITABLY	ISEIKONIC	ISOBUTANE
IRIDOTOMY	IRONIST	IRRITANCY	ISENERGIC	ISOBUTENE
IRIDS	IRONISTS	IRRITANT	ISH	ISOBUTYL
IRING	IRONIZE	IRRITANTS	ISHES	ISOBUTYLS
IRIS	IRONIZED	IRRITATE	ISINGLASS	ISOCHASM
IRISATE	IRONIZES	IRRITATED	ISIT	ISOCHASMS
IRISATED	IRONIZING	IRRITATES	ISLAND	ISOCHEIM
IRISATES	IRONLESS	IRRITATOR	ISLANDED	ISOCHEIMS
IRISATING	IRONLIKE	IRRUPT	ISLANDER	ISOCHIMAL
IRISATION	IRONMAN	IRRUPTED	ISLANDERS	ISOCHIME
IRISCOPE	IRONMEN	IRRUPTING	ISLANDING	ISOCHIMES
IRISCOPES	IRONNESS	IRRUPTION	ISLANDS	ISOCHOR
IRISED	IRONS	IRRUPTIVE	ISLE	ISOCHORE
IRISES	IRONSIDE	IRRUPTS	ISLED	ISOCHORES
IRISING	IRONSIDES	IRUKANDJI	ISLELESS	ISOCHORIC
IRITIC	IRONSMITH	IS	ISLEMAN	ISOCHORS
IRITIS	IRONSTONE	ISABEL	ISLEMEN	ISOCHRON
IRITISES	IRONWARE	ISABELLA	ISLES	ISOCHRONE

ISOCHRONS
ISOCLINAL
ISOCLINE
ISOCLINES
ISOCLINIC
ISOCRACY
ISOCRATIC
ISOCRYMAL
ISOCRYME
ISOCRYMES
ISOCYANIC
ISOCYCLIC
ISODICA
ISODICON
ISODOMA
ISODOMON
ISODOMOUS
ISODOMUM
ISODONT
ISODONTAL
ISODONTS
ISODOSE
ISODOSES
ISOENZYME
ISOETES
ISOFORM
ISOFORMS
ISOGAMETE
ISOGAMIC
ISOGAMIES
ISOGAMOUS
ISOGAMY
ISOGENEIC
ISOGENIC
ISOGENIES
ISOGENOUS
ISOGENY
ISOGLOSS
ISOGON
ISOGONAL
ISOGONALS
ISOGONE
ISOGONES
ISOGONIC
ISOGONICS
ISOGONIES
ISOGONS

ISOGONY
ISOGRAFT
ISOGRAFTS
ISOGRAM
ISOGRAMS
ISOGRAPH
ISOGRAPHS
ISOGRIV
ISOGRIVS
ISOHEL
ISOHELS
ISOHYDRIC
ISOHYET
ISOHYETAL
ISOHYETS
ISOKONT
ISOKONTAN
ISOKONTS
ISOLABLE
ISOLATE
ISOLATED
ISOLATES
ISOLATING
ISOLATION
ISOLATIVE
ISOLATOR
ISOLATORS
ISOLEAD
ISOLEADS
ISOLEX
ISOLEXES
ISOLINE
ISOLINES
ISOLOG
ISOLOGOUS
ISOLOGS
ISOLOGUE
ISOLOGUES
ISOMER
ISOMERASE
ISOMERE
ISOMERES
ISOMERIC
ISOMERISE
ISOMERISM
ISOMERIZE
ISOMEROUS

ISOMERS
ISOMETRIC
ISOMETRY
ISOMORPH
ISOMORPHS
ISONIAZID
ISONOME
ISONOMES
ISONOMIC
ISONOMIES
ISONOMOUS
ISONOMY
ISOOCTANE
ISOPACH
ISOPACHS
ISOPHONE
ISOPHONES
ISOPHOTAL
ISOPHOTE
ISOPHOTES
ISOPLETH
ISOPLETHS
ISOPOD
ISOPODAN
ISOPODANS
ISOPODOUS
ISOPODS
ISOPOLITY
ISOPRENE
ISOPRENES
ISOPROPYL
ISOPTERAN
ISOPYCNAL
ISOPYCNIC
ISOS
ISOSCELES
ISOSMOTIC
ISOSPIN
ISOSPINS
ISOSPORY
ISOSTACY
ISOSTASY
ISOSTATIC
ISOSTERIC
ISOTACH
ISOTACHS
ISOTACTIC

ISOTHERAL
ISOTHERE
ISOTHERES
ISOTHERM
ISOTHERMS
ISOTONE
ISOTONES
ISOTONIC
ISOTOPE
ISOTOPES
ISOTOPIC
ISOTOPIES
ISOTOPY
ISOTRON
ISOTRONS
ISOTROPIC
ISOTROPY
ISOTYPE
ISOTYPES
ISOTYPIC
ISOZYME
ISOZYMES
ISOZYMIC
ISPAGHULA
ISSEI
ISSEIS
ISSUABLE
ISSUABLY
ISSUANCE
ISSUANCES
ISSUANT
ISSUE
ISSUED
ISSUELESS
ISSUER
ISSUERS
ISSUES
ISSUING
ISTANA
ISTANAS
ISTHMI
ISTHMIAN
ISTHMIANS
ISTHMIC
ISTHMOID
ISTHMUS
ISTHMUSES

ISTLE
ISTLES
IT
ITA
ITACISM
ITACISMS
ITACONIC
ITALIC
ITALICISE
ITALICIZE
ITALICS
ITAS
ITCH
ITCHED
ITCHES
ITCHIER
ITCHIEST
ITCHILY
ITCHINESS
ITCHING
ITCHINGS
ITCHWEED
ITCHWEEDS
ITCHY
ITEM
ITEMED
ITEMING
ITEMISE
ITEMISED
ITEMISER
ITEMISERS
ITEMISES
ITEMISING
ITEMIZE
ITEMIZED
ITEMIZER
ITEMIZERS
ITEMIZES
ITEMIZING
ITEMS
ITERANCE
ITERANCES
ITERANT
ITERATE
ITERATED
ITERATES
ITERATING

ITERATION

ITERATION
ITERATIVE
ITERUM
ITHER
ITINERACY
ITINERANT
ITINERARY
ITINERATE
ITS
ITSELF

IURE
IVIED
IVIES
IVORIED
IVORIES
IVORIST
IVORISTS
IVORY
IVORYBILL
IVORYLIKE

IVORYWOOD
IVRESSE
IVRESSES
IVY
IVYLEAF
IVYLIKE
IWI
IWIS
IXIA
IXIAS

IXNAY
IXODIASES
IXODIASIS
IXODID
IXODIDS
IXORA
IXORAS
IXTLE
IXTLES
IZAR

IZARD
IZARDS
IZARS
IZVESTIA
IZVESTIAS
IZVESTIYA
IZZARD
IZZARDS
IZZAT
IZZATS

J

JA	JACK	JACKS	JADISH	JAGLESS
JAAP	JACKAL	JACKSCREW	JADISHLY	JAGRA
JAAPS	JACKALLED	JACKSHAFT	JADITIC	JAGRAS
JAB	JACKALS	JACKSIE	JAEGER	JAGS
JABBED	JACKAROO	JACKSIES	JAEGERS	JAGUAR
JABBER	JACKAROOS	JACKSMELT	JAFA	JAGUARS
JABBERED	JACKASS	JACKSMITH	JAFAS	JAI
JABBERER	JACKASSES	JACKSNIPE	JAFFA	JAIL
JABBERERS	JACKBOOT	JACKSTAY	JAFFAS	JAILABLE
JABBERING	JACKBOOTS	JACKSTAYS	JAG	JAILBAIT
JABBERS	JACKDAW	JACKSTONE	JAGA	JAILBAITS
JABBING	JACKDAWS	JACKSTRAW	JAGAED	JAILBIRD
JABBINGLY	JACKED	JACKSY	JAGAING	JAILBIRDS
JABBLE	JACKEEN	JACKY	JAGAS	JAILBREAK
JABBLED	JACKEENS	JACOBIN	JAGER	JAILBROKE
JABBLES	JACKER	JACOBINS	JAGERS	JAILED
JABBLING	JACKEROO	JACOBUS	JAGG	JAILER
JABERS	JACKEROOS	JACOBUSES	JAGGARIES	JAILERESS
JABIRU	JACKERS	JACONET	JAGGARY	JAILERS
JABIRUS	JACKET	JACONETS	JAGGED	JAILHOUSE
JABORANDI	JACKETED	JACQUARD	JAGGEDER	JAILING
JABOT	JACKETING	JACQUARDS	JAGGEDEST	JAILLESS
JABOTS	JACKETS	JACQUERIE	JAGGEDLY	JAILOR
JABS	JACKFISH	JACTATION	JAGGER	JAILORESS
JACAL	JACKFRUIT	JACULATE	JAGGERIES	JAILORS
JACALES	JACKIES	JACULATED	JAGGERS	JAILS
JACALS	JACKING	JACULATES	JAGGERY	JAK
JACAMAR	JACKINGS	JACULATOR	JAGGHERY	JAKE
JACAMARS	JACKKNIFE	JACUZZI	JAGGIER	JAKES
JACANA	JACKLEG	JACUZZIS	JAGGIES	JAKESES
JACANAS	JACKLEGS	JADE	JAGGIEST	JAKEY
JACARANDA	JACKLIGHT	JADED	JAGGING	JAKEYS
JACARE	JACKLING	JADEDLY	JAGGS	JAKFRUIT
JACARES	JACKLINGS	JADEDNESS	JAGGY	JAKFRUITS
JACCHUS	JACKMAN	JADEITE	JAGHIR	JAKS
JACCHUSES	JACKMEN	JADEITES	JAGHIRDAR	JALABIB
JACENT	JACKPLANE	JADELIKE	JAGHIRE	JALAP
JACINTH	JACKPOT	JADERIES	JAGHIRES	JALAPENO
JACINTHE	JACKPOTS	JADERY	JAGHIRS	JALAPENOS
JACINTHES	JACKROLL	JADES	JAGIR	JALAPIC
JACINTHS	JACKROLLS	JADING	JAGIRS	JALAPIN

JALAPINS	JAMBIYAS	JANE	JAPANISED	JARHEADS
JALAPS	JAMBO	JANES	JAPANISES	JARINA
JALEBI	JAMBOK	JANGLE	JAPANIZE	JARINAS
JALEBIS	JAMBOKKED	JANGLED	JAPANIZED	JARK
JALFREZI	JAMBOKS	JANGLER	JAPANIZES	JARKMAN
JALFREZIS	JAMBOLAN	JANGLERS	JAPANNED	JARKMEN
JALLEBI	JAMBOLANA	JANGLES	JAPANNER	JARKS
JALLEBIS	JAMBOLANS	JANGLIER	JAPANNERS	JARL
JALOP	JAMBONE	JANGLIEST	JAPANNING	JARLDOM
JALOPIES	JAMBONES	JANGLING	JAPANS	JARLDOMS
JALOPPIES	JAMBOOL	JANGLINGS	JAPE	JARLS
JALOPPY	JAMBOOLS	JANGLY	JAPED	JARLSBERG
JALOPS	JAMBOREE	JANIFORM	JAPER	JAROOL
JALOPY	JAMBOREES	JANISARY	JAPERIES	JAROOLS
JALOUSE	JAMBS	JANISSARY	JAPERS	JAROSITE
JALOUSED	JAMBU	JANITOR	JAPERY	JAROSITES
JALOUSES	JAMBUL	JANITORS	JAPES	JAROVISE
JALOUSIE	JAMBULS	JANITRESS	JAPING	JAROVISED
JALOUSIED	JAMBUS	JANITRIX	JAPINGLY	JAROVISES
JALOUSIES	JAMDANI	JANIZAR	JAPINGS	JAROVIZE
JALOUSING	JAMDANIS	JANIZARS	JAPONICA	JAROVIZED
JAM	JAMES	JANIZARY	JAPONICAS	JAROVIZES
JAMAAT	JAMESES	JANKER	JAPPED	JARP
JAMAATS	JAMJAR	JANKERS	JAPPING	JARPED
JAMADAR	JAMJARS	JANN	JAPS	JARPING
JAMADARS	JAMLIKE	JANNEY	JAR	JARPS
JAMB	JAMMABLE	JANNEYED	JARARACA	JARRAH
JAMBALAYA	JAMMED	JANNEYING	JARARACAS	JARRAHS
JAMBART	JAMMER	JANNEYS	JARARAKA	JARRED
JAMBARTS	JAMMERS	JANNIED	JARARAKAS	JARRING
JAMBE	JAMMIER	JANNIES	JARFUL	JARRINGLY
JAMBEAU	JAMMIES	JANNOCK	JARFULS	JARRINGS
JAMBEAUS	JAMMIEST	JANNOCKS	JARGON	JARS
JAMBEAUX	JAMMING	JANNS	JARGONED	JARSFUL
JAMBED	JAMMINGS	JANNY	JARGONEER	JARTA
JAMBEE	JAMMY	JANNYING	JARGONEL	JARTAS
JAMBEES	JAMON	JANNYINGS	JARGONELS	JARUL
JAMBER	JAMPACKED	JANSKY	JARGONING	JARULS
JAMBERS	JAMPAN	JANSKYS	JARGONISE	JARVEY
JAMBES	JAMPANEE	JANTEE	JARGONISH	JARVEYS
JAMBEUX	JAMPANEES	JANTIER	JARGONIST	JARVIE
JAMBIER	JAMPANI	JANTIES	JARGONIZE	JARVIES
JAMBIERS	JAMPANIS	JANTIEST	JARGONS	JASEY
JAMBING	JAMPANS	JANTY	JARGONY	JASEYS
JAMBIYA	JAMPOT	JAP	JARGOON	JASIES
JAMBIYAH	JAMPOTS	JAPAN	JARGOONS	JASMIN
JAMBIYAHS	JAMS	JAPANISE	JARHEAD	JASMINE

JASMINES	JAUNTIER	JAXIES	JEANS	JEGGINGS
JASMINS	JAUNTIES	JAXY	JEAT	JEHAD
JASMONATE	JAUNTIEST	JAY	JEATS	JEHADEEN
JASP	JAUNTILY	JAYBIRD	JEBEL	JEHADI
JASPE	JAUNTING	JAYBIRDS	JEBELS	JEHADIS
JASPER	JAUNTS	JAYCEE	JEDI	JEHADISM
JASPERISE	JAUNTY	JAYCEES	JEDIS	JEHADISMS
JASPERIZE	JAUP	JAYGEE	JEE	JEHADIST
JASPEROUS	JAUPED	JAYGEES	JEED	JEHADISTS
JASPERS	JAUPING	JAYHAWKER	JEEING	JEHADS
JASPERY	JAUPS	JAYS	JEEL	JEHU
JASPES	JAVA	JAYVEE	JEELED	JEHUS
JASPIDEAN	JAVAS	JAYVEES	JEELIE	JEJUNA
JASPILITE	JAVEL	JAYWALK	JEELIED	JEJUNAL
JASPIS	JAVELIN	JAYWALKED	JEELIEING	JEJUNE
JASPISES	JAVELINA	JAYWALKER	JEELIES	JEJUNELY
JASPS	JAVELINAS	JAYWALKS	JEELING	JEJUNITY
JASS	JAVELINED	JAZERANT	JEELS	JEJUNUM
JASSES	JAVELINS	JAZERANTS	JEELY	JEJUNUMS
JASSID	JAVELS	JAZIES	JEELYING	JELAB
JASSIDS	JAW	JAZY	JEEP	JELABS
JASY	JAWAN	JAZZ	JEEPED	JELL
JATAKA	JAWANS	JAZZBO	JEEPERS	JELLABA
JATAKAS	JAWARI	JAZZBOS	JEEPING	JELLABAH
JATO	JAWARIS	JAZZED	JEEPNEY	JELLABAHS
JATOS	JAWBATION	JAZZER	JEEPNEYS	JELLABAS
JATROPHA	JAWBONE	JAZZERS	JEEPS	JELLED
JATROPHAS	JAWBONED	JAZZES	JEER	JELLIED
JAUK	JAWBONER	JAZZIER	JEERED	JELLIES
JAUKED	JAWBONERS	JAZZIEST	JEERER	JELLIFIED
JAUKING	JAWBONES	JAZZILY	JEERERS	JELLIFIES
JAUKS	JAWBONING	JAZZINESS	JEERING	JELLIFY
JAUNCE	JAWBOX	JAZZING	JEERINGLY	JELLING
JAUNCED	JAWBOXES	JAZZLIKE	JEERINGS	JELLO
JAUNCES	JAWED	JAZZMAN	JEERS	JELLOS
JAUNCING	JAWFALL	JAZZMEN	JEES	JELLS
JAUNDICE	JAWFALLS	JAZZY	JEESLY	JELLY
JAUNDICED	JAWHOLE	JEALOUS	JEEZ	JELLYBEAN
JAUNDICES	JAWHOLES	JEALOUSE	JEEZE	JELLYFISH
JAUNSE	JAWING	JEALOUSED	JEEZELY	JELLYING
JAUNSED	JAWINGS	JEALOUSES	JEEZLY	JELLYLIKE
JAUNSES	JAWLESS	JEALOUSLY	JEFE	JELLYROLL
JAUNSING	JAWLIKE	JEALOUSY	JEFES	JELUTONG
JAUNT	JAWLINE	JEAN	JEFF	JELUTONGS
JAUNTED	JAWLINES	JEANED	JEFFED	JEMADAR
JAUNTEE	JAWS	JEANETTE	JEFFING	JEMADARS
JAUNTIE	JAXIE	JEANETTES	JEFFS	JEMBE

JEMBES	JERKIEST	JESTBOOKS	JETTIES	JIAO
JEMIDAR	JERKILY	JESTED	JETTIEST	JIAOS
JEMIDARS	JERKIN	JESTEE	JETTINESS	JIB
JEMIMA	JERKINESS	JESTEES	JETTING	JIBB
JEMIMAS	JERKING	JESTER	JETTISON	JIBBA
JEMMIED	JERKINGLY	JESTERS	JETTISONS	JIBBAH
JEMMIER	JERKINGS	JESTFUL	JETTON	JIBBAHS
JEMMIES	JERKINS	JESTING	JETTONS	JIBBAS
JEMMIEST	JERKS	JESTINGLY	JETTY	JIBBED
JEMMINESS	JERKWATER	JESTINGS	JETTYING	JIBBER
JEMMY	JERKY	JESTS	JETWAY	JIBBERED
JEMMYING	JEROBOAM	JESUIT	JETWAYS	JIBBERING
JENNET	JEROBOAMS	JESUITIC	JEU	JIBBERS
JENNETING	JERQUE	JESUITISM	JEUNE	JIBBING
JENNETS	JERQUED	JESUITRY	JEUX	JIBBINGS
JENNIES	JERQUER	JESUITS	JEW	JIBBONS
JENNY	JERQUERS	JESUS	JEWED	JIBBOOM
JEOFAIL	JERQUES	JET	JEWEL	JIBBOOMS
JEOFAILS	JERQUING	JETBEAD	JEWELED	JIBBS
JEON	JERQUINGS	JETBEADS	JEWELER	JIBE
JEONS	JERREED	JETE	JEWELERS	JIBED
JEOPARD	JERREEDS	JETES	JEWELFISH	JIBER
JEOPARDED	JERRICAN	JETFOIL	JEWELING	JIBERS
JEOPARDER	JERRICANS	JETFOILS	JEWELLED	JIBES
JEOPARDS	JERRID	JETLAG	JEWELLER	JIBING
JEOPARDY	JERRIDS	JETLAGS	JEWELLERS	JIBINGLY
JEQUERITY	JERRIES	JETLIKE	JEWELLERY	JIBS
JEQUIRITY	JERRY	JETLINER	JEWELLIKE	JICAMA
JERBIL	JERRYCAN	JETLINERS	JEWELLING	JICAMAS
JERBILS	JERRYCANS	JETON	JEWELRIES	JICKAJOG
JERBOA	JERSEY	JETONS	JEWELRY	JICKAJOGS
JERBOAS	JERSEYED	JETPACK	JEWELS	JIFF
JEREED	JERSEYS	JETPACKS	JEWELWEED	JIFFIES
JEREEDS	JESS	JETPORT	JEWFISH	JIFFS
JEREMIAD	JESSAMIES	JETPORTS	JEWFISHES	JIFFY
JEREMIADS	JESSAMINE	JETS	JEWIE	JIG
JEREPIGO	JESSAMY	JETSAM	JEWIES	JIGABOO
JEREPIGOS	JESSANT	JETSAMS	JEWING	JIGABOOS
JERFALCON	JESSE	JETSOM	JEWS	JIGAJIG
JERID	JESSED	JETSOMS	JEZAIL	JIGAJIGS
JERIDS	JESSERANT	JETSON	JEZAILS	JIGAJOG
JERK	JESSES	JETSONS	JEZEBEL	JIGAJOGS
JERKED	JESSIE	JETSTREAM	JEZEBELS	JIGAMAREE
JERKER	JESSIES	JETTATURA	JHALA	JIGGED
JERKERS	JESSING	JETTED	JHALAS	JIGGER
JERKIER	JEST	JETTIED	JHATKA	JIGGERED
JERKIES	JESTBOOK	JETTIER	JHATKAS	JIGGERING

JIGGERS	JILLIONS	JINGLIER	JIRRE	JOBBERS
JIGGIER	JILLIONTH	JINGLIEST	JISM	JOBBERY
JIGGIEST	JILLS	JINGLING	JISMS	JOBBIE
JIGGING	JILT	JINGLY	JISSOM	JOBBIES
JIGGINGS	JILTED	JINGO	JISSOMS	JOBBING
JIGGISH	JILTER	JINGOES	JITNEY	JOBBINGS
JIGGLE	JILTERS	JINGOISH	JITNEYS	JOBCENTRE
JIGGLED	JILTING	JINGOISM	JITTER	JOBE
JIGGLES	JILTS	JINGOISMS	JITTERBUG	JOBED
JIGGLIER	JIMCRACK	JINGOIST	JITTERED	JOBERNOWL
JIGGLIEST	JIMCRACKS	JINGOISTS	JITTERIER	JOBES
JIGGLING	JIMINY	JINJILI	JITTERING	JOBHOLDER
JIGGLY	JIMJAM	JINJILIS	JITTERS	JOBING
JIGGUMBOB	JIMJAMS	JINK	JITTERY	JOBLESS
JIGGY	JIMMIE	JINKED	JIUJITSU	JOBNAME
JIGJIG	JIMMIED	JINKER	JIUJITSUS	JOBNAMES
JIGJIGGED	JIMMIES	JINKERED	JIUJUTSU	JOBS
JIGJIGS	JIMMINY	JINKERING	JIUJUTSUS	JOBSEEKER
JIGLIKE	JIMMY	JINKERS	JIVE	JOBSHARE
JIGOT	JIMMYING	JINKING	JIVEASS	JOBSHARES
JIGOTS	JIMP	JINKS	JIVEASSES	JOBSWORTH
JIGS	JIMPER	JINN	JIVED	JOCK
JIGSAW	JIMPEST	JINNE	JIVER	JOCKDOM
JIGSAWED	JIMPIER	JINNEE	JIVERS	JOCKDOMS
JIGSAWING	JIMPIEST	JINNI	JIVES	JOCKETTE
JIGSAWN	JIMPLY	JINNIS	JIVEST	JOCKETTES
JIGSAWS	JIMPNESS	JINNS	JIVEY	JOCKEY
JIHAD	JIMPSON	JINRIKSHA	JIVIER	JOCKEYED
JIHADEEN	JIMPY	JINS	JIVIEST	JOCKEYING
JIHADI	JIMSON	JINX	JIVING	JOCKEYISH
JIHADIS	JIMSONS	JINXED	JIVY	JOCKEYISM
JIHADISM	JIN	JINXES	JIZ	JOCKEYS
JIHADISMS	JINGAL	JINXING	JIZZ	JOCKIER
JIHADIST	JINGALL	JIPIJAPA	JIZZES	JOCKIEST
JIHADISTS	JINGALLS	JIPIJAPAS	JNANA	JOCKISH
JIHADS	JINGALS	JIPYAPA	JNANAS	JOCKNEY
JILBAB	JINGBANG	JIPYAPAS	JO	JOCKNEYS
JILBABS	JINGBANGS	JIRBLE	JOANNA	JOCKO
JILGIE	JINGKO	JIRBLED	JOANNAS	JOCKOS
JILGIES	JINGKOES	JIRBLES	JOANNES	JOCKS
JILL	JINGLE	JIRBLING	JOANNESES	JOCKSTRAP
JILLAROO	JINGLED	JIRD	JOB	JOCKTELEG
JILLAROOS	JINGLER	JIRDS	JOBATION	JOCKY
JILLET	JINGLERS	JIRGA	JOBATIONS	JOCO
JILLETS	JINGLES	JIRGAS	JOBBED	JOCOS
JILLFLIRT	JINGLET	JIRKINET	JOBBER	JOCOSE
JILLION	JINGLETS	JIRKINETS	JOBBERIES	JOCOSELY

JOCOSITY	JOINED	JOKINGS	JOLTHEAD	JOSEPHS
JOCULAR	JOINER	JOKOL	JOLTHEADS	JOSH
JOCULARLY	JOINERIES	JOKY	JOLTIER	JOSHED
JOCULATOR	JOINERS	JOL	JOLTIEST	JOSHER
JOCUND	JOINERY	JOLE	JOLTILY	JOSHERS
JOCUNDITY	JOINING	JOLED	JOLTING	JOSHES
JOCUNDLY	JOININGS	JOLES	JOLTINGLY	JOSHING
JODEL	JOINS	JOLING	JOLTINGS	JOSHINGLY
JODELLED	JOINT	JOLIOTIUM	JOLTS	JOSHINGS
JODELLING	JOINTED	JOLL	JOLTY	JOSKIN
JODELS	JOINTEDLY	JOLLED	JOMO	JOSKINS
JODHPUR	JOINTER	JOLLER	JOMON	JOSS
JODHPURS	JOINTERS	JOLLERS	JOMONS	JOSSER
JOE	JOINTING	JOLLEY	JOMOS	JOSSERS
JOES	JOINTINGS	JOLLEYER	JONCANOE	JOSSES
JOEY	JOINTLESS	JOLLEYERS	JONCANOES	JOSTLE
JOEYS	JOINTLY	JOLLEYING	JONES	JOSTLED
JOG	JOINTNESS	JOLLEYS	JONESED	JOSTLER
JOGGED	JOINTRESS	JOLLIED	JONESES	JOSTLERS
JOGGER	JOINTS	JOLLIER	JONESING	JOSTLES
JOGGERS	JOINTURE	JOLLIERS	JONG	JOSTLING
JOGGING	JOINTURED	JOLLIES	JONGLEUR	JOSTLINGS
JOGGINGS	JOINTURES	JOLLIEST	JONGLEURS	JOT
JOGGLE	JOINTWEED	JOLLIFIED	JONGS	JOTA
JOGGLED	JOINTWORM	JOLLIFIES	JONNOCK	JOTAS
JOGGLER	JOIST	JOLLIFY	JONNYCAKE	JOTS
JOGGLERS	JOISTED	JOLLILY	JONQUIL	JOTTED
JOGGLES	JOISTING	JOLLIMENT	JONQUILS	JOTTER
JOGGLING	JOISTS	JOLLINESS	JONTIES	JOTTERS
JOGPANTS	JOJOBA	JOLLING	JONTY	JOTTIER
JOGS	JOJOBAS	JOLLITIES	JOOK	JOTTIEST
JOGTROT	JOKE	JOLLITY	JOOKED	JOTTING
JOGTROTS	JOKED	JOLLOP	JOOKERIES	JOTTINGS
JOHANNES	JOKER	JOLLOPS	JOOKERY	JOTTY
JOHN	JOKERS	JOLLS	JOOKING	JOTUN
JOHNBOAT	JOKES	JOLLY	JOOKS	JOTUNN
JOHNBOATS	JOKESMITH	JOLLYBOAT	JOR	JOTUNNS
JOHNNIE	JOKESOME	JOLLYER	JORAM	JOTUNS
JOHNNIES	JOKESTER	JOLLYERS	JORAMS	JOUAL
JOHNNY	JOKESTERS	JOLLYHEAD	JORDAN	JOUALS
JOHNS	JOKEY	JOLLYING	JORDANS	JOUGS
JOHNSON	JOKIER	JOLLYINGS	JORDELOO	JOUISANCE
JOHNSONS	JOKIEST	JOLS	JORDELOOS	JOUK
JOIN	JOKILY	JOLT	JORS	JOUKED
JOINABLE	JOKINESS	JOLTED	JORUM	JOUKERIES
JOINDER	JOKING	JOLTER	JORUMS	JOUKERY
JOINDERS	JOKINGLY	JOLTERS	JOSEPH	JOUKING

JOUKS	JOWLINESS	JUBILATES	JUDS	JUICINESS
JOULE	JOWLING	JUBILE	JUDY	JUICING
JOULED	JOWLS	JUBILEE	JUG	JUICY
JOULES	JOWLY	JUBILEES	JUGA	JUJITSU
JOULING	JOWS	JUBILES	JUGAL	JUJITSUS
JOUNCE	JOY	JUCO	JUGALS	JUJU
JOUNCED	JOYANCE	JUCOS	JUGATE	JUJUBE
JOUNCES	JOYANCES	JUD	JUGFUL	JUJUBES
JOUNCIER	JOYED	JUDAS	JUGFULS	JUJUISM
JOUNCIEST	JOYFUL	JUDASES	JUGGED	JUJUISMS
JOUNCING	JOYFULLER	JUDDER	JUGGING	JUJUIST
JOUNCY	JOYFULLY	JUDDERED	JUGGINGS	JUJUISTS
JOUR	JOYING	JUDDERING	JUGGINS	JUJUS
JOURNAL	JOYLESS	JUDDERS	JUGGINSES	JUJUTSU
JOURNALED	JOYLESSLY	JUDDERY	JUGGLE	JUJUTSUS
JOURNALS	JOYOUS	JUDGE	JUGGLED	JUKE
JOURNEY	JOYOUSLY	JUDGEABLE	JUGGLER	JUKEBOX
JOURNEYED	JOYPAD	JUDGED	JUGGLERS	JUKEBOXES
JOURNEYER	JOYPADS	JUDGELESS	JUGGLERY	JUKED
JOURNEYS	JOYPOP	JUDGELIKE	JUGGLES	JUKES
JOURNO	JOYPOPPED	JUDGEMENT	JUGGLING	JUKING
JOURNOS	JOYPOPPER	JUDGER	JUGGLINGS	JUKSKEI
JOURS	JOYPOPS	JUDGERS	JUGHEAD	JUKSKEIS
JOUST	JOYRIDDEN	JUDGES	JUGHEADS	JUKU
JOUSTED	JOYRIDE	JUDGESHIP	JUGLET	JUKUS
JOUSTER	JOYRIDER	JUDGING	JUGLETS	JULEP
JOUSTERS	JOYRIDERS	JUDGINGLY	JUGS	JULEPS
JOUSTING	JOYRIDES	JUDGINGS	JUGSFUL	JULIENNE
JOUSTINGS	JOYRIDING	JUDGMATIC	JUGULA	JULIENNED
JOUSTS	JOYRODE	JUDGMENT	JUGULAR	JULIENNES
JOVIAL	JOYS	JUDGMENTS	JUGULARS	JULIET
JOVIALITY	JOYSTICK	JUDICABLE	JUGULATE	JULIETS
JOVIALLY	JOYSTICKS	JUDICARE	JUGULATED	JUMAR
JOVIALTY	JUBA	JUDICARES	JUGULATES	JUMARED
JOW	JUBAS	JUDICATOR	JUGULUM	JUMARING
JOWAR	JUBATE	JUDICIAL	JUGUM	JUMARRED
JOWARI	JUBBAH	JUDICIARY	JUGUMS	JUMARRING
JOWARIS	JUBBAHS	JUDICIOUS	JUICE	JUMARS
JOWARS	JUBE	JUDIES	JUICED	JUMART
JOWED	JUBES	JUDO	JUICEHEAD	JUMARTS
JOWING	JUBHAH	JUDOGI	JUICELESS	JUMBAL
JOWL	JUBHAHS	JUDOGIS	JUICER	JUMBALS
JOWLED	JUBILANCE	JUDOIST	JUICERS	JUMBIE
JOWLER	JUBILANCY	JUDOISTS	JUICES	JUMBIES
JOWLERS	JUBILANT	JUDOKA	JUICIER	JUMBLE
JOWLIER	JUBILATE	JUDOKAS	JUICIEST	JUMBLED
JOWLIEST	JUBILATED	JUDOS	JUICILY	JUMBLER

JUMBLERS	JUMPSUIT	JUNKED	JURASSIC	JUSTIFIED
JUMBLES	JUMPSUITS	JUNKER	JURAT	JUSTIFIER
JUMBLIER	JUMPY	JUNKERS	JURATORY	JUSTIFIES
JUMBLIEST	JUN	JUNKET	JURATS	JUSTIFY
JUMBLING	JUNCATE	JUNKETED	JURE	JUSTING
JUMBLY	JUNCATES	JUNKETEER	JUREL	JUSTLE
JUMBO	JUNCO	JUNKETER	JURELS	JUSTLED
JUMBOISE	JUNCOES	JUNKETERS	JURES	JUSTLES
JUMBOISED	JUNCOS	JUNKETING	JURIDIC	JUSTLING
JUMBOISES	JUNCTION	JUNKETS	JURIDICAL	JUSTLY
JUMBOIZE	JUNCTIONS	JUNKETTED	JURIED	JUSTNESS
JUMBOIZED	JUNCTURAL	JUNKETTER	JURIES	JUSTS
JUMBOIZES	JUNCTURE	JUNKIE	JURIST	JUT
JUMBOS	JUNCTURES	JUNKIER	JURISTIC	JUTE
JUMBUCK	JUNCUS	JUNKIES	JURISTS	JUTELIKE
JUMBUCKS	JUNCUSES	JUNKIEST	JUROR	JUTES
JUMBY	JUNEATING	JUNKINESS	JURORS	JUTS
JUMELLE	JUNGLE	JUNKING	JURY	JUTTED
JUMELLES	JUNGLED	JUNKMAN	JURYING	JUTTIED
JUMP	JUNGLEGYM	JUNKMEN	JURYLESS	JUTTIER
JUMPABLE	JUNGLES	JUNKS	JURYMAST	JUTTIES
JUMPED	JUNGLI	JUNKY	JURYMASTS	JUTTIEST
JUMPER	JUNGLIER	JUNKYARD	JURYMEN	JUTTING
JUMPERS	JUNGLIEST	JUNKYARDS	JURYWOMAN	JUTTINGLY
JUMPIER	JUNGLIS	JUNTA	JURYWOMEN	JUTTY
JUMPIEST	JUNGLIST	JUNTAS	JUS	JUTTYING
JUMPILY	JUNGLISTS	JUNTO	JUSSIVE	JUVE
JUMPINESS	JUNGLY	JUNTOS	JUSSIVES	JUVENAL
JUMPING	JUNIOR	JUPATI	JUST	JUVENALS
JUMPINGLY	JUNIORATE	JUPATIS	JUSTED	JUVENILE
JUMPINGS	JUNIORED	JUPE	JUSTER	JUVENILES
JUMPOFF	JUNIORING	JUPES	JUSTERS	JUVENILIA
JUMPOFFS	JUNIORITY	JUPON	JUSTEST	JUVES
JUMPROPE	JUNIORS	JUPONS	JUSTICE	JUVIE
JUMPROPES	JUNIPER	JURA	JUSTICER	JUVIES
JUMPS	JUNIPERS	JURAL	JUSTICERS	JUXTAPOSE
JUMPSHOT	JUNK	JURALLY	JUSTICES	JYMOLD
JUMPSHOTS	JUNKANOO	JURANT	JUSTICIAR	JYNX
JUMPSIES	JUNKANOOS	JURANTS		JYNXES

K

KA
KAAL
KAAMA
KAAMAS
KAAS
KAB
KABAB
KABABBED
KABABBING
KABABS
KABADDI
KABADDIS
KABAKA
KABAKAS
KABALA
KABALAS
KABALISM
KABALISMS
KABALIST
KABALISTS
KABAR
KABARS
KABAYA
KABAYAS
KABBALA
KABBALAH
KABBALAHS
KABBALAS
KABBALISM
KABBALIST
KABELE
KABELES
KABELJOU
KABELJOUS
KABELJOUW
KABIKI
KABIKIS
KABLOOEY
KABLOOIE
KABLOONA
KABLOONAS

KABLOONAT
KABOB
KABOBBED
KABOBBING
KABOBS
KABOCHA
KABOCHAS
KABOODLE
KABOODLES
KABOOM
KABOOMS
KABS
KABUKI
KABUKIS
KACCHA
KACCHAS
KACHA
KACHAHRI
KACHAHRIS
KACHCHA
KACHERI
KACHERIS
KACHINA
KACHINAS
KACHORI
KACHORIS
KACHUMBER
KACK
KACKS
KADAI
KADAIS
KADAITCHA
KADDISH
KADDISHES
KADDISHIM
KADE
KADES
KADI
KADIS
KAE
KAED

KAEING
KAES
KAF
KAFFIR
KAFFIRS
KAFFIYAH
KAFFIYAHS
KAFFIYEH
KAFFIYEHS
KAFILA
KAFILAS
KAFIR
KAFIRS
KAFS
KAFTAN
KAFTANS
KAFUFFLE
KAFUFFLES
KAGO
KAGOOL
KAGOOLS
KAGOS
KAGOUL
KAGOULE
KAGOULES
KAGOULS
KAGU
KAGUS
KAHAL
KAHALS
KAHAWAI
KAHAWAIS
KAHIKATEA
KAHIKATOA
KAHUNA
KAHUNAS
KAI
KAIAK
KAIAKED
KAIAKING
KAIAKS

KAID
KAIDS
KAIE
KAIES
KAIF
KAIFS
KAIK
KAIKA
KAIKAI
KAIKAIS
KAIKAS
KAIKAWAKA
KAIKOMAKO
KAIKS
KAIL
KAILS
KAILYAIRD
KAILYARD
KAILYARDS
KAIM
KAIMAKAM
KAIMAKAMS
KAIMS
KAIN
KAING
KAINGA
KAINGAS
KAINIT
KAINITE
KAINITES
KAINITS
KAINS
KAIROMONE
KAIS
KAISER
KAISERDOM
KAISERIN
KAISERINS
KAISERISM
KAISERS
KAIZEN

KAIZENS
KAJAWAH
KAJAWAHS
KAJEPUT
KAJEPUTS
KAK
KAKA
KAKAPO
KAKAPOS
KAKARIKI
KAKARIKIS
KAKAS
KAKEMONO
KAKEMONOS
KAKI
KAKIEMON
KAKIEMONS
KAKIS
KAKIVAK
KAKIVAKS
KAKODYL
KAKODYLS
KAKS
KAKURO
KAKUROS
KALAM
KALAMATA
KALAMATAS
KALAMDAN
KALAMDANS
KALAMKARI
KALAMS
KALANCHOE
KALE
KALENDAR
KALENDARS
KALENDS
KALES
KALEWIFE
KALEWIVES
KALEYARD

KALEYARDS

KALEYARDS	KAMA	KANAES	KAOLIN	KARANGAS
KALI	KAMAAINA	KANAKA	KAOLINE	KARAOKE
KALIAN	KAMAAINAS	KANAKAS	KAOLINES	KARAOKES
KALIANS	KAMACITE	KANAMYCIN	KAOLINIC	KARAS
KALIF	KAMACITES	KANAS	KAOLINISE	KARAT
KALIFATE	KAMAHI	KANBAN	KAOLINITE	KARATE
KALIFATES	KAMAHIS	KANBANS	KAOLINIZE	KARATEIST
KALIFS	KAMALA	KANDIES	KAOLINS	KARATEKA
KALIMBA	KAMALAS	KANDY	KAON	KARATEKAS
KALIMBAS	KAMAS	KANE	KAONIC	KARATES
KALINITE	KAME	KANEH	KAONS	KARATS
KALINITES	KAMEES	KANEHS	KAPA	KAREAREA
KALIPH	KAMEESES	KANES	KAPAS	KAREAREAS
KALIPHATE	KAMEEZ	KANG	KAPEEK	KARENGO
KALIPHS	KAMEEZES	KANGA	KAPEYKA	KARENGOS
KALIS	KAMELA	KANGAROO	KAPH	KARITE
KALIUM	KAMELAS	KANGAROOS	KAPHS	KARITES
KALIUMS	KAMERAD	KANGAS	KAPOK	KARK
KALLIDIN	KAMERADED	KANGHA	KAPOKS	KARKED
KALLIDINS	KAMERADS	KANGHAS	KAPOW	KARKING
KALLITYPE	KAMES	KANGS	KAPOWS	KARKS
KALMIA	KAMI	KANJI	KAPPA	KARMA
KALMIAS	KAMICHI	KANJIS	KAPPAS	KARMAS
KALONG	KAMICHIS	KANS	KAPU	KARMIC
KALONGS	KAMIK	KANSES	KAPUKA	KARN
KALOOKI	KAMIKAZE	KANT	KAPUKAS	KARNS
KALOOKIE	KAMIKAZES	KANTAR	KAPUS	KARO
KALOOKIES	KAMIKS	KANTARS	KAPUT	KAROO
KALOOKIS	KAMILA	KANTED	KAPUTT	KAROOS
KALOTYPE	KAMILAS	KANTELA	KARA	KARORO
KALOTYPES	KAMIS	KANTELAS	KARABINER	KAROROS
KALPA	KAMISES	KANTELE	KARAHI	KAROS
KALPAC	KAMME	KANTELES	KARAHIS	KAROSHI
KALPACS	KAMOKAMO	KANTEN	KARAISM	KAROSHIS
KALPAK	KAMOKAMOS	KANTENS	KARAISMS	KAROSS
KALPAKS	KAMOTIK	KANTHA	KARAIT	KAROSSES
KALPAS	KAMOTIKS	KANTHAS	KARAITS	KARRI
KALPIS	KAMOTIQ	KANTIKOY	KARAKA	KARRIS
KALPISES	KAMOTIQS	KANTIKOYS	KARAKAS	KARROO
KALSOMINE	KAMPONG	KANTING	KARAKIA	KARROOS
KALUKI	KAMPONGS	KANTS	KARAKIAS	KARSEY
KALUKIS	KAMSEEN	KANUKA	KARAKUL	KARSEYS
KALUMPIT	KAMSEENS	KANUKAS	KARAKULS	KARSIES
KALUMPITS	KAMSIN	KANZU	KARAMU	KARST
KALYPTRA	KAMSINS	KANZUS	KARAMUS	KARSTIC
KALYPTRAS	KANA	KAOLIANG	KARANGA	KARSTIFY
KAM	KANAE	KAOLIANGS	KARANGAED	KARSTS

KARSY	KATANAS	KAVA	KAZI	KECKSIES
KART	KATAS	KAVAKAVA	KAZILLION	KECKSY
KARTER	KATCHINA	KAVAKAVAS	KAZIS	KED
KARTERS	KATCHINAS	KAVAL	KAZOO	KEDDAH
KARTING	KATCINA	KAVALS	KAZOOS	KEDDAHS
KARTINGS	KATCINAS	KAVAS	KBAR	KEDGE
KARTS	KATHAK	KAVASS	KBARS	KEDGED
KARYOGAMY	KATHAKALI	KAVASSES	KEA	KEDGER
KARYOGRAM	KATHAKS	KAW	KEAS	KEDGEREE
KARYOLOGY	KATHARSES	KAWA	KEASAR	KEDGEREES
KARYON	KATHARSIS	KAWAII	KEASARS	KEDGERS
KARYONS	KATHODAL	KAWAIIS	KEAVIE	KEDGES
KARYOSOME	KATHODE	KAWAKAWA	KEAVIES	KEDGIER
KARYOTIN	KATHODES	KAWAKAWAS	KEB	KEDGIEST
KARYOTINS	KATHODIC	KAWAS	KEBAB	KEDGING
KARYOTYPE	KATHUMP	KAWAU	KEBABBED	KEDGY
KARZIES	KATHUMPS	KAWAUS	KEBABBING	KEDS
KARZY	KATI	KAWED	KEBABS	KEECH
KAS	KATION	KAWING	KEBAR	KEECHES
KASBAH	KATIONS	KAWS	KEBARS	KEEF
KASBAHS	KATIPO	KAY	KEBBED	KEEFS
KASHA	KATIPOS	KAYAK	KEBBIE	KEEK
KASHAS	KATIS	KAYAKED	KEBBIES	KEEKED
KASHER	KATORGA	KAYAKER	KEBBING	KEEKER
KASHERED	KATORGAS	KAYAKERS	KEBBOCK	KEEKERS
KASHERING	KATS	KAYAKING	KEBBOCKS	KEEKING
KASHERS	KATSINA	KAYAKINGS	KEBBUCK	KEEKS
KASHMIR	KATSINAM	KAYAKS	KEBBUCKS	KEEL
KASHMIRS	KATSINAS	KAYLE	KEBELE	KEELAGE
KASHRUS	KATSURA	KAYLES	KEBELES	KEELAGES
KASHRUSES	KATSURAS	KAYLIED	KEBLAH	KEELBOAT
KASHRUT	KATTI	KAYO	KEBLAHS	KEELBOATS
KASHRUTH	KATTIS	KAYOED	KEBOB	KEELED
KASHRUTHS	KATYDID	KAYOES	KEBOBBED	KEELER
KASHRUTS	KATYDIDS	KAYOING	KEBOBBING	KEELERS
KASME	KAUGH	KAYOINGS	KEBOBS	KEELHALE
KAT	KAUGHS	KAYOS	KEBS	KEELHALED
KATA	KAUMATUA	KAYS	KECK	KEELHALES
KATABASES	KAUMATUAS	KAZACHKI	KECKED	KEELHAUL
KATABASIS	KAUPAPA	KAZACHOC	KECKING	KEELHAULS
KATABATIC	KAUPAPAS	KAZACHOCS	KECKLE	KEELIE
KATABOLIC	KAURI	KAZACHOK	KECKLED	KEELIES
KATAKANA	KAURIES	KAZACHOKS	KECKLES	KEELING
KATAKANAS	KAURIS	KAZATSKI	KECKLING	KEELINGS
KATAL	KAURU	KAZATSKY	KECKLINGS	KEELIVINE
KATALS	KAURUS	KAZATZKA	KECKS	KEELLESS
KATANA	KAURY	KAZATZKAS	KECKSES	KEELMAN

K

KEELMEN	KEFIRS	KELLS	KEMPT	KENTS
KEELS	KEFS	KELLY	KEMPY	KEP
KEELSON	KEFTEDES	KELOID	KEN	KEPHALIC
KEELSONS	KEFUFFLE	KELOIDAL	KENAF	KEPHALICS
KEELYVINE	KEFUFFLED	KELOIDS	KENAFS	KEPHALIN
KEEMA	KEFUFFLES	KELP	KENCH	KEPHALINS
KEEMAS	KEG	KELPED	KENCHES	KEPHIR
KEEN	KEGELER	KELPER	KENDO	KEPHIRS
KEENED	KEGELERS	KELPERS	KENDOIST	KEPI
KEENER	KEGGED	KELPFISH	KENDOISTS	KEPIS
KEENERS	KEGGER	KELPIE	KENDOS	KEPPED
KEENEST	KEGGERS	KELPIES	KENNED	KEPPEN
KEENING	KEGGING	KELPING	KENNEL	KEPPING
KEENINGS	KEGLER	KELPS	KENNELED	KEPPIT
KEENLY	KEGLERS	KELPY	KENNELING	KEPS
KEENNESS	KEGLING	KELSON	KENNELLED	KEPT
KEENO	KEGLINGS	KELSONS	KENNELMAN	KERAMIC
KEENOS	KEGS	KELT	KENNELMEN	KERAMICS
KEENS	KEHUA	KELTER	KENNELS	KERATIN
KEEP	KEHUAS	KELTERS	KENNER	KERATINS
KEEPABLE	KEIGHT	KELTIE	KENNERS	KERATITIS
KEEPER	KEIR	KELTIES	KENNET	KERATOID
KEEPERS	KEIREN	KELTS	KENNETS	KERATOMA
KEEPING	KEIRENS	KELTY	KENNETT	KERATOMAS
KEEPINGS	KEIRETSU	KELVIN	KENNETTED	KERATOSE
KEEPNET	KEIRETSUS	KELVINS	KENNETTS	KERATOSES
KEEPNETS	KEIRIN	KEMB	KENNING	KERATOSIC
KEEPS	KEIRINS	KEMBED	KENNINGS	KERATOSIS
KEEPSAKE	KEIRS	KEMBING	KENO	KERATOTIC
KEEPSAKES	KEISTER	KEMBLA	KENOS	KERB
KEEPSAKY	KEISTERS	KEMBLAS	KENOSES	KERBAYA
KEESHOND	KEITLOA	KEMBO	KENOSIS	KERBAYAS
KEESHONDS	KEITLOAS	KEMBOED	KENOSISES	KERBED
KEESTER	KEKENO	KEMBOING	KENOTIC	KERBING
KEESTERS	KEKENOS	KEMBOS	KENOTICS	KERBINGS
KEET	KEKERENGU	KEMBS	KENOTRON	KERBS
KEETS	KEKS	KEMP	KENOTRONS	KERBSIDE
KEEVE	KEKSYE	KEMPED	KENS	KERBSIDES
KEEVES	KEKSYES	KEMPER	KENSPECK	KERBSTONE
KEF	KELEP	KEMPERS	KENT	KERCHIEF
KEFFEL	KELEPS	KEMPIER	KENTE	KERCHIEFS
KEFFELS	KELIM	KEMPIEST	KENTED	KERCHOO
KEFFIYAH	KELIMS	KEMPING	KENTES	KEREL
KEFFIYAHS	KELL	KEMPINGS	KENTIA	KERELS
KEFFIYEH	KELLAUT	KEMPLE	KENTIAS	KERERU
KEFFIYEHS	KELLAUTS	KEMPLES	KENTING	KERERUS
KEFIR	KELLIES	KEMPS	KENTLEDGE	KERF

KERFED	KERRIAS	KETONURIA	KEYLINES	KHALIFAS
KERFING	KERRIES	KETOSE	KEYLOGGER	KHALIFAT
KERFLOOEY	KERRY	KETOSES	KEYNOTE	KHALIFATE
KERFS	KERSEY	KETOSIS	KEYNOTED	KHALIFATS
KERFUFFLE	KERSEYS	KETOTIC	KEYNOTER	KHALIFS
KERKIER	KERVE	KETOXIME	KEYNOTERS	KHAMSEEN
KERKIEST	KERVED	KETOXIMES	KEYNOTES	KHAMSEENS
KERKY	KERVES	KETS	KEYNOTING	KHAMSIN
KERMA	KERVING	KETTLE	KEYPAD	KHAMSINS
KERMAS	KERYGMA	KETTLED	KEYPADS	KHAN
KERMES	KERYGMAS	KETTLEFUL	KEYPAL	KHANATE
KERMESES	KERYGMATA	KETTLES	KEYPALS	KHANATES
KERMESITE	KESAR	KETTLING	KEYPRESS	KHANDA
KERMESS	KESARS	KETUBAH	KEYPUNCH	KHANDAS
KERMESSE	KESH	KETUBAHS	KEYRING	KHANGA
KERMESSES	KESHES	KETUBOT	KEYRINGS	KHANGAS
KERMIS	KEST	KETUBOTH	KEYS	KHANJAR
KERMISES	KESTING	KEVEL	KEYSET	KHANJARS
KERMODE	KESTREL	KEVELS	KEYSETS	KHANS
KERMODES	KESTRELS	KEVIL	KEYSTER	KHANSAMA
KERN	KESTS	KEVILS	KEYSTERS	KHANSAMAH
KERNE	KET	KEWL	KEYSTONE	KHANSAMAS
KERNED	KETA	KEWLER	KEYSTONED	KHANUM
KERNEL	KETAINE	KEWLEST	KEYSTONES	KHANUMS
KERNELED	KETAMINE	KEWPIE	KEYSTROKE	KHAPH
KERNELING	KETAMINES	KEWPIES	KEYWAY	KHAPHS
KERNELLED	KETAS	KEX	KEYWAYS	KHARIF
KERNELLY	KETCH	KEXES	KEYWORD	KHARIFS
KERNELS	KETCHES	KEY	KEYWORDS	KHAT
KERNES	KETCHING	KEYBOARD	KEYWORKER	KHATS
KERNING	KETCHUP	KEYBOARDS	KGOTLA	KHAYA
KERNINGS	KETCHUPS	KEYBUGLE	KGOTLAS	KHAYAL
KERNISH	KETCHUPY	KEYBUGLES	KHADDAR	KHAYALS
KERNITE	KETE	KEYBUTTON	KHADDARS	KHAYAS
KERNITES	KETENE	KEYCARD	KHADI	KHAZEN
KERNS	KETENES	KEYCARDS	KHADIS	KHAZENIM
KERO	KETES	KEYED	KHAF	KHAZENS
KEROGEN	KETMIA	KEYER	KHAFS	KHAZI
KEROGENS	KETMIAS	KEYERS	KHAKI	KHAZIS
KEROS	KETO	KEYFRAME	KHAKILIKE	KHEDA
KEROSENE	KETOGENIC	KEYFRAMES	KHAKIS	KHEDAH
KEROSENES	KETOL	KEYHOLE	KHALAT	KHEDAHS
KEROSINE	KETOLS	KEYHOLES	KHALATS	KHEDAS
KEROSINES	KETONE	KEYING	KHALIF	KHEDIVA
KERPLUNK	KETONEMIA	KEYINGS	KHALIFA	KHEDIVAL
KERPLUNKS	KETONES	KEYLESS	KHALIFAH	KHEDIVAS
KERRIA	KETONIC	KEYLINE	KHALIFAHS	KHEDIVATE

K

KHEDIVE	KIBBE	KICKBOXES	KIDEL	KIERS
KHEDIVES	KIBBEH	KICKDOWN	KIDELS	KIESELGUR
KHEDIVIAL	KIBBEHS	KICKDOWNS	KIDGE	KIESERITE
KHET	KIBBES	KICKED	KIDGIE	KIESTER
KHETH	KIBBI	KICKER	KIDGIER	KIESTERS
KHETHS	KIBBIS	KICKERS	KIDGIEST	KIEV
KHETS	KIBBITZ	KICKFLIP	KIDGLOVE	KIEVE
KHI	KIBBITZED	KICKFLIPS	KIDLET	KIEVES
KHILAFAT	KIBBITZER	KICKIER	KIDLETS	KIEVS
KHILAFATS	KIBBITZES	KICKIEST	KIDLIKE	KIF
KHILAT	KIBBLE	KICKING	KIDLING	KIFF
KHILATS	KIBBLED	KICKINGS	KIDLINGS	KIFS
KHILIM	KIBBLES	KICKOFF	KIDLIT	KIGHT
KHILIMS	KIBBLING	KICKOFFS	KIDLITS	KIGHTS
KHIMAR	KIBBUTZ	KICKOUT	KIDNAP	KIKE
KHIMARS	KIBBUTZIM	KICKOUTS	KIDNAPED	KIKES
KHIRKAH	KIBE	KICKS	KIDNAPEE	KIKOI
KHIRKAHS	KIBEI	KICKSHAW	KIDNAPEES	KIKOIS
KHIS	KIBEIS	KICKSHAWS	KIDNAPER	KIKUMON
KHODJA	KIBES	KICKSTAND	KIDNAPERS	KIKUMONS
KHODJAS	KIBITKA	KICKSTART	KIDNAPING	KIKUYU
KHOJA	KIBITKAS	KICKUP	KIDNAPPED	KIKUYUS
KHOJAS	KIBITZ	KICKUPS	KIDNAPPEE	KILD
KHOR	KIBITZED	KICKY	KIDNAPPER	KILDERKIN
KHORS	KIBITZER	KID	KIDNAPS	KILERG
KHOTBAH	KIBITZERS	KIDDED	KIDNEY	KILERGS
KHOTBAHS	KIBITZES	KIDDER	KIDNEYS	KILEY
KHOTBEH	KIBITZING	KIDDERS	KIDOLOGY	KILEYS
KHOTBEHS	KIBLA	KIDDIE	KIDS	KILIM
KHOUM	KIBLAH	KIDDIED	KIDSKIN	KILIMS
KHOUMS	KIBLAHS	KIDDIER	KIDSKINS	KILL
KHUD	KIBLAS	KIDDIERS	KIDSTAKES	KILLABLE
KHUDS	KIBOSH	KIDDIES	KIDULT	KILLADAR
KHURTA	KIBOSHED	KIDDING	KIDULTS	KILLADARS
KHURTAS	KIBOSHES	KIDDINGLY	KIDVID	KILLAS
KHUSKHUS	KIBOSHING	KIDDINGS	KIDVIDS	KILLASES
KHUTBAH	KICK	KIDDISH	KIEF	KILLCOW
KHUTBAHS	KICKABLE	KIDDLE	KIEFS	KILLCOWS
KI	KICKABOUT	KIDDLES	KIEKIE	KILLCROP
KIAAT	KICKBACK	KIDDO	KIEKIES	KILLCROPS
KIAATS	KICKBACKS	KIDDOES	KIELBASA	KILLDEE
KIACK	KICKBALL	KIDDOS	KIELBASAS	KILLDEER
KIACKS	KICKBALLS	KIDDUSH	KIELBASI	KILLDEERS
KIANG	KICKBOARD	KIDDUSHES	KIELBASY	KILLDEES
KIANGS	KICKBOX	KIDDY	KIER	KILLED
KIAUGH	KICKBOXED	KIDDYING	KIERIE	KILLER
KIAUGHS	KICKBOXER	KIDDYWINK	KIERIES	KILLERS

K

KILLICK	KILOPOND	KINCHIN	KINFOLKS	KINKAJOUS
KILLICKS	KILOPONDS	KINCHINS	KING	KINKED
KILLIE	KILORAD	KINCOB	KINGBIRD	KINKIER
KILLIES	KILORADS	KINCOBS	KINGBIRDS	KINKIEST
KILLIFISH	KILOS	KIND	KINGBOLT	KINKILY
KILLING	KILOTON	KINDA	KINGBOLTS	KINKINESS
KILLINGLY	KILOTONNE	KINDED	KINGCRAFT	KINKING
KILLINGS	KILOTONS	KINDER	KINGCUP	KINKLE
KILLJOY	KILOVOLT	KINDERS	KINGCUPS	KINKLES
KILLJOYS	KILOVOLTS	KINDEST	KINGDOM	KINKS
KILLOCK	KILOWATT	KINDIE	KINGDOMED	KINKY
KILLOCKS	KILOWATTS	KINDIES	KINGDOMS	KINLESS
KILLOGIE	KILP	KINDING	KINGED	KINO
KILLOGIES	KILPS	KINDLE	KINGFISH	KINONE
KILLS	KILT	KINDLED	KINGHOOD	KINONES
KILLUT	KILTED	KINDLER	KINGHOODS	KINOS
KILLUTS	KILTER	KINDLERS	KINGING	KINRED
KILN	KILTERS	KINDLES	KINGKLIP	KINREDS
KILNED	KILTIE	KINDLESS	KINGKLIPS	KINS
KILNING	KILTIES	KINDLIER	KINGLE	KINSFOLK
KILNS	KILTING	KINDLIEST	KINGLES	KINSFOLKS
KILO	KILTINGS	KINDLILY	KINGLESS	KINSHIP
KILOBAR	KILTLIKE	KINDLING	KINGLET	KINSHIPS
KILOBARS	KILTS	KINDLINGS	KINGLETS	KINSMAN
KILOBASE	KILTY	KINDLY	KINGLIER	KINSMEN
KILOBASES	KIMBO	KINDNESS	KINGLIEST	KINSWOMAN
KILOBAUD	KIMBOED	KINDRED	KINGLIKE	KINSWOMEN
KILOBAUDS	KIMBOING	KINDREDS	KINGLING	KINTLEDGE
KILOBIT	KIMBOS	KINDS	KINGLINGS	KIORE
KILOBITS	KIMCHEE	KINDY	KINGLY	KIORES
KILOBYTE	KIMCHEES	KINE	KINGMAKER	KIOSK
KILOBYTES	KIMCHI	KINEMA	KINGPIN	KIOSKS
KILOCURIE	KIMCHIS	KINEMAS	KINGPINS	KIP
KILOCYCLE	KIMMER	KINEMATIC	KINGPOST	KIPE
KILOGAUSS	KIMMERS	KINES	KINGPOSTS	KIPES
KILOGRAM	KIMONO	KINESCOPE	KINGS	KIPP
KILOGRAMS	KIMONOED	KINESES	KINGSHIP	KIPPA
KILOGRAY	KIMONOS	KINESIC	KINGSHIPS	KIPPAGE
KILOGRAYS	KIN	KINESICS	KINGSIDE	KIPPAGES
KILOHERTZ	KINA	KINESIS	KINGSIDES	KIPPAH
KILOJOULE	KINAKINA	KINESISES	KINGSNAKE	KIPPAHS
KILOLITER	KINAKINAS	KINETIC	KINGWOOD	KIPPAS
KILOLITRE	KINARA	KINETICAL	KINGWOODS	KIPPED
KILOMETER	KINARAS	KINETICS	KININ	KIPPEN
KILOMETRE	KINAS	KINETIN	KININS	KIPPER
KILOMOLE	KINASE	KINETINS	KINK	KIPPERED
KILOMOLES	KINASES	KINFOLK	KINKAJOU	KIPPERER

KIPPERERS	KIRTAN	KITBAGS	KITTIWAKE	KLEPHTISM
KIPPERING	KIRTANS	KITCHEN	KITTLE	KLEPHTS
KIPPERS	KIRTLE	KITCHENED	KITTLED	KLEPTO
KIPPING	KIRTLED	KITCHENER	KITTLER	KLEPTOS
KIPPS	KIRTLES	KITCHENET	KITTLES	KLETT
KIPS	KIS	KITCHENS	KITTLEST	KLETTS
KIPSKIN	KISAN	KITE	KITTLIER	KLEZMER
KIPSKINS	KISANS	KITEBOARD	KITTLIEST	KLEZMERS
KIPUNJI	KISH	KITED	KITTLING	KLEZMORIM
KIPUNJIS	KISHES	KITELIKE	KITTLY	KLICK
KIR	KISHKA	KITENGE	KITTUL	KLICKS
KIRANA	KISHKAS	KITENGES	KITTULS	KLIEG
KIRANAS	KISHKE	KITER	KITTY	KLIEGS
KIRBEH	KISHKES	KITERS	KITUL	KLIK
KIRBEHS	KISKADEE	KITES	KITULS	KLIKS
KIRBIGRIP	KISKADEES	KITH	KIVA	KLINKER
KIRBY	KISMAT	KITHARA	KIVAS	KLINKERS
KIRIGAMI	KISMATS	KITHARAS	KIWI	KLINOSTAT
KIRIGAMIS	KISMET	KITHE	KIWIFRUIT	KLIPDAS
KIRIMON	KISMETIC	KITHED	KIWIS	KLIPDASES
KIRIMONS	KISMETS	KITHES	KLANG	KLISTER
KIRK	KISS	KITHING	KLANGS	KLISTERS
KIRKED	KISSABLE	KITHS	KLAP	KLONDIKE
KIRKING	KISSABLY	KITING	KLAPPED	KLONDIKED
KIRKINGS	KISSAGRAM	KITINGS	KLAPPING	KLONDIKER
KIRKMAN	KISSED	KITLING	KLAPS	KLONDIKES
KIRKMEN	KISSEL	KITLINGS	KLATCH	KLONDYKE
KIRKS	KISSELS	KITS	KLATCHES	KLONDYKED
KIRKTON	KISSER	KITSCH	KLATSCH	KLONDYKER
KIRKTONS	KISSERS	KITSCHES	KLATSCHES	KLONDYKES
KIRKWARD	KISSES	KITSCHIER	KLAVERN	KLONG
KIRKYAIRD	KISSIER	KITSCHIFY	KLAVERNS	KLONGS
KIRKYARD	KISSIEST	KITSCHILY	KLAVIER	KLOOCH
KIRKYARDS	KISSING	KITSCHY	KLAVIERS	KLOOCHES
KIRMESS	KISSINGS	KITSET	KLAXON	KLOOCHMAN
KIRMESSES	KISSOGRAM	KITSETS	KLAXONED	KLOOCHMEN
KIRN	KISSY	KITTED	KLAXONING	KLOOF
KIRNED	KIST	KITTEL	KLAXONS	KLOOFS
KIRNING	KISTED	KITTELS	KLEAGLE	KLOOTCH
KIRNS	KISTFUL	KITTEN	KLEAGLES	KLOOTCHES
KIRPAN	KISTFULS	KITTENED	KLEENEX	KLUDGE
KIRPANS	KISTING	KITTENING	KLEENEXES	KLUDGED
KIRRI	KISTS	KITTENISH	KLEFTIKO	KLUDGES
KIRRIS	KISTVAEN	KITTENS	KLEFTIKOS	KLUDGEY
KIRS	KISTVAENS	KITTENY	KLENDUSIC	KLUDGIER
KIRSCH	KIT	KITTIES	KLEPHT	KLUDGIEST
KIRSCHES	KITBAG	KITTING	KLEPHTIC	KLUDGING

K

KLUDGY	KNARL	KNEEPAN	KNISHES	KNOCKINGS
KLUGE	KNARLIER	KNEEPANS	KNIT	KNOCKLESS
KLUGED	KNARLIEST	KNEEPIECE	KNITBONE	KNOCKOFF
KLUGES	KNARLS	KNEEROOM	KNITBONES	KNOCKOFFS
KLUGING	KNARLY	KNEEROOMS	KNITCH	KNOCKOUT
KLUTZ	KNARRED	KNEES	KNITCHES	KNOCKOUTS
KLUTZES	KNARRIER	KNEESIES	KNITS	KNOCKS
KLUTZIER	KNARRIEST	KNEESOCK	KNITTABLE	KNOLL
KLUTZIEST	KNARRING	KNEESOCKS	KNITTED	KNOLLED
KLUTZY	KNARRY	KNEIDEL	KNITTER	KNOLLER
KLYSTRON	KNARS	KNEIDELS	KNITTERS	KNOLLERS
KLYSTRONS	KNAUR	KNEIDLACH	KNITTING	KNOLLIER
KNACK	KNAURS	KNELL	KNITTINGS	KNOLLIEST
KNACKED	KNAVE	KNELLED	KNITTLE	KNOLLING
KNACKER	KNAVERIES	KNELLING	KNITTLES	KNOLLS
KNACKERED	KNAVERY	KNELLS	KNITWEAR	KNOLLY
KNACKERS	KNAVES	KNELT	KNITWEARS	KNOP
KNACKERY	KNAVESHIP	KNESSET	KNIVE	KNOPPED
KNACKIER	KNAVISH	KNESSETS	KNIVED	KNOPS
KNACKIEST	KNAVISHLY	KNEVELL	KNIVES	KNOSP
KNACKING	KNAWE	KNEVELLED	KNIVING	KNOSPS
KNACKISH	KNAWEL	KNEVELLS	KNOB	KNOT
KNACKS	KNAWELS	KNEW	KNOBBED	KNOTGRASS
KNACKY	KNAWES	KNICKER	KNOBBER	KNOTHEAD
KNAG	KNEAD	KNICKERED	KNOBBERS	KNOTHEADS
KNAGGIER	KNEADABLE	KNICKERS	KNOBBIER	KNOTHOLE
KNAGGIEST	KNEADED	KNICKS	KNOBBIEST	KNOTHOLES
KNAGGY	KNEADER	KNIFE	KNOBBING	KNOTLESS
KNAGS	KNEADERS	KNIFED	KNOBBLE	KNOTLIKE
KNAIDEL	KNEADING	KNIFELESS	KNOBBLED	KNOTS
KNAIDELS	KNEADS	KNIFELIKE	KNOBBLES	KNOTTED
KNAIDLACH	KNEE	KNIFEMAN	KNOBBLIER	KNOTTER
KNAP	KNEECAP	KNIFEMEN	KNOBBLING	KNOTTERS
KNAPPED	KNEECAPS	KNIFER	KNOBBLY	KNOTTIER
KNAPPER	KNEED	KNIFEREST	KNOBBY	KNOTTIEST
KNAPPERS	KNEEHOLE	KNIFERS	KNOBHEAD	KNOTTILY
KNAPPING	KNEEHOLES	KNIFES	KNOBHEADS	KNOTTING
KNAPPLE	KNEEING	KNIFING	KNOBLIKE	KNOTTINGS
KNAPPLED	KNEEJERK	KNIFINGS	KNOBS	KNOTTY
KNAPPLES	KNEEL	KNIGHT	KNOBSTICK	KNOTWEED
KNAPPLING	KNEELED	KNIGHTAGE	KNOCK	KNOTWEEDS
KNAPS	KNEELER	KNIGHTED	KNOCKBACK	KNOTWORK
KNAPSACK	KNEELERS	KNIGHTING	KNOCKDOWN	KNOTWORKS
KNAPSACKS	KNEELING	KNIGHTLY	KNOCKED	KNOUT
KNAPWEED	KNEELS	KNIGHTS	KNOCKER	KNOUTED
KNAPWEEDS	KNEEPAD	KNIPHOFIA	KNOCKERS	KNOUTING
KNAR	KNEEPADS	KNISH	KNOCKING	KNOUTS

K

KNOW	KNUT	KOHLRABIS	KOLKHOZ	KOOKIER
KNOWABLE	KNUTS	KOHLS	KOLKHOZES	KOOKIEST
KNOWE	KO	KOI	KOLKHOZY	KOOKILY
KNOWER	KOA	KOINE	KOLKOZ	KOOKINESS
KNOWERS	KOALA	KOINES	KOLKOZES	KOOKING
KNOWES	KOALAS	KOIS	KOLKOZY	KOOKS
KNOWHOW	KOAN	KOJI	KOLO	KOOKUM
KNOWHOWS	KOANS	KOJIS	KOLOS	KOOKUMS
KNOWING	KOAP	KOKA	KOMATIK	KOOKY
KNOWINGER	KOAPS	KOKAKO	KOMATIKS	KOOLAH
KNOWINGLY	KOAS	KOKAKOS	KOMBU	KOOLAHS
KNOWINGS	KOB	KOKAM	KOMBUS	KOORI
KNOWLEDGE	KOBAN	KOKAMS	KOMISSAR	KOORIES
KNOWN	KOBANG	KOKANEE	KOMISSARS	KOORIS
KNOWNS	KOBANGS	KOKANEES	KOMITAJI	KOP
KNOWS	KOBANS	KOKAS	KOMITAJIS	KOPASETIC
KNUB	KOBO	KOKER	KOMONDOR	KOPECK
KNUBBIER	KOBOLD	KOKERS	KOMONDORS	KOPECKS
KNUBBIEST	KOBOLDS	KOKIRI	KON	KOPEK
KNUBBLE	KOBOS	KOKIRIS	KONAKI	KOPEKS
KNUBBLED	KOBS	KOKOBEH	KONAKIS	KOPH
KNUBBLES	KOCHIA	KOKOPU	KONBU	KOPHS
KNUBBLIER	KOCHIAS	KOKOPUS	KONBUS	KOPIYKA
KNUBBLING	KOEKOEA	KOKOWAI	KOND	KOPIYKAS
KNUBBLY	KOEKOEAS	KOKOWAIS	KONDO	KOPIYOK
KNUBBY	KOEL	KOKRA	KONDOS	KOPJE
KNUBS	KOELS	KOKRAS	KONEKE	KOPJES
KNUCKLE	KOFF	KOKUM	KONEKES	KOPPA
KNUCKLED	KOFFS	KOKUMS	KONFYT	KOPPAS
KNUCKLER	KOFTA	KOLA	KONFYTS	KOPPIE
KNUCKLERS	KOFTAS	KOLACKIES	KONGONI	KOPPIES
KNUCKLES	KOFTGAR	KOLACKY	KONIMETER	KOPS
KNUCKLIER	KOFTGARI	KOLAS	KONINI	KOR
KNUCKLING	KOFTGARIS	KOLBASI	KONINIS	KORA
KNUCKLY	KOFTGARS	KOLBASIS	KONIOLOGY	KORAI
KNUR	KOFTWORK	KOLBASSA	KONISCOPE	KORARI
KNURL	KOFTWORKS	KOLBASSAS	KONK	KORARIS
KNURLED	KOGAL	KOLBASSI	KONKED	KORAS
KNURLIER	KOGALS	KOLBASSIS	KONKING	KORAT
KNURLIEST	KOHA	KOLHOZ	KONKS	KORATS
KNURLING	KOHANIM	KOLHOZES	KONNING	KORE
KNURLINGS	KOHAS	KOLHOZY	KONS	KORERO
KNURLS	KOHEKOHE	KOLINSKI	KOODOO	KOREROED
KNURLY	KOHEKOHES	KOLINSKY	KOODOOS	KOREROING
KNURR	KOHEN	KOLKHOS	KOOK	KOREROS
KNURRS	KOHL	KOLKHOSES	KOOKED	KORES
KNURS	KOHLRABI	KOLKHOSY	KOOKIE	KORFBALL

KORFBALLS	KOTUKU	KRAKENS	KRIMMERS	KUBASA
KORIMAKO	KOTUKUS	KRAKOWIAK	KRIS	KUBASAS
KORIMAKOS	KOTWAL	KRAMERIA	KRISED	KUBIE
KORKIR	KOTWALS	KRAMERIAS	KRISES	KUBIES
KORKIRS	KOULAN	KRANG	KRISING	KUCCHA
KORMA	KOULANS	KRANGS	KROMESKY	KUCCHAS
KORMAS	KOUMIS	KRANS	KRONA	KUCHCHA
KORO	KOUMISES	KRANSES	KRONE	KUCHEN
KOROMIKO	KOUMISS	KRANTZ	KRONEN	KUCHENS
KOROMIKOS	KOUMISSES	KRANTZES	KRONER	KUDLIK
KORORA	KOUMYS	KRANZ	KRONOR	KUDLIKS
KORORAS	KOUMYSES	KRANZES	KRONUR	KUDO
KOROS	KOUMYSS	KRATER	KROON	KUDOS
KOROWAI	KOUMYSSES	KRATERS	KROONI	KUDOSES
KOROWAIS	KOUPREY	KRAUT	KROONS	KUDU
KORS	KOUPREYS	KRAUTS	KRUBI	KUDUS
KORU	KOURA	KRAY	KRUBIS	KUDZU
KORUN	KOURAS	KRAYS	KRUBUT	KUDZUS
KORUNA	KOURBASH	KREASOTE	KRUBUTS	KUE
KORUNAS	KOUROI	KREASOTED	KRULLER	KUEH
KORUNY	KOUROS	KREASOTES	KRULLERS	KUES
KORUS	KOUSKOUS	KREATINE	KRUMHORN	KUFI
KOS	KOUSSO	KREATINES	KRUMHORNS	KUFIS
KOSES	KOUSSOS	KREEP	KRUMKAKE	KUFIYAH
KOSHER	KOW	KREEPS	KRUMKAKES	KUFIYAHS
KOSHERED	KOWHAI	KREESE	KRUMMHOLZ	KUGEL
KOSHERING	KOWHAIS	KREESED	KRUMMHORN	KUGELS
KOSHERS	KOWS	KREESES	KRUMPER	KUIA
KOSMOS	KOWTOW	KREESING	KRUMPERS	KUIAS
KOSMOSES	KOWTOWED	KREMLIN	KRUMPING	KUKRI
KOSS	KOWTOWER	KREMLINS	KRUMPINGS	KUKRIS
KOSSES	KOWTOWERS	KRENG	KRUNK	KUKU
KOTARE	KOWTOWING	KRENGS	KRUNKED	KUKUS
KOTARES	KOWTOWS	KREOSOTE	KRUNKS	KULA
KOTCH	KRAAL	KREOSOTED	KRYOLITE	KULAK
KOTCHED	KRAALED	KREOSOTES	KRYOLITES	KULAKI
KOTCHES	KRAALING	KREPLACH	KRYOLITH	KULAKS
KOTCHING	KRAALS	KREPLECH	KRYOLITHS	KULAN
KOTO	KRAB	KREUTZER	KRYOMETER	KULANS
KOTOS	KRABS	KREUTZERS	KRYPSES	KULAS
KOTOW	KRAFT	KREUZER	KRYPSIS	KULBASA
KOTOWED	KRAFTS	KREUZERS	KRYPTON	KULBASAS
KOTOWER	KRAI	KREWE	KRYPTONS	KULFI
KOTOWERS	KRAIS	KREWES	KRYTRON	KULFIS
KOTOWING	KRAIT	KRILL	KRYTRONS	KULTUR
KOTOWS	KRAITS	KRILLS	KSAR	KULTURS
KOTTABOS	KRAKEN	KRIMMER	KSARS	KUMARA

KUMARAHOU	KURBASHED	KUTUS	KYANGS	KYLLOSIS
KUMARAS	KURBASHES	KUVASZ	KYANISE	KYLOE
KUMARI	KURFUFFLE	KUVASZOK	KYANISED	KYLOES
KUMARIS	KURGAN	KUZU	KYANISES	KYMOGRAM
KUMBALOI	KURGANS	KUZUS	KYANISING	KYMOGRAMS
KUMERA	KURI	KVAS	KYANITE	KYMOGRAPH
KUMERAS	KURIS	KVASES	KYANITES	KYND
KUMIKUMI	KURRAJONG	KVASS	KYANITIC	KYNDE
KUMIKUMIS	KURRE	KVASSES	KYANIZE	KYNDED
KUMIS	KURRES	KVELL	KYANIZED	KYNDES
KUMISES	KURSAAL	KVELLED	KYANIZES	KYNDING
KUMISS	KURSAALS	KVELLING	KYANIZING	KYNDS
KUMISSES	KURTA	KVELLS	KYAR	KYNE
KUMITE	KURTAS	KVETCH	KYARS	KYOGEN
KUMITES	KURTOSES	KVETCHED	KYAT	KYOGENS
KUMKUM	KURTOSIS	KVETCHER	KYATS	KYPE
KUMKUMS	KURU	KVETCHERS	KYBO	KYPES
KUMMEL	KURUS	KVETCHES	KYBOS	KYPHOSES
KUMMELS	KURUSH	KVETCHIER	KYBOSH	KYPHOSIS
KUMQUAT	KURUSHES	KVETCHILY	KYBOSHED	KYPHOTIC
KUMQUATS	KURVEY	KVETCHING	KYBOSHES	KYRIE
KUMYS	KURVEYED	KVETCHY	KYBOSHING	KYRIELLE
KUMYSES	KURVEYING	KWACHA	KYDST	KYRIELLES
KUNA	KURVEYOR	KWACHAS	KYE	KYRIES
KUNDALINI	KURVEYORS	KWAITO	KYES	KYTE
KUNE	KURVEYS	KWAITOS	KYLE	KYTES
KUNEKUNE	KUSSO	KWANZA	KYLES	KYTHE
KUNEKUNES	KUSSOS	KWANZAS	KYLICES	KYTHED
KUNJOOS	KUTA	KWELA	KYLIE	KYTHES
KUNKAR	KUTAS	KWELAS	KYLIES	KYTHING
KUNKARS	KUTCH	KY	KYLIKES	KYU
KUNKUR	KUTCHA	KYACK	KYLIN	KYUS
KUNKURS	KUTCHES	KYACKS	KYLINS	
KUNZITE	KUTI	KYAK	KYLIX	
KUNZITES	KUTIS	KYAKS	KYLIXES	
KURBASH	KUTU	KYANG	KYLLOSES	

L

LA	LABIATE	LABRIDS	LACEWOODS	LACQUEY
LAAGER	LABIATED	LABROID	LACEWORK	LACQUEYED
LAAGERED	LABIATES	LABROIDS	LACEWORKS	LACQUEYS
LAAGERING	LABILE	LABROSE	LACEY	LACRIMAL
LAAGERS	LABILITY	LABRUM	LACHES	LACRIMALS
LAARI	LABIS	LABRUMS	LACHESES	LACRIMARY
LAARIS	LABISES	LABRUSCA	LACHRYMAL	LACRIMOSO
LAB	LABIUM	LABRUSCAS	LACIER	LACROSSE
LABARA	LABLAB	LABRYS	LACIEST	LACROSSES
LABARUM	LABLABS	LABRYSES	LACILY	LACRYMAL
LABARUMS	LABOR	LABS	LACINESS	LACRYMALS
LABDA	LABORED	LABURNUM	LACING	LACS
LABDACISM	LABOREDLY	LABURNUMS	LACINGS	LACTAM
LABDANUM	LABORER	LABYRINTH	LACINIA	LACTAMS
LABDANUMS	LABORERS	LAC	LACINIAE	LACTARIAN
LABDAS	LABORING	LACCOLITE	LACINIATE	LACTARY
LABEL	LABORIOUS	LACCOLITH	LACK	LACTASE
LABELABLE	LABORISM	LACE	LACKADAY	LACTASES
LABELED	LABORISMS	LACEBARK	LACKED	LACTATE
LABELER	LABORIST	LACEBARKS	LACKER	LACTATED
LABELERS	LABORISTS	LACED	LACKERED	LACTATES
LABELING	LABORITE	LACELESS	LACKERING	LACTATING
LABELLA	LABORITES	LACELIKE	LACKERS	LACTATION
LABELLATE	LABORS	LACEMAKER	LACKEY	LACTEAL
LABELLED	LABORSOME	LACER	LACKEYED	LACTEALLY
LABELLER	LABOUR	LACERABLE	LACKEYING	LACTEALS
LABELLERS	LABOURED	LACERANT	LACKEYS	LACTEAN
LABELLING	LABOURER	LACERATE	LACKING	LACTEOUS
LABELLIST	LABOURERS	LACERATED	LACKLAND	LACTIC
LABELLOID	LABOURING	LACERATES	LACKLANDS	LACTIFIC
LABELLUM	LABOURISM	LACERS	LACKS	LACTITOL
LABELMATE	LABOURIST	LACERTIAN	LACMUS	LACTITOLS
LABELS	LABOURITE	LACERTID	LACMUSES	LACTIVISM
LABIA	LABOURS	LACERTIDS	LACONIC	LACTIVIST
LABIAL	LABRA	LACERTINE	LACONICAL	LACTONE
LABIALISE	LABRADOR	LACES	LACONISM	LACTONES
LABIALISM	LABRADORS	LACET	LACONISMS	LACTONIC
LABIALITY	LABRAL	LACETS	LACQUER	LACTOSE
LABIALIZE	LABRET	LACEWING	LACQUERED	LACTOSES
LABIALLY	LABRETS	LACEWINGS	LACQUERER	LACUNA
LABIALS	LABRID	LACEWOOD	LACQUERS	LACUNAE

LACUNAL	LADINO	LAERED	LAGUNAS	LAIPSE
LACUNAR	LADINOS	LAERING	LAGUNE	LAIPSED
LACUNARIA	LADLE	LAERS	LAGUNES	LAIPSES
LACUNARS	LADLED	LAESIE	LAH	LAIPSING
LACUNARY	LADLEFUL	LAETARE	LAHAL	LAIR
LACUNAS	LADLEFULS	LAETARES	LAHALS	LAIRAGE
LACUNATE	LADLER	LAETRILE	LAHAR	LAIRAGES
LACUNE	LADLERS	LAETRILES	LAHARS	LAIRD
LACUNES	LADLES	LAEVIGATE	LAHS	LAIRDLIER
LACUNOSE	LADLING	LAEVO	LAIC	LAIRDLY
LACY	LADRON	LAEVULIN	LAICAL	LAIRDS
LAD	LADRONE	LAEVULINS	LAICALLY	LAIRDSHIP
LADANUM	LADRONES	LAEVULOSE	LAICH	LAIRED
LADANUMS	LADRONS	LAG	LAICHS	LAIRIER
LADDER	LADS	LAGAN	LAICISE	LAIRIEST
LADDERED	LADY	LAGANS	LAICISED	LAIRING
LADDERING	LADYBIRD	LAGENA	LAICISES	LAIRISE
LADDERS	LADYBIRDS	LAGENAS	LAICISING	LAIRISED
LADDERY	LADYBOY	LAGEND	LAICISM	LAIRISES
LADDIE	LADYBOYS	LAGENDS	LAICISMS	LAIRISING
LADDIER	LADYBUG	LAGER	LAICITIES	LAIRIZE
LADDIES	LADYBUGS	LAGERED	LAICITY	LAIRIZED
LADDIEST	LADYCOW	LAGERING	LAICIZE	LAIRIZES
LADDISH	LADYCOWS	LAGERS	LAICIZED	LAIRIZING
LADDISM	LADYFIED	LAGGARD	LAICIZES	LAIRS
LADDISMS	LADYFIES	LAGGARDLY	LAICIZING	LAIRY
LADDY	LADYFISH	LAGGARDS	LAICS	LAISSE
LADE	LADYFLIES	LAGGED	LAID	LAISSES
LADED	LADYFLY	LAGGEN	LAIDED	LAITANCE
LADEN	LADYFY	LAGGENS	LAIDING	LAITANCES
LADENED	LADYFYING	LAGGER	LAIDLIER	LAITH
LADENING	LADYHOOD	LAGGERS	LAIDLIEST	LAITHLY
LADENS	LADYHOODS	LAGGIN	LAIDLY	LAITIES
LADER	LADYISH	LAGGING	LAIDS	LAITY
LADERS	LADYISM	LAGGINGLY	LAIGH	LAKE
LADES	LADYISMS	LAGGINGS	LAIGHER	LAKEBED
LADETTE	LADYKIN	LAGGINS	LAIGHEST	LAKEBEDS
LADETTES	LADYKINS	LAGNAPPE	LAIGHS	LAKED
LADHOOD	LADYLIKE	LAGNAPPES	LAIK	LAKEFILL
LADHOODS	LADYLOVE	LAGNIAPPE	LAIKA	LAKEFILLS
LADIES	LADYLOVES	LAGOMORPH	LAIKAS	LAKEFRONT
LADIFIED	LADYNESS	LAGOON	LAIKED	LAKEHEAD
LADIFIES	LADYPALM	LAGOONAL	LAIKER	LAKEHEADS
LADIFY	LADYPALMS	LAGOONS	LAIKERS	LAKELAND
LADIFYING	LADYSHIP	LAGRIMOSO	LAIKING	LAKELANDS
LADING	LADYSHIPS	LAGS	LAIKS	LAKELET
LADINGS	LAER	LAGUNA	LAIN	LAKELETS

LAKELIKE	LAMANTINS	LAMEDH	LAMINOSE	LAMPPOST
LAKEPORT	LAMAS	LAMEDHS	LAMINOUS	LAMPPOSTS
LAKEPORTS	LAMASERAI	LAMEDS	LAMISH	LAMPREY
LAKER	LAMASERY	LAMELLA	LAMISTER	LAMPREYS
LAKERS	LAMB	LAMELLAE	LAMISTERS	LAMPS
LAKES	LAMBADA	LAMELLAR	LAMITER	LAMPSHADE
LAKESHORE	LAMBADAS	LAMELLAS	LAMITERS	LAMPSHELL
LAKESIDE	LAMBAST	LAMELLATE	LAMMED	LAMPSTAND
LAKESIDES	LAMBASTE	LAMELLOID	LAMMER	LAMPUKA
LAKEVIEW	LAMBASTED	LAMELLOSE	LAMMERS	LAMPUKAS
LAKEWARD	LAMBASTES	LAMELY	LAMMIE	LAMPUKI
LAKEWARDS	LAMBASTS	LAMENESS	LAMMIES	LAMPUKIS
LAKH	LAMBDA	LAMENT	LAMMIGER	LAMPYRID
LAKHS	LAMBDAS	LAMENTED	LAMMIGERS	LAMPYRIDS
LAKIER	LAMBDOID	LAMENTER	LAMMING	LAMS
LAKIEST	LAMBED	LAMENTERS	LAMMINGS	LAMSTER
LAKIN	LAMBENCY	LAMENTING	LAMMY	LAMSTERS
LAKING	LAMBENT	LAMENTS	LAMP	LANA
LAKINGS	LAMBENTLY	LAMER	LAMPAD	LANAI
LAKINS	LAMBER	LAMES	LAMPADARY	LANAIS
LAKISH	LAMBERS	LAMEST	LAMPADIST	LANAS
LAKSA	LAMBERT	LAMETER	LAMPADS	LANATE
LAKSAS	LAMBERTS	LAMETERS	LAMPAS	LANATED
LAKY	LAMBIE	LAMIA	LAMPASES	LANCE
LALANG	LAMBIER	LAMIAE	LAMPASSE	LANCED
LALANGS	LAMBIES	LAMIAS	LAMPASSES	LANCEGAY
LALDIE	LAMBIEST	LAMIGER	LAMPBLACK	LANCEGAYS
LALDIES	LAMBING	LAMIGERS	LAMPBRUSH	LANCEJACK
LALDY	LAMBINGS	LAMINA	LAMPED	LANCELET
LALIQUE	LAMBITIVE	LAMINABLE	LAMPER	LANCELETS
LALIQUES	LAMBKILL	LAMINAE	LAMPERN	LANCEOLAR
LALL	LAMBKILLS	LAMINAL	LAMPERNS	LANCER
LALLAN	LAMBKIN	LAMINALS	LAMPERS	LANCERS
LALLAND	LAMBKINS	LAMINAR	LAMPERSES	LANCES
LALLANDS	LAMBLIKE	LAMINARIA	LAMPHOLE	LANCET
LALLANS	LAMBLING	LAMINARIN	LAMPHOLES	LANCETED
LALLATION	LAMBLINGS	LAMINARY	LAMPING	LANCETS
LALLED	LAMBOYS	LAMINAS	LAMPINGS	LANCEWOOD
LALLING	LAMBRUSCO	LAMINATE	LAMPION	LANCH
LALLINGS	LAMBS	LAMINATED	LAMPIONS	LANCHED
LALLS	LAMBSKIN	LAMINATES	LAMPLESS	LANCHES
LALLYGAG	LAMBSKINS	LAMINATOR	LAMPLIGHT	LANCHING
LALLYGAGS	LAMBSWOOL	LAMING	LAMPLIT	LANCIERS
LAM	LAMBY	LAMINGTON	LAMPOON	LANCIFORM
LAMA	LAME	LAMININ	LAMPOONED	LANCINATE
LAMAISTIC	LAMEBRAIN	LAMININS	LAMPOONER	LANCING
LAMANTIN	LAMED	LAMINITIS	LAMPOONS	LAND

LANDAMMAN	LANDRAILS	LANGSPELS	LANOLINE	LAPIDIST
LANDAU	LANDS	LANGSPIEL	LANOLINES	LAPIDISTS
LANDAULET	LANDSCAPE	LANGSPIL	LANOLINS	LAPILLI
LANDAUS	LANDSHARK	LANGSPILS	LANOSE	LAPILLUS
LANDBOARD	LANDSIDE	LANGSYNE	LANOSITY	LAPIN
LANDDAMNE	LANDSIDES	LANGSYNES	LANT	LAPINS
LANDDROS	LANDSKIP	LANGUAGE	LANTANA	LAPIS
LANDDROST	LANDSKIPS	LANGUAGED	LANTANAS	LAPISES
LANDE	LANDSLEIT	LANGUAGES	LANTERLOO	LAPJE
LANDED	LANDSLID	LANGUE	LANTERN	LAPJES
LANDER	LANDSLIDE	LANGUED	LANTERNED	LAPPED
LANDERS	LANDSLIP	LANGUES	LANTERNS	LAPPEL
LANDES	LANDSLIPS	LANGUET	LANTHANON	LAPPELS
LANDFALL	LANDSMAN	LANGUETS	LANTHANUM	LAPPER
LANDFALLS	LANDSMEN	LANGUETTE	LANTHORN	LAPPERED
LANDFAST	LANDWARD	LANGUID	LANTHORNS	LAPPERING
LANDFILL	LANDWARDS	LANGUIDLY	LANTS	LAPPERS
LANDFILLS	LANDWASH	LANGUISH	LANTSKIP	LAPPET
LANDFORCE	LANDWIND	LANGUOR	LANTSKIPS	LAPPETED
LANDFORM	LANDWINDS	LANGUORS	LANUGO	LAPPETS
LANDFORMS	LANE	LANGUR	LANUGOS	LAPPIE
LANDGRAB	LANELY	LANGURS	LANX	LAPPIES
LANDGRABS	LANES	LANIARD	LANYARD	LAPPING
LANDGRAVE	LANEWAY	LANIARDS	LANYARDS	LAPPINGS
LANDING	LANEWAYS	LANIARIES	LAODICEAN	LAPS
LANDINGS	LANG	LANIARY	LAOGAI	LAPSABLE
LANDLADY	LANGAHA	LANITAL	LAOGAIS	LAPSANG
LANDLER	LANGAHAS	LANITALS	LAP	LAPSANGS
LANDLERS	LANGAR	LANK	LAPBOARD	LAPSE
LANDLESS	LANGARS	LANKED	LAPBOARDS	LAPSED
LANDLINE	LANGER	LANKER	LAPDOG	LAPSER
LANDLINES	LANGERED	LANKEST	LAPDOGS	LAPSERS
LANDLOPER	LANGERS	LANKIER	LAPEL	LAPSES
LANDLORD	LANGEST	LANKIEST	LAPELED	LAPSIBLE
LANDLORDS	LANGLAUF	LANKILY	LAPELLED	LAPSING
LANDMAN	LANGLAUFS	LANKINESS	LAPELS	LAPSTONE
LANDMARK	LANGLEY	LANKING	LAPFUL	LAPSTONES
LANDMARKS	LANGLEYS	LANKLY	LAPFULS	LAPSTRAKE
LANDMASS	LANGOUSTE	LANKNESS	LAPHELD	LAPSTREAK
LANDMEN	LANGRAGE	LANKS	LAPIDARY	LAPSUS
LANDMINE	LANGRAGES	LANKY	LAPIDATE	LAPTOP
LANDMINED	LANGREL	LANNER	LAPIDATED	LAPTOPS
LANDMINES	LANGRELS	LANNERET	LAPIDATES	LAPTRAY
LANDOWNER	LANGRIDGE	LANNERETS	LAPIDEOUS	LAPTRAYS
LANDRACE	LANGSHAN	LANNERS	LAPIDES	LAPWING
LANDRACES	LANGSHANS	LANOLATED	LAPIDIFIC	LAPWINGS
LANDRAIL	LANGSPEL	LANOLIN	LAPIDIFY	LAPWORK

LAPWORKS	LARGESSES	LARRIKINS	LASHING	LAT
LAQUEARIA	LARGEST	LARRUP	LASHINGLY	LATAH
LAR	LARGHETTO	LARRUPED	LASHINGS	LATAHS
LARBOARD	LARGISH	LARRUPER	LASHINS	LATAKIA
LARBOARDS	LARGITION	LARRUPERS	LASHKAR	LATAKIAS
LARCENER	LARGO	LARRUPING	LASHKARS	LATCH
LARCENERS	LARGOS	LARRUPS	LASHLESS	LATCHED
LARCENIES	LARI	LARS	LASING	LATCHES
LARCENIST	LARIAT	LARUM	LASINGS	LATCHET
LARCENOUS	LARIATED	LARUMS	LASKET	LATCHETS
LARCENY	LARIATING	LARVA	LASKETS	LATCHING
LARCH	LARIATS	LARVAE	LASQUE	LATCHKEY
LARCHEN	LARIGAN	LARVAL	LASQUES	LATCHKEYS
LARCHES	LARIGANS	LARVAS	LASS	LATE
LARD	LARINE	LARVATE	LASSES	LATECOMER
LARDALITE	LARIS	LARVATED	LASSI	LATED
LARDED	LARK	LARVICIDE	LASSIE	LATEEN
LARDER	LARKED	LARVIFORM	LASSIES	LATEENER
LARDERER	LARKER	LARVIKITE	LASSIS	LATEENERS
LARDERERS	LARKERS	LARYNGAL	LASSITUDE	LATEENS
LARDERS	LARKIER	LARYNGALS	LASSLORN	LATELY
LARDIER	LARKIEST	LARYNGEAL	LASSO	LATEN
LARDIEST	LARKINESS	LARYNGES	LASSOCK	LATENCE
LARDING	LARKING	LARYNX	LASSOCKS	LATENCES
LARDLIKE	LARKISH	LARYNXES	LASSOED	LATENCIES
LARDON	LARKS	LAS	LASSOER	LATENCY
LARDONS	LARKSOME	LASAGNA	LASSOERS	LATENED
LARDOON	LARKSPUR	LASAGNAS	LASSOES	LATENESS
LARDOONS	LARKSPURS	LASAGNE	LASSOING	LATENING
LARDS	LARKY	LASAGNES	LASSOINGS	LATENS
LARDY	LARMIER	LASCAR	LASSOS	LATENT
LARE	LARMIERS	LASCARS	LASSU	LATENTLY
LAREE	LARN	LASE	LASSUS	LATENTS
LAREES	LARNAKES	LASED	LASSY	LATER
LARES	LARNAX	LASER	LAST	LATERAD
LARGANDO	LARNED	LASERDISC	LASTAGE	LATERAL
LARGE	LARNEY	LASERDISK	LASTAGES	LATERALED
LARGELY	LARNEYS	LASERED	LASTBORN	LATERALLY
LARGEN	LARNIER	LASERING	LASTBORNS	LATERALS
LARGENED	LARNIEST	LASERS	LASTED	LATERBORN
LARGENESS	LARNING	LASERWORT	LASTER	LATERISE
LARGENING	LARNS	LASES	LASTERS	LATERISED
LARGENS	LARNT	LASH	LASTING	LATERISES
LARGER	LAROID	LASHED	LASTINGLY	LATERITE
LARGES	LARRIGAN	LASHER	LASTINGS	LATERITES
LARGESS	LARRIGANS	LASHERS	LASTLY	LATERITIC
LARGESSE	LARRIKIN	LASHES	LASTS	LATERIZE

L

LATERIZED	LATIGOS	LATTICING	LAUNCED	LAVALIERS
LATERIZES	LATILLA	LATTICINI	LAUNCES	LAVALIKE
LATESCENT	LATILLAS	LATTICINO	LAUNCH	LAVANDIN
LATEST	LATIMERIA	LATTIN	LAUNCHED	LAVANDINS
LATESTS	LATINA	LATTINS	LAUNCHER	LAVAS
LATEWAKE	LATINAS	LATU	LAUNCHERS	LAVASH
LATEWAKES	LATINISE	LATUS	LAUNCHES	LAVASHES
LATEWOOD	LATINISED	LAUAN	LAUNCHING	LAVATERA
LATEWOODS	LATINISES	LAUANS	LAUNCHPAD	LAVATERAS
LATEX	LATINITY	LAUCH	LAUNCING	LAVATION
LATEXES	LATINIZE	LAUCHING	LAUND	LAVATIONS
LATH	LATINIZED	LAUCHS	LAUNDER	LAVATORY
LATHE	LATINIZES	LAUD	LAUNDERED	LAVE
LATHED	LATINO	LAUDABLE	LAUNDERER	LAVED
LATHEE	LATINOS	LAUDABLY	LAUNDERERS	LAVEER
LATHEES	LATISH	LAUDANUM	LAUNDERS	LAVEERED
LATHEN	LATITANCY	LAUDANUMS	LAUNDRESS	LAVEERING
LATHER	LATITANT	LAUDATION	LAUNDRIES	LAVEERS
LATHERED	LATITAT	LAUDATIVE	LAUNDRY	LAVEMENT
LATHERER	LATITATS	LAUDATOR	LAUNDS	LAVEMENTS
LATHERERS	LATITUDE	LAUDATORS	LAURA	LAVENDER
LATHERIER	LATITUDES	LAUDATORY	LAURAE	LAVENDERS
LATHERING	LATKE	LAUDED	LAURAS	LAVER
LATHERS	LATKES	LAUDER	LAUREATE	LAVEROCK
LATHERY	LATOSOL	LAUDERS	LAUREATED	LAVEROCKS
LATHES	LATOSOLIC	LAUDING	LAUREATES	LAVERS
LATHI	LATOSOLS	LAUDS	LAUREL	LAVES
LATHIER	LATRANT	LAUF	LAURELED	LAVING
LATHIEST	LATRATION	LAUFS	LAURELING	LAVISH
LATHING	LATRIA	LAUGH	LAURELLED	LAVISHED
LATHINGS	LATRIAS	LAUGHABLE	LAURELS	LAVISHER
LATHIS	LATRINE	LAUGHABLY	LAURIC	LAVISHERS
LATHLIKE	LATRINES	LAUGHED	LAURYL	LAVISHES
LATHS	LATROCINY	LAUGHER	LAURYLS	LAVISHEST
LATHWORK	LATRON	LAUGHERS	LAUWINE	LAVISHING
LATHWORKS	LATRONS	LAUGHFUL	LAUWINES	LAVISHLY
LATHY	LATS	LAUGHIER	LAV	LAVOLT
LATHYRISM	LATTE	LAUGHIEST	LAVA	LAVOLTA
LATHYRUS	LATTEN	LAUGHING	LAVABO	LAVOLTAED
LATI	LATTENS	LAUGHINGS	LAVABOES	LAVOLTAS
LATICES	LATTER	LAUGHLINE	LAVABOS	LAVOLTED
LATICIFER	LATTERLY	LAUGHS	LAVAFORM	LAVOLTING
LATICLAVE	LATTERS	LAUGHSOME	LAVAGE	LAVOLTS
LATIFONDI	LATTES	LAUGHTER	LAVAGES	LAVRA
LATIFONDO	LATTICE	LAUGHTERS	LAVALAVA	LAVRAS
LATIGO	LATTICED	LAUGHY	LAVALAVAS	LAVROCK
LATIGOES	LATTICES	LAUNCE	LAVALIER	LAVROCKS
			LAVALIERE	

LAVS	LAWSUITS	LAYINS	LAZULI	LEADMAN
LAVVIES	LAWYER	LAYLOCK	LAZULIS	LEADMEN
LAVVY	LAWYERED	LAYLOCKS	LAZULITE	LEADOFF
LAW	LAWYERING	LAYMAN	LAZULITES	LEADOFFS
LAWBOOK	LAWYERLY	LAYMANISE	LAZURITE	LEADPLANT
LAWBOOKS	LAWYERS	LAYMANIZE	LAZURITES	LEADS
LAWCOURT	LAX	LAYMEN	LAZY	LEADSCREW
LAWCOURTS	LAXATION	LAYOFF	LAZYBONES	LEADSMAN
LAWED	LAXATIONS	LAYOFFS	LAZYING	LEADSMEN
LAWER	LAXATIVE	LAYOUT	LAZYISH	LEADWORK
LAWEST	LAXATIVES	LAYOUTS	LAZZARONE	LEADWORKS
LAWFARE	LAXATOR	LAYOVER	LAZZARONI	LEADWORT
LAWFARES	LAXATORS	LAYOVERS	LAZZI	LEADWORTS
LAWFUL	LAXER	LAYPEOPLE	LAZZO	LEADY
LAWFULLY	LAXES	LAYPERSON	LEA	LEAF
LAWGIVER	LAXEST	LAYS	LEACH	LEAFAGE
LAWGIVERS	LAXISM	LAYSHAFT	LEACHABLE	LEAFAGES
LAWGIVING	LAXISMS	LAYSHAFTS	LEACHATE	LEAFBUD
LAWIN	LAXIST	LAYSTALL	LEACHATES	LEAFBUDS
LAWINE	LAXISTS	LAYSTALLS	LEACHED	LEAFED
LAWINES	LAXITIES	LAYTIME	LEACHER	LEAFERIES
LAWING	LAXITY	LAYTIMES	LEACHERS	LEAFERY
LAWINGS	LAXLY	LAYUP	LEACHES	LEAFIER
LAWINS	LAXNESS	LAYUPS	LEACHIER	LEAFIEST
LAWK	LAXNESSES	LAYWOMAN	LEACHIEST	LEAFINESS
LAWKS	LAY	LAYWOMEN	LEACHING	LEAFING
LAWLAND	LAYABOUT	LAZAR	LEACHINGS	LEAFLESS
LAWLANDS	LAYABOUTS	LAZARET	LEACHOUR	LEAFLET
LAWLESS	LAYAWAY	LAZARETS	LEACHOURS	LEAFLETED
LAWLESSLY	LAYAWAYS	LAZARETTE	LEACHY	LEAFLETER
LAWLIKE	LAYBACK	LAZARETTO	LEAD	LEAFLETS
LAWMAKER	LAYBACKED	LAZARS	LEADABLE	LEAFLIKE
LAWMAKERS	LAYBACKS	LAZE	LEADED	LEAFMOLD
LAWMAKING	LAYDEEZ	LAZED	LEADEN	LEAFMOLDS
LAWMAN	LAYED	LAZES	LEADENED	LEAFROLL
LAWMEN	LAYER	LAZIED	LEADENING	LEAFROLLS
LAWMONGER	LAYERAGE	LAZIER	LEADENLY	LEAFS
LAWN	LAYERAGES	LAZIES	LEADENS	LEAFSTALK
LAWNED	LAYERED	LAZIEST	LEADER	LEAFWORM
LAWNIER	LAYERING	LAZILY	LEADERENE	LEAFWORMS
LAWNIEST	LAYERINGS	LAZINESS	LEADERS	LEAFY
LAWNING	LAYERS	LAZING	LEADIER	LEAGUE
LAWNMOWER	LAYETTE	LAZO	LEADIEST	LEAGUED
LAWNS	LAYETTES	LAZOED	LEADING	LEAGUER
LAWNY	LAYIN	LAZOES	LEADINGLY	LEAGUERED
LAWS	LAYING	LAZOING	LEADINGS	LEAGUERS
LAWSUIT	LAYINGS	LAZOS	LEADLESS	LEAGUES

LEAGUING
LEAK
LEAKAGE
LEAKAGES
LEAKED
LEAKER
LEAKERS
LEAKIER
LEAKIEST
LEAKILY
LEAKINESS
LEAKING
LEAKLESS
LEAKPROOF
LEAKS
LEAKY
LEAL
LEALER
LEALEST
LEALLY
LEALTIES
LEALTY
LEAM
LEAMED
LEAMING
LEAMS
LEAN
LEANED
LEANER
LEANERS
LEANEST
LEANING
LEANINGS
LEANLY
LEANNESS
LEANS
LEANT
LEANY
LEAP
LEAPED
LEAPER
LEAPEROUS
LEAPERS
LEAPFROG
LEAPFROGS
LEAPING
LEAPOROUS

LEAPROUS
LEAPS
LEAPT
LEAR
LEARE
LEARED
LEARES
LEARIER
LEARIEST
LEARINESS
LEARING
LEARN
LEARNABLE
LEARNED
LEARNEDLY
LEARNER
LEARNERS
LEARNING
LEARNINGS
LEARNS
LEARNT
LEARS
LEARY
LEAS
LEASABLE
LEASE
LEASEBACK
LEASED
LEASEHOLD
LEASER
LEASERS
LEASES
LEASH
LEASHED
LEASHES
LEASHING
LEASING
LEASINGS
LEASOW
LEASOWE
LEASOWED
LEASOWES
LEASOWING
LEASOWS
LEAST
LEASTS
LEASTWAYS

LEASTWISE
LEASURE
LEASURES
LEAT
LEATHER
LEATHERED
LEATHERN
LEATHERS
LEATHERY
LEATS
LEAVE
LEAVED
LEAVEN
LEAVENED
LEAVENER
LEAVENERS
LEAVENING
LEAVENOUS
LEAVENS
LEAVER
LEAVERS
LEAVES
LEAVIER
LEAVIEST
LEAVING
LEAVINGS
LEAVY
LEAZE
LEAZES
LEBBEK
LEBBEKS
LEBEN
LEBENS
LEBKUCHEN
LECANORA
LECANORAS
LECCIES
LECCY
LECH
LECHAIM
LECHAIMS
LECHAYIM
LECHAYIMS
LECHED
LECHER
LECHERED
LECHERIES

LECHERING
LECHEROUS
LECHERS
LECHERY
LECHES
LECHING
LECHWE
LECHWES
LECITHIN
LECITHINS
LECTERN
LECTERNS
LECTIN
LECTINS
LECTION
LECTIONS
LECTOR
LECTORATE
LECTORS
LECTOTYPE
LECTRESS
LECTURE
LECTURED
LECTURER
LECTURERS
LECTURES
LECTURING
LECTURN
LECTURNS
LECYTHI
LECYTHIS
LECYTHUS
LED
LEDDEN
LEDDENS
LEDE
LEDES
LEDGE
LEDGED
LEDGER
LEDGERED
LEDGERING
LEDGERS
LEDGES
LEDGIER
LEDGIEST
LEDGY

LEDUM
LEDUMS
LEE
LEEAR
LEEARS
LEEBOARD
LEEBOARDS
LEECH
LEECHDOM
LEECHDOMS
LEECHED
LEECHEE
LEECHEES
LEECHES
LEECHING
LEECHLIKE
LEED
LEEING
LEEK
LEEKS
LEEP
LEEPED
LEEPING
LEEPS
LEER
LEERED
LEERIER
LEERIEST
LEERILY
LEERINESS
LEERING
LEERINGLY
LEERINGS
LEERS
LEERY
LEES
LEESE
LEESES
LEESING
LEET
LEETLE
LEETS
LEETSPEAK
LEEWARD
LEEWARDLY
LEEWARDS
LEEWAY

LEEWAYS	LEGATEES	LEGIBLE	LEHAYIM	LEKYTHI
LEEZE	LEGATES	LEGIBLY	LEHAYIMS	LEKYTHOI
LEFT	LEGATINE	LEGION	LEHR	LEKYTHOS
LEFTE	LEGATING	LEGIONARY	LEHRJAHRE	LEKYTHUS
LEFTER	LEGATION	LEGIONED	LEHRS	LEMAN
LEFTEST	LEGATIONS	LEGIONS	LEHUA	LEMANS
LEFTIE	LEGATO	LEGISLATE	LEHUAS	LEME
LEFTIES	LEGATOR	LEGIST	LEI	LEMED
LEFTISH	LEGATORS	LEGISTS	LEIDGER	LEMEL
LEFTISM	LEGATOS	LEGIT	LEIDGERS	LEMELS
LEFTISMS	LEGEND	LEGITIM	LEIGER	LEMES
LEFTIST	LEGENDARY	LEGITIMS	LEIGERS	LEMING
LEFTISTS	LEGENDISE	LEGITS	LEIOMYOMA	LEMMA
LEFTMOST	LEGENDIST	LEGLAN	LEIPOA	LEMMAS
LEFTMOSTS	LEGENDIZE	LEGLANS	LEIPOAS	LEMMATA
LEFTOVER	LEGENDRY	LEGLEN	LEIR	LEMMATISE
LEFTOVERS	LEGENDS	LEGLENS	LEIRED	LEMMATIZE
LEFTS	LEGER	LEGLESS	LEIRING	LEMME
LEFTWARD	LEGERING	LEGLET	LEIRS	LEMMING
LEFTWARDS	LEGERINGS	LEGLETS	LEIS	LEMMINGS
LEFTWING	LEGERITY	LEGLIKE	LEISH	LEMNISCAL
LEFTY	LEGERS	LEGLIN	LEISHER	LEMNISCI
LEG	LEGES	LEGLINS	LEISHEST	LEMNISCUS
LEGACIES	LEGGE	LEGMAN	LEISLER	LEMON
LEGACY	LEGGED	LEGMEN	LEISLERS	LEMONADE
LEGAL	LEGGER	LEGONG	LEISTER	LEMONADES
LEGALESE	LEGGERS	LEGONGS	LEISTERED	LEMONED
LEGALESES	LEGGES	LEGROOM	LEISTERS	LEMONFISH
LEGALISE	LEGGIE	LEGROOMS	LEISURE	LEMONIER
LEGALISED	LEGGIER	LEGS	LEISURED	LEMONIEST
LEGALISER	LEGGIERO	LEGSIDE	LEISURELY	LEMONING
LEGALISES	LEGGIES	LEGSIDES	LEISURES	LEMONISH
LEGALISM	LEGGIEST	LEGUAAN	LEISURING	LEMONLIKE
LEGALISMS	LEGGIN	LEGUAANS	LEITMOTIF	LEMONS
LEGALIST	LEGGINESS	LEGUAN	LEITMOTIV	LEMONWOOD
LEGALISTS	LEGGING	LEGUANS	LEK	LEMONY
LEGALITY	LEGGINGED	LEGUME	LEKE	LEMPIRA
LEGALIZE	LEGGINGS	LEGUMES	LEKGOTLA	LEMPIRAS
LEGALIZED	LEGGINS	LEGUMIN	LEKGOTLAS	LEMUR
LEGALIZER	LEGGISM	LEGUMINS	LEKKED	LEMURES
LEGALIZES	LEGGISMS	LEGWARMER	LEKKER	LEMURIAN
LEGALLY	LEGGO	LEGWEAR	LEKKING	LEMURIANS
LEGALS	LEGGY	LEGWEARS	LEKKINGS	LEMURINE
LEGATARY	LEGHOLD	LEGWORK	LEKS	LEMURINES
LEGATE	LEGHOLDS	LEGWORKS	LEKU	LEMURLIKE
LEGATED	LEGHORN	LEHAIM	LEKVAR	LEMUROID
LEGATEE	LEGHORNS	LEHAIMS	LEKVARS	LEMUROIDS

LEMURS

LEMURS
LEND
LENDABLE
LENDER
LENDERS
LENDING
LENDINGS
LENDS
LENES
LENG
LENGED
LENGER
LENGEST
LENGING
LENGS
LENGTH
LENGTHEN
LENGTHENS
LENGTHFUL
LENGTHIER
LENGTHILY
LENGTHMAN
LENGTHMEN
LENGTHS
LENGTHY
LENIENCE
LENIENCES
LENIENCY
LENIENT
LENIENTLY
LENIENTS
LENIFIED
LENIFIES
LENIFY
LENIFYING
LENIS
LENITE
LENITED
LENITES
LENITIES
LENITING
LENITION
LENITIONS
LENITIVE
LENITIVES
LENITY
LENO

LENOS
LENS
LENSE
LENSED
LENSES
LENSING
LENSINGS
LENSLESS
LENSMAN
LENSMEN
LENT
LENTANDO
LENTEN
LENTI
LENTIC
LENTICEL
LENTICELS
LENTICLE
LENTICLES
LENTICULE
LENTIFORM
LENTIGO
LENTIL
LENTILS
LENTISC
LENTISCS
LENTISK
LENTISKS
LENTO
LENTOID
LENTOIDS
LENTOR
LENTORS
LENTOS
LENTOUS
LENVOY
LENVOYS
LEONE
LEONES
LEONINE
LEOPARD
LEOPARDS
LEOTARD
LEOTARDED
LEOTARDS
LEP
LEPER

LEPERS
LEPID
LEPIDOTE
LEPIDOTES
LEPORID
LEPORIDAE
LEPORIDS
LEPORINE
LEPPED
LEPPING
LEPRA
LEPRAS
LEPROSE
LEPROSERY
LEPROSIES
LEPROSITY
LEPROSY
LEPROTIC
LEPROUS
LEPROUSLY
LEPS
LEPT
LEPTA
LEPTIN
LEPTINS
LEPTOME
LEPTOMES
LEPTON
LEPTONIC
LEPTONS
LEPTOPHOS
LEPTOSOME
LEPTOTENE
LEQUEAR
LEQUEARS
LERE
LERED
LERES
LERING
LERNAEAN
LERP
LERPS
LES
LESBIAN
LESBIANS
LESBIC
LESBIGAY

LESBIGAYS
LESBO
LESBOS
LESES
LESION
LESIONED
LESIONING
LESIONS
LESPEDEZA
LESS
LESSEE
LESSEES
LESSEN
LESSENED
LESSENING
LESSENS
LESSER
LESSES
LESSON
LESSONED
LESSONING
LESSONS
LESSOR
LESSORS
LEST
LESTED
LESTING
LESTS
LESULA
LESULAS
LET
LETCH
LETCHED
LETCHES
LETCHING
LETCHINGS
LETDOWN
LETDOWNS
LETHAL
LETHALITY
LETHALLY
LETHALS
LETHARGIC
LETHARGY
LETHE
LETHEAN
LETHEE

LETHEES
LETHES
LETHIED
LETOUT
LETOUTS
LETROZOLE
LETS
LETTABLE
LETTED
LETTER
LETTERBOX
LETTERED
LETTERER
LETTERERS
LETTERING
LETTERMAN
LETTERMEN
LETTERN
LETTERNS
LETTERS
LETTERSET
LETTING
LETTINGS
LETTRE
LETTRES
LETTUCE
LETTUCES
LETUP
LETUPS
LEU
LEUCAEMIA
LEUCAEMIC
LEUCEMIA
LEUCEMIAS
LEUCEMIC
LEUCH
LEUCHEN
LEUCIN
LEUCINE
LEUCINES
LEUCINS
LEUCISTIC
LEUCITE
LEUCITES
LEUCITIC
LEUCO
LEUCOCYTE

LEUCOMA	LEVEE	LEVITATOR	LEXIGRAM	LIBATED
LEUCOMAS	LEVEED	LEVITE	LEXIGRAMS	LIBATES
LEUCON	LEVEEING	LEVITES	LEXIS	LIBATING
LEUCONS	LEVEES	LEVITIC	LEXISES	LIBATION
LEUCOSES	LEVEL	LEVITICAL	LEY	LIBATIONS
LEUCOSIN	LEVELED	LEVITIES	LEYLANDI	LIBATORY
LEUCOSINS	LEVELER	LEVITY	LEYLANDII	LIBBARD
LEUCOSIS	LEVELERS	LEVO	LEYLANDIS	LIBBARDS
LEUCOTIC	LEVELING	LEVODOPA	LEYS	LIBBED
LEUCOTOME	LEVELLED	LEVODOPAS	LEZ	LIBBER
LEUCOTOMY	LEVELLER	LEVOGYRE	LEZES	LIBBERS
LEUD	LEVELLERS	LEVOGYRES	LEZZ	LIBBING
LEUDES	LEVELLEST	LEVS	LEZZA	LIBECCHIO
LEUDS	LEVELLING	LEVULIN	LEZZAS	LIBECCIO
LEUGH	LEVELLY	LEVULINS	LEZZES	LIBECCIOS
LEUGHEN	LEVELNESS	LEVULOSE	LEZZIE	LIBEL
LEUKAEMIA	LEVELS	LEVULOSES	LEZZIES	LIBELANT
LEUKAEMIC	LEVER	LEVY	LEZZY	LIBELANTS
LEUKEMIA	LEVERAGE	LEVYING	LI	LIBELED
LEUKEMIAS	LEVERAGED	LEW	LIABILITY	LIBELEE
LEUKEMIC	LEVERAGES	LEWD	LIABLE	LIBELEES
LEUKEMICS	LEVERED	LEWDER	LIAISE	LIBELER
LEUKEMOID	LEVERET	LEWDEST	LIAISED	LIBELERS
LEUKOCYTE	LEVERETS	LEWDLY	LIAISES	LIBELING
LEUKOMA	LEVERING	LEWDNESS	LIAISING	LIBELINGS
LEUKOMAS	LEVERS	LEWDSBIES	LIAISON	LIBELIST
LEUKON	LEVES	LEWDSBY	LIAISONS	LIBELISTS
LEUKONS	LEVIABLE	LEWDSTER	LIANA	LIBELLANT
LEUKOSES	LEVIATHAN	LEWDSTERS	LIANAS	LIBELLED
LEUKOSIS	LEVIED	LEWIS	LIANE	LIBELLEE
LEUKOTIC	LEVIER	LEWISES	LIANES	LIBELLEES
LEUKOTOME	LEVIERS	LEWISIA	LIANG	LIBELLER
LEUKOTOMY	LEVIES	LEWISIAS	LIANGS	LIBELLERS
LEV	LEVIGABLE	LEWISITE	LIANOID	LIBELLING
LEVA	LEVIGATE	LEWISITES	LIAR	LIBELLOUS
LEVANT	LEVIGATED	LEWISSON	LIARD	LIBELOUS
LEVANTED	LEVIGATES	LEWISSONS	LIARDS	LIBELS
LEVANTER	LEVIGATOR	LEX	LIARS	LIBER
LEVANTERS	LEVIN	LEXEME	LIART	LIBERAL
LEVANTINE	LEVINS	LEXEMES	LIAS	LIBERALLY
LEVANTING	LEVIRATE	LEXEMIC	LIASES	LIBERALS
LEVANTS	LEVIRATES	LEXES	LIASSIC	LIBERATE
LEVAS	LEVIRATIC	LEXICA	LIATRIS	LIBERATED
LEVATOR	LEVIS	LEXICAL	LIATRISES	LIBERATES
LEVATORES	LEVITATE	LEXICALLY	LIB	LIBERATOR
LEVATORS	LEVITATED	LEXICON	LIBANT	LIBERO
LEVE	LEVITATES	LEXICONS	LIBATE	LIBEROS

LIBERS	LICENSES	LICKING	LIENORS	LIFEWORK
LIBERTIES	LICENSING	LICKINGS	LIENS	LIFEWORKS
LIBERTINE	LICENSOR	LICKPENNY	LIENTERIC	LIFEWORLD
LIBERTY	LICENSORS	LICKS	LIENTERY	LIFT
LIBIDINAL	LICENSURE	LICKSPIT	LIER	LIFTABLE
LIBIDO	LICENTE	LICKSPITS	LIERNE	LIFTBACK
LIBIDOS	LICH	LICORICE	LIERNES	LIFTBACKS
LIBKEN	LICHANOS	LICORICES	LIERS	LIFTBOY
LIBKENS	LICHEE	LICTOR	LIES	LIFTBOYS
LIBLAB	LICHEES	LICTORIAN	LIEU	LIFTED
LIBLABS	LICHEN	LICTORS	LIEUS	LIFTER
LIBRA	LICHENED	LID	LIEVE	LIFTERS
LIBRAE	LICHENIN	LIDAR	LIEVER	LIFTGATE
LIBRAIRE	LICHENING	LIDARS	LIEVES	LIFTGATES
LIBRAIRES	LICHENINS	LIDDED	LIEVEST	LIFTING
LIBRAIRIE	LICHENISM	LIDDING	LIFE	LIFTMAN
LIBRARIAN	LICHENIST	LIDDINGS	LIFEBELT	LIFTMEN
LIBRARIES	LICHENOID	LIDGER	LIFEBELTS	LIFTOFF
LIBRARY	LICHENOSE	LIDGERS	LIFEBLOOD	LIFTOFFS
LIBRAS	LICHENOUS	LIDLESS	LIFEBOAT	LIFTS
LIBRATE	LICHENS	LIDO	LIFEBOATS	LIFULL
LIBRATED	LICHES	LIDOCAINE	LIFEBUOY	LIG
LIBRATES	LICHGATE	LIDOS	LIFEBUOYS	LIGAMENT
LIBRATING	LICHGATES	LIDS	LIFECARE	LIGAMENTS
LIBRATION	LICHI	LIE	LIFECARES	LIGAN
LIBRATORY	LICHIS	LIED	LIFEFUL	LIGAND
LIBRETTI	LICHT	LIEDER	LIFEGUARD	LIGANDS
LIBRETTO	LICHTED	LIEF	LIFEHACK	LIGANS
LIBRETTOS	LICHTER	LIEFER	LIFEHACKS	LIGASE
LIBRI	LICHTEST	LIEFEST	LIFEHOLD	LIGASES
LIBRIFORM	LICHTING	LIEFLY	LIFELESS	LIGATE
LIBS	LICHTLIED	LIEFS	LIFELIKE	LIGATED
LICE	LICHTLIES	LIEGE	LIFELINE	LIGATES
LICENCE	LICHTLY	LIEGEDOM	LIFELINES	LIGATING
LICENCED	LICHTS	LIEGEDOMS	LIFELONG	LIGATION
LICENCEE	LICHWAKE	LIEGELESS	LIFER	LIGATIONS
LICENCEES	LICHWAKES	LIEGEMAN	LIFERS	LIGATIVE
LICENCER	LICHWAY	LIEGEMEN	LIFES	LIGATURE
LICENCERS	LICHWAYS	LIEGER	LIFESAVER	LIGATURED
LICENCES	LICIT	LIEGERS	LIFESOME	LIGATURES
LICENCING	LICITLY	LIEGES	LIFESPAN	LIGER
LICENSE	LICITNESS	LIEN	LIFESPANS	LIGERS
LICENSED	LICK	LIENABLE	LIFESTYLE	LIGGE
LICENSEE	LICKED	LIENAL	LIFETIME	LIGGED
LICENSEES	LICKER	LIENEE	LIFETIMES	LIGGER
LICENSER	LICKERISH	LIENEES	LIFEWAY	LIGGERS
LICENSERS	LICKERS	LIENOR	LIFEWAYS	LIGGES

LIGGING	LIGNITIC	LIKINS	LIMBER	LIMIER
LIGGINGS	LIGNOSE	LIKUTA	LIMBERED	LIMIEST
LIGHT	LIGNOSES	LILAC	LIMBERER	LIMINA
LIGHTBULB	LIGNUM	LILACS	LIMBEREST	LIMINAL
LIGHTED	LIGNUMS	LILANGENI	LIMBERING	LIMINESS
LIGHTEN	LIGROIN	LILIED	LIMBERLY	LIMING
LIGHTENED	LIGROINE	LILIES	LIMBERS	LIMINGS
LIGHTENER	LIGROINES	LILL	LIMBI	LIMIT
LIGHTENS	LIGROINS	LILLED	LIMBIC	LIMITABLE
LIGHTER	LIGS	LILLING	LIMBIER	LIMITARY
LIGHTERED	LIGULA	LILLIPUT	LIMBIEST	LIMITED
LIGHTERS	LIGULAE	LILLIPUTS	LIMBING	LIMITEDLY
LIGHTEST	LIGULAR	LILLS	LIMBLESS	LIMITEDS
LIGHTFACE	LIGULAS	LILO	LIMBMEAL	LIMITER
LIGHTFAST	LIGULATE	LILOS	LIMBO	LIMITERS
LIGHTFUL	LIGULATED	LILT	LIMBOED	LIMITES
LIGHTING	LIGULE	LILTED	LIMBOES	LIMITING
LIGHTINGS	LIGULES	LILTING	LIMBOING	LIMITINGS
LIGHTISH	LIGULOID	LILTINGLY	LIMBOS	LIMITLESS
LIGHTLESS	LIGURE	LILTS	LIMBOUS	LIMITS
LIGHTLIED	LIGURES	LILY	LIMBS	LIMMA
LIGHTLIES	LIKABLE	LILYLIKE	LIMBUS	LIMMAS
LIGHTLY	LIKABLY	LIMA	LIMBUSES	LIMMER
LIGHTNESS	LIKE	LIMACEL	LIMBY	LIMMERS
LIGHTNING	LIKEABLE	LIMACELS	LIME	LIMN
LIGHTS	LIKEABLY	LIMACEOUS	LIMEADE	LIMNAEID
LIGHTSHIP	LIKED	LIMACES	LIMEADES	LIMNAEIDS
LIGHTSOME	LIKELIER	LIMACINE	LIMED	LIMNED
LIGHTWAVE	LIKELIEST	LIMACON	LIMEKILN	LIMNER
LIGHTWOOD	LIKELY	LIMACONS	LIMEKILNS	LIMNERS
LIGNAGE	LIKEN	LIMAIL	LIMELESS	LIMNETIC
LIGNAGES	LIKENED	LIMAILS	LIMELIGHT	LIMNIC
LIGNALOES	LIKENESS	LIMAN	LIMELIT	LIMNING
LIGNAN	LIKENING	LIMANS	LIMEN	LIMNOLOGY
LIGNANS	LIKENS	LIMAS	LIMENS	LIMNS
LIGNE	LIKER	LIMATION	LIMEPIT	LIMO
LIGNEOUS	LIKERS	LIMATIONS	LIMEPITS	LIMONENE
LIGNES	LIKES	LIMAX	LIMERENCE	LIMONENES
LIGNICOLE	LIKEST	LIMB	LIMERICK	LIMONITE
LIGNIFIED	LIKEWAKE	LIMBA	LIMERICKS	LIMONITES
LIGNIFIES	LIKEWAKES	LIMBAS	LIMES	LIMONITIC
LIGNIFORM	LIKEWALK	LIMBATE	LIMESCALE	LIMONIUM
LIGNIFY	LIKEWALKS	LIMBEC	LIMESTONE	LIMONIUMS
LIGNIN	LIKEWISE	LIMBECK	LIMEWASH	LIMOS
LIGNINS	LIKIN	LIMBECKS	LIMEWATER	LIMOSES
LIGNITE	LIKING	LIMBECS	LIMEY	LIMOSIS
LIGNITES	LIKINGS	LIMBED	LIMEYS	LIMOUS

LIMOUSINE	LINCRUSTA	LINER	LINGUINE	LINKSLAND
LIMP	LINCTURE	LINERLESS	LINGUINES	LINKSMAN
LIMPA	LINCTURES	LINERS	LINGUINI	LINKSMEN
LIMPAS	LINCTUS	LINES	LINGUINIS	LINKSPAN
LIMPED	LINCTUSES	LINESMAN	LINGUISA	LINKSPANS
LIMPER	LIND	LINESMEN	LINGUISAS	LINKSTER
LIMPERS	LINDANE	LINEUP	LINGUIST	LINKSTERS
LIMPEST	LINDANES	LINEUPS	LINGUISTS	LINKUP
LIMPET	LINDEN	LINEY	LINGULA	LINKUPS
LIMPETS	LINDENS	LING	LINGULAE	LINKWORK
LIMPID	LINDIED	LINGA	LINGULAR	LINKWORKS
LIMPIDITY	LINDIES	LINGAM	LINGULAS	LINKY
LIMPIDLY	LINDS	LINGAMS	LINGULATE	LINN
LIMPING	LINDWORM	LINGAS	LINGY	LINNED
LIMPINGLY	LINDWORMS	LINGBERRY	LINHAY	LINNET
LIMPINGS	LINDY	LINGCOD	LINHAYS	LINNETS
LIMPKIN	LINDYING	LINGCODS	LINIER	LINNEY
LIMPKINS	LINE	LINGEL	LINIEST	LINNEYS
LIMPLY	LINEABLE	LINGELS	LINIMENT	LINNIES
LIMPNESS	LINEAGE	LINGER	LINIMENTS	LINNING
LIMPS	LINEAGES	LINGERED	LININ	LINNS
LIMPSEY	LINEAL	LINGERER	LINING	LINNY
LIMPSIER	LINEALITY	LINGERERS	LININGS	LINO
LIMPSIEST	LINEALLY	LINGERIE	LININS	LINOCUT
LIMPSY	LINEAMENT	LINGERIES	LINISH	LINOCUTS
LIMULI	LINEAR	LINGERING	LINISHED	LINOLEATE
LIMULOID	LINEARISE	LINGERS	LINISHER	LINOLEIC
LIMULOIDS	LINEARITY	LINGIER	LINISHERS	LINOLENIC
LIMULUS	LINEARIZE	LINGIEST	LINISHES	LINOLEUM
LIMULUSES	LINEARLY	LINGLE	LINISHING	LINOLEUMS
LIMY	LINEATE	LINGLES	LINK	LINOS
LIN	LINEATED	LINGO	LINKABLE	LINOTYPE
LINABLE	LINEATION	LINGOES	LINKAGE	LINOTYPED
LINAC	LINEBRED	LINGOS	LINKAGES	LINOTYPER
LINACS	LINECUT	LINGOT	LINKBOY	LINOTYPES
LINAGE	LINECUTS	LINGOTS	LINKBOYS	LINS
LINAGES	LINED	LINGS	LINKED	LINSANG
LINALOL	LINELESS	LINGSTER	LINKER	LINSANGS
LINALOLS	LINELIKE	LINGSTERS	LINKERS	LINSEED
LINALOOL	LINEMAN	LINGUA	LINKIER	LINSEEDS
LINALOOLS	LINEMATE	LINGUAE	LINKIEST	LINSEY
LINCH	LINEMATES	LINGUAL	LINKING	LINSEYS
LINCHES	LINEMEN	LINGUALLY	LINKMAN	LINSTOCK
LINCHET	LINEN	LINGUALS	LINKMEN	LINSTOCKS
LINCHETS	LINENS	LINGUAS	LINKROT	LINT
LINCHPIN	LINENY	LINGUICA	LINKROTS	LINTED
LINCHPINS	LINEOLATE	LINGUICAS	LINKS	LINTEL

LINTELED
LINTELLED
LINTELS
LINTER
LINTERS
LINTIE
LINTIER
LINTIES
LINTIEST
LINTING
LINTINGS
LINTLESS
LINTOL
LINTOLS
LINTS
LINTSEED
LINTSEEDS
LINTSTOCK
LINTWHITE
LINTY
LINUM
LINUMS
LINURON
LINURONS
LINUX
LINUXES
LINY
LION
LIONCEL
LIONCELLE
LIONCELS
LIONEL
LIONELS
LIONESS
LIONESSES
LIONET
LIONETS
LIONFISH
LIONHEAD
LIONHEADS
LIONISE
LIONISED
LIONISER
LIONISERS
LIONISES
LIONISING
LIONISM

LIONISMS
LIONIZE
LIONIZED
LIONIZER
LIONIZERS
LIONIZES
LIONIZING
LIONLIKE
LIONLY
LIONS
LIP
LIPA
LIPAEMIA
LIPAEMIAS
LIPARITE
LIPARITES
LIPAS
LIPASE
LIPASES
LIPE
LIPECTOMY
LIPEMIA
LIPEMIAS
LIPES
LIPGLOSS
LIPID
LIPIDE
LIPIDES
LIPIDIC
LIPIDS
LIPIN
LIPINS
LIPLESS
LIPLIKE
LIPLINER
LIPLINERS
LIPO
LIPOCYTE
LIPOCYTES
LIPOGRAM
LIPOGRAMS
LIPOIC
LIPOID
LIPOIDAL
LIPOIDS
LIPOLITIC
LIPOLYSES

LIPOLYSIS
LIPOLYTIC
LIPOMA
LIPOMAS
LIPOMATA
LIPOPLAST
LIPOS
LIPOSOMAL
LIPOSOME
LIPOSOMES
LIPOSUCK
LIPOSUCKS
LIPOTROPY
LIPPED
LIPPEN
LIPPENED
LIPPENING
LIPPENS
LIPPER
LIPPERED
LIPPERING
LIPPERS
LIPPIE
LIPPIER
LIPPIES
LIPPIEST
LIPPINESS
LIPPING
LIPPINGS
LIPPITUDE
LIPPY
LIPREAD
LIPREADER
LIPREADS
LIPS
LIPSALVE
LIPSALVES
LIPSTICK
LIPSTICKS
LIPURIA
LIPURIAS
LIQUABLE
LIQUATE
LIQUATED
LIQUATES
LIQUATING
LIQUATION

LIQUEFIED
LIQUEFIER
LIQUEFIES
LIQUEFY
LIQUESCE
LIQUESCED
LIQUESCES
LIQUEUR
LIQUEURED
LIQUEURS
LIQUID
LIQUIDATE
LIQUIDISE
LIQUIDITY
LIQUIDIZE
LIQUIDLY
LIQUIDS
LIQUIDUS
LIQUIDY
LIQUIFIED
LIQUIFIER
LIQUIFIES
LIQUIFY
LIQUITAB
LIQUITABS
LIQUOR
LIQUORED
LIQUORICE
LIQUORING
LIQUORISH
LIQUORS
LIRA
LIRAS
LIRE
LIRI
LIRIOPE
LIRIOPES
LIRIPIPE
LIRIPIPES
LIRIPOOP
LIRIPOOPS
LIRK
LIRKED
LIRKING
LIRKS
LIROT
LIROTH

LIS
LISENTE
LISK
LISKS
LISLE
LISLES
LISP
LISPED
LISPER
LISPERS
LISPING
LISPINGLY
LISPINGS
LISPOUND
LISPOUNDS
LISPS
LISPUND
LISPUNDS
LISSES
LISSOM
LISSOME
LISSOMELY
LISSOMLY
LIST
LISTABLE
LISTBOX
LISTBOXES
LISTED
LISTEE
LISTEES
LISTEL
LISTELS
LISTEN
LISTENED
LISTENER
LISTENERS
LISTENING
LISTENS
LISTER
LISTERIA
LISTERIAL
LISTERIAS
LISTERS
LISTETH
LISTFUL
LISTING
LISTINGS

L

LISTLESS
LISTS
LISTSERV
LISTSERVS
LIT
LITAI
LITANIES
LITANY
LITAS
LITCHI
LITCHIS
LITE
LITED
LITENESS
LITER
LITERACY
LITERAL
LITERALLY
LITERALS
LITERARY
LITERATE
LITERATES
LITERATI
LITERATIM
LITERATO
LITERATOR
LITERATUS
LITEROSE
LITERS
LITES
LITEST
LITH
LITHARGE
LITHARGES
LITHATE
LITHATES
LITHE
LITHED
LITHELY
LITHEMIA
LITHEMIAS
LITHEMIC
LITHENESS
LITHER
LITHERLY
LITHES
LITHESOME

LITHEST
LITHIA
LITHIAS
LITHIASES
LITHIASIS
LITHIC
LITHIFIED
LITHIFIES
LITHIFY
LITHING
LITHISTID
LITHITE
LITHITES
LITHIUM
LITHIUMS
LITHO
LITHOCYST
LITHOED
LITHOES
LITHOID
LITHOIDAL
LITHOING
LITHOLOGY
LITHOPONE
LITHOPS
LITHOS
LITHOSOL
LITHOSOLS
LITHOTOME
LITHOTOMY
LITHS
LITIGABLE
LITIGANT
LITIGANTS
LITIGATE
LITIGATED
LITIGATES
LITIGATOR
LITIGIOUS
LITING
LITMUS
LITMUSES
LITORAL
LITOTES
LITOTIC
LITRE
LITREAGE

LITREAGES
LITRES
LITS
LITTEN
LITTER
LITTERBAG
LITTERBUG
LITTERED
LITTERER
LITTERERS
LITTERING
LITTERS
LITTERY
LITTLE
LITTLER
LITTLES
LITTLEST
LITTLIE
LITTLIES
LITTLIN
LITTLING
LITTLINGS
LITTLINS
LITTLISH
LITTORAL
LITTORALS
LITU
LITURGIC
LITURGICS
LITURGIES
LITURGISM
LITURGIST
LITURGY
LITUUS
LITUUSES
LIVABLE
LIVE
LIVEABLE
LIVEBLOG
LIVEBLOGS
LIVED
LIVEDO
LIVEDOS
LIVELIER
LIVELIEST
LIVELILY
LIVELOD

LIVELODS
LIVELONG
LIVELONGS
LIVELOOD
LIVELOODS
LIVELY
LIVEN
LIVENED
LIVENER
LIVENERS
LIVENESS
LIVENING
LIVENS
LIVER
LIVERED
LIVERIED
LIVERIES
LIVERING
LIVERINGS
LIVERISH
LIVERLEAF
LIVERLESS
LIVERS
LIVERWORT
LIVERY
LIVERYMAN
LIVERYMEN
LIVES
LIVEST
LIVESTOCK
LIVETRAP
LIVETRAPS
LIVEWARE
LIVEWARES
LIVEWELL
LIVEWELLS
LIVEYER
LIVEYERE
LIVEYERES
LIVEYERS
LIVID
LIVIDER
LIVIDEST
LIVIDITY
LIVIDLY
LIVIDNESS
LIVIER

LIVIERS
LIVING
LIVINGLY
LIVINGS
LIVOR
LIVORS
LIVRAISON
LIVRE
LIVRES
LIVYER
LIVYERS
LIXIVIA
LIXIVIAL
LIXIVIATE
LIXIVIOUS
LIXIVIUM
LIXIVIUMS
LIZARD
LIZARDS
LIZZIE
LIZZIES
LLAMA
LLAMAS
LLANERO
LLANEROS
LLANO
LLANOS
LO
LOACH
LOACHES
LOAD
LOADABLE
LOADED
LOADEN
LOADENED
LOADENING
LOADENS
LOADER
LOADERS
LOADING
LOADINGS
LOADS
LOADSPACE
LOADSTAR
LOADSTARS
LOADSTONE
LOAF

LOAFED	LOAVED	LOBOLAS	LOCALIZES	LOCKETS
LOAFER	LOAVES	LOBOLO	LOCALLY	LOCKFAST
LOAFERISH	LOAVING	LOBOLOS	LOCALNESS	LOCKFUL
LOAFERS	LOB	LOBOS	LOCALS	LOCKFULS
LOAFING	LOBAR	LOBOSE	LOCATABLE	LOCKHOUSE
LOAFINGS	LOBATE	LOBOTOMY	LOCATE	LOCKING
LOAFS	LOBATED	LOBS	LOCATED	LOCKINGS
LOAM	LOBATELY	LOBSCOUSE	LOCATER	LOCKJAW
LOAMED	LOBATION	LOBSTER	LOCATERS	LOCKJAWS
LOAMIER	LOBATIONS	LOBSTERED	LOCATES	LOCKLESS
LOAMIEST	LOBBED	LOBSTERER	LOCATING	LOCKMAKER
LOAMINESS	LOBBER	LOBSTERS	LOCATION	LOCKMAN
LOAMING	LOBBERS	LOBSTICK	LOCATIONS	LOCKMEN
LOAMLESS	LOBBIED	LOBSTICKS	LOCATIVE	LOCKNUT
LOAMS	LOBBIES	LOBTAIL	LOCATIVES	LOCKNUTS
LOAMY	LOBBING	LOBTAILED	LOCATOR	LOCKOUT
LOAN	LOBBY	LOBTAILS	LOCATORS	LOCKOUTS
LOANABLE	LOBBYER	LOBULAR	LOCAVORE	LOCKPICK
LOANBACK	LOBBYERS	LOBULARLY	LOCAVORES	LOCKPICKS
LOANBACKS	LOBBYGOW	LOBULATE	LOCELLATE	LOCKRAM
LOANED	LOBBYGOWS	LOBULATED	LOCH	LOCKRAMS
LOANEE	LOBBYING	LOBULE	LOCHAN	LOCKS
LOANEES	LOBBYINGS	LOBULES	LOCHANS	LOCKSET
LOANER	LOBBYISM	LOBULI	LOCHE	LOCKSETS
LOANERS	LOBBYISMS	LOBULOSE	LOCHES	LOCKSMAN
LOANING	LOBBYIST	LOBULUS	LOCHIA	LOCKSMEN
LOANINGS	LOBBYISTS	LOBUS	LOCHIAL	LOCKSMITH
LOANS	LOBE	LOBWORM	LOCHIAS	LOCKSTEP
LOANSHIFT	LOBECTOMY	LOBWORMS	LOCHS	LOCKSTEPS
LOANWORD	LOBED	LOCA	LOCI	LOCKUP
LOANWORDS	LOBEFIN	LOCAL	LOCIE	LOCKUPS
LOAST	LOBEFINS	LOCALE	LOCIES	LOCO
LOATH	LOBELESS	LOCALES	LOCIS	LOCOED
LOATHE	LOBELET	LOCALISE	LOCK	LOCOES
LOATHED	LOBELETS	LOCALISED	LOCKABLE	LOCOFOCO
LOATHER	LOBELIA	LOCALISER	LOCKAGE	LOCOFOCOS
LOATHERS	LOBELIAS	LOCALISES	LOCKAGES	LOCOING
LOATHES	LOBELINE	LOCALISM	LOCKAWAY	LOCOISM
LOATHEST	LOBELINES	LOCALISMS	LOCKAWAYS	LOCOISMS
LOATHFUL	LOBES	LOCALIST	LOCKBOX	LOCOMAN
LOATHING	LOBI	LOCALISTS	LOCKBOXES	LOCOMEN
LOATHINGS	LOBING	LOCALITE	LOCKDOWN	LOCOMOTE
LOATHLY	LOBINGS	LOCALITES	LOCKDOWNS	LOCOMOTED
LOATHNESS	LOBIPED	LOCALITY	LOCKED	LOCOMOTES
LOATHSOME	LOBLOLLY	LOCALIZE	LOCKER	LOCOMOTOR
LOATHY	LOBO	LOCALIZED	LOCKERS	LOCOPLANT
LOAVE	LOBOLA	LOCALIZER	LOCKET	LOCOS

LOCOWEED	LODICULAE	LOGGIE	LOGO	LOIPEN
LOCOWEEDS	LODICULE	LOGGIER	LOGOED	LOIR
LOCULAR	LODICULES	LOGGIEST	LOGOFF	LOIRS
LOCULATE	LODS	LOGGING	LOGOFFS	LOITER
LOCULATED	LOERIE	LOGGINGS	LOGOGRAM	LOITERED
LOCULE	LOERIES	LOGGISH	LOGOGRAMS	LOITERER
LOCULED	LOESS	LOGGY	LOGOGRAPH	LOITERERS
LOCULES	LOESSAL	LOGIA	LOGOGRIPH	LOITERING
LOCULI	LOESSES	LOGIC	LOGOI	LOITERS
LOCULUS	LOESSIAL	LOGICAL	LOGOMACH	LOKE
LOCUM	LOESSIC	LOGICALLY	LOGOMACHS	LOKES
LOCUMS	LOFT	LOGICIAN	LOGOMACHY	LOKSHEN
LOCUPLETE	LOFTED	LOGICIANS	LOGON	LOLIGO
LOCUS	LOFTER	LOGICISE	LOGONS	LOLIGOS
LOCUST	LOFTERS	LOGICISED	LOGOPEDIC	LOLIUM
LOCUSTA	LOFTIER	LOGICISES	LOGOPHILE	LOLIUMS
LOCUSTAE	LOFTIEST	LOGICISM	LOGORRHEA	LOLL
LOCUSTAL	LOFTILY	LOGICISMS	LOGOS	LOLLED
LOCUSTED	LOFTINESS	LOGICIST	LOGOTHETE	LOLLER
LOCUSTING	LOFTING	LOGICISTS	LOGOTYPE	LOLLERS
LOCUSTS	LOFTLESS	LOGICIZE	LOGOTYPES	LOLLIES
LOCUTION	LOFTLIKE	LOGICIZED	LOGOTYPY	LOLLING
LOCUTIONS	LOFTS	LOGICIZES	LOGOUT	LOLLINGLY
LOCUTORY	LOFTSMAN	LOGICLESS	LOGOUTS	LOLLIPOP
LOD	LOFTSMEN	LOGICS	LOGROLL	LOLLIPOPS
LODE	LOFTY	LOGIE	LOGROLLED	LOLLOP
LODEN	LOG	LOGIER	LOGROLLER	LOLLOPED
LODENS	LOGAN	LOGIES	LOGROLLS	LOLLOPING
LODES	LOGANIA	LOGIEST	LOGS	LOLLOPS
LODESMAN	LOGANIAS	LOGILY	LOGWAY	LOLLOPY
LODESMEN	LOGANS	LOGIN	LOGWAYS	LOLLS
LODESTAR	LOGAOEDIC	LOGINESS	LOGWOOD	LOLLY
LODESTARS	LOGARITHM	LOGINS	LOGWOODS	LOLLYGAG
LODESTONE	LOGBOARD	LOGION	LOGY	LOLLYGAGS
LODGE	LOGBOARDS	LOGIONS	LOHAN	LOLLYPOP
LODGEABLE	LOGBOOK	LOGISTIC	LOHANS	LOLLYPOPS
LODGED	LOGBOOKS	LOGISTICS	LOIASES	LOLOG
LODGEMENT	LOGE	LOGJAM	LOIASIS	LOLOGS
LODGEPOLE	LOGES	LOGJAMMED	LOIASISES	LOLZ
LODGER	LOGGAT	LOGJAMS	LOID	LOMA
LODGERS	LOGGATS	LOGJUICE	LOIDED	LOMAS
LODGES	LOGGED	LOGJUICES	LOIDING	LOMATA
LODGING	LOGGER	LOGLINE	LOIDS	LOME
LODGINGS	LOGGERS	LOGLINES	LOIN	LOMED
LODGMENT	LOGGETS	LOGLOG	LOINCLOTH	LOMEIN
LODGMENTS	LOGGIA	LOGLOGS	LOINS	LOMEINS
LODICULA	LOGGIAS	LOGNORMAL	LOIPE	LOMENT

LOMENTA
LOMENTS
LOMENTUM
LOMENTUMS
LOMES
LOMING
LOMPISH
LONE
LONELIER
LONELIEST
LONELILY
LONELY
LONENESS
LONER
LONERS
LONESOME
LONESOMES
LONG
LONGA
LONGAEVAL
LONGAN
LONGANS
LONGAS
LONGBOARD
LONGBOAT
LONGBOATS
LONGBOW
LONGBOWS
LONGCASE
LONGCLOTH
LONGE
LONGED
LONGEING
LONGER
LONGERON
LONGERONS
LONGERS
LONGES
LONGEST
LONGEVAL
LONGEVITY
LONGEVOUS
LONGHAIR
LONGHAIRS
LONGHAND
LONGHANDS
LONGHEAD

LONGHEADS
LONGHORN
LONGHORNS
LONGHOUSE
LONGICORN
LONGIES
LONGING
LONGINGLY
LONGINGS
LONGISH
LONGITUDE
LONGJUMP
LONGJUMPS
LONGLEAF
LONGLINE
LONGLINES
LONGLIST
LONGLISTS
LONGLY
LONGNECK
LONGNECKS
LONGNESS
LONGS
LONGSHIP
LONGSHIPS
LONGSHORE
LONGSOME
LONGSPUR
LONGSPURS
LONGTIME
LONGUEUR
LONGUEURS
LONGWALL
LONGWALLS
LONGWAYS
LONGWISE
LONGWORM
LONGWORMS
LONICERA
LONICERAS
LOO
LOOBIER
LOOBIES
LOOBIEST
LOOBILY
LOOBY
LOOED

LOOEY
LOOEYS
LOOF
LOOFA
LOOFAH
LOOFAHS
LOOFAS
LOOFFUL
LOOFFULS
LOOFS
LOOIE
LOOIES
LOOING
LOOK
LOOKALIKE
LOOKDOWN
LOOKDOWNS
LOOKED
LOOKER
LOOKERS
LOOKIE
LOOKING
LOOKISM
LOOKISMS
LOOKIST
LOOKISTS
LOOKIT
LOOKOUT
LOOKOUTS
LOOKOVER
LOOKOVERS
LOOKS
LOOKSISM
LOOKSISMS
LOOKUP
LOOKUPS
LOOKY
LOOM
LOOMED
LOOMING
LOOMS
LOON
LOONEY
LOONEYS
LOONIE
LOONIER
LOONIES

LOONIEST
LOONILY
LOONINESS
LOONING
LOONINGS
LOONS
LOONY
LOOP
LOOPED
LOOPER
LOOPERS
LOOPHOLE
LOOPHOLED
LOOPHOLES
LOOPIER
LOOPIEST
LOOPILY
LOOPINESS
LOOPING
LOOPINGS
LOOPS
LOOPY
LOOR
LOORD
LOORDS
LOOS
LOOSE
LOOSEBOX
LOOSED
LOOSELY
LOOSEN
LOOSENED
LOOSENER
LOOSENERS
LOOSENESS
LOOSENING
LOOSENS
LOOSER
LOOSES
LOOSEST
LOOSIE
LOOSIES
LOOSING
LOOSINGS
LOOT
LOOTED
LOOTEN

LOOTER
LOOTERS
LOOTING
LOOTINGS
LOOTS
LOOVES
LOP
LOPE
LOPED
LOPER
LOPERS
LOPES
LOPGRASS
LOPHODONT
LOPING
LOPINGLY
LOPOLITH
LOPOLITHS
LOPPED
LOPPER
LOPPERED
LOPPERING
LOPPERS
LOPPET
LOPPETS
LOPPIER
LOPPIES
LOPPIEST
LOPPING
LOPPINGS
LOPPY
LOPS
LOPSIDED
LOPSTICK
LOPSTICKS
LOQUACITY
LOQUAT
LOQUATS
LOQUITUR
LOR
LORAL
LORAN
LORANS
LORATE
LORAZEPAM
LORCHA
LORCHAS

L

LORD
LORDED
LORDING
LORDINGS
LORDKIN
LORDKINS
LORDLESS
LORDLIER
LORDLIEST
LORDLIKE
LORDLING
LORDLINGS
LORDLY
LORDOMA
LORDOMAS
LORDOSES
LORDOSIS
LORDOTIC
LORDS
LORDSHIP
LORDSHIPS
LORDY
LORE
LOREAL
LOREL
LORELS
LORES
LORETTE
LORETTES
LORGNETTE
LORGNON
LORGNONS
LORIC
LORICA
LORICAE
LORICAS
LORICATE
LORICATED
LORICATES
LORICS
LORIES
LORIKEET
LORIKEETS
LORIMER
LORIMERS
LORINER
LORINERS

LORING
LORINGS
LORIOT
LORIOTS
LORIS
LORISES
LORN
LORNNESS
LORRELL
LORRELLS
LORRIES
LORRY
LORY
LOS
LOSABLE
LOSE
LOSED
LOSEL
LOSELS
LOSEN
LOSER
LOSERS
LOSES
LOSH
LOSING
LOSINGEST
LOSINGLY
LOSINGS
LOSS
LOSSES
LOSSIER
LOSSIEST
LOSSLESS
LOSSMAKER
LOSSY
LOST
LOSTNESS
LOT
LOTA
LOTAH
LOTAHS
LOTAS
LOTE
LOTES
LOTH

LOTHARIO
LOTHARIOS
LOTHEFULL
LOTHER
LOTHEST
LOTHFULL
LOTHNESS
LOTHSOME
LOTI
LOTIC
LOTION
LOTIONS
LOTO
LOTOS
LOTOSES
LOTS
LOTSA
LOTTA
LOTTE
LOTTED
LOTTER
LOTTERIES
LOTTERS
LOTTERY
LOTTES
LOTTING
LOTTO
LOTTOS
LOTUS
LOTUSES
LOTUSLAND
LOU
LOUCHE
LOUCHELY
LOUCHER
LOUCHEST
LOUD
LOUDEN
LOUDENED
LOUDENING
LOUDENS
LOUDER
LOUDEST
LOUDISH
LOUDLIER
LOUDLIEST
LOUDLY

LOUDMOUTH
LOUDNESS
LOUED
LOUGH
LOUGHS
LOUIE
LOUIES
LOUING
LOUIS
LOUMA
LOUMAS
LOUN
LOUND
LOUNDED
LOUNDER
LOUNDERED
LOUNDERS
LOUNDING
LOUNDS
LOUNED
LOUNGE
LOUNGED
LOUNGER
LOUNGERS
LOUNGES
LOUNGEY
LOUNGIER
LOUNGIEST
LOUNGING
LOUNGINGS
LOUNGY
LOUNING
LOUNS
LOUP
LOUPE
LOUPED
LOUPEN
LOUPES
LOUPING
LOUPIT
LOUPS
LOUR
LOURE
LOURED
LOURES
LOURIE
LOURIER

LOURIES
LOURIEST
LOURING
LOURINGLY
LOURINGS
LOURS
LOURY
LOUS
LOUSE
LOUSED
LOUSER
LOUSERS
LOUSES
LOUSEWORT
LOUSIER
LOUSIEST
LOUSILY
LOUSINESS
LOUSING
LOUSINGS
LOUSY
LOUT
LOUTED
LOUTERIES
LOUTERY
LOUTING
LOUTISH
LOUTISHLY
LOUTS
LOUVAR
LOUVARS
LOUVER
LOUVERED
LOUVERS
LOUVRE
LOUVRED
LOUVRES
LOVABLE
LOVABLY
LOVAGE
LOVAGES
LOVAT
LOVATS
LOVE
LOVEABLE
LOVEABLY
LOVEBIRD

LOVEBIRDS
LOVEBITE
LOVEBITES
LOVEBUG
LOVEBUGS
LOVED
LOVEFEST
LOVEFESTS
LOVELESS
LOVELIER
LOVELIES
LOVELIEST
LOVELIGHT
LOVELILY
LOVELOCK
LOVELOCKS
LOVELORN
LOVELY
LOVEMAKER
LOVER
LOVERED
LOVERLESS
LOVERLY
LOVERS
LOVES
LOVESEAT
LOVESEATS
LOVESICK
LOVESOME
LOVEVINE
LOVEVINES
LOVEY
LOVEYS
LOVIE
LOVIER
LOVIES
LOVIEST
LOVING
LOVINGLY
LOVINGS
LOW
LOWAN
LOWANS
LOWBALL
LOWBALLED
LOWBALLS
LOWBORN

LOWBOY
LOWBOYS
LOWBRED
LOWBROW
LOWBROWED
LOWBROWS
LOWBUSH
LOWBUSHES
LOWDOWN
LOWDOWNS
LOWE
LOWED
LOWER
LOWERABLE
LOWERCASE
LOWERED
LOWERIER
LOWERIEST
LOWERING
LOWERINGS
LOWERMOST
LOWERS
LOWERY
LOWES
LOWEST
LOWING
LOWINGS
LOWISH
LOWLAND
LOWLANDER
LOWLANDS
LOWLIER
LOWLIEST
LOWLIFE
LOWLIFER
LOWLIFERS
LOWLIFES
LOWLIGHT
LOWLIGHTS
LOWLIHEAD
LOWLILY
LOWLINESS
LOWLIVES
LOWLY
LOWN
LOWND
LOWNDED

LOWNDING
LOWNDS
LOWNE
LOWNED
LOWNES
LOWNESS
LOWNESSES
LOWNING
LOWNS
LOWP
LOWPASS
LOWPED
LOWPING
LOWPS
LOWRIDER
LOWRIDERS
LOWRIE
LOWRIES
LOWRY
LOWS
LOWSE
LOWSED
LOWSENING
LOWSER
LOWSES
LOWSEST
LOWSING
LOWSIT
LOWT
LOWTED
LOWTING
LOWTS
LOWVELD
LOWVELDS
LOX
LOXED
LOXES
LOXING
LOXODROME
LOXODROMY
LOXYGEN
LOXYGENS
LOY
LOYAL
LOYALER
LOYALEST
LOYALISM

LOYALISMS
LOYALIST
LOYALISTS
LOYALLER
LOYALLEST
LOYALLY
LOYALNESS
LOYALTIES
LOYALTY
LOYS
LOZELL
LOZELLS
LOZEN
LOZENGE
LOZENGED
LOZENGES
LOZENGY
LOZENS
LUACH
LUAU
LUAUS
LUBBARD
LUBBARDS
LUBBER
LUBBERLY
LUBBERS
LUBE
LUBED
LUBES
LUBFISH
LUBFISHES
LUBING
LUBRA
LUBRAS
LUBRIC
LUBRICAL
LUBRICANT
LUBRICATE
LUBRICITY
LUBRICOUS
LUCARNE
LUCARNES
LUCE
LUCENCE
LUCENCES
LUCENCIES
LUCENCY

LUCENT
LUCENTLY
LUCERN
LUCERNE
LUCERNES
LUCERNS
LUCES
LUCHOT
LUCHOTH
LUCID
LUCIDER
LUCIDEST
LUCIDITY
LUCIDLY
LUCIDNESS
LUCIFER
LUCIFERIN
LUCIFERS
LUCIGEN
LUCIGENS
LUCITE
LUCITES
LUCK
LUCKED
LUCKEN
LUCKIE
LUCKIER
LUCKIES
LUCKIEST
LUCKILY
LUCKINESS
LUCKING
LUCKLESS
LUCKPENNY
LUCKS
LUCKY
LUCRATIVE
LUCRE
LUCRES
LUCTATION
LUCUBRATE
LUCULENT
LUCUMA
LUCUMAS
LUCUMO
LUCUMONES
LUCUMOS

L

LUD	LUGWORM	LUMINAIRE	LUNA	LUNGED
LUDE	LUGWORMS	LUMINAL	LUNACIES	LUNGEE
LUDERICK	LUIT	LUMINANCE	LUNACY	LUNGEES
LUDERICKS	LUITEN	LUMINANT	LUNANAUT	LUNGEING
LUDES	LUKE	LUMINANTS	LUNANAUTS	LUNGER
LUDIC	LUKEWARM	LUMINARIA	LUNAR	LUNGERS
LUDICALLY	LULIBUB	LUMINARY	LUNARIAN	LUNGES
LUDICROUS	LULIBUBS	LUMINE	LUNARIANS	LUNGFISH
LUDO	LULL	LUMINED	LUNARIES	LUNGFUL
LUDOS	LULLABIED	LUMINES	LUNARIST	LUNGFULS
LUDS	LULLABIES	LUMINESCE	LUNARISTS	LUNGI
LUDSHIP	LULLABY	LUMINING	LUNARNAUT	LUNGIE
LUDSHIPS	LULLED	LUMINISM	LUNARS	LUNGIES
LUES	LULLER	LUMINISMS	LUNARY	LUNGING
LUETIC	LULLERS	LUMINIST	LUNAS	LUNGIS
LUETICS	LULLING	LUMINISTS	LUNATE	LUNGLESS
LUFF	LULLS	LUMINOUS	LUNATED	LUNGS
LUFFA	LULU	LUMME	LUNATELY	LUNGWORM
LUFFAS	LULUS	LUMMIER	LUNATES	LUNGWORMS
LUFFED	LULZ	LUMMIEST	LUNATIC	LUNGWORT
LUFFING	LUM	LUMMOX	LUNATICAL	LUNGWORTS
LUFFS	LUMA	LUMMOXES	LUNATICS	LUNGYI
LUG	LUMAS	LUMMY	LUNATION	LUNGYIS
LUGE	LUMBAGO	LUMP	LUNATIONS	LUNIER
LUGED	LUMBAGOS	LUMPED	LUNCH	LUNIES
LUGEING	LUMBANG	LUMPEN	LUNCHBOX	LUNIEST
LUGEINGS	LUMBANGS	LUMPENLY	LUNCHED	LUNINESS
LUGER	LUMBAR	LUMPENS	LUNCHEON	LUNISOLAR
LUGERS	LUMBARS	LUMPER	LUNCHEONS	LUNITIDAL
LUGES	LUMBER	LUMPERS	LUNCHER	LUNK
LUGGABLE	LUMBERED	LUMPFISH	LUNCHERS	LUNKER
LUGGABLES	LUMBERER	LUMPIA	LUNCHES	LUNKERS
LUGGAGE	LUMBERERS	LUMPIAS	LUNCHING	LUNKHEAD
LUGGAGES	LUMBERING	LUMPIER	LUNCHMEAT	LUNKHEADS
LUGGED	LUMBERLY	LUMPIEST	LUNCHPAIL	LUNKS
LUGGER	LUMBERMAN	LUMPILY	LUNCHROOM	LUNS
LUGGERS	LUMBERMEN	LUMPINESS	LUNCHTIME	LUNT
LUGGIE	LUMBERS	LUMPING	LUNE	LUNTED
LUGGIES	LUMBI	LUMPINGLY	LUNES	LUNTING
LUGGING	LUMBRICAL	LUMPISH	LUNET	LUNTS
LUGHOLE	LUMBRICI	LUMPISHLY	LUNETS	LUNULA
LUGHOLES	LUMBRICUS	LUMPKIN	LUNETTE	LUNULAE
LUGING	LUMBUS	LUMPKINS	LUNETTES	LUNULAR
LUGINGS	LUMEN	LUMPS	LUNG	LUNULATE
LUGS	LUMENAL	LUMPY	LUNGAN	LUNULATED
LUGSAIL	LUMENS	LUMS	LUNGANS	LUNULE
LUGSAILS	LUMINA	LUN	LUNGE	LUNULES

LUNY	LURING	LUSTIEST	LUTER	LUXURIES
LUNYIE	LURINGLY	LUSTIHEAD	LUTERS	LUXURIOUS
LUNYIES	LURINGS	LUSTIHOOD	LUTES	LUXURIST
LUPANAR	LURK	LUSTILY	LUTESCENT	LUXURISTS
LUPANARS	LURKED	LUSTINESS	LUTETIUM	LUXURY
LUPIN	LURKER	LUSTING	LUTETIUMS	LUZ
LUPINE	LURKERS	LUSTIQUE	LUTEUM	LUZERN
LUPINES	LURKING	LUSTLESS	LUTFISK	LUZERNS
LUPINS	LURKINGLY	LUSTRA	LUTFISKS	LUZZES
LUPOID	LURKINGS	LUSTRAL	LUTHERN	LWEI
LUPOUS	LURKS	LUSTRATE	LUTHERNS	LWEIS
LUPPEN	LURRIES	LUSTRATED	LUTHIER	LYAM
LUPULIN	LURRY	LUSTRATES	LUTHIERS	LYAMS
LUPULINE	LURS	LUSTRE	LUTING	LYARD
LUPULINIC	LURVE	LUSTRED	LUTINGS	LYART
LUPULINS	LURVES	LUSTRES	LUTIST	LYASE
LUPUS	LUSCIOUS	LUSTRINE	LUTISTS	LYASES
LUPUSES	LUSER	LUSTRINES	LUTITE	LYCAENID
LUR	LUSERS	LUSTRING	LUTITES	LYCAENIDS
LURCH	LUSH	LUSTRINGS	LUTTEN	LYCEA
LURCHED	LUSHED	LUSTROUS	LUTZ	LYCEE
LURCHER	LUSHER	LUSTRUM	LUTZES	LYCEES
LURCHERS	LUSHERS	LUSTRUMS	LUV	LYCEUM
LURCHES	LUSHES	LUSTS	LUVS	LYCEUMS
LURCHING	LUSHEST	LUSTY	LUVVED	LYCH
LURDAN	LUSHIER	LUSUS	LUVVIE	LYCHEE
LURDANE	LUSHIES	LUSUSES	LUVVIEDOM	LYCHEES
LURDANES	LUSHIEST	LUTANIST	LUVVIES	LYCHES
LURDANS	LUSHING	LUTANISTS	LUVVING	LYCHGATE
LURDEN	LUSHLY	LUTE	LUVVY	LYCHGATES
LURDENS	LUSHNESS	LUTEA	LUX	LYCHNIS
LURE	LUSHY	LUTEAL	LUXATE	LYCHNISES
LURED	LUSK	LUTECIUM	LUXATED	LYCOPENE
LURER	LUSKED	LUTECIUMS	LUXATES	LYCOPENES
LURERS	LUSKING	LUTED	LUXATING	LYCOPOD
LURES	LUSKISH	LUTEFISK	LUXATION	LYCOPODS
LUREX	LUSKS	LUTEFISKS	LUXATIONS	LYCOPSID
LUREXES	LUST	LUTEIN	LUXE	LYCOPSIDS
LURGI	LUSTED	LUTEINISE	LUXED	LYCRA
LURGIES	LUSTER	LUTEINIZE	LUXER	LYCRAS
LURGIS	LUSTERED	LUTEINS	LUXES	LYDDITE
LURGY	LUSTERING	LUTENIST	LUXEST	LYDDITES
LURID	LUSTERS	LUTENISTS	LUXING	LYE
LURIDER	LUSTFUL	LUTEOLIN	LUXMETER	LYES
LURIDEST	LUSTFULLY	LUTEOLINS	LUXMETERS	LYFULL
LURIDLY	LUSTICK	LUTEOLOUS	LUXURIANT	LYING
LURIDNESS	LUSTIER	LUTEOUS	LUXURIATE	LYINGLY

LYINGS
LYKEWAKE
LYKEWAKES
LYKEWALK
LYKEWALKS
LYM
LYME
LYMES
LYMITER
LYMITERS
LYMPH
LYMPHAD
LYMPHADS
LYMPHATIC
LYMPHOID
LYMPHOMA
LYMPHOMAS
LYMPHOUS
LYMPHS
LYMS
LYNAGE
LYNAGES
LYNCEAN
LYNCH

LYNCHED
LYNCHER
LYNCHERS
LYNCHES
LYNCHET
LYNCHETS
LYNCHING
LYNCHINGS
LYNCHPIN
LYNCHPINS
LYNE
LYNES
LYNX
LYNXES
LYNXLIKE
LYOLYSES
LYOLYSIS
LYOMEROUS
LYONNAISE
LYOPHIL
LYOPHILE
LYOPHILED
LYOPHILIC
LYOPHOBE

LYOPHOBIC
LYRA
LYRATE
LYRATED
LYRATELY
LYRE
LYREBIRD
LYREBIRDS
LYRES
LYRIC
LYRICAL
LYRICALLY
LYRICISE
LYRICISED
LYRICISES
LYRICISM
LYRICISMS
LYRICIST
LYRICISTS
LYRICIZE
LYRICIZED
LYRICIZES
LYRICON
LYRICONS

LYRICS
LYRIFORM
LYRISM
LYRISMS
LYRIST
LYRISTS
LYSATE
LYSATES
LYSE
LYSED
LYSERGIC
LYSERGIDE
LYSES
LYSIGENIC
LYSIMETER
LYSIN
LYSINE
LYSINES
LYSING
LYSINS
LYSIS
LYSOGEN
LYSOGENIC
LYSOGENS

LYSOGENY
LYSOL
LYSOLS
LYSOSOMAL
LYSOSOME
LYSOSOMES
LYSOZYME
LYSOZYMES
LYSSA
LYSSAS
LYTE
LYTED
LYTES
LYTHE
LYTHES
LYTHRUM
LYTHRUMS
LYTIC
LYTICALLY
LYTING
LYTTA
LYTTAE
LYTTAS

M

MA	MACAROON	MACHETES	MACOYAS	MACULED
MAA	MACAROONS	MACHI	MACRAME	MACULES
MAAED	MACASSAR	MACHINATE	MACRAMES	MACULING
MAAING	MACASSARS	MACHINE	MACRAMI	MACULOSE
MAAR	MACAW	MACHINED	MACRAMIS	MACUMBA
MAARE	MACAWS	MACHINERY	MACRO	MACUMBAS
MAARS	MACCABAW	MACHINES	MACROBIAN	MAD
MAAS	MACCABAWS	MACHINIMA	MACROCODE	MADAFU
MAASES	MACCABOY	MACHINING	MACROCOPY	MADAFUS
MAATJES	MACCABOYS	MACHINIST	MACROCOSM	MADAM
MABE	MACCARONI	MACHISMO	MACROCYST	MADAME
MABELA	MACCHIA	MACHISMOS	MACROCYTE	MADAMED
MABELAS	MACCHIATO	MACHMETER	MACRODOME	MADAMES
MABES	MACCHIE	MACHO	MACRODONT	MADAMING
MAC	MACCOBOY	MACHOISM	MACROGLIA	MADAMS
MACABER	MACCOBOYS	MACHOISMS	MACROLIDE	MADAROSES
MACABRE	MACE	MACHOS	MACROLOGY	MADAROSIS
MACABRELY	MACED	MACHREE	MACROMERE	MADBRAIN
MACACO	MACEDOINE	MACHREES	MACROMOLE	MADBRAINS
MACACOS	MACER	MACHS	MACRON	MADCAP
MACADAM	MACERAL	MACHZOR	MACRONS	MADCAPS
MACADAMED	MACERALS	MACHZORIM	MACROPOD	MADDED
MACADAMIA	MACERATE	MACHZORS	MACROPODS	MADDEN
MACADAMS	MACERATED	MACING	MACROPSIA	MADDENED
MACAHUBA	MACERATER	MACINTOSH	MACROS	MADDENING
MACAHUBAS	MACERATES	MACK	MACROTOUS	MADDENS
MACALLUM	MACERATOR	MACKEREL	MACRURAL	MADDER
MACALLUMS	MACERS	MACKERELS	MACRURAN	MADDERS
MACAQUE	MACES	MACKINAW	MACRURANS	MADDEST
MACAQUES	MACH	MACKINAWS	MACRUROID	MADDING
MACARISE	MACHACA	MACKLE	MACRUROUS	MADDINGLY
MACARISED	MACHACAS	MACKLED	MACS	MADDISH
MACARISES	MACHAIR	MACKLES	MACTATION	MADDOCK
MACARISM	MACHAIRS	MACKLING	MACULA	MADDOCKS
MACARISMS	MACHAN	MACKS	MACULAE	MADE
MACARIZE	MACHANS	MACLE	MACULAR	MADEFIED
MACARIZED	MACHE	MACLED	MACULAS	MADEFIES
MACARIZES	MACHER	MACLES	MACULATE	MADEFY
MACARONI	MACHERS	MACON	MACULATED	MADEFYING
MACARONIC	MACHES	MACONS	MACULATES	MADEIRA
MACARONIS	MACHETE	MACOYA	MACULE	MADEIRAS

MADELEINE	MADS	MAFTIR	MAGISTERY	MAGNONS
MADERISE	MADTOM	MAFTIRS	MAGISTRAL	MAGNOX
MADERISED	MADTOMS	MAG	MAGLEV	MAGNOXES
MADERISES	MADURO	MAGAININ	MAGLEVS	MAGNUM
MADERIZE	MADUROS	MAGAININS	MAGMA	MAGNUMS
MADERIZED	MADWOMAN	MAGALOG	MAGMAS	MAGNUS
MADERIZES	MADWOMEN	MAGALOGS	MAGMATA	MAGOT
MADEUPPY	MADWORT	MAGALOGUE	MAGMATIC	MAGOTS
MADGE	MADWORTS	MAGAZINE	MAGMATISM	MAGPIE
MADGES	MADZOON	MAGAZINES	MAGNALIUM	MAGPIES
MADHOUSE	MADZOONS	MAGDALEN	MAGNATE	MAGS
MADHOUSES	MAE	MAGDALENE	MAGNATES	MAGSMAN
MADID	MAELID	MAGDALENS	MAGNES	MAGSMEN
MADISON	MAELIDS	MAGE	MAGNESES	MAGUEY
MADISONS	MAELSTROM	MAGENTA	MAGNESIA	MAGUEYS
MADLING	MAENAD	MAGENTAS	MAGNESIAL	MAGUS
MADLINGS	MAENADES	MAGES	MAGNESIAN	MAGYAR
MADLY	MAENADIC	MAGESHIP	MAGNESIAS	MAHA
MADMAN	MAENADISM	MAGESHIPS	MAGNESIC	MAHANT
MADMEN	MAENADS	MAGG	MAGNESITE	MAHANTS
MADNESS	MAERL	MAGGED	MAGNESIUM	MAHARAJA
MADNESSES	MAERLS	MAGGIE	MAGNET	MAHARAJAH
MADONNA	MAES	MAGGIES	MAGNETAR	MAHARAJAS
MADONNAS	MAESTOSO	MAGGING	MAGNETARS	MAHARANEE
MADOQUA	MAESTOSOS	MAGGOT	MAGNETIC	MAHARANI
MADOQUAS	MAESTRI	MAGGOTIER	MAGNETICS	MAHARANIS
MADRAS	MAESTRO	MAGGOTS	MAGNETISE	MAHARISHI
MADRASA	MAESTROS	MAGGOTY	MAGNETISM	MAHATMA
MADRASAH	MAFFIA	MAGGS	MAGNETIST	MAHATMAS
MADRASAHS	MAFFIAS	MAGI	MAGNETITE	MAHEWU
MADRASAS	MAFFICK	MAGIAN	MAGNETIZE	MAHEWUS
MADRASES	MAFFICKED	MAGIANISM	MAGNETO	MAHIMAHI
MADRASSA	MAFFICKER	MAGIANS	MAGNETON	MAHIMAHIS
MADRASSAH	MAFFICKS	MAGIC	MAGNETONS	MAHJONG
MADRASSAS	MAFFLED	MAGICAL	MAGNETOS	MAHJONGG
MADRE	MAFFLIN	MAGICALLY	MAGNETRON	MAHJONGGS
MADREPORE	MAFFLING	MAGICIAN	MAGNETS	MAHJONGS
MADRES	MAFFLINGS	MAGICIANS	MAGNIFIC	MAHLSTICK
MADRIGAL	MAFFLINS	MAGICKED	MAGNIFICO	MAHMAL
MADRIGALS	MAFIA	MAGICKING	MAGNIFIED	MAHMALS
MADRILENE	MAFIAS	MAGICS	MAGNIFIER	MAHOE
MADRONA	MAFIC	MAGILP	MAGNIFIES	MAHOES
MADRONAS	MAFICS	MAGILPS	MAGNIFY	MAHOGANY
MADRONE	MAFIOSI	MAGISM	MAGNITUDE	MAHONIA
MADRONES	MAFIOSO	MAGISMS	MAGNOLIA	MAHONIAS
MADRONO	MAFIOSOS	MAGISTER	MAGNOLIAS	MAHOUT
MADRONOS	MAFTED	MAGISTERS	MAGNON	MAHOUTS

MAHSEER
MAHSEERS
MAHSIR
MAHSIRS
MAHUA
MAHUANG
MAHUANGS
MAHUAS
MAHWA
MAHWAS
MAHZOR
MAHZORIM
MAHZORS
MAIASAUR
MAIASAURA
MAIASAURS
MAID
MAIDAN
MAIDANS
MAIDED
MAIDEN
MAIDENISH
MAIDENLY
MAIDENS
MAIDHOOD
MAIDHOODS
MAIDING
MAIDISH
MAIDISM
MAIDISMS
MAIDLESS
MAIDS
MAIEUTIC
MAIEUTICS
MAIGRE
MAIGRES
MAIHEM
MAIHEMS
MAIK
MAIKO
MAIKOS
MAIKS
MAIL
MAILABLE
MAILBAG
MAILBAGS
MAILBOAT

MAILBOATS
MAILBOX
MAILBOXES
MAILCAR
MAILCARS
MAILCOACH
MAILE
MAILED
MAILER
MAILERS
MAILES
MAILGRAM
MAILGRAMS
MAILING
MAILINGS
MAILL
MAILLESS
MAILLOT
MAILLOTS
MAILLS
MAILMAN
MAILMEN
MAILMERGE
MAILPOUCH
MAILROOM
MAILROOMS
MAILS
MAILSACK
MAILSACKS
MAILSHOT
MAILSHOTS
MAILVAN
MAILVANS
MAIM
MAIMED
MAIMER
MAIMERS
MAIMING
MAIMINGS
MAIMS
MAIN
MAINBOOM
MAINBOOMS
MAINBRACE
MAINDOOR
MAINDOORS
MAINED

MAINER
MAINEST
MAINFRAME
MAINING
MAINLAND
MAINLANDS
MAINLINE
MAINLINED
MAINLINER
MAINLINES
MAINLY
MAINMAST
MAINMASTS
MAINOR
MAINORS
MAINOUR
MAINOURS
MAINPRISE
MAINS
MAINSAIL
MAINSAILS
MAINSHEET
MAINSTAY
MAINSTAYS
MAINTAIN
MAINTAINS
MAINTOP
MAINTOPS
MAINYARD
MAINYARDS
MAIOLICA
MAIOLICAS
MAIR
MAIRE
MAIREHAU
MAIREHAUS
MAIRES
MAIRS
MAISE
MAISES
MAIST
MAISTER
MAISTERED
MAISTERS
MAISTRIES
MAISTRING
MAISTRY

MAISTS
MAIZE
MAIZES
MAJAGUA
MAJAGUAS
MAJESTIC
MAJESTIES
MAJESTY
MAJLIS
MAJLISES
MAJOLICA
MAJOLICAS
MAJOR
MAJORAT
MAJORATS
MAJORDOMO
MAJORED
MAJORETTE
MAJORING
MAJORITY
MAJORLY
MAJORS
MAJORSHIP
MAJUSCULE
MAK
MAKABLE
MAKAR
MAKARS
MAKE
MAKEABLE
MAKEBATE
MAKEBATES
MAKEFAST
MAKEFASTS
MAKELESS
MAKEOVER
MAKEOVERS
MAKER
MAKEREADY
MAKERS
MAKES
MAKESHIFT
MAKEUP
MAKEUPS
MAKHANI
MAKI
MAKIMONO

MAKIMONOS
MAKING
MAKINGS
MAKIS
MAKO
MAKOS
MAKS
MAKUTA
MAKUTU
MAKUTUED
MAKUTUING
MAKUTUS
MAL
MALA
MALACCA
MALACCAS
MALACHITE
MALACIA
MALACIAS
MALADIES
MALADROIT
MALADY
MALAGUENA
MALAISE
MALAISES
MALAM
MALAMS
MALAMUTE
MALAMUTES
MALANDER
MALANDERS
MALANGA
MALANGAS
MALAPERT
MALAPERTS
MALAPROP
MALAPROPS
MALAR
MALARIA
MALARIAL
MALARIAN
MALARIAS
MALARIOUS
MALARKEY
MALARKEYS
MALARKIES
MALARKY

M

MALAROMA
MALAROMAS
MALARS
MALAS
MALATE
MALATES
MALATHION
MALAX
MALAXAGE
MALAXAGES
MALAXATE
MALAXATED
MALAXATES
MALAXATOR
MALAXED
MALAXES
MALAXING
MALE
MALEATE
MALEATES
MALEDICT
MALEDICTS
MALEFFECT
MALEFIC
MALEFICE
MALEFICES
MALEIC
MALEMIUT
MALEMIUTS
MALEMUTE
MALEMUTES
MALENESS
MALENGINE
MALES
MALFED
MALFORMED
MALGRADO
MALGRE
MALGRED
MALGRES
MALGRING
MALI
MALIBU
MALIC
MALICE
MALICED
MALICES

MALICHO
MALICHOS
MALICING
MALICIOUS
MALIGN
MALIGNANT
MALIGNED
MALIGNER
MALIGNERS
MALIGNING
MALIGNITY
MALIGNLY
MALIGNS
MALIHINI
MALIHINIS
MALIK
MALIKS
MALINE
MALINES
MALINGER
MALINGERS
MALINGERY
MALIS
MALISM
MALISMS
MALISON
MALISONS
MALIST
MALKIN
MALKINS
MALL
MALLAM
MALLAMS
MALLANDER
MALLARD
MALLARDS
MALLCORE
MALLCORES
MALLEABLE
MALLEABLY
MALLEATE
MALLEATED
MALLEATES
MALLECHO
MALLECHOS
MALLED
MALLEE

MALLEES
MALLEI
MALLEMUCK
MALLENDER
MALLEOLAR
MALLEOLI
MALLEOLUS
MALLET
MALLETS
MALLEUS
MALLEUSES
MALLING
MALLINGS
MALLOW
MALLOWS
MALLS
MALM
MALMAG
MALMAGS
MALMIER
MALMIEST
MALMS
MALMSEY
MALMSEYS
MALMSTONE
MALMY
MALODOR
MALODORS
MALODOUR
MALODOURS
MALONATE
MALONATES
MALONIC
MALOTI
MALPIGHIA
MALPOSED
MALS
MALSTICK
MALSTICKS
MALT
MALTALENT
MALTASE
MALTASES
MALTED
MALTEDS
MALTESE
MALTHA

MALTHAS
MALTIER
MALTIEST
MALTINESS
MALTING
MALTINGS
MALTMAN
MALTMEN
MALTOL
MALTOLS
MALTOSE
MALTOSES
MALTREAT
MALTREATS
MALTS
MALTSTER
MALTSTERS
MALTWORM
MALTWORMS
MALTY
MALUS
MALUSES
MALVA
MALVAS
MALVASIA
MALVASIAN
MALVASIAS
MALVESIE
MALVESIES
MALVOISIE
MALWA
MALWARE
MALWARES
MALWAS
MAM
MAMA
MAMAGUY
MAMAGUYED
MAMAGUYS
MAMAKAU
MAMAKAUS
MAMAKO
MAMAKOS
MAMAKU
MAMAKUS
MAMALIGA
MAMALIGAS

MAMAS
MAMASAN
MAMASANS
MAMATEEK
MAMATEEKS
MAMBA
MAMBAS
MAMBO
MAMBOED
MAMBOES
MAMBOING
MAMBOS
MAMEE
MAMEES
MAMELON
MAMELONS
MAMELUCO
MAMELUCOS
MAMELUKE
MAMELUKES
MAMEY
MAMEYES
MAMEYS
MAMIE
MAMIES
MAMILLA
MAMILLAE
MAMILLAR
MAMILLARY
MAMILLATE
MAMLUK
MAMLUKS
MAMMA
MAMMAE
MAMMAL
MAMMALIAN
MAMMALITY
MAMMALOGY
MAMMALS
MAMMARIES
MAMMARY
MAMMAS
MAMMATE
MAMMATI
MAMMATUS
MAMMEE
MAMMEES

MAMMER	MANAGE	MANDARINS	MANED	MANGLE
MAMMERED	MANAGED	MANDATARY	MANEGE	MANGLED
MAMMERING	MANAGER	MANDATE	MANEGED	MANGLER
MAMMERS	MANAGERS	MANDATED	MANEGES	MANGLERS
MAMMET	MANAGES	MANDATES	MANEGING	MANGLES
MAMMETRY	MANAGING	MANDATING	MANEH	MANGLING
MAMMETS	MANAIA	MANDATOR	MANEHS	MANGO
MAMMEY	MANAIAS	MANDATORS	MANELESS	MANGOES
MAMMEYS	MANAKIN	MANDATORY	MANENT	MANGOLD
MAMMIE	MANAKINS	MANDI	MANES	MANGOLDS
MAMMIES	MANANA	MANDIBLE	MANET	MANGONEL
MAMMIFER	MANANAS	MANDIBLES	MANEUVER	MANGONELS
MAMMIFERS	MANAS	MANDILION	MANEUVERS	MANGOS
MAMMIFORM	MANAT	MANDIOC	MANFUL	MANGOSTAN
MAMMILLA	MANATEE	MANDIOCA	MANFULLY	MANGOUSTE
MAMMILLAE	MANATEES	MANDIOCAS	MANG	MANGROVE
MAMMILLAR	MANATI	MANDIOCCA	MANGA	MANGROVES
MAMMITIS	MANATIS	MANDIOCS	MANGABEY	MANGS
MAMMOCK	MANATOID	MANDIR	MANGABEYS	MANGULATE
MAMMOCKED	MANATS	MANDIRA	MANGABIES	MANGY
MAMMOCKS	MANATU	MANDIRAS	MANGABY	MANHANDLE
MAMMOGRAM	MANATUS	MANDIRS	MANGAL	MANHATTAN
MAMMON	MANAWA	MANDIS	MANGALS	MANHOLE
MAMMONISH	MANAWAS	MANDOLA	MANGANATE	MANHOLES
MAMMONISM	MANBAG	MANDOLAS	MANGANESE	MANHOOD
MAMMONIST	MANBAGS	MANDOLIN	MANGANIC	MANHOODS
MAMMONITE	MANBAND	MANDOLINE	MANGANIN	MANHUNT
MAMMONS	MANBANDS	MANDOLINS	MANGANINS	MANHUNTER
MAMMOTH	MANCALA	MANDOM	MANGANITE	MANHUNTS
MAMMOTHS	MANCALAS	MANDOMS	MANGANOUS	MANI
MAMMY	MANCANDO	MANDORA	MANGAS	MANIA
MAMPARA	MANCHE	MANDORAS	MANGE	MANIAC
MAMPARAS	MANCHES	MANDORLA	MANGEAO	MANIACAL
MAMPOER	MANCHET	MANDORLAS	MANGEAOS	MANIACS
MAMPOERS	MANCHETS	MANDRAKE	MANGED	MANIAS
MAMS	MANCIPATE	MANDRAKES	MANGEL	MANIC
MAMSELLE	MANCIPLE	MANDREL	MANGELS	MANICALLY
MAMSELLES	MANCIPLES	MANDRELS	MANGER	MANICOTTI
MAMZER	MANCUS	MANDRIL	MANGERS	MANICS
MAMZERIM	MANCUSES	MANDRILL	MANGES	MANICURE
MAMZERS	MAND	MANDRILLS	MANGETOUT	MANICURED
MAN	MANDALA	MANDRILS	MANGEY	MANICURES
MANA	MANDALAS	MANDUCATE	MANGIER	MANIES
MANACLE	MANDALIC	MANDYLION	MANGIEST	MANIFEST
MANACLED	MANDAMUS	MANE	MANGILY	MANIFESTO
MANACLES	MANDARIN	MANEB	MANGINESS	MANIFESTS
MANACLING	MANDARINE	MANEBS	MANGING	MANIFOLD

M

MANIFOLDS	MANMADE	MANRIDER	MANTLE	MANURING
MANIFORM	MANNA	MANRIDERS	MANTLED	MANURINGS
MANIHOC	MANNAN	MANRIDING	MANTLES	MANUS
MANIHOCS	MANNANS	MANROPE	MANTLET	MANWARD
MANIHOT	MANNAS	MANROPES	MANTLETS	MANWARDS
MANIHOTS	MANNED	MANS	MANTLING	MANWISE
MANIKIN	MANNEQUIN	MANSARD	MANTLINGS	MANY
MANIKINS	MANNER	MANSARDED	MANTO	MANYATA
MANILA	MANNERED	MANSARDS	MANTOES	MANYATAS
MANILAS	MANNERISM	MANSCAPE	MANTOS	MANYATTA
MANILLA	MANNERIST	MANSCAPED	MANTRA	MANYATTAS
MANILLAS	MANNERLY	MANSCAPES	MANTRAM	MANYFOLD
MANILLE	MANNERS	MANSE	MANTRAMS	MANYPLIES
MANILLES	MANNIKIN	MANSES	MANTRAP	MANZANITA
MANIOC	MANNIKINS	MANSHIFT	MANTRAPS	MANZELLO
MANIOCA	MANNING	MANSHIFTS	MANTRAS	MANZELLOS
MANIOCAS	MANNISH	MANSION	MANTRIC	MAOMAO
MANIOCS	MANNISHLY	MANSIONS	MANTUA	MAOMAOS
MANIPLE	MANNITE	MANSLAYER	MANTUAS	MAORMOR
MANIPLES	MANNITES	MANSONRY	MANTY	MAORMORS
MANIPLIES	MANNITIC	MANSUETE	MANTYHOSE	MAP
MANIPULAR	MANNITOL	MANSWORN	MANUAL	MAPAU
MANIS	MANNITOLS	MANSWORNS	MANUALLY	MAPAUS
MANISES	MANNOSE	MANTA	MANUALS	MAPLE
MANITO	MANNOSES	MANTAS	MANUARY	MAPLELIKE
MANITOS	MANO	MANTEAU	MANUBRIA	MAPLES
MANITOU	MANOAO	MANTEAUS	MANUBRIAL	MAPLESS
MANITOUS	MANOAOS	MANTEAUX	MANUBRIUM	MAPLIKE
MANITU	MANOES	MANTEEL	MANUCODE	MAPMAKER
MANITUS	MANOEUVRE	MANTEELS	MANUCODES	MAPMAKERS
MANJACK	MANOMETER	MANTEL	MANUHIRI	MAPMAKING
MANJACKS	MANOMETRY	MANTELET	MANUHIRIS	MAPPABLE
MANKIER	MANOR	MANTELETS	MANUKA	MAPPED
MANKIEST	MANORIAL	MANTELS	MANUKAS	MAPPEMOND
MANKIND	MANORS	MANTES	MANUL	MAPPER
MANKINDS	MANOS	MANTIC	MANULS	MAPPERIES
MANKINI	MANOSCOPY	MANTICORA	MANUMEA	MAPPERS
MANKINIS	MANPACK	MANTICORE	MANUMEAS	MAPPERY
MANKY	MANPACKS	MANTID	MANUMIT	MAPPING
MANLESS	MANPOWER	MANTIDS	MANUMITS	MAPPINGS
MANLIER	MANPOWERS	MANTIES	MANURANCE	MAPPIST
MANLIEST	MANQUE	MANTILLA	MANURE	MAPPISTS
MANLIKE	MANQUES	MANTILLAS	MANURED	MAPS
MANLIKELY	MANRED	MANTIS	MANURER	MAPSTICK
MANLILY	MANREDS	MANTISES	MANURERS	MAPSTICKS
MANLINESS	MANRENT	MANTISSA	MANURES	MAPWISE
MANLY	MANRENTS	MANTISSAS	MANURIAL	MAQUETTE

MAQUETTES	MARBLED	MARDYING	MARIGRAM	MARKETED
MAQUI	MARBLEISE	MARE	MARIGRAMS	MARKETEER
MAQUILA	MARBLEIZE	MAREMMA	MARIGRAPH	MARKETER
MAQUILAS	MARBLER	MAREMMAS	MARIHUANA	MARKETERS
MAQUIS	MARBLERS	MAREMME	MARIJUANA	MARKETING
MAQUISARD	MARBLES	MARENGO	MARIMBA	MARKETISE
MAR	MARBLIER	MARERO	MARIMBAS	MARKETIZE
MARA	MARBLIEST	MAREROS	MARIMBIST	MARKETS
MARABI	MARBLING	MARES	MARINA	MARKHOOR
MARABIS	MARBLINGS	MARESCHAL	MARINADE	MARKHOORS
MARABOU	MARBLY	MARG	MARINADED	MARKHOR
MARABOUS	MARC	MARGARIC	MARINADES	MARKHORS
MARABOUT	MARCASITE	MARGARIN	MARINARA	MARKING
MARABOUTS	MARCATO	MARGARINE	MARINARAS	MARKINGS
MARABUNTA	MARCATOS	MARGARINS	MARINAS	MARKKA
MARACA	MARCEL	MARGARITA	MARINATE	MARKKAA
MARACAS	MARCELLA	MARGARITE	MARINATED	MARKKAS
MARAE	MARCELLAS	MARGATE	MARINATES	MARKMAN
MARAES	MARCELLED	MARGATES	MARINE	MARKMEN
MARAGING	MARCELLER	MARGAY	MARINER	MARKS
MARAGINGS	MARCELS	MARGAYS	MARINERA	MARKSMAN
MARAH	MARCH	MARGE	MARINERAS	MARKSMEN
MARAHS	MARCHED	MARGENT	MARINERS	MARKUP
MARANATHA	MARCHEN	MARGENTED	MARINES	MARKUPS
MARANTA	MARCHER	MARGENTS	MARINIERE	MARL
MARANTAS	MARCHERS	MARGES	MARIPOSA	MARLE
MARARI	MARCHES	MARGIN	MARIPOSAS	MARLED
MARARIS	MARCHESA	MARGINAL	MARISCHAL	MARLES
MARAS	MARCHESAS	MARGINALS	MARISH	MARLIER
MARASCA	MARCHESE	MARGINATE	MARISHES	MARLIEST
MARASCAS	MARCHESI	MARGINED	MARITAGE	MARLIN
MARASMIC	MARCHING	MARGINING	MARITAGES	MARLINE
MARASMOID	MARCHLAND	MARGINS	MARITAL	MARLINES
MARASMUS	MARCHLIKE	MARGOSA	MARITALLY	MARLING
MARATHON	MARCHMAN	MARGOSAS	MARITIME	MARLINGS
MARATHONS	MARCHMEN	MARGRAVE	MARJORAM	MARLINS
MARAUD	MARCHPANE	MARGRAVES	MARJORAMS	MARLITE
MARAUDED	MARCONI	MARGS	MARK	MARLITES
MARAUDER	MARCONIED	MARIA	MARKA	MARLITIC
MARAUDERS	MARCONIS	MARIACHI	MARKAS	MARLS
MARAUDING	MARCS	MARIACHIS	MARKDOWN	MARLSTONE
MARAUDS	MARD	MARIALITE	MARKDOWNS	MARLY
MARAVEDI	MARDIED	MARID	MARKED	MARM
MARAVEDIS	MARDIER	MARIDS	MARKEDLY	MARMALADE
MARBELISE	MARDIES	MARIES	MARKER	MARMALISE
MARBELIZE	MARDIEST	MARIGOLD	MARKERS	MARMALIZE
MARBLE	MARDY	MARIGOLDS	MARKET	MARMARISE

M

MARMARIZE	MARRELS	MARSHLAND	MARTYRIUM	MASCULY
MARMELISE	MARRER	MARSHLIKE	MARTYRIZE	MASE
MARMELIZE	MARRERS	MARSHWORT	MARTYRLY	MASED
MARMEM	MARRI	MARSHY	MARTYRS	MASER
MARMITE	MARRIAGE	MARSPORT	MARTYRY	MASERS
MARMITES	MARRIAGES	MARSPORTS	MARVEL	MASES
MARMOREAL	MARRIED	MARSQUAKE	MARVELED	MASH
MARMOREAN	MARRIEDS	MARSUPIA	MARVELER	MASHALLAH
MARMOSE	MARRIER	MARSUPIAL	MARVELERS	MASHED
MARMOSES	MARRIERS	MARSUPIAN	MARVELING	MASHER
MARMOSET	MARRIES	MARSUPIUM	MARVELLED	MASHERS
MARMOSETS	MARRING	MART	MARVELOUS	MASHES
MARMOT	MARRIS	MARTAGON	MARVELS	MASHGIACH
MARMOTS	MARRON	MARTAGONS	MARVER	MASHGIAH
MARMS	MARRONS	MARTED	MARVERED	MASHGIHIM
MAROCAIN	MARROW	MARTEL	MARVERING	MASHIACH
MAROCAINS	MARROWED	MARTELLED	MARVERS	MASHIACHS
MARON	MARROWFAT	MARTELLO	MARVIER	MASHIE
MARONS	MARROWING	MARTELLOS	MARVIEST	MASHIER
MAROON	MARROWISH	MARTELS	MARVY	MASHIES
MAROONED	MARROWS	MARTEN	MARXISANT	MASHIEST
MAROONER	MARROWSKY	MARTENS	MARY	MASHING
MAROONERS	MARROWY	MARTEXT	MARYBUD	MASHINGS
MAROONING	MARRUM	MARTEXTS	MARYBUDS	MASHLAM
MAROONS	MARRUMS	MARTIAL	MARYJANE	MASHLAMS
MAROQUIN	MARRY	MARTIALLY	MARYJANES	MASHLIM
MAROQUINS	MARRYING	MARTIALS	MARZIPAN	MASHLIMS
MAROR	MARRYINGS	MARTIAN	MARZIPANS	MASHLIN
MARORS	MARS	MARTIANS	MAS	MASHLINS
MARPLOT	MARSALA	MARTIN	MASA	MASHLOCH
MARPLOTS	MARSALAS	MARTINET	MASALA	MASHLOCHS
MARQUE	MARSE	MARTINETS	MASALAS	MASHLUM
MARQUEE	MARSEILLE	MARTING	MASAS	MASHLUMS
MARQUEES	MARSES	MARTINGAL	MASCARA	MASHMAN
MARQUES	MARSH	MARTINI	MASCARAED	MASHMEN
MARQUESS	MARSHAL	MARTINIS	MASCARAS	MASHUA
MARQUETRY	MARSHALCY	MARTINS	MASCARON	MASHUAS
MARQUIS	MARSHALED	MARTLET	MASCARONS	MASHUP
MARQUISE	MARSHALER	MARTLETS	MASCLE	MASHUPS
MARQUISES	MARSHALL	MARTS	MASCLED	MASHY
MARRA	MARSHALLS	MARTYR	MASCLES	MASING
MARRAM	MARSHALS	MARTYRDOM	MASCON	MASJID
MARRAMS	MARSHBUCK	MARTYRED	MASCONS	MASJIDS
MARRANO	MARSHED	MARTYRIA	MASCOT	MASK
MARRANOS	MARSHES	MARTYRIES	MASCOTS	MASKABLE
MARRAS	MARSHIER	MARTYRING	MASCULINE	MASKED
MARRED	MARSHIEST	MARTYRISE	MASCULIST	MASKEG

MASKEGS	MASSETER	MASTICHE	MATAMATAS	MATEYNESS
MASKER	MASSETERS	MASTICHES	MATAMBALA	MATEYS
MASKERS	MASSEUR	MASTICHS	MATATA	MATFELLON
MASKING	MASSEURS	MASTICOT	MATATAS	MATFELON
MASKINGS	MASSEUSE	MASTICOTS	MATATU	MATFELONS
MASKLIKE	MASSEUSES	MASTICS	MATATUS	MATGRASS
MASKS	MASSICOT	MASTIER	MATCH	MATH
MASLIN	MASSICOTS	MASTIEST	MATCHABLE	MATHESES
MASLINS	MASSIER	MASTIFF	MATCHBOOK	MATHESIS
MASOCHISM	MASSIEST	MASTIFFS	MATCHBOX	MATHS
MASOCHIST	MASSIF	MASTING	MATCHED	MATICO
MASON	MASSIFS	MASTITIC	MATCHER	MATICOS
MASONED	MASSINESS	MASTITIS	MATCHERS	MATIER
MASONIC	MASSING	MASTIX	MATCHES	MATIES
MASONING	MASSIVE	MASTIXES	MATCHET	MATIEST
MASONITE	MASSIVELY	MASTLESS	MATCHETS	MATILDA
MASONITES	MASSIVES	MASTLIKE	MATCHING	MATILDAS
MASONRIED	MASSLESS	MASTODON	MATCHLESS	MATILY
MASONRIES	MASSOOLA	MASTODONS	MATCHLOCK	MATIN
MASONRY	MASSOOLAS	MASTODONT	MATCHMADE	MATINAL
MASONS	MASSTIGE	MASTOID	MATCHMAKE	MATINEE
MASOOLAH	MASSTIGES	MASTOIDAL	MATCHMARK	MATINEES
MASOOLAHS	MASSY	MASTOIDS	MATCHPLAY	MATINESS
MASQUE	MASSYMORE	MASTOPEXY	MATCHUP	MATING
MASQUER	MAST	MASTS	MATCHUPS	MATINGS
MASQUERS	MASTABA	MASTY	MATCHWOOD	MATINS
MASQUES	MASTABAH	MASU	MATE	MATIPO
MASS	MASTABAHS	MASULA	MATED	MATIPOS
MASSA	MASTABAS	MASULAS	MATELASSE	MATJES
MASSACRE	MASTED	MASURIUM	MATELESS	MATLESS
MASSACRED	MASTER	MASURIUMS	MATELOT	MATLO
MASSACRER	MASTERATE	MASUS	MATELOTE	MATLOS
MASSACRES	MASTERDOM	MAT	MATELOTES	MATLOW
MASSAGE	MASTERED	MATACHIN	MATELOTS	MATLOWS
MASSAGED	MASTERFUL	MATACHINA	MATELOTTE	MATOKE
MASSAGER	MASTERIES	MATACHINI	MATER	MATOKES
MASSAGERS	MASTERING	MATACHINS	MATERIAL	MATOOKE
MASSAGES	MASTERLY	MATADOR	MATERIALS	MATOOKES
MASSAGING	MASTERS	MATADORA	MATERIEL	MATRASS
MASSAGIST	MASTERY	MATADORAS	MATERIELS	MATRASSES
MASSAS	MASTFUL	MATADORE	MATERNAL	MATRES
MASSCULT	MASTHEAD	MATADORES	MATERNITY	MATRIARCH
MASSCULTS	MASTHEADS	MATADORS	MATERS	MATRIC
MASSE	MASTHOUSE	MATAGOURI	MATES	MATRICE
MASSED	MASTIC	MATAI	MATESHIP	MATRICES
MASSEDLY	MASTICATE	MATAIS	MATESHIPS	MATRICIDE
MASSES	MASTICH	MATAMATA	MATEY	MATRICS

M

MATRICULA	MATTS	MAULGRED	MAUVES	MAWTHERS
MATRILINY	MATURABLE	MAULGRES	MAUVEST	MAX
MATRIMONY	MATURATE	MAULGRING	MAUVIN	MAXED
MATRIX	MATURATED	MAULING	MAUVINE	MAXES
MATRIXES	MATURATES	MAULINGS	MAUVINES	MAXI
MATRON	MATURE	MAULS	MAUVINS	MAXIBOAT
MATRONAGE	MATURED	MAULSTICK	MAUZIER	MAXIBOATS
MATRONAL	MATURELY	MAULVI	MAUZIEST	MAXICOAT
MATRONISE	MATURER	MAULVIS	MAUZY	MAXICOATS
MATRONIZE	MATURERS	MAUMET	MAVEN	MAXIDRESS
MATRONLY	MATURES	MAUMETRY	MAVENS	MAXILLA
MATRONS	MATUREST	MAUMETS	MAVERICK	MAXILLAE
MATROSS	MATURING	MAUN	MAVERICKS	MAXILLAR
MATROSSES	MATURITY	MAUND	MAVIE	MAXILLARY
MATS	MATUTINAL	MAUNDED	MAVIES	MAXILLAS
MATSAH	MATUTINE	MAUNDER	MAVIN	MAXILLULA
MATSAHS	MATWEED	MAUNDERED	MAVINS	MAXIM
MATSURI	MATWEEDS	MAUNDERER	MAVIS	MAXIMA
MATSURIS	MATY	MAUNDERS	MAVISES	MAXIMAL
MATSUTAKE	MATZA	MAUNDIES	MAVOURNIN	MAXIMALLY
MATT	MATZAH	MAUNDING	MAW	MAXIMALS
MATTAMORE	MATZAHS	MAUNDS	MAWBOUND	MAXIMAND
MATTE	MATZAS	MAUNDY	MAWED	MAXIMANDS
MATTED	MATZO	MAUNGIER	MAWGER	MAXIMIN
MATTEDLY	MATZOH	MAUNGIEST	MAWING	MAXIMINS
MATTER	MATZOHS	MAUNGY	MAWK	MAXIMISE
MATTERED	MATZOON	MAUNNA	MAWKIER	MAXIMISED
MATTERFUL	MATZOONS	MAURI	MAWKIEST	MAXIMISER
MATTERING	MATZOS	MAURIS	MAWKIN	MAXIMISES
MATTERS	MATZOT	MAUSIER	MAWKINS	MAXIMIST
MATTERY	MATZOTH	MAUSIEST	MAWKISH	MAXIMISTS
MATTES	MAUBIES	MAUSOLEA	MAWKISHLY	MAXIMITE
MATTIE	MAUBY	MAUSOLEAN	MAWKS	MAXIMITES
MATTIES	MAUD	MAUSOLEUM	MAWKY	MAXIMIZE
MATTIFIED	MAUDLIN	MAUSY	MAWMET	MAXIMIZED
MATTIFIES	MAUDLINLY	MAUT	MAWMETRY	MAXIMIZER
MATTIFY	MAUDS	MAUTHER	MAWMETS	MAXIMIZES
MATTIN	MAUGER	MAUTHERS	MAWN	MAXIMS
MATTING	MAUGRE	MAUTS	MAWNS	MAXIMUM
MATTINGS	MAUGRED	MAUVAIS	MAWPUS	MAXIMUMLY
MATTINS	MAUGRES	MAUVAISE	MAWPUSES	MAXIMUMS
MATTOCK	MAUGRING	MAUVE	MAWR	MAXIMUS
MATTOCKS	MAUL	MAUVEIN	MAWRS	MAXIMUSES
MATTOID	MAULED	MAUVEINE	MAWS	MAXING
MATTOIDS	MAULER	MAUVEINES	MAWSEED	MAXIS
MATTRASS	MAULERS	MAUVEINS	MAWSEEDS	MAXIXE
MATTRESS	MAULGRE	MAUVER	MAWTHER	MAXIXES

MAXWELL	MAYWEED	MEACOCKS	MEANIE	MEATHS
MAXWELLS	MAYWEEDS	MEAD	MEANIES	MEATIER
MAY	MAZAEDIA	MEADOW	MEANING	MEATIEST
MAYA	MAZAEDIUM	MEADOWS	MEANINGLY	MEATILY
MAYAN	MAZARD	MEADOWY	MEANINGS	MEATINESS
MAYAPPLE	MAZARDS	MEADS	MEANLY	MEATLESS
MAYAPPLES	MAZARINE	MEAGER	MEANNESS	MEATLOAF
MAYAS	MAZARINES	MEAGERER	MEANS	MEATMAN
MAYBE	MAZE	MEAGEREST	MEANT	MEATMEN
MAYBES	MAZED	MEAGERLY	MEANTIME	MEATS
MAYBIRD	MAZEDLY	MEAGRE	MEANTIMES	MEATSPACE
MAYBIRDS	MAZEDNESS	MEAGRELY	MEANWHILE	MEATUS
MAYBUSH	MAZEFUL	MEAGRER	MEANY	MEATUSES
MAYBUSHES	MAZELIKE	MEAGRES	MEARE	MEATY
MAYDAY	MAZELTOV	MEAGREST	MEARES	MEAWES
MAYDAYS	MAZEMENT	MEAL	MEARING	MEAZEL
MAYED	MAZEMENTS	MEALED	MEASE	MEAZELS
MAYEST	MAZER	MEALER	MEASED	MEBOS
MAYFISH	MAZERS	MEALERS	MEASES	MEBOSES
MAYFISHES	MAZES	MEALIE	MEASING	MECCA
MAYFLIES	MAZEY	MEALIER	MEASLE	MECCAS
MAYFLOWER	MAZHBI	MEALIEST	MEASLED	MECH
MAYFLY	MAZHBIS	MEALINESS	MEASLES	MECHANIC
MAYHAP	MAZIER	MEALING	MEASLIER	MECHANICS
MAYHAPPEN	MAZIEST	MEALLESS	MEASLIEST	MECHANISE
MAYHEM	MAZILY	MEALS	MEASLING	MECHANISM
MAYHEMS	MAZINESS	MEALTIME	MEASLY	MECHANIST
MAYING	MAZING	MEALTIMES	MEASURE	MECHANIZE
MAYINGS	MAZOURKA	MEALWORM	MEASURED	MECHITZA
MAYO	MAZOURKAS	MEALWORMS	MEASURER	MECHITZAS
MAYOR	MAZOUT	MEALY	MEASURERS	MECHITZOT
MAYORAL	MAZOUTS	MEALYBUG	MEASURES	MECHOUI
MAYORALTY	MAZUMA	MEALYBUGS	MEASURING	MECHOUIS
MAYORESS	MAZUMAS	MEAN	MEAT	MECHS
MAYORS	MAZURKA	MEANDER	MEATAL	MECK
MAYORSHIP	MAZURKAS	MEANDERED	MEATAXE	MECKS
MAYOS	MAZUT	MEANDERER	MEATAXES	MECLIZINE
MAYPOLE	MAZUTS	MEANDERS	MEATBALL	MECONATE
MAYPOLES	MAZY	MEANDRIAN	MEATBALLS	MECONATES
MAYPOP	MAZZARD	MEANDROUS	MEATED	MECONIC
MAYPOPS	MAZZARDS	MEANE	MEATH	MECONIN
MAYS	MBAQANGA	MEANED	MEATHE	MECONINS
MAYST	MBAQANGAS	MEANER	MEATHEAD	MECONIUM
MAYSTER	MBIRA	MEANERS	MEATHEADS	MECONIUMS
MAYSTERS	MBIRAS	MEANES	MEATHES	MED
MAYVIN	ME	MEANEST	MEATHOOK	MEDACCA
MAYVINS	MEACOCK	MEANEST	MEATHOOKS	MEDACCAS

M

MEDAILLON	MEDIATELY	MEDITATED	MEEKEST	MEGAFLOP
MEDAKA	MEDIATES	MEDITATES	MEEKLY	MEGAFLOPS
MEDAKAS	MEDIATING	MEDITATOR	MEEKNESS	MEGAFLORA
MEDAL	MEDIATION	MEDIUM	MEEMIE	MEGAFOG
MEDALED	MEDIATISE	MEDIUMS	MEEMIES	MEGAFOGS
MEDALET	MEDIATIVE	MEDIUS	MEER	MEGAGAUSS
MEDALETS	MEDIATIZE	MEDIUSES	MEERCAT	MEGAHERTZ
MEDALING	MEDIATOR	MEDIVAC	MEERCATS	MEGAHIT
MEDALIST	MEDIATORS	MEDIVACED	MEERED	MEGAHITS
MEDALISTS	MEDIATORY	MEDIVACS	MEERING	MEGAJOULE
MEDALLED	MEDIATRIX	MEDLAR	MEERKAT	MEGALITH
MEDALLIC	MEDIC	MEDLARS	MEERKATS	MEGALITHS
MEDALLING	MEDICABLE	MEDLE	MEERS	MEGALITRE
MEDALLION	MEDICABLY	MEDLED	MEES	MEGALODON
MEDALLIST	MEDICAID	MEDLES	MEET	MEGALOPIC
MEDALPLAY	MEDICAIDS	MEDLEY	MEETER	MEGALOPS
MEDALS	MEDICAL	MEDLEYS	MEETERS	MEGAMALL
MEDCINAL	MEDICALLY	MEDLING	MEETEST	MEGAMALLS
MEDDLE	MEDICALS	MEDRESA	MEETING	MEGAPHONE
MEDDLED	MEDICANT	MEDRESAS	MEETINGS	MEGAPHYLL
MEDDLER	MEDICANTS	MEDRESE	MEETLY	MEGAPIXEL
MEDDLERS	MEDICARE	MEDRESES	MEETNESS	MEGAPLEX
MEDDLES	MEDICARES	MEDRESSEH	MEETS	MEGAPOD
MEDDLING	MEDICATE	MEDS	MEFF	MEGAPODE
MEDDLINGS	MEDICATED	MEDULLA	MEFFS	MEGAPODES
MEDEVAC	MEDICATES	MEDULLAE	MEG	MEGAPODS
MEDEVACED	MEDICIDE	MEDULLAR	MEGA	MEGAQUAKE
MEDEVACS	MEDICIDES	MEDULLARY	MEGABAR	MEGARA
MEDFLIES	MEDICINAL	MEDULLAS	MEGABARS	MEGARAD
MEDFLY	MEDICINE	MEDULLATE	MEGABIT	MEGARADS
MEDIA	MEDICINED	MEDUSA	MEGABITS	MEGARON
MEDIACIES	MEDICINER	MEDUSAE	MEGABUCK	MEGARONS
MEDIACY	MEDICINES	MEDUSAL	MEGABUCKS	MEGASCOPE
MEDIAD	MEDICK	MEDUSAN	MEGABYTE	MEGASPORE
MEDIAE	MEDICKS	MEDUSANS	MEGABYTES	MEGASS
MEDIAEVAL	MEDICO	MEDUSAS	MEGACITY	MEGASSE
MEDIAL	MEDICOS	MEDUSOID	MEGACURIE	MEGASSES
MEDIALLY	MEDICS	MEDUSOIDS	MEGACYCLE	MEGASTAR
MEDIALS	MEDIEVAL	MEE	MEGADEAL	MEGASTARS
MEDIAN	MEDIEVALS	MEED	MEGADEALS	MEGASTORE
MEDIANLY	MEDIGAP	MEEDS	MEGADEATH	MEGASTORM
MEDIANS	MEDIGAPS	MEEK	MEGADOSE	MEGATHERE
MEDIANT	MEDII	MEEKEN	MEGADOSES	MEGATON
MEDIANTS	MEDINA	MEEKENED	MEGADYNE	MEGATONIC
MEDIAS	MEDINAS	MEEKENING	MEGADYNES	MEGATONS
MEDIATE	MEDIOCRE	MEEKENS	MEGAFARAD	MEGAVOLT
MEDIATED	MEDITATE	MEEKER	MEGAFAUNA	MEGAVOLTS

MEGAWATT	MEJLISES	MELAPHYRE	MELLOWED	MELTAGE
MEGAWATTS	MEKKA	MELAS	MELLOWER	MELTAGES
MEGILLA	MEKKAS	MELASTOME	MELLOWEST	MELTDOWN
MEGILLAH	MEKOMETER	MELATONIN	MELLOWING	MELTDOWNS
MEGILLAHS	MEL	MELBA	MELLOWLY	MELTED
MEGILLAS	MELA	MELD	MELLOWS	MELTEMI
MEGILLOTH	MELAENA	MELDED	MELLOWY	MELTEMIS
MEGILP	MELAENAS	MELDER	MELLS	MELTER
MEGILPH	MELALEUCA	MELDERS	MELOCOTON	MELTERS
MEGILPHS	MELAMDIM	MELDING	MELODEON	MELTIER
MEGILPS	MELAMED	MELDS	MELODEONS	MELTIEST
MEGOHM	MELAMINE	MELEE	MELODIA	MELTING
MEGOHMS	MELAMINES	MELEES	MELODIAS	MELTINGLY
MEGRIM	MELAMPODE	MELENA	MELODIC	MELTINGS
MEGRIMS	MELANGE	MELENAS	MELODICA	MELTITH
MEGS	MELANGES	MELIC	MELODICAS	MELTITHS
MEH	MELANIAN	MELICK	MELODICS	MELTON
MEHNDI	MELANIANS	MELICKS	MELODIES	MELTONS
MEHNDIS	MELANIC	MELICS	MELODION	MELTS
MEIBOMIAN	MELANICS	MELIK	MELODIONS	MELTWATER
MEIKLE	MELANIN	MELIKS	MELODIOUS	MELTY
MEIN	MELANINS	MELILITE	MELODISE	MELUNGEON
MEINED	MELANISE	MELILITES	MELODISED	MEM
MEINEY	MELANISED	MELILOT	MELODISER	MEMBER
MEINEYS	MELANISES	MELILOTS	MELODISES	MEMBERED
MEINIE	MELANISM	MELINITE	MELODIST	MEMBERS
MEINIES	MELANISMS	MELINITES	MELODISTS	MEMBRAL
MEINING	MELANIST	MELIORATE	MELODIZE	MEMBRANAL
MEINS	MELANISTS	MELIORISM	MELODIZED	MEMBRANE
MEINT	MELANITE	MELIORIST	MELODIZER	MEMBRANED
MEINY	MELANITES	MELIORITY	MELODIZES	MEMBRANES
MEIOCYTE	MELANITIC	MELISMA	MELODRAMA	MEME
MEIOCYTES	MELANIZE	MELISMAS	MELODRAME	MEMENTO
MEIOFAUNA	MELANIZED	MELISMATA	MELODY	MEMENTOES
MEIONITE	MELANIZES	MELITTIN	MELOID	MEMENTOS
MEIONITES	MELANO	MELITTINS	MELOIDS	MEMES
MEIOSES	MELANOID	MELL	MELOMANIA	MEMETIC
MEIOSIS	MELANOIDS	MELLAY	MELOMANIC	MEMETICS
MEIOSPORE	MELANOMA	MELLAYS	MELON	MEMO
MEIOTIC	MELANOMAS	MELLED	MELONGENE	MEMOIR
MEISHI	MELANOS	MELLIFIC	MELONS	MEMOIRISM
MEISHIS	MELANOSES	MELLING	MELONY	MEMOIRIST
MEISTER	MELANOSIS	MELLITE	MELOXICAM	MEMOIRS
MEISTERS	MELANOTIC	MELLITES	MELPHALAN	MEMORABLE
MEITH	MELANOUS	MELLITIC	MELS	MEMORABLY
MEITHS	MELANURIA	MELLOTRON	MELT	MEMORANDA
MEJLIS	MELANURIC	MELLOW	MELTABLE	MEMORIAL

MEMORIALS	MENDS	MENSAS	MENTORIAL	MERCHETS
MEMORIES	MENE	MENSCH	MENTORING	MERCHILD
MEMORISE	MENED	MENSCHEN	MENTORS	MERCIABLE
MEMORISED	MENEER	MENSCHES	MENTOS	MERCIES
MEMORISER	MENEERS	MENSCHIER	MENTUM	MERCIFIDE
MEMORISES	MENES	MENSCHY	MENU	MERCIFIED
MEMORITER	MENFOLK	MENSE	MENUDO	MERCIFIES
MEMORIZE	MENFOLKS	MENSED	MENUDOS	MERCIFUL
MEMORIZED	MENG	MENSEFUL	MENUISIER	MERCIFY
MEMORIZER	MENGE	MENSELESS	MENUS	MERCILESS
MEMORIZES	MENGED	MENSES	MENYIE	MERCS
MEMORY	MENGES	MENSH	MENYIES	MERCURATE
MEMOS	MENGING	MENSHED	MEOU	MERCURIAL
MEMS	MENGS	MENSHEN	MEOUED	MERCURIC
MEMSAHIB	MENHADEN	MENSHES	MEOUING	MERCURIES
MEMSAHIBS	MENHADENS	MENSHING	MEOUS	MERCURISE
MEN	MENHIR	MENSING	MEOW	MERCURIZE
MENACE	MENHIRS	MENSTRUA	MEOWED	MERCUROUS
MENACED	MENIAL	MENSTRUAL	MEOWING	MERCURY
MENACER	MENIALLY	MENSTRUUM	MEOWS	MERCY
MENACERS	MENIALS	MENSUAL	MEPACRINE	MERDE
MENACES	MENILITE	MENSURAL	MEPHITIC	MERDES
MENACING	MENILITES	MENSWEAR	MEPHITIS	MERE
MENAD	MENING	MENSWEARS	MEPHITISM	MERED
MENADIONE	MENINGEAL	MENT	MERANTI	MEREL
MENADS	MENINGES	MENTA	MERANTIS	MERELL
MENAGE	MENINX	MENTAL	MERBROMIN	MERELLS
MENAGED	MENISCAL	MENTALESE	MERC	MERELS
MENAGERIE	MENISCATE	MENTALISM	MERCADO	MERELY
MENAGES	MENISCI	MENTALIST	MERCADOS	MERENGUE
MENAGING	MENISCOID	MENTALITY	MERCAPTAN	MERENGUES
MENARCHE	MENISCUS	MENTALLY	MERCAPTO	MEREOLOGY
MENARCHES	MENO	MENTATION	MERCAT	MERER
MENAZON	MENOLOGY	MENTEE	MERCATS	MERES
MENAZONS	MENOMINEE	MENTEES	MERCENARY	MERESMAN
MEND	MENOMINI	MENTHENE	MERCER	MERESMEN
MENDABLE	MENOMINIS	MENTHENES	MERCERIES	MEREST
MENDACITY	MENOPAUSE	MENTHOL	MERCERISE	MERESTONE
MENDED	MENOPOLIS	MENTHOLS	MERCERIZE	MERFOLK
MENDER	MENOPOME	MENTICIDE	MERCERS	MERFOLKS
MENDERS	MENOPOMES	MENTION	MERCERY	MERGANSER
MENDICANT	MENORAH	MENTIONED	MERCES	MERGE
MENDICITY	MENORAHS	MENTIONER	MERCH	MERGED
MENDIGO	MENORRHEA	MENTIONS	MERCHANT	MERGEE
MENDIGOS	MENSA	MENTO	MERCHANTS	MERGEES
MENDING	MENSAE	MENTOR	MERCHES	MERGENCE
MENDINGS	MENSAL	MENTORED	MERCHET	MERGENCES

MERGER	MERLOT	MESALLY	MESIAN	MESPRISE
MERGERS	MERLOTS	MESARAIC	MESIC	MESPRISES
MERGES	MERLS	MESARCH	MESICALLY	MESPRIZE
MERGING	MERMAID	MESAS	MESMERIC	MESPRIZES
MERGINGS	MERMAIDEN	MESCAL	MESMERISE	MESQUIN
MERGUEZ	MERMAIDS	MESCALIN	MESMERISM	MESQUINE
MERI	MERMAN	MESCALINE	MESMERIST	MESQUIT
MERICARP	MERMEN	MESCALINS	MESMERIZE	MESQUITE
MERICARPS	MEROCRINE	MESCALISM	MESNALTY	MESQUITES
MERIDIAN	MEROGONY	MESCALS	MESNE	MESQUITS
MERIDIANS	MEROISTIC	MESCLUM	MESNES	MESS
MERIL	MEROME	MESCLUMS	MESOBLAST	MESSAGE
MERILS	MEROMES	MESCLUN	MESOCARP	MESSAGED
MERIMAKE	MERONYM	MESCLUNS	MESOCARPS	MESSAGES
MERIMAKES	MERONYMS	MESDAMES	MESOCRANY	MESSAGING
MERING	MERONYMY	MESE	MESODERM	MESSALINE
MERINGS	MEROPIA	MESEEMED	MESODERMS	MESSAN
MERINGUE	MEROPIAS	MESEEMETH	MESOGLEA	MESSANS
MERINGUES	MEROPIC	MESEEMS	MESOGLEAL	MESSED
MERINO	MEROPIDAN	MESEL	MESOGLEAS	MESSENGER
MERINOS	MEROSOME	MESELED	MESOGLOEA	MESSES
MERIS	MEROSOMES	MESELS	MESOLITE	MESSIAH
MERISES	MEROZOITE	MESENTERA	MESOLITES	MESSIAHS
MERISIS	MERPEOPLE	MESENTERY	MESOMERE	MESSIANIC
MERISM	MERRIE	MESES	MESOMERES	MESSIAS
MERISMS	MERRIER	MESETA	MESOMORPH	MESSIASES
MERISTEM	MERRIES	MESETAS	MESON	MESSIER
MERISTEMS	MERRIEST	MESH	MESONIC	MESSIEST
MERISTIC	MERRILY	MESHED	MESONS	MESSIEURS
MERIT	MERRIMENT	MESHES	MESOPAUSE	MESSILY
MERITED	MERRINESS	MESHIER	MESOPHILE	MESSINESS
MERITING	MERRY	MESHIEST	MESOPHYL	MESSING
MERITLESS	MERRYMAN	MESHING	MESOPHYLL	MESSMAN
MERITS	MERRYMEN	MESHINGS	MESOPHYLS	MESSMATE
MERK	MERSALYL	MESHUGA	MESOPHYTE	MESSMATES
MERKIN	MERSALYLS	MESHUGAAS	MESOSAUR	MESSMEN
MERKINS	MERSE	MESHUGAH	MESOSAURS	MESSUAGE
MERKS	MERSES	MESHUGAS	MESOSCALE	MESSUAGES
MERL	MERSION	MESHUGGA	MESOSOME	MESSY
MERLE	MERSIONS	MESHUGGAH	MESOSOMES	MESTEE
MERLES	MERYCISM	MESHUGGE	MESOTRON	MESTEES
MERLIN	MERYCISMS	MESHWORK	MESOTRONS	MESTER
MERLING	MES	MESHWORKS	MESOZOAN	MESTERS
MERLINGS	MESA	MESHY	MESOZOANS	MESTESO
MERLINS	MESAIL	MESIAD	MESOZOIC	MESTESOES
MERLON	MESAILS	MESIAL	MESPIL	MESTESOS
MERLONS	MESAL	MESIALLY	MESPILS	MESTINO

M

MESTINOES	METALLING	METCAST	METHODIST	METOPON
MESTINOS	METALLISE	METCASTS	METHODIZE	METOPONS
MESTIZA	METALLIST	METE	METHODS	METOPRYL
MESTIZAS	METALLIZE	METED	METHOS	METOPRYLS
MESTIZO	METALLOID	METEOR	METHOUGHT	METRALGIA
MESTIZOES	METALLY	METEORIC	METHOXIDE	METRAZOL
MESTIZOS	METALMARK	METEORISM	METHOXIES	METRAZOLS
MESTO	METALS	METEORIST	METHOXY	METRE
MESTOM	METALWARE	METEORITE	METHOXYL	METRED
MESTOME	METALWORK	METEOROID	METHOXYLS	METRES
MESTOMES	METAMALE	METEOROUS	METHS	METRIC
MESTOMS	METAMALES	METEORS	METHYL	METRICAL
MESTRANOL	METAMER	METEPA	METHYLAL	METRICATE
MET	METAMERAL	METEPAS	METHYLALS	METRICIAN
META	METAMERE	METER	METHYLASE	METRICISE
METABASES	METAMERES	METERAGE	METHYLATE	METRICISM
METABASIS	METAMERIC	METERAGES	METHYLENE	METRICIST
METABATIC	METAMERS	METERED	METHYLIC	METRICIZE
METABOLIC	METAMICT	METERING	METHYLS	METRICS
METABOLY	METANOIA	METERS	METHYSES	METRIFIED
METACARPI	METANOIAS	METES	METHYSIS	METRIFIER
METADATA	METAPELET	METESTICK	METHYSTIC	METRIFIES
METADATAS	METAPHASE	METESTRUS	METIC	METRIFY
METAFILE	METAPHOR	METEWAND	METICAIS	METRING
METAFILES	METAPHORS	METEWANDS	METICAL	METRIST
METAGE	METAPLASM	METEYARD	METICALS	METRISTS
METAGENIC	METAPLOT	METEYARDS	METICS	METRITIS
METAGES	METARCHON	METFORMIN	METIER	METRO
METAIRIE	METASOMA	METH	METIERS	METROLOGY
METAIRIES	METASOMAS	METHADON	METIF	METRONOME
METAL	METATAG	METHADONE	METIFS	METROPLEX
METALED	METATAGS	METHADONS	METING	METROS
METALHEAD	METATARSI	METHANAL	METIS	METS
METALING	METATE	METHANALS	METISSE	METTLE
METALISE	METATES	METHANE	METISSES	METTLED
METALISED	METAVERSE	METHANES	METOL	METTLES
METALISES	METAXYLEM	METHANOIC	METOLS	METUMP
METALIST	METAYAGE	METHANOL	METONYM	METUMPS
METALISTS	METAYAGES	METHANOLS	METONYMIC	MEU
METALIZE	METAYER	METHEGLIN	METONYMS	MEUNIERE
METALIZED	METAYERS	METHINK	METONYMY	MEUS
METALIZES	METAZOA	METHINKS	METOPAE	MEUSE
METALLED	METAZOAL	METHO	METOPE	MEUSED
METALLIC	METAZOAN	METHOD	METOPES	MEUSES
METALLICS	METAZOANS	METHODIC	METOPIC	MEUSING
METALLIKE	METAZOIC	METHODISE	METOPISM	MEVE
METALLINE	METAZOON	METHODISM	METOPISMS	MEVED

MEVES	MGANGA	MICELLAS	MICROBLOG	MICROTOME
MEVING	MGANGAS	MICELLE	MICROBREW	MICROTOMY
MEVROU	MHO	MICELLES	MICROBUS	MICROTONE
MEVROUS	MHORR	MICELLS	MICROCAP	MICROVOLT
MEW	MHORRS	MICH	MICROCAR	MICROWATT
MEWED	MHOS	MICHAEL	MICROCARD	MICROWAVE
MEWING	MI	MICHAELS	MICROCARS	MICROWIRE
MEWL	MIAOU	MICHE	MICROCHIP	MICRURGY
MEWLED	MIAOUED	MICHED	MICROCODE	MICS
MEWLER	MIAOUING	MICHER	MICROCOPY	MICTION
MEWLERS	MIAOUS	MICHERS	MICROCOSM	MICTIONS
MEWLING	MIAOW	MICHES	MICROCYTE	MICTURATE
MEWLS	MIAOWED	MICHIGAN	MICRODONT	MID
MEWS	MIAOWING	MICHIGANS	MICRODOT	MIDAIR
MEWSED	MIAOWS	MICHING	MICRODOTS	MIDAIRS
MEWSES	MIASM	MICHINGS	MICROFILM	MIDBAND
MEWSING	MIASMA	MICHT	MICROFORM	MIDBRAIN
MEYNT	MIASMAL	MICHTS	MICROGLIA	MIDBRAINS
MEZAIL	MIASMAS	MICK	MICROGRAM	MIDCAP
MEZAILS	MIASMATA	MICKERIES	MICROHM	MIDCOURSE
MEZCAL	MIASMATIC	MICKERY	MICROHMS	MIDCULT
MEZCALINE	MIASMIC	MICKEY	MICROINCH	MIDCULTS
MEZCALS	MIASMOUS	MICKEYED	MICROJET	MIDDAY
MEZE	MIASMS	MICKEYING	MICROJETS	MIDDAYS
MEZEREON	MIAUL	MICKEYS	MICROLITE	MIDDEN
MEZEREONS	MIAULED	MICKIES	MICROLITH	MIDDENS
MEZEREUM	MIAULING	MICKLE	MICROLOAN	MIDDEST
MEZEREUMS	MIAULS	MICKLER	MICROLOGY	MIDDIE
MEZES	MIB	MICKLES	MICROLUX	MIDDIES
MEZQUIT	MIBS	MICKLEST	MICROMERE	MIDDLE
MEZQUITE	MIBUNA	MICKS	MICROMESH	MIDDLED
MEZQUITES	MIBUNAS	MICKY	MICROMHO	MIDDLEMAN
MEZQUITS	MIC	MICO	MICROMHOS	MIDDLEMEN
MEZUZA	MICA	MICOS	MICROMINI	MIDDLER
MEZUZAH	MICACEOUS	MICRA	MICROMOLE	MIDDLERS
MEZUZAHS	MICAS	MICRIFIED	MICROMORT	MIDDLES
MEZUZAS	MICATE	MICRIFIES	MICRON	MIDDLING
MEZUZOT	MICATED	MICRIFY	MICRONISE	MIDDLINGS
MEZUZOTH	MICATES	MICRO	MICRONIZE	MIDDORSAL
MEZZ	MICATING	MICROBAR	MICRONS	MIDDY
MEZZALUNA	MICAWBER	MICROBARS	MICROPORE	MIDFIELD
MEZZANINE	MICAWBERS	MICROBE	MICROPSIA	MIDFIELDS
MEZZE	MICE	MICROBEAM	MICROPUMP	MIDGE
MEZZES	MICELL	MICROBES	MICROPYLE	MIDGES
MEZZO	MICELLA	MICROBIAL	MICROS	MIDGET
MEZZOS	MICELLAE	MICROBIAN	MICROSITE	MIDGETS
MEZZOTINT	MICELLAR	MICROBIC	MICROSOME	MIDGIE

M

MIDGIER	MIDSEASON	MIFF	MIHIING	MILDING
MIDGIES	MIDSHIP	MIFFED	MIHIS	MILDISH
MIDGIEST	MIDSHIPS	MIFFIER	MIHRAB	MILDLY
MIDGUT	MIDSHORE	MIFFIEST	MIHRABS	MILDNESS
MIDGUTS	MIDSIZE	MIFFILY	MIJNHEER	MILDS
MIDGY	MIDSIZED	MIFFINESS	MIJNHEERS	MILE
MIDI	MIDSOLE	MIFFING	MIKADO	MILEAGE
MIDINETTE	MIDSOLES	MIFFS	MIKADOS	MILEAGES
MIDIRON	MIDSPACE	MIFFY	MIKE	MILEPOST
MIDIRONS	MIDSPACES	MIFTY	MIKED	MILEPOSTS
MIDIS	MIDST	MIG	MIKES	MILER
MIDISKIRT	MIDSTORY	MIGAWD	MIKING	MILERS
MIDLAND	MIDSTREAM	MIGG	MIKRA	MILES
MIDLANDER	MIDSTS	MIGGLE	MIKRON	MILESIAN
MIDLANDS	MIDSUMMER	MIGGLES	MIKRONS	MILESIMO
MIDLEG	MIDTERM	MIGGS	MIKVA	MILESIMOS
MIDLEGS	MIDTERMS	MIGHT	MIKVAH	MILESTONE
MIDLIFE	MIDTOWN	MIGHTEST	MIKVAHS	MILF
MIDLIFER	MIDTOWNS	MIGHTFUL	MIKVAS	MILFOIL
MIDLIFERS	MIDWATCH	MIGHTIER	MIKVEH	MILFOILS
MIDLINE	MIDWATER	MIGHTIEST	MIKVEHS	MILFS
MIDLINES	MIDWATERS	MIGHTILY	MIKVOS	MILIA
MIDLIST	MIDWAY	MIGHTS	MIKVOT	MILIARIA
MIDLISTS	MIDWAYS	MIGHTST	MIKVOTH	MILIARIAL
MIDLIVES	MIDWEEK	MIGHTY	MIL	MILIARIAS
MIDMONTH	MIDWEEKLY	MIGMATITE	MILADI	MILIARY
MIDMONTHS	MIDWEEKS	MIGNON	MILADIES	MILIEU
MIDMOST	MIDWIFE	MIGNONNE	MILADIS	MILIEUS
MIDMOSTS	MIDWIFED	MIGNONNES	MILADY	MILIEUX
MIDNIGHT	MIDWIFERY	MIGNONS	MILAGE	MILING
MIDNIGHTS	MIDWIFES	MIGRAINE	MILAGES	MILINGS
MIDNOON	MIDWIFING	MIGRAINES	MILCH	MILITANCE
MIDNOONS	MIDWINTER	MIGRANT	MILCHIG	MILITANCY
MIDPAY	MIDWIVE	MIGRANTS	MILCHIK	MILITANT
MIDPOINT	MIDWIVED	MIGRATE	MILD	MILITANTS
MIDPOINTS	MIDWIVES	MIGRATED	MILDED	MILITAR
MIDRANGE	MIDWIVING	MIGRATES	MILDEN	MILITARIA
MIDRANGES	MIDYEAR	MIGRATING	MILDENED	MILITARY
MIDRASH	MIDYEARS	MIGRATION	MILDENING	MILITATE
MIDRASHIC	MIELIE	MIGRATOR	MILDENS	MILITATED
MIDRASHIM	MIELIES	MIGRATORS	MILDER	MILITATES
MIDRASHOT	MIEN	MIGRATORY	MILDEST	MILITIA
MIDRIB	MIENS	MIGS	MILDEW	MILITIAS
MIDRIBS	MIEVE	MIHA	MILDEWED	MILIUM
MIDRIFF	MIEVED	MIHAS	MILDEWING	MILK
MIDRIFFS	MIEVES	MIHI	MILDEWS	MILKED
MIDS	MIEVING	MIHIED	MILDEWY	MILKEN

MILKER	MILLEPEDS	MILLIPED	MILTONIAS	MIMSIER
MILKERS	MILLEPORE	MILLIPEDE	MILTS	MIMSIEST
MILKFISH	MILLER	MILLIPEDS	MILTY	MIMSY
MILKIER	MILLERITE	MILLIREM	MILTZ	MIMULUS
MILKIEST	MILLERS	MILLIREMS	MILTZES	MIMULUSES
MILKILY	MILLES	MILLIVOLT	MILVINE	MINA
MILKINESS	MILLET	MILLIWATT	MIM	MINABLE
MILKING	MILLETS	MILLOCRAT	MIMBAR	MINACIOUS
MILKINGS	MILLHAND	MILLPOND	MIMBARS	MINACITY
MILKLESS	MILLHANDS	MILLPONDS	MIME	MINAE
MILKLIKE	MILLHOUSE	MILLRACE	MIMED	MINAR
MILKMAID	MILLIAMP	MILLRACES	MIMEO	MINARET
MILKMAIDS	MILLIAMPS	MILLRIND	MIMEOED	MINARETED
MILKMAN	MILLIARD	MILLRINDS	MIMEOING	MINARETS
MILKMEN	MILLIARDS	MILLRUN	MIMEOS	MINARS
MILKO	MILLIARE	MILLRUNS	MIMER	MINAS
MILKOS	MILLIARES	MILLS	MIMERS	MINATORY
MILKS	MILLIARY	MILLSCALE	MIMES	MINBAR
MILKSHAKE	MILLIBAR	MILLSTONE	MIMESES	MINBARS
MILKSHED	MILLIBARS	MILLTAIL	MIMESIS	MINCE
MILKSHEDS	MILLIE	MILLTAILS	MIMESISES	MINCED
MILKSOP	MILLIEME	MILLWHEEL	MIMESTER	MINCEMEAT
MILKSOPPY	MILLIEMES	MILLWORK	MIMESTERS	MINCER
MILKSOPS	MILLIER	MILLWORKS	MIMETIC	MINCERS
MILKTOAST	MILLIERS	MILNEB	MIMETICAL	MINCES
MILKWEED	MILLIES	MILNEBS	MIMETITE	MINCEUR
MILKWEEDS	MILLIGAL	MILO	MIMETITES	MINCIER
MILKWOOD	MILLIGALS	MILOMETER	MIMIC	MINCIEST
MILKWOODS	MILLIGRAM	MILOR	MIMICAL	MINCING
MILKWORT	MILLILUX	MILORD	MIMICKED	MINCINGLY
MILKWORTS	MILLIME	MILORDS	MIMICKER	MINCY
MILKY	MILLIMES	MILORS	MIMICKERS	MIND
MILL	MILLIMHO	MILOS	MIMICKING	MINDED
MILLABLE	MILLIMHOS	MILPA	MIMICRIES	MINDEDLY
MILLAGE	MILLIMOLE	MILPAS	MIMICRY	MINDER
MILLAGES	MILLINE	MILREIS	MIMICS	MINDERS
MILLBOARD	MILLINER	MILS	MIMING	MINDFUCK
MILLCAKE	MILLINERS	MILSEY	MIMIVIRUS	MINDFUCKS
MILLCAKES	MILLINERY	MILSEYS	MIMMER	MINDFUL
MILLDAM	MILLINES	MILT	MIMMEST	MINDFULLY
MILLDAMS	MILLING	MILTED	MIMMICK	MINDING
MILLE	MILLINGS	MILTER	MIMMICKED	MINDINGS
MILLED	MILLIOHM	MILTERS	MIMMICKS	MINDLESS
MILLENARY	MILLIOHMS	MILTIER	MIMOSA	MINDS
MILLENNIA	MILLION	MILTIEST	MIMOSAE	MINDSET
MILLEPED	MILLIONS	MILTING	MIMOSAS	MINDSETS
MILLEPEDE	MILLIONTH	MILTONIA	MIMSEY	MINDSHARE

MINE	MINIBIKE	MINIMILLS	MINIUMS	MINTERS
MINEABLE	MINIBIKER	MINIMISE	MINIVAN	MINTIER
MINED	MINIBIKES	MINIMISED	MINIVANS	MINTIEST
MINEFIELD	MINIBREAK	MINIMISER	MINIVER	MINTING
MINELAYER	MINIBUS	MINIMISES	MINIVERS	MINTS
MINEOLA	MINIBUSES	MINIMISM	MINIVET	MINTY
MINEOLAS	MINICAB	MINIMISMS	MINIVETS	MINUEND
MINER	MINICABS	MINIMIST	MINK	MINUENDS
MINERAL	MINICAM	MINIMISTS	MINKE	MINUET
MINERALS	MINICAMP	MINIMIZE	MINKES	MINUETED
MINERS	MINICAMPS	MINIMIZED	MINKS	MINUETING
MINES	MINICAMS	MINIMIZER	MINNEOLA	MINUETS
MINESHAFT	MINICAR	MINIMIZES	MINNEOLAS	MINUS
MINESTONE	MINICARS	MINIMOTO	MINNICK	MINUSCULE
MINETTE	MINICOM	MINIMOTOS	MINNICKED	MINUSES
MINETTES	MINICOMS	MINIMS	MINNICKS	MINUTE
MINEVER	MINIDISC	MINIMUM	MINNIE	MINUTED
MINEVERS	MINIDISCS	MINIMUMS	MINNIES	MINUTELY
MING	MINIDISH	MINIMUS	MINNOCK	MINUTEMAN
MINGE	MINIDISK	MINIMUSES	MINNOCKED	MINUTEMEN
MINGED	MINIDISKS	MINING	MINNOCKS	MINUTER
MINGER	MINIDRESS	MININGS	MINNOW	MINUTES
MINGERS	MINIER	MINION	MINNOWS	MINUTEST
MINGES	MINIEST	MINIONS	MINNY	MINUTIA
MINGIER	MINIFIED	MINIPARK	MINO	MINUTIAE
MINGIEST	MINIFIES	MINIPARKS	MINOR	MINUTIAL
MINGILY	MINIFY	MINIPILL	MINORCA	MINUTING
MINGINESS	MINIFYING	MINIPILLS	MINORCAS	MINUTIOSE
MINGING	MINIGOLF	MINIRUGBY	MINORED	MINX
MINGLE	MINIGOLFS	MINIS	MINORING	MINXES
MINGLED	MINIKIN	MINISCULE	MINORITY	MINXISH
MINGLER	MINIKINS	MINISH	MINORS	MINY
MINGLERS	MINILAB	MINISHED	MINORSHIP	MINYAN
MINGLES	MINILABS	MINISHES	MINOS	MINYANIM
MINGLING	MINIM	MINISHING	MINOTAUR	MINYANS
MINGLINGS	MINIMA	MINISKI	MINOXIDIL	MIOCENE
MINGS	MINIMAL	MINISKIRT	MINSHUKU	MIOMBO
MINGY	MINIMALLY	MINISKIS	MINSHUKUS	MIOMBOS
MINI	MINIMALS	MINISODE	MINSTER	MIOSES
MINIATE	MINIMART	MINISODES	MINSTERS	MIOSIS
MINIATED	MINIMARTS	MINISTATE	MINSTREL	MIOSISES
MINIATES	MINIMAX	MINISTER	MINSTRELS	MIOTIC
MINIATING	MINIMAXED	MINISTERS	MINT	MIOTICS
MINIATION	MINIMAXES	MINISTRY	MINTAGE	MIPS
MINIATURE	MINIMENT	MINITOWER	MINTAGES	MIQUELET
MINIBAR	MINIMENTS	MINITRACK	MINTED	MIQUELETS
MINIBARS	MINIMILL	MINIUM	MINTER	MIR

MIRABELLE	MIRLITON	MISALLIES	MISBRANDS	MISCOPIED
MIRABILIA	MIRLITONS	MISALLOT	MISBUILD	MISCOPIES
MIRABILIS	MIRLY	MISALLOTS	MISBUILDS	MISCOPY
MIRABLE	MIRO	MISALLY	MISBUILT	MISCOUNT
MIRACIDIA	MIROMIRO	MISALTER	MISBUTTON	MISCOUNTS
MIRACLE	MIROMIROS	MISALTERS	MISCALL	MISCREANT
MIRACLES	MIROS	MISANDRY	MISCALLED	MISCREATE
MIRADOR	MIRROR	MISAPPLY	MISCALLER	MISCREDIT
MIRADORS	MIRRORED	MISARRAY	MISCALLS	MISCREED
MIRAGE	MIRRORING	MISARRAYS	MISCARRY	MISCREEDS
MIRAGES	MIRRORS	MISASSAY	MISCAST	MISCUE
MIRANDISE	MIRS	MISASSAYS	MISCASTS	MISCUED
MIRANDIZE	MIRTH	MISASSIGN	MISCEGEN	MISCUEING
MIRBANE	MIRTHFUL	MISATE	MISCEGENE	MISCUES
MIRBANES	MIRTHLESS	MISATONE	MISCEGENS	MISCUING
MIRCHI	MIRTHS	MISATONED	MISCEGINE	MISCUT
MIRE	MIRV	MISATONES	MISCH	MISCUTS
MIRED	MIRVED	MISAUNTER	MISCHANCE	MISDATE
MIREPOIX	MIRVING	MISAVER	MISCHANCY	MISDATED
MIRES	MIRVS	MISAVERS	MISCHARGE	MISDATES
MIREX	MIRY	MISAVISED	MISCHIEF	MISDATING
MIREXES	MIRZA	MISAWARD	MISCHIEFS	MISDEAL
MIRI	MIRZAS	MISAWARDS	MISCHOICE	MISDEALER
MIRID	MIS	MISBECAME	MISCHOOSE	MISDEALS
MIRIDS	MISACT	MISBECOME	MISCHOSE	MISDEALT
MIRIER	MISACTED	MISBEGAN	MISCHOSEN	MISDEED
MIRIEST	MISACTING	MISBEGIN	MISCIBLE	MISDEEDS
MIRIFIC	MISACTS	MISBEGINS	MISCITE	MISDEEM
MIRIFICAL	MISADAPT	MISBEGOT	MISCITED	MISDEEMED
MIRIN	MISADAPTS	MISBEGUN	MISCITES	MISDEEMS
MIRINESS	MISADD	MISBEHAVE	MISCITING	MISDEFINE
MIRING	MISADDED	MISBELIEF	MISCLAIM	MISDEMEAN
MIRINS	MISADDING	MISBESEEM	MISCLAIMS	MISDEMPT
MIRITI	MISADDS	MISBESTOW	MISCLASS	MISDESERT
MIRITIS	MISADJUST	MISBIAS	MISCODE	MISDIAL
MIRK	MISADVICE	MISBIASED	MISCODED	MISDIALED
MIRKER	MISADVISE	MISBIASES	MISCODES	MISDIALS
MIRKEST	MISAGENT	MISBILL	MISCODING	MISDID
MIRKIER	MISAGENTS	MISBILLED	MISCOIN	MISDIET
MIRKIEST	MISAIM	MISBILLS	MISCOINED	MISDIETED
MIRKILY	MISAIMED	MISBIND	MISCOINS	MISDIETS
MIRKINESS	MISAIMING	MISBINDS	MISCOLOR	MISDIGHT
MIRKS	MISAIMS	MISBIRTH	MISCOLORS	MISDIGHTS
MIRKY	MISALIGN	MISBIRTHS	MISCOLOUR	MISDIRECT
MIRLIER	MISALIGNS	MISBORN	MISCOOK	MISDIVIDE
MIRLIEST	MISALLEGE	MISBOUND	MISCOOKED	MISDO
MIRLIGOES	MISALLIED	MISBRAND	MISCOOKS	MISDOER

MISDOERS	MISES	MISGIVES	MISINFERS	MISLEARED
MISDOES	MISESTEEM	MISGIVING	MISINFORM	MISLEARN
MISDOING	MISEVENT	MISGO	MISINTEND	MISLEARNS
MISDOINGS	MISEVENTS	MISGOES	MISINTER	MISLEARNT
MISDONE	MISFAITH	MISGOING	MISINTERS	MISLED
MISDONNE	MISFAITHS	MISGONE	MISJOIN	MISLEEKE
MISDOUBT	MISFALL	MISGOTTEN	MISJOINED	MISLEEKED
MISDOUBTS	MISFALLEN	MISGOVERN	MISJOINS	MISLEEKES
MISDRAW	MISFALLS	MISGRADE	MISJUDGE	MISLETOE
MISDRAWN	MISFALNE	MISGRADED	MISJUDGED	MISLETOES
MISDRAWS	MISFARE	MISGRADES	MISJUDGER	MISLIE
MISDREAD	MISFARED	MISGRAFF	MISJUDGES	MISLIES
MISDREADS	MISFARES	MISGRAFT	MISKAL	MISLIGHT
MISDREW	MISFARING	MISGRAFTS	MISKALS	MISLIGHTS
MISDRIVE	MISFEASOR	MISGREW	MISKEEP	MISLIKE
MISDRIVEN	MISFED	MISGROW	MISKEEPS	MISLIKED
MISDRIVES	MISFEED	MISGROWN	MISKEN	MISLIKER
MISDROVE	MISFEEDS	MISGROWS	MISKENNED	MISLIKERS
MISE	MISFEIGN	MISGROWTH	MISKENS	MISLIKES
MISEASE	MISFEIGNS	MISGUESS	MISKENT	MISLIKING
MISEASES	MISFELL	MISGUGGLE	MISKEPT	MISLIPPEN
MISEAT	MISFIELD	MISGUIDE	MISKEY	MISLIT
MISEATEN	MISFIELDS	MISGUIDED	MISKEYED	MISLIVE
MISEATING	MISFILE	MISGUIDER	MISKEYING	MISLIVED
MISEATS	MISFILED	MISGUIDES	MISKEYS	MISLIVES
MISEDIT	MISFILES	MISHANDLE	MISKICK	MISLIVING
MISEDITED	MISFILING	MISHANTER	MISKICKED	MISLOCATE
MISEDITS	MISFIRE	MISHAP	MISKICKS	MISLODGE
MISEMPLOY	MISFIRED	MISHAPPED	MISKNEW	MISLODGED
MISENROL	MISFIRES	MISHAPPEN	MISKNOW	MISLODGES
MISENROLL	MISFIRING	MISHAPS	MISKNOWN	MISLUCK
MISENROLS	MISFIT	MISHAPT	MISKNOWS	MISLUCKED
MISENTER	MISFITS	MISHEAR	MISLABEL	MISLUCKS
MISENTERS	MISFITTED	MISHEARD	MISLABELS	MISLYING
MISENTRY	MISFOCUS	MISHEARS	MISLABOR	MISMADE
MISER	MISFORM	MISHEGAAS	MISLABORS	MISMAKE
MISERABLE	MISFORMED	MISHEGOSS	MISLABOUR	MISMAKES
MISERABLY	MISFORMS	MISHIT	MISLAID	MISMAKING
MISERE	MISFRAME	MISHITS	MISLAIN	MISMANAGE
MISERERE	MISFRAMED	MISHMASH	MISLAY	MISMARK
MISERERES	MISFRAMES	MISHMEE	MISLAYER	MISMARKED
MISERES	MISGAUGE	MISHMEES	MISLAYERS	MISMARKS
MISERIES	MISGAUGED	MISHMI	MISLAYING	MISMARRY
MISERLIER	MISGAUGES	MISHMIS	MISLAYS	MISMATCH
MISERLY	MISGAVE	MISHMOSH	MISLEAD	MISMATE
MISERS	MISGIVE	MISHUGAS	MISLEADER	MISMATED
MISERY	MISGIVEN	MISINFER	MISLEADS	MISMATES

MISMATING	MISPHRASE	MISREADS	MISSENDS	MISSPEAK
MISMEET	MISPICKEL	MISRECKON	MISSENSE	MISSPEAKS
MISMEETS	MISPLACE	MISRECORD	MISSENSED	MISSPELL
MISMET	MISPLACED	MISREFER	MISSENSES	MISSPELLS
MISMETRE	MISPLACES	MISREFERS	MISSENT	MISSPELT
MISMETRED	MISPLAN	MISREGARD	MISSES	MISSPEND
MISMETRES	MISPLANS	MISRELATE	MISSET	MISSPENDS
MISMOVE	MISPLANT	MISRELIED	MISSETS	MISSPENT
MISMOVED	MISPLANTS	MISRELIES	MISSHAPE	MISSPOKE
MISMOVES	MISPLAY	MISRELY	MISSHAPED	MISSPOKEN
MISMOVING	MISPLAYED	MISRENDER	MISSHAPEN	MISSTAMP
MISNAME	MISPLAYS	MISREPORT	MISSHAPER	MISSTAMPS
MISNAMED	MISPLEAD	MISRHYMED	MISSHAPES	MISSTART
MISNAMES	MISPLEADS	MISROUTE	MISSHOD	MISSTARTS
MISNAMING	MISPLEASE	MISROUTED	MISSHOOD	MISSTATE
MISNOMER	MISPLED	MISROUTES	MISSHOODS	MISSTATED
MISNOMERS	MISPOINT	MISRULE	MISSIER	MISSTATES
MISNUMBER	MISPOINTS	MISRULED	MISSIES	MISSTEER
MISO	MISPOISE	MISRULES	MISSIEST	MISSTEERS
MISOCLERE	MISPOISED	MISRULING	MISSILE	MISSTEP
MISOGAMIC	MISPOISES	MISS	MISSILEER	MISSTEPS
MISOGAMY	MISPRAISE	MISSA	MISSILERY	MISSTOP
MISOGYNIC	MISPRICE	MISSABLE	MISSILES	MISSTOPS
MISOGYNY	MISPRICED	MISSAE	MISSILRY	MISSTRIKE
MISOLOGY	MISPRICES	MISSAID	MISSING	MISSTRUCK
MISONEISM	MISPRINT	MISSAL	MISSINGLY	MISSTYLE
MISONEIST	MISPRINTS	MISSALS	MISSION	MISSTYLED
MISORDER	MISPRISE	MISSAW	MISSIONAL	MISSTYLES
MISORDERS	MISPRISED	MISSAY	MISSIONED	MISSUIT
MISORIENT	MISPRISES	MISSAYING	MISSIONER	MISSUITED
MISOS	MISPRIZE	MISSAYS	MISSIONS	MISSUITS
MISPAGE	MISPRIZED	MISSEAT	MISSIS	MISSUS
MISPAGED	MISPRIZER	MISSEATED	MISSISES	MISSUSES
MISPAGES	MISPRIZES	MISSEATS	MISSISH	MISSY
MISPAGING	MISPROUD	MISSED	MISSIVE	MIST
MISPAINT	MISQUOTE	MISSEE	MISSIVES	MISTAKE
MISPAINTS	MISQUOTED	MISSEEING	MISSOLD	MISTAKEN
MISPARSE	MISQUOTER	MISSEEM	MISSORT	MISTAKER
MISPARSED	MISQUOTES	MISSEEMED	MISSORTED	MISTAKERS
MISPARSES	MISRAISE	MISSEEMS	MISSORTS	MISTAKES
MISPART	MISRAISED	MISSEEN	MISSOUND	MISTAKING
MISPARTED	MISRAISES	MISSEES	MISSOUNDS	MISTAL
MISPARTS	MISRATE	MISSEL	MISSOUT	MISTALS
MISPATCH	MISRATED	MISSELL	MISSOUTS	MISTAUGHT
MISPEN	MISRATES	MISSELLS	MISSPACE	MISTBOW
MISPENNED	MISRATING	MISSELS	MISSPACED	MISTBOWS
MISPENS	MISREAD	MISSEND	MISSPACES	MISTEACH

MISTED	MISTOUCH	MISWEENS	MITOGENIC	MIXINGS
MISTELL	MISTRACE	MISWEND	MITOGENS	MIXMASTER
MISTELLS	MISTRACED	MISWENDS	MITOMYCIN	MIXOLOGY
MISTEMPER	MISTRACES	MISWENT	MITOSES	MIXT
MISTEND	MISTRAIN	MISWORD	MITOSIS	MIXTAPE
MISTENDED	MISTRAINS	MISWORDED	MITOTIC	MIXTAPES
MISTENDS	MISTRAL	MISWORDS	MITRAILLE	MIXTE
MISTER	MISTRALS	MISWRIT	MITRAL	MIXTION
MISTERED	MISTREAT	MISWRITE	MITRE	MIXTIONS
MISTERIES	MISTREATS	MISWRITES	MITRED	MIXTURE
MISTERING	MISTRESS	MISWROTE	MITRES	MIXTURES
MISTERM	MISTRIAL	MISYOKE	MITREWORT	MIXUP
MISTERMED	MISTRIALS	MISYOKED	MITRIFORM	MIXUPS
MISTERMS	MISTRUST	MISYOKES	MITRING	MIXY
MISTERS	MISTRUSTS	MISYOKING	MITSVAH	MIZ
MISTERY	MISTRUTH	MITCH	MITSVAHS	MIZEN
MISTEUK	MISTRUTHS	MITCHED	MITSVOTH	MIZENMAST
MISTFUL	MISTRYST	MITCHES	MITT	MIZENS
MISTHINK	MISTRYSTS	MITCHING	MITTEN	MIZMAZE
MISTHINKS	MISTS	MITE	MITTENED	MIZMAZES
MISTHREW	MISTUNE	MITER	MITTENS	MIZUNA
MISTHROW	MISTUNED	MITERED	MITTIMUS	MIZUNAS
MISTHROWN	MISTUNES	MITERER	MITTS	MIZZ
MISTHROWS	MISTUNING	MITERERS	MITUMBA	MIZZEN
MISTICO	MISTUTOR	MITERING	MITUMBAS	MIZZENS
MISTICOS	MISTUTORS	MITERS	MITY	MIZZES
MISTIER	MISTY	MITERWORT	MITZVAH	MIZZLE
MISTIEST	MISTYPE	MITES	MITZVAHS	MIZZLED
MISTIGRIS	MISTYPED	MITHER	MITZVOTH	MIZZLES
MISTILY	MISTYPES	MITHERED	MIURUS	MIZZLIER
MISTIME	MISTYPING	MITHERING	MIURUSES	MIZZLIEST
MISTIMED	MISUNION	MITHERS	MIX	MIZZLING
MISTIMES	MISUNIONS	MITICIDAL	MIXABLE	MIZZLINGS
MISTIMING	MISUSAGE	MITICIDE	MIXDOWN	MIZZLY
MISTINESS	MISUSAGES	MITICIDES	MIXDOWNS	MIZZONITE
MISTING	MISUSE	MITIER	MIXED	MIZZY
MISTINGS	MISUSED	MITIEST	MIXEDLY	MM
MISTITLE	MISUSER	MITIGABLE	MIXEDNESS	MMM
MISTITLED	MISUSERS	MITIGANT	MIXEN	MNA
MISTITLES	MISUSES	MITIGANTS	MIXENS	MNAS
MISTLE	MISUSING	MITIGATE	MIXER	MNEME
MISTLED	MISUST	MITIGATED	MIXERS	MNEMES
MISTLES	MISVALUE	MITIGATES	MIXES	MNEMIC
MISTLETOE	MISVALUED	MITIGATOR	MIXIBLE	MNEMON
MISTLING	MISVALUES	MITIS	MIXIER	MNEMONIC
MISTOLD	MISWEEN	MITISES	MIXIEST	MNEMONICS
MISTOOK	MISWEENED	MITOGEN	MIXING	MNEMONIST

MNEMONS	MOBIES	MOCHILAS	MODDED	MODERNS
MO	MOBILE	MOCHINESS	MODDER	MODERS
MOA	MOBILES	MOCHING	MODDERS	MODES
MOAI	MOBILISE	MOCHIS	MODDING	MODEST
MOAN	MOBILISED	MOCHS	MODDINGS	MODESTER
MOANED	MOBILISER	MOCHY	MODE	MODESTEST
MOANER	MOBILISES	MOCK	MODEL	MODESTIES
MOANERS	MOBILITY	MOCKABLE	MODELED	MODESTLY
MOANFUL	MOBILIZE	MOCKADO	MODELER	MODESTY
MOANFULLY	MOBILIZED	MOCKADOES	MODELERS	MODGE
MOANING	MOBILIZER	MOCKAGE	MODELING	MODGED
MOANINGLY	MOBILIZES	MOCKAGES	MODELINGS	MODGES
MOANINGS	MOBISODE	MOCKED	MODELIST	MODGING
MOANS	MOBISODES	MOCKER	MODELISTS	MODI
MOAS	MOBLE	MOCKERED	MODELLED	MODICA
MOAT	MOBLED	MOCKERIES	MODELLER	MODICUM
MOATED	MOBLES	MOCKERING	MODELLERS	MODICUMS
MOATING	MOBLING	MOCKERNUT	MODELLI	MODIFIED
MOATLIKE	MOBLOG	MOCKERS	MODELLING	MODIFIER
MOATS	MOBLOGGER	MOCKERY	MODELLIST	MODIFIERS
MOB	MOBLOGS	MOCKING	MODELLO	MODIFIES
MOBBED	MOBOCRACY	MOCKINGLY	MODELLOS	MODIFY
MOBBER	MOBOCRAT	MOCKINGS	MODELS	MODIFYING
MOBBERS	MOBOCRATS	MOCKNEY	MODEM	MODII
MOBBIE	MOBS	MOCKNEYS	MODEMED	MODILLION
MOBBIES	MOBSMAN	MOCKS	MODEMING	MODIOLAR
MOBBING	MOBSMEN	MOCKTAIL	MODEMS	MODIOLI
MOBBINGS	MOBSTER	MOCKTAILS	MODENA	MODIOLUS
MOBBISH	MOBSTERS	MOCKUP	MODENAS	MODISH
MOBBISHLY	MOBY	MOCKUPS	MODER	MODISHLY
MOBBISM	MOC	MOCOCK	MODERATE	MODIST
MOBBISMS	MOCASSIN	MOCOCKS	MODERATED	MODISTE
MOBBLE	MOCASSINS	MOCS	MODERATES	MODISTES
MOBBLED	MOCCASIN	MOCUCK	MODERATO	MODISTS
MOBBLES	MOCCASINS	MOCUCKS	MODERATOR	MODIUS
MOBBLING	MOCCIES	MOCUDDUM	MODERATOS	MODIWORT
MOBBY	MOCH	MOCUDDUMS	MODERN	MODIWORTS
MOBCAP	MOCHA	MOD	MODERNE	MODS
MOBCAPS	MOCHAS	MODAFINIL	MODERNER	MODULAR
MOBCAST	MOCHED	MODAL	MODERNES	MODULARLY
MOBCASTED	MOCHELL	MODALISM	MODERNEST	MODULARS
MOBCASTS	MOCHELLS	MODALISMS	MODERNISE	MODULATE
MOBE	MOCHI	MODALIST	MODERNISM	MODULATED
MOBES	MOCHIE	MODALISTS	MODERNIST	MODULATES
MOBEY	MOCHIER	MODALITY	MODERNITY	MODULATOR
MOBEYS	MOCHIEST	MODALLY	MODERNIZE	MODULE
MOBIE	MOCHILA	MODALS	MODERNLY	MODULES

MODULI	MOHOS	MOISTURE	MOLDED	MOLLAS
MODULO	MOHR	MOISTURES	MOLDER	MOLLIE
MODULUS	MOHRS	MOIT	MOLDERED	MOLLIES
MODUS	MOHUA	MOITHER	MOLDERING	MOLLIFIED
MOE	MOHUAS	MOITHERED	MOLDERS	MOLLIFIER
MOELLON	MOHUR	MOITHERS	MOLDIER	MOLLIFIES
MOELLONS	MOHURS	MOITS	MOLDIEST	MOLLIFY
MOER	MOI	MOJAHEDIN	MOLDINESS	MOLLITIES
MOERED	MOIDER	MOJARRA	MOLDING	MOLLS
MOERING	MOIDERED	MOJARRAS	MOLDINGS	MOLLUSC
MOERS	MOIDERING	MOJITO	MOLDS	MOLLUSCA
MOES	MOIDERS	MOJITOS	MOLDWARP	MOLLUSCAN
MOFETTE	MOIDORE	MOJO	MOLDWARPS	MOLLUSCS
MOFETTES	MOIDORES	MOJOES	MOLDY	MOLLUSCUM
MOFFETTE	MOIETIES	MOJOS	MOLE	MOLLUSK
MOFFETTES	MOIETY	MOKADDAM	MOLECAST	MOLLUSKAN
MOFFIE	MOIL	MOKADDAMS	MOLECASTS	MOLLUSKS
MOFFIES	MOILE	MOKE	MOLECULAR	MOLLY
MOFO	MOILED	MOKES	MOLECULE	MOLLYHAWK
MOFOS	MOILER	MOKI	MOLECULES	MOLLYMAWK
MOFUSSIL	MOILERS	MOKIHI	MOLED	MOLOCH
MOFUSSILS	MOILES	MOKIHIS	MOLEHILL	MOLOCHISE
MOG	MOILING	MOKIS	MOLEHILLS	MOLOCHIZE
MOGGAN	MOILINGLY	MOKO	MOLEHUNT	MOLOCHS
MOGGANS	MOILS	MOKOMOKO	MOLEHUNTS	MOLOSSI
MOGGED	MOINEAU	MOKOMOKOS	MOLES	MOLOSSUS
MOGGIE	MOINEAUS	MOKOPUNA	MOLESKIN	MOLS
MOGGIES	MOIRA	MOKOPUNAS	MOLESKINS	MOLT
MOGGING	MOIRAI	MOKORO	MOLEST	MOLTED
MOGGY	MOIRE	MOKOROS	MOLESTED	MOLTEN
MOGHUL	MOIRES	MOKOS	MOLESTER	MOLTENLY
MOGHULS	MOISER	MOKSHA	MOLESTERS	MOLTER
MOGS	MOISERS	MOKSHAS	MOLESTFUL	MOLTERS
MOGUL	MOIST	MOL	MOLESTING	MOLTING
MOGULED	MOISTED	MOLA	MOLESTS	MOLTO
MOGULS	MOISTEN	MOLAL	MOLIES	MOLTS
MOHAIR	MOISTENED	MOLALITY	MOLIMEN	MOLY
MOHAIRS	MOISTENER	MOLAR	MOLIMENS	MOLYBDATE
MOHALIM	MOISTENS	MOLARITY	MOLINE	MOLYBDIC
MOHAWK	MOISTER	MOLARS	MOLINES	MOLYBDOUS
MOHAWKS	MOISTEST	MOLAS	MOLINET	MOLYS
MOHEL	MOISTFUL	MOLASSE	MOLINETS	MOM
MOHELIM	MOISTIFY	MOLASSES	MOLING	MOME
MOHELS	MOISTING	MOLD	MOLL	MOMENT
MOHICAN	MOISTLY	MOLDABLE	MOLLA	MOMENTA
MOHICANS	MOISTNESS	MOLDAVITE	MOLLAH	MOMENTANY
MOHO	MOISTS	MOLDBOARD	MOLLAHS	MOMENTARY

MOMENTLY	MONADS	MONERGISM	MONGRELS	MONKEYPOT
MOMENTO	MONAL	MONERON	MONGS	MONKEYPOX
MOMENTOES	MONALS	MONETARY	MONGST	MONKEYS
MOMENTOS	MONAMINE	MONETH	MONIAL	MONKFISH
MOMENTOUS	MONAMINES	MONETHS	MONIALS	MONKHOOD
MOMENTS	MONANDRY	MONETISE	MONIC	MONKHOODS
MOMENTUM	MONARCH	MONETISED	MONICKER	MONKISH
MOMENTUMS	MONARCHAL	MONETISES	MONICKERS	MONKISHLY
MOMES	MONARCHIC	MONETIZE	MONIE	MONKS
MOMI	MONARCHS	MONETIZED	MONIED	MONKSHOOD
MOMISM	MONARCHY	MONETIZES	MONIES	MONO
MOMISMS	MONARDA	MONEY	MONIKER	MONOACID
MOMMA	MONARDAS	MONEYBAG	MONIKERED	MONOACIDS
MOMMAS	MONAS	MONEYBAGS	MONIKERS	MONOAMINE
MOMMET	MONASES	MONEYBOX	MONILIA	MONOAO
MOMMETS	MONASTERY	MONEYED	MONILIAE	MONOAOS
MOMMIES	MONASTIC	MONEYER	MONILIAL	MONOBASIC
MOMMY	MONASTICS	MONEYERS	MONILIAS	MONOBLOC
MOMOIR	MONATOMIC	MONEYLESS	MONIMENT	MONOBROW
MOMOIRS	MONAUL	MONEYMAN	MONIMENTS	MONOBROWS
MOMS	MONAULS	MONEYMEN	MONIPLIES	MONOCARP
MOMSER	MONAURAL	MONEYS	MONISH	MONOCARPS
MOMSERS	MONAXIAL	MONEYWORT	MONISHED	MONOCEROS
MOMUS	MONAXON	MONG	MONISHES	MONOCHORD
MOMUSES	MONAXONIC	MONGCORN	MONISHING	MONOCLE
MOMZER	MONAXONS	MONGCORNS	MONISM	MONOCLED
MOMZERIM	MONAZITE	MONGED	MONISMS	MONOCLES
MOMZERS	MONAZITES	MONGEESE	MONIST	MONOCLINE
MON	MONDAIN	MONGER	MONISTIC	MONOCOQUE
MONA	MONDAINE	MONGERED	MONISTS	MONOCOT
MONACHAL	MONDAINES	MONGERIES	MONITION	MONOCOTS
MONACHISM	MONDAINS	MONGERING	MONITIONS	MONOCOTYL
MONACHIST	MONDE	MONGERS	MONITIVE	MONOCRACY
MONACID	MONDES	MONGERY	MONITOR	MONOCRAT
MONACIDIC	MONDIAL	MONGO	MONITORED	MONOCRATS
MONACIDS	MONDO	MONGOE	MONITORS	MONOCROP
MONACT	MONDOS	MONGOES	MONITORY	MONOCROPS
MONACTINE	MONECIAN	MONGOL	MONITRESS	MONOCULAR
MONACTS	MONECIOUS	MONGOLIAN	MONK	MONOCYCLE
MONAD	MONELLIN	MONGOLISM	MONKERIES	MONOCYTE
MONADAL	MONELLINS	MONGOLOID	MONKERY	MONOCYTES
MONADES	MONEME	MONGOLS	MONKEY	MONOCYTIC
MONADIC	MONEMES	MONGOOSE	MONKEYED	MONODIC
MONADICAL	MONER	MONGOOSES	MONKEYING	MONODICAL
MONADISM	MONERA	MONGOS	MONKEYISH	MONODIES
MONADISMS	MONERAN	MONGREL	MONKEYISM	MONODIST
MONADNOCK	MONERANS	MONGRELLY	MONKEYPOD	MONODISTS

MONODONT	MONOMERS	MONOSTELY	MONTARIA	MOODINESS
MONODRAMA	MONOMETER	MONOSTICH	MONTARIAS	MOODS
MONODY	MONOMIAL	MONOSTOME	MONTE	MOODY
MONOECIES	MONOMIALS	MONOSTYLE	MONTEITH	MOODYING
MONOECISM	MONOMODE	MONOSY	MONTEITHS	MOOED
MONOECY	MONONYM	MONOTASK	MONTEM	MOOI
MONOESTER	MONONYMS	MONOTASKS	MONTEMS	MOOING
MONOFIL	MONOPHAGY	MONOTINT	MONTERO	MOOK
MONOFILS	MONOPHASE	MONOTINTS	MONTEROS	MOOKS
MONOFUEL	MONOPHONY	MONOTONE	MONTES	MOOKTAR
MONOFUELS	MONOPHYLY	MONOTONED	MONTH	MOOKTARS
MONOGAMIC	MONOPITCH	MONOTONES	MONTHLIES	MOOL
MONOGAMY	MONOPLANE	MONOTONIC	MONTHLING	MOOLA
MONOGENIC	MONOPLOID	MONOTONY	MONTHLONG	MOOLAH
MONOGENY	MONOPOD	MONOTREME	MONTHLY	MOOLAHS
MONOGERM	MONOPODE	MONOTROCH	MONTHS	MOOLAS
MONOGLOT	MONOPODES	MONOTYPE	MONTICLE	MOOLED
MONOGLOTS	MONOPODIA	MONOTYPES	MONTICLES	MOOLEY
MONOGONY	MONOPODS	MONOTYPIC	MONTICULE	MOOLEYS
MONOGRAM	MONOPODY	MONOVULAR	MONTIES	MOOLI
MONOGRAMS	MONOPOLE	MONOXIDE	MONTRE	MOOLIES
MONOGRAPH	MONOPOLES	MONOXIDES	MONTRES	MOOLING
MONOGYNY	MONOPOLY	MONOXYLON	MONTURE	MOOLIS
MONOHULL	MONOPSONY	MONS	MONTURES	MOOLOO
MONOHULLS	MONOPTERA	MONSIEUR	MONTY	MOOLOOS
MONOICOUS	MONOPTOTE	MONSIGNOR	MONUMENT	MOOLS
MONOKINE	MONOPULSE	MONSOON	MONUMENTS	MOOLVI
MONOKINES	MONORAIL	MONSOONAL	MONURON	MOOLVIE
MONOKINI	MONORAILS	MONSOONS	MONURONS	MOOLVIES
MONOKINIS	MONORCHID	MONSTER	MONY	MOOLVIS
MONOLATER	MONORHINE	MONSTERA	MONYPLIES	MOOLY
MONOLATRY	MONORHYME	MONSTERAS	MONZONITE	MOON
MONOLAYER	MONOS	MONSTERED	MOO	MOONBEAM
MONOLINE	MONOSEMIC	MONSTERS	MOOBIES	MOONBEAMS
MONOLITH	MONOSEMY	MONSTROUS	MOOBS	MOONBLIND
MONOLITHS	MONOSES	MONTADALE	MOOCH	MOONBOOTS
MONOLOG	MONOSIES	MONTAGE	MOOCHED	MOONBOW
MONOLOGIC	MONOSIS	MONTAGED	MOOCHER	MOONBOWS
MONOLOGS	MONOSKI	MONTAGES	MOOCHERS	MOONCAKE
MONOLOGUE	MONOSKIED	MONTAGING	MOOCHES	MOONCAKES
MONOLOGY	MONOSKIER	MONTAN	MOOCHING	MOONCALF
MONOMACHY	MONOSKIS	MONTANE	MOOD	MOONCHILD
MONOMANIA	MONOSOME	MONTANES	MOODIED	MOONCRAFT
MONOMARK	MONOSOMES	MONTANT	MOODIER	MOONDOG
MONOMARKS	MONOSOMIC	MONTANTO	MOODIES	MOONDOGS
MONOMER	MONOSOMY	MONTANTOS	MOODIEST	MOONDUST
MONOMERIC	MONOSTELE	MONTANTS	MOODILY	MOONDUSTS

MOONED	MOONSHINE	MOORWORTS	MOPING	MORALIZER
MOONER	MOONSHINY	MOORY	MOPINGLY	MORALIZES
MOONERS	MOONSHIP	MOOS	MOPISH	MORALL
MOONEYE	MOONSHIPS	MOOSE	MOPISHLY	MORALLED
MOONEYES	MOONSHOT	MOOSEBIRD	MOPOKE	MORALLER
MOONFACE	MOONSHOTS	MOOSEWOOD	MOPOKES	MORALLERS
MOONFACED	MOONSTONE	MOOSEYARD	MOPPED	MORALLING
MOONFACES	MOONWALK	MOOT	MOPPER	MORALLS
MOONFISH	MOONWALKS	MOOTABLE	MOPPERS	MORALLY
MOONG	MOONWARD	MOOTED	MOPPET	MORALS
MOONGATE	MOONWARDS	MOOTER	MOPPETS	MORAS
MOONGATES	MOONWORT	MOOTERS	MOPPIER	MORASS
MOONIER	MOONWORTS	MOOTEST	MOPPIEST	MORASSES
MOONIES	MOONY	MOOTING	MOPPING	MORASSY
MOONIEST	MOOP	MOOTINGS	MOPPY	MORAT
MOONILY	MOOPED	MOOTMAN	MOPS	MORATORIA
MOONINESS	MOOPING	MOOTMEN	MOPSIES	MORATORY
MOONING	MOOPS	MOOTNESS	MOPSTICK	MORATS
MOONISH	MOOR	MOOTS	MOPSTICKS	MORAY
MOONISHLY	MOORAGE	MOOVE	MOPSY	MORAYS
MOONLESS	MOORAGES	MOOVED	MOPUS	MORBID
MOONLET	MOORBURN	MOOVES	MOPUSES	MORBIDER
MOONLETS	MOORBURNS	MOOVING	MOPY	MORBIDEST
MOONLIGHT	MOORCOCK	MOP	MOQUETTE	MORBIDITY
MOONLIKE	MOORCOCKS	MOPANE	MOQUETTES	MORBIDLY
MOONLIT	MOORED	MOPANES	MOR	MORBIFIC
MOONPHASE	MOORFOWL	MOPANI	MORA	MORBILLI
MOONPORT	MOORFOWLS	MOPANIS	MORACEOUS	MORBUS
MOONPORTS	MOORHEN	MOPBOARD	MORAE	MORBUSES
MOONQUAKE	MOORHENS	MOPBOARDS	MORAINAL	MORCEAU
MOONRAKER	MOORIER	MOPE	MORAINE	MORCEAUX
MOONRISE	MOORIEST	MOPED	MORAINES	MORCHA
MOONRISES	MOORILL	MOPEDS	MORAINIC	MORCHAS
MOONROCK	MOORILLS	MOPEHAWK	MORAL	MORDACITY
MOONROCKS	MOORING	MOPEHAWKS	MORALE	MORDANCY
MOONROOF	MOORINGS	MOPER	MORALES	MORDANT
MOONROOFS	MOORISH	MOPERIES	MORALISE	MORDANTED
MOONS	MOORLAND	MOPERS	MORALISED	MORDANTLY
MOONSAIL	MOORLANDS	MOPERY	MORALISER	MORDANTS
MOONSAILS	MOORLOG	MOPES	MORALISES	MORDENT
MOONSCAPE	MOORLOGS	MOPEY	MORALISM	MORDENTS
MOONSEED	MOORMAN	MOPHEAD	MORALISMS	MORE
MOONSEEDS	MOORMEN	MOPHEADS	MORALIST	MOREEN
MOONSET	MOORS	MOPIER	MORALISTS	MOREENS
MOONSETS	MOORVA	MOPIEST	MORALITY	MOREISH
MOONSHEE	MOORVAS	MOPILY	MORALIZE	MOREL
MOONSHEES	MOORWORT	MOPINESS	MORALIZED	MORELLE

M

MORELLES	MORNS	MORRICES	MORTICED	MOSELLE
MORELLO	MOROCCO	MORRION	MORTICER	MOSELLES
MORELLOS	MOROCCOS	MORRIONS	MORTICERS	MOSES
MORELS	MORON	MORRIS	MORTICES	MOSEY
MORENDO	MORONIC	MORRISED	MORTICIAN	MOSEYED
MORENDOS	MORONISM	MORRISES	MORTICING	MOSEYING
MORENESS	MORONISMS	MORRISING	MORTIFIC	MOSEYS
MOREOVER	MORONITY	MORRO	MORTIFIED	MOSH
MOREPORK	MORONS	MORROS	MORTIFIER	MOSHAV
MOREPORKS	MOROSE	MORROW	MORTIFIES	MOSHAVIM
MORES	MOROSELY	MORROWS	MORTIFY	MOSHED
MORESQUE	MOROSER	MORS	MORTISE	MOSHER
MORESQUES	MOROSEST	MORSAL	MORTISED	MOSHERS
MORGAN	MOROSITY	MORSALS	MORTISER	MOSHES
MORGANITE	MORPH	MORSE	MORTISERS	MOSHING
MORGANS	MORPHEAN	MORSEL	MORTISES	MOSHINGS
MORGAY	MORPHED	MORSELED	MORTISING	MOSING
MORGAYS	MORPHEME	MORSELING	MORTLING	MOSK
MORGEN	MORPHEMES	MORSELLED	MORTLINGS	MOSKONFYT
MORGENS	MORPHEMIC	MORSELS	MORTMAIN	MOSKS
MORGUE	MORPHETIC	MORSES	MORTMAINS	MOSLINGS
MORGUES	MORPHEW	MORSURE	MORTS	MOSQUE
MORIA	MORPHEWS	MORSURES	MORTSAFE	MOSQUES
MORIAS	MORPHIA	MORT	MORTSAFES	MOSQUITO
MORIBUND	MORPHIAS	MORTAL	MORTUARY	MOSQUITOS
MORICHE	MORPHIC	MORTALISE	MORULA	MOSS
MORICHES	MORPHIN	MORTALITY	MORULAE	MOSSBACK
MORION	MORPHINE	MORTALIZE	MORULAR	MOSSBACKS
MORIONS	MORPHINES	MORTALLY	MORULAS	MOSSED
MORISCO	MORPHING	MORTALS	MORWONG	MOSSER
MORISCOES	MORPHINGS	MORTAR	MORWONGS	MOSSERS
MORISCOS	MORPHINIC	MORTARED	MORYAH	MOSSES
MORISH	MORPHINS	MORTARING	MOS	MOSSGROWN
MORKIN	MORPHO	MORTARMAN	MOSAIC	MOSSIE
MORKINS	MORPHOGEN	MORTARMEN	MOSAICISM	MOSSIER
MORLING	MORPHOS	MORTARS	MOSAICIST	MOSSIES
MORLINGS	MORPHOSES	MORTARY	MOSAICKED	MOSSIEST
MORMAOR	MORPHOSIS	MORTBELL	MOSAICS	MOSSINESS
MORMAORS	MORPHOTIC	MORTBELLS	MOSASAUR	MOSSING
MORN	MORPHS	MORTCLOTH	MOSASAURI	MOSSLAND
MORNAY	MORRA	MORTGAGE	MOSASAURS	MOSSLANDS
MORNAYS	MORRAS	MORTGAGED	MOSCATO	MOSSLIKE
MORNE	MORRELL	MORTGAGEE	MOSCATOS	MOSSO
MORNED	MORRELLS	MORTGAGER	MOSCHATE	MOSSPLANT
MORNES	MORRHUA	MORTGAGES	MOSCHATEL	MOSSY
MORNING	MORRHUAS	MORTGAGOR	MOSE	MOST
MORNINGS	MORRICE	MORTICE	MOSED	MOSTE

MOSTEST	MOTION	MOTORISED	MOU	MOULTERS
MOSTESTS	MOTIONAL	MOTORISES	MOUCH	MOULTING
MOSTLY	MOTIONED	MOTORIST	MOUCHARD	MOULTINGS
MOSTS	MOTIONER	MOTORISTS	MOUCHARDS	MOULTS
MOSTWHAT	MOTIONERS	MOTORIUM	MOUCHED	MOUND
MOT	MOTIONING	MOTORIUMS	MOUCHER	MOUNDBIRD
MOTE	MOTIONIST	MOTORIZE	MOUCHERS	MOUNDED
MOTED	MOTIONS	MOTORIZED	MOUCHES	MOUNDING
MOTEL	MOTIS	MOTORIZES	MOUCHING	MOUNDS
MOTELIER	MOTIVATE	MOTORLESS	MOUCHOIR	MOUNSEER
MOTELIERS	MOTIVATED	MOTORMAN	MOUCHOIRS	MOUNSEERS
MOTELS	MOTIVATES	MOTORMEN	MOUDIWART	MOUNT
MOTEN	MOTIVATOR	MOTORS	MOUDIWORT	MOUNTABLE
MOTES	MOTIVE	MOTORSHIP	MOUE	MOUNTAIN
MOTET	MOTIVED	MOTORWAY	MOUES	MOUNTAINS
MOTETS	MOTIVES	MOTORWAYS	MOUFFLON	MOUNTAINY
MOTETT	MOTIVIC	MOTORY	MOUFFLONS	MOUNTANT
MOTETTIST	MOTIVING	MOTOSCAFI	MOUFLON	MOUNTANTS
MOTETTS	MOTIVITY	MOTOSCAFO	MOUFLONS	MOUNTED
MOTEY	MOTLEY	MOTS	MOUGHT	MOUNTER
MOTEYS	MOTLEYER	MOTSER	MOUILLE	MOUNTERS
MOTH	MOTLEYEST	MOTSERS	MOUJIK	MOUNTING
MOTHBALL	MOTLEYS	MOTT	MOUJIKS	MOUNTINGS
MOTHBALLS	MOTLIER	MOTTE	MOULAGE	MOUNTS
MOTHED	MOTLIEST	MOTTES	MOULAGES	MOUP
MOTHER	MOTMOT	MOTTIER	MOULD	MOUPED
MOTHERED	MOTMOTS	MOTTIES	MOULDABLE	MOUPING
MOTHERESE	MOTOCROSS	MOTTIEST	MOULDED	MOUPS
MOTHERING	MOTOR	MOTTLE	MOULDER	MOURN
MOTHERLY	MOTORABLE	MOTTLED	MOULDERED	MOURNED
MOTHERS	MOTORAIL	MOTTLER	MOULDERS	MOURNER
MOTHERY	MOTORAILS	MOTTLERS	MOULDIER	MOURNERS
MOTHIER	MOTORBIKE	MOTTLES	MOULDIEST	MOURNFUL
MOTHIEST	MOTORBOAT	MOTTLING	MOULDING	MOURNING
MOTHLIKE	MOTORBUS	MOTTLINGS	MOULDINGS	MOURNINGS
MOTHPROOF	MOTORCADE	MOTTO	MOULDS	MOURNIVAL
MOTHS	MOTORCAR	MOTTOED	MOULDWARP	MOURNS
MOTHY	MOTORCARS	MOTTOES	MOULDY	MOUS
MOTI	MOTORDOM	MOTTOS	MOULIN	MOUSAKA
MOTIER	MOTORDOMS	MOTTS	MOULINET	MOUSAKAS
MOTIEST	MOTORED	MOTTY	MOULINETS	MOUSE
MOTIF	MOTORHOME	MOTU	MOULINS	MOUSEBIRD
MOTIFIC	MOTORIAL	MOTUCA	MOULS	MOUSED
MOTIFS	MOTORIC	MOTUCAS	MOULT	MOUSEKIN
MOTILE	MOTORING	MOTUS	MOULTED	MOUSEKINS
MOTILES	MOTORINGS	MOTZA	MOULTEN	MOUSELIKE
MOTILITY	MOTORISE	MOTZAS	MOULTER	MOUSEMAT

M

MOUSEMATS	MOUTERING	MOVIEOLAS	MOZETTE	MUCIN
MOUSEOVER	MOUTERS	MOVIES	MOZING	MUCINOGEN
MOUSEPAD	MOUTH	MOVING	MOZO	MUCINOID
MOUSEPADS	MOUTHABLE	MOVINGLY	MOZOS	MUCINOUS
MOUSER	MOUTHED	MOVIOLA	MOZZ	MUCINS
MOUSERIES	MOUTHER	MOVIOLAS	MOZZES	MUCK
MOUSERS	MOUTHERS	MOW	MOZZETTA	MUCKAMUCK
MOUSERY	MOUTHFEEL	MOWA	MOZZETTAS	MUCKED
MOUSES	MOUTHFUL	MOWAS	MOZZETTE	MUCKENDER
MOUSETAIL	MOUTHFULS	MOWBURN	MOZZIE	MUCKER
MOUSETRAP	MOUTHIER	MOWBURNED	MOZZIES	MUCKERED
MOUSEY	MOUTHIEST	MOWBURNS	MOZZLE	MUCKERING
MOUSIE	MOUTHILY	MOWBURNT	MOZZLED	MUCKERISH
MOUSIER	MOUTHING	MOWDIE	MOZZLES	MUCKERS
MOUSIES	MOUTHLESS	MOWDIES	MOZZLING	MUCKHEAP
MOUSIEST	MOUTHLIKE	MOWED	MPRET	MUCKHEAPS
MOUSILY	MOUTHPART	MOWER	MPRETS	MUCKIER
MOUSINESS	MOUTHS	MOWERS	MRIDAMGAM	MUCKIEST
MOUSING	MOUTHWASH	MOWING	MRIDANG	MUCKILY
MOUSINGS	MOUTHY	MOWINGS	MRIDANGA	MUCKINESS
MOUSLE	MOUTON	MOWN	MRIDANGAM	MUCKING
MOUSLED	MOUTONNEE	MOWRA	MRIDANGAS	MUCKLE
MOUSLES	MOUTONS	MOWRAS	MRIDANGS	MUCKLES
MOUSLING	MOVABLE	MOWS	MU	MUCKLUCK
MOUSME	MOVABLES	MOXA	MUCATE	MUCKLUCKS
MOUSMEE	MOVABLY	MOXAS	MUCATES	MUCKRAKE
MOUSMEES	MOVANT	MOXIE	MUCH	MUCKRAKED
MOUSMES	MOVANTS	MOXIES	MUCHACHA	MUCKRAKER
MOUSSAKA	MOVE	MOY	MUCHACHAS	MUCKRAKES
MOUSSAKAS	MOVEABLE	MOYA	MUCHACHO	MUCKS
MOUSSE	MOVEABLES	MOYAS	MUCHACHOS	MUCKSWEAT
MOUSSED	MOVEABLY	MOYGASHEL	MUCHEL	MUCKWORM
MOUSSES	MOVED	MOYITIES	MUCHELL	MUCKWORMS
MOUSSEUX	MOVELESS	MOYITY	MUCHELLS	MUCKY
MOUSSING	MOVEMENT	MOYL	MUCHELS	MUCKYMUCK
MOUST	MOVEMENTS	MOYLE	MUCHES	MUCLUC
MOUSTACHE	MOVER	MOYLED	MUCHLY	MUCLUCS
MOUSTED	MOVERS	MOYLES	MUCHNESS	MUCOID
MOUSTING	MOVES	MOYLING	MUCHO	MUCOIDAL
MOUSTS	MOVIE	MOYLS	MUCIC	MUCOIDS
MOUSY	MOVIEDOM	MOYS	MUCID	MUCOLYTIC
MOUTAN	MOVIEDOMS	MOZ	MUCIDITY	MUCOR
MOUTANS	MOVIEGOER	MOZE	MUCIDNESS	MUCORS
MOUTER	MOVIELAND	MOZED	MUCIGEN	MUCOSA
MOUTERED	MOVIEOKE	MOZES	MUCIGENS	MUCOSAE
MOUTERER	MOVIEOKES	MOZETTA	MUCILAGE	MUCOSAL
MOUTERERS	MOVIEOLA	MOZETTAS	MUCILAGES	MUCOSAS

MUCOSE	MUDEYES	MUDSCOWS	MUGGARS	MUJIK
MUCOSITY	MUDFISH	MUDSILL	MUGGAS	MUJIKS
MUCOUS	MUDFISHES	MUDSILLS	MUGGED	MUKHTAR
MUCRO	MUDFLAP	MUDSLIDE	MUGGEE	MUKHTARS
MUCRONATE	MUDFLAPS	MUDSLIDES	MUGGEES	MUKLUK
MUCRONES	MUDFLAT	MUDSLING	MUGGER	MUKLUKS
MUCROS	MUDFLATS	MUDSLINGS	MUGGERS	MUKTUK
MUCULENT	MUDFLOW	MUDSLUNG	MUGGIER	MUKTUKS
MUCUS	MUDFLOWS	MUDSTONE	MUGGIEST	MULATRESS
MUCUSES	MUDGE	MUDSTONES	MUGGILY	MULATTA
MUD	MUDGED	MUDWORT	MUGGINESS	MULATTAS
MUDBANK	MUDGER	MUDWORTS	MUGGING	MULATTO
MUDBANKS	MUDGERS	MUEDDIN	MUGGINGS	MULATTOES
MUDBATH	MUDGES	MUEDDINS	MUGGINS	MULATTOS
MUDBATHS	MUDGING	MUENSTER	MUGGINSES	MULBERRY
MUDBUG	MUDGUARD	MUENSTERS	MUGGISH	MULCH
MUDBUGS	MUDGUARDS	MUESLI	MUGGLE	MULCHED
MUDCAP	MUDHEN	MUESLIS	MUGGLES	MULCHES
MUDCAPPED	MUDHENS	MUEZZIN	MUGGS	MULCHING
MUDCAPS	MUDHOLE	MUEZZINS	MUGGUR	MULCT
MUDCAT	MUDHOLES	MUFF	MUGGURS	MULCTED
MUDCATS	MUDHOOK	MUFFED	MUGGY	MULCTING
MUDDED	MUDHOOKS	MUFFETTEE	MUGHAL	MULCTS
MUDDER	MUDHOPPER	MUFFIN	MUGHALS	MULE
MUDDERS	MUDIR	MUFFINEER	MUGS	MULED
MUDDIED	MUDIRIA	MUFFING	MUGSHOT	MULES
MUDDIER	MUDIRIAS	MUFFINS	MUGSHOTS	MULESED
MUDDIES	MUDIRIEH	MUFFISH	MUGWORT	MULESES
MUDDIEST	MUDIRIEHS	MUFFLE	MUGWORTS	MULESING
MUDDILY	MUDIRS	MUFFLED	MUGWUMP	MULESINGS
MUDDINESS	MUDLARK	MUFFLER	MUGWUMPS	MULETA
MUDDING	MUDLARKED	MUFFLERED	MUHLIES	MULETAS
MUDDLE	MUDLARKS	MUFFLERS	MUHLY	MULETEER
MUDDLED	MUDLOGGER	MUFFLES	MUID	MULETEERS
MUDDLER	MUDPACK	MUFFLING	MUIDS	MULEY
MUDDLERS	MUDPACKS	MUFFS	MUIL	MULEYS
MUDDLES	MUDPIE	MUFLON	MUILS	MULGA
MUDDLIER	MUDPIES	MUFLONS	MUIR	MULGAS
MUDDLIEST	MUDPUPPY	MUFTI	MUIRBURN	MULIE
MUDDLING	MUDRA	MUFTIS	MUIRBURNS	MULIES
MUDDLINGS	MUDRAS	MUG	MUIRS	MULING
MUDDLY	MUDROCK	MUGEARITE	MUIST	MULISH
MUDDY	MUDROCKS	MUGFUL	MUISTED	MULISHLY
MUDDYING	MUDROOM	MUGFULS	MUISTING	MULL
MUDEJAR	MUDROOMS	MUGG	MUISTS	MULLA
MUDEJARES	MUDS	MUGGA	MUJAHEDIN	MULLAH
MUDEYE	MUDSCOW	MUGGAR	MUJAHIDIN	MULLAHED

MULLAHING	MULTICAR	MULTISTEP	MUMMIFORM	MUNDICS
MULLAHISM	MULTICAST	MULTITASK	MUMMIFY	MUNDIFIED
MULLAHS	MULTICELL	MULTITON	MUMMING	MUNDIFIES
MULLARKY	MULTICIDE	MULTITONE	MUMMINGS	MUNDIFY
MULLAS	MULTICITY	MULTITOOL	MUMMOCK	MUNDUNGO
MULLED	MULTICOPY	MULTITUDE	MUMMOCKS	MUNDUNGOS
MULLEIN	MULTIDAY	MULTIUNIT	MUMMS	MUNDUNGUS
MULLEINS	MULTIDISC	MULTIUSE	MUMMY	MUNG
MULLEN	MULTIDRUG	MULTIUSER	MUMMYING	MUNGA
MULLENS	MULTIFID	MULTIWALL	MUMP	MUNGAS
MULLER	MULTIFIL	MULTIWAY	MUMPED	MUNGCORN
MULLERED	MULTIFILS	MULTIYEAR	MUMPER	MUNGCORNS
MULLERING	MULTIFOIL	MULTUM	MUMPERS	MUNGE
MULLERS	MULTIFOLD	MULTUMS	MUMPING	MUNGED
MULLET	MULTIFORM	MULTURE	MUMPISH	MUNGES
MULLETS	MULTIGERM	MULTURED	MUMPISHLY	MUNGING
MULLEY	MULTIGRID	MULTURER	MUMPS	MUNGO
MULLEYS	MULTIGYM	MULTURERS	MUMPSIMUS	MUNGOES
MULLIGAN	MULTIGYMS	MULTURES	MUMS	MUNGOOSE
MULLIGANS	MULTIHUED	MULTURING	MUMSIER	MUNGOOSES
MULLING	MULTIHULL	MUM	MUMSIES	MUNGOS
MULLION	MULTIJET	MUMBLE	MUMSIEST	MUNGS
MULLIONED	MULTILANE	MUMBLED	MUMSINESS	MUNI
MULLIONS	MULTILINE	MUMBLER	MUMSY	MUNICIPAL
MULLITE	MULTILOBE	MUMBLERS	MUMU	MUNIFIED
MULLITES	MULTIMODE	MUMBLES	MUMUS	MUNIFIES
MULLOCK	MULTIPACK	MUMBLIER	MUN	MUNIFY
MULLOCKS	MULTIPAGE	MUMBLIEST	MUNCH	MUNIFYING
MULLOCKY	MULTIPARA	MUMBLING	MUNCHABLE	MUNIMENT
MULLOWAY	MULTIPART	MUMBLINGS	MUNCHED	MUNIMENTS
MULLOWAYS	MULTIPATH	MUMBLY	MUNCHER	MUNIS
MULLS	MULTIPED	MUMCHANCE	MUNCHERS	MUNITE
MULMUL	MULTIPEDE	MUMM	MUNCHES	MUNITED
MULMULL	MULTIPEDS	MUMMED	MUNCHIE	MUNITES
MULMULLS	MULTIPION	MUMMER	MUNCHIER	MUNITING
MULMULS	MULTIPLE	MUMMERED	MUNCHIES	MUNITION
MULSE	MULTIPLES	MUMMERIES	MUNCHIEST	MUNITIONS
MULSES	MULTIPLET	MUMMERING	MUNCHING	MUNNION
MULSH	MULTIPLEX	MUMMERS	MUNCHKIN	MUNNIONS
MULSHED	MULTIPLY	MUMMERY	MUNCHKINS	MUNS
MULSHES	MULTIPOLE	MUMMIA	MUNCHY	MUNSHI
MULSHING	MULTIPORT	MUMMIAS	MUNDANE	MUNSHIS
MULTEITY	MULTIRISK	MUMMICHOG	MUNDANELY	MUNSTER
MULTIAGE	MULTIROLE	MUMMIED	MUNDANER	MUNSTERS
MULTIATOM	MULTIROOM	MUMMIES	MUNDANEST	MUNT
MULTIBAND	MULTISITE	MUMMIFIED	MUNDANITY	MUNTED
MULTIBANK	MULTISIZE	MUMMIFIES	MUNDIC	MUNTER

MUNTERS	MURDEROUS	MURLIER	MURRINS	MUSCLY
MUNTIN	MURDERS	MURLIEST	MURRION	MUSCOID
MUNTINED	MURE	MURLIN	MURRIONS	MUSCOIDS
MUNTING	MURED	MURLING	MURRIS	MUSCOLOGY
MUNTINGS	MUREIN	MURLINS	MURRS	MUSCONE
MUNTINS	MUREINS	MURLS	MURRY	MUSCONES
MUNTJAC	MURENA	MURLY	MURTHER	MUSCOSE
MUNTJACS	MURENAS	MURMUR	MURTHERED	MUSCOVADO
MUNTJAK	MURES	MURMURED	MURTHERER	MUSCOVITE
MUNTJAKS	MUREX	MURMURER	MURTHERS	MUSCOVY
MUNTRIE	MUREXES	MURMURERS	MURTI	MUSCULAR
MUNTRIES	MURGEON	MURMURING	MURTIS	MUSCULOUS
MUNTS	MURGEONED	MURMUROUS	MURVA	MUSE
MUNTU	MURGEONS	MURMURS	MURVAS	MUSED
MUNTUS	MURIATE	MURPHIES	MUS	MUSEFUL
MUON	MURIATED	MURPHY	MUSACEOUS	MUSEFULLY
MUONIC	MURIATES	MURR	MUSANG	MUSEOLOGY
MUONIUM	MURIATIC	MURRA	MUSANGS	MUSER
MUONIUMS	MURICATE	MURRAGH	MUSAR	MUSERS
MUONS	MURICATED	MURRAGHS	MUSARS	MUSES
MUPPET	MURICES	MURRAIN	MUSCA	MUSET
MUPPETS	MURID	MURRAINED	MUSCADEL	MUSETS
MUQADDAM	MURIDS	MURRAINS	MUSCADELS	MUSETTE
MUQADDAMS	MURIFORM	MURRAM	MUSCADET	MUSETTES
MURA	MURINE	MURRAMS	MUSCADETS	MUSEUM
MURAENA	MURINES	MURRAS	MUSCADIN	MUSEUMS
MURAENAS	MURING	MURRAY	MUSCADINE	MUSH
MURAENID	MURK	MURRAYS	MUSCADINS	MUSHA
MURAENIDS	MURKED	MURRE	MUSCAE	MUSHED
MURAGE	MURKER	MURREE	MUSCARINE	MUSHER
MURAGES	MURKEST	MURREES	MUSCAT	MUSHERS
MURAL	MURKIER	MURRELET	MUSCATEL	MUSHES
MURALED	MURKIEST	MURRELETS	MUSCATELS	MUSHIER
MURALIST	MURKILY	MURREN	MUSCATS	MUSHIEST
MURALISTS	MURKINESS	MURRENS	MUSCAVADO	MUSHILY
MURALLED	MURKING	MURRES	MUSCID	MUSHINESS
MURALS	MURKISH	MURREY	MUSCIDS	MUSHING
MURAS	MURKLY	MURREYS	MUSCLE	MUSHINGS
MURDABAD	MURKS	MURRHA	MUSCLED	MUSHMOUTH
MURDER	MURKSOME	MURRHAS	MUSCLEMAN	MUSHRAT
MURDERED	MURKY	MURRHINE	MUSCLEMEN	MUSHRATS
MURDEREE	MURL	MURRHINES	MUSCLES	MUSHROOM
MURDEREES	MURLAIN	MURRI	MUSCLEY	MUSHROOMS
MURDERER	MURLAINS	MURRIES	MUSCLIER	MUSHY
MURDERERS	MURLAN	MURRIN	MUSCLIEST	MUSIC
MURDERESS	MURLANS	MURRINE	MUSCLING	MUSICAL
MURDERING	MURLED	MURRINES	MUSCLINGS	MUSICALE

M

MUSICALES	MUSKOXEN	MUSTEES	MUTE	MUTUAL
MUSICALLY	MUSKRAT	MUSTELID	MUTED	MUTUALISE
MUSICALS	MUSKRATS	MUSTELIDS	MUTEDLY	MUTUALISM
MUSICIAN	MUSKROOT	MUSTELINE	MUTELY	MUTUALIST
MUSICIANS	MUSKROOTS	MUSTER	MUTENESS	MUTUALITY
MUSICK	MUSKS	MUSTERED	MUTER	MUTUALIZE
MUSICKED	MUSKY	MUSTERER	MUTES	MUTUALLY
MUSICKER	MUSLIN	MUSTERERS	MUTEST	MUTUALS
MUSICKERS	MUSLINED	MUSTERING	MUTHA	MUTUCA
MUSICKING	MUSLINET	MUSTERS	MUTHAS	MUTUCAS
MUSICKS	MUSLINETS	MUSTH	MUTI	MUTUEL
MUSICLESS	MUSLINS	MUSTHS	MUTICATE	MUTUELS
MUSICS	MUSMON	MUSTIER	MUTICOUS	MUTULAR
MUSIMON	MUSMONS	MUSTIEST	MUTILATE	MUTULE
MUSIMONS	MUSO	MUSTILY	MUTILATED	MUTULES
MUSING	MUSOS	MUSTINESS	MUTILATES	MUTUUM
MUSINGLY	MUSPIKE	MUSTING	MUTILATOR	MUTUUMS
MUSINGS	MUSPIKES	MUSTS	MUTINE	MUUMUU
MUSIT	MUSQUASH	MUSTY	MUTINED	MUUMUUS
MUSITS	MUSROL	MUT	MUTINEER	MUX
MUSIVE	MUSROLS	MUTABLE	MUTINEERS	MUXED
MUSJID	MUSS	MUTABLY	MUTINES	MUXES
MUSJIDS	MUSSE	MUTAGEN	MUTING	MUXING
MUSK	MUSSED	MUTAGENIC	MUTINIED	MUZAK
MUSKED	MUSSEL	MUTAGENS	MUTINIES	MUZAKS
MUSKEG	MUSSELLED	MUTANDA	MUTINING	MUZAKY
MUSKEGS	MUSSELS	MUTANDUM	MUTINOUS	MUZHIK
MUSKET	MUSSES	MUTANT	MUTINY	MUZHIKS
MUSKETEER	MUSSIER	MUTANTS	MUTINYING	MUZJIK
MUSKETOON	MUSSIEST	MUTASE	MUTIS	MUZJIKS
MUSKETRY	MUSSILY	MUTASES	MUTISM	MUZZ
MUSKETS	MUSSINESS	MUTATE	MUTISMS	MUZZED
MUSKIE	MUSSING	MUTATED	MUTON	MUZZES
MUSKIER	MUSSITATE	MUTATES	MUTONS	MUZZIER
MUSKIES	MUSSY	MUTATING	MUTOSCOPE	MUZZIEST
MUSKIEST	MUST	MUTATION	MUTS	MUZZILY
MUSKILY	MUSTACHE	MUTATIONS	MUTT	MUZZINESS
MUSKINESS	MUSTACHED	MUTATIVE	MUTTER	MUZZING
MUSKING	MUSTACHES	MUTATOR	MUTTERED	MUZZLE
MUSKIT	MUSTACHIO	MUTATORS	MUTTERER	MUZZLED
MUSKITS	MUSTANG	MUTATORY	MUTTERERS	MUZZLER
MUSKLE	MUSTANGS	MUTCH	MUTTERING	MUZZLERS
MUSKLES	MUSTARD	MUTCHED	MUTTERS	MUZZLES
MUSKMELON	MUSTARDS	MUTCHES	MUTTON	MUZZLING
MUSKONE	MUSTARDY	MUTCHING	MUTTONS	MUZZY
MUSKONES	MUSTED	MUTCHKIN	MUTTONY	MVULE
MUSKOX	MUSTEE	MUTCHKINS	MUTTS	MVULES

MWAH	MYELINES	MYOGRAPHS	MYOTONIAS	MYSTIC
MWALIMU	MYELINIC	MYOGRAPHY	MYOTONIC	MYSTICAL
MWALIMUS	MYELINS	MYOID	MYOTUBE	MYSTICETE
MY	MYELITES	MYOIDS	MYOTUBES	MYSTICISM
MYAL	MYELITIS	MYOLOGIC	MYRBANE	MYSTICLY
MYALGIA	MYELOCYTE	MYOLOGIES	MYRBANES	MYSTICS
MYALGIAS	MYELOGRAM	MYOLOGIST	MYRIAD	MYSTIFIED
MYALGIC	MYELOID	MYOLOGY	MYRIADS	MYSTIFIER
MYALISM	MYELOMA	MYOMA	MYRIADTH	MYSTIFIES
MYALISMS	MYELOMAS	MYOMANCY	MYRIADTHS	MYSTIFY
MYALIST	MYELOMATA	MYOMANTIC	MYRIAPOD	MYSTIQUE
MYALISTS	MYELON	MYOMAS	MYRIAPODS	MYSTIQUES
MYALL	MYELONS	MYOMATA	MYRICA	MYTH
MYALLS	MYGALE	MYOMATOUS	MYRICAS	MYTHI
MYASES	MYGALES	MYOMERE	MYRINGA	MYTHIC
MYASIS	MYIASES	MYOMERES	MYRINGAS	MYTHICAL
MYC	MYIASIS	MYONEURAL	MYRIOPOD	MYTHICISE
MYCELE	MYIOPHILY	MYOPATHIC	MYRIOPODS	MYTHICISM
MYCELES	MYLAR	MYOPATHY	MYRIORAMA	MYTHICIST
MYCELIA	MYLARS	MYOPE	MYRISTIC	MYTHICIZE
MYCELIAL	MYLODON	MYOPES	MYRMECOID	MYTHIER
MYCELIAN	MYLODONS	MYOPHILY	MYRMIDON	MYTHIEST
MYCELIUM	MYLODONT	MYOPIA	MYRMIDONS	MYTHISE
MYCELLA	MYLODONTS	MYOPIAS	MYROBALAN	MYTHISED
MYCELLAS	MYLOHYOID	MYOPIC	MYRRH	MYTHISES
MYCELOID	MYLONITE	MYOPICS	MYRRHIC	MYTHISING
MYCETES	MYLONITES	MYOPIES	MYRRHINE	MYTHISM
MYCETOMA	MYLONITIC	MYOPS	MYRRHOL	MYTHISMS
MYCETOMAS	MYNA	MYOPSES	MYRRHOLS	MYTHIST
MYCOBIONT	MYNAH	MYOPY	MYRRHS	MYTHISTS
MYCOFLORA	MYNAHS	MYOSCOPE	MYRRHY	MYTHIZE
MYCOLOGIC	MYNAS	MYOSCOPES	MYRTLE	MYTHIZED
MYCOLOGY	MYNHEER	MYOSES	MYRTLES	MYTHIZES
MYCOPHAGY	MYNHEERS	MYOSIN	MYSELF	MYTHIZING
MYCOPHILE	MYOBLAST	MYOSINS	MYSID	MYTHMAKER
MYCORHIZA	MYOBLASTS	MYOSIS	MYSIDS	MYTHOI
MYCOSES	MYOCARDIA	MYOSISES	MYSOST	MYTHOLOGY
MYCOSIS	MYOCLONIC	MYOSITIS	MYSOSTS	MYTHOMANE
MYCOTIC	MYOCLONUS	MYOSOTE	MYSPACE	MYTHOPEIC
MYCOTOXIN	MYOFIBRIL	MYOSOTES	MYSPACED	MYTHOPOET
MYCOVIRUS	MYOGEN	MYOSOTIS	MYSPACES	MYTHOS
MYCS	MYOGENIC	MYOSTATIN	MYSPACING	MYTHS
MYDRIASES	MYOGENS	MYOTIC	MYSTAGOG	MYTHUS
MYDRIASIS	MYOGLOBIN	MYOTICS	MYSTAGOGS	MYTHY
MYDRIATIC	MYOGRAM	MYOTOME	MYSTAGOGY	MYTILOID
MYELIN	MYOGRAMS	MYOTOMES	MYSTERIES	MYXAMEBA
MYELINE	MYOGRAPH	MYOTONIA	MYSTERY	MYXAMEBAE

MYXAMEBAS

MYXAMEBAS	MYXEDEMIC	MYXOEDEMA	MYXOMATA	MZEE
MYXAMOEBA	MYXO	MYXOID	MYXOS	MZEES
MYXEDEMA	MYXOCYTE	MYXOMA	MYXOVIRAL	MZUNGU
MYXEDEMAS	MYXOCYTES	MYXOMAS	MYXOVIRUS	MZUNGUS

N

NA	NACKETS	NAGARIS	NAILFILE	NAKFA
NAAM	NACRE	NAGAS	NAILFILES	NAKFAS
NAAMS	NACRED	NAGGED	NAILFOLD	NALA
NAAN	NACREOUS	NAGGER	NAILFOLDS	NALAS
NAANS	NACRES	NAGGERS	NAILHEAD	NALED
NAARTJE	NACRITE	NAGGIER	NAILHEADS	NALEDS
NAARTJES	NACRITES	NAGGIEST	NAILING	NALIDIXIC
NAARTJIE	NACROUS	NAGGING	NAILINGS	NALLA
NAARTJIES	NADA	NAGGINGLY	NAILLESS	NALLAH
NAB	NADAS	NAGGINGS	NAILS	NALLAHS
NABBED	NADIR	NAGGY	NAILSET	NALLAS
NABBER	NADIRAL	NAGMAAL	NAILSETS	NALOXONE
NABBERS	NADIRS	NAGMAALS	NAIN	NALOXONES
NABBING	NADORS	NAGOR	NAINSELL	NAM
NABE	NADS	NAGORS	NAINSELLS	NAMABLE
NABES	NAE	NAGS	NAINSOOK	NAMASKAR
NABIS	NAEBODIES	NAGWARE	NAINSOOKS	NAMASKARS
NABK	NAEBODY	NAGWARES	NAIRA	NAMASTE
NABKS	NAES	NAH	NAIRAS	NAMASTES
NABLA	NAETHING	NAHAL	NAIRU	NAMAYCUSH
NABLAS	NAETHINGS	NAHALS	NAIRUS	NAME
NABOB	NAEVE	NAIAD	NAISSANCE	NAMEABLE
NABOBERY	NAEVES	NAIADES	NAISSANT	NAMECHECK
NABOBESS	NAEVI	NAIADS	NAIVE	NAMED
NABOBISH	NAEVOID	NAIANT	NAIVELY	NAMELESS
NABOBISM	NAEVUS	NAIF	NAIVENESS	NAMELY
NABOBISMS	NAFF	NAIFER	NAIVER	NAMEPLATE
NABOBS	NAFFED	NAIFEST	NAIVES	NAMER
NABS	NAFFER	NAIFLY	NAIVEST	NAMERS
NACARAT	NAFFEST	NAIFNESS	NAIVETE	NAMES
NACARATS	NAFFING	NAIFS	NAIVETES	NAMESAKE
NACELLE	NAFFLY	NAIK	NAIVETIES	NAMESAKES
NACELLES	NAFFNESS	NAIKS	NAIVETY	NAMETAG
NACH	NAFFS	NAIL	NAIVIST	NAMETAGS
NACHAS	NAG	NAILBITER	NAKED	NAMETAPE
NACHE	NAGA	NAILBRUSH	NAKEDER	NAMETAPES
NACHES	NAGANA	NAILED	NAKEDEST	NAMING
NACHO	NAGANAS	NAILER	NAKEDLY	NAMINGS
NACHOS	NAGAPIE	NAILERIES	NAKEDNESS	NAMMA
NACHTMAAL	NAGAPIES	NAILERS	NAKER	NAMS
NACKET	NAGARI	NAILERY	NAKERS	NAMU

NAMUS	NANODOT	NAPHTHYL	NARCIST	NARKIER
NAN	NANODOTS	NAPHTHYLS	NARCISTIC	NARKIEST
NANA	NANOGRAM	NAPHTOL	NARCISTS	NARKING
NANAS	NANOGRAMS	NAPHTOLS	NARCO	NARKS
NANCE	NANOGRASS	NAPIFORM	NARCOMA	NARKY
NANCES	NANOMETER	NAPING	NARCOMAS	NARQUOIS
NANCIES	NANOMETRE	NAPKIN	NARCOMATA	NARRAS
NANCIFIED	NANOOK	NAPKINS	NARCOS	NARRASES
NANCY	NANOOKS	NAPLESS	NARCOSE	NARRATE
NANDIN	NANOPORE	NAPOLEON	NARCOSES	NARRATED
NANDINA	NANOPORES	NAPOLEONS	NARCOSIS	NARRATER
NANDINAS	NANOS	NAPOO	NARCOTIC	NARRATERS
NANDINE	NANOSCALE	NAPOOED	NARCOTICS	NARRATES
NANDINES	NANOTECH	NAPOOING	NARCOTINE	NARRATING
NANDINS	NANOTECHS	NAPOOS	NARCOTISE	NARRATION
NANDOO	NANOTESLA	NAPPA	NARCOTISM	NARRATIVE
NANDOOS	NANOTUBE	NAPPAS	NARCOTIST	NARRATOR
NANDU	NANOTUBES	NAPPE	NARCOTIZE	NARRATORS
NANDUS	NANOWATT	NAPPED	NARCS	NARRATORY
NANE	NANOWATTS	NAPPER	NARD	NARRE
NANG	NANOWIRE	NAPPERS	NARDED	NARROW
NANISM	NANOWIRES	NAPPES	NARDINE	NARROWED
NANISMS	NANOWORLD	NAPPIE	NARDING	NARROWER
NANITE	NANS	NAPPIER	NARDOO	NARROWEST
NANITES	NANUA	NAPPIES	NARDOOS	NARROWING
NANKEEN	NANUAS	NAPPIEST	NARDS	NARROWISH
NANKEENS	NAOI	NAPPINESS	NARE	NARROWLY
NANKIN	NAOS	NAPPING	NARES	NARROWS
NANKINS	NAOSES	NAPPY	NARGHILE	NARTHEX
NANNA	NAP	NAPRON	NARGHILES	NARTHEXES
NANNAS	NAPA	NAPRONS	NARGHILLY	NARTJIE
NANNIE	NAPALM	NAPROXEN	NARGHILY	NARTJIES
NANNIED	NAPALMED	NAPROXENS	NARGILE	NARWAL
NANNIES	NAPALMING	NAPS	NARGILEH	NARWALS
NANNY	NAPALMS	NARAS	NARGILEHS	NARWHAL
NANNYGAI	NAPAS	NARASES	NARGILES	NARWHALE
NANNYGAIS	NAPE	NARC	NARGILIES	NARWHALES
NANNYING	NAPED	NARCEEN	NARGILY	NARWHALS
NANNYINGS	NAPERIES	NARCEENS	NARGUILEH	NARY
NANNYISH	NAPERY	NARCEIN	NARIAL	NAS
NANO	NAPES	NARCEINE	NARIC	NASAL
NANOBE	NAPHTHA	NARCEINES	NARICORN	NASALISE
NANOBEE	NAPHTHAS	NARCEINS	NARICORNS	NASALISED
NANOBEES	NAPHTHENE	NARCISM	NARINE	NASALISES
NANOBES	NAPHTHOL	NARCISMS	NARIS	NASALISM
NANOBOT	NAPHTHOLS	NARCISSI	NARK	NASALISMS
NANOBOTS	NAPHTHOUS	NARCISSUS	NARKED	NASALITY

NASALIZE	NATIFORM	NAUGAHYDE	NAVE	NAZIFIES
NASALIZED	NATION	NAUGHT	NAVEL	NAZIFY
NASALIZES	NATIONAL	NAUGHTIER	NAVELS	NAZIFYING
NASALLY	NATIONALS	NAUGHTIES	NAVELWORT	NAZIR
NASALS	NATIONS	NAUGHTILY	NAVES	NAZIRS
NASARD	NATIS	NAUGHTS	NAVETTE	NAZIS
NASARDS	NATIVE	NAUGHTY	NAVETTES	NE
NASCENCE	NATIVELY	NAUMACHIA	NAVEW	NEAFE
NASCENCES	NATIVES	NAUMACHY	NAVEWS	NEAFES
NASCENCY	NATIVISM	NAUNT	NAVICERT	NEAFFE
NASCENT	NATIVISMS	NAUNTS	NAVICERTS	NEAFFES
NASEBERRY	NATIVIST	NAUPLIAL	NAVICULA	NEAL
NASHGAB	NATIVISTS	NAUPLII	NAVICULAR	NEALED
NASHGABS	NATIVITY	NAUPLIOID	NAVICULAS	NEALING
NASHI	NATRIUM	NAUPLIUS	NAVIES	NEALS
NASHIS	NATRIUMS	NAUSEA	NAVIGABLE	NEANIC
NASIAL	NATROLITE	NAUSEANT	NAVIGABLY	NEAP
NASION	NATRON	NAUSEANTS	NAVIGATE	NEAPED
NASIONS	NATRONS	NAUSEAS	NAVIGATED	NEAPING
NASSELLA	NATS	NAUSEATE	NAVIGATES	NEAPS
NASTALIK	NATTER	NAUSEATED	NAVIGATOR	NEAR
NASTALIKS	NATTERED	NAUSEATES	NAVS	NEARBY
NASTIC	NATTERER	NAUSEOUS	NAVVIED	NEARED
NASTIER	NATTERERS	NAUTCH	NAVVIES	NEARER
NASTIES	NATTERING	NAUTCHES	NAVVY	NEAREST
NASTIEST	NATTERS	NAUTIC	NAVVYING	NEARING
NASTILY	NATTERY	NAUTICAL	NAVY	NEARISH
NASTINESS	NATTIER	NAUTICS	NAW	NEARLIER
NASTY	NATTIEST	NAUTILI	NAWAB	NEARLIEST
NASUTE	NATTILY	NAUTILOID	NAWABS	NEARLY
NASUTES	NATTINESS	NAUTILUS	NAY	NEARNESS
NAT	NATTY	NAV	NAYS	NEARS
NATAL	NATURA	NAVAID	NAYSAID	NEARSHORE
NATALITY	NATURAE	NAVAIDS	NAYSAY	NEARSIDE
NATANT	NATURAL	NAVAL	NAYSAYER	NEARSIDES
NATANTLY	NATURALLY	NAVALISM	NAYSAYERS	NEAT
NATATION	NATURALS	NAVALISMS	NAYSAYING	NEATEN
NATATIONS	NATURE	NAVALLY	NAYSAYS	NEATENED
NATATORIA	NATURED	NAVAR	NAYTHLES	NEATENING
NATATORY	NATURES	NAVARCH	NAYWARD	NEATENS
NATCH	NATURING	NAVARCHS	NAYWARDS	NEATER
NATCHES	NATURISM	NAVARCHY	NAYWORD	NEATEST
NATES	NATURISMS	NAVARHO	NAYWORDS	NEATH
NATHELESS	NATURIST	NAVARHOS	NAZE	NEATHERD
NATHEMO	NATURISTS	NAVARIN	NAZES	NEATHERDS
NATHEMORE	NAUCH	NAVARINS	NAZI	NEATLY
NATHLESS	NAUCHES	NAVARS	NAZIFIED	NEATNESS

NEATNIK	NECESSITY	NECROTIZE	NEEDLINGS	NEGATRON
NEATNIKS	NECK	NECROTOMY	NEEDLY	NEGATRONS
NEATS	NECKATEE	NECTAR	NEEDMENT	NEGLECT
NEB	NECKATEES	NECTAREAL	NEEDMENTS	NEGLECTED
NEBBED	NECKBAND	NECTAREAN	NEEDS	NEGLECTER
NEBBICH	NECKBANDS	NECTARED	NEEDY	NEGLECTOR
NEBBICHS	NECKBEEF	NECTARIAL	NEELD	NEGLECTS
NEBBING	NECKBEEFS	NECTARIED	NEELDS	NEGLIGE
NEBBISH	NECKCLOTH	NECTARIES	NEELE	NEGLIGEE
NEBBISHE	NECKED	NECTARINE	NEELES	NEGLIGEES
NEBBISHER	NECKER	NECTAROUS	NEEM	NEGLIGENT
NEBBISHES	NECKERS	NECTARS	NEEMB	NEGLIGES
NEBBISHY	NECKGEAR	NECTARY	NEEMBS	NEGOCIANT
NEBBUK	NECKGEARS	NED	NEEMS	NEGOTIANT
NEBBUKS	NECKING	NEDDIER	NEEP	NEGOTIATE
NEBECK	NECKINGS	NEDDIES	NEEPS	NEGRESS
NEBECKS	NECKLACE	NEDDIEST	NEESBERRY	NEGRESSES
NEBEK	NECKLACED	NEDDISH	NEESE	NEGRITUDE
NEBEKS	NECKLACES	NEDDY	NEESED	NEGRO
NEBEL	NECKLESS	NEDETTE	NEESES	NEGROES
NEBELS	NECKLET	NEDETTES	NEESING	NEGROHEAD
NEBENKERN	NECKLETS	NEDS	NEEZE	NEGROID
NEBISH	NECKLIKE	NEE	NEEZED	NEGROIDAL
NEBISHES	NECKLINE	NEED	NEEZES	NEGROIDS
NEBRIS	NECKLINES	NEEDED	NEEZING	NEGROISM
NEBRISES	NECKPIECE	NEEDER	NEF	NEGROISMS
NEBS	NECKS	NEEDERS	NEFANDOUS	NEGRONI
NEBULA	NECKSHOT	NEEDFIRE	NEFARIOUS	NEGRONIS
NEBULAE	NECKSHOTS	NEEDFIRES	NEFAST	NEGROPHIL
NEBULAR	NECKTIE	NEEDFUL	NEFS	NEGS
NEBULAS	NECKTIES	NEEDFULLY	NEG	NEGUS
NEBULE	NECKVERSE	NEEDFULS	NEGATE	NEGUSES
NEBULES	NECKWEAR	NEEDIER	NEGATED	NEIF
NEBULISE	NECKWEARS	NEEDIEST	NEGATER	NEIFS
NEBULISED	NECKWEED	NEEDILY	NEGATERS	NEIGH
NEBULISER	NECKWEEDS	NEEDINESS	NEGATES	NEIGHBOR
NEBULISES	NECROLOGY	NEEDING	NEGATING	NEIGHBORS
NEBULIUM	NECROPHIL	NEEDLE	NEGATION	NEIGHBOUR
NEBULIUMS	NECROPOLI	NEEDLED	NEGATIONS	NEIGHED
NEBULIZE	NECROPSY	NEEDLEFUL	NEGATIVE	NEIGHING
NEBULIZED	NECROSE	NEEDLER	NEGATIVED	NEIGHINGS
NEBULIZER	NECROSED	NEEDLERS	NEGATIVES	NEIGHS
NEBULIZES	NECROSES	NEEDLES	NEGATON	NEINEI
NEBULOSE	NECROSING	NEEDLESS	NEGATONS	NEINEIS
NEBULOUS	NECROSIS	NEEDLIER	NEGATOR	NEIST
NEBULY	NECROTIC	NEEDLIEST	NEGATORS	NEITHER
NECESSARY	NECROTISE	NEEDLING	NEGATORY	NEIVE

NEIVES	NEOCONS	NEOSOULS	NEPIONIC	NERVELET
NEK	NEOCORTEX	NEOTEINIA	NEPIT	NERVELETS
NEKS	NEODYMIUM	NEOTENIC	NEPITS	NERVER
NEKTON	NEOGENE	NEOTENIES	NEPOTIC	NERVERS
NEKTONIC	NEOGOTHIC	NEOTENOUS	NEPOTISM	NERVES
NEKTONS	NEOLITH	NEOTENY	NEPOTISMS	NERVIER
NELIES	NEOLITHIC	NEOTERIC	NEPOTIST	NERVIEST
NELIS	NEOLITHS	NEOTERICS	NEPOTISTS	NERVILY
NELLIE	NEOLOGIAN	NEOTERISE	NEPS	NERVINE
NELLIES	NEOLOGIC	NEOTERISM	NEPTUNIUM	NERVINES
NELLY	NEOLOGIES	NEOTERIST	NERAL	NERVINESS
NELSON	NEOLOGISE	NEOTERIZE	NERALS	NERVING
NELSONS	NEOLOGISM	NEOTOXIN	NERD	NERVINGS
NELUMBIUM	NEOLOGIST	NEOTOXINS	NERDIC	NERVOSITY
NELUMBO	NEOLOGIZE	NEOTROPIC	NERDICS	NERVOUS
NELUMBOS	NEOLOGY	NEOTYPE	NERDIER	NERVOUSLY
NEMA	NEOMORPH	NEOTYPES	NERDIEST	NERVULAR
NEMAS	NEOMORPHS	NEP	NERDINESS	NERVULE
NEMATIC	NEOMYCIN	NEPENTHE	NERDISH	NERVULES
NEMATICS	NEOMYCINS	NEPENTHES	NERDS	NERVURE
NEMATODE	NEON	NEPER	NERDY	NERVURES
NEMATODES	NEONATAL	NEPERS	NEREID	NERVY
NEMATOID	NEONATE	NEPETA	NEREIDES	NESCIENCE
NEMERTEAN	NEONATES	NEPETAS	NEREIDS	NESCIENT
NEMERTIAN	NEONED	NEPHALISM	NEREIS	NESCIENTS
NEMERTINE	NEONOMIAN	NEPHALIST	NERINE	NESH
NEMESES	NEONS	NEPHELINE	NERINES	NESHER
NEMESIA	NEOPAGAN	NEPHELITE	NERITE	NESHEST
NEMESIAS	NEOPAGANS	NEPHEW	NERITES	NESHNESS
NEMESIS	NEOPHILE	NEPHEWS	NERITIC	NESS
NEMN	NEOPHILES	NEPHOGRAM	NERK	NESSES
NEMNED	NEOPHILIA	NEPHOLOGY	NERKA	NEST
NEMNING	NEOPHOBE	NEPHRALGY	NERKAS	NESTABLE
NEMNS	NEOPHOBES	NEPHRIC	NERKS	NESTED
NEMOPHILA	NEOPHOBIA	NEPHRIDIA	NEROL	NESTER
NEMORAL	NEOPHOBIC	NEPHRISM	NEROLI	NESTERS
NEMOROUS	NEOPHYTE	NEPHRISMS	NEROLIS	NESTFUL
NEMPT	NEOPHYTES	NEPHRITE	NEROLS	NESTFULS
NENE	NEOPHYTIC	NEPHRITES	NERTS	NESTING
NENES	NEOPILINA	NEPHRITIC	NERTZ	NESTINGS
NENNIGAI	NEOPLASIA	NEPHRITIS	NERVAL	NESTLE
NENNIGAIS	NEOPLASM	NEPHROID	NERVATE	NESTLED
NENUPHAR	NEOPLASMS	NEPHRON	NERVATION	NESTLER
NENUPHARS	NEOPLASTY	NEPHRONS	NERVATURE	NESTLERS
NEOBLAST	NEOPRENE	NEPHROSES	NERVE	NESTLES
NEOBLASTS	NEOPRENES	NEPHROSIS	NERVED	NESTLIKE
NEOCON	NEOSOUL	NEPHROTIC	NERVELESS	NESTLING

N

NESTLINGS	NETTING	NEUROIDS	NEVER	NEWSCASTS
NESTMATE	NETTINGS	NEUROLOGY	NEVERMIND	NEWSCLIP
NESTMATES	NETTLE	NEUROMA	NEVERMORE	NEWSCLIPS
NESTOR	NETTLED	NEUROMAS	NEVES	NEWSDESK
NESTORS	NETTLER	NEUROMAST	NEVI	NEWSDESKS
NESTS	NETTLERS	NEUROMATA	NEVOID	NEWSED
NET	NETTLES	NEURON	NEVUS	NEWSES
NETBALL	NETTLIER	NEURONAL	NEW	NEWSFEED
NETBALLER	NETTLIEST	NEURONE	NEWB	NEWSFEEDS
NETBALLS	NETTLING	NEURONES	NEWBIE	NEWSFLASH
NETBOOK	NETTLY	NEURONIC	NEWBIES	NEWSGIRL
NETBOOKS	NETTS	NEURONS	NEWBORN	NEWSGIRLS
NETE	NETTY	NEUROPATH	NEWBORNS	NEWSGROUP
NETES	NETWORK	NEUROPIL	NEWBS	NEWSHAWK
NETFUL	NETWORKED	NEUROPILS	NEWCOME	NEWSHAWKS
NETFULS	NETWORKER	NEUROSAL	NEWCOMER	NEWSHOUND
NETHEAD	NETWORKS	NEUROSES	NEWCOMERS	NEWSIE
NETHEADS	NEUK	NEUROSIS	NEWED	NEWSIER
NETHELESS	NEUKS	NEUROTIC	NEWEL	NEWSIES
NETHER	NEUM	NEUROTICS	NEWELL	NEWSIEST
NETIZEN	NEUMATIC	NEUROTOMY	NEWELLED	NEWSINESS
NETIZENS	NEUME	NEURULA	NEWELLS	NEWSING
NETLESS	NEUMES	NEURULAE	NEWELS	NEWSLESS
NETLIKE	NEUMIC	NEURULAR	NEWER	NEWSMAKER
NETMINDER	NEUMS	NEURULAS	NEWEST	NEWSMAN
NETOP	NEURAL	NEUSTIC	NEWFANGLE	NEWSMEN
NETOPS	NEURALGIA	NEUSTON	NEWFOUND	NEWSPAPER
NETROOT	NEURALGIC	NEUSTONIC	NEWIE	NEWSPEAK
NETROOTS	NEURALLY	NEUSTONS	NEWIES	NEWSPEAKS
NETS	NEURATION	NEUTER	NEWING	NEWSPRINT
NETSPEAK	NEURAXON	NEUTERED	NEWISH	NEWSREEL
NETSPEAKS	NEURAXONS	NEUTERING	NEWISHLY	NEWSREELS
NETSUKE	NEURILITY	NEUTERS	NEWLY	NEWSROOM
NETSUKES	NEURINE	NEUTRAL	NEWLYWED	NEWSROOMS
NETSURF	NEURINES	NEUTRALLY	NEWLYWEDS	NEWSSHEET
NETSURFED	NEURISM	NEUTRALS	NEWMARKET	NEWSSTAND
NETSURFER	NEURISMS	NEUTRETTO	NEWMOWN	NEWSTRADE
NETSURFS	NEURITE	NEUTRINO	NEWNESS	NEWSWIRE
NETT	NEURITES	NEUTRINOS	NEWNESSES	NEWSWIRES
NETTABLE	NEURITIC	NEUTRON	NEWS	NEWSWOMAN
NETTED	NEURITICS	NEUTRONIC	NEWSAGENT	NEWSWOMEN
NETTER	NEURITIS	NEUTRONS	NEWSBEAT	NEWSY
NETTERS	NEUROCHIP	NEVE	NEWSBEATS	NEWT
NETTIE	NEUROCOEL	NEVEL	NEWSBOY	NEWTON
NETTIER	NEUROGLIA	NEVELLED	NEWSBOYS	NEWTONS
NETTIES	NEUROGRAM	NEVELLING	NEWSBREAK	NEWTS
NETTIEST	NEUROID	NEVELS	NEWSCAST	NEWWAVER

NEWWAVERS	NIBLIKE	NICKLES	NIDERING	NIFFERING
NEXT	NIBS	NICKLING	NIDERINGS	NIFFERS
NEXTDOOR	NICAD	NICKNACK	NIDERLING	NIFFIER
NEXTLY	NICADS	NICKNACKS	NIDES	NIFFIEST
NEXTNESS	NICCOLITE	NICKNAME	NIDGET	NIFFING
NEXTS	NICE	NICKNAMED	NIDGETED	NIFFNAFF
NEXUS	NICEISH	NICKNAMER	NIDGETING	NIFFNAFFS
NEXUSES	NICELY	NICKNAMES	NIDGETS	NIFFS
NGAI	NICENESS	NICKPOINT	NIDI	NIFFY
NGAIO	NICER	NICKS	NIDIFIED	NIFTIER
NGAIOS	NICEST	NICKSTICK	NIDIFIES	NIFTIES
NGANA	NICETIES	NICKUM	NIDIFY	NIFTIEST
NGANAS	NICETY	NICKUMS	NIDIFYING	NIFTILY
NGARARA	NICHE	NICOISE	NIDING	NIFTINESS
NGARARAS	NICHED	NICOL	NIDINGS	NIFTY
NGATI	NICHER	NICOLS	NIDOR	NIGELLA
NGATIS	NICHERED	NICOMPOOP	NIDOROUS	NIGELLAS
NGOMA	NICHERING	NICOTIAN	NIDORS	NIGER
NGOMAS	NICHERS	NICOTIANA	NIDS	NIGERS
NGULTRUM	NICHES	NICOTIANS	NIDUS	NIGGARD
NGULTRUMS	NICHING	NICOTIN	NIDUSES	NIGGARDED
NGWEE	NICHROME	NICOTINE	NIE	NIGGARDLY
NGWEES	NICHROMES	NICOTINED	NIECE	NIGGARDS
NHANDU	NICHT	NICOTINES	NIECES	NIGGER
NHANDUS	NICHTS	NICOTINIC	NIED	NIGGERDOM
NIACIN	NICISH	NICOTINS	NIEF	NIGGERED
NIACINS	NICK	NICTATE	NIEFS	NIGGERING
NIAGARA	NICKAR	NICTATED	NIELLATED	NIGGERISH
NIAGARAS	NICKARS	NICTATES	NIELLI	NIGGERISM
NIAISERIE	NICKED	NICTATING	NIELLIST	NIGGERS
NIALAMIDE	NICKEL	NICTATION	NIELLISTS	NIGGERY
NIB	NICKELED	NICTITANT	NIELLO	NIGGLE
NIBBED	NICKELIC	NICTITATE	NIELLOED	NIGGLED
NIBBING	NICKELINE	NID	NIELLOING	NIGGLER
NIBBLE	NICKELING	NIDAL	NIELLOS	NIGGLERS
NIBBLED	NICKELISE	NIDAMENTA	NIENTE	NIGGLES
NIBBLER	NICKELIZE	NIDATE	NIES	NIGGLIER
NIBBLERS	NICKELLED	NIDATED	NIEVE	NIGGLIEST
NIBBLES	NICKELOUS	NIDATES	NIEVEFUL	NIGGLING
NIBBLIES	NICKELS	NIDATING	NIEVEFULS	NIGGLINGS
NIBBLING	NICKER	NIDATION	NIEVES	NIGGLY
NIBBLINGS	NICKERED	NIDATIONS	NIFE	NIGH
NIBBLY	NICKERING	NIDDERING	NIFES	NIGHED
NIBLET	NICKERS	NIDDICK	NIFF	NIGHER
NIBLETS	NICKING	NIDDICKS	NIFFED	NIGHEST
NIBLICK	NICKLE	NIDE	NIFFER	NIGHING
NIBLICKS	NICKLED	NIDED	NIFFERED	NIGHLY

NIGHNESS
NIGHS
NIGHT
NIGHTBIRD
NIGHTCAP
NIGHTCAPS
NIGHTCLUB
NIGHTED
NIGHTFALL
NIGHTFIRE
NIGHTGEAR
NIGHTGLOW
NIGHTGOWN
NIGHTHAWK
NIGHTIE
NIGHTIES
NIGHTJAR
NIGHTJARS
NIGHTLESS
NIGHTLIFE
NIGHTLIKE
NIGHTLONG
NIGHTLY
NIGHTMARE
NIGHTMARY
NIGHTS
NIGHTSIDE
NIGHTSPOT
NIGHTTIDE
NIGHTTIME
NIGHTWARD
NIGHTWEAR
NIGHTY
NIGIRI
NIGIRIS
NIGRICANT
NIGRIFIED
NIGRIFIES
NIGRIFY
NIGRITUDE
NIGROSIN
NIGROSINE
NIGROSINS
NIHIL
NIHILISM
NIHILISMS
NIHILIST

NIHILISTS
NIHILITY
NIHILS
NIHONGA
NIHONGAS
NIKAB
NIKABS
NIKAH
NIKAHS
NIKAU
NIKAUS
NIL
NILGAI
NILGAIS
NILGAU
NILGAUS
NILGHAI
NILGHAIS
NILGHAU
NILGHAUS
NILL
NILLED
NILLING
NILLS
NILPOTENT
NILS
NIM
NIMB
NIMBED
NIMBI
NIMBLE
NIMBLER
NIMBLESSE
NIMBLEST
NIMBLEWIT
NIMBLY
NIMBS
NIMBUS
NIMBUSED
NIMBUSES
NIMBYISM
NIMBYISMS
NIMBYNESS
NIMIETIES
NIMIETY
NIMIOUS
NIMMED

NIMMER
NIMMERS
NIMMING
NIMONIC
NIMPS
NIMROD
NIMRODS
NIMS
NINCOM
NINCOMS
NINCUM
NINCUMS
NINE
NINEBARK
NINEBARKS
NINEFOLD
NINEHOLES
NINEPENCE
NINEPENNY
NINEPIN
NINEPINS
NINER
NINERS
NINES
NINESCORE
NINETEEN
NINETEENS
NINETIES
NINETIETH
NINETY
NINHYDRIN
NINJA
NINJAS
NINJITSU
NINJITSUS
NINJUTSU
NINJUTSUS
NINNIES
NINNY
NINNYISH
NINON
NINONS
NINTH
NINTHLY
NINTHS
NIOBATE
NIOBATES

NIOBIC
NIOBITE
NIOBITES
NIOBIUM
NIOBIUMS
NIOBOUS
NIP
NIPA
NIPAS
NIPCHEESE
NIPPED
NIPPER
NIPPERED
NIPPERING
NIPPERKIN
NIPPERS
NIPPIER
NIPPIEST
NIPPILY
NIPPINESS
NIPPING
NIPPINGLY
NIPPLE
NIPPLED
NIPPLES
NIPPLING
NIPPY
NIPS
NIPTER
NIPTERS
NIQAAB
NIQAABS
NIQAB
NIQABS
NIRAMIAI
NIRAMIAIS
NIRL
NIRLED
NIRLIE
NIRLIER
NIRLIEST
NIRLING
NIRLIT
NIRLS
NIRLY
NIRVANA
NIRVANAS

NIRVANIC
NIS
NISBERRY
NISEI
NISEIS
NISGUL
NISGULS
NISH
NISHES
NISI
NISSE
NISSES
NISUS
NIT
NITCHIE
NITCHIES
NITE
NITER
NITERIE
NITERIES
NITERS
NITERY
NITES
NITHER
NITHERED
NITHERING
NITHERS
NITHING
NITHINGS
NITID
NITINOL
NITINOLS
NITON
NITONS
NITPICK
NITPICKED
NITPICKER
NITPICKS
NITPICKY
NITRAMINE
NITRATE
NITRATED
NITRATES
NITRATINE
NITRATING
NITRATION
NITRATOR

NITRATORS	NIVEOUS	NOBLY	NODALISES	NOGAKU
NITRE	NIX	NOBODIES	NODALITY	NOGG
NITREOUS	NIXE	NOBODY	NODALIZE	NOGGED
NITRES	NIXED	NOBS	NODALIZED	NOGGIN
NITRIC	NIXER	NOCAKE	NODALIZES	NOGGING
NITRID	NIXERS	NOCAKES	NODALLY	NOGGINGS
NITRIDE	NIXES	NOCEBO	NODATED	NOGGINS
NITRIDED	NIXIE	NOCEBOS	NODATION	NOGGS
NITRIDES	NIXIES	NOCENT	NODATIONS	NOGS
NITRIDING	NIXING	NOCENTLY	NODDED	NOH
NITRIDS	NIXY	NOCENTS	NODDER	NOHOW
NITRIFIED	NIZAM	NOCHEL	NODDERS	NOHOWISH
NITRIFIER	NIZAMATE	NOCHELED	NODDIER	NOIL
NITRIFIES	NIZAMATES	NOCHELING	NODDIES	NOILIER
NITRIFY	NIZAMS	NOCHELLED	NODDIEST	NOILIES
NITRIL	NKOSI	NOCHELS	NODDING	NOILIEST
NITRILE	NKOSIS	NOCK	NODDINGLY	NOILS
NITRILES	NO	NOCKED	NODDINGS	NOILY
NITRILS	NOAH	NOCKET	NODDLE	NOINT
NITRITE	NOAHS	NOCKETS	NODDLED	NOINTED
NITRITES	NOB	NOCKING	NODDLES	NOINTER
NITRO	NOBBIER	NOCKS	NODDLING	NOINTERS
NITROGEN	NOBBIEST	NOCTILIO	NODDY	NOINTING
NITROGENS	NOBBILY	NOCTILIOS	NODE	NOINTS
NITROLIC	NOBBINESS	NOCTILUCA	NODES	NOIR
NITROS	NOBBLE	NOCTUA	NODI	NOIRISH
NITROSO	NOBBLED	NOCTUARY	NODICAL	NOIRS
NITROSYL	NOBBLER	NOCTUAS	NODOSE	NOISE
NITROSYLS	NOBBLERS	NOCTUID	NODOSITY	NOISED
NITROUS	NOBBLES	NOCTUIDS	NODOUS	NOISEFUL
NITROX	NOBBLING	NOCTULE	NODS	NOISELESS
NITROXES	NOBBUT	NOCTULES	NODULAR	NOISENIK
NITROXYL	NOBBY	NOCTUOID	NODULATED	NOISENIKS
NITROXYLS	NOBELIUM	NOCTUOIDS	NODULE	NOISES
NITRY	NOBELIUMS	NOCTURIA	NODULED	NOISETTE
NITRYL	NOBILESSE	NOCTURIAS	NODULES	NOISETTES
NITRYLS	NOBILIARY	NOCTURN	NODULOSE	NOISIER
NITS	NOBILITY	NOCTURNAL	NODULOUS	NOISIEST
NITTIER	NOBLE	NOCTURNE	NODUS	NOISILY
NITTIEST	NOBLEMAN	NOCTURNES	NOEL	NOISINESS
NITTY	NOBLEMEN	NOCTURNS	NOELS	NOISING
NITWIT	NOBLENESS	NOCUOUS	NOES	NOISOME
NITWITS	NOBLER	NOCUOUSLY	NOESES	NOISOMELY
NITWITTED	NOBLES	NOD	NOESIS	NOISY
NIVAL	NOBLESSE	NODAL	NOESISES	NOLE
NIVATION	NOBLESSES	NODALISE	NOETIC	NOLES
NIVATIONS	NOBLEST	NODALISED	NOG	NOLITION

NOLITIONS	NOMISTIC	NONBASIC	NONCYCLIC	NONFADING
NOLL	NOMOCRACY	NONBEING	NONDAIRY	NONFAMILY
NOLLS	NOMOGENY	NONBEINGS	NONDANCE	NONFAN
NOLO	NOMOGRAM	NONBELIEF	NONDANCER	NONFANS
NOLOS	NOMOGRAMS	NONBINARY	NONDANCES	NONFARM
NOM	NOMOGRAPH	NONBITING	NONDEGREE	NONFARMER
NOMA	NOMOI	NONBLACK	NONDEMAND	NONFAT
NOMAD	NOMOLOGIC	NONBLACKS	NONDESERT	NONFATAL
NOMADE	NOMOLOGY	NONBODIES	NONDOCTOR	NONFATTY
NOMADES	NOMOS	NONBODY	NONDOLLAR	NONFEUDAL
NOMADIC	NOMOTHETE	NONBONDED	NONDRIP	NONFILIAL
NOMADIES	NOMS	NONBOOK	NONDRIVER	NONFINAL
NOMADISE	NON	NONBOOKS	NONDRUG	NONFINITE
NOMADISED	NONA	NONBRAND	NONDRYING	NONFISCAL
NOMADISES	NONACID	NONBUYING	NONE	NONFLUID
NOMADISM	NONACIDIC	NONCAKING	NONEDIBLE	NONFLUIDS
NOMADISMS	NONACIDS	NONCAMPUS	NONEGO	NONFLYING
NOMADIZE	NONACTING	NONCAREER	NONEGOS	NONFOCAL
NOMADIZED	NONACTION	NONCASH	NONELECT	NONFOOD
NOMADIZES	NONACTIVE	NONCASUAL	NONELITE	NONFOODS
NOMADS	NONACTOR	NONCAUSAL	NONEMPTY	NONFORMAL
NOMADY	NONACTORS	NONCE	NONENDING	NONFOSSIL
NOMARCH	NONADDICT	NONCEREAL	NONENERGY	NONFROZEN
NOMARCHS	NONADULT	NONCES	NONENTITY	NONFUEL
NOMARCHY	NONADULTS	NONCHURCH	NONENTRY	NONFUELS
NOMAS	NONAGE	NONCLASS	NONEQUAL	NONFUNDED
NOMBLES	NONAGED	NONCLING	NONEQUALS	NONG
NOMBRIL	NONAGES	NONCODING	NONEROTIC	NONGAME
NOMBRILS	NONAGON	NONCOITAL	NONES	NONGAY
NOME	NONAGONAL	NONCOKING	NONESUCH	NONGAYS
NOMEN	NONAGONS	NONCOLA	NONET	NONGHETTO
NOMENS	NONANE	NONCOLAS	NONETHNIC	NONGLARE
NOMES	NONANES	NONCOLOR	NONETS	NONGLARES
NOMIC	NONANIMAL	NONCOLORS	NONETTE	NONGLAZED
NOMINA	NONANOIC	NONCOLOUR	NONETTES	NONGLOSSY
NOMINABLE	NONANSWER	NONCOM	NONETTI	NONGOLFER
NOMINAL	NONARABLE	NONCOMBAT	NONETTO	NONGRADED
NOMINALLY	NONARIES	NONCOMS	NONETTOS	NONGREASY
NOMINALS	NONART	NONCONCUR	NONEVENT	NONGREEN
NOMINATE	NONARTIST	NONCORE	NONEVENTS	NONGROWTH
NOMINATED	NONARTS	NONCOUNT	NONEXEMPT	NONGS
NOMINATES	NONARY	NONCOUNTY	NONEXOTIC	NONGUEST
NOMINATOR	NONAS	NONCREDIT	NONEXPERT	NONGUESTS
NOMINEE	NONATOMIC	NONCRIME	NONEXTANT	NONGUILT
NOMINEES	NONAUTHOR	NONCRIMES	NONFACT	NONGUILTS
NOMISM	NONBANK	NONCRISES	NONFACTOR	NONHARDY
NOMISMS	NONBANKS	NONCRISIS	NONFACTS	NONHEME

NONHERO	NONLOCALS	NONOWNER	NONRIGID	NONSTYLES
NONHEROES	NONLOVING	NONOWNERS	NONRIOTER	NONSUCH
NONHEROIC	NONLOYAL	NONPAGAN	NONRIVAL	NONSUCHES
NONHOME	NONLYRIC	NONPAGANS	NONRIVALS	NONSUGAR
NONHUMAN	NONMAJOR	NONPAID	NONROYAL	NONSUGARS
NONHUMANS	NONMAJORS	NONPAPAL	NONROYALS	NONSUIT
NONHUNTER	NONMAN	NONPAPIST	NONRUBBER	NONSUITED
NONI	NONMANUAL	NONPAR	NONRULING	NONSUITS
NONIDEAL	NONMARKET	NONPAREIL	NONRUN	NONSYSTEM
NONILLION	NONMATURE	NONPARENT	NONRUNNER	NONTALKER
NONIMAGE	NONMEAT	NONPARITY	NONRURAL	NONTARGET
NONIMAGES	NONMEATS	NONPAROUS	NONSACRED	NONTARIFF
NONIMMUNE	NONMEMBER	NONPARTY	NONSALINE	NONTAX
NONIMPACT	NONMEN	NONPAST	NONSCHOOL	NONTAXES
NONINERT	NONMENTAL	NONPASTS	NONSECRET	NONTHEIST
NONINJURY	NONMETAL	NONPAYING	NONSECURE	NONTIDAL
NONINSECT	NONMETALS	NONPEAK	NONSELF	NONTITLE
NONIONIC	NONMETRIC	NONPEAKS	NONSELVES	NONTONAL
NONIRON	NONMETRO	NONPERSON	NONSENSE	NONTONIC
NONIS	NONMOBILE	NONPLANAR	NONSENSES	NONTOXIC
NONISSUE	NONMODAL	NONPLAY	NONSERIAL	NONTRAGIC
NONISSUES	NONMODERN	NONPLAYER	NONSEXIST	NONTRIBAL
NONJOINER	NONMONEY	NONPLAYS	NONSEXUAL	NONTRUMP
NONJURIES	NONMORAL	NONPLIANT	NONSHRINK	NONTRUTH
NONJURING	NONMORTAL	NONPLUS	NONSIGNER	NONTRUTHS
NONJUROR	NONMOTILE	NONPLUSED	NONSKATER	NONUNION
NONJURORS	NONMOVING	NONPLUSES	NONSKED	NONUNIONS
NONJURY	NONMUSIC	NONPOETIC	NONSKEDS	NONUNIQUE
NONKOSHER	NONMUSICS	NONPOINT	NONSKID	NONUPLE
NONLABOR	NONMUTANT	NONPOLAR	NONSKIER	NONUPLES
NONLABOUR	NONMUTUAL	NONPOLICE	NONSKIERS	NONUPLET
NONLAWYER	NONNASAL	NONPOOR	NONSLIP	NONUPLETS
NONLEADED	NONNATIVE	NONPOORS	NONSMOKER	NONURBAN
NONLEAFY	NONNAVAL	NONPOROUS	NONSOCIAL	NONURGENT
NONLEAGUE	NONNEURAL	NONPOSTAL	NONSOLAR	NONUSABLE
NONLEGAL	NONNEWS	NONPRINT	NONSOLID	NONUSE
NONLEGUME	NONNIES	NONPROFIT	NONSOLIDS	NONUSER
NONLETHAL	NONNOBLE	NONPROS	NONSPEECH	NONUSERS
NONLEVEL	NONNORMAL	NONPROVEN	NONSTAPLE	NONUSES
NONLIABLE	NONNOVEL	NONPUBLIC	NONSTATIC	NONUSING
NONLIFE	NONNOVELS	NONQUOTA	NONSTEADY	NONVACANT
NONLINEAL	NONNY	NONRACIAL	NONSTICK	NONVALID
NONLINEAR	NONOBESE	NONRANDOM	NONSTICKY	NONVECTOR
NONLIQUID	NONOHMIC	NONRATED	NONSTOP	NONVENOUS
NONLIVES	NONOILY	NONREADER	NONSTOPS	NONVERBAL
NONLIVING	NONORAL	NONRETURN	NONSTORY	NONVESTED
NONLOCAL	NONORALLY	NONRHOTIC	NONSTYLE	NONVIABLE

N

NONVIEWER	NOOKIE	NORIS	NORTHMOST	NOSINESS
NONVIRAL	NOOKIER	NORITE	NORTHS	NOSING
NONVIRGIN	NOOKIES	NORITES	NORTHWARD	NOSINGS
NONVIRILE	NOOKIEST	NORITIC	NORTHWEST	NOSODE
NONVISUAL	NOOKLIKE	NORK	NORWARD	NOSODES
NONVITAL	NOOKS	NORKS	NORWARDS	NOSOLOGIC
NONVOCAL	NOOKY	NORLAND	NOS	NOSOLOGY
NONVOCALS	NOOLOGIES	NORLANDS	NOSE	NOSTALGIA
NONVOTER	NOOLOGY	NORM	NOSEAN	NOSTALGIC
NONVOTERS	NOOMETRY	NORMA	NOSEANS	NOSTOC
NONVOTING	NOON	NORMAL	NOSEBAG	NOSTOCS
NONWAGE	NOONDAY	NORMALCY	NOSEBAGS	NOSTOI
NONWAR	NOONDAYS	NORMALISE	NOSEBAND	NOSTOLOGY
NONWARS	NOONED	NORMALITY	NOSEBANDS	NOSTOS
NONWHITE	NOONER	NORMALIZE	NOSEBLEED	NOSTRIL
NONWHITES	NOONERS	NORMALLY	NOSED	NOSTRILS
NONWINGED	NOONING	NORMALS	NOSEDIVE	NOSTRO
NONWOODY	NOONINGS	NORMAN	NOSEDIVED	NOSTRUM
NONWOOL	NOONS	NORMANDE	NOSEDIVES	NOSTRUMS
NONWORD	NOONTIDE	NORMANDES	NOSEDOVE	NOSY
NONWORDS	NOONTIDES	NORMANS	NOSEGAY	NOT
NONWORK	NOONTIME	NORMAS	NOSEGAYS	NOTA
NONWORKER	NOONTIMES	NORMATIVE	NOSEGUARD	NOTABILIA
NONWORKS	NOOP	NORMED	NOSELESS	NOTABLE
NONWOVEN	NOOPS	NORMLESS	NOSELIKE	NOTABLES
NONWOVENS	NOOSE	NORMS	NOSELITE	NOTABLY
NONWRITER	NOOSED	NOROVIRUS	NOSELITES	NOTAEUM
NONYL	NOOSER	NORSEL	NOSEPIECE	NOTAEUMS
NONYLS	NOOSERS	NORSELLED	NOSER	NOTAIRE
NONZERO	NOOSES	NORSELLER	NOSERS	NOTAIRES
NOO	NOOSING	NORSELS	NOSES	NOTAL
NOOB	NOOSPHERE	NORTENA	NOSEWHEEL	NOTANDA
NOOBS	NOOTROPIC	NORTENAS	NOSEY	NOTANDUM
NOODGE	NOPAL	NORTENO	NOSEYS	NOTAPHILY
NOODGED	NOPALES	NORTENOS	NOSH	NOTARIAL
NOODGES	NOPALITO	NORTH	NOSHED	NOTARIES
NOODGING	NOPALITOS	NORTHEAST	NOSHER	NOTARISE
NOODLE	NOPALS	NORTHED	NOSHERIE	NOTARISED
NOODLED	NOPE	NORTHER	NOSHERIES	NOTARISES
NOODLEDOM	NOPLACE	NORTHERED	NOSHERS	NOTARIZE
NOODLES	NOR	NORTHERLY	NOSHERY	NOTARIZED
NOODLING	NORDIC	NORTHERN	NOSHES	NOTARIZES
NOODLINGS	NORI	NORTHERNS	NOSHING	NOTARY
NOOGIE	NORIA	NORTHERS	NOSIER	NOTATE
NOOGIES	NORIAS	NORTHING	NOSIES	NOTATED
NOOIT	NORIMON	NORTHINGS	NOSIEST	NOTATES
NOOK	NORIMONS	NORTHLAND	NOSILY	NOTATING

NOTATION	NOTIFIER	NOURICE	NOVELISM	NOWISE
NOTATIONS	NOTIFIERS	NOURICES	NOVELISMS	NOWL
NOTATOR	NOTIFIES	NOURISH	NOVELIST	NOWLS
NOTATORS	NOTIFY	NOURISHED	NOVELISTS	NOWN
NOTCH	NOTIFYING	NOURISHER	NOVELIZE	NOWNESS
NOTCHBACK	NOTING	NOURISHES	NOVELIZED	NOWNESSES
NOTCHED	NOTION	NOURITURE	NOVELIZER	NOWS
NOTCHEL	NOTIONAL	NOURSLE	NOVELIZES	NOWT
NOTCHELED	NOTIONIST	NOURSLED	NOVELLA	NOWTIER
NOTCHELS	NOTIONS	NOURSLES	NOVELLAE	NOWTIEST
NOTCHER	NOTITIA	NOURSLING	NOVELLAS	NOWTS
NOTCHERS	NOTITIAE	NOUS	NOVELLE	NOWTY
NOTCHES	NOTITIAS	NOUSELL	NOVELLY	NOWY
NOTCHIER	NOTOCHORD	NOUSELLED	NOVELS	NOX
NOTCHIEST	NOTORIETY	NOUSELLS	NOVELTIES	NOXAL
NOTCHING	NOTORIOUS	NOUSES	NOVELTY	NOXES
NOTCHINGS	NOTORNIS	NOUSLE	NOVEMBER	NOXIOUS
NOTCHY	NOTOUR	NOUSLED	NOVEMBERS	NOXIOUSLY
NOTE	NOTT	NOUSLES	NOVENA	NOY
NOTEBOOK	NOTTURNI	NOUSLING	NOVENAE	NOYADE
NOTEBOOKS	NOTTURNO	NOUT	NOVENARY	NOYADES
NOTECARD	NOTUM	NOUVEAU	NOVENAS	NOYANCE
NOTECARDS	NOUGAT	NOUVEAUX	NOVENNIAL	NOYANCES
NOTECASE	NOUGATINE	NOUVELLE	NOVERCAL	NOYAU
NOTECASES	NOUGATS	NOUVELLES	NOVERINT	NOYAUS
NOTED	NOUGHT	NOVA	NOVERINTS	NOYAUX
NOTEDLY	NOUGHTIES	NOVAE	NOVICE	NOYED
NOTEDNESS	NOUGHTS	NOVALIA	NOVICES	NOYES
NOTELESS	NOUL	NOVALIKE	NOVICIATE	NOYESES
NOTELET	NOULD	NOVAS	NOVITIATE	NOYING
NOTELETS	NOULDE	NOVATE	NOVITIES	NOYOUS
NOTEPAD	NOULE	NOVATED	NOVITY	NOYS
NOTEPADS	NOULES	NOVATES	NOVOCAINE	NOYSOME
NOTEPAPER	NOULS	NOVATING	NOVODAMUS	NOZZER
NOTER	NOUMENA	NOVATION	NOVUM	NOZZERS
NOTERS	NOUMENAL	NOVATIONS	NOVUMS	NOZZLE
NOTES	NOUMENON	NOVEL	NOW	NOZZLES
NOTHER	NOUN	NOVELDOM	NOWADAYS	NTH
NOTHING	NOUNAL	NOVELDOMS	NOWAY	NU
NOTHINGS	NOUNALLY	NOVELESE	NOWAYS	NUANCE
NOTICE	NOUNIER	NOVELESES	NOWCAST	NUANCED
NOTICED	NOUNIEST	NOVELETTE	NOWCASTS	NUANCES
NOTICER	NOUNLESS	NOVELISE	NOWED	NUANCING
NOTICERS	NOUNS	NOVELISED	NOWHENCE	NUB
NOTICES	NOUNY	NOVELISER	NOWHERE	NUBBED
NOTICING	NOUP	NOVELISES	NOWHERES	NUBBIER
NOTIFIED	NOUPS	NOVELISH	NOWHITHER	NUBBIEST

NUBBIN	NUCLEOID	NUDZHED	NUMBED	NUMMULARY
NUBBINESS	NUCLEOIDS	NUDZHES	NUMBER	NUMMULINE
NUBBING	NUCLEOLAR	NUDZHING	NUMBERED	NUMMULITE
NUBBINGS	NUCLEOLE	NUFF	NUMBERER	NUMMY
NUBBINS	NUCLEOLES	NUFFIN	NUMBERERS	NUMNAH
NUBBLE	NUCLEOLI	NUFFINS	NUMBERING	NUMNAHS
NUBBLED	NUCLEOLUS	NUFFS	NUMBERS	NUMPKIN
NUBBLES	NUCLEON	NUG	NUMBEST	NUMPKINS
NUBBLIER	NUCLEONIC	NUGAE	NUMBFISH	NUMPTIES
NUBBLIEST	NUCLEONS	NUGATORY	NUMBHEAD	NUMPTY
NUBBLING	NUCLEUS	NUGGAR	NUMBHEADS	NUMSKULL
NUBBLY	NUCLEUSES	NUGGARS	NUMBING	NUMSKULLS
NUBBY	NUCLIDE	NUGGET	NUMBINGLY	NUN
NUBECULA	NUCLIDES	NUGGETED	NUMBLES	NUNATAK
NUBECULAE	NUCLIDIC	NUGGETING	NUMBLY	NUNATAKER
NUBIA	NUCULE	NUGGETS	NUMBNESS	NUNATAKS
NUBIAS	NUCULES	NUGGETTED	NUMBNUT	NUNCHAKU
NUBIFORM	NUDATION	NUGGETY	NUMBNUTS	NUNCHAKUS
NUBILE	NUDATIONS	NUGS	NUMBS	NUNCHEON
NUBILITY	NUDDIES	NUISANCE	NUMBSKULL	NUNCHEONS
NUBILOSE	NUDDY	NUISANCER	NUMCHUCK	NUNCHUCKS
NUBILOUS	NUDE	NUISANCES	NUMCHUCKS	NUNCHUK
NUBS	NUDELY	NUKE	NUMDAH	NUNCHUKS
NUBUCK	NUDENESS	NUKED	NUMDAHS	NUNCIO
NUBUCKS	NUDER	NUKES	NUMEN	NUNCIOS
NUCELLAR	NUDES	NUKING	NUMERABLE	NUNCLE
NUCELLI	NUDEST	NULL	NUMERABLY	NUNCLES
NUCELLUS	NUDGE	NULLA	NUMERACY	NUNCUPATE
NUCHA	NUDGED	NULLAH	NUMERAIRE	NUNDINAL
NUCHAE	NUDGER	NULLAHS	NUMERAL	NUNDINE
NUCHAL	NUDGERS	NULLAS	NUMERALLY	NUNDINES
NUCHALS	NUDGES	NULLED	NUMERALS	NUNHOOD
NUCLEAL	NUDGING	NULLIFIED	NUMERARY	NUNHOODS
NUCLEAR	NUDICAUL	NULLIFIER	NUMERATE	NUNLIKE
NUCLEASE	NUDIE	NULLIFIES	NUMERATED	NUNNATION
NUCLEASES	NUDIES	NULLIFY	NUMERATES	NUNNERIES
NUCLEATE	NUDISM	NULLING	NUMERATOR	NUNNERY
NUCLEATED	NUDISMS	NULLINGS	NUMERIC	NUNNISH
NUCLEATES	NUDIST	NULLIPARA	NUMERICAL	NUNNY
NUCLEATOR	NUDISTS	NULLIPORE	NUMERICS	NUNS
NUCLEI	NUDITIES	NULLITIES	NUMEROUS	NUNSHIP
NUCLEIC	NUDITY	NULLITY	NUMINA	NUNSHIPS
NUCLEIDE	NUDNICK	NULLNESS	NUMINOUS	NUPTIAL
NUCLEIDES	NUDNICKS	NULLS	NUMMARY	NUPTIALLY
NUCLEIN	NUDNIK	NUMB	NUMMIER	NUPTIALS
NUCLEINIC	NUDNIKS	NUMBAT	NUMMIEST	NUR
NUCLEINS	NUDZH	NUMBATS	NUMMULAR	NURAGHE

NURAGHI	NURTURAL	NUTLOAF	NUTTINESS	NYLON
NURAGHIC	NURTURANT	NUTLOAVES	NUTTING	NYLONED
NURD	NURTURE	NUTMEAL	NUTTINGS	NYLONS
NURDIER	NURTURED	NUTMEALS	NUTTY	NYM
NURDIEST	NURTURER	NUTMEAT	NUTWOOD	NYMPH
NURDISH	NURTURERS	NUTMEATS	NUTWOODS	NYMPHA
NURDLE	NURTURES	NUTMEG	NUZZER	NYMPHAE
NURDLED	NURTURING	NUTMEGGED	NUZZERS	NYMPHAEA
NURDLES	NUS	NUTMEGGY	NUZZLE	NYMPHAEAS
NURDLING	NUT	NUTMEGS	NUZZLED	NYMPHAEUM
NURDS	NUTANT	NUTPECKER	NUZZLER	NYMPHAL
NURDY	NUTARIAN	NUTPICK	NUZZLERS	NYMPHALID
NURHAG	NUTARIANS	NUTPICKS	NUZZLES	NYMPHEAN
NURHAGS	NUTATE	NUTRIA	NUZZLING	NYMPHED
NURL	NUTATED	NUTRIAS	NY	NYMPHET
NURLED	NUTATES	NUTRIENT	NYAFF	NYMPHETIC
NURLING	NUTATING	NUTRIENTS	NYAFFED	NYMPHETS
NURLS	NUTATION	NUTRIMENT	NYAFFING	NYMPHETTE
NURR	NUTATIONS	NUTRITION	NYAFFS	NYMPHIC
NURRS	NUTBAR	NUTRITIVE	NYAH	NYMPHICAL
NURS	NUTBARS	NUTS	NYALA	NYMPHING
NURSE	NUTBROWN	NUTSEDGE	NYALAS	NYMPHISH
NURSED	NUTBUTTER	NUTSEDGES	NYANZA	NYMPHLIKE
NURSELIKE	NUTCASE	NUTSHELL	NYANZAS	NYMPHLY
NURSELING	NUTCASES	NUTSHELLS	NYAS	NYMPHO
NURSEMAID	NUTGALL	NUTSIER	NYASES	NYMPHOS
NURSER	NUTGALLS	NUTSIEST	NYBBLE	NYMPHS
NURSERIES	NUTGRASS	NUTSO	NYBBLES	NYS
NURSERS	NUTHATCH	NUTSOS	NYCTALOPE	NYSSA
NURSERY	NUTHIN	NUTSY	NYCTALOPS	NYSSAS
NURSES	NUTHOUSE	NUTTED	NYE	NYSTAGMIC
NURSING	NUTHOUSES	NUTTER	NYED	NYSTAGMUS
NURSINGS	NUTJOB	NUTTERIES	NYES	NYSTATIN
NURSLE	NUTJOBBER	NUTTERS	NYING	NYSTATINS
NURSLED	NUTJOBS	NUTTERY	NYLGHAI	
NURSLES	NUTLET	NUTTIER	NYLGHAIS	
NURSLING	NUTLETS	NUTTIEST	NYLGHAU	
NURSLINGS	NUTLIKE	NUTTILY	NYLGHAUS	

N

O

OAF
OAFISH
OAFISHLY
OAFS
OAK
OAKED
OAKEN
OAKENSHAW
OAKER
OAKERS
OAKIER
OAKIES
OAKIEST
OAKINESS
OAKLEAF
OAKLEAVES
OAKLIKE
OAKLING
OAKLINGS
OAKMOSS
OAKMOSSES
OAKS
OAKUM
OAKUMS
OAKWOOD
OAKWOODS
OAKY
OANSHAGH
OANSHAGHS
OAR
OARAGE
OARAGES
OARED
OARFISH
OARFISHES
OARIER
OARIEST
OARING
OARLESS
OARLIKE
OARLOCK

OARLOCKS
OARS
OARSMAN
OARSMEN
OARSWOMAN
OARSWOMEN
OARWEED
OARWEEDS
OARY
OASES
OASIS
OAST
OASTHOUSE
OASTS
OAT
OATCAKE
OATCAKES
OATEN
OATER
OATERS
OATH
OATHABLE
OATHS
OATIER
OATIEST
OATLIKE
OATMEAL
OATMEALS
OATS
OATY
OAVES
OB
OBA
OBANG
OBANGS
OBAS
OBBLIGATI
OBBLIGATO
OBCONIC
OBCONICAL
OBCORDATE

OBDURACY
OBDURATE
OBDURATED
OBDURATES
OBDURE
OBDURED
OBDURES
OBDURING
OBE
OBEAH
OBEAHED
OBEAHING
OBEAHISM
OBEAHISMS
OBEAHS
OBECHE
OBECHES
OBEDIENCE
OBEDIENT
OBEISANCE
OBEISANT
OBEISM
OBEISMS
OBELI
OBELIA
OBELIAS
OBELION
OBELISCAL
OBELISE
OBELISED
OBELISES
OBELISING
OBELISK
OBELISKS
OBELISM
OBELISMS
OBELIZE
OBELIZED
OBELIZES
OBELIZING
OBELUS

OBENTO
OBENTOS
OBES
OBESE
OBESELY
OBESENESS
OBESER
OBESEST
OBESITIES
OBESITY
OBESOGEN
OBESOGENS
OBEY
OBEYABLE
OBEYED
OBEYER
OBEYERS
OBEYING
OBEYS
OBFUSCATE
OBI
OBIA
OBIAS
OBIED
OBIING
OBIISM
OBIISMS
OBIIT
OBIS
OBIT
OBITAL
OBITER
OBITS
OBITUAL
OBITUARY
OBJECT
OBJECTED
OBJECTIFY
OBJECTING
OBJECTION
OBJECTIVE

OBJECTOR
OBJECTORS
OBJECTS
OBJET
OBJETS
OBJURE
OBJURED
OBJURES
OBJURGATE
OBJURING
OBLAST
OBLASTI
OBLASTS
OBLATE
OBLATELY
OBLATES
OBLATION
OBLATIONS
OBLATORY
OBLIGABLE
OBLIGANT
OBLIGANTS
OBLIGATE
OBLIGATED
OBLIGATES
OBLIGATI
OBLIGATO
OBLIGATOR
OBLIGATOS
OBLIGE
OBLIGED
OBLIGEE
OBLIGEES
OBLIGER
OBLIGERS
OBLIGES
OBLIGING
OBLIGOR
OBLIGORS
OBLIQUE
OBLIQUED

OBLIQUELY	OBSCUREST	OBTAINING	OBVERTS	OCCULTERS
OBLIQUER	OBSCURING	OBTAINS	OBVIABLE	OCCULTING
OBLIQUES	OBSCURITY	OBTECT	OBVIATE	OCCULTISM
OBLIQUEST	OBSECRATE	OBTECTED	OBVIATED	OCCULTIST
OBLIQUID	OBSEQUENT	OBTEMPER	OBVIATES	OCCULTLY
OBLIQUING	OBSEQUIAL	OBTEMPERS	OBVIATING	OCCULTS
OBLIQUITY	OBSEQUIE	OBTEND	OBVIATION	OCCUPANCE
OBLIVION	OBSEQUIES	OBTENDED	OBVIATOR	OCCUPANCY
OBLIVIONS	OBSEQUY	OBTENDING	OBVIATORS	OCCUPANT
OBLIVIOUS	OBSERVANT	OBTENDS	OBVIOUS	OCCUPANTS
OBLONG	OBSERVE	OBTENTION	OBVIOUSLY	OCCUPATE
OBLONGLY	OBSERVED	OBTEST	OBVOLUTE	OCCUPATED
OBLONGS	OBSERVER	OBTESTED	OBVOLUTED	OCCUPATES
OBLOQUIAL	OBSERVERS	OBTESTING	OBVOLVENT	OCCUPIED
OBLOQUIES	OBSERVES	OBTESTS	OBVS	OCCUPIER
OBLOQUY	OBSERVING	OBTRUDE	OCA	OCCUPIERS
OBNOXIOUS	OBSESS	OBTRUDED	OCARINA	OCCUPIES
OBO	OBSESSED	OBTRUDER	OCARINAS	OCCUPY
OBOE	OBSESSES	OBTRUDERS	OCAS	OCCUPYING
OBOES	OBSESSING	OBTRUDES	OCCAM	OCCUR
OBOIST	OBSESSION	OBTRUDING	OCCAMIES	OCCURRED
OBOISTS	OBSESSIVE	OBTRUSION	OCCAMS	OCCURRENT
OBOL	OBSESSOR	OBTRUSIVE	OCCAMY	OCCURRING
OBOLARY	OBSESSORS	OBTUND	OCCASION	OCCURS
OBOLE	OBSIDIAN	OBTUNDED	OCCASIONS	OCCY
OBOLES	OBSIDIANS	OBTUNDENT	OCCIDENT	OCEAN
OBOLI	OBSIGN	OBTUNDING	OCCIDENTS	OCEANARIA
OBOLS	OBSIGNATE	OBTUNDITY	OCCIES	OCEANAUT
OBOLUS	OBSIGNED	OBTUNDS	OCCIPITA	OCEANAUTS
OBOS	OBSIGNING	OBTURATE	OCCIPITAL	OCEANIC
OBOVATE	OBSIGNS	OBTURATED	OCCIPUT	OCEANID
OBOVATELY	OBSOLESCE	OBTURATES	OCCIPUTS	OCEANIDES
OBOVOID	OBSOLETE	OBTURATOR	OCCLUDE	OCEANIDS
OBREPTION	OBSOLETED	OBTUSE	OCCLUDED	OCEANS
OBS	OBSOLETES	OBTUSELY	OCCLUDENT	OCELLAR
OBSCENE	OBSTACLE	OBTUSER	OCCLUDER	OCELLATE
OBSCENELY	OBSTACLES	OBTUSEST	OCCLUDERS	OCELLATED
OBSCENER	OBSTETRIC	OBTUSITY	OCCLUDES	OCELLI
OBSCENEST	OBSTINACY	OBUMBRATE	OCCLUDING	OCELLUS
OBSCENITY	OBSTINATE	OBVENTION	OCCLUSAL	OCELOID
OBSCURANT	OBSTRUCT	OBVERSE	OCCLUSION	OCELOT
OBSCURE	OBSTRUCTS	OBVERSELY	OCCLUSIVE	OCELOTS
OBSCURED	OBSTRUENT	OBVERSES	OCCLUSOR	OCH
OBSCURELY	OBTAIN	OBVERSION	OCCLUSORS	OCHE
OBSCURER	OBTAINED	OBVERT	OCCULT	OCHER
OBSCURERS	OBTAINER	OBVERTED	OCCULTED	OCHERED
OBSCURES	OBTAINERS	OBVERTING	OCCULTER	OCHERING

O

OCHERISH	OCTAMETER	OCTOPUS	ODDBALLS	ODONTOMA
OCHEROID	OCTAN	OCTOPUSES	ODDER	ODONTOMAS
OCHEROUS	OCTANE	OCTOPUSH	ODDEST	ODOR
OCHERS	OCTANES	OCTOROON	ODDISH	ODORANT
OCHERY	OCTANGLE	OCTOROONS	ODDITIES	ODORANTS
OCHES	OCTANGLES	OCTOSTYLE	ODDITY	ODORATE
OCHIDORE	OCTANOL	OCTOTHORP	ODDLY	ODORED
OCHIDORES	OCTANOLS	OCTROI	ODDMENT	ODORFUL
OCHLOCRAT	OCTANS	OCTROIS	ODDMENTS	ODORISE
OCHONE	OCTANT	OCTUOR	ODDNESS	ODORISED
OCHRE	OCTANTAL	OCTUORS	ODDNESSES	ODORISER
OCHREA	OCTANTS	OCTUPLE	ODDS	ODORISERS
OCHREAE	OCTAPLA	OCTUPLED	ODDSMAKER	ODORISES
OCHREAS	OCTAPLAS	OCTUPLES	ODDSMAN	ODORISING
OCHREATE	OCTAPLOID	OCTUPLET	ODDSMEN	ODORIZE
OCHRED	OCTAPODIC	OCTUPLETS	ODE	ODORIZED
OCHREOUS	OCTAPODY	OCTUPLEX	ODEA	ODORIZER
OCHRES	OCTARCHY	OCTUPLING	ODEON	ODORIZERS
OCHREY	OCTAROON	OCTUPLY	ODEONS	ODORIZES
OCHRING	OCTAROONS	OCTYL	ODES	ODORIZING
OCHROID	OCTAS	OCTYLS	ODEUM	ODORLESS
OCHROUS	OCTASTICH	OCULAR	ODEUMS	ODOROUS
OCHRY	OCTASTYLE	OCULARIST	ODIC	ODOROUSLY
OCICAT	OCTAVAL	OCULARLY	ODIFEROUS	ODORS
OCICATS	OCTAVE	OCULARS	ODIOUS	ODOUR
OCKER	OCTAVES	OCULATE	ODIOUSLY	ODOURED
OCKERISM	OCTAVO	OCULATED	ODISM	ODOURFUL
OCKERISMS	OCTAVOS	OCULI	ODISMS	ODOURLESS
OCKERS	OCTENNIAL	OCULIST	ODIST	ODOURS
OCKODOLS	OCTET	OCULISTS	ODISTS	ODS
OCOTILLO	OCTETS	OCULUS	ODIUM	ODSO
OCOTILLOS	OCTETT	OD	ODIUMS	ODYL
OCREA	OCTETTE	ODA	ODOGRAPH	ODYLE
OCREAE	OCTETTES	ODAH	ODOGRAPHS	ODYLES
OCREAS	OCTETTS	ODAHS	ODOMETER	ODYLISM
OCREATE	OCTILLION	ODAL	ODOMETERS	ODYLISMS
OCTA	OCTOFID	ODALIQUE	ODOMETRY	ODYLS
OCTACHORD	OCTOHEDRA	ODALIQUES	ODONATA	ODYSSEAN
OCTAD	OCTONARII	ODALISK	ODONATE	ODYSSEY
OCTADIC	OCTONARY	ODALISKS	ODONATES	ODYSSEYS
OCTADS	OCTOPI	ODALISQUE	ODONATIST	ODZOOKS
OCTAGON	OCTOPLOID	ODALLER	ODONTALGY	OE
OCTAGONAL	OCTOPOD	ODALLERS	ODONTIC	OECIST
OCTAGONS	OCTOPODAN	ODALS	ODONTIST	OECISTS
OCTAHEDRA	OCTOPODES	ODAS	ODONTISTS	OECOLOGIC
OCTAL	OCTOPODS	ODD	ODONTOID	OECOLOGY
OCTALS	OCTOPOID	ODDBALL	ODONTOIDS	OECUMENIC

OEDEMA	OFFA	OFFICIOUS	OFTENER	OHIAS
OEDEMAS	OFFAL	OFFIE	OFTENEST	OHING
OEDEMATA	OFFALS	OFFIES	OFTENNESS	OHM
OEDIPAL	OFFBEAT	OFFING	OFTER	OHMAGE
OEDIPALLY	OFFBEATS	OFFINGS	OFTEST	OHMAGES
OEDIPEAN	OFFCAST	OFFISH	OFTTIMES	OHMIC
OEDOMETER	OFFCASTS	OFFISHLY	OGAM	OHMICALLY
OEILLADE	OFFCUT	OFFKEY	OGAMIC	OHMMETER
OEILLADES	OFFCUTS	OFFLINE	OGAMS	OHMMETERS
OENANTHIC	OFFED	OFFLOAD	OGDOAD	OHMS
OENOLOGY	OFFENCE	OFFLOADED	OGDOADS	OHO
OENOMANCY	OFFENCES	OFFLOADS	OGEE	OHONE
OENOMANIA	OFFEND	OFFPEAK	OGEED	OHS
OENOMEL	OFFENDED	OFFPRINT	OGEES	OI
OENOMELS	OFFENDER	OFFPRINTS	OGGIN	OIDIA
OENOMETER	OFFENDERS	OFFPUT	OGGINS	OIDIOID
OENOPHIL	OFFENDING	OFFPUTS	OGHAM	OIDIUM
OENOPHILE	OFFENDS	OFFRAMP	OGHAMIC	OIK
OENOPHILS	OFFENSE	OFFRAMPS	OGHAMIST	OIKIST
OENOPHILY	OFFENSES	OFFS	OGHAMISTS	OIKISTS
OENOTHERA	OFFENSIVE	OFFSADDLE	OGHAMS	OIKS
OERLIKON	OFFER	OFFSCREEN	OGIVAL	OIL
OERLIKONS	OFFERABLE	OFFSCUM	OGIVE	OILBIRD
OERSTED	OFFERED	OFFSCUMS	OGIVES	OILBIRDS
OERSTEDS	OFFEREE	OFFSEASON	OGLE	OILCAMP
OES	OFFEREES	OFFSET	OGLED	OILCAMPS
OESOPHAGI	OFFERER	OFFSETS	OGLER	OILCAN
OESTRAL	OFFERERS	OFFSHOOT	OGLERS	OILCANS
OESTRIN	OFFERING	OFFSHOOTS	OGLES	OILCLOTH
OESTRINS	OFFERINGS	OFFSHORE	OGLING	OILCLOTHS
OESTRIOL	OFFEROR	OFFSHORED	OGLINGS	OILCUP
OESTRIOLS	OFFERORS	OFFSHORES	OGMIC	OILCUPS
OESTROGEN	OFFERS	OFFSIDE	OGRE	OILED
OESTRONE	OFFERTORY	OFFSIDER	OGREISH	OILER
OESTRONES	OFFHAND	OFFSIDERS	OGREISHLY	OILERIES
OESTROUS	OFFHANDED	OFFSIDES	OGREISM	OILERS
OESTRUAL	OFFICE	OFFSPRING	OGREISMS	OILERY
OESTRUM	OFFICER	OFFSTAGE	OGRES	OILFIELD
OESTRUMS	OFFICERED	OFFSTAGES	OGRESS	OILFIELDS
OESTRUS	OFFICERS	OFFTAKE	OGRESSES	OILFIRED
OESTRUSES	OFFICES	OFFTAKES	OGRISH	OILGAS
OEUVRE	OFFICIAL	OFFTRACK	OGRISHLY	OILGASES
OEUVRES	OFFICIALS	OFFY	OGRISM	OILHOLE
OF	OFFICIANT	OFLAG	OGRISMS	OILHOLES
OFAY	OFFICIARY	OFLAGS	OH	OILIER
OFAYS	OFFICIATE	OFT	OHED	OILIEST
OFF	OFFICINAL	OFTEN	OHIA	OILILY

O

OILINESS	OKAYED	OLEATE	OLIGOCENE	OLOGOANED
OILING	OKAYING	OLEATES	OLIGOGENE	OLOGOANS
OILLET	OKAYS	OLECRANAL	OLIGOMER	OLOGY
OILLETS	OKE	OLECRANON	OLIGOMERS	OLOLIUQUI
OILMAN	OKEH	OLEFIANT	OLIGOPOLY	OLOROSO
OILMEN	OKEHS	OLEFIN	OLIGURIA	OLOROSOS
OILNUT	OKES	OLEFINE	OLIGURIAS	OLPAE
OILNUTS	OKEYDOKE	OLEFINES	OLIGURIC	OLPE
OILPAN	OKEYDOKEY	OLEFINIC	OLINGO	OLPES
OILPANS	OKIMONO	OLEFINS	OLINGOS	OLYCOOK
OILPAPER	OKIMONOS	OLEIC	OLINGUITO	OLYCOOKS
OILPAPERS	OKRA	OLEIN	OLIO	OLYKOEK
OILPROOF	OKRAS	OLEINE	OLIOS	OLYKOEKS
OILS	OKTA	OLEINES	OLIPHANT	OLYMPIAD
OILSEED	OKTAS	OLEINS	OLIPHANTS	OLYMPIADS
OILSEEDS	OLD	OLENT	OLITORIES	OLYMPICS
OILSKIN	OLDE	OLEO	OLITORY	OM
OILSKINS	OLDEN	OLEOGRAPH	OLIVARY	OMA
OILSTONE	OLDENED	OLEORESIN	OLIVE	OMADHAUN
OILSTONES	OLDENING	OLEOS	OLIVENITE	OMADHAUNS
OILTIGHT	OLDENS	OLES	OLIVER	OMAS
OILWAY	OLDER	OLESTRA	OLIVERS	OMASA
OILWAYS	OLDEST	OLESTRAS	OLIVES	OMASAL
OILY	OLDIE	OLEUM	OLIVET	OMASUM
OINK	OLDIES	OLEUMS	OLIVETS	OMBER
OINKED	OLDISH	OLFACT	OLIVEWOOD	OMBERS
OINKING	OLDNESS	OLFACTED	OLIVINE	OMBRE
OINKS	OLDNESSES	OLFACTING	OLIVINES	OMBRELLA
OINOLOGY	OLDS	OLFACTION	OLIVINIC	OMBRELLAS
OINOMEL	OLDSQUAW	OLFACTIVE	OLLA	OMBRES
OINOMELS	OLDSQUAWS	OLFACTORY	OLLAMH	OMBROPHIL
OINT	OLDSTER	OLFACTS	OLLAMHS	OMBU
OINTED	OLDSTERS	OLIBANUM	OLLAS	OMBUDSMAN
OINTING	OLDSTYLE	OLIBANUMS	OLLAV	OMBUDSMEN
OINTMENT	OLDSTYLES	OLICOOK	OLLAVS	OMBUS
OINTMENTS	OLDWIFE	OLICOOKS	OLLER	OMEGA
OINTS	OLDWIVES	OLID	OLLERS	OMEGAS
OIS	OLDY	OLIGAEMIA	OLLIE	OMELET
OITICICA	OLE	OLIGAEMIC	OLLIED	OMELETS
OITICICAS	OLEA	OLIGARCH	OLLIEING	OMELETTE
OJIME	OLEACEOUS	OLIGARCHS	OLLIES	OMELETTES
OJIMES	OLEANDER	OLIGARCHY	OLM	OMEN
OKA	OLEANDERS	OLIGEMIA	OLMS	OMENED
OKAPI	OLEARIA	OLIGEMIAS	OLOGIES	OMENING
OKAPIS	OLEARIAS	OLIGEMIC	OLOGIST	OMENS
OKAS	OLEASTER	OLIGIST	OLOGISTS	OMENTA
OKAY	OLEASTERS	OLIGISTS	OLOGOAN	OMENTAL

O

OMENTUM	OMNIUMS	ONCOGENS	ONEYER	ONRUSH
OMENTUMS	OMNIVORA	ONCOLOGIC	ONEYERS	ONRUSHES
OMER	OMNIVORE	ONCOLOGY	ONEYRE	ONRUSHING
OMERS	OMNIVORES	ONCOLYSES	ONEYRES	ONS
OMERTA	OMNIVORY	ONCOLYSIS	ONFALL	ONSCREEN
OMERTAS	OMOHYOID	ONCOLYTIC	ONFALLS	ONSET
OMICRON	OMOHYOIDS	ONCOME	ONFLOW	ONSETS
OMICRONS	OMOPHAGIA	ONCOMES	ONFLOWS	ONSETTER
OMIGOD	OMOPHAGIC	ONCOMETER	ONGAONGA	ONSETTERS
OMIKRON	OMOPHAGY	ONCOMICE	ONGAONGAS	ONSETTING
OMIKRONS	OMOPHORIA	ONCOMING	ONGOING	ONSHORE
OMINOUS	OMOPLATE	ONCOMINGS	ONGOINGS	ONSHORING
OMINOUSLY	OMOPLATES	ONCOMOUSE	ONIE	ONSIDE
OMISSIBLE	OMOV	ONCOST	ONION	ONSIDES
OMISSION	OMOVS	ONCOSTMAN	ONIONED	ONSLAUGHT
OMISSIONS	OMPHACITE	ONCOSTMEN	ONIONIER	ONST
OMISSIVE	OMPHALI	ONCOSTS	ONIONIEST	ONSTAGE
OMIT	OMPHALIC	ONCOTOMY	ONIONING	ONSTEAD
OMITS	OMPHALOI	ONCOVIRUS	ONIONS	ONSTEADS
OMITTANCE	OMPHALOID	ONCUS	ONIONSKIN	ONSTREAM
OMITTED	OMPHALOS	ONDATRA	ONIONY	ONTIC
OMITTER	OMRAH	ONDATRAS	ONIRIC	ONTICALLY
OMITTERS	OMRAHS	ONDINE	ONISCOID	ONTO
OMITTING	OMS	ONDINES	ONIUM	ONTOGENIC
OMLAH	ON	ONDING	ONIUMS	ONTOGENY
OMLAHS	ONAGER	ONDINGS	ONKUS	ONTOLOGIC
OMMATEA	ONAGERS	ONDOGRAM	ONLAY	ONTOLOGY
OMMATEUM	ONAGRI	ONDOGRAMS	ONLAYS	ONUS
OMMATIDIA	ONANISM	ONDOGRAPH	ONLIEST	ONUSES
OMNEITIES	ONANISMS	ONE	ONLINE	ONWARD
OMNEITY	ONANIST	ONEFOLD	ONLINER	ONWARDLY
OMNIANA	ONANISTIC	ONEIRIC	ONLINERS	ONWARDS
OMNIARCH	ONANISTS	ONELY	ONLOAD	ONY
OMNIARCHS	ONBEAT	ONENESS	ONLOADED	ONYCHA
OMNIBUS	ONBEATS	ONENESSES	ONLOADING	ONYCHAS
OMNIBUSES	ONBOARD	ONER	ONLOADS	ONYCHIA
OMNIETIES	ONCE	ONERIER	ONLOOKER	ONYCHIAS
OMNIETY	ONCER	ONERIEST	ONLOOKERS	ONYCHITE
OMNIFIC	ONCERS	ONEROUS	ONLOOKING	ONYCHITES
OMNIFIED	ONCES	ONEROUSLY	ONLY	ONYCHITIS
OMNIFIES	ONCET	ONERS	ONNED	ONYCHIUM
OMNIFORM	ONCIDIUM	ONERY	ONNING	ONYCHIUMS
OMNIFY	ONCIDIUMS	ONES	ONO	ONYMOUS
OMNIFYING	ONCOGEN	ONESELF	ONOMAST	ONYX
OMNIMODE	ONCOGENE	ONESIE	ONOMASTIC	ONYXES
OMNIRANGE	ONCOGENES	ONESIES	ONOMASTS	OO
OMNIUM	ONCOGENIC	ONETIME	ONOS	OOBIT

OOBITS	OOLOGIES	OOSIEST	OPAQUE	OPERATISE
OOCYST	OOLOGIST	OOSPERM	OPAQUED	OPERATIVE
OOCYSTS	OOLOGISTS	OOSPERMS	OPAQUELY	OPERATIZE
OOCYTE	OOLOGY	OOSPHERE	OPAQUER	OPERATOR
OOCYTES	OOLONG	OOSPHERES	OPAQUES	OPERATORS
OODLES	OOLONGS	OOSPORE	OPAQUEST	OPERCELE
OODLINS	OOM	OOSPORES	OPAQUING	OPERCELES
OOF	OOMIAC	OOSPORIC	OPAS	OPERCULA
OOFIER	OOMIACK	OOSPOROUS	OPCODE	OPERCULAR
OOFIEST	OOMIACKS	OOSY	OPCODES	OPERCULE
OOFS	OOMIACS	OOT	OPE	OPERCULES
OOFTISH	OOMIAK	OOTHECA	OPED	OPERCULUM
OOFTISHES	OOMIAKS	OOTHECAE	OPEN	OPERETTA
OOFY	OOMPAH	OOTHECAL	OPENABLE	OPERETTAS
OOGAMETE	OOMPAHED	OOTID	OPENCAST	OPERON
OOGAMETES	OOMPAHING	OOTIDS	OPENED	OPERONS
OOGAMIES	OOMPAHS	OOTS	OPENER	OPEROSE
OOGAMOUS	OOMPH	OOZE	OPENERS	OPEROSELY
OOGAMY	OOMPHS	OOZED	OPENEST	OPEROSITY
OOGENESES	OOMS	OOZES	OPENING	OPES
OOGENESIS	OOMYCETE	OOZIER	OPENINGS	OPGEFOK
OOGENETIC	OOMYCETES	OOZIEST	OPENLY	OPHIDIAN
OOGENIES	OON	OOZILY	OPENNESS	OPHIDIANS
OOGENY	OONS	OOZINESS	OPENS	OPHIOLITE
OOGONIA	OONT	OOZING	OPENSIDE	OPHIOLOGY
OOGONIAL	OONTS	OOZY	OPENSIDES	OPHITE
OOGONIUM	OOP	OP	OPENWORK	OPHITES
OOGONIUMS	OOPED	OPA	OPENWORKS	OPHITIC
OOH	OOPHORON	OPACIFIED	OPEPE	OPHIURA
OOHED	OOPHORONS	OPACIFIER	OPEPES	OPHIURAN
OOHING	OOPHYTE	OPACIFIES	OPERA	OPHIURANS
OOHINGS	OOPHYTES	OPACIFY	OPERABLE	OPHIURAS
OOHS	OOPHYTIC	OPACITIES	OPERABLY	OPHIURID
OOIDAL	OOPING	OPACITY	OPERAGOER	OPHIURIDS
OOLACHAN	OOPS	OPACOUS	OPERAND	OPHIUROID
OOLACHANS	OOR	OPAH	OPERANDS	OPIATE
OOLAKAN	OORALI	OPAHS	OPERANT	OPIATED
OOLAKANS	OORALIS	OPAL	OPERANTLY	OPIATES
OOLICHAN	OORIAL	OPALED	OPERANTS	OPIATING
OOLICHANS	OORIALS	OPALESCE	OPERAS	OPIFICER
OOLITE	OORIE	OPALESCED	OPERATE	OPIFICERS
OOLITES	OORIER	OPALESCES	OPERATED	OPINABLE
OOLITH	OORIEST	OPALINE	OPERATES	OPINE
OOLITHS	OOS	OPALINES	OPERATIC	OPINED
OOLITIC	OOSE	OPALISED	OPERATICS	OPINES
OOLOGIC	OOSES	OPALIZED	OPERATING	OPING
OOLOGICAL	OOSIER	OPALS	OPERATION	OPINICUS

OPINING	OPPUGNER	OPTIMISED	OQUASSA	ORARIONS
OPINION	OPPUGNERS	OPTIMISER	OQUASSAS	ORARIUM
OPINIONED	OPPUGNING	OPTIMISES	OR	ORARIUMS
OPINIONS	OPPUGNS	OPTIMISM	ORA	ORATE
OPIOID	OPS	OPTIMISMS	ORACH	ORATED
OPIOIDS	OPSIMATH	OPTIMIST	ORACHE	ORATES
OPIUM	OPSIMATHS	OPTIMISTS	ORACHES	ORATING
OPIUMISM	OPSIMATHY	OPTIMIZE	ORACIES	ORATION
OPIUMISMS	OPSIN	OPTIMIZED	ORACLE	ORATIONS
OPIUMS	OPSINS	OPTIMIZER	ORACLED	ORATOR
OPOBALSAM	OPSOMANIA	OPTIMIZES	ORACLES	ORATORIAL
OPODELDOC	OPSONIC	OPTIMUM	ORACLING	ORATORIAN
OPOPANAX	OPSONIFY	OPTIMUMS	ORACULAR	ORATORIES
OPORICE	OPSONIN	OPTING	ORACULOUS	ORATORIO
OPORICES	OPSONINS	OPTION	ORACY	ORATORIOS
OPOSSUM	OPSONISE	OPTIONAL	ORAD	ORATORS
OPOSSUMS	OPSONISED	OPTIONALS	ORAGIOUS	ORATORY
OPPIDAN	OPSONISES	OPTIONED	ORAL	ORATRESS
OPPIDANS	OPSONIUM	OPTIONEE	ORALISM	ORATRICES
OPPILANT	OPSONIUMS	OPTIONEES	ORALISMS	ORATRIX
OPPILATE	OPSONIZE	OPTIONING	ORALIST	ORATRIXES
OPPILATED	OPSONIZED	OPTIONS	ORALISTS	ORATURE
OPPILATES	OPSONIZES	OPTOLOGY	ORALITIES	ORATURES
OPPO	OPT	OPTOMETER	ORALITY	ORB
OPPONENCY	OPTANT	OPTOMETRY	ORALLY	ORBED
OPPONENS	OPTANTS	OPTOPHONE	ORALS	ORBICULAR
OPPONENT	OPTATIVE	OPTRONIC	ORANG	ORBIER
OPPONENTS	OPTATIVES	OPTRONICS	ORANGE	ORBIEST
OPPORTUNE	OPTED	OPTS	ORANGEADE	ORBING
OPPOS	OPTER	OPULENCE	ORANGER	ORBIT
OPPOSABLE	OPTERS	OPULENCES	ORANGERIE	ORBITA
OPPOSABLY	OPTIC	OPULENCY	ORANGERY	ORBITAL
OPPOSE	OPTICAL	OPULENT	ORANGES	ORBITALLY
OPPOSED	OPTICALLY	OPULENTLY	ORANGEST	ORBITALS
OPPOSER	OPTICIAN	OPULUS	ORANGEY	ORBITAS
OPPOSERS	OPTICIANS	OPULUSES	ORANGIER	ORBITED
OPPOSES	OPTICIST	OPUNTIA	ORANGIEST	ORBITER
OPPOSING	OPTICISTS	OPUNTIAS	ORANGISH	ORBITERS
OPPOSITE	OPTICS	OPUS	ORANGS	ORBITIES
OPPOSITES	OPTIMA	OPUSCLE	ORANGUTAN	ORBITING
OPPRESS	OPTIMAL	OPUSCLES	ORANGY	ORBITS
OPPRESSED	OPTIMALLY	OPUSCULA	ORANT	ORBITY
OPPRESSES	OPTIMATE	OPUSCULAR	ORANTS	ORBLESS
OPPRESSOR	OPTIMATES	OPUSCULE	ORARIA	ORBS
OPPUGN	OPTIME	OPUSCULES	ORARIAN	ORBY
OPPUGNANT	OPTIMES	OPUSCULUM	ORARIANS	ORC
OPPUGNED	OPTIMISE	OPUSES	ORARION	ORCA

O

ORCAS	ORDERED	OREODONT	ORGANUMS	ORIENTERS
ORCEIN	ORDERER	OREODONTS	ORGANZA	ORIENTING
ORCEINS	ORDERERS	OREOLOGY	ORGANZAS	ORIENTS
ORCHARD	ORDERING	OREPEARCH	ORGANZINE	ORIFEX
ORCHARDS	ORDERINGS	ORES	ORGASM	ORIFEXES
ORCHAT	ORDERLESS	ORESTUNCK	ORGASMED	ORIFICE
ORCHATS	ORDERLIES	OREWEED	ORGASMIC	ORIFICES
ORCHEL	ORDERLY	OREWEEDS	ORGASMING	ORIFICIAL
ORCHELLA	ORDERS	OREXIN	ORGASMS	ORIFLAMME
ORCHELLAS	ORDINAIRE	OREXINS	ORGASTIC	ORIGAMI
ORCHELS	ORDINAL	OREXIS	ORGEAT	ORIGAMIS
ORCHESES	ORDINALLY	OREXISES	ORGEATS	ORIGAN
ORCHESIS	ORDINALS	ORF	ORGIA	ORIGANE
ORCHESTIC	ORDINANCE	ORFE	ORGIAC	ORIGANES
ORCHESTRA	ORDINAND	ORFES	ORGIAS	ORIGANS
ORCHID	ORDINANDS	ORFRAY	ORGIAST	ORIGANUM
ORCHIDIST	ORDINANT	ORFRAYS	ORGIASTIC	ORIGANUMS
ORCHIDS	ORDINANTS	ORFS	ORGIASTS	ORIGIN
ORCHIL	ORDINAR	ORG	ORGIC	ORIGINAL
ORCHILLA	ORDINARS	ORGAN	ORGIES	ORIGINALS
ORCHILLAS	ORDINARY	ORGANA	ORGILLOUS	ORIGINATE
ORCHILS	ORDINATE	ORGANDIE	ORGONE	ORIGINS
ORCHIS	ORDINATED	ORGANDIES	ORGONES	ORIHOU
ORCHISES	ORDINATES	ORGANDY	ORGS	ORIHOUS
ORCHITIC	ORDINEE	ORGANELLE	ORGUE	ORILLION
ORCHITIS	ORDINEES	ORGANIC	ORGUES	ORILLIONS
ORCIN	ORDINES	ORGANICAL	ORGULOUS	ORINASAL
ORCINE	ORDNANCE	ORGANICS	ORGY	ORINASALS
ORCINES	ORDNANCES	ORGANISE	ORIBATID	ORIOLE
ORCINOL	ORDO	ORGANISED	ORIBATIDS	ORIOLES
ORCINOLS	ORDOS	ORGANISER	ORIBI	ORISHA
ORCINS	ORDS	ORGANISES	ORIBIS	ORISHAS
ORCS	ORDURE	ORGANISM	ORICALCHE	ORISON
ORD	ORDURES	ORGANISMS	ORICHALC	ORISONS
ORDAIN	ORDUROUS	ORGANIST	ORICHALCS	ORIXA
ORDAINED	ORE	ORGANISTS	ORIEL	ORIXAS
ORDAINER	OREAD	ORGANITY	ORIELLED	ORLE
ORDAINERS	OREADES	ORGANIZE	ORIELS	ORLEANS
ORDAINING	OREADS	ORGANIZED	ORIENCIES	ORLEANSES
ORDAINS	OREBODIES	ORGANIZER	ORIENCY	ORLES
ORDALIAN	OREBODY	ORGANIZES	ORIENT	ORLISTAT
ORDALIUM	ORECTIC	ORGANON	ORIENTAL	ORLISTATS
ORDALIUMS	ORECTIVE	ORGANONS	ORIENTALS	ORLON
ORDEAL	OREGANO	ORGANOSOL	ORIENTATE	ORLONS
ORDEALS	OREGANOS	ORGANOTIN	ORIENTED	ORLOP
ORDER	OREIDE	ORGANS	ORIENTEER	ORLOPS
ORDERABLE	OREIDES	ORGANUM	ORIENTER	ORMER

ORMERS	ORPHREYED	ORTHROSES	OSMATIC	OSSETRA
ORMOLU	ORPHREYS	ORTOLAN	OSMETERIA	OSSETRAS
ORMOLUS	ORPIMENT	ORTOLANS	OSMIATE	OSSIA
ORNAMENT	ORPIMENTS	ORTS	OSMIATES	OSSIAS
ORNAMENTS	ORPIN	ORVAL	OSMIC	OSSICLE
ORNATE	ORPINE	ORVALS	OSMICALLY	OSSICLES
ORNATELY	ORPINES	ORYX	OSMICS	OSSICULAR
ORNATER	ORPINS	ORYXES	OSMIOUS	OSSIFIC
ORNATEST	ORRA	ORZO	OSMIUM	OSSIFIED
ORNERIER	ORRAMAN	ORZOS	OSMIUMS	OSSIFIER
ORNERIEST	ORRAMEN	OS	OSMOL	OSSIFIERS
ORNERY	ORRERIES	OSAR	OSMOLAL	OSSIFIES
ORNIS	ORRERY	OSCAR	OSMOLAR	OSSIFRAGA
ORNISES	ORRICE	OSCARS	OSMOLE	OSSIFRAGE
ORNITHES	ORRICES	OSCHEAL	OSMOLES	OSSIFY
ORNITHIC	ORRIS	OSCILLATE	OSMOLS	OSSIFYING
ORNITHINE	ORRISES	OSCINE	OSMOMETER	OSSOBUCO
ORNITHOID	ORRISROOT	OSCINES	OSMOMETRY	OSSOBUCOS
OROGEN	ORS	OSCININE	OSMOSE	OSSUARIES
OROGENIC	ORSEILLE	OSCITANCE	OSMOSED	OSSUARY
OROGENIES	ORSEILLES	OSCITANCY	OSMOSES	OSTEAL
OROGENS	ORSELLIC	OSCITANT	OSMOSING	OSTEITIC
OROGENY	ORT	OSCITATE	OSMOSIS	OSTEITIS
OROGRAPHY	ORTANIQUE	OSCITATED	OSMOTIC	OSTENSIVE
OROIDE	ORTHIAN	OSCITATES	OSMOUS	OSTENSORY
OROIDES	ORTHICON	OSCULA	OSMUND	OSTENT
OROLOGIES	ORTHICONS	OSCULANT	OSMUNDA	OSTENTED
OROLOGIST	ORTHO	OSCULAR	OSMUNDAS	OSTENTING
OROLOGY	ORTHOAXES	OSCULATE	OSMUNDINE	OSTENTS
OROMETER	ORTHOAXIS	OSCULATED	OSMUNDS	OSTEOCYTE
OROMETERS	ORTHODOX	OSCULATES	OSNABURG	OSTEODERM
ORONASAL	ORTHODOXY	OSCULE	OSNABURGS	OSTEOGEN
OROPESA	ORTHOEPIC	OSCULES	OSPREY	OSTEOGENS
OROPESAS	ORTHOEPY	OSCULUM	OSPREYS	OSTEOGENY
OROTUND	ORTHOPEDY	OSE	OSSA	OSTEOID
ORPHAN	ORTHOPOD	OSES	OSSARIUM	OSTEOIDS
ORPHANAGE	ORTHOPODS	OSETRA	OSSARIUMS	OSTEOLOGY
ORPHANED	ORTHOPTER	OSETRAS	OSSATURE	OSTEOMA
ORPHANING	ORTHOPTIC	OSHAC	OSSATURES	OSTEOMAS
ORPHANISM	ORTHOS	OSHACS	OSSEIN	OSTEOMATA
ORPHANS	ORTHOSES	OSIER	OSSEINS	OSTEOPATH
ORPHARION	ORTHOSIS	OSIERED	OSSELET	OSTEOSES
ORPHIC	ORTHOTIC	OSIERIES	OSSELETS	OSTEOSIS
ORPHICAL	ORTHOTICS	OSIERS	OSSEOUS	OSTEOTOME
ORPHISM	ORTHOTIST	OSIERY	OSSEOUSLY	OSTEOTOMY
ORPHISMS	ORTHOTONE	OSMATE	OSSETER	OSTIA
ORPHREY	ORTHROS	OSMATES	OSSETERS	OSTIAL

OSTIARIES	OTARINE	OUABAIN	OULDEST	OUSTERS
OSTIARY	OTARY	OUABAINS	OULK	OUSTING
OSTIATE	OTHER	OUAKARI	OULKS	OUSTITI
OSTINATI	OTHERNESS	OUAKARIS	OULONG	OUSTITIS
OSTINATO	OTHERS	OUBAAS	OULONGS	OUSTS
OSTINATOS	OTHERWISE	OUBAASES	OUMA	OUT
OSTIOLAR	OTIC	OUBIT	OUMAS	OUTA
OSTIOLATE	OTIOSE	OUBITS	OUNCE	OUTACT
OSTIOLE	OTIOSELY	OUBLIETTE	OUNCES	OUTACTED
OSTIOLES	OTIOSITY	OUCH	OUNDIER	OUTACTING
OSTIUM	OTITIC	OUCHED	OUNDIEST	OUTACTS
OSTLER	OTITIDES	OUCHES	OUNDY	OUTADD
OSTLERESS	OTITIS	OUCHING	OUP	OUTADDED
OSTLERS	OTITISES	OUCHT	OUPA	OUTADDING
OSTMARK	OTOCYST	OUCHTS	OUPAS	OUTADDS
OSTMARKS	OTOCYSTIC	OUD	OUPED	OUTAGE
OSTOMATE	OTOCYSTS	OUDS	OUPH	OUTAGES
OSTOMATES	OTOLITH	OUENS	OUPHE	OUTARGUE
OSTOMIES	OTOLITHIC	OUGHLIED	OUPHES	OUTARGUED
OSTOMY	OTOLITHS	OUGHLIES	OUPHS	OUTARGUES
OSTOSES	OTOLOGIC	OUGHLY	OUPING	OUTASIGHT
OSTOSIS	OTOLOGIES	OUGHLYING	OUPS	OUTASITE
OSTOSISES	OTOLOGIST	OUGHT	OUR	OUTASK
OSTRACA	OTOLOGY	OUGHTED	OURALI	OUTASKED
OSTRACEAN	OTOPLASTY	OUGHTING	OURALIS	OUTASKING
OSTRACISE	OTORRHOEA	OUGHTNESS	OURANG	OUTASKS
OSTRACISM	OTOSCOPE	OUGHTS	OURANGS	OUTATE
OSTRACIZE	OTOSCOPES	OUGIYA	OURARI	OUTBACK
OSTRACOD	OTOSCOPIC	OUGIYAS	OURARIS	OUTBACKER
OSTRACODE	OTOSCOPY	OUGLIE	OUREBI	OUTBACKS
OSTRACODS	OTOTOXIC	OUGLIED	OUREBIS	OUTBAKE
OSTRACON	OTTAR	OUGLIEING	OURIE	OUTBAKED
OSTRAKA	OTTARS	OUGLIES	OURIER	OUTBAKES
OSTRAKON	OTTAVA	OUGUIYA	OURIEST	OUTBAKING
OSTREGER	OTTAVAS	OUGUIYAS	OURN	OUTBAR
OSTREGERS	OTTAVINO	OUIJA	OUROBOROS	OUTBARK
OSTRICH	OTTAVINOS	OUIJAS	OUROLOGY	OUTBARKED
OSTRICHES	OTTER	OUISTITI	OUROSCOPY	OUTBARKS
OTAKU	OTTERED	OUISTITIS	OURS	OUTBARRED
OTAKUS	OTTERING	OUK	OURSELF	OUTBARS
OTALGIA	OTTERS	OUKS	OURSELVES	OUTBAWL
OTALGIAS	OTTO	OULACHON	OUS	OUTBAWLED
OTALGIC	OTTOMAN	OULACHONS	OUSEL	OUTBAWLS
OTALGIES	OTTOMANS	OULAKAN	OUSELS	OUTBEAM
OTALGY	OTTOS	OULAKANS	OUST	OUTBEAMED
OTARID	OTTRELITE	OULD	OUSTED	OUTBEAMS
OTARIES	OU	OULDER	OUSTER	OUTBEG

OUTBEGGED	OUTBUILD	OUTCLIMB	OUTDODGE	OUTEATS
OUTBEGS	OUTBUILDS	OUTCLIMBS	OUTDODGED	OUTECHO
OUTBID	OUTBUILT	OUTCLOMB	OUTDODGES	OUTECHOED
OUTBIDDEN	OUTBULGE	OUTCOACH	OUTDOER	OUTECHOES
OUTBIDDER	OUTBULGED	OUTCOME	OUTDOERS	OUTED
OUTBIDS	OUTBULGES	OUTCOMES	OUTDOES	OUTEDGE
OUTBITCH	OUTBULK	OUTCOOK	OUTDOING	OUTEDGES
OUTBLAZE	OUTBULKED	OUTCOOKED	OUTDONE	OUTER
OUTBLAZED	OUTBULKS	OUTCOOKS	OUTDOOR	OUTERCOAT
OUTBLAZES	OUTBULLY	OUTCOUNT	OUTDOORS	OUTERMOST
OUTBLEAT	OUTBURN	OUTCOUNTS	OUTDOORSY	OUTERS
OUTBLEATS	OUTBURNED	OUTCRAFTY	OUTDRAG	OUTERWEAR
OUTBLESS	OUTBURNS	OUTCRAWL	OUTDRAGS	OUTFABLE
OUTBLOOM	OUTBURNT	OUTCRAWLS	OUTDRANK	OUTFABLED
OUTBLOOMS	OUTBURST	OUTCRIED	OUTDRAW	OUTFABLES
OUTBLUFF	OUTBURSTS	OUTCRIES	OUTDRAWN	OUTFACE
OUTBLUFFS	OUTBUY	OUTCROP	OUTDRAWS	OUTFACED
OUTBLUSH	OUTBUYING	OUTCROPS	OUTDREAM	OUTFACES
OUTBOARD	OUTBUYS	OUTCROSS	OUTDREAMS	OUTFACING
OUTBOARDS	OUTBY	OUTCROW	OUTDREAMT	OUTFALL
OUTBOAST	OUTBYE	OUTCROWD	OUTDRESS	OUTFALLS
OUTBOASTS	OUTCALL	OUTCROWDS	OUTDREW	OUTFAST
OUTBOUGHT	OUTCALLED	OUTCROWED	OUTDRINK	OUTFASTED
OUTBOUND	OUTCALLS	OUTCROWS	OUTDRINKS	OUTFASTS
OUTBOUNDS	OUTCAPER	OUTCRY	OUTDRIVE	OUTFAWN
OUTBOX	OUTCAPERS	OUTCRYING	OUTDRIVEN	OUTFAWNED
OUTBOXED	OUTCAST	OUTCURSE	OUTDRIVES	OUTFAWNS
OUTBOXES	OUTCASTE	OUTCURSED	OUTDROP	OUTFEAST
OUTBOXING	OUTCASTED	OUTCURSES	OUTDROPS	OUTFEASTS
OUTBRAG	OUTCASTES	OUTCURVE	OUTDROVE	OUTFEEL
OUTBRAGS	OUTCASTS	OUTCURVES	OUTDRUNK	OUTFEELS
OUTBRAVE	OUTCATCH	OUTDANCE	OUTDUEL	OUTFELT
OUTBRAVED	OUTCAUGHT	OUTDANCED	OUTDUELED	OUTFENCE
OUTBRAVES	OUTCAVIL	OUTDANCES	OUTDUELS	OUTFENCED
OUTBRAWL	OUTCAVILS	OUTDARE	OUTDURE	OUTFENCES
OUTBRAWLS	OUTCHARGE	OUTDARED	OUTDURED	OUTFIELD
OUTBRAZEN	OUTCHARM	OUTDARES	OUTDURES	OUTFIELDS
OUTBREAK	OUTCHARMS	OUTDARING	OUTDURING	OUTFIGHT
OUTBREAKS	OUTCHEAT	OUTDATE	OUTDWELL	OUTFIGHTS
OUTBRED	OUTCHEATS	OUTDATED	OUTDWELLS	OUTFIGURE
OUTBREED	OUTCHID	OUTDATES	OUTDWELT	OUTFIND
OUTBREEDS	OUTCHIDE	OUTDATING	OUTEARN	OUTFINDS
OUTBRIBE	OUTCHIDED	OUTDAZZLE	OUTEARNED	OUTFIRE
OUTBRIBED	OUTCHIDES	OUTDEBATE	OUTEARNS	OUTFIRED
OUTBRIBES	OUTCITIES	OUTDESIGN	OUTEAT	OUTFIRES
OUTBROKE	OUTCITY	OUTDID	OUTEATEN	OUTFIRING
OUTBROKEN	OUTCLASS	OUTDO	OUTEATING	OUTFISH

OUTFISHED	OUTGATE	OUTGUNNED	OUTJOCKEY	OUTLEAPS
OUTFISHES	OUTGATES	OUTGUNS	OUTJUGGLE	OUTLEAPT
OUTFIT	OUTGAVE	OUTGUSH	OUTJUMP	OUTLEARN
OUTFITS	OUTGAZE	OUTGUSHED	OUTJUMPED	OUTLEARNS
OUTFITTED	OUTGAZED	OUTGUSHES	OUTJUMPS	OUTLEARNT
OUTFITTER	OUTGAZES	OUTHANDLE	OUTJUT	OUTLED
OUTFLANK	OUTGAZING	OUTHAUL	OUTJUTS	OUTLER
OUTFLANKS	OUTGIVE	OUTHAULER	OUTJUTTED	OUTLERS
OUTFLASH	OUTGIVEN	OUTHAULS	OUTKEEP	OUTLET
OUTFLEW	OUTGIVES	OUTHEAR	OUTKEEPS	OUTLETS
OUTFLIES	OUTGIVING	OUTHEARD	OUTKEPT	OUTLIE
OUTFLING	OUTGLARE	OUTHEARS	OUTKICK	OUTLIED
OUTFLINGS	OUTGLARED	OUTHER	OUTKICKED	OUTLIER
OUTFLOAT	OUTGLARES	OUTHIRE	OUTKICKS	OUTLIERS
OUTFLOATS	OUTGLEAM	OUTHIRED	OUTKILL	OUTLIES
OUTFLOW	OUTGLEAMS	OUTHIRES	OUTKILLED	OUTLINE
OUTFLOWED	OUTGLOW	OUTHIRING	OUTKILLS	OUTLINEAR
OUTFLOWN	OUTGLOWED	OUTHIT	OUTKISS	OUTLINED
OUTFLOWS	OUTGLOWS	OUTHITS	OUTKISSED	OUTLINER
OUTFLUNG	OUTGNAW	OUTHOMER	OUTKISSES	OUTLINERS
OUTFLUSH	OUTGNAWED	OUTHOMERS	OUTLAID	OUTLINES
OUTFLY	OUTGNAWN	OUTHOUSE	OUTLAIN	OUTLINING
OUTFLYING	OUTGNAWS	OUTHOUSES	OUTLAND	OUTLIVE
OUTFOOL	OUTGO	OUTHOWL	OUTLANDER	OUTLIVED
OUTFOOLED	OUTGOER	OUTHOWLED	OUTLANDS	OUTLIVER
OUTFOOLS	OUTGOERS	OUTHOWLS	OUTLASH	OUTLIVERS
OUTFOOT	OUTGOES	OUTHUMOR	OUTLASHED	OUTLIVES
OUTFOOTED	OUTGOING	OUTHUMORS	OUTLASHES	OUTLIVING
OUTFOOTS	OUTGOINGS	OUTHUMOUR	OUTLAST	OUTLOOK
OUTFOUGHT	OUTGONE	OUTHUNT	OUTLASTED	OUTLOOKED
OUTFOUND	OUTGREW	OUTHUNTED	OUTLASTS	OUTLOOKS
OUTFOX	OUTGRIN	OUTHUNTS	OUTLAUGH	OUTLOVE
OUTFOXED	OUTGRINS	OUTHUSTLE	OUTLAUGHS	OUTLOVED
OUTFOXES	OUTGROSS	OUTHYRE	OUTLAUNCE	OUTLOVES
OUTFOXING	OUTGROUP	OUTHYRED	OUTLAUNCH	OUTLOVING
OUTFROWN	OUTGROUPS	OUTHYRES	OUTLAW	OUTLUSTRE
OUTFROWNS	OUTGROW	OUTHYRING	OUTLAWED	OUTLYING
OUTFUMBLE	OUTGROWN	OUTING	OUTLAWING	OUTMAN
OUTGAIN	OUTGROWS	OUTINGS	OUTLAWRY	OUTMANNED
OUTGAINED	OUTGROWTH	OUTJEST	OUTLAWS	OUTMANS
OUTGAINS	OUTGUARD	OUTJESTED	OUTLAY	OUTMANTLE
OUTGALLOP	OUTGUARDS	OUTJESTS	OUTLAYING	OUTMARCH
OUTGAMBLE	OUTGUESS	OUTJET	OUTLAYS	OUTMASTER
OUTGAS	OUTGUIDE	OUTJETS	OUTLEAD	OUTMATCH
OUTGASES	OUTGUIDED	OUTJINX	OUTLEADS	OUTMODE
OUTGASSED	OUTGUIDES	OUTJINXED	OUTLEAP	OUTMODED
OUTGASSES	OUTGUN	OUTJINXES	OUTLEAPED	OUTMODES

OUTMODING	OUTPLAYS	OUTPUTS	OUTREMER	OUTRUSH
OUTMOST	OUTPLOD	OUTPUTTED	OUTREMERS	OUTRUSHED
OUTMOVE	OUTPLODS	OUTQUOTE	OUTRIDDEN	OUTRUSHES
OUTMOVED	OUTPLOT	OUTQUOTED	OUTRIDE	OUTS
OUTMOVES	OUTPLOTS	OUTQUOTES	OUTRIDER	OUTSAID
OUTMOVING	OUTPOINT	OUTRACE	OUTRIDERS	OUTSAIL
OUTMUSCLE	OUTPOINTS	OUTRACED	OUTRIDES	OUTSAILED
OUTNAME	OUTPOLL	OUTRACES	OUTRIDING	OUTSAILS
OUTNAMED	OUTPOLLED	OUTRACING	OUTRIG	OUTSANG
OUTNAMES	OUTPOLLS	OUTRAGE	OUTRIGGED	OUTSAT
OUTNAMING	OUTPORT	OUTRAGED	OUTRIGGER	OUTSAVOR
OUTNESS	OUTPORTER	OUTRAGES	OUTRIGHT	OUTSAVORS
OUTNESSES	OUTPORTS	OUTRAGING	OUTRIGS	OUTSAVOUR
OUTNIGHT	OUTPOST	OUTRAISE	OUTRING	OUTSAW
OUTNIGHTS	OUTPOSTS	OUTRAISED	OUTRINGS	OUTSAY
OUTNUMBER	OUTPOUR	OUTRAISES	OUTRIVAL	OUTSAYING
OUTOFFICE	OUTPOURED	OUTRAN	OUTRIVALS	OUTSAYS
OUTPACE	OUTPOURER	OUTRANCE	OUTRO	OUTSCHEME
OUTPACED	OUTPOURS	OUTRANCES	OUTROAR	OUTSCOLD
OUTPACES	OUTPOWER	OUTRANG	OUTROARED	OUTSCOLDS
OUTPACING	OUTPOWERS	OUTRANGE	OUTROARS	OUTSCOOP
OUTPAINT	OUTPRAY	OUTRANGED	OUTROCK	OUTSCOOPS
OUTPAINTS	OUTPRAYED	OUTRANGES	OUTROCKED	OUTSCORE
OUTPART	OUTPRAYS	OUTRANK	OUTROCKS	OUTSCORED
OUTPARTS	OUTPREACH	OUTRANKED	OUTRODE	OUTSCORES
OUTPASS	OUTPREEN	OUTRANKS	OUTROLL	OUTSCORN
OUTPASSED	OUTPREENS	OUTRATE	OUTROLLED	OUTSCORNS
OUTPASSES	OUTPRESS	OUTRATED	OUTROLLS	OUTSCREAM
OUTPEEP	OUTPRICE	OUTRATES	OUTROOP	OUTSEE
OUTPEEPED	OUTPRICED	OUTRATING	OUTROOPER	OUTSEEING
OUTPEEPS	OUTPRICES	OUTRAVE	OUTROOPS	OUTSEEN
OUTPEER	OUTPRIZE	OUTRAVED	OUTROOT	OUTSEES
OUTPEERED	OUTPRIZED	OUTRAVES	OUTROOTED	OUTSELL
OUTPEERS	OUTPRIZES	OUTRAVING	OUTROOTS	OUTSELLS
OUTPEOPLE	OUTPSYCH	OUTRE	OUTROPE	OUTSERT
OUTPITCH	OUTPSYCHS	OUTREACH	OUTROPER	OUTSERTS
OUTPITIED	OUTPULL	OUTREAD	OUTROPERS	OUTSERVE
OUTPITIES	OUTPULLED	OUTREADS	OUTROPES	OUTSERVED
OUTPITY	OUTPULLS	OUTREASON	OUTROS	OUTSERVES
OUTPLACE	OUTPUNCH	OUTRECKON	OUTROW	OUTSET
OUTPLACED	OUTPUPIL	OUTRED	OUTROWED	OUTSETS
OUTPLACER	OUTPUPILS	OUTREDDED	OUTROWING	OUTSHAME
OUTPLACES	OUTPURSUE	OUTREDDEN	OUTROWS	OUTSHAMED
OUTPLAN	OUTPUSH	OUTREDS	OUTRUN	OUTSHAMES
OUTPLANS	OUTPUSHED	OUTREIGN	OUTRUNG	OUTSHINE
OUTPLAY	OUTPUSHES	OUTREIGNS	OUTRUNNER	OUTSHINED
OUTPLAYED	OUTPUT	OUTRELIEF	OUTRUNS	OUTSHINES

O

OUTSHONE	OUTSOAR	OUTSTRAIN	OUTTASKS	OUTVOICES
OUTSHOOT	OUTSOARED	OUTSTRIDE	OUTTELL	OUTVOTE
OUTSHOOTS	OUTSOARS	OUTSTRIKE	OUTTELLS	OUTVOTED
OUTSHOT	OUTSOLD	OUTSTRIP	OUTTHANK	OUTVOTER
OUTSHOTS	OUTSOLE	OUTSTRIPS	OUTTHANKS	OUTVOTERS
OUTSHOUT	OUTSOLES	OUTSTRIVE	OUTTHIEVE	OUTVOTES
OUTSHOUTS	OUTSOURCE	OUTSTRODE	OUTTHINK	OUTVOTING
OUTSIDE	OUTSPAN	OUTSTROKE	OUTTHINKS	OUTVYING
OUTSIDER	OUTSPANS	OUTSTROVE	OUTTHREW	OUTWAIT
OUTSIDERS	OUTSPEAK	OUTSTRUCK	OUTTHROB	OUTWAITED
OUTSIDES	OUTSPEAKS	OUTSTUDY	OUTTHROBS	OUTWAITS
OUTSIGHT	OUTSPED	OUTSTUNT	OUTTHROW	OUTWALK
OUTSIGHTS	OUTSPEED	OUTSTUNTS	OUTTHROWN	OUTWALKED
OUTSIN	OUTSPEEDS	OUTSULK	OUTTHROWS	OUTWALKS
OUTSING	OUTSPELL	OUTSULKED	OUTTHRUST	OUTWAR
OUTSINGS	OUTSPELLS	OUTSULKS	OUTTOLD	OUTWARD
OUTSINNED	OUTSPELT	OUTSUM	OUTTONGUE	OUTWARDLY
OUTSINS	OUTSPEND	OUTSUMMED	OUTTOOK	OUTWARDS
OUTSIT	OUTSPENDS	OUTSUMS	OUTTOP	OUTWARRED
OUTSITS	OUTSPENT	OUTSUNG	OUTTOPPED	OUTWARS
OUTSIZE	OUTSPOKE	OUTSWAM	OUTTOPS	OUTWASH
OUTSIZED	OUTSPOKEN	OUTSWARE	OUTTOWER	OUTWASHES
OUTSIZES	OUTSPORT	OUTSWEAR	OUTTOWERS	OUTWASTE
OUTSKATE	OUTSPORTS	OUTSWEARS	OUTTRADE	OUTWASTED
OUTSKATED	OUTSPRANG	OUTSWEEP	OUTTRADED	OUTWASTES
OUTSKATES	OUTSPREAD	OUTSWEEPS	OUTTRADES	OUTWATCH
OUTSKIRT	OUTSPRING	OUTSWELL	OUTTRAVEL	OUTWEAR
OUTSKIRTS	OUTSPRINT	OUTSWELLS	OUTTRICK	OUTWEARS
OUTSLEEP	OUTSPRUNG	OUTSWEPT	OUTTRICKS	OUTWEARY
OUTSLEEPS	OUTSTAND	OUTSWIM	OUTTROT	OUTWEED
OUTSLEPT	OUTSTANDS	OUTSWIMS	OUTTROTS	OUTWEEDED
OUTSLICK	OUTSTARE	OUTSWING	OUTTRUMP	OUTWEEDS
OUTSLICKS	OUTSTARED	OUTSWINGS	OUTTRUMPS	OUTWEEP
OUTSMART	OUTSTARES	OUTSWORE	OUTTURN	OUTWEEPS
OUTSMARTS	OUTSTART	OUTSWORN	OUTTURNS	OUTWEIGH
OUTSMELL	OUTSTARTS	OUTSWUM	OUTVALUE	OUTWEIGHS
OUTSMELLS	OUTSTATE	OUTSWUNG	OUTVALUED	OUTWELL
OUTSMELT	OUTSTATED	OUTTA	OUTVALUES	OUTWELLED
OUTSMILE	OUTSTATES	OUTTAKE	OUTVAUNT	OUTWELLS
OUTSMILED	OUTSTAY	OUTTAKEN	OUTVAUNTS	OUTWENT
OUTSMILES	OUTSTAYED	OUTTAKES	OUTVENOM	OUTWEPT
OUTSMOKE	OUTSTAYS	OUTTAKING	OUTVENOMS	OUTWHIRL
OUTSMOKED	OUTSTEER	OUTTALK	OUTVIE	OUTWHIRLS
OUTSMOKES	OUTSTEERS	OUTTALKED	OUTVIED	OUTWICK
OUTSNORE	OUTSTEP	OUTTALKS	OUTVIES	OUTWICKED
OUTSNORED	OUTSTEPS	OUTTASK	OUTVOICE	OUTWICKS
OUTSNORES	OUTSTOOD	OUTTASKED	OUTVOICED	OUTWILE

OUTWILED	OUVRAGE	OVENWARE	OVERBLOW	OVERCLAIM
OUTWILES	OUVRAGES	OVENWARES	OVERBLOWN	OVERCLASS
OUTWILING	OUVRIER	OVENWOOD	OVERBLOWS	OVERCLEAN
OUTWILL	OUVRIERE	OVENWOODS	OVERBOARD	OVERCLEAR
OUTWILLED	OUVRIERES	OVER	OVERBOIL	OVERCLOCK
OUTWILLS	OUVRIERS	OVERABLE	OVERBOILS	OVERCLOSE
OUTWIN	OUZEL	OVERACT	OVERBOLD	OVERCLOUD
OUTWIND	OUZELS	OVERACTED	OVERBOOK	OVERCLOY
OUTWINDED	OUZO	OVERACTS	OVERBOOKS	OVERCLOYS
OUTWINDS	OUZOS	OVERACUTE	OVERBOOT	OVERCLUB
OUTWING	OVA	OVERAGE	OVERBOOTS	OVERCLUBS
OUTWINGED	OVAL	OVERAGED	OVERBORE	OVERCOACH
OUTWINGS	OVALBUMIN	OVERAGES	OVERBORN	OVERCOAT
OUTWINS	OVALITIES	OVERALERT	OVERBORNE	OVERCOATS
OUTWISH	OVALITY	OVERALL	OVERBOUND	OVERCOLD
OUTWISHED	OVALLY	OVERALLED	OVERBRAKE	OVERCOLOR
OUTWISHES	OVALNESS	OVERALLS	OVERBRED	OVERCOME
OUTWIT	OVALS	OVERAPT	OVERBREED	OVERCOMER
OUTWITH	OVARIAL	OVERARCH	OVERBRIEF	OVERCOMES
OUTWITS	OVARIAN	OVERARM	OVERBRIM	OVERCOOK
OUTWITTED	OVARIES	OVERARMED	OVERBRIMS	OVERCOOKS
OUTWON	OVARIOLE	OVERARMS	OVERBROAD	OVERCOOL
OUTWORE	OVARIOLES	OVERATE	OVERBROW	OVERCOOLS
OUTWORK	OVARIOUS	OVERAWE	OVERBROWS	OVERCOUNT
OUTWORKED	OVARITIS	OVERAWED	OVERBUILD	OVERCOVER
OUTWORKER	OVARY	OVERAWES	OVERBUILT	OVERCOY
OUTWORKS	OVATE	OVERAWING	OVERBULK	OVERCRAM
OUTWORN	OVATED	OVERBAKE	OVERBULKS	OVERCRAMS
OUTWORTH	OVATELY	OVERBAKED	OVERBURN	OVERCRAW
OUTWORTHS	OVATES	OVERBAKES	OVERBURNS	OVERCRAWS
OUTWOUND	OVATING	OVERBANK	OVERBURNT	OVERCROP
OUTWREST	OVATION	OVERBANKS	OVERBUSY	OVERCROPS
OUTWRESTS	OVATIONAL	OVERBEAR	OVERBUY	OVERCROW
OUTWRIT	OVATIONS	OVERBEARS	OVERBUYS	OVERCROWD
OUTWRITE	OVATOR	OVERBEAT	OVERBY	OVERCROWS
OUTWRITES	OVATORS	OVERBEATS	OVERCALL	OVERCURE
OUTWROTE	OVEL	OVERBED	OVERCALLS	OVERCURED
OUTYELL	OVELS	OVERBET	OVERCAME	OVERCURES
OUTYELLED	OVEN	OVERBETS	OVERCARRY	OVERCUT
OUTYELLS	OVENABLE	OVERBID	OVERCAST	OVERCUTS
OUTYELP	OVENBIRD	OVERBIDS	OVERCASTS	OVERDARE
OUTYELPED	OVENBIRDS	OVERBIG	OVERCATCH	OVERDARED
OUTYELPS	OVENED	OVERBILL	OVERCHEAP	OVERDARES
OUTYIELD	OVENING	OVERBILLS	OVERCHECK	OVERDATED
OUTYIELDS	OVENLIKE	OVERBITE	OVERCHILL	OVERDEAR
OUVERT	OVENPROOF	OVERBITES	OVERCIVIL	OVERDECK
OUVERTE	OVENS	OVERBLEW	OVERCLAD	OVERDECKS

O

OVERDID	OVEREGGED	OVERGANG	OVERHAPPY	OVERJUST
OVERDIGHT	OVEREGGS	OVERGANGS	OVERHARD	OVERKEEN
OVERDO	OVEREMOTE	OVERGAVE	OVERHASTE	OVERKEEP
OVERDOER	OVEREQUIP	OVERGEAR	OVERHASTY	OVERKEEPS
OVERDOERS	OVEREXERT	OVERGEARS	OVERHATE	OVERKEPT
OVERDOES	OVEREYE	OVERGET	OVERHATED	OVERKEST
OVERDOG	OVEREYED	OVERGETS	OVERHATES	OVERKILL
OVERDOGS	OVEREYES	OVERGILD	OVERHAUL	OVERKILLS
OVERDOING	OVEREYING	OVERGILDS	OVERHAULS	OVERKIND
OVERDONE	OVERFALL	OVERGILT	OVERHEAD	OVERKING
OVERDOSE	OVERFALLS	OVERGIRD	OVERHEADS	OVERKINGS
OVERDOSED	OVERFAR	OVERGIRDS	OVERHEAP	OVERKNEE
OVERDOSES	OVERFAST	OVERGIRT	OVERHEAPS	OVERLABOR
OVERDRAFT	OVERFAT	OVERGIVE	OVERHEAR	OVERLADE
OVERDRANK	OVERFAVOR	OVERGIVEN	OVERHEARD	OVERLADED
OVERDRAW	OVERFEAR	OVERGIVES	OVERHEARS	OVERLADEN
OVERDRAWN	OVERFEARS	OVERGLAD	OVERHEAT	OVERLADES
OVERDRAWS	OVERFED	OVERGLAZE	OVERHEATS	OVERLAID
OVERDRESS	OVERFEED	OVERGLOOM	OVERHELD	OVERLAIN
OVERDREW	OVERFEEDS	OVERGO	OVERHENT	OVERLAND
OVERDRIED	OVERFELL	OVERGOAD	OVERHENTS	OVERLANDS
OVERDRIES	OVERFILL	OVERGOADS	OVERHIGH	OVERLAP
OVERDRINK	OVERFILLS	OVERGOES	OVERHIT	OVERLAPS
OVERDRIVE	OVERFINE	OVERGOING	OVERHITS	OVERLARD
OVERDROVE	OVERFISH	OVERGONE	OVERHOLD	OVERLARDS
OVERDRUNK	OVERFIT	OVERGORGE	OVERHOLDS	OVERLARGE
OVERDRY	OVERFLEW	OVERGOT	OVERHOLY	OVERLATE
OVERDUB	OVERFLIES	OVERGRADE	OVERHONOR	OVERLAX
OVERDUBS	OVERFLOOD	OVERGRAIN	OVERHOPE	OVERLAY
OVERDUE	OVERFLOW	OVERGRASS	OVERHOPED	OVERLAYS
OVERDUST	OVERFLOWN	OVERGRAZE	OVERHOPES	OVERLEAF
OVERDUSTS	OVERFLOWS	OVERGREAT	OVERHOT	OVERLEAP
OVERDYE	OVERFLUSH	OVERGREEN	OVERHUNG	OVERLEAPS
OVERDYED	OVERFLY	OVERGREW	OVERHUNT	OVERLEAPT
OVERDYER	OVERFOCUS	OVERGROW	OVERHUNTS	OVERLEARN
OVERDYERS	OVERFOLD	OVERGROWN	OVERHYPE	OVERLEND
OVERDYES	OVERFOLDS	OVERGROWS	OVERHYPED	OVERLENDS
OVEREAGER	OVERFOND	OVERHAILE	OVERHYPES	OVERLENT
OVEREASY	OVERFOUL	OVERHAIR	OVERIDLE	OVERLET
OVEREAT	OVERFRANK	OVERHAIRS	OVERING	OVERLETS
OVEREATEN	OVERFREE	OVERHALE	OVERINKED	OVERLEWD
OVEREATER	OVERFULL	OVERHALED	OVERISSUE	OVERLIE
OVEREATS	OVERFUND	OVERHALES	OVERJOY	OVERLIER
OVERED	OVERFUNDS	OVERHAND	OVERJOYED	OVERLIERS
OVEREDIT	OVERFUSSY	OVERHANDS	OVERJOYS	OVERLIES
OVEREDITS	OVERGALL	OVERHANG	OVERJUMP	OVERLIGHT
OVEREGG	OVERGALLS	OVERHANGS	OVERJUMPS	OVERLIT

OVERLIVE	OVERNET	OVERQUICK	OVERSALTS	OVERSLEPT
OVERLIVED	OVERNETS	OVERRACK	OVERSAUCE	OVERSLIP
OVERLIVES	OVERNEW	OVERRACKS	OVERSAVE	OVERSLIPS
OVERLOAD	OVERNICE	OVERRAKE	OVERSAVED	OVERSLIPT
OVERLOADS	OVERNIGHT	OVERRAKED	OVERSAVES	OVERSLOW
OVERLOCK	OVERPACK	OVERRAKES	OVERSAW	OVERSMAN
OVERLOCKS	OVERPACKS	OVERRAN	OVERSCALE	OVERSMEN
OVERLONG	OVERPAGE	OVERRANK	OVERSCORE	OVERSMOKE
OVERLOOK	OVERPAID	OVERRANKS	OVERSEA	OVERSOAK
OVERLOOKS	OVERPAINT	OVERRASH	OVERSEAS	OVERSOAKS
OVERLORD	OVERPART	OVERRATE	OVERSEE	OVERSOFT
OVERLORDS	OVERPARTS	OVERRATED	OVERSEED	OVERSOLD
OVERLOUD	OVERPASS	OVERRATES	OVERSEEDS	OVERSOON
OVERLOVE	OVERPAST	OVERREACH	OVERSEEN	OVERSOUL
OVERLOVED	OVERPAY	OVERREACT	OVERSEER	OVERSOULS
OVERLOVES	OVERPAYS	OVERREAD	OVERSEERS	OVERSOW
OVERLUSH	OVERPEDAL	OVERREADS	OVERSEES	OVERSOWED
OVERLUSTY	OVERPEER	OVERRED	OVERSELL	OVERSOWN
OVERLY	OVERPEERS	OVERREDS	OVERSELLS	OVERSOWS
OVERLYING	OVERPERCH	OVERREN	OVERSET	OVERSPEND
OVERMAN	OVERPERT	OVERRENS	OVERSETS	OVERSPENT
OVERMANS	OVERPITCH	OVERRICH	OVERSEW	OVERSPICE
OVERMANY	OVERPLAID	OVERRIDE	OVERSEWED	OVERSPILL
OVERMAST	OVERPLAN	OVERRIDER	OVERSEWN	OVERSPILT
OVERMASTS	OVERPLANS	OVERRIDES	OVERSEWS	OVERSPIN
OVERMATCH	OVERPLANT	OVERRIFE	OVERSEXED	OVERSPINS
OVERMEEK	OVERPLAST	OVERRIGID	OVERSHADE	OVERSTAFF
OVERMELT	OVERPLAY	OVERRIPE	OVERSHARP	OVERSTAIN
OVERMELTS	OVERPLAYS	OVERRIPEN	OVERSHINE	OVERSTAND
OVERMEN	OVERPLIED	OVERROAST	OVERSHIRT	OVERSTANK
OVERMERRY	OVERPLIES	OVERRODE	OVERSHOE	OVERSTARE
OVERMILD	OVERPLOT	OVERRUDE	OVERSHOES	OVERSTATE
OVERMILK	OVERPLOTS	OVERRUFF	OVERSHONE	OVERSTAY
OVERMILKS	OVERPLUS	OVERRUFFS	OVERSHOOT	OVERSTAYS
OVERMINE	OVERPLY	OVERRULE	OVERSHOT	OVERSTEER
OVERMINED	OVERPOISE	OVERRULED	OVERSHOTS	OVERSTEP
OVERMINES	OVERPOST	OVERRULER	OVERSICK	OVERSTEPS
OVERMIX	OVERPOSTS	OVERRULES	OVERSIDE	OVERSTINK
OVERMIXED	OVERPOWER	OVERRUN	OVERSIDES	OVERSTIR
OVERMIXES	OVERPRESS	OVERRUNS	OVERSIGHT	OVERSTIRS
OVERMOUNT	OVERPRICE	OVERS	OVERSIZE	OVERSTOCK
OVERMUCH	OVERPRINT	OVERSAD	OVERSIZED	OVERSTOOD
OVERNAME	OVERPRIZE	OVERSAIL	OVERSIZES	OVERSTORY
OVERNAMED	OVERPROOF	OVERSAILS	OVERSKIP	OVERSTREW
OVERNAMES	OVERPROUD	OVERSALE	OVERSKIPS	OVERSTUDY
OVERNEAR	OVERPUMP	OVERSALES	OVERSKIRT	OVERSTUFF
OVERNEAT	OVERPUMPS	OVERSALT	OVERSLEEP	OVERSTUNK

OVERSUDS	OVERTIRED	OVERWARMS	OVIDUCTAL	OWERBY
OVERSUP	OVERTIRES	OVERWARY	OVIDUCTS	OWERLOUP
OVERSUPS	OVERTLY	OVERWASH	OVIFEROUS	OWERLOUPS
OVERSURE	OVERTNESS	OVERWATCH	OVIFORM	OWES
OVERSWAM	OVERTOIL	OVERWATER	OVIGEROUS	OWING
OVERSWAY	OVERTOILS	OVERWEAK	OVINE	OWL
OVERSWAYS	OVERTONE	OVERWEAR	OVINES	OWLED
OVERSWEAR	OVERTONES	OVERWEARS	OVIPARA	OWLER
OVERSWEET	OVERTOOK	OVERWEARY	OVIPARITY	OWLERIES
OVERSWELL	OVERTOP	OVERWEEN	OVIPAROUS	OWLERS
OVERSWIM	OVERTOPS	OVERWEENS	OVIPOSIT	OWLERY
OVERSWIMS	OVERTOWER	OVERWEIGH	OVIPOSITS	OWLET
OVERSWING	OVERTRADE	OVERWENT	OVIRAPTOR	OWLETS
OVERSWORE	OVERTRAIN	OVERWET	OVISAC	OWLIER
OVERSWORN	OVERTREAT	OVERWETS	OVISACS	OWLIEST
OVERSWUM	OVERTRICK	OVERWHELM	OVIST	OWLING
OVERSWUNG	OVERTRIM	OVERWIDE	OVISTS	OWLISH
OVERT	OVERTRIMS	OVERWILY	OVOID	OWLISHLY
OVERTAKE	OVERTRIP	OVERWIND	OVOIDAL	OWLLIKE
OVERTAKEN	OVERTRIPS	OVERWINDS	OVOIDALS	OWLS
OVERTAKES	OVERTRUMP	OVERWING	OVOIDS	OWLY
OVERTALK	OVERTRUST	OVERWINGS	OVOLI	OWN
OVERTALKS	OVERTURE	OVERWISE	OVOLO	OWNABLE
OVERTAME	OVERTURED	OVERWORD	OVOLOS	OWNED
OVERTART	OVERTURES	OVERWORDS	OVONIC	OWNER
OVERTASK	OVERTURN	OVERWORE	OVONICS	OWNERLESS
OVERTASKS	OVERTURNS	OVERWORK	OVOTESTES	OWNERS
OVERTAX	OVERTYPE	OVERWORKS	OVOTESTIS	OWNERSHIP
OVERTAXED	OVERTYPED	OVERWORN	OVULAR	OWNING
OVERTAXES	OVERTYPES	OVERWOUND	OVULARY	OWNS
OVERTEACH	OVERURGE	OVERWRAP	OVULATE	OWNSOME
OVERTEEM	OVERURGED	OVERWRAPS	OVULATED	OWNSOMES
OVERTEEMS	OVERURGES	OVERWREST	OVULATES	OWRE
OVERTHICK	OVERUSE	OVERWRITE	OVULATING	OWRECAME
OVERTHIN	OVERUSED	OVERWROTE	OVULATION	OWRECOME
OVERTHINK	OVERUSES	OVERYEAR	OVULATORY	OWRECOMES
OVERTHREW	OVERUSING	OVERYEARS	OVULE	OWRELAY
OVERTHROW	OVERVALUE	OVERZEAL	OVULES	OWRELAYS
OVERTIGHT	OVERVEIL	OVERZEALS	OVUM	OWRES
OVERTIME	OVERVEILS	OVIBOS	OW	OWREWORD
OVERTIMED	OVERVIEW	OVIBOSES	OWCHE	OWREWORDS
OVERTIMER	OVERVIEWS	OVIBOVINE	OWCHES	OWRIE
OVERTIMES	OVERVIVID	OVICIDAL	OWE	OWRIER
OVERTIMID	OVERVOTE	OVICIDE	OWED	OWRIEST
OVERTIP	OVERVOTED	OVICIDES	OWELTIES	OWSE
OVERTIPS	OVERVOTES	OVIDUCAL	OWELTY	OWSEN
OVERTIRE	OVERWARM	OVIDUCT	OWER	OWT

OWTS	OXHERD	OXIMETER	OXYMORA	OYSTERMEN
OX	OXHERDS	OXIMETERS	OXYMORON	OYSTERS
OXACILLIN	OXHIDE	OXIMETRY	OXYMORONS	OYSTRIGE
OXALATE	OXHIDES	OXIMS	OXYNTIC	OYSTRIGES
OXALATED	OXIC	OXLAND	OXYPHIL	OZAENA
OXALATES	OXID	OXLANDS	OXYPHILE	OZAENAS
OXALATING	OXIDABLE	OXLIKE	OXYPHILES	OZALID
OXALIC	OXIDANT	OXLIP	OXYPHILIC	OZALIDS
OXALIS	OXIDANTS	OXLIPS	OXYPHILS	OZEKI
OXALISES	OXIDASE	OXO	OXYSALT	OZEKIS
OXAZEPAM	OXIDASES	OXONIUM	OXYSALTS	OZOCERITE
OXAZEPAMS	OXIDASIC	OXONIUMS	OXYSOME	OZOKERITE
OXAZINE	OXIDATE	OXPECKER	OXYSOMES	OZONATE
OXAZINES	OXIDATED	OXPECKERS	OXYTOCIC	OZONATED
OXAZOLE	OXIDATES	OXSLIP	OXYTOCICS	OZONATES
OXAZOLES	OXIDATING	OXSLIPS	OXYTOCIN	OZONATING
OXBLOOD	OXIDATION	OXTAIL	OXYTOCINS	OZONATION
OXBLOODS	OXIDATIVE	OXTAILS	OXYTONE	OZONE
OXBOW	OXIDE	OXTER	OXYTONES	OZONES
OXBOWS	OXIDES	OXTERED	OXYTONIC	OZONIC
OXCART	OXIDIC	OXTERING	OXYTROPE	OZONIDE
OXCARTS	OXIDISE	OXTERS	OXYTROPES	OZONIDES
OXEN	OXIDISED	OXTONGUE	OY	OZONISE
OXER	OXIDISER	OXTONGUES	OYE	OZONISED
OXERS	OXIDISERS	OXY	OYER	OZONISER
OXES	OXIDISES	OXYACID	OYERS	OZONISERS
OXEYE	OXIDISING	OXYACIDS	OYES	OZONISES
OXEYES	OXIDIZE	OXYCODONE	OYESES	OZONISING
OXFORD	OXIDIZED	OXYGEN	OYESSES	OZONIZE
OXFORDS	OXIDIZER	OXYGENASE	OYEZ	OZONIZED
OXGANG	OXIDIZERS	OXYGENATE	OYEZES	OZONIZER
OXGANGS	OXIDIZES	OXYGENIC	OYS	OZONIZERS
OXGATE	OXIDIZING	OXYGENISE	OYSTER	OZONIZES
OXGATES	OXIDS	OXYGENIZE	OYSTERED	OZONIZING
OXHEAD	OXIES	OXYGENOUS	OYSTERER	OZONOUS
OXHEADS	OXIM	OXYGENS	OYSTERERS	OZZIE
OXHEART	OXIME	OXYMEL	OYSTERING	OZZIES
OXHEARTS	OXIMES	OXYMELS	OYSTERMAN	

O

P

PA
PAAL
PAALS
PAAN
PAANS
PABLUM
PABLUMS
PABOUCHE
PABOUCHES
PABULAR
PABULOUS
PABULUM
PABULUMS
PAC
PACA
PACABLE
PACAS
PACATION
PACATIONS
PACE
PACED
PACEMAKER
PACEMAN
PACEMEN
PACER
PACERS
PACES
PACEWAY
PACEWAYS
PACEY
PACHA
PACHADOM
PACHADOMS
PACHAK
PACHAKS
PACHALIC
PACHALICS
PACHAS
PACHINKO
PACHINKOS
PACHISI

PACHISIS
PACHOULI
PACHOULIS
PACHUCO
PACHUCOS
PACHYDERM
PACHYTENE
PACIER
PACIEST
PACIFIC
PACIFICAE
PACIFICAL
PACIFIED
PACIFIER
PACIFIERS
PACIFIES
PACIFISM
PACIFISMS
PACIFIST
PACIFISTS
PACIFY
PACIFYING
PACING
PACINGS
PACK
PACKABLE
PACKAGE
PACKAGED
PACKAGER
PACKAGERS
PACKAGES
PACKAGING
PACKBOARD
PACKCLOTH
PACKED
PACKER
PACKERS
PACKET
PACKETED
PACKETING
PACKETS

PACKFONG
PACKFONGS
PACKFRAME
PACKHORSE
PACKING
PACKINGS
PACKLY
PACKMAN
PACKMEN
PACKMULE
PACKMULES
PACKNESS
PACKS
PACKSACK
PACKSACKS
PACKSHEET
PACKSTAFF
PACKWAX
PACKWAXES
PACKWAY
PACKWAYS
PACO
PACOS
PACS
PACT
PACTA
PACTION
PACTIONAL
PACTIONED
PACTIONS
PACTS
PACTUM
PACY
PACZKI
PACZKIS
PAD
PADANG
PADANGS
PADAUK
PADAUKS
PADDED

PADDER
PADDERS
PADDIES
PADDING
PADDINGS
PADDLE
PADDLED
PADDLER
PADDLERS
PADDLES
PADDLING
PADDLINGS
PADDOCK
PADDOCKED
PADDOCKS
PADDY
PADDYWACK
PADELLA
PADELLAS
PADEMELON
PADERERO
PADEREROS
PADI
PADIS
PADISHAH
PADISHAHS
PADKOS
PADLE
PADLES
PADLOCK
PADLOCKED
PADLOCKS
PADMA
PADMAS
PADNAG
PADNAGS
PADOUK
PADOUKS
PADRE
PADRES
PADRI

PADRONA
PADRONAS
PADRONE
PADRONES
PADRONI
PADRONISM
PADS
PADSAW
PADSAWS
PADSHAH
PADSHAHS
PADUASOY
PADUASOYS
PADYMELON
PAEAN
PAEANISM
PAEANISMS
PAEANS
PAEDERAST
PAEDEUTIC
PAEDIATRY
PAEDO
PAEDOLOGY
PAEDOS
PAELLA
PAELLAS
PAENULA
PAENULAE
PAENULAS
PAEON
PAEONIC
PAEONICS
PAEONIES
PAEONS
PAEONY
PAESAN
PAESANI
PAESANO
PAESANOS
PAESANS
PAGAN

PAGANDOM	PAGRIS	PAINTBALL	PAITRICKS	PALAMINOS
PAGANDOMS	PAGURIAN	PAINTBOX	PAJAMA	PALAMPORE
PAGANISE	PAGURIANS	PAINTED	PAJAMAED	PALANKEEN
PAGANISED	PAGURID	PAINTER	PAJAMAS	PALANQUIN
PAGANISER	PAGURIDS	PAINTERLY	PAJOCK	PALAPA
PAGANISES	PAH	PAINTERS	PAJOCKE	PALAPAS
PAGANISH	PAHAUTEA	PAINTIER	PAJOCKES	PALAS
PAGANISM	PAHAUTEAS	PAINTIEST	PAJOCKS	PALASES
PAGANISMS	PAHLAVI	PAINTING	PAK	PALATABLE
PAGANIST	PAHLAVIS	PAINTINGS	PAKAHI	PALATABLY
PAGANISTS	PAHOEHOE	PAINTPOT	PAKAHIS	PALATAL
PAGANIZE	PAHOEHOES	PAINTPOTS	PAKAPOO	PALATALLY
PAGANIZED	PAHS	PAINTRESS	PAKAPOOS	PALATALS
PAGANIZER	PAID	PAINTS	PAKEHA	PALATE
PAGANIZES	PAIDEUTIC	PAINTURE	PAKEHAS	PALATED
PAGANS	PAIDLE	PAINTURES	PAKFONG	PALATES
PAGE	PAIDLES	PAINTWORK	PAKFONGS	PALATIAL
PAGEANT	PAIGLE	PAINTY	PAKIHI	PALATINE
PAGEANTRY	PAIGLES	PAIOCK	PAKIHIS	PALATINES
PAGEANTS	PAIK	PAIOCKE	PAKKA	PALATING
PAGEBOY	PAIKED	PAIOCKES	PAKOKO	PALAVER
PAGEBOYS	PAIKING	PAIOCKS	PAKOKOS	PALAVERED
PAGED	PAIKS	PAIR	PAKORA	PALAVERER
PAGEFUL	PAIL	PAIRE	PAKORAS	PALAVERS
PAGEFULS	PAILFUL	PAIRED	PAKS	PALAY
PAGEHOOD	PAILFULS	PAIRER	PAKTHONG	PALAYS
PAGEHOODS	PAILLARD	PAIRES	PAKTHONGS	PALAZZI
PAGER	PAILLARDS	PAIREST	PAKTONG	PALAZZO
PAGERS	PAILLASSE	PAIRIAL	PAKTONGS	PALAZZOS
PAGES	PAILLETTE	PAIRIALS	PAL	PALE
PAGEVIEW	PAILLON	PAIRING	PALABRA	PALEA
PAGEVIEWS	PAILLONS	PAIRINGS	PALABRAS	PALEAE
PAGINAL	PAILS	PAIRS	PALACE	PALEAL
PAGINATE	PAILSFUL	PAIRWISE	PALACED	PALEATE
PAGINATED	PAIN	PAIS	PALACES	PALEBUCK
PAGINATES	PAINCH	PAISA	PALADIN	PALEBUCKS
PAGING	PAINCHES	PAISAN	PALADINS	PALED
PAGINGS	PAINED	PAISANA	PALAEOSOL	PALEFACE
PAGLE	PAINFUL	PAISANAS	PALAESTRA	PALEFACES
PAGLES	PAINFULLY	PAISANO	PALAFITTE	PALELY
PAGOD	PAINIM	PAISANOS	PALAGI	PALEMPORE
PAGODA	PAINIMS	PAISANS	PALAGIS	PALENESS
PAGODAS	PAINING	PAISAS	PALAIS	PALEOCENE
PAGODITE	PAINLESS	PAISE	PALAMA	PALEOCON
PAGODITES	PAINS	PAISLEY	PALAMAE	PALEOCONS
PAGODS	PAINT	PAISLEYS	PALAMATE	PALEOGENE
PAGRI	PAINTABLE	PAITRICK	PALAMINO	PALEOLITH

PALEOLOGY
PALEOSOL
PALEOSOLS
PALEOZOIC
PALER
PALES
PALEST
PALESTRA
PALESTRAE
PALESTRAL
PALESTRAS
PALET
PALETOT
PALETOTS
PALETS
PALETTE
PALETTES
PALEWAYS
PALEWISE
PALFREY
PALFREYED
PALFREYS
PALI
PALIER
PALIEST
PALIFORM
PALIKAR
PALIKARS
PALILALIA
PALILLOGY
PALIMONY
PALING
PALINGS
PALINKA
PALINKAS
PALINODE
PALINODES
PALINODY
PALINOPIA
PALIS
PALISADE
PALISADED
PALISADES
PALISADO
PALISH
PALKEE
PALKEES

PALKI
PALKIS
PALL
PALLA
PALLADIA
PALLADIC
PALLADIUM
PALLADOUS
PALLAE
PALLAH
PALLAHS
PALLED
PALLET
PALLETED
PALLETING
PALLETISE
PALLETIZE
PALLETS
PALLETTE
PALLETTES
PALLIA
PALLIAL
PALLIARD
PALLIARDS
PALLIASSE
PALLIATE
PALLIATED
PALLIATES
PALLIATOR
PALLID
PALLIDER
PALLIDEST
PALLIDITY
PALLIDLY
PALLIED
PALLIER
PALLIES
PALLIEST
PALLING
PALLIUM
PALLIUMS
PALLONE
PALLONES
PALLOR
PALLORS
PALLS
PALLY

PALLYING
PALM
PALMAR
PALMARIAN
PALMARY
PALMATE
PALMATED
PALMATELY
PALMATION
PALMBALL
PALMBALLS
PALMED
PALMER
PALMERS
PALMETTE
PALMETTES
PALMETTO
PALMETTOS
PALMFUL
PALMFULS
PALMHOUSE
PALMIE
PALMIER
PALMIERS
PALMIES
PALMIEST
PALMIET
PALMIETS
PALMING
PALMIPED
PALMIPEDE
PALMIPEDS
PALMIST
PALMISTER
PALMISTRY
PALMISTS
PALMITATE
PALMITIC
PALMITIN
PALMITINS
PALMLIKE
PALMS
PALMTOP
PALMTOPS
PALMY
PALMYRA
PALMYRAS

PALOLO
PALOLOS
PALOMINO
PALOMINOS
PALOOKA
PALOOKAS
PALOVERDE
PALP
PALPABLE
PALPABLY
PALPAL
PALPATE
PALPATED
PALPATES
PALPATING
PALPATION
PALPATOR
PALPATORS
PALPATORY
PALPEBRA
PALPEBRAE
PALPEBRAL
PALPEBRAS
PALPED
PALPI
PALPING
PALPITANT
PALPITATE
PALPS
PALPUS
PALPUSES
PALS
PALSA
PALSAS
PALSGRAVE
PALSHIP
PALSHIPS
PALSIED
PALSIER
PALSIES
PALSIEST
PALSTAFF
PALSTAFFS
PALSTAVE
PALSTAVES
PALSY
PALSYING

PALSYLIKE
PALTER
PALTERED
PALTERER
PALTERERS
PALTERING
PALTERS
PALTRIER
PALTRIEST
PALTRILY
PALTRY
PALUDAL
PALUDIC
PALUDINAL
PALUDINE
PALUDISM
PALUDISMS
PALUDOSE
PALUDOUS
PALUSTRAL
PALY
PAM
PAMPA
PAMPAS
PAMPASES
PAMPEAN
PAMPEANS
PAMPER
PAMPERED
PAMPERER
PAMPERERS
PAMPERING
PAMPERO
PAMPEROS
PAMPERS
PAMPHLET
PAMPHLETS
PAMPHREY
PAMPHREYS
PAMPOEN
PAMPOENS
PAMPOOTIE
PAMS
PAN
PANACEA
PANACEAN
PANACEAS

PANACHAEA	PANDATION	PANEITY	PANGRAMS	PANNER
PANACHE	PANDECT	PANEL	PANGS	PANNERS
PANACHES	PANDECTS	PANELED	PANHANDLE	PANNES
PANADA	PANDEMIA	PANELESS	PANHUMAN	PANNICK
PANADAS	PANDEMIAN	PANELING	PANIC	PANNICKS
PANAMA	PANDEMIAS	PANELINGS	PANICALLY	PANNICLE
PANAMAS	PANDEMIC	PANELISED	PANICK	PANNICLES
PANARIES	PANDEMICS	PANELIST	PANICKED	PANNIER
PANARY	PANDER	PANELISTS	PANICKIER	PANNIERED
PANATELA	PANDERED	PANELIZED	PANICKING	PANNIERS
PANATELAS	PANDERER	PANELLED	PANICKS	PANNIKEL
PANATELLA	PANDERERS	PANELLING	PANICKY	PANNIKELL
PANAX	PANDERESS	PANELLIST	PANICLE	PANNIKELS
PANAXES	PANDERING	PANELS	PANICLED	PANNIKIN
PANBROIL	PANDERISM	PANES	PANICLES	PANNIKINS
PANBROILS	PANDERLY	PANETELA	PANICS	PANNING
PANCAKE	PANDEROUS	PANETELAS	PANICUM	PANNINGS
PANCAKED	PANDERS	PANETELLA	PANICUMS	PANNIST
PANCAKES	PANDIED	PANETTONE	PANIER	PANNISTS
PANCAKING	PANDIES	PANETTONI	PANIERS	PANNOSE
PANCE	PANDIT	PANFISH	PANIM	PANNUS
PANCES	PANDITS	PANFISHED	PANIMS	PANNUSES
PANCETTA	PANDOOR	PANFISHES	PANING	PANOCHA
PANCETTAS	PANDOORS	PANFORTE	PANINI	PANOCHAS
PANCHAX	PANDORA	PANFORTES	PANINIS	PANOCHE
PANCHAXES	PANDORAS	PANFRIED	PANINO	PANOCHES
PANCHAYAT	PANDORE	PANFRIES	PANISC	PANOISTIC
PANCHEON	PANDORES	PANFRY	PANISCS	PANOPLIED
PANCHEONS	PANDOUR	PANFRYING	PANISK	PANOPLIES
PANCHION	PANDOURS	PANFUL	PANISKS	PANOPLY
PANCHIONS	PANDOWDY	PANFULS	PANISLAM	PANOPTIC
PANCOSMIC	PANDROP	PANG	PANISLAMS	PANORAMA
PANCRATIA	PANDROPS	PANGA	PANJANDRA	PANORAMAS
PANCRATIC	PANDS	PANGAMIC	PANKO	PANORAMIC
PANCREAS	PANDURA	PANGAMIES	PANKOS	PANPIPE
PAND	PANDURAS	PANGAMY	PANLIKE	PANPIPES
PANDA	PANDURATE	PANGAS	PANLOGISM	PANS
PANDAN	PANDY	PANGED	PANMICTIC	PANSEXUAL
PANDANI	PANDYING	PANGEN	PANMIXES	PANSIED
PANDANIS	PANE	PANGENE	PANMIXIA	PANSIES
PANDANS	PANED	PANGENES	PANMIXIAS	PANSOPHIC
PANDANUS	PANEER	PANGENS	PANMIXIS	PANSOPHY
PANDAR	PANEERS	PANGING	PANNAGE	PANSPERMY
PANDARED	PANEGOISM	PANGLESS	PANNAGES	PANSTICK
PANDARING	PANEGYRIC	PANGOLIN	PANNE	PANSTICKS
PANDARS	PANEGYRY	PANGOLINS	PANNED	PANSY
PANDAS	PANEITIES	PANGRAM	PANNELLED	PANT

P

PANTABLE	PANTOUMS	PAPAUMAS	PAPISHER	PAPYRUS
PANTABLES	PANTRIES	PAPAVER	PAPISHERS	PAPYRUSES
PANTAGAMY	PANTROPIC	PAPAVERS	PAPISHES	PAR
PANTALEON	PANTRY	PAPAW	PAPISM	PARA
PANTALET	PANTRYMAN	PAPAWS	PAPISMS	PARABASES
PANTALETS	PANTRYMEN	PAPAYA	PAPIST	PARABASIS
PANTALON	PANTS	PAPAYAN	PAPISTIC	PARABEMA
PANTALONE	PANTSUIT	PAPAYAS	PAPISTRY	PARABEN
PANTALONS	PANTSUITS	PAPE	PAPISTS	PARABENS
PANTALOON	PANTUN	PAPER	PAPOOSE	PARABLAST
PANTDRESS	PANTUNS	PAPERBACK	PAPOOSES	PARABLE
PANTED	PANTY	PAPERBARK	PAPPADAM	PARABLED
PANTER	PANTYHOSE	PAPERBOY	PAPPADAMS	PARABLES
PANTERS	PANZER	PAPERBOYS	PAPPADOM	PARABLING
PANTHEISM	PANZERS	PAPERCLIP	PAPPADOMS	PARABOLA
PANTHEIST	PANZOOTIC	PAPERED	PAPPADUM	PARABOLAE
PANTHENOL	PAOLI	PAPERER	PAPPADUMS	PARABOLAS
PANTHEON	PAOLO	PAPERERS	PAPPED	PARABOLE
PANTHEONS	PAP	PAPERGIRL	PAPPI	PARABOLES
PANTHER	PAPA	PAPERIER	PAPPIER	PARABOLIC
PANTHERS	PAPABLE	PAPERIEST	PAPPIES	PARABRAKE
PANTIE	PAPACIES	PAPERING	PAPPIEST	PARACHOR
PANTIES	PAPACY	PAPERINGS	PAPPING	PARACHORS
PANTIHOSE	PAPADAM	PAPERLESS	PAPPOOSE	PARACHUTE
PANTILE	PAPADAMS	PAPERS	PAPPOOSES	PARACLETE
PANTILED	PAPADOM	PAPERWARE	PAPPOSE	PARACME
PANTILES	PAPADOMS	PAPERWORK	PAPPOUS	PARACMES
PANTILING	PAPADUM	PAPERY	PAPPUS	PARACRINE
PANTINE	PAPADUMS	PAPES	PAPPUSES	PARACUSES
PANTINES	PAPAIN	PAPETERIE	PAPPY	PARACUSIS
PANTING	PAPAINS	PAPHIAN	PAPRICA	PARADE
PANTINGLY	PAPAL	PAPHIANS	PAPRICAS	PARADED
PANTINGS	PAPALISE	PAPILIO	PAPRIKA	PARADER
PANTLEG	PAPALISED	PAPILIOS	PAPRIKAS	PARADERS
PANTLEGS	PAPALISES	PAPILLA	PAPS	PARADES
PANTLER	PAPALISM	PAPILLAE	PAPULA	PARADIGM
PANTLERS	PAPALISMS	PAPILLAR	PAPULAE	PARADIGMS
PANTO	PAPALIST	PAPILLARY	PAPULAR	PARADING
PANTOFFLE	PAPALISTS	PAPILLATE	PAPULAS	PARADISAL
PANTOFLE	PAPALIZE	PAPILLOMA	PAPULE	PARADISE
PANTOFLES	PAPALIZED	PAPILLON	PAPULES	PARADISES
PANTOMIME	PAPALIZES	PAPILLONS	PAPULOSE	PARADISIC
PANTON	PAPALLY	PAPILLOSE	PAPULOUS	PARADOR
PANTONS	PAPARAZZI	PAPILLOTE	PAPYRAL	PARADORES
PANTOS	PAPARAZZO	PAPILLOUS	PAPYRI	PARADORS
PANTOUFLE	PAPAS	PAPILLULE	PAPYRIAN	PARADOS
PANTOUM	PAPAUMA	PAPISH	PAPYRINE	PARADOSES

PARADOX	PARALOGY	PARAPET	PARAZOAN	PARDIE
PARADOXAL	PARALYSE	PARAPETED	PARAZOANS	PARDINE
PARADOXER	PARALYSED	PARAPETS	PARAZOON	PARDNER
PARADOXES	PARALYSER	PARAPH	PARBAKE	PARDNERS
PARADOXY	PARALYSES	PARAPHED	PARBAKED	PARDON
PARADROP	PARALYSIS	PARAPHING	PARBAKES	PARDONED
PARADROPS	PARALYTIC	PARAPHS	PARBAKING	PARDONER
PARAE	PARALYZE	PARAPODIA	PARBOIL	PARDONERS
PARAFFIN	PARALYZED	PARAQUAT	PARBOILED	PARDONING
PARAFFINE	PARALYZER	PARAQUATS	PARBOILS	PARDONS
PARAFFINS	PARALYZES	PARAQUET	PARBREAK	PARDS
PARAFFINY	PARAMATTA	PARAQUETS	PARBREAKS	PARDY
PARAFFLE	PARAMECIA	PARAQUITO	PARBUCKLE	PARE
PARAFFLES	PARAMEDIC	PARARHYME	PARCEL	PARECIOUS
PARAFLE	PARAMENT	PARAS	PARCELED	PARECISM
PARAFLES	PARAMENTA	PARASAIL	PARCELING	PARECISMS
PARAFOIL	PARAMENTS	PARASAILS	PARCELLED	PARED
PARAFOILS	PARAMESE	PARASANG	PARCELS	PAREGORIC
PARAFORM	PARAMESES	PARASANGS	PARCENARY	PAREIRA
PARAFORMS	PARAMETER	PARASCEVE	PARCENER	PAREIRAS
PARAGE	PARAMO	PARASHAH	PARCENERS	PARELLA
PARAGES	PARAMORPH	PARASHAHS	PARCH	PARELLAS
PARAGLIDE	PARAMOS	PARASHOT	PARCHED	PARELLE
PARAGOGE	PARAMOUNT	PARASHOTH	PARCHEDLY	PARELLES
PARAGOGES	PARAMOUR	PARASITE	PARCHEESI	PAREN
PARAGOGIC	PARAMOURS	PARASITES	PARCHES	PARENESES
PARAGOGUE	PARAMYLUM	PARASITIC	PARCHESI	PARENESIS
PARAGON	PARANETE	PARASOL	PARCHESIS	PARENS
PARAGONED	PARANETES	PARASOLED	PARCHING	PARENT
PARAGONS	PARANG	PARASOLS	PARCHISI	PARENTAGE
PARAGRAM	PARANGS	PARATAXES	PARCHISIS	PARENTAL
PARAGRAMS	PARANOEA	PARATAXIS	PARCHMENT	PARENTED
PARAGRAPH	PARANOEAS	PARATHA	PARCIMONY	PARENTING
PARAKEET	PARANOEIC	PARATHAS	PARCLOSE	PARENTS
PARAKEETS	PARANOIA	PARATHION	PARCLOSES	PAREO
PARAKELIA	PARANOIAC	PARATONIC	PARD	PAREOS
PARAKITE	PARANOIAS	PARATROOP	PARDAH	PARER
PARAKITES	PARANOIC	PARAVAIL	PARDAHS	PARERA
PARALALIA	PARANOICS	PARAVANE	PARDAL	PARERAS
PARALEGAL	PARANOID	PARAVANES	PARDALE	PARERGA
PARALEXIA	PARANOIDS	PARAVANT	PARDALES	PARERGON
PARALEXIC	PARANYM	PARAVANTS	PARDALIS	PARERS
PARALLAX	PARANYMPH	PARAVAUNT	PARDALOTE	PARES
PARALLEL	PARANYMS	PARAWING	PARDALS	PARESES
PARALLELS	PARAPARA	PARAWINGS	PARDED	PARESIS
PARALOGIA	PARAPARAS	PARAXIAL	PARDEE	PARETIC
PARALOGUE	PARAPENTE	PARAZOA	PARDI	PARETICS

P

PAREU	PARISES	PARKY	PAROEMIAC	PARPENTS
PAREUS	PARISH	PARLANCE	PAROEMIAL	PARPING
PAREV	PARISHAD	PARLANCES	PAROEMIAS	PARPOINT
PAREVE	PARISHADS	PARLANDO	PAROICOUS	PARPOINTS
PARFAIT	PARISHEN	PARLANTE	PAROL	PARPS
PARFAITS	PARISHENS	PARLAY	PAROLABLE	PARQUET
PARFLECHE	PARISHES	PARLAYED	PAROLE	PARQUETED
PARFLESH	PARISON	PARLAYING	PAROLED	PARQUETRY
PARFOCAL	PARISONS	PARLAYS	PAROLEE	PARQUETS
PARGANA	PARITIES	PARLE	PAROLEES	PARR
PARGANAS	PARITOR	PARLED	PAROLES	PARRA
PARGASITE	PARITORS	PARLEMENT	PAROLING	PARRAKEET
PARGE	PARITY	PARLES	PAROLS	PARRAL
PARGED	PARK	PARLEY	PARONYM	PARRALS
PARGES	PARKA	PARLEYED	PARONYMIC	PARRAS
PARGET	PARKADE	PARLEYER	PARONYMS	PARRED
PARGETED	PARKADES	PARLEYERS	PARONYMY	PARREL
PARGETER	PARKAS	PARLEYING	PAROQUET	PARRELS
PARGETERS	PARKED	PARLEYS	PAROQUETS	PARRHESIA
PARGETING	PARKEE	PARLEYVOO	PARORE	PARRICIDE
PARGETS	PARKEES	PARLIES	PARORES	PARRIDGE
PARGETTED	PARKER	PARLING	PAROSMIA	PARRIDGES
PARGETTER	PARKERS	PARLOR	PAROSMIAS	PARRIED
PARGING	PARKETTE	PARLORS	PAROTIC	PARRIER
PARGINGS	PARKETTES	PARLOUR	PAROTID	PARRIERS
PARGO	PARKI	PARLOURS	PAROTIDES	PARRIES
PARGOES	PARKIE	PARLOUS	PAROTIDS	PARRING
PARGOS	PARKIER	PARLOUSLY	PAROTIS	PARRITCH
PARGYLINE	PARKIES	PARLY	PAROTISES	PARROCK
PARHELIA	PARKIEST	PARMESAN	PAROTITIC	PARROCKED
PARHELIC	PARKIN	PARMESANS	PAROTITIS	PARROCKS
PARHELION	PARKING	PAROCHIAL	PAROTOID	PARROKET
PARHYPATE	PARKINGS	PAROCHIN	PAROTOIDS	PARROKETS
PARIAH	PARKINS	PAROCHINE	PAROUS	PARROQUET
PARIAHS	PARKIS	PAROCHINS	PAROUSIA	PARROT
PARIAL	PARKISH	PARODIC	PAROUSIAS	PARROTED
PARIALS	PARKLAND	PARODICAL	PAROXYSM	PARROTER
PARIAN	PARKLANDS	PARODIED	PAROXYSMS	PARROTERS
PARIANS	PARKLIKE	PARODIES	PARP	PARROTING
PARIES	PARKLY	PARODIST	PARPANE	PARROTRY
PARIETAL	PARKOUR	PARODISTS	PARPANES	PARROTS
PARIETALS	PARKOURS	PARODOI	PARPED	PARROTY
PARIETES	PARKS	PARODOS	PARPEN	PARRS
PARING	PARKWARD	PARODY	PARPEND	PARRY
PARINGS	PARKWARDS	PARODYING	PARPENDS	PARRYING
PARIS	PARKWAY	PAROECISM	PARPENS	PARS
PARISCHAN	PARKWAYS	PAROEMIA	PARPENT	PARSABLE

PARSE	PARTIES	PARURESIS	PASHM	PASSERBY
PARSEC	PARTIM	PARVE	PASHMINA	PASSERINE
PARSECS	PARTING	PARVENU	PASHMINAS	PASSERS
PARSED	PARTINGS	PARVENUE	PASHMS	PASSERSBY
PARSER	PARTIS	PARVENUES	PASKA	PASSES
PARSERS	PARTISAN	PARVENUS	PASKAS	PASSIBLE
PARSES	PARTISANS	PARVIS	PASKHA	PASSIBLY
PARSIMONY	PARTITA	PARVISE	PASKHAS	PASSIM
PARSING	PARTITAS	PARVISES	PASODOBLE	PASSING
PARSINGS	PARTITE	PARVO	PASPALUM	PASSINGLY
PARSLEY	PARTITION	PARVOLIN	PASPALUMS	PASSINGS
PARSLEYED	PARTITIVE	PARVOLINE	PASPIES	PASSION
PARSLEYS	PARTITURA	PARVOLINS	PASPY	PASSIONAL
PARSLIED	PARTIZAN	PARVOS	PASQUIL	PASSIONED
PARSNEP	PARTIZANS	PAS	PASQUILER	PASSIONS
PARSNEPS	PARTLET	PASCAL	PASQUILS	PASSIVATE
PARSNIP	PARTLETS	PASCALS	PASS	PASSIVE
PARSNIPS	PARTLY	PASCHAL	PASSABLE	PASSIVELY
PARSON	PARTNER	PASCHALS	PASSABLY	PASSIVES
PARSONAGE	PARTNERED	PASCUAL	PASSADE	PASSIVISM
PARSONIC	PARTNERS	PASCUALS	PASSADES	PASSIVIST
PARSONISH	PARTON	PASE	PASSADO	PASSIVITY
PARSONS	PARTONS	PASEAR	PASSADOES	PASSKEY
PART	PARTOOK	PASEARED	PASSADOS	PASSKEYS
PARTAKE	PARTRIDGE	PASEARING	PASSAGE	PASSLESS
PARTAKEN	PARTS	PASEARS	PASSAGED	PASSMAN
PARTAKER	PARTURE	PASELA	PASSAGER	PASSMEN
PARTAKERS	PARTURES	PASELAS	PASSAGES	PASSMENT
PARTAKES	PARTWAY	PASEO	PASSAGING	PASSMENTS
PARTAKING	PARTWORK	PASEOS	PASSALONG	PASSOUT
PARTAN	PARTWORKS	PASES	PASSAMENT	PASSOUTS
PARTANS	PARTY	PASH	PASSANT	PASSOVER
PARTED	PARTYER	PASHA	PASSATA	PASSOVERS
PARTER	PARTYERS	PASHADOM	PASSATAS	PASSPORT
PARTERRE	PARTYGOER	PASHADOMS	PASSBAND	PASSPORTS
PARTERRES	PARTYING	PASHALIC	PASSBANDS	PASSUS
PARTERS	PARTYINGS	PASHALICS	PASSBOOK	PASSUSES
PARTI	PARTYISM	PASHALIK	PASSBOOKS	PASSWORD
PARTIAL	PARTYISMS	PASHALIKS	PASSE	PASSWORDS
PARTIALLY	PARULIDES	PASHAS	PASSED	PAST
PARTIALS	PARULIS	PASHED	PASSEE	PASTA
PARTIBLE	PARULISES	PASHES	PASSEL	PASTALIKE
PARTICLE	PARURA	PASHIM	PASSELS	PASTANCE
PARTICLES	PARURAS	PASHIMS	PASSEMENT	PASTANCES
PARTIED	PARURE	PASHING	PASSENGER	PASTAS
PARTIER	PARURES	PASHKA	PASSEPIED	PASTE
PARTIERS	PARURESES	PASHKAS	PASSER	PASTED

PASTEDOWN	PASTORLY	PATE	PATHS	PATRIALS
PASTEL	PASTORS	PATED	PATHWAY	PATRIARCH
PASTELIST	PASTRAMI	PATELLA	PATHWAYS	PATRIATE
PASTELS	PASTRAMIS	PATELLAE	PATIBLE	PATRIATED
PASTER	PASTRIES	PATELLAR	PATIENCE	PATRIATES
PASTERN	PASTROMI	PATELLAS	PATIENCES	PATRICIAN
PASTERNS	PASTROMIS	PATELLATE	PATIENT	PATRICIDE
PASTERS	PASTRY	PATEN	PATIENTED	PATRICK
PASTES	PASTS	PATENCIES	PATIENTER	PATRICKS
PASTEUP	PASTURAGE	PATENCY	PATIENTLY	PATRICO
PASTEUPS	PASTURAL	PATENS	PATIENTS	PATRICOES
PASTICCI	PASTURE	PATENT	PATIKI	PATRICOS
PASTICCIO	PASTURED	PATENTED	PATIKIS	PATRILINY
PASTICHE	PASTURER	PATENTEE	PATIN	PATRIMONY
PASTICHES	PASTURERS	PATENTEES	PATINA	PATRIOT
PASTIE	PASTURES	PATENTING	PATINAE	PATRIOTIC
PASTIER	PASTURING	PATENTLY	PATINAED	PATRIOTS
PASTIES	PASTY	PATENTOR	PATINAS	PATRISTIC
PASTIEST	PAT	PATENTORS	PATINATE	PATROL
PASTIL	PATACA	PATENTS	PATINATED	PATROLLED
PASTILLE	PATACAS	PATER	PATINATES	PATROLLER
PASTILLES	PATAGIA	PATERA	PATINE	PATROLMAN
PASTILS	PATAGIAL	PATERAE	PATINED	PATROLMEN
PASTILY	PATAGIUM	PATERCOVE	PATINES	PATROLOGY
PASTIME	PATAKA	PATERERO	PATINING	PATROLS
PASTIMES	PATAKAS	PATEREROS	PATINISE	PATRON
PASTINA	PATAMAR	PATERNAL	PATINISED	PATRONAGE
PASTINAS	PATAMARS	PATERNITY	PATINISES	PATRONAL
PASTINESS	PATBALL	PATERS	PATINIZE	PATRONESS
PASTING	PATBALLS	PATES	PATINIZED	PATRONISE
PASTINGS	PATCH	PATH	PATINIZES	PATRONIZE
PASTIS	PATCHABLE	PATHED	PATINS	PATRONLY
PASTISES	PATCHED	PATHETIC	PATIO	PATRONNE
PASTITSIO	PATCHER	PATHETICS	PATIOS	PATRONNES
PASTITSO	PATCHERS	PATHIC	PATISSIER	PATRONS
PASTITSOS	PATCHERY	PATHICS	PATKA	PATROON
PASTLESS	PATCHES	PATHING	PATKAS	PATROONS
PASTNESS	PATCHIER	PATHLESS	PATLY	PATS
PASTOR	PATCHIEST	PATHNAME	PATNESS	PATSIES
PASTORAL	PATCHILY	PATHNAMES	PATNESSES	PATSY
PASTORALE	PATCHING	PATHOGEN	PATOIS	PATTAMAR
PASTORALI	PATCHINGS	PATHOGENE	PATONCE	PATTAMARS
PASTORALS	PATCHOCKE	PATHOGENS	PATOOT	PATTE
PASTORATE	PATCHOULI	PATHOGENY	PATOOTIE	PATTED
PASTORED	PATCHOULY	PATHOLOGY	PATOOTIES	PATTEE
PASTORING	PATCHWORK	PATHOS	PATOOTS	PATTEN
PASTORIUM	PATCHY	PATHOSES	PATRIAL	PATTENED

PATTENING	PAULS	PAVENS	PAWKINESS	PAYER
PATTENS	PAUNCE	PAVER	PAWKS	PAYERS
PATTER	PAUNCES	PAVERS	PAWKY	PAYESS
PATTERED	PAUNCH	PAVES	PAWL	PAYFONE
PATTERER	PAUNCHED	PAVID	PAWLS	PAYFONES
PATTERERS	PAUNCHES	PAVILION	PAWN	PAYGRADE
PATTERING	PAUNCHIER	PAVILIONS	PAWNABLE	PAYGRADES
PATTERN	PAUNCHING	PAVILLON	PAWNAGE	PAYING
PATTERNED	PAUNCHY	PAVILLONS	PAWNAGES	PAYINGS
PATTERNS	PAUPER	PAVIN	PAWNCE	PAYLIST
PATTERS	PAUPERDOM	PAVING	PAWNCES	PAYLISTS
PATTES	PAUPERED	PAVINGS	PAWNED	PAYLOAD
PATTEST	PAUPERESS	PAVINS	PAWNEE	PAYLOADS
PATTIE	PAUPERING	PAVIOR	PAWNEES	PAYMASTER
PATTIES	PAUPERISE	PAVIORS	PAWNER	PAYMENT
PATTING	PAUPERISM	PAVIOUR	PAWNERS	PAYMENTS
PATTLE	PAUPERIZE	PAVIOURS	PAWNING	PAYNIM
PATTLES	PAUPERS	PAVIS	PAWNOR	PAYNIMRY
PATTRESS	PAUPIETTE	PAVISE	PAWNORS	PAYNIMS
PATTY	PAURAQUE	PAVISER	PAWNS	PAYOFF
PATTYPAN	PAURAQUES	PAVISERS	PAWNSHOP	PAYOFFS
PATTYPANS	PAUROPOD	PAVISES	PAWNSHOPS	PAYOLA
PATU	PAUROPODS	PAVISSE	PAWPAW	PAYOLAS
PATULENT	PAUSAL	PAVISSES	PAWPAWS	PAYOR
PATULIN	PAUSE	PAVLOVA	PAWS	PAYORS
PATULINS	PAUSED	PAVLOVAS	PAX	PAYOUT
PATULOUS	PAUSEFUL	PAVONAZZO	PAXES	PAYOUTS
PATUS	PAUSELESS	PAVONE	PAXIUBA	PAYPHONE
PATUTUKI	PAUSER	PAVONES	PAXIUBAS	PAYPHONES
PATUTUKIS	PAUSERS	PAVONIAN	PAXWAX	PAYROLL
PATY	PAUSES	PAVONINE	PAXWAXES	PAYROLLS
PATZER	PAUSING	PAVS	PAY	PAYS
PATZERS	PAUSINGLY	PAW	PAYABLE	PAYSAGE
PAUA	PAUSINGS	PAWA	PAYABLES	PAYSAGES
PAUAS	PAV	PAWAS	PAYABLY	PAYSAGIST
PAUCAL	PAVAGE	PAWAW	PAYBACK	PAYSD
PAUCALS	PAVAGES	PAWAWED	PAYBACKS	PAYSLIP
PAUCITIES	PAVAN	PAWAWING	PAYCHECK	PAYSLIPS
PAUCITY	PAVANE	PAWAWS	PAYCHECKS	PAYWALL
PAUGHTIER	PAVANES	PAWED	PAYCHEQUE	PAYWALLS
PAUGHTY	PAVANS	PAWER	PAYDAY	PAZAZZ
PAUL	PAVE	PAWERS	PAYDAYS	PAZAZZES
PAULDRON	PAVED	PAWING	PAYDOWN	PAZZAZZ
PAULDRONS	PAVEED	PAWK	PAYDOWNS	PAZZAZZES
PAULIN	PAVEMENT	PAWKIER	PAYED	PE
PAULINS	PAVEMENTS	PAWKIEST	PAYEE	PEA
PAULOWNIA	PAVEN	PAWKILY	PAYEES	PEABERRY

PEABRAIN	PEAKINGS	PEARMAIN	PEAZED	PECORINO
PEABRAINS	PEAKISH	PEARMAINS	PEAZES	PECORINOS
PEACE	PEAKLESS	PEARS	PEAZING	PECS
PEACEABLE	PEAKLIKE	PEARST	PEBA	PECTASE
PEACEABLY	PEAKS	PEART	PEBAS	PECTASES
PEACED	PEAKY	PEARTER	PEBBLE	PECTATE
PEACEFUL	PEAL	PEARTEST	PEBBLED	PECTATES
PEACELESS	PEALED	PEARTLY	PEBBLES	PECTEN
PEACENIK	PEALIKE	PEARTNESS	PEBBLIER	PECTENS
PEACENIKS	PEALING	PEARWOOD	PEBBLIEST	PECTIC
PEACES	PEALS	PEARWOODS	PEBBLING	PECTIN
PEACETIME	PEAN	PEAS	PEBBLINGS	PECTINAL
PEACH	PEANED	PEASANT	PEBBLY	PECTINALS
PEACHBLOW	PEANING	PEASANTRY	PEBRINE	PECTINATE
PEACHED	PEANS	PEASANTS	PEBRINES	PECTINEAL
PEACHER	PEANUT	PEASANTY	PEC	PECTINES
PEACHERS	PEANUTS	PEASCOD	PECAN	PECTINOUS
PEACHES	PEANUTTY	PEASCODS	PECANS	PECTINS
PEACHICK	PEAPOD	PEASE	PECCABLE	PECTISE
PEACHICKS	PEAPODS	PEASECOD	PECCANCY	PECTISED
PEACHIER	PEAR	PEASECODS	PECCANT	PECTISES
PEACHIEST	PEARCE	PEASED	PECCANTLY	PECTISING
PEACHILY	PEARCED	PEASEN	PECCARIES	PECTIZE
PEACHING	PEARCES	PEASES	PECCARY	PECTIZED
PEACHY	PEARCING	PEASING	PECCAVI	PECTIZES
PEACING	PEARE	PEASON	PECCAVIS	PECTIZING
PEACOAT	PEARES	PEASOUPER	PECH	PECTOLITE
PEACOATS	PEARL	PEAT	PECHAN	PECTORAL
PEACOCK	PEARLASH	PEATARIES	PECHANS	PECTORALS
PEACOCKED	PEARLED	PEATARY	PECHED	PECTOSE
PEACOCKS	PEARLER	PEATERIES	PECHING	PECTOSES
PEACOCKY	PEARLERS	PEATERY	PECHS	PECULATE
PEACOD	PEARLIER	PEATIER	PECK	PECULATED
PEACODS	PEARLIES	PEATIEST	PECKE	PECULATES
PEAFOWL	PEARLIEST	PEATLAND	PECKED	PECULATOR
PEAFOWLS	PEARLIN	PEATLANDS	PECKER	PECULIA
PEAG	PEARLING	PEATMAN	PECKERS	PECULIAR
PEAGE	PEARLINGS	PEATMEN	PECKES	PECULIARS
PEAGES	PEARLINS	PEATS	PECKIER	PECULIUM
PEAGS	PEARLISED	PEATSHIP	PECKIEST	PECUNIARY
PEAHEN	PEARLITE	PEATSHIPS	PECKING	PECUNIOUS
PEAHENS	PEARLITES	PEATY	PECKINGS	PED
PEAK	PEARLITIC	PEAVEY	PECKISH	PEDAGOG
PEAKED	PEARLIZED	PEAVEYS	PECKISHLY	PEDAGOGIC
PEAKIER	PEARLS	PEAVIES	PECKS	PEDAGOGS
PEAKIEST	PEARLWORT	PEAVY	PECKY	PEDAGOGUE
PEAKING	PEARLY	PEAZE	PECORINI	PEDAGOGY

PEDAL	PEDESIS	PEDREROES	PEEP	PEEWITS
PEDALBOAT	PEDESTAL	PEDREROS	PEEPBO	PEG
PEDALCAR	PEDESTALS	PEDRO	PEEPBOS	PEGASUS
PEDALCARS	PEDETIC	PEDROS	PEEPE	PEGASUSES
PEDALED	PEDIATRIC	PEDS	PEEPED	PEGBOARD
PEDALER	PEDICAB	PEDUNCLE	PEEPER	PEGBOARDS
PEDALERS	PEDICABS	PEDUNCLED	PEEPERS	PEGBOX
PEDALFER	PEDICEL	PEDUNCLES	PEEPES	PEGBOXES
PEDALFERS	PEDICELS	PEDWAY	PEEPHOLE	PEGGED
PEDALIER	PEDICLE	PEDWAYS	PEEPHOLES	PEGGIER
PEDALIERS	PEDICLED	PEE	PEEPING	PEGGIES
PEDALING	PEDICLES	PEEBEEN	PEEPS	PEGGIEST
PEDALLED	PEDICULAR	PEEBEENS	PEEPSHOW	PEGGING
PEDALLER	PEDICULI	PEECE	PEEPSHOWS	PEGGINGS
PEDALLERS	PEDICULUS	PEECES	PEEPTOE	PEGGY
PEDALLING	PEDICURE	PEED	PEEPUL	PEGH
PEDALO	PEDICURED	PEEING	PEEPULS	PEGHED
PEDALOES	PEDICURES	PEEK	PEER	PEGHING
PEDALOS	PEDIFORM	PEEKABO	PEERAGE	PEGHS
PEDALS	PEDIGREE	PEEKABOO	PEERAGES	PEGLEGGED
PEDANT	PEDIGREED	PEEKABOOS	PEERED	PEGLESS
PEDANTIC	PEDIGREES	PEEKABOS	PEERESS	PEGLIKE
PEDANTISE	PEDIMENT	PEEKAPOO	PEERESSES	PEGMATITE
PEDANTISM	PEDIMENTS	PEEKAPOOS	PEERIE	PEGS
PEDANTIZE	PEDIPALP	PEEKED	PEERIER	PEGTOP
PEDANTRY	PEDIPALPI	PEEKING	PEERIES	PEGTOPS
PEDANTS	PEDIPALPS	PEEKS	PEERIEST	PEH
PEDATE	PEDLAR	PEEL	PEERING	PEHS
PEDATELY	PEDLARIES	PEELABLE	PEERLESS	PEIGNOIR
PEDATIFID	PEDLARS	PEELED	PEERS	PEIGNOIRS
PEDDER	PEDLARY	PEELER	PEERY	PEIN
PEDDERS	PEDLER	PEELERS	PEES	PEINCT
PEDDLE	PEDLERIES	PEELING	PEESWEEP	PEINCTED
PEDDLED	PEDLERS	PEELINGS	PEESWEEPS	PEINCTING
PEDDLER	PEDLERY	PEELS	PEETWEET	PEINCTS
PEDDLERS	PEDOCAL	PEEN	PEETWEETS	PEINED
PEDDLERY	PEDOCALIC	PEENED	PEEVE	PEINING
PEDDLES	PEDOCALS	PEENGE	PEEVED	PEINS
PEDDLING	PEDOGENIC	PEENGED	PEEVER	PEIRASTIC
PEDDLINGS	PEDOLOGIC	PEENGEING	PEEVERS	PEISE
PEDERAST	PEDOLOGY	PEENGES	PEEVES	PEISED
PEDERASTS	PEDOMETER	PEENGING	PEEVING	PEISES
PEDERASTY	PEDOPHILE	PEENING	PEEVISH	PEISHWA
PEDERERO	PEDORTHIC	PEENINGS	PEEVISHLY	PEISHWAH
PEDEREROS	PEDRAIL	PEENS	PEEWEE	PEISHWAHS
PEDES	PEDRAILS	PEEOY	PEEWEES	PEISHWAS
PEDESES	PEDRERO	PEEOYS	PEEWIT	PEISING

PEIZE	PELLACH	PELORIZED	PEMPHIGUS	PENDICLE
PEIZED	PELLACHS	PELORUS	PEMPHIX	PENDICLER
PEIZES	PELLACK	PELORUSES	PEMPHIXES	PENDICLES
PEIZING	PELLACKS	PELORY	PEN	PENDING
PEJORATE	PELLAGRA	PELOTA	PENAL	PENDRAGON
PEJORATED	PELLAGRAS	PELOTAS	PENALISE	PENDS
PEJORATES	PELLAGRIN	PELOTON	PENALISED	PENDU
PEKAN	PELLED	PELOTONS	PENALISES	PENDULAR
PEKANS	PELLET	PELS	PENALITY	PENDULATE
PEKE	PELLETAL	PELT	PENALIZE	PENDULE
PEKEPOO	PELLETED	PELTA	PENALIZED	PENDULES
PEKEPOOS	PELLETIFY	PELTAE	PENALIZES	PENDULINE
PEKES	PELLETING	PELTAS	PENALLY	PENDULOUS
PEKIN	PELLETISE	PELTAST	PENALTIES	PENDULUM
PEKINS	PELLETIZE	PELTASTS	PENALTY	PENDULUMS
PEKOE	PELLETS	PELTATE	PENANCE	PENE
PEKOES	PELLICLE	PELTATELY	PENANCED	PENED
PEL	PELLICLES	PELTATION	PENANCES	PENEPLAIN
PELA	PELLING	PELTED	PENANCING	PENEPLANE
PELAGE	PELLITORY	PELTER	PENANG	PENES
PELAGES	PELLMELL	PELTERED	PENANGS	PENETRANT
PELAGIAL	PELLMELLS	PELTERING	PENATES	PENETRATE
PELAGIALS	PELLOCK	PELTERS	PENCE	PENFOLD
PELAGIAN	PELLOCKS	PELTING	PENCEL	PENFOLDS
PELAGIANS	PELLS	PELTINGLY	PENCELS	PENFUL
PELAGIC	PELLUCID	PELTINGS	PENCES	PENFULS
PELAGICS	PELLUM	PELTLESS	PENCHANT	PENGO
PELAS	PELLUMS	PELTRIES	PENCHANTS	PENGOS
PELAU	PELMA	PELTRY	PENCIL	PENGUIN
PELAUS	PELMANISM	PELTS	PENCILED	PENGUINRY
PELE	PELMAS	PELVES	PENCILER	PENGUINS
PELECYPOD	PELMATIC	PELVIC	PENCILERS	PENHOLDER
PELERINE	PELMET	PELVICS	PENCILING	PENI
PELERINES	PELMETS	PELVIFORM	PENCILLED	PENIAL
PELES	PELOID	PELVIS	PENCILLER	PENICIL
PELF	PELOIDS	PELVISES	PENCILS	PENICILLI
PELFS	PELOLOGY	PEMBINA	PENCRAFT	PENICILS
PELHAM	PELON	PEMBINAS	PENCRAFTS	PENIE
PELHAMS	PELONS	PEMBROKE	PEND	PENIES
PELICAN	PELORIA	PEMBROKES	PENDANT	PENILE
PELICANS	PELORIAN	PEMICAN	PENDANTLY	PENILL
PELISSE	PELORIAS	PEMICANS	PENDANTS	PENILLION
PELISSES	PELORIC	PEMMICAN	PENDED	PENING
PELITE	PELORIES	PEMMICANS	PENDENCY	PENINSULA
PELITES	PELORISED	PEMOLINE	PENDENT	PENIS
PELITIC	PELORISM	PEMOLINES	PENDENTLY	PENISES
PELL	PELORISMS	PEMPHIGI	PENDENTS	PENISTONE

PENITENCE	PENNON	PENTACLE	PENTOSIDE	PEPERINOS
PENITENCY	PENNONCEL	PENTACLES	PENTOXIDE	PEPEROMIA
PENITENT	PENNONED	PENTACT	PENTROOF	PEPERONI
PENITENTS	PENNONS	PENTACTS	PENTROOFS	PEPERONIS
PENK	PENNY	PENTAD	PENTS	PEPFUL
PENKNIFE	PENNYBOY	PENTADIC	PENTYL	PEPINO
PENKNIVES	PENNYBOYS	PENTADS	PENTYLENE	PEPINOS
PENKS	PENNYFEE	PENTAGON	PENTYLS	PEPITA
PENLIGHT	PENNYFEES	PENTAGONS	PENUCHE	PEPITAS
PENLIGHTS	PENNYLAND	PENTAGRAM	PENUCHES	PEPLA
PENLITE	PENNYWISE	PENTALOGY	PENUCHI	PEPLOS
PENLITES	PENNYWORT	PENTALPHA	PENUCHIS	PEPLOSES
PENMAN	PENOCHE	PENTAMERY	PENUCHLE	PEPLUM
PENMEN	PENOCHES	PENTANE	PENUCHLES	PEPLUMED
PENNA	PENOLOGY	PENTANES	PENUCKLE	PEPLUMS
PENNAE	PENONCEL	PENTANGLE	PENUCKLES	PEPLUS
PENNAL	PENONCELS	PENTANOIC	PENULT	PEPLUSES
PENNALISM	PENPOINT	PENTANOL	PENULTIMA	PEPO
PENNALS	PENPOINTS	PENTANOLS	PENULTS	PEPONIDA
PENNAME	PENPUSHER	PENTAPODY	PENUMBRA	PEPONIDAS
PENNAMES	PENS	PENTARCH	PENUMBRAE	PEPONIUM
PENNANT	PENSEE	PENTARCHS	PENUMBRAL	PEPONIUMS
PENNANTS	PENSEES	PENTARCHY	PENUMBRAS	PEPOS
PENNATE	PENSEL	PENTATHLA	PENURIES	PEPPED
PENNATED	PENSELS	PENTENE	PENURIOUS	PEPPER
PENNATULA	PENSEROSO	PENTENES	PENURY	PEPPERBOX
PENNE	PENSIL	PENTHIA	PENWIPER	PEPPERED
PENNED	PENSILE	PENTHIAS	PENWIPERS	PEPPERER
PENNEECH	PENSILITY	PENTHOUSE	PENWOMAN	PEPPERERS
PENNEECHS	PENSILS	PENTICE	PENWOMEN	PEPPERIER
PENNEECK	PENSION	PENTICED	PEON	PEPPERING
PENNEECKS	PENSIONE	PENTICES	PEONAGE	PEPPERONI
PENNER	PENSIONED	PENTICING	PEONAGES	PEPPERS
PENNERS	PENSIONER	PENTISE	PEONES	PEPPERY
PENNES	PENSIONES	PENTISED	PEONIES	PEPPIER
PENNI	PENSIONI	PENTISES	PEONISM	PEPPIEST
PENNIA	PENSIONS	PENTISING	PEONISMS	PEPPILY
PENNIED	PENSIVE	PENTITI	PEONS	PEPPINESS
PENNIES	PENSIVELY	PENTITO	PEONY	PEPPING
PENNIFORM	PENSTEMON	PENTODE	PEOPLE	PEPPY
PENNILESS	PENSTER	PENTODES	PEOPLED	PEPS
PENNILL	PENSTERS	PENTOMIC	PEOPLER	PEPSI
PENNINE	PENSTOCK	PENTOSAN	PEOPLERS	PEPSIN
PENNINES	PENSTOCKS	PENTOSANE	PEOPLES	PEPSINATE
PENNING	PENSUM	PENTOSANS	PEOPLING	PEPSINE
PENNINITE	PENSUMS	PENTOSE	PEP	PEPSINES
PENNIS	PENT	PENTOSES	PEPERINO	PEPSINS

P

PEPSIS
PEPTALK
PEPTALKED
PEPTALKS
PEPTIC
PEPTICITY
PEPTICS
PEPTID
PEPTIDASE
PEPTIDE
PEPTIDES
PEPTIDIC
PEPTIDS
PEPTISE
PEPTISED
PEPTISER
PEPTISERS
PEPTISES
PEPTISING
PEPTIZE
PEPTIZED
PEPTIZER
PEPTIZERS
PEPTIZES
PEPTIZING
PEPTONE
PEPTONES
PEPTONIC
PEPTONISE
PEPTONIZE
PEQUISTE
PEQUISTES
PER
PERACID
PERACIDS
PERACUTE
PERAEA
PERAEON
PERAEONS
PERAEOPOD
PERAI
PERAIS
PERBORATE
PERC
PERCALE
PERCALES
PERCALINE

PERCASE
PERCE
PERCEABLE
PERCEANT
PERCED
PERCEIVE
PERCEIVED
PERCEIVER
PERCEIVES
PERCEN
PERCENT
PERCENTAL
PERCENTS
PERCEPT
PERCEPTS
PERCES
PERCH
PERCHANCE
PERCHED
PERCHER
PERCHERON
PERCHERS
PERCHERY
PERCHES
PERCHING
PERCHINGS
PERCID
PERCIDS
PERCIFORM
PERCINE
PERCINES
PERCING
PERCOCT
PERCOCTED
PERCOCTS
PERCOID
PERCOIDS
PERCOLATE
PERCOLIN
PERCOLINS
PERCS
PERCUSS
PERCUSSED
PERCUSSES
PERCUSSOR
PERDENDO
PERDIE

PERDITION
PERDU
PERDUE
PERDUES
PERDURE
PERDURED
PERDURES
PERDURING
PERDUS
PERDY
PERE
PEREA
PEREGAL
PEREGALS
PEREGRIN
PEREGRINE
PEREGRINS
PEREIA
PEREION
PEREIONS
PEREIOPOD
PEREIRA
PEREIRAS
PERENNATE
PERENNIAL
PERENNITY
PERENTIE
PERENTIES
PERENTY
PEREON
PEREONS
PEREOPOD
PEREOPODS
PERES
PERFAY
PERFECT
PERFECTA
PERFECTAS
PERFECTED
PERFECTER
PERFECTI
PERFECTLY
PERFECTO
PERFECTOR
PERFECTOS
PERFECTS
PERFERVID

PERFERVOR
PERFET
PERFIDIES
PERFIDY
PERFIN
PERFING
PERFINGS
PERFINS
PERFORANS
PERFORANT
PERFORATE
PERFORCE
PERFORM
PERFORMED
PERFORMER
PERFORMS
PERFUME
PERFUMED
PERFUMER
PERFUMERS
PERFUMERY
PERFUMES
PERFUMIER
PERFUMING
PERFUMY
PERFUSATE
PERFUSE
PERFUSED
PERFUSES
PERFUSING
PERFUSION
PERFUSIVE
PERGOLA
PERGOLAS
PERGUNNAH
PERHAPS
PERHAPSES
PERI
PERIAGUA
PERIAGUAS
PERIAKTOI
PERIAKTOS
PERIANTH
PERIANTHS
PERIAPSES
PERIAPSIS
PERIAPT

PERIAPTS
PERIBLAST
PERIBLEM
PERIBLEMS
PERIBOLI
PERIBOLOI
PERIBOLOS
PERIBOLUS
PERICARP
PERICARPS
PERICLASE
PERICLINE
PERICON
PERICONES
PERICOPAE
PERICOPAL
PERICOPE
PERICOPES
PERICOPIC
PERICYCLE
PERIDERM
PERIDERMS
PERIDIA
PERIDIAL
PERIDINIA
PERIDIUM
PERIDIUMS
PERIDOT
PERIDOTE
PERIDOTES
PERIDOTIC
PERIDOTS
PERIDROME
PERIGEAL
PERIGEAN
PERIGEE
PERIGEES
PERIGON
PERIGONE
PERIGONES
PERIGONIA
PERIGONS
PERIGYNY
PERIHELIA
PERIKARYA
PERIL
PERILED

PERILING	PERIQUE	PERLITES	PEROG	PERRUQUES
PERILLA	PERIQUES	PERLITIC	PEROGI	PERRY
PERILLAS	PERIS	PERLOUS	PEROGIE	PERSALT
PERILLED	PERISARC	PERM	PEROGIES	PERSALTS
PERILLING	PERISARCS	PERMABEAR	PEROGIS	PERSANT
PERILOUS	PERISCIAN	PERMABULL	PEROGS	PERSAUNT
PERILS	PERISCOPE	PERMALINK	PEROGY	PERSE
PERILUNE	PERISH	PERMALLOY	PERONE	PERSECUTE
PERILUNES	PERISHED	PERMANENT	PERONEAL	PERSEITY
PERILYMPH	PERISHER	PERMATAN	PERONES	PERSELINE
PERIMETER	PERISHERS	PERMATANS	PERONEUS	PERSES
PERIMETRY	PERISHES	PERMEABLE	PERORAL	PERSEVERE
PERIMORPH	PERISHING	PERMEABLY	PERORALLY	PERSICO
PERIMYSIA	PERISPERM	PERMEANCE	PERORATE	PERSICOS
PERINAEUM	PERISTOME	PERMEANT	PERORATED	PERSICOT
PERINATAL	PERISTYLE	PERMEANTS	PERORATES	PERSICOTS
PERINEA	PERITI	PERMEASE	PERORATOR	PERSIENNE
PERINEAL	PERITONEA	PERMEASES	PEROVSKIA	PERSIMMON
PERINEUM	PERITRACK	PERMEATE	PEROXID	PERSING
PERINEUMS	PERITRICH	PERMEATED	PEROXIDE	PERSIST
PERIOD	PERITUS	PERMEATES	PEROXIDED	PERSISTED
PERIODATE	PERIWIG	PERMEATOR	PEROXIDES	PERSISTER
PERIODED	PERIWIGS	PERMED	PEROXIDIC	PERSISTS
PERIODIC	PERJINK	PERMIAN	PEROXIDS	PERSON
PERIODID	PERJURE	PERMIE	PEROXO	PERSONA
PERIODIDE	PERJURED	PERMIES	PEROXY	PERSONAE
PERIODIDS	PERJURER	PERMING	PERP	PERSONAGE
PERIODING	PERJURERS	PERMIT	PERPEND	PERSONAL
PERIODISE	PERJURES	PERMITS	PERPENDED	PERSONALS
PERIODIZE	PERJURIES	PERMITTED	PERPENDS	PERSONAS
PERIODS	PERJURING	PERMITTEE	PERPENT	PERSONATE
PERIOST	PERJUROUS	PERMITTER	PERPENTS	PERSONIFY
PERIOSTEA	PERJURY	PERMS	PERPETUAL	PERSONISE
PERIOSTS	PERK	PERMUTATE	PERPLEX	PERSONIZE
PERIOTIC	PERKED	PERMUTE	PERPLEXED	PERSONNED
PERIOTICS	PERKIER	PERMUTED	PERPLEXER	PERSONNEL
PERIPATUS	PERKIEST	PERMUTES	PERPLEXES	PERSONS
PERIPETIA	PERKILY	PERMUTING	PERPS	PERSPEX
PERIPETY	PERKIN	PERN	PERRADIAL	PERSPEXES
PERIPHERY	PERKINESS	PERNANCY	PERRADII	PERSPIRE
PERIPLASM	PERKING	PERNED	PERRADIUS	PERSPIRED
PERIPLAST	PERKINS	PERNING	PERRIER	PERSPIRES
PERIPLUS	PERKISH	PERNIO	PERRIERS	PERSPIRY
PERIPROCT	PERKS	PERNIONES	PERRIES	PERST
PERIPTER	PERKY	PERNOD	PERRON	PERSUADE
PERIPTERS	PERLEMOEN	PERNODS	PERRONS	PERSUADED
PERIPTERY	PERLITE	PERNS	PERRUQUE	PERSUADER

P

PERSUADES	PERUSES	PESKIEST	PETALISM	PETIOLULE
PERSUE	PERUSING	PESKILY	PETALISMS	PETIT
PERSUED	PERV	PESKINESS	PETALLED	PETITE
PERSUES	PERVADE	PESKY	PETALLIKE	PETITES
PERSUING	PERVADED	PESO	PETALODIC	PETITION
PERSWADE	PERVADER	PESOS	PETALODY	PETITIONS
PERSWADED	PERVADERS	PESSARIES	PETALOID	PETITORY
PERSWADES	PERVADES	PESSARY	PETALOUS	PETNAP
PERT	PERVADING	PESSIMA	PETALS	PETNAPER
PERTAIN	PERVASION	PESSIMAL	PETANQUE	PETNAPERS
PERTAINED	PERVASIVE	PESSIMISM	PETANQUES	PETNAPING
PERTAINS	PERVE	PESSIMIST	PETAR	PETNAPPED
PERTAKE	PERVED	PESSIMUM	PETARA	PETNAPPER
PERTAKEN	PERVERSE	PEST	PETARAS	PETNAPS
PERTAKES	PERVERSER	PESTER	PETARD	PETRALE
PERTAKING	PERVERT	PESTERED	PETARDS	PETRALES
PERTER	PERVERTED	PESTERER	PETARIES	PETRARIES
PERTEST	PERVERTER	PESTERERS	PETARS	PETRARY
PERTHITE	PERVERTS	PESTERING	PETARY	PETRE
PERTHITES	PERVES	PESTEROUS	PETASOS	PETREL
PERTHITIC	PERVIATE	PESTERS	PETASOSES	PETRELS
PERTINENT	PERVIATED	PESTFUL	PETASUS	PETRES
PERTLY	PERVIATES	PESTHOLE	PETASUSES	PETRI
PERTNESS	PERVICACY	PESTHOLES	PETAURINE	PETRICHOR
PERTOOK	PERVIER	PESTHOUSE	PETAURIST	PETRIFIC
PERTS	PERVIEST	PESTICIDE	PETCHARY	PETRIFIED
PERTURB	PERVING	PESTIER	PETCOCK	PETRIFIER
PERTURBED	PERVIOUS	PESTIEST	PETCOCKS	PETRIFIES
PERTURBER	PERVO	PESTILENT	PETECHIA	PETRIFY
PERTURBS	PERVOS	PESTLE	PETECHIAE	PETROGENY
PERTUSATE	PERVS	PESTLED	PETECHIAL	PETROGRAM
PERTUSE	PERVY	PESTLES	PETER	PETROL
PERTUSED	PES	PESTLING	PETERED	PETROLAGE
PERTUSION	PESADE	PESTO	PETERING	PETROLEUM
PERTUSSAL	PESADES	PESTOLOGY	PETERMAN	PETROLEUR
PERTUSSES	PESANT	PESTOS	PETERMEN	PETROLIC
PERTUSSIS	PESANTE	PESTS	PETERS	PETROLLED
PERUKE	PESANTS	PESTY	PETERSHAM	PETROLOGY
PERUKED	PESAUNT	PET	PETHER	PETROLS
PERUKES	PESAUNTS	PETABYTE	PETHERS	PETRONEL
PERUSABLE	PESETA	PETABYTES	PETHIDINE	PETRONELS
PERUSAL	PESETAS	PETAFLOP	PETILLANT	PETROSAL
PERUSALS	PESEWA	PETAFLOPS	PETIOLAR	PETROSALS
PERUSE	PESEWAS	PETAHERTZ	PETIOLATE	PETROUS
PERUSED	PESHWA	PETAL	PETIOLE	PETS
PERUSER	PESHWAS	PETALED	PETIOLED	PETSAI
PERUSERS	PESKIER	PETALINE	PETIOLES	PETSAIS

PETTABLE	PEYOTES	PHALANGES	PHARMING	PHEEZING
PETTED	PEYOTISM	PHALANGID	PHARMINGS	PHELLEM
PETTEDLY	PEYOTISMS	PHALANX	PHARMS	PHELLEMS
PETTER	PEYOTIST	PHALANXES	PHAROS	PHELLOGEN
PETTERS	PEYOTISTS	PHALAROPE	PHAROSES	PHELLOID
PETTI	PEYOTL	PHALLI	PHARYNGAL	PHELONIA
PETTICOAT	PEYOTLS	PHALLIC	PHARYNGES	PHELONION
PETTIER	PEYSE	PHALLIN	PHARYNX	PHENACITE
PETTIES	PEYSED	PHALLINS	PHARYNXES	PHENAKISM
PETTIEST	PEYSES	PHALLISM	PHASE	PHENAKITE
PETTIFOG	PEYSING	PHALLISMS	PHASEAL	PHENATE
PETTIFOGS	PEYTRAL	PHALLIST	PHASED	PHENATES
PETTILY	PEYTRALS	PHALLISTS	PHASEDOWN	PHENAZIN
PETTINESS	PEYTREL	PHALLOID	PHASELESS	PHENAZINE
PETTING	PEYTRELS	PHALLUS	PHASEOLIN	PHENAZINS
PETTINGS	PEZANT	PHALLUSES	PHASEOUT	PHENE
PETTISH	PEZANTS	PHANG	PHASEOUTS	PHENES
PETTISHLY	PEZIZOID	PHANGED	PHASER	PHENETIC
PETTITOES	PFENNIG	PHANGING	PHASERS	PHENETICS
PETTLE	PFENNIGE	PHANGS	PHASES	PHENETOL
PETTLED	PFENNIGS	PHANSIGAR	PHASIC	PHENETOLE
PETTLES	PFENNING	PHANTASIM	PHASING	PHENETOLS
PETTLING	PFENNINGS	PHANTASM	PHASINGS	PHENGITE
PETTO	PFFT	PHANTASMA	PHASIS	PHENGITES
PETTY	PFUI	PHANTASMS	PHASMID	PHENIC
PETULANCE	PHABLET	PHANTAST	PHASMIDS	PHENIX
PETULANCY	PHABLETS	PHANTASTS	PHASOR	PHENIXES
PETULANT	PHACELIA	PHANTASY	PHASORS	PHENOCOPY
PETUNIA	PHACELIAS	PHANTOM	PHAT	PHENOGAM
PETUNIAS	PHACOID	PHANTOMS	PHATIC	PHENOGAMS
PETUNTSE	PHACOIDAL	PHANTOMY	PHATTER	PHENOL
PETUNTSES	PHACOLITE	PHANTOSME	PHATTEST	PHENOLATE
PETUNTZE	PHACOLITH	PHARAOH	PHEASANT	PHENOLIC
PETUNTZES	PHAEIC	PHARAOHS	PHEASANTS	PHENOLICS
PEW	PHAEISM	PHARAONIC	PHEAZAR	PHENOLOGY
PEWEE	PHAEISMS	PHARE	PHEAZARS	PHENOLS
PEWEES	PHAENOGAM	PHARES	PHEER	PHENOM
PEWHOLDER	PHAETON	PHARISAIC	PHEERE	PHENOME
PEWIT	PHAETONS	PHARISEE	PHEERES	PHENOMENA
PEWITS	PHAGE	PHARISEES	PHEERS	PHENOMES
PEWS	PHAGEDENA	PHARM	PHEESE	PHENOMS
PEWTER	PHAGES	PHARMA	PHEESED	PHENOTYPE
PEWTERER	PHAGOCYTE	PHARMACY	PHEESES	PHENOXIDE
PEWTERERS	PHAGOSOME	PHARMAS	PHEESING	PHENOXY
PEWTERS	PHALANGAL	PHARMED	PHEEZE	PHENYL
PEWTERY	PHALANGE	PHARMER	PHEEZED	PHENYLENE
PEYOTE	PHALANGER	PHARMERS	PHEEZES	PHENYLIC

P

PHENYLS	PHILTRING	PHOCA	PHONIED	PHOSPHORS
PHENYTOIN	PHILTRUM	PHOCAE	PHONIER	PHOSSY
PHEON	PHIMOSES	PHOCAS	PHONIES	PHOT
PHEONS	PHIMOSIS	PHOCINE	PHONIEST	PHOTIC
PHERESES	PHIMOTIC	PHOCOMELY	PHONILY	PHOTICS
PHERESIS	PHINNOCK	PHOEBE	PHONINESS	PHOTINIA
PHEROMONE	PHINNOCKS	PHOEBES	PHONING	PHOTINIAS
PHESE	PHIS	PHOEBUS	PHONMETER	PHOTINO
PHESED	PHISH	PHOEBUSES	PHONO	PHOTINOS
PHESES	PHISHED	PHOENIX	PHONOGRAM	PHOTISM
PHESING	PHISHER	PHOENIXES	PHONOLITE	PHOTISMS
PHEW	PHISHERS	PHOH	PHONOLOGY	PHOTO
PHI	PHISHES	PHOLADES	PHONON	PHOTOBLOG
PHIAL	PHISHING	PHOLAS	PHONONS	PHOTOBOMB
PHIALLED	PHISHINGS	PHON	PHONOPORE	PHOTOCALL
PHIALLING	PHISNOMY	PHONAL	PHONOS	PHOTOCARD
PHIALS	PHIZ	PHONATE	PHONOTYPE	PHOTOCELL
PHILABEG	PHIZES	PHONATED	PHONOTYPY	PHOTOCOPY
PHILABEGS	PHIZOG	PHONATES	PHONS	PHOTODISK
PHILAMOT	PHIZOGS	PHONATHON	PHONY	PHOTOED
PHILAMOTS	PHIZZ	PHONATING	PHONYING	PHOTOFIT
PHILANDER	PHIZZES	PHONATION	PHOOEY	PHOTOFITS
PHILATELY	PHLEBITIC	PHONATORY	PHORATE	PHOTOG
PHILAVERY	PHLEBITIS	PHONE	PHORATES	PHOTOGEN
PHILHORSE	PHLEGM	PHONECAM	PHORESIES	PHOTOGENE
PHILIBEG	PHLEGMIER	PHONECAMS	PHORESY	PHOTOGENS
PHILIBEGS	PHLEGMON	PHONECARD	PHORETIC	PHOTOGENY
PHILIPPIC	PHLEGMONS	PHONED	PHORMINX	PHOTOGRAM
PHILISTIA	PHLEGMS	PHONEME	PHORMIUM	PHOTOGS
PHILLABEG	PHLEGMY	PHONEMES	PHORMIUMS	PHOTOING
PHILLIBEG	PHLOEM	PHONEMIC	PHORONID	PHOTOLYSE
PHILOGYNY	PHLOEMS	PHONEMICS	PHORONIDS	PHOTOLYZE
PHILOLOGY	PHLOMIS	PHONER	PHOS	PHOTOMAP
PHILOMATH	PHLOMISES	PHONERS	PHOSGENE	PHOTOMAPS
PHILOMEL	PHLORIZIN	PHONES	PHOSGENES	PHOTOMASK
PHILOMELA	PHLOX	PHONETIC	PHOSPHATE	PHOTON
PHILOMELS	PHLOXES	PHONETICS	PHOSPHENE	PHOTONIC
PHILOMOT	PHLYCTENA	PHONETISE	PHOSPHID	PHOTONICS
PHILOMOTS	PHO	PHONETISM	PHOSPHIDE	PHOTONS
PHILOPENA	PHOBIA	PHONETIST	PHOSPHIDS	PHOTOPHIL
PHILTER	PHOBIAS	PHONETIZE	PHOSPHIN	PHOTOPIA
PHILTERED	PHOBIC	PHONEY	PHOSPHINE	PHOTOPIAS
PHILTERS	PHOBICS	PHONEYED	PHOSPHINS	PHOTOPIC
PHILTRA	PHOBISM	PHONEYING	PHOSPHITE	PHOTOPLAY
PHILTRE	PHOBISMS	PHONEYS	PHOSPHOR	PHOTOPSIA
PHILTRED	PHOBIST	PHONIC	PHOSPHORE	PHOTOPSY
PHILTRES	PHOBISTS	PHONICS	PHOSPHORI	PHOTOS

PHOTOSCAN	PHRENSY	PHYLLOID	PHYTOSES	PIASTERS
PHOTOSET	PHRENTICK	PHYLLOIDS	PHYTOSIS	PIASTRE
PHOTOSETS	PHRYGANA	PHYLLOME	PHYTOTOMY	PIASTRES
PHOTOSHOP	PHRYGANAS	PHYLLOMES	PHYTOTRON	PIAZZA
PHOTOSTAT	PHT	PHYLLOMIC	PI	PIAZZAS
PHOTOTAXY	PHTHALATE	PHYLLOPOD	PIA	PIAZZE
PHOTOTUBE	PHTHALEIN	PHYLLOS	PIACEVOLE	PIAZZIAN
PHOTOTYPE	PHTHALIC	PHYLOGENY	PIACULAR	PIBAL
PHOTOTYPY	PHTHALIN	PHYLON	PIAFFE	PIBALS
PHOTS	PHTHALINS	PHYLUM	PIAFFED	PIBROCH
PHPHT	PHTHISES	PHYSALIA	PIAFFER	PIBROCHS
PHRASAL	PHTHISIC	PHYSALIAS	PIAFFERS	PIC
PHRASALLY	PHTHISICS	PHYSALIS	PIAFFES	PICA
PHRASE	PHTHISIS	PHYSED	PIAFFING	PICACHO
PHRASED	PHUT	PHYSEDS	PIAL	PICACHOS
PHRASEMAN	PHUTS	PHYSES	PIAN	PICADILLO
PHRASEMEN	PHUTTED	PHYSETER	PIANETTE	PICADOR
PHRASER	PHUTTING	PHYSETERS	PIANETTES	PICADORES
PHRASERS	PHWOAH	PHYSIATRY	PIANI	PICADORS
PHRASES	PHWOAR	PHYSIC	PIANIC	PICAL
PHRASIER	PHYCOCYAN	PHYSICAL	PIANINO	PICAMAR
PHRASIEST	PHYCOLOGY	PHYSICALS	PIANINOS	PICAMARS
PHRASING	PHYLA	PHYSICIAN	PIANISM	PICANINNY
PHRASINGS	PHYLACTIC	PHYSICISM	PIANISMS	PICANTE
PHRASY	PHYLAE	PHYSICIST	PIANIST	PICARA
PHRATRAL	PHYLAR	PHYSICKED	PIANISTE	PICARAS
PHRATRIC	PHYLARCH	PHYSICKY	PIANISTES	PICARIAN
PHRATRIES	PHYLARCHS	PHYSICS	PIANISTIC	PICARIANS
PHRATRY	PHYLARCHY	PHYSIO	PIANISTS	PICARO
PHREAK	PHYLAXIS	PHYSIOS	PIANO	PICAROON
PHREAKED	PHYLE	PHYSIQUE	PIANOLA	PICAROONS
PHREAKER	PHYLESES	PHYSIQUED	PIANOLAS	PICAROS
PHREAKERS	PHYLESIS	PHYSIQUES	PIANOLIST	PICAS
PHREAKING	PHYLETIC	PHYSIS	PIANOS	PICAYUNE
PHREAKS	PHYLETICS	PHYTANE	PIANS	PICAYUNES
PHREATIC	PHYLIC	PHYTANES	PIARIST	PICCADILL
PHRENESES	PHYLLARY	PHYTIN	PIARISTS	PICCANIN
PHRENESIS	PHYLLID	PHYTINS	PIAS	PICCANINS
PHRENETIC	PHYLLIDS	PHYTOGENY	PIASABA	PICCATA
PHRENIC	PHYLLITE	PHYTOID	PIASABAS	PICCATAS
PHRENICS	PHYLLITES	PHYTOL	PIASAVA	PICCIES
PHRENISM	PHYLLITIC	PHYTOLITH	PIASAVAS	PICCOLO
PHRENISMS	PHYLLO	PHYTOLOGY	PIASSABA	PICCOLOS
PHRENITIC	PHYLLODE	PHYTOLS	PIASSABAS	PICCY
PHRENITIS	PHYLLODES	PHYTON	PIASSAVA	PICE
PHRENSIED	PHYLLODIA	PHYTONIC	PIASSAVAS	PICENE
PHRENSIES	PHYLLODY	PHYTONS	PIASTER	PICENES

P

PICEOUS	PICKLED	PICOTEES	PIDGEON	PIEPLANTS
PICHOLINE	PICKLER	PICOTING	PIDGEONS	PIEPOWDER
PICHURIM	PICKLERS	PICOTITE	PIDGIN	PIER
PICHURIMS	PICKLES	PICOTITES	PIDGINISE	PIERAGE
PICIFORM	PICKLING	PICOTS	PIDGINIZE	PIERAGES
PICINE	PICKLOCK	PICOWAVE	PIDGINS	PIERCE
PICK	PICKLOCKS	PICOWAVED	PIE	PIERCED
PICKABACK	PICKMAW	PICOWAVES	PIEBALD	PIERCER
PICKABLE	PICKMAWS	PICQUET	PIEBALDS	PIERCERS
PICKADIL	PICKNEY	PICQUETED	PIECE	PIERCES
PICKADILL	PICKNEYS	PICQUETS	PIECED	PIERCING
PICKADILS	PICKOFF	PICRA	PIECELESS	PIERCINGS
PICKAPACK	PICKOFFS	PICRAS	PIECEMEAL	PIERHEAD
PICKAROON	PICKPROOF	PICRATE	PIECEN	PIERHEADS
PICKAX	PICKS	PICRATED	PIECENED	PIERID
PICKAXE	PICKTHANK	PICRATES	PIECENER	PIERIDINE
PICKAXED	PICKUP	PICRIC	PIECENERS	PIERIDS
PICKAXES	PICKUPS	PICRITE	PIECENING	PIERIS
PICKAXING	PICKWICK	PICRITES	PIECENS	PIERISES
PICKBACK	PICKWICKS	PICRITIC	PIECER	PIEROG
PICKBACKS	PICKY	PICS	PIECERS	PIEROGI
PICKED	PICLORAM	PICTARNIE	PIECES	PIEROGIES
PICKEER	PICLORAMS	PICTOGRAM	PIECEWISE	PIEROGS
PICKEERED	PICNIC	PICTORIAL	PIECEWORK	PIERRETTE
PICKEERER	PICNICKED	PICTURAL	PIECING	PIERROT
PICKEERS	PICNICKER	PICTURALS	PIECINGS	PIERROTS
PICKER	PICNICKY	PICTURE	PIECRUST	PIERS
PICKEREL	PICNICS	PICTURED	PIECRUSTS	PIERST
PICKERELS	PICOCURIE	PICTURES	PIED	PIERT
PICKERIES	PICOFARAD	PICTURING	PIEDFORT	PIERTS
PICKERS	PICOGRAM	PICTURISE	PIEDFORTS	PIES
PICKERY	PICOGRAMS	PICTURIZE	PIEDISH	PIET
PICKET	PICOLIN	PICUL	PIEDISHES	PIETA
PICKETED	PICOLINE	PICULET	PIEDMONT	PIETAS
PICKETER	PICOLINES	PICULETS	PIEDMONTS	PIETIES
PICKETERS	PICOLINIC	PICULS	PIEDNESS	PIETISM
PICKETING	PICOLINS	PIDDLE	PIEFORT	PIETISMS
PICKETS	PICOMETER	PIDDLED	PIEFORTS	PIETIST
PICKIER	PICOMETRE	PIDDLER	PIEHOLE	PIETISTIC
PICKIEST	PICOMOLE	PIDDLERS	PIEHOLES	PIETISTS
PICKILY	PICOMOLES	PIDDLES	PIEING	PIETS
PICKIN	PICONG	PIDDLIER	PIEINGS	PIETY
PICKINESS	PICONGS	PIDDLIEST	PIEMAN	PIEZO
PICKING	PICOT	PIDDLING	PIEMEN	PIFFERARI
PICKINGS	PICOTE	PIDDLY	PIEND	PIFFERARO
PICKINS	PICOTED	PIDDOCK	PIENDS	PIFFERO
PICKLE	PICOTEE	PIDDOCKS	PIEPLANT	PIFFEROS

PIFFLE	PIGLING	PIGTAILED	PILAW	PILIFORM
PIFFLED	PIGLINGS	PIGTAILS	PILAWS	PILING
PIFFLER	PIGMAEAN	PIGWASH	PILCH	PILINGS
PIFFLERS	PIGMAN	PIGWASHES	PILCHARD	PILINUT
PIFFLES	PIGMEAN	PIGWEED	PILCHARDS	PILINUTS
PIFFLING	PIGMEAT	PIGWEEDS	PILCHER	PILIS
PIG	PIGMEATS	PIHOIHOI	PILCHERS	PILL
PIGBOAT	PIGMEN	PIHOIHOIS	PILCHES	PILLAGE
PIGBOATS	PIGMENT	PIING	PILCORN	PILLAGED
PIGEON	PIGMENTAL	PIKA	PILCORNS	PILLAGER
PIGEONED	PIGMENTED	PIKAKE	PILCROW	PILLAGERS
PIGEONING	PIGMENTS	PIKAKES	PILCROWS	PILLAGES
PIGEONITE	PIGMIES	PIKAS	PILE	PILLAGING
PIGEONRY	PIGMOID	PIKAU	PILEA	PILLAR
PIGEONS	PIGMOIDS	PIKAUS	PILEAS	PILLARED
PIGFACE	PIGMY	PIKE	PILEATE	PILLARING
PIGFACES	PIGNERATE	PIKED	PILEATED	PILLARIST
PIGFEED	PIGNOLI	PIKELET	PILED	PILLARS
PIGFEEDS	PIGNOLIA	PIKELETS	PILEI	PILLAU
PIGFISH	PIGNOLIAS	PIKEMAN	PILELESS	PILLAUS
PIGFISHES	PIGNOLIS	PIKEMEN	PILEOUS	PILLBOX
PIGGED	PIGNORA	PIKEPERCH	PILER	PILLBOXES
PIGGERIES	PIGNORATE	PIKER	PILERS	PILLBUG
PIGGERY	PIGNUS	PIKERS	PILES	PILLBUGS
PIGGIE	PIGNUT	PIKES	PILEUM	PILLED
PIGGIER	PIGNUTS	PIKESTAFF	PILEUP	PILLHEAD
PIGGIES	PIGOUT	PIKEY	PILEUPS	PILLHEADS
PIGGIEST	PIGOUTS	PIKEYS	PILEUS	PILLICOCK
PIGGIN	PIGPEN	PIKI	PILEWORK	PILLIE
PIGGINESS	PIGPENS	PIKING	PILEWORKS	PILLIES
PIGGING	PIGS	PIKINGS	PILEWORT	PILLING
PIGGINGS	PIGSCONCE	PIKIS	PILEWORTS	PILLINGS
PIGGINS	PIGSKIN	PIKUL	PILFER	PILLION
PIGGISH	PIGSKINS	PIKULS	PILFERAGE	PILLIONED
PIGGISHLY	PIGSNEY	PILA	PILFERED	PILLIONS
PIGGY	PIGSNEYS	PILAE	PILFERER	PILLOCK
PIGGYBACK	PIGSNIE	PILAF	PILFERERS	PILLOCKS
PIGHEADED	PIGSNIES	PILAFF	PILFERIES	PILLORIED
PIGHT	PIGSNY	PILAFFS	PILFERING	PILLORIES
PIGHTED	PIGSTICK	PILAFS	PILFERS	PILLORISE
PIGHTING	PIGSTICKS	PILAO	PILFERY	PILLORIZE
PIGHTLE	PIGSTIES	PILAOS	PILGARLIC	PILLORY
PIGHTLES	PIGSTUCK	PILAR	PILGRIM	PILLOW
PIGHTS	PIGSTY	PILASTER	PILGRIMED	PILLOWED
PIGLET	PIGSWILL	PILASTERS	PILGRIMER	PILLOWING
PIGLETS	PIGSWILLS	PILAU	PILGRIMS	PILLOWS
PIGLIKE	PIGTAIL	PILAUS	PILI	PILLOWY

PILLS	PIMP	PINCHECK	PINFALL	PINK
PILLWORM	PIMPED	PINCHECKS	PINFALLS	PINKED
PILLWORMS	PIMPERNEL	PINCHED	PINFISH	PINKEN
PILLWORT	PIMPING	PINCHER	PINFISHES	PINKENED
PILLWORTS	PIMPINGS	PINCHERS	PINFOLD	PINKENING
PILOMOTOR	PIMPLE	PINCHES	PINFOLDED	PINKENS
PILONIDAL	PIMPLED	PINCHFIST	PINFOLDS	PINKER
PILOSE	PIMPLES	PINCHGUT	PING	PINKERS
PILOSITY	PIMPLIER	PINCHGUTS	PINGED	PINKERTON
PILOT	PIMPLIEST	PINCHING	PINGER	PINKEST
PILOTAGE	PIMPLY	PINCHINGS	PINGERS	PINKEY
PILOTAGES	PIMPS	PINCURL	PINGING	PINKEYE
PILOTED	PIN	PINCURLS	PINGLE	PINKEYES
PILOTFISH	PINA	PINDAN	PINGLED	PINKEYS
PILOTING	PINACEOUS	PINDANS	PINGLER	PINKIE
PILOTINGS	PINACOID	PINDAREE	PINGLERS	PINKIER
PILOTIS	PINACOIDS	PINDAREES	PINGLES	PINKIES
PILOTLESS	PINAFORE	PINDARI	PINGLING	PINKIEST
PILOTMAN	PINAFORED	PINDARIS	PINGO	PINKINESS
PILOTMEN	PINAFORES	PINDER	PINGOES	PINKING
PILOTS	PINAKOID	PINDERS	PINGOS	PINKINGS
PILOUS	PINAKOIDS	PINDLING	PINGPONG	PINKISH
PILOW	PINANG	PINDOWN	PINGPONGS	PINKLY
PILOWS	PINANGS	PINDOWNS	PINGRASS	PINKNESS
PILSENER	PINAS	PINE	PINGS	PINKO
PILSENERS	PINASTER	PINEAL	PINGUEFY	PINKOES
PILSNER	PINASTERS	PINEALS	PINGUID	PINKOS
PILSNERS	PINATA	PINEAPPLE	PINGUIN	PINKROOT
PILULA	PINATAS	PINECONE	PINGUINS	PINKROOTS
PILULAE	PINBALL	PINECONES	PINHEAD	PINKS
PILULAR	PINBALLED	PINED	PINHEADED	PINKY
PILULAS	PINBALLS	PINEDROPS	PINHEADS	PINLESS
PILULE	PINBOARD	PINELAND	PINHOLE	PINNA
PILULES	PINBOARDS	PINELANDS	PINHOLES	PINNACE
PILUM	PINBONE	PINELIKE	PINHOOKER	PINNACES
PILUS	PINBONES	PINENE	PINIER	PINNACLE
PILY	PINCASE	PINENES	PINIES	PINNACLED
PIMA	PINCASES	PINERIES	PINIEST	PINNACLES
PIMAS	PINCER	PINERY	PINING	PINNAE
PIMENT	PINCERED	PINES	PINION	PINNAL
PIMENTO	PINCERING	PINESAP	PINIONED	PINNAS
PIMENTON	PINCERS	PINESAPS	PINIONING	PINNATE
PIMENTONS	PINCH	PINETA	PINIONS	PINNATED
PIMENTOS	PINCHBECK	PINETUM	PINITE	PINNATELY
PIMENTS	PINCHBUG	PINEWOOD	PINITES	PINNATION
PIMIENTO	PINCHBUGS	PINEWOODS	PINITOL	PINNED
PIMIENTOS	PINCHCOCK	PINEY	PINITOLS	PINNER

PINNERS	PINSWELLS	PIOLET	PIPELINE	PIPULS
PINNET	PINT	PIOLETS	PIPELINED	PIPY
PINNETS	PINTA	PION	PIPELINES	PIQUANCE
PINNIE	PINTABLE	PIONED	PIPER	PIQUANCES
PINNIES	PINTABLES	PIONEER	PIPERIC	PIQUANCY
PINNING	PINTADA	PIONEERED	PIPERINE	PIQUANT
PINNINGS	PINTADAS	PIONEERS	PIPERINES	PIQUANTLY
PINNIPED	PINTADERA	PIONER	PIPERONAL	PIQUE
PINNIPEDE	PINTADO	PIONERS	PIPERS	PIQUED
PINNIPEDS	PINTADOES	PIONEY	PIPES	PIQUES
PINNOCK	PINTADOS	PIONEYS	PIPESTEM	PIQUET
PINNOCKS	PINTAIL	PIONIC	PIPESTEMS	PIQUETED
PINNOED	PINTAILED	PIONIES	PIPESTONE	PIQUETING
PINNULA	PINTAILS	PIONING	PIPET	PIQUETS
PINNULAE	PINTANO	PIONINGS	PIPETS	PIQUILLO
PINNULAR	PINTANOS	PIONS	PIPETTE	PIQUILLOS
PINNULAS	PINTAS	PIONY	PIPETTED	PIQUING
PINNULATE	PINTLE	PIOPIO	PIPETTES	PIR
PINNULE	PINTLES	PIOPIOS	PIPETTING	PIRACETAM
PINNULES	PINTO	PIOSITIES	PIPEWORK	PIRACIES
PINNY	PINTOES	PIOSITY	PIPEWORKS	PIRACY
PINOCHLE	PINTOS	PIOTED	PIPEWORT	PIRAGUA
PINOCHLES	PINTS	PIOUS	PIPEWORTS	PIRAGUAS
PINOCLE	PINTSIZE	PIOUSLY	PIPI	PIRAI
PINOCLES	PINTSIZED	PIOUSNESS	PIPIER	PIRAIS
PINOCYTIC	PINTUCK	PIOY	PIPIEST	PIRANA
PINOLE	PINTUCKED	PIOYE	PIPINESS	PIRANAS
PINOLES	PINTUCKS	PIOYES	PIPING	PIRANHA
PINON	PINUP	PIOYS	PIPINGLY	PIRANHAS
PINONES	PINUPS	PIP	PIPINGS	PIRARUCU
PINONS	PINWALE	PIPA	PIPIS	PIRARUCUS
PINOT	PINWALES	PIPAGE	PIPISTREL	PIRATE
PINOTAGE	PINWEED	PIPAGES	PIPIT	PIRATED
PINOTAGES	PINWEEDS	PIPAL	PIPITS	PIRATES
PINOTS	PINWHEEL	PIPALS	PIPKIN	PIRATIC
PINPOINT	PINWHEELS	PIPAS	PIPKINS	PIRATICAL
PINPOINTS	PINWORK	PIPE	PIPLESS	PIRATING
PINPRICK	PINWORKS	PIPEAGE	PIPPED	PIRATINGS
PINPRICKS	PINWORM	PIPEAGES	PIPPIER	PIRAYA
PINS	PINWORMS	PIPECLAY	PIPPIEST	PIRAYAS
PINSCHER	PINWRENCH	PIPECLAYS	PIPPIN	PIRIFORM
PINSCHERS	PINXIT	PIPED	PIPPING	PIRL
PINSETTER	PINY	PIPEFISH	PIPPINS	PIRLICUE
PINSPOT	PINYIN	PIPEFUL	PIPPY	PIRLICUED
PINSPOTS	PINYINS	PIPEFULS	PIPS	PIRLICUES
PINSTRIPE	PINYON	PIPELESS	PIPSQUEAK	PIRLS
PINSWELL	PINYONS	PIPELIKE	PIPUL	PIRN

P

PIRNIE	PISHOGE	PISTOLEER	PITEOUSLY	PITTANCES
PIRNIES	PISHOGES	PISTOLERO	PITFALL	PITTAS
PIRNIT	PISHOGUE	PISTOLES	PITFALLS	PITTED
PIRNS	PISHOGUES	PISTOLET	PITH	PITTEN
PIROG	PISIFORM	PISTOLETS	PITHBALL	PITTER
PIROGEN	PISIFORMS	PISTOLIER	PITHBALLS	PITTERED
PIROGHI	PISKIES	PISTOLING	PITHEAD	PITTERING
PIROGI	PISKY	PISTOLLED	PITHEADS	PITTERS
PIROGIES	PISMIRE	PISTOLS	PITHECOID	PITTING
PIROGUE	PISMIRES	PISTON	PITHED	PITTINGS
PIROGUES	PISO	PISTONS	PITHFUL	PITTITE
PIROJKI	PISOLITE	PISTOU	PITHIER	PITTITES
PIROPLASM	PISOLITES	PISTOUS	PITHIEST	PITUITA
PIROQUE	PISOLITH	PIT	PITHILY	PITUITARY
PIROQUES	PISOLITHS	PITA	PITHINESS	PITUITAS
PIROSHKI	PISOLITIC	PITAHAYA	PITHING	PITUITE
PIROUETTE	PISOS	PITAHAYAS	PITHLESS	PITUITES
PIROZHKI	PISS	PITAPAT	PITHLIKE	PITUITRIN
PIROZHOK	PISSANT	PITAPATS	PITHOI	PITURI
PIRS	PISSANTS	PITARA	PITHOS	PITURIS
PIS	PISSED	PITARAH	PITHS	PITY
PISCARIES	PISSER	PITARAHS	PITHY	PITYING
PISCARY	PISSERS	PITARAS	PITIABLE	PITYINGLY
PISCATOR	PISSES	PITAS	PITIABLY	PITYROID
PISCATORS	PISSHEAD	PITAYA	PITIED	PIU
PISCATORY	PISSHEADS	PITAYAS	PITIER	PIUM
PISCATRIX	PISSHOLE	PITCH	PITIERS	PIUMS
PISCIFORM	PISSHOLES	PITCHBEND	PITIES	PIUPIU
PISCINA	PISSIER	PITCHED	PITIETH	PIUPIUS
PISCINAE	PISSIEST	PITCHER	PITIFUL	PIVOT
PISCINAL	PISSING	PITCHERS	PITIFULLY	PIVOTABLE
PISCINAS	PISSOIR	PITCHES	PITIKINS	PIVOTAL
PISCINE	PISSOIRS	PITCHFORK	PITILESS	PIVOTALLY
PISCINES	PISSY	PITCHIER	PITMAN	PIVOTED
PISCIVORE	PISTACHE	PITCHIEST	PITMANS	PIVOTER
PISCO	PISTACHES	PITCHILY	PITMEN	PIVOTERS
PISCOS	PISTACHIO	PITCHING	PITON	PIVOTING
PISE	PISTAREEN	PITCHINGS	PITONS	PIVOTINGS
PISES	PISTE	PITCHMAN	PITOT	PIVOTMAN
PISH	PISTED	PITCHMEN	PITOTS	PIVOTMEN
PISHED	PISTES	PITCHOUT	PITPROP	PIVOTS
PISHEOG	PISTIL	PITCHOUTS	PITPROPS	PIX
PISHEOGS	PISTILLAR	PITCHPINE	PITS	PIXEL
PISHER	PISTILS	PITCHPIPE	PITSAW	PIXELATE
PISHERS	PISTOL	PITCHPOLE	PITSAWS	PIXELATED
PISHES	PISTOLE	PITCHY	PITTA	PIXELATES
PISHING	PISTOLED	PITEOUS	PITTANCE	PIXELLATE

PIXELS	PLACATES	PLACKS	PLAINSONG	PLANGENCY
PIXES	PLACATING	PLACODERM	PLAINT	PLANGENT
PIXIE	PLACATION	PLACOID	PLAINTEXT	PLANIGRAM
PIXIEISH	PLACATIVE	PLACOIDS	PLAINTFUL	PLANING
PIXIES	PLACATORY	PLAFOND	PLAINTIFF	PLANISH
PIXILATE	PLACCAT	PLAFONDS	PLAINTIVE	PLANISHED
PIXILATED	PLACCATE	PLAGAL	PLAINTS	PLANISHER
PIXILATES	PLACCATES	PLAGE	PLAINWORK	PLANISHES
PIXILLATE	PLACCATS	PLAGES	PLAISTER	PLANK
PIXINESS	PLACE	PLAGIARY	PLAISTERS	PLANKED
PIXY	PLACEABLE	PLAGIUM	PLAIT	PLANKING
PIXYISH	PLACEBO	PLAGIUMS	PLAITED	PLANKINGS
PIZAZZ	PLACEBOES	PLAGUE	PLAITER	PLANKS
PIZAZZES	PLACEBOS	PLAGUED	PLAITERS	PLANKTER
PIZAZZY	PLACED	PLAGUER	PLAITING	PLANKTERS
PIZE	PLACEKICK	PLAGUERS	PLAITINGS	PLANKTIC
PIZED	PLACELESS	PLAGUES	PLAITS	PLANKTON
PIZES	PLACEMAN	PLAGUEY	PLAN	PLANKTONS
PIZING	PLACEMAT	PLAGUIER	PLANAR	PLANLESS
PIZZA	PLACEMATS	PLAGUIEST	PLANARIA	PLANNED
PIZZAIOLA	PLACEMEN	PLAGUILY	PLANARIAN	PLANNER
PIZZALIKE	PLACEMENT	PLAGUING	PLANARIAS	PLANNERS
PIZZAS	PLACENTA	PLAGUY	PLANARITY	PLANNING
PIZZAZ	PLACENTAE	PLAICE	PLANATE	PLANNINGS
PIZZAZES	PLACENTAL	PLAICES	PLANATION	PLANOGRAM
PIZZAZZ	PLACENTAS	PLAID	PLANCH	PLANOSOL
PIZZAZZES	PLACER	PLAIDED	PLANCHE	PLANOSOLS
PIZZAZZY	PLACERS	PLAIDING	PLANCHED	PLANS
PIZZELLE	PLACES	PLAIDINGS	PLANCHES	PLANT
PIZZELLES	PLACET	PLAIDMAN	PLANCHET	PLANTA
PIZZERIA	PLACETS	PLAIDMEN	PLANCHETS	PLANTABLE
PIZZERIAS	PLACID	PLAIDS	PLANCHING	PLANTAE
PIZZICATI	PLACIDER	PLAIN	PLANE	PLANTAGE
PIZZICATO	PLACIDEST	PLAINANT	PLANED	PLANTAGES
PIZZLE	PLACIDITY	PLAINANTS	PLANELOAD	PLANTAIN
PIZZLES	PLACIDLY	PLAINED	PLANENESS	PLANTAINS
PLAAS	PLACING	PLAINER	PLANER	PLANTAR
PLAASES	PLACINGS	PLAINEST	PLANERS	PLANTAS
PLACABLE	PLACIT	PLAINFUL	PLANES	PLANTED
PLACABLY	PLACITA	PLAINING	PLANESIDE	PLANTER
PLACARD	PLACITORY	PLAININGS	PLANET	PLANTERS
PLACARDED	PLACITS	PLAINISH	PLANETARY	PLANTING
PLACARDS	PLACITUM	PLAINLY	PLANETIC	PLANTINGS
PLACATE	PLACK	PLAINNESS	PLANETOID	PLANTLESS
PLACATED	PLACKET	PLAINS	PLANETS	PLANTLET
PLACATER	PLACKETS	PLAINSMAN	PLANFORM	PLANTLETS
PLACATERS	PLACKLESS	PLAINSMEN	PLANFORMS	PLANTLIKE

P

PLANTLING	PLASMODIA	PLATELETS	PLATYSMAS	PLAYINGS
PLANTS	PLASMOID	PLATELIKE	PLAUDIT	PLAYLAND
PLANTSMAN	PLASMOIDS	PLATEMAN	PLAUDITE	PLAYLANDS
PLANTSMEN	PLASMON	PLATEMARK	PLAUDITS	PLAYLESS
PLANTULE	PLASMONS	PLATEMEN	PLAUSIBLE	PLAYLET
PLANTULES	PLASMS	PLATEN	PLAUSIBLY	PLAYLETS
PLANULA	PLAST	PLATENS	PLAUSIVE	PLAYLIKE
PLANULAE	PLASTE	PLATER	PLAUSTRAL	PLAYLIST
PLANULAR	PLASTER	PLATERS	PLAY	PLAYLISTS
PLANULATE	PLASTERED	PLATES	PLAYA	PLAYMAKER
PLANULOID	PLASTERER	PLATESFUL	PLAYABLE	PLAYMATE
PLANURIA	PLASTERS	PLATFORM	PLAYACT	PLAYMATES
PLANURIAS	PLASTERY	PLATFORMS	PLAYACTED	PLAYOFF
PLANURIES	PLASTIC	PLATIER	PLAYACTOR	PLAYOFFS
PLANURY	PLASTICKY	PLATIES	PLAYACTS	PLAYPEN
PLANXTIES	PLASTICLY	PLATIEST	PLAYAS	PLAYPENS
PLANXTY	PLASTICS	PLATINA	PLAYBACK	PLAYROOM
PLAP	PLASTID	PLATINAS	PLAYBACKS	PLAYROOMS
PLAPPED	PLASTIDS	PLATING	PLAYBILL	PLAYS
PLAPPING	PLASTIQUE	PLATINGS	PLAYBILLS	PLAYSET
PLAPS	PLASTISOL	PLATINIC	PLAYBOOK	PLAYSETS
PLAQUE	PLASTRAL	PLATINISE	PLAYBOOKS	PLAYSLIP
PLAQUES	PLASTRON	PLATINIZE	PLAYBOY	PLAYSLIPS
PLAQUETTE	PLASTRONS	PLATINOID	PLAYBOYS	PLAYSOME
PLASH	PLASTRUM	PLATINOUS	PLAYBUS	PLAYSUIT
PLASHED	PLASTRUMS	PLATINUM	PLAYBUSES	PLAYSUITS
PLASHER	PLAT	PLATINUMS	PLAYDATE	PLAYTHING
PLASHERS	PLATAN	PLATITUDE	PLAYDATES	PLAYTIME
PLASHES	PLATANE	PLATONIC	PLAYDAY	PLAYTIMES
PLASHET	PLATANES	PLATONICS	PLAYDAYS	PLAYWEAR
PLASHETS	PLATANNA	PLATONISM	PLAYDOUGH	PLAYWEARS
PLASHIER	PLATANNAS	PLATOON	PLAYDOWN	PLAZA
PLASHIEST	PLATANS	PLATOONED	PLAYDOWNS	PLAZAS
PLASHING	PLATBAND	PLATOONS	PLAYED	PLEA
PLASHINGS	PLATBANDS	PLATS	PLAYER	PLEACH
PLASHY	PLATE	PLATT	PLAYERS	PLEACHED
PLASM	PLATEASM	PLATTED	PLAYFIELD	PLEACHES
PLASMA	PLATEASMS	PLATTER	PLAYFUL	PLEACHING
PLASMAGEL	PLATEAU	PLATTERS	PLAYFULLY	PLEAD
PLASMAS	PLATEAUED	PLATTING	PLAYGIRL	PLEADABLE
PLASMASOL	PLATEAUS	PLATTINGS	PLAYGIRLS	PLEADED
PLASMATIC	PLATEAUX	PLATY	PLAYGOER	PLEADER
PLASMIC	PLATED	PLATYFISH	PLAYGOERS	PLEADERS
PLASMID	PLATEFUL	PLATYPI	PLAYGOING	PLEADING
PLASMIDS	PLATEFULS	PLATYPUS	PLAYGROUP	PLEADINGS
PLASMIN	PLATELESS	PLATYS	PLAYHOUSE	PLEADS
PLASMINS	PLATELET	PLATYSMA	PLAYING	PLEAED

P

PLEAING
PLEAS
PLEASABLE
PLEASANCE
PLEASANT
PLEASE
PLEASED
PLEASEDLY
PLEASEMAN
PLEASEMEN
PLEASER
PLEASERS
PLEASES
PLEASETH
PLEASING
PLEASINGS
PLEASURE
PLEASURED
PLEASURER
PLEASURES
PLEAT
PLEATED
PLEATER
PLEATERS
PLEATHER
PLEATHERS
PLEATING
PLEATINGS
PLEATLESS
PLEATS
PLEB
PLEBBIER
PLEBBIEST
PLEBBY
PLEBE
PLEBEAN
PLEBEIAN
PLEBEIANS
PLEBES
PLEBIFIED
PLEBIFIES
PLEBIFY
PLEBS
PLECTRA
PLECTRE
PLECTRES
PLECTRON

PLECTRONS
PLECTRUM
PLECTRUMS
PLED
PLEDGABLE
PLEDGE
PLEDGED
PLEDGEE
PLEDGEES
PLEDGEOR
PLEDGEORS
PLEDGER
PLEDGERS
PLEDGES
PLEDGET
PLEDGETS
PLEDGING
PLEDGOR
PLEDGORS
PLEIAD
PLEIADES
PLEIADS
PLEIOCENE
PLEIOMERY
PLEIOTAXY
PLENA
PLENARIES
PLENARILY
PLENARTY
PLENARY
PLENCH
PLENCHES
PLENILUNE
PLENIPO
PLENIPOES
PLENIPOS
PLENISH
PLENISHED
PLENISHER
PLENISHES
PLENISM
PLENISMS
PLENIST
PLENISTS
PLENITUDE
PLENTEOUS
PLENTIES

PLENTIFUL
PLENTY
PLENUM
PLENUMS
PLEON
PLEONAL
PLEONASM
PLEONASMS
PLEONAST
PLEONASTE
PLEONASTS
PLEONEXIA
PLEONIC
PLEONS
PLEOPOD
PLEOPODS
PLERION
PLERIONS
PLEROMA
PLEROMAS
PLEROME
PLEROMES
PLESH
PLESHES
PLESSOR
PLESSORS
PLETHORA
PLETHORAS
PLETHORIC
PLEUCH
PLEUCHED
PLEUCHING
PLEUCHS
PLEUGH
PLEUGHED
PLEUGHING
PLEUGHS
PLEURA
PLEURAE
PLEURAL
PLEURAS
PLEURISY
PLEURITIC
PLEURITIS
PLEURON
PLEURONIA
PLEUSTON

PLEUSTONS
PLEW
PLEWS
PLEX
PLEXAL
PLEXED
PLEXES
PLEXIFORM
PLEXING
PLEXOR
PLEXORS
PLEXURE
PLEXURES
PLEXUS
PLEXUSES
PLIABLE
PLIABLY
PLIANCIES
PLIANCY
PLIANT
PLIANTLY
PLICA
PLICAE
PLICAL
PLICAS
PLICATE
PLICATED
PLICATELY
PLICATES
PLICATING
PLICATION
PLICATURE
PLIE
PLIED
PLIER
PLIERS
PLIES
PLIGHT
PLIGHTED
PLIGHTER
PLIGHTERS
PLIGHTFUL
PLIGHTING
PLIGHTS
PLIM
PLIMMED
PLIMMING

PLIMS
PLIMSOL
PLIMSOLE
PLIMSOLES
PLIMSOLL
PLIMSOLLS
PLIMSOLS
PLING
PLINGED
PLINGING
PLINGS
PLINK
PLINKED
PLINKER
PLINKERS
PLINKIER
PLINKIEST
PLINKING
PLINKINGS
PLINKS
PLINKY
PLINTH
PLINTHS
PLIOCENE
PLIOFILM
PLIOFILMS
PLIOSAUR
PLIOSAURS
PLIOTRON
PLIOTRONS
PLISKIE
PLISKIER
PLISKIES
PLISKIEST
PLISKY
PLISSE
PLISSES
PLOAT
PLOATED
PLOATING
PLOATS
PLOD
PLODDED
PLODDER
PLODDERS
PLODDING
PLODDINGS

P

PLODGE	PLOTTAGES	PLOWHEADS	PLUGGING	PLUMELETS
PLODGED	PLOTTED	PLOWING	PLUGGINGS	PLUMELIKE
PLODGES	PLOTTER	PLOWINGS	PLUGHOLE	PLUMERIA
PLODGING	PLOTTERED	PLOWLAND	PLUGHOLES	PLUMERIAS
PLODS	PLOTTERS	PLOWLANDS	PLUGLESS	PLUMERIES
PLOIDIES	PLOTTIE	PLOWMAN	PLUGOLA	PLUMERY
PLOIDY	PLOTTIER	PLOWMEN	PLUGOLAS	PLUMES
PLONG	PLOTTIES	PLOWS	PLUGS	PLUMIER
PLONGD	PLOTTIEST	PLOWSHARE	PLUGUGLY	PLUMIEST
PLONGE	PLOTTING	PLOWSTAFF	PLUM	PLUMING
PLONGED	PLOTTINGS	PLOWTAIL	PLUMAGE	PLUMIPED
PLONGES	PLOTTY	PLOWTAILS	PLUMAGED	PLUMIPEDS
PLONGING	PLOTZ	PLOWTER	PLUMAGES	PLUMIST
PLONGS	PLOTZED	PLOWTERED	PLUMATE	PLUMISTS
PLONK	PLOTZES	PLOWTERS	PLUMB	PLUMLIKE
PLONKED	PLOTZING	PLOWWISE	PLUMBABLE	PLUMMER
PLONKER	PLOUGH	PLOY	PLUMBAGO	PLUMMEST
PLONKERS	PLOUGHBOY	PLOYE	PLUMBAGOS	PLUMMET
PLONKIER	PLOUGHED	PLOYED	PLUMBATE	PLUMMETED
PLONKIEST	PLOUGHER	PLOYES	PLUMBATES	PLUMMETS
PLONKING	PLOUGHERS	PLOYING	PLUMBED	PLUMMIER
PLONKINGS	PLOUGHING	PLOYS	PLUMBEOUS	PLUMMIEST
PLONKO	PLOUGHMAN	PLU	PLUMBER	PLUMMY
PLONKOS	PLOUGHMEN	PLUCK	PLUMBERS	PLUMOSE
PLONKS	PLOUGHS	PLUCKED	PLUMBERY	PLUMOSELY
PLONKY	PLOUK	PLUCKER	PLUMBIC	PLUMOSITY
PLOOK	PLOUKIE	PLUCKERS	PLUMBING	PLUMOUS
PLOOKIE	PLOUKIER	PLUCKIER	PLUMBINGS	PLUMP
PLOOKIER	PLOUKIEST	PLUCKIEST	PLUMBISM	PLUMPED
PLOOKIEST	PLOUKS	PLUCKILY	PLUMBISMS	PLUMPEN
PLOOKS	PLOUKY	PLUCKING	PLUMBITE	PLUMPENED
PLOOKY	PLOUTER	PLUCKS	PLUMBITES	PLUMPENS
PLOP	PLOUTERED	PLUCKY	PLUMBLESS	PLUMPER
PLOPPED	PLOUTERS	PLUE	PLUMBNESS	PLUMPERS
PLOPPING	PLOVER	PLUES	PLUMBOUS	PLUMPEST
PLOPS	PLOVERS	PLUFF	PLUMBS	PLUMPIE
PLOSION	PLOVERY	PLUFFED	PLUMBUM	PLUMPIER
PLOSIONS	PLOW	PLUFFIER	PLUMBUMS	PLUMPIEST
PLOSIVE	PLOWABLE	PLUFFIEST	PLUMCAKE	PLUMPING
PLOSIVES	PLOWBACK	PLUFFING	PLUMCAKES	PLUMPISH
PLOT	PLOWBACKS	PLUFFS	PLUMCOT	PLUMPLY
PLOTFUL	PLOWBOY	PLUFFY	PLUMCOTS	PLUMPNESS
PLOTLESS	PLOWBOYS	PLUG	PLUMDAMAS	PLUMPS
PLOTLINE	PLOWED	PLUGBOARD	PLUME	PLUMPY
PLOTLINES	PLOWER	PLUGGED	PLUMED	PLUMS
PLOTS	PLOWERS	PLUGGER	PLUMELESS	PLUMULA
PLOTTAGE	PLOWHEAD	PLUGGERS	PLUMELET	PLUMULAE

PLUMULAR	PLUSHER	PNEUMONIA	POCKIES	PODGES
PLUMULATE	PLUSHES	PNEUMONIC	POCKIEST	PODGIER
PLUMULE	PLUSHEST	PO	POCKILY	PODGIEST
PLUMULES	PLUSHIER	POA	POCKING	PODGILY
PLUMULOSE	PLUSHIEST	POACEOUS	POCKMANKY	PODGINESS
PLUMY	PLUSHILY	POACH	POCKMARK	PODGY
PLUNDER	PLUSHLY	POACHABLE	POCKMARKS	PODIA
PLUNDERED	PLUSHNESS	POACHED	POCKPIT	PODIAL
PLUNDERER	PLUSHY	POACHER	POCKPITS	PODIATRIC
PLUNDERS	PLUSING	POACHERS	POCKS	PODIATRY
PLUNGE	PLUSSAGE	POACHES	POCKY	PODITE
PLUNGED	PLUSSAGES	POACHIER	POCO	PODITES
PLUNGER	PLUSSED	POACHIEST	POCOSEN	PODITIC
PLUNGERS	PLUSSES	POACHING	POCOSENS	PODIUM
PLUNGES	PLUSSING	POACHINGS	POCOSIN	PODIUMED
PLUNGING	PLUTEAL	POACHY	POCOSINS	PODIUMING
PLUNGINGS	PLUTEI	POAKA	POCOSON	PODIUMS
PLUNK	PLUTEUS	POAKAS	POCOSONS	PODLEY
PLUNKED	PLUTEUSES	POAKE	POD	PODLEYS
PLUNKER	PLUTOCRAT	POAKES	PODAGRA	PODLIKE
PLUNKERS	PLUTOID	POAS	PODAGRAL	PODOCARP
PLUNKIER	PLUTOIDS	POBLANO	PODAGRAS	PODOCARPS
PLUNKIEST	PLUTOLOGY	POBLANOS	PODAGRIC	PODOLOGY
PLUNKING	PLUTON	POBOY	PODAGROUS	PODOMERE
PLUNKS	PLUTONIAN	POBOYS	PODAL	PODOMERES
PLUNKY	PLUTONIC	POCHARD	PODALIC	PODS
PLUOT	PLUTONISM	POCHARDS	PODARGUS	PODSOL
PLUOTS	PLUTONIUM	POCHAY	PODCAST	PODSOLIC
PLURAL	PLUTONOMY	POCHAYED	PODCASTED	PODSOLISE
PLURALISE	PLUTONS	POCHAYING	PODCASTER	PODSOLIZE
PLURALISM	PLUVIAL	POCHAYS	PODCASTS	PODSOLS
PLURALIST	PLUVIALS	POCHETTE	PODDED	PODUNK
PLURALITY	PLUVIAN	POCHETTES	PODDIE	PODUNKS
PLURALIZE	PLUVIANS	POCHOIR	PODDIER	PODZOL
PLURALLY	PLUVIOSE	POCHOIRS	PODDIES	PODZOLIC
PLURALS	PLUVIOUS	POCK	PODDIEST	PODZOLISE
PLURIPARA	PLUVIUS	POCKARD	PODDING	PODZOLIZE
PLURISIE	PLY	POCKARDS	PODDLE	PODZOLS
PLURISIES	PLYER	POCKED	PODDLED	POECHORE
PLURRY	PLYERS	POCKET	PODDLES	POECHORES
PLUS	PLYING	POCKETED	PODDLING	POEM
PLUSAGE	PLYINGLY	POCKETER	PODDY	POEMATIC
PLUSAGES	PLYWOOD	POCKETERS	PODESTA	POEMS
PLUSED	PLYWOODS	POCKETFUL	PODESTAS	POENOLOGY
PLUSES	PNEUMA	POCKETING	PODEX	POEP
PLUSH	PNEUMAS	POCKETS	PODEXES	POEPED
PLUSHED	PNEUMATIC	POCKIER	PODGE	POEPING

POEPOL	POGO	POINTELS	POKEFULS	POLEAXE
POEPOLS	POGOED	POINTER	POKELOGAN	POLEAXED
POEPS	POGOER	POINTERS	POKER	POLEAXES
POESIED	POGOERS	POINTES	POKERISH	POLEAXING
POESIES	POGOES	POINTIER	POKEROOT	POLECAT
POESY	POGOING	POINTIEST	POKEROOTS	POLECATS
POESYING	POGONIA	POINTILLE	POKERS	POLED
POET	POGONIAS	POINTING	POKERWORK	POLEIS
POETASTER	POGONIP	POINTINGS	POKES	POLELESS
POETASTRY	POGONIPS	POINTLESS	POKEWEED	POLEMARCH
POETESS	POGOS	POINTMAN	POKEWEEDS	POLEMIC
POETESSES	POGROM	POINTMEN	POKEY	POLEMICAL
POETIC	POGROMED	POINTS	POKEYS	POLEMICS
POETICAL	POGROMING	POINTSMAN	POKIE	POLEMISE
POETICALS	POGROMIST	POINTSMEN	POKIER	POLEMISED
POETICISE	POGROMS	POINTY	POKIES	POLEMISES
POETICISM	POGY	POIS	POKIEST	POLEMIST
POETICIZE	POH	POISE	POKILY	POLEMISTS
POETICS	POHED	POISED	POKINESS	POLEMIZE
POETICULE	POHING	POISER	POKING	POLEMIZED
POETISE	POHIRI	POISERS	POKY	POLEMIZES
POETISED	POHIRIS	POISES	POL	POLENTA
POETISER	POHS	POISHA	POLACCA	POLENTAS
POETISERS	POI	POISHAS	POLACCAS	POLER
POETISES	POIGNADO	POISING	POLACK	POLERS
POETISING	POIGNANCE	POISON	POLACKS	POLES
POETIZE	POIGNANCY	POISONED	POLACRE	POLESTAR
POETIZED	POIGNANT	POISONER	POLACRES	POLESTARS
POETIZER	POILU	POISONERS	POLAR	POLEWARD
POETIZERS	POILUS	POISONING	POLARISE	POLEY
POETIZES	POINADO	POISONOUS	POLARISED	POLEYN
POETIZING	POINADOES	POISONS	POLARISER	POLEYNS
POETLESS	POINCIANA	POISSON	POLARISES	POLEYS
POETRESSE	POIND	POISSONS	POLARITY	POLIANITE
POETRIES	POINDED	POITIN	POLARIZE	POLICE
POETRY	POINDER	POITINS	POLARIZED	POLICED
POETS	POINDERS	POITREL	POLARIZER	POLICEMAN
POETSHIP	POINDING	POITRELS	POLARIZES	POLICEMEN
POETSHIPS	POINDINGS	POITRINE	POLARON	POLICER
POFFLE	POINDS	POITRINES	POLARONS	POLICERS
POFFLES	POINT	POKABLE	POLARS	POLICES
POGEY	POINTABLE	POKAL	POLDER	POLICIER
POGEYS	POINTE	POKALS	POLDERED	POLICIERS
POGGE	POINTED	POKE	POLDERING	POLICIES
POGGES	POINTEDLY	POKEBERRY	POLDERS	POLICING
POGIES	POINTEL	POKED	POLE	POLICINGS
	POINTELLE	POKEFUL	POLEAX	POLICY

POLIES	POLLARDS	POLLUTANT	POLYACT	POLYGRAPH
POLING	POLLAXE	POLLUTE	POLYADIC	POLYGYNE
POLINGS	POLLAXED	POLLUTED	POLYAMIDE	POLYGYNY
POLIO	POLLAXES	POLLUTER	POLYAMINE	POLYHEDRA
POLIOS	POLLAXING	POLLUTERS	POLYAMORY	POLYIMIDE
POLIS	POLLED	POLLUTES	POLYANDRY	POLYLEMMA
POLISES	POLLEE	POLLUTING	POLYANTHA	POLYMASTY
POLISH	POLLEES	POLLUTION	POLYANTHI	POLYMATH
POLISHED	POLLEN	POLLUTIVE	POLYARCH	POLYMATHS
POLISHER	POLLENATE	POLLY	POLYARCHY	POLYMATHY
POLISHERS	POLLENED	POLLYANNA	POLYAXIAL	POLYMER
POLISHES	POLLENING	POLLYWIG	POLYAXON	POLYMERIC
POLISHING	POLLENS	POLLYWIGS	POLYAXONS	POLYMERS
POLITBURO	POLLENT	POLLYWOG	POLYBAG	POLYMERY
POLITE	POLLER	POLLYWOGS	POLYBAGS	POLYMORPH
POLITELY	POLLERS	POLO	POLYBASIC	POLYMYXIN
POLITER	POLLEX	POLOIDAL	POLYBRID	POLYNIA
POLITESSE	POLLICAL	POLOIST	POLYBRIDS	POLYNIAS
POLITEST	POLLICES	POLOISTS	POLYCARPY	POLYNYA
POLITIC	POLLICIE	POLONAISE	POLYCHETE	POLYNYAS
POLITICAL	POLLICIES	POLONIE	POLYCONIC	POLYNYI
POLITICK	POLLICY	POLONIES	POLYCOT	POLYOL
POLITICKS	POLLIES	POLONISE	POLYCOTS	POLYOLS
POLITICLY	POLLINATE	POLONISED	POLYDEMIC	POLYOMA
POLITICO	POLLING	POLONISES	POLYDRUG	POLYOMAS
POLITICOS	POLLINGS	POLONISM	POLYENE	POLYOMINO
POLITICS	POLLINIA	POLONISMS	POLYENES	POLYONYM
POLITIES	POLLINIC	POLONIUM	POLYENIC	POLYONYMS
POLITIQUE	POLLINISE	POLONIUMS	POLYESTER	POLYONYMY
POLITY	POLLINIUM	POLONIZE	POLYGALA	POLYP
POLJE	POLLINIZE	POLONIZED	POLYGALAS	POLYPARIA
POLJES	POLLIST	POLONIZES	POLYGAM	POLYPARY
POLK	POLLISTS	POLONY	POLYGAMIC	POLYPE
POLKA	POLLIWIG	POLOS	POLYGAMS	POLYPED
POLKAED	POLLIWIGS	POLS	POLYGAMY	POLYPEDS
POLKAING	POLLIWOG	POLT	POLYGENE	POLYPES
POLKAS	POLLIWOGS	POLTED	POLYGENES	POLYPHAGY
POLKED	POLLMAN	POLTFEET	POLYGENIC	POLYPHASE
POLKING	POLLMEN	POLTFOOT	POLYGENY	POLYPHON
POLKS	POLLOCK	POLTING	POLYGLOT	POLYPHONE
POLL	POLLOCKS	POLTROON	POLYGLOTS	POLYPHONS
POLLACK	POLLS	POLTROONS	POLYGLOTT	POLYPHONY
POLLACKS	POLLSTER	POLTS	POLYGON	POLYPI
POLLAN	POLLSTERS	POLVERINE	POLYGONAL	POLYPIDE
POLLANS	POLLTAKER	POLY	POLYGONS	POLYPIDES
POLLARD	POLLUCITE	POLYACID	POLYGONUM	POLYPIDOM
POLLARDED	POLLUSION	POLYACIDS	POLYGONY	POLYPILL

POLYPILLS	POLYZOARY	POMPANOS	PONDED	PONK
POLYPINE	POLYZOIC	POMPELO	PONDER	PONKED
POLYPITE	POLYZONAL	POMPELOS	PONDERAL	PONKING
POLYPITES	POLYZOOID	POMPEY	PONDERATE	PONKS
POLYPLOID	POLYZOON	POMPEYED	PONDERED	PONS
POLYPNEA	POM	POMPEYING	PONDERER	PONT
POLYPNEAS	POMACE	POMPEYS	PONDERERS	PONTAGE
POLYPNEIC	POMACEOUS	POMPHOLYX	PONDERING	PONTAGES
POLYPOD	POMACES	POMPIER	PONDEROSA	PONTAL
POLYPODS	POMADE	POMPIERS	PONDEROUS	PONTES
POLYPODY	POMADED	POMPILID	PONDERS	PONTIANAC
POLYPOID	POMADES	POMPILIDS	PONDING	PONTIANAK
POLYPORE	POMADING	POMPION	PONDOK	PONTIC
POLYPORES	POMANDER	POMPIONS	PONDOKKIE	PONTIE
POLYPOSES	POMANDERS	POMPOM	PONDOKS	PONTIES
POLYPOSIS	POMATO	POMPOMS	PONDS	PONTIFEX
POLYPOUS	POMATOES	POMPON	PONDWEED	PONTIFF
POLYPS	POMATUM	POMPONS	PONDWEEDS	PONTIFFS
POLYPTYCH	POMATUMS	POMPOON	PONE	PONTIFIC
POLYPUS	POMBE	POMPOONS	PONENT	PONTIFICE
POLYPUSES	POMBES	POMPOSITY	PONENTS	PONTIFIED
POLYS	POME	POMPOSO	PONES	PONTIFIES
POLYSEME	POMELO	POMPOUS	PONEY	PONTIFY
POLYSEMES	POMELOS	POMPOUSLY	PONEYS	PONTIL
POLYSEMIC	POMEROY	POMPS	PONG	PONTILE
POLYSEMY	POMEROYS	POMROY	PONGA	PONTILES
POLYSOME	POMES	POMROYS	PONGAL	PONTILS
POLYSOMES	POMFRET	POMS	PONGALS	PONTINE
POLYSOMIC	POMFRETS	POMWATER	PONGAS	PONTLEVIS
POLYSOMY	POMMEE	POMWATERS	PONGED	PONTON
POLYSTYLE	POMMEL	PONCE	PONGEE	PONTONEER
POLYTENE	POMMELE	PONCEAU	PONGEES	PONTONIER
POLYTENY	POMMELED	PONCEAUS	PONGID	PONTONS
POLYTHENE	POMMELING	PONCEAUX	PONGIDS	PONTOON
POLYTONAL	POMMELLED	PONCED	PONGIER	PONTOONED
POLYTYPE	POMMELS	PONCES	PONGIEST	PONTOONER
POLYTYPED	POMMETTY	PONCEY	PONGING	PONTOONS
POLYTYPES	POMMIE	PONCHO	PONGO	PONTS
POLYTYPIC	POMMIES	PONCHOED	PONGOES	PONTY
POLYURIA	POMMY	PONCHOS	PONGOS	PONY
POLYURIAS	POMO	PONCIER	PONGS	PONYING
POLYURIC	POMOERIUM	PONCIEST	PONGY	PONYSKIN
POLYVINYL	POMOLOGY	PONCING	PONIARD	PONYSKINS
POLYWATER	POMOS	PONCY	PONIARDED	PONYTAIL
POLYZOA	POMP	POND	PONIARDS	PONYTAILS
POLYZOAN	POMPADOUR	PONDAGE	PONIED	PONZU
POLYZOANS	POMPANO	PONDAGES	PONIES	PONZUS

POO	POOLS	POOTING	POPINJAYS	POPPYCOCK
POOBAH	POOLSIDE	POOTLE	POPISH	POPPYHEAD
POOBAHS	POOLSIDES	POOTLED	POPISHLY	POPRIN
POOCH	POON	POOTLES	POPJOY	POPS
POOCHED	POONAC	POOTLING	POPJOYED	POPSICLE
POOCHES	POONACS	POOTS	POPJOYING	POPSICLES
POOCHING	POONCE	POOVE	POPJOYS	POPSIE
POOD	POONCED	POOVERIES	POPLAR	POPSIES
POODLE	POONCES	POOVERY	POPLARS	POPSOCK
POODLES	POONCING	POOVES	POPLIN	POPSOCKS
POODS	POONS	POOVIER	POPLINS	POPSTER
POOED	POONTANG	POOVIEST	POPLITEAL	POPSTERS
POOF	POONTANGS	POOVY	POPLITEI	POPSTREL
POOFIER	POOP	POP	POPLITEUS	POPSTRELS
POOFIEST	POOPED	POPADUM	POPLITIC	POPSY
POOFS	POOPER	POPADUMS	POPOUT	POPULACE
POOFTAH	POOPERS	POPCORN	POPOUTS	POPULACES
POOFTAHS	POOPIER	POPCORNS	POPOVER	POPULAR
POOFTER	POOPIEST	POPE	POPOVERS	POPULARLY
POOFTERS	POOPING	POPEDOM	POPPA	POPULARS
POOFY	POOPS	POPEDOMS	POPPADOM	POPULATE
POOGYE	POOPY	POPEHOOD	POPPADOMS	POPULATED
POOGYES	POOR	POPEHOODS	POPPADUM	POPULATES
POOH	POORBOX	POPELESS	POPPADUMS	POPULISM
POOHED	POORBOXES	POPELIKE	POPPAS	POPULISMS
POOHING	POORER	POPELING	POPPED	POPULIST
POOHS	POOREST	POPELINGS	POPPER	POPULISTS
POOING	POORHOUSE	POPERA	POPPERING	POPULOUS
POOJA	POORI	POPERAS	POPPERS	PORAE
POOJAH	POORIS	POPERIES	POPPET	PORAES
POOJAHS	POORISH	POPERIN	POPPETS	PORAL
POOJAS	POORLIER	POPERINS	POPPIED	PORANGI
POOK	POORLIEST	POPERY	POPPIER	PORBEAGLE
POOKA	POORLY	POPES	POPPIES	PORCELAIN
POOKAS	POORMOUTH	POPESEYE	POPPIEST	PORCH
POOKING	POORNESS	POPESHIP	POPPING	PORCHED
POOKIT	POORT	POPESHIPS	POPPISH	PORCHES
POOKS	POORTITH	POPETTE	POPPIT	PORCHETTA
POOL	POORTITHS	POPETTES	POPPITS	PORCINE
POOLED	POORTS	POPEYED	POPPLE	PORCINI
POOLER	POORWILL	POPGUN	POPPLED	PORCINIS
POOLERS	POORWILLS	POPGUNS	POPPLES	PORCINO
POOLHALL	POOS	POPINAC	POPPLIER	PORCUPINE
POOLHALLS	POOT	POPINACK	POPPLIEST	PORCUPINY
POOLING	POOTED	POPINACKS	POPPLING	PORE
POOLROOM	POOTER	POPINACS	POPPLY	PORED
POOLROOMS	POOTERS	POPINJAY	POPPY	PORER

PORERS	PORNO	PORTAGING	PORTIERE	POSABLE
PORES	PORNOMAG	PORTAGUE	PORTIERED	POSADA
PORGE	PORNOMAGS	PORTAGUES	PORTIERES	POSADAS
PORGED	PORNOS	PORTAL	PORTIEST	POSAUNE
PORGES	PORNS	PORTALED	PORTIGUE	POSAUNES
PORGIE	PORNY	PORTALS	PORTIGUES	POSE
PORGIES	POROGAMIC	PORTANCE	PORTING	POSEABLE
PORGING	POROGAMY	PORTANCES	PORTION	POSED
PORGY	POROMERIC	PORTAPACK	PORTIONED	POSER
PORIER	POROSCOPE	PORTAPAK	PORTIONER	POSERISH
PORIEST	POROSCOPY	PORTAPAKS	PORTIONS	POSERS
PORIFER	POROSE	PORTAS	PORTLAND	POSES
PORIFERAL	POROSES	PORTASES	PORTLANDS	POSEUR
PORIFERAN	POROSIS	PORTATE	PORTLAST	POSEURS
PORIFERS	POROSITY	PORTATILE	PORTLASTS	POSEUSE
PORIN	POROUS	PORTATIVE	PORTLESS	POSEUSES
PORINA	POROUSLY	PORTED	PORTLIER	POSEY
PORINAS	PORPESS	PORTEND	PORTLIEST	POSH
PORINESS	PORPESSE	PORTENDED	PORTLY	POSHED
PORING	PORPESSES	PORTENDS	PORTMAN	POSHER
PORINS	PORPHYRIA	PORTENT	PORTMEN	POSHES
PORISM	PORPHYRIC	PORTENTS	PORTOISE	POSHEST
PORISMS	PORPHYRIN	PORTEOUS	PORTOISES	POSHING
PORISTIC	PORPHYRIO	PORTER	PORTOLAN	POSHLY
PORK	PORPHYRY	PORTERAGE	PORTOLANI	POSHNESS
PORKED	PORPOISE	PORTERED	PORTOLANO	POSHO
PORKER	PORPOISED	PORTERESS	PORTOLANS	POSHOS
PORKERS	PORPOISES	PORTERING	PORTOUS	POSHTEEN
PORKIER	PORPORATE	PORTERLY	PORTOUSES	POSHTEENS
PORKIES	PORRECT	PORTERS	PORTRAIT	POSIDRIVE
PORKIEST	PORRECTED	PORTESS	PORTRAITS	POSIER
PORKINESS	PORRECTS	PORTESSE	PORTRAY	POSIES
PORKING	PORRENGER	PORTESSES	PORTRAYAL	POSIEST
PORKLING	PORRIDGE	PORTFIRE	PORTRAYED	POSIGRADE
PORKLINGS	PORRIDGES	PORTFIRES	PORTRAYER	POSING
PORKPIE	PORRIDGY	PORTFOLIO	PORTRAYS	POSINGLY
PORKPIES	PORRIGO	PORTHOLE	PORTREEVE	POSINGS
PORKS	PORRIGOS	PORTHOLES	PORTRESS	POSIT
PORKWOOD	PORRINGER	PORTHORS	PORTS	POSITED
PORKWOODS	PORT	PORTHOS	PORTSIDE	POSITIF
PORKY	PORTA	PORTHOSES	PORTULACA	POSITIFS
PORLOCK	PORTABLE	PORTHOUSE	PORTULAN	POSITING
PORLOCKED	PORTABLES	PORTICO	PORTULANS	POSITION
PORLOCKS	PORTABLY	PORTICOED	PORTY	POSITIONS
PORN	PORTAGE	PORTICOES	PORWIGGLE	POSITIVE
PORNIER	PORTAGED	PORTICOS	PORY	POSITIVER
PORNIEST	PORTAGES	PORTIER	POS	POSITIVES

POSITON
POSITONS
POSITRON
POSITRONS
POSITS
POSNET
POSNETS
POSOLE
POSOLES
POSOLOGIC
POSOLOGY
POSS
POSSE
POSSED
POSSER
POSSERS
POSSES
POSSESS
POSSESSED
POSSESSES
POSSESSOR
POSSET
POSSETED
POSSETING
POSSETS
POSSIBLE
POSSIBLER
POSSIBLES
POSSIBLY
POSSIE
POSSIES
POSSING
POSSUM
POSSUMED
POSSUMING
POSSUMS
POST
POSTAGE
POSTAGES
POSTAL
POSTALLY
POSTALS
POSTANAL
POSTAXIAL
POSTBAG
POSTBAGS
POSTBASE

POSTBASES
POSTBOX
POSTBOXES
POSTBOY
POSTBOYS
POSTBURN
POSTBUS
POSTBUSES
POSTCARD
POSTCARDS
POSTCAVA
POSTCAVAE
POSTCAVAL
POSTCAVAS
POSTCODE
POSTCODED
POSTCODES
POSTCOUP
POSTCRASH
POSTDATE
POSTDATED
POSTDATES
POSTDIVE
POSTDOC
POSTDOCS
POSTDRUG
POSTED
POSTEEN
POSTEENS
POSTER
POSTERED
POSTERING
POSTERIOR
POSTERISE
POSTERITY
POSTERIZE
POSTERN
POSTERNS
POSTERS
POSTFACE
POSTFACES
POSTFAULT
POSTFIRE
POSTFIX
POSTFIXAL
POSTFIXED
POSTFIXES

POSTFORM
POSTFORMS
POSTGAME
POSTGRAD
POSTGRADS
POSTHASTE
POSTHEAT
POSTHEATS
POSTHOLE
POSTHOLES
POSTHORSE
POSTHOUSE
POSTICAL
POSTICHE
POSTICHES
POSTICOUS
POSTIE
POSTIES
POSTIL
POSTILED
POSTILING
POSTILION
POSTILLED
POSTILLER
POSTILS
POSTIN
POSTING
POSTINGS
POSTINS
POSTIQUE
POSTIQUES
POSTLUDE
POSTLUDES
POSTMAN
POSTMARK
POSTMARKS
POSTMEN
POSTNASAL
POSTNATAL
POSTNATI
POSTOP
POSTOPS
POSTORAL
POSTPAID
POSTPONE
POSTPONED
POSTPONER

POSTPONES
POSTPOSE
POSTPOSED
POSTPOSES
POSTPUNK
POSTPUNKS
POSTRACE
POSTRIDER
POSTRIOT
POSTS
POSTSHOW
POSTSYNC
POSTSYNCS
POSTTAX
POSTTEEN
POSTTEENS
POSTTEST
POSTTESTS
POSTTRIAL
POSTULANT
POSTULATA
POSTULATE
POSTURAL
POSTURE
POSTURED
POSTURER
POSTURERS
POSTURES
POSTURING
POSTURISE
POSTURIST
POSTURIZE
POSTVIRAL
POSTWAR
POSTWOMAN
POSTWOMEN
POSY
POT
POTABLE
POTABLES
POTAE
POTAES
POTAGE
POTAGER
POTAGERS
POTAGES
POTALE

POTALES
POTAMIC
POTASH
POTASHED
POTASHES
POTASHING
POTASS
POTASSA
POTASSAS
POTASSES
POTASSIC
POTASSIUM
POTATION
POTATIONS
POTATO
POTATOBUG
POTATOES
POTATORY
POTBELLY
POTBOIL
POTBOILED
POTBOILER
POTBOILS
POTBOUND
POTBOY
POTBOYS
POTCH
POTCHE
POTCHED
POTCHER
POTCHERS
POTCHES
POTCHING
POTE
POTED
POTEEN
POTEENS
POTENCE
POTENCES
POTENCIES
POTENCY
POTENT
POTENTATE
POTENTIAL
POTENTISE
POTENTIZE
POTENTLY

P

POTENTS	POTLINES	POTTINESS	POUKIT	POUNDERS
POTES	POTLUCK	POTTING	POUKS	POUNDING
POTFUL	POTLUCKS	POTTINGAR	POULAINE	POUNDINGS
POTFULS	POTMAN	POTTINGER	POULAINES	POUNDS
POTGUN	POTMEN	POTTLE	POULARD	POUPE
POTGUNS	POTOMETER	POTTLES	POULARDE	POUPED
POTHEAD	POTOO	POTTO	POULARDES	POUPES
POTHEADS	POTOOS	POTTOS	POULARDS	POUPING
POTHECARY	POTOROO	POTTS	POULDER	POUPT
POTHEEN	POTOROOS	POTTY	POULDERS	POUR
POTHEENS	POTPIE	POTWALLER	POULDRE	POURABLE
POTHER	POTPIES	POTZER	POULDRES	POURBOIRE
POTHERB	POTPOURRI	POTZERS	POULDRON	POURED
POTHERBS	POTS	POUCH	POULDRONS	POURER
POTHERED	POTSHARD	POUCHED	POULE	POURERS
POTHERING	POTSHARDS	POUCHES	POULES	POURIE
POTHERS	POTSHARE	POUCHFUL	POULP	POURIES
POTHERY	POTSHARES	POUCHFULS	POULPE	POURING
POTHOLDER	POTSHERD	POUCHIER	POULPES	POURINGLY
POTHOLE	POTSHERDS	POUCHIEST	POULPS	POURINGS
POTHOLED	POTSHOP	POUCHING	POULT	POURPOINT
POTHOLER	POTSHOPS	POUCHY	POULTER	POURS
POTHOLERS	POTSHOT	POUDER	POULTERER	POURSEW
POTHOLES	POTSHOTS	POUDERS	POULTERERS	POURSEWED
POTHOLING	POTSIE	POUDRE	POULTICE	POURSEWS
POTHOOK	POTSIES	POUDRES	POULTICED	POURSUE
POTHOOKS	POTSTONE	POUF	POULTICES	POURSUED
POTHOS	POTSTONES	POUFED	POULTRIES	POURSUES
POTHOUSE	POTSY	POUFF	POULTRY	POURSUING
POTHOUSES	POTT	POUFFE	POULTS	POURSUIT
POTHUNTER	POTTABLE	POUFFED	POUNCE	POURSUITS
POTICARY	POTTAGE	POUFFES	POUNCED	POURTRAY
POTICHE	POTTAGES	POUFFIER	POUNCER	POURTRAYD
POTICHES	POTTED	POUFFIEST	POUNCERS	POURTRAYS
POTIN	POTTEEN	POUFFING	POUNCES	POUSADA
POTING	POTTEENS	POUFFS	POUNCET	POUSADAS
POTINS	POTTER	POUFFY	POUNCETS	POUSOWDIE
POTION	POTTERED	POUFING	POUNCHING	POUSSE
POTIONS	POTTERER	POUFS	POUNCING	POUSSES
POTJIE	POTTERERS	POUFTAH	POUND	POUSSETTE
POTJIES	POTTERIES	POUFTAHS	POUNDAGE	POUSSIE
POTLACH	POTTERING	POUFTER	POUNDAGES	POUSSIES
POTLACHE	POTTERS	POUFTERS	POUNDAL	POUSSIN
POTLACHES	POTTERY	POUK	POUNDALS	POUSSINS
POTLATCH	POTTIER	POUKE	POUNDCAKE	POUT
POTLIKE	POTTIES	POUKES	POUNDED	POUTASSOU
POTLINE	POTTIEST	POUKING	POUNDER	POUTED

POUTER	POWNDING	POZIDRIVE	PRAETOR	PRANKIER
POUTERS	POWNDS	POZOLE	PRAETORS	PRANKIEST
POUTFUL	POWNEY	POZOLES	PRAGMATIC	PRANKING
POUTHER	POWNEYS	POZZ	PRAHU	PRANKINGS
POUTHERED	POWNIE	POZZIES	PRAHUS	PRANKISH
POUTHERS	POWNIES	POZZOLAN	PRAIRIE	PRANKLE
POUTIER	POWNS	POZZOLANA	PRAIRIED	PRANKLED
POUTIEST	POWNY	POZZOLANS	PRAIRIES	PRANKLES
POUTINE	POWRE	POZZY	PRAISE	PRANKLING
POUTINES	POWRED	PRAAM	PRAISEACH	PRANKS
POUTING	POWRES	PRAAMS	PRAISED	PRANKSOME
POUTINGLY	POWRING	PRABBLE	PRAISEFUL	PRANKSTER
POUTINGS	POWS	PRABBLES	PRAISER	PRANKY
POUTS	POWSOWDY	PRACHARAK	PRAISERS	PRAO
POUTY	POWTER	PRACTIC	PRAISES	PRAOS
POVERTIES	POWTERED	PRACTICAL	PRAISING	PRASE
POVERTY	POWTERING	PRACTICE	PRAISINGS	PRASES
POW	POWTERS	PRACTICED	PRAJNA	PRAT
POWAN	POWWAW	PRACTICER	PRAJNAS	PRATE
POWANS	POWWOW	PRACTICES	PRALINE	PRATED
POWDER	POWWOWED	PRACTICK	PRALINES	PRATER
POWDERED	POWWOWING	PRACTICKS	PRAM	PRATERS
POWDERER	POWWOWS	PRACTICS	PRAMS	PRATES
POWDERERS	POX	PRACTICUM	PRANA	PRATFALL
POWDERIER	POXED	PRACTIQUE	PRANAS	PRATFALLS
POWDERING	POXES	PRACTISE	PRANAYAMA	PRATFELL
POWDERS	POXIER	PRACTISED	PRANCE	PRATIE
POWDERY	POXIEST	PRACTISER	PRANCED	PRATIES
POWELLISE	POXING	PRACTISES	PRANCER	PRATING
POWELLITE	POXVIRUS	PRACTIVE	PRANCERS	PRATINGLY
POWELLIZE	POXY	PRACTOLOL	PRANCES	PRATINGS
POWER	POYNANT	PRAD	PRANCING	PRATIQUE
POWERBOAT	POYNT	PRADS	PRANCINGS	PRATIQUES
POWERED	POYNTED	PRAEAMBLE	PRANCK	PRATS
POWERFUL	POYNTING	PRAECIPE	PRANCKE	PRATT
POWERING	POYNTS	PRAECIPES	PRANCKED	PRATTED
POWERLESS	POYOU	PRAECOCES	PRANCKES	PRATTING
POWERPLAY	POYOUS	PRAEDIAL	PRANCKING	PRATTLE
POWERS	POYSE	PRAEDIALS	PRANCKS	PRATTLED
POWFAGGED	POYSED	PRAEFECT	PRANDIAL	PRATTLER
POWHIRI	POYSES	PRAEFECTS	PRANG	PRATTLERS
POWHIRIS	POYSING	PRAELECT	PRANGED	PRATTLES
POWIN	POYSON	PRAELECTS	PRANGING	PRATTLING
POWINS	POYSONED	PRAELUDIA	PRANGS	PRATTS
POWN	POYSONING	PRAENOMEN	PRANK	PRATY
POWND	POYSONS	PRAESES	PRANKED	PRAU
POWNDED	POZ	PRAESIDIA	PRANKFUL	PRAUNCE

PRAUNCED	PREACTING	PREBAKED	PRECAVA	PRECISEST
PRAUNCES	PREACTS	PREBAKES	PRECAVAE	PRECISIAN
PRAUNCING	PREADAMIC	PREBAKING	PRECAVAL	PRECISING
PRAUS	PREADAPT	PREBASAL	PRECEDE	PRECISION
PRAVITIES	PREADAPTS	PREBATTLE	PRECEDED	PRECISIVE
PRAVITY	PREADJUST	PREBEND	PRECEDENT	PRECITED
PRAWLE	PREADMIT	PREBENDAL	PRECEDES	PRECLEAN
PRAWLES	PREADMITS	PREBENDS	PRECEDING	PRECLEANS
PRAWLIN	PREADOPT	PREBID	PRECEESE	PRECLEAR
PRAWLINS	PREADOPTS	PREBIDDEN	PRECENSOR	PRECLEARS
PRAWN	PREADULT	PREBIDS	PRECENT	PRECLUDE
PRAWNED	PREADULTS	PREBILL	PRECENTED	PRECLUDED
PRAWNER	PREAGED	PREBILLED	PRECENTOR	PRECLUDES
PRAWNERS	PREALLOT	PREBILLS	PRECENTS	PRECOCIAL
PRAWNING	PREALLOTS	PREBIND	PRECEPIT	PRECOCITY
PRAWNS	PREALTER	PREBINDS	PRECEPITS	PRECODE
PRAXES	PREALTERS	PREBIOTIC	PRECEPT	PRECODED
PRAXIS	PREAMBLE	PREBIRTH	PRECEPTOR	PRECODES
PRAXISES	PREAMBLED	PREBIRTHS	PRECEPTS	PRECODING
PRAY	PREAMBLES	PREBLESS	PRECES	PRECOITAL
PRAYED	PREAMP	PREBOARD	PRECESS	PRECONISE
PRAYER	PREAMPS	PREBOARDS	PRECESSED	PRECONIZE
PRAYERFUL	PREANAL	PREBOIL	PRECESSES	PRECOOK
PRAYERS	PREAPPLY	PREBOILED	PRECHARGE	PRECOOKED
PRAYING	PREARM	PREBOILS	PRECHECK	PRECOOKER
PRAYINGLY	PREARMED	PREBOOK	PRECHECKS	PRECOOKS
PRAYINGS	PREARMING	PREBOOKED	PRECHILL	PRECOOL
PRAYS	PREARMS	PREBOOKS	PRECHILLS	PRECOOLED
PRE	PREASE	PREBOOM	PRECHOOSE	PRECOOLS
PREABSORB	PREASED	PREBORN	PRECHOSE	PRECOUP
PREACCUSE	PREASES	PREBOUGHT	PRECHOSEN	PRECRASH
PREACE	PREASING	PREBOUND	PRECIEUSE	PRECREASE
PREACED	PREASSE	PREBUDGET	PRECIEUX	PRECRISIS
PREACES	PREASSED	PREBUILD	PRECINCT	PRECURE
PREACH	PREASSES	PREBUILDS	PRECINCTS	PRECURED
PREACHED	PREASSIGN	PREBUILT	PRECIOUS	PRECURES
PREACHER	PREASSING	PREBUTTAL	PRECIP	PRECURING
PREACHERS	PREASSURE	PREBUY	PRECIPE	PRECURRER
PREACHES	PREATOMIC	PREBUYING	PRECIPES	PRECURSE
PREACHIER	PREATTUNE	PREBUYS	PRECIPICE	PRECURSED
PREACHIFY	PREAUDIT	PRECANCEL	PRECIPS	PRECURSES
PREACHILY	PREAUDITS	PRECANCER	PRECIS	PRECURSOR
PREACHING	PREAVER	PRECAST	PRECISE	PRECUT
PREACHY	PREAVERS	PRECASTS	PRECISED	PRECUTS
PREACING	PREAXIAL	PRECATIVE	PRECISELY	PRECYCLE
PREACT	PREBADE	PRECATORY	PRECISER	PRECYCLED
PREACTED	PREBAKE	PRECAUDAL	PRECISES	PRECYCLES

PREDACITY	PREDRILLS	PREFACER	PREFUND	PREJUDGES
PREDATE	PREDRY	PREFACERS	PREFUNDED	PREJUDICE
PREDATED	PREDRYING	PREFACES	PREFUNDS	PREJUDIZE
PREDATES	PREDUSK	PREFACIAL	PREGAME	PRELACIES
PREDATING	PREDUSKS	PREFACING	PREGAMES	PRELACY
PREDATION	PREDY	PREFADE	PREGGERS	PRELATE
PREDATISM	PREDYING	PREFADED	PREGGIER	PRELATES
PREDATIVE	PREE	PREFADES	PREGGIEST	PRELATESS
PREDATOR	PREED	PREFADING	PREGGY	PRELATIAL
PREDATORS	PREEDIT	PREFARD	PREGNABLE	PRELATIC
PREDATORY	PREEDITED	PREFATORY	PREGNANCE	PRELATIES
PREDAWN	PREEDITS	PREFECT	PREGNANCY	PRELATION
PREDAWNS	PREEING	PREFECTS	PREGNANT	PRELATISE
PREDEATH	PREELECT	PREFER	PREGROWTH	PRELATISH
PREDEATHS	PREELECTS	PREFERRED	PREGUIDE	PRELATISM
PREDEBATE	PREEMIE	PREFERRER	PREGUIDED	PRELATIST
PREDEDUCT	PREEMIES	PREFERS	PREGUIDES	PRELATIZE
PREDEFINE	PREEMPT	PREFEUDAL	PREHAB	PRELATURE
PREDELLA	PREEMPTED	PREFIGHT	PREHABS	PRELATY
PREDELLAS	PREEMPTOR	PREFIGURE	PREHALLUX	PRELAUNCH
PREDELLE	PREEMPTS	PREFILE	PREHANDLE	PRELAW
PREDESIGN	PREEN	PREFILED	PREHARDEN	PRELECT
PREDEVOTE	PREENACT	PREFILES	PREHEAT	PRELECTED
PREDIAL	PREENACTS	PREFILING	PREHEATED	PRELECTOR
PREDIALS	PREENED	PREFILLED	PREHEATER	PRELECTS
PREDICANT	PREENER	PREFIRE	PREHEATS	PRELEGAL
PREDICATE	PREENERS	PREFIRED	PREHEND	PRELIFE
PREDICT	PREENING	PREFIRES	PREHENDED	PRELIM
PREDICTED	PREENS	PREFIRING	PREHENDS	PRELIMIT
PREDICTER	PREERECT	PREFIX	PREHENSOR	PRELIMITS
PREDICTOR	PREERECTS	PREFIXAL	PREHIRING	PRELIMS
PREDICTS	PREES	PREFIXED	PREHNITE	PRELIVES
PREDIED	PREEVE	PREFIXES	PREHNITES	PRELOAD
PREDIES	PREEVED	PREFIXING	PREHUMAN	PRELOADED
PREDIGEST	PREEVES	PREFIXION	PREHUMANS	PRELOADS
PREDIKANT	PREEVING	PREFLAME	PREIF	PRELOCATE
PREDILECT	PREEXCITE	PREFLIGHT	PREIFE	PRELOVED
PREDINNER	PREEXEMPT	PREFOCUS	PREIFES	PRELUDE
PREDIVE	PREEXILIC	PREFORM	PREIFS	PRELUDED
PREDOOM	PREEXIST	PREFORMAT	PREIMPOSE	PRELUDER
PREDOOMED	PREEXISTS	PREFORMED	PREINFORM	PRELUDERS
PREDOOMS	PREEXPOSE	PREFORMS	PREINSERT	PRELUDES
PREDRAFT	PREFAB	PREFRANK	PREINVITE	PRELUDI
PREDRAFTS	PREFABBED	PREFRANKS	PREJINK	PRELUDIAL
PREDRIED	PREFABS	PREFREEZE	PREJUDGE	PRELUDING
PREDRIES	PREFACE	PREFROZE	PREJUDGED	PRELUDIO
PREDRILL	PREFACED	PREFROZEN	PREJUDGER	PRELUNCH

P

PRELUSION	PREMORAL	PREOPTION	PREPOTENT	PRESAGED
PRELUSIVE	PREMORSE	PREORAL	PREPPED	PRESAGER
PRELUSORY	PREMOSAIC	PREORDAIN	PREPPIE	PRESAGERS
PREM	PREMOTION	PREORDER	PREPPIER	PRESAGES
PREMADE	PREMOTOR	PREORDERS	PREPPIES	PRESAGING
PREMAN	PREMOULD	PREOWNED	PREPPIEST	PRESALE
PREMARKET	PREMOULDS	PREP	PREPPILY	PRESALES
PREMATURE	PREMOULT	PREPACK	PREPPING	PRESBYOPE
PREMEAL	PREMOVE	PREPACKED	PREPPY	PRESBYOPY
PREMED	PREMOVED	PREPACKS	PREPREG	PRESBYTE
PREMEDIC	PREMOVES	PREPAID	PREPREGS	PRESBYTER
PREMEDICS	PREMOVING	PREPARE	PREPRESS	PRESBYTES
PREMEDS	PREMS	PREPARED	PREPRICE	PRESBYTIC
PREMEET	PREMUNE	PREPARER	PREPRICED	PRESCHOOL
PREMEN	PREMY	PREPARERS	PREPRICES	PRESCIENT
PREMERGER	PRENAME	PREPARES	PREPRINT	PRESCIND
PREMIA	PRENAMES	PREPARING	PREPRINTS	PRESCINDS
PREMIE	PRENASAL	PREPASTE	PREPS	PRESCIOUS
PREMIER	PRENASALS	PREPASTED	PREPUBES	PRESCORE
PREMIERE	PRENATAL	PREPASTES	PREPUBIS	PRESCORED
PREMIERED	PRENATALS	PREPAVE	PREPUCE	PRESCORES
PREMIERES	PRENEED	PREPAVED	PREPUCES	PRESCREEN
PREMIERS	PRENOMEN	PREPAVES	PREPUEBLO	PRESCRIBE
PREMIES	PRENOMENS	PREPAVING	PREPUNCH	PRESCRIPT
PREMISE	PRENOMINA	PREPAY	PREPUPA	PRESCUTA
PREMISED	PRENOON	PREPAYING	PREPUPAE	PRESCUTUM
PREMISES	PRENOTIFY	PREPAYS	PREPUPAL	PRESE
PREMISING	PRENOTION	PREPENSE	PREPUPAS	PRESEASON
PREMISS	PRENT	PREPENSED	PREPUTIAL	PRESELECT
PREMISSED	PRENTED	PREPENSES	PREQUEL	PRESELL
PREMISSES	PRENTICE	PREPILL	PREQUELS	PRESELLS
PREMIUM	PRENTICED	PREPLACE	PRERACE	PRESENCE
PREMIUMS	PRENTICES	PREPLACED	PRERADIO	PRESENCES
PREMIX	PRENTING	PREPLACES	PRERECORD	PRESENILE
PREMIXED	PRENTS	PREPLAN	PRERECTAL	PRESENT
PREMIXES	PRENUBILE	PREPLANS	PREREFORM	PRESENTED
PREMIXING	PRENUMBER	PREPLANT	PRERENAL	PRESENTEE
PREMIXT	PRENUP	PREPOLLEX	PRERETURN	PRESENTER
PREMODERN	PRENUPS	PREPONE	PREREVIEW	PRESENTLY
PREMODIFY	PRENZIE	PREPONED	PRERINSE	PRESENTS
PREMOLAR	PREOBTAIN	PREPONES	PRERINSED	PRESERVE
PREMOLARS	PREOCCUPY	PREPONING	PRERINSES	PRESERVED
PREMOLD	PREOCULAR	PREPOSE	PRERIOT	PRESERVER
PREMOLDED	PREON	PREPOSED	PREROCK	PRESERVES
PREMOLDS	PREONS	PREPOSES	PRERUPT	PRESES
PREMOLT	PREOP	PREPOSING	PRESA	PRESET
PREMONISH	PREOPS	PREPOSTOR	PRESAGE	PRESETS

PRESETTLE	PRESSER	PRESUMER	PRETRAVEL	PREVERBAL
PRESHAPE	PRESSERS	PRESUMERS	PRETREAT	PREVERBS
PRESHAPED	PRESSES	PRESUMES	PRETREATS	PREVES
PRESHAPES	PRESSFAT	PRESUMING	PRETRIAL	PREVIABLE
PRESHIP	PRESSFATS	PRESUMMIT	PRETRIALS	PREVIEW
PRESHIPS	PRESSFUL	PRESURVEY	PRETRIM	PREVIEWED
PRESHOW	PRESSFULS	PRETAPE	PRETRIMS	PREVIEWER
PRESHOWED	PRESSGANG	PRETAPED	PRETTIED	PREVIEWS
PRESHOWN	PRESSIE	PRETAPES	PRETTIER	PREVING
PRESHOWS	PRESSIES	PRETAPING	PRETTIES	PREVIOUS
PRESHRANK	PRESSING	PRETASTE	PRETTIEST	PREVISE
PRESHRINK	PRESSINGS	PRETASTED	PRETTIFY	PREVISED
PRESHRUNK	PRESSION	PRETASTES	PRETTILY	PREVISES
PRESIDE	PRESSIONS	PRETAX	PRETTY	PREVISING
PRESIDED	PRESSMAN	PRETEEN	PRETTYING	PREVISION
PRESIDENT	PRESSMARK	PRETEENS	PRETTYISH	PREVISIT
PRESIDER	PRESSMEN	PRETELL	PRETTYISM	PREVISITS
PRESIDERS	PRESSOR	PRETELLS	PRETYPE	PREVISOR
PRESIDES	PRESSORS	PRETENCE	PRETYPED	PREVISORS
PRESIDIA	PRESSROOM	PRETENCES	PRETYPES	PREVUE
PRESIDIAL	PRESSRUN	PRETEND	PRETYPING	PREVUED
PRESIDING	PRESSRUNS	PRETENDED	PRETZEL	PREVUES
PRESIDIO	PRESSURE	PRETENDER	PRETZELS	PREVUING
PRESIDIOS	PRESSURED	PRETENDS	PREUNION	PREWAR
PRESIDIUM	PRESSURES	PRETENSE	PREUNIONS	PREWARM
PRESIFT	PRESSWORK	PRETENSES	PREUNITE	PREWARMED
PRESIFTED	PRESSY	PRETERIST	PREUNITED	PREWARMS
PRESIFTS	PREST	PRETERIT	PREUNITES	PREWARN
PRESIGNAL	PRESTAMP	PRETERITE	PREVAIL	PREWARNED
PRESLEEP	PRESTAMPS	PRETERITS	PREVAILED	PREWARNS
PRESLICE	PRESTED	PRETERM	PREVAILER	PREWASH
PRESLICED	PRESTER	PRETERMIT	PREVAILS	PREWASHED
PRESLICES	PRESTERNA	PRETERMS	PREVALENT	PREWASHES
PRESOAK	PRESTERS	PRETEST	PREVALUE	PREWEIGH
PRESOAKED	PRESTIGE	PRETESTED	PREVALUED	PREWEIGHS
PRESOAKS	PRESTIGES	PRETESTS	PREVALUES	PREWIRE
PRESOLD	PRESTING	PRETEXT	PREVE	PREWIRED
PRESOLVE	PRESTO	PRETEXTED	PREVED	PREWIRES
PRESOLVED	PRESTORE	PRETEXTS	PREVENE	PREWIRING
PRESOLVES	PRESTORED	PRETOLD	PREVENED	PREWORK
PRESONG	PRESTORES	PRETONIC	PREVENES	PREWORKED
PRESORT	PRESTOS	PRETOR	PREVENING	PREWORKS
PRESORTED	PRESTRESS	PRETORIAL	PREVENT	PREWORN
PRESORTS	PRESTRIKE	PRETORIAN	PREVENTED	PREWRAP
PRESPLIT	PRESTS	PRETORS	PREVENTER	PREWRAPS
PRESS	PRESUME	PRETRAIN	PREVENTS	PREWYN
PRESSED	PRESUMED	PRETRAINS	PREVERB	PREWYNS

PREX	PRICKIER	PRIGGING	PRIMING	PRINCIPI
PREXES	PRICKIEST	PRIGGINGS	PRIMINGS	PRINCIPIA
PREXIE	PRICKING	PRIGGISH	PRIMIPARA	PRINCIPLE
PREXIES	PRICKINGS	PRIGGISM	PRIMITIAE	PRINCOCK
PREXY	PRICKLE	PRIGGISMS	PRIMITIAL	PRINCOCKS
PREY	PRICKLED	PRIGS	PRIMITIAS	PRINCOX
PREYED	PRICKLES	PRILL	PRIMITIVE	PRINCOXES
PREYER	PRICKLIER	PRILLED	PRIMLY	PRINK
PREYERS	PRICKLING	PRILLING	PRIMMED	PRINKED
PREYFUL	PRICKLY	PRILLS	PRIMMER	PRINKER
PREYING	PRICKS	PRIM	PRIMMERS	PRINKERS
PREYS	PRICKWOOD	PRIMA	PRIMMEST	PRINKING
PREZ	PRICKY	PRIMACIES	PRIMMING	PRINKS
PREZES	PRICY	PRIMACY	PRIMNESS	PRINT
PREZZIE	PRIDE	PRIMAEVAL	PRIMO	PRINTABLE
PREZZIES	PRIDED	PRIMAGE	PRIMORDIA	PRINTED
PRIAL	PRIDEFUL	PRIMAGES	PRIMOS	PRINTER
PRIALS	PRIDELESS	PRIMAL	PRIMP	PRINTERS
PRIAPEAN	PRIDES	PRIMALITY	PRIMPED	PRINTERY
PRIAPI	PRIDIAN	PRIMALLY	PRIMPING	PRINTHEAD
PRIAPIC	PRIDING	PRIMARIES	PRIMPS	PRINTING
PRIAPISM	PRIED	PRIMARILY	PRIMROSE	PRINTINGS
PRIAPISMS	PRIEDIEU	PRIMARY	PRIMROSED	PRINTLESS
PRIAPUS	PRIEDIEUS	PRIMAS	PRIMROSES	PRINTOUT
PRIAPUSES	PRIEDIEUX	PRIMATAL	PRIMROSY	PRINTOUTS
PRIBBLE	PRIEF	PRIMATALS	PRIMS	PRINTS
PRIBBLES	PRIEFE	PRIMATE	PRIMSIE	PRION
PRICE	PRIEFES	PRIMATES	PRIMSIER	PRIONS
PRICEABLE	PRIEFS	PRIMATIAL	PRIMSIEST	PRIOR
PRICED	PRIER	PRIMATIC	PRIMULA	PRIORATE
PRICELESS	PRIERS	PRIMAVERA	PRIMULAS	PRIORATES
PRICER	PRIES	PRIME	PRIMULINE	PRIORESS
PRICERS	PRIEST	PRIMED	PRIMUS	PRIORIES
PRICES	PRIESTED	PRIMELY	PRIMUSES	PRIORITY
PRICEY	PRIESTESS	PRIMENESS	PRIMY	PRIORLY
PRICIER	PRIESTING	PRIMER	PRINCE	PRIORS
PRICIEST	PRIESTLY	PRIMERO	PRINCED	PRIORSHIP
PRICILY	PRIESTS	PRIMEROS	PRINCEDOM	PRIORY
PRICINESS	PRIEVE	PRIMERS	PRINCEKIN	PRISAGE
PRICING	PRIEVED	PRIMES	PRINCELET	PRISAGES
PRICINGS	PRIEVES	PRIMETIME	PRINCELY	PRISE
PRICK	PRIEVING	PRIMEUR	PRINCES	PRISED
PRICKED	PRIG	PRIMEURS	PRINCESS	PRISER
PRICKER	PRIGGED	PRIMEVAL	PRINCESSE	PRISERE
PRICKERS	PRIGGER	PRIMI	PRINCING	PRISERES
PRICKET	PRIGGERS	PRIMINE	PRINCIPAL	PRISERS
PRICKETS	PRIGGERY	PRIMINES	PRINCIPE	PRISES

PRISING	PRIVIES	PROBIT	PROCTORS	PROEM
PRISM	PRIVIEST	PROBITIES	PROCURACY	PROEMBRYO
PRISMATIC	PRIVILEGE	PROBITS	PROCURAL	PROEMIAL
PRISMOID	PRIVILY	PROBITY	PROCURALS	PROEMS
PRISMOIDS	PRIVITIES	PROBLEM	PROCURE	PROENZYME
PRISMS	PRIVITY	PROBLEMS	PROCURED	PROESTRUS
PRISMY	PRIVY	PROBOSCIS	PROCURER	PROETTE
PRISON	PRIZABLE	PROBS	PROCURERS	PROETTES
PRISONED	PRIZE	PROCACITY	PROCURES	PROF
PRISONER	PRIZED	PROCAINE	PROCURESS	PROFACE
PRISONERS	PRIZEMAN	PROCAINES	PROCUREUR	PROFAMILY
PRISONING	PRIZEMEN	PROCAMBIA	PROCURING	PROFANE
PRISONOUS	PRIZER	PROCARP	PROCYONID	PROFANED
PRISONS	PRIZERS	PROCARPS	PROD	PROFANELY
PRISS	PRIZES	PROCARYON	PRODDED	PROFANER
PRISSED	PRIZING	PROCEDURE	PRODDER	PROFANERS
PRISSES	PRO	PROCEED	PRODDERS	PROFANES
PRISSIER	PROA	PROCEEDED	PRODDING	PROFANING
PRISSIES	PROACTION	PROCEEDER	PRODDINGS	PROFANITY
PRISSIEST	PROACTIVE	PROCEEDS	PRODIGAL	PROFESS
PRISSILY	PROAS	PROCERITY	PRODIGALS	PROFESSED
PRISSING	PROB	PROCESS	PRODIGIES	PROFESSES
PRISSY	PROBABLE	PROCESSED	PRODIGY	PROFESSOR
PRISTANE	PROBABLES	PROCESSER	PRODITOR	PROFFER
PRISTANES	PROBABLY	PROCESSES	PRODITORS	PROFFERED
PRISTINE	PROBALL	PROCESSOR	PRODITORY	PROFFERER
PRITHEE	PROBAND	PROCHAIN	PRODNOSE	PROFFERS
PRIVACIES	PROBANDS	PROCHEIN	PRODNOSED	PROFILE
PRIVACY	PROBANG	PROCHOICE	PRODNOSES	PROFILED
PRIVADO	PROBANGS	PROCHURCH	PRODROMA	PROFILER
PRIVADOES	PROBATE	PROCIDENT	PRODROMAL	PROFILERS
PRIVADOS	PROBATED	PROCINCT	PRODROME	PROFILES
PRIVATE	PROBATES	PROCINCTS	PRODROMES	PROFILING
PRIVATEER	PROBATING	PROCLAIM	PRODROMI	PROFILIST
PRIVATELY	PROBATION	PROCLAIMS	PRODROMIC	PROFIT
PRIVATER	PROBATIVE	PROCLISES	PRODROMUS	PROFITED
PRIVATES	PROBATORY	PROCLISIS	PRODRUG	PROFITEER
PRIVATEST	PROBE	PROCLITIC	PRODRUGS	PROFITER
PRIVATION	PROBEABLE	PROCLIVE	PRODS	PROFITERS
PRIVATISE	PROBED	PROCONSUL	PRODUCE	PROFITING
PRIVATISM	PROBER	PROCREANT	PRODUCED	PROFITS
PRIVATIST	PROBERS	PROCREATE	PRODUCER	PROFLUENT
PRIVATIVE	PROBES	PROCTAL	PRODUCERS	PROFORMA
PRIVATIZE	PROBING	PROCTITIS	PRODUCES	PROFOUND
PRIVET	PROBINGLY	PROCTODEA	PRODUCING	PROFOUNDS
PRIVETS	PROBINGS	PROCTOR	PRODUCT	PROFS
PRIVIER	PROBIOTIC	PROCTORED	PRODUCTS	PROFUSE

P

PROFUSELY	PROJET	PROLIXLY	PROMMERS	PRONEUR
PROFUSER	PROJETS	PROLL	PROMO	PRONEURS
PROFUSERS	PROKARYON	PROLLED	PROMODERN	PRONG
PROFUSION	PROKARYOT	PROLLER	PROMOED	PRONGBUCK
PROFUSIVE	PROKE	PROLLERS	PROMOING	PRONGED
PROG	PROKED	PROLLING	PROMOS	PRONGHORN
PROGENIES	PROKER	PROLLS	PROMOTE	PRONGING
PROGENY	PROKERS	PROLLY	PROMOTED	PRONGS
PROGERIA	PROKES	PROLOG	PROMOTER	PRONK
PROGERIAS	PROKING	PROLOGED	PROMOTERS	PRONKED
PROGESTIN	PROLABOR	PROLOGING	PROMOTES	PRONKING
PROGGED	PROLABOUR	PROLOGISE	PROMOTING	PRONKINGS
PROGGER	PROLACTIN	PROLOGIST	PROMOTION	PRONKS
PROGGERS	PROLAMIN	PROLOGIZE	PROMOTIVE	PRONOTA
PROGGING	PROLAMINE	PROLOGS	PROMOTOR	PRONOTAL
PROGGINS	PROLAMINS	PROLOGUE	PROMOTORS	PRONOTUM
PROGNOSE	PROLAN	PROLOGUED	PROMPT	PRONOUN
PROGNOSED	PROLANS	PROLOGUES	PROMPTED	PRONOUNCE
PROGNOSES	PROLAPSE	PROLONG	PROMPTER	PRONOUNS
PROGNOSIS	PROLAPSED	PROLONGE	PROMPTERS	PRONTO
PROGRADE	PROLAPSES	PROLONGED	PROMPTEST	PRONUCLEI
PROGRADED	PROLAPSUS	PROLONGER	PROMPTING	PRONUNCIO
PROGRADES	PROLATE	PROLONGES	PROMPTLY	PROO
PROGRAM	PROLATED	PROLONGS	PROMPTS	PROOEMION
PROGRAMED	PROLATELY	PROLUSION	PROMPTURE	PROOEMIUM
PROGRAMER	PROLATES	PROLUSORY	PROMS	PROOF
PROGRAMME	PROLATING	PROM	PROMULGE	PROOFED
PROGRAMS	PROLATION	PROMACHOS	PROMULGED	PROOFER
PROGRESS	PROLATIVE	PROMENADE	PROMULGES	PROOFERS
PROGS	PROLE	PROMETAL	PROMUSCES	PROOFING
PROGUN	PROLED	PROMETALS	PROMUSCIS	PROOFINGS
PROHIBIT	PROLEG	PROMETRIC	PRONAOI	PROOFLESS
PROHIBITS	PROLEGS	PROMINE	PRONAOS	PROOFREAD
PROIGN	PROLEPSES	PROMINENT	PRONATE	PROOFROOM
PROIGNED	PROLEPSIS	PROMINES	PRONATED	PROOFS
PROIGNING	PROLEPTIC	PROMISE	PRONATES	PROOTIC
PROIGNS	PROLER	PROMISED	PRONATING	PROOTICS
PROIN	PROLERS	PROMISEE	PRONATION	PROP
PROINE	PROLES	PROMISEES	PRONATOR	PROPAGATE
PROINED	PROLETARY	PROMISER	PRONATORS	PROPAGE
PROINES	PROLICIDE	PROMISERS	PRONE	PROPAGED
PROINING	PROLIFIC	PROMISES	PRONELY	PROPAGES
PROINS	PROLINE	PROMISING	PRONENESS	PROPAGING
PROJECT	PROLINES	PROMISOR	PRONEPHRA	PROPAGULA
PROJECTED	PROLING	PROMISORS	PRONER	PROPAGULE
PROJECTOR	PROLIX	PROMISSOR	PRONES	PROPALE
PROJECTS	PROLIXITY	PROMMER	PRONEST	PROPALED

PROPALES	PROPINES	PROPYLS	PROSIFIED	PROTAMIN
PROPALING	PROPINING	PROPYNE	PROSIFIES	PROTAMINE
PROPANE	PROPIONIC	PROPYNES	PROSIFY	PROTAMINS
PROPANES	PROPJET	PRORATE	PROSILY	PROTANDRY
PROPANOIC	PROPJETS	PRORATED	PROSIMIAN	PROTANOPE
PROPANOL	PROPMAN	PRORATES	PROSINESS	PROTASES
PROPANOLS	PROPMEN	PRORATING	PROSING	PROTASIS
PROPANONE	PROPODEON	PRORATION	PROSINGS	PROTATIC
PROPEL	PROPODEUM	PRORE	PROSIT	PROTEA
PROPELLED	PROPOLIS	PRORECTOR	PROSO	PROTEAN
PROPELLER	PROPONE	PROREFORM	PROSOCIAL	PROTEANS
PROPELLOR	PROPONED	PRORES	PROSODIAL	PROTEAS
PROPELS	PROPONENT	PROROGATE	PROSODIAN	PROTEASE
PROPENAL	PROPONES	PROROGUE	PROSODIC	PROTEASES
PROPENALS	PROPONING	PROROGUED	PROSODIES	PROTECT
PROPEND	PROPOSAL	PROROGUES	PROSODIST	PROTECTED
PROPENDED	PROPOSALS	PROS	PROSODY	PROTECTER
PROPENDS	PROPOSE	PROSAIC	PROSOMA	PROTECTOR
PROPENE	PROPOSED	PROSAICAL	PROSOMAL	PROTECTS
PROPENES	PROPOSER	PROSAISM	PROSOMAS	PROTEGE
PROPENOIC	PROPOSERS	PROSAISMS	PROSOMATA	PROTEGEE
PROPENOL	PROPOSES	PROSAIST	PROSOPON	PROTEGEES
PROPENOLS	PROPOSING	PROSAISTS	PROSOPONS	PROTEGES
PROPENSE	PROPOSITA	PROSATEUR	PROSOS	PROTEI
PROPENYL	PROPOSITI	PROSCENIA	PROSPECT	PROTEID
PROPENYLS	PROPOUND	PROSCRIBE	PROSPECTS	PROTEIDE
PROPER	PROPOUNDS	PROSCRIPT	PROSPER	PROTEIDES
PROPERDIN	PROPPANT	PROSE	PROSPERED	PROTEIDS
PROPERER	PROPPANTS	PROSECCO	PROSPERS	PROTEIN
PROPEREST	PROPPED	PROSECCOS	PROSS	PROTEINIC
PROPERLY	PROPPING	PROSECT	PROSSES	PROTEINS
PROPERS	PROPRETOR	PROSECTED	PROSSIE	PROTEND
PROPERTY	PROPRIA	PROSECTOR	PROSSIES	PROTENDED
PROPHAGE	PROPRIETY	PROSECTS	PROST	PROTENDS
PROPHAGES	PROPRIUM	PROSECUTE	PROSTATE	PROTENSE
PROPHASE	PROPS	PROSED	PROSTATES	PROTENSES
PROPHASES	PROPTOSES	PROSELIKE	PROSTATIC	PROTEOME
PROPHASIC	PROPTOSIS	PROSELYTE	PROSTERNA	PROTEOMES
PROPHECY	PROPULSOR	PROSEMAN	PROSTIE	PROTEOMIC
PROPHESY	PROPYL	PROSEMEN	PROSTIES	PROTEOSE
PROPHET	PROPYLA	PROSER	PROSTOMIA	PROTEOSES
PROPHETIC	PROPYLAEA	PROSERS	PROSTRATE	PROTEST
PROPHETS	PROPYLENE	PROSES	PROSTYLE	PROTESTED
PROPHYLL	PROPYLIC	PROSEUCHA	PROSTYLES	PROTESTER
PROPHYLLS	PROPYLITE	PROSEUCHE	PROSUMER	PROTESTOR
PROPINE	PROPYLON	PROSIER	PROSUMERS	PROTESTS
PROPINED	PROPYLONS	PROSIEST	PROSY	PROTEUS

P

PROTEUSES	PROTURANS	PROVIDE	PROWLERS	PRUNES
PROTHALLI	PROTYL	PROVIDED	PROWLING	PRUNEY
PROTHESES	PROTYLE	PROVIDENT	PROWLINGS	PRUNIER
PROTHESIS	PROTYLES	PROVIDER	PROWLS	PRUNIEST
PROTHETIC	PROTYLS	PROVIDERS	PROWS	PRUNING
PROTHORAX	PROUD	PROVIDES	PROXEMIC	PRUNINGS
PROTHYL	PROUDER	PROVIDING	PROXEMICS	PRUNT
PROTHYLS	PROUDEST	PROVIDOR	PROXIES	PRUNTED
PROTIST	PROUDFUL	PROVIDORS	PROXIMAL	PRUNTS
PROTISTAN	PROUDISH	PROVINCE	PROXIMATE	PRUNUS
PROTISTIC	PROUDLY	PROVINCES	PROXIMITY	PRUNUSES
PROTISTS	PROUDNESS	PROVINE	PROXIMO	PRURIENCE
PROTIUM	PROUL	PROVINED	PROXY	PRURIENCY
PROTIUMS	PROULED	PROVINES	PROYN	PRURIENT
PROTO	PROULER	PROVING	PROYNE	PRURIGO
PROTOAVIS	PROULERS	PROVINGS	PROYNED	PRURIGOS
PROTOCOL	PROULING	PROVINING	PROYNES	PRURITIC
PROTOCOLS	PROULS	PROVIRAL	PROYNING	PRURITUS
PROTODERM	PROUNION	PROVIRUS	PROYNS	PRUSIK
PROTOGINE	PROUSTITE	PROVISION	PROZYMITE	PRUSIKED
PROTOGYNY	PROVABLE	PROVISO	PRUDE	PRUSIKING
PROTON	PROVABLY	PROVISOES	PRUDENCE	PRUSIKS
PROTONATE	PROVAND	PROVISOR	PRUDENCES	PRUSSIAN
PROTONEMA	PROVANDS	PROVISORS	PRUDENT	PRUSSIATE
PROTONIC	PROVANT	PROVISORY	PRUDENTLY	PRUSSIC
PROTONS	PROVANTED	PROVISOS	PRUDERIES	PRUTA
PROTOPOD	PROVANTS	PROVOCANT	PRUDERY	PRUTAH
PROTOPODS	PROVE	PROVOKE	PRUDES	PRUTOT
PROTORE	PROVEABLE	PROVOKED	PRUDISH	PRUTOTH
PROTORES	PROVEABLY	PROVOKER	PRUDISHLY	PRY
PROTOSTAR	PROVED	PROVOKERS	PRUH	PRYER
PROTOTYPE	PROVEDOR	PROVOKES	PRUINA	PRYERS
PROTOXID	PROVEDORE	PROVOKING	PRUINAS	PRYING
PROTOXIDE	PROVEDORS	PROVOLONE	PRUINE	PRYINGLY
PROTOXIDS	PROVEN	PROVOST	PRUINES	PRYINGS
PROTOZOA	PROVEND	PROVOSTRY	PRUINOSE	PRYS
PROTOZOAL	PROVENDER	PROVOSTS	PRUNABLE	PRYSE
PROTOZOAN	PROVENDS	PROW	PRUNE	PRYSED
PROTOZOIC	PROVENLY	PROWAR	PRUNED	PRYSES
PROTOZOON	PROVER	PROWER	PRUNELLA	PRYSING
PROTRACT	PROVERB	PROWESS	PRUNELLAS	PRYTANEA
PROTRACTS	PROVERBED	PROWESSED	PRUNELLE	PRYTANEUM
PROTRADE	PROVERBS	PROWESSES	PRUNELLES	PRYTHEE
PROTRUDE	PROVERS	PROWEST	PRUNELLO	PSALM
PROTRUDED	PROVES	PROWL	PRUNELLOS	PSALMBOOK
PROTRUDES	PROVIANT	PROWLED	PRUNER	PSALMED
PROTURAN	PROVIANTS	PROWLER	PRUNERS	PSALMIC

PSALMING	PSION	PSYLLID	PTYALIZE	PUCEST
PSALMIST	PSIONIC	PSYLLIDS	PTYALIZED	PUCK
PSALMISTS	PSIONICS	PSYLLIUM	PTYALIZES	PUCKA
PSALMODIC	PSIONS	PSYLLIUMS	PTYXES	PUCKED
PSALMODY	PSIS	PSYOP	PTYXIS	PUCKER
PSALMS	PSOAE	PSYOPS	PTYXISES	PUCKERED
PSALTER	PSOAI	PSYWAR	PUB	PUCKERER
PSALTERIA	PSOAS	PSYWARS	PUBBED	PUCKERERS
PSALTERS	PSOASES	PTARMIC	PUBBING	PUCKERIER
PSALTERY	PSOATIC	PTARMICS	PUBBINGS	PUCKERIES
PSALTRESS	PSOCID	PTARMIGAN	PUBCO	PUCKERING
PSALTRIES	PSOCIDS	PTERIA	PUBCOS	PUCKEROOD
PSALTRY	PSORA	PTERIDINE	PUBE	PUCKERS
PSAMMITE	PSORALEA	PTERIN	PUBERAL	PUCKERY
PSAMMITES	PSORALEAS	PTERINS	PUBERTAL	PUCKFIST
PSAMMITIC	PSORALEN	PTERION	PUBERTIES	PUCKFISTS
PSAMMON	PSORALENS	PTEROIC	PUBERTY	PUCKING
PSAMMONS	PSORAS	PTEROPOD	PUBES	PUCKISH
PSCHENT	PSORIASES	PTEROPODS	PUBESCENT	PUCKISHLY
PSCHENTS	PSORIASIS	PTEROSAUR	PUBIC	PUCKLE
PSELLISM	PSORIATIC	PTERYGIA	PUBIS	PUCKLES
PSELLISMS	PSORIC	PTERYGIAL	PUBISES	PUCKOUT
PSEPHISM	PSST	PTERYGIUM	PUBLIC	PUCKOUTS
PSEPHISMS	PST	PTERYGOID	PUBLICAN	PUCKS
PSEPHITE	PSYCH	PTERYLA	PUBLICANS	PUCKSTER
PSEPHITES	PSYCHE	PTERYLAE	PUBLICISE	PUCKSTERS
PSEPHITIC	PSYCHED	PTILOSES	PUBLICIST	PUD
PSEUD	PSYCHES	PTILOSIS	PUBLICITY	PUDDEN
PSEUDAXES	PSYCHIC	PTISAN	PUBLICIZE	PUDDENING
PSEUDAXIS	PSYCHICAL	PTISANS	PUBLICLY	PUDDENS
PSEUDERY	PSYCHICS	PTOMAIN	PUBLICS	PUDDER
PSEUDISH	PSYCHING	PTOMAINE	PUBLISH	PUDDERED
PSEUDO	PSYCHISM	PTOMAINES	PUBLISHED	PUDDERING
PSEUDONYM	PSYCHISMS	PTOMAINIC	PUBLISHER	PUDDERS
PSEUDOPOD	PSYCHIST	PTOMAINS	PUBLISHES	PUDDIER
PSEUDOS	PSYCHISTS	PTOOEY	PUBS	PUDDIES
PSEUDS	PSYCHO	PTOSES	PUCAN	PUDDIEST
PSHAW	PSYCHOGAS	PTOSIS	PUCANS	PUDDING
PSHAWED	PSYCHOID	PTOTIC	PUCCOON	PUDDINGS
PSHAWING	PSYCHOIDS	PTUI	PUCCOONS	PUDDINGY
PSHAWS	PSYCHOS	PTYALIN	PUCE	PUDDLE
PSI	PSYCHOSES	PTYALINS	PUCELAGE	PUDDLED
PSILOCIN	PSYCHOSIS	PTYALISE	PUCELAGES	PUDDLER
PSILOCINS	PSYCHOTIC	PTYALISED	PUCELLE	PUDDLERS
PSILOSES	PSYCHS	PTYALISES	PUCELLES	PUDDLES
PSILOSIS	PSYLLA	PTYALISM	PUCER	PUDDLIER
PSILOTIC	PSYLLAS	PTYALISMS	PUCES	PUDDLIEST

P

PUDDLING	PUERPERIA	PUGGREE	PUKERS	PULLETS
PUDDLINGS	PUERS	PUGGREES	PUKES	PULLEY
PUDDLY	PUFF	PUGGRIES	PUKEY	PULLEYED
PUDDOCK	PUFFA	PUGGRY	PUKIER	PULLEYING
PUDDOCKS	PUFFBACK	PUGGY	PUKIEST	PULLEYS
PUDDY	PUFFBACKS	PUGH	PUKING	PULLI
PUDENCIES	PUFFBALL	PUGIL	PUKKA	PULLIES
PUDENCY	PUFFBALLS	PUGILISM	PUKKAH	PULLING
PUDENDA	PUFFBIRD	PUGILISMS	PUKU	PULLMAN
PUDENDAL	PUFFBIRDS	PUGILIST	PUKUS	PULLMANS
PUDENDOUS	PUFFED	PUGILISTS	PUKY	PULLORUM
PUDENDUM	PUFFER	PUGILS	PUL	PULLOUT
PUDENT	PUFFERIES	PUGMARK	PULA	PULLOUTS
PUDEUR	PUFFERS	PUGMARKS	PULAO	PULLOVER
PUDEURS	PUFFERY	PUGNACITY	PULAOS	PULLOVERS
PUDGE	PUFFIER	PUGREE	PULAS	PULLS
PUDGES	PUFFIEST	PUGREES	PULDRON	PULLULATE
PUDGIER	PUFFILY	PUGS	PULDRONS	PULLUP
PUDGIEST	PUFFIN	PUH	PULE	PULLUPS
PUDGILY	PUFFINESS	PUHA	PULED	PULLUS
PUDGINESS	PUFFING	PUHAS	PULER	PULLY
PUDGY	PUFFINGLY	PUIR	PULERS	PULMO
PUDIBUND	PUFFINGS	PUIRER	PULES	PULMONARY
PUDIC	PUFFINS	PUIREST	PULI	PULMONATE
PUDICITY	PUFFS	PUIRTITH	PULICENE	PULMONES
PUDOR	PUFFY	PUIRTITHS	PULICIDE	PULMONIC
PUDORS	PUFTALOON	PUISNE	PULICIDES	PULMONICS
PUDS	PUG	PUISNES	PULIER	PULMOTOR
PUDSEY	PUGAREE	PUISNY	PULIEST	PULMOTORS
PUDSIER	PUGAREES	PUISSANCE	PULIK	PULP
PUDSIES	PUGGAREE	PUISSANT	PULING	PULPAL
PUDSIEST	PUGGAREES	PUISSAUNT	PULINGLY	PULPALLY
PUDSY	PUGGED	PUJA	PULINGS	PULPBOARD
PUDU	PUGGERIES	PUJAH	PULIS	PULPED
PUDUS	PUGGERY	PUJAHS	PULK	PULPER
PUEBLO	PUGGIE	PUJARI	PULKA	PULPERS
PUEBLOS	PUGGIER	PUJARIS	PULKAS	PULPIER
PUER	PUGGIES	PUJAS	PULKHA	PULPIEST
PUERED	PUGGIEST	PUKA	PULKHAS	PULPIFIED
PUERILE	PUGGINESS	PUKAS	PULKS	PULPIFIES
PUERILELY	PUGGING	PUKATEA	PULL	PULPIFY
PUERILISM	PUGGINGS	PUKATEAS	PULLBACK	PULPILY
PUERILITY	PUGGISH	PUKE	PULLBACKS	PULPINESS
PUERING	PUGGLE	PUKED	PULLED	PULPING
PUERPERA	PUGGLED	PUKEKO	PULLER	PULPINGS
PUERPERAE	PUGGLES	PUKEKOS	PULLERS	PULPIT
PUERPERAL	PUGGLING	PUKER	PULLET	PULPITAL

PULPITED	PULSIONS	PUMAS	PUNAANI	PUNCTURES
PULPITEER	PULSOJET	PUMELO	PUNAANY	PUNDIT
PULPITER	PULSOJETS	PUMELOS	PUNALUA	PUNDITIC
PULPITERS	PULTAN	PUMICATE	PUNALUAN	PUNDITRY
PULPITRY	PULTANS	PUMICATED	PUNALUAS	PUNDITS
PULPITS	PULTON	PUMICATES	PUNANI	PUNDONOR
PULPITUM	PULTONS	PUMICE	PUNANY	PUNG
PULPITUMS	PULTOON	PUMICED	PUNAS	PUNGA
PULPLESS	PULTOONS	PUMICEOUS	PUNCE	PUNGAS
PULPMILL	PULTRUDE	PUMICER	PUNCED	PUNGENCE
PULPMILLS	PULTRUDED	PUMICERS	PUNCES	PUNGENCES
PULPOUS	PULTRUDES	PUMICES	PUNCH	PUNGENCY
PULPS	PULTUN	PUMICING	PUNCHBAG	PUNGENT
PULPSTONE	PULTUNS	PUMICITE	PUNCHBAGS	PUNGENTLY
PULPWOOD	PULTURE	PUMICITES	PUNCHBALL	PUNGLE
PULPWOODS	PULTURES	PUMIE	PUNCHBOWL	PUNGLED
PULPY	PULU	PUMIES	PUNCHED	PUNGLES
PULQUE	PULUS	PUMMEL	PUNCHEON	PUNGLING
PULQUES	PULVER	PUMMELED	PUNCHEONS	PUNGS
PULS	PULVERED	PUMMELING	PUNCHER	PUNIER
PULSANT	PULVERINE	PUMMELLED	PUNCHERS	PUNIEST
PULSAR	PULVERING	PUMMELO	PUNCHES	PUNILY
PULSARS	PULVERISE	PUMMELOS	PUNCHIER	PUNINESS
PULSATE	PULVERIZE	PUMMELS	PUNCHIEST	PUNISH
PULSATED	PULVEROUS	PUMP	PUNCHILY	PUNISHED
PULSATES	PULVERS	PUMPABLE	PUNCHING	PUNISHER
PULSATILE	PULVIL	PUMPED	PUNCHLESS	PUNISHERS
PULSATING	PULVILIO	PUMPER	PUNCHLINE	PUNISHES
PULSATION	PULVILIOS	PUMPERS	PUNCHOUT	PUNISHING
PULSATIVE	PULVILLAR	PUMPHOOD	PUNCHOUTS	PUNITION
PULSATOR	PULVILLE	PUMPHOODS	PUNCHY	PUNITIONS
PULSATORS	PULVILLED	PUMPING	PUNCING	PUNITIVE
PULSATORY	PULVILLES	PUMPINGS	PUNCTA	PUNITORY
PULSE	PULVILLI	PUMPION	PUNCTATE	PUNJI
PULSEBEAT	PULVILLIO	PUMPIONS	PUNCTATED	PUNJIED
PULSED	PULVILLUS	PUMPJACK	PUNCTATOR	PUNJIES
PULSEJET	PULVILS	PUMPJACKS	PUNCTILIO	PUNJIING
PULSEJETS	PULVINAR	PUMPKIN	PUNCTO	PUNJIS
PULSELESS	PULVINARS	PUMPKING	PUNCTOS	PUNK
PULSER	PULVINATE	PUMPKINGS	PUNCTUAL	PUNKA
PULSERS	PULVINI	PUMPKINS	PUNCTUATE	PUNKAH
PULSES	PULVINULE	PUMPLESS	PUNCTULE	PUNKAHS
PULSIDGE	PULVINUS	PUMPLIKE	PUNCTULES	PUNKAS
PULSIDGES	PULWAR	PUMPS	PUNCTUM	PUNKER
PULSIFIC	PULWARS	PUMY	PUNCTURE	PUNKERS
PULSING	PULY	PUN	PUNCTURED	PUNKEST
PULSION	PUMA	PUNA	PUNCTURER	PUNKETTE

P

PUNKETTES	PUPARIAL	PURANA	PURI	PURPIE
PUNKEY	PUPARIUM	PURANAS	PURIFIED	PURPIES
PUNKEYS	PUPAS	PURANIC	PURIFIER	PURPLE
PUNKIE	PUPATE	PURBLIND	PURIFIERS	PURPLED
PUNKIER	PUPATED	PURCHASE	PURIFIES	PURPLER
PUNKIES	PUPATES	PURCHASED	PURIFY	PURPLES
PUNKIEST	PUPATING	PURCHASER	PURIFYING	PURPLEST
PUNKIN	PUPATION	PURCHASES	PURIN	PURPLIER
PUNKINESS	PUPATIONS	PURDA	PURINE	PURPLIEST
PUNKINS	PUPFISH	PURDAH	PURINES	PURPLING
PUNKISH	PUPFISHES	PURDAHED	PURING	PURPLISH
PUNKS	PUPIL	PURDAHS	PURINS	PURPLY
PUNKY	PUPILAGE	PURDAS	PURIRI	PURPORT
PUNNED	PUPILAGES	PURDONIUM	PURIRIS	PURPORTED
PUNNER	PUPILAR	PURE	PURIS	PURPORTS
PUNNERS	PUPILARY	PUREBLOOD	PURISM	PURPOSE
PUNNET	PUPILLAGE	PUREBRED	PURISMS	PURPOSED
PUNNETS	PUPILLAR	PUREBREDS	PURIST	PURPOSELY
PUNNIER	PUPILLARY	PURED	PURISTIC	PURPOSES
PUNNIEST	PUPILLATE	PUREE	PURISTS	PURPOSING
PUNNING	PUPILS	PUREED	PURITAN	PURPOSIVE
PUNNINGLY	PUPILSHIP	PUREEING	PURITANIC	PURPURA
PUNNINGS	PUPPED	PUREES	PURITANS	PURPURAS
PUNNY	PUPPET	PURELY	PURITIES	PURPURE
PUNS	PUPPETEER	PURENESS	PURITY	PURPUREAL
PUNSTER	PUPPETRY	PURER	PURL	PURPURES
PUNSTERS	PUPPETS	PURES	PURLED	PURPURIC
PUNT	PUPPIED	PUREST	PURLER	PURPURIN
PUNTED	PUPPIES	PURFLE	PURLERS	PURPURINS
PUNTEE	PUPPING	PURFLED	PURLICUE	PURPY
PUNTEES	PUPPODUM	PURFLER	PURLICUED	PURR
PUNTER	PUPPODUMS	PURFLERS	PURLICUES	PURRED
PUNTERS	PUPPY	PURFLES	PURLIEU	PURRING
PUNTIES	PUPPYDOM	PURFLING	PURLIEUS	PURRINGLY
PUNTING	PUPPYDOMS	PURFLINGS	PURLIEUX	PURRINGS
PUNTO	PUPPYHOOD	PURFLY	PURLIN	PURRS
PUNTOS	PUPPYING	PURGATION	PURLINE	PURS
PUNTS	PUPPYISH	PURGATIVE	PURLINES	PURSE
PUNTSMAN	PUPPYISM	PURGATORY	PURLING	PURSED
PUNTSMEN	PUPPYISMS	PURGE	PURLINGS	PURSEFUL
PUNTY	PUPPYLIKE	PURGEABLE	PURLINS	PURSEFULS
PUNY	PUPS	PURGED	PURLOIN	PURSELIKE
PUP	PUPU	PURGER	PURLOINED	PURSER
PUPA	PUPUNHA	PURGERS	PURLOINER	PURSERS
PUPAE	PUPUNHAS	PURGES	PURLOINS	PURSES
PUPAL	PUPUS	PURGING	PURLS	PURSEW
PUPARIA	PUR	PURGINGS	PUROMYCIN	PURSEWED

PURSEWING	PUSHBALL	PUSSIEST	PUTONS	PUTZED
PURSEWS	PUSHBALLS	PUSSLEY	PUTOUT	PUTZES
PURSIER	PUSHBIKE	PUSSLEYS	PUTOUTS	PUTZING
PURSIEST	PUSHBIKES	PUSSLIES	PUTREFIED	PUY
PURSILY	PUSHCART	PUSSLIKE	PUTREFIER	PUYS
PURSINESS	PUSHCARTS	PUSSLY	PUTREFIES	PUZEL
PURSING	PUSHCHAIR	PUSSY	PUTREFY	PUZELS
PURSLAIN	PUSHDOWN	PUSSYCAT	PUTRID	PUZZEL
PURSLAINS	PUSHDOWNS	PUSSYCATS	PUTRIDER	PUZZELS
PURSLANE	PUSHED	PUSSYFOOT	PUTRIDEST	PUZZLE
PURSLANES	PUSHER	PUSSYTOES	PUTRIDITY	PUZZLED
PURSUABLE	PUSHERS	PUSTULANT	PUTRIDLY	PUZZLEDLY
PURSUAL	PUSHES	PUSTULAR	PUTS	PUZZLEDOM
PURSUALS	PUSHFUL	PUSTULATE	PUTSCH	PUZZLER
PURSUANCE	PUSHFULLY	PUSTULE	PUTSCHES	PUZZLERS
PURSUANT	PUSHIER	PUSTULED	PUTSCHIST	PUZZLES
PURSUE	PUSHIEST	PUSTULES	PUTT	PUZZLING
PURSUED	PUSHILY	PUSTULOUS	PUTTED	PUZZOLANA
PURSUER	PUSHINESS	PUT	PUTTEE	PWN
PURSUERS	PUSHING	PUTAMEN	PUTTEES	PWNED
PURSUES	PUSHINGLY	PUTAMENS	PUTTEN	PWNING
PURSUING	PUSHOVER	PUTAMINA	PUTTER	PWNS
PURSUINGS	PUSHOVERS	PUTATIVE	PUTTERED	PYA
PURSUIT	PUSHPIN	PUTCHEON	PUTTERER	PYAEMIA
PURSUITS	PUSHPINS	PUTCHEONS	PUTTERERS	PYAEMIAS
PURSY	PUSHPIT	PUTCHER	PUTTERING	PYAEMIC
PURTIER	PUSHPITS	PUTCHERS	PUTTERS	PYAS
PURTIEST	PUSHROD	PUTCHOCK	PUTTI	PYAT
PURTRAID	PUSHRODS	PUTCHOCKS	PUTTIE	PYATS
PURTRAYD	PUSHUP	PUTCHUK	PUTTIED	PYCNIC
PURTY	PUSHUPS	PUTCHUKS	PUTTIER	PYCNIDIA
PURULENCE	PUSHY	PUTDOWN	PUTTIERS	PYCNIDIAL
PURULENCY	PUSLE	PUTDOWNS	PUTTIES	PYCNIDIUM
PURULENT	PUSLED	PUTEAL	PUTTING	PYCNITE
PURVEY	PUSLES	PUTEALS	PUTTINGS	PYCNITES
PURVEYED	PUSLEY	PUTELI	PUTTO	PYCNON
PURVEYING	PUSLEYS	PUTELIS	PUTTOCK	PYCNONS
PURVEYOR	PUSLIKE	PUTID	PUTTOCKS	PYCNOSES
PURVEYORS	PUSLING	PUTLOCK	PUTTS	PYCNOSIS
PURVEYS	PUSS	PUTLOCKS	PUTTY	PYCNOSOME
PURVIEW	PUSSEL	PUTLOG	PUTTYING	PYCNOTIC
PURVIEWS	PUSSELS	PUTLOGS	PUTTYLESS	PYE
PUS	PUSSER	PUTOFF	PUTTYLIKE	PYEBALD
PUSES	PUSSERS	PUTOFFS	PUTTYROOT	PYEBALDS
PUSH	PUSSES	PUTOIS	PUTURE	PYEING
PUSHBACK	PUSSIER	PUTON	PUTURES	PYELITIC
PUSHBACKS	PUSSIES	PUTONGHUA	PUTZ	PYELITIS

P

PYELOGRAM	PYLORIC	PYRANS	PYROHIES	PYROSTAT
PYEMIA	PYLORUS	PYRAZOLE	PYROHY	PYROSTATS
PYEMIAS	PYLORUSES	PYRAZOLES	PYROLA	PYROXENE
PYEMIC	PYNE	PYRE	PYROLAS	PYROXENES
PYENGADU	PYNED	PYRENE	PYROLATER	PYROXENIC
PYENGADUS	PYNES	PYRENEITE	PYROLATRY	PYROXYLE
PYES	PYNING	PYRENES	PYROLISE	PYROXYLES
PYET	PYODERMA	PYRENOID	PYROLISED	PYROXYLIC
PYETS	PYODERMAS	PYRENOIDS	PYROLISES	PYROXYLIN
PYGAL	PYODERMIC	PYRES	PYROLIZE	PYRRHIC
PYGALS	PYOGENIC	PYRETHRIN	PYROLIZED	PYRRHICS
PYGARG	PYOID	PYRETHRUM	PYROLIZES	PYRRHOUS
PYGARGS	PYONER	PYRETIC	PYROLOGY	PYRROL
PYGARGUS	PYONERS	PYREX	PYROLYSE	PYRROLE
PYGIDIA	PYONINGS	PYREXES	PYROLYSED	PYRROLES
PYGIDIAL	PYORRHEA	PYREXIA	PYROLYSER	PYRROLIC
PYGIDIUM	PYORRHEAL	PYREXIAL	PYROLYSES	PYRROLS
PYGIDIUMS	PYORRHEAS	PYREXIAS	PYROLYSIS	PYRUVATE
PYGMAEAN	PYORRHEIC	PYREXIC	PYROLYTIC	PYRUVATES
PYGMEAN	PYORRHOEA	PYRIC	PYROLYZE	PYRUVIC
PYGMIES	PYOSES	PYRIDIC	PYROLYZED	PYSANKA
PYGMOID	PYOSIS	PYRIDINE	PYROLYZER	PYSANKY
PYGMOIDS	PYOT	PYRIDINES	PYROLYZES	PYTHIUM
PYGMY	PYOTS	PYRIDOXAL	PYROMANCY	PYTHIUMS
PYGMYISH	PYRACANTH	PYRIDOXIN	PYROMANIA	PYTHON
PYGMYISM	PYRAL	PYRIFORM	PYROMETER	PYTHONESS
PYGMYISMS	PYRALID	PYRITE	PYROMETRY	PYTHONIC
PYGOSTYLE	PYRALIDID	PYRITES	PYRONE	PYTHONS
PYIC	PYRALIDS	PYRITIC	PYRONES	PYURIA
PYIN	PYRALIS	PYRITICAL	PYRONIN	PYURIAS
PYINKADO	PYRALISES	PYRITISE	PYRONINE	PYX
PYINKADOS	PYRAMID	PYRITISED	PYRONINES	PYXED
PYINS	PYRAMIDAL	PYRITISES	PYRONINS	PYXES
PYJAMA	PYRAMIDED	PYRITIZE	PYROPE	PYXIDES
PYJAMAED	PYRAMIDES	PYRITIZED	PYROPES	PYXIDIA
PYJAMAS	PYRAMIDIA	PYRITIZES	PYROPHONE	PYXIDIUM
PYKNIC	PYRAMIDIC	PYRITOUS	PYROPUS	PYXIE
PYKNICS	PYRAMIDON	PYRO	PYROPUSES	PYXIES
PYKNOSES	PYRAMIDS	PYROCERAM	PYROS	PYXING
PYKNOSIS	PYRAMIS	PYROCLAST	PYROSCOPE	PYXIS
PYKNOSOME	PYRAMISES	PYROGEN	PYROSES	PZAZZ
PYKNOTIC	PYRAN	PYROGENIC	PYROSIS	PZAZZES
PYLON	PYRANOID	PYROGENS	PYROSISES	
PYLONS	PYRANOSE	PYROGIES	PYROSOME	
PYLORI	PYRANOSES	PYROGY	PYROSOMES	

Q

QABALA
QABALAH
QABALAHS
QABALAS
QABALISM
QABALISMS
QABALIST
QABALISTS
QADI
QADIS
QAID
QAIDS
QAIMAQAM
QAIMAQAMS
QAJAQ
QAJAQS
QALAMDAN
QALAMDANS
QAMUTIK
QAMUTIKS
QANAT
QANATS
QASIDA
QASIDAS
QAT
QATS
QAWWAL
QAWWALI
QAWWALIS
QAWWALS
QI
QIBLA
QIBLAS
QIGONG
QIGONGS
QIN
QINDAR
QINDARKA
QINDARS
QINGHAOSU
QINS

QINTAR
QINTARKA
QINTARS
QIS
QIVIUT
QIVIUTS
QOPH
QOPHS
QORMA
QORMAS
QUA
QUAALUDE
QUAALUDES
QUACK
QUACKED
QUACKER
QUACKERS
QUACKERY
QUACKIER
QUACKIEST
QUACKING
QUACKISH
QUACKISM
QUACKISMS
QUACKLE
QUACKLED
QUACKLES
QUACKLING
QUACKS
QUACKY
QUAD
QUADDED
QUADDING
QUADDINGS
QUADPLAY
QUADPLAYS
QUADPLEX
QUADRANS
QUADRANT
QUADRANTS
QUADRAT

QUADRATE
QUADRATED
QUADRATES
QUADRATI
QUADRATIC
QUADRATS
QUADRATUS
QUADRELLA
QUADRIC
QUADRICEP
QUADRICS
QUADRIFID
QUADRIGA
QUADRIGAE
QUADRIGAS
QUADRILLE
QUADRIVIA
QUADROON
QUADROONS
QUADRUMAN
QUADRUPED
QUADRUPLE
QUADRUPLY
QUADS
QUAERE
QUAERED
QUAEREING
QUAERES
QUAERITUR
QUAESITUM
QUAESTOR
QUAESTORS
QUAFF
QUAFFABLE
QUAFFED
QUAFFER
QUAFFERS
QUAFFING
QUAFFS
QUAG
QUAGGA

QUAGGAS
QUAGGIER
QUAGGIEST
QUAGGY
QUAGMIRE
QUAGMIRED
QUAGMIRES
QUAGMIRY
QUAGS
QUAHAUG
QUAHAUGS
QUAHOG
QUAHOGS
QUAI
QUAICH
QUAICHES
QUAICHS
QUAIGH
QUAIGHS
QUAIL
QUAILED
QUAILING
QUAILINGS
QUAILS
QUAINT
QUAINTER
QUAINTEST
QUAINTLY
QUAIR
QUAIRS
QUAIS
QUAKE
QUAKED
QUAKER
QUAKERS
QUAKES
QUAKIER
QUAKIEST
QUAKILY
QUAKINESS
QUAKING

QUAKINGLY
QUAKINGS
QUAKY
QUALE
QUALIA
QUALIFIED
QUALIFIER
QUALIFIES
QUALIFY
QUALITIED
QUALITIES
QUALITY
QUALM
QUALMIER
QUALMIEST
QUALMING
QUALMINGS
QUALMISH
QUALMLESS
QUALMS
QUALMY
QUAMASH
QUAMASHES
QUANDANG
QUANDANGS
QUANDARY
QUANDONG
QUANDONGS
QUANGO
QUANGOS
QUANNET
QUANNETS
QUANT
QUANTA
QUANTAL
QUANTALLY
QUANTED
QUANTIC
QUANTICAL
QUANTICS
QUANTIFY

QUANTILE	QUARTERLY	QUAT	QUEASILY	QUEERNESS
QUANTILES	QUARTERN	QUATCH	QUEASY	QUEERS
QUANTING	QUARTERNS	QUATCHED	QUEAZIER	QUEEST
QUANTISE	QUARTERS	QUATCHES	QUEAZIEST	QUEESTS
QUANTISED	QUARTES	QUATCHING	QUEAZY	QUEINT
QUANTISER	QUARTET	QUATE	QUEBEC	QUELCH
QUANTISES	QUARTETS	QUATES	QUEBECS	QUELCHED
QUANTITY	QUARTETT	QUATORZE	QUEBRACHO	QUELCHES
QUANTIZE	QUARTETTE	QUATORZES	QUEECHIER	QUELCHING
QUANTIZED	QUARTETTI	QUATRAIN	QUEECHY	QUELEA
QUANTIZER	QUARTETTO	QUATRAINS	QUEEN	QUELEAS
QUANTIZES	QUARTETTS	QUATRE	QUEENCAKE	QUELL
QUANTONG	QUARTIC	QUATRES	QUEENCUP	QUELLABLE
QUANTONGS	QUARTICS	QUATS	QUEENCUPS	QUELLED
QUANTS	QUARTIER	QUATTED	QUEENDOM	QUELLER
QUANTUM	QUARTIERS	QUATTING	QUEENDOMS	QUELLERS
QUANTUMS	QUARTILE	QUAVER	QUEENED	QUELLING
QUARE	QUARTILES	QUAVERED	QUEENFISH	QUELLS
QUARENDEN	QUARTO	QUAVERER	QUEENHOOD	QUEME
QUARENDER	QUARTOS	QUAVERERS	QUEENIE	QUEMED
QUARER	QUARTS	QUAVERIER	QUEENIER	QUEMES
QUAREST	QUARTZ	QUAVERING	QUEENIES	QUEMING
QUARK	QUARTZES	QUAVERS	QUEENIEST	QUENA
QUARKS	QUARTZIER	QUAVERY	QUEENING	QUENAS
QUARREL	QUARTZITE	QUAY	QUEENINGS	QUENCH
QUARRELED	QUARTZOSE	QUAYAGE	QUEENITE	QUENCHED
QUARRELER	QUARTZOUS	QUAYAGES	QUEENITES	QUENCHER
QUARRELS	QUARTZY	QUAYD	QUEENLESS	QUENCHERS
QUARRIAN	QUASAR	QUAYLIKE	QUEENLET	QUENCHES
QUARRIANS	QUASARS	QUAYS	QUEENLETS	QUENCHING
QUARRIED	QUASH	QUAYSIDE	QUEENLIER	QUENELLE
QUARRIER	QUASHED	QUAYSIDES	QUEENLY	QUENELLES
QUARRIERS	QUASHEE	QUAZZIER	QUEENS	QUEP
QUARRIES	QUASHEES	QUAZZIEST	QUEENSHIP	QUERCETIC
QUARRION	QUASHER	QUAZZY	QUEENSIDE	QUERCETIN
QUARRIONS	QUASHERS	QUBIT	QUEENY	QUERCETUM
QUARRY	QUASHES	QUBITS	QUEER	QUERCINE
QUARRYING	QUASHIE	QUBYTE	QUEERCORE	QUERCITIN
QUARRYMAN	QUASHIES	QUBYTES	QUEERDOM	QUERIDA
QUARRYMEN	QUASHING	QUEACH	QUEERDOMS	QUERIDAS
QUART	QUASI	QUEACHES	QUEERED	QUERIED
QUARTAN	QUASS	QUEACHIER	QUEERER	QUERIER
QUARTANS	QUASSES	QUEACHY	QUEEREST	QUERIERS
QUARTE	QUASSIA	QUEAN	QUEERING	QUERIES
QUARTER	QUASSIAS	QUEANS	QUEERISH	QUERIMONY
QUARTERED	QUASSIN	QUEASIER	QUEERITY	QUERIST
QUARTERER	QUASSINS	QUEASIEST	QUEERLY	QUERISTS

QUERN	QUEZAL	QUIDDLERS	QUILLAIS	QUINIDINE
QUERNS	QUEZALES	QUIDDLES	QUILLAJA	QUINIE
QUERULOUS	QUEZALS	QUIDDLING	QUILLAJAS	QUINIELA
QUERY	QUIBBLE	QUIDNUNC	QUILLBACK	QUINIELAS
QUERYING	QUIBBLED	QUIDNUNCS	QUILLED	QUINIES
QUERYINGS	QUIBBLER	QUIDS	QUILLET	QUININ
QUEST	QUIBBLERS	QUIESCE	QUILLETS	QUININA
QUESTANT	QUIBBLES	QUIESCED	QUILLING	QUININAS
QUESTANTS	QUIBBLING	QUIESCENT	QUILLINGS	QUININE
QUESTED	QUIBLIN	QUIESCES	QUILLMAN	QUININES
QUESTER	QUIBLINS	QUIESCING	QUILLMEN	QUININS
QUESTERS	QUICH	QUIET	QUILLON	QUINNAT
QUESTING	QUICHE	QUIETED	QUILLONS	QUINNATS
QUESTINGS	QUICHED	QUIETEN	QUILLOW	QUINO
QUESTION	QUICHES	QUIETENED	QUILLOWS	QUINOA
QUESTIONS	QUICHING	QUIETENER	QUILLS	QUINOAS
QUESTOR	QUICK	QUIETENS	QUILLWORK	QUINOID
QUESTORS	QUICKBEAM	QUIETER	QUILLWORT	QUINOIDAL
QUESTRIST	QUICKEN	QUIETERS	QUILT	QUINOIDS
QUESTS	QUICKENED	QUIETEST	QUILTED	QUINOL
QUETCH	QUICKENER	QUIETING	QUILTER	QUINOLIN
QUETCHED	QUICKENS	QUIETINGS	QUILTERS	QUINOLINE
QUETCHES	QUICKER	QUIETISM	QUILTING	QUINOLINS
QUETCHING	QUICKEST	QUIETISMS	QUILTINGS	QUINOLONE
QUETHE	QUICKFIRE	QUIETIST	QUILTS	QUINOLS
QUETHES	QUICKIE	QUIETISTS	QUIM	QUINONE
QUETHING	QUICKIES	QUIETIVE	QUIMS	QUINONES
QUETSCH	QUICKLIME	QUIETIVES	QUIN	QUINONOID
QUETSCHES	QUICKLY	QUIETLY	QUINA	QUINOS
QUETZAL	QUICKNESS	QUIETNESS	QUINARIES	QUINQUINA
QUETZALES	QUICKS	QUIETS	QUINARY	QUINS
QUETZALS	QUICKSAND	QUIETSOME	QUINAS	QUINSIED
QUEUE	QUICKSET	QUIETUDE	QUINATE	QUINSIES
QUEUED	QUICKSETS	QUIETUDES	QUINCE	QUINSY
QUEUEING	QUICKSTEP	QUIETUS	QUINCES	QUINT
QUEUEINGS	QUICKY	QUIETUSES	QUINCHE	QUINTA
QUEUER	QUID	QUIFF	QUINCHED	QUINTAIN
QUEUERS	QUIDAM	QUIFFED	QUINCHES	QUINTAINS
QUEUES	QUIDAMS	QUIFFS	QUINCHING	QUINTAL
QUEUING	QUIDDANY	QUIGHT	QUINCUNX	QUINTALS
QUEUINGS	QUIDDIT	QUIGHTED	QUINE	QUINTAN
QUEY	QUIDDITCH	QUIGHTING	QUINELA	QUINTANS
QUEYN	QUIDDITS	QUIGHTS	QUINELAS	QUINTAR
QUEYNIE	QUIDDITY	QUILL	QUINELLA	QUINTARS
QUEYNIES	QUIDDLE	QUILLAI	QUINELLAS	QUINTAS
QUEYNS	QUIDDLED	QUILLAIA	QUINES	QUINTE
QUEYS	QUIDDLER	QUILLAIAS	QUINIC	QUINTES

Q

QUINTET	QUIPSTERS	QUITTAL	QUODDED	QUOPPED
QUINTETS	QUIPU	QUITTALS	QUODDING	QUOPPING
QUINTETT	QUIPUS	QUITTANCE	QUODLIBET	QUOPS
QUINTETTE	QUIRE	QUITTED	QUODLIN	QUORATE
QUINTETTI	QUIRED	QUITTER	QUODLINS	QUORUM
QUINTETTO	QUIRES	QUITTERS	QUODS	QUORUMS
QUINTETTS	QUIRING	QUITTING	QUOHOG	QUOTA
QUINTIC	QUIRISTER	QUITTOR	QUOHOGS	QUOTABLE
QUINTICS	QUIRK	QUITTORS	QUOIF	QUOTABLY
QUINTILE	QUIRKED	QUIVER	QUOIFED	QUOTAS
QUINTILES	QUIRKIER	QUIVERED	QUOIFING	QUOTATION
QUINTIN	QUIRKIEST	QUIVERER	QUOIFS	QUOTATIVE
QUINTINS	QUIRKILY	QUIVERERS	QUOIN	QUOTE
QUINTROON	QUIRKING	QUIVERFUL	QUOINED	QUOTED
QUINTS	QUIRKISH	QUIVERIER	QUOINING	QUOTER
QUINTUPLE	QUIRKS	QUIVERING	QUOININGS	QUOTERS
QUINTUPLY	QUIRKY	QUIVERISH	QUOINS	QUOTES
QUINZE	QUIRT	QUIVERS	QUOIST	QUOTH
QUINZES	QUIRTED	QUIVERY	QUOISTS	QUOTHA
QUINZHEE	QUIRTING	QUIXOTE	QUOIT	QUOTIDIAN
QUINZHEES	QUIRTS	QUIXOTES	QUOITED	QUOTIENT
QUINZIE	QUISLING	QUIXOTIC	QUOITER	QUOTIENTS
QUINZIES	QUISLINGS	QUIXOTISM	QUOITERS	QUOTING
QUIP	QUIST	QUIXOTRY	QUOITING	QUOTITION
QUIPO	QUISTS	QUIZ	QUOITS	QUOTUM
QUIPOS	QUIT	QUIZZED	QUOKKA	QUOTUMS
QUIPPED	QUITCH	QUIZZER	QUOKKAS	QURSH
QUIPPER	QUITCHED	QUIZZERS	QUOLL	QURSHES
QUIPPERS	QUITCHES	QUIZZERY	QUOLLS	QURUSH
QUIPPIER	QUITCHING	QUIZZES	QUOMODO	QURUSHES
QUIPPIEST	QUITCLAIM	QUIZZICAL	QUOMODOS	QUYTE
QUIPPING	QUITE	QUIZZIFY	QUONDAM	QUYTED
QUIPPISH	QUITED	QUIZZING	QUONK	QUYTES
QUIPPU	QUITES	QUIZZINGS	QUONKED	QUYTING
QUIPPUS	QUITING	QULLIQ	QUONKING	QWERTIES
QUIPPY	QUITRENT	QULLIQS	QUONKS	QWERTY
QUIPS	QUITRENTS	QUOAD	QUOOKE	QWERTYS
QUIPSTER	QUITS	QUOD	QUOP	

R

RABANNA	RABBITS	RACEMES	RACIAL	RACKLES
RABANNAS	RABBITY	RACEMIC	RACIALISE	RACKS
RABASKA	RABBLE	RACEMISE	RACIALISM	RACKWORK
RABASKAS	RABBLED	RACEMISED	RACIALIST	RACKWORKS
RABAT	RABBLER	RACEMISES	RACIALIZE	RACLETTE
RABATINE	RABBLERS	RACEMISM	RACIALLY	RACLETTES
RABATINES	RABBLES	RACEMISMS	RACIATION	RACLOIR
RABATMENT	RABBLING	RACEMIZE	RACIER	RACLOIRS
RABATO	RABBLINGS	RACEMIZED	RACIEST	RACON
RABATOES	RABBONI	RACEMIZES	RACILY	RACONS
RABATOS	RABBONIS	RACEMOID	RACINESS	RACONTEUR
RABATS	RABI	RACEMOSE	RACING	RACOON
RABATTE	RABIC	RACEMOUS	RACINGS	RACOONS
RABATTED	RABID	RACEPATH	RACINO	RACQUET
RABATTES	RABIDER	RACEPATHS	RACINOS	RACQUETED
RABATTING	RABIDEST	RACER	RACISM	RACQUETS
RABBET	RABIDITY	RACERS	RACISMS	RACY
RABBETED	RABIDLY	RACES	RACIST	RAD
RABBETING	RABIDNESS	RACETRACK	RACISTS	RADAR
RABBETS	RABIES	RACEWALK	RACK	RADARS
RABBI	RABIETIC	RACEWALKS	RACKED	RADDED
RABBIES	RABIS	RACEWAY	RACKER	RADDER
RABBIN	RACA	RACEWAYS	RACKERS	RADDEST
RABBINATE	RACAHOUT	RACH	RACKET	RADDING
RABBINIC	RACAHOUTS	RACHE	RACKETED	RADDLE
RABBINICS	RACCAHOUT	RACHES	RACKETEER	RADDLED
RABBINISM	RACCOON	RACHET	RACKETER	RADDLEMAN
RABBINIST	RACCOONS	RACHETED	RACKETERS	RADDLEMEN
RABBINITE	RACE	RACHETING	RACKETIER	RADDLES
RABBINS	RACEABLE	RACHETS	RACKETING	RADDLING
RABBIS	RACECARD	RACHIAL	RACKETRY	RADDOCKE
RABBIT	RACECARDS	RACHIDES	RACKETS	RADDOCKES
RABBITED	RACED	RACHIDIAL	RACKETT	RADE
RABBITER	RACEGOER	RACHIDIAN	RACKETTS	RADGE
RABBITERS	RACEGOERS	RACHILLA	RACKETY	RADGER
RABBITING	RACEGOING	RACHILLAE	RACKFUL	RADGES
RABBITO	RACEHORSE	RACHILLAS	RACKFULS	RADGEST
RABBITOH	RACEMATE	RACHIS	RACKING	RADIABLE
RABBITOHS	RACEMATES	RACHISES	RACKINGLY	RADIAL
RABBITOS	RACEME	RACHITIC	RACKINGS	RADIALE
RABBITRY	RACEMED	RACHITIS	RACKLE	RADIALIA

RADIALISE	RADIOGOLD	RAFFS	RAGGINGS	RAGWHEELS
RADIALITY	RADIOGRAM	RAFT	RAGGLE	RAGWORK
RADIALIZE	RADIOING	RAFTED	RAGGLED	RAGWORKS
RADIALLY	RADIOLOGY	RAFTER	RAGGLES	RAGWORM
RADIALS	RADIOMAN	RAFTERED	RAGGLING	RAGWORMS
RADIAN	RADIOMEN	RAFTERING	RAGGS	RAGWORT
RADIANCE	RADIONICS	RAFTERS	RAGGY	RAGWORTS
RADIANCES	RADIOS	RAFTING	RAGHEAD	RAH
RADIANCY	RADIOTHON	RAFTINGS	RAGHEADS	RAHED
RADIANS	RADISH	RAFTMAN	RAGI	RAHING
RADIANT	RADISHES	RAFTMEN	RAGING	RAHS
RADIANTLY	RADIUM	RAFTS	RAGINGLY	RAHUI
RADIANTS	RADIUMS	RAFTSMAN	RAGINGS	RAHUIS
RADIATA	RADIUS	RAFTSMEN	RAGINI	RAI
RADIATAS	RADIUSED	RAG	RAGINIS	RAIA
RADIATE	RADIUSES	RAGA	RAGIS	RAIAS
RADIATED	RADIUSING	RAGAS	RAGLAN	RAID
RADIATELY	RADIX	RAGBAG	RAGLANS	RAIDED
RADIATES	RADIXES	RAGBAGS	RAGMAN	RAIDER
RADIATING	RADOME	RAGBOLT	RAGMANS	RAIDERS
RADIATION	RADOMES	RAGBOLTS	RAGMEN	RAIDING
RADIATIVE	RADON	RAGDE	RAGMENT	RAIDINGS
RADIATOR	RADONS	RAGE	RAGMENTS	RAIDS
RADIATORS	RADS	RAGED	RAGOUT	RAIK
RADIATORY	RADULA	RAGEE	RAGOUTED	RAIKED
RADICAL	RADULAE	RAGEES	RAGOUTING	RAIKING
RADICALLY	RADULAR	RAGEFUL	RAGOUTS	RAIKS
RADICALS	RADULAS	RAGER	RAGPICKER	RAIL
RADICAND	RADULATE	RAGERS	RAGS	RAILAGE
RADICANDS	RADWASTE	RAGES	RAGSTONE	RAILAGES
RADICANT	RADWASTES	RAGG	RAGSTONES	RAILBED
RADICATE	RAFALE	RAGGA	RAGTAG	RAILBEDS
RADICATED	RAFALES	RAGGAS	RAGTAGS	RAILBIRD
RADICATES	RAFF	RAGGED	RAGTAIL	RAILBIRDS
RADICCHIO	RAFFIA	RAGGEDER	RAGTIME	RAILBUS
RADICEL	RAFFIAS	RAGGEDEST	RAGTIMER	RAILBUSES
RADICELS	RAFFINATE	RAGGEDIER	RAGTIMERS	RAILCAR
RADICES	RAFFINOSE	RAGGEDLY	RAGTIMES	RAILCARD
RADICLE	RAFFISH	RAGGEDY	RAGTOP	RAILCARDS
RADICLES	RAFFISHLY	RAGGEE	RAGTOPS	RAILCARS
RADICULAR	RAFFLE	RAGGEES	RAGU	RAILE
RADICULE	RAFFLED	RAGGERIES	RAGULED	RAILED
RADICULES	RAFFLER	RAGGERY	RAGULY	RAILER
RADII	RAFFLERS	RAGGIER	RAGUS	RAILERS
RADIO	RAFFLES	RAGGIES	RAGWEED	RAILES
RADIOED	RAFFLESIA	RAGGIEST	RAGWEEDS	RAILHEAD
RADIOES	RAFFLING	RAGGING	RAGWHEEL	RAILHEADS

RAILING	RAINOUTS	RAJES	RALPH	RAMILIES
RAILINGLY	RAINPROOF	RAKE	RALPHED	RAMILLIE
RAILINGS	RAINS	RAKED	RALPHING	RAMILLIES
RAILLERY	RAINSPOUT	RAKEE	RALPHS	RAMIN
RAILLESS	RAINSTICK	RAKEES	RAM	RAMINS
RAILLIES	RAINSTORM	RAKEHELL	RAMADA	RAMIS
RAILLY	RAINSUIT	RAKEHELLS	RAMADAS	RAMJET
RAILMAN	RAINSUITS	RAKEHELLY	RAMAKIN	RAMJETS
RAILMEN	RAINSWEPT	RAKEOFF	RAMAKINS	RAMMED
RAILROAD	RAINTIGHT	RAKEOFFS	RAMAL	RAMMEL
RAILROADS	RAINWASH	RAKER	RAMATE	RAMMELS
RAILS	RAINWATER	RAKERIES	RAMBLA	RAMMER
RAILWAY	RAINWEAR	RAKERS	RAMBLAS	RAMMERS
RAILWAYS	RAINWEARS	RAKERY	RAMBLE	RAMMIER
RAILWOMAN	RAINY	RAKES	RAMBLED	RAMMIES
RAILWOMEN	RAIRD	RAKESHAME	RAMBLER	RAMMIEST
RAIMENT	RAIRDS	RAKI	RAMBLERS	RAMMING
RAIMENTS	RAIS	RAKIA	RAMBLES	RAMMISH
RAIN	RAISABLE	RAKIAS	RAMBLING	RAMMISHLY
RAINBAND	RAISE	RAKIJA	RAMBLINGS	RAMMLE
RAINBANDS	RAISEABLE	RAKIJAS	RAMBUTAN	RAMMLES
RAINBIRD	RAISED	RAKING	RAMBUTANS	RAMMY
RAINBIRDS	RAISER	RAKINGS	RAMCAT	RAMONA
RAINBOW	RAISERS	RAKIS	RAMCATS	RAMONAS
RAINBOWED	RAISES	RAKISH	RAMEAL	RAMOSE
RAINBOWS	RAISIN	RAKISHLY	RAMEE	RAMOSELY
RAINBOWY	RAISING	RAKSHAS	RAMEES	RAMOSITY
RAINCHECK	RAISINGS	RAKSHASA	RAMEKIN	RAMOUS
RAINCOAT	RAISINS	RAKSHASAS	RAMEKINS	RAMOUSLY
RAINCOATS	RAISINY	RAKSHASES	RAMEN	RAMP
RAINDATE	RAISONNE	RAKU	RAMENS	RAMPAGE
RAINDATES	RAIT	RAKUS	RAMENTA	RAMPAGED
RAINDROP	RAITA	RALE	RAMENTUM	RAMPAGER
RAINDROPS	RAITAS	RALES	RAMEOUS	RAMPAGERS
RAINE	RAITED	RALLIED	RAMEQUIN	RAMPAGES
RAINED	RAITING	RALLIER	RAMEQUINS	RAMPAGING
RAINES	RAITS	RALLIERS	RAMET	RAMPANCY
RAINFALL	RAIYAT	RALLIES	RAMETS	RAMPANT
RAINFALLS	RAIYATS	RALLIFORM	RAMI	RAMPANTLY
RAINIER	RAJ	RALLINE	RAMIE	RAMPART
RAINIEST	RAJA	RALLY	RAMIES	RAMPARTED
RAINILY	RAJAH	RALLYE	RAMIFIED	RAMPARTS
RAININESS	RAJAHS	RALLYES	RAMIFIES	RAMPAUGE
RAINING	RAJAHSHIP	RALLYING	RAMIFORM	RAMPAUGED
RAINLESS	RAJAS	RALLYINGS	RAMIFY	RAMPAUGES
RAINMAKER	RAJASHIP	RALLYIST	RAMIFYING	RAMPED
RAINOUT	RAJASHIPS	RALLYISTS	RAMILIE	RAMPER

R

RAMPERS	RANCES	RANDLORDS	RANKES	RANZEL
RAMPICK	RANCH	RANDOM	RANKEST	RANZELMAN
RAMPICKED	RANCHED	RANDOMISE	RANKING	RANZELMEN
RAMPICKS	RANCHER	RANDOMIZE	RANKINGS	RANZELS
RAMPIKE	RANCHERA	RANDOMLY	RANKISH	RAOULIA
RAMPIKES	RANCHERAS	RANDOMS	RANKISM	RAOULIAS
RAMPING	RANCHERIA	RANDON	RANKISMS	RAP
RAMPINGS	RANCHERIE	RANDONS	RANKIST	RAPACIOUS
RAMPION	RANCHERO	RANDS	RANKISTS	RAPACITY
RAMPIONS	RANCHEROS	RANDY	RANKLE	RAPE
RAMPIRE	RANCHERS	RANEE	RANKLED	RAPED
RAMPIRED	RANCHES	RANEES	RANKLES	RAPER
RAMPIRES	RANCHING	RANG	RANKLESS	RAPERS
RAMPOLE	RANCHINGS	RANGA	RANKLING	RAPES
RAMPOLES	RANCHLESS	RANGAS	RANKLY	RAPESEED
RAMPS	RANCHLIKE	RANGATIRA	RANKNESS	RAPESEEDS
RAMPSMAN	RANCHMAN	RANGE	RANKS	RAPHAE
RAMPSMEN	RANCHMEN	RANGED	RANKSHIFT	RAPHANIA
RAMROD	RANCHO	RANGELAND	RANPIKE	RAPHANIAS
RAMRODDED	RANCHOS	RANGER	RANPIKES	RAPHE
RAMRODS	RANCID	RANGERS	RANSACK	RAPHES
RAMS	RANCIDER	RANGES	RANSACKED	RAPHIA
RAMSHORN	RANCIDEST	RANGI	RANSACKER	RAPHIAS
RAMSHORNS	RANCIDITY	RANGIER	RANSACKS	RAPHIDE
RAMSON	RANCIDLY	RANGIEST	RANSEL	RAPHIDES
RAMSONS	RANCING	RANGILY	RANSELS	RAPHIS
RAMSTAM	RANCOR	RANGINESS	RANSHAKLE	RAPID
RAMTIL	RANCORED	RANGING	RANSOM	RAPIDER
RAMTILLA	RANCOROUS	RANGINGS	RANSOMED	RAPIDEST
RAMTILLAS	RANCORS	RANGIORA	RANSOMER	RAPIDITY
RAMTILS	RANCOUR	RANGIORAS	RANSOMERS	RAPIDLY
RAMULAR	RANCOURED	RANGIS	RANSOMING	RAPIDNESS
RAMULI	RANCOURS	RANGOLI	RANSOMS	RAPIDS
RAMULOSE	RAND	RANGOLIS	RANT	RAPIER
RAMULOUS	RANDAN	RANGS	RANTED	RAPIERED
RAMULUS	RANDANS	RANGY	RANTER	RAPIERS
RAMUS	RANDED	RANI	RANTERISM	RAPINE
RAN	RANDEM	RANID	RANTERS	RAPINES
RANA	RANDEMS	RANIDS	RANTING	RAPING
RANARIAN	RANDIE	RANIFORM	RANTINGLY	RAPINI
RANARIUM	RANDIER	RANINE	RANTINGS	RAPINIS
RANARIUMS	RANDIES	RANIS	RANTIPOLE	RAPIST
RANAS	RANDIEST	RANK	RANTS	RAPISTS
RANCE	RANDILY	RANKE	RANULA	RAPLOCH
RANCED	RANDINESS	RANKED	RANULAR	RAPLOCHS
RANCEL	RANDING	RANKER	RANULAS	RAPPAREE
RANCELS	RANDLORD	RANKERS	RANUNCULI	RAPPAREES

RAPPE	RARERIPE	RASMALAI	RATAFIAS	RATHERISH
RAPPED	RARERIPES	RASMALAIS	RATAL	RATHEST
RAPPEE	RARES	RASORIAL	RATALS	RATHOLE
RAPPEES	RAREST	RASP	RATAN	RATHOLES
RAPPEL	RARIFIED	RASPATORY	RATANIES	RATHOUSE
RAPPELED	RARIFIES	RASPBERRY	RATANS	RATHOUSES
RAPPELING	RARIFY	RASPED	RATANY	RATHRIPE
RAPPELLED	RARIFYING	RASPER	RATAPLAN	RATHRIPES
RAPPELS	RARING	RASPERS	RATAPLANS	RATHS
RAPPEN	RARITIES	RASPIER	RATAS	RATICIDE
RAPPER	RARITY	RASPIEST	RATATAT	RATICIDES
RAPPERS	RARK	RASPINESS	RATATATS	RATIFIED
RAPPES	RARKED	RASPING	RATBAG	RATIFIER
RAPPING	RARKING	RASPINGLY	RATBAGS	RATIFIERS
RAPPINGS	RARKS	RASPINGS	RATBITE	RATIFIES
RAPPINI	RAS	RASPISH	RATCH	RATIFY
RAPPORT	RASBORA	RASPS	RATCHED	RATIFYING
RAPPORTS	RASBORAS	RASPY	RATCHES	RATINE
RAPS	RASCAILLE	RASSE	RATCHET	RATINES
RAPT	RASCAL	RASSES	RATCHETED	RATING
RAPTLY	RASCALDOM	RASSLE	RATCHETS	RATINGS
RAPTNESS	RASCALISM	RASSLED	RATCHING	RATIO
RAPTOR	RASCALITY	RASSLER	RATE	RATION
RAPTORIAL	RASCALLY	RASSLERS	RATEABLE	RATIONAL
RAPTORS	RASCALS	RASSLES	RATEABLES	RATIONALE
RAPTURE	RASCASSE	RASSLING	RATEABLY	RATIONALS
RAPTURED	RASCASSES	RAST	RATED	RATIONED
RAPTURES	RASCHEL	RASTA	RATEEN	RATIONING
RAPTURING	RASCHELS	RASTAFARI	RATEENS	RATIONS
RAPTURISE	RASE	RASTER	RATEL	RATIOS
RAPTURIST	RASED	RASTERED	RATELS	RATITE
RAPTURIZE	RASER	RASTERING	RATEMETER	RATITES
RAPTUROUS	RASERS	RASTERISE	RATEPAYER	RATLIKE
RARE	RASES	RASTERIZE	RATER	RATLIN
RAREBIT	RASH	RASTERS	RATERS	RATLINE
RAREBITS	RASHED	RASTRUM	RATES	RATLINES
RARED	RASHER	RASTRUMS	RATFINK	RATLING
RAREE	RASHERS	RASURE	RATFINKS	RATLINGS
RAREFIED	RASHES	RASURES	RATFISH	RATLINS
RAREFIER	RASHEST	RAT	RATFISHES	RATO
RAREFIERS	RASHIE	RATA	RATH	RATOO
RAREFIES	RASHIES	RATABLE	RATHA	RATOON
RAREFY	RASHING	RATABLES	RATHAS	RATOONED
RAREFYING	RASHLIKE	RATABLY	RATHE	RATOONER
RARELY	RASHLY	RATAFEE	RATHER	RATOONERS
RARENESS	RASHNESS	RATAFEES	RATHEREST	RATOONING
RARER	RASING	RATAFIA	RATHERIPE	RATOONS

R

RATOOS
RATOS
RATPACK
RATPACKS
RATPROOF
RATS
RATSBANE
RATSBANES
RATTAIL
RATTAILED
RATTAILS
RATTAN
RATTANS
RATTED
RATTEEN
RATTEENS
RATTEN
RATTENED
RATTENER
RATTENERS
RATTENING
RATTENS
RATTER
RATTERIES
RATTERS
RATTERY
RATTIER
RATTIEST
RATTILY
RATTINESS
RATTING
RATTINGS
RATTISH
RATTLE
RATTLEBAG
RATTLEBOX
RATTLED
RATTLER
RATTLERS
RATTLES
RATTLIER
RATTLIEST
RATTLIN
RATTLINE
RATTLINES
RATTLING
RATTLINGS

RATTLINS
RATTLY
RATTON
RATTONS
RATTOON
RATTOONED
RATTOONS
RATTRAP
RATTRAPS
RATTY
RATU
RATUS
RAUCID
RAUCITIES
RAUCITY
RAUCLE
RAUCLER
RAUCLEST
RAUCOUS
RAUCOUSLY
RAUGHT
RAUN
RAUNCH
RAUNCHED
RAUNCHES
RAUNCHIER
RAUNCHILY
RAUNCHING
RAUNCHY
RAUNGE
RAUNGED
RAUNGES
RAUNGING
RAUNS
RAUPATU
RAUPATUS
RAUPO
RAUPOS
RAURIKI
RAURIKIS
RAUWOLFIA
RAV
RAVAGE
RAVAGED
RAVAGER
RAVAGERS
RAVAGES

RAVAGING
RAVE
RAVED
RAVEL
RAVELED
RAVELER
RAVELERS
RAVELIN
RAVELING
RAVELINGS
RAVELINS
RAVELLED
RAVELLER
RAVELLERS
RAVELLING
RAVELLY
RAVELMENT
RAVELS
RAVEN
RAVENED
RAVENER
RAVENERS
RAVENING
RAVENINGS
RAVENLIKE
RAVENOUS
RAVENS
RAVER
RAVERS
RAVES
RAVEY
RAVIER
RAVIEST
RAVIGOTE
RAVIGOTES
RAVIGOTTE
RAVIN
RAVINE
RAVINED
RAVINES
RAVING
RAVINGLY
RAVINGS
RAVINING
RAVINS
RAVIOLI
RAVIOLIS

RAVISH
RAVISHED
RAVISHER
RAVISHERS
RAVISHES
RAVISHING
RAVS
RAW
RAWARU
RAWARUS
RAWBONE
RAWBONED
RAWER
RAWEST
RAWHEAD
RAWHEADS
RAWHIDE
RAWHIDED
RAWHIDES
RAWHIDING
RAWIN
RAWING
RAWINGS
RAWINS
RAWISH
RAWLY
RAWMAISH
RAWN
RAWNESS
RAWNESSES
RAWNS
RAWS
RAX
RAXED
RAXES
RAXING
RAY
RAYA
RAYAH
RAYAHS
RAYAS
RAYED
RAYGRASS
RAYING
RAYLE
RAYLED
RAYLES

RAYLESS
RAYLESSLY
RAYLET
RAYLETS
RAYLIKE
RAYLING
RAYNE
RAYNES
RAYON
RAYONS
RAYS
RAZE
RAZED
RAZEE
RAZEED
RAZEEING
RAZEES
RAZER
RAZERS
RAZES
RAZING
RAZMATAZ
RAZOO
RAZOOS
RAZOR
RAZORABLE
RAZORBACK
RAZORBILL
RAZORCLAM
RAZORED
RAZORFISH
RAZORING
RAZORS
RAZURE
RAZURES
RAZZ
RAZZBERRY
RAZZED
RAZZES
RAZZIA
RAZZIAS
RAZZING
RAZZINGS
RAZZLE
RAZZLES
RE
REABSORB

R

REABSORBS	READER	REAKING	REALTERS	REAPPLIED
REACCEDE	READERLY	REAKS	REALTIE	REAPPLIES
REACCEDED	READERS	REAL	REALTIES	REAPPLY
REACCEDES	READIED	REALER	REALTIME	REAPPOINT
REACCENT	READIER	REALES	REALTONE	REAPPROVE
REACCENTS	READIES	REALEST	REALTONES	REAPS
REACCEPT	READIEST	REALGAR	REALTOR	REAR
REACCEPTS	READILY	REALGARS	REALTORS	REARED
REACCLAIM	READINESS	REALIA	REALTY	REARER
REACCUSE	READING	REALIGN	REAM	REARERS
REACCUSED	READINGS	REALIGNED	REAME	REARGUARD
REACCUSES	READJUST	REALIGNS	REAMED	REARGUE
REACH	READJUSTS	REALISE	REAMEND	REARGUED
REACHABLE	README	REALISED	REAMENDED	REARGUES
REACHED	READMIT	REALISER	REAMENDS	REARGUING
REACHER	READMITS	REALISERS	REAMER	REARHORSE
REACHERS	READOPT	REALISES	REAMERS	REARING
REACHES	READOPTED	REALISING	REAMES	REARINGS
REACHING	READOPTS	REALISM	REAMIER	REARISE
REACHLESS	READORN	REALISMS	REAMIEST	REARISEN
REACQUIRE	READORNED	REALIST	REAMING	REARISES
REACT	READORNS	REALISTIC	REAMS	REARISING
REACTANCE	READOUT	REALISTS	REAMY	REARLY
REACTANT	READOUTS	REALITIES	REAN	REARM
REACTANTS	READS	REALITY	REANALYSE	REARMED
REACTED	READVANCE	REALIZE	REANALYZE	REARMICE
REACTING	READVISE	REALIZED	REANIMATE	REARMING
REACTION	READVISED	REALIZER	REANNEX	REARMOST
REACTIONS	READVISES	REALIZERS	REANNEXED	REARMOUSE
REACTIVE	READY	REALIZES	REANNEXES	REARMS
REACTOR	READYING	REALIZING	REANOINT	REAROSE
REACTORS	READYMADE	REALLIE	REANOINTS	REAROUSAL
REACTS	REAEDIFY	REALLIED	REANS	REAROUSE
REACTUATE	REAEDIFYE	REALLIES	REANSWER	REAROUSED
READ	REAFFIRM	REALLOT	REANSWERS	REAROUSES
READABLE	REAFFIRMS	REALLOTS	REAP	REARRANGE
READABLY	REAFFIX	REALLY	REAPABLE	REARREST
READAPT	REAFFIXED	REALLYING	REAPED	REARRESTS
READAPTED	REAFFIXES	REALM	REAPER	REARS
READAPTS	REAGENCY	REALMLESS	REAPERS	REARWARD
READD	REAGENT	REALMS	REAPHOOK	REARWARDS
READDED	REAGENTS	REALNESS	REAPHOOKS	REASCEND
READDICT	REAGIN	REALO	REAPING	REASCENDS
READDICTS	REAGINIC	REALOS	REAPINGS	REASCENT
READDING	REAGINS	REALS	REAPPAREL	REASCENTS
READDRESS	REAK	REALTER	REAPPEAR	REASON
READDS	REAKED	REALTERED	REAPPEARS	REASONED

REASONER	REAVOWED	REBEC	REBOANT	REBRANDS
REASONERS	REAVOWING	REBECK	REBOARD	REBRED
REASONING	REAVOWS	REBECKS	REBOARDED	REBREED
REASONS	REAWAKE	REBECS	REBOARDS	REBREEDS
REASSAIL	REAWAKED	REBEGAN	REBOATION	REBS
REASSAILS	REAWAKEN	REBEGIN	REBODIED	REBUFF
REASSERT	REAWAKENS	REBEGINS	REBODIES	REBUFFED
REASSERTS	REAWAKES	REBEGUN	REBODY	REBUFFING
REASSESS	REAWAKING	REBEL	REBODYING	REBUFFS
REASSIGN	REAWOKE	REBELDOM	REBOIL	REBUILD
REASSIGNS	REAWOKEN	REBELDOMS	REBOILED	REBUILDED
REASSORT	REB	REBELLED	REBOILING	REBUILDS
REASSORTS	REBACK	REBELLER	REBOILS	REBUILT
REASSUME	REBACKED	REBELLERS	REBOOK	REBUKABLE
REASSUMED	REBACKING	REBELLING	REBOOKED	REBUKE
REASSUMES	REBACKS	REBELLION	REBOOKING	REBUKED
REASSURE	REBADGE	REBELLOW	REBOOKS	REBUKEFUL
REASSURED	REBADGED	REBELLOWS	REBOOT	REBUKER
REASSURER	REBADGES	REBELS	REBOOTED	REBUKERS
REASSURES	REBADGING	REBID	REBOOTING	REBUKES
REAST	REBAIT	REBIDDEN	REBOOTS	REBUKING
REASTED	REBAITED	REBIDDING	REBOP	REBURIAL
REASTIER	REBAITING	REBIDS	REBOPS	REBURIALS
REASTIEST	REBAITS	REBILL	REBORE	REBURIED
REASTING	REBALANCE	REBILLED	REBORED	REBURIES
REASTS	REBAPTISE	REBILLING	REBORES	REBURY
REASTY	REBAPTISM	REBILLS	REBORING	REBURYING
REATA	REBAPTIZE	REBIND	REBORN	REBUS
REATAS	REBAR	REBINDING	REBORROW	REBUSES
REATE	REBARS	REBINDS	REBORROWS	REBUT
REATES	REBASE	REBIRTH	REBOTTLE	REBUTMENT
REATTACH	REBASED	REBIRTHER	REBOTTLED	REBUTS
REATTACK	REBASES	REBIRTHS	REBOTTLES	REBUTTAL
REATTACKS	REBASING	REBIT	REBOUGHT	REBUTTALS
REATTAIN	REBATABLE	REBITE	REBOUND	REBUTTED
REATTAINS	REBATE	REBITES	REBOUNDED	REBUTTER
REATTEMPT	REBATED	REBITING	REBOUNDER	REBUTTERS
REAVAIL	REBATER	REBITTEN	REBOUNDS	REBUTTING
REAVAILED	REBATERS	REBLEND	REBOZO	REBUTTON
REAVAILS	REBATES	REBLENDED	REBOZOS	REBUTTONS
REAVE	REBATING	REBLENDS	REBRACE	REBUY
REAVED	REBATO	REBLENT	REBRACED	REBUYING
REAVER	REBATOES	REBLOCHON	REBRACES	REBUYS
REAVERS	REBATOS	REBLOOM	REBRACING	REC
REAVES	REBBE	REBLOOMED	REBRANCH	RECAL
REAVING	REBBES	REBLOOMS	REBRAND	RECALESCE
REAVOW	REBBETZIN	REBLOSSOM	REBRANDED	RECALL

RECALLED	RECCO	RECESSES	RECIT	RECLINER
RECALLER	RECCOS	RECESSING	RECITABLE	RECLINERS
RECALLERS	RECCY	RECESSION	RECITAL	RECLINES
RECALLING	RECCYING	RECESSIVE	RECITALS	RECLINING
RECALLS	RECEDE	RECHANGE	RECITE	RECLOSE
RECALMENT	RECEDED	RECHANGED	RECITED	RECLOSED
RECALS	RECEDES	RECHANGES	RECITER	RECLOSES
RECAMIER	RECEDING	RECHANNEL	RECITERS	RECLOSING
RECAMIERS	RECEIPT	RECHARGE	RECITES	RECLOTHE
RECANE	RECEIPTED	RECHARGED	RECITING	RECLOTHED
RECANED	RECEIPTOR	RECHARGER	RECITS	RECLOTHES
RECANES	RECEIPTS	RECHARGES	RECK	RECLUSE
RECANING	RECEIVAL	RECHART	RECKAN	RECLUSELY
RECANT	RECEIVALS	RECHARTED	RECKANS	RECLUSES
RECANTED	RECEIVE	RECHARTER	RECKED	RECLUSION
RECANTER	RECEIVED	RECHARTS	RECKING	RECLUSIVE
RECANTERS	RECEIVER	RECHATE	RECKLESS	RECLUSORY
RECANTING	RECEIVERS	RECHATES	RECKLING	RECOAL
RECANTS	RECEIVES	RECHAUFFE	RECKLINGS	RECOALED
RECAP	RECEIVING	RECHEAT	RECKON	RECOALING
RECAPPED	RECEMENT	RECHEATED	RECKONED	RECOALS
RECAPPING	RECEMENTS	RECHEATS	RECKONER	RECOAT
RECAPS	RECENCIES	RECHECK	RECKONERS	RECOATED
RECAPTION	RECENCY	RECHECKED	RECKONING	RECOATING
RECAPTOR	RECENSE	RECHECKS	RECKONS	RECOATS
RECAPTORS	RECENSED	RECHERCHE	RECKS	RECOCK
RECAPTURE	RECENSES	RECHEW	RECLAD	RECOCKED
RECARPET	RECENSING	RECHEWED	RECLADDED	RECOCKING
RECARPETS	RECENSION	RECHEWING	RECLADS	RECOCKS
RECARRIED	RECENSOR	RECHEWS	RECLAIM	RECODE
RECARRIES	RECENSORS	RECHIE	RECLAIMED	RECODED
RECARRY	RECENT	RECHIP	RECLAIMER	RECODES
RECAST	RECENTER	RECHIPPED	RECLAIMS	RECODIFY
RECASTING	RECENTEST	RECHIPS	RECLAME	RECODING
RECASTS	RECENTLY	RECHLESSE	RECLAMES	RECOGNISE
RECATALOG	RECENTRE	RECHOOSE	RECLASP	RECOGNIZE
RECATCH	RECENTRED	RECHOOSES	RECLASPED	RECOIL
RECATCHES	RECENTRES	RECHOSE	RECLASPS	RECOILED
RECAUGHT	RECEPT	RECHOSEN	RECLEAN	RECOILER
RECAUTION	RECEPTION	RECIPE	RECLEANED	RECOILERS
RECCE	RECEPTIVE	RECIPES	RECLEANS	RECOILING
RECCED	RECEPTOR	RECIPIENT	RECLIMB	RECOILS
RECCEED	RECEPTORS	RECIRCLE	RECLIMBED	RECOIN
RECCEING	RECEPTS	RECIRCLED	RECLIMBS	RECOINAGE
RECCES	RECERTIFY	RECIRCLES	RECLINATE	RECOINED
RECCIED	RECESS	RECISION	RECLINE	RECOINING
RECCIES	RECESSED	RECISIONS	RECLINED	RECOINS

R

RECOLLECT	RECOOKS	RECOYLE	RECTORATE	RECUSING
RECOLLET	RECOPIED	RECOYLED	RECTORESS	RECUT
RECOLLETS	RECOPIES	RECOYLES	RECTORIAL	RECUTS
RECOLOR	RECOPY	RECOYLING	RECTORIES	RECUTTING
RECOLORED	RECOPYING	RECRATE	RECTORS	RECYCLATE
RECOLORS	RECORD	RECRATED	RECTORY	RECYCLE
RECOLOUR	RECORDED	RECRATES	RECTOS	RECYCLED
RECOLOURS	RECORDER	RECRATING	RECTRESS	RECYCLER
RECOMB	RECORDERS	RECREANCE	RECTRICES	RECYCLERS
RECOMBED	RECORDING	RECREANCY	RECTRIX	RECYCLES
RECOMBINE	RECORDIST	RECREANT	RECTUM	RECYCLING
RECOMBING	RECORDS	RECREANTS	RECTUMS	RECYCLIST
RECOMBS	RECORK	RECREATE	RECTUS	RED
RECOMFORT	RECORKED	RECREATED	RECUILE	REDACT
RECOMMEND	RECORKING	RECREATES	RECUILED	REDACTED
RECOMMIT	RECORKS	RECREATOR	RECUILES	REDACTING
RECOMMITS	RECOUNT	RECREMENT	RECUILING	REDACTION
RECOMPACT	RECOUNTAL	RECROSS	RECULE	REDACTOR
RECOMPILE	RECOUNTED	RECROSSED	RECULED	REDACTORS
RECOMPOSE	RECOUNTER	RECROSSES	RECULES	REDACTS
RECOMPUTE	RECOUNTS	RECROWN	RECULING	REDAMAGE
RECON	RECOUP	RECROWNED	RECUMBENT	REDAMAGED
RECONCILE	RECOUPE	RECROWNS	RECUR	REDAMAGES
RECONDITE	RECOUPED	RECRUIT	RECURE	REDAN
RECONDUCT	RECOUPES	RECRUITAL	RECURED	REDANS
RECONFER	RECOUPING	RECRUITED	RECURES	REDARGUE
RECONFERS	RECOUPLE	RECRUITER	RECURING	REDARGUED
RECONFINE	RECOUPLED	RECRUITS	RECURRED	REDARGUES
RECONFIRM	RECOUPLES	RECS	RECURRENT	REDATE
RECONNECT	RECOUPS	RECTA	RECURRING	REDATED
RECONNED	RECOURE	RECTAL	RECURS	REDATES
RECONNING	RECOURED	RECTALLY	RECURSION	REDATING
RECONQUER	RECOURES	RECTANGLE	RECURSIVE	REDBACK
RECONS	RECOURING	RECTI	RECURVATE	REDBACKS
RECONSIGN	RECOURSE	RECTIFIED	RECURVE	REDBAIT
RECONSOLE	RECOURSED	RECTIFIER	RECURVED	REDBAITED
RECONSULT	RECOURSES	RECTIFIES	RECURVES	REDBAITER
RECONTACT	RECOVER	RECTIFY	RECURVING	REDBAITS
RECONTOUR	RECOVERED	RECTION	RECUSAL	REDBAY
RECONVENE	RECOVEREE	RECTIONS	RECUSALS	REDBAYS
RECONVERT	RECOVERER	RECTITIC	RECUSANCE	REDBELLY
RECONVEY	RECOVEROR	RECTITIS	RECUSANCY	REDBIRD
RECONVEYS	RECOVERS	RECTITUDE	RECUSANT	REDBIRDS
RECONVICT	RECOVERY	RECTO	RECUSANTS	REDBONE
RECOOK	RECOWER	RECTOCELE	RECUSE	REDBONES
RECOOKED	RECOWERED	RECTOR	RECUSED	REDBREAST
RECOOKING	RECOWERS	RECTORAL	RECUSES	REDBRICK

REDBRICKS
REDBUD
REDBUDS
REDBUG
REDBUGS
REDCAP
REDCAPS
REDCOAT
REDCOATS
REDD
REDDED
REDDEN
REDDENDA
REDDENDO
REDDENDOS
REDDENDUM
REDDENED
REDDENING
REDDENS
REDDER
REDDERS
REDDEST
REDDIER
REDDIEST
REDDING
REDDINGS
REDDISH
REDDISHLY
REDDLE
REDDLED
REDDLEMAN
REDDLEMEN
REDDLES
REDDLING
REDDS
REDDY
REDE
REDEAL
REDEALING
REDEALS
REDEALT
REDEAR
REDEARS
REDECIDE
REDECIDED
REDECIDES
REDECRAFT

REDED
REDEEM
REDEEMED
REDEEMER
REDEEMERS
REDEEMING
REDEEMS
REDEFEAT
REDEFEATS
REDEFECT
REDEFECTS
REDEFIED
REDEFIES
REDEFINE
REDEFINED
REDEFINES
REDEFY
REDEFYING
REDELESS
REDELIVER
REDEMAND
REDEMANDS
REDENIED
REDENIES
REDENY
REDENYING
REDEPLOY
REDEPLOYS
REDEPOSIT
REDES
REDESCEND
REDESIGN
REDESIGNS
REDEVELOP
REDEYE
REDEYES
REDFIN
REDFINS
REDFISH
REDFISHES
REDFOOT
REDFOOTS
REDHANDED
REDHEAD
REDHEADED
REDHEADS
REDHORSE

REDHORSES
REDIA
REDIAE
REDIAL
REDIALED
REDIALING
REDIALLED
REDIALS
REDIAS
REDICTATE
REDID
REDIGEST
REDIGESTS
REDIGRESS
REDING
REDINGOTE
REDIP
REDIPPED
REDIPPING
REDIPS
REDIPT
REDIRECT
REDIRECTS
REDISCUSS
REDISPLAY
REDISPOSE
REDISTIL
REDISTILL
REDISTILS
REDIVIDE
REDIVIDED
REDIVIDES
REDIVIVUS
REDIVORCE
REDLEG
REDLEGS
REDLINE
REDLINED
REDLINER
REDLINERS
REDLINES
REDLINING
REDLY
REDNECK
REDNECKED
REDNECKS
REDNESS

REDNESSES
REDO
REDOCK
REDOCKED
REDOCKING
REDOCKS
REDOES
REDOING
REDOLENCE
REDOLENCY
REDOLENT
REDON
REDONE
REDONNED
REDONNING
REDONS
REDOS
REDOUBLE
REDOUBLED
REDOUBLER
REDOUBLES
REDOUBT
REDOUBTED
REDOUBTS
REDOUND
REDOUNDED
REDOUNDS
REDOUT
REDOUTS
REDOWA
REDOWAS
REDOX
REDOXES
REDPOLL
REDPOLLS
REDRAFT
REDRAFTED
REDRAFTS
REDRAW
REDRAWER
REDRAWERS
REDRAWING
REDRAWN
REDRAWS
REDREAM
REDREAMED
REDREAMS

REDREAMT
REDRESS
REDRESSAL
REDRESSED
REDRESSER
REDRESSES
REDRESSOR
REDREW
REDRIED
REDRIES
REDRILL
REDRILLED
REDRILLS
REDRIVE
REDRIVEN
REDRIVES
REDRIVING
REDROOT
REDROOTS
REDROVE
REDRY
REDRYING
REDS
REDSEAR
REDSHANK
REDSHANKS
REDSHARE
REDSHIFT
REDSHIFTS
REDSHIRE
REDSHIRT
REDSHIRTS
REDSHORT
REDSKIN
REDSKINS
REDSTART
REDSTARTS
REDSTREAK
REDTAIL
REDTAILS
REDTOP
REDTOPS
REDUB
REDUBBED
REDUBBING
REDUBS
REDUCE

R

REDUCED	REECHOES	REEFING	REENACTED	REEVOKING
REDUCER	REECHOING	REEFINGS	REENACTOR	REEXAMINE
REDUCERS	REECHY	REEFS	REENACTS	REEXECUTE
REDUCES	REED	REEFY	REENDOW	REEXHIBIT
REDUCIBLE	REEDBED	REEJECT	REENDOWED	REEXPEL
REDUCIBLY	REEDBEDS	REEJECTED	REENDOWS	REEXPELS
REDUCING	REEDBIRD	REEJECTS	REENFORCE	REEXPLAIN
REDUCTANT	REEDBIRDS	REEK	REENGAGE	REEXPLORE
REDUCTASE	REEDBUCK	REEKED	REENGAGED	REEXPORT
REDUCTION	REEDBUCKS	REEKER	REENGAGES	REEXPORTS
REDUCTIVE	REEDE	REEKERS	REENGRAVE	REEXPOSE
REDUCTOR	REEDED	REEKIE	REENJOY	REEXPOSED
REDUCTORS	REEDEN	REEKIER	REENJOYED	REEXPOSES
REDUIT	REEDER	REEKIEST	REENJOYS	REEXPRESS
REDUITS	REEDERS	REEKING	REENLARGE	REF
REDUNDANT	REEDES	REEKINGLY	REENLIST	REFACE
REDUVIID	REEDIER	REEKS	REENLISTS	REFACED
REDUVIIDS	REEDIEST	REEKY	REENROLL	REFACES
REDUX	REEDIFIED	REEL	REENROLLS	REFACING
REDWARE	REEDIFIES	REELABLE	REENS	REFALL
REDWARES	REEDIFY	REELECT	REENSLAVE	REFALLEN
REDWATER	REEDILY	REELECTED	REENTER	REFALLING
REDWATERS	REEDINESS	REELECTS	REENTERED	REFALLS
REDWING	REEDING	REELED	REENTERS	REFASHION
REDWINGS	REEDINGS	REELER	REENTRANT	REFASTEN
REDWOOD	REEDIT	REELERS	REENTRIES	REFASTENS
REDWOODS	REEDITED	REELEVATE	REENTRY	REFECT
REDYE	REEDITING	REELING	REEQUIP	REFECTED
REDYED	REEDITION	REELINGLY	REEQUIPS	REFECTING
REDYEING	REEDITS	REELINGS	REERECT	REFECTION
REDYES	REEDLIKE	REELMAN	REERECTED	REFECTIVE
REE	REEDLING	REELMEN	REERECTS	REFECTORY
REEARN	REEDLINGS	REELS	REES	REFECTS
REEARNED	REEDMAN	REEMBARK	REEST	REFED
REEARNING	REEDMEN	REEMBARKS	REESTED	REFEED
REEARNS	REEDS	REEMBODY	REESTIER	REFEEDING
REEBOK	REEDSTOP	REEMBRACE	REESTIEST	REFEEDS
REEBOKS	REEDSTOPS	REEMERGE	REESTING	REFEEL
REECH	REEDUCATE	REEMERGED	REESTS	REFEELING
REECHED	REEDY	REEMERGES	REESTY	REFEELS
REECHES	REEF	REEMIT	REEVE	REFEL
REECHIE	REEFABLE	REEMITS	REEVED	REFELL
REECHIER	REEFED	REEMITTED	REEVES	REFELLED
REECHIEST	REEFER	REEMPLOY	REEVING	REFELLING
REECHING	REEFERS	REEMPLOYS	REEVOKE	REFELS
REECHO	REEFIER	REEN	REEVOKED	REFELT
REECHOED	REEFIEST	REENACT	REEVOKES	REFENCE

REFENCED	REFINDING	REFLEXIVE	REFORMED	REFUELED
REFENCES	REFINDS	REFLEXLY	REFORMER	REFUELING
REFENCING	REFINE	REFLIES	REFORMERS	REFUELLED
REFER	REFINED	REFLOAT	REFORMING	REFUELS
REFERABLE	REFINEDLY	REFLOATED	REFORMISM	REFUGE
REFEREE	REFINER	REFLOATS	REFORMIST	REFUGED
REFEREED	REFINERS	REFLOOD	REFORMS	REFUGEE
REFEREES	REFINERY	REFLOODED	REFORTIFY	REFUGEES
REFERENCE	REFINES	REFLOODS	REFOUGHT	REFUGES
REFERENDA	REFINING	REFLOW	REFOUND	REFUGIA
REFERENT	REFININGS	REFLOWED	REFOUNDED	REFUGING
REFERENTS	REFINISH	REFLOWER	REFOUNDER	REFUGIUM
REFERRAL	REFIRE	REFLOWERS	REFOUNDS	REFULGENT
REFERRALS	REFIRED	REFLOWING	REFRACT	REFUND
REFERRED	REFIRES	REFLOWN	REFRACTED	REFUNDED
REFERRER	REFIRING	REFLOWS	REFRACTOR	REFUNDER
REFERRERS	REFIS	REFLUENCE	REFRACTS	REFUNDERS
REFERRING	REFIT	REFLUENT	REFRAIN	REFUNDING
REFERS	REFITMENT	REFLUX	REFRAINED	REFUNDS
REFFED	REFITS	REFLUXED	REFRAINER	REFURB
REFFING	REFITTED	REFLUXES	REFRAINS	REFURBED
REFFINGS	REFITTING	REFLUXING	REFRAME	REFURBING
REFFO	REFIX	REFLY	REFRAMED	REFURBISH
REFFOS	REFIXED	REFLYING	REFRAMES	REFURBS
REFI	REFIXES	REFOCUS	REFRAMING	REFURNISH
REFIGHT	REFIXING	REFOCUSED	REFREEZE	REFUSABLE
REFIGHTS	REFLAG	REFOCUSES	REFREEZES	REFUSAL
REFIGURE	REFLAGGED	REFOLD	REFRESH	REFUSALS
REFIGURED	REFLAGS	REFOLDED	REFRESHED	REFUSE
REFIGURES	REFLATE	REFOLDING	REFRESHEN	REFUSED
REFILE	REFLATED	REFOLDS	REFRESHER	REFUSENIK
REFILED	REFLATES	REFOOT	REFRESHES	REFUSER
REFILES	REFLATING	REFOOTED	REFRIED	REFUSERS
REFILING	REFLATION	REFOOTING	REFRIES	REFUSES
REFILL	REFLECT	REFOOTS	REFRINGE	REFUSING
REFILLED	REFLECTED	REFOREST	REFRINGED	REFUSION
REFILLING	REFLECTER	REFORESTS	REFRINGES	REFUSIONS
REFILLS	REFLECTOR	REFORGE	REFRONT	REFUSNIK
REFILM	REFLECTS	REFORGED	REFRONTED	REFUSNIKS
REFILMED	REFLET	REFORGES	REFRONTS	REFUTABLE
REFILMING	REFLETS	REFORGING	REFROZE	REFUTABLY
REFILMS	REFLEW	REFORM	REFROZEN	REFUTAL
REFILTER	REFLEX	REFORMADE	REFRY	REFUTALS
REFILTERS	REFLEXED	REFORMADO	REFRYING	REFUTE
REFINABLE	REFLEXES	REFORMAT	REFS	REFUTED
REFINANCE	REFLEXING	REFORMATE	REFT	REFUTER
REFIND	REFLEXION	REFORMATS	REFUEL	REFUTERS

R

REFUTES	REGEARED	REGINAE	REGOLITHS	REGRINDS
REFUTING	REGEARING	REGINAL	REGORGE	REGROOM
REG	REGEARS	REGINAS	REGORGED	REGROOMED
REGAIN	REGELATE	REGION	REGORGES	REGROOMS
REGAINED	REGELATED	REGIONAL	REGORGING	REGROOVE
REGAINER	REGELATES	REGIONALS	REGOS	REGROOVED
REGAINERS	REGENCE	REGIONARY	REGOSOL	REGROOVES
REGAINING	REGENCES	REGIONS	REGOSOLS	REGROUND
REGAINS	REGENCIES	REGISSEUR	REGRADE	REGROUP
REGAL	REGENCY	REGISTER	REGRADED	REGROUPED
REGALE	REGENT	REGISTERS	REGRADES	REGROUPS
REGALED	REGENTAL	REGISTRAR	REGRADING	REGROW
REGALER	REGENTS	REGISTRY	REGRAFT	REGROWING
REGALERS	REGES	REGIUS	REGRAFTED	REGROWN
REGALES	REGEST	REGIVE	REGRAFTS	REGROWS
REGALIA	REGESTED	REGIVEN	REGRANT	REGROWTH
REGALIAN	REGESTING	REGIVES	REGRANTED	REGROWTHS
REGALIAS	REGESTS	REGIVING	REGRANTS	REGS
REGALING	REGGAE	REGLAZE	REGRATE	REGUERDON
REGALISM	REGGAES	REGLAZED	REGRATED	REGULA
REGALISMS	REGGAETON	REGLAZES	REGRATER	REGULABLE
REGALIST	REGGO	REGLAZING	REGRATERS	REGULAE
REGALISTS	REGGOS	REGLET	REGRATES	REGULAR
REGALITY	REGICIDAL	REGLETS	REGRATING	REGULARLY
REGALLY	REGICIDE	REGLORIFY	REGRATOR	REGULARS
REGALNESS	REGICIDES	REGLOSS	REGRATORS	REGULATE
REGALS	REGIE	REGLOSSED	REGREDE	REGULATED
REGAR	REGIES	REGLOSSES	REGREDED	REGULATES
REGARD	REGIFT	REGLOW	REGREDES	REGULATOR
REGARDANT	REGIFTED	REGLOWED	REGREDING	REGULI
REGARDED	REGIFTER	REGLOWING	REGREEN	REGULINE
REGARDER	REGIFTERS	REGLOWS	REGREENED	REGULISE
REGARDERS	REGIFTING	REGLUE	REGREENS	REGULISED
REGARDFUL	REGIFTS	REGLUED	REGREET	REGULISES
REGARDING	REGILD	REGLUES	REGREETED	REGULIZE
REGARDS	REGILDED	REGLUING	REGREETS	REGULIZED
REGARS	REGILDING	REGMA	REGRESS	REGULIZES
REGATHER	REGILDS	REGMAKER	REGRESSED	REGULO
REGATHERS	REGILT	REGMAKERS	REGRESSES	REGULOS
REGATTA	REGIME	REGMATA	REGRESSOR	REGULUS
REGATTAS	REGIMEN	REGNA	REGRET	REGULUSES
REGAUGE	REGIMENS	REGNAL	REGRETFUL	REGUR
REGAUGED	REGIMENT	REGNANCY	REGRETS	REGURS
REGAUGES	REGIMENTS	REGNANT	REGRETTED	REH
REGAUGING	REGIMES	REGNUM	REGRETTER	REHAB
REGAVE	REGIMINAL	REGO	REGREW	REHABBED
REGEAR	REGINA	REGOLITH	REGRIND	REHABBER

REHABBERS	REHIRES	REIMPORT	REINKED	REIST
REHABBING	REHIRING	REIMPORTS	REINKING	REISTAFEL
REHABS	REHOBOAM	REIMPOSE	REINKS	REISTED
REHAMMER	REHOBOAMS	REIMPOSED	REINLESS	REISTING
REHAMMERS	REHOME	REIMPOSES	REINS	REISTS
REHANDLE	REHOMED	REIN	REINSERT	REITBOK
REHANDLED	REHOMES	REINCITE	REINSERTS	REITBOKS
REHANDLES	REHOMING	REINCITED	REINSMAN	REITER
REHANG	REHOMINGS	REINCITES	REINSMEN	REITERANT
REHANGED	REHOUSE	REINCUR	REINSPECT	REITERATE
REHANGING	REHOUSED	REINCURS	REINSPIRE	REITERED
REHANGS	REHOUSES	REINDEER	REINSTAL	REITERING
REHARDEN	REHOUSING	REINDEERS	REINSTALL	REITERS
REHARDENS	REHS	REINDEX	REINSTALS	REIVE
REHASH	REHUNG	REINDEXED	REINSTATE	REIVED
REHASHED	REHYDRATE	REINDEXES	REINSURE	REIVER
REHASHES	REI	REINDICT	REINSURED	REIVERS
REHASHING	REIF	REINDICTS	REINSURER	REIVES
REHEAR	REIFIED	REINDUCE	REINSURES	REIVING
REHEARD	REIFIER	REINDUCED	REINTER	REIVINGS
REHEARING	REIFIERS	REINDUCES	REINTERS	REJACKET
REHEARS	REIFIES	REINDUCT	REINVADE	REJACKETS
REHEARSAL	REIFS	REINDUCTS	REINVADED	REJECT
REHEARSE	REIFY	REINED	REINVADES	REJECTED
REHEARSED	REIFYING	REINETTE	REINVENT	REJECTEE
REHEARSER	REIGN	REINETTES	REINVENTS	REJECTEES
REHEARSES	REIGNED	REINFECT	REINVEST	REJECTER
REHEAT	REIGNING	REINFECTS	REINVESTS	REJECTERS
REHEATED	REIGNITE	REINFLAME	REINVITE	REJECTING
REHEATER	REIGNITED	REINFLATE	REINVITED	REJECTION
REHEATERS	REIGNITES	REINFORCE	REINVITES	REJECTIVE
REHEATING	REIGNS	REINFORM	REINVOKE	REJECTOR
REHEATS	REIK	REINFORMS	REINVOKED	REJECTORS
REHEEL	REIKI	REINFUND	REINVOKES	REJECTS
REHEELED	REIKIS	REINFUNDS	REINVOLVE	REJIG
REHEELING	REIKS	REINFUSE	REIRD	REJIGGED
REHEELS	REILLUME	REINFUSED	REIRDS	REJIGGER
REHEM	REILLUMED	REINFUSES	REIS	REJIGGERS
REHEMMED	REILLUMES	REINHABIT	REISES	REJIGGING
REHEMMING	REIMAGE	REINING	REISHI	REJIGS
REHEMS	REIMAGED	REINJECT	REISHIS	REJOICE
REHINGE	REIMAGES	REINJECTS	REISSUE	REJOICED
REHINGED	REIMAGINE	REINJURE	REISSUED	REJOICER
REHINGES	REIMAGING	REINJURED	REISSUER	REJOICERS
REHINGING	REIMBURSE	REINJURES	REISSUERS	REJOICES
REHIRE	REIMMERSE	REINJURY	REISSUES	REJOICING
REHIRED	REIMPLANT	REINK	REISSUING	REJOIN

R

REJOINDER	RELAND	RELEARNS	RELIE	RELIVE
REJOINED	RELANDED	RELEARNT	RELIED	RELIVED
REJOINING	RELANDING	RELEASE	RELIEF	RELIVER
REJOINS	RELANDS	RELEASED	RELIEFS	RELIVERED
REJON	RELAPSE	RELEASEE	RELIER	RELIVERS
REJONEO	RELAPSED	RELEASEES	RELIERS	RELIVES
REJONEOS	RELAPSER	RELEASER	RELIES	RELIVING
REJONES	RELAPSERS	RELEASERS	RELIEVE	RELLENO
REJOURN	RELAPSES	RELEASES	RELIEVED	RELLENOS
REJOURNED	RELAPSING	RELEASING	RELIEVER	RELLIE
REJOURNS	RELATA	RELEASOR	RELIEVERS	RELLIES
REJUDGE	RELATABLE	RELEASORS	RELIEVES	RELLISH
REJUDGED	RELATE	RELEGABLE	RELIEVING	RELLISHED
REJUDGES	RELATED	RELEGATE	RELIEVO	RELLISHES
REJUDGING	RELATEDLY	RELEGATED	RELIEVOS	RELOAD
REJUGGLE	RELATER	RELEGATES	RELIGHT	RELOADED
REJUGGLED	RELATERS	RELEND	RELIGHTED	RELOADER
REJUGGLES	RELATES	RELENDING	RELIGHTS	RELOADERS
REJUSTIFY	RELATING	RELENDS	RELIGIEUX	RELOADING
REKE	RELATION	RELENT	RELIGION	RELOADS
REKED	RELATIONS	RELENTED	RELIGIONS	RELOAN
REKES	RELATIVAL	RELENTING	RELIGIOSE	RELOANED
REKEY	RELATIVE	RELENTS	RELIGIOSO	RELOANING
REKEYED	RELATIVES	RELET	RELIGIOUS	RELOANS
REKEYING	RELATOR	RELETS	RELINE	RELOCATE
REKEYS	RELATORS	RELETTER	RELINED	RELOCATED
REKINDLE	RELATUM	RELETTERS	RELINES	RELOCATEE
REKINDLED	RELAUNCH	RELETTING	RELINING	RELOCATES
REKINDLES	RELAUNDER	RELEVANCE	RELINK	RELOCATOR
REKING	RELAX	RELEVANCY	RELINKED	RELOCK
REKNIT	RELAXABLE	RELEVANT	RELINKING	RELOCKED
REKNITS	RELAXANT	RELEVE	RELINKS	RELOCKING
REKNITTED	RELAXANTS	RELEVES	RELIQUARY	RELOCKS
REKNOT	RELAXED	RELIABLE	RELIQUE	RELOOK
REKNOTS	RELAXEDLY	RELIABLES	RELIQUEFY	RELOOKED
REKNOTTED	RELAXER	RELIABLY	RELIQUES	RELOOKING
RELABEL	RELAXERS	RELIANCE	RELIQUIAE	RELOOKS
RELABELED	RELAXES	RELIANCES	RELISH	RELUCENT
RELABELS	RELAXIN	RELIANT	RELISHED	RELUCT
RELACE	RELAXING	RELIANTLY	RELISHES	RELUCTANT
RELACED	RELAXINS	RELIC	RELISHING	RELUCTATE
RELACES	RELAY	RELICENSE	RELIST	RELUCTED
RELACHE	RELAYED	RELICS	RELISTED	RELUCTING
RELACHES	RELAYING	RELICT	RELISTING	RELUCTS
RELACING	RELAYS	RELICTION	RELISTS	RELUME
RELACQUER	RELEARN	RELICTS	RELIT	RELUMED
RELAID	RELEARNED	RELIDE	RELIVABLE	RELUMES

RELUMINE	REMARKER	REMEIDED	REMISSION	REMORSES
RELUMINED	REMARKERS	REMEIDING	REMISSIVE	REMOTE
RELUMINES	REMARKET	REMEIDS	REMISSLY	REMOTELY
RELUMING	REMARKETS	REMELT	REMISSORY	REMOTER
RELY	REMARKING	REMELTED	REMIT	REMOTES
RELYING	REMARKS	REMELTING	REMITMENT	REMOTEST
REM	REMARQUE	REMELTS	REMITS	REMOTION
REMADE	REMARQUED	REMEMBER	REMITTAL	REMOTIONS
REMADES	REMARQUES	REMEMBERS	REMITTALS	REMOUD
REMAIL	REMARRIED	REMEN	REMITTED	REMOULADE
REMAILED	REMARRIES	REMEND	REMITTEE	REMOULD
REMAILER	REMARRY	REMENDED	REMITTEES	REMOULDED
REMAILERS	REMASTER	REMENDING	REMITTENT	REMOULDS
REMAILING	REMASTERS	REMENDS	REMITTER	REMOUNT
REMAILS	REMATCH	REMENS	REMITTERS	REMOUNTED
REMAIN	REMATCHED	REMERCIED	REMITTING	REMOUNTS
REMAINDER	REMATCHES	REMERCIES	REMITTOR	REMOVABLE
REMAINED	REMATE	REMERCY	REMITTORS	REMOVABLY
REMAINING	REMATED	REMERGE	REMIX	REMOVAL
REMAINS	REMATES	REMERGED	REMIXED	REMOVALS
REMAKE	REMATING	REMERGES	REMIXER	REMOVE
REMAKER	REMBLAI	REMERGING	REMIXERS	REMOVED
REMAKERS	REMBLAIS	REMET	REMIXES	REMOVEDLY
REMAKES	REMBLE	REMEX	REMIXING	REMOVER
REMAKING	REMBLED	REMIGATE	REMIXT	REMOVERS
REMAN	REMBLES	REMIGATED	REMIXTURE	REMOVES
REMAND	REMBLING	REMIGATES	REMNANT	REMOVING
REMANDED	REMEAD	REMIGES	REMNANTAL	REMS
REMANDING	REMEADED	REMIGIAL	REMNANTS	REMUAGE
REMANDS	REMEADING	REMIGRATE	REMODEL	REMUAGES
REMANENCE	REMEADS	REMIND	REMODELED	REMUDA
REMANENCY	REMEASURE	REMINDED	REMODELER	REMUDAS
REMANENT	REMEDE	REMINDER	REMODELS	REMUEUR
REMANENTS	REMEDED	REMINDERS	REMODIFY	REMUEURS
REMANET	REMEDES	REMINDFUL	REMOISTEN	REMURMUR
REMANETS	REMEDIAL	REMINDING	REMOLADE	REMURMURS
REMANIE	REMEDIAT	REMINDS	REMOLADES	REN
REMANIES	REMEDIATE	REMINISCE	REMOLD	RENAGUE
REMANNED	REMEDIED	REMINT	REMOLDED	RENAGUED
REMANNING	REMEDIES	REMINTED	REMOLDING	RENAGUES
REMANS	REMEDING	REMINTING	REMOLDS	RENAGUING
REMAP	REMEDY	REMINTS	REMONTANT	RENAIL
REMAPPED	REMEDYING	REMISE	REMONTOIR	RENAILED
REMAPPING	REMEET	REMISED	REMORA	RENAILING
REMAPS	REMEETING	REMISES	REMORAS	RENAILS
REMARK	REMEETS	REMISING	REMORID	RENAL
REMARKED	REMEID	REMISS	REMORSE	RENAME

RENAMED	RENEGUING	RENNE	RENVERSED	REORIENTS
RENAMES	RENEST	RENNED	RENVERSES	REOS
RENAMING	RENESTED	RENNES	RENVERST	REOUTFIT
RENASCENT	RENESTING	RENNET	RENVOI	REOUTFITS
RENATURE	RENESTS	RENNETS	RENVOIS	REOVIRUS
RENATURED	RENEW	RENNIN	RENVOY	REOXIDISE
RENATURES	RENEWABLE	RENNING	RENVOYS	REOXIDIZE
RENAY	RENEWABLY	RENNINGS	RENY	REP
RENAYED	RENEWAL	RENNINS	RENYING	REPACIFY
RENAYING	RENEWALS	RENO	REO	REPACK
RENAYS	RENEWED	RENOGRAM	REOBJECT	REPACKAGE
RENCONTRE	RENEWEDLY	RENOGRAMS	REOBJECTS	REPACKED
REND	RENEWER	RENOS	REOBSERVE	REPACKING
RENDED	RENEWERS	RENOTIFY	REOBTAIN	REPACKS
RENDER	RENEWING	RENOUNCE	REOBTAINS	REPAID
RENDERED	RENEWINGS	RENOUNCED	REOCCUPY	REPAINT
RENDERER	RENEWS	RENOUNCER	REOCCUR	REPAINTED
RENDERERS	RENEY	RENOUNCES	REOCCURS	REPAINTS
RENDERING	RENEYED	RENOVATE	REOFFEND	REPAIR
RENDERS	RENEYING	RENOVATED	REOFFENDS	REPAIRED
RENDIBLE	RENEYS	RENOVATES	REOFFER	REPAIRER
RENDING	RENFIERST	RENOVATOR	REOFFERED	REPAIRERS
RENDITION	RENFORCE	RENOWN	REOFFERS	REPAIRING
RENDS	RENFORCED	RENOWNED	REOIL	REPAIRMAN
RENDZINA	RENFORCES	RENOWNER	REOILED	REPAIRMEN
RENDZINAS	RENFORST	RENOWNERS	REOILING	REPAIRS
RENEAGUE	RENGA	RENOWNING	REOILS	REPAND
RENEAGUED	RENGAS	RENOWNS	REOPEN	REPANDLY
RENEAGUES	RENIED	RENS	REOPENED	REPANEL
RENEGADE	RENIES	RENT	REOPENER	REPANELED
RENEGADED	RENIFORM	RENTABLE	REOPENERS	REPANELS
RENEGADES	RENIG	RENTAL	REOPENING	REPAPER
RENEGADO	RENIGGED	RENTALLER	REOPENS	REPAPERED
RENEGADOS	RENIGGING	RENTALS	REOPERATE	REPAPERS
RENEGATE	RENIGS	RENTE	REOPPOSE	REPARABLE
RENEGATES	RENIN	RENTED	REOPPOSED	REPARABLY
RENEGE	RENINS	RENTER	REOPPOSES	REPARK
RENEGED	RENITENCE	RENTERS	REORDAIN	REPARKED
RENEGER	RENITENCY	RENTES	REORDAINS	REPARKING
RENEGERS	RENITENT	RENTIER	REORDER	REPARKS
RENEGES	RENK	RENTIERS	REORDERED	REPARTEE
RENEGING	RENKER	RENTING	REORDERS	REPARTEED
RENEGUE	RENKEST	RENTINGS	REORG	REPARTEES
RENEGUED	RENMINBI	RENTS	REORGED	REPASS
RENEGUER	RENMINBIS	RENUMBER	REORGING	REPASSAGE
RENEGUERS	RENNASE	RENUMBERS	REORGS	REPASSED
RENEGUES	RENNASES	RENVERSE	REORIENT	REPASSES

REPASSING	REPENTER	REPLAN	REPLOTS	REPOSEFUL
REPAST	REPENTERS	REPLANNED	REPLOTTED	REPOSER
REPASTED	REPENTING	REPLANS	REPLOUGH	REPOSERS
REPASTING	REPENTS	REPLANT	REPLOUGHS	REPOSES
REPASTS	REPEOPLE	REPLANTED	REPLOW	REPOSING
REPASTURE	REPEOPLED	REPLANTS	REPLOWED	REPOSIT
REPATCH	REPEOPLES	REPLASTER	REPLOWING	REPOSITED
REPATCHED	REPERCUSS	REPLATE	REPLOWS	REPOSITOR
REPATCHES	REPEREPE	REPLATED	REPLUM	REPOSITS
REPATTERN	REPEREPES	REPLATES	REPLUMB	REPOSSESS
REPAVE	REPERK	REPLATING	REPLUMBED	REPOST
REPAVED	REPERKED	REPLAY	REPLUMBS	REPOSTED
REPAVES	REPERKING	REPLAYED	REPLUNGE	REPOSTING
REPAVING	REPERKS	REPLAYING	REPLUNGED	REPOSTS
REPAY	REPERTORY	REPLAYS	REPLUNGES	REPOSURE
REPAYABLE	REPERUSAL	REPLEAD	REPLY	REPOSURES
REPAYING	REPERUSE	REPLEADED	REPLYING	REPOT
REPAYMENT	REPERUSED	REPLEADER	REPO	REPOTS
REPAYS	REPERUSES	REPLEADS	REPOINT	REPOTTED
REPEAL	REPETEND	REPLED	REPOINTED	REPOTTING
REPEALED	REPETENDS	REPLEDGE	REPOINTS	REPOUR
REPEALER	REPHRASE	REPLEDGED	REPOLISH	REPOURED
REPEALERS	REPHRASED	REPLEDGES	REPOLL	REPOURING
REPEALING	REPHRASES	REPLENISH	REPOLLED	REPOURS
REPEALS	REPIGMENT	REPLETE	REPOLLING	REPOUSSE
REPEAT	REPIN	REPLETED	REPOLLS	REPOUSSES
REPEATED	REPINE	REPLETELY	REPOMAN	REPOWER
REPEATER	REPINED	REPLETES	REPOMEN	REPOWERED
REPEATERS	REPINER	REPLETING	REPONE	REPOWERS
REPEATING	REPINERS	REPLETION	REPONED	REPP
REPEATS	REPINES	REPLEVIED	REPONES	REPPED
REPECHAGE	REPINING	REPLEVIES	REPONING	REPPING
REPEG	REPININGS	REPLEVIN	REPORT	REPPINGS
REPEGGED	REPINNED	REPLEVINS	REPORTAGE	REPPS
REPEGGING	REPINNING	REPLEVY	REPORTED	REPREEVE
REPEGS	REPINS	REPLICA	REPORTER	REPREEVED
REPEL	REPIQUE	REPLICANT	REPORTERS	REPREEVES
REPELLANT	REPIQUED	REPLICAS	REPORTING	REPREHEND
REPELLED	REPIQUES	REPLICASE	REPORTS	REPRESENT
REPELLENT	REPIQUING	REPLICATE	REPOS	REPRESS
REPELLER	REPLA	REPLICON	REPOSAL	REPRESSED
REPELLERS	REPLACE	REPLICONS	REPOSALL	REPRESSER
REPELLING	REPLACED	REPLIED	REPOSALLS	REPRESSES
REPELS	REPLACER	REPLIER	REPOSALS	REPRESSOR
REPENT	REPLACERS	REPLIERS	REPOSE	REPRICE
REPENTANT	REPLACES	REPLIES	REPOSED	REPRICED
REPENTED	REPLACING	REPLOT	REPOSEDLY	REPRICES

R

REPRICING	REPROVALS	REPURE	REQUITED	RERENTS
REPRIEFE	REPROVE	REPURED	REQUITER	REREPEAT
REPRIEFES	REPROVED	REPURES	REQUITERS	REREPEATS
REPRIEVAL	REPROVER	REPURIFY	REQUITES	REREVIEW
REPRIEVE	REPROVERS	REPURING	REQUITING	REREVIEWS
REPRIEVED	REPROVES	REPURPOSE	REQUITS	REREVISE
REPRIEVER	REPROVING	REPURSUE	REQUITTED	REREVISED
REPRIEVES	REPRYVE	REPURSUED	REQUOTE	REREVISES
REPRIMAND	REPRYVED	REPURSUES	REQUOTED	REREWARD
REPRIME	REPRYVES	REPUTABLE	REQUOTES	REREWARDS
REPRIMED	REPRYVING	REPUTABLY	REQUOTING	RERIG
REPRIMES	REPS	REPUTE	REQUOYLE	RERIGGED
REPRIMING	REPTANT	REPUTED	REQUOYLED	RERIGGING
REPRINT	REPTATION	REPUTEDLY	REQUOYLES	RERIGS
REPRINTED	REPTILE	REPUTES	RERACK	RERISE
REPRINTER	REPTILES	REPUTING	RERACKED	RERISEN
REPRINTS	REPTILIA	REPUTINGS	RERACKING	RERISES
REPRISAL	REPTILIAN	REQUALIFY	RERACKS	RERISING
REPRISALS	REPTILIUM	REQUERE	RERADIATE	REROLL
REPRISE	REPTILOID	REQUERED	RERAIL	REROLLED
REPRISED	REPUBLIC	REQUERES	RERAILED	REROLLER
REPRISES	REPUBLICS	REQUERING	RERAILING	REROLLERS
REPRISING	REPUBLISH	REQUEST	RERAILS	REROLLING
REPRIVE	REPUDIATE	REQUESTED	RERAISE	REROLLS
REPRIVED	REPUGN	REQUESTER	RERAISED	REROOF
REPRIVES	REPUGNANT	REQUESTOR	RERAISES	REROOFED
REPRIVING	REPUGNED	REQUESTS	RERAISING	REROOFING
REPRIZE	REPUGNING	REQUICKEN	RERAN	REROOFS
REPRIZED	REPUGNS	REQUIEM	REREAD	REROSE
REPRIZES	REPULP	REQUIEMS	REREADING	REROUTE
REPRIZING	REPULPED	REQUIGHT	REREADS	REROUTED
REPRO	REPULPING	REQUIGHTS	REREBRACE	REROUTES
REPROACH	REPULPS	REQUIN	RERECORD	REROUTING
REPROBACY	REPULSE	REQUINS	RERECORDS	RERUN
REPROBATE	REPULSED	REQUINTO	REREDOS	RERUNNING
REPROBE	REPULSER	REQUINTOS	REREDOSES	RERUNS
REPROBED	REPULSERS	REQUIRE	REREDOSSE	RES
REPROBES	REPULSES	REQUIRED	RERELEASE	RESADDLE
REPROBING	REPULSING	REQUIRER	REREMAI	RESADDLED
REPROCESS	REPULSION	REQUIRERS	REREMAIS	RESADDLES
REPRODUCE	REPULSIVE	REQUIRES	REREMICE	RESAID
REPROGRAM	REPUMP	REQUIRING	REREMIND	RESAIL
REPROOF	REPUMPED	REQUISITE	REREMINDS	RESAILED
REPROOFED	REPUMPING	REQUIT	REREMOUSE	RESAILING
REPROOFS	REPUMPS	REQUITAL	RERENT	RESAILS
REPROS	REPUNIT	REQUITALS	RERENTED	RESALABLE
REPROVAL	REPUNITS	REQUITE	RERENTING	RESALE

RESALES	RESEAL	RESEMBLE	RESHARPEN	RESIDING
RESALGAR	RESEALED	RESEMBLED	RESHAVE	RESIDS
RESALGARS	RESEALING	RESEMBLER	RESHAVED	RESIDUA
RESALUTE	RESEALS	RESEMBLES	RESHAVEN	RESIDUAL
RESALUTED	RESEARCH	RESEND	RESHAVES	RESIDUALS
RESALUTES	RESEASON	RESENDING	RESHAVING	RESIDUARY
RESAMPLE	RESEASONS	RESENDS	RESHES	RESIDUE
RESAMPLED	RESEAT	RESENT	RESHINE	RESIDUES
RESAMPLES	RESEATED	RESENTED	RESHINED	RESIDUOUS
RESAT	RESEATING	RESENTER	RESHINES	RESIDUUM
RESAW	RESEATS	RESENTERS	RESHINGLE	RESIDUUMS
RESAWED	RESEAU	RESENTFUL	RESHINING	RESIFT
RESAWING	RESEAUS	RESENTING	RESHIP	RESIFTED
RESAWN	RESEAUX	RESENTIVE	RESHIPPED	RESIFTING
RESAWS	RESECT	RESENTS	RESHIPPER	RESIFTS
RESAY	RESECTED	RESERPINE	RESHIPS	RESIGHT
RESAYING	RESECTING	RESERVE	RESHOD	RESIGHTED
RESAYS	RESECTION	RESERVED	RESHOE	RESIGHTS
RESCALE	RESECTS	RESERVER	RESHOED	RESIGN
RESCALED	RESECURE	RESERVERS	RESHOEING	RESIGNED
RESCALES	RESECURED	RESERVES	RESHOES	RESIGNER
RESCALING	RESECURES	RESERVICE	RESHONE	RESIGNERS
RESCHOOL	RESEDA	RESERVING	RESHOOT	RESIGNING
RESCHOOLS	RESEDAS	RESERVIST	RESHOOTS	RESIGNS
RESCIND	RESEE	RESERVOIR	RESHOT	RESILE
RESCINDED	RESEED	RESES	RESHOW	RESILED
RESCINDER	RESEEDED	RESET	RESHOWED	RESILES
RESCINDS	RESEEDING	RESETS	RESHOWER	RESILIENT
RESCORE	RESEEDS	RESETTED	RESHOWERS	RESILIN
RESCORED	RESEEING	RESETTER	RESHOWING	RESILING
RESCORES	RESEEK	RESETTERS	RESHOWN	RESILINS
RESCORING	RESEEKING	RESETTING	RESHOWS	RESILVER
RESCREEN	RESEEKS	RESETTLE	RESHUFFLE	RESILVERS
RESCREENS	RESEEN	RESETTLED	RESIANCE	RESIN
RESCRIPT	RESEES	RESETTLES	RESIANCES	RESINATA
RESCRIPTS	RESEIZE	RESEW	RESIANT	RESINATAS
RESCUABLE	RESEIZED	RESEWED	RESIANTS	RESINATE
RESCUE	RESEIZES	RESEWING	RESID	RESINATED
RESCUED	RESEIZING	RESEWN	RESIDE	RESINATES
RESCUEE	RESEIZURE	RESEWS	RESIDED	RESINED
RESCUEES	RESELECT	RESH	RESIDENCE	RESINER
RESCUER	RESELECTS	RESHAPE	RESIDENCY	RESINERS
RESCUERS	RESELL	RESHAPED	RESIDENT	RESINIFY
RESCUES	RESELLER	RESHAPER	RESIDENTS	RESINING
RESCUING	RESELLERS	RESHAPERS	RESIDER	RESINISE
RESCULPT	RESELLING	RESHAPES	RESIDERS	RESINISED
RESCULPTS	RESELLS	RESHAPING	RESIDES	RESINISES

R

RESINIZE	RESKUES	RESONATES	RESPIRED	RESTABLES
RESINIZED	RESKUING	RESONATOR	RESPIRES	RESTACK
RESINIZES	RESLATE	RESORB	RESPIRING	RESTACKED
RESINLIKE	RESLATED	RESORBED	RESPITE	RESTACKS
RESINOID	RESLATES	RESORBENT	RESPITED	RESTAFF
RESINOIDS	RESLATING	RESORBING	RESPITES	RESTAFFED
RESINOSES	RESMELT	RESORBS	RESPITING	RESTAFFS
RESINOSIS	RESMELTED	RESORCIN	RESPLEND	RESTAGE
RESINOUS	RESMELTS	RESORCINS	RESPLENDS	RESTAGED
RESINS	RESMOOTH	RESORT	RESPLICE	RESTAGES
RESINY	RESMOOTHS	RESORTED	RESPLICED	RESTAGING
RESIST	RESNATRON	RESORTER	RESPLICES	RESTAMP
RESISTANT	RESOAK	RESORTERS	RESPLIT	RESTAMPED
RESISTED	RESOAKED	RESORTING	RESPLITS	RESTAMPS
RESISTENT	RESOAKING	RESORTS	RESPOKE	RESTART
RESISTER	RESOAKS	RESOUGHT	RESPOKEN	RESTARTED
RESISTERS	RESOD	RESOUND	RESPOND	RESTARTER
RESISTING	RESODDED	RESOUNDED	RESPONDED	RESTARTS
RESISTIVE	RESODDING	RESOUNDS	RESPONDER	RESTATE
RESISTOR	RESODS	RESOURCE	RESPONDS	RESTATED
RESISTORS	RESOFTEN	RESOURCED	RESPONSA	RESTATES
RESISTS	RESOFTENS	RESOURCES	RESPONSE	RESTATING
RESIT	RESOJET	RESOW	RESPONSER	RESTATION
RESITE	RESOJETS	RESOWED	RESPONSES	RESTED
RESITED	RESOLD	RESOWING	RESPONSOR	RESTEM
RESITES	RESOLDER	RESOWN	RESPONSUM	RESTEMMED
RESITING	RESOLDERS	RESOWS	RESPOOL	RESTEMS
RESITS	RESOLE	RESPACE	RESPOOLED	RESTER
RESITTING	RESOLED	RESPACED	RESPOOLS	RESTERS
RESITUATE	RESOLES	RESPACES	RESPOT	RESTFUL
RESIZE	RESOLING	RESPACING	RESPOTS	RESTFULLY
RESIZED	RESOLUBLE	RESPADE	RESPOTTED	RESTIER
RESIZES	RESOLUTE	RESPADED	RESPRANG	RESTIEST
RESIZING	RESOLUTER	RESPADES	RESPRAY	RESTIFF
RESKETCH	RESOLUTES	RESPADING	RESPRAYED	RESTIFORM
RESKEW	RESOLVE	RESPEAK	RESPRAYS	RESTING
RESKEWED	RESOLVED	RESPEAKS	RESPREAD	RESTINGS
RESKEWING	RESOLVENT	RESPECIFY	RESPREADS	RESTITCH
RESKEWS	RESOLVER	RESPECT	RESPRING	RESTITUTE
RESKILL	RESOLVERS	RESPECTED	RESPRINGS	RESTIVE
RESKILLED	RESOLVES	RESPECTER	RESPROUT	RESTIVELY
RESKILLS	RESOLVING	RESPECTS	RESPROUTS	RESTLESS
RESKIN	RESONANCE	RESPELL	RESPRUNG	RESTO
RESKINNED	RESONANT	RESPELLED	RESSALDAR	RESTOCK
RESKINS	RESONANTS	RESPELLS	REST	RESTOCKED
RESKUE	RESONATE	RESPELT	RESTABLE	RESTOCKS
RESKUED	RESONATED	RESPIRE	RESTABLED	RESTOKE

RESTOKED	RESUBJECT	RETAGGED	RETASTING	RETIA
RESTOKES	RESUBMIT	RETAGGING	RETAUGHT	RETIAL
RESTOKING	RESUBMITS	RETAGS	RETAX	RETIARII
RESTORAL	RESULT	RETAIL	RETAXED	RETIARIUS
RESTORALS	RESULTANT	RETAILED	RETAXES	RETIARY
RESTORE	RESULTED	RETAILER	RETAXING	RETICELLA
RESTORED	RESULTFUL	RETAILERS	RETCH	RETICENCE
RESTORER	RESULTING	RETAILING	RETCHED	RETICENCY
RESTORERS	RESULTS	RETAILOR	RETCHES	RETICENT
RESTORES	RESUMABLE	RETAILORS	RETCHING	RETICLE
RESTORING	RESUME	RETAILS	RETCHINGS	RETICLES
RESTOS	RESUMED	RETAIN	RETCHLESS	RETICULA
RESTRAIN	RESUMER	RETAINED	RETE	RETICULAR
RESTRAINS	RESUMERS	RETAINER	RETEACH	RETICULE
RESTRAINT	RESUMES	RETAINERS	RETEACHES	RETICULES
RESTRESS	RESUMING	RETAINING	RETEAM	RETICULUM
RESTRETCH	RESUMMON	RETAINS	RETEAMED	RETIE
RESTRICT	RESUMMONS	RETAKE	RETEAMING	RETIED
RESTRICTS	RESUPINE	RETAKEN	RETEAMS	RETIEING
RESTRIKE	RESUPPLY	RETAKER	RETEAR	RETIES
RESTRIKES	RESURFACE	RETAKERS	RETEARING	RETIFORM
RESTRING	RESURGE	RETAKES	RETEARS	RETIGHTEN
RESTRINGE	RESURGED	RETAKING	RETELL	RETILE
RESTRINGS	RESURGENT	RETAKINGS	RETELLER	RETILED
RESTRIVE	RESURGES	RETALIATE	RETELLERS	RETILES
RESTRIVEN	RESURGING	RETALLIED	RETELLING	RETILING
RESTRIVES	RESURRECT	RETALLIES	RETELLS	RETIME
RESTROOM	RESURVEY	RETALLY	RETEM	RETIMED
RESTROOMS	RESURVEYS	RETAMA	RETEMPER	RETIMES
RESTROVE	RESUS	RETAMAS	RETEMPERS	RETIMING
RESTRUCK	RESUSES	RETAPE	RETEMS	RETINA
RESTRUNG	RESUSPEND	RETAPED	RETENE	RETINAE
RESTS	RESUSSES	RETAPES	RETENES	RETINAL
RESTUDIED	RESWALLOW	RETAPING	RETENTION	RETINALS
RESTUDIES	RET	RETARD	RETENTIVE	RETINAS
RESTUDY	RETABLE	RETARDANT	RETEST	RETINE
RESTUFF	RETABLES	RETARDATE	RETESTED	RETINENE
RESTUFFED	RETABLO	RETARDED	RETESTIFY	RETINENES
RESTUFFS	RETABLOS	RETARDER	RETESTING	RETINES
RESTUMP	RETACK	RETARDERS	RETESTS	RETINITE
RESTUMPED	RETACKED	RETARDING	RETEXTURE	RETINITES
RESTUMPS	RETACKING	RETARDS	RETHINK	RETINITIS
RESTY	RETACKLE	RETARGET	RETHINKER	RETINOIC
RESTYLE	RETACKLED	RETARGETS	RETHINKS	RETINOID
RESTYLED	RETACKLES	RETASTE	RETHOUGHT	RETINOIDS
RESTYLES	RETACKS	RETASTED	RETHREAD	RETINOL
RESTYLING	RETAG	RETASTES	RETHREADS	RETINOLS

R

RETINT	RETOTALED	RETREADS	RETTERY	REUPTAKE
RETINTED	RETOTALS	RETREAT	RETTING	REUPTAKEN
RETINTING	RETOUCH	RETREATED	RETUND	REUPTAKES
RETINTS	RETOUCHED	RETREATER	RETUNDED	REUPTOOK
RETINUE	RETOUCHER	RETREATS	RETUNDING	REURGE
RETINUED	RETOUCHES	RETREE	RETUNDS	REURGED
RETINUES	RETOUR	RETREES	RETUNE	REURGES
RETINULA	RETOURED	RETRENCH	RETUNED	REURGING
RETINULAE	RETOURING	RETRIAL	RETUNES	REUSABLE
RETINULAR	RETOURS	RETRIALS	RETUNING	REUSABLES
RETINULAS	RETOX	RETRIBUTE	RETURF	REUSE
RETIRACY	RETOXED	RETRIED	RETURFED	REUSED
RETIRAL	RETOXES	RETRIES	RETURFING	REUSES
RETIRALS	RETOXING	RETRIEVAL	RETURFS	REUSING
RETIRANT	RETRACE	RETRIEVE	RETURN	REUTILISE
RETIRANTS	RETRACED	RETRIEVED	RETURNED	REUTILIZE
RETIRE	RETRACER	RETRIEVER	RETURNEE	REUTTER
RETIRED	RETRACERS	RETRIEVES	RETURNEES	REUTTERED
RETIREDLY	RETRACES	RETRIM	RETURNER	REUTTERS
RETIREE	RETRACING	RETRIMMED	RETURNERS	REV
RETIREES	RETRACK	RETRIMS	RETURNIK	REVALENTA
RETIRER	RETRACKED	RETRO	RETURNIKS	REVALUATE
RETIRERS	RETRACKS	RETROACT	RETURNING	REVALUE
RETIRES	RETRACT	RETROACTS	RETURNS	REVALUED
RETIRING	RETRACTED	RETROCEDE	RETUSE	REVALUES
RETITLE	RETRACTOR	RETROD	RETWEET	REVALUING
RETITLED	RETRACTS	RETRODDEN	RETWEETED	REVAMP
RETITLES	RETRAICT	RETRODICT	RETWEETS	REVAMPED
RETITLING	RETRAICTS	RETROFIRE	RETWIST	REVAMPER
RETOLD	RETRAIN	RETROFIT	RETWISTED	REVAMPERS
RETOOK	RETRAINED	RETROFITS	RETWISTS	REVAMPING
RETOOL	RETRAINEE	RETROFLEX	RETYING	REVAMPS
RETOOLED	RETRAINS	RETROJECT	RETYPE	REVANCHE
RETOOLING	RETRAIT	RETRONYM	RETYPED	REVANCHES
RETOOLS	RETRAITE	RETRONYMS	RETYPES	REVARNISH
RETORE	RETRAITES	RETROPACK	RETYPING	REVEAL
RETORN	RETRAITS	RETRORSE	REUNIFIED	REVEALED
RETORSION	RETRAITT	RETROS	REUNIFIES	REVEALER
RETORT	RETRAITTS	RETROUSSE	REUNIFY	REVEALERS
RETORTED	RETRAL	RETROVERT	REUNION	REVEALING
RETORTER	RETRALLY	RETRY	REUNIONS	REVEALS
RETORTERS	RETRATE	RETRYING	REUNITE	REVEHENT
RETORTING	RETRATED	RETS	REUNITED	REVEILLE
RETORTION	RETRATES	RETSINA	REUNITER	REVEILLES
RETORTIVE	RETRATING	RETSINAS	REUNITERS	REVEL
RETORTS	RETREAD	RETTED	REUNITES	REVELATOR
RETOTAL	RETREADED	RETTERIES	REUNITING	REVELED

REVELER	REVERS	REVIEWER	REVOICES	REWARD
REVELERS	REVERSAL	REVIEWERS	REVOICING	REWARDED
REVELING	REVERSALS	REVIEWING	REVOKABLE	REWARDER
REVELLED	REVERSE	REVIEWS	REVOKABLY	REWARDERS
REVELLER	REVERSED	REVILE	REVOKE	REWARDFUL
REVELLERS	REVERSELY	REVILED	REVOKED	REWARDING
REVELLING	REVERSER	REVILER	REVOKER	REWARDS
REVELMENT	REVERSERS	REVILERS	REVOKERS	REWAREWA
REVELRIES	REVERSES	REVILES	REVOKES	REWAREWAS
REVELROUS	REVERSI	REVILING	REVOKING	REWARM
REVELRY	REVERSING	REVILINGS	REVOLT	REWARMED
REVELS	REVERSION	REVIOLATE	REVOLTED	REWARMING
REVENANT	REVERSIS	REVISABLE	REVOLTER	REWARMS
REVENANTS	REVERSO	REVISAL	REVOLTERS	REWASH
REVENGE	REVERSOS	REVISALS	REVOLTING	REWASHED
REVENGED	REVERT	REVISE	REVOLTS	REWASHES
REVENGER	REVERTANT	REVISED	REVOLUTE	REWASHING
REVENGERS	REVERTED	REVISER	REVOLVE	REWATER
REVENGES	REVERTER	REVISERS	REVOLVED	REWATERED
REVENGING	REVERTERS	REVISES	REVOLVER	REWATERS
REVENGIVE	REVERTING	REVISING	REVOLVERS	REWAX
REVENUAL	REVERTIVE	REVISION	REVOLVES	REWAXED
REVENUE	REVERTS	REVISIONS	REVOLVING	REWAXES
REVENUED	REVERY	REVISIT	REVOTE	REWAXING
REVENUER	REVEST	REVISITED	REVOTED	REWEAR
REVENUERS	REVESTED	REVISITS	REVOTES	REWEARING
REVENUES	REVESTING	REVISOR	REVOTING	REWEARS
REVERABLE	REVESTRY	REVISORS	REVS	REWEAVE
REVERB	REVESTS	REVISORY	REVUE	REWEAVED
REVERBED	REVET	REVIVABLE	REVUES	REWEAVES
REVERBING	REVETMENT	REVIVABLY	REVUIST	REWEAVING
REVERBS	REVETS	REVIVAL	REVUISTS	REWED
REVERE	REVETTED	REVIVALS	REVULSED	REWEDDED
REVERED	REVETTING	REVIVE	REVULSION	REWEDDING
REVERENCE	REVEUR	REVIVED	REVULSIVE	REWEDS
REVEREND	REVEURS	REVIVER	REVVED	REWEIGH
REVERENDS	REVEUSE	REVIVERS	REVVING	REWEIGHED
REVERENT	REVEUSES	REVIVES	REVYING	REWEIGHS
REVERER	REVIBRATE	REVIVIFY	REW	REWELD
REVERERS	REVICTUAL	REVIVING	REWAKE	REWELDED
REVERES	REVIE	REVIVINGS	REWAKED	REWELDING
REVERIE	REVIED	REVIVOR	REWAKEN	REWELDS
REVERIES	REVIES	REVIVORS	REWAKENED	REWET
REVERIFY	REVIEW	REVOCABLE	REWAKENS	REWETS
REVERING	REVIEWAL	REVOCABLY	REWAKES	REWETTED
REVERIST	REVIEWALS	REVOICE	REWAKING	REWETTING
REVERISTS	REVIEWED	REVOICED	REWAN	REWIDEN

REWIDENED	REWROTE	RHAPHE	RHETORS	RHIZOPOD
REWIDENS	REWROUGHT	RHAPHES	RHEUM	RHIZOPODS
REWILD	REWS	RHAPHIDE	RHEUMATIC	RHIZOPUS
REWILDED	REWTH	RHAPHIDES	RHEUMATIZ	RHIZOTOMY
REWILDING	REWTHS	RHAPHIS	RHEUMED	RHO
REWILDS	REX	RHAPONTIC	RHEUMIC	RHODAMIN
REWIN	REXES	RHAPSODE	RHEUMIER	RHODAMINE
REWIND	REXINE	RHAPSODES	RHEUMIEST	RHODAMINS
REWINDED	REXINES	RHAPSODIC	RHEUMS	RHODANATE
REWINDER	REYNARD	RHAPSODY	RHEUMY	RHODANIC
REWINDERS	REYNARDS	RHATANIES	RHEXES	RHODANISE
REWINDING	REZ	RHATANY	RHEXIS	RHODANIZE
REWINDS	REZERO	RHEA	RHEXISES	RHODIC
REWINNING	REZEROED	RHEAS	RHIES	RHODIE
REWINS	REZEROES	RHEBOK	RHIGOLENE	RHODIES
REWIRABLE	REZEROING	RHEBOKS	RHIME	RHODINAL
REWIRE	REZEROS	RHEMATIC	RHIMES	RHODINALS
REWIRED	REZES	RHEME	RHINAL	RHODIUM
REWIRES	REZONE	RHEMES	RHINE	RHODIUMS
REWIRING	REZONED	RHENIUM	RHINES	RHODOLITE
REWIRINGS	REZONES	RHENIUMS	RHINITIC	RHODONITE
REWOKE	REZONING	RHEOBASE	RHINITIS	RHODOPSIN
REWOKEN	REZZES	RHEOBASES	RHINO	RHODORA
REWON	RHABDOID	RHEOBASIC	RHINOCERI	RHODORAS
REWORD	RHABDOIDS	RHEOCHORD	RHINOLITH	RHODOUS
REWORDED	RHABDOM	RHEOCORD	RHINOLOGY	RHODY
REWORDING	RHABDOMAL	RHEOCORDS	RHINOS	RHOEADINE
REWORDS	RHABDOME	RHEOLOGIC	RHIPIDATE	RHOMB
REWORE	RHABDOMES	RHEOLOGY	RHIPIDION	RHOMBI
REWORK	RHABDOMS	RHEOMETER	RHIPIDIUM	RHOMBIC
REWORKED	RHABDUS	RHEOMETRY	RHIZIC	RHOMBICAL
REWORKING	RHABDUSES	RHEOPHIL	RHIZINE	RHOMBOI
REWORKS	RHACHIAL	RHEOPHILE	RHIZINES	RHOMBOID
REWORN	RHACHIDES	RHEOSTAT	RHIZOBIA	RHOMBOIDS
REWOUND	RHACHILLA	RHEOSTATS	RHIZOBIAL	RHOMBOS
REWOVE	RHACHIS	RHEOTAXES	RHIZOBIUM	RHOMBS
REWOVEN	RHACHISES	RHEOTAXIS	RHIZOCARP	RHOMBUS
REWRAP	RHACHITIS	RHEOTOME	RHIZOCAUL	RHOMBUSES
REWRAPPED	RHAGADES	RHEOTOMES	RHIZOID	RHONCHAL
REWRAPS	RHAMNOSE	RHEOTROPE	RHIZOIDAL	RHONCHI
REWRAPT	RHAMNOSES	RHESUS	RHIZOIDS	RHONCHIAL
REWRITE	RHAMNUS	RHESUSES	RHIZOMA	RHONCHUS
REWRITER	RHAMNUSES	RHETOR	RHIZOMATA	RHONCUS
REWRITERS	RHAMPHOID	RHETORIC	RHIZOME	RHONCUSES
REWRITES	RHANJA	RHETORICS	RHIZOMES	RHONE
REWRITING	RHANJAS	RHETORISE	RHIZOMIC	RHONES
REWRITTEN	RHAPHAE	RHETORIZE	RHIZOPI	RHOPALIC

RHOPALISM	RHYTHMUS	RIBBINGS	RICEBIRDS	RICKETILY
RHOS	RHYTIDOME	RIBBIT	RICED	RICKETS
RHOTACISE	RHYTINA	RIBBITS	RICEFIELD	RICKETTY
RHOTACISM	RHYTINAS	RIBBON	RICER	RICKETY
RHOTACIST	RHYTON	RIBBONED	RICERCAR	RICKEY
RHOTACIZE	RHYTONS	RIBBONING	RICERCARE	RICKEYS
RHOTIC	RIA	RIBBONRY	RICERCARI	RICKING
RHOTICITY	RIAD	RIBBONS	RICERCARS	RICKLE
RHUBARB	RIADS	RIBBONY	RICERCATA	RICKLES
RHUBARBED	RIAL	RIBBY	RICERS	RICKLIER
RHUBARBS	RIALS	RIBCAGE	RICES	RICKLIEST
RHUBARBY	RIALTO	RIBCAGES	RICEY	RICKLY
RHUMB	RIALTOS	RIBES	RICH	RICKRACK
RHUMBA	RIANCIES	RIBEYE	RICHED	RICKRACKS
RHUMBAED	RIANCY	RIBEYES	RICHEN	RICKS
RHUMBAING	RIANT	RIBGRASS	RICHENED	RICKSHA
RHUMBAS	RIANTLY	RIBIBE	RICHENING	RICKSHAS
RHUMBS	RIAS	RIBIBES	RICHENS	RICKSHAW
RHUS	RIATA	RIBIBLE	RICHER	RICKSHAWS
RHUSES	RIATAS	RIBIBLES	RICHES	RICKSTAND
RHY	RIB	RIBIER	RICHESSE	RICKSTICK
RHYME	RIBA	RIBIERS	RICHESSES	RICKYARD
RHYMED	RIBALD	RIBLESS	RICHEST	RICKYARDS
RHYMELESS	RIBALDER	RIBLET	RICHING	RICOCHET
RHYMER	RIBALDEST	RIBLETS	RICHLY	RICOCHETS
RHYMERS	RIBALDLY	RIBLIKE	RICHNESS	RICOTTA
RHYMES	RIBALDRY	RIBOSE	RICHT	RICOTTAS
RHYMESTER	RIBALDS	RIBOSES	RICHTED	RICRAC
RHYMING	RIBAND	RIBOSOMAL	RICHTER	RICRACS
RHYMIST	RIBANDS	RIBOSOME	RICHTEST	RICTAL
RHYMISTS	RIBAS	RIBOSOMES	RICHTING	RICTUS
RHYNE	RIBATTUTA	RIBOZYMAL	RICHTS	RICTUSES
RHYNES	RIBAUD	RIBOZYME	RICHWEED	RICY
RHYOLITE	RIBAUDRED	RIBOZYMES	RICHWEEDS	RID
RHYOLITES	RIBAUDRY	RIBS	RICIER	RIDABLE
RHYOLITIC	RIBAUDS	RIBSTON	RICIEST	RIDDANCE
RHYTA	RIBAVIRIN	RIBSTONE	RICIN	RIDDANCES
RHYTHM	RIBBAND	RIBSTONES	RICING	RIDDED
RHYTHMAL	RIBBANDS	RIBSTONS	RICINS	RIDDEN
RHYTHMED	RIBBED	RIBULOSE	RICINUS	RIDDER
RHYTHMI	RIBBER	RIBULOSES	RICINUSES	RIDDERS
RHYTHMIC	RIBBERS	RIBWORK	RICK	RIDDING
RHYTHMICS	RIBBIE	RIBWORKS	RICKED	RIDDLE
RHYTHMISE	RIBBIER	RIBWORT	RICKER	RIDDLED
RHYTHMIST	RIBBIES	RIBWORTS	RICKERS	RIDDLER
RHYTHMIZE	RIBBIEST	RICE	RICKET	RIDDLERS
RHYTHMS	RIBBING	RICEBIRD	RICKETIER	RIDDLES

R

RIDDLING	RIDOTTOS	RIFLERS	RIGHTIES	RIGORS
RIDDLINGS	RIDS	RIFLERY	RIGHTIEST	RIGOUR
RIDE	RIEL	RIFLES	RIGHTING	RIGOURS
RIDEABLE	RIELS	RIFLING	RIGHTINGS	RIGOUT
RIDENT	RIEM	RIFLINGS	RIGHTISH	RIGOUTS
RIDER	RIEMPIE	RIFLIP	RIGHTISM	RIGS
RIDERED	RIEMPIES	RIFLIPS	RIGHTISMS	RIGSDALER
RIDERLESS	RIEMS	RIFS	RIGHTIST	RIGWIDDIE
RIDERS	RIESLING	RIFT	RIGHTISTS	RIGWOODIE
RIDERSHIP	RIESLINGS	RIFTE	RIGHTLESS	RIJSTAFEL
RIDES	RIEVE	RIFTED	RIGHTLY	RIKISHA
RIDGE	RIEVER	RIFTIER	RIGHTMOST	RIKISHAS
RIDGEBACK	RIEVERS	RIFTIEST	RIGHTNESS	RIKISHI
RIDGED	RIEVES	RIFTING	RIGHTO	RIKSHAW
RIDGEL	RIEVING	RIFTLESS	RIGHTS	RIKSHAWS
RIDGELIKE	RIF	RIFTS	RIGHTSIZE	RILE
RIDGELINE	RIFAMPIN	RIFTY	RIGHTWARD	RILED
RIDGELING	RIFAMPINS	RIG	RIGHTY	RILES
RIDGELS	RIFAMYCIN	RIGADOON	RIGID	RILEY
RIDGEPOLE	RIFE	RIGADOONS	RIGIDER	RILIER
RIDGER	RIFELY	RIGATONI	RIGIDEST	RILIEST
RIDGERS	RIFENESS	RIGATONIS	RIGIDIFY	RILIEVI
RIDGES	RIFER	RIGAUDON	RIGIDISE	RILIEVO
RIDGETOP	RIFEST	RIGAUDONS	RIGIDISED	RILING
RIDGETOPS	RIFF	RIGG	RIGIDISES	RILL
RIDGETREE	RIFFAGE	RIGGALD	RIGIDITY	RILLE
RIDGEWAY	RIFFAGES	RIGGALDS	RIGIDIZE	RILLED
RIDGEWAYS	RIFFED	RIGGED	RIGIDIZED	RILLES
RIDGIER	RIFFING	RIGGER	RIGIDIZES	RILLET
RIDGIEST	RIFFLE	RIGGERS	RIGIDLY	RILLETS
RIDGIL	RIFFLED	RIGGING	RIGIDNESS	RILLETTES
RIDGILS	RIFFLER	RIGGINGS	RIGIDS	RILLING
RIDGING	RIFFLERS	RIGGISH	RIGLIN	RILLMARK
RIDGINGS	RIFFLES	RIGGS	RIGLING	RILLMARKS
RIDGLING	RIFFLING	RIGHT	RIGLINGS	RILLS
RIDGLINGS	RIFFOLA	RIGHTABLE	RIGLINS	RIM
RIDGY	RIFFOLAS	RIGHTABLY	RIGMAROLE	RIMA
RIDIC	RIFFRAFF	RIGHTED	RIGOL	RIMAE
RIDICULE	RIFFRAFFS	RIGHTEN	RIGOLL	RIMAYE
RIDICULED	RIFFS	RIGHTENED	RIGOLLS	RIMAYES
RIDICULER	RIFLE	RIGHTENS	RIGOLS	RIME
RIDICULES	RIFLEBIRD	RIGHTEOUS	RIGOR	RIMED
RIDING	RIFLED	RIGHTER	RIGORISM	RIMELESS
RIDINGS	RIFLEMAN	RIGHTERS	RIGORISMS	RIMER
RIDLEY	RIFLEMEN	RIGHTEST	RIGORIST	RIMERS
RIDLEYS	RIFLER	RIGHTFUL	RIGORISTS	RIMES
RIDOTTO	RIFLERIES	RIGHTIER	RIGOROUS	RIMESTER

RIMESTERS	RINGBOLT	RINGWORK	RIPECK	RIPPLING
RIMFIRE	RINGBOLTS	RINGWORKS	RIPECKS	RIPPLINGS
RIMFIRES	RINGBONE	RINGWORM	RIPED	RIPPLY
RIMIER	RINGBONES	RINGWORMS	RIPELY	RIPPS
RIMIEST	RINGDOVE	RINK	RIPEN	RIPRAP
RIMINESS	RINGDOVES	RINKED	RIPENED	RIPRAPPED
RIMING	RINGED	RINKHALS	RIPENER	RIPRAPS
RIMLAND	RINGENT	RINKING	RIPENERS	RIPS
RIMLANDS	RINGER	RINKS	RIPENESS	RIPSAW
RIMLESS	RINGERS	RINKSIDE	RIPENING	RIPSAWED
RIMMED	RINGETTE	RINKSIDES	RIPENS	RIPSAWING
RIMMER	RINGETTES	RINNING	RIPER	RIPSAWN
RIMMERS	RINGGIT	RINS	RIPERS	RIPSAWS
RIMMING	RINGGITS	RINSABLE	RIPES	RIPSTOP
RIMMINGS	RINGHALS	RINSE	RIPEST	RIPSTOPS
RIMOSE	RINGING	RINSEABLE	RIPIENI	RIPT
RIMOSELY	RINGINGLY	RINSED	RIPIENIST	RIPTIDE
RIMOSITY	RINGINGS	RINSER	RIPIENO	RIPTIDES
RIMOUS	RINGLESS	RINSERS	RIPIENOS	RIRORIRO
RIMPLE	RINGLET	RINSES	RIPING	RIRORIROS
RIMPLED	RINGLETED	RINSIBLE	RIPOFF	RISALDAR
RIMPLES	RINGLETS	RINSING	RIPOFFS	RISALDARS
RIMPLING	RINGLETY	RINSINGS	RIPOST	RISE
RIMROCK	RINGLIKE	RIOJA	RIPOSTE	RISEN
RIMROCKS	RINGMAN	RIOJAS	RIPOSTED	RISER
RIMS	RINGMEN	RIOT	RIPOSTES	RISERS
RIMSHOT	RINGNECK	RIOTED	RIPOSTING	RISES
RIMSHOTS	RINGNECKS	RIOTER	RIPOSTS	RISHI
RIMU	RINGS	RIOTERS	RIPP	RISHIS
RIMUS	RINGSIDE	RIOTING	RIPPABLE	RISIBLE
RIMY	RINGSIDER	RIOTINGS	RIPPED	RISIBLES
RIN	RINGSIDES	RIOTISE	RIPPER	RISIBLY
RIND	RINGSTAND	RIOTISES	RIPPERS	RISING
RINDED	RINGSTER	RIOTIZE	RIPPIER	RISINGS
RINDIER	RINGSTERS	RIOTIZES	RIPPIERS	RISK
RINDIEST	RINGTAIL	RIOTOUS	RIPPING	RISKED
RINDING	RINGTAILS	RIOTOUSLY	RIPPINGLY	RISKER
RINDLESS	RINGTAW	RIOTRIES	RIPPINGS	RISKERS
RINDS	RINGTAWS	RIOTRY	RIPPLE	RISKFUL
RINDY	RINGTONE	RIOTS	RIPPLED	RISKIER
RINE	RINGTONES	RIP	RIPPLER	RISKIEST
RINES	RINGTOSS	RIPARIAL	RIPPLERS	RISKILY
RING	RINGWAY	RIPARIAN	RIPPLES	RISKINESS
RINGBARK	RINGWAYS	RIPARIANS	RIPPLET	RISKING
RINGBARKS	RINGWISE	RIPCORD	RIPPLETS	RISKLESS
RINGBIT	RINGWOMB	RIPCORDS	RIPPLIER	RISKS
RINGBITS	RINGWOMBS	RIPE	RIPPLIEST	RISKY

R

RISOLUTO	RITZ	RIVERHEAD	RIZZARS	ROADWORKS
RISORII	RITZES	RIVERINE	RIZZART	ROAM
RISORIUS	RITZIER	RIVERLESS	RIZZARTS	ROAMED
RISOTTO	RITZIEST	RIVERLIKE	RIZZER	ROAMER
RISOTTOS	RITZILY	RIVERMAN	RIZZERED	ROAMERS
RISP	RITZINESS	RIVERMEN	RIZZERING	ROAMING
RISPED	RITZY	RIVERS	RIZZERS	ROAMINGS
RISPETTI	RIVA	RIVERSIDE	RIZZOR	ROAMS
RISPETTO	RIVAGE	RIVERWALK	RIZZORED	ROAN
RISPING	RIVAGES	RIVERWARD	RIZZORING	ROANPIPE
RISPINGS	RIVAL	RIVERWAY	RIZZORS	ROANPIPES
RISPS	RIVALED	RIVERWAYS	ROACH	ROANS
RISQUE	RIVALESS	RIVERWEED	ROACHED	ROAR
RISQUES	RIVALING	RIVERY	ROACHES	ROARED
RISSOLE	RIVALISE	RIVES	ROACHING	ROARER
RISSOLES	RIVALISED	RIVET	ROAD	ROARERS
RISTRA	RIVALISES	RIVETED	ROADBED	ROARIE
RISTRAS	RIVALITY	RIVETER	ROADBEDS	ROARIER
RISUS	RIVALIZE	RIVETERS	ROADBLOCK	ROARIEST
RISUSES	RIVALIZED	RIVETING	ROADCRAFT	ROARING
RIT	RIVALIZES	RIVETINGS	ROADEO	ROARINGLY
RITARD	RIVALLED	RIVETS	ROADEOS	ROARINGS
RITARDS	RIVALLESS	RIVETTED	ROADHOG	ROARMING
RITE	RIVALLING	RIVETTING	ROADHOGS	ROARS
RITELESS	RIVALRIES	RIVIERA	ROADHOUSE	ROARY
RITENUTO	RIVALROUS	RIVIERAS	ROADIE	ROAST
RITENUTOS	RIVALRY	RIVIERE	ROADIES	ROASTED
RITES	RIVALS	RIVIERES	ROADING	ROASTER
RITONAVIR	RIVALSHIP	RIVING	ROADINGS	ROASTERS
RITORNEL	RIVAS	RIVLIN	ROADKILL	ROASTIE
RITORNELL	RIVE	RIVLINS	ROADKILLS	ROASTIES
RITORNELS	RIVED	RIVO	ROADLESS	ROASTING
RITS	RIVEL	RIVULET	ROADMAN	ROASTINGS
RITT	RIVELLED	RIVULETS	ROADMEN	ROASTS
RITTED	RIVELLING	RIVULOSE	ROADS	ROATE
RITTER	RIVELS	RIVULUS	ROADSHOW	ROATED
RITTERS	RIVEN	RIVULUSES	ROADSHOWS	ROATES
RITTING	RIVER	RIYAL	ROADSIDE	ROATING
RITTS	RIVERAIN	RIYALS	ROADSIDES	ROB
RITUAL	RIVERAINS	RIZ	ROADSMAN	ROBALO
RITUALISE	RIVERBANK	RIZA	ROADSMEN	ROBALOS
RITUALISM	RIVERBED	RIZARD	ROADSTEAD	ROBAND
RITUALIST	RIVERBEDS	RIZARDS	ROADSTER	ROBANDS
RITUALIZE	RIVERBOAT	RIZAS	ROADSTERS	ROBATA
RITUALLY	RIVERED	RIZZAR	ROADWAY	ROBATAS
RITUALS	RIVERET	RIZZARED	ROADWAYS	ROBBED
RITUXIMAB	RIVERETS	RIZZARING	ROADWORK	ROBBER

ROBBERIES	ROCAMBOLE	ROCKOONS	RODSTER	ROILY
ROBBERS	ROCH	ROCKROSE	RODSTERS	ROIN
ROBBERY	ROCHES	ROCKROSES	ROE	ROINED
ROBBIN	ROCHET	ROCKS	ROEBUCK	ROINING
ROBBING	ROCHETS	ROCKSHAFT	ROEBUCKS	ROINISH
ROBBINS	ROCK	ROCKSLIDE	ROED	ROINS
ROBE	ROCKABIES	ROCKWATER	ROEMER	ROIST
ROBED	ROCKABLE	ROCKWEED	ROEMERS	ROISTED
ROBES	ROCKABY	ROCKWEEDS	ROENTGEN	ROISTER
ROBIN	ROCKABYE	ROCKWOOL	ROENTGENS	ROISTERED
ROBING	ROCKABYES	ROCKWOOLS	ROES	ROISTERER
ROBINGS	ROCKAWAY	ROCKWORK	ROESTI	ROISTERS
ROBINIA	ROCKAWAYS	ROCKWORKS	ROESTIS	ROISTING
ROBINIAS	ROCKBOUND	ROCKY	ROESTONE	ROISTS
ROBINS	ROCKCRESS	ROCOCO	ROESTONES	ROJAK
ROBLE	ROCKED	ROCOCOS	ROGALLO	ROJAKS
ROBLES	ROCKER	ROCQUET	ROGALLOS	ROJI
ROBOCALL	ROCKERIES	ROCQUETS	ROGATION	ROJIS
ROBOCALLS	ROCKERS	ROCS	ROGATIONS	ROK
ROBORANT	ROCKERY	ROD	ROGATORY	ROKE
ROBORANTS	ROCKET	RODDED	ROGER	ROKED
ROBOT	ROCKETED	RODDING	ROGERED	ROKELAY
ROBOTIC	ROCKETEER	RODDINGS	ROGERING	ROKELAYS
ROBOTICS	ROCKETER	RODE	ROGERINGS	ROKER
ROBOTISE	ROCKETERS	RODED	ROGERS	ROKERS
ROBOTISED	ROCKETING	RODENT	ROGNON	ROKES
ROBOTISES	ROCKETRY	RODENTS	ROGNONS	ROKIER
ROBOTISM	ROCKETS	RODEO	ROGUE	ROKIEST
ROBOTISMS	ROCKFALL	RODEOED	ROGUED	ROKING
ROBOTIZE	ROCKFALLS	RODEOING	ROGUEING	ROKKAKU
ROBOTIZED	ROCKFISH	RODEOS	ROGUER	ROKS
ROBOTIZES	ROCKHOUND	RODES	ROGUERIES	ROKY
ROBOTRIES	ROCKIER	RODEWAY	ROGUERS	ROLAG
ROBOTRY	ROCKIERS	RODEWAYS	ROGUERY	ROLAGS
ROBOTS	ROCKIEST	RODFISHER	ROGUES	ROLAMITE
ROBS	ROCKILY	RODGERSIA	ROGUESHIP	ROLAMITES
ROBURITE	ROCKINESS	RODING	ROGUING	ROLE
ROBURITES	ROCKING	RODINGS	ROGUISH	ROLES
ROBUST	ROCKINGLY	RODLESS	ROGUISHLY	ROLF
ROBUSTA	ROCKINGS	RODLIKE	ROGUY	ROLFED
ROBUSTAS	ROCKLAY	RODMAN	ROID	ROLFER
ROBUSTER	ROCKLAYS	RODMEN	ROIL	ROLFERS
ROBUSTEST	ROCKLESS	RODNEY	ROILED	ROLFING
ROBUSTLY	ROCKLIKE	RODNEYS	ROILIER	ROLFINGS
ROC	ROCKLING	RODS	ROILIEST	ROLFS
ROCAILLE	ROCKLINGS	RODSMAN	ROILING	ROLL
ROCAILLES	ROCKOON	RODSMEN	ROILS	ROLLABLE

R

ROLLAWAY	ROMANCED	RONDEL	ROODS	ROOMFULS
ROLLAWAYS	ROMANCER	RONDELET	ROOF	ROOMIE
ROLLBACK	ROMANCERS	RONDELETS	ROOFED	ROOMIER
ROLLBACKS	ROMANCES	RONDELLE	ROOFER	ROOMIES
ROLLBAR	ROMANCING	RONDELLES	ROOFERS	ROOMIEST
ROLLBARS	ROMANESCO	RONDELS	ROOFIE	ROOMILY
ROLLED	ROMANISE	RONDES	ROOFIER	ROOMINESS
ROLLER	ROMANISED	RONDINO	ROOFIES	ROOMING
ROLLERS	ROMANISES	RONDINOS	ROOFIEST	ROOMMATE
ROLLICK	ROMANIZE	RONDO	ROOFING	ROOMMATES
ROLLICKED	ROMANIZED	RONDOS	ROOFINGS	ROOMS
ROLLICKS	ROMANIZES	RONDURE	ROOFLESS	ROOMSFUL
ROLLICKY	ROMANO	RONDURES	ROOFLIKE	ROOMSOME
ROLLIE	ROMANOS	RONE	ROOFLINE	ROOMY
ROLLIES	ROMANS	RONEO	ROOFLINES	ROON
ROLLING	ROMANTIC	RONEOED	ROOFS	ROONS
ROLLINGS	ROMANTICS	RONEOING	ROOFSCAPE	ROOP
ROLLMOP	ROMANZA	RONEOS	ROOFTOP	ROOPED
ROLLMOPS	ROMANZAS	RONEPIPE	ROOFTOPS	ROOPIER
ROLLNECK	ROMAUNT	RONEPIPES	ROOFTREE	ROOPIEST
ROLLNECKS	ROMAUNTS	RONES	ROOFTREES	ROOPING
ROLLOCK	ROMCOM	RONG	ROOFY	ROOPIT
ROLLOCKS	ROMCOMS	RONGGENG	ROOIBOS	ROOPS
ROLLOUT	ROMELDALE	RONGGENGS	ROOIBOSES	ROOPY
ROLLOUTS	ROMEO	RONIN	ROOIKAT	ROORBACH
ROLLOVER	ROMEOS	RONINS	ROOIKATS	ROORBACHS
ROLLOVERS	ROMNEYA	RONION	ROOINEK	ROORBACK
ROLLS	ROMNEYAS	RONIONS	ROOINEKS	ROORBACKS
ROLLTOP	ROMP	RONNE	ROOK	ROOS
ROLLUP	ROMPED	RONNEL	ROOKED	ROOSA
ROLLUPS	ROMPER	RONNELS	ROOKERIES	ROOSAS
ROLLWAY	ROMPERS	RONNIE	ROOKERY	ROOSE
ROLLWAYS	ROMPING	RONNIES	ROOKIE	ROOSED
ROM	ROMPINGLY	RONNING	ROOKIER	ROOSER
ROMA	ROMPISH	RONT	ROOKIES	ROOSERS
ROMAGE	ROMPISHLY	RONTE	ROOKIEST	ROOSES
ROMAGES	ROMPS	RONTES	ROOKING	ROOSING
ROMAIKA	ROMS	RONTGEN	ROOKISH	ROOST
ROMAIKAS	RONCADOR	RONTGENS	ROOKS	ROOSTED
ROMAINE	RONCADORS	RONTS	ROOKY	ROOSTER
ROMAINES	RONDACHE	RONYON	ROOM	ROOSTERS
ROMAJI	RONDACHES	RONYONS	ROOMED	ROOSTING
ROMAJIS	RONDAVEL	RONZ	ROOMER	ROOSTS
ROMAL	RONDAVELS	RONZER	ROOMERS	ROOT
ROMALS	RONDE	RONZERS	ROOMETTE	ROOTAGE
ROMAN	RONDEAU	ROO	ROOMETTES	ROOTAGES
ROMANCE	RONDEAUX	ROOD	ROOMFUL	ROOTBALL

R

ROOTBALLS	ROPEWAY	ROSAKERS	ROSERY	ROSITS
ROOTBOUND	ROPEWAYS	ROSALIA	ROSES	ROSMARINE
ROOTCAP	ROPEWORK	ROSALIAS	ROSESLUG	ROSOGLIO
ROOTCAPS	ROPEWORKS	ROSANILIN	ROSESLUGS	ROSOGLIOS
ROOTED	ROPEY	ROSARIA	ROSET	ROSOLIO
ROOTEDLY	ROPIER	ROSARIAN	ROSETED	ROSOLIOS
ROOTER	ROPIEST	ROSARIANS	ROSETING	ROSSER
ROOTERS	ROPILY	ROSARIES	ROSETS	ROSSERS
ROOTHOLD	ROPINESS	ROSARIUM	ROSETTE	ROST
ROOTHOLDS	ROPING	ROSARIUMS	ROSETTED	ROSTED
ROOTIER	ROPINGS	ROSARY	ROSETTES	ROSTELLA
ROOTIES	ROPY	ROSBIF	ROSETTING	ROSTELLAR
ROOTIEST	ROQUE	ROSBIFS	ROSETTY	ROSTELLUM
ROOTINESS	ROQUES	ROSCID	ROSETY	ROSTER
ROOTING	ROQUET	ROSCOE	ROSEWATER	ROSTERED
ROOTINGS	ROQUETED	ROSCOES	ROSEWOOD	ROSTERING
ROOTKIT	ROQUETING	ROSE	ROSEWOODS	ROSTERS
ROOTKITS	ROQUETS	ROSEAL	ROSHAMBO	ROSTI
ROOTLE	ROQUETTE	ROSEATE	ROSHAMBOS	ROSTING
ROOTLED	ROQUETTES	ROSEATELY	ROSHI	ROSTIS
ROOTLES	RORAL	ROSEBAY	ROSHIS	ROSTRA
ROOTLESS	RORE	ROSEBAYS	ROSIED	ROSTRAL
ROOTLET	RORES	ROSEBED	ROSIER	ROSTRALLY
ROOTLETS	RORIC	ROSEBEDS	ROSIERE	ROSTRATE
ROOTLIKE	RORID	ROSEBOWL	ROSIERES	ROSTRATED
ROOTLING	RORIE	ROSEBOWLS	ROSIERS	ROSTRUM
ROOTS	RORIER	ROSEBUD	ROSIES	ROSTRUMS
ROOTSIER	RORIEST	ROSEBUDS	ROSIEST	ROSTS
ROOTSIEST	RORQUAL	ROSEBUSH	ROSILY	ROSULA
ROOTSTALK	RORQUALS	ROSED	ROSIN	ROSULAS
ROOTSTOCK	RORT	ROSEFINCH	ROSINATE	ROSULATE
ROOTSY	RORTED	ROSEFISH	ROSINATES	ROSY
ROOTWORM	RORTER	ROSEHIP	ROSINED	ROSYING
ROOTWORMS	RORTERS	ROSEHIPS	ROSINER	ROT
ROOTY	RORTIER	ROSELESS	ROSINERS	ROTA
ROPABLE	RORTIEST	ROSELIKE	ROSINESS	ROTACHUTE
ROPE	RORTING	ROSELLA	ROSING	ROTAL
ROPEABLE	RORTINGS	ROSELLAS	ROSINING	ROTAMETER
ROPED	RORTS	ROSELLE	ROSINOL	ROTAN
ROPELIKE	RORTY	ROSELLES	ROSINOLS	ROTANS
ROPER	RORY	ROSEMARY	ROSINOUS	ROTAPLANE
ROPERIES	ROSACE	ROSEOLA	ROSINS	ROTARIES
ROPERS	ROSACEA	ROSEOLAR	ROSINWEED	ROTARY
ROPERY	ROSACEAS	ROSEOLAS	ROSINY	ROTAS
ROPES	ROSACEOUS	ROSERIES	ROSIT	ROTATABLE
ROPEWALK	ROSACES	ROSEROOT	ROSITED	ROTATE
ROPEWALKS	ROSAKER	ROSEROOTS	ROSITING	ROTATED

ROTATES	ROTOR	ROUCHINGS	ROULADES	ROUNDURE
ROTATING	ROTORS	ROUCOU	ROULE	ROUNDURES
ROTATION	ROTOS	ROUCOUS	ROULEAU	ROUNDWOOD
ROTATIONS	ROTOSCOPE	ROUE	ROULEAUS	ROUNDWORM
ROTATIVE	ROTOTILL	ROUEN	ROULEAUX	ROUP
ROTATOR	ROTOTILLS	ROUENS	ROULES	ROUPED
ROTATORES	ROTOVATE	ROUES	ROULETTE	ROUPET
ROTATORS	ROTOVATED	ROUGE	ROULETTED	ROUPIER
ROTATORY	ROTOVATES	ROUGED	ROULETTES	ROUPIEST
ROTAVATE	ROTOVATOR	ROUGES	ROULS	ROUPILY
ROTAVATED	ROTPROOF	ROUGH	ROUM	ROUPING
ROTAVATES	ROTS	ROUGHAGE	ROUMING	ROUPIT
ROTAVATOR	ROTTAN	ROUGHAGES	ROUMINGS	ROUPS
ROTAVIRUS	ROTTANS	ROUGHBACK	ROUMS	ROUPY
ROTCH	ROTTE	ROUGHCAST	ROUNCE	ROUSABLE
ROTCHE	ROTTED	ROUGHDRY	ROUNCES	ROUSANT
ROTCHES	ROTTEN	ROUGHED	ROUNCEVAL	ROUSE
ROTCHIE	ROTTENER	ROUGHEN	ROUNCIES	ROUSED
ROTCHIES	ROTTENEST	ROUGHENED	ROUNCY	ROUSEMENT
ROTE	ROTTENLY	ROUGHENS	ROUND	ROUSER
ROTED	ROTTENS	ROUGHER	ROUNDARCH	ROUSERS
ROTENONE	ROTTER	ROUGHERS	ROUNDBALL	ROUSES
ROTENONES	ROTTERS	ROUGHEST	ROUNDED	ROUSING
ROTES	ROTTES	ROUGHHEW	ROUNDEDLY	ROUSINGLY
ROTGRASS	ROTTING	ROUGHHEWN	ROUNDEL	ROUSSEAU
ROTGUT	ROTULA	ROUGHHEWS	ROUNDELAY	ROUSSEAUS
ROTGUTS	ROTULAE	ROUGHIE	ROUNDELS	ROUSSETTE
ROTHER	ROTULAS	ROUGHIES	ROUNDER	ROUST
ROTHERS	ROTUND	ROUGHING	ROUNDERS	ROUSTED
ROTI	ROTUNDA	ROUGHINGS	ROUNDEST	ROUSTER
ROTIFER	ROTUNDAS	ROUGHISH	ROUNDHAND	ROUSTERS
ROTIFERAL	ROTUNDATE	ROUGHLEG	ROUNDHEEL	ROUSTING
ROTIFERAN	ROTUNDED	ROUGHLEGS	ROUNDING	ROUSTS
ROTIFERS	ROTUNDER	ROUGHLY	ROUNDINGS	ROUT
ROTIFORM	ROTUNDEST	ROUGHNECK	ROUNDISH	ROUTE
ROTING	ROTUNDING	ROUGHNESS	ROUNDLE	ROUTED
ROTINI	ROTUNDITY	ROUGHOUT	ROUNDLES	ROUTEING
ROTINIS	ROTUNDLY	ROUGHOUTS	ROUNDLET	ROUTEMAN
ROTIS	ROTUNDS	ROUGHS	ROUNDLETS	ROUTEMEN
ROTL	ROTURIER	ROUGHSHOD	ROUNDLY	ROUTER
ROTLS	ROTURIERS	ROUGHT	ROUNDNESS	ROUTERS
ROTO	ROUBLE	ROUGHY	ROUNDS	ROUTES
ROTOGRAPH	ROUBLES	ROUGING	ROUNDSMAN	ROUTEWAY
ROTOLO	ROUCHE	ROUILLE	ROUNDSMEN	ROUTEWAYS
ROTOLOS	ROUCHED	ROUILLES	ROUNDTRIP	ROUTH
ROTON	ROUCHES	ROUL	ROUNDUP	ROUTHIE
ROTONS	ROUCHING	ROULADE	ROUNDUPS	ROUTHIER

ROUTHIEST	ROWELING	ROYALMAST	RUBBER	RUBELS
ROUTHS	ROWELLED	ROYALS	RUBBERED	RUBEOLA
ROUTINE	ROWELLING	ROYALTIES	RUBBERIER	RUBEOLAR
ROUTINEER	ROWELS	ROYALTY	RUBBERING	RUBEOLAS
ROUTINELY	ROWEN	ROYNE	RUBBERISE	RUBES
ROUTINES	ROWENS	ROYNED	RUBBERIZE	RUBESCENT
ROUTING	ROWER	ROYNES	RUBBERS	RUBICELLE
ROUTINGS	ROWERS	ROYNING	RUBBERY	RUBICON
ROUTINISE	ROWIE	ROYNISH	RUBBET	RUBICONED
ROUTINISM	ROWIES	ROYST	RUBBIDIES	RUBICONS
ROUTINIST	ROWING	ROYSTED	RUBBIDY	RUBICUND
ROUTINIZE	ROWINGS	ROYSTER	RUBBIES	RUBIDIC
ROUTOUS	ROWLOCK	ROYSTERED	RUBBING	RUBIDIUM
ROUTOUSLY	ROWLOCKS	ROYSTERER	RUBBINGS	RUBIDIUMS
ROUTS	ROWME	ROYSTERS	RUBBISH	RUBIED
ROUX	ROWMES	ROYSTING	RUBBISHED	RUBIER
ROVE	ROWND	ROYSTS	RUBBISHES	RUBIES
ROVED	ROWNDED	ROZELLE	RUBBISHLY	RUBIEST
ROVEN	ROWNDELL	ROZELLES	RUBBISHY	RUBIFIED
ROVER	ROWNDELLS	ROZET	RUBBIT	RUBIFIES
ROVERS	ROWNDING	ROZETED	RUBBITIES	RUBIFY
ROVES	ROWNDS	ROZETING	RUBBITY	RUBIFYING
ROVING	ROWOVER	ROZETS	RUBBLE	RUBIGO
ROVINGLY	ROWOVERS	ROZIT	RUBBLED	RUBIGOS
ROVINGS	ROWS	ROZITED	RUBBLES	RUBIN
ROW	ROWT	ROZITING	RUBBLIER	RUBINE
ROWABLE	ROWTED	ROZITS	RUBBLIEST	RUBINEOUS
ROWAN	ROWTH	ROZZER	RUBBLING	RUBINES
ROWANS	ROWTHS	ROZZERS	RUBBLY	RUBINS
ROWBOAT	ROWTING	RUANA	RUBBOARD	RUBIOUS
ROWBOATS	ROWTS	RUANAS	RUBBOARDS	RUBLE
ROWDEDOW	ROYAL	RUB	RUBBY	RUBLES
ROWDEDOWS	ROYALET	RUBABOO	RUBBYDUB	RUBLI
ROWDIER	ROYALETS	RUBABOOS	RUBBYDUBS	RUBOFF
ROWDIES	ROYALISE	RUBACE	RUBDOWN	RUBOFFS
ROWDIEST	ROYALISED	RUBACES	RUBDOWNS	RUBOUT
ROWDILY	ROYALISES	RUBAI	RUBE	RUBOUTS
ROWDINESS	ROYALISM	RUBAIS	RUBEFIED	RUBRIC
ROWDY	ROYALISMS	RUBAIYAT	RUBEFIES	RUBRICAL
ROWDYDOW	ROYALIST	RUBASSE	RUBEFY	RUBRICATE
ROWDYDOWS	ROYALISTS	RUBASSES	RUBEFYING	RUBRICIAN
ROWDYISH	ROYALIZE	RUBATI	RUBEL	RUBRICS
ROWDYISM	ROYALIZED	RUBATO	RUBELLA	RUBS
ROWDYISMS	ROYALIZES	RUBATOS	RUBELLAN	RUBSTONE
ROWED	ROYALLER	RUBBABOO	RUBELLANS	RUBSTONES
ROWEL	ROYALLEST	RUBBABOOS	RUBELLAS	RUBUS
ROWELED	ROYALLY	RUBBED	RUBELLITE	RUBUSES

R

RUBY	RUDDING	RUELLIA	RUGGEDIZE	RULERED
RUBYING	RUDDLE	RUELLIAS	RUGGEDLY	RULERING
RUBYLIKE	RUDDLED	RUER	RUGGELACH	RULERS
RUC	RUDDLEMAN	RUERS	RUGGER	RULERSHIP
RUCHE	RUDDLEMEN	RUES	RUGGERS	RULES
RUCHED	RUDDLES	RUFESCENT	RUGGIER	RULESSE
RUCHES	RUDDLING	RUFF	RUGGIEST	RULIER
RUCHING	RUDDOCK	RUFFE	RUGGING	RULIEST
RUCHINGS	RUDDOCKS	RUFFED	RUGGINGS	RULING
RUCK	RUDDS	RUFFES	RUGGY	RULINGS
RUCKED	RUDDY	RUFFIAN	RUGLIKE	RULLION
RUCKING	RUDDYING	RUFFIANED	RUGOLA	RULLIONS
RUCKLE	RUDE	RUFFIANLY	RUGOLAS	RULLOCK
RUCKLED	RUDELY	RUFFIANS	RUGOSA	RULLOCKS
RUCKLES	RUDENESS	RUFFIN	RUGOSAS	RULY
RUCKLING	RUDER	RUFFING	RUGOSE	RUM
RUCKMAN	RUDERAL	RUFFINS	RUGOSELY	RUMAKI
RUCKMEN	RUDERALS	RUFFLE	RUGOSITY	RUMAKIS
RUCKS	RUDERIES	RUFFLED	RUGOUS	RUMAL
RUCKSACK	RUDERY	RUFFLER	RUGRAT	RUMALS
RUCKSACKS	RUDES	RUFFLERS	RUGRATS	RUMBA
RUCKSEAT	RUDESBIES	RUFFLES	RUGS	RUMBAED
RUCKSEATS	RUDESBY	RUFFLIER	RUGULOSE	RUMBAING
RUCKUS	RUDEST	RUFFLIEST	RUIN	RUMBAS
RUCKUSES	RUDI	RUFFLIKE	RUINABLE	RUMBELOW
RUCOLA	RUDIE	RUFFLING	RUINATE	RUMBELOWS
RUCOLAS	RUDIES	RUFFLINGS	RUINATED	RUMBLE
RUCS	RUDIMENT	RUFFLY	RUINATES	RUMBLED
RUCTATION	RUDIMENTS	RUFFS	RUINATING	RUMBLER
RUCTION	RUDIS	RUFIYAA	RUINATION	RUMBLERS
RUCTIONS	RUDISH	RUFIYAAS	RUINED	RUMBLES
RUCTIOUS	RUDIST	RUFOUS	RUINER	RUMBLIER
RUD	RUDISTID	RUFOUSES	RUINERS	RUMBLIEST
RUDACEOUS	RUDISTIDS	RUG	RUING	RUMBLING
RUDAS	RUDISTS	RUGA	RUINGS	RUMBLINGS
RUDASES	RUDS	RUGAE	RUINING	RUMBLY
RUDBECKIA	RUDY	RUGAL	RUININGS	RUMBO
RUDD	RUE	RUGALACH	RUINOUS	RUMBOS
RUDDED	RUED	RUGATE	RUINOUSLY	RUMDUM
RUDDER	RUEDA	RUGBIES	RUINS	RUMDUMS
RUDDERS	RUEDAS	RUGBY	RUKH	RUME
RUDDIED	RUEFUL	RUGELACH	RUKHS	RUMEN
RUDDIER	RUEFULLY	RUGELACHS	RULABLE	RUMENS
RUDDIES	RUEING	RUGGED	RULE	RUMES
RUDDIEST	RUEINGS	RUGGEDER	RULED	RUMINA
RUDDILY	RUELLE	RUGGEDEST	RULELESS	RUMINAL
RUDDINESS	RUELLES	RUGGEDISE	RULER	RUMINANT

RUMINANTS
RUMINATE
RUMINATED
RUMINATES
RUMINATOR
RUMKIN
RUMKINS
RUMLY
RUMMAGE
RUMMAGED
RUMMAGER
RUMMAGERS
RUMMAGES
RUMMAGING
RUMMER
RUMMERS
RUMMEST
RUMMIER
RUMMIES
RUMMIEST
RUMMILY
RUMMINESS
RUMMISH
RUMMISHED
RUMMISHES
RUMMY
RUMNESS
RUMNESSES
RUMOR
RUMORED
RUMORER
RUMORERS
RUMORING
RUMOROUS
RUMORS
RUMOUR
RUMOURED
RUMOURER
RUMOURERS
RUMOURING
RUMOURS
RUMP
RUMPED
RUMPIES
RUMPING
RUMPLE
RUMPLED

RUMPLES
RUMPLESS
RUMPLIER
RUMPLIEST
RUMPLING
RUMPLY
RUMPO
RUMPOS
RUMPOT
RUMPOTS
RUMPS
RUMPUS
RUMPUSES
RUMPY
RUMRUNNER
RUMS
RUN
RUNABOUT
RUNABOUTS
RUNAGATE
RUNAGATES
RUNANGA
RUNANGAS
RUNAROUND
RUNAWAY
RUNAWAYS
RUNBACK
RUNBACKS
RUNCH
RUNCHES
RUNCIBLE
RUNCINATE
RUND
RUNDALE
RUNDALES
RUNDLE
RUNDLED
RUNDLES
RUNDLET
RUNDLETS
RUNDOWN
RUNDOWNS
RUNDS
RUNE
RUNECRAFT
RUNED
RUNELIKE

RUNES
RUNFLAT
RUNFLATS
RUNG
RUNGED
RUNGLESS
RUNGS
RUNIC
RUNKLE
RUNKLED
RUNKLES
RUNKLING
RUNLESS
RUNLET
RUNLETS
RUNNABLE
RUNNEL
RUNNELS
RUNNER
RUNNERS
RUNNET
RUNNETS
RUNNIER
RUNNIEST
RUNNINESS
RUNNING
RUNNINGLY
RUNNINGS
RUNNION
RUNNIONS
RUNNY
RUNOFF
RUNOFFS
RUNOUT
RUNOUTS
RUNOVER
RUNOVERS
RUNPROOF
RUNRIG
RUNRIGS
RUNROUND
RUNROUNDS
RUNS
RUNT
RUNTED
RUNTIER
RUNTIEST

RUNTINESS
RUNTISH
RUNTISHLY
RUNTS
RUNTY
RUNWAY
RUNWAYS
RUPEE
RUPEES
RUPIA
RUPIAH
RUPIAHS
RUPIAS
RUPTURE
RUPTURED
RUPTURES
RUPTURING
RURAL
RURALISE
RURALISED
RURALISES
RURALISM
RURALISMS
RURALIST
RURALISTS
RURALITE
RURALITES
RURALITY
RURALIZE
RURALIZED
RURALIZES
RURALLY
RURALNESS
RURALS
RURBAN
RURP
RURPS
RURU
RURUS
RUSA
RUSALKA
RUSALKAS
RUSAS
RUSCUS
RUSCUSES
RUSE
RUSES

RUSH
RUSHED
RUSHEE
RUSHEES
RUSHEN
RUSHER
RUSHERS
RUSHES
RUSHIER
RUSHIEST
RUSHINESS
RUSHING
RUSHINGS
RUSHLIGHT
RUSHLIKE
RUSHY
RUSINE
RUSK
RUSKS
RUSMA
RUSMAS
RUSSE
RUSSEL
RUSSELS
RUSSET
RUSSETED
RUSSETING
RUSSETS
RUSSETY
RUSSIA
RUSSIAS
RUSSIFIED
RUSSIFIES
RUSSIFY
RUSSULA
RUSSULAE
RUSSULAS
RUST
RUSTABLE
RUSTED
RUSTIC
RUSTICAL
RUSTICALS
RUSTICANA
RUSTICATE
RUSTICIAL
RUSTICISE

R

RUSTICISM	RUSTPROOF	RUTILATED	RYAL	RYKING
RUSTICITY	RUSTRE	RUTILE	RYALS	RYMME
RUSTICIZE	RUSTRED	RUTILES	RYAS	RYMMED
RUSTICLY	RUSTRES	RUTIN	RYBAT	RYMMES
RUSTICS	RUSTS	RUTINS	RYBATS	RYMMING
RUSTIER	RUSTY	RUTS	RYBAUDRYE	RYND
RUSTIEST	RUT	RUTTED	RYE	RYNDS
RUSTILY	RUTABAGA	RUTTER	RYEBREAD	RYOKAN
RUSTINESS	RUTABAGAS	RUTTERS	RYEBREADS	RYOKANS
RUSTING	RUTACEOUS	RUTTIER	RYEFLOUR	RYOT
RUSTINGS	RUTH	RUTTIEST	RYEFLOURS	RYOTS
RUSTLE	RUTHENIC	RUTTILY	RYEGRASS	RYOTWARI
RUSTLED	RUTHENIUM	RUTTINESS	RYEPECK	RYOTWARIS
RUSTLER	RUTHER	RUTTING	RYEPECKS	RYPE
RUSTLERS	RUTHFUL	RUTTINGS	RYES	RYPECK
RUSTLES	RUTHFULLY	RUTTISH	RYFE	RYPECKS
RUSTLESS	RUTHLESS	RUTTISHLY	RYKE	RYPER
RUSTLING	RUTHS	RUTTY	RYKED	RYU
RUSTLINGS	RUTILANT	RYA	RYKES	RYUS

S

SAAG	SABINS	SAC	SACKER	SACRISTS
SAAGS	SABIR	SACATON	SACKERS	SACRISTY
SAB	SABIRS	SACATONS	SACKFUL	SACRUM
SABADILLA	SABKHA	SACBUT	SACKFULS	SACRUMS
SABAL	SABKHAH	SACBUTS	SACKING	SACS
SABALS	SABKHAHS	SACCADE	SACKINGS	SAD
SABATON	SABKHAS	SACCADES	SACKLESS	SADDED
SABATONS	SABKHAT	SACCADIC	SACKLIKE	SADDEN
SABAYON	SABKHATS	SACCATE	SACKLOAD	SADDENED
SABAYONS	SABLE	SACCHARIC	SACKLOADS	SADDENING
SABBAT	SABLED	SACCHARIN	SACKS	SADDENS
SABBATH	SABLEFISH	SACCHARUM	SACKSFUL	SADDER
SABBATHS	SABLES	SACCIFORM	SACLESS	SADDEST
SABBATIC	SABLING	SACCOI	SACLIKE	SADDHU
SABBATICS	SABOT	SACCOS	SACQUE	SADDHUS
SABBATINE	SABOTAGE	SACCOSES	SACQUES	SADDIE
SABBATISE	SABOTAGED	SACCULAR	SACRA	SADDIES
SABBATISM	SABOTAGES	SACCULATE	SACRAL	SADDING
SABBATIZE	SABOTED	SACCULE	SACRALGIA	SADDISH
SABBATS	SABOTEUR	SACCULES	SACRALISE	SADDLE
SABBED	SABOTEURS	SACCULI	SACRALITY	SADDLEBAG
SABBING	SABOTIER	SACCULUS	SACRALIZE	SADDLEBOW
SABBINGS	SABOTIERS	SACELLA	SACRALS	SADDLED
SABE	SABOTS	SACELLUM	SACRAMENT	SADDLER
SABED	SABRA	SACHEM	SACRARIA	SADDLERS
SABEING	SABRAS	SACHEMDOM	SACRARIAL	SADDLERY
SABELLA	SABRE	SACHEMIC	SACRARIUM	SADDLES
SABELLAS	SABRED	SACHEMS	SACRED	SADDLING
SABER	SABRELIKE	SACHET	SACREDER	SADDO
SABERED	SABRES	SACHETED	SACREDEST	SADDOES
SABERING	SABREUR	SACHETS	SACREDLY	SADDOS
SABERLIKE	SABREURS	SACK	SACRIFICE	SADE
SABERS	SABREWING	SACKABLE	SACRIFIDE	SADES
SABES	SABRING	SACKAGE	SACRIFIED	SADHANA
SABHA	SABS	SACKAGED	SACRIFIES	SADHANAS
SABHAS	SABULINE	SACKAGES	SACRIFY	SADHE
SABICU	SABULOSE	SACKAGING	SACRILEGE	SADHES
SABICUS	SABULOUS	SACKBUT	SACRING	SADHU
SABIN	SABURRA	SACKBUTS	SACRINGS	SADHUS
SABINE	SABURRAL	SACKCLOTH	SACRIST	SADI
SABINES	SABURRAS	SACKED	SACRISTAN	SADIRON

S

SADIRONS
SADIS
SADISM
SADISMS
SADIST
SADISTIC
SADISTS
SADLY
SADNESS
SADNESSES
SADO
SADOS
SADS
SADZA
SADZAS
SAE
SAECULA
SAECULUM
SAECULUMS
SAETER
SAETERS
SAFARI
SAFARIED
SAFARIING
SAFARIS
SAFARIST
SAFARISTS
SAFE
SAFED
SAFEGUARD
SAFELIGHT
SAFELY
SAFENESS
SAFER
SAFES
SAFEST
SAFETIED
SAFETIES
SAFETY
SAFETYING
SAFETYMAN
SAFETYMEN
SAFFIAN
SAFFIANS
SAFFLOWER
SAFFRON
SAFFRONED

SAFFRONS
SAFFRONY
SAFING
SAFRANIN
SAFRANINE
SAFRANINS
SAFROL
SAFROLE
SAFROLES
SAFROLS
SAFRONAL
SAFRONALS
SAFT
SAFTER
SAFTEST
SAG
SAGA
SAGACIOUS
SAGACITY
SAGAMAN
SAGAMEN
SAGAMORE
SAGAMORES
SAGANASH
SAGAPENUM
SAGAS
SAGATHIES
SAGATHY
SAGBUT
SAGBUTS
SAGE
SAGEBRUSH
SAGEHOOD
SAGEHOODS
SAGELY
SAGENE
SAGENES
SAGENESS
SAGENITE
SAGENITES
SAGENITIC
SAGER
SAGES
SAGEST
SAGGAR
SAGGARD
SAGGARDS

SAGGARED
SAGGARING
SAGGARS
SAGGED
SAGGER
SAGGERED
SAGGERING
SAGGERS
SAGGIER
SAGGIEST
SAGGING
SAGGINGS
SAGGY
SAGIER
SAGIEST
SAGINATE
SAGINATED
SAGINATES
SAGITTA
SAGITTAL
SAGITTARY
SAGITTAS
SAGITTATE
SAGO
SAGOIN
SAGOINS
SAGOS
SAGOUIN
SAGOUINS
SAGRADA
SAGS
SAGUARO
SAGUAROS
SAGUIN
SAGUINS
SAGUM
SAGY
SAHEB
SAHEBS
SAHIB
SAHIBA
SAHIBAH
SAHIBAHS
SAHIBAS
SAHIBS
SAHIWAL
SAHIWALS

SAHUARO
SAHUAROS
SAI
SAIBLING
SAIBLINGS
SAIC
SAICE
SAICES
SAICK
SAICKS
SAICS
SAID
SAIDEST
SAIDS
SAIDST
SAIGA
SAIGAS
SAIKEI
SAIKEIS
SAIKLESS
SAIL
SAILABLE
SAILBOARD
SAILBOAT
SAILBOATS
SAILCLOTH
SAILED
SAILER
SAILERS
SAILFISH
SAILING
SAILINGS
SAILLESS
SAILMAKER
SAILOR
SAILORING
SAILORLY
SAILORS
SAILPAST
SAILPASTS
SAILPLANE
SAILROOM
SAILROOMS
SAILS
SAIM
SAIMIN
SAIMINS

SAIMIRI
SAIMIRIS
SAIMS
SAIN
SAINE
SAINED
SAINFOIN
SAINFOINS
SAINING
SAINS
SAINT
SAINTDOM
SAINTDOMS
SAINTED
SAINTESS
SAINTFOIN
SAINTHOOD
SAINTING
SAINTISH
SAINTISM
SAINTISMS
SAINTLESS
SAINTLIER
SAINTLIKE
SAINTLILY
SAINTLING
SAINTLY
SAINTS
SAINTSHIP
SAIQUE
SAIQUES
SAIR
SAIRED
SAIRER
SAIREST
SAIRING
SAIRS
SAIS
SAIST
SAITH
SAITHE
SAITHES
SAITHS
SAIYID
SAIYIDS
SAJOU
SAJOUS

SAKAI	SALARIAT	SALICINS	SALLIED	SALPIDS
SAKAIS	SALARIATS	SALICYLIC	SALLIER	SALPIFORM
SAKE	SALARIED	SALIENCE	SALLIERS	SALPINGES
SAKER	SALARIES	SALIENCES	SALLIES	SALPINX
SAKERET	SALARY	SALIENCY	SALLOW	SALPINXES
SAKERETS	SALARYING	SALIENT	SALLOWED	SALPS
SAKERS	SALARYMAN	SALIENTLY	SALLOWER	SALS
SAKES	SALARYMEN	SALIENTS	SALLOWEST	SALSA
SAKI	SALAT	SALIFIED	SALLOWING	SALSAED
SAKIA	SALATS	SALIFIES	SALLOWISH	SALSAING
SAKIAS	SALBAND	SALIFY	SALLOWLY	SALSAS
SAKIEH	SALBANDS	SALIFYING	SALLOWS	SALSE
SAKIEHS	SALCHOW	SALIGOT	SALLOWY	SALSES
SAKIS	SALCHOWS	SALIGOTS	SALLY	SALSIFIES
SAKIYEH	SALE	SALIMETER	SALLYING	SALSIFY
SAKIYEHS	SALEABLE	SALIMETRY	SALLYPORT	SALSILLA
SAKKOI	SALEABLY	SALINA	SALMI	SALSILLAS
SAKKOS	SALEP	SALINAS	SALMIS	SALT
SAKKOSES	SALEPS	SALINE	SALMON	SALTANDO
SAKSAUL	SALERATUS	SALINES	SALMONET	SALTANDOS
SAKSAULS	SALERING	SALINISE	SALMONETS	SALTANT
SAKTI	SALERINGS	SALINISED	SALMONID	SALTANTS
SAKTIS	SALEROOM	SALINISES	SALMONIDS	SALTATE
SAL	SALEROOMS	SALINITY	SALMONOID	SALTATED
SALAAM	SALES	SALINIZE	SALMONS	SALTATES
SALAAMED	SALESGIRL	SALINIZED	SALMONY	SALTATING
SALAAMING	SALESLADY	SALINIZES	SALOL	SALTATION
SALAAMS	SALESMAN	SALIVA	SALOLS	SALTATO
SALABLE	SALESMEN	SALIVAL	SALOMETER	SALTATORY
SALABLY	SALESROOM	SALIVARY	SALON	SALTATOS
SALACIOUS	SALET	SALIVAS	SALONS	SALTBOX
SALACITY	SALETS	SALIVATE	SALOON	SALTBOXES
SALAD	SALEWD	SALIVATED	SALOONS	SALTBUSH
SALADANG	SALEYARD	SALIVATES	SALOOP	SALTCAT
SALADANGS	SALEYARDS	SALIVATOR	SALOOPS	SALTCATS
SALADE	SALFERN	SALIX	SALOP	SALTCHUCK
SALADES	SALFERNS	SALL	SALOPIAN	SALTED
SALADING	SALIAUNCE	SALLAD	SALOPS	SALTER
SALADINGS	SALIC	SALLADS	SALP	SALTERIES
SALADS	SALICES	SALLAL	SALPA	SALTERN
SALAL	SALICET	SALLALS	SALPAE	SALTERNS
SALALS	SALICETA	SALLE	SALPAS	SALTERS
SALAMI	SALICETS	SALLEE	SALPIAN	SALTERY
SALAMIS	SALICETUM	SALLEES	SALPIANS	SALTEST
SALAMON	SALICIN	SALLES	SALPICON	SALTFISH
SALAMONS	SALICINE	SALLET	SALPICONS	SALTIE
SALANGANE	SALICINES	SALLETS	SALPID	SALTIER

S

SALTIERS	SALUTERS	SAMARITAN	SAMISEN	SAMSHOO
SALTIES	SALUTES	SAMARIUM	SAMISENS	SAMSHOOS
SALTIEST	SALUTING	SAMARIUMS	SAMITE	SAMSHU
SALTILY	SALVABLE	SAMAS	SAMITES	SAMSHUS
SALTINE	SALVABLY	SAMBA	SAMITHI	SAMSKARA
SALTINES	SALVAGE	SAMBAED	SAMITHIS	SAMSKARAS
SALTINESS	SALVAGED	SAMBAING	SAMITI	SAMURAI
SALTING	SALVAGEE	SAMBAL	SAMITIS	SAMURAIS
SALTINGS	SALVAGEES	SAMBALS	SAMIZDAT	SAN
SALTIRE	SALVAGER	SAMBAR	SAMIZDATS	SANATIVE
SALTIRES	SALVAGERS	SAMBARS	SAMLET	SANATORIA
SALTISH	SALVAGES	SAMBAS	SAMLETS	SANATORY
SALTISHLY	SALVAGING	SAMBHAR	SAMLOR	SANBENITO
SALTLESS	SALVARSAN	SAMBHARS	SAMLORS	SANCAI
SALTLIKE	SALVATION	SAMBHUR	SAMMED	SANCAIS
SALTLY	SALVATORY	SAMBHURS	SAMMIES	SANCHO
SALTNESS	SALVE	SAMBO	SAMMING	SANCHOS
SALTO	SALVED	SAMBOES	SAMMY	SANCTA
SALTOED	SALVER	SAMBOS	SAMNITIS	SANCTIFY
SALTOING	SALVERS	SAMBUCA	SAMOSA	SANCTION
SALTOS	SALVES	SAMBUCAS	SAMOSAS	SANCTIONS
SALTPAN	SALVETE	SAMBUKE	SAMOVAR	SANCTITY
SALTPANS	SALVETES	SAMBUKES	SAMOVARS	SANCTUARY
SALTPETER	SALVIA	SAMBUR	SAMOYED	SANCTUM
SALTPETRE	SALVIAS	SAMBURS	SAMOYEDS	SANCTUMS
SALTS	SALVIFIC	SAME	SAMP	SAND
SALTUS	SALVING	SAMECH	SAMPAN	SANDABLE
SALTUSES	SALVINGS	SAMECHS	SAMPANS	SANDAL
SALTWATER	SALVO	SAMEK	SAMPHIRE	SANDALED
SALTWORK	SALVOED	SAMEKH	SAMPHIRES	SANDALING
SALTWORKS	SALVOES	SAMEKHS	SAMPI	SANDALLED
SALTWORT	SALVOING	SAMEKS	SAMPIRE	SANDALS
SALTWORTS	SALVOR	SAMEL	SAMPIRES	SANDARAC
SALTY	SALVORS	SAMELY	SAMPIS	SANDARACH
SALUBRITY	SALVOS	SAMEN	SAMPLE	SANDARACS
SALUE	SALWAR	SAMENESS	SAMPLED	SANDBAG
SALUED	SALWARS	SAMES	SAMPLER	SANDBAGS
SALUES	SAM	SAMEY	SAMPLERS	SANDBANK
SALUING	SAMA	SAMEYNESS	SAMPLERY	SANDBANKS
SALUKI	SAMAAN	SAMFOO	SAMPLES	SANDBAR
SALUKIS	SAMAANS	SAMFOOS	SAMPLING	SANDBARS
SALURETIC	SAMADHI	SAMFU	SAMPLINGS	SANDBLAST
SALUT	SAMADHIS	SAMFUS	SAMPS	SANDBOX
SALUTARY	SAMAN	SAMIEL	SAMS	SANDBOXES
SALUTE	SAMANS	SAMIELS	SAMSARA	SANDBOY
SALUTED	SAMARA	SAMIER	SAMSARAS	SANDBOYS
SALUTER	SAMARAS	SAMIEST	SAMSARIC	SANDBUR

SANDBURR	SANDPUMP	SANGLIERS	SANKOS	SANTON
SANDBURRS	SANDPUMPS	SANGO	SANNIE	SANTONICA
SANDBURS	SANDS	SANGOMA	SANNIES	SANTONIN
SANDCRACK	SANDSHOE	SANGOMAS	SANNOP	SANTONINS
SANDDAB	SANDSHOES	SANGOS	SANNOPS	SANTONS
SANDDABS	SANDSOAP	SANGRAIL	SANNUP	SANTOOR
SANDED	SANDSOAPS	SANGRAILS	SANNUPS	SANTOORS
SANDEK	SANDSPIT	SANGREAL	SANNYASI	SANTOS
SANDEKS	SANDSPITS	SANGREALS	SANNYASIN	SANTOUR
SANDER	SANDSPOUT	SANGRIA	SANNYASIS	SANTOURS
SANDERS	SANDSPUR	SANGRIAS	SANPAN	SANTS
SANDERSES	SANDSPURS	SANGS	SANPANS	SANTUR
SANDFISH	SANDSTONE	SANGUIFY	SANPRO	SANTURS
SANDFLIES	SANDSTORM	SANGUINE	SANPROS	SANYASI
SANDFLY	SANDWICH	SANGUINED	SANS	SANYASIS
SANDGLASS	SANDWORM	SANGUINES	SANSA	SAOLA
SANDHEAP	SANDWORMS	SANICLE	SANSAR	SAOLAS
SANDHEAPS	SANDWORT	SANICLES	SANSARS	SAOUARI
SANDHI	SANDWORTS	SANIDINE	SANSAS	SAOUARIS
SANDHILL	SANDY	SANIDINES	SANSEI	SAP
SANDHILLS	SANDYISH	SANIES	SANSEIS	SAPAJOU
SANDHIS	SANE	SANIFIED	SANSERIF	SAPAJOUS
SANDHOG	SANED	SANIFIES	SANSERIFS	SAPAN
SANDHOGS	SANELY	SANIFY	SANT	SAPANS
SANDIER	SANENESS	SANIFYING	SANTAL	SAPANWOOD
SANDIEST	SANER	SANING	SANTALIC	SAPEGO
SANDINESS	SANES	SANIOUS	SANTALIN	SAPEGOES
SANDING	SANEST	SANITARIA	SANTALINS	SAPELE
SANDINGS	SANG	SANITARY	SANTALOL	SAPELES
SANDIVER	SANGA	SANITATE	SANTALOLS	SAPFUL
SANDIVERS	SANGAR	SANITATED	SANTALS	SAPHEAD
SANDLESS	SANGAREE	SANITATES	SANTERA	SAPHEADED
SANDLIKE	SANGAREES	SANITIES	SANTERAS	SAPHEADS
SANDLING	SANGARS	SANITISE	SANTERIA	SAPHENA
SANDLINGS	SANGAS	SANITISED	SANTERIAS	SAPHENAE
SANDLOT	SANGEET	SANITISER	SANTERO	SAPHENAS
SANDLOTS	SANGEETS	SANITISES	SANTEROS	SAPHENOUS
SANDMAN	SANGER	SANITIZE	SANTIM	SAPID
SANDMEN	SANGERS	SANITIZED	SANTIMI	SAPIDITY
SANDPAPER	SANGFROID	SANITIZER	SANTIMS	SAPIDLESS
SANDPEEP	SANGH	SANITIZES	SANTIMU	SAPIDNESS
SANDPEEPS	SANGHA	SANITORIA	SANTIR	SAPIENCE
SANDPILE	SANGHAS	SANITY	SANTIRS	SAPIENCES
SANDPILES	SANGHAT	SANJAK	SANTO	SAPIENCY
SANDPIPER	SANGHATS	SANJAKS	SANTOL	SAPIENS
SANDPIT	SANGHS	SANK	SANTOLINA	SAPIENT
SANDPITS	SANGLIER	SANKO	SANTOLS	SAPIENTLY

S

SAPIENTS	SAPPLES	SARCODES	SARI	SARSENETS
SAPLESS	SAPPLING	SARCODIC	SARIN	SARSENS
SAPLING	SAPPY	SARCOID	SARING	SARSNET
SAPLINGS	SAPRAEMIA	SARCOIDS	SARINS	SARSNETS
SAPODILLA	SAPRAEMIC	SARCOLOGY	SARIS	SARTOR
SAPOGENIN	SAPREMIA	SARCOMA	SARK	SARTORIAL
SAPONARIA	SAPREMIAS	SARCOMAS	SARKIER	SARTORIAN
SAPONATED	SAPREMIC	SARCOMATA	SARKIEST	SARTORII
SAPONIFY	SAPROBE	SARCOMERE	SARKILY	SARTORIUS
SAPONIN	SAPROBES	SARCONET	SARKINESS	SARTORS
SAPONINE	SAPROBIAL	SARCONETS	SARKING	SARUS
SAPONINES	SAPROBIC	SARCOPTIC	SARKINGS	SARUSES
SAPONINS	SAPROLITE	SARCOSOME	SARKS	SASANQUA
SAPONITE	SAPROPEL	SARCOUS	SARKY	SASANQUAS
SAPONITES	SAPROPELS	SARD	SARMENT	SASARARA
SAPOR	SAPROZOIC	SARDANA	SARMENTA	SASARARAS
SAPORIFIC	SAPS	SARDANAS	SARMENTS	SASER
SAPOROUS	SAPSAGO	SARDAR	SARMENTUM	SASERS
SAPORS	SAPSAGOS	SARDARS	SARMIE	SASH
SAPOTA	SAPSUCKER	SARDEL	SARMIES	SASHAY
SAPOTAS	SAPUCAIA	SARDELLE	SARNEY	SASHAYED
SAPOTE	SAPUCAIAS	SARDELLES	SARNEYS	SASHAYING
SAPOTES	SAPWOOD	SARDELS	SARNIE	SASHAYS
SAPOUR	SAPWOODS	SARDINE	SARNIES	SASHED
SAPOURS	SAR	SARDINED	SAROD	SASHES
SAPPAN	SARABAND	SARDINES	SARODE	SASHIMI
SAPPANS	SARABANDE	SARDINING	SARODES	SASHIMIS
SAPPED	SARABANDS	SARDIUS	SARODIST	SASHING
SAPPER	SARAFAN	SARDIUSES	SARODISTS	SASHLESS
SAPPERS	SARAFANS	SARDONIAN	SARODS	SASIN
SAPPHIC	SARAN	SARDONIC	SARONG	SASINE
SAPPHICS	SARANGI	SARDONYX	SARONGS	SASINES
SAPPHIRE	SARANGIS	SARDS	SARONIC	SASINS
SAPPHIRED	SARANS	SARED	SAROS	SASKATOON
SAPPHIRES	SARAPE	SAREE	SAROSES	SASQUATCH
SAPPHISM	SARAPES	SAREES	SARPANCH	SASS
SAPPHISMS	SARBACANE	SARGASSA	SARRASIN	SASSABIES
SAPPHIST	SARCASM	SARGASSO	SARRASINS	SASSABY
SAPPHISTS	SARCASMS	SARGASSOS	SARRAZIN	SASSAFRAS
SAPPIER	SARCASTIC	SARGASSUM	SARRAZINS	SASSARARA
SAPPIEST	SARCENET	SARGE	SARS	SASSE
SAPPILY	SARCENETS	SARGES	SARSAR	SASSED
SAPPINESS	SARCINA	SARGO	SARSARS	SASSES
SAPPING	SARCINAE	SARGOS	SARSDEN	SASSIER
SAPPINGS	SARCINAS	SARGOSES	SARSDENS	SASSIES
SAPPLE	SARCOCARP	SARGUS	SARSEN	SASSIEST
SAPPLED	SARCODE	SARGUSES	SARSENET	SASSILY

S

SASSINESS	SATIATE	SATRAPIES	SAUCEPOTS	SAURIANS
SASSING	SATIATED	SATRAPS	SAUCER	SAURIES
SASSOLIN	SATIATES	SATRAPY	SAUCERFUL	SAUROID
SASSOLINS	SATIATING	SATSANG	SAUCERS	SAUROIDS
SASSOLITE	SATIATION	SATSANGS	SAUCES	SAUROPOD
SASSWOOD	SATIETIES	SATSUMA	SAUCH	SAUROPODS
SASSWOODS	SATIETY	SATSUMAS	SAUCHS	SAURY
SASSY	SATIN	SATURABLE	SAUCIER	SAUSAGE
SASSYWOOD	SATINED	SATURANT	SAUCIERS	SAUSAGES
SASTRA	SATINET	SATURANTS	SAUCIEST	SAUT
SASTRAS	SATINETS	SATURATE	SAUCILY	SAUTE
SASTRUGA	SATINETTA	SATURATED	SAUCINESS	SAUTED
SASTRUGI	SATINETTE	SATURATER	SAUCING	SAUTEED
SAT	SATING	SATURATES	SAUCISSE	SAUTEEING
SATAI	SATINING	SATURATOR	SAUCISSES	SAUTEING
SATAIS	SATINPOD	SATURNIC	SAUCISSON	SAUTERNE
SATANG	SATINPODS	SATURNIID	SAUCY	SAUTERNES
SATANGS	SATINS	SATURNINE	SAUFGARD	SAUTES
SATANIC	SATINWOOD	SATURNISM	SAUFGARDS	SAUTING
SATANICAL	SATINY	SATURNIST	SAUGER	SAUTOIR
SATANISM	SATIRE	SATYR	SAUGERS	SAUTOIRE
SATANISMS	SATIRES	SATYRA	SAUGH	SAUTOIRES
SATANIST	SATIRIC	SATYRAL	SAUGHS	SAUTOIRS
SATANISTS	SATIRICAL	SATYRALS	SAUGHY	SAUTS
SATANITY	SATIRISE	SATYRAS	SAUL	SAV
SATARA	SATIRISED	SATYRE	SAULGE	SAVABLE
SATARAS	SATIRISER	SATYRES	SAULGES	SAVAGE
SATAY	SATIRISES	SATYRESS	SAULIE	SAVAGED
SATAYS	SATIRIST	SATYRIC	SAULIES	SAVAGEDOM
SATCHEL	SATIRISTS	SATYRICAL	SAULS	SAVAGELY
SATCHELED	SATIRIZE	SATYRID	SAULT	SAVAGER
SATCHELS	SATIRIZED	SATYRIDS	SAULTS	SAVAGERY
SATCOM	SATIRIZER	SATYRISK	SAUNA	SAVAGES
SATCOMS	SATIRIZES	SATYRISKS	SAUNAED	SAVAGEST
SATE	SATIS	SATYRLIKE	SAUNAING	SAVAGING
SATED	SATISFICE	SATYRS	SAUNAS	SAVAGISM
SATEDNESS	SATISFIED	SAU	SAUNT	SAVAGISMS
SATEEN	SATISFIER	SAUBA	SAUNTED	SAVANNA
SATEENS	SATISFIES	SAUBAS	SAUNTER	SAVANNAH
SATELESS	SATISFY	SAUCE	SAUNTERED	SAVANNAHS
SATELLES	SATIVE	SAUCEBOAT	SAUNTERER	SAVANNAS
SATELLITE	SATNAV	SAUCEBOX	SAUNTERS	SAVANT
SATEM	SATNAVS	SAUCED	SAUNTING	SAVANTE
SATES	SATORI	SAUCELESS	SAUNTS	SAVANTES
SATI	SATORIS	SAUCEPAN	SAUREL	SAVANTS
SATIABLE	SATRAP	SAUCEPANS	SAURELS	SAVARIN
SATIABLY	SATRAPAL	SAUCEPOT	SAURIAN	SAVARINS

SAVATE
SAVATES
SAVE
SAVEABLE
SAVED
SAVEGARD
SAVEGARDS
SAVELOY
SAVELOYS
SAVER
SAVERS
SAVES
SAVEY
SAVEYED
SAVEYING
SAVEYS
SAVIN
SAVINE
SAVINES
SAVING
SAVINGLY
SAVINGS
SAVINS
SAVIOR
SAVIORS
SAVIOUR
SAVIOURS
SAVOR
SAVORED
SAVORER
SAVORERS
SAVORIER
SAVORIES
SAVORIEST
SAVORILY
SAVORING
SAVORLESS
SAVOROUS
SAVORS
SAVORY
SAVOUR
SAVOURED
SAVOURER
SAVOURERS
SAVOURIER
SAVOURIES
SAVOURILY

SAVOURING
SAVOURLY
SAVOURS
SAVOURY
SAVOY
SAVOYARD
SAVOYARDS
SAVOYS
SAVS
SAVVEY
SAVVEYED
SAVVEYING
SAVVEYS
SAVVIED
SAVVIER
SAVVIES
SAVVIEST
SAVVILY
SAVVINESS
SAVVY
SAVVYING
SAW
SAWAH
SAWAHS
SAWBILL
SAWBILLS
SAWBLADE
SAWBLADES
SAWBONES
SAWBUCK
SAWBUCKS
SAWDER
SAWDERED
SAWDERING
SAWDERS
SAWDUST
SAWDUSTED
SAWDUSTS
SAWDUSTY
SAWED
SAWER
SAWERS
SAWFISH
SAWFISHES
SAWFLIES
SAWFLY
SAWGRASS

SAWHORSE
SAWHORSES
SAWING
SAWINGS
SAWLIKE
SAWLOG
SAWLOGS
SAWMILL
SAWMILLS
SAWN
SAWNEY
SAWNEYS
SAWPIT
SAWPITS
SAWS
SAWSHARK
SAWSHARKS
SAWTEETH
SAWTIMBER
SAWTOOTH
SAWYER
SAWYERS
SAX
SAXATILE
SAXAUL
SAXAULS
SAXE
SAXES
SAXHORN
SAXHORNS
SAXICOLE
SAXIFRAGE
SAXIST
SAXISTS
SAXITOXIN
SAXMAN
SAXMEN
SAXONIES
SAXONITE
SAXONITES
SAXONY
SAXOPHONE
SAXTUBA
SAXTUBAS
SAY
SAYABLE
SAYED

SAYEDS
SAYER
SAYERS
SAYEST
SAYID
SAYIDS
SAYING
SAYINGS
SAYNE
SAYON
SAYONARA
SAYONARAS
SAYONS
SAYS
SAYST
SAYYID
SAYYIDS
SAZ
SAZERAC
SAZERACS
SAZHEN
SAZHENS
SAZZES
SBIRRI
SBIRRO
SCAB
SCABBARD
SCABBARDS
SCABBED
SCABBIER
SCABBIEST
SCABBILY
SCABBING
SCABBLE
SCABBLED
SCABBLES
SCABBLING
SCABBY
SCABIES
SCABIETIC
SCABIOSA
SCABIOSAS
SCABIOUS
SCABLAND
SCABLANDS
SCABLIKE

SCABRID
SCABROUS
SCABS
SCAD
SCADS
SCAFF
SCAFFED
SCAFFIE
SCAFFIER
SCAFFIES
SCAFFIEST
SCAFFING
SCAFFOLD
SCAFFOLDS
SCAFFS
SCAFFY
SCAG
SCAGGED
SCAGGING
SCAGLIA
SCAGLIAS
SCAGLIOLA
SCAGS
SCAIL
SCAILED
SCAILING
SCAILS
SCAITH
SCAITHED
SCAITHING
SCAITHS
SCALA
SCALABLE
SCALABLY
SCALADE
SCALADES
SCALADO
SCALADOS
SCALAE
SCALAGE
SCALAGES
SCALAR
SCALARE
SCALARES
SCALARS
SCALATION
SCALAWAG

SCALAWAGS	SCALLOPS	SCAMSTER	SCAPED	SCAREY
SCALD	SCALLS	SCAMSTERS	SCAPEGOAT	SCARF
SCALDED	SCALLY	SCAMTO	SCAPELESS	SCARFED
SCALDER	SCALLYWAG	SCAMTOS	SCAPEMENT	SCARFER
SCALDERS	SCALOGRAM	SCAN	SCAPES	SCARFERS
SCALDFISH	SCALP	SCAND	SCAPHOID	SCARFING
SCALDHEAD	SCALPED	SCANDAL	SCAPHOIDS	SCARFINGS
SCALDIC	SCALPEL	SCANDALED	SCAPHOPOD	SCARFISH
SCALDING	SCALPELS	SCANDALS	SCAPI	SCARFPIN
SCALDINGS	SCALPER	SCANDENT	SCAPING	SCARFPINS
SCALDINI	SCALPERS	SCANDIA	SCAPOLITE	SCARFS
SCALDINO	SCALPING	SCANDIAS	SCAPOSE	SCARFSKIN
SCALDS	SCALPINGS	SCANDIC	SCAPPLE	SCARFWISE
SCALDSHIP	SCALPINS	SCANDIUM	SCAPPLED	SCARIER
SCALE	SCALPLESS	SCANDIUMS	SCAPPLES	SCARIEST
SCALEABLE	SCALPRUM	SCANNABLE	SCAPPLING	SCARIFIED
SCALEABLY	SCALPRUMS	SCANNED	SCAPULA	SCARIFIER
SCALED	SCALPS	SCANNER	SCAPULAE	SCARIFIES
SCALELESS	SCALY	SCANNERS	SCAPULAR	SCARIFY
SCALELIKE	SCAM	SCANNING	SCAPULARS	SCARILY
SCALENE	SCAMBLE	SCANNINGS	SCAPULARY	SCARINESS
SCALENES	SCAMBLED	SCANS	SCAPULAS	SCARING
SCALENI	SCAMBLER	SCANSION	SCAPUS	SCARIOSE
SCALENUS	SCAMBLERS	SCANSIONS	SCAR	SCARIOUS
SCALEPAN	SCAMBLES	SCANT	SCARAB	SCARLESS
SCALEPANS	SCAMBLING	SCANTED	SCARABAEI	SCARLET
SCALER	SCAMEL	SCANTER	SCARABEE	SCARLETED
SCALERS	SCAMELS	SCANTEST	SCARABEES	SCARLETS
SCALES	SCAMMED	SCANTIER	SCARABOID	SCARMOGE
SCALETAIL	SCAMMER	SCANTIES	SCARABS	SCARMOGES
SCALEUP	SCAMMERS	SCANTIEST	SCARCE	SCARP
SCALEUPS	SCAMMING	SCANTILY	SCARCELY	SCARPA
SCALEWORK	SCAMMONY	SCANTING	SCARCER	SCARPAED
SCALIER	SCAMP	SCANTITY	SCARCEST	SCARPAING
SCALIEST	SCAMPED	SCANTLE	SCARCITY	SCARPAS
SCALINESS	SCAMPER	SCANTLED	SCARE	SCARPED
SCALING	SCAMPERED	SCANTLES	SCARECROW	SCARPER
SCALINGS	SCAMPERER	SCANTLING	SCARED	SCARPERED
SCALL	SCAMPERS	SCANTLY	SCAREDER	SCARPERS
SCALLAWAG	SCAMPI	SCANTNESS	SCAREDEST	SCARPETTI
SCALLED	SCAMPIES	SCANTS	SCAREDIES	SCARPETTO
SCALLIES	SCAMPING	SCANTY	SCAREDY	SCARPH
SCALLION	SCAMPINGS	SCAPA	SCAREHEAD	SCARPHED
SCALLIONS	SCAMPIS	SCAPAED	SCARER	SCARPHING
SCALLOP	SCAMPISH	SCAPAING	SCARERS	SCARPHS
SCALLOPED	SCAMPS	SCAPAS	SCARES	SCARPINES
SCALLOPER	SCAMS	SCAPE	SCAREWARE	SCARPING

S

SCARPINGS	SCATTINGS	SCENA	SCERNED	SCHIEDAM
SCARPS	SCATTS	SCENARIES	SCERNES	SCHIEDAMS
SCARRE	SCATTY	SCENARIO	SCERNING	SCHILLER
SCARRED	SCAUD	SCENARIOS	SCHANSE	SCHILLERS
SCARRES	SCAUDED	SCENARISE	SCHANSES	SCHILLING
SCARRIER	SCAUDING	SCENARIST	SCHANTZE	SCHIMMEL
SCARRIEST	SCAUDS	SCENARIZE	SCHANTZES	SCHIMMELS
SCARRING	SCAUP	SCENARY	SCHANZE	SCHISM
SCARRINGS	SCAUPED	SCENAS	SCHANZES	SCHISMA
SCARRY	SCAUPER	SCEND	SCHAPPE	SCHISMAS
SCARS	SCAUPERS	SCENDED	SCHAPPED	SCHISMS
SCART	SCAUPING	SCENDING	SCHAPPES	SCHIST
SCARTED	SCAUPS	SCENDS	SCHAPSKA	SCHISTOSE
SCARTH	SCAUR	SCENE	SCHAPSKAS	SCHISTOUS
SCARTHS	SCAURED	SCENED	SCHATCHEN	SCHISTS
SCARTING	SCAURIES	SCENEMAN	SCHAV	SCHIZIER
SCARTS	SCAURING	SCENEMEN	SCHAVS	SCHIZIEST
SCARVED	SCAURS	SCENERIES	SCHECHITA	SCHIZO
SCARVES	SCAURY	SCENERY	SCHEDULAR	SCHIZOID
SCARY	SCAVAGE	SCENES	SCHEDULE	SCHIZOIDS
SCAT	SCAVAGED	SCENESTER	SCHEDULED	SCHIZONT
SCATBACK	SCAVAGER	SCENIC	SCHEDULER	SCHIZONTS
SCATBACKS	SCAVAGERS	SCENICAL	SCHEDULES	SCHIZOPOD
SCATCH	SCAVAGES	SCENICS	SCHEELITE	SCHIZOS
SCATCHES	SCAVAGING	SCENING	SCHELLIES	SCHIZY
SCATH	SCAVENGE	SCENT	SCHELLUM	SCHIZZIER
SCATHE	SCAVENGED	SCENTED	SCHELLUMS	SCHIZZY
SCATHED	SCAVENGER	SCENTFUL	SCHELLY	SCHLAGER
SCATHEFUL	SCAVENGES	SCENTING	SCHELM	SCHLAGERS
SCATHES	SCAW	SCENTINGS	SCHELMS	SCHLEMIEL
SCATHING	SCAWS	SCENTLESS	SCHEMA	SCHLEMIHL
SCATHS	SCAWTITE	SCENTS	SCHEMAS	SCHLEP
SCATOLE	SCAWTITES	SCEPSIS	SCHEMATA	SCHLEPP
SCATOLES	SCAZON	SCEPSISES	SCHEMATIC	SCHLEPPED
SCATOLOGY	SCAZONS	SCEPTER	SCHEME	SCHLEPPER
SCATS	SCAZONTES	SCEPTERED	SCHEMED	SCHLEPPS
SCATT	SCAZONTIC	SCEPTERS	SCHEMER	SCHLEPPY
SCATTED	SCEAT	SCEPTIC	SCHEMERS	SCHLEPS
SCATTER	SCEATT	SCEPTICAL	SCHEMES	SCHLICH
SCATTERED	SCEATTAS	SCEPTICS	SCHEMIE	SCHLICHS
SCATTERER	SCEDULE	SCEPTRAL	SCHEMIES	SCHLIERE
SCATTERS	SCEDULED	SCEPTRE	SCHEMING	SCHLIEREN
SCATTERY	SCEDULES	SCEPTRED	SCHEMINGS	SCHLIERIC
SCATTIER	SCEDULING	SCEPTRES	SCHERZI	SCHLOCK
SCATTIEST	SCELERAT	SCEPTRING	SCHERZO	SCHLOCKER
SCATTILY	SCELERATE	SCEPTRY	SCHERZOS	SCHLOCKS
SCATTING	SCELERATS	SCERNE	SCHIAVONE	SCHLOCKY

SCHLONG	SCHMOS	SCHOOLES	SCHVITZES	SCION
SCHLONGS	SCHMUCK	SCHOOLIE	SCHWA	SCIONS
SCHLOSS	SCHMUCKED	SCHOOLIES	SCHWAG	SCIOPHYTE
SCHLOSSES	SCHMUCKS	SCHOOLING	SCHWAGS	SCIOSOPHY
SCHLUB	SCHMUCKY	SCHOOLKID	SCHWARTZE	SCIROC
SCHLUBS	SCHMUTTER	SCHOOLMAN	SCHWAS	SCIROCCO
SCHLUMP	SCHMUTZ	SCHOOLMEN	SCIAENID	SCIROCCOS
SCHLUMPED	SCHMUTZES	SCHOOLS	SCIAENIDS	SCIROCS
SCHLUMPS	SCHNAPPER	SCHOONER	SCIAENOID	SCIRRHI
SCHLUMPY	SCHNAPPS	SCHOONERS	SCIAMACHY	SCIRRHOID
SCHMALTZ	SCHNAPS	SCHORL	SCIARID	SCIRRHOUS
SCHMALTZY	SCHNAPSES	SCHORLS	SCIARIDS	SCIRRHUS
SCHMALZ	SCHNAUZER	SCHOUT	SCIATIC	SCISSEL
SCHMALZES	SCHNECKE	SCHOUTS	SCIATICA	SCISSELS
SCHMALZY	SCHNECKEN	SCHRIK	SCIATICAL	SCISSIL
SCHMATTE	SCHNELL	SCHRIKS	SCIATICAS	SCISSILE
SCHMATTES	SCHNITZEL	SCHROD	SCIATICS	SCISSILS
SCHMEAR	SCHNOOK	SCHRODS	SCIENCE	SCISSION
SCHMEARED	SCHNOOKS	SCHTICK	SCIENCED	SCISSIONS
SCHMEARS	SCHNORKEL	SCHTICKS	SCIENCES	SCISSOR
SCHMECK	SCHNORR	SCHTIK	SCIENT	SCISSORED
SCHMECKED	SCHNORRED	SCHTIKS	SCIENTER	SCISSORER
SCHMECKER	SCHNORRER	SCHTOOK	SCIENTIAL	SCISSORS
SCHMECKS	SCHNORRS	SCHTOOKS	SCIENTISE	SCISSURE
SCHMEER	SCHNOZ	SCHTOOM	SCIENTISM	SCISSURES
SCHMEERED	SCHNOZES	SCHTUCK	SCIENTIST	SCIURID
SCHMEERS	SCHNOZZ	SCHTUCKS	SCIENTIZE	SCIURIDS
SCHMELZ	SCHNOZZES	SCHTUM	SCILICET	SCIURINE
SCHMELZE	SCHNOZZLE	SCHTUP	SCILLA	SCIURINES
SCHMELZES	SCHOLAR	SCHTUPPED	SCILLAS	SCIUROID
SCHMICK	SCHOLARCH	SCHTUPS	SCIMETAR	SCLAFF
SCHMICKER	SCHOLARLY	SCHUIT	SCIMETARS	SCLAFFED
SCHMO	SCHOLARS	SCHUITS	SCIMITAR	SCLAFFER
SCHMOCK	SCHOLIA	SCHUL	SCIMITARS	SCLAFFERS
SCHMOCKS	SCHOLIAST	SCHULN	SCIMITER	SCLAFFING
SCHMOE	SCHOLION	SCHULS	SCIMITERS	SCLAFFS
SCHMOES	SCHOLIUM	SCHUSS	SCINCOID	SCLATE
SCHMOOS	SCHOLIUMS	SCHUSSED	SCINCOIDS	SCLATED
SCHMOOSE	SCHOOL	SCHUSSER	SCINTILLA	SCLATES
SCHMOOSED	SCHOOLBAG	SCHUSSERS	SCIOLISM	SCLATING
SCHMOOSES	SCHOOLBOY	SCHUSSES	SCIOLISMS	SCLAUNDER
SCHMOOZ	SCHOOLDAY	SCHUSSING	SCIOLIST	SCLAVE
SCHMOOZE	SCHOOLE	SCHUYT	SCIOLISTS	SCLAVES
SCHMOOZED	SCHOOLED	SCHUYTS	SCIOLOUS	SCLERA
SCHMOOZER	SCHOOLER	SCHVARTZE	SCIOLTO	SCLERAE
SCHMOOZES	SCHOOLERS	SCHVITZ	SCIOMACHY	SCLERAL
SCHMOOZY	SCHOOLERY	SCHVITZED	SCIOMANCY	SCLERAS

S

SCLERE
SCLEREID
SCLEREIDE
SCLEREIDS
SCLEREMA
SCLEREMAS
SCLERES
SCLERITE
SCLERITES
SCLERITIC
SCLERITIS
SCLEROID
SCLEROMA
SCLEROMAS
SCLEROSAL
SCLEROSE
SCLEROSED
SCLEROSES
SCLEROSIS
SCLEROTAL
SCLEROTIA
SCLEROTIC
SCLEROTIN
SCLEROUS
SCLIFF
SCLIFFS
SCLIM
SCLIMMED
SCLIMMING
SCLIMS
SCODIER
SCODIEST
SCODY
SCOFF
SCOFFED
SCOFFER
SCOFFERS
SCOFFING
SCOFFINGS
SCOFFLAW
SCOFFLAWS
SCOFFS
SCOG
SCOGGED
SCOGGING
SCOGS
SCOINSON

SCOINSONS
SCOLD
SCOLDABLE
SCOLDED
SCOLDER
SCOLDERS
SCOLDING
SCOLDINGS
SCOLDS
SCOLECES
SCOLECID
SCOLECIDS
SCOLECITE
SCOLECOID
SCOLEX
SCOLIA
SCOLICES
SCOLIOMA
SCOLIOMAS
SCOLION
SCOLIOSES
SCOLIOSIS
SCOLIOTIC
SCOLLOP
SCOLLOPED
SCOLLOPS
SCOLYTID
SCOLYTIDS
SCOLYTOID
SCOMBRID
SCOMBRIDS
SCOMBROID
SCOMFISH
SCONCE
SCONCED
SCONCES
SCONCHEON
SCONCING
SCONE
SCONES
SCONTION
SCONTIONS
SCOOBIES
SCOOBY
SCOOCH
SCOOCHED
SCOOCHES

SCOOCHING
SCOOG
SCOOGED
SCOOGING
SCOOGS
SCOOP
SCOOPABLE
SCOOPED
SCOOPER
SCOOPERS
SCOOPFUL
SCOOPFULS
SCOOPING
SCOOPINGS
SCOOPS
SCOOPSFUL
SCOOSH
SCOOSHED
SCOOSHES
SCOOSHING
SCOOT
SCOOTCH
SCOOTCHED
SCOOTCHES
SCOOTED
SCOOTER
SCOOTERED
SCOOTERS
SCOOTING
SCOOTS
SCOP
SCOPA
SCOPAE
SCOPAS
SCOPATE
SCOPE
SCOPED
SCOPELID
SCOPELIDS
SCOPELOID
SCOPES
SCOPING
SCOPOLINE
SCOPS
SCOPULA
SCOPULAE
SCOPULAS

SCOPULATE
SCORBUTIC
SCORCH
SCORCHED
SCORCHER
SCORCHERS
SCORCHES
SCORCHING
SCORDATO
SCORE
SCORECARD
SCORED
SCORELESS
SCORELINE
SCOREPAD
SCOREPADS
SCORER
SCORERS
SCORES
SCORIA
SCORIAC
SCORIAE
SCORIFIED
SCORIFIER
SCORIFIES
SCORIFY
SCORING
SCORINGS
SCORIOUS
SCORN
SCORNED
SCORNER
SCORNERS
SCORNFUL
SCORNING
SCORNINGS
SCORNS
SCORODITE
SCORPER
SCORPERS
SCORPIOID
SCORPION
SCORPIONS
SCORRENDO
SCORSE
SCORSED
SCORSER

SCORSERS
SCORSES
SCORSING
SCOT
SCOTCH
SCOTCHED
SCOTCHES
SCOTCHING
SCOTER
SCOTERS
SCOTIA
SCOTIAS
SCOTOMA
SCOTOMAS
SCOTOMATA
SCOTOMIA
SCOTOMIAS
SCOTOMIES
SCOTOMY
SCOTOPHIL
SCOTOPIA
SCOTOPIAS
SCOTOPIC
SCOTS
SCOTTIE
SCOTTIES
SCOUG
SCOUGED
SCOUGING
SCOUGS
SCOUNDREL
SCOUP
SCOUPED
SCOUPING
SCOUPS
SCOUR
SCOURED
SCOURER
SCOURERS
SCOURGE
SCOURGED
SCOURGER
SCOURGERS
SCOURGES
SCOURGING
SCOURIE
SCOURIES

SCOURING	SCOWTHS	SCRANNELS	SCRAUGHED	SCREAMS
SCOURINGS	SCOZZA	SCRANNIER	SCRAUGHS	SCREE
SCOURS	SCOZZAS	SCRANNY	SCRAVEL	SCREECH
SCOURSE	SCRAB	SCRANS	SCRAVELED	SCREECHED
SCOURSED	SCRABBED	SCRAP	SCRAVELS	SCREECHER
SCOURSES	SCRABBING	SCRAPABLE	SCRAW	SCREECHES
SCOURSING	SCRABBLE	SCRAPBOOK	SCRAWB	SCREECHY
SCOUSE	SCRABBLED	SCRAPE	SCRAWBED	SCREED
SCOUSER	SCRABBLER	SCRAPED	SCRAWBING	SCREEDED
SCOUSERS	SCRABBLES	SCRAPEGUT	SCRAWBS	SCREEDER
SCOUSES	SCRABBLY	SCRAPER	SCRAWL	SCREEDERS
SCOUT	SCRABS	SCRAPERS	SCRAWLED	SCREEDING
SCOUTED	SCRAE	SCRAPES	SCRAWLER	SCREEDS
SCOUTER	SCRAES	SCRAPHEAP	SCRAWLERS	SCREEN
SCOUTERS	SCRAG	SCRAPIE	SCRAWLIER	SCREENED
SCOUTH	SCRAGGED	SCRAPIES	SCRAWLING	SCREENER
SCOUTHER	SCRAGGIER	SCRAPING	SCRAWLS	SCREENERS
SCOUTHERS	SCRAGGILY	SCRAPINGS	SCRAWLY	SCREENFUL
SCOUTHERY	SCRAGGING	SCRAPPAGE	SCRAWM	SCREENIE
SCOUTHS	SCRAGGLY	SCRAPPED	SCRAWMED	SCREENIES
SCOUTING	SCRAGGY	SCRAPPER	SCRAWMING	SCREENING
SCOUTINGS	SCRAGS	SCRAPPERS	SCRAWMS	SCREENS
SCOUTS	SCRAICH	SCRAPPIER	SCRAWNIER	SCREES
SCOW	SCRAICHED	SCRAPPILY	SCRAWNILY	SCREET
SCOWDER	SCRAICHS	SCRAPPING	SCRAWNY	SCREETED
SCOWDERED	SCRAIGH	SCRAPPLE	SCRAWP	SCREETING
SCOWDERS	SCRAIGHED	SCRAPPLES	SCRAWPED	SCREETS
SCOWED	SCRAIGHS	SCRAPPY	SCRAWPING	SCREEVE
SCOWING	SCRAM	SCRAPS	SCRAWPS	SCREEVED
SCOWL	SCRAMB	SCRAPYARD	SCRAWS	SCREEVER
SCOWLED	SCRAMBED	SCRAT	SCRAY	SCREEVERS
SCOWLER	SCRAMBING	SCRATCH	SCRAYE	SCREEVES
SCOWLERS	SCRAMBLE	SCRATCHED	SCRAYES	SCREEVING
SCOWLING	SCRAMBLED	SCRATCHER	SCRAYS	SCREICH
SCOWLS	SCRAMBLER	SCRATCHES	SCREAK	SCREICHED
SCOWP	SCRAMBLES	SCRATCHIE	SCREAKED	SCREICHS
SCOWPED	SCRAMBS	SCRATCHY	SCREAKIER	SCREIGH
SCOWPING	SCRAMJET	SCRATS	SCREAKING	SCREIGHED
SCOWPS	SCRAMJETS	SCRATTED	SCREAKS	SCREIGHS
SCOWRER	SCRAMMED	SCRATTING	SCREAKY	SCREW
SCOWRERS	SCRAMMING	SCRATTLE	SCREAM	SCREWABLE
SCOWRIE	SCRAMS	SCRATTLED	SCREAMED	SCREWBALL
SCOWRIES	SCRAN	SCRATTLES	SCREAMER	SCREWBEAN
SCOWS	SCRANCH	SCRAUCH	SCREAMERS	SCREWED
SCOWTH	SCRANCHED	SCRAUCHED	SCREAMING	SCREWER
SCOWTHER	SCRANCHES	SCRAUCHS	SCREAMO	SCREWERS
SCOWTHERS	SCRANNEL	SCRAUGH	SCREAMOS	SCREWIER

S

SCREWIEST	SCRIMMAGE	SCRODDLED	SCROUNGE	SCRUMPING
SCREWING	SCRIMP	SCRODS	SCROUNGED	SCRUMPLE
SCREWINGS	SCRIMPED	SCROFULA	SCROUNGER	SCRUMPLED
SCREWLIKE	SCRIMPER	SCROFULAS	SCROUNGES	SCRUMPLES
SCREWS	SCRIMPERS	SCROG	SCROUNGY	SCRUMPOX
SCREWTOP	SCRIMPIER	SCROGGIE	SCROW	SCRUMPS
SCREWTOPS	SCRIMPILY	SCROGGIER	SCROWDGE	SCRUMPY
SCREWUP	SCRIMPING	SCROGGIN	SCROWDGED	SCRUMS
SCREWUPS	SCRIMPIT	SCROGGINS	SCROWDGES	SCRUNCH
SCREWWORM	SCRIMPLY	SCROGGY	SCROWL	SCRUNCHED
SCREWY	SCRIMPS	SCROGS	SCROWLE	SCRUNCHES
SCRIBABLE	SCRIMPY	SCROLL	SCROWLED	SCRUNCHIE
SCRIBAL	SCRIMS	SCROLLED	SCROWLES	SCRUNCHY
SCRIBBLE	SCRIMSHAW	SCROLLER	SCROWLING	SCRUNT
SCRIBBLED	SCRIMURE	SCROLLERS	SCROWLS	SCRUNTIER
SCRIBBLER	SCRIMURES	SCROLLING	SCROWS	SCRUNTS
SCRIBBLES	SCRINE	SCROLLS	SCROYLE	SCRUNTY
SCRIBBLY	SCRINES	SCROME	SCROYLES	SCRUPLE
SCRIBE	SCRIP	SCROMED	SCRUB	SCRUPLED
SCRIBED	SCRIPPAGE	SCROMES	SCRUBBED	SCRUPLER
SCRIBER	SCRIPS	SCROMING	SCRUBBER	SCRUPLERS
SCRIBERS	SCRIPT	SCROOCH	SCRUBBERS	SCRUPLES
SCRIBES	SCRIPTED	SCROOCHED	SCRUBBIER	SCRUPLING
SCRIBING	SCRIPTER	SCROOCHES	SCRUBBILY	SCRUTABLE
SCRIBINGS	SCRIPTERS	SCROOGE	SCRUBBING	SCRUTATOR
SCRIBISM	SCRIPTING	SCROOGED	SCRUBBY	SCRUTINY
SCRIBISMS	SCRIPTORY	SCROOGES	SCRUBLAND	SCRUTO
SCRIECH	SCRIPTS	SCROOGING	SCRUBS	SCRUTOIRE
SCRIECHED	SCRIPTURE	SCROOP	SCRUFF	SCRUTOS
SCRIECHS	SCRITCH	SCROOPED	SCRUFFED	SCRUZE
SCRIED	SCRITCHED	SCROOPING	SCRUFFIER	SCRUZED
SCRIENE	SCRITCHES	SCROOPS	SCRUFFILY	SCRUZES
SCRIENES	SCRIVE	SCROOTCH	SCRUFFING	SCRUZING
SCRIES	SCRIVED	SCRORP	SCRUFFS	SCRY
SCRIEVE	SCRIVENER	SCRORPS	SCRUFFY	SCRYDE
SCRIEVED	SCRIVES	SCROTA	SCRUM	SCRYER
SCRIEVES	SCRIVING	SCROTAL	SCRUMDOWN	SCRYERS
SCRIEVING	SCROB	SCROTE	SCRUMMAGE	SCRYING
SCRIGGLE	SCROBBED	SCROTES	SCRUMMED	SCRYINGS
SCRIGGLED	SCROBBING	SCROTUM	SCRUMMIE	SCRYNE
SCRIGGLES	SCROBBLE	SCROTUMS	SCRUMMIER	SCRYNES
SCRIGGLY	SCROBBLED	SCROUGE	SCRUMMIES	SCUBA
SCRIKE	SCROBBLES	SCROUGED	SCRUMMING	SCUBAED
SCRIKED	SCROBE	SCROUGER	SCRUMMY	SCUBAING
SCRIKES	SCROBES	SCROUGERS	SCRUMP	SCUBAS
SCRIKING	SCROBS	SCROUGES	SCRUMPED	SCUCHIN
SCRIM	SCROD	SCROUGING	SCRUMPIES	SCUCHINS

SCUD	SCULLERY	SCUMMY	SCURVY	SCUZZY
SCUDDALER	SCULLES	SCUMS	SCUSE	SCYBALA
SCUDDED	SCULLING	SCUNCHEON	SCUSED	SCYBALOUS
SCUDDER	SCULLINGS	SCUNDERED	SCUSES	SCYBALUM
SCUDDERS	SCULLION	SCUNGE	SCUSING	SCYE
SCUDDING	SCULLIONS	SCUNGED	SCUT	SCYES
SCUDDLE	SCULLS	SCUNGES	SCUTA	SCYPHATE
SCUDDLED	SCULP	SCUNGIER	SCUTAGE	SCYPHI
SCUDDLES	SCULPED	SCUNGIEST	SCUTAGES	SCYPHUS
SCUDDLING	SCULPIN	SCUNGILE	SCUTAL	SCYTALE
SCUDI	SCULPING	SCUNGILI	SCUTATE	SCYTALES
SCUDLER	SCULPINS	SCUNGILLE	SCUTATION	SCYTHE
SCUDLERS	SCULPS	SCUNGILLI	SCUTCH	SCYTHED
SCUDO	SCULPSIT	SCUNGING	SCUTCHED	SCYTHEMAN
SCUDS	SCULPT	SCUNGY	SCUTCHEON	SCYTHEMEN
SCUFF	SCULPTED	SCUNNER	SCUTCHER	SCYTHER
SCUFFED	SCULPTING	SCUNNERED	SCUTCHERS	SCYTHERS
SCUFFER	SCULPTOR	SCUNNERS	SCUTCHES	SCYTHES
SCUFFERS	SCULPTORS	SCUP	SCUTCHING	SCYTHING
SCUFFING	SCULPTS	SCUPPAUG	SCUTE	SDAINE
SCUFFLE	SCULPTURE	SCUPPAUGS	SCUTELLA	SDAINED
SCUFFLED	SCULS	SCUPPER	SCUTELLAR	SDAINES
SCUFFLER	SCULTCH	SCUPPERED	SCUTELLUM	SDAINING
SCUFFLERS	SCULTCHES	SCUPPERS	SCUTES	SDAYN
SCUFFLES	SCUM	SCUPS	SCUTIFORM	SDAYNED
SCUFFLING	SCUMBAG	SCUR	SCUTIGER	SDAYNING
SCUFFS	SCUMBAGS	SCURF	SCUTIGERS	SDAYNS
SCUFT	SCUMBALL	SCURFIER	SCUTS	SDEIGN
SCUFTS	SCUMBALLS	SCURFIEST	SCUTTER	SDEIGNE
SCUG	SCUMBER	SCURFS	SCUTTERED	SDEIGNED
SCUGGED	SCUMBERED	SCURFY	SCUTTERS	SDEIGNES
SCUGGING	SCUMBERS	SCURRED	SCUTTLE	SDEIGNING
SCUGS	SCUMBLE	SCURRIED	SCUTTLED	SDEIGNS
SCUL	SCUMBLED	SCURRIER	SCUTTLER	SDEIN
SCULCH	SCUMBLES	SCURRIERS	SCUTTLERS	SDEINED
SCULCHES	SCUMBLING	SCURRIES	SCUTTLES	SDEINING
SCULK	SCUMFISH	SCURRIL	SCUTTLING	SDEINS
SCULKED	SCUMLESS	SCURRILE	SCUTUM	SEA
SCULKER	SCUMLIKE	SCURRING	SCUTWORK	SEABAG
SCULKERS	SCUMMED	SCURRIOUR	SCUTWORKS	SEABAGS
SCULKING	SCUMMER	SCURRY	SCUZZ	SEABANK
SCULKS	SCUMMERS	SCURRYING	SCUZZBAG	SEABANKS
SCULL	SCUMMIER	SCURS	SCUZZBAGS	SEABEACH
SCULLE	SCUMMIEST	SCURVIER	SCUZZBALL	SEABED
SCULLED	SCUMMILY	SCURVIES	SCUZZES	SEABEDS
SCULLER	SCUMMING	SCURVIEST	SCUZZIER	SEABIRD
SCULLERS	SCUMMINGS	SCURVILY	SCUZZIEST	SEABIRDS

S

SEABLITE	SEAKALE	SEAMINESS	SEARINGLY	SEATMATE
SEABLITES	SEAKALES	SEAMING	SEARINGS	SEATMATES
SEABOARD	SEAL	SEAMINGS	SEARNESS	SEATRAIN
SEABOARDS	SEALABLE	SEAMLESS	SEAROBIN	SEATRAINS
SEABOOT	SEALANT	SEAMLIKE	SEAROBINS	SEATROUT
SEABOOTS	SEALANTS	SEAMOUNT	SEARS	SEATROUTS
SEABORNE	SEALCH	SEAMOUNTS	SEAS	SEATS
SEABOTTLE	SEALCHS	SEAMS	SEASCAPE	SEATWORK
SEACOAST	SEALED	SEAMSET	SEASCAPES	SEATWORKS
SEACOASTS	SEALER	SEAMSETS	SEASCOUT	SEAWALL
SEACOCK	SEALERIES	SEAMSTER	SEASCOUTS	SEAWALLED
SEACOCKS	SEALERS	SEAMSTERS	SEASE	SEAWALLS
SEACRAFT	SEALERY	SEAMY	SEASED	SEAWAN
SEACRAFTS	SEALGH	SEAN	SEASES	SEAWANS
SEACUNNY	SEALGHS	SEANCE	SEASHELL	SEAWANT
SEADOG	SEALIFT	SEANCES	SEASHELLS	SEAWANTS
SEADOGS	SEALIFTED	SEANED	SEASHORE	SEAWARD
SEADROME	SEALIFTS	SEANING	SEASHORES	SEAWARDLY
SEADROMES	SEALINE	SEANNACHY	SEASICK	SEAWARDS
SEAFARER	SEALINES	SEANS	SEASICKER	SEAWARE
SEAFARERS	SEALING	SEAPIECE	SEASIDE	SEAWARES
SEAFARING	SEALINGS	SEAPIECES	SEASIDES	SEAWATER
SEAFLOOR	SEALLIKE	SEAPLANE	SEASING	SEAWATERS
SEAFLOORS	SEALPOINT	SEAPLANES	SEASON	SEAWAY
SEAFOAM	SEALS	SEAPORT	SEASONAL	SEAWAYS
SEAFOAMS	SEALSKIN	SEAPORTS	SEASONALS	SEAWEED
SEAFOLK	SEALSKINS	SEAQUAKE	SEASONED	SEAWEEDS
SEAFOLKS	SEALWAX	SEAQUAKES	SEASONER	SEAWEEDY
SEAFOOD	SEALWAXES	SEAQUARIA	SEASONERS	SEAWIFE
SEAFOODS	SEALYHAM	SEAR	SEASONING	SEAWIVES
SEAFOWL	SEALYHAMS	SEARAT	SEASONS	SEAWOMAN
SEAFOWLS	SEAM	SEARATS	SEASPEAK	SEAWOMEN
SEAFRONT	SEAMAID	SEARCE	SEASPEAKS	SEAWORM
SEAFRONTS	SEAMAIDS	SEARCED	SEASTRAND	SEAWORMS
SEAGIRT	SEAMAN	SEARCES	SEASURE	SEAWORTHY
SEAGOING	SEAMANLY	SEARCH	SEASURES	SEAZE
SEAGRASS	SEAMARK	SEARCHED	SEAT	SEAZED
SEAGULL	SEAMARKS	SEARCHER	SEATBACK	SEAZES
SEAGULLS	SEAME	SEARCHERS	SEATBACKS	SEAZING
SEAHAWK	SEAMED	SEARCHES	SEATBELT	SEBACEOUS
SEAHAWKS	SEAMEN	SEARCHING	SEATBELTS	SEBACIC
SEAHOG	SEAMER	SEARCING	SEATED	SEBASIC
SEAHOGS	SEAMERS	SEARE	SEATER	SEBATE
SEAHORSE	SEAMES	SEARED	SEATERS	SEBATES
SEAHORSES	SEAMFREE	SEARER	SEATING	SEBESTEN
SEAHOUND	SEAMIER	SEAREST	SEATINGS	SEBESTENS
SEAHOUNDS	SEAMIEST	SEARING	SEATLESS	SEBIFIC

S

SEBORRHEA	SECONALS	SECTILITY	SEDATION	SEEDBED
SEBUM	SECOND	SECTION	SEDATIONS	SEEDBEDS
SEBUMS	SECONDARY	SECTIONAL	SEDATIVE	SEEDBOX
SEBUNDIES	SECONDE	SECTIONED	SEDATIVES	SEEDBOXES
SEBUNDY	SECONDED	SECTIONS	SEDENT	SEEDCAKE
SEC	SECONDEE	SECTOR	SEDENTARY	SEEDCAKES
SECALOSE	SECONDEES	SECTORAL	SEDER	SEEDCASE
SECALOSES	SECONDER	SECTORED	SEDERS	SEEDCASES
SECANT	SECONDERS	SECTORIAL	SEDERUNT	SEEDEATER
SECANTLY	SECONDES	SECTORING	SEDERUNTS	SEEDED
SECANTS	SECONDI	SECTORISE	SEDES	SEEDER
SECATEUR	SECONDING	SECTORIZE	SEDGE	SEEDERS
SECATEURS	SECONDLY	SECTORS	SEDGED	SEEDHEAD
SECCO	SECONDO	SECTS	SEDGELAND	SEEDHEADS
SECCOS	SECONDS	SECULA	SEDGES	SEEDIER
SECEDE	SECPAR	SECULAR	SEDGIER	SEEDIEST
SECEDED	SECPARS	SECULARLY	SEDGIEST	SEEDILY
SECEDER	SECRECIES	SECULARS	SEDGY	SEEDINESS
SECEDERS	SECRECY	SECULUM	SEDILE	SEEDING
SECEDES	SECRET	SECULUMS	SEDILIA	SEEDINGS
SECEDING	SECRETA	SECUND	SEDILIUM	SEEDLESS
SECERN	SECRETAGE	SECUNDINE	SEDIMENT	SEEDLIKE
SECERNED	SECRETARY	SECUNDLY	SEDIMENTS	SEEDLING
SECERNENT	SECRETE	SECUNDUM	SEDITION	SEEDLINGS
SECERNING	SECRETED	SECURABLE	SEDITIONS	SEEDLIP
SECERNS	SECRETER	SECURANCE	SEDITIOUS	SEEDLIPS
SECESH	SECRETES	SECURE	SEDUCE	SEEDMAN
SECESHER	SECRETEST	SECURED	SEDUCED	SEEDMEN
SECESHERS	SECRETIN	SECURELY	SEDUCER	SEEDNESS
SECESHES	SECRETING	SECURER	SEDUCERS	SEEDPOD
SECESSION	SECRETINS	SECURERS	SEDUCES	SEEDPODS
SECH	SECRETION	SECURES	SEDUCIBLE	SEEDS
SECHS	SECRETIVE	SECUREST	SEDUCING	SEEDSMAN
SECKEL	SECRETLY	SECURING	SEDUCINGS	SEEDSMEN
SECKELS	SECRETOR	SECURITAN	SEDUCIVE	SEEDSTOCK
SECKLE	SECRETORS	SECURITY	SEDUCTION	SEEDTIME
SECKLES	SECRETORY	SED	SEDUCTIVE	SEEDTIMES
SECLUDE	SECRETS	SEDAN	SEDUCTOR	SEEDY
SECLUDED	SECS	SEDANS	SEDUCTORS	SEEING
SECLUDES	SECT	SEDARIM	SEDULITY	SEEINGS
SECLUDING	SECTARIAL	SEDATE	SEDULOUS	SEEK
SECLUSION	SECTARIAN	SEDATED	SEDUM	SEEKER
SECLUSIVE	SECTARIES	SEDATELY	SEDUMS	SEEKERS
SECO	SECTARY	SEDATER	SEE	SEEKING
SECODONT	SECTATOR	SEDATES	SEEABLE	SEEKS
SECODONTS	SECTATORS	SEDATEST	SEECATCH	SEEL
SECONAL	SECTILE	SEDATING	SEED	SEELD

S

SEELED	SEETHINGS	SEIGNEUR	SEITANS	SELECTEES
SEELIE	SEEWING	SEIGNEURS	SEITEN	SELECTING
SEELIER	SEEWINGS	SEIGNEURY	SEITENS	SELECTION
SEELIEST	SEFER	SEIGNIOR	SEITIES	SELECTIVE
SEELING	SEG	SEIGNIORS	SEITY	SELECTLY
SEELINGS	SEGAR	SEIGNIORY	SEIZA	SELECTMAN
SEELS	SEGARS	SEIGNORAL	SEIZABLE	SELECTMEN
SEELY	SEGETAL	SEIGNORY	SEIZAS	SELECTOR
SEEM	SEGGAR	SEIK	SEIZE	SELECTORS
SEEMED	SEGGARS	SEIKER	SEIZED	SELECTS
SEEMER	SEGHOL	SEIKEST	SEIZER	SELENATE
SEEMERS	SEGHOLATE	SEIL	SEIZERS	SELENATES
SEEMING	SEGHOLS	SEILED	SEIZES	SELENIAN
SEEMINGLY	SEGMENT	SEILING	SEIZIN	SELENIC
SEEMINGS	SEGMENTAL	SEILS	SEIZING	SELENIDE
SEEMLESS	SEGMENTED	SEINE	SEIZINGS	SELENIDES
SEEMLIER	SEGMENTS	SEINED	SEIZINS	SELENIOUS
SEEMLIEST	SEGNI	SEINER	SEIZOR	SELENITE
SEEMLIHED	SEGNO	SEINERS	SEIZORS	SELENITES
SEEMLY	SEGNOS	SEINES	SEIZURE	SELENITIC
SEEMLYHED	SEGO	SEINING	SEIZURES	SELENIUM
SEEMS	SEGOL	SEININGS	SEJANT	SELENIUMS
SEEN	SEGOLATE	SEIR	SEJEANT	SELENOSES
SEEP	SEGOLATES	SEIRS	SEKOS	SELENOSIS
SEEPAGE	SEGOLS	SEIS	SEKOSES	SELENOUS
SEEPAGES	SEGOS	SEISABLE	SEKT	SELES
SEEPED	SEGREANT	SEISE	SEKTS	SELF
SEEPIER	SEGREGANT	SEISED	SEL	SELFDOM
SEEPIEST	SEGREGATE	SEISER	SELACHIAN	SELFDOMS
SEEPING	SEGS	SEISERS	SELADANG	SELFED
SEEPS	SEGUE	SEISES	SELADANGS	SELFHEAL
SEEPY	SEGUED	SEISIN	SELAH	SELFHEALS
SEER	SEGUEING	SEISING	SELAHS	SELFHOOD
SEERESS	SEGUES	SEISINGS	SELAMLIK	SELFHOODS
SEERESSES	SEGUGIO	SEISINS	SELAMLIKS	SELFIE
SEERS	SEGUGIOS	SEISM	SELCOUTH	SELFIES
SEES	SEHRI	SEISMAL	SELD	SELFING
SEESAW	SEHRIS	SEISMIC	SELDOM	SELFINGS
SEESAWED	SEI	SEISMICAL	SELDOMLY	SELFISH
SEESAWING	SEICENTO	SEISMISM	SELDSEEN	SELFISHLY
SEESAWS	SEICENTOS	SEISMISMS	SELDSHOWN	SELFISM
SEETHE	SEICHE	SEISMS	SELE	SELFISMS
SEETHED	SEICHES	SEISOR	SELECT	SELFIST
SEETHER	SEIDEL	SEISORS	SELECTA	SELFISTS
SEETHERS	SEIDELS	SEISURE	SELECTAS	SELFLESS
SEETHES	SEIF	SEISURES	SELECTED	SELFNESS
SEETHING	SEIFS	SEITAN	SELECTEE	SELFS

SELFSAME	SEMANTRON	SEMIDWARF	SEMIOSIS	SEMPLICE
SELFWARD	SEMAPHORE	SEMIE	SEMIOTIC	SEMPRE
SELFWARDS	SEMATIC	SEMIERECT	SEMIOTICS	SEMPSTER
SELICTAR	SEMBLABLE	SEMIES	SEMIOVAL	SEMPSTERS
SELICTARS	SEMBLABLY	SEMIFINAL	SEMIPED	SEMSEM
SELKIE	SEMBLANCE	SEMIFIT	SEMIPEDS	SEMSEMS
SELKIES	SEMBLANT	SEMIFLUID	SEMIPIOUS	SEMUNCIA
SELL	SEMBLANTS	SEMIGALA	SEMIPLUME	SEMUNCIAE
SELLA	SEMBLE	SEMIGALAS	SEMIPOLAR	SEMUNCIAL
SELLABLE	SEMBLED	SEMIGLOBE	SEMIPRO	SEMUNCIAS
SELLAE	SEMBLES	SEMIGLOSS	SEMIPROS	SEN
SELLAS	SEMBLING	SEMIGROUP	SEMIRAW	SENA
SELLE	SEME	SEMIHARD	SEMIRIGID	SENARIES
SELLER	SEMEE	SEMIHIGH	SEMIROUND	SENARII
SELLERS	SEMEED	SEMIHOBO	SEMIRURAL	SENARIUS
SELLES	SEMEIA	SEMIHOBOS	SEMIS	SENARY
SELLING	SEMEION	SEMILLON	SEMISES	SENAS
SELLINGS	SEMEIOTIC	SEMILLONS	SEMISOFT	SENATE
SELLOFF	SEMEME	SEMILOG	SEMISOLID	SENATES
SELLOFFS	SEMEMES	SEMILUNAR	SEMISOLUS	SENATOR
SELLOTAPE	SEMEMIC	SEMILUNE	SEMISTIFF	SENATORS
SELLOUT	SEMEN	SEMILUNES	SEMISWEET	SEND
SELLOUTS	SEMENS	SEMIMAT	SEMITAR	SENDABLE
SELLS	SEMES	SEMIMATT	SEMITARS	SENDAL
SELS	SEMESTER	SEMIMATTE	SEMITAUR	SENDALS
SELSYN	SEMESTERS	SEMIMETAL	SEMITAURS	SENDED
SELSYNS	SEMESTRAL	SEMIMICRO	SEMITIST	SENDER
SELTZER	SEMI	SEMIMILD	SEMITISTS	SENDERS
SELTZERS	SEMIANGLE	SEMIMOIST	SEMITONAL	SENDING
SELVA	SEMIARID	SEMIMUTE	SEMITONE	SENDINGS
SELVAGE	SEMIBALD	SEMIMUTES	SEMITONES	SENDOFF
SELVAGED	SEMIBOLD	SEMINA	SEMITONIC	SENDOFFS
SELVAGEE	SEMIBOLDS	SEMINAL	SEMITRUCK	SENDS
SELVAGEES	SEMIBREVE	SEMINALLY	SEMIURBAN	SENDUP
SELVAGES	SEMIBULL	SEMINAR	SEMIVOCAL	SENDUPS
SELVAGING	SEMIBULLS	SEMINARS	SEMIVOWEL	SENE
SELVAS	SEMICOLON	SEMINARY	SEMIWATER	SENECA
SELVEDGE	SEMICOMA	SEMINATE	SEMIWILD	SENECAS
SELVEDGED	SEMICOMAS	SEMINATED	SEMIWORKS	SENECIO
SELVEDGES	SEMICURED	SEMINATES	SEMMIT	SENECIOS
SELVES	SEMIDEAF	SEMINOMA	SEMMITS	SENEGA
SEMAINIER	SEMIDEIFY	SEMINOMAD	SEMOLINA	SENEGAS
SEMANTEME	SEMIDOME	SEMINOMAS	SEMOLINAS	SENES
SEMANTIC	SEMIDOMED	SEMINUDE	SEMPER	SENESCE
SEMANTICS	SEMIDOMES	SEMIOLOGY	SEMPLE	SENESCED
SEMANTIDE	SEMIDRIER	SEMIOPEN	SEMPLER	SENESCENT
SEMANTRA	SEMIDRY	SEMIOSES	SEMPLEST	SENESCES

S

SENESCHAL	SENSATION	SENTIENCE	SEPIUMS	SEPTUPLES
SENESCING	SENSE	SENTIENCY	SEPMAG	SEPTUPLET
SENGI	SENSED	SENTIENT	SEPOY	SEPULCHER
SENGIS	SENSEFUL	SENTIENTS	SEPOYS	SEPULCHRE
SENGREEN	SENSEI	SENTIMENT	SEPPUKU	SEPULTURE
SENGREENS	SENSEIS	SENTIMO	SEPPUKUS	SEQUACITY
SENHOR	SENSELESS	SENTIMOS	SEPS	SEQUEL
SENHORA	SENSES	SENTINEL	SEPSES	SEQUELA
SENHORAS	SENSI	SENTINELS	SEPSIS	SEQUELAE
SENHORES	SENSIBLE	SENTING	SEPT	SEQUELISE
SENHORITA	SENSIBLER	SENTRIES	SEPTA	SEQUELIZE
SENHORS	SENSIBLES	SENTRY	SEPTAGE	SEQUELS
SENILE	SENSIBLY	SENTS	SEPTAGES	SEQUENCE
SENILELY	SENSILE	SENVIES	SEPTAL	SEQUENCED
SENILES	SENSILLA	SENVY	SEPTARIA	SEQUENCER
SENILITY	SENSILLAE	SENZA	SEPTARIAN	SEQUENCES
SENIOR	SENSILLUM	SEPAD	SEPTARIUM	SEQUENCY
SENIORITY	SENSING	SEPADDED	SEPTATE	SEQUENT
SENIORS	SENSINGS	SEPADDING	SEPTATION	SEQUENTLY
SENITI	SENSIS	SEPADS	SEPTEMFID	SEQUENTS
SENITIS	SENSISM	SEPAL	SEPTEMVIR	SEQUESTER
SENNA	SENSISMS	SEPALED	SEPTENARY	SEQUESTRA
SENNACHIE	SENSIST	SEPALINE	SEPTENNIA	SEQUIN
SENNAS	SENSISTS	SEPALLED	SEPTET	SEQUINED
SENNET	SENSITISE	SEPALODY	SEPTETS	SEQUINING
SENNETS	SENSITIVE	SEPALOID	SEPTETTE	SEQUINNED
SENNIGHT	SENSITIZE	SEPALOUS	SEPTETTES	SEQUINS
SENNIGHTS	SENSOR	SEPALS	SEPTIC	SEQUITUR
SENNIT	SENSORIA	SEPARABLE	SEPTICAL	SEQUITURS
SENNITS	SENSORIAL	SEPARABLY	SEPTICITY	SEQUOIA
SENOPIA	SENSORILY	SEPARATA	SEPTICS	SEQUOIAS
SENOPIAS	SENSORIUM	SEPARATE	SEPTIFORM	SER
SENOR	SENSORS	SEPARATED	SEPTIMAL	SERA
SENORA	SENSORY	SEPARATES	SEPTIME	SERAC
SENORAS	SENSUAL	SEPARATOR	SEPTIMES	SERACS
SENORES	SENSUALLY	SEPARATUM	SEPTIMOLE	SERAFILE
SENORITA	SENSUM	SEPHEN	SEPTLEVA	SERAFILES
SENORITAS	SENSUOUS	SEPHENS	SEPTLEVAS	SERAFIN
SENORS	SENT	SEPIA	SEPTORIA	SERAFINS
SENRYU	SENTE	SEPIAS	SEPTORIAS	SERAGLIO
SENS	SENTED	SEPIC	SEPTS	SERAGLIOS
SENSA	SENTENCE	SEPIMENT	SEPTUM	SERAI
SENSATE	SENTENCED	SEPIMENTS	SEPTUMS	SERAIL
SENSATED	SENTENCER	SEPIOLITE	SEPTUOR	SERAILS
SENSATELY	SENTENCES	SEPIOST	SEPTUORS	SERAIS
SENSATES	SENTENTIA	SEPIOSTS	SEPTUPLE	SERAL
SENSATING	SENTI	SEPIUM	SEPTUPLED	SERANG

S

SERANGS
SERAPE
SERAPES
SERAPH
SERAPHIC
SERAPHIM
SERAPHIMS
SERAPHIN
SERAPHINE
SERAPHINS
SERAPHS
SERASKIER
SERDAB
SERDABS
SERE
SERED
SEREIN
SEREINS
SERENADE
SERENADED
SERENADER
SERENADES
SERENATA
SERENATAS
SERENATE
SERENATED
SERENATES
SERENE
SERENED
SERENELY
SERENER
SERENES
SERENEST
SERENING
SERENITY
SERER
SERES
SEREST
SERF
SERFAGE
SERFAGES
SERFDOM
SERFDOMS
SERFHOOD
SERFHOODS
SERFISH
SERFLIKE

SERFS
SERFSHIP
SERFSHIPS
SERGE
SERGEANCY
SERGEANT
SERGEANTS
SERGEANTY
SERGED
SERGER
SERGERS
SERGES
SERGING
SERGINGS
SERIAL
SERIALISE
SERIALISM
SERIALIST
SERIALITY
SERIALIZE
SERIALLY
SERIALS
SERIATE
SERIATED
SERIATELY
SERIATES
SERIATIM
SERIATING
SERIATION
SERIC
SERICEOUS
SERICIN
SERICINS
SERICITE
SERICITES
SERICITIC
SERICON
SERICONS
SERIEMA
SERIEMAS
SERIES
SERIF
SERIFED
SERIFFED
SERIFS
SERIGRAPH
SERIN

SERINE
SERINES
SERINETTE
SERING
SERINGA
SERINGAS
SERINS
SERIOUS
SERIOUSLY
SERIPH
SERIPHS
SERJEANCY
SERJEANT
SERJEANTS
SERJEANTY
SERK
SERKALI
SERKALIS
SERKS
SERMON
SERMONED
SERMONEER
SERMONER
SERMONERS
SERMONET
SERMONETS
SERMONIC
SERMONING
SERMONISE
SERMONIZE
SERMONS
SEROGROUP
SEROLOGIC
SEROLOGY
SERON
SERONS
SEROON
SEROONS
SEROPUS
SEROPUSES
SEROSA
SEROSAE
SEROSAL
SEROSAS
SEROSITY
SEROTINAL
SEROTINE

SEROTINES
SEROTINY
SEROTONIN
SEROTYPE
SEROTYPED
SEROTYPES
SEROTYPIC
SEROUS
SEROVAR
SEROVARS
SEROW
SEROWS
SERPENT
SERPENTRY
SERPENTS
SERPIGO
SERPIGOES
SERPIGOS
SERPULA
SERPULAE
SERPULAS
SERPULID
SERPULIDS
SERPULITE
SERR
SERRA
SERRAE
SERRAN
SERRANID
SERRANIDS
SERRANO
SERRANOID
SERRANOS
SERRANS
SERRAS
SERRATE
SERRATED
SERRATES
SERRATI
SERRATING
SERRATION
SERRATURE
SERRATUS
SERRE
SERRED
SERREFILE
SERRES

SERRICORN
SERRIED
SERRIEDLY
SERRIES
SERRIFORM
SERRING
SERRS
SERRULATE
SERRY
SERRYING
SERS
SERUEWE
SERUEWED
SERUEWES
SERUEWING
SERUM
SERUMAL
SERUMS
SERVABLE
SERVAL
SERVALS
SERVANT
SERVANTED
SERVANTRY
SERVANTS
SERVE
SERVEABLE
SERVED
SERVER
SERVERIES
SERVERS
SERVERY
SERVES
SERVEWE
SERVEWED
SERVEWES
SERVEWING
SERVICE
SERVICED
SERVICER
SERVICERS
SERVICES
SERVICING
SERVIENT
SERVIETTE
SERVILE
SERVILELY

S

SERVILES	SESTETTS	SETTLINGS	SEWABLE	SEXISMS
SERVILISM	SESTINA	SETTLOR	SEWAGE	SEXIST
SERVILITY	SESTINAS	SETTLORS	SEWAGES	SEXISTS
SERVING	SESTINE	SETTS	SEWAN	SEXLESS
SERVINGS	SESTINES	SETUALE	SEWANS	SEXLESSLY
SERVITOR	SESTON	SETUALES	SEWAR	SEXLINKED
SERVITORS	SESTONS	SETULE	SEWARS	SEXOLOGIC
SERVITUDE	SET	SETULES	SEWED	SEXOLOGY
SERVLET	SETA	SETULOSE	SEWEL	SEXPERT
SERVLETS	SETACEOUS	SETULOUS	SEWELLEL	SEXPERTS
SERVO	SETAE	SETUP	SEWELLELS	SEXPOT
SERVOS	SETAL	SETUPS	SEWELS	SEXPOTS
SERVQUAL	SETBACK	SETWALL	SEWEN	SEXT
SERVQUALS	SETBACKS	SETWALLS	SEWENS	SEXTAIN
SESAME	SETENANT	SEV	SEWER	SEXTAINS
SESAMES	SETENANTS	SEVEN	SEWERAGE	SEXTAN
SESAMOID	SETIFORM	SEVENFOLD	SEWERAGES	SEXTANS
SESAMOIDS	SETLINE	SEVENS	SEWERED	SEXTANSES
SESE	SETLINES	SEVENTEEN	SEWERING	SEXTANT
SESELI	SETNESS	SEVENTH	SEWERINGS	SEXTANTAL
SESELIS	SETNESSES	SEVENTHLY	SEWERLESS	SEXTANTS
SESEY	SETOFF	SEVENTHS	SEWERLIKE	SEXTARII
SESH	SETOFFS	SEVENTIES	SEWERS	SEXTARIUS
SESHES	SETON	SEVENTY	SEWIN	SEXTED
SESS	SETONS	SEVER	SEWING	SEXTET
SESSA	SETOSE	SEVERABLE	SEWINGS	SEXTETS
SESSED	SETOUS	SEVERAL	SEWINS	SEXTETT
SESSES	SETOUT	SEVERALLY	SEWN	SEXTETTE
SESSILE	SETOUTS	SEVERALS	SEWS	SEXTETTES
SESSILITY	SETS	SEVERALTY	SEX	SEXTETTS
SESSING	SETSCREW	SEVERANCE	SEXAHOLIC	SEXTILE
SESSION	SETSCREWS	SEVERE	SEXED	SEXTILES
SESSIONAL	SETT	SEVERED	SEXENNIAL	SEXTING
SESSIONS	SETTEE	SEVERELY	SEXER	SEXTINGS
SESSPOOL	SETTEES	SEVERER	SEXERCISE	SEXTO
SESSPOOLS	SETTER	SEVEREST	SEXERS	SEXTOLET
SESTERCE	SETTERED	SEVERIES	SEXES	SEXTOLETS
SESTERCES	SETTERING	SEVERING	SEXFID	SEXTON
SESTERTIA	SETTERS	SEVERITY	SEXFOIL	SEXTONESS
SESTERTII	SETTING	SEVERS	SEXFOILS	SEXTONS
SESTET	SETTINGS	SEVERY	SEXIER	SEXTOS
SESTETS	SETTLE	SEVICHE	SEXIEST	SEXTS
SESTETT	SETTLED	SEVICHES	SEXILY	SEXTUOR
SESTETTE	SETTLER	SEVRUGA	SEXINESS	SEXTUORS
SESTETTES	SETTLERS	SEVRUGAS	SEXING	SEXTUPLE
SESTETTO	SETTLES	SEVS	SEXINGS	SEXTUPLED
SESTETTOS	SETTLING	SEW	SEXISM	SEXTUPLES

SEXTUPLET	SHACKLER	SHADRACH	SHAIRD	SHALLOP
SEXTUPLY	SHACKLERS	SHADRACHS	SHAIRDS	SHALLOPS
SEXUAL	SHACKLES	SHADS	SHAIRN	SHALLOT
SEXUALISE	SHACKLING	SHADUF	SHAIRNS	SHALLOTS
SEXUALISM	SHACKO	SHADUFS	SHAITAN	SHALLOW
SEXUALIST	SHACKOES	SHADY	SHAITANS	SHALLOWED
SEXUALITY	SHACKOS	SHAFT	SHAKABLE	SHALLOWER
SEXUALIZE	SHACKS	SHAFTED	SHAKE	SHALLOWLY
SEXUALLY	SHACKY	SHAFTER	SHAKEABLE	SHALLOWS
SEXVALENT	SHAD	SHAFTERS	SHAKED	SHALM
SEXY	SHADBERRY	SHAFTING	SHAKEDOWN	SHALMS
SEY	SHADBLOW	SHAFTINGS	SHAKEN	SHALOM
SEYEN	SHADBLOWS	SHAFTLESS	SHAKEOUT	SHALOMS
SEYENS	SHADBUSH	SHAFTS	SHAKEOUTS	SHALOT
SEYS	SHADCHAN	SHAG	SHAKER	SHALOTS
SEYSURE	SHADCHANS	SHAGBARK	SHAKERS	SHALT
SEYSURES	SHADDOCK	SHAGBARKS	SHAKES	SHALWAR
SEZ	SHADDOCKS	SHAGGABLE	SHAKEUP	SHALWARS
SFERICS	SHADDUP	SHAGGED	SHAKEUPS	SHALY
SFORZANDI	SHADE	SHAGGER	SHAKIER	SHAM
SFORZANDO	SHADED	SHAGGERS	SHAKIEST	SHAMA
SFORZATI	SHADELESS	SHAGGIER	SHAKILY	SHAMABLE
SFORZATO	SHADER	SHAGGIEST	SHAKINESS	SHAMABLY
SFORZATOS	SHADERS	SHAGGILY	SHAKING	SHAMAL
SFUMATO	SHADES	SHAGGING	SHAKINGS	SHAMALS
SFUMATOS	SHADFLIES	SHAGGY	SHAKO	SHAMAN
SGRAFFITI	SHADFLY	SHAGPILE	SHAKOES	SHAMANIC
SGRAFFITO	SHADIER	SHAGREEN	SHAKOS	SHAMANISM
SH	SHADIEST	SHAGREENS	SHAKT	SHAMANIST
SHA	SHADILY	SHAGROON	SHAKUDO	SHAMANS
SHABASH	SHADINESS	SHAGROONS	SHAKUDOS	SHAMAS
SHABBATOT	SHADING	SHAGS	SHAKY	SHAMATEUR
SHABBIER	SHADINGS	SHAH	SHALE	SHAMBA
SHABBIEST	SHADKHAN	SHAHADA	SHALED	SHAMBAS
SHABBILY	SHADKHANS	SHAHADAH	SHALELIKE	SHAMBLE
SHABBLE	SHADOOF	SHAHADAHS	SHALES	SHAMBLED
SHABBLES	SHADOOFS	SHAHADAS	SHALEY	SHAMBLES
SHABBY	SHADOW	SHAHDOM	SHALIER	SHAMBLIER
SHABRACK	SHADOWBOX	SHAHDOMS	SHALIEST	SHAMBLING
SHABRACKS	SHADOWED	SHAHEED	SHALING	SHAMBLY
SHACK	SHADOWER	SHAHEEDS	SHALL	SHAMBOLIC
SHACKED	SHADOWERS	SHAHID	SHALLI	SHAME
SHACKIER	SHADOWIER	SHAHIDS	SHALLIS	SHAMEABLE
SHACKIEST	SHADOWILY	SHAHS	SHALLON	SHAMEABLY
SHACKING	SHADOWING	SHAHTOOSH	SHALLONS	SHAMED
SHACKLE	SHADOWS	SHAIKH	SHALLOON	SHAMEFAST
SHACKLED	SHADOWY	SHAIKHS	SHALLOONS	SHAMEFUL

S

SHAMELESS	SHANDIES	SHARABLE	SHARPENED	SHAVABLE
SHAMER	SHANDRIES	SHARD	SHARPENER	SHAVE
SHAMERS	SHANDRY	SHARDED	SHARPENS	SHAVEABLE
SHAMES	SHANDS	SHARDS	SHARPER	SHAVED
SHAMIANA	SHANDY	SHARE	SHARPERS	SHAVELING
SHAMIANAH	SHANGHAI	SHAREABLE	SHARPEST	SHAVEN
SHAMIANAS	SHANGHAIS	SHARECROP	SHARPIE	SHAVER
SHAMINA	SHANK	SHARED	SHARPIES	SHAVERS
SHAMINAS	SHANKBONE	SHAREMAN	SHARPING	SHAVES
SHAMING	SHANKED	SHAREMEN	SHARPINGS	SHAVETAIL
SHAMISEN	SHANKING	SHARER	SHARPISH	SHAVIE
SHAMISENS	SHANKS	SHARERS	SHARPLY	SHAVIES
SHAMMAS	SHANNIES	SHARES	SHARPNESS	SHAVING
SHAMMASH	SHANNY	SHARESMAN	SHARPS	SHAVINGS
SHAMMASIM	SHANS	SHARESMEN	SHARPY	SHAW
SHAMMED	SHANTEY	SHAREWARE	SHASH	SHAWARMA
SHAMMER	SHANTEYS	SHARIA	SHASHED	SHAWARMAS
SHAMMERS	SHANTI	SHARIAH	SHASHES	SHAWED
SHAMMES	SHANTIES	SHARIAHS	SHASHING	SHAWING
SHAMMIED	SHANTIH	SHARIAS	SHASHLICK	SHAWL
SHAMMIES	SHANTIHS	SHARIAT	SHASHLIK	SHAWLED
SHAMMING	SHANTIS	SHARIATS	SHASHLIKS	SHAWLEY
SHAMMOS	SHANTUNG	SHARIF	SHASLIK	SHAWLEYS
SHAMMOSIM	SHANTUNGS	SHARIFIAN	SHASLIKS	SHAWLIE
SHAMMY	SHANTY	SHARIFS	SHASTA	SHAWLIES
SHAMMYING	SHANTYMAN	SHARING	SHASTAS	SHAWLING
SHAMOIS	SHANTYMEN	SHARINGS	SHASTER	SHAWLINGS
SHAMOISED	SHAPABLE	SHARK	SHASTERS	SHAWLLESS
SHAMOISES	SHAPE	SHARKED	SHASTRA	SHAWLS
SHAMOS	SHAPEABLE	SHARKER	SHASTRAS	SHAWM
SHAMOSIM	SHAPED	SHARKERS	SHAT	SHAWMS
SHAMOY	SHAPELESS	SHARKING	SHATOOSH	SHAWN
SHAMOYED	SHAPELIER	SHARKINGS	SHATTER	SHAWS
SHAMOYING	SHAPELY	SHARKISH	SHATTERED	SHAY
SHAMOYS	SHAPEN	SHARKLIKE	SHATTERER	SHAYA
SHAMPOO	SHAPENED	SHARKS	SHATTERS	SHAYAS
SHAMPOOED	SHAPENING	SHARKSKIN	SHATTERY	SHAYKH
SHAMPOOER	SHAPENS	SHARN	SHAUCHLE	SHAYKHS
SHAMPOOS	SHAPER	SHARNIER	SHAUCHLED	SHAYS
SHAMROCK	SHAPERS	SHARNIES	SHAUCHLES	SHAZAM
SHAMROCKS	SHAPES	SHARNIEST	SHAUCHLY	SHCHI
SHAMS	SHAPEUP	SHARNS	SHAUGH	SHCHIS
SHAMUS	SHAPEUPS	SHARNY	SHAUGHS	SHE
SHAMUSES	SHAPEWEAR	SHARON	SHAUL	SHEA
SHAN	SHAPING	SHARP	SHAULED	SHEADING
SHANACHIE	SHAPINGS	SHARPED	SHAULING	SHEADINGS
SHAND	SHAPS	SHARPEN	SHAULS	SHEAF

SHEAFED
SHEAFIER
SHEAFIEST
SHEAFING
SHEAFLIKE
SHEAFS
SHEAFY
SHEAL
SHEALED
SHEALING
SHEALINGS
SHEALS
SHEAR
SHEARED
SHEARER
SHEARERS
SHEARING
SHEARINGS
SHEARLEG
SHEARLEGS
SHEARLING
SHEARMAN
SHEARMEN
SHEARS
SHEAS
SHEATFISH
SHEATH
SHEATHE
SHEATHED
SHEATHER
SHEATHERS
SHEATHES
SHEATHIER
SHEATHING
SHEATHS
SHEATHY
SHEAVE
SHEAVED
SHEAVES
SHEAVING
SHEBANG
SHEBANGS
SHEBEAN
SHEBEANS
SHEBEEN
SHEBEENED
SHEBEENER

SHEBEENS
SHECHITA
SHECHITAH
SHECHITAS
SHED
SHEDABLE
SHEDDABLE
SHEDDED
SHEDDER
SHEDDERS
SHEDDING
SHEDDINGS
SHEDFUL
SHEDFULS
SHEDHAND
SHEDHANDS
SHEDLIKE
SHEDLOAD
SHEDLOADS
SHEDS
SHEEL
SHEELED
SHEELING
SHEELS
SHEEN
SHEENED
SHEENEY
SHEENEYS
SHEENFUL
SHEENIE
SHEENIER
SHEENIES
SHEENIEST
SHEENING
SHEENS
SHEENY
SHEEP
SHEEPCOT
SHEEPCOTE
SHEEPCOTS
SHEEPDOG
SHEEPDOGS
SHEEPFOLD
SHEEPHEAD
SHEEPIER
SHEEPIEST
SHEEPISH

SHEEPLE
SHEEPLIKE
SHEEPMAN
SHEEPMEN
SHEEPO
SHEEPOS
SHEEPSKIN
SHEEPWALK
SHEEPY
SHEER
SHEERED
SHEERER
SHEEREST
SHEERING
SHEERLEG
SHEERLEGS
SHEERLY
SHEERNESS
SHEERS
SHEESH
SHEESHA
SHEESHAS
SHEET
SHEETED
SHEETER
SHEETERS
SHEETFED
SHEETIER
SHEETIEST
SHEETING
SHEETINGS
SHEETLESS
SHEETLIKE
SHEETROCK
SHEETS
SHEETY
SHEEVE
SHEEVES
SHEGETZ
SHEHITA
SHEHITAH
SHEHITAHS
SHEHITAS
SHEHNAI
SHEHNAIS
SHEIK
SHEIKDOM

SHEIKDOMS
SHEIKH
SHEIKHA
SHEIKHAS
SHEIKHDOM
SHEIKHS
SHEIKS
SHEILA
SHEILAS
SHEILING
SHEILINGS
SHEITAN
SHEITANS
SHEITEL
SHEITELS
SHEKALIM
SHEKEL
SHEKELIM
SHEKELS
SHELDDUCK
SHELDRAKE
SHELDUCK
SHELDUCKS
SHELF
SHELFED
SHELFFUL
SHELFFULS
SHELFIER
SHELFIEST
SHELFING
SHELFLIKE
SHELFROOM
SHELFS
SHELFY
SHELL
SHELLAC
SHELLACK
SHELLACKS
SHELLACS
SHELLBACK
SHELLBARK
SHELLDUCK
SHELLED
SHELLER
SHELLERS
SHELLFIRE
SHELLFISH

SHELLFUL
SHELLFULS
SHELLIER
SHELLIEST
SHELLING
SHELLINGS
SHELLS
SHELLWORK
SHELLY
SHELTA
SHELTAS
SHELTER
SHELTERED
SHELTERER
SHELTERS
SHELTERY
SHELTIE
SHELTIES
SHELTY
SHELVE
SHELVED
SHELVER
SHELVERS
SHELVES
SHELVIER
SHELVIEST
SHELVING
SHELVINGS
SHELVY
SHEMALE
SHEMALES
SHEMOZZLE
SHEN
SHENAI
SHENAIS
SHEND
SHENDING
SHENDS
SHENT
SHEOL
SHEOLS
SHEPHERD
SHEPHERDS
SHEQALIM
SHEQEL
SHEQELS
SHERANG

S

SHERANGS	SHEUGHS	SHIEST	SHILLED	SHINGLY
SHERBERT	SHEVA	SHIFT	SHILLELAH	SHINGUARD
SHERBERTS	SHEVAS	SHIFTABLE	SHILLING	SHINIER
SHERBET	SHEW	SHIFTED	SHILLINGS	SHINIES
SHERBETS	SHEWBREAD	SHIFTER	SHILLS	SHINIEST
SHERD	SHEWED	SHIFTERS	SHILPIT	SHINILY
SHERDS	SHEWEL	SHIFTIER	SHILY	SHININESS
SHERE	SHEWELS	SHIFTIEST	SHIM	SHINING
SHEREEF	SHEWER	SHIFTILY	SHIMAAL	SHININGLY
SHEREEFS	SHEWERS	SHIFTING	SHIMAALS	SHINJU
SHERIA	SHEWING	SHIFTINGS	SHIMMED	SHINJUS
SHERIAS	SHEWN	SHIFTLESS	SHIMMER	SHINKIN
SHERIAT	SHEWS	SHIFTS	SHIMMERED	SHINKINS
SHERIATS	SHH	SHIFTWORK	SHIMMERS	SHINLEAF
SHERIF	SHHH	SHIFTY	SHIMMERY	SHINLEAFS
SHERIFF	SHIAI	SHIGELLA	SHIMMEY	SHINNE
SHERIFFS	SHIAIS	SHIGELLAE	SHIMMEYS	SHINNED
SHERIFIAN	SHIATSU	SHIGELLAS	SHIMMIED	SHINNERY
SHERIFS	SHIATSUS	SHIITAKE	SHIMMIES	SHINNES
SHERLOCK	SHIATZU	SHIITAKES	SHIMMING	SHINNEY
SHERLOCKS	SHIATZUS	SHIKAR	SHIMMY	SHINNEYED
SHERO	SHIBAH	SHIKARA	SHIMMYING	SHINNEYS
SHEROES	SHIBAHS	SHIKARAS	SHIMOZZLE	SHINNIED
SHEROOT	SHIBUICHI	SHIKAREE	SHIMS	SHINNIES
SHEROOTS	SHICKER	SHIKAREES	SHIN	SHINNING
SHERPA	SHICKERED	SHIKARI	SHINBONE	SHINNY
SHERPAS	SHICKERS	SHIKARIS	SHINBONES	SHINNYING
SHERRIED	SHICKSA	SHIKARRED	SHINDIES	SHINOLA
SHERRIES	SHICKSAS	SHIKARS	SHINDIG	SHINOLAS
SHERRIS	SHIDDER	SHIKKER	SHINDIGS	SHINS
SHERRISES	SHIDDERS	SHIKKERED	SHINDY	SHINTIED
SHERRY	SHIDDUCH	SHIKKERS	SHINDYS	SHINTIES
SHERWANI	SHIED	SHIKRA	SHINE	SHINTY
SHERWANIS	SHIEL	SHIKRAS	SHINED	SHINTYING
SHES	SHIELD	SHIKSA	SHINELESS	SHINY
SHET	SHIELDED	SHIKSAS	SHINER	SHIP
SHETLAND	SHIELDER	SHIKSE	SHINERS	SHIPBOARD
SHETLANDS	SHIELDERS	SHIKSEH	SHINES	SHIPBORNE
SHETS	SHIELDING	SHIKSEHS	SHINESS	SHIPFUL
SHETTING	SHIELDS	SHIKSES	SHINESSES	SHIPFULS
SHEUCH	SHIELED	SHILINGI	SHINGLE	SHIPLAP
SHEUCHED	SHIELING	SHILINGIS	SHINGLED	SHIPLAPS
SHEUCHING	SHIELINGS	SHILL	SHINGLER	SHIPLESS
SHEUCHS	SHIELS	SHILLABER	SHINGLERS	SHIPLOAD
SHEUGH	SHIER	SHILLALA	SHINGLES	SHIPLOADS
SHEUGHED	SHIERS	SHILLALAH	SHINGLIER	SHIPMAN
SHEUGHING	SHIES	SHILLALAS	SHINGLING	SHIPMATE

SHIPMATES	SHIRKERS	SHITHEELS	SHIVITI	SHMEARING
SHIPMEN	SHIRKING	SHITHOLE	SHIVITIS	SHMEARS
SHIPMENT	SHIRKS	SHITHOLES	SHIVOO	SHMEER
SHIPMENTS	SHIRR	SHITHOUSE	SHIVOOS	SHMEERED
SHIPOWNER	SHIRRA	SHITING	SHIVS	SHMEERING
SHIPPABLE	SHIRRALEE	SHITLESS	SHIVVED	SHMEERS
SHIPPED	SHIRRAS	SHITLIST	SHIVVING	SHMEK
SHIPPEN	SHIRRED	SHITLISTS	SHIZZLE	SHMEKS
SHIPPENS	SHIRRING	SHITLOAD	SHIZZLES	SHMO
SHIPPER	SHIRRINGS	SHITLOADS	SHKOTZIM	SHMOCK
SHIPPERS	SHIRRS	SHITS	SHLEMIEHL	SHMOCKS
SHIPPIE	SHIRS	SHITTAH	SHLEMIEL	SHMOE
SHIPPIES	SHIRT	SHITTAHS	SHLEMIELS	SHMOES
SHIPPING	SHIRTBAND	SHITTED	SHLEP	SHMOOSE
SHIPPINGS	SHIRTED	SHITTER	SHLEPP	SHMOOSED
SHIPPO	SHIRTIER	SHITTERS	SHLEPPED	SHMOOSES
SHIPPON	SHIRTIEST	SHITTIER	SHLEPPER	SHMOOSING
SHIPPONS	SHIRTILY	SHITTIEST	SHLEPPERS	SHMOOZE
SHIPPOS	SHIRTING	SHITTILY	SHLEPPIER	SHMOOZED
SHIPPOUND	SHIRTINGS	SHITTIM	SHLEPPING	SHMOOZER
SHIPS	SHIRTLESS	SHITTIMS	SHLEPPS	SHMOOZERS
SHIPSHAPE	SHIRTS	SHITTING	SHLEPPY	SHMOOZES
SHIPSIDE	SHIRTTAIL	SHITTY	SHLEPS	SHMOOZIER
SHIPSIDES	SHIRTY	SHITWORK	SHLIMAZEL	SHMOOZING
SHIPTIME	SHISH	SHITWORKS	SHLOCK	SHMOOZY
SHIPTIMES	SHISHA	SHITZU	SHLOCKIER	SHMUCK
SHIPWAY	SHISHAS	SHITZUS	SHLOCKS	SHMUCKIER
SHIPWAYS	SHISO	SHIUR	SHLOCKY	SHMUCKS
SHIPWORM	SHISOS	SHIURIM	SHLONG	SHMUCKY
SHIPWORMS	SHIST	SHIV	SHLONGS	SHNAPPS
SHIPWRECK	SHISTS	SHIVA	SHLOSHIM	SHNAPS
SHIPYARD	SHIT	SHIVAH	SHLOSHIMS	SHNOOK
SHIPYARDS	SHITAKE	SHIVAHS	SHLUB	SHNOOKS
SHIR	SHITAKES	SHIVAREE	SHLUBS	SHNORRER
SHIRALEE	SHITBAG	SHIVAREED	SHLUMP	SHNORRERS
SHIRALEES	SHITBAGS	SHIVAREES	SHLUMPED	SHO
SHIRAZ	SHITCAN	SHIVAS	SHLUMPIER	SHOAL
SHIRAZES	SHITCANS	SHIVE	SHLUMPING	SHOALED
SHIRE	SHITE	SHIVER	SHLUMPS	SHOALER
SHIRED	SHITED	SHIVERED	SHLUMPY	SHOALEST
SHIREMAN	SHITES	SHIVERER	SHMALTZ	SHOALIER
SHIREMEN	SHITFACE	SHIVERERS	SHMALTZES	SHOALIEST
SHIRES	SHITFACED	SHIVERIER	SHMALTZY	SHOALING
SHIRING	SHITFACES	SHIVERING	SHMATTE	SHOALINGS
SHIRK	SHITHEAD	SHIVERS	SHMATTES	SHOALNESS
SHIRKED	SHITHEADS	SHIVERY	SHMEAR	SHOALS
SHIRKER	SHITHEEL	SHIVES	SHMEARED	SHOALWISE

S

SHOALY	SHOESHINE	SHOOGLY	SHOPLESS	SHORTARM
SHOAT	SHOETREE	SHOOING	SHOPLIFT	SHORTARSE
SHOATS	SHOETREES	SHOOK	SHOPLIFTS	SHORTCAKE
SHOCHET	SHOFAR	SHOOKS	SHOPMAN	SHORTCUT
SHOCHETIM	SHOFARS	SHOOL	SHOPMEN	SHORTCUTS
SHOCHETS	SHOFROTH	SHOOLE	SHOPPE	SHORTED
SHOCHU	SHOG	SHOOLED	SHOPPED	SHORTEN
SHOCHUS	SHOGGED	SHOOLES	SHOPPER	SHORTENED
SHOCK	SHOGGING	SHOOLING	SHOPPERS	SHORTENER
SHOCKABLE	SHOGGLE	SHOOLS	SHOPPES	SHORTENS
SHOCKED	SHOGGLED	SHOON	SHOPPIER	SHORTER
SHOCKER	SHOGGLES	SHOORA	SHOPPIES	SHORTEST
SHOCKERS	SHOGGLIER	SHOORAS	SHOPPIEST	SHORTFALL
SHOCKING	SHOGGLING	SHOOS	SHOPPING	SHORTGOWN
SHOCKS	SHOGGLY	SHOOSH	SHOPPINGS	SHORTHAIR
SHOD	SHOGI	SHOOSHED	SHOPPY	SHORTHAND
SHODDEN	SHOGIS	SHOOSHES	SHOPS	SHORTHEAD
SHODDIER	SHOGS	SHOOSHING	SHOPTALK	SHORTHOLD
SHODDIES	SHOGUN	SHOOT	SHOPTALKS	SHORTHORN
SHODDIEST	SHOGUNAL	SHOOTABLE	SHOPWOMAN	SHORTIA
SHODDILY	SHOGUNATE	SHOOTDOWN	SHOPWOMEN	SHORTIAS
SHODDY	SHOGUNS	SHOOTER	SHOPWORN	SHORTIE
SHODER	SHOJI	SHOOTERS	SHORAN	SHORTIES
SHODERS	SHOJIS	SHOOTIE	SHORANS	SHORTING
SHOE	SHOJO	SHOOTIES	SHORE	SHORTISH
SHOEBILL	SHOLA	SHOOTING	SHOREBIRD	SHORTLIST
SHOEBILLS	SHOLAS	SHOOTINGS	SHORED	SHORTLY
SHOEBLACK	SHOLOM	SHOOTIST	SHORELESS	SHORTNESS
SHOEBOX	SHOLOMS	SHOOTISTS	SHORELINE	SHORTS
SHOEBOXES	SHONE	SHOOTOUT	SHOREMAN	SHORTSTOP
SHOEBRUSH	SHONEEN	SHOOTOUTS	SHOREMEN	SHORTWAVE
SHOED	SHONEENS	SHOOTS	SHORER	SHORTY
SHOEHORN	SHONKIER	SHOP	SHORERS	SHOT
SHOEHORNS	SHONKIEST	SHOPBOARD	SHORES	SHOTE
SHOEING	SHONKY	SHOPBOT	SHORESIDE	SHOTES
SHOEINGS	SHOO	SHOPBOTS	SHORESMAN	SHOTFIRER
SHOELACE	SHOOED	SHOPBOY	SHORESMEN	SHOTGUN
SHOELACES	SHOOFLIES	SHOPBOYS	SHOREWARD	SHOTGUNS
SHOELESS	SHOOFLY	SHOPE	SHOREWEED	SHOTHOLE
SHOEMAKER	SHOOGIE	SHOPFRONT	SHORING	SHOTHOLES
SHOEPAC	SHOOGIED	SHOPFUL	SHORINGS	SHOTMAKER
SHOEPACK	SHOOGIES	SHOPFULS	SHORL	SHOTPROOF
SHOEPACKS	SHOOGLE	SHOPGIRL	SHORLS	SHOTS
SHOEPACS	SHOOGLED	SHOPGIRLS	SHORN	SHOTT
SHOER	SHOOGLES	SHOPHAR	SHORT	SHOTTE
SHOERS	SHOOGLIER	SHOPHARS	SHORTAGE	SHOTTED
SHOES	SHOOGLING	SHOPHROTH	SHORTAGES	SHOTTEN

SHOTTES	SHOWBIZ	SHOWPIECE	SHREWMICE	SHRINING
SHOTTING	SHOWBIZZY	SHOWPLACE	SHREWS	SHRINK
SHOTTLE	SHOWBOAT	SHOWRING	SHRI	SHRINKAGE
SHOTTLES	SHOWBOATS	SHOWRINGS	SHRIECH	SHRINKER
SHOTTS	SHOWBOX	SHOWROOM	SHRIECHED	SHRINKERS
SHOUGH	SHOWBOXES	SHOWROOMS	SHRIECHES	SHRINKING
SHOUGHS	SHOWBREAD	SHOWS	SHRIEK	SHRINKS
SHOULD	SHOWCASE	SHOWTIME	SHRIEKED	SHRIS
SHOULDER	SHOWCASED	SHOWTIMES	SHRIEKER	SHRITCH
SHOULDERS	SHOWCASES	SHOWY	SHRIEKERS	SHRITCHED
SHOULDEST	SHOWD	SHOWYARD	SHRIEKIER	SHRITCHES
SHOULDST	SHOWDED	SHOWYARDS	SHRIEKING	SHRIVE
SHOUSE	SHOWDING	SHOYU	SHRIEKS	SHRIVED
SHOUSES	SHOWDOWN	SHOYUS	SHRIEKY	SHRIVEL
SHOUT	SHOWDOWNS	SHRADDHA	SHRIEVAL	SHRIVELED
SHOUTED	SHOWDS	SHRADDHAS	SHRIEVE	SHRIVELS
SHOUTER	SHOWED	SHRANK	SHRIEVED	SHRIVEN
SHOUTERS	SHOWER	SHRAPNEL	SHRIEVES	SHRIVER
SHOUTHER	SHOWERED	SHRAPNELS	SHRIEVING	SHRIVERS
SHOUTHERS	SHOWERER	SHRED	SHRIFT	SHRIVES
SHOUTIER	SHOWERERS	SHREDDED	SHRIFTS	SHRIVING
SHOUTIEST	SHOWERFUL	SHREDDER	SHRIGHT	SHRIVINGS
SHOUTING	SHOWERIER	SHREDDERS	SHRIGHTS	SHROFF
SHOUTINGS	SHOWERING	SHREDDIER	SHRIKE	SHROFFAGE
SHOUTLINE	SHOWERS	SHREDDING	SHRIKED	SHROFFED
SHOUTOUT	SHOWERY	SHREDDY	SHRIKES	SHROFFING
SHOUTOUTS	SHOWGHE	SHREDLESS	SHRIKING	SHROFFS
SHOUTS	SHOWGHES	SHREDS	SHRILL	SHROOM
SHOUTY	SHOWGIRL	SHREEK	SHRILLED	SHROOMED
SHOVE	SHOWGIRLS	SHREEKED	SHRILLER	SHROOMER
SHOVED	SHOWGOER	SHREEKING	SHRILLEST	SHROOMERS
SHOVEL	SHOWGOERS	SHREEKS	SHRILLIER	SHROOMING
SHOVELED	SHOWIER	SHREIK	SHRILLING	SHROOMS
SHOVELER	SHOWIEST	SHREIKED	SHRILLS	SHROUD
SHOVELERS	SHOWILY	SHREIKING	SHRILLY	SHROUDED
SHOVELFUL	SHOWINESS	SHREIKS	SHRIMP	SHROUDIER
SHOVELING	SHOWING	SHREW	SHRIMPED	SHROUDING
SHOVELLED	SHOWINGS	SHREWD	SHRIMPER	SHROUDS
SHOVELLER	SHOWJUMP	SHREWDER	SHRIMPERS	SHROUDY
SHOVELS	SHOWJUMPS	SHREWDEST	SHRIMPIER	SHROVE
SHOVER	SHOWMAN	SHREWDIE	SHRIMPING	SHROVED
SHOVERS	SHOWMANCE	SHREWDIES	SHRIMPS	SHROVES
SHOVES	SHOWMANLY	SHREWDLY	SHRIMPY	SHROVING
SHOVING	SHOWMEN	SHREWED	SHRINAL	SHROW
SHOVINGS	SHOWN	SHREWING	SHRINE	SHROWD
SHOW	SHOWOFF	SHREWISH	SHRINED	SHROWED
SHOWABLE	SHOWOFFS	SHREWLIKE	SHRINES	SHROWING

S

SHROWS	SHUCKINGS	SHURIKEN	SHYEST	SIBILOUS
SHRUB	SHUCKS	SHURIKENS	SHYING	SIBLING
SHRUBBED	SHUDDER	SHUSH	SHYISH	SIBLINGS
SHRUBBERY	SHUDDERED	SHUSHED	SHYLOCK	SIBS
SHRUBBIER	SHUDDERS	SHUSHER	SHYLOCKED	SIBSHIP
SHRUBBING	SHUDDERY	SHUSHERS	SHYLOCKS	SIBSHIPS
SHRUBBY	SHUFFLE	SHUSHES	SHYLY	SIBYL
SHRUBLAND	SHUFFLED	SHUSHING	SHYNESS	SIBYLIC
SHRUBLESS	SHUFFLER	SHUT	SHYNESSES	SIBYLLIC
SHRUBLIKE	SHUFFLERS	SHUTDOWN	SHYPOO	SIBYLLINE
SHRUBS	SHUFFLES	SHUTDOWNS	SHYPOOS	SIBYLS
SHRUG	SHUFFLING	SHUTE	SHYSTER	SIC
SHRUGGED	SHUFTI	SHUTED	SHYSTERS	SICARIO
SHRUGGING	SHUFTIES	SHUTES	SI	SICARIOS
SHRUGS	SHUFTIS	SHUTEYE	SIAL	SICCAN
SHRUNK	SHUFTY	SHUTEYES	SIALIC	SICCAR
SHRUNKEN	SHUGGIES	SHUTING	SIALID	SICCATIVE
SHTCHI	SHUGGY	SHUTOFF	SIALIDAN	SICCED
SHTCHIS	SHUL	SHUTOFFS	SIALIDANS	SICCING
SHTETEL	SHULE	SHUTOUT	SIALIDS	SICCITIES
SHTETELS	SHULED	SHUTOUTS	SIALOGRAM	SICCITY
SHTETL	SHULES	SHUTS	SIALOID	SICE
SHTETLACH	SHULING	SHUTTER	SIALOLITH	SICES
SHTETLS	SHULN	SHUTTERED	SIALON	SICH
SHTICK	SHULS	SHUTTERS	SIALONS	SICHT
SHTICKIER	SHUMAI	SHUTTING	SIALS	SICHTED
SHTICKS	SHUN	SHUTTLE	SIAMANG	SICHTING
SHTICKY	SHUNLESS	SHUTTLED	SIAMANGS	SICHTS
SHTIK	SHUNNABLE	SHUTTLER	SIAMESE	SICILIANA
SHTIKS	SHUNNED	SHUTTLERS	SIAMESED	SICILIANE
SHTOOK	SHUNNER	SHUTTLES	SIAMESES	SICILIANO
SHTOOKS	SHUNNERS	SHUTTLING	SIAMESING	SICK
SHTOOM	SHUNNING	SHVARTZE	SIAMEZE	SICKBAY
SHTUCK	SHUNPIKE	SHVARTZES	SIAMEZED	SICKBAYS
SHTUCKS	SHUNPIKED	SHVITZ	SIAMEZES	SICKBED
SHTUM	SHUNPIKER	SHVITZED	SIAMEZING	SICKBEDS
SHTUMM	SHUNPIKES	SHVITZES	SIB	SICKED
SHTUP	SHUNS	SHVITZING	SIBB	SICKEE
SHTUPPED	SHUNT	SHWA	SIBBS	SICKEES
SHTUPPING	SHUNTED	SHWANPAN	SIBILANCE	SICKEN
SHTUPS	SHUNTER	SHWANPANS	SIBILANCY	SICKENED
SHUBUNKIN	SHUNTERS	SHWAS	SIBILANT	SICKENER
SHUCK	SHUNTING	SHWESHWE	SIBILANTS	SICKENERS
SHUCKED	SHUNTINGS	SHWESHWES	SIBILATE	SICKENING
SHUCKER	SHUNTS	SHY	SIBILATED	SICKENS
SHUCKERS	SHURA	SHYER	SIBILATES	SICKER
SHUCKING	SHURAS	SHYERS	SIBILATOR	SICKERLY

SICKEST	SIDEARMED	SIDEREAL	SIDLINGLY	SIFFLEUSE
SICKIE	SIDEARMS	SIDERITE	SIECLE	SIFFLING
SICKIES	SIDEBAND	SIDERITES	SIECLES	SIFREI
SICKING	SIDEBANDS	SIDERITIC	SIEGE	SIFT
SICKISH	SIDEBAR	SIDEROAD	SIEGED	SIFTED
SICKISHLY	SIDEBARS	SIDEROADS	SIEGER	SIFTER
SICKLE	SIDEBOARD	SIDEROSES	SIEGERS	SIFTERS
SICKLED	SIDEBONE	SIDEROSIS	SIEGES	SIFTING
SICKLEMAN	SIDEBONES	SIDEROTIC	SIEGING	SIFTINGLY
SICKLEMEN	SIDEBURN	SIDERS	SIELD	SIFTINGS
SICKLEMIA	SIDEBURNS	SIDES	SIEMENS	SIFTS
SICKLEMIC	SIDECAR	SIDESHOOT	SIEMENSES	SIG
SICKLES	SIDECARS	SIDESHOW	SIEN	SIGANID
SICKLIED	SIDECHECK	SIDESHOWS	SIENITE	SIGANIDS
SICKLIER	SIDED	SIDESLIP	SIENITES	SIGH
SICKLIES	SIDEDLY	SIDESLIPS	SIENNA	SIGHED
SICKLIEST	SIDEDNESS	SIDESMAN	SIENNAS	SIGHER
SICKLILY	SIDEDRESS	SIDESMEN	SIENS	SIGHERS
SICKLING	SIDEHILL	SIDESPIN	SIENT	SIGHFUL
SICKLY	SIDEHILLS	SIDESPINS	SIENTS	SIGHING
SICKLYING	SIDEKICK	SIDESTEP	SIEROZEM	SIGHINGLY
SICKNESS	SIDEKICKS	SIDESTEPS	SIEROZEMS	SIGHINGS
SICKNURSE	SIDELESS	SIDESWIPE	SIERRA	SIGHLESS
SICKO	SIDELIGHT	SIDETABLE	SIERRAN	SIGHLIKE
SICKOS	SIDELINE	SIDETRACK	SIERRAS	SIGHS
SICKOUT	SIDELINED	SIDEWALK	SIES	SIGHT
SICKOUTS	SIDELINER	SIDEWALKS	SIESTA	SIGHTABLE
SICKROOM	SIDELINES	SIDEWALL	SIESTAS	SIGHTED
SICKROOMS	SIDELING	SIDEWALLS	SIETH	SIGHTER
SICKS	SIDELINGS	SIDEWARD	SIETHS	SIGHTERS
SICKY	SIDELOCK	SIDEWARDS	SIEUR	SIGHTING
SICLIKE	SIDELOCKS	SIDEWAY	SIEURS	SIGHTINGS
SICS	SIDELONG	SIDEWAYS	SIEVE	SIGHTLESS
SIDA	SIDEMAN	SIDEWHEEL	SIEVED	SIGHTLIER
SIDALCEA	SIDEMEAT	SIDEWISE	SIEVELIKE	SIGHTLINE
SIDALCEAS	SIDEMEATS	SIDH	SIEVERT	SIGHTLY
SIDAS	SIDEMEN	SIDHA	SIEVERTS	SIGHTS
SIDDHA	SIDENOTE	SIDHAS	SIEVES	SIGHTSAW
SIDDHAS	SIDENOTES	SIDHE	SIEVING	SIGHTSEE
SIDDHI	SIDEPATH	SIDING	SIF	SIGHTSEEN
SIDDHIS	SIDEPATHS	SIDINGS	SIFAKA	SIGHTSEER
SIDDHUISM	SIDEPIECE	SIDLE	SIFAKAS	SIGHTSEES
SIDDUR	SIDER	SIDLED	SIFFLE	SIGHTSMAN
SIDDURIM	SIDERAL	SIDLER	SIFFLED	SIGHTSMEN
SIDDURS	SIDERATE	SIDLERS	SIFFLES	SIGIL
SIDE	SIDERATED	SIDLES	SIFFLEUR	SIGILLARY
SIDEARM	SIDERATES	SIDLING	SIFFLEURS	SIGILLATE

SIGILS	SIGNER	SIKE	SILICATES	SILKOLINE
SIGISBEI	SIGNERS	SIKER	SILICEOUS	SILKS
SIGISBEO	SIGNET	SIKES	SILICIC	SILKTAIL
SIGLA	SIGNETED	SIKORSKY	SILICIDE	SILKTAILS
SIGLAS	SIGNETING	SIKSIK	SILICIDES	SILKWEED
SIGLOI	SIGNETS	SIKSIKS	SILICIFY	SILKWEEDS
SIGLOS	SIGNEUR	SILAGE	SILICIOUS	SILKWORM
SIGLUM	SIGNEURIE	SILAGED	SILICIUM	SILKWORMS
SIGMA	SIGNIEUR	SILAGEING	SILICIUMS	SILKY
SIGMAS	SIGNIEURS	SILAGES	SILICLE	SILL
SIGMATE	SIGNIFICS	SILAGING	SILICLES	SILLABUB
SIGMATED	SIGNIFIED	SILANE	SILICON	SILLABUBS
SIGMATES	SIGNIFIER	SILANES	SILICONE	SILLADAR
SIGMATIC	SIGNIFIES	SILASTIC	SILICONES	SILLADARS
SIGMATING	SIGNIFY	SILASTICS	SILICONS	SILLER
SIGMATION	SIGNING	SILD	SILICOSES	SILLERS
SIGMATISM	SIGNINGS	SILDS	SILICOSIS	SILLIBUB
SIGMATRON	SIGNIOR	SILE	SILICOTIC	SILLIBUBS
SIGMOID	SIGNIORI	SILED	SILICULA	SILLIER
SIGMOIDAL	SIGNIORS	SILEN	SILICULAE	SILLIES
SIGMOIDS	SIGNIORY	SILENCE	SILICULAS	SILLIEST
SIGN	SIGNLESS	SILENCED	SILICULE	SILLILY
SIGNA	SIGNOR	SILENCER	SILICULES	SILLINESS
SIGNABLE	SIGNORA	SILENCERS	SILING	SILLOCK
SIGNAGE	SIGNORAS	SILENCES	SILIQUA	SILLOCKS
SIGNAGES	SIGNORE	SILENCING	SILIQUAE	SILLS
SIGNAL	SIGNORES	SILENE	SILIQUAS	SILLY
SIGNALED	SIGNORI	SILENES	SILIQUE	SILO
SIGNALER	SIGNORIA	SILENI	SILIQUES	SILOED
SIGNALERS	SIGNORIAL	SILENS	SILIQUOSE	SILOING
SIGNALING	SIGNORIAS	SILENT	SILIQUOUS	SILOS
SIGNALISE	SIGNORIES	SILENTER	SILK	SILOXANE
SIGNALIZE	SIGNORINA	SILENTEST	SILKALENE	SILOXANES
SIGNALLED	SIGNORINE	SILENTLY	SILKALINE	SILPHIA
SIGNALLER	SIGNORINI	SILENTS	SILKED	SILPHIUM
SIGNALLY	SIGNORINO	SILENUS	SILKEN	SILPHIUMS
SIGNALMAN	SIGNORS	SILER	SILKENED	SILT
SIGNALMEN	SIGNORY	SILERS	SILKENING	SILTATION
SIGNALS	SIGNPOST	SILES	SILKENS	SILTED
SIGNARIES	SIGNPOSTS	SILESIA	SILKIE	SILTIER
SIGNARY	SIGNS	SILESIAS	SILKIER	SILTIEST
SIGNATORY	SIGS	SILEX	SILKIES	SILTING
SIGNATURE	SIJO	SILEXES	SILKIEST	SILTS
SIGNBOARD	SIJOS	SILICA	SILKILY	SILTSTONE
SIGNED	SIK	SILICAS	SILKINESS	SILTY
SIGNEE	SIKA	SILICATE	SILKING	SILURIAN
SIGNEES	SIKAS	SILICATED	SILKLIKE	SILURID

SILURIDS	SIMI	SIMOOMS	SIMULATE	SINFUL
SILURIST	SIMIAL	SIMOON	SIMULATED	SINFULLY
SILURISTS	SIMIAN	SIMOONS	SIMULATES	SING
SILUROID	SIMIANS	SIMORG	SIMULATOR	SINGABLE
SILUROIDS	SIMILAR	SIMORGS	SIMULCAST	SINGALONG
SILVA	SIMILARLY	SIMP	SIMULIUM	SINGE
SILVAE	SIMILE	SIMPAI	SIMULIUMS	SINGED
SILVAN	SIMILES	SIMPAIS	SIMULS	SINGEING
SILVANS	SIMILISE	SIMPATICO	SIMURG	SINGER
SILVAS	SIMILISED	SIMPER	SIMURGH	SINGERS
SILVATIC	SIMILISES	SIMPERED	SIMURGHS	SINGES
SILVER	SIMILIZE	SIMPERER	SIMURGS	SINGING
SILVERED	SIMILIZED	SIMPERERS	SIN	SINGINGLY
SILVERER	SIMILIZES	SIMPERING	SINAPISM	SINGINGS
SILVERERS	SIMILOR	SIMPERS	SINAPISMS	SINGLE
SILVEREYE	SIMILORS	SIMPKIN	SINCE	SINGLED
SILVERIER	SIMIOID	SIMPKINS	SINCERE	SINGLEDOM
SILVERING	SIMIOUS	SIMPLE	SINCERELY	SINGLES
SILVERISE	SIMIS	SIMPLED	SINCERER	SINGLET
SILVERIZE	SIMITAR	SIMPLER	SINCEREST	SINGLETON
SILVERLY	SIMITARS	SIMPLERS	SINCERITY	SINGLETS
SILVERN	SIMKIN	SIMPLES	SINCIPITA	SINGLING
SILVERS	SIMKINS	SIMPLESSE	SINCIPUT	SINGLINGS
SILVERTIP	SIMLIN	SIMPLEST	SINCIPUTS	SINGLY
SILVERY	SIMLINS	SIMPLETON	SIND	SINGS
SILVEX	SIMMER	SIMPLEX	SINDED	SINGSONG
SILVEXES	SIMMERED	SIMPLEXES	SINDING	SINGSONGS
SILVICAL	SIMMERING	SIMPLICES	SINDINGS	SINGSONGY
SILVICS	SIMMERS	SIMPLICIA	SINDON	SINGSPIEL
SILYMARIN	SIMNEL	SIMPLIFY	SINDONS	SINGULAR
SIM	SIMNELS	SIMPLING	SINDS	SINGULARS
SIMA	SIMOLEON	SIMPLINGS	SINE	SINGULARY
SIMAR	SIMOLEONS	SIMPLISM	SINECURE	SINGULT
SIMAROUBA	SIMONIAC	SIMPLISMS	SINECURES	SINGULTS
SIMARRE	SIMONIACS	SIMPLIST	SINED	SINGULTUS
SIMARRES	SIMONIES	SIMPLISTE	SINES	SINH
SIMARS	SIMONIOUS	SIMPLISTS	SINEW	SINHS
SIMARUBA	SIMONISE	SIMPLY	SINEWED	SINICAL
SIMARUBAS	SIMONISED	SIMPS	SINEWIER	SINICISE
SIMAS	SIMONISES	SIMS	SINEWIEST	SINICISED
SIMATIC	SIMONIST	SIMUL	SINEWING	SINICISES
SIMAZINE	SIMONISTS	SIMULACRA	SINEWLESS	SINICIZE
SIMAZINES	SIMONIZE	SIMULACRE	SINEWS	SINICIZED
SIMBA	SIMONIZED	SIMULANT	SINEWY	SINICIZES
SIMBAS	SIMONIZES	SIMULANTS	SINFONIA	SINING
SIMCHA	SIMONY	SIMULAR	SINFONIAS	SINISTER
SIMCHAS	SIMOOM	SIMULARS	SINFONIE	SINISTRAL

S

SINK	SINUATING	SIRE	SIRRAHS	SISTRA
SINKABLE	SINUATION	SIRED	SIRRAS	SISTROID
SINKAGE	SINUITIS	SIREE	SIRRED	SISTRUM
SINKAGES	SINUOSE	SIREES	SIRREE	SISTRUMS
SINKER	SINUOSITY	SIREN	SIRREES	SISTS
SINKERS	SINUOUS	SIRENIAN	SIRRING	SIT
SINKFUL	SINUOUSLY	SIRENIANS	SIRS	SITAR
SINKFULS	SINUS	SIRENIC	SIRTUIN	SITARIST
SINKHOLE	SINUSES	SIRENISE	SIRTUINS	SITARISTS
SINKHOLES	SINUSITIS	SIRENISED	SIRUP	SITARS
SINKIER	SINUSLIKE	SIRENISES	SIRUPED	SITATUNGA
SINKIEST	SINUSOID	SIRENIZE	SIRUPIER	SITCOM
SINKING	SINUSOIDS	SIRENIZED	SIRUPIEST	SITCOMS
SINKINGS	SIP	SIRENIZES	SIRUPING	SITE
SINKS	SIPE	SIRENS	SIRUPS	SITED
SINKY	SIPED	SIRES	SIRUPY	SITELLA
SINLESS	SIPES	SIRGANG	SIRVENTE	SITELLAS
SINLESSLY	SIPHON	SIRGANGS	SIRVENTES	SITES
SINNED	SIPHONAGE	SIRI	SIS	SITFAST
SINNER	SIPHONAL	SIRIASES	SISAL	SITFASTS
SINNERED	SIPHONATE	SIRIASIS	SISALS	SITH
SINNERING	SIPHONED	SIRIH	SISERARY	SITHE
SINNERS	SIPHONET	SIRIHS	SISES	SITHED
SINNET	SIPHONETS	SIRING	SISKIN	SITHEE
SINNETS	SIPHONIC	SIRINGS	SISKINS	SITHEN
SINNING	SIPHONING	SIRIS	SISS	SITHENCE
SINNINGIA	SIPHONS	SIRKAR	SISSES	SITHENS
SINOLOGUE	SIPHUNCLE	SIRKARS	SISSIER	SITHES
SINOLOGY	SIPING	SIRLOIN	SISSIES	SITHING
SINOPIA	SIPPABLE	SIRLOINS	SISSIEST	SITING
SINOPIAS	SIPPED	SIRNAME	SISSIFIED	SITINGS
SINOPIE	SIPPER	SIRNAMED	SISSINESS	SITIOLOGY
SINOPIS	SIPPERS	SIRNAMES	SISSOO	SITKA
SINOPISES	SIPPET	SIRNAMING	SISSOOS	SITKAMER
SINOPITE	SIPPETS	SIROC	SISSY	SITKAMERS
SINOPITES	SIPPING	SIROCCO	SISSYISH	SITOLOGY
SINS	SIPPLE	SIROCCOS	SISSYNESS	SITREP
SINSYNE	SIPPLED	SIROCS	SIST	SITREPS
SINTER	SIPPLES	SIRONISE	SISTA	SITS
SINTERED	SIPPLING	SIRONISED	SISTAS	SITTAR
SINTERING	SIPPY	SIRONISES	SISTED	SITTARS
SINTERS	SIPS	SIRONIZE	SISTER	SITTELLA
SINTERY	SIR	SIRONIZED	SISTERED	SITTELLAS
SINUATE	SIRCAR	SIRONIZES	SISTERING	SITTEN
SINUATED	SIRCARS	SIROSET	SISTERLY	SITTER
SINUATELY	SIRDAR	SIRRA	SISTERS	SITTERS
SINUATES	SIRDARS	SIRRAH	SISTING	SITTINE

SITTINES	SIXTEENTH	SJAMBOKS	SKATS	SKEEVY
SITTING	SIXTES	SJOE	SKATT	SKEG
SITTINGS	SIXTH	SKA	SKATTS	SKEGG
SITUATE	SIXTHLY	SKAG	SKAW	SKEGGER
SITUATED	SIXTHS	SKAGS	SKAWS	SKEGGERS
SITUATES	SIXTIES	SKAIL	SKEAN	SKEGGS
SITUATING	SIXTIETH	SKAILED	SKEANE	SKEGS
SITUATION	SIXTIETHS	SKAILING	SKEANES	SKEIGH
SITULA	SIXTY	SKAILS	SKEANS	SKEIGHER
SITULAE	SIXTYISH	SKAITH	SKEAR	SKEIGHEST
SITUP	SIZABLE	SKAITHED	SKEARED	SKEIN
SITUPS	SIZABLY	SKAITHING	SKEARIER	SKEINED
SITUS	SIZAR	SKAITHS	SKEARIEST	SKEINING
SITUSES	SIZARS	SKALD	SKEARING	SKEINS
SITUTUNGA	SIZARSHIP	SKALDIC	SKEARS	SKELDER
SITZ	SIZE	SKALDS	SKEARY	SKELDERED
SITZKRIEG	SIZEABLE	SKALDSHIP	SKED	SKELDERS
SITZMARK	SIZEABLY	SKANGER	SKEDADDLE	SKELETAL
SITZMARKS	SIZED	SKANGERS	SKEDDED	SKELETON
SIVER	SIZEISM	SKANK	SKEDDING	SKELETONS
SIVERS	SIZEISMS	SKANKED	SKEDS	SKELF
SIWASH	SIZEIST	SKANKER	SKEE	SKELFS
SIWASHED	SIZEISTS	SKANKERS	SKEECHAN	SKELL
SIWASHES	SIZEL	SKANKIER	SKEECHANS	SKELLIE
SIWASHING	SIZELS	SKANKIEST	SKEED	SKELLIED
SIX	SIZER	SKANKING	SKEEF	SKELLIER
SIXAIN	SIZERS	SKANKINGS	SKEEING	SKELLIES
SIXAINE	SIZES	SKANKS	SKEELIER	SKELLIEST
SIXAINES	SIZIER	SKANKY	SKEELIEST	SKELLOCH
SIXAINS	SIZIEST	SKART	SKEELY	SKELLOCHS
SIXER	SIZINESS	SKARTH	SKEEN	SKELLS
SIXERS	SIZING	SKARTHS	SKEENS	SKELLUM
SIXES	SIZINGS	SKARTS	SKEER	SKELLUMS
SIXFOLD	SIZISM	SKAS	SKEERED	SKELLY
SIXISH	SIZISMS	SKAT	SKEERIER	SKELLYING
SIXMO	SIZIST	SKATE	SKEERIEST	SKELM
SIXMOS	SIZISTS	SKATED	SKEERING	SKELMS
SIXPENCE	SIZY	SKATEPARK	SKEERS	SKELP
SIXPENCES	SIZZLE	SKATER	SKEERY	SKELPED
SIXPENNY	SIZZLED	SKATERS	SKEES	SKELPING
SIXSCORE	SIZZLER	SKATES	SKEESICKS	SKELPINGS
SIXSCORES	SIZZLERS	SKATING	SKEET	SKELPIT
SIXTE	SIZZLES	SKATINGS	SKEETER	SKELPS
SIXTEEN	SIZZLING	SKATOL	SKEETERS	SKELTER
SIXTEENER	SIZZLINGS	SKATOLE	SKEETS	SKELTERED
SIXTEENMO	SJAMBOK	SKATOLES	SKEEVIER	SKELTERS
SIXTEENS	SJAMBOKED	SKATOLS	SKEEVIEST	SKELUM

S

SKELUMS	SKEWBALDS	SKIDPAD	SKILLS	SKINNIEST
SKEN	SKEWED	SKIDPADS	SKILLY	SKINNING
SKENE	SKEWER	SKIDPAN	SKIM	SKINNY
SKENES	SKEWERED	SKIDPANS	SKIMBOARD	SKINS
SKENNED	SKEWERING	SKIDPROOF	SKIMMED	SKINSUIT
SKENNING	SKEWERS	SKIDS	SKIMMER	SKINSUITS
SKENS	SKEWEST	SKIDWAY	SKIMMERS	SKINT
SKEO	SKEWING	SKIDWAYS	SKIMMIA	SKINTER
SKEOES	SKEWNESS	SKIED	SKIMMIAS	SKINTEST
SKEOS	SKEWS	SKIER	SKIMMING	SKINTIGHT
SKEP	SKEWWHIFF	SKIERS	SKIMMINGS	SKIO
SKEPFUL	SKI	SKIES	SKIMO	SKIOES
SKEPFULS	SKIABLE	SKIEY	SKIMOBILE	SKIORER
SKEPPED	SKIAGRAM	SKIEYER	SKIMOS	SKIORERS
SKEPPING	SKIAGRAMS	SKIEYEST	SKIMP	SKIORING
SKEPS	SKIAGRAPH	SKIFF	SKIMPED	SKIORINGS
SKEPSIS	SKIAMACHY	SKIFFED	SKIMPIER	SKIOS
SKEPSISES	SKIASCOPE	SKIFFING	SKIMPIEST	SKIP
SKEPTIC	SKIASCOPY	SKIFFLE	SKIMPILY	SKIPJACK
SKEPTICAL	SKIATRON	SKIFFLED	SKIMPING	SKIPJACKS
SKEPTICS	SKIATRONS	SKIFFLES	SKIMPS	SKIPLANE
SKER	SKIBOB	SKIFFLESS	SKIMPY	SKIPLANES
SKERRED	SKIBOBBED	SKIFFLING	SKIMS	SKIPPABLE
SKERRICK	SKIBOBBER	SKIFFS	SKIN	SKIPPED
SKERRICKS	SKIBOBS	SKIING	SKINCARE	SKIPPER
SKERRIES	SKID	SKIINGS	SKINCARES	SKIPPERED
SKERRING	SKIDDED	SKIJORER	SKINFLICK	SKIPPERS
SKERRY	SKIDDER	SKIJORERS	SKINFLINT	SKIPPET
SKERS	SKIDDERS	SKIJORING	SKINFOOD	SKIPPETS
SKET	SKIDDIER	SKIJUMPER	SKINFOODS	SKIPPIER
SKETCH	SKIDDIEST	SKIKJORER	SKINFUL	SKIPPIEST
SKETCHED	SKIDDING	SKILFUL	SKINFULS	SKIPPING
SKETCHER	SKIDDINGS	SKILFULL	SKINHEAD	SKIPPINGS
SKETCHERS	SKIDDOO	SKILFULLY	SKINHEADS	SKIPPY
SKETCHES	SKIDDOOED	SKILL	SKINK	SKIPS
SKETCHIER	SKIDDOOS	SKILLED	SKINKED	SKIRL
SKETCHILY	SKIDDY	SKILLESS	SKINKER	SKIRLED
SKETCHING	SKIDLID	SKILLET	SKINKERS	SKIRLING
SKETCHPAD	SKIDLIDS	SKILLETS	SKINKING	SKIRLINGS
SKETCHY	SKIDMARK	SKILLFUL	SKINKS	SKIRLS
SKETS	SKIDMARKS	SKILLIER	SKINLESS	SKIRMISH
SKETTED	SKIDOO	SKILLIES	SKINLIKE	SKIRR
SKETTING	SKIDOOED	SKILLIEST	SKINNED	SKIRRED
SKEW	SKIDOOER	SKILLING	SKINNER	SKIRRET
SKEWBACK	SKIDOOERS	SKILLINGS	SKINNERS	SKIRRETS
SKEWBACKS	SKIDOOING	SKILLION	SKINNIER	SKIRRING
SKEWBALD	SKIDOOS	SKILLIONS	SKINNIES	SKIRRS

SKIRT	SKLATE	SKOOSHES	SKUDLER	SKYBOXES
SKIRTED	SKLATED	SKOOSHING	SKUDLERS	SKYBRIDGE
SKIRTER	SKLATES	SKORT	SKUG	SKYCAP
SKIRTERS	SKLATING	SKORTS	SKUGGED	SKYCAPS
SKIRTING	SKLENT	SKOSH	SKUGGING	SKYCLAD
SKIRTINGS	SKLENTED	SKOSHES	SKUGS	SKYDIVE
SKIRTLESS	SKLENTING	SKRAN	SKULK	SKYDIVED
SKIRTLIKE	SKLENTS	SKRANS	SKULKED	SKYDIVER
SKIRTS	SKLIFF	SKREEGH	SKULKER	SKYDIVERS
SKIS	SKLIFFED	SKREEGHED	SKULKERS	SKYDIVES
SKIT	SKLIFFING	SKREEGHS	SKULKING	SKYDIVING
SKITCH	SKLIFFS	SKREEN	SKULKINGS	SKYDOVE
SKITCHED	SKLIM	SKREENS	SKULKS	SKYED
SKITCHES	SKLIMMED	SKREIGH	SKULL	SKYER
SKITCHING	SKLIMMING	SKREIGHED	SKULLCAP	SKYERS
SKITE	SKLIMS	SKREIGHS	SKULLCAPS	SKYEY
SKITED	SKOAL	SKRIECH	SKULLED	SKYF
SKITES	SKOALED	SKRIECHED	SKULLING	SKYFED
SKITING	SKOALING	SKRIECHS	SKULLS	SKYFING
SKITS	SKOALS	SKRIED	SKULPIN	SKYFS
SKITTER	SKOFF	SKRIEGH	SKULPINS	SKYGLOW
SKITTERED	SKOFFED	SKRIEGHED	SKUMMER	SKYGLOWS
SKITTERS	SKOFFING	SKRIEGHS	SKUMMERED	SKYHOME
SKITTERY	SKOFFS	SKRIES	SKUMMERS	SKYHOMES
SKITTISH	SKOG	SKRIK	SKUNK	SKYHOOK
SKITTLE	SKOGGED	SKRIKE	SKUNKBIRD	SKYHOOKS
SKITTLED	SKOGGING	SKRIKED	SKUNKED	SKYIER
SKITTLES	SKOGS	SKRIKES	SKUNKIER	SKYIEST
SKITTLING	SKOKIAAN	SKRIKING	SKUNKIEST	SKYING
SKIVE	SKOKIAANS	SKRIKS	SKUNKING	SKYISH
SKIVED	SKOL	SKRIMMAGE	SKUNKS	SKYJACK
SKIVER	SKOLED	SKRIMP	SKUNKWEED	SKYJACKED
SKIVERED	SKOLIA	SKRIMPED	SKUNKY	SKYJACKER
SKIVERING	SKOLING	SKRIMPING	SKURRIED	SKYJACKS
SKIVERS	SKOLION	SKRIMPS	SKURRIES	SKYLAB
SKIVES	SKOLLED	SKRONK	SKURRY	SKYLABS
SKIVIE	SKOLLIE	SKRONKS	SKURRYING	SKYLARK
SKIVIER	SKOLLIES	SKRUMP	SKUTTLE	SKYLARKED
SKIVIEST	SKOLLING	SKRUMPED	SKUTTLED	SKYLARKER
SKIVING	SKOLLY	SKRUMPING	SKUTTLES	SKYLARKS
SKIVINGS	SKOLS	SKRUMPS	SKUTTLING	SKYLESS
SKIVVIED	SKOOKUM	SKRY	SKY	SKYLIGHT
SKIVVIES	SKOOKUMS	SKRYER	SKYBOARD	SKYLIGHTS
SKIVVY	SKOOL	SKRYERS	SKYBOARDS	SKYLIKE
SKIVVYING	SKOOLS	SKRYING	SKYBORN	SKYLINE
SKIVY	SKOOSH	SKUA	SKYBORNE	SKYLINES
SKIWEAR	SKOOSHED	SKUAS	SKYBOX	SKYLIT

S

SKYMAN	SLABBY	SLAKED	SLANTIER	SLATHERED
SKYMEN	SLABLIKE	SLAKELESS	SLANTIEST	SLATHERS
SKYPHOI	SLABS	SLAKER	SLANTING	SLATIER
SKYPHOS	SLABSTONE	SLAKERS	SLANTLY	SLATIEST
SKYR	SLACK	SLAKES	SLANTS	SLATINESS
SKYRE	SLACKED	SLAKING	SLANTWAYS	SLATING
SKYRED	SLACKEN	SLALOM	SLANTWISE	SLATINGS
SKYRES	SLACKENED	SLALOMED	SLANTY	SLATS
SKYRING	SLACKENER	SLALOMER	SLAP	SLATTED
SKYRMION	SLACKENS	SLALOMERS	SLAPDASH	SLATTER
SKYRMIONS	SLACKER	SLALOMING	SLAPHAPPY	SLATTERED
SKYROCKET	SLACKERS	SLALOMIST	SLAPHEAD	SLATTERN
SKYRS	SLACKEST	SLALOMS	SLAPHEADS	SLATTERNS
SKYSAIL	SLACKING	SLAM	SLAPJACK	SLATTERS
SKYSAILS	SLACKLY	SLAMDANCE	SLAPJACKS	SLATTERY
SKYSCAPE	SLACKNESS	SLAMMAKIN	SLAPPED	SLATTING
SKYSCAPES	SLACKS	SLAMMED	SLAPPER	SLATTINGS
SKYSURF	SLADANG	SLAMMER	SLAPPERS	SLATY
SKYSURFED	SLADANGS	SLAMMERS	SLAPPING	SLAUGHTER
SKYSURFER	SLADE	SLAMMING	SLAPPINGS	SLAVE
SKYSURFS	SLADES	SLAMMINGS	SLAPS	SLAVED
SKYTE	SLAE	SLAMS	SLAPSHOT	SLAVER
SKYTED	SLAES	SLANDER	SLAPSHOTS	SLAVERED
SKYTES	SLAG	SLANDERED	SLAPSTICK	SLAVERER
SKYTING	SLAGGED	SLANDERER	SLART	SLAVERERS
SKYWALK	SLAGGIER	SLANDERS	SLARTED	SLAVERIES
SKYWALKS	SLAGGIEST	SLANE	SLARTING	SLAVERING
SKYWARD	SLAGGING	SLANES	SLARTS	SLAVERS
SKYWARDS	SLAGGINGS	SLANG	SLASH	SLAVERY
SKYWATCH	SLAGGY	SLANGED	SLASHED	SLAVES
SKYWAY	SLAGS	SLANGER	SLASHER	SLAVEY
SKYWAYS	SLAHAL	SLANGERS	SLASHERS	SLAVEYS
SKYWRITE	SLAHALS	SLANGIER	SLASHES	SLAVING
SKYWRITER	SLAID	SLANGIEST	SLASHFEST	SLAVISH
SKYWRITES	SLAIDS	SLANGILY	SLASHING	SLAVISHLY
SKYWROTE	SLAIN	SLANGING	SLASHINGS	SLAVOCRAT
SLAB	SLAINTE	SLANGINGS	SLAT	SLAVOPHIL
SLABBED	SLAIRG	SLANGISH	SLATCH	SLAW
SLABBER	SLAIRGED	SLANGS	SLATCHES	SLAWS
SLABBERED	SLAIRGING	SLANGUAGE	SLATE	SLAY
SLABBERER	SLAIRGS	SLANGULAR	SLATED	SLAYABLE
SLABBERS	SLAISTER	SLANGY	SLATELIKE	SLAYED
SLABBERY	SLAISTERS	SLANK	SLATER	SLAYER
SLABBIER	SLAISTERY	SLANT	SLATERS	SLAYERS
SLABBIEST	SLAKABLE	SLANTED	SLATES	SLAYING
SLABBING	SLAKE	SLANTER	SLATEY	SLAYINGS
SLABBINGS	SLAKEABLE	SLANTERS	SLATHER	SLAYS

SLEAVE	SLEEKIER	SLEEVING	SLICKEST	SLIMES
SLEAVED	SLEEKIEST	SLEEVINGS	SLICKING	SLIMIER
SLEAVES	SLEEKING	SLEEZIER	SLICKINGS	SLIMIEST
SLEAVING	SLEEKINGS	SLEEZIEST	SLICKLY	SLIMILY
SLEAZE	SLEEKIT	SLEEZY	SLICKNESS	SLIMINESS
SLEAZEBAG	SLEEKLY	SLEIDED	SLICKROCK	SLIMING
SLEAZED	SLEEKNESS	SLEIGH	SLICKS	SLIMLINE
SLEAZES	SLEEKS	SLEIGHED	SLICKSTER	SLIMLY
SLEAZIER	SLEEKY	SLEIGHER	SLID	SLIMMED
SLEAZIEST	SLEEP	SLEIGHERS	SLIDABLE	SLIMMER
SLEAZILY	SLEEPAWAY	SLEIGHING	SLIDDEN	SLIMMERS
SLEAZING	SLEEPER	SLEIGHS	SLIDDER	SLIMMEST
SLEAZO	SLEEPERS	SLEIGHT	SLIDDERED	SLIMMING
SLEAZOID	SLEEPERY	SLEIGHTS	SLIDDERS	SLIMMINGS
SLEAZOIDS	SLEEPIER	SLENDER	SLIDDERY	SLIMMISH
SLEAZOS	SLEEPIEST	SLENDERER	SLIDE	SLIMNESS
SLEAZY	SLEEPILY	SLENDERLY	SLIDED	SLIMPSIER
SLEB	SLEEPING	SLENTER	SLIDER	SLIMPSY
SLEBS	SLEEPINGS	SLENTERS	SLIDERS	SLIMS
SLED	SLEEPLESS	SLEPT	SLIDES	SLIMSIER
SLEDDED	SLEEPLIKE	SLEUTH	SLIDEWAY	SLIMSIEST
SLEDDER	SLEEPOUT	SLEUTHED	SLIDEWAYS	SLIMSY
SLEDDERS	SLEEPOUTS	SLEUTHING	SLIDING	SLIMY
SLEDDING	SLEEPOVER	SLEUTHS	SLIDINGLY	SLING
SLEDDINGS	SLEEPRY	SLEW	SLIDINGS	SLINGBACK
SLEDED	SLEEPS	SLEWED	SLIER	SLINGER
SLEDGE	SLEEPSUIT	SLEWING	SLIEST	SLINGERS
SLEDGED	SLEEPWALK	SLEWS	SLIEVE	SLINGING
SLEDGER	SLEEPWEAR	SLEY	SLIEVES	SLINGS
SLEDGERS	SLEEPY	SLEYS	SLIGHT	SLINGSHOT
SLEDGES	SLEER	SLICE	SLIGHTED	SLINK
SLEDGING	SLEEST	SLICEABLE	SLIGHTER	SLINKED
SLEDGINGS	SLEET	SLICED	SLIGHTERS	SLINKER
SLEDS	SLEETED	SLICER	SLIGHTEST	SLINKERS
SLEE	SLEETIER	SLICERS	SLIGHTING	SLINKIER
SLEECH	SLEETIEST	SLICES	SLIGHTISH	SLINKIEST
SLEECHES	SLEETING	SLICING	SLIGHTLY	SLINKILY
SLEECHIER	SLEETS	SLICINGS	SLIGHTS	SLINKING
SLEECHY	SLEETY	SLICK	SLILY	SLINKS
SLEEK	SLEEVE	SLICKED	SLIM	SLINKSKIN
SLEEKED	SLEEVED	SLICKEN	SLIMDOWN	SLINKWEED
SLEEKEN	SLEEVEEN	SLICKENED	SLIMDOWNS	SLINKY
SLEEKENED	SLEEVEENS	SLICKENER	SLIME	SLINTER
SLEEKENS	SLEEVELET	SLICKENS	SLIMEBAG	SLINTERS
SLEEKER	SLEEVER	SLICKER	SLIMEBAGS	SLIOTAR
SLEEKERS	SLEEVERS	SLICKERED	SLIMEBALL	SLIOTARS
SLEEKEST	SLEEVES	SLICKERS	SLIMED	SLIP

SLIPCASE	SLISH	SLOBLANDS	SLOOSHING	SLOTTERS
SLIPCASED	SLISHES	SLOBS	SLOOT	SLOTTING
SLIPCASES	SLIT	SLOCKEN	SLOOTS	SLOUCH
SLIPCOVER	SLITHER	SLOCKENED	SLOP	SLOUCHED
SLIPDRESS	SLITHERED	SLOCKENS	SLOPE	SLOUCHER
SLIPE	SLITHERS	SLOE	SLOPED	SLOUCHERS
SLIPED	SLITHERY	SLOEBUSH	SLOPER	SLOUCHES
SLIPES	SLITLESS	SLOES	SLOPERS	SLOUCHIER
SLIPFORM	SLITLIKE	SLOETHORN	SLOPES	SLOUCHILY
SLIPFORMS	SLITS	SLOETREE	SLOPEWISE	SLOUCHING
SLIPING	SLITTED	SLOETREES	SLOPIER	SLOUCHY
SLIPKNOT	SLITTER	SLOG	SLOPIEST	SLOUGH
SLIPKNOTS	SLITTERS	SLOGAN	SLOPING	SLOUGHED
SLIPLESS	SLITTIER	SLOGANED	SLOPINGLY	SLOUGHI
SLIPNOOSE	SLITTIEST	SLOGANEER	SLOPPED	SLOUGHIER
SLIPOUT	SLITTING	SLOGANISE	SLOPPIER	SLOUGHING
SLIPOUTS	SLITTY	SLOGANIZE	SLOPPIEST	SLOUGHIS
SLIPOVER	SLIVE	SLOGANS	SLOPPILY	SLOUGHS
SLIPOVERS	SLIVED	SLOGGED	SLOPPING	SLOUGHY
SLIPPAGE	SLIVEN	SLOGGER	SLOPPY	SLOVE
SLIPPAGES	SLIVER	SLOGGERS	SLOPS	SLOVEN
SLIPPED	SLIVERED	SLOGGING	SLOPWORK	SLOVENLY
SLIPPER	SLIVERER	SLOGS	SLOPWORKS	SLOVENRY
SLIPPERED	SLIVERERS	SLOID	SLOPY	SLOVENS
SLIPPERS	SLIVERING	SLOIDS	SLORM	SLOW
SLIPPERY	SLIVERS	SLOJD	SLORMED	SLOWBACK
SLIPPIER	SLIVES	SLOJDS	SLORMING	SLOWBACKS
SLIPPIEST	SLIVING	SLOKEN	SLORMS	SLOWCOACH
SLIPPILY	SLIVOVIC	SLOKENED	SLOSH	SLOWDOWN
SLIPPING	SLIVOVICA	SLOKENING	SLOSHED	SLOWDOWNS
SLIPPY	SLIVOVITZ	SLOKENS	SLOSHES	SLOWED
SLIPRAIL	SLIVOWITZ	SLOMMOCK	SLOSHIER	SLOWER
SLIPRAILS	SLOAN	SLOMMOCKS	SLOSHIEST	SLOWEST
SLIPS	SLOANS	SLOMO	SLOSHING	SLOWING
SLIPSHEET	SLOB	SLOMOS	SLOSHINGS	SLOWINGS
SLIPSHOD	SLOBBED	SLOOM	SLOSHY	SLOWISH
SLIPSLOP	SLOBBER	SLOOMED	SLOT	SLOWLY
SLIPSLOPS	SLOBBERED	SLOOMIER	SLOTBACK	SLOWNESS
SLIPSOLE	SLOBBERER	SLOOMIEST	SLOTBACKS	SLOWPOKE
SLIPSOLES	SLOBBERS	SLOOMING	SLOTH	SLOWPOKES
SLIPT	SLOBBERY	SLOOMS	SLOTHED	SLOWS
SLIPUP	SLOBBIER	SLOOMY	SLOTHFUL	SLOWWORM
SLIPUPS	SLOBBIEST	SLOOP	SLOTHING	SLOWWORMS
SLIPWARE	SLOBBING	SLOOPS	SLOTHS	SLOYD
SLIPWARES	SLOBBISH	SLOOSH	SLOTS	SLOYDS
SLIPWAY	SLOBBY	SLOOSHED	SLOTTED	SLUB
SLIPWAYS	SLOBLAND	SLOOSHES	SLOTTER	SLUBB

SLUBBED	SLUICIER	SLURPED	SLYNESSES	SMALTITE
SLUBBER	SLUICIEST	SLURPER	SLYPE	SMALTITES
SLUBBERED	SLUICING	SLURPERS	SLYPES	SMALTO
SLUBBERS	SLUICY	SLURPIER	SMA	SMALTOS
SLUBBIER	SLUING	SLURPIEST	SMAAK	SMALTS
SLUBBIEST	SLUIT	SLURPING	SMAAKED	SMARAGD
SLUBBING	SLUITS	SLURPS	SMAAKING	SMARAGDE
SLUBBINGS	SLUM	SLURPY	SMAAKS	SMARAGDES
SLUBBS	SLUMBER	SLURRED	SMACK	SMARAGDS
SLUBBY	SLUMBERED	SLURRIED	SMACKDOWN	SMARM
SLUBS	SLUMBERER	SLURRIES	SMACKED	SMARMED
SLUDGE	SLUMBERS	SLURRING	SMACKER	SMARMIER
SLUDGED	SLUMBERY	SLURRY	SMACKERS	SMARMIEST
SLUDGES	SLUMBROUS	SLURRYING	SMACKHEAD	SMARMILY
SLUDGIER	SLUMBRY	SLURS	SMACKING	SMARMING
SLUDGIEST	SLUMGUM	SLURVE	SMACKINGS	SMARMS
SLUDGING	SLUMGUMS	SLURVES	SMACKS	SMARMY
SLUDGY	SLUMISM	SLUSE	SMAIK	SMART
SLUE	SLUMISMS	SLUSES	SMAIKS	SMARTARSE
SLUED	SLUMLORD	SLUSH	SMALL	SMARTASS
SLUEING	SLUMLORDS	SLUSHED	SMALLAGE	SMARTED
SLUES	SLUMMED	SLUSHES	SMALLAGES	SMARTEN
SLUFF	SLUMMER	SLUSHIER	SMALLBOY	SMARTENED
SLUFFED	SLUMMERS	SLUSHIES	SMALLBOYS	SMARTENS
SLUFFING	SLUMMIER	SLUSHIEST	SMALLED	SMARTER
SLUFFS	SLUMMIEST	SLUSHILY	SMALLER	SMARTEST
SLUG	SLUMMING	SLUSHING	SMALLEST	SMARTIE
SLUGABED	SLUMMINGS	SLUSHY	SMALLING	SMARTIES
SLUGABEDS	SLUMMOCK	SLUT	SMALLISH	SMARTING
SLUGFEST	SLUMMOCKS	SLUTCH	SMALLNESS	SMARTISH
SLUGFESTS	SLUMMY	SLUTCHES	SMALLPOX	SMARTLY
SLUGGABED	SLUMP	SLUTCHIER	SMALLS	SMARTNESS
SLUGGARD	SLUMPED	SLUTCHY	SMALLSAT	SMARTS
SLUGGARDS	SLUMPIER	SLUTS	SMALLSATS	SMARTWEED
SLUGGED	SLUMPIEST	SLUTTERY	SMALLTIME	SMARTY
SLUGGER	SLUMPING	SLUTTIER	SMALM	SMASH
SLUGGERS	SLUMPS	SLUTTIEST	SMALMED	SMASHABLE
SLUGGING	SLUMPY	SLUTTILY	SMALMIER	SMASHED
SLUGGISH	SLUMS	SLUTTISH	SMALMIEST	SMASHER
SLUGHORN	SLUNG	SLUTTY	SMALMILY	SMASHEROO
SLUGHORNE	SLUNGSHOT	SLY	SMALMING	SMASHERS
SLUGHORNS	SLUNK	SLYBOOTS	SMALMS	SMASHES
SLUGS	SLUR	SLYER	SMALMY	SMASHING
SLUICE	SLURB	SLYEST	SMALT	SMASHINGS
SLUICED	SLURBAN	SLYISH	SMALTI	SMASHUP
SLUICES	SLURBS	SLYLY	SMALTINE	SMASHUPS
SLUICEWAY	SLURP	SLYNESS	SMALTINES	SMATCH

S

SMATCHED	SMEIKS	SMIDGEONS	SMIRRED	SMOKABLE
SMATCHES	SMEKE	SMIDGES	SMIRRIER	SMOKE
SMATCHING	SMEKED	SMIDGIN	SMIRRIEST	SMOKEABLE
SMATTER	SMEKES	SMIDGINS	SMIRRING	SMOKEBOX
SMATTERED	SMEKING	SMIERCASE	SMIRRS	SMOKEBUSH
SMATTERER	SMELL	SMIGHT	SMIRRY	SMOKED
SMATTERS	SMELLABLE	SMIGHTING	SMIRS	SMOKEHO
SMAZE	SMELLED	SMIGHTS	SMIRTING	SMOKEHOOD
SMAZES	SMELLER	SMILAX	SMIRTINGS	SMOKEHOS
SMEAR	SMELLERS	SMILAXES	SMIT	SMOKEJACK
SMEARCASE	SMELLIER	SMILE	SMITE	SMOKELESS
SMEARED	SMELLIES	SMILED	SMITER	SMOKELIKE
SMEARER	SMELLIEST	SMILEFUL	SMITERS	SMOKEPOT
SMEARERS	SMELLING	SMILELESS	SMITES	SMOKEPOTS
SMEARIER	SMELLINGS	SMILER	SMITH	SMOKER
SMEARIEST	SMELLS	SMILERS	SMITHED	SMOKERS
SMEARILY	SMELLY	SMILES	SMITHERS	SMOKES
SMEARING	SMELT	SMILET	SMITHERY	SMOKEY
SMEARS	SMELTED	SMILETS	SMITHIED	SMOKEYS
SMEARY	SMELTER	SMILEY	SMITHIES	SMOKIE
SMEATH	SMELTERS	SMILEYS	SMITHING	SMOKIER
SMEATHS	SMELTERY	SMILIER	SMITHINGS	SMOKIES
SMECTIC	SMELTING	SMILIES	SMITHS	SMOKIEST
SMECTITE	SMELTINGS	SMILIEST	SMITHY	SMOKILY
SMECTITES	SMELTS	SMILING	SMITHYING	SMOKINESS
SMECTITIC	SMERK	SMILINGLY	SMITING	SMOKING
SMEDDUM	SMERKED	SMILINGS	SMITS	SMOKINGS
SMEDDUMS	SMERKING	SMILODON	SMITTED	SMOKO
SMEE	SMERKS	SMILODONS	SMITTEN	SMOKOS
SMEECH	SMEUSE	SMIR	SMITTING	SMOKY
SMEECHED	SMEUSES	SMIRCH	SMITTLE	SMOLDER
SMEECHES	SMEW	SMIRCHED	SMOCK	SMOLDERED
SMEECHING	SMEWS	SMIRCHER	SMOCKED	SMOLDERS
SMEEK	SMICKER	SMIRCHERS	SMOCKING	SMOLT
SMEEKED	SMICKERED	SMIRCHES	SMOCKINGS	SMOLTS
SMEEKING	SMICKERS	SMIRCHING	SMOCKLIKE	SMOOCH
SMEEKS	SMICKET	SMIRK	SMOCKS	SMOOCHED
SMEES	SMICKETS	SMIRKED	SMOG	SMOOCHER
SMEETH	SMICKLY	SMIRKER	SMOGGIER	SMOOCHERS
SMEETHED	SMIDDIED	SMIRKERS	SMOGGIEST	SMOOCHES
SMEETHING	SMIDDIES	SMIRKIER	SMOGGY	SMOOCHIER
SMEETHS	SMIDDY	SMIRKIEST	SMOGLESS	SMOOCHING
SMEGMA	SMIDDYING	SMIRKILY	SMOGS	SMOOCHY
SMEGMAS	SMIDGE	SMIRKING	SMOILE	SMOODGE
SMEIK	SMIDGEN	SMIRKS	SMOILED	SMOODGED
SMEIKED	SMIDGENS	SMIRKY	SMOILES	SMOODGES
SMEIKING	SMIDGEON	SMIRR	SMOILING	SMOODGING

SMOOGE	SMOTHERY	SMUGGLERS	SNACKIEST	SNAKEWEED
SMOOGED	SMOUCH	SMUGGLES	SNACKING	SNAKEWISE
SMOOGES	SMOUCHED	SMUGGLING	SNACKS	SNAKEWOOD
SMOOGING	SMOUCHES	SMUGLY	SNACKY	SNAKEY
SMOOR	SMOUCHING	SMUGNESS	SNAFFLE	SNAKIER
SMOORED	SMOULDER	SMUGS	SNAFFLED	SNAKIEST
SMOORING	SMOULDERS	SMUR	SNAFFLES	SNAKILY
SMOORS	SMOULDRY	SMURFING	SNAFFLING	SNAKINESS
SMOOSH	SMOUSE	SMURFINGS	SNAFU	SNAKING
SMOOSHED	SMOUSED	SMURRED	SNAFUED	SNAKISH
SMOOSHES	SMOUSER	SMURRIER	SNAFUING	SNAKY
SMOOSHING	SMOUSERS	SMURRIEST	SNAFUS	SNAP
SMOOT	SMOUSES	SMURRING	SNAG	SNAPBACK
SMOOTED	SMOUSING	SMURRY	SNAGGED	SNAPBACKS
SMOOTH	SMOUT	SMURS	SNAGGER	SNAPHANCE
SMOOTHE	SMOUTED	SMUSH	SNAGGERS	SNAPLESS
SMOOTHED	SMOUTING	SMUSHED	SNAGGIER	SNAPLINK
SMOOTHEN	SMOUTS	SMUSHES	SNAGGIEST	SNAPLINKS
SMOOTHENS	SMOWT	SMUSHING	SNAGGING	SNAPPABLE
SMOOTHER	SMOWTS	SMUT	SNAGGLE	SNAPPED
SMOOTHERS	SMOYLE	SMUTCH	SNAGGLES	SNAPPER
SMOOTHES	SMOYLED	SMUTCHED	SNAGGY	SNAPPERED
SMOOTHEST	SMOYLES	SMUTCHES	SNAGLIKE	SNAPPERS
SMOOTHIE	SMOYLING	SMUTCHIER	SNAGS	SNAPPIER
SMOOTHIES	SMRITI	SMUTCHING	SNAIL	SNAPPIEST
SMOOTHING	SMRITIS	SMUTCHY	SNAILED	SNAPPILY
SMOOTHISH	SMUDGE	SMUTS	SNAILERY	SNAPPING
SMOOTHLY	SMUDGED	SMUTTED	SNAILFISH	SNAPPINGS
SMOOTHS	SMUDGEDLY	SMUTTIER	SNAILIER	SNAPPISH
SMOOTHY	SMUDGER	SMUTTIEST	SNAILIEST	SNAPPY
SMOOTING	SMUDGERS	SMUTTILY	SNAILING	SNAPS
SMOOTS	SMUDGES	SMUTTING	SNAILLIKE	SNAPSHOT
SMORBROD	SMUDGIER	SMUTTY	SNAILS	SNAPSHOTS
SMORBRODS	SMUDGIEST	SMYTRIE	SNAILY	SNAPTIN
SMORE	SMUDGILY	SMYTRIES	SNAKE	SNAPTINS
SMORED	SMUDGING	SNAB	SNAKEBIRD	SNAPWEED
SMORES	SMUDGINGS	SNABBLE	SNAKEBIT	SNAPWEEDS
SMORG	SMUDGY	SNABBLED	SNAKEBITE	SNAR
SMORGS	SMUG	SNABBLES	SNAKED	SNARE
SMORING	SMUGGED	SNABBLING	SNAKEFISH	SNARED
SMORZANDO	SMUGGER	SNABS	SNAKEHEAD	SNARELESS
SMORZATO	SMUGGERY	SNACK	SNAKELIKE	SNARER
SMOTE	SMUGGEST	SNACKED	SNAKEPIT	SNARERS
SMOTHER	SMUGGING	SNACKER	SNAKEPITS	SNARES
SMOTHERED	SMUGGLE	SNACKERS	SNAKEROOT	SNARF
SMOTHERER	SMUGGLED	SNACKETTE	SNAKES	SNARFED
SMOTHERS	SMUGGLER	SNACKIER	SNAKESKIN	SNARFING

S

SNARFLE	SNATHS	SNEE	SNICKERED	SNIFTIEST
SNARFLED	SNAW	SNEED	SNICKERER	SNIFTING
SNARFLES	SNAWED	SNEEING	SNICKERS	SNIFTS
SNARFLING	SNAWING	SNEER	SNICKERY	SNIFTY
SNARFS	SNAWS	SNEERED	SNICKET	SNIG
SNARIER	SNAZZIER	SNEERER	SNICKETS	SNIGGED
SNARIEST	SNAZZIEST	SNEERERS	SNICKING	SNIGGER
SNARING	SNAZZILY	SNEERFUL	SNICKS	SNIGGERED
SNARINGS	SNAZZY	SNEERIER	SNIDE	SNIGGERER
SNARK	SNEAD	SNEERIEST	SNIDED	SNIGGERS
SNARKIER	SNEADS	SNEERING	SNIDELY	SNIGGING
SNARKIEST	SNEAK	SNEERINGS	SNIDENESS	SNIGGLE
SNARKILY	SNEAKBOX	SNEERS	SNIDER	SNIGGLED
SNARKS	SNEAKED	SNEERY	SNIDES	SNIGGLER
SNARKY	SNEAKER	SNEES	SNIDEST	SNIGGLERS
SNARL	SNEAKERED	SNEESH	SNIDEY	SNIGGLES
SNARLED	SNEAKERS	SNEESHAN	SNIDIER	SNIGGLING
SNARLER	SNEAKEUP	SNEESHANS	SNIDIEST	SNIGLET
SNARLERS	SNEAKEUPS	SNEESHED	SNIDING	SNIGLETS
SNARLIER	SNEAKIER	SNEESHES	SNIES	SNIGS
SNARLIEST	SNEAKIEST	SNEESHIN	SNIFF	SNIP
SNARLING	SNEAKILY	SNEESHING	SNIFFABLE	SNIPE
SNARLINGS	SNEAKING	SNEESHINS	SNIFFED	SNIPED
SNARLS	SNEAKISH	SNEEZE	SNIFFER	SNIPEFISH
SNARLY	SNEAKS	SNEEZED	SNIFFERS	SNIPELIKE
SNARRED	SNEAKSBY	SNEEZER	SNIFFIER.	SNIPER
SNARRING	SNEAKY	SNEEZERS	SNIFFIEST	SNIPERS
SNARS	SNEAP	SNEEZES	SNIFFILY	SNIPES
SNARY	SNEAPED	SNEEZIER	SNIFFING	SNIPIER
SNASH	SNEAPING	SNEEZIEST	SNIFFINGS	SNIPIEST
SNASHED	SNEAPS	SNEEZING	SNIFFISH	SNIPING
SNASHES	SNEATH	SNEEZINGS	SNIFFLE	SNIPINGS
SNASHING	SNEATHS	SNEEZY	SNIFFLED	SNIPPED
SNASTE	SNEB	SNELL	SNIFFLER	SNIPPER
SNASTES	SNEBBE	SNELLED	SNIFFLERS	SNIPPERS
SNATCH	SNEBBED	SNELLER	SNIFFLES	SNIPPET
SNATCHED	SNEBBES	SNELLEST	SNIFFLIER	SNIPPETS
SNATCHER	SNEBBING	SNELLING	SNIFFLING	SNIPPETY
SNATCHERS	SNEBS	SNELLS	SNIFFLY	SNIPPIER
SNATCHES	SNECK	SNELLY	SNIFFS	SNIPPIEST
SNATCHIER	SNECKED	SNIB	SNIFFY	SNIPPILY
SNATCHILY	SNECKING	SNIBBED	SNIFT	SNIPPING
SNATCHING	SNECKS	SNIBBING	SNIFTED	SNIPPINGS
SNATCHY	SNED	SNIBS	SNIFTER	SNIPPY
SNATH	SNEDDED	SNICK	SNIFTERED	SNIPS
SNATHE	SNEDDING	SNICKED	SNIFTERS	SNIPY
SNATHES	SNEDS	SNICKER	SNIFTIER	SNIRT

SNIRTED	SNODDING	SNOOTIER	SNOTTERS	SNOWDROPS
SNIRTING	SNODDIT	SNOOTIEST	SNOTTERY	SNOWED
SNIRTLE	SNODS	SNOOTILY	SNOTTIE	SNOWFALL
SNIRTLED	SNOEK	SNOOTING	SNOTTIER	SNOWFALLS
SNIRTLES	SNOEKS	SNOOTS	SNOTTIES	SNOWFIELD
SNIRTLING	SNOEP	SNOOTY	SNOTTIEST	SNOWFLAKE
SNIRTS	SNOG	SNOOZE	SNOTTILY	SNOWFLEA
SNIT	SNOGGED	SNOOZED	SNOTTING	SNOWFLEAS
SNITCH	SNOGGER	SNOOZER	SNOTTY	SNOWFLECK
SNITCHED	SNOGGERS	SNOOZERS	SNOUT	SNOWFLICK
SNITCHER	SNOGGING	SNOOZES	SNOUTED	SNOWGLOBE
SNITCHERS	SNOGS	SNOOZIER	SNOUTIER	SNOWIER
SNITCHES	SNOKE	SNOOZIEST	SNOUTIEST	SNOWIEST
SNITCHIER	SNOKED	SNOOZING	SNOUTING	SNOWILY
SNITCHING	SNOKES	SNOOZLE	SNOUTISH	SNOWINESS
SNITCHY	SNOKING	SNOOZLED	SNOUTLESS	SNOWING
SNITS	SNOOD	SNOOZLES	SNOUTLIKE	SNOWISH
SNITTIER	SNOODED	SNOOZLING	SNOUTS	SNOWK
SNITTIEST	SNOODING	SNOOZY	SNOUTY	SNOWKED
SNITTY	SNOODS	SNORE	SNOW	SNOWKING
SNIVEL	SNOOK	SNORED	SNOWBALL	SNOWKS
SNIVELED	SNOOKED	SNORER	SNOWBALLS	SNOWLAND
SNIVELER	SNOOKER	SNORERS	SNOWBANK	SNOWLANDS
SNIVELERS	SNOOKERED	SNORES	SNOWBANKS	SNOWLESS
SNIVELING	SNOOKERS	SNORING	SNOWBELL	SNOWLIKE
SNIVELLED	SNOOKING	SNORINGS	SNOWBELLS	SNOWLINE
SNIVELLER	SNOOKS	SNORKEL	SNOWBELT	SNOWLINES
SNIVELLY	SNOOL	SNORKELED	SNOWBELTS	SNOWMAKER
SNIVELS	SNOOLED	SNORKELER	SNOWBERRY	SNOWMAN
SNIVELY	SNOOLING	SNORKELS	SNOWBIRD	SNOWMELT
SNOB	SNOOLS	SNORT	SNOWBIRDS	SNOWMELTS
SNOBBERY	SNOOP	SNORTED	SNOWBLINK	SNOWMEN
SNOBBIER	SNOOPED	SNORTER	SNOWBOARD	SNOWMOLD
SNOBBIEST	SNOOPER	SNORTERS	SNOWBOOT	SNOWMOLDS
SNOBBILY	SNOOPERS	SNORTIER	SNOWBOOTS	SNOWMOULD
SNOBBISH	SNOOPIER	SNORTIEST	SNOWBOUND	SNOWPACK
SNOBBISM	SNOOPIEST	SNORTING	SNOWBRUSH	SNOWPACKS
SNOBBISMS	SNOOPILY	SNORTINGS	SNOWBUSH	SNOWPLOW
SNOBBY	SNOOPING	SNORTS	SNOWCAP	SNOWPLOWS
SNOBLING	SNOOPS	SNORTY	SNOWCAPS	SNOWS
SNOBLINGS	SNOOPY	SNOT	SNOWCAT	SNOWSCAPE
SNOBS	SNOOSE	SNOTRAG	SNOWCATS	SNOWSHED
SNOCOACH	SNOOSES	SNOTRAGS	SNOWCLONE	SNOWSHEDS
SNOD	SNOOT	SNOTS	SNOWDOME	SNOWSHOE
SNODDED	SNOOTED	SNOTTED	SNOWDOMES	SNOWSHOED
SNODDER	SNOOTFUL	SNOTTER	SNOWDRIFT	SNOWSHOER
SNODDEST	SNOOTFULS	SNOTTERED	SNOWDROP	SNOWSHOES

S

SNOWSLIDE	SNUG	SOAPBOXED	SOBBINGLY	SOCIATE
SNOWSLIP	SNUGGED	SOAPBOXES	SOBBINGS	SOCIATES
SNOWSLIPS	SNUGGER	SOAPDISH	SOBEIT	SOCIATION
SNOWSTORM	SNUGGERIE	SOAPED	SOBER	SOCIATIVE
SNOWSUIT	SNUGGERY	SOAPER	SOBERED	SOCIETAL
SNOWSUITS	SNUGGEST	SOAPERS	SOBERER	SOCIETIES
SNOWY	SNUGGIES	SOAPFISH	SOBEREST	SOCIETY
SNUB	SNUGGING	SOAPIE	SOBERING	SOCIOGRAM
SNUBBE	SNUGGLE	SOAPIER	SOBERISE	SOCIOLECT
SNUBBED	SNUGGLED	SOAPIES	SOBERISED	SOCIOLOGY
SNUBBER	SNUGGLES	SOAPIEST	SOBERISES	SOCIOPATH
SNUBBERS	SNUGGLIER	SOAPILY	SOBERIZE	SOCK
SNUBBES	SNUGGLING	SOAPINESS	SOBERIZED	SOCKED
SNUBBIER	SNUGGLY	SOAPING	SOBERIZES	SOCKET
SNUBBIEST	SNUGLY	SOAPLAND	SOBERLY	SOCKETED
SNUBBING	SNUGNESS	SOAPLANDS	SOBERNESS	SOCKETING
SNUBBINGS	SNUGS	SOAPLESS	SOBERS	SOCKETS
SNUBBISH	SNUSH	SOAPLIKE	SOBFUL	SOCKETTE
SNUBBY	SNUSHED	SOAPROOT	SOBOLE	SOCKETTES
SNUBFIN	SNUSHES	SOAPROOTS	SOBOLES	SOCKEYE
SNUBNESS	SNUSHING	SOAPS	SOBRIETY	SOCKEYES
SNUBS	SNUZZLE	SOAPSTONE	SOBRIQUET	SOCKING
SNUCK	SNUZZLED	SOAPSUDS	SOBS	SOCKLESS
SNUDGE	SNUZZLES	SOAPSUDSY	SOC	SOCKMAN
SNUDGED	SNUZZLING	SOAPWORT	SOCA	SOCKMEN
SNUDGES	SNY	SOAPWORTS	SOCAGE	SOCKO
SNUDGING	SNYE	SOAPY	SOCAGER	SOCKS
SNUFF	SNYES	SOAR	SOCAGERS	SOCLE
SNUFFBOX	SO	SOARAWAY	SOCAGES	SOCLES
SNUFFED	SOAK	SOARE	SOCAS	SOCMAN
SNUFFER	SOAKAGE	SOARED	SOCCAGE	SOCMEN
SNUFFERS	SOAKAGES	SOARER	SOCCAGES	SOCS
SNUFFIER	SOAKAWAY	SOARERS	SOCCER	SOD
SNUFFIEST	SOAKAWAYS	SOARES	SOCCERS	SODA
SNUFFILY	SOAKED	SOARING	SOCES	SODAIC
SNUFFING	SOAKEN	SOARINGLY	SOCIABLE	SODAIN
SNUFFINGS	SOAKER	SOARINGS	SOCIABLES	SODAINE
SNUFFLE	SOAKERS	SOARS	SOCIABLY	SODALESS
SNUFFLED	SOAKING	SOAVE	SOCIAL	SODALIST
SNUFFLER	SOAKINGLY	SOAVES	SOCIALISE	SODALISTS
SNUFFLERS	SOAKINGS	SOB	SOCIALISM	SODALITE
SNUFFLES	SOAKS	SOBA	SOCIALIST	SODALITES
SNUFFLIER	SOAP	SOBAS	SOCIALITE	SODALITY
SNUFFLING	SOAPBARK	SOBBED	SOCIALITY	SODAMIDE
SNUFFLY	SOAPBARKS	SOBBER	SOCIALIZE	SODAMIDES
SNUFFS	SOAPBERRY	SOBBERS	SOCIALLY	SODAS
SNUFFY	SOAPBOX	SOBBING	SOCIALS	SODBUSTER

S

SODDED	SOFTA	SOGGY	SOLA	SOLATIUM
SODDEN	SOFTAS	SOGS	SOLACE	SOLD
SODDENED	SOFTBACK	SOH	SOLACED	SOLDADO
SODDENING	SOFTBACKS	SOHO	SOLACER	SOLDADOES
SODDENLY	SOFTBALL	SOHS	SOLACERS	SOLDADOS
SODDENS	SOFTBALLS	SOHUR	SOLACES	SOLDAN
SODDIE	SOFTBOUND	SOHURS	SOLACING	SOLDANS
SODDIER	SOFTCORE	SOIGNE	SOLACIOUS	SOLDE
SODDIES	SOFTCOVER	SOIGNEE	SOLAH	SOLDER
SODDIEST	SOFTED	SOIL	SOLAHS	SOLDERED
SODDING	SOFTEN	SOILAGE	SOLAN	SOLDERER
SODDY	SOFTENED	SOILAGES	SOLAND	SOLDERERS
SODGER	SOFTENER	SOILBORNE	SOLANDER	SOLDERING
SODGERED	SOFTENERS	SOILED	SOLANDERS	SOLDERS
SODGERING	SOFTENING	SOILIER	SOLANDS	SOLDES
SODGERS	SOFTENS	SOILIEST	SOLANIN	SOLDI
SODIC	SOFTER	SOILINESS	SOLANINE	SOLDIER
SODICITY	SOFTEST	SOILING	SOLANINES	SOLDIERED
SODIUM	SOFTGOODS	SOILINGS	SOLANINS	SOLDIERLY
SODIUMS	SOFTHEAD	SOILLESS	SOLANO	SOLDIERS
SODOM	SOFTHEADS	SOILS	SOLANOS	SOLDIERY
SODOMIES	SOFTIE	SOILURE	SOLANS	SOLDO
SODOMISE	SOFTIES	SOILURES	SOLANUM	SOLDS
SODOMISED	SOFTING	SOILY	SOLANUMS	SOLE
SODOMISES	SOFTISH	SOIREE	SOLAR	SOLECISE
SODOMIST	SOFTLING	SOIREES	SOLARIA	SOLECISED
SODOMISTS	SOFTLINGS	SOJA	SOLARISE	SOLECISES
SODOMITE	SOFTLY	SOJAS	SOLARISED	SOLECISM
SODOMITES	SOFTNESS	SOJOURN	SOLARISES	SOLECISMS
SODOMITIC	SOFTS	SOJOURNED	SOLARISM	SOLECIST
SODOMIZE	SOFTSCAPE	SOJOURNER	SOLARISMS	SOLECISTS
SODOMIZED	SOFTSHELL	SOJOURNS	SOLARIST	SOLECIZE
SODOMIZES	SOFTWARE	SOJU	SOLARISTS	SOLECIZED
SODOMS	SOFTWARES	SOJUS	SOLARIUM	SOLECIZES
SODOMY	SOFTWOOD	SOKAH	SOLARIUMS	SOLED
SODS	SOFTWOODS	SOKAHS	SOLARIZE	SOLEI
SOEVER	SOFTY	SOKAIYA	SOLARIZED	SOLEIN
SOFA	SOG	SOKE	SOLARIZES	SOLELESS
SOFABED	SOGER	SOKEMAN	SOLARS	SOLELY
SOFABEDS	SOGERS	SOKEMANRY	SOLAS	SOLEMN
SOFAR	SOGGED	SOKEMEN	SOLATE	SOLEMNER
SOFARS	SOGGIER	SOKEN	SOLATED	SOLEMNESS
SOFAS	SOGGIEST	SOKENS	SOLATES	SOLEMNEST
SOFFIONI	SOGGILY	SOKES	SOLATIA	SOLEMNIFY
SOFFIT	SOGGINESS	SOKOL	SOLATING	SOLEMNISE
SOFFITS	SOGGING	SOKOLS	SOLATION	SOLEMNITY
SOFT	SOGGINGS	SOL	SOLATIONS	SOLEMNIZE

S

SOLEMNLY	SOLIDISTS	SOLONS	SOMATISMS	SOMITES
SOLENESS	SOLIDITY	SOLOS	SOMATIST	SOMITIC
SOLENETTE	SOLIDLY	SOLPUGID	SOMATISTS	SOMMELIER
SOLENODON	SOLIDNESS	SOLPUGIDS	SOMBER	SOMNIAL
SOLENOID	SOLIDS	SOLS	SOMBERED	SOMNIATE
SOLENOIDS	SOLIDUM	SOLSTICE	SOMBERER	SOMNIATED
SOLEPLATE	SOLIDUMS	SOLSTICES	SOMBEREST	SOMNIATES
SOLEPRINT	SOLIDUS	SOLUBLE	SOMBERING	SOMNIFIC
SOLER	SOLILOQUY	SOLUBLES	SOMBERLY	SOMNOLENT
SOLERA	SOLING	SOLUBLY	SOMBERS	SOMONI
SOLERAS	SOLION	SOLUM	SOMBRE	SOMONIS
SOLERET	SOLIONS	SOLUMS	SOMBRED	SOMS
SOLERETS	SOLIPED	SOLUNAR	SOMBRELY	SOMY
SOLERS	SOLIPEDS	SOLUS	SOMBRER	SON
SOLES	SOLIPSISM	SOLUSES	SOMBRERO	SONANCE
SOLEUS	SOLIPSIST	SOLUTAL	SOMBREROS	SONANCES
SOLEUSES	SOLIQUID	SOLUTE	SOMBRES	SONANCIES
SOLFATARA	SOLIQUIDS	SOLUTES	SOMBREST	SONANCY
SOLFEGE	SOLITAIRE	SOLUTION	SOMBRING	SONANT
SOLFEGES	SOLITARY	SOLUTIONS	SOMBROUS	SONANTAL
SOLFEGGI	SOLITO	SOLUTIVE	SOME	SONANTIC
SOLFEGGIO	SOLITON	SOLUTIVES	SOMEBODY	SONANTS
SOLFERINO	SOLITONS	SOLVABLE	SOMEDAY	SONAR
SOLGEL	SOLITUDE	SOLVATE	SOMEDEAL	SONARMAN
SOLI	SOLITUDES	SOLVATED	SOMEDEALS	SONARMEN
SOLICIT	SOLIVE	SOLVATES	SOMEDELE	SONARS
SOLICITED	SOLIVES	SOLVATING	SOMEGATE	SONATA
SOLICITOR	SOLLAR	SOLVATION	SOMEHOW	SONATAS
SOLICITS	SOLLARED	SOLVE	SOMEONE	SONATINA
SOLICITY	SOLLARING	SOLVED	SOMEONES	SONATINAS
SOLID	SOLLARS	SOLVENCY	SOMEPLACE	SONATINE
SOLIDAGO	SOLLER	SOLVENT	SOMERSET	SONCE
SOLIDAGOS	SOLLERET	SOLVENTLY	SOMERSETS	SONCES
SOLIDARE	SOLLERETS	SOLVENTS	SOMETHING	SONDAGE
SOLIDARES	SOLLERS	SOLVER	SOMETIME	SONDAGES
SOLIDARY	SOLLICKER	SOLVERS	SOMETIMES	SONDE
SOLIDATE	SOLO	SOLVES	SOMEWAY	SONDELI
SOLIDATED	SOLOED	SOLVING	SOMEWAYS	SONDELIS
SOLIDATES	SOLOES	SOM	SOMEWHAT	SONDER
SOLIDER	SOLOING	SOMA	SOMEWHATS	SONDERS
SOLIDEST	SOLOIST	SOMAN	SOMEWHEN	SONDES
SOLIDI	SOLOISTIC	SOMANS	SOMEWHERE	SONE
SOLIDIFY	SOLOISTS	SOMAS	SOMEWHILE	SONERI
SOLIDISH	SOLON	SOMASCOPE	SOMEWHY	SONERIS
SOLIDISM	SOLONCHAK	SOMATA	SOMEWISE	SONES
SOLIDISMS	SOLONETS	SOMATIC	SOMITAL	SONG
SOLIDIST	SOLONETZ	SOMATISM	SOMITE	SONGBIRD

SONGBIRDS	SONOGRAM	SOOM	SOOTY	SORB
SONGBOOK	SONOGRAMS	SOOMED	SOP	SORBABLE
SONGBOOKS	SONOGRAPH	SOOMING	SOPAPILLA	SORBARIA
SONGCRAFT	SONOMETER	SOOMS	SOPH	SORBARIAS
SONGFEST	SONORANT	SOON	SOPHERIC	SORBATE
SONGFESTS	SONORANTS	SOONER	SOPHERIM	SORBATES
SONGFUL	SONORITY	SOONERS	SOPHIES	SORBED
SONGFULLY	SONOROUS	SOONEST	SOPHISM	SORBENT
SONGKOK	SONOVOX	SOONISH	SOPHISMS	SORBENTS
SONGKOKS	SONOVOXES	SOOP	SOPHIST	SORBET
SONGLESS	SONS	SOOPED	SOPHISTER	SORBETS
SONGLIKE	SONSE	SOOPING	SOPHISTIC	SORBIC
SONGMAN	SONSES	SOOPINGS	SOPHISTRY	SORBING
SONGMEN	SONSHIP	SOOPS	SOPHISTS	SORBITAN
SONGOLOLO	SONSHIPS	SOOPSTAKE	SOPHOMORE	SORBITANS
SONGS	SONSIE	SOOT	SOPHS	SORBITE
SONGSHEET	SONSIER	SOOTE	SOPHY	SORBITES
SONGSMITH	SONSIEST	SOOTED	SOPITE	SORBITIC
SONGSTER	SONSY	SOOTERKIN	SOPITED	SORBITISE
SONGSTERS	SONTAG	SOOTES	SOPITES	SORBITIZE
SONHOOD	SONTAGS	SOOTFLAKE	SOPITING	SORBITOL
SONHOODS	SONTIES	SOOTH	SOPOR	SORBITOLS
SONIC	SOOCHONG	SOOTHE	SOPORIFIC	SORBO
SONICALLY	SOOCHONGS	SOOTHED	SOPOROSE	SORBOSE
SONICATE	SOOEY	SOOTHER	SOPOROUS	SORBOSES
SONICATED	SOOGEE	SOOTHERED	SOPORS	SORBS
SONICATES	SOOGEED	SOOTHERS	SOPPED	SORBUS
SONICATOR	SOOGEEING	SOOTHES	SOPPIER	SORBUSES
SONICS	SOOGEES	SOOTHEST	SOPPIEST	SORCERER
SONLESS	SOOGIE	SOOTHFAST	SOPPILY	SORCERERS
SONLIKE	SOOGIED	SOOTHFUL	SOPPINESS	SORCERESS
SONLY	SOOGIEING	SOOTHING	SOPPING	SORCERIES
SONNE	SOOGIES	SOOTHINGS	SOPPINGS	SORCEROUS
SONNES	SOOJEY	SOOTHLICH	SOPPY	SORCERY
SONNET	SOOJEYS	SOOTHLY	SOPRA	SORD
SONNETARY	SOOK	SOOTHS	SOPRANI	SORDA
SONNETED	SOOKED	SOOTHSAID	SOPRANINI	SORDED
SONNETEER	SOOKING	SOOTHSAY	SOPRANINO	SORDES
SONNETING	SOOKS	SOOTHSAYS	SOPRANIST	SORDID
SONNETISE	SOOL	SOOTIER	SOPRANO	SORDIDER
SONNETIZE	SOOLE	SOOTIEST	SOPRANOS	SORDIDEST
SONNETS	SOOLED	SOOTILY	SOPS	SORDIDLY
SONNETTED	SOOLER	SOOTINESS	SORA	SORDINE
SONNIES	SOOLERS	SOOTING	SORAGE	SORDINES
SONNY	SOOLES	SOOTINGS	SORAGES	SORDING
SONOBUOY	SOOLING	SOOTLESS	SORAL	SORDINI
SONOBUOYS	SOOLS	SOOTS	SORAS	SORDINO

S

SORDO	SORNS	SORTANCES	SOUBISES	SOUMS
SORDOR	SOROBAN	SORTATION	SOUBRETTE	SOUND
SORDORS	SOROBANS	SORTED	SOUCAR	SOUNDABLE
SORDS	SOROCHE	SORTER	SOUCARS	SOUNDBITE
SORE	SOROCHES	SORTERS	SOUCE	SOUNDBOX
SORED	SORORAL	SORTES	SOUCED	SOUNDCARD
SOREDIA	SORORALLY	SORTIE	SOUCES	SOUNDED
SOREDIAL	SORORATE	SORTIED	SOUCHONG	SOUNDER
SOREDIATE	SORORATES	SORTIEING	SOUCHONGS	SOUNDERS
SOREDIUM	SORORIAL	SORTIES	SOUCING	SOUNDEST
SOREE	SORORISE	SORTILEGE	SOUCT	SOUNDING
SOREES	SORORISED	SORTILEGY	SOUDAN	SOUNDINGS
SOREHEAD	SORORISES	SORTING	SOUDANS	SOUNDLESS
SOREHEADS	SORORITY	SORTINGS	SOUFFLE	SOUNDLY
SOREHON	SORORIZE	SORTITION	SOUFFLED	SOUNDMAN
SOREHONS	SORORIZED	SORTMENT	SOUFFLEED	SOUNDMEN
SOREL	SORORIZES	SORTMENTS	SOUFFLES	SOUNDNESS
SORELL	SOROSES	SORTS	SOUGH	SOUNDPOST
SORELLS	SOROSIS	SORUS	SOUGHED	SOUNDS
SORELS	SOROSISES	SOS	SOUGHING	SOUP
SORELY	SORPTION	SOSATIE	SOUGHS	SOUPCON
SORENESS	SORPTIONS	SOSATIES	SOUGHT	SOUPCONS
SORER	SORPTIVE	SOSS	SOUK	SOUPED
SORES	SORRA	SOSSED	SOUKED	SOUPER
SOREST	SORRAS	SOSSES	SOUKING	SOUPERS
SOREX	SORREL	SOSSING	SOUKOUS	SOUPFIN
SOREXES	SORRELS	SOSSINGS	SOUKOUSES	SOUPFINS
SORGHO	SORRIER	SOSTENUTI	SOUKS	SOUPIER
SORGHOS	SORRIEST	SOSTENUTO	SOUL	SOUPIEST
SORGHUM	SORRILY	SOT	SOULDAN	SOUPILY
SORGHUMS	SORRINESS	SOTERIAL	SOULDANS	SOUPING
SORGO	SORROW	SOTH	SOULDIER	SOUPLE
SORGOS	SORROWED	SOTHS	SOULDIERS	SOUPLED
SORI	SORROWER	SOTOL	SOULED	SOUPLES
SORICINE	SORROWERS	SOTOLS	SOULFUL	SOUPLESS
SORICOID	SORROWFUL	SOTS	SOULFULLY	SOUPLIKE
SORING	SORROWING	SOTTED	SOULLESS	SOUPLING
SORINGS	SORROWS	SOTTEDLY	SOULLIKE	SOUPS
SORITES	SORRY	SOTTING	SOULMATE	SOUPSPOON
SORITIC	SORRYISH	SOTTINGS	SOULMATES	SOUPY
SORITICAL	SORT	SOTTISH	SOULS	SOUR
SORN	SORTA	SOTTISHLY	SOULSTER	SOURBALL
SORNED	SORTABLE	SOTTISIER	SOULSTERS	SOURBALLS
SORNER	SORTABLY	SOU	SOUM	SOURCE
SORNERS	SORTAL	SOUARI	SOUMED	SOURCED
SORNING	SORTALS	SOUARIS	SOUMING	SOURCEFUL
SORNINGS	SORTANCE	SOUBISE	SOUMINGS	SOURCES

SOURCING
SOURCINGS
SOURDINE
SOURDINES
SOURDOUGH
SOURED
SOURER
SOUREST
SOURGUM
SOURGUMS
SOURING
SOURINGS
SOURISH
SOURISHLY
SOURLY
SOURNESS
SOUROCK
SOUROCKS
SOURPUSS
SOURS
SOURSE
SOURSES
SOURSOP
SOURSOPS
SOURVELD
SOURVELDS
SOURWOOD
SOURWOODS
SOUS
SOUSE
SOUSED
SOUSER
SOUSERS
SOUSES
SOUSING
SOUSINGS
SOUSLIK
SOUSLIKS
SOUT
SOUTACHE
SOUTACHES
SOUTANE
SOUTANES
SOUTAR
SOUTARS
SOUTENEUR
SOUTER

SOUTERLY
SOUTERS
SOUTH
SOUTHEAST
SOUTHED
SOUTHER
SOUTHERED
SOUTHERLY
SOUTHERN
SOUTHERNS
SOUTHERS
SOUTHING
SOUTHINGS
SOUTHLAND
SOUTHMOST
SOUTHPAW
SOUTHPAWS
SOUTHRON
SOUTHRONS
SOUTHS
SOUTHSAID
SOUTHSAY
SOUTHSAYS
SOUTHWARD
SOUTHWEST
SOUTIE
SOUTIES
SOUTPIEL
SOUTPIELS
SOUTS
SOUVENIR
SOUVENIRS
SOUVLAKI
SOUVLAKIA
SOUVLAKIS
SOV
SOVENANCE
SOVEREIGN
SOVIET
SOVIETIC
SOVIETISE
SOVIETISM
SOVIETIST
SOVIETIZE
SOVIETS
SOVKHOZ
SOVKHOZES

SOVKHOZY
SOVRAN
SOVRANLY
SOVRANS
SOVRANTY
SOVS
SOW
SOWABLE
SOWANS
SOWAR
SOWARREE
SOWARREES
SOWARRIES
SOWARRY
SOWARS
SOWBACK
SOWBACKS
SOWBELLY
SOWBREAD
SOWBREADS
SOWBUG
SOWBUGS
SOWCAR
SOWCARS
SOWCE
SOWCED
SOWCES
SOWCING
SOWDER
SOWDERS
SOWED
SOWENS
SOWER
SOWERS
SOWF
SOWFED
SOWFF
SOWFFED
SOWFFING
SOWFFS
SOWFING
SOWFS
SOWING
SOWINGS
SOWL
SOWLE
SOWLED

SOWLES
SOWLING
SOWLS
SOWM
SOWMED
SOWMING
SOWMS
SOWN
SOWND
SOWNDED
SOWNDING
SOWNDS
SOWNE
SOWNES
SOWP
SOWPED
SOWPING
SOWPS
SOWS
SOWSE
SOWSED
SOWSES
SOWSING
SOWSSE
SOWSSED
SOWSSES
SOWSSING
SOWTER
SOWTERS
SOWTH
SOWTHED
SOWTHING
SOWTHS
SOX
SOY
SOYA
SOYAS
SOYBEAN
SOYBEANS
SOYLE
SOYLED
SOYLES
SOYLING
SOYMEAL
SOYMEALS
SOYMILK
SOYMILKS

SOYS
SOYUZ
SOYUZES
SOZ
SOZIN
SOZINE
SOZINES
SOZINS
SOZZLE
SOZZLED
SOZZLES
SOZZLIER
SOZZLIEST
SOZZLING
SOZZLY
SPA
SPACE
SPACEBAND
SPACED
SPACELAB
SPACELABS
SPACELESS
SPACEMAN
SPACEMEN
SPACEPORT
SPACER
SPACERS
SPACES
SPACESHIP
SPACESUIT
SPACEWALK
SPACEWARD
SPACEY
SPACIAL
SPACIALLY
SPACIER
SPACIEST
SPACINESS
SPACING
SPACINGS
SPACIOUS
SPACKLE
SPACKLED
SPACKLES
SPACKLING
SPACY
SPADASSIN

S

SPADE	SPAGGING	SPALTING	SPANGS	SPARIDS
SPADED	SPAGHETTI	SPALTS	SPANIEL	SPARING
SPADEFISH	SPAGIRIC	SPAM	SPANIELS	SPARINGLY
SPADEFUL	SPAGIRIST	SPAMBOT	SPANING	SPARK
SPADEFULS	SPAGS	SPAMBOTS	SPANK	SPARKE
SPADELIKE	SPAGYRIC	SPAMMED	SPANKED	SPARKED
SPADEMAN	SPAGYRICS	SPAMMER	SPANKER	SPARKER
SPADEMEN	SPAGYRIST	SPAMMERS	SPANKERS	SPARKERS
SPADER	SPAHEE	SPAMMIE	SPANKING	SPARKES
SPADERS	SPAHEES	SPAMMIER	SPANKINGS	SPARKIE
SPADES	SPAHI	SPAMMIES	SPANKS	SPARKIER
SPADESMAN	SPAHIS	SPAMMIEST	SPANLESS	SPARKIES
SPADESMEN	SPAIL	SPAMMING	SPANNED	SPARKIEST
SPADEWORK	SPAILS	SPAMMINGS	SPANNER	SPARKILY
SPADGER	SPAIN	SPAMMY	SPANNERS	SPARKING
SPADGERS	SPAINED	SPAMS	SPANNING	SPARKISH
SPADICES	SPAING	SPAN	SPANS	SPARKLE
SPADILLE	SPAINGS	SPANAEMIA	SPANSPEK	SPARKLED
SPADILLES	SPAINING	SPANAEMIC	SPANSPEKS	SPARKLER
SPADILLIO	SPAINS	SPANCEL	SPANSULE	SPARKLERS
SPADILLO	SPAIRGE	SPANCELED	SPANSULES	SPARKLES
SPADILLOS	SPAIRGED	SPANCELS	SPANWORM	SPARKLESS
SPADING	SPAIRGES	SPANDEX	SPANWORMS	SPARKLET
SPADIX	SPAIRGING	SPANDEXED	SPAR	SPARKLETS
SPADIXES	SPAIT	SPANDEXES	SPARABLE	SPARKLIER
SPADO	SPAITS	SPANDREL	SPARABLES	SPARKLIES
SPADOES	SPAKE	SPANDRELS	SPARAXIS	SPARKLING
SPADONES	SPALD	SPANDRIL	SPARD	SPARKLY
SPADOS	SPALDEEN	SPANDRILS	SPARE	SPARKPLUG
SPADROON	SPALDEENS	SPANE	SPAREABLE	SPARKS
SPADROONS	SPALDS	SPANED	SPARED	SPARKY
SPAE	SPALE	SPANES	SPARELESS	SPARLIKE
SPAED	SPALES	SPANG	SPARELY	SPARLING
SPAEING	SPALL	SPANGED	SPARENESS	SPARLINGS
SPAEINGS	SPALLABLE	SPANGHEW	SPARER	SPAROID
SPAEMAN	SPALLE	SPANGHEWS	SPARERIB	SPAROIDS
SPAEMEN	SPALLED	SPANGING	SPARERIBS	SPARRE
SPAER	SPALLER	SPANGLE	SPARERS	SPARRED
SPAERS	SPALLERS	SPANGLED	SPARES	SPARRER
SPAES	SPALLES	SPANGLER	SPAREST	SPARRERS
SPAETZLE	SPALLING	SPANGLERS	SPARGE	SPARRES
SPAETZLES	SPALLINGS	SPANGLES	SPARGED	SPARRIER
SPAEWIFE	SPALLS	SPANGLET	SPARGER	SPARRIEST
SPAEWIVES	SPALPEEN	SPANGLETS	SPARGERS	SPARRING
SPAG	SPALPEENS	SPANGLIER	SPARGES	SPARRINGS
SPAGERIC	SPALT	SPANGLING	SPARGING	SPARROW
SPAGGED	SPALTED	SPANGLY	SPARID	SPARROWS

SPARRY	SPATS	SPAYED	SPECCED	SPECTERS
SPARS	SPATTED	SPAYING	SPECCIER	SPECTING
SPARSE	SPATTEE	SPAYS	SPECCIES	SPECTRA
SPARSEDLY	SPATTEES	SPAZ	SPECCIEST	SPECTRAL
SPARSELY	SPATTER	SPAZA	SPECCING	SPECTRE
SPARSER	SPATTERED	SPAZZ	SPECCY	SPECTRES
SPARSEST	SPATTERS	SPAZZED	SPECIAL	SPECTRIN
SPARSITY	SPATTING	SPAZZES	SPECIALER	SPECTRINS
SPART	SPATULA	SPAZZING	SPECIALLY	SPECTRUM
SPARTAN	SPATULAR	SPEAK	SPECIALS	SPECTRUMS
SPARTANS	SPATULAS	SPEAKABLE	SPECIALTY	SPECTS
SPARTEINE	SPATULATE	SPEAKEASY	SPECIATE	SPECULA
SPARTERIE	SPATULE	SPEAKER	SPECIATED	SPECULAR
SPARTH	SPATULES	SPEAKERS	SPECIATES	SPECULATE
SPARTHE	SPATZLE	SPEAKING	SPECIE	SPECULUM
SPARTHES	SPATZLES	SPEAKINGS	SPECIES	SPECULUMS
SPARTHS	SPAUL	SPEAKOUT	SPECIFIC	SPED
SPARTICLE	SPAULD	SPEAKOUTS	SPECIFICS	SPEECH
SPARTINA	SPAULDS	SPEAKS	SPECIFIED	SPEECHED
SPARTINAS	SPAULS	SPEAL	SPECIFIER	SPEECHES
SPARTS	SPAVIE	SPEALS	SPECIFIES	SPEECHFUL
AS	SPAVIES	SPEAN	SPECIFY	SPEECHIFY
ASM	SPAVIET	SPEANED	SPECIMEN	SPEECHING
PASMATIC	SPAVIN	SPEANING	SPECIMENS	SPEED
SPASMED	SPAVINED	SPEANS	SPECIOUS	SPEEDBALL
SPASMIC	SPAVINS	SPEAR	SPECK	SPEEDBOAT
SPASMING	SPAW	SPEARED	SPECKED	SPEEDED
SPASMODIC	SPAWL	SPEARER	SPECKIER	SPEEDER
SPASMS	SPAWLED	SPEARERS	SPECKIES	SPEEDERS
SPASTIC	SPAWLING	SPEARFISH	SPECKIEST	SPEEDFUL
SPASTICS	SPAWLS	SPEARGUN	SPECKING	SPEEDIER
SPAT	SPAWN	SPEARGUNS	SPECKLE	SPEEDIEST
SPATE	SPAWNED	SPEARHEAD	SPECKLED	SPEEDILY
SPATES	SPAWNER	SPEARIER	SPECKLES	SPEEDING
SPATFALL	SPAWNERS	SPEARIEST	SPECKLESS	SPEEDINGS
SPATFALLS	SPAWNIER	SPEARING	SPECKLING	SPEEDLESS
SPATHAL	SPAWNIEST	SPEARINGS	SPECKS	SPEEDO
SPATHE	SPAWNING	SPEARLIKE	SPECKY	SPEEDOS
SPATHED	SPAWNINGS	SPEARMAN	SPECS	SPEEDREAD
SPATHES	SPAWNS	SPEARMEN	SPECT	SPEEDS
SPATHIC	SPAWNY	SPEARMINT	SPECTACLE	SPEEDSTER
SPATHOSE	SPAWS	SPEARS	SPECTATE	SPEEDUP
SPATIAL	SPAY	SPEARWORT	SPECTATED	SPEEDUPS
SPATIALLY	SPAYAD	SPEARY	SPECTATES	SPEEDWALK
SPATLESE	SPAYADS	SPEAT	SPECTATOR	SPEEDWAY
SPATLESEN	SPAYD	SPEATS	SPECTED	SPEEDWAYS
SPATLESES	SPAYDS	SPEC	SPECTER	SPEEDWELL

S

SPEEDY	SPELLABLE	SPERMATIA	SPHAGNUM	SPICAS
SPEEL	SPELLBIND	SPERMATIC	SPHAGNUMS	SPICATE
SPEELED	SPELLDOWN	SPERMATID	SPHAIREE	SPICATED
SPEELER	SPELLED	SPERMIC	SPHAIREES	SPICCATO
SPEELERS	SPELLER	SPERMINE	SPHEAR	SPICCATOS
SPEELING	SPELLERS	SPERMINES	SPHEARE	SPICE
SPEELS	SPELLFUL	SPERMOUS	SPHEARES	SPICEBUSH
SPEER	SPELLICAN	SPERMS	SPHEARS	SPICED
SPEERED	SPELLING	SPERRE	SPHENDONE	SPICELESS
SPEERING	SPELLINGS	SPERRED	SPHENE	SPICER
SPEERINGS	SPELLS	SPERRES	SPHENES	SPICERIES
SPEERS	SPELT	SPERRING	SPHENIC	SPICERS
SPEIL	SPELTER	SPERSE	SPHENODON	SPICERY
SPEILED	SPELTERS	SPERSED	SPHENOID	SPICES
SPEILING	SPELTS	SPERSES	SPHENOIDS	SPICEY
SPEILS	SPELTZ	SPERSING	SPHERAL	SPICIER
SPEIR	SPELTZES	SPERST	SPHERE	SPICIEST
SPEIRED	SPELUNK	SPERTHE	SPHERED	SPICILEGE
SPEIRING	SPELUNKED	SPERTHES	SPHERES	SPICILY
SPEIRINGS	SPELUNKER	SPET	SPHERIC	SPICINESS
SPEIRS	SPELUNKS	SPETCH	SPHERICAL	SPICING
SPEISE	SPENCE	SPETCHED	SPHERICS	SPICK
SPEISES	SPENCER	SPETCHES	SPHERIER	SPICKER
SPEISS	SPENCERS	SPETCHING	SPHERIEST	SPICKEST
SPEISSES	SPENCES	SPETS	SPHERING	SPICKNEL
SPEK	SPEND	SPETSNAZ	SPHEROID	SPICKNELS
SPEKBOOM	SPENDABLE	SPETTING	SPHEROIDS	SPICKS
SPEKBOOMS	SPENDALL	SPETZNAZ	SPHERULAR	SPICS
SPEKS	SPENDALLS	SPEUG	SPHERULE	SPICULA
SPELAEAN	SPENDER	SPEUGS	SPHERULES	SPICULAE
SPELD	SPENDERS	SPEW	SPHERY	SPICULAR
SPELDED	SPENDIER	SPEWED	SPHINCTER	SPICULATE
SPELDER	SPENDIEST	SPEWER	SPHINGES	SPICULE
SPELDERED	SPENDING	SPEWERS	SPHINGID	SPICULES
SPELDERS	SPENDINGS	SPEWIER	SPHINGIDS	SPICULUM
SPELDIN	SPENDS	SPEWIEST	SPHINX	SPICY
SPELDING	SPENDY	SPEWINESS	SPHINXES	SPIDE
SPELDINGS	SPENSE	SPEWING	SPHYGMIC	SPIDER
SPELDINS	SPENSES	SPEWS	SPHYGMOID	SPIDERED
SPELDRIN	SPENT	SPEWY	SPHYGMUS	SPIDERIER
SPELDRING	SPEOS	SPHACELUS	SPHYNX	SPIDERING
SPELDRINS	SPEOSES	SPHAER	SPHYNXES	SPIDERISH
SPELDS	SPERLING	SPHAERE	SPIAL	SPIDERMAN
SPELEAN	SPERLINGS	SPHAERES	SPIALS	SPIDERMEN
SPELK	SPERM	SPHAERITE	SPIC	SPIDERS
SPELKS	SPERMARIA	SPHAERS	SPICA	SPIDERWEB
SPELL	SPERMARY	SPHAGNOUS	SPICAE	SPIDERY

SPIDES	SPIKERS	SPINACENE	SPINNER	SPIRAEAS
SPIE	SPIKERY	SPINACH	SPINNERET	SPIRAL
SPIED	SPIKES	SPINACHES	SPINNERS	SPIRALED
SPIEGEL	SPIKEY	SPINACHY	SPINNERY	SPIRALING
SPIEGELS	SPIKIER	SPINAE	SPINNET	SPIRALISM
SPIEL	SPIKIEST	SPINAGE	SPINNETS	SPIRALIST
SPIELED	SPIKILY	SPINAGES	SPINNEY	SPIRALITY
SPIELER	SPIKINESS	SPINAL	SPINNEYS	SPIRALLED
SPIELERS	SPIKING	SPINALLY	SPINNIER	SPIRALLY
SPIELING	SPIKS	SPINALS	SPINNIES	SPIRALS
SPIELS	SPIKY	SPINAR	SPINNIEST	SPIRANT
SPIER	SPILE	SPINARS	SPINNING	SPIRANTS
SPIERED	SPILED	SPINAS	SPINNINGS	SPIRASTER
SPIERING	SPILES	SPINATE	SPINNY	SPIRATED
SPIERS	SPILIKIN	SPINDLE	SPINODE	SPIRATION
SPIES	SPILIKINS	SPINDLED	SPINODES	SPIRE
SPIF	SPILING	SPINDLER	SPINOFF	SPIREA
SPIFF	SPILINGS	SPINDLERS	SPINOFFS	SPIREAS
SPIFFED	SPILITE	SPINDLES	SPINONE	SPIRED
SPIFFIED	SPILITES	SPINDLIER	SPINONI	SPIRELESS
SPIFFIER	SPILITIC	SPINDLING	SPINOR	SPIRELET
SPIFFIES	SPILL	SPINDLY	SPINORS	SPIRELETS
SPIFFIEST	SPILLABLE	SPINDRIFT	SPINOSE	SPIREM
SPIFFILY	SPILLAGE	SPINE	SPINOSELY	SPIREME
SPIFFING	SPILLAGES	SPINED	SPINOSITY	SPIREMES
SPIFFS	SPILLED	SPINEL	SPINOUS	SPIREMS
SPIFFY	SPILLER	SPINELESS	SPINOUT	SPIRES
SPIFFYING	SPILLERS	SPINELIKE	SPINOUTS	SPIREWISE
SPIFS	SPILLIKIN	SPINELLE	SPINS	SPIRIC
SPIGHT	SPILLING	SPINELLES	SPINSTER	SPIRICS
SPIGHTED	SPILLINGS	SPINELS	SPINSTERS	SPIRIER
SPIGHTING	SPILLOVER	SPINES	SPINTEXT	SPIRIEST
SPIGHTS	SPILLS	SPINET	SPINTEXTS	SPIRILLA
SPIGNEL	SPILLWAY	SPINETS	SPINTO	SPIRILLAR
SPIGNELS	SPILLWAYS	SPINETTE	SPINTOS	SPIRILLUM
SPIGOT	SPILOSITE	SPINETTES	SPINULA	SPIRING
SPIGOTS	SPILT	SPINIER	SPINULAE	SPIRIT
SPIK	SPILTH	SPINIEST	SPINULATE	SPIRITED
SPIKE	SPILTHS	SPINIFEX	SPINULE	SPIRITFUL
SPIKED	SPIM	SPINIFORM	SPINULES	SPIRITING
SPIKEFISH	SPIMMER	SPININESS	SPINULOSE	SPIRITISM
SPIKELET	SPIMMERS	SPINK	SPINULOUS	SPIRITIST
SPIKELETS	SPIMMING	SPINKED	SPINY	SPIRITOSO
SPIKELIKE	SPIMMINGS	SPINKING	SPIRACLE	SPIRITOUS
SPIKENARD	SPIMS	SPINKS	SPIRACLES	SPIRITS
SPIKER	SPIN	SPINLESS	SPIRACULA	SPIRITUAL
SPIKERIES	SPINA	SPINNAKER	SPIRAEA	SPIRITUEL

S

SPIRITUS	SPITTY	SPLENETIC	SPLODGIER	SPOFFISH
SPIRITY	SPITZ	SPLENIA	SPLODGILY	SPOFFY
SPIRLING	SPITZES	SPLENIAL	SPLODGING	SPOIL
SPIRLINGS	SPIV	SPLENIC	SPLODGY	SPOILABLE
SPIROGRAM	SPIVS	SPLENII	SPLOG	SPOILAGE
SPIROGYRA	SPIVVERY	SPLENITIS	SPLOGS	SPOILAGES
SPIROID	SPIVVIER	SPLENIUM	SPLOOSH	SPOILED
SPIRT	SPIVVIEST	SPLENIUMS	SPLOOSHED	SPOILER
SPIRTED	SPIVVISH	SPLENIUS	SPLOOSHES	SPOILERS
SPIRTING	SPIVVY	SPLENT	SPLORE	SPOILFIVE
SPIRTLE	SPLAKE	SPLENTS	SPLORES	SPOILFUL
SPIRTLES	SPLAKES	SPLEUCHAN	SPLOSH	SPOILING
SPIRTS	SPLASH	SPLICE	SPLOSHED	SPOILS
SPIRULA	SPLASHED	SPLICED	SPLOSHES	SPOILSMAN
SPIRULAE	SPLASHER	SPLICER	SPLOSHING	SPOILSMEN
SPIRULAS	SPLASHERS	SPLICERS	SPLOTCH	SPOILT
SPIRULINA	SPLASHES	SPLICES	SPLOTCHED	SPOKE
SPIRY	SPLASHIER	SPLICING	SPLOTCHES	SPOKED
SPIT	SPLASHILY	SPLICINGS	SPLOTCHY	SPOKEN
SPITAL	SPLASHING	SPLIFF	SPLURGE	SPOKES
SPITALS	SPLASHY	SPLIFFS	SPLURGED	SPOKESMAN
SPITBALL	SPLAT	SPLINE	SPLURGER	SPOKESMEN
SPITBALLS	SPLATCH	SPLINED	SPLURGERS	SPOKEWISE
SPITCHER	SPLATCHED	SPLINES	SPLURGES	SPOKING
SPITCHERS	SPLATCHES	SPLINING	SPLURGIER	SPOLIATE
SPITE	SPLATS	SPLINT	SPLURGING	SPOLIATED
SPITED	SPLATTED	SPLINTED	SPLURGY	SPOLIATES
SPITEFUL	SPLATTER	SPLINTER	SPLURT	SPOLIATOR
SPITES	SPLATTERS	SPLINTERS	SPLURTED	SPONDAIC
SPITFIRE	SPLATTING	SPLINTERY	SPLURTING	SPONDAICS
SPITFIRES	SPLAY	SPLINTING	SPLURTS	SPONDEE
SPITING	SPLAYED	SPLINTS	SPLUTTER	SPONDEES
SPITS	SPLAYFEET	SPLISH	SPLUTTERS	SPONDULIX
SPITTED	SPLAYFOOT	SPLISHED	SPLUTTERY	SPONDYL
SPITTEN	SPLAYING	SPLISHES	SPOD	SPONDYLS
SPITTER	SPLAYS	SPLISHING	SPODDIER	SPONGE
SPITTERS	SPLEEN	SPLIT	SPODDIEST	SPONGEBAG
SPITTIER	SPLEENFUL	SPLITS	SPODDY	SPONGED
SPITTIEST	SPLEENIER	SPLITTED	SPODE	SPONGEING
SPITTING	SPLEENISH	SPLITTER	SPODES	SPONGEOUS
SPITTINGS	SPLEENS	SPLITTERS	SPODIUM	SPONGER
SPITTLE	SPLEENY	SPLITTING	SPODIUMS	SPONGERS
SPITTLES	SPLENDENT	SPLITTISM	SPODOGRAM	SPONGES
SPITTLIER	SPLENDID	SPLITTIST	SPODOSOL	SPONGIER
SPITTLY	SPLENDOR	SPLODGE	SPODOSOLS	SPONGIEST
SPITTOON	SPLENDORS	SPLODGED	SPODS	SPONGILY
SPITTOONS	SPLENDOUR	SPLODGES	SPODUMENE	SPONGIN

SPONGING	SPOOLS	SPORING	SPOT	SPRAGGING
SPONGINS	SPOOM	SPORK	SPOTLESS	SPRAGS
SPONGIOSE	SPOOMED	SPORKS	SPOTLIGHT	SPRAID
SPONGIOUS	SPOOMING	SPOROCARP	SPOTLIT	SPRAIN
SPONGOID	SPOOMS	SPOROCYST	SPOTS	SPRAINED
SPONGY	SPOON	SPOROCYTE	SPOTTABLE	SPRAINING
SPONSAL	SPOONBAIT	SPOROGENY	SPOTTED	SPRAINS
SPONSALIA	SPOONBILL	SPOROGONY	SPOTTER	SPRAINT
SPONSIBLE	SPOONED	SPOROID	SPOTTERS	SPRAINTS
SPONSING	SPOONER	SPOROPHYL	SPOTTIE	SPRANG
SPONSINGS	SPOONERS	SPOROZOA	SPOTTIER	SPRANGLE
SPONSION	SPOONEY	SPOROZOAL	SPOTTIES	SPRANGLED
SPONSIONS	SPOONEYS	SPOROZOAN	SPOTTIEST	SPRANGLES
SPONSON	SPOONFED	SPOROZOIC	SPOTTILY	SPRANGS
SPONSONS	SPOONFUL	SPOROZOON	SPOTTING	SPRAT
SPONSOR	SPOONFULS	SPORRAN	SPOTTINGS	SPRATS
SPONSORED	SPOONHOOK	SPORRANS	SPOTTY	SPRATTLE
SPONSORS	SPOONIER	SPORT	SPOUSAGE	SPRATTLED
SPONTOON	SPOONIES	SPORTABLE	SPOUSAGES	SPRATTLES
SPONTOONS	SPOONIEST	SPORTANCE	SPOUSAL	SPRAUCHLE
SPOOF	SPOONILY	SPORTBIKE	SPOUSALLY	SPRAUNCY
SPOOFED	SPOONING	SPORTED	SPOUSALS	SPRAWL
SPOOFER	SPOONS	SPORTER	SPOUSE	SPRAWLED
SPOOFERS	SPOONSFUL	SPORTERS	SPOUSED	SPRAWLER
SPOOFERY	SPOONWAYS	SPORTFUL	SPOUSES	SPRAWLERS
SPOOFIER	SPOONWISE	SPORTIER	SPOUSING	SPRAWLIER
SPOOFIEST	SPOONWORM	SPORTIES	SPOUT	SPRAWLING
SPOOFING	SPOONY	SPORTIEST	SPOUTED	SPRAWLS
SPOOFINGS	SPOOR	SPORTIF	SPOUTER	SPRAWLY
SPOOFS	SPOORED	SPORTIFS	SPOUTERS	SPRAY
SPOOFY	SPOORER	SPORTILY	SPOUTIER	SPRAYED
SPOOK	SPOORERS	SPORTING	SPOUTIEST	SPRAYER
SPOOKED	SPOORING	SPORTIVE	SPOUTING	SPRAYERS
SPOOKERY	SPOORS	SPORTLESS	SPOUTINGS	SPRAYEY
SPOOKIER	SPOOT	SPORTS	SPOUTLESS	SPRAYIER
SPOOKIEST	SPOOTS	SPORTSMAN	SPOUTS	SPRAYIEST
SPOOKILY	SPORADIC	SPORTSMEN	SPOUTY	SPRAYING
SPOOKING	SPORAL	SPORTY	SPRACK	SPRAYINGS
SPOOKISH	SPORANGIA	SPORULAR	SPRACKLE	SPRAYS
SPOOKS	SPORE	SPORULATE	SPRACKLED	SPREAD
SPOOKY	SPORED	SPORULE	SPRACKLES	SPREADER
SPOOL	SPORES	SPORULES	SPRAD	SPREADERS
SPOOLED	SPORICIDE	SPOSH	SPRADDLE	SPREADING
SPOOLER	SPORIDESM	SPOSHES	SPRADDLED	SPREADS
SPOOLERS	SPORIDIA	SPOSHIER	SPRADDLES	SPREAGH
SPOOLING	SPORIDIAL	SPOSHIEST	SPRAG	SPREAGHS
SPOOLINGS	SPORIDIUM	SPOSHY	SPRAGGED	SPREATHE

SPREATHED	SPRIGS	SPROCKET	SPUDDER	SPUMONES
SPREATHES	SPRIGTAIL	SPROCKETS	SPUDDERS	SPUMONI
SPREAZE	SPRING	SPROD	SPUDDIER	SPUMONIS
SPREAZED	SPRINGAL	SPRODS	SPUDDIEST	SPUMOUS
SPREAZES	SPRINGALD	SPROG	SPUDDING	SPUMY
SPREAZING	SPRINGALS	SPROGLET	SPUDDINGS	SPUN
SPRECHERY	SPRINGBOK	SPROGLETS	SPUDDLE	SPUNGE
SPRECKLED	SPRINGE	SPROGS	SPUDDLES	SPUNGES
SPRED	SPRINGED	SPRONG	SPUDDY	SPUNK
SPREDD	SPRINGER	SPROUT	SPUDGEL	SPUNKED
SPREDDE	SPRINGERS	SPROUTED	SPUDGELS	SPUNKIE
SPREDDEN	SPRINGES	SPROUTING	SPUDS	SPUNKIER
SPREDDES	SPRINGIER	SPROUTS	SPUE	SPUNKIES
SPREDDING	SPRINGILY	SPRUCE	SPUED	SPUNKIEST
SPREDDS	SPRINGING	SPRUCED	SPUEING	SPUNKILY
SPREDS	SPRINGLE	SPRUCELY	SPUER	SPUNKING
SPREE	SPRINGLES	SPRUCER	SPUERS	SPUNKS
SPREED	SPRINGLET	SPRUCES	SPUES	SPUNKY
SPREEING	SPRINGS	SPRUCEST	SPUG	SPUNYARN
SPREES	SPRINGY	SPRUCIER	SPUGGIES	SPUNYARNS
SPREETHE	SPRINKLE	SPRUCIEST	SPUGGY	SPUR
SPREETHED	SPRINKLED	SPRUCING	SPUGS	SPURDOG
SPREETHES	SPRINKLER	SPRUCY	SPUILZIE	SPURDOGS
SPREEZE	SPRINKLES	SPRUE	SPUILZIED	SPURGALL
SPREEZED	SPRINT	SPRUES	SPUILZIES	SPURGALLS
SPREEZES	SPRINTED	SPRUG	SPUING	SPURGE
SPREEZING	SPRINTER	SPRUGS	SPULE	SPURGES
SPREKELIA	SPRINTERS	SPRUIK	SPULES	SPURIAE
SPRENT	SPRINTING	SPRUIKED	SPULYE	SPURIOUS
SPRENTED	SPRINTS	SPRUIKER	SPULYED	SPURLESS
SPRENTING	SPRIT	SPRUIKERS	SPULYEING	SPURLING
SPRENTS	SPRITE	SPRUIKING	SPULYES	SPURLINGS
SPREW	SPRITEFUL	SPRUIKS	SPULYIE	SPURN
SPREWS	SPRITELY	SPRUIT	SPULYIED	SPURNE
SPRIER	SPRITES	SPRUITS	SPULYIES	SPURNED
SPRIEST	SPRITS	SPRUNG	SPULZIE	SPURNER
SPRIG	SPRITSAIL	SPRUSH	SPULZIED	SPURNERS
SPRIGGED	SPRITZ	SPRUSHED	SPULZIES	SPURNES
SPRIGGER	SPRITZED	SPRUSHES	SPUMANTE	SPURNING
SPRIGGERS	SPRITZER	SPRUSHING	SPUMANTES	SPURNINGS
SPRIGGIER	SPRITZERS	SPRY	SPUME	SPURNS
SPRIGGING	SPRITZES	SPRYER	SPUMED	SPURRED
SPRIGGY	SPRITZIER	SPRYEST	SPUMES	SPURRER
SPRIGHT	SPRITZIG	SPRYLY	SPUMIER	SPURRERS
SPRIGHTED	SPRITZIGS	SPRYNESS	SPUMIEST	SPURREY
SPRIGHTLY	SPRITZING	SPUD	SPUMING	SPURREYS
SPRIGHTS	SPRITZY	SPUDDED	SPUMONE	SPURRIER

SPURRIERS	SQUABBEST	SQUAMAE	SQUATTERS	SQUEEZERS
SPURRIES	SQUABBIER	SQUAMATE	SQUATTEST	SQUEEZES
SPURRIEST	SQUABBING	SQUAMATES	SQUATTIER	SQUEEZIER
SPURRING	SQUABBISH	SQUAME	SQUATTILY	SQUEEZING
SPURRINGS	SQUABBLE	SQUAMELLA	SQUATTING	SQUEEZY
SPURRY	SQUABBLED	SQUAMES	SQUATTLE	SQUEG
SPURS	SQUABBLER	SQUAMOSAL	SQUATTLED	SQUEGGED
SPURT	SQUABBLES	SQUAMOSE	SQUATTLES	SQUEGGER
SPURTED	SQUABBY	SQUAMOUS	SQUATTY	SQUEGGERS
SPURTER	SQUABS	SQUAMULA	SQUAW	SQUEGGING
SPURTERS	SQUACCO	SQUAMULAS	SQUAWBUSH	SQUEGS
SPURTING	SQUACCOS	SQUAMULE	SQUAWFISH	SQUELCH
SPURTLE	SQUAD	SQUAMULES	SQUAWK	SQUELCHED
SPURTLES	SQUADDED	SQUANDER	SQUAWKED	SQUELCHER
SPURTS	SQUADDIE	SQUANDERS	SQUAWKER	SQUELCHES
SPURWAY	SQUADDIES	SQUARE	SQUAWKERS	SQUELCHY
SPURWAYS	SQUADDING	SQUARED	SQUAWKIER	SQUIB
SPUTA	SQUADDY	SQUARELY	SQUAWKING	SQUIBBED
SPUTNIK	SQUADOOSH	SQUARER	SQUAWKS	SQUIBBER
SPUTNIKS	SQUADRON	SQUARERS	SQUAWKY	SQUIBBERS
SPUTTER	SQUADRONE	SQUARES	SQUAWMAN	SQUIBBING
SPUTTERED	SQUADRONS	SQUAREST	SQUAWMEN	SQUIBS
SPUTTERER	SQUADS	SQUARIAL	SQUAWROOT	SQUID
SPUTTERS	SQUAIL	SQUARIALS	SQUAWS	SQUIDDED
SPUTTERY	SQUAILED	SQUARING	SQUEAK	SQUIDDING
SPUTUM	SQUAILER	SQUARINGS	SQUEAKED	SQUIDGE
SPY	SQUAILERS	SQUARISH	SQUEAKER	SQUIDGED
SPYAL	SQUAILING	SQUARK	SQUEAKERS	SQUIDGES
SPYALS	SQUAILS	SQUARKS	SQUEAKERY	SQUIDGIER
SPYCAM	SQUALENE	SQUARROSE	SQUEAKIER	SQUIDGING
SPYCAMS	SQUALENES	SQUARSON	SQUEAKILY	SQUIDGY
SPYGLASS	SQUALID	SQUARSONS	SQUEAKING	SQUIDS
SPYHOLE	SQUALIDER	SQUASH	SQUEAKS	SQUIER
SPYHOLES	SQUALIDLY	SQUASHED	SQUEAKY	SQUIERS
SPYING	SQUALL	SQUASHER	SQUEAL	SQUIFF
SPYINGS	SQUALLED	SQUASHERS	SQUEALED	SQUIFFED
SPYMASTER	SQUALLER	SQUASHES	SQUEALER	SQUIFFER
SPYPLANE	SQUALLERS	SQUASHIER	SQUEALERS	SQUIFFERS
SPYPLANES	SQUALLIER	SQUASHILY	SQUEALING	SQUIFFIER
SPYRE	SQUALLING	SQUASHING	SQUEALS	SQUIFFY
SPYRES	SQUALLISH	SQUASHY	SQUEAMISH	SQUIGGLE
SPYWARE	SQUALLS	SQUAT	SQUEEGEE	SQUIGGLED
SPYWARES	SQUALLY	SQUATLY	SQUEEGEED	SQUIGGLER
SQUAB	SQUALOID	SQUATNESS	SQUEEGEES	SQUIGGLES
SQUABASH	SQUALOR	SQUATS	SQUEEZE	SQUIGGLY
SQUABBED	SQUALORS	SQUATTED	SQUEEZED	SQUILGEE
SQUABBER	SQUAMA	SQUATTER	SQUEEZER	SQUILGEED

S

SQUILGEES	SQUIRMER	STAB	STACTE	STAGGER
SQUILL	SQUIRMERS	STABBED	STACTES	STAGGERED
SQUILLA	SQUIRMIER	STABBER	STADDA	STAGGERER
SQUILLAE	SQUIRMING	STABBERS	STADDAS	STAGGERS
SQUILLAS	SQUIRMS	STABBING	STADDLE	STAGGERY
SQUILLION	SQUIRMY	STABBINGS	STADDLES	STAGGIE
SQUILLS	SQUIRR	STABILATE	STADE	STAGGIER
SQUINANCY	SQUIRRED	STABILE	STADES	STAGGIES
SQUINCH	SQUIRREL	STABILES	STADIA	STAGGIEST
SQUINCHED	SQUIRRELS	STABILISE	STADIAL	STAGGING
SQUINCHES	SQUIRRELY	STABILITY	STADIALS	STAGGY
SQUINIED	SQUIRRING	STABILIZE	STADIAS	STAGHORN
SQUINIES	SQUIRRS	STABLE	STADIUM	STAGHORNS
SQUINNIED	SQUIRT	STABLEBOY	STADIUMS	STAGHOUND
SQUINNIER	SQUIRTED	STABLED	STAFF	STAGIER
SQUINNIES	SQUIRTER	STABLEMAN	STAFFAGE	STAGIEST
SQUINNY	SQUIRTERS	STABLEMEN	STAFFAGES	STAGILY
SQUINT	SQUIRTING	STABLER	STAFFED	STAGINESS
SQUINTED	SQUIRTS	STABLERS	STAFFER	STAGING
SQUINTER	SQUISH	STABLES	STAFFERS	STAGINGS
SQUINTERS	SQUISHED	STABLEST	STAFFING	STAGNANCE
SQUINTEST	SQUISHES	STABLING	STAFFINGS	STAGNANCY
SQUINTIER	SQUISHIER	STABLINGS	STAFFMAN	STAGNANT
SQUINTING	SQUISHING	STABLISH	STAFFMEN	STAGNATE
SQUINTS	SQUISHY	STABLY	STAFFROOM	STAGNATED
SQUINTY	SQUIT	STABS	STAFFS	STAGNATES
SQUINY	SQUITCH	STACATION	STAG	STAGS
SQUINYING	SQUITCHES	STACCATI	STAGE	STAGY
SQUIRAGE	SQUITS	STACCATO	STAGEABLE	STAID
SQUIRAGES	SQUITTERS	STACCATOS	STAGED	STAIDER
SQUIRALTY	SQUIZ	STACHYS	STAGEFUL	STAIDEST
SQUIRARCH	SQUIZZES	STACHYSES	STAGEFULS	STAIDLY
SQUIRE	SQUOOSH	STACK	STAGEHAND	STAIDNESS
SQUIREAGE	SQUOOSHED	STACKABLE	STAGELIKE	STAIG
SQUIRED	SQUOOSHES	STACKED	STAGER	STAIGS
SQUIREDOM	SQUOOSHY	STACKER	STAGERIES	STAIN
SQUIREEN	SQUUSH	STACKERS	STAGERS	STAINABLE
SQUIREENS	SQUUSHED	STACKET	STAGERY	STAINED
SQUIRELY	SQUUSHES	STACKETS	STAGES	STAINER
SQUIRES	SQUUSHING	STACKING	STAGETTE	STAINERS
SQUIRESS	SRADDHA	STACKINGS	STAGETTES	STAINING
SQUIRING	SRADDHAS	STACKLESS	STAGEY	STAININGS
SQUIRISH	SRADHA	STACKROOM	STAGGARD	STAINLESS
SQUIRL	SRADHAS	STACKS	STAGGARDS	STAINS
SQUIRLS	SRI	STACKUP	STAGGART	STAIR
SQUIRM	SRIS	STACKUPS	STAGGARTS	STAIRCASE
SQUIRMED	ST	STACKYARD	STAGGED	STAIRED

STAIRFOOT	STALKLESS	STAMPEDOS	STANDUPS	STAPEDII
STAIRHEAD	STALKLIKE	STAMPER	STANE	STAPEDIUS
STAIRLESS	STALKO	STAMPERS	STANED	STAPELIA
STAIRLIFT	STALKOES	STAMPING	STANES	STAPELIAS
STAIRLIKE	STALKOS	STAMPINGS	STANG	STAPES
STAIRS	STALKS	STAMPLESS	STANGED	STAPH
STAIRSTEP	STALKY	STAMPS	STANGING	STAPHS
STAIRWAY	STALL	STANCE	STANGS	STAPLE
STAIRWAYS	STALLAGE	STANCES	STANHOPE	STAPLED
STAIRWELL	STALLAGES	STANCH	STANHOPES	STAPLER
STAIRWISE	STALLED	STANCHED	STANIEL	STAPLERS
STAIRWORK	STALLING	STANCHEL	STANIELS	STAPLES
STAITH	STALLINGS	STANCHELS	STANINE	STAPLING
STAITHE	STALLION	STANCHER	STANINES	STAPLINGS
STAITHES	STALLIONS	STANCHERS	STANING	STAPPED
STAITHS	STALLMAN	STANCHES	STANK	STAPPING
STAKE	STALLMEN	STANCHEST	STANKED	STAPPLE
STAKED	STALLS	STANCHING	STANKING	STAPPLES
STAKEOUT	STALWART	STANCHION	STANKS	STAPS
STAKEOUTS	STALWARTS	STANCHLY	STANNARY	STAR
STAKER	STALWORTH	STANCK	STANNATE	STARAGEN
STAKERS	STAMEN	STAND	STANNATES	STARAGENS
STAKES	STAMENED	STANDARD	STANNATOR	STARBOARD
STAKING	STAMENS	STANDARDS	STANNEL	STARBURST
STALACTIC	STAMINA	STANDAWAY	STANNELS	STARCH
STALAG	STAMINAL	STANDBY	STANNIC	STARCHED
STALAGMA	STAMINAS	STANDBYS	STANNITE	STARCHER
STALAGMAS	STAMINATE	STANDDOWN	STANNITES	STARCHERS
STALAGS	STAMINEAL	STANDEE	STANNOUS	STARCHES
STALE	STAMINODE	STANDEES	STANNUM	STARCHIER
STALED	STAMINODY	STANDEN	STANNUMS	STARCHILY
STALELY	STAMINOID	STANDER	STANOL	STARCHING
STALEMATE	STAMMEL	STANDERS	STANOLS	STARCHY
STALENESS	STAMMELS	STANDFAST	STANYEL	STARDOM
STALER	STAMMER	STANDGALE	STANYELS	STARDOMS
STALES	STAMMERED	STANDING	STANZA	STARDRIFT
STALEST	STAMMERER	STANDINGS	STANZAED	STARDUST
STALING	STAMMERS	STANDISH	STANZAIC	STARDUSTS
STALK	STAMNOI	STANDOFF	STANZAS	STARE
STALKED	STAMNOS	STANDOFFS	STANZE	STARED
STALKER	STAMP	STANDOUT	STANZES	STARER
STALKERS	STAMPED	STANDOUTS	STANZO	STARERS
STALKIER	STAMPEDE	STANDOVER	STANZOES	STARES
STALKIEST	STAMPEDED	STANDPAT	STANZOS	STARETS
STALKILY	STAMPEDER	STANDPIPE	STAP	STARETSES
STALKING	STAMPEDES	STANDS	STAPEDES	STARETZ
STALKINGS	STAMPEDO	STANDUP	STAPEDIAL	STARETZES

S

STARFISH	STARRINGS	STASIMA	STATIVE	STAYED
STARFRUIT	STARRS	STASIMON	STATIVES	STAYER
STARGAZE	STARRY	STASIS	STATOCYST	STAYERS
STARGAZED	STARS	STAT	STATOLITH	STAYING
STARGAZER	STARSHINE	STATABLE	STATOR	STAYLESS
STARGAZES	STARSHIP	STATAL	STATORS	STAYMAKER
STARGAZEY	STARSHIPS	STATANT	STATS	STAYNE
STARING	STARSPOT	STATE	STATTO	STAYNED
STARINGLY	STARSPOTS	STATEABLE	STATTOS	STAYNES
STARINGS	STARSTONE	STATED	STATUA	STAYNING
STARK	START	STATEDLY	STATUARY	STAYRE
STARKED	STARTED	STATEHOOD	STATUAS	STAYRES
STARKEN	STARTER	STATELESS	STATUE	STAYS
STARKENED	STARTERS	STATELET	STATUED	STAYSAIL
STARKENS	STARTFUL	STATELETS	STATUES	STAYSAILS
STARKER	STARTING	STATELIER	STATUETTE	STEAD
STARKERS	STARTINGS	STATELILY	STATURE	STEADED
STARKEST	STARTISH	STATELY	STATURED	STEADFAST
STARKING	STARTLE	STATEMENT	STATURES	STEADIED
STARKLY	STARTLED	STATER	STATUS	STEADIER
STARKNESS	STARTLER	STATEROOM	STATUSES	STEADIERS
STARKS	STARTLERS	STATERS	STATUSY	STEADIES
STARLESS	STARTLES	STATES	STATUTE	STEADIEST
STARLET	STARTLING	STATESIDE	STATUTES	STEADILY
STARLETS	STARTLISH	STATESMAN	STATUTORY	STEADING
STARLIGHT	STARTLY	STATESMEN	STAUMREL	STEADINGS
STARLIKE	STARTS	STATEWIDE	STAUMRELS	STEADS
STARLING	STARTSY	STATIC	STAUN	STEADY
STARLINGS	STARTUP	STATICAL	STAUNCH	STEADYING
STARLIT	STARTUPS	STATICE	STAUNCHED	STEAK
STARN	STARVE	STATICES	STAUNCHER	STEAKS
STARNED	STARVED	STATICKY	STAUNCHES	STEAL
STARNIE	STARVER	STATICS	STAUNCHLY	STEALABLE
STARNIES	STARVERS	STATIM	STAUNING	STEALAGE
STARNING	STARVES	STATIN	STAUNS	STEALAGES
STARNOSE	STARVING	STATING	STAVE	STEALE
STARNOSES	STARVINGS	STATINS	STAVED	STEALED
STARNS	STARWORT	STATION	STAVES	STEALER
STAROSTA	STARWORTS	STATIONAL	STAVING	STEALERS
STAROSTAS	STASES	STATIONED	STAVUDINE	STEALES
STAROSTY	STASH	STATIONER	STAW	STEALING
STARR	STASHED	STATIONS	STAWED	STEALINGS
STARRED	STASHES	STATISM	STAWING	STEALS
STARRIER	STASHIE	STATISMS	STAWS	STEALT
STARRIEST	STASHIES	STATIST	STAY	STEALTH
STARRILY	STASHING	STATISTIC	STAYAWAY	STEALTHED
STARRING	STASIDION	STATISTS	STAYAWAYS	STEALTHS

S

STEALTHY	STEATITES	STEELING	STEERAGE	STELENE
STEAM	STEATITIC	STEELINGS	STEERAGES	STELES
STEAMBOAT	STEATOMA	STEELMAN	STEERED	STELIC
STEAMED	STEATOMAS	STEELMEN	STEERER	STELL
STEAMER	STEATOSES	STEELS	STEERERS	STELLA
STEAMERED	STEATOSIS	STEELWARE	STEERIER	STELLAR
STEAMERS	STED	STEELWORK	STEERIES	STELLAS
STEAMIE	STEDD	STEELY	STEERIEST	STELLATE
STEAMIER	STEDDE	STEELYARD	STEERING	STELLATED
STEAMIES	STEDDED	STEEM	STEERINGS	STELLED
STEAMIEST	STEDDES	STEEMED	STEERLING	STELLERID
STEAMILY	STEDDIED	STEEMING	STEERS	STELLIFY
STEAMING	STEDDIES	STEEMS	STEERSMAN	STELLING
STEAMINGS	STEDDING	STEEN	STEERSMEN	STELLIO
STEAMPUNK	STEDDS	STEENBOK	STEERY	STELLION
STEAMROLL	STEDDY	STEENBOKS	STEEVE	STELLIONS
STEAMS	STEDDYING	STEENBRAS	STEEVED	STELLITE
STEAMSHIP	STEDE	STEENBUCK	STEEVELY	STELLITES
STEAMY	STEDED	STEENED	STEEVER	STELLS
STEAN	STEDES	STEENING	STEEVES	STELLULAR
STEANE	STEDFAST	STEENINGS	STEEVEST	STEM
STEANED	STEDING	STEENKIRK	STEEVING	STEMBOK
STEANES	STEDS	STEENS	STEEVINGS	STEMBOKS
STEANING	STEED	STEEP	STEGNOSES	STEMBUCK
STEANINGS	STEEDED	STEEPED	STEGNOSIS	STEMBUCKS
STEANS	STEEDIED	STEEPEN	STEGNOTIC	STEME
STEAPSIN	STEEDIES	STEEPENED	STEGODON	STEMED
STEAPSINS	STEEDING	STEEPENS	STEGODONS	STEMES
STEAR	STEEDLIKE	STEEPER	STEGODONT	STEMHEAD
STEARAGE	STEEDS	STEEPERS	STEGOMYIA	STEMHEADS
STEARAGES	STEEDY	STEEPEST	STEGOSAUR	STEMING
STEARATE	STEEDYING	STEEPEUP	STEIL	STEMLESS
STEARATES	STEEK	STEEPIER	STEILS	STEMLET
STEARD	STEEKED	STEEPIEST	STEIN	STEMLETS
STEARE	STEEKING	STEEPING	STEINBOCK	STEMLIKE
STEARED	STEEKIT	STEEPISH	STEINBOK	STEMMA
STEARES	STEEKS	STEEPLE	STEINBOKS	STEMMAS
STEARIC	STEEL	STEEPLED	STEINED	STEMMATA
STEARIN	STEELBOW	STEEPLES	STEINING	STEMMATIC
STEARINE	STEELBOWS	STEEPLING	STEININGS	STEMME
STEARINES	STEELD	STEEPLY	STEINKIRK	STEMMED
STEARING	STEELED	STEEPNESS	STEINS	STEMMER
STEARINS	STEELHEAD	STEEPS	STELA	STEMMERS
STEARS	STEELIE	STEEPUP	STELAE	STEMMERY
STEARSMAN	STEELIER	STEEPY	STELAI	STEMMES
STEARSMEN	STEELIES	STEER	STELAR	STEMMIER
STEATITE	STEELIEST	STEERABLE	STELE	STEMMIEST

S

STEMMING	STENOTYPY	STEREOING	STEROIDAL	STEYEST
STEMMINGS	STENS	STEREOME	STEROIDS	STEYS
STEMMY	STENT	STEREOMES	STEROL	STHENIA
STEMPEL	STENTED	STEREOS	STEROLS	STHENIAS
STEMPELS	STENTING	STERES	STERTOR	STHENIC
STEMPLE	STENTOR	STERIC	STERTORS	STIBBLE
STEMPLES	STENTORS	STERICAL	STERVE	STIBBLER
STEMS	STENTOUR	STERIGMA	STERVED	STIBBLERS
STEMSON	STENTOURS	STERIGMAS	STERVES	STIBBLES
STEMSONS	STENTS	STERILANT	STERVING	STIBIAL
STEMWARE	STEP	STERILE	STET	STIBINE
STEMWARES	STEPBAIRN	STERILELY	STETS	STIBINES
STEN	STEPCHILD	STERILISE	STETSON	STIBIUM
STENCH	STEPDAD	STERILITY	STETSONS	STIBIUMS
STENCHED	STEPDADS	STERILIZE	STETTED	STIBNITE
STENCHES	STEPDAME	STERLET	STETTING	STIBNITES
STENCHFUL	STEPDAMES	STERLETS	STEVEDORE	STICCADO
STENCHIER	STEPHANE	STERLING	STEVEN	STICCADOS
STENCHING	STEPHANES	STERLINGS	STEVENS	STICCATO
STENCHY	STEPLESS	STERN	STEVIA	STICCATOS
STENCIL	STEPLIKE	STERNA	STEVIAS	STICH
STENCILED	STEPMOM	STERNAGE	STEW	STICHARIA
STENCILER	STEPMOMS	STERNAGES	STEWABLE	STICHERA
STENCILS	STEPNEY	STERNAL	STEWARD	STICHERON
STEND	STEPNEYS	STERNEBRA	STEWARDED	STICHIC
STENDED	STEPOVER	STERNED	STEWARDRY	STICHIDIA
STENDING	STEPOVERS	STERNER	STEWARDS	STICHOI
STENDS	STEPPE	STERNEST	STEWARTRY	STICHOS
STENGAH	STEPPED	STERNFAST	STEWBUM	STICHS
STENGAHS	STEPPER	STERNING	STEWBUMS	STICK
STENLOCK	STEPPERS	STERNITE	STEWED	STICKABLE
STENLOCKS	STEPPES	STERNITES	STEWER	STICKBALL
STENNED	STEPPING	STERNITIC	STEWERS	STICKED
STENNING	STEPS	STERNLY	STEWIER	STICKER
STENO	STEPSON	STERNMOST	STEWIEST	STICKERED
STENOBATH	STEPSONS	STERNNESS	STEWING	STICKERS
STENOKIES	STEPSTOOL	STERNPORT	STEWINGS	STICKFUL
STENOKOUS	STEPT	STERNPOST	STEWPAN	STICKFULS
STENOKY	STEPWISE	STERNS	STEWPANS	STICKIE
STENOPAIC	STERADIAN	STERNSON	STEWPOND	STICKIED
STENOS	STERANE	STERNSONS	STEWPONDS	STICKIER
STENOSED	STERANES	STERNUM	STEWPOT	STICKIES
STENOSES	STERCORAL	STERNUMS	STEWPOTS	STICKIEST
STENOSING	STERCULIA	STERNWARD	STEWS	STICKILY
STENOSIS	STERE	STERNWAY	STEWY	STICKING
STENOTIC	STEREO	STERNWAYS	STEY	STICKINGS
STENOTYPE	STEREOED	STEROID	STEYER	STICKIT

STICKJAW	STIFFING	STILLION	STINGIER	STIPE
STICKJAWS	STIFFISH	STILLIONS	STINGIES	STIPED
STICKLE	STIFFLY	STILLMAN	STINGIEST	STIPEL
STICKLED	STIFFNESS	STILLMEN	STINGILY	STIPELS
STICKLER	STIFFS	STILLNESS	STINGING	STIPEND
STICKLERS	STIFFWARE	STILLROOM	STINGINGS	STIPENDS
STICKLES	STIFFY	STILLS	STINGLESS	STIPES
STICKLIKE	STIFLE	STILLSON	STINGO	STIPIFORM
STICKLING	STIFLED	STILLSONS	STINGOS	STIPITATE
STICKMAN	STIFLER	STILLY	STINGRAY	STIPITES
STICKMEN	STIFLERS	STILT	STINGRAYS	STIPPLE
STICKOUT	STIFLES	STILTBIRD	STINGS	STIPPLED
STICKOUTS	STIFLING	STILTED	STINGY	STIPPLER
STICKPIN	STIFLINGS	STILTEDLY	STINK	STIPPLERS
STICKPINS	STIGMA	STILTER	STINKARD	STIPPLES
STICKS	STIGMAL	STILTERS	STINKARDS	STIPPLING
STICKSEED	STIGMAS	STILTIER	STINKBIRD	STIPULAR
STICKUM	STIGMATA	STILTIEST	STINKBUG	STIPULARY
STICKUMS	STIGMATIC	STILTING	STINKBUGS	STIPULATE
STICKUP	STIGME	STILTINGS	STINKER	STIPULE
STICKUPS	STIGMES	STILTISH	STINKEROO	STIPULED
STICKWEED	STILB	STILTS	STINKERS	STIPULES
STICKWORK	STILBENE	STILTY	STINKHORN	STIR
STICKY	STILBENES	STIM	STINKIER	STIRABOUT
STICKYING	STILBITE	STIME	STINKIEST	STIRE
STICTION	STILBITES	STIMED	STINKING	STIRED
STICTIONS	STILBS	STIMES	STINKO	STIRES
STIDDIE	STILE	STIMIE	STINKPOT	STIRING
STIDDIED	STILED	STIMIED	STINKPOTS	STIRK
STIDDIES	STILES	STIMIES	STINKS	STIRKS
STIE	STILET	STIMING	STINKWEED	STIRLESS
STIED	STILETS	STIMS	STINKWOOD	STIRP
STIES	STILETTO	STIMULANT	STINKY	STIRPES
STIEVE	STILETTOS	STIMULATE	STINT	STIRPS
STIEVELY	STILING	STIMULI	STINTED	STIRRA
STIEVER	STILL	STIMULUS	STINTEDLY	STIRRABLE
STIEVEST	STILLAGE	STIMY	STINTER	STIRRAH
STIFF	STILLAGES	STIMYING	STINTERS	STIRRAHS
STIFFED	STILLBORN	STING	STINTIER	STIRRAS
STIFFEN	STILLED	STINGAREE	STINTIEST	STIRRE
STIFFENED	STILLER	STINGBULL	STINTING	STIRRED
STIFFENER	STILLERS	STINGE	STINTINGS	STIRRER
STIFFENS	STILLEST	STINGED	STINTLESS	STIRRERS
STIFFER	STILLIER	STINGER	STINTS	STIRRES
STIFFEST	STILLIEST	STINGERS	STINTY	STIRRING
STIFFIE	STILLING	STINGES	STIPA	STIRRINGS
STIFFIES	STILLINGS	STINGFISH	STIPAS	STIRRUP

S

STIRRUPS	STOCKCARS	STOIC	STOMACHER	STONELESS
STIRS	STOCKED	STOICAL	STOMACHIC	STONELIKE
STISHIE	STOCKER	STOICALLY	STOMACHS	STONEN
STISHIES	STOCKERS	STOICISM	STOMACHY	STONER
STITCH	STOCKFISH	STOICISMS	STOMACK	STONERAG
STITCHED	STOCKHORN	STOICS	STOMACKS	STONERAGS
STITCHER	STOCKIER	STOIT	STOMAL	STONERAW
STITCHERS	STOCKIEST	STOITED	STOMAS	STONERAWS
STITCHERY	STOCKILY	STOITER	STOMATA	STONERN
STITCHES	STOCKINET	STOITERED	STOMATAL	STONERS
STITCHING	STOCKING	STOITERS	STOMATE	STONES
STITHIED	STOCKINGS	STOITING	STOMATES	STONESHOT
STITHIES	STOCKISH	STOITS	STOMATIC	STONEWALL
STITHY	STOCKIST	STOKE	STOMATOUS	STONEWARE
STITHYING	STOCKISTS	STOKED	STOMIA	STONEWASH
STIVE	STOCKLESS	STOKEHOLD	STOMIUM	STONEWORK
STIVED	STOCKLIST	STOKEHOLE	STOMIUMS	STONEWORT
STIVER	STOCKLOCK	STOKER	STOMODAEA	STONEY
STIVERS	STOCKMAN	STOKERS	STOMODEA	STONG
STIVES	STOCKMEN	STOKES	STOMODEAL	STONIED
STIVIER	STOCKPILE	STOKESIA	STOMODEUM	STONIER
STIVIEST	STOCKPOT	STOKESIAS	STOMP	STONIES
STIVING	STOCKPOTS	STOKING	STOMPED	STONIEST
STIVY	STOCKROOM	STOKVEL	STOMPER	STONILY
STOA	STOCKS	STOKVELS	STOMPERS	STONINESS
STOAE	STOCKTAKE	STOLE	STOMPIE	STONING
STOAI	STOCKTOOK	STOLED	STOMPIER	STONINGS
STOAS	STOCKWORK	STOLEN	STOMPIES	STONISH
STOAT	STOCKY	STOLES	STOMPIEST	STONISHED
STOATS	STOCKYARD	STOLID	STOMPING	STONISHES
STOB	STODGE	STOLIDER	STOMPS	STONK
STOBBED	STODGED	STOLIDEST	STOMPY	STONKED
STOBBING	STODGER	STOLIDITY	STONABLE	STONKER
STOBIE	STODGERS	STOLIDLY	STOND	STONKERED
STOBS	STODGES	STOLLEN	STONDS	STONKERS
STOCCADO	STODGIER	STOLLENS	STONE	STONKING
STOCCADOS	STODGIEST	STOLN	STONEABLE	STONKS
STOCCATA	STODGILY	STOLON	STONEBOAT	STONN
STOCCATAS	STODGING	STOLONATE	STONECAST	STONNE
STOCIOUS	STODGY	STOLONIC	STONECHAT	STONNED
STOCK	STOEP	STOLONS	STONECROP	STONNES
STOCKADE	STOEPS	STOLPORT	STONECUT	STONNING
STOCKADED	STOGEY	STOLPORTS	STONECUTS	STONNS
STOCKADES	STOGEYS	STOMA	STONED	STONY
STOCKAGE	STOGIE	STOMACH	STONEFISH	STONYING
STOCKAGES	STOGIES	STOMACHAL	STONEFLY	STOOD
STOCKCAR	STOGY	STOMACHED	STONEHAND	STOODEN

STOOGE	STOPCOCKS	STORERS	STOTINS	STOUTS
STOOGED	STOPE	STORES	STOTIOUS	STOVAINE
STOOGES	STOPED	STORESHIP	STOTS	STOVAINES
STOOGING	STOPER	STOREWIDE	STOTT	STOVE
STOOK	STOPERS	STOREY	STOTTED	STOVED
STOOKED	STOPES	STOREYED	STOTTER	STOVEPIPE
STOOKER	STOPGAP	STOREYS	STOTTERED	STOVER
STOOKERS	STOPGAPS	STORGE	STOTTERS	STOVERS
STOOKIE	STOPING	STORGES	STOTTIE	STOVES
STOOKIES	STOPINGS	STORIATED	STOTTIES	STOVETOP
STOOKING	STOPLESS	STORIED	STOTTING	STOVETOPS
STOOKINGS	STOPLIGHT	STORIES	STOTTS	STOVIES
STOOKS	STOPOFF	STORIETTE	STOTTY	STOVING
STOOL	STOPOFFS	STORING	STOUN	STOVINGS
STOOLBALL	STOPOVER	STORK	STOUND	STOW
STOOLED	STOPOVERS	STORKS	STOUNDED	STOWABLE
STOOLIE	STOPPABLE	STORM	STOUNDING	STOWAGE
STOOLIES	STOPPAGE	STORMBIRD	STOUNDS	STOWAGES
STOOLING	STOPPAGES	STORMCOCK	STOUNING	STOWAWAY
STOOLS	STOPPED	STORMED	STOUNS	STOWAWAYS
STOOLY	STOPPER	STORMER	STOUP	STOWDOWN
STOOP	STOPPERED	STORMERS	STOUPS	STOWDOWNS
STOOPBALL	STOPPERS	STORMFUL	STOUR	STOWED
STOOPE	STOPPING	STORMIER	STOURE	STOWER
STOOPED	STOPPINGS	STORMIEST	STOURES	STOWERS
STOOPER	STOPPLE	STORMILY	STOURIE	STOWING
STOOPERS	STOPPLED	STORMING	STOURIER	STOWINGS
STOOPES	STOPPLES	STORMINGS	STOURIEST	STOWLINS
STOOPING	STOPPLING	STORMLESS	STOURS	STOWN
STOOPS	STOPS	STORMLIKE	STOURY	STOWND
STOOR	STOPT	STORMS	STOUSH	STOWNDED
STOORS	STOPWATCH	STORMY	STOUSHED	STOWNDING
STOOSHIE	STOPWORD	STORNELLI	STOUSHES	STOWNDS
STOOSHIES	STOPWORDS	STORNELLO	STOUSHIE	STOWNLINS
STOOZE	STORABLE	STORY	STOUSHIES	STOWP
STOOZED	STORABLES	STORYBOOK	STOUSHING	STOWPS
STOOZER	STORAGE	STORYETTE	STOUT	STOWRE
STOOZERS	STORAGES	STORYING	STOUTEN	STOWRES
STOOZES	STORAX	STORYINGS	STOUTENED	STOWS
STOOZING	STORAXES	STORYLINE	STOUTENS	STRABISM
STOOZINGS	STORE	STOSS	STOUTER	STRABISMS
STOP	STORECARD	STOSSES	STOUTEST	STRACK
STOPBAND	STORED	STOT	STOUTH	STRAD
STOPBANDS	STOREMAN	STOTIN	STOUTHS	STRADDLE
STOPBANK	STOREMEN	STOTINKA	STOUTISH	STRADDLED
STOPBANKS	STORER	STOTINKI	STOUTLY	STRADDLER
STOPCOCK	STOREROOM	STOTINOV	STOUTNESS	STRADDLES

S

STRADIOT	STRAK	STRASSES	STRAYLING	STREIGNE
STRADIOTS	STRAKE	STRATA	STRAYS	STREIGNED
STRADS	STRAKED	STRATAGEM	STRAYVE	STREIGNES
STRAE	STRAKES	STRATAL	STRAYVED	STRELITZ
STRAES	STRAMACON	STRATAS	STRAYVES	STRELITZI
STRAFE	STRAMASH	STRATEGIC	STRAYVING	STRENE
STRAFED	STRAMAZON	STRATEGY	STREAK	STRENES
STRAFER	STRAMMEL	STRATH	STREAKED	STRENGTH
STRAFERS	STRAMMELS	STRATHS	STREAKER	STRENGTHS
STRAFES	STRAMONY	STRATI	STREAKERS	STRENUITY
STRAFF	STRAMP	STRATIFY	STREAKIER	STRENUOUS
STRAFFED	STRAMPED	STRATONIC	STREAKILY	STREP
STRAFFING	STRAMPING	STRATOSE	STREAKING	STREPENT
STRAFFS	STRAMPS	STRATOUS	STREAKS	STREPS
STRAFING	STRAND	STRATUM	STREAKY	STRESS
STRAFINGS	STRANDED	STRATUMS	STREAM	STRESSED
STRAG	STRANDER	STRATUS	STREAMBED	STRESSES
STRAGGLE	STRANDERS	STRATUSES	STREAMED	STRESSFUL
STRAGGLED	STRANDING	STRAUCHT	STREAMER	STRESSIER
STRAGGLER	STRANDS	STRAUCHTS	STREAMERS	STRESSING
STRAGGLES	STRANG	STRAUGHT	STREAMIER	STRESSOR
STRAGGLY	STRANGE	STRAUGHTS	STREAMING	STRESSORS
STRAGS	STRANGELY	STRAUNGE	STREAMLET	STRESSY
STRAICHT	STRANGER	STRAVAGE	STREAMS	STRETCH
STRAIGHT	STRANGERS	STRAVAGED	STREAMY	STRETCHED
STRAIGHTS	STRANGES	STRAVAGES	STREEK	STRETCHER
STRAIK	STRANGEST	STRAVAIG	STREEKED	STRETCHES
STRAIKED	STRANGLE	STRAVAIGS	STREEKER	STRETCHY
STRAIKING	STRANGLED	STRAW	STREEKERS	STRETTA
STRAIKS	STRANGLER	STRAWED	STREEKING	STRETTAS
STRAIN	STRANGLES	STRAWEN	STREEKS	STRETTE
STRAINED	STRANGURY	STRAWHAT	STREEL	STRETTI
STRAINER	STRAP	STRAWIER	STREELED	STRETTO
STRAINERS	STRAPHANG	STRAWIEST	STREELING	STRETTOS
STRAINING	STRAPHUNG	STRAWING	STREELS	STREUSEL
STRAINS	STRAPLESS	STRAWLESS	STREET	STREUSELS
STRAINT	STRAPLINE	STRAWLIKE	STREETAGE	STREW
STRAINTS	STRAPPADO	STRAWN	STREETBOY	STREWAGE
STRAIT	STRAPPED	STRAWS	STREETCAR	STREWAGES
STRAITED	STRAPPER	STRAWWORM	STREETED	STREWED
STRAITEN	STRAPPERS	STRAWY	STREETFUL	STREWER
STRAITENS	STRAPPIER	STRAY	STREETIER	STREWERS
STRAITER	STRAPPING	STRAYED	STREETING	STREWING
STRAITEST	STRAPPY	STRAYER	STREETS	STREWINGS
STRAITING	STRAPS	STRAYERS	STREETY	STREWMENT
STRAITLY	STRAPWORT	STRAYING	STREIGHT	STREWN
STRAITS	STRASS	STRAYINGS	STREIGHTS	STREWS

STREWTH	STRIFTS	STRIPING	STROKED	STROPHOID
STRIA	STRIG	STRIPINGS	STROKEN	STROPHULI
STRIAE	STRIGA	STRIPLING	STROKER	STROPPED
STRIATA	STRIGAE	STRIPPED	STROKERS	STROPPER
STRIATAL	STRIGATE	STRIPPER	STROKES	STROPPERS
STRIATE	STRIGGED	STRIPPERS	STROKING	STROPPIER
STRIATED	STRIGGING	STRIPPING	STROKINGS	STROPPILY
STRIATES	STRIGIL	STRIPS	STROLL	STROPPING
STRIATING	STRIGILS	STRIPT	STROLLED	STROPPY
STRIATION	STRIGINE	STRIPY	STROLLER	STROPS
STRIATUM	STRIGOSE	STRIVE	STROLLERS	STROSSERS
STRIATUMS	STRIGS	STRIVED	STROLLING	STROUD
STRIATURE	STRIKE	STRIVEN	STROLLS	STROUDING
STRICH	STRIKEOUT	STRIVER	STROMA	STROUDS
STRICHES	STRIKER	STRIVERS	STROMAL	STROUP
STRICK	STRIKERS	STRIVES	STROMATA	STROUPACH
STRICKEN	STRIKES	STRIVING	STROMATIC	STROUPAN
STRICKLE	STRIKING	STRIVINGS	STROMB	STROUPANS
STRICKLED	STRIKINGS	STROAM	STROMBS	STROUPS
STRICKLES	STRIM	STROAMED	STROMBUS	STROUT
STRICKS	STRIMMED	STROAMING	STROND	STROUTED
STRICT	STRIMMING	STROAMS	STRONDS	STROUTING
STRICTER	STRIMS	STROBE	STRONG	STROUTS
STRICTEST	STRINE	STROBED	STRONGARM	STROVE
STRICTION	STRINES	STROBES	STRONGBOX	STROW
STRICTISH	STRING	STROBIC	STRONGER	STROWED
STRICTLY	STRINGED	STROBIL	STRONGEST	STROWER
STRICTURE	STRINGENT	STROBILA	STRONGISH	STROWERS
STRIDDEN	STRINGER	STROBILAE	STRONGLY	STROWING
STRIDDLE	STRINGERS	STROBILAR	STRONGMAN	STROWINGS
STRIDDLED	STRINGIER	STROBILE	STRONGMEN	STROWN
STRIDDLES	STRINGILY	STROBILES	STRONGYL	STROWS
STRIDE	STRINGING	STROBILI	STRONGYLE	STROY
STRIDENCE	STRINGS	STROBILS	STRONGYLS	STROYED
STRIDENCY	STRINGY	STROBILUS	STRONTIA	STROYER
STRIDENT	STRINKLE	STROBING	STRONTIAN	STROYERS
STRIDER	STRINKLED	STROBINGS	STRONTIAS	STROYING
STRIDERS	STRINKLES	STRODDLE	STRONTIC	STROYS
STRIDES	STRIP	STRODDLED	STRONTIUM	STRUCK
STRIDING	STRIPE	STRODDLES	STROOK	STRUCKEN
STRIDLING	STRIPED	STRODE	STROOKE	STRUCTURE
STRIDOR	STRIPER	STRODLE	STROOKEN	STRUDEL
STRIDORS	STRIPERS	STRODLED	STROOKES	STRUDELS
STRIFE	STRIPES	STRODLES	STROP	STRUGGLE
STRIFEFUL	STRIPEY	STRODLING	STROPHE	STRUGGLED
STRIFES	STRIPIER	STROKABLE	STROPHES	STRUGGLER
STRIFT	STRIPIEST	STROKE	STROPHIC	STRUGGLES

S

STRUM	STUCCO	STUFFER	STUMPING	STURDIED
STRUMA	STUCCOED	STUFFERS	STUMPINGS	STURDIER
STRUMAE	STUCCOER	STUFFIER	STUMPS	STURDIES
STRUMAS	STUCCOERS	STUFFIEST	STUMPWORK	STURDIEST
STRUMATIC	STUCCOES	STUFFILY	STUMPY	STURDILY
STRUMITIS	STUCCOING	STUFFING	STUMS	STURDY
STRUMMED	STUCCOS	STUFFINGS	STUN	STURE
STRUMMEL	STUCK	STUFFLESS	STUNG	STURGEON
STRUMMELS	STUCKS	STUFFS	STUNK	STURGEONS
STRUMMER	STUD	STUFFY	STUNKARD	STURMER
STRUMMERS	STUDBOOK	STUGGIER	STUNNED	STURMERS
STRUMMING	STUDBOOKS	STUGGIEST	STUNNER	STURNINE
STRUMOSE	STUDDED	STUGGY	STUNNERS	STURNOID
STRUMOUS	STUDDEN	STUIVER	STUNNING	STURNUS
STRUMPET	STUDDIE	STUIVERS	STUNNINGS	STURNUSES
STRUMPETS	STUDDIES	STUKKEND	STUNS	STURT
STRUMS	STUDDING	STULL	STUNSAIL	STURTED
STRUNG	STUDDINGS	STULLS	STUNSAILS	STURTING
STRUNT	STUDDLE	STULM	STUNT	STURTS
STRUNTED	STUDDLES	STULMS	STUNTED	STUSHIE
STRUNTING	STUDE	STULTIFY	STUNTING	STUSHIES
STRUNTS	STUDENT	STUM	STUNTMAN	STUTTER
STRUT	STUDENTRY	STUMBLE	STUNTMEN	STUTTERED
STRUTS	STUDENTS	STUMBLED	STUNTS	STUTTERER
STRUTTED	STUDENTY	STUMBLER	STUPA	STUTTERS
STRUTTER	STUDFARM	STUMBLERS	STUPAS	STY
STRUTTERS	STUDFARMS	STUMBLES	STUPE	STYE
STRUTTING	STUDFISH	STUMBLIER	STUPED	STYED
STRYCHNIA	STUDHORSE	STUMBLING	STUPEFIED	STYES
STRYCHNIC	STUDIED	STUMBLY	STUPEFIER	STYGIAN
STUB	STUDIEDLY	STUMER	STUPEFIES	STYING
STUBBED	STUDIER	STUMERS	STUPEFY	STYLAR
STUBBIE	STUDIERS	STUMM	STUPENT	STYLATE
STUBBIER	STUDIES	STUMMED	STUPES	STYLE
STUBBIES	STUDIO	STUMMEL	STUPID	STYLEBOOK
STUBBIEST	STUDIOS	STUMMELS	STUPIDER	STYLED
STUBBILY	STUDIOUS	STUMMING	STUPIDEST	STYLEE
STUBBING	STUDLIER	STUMP	STUPIDITY	STYLEES
STUBBLE	STUDLIEST	STUMPAGE	STUPIDLY	STYLELESS
STUBBLED	STUDLY	STUMPAGES	STUPIDS	STYLER
STUBBLES	STUDS	STUMPED	STUPING	STYLERS
STUBBLIER	STUDWORK	STUMPER	STUPOR	STYLES
STUBBLY	STUDWORKS	STUMPERS	STUPOROUS	STYLET
STUBBORN	STUDY	STUMPIER	STUPORS	STYLETS
STUBBORNS	STUDYING	STUMPIES	STUPRATE	STYLI
STUBBY	STUFF	STUMPIEST	STUPRATED	STYLIE
STUBS	STUFFED	STUMPILY	STUPRATES	STYLIER

STYLIEST
STYLIFORM
STYLING
STYLINGS
STYLISE
STYLISED
STYLISER
STYLISERS
STYLISES
STYLISH
STYLISHLY
STYLISING
STYLIST
STYLISTIC
STYLISTS
STYLITE
STYLITES
STYLITIC
STYLITISM
STYLIZE
STYLIZED
STYLIZER
STYLIZERS
STYLIZES
STYLIZING
STYLO
STYLOBATE
STYLOID
STYLOIDS
STYLOLITE
STYLOPES
STYLOPID
STYLOPIDS
STYLOPISE
STYLOPIZE
STYLOPS
STYLOS
STYLUS
STYLUSES
STYME
STYMED
STYMES
STYMIE
STYMIED
STYMIEING
STYMIES
STYMING

STYMY
STYMYING
STYPSIS
STYPSISES
STYPTIC
STYPTICAL
STYPTICS
STYRAX
STYRAXES
STYRE
STYRED
STYRENE
STYRENES
STYRES
STYRING
STYROFOAM
STYTE
STYTED
STYTES
STYTING
SUABILITY
SUABLE
SUABLY
SUASIBLE
SUASION
SUASIONS
SUASIVE
SUASIVELY
SUASORY
SUAVE
SUAVELY
SUAVENESS
SUAVER
SUAVEST
SUAVITIES
SUAVITY
SUB
SUBA
SUBABBOT
SUBABBOTS
SUBACID
SUBACIDLY
SUBACRID
SUBACT
SUBACTED
SUBACTING
SUBACTION

SUBACTS
SUBACUTE
SUBADAR
SUBADARS
SUBADULT
SUBADULTS
SUBAERIAL
SUBAGENCY
SUBAGENT
SUBAGENTS
SUBAH
SUBAHDAR
SUBAHDARS
SUBAHDARY
SUBAHS
SUBAHSHIP
SUBALAR
SUBALPINE
SUBALTERN
SUBAPICAL
SUBAQUA
SUBARCTIC
SUBAREA
SUBAREAS
SUBARID
SUBAS
SUBASTRAL
SUBATOM
SUBATOMIC
SUBATOMS
SUBAUDIO
SUBAURAL
SUBAXIAL
SUBBASAL
SUBBASE
SUBBASES
SUBBASIN
SUBBASINS
SUBBASS
SUBBASSES
SUBBED
SUBBIE
SUBBIES
SUBBING
SUBBINGS
SUBBLOCK
SUBBLOCKS

SUBBRANCH
SUBBREED
SUBBREEDS
SUBBUREAU
SUBBY
SUBCANTOR
SUBCASTE
SUBCASTES
SUBCAUDAL
SUBCAUSE
SUBCAUSES
SUBCAVITY
SUBCELL
SUBCELLAR
SUBCELLS
SUBCENTER
SUBCENTRE
SUBCHASER
SUBCHIEF
SUBCHIEFS
SUBCHORD
SUBCHORDS
SUBCLAIM
SUBCLAIMS
SUBCLAN
SUBCLANS
SUBCLASS
SUBCLAUSE
SUBCLERK
SUBCLERKS
SUBCLIMAX
SUBCODE
SUBCODES
SUBCOLONY
SUBCONSUL
SUBCOOL
SUBCOOLED
SUBCOOLS
SUBCORTEX
SUBCOSTA
SUBCOSTAE
SUBCOSTAL
SUBCOUNTY
SUBCRUST
SUBCRUSTS
SUBCULT
SUBCULTS

SUBCUTES
SUBCUTIS
SUBDEACON
SUBDEALER
SUBDEAN
SUBDEANS
SUBDEB
SUBDEBS
SUBDEPOT
SUBDEPOTS
SUBDEPUTY
SUBDERMAL
SUBDEW
SUBDEWED
SUBDEWING
SUBDEWS
SUBDIVIDE
SUBDOLOUS
SUBDORSAL
SUBDUABLE
SUBDUABLY
SUBDUAL
SUBDUALS
SUBDUCE
SUBDUCED
SUBDUCES
SUBDUCING
SUBDUCT
SUBDUCTED
SUBDUCTS
SUBDUE
SUBDUED
SUBDUEDLY
SUBDUER
SUBDUERS
SUBDUES
SUBDUING
SUBDUPLE
SUBDURAL
SUBDWARF
SUBDWARFS
SUBECHO
SUBECHOES
SUBEDAR
SUBEDARS
SUBEDIT
SUBEDITED

S

SUBEDITOR	SUBGENRES	SUBLATING	SUBMERGED	SUBPAR
SUBEDITS	SUBGENUS	SUBLATION	SUBMERGES	SUBPART
SUBENTIRE	SUBGOAL	SUBLEASE	SUBMERSE	SUBPARTS
SUBENTRY	SUBGOALS	SUBLEASED	SUBMERSED	SUBPENA
SUBEPOCH	SUBGRADE	SUBLEASES	SUBMERSES	SUBPENAED
SUBEPOCHS	SUBGRADES	SUBLESSEE	SUBMICRON	SUBPENAS
SUBEQUAL	SUBGRAPH	SUBLESSOR	SUBMISS	SUBPERIOD
SUBER	SUBGRAPHS	SUBLET	SUBMISSLY	SUBPHASE
SUBERATE	SUBGROUP	SUBLETHAL	SUBMIT	SUBPHASES
SUBERATES	SUBGROUPS	SUBLETS	SUBMITS	SUBPHYLA
SUBERECT	SUBGUM	SUBLETTER	SUBMITTAL	SUBPHYLAR
SUBEREOUS	SUBGUMS	SUBLEVEL	SUBMITTED	SUBPHYLUM
SUBERIC	SUBHA	SUBLEVELS	SUBMITTER	SUBPLOT
SUBERIN	SUBHAS	SUBLIMATE	SUBMUCOSA	SUBPLOTS
SUBERINS	SUBHEAD	SUBLIME	SUBMUCOUS	SUBPOENA
SUBERISE	SUBHEADS	SUBLIMED	SUBNASAL	SUBPOENAS
SUBERISED	SUBHEDRAL	SUBLIMELY	SUBNET	SUBPOLAR
SUBERISES	SUBHUMAN	SUBLIMER	SUBNETS	SUBPOTENT
SUBERIZE	SUBHUMANS	SUBLIMERS	SUBNEURAL	SUBPRIME
SUBERIZED	SUBHUMID	SUBLIMES	SUBNICHE	SUBPRIMES
SUBERIZES	SUBIDEA	SUBLIMEST	SUBNICHES	SUBPRIOR
SUBEROSE	SUBIDEAS	SUBLIMING	SUBNIVEAL	SUBPRIORS
SUBEROUS	SUBIMAGO	SUBLIMISE	SUBNIVEAN	SUBPUBIC
SUBERS	SUBIMAGOS	SUBLIMIT	SUBNODAL	SUBRACE
SUBFAMILY	SUBINCISE	SUBLIMITS	SUBNORMAL	SUBRACES
SUBFEU	SUBINDEX	SUBLIMITY	SUBNUCLEI	SUBREGION
SUBFEUED	SUBINFEUD	SUBLIMIZE	SUBOCEAN	SUBRENT
SUBFEUING	SUBITEM	SUBLINE	SUBOCTAVE	SUBRENTED
SUBFEUS	SUBITEMS	SUBLINEAR	SUBOCULAR	SUBRENTS
SUBFIELD	SUBITISE	SUBLINES	SUBOFFICE	SUBRING
SUBFIELDS	SUBITISED	SUBLOT	SUBOPTIC	SUBRINGS
SUBFILE	SUBITISES	SUBLOTS	SUBORAL	SUBROGATE
SUBFILES	SUBITIZE	SUBLUNAR	SUBORDER	SUBRULE
SUBFIX	SUBITIZED	SUBLUNARY	SUBORDERS	SUBRULES
SUBFIXES	SUBITIZES	SUBLUNATE	SUBORN	SUBS
SUBFLOOR	SUBITO	SUBLUXATE	SUBORNED	SUBSACRAL
SUBFLOORS	SUBJACENT	SUBMAN	SUBORNER	SUBSALE
SUBFLUID	SUBJECT	SUBMARINE	SUBORNERS	SUBSALES
SUBFOSSIL	SUBJECTED	SUBMARKET	SUBORNING	SUBSAMPLE
SUBFRAME	SUBJECTS	SUBMATRIX	SUBORNS	SUBSCALE
SUBFRAMES	SUBJOIN	SUBMEN	SUBOSCINE	SUBSCALES
SUBFUSC	SUBJOINED	SUBMENTA	SUBOVAL	SUBSCHEMA
SUBFUSCS	SUBJOINS	SUBMENTAL	SUBOVATE	SUBSCRIBE
SUBFUSK	SUBJUGATE	SUBMENTUM	SUBOXIDE	SUBSCRIPT
SUBFUSKS	SUBLATE	SUBMENU	SUBOXIDES	SUBSEA
SUBGENERA	SUBLATED	SUBMENUS	SUBPANEL	SUBSECIVE
SUBGENRE	SUBLATES	SUBMERGE	SUBPANELS	SUBSECT

SUBSECTOR	SUBSONIC	SUBTILELY	SUBUCULAS	SUCCAH
SUBSECTS	SUBSPACE	SUBTILER	SUBULATE	SUCCAHS
SUBSELLIA	SUBSPACES	SUBTILEST	SUBUNIT	SUCCEDENT
SUBSENSE	SUBSTAGE	SUBTILIN	SUBUNITS	SUCCEED
SUBSENSES	SUBSTAGES	SUBTILINS	SUBURB	SUCCEEDED
SUBSERE	SUBSTANCE	SUBTILISE	SUBURBAN	SUCCEEDER
SUBSERES	SUBSTATE	SUBTILITY	SUBURBANS	SUCCEEDS
SUBSERIES	SUBSTATES	SUBTILIZE	SUBURBED	SUCCENTOR
SUBSERVE	SUBSTRACT	SUBTILTY	SUBURBIA	SUCCES
SUBSERVED	SUBSTRATA	SUBTITLE	SUBURBIAS	SUCCESS
SUBSERVES	SUBSTRATE	SUBTITLED	SUBURBS	SUCCESSES
SUBSET	SUBSTRUCT	SUBTITLES	SUBURSINE	SUCCESSOR
SUBSETS	SUBSTYLAR	SUBTLE	SUBVASSAL	SUCCI
SUBSHAFT	SUBSTYLE	SUBTLER	SUBVENE	SUCCINATE
SUBSHAFTS	SUBSTYLES	SUBTLEST	SUBVENED	SUCCINCT
SUBSHELL	SUBSULTUS	SUBTLETY	SUBVENES	SUCCINIC
SUBSHELLS	SUBSUME	SUBTLY	SUBVENING	SUCCINITE
SUBSHRUB	SUBSUMED	SUBTONE	SUBVERSAL	SUCCINYL
SUBSHRUBS	SUBSUMES	SUBTONES	SUBVERSE	SUCCINYLS
SUBSIDE	SUBSUMING	SUBTONIC	SUBVERSED	SUCCISE
SUBSIDED	SUBSYSTEM	SUBTONICS	SUBVERSES	SUCCOR
SUBSIDER	SUBTACK	SUBTOPIA	SUBVERST	SUCCORED
SUBSIDERS	SUBTACKS	SUBTOPIAN	SUBVERT	SUCCORER
SUBSIDES	SUBTALAR	SUBTOPIAS	SUBVERTED	SUCCORERS
SUBSIDIES	SUBTASK	SUBTOPIC	SUBVERTER	SUCCORIES
SUBSIDING	SUBTASKS	SUBTOPICS	SUBVERTS	SUCCORING
SUBSIDISE	SUBTAXA	SUBTORRID	SUBVICAR	SUCCORS
SUBSIDIZE	SUBTAXON	SUBTOTAL	SUBVICARS	SUCCORY
SUBSIDY	SUBTAXONS	SUBTOTALS	SUBVIRAL	SUCCOS
SUBSIST	SUBTEEN	SUBTRACT	SUBVIRUS	SUCCOSE
SUBSISTED	SUBTEENS	SUBTRACTS	SUBVISUAL	SUCCOT
SUBSISTER	SUBTENANT	SUBTRADE	SUBVOCAL	SUCCOTASH
SUBSISTS	SUBTEND	SUBTRADES	SUBWARDEN	SUCCOTH
SUBSITE	SUBTENDED	SUBTREND	SUBWAY	SUCCOUR
SUBSITES	SUBTENDS	SUBTRENDS	SUBWAYED	SUCCOURED
SUBSIZAR	SUBTENSE	SUBTRIBE	SUBWAYING	SUCCOURER
SUBSIZARS	SUBTENSES	SUBTRIBES	SUBWAYS	SUCCOURS
SUBSKILL	SUBTENURE	SUBTRIST	SUBWOOFER	SUCCOUS
SUBSKILLS	SUBTEST	SUBTROPIC	SUBWORLD	SUCCUBA
SUBSOCIAL	SUBTESTS	SUBTRUDE	SUBWORLDS	SUCCUBAE
SUBSOIL	SUBTEXT	SUBTRUDED	SUBWRITER	SUCCUBAS
SUBSOILED	SUBTEXTS	SUBTRUDES	SUBZERO	SUCCUBI
SUBSOILER	SUBTHEME	SUBTUNIC	SUBZONAL	SUCCUBINE
SUBSOILS	SUBTHEMES	SUBTUNICS	SUBZONE	SUCCUBOUS
SUBSOLAR	SUBTIDAL	SUBTYPE	SUBZONES	SUCCUBUS
SUBSONG	SUBTIL	SUBTYPES	SUCCADE	SUCCULENT
SUBSONGS	SUBTILE	SUBUCULA	SUCCADES	SUCCUMB

S

SUCCUMBED	SUCRIER	SUDSERS	SUFFICING	SUGGINGS
SUCCUMBER	SUCRIERS	SUDSES	SUFFIX	SUGH
SUCCUMBS	SUCROSE	SUDSIER	SUFFIXAL	SUGHED
SUCCURSAL	SUCROSES	SUDSIEST	SUFFIXED	SUGHING
SUCCUS	SUCTION	SUDSING	SUFFIXES	SUGHS
SUCCUSS	SUCTIONAL	SUDSLESS	SUFFIXING	SUGO
SUCCUSSED	SUCTIONED	SUDSY	SUFFIXION	SUGOS
SUCCUSSES	SUCTIONS	SUE	SUFFLATE	SUGS
SUCH	SUCTORIAL	SUEABLE	SUFFLATED	SUHUR
SUCHLIKE	SUCTORIAN	SUED	SUFFLATES	SUHURS
SUCHNESS	SUCURUJU	SUEDE	SUFFOCATE	SUI
SUCHWISE	SUCURUJUS	SUEDED	SUFFRAGAN	SUICIDAL
SUCK	SUD	SUEDES	SUFFRAGE	SUICIDE
SUCKED	SUDAMEN	SUEDETTE	SUFFRAGES	SUICIDED
SUCKEN	SUDAMENS	SUEDETTES	SUFFUSE	SUICIDES
SUCKENER	SUDAMINA	SUEDING	SUFFUSED	SUICIDING
SUCKENERS	SUDAMINAL	SUENT	SUFFUSES	SUID
SUCKENS	SUDARIA	SUER	SUFFUSING	SUIDIAN
SUCKER	SUDARIES	SUERS	SUFFUSION	SUIDIANS
SUCKERED	SUDARIUM	SUES	SUFFUSIVE	SUIDS
SUCKERING	SUDARY	SUET	SUG	SUILLINE
SUCKERS	SUDATE	SUETE	SUGAN	SUING
SUCKET	SUDATED	SUETES	SUGANS	SUINGS
SUCKETS	SUDATES	SUETIER	SUGAR	SUINT
SUCKFISH	SUDATING	SUETIEST	SUGARALLY	SUINTS
SUCKHOLE	SUDATION	SUETS	SUGARBUSH	SUIPLAP
SUCKHOLED	SUDATIONS	SUETTIER	SUGARCANE	SUIPLAPS
SUCKHOLES	SUDATORIA	SUETTIEST	SUGARCOAT	SUIT
SUCKIER	SUDATORY	SUETTY	SUGARED	SUITABLE
SUCKIEST	SUDD	SUETY	SUGARER	SUITABLY
SUCKING	SUDDEN	SUFFARI	SUGARERS	SUITCASE
SUCKINGS	SUDDENLY	SUFFARIS	SUGARIER	SUITCASES
SUCKLE	SUDDENS	SUFFECT	SUGARIEST	SUITE
SUCKLED	SUDDENTY	SUFFECTS	SUGARING	SUITED
SUCKLER	SUDDER	SUFFER	SUGARINGS	SUITER
SUCKLERS	SUDDERS	SUFFERED	SUGARLESS	SUITERS
SUCKLES	SUDDS	SUFFERER	SUGARLIKE	SUITES
SUCKLESS	SUDOKU	SUFFERERS	SUGARLOAF	SUITING
SUCKLING	SUDOKUS	SUFFERING	SUGARPLUM	SUITINGS
SUCKLINGS	SUDOR	SUFFERS	SUGARS	SUITLIKE
SUCKS	SUDORAL	SUFFETE	SUGARY	SUITOR
SUCKY	SUDORIFIC	SUFFETES	SUGGED	SUITORED
SUCRALOSE	SUDOROUS	SUFFICE	SUGGEST	SUITORING
SUCRASE	SUDORS	SUFFICED	SUGGESTED	SUITORS
SUCRASES	SUDS	SUFFICER	SUGGESTER	SUITRESS
SUCRE	SUDSED	SUFFICERS	SUGGESTS	SUITS
SUCRES	SUDSER	SUFFICES	SUGGING	SUIVANTE

SUIVANTES	SULFONE	SULPHAS	SUMIS	SUMMONING
SUIVEZ	SULFONES	SULPHATE	SUMLESS	SUMMONS
SUJEE	SULFONIC	SULPHATED	SUMMA	SUMMONSED
SUJEES	SULFONIUM	SULPHATES	SUMMABLE	SUMMONSES
SUK	SULFONYL	SULPHATIC	SUMMAE	SUMO
SUKH	SULFONYLS	SULPHID	SUMMAND	SUMOIST
SUKHS	SULFOXIDE	SULPHIDE	SUMMANDS	SUMOISTS
SUKIYAKI	SULFUR	SULPHIDES	SUMMAR	SUMOS
SUKIYAKIS	SULFURATE	SULPHIDS	SUMMARIES	SUMOTORI
SUKKAH	SULFURED	SULPHINYL	SUMMARILY	SUMOTORIS
SUKKAHS	SULFURET	SULPHITE	SUMMARISE	SUMP
SUKKOS	SULFURETS	SULPHITES	SUMMARIST	SUMPH
SUKKOT	SULFURIC	SULPHITIC	SUMMARIZE	SUMPHISH
SUKKOTH	SULFURING	SULPHONE	SUMMARY	SUMPHS
SUKS	SULFURISE	SULPHONES	SUMMAS	SUMPIT
SUKUK	SULFURIZE	SULPHONIC	SUMMAT	SUMPITAN
SUKUKS	SULFUROUS	SULPHONYL	SUMMATE	SUMPITANS
SULCAL	SULFURS	SULPHS	SUMMATED	SUMPITS
SULCALISE	SULFURY	SULPHUR	SUMMATES	SUMPS
SULCALIZE	SULFURYL	SULPHURED	SUMMATING	SUMPSIMUS
SULCATE	SULFURYLS	SULPHURET	SUMMATION	SUMPTER
SULCATED	SULK	SULPHURIC	SUMMATIVE	SUMPTERS
SULCATION	SULKED	SULPHURS	SUMMATS	SUMPTUARY
SULCI	SULKER	SULPHURY	SUMMED	SUMPTUOUS
SULCUS	SULKERS	SULPHURYL	SUMMER	SUMPWEED
SULDAN	SULKIER	SULTAN	SUMMERED	SUMPWEEDS
SULDANS	SULKIES	SULTANA	SUMMERIER	SUMS
SULFA	SULKIEST	SULTANAS	SUMMERING	SUMY
SULFAS	SULKILY	SULTANATE	SUMMERLY	SUN
SULFATASE	SULKINESS	SULTANESS	SUMMERS	SUNBACK
SULFATE	SULKING	SULTANIC	SUMMERSET	SUNBAKE
SULFATED	SULKS	SULTANS	SUMMERY	SUNBAKED
SULFATES	SULKY	SULTRIER	SUMMING	SUNBAKES
SULFATIC	SULLAGE	SULTRIEST	SUMMINGS	SUNBAKING
SULFATING	SULLAGES	SULTRILY	SUMMIST	SUNBATH
SULFATION	SULLEN	SULTRY	SUMMISTS	SUNBATHE
SULFID	SULLENER	SULU	SUMMIT	SUNBATHED
SULFIDE	SULLENEST	SULUS	SUMMITAL	SUNBATHER
SULFIDES	SULLENLY	SUM	SUMMITED	SUNBATHES
SULFIDS	SULLENS	SUMAC	SUMMITEER	SUNBATHS
SULFINYL	SULLIABLE	SUMACH	SUMMITING	SUNBEAM
SULFINYLS	SULLIED	SUMACHS	SUMMITRY	SUNBEAMED
SULFITE	SULLIES	SUMACS	SUMMITS	SUNBEAMS
SULFITES	SULLY	SUMATRA	SUMMON	SUNBEAMY
SULFITIC	SULLYING	SUMATRAS	SUMMONED	SUNBEAT
SULFO	SULPH	SUMBITCH	SUMMONER	SUNBEATEN
SULFONATE	SULPHA	SUMI	SUMMONERS	SUNBED

SUNBEDS	SUNDRAS	SUNNA	SUNTAN	SUPERCOPS
SUNBELT	SUNDRESS	SUNNAH	SUNTANNED	SUPERCOW
SUNBELTS	SUNDRI	SUNNAHS	SUNTANS	SUPERCOWS
SUNBERRY	SUNDRIES	SUNNAS	SUNTRAP	SUPERCUTE
SUNBIRD	SUNDRILY	SUNNED	SUNTRAPS	SUPERED
SUNBIRDS	SUNDRIS	SUNNIER	SUNUP	SUPEREGO
SUNBLIND	SUNDROPS	SUNNIES	SUNUPS	SUPEREGOS
SUNBLINDS	SUNDRY	SUNNIEST	SUNWARD	SUPERETTE
SUNBLOCK	SUNFAST	SUNNILY	SUNWARDS	SUPERFAN
SUNBLOCKS	SUNFISH	SUNNINESS	SUNWISE	SUPERFANS
SUNBONNET	SUNFISHES	SUNNING	SUP	SUPERFARM
SUNBOW	SUNFLOWER	SUNNS	SUPAWN	SUPERFAST
SUNBOWS	SUNG	SUNNY	SUPAWNS	SUPERFINE
SUNBRIGHT	SUNGAR	SUNPORCH	SUPE	SUPERFIRM
SUNBURN	SUNGARS	SUNPROOF	SUPER	SUPERFIT
SUNBURNED	SUNGAZER	SUNRAY	SUPERABLE	SUPERFIX
SUNBURNS	SUNGAZERS	SUNRAYS	SUPERABLY	SUPERFLUX
SUNBURNT	SUNGAZING	SUNRISE	SUPERADD	SUPERFLY
SUNBURST	SUNGLASS	SUNRISES	SUPERADDS	SUPERFOOD
SUNBURSTS	SUNGLOW	SUNRISING	SUPERATE	SUPERFUND
SUNCARE	SUNGLOWS	SUNROOF	SUPERATED	SUPERFUSE
SUNCARES	SUNGREBE	SUNROOFS	SUPERATES	SUPERGENE
SUNCHOKE	SUNGREBES	SUNROOM	SUPERATOM	SUPERGLUE
SUNCHOKES	SUNHAT	SUNROOMS	SUPERB	SUPERGOOD
SUNDAE	SUNHATS	SUNS	SUPERBAD	SUPERGUN
SUNDAES	SUNI	SUNSCALD	SUPERBANK	SUPERGUNS
SUNDARI	SUNIS	SUNSCALDS	SUPERBER	SUPERHEAT
SUNDARIS	SUNK	SUNSCREEN	SUPERBEST	SUPERHERO
SUNDECK	SUNKEN	SUNSEEKER	SUPERBIKE	SUPERHET
SUNDECKS	SUNKER	SUNSET	SUPERBITY	SUPERHETS
SUNDER	SUNKERS	SUNSETS	SUPERBLY	SUPERHIGH
SUNDERED	SUNKET	SUNSHADE	SUPERBOLD	SUPERHIT
SUNDERER	SUNKETS	SUNSHADES	SUPERBOMB	SUPERHITS
SUNDERERS	SUNKIE	SUNSHINE	SUPERBRAT	SUPERHIVE
SUNDERING	SUNKIES	SUNSHINES	SUPERBUG	SUPERHOT
SUNDERS	SUNKS	SUNSHINY	SUPERBUGS	SUPERHYPE
SUNDEW	SUNLAMP	SUNSPECS	SUPERCAR	SUPERING
SUNDEWS	SUNLAMPS	SUNSPOT	SUPERCARS	SUPERIOR
SUNDIAL	SUNLAND	SUNSPOTS	SUPERCEDE	SUPERIORS
SUNDIALS	SUNLANDS	SUNSTAR	SUPERCELL	SUPERJET
SUNDOG	SUNLESS	SUNSTARS	SUPERCHIC	SUPERJETS
SUNDOGS	SUNLESSLY	SUNSTONE	SUPERCITY	SUPERJOCK
SUNDOWN	SUNLIGHT	SUNSTONES	SUPERCLUB	SUPERLAIN
SUNDOWNED	SUNLIGHTS	SUNSTROKE	SUPERCOIL	SUPERLAY
SUNDOWNER	SUNLIKE	SUNSTRUCK	SUPERCOLD	SUPERLIE
SUNDOWNS	SUNLIT	SUNSUIT	SUPERCOOL	SUPERLIES
SUNDRA	SUNN	SUNSUITS	SUPERCOP	SUPERLOAD

S

SUPERLONG	SUPERWAIF	SUPPOSAL	SURBED	SURFEITS
SUPERLOO	SUPERWAVE	SUPPOSALS	SURBEDDED	SURFER
SUPERLOOS	SUPERWEED	SUPPOSE	SURBEDS	SURFERS
SUPERMALE	SUPERWIDE	SUPPOSED	SURBET	SURFFISH
SUPERMAN	SUPERWIFE	SUPPOSER	SURCEASE	SURFICIAL
SUPERMART	SUPES	SUPPOSERS	SURCEASED	SURFIE
SUPERMAX	SUPINATE	SUPPOSES	SURCEASES	SURFIER
SUPERMEN	SUPINATED	SUPPOSING	SURCHARGE	SURFIES
SUPERMIND	SUPINATES	SUPPRESS	SURCINGLE	SURFIEST
SUPERMINI	SUPINATOR	SUPPURATE	SURCOAT	SURFING
SUPERMOM	SUPINE	SUPRA	SURCOATS	SURFINGS
SUPERMOMS	SUPINELY	SUPREMA	SURCULI	SURFLIKE
SUPERMOTO	SUPINES	SUPREMACY	SURCULOSE	SURFMAN
SUPERNAL	SUPLEX	SUPREME	SURCULUS	SURFMEN
SUPERNATE	SUPLEXES	SUPREMELY	SURD	SURFPERCH
SUPERNOVA	SUPPAWN	SUPREMER	SURDITIES	SURFRIDE
SUPERPIMP	SUPPAWNS	SUPREMES	SURDITY	SURFRIDER
SUPERPLUS	SUPPEAGO	SUPREMEST	SURDS	SURFRIDES
SUPERPORT	SUPPED	SUPREMITY	SURE	SURFRODE
SUPERPOSE	SUPPER	SUPREMO	SURED	SURFS
SUPERPRO	SUPPERED	SUPREMOS	SUREFIRE	SURFSIDE
SUPERPROS	SUPPERING	SUPREMUM	SURELY	SURFY
SUPERRACE	SUPPERS	SUPREMUMS	SURENESS	SURGE
SUPERREAL	SUPPING	SUPS	SURER	SURGED
SUPERRICH	SUPPLANT	SUQ	SURES	SURGEFUL
SUPERROAD	SUPPLANTS	SUQS	SUREST	SURGELESS
SUPERS	SUPPLE	SUR	SURETIED	SURGENT
SUPERSAFE	SUPPLED	SURA	SURETIES	SURGEON
SUPERSALE	SUPPLELY	SURAH	SURETY	SURGEONCY
SUPERSALT	SUPPLER	SURAHS	SURETYING	SURGEONS
SUPERSAUR	SUPPLES	SURAL	SURF	SURGER
SUPERSEDE	SUPPLEST	SURAMIN	SURFABLE	SURGERIES
SUPERSELL	SUPPLIAL	SURAMINS	SURFACE	SURGERS
SUPERSEX	SUPPLIALS	SURANCE	SURFACED	SURGERY
SUPERSHOW	SUPPLIANT	SURANCES	SURFACER	SURGES
SUPERSIZE	SUPPLICAT	SURAS	SURFACERS	SURGICAL
SUPERSOFT	SUPPLIED	SURAT	SURFACES	SURGIER
SUPERSOLD	SUPPLIER	SURATS	SURFACING	SURGIEST
SUPERSPY	SUPPLIERS	SURBAHAR	SURFBIRD	SURGING
SUPERSTAR	SUPPLIES	SURBAHARS	SURFBIRDS	SURGINGS
SUPERSTUD	SUPPLING	SURBASE	SURFBOARD	SURGY
SUPERTAX	SUPPLY	SURBASED	SURFBOAT	SURICATE
SUPERTHIN	SUPPLYING	SURBASES	SURFBOATS	SURICATES
SUPERTRAM	SUPPORT	SURBATE	SURFED	SURIMI
SUPERUSER	SUPPORTED	SURBATED	SURFEIT	SURIMIS
SUPERVENE	SUPPORTER	SURBATES	SURFEITED	SURING
SUPERVISE	SUPPORTS	SURBATING	SURFEITER	SURLIER

S

SURLIEST	SURRAS	SURVIVER	SUSURROUS	SWABBIE
SURLILY	SURREAL	SURVIVERS	SUSURRUS	SWABBIES
SURLINESS	SURREALLY	SURVIVES	SUSUS	SWABBING
SURLOIN	SURREALS	SURVIVING	SUTILE	SWABBY
SURLOINS	SURREBUT	SURVIVOR	SUTLER	SWABS
SURLY	SURREBUTS	SURVIVORS	SUTLERIES	SWACK
SURMASTER	SURREINED	SUS	SUTLERS	SWACKED
SURMISAL	SURREJOIN	SUSCEPTOR	SUTLERY	SWACKING
SURMISALS	SURRENDER	SUSCITATE	SUTOR	SWACKS
SURMISE	SURRENDRY	SUSED	SUTORIAL	SWAD
SURMISED	SURREY	SUSES	SUTORIAN	SWADDIE
SURMISER	SURREYS	SUSHI	SUTORS	SWADDIES
SURMISERS	SURROGACY	SUSHIS	SUTRA	SWADDLE
SURMISES	SURROGATE	SUSING	SUTRAS	SWADDLED
SURMISING	SURROUND	SUSLIK	SUTTA	SWADDLER
SURMOUNT	SURROUNDS	SUSLIKS	SUTTAS	SWADDLERS
SURMOUNTS	SURROYAL	SUSPECT	SUTTEE	SWADDLES
SURMULLET	SURROYALS	SUSPECTED	SUTTEEISM	SWADDLING
SURNAME	SURTAX	SUSPECTER	SUTTEES	SWADDY
SURNAMED	SURTAXED	SUSPECTS	SUTTLE	SWADS
SURNAMER	SURTAXES	SUSPENCE	SUTTLED	SWAG
SURNAMERS	SURTAXING	SUSPEND	SUTTLES	SWAGE
SURNAMES	SURTITLE	SUSPENDED	SUTTLETIE	SWAGED
SURNAMING	SURTITLES	SUSPENDER	SUTTLING	SWAGER
SURPASS	SURTOUT	SUSPENDS	SUTTLY	SWAGERS
SURPASSED	SURTOUTS	SUSPENS	SUTURAL	SWAGES
SURPASSER	SURUCUCU	SUSPENSE	SUTURALLY	SWAGGED
SURPASSES	SURUCUCUS	SUSPENSER	SUTURE	SWAGGER
SURPLICE	SURVEIL	SUSPENSES	SUTURED	SWAGGERED
SURPLICED	SURVEILED	SUSPENSOR	SUTURES	SWAGGERER
SURPLICES	SURVEILLE	SUSPICION	SUTURING	SWAGGERS
SURPLUS	SURVEILS	SUSPIRE	SUZERAIN	SWAGGIE
SURPLUSED	SURVEY	SUSPIRED	SUZERAINS	SWAGGIES
SURPLUSES	SURVEYAL	SUSPIRES	SVARAJ	SWAGGING
SURPRINT	SURVEYALS	SUSPIRING	SVARAJES	SWAGING
SURPRINTS	SURVEYED	SUSS	SVASTIKA	SWAGMAN
SURPRISAL	SURVEYING	SUSSED	SVASTIKAS	SWAGMEN
SURPRISE	SURVEYOR	SUSSES	SVEDBERG	SWAGS
SURPRISED	SURVEYORS	SUSSING	SVEDBERGS	SWAGSHOP
SURPRISER	SURVEYS	SUSTAIN	SVELTE	SWAGSHOPS
SURPRISES	SURVIEW	SUSTAINED	SVELTELY	SWAGSMAN
SURPRIZE	SURVIEWED	SUSTAINER	SVELTER	SWAGSMEN
SURPRIZED	SURVIEWS	SUSTAINS	SVELTEST	SWAIL
SURPRIZES	SURVIVAL	SUSTINENT	SWAB	SWAILS
SURQUEDRY	SURVIVALS	SUSU	SWABBED	SWAIN
SURQUEDY	SURVIVE	SUSURRANT	SWABBER	SWAINING
SURRA	SURVIVED	SUSURRATE	SWABBERS	SWAININGS

S

SWAINISH	SWANKIER	SWARDING	SWATHE	SWEARERS
SWAINS	SWANKIES	SWARDS	SWATHED	SWEARIER
SWALE	SWANKIEST	SWARDY	SWATHER	SWEARIEST
SWALED	SWANKILY	SWARE	SWATHERS	SWEARING
SWALES	SWANKING	SWARF	SWATHES	SWEARINGS
SWALIER	SWANKPOT	SWARFED	SWATHIER	SWEARS
SWALIEST	SWANKPOTS	SWARFING	SWATHIEST	SWEARWORD
SWALING	SWANKS	SWARFS	SWATHING	SWEARY
SWALINGS	SWANKY	SWARM	SWATHS	SWEAT
SWALLET	SWANLIKE	SWARMED	SWATHY	SWEATBAND
SWALLETS	SWANNED	SWARMER	SWATS	SWEATBOX
SWALLIES	SWANNERY	SWARMERS	SWATTED	SWEATED
SWALLOW	SWANNIE	SWARMING	SWATTER	SWEATER
SWALLOWED	SWANNIER	SWARMINGS	SWATTERED	SWEATERED
SWALLOWER	SWANNIES	SWARMS	SWATTERS	SWEATERS
SWALLOWS	SWANNIEST	SWART	SWATTIER	SWEATIER
SWALLY	SWANNING	SWARTH	SWATTIEST	SWEATIEST
SWALY	SWANNINGS	SWARTHIER	SWATTING	SWEATILY
SWAM	SWANNY	SWARTHILY	SWATTINGS	SWEATING
SWAMI	SWANPAN	SWARTHS	SWATTY	SWEATINGS
SWAMIES	SWANPANS	SWARTHY	SWAY	SWEATLESS
SWAMIS	SWANS	SWARTNESS	SWAYABLE	SWEATS
SWAMP	SWANSDOWN	SWARTY	SWAYBACK	SWEATSHOP
SWAMPED	SWANSKIN	SWARVE	SWAYBACKS	SWEATSUIT
SWAMPER	SWANSKINS	SWARVED	SWAYED	SWEATY
SWAMPERS	SWANSONG	SWARVES	SWAYER	SWEDE
SWAMPIER	SWANSONGS	SWARVING	SWAYERS	SWEDES
SWAMPIEST	SWAP	SWASH	SWAYFUL	SWEDGER
SWAMPING	SWAPFILE	SWASHED	SWAYING	SWEDGERS
SWAMPISH	SWAPFILES	SWASHER	SWAYINGS	SWEE
SWAMPLAND	SWAPPED	SWASHERS	SWAYL	SWEED
SWAMPLESS	SWAPPER	SWASHES	SWAYLED	SWEEING
SWAMPS	SWAPPERS	SWASHIER	SWAYLING	SWEEL
SWAMPY	SWAPPING	SWASHIEST	SWAYLINGS	SWEELED
SWAMY	SWAPPINGS	SWASHING	SWAYLS	SWEELING
SWAN	SWAPS	SWASHINGS	SWAYS	SWEELS
SWANG	SWAPT	SWASHWORK	SWAZZLE	SWEENEY
SWANHERD	SWAPTION	SWASHY	SWAZZLES	SWEENEYS
SWANHERDS	SWAPTIONS	SWASTICA	SWEAL	SWEENIES
SWANK	SWARAJ	SWASTICAS	SWEALED	SWEENY
SWANKED	SWARAJES	SWASTIKA	SWEALING	SWEEP
SWANKER	SWARAJISM	SWASTIKAS	SWEALINGS	SWEEPBACK
SWANKERS	SWARAJIST	SWAT	SWEALS	SWEEPER
SWANKEST	SWARD	SWATCH	SWEAR	SWEEPERS
SWANKEY	SWARDED	SWATCHES	SWEARD	SWEEPIER
SWANKEYS	SWARDIER	SWATH	SWEARDS	SWEEPIEST
SWANKIE	SWARDIEST	SWATHABLE	SWEARER	SWEEPING

S

SWEEPINGS
SWEEPS
SWEEPY
SWEER
SWEERED
SWEERING
SWEERS
SWEERT
SWEES
SWEET
SWEETCORN
SWEETED
SWEETEN
SWEETENED
SWEETENER
SWEETENS
SWEETER
SWEETEST
SWEETFISH
SWEETIE
SWEETIES
SWEETING
SWEETINGS
SWEETISH
SWEETLIP
SWEETLIPS
SWEETLY
SWEETMAN
SWEETMEAL
SWEETMEAT
SWEETMEN
SWEETNESS
SWEETS
SWEETSHOP
SWEETSOP
SWEETSOPS
SWEETVELD
SWEETWOOD
SWEETY
SWEIR
SWEIRED
SWEIRER
SWEIREST
SWEIRING
SWEIRNESS
SWEIRS
SWEIRT

SWELCHIE
SWELCHIES
SWELL
SWELLDOM
SWELLDOMS
SWELLED
SWELLER
SWELLERS
SWELLEST
SWELLFISH
SWELLHEAD
SWELLING
SWELLINGS
SWELLISH
SWELLS
SWELT
SWELTED
SWELTER
SWELTERED
SWELTERS
SWELTING
SWELTRIER
SWELTRY
SWELTS
SWEPT
SWEPTBACK
SWEPTWING
SWERF
SWERFED
SWERFING
SWERFS
SWERVABLE
SWERVE
SWERVED
SWERVER
SWERVERS
SWERVES
SWERVING
SWERVINGS
SWEVEN
SWEVENS
SWEY
SWEYED
SWEYING
SWEYS
SWIDDEN
SWIDDENS

SWIES
SWIFT
SWIFTED
SWIFTER
SWIFTERS
SWIFTEST
SWIFTIE
SWIFTIES
SWIFTING
SWIFTLET
SWIFTLETS
SWIFTLY
SWIFTNESS
SWIFTS
SWIFTY
SWIG
SWIGGED
SWIGGER
SWIGGERS
SWIGGING
SWIGS
SWILE
SWILER
SWILERS
SWILES
SWILING
SWILINGS
SWILL
SWILLED
SWILLER
SWILLERS
SWILLING
SWILLINGS
SWILLS
SWIM
SWIMMABLE
SWIMMER
SWIMMERET
SWIMMERS
SWIMMIER
SWIMMIEST
SWIMMILY
SWIMMING
SWIMMINGS
SWIMMY
SWIMS
SWIMSUIT

SWIMSUITS
SWIMWEAR
SWIMWEARS
SWINDGE
SWINDGED
SWINDGES
SWINDGING
SWINDLE
SWINDLED
SWINDLER
SWINDLERS
SWINDLES
SWINDLING
SWINE
SWINEHERD
SWINEHOOD
SWINELIKE
SWINEPOX
SWINERIES
SWINERY
SWINES
SWING
SWINGARM
SWINGARMS
SWINGBEAT
SWINGBIN
SWINGBINS
SWINGBOAT
SWINGBY
SWINGBYS
SWINGE
SWINGED
SWINGEING
SWINGER
SWINGERS
SWINGES
SWINGIER
SWINGIEST
SWINGING
SWINGINGS
SWINGISM
SWINGISMS
SWINGLE
SWINGLED
SWINGLES
SWINGLING
SWINGMAN

SWINGMEN
SWINGS
SWINGTAIL
SWINGTREE
SWINGY
SWINISH
SWINISHLY
SWINK
SWINKED
SWINKER
SWINKERS
SWINKING
SWINKS
SWINNEY
SWINNEYS
SWIPE
SWIPED
SWIPER
SWIPERS
SWIPES
SWIPEY
SWIPIER
SWIPIEST
SWIPING
SWIPLE
SWIPLES
SWIPPLE
SWIPPLES
SWIRE
SWIRES
SWIRL
SWIRLED
SWIRLIER
SWIRLIEST
SWIRLING
SWIRLS
SWIRLY
SWISH
SWISHED
SWISHER
SWISHERS
SWISHES
SWISHEST
SWISHIER
SWISHIEST
SWISHING
SWISHINGS

SWISHY	SWOB	SWORDER	SYBBE	SYLLABICS
SWISS	SWOBBED	SWORDERS	SYBBES	SYLLABIFY
SWISSES	SWOBBER	SWORDFISH	SYBIL	SYLLABISE
SWISSING	SWOBBERS	SWORDING	SYBILS	SYLLABISM
SWISSINGS	SWOBBING	SWORDLESS	SYBO	SYLLABIZE
SWITCH	SWOBS	SWORDLIKE	SYBOE	SYLLABLE
SWITCHED	SWOFFER	SWORDMAN	SYBOES	SYLLABLED
SWITCHEL	SWOFFERS	SWORDMEN	SYBOTIC	SYLLABLES
SWITCHELS	SWOFFING	SWORDPLAY	SYBOTISM	SYLLABUB
SWITCHER	SWOFFINGS	SWORDS	SYBOTISMS	SYLLABUBS
SWITCHERS	SWOLLEN	SWORDSMAN	SYBOW	SYLLABUS
SWITCHES	SWOLLENLY	SWORDSMEN	SYBOWS	SYLLEPSES
SWITCHIER	SWOLN	SWORDTAIL	SYCAMINE	SYLLEPSIS
SWITCHING	SWOON	SWORE	SYCAMINES	SYLLEPTIC
SWITCHMAN	SWOONED	SWORN	SYCAMORE	SYLLOGE
SWITCHMEN	SWOONER	SWOT	SYCAMORES	SYLLOGES
SWITCHY	SWOONERS	SWOTS	SYCE	SYLLOGISE
SWITH	SWOONIER	SWOTTED	SYCEE	SYLLOGISM
SWITHE	SWOONIEST	SWOTTER	SYCEES	SYLLOGIST
SWITHER	SWOONING	SWOTTERS	SYCES	SYLLOGIZE
SWITHERED	SWOONINGS	SWOTTIER	SYCOMORE	SYLPH
SWITHERS	SWOONS	SWOTTIEST	SYCOMORES	SYLPHIC
SWITHLY	SWOONY	SWOTTING	SYCON	SYLPHID
SWITS	SWOOP	SWOTTINGS	SYCONIA	SYLPHIDE
SWITSES	SWOOPED	SWOTTY	SYCONIUM	SYLPHIDES
SWIVE	SWOOPER	SWOUN	SYCONOID	SYLPHIDS
SWIVED	SWOOPERS	SWOUND	SYCONS	SYLPHIER
SWIVEL	SWOOPIER	SWOUNDED	SYCOPHANT	SYLPHIEST
SWIVELED	SWOOPIEST	SWOUNDING	SYCOSES	SYLPHINE
SWIVELING	SWOOPING	SWOUNDS	SYCOSIS	SYLPHISH
SWIVELLED	SWOOPS	SWOUNE	SYE	SYLPHLIKE
SWIVELS	SWOOPY	SWOUNED	SYED	SYLPHS
SWIVES	SWOOSH	SWOUNES	SYEING	SYLPHY
SWIVET	SWOOSHED	SWOUNING	SYEN	SYLVA
SWIVETS	SWOOSHES	SWOUNS	SYENITE	SYLVAE
SWIVING	SWOOSHING	SWOWND	SYENITES	SYLVAN
SWIZ	SWOP	SWOWNDS	SYENITIC	SYLVANER
SWIZZ	SWOPPED	SWOWNE	SYENS	SYLVANERS
SWIZZED	SWOPPER	SWOWNES	SYENS	SYLVANITE
SWIZZES	SWOPPERS	SWOZZLE	SYES	SYLVANS
SWIZZING	SWOPPING	SWOZZLES	SYKE	SYLVAS
SWIZZLE	SWOPPINGS	SWUM	SYKER	SYLVATIC
SWIZZLED	SWOPS	SWUNG	SYKES	SYLVIA
SWIZZLER	SWOPT	SWY	SYLI	SYLVIAS
SWIZZLERS	SWORD	SYBARITE	SYLIS	SYLVIINE
SWIZZLES	SWORDBILL	SYBARITES	SYLLABARY	SYLVIN
SWIZZLING	SWORDED	SYBARITIC	SYLLABI	SYLVINE
			SYLLABIC	

S

SYLVINES	SYMPHILY	SYNAPTES	SYNDETONS	SYNGASES
SYLVINITE	SYMPHONIC	SYNAPTIC	SYNDETS	SYNGASSES
SYLVINS	SYMPHONY	SYNARCHY	SYNDIC	SYNGENEIC
SYLVITE	SYMPHYSES	SYNASTRY	SYNDICAL	SYNGENIC
SYLVITES	SYMPHYSIS	SYNAXARIA	SYNDICATE	SYNGRAPH
SYMAR	SYMPHYTIC	SYNAXES	SYNDICS	SYNGRAPHS
SYMARS	SYMPLAST	SYNAXIS	SYNDING	SYNING
SYMBION	SYMPLASTS	SYNBIOTIC	SYNDINGS	SYNIZESES
SYMBIONS	SYMPLOCE	SYNC	SYNDROME	SYNIZESIS
SYMBIONT	SYMPLOCES	SYNCARP	SYNDROMES	SYNKARYA
SYMBIONTS	SYMPODIA	SYNCARPS	SYNDROMIC	SYNKARYON
SYMBIOSES	SYMPODIAL	SYNCARPY	SYNDS	SYNOD
SYMBIOSIS	SYMPODIUM	SYNCED	SYNE	SYNODAL
SYMBIOT	SYMPOSIA	SYNCH	SYNECHIA	SYNODALS
SYMBIOTE	SYMPOSIAC	SYNCHED	SYNECHIAS	SYNODIC
SYMBIOTES	SYMPOSIAL	SYNCHING	SYNECIOUS	SYNODICAL
SYMBIOTIC	SYMPOSIUM	SYNCHRO	SYNECTIC	SYNODS
SYMBIOTS	SYMPTOM	SYNCHRONY	SYNECTICS	SYNODSMAN
SYMBOL	SYMPTOMS	SYNCHROS	SYNED	SYNODSMEN
SYMBOLE	SYMPTOSES	SYNCHS	SYNEDRIA	SYNOECETE
SYMBOLED	SYMPTOSIS	SYNCHYSES	SYNEDRIAL	SYNOECISE
SYMBOLES	SYMPTOTIC	SYNCHYSIS	SYNEDRION	SYNOECISM
SYMBOLIC	SYN	SYNCING	SYNEDRIUM	SYNOECIZE
SYMBOLICS	SYNAGOG	SYNCLINAL	SYNERESES	SYNOEKETE
SYMBOLING	SYNAGOGAL	SYNCLINE	SYNERESIS	SYNOICOUS
SYMBOLISE	SYNAGOGS	SYNCLINES	SYNERGIA	SYNONYM
SYMBOLISM	SYNAGOGUE	SYNCOM	SYNERGIAS	SYNONYME
SYMBOLIST	SYNALEPHA	SYNCOMS	SYNERGIC	SYNONYMES
SYMBOLIZE	SYNANDRIA	SYNCOPAL	SYNERGID	SYNONYMIC
SYMBOLLED	SYNANGIA	SYNCOPATE	SYNERGIDS	SYNONYMS
SYMBOLOGY	SYNANGIUM	SYNCOPE	SYNERGIES	SYNONYMY
SYMBOLS	SYNANON	SYNCOPES	SYNERGISE	SYNOPSES
SYMITAR	SYNANONS	SYNCOPIC	SYNERGISM	SYNOPSIS
SYMITARE	SYNANTHIC	SYNCOPTIC	SYNERGIST	SYNOPSISE
SYMITARES	SYNANTHY	SYNCRETIC	SYNERGIZE	SYNOPSIZE
SYMITARS	SYNAPHEA	SYNCS	SYNERGY	SYNOPTIC
SYMMETRAL	SYNAPHEAS	SYNCYTIA	SYNES	SYNOPTICS
SYMMETRIC	SYNAPHEIA	SYNCYTIAL	SYNESES	SYNOPTIST
SYMMETRY	SYNAPSE	SYNCYTIUM	SYNESIS	SYNOVIA
SYMPATHIN	SYNAPSED	SYND	SYNESISES	SYNOVIAL
SYMPATHY	SYNAPSES	SYNDACTYL	SYNFUEL	SYNOVIAS
SYMPATICO	SYNAPSID	SYNDED	SYNFUELS	SYNOVITIC
SYMPATRIC	SYNAPSIDS	SYNDESES	SYNGAMIC	SYNOVITIS
SYMPATRY	SYNAPSING	SYNDESIS	SYNGAMIES	SYNROC
SYMPETALY	SYNAPSIS	SYNDET	SYNGAMOUS	SYNROCS
SYMPHILE	SYNAPTASE	SYNDETIC	SYNGAMY	SYNTACTIC
SYMPHILES	SYNAPTE	SYNDETON	SYNGAS	SYNTAGM

SYNTAGMA
SYNTAGMAS
SYNTAGMIC
SYNTAGMS
SYNTAN
SYNTANS
SYNTAX
SYNTAXES
SYNTECTIC
SYNTENIC
SYNTENIES
SYNTENY
SYNTEXIS
SYNTH
SYNTHASE
SYNTHASES
SYNTHESES
SYNTHESIS
SYNTHETIC
SYNTHON
SYNTHONS
SYNTHPOP
SYNTHPOPS
SYNTHRONI

SYNTHS
SYNTONE
SYNTONES
SYNTONIC
SYNTONIES
SYNTONIN
SYNTONINS
SYNTONISE
SYNTONIZE
SYNTONOUS
SYNTONY
SYNTYPE
SYNTYPES
SYNURA
SYNURAE
SYPE
SYPED
SYPES
SYPH
SYPHER
SYPHERED
SYPHERING
SYPHERS
SYPHILIS

SYPHILISE
SYPHILIZE
SYPHILOID
SYPHILOMA
SYPHON
SYPHONAL
SYPHONED
SYPHONIC
SYPHONING
SYPHONS
SYPHS
SYPING
SYRAH
SYRAHS
SYREN
SYRENS
SYRETTE
SYRETTES
SYRINGA
SYRINGAS
SYRINGE
SYRINGEAL
SYRINGED
SYRINGES

SYRINGING
SYRINX
SYRINXES
SYRPHIAN
SYRPHIANS
SYRPHID
SYRPHIDS
SYRTES
SYRTIS
SYRUP
SYRUPED
SYRUPIER
SYRUPIEST
SYRUPING
SYRUPLIKE
SYRUPS
SYRUPY
SYSADMIN
SYSADMINS
SYSOP
SYSOPS
SYSSITIA
SYSSITIAS
SYSTALTIC

SYSTEM
SYSTEMED
SYSTEMIC
SYSTEMICS
SYSTEMISE
SYSTEMIZE
SYSTEMS
SYSTOLE
SYSTOLES
SYSTOLIC
SYSTYLE
SYSTYLES
SYTHE
SYTHES
SYVER
SYVERS
SYZYGAL
SYZYGETIC
SYZYGIAL
SYZYGIES
SYZYGY

S

T

TA	TABERED	TABLINGS	TABRETS	TACHO
TAAL	TABERING	TABLOID	TABS	TACHOGRAM
TAALS	TABERS	TABLOIDS	TABU	TACHOS
TAATA	TABES	TABLOIDY	TABUED	TACHS
TAATAS	TABESCENT	TABOGGAN	TABUING	TACHYLITE
TAB	TABETIC	TABOGGANS	TABULA	TACHYLYTE
TABANID	TABETICS	TABOO	TABULABLE	TACHYON
TABANIDS	TABI	TABOOED	TABULAE	TACHYONIC
TABARD	TABID	TABOOING	TABULAR	TACHYONS
TABARDED	TABINET	TABOOLEY	TABULARLY	TACHYPNEA
TABARDS	TABINETS	TABOOLEYS	TABULATE	TACIT
TABARET	TABIS	TABOOS	TABULATED	TACITLY
TABARETS	TABLA	TABOR	TABULATES	TACITNESS
TABASHEER	TABLAS	TABORED	TABULATOR	TACITURN
TABASHIR	TABLATURE	TABORER	TABULI	TACK
TABASHIRS	TABLE	TABORERS	TABULIS	TACKBOARD
TABBED	TABLEAU	TABORET	TABUN	TACKED
TABBIED	TABLEAUS	TABORETS	TABUNS	TACKER
TABBIES	TABLEAUX	TABORIN	TABUS	TACKERS
TABBINET	TABLED	TABORINE	TACAHOUT	TACKET
TABBINETS	TABLEFUL	TABORINES	TACAHOUTS	TACKETS
TABBING	TABLEFULS	TABORING	TACAMAHAC	TACKETY
TABBINGS	TABLELAND	TABORINS	TACAN	TACKEY
TABBIS	TABLELESS	TABORS	TACANS	TACKIER
TABBISES	TABLEMAT	TABOULEH	TACE	TACKIES
TABBOULEH	TABLEMATE	TABOULEHS	TACES	TACKIEST
TABBOULI	TABLEMATS	TABOULI	TACET	TACKIFIED
TABBOULIS	TABLES	TABOULIS	TACH	TACKIFIER
TABBY	TABLESFUL	TABOUR	TACHE	TACKIFIES
TABBYHOOD	TABLET	TABOURED	TACHES	TACKIFY
TABBYING	TABLETED	TABOURER	TACHINA	TACKILY
TABEFIED	TABLETING	TABOURERS	TACHINID	TACKINESS
TABEFIES	TABLETOP	TABOURET	TACHINIDS	TACKING
TABEFY	TABLETOPS	TABOURETS	TACHISM	TACKINGS
TABEFYING	TABLETS	TABOURIN	TACHISME	TACKLE
TABELLION	TABLETTED	TABOURING	TACHISMES	TACKLED
TABER	TABLEWARE	TABOURINS	TACHISMS	TACKLER
TABERD	TABLEWISE	TABOURS	TACHIST	TACKLERS
TABERDAR	TABLIER	TABRERE	TACHISTE	TACKLES
TABERDARS	TABLIERS	TABRERES	TACHISTES	TACKLESS
TABERDS	TABLING	TABRET	TACHISTS	TACKLING

TACKLINGS
TACKS
TACKSMAN
TACKSMEN
TACKY
TACMAHACK
TACNODE
TACNODES
TACO
TACONITE
TACONITES
TACOS
TACRINE
TACRINES
TACT
TACTFUL
TACTFULLY
TACTIC
TACTICAL
TACTICIAN
TACTICITY
TACTICS
TACTILE
TACTILELY
TACTILIST
TACTILITY
TACTION
TACTIONS
TACTISM
TACTISMS
TACTLESS
TACTS
TACTUAL
TACTUALLY
TAD
TADDIE
TADDIES
TADPOLE
TADPOLES
TADS
TAE
TAED
TAEDIUM
TAEDIUMS
TAEING
TAEKWONDO
TAEL

TAELS
TAENIA
TAENIAE
TAENIAS
TAENIASES
TAENIASIS
TAENIATE
TAENIOID
TAENITE
TAENITES
TAES
TAFFAREL
TAFFARELS
TAFFEREL
TAFFERELS
TAFFETA
TAFFETAS
TAFFETY
TAFFIA
TAFFIAS
TAFFIES
TAFFRAIL
TAFFRAILS
TAFFY
TAFIA
TAFIAS
TAG
TAGALONG
TAGALONGS
TAGAREEN
TAGAREENS
TAGBOARD
TAGBOARDS
TAGETES
TAGGANT
TAGGANTS
TAGGED
TAGGEE
TAGGEES
TAGGER
TAGGERS
TAGGIER
TAGGIEST
TAGGING
TAGGINGS
TAGGY
TAGHAIRM

TAGHAIRMS
TAGINE
TAGINES
TAGLESS
TAGLIKE
TAGLINE
TAGLINES
TAGLIONI
TAGLIONIS
TAGMA
TAGMATA
TAGMEME
TAGMEMES
TAGMEMIC
TAGMEMICS
TAGRAG
TAGRAGS
TAGS
TAGUAN
TAGUANS
TAHA
TAHAS
TAHINA
TAHINAS
TAHINI
TAHINIS
TAHR
TAHRS
TAHSIL
TAHSILDAR
TAHSILS
TAI
TAIAHA
TAIAHAS
TAIG
TAIGA
TAIGAS
TAIGLACH
TAIGLE
TAIGLED
TAIGLES
TAIGLING
TAIGS
TAIHOA
TAIKO
TAIKONAUT
TAIKOS

TAIL
TAILARD
TAILARDS
TAILBACK
TAILBACKS
TAILBOARD
TAILBONE
TAILBONES
TAILCOAT
TAILCOATS
TAILED
TAILENDER
TAILER
TAILERON
TAILERONS
TAILERS
TAILFAN
TAILFANS
TAILFIN
TAILFINS
TAILFLIES
TAILFLY
TAILGATE
TAILGATED
TAILGATER
TAILGATES
TAILHOOK
TAILHOOKS
TAILING
TAILINGS
TAILLAMP
TAILLAMPS
TAILLE
TAILLES
TAILLESS
TAILLEUR
TAILLEURS
TAILLIE
TAILLIES
TAILLIGHT
TAILLIKE
TAILOR
TAILORED
TAILORESS
TAILORING
TAILORS
TAILPIECE

TAILPIPE
TAILPIPED
TAILPIPES
TAILPLANE
TAILRACE
TAILRACES
TAILS
TAILSKID
TAILSKIDS
TAILSLIDE
TAILSPIN
TAILSPINS
TAILSPUN
TAILSTOCK
TAILWATER
TAILWHEEL
TAILWIND
TAILWINDS
TAILYE
TAILYES
TAILZIE
TAILZIES
TAIN
TAINS
TAINT
TAINTED
TAINTING
TAINTLESS
TAINTS
TAINTURE
TAINTURES
TAIPAN
TAIPANS
TAIRA
TAIRAS
TAIS
TAISCH
TAISCHES
TAISH
TAISHES
TAIT
TAITS
TAIVER
TAIVERED
TAIVERING
TAIVERS
TAIVERT

T

TAJ	TALAKS	TALERS	TALLAGING	TALLY
TAJES	TALANT	TALES	TALLAISIM	TALLYHO
TAJINE	TALANTS	TALESMAN	TALLAT	TALLYHOED
TAJINES	TALAPOIN	TALESMEN	TALLATS	TALLYHOES
TAK	TALAPOINS	TALEYSIM	TALLBOY	TALLYHOS
TAKA	TALAQ	TALI	TALLBOYS	TALLYING
TAKABLE	TALAQS	TALIGRADE	TALLENT	TALLYMAN
TAKAHE	TALAR	TALION	TALLENTS	TALLYMEN
TAKAHES	TALARIA	TALIONIC	TALLER	TALLYSHOP
TAKAMAKA	TALARS	TALIONS	TALLEST	TALMA
TAKAMAKAS	TALAS	TALIPAT	TALLET	TALMAS
TAKAS	TALAUNT	TALIPATS	TALLETS	TALMUD
TAKE	TALAUNTS	TALIPED	TALLGRASS	TALMUDIC
TAKEABLE	TALAYOT	TALIPEDS	TALLIABLE	TALMUDISM
TAKEAWAY	TALAYOTS	TALIPES	TALLIATE	TALMUDS
TAKEAWAYS	TALBOT	TALIPOT	TALLIATED	TALON
TAKEDOWN	TALBOTS	TALIPOTS	TALLIATES	TALONED
TAKEDOWNS	TALBOTYPE	TALISMAN	TALLIED	TALONS
TAKEN	TALC	TALISMANS	TALLIER	TALOOKA
TAKEOFF	TALCED	TALK	TALLIERS	TALOOKAS
TAKEOFFS	TALCIER	TALKABLE	TALLIES	TALPA
TAKEOUT	TALCIEST	TALKATHON	TALLIS	TALPAE
TAKEOUTS	TALCING	TALKATIVE	TALLISES	TALPAS
TAKEOVER	TALCKED	TALKBACK	TALLISH	TALUK
TAKEOVERS	TALCKIER	TALKBACKS	TALLISIM	TALUKA
TAKER	TALCKIEST	TALKBOX	TALLIT	TALUKAS
TAKERS	TALCKING	TALKBOXES	TALLITES	TALUKDAR
TAKES	TALCKY	TALKED	TALLITH	TALUKDARS
TAKEUP	TALCOSE	TALKER	TALLITHES	TALUKS
TAKEUPS	TALCOUS	TALKERS	TALLITHIM	TALUS
TAKHI	TALCS	TALKFEST	TALLITHS	TALUSES
TAKHIS	TALCUM	TALKFESTS	TALLITIM	TALWEG
TAKI	TALCUMED	TALKIE	TALLITOT	TALWEGS
TAKIER	TALCUMING	TALKIER	TALLITOTH	TAM
TAKIEST	TALCUMS	TALKIES	TALLITS	TAMABLE
TAKIN	TALCY	TALKIEST	TALLNESS	TAMAL
TAKING	TALE	TALKINESS	TALLOL	TAMALE
TAKINGLY	TALEA	TALKING	TALLOLS	TAMALES
TAKINGS	TALEAE	TALKINGS	TALLOT	TAMALS
TAKINS	TALEFUL	TALKS	TALLOTS	TAMANDU
TAKIS	TALEGALLA	TALKTIME	TALLOW	TAMANDUA
TAKKIES	TALEGGIO	TALKTIMES	TALLOWED	TAMANDUAS
TAKKY	TALEGGIOS	TALKY	TALLOWING	TAMANDUS
TAKS	TALENT	TALL	TALLOWISH	TAMANOIR
TAKY	TALENTED	TALLAGE	TALLOWS	TAMANOIRS
TALA	TALENTS	TALLAGED	TALLOWY	TAMANU
TALAK	TALER	TALLAGES	TALLS	TAMANUS

TAMARA	TAMENESS	TAMWORTHS	TANGIEST	TANKFUL
TAMARACK	TAMER	TAN	TANGINESS	TANKFULS
TAMARACKS	TAMERS	TANA	TANGING	TANKIA
TAMARAO	TAMES	TANADAR	TANGIS	TANKIAS
TAMARAOS	TAMEST	TANADARS	TANGLE	TANKIES
TAMARAS	TAMIN	TANAGER	TANGLED	TANKING
TAMARAU	TAMINE	TANAGERS	TANGLER	TANKINGS
TAMARAUS	TAMINES	TANAGRA	TANGLERS	TANKINI
TAMARI	TAMING	TANAGRAS	TANGLES	TANKINIS
TAMARILLO	TAMINGS	TANAGRINE	TANGLIER	TANKLESS
TAMARIN	TAMINS	TANAISTE	TANGLIEST	TANKLIKE
TAMARIND	TAMIS	TANAISTES	TANGLING	TANKS
TAMARINDS	TAMISE	TANALISED	TANGLINGS	TANKSHIP
TAMARINS	TAMISES	TANALIZED	TANGLY	TANKSHIPS
TAMARIS	TAMMAR	TANAS	TANGO	TANKY
TAMARISK	TAMMARS	TANBARK	TANGOED	TANLING
TAMARISKS	TAMMIE	TANBARKS	TANGOES	TANLINGS
TAMASHA	TAMMIED	TANDEM	TANGOING	TANNA
TAMASHAS	TAMMIES	TANDEMS	TANGOIST	TANNABLE
TAMBAC	TAMMY	TANDOOR	TANGOISTS	TANNAGE
TAMBACS	TAMMYING	TANDOORI	TANGOLIKE	TANNAGES
TAMBAK	TAMOXIFEN	TANDOORIS	TANGOS	TANNAH
TAMBAKS	TAMP	TANDOORS	TANGRAM	TANNAHS
TAMBALA	TAMPALA	TANE	TANGRAMS	TANNAS
TAMBALAS	TAMPALAS	TANG	TANGS	TANNATE
TAMBER	TAMPAN	TANGA	TANGUN	TANNATES
TAMBERS	TAMPANS	TANGAS	TANGUNS	TANNED
TAMBOUR	TAMPED	TANGED	TANGY	TANNER
TAMBOURA	TAMPER	TANGELO	TANH	TANNERIES
TAMBOURAS	TAMPERED	TANGELOS	TANHS	TANNERS
TAMBOURED	TAMPERER	TANGENCE	TANIST	TANNERY
TAMBOURER	TAMPERERS	TANGENCES	TANISTRY	TANNEST
TAMBOURIN	TAMPERING	TANGENCY	TANISTS	TANNIC
TAMBOURS	TAMPERS	TANGENT	TANIWHA	TANNIE
TAMBUR	TAMPING	TANGENTAL	TANIWHAS	TANNIES
TAMBURA	TAMPINGS	TANGENTS	TANK	TANNIN
TAMBURAS	TAMPION	TANGERINE	TANKA	TANNING
TAMBURIN	TAMPIONS	TANGHIN	TANKAGE	TANNINGS
TAMBURINS	TAMPON	TANGHININ	TANKAGES	TANNINS
TAMBURS	TAMPONADE	TANGHINS	TANKARD	TANNISH
TAME	TAMPONAGE	TANGI	TANKARDS	TANNOY
TAMEABLE	TAMPONED	TANGIBLE	TANKAS	TANNOYED
TAMED	TAMPONING	TANGIBLES	TANKED	TANNOYING
TAMEIN	TAMPONS	TANGIBLY	TANKER	TANNOYS
TAMEINS	TAMPS	TANGIE	TANKERED	TANOREXIC
TAMELESS	TAMS	TANGIER	TANKERING	TANREC
TAMELY	TAMWORTH	TANGIES	TANKERS	TANRECS

T

TANS	TAPADERA	TAPIOCA	TAR	TARGAS
TANSIES	TAPADERAS	TAPIOCAS	TARA	TARGE
TANSY	TAPADERO	TAPIR	TARABISH	TARGED
TANTALATE	TAPADEROS	TAPIROID	TARAIRE	TARGES
TANTALIC	TAPALO	TAPIROIDS	TARAIRES	TARGET
TANTALISE	TAPALOS	TAPIRS	TARAKIHI	TARGETED
TANTALISM	TAPAS	TAPIS	TARAKIHIS	TARGETEER
TANTALITE	TAPE	TAPISES	TARAMA	TARGETING
TANTALIZE	TAPEABLE	TAPIST	TARAMAS	TARGETS
TANTALOUS	TAPED	TAPISTS	TARAMEA	TARGING
TANTALUM	TAPELESS	TAPLASH	TARAMEAS	TARIFF
TANTALUMS	TAPELIKE	TAPLASHES	TARAND	TARIFFED
TANTALUS	TAPELINE	TAPLESS	TARANDS	TARIFFING
TANTARA	TAPELINES	TAPPA	TARANTARA	TARIFFS
TANTARARA	TAPEN	TAPPABLE	TARANTAS	TARING
TANTARAS	TAPENADE	TAPPAS	TARANTASS	TARINGS
TANTI	TAPENADES	TAPPED	TARANTISM	TARLATAN
TANTIVIES	TAPER	TAPPER	TARANTIST	TARLATANS
TANTIVY	TAPERED	TAPPERS	TARANTULA	TARLETAN
TANTO	TAPERER	TAPPET	TARAS	TARLETANS
TANTONIES	TAPERERS	TAPPETS	TARAXACUM	TARMAC
TANTONY	TAPERING	TAPPICE	TARBOGGIN	TARMACKED
TANTOS	TAPERINGS	TAPPICED	TARBOOSH	TARMACS
TANTRA	TAPERNESS	TAPPICES	TARBOUCHE	TARN
TANTRAS	TAPERS	TAPPICING	TARBOUSH	TARNAL
TANTRIC	TAPERWISE	TAPPING	TARBOY	TARNALLY
TANTRISM	TAPES	TAPPINGS	TARBOYS	TARNATION
TANTRISMS	TAPESTRY	TAPPIT	TARBUSH	TARNISH
TANTRIST	TAPET	TAPROOM	TARBUSHES	TARNISHED
TANTRISTS	TAPETA	TAPROOMS	TARCEL	TARNISHER
TANTRUM	TAPETAL	TAPROOT	TARCELS	TARNISHES
TANTRUMS	TAPETED	TAPROOTED	TARDIED	TARNS
TANUKI	TAPETI	TAPROOTS	TARDIER	TARO
TANUKIS	TAPETING	TAPS	TARDIES	TAROC
TANYARD	TAPETIS	TAPSMAN	TARDIEST	TAROCS
TANYARDS	TAPETS	TAPSMEN	TARDILY	TAROK
TANZANITE	TAPETUM	TAPSTER	TARDINESS	TAROKS
TAO	TAPETUMS	TAPSTERS	TARDIVE	TAROS
TAONGA	TAPEWORM	TAPSTRESS	TARDO	TAROT
TAONGAS	TAPEWORMS	TAPSTRIES	TARDY	TAROTS
TAOS	TAPHOLE	TAPSTRY	TARDYING	TARP
TAP	TAPHOLES	TAPU	TARDYON	TARPAN
TAPA	TAPHONOMY	TAPUED	TARDYONS	TARPANS
TAPACOLO	TAPHOUSE	TAPUING	TARE	TARPAPER
TAPACOLOS	TAPHOUSES	TAPUS	TARED	TARPAPERS
TAPACULO	TAPING	TAQUERIA	TARES	TARPAULIN
TAPACULOS	TAPINGS	TAQUERIAS	TARGA	TARPON

TARPONS	TARTANAS	TARZAN	TASSES	TATOUAY
TARPS	TARTANE	TARZANS	TASSET	TATOUAYS
TARRAGON	TARTANED	TAS	TASSETS	TATOUS
TARRAGONS	TARTANES	TASAR	TASSIE	TATS
TARRAS	TARTANRY	TASARS	TASSIES	TATSOI
TARRASES	TARTANS	TASBIH	TASSO	TATSOIS
TARRE	TARTAR	TASBIHS	TASSOS	TATT
TARRED	TARTARE	TASE	TASSWAGE	TATTED
TARRES	TARTARES	TASED	TASTABLE	TATTER
TARRIANCE	TARTARIC	TASER	TASTE	TATTERED
TARRIED	TARTARISE	TASERED	TASTEABLE	TATTERING
TARRIER	TARTARIZE	TASERING	TASTED	TATTERS
TARRIERS	TARTARLY	TASERS	TASTEFUL	TATTERY
TARRIES	TARTAROUS	TASES	TASTELESS	TATTIE
TARRIEST	TARTARS	TASH	TASTER	TATTIER
TARRINESS	TARTED	TASHED	TASTERS	TATTIES
TARRING	TARTER	TASHES	TASTES	TATTIEST
TARRINGS	TARTEST	TASHING	TASTEVIN	TATTILY
TARROCK	TARTIER	TASIMETER	TASTEVINS	TATTINESS
TARROCKS	TARTIEST	TASIMETRY	TASTIER	TATTING
TARROW	TARTILY	TASING	TASTIEST	TATTINGS
TARROWED	TARTINE	TASK	TASTILY	TATTLE
TARROWING	TARTINES	TASKBAR	TASTINESS	TATTLED
TARROWS	TARTINESS	TASKBARS	TASTING	TATTLER
TARRY	TARTING	TASKED	TASTINGS	TATTLERS
TARRYING	TARTISH	TASKER	TASTY	TATTLES
TARS	TARTISHLY	TASKERS	TAT	TATTLING
TARSAL	TARTLET	TASKING	TATAHASH	TATTLINGS
TARSALGIA	TARTLETS	TASKINGS	TATAMI	TATTOO
TARSALS	TARTLY	TASKLESS	TATAMIS	TATTOOED
TARSEAL	TARTNESS	TASKS	TATAR	TATTOOER
TARSEALS	TARTRATE	TASKWORK	TATARS	TATTOOERS
TARSEL	TARTRATED	TASKWORKS	TATE	TATTOOING
TARSELS	TARTRATES	TASLET	TATER	TATTOOIST
TARSI	TARTS	TASLETS	TATERS	TATTOOS
TARSIA	TARTUFE	TASS	TATES	TATTOW
TARSIAS	TARTUFES	TASSA	TATH	TATTOWED
TARSIER	TARTUFFE	TASSAS	TATHATA	TATTOWING
TARSIERS	TARTUFFES	TASSE	TATHATAS	TATTOWS
TARSIOID	TARTUFI	TASSEL	TATHED	TATTS
TARSIOIDS	TARTUFO	TASSELED	TATHING	TATTY
TARSIPED	TARTUFOS	TASSELING	TATHS	TATU
TARSIPEDS	TARTY	TASSELL	TATIE	TATUED
TARSUS	TARWEED	TASSELLED	TATIES	TATUING
TART	TARWEEDS	TASSELLS	TATLER	TATUS
TARTAN	TARWHINE	TASSELLY	TATLERS	TAU
TARTANA	TARWHINES	TASSELS	TATOU	TAUBE

TAUBES	TAUTOMER	TAWNEY	TAXIING	TCHOTCHKE
TAUGHT	TAUTOMERS	TAWNEYS	TAXIMAN	TE
TAUHINU	TAUTONYM	TAWNIER	TAXIMEN	TEA
TAUHINUS	TAUTONYMS	TAWNIES	TAXIMETER	TEABAG
TAUHOU	TAUTONYMY	TAWNIEST	TAXING	TEABAGS
TAUHOUS	TAUTS	TAWNILY	TAXINGLY	TEABERRY
TAUIWI	TAV	TAWNINESS	TAXINGS	TEABOARD
TAUIWIS	TAVA	TAWNY	TAXIPLANE	TEABOARDS
TAULD	TAVAH	TAWPIE	TAXIS	TEABOWL
TAUNT	TAVAHS	TAWPIES	TAXISES	TEABOWLS
TAUNTED	TAVAS	TAWS	TAXITE	TEABOX
TAUNTER	TAVER	TAWSE	TAXITES	TEABOXES
TAUNTERS	TAVERED	TAWSED	TAXITIC	TEABREAD
TAUNTING	TAVERING	TAWSES	TAXIWAY	TEABREADS
TAUNTINGS	TAVERN	TAWSING	TAXIWAYS	TEACAKE
TAUNTS	TAVERNA	TAWT	TAXLESS	TEACAKES
TAUON	TAVERNAS	TAWTED	TAXMAN	TEACART
TAUONS	TAVERNER	TAWTIE	TAXMEN	TEACARTS
TAUPATA	TAVERNERS	TAWTIER	TAXOL	TEACH
TAUPATAS	TAVERNS	TAWTIEST	TAXOLS	TEACHABLE
TAUPE	TAVERS	TAWTING	TAXON	TEACHABLY
TAUPES	TAVERT	TAWTS	TAXONOMER	TEACHER
TAUPIE	TAVS	TAX	TAXONOMIC	TEACHERLY
TAUPIES	TAW	TAXA	TAXONOMY	TEACHERS
TAUREAN	TAWA	TAXABLE	TAXONS	TEACHES
TAURIC	TAWAI	TAXABLES	TAXOR	TEACHIE
TAURIFORM	TAWAIS	TAXABLY	TAXORS	TEACHING
TAURINE	TAWAS	TAXACEOUS	TAXPAID	TEACHINGS
TAURINES	TAWDRIER	TAXAMETER	TAXPAYER	TEACHLESS
TAUS	TAWDRIES	TAXATION	TAXPAYERS	TEACUP
TAUT	TAWDRIEST	TAXATIONS	TAXPAYING	TEACUPFUL
TAUTAUG	TAWDRILY	TAXATIVE	TAXUS	TEACUPS
TAUTAUGS	TAWDRY	TAXED	TAXWISE	TEAD
TAUTED	TAWED	TAXEME	TAXYING	TEADE
TAUTEN	TAWER	TAXEMES	TAY	TEADES
TAUTENED	TAWERIES	TAXEMIC	TAYASSUID	TEADS
TAUTENING	TAWERS	TAXER	TAYBERRY	TEAED
TAUTENS	TAWERY	TAXERS	TAYRA	TEAGLE
TAUTER	TAWHAI	TAXES	TAYRAS	TEAGLED
TAUTEST	TAWHAIS	TAXI	TAYS	TEAGLES
TAUTING	TAWHIRI	TAXIARCH	TAZZA	TEAGLING
TAUTIT	TAWHIRIS	TAXIARCHS	TAZZAS	TEAHOUSE
TAUTLY	TAWIE	TAXICAB	TAZZE	TEAHOUSES
TAUTNESS	TAWIER	TAXICABS	TCHICK	TEAING
TAUTOG	TAWIEST	TAXIDERMY	TCHICKED	TEAK
TAUTOGS	TAWING	TAXIED	TCHICKING	TEAKETTLE
TAUTOLOGY	TAWINGS	TAXIES	TCHICKS	TEAKS

TEAKWOOD	TEARLESS	TEAZING	TEDDERED	TEENERS
TEAKWOODS	TEARLIKE	TEAZLE	TEDDERING	TEENES
TEAL	TEAROOM	TEAZLED	TEDDERS	TEENFUL
TEALIGHT	TEAROOMS	TEAZLES	TEDDIE	TEENIER
TEALIGHTS	TEARS	TEAZLING	TEDDIES	TEENIEST
TEALIKE	TEARSHEET	TEBBAD	TEDDING	TEENING
TEALS	TEARSTAIN	TEBBADS	TEDDY	TEENS
TEAM	TEARSTRIP	TEC	TEDIER	TEENSIER
TEAMAKER	TEARY	TECH	TEDIEST	TEENSIEST
TEAMAKERS	TEAS	TECHED	TEDIOSITY	TEENSY
TEAMED	TEASABLE	TECHIE	TEDIOUS	TEENTIER
TEAMER	TEASE	TECHIER	TEDIOUSLY	TEENTIEST
TEAMERS	TEASED	TECHIES	TEDISOME	TEENTSIER
TEAMING	TEASEL	TECHIEST	TEDIUM	TEENTSY
TEAMINGS	TEASELED	TECHILY	TEDIUMS	TEENTY
TEAMMATE	TEASELER	TECHINESS	TEDS	TEENY
TEAMMATES	TEASELERS	TECHNIC	TEDY	TEENYBOP
TEAMS	TEASELING	TECHNICAL	TEE	TEEPEE
TEAMSTER	TEASELLED	TECHNICS	TEED	TEEPEES
TEAMSTERS	TEASELLER	TECHNIKON	TEEING	TEER
TEAMWISE	TEASELS	TECHNIQUE	TEEK	TEERED
TEAMWORK	TEASER	TECHNO	TEEL	TEERING
TEAMWORKS	TEASERS	TECHNOID	TEELS	TEERS
TEAPOT	TEASES	TECHNOIDS	TEEM	TEES
TEAPOTS	TEASHOP	TECHNOPOP	TEEMED	TEETER
TEAPOY	TEASHOPS	TECHNOS	TEEMER	TEETERED
TEAPOYS	TEASING	TECHS	TEEMERS	TEETERING
TEAR	TEASINGLY	TECHY	TEEMFUL	TEETERS
TEARABLE	TEASINGS	TECKEL	TEEMING	TEETH
TEARAWAY	TEASPOON	TECKELS	TEEMINGLY	TEETHE
TEARAWAYS	TEASPOONS	TECS	TEEMLESS	TEETHED
TEARDOWN	TEAT	TECTA	TEEMS	TEETHER
TEARDOWNS	TEATASTER	TECTAL	TEEN	TEETHERS
TEARDROP	TEATED	TECTIFORM	TEENAGE	TEETHES
TEARDROPS	TEATIME	TECTITE	TEENAGED	TEETHING
TEARED	TEATIMES	TECTITES	TEENAGER	TEETHINGS
TEARER	TEATS	TECTONIC	TEENAGERS	TEETHLESS
TEARERS	TEAWARE	TECTONICS	TEENAGES	TEETOTAL
TEARFUL	TEAWARES	TECTONISM	TEEND	TEETOTALS
TEARFULLY	TEAZE	TECTORIAL	TEENDED	TEETOTUM
TEARGAS	TEAZED	TECTRICES	TEENDING	TEETOTUMS
TEARGASES	TEAZEL	TECTRIX	TEENDOM	TEEVEE
TEARIER	TEAZELED	TECTUM	TEENDOMS	TEEVEES
TEARIEST	TEAZELING	TECTUMS	TEENDS	TEF
TEARILY	TEAZELLED	TED	TEENE	TEFF
TEARINESS	TEAZELS	TEDDED	TEENED	TEFFS
TEARING	TEAZES	TEDDER	TEENER	TEFILLAH

TEFILLIN	TEKNONYMY	TELEMEN	TELETEXTS	TELLIES
TEFLON	TEKTITE	TELEMETER	TELETHON	TELLIN
TEFLONS	TEKTITES	TELEMETRY	TELETHONS	TELLING
TEFS	TEKTITIC	TELEOLOGY	TELETRON	TELLINGLY
TEG	TEL	TELEONOMY	TELETRONS	TELLINGS
TEGG	TELA	TELEOSAUR	TELETYPE	TELLINOID
TEGGS	TELAE	TELEOST	TELETYPED	TELLINS
TEGMEN	TELAMON	TELEOSTS	TELETYPES	TELLS
TEGMENTA	TELAMONES	TELEPATH	TELEVIEW	TELLTALE
TEGMENTAL	TELAMONS	TELEPATHS	TELEVIEWS	TELLTALES
TEGMENTUM	TELARY	TELEPATHY	TELEVISE	TELLURAL
TEGMINA	TELCO	TELEPHEME	TELEVISED	TELLURATE
TEGMINAL	TELCOS	TELEPHONE	TELEVISER	TELLURIAN
TEGS	TELD	TELEPHONY	TELEVISES	TELLURIC
TEGU	TELE	TELEPHOTO	TELEVISOR	TELLURIDE
TEGUA	TELECAST	TELEPIC	TELEWORK	TELLURION
TEGUAS	TELECASTS	TELEPICS	TELEWORKS	TELLURISE
TEGUEXIN	TELECHIR	TELEPLAY	TELEX	TELLURITE
TEGUEXINS	TELECHIRS	TELEPLAYS	TELEXED	TELLURIUM
TEGULA	TELECINE	TELEPOINT	TELEXES	TELLURIZE
TEGULAE	TELECINES	TELEPORT	TELEXING	TELLUROUS
TEGULAR	TELECOM	TELEPORTS	TELFER	TELLUS
TEGULARLY	TELECOMM	TELEPRINT	TELFERAGE	TELLUSES
TEGULATED	TELECOMMS	TELERAN	TELFERED	TELLY
TEGUMEN	TELECOMS	TELERANS	TELFERIC	TELLYS
TEGUMENT	TELECON	TELERGIC	TELFERING	TELNET
TEGUMENTS	TELECONS	TELERGIES	TELFERS	TELNETED
TEGUMINA	TELECOPY	TELERGY	TELFORD	TELNETING
TEGUS	TELEDU	TELES	TELFORDS	TELNETS
TEHR	TELEDUS	TELESALE	TELIA	TELNETTED
TEHRS	TELEFAX	TELESALES	TELIAL	TELOI
TEHSIL	TELEFAXED	TELESCOPE	TELIC	TELOME
TEHSILDAR	TELEFAXES	TELESCOPY	TELICALLY	TELOMERE
TEHSILS	TELEFILM	TELESEME	TELICITY	TELOMERES
TEIGLACH	TELEFILMS	TELESEMES	TELIUM	TELOMES
TEIID	TELEGA	TELESES	TELL	TELOMIC
TEIIDS	TELEGAS	TELESHOP	TELLABLE	TELOPHASE
TEIL	TELEGENIC	TELESHOPS	TELLAR	TELOS
TEILS	TELEGONIC	TELESIS	TELLARED	TELOTAXES
TEIN	TELEGONY	TELESM	TELLARING	TELOTAXIS
TEIND	TELEGRAM	TELESMS	TELLARS	TELPHER
TEINDED	TELEGRAMS	TELESTIC	TELLEN	TELPHERED
TEINDING	TELEGRAPH	TELESTICH	TELLENS	TELPHERIC
TEINDS	TELEMAN	TELESTICS	TELLER	TELPHERS
TEINS	TELEMARK	TELETEX	TELLERED	TELS
TEKKIE	TELEMARKS	TELETEXES	TELLERING	TELSON
TEKKIES	TELEMATIC	TELETEXT	TELLERS	TELSONIC

TELSONS	TEMPORIZE	TENDANCES	TENESI	TENOROONS
TELT	TEMPOS	TENDED	TENESMIC	TENORS
TEMAZEPAM	TEMPS	TENDENCE	TENESMUS	TENOTOMY
TEMBLOR	TEMPT	TENDENCES	TENET	TENOUR
TEMBLORES	TEMPTABLE	TENDENCY	TENETS	TENOURS
TEMBLORS	TEMPTED	TENDENZ	TENFOLD	TENPENCE
TEME	TEMPTER	TENDENZEN	TENFOLDS	TENPENCES
TEMED	TEMPTERS	TENDER	TENGE	TENPENNY
TEMENE	TEMPTING	TENDERED	TENGES	TENPIN
TEMENOS	TEMPTINGS	TENDERER	TENIA	TENPINS
TEMERITY	TEMPTRESS	TENDERERS	TENIACIDE	TENREC
TEMEROUS	TEMPTS	TENDEREST	TENIAE	TENRECS
TEMES	TEMPURA	TENDERING	TENIAFUGE	TENS
TEMP	TEMPURAS	TENDERISE	TENIAS	TENSE
TEMPED	TEMS	TENDERIZE	TENIASES	TENSED
TEMPEH	TEMSE	TENDERLY	TENIASIS	TENSELESS
TEMPEHS	TEMSED	TENDERS	TENIOID	TENSELY
TEMPER	TEMSES	TENDING	TENNE	TENSENESS
TEMPERA	TEMSING	TENDINOUS	TENNER	TENSER
TEMPERAS	TEMULENCE	TENDON	TENNERS	TENSES
TEMPERATE	TEMULENCY	TENDONS	TENNES	TENSEST
TEMPERED	TEMULENT	TENDRE	TENNESI	TENSIBLE
TEMPERER	TEN	TENDRES	TENNIES	TENSIBLY
TEMPERERS	TENABLE	TENDRESSE	TENNIS	TENSILE
TEMPERING	TENABLY	TENDRIL	TENNISES	TENSILELY
TEMPERS	TENACE	TENDRILED	TENNIST	TENSILITY
TEMPEST	TENACES	TENDRILLY	TENNISTS	TENSING
TEMPESTED	TENACIOUS	TENDRILS	TENNO	TENSION
TEMPESTS	TENACITY	TENDRON	TENNOS	TENSIONAL
TEMPI	TENACULA	TENDRONS	TENNY	TENSIONED
TEMPING	TENACULUM	TENDS	TENON	TENSIONER
TEMPINGS	TENAIL	TENDU	TENONED	TENSIONS
TEMPLAR	TENAILLE	TENDUS	TENONER	TENSITIES
TEMPLARS	TENAILLES	TENE	TENONERS	TENSITY
TEMPLATE	TENAILLON	TENEBRAE	TENONING	TENSIVE
TEMPLATES	TENAILS	TENEBRIO	TENONS	TENSON
TEMPLE	TENANCIES	TENEBRIOS	TENOR	TENSONS
TEMPLED	TENANCY	TENEBRISM	TENORINI	TENSOR
TEMPLES	TENANT	TENEBRIST	TENORINO	TENSORIAL
TEMPLET	TENANTED	TENEBRITY	TENORIST	TENSORS
TEMPLETS	TENANTING	TENEBROSE	TENORISTS	TENT
TEMPO	TENANTRY	TENEBROUS	TENORITE	TENTACLE
TEMPORAL	TENANTS	TENEMENT	TENORITES	TENTACLED
TEMPORALS	TENCH	TENEMENTS	TENORLESS	TENTACLES
TEMPORARY	TENCHES	TENENDUM	TENORMAN	TENTACULA
TEMPORE	TEND	TENENDUMS	TENORMEN	TENTAGE
TEMPORISE	TENDANCE	TENES	TENOROON	TENTAGES

TENTATION	TENZON	TERAGLINS	TEREDOS	TERN
TENTATIVE	TENZONS	TERAHERTZ	TEREFA	TERNAL
TENTED	TEOCALLI	TERAI	TEREFAH	TERNARIES
TENTER	TEOCALLIS	TERAIS	TEREK	TERNARY
TENTERED	TEOPAN	TERAKIHI	TEREKS	TERNATE
TENTERING	TEOPANS	TERAKIHIS	TERES	TERNATELY
TENTERS	TEOSINTE	TERAOHM	TERESES	TERNE
TENTFUL	TEOSINTES	TERAOHMS	TERETE	TERNED
TENTFULS	TEPA	TERAPH	TERETES	TERNES
TENTH	TEPACHE	TERAPHIM	TERF	TERNING
TENTHLY	TEPACHES	TERAPHIMS	TERFE	TERNION
TENTHS	TEPAL	TERAS	TERFES	TERNIONS
TENTIE	TEPALS	TERATA	TERFS	TERNS
TENTIER	TEPAS	TERATISM	TERGA	TERPENE
TENTIEST	TEPEE	TERATISMS	TERGAL	TERPENES
TENTIGO	TEPEES	TERATOGEN	TERGITE	TERPENIC
TENTIGOS	TEPEFIED	TERATOID	TERGITES	TERPENOID
TENTING	TEPEFIES	TERATOMA	TERGUM	TERPINEOL
TENTINGS	TEPEFY	TERATOMAS	TERIYAKI	TERPINOL
TENTLESS	TEPEFYING	TERAWATT	TERIYAKIS	TERPINOLS
TENTLIKE	TEPHIGRAM	TERAWATTS	TERM	TERRA
TENTMAKER	TEPHILLAH	TERBIA	TERMAGANT	TERRACE
TENTORIA	TEPHILLIN	TERBIAS	TERMED	TERRACED
TENTORIAL	TEPHRA	TERBIC	TERMER	TERRACES
TENTORIUM	TEPHRAS	TERBIUM	TERMERS	TERRACING
TENTPOLE	TEPHRITE	TERBIUMS	TERMINAL	TERRAE
TENTPOLES	TEPHRITES	TERCE	TERMINALS	TERRAFORM
TENTS	TEPHRITIC	TERCEL	TERMINATE	TERRAIN
TENTWISE	TEPHROITE	TERCELET	TERMINER	TERRAINS
TENTY	TEPID	TERCELETS	TERMINERS	TERRAMARA
TENUE	TEPIDARIA	TERCELS	TERMING	TERRAMARE
TENUES	TEPIDER	TERCES	TERMINI	TERRANE
TENUIOUS	TEPIDEST	TERCET	TERMINISM	TERRANES
TENUIS	TEPIDITY	TERCETS	TERMINIST	TERRAPIN
TENUITIES	TEPIDLY	TERCIO	TERMINUS	TERRAPINS
TENUITY	TEPIDNESS	TERCIOS	TERMITARY	TERRARIA
TENUOUS	TEPOY	TEREBENE	TERMITE	TERRARIUM
TENUOUSLY	TEPOYS	TEREBENES	TERMITES	TERRAS
TENURABLE	TEQUILA	TEREBIC	TERMITIC	TERRASES
TENURE	TEQUILAS	TEREBINTH	TERMLESS	TERRASSE
TENURED	TEQUILLA	TEREBRA	TERMLIES	TERRAZZO
TENURES	TEQUILLAS	TEREBRAE	TERMLY	TERRAZZOS
TENURIAL	TERABYTE	TEREBRANT	TERMOR	TERREEN
TENURING	TERABYTES	TEREBRAS	TERMORS	TERREENS
TENUTI	TERAFLOP	TEREBRATE	TERMS	TERRELLA
TENUTO	TERAFLOPS	TEREDINES	TERMTIME	TERRELLAS
TENUTOS	TERAGLIN	TEREDO	TERMTIMES	TERRENE

TERRENELY	TERTIUSES	TESTERN	TETCHED	TETROSE
TERRENES	TERTS	TESTERNED	TETCHIER	TETROSES
TERRET	TERVALENT	TESTERNS	TETCHIEST	TETROXID
TERRETS	TERYLENE	TESTERS	TETCHILY	TETROXIDE
TERRIBLE	TERYLENES	TESTES	TETCHY	TETROXIDS
TERRIBLES	TERZETTA	TESTICLE	TETE	TETRYL
TERRIBLY	TERZETTAS	TESTICLES	TETES	TETRYLS
TERRICOLE	TERZETTI	TESTIER	TETH	TETS
TERRIER	TERZETTO	TESTIEST	TETHER	TETTER
TERRIERS	TERZETTOS	TESTIFIED	TETHERED	TETTERED
TERRIES	TES	TESTIFIER	TETHERING	TETTERING
TERRIFIC	TESLA	TESTIFIES	TETHERS	TETTEROUS
TERRIFIED	TESLAS	TESTIFY	TETHS	TETTERS
TERRIFIER	TESSELATE	TESTILY	TETOTUM	TETTIX
TERRIFIES	TESSELLA	TESTIMONY	TETOTUMS	TETTIXES
TERRIFY	TESSELLAE	TESTINESS	TETRA	TEUCH
TERRINE	TESSELLAR	TESTING	TETRACID	TEUCHAT
TERRINES	TESSERA	TESTINGS	TETRACIDS	TEUCHATS
TERRIT	TESSERACT	TESTIS	TETRACT	TEUCHER
TERRITORY	TESSERAE	TESTON	TETRACTS	TEUCHEST
TERRITS	TESSERAL	TESTONS	TETRAD	TEUCHTER
TERROIR	TESSITURA	TESTOON	TETRADIC	TEUCHTERS
TERROIRS	TESSITURE	TESTOONS	TETRADITE	TEUGH
TERROR	TEST	TESTRIL	TETRADS	TEUGHER
TERRORFUL	TESTA	TESTRILL	TETRAGON	TEUGHEST
TERRORISE	TESTABLE	TESTRILLS	TETRAGONS	TEUGHLY
TERRORISM	TESTACEAN	TESTRILS	TETRAGRAM	TEUTONISE
TERRORIST	TESTACIES	TESTS	TETRALOGY	TEUTONIZE
TERRORIZE	TESTACY	TESTUDO	TETRAMER	TEVATRON
TERRORS	TESTAE	TESTUDOS	TETRAMERS	TEVATRONS
TERRY	TESTAMENT	TESTY	TETRAPLA	TEW
TERSE	TESTAMUR	TET	TETRAPLAS	TEWART
TERSELY	TESTAMURS	TETANAL	TETRAPOD	TEWARTS
TERSENESS	TESTATE	TETANIC	TETRAPODS	TEWED
TERSER	TESTATES	TETANICAL	TETRAPODY	TEWEL
TERSEST	TESTATION	TETANICS	TETRARCH	TEWELS
TERSION	TESTATOR	TETANIES	TETRARCHS	TEWHIT
TERSIONS	TESTATORS	TETANISE	TETRARCHY	TEWHITS
TERTIA	TESTATRIX	TETANISED	TETRAS	TEWING
TERTIAL	TESTATUM	TETANISES	TETRAXON	TEWIT
TERTIALS	TESTATUMS	TETANIZE	TETRAXONS	TEWITS
TERTIAN	TESTCROSS	TETANIZED	TETRI	TEWS
TERTIANS	TESTE	TETANIZES	TETRIS	TEX
TERTIARY	TESTED	TETANOID	TETRODE	TEXAS
TERTIAS	TESTEE	TETANUS	TETRODES	TEXASES
TERTIUM	TESTEES	TETANUSES	TETRONAL	TEXES
TERTIUS	TESTER	TETANY	TETRONALS	TEXT

TEXTBOOK	THALIS	THANKYOU	THEATRICS	THELF
TEXTBOOKS	THALLI	THANKYOUS	THEAVE	THELITIS
TEXTED	THALLIC	THANNA	THEAVES	THELVES
TEXTER	THALLINE	THANNAH	THEBAINE	THELYTOKY
TEXTERS	THALLIOUS	THANNAHS	THEBAINES	THEM
TEXTILE	THALLIUM	THANNAS	THEBE	THEMA
TEXTILES	THALLIUMS	THANS	THEBES	THEMATA
TEXTING	THALLOID	THANX	THECA	THEMATIC
TEXTINGS	THALLOUS	THAR	THECAE	THEMATICS
TEXTISM	THALLUS	THARM	THECAL	THEME
TEXTISMS	THALLUSES	THARMS	THECATE	THEMED
TEXTLESS	THALWEG	THARS	THECODONT	THEMELESS
TEXTONYM	THALWEGS	THAT	THEE	THEMES
TEXTONYMS	THAN	THATAWAY	THEED	THEMING
TEXTORIAL	THANA	THATCH	THEEING	THEMSELF
TEXTPHONE	THANADAR	THATCHED	THEEK	THEN
TEXTS	THANADARS	THATCHER	THEEKED	THENABOUT
TEXTSPEAK	THANAGE	THATCHERS	THEEKING	THENAGE
TEXTUAL	THANAGES	THATCHES	THEEKS	THENAGES
TEXTUALLY	THANAH	THATCHIER	THEELIN	THENAL
TEXTUARY	THANAHS	THATCHING	THEELINS	THENAR
TEXTURAL	THANAS	THATCHT	THEELOL	THENARS
TEXTURE	THANATISM	THATCHY	THEELOLS	THENCE
TEXTURED	THANATIST	THATNESS	THEES	THENS
TEXTURES	THANATOID	THAUMATIN	THEFT	THEOCON
TEXTURING	THANATOS	THAW	THEFTLESS	THEOCONS
TEXTURISE	THANE	THAWED	THEFTS	THEOCRACY
TEXTURIZE	THANEDOM	THAWER	THEFTUOUS	THEOCRASY
THACK	THANEDOMS	THAWERS	THEGITHER	THEOCRAT
THACKED	THANEHOOD	THAWIER	THEGN	THEOCRATS
THACKING	THANES	THAWIEST	THEGNLY	THEODICY
THACKS	THANESHIP	THAWING	THEGNS	THEOGONIC
THAE	THANG	THAWINGS	THEIC	THEOGONY
THAGI	THANGKA	THAWLESS	THEICS	THEOLOG
THAGIS	THANGKAS	THAWS	THEIN	THEOLOGER
THAIM	THANGS	THAWY	THEINE	THEOLOGIC
THAIRM	THANK	THE	THEINES	THEOLOGS
THAIRMS	THANKED	THEACEOUS	THEINS	THEOLOGUE
THALAMI	THANKEE	THEANDRIC	THEIR	THEOLOGY
THALAMIC	THANKER	THEARCHIC	THEIRS	THEOMACHY
THALAMUS	THANKERS	THEARCHY	THEIRSELF	THEOMANCY
THALASSIC	THANKFUL	THEATER	THEISM	THEOMANIA
THALE	THANKING	THEATERS	THEISMS	THEONOMY
THALER	THANKINGS	THEATRAL	THEIST	THEOPATHY
THALERS	THANKIT	THEATRE	THEISTIC	THEOPHAGY
THALI	THANKLESS	THEATRES	THEISTS	THEOPHANY
THALIAN	THANKS	THEATRIC	THELEMENT	THEORBIST

THEORBO	THEREOF	THESES	THIBETS	THIGHBONE
THEORBOS	THEREON	THESIS	THIBLE	THIGHED
THEOREM	THEREOUT	THESP	THIBLES	THIGHS
THEOREMIC	THERES	THESPIAN	THICK	THIGS
THEOREMS	THERETO	THESPIANS	THICKED	THILK
THEORETIC	THEREUNTO	THESPS	THICKEN	THILL
THEORIC	THEREUPON	THETA	THICKENED	THILLER
THEORICS	THEREWITH	THETAS	THICKENER	THILLERS
THEORIES	THERIAC	THETCH	THICKENS	THILLS
THEORIQUE	THERIACA	THETCHED	THICKER	THIMBLE
THEORISE	THERIACAL	THETCHES	THICKEST	THIMBLED
THEORISED	THERIACAS	THETCHING	THICKET	THIMBLES
THEORISER	THERIACS	THETE	THICKETED	THIMBLING
THEORISES	THERIAN	THETES	THICKETS	THIN
THEORIST	THERIANS	THETHER	THICKETY	THINCLAD
THEORISTS	THERM	THETIC	THICKHEAD	THINCLADS
THEORIZE	THERMAE	THETICAL	THICKIE	THINDOWN
THEORIZED	THERMAL	THEURGIC	THICKIES	THINDOWNS
THEORIZER	THERMALLY	THEURGIES	THICKING	THINE
THEORIZES	THERMALS	THEURGIST	THICKISH	THING
THEORY	THERME	THEURGY	THICKLEAF	THINGAMY
THEOSOPH	THERMEL	THEW	THICKLY	THINGHOOD
THEOSOPHS	THERMELS	THEWED	THICKNESS	THINGIER
THEOSOPHY	THERMES	THEWES	THICKO	THINGIES
THEOTOKOI	THERMETTE	THEWIER	THICKOES	THINGIEST
THEOTOKOS	THERMIC	THEWIEST	THICKOS	THINGNESS
THEOW	THERMICAL	THEWLESS	THICKS	THINGS
THEOWS	THERMIDOR	THEWS	THICKSET	THINGUMMY
THERALITE	THERMION	THEWY	THICKSETS	THINGY
THERAPIES	THERMIONS	THEY	THICKSKIN	THINK
THERAPIST	THERMIT	THIAMIN	THICKY	THINKABLE
THERAPSID	THERMITE	THIAMINE	THIEF	THINKABLY
THERAPY	THERMITES	THIAMINES	THIEFLIKE	THINKER
THERBLIG	THERMITS	THIAMINS	THIEVE	THINKERS
THERBLIGS	THERMOS	THIASUS	THIEVED	THINKING
THERE	THERMOSES	THIASUSES	THIEVERY	THINKINGS
THEREAT	THERMOSET	THIAZIDE	THIEVES	THINKS
THEREAWAY	THERMOTIC	THIAZIDES	THIEVING	THINLY
THEREBY	THERMS	THIAZIN	THIEVINGS	THINNED
THEREFOR	THEROID	THIAZINE	THIEVISH	THINNER
THEREFORE	THEROLOGY	THIAZINES	THIG	THINNERS
THEREFROM	THEROPOD	THIAZINS	THIGGER	THINNESS
THEREIN	THEROPODS	THIAZOL	THIGGERS	THINNEST
THEREINTO	THESAURAL	THIAZOLE	THIGGING	THINNING
THEREMIN	THESAURI	THIAZOLES	THIGGINGS	THINNINGS
THEREMINS	THESAURUS	THIAZOLS	THIGGIT	THINNISH
THERENESS	THESE	THIBET	THIGH	THINS

T

THIO	THIRSTING	THORACES	THOUSAND	THREADFIN
THIOFURAN	THIRSTS	THORACIC	THOUSANDS	THREADIER
THIOL	THIRSTY	THORAX	THOWEL	THREADING
THIOLIC	THIRTEEN	THORAXES	THOWELS	THREADS
THIOLS	THIRTEENS	THORIA	THOWL	THREADY
THIONATE	THIRTIES	THORIAS	THOWLESS	THREAP
THIONATES	THIRTIETH	THORIC	THOWLS	THREAPED
THIONIC	THIRTY	THORITE	THRAE	THREAPER
THIONIN	THIRTYISH	THORITES	THRAIPING	THREAPERS
THIONINE	THIS	THORIUM	THRALDOM	THREAPING
THIONINES	THISAWAY	THORIUMS	THRALDOMS	THREAPIT
THIONINS	THISNESS	THORN	THRALL	THREAPS
THIONYL	THISTLE	THORNBACK	THRALLDOM	THREAT
THIONYLS	THISTLES	THORNBILL	THRALLED	THREATED
THIOPHEN	THISTLIER	THORNBIRD	THRALLING	THREATEN
THIOPHENE	THISTLY	THORNBUSH	THRALLS	THREATENS
THIOPHENS	THITHER	THORNED	THRANG	THREATFUL
THIOPHIL	THITHERTO	THORNIER	THRANGED	THREATING
THIOTEPA	THIVEL	THORNIEST	THRANGING	THREATS
THIOTEPAS	THIVELS	THORNILY	THRANGS	THREAVE
THIOUREA	THLIPSES	THORNING	THRAPPLE	THREAVES
THIOUREAS	THLIPSIS	THORNLESS	THRAPPLED	THREE
THIR	THO	THORNLIKE	THRAPPLES	THREEFOLD
THIRAM	THOFT	THORNS	THRASH	THREENESS
THIRAMS	THOFTS	THORNSET	THRASHED	THREEP
THIRD	THOLE	THORNTREE	THRASHER	THREEPEAT
THIRDED	THOLED	THORNY	THRASHERS	THREEPED
THIRDHAND	THOLEIITE	THORO	THRASHES	THREEPER
THIRDING	THOLEPIN	THORON	THRASHIER	THREEPERS
THIRDINGS	THOLEPINS	THORONS	THRASHING	THREEPING
THIRDLY	THOLES	THOROUGH	THRASHY	THREEPIT
THIRDS	THOLI	THOROUGHS	THRASONIC	THREEPS
THIRDSMAN	THOLING	THORP	THRAVE	THREEQUEL
THIRDSMEN	THOLOBATE	THORPE	THRAVES	THREES
THIRL	THOLOI	THORPES	THRAW	THREESOME
THIRLAGE	THOLOS	THORPS	THRAWARD	THRENE
THIRLAGES	THOLUS	THOSE	THRAWART	THRENES
THIRLED	THON	THOTHER	THRAWED	THRENETIC
THIRLING	THONDER	THOU	THRAWING	THRENODE
THIRLS	THONG	THOUED	THRAWN	THRENODES
THIRST	THONGED	THOUGH	THRAWNLY	THRENODIC
THIRSTED	THONGIER	THOUGHT	THRAWS	THRENODY
THIRSTER	THONGIEST	THOUGHTED	THREAD	THRENOS
THIRSTERS	THONGING	THOUGHTEN	THREADED	THRENOSES
THIRSTFUL	THONGS	THOUGHTS	THREADEN	THREONINE
THIRSTIER	THONGY	THOUING	THREADER	THRESH
THIRSTILY	THORACAL	THOUS	THREADERS	THRESHED

THRESHEL	THRIVEN	THROTTLED	THRUWAYS	THUMPER
THRESHELS	THRIVER	THROTTLER	THRYMSA	THUMPERS
THRESHER	THRIVERS	THROTTLES	THRYMSAS	THUMPING
THRESHERS	THRIVES	THROUGH	THUD	THUMPS
THRESHES	THRIVING	THROUGHLY	THUDDED	THUNDER
THRESHING	THRIVINGS	THROVE	THUDDING	THUNDERED
THRESHOLD	THRO	THROW	THUDDINGS	THUNDERER
THRETTIES	THROAT	THROWAWAY	THUDS	THUNDERS
THRETTY	THROATED	THROWBACK	THUG	THUNDERY
THREW	THROATIER	THROWDOWN	THUGGEE	THUNDROUS
THRICE	THROATILY	THROWE	THUGGEES	THUNK
THRID	THROATING	THROWER	THUGGERY	THUNKED
THRIDACE	THROATS	THROWERS	THUGGISH	THUNKING
THRIDACES	THROATY	THROWES	THUGGISM	THUNKS
THRIDDED	THROB	THROWING	THUGGISMS	THURIBLE
THRIDDING	THROBBED	THROWINGS	THUGGO	THURIBLES
THRIDS	THROBBER	THROWN	THUGGOS	THURIFER
THRIFT	THROBBERS	THROWOVER	THUGS	THURIFERS
THRIFTIER	THROBBING	THROWS	THUJA	THURIFIED
THRIFTILY	THROBLESS	THROWSTER	THUJAS	THURIFIES
THRIFTS	THROBS	THRU	THULIA	THURIFY
THRIFTY	THROE	THRUM	THULIAS	THURL
THRILL	THROED	THRUMMED	THULITE	THURLS
THRILLANT	THROEING	THRUMMER	THULITES	THUS
THRILLED	THROES	THRUMMERS	THULIUM	THUSES
THRILLER	THROMBI	THRUMMIER	THULIUMS	THUSLY
THRILLERS	THROMBIN	THRUMMING	THUMB	THUSNESS
THRILLIER	THROMBINS	THRUMMY	THUMBED	THUSWISE
THRILLING	THROMBOSE	THRUMS	THUMBHOLE	THUYA
THRILLS	THROMBUS	THRUPENNY	THUMBIER	THUYAS
THRILLY	THRONE	THRUPUT	THUMBIEST	THWACK
THRIMSA	THRONED	THRUPUTS	THUMBING	THWACKED
THRIMSAS	THRONES	THRUSH	THUMBKIN	THWACKER
THRIP	THRONG	THRUSHES	THUMBKINS	THWACKERS
THRIPS	THRONGED	THRUST	THUMBLESS	THWACKING
THRIPSES	THRONGFUL	THRUSTED	THUMBLIKE	THWACKS
THRISSEL	THRONGING	THRUSTER	THUMBLING	THWAITE
THRISSELS	THRONGS	THRUSTERS	THUMBNAIL	THWAITES
THRIST	THRONING	THRUSTFUL	THUMBNUT	THWART
THRISTED	THRONNER	THRUSTING	THUMBNUTS	THWARTED
THRISTING	THRONNERS	THRUSTOR	THUMBPOT	THWARTER
THRISTLE	THROPPLE	THRUSTORS	THUMBPOTS	THWARTERS
THRISTLES	THROPPLED	THRUSTS	THUMBS	THWARTING
THRISTS	THROPPLES	THRUTCH	THUMBTACK	THWARTLY
THRISTY	THROSTLE	THRUTCHED	THUMBY	THWARTS
THRIVE	THROSTLES	THRUTCHES	THUMP	THY
THRIVED	THROTTLE	THRUWAY	THUMPED	THYINE

THYLACINE	TIARAED	TICKLIEST	TIDELINE	TIERCEL
THYLAKOID	TIARAS	TICKLING	TIDELINES	TIERCELET
THYLOSE	TIARS	TICKLINGS	TIDEMARK	TIERCELS
THYLOSES	TIBIA	TICKLISH	TIDEMARKS	TIERCERON
THYLOSIS	TIBIAE	TICKLY	TIDEMILL	TIERCES
THYME	TIBIAL	TICKS	TIDEMILLS	TIERCET
THYMES	TIBIALES	TICKSEED	TIDERIP	TIERCETS
THYMEY	TIBIALIS	TICKSEEDS	TIDERIPS	TIERED
THYMI	TIBIAS	TICKTACK	TIDES	TIERING
THYMIC	TIC	TICKTACKS	TIDESMAN	TIERS
THYMIDINE	TICAL	TICKTOCK	TIDESMEN	TIES
THYMIER	TICALS	TICKTOCKS	TIDEWATER	TIETAC
THYMIEST	TICCA	TICKY	TIDEWAVE	TIETACK
THYMINE	TICCED	TICS	TIDEWAVES	TIETACKS
THYMINES	TICCING	TICTAC	TIDEWAY	TIETACS
THYMOCYTE	TICE	TICTACKED	TIDEWAYS	TIFF
THYMOL	TICED	TICTACS	TIDIED	TIFFANIES
THYMOLS	TICES	TICTOC	TIDIER	TIFFANY
THYMOMA	TICH	TICTOCKED	TIDIERS	TIFFED
THYMOMAS	TICHES	TICTOCS	TIDIES	TIFFIN
THYMOMATA	TICHIER	TID	TIDIEST	TIFFINED
THYMOSIN	TICHIEST	TIDAL	TIDILY	TIFFING
THYMOSINS	TICHY	TIDALLY	TIDINESS	TIFFINGS
THYMUS	TICING	TIDBIT	TIDING	TIFFINING
THYMUSES	TICK	TIDBITS	TIDINGS	TIFFINS
THYMY	TICKED	TIDDIER	TIDIVATE	TIFFS
THYRATRON	TICKEN	TIDDIES	TIDIVATED	TIFOSI
THYREOID	TICKENS	TIDDIEST	TIDIVATES	TIFOSO
THYREOIDS	TICKER	TIDDLE	TIDS	TIFOSOS
THYRISTOR	TICKERS	TIDDLED	TIDY	TIFT
THYROID	TICKET	TIDDLER	TIDYING	TIFTED
THYROIDAL	TICKETED	TIDDLERS	TIDYTIPS	TIFTING
THYROIDS	TICKETING	TIDDLES	TIE	TIFTS
THYROXIN	TICKETS	TIDDLEY	TIEBACK	TIG
THYROXINE	TICKEY	TIDDLEYS	TIEBACKS	TIGE
THYROXINS	TICKEYS	TIDDLIER	TIEBREAK	TIGER
THYRSE	TICKIES	TIDDLIES	TIEBREAKS	TIGEREYE
THYRSES	TICKING	TIDDLIEST	TIECLASP	TIGEREYES
THYRSI	TICKINGS	TIDDLING	TIECLASPS	TIGERISH
THYRSOID	TICKLACE	TIDDLY	TIED	TIGERISM
THYRSUS	TICKLACES	TIDDY	TIEING	TIGERISMS
THYSELF	TICKLE	TIDE	TIELESS	TIGERLIKE
TI	TICKLED	TIDED	TIEPIN	TIGERLY
TIAN	TICKLER	TIDELAND	TIEPINS	TIGERS
TIANS	TICKLERS	TIDELANDS	TIER	TIGERWOOD
TIAR	TICKLES	TIDELESS	TIERCE	TIGERY
TIARA	TICKLIER	TIDELIKE	TIERCED	TIGES

TIGGED	TIKIED	TILLS	TIMELIER	TIMPANAS
TIGGER	TIKIING	TILLY	TIMELIEST	TIMPANI
TIGGERED	TIKIS	TILS	TIMELINE	TIMPANIST
TIGGERING	TIKKA	TILT	TIMELINES	TIMPANO
TIGGERS	TIKKAS	TILTABLE	TIMELY	TIMPANUM
TIGGING	TIKOLOSHE	TILTED	TIMENOGUY	TIMPANUMS
TIGHT	TIKS	TILTER	TIMEOUS	TIMPS
TIGHTASS	TIKTAALIK	TILTERS	TIMEOUSLY	TIN
TIGHTEN	TIL	TILTH	TIMEOUT	TINA
TIGHTENED	TILAK	TILTHS	TIMEOUTS	TINAJA
TIGHTENER	TILAKS	TILTING	TIMEPASS	TINAJAS
TIGHTENS	TILAPIA	TILTINGS	TIMEPIECE	TINAMOU
TIGHTER	TILAPIAS	TILTMETER	TIMER	TINAMOUS
TIGHTEST	TILBURIES	TILTROTOR	TIMERS	TINAS
TIGHTISH	TILBURY	TILTS	TIMES	TINCAL
TIGHTKNIT	TILDE	TILTYARD	TIMESAVER	TINCALS
TIGHTLY	TILDES	TILTYARDS	TIMESCALE	TINCHEL
TIGHTNESS	TILE	TIMARAU	TIMESHARE	TINCHELS
TIGHTROPE	TILED	TIMARAUS	TIMESTAMP	TINCT
TIGHTS	TILEFISH	TIMARIOT	TIMETABLE	TINCTED
TIGHTWAD	TILELIKE	TIMARIOTS	TIMEWORK	TINCTING
TIGHTWADS	TILER	TIMBAL	TIMEWORKS	TINCTS
TIGHTWIRE	TILERIES	TIMBALE	TIMEWORN	TINCTURE
TIGLIC	TILERS	TIMBALES	TIMID	TINCTURED
TIGLON	TILERY	TIMBALS	TIMIDER	TINCTURES
TIGLONS	TILES	TIMBER	TIMIDEST	TIND
TIGNON	TILING	TIMBERED	TIMIDITY	TINDAL
TIGNONS	TILINGS	TIMBERING	TIMIDLY	TINDALS
TIGON	TILL	TIMBERMAN	TIMIDNESS	TINDED
TIGONS	TILLABLE	TIMBERMEN	TIMING	TINDER
TIGRESS	TILLAGE	TIMBERS	TIMINGS	TINDERBOX
TIGRESSES	TILLAGES	TIMBERY	TIMIST	TINDERS
TIGRIDIA	TILLED	TIMBO	TIMISTS	TINDERY
TIGRIDIAS	TILLER	TIMBOS	TIMOCRACY	TINDING
TIGRINE	TILLERED	TIMBRAL	TIMOLOL	TINDS
TIGRISH	TILLERING	TIMBRE	TIMOLOLS	TINE
TIGRISHLY	TILLERMAN	TIMBREL	TIMON	TINEA
TIGROID	TILLERMEN	TIMBRELS	TIMONEER	TINEAL
TIGS	TILLERS	TIMBRES	TIMONEERS	TINEAS
TIK	TILLICUM	TIME	TIMONS	TINED
TIKA	TILLICUMS	TIMEBOMB	TIMOROUS	TINEID
TIKANGA	TILLIER	TIMEBOMBS	TIMORSOME	TINEIDS
TIKANGAS	TILLIEST	TIMECARD	TIMOTHIES	TINES
TIKAS	TILLING	TIMECARDS	TIMOTHY	TINFOIL
TIKE	TILLINGS	TIMED	TIMOUS	TINFOILS
TIKES	TILLITE	TIMEFRAME	TIMOUSLY	TINFUL
TIKI	TILLITES	TIMELESS	TIMPANA	TINFULS

TING	TINKLINGS	TINTIEST	TIPS	TIREMAKER
TINGE	TINKLY	TINTINESS	TIPSHEET	TIRES
TINGED	TINKS	TINTING	TIPSHEETS	TIRESOME
TINGEING	TINLIKE	TINTINGS	TIPSIER	TIREWOMAN
TINGES	TINMAN	TINTLESS	TIPSIEST	TIREWOMEN
TINGING	TINMEN	TINTOOKIE	TIPSIFIED	TIRING
TINGLE	TINNED	TINTS	TIPSIFIES	TIRINGS
TINGLED	TINNER	TINTY	TIPSIFY	TIRITI
TINGLER	TINNERS	TINTYPE	TIPSILY	TIRITIS
TINGLERS	TINNIE	TINTYPES	TIPSINESS	TIRL
TINGLES	TINNIER	TINWARE	TIPSTAFF	TIRLED
TINGLIER	TINNIES	TINWARES	TIPSTAFFS	TIRLING
TINGLIEST	TINNIEST	TINWORK	TIPSTAVES	TIRLS
TINGLING	TINNILY	TINWORKS	TIPSTER	TIRO
TINGLINGS	TINNINESS	TINY	TIPSTERS	TIROES
TINGLISH	TINNING	TIP	TIPSTOCK	TIRONIC
TINGLY	TINNINGS	TIPCART	TIPSTOCKS	TIROS
TINGS	TINNITUS	TIPCARTS	TIPSY	TIRR
TINGUAITE	TINNY	TIPCAT	TIPT	TIRRED
TINHORN	TINPLATE	TIPCATS	TIPTOE	TIRRING
TINHORNS	TINPLATED	TIPI	TIPTOED	TIRRIT
TINIER	TINPLATES	TIPIS	TIPTOEING	TIRRITS
TINIES	TINPOT	TIPLESS	TIPTOES	TIRRIVEE
TINIEST	TINPOTS	TIPOFF	TIPTOP	TIRRIVEES
TINILY	TINS	TIPOFFS	TIPTOPS	TIRRIVIE
TININESS	TINSEL	TIPPABLE	TIPTRONIC	TIRRIVIES
TINING	TINSELED	TIPPED	TIPULA	TIRRS
TINK	TINSELING	TIPPEE	TIPULAS	TIS
TINKED	TINSELLED	TIPPEES	TIPUNA	TISANE
TINKER	TINSELLY	TIPPER	TIPUNAS	TISANES
TINKERED	TINSELRY	TIPPERS	TIRADE	TISICK
TINKERER	TINSELS	TIPPET	TIRADES	TISICKS
TINKERERS	TINSELY	TIPPETS	TIRAGE	TISSUAL
TINKERING	TINSEY	TIPPIER	TIRAGES	TISSUE
TINKERMAN	TINSEYS	TIPPIEST	TIRAMISU	TISSUED
TINKERMEN	TINSMITH	TIPPING	TIRAMISUS	TISSUES
TINKERS	TINSMITHS	TIPPINGS	TIRASSE	TISSUEY
TINKERTOY	TINSNIPS	TIPPLE	TIRASSES	TISSUING
TINKING	TINSTONE	TIPPLED	TIRE	TISSULAR
TINKLE	TINSTONES	TIPPLER	TIRED	TISWAS
TINKLED	TINT	TIPPLERS	TIREDER	TISWASES
TINKLER	TINTACK	TIPPLES	TIREDEST	TIT
TINKLERS	TINTACKS	TIPPLING	TIREDLY	TITAN
TINKLES	TINTED	TIPPY	TIREDNESS	TITANATE
TINKLIER	TINTER	TIPPYTOE	TIRELESS	TITANATES
TINKLIEST	TINTERS	TIPPYTOED	TIRELING	TITANESS
TINKLING	TINTIER	TIPPYTOES	TIRELINGS	TITANIA

TITANIAS	TITLE	TITTUP	TMESIS	TOBOGGINS
TITANIC	TITLED	TITTUPED	TO	TOBY
TITANIS	TITLELESS	TITTUPING	TOAD	TOC
TITANISES	TITLER	TITTUPPED	TOADEATER	TOCCATA
TITANISM	TITLERS	TITTUPPY	TOADFISH	TOCCATAS
TITANISMS	TITLES	TITTUPS	TOADFLAX	TOCCATE
TITANITE	TITLING	TITTUPY	TOADGRASS	TOCCATINA
TITANITES	TITLINGS	TITTY	TOADIED	TOCHER
TITANIUM	TITLIST	TITUBANCY	TOADIES	TOCHERED
TITANIUMS	TITLISTS	TITUBANT	TOADISH	TOCHERING
TITANOUS	TITMAN	TITUBATE	TOADLESS	TOCHERS
TITANS	TITMEN	TITUBATED	TOADLET	TOCK
TITBIT	TITMICE	TITUBATES	TOADLETS	TOCKED
TITBITS	TITMOSE	TITULAR	TOADLIKE	TOCKIER
TITCH	TITMOUSE	TITULARLY	TOADRUSH	TOCKIEST
TITCHES	TITOKI	TITULARS	TOADS	TOCKING
TITCHIE	TITOKIS	TITULARY	TOADSTONE	TOCKLEY
TITCHIER	TITRABLE	TITULE	TOADSTOOL	TOCKLEYS
TITCHIEST	TITRANT	TITULED	TOADY	TOCKS
TITCHY	TITRANTS	TITULES	TOADYING	TOCKY
TITE	TITRATE	TITULI	TOADYINGS	TOCO
TITELY	TITRATED	TITULING	TOADYISH	TOCOLOGY
TITER	TITRATES	TITULUS	TOADYISM	TOCOS
TITERS	TITRATING	TITUP	TOADYISMS	TOCS
TITFER	TITRATION	TITUPED	TOAST	TOCSIN
TITFERS	TITRATOR	TITUPING	TOASTED	TOCSINS
TITHABLE	TITRATORS	TITUPPED	TOASTER	TOD
TITHE	TITRE	TITUPPING	TOASTERS	TODAY
TITHED	TITRES	TITUPS	TOASTIE	TODAYS
TITHER	TITS	TITUPY	TOASTIER	TODDE
TITHERS	TITTED	TIVY	TOASTIES	TODDED
TITHES	TITTER	TIX	TOASTIEST	TODDES
TITHING	TITTERED	TIYIN	TOASTING	TODDIES
TITHINGS	TITTERER	TIYINS	TOASTINGS	TODDING
TITHONIA	TITTERERS	TIYN	TOASTS	TODDLE
TITHONIAS	TITTERING	TIYNS	TOASTY	TODDLED
TITI	TITTERS	TIZ	TOAZE	TODDLER
TITIAN	TITTIE	TIZES	TOAZED	TODDLERS
TITIANS	TITTIES	TIZWAS	TOAZES	TODDLES
TITILLATE	TITTING	TIZWASES	TOAZING	TODDLING
TITIS	TITTISH	TIZZ	TOBACCO	TODDY
TITIVATE	TITTIVATE	TIZZES	TOBACCOES	TODGER
TITIVATED	TITTLE	TIZZIES	TOBACCOS	TODGERS
TITIVATES	TITTLEBAT	TIZZY	TOBIES	TODIES
TITIVATOR	TITTLED	TJANTING	TOBOGGAN	TODS
TITLARK	TITTLES	TJANTINGS	TOBOGGANS	TODY
TITLARKS	TITTLING	TMESES	TOBOGGIN	TOE

TOEA	TOFUTTIS	TOILETTES	TOKOMAK	TOLLBARS
TOEAS	TOG	TOILFUL	TOKOMAKS	TOLLBOOTH
TOEBIE	TOGA	TOILFULLY	TOKONOMA	TOLLDISH
TOEBIES	TOGAE	TOILINET	TOKONOMAS	TOLLED
TOECAP	TOGAED	TOILINETS	TOKOS	TOLLER
TOECAPS	TOGAS	TOILING	TOKOTOKO	TOLLERS
TOECLIP	TOGATE	TOILINGS	TOKOTOKOS	TOLLEY
TOECLIPS	TOGATED	TOILLESS	TOKTOKKIE	TOLLEYS
TOED	TOGAVIRUS	TOILS	TOLA	TOLLGATE
TOEHOLD	TOGE	TOILSOME	TOLAN	TOLLGATED
TOEHOLDS	TOGED	TOILWORN	TOLANE	TOLLGATES
TOEIER	TOGES	TOING	TOLANES	TOLLHOUSE
TOEIEST	TOGETHER	TOINGS	TOLANS	TOLLIE
TOEING	TOGGED	TOISE	TOLAR	TOLLIES
TOELESS	TOGGER	TOISEACH	TOLARJEV	TOLLING
TOELIKE	TOGGERED	TOISEACHS	TOLARJI	TOLLINGS
TOENAIL	TOGGERIES	TOISECH	TOLARS	TOLLMAN
TOENAILED	TOGGERING	TOISECHS	TOLAS	TOLLMEN
TOENAILS	TOGGERS	TOISES	TOLBOOTH	TOLLS
TOEPIECE	TOGGERY	TOISON	TOLBOOTHS	TOLLWAY
TOEPIECES	TOGGING	TOISONS	TOLD	TOLLWAYS
TOEPLATE	TOGGLE	TOIT	TOLE	TOLLY
TOEPLATES	TOGGLED	TOITED	TOLED	TOLSEL
TOERAG	TOGGLER	TOITING	TOLEDO	TOLSELS
TOERAGGER	TOGGLERS	TOITOI	TOLEDOS	TOLSEY
TOERAGS	TOGGLES	TOITOIS	TOLERABLE	TOLSEYS
TOES	TOGGLING	TOITS	TOLERABLY	TOLT
TOESHOE	TOGS	TOKAMAK	TOLERANCE	TOLTER
TOESHOES	TOGUE	TOKAMAKS	TOLERANT	TOLTERED
TOETOE	TOGUES	TOKAY	TOLERATE	TOLTERING
TOETOES	TOHEROA	TOKAYS	TOLERATED	TOLTERS
TOEY	TOHEROAS	TOKE	TOLERATES	TOLTS
TOFF	TOHO	TOKED	TOLERATOR	TOLU
TOFFEE	TOHUNGA	TOKEN	TOLES	TOLUATE
TOFFEES	TOHUNGAS	TOKENED	TOLEWARE	TOLUATES
TOFFIER	TOIL	TOKENING	TOLEWARES	TOLUENE
TOFFIES	TOILE	TOKENISM	TOLIDIN	TOLUENES
TOFFIEST	TOILED	TOKENISMS	TOLIDINE	TOLUIC
TOFFISH	TOILER	TOKENS	TOLIDINES	TOLUID
TOFFS	TOILERS	TOKER	TOLIDINS	TOLUIDE
TOFFY	TOILES	TOKERS	TOLING	TOLUIDES
TOFORE	TOILET	TOKES	TOLINGS	TOLUIDIDE
TOFT	TOILETED	TOKING	TOLL	TOLUIDIN
TOFTS	TOILETING	TOKO	TOLLABLE	TOLUIDINE
TOFU	TOILETRY	TOKOLOGY	TOLLAGE	TOLUIDINS
TOFUS	TOILETS	TOKOLOSHE	TOLLAGES	TOLUIDS
TOFUTTI	TOILETTE	TOKOLOSHI	TOLLBAR	TOLUOL

TOLUOLE	TOMCATTED	TONALITY	TONICITY	TONSILLAR
TOLUOLES	TOMCOD	TONALLY	TONICS	TONSILS
TOLUOLS	TOMCODS	TONANT	TONIER	TONSOR
TOLUS	TOME	TONDI	TONIES	TONSORIAL
TOLUYL	TOMENTA	TONDINI	TONIEST	TONSORS
TOLUYLS	TOMENTOSE	TONDINO	TONIFIED	TONSURE
TOLYL	TOMENTOUS	TONDINOS	TONIFIES	TONSURED
TOLYLS	TOMENTUM	TONDO	TONIFY	TONSURES
TOLZEY	TOMES	TONDOS	TONIFYING	TONSURING
TOLZEYS	TOMFOOL	TONE	TONIGHT	TONTINE
TOM	TOMFOOLED	TONEARM	TONIGHTS	TONTINER
TOMAHAWK	TOMFOOLS	TONEARMS	TONING	TONTINERS
TOMAHAWKS	TOMIA	TONED	TONINGS	TONTINES
TOMALLEY	TOMIAL	TONELESS	TONISH	TONUS
TOMALLEYS	TOMIUM	TONEME	TONISHLY	TONUSES
TOMAN	TOMMED	TONEMES	TONITE	TONY
TOMANS	TOMMIED	TONEMIC	TONITES	TOO
TOMATILLO	TOMMIES	TONEPAD	TONK	TOOART
TOMATO	TOMMING	TONEPADS	TONKA	TOOARTS
TOMATOES	TOMMY	TONER	TONKED	TOODLE
TOMATOEY	TOMMYCOD	TONERS	TONKER	TOODLED
TOMB	TOMMYCODS	TONES	TONKERS	TOODLES
TOMBAC	TOMMYING	TONETIC	TONKING	TOODLING
TOMBACK	TOMMYROT	TONETICS	TONKS	TOOK
TOMBACKS	TOMMYROTS	TONETTE	TONLET	TOOL
TOMBACS	TOMO	TONETTES	TONLETS	TOOLBAG
TOMBAK	TOMOGRAM	TONEY	TONNAG	TOOLBAGS
TOMBAKS	TOMOGRAMS	TONG	TONNAGE	TOOLBAR
TOMBAL	TOMOGRAPH	TONGA	TONNAGES	TOOLBARS
TOMBED	TOMORROW	TONGAS	TONNAGS	TOOLBOX
TOMBIC	TOMORROWS	TONGED	TONNE	TOOLBOXES
TOMBING	TOMOS	TONGER	TONNEAU	TOOLCASE
TOMBLESS	TOMPION	TONGERS	TONNEAUS	TOOLCASES
TOMBLIKE	TOMPIONS	TONGING	TONNEAUX	TOOLCHEST
TOMBOC	TOMPON	TONGMAN	TONNELL	TOOLED
TOMBOCS	TOMPONED	TONGMEN	TONNELLS	TOOLER
TOMBOLA	TOMPONING	TONGS	TONNER	TOOLERS
TOMBOLAS	TOMPONS	TONGSTER	TONNERS	TOOLHEAD
TOMBOLO	TOMPOT	TONGSTERS	TONNES	TOOLHEADS
TOMBOLOS	TOMS	TONGUE	TONNISH	TOOLHOUSE
TOMBOY	TOMTIT	TONGUED	TONNISHLY	TOOLIE
TOMBOYISH	TOMTITS	TONGUELET	TONOMETER	TOOLIES
TOMBOYS	TON	TONGUES	TONOMETRY	TOOLING
TOMBS	TONAL	TONGUING	TONOPLAST	TOOLINGS
TOMBSTONE	TONALITE	TONGUINGS	TONS	TOOLKIT
TOMCAT	TONALITES	TONIC	TONSIL	TOOLKITS
TOMCATS	TONALITIC	TONICALLY	TONSILAR	TOOLLESS

T

TOOLMAKER	TOOTHS	TOPHI	TOPONYMY	TOR
TOOLMAN	TOOTHSOME	TOPHS	TOPOS	TORA
TOOLMEN	TOOTHWASH	TOPHUS	TOPOTYPE	TORAH
TOOLPUSH	TOOTHWORT	TOPI	TOPOTYPES	TORAHS
TOOLROOM	TOOTHY	TOPIARIAN	TOPPED	TORAN
TOOLROOMS	TOOTING	TOPIARIES	TOPPER	TORANA
TOOLS	TOOTLE	TOPIARIST	TOPPERS	TORANAS
TOOLSET	TOOTLED	TOPIARY	TOPPIER	TORANS
TOOLSETS	TOOTLER	TOPIC	TOPPIEST	TORAS
TOOLSHED	TOOTLERS	TOPICAL	TOPPING	TORBANITE
TOOLSHEDS	TOOTLES	TOPICALLY	TOPPINGLY	TORC
TOOLTIP	TOOTLING	TOPICALS	TOPPINGS	TORCH
TOOLTIPS	TOOTS	TOPICS	TOPPLE	TORCHABLE
TOOM	TOOTSED	TOPING	TOPPLED	TORCHED
TOOMED	TOOTSES	TOPIS	TOPPLES	TORCHER
TOOMER	TOOTSIE	TOPKICK	TOPPLING	TORCHERE
TOOMEST	TOOTSIES	TOPKICKS	TOPPY	TORCHERES
TOOMING	TOOTSING	TOPKNOT	TOPS	TORCHERS
TOOMS	TOOTSY	TOPKNOTS	TOPSAIL	TORCHES
TOON	TOP	TOPLESS	TOPSAILS	TORCHIER
TOONIE	TOPALGIA	TOPLINE	TOPSCORE	TORCHIERE
TOONIES	TOPALGIAS	TOPLINED	TOPSCORED	TORCHIERS
TOONS	TOPARCH	TOPLINER	TOPSCORES	TORCHIEST
TOORIE	TOPARCHS	TOPLINERS	TOPSIDE	TORCHING
TOORIES	TOPARCHY	TOPLINES	TOPSIDER	TORCHINGS
TOOSHIE	TOPAZ	TOPLINING	TOPSIDERS	TORCHLIKE
TOOSHIER	TOPAZES	TOPLOFTY	TOPSIDES	TORCHLIT
TOOSHIEST	TOPAZINE	TOPMAKER	TOPSMAN	TORCHON
TOOT	TOPCOAT	TOPMAKERS	TOPSMEN	TORCHONS
TOOTED	TOPCOATS	TOPMAKING	TOPSOIL	TORCHWOOD
TOOTER	TOPCROSS	TOPMAN	TOPSOILED	TORCHY
TOOTERS	TOPE	TOPMAST	TOPSOILS	TORCS
TOOTH	TOPECTOMY	TOPMASTS	TOPSPIN	TORCULAR
TOOTHACHE	TOPED	TOPMEN	TOPSPINS	TORCULARS
TOOTHCOMB	TOPEE	TOPMINNOW	TOPSTITCH	TORDION
TOOTHED	TOPEES	TOPMOST	TOPSTONE	TORDIONS
TOOTHFISH	TOPEK	TOPNOTCH	TOPSTONES	TORE
TOOTHFUL	TOPEKS	TOPO	TOPWATER	TOREADOR
TOOTHFULS	TOPER	TOPOGRAPH	TOPWORK	TOREADORS
TOOTHIER	TOPERS	TOPOI	TOPWORKED	TORERO
TOOTHIEST	TOPES	TOPOLOGIC	TOPWORKS	TOREROS
TOOTHILY	TOPFLIGHT	TOPOLOGY	TOQUE	TORES
TOOTHING	TOPFUL	TOPOMETRY	TOQUES	TOREUTIC
TOOTHINGS	TOPFULL	TOPONYM	TOQUET	TOREUTICS
TOOTHLESS	TOPH	TOPONYMAL	TOQUETS	TORGOCH
TOOTHLIKE	TOPHE	TOPONYMIC	TOQUILLA	TORGOCHS
TOOTHPICK	TOPHES	TOPONYMS	TOQUILLAS	TORI

TORIC	TORPOR	TORT	TOSA	TOTALISER
TORICS	TORPORS	TORTA	TOSAS	TOTALISES
TORIES	TORQUATE	TORTAS	TOSE	TOTALISM
TORII	TORQUATED	TORTE	TOSED	TOTALISMS
TORMENT	TORQUE	TORTELLI	TOSES	TOTALIST
TORMENTA	TORQUED	TORTELLIS	TOSH	TOTALISTS
TORMENTED	TORQUER	TORTEN	TOSHACH	TOTALITY
TORMENTER	TORQUERS	TORTES	TOSHACHS	TOTALIZE
TORMENTIL	TORQUES	TORTIE	TOSHED	TOTALIZED
TORMENTOR	TORQUESES	TORTIES	TOSHER	TOTALIZER
TORMENTS	TORQUEY	TORTILE	TOSHERS	TOTALIZES
TORMENTUM	TORQUIER	TORTILITY	TOSHES	TOTALLED
TORMINA	TORQUIEST	TORTILLA	TOSHIER	TOTALLING
TORMINAL	TORQUING	TORTILLAS	TOSHIEST	TOTALLY
TORMINOUS	TORR	TORTILLON	TOSHING	TOTALS
TORN	TORREFIED	TORTIOUS	TOSHY	TOTANUS
TORNADE	TORREFIES	TORTIVE	TOSING	TOTANUSES
TORNADES	TORREFY	TORTOISE	TOSS	TOTAQUINE
TORNADIC	TORRENT	TORTOISES	TOSSED	TOTARA
TORNADO	TORRENTS	TORTONI	TOSSEN	TOTARAS
TORNADOES	TORRET	TORTONIS	TOSSER	TOTE
TORNADOS	TORRETS	TORTRICES	TOSSERS	TOTEABLE
TORNILLO	TORRID	TORTRICID	TOSSES	TOTED
TORNILLOS	TORRIDER	TORTRIX	TOSSIER	TOTEM
TORO	TORRIDEST	TORTRIXES	TOSSIEST	TOTEMIC
TOROID	TORRIDITY	TORTS	TOSSILY	TOTEMISM
TOROIDAL	TORRIDLY	TORTUOUS	TOSSING	TOTEMISMS
TOROIDS	TORRIFIED	TORTURE	TOSSINGS	TOTEMIST
TOROS	TORRIFIES	TORTURED	TOSSPOT	TOTEMISTS
TOROSE	TORRIFY	TORTURER	TOSSPOTS	TOTEMITE
TOROSITY	TORRS	TORTURERS	TOSSUP	TOTEMITES
TOROT	TORS	TORTURES	TOSSUPS	TOTEMS
TOROTH	TORSADE	TORTURING	TOSSY	TOTER
TOROUS	TORSADES	TORTUROUS	TOST	TOTERS
TORPEDO	TORSE	TORULA	TOSTADA	TOTES
TORPEDOED	TORSEL	TORULAE	TOSTADAS	TOTHER
TORPEDOER	TORSELS	TORULAS	TOSTADO	TOTHERS
TORPEDOES	TORSES	TORULI	TOSTADOS	TOTIENT
TORPEDOS	TORSI	TORULIN	TOSTONE	TOTIENTS
TORPEFIED	TORSION	TORULINS	TOSTONES	TOTING
TORPEFIES	TORSIONAL	TORULOSE	TOT	TOTITIVE
TORPEFY	TORSIONS	TORULOSES	TOTABLE	TOTITIVES
TORPID	TORSIVE	TORULOSIS	TOTAL	TOTS
TORPIDITY	TORSK	TORULUS	TOTALED	TOTTED
TORPIDLY	TORSKS	TORUS	TOTALING	TOTTER
TORPIDS	TORSO	TORUSES	TOTALISE	TOTTERED
TORPITUDE	TORSOS	TORY	TOTALISED	TOTTERER

TOTTERERS	TOUGHER	TOURNEYER	TOVARISH	TOWLINES
TOTTERING	TOUGHEST	TOURNEYS	TOW	TOWMON
TOTTERS	TOUGHIE	TOURNURE	TOWABLE	TOWMOND
TOTTERY	TOUGHIES	TOURNURES	TOWAGE	TOWMONDS
TOTTIE	TOUGHING	TOURS	TOWAGES	TOWMONS
TOTTIER	TOUGHISH	TOURTIERE	TOWARD	TOWMONT
TOTTIES	TOUGHLY	TOUSE	TOWARDLY	TOWMONTS
TOTTIEST	TOUGHNESS	TOUSED	TOWARDS	TOWN
TOTTING	TOUGHS	TOUSER	TOWAWAY	TOWNEE
TOTTINGS	TOUGHY	TOUSERS	TOWAWAYS	TOWNEES
TOTTRING	TOUK	TOUSES	TOWBAR	TOWNFOLK
TOTTY	TOUKED	TOUSIER	TOWBARS	TOWNHALL
TOUCAN	TOUKING	TOUSIEST	TOWBOAT	TOWNHOME
TOUCANET	TOUKS	TOUSING	TOWBOATS	TOWNHOMES
TOUCANETS	TOULADI	TOUSINGS	TOWED	TOWNHOUSE
TOUCANS	TOULADIS	TOUSLE	TOWEL	TOWNIE
TOUCH	TOUN	TOUSLED	TOWELED	TOWNIER
TOUCHABLE	TOUNS	TOUSLES	TOWELETTE	TOWNIES
TOUCHBACK	TOUPEE	TOUSLING	TOWELHEAD	TOWNIEST
TOUCHDOWN	TOUPEED	TOUSTIE	TOWELING	TOWNISH
TOUCHE	TOUPEES	TOUSTIER	TOWELINGS	TOWNLAND
TOUCHED	TOUPET	TOUSTIEST	TOWELLED	TOWNLANDS
TOUCHER	TOUPETS	TOUSY	TOWELLING	TOWNLESS
TOUCHERS	TOUPIE	TOUT	TOWELS	TOWNLET
TOUCHES	TOUPIES	TOUTED	TOWER	TOWNLETS
TOUCHHOLE	TOUR	TOUTER	TOWERED	TOWNLIER
TOUCHIER	TOURACO	TOUTERS	TOWERIER	TOWNLIEST
TOUCHIEST	TOURACOS	TOUTIE	TOWERIEST	TOWNLING
TOUCHILY	TOURED	TOUTIER	TOWERING	TOWNLINGS
TOUCHING	TOURER	TOUTIEST	TOWERLESS	TOWNLY
TOUCHINGS	TOURERS	TOUTING	TOWERLIKE	TOWNS
TOUCHLESS	TOURIE	TOUTON	TOWERS	TOWNSCAPE
TOUCHLINE	TOURIES	TOUTONS	TOWERY	TOWNSFOLK
TOUCHMARK	TOURING	TOUTS	TOWHEAD	TOWNSHIP
TOUCHPAD	TOURINGS	TOUZE	TOWHEADED	TOWNSHIPS
TOUCHPADS	TOURISM	TOUZED	TOWHEADS	TOWNSITE
TOUCHTONE	TOURISMS	TOUZES	TOWHEE	TOWNSITES
TOUCHUP	TOURIST	TOUZIER	TOWHEES	TOWNSKIP
TOUCHUPS	TOURISTA	TOUZIEST	TOWIE	TOWNSKIPS
TOUCHWOOD	TOURISTAS	TOUZING	TOWIER	TOWNSMAN
TOUCHY	TOURISTED	TOUZLE	TOWIES	TOWNSMEN
TOUGH	TOURISTIC	TOUZLED	TOWIEST	TOWNWARD
TOUGHED	TOURISTS	TOUZLES	TOWING	TOWNWEAR
TOUGHEN	TOURISTY	TOUZLING	TOWINGS	TOWNWEARS
TOUGHENED	TOURNEDOS	TOUZY	TOWKAY	TOWNY
TOUGHENER	TOURNEY	TOVARICH	TOWKAYS	TOWPATH
TOUGHENS	TOURNEYED	TOVARISCH	TOWLINE	TOWPATHS

TOWPLANE	TOXINES	TRABEATE	TRACKED	TRADER
TOWPLANES	TOXINS	TRABEATED	TRACKER	TRADERS
TOWROPE	TOXOCARA	TRABECULA	TRACKERS	TRADES
TOWROPES	TOXOCARAL	TRABS	TRACKIE	TRADESMAN
TOWS	TOXOCARAS	TRACE	TRACKIES	TRADESMEN
TOWSACK	TOXOID	TRACEABLE	TRACKING	TRADING
TOWSACKS	TOXOIDS	TRACEABLY	TRACKINGS	TRADINGS
TOWSE	TOXOPHILY	TRACED	TRACKLESS	TRADITION
TOWSED	TOY	TRACELESS	TRACKMAN	TRADITIVE
TOWSER	TOYBOX	TRACER	TRACKMEN	TRADITOR
TOWSERS	TOYBOXES	TRACERIED	TRACKPAD	TRADITORS
TOWSES	TOYCHEST	TRACERIES	TRACKPADS	TRADS
TOWSIER	TOYCHESTS	TRACERS	TRACKROAD	TRADUCE
TOWSIEST	TOYED	TRACERY	TRACKS	TRADUCED
TOWSING	TOYER	TRACES	TRACKSIDE	TRADUCER
TOWSY	TOYERS	TRACEUR	TRACKSUIT	TRADUCERS
TOWT	TOYETIC	TRACEURS	TRACKWAY	TRADUCES
TOWTED	TOYING	TRACHEA	TRACKWAYS	TRADUCIAN
TOWTING	TOYINGS	TRACHEAE	TRACT	TRADUCING
TOWTS	TOYISH	TRACHEAL	TRACTABLE	TRAFFIC
TOWY	TOYISHLY	TRACHEARY	TRACTABLY	TRAFFICKY
TOWZE	TOYLAND	TRACHEAS	TRACTATE	TRAFFICS
TOWZED	TOYLANDS	TRACHEATE	TRACTATES	TRAGAL
TOWZES	TOYLESOME	TRACHEID	TRACTATOR	TRAGEDIAN
TOWZIER	TOYLESS	TRACHEIDE	TRACTED	TRAGEDIES
TOWZIEST	TOYLIKE	TRACHEIDS	TRACTILE	TRAGEDY
TOWZING	TOYLSOM	TRACHEOLE	TRACTING	TRAGELAPH
TOWZY	TOYMAN	TRACHINUS	TRACTION	TRAGI
TOXAEMIA	TOYMEN	TRACHITIS	TRACTIONS	TRAGIC
TOXAEMIAS	TOYO	TRACHLE	TRACTIVE	TRAGICAL
TOXAEMIC	TOYON	TRACHLED	TRACTOR	TRAGICS
TOXAPHENE	TOYONS	TRACHLES	TRACTORS	TRAGOPAN
TOXEMIA	TOYOS	TRACHLING	TRACTRIX	TRAGOPANS
TOXEMIAS	TOYS	TRACHOMA	TRACTS	TRAGULE
TOXEMIC	TOYSHOP	TRACHOMAS	TRACTUS	TRAGULES
TOXIC	TOYSHOPS	TRACHYTE	TRACTUSES	TRAGULINE
TOXICAL	TOYSOME	TRACHYTES	TRAD	TRAGUS
TOXICALLY	TOYTOWN	TRACHYTIC	TRADABLE	TRAHISON
TOXICANT	TOYTOWNS	TRACING	TRADE	TRAHISONS
TOXICANTS	TOYWOMAN	TRACINGS	TRADEABLE	TRAIK
TOXICITY	TOYWOMEN	TRACK	TRADED	TRAIKED
TOXICOSES	TOZE	TRACKABLE	TRADEFUL	TRAIKING
TOXICOSIS	TOZED	TRACKAGE	TRADELESS	TRAIKIT
TOXICS	TOZES	TRACKAGES	TRADEMARK	TRAIKS
TOXIGENIC	TOZIE	TRACKBALL	TRADENAME	TRAIL
TOXIN	TOZIES	TRACKBED	TRADEOFF	TRAILABLE
TOXINE	TOZING	TRACKBEDS	TRADEOFFS	TRAILED

TRAILER	TRAMELLED	TRANCHES	TRANSGENE	TRAPDOORS
TRAILERED	TRAMELLS	TRANCHET	TRANSHIP	TRAPE
TRAILERS	TRAMELS	TRANCHETS	TRANSHIPS	TRAPED
TRAILHEAD	TRAMLESS	TRANCIER	TRANSHUME	TRAPES
TRAILING	TRAMLINE	TRANCIEST	TRANSIENT	TRAPESED
TRAILLESS	TRAMLINED	TRANCING	TRANSIRE	TRAPESES
TRAILS	TRAMLINES	TRANECT	TRANSIRES	TRAPESING
TRAILSIDE	TRAMMED	TRANECTS	TRANSIT	TRAPEZE
TRAIN	TRAMMEL	TRANGAM	TRANSITED	TRAPEZED
TRAINABLE	TRAMMELED	TRANGAMS	TRANSITS	TRAPEZES
TRAINBAND	TRAMMELER	TRANGLE	TRANSLATE	TRAPEZIA
TRAINED	TRAMMELS	TRANGLES	TRANSMEW	TRAPEZIAL
TRAINEE	TRAMMIE	TRANK	TRANSMEWS	TRAPEZII
TRAINEES	TRAMMIES	TRANKED	TRANSMIT	TRAPEZING
TRAINER	TRAMMING	TRANKING	TRANSMITS	TRAPEZIST
TRAINERS	TRAMP	TRANKS	TRANSMOVE	TRAPEZIUM
TRAINFUL	TRAMPED	TRANKUM	TRANSMUTE	TRAPEZIUS
TRAINFULS	TRAMPER	TRANKUMS	TRANSOM	TRAPEZOID
TRAINING	TRAMPERS	TRANNIE	TRANSOMED	TRAPFALL
TRAININGS	TRAMPET	TRANNIES	TRANSOMS	TRAPFALLS
TRAINLESS	TRAMPETS	TRANNY	TRANSONIC	TRAPING
TRAINLOAD	TRAMPETTE	TRANQ	TRANSPIRE	TRAPLIKE
TRAINMAN	TRAMPIER	TRANQS	TRANSPORT	TRAPLINE
TRAINMEN	TRAMPIEST	TRANQUIL	TRANSPOSE	TRAPLINES
TRAINS	TRAMPING	TRANS	TRANSSHIP	TRAPNEST
TRAINWAY	TRAMPINGS	TRANSACT	TRANSUDE	TRAPNESTS
TRAINWAYS	TRAMPISH	TRANSACTS	TRANSUDED	TRAPPEAN
TRAIPSE	TRAMPLE	TRANSAXLE	TRANSUDES	TRAPPED
TRAIPSED	TRAMPLED	TRANSCEND	TRANSUME	TRAPPER
TRAIPSES	TRAMPLER	TRANSCODE	TRANSUMED	TRAPPERS
TRAIPSING	TRAMPLERS	TRANSDUCE	TRANSUMES	TRAPPIER
TRAIT	TRAMPLES	TRANSE	TRANSUMPT	TRAPPIEST
TRAITOR	TRAMPLING	TRANSECT	TRANSVEST	TRAPPING
TRAITORLY	TRAMPOLIN	TRANSECTS	TRANT	TRAPPINGS
TRAITORS	TRAMPS	TRANSENNA	TRANTED	TRAPPOSE
TRAITRESS	TRAMPY	TRANSEPT	TRANTER	TRAPPOUS
TRAITS	TRAMROAD	TRANSEPTS	TRANTERS	TRAPPY
TRAJECT	TRAMROADS	TRANSES	TRANTING	TRAPROCK
TRAJECTED	TRAMS	TRANSEUNT	TRANTS	TRAPROCKS
TRAJECTS	TRAMWAY	TRANSFARD	TRAP	TRAPS
TRAM	TRAMWAYS	TRANSFECT	TRAPAN	TRAPSE
TRAMCAR	TRANCE	TRANSFER	TRAPANNED	TRAPSED
TRAMCARS	TRANCED	TRANSFERS	TRAPANNER	TRAPSES
TRAMEL	TRANCEDLY	TRANSFIX	TRAPANS	TRAPSING
TRAMELED	TRANCES	TRANSFIXT	TRAPBALL	TRAPT
TRAMELING	TRANCEY	TRANSFORM	TRAPBALLS	TRAPUNTO
TRAMELL	TRANCHE	TRANSFUSE	TRAPDOOR	TRAPUNTOS

TRASH	TRAVERSED	TREAD	TRECENTOS	TREIF
TRASHCAN	TRAVERSER	TREADED	TRECK	TREIFA
TRASHCANS	TRAVERSES	TREADER	TRECKED	TREILLAGE
TRASHED	TRAVERTIN	TREADERS	TRECKING	TREILLE
TRASHER	TRAVES	TREADING	TRECKS	TREILLES
TRASHERS	TRAVESTY	TREADINGS	TREDDLE	TREK
TRASHERY	TRAVIS	TREADLE	TREDDLED	TREKKED
TRASHES	TRAVISES	TREADLED	TREDDLES	TREKKER
TRASHIER	TRAVOIS	TREADLER	TREDDLING	TREKKERS
TRASHIEST	TRAVOISE	TREADLERS	TREDILLE	TREKKING
TRASHILY	TRAVOISES	TREADLES	TREDILLES	TREKKINGS
TRASHING	TRAWL	TREADLESS	TREDRILLE	TREKS
TRASHMAN	TRAWLED	TREADLING	TREE	TRELLIS
TRASHMEN	TRAWLER	TREADMILL	TREED	TRELLISED
TRASHTRIE	TRAWLERS	TREADS	TREEHOUSE	TRELLISES
TRASHY	TRAWLEY	TREAGUE	TREEING	TREM
TRASS	TRAWLEYS	TREAGUES	TREELAWN	TREMA
TRASSES	TRAWLING	TREASON	TREELAWNS	TREMAS
TRAT	TRAWLINGS	TREASONS	TREELESS	TREMATIC
TRATS	TRAWLNET	TREASURE	TREELIKE	TREMATODE
TRATT	TRAWLNETS	TREASURED	TREELINE	TREMATOID
TRATTORIA	TRAWLS	TREASURER	TREELINES	TREMBLANT
TRATTORIE	TRAY	TREASURES	TREEN	TREMBLE
TRATTS	TRAYBAKE	TREASURY	TREENAIL	TREMBLED
TRAUCHLE	TRAYBAKES	TREAT	TREENAILS	TREMBLER
TRAUCHLED	TRAYBIT	TREATABLE	TREENS	TREMBLERS
TRAUCHLES	TRAYBITS	TREATED	TREENWARE	TREMBLES
TRAUMA	TRAYCLOTH	TREATER	TREES	TREMBLIER
TRAUMAS	TRAYF	TREATERS	TREESHIP	TREMBLING
TRAUMATA	TRAYFUL	TREATIES	TREESHIPS	TREMBLOR
TRAUMATIC	TRAYFULS	TREATING	TREETOP	TREMBLORS
TRAVAIL	TRAYNE	TREATINGS	TREETOPS	TREMBLY
TRAVAILED	TRAYNED	TREATISE	TREEWARE	TREMIE
TRAVAILS	TRAYNES	TREATISES	TREEWARES	TREMIES
TRAVE	TRAYNING	TREATMENT	TREEWAX	TREMOLANT
TRAVEL	TRAYS	TREATS	TREEWAXES	TREMOLITE
TRAVELED	TRAZODONE	TREATY	TREF	TREMOLO
TRAVELER	TREACHER	TREBBIANO	TREFA	TREMOLOS
TRAVELERS	TREACHERS	TREBLE	TREFAH	TREMOR
TRAVELING	TREACHERY	TREBLED	TREFOIL	TREMORED
TRAVELLED	TREACHOUR	TREBLES	TREFOILED	TREMORING
TRAVELLER	TREACLE	TREBLING	TREFOILS	TREMOROUS
TRAVELOG	TREACLED	TREBLINGS	TREGETOUR	TREMORS
TRAVELOGS	TREACLES	TREBLY	TREGGINGS	TREMS
TRAVELS	TREACLIER	TREBUCHET	TREHALA	TREMULANT
TRAVERSAL	TREACLING	TREBUCKET	TREHALAS	TREMULATE
TRAVERSE	TREACLY	TRECENTO	TREHALOSE	TREMULOUS

TRENAIL	TRESSELS	TRIACTS	TRIAZOLE	TRICES
TRENAILS	TRESSES	TRIAD	TRIAZOLES	TRICHINA
TRENCH	TRESSIER	TRIADIC	TRIAZOLIC	TRICHINAE
TRENCHAND	TRESSIEST	TRIADICS	TRIBADE	TRICHINAL
TRENCHANT	TRESSING	TRIADISM	TRIBADES	TRICHINAS
TRENCHARD	TRESSOUR	TRIADISMS	TRIBADIC	TRICHITE
TRENCHED	TRESSOURS	TRIADIST	TRIBADIES	TRICHITES
TRENCHER	TRESSURE	TRIADISTS	TRIBADISM	TRICHITIC
TRENCHERS	TRESSURED	TRIADS	TRIBADY	TRICHOID
TRENCHES	TRESSURES	TRIAGE	TRIBAL	TRICHOME
TRENCHING	TRESSY	TRIAGED	TRIBALISM	TRICHOMES
TREND	TREST	TRIAGES	TRIBALIST	TRICHOMIC
TRENDED	TRESTLE	TRIAGING	TRIBALLY	TRICHORD
TRENDIER	TRESTLES	TRIAL	TRIBALS	TRICHORDS
TRENDIES	TRESTS	TRIALED	TRIBASIC	TRICHOSES
TRENDIEST	TRET	TRIALING	TRIBBLE	TRICHOSIS
TRENDIFY	TRETINOIN	TRIALISM	TRIBBLES	TRICHROIC
TRENDILY	TRETS	TRIALISMS	TRIBE	TRICHROME
TRENDING	TREVALLY	TRIALIST	TRIBELESS	TRICING
TRENDOID	TREVALLYS	TRIALISTS	TRIBES	TRICITIES
TRENDOIDS	TREVET	TRIALITY	TRIBESMAN	TRICITY
TRENDS	TREVETS	TRIALLED	TRIBESMEN	TRICK
TRENDY	TREVIS	TRIALLING	TRIBLET	TRICKED
TRENDYISM	TREVISES	TRIALLIST	TRIBLETS	TRICKER
TRENISE	TREVISS	TRIALOGUE	TRIBOLOGY	TRICKERS
TRENISES	TREVISSES	TRIALS	TRIBRACH	TRICKERY
TRENTAL	TREW	TRIALWARE	TRIBRACHS	TRICKIE
TRENTALS	TREWS	TRIANGLE	TRIBULATE	TRICKIER
TREPAN	TREWSMAN	TRIANGLED	TRIBUNAL	TRICKIEST
TREPANG	TREWSMEN	TRIANGLES	TRIBUNALS	TRICKILY
TREPANGS	TREY	TRIAPSAL	TRIBUNARY	TRICKING
TREPANNED	TREYBIT	TRIARCH	TRIBUNATE	TRICKINGS
TREPANNER	TREYBITS	TRIARCHS	TRIBUNE	TRICKISH
TREPANS	TREYF	TRIARCHY	TRIBUNES	TRICKLE
TREPHINE	TREYFA	TRIASSIC	TRIBUTARY	TRICKLED
TREPHINED	TREYS	TRIATHLON	TRIBUTE	TRICKLES
TREPHINER	TREZ	TRIATIC	TRIBUTER	TRICKLESS
TREPHINES	TREZES	TRIATICS	TRIBUTERS	TRICKLET
TREPID	TRIABLE	TRIATOMIC	TRIBUTES	TRICKLETS
TREPIDANT	TRIAC	TRIAXIAL	TRICAR	TRICKLIER
TREPONEMA	TRIACID	TRIAXIALS	TRICARS	TRICKLING
TREPONEME	TRIACIDS	TRIAXON	TRICE	TRICKLY
TRES	TRIACS	TRIAXONS	TRICED	TRICKS
TRESPASS	TRIACT	TRIAZIN	TRICEP	TRICKSIER
TRESS	TRIACTINE	TRIAZINE	TRICEPS	TRICKSILY
TRESSED	TRIACTOR	TRIAZINES	TRICEPSES	TRICKSOME
TRESSEL	TRIACTORS	TRIAZINS	TRICERION	TRICKSTER

TRICKSY	TRIENNIA	TRIGGER	TRILITHS	TRIMOTOR
TRICKY	TRIENNIAL	TRIGGERED	TRILL	TRIMOTORS
TRICLAD	TRIENNIUM	TRIGGERS	TRILLED	TRIMPHONE
TRICLADS	TRIENS	TRIGGEST	TRILLER	TRIMPOT
TRICLINIA	TRIENTES	TRIGGING	TRILLERS	TRIMPOTS
TRICLINIC	TRIER	TRIGLOT	TRILLING	TRIMS
TRICLOSAN	TRIERARCH	TRIGLOTS	TRILLINGS	TRIMTAB
TRICOLOR	TRIERS	TRIGLY	TRILLION	TRIMTABS
TRICOLORS	TRIES	TRIGLYPH	TRILLIONS	TRIN
TRICOLOUR	TRIETERIC	TRIGLYPHS	TRILLIUM	TRINAL
TRICORN	TRIETHYL	TRIGNESS	TRILLIUMS	TRINARY
TRICORNE	TRIFACIAL	TRIGO	TRILLO	TRINDLE
TRICORNES	TRIFECTA	TRIGON	TRILLOES	TRINDLED
TRICORNS	TRIFECTAS	TRIGONAL	TRILLS	TRINDLES
TRICOT	TRIFF	TRIGONIC	TRILOBAL	TRINDLING
TRICOTINE	TRIFFER	TRIGONOUS	TRILOBATE	TRINE
TRICOTS	TRIFFEST	TRIGONS	TRILOBE	TRINED
TRICROTIC	TRIFFIC	TRIGOS	TRILOBED	TRINES
TRICTRAC	TRIFFID	TRIGRAM	TRILOBES	TRINGLE
TRICTRACS	TRIFFIDS	TRIGRAMS	TRILOBITE	TRINGLES
TRICUSPID	TRIFFIDY	TRIGRAPH	TRILOGIES	TRINING
TRICYCLE	TRIFID	TRIGRAPHS	TRILOGY	TRINITIES
TRICYCLED	TRIFLE	TRIGS	TRIM	TRINITRIN
TRICYCLER	TRIFLED	TRIGYNIAN	TRIMARAN	TRINITY
TRICYCLES	TRIFLER	TRIGYNOUS	TRIMARANS	TRINKET
TRICYCLIC	TRIFLERS	TRIHEDRA	TRIMER	TRINKETED
TRIDACNA	TRIFLES	TRIHEDRAL	TRIMERIC	TRINKETER
TRIDACNAS	TRIFLING	TRIHEDRON	TRIMERISM	TRINKETRY
TRIDACTYL	TRIFLINGS	TRIHYBRID	TRIMEROUS	TRINKETS
TRIDARN	TRIFOCAL	TRIHYDRIC	TRIMERS	TRINKUM
TRIDARNS	TRIFOCALS	TRIJET	TRIMESTER	TRINKUMS
TRIDE	TRIFOLD	TRIJETS	TRIMETER	TRINODAL
TRIDENT	TRIFOLIES	TRIJUGATE	TRIMETERS	TRINOMIAL
TRIDENTAL	TRIFOLIUM	TRIJUGOUS	TRIMETHYL	TRINS
TRIDENTED	TRIFOLY	TRIKE	TRIMETRIC	TRIO
TRIDENTS	TRIFORIA	TRIKES	TRIMIX	TRIODE
TRIDUAN	TRIFORIAL	TRILBIED	TRIMIXES	TRIODES
TRIDUUM	TRIFORIUM	TRILBIES	TRIMLY	TRIOL
TRIDUUMS	TRIFORM	TRILBY	TRIMMED	TRIOLEIN
TRIDYMITE	TRIFORMED	TRILBYS	TRIMMER	TRIOLEINS
TRIE	TRIG	TRILD	TRIMMERS	TRIOLET
TRIECIOUS	TRIGAMIES	TRILEMMA	TRIMMEST	TRIOLETS
TRIED	TRIGAMIST	TRILEMMAS	TRIMMING	TRIOLS
TRIELLA	TRIGAMOUS	TRILINEAR	TRIMMINGS	TRIONES
TRIELLAS	TRIGAMY	TRILITH	TRIMNESS	TRIONYM
TRIENE	TRIGEMINI	TRILITHIC	TRIMORPH	TRIONYMAL
TRIENES	TRIGGED	TRILITHON	TRIMORPHS	TRIONYMS

T

TRIOR	TRIPMAN	TRIPWIRES	TRITELY	TRIVETS
TRIORS	TRIPMEN	TRIPY	TRITENESS	TRIVIA
TRIOS	TRIPOD	TRIQUETRA	TRITER	TRIVIAL
TRIOSE	TRIPODAL	TRIRADIAL	TRITES	TRIVIALLY
TRIOSES	TRIPODIC	TRIREME	TRITEST	TRIVIUM
TRIOXID	TRIPODIES	TRIREMES	TRITHEISM	TRIVIUMS
TRIOXIDE	TRIPODS	TRISAGION	TRITHEIST	TRIWEEKLY
TRIOXIDES	TRIPODY	TRISCELE	TRITHING	TRIZONAL
TRIOXIDS	TRIPOLI	TRISCELES	TRITHINGS	TRIZONE
TRIOXYGEN	TRIPOLIS	TRISECT	TRITIATE	TRIZONES
TRIP	TRIPOS	TRISECTED	TRITIATED	TROAD
TRIPACK	TRIPOSES	TRISECTOR	TRITIATES	TROADE
TRIPACKS	TRIPPANT	TRISECTS	TRITICAL	TROADES
TRIPART	TRIPPED	TRISEME	TRITICALE	TROADS
TRIPE	TRIPPER	TRISEMES	TRITICISM	TROAK
TRIPEDAL	TRIPPERS	TRISEMIC	TRITICUM	TROAKED
TRIPERIES	TRIPPERY	TRISERIAL	TRITICUMS	TROAKING
TRIPERY	TRIPPET	TRISHAW	TRITIDE	TROAKS
TRIPES	TRIPPETS	TRISHAWS	TRITIDES	TROAT
TRIPEY	TRIPPIER	TRISKELE	TRITIUM	TROATED
TRIPHASE	TRIPPIEST	TRISKELES	TRITIUMS	TROATING
TRIPHONE	TRIPPING	TRISKELIA	TRITOMA	TROATS
TRIPHONES	TRIPPINGS	TRISMIC	TRITOMAS	TROCAR
TRIPIER	TRIPPLE	TRISMUS	TRITON	TROCARS
TRIPIEST	TRIPPLED	TRISMUSES	TRITONE	TROCHAIC
TRIPITAKA	TRIPPLER	TRISODIUM	TRITONES	TROCHAICS
TRIPLANE	TRIPPLERS	TRISOME	TRITONIA	TROCHAL
TRIPLANES	TRIPPLES	TRISOMES	TRITONIAS	TROCHAR
TRIPLE	TRIPPLING	TRISOMIC	TRITONS	TROCHARS
TRIPLED	TRIPPY	TRISOMICS	TRITURATE	TROCHE
TRIPLES	TRIPS	TRISOMIES	TRIUMPH	TROCHEE
TRIPLET	TRIPSES	TRISOMY	TRIUMPHAL	TROCHEES
TRIPLETS	TRIPSIS	TRIST	TRIUMPHED	TROCHES
TRIPLEX	TRIPTAN	TRISTATE	TRIUMPHER	TROCHI
TRIPLEXED	TRIPTANE	TRISTE	TRIUMPHS	TROCHIL
TRIPLEXES	TRIPTANES	TRISTESSE	TRIUMVIR	TROCHILI
TRIPLIED	TRIPTANS	TRISTEZA	TRIUMVIRI	TROCHILIC
TRIPLIES	TRIPTOTE	TRISTEZAS	TRIUMVIRS	TROCHILS
TRIPLING	TRIPTOTES	TRISTFUL	TRIUMVIRY	TROCHILUS
TRIPLINGS	TRIPTYCA	TRISTICH	TRIUNE	TROCHISK
TRIPLITE	TRIPTYCAS	TRISTICHS	TRIUNES	TROCHISKS
TRIPLITES	TRIPTYCH	TRISUL	TRIUNITY	TROCHITE
TRIPLOID	TRIPTYCHS	TRISULA	TRIVALENT	TROCHITES
TRIPLOIDS	TRIPTYQUE	TRISULAS	TRIVALVE	TROCHLEA
TRIPLOIDY	TRIPUDIA	TRISULS	TRIVALVED	TROCHLEAE
TRIPLY	TRIPUDIUM	TRITANOPE	TRIVALVES	TROCHLEAR
TRIPLYING	TRIPWIRE	TRITE	TRIVET	TROCHLEAS

TROCHOID	TROLLEY	TROOPIALS	TROTLINE	TROUSERS
TROCHOIDS	TROLLEYED	TROOPING	TROTLINES	TROUSES
TROCHUS	TROLLEYS	TROOPS	TROTS	TROUSSEAU
TROCHUSES	TROLLIED	TROOPSHIP	TROTTED	TROUT
TROCK	TROLLIES	TROOSTITE	TROTTER	TROUTER
TROCKED	TROLLING	TROOZ	TROTTERS	TROUTERS
TROCKEN	TROLLINGS	TROP	TROTTING	TROUTFUL
TROCKING	TROLLISH	TROPAEOLA	TROTTINGS	TROUTIER
TROCKS	TROLLIUS	TROPARIA	TROTTOIR	TROUTIEST
TROD	TROLLOP	TROPARION	TROTTOIRS	TROUTING
TRODDEN	TROLLOPED	TROPE	TROTYL	TROUTINGS
TRODE	TROLLOPEE	TROPED	TROTYLS	TROUTLESS
TRODES	TROLLOPS	TROPEOLIN	TROU	TROUTLET
TRODS	TROLLOPY	TROPES	TROUBLE	TROUTLETS
TROELIE	TROLLS	TROPHESY	TROUBLED	TROUTLING
TROELIES	TROLLY	TROPHI	TROUBLER	TROUTS
TROELY	TROLLYING	TROPHIC	TROUBLERS	TROUTY
TROFFER	TROMBONE	TROPHIED	TROUBLES	TROUVERE
TROFFERS	TROMBONES	TROPHIES	TROUBLING	TROUVERES
TROG	TROMINO	TROPHY	TROUBLOUS	TROUVEUR
TROGGED	TROMINOES	TROPHYING	TROUCH	TROUVEURS
TROGGING	TROMINOS	TROPIC	TROUCHES	TROVE
TROGGS	TROMMEL	TROPICAL	TROUGH	TROVER
TROGON	TROMMELS	TROPICALS	TROUGHED	TROVERS
TROGONS	TROMP	TROPICS	TROUGHING	TROVES
TROGS	TROMPE	TROPIN	TROUGHS	TROW
TROIKA	TROMPED	TROPINE	TROULE	TROWED
TROIKAS	TROMPES	TROPINES	TROULED	TROWEL
TROILISM	TROMPING	TROPING	TROULES	TROWELED
TROILISMS	TROMPS	TROPINS	TROULING	TROWELER
TROILIST	TRON	TROPISM	TROUNCE	TROWELERS
TROILISTS	TRONA	TROPISMS	TROUNCED	TROWELING
TROILITE	TRONAS	TROPIST	TROUNCER	TROWELLED
TROILITES	TRONC	TROPISTIC	TROUNCERS	TROWELLER
TROILUS	TRONCS	TROPISTS	TROUNCES	TROWELS
TROILUSES	TRONE	TROPOLOGY	TROUNCING	TROWING
TROIS	TRONES	TROPONIN	TROUPE	TROWS
TROKE	TRONK	TROPONINS	TROUPED	TROWSERS
TROKED	TRONKS	TROPPO	TROUPER	TROWTH
TROKES	TRONS	TROSSERS	TROUPERS	TROWTHS
TROKING	TROOLIE	TROT	TROUPES	TROY
TROLAND	TROOLIES	TROTH	TROUPIAL	TROYS
TROLANDS	TROOP	TROTHED	TROUPIALS	TRUANCIES
TROLL	TROOPED	TROTHFUL	TROUPING	TRUANCY
TROLLED	TROOPER	TROTHING	TROUSE	TRUANT
TROLLER	TROOPERS	TROTHLESS	TROUSER	TRUANTED
TROLLERS	TROOPIAL	TROTHS	TROUSERED	TRUANTING

TRUANTLY	TRUDGERS	TRUMPINGS	TRUSTFUL	TRYSTES
TRUANTRY	TRUDGES	TRUMPLESS	TRUSTIER	TRYSTING
TRUANTS	TRUDGING	TRUMPS	TRUSTIES	TRYSTS
TRUCAGE	TRUDGINGS	TRUNCAL	TRUSTIEST	TRYWORKS
TRUCAGES	TRUE	TRUNCATE	TRUSTILY	TSADDIK
TRUCE	TRUEBLUE	TRUNCATED	TRUSTING	TSADDIKIM
TRUCED	TRUEBLUES	TRUNCATES	TRUSTLESS	TSADDIKS
TRUCELESS	TRUEBORN	TRUNCHEON	TRUSTOR	TSADDIQ
TRUCES	TRUEBRED	TRUNDLE	TRUSTORS	TSADDIQIM
TRUCHMAN	TRUED	TRUNDLED	TRUSTS	TSADDIQS
TRUCHMANS	TRUEING	TRUNDLER	TRUSTY	TSADE
TRUCHMEN	TRUELOVE	TRUNDLERS	TRUTH	TSADES
TRUCIAL	TRUELOVES	TRUNDLES	TRUTHER	TSADI
TRUCING	TRUEMAN	TRUNDLING	TRUTHERS	TSADIK
TRUCK	TRUEMEN	TRUNK	TRUTHFUL	TSADIKS
TRUCKABLE	TRUENESS	TRUNKED	TRUTHIER	TSADIS
TRUCKAGE	TRUEPENNY	TRUNKFISH	TRUTHIEST	TSAMBA
TRUCKAGES	TRUER	TRUNKFUL	TRUTHLESS	TSAMBAS
TRUCKED	TRUES	TRUNKFULS	TRUTHLIKE	TSANTSA
TRUCKER	TRUEST	TRUNKING	TRUTHS	TSANTSAS
TRUCKERS	TRUFFE	TRUNKINGS	TRUTHY	TSAR
TRUCKFUL	TRUFFES	TRUNKLESS	TRY	TSARDOM
TRUCKFULS	TRUFFLE	TRUNKS	TRYE	TSARDOMS
TRUCKIE	TRUFFLED	TRUNKWORK	TRYER	TSAREVICH
TRUCKIES	TRUFFLES	TRUNNEL	TRYERS	TSAREVNA
TRUCKING	TRUFFLING	TRUNNELS	TRYING	TSAREVNAS
TRUCKINGS	TRUG	TRUNNION	TRYINGLY	TSARINA
TRUCKLE	TRUGO	TRUNNIONS	TRYINGS	TSARINAS
TRUCKLED	TRUGOS	TRUQUAGE	TRYKE	TSARISM
TRUCKLER	TRUGS	TRUQUAGES	TRYKES	TSARISMS
TRUCKLERS	TRUING	TRUQUEUR	TRYMA	TSARIST
TRUCKLES	TRUISM	TRUQUEURS	TRYMATA	TSARISTS
TRUCKLINE	TRUISMS	TRUSS	TRYOUT	TSARITSA
TRUCKLING	TRUISTIC	TRUSSED	TRYOUTS	TSARITSAS
TRUCKLOAD	TRULL	TRUSSER	TRYP	TSARITZA
TRUCKMAN	TRULLS	TRUSSERS	TRYPAN	TSARITZAS
TRUCKMEN	TRULY	TRUSSES	TRYPS	TSARS
TRUCKS	TRUMEAU	TRUSSING	TRYPSIN	TSATSKE
TRUCKSTOP	TRUMEAUX	TRUSSINGS	TRYPSINS	TSATSKES
TRUCULENT	TRUMP	TRUST	TRYPTIC	TSESSEBE
TRUDGE	TRUMPED	TRUSTABLE	TRYSAIL	TSESSEBES
TRUDGED	TRUMPERY	TRUSTED	TRYSAILS	TSETSE
TRUDGEN	TRUMPET	TRUSTEE	TRYST	TSETSES
TRUDGENS	TRUMPETED	TRUSTEED	TRYSTE	TSIGANE
TRUDGEON	TRUMPETER	TRUSTEES	TRYSTED	TSIGANES
TRUDGEONS	TRUMPETS	TRUSTER	TRYSTER	TSIMMES
TRUDGER	TRUMPING	TRUSTERS	TRYSTERS	TSITSITH

TSK	TUBAR	TUBFULS	TUCKET	TUGLESS
TSKED	TUBAS	TUBICOLAR	TUCKETS	TUGRA
TSKING	TUBATE	TUBICOLE	TUCKING	TUGRAS
TSKS	TUBBABLE	TUBICOLES	TUCKINGS	TUGRIK
TSKTSK	TUBBED	TUBIFEX	TUCKS	TUGRIKS
TSKTSKED	TUBBER	TUBIFEXES	TUCKSHOP	TUGS
TSKTSKING	TUBBERS	TUBIFICID	TUCKSHOPS	TUI
TSKTSKS	TUBBIER	TUBIFORM	TUCOTUCO	TUILE
TSOORIS	TUBBIEST	TUBING	TUCOTUCOS	TUILES
TSORES	TUBBINESS	TUBINGS	TUCUTUCO	TUILLE
TSORIS	TUBBING	TUBIST	TUCUTUCOS	TUILLES
TSORRISS	TUBBINGS	TUBISTS	TUCUTUCU	TUILLETTE
TSOTSI	TUBBISH	TUBLIKE	TUCUTUCUS	TUILYIE
TSOTSIS	TUBBY	TUBS	TUFA	TUILYIED
TSOURIS	TUBE	TUBULAR	TUFACEOUS	TUILYIES
TSOURISES	TUBECTOMY	TUBULARLY	TUFAS	TUILZIE
TSUBA	TUBED	TUBULARS	TUFF	TUILZIED
TSUBAS	TUBEFUL	TUBULATE	TUFFE	TUILZIES
TSUBO	TUBEFULS	TUBULATED	TUFFES	TUINA
TSUBOS	TUBELESS	TUBULATES	TUFFET	TUINAS
TSUNAMI	TUBELIKE	TUBULATOR	TUFFETS	TUIS
TSUNAMIC	TUBENOSE	TUBULE	TUFFS	TUISM
TSUNAMIS	TUBENOSES	TUBULES	TUFOLI	TUISMS
TSURIS	TUBER	TUBULIN	TUFT	TUITION
TSURISES	TUBERCLE	TUBULINS	TUFTED	TUITIONAL
TSUTSUMU	TUBERCLED	TUBULOSE	TUFTER	TUITIONS
TSUTSUMUS	TUBERCLES	TUBULOUS	TUFTERS	TUKTOO
TUAN	TUBERCULA	TUBULURE	TUFTIER	TUKTOOS
TUANS	TUBERCULE	TUBULURES	TUFTIEST	TUKTU
TUART	TUBEROID	TUCHIS	TUFTILY	TUKTUS
TUARTS	TUBEROIDS	TUCHISES	TUFTING	TULADI
TUATARA	TUBEROSE	TUCHUN	TUFTINGS	TULADIS
TUATARAS	TUBEROSES	TUCHUNS	TUFTS	TULAREMIA
TUATERA	TUBEROUS	TUCHUS	TUFTY	TULAREMIC
TUATERAS	TUBERS	TUCHUSES	TUG	TULBAN
TUATH	TUBES	TUCK	TUGBOAT	TULBANS
TUATHS	TUBEWELL	TUCKAHOE	TUGBOATS	TULCHAN
TUATUA	TUBEWELLS	TUCKAHOES	TUGGED	TULCHANS
TUATUAS	TUBEWORK	TUCKBOX	TUGGER	TULE
TUB	TUBEWORKS	TUCKBOXES	TUGGERS	TULES
TUBA	TUBEWORM	TUCKED	TUGGING	TULIP
TUBAE	TUBEWORMS	TUCKER	TUGGINGLY	TULIPANT
TUBAGE	TUBFAST	TUCKERBAG	TUGGINGS	TULIPANTS
TUBAGES	TUBFASTS	TUCKERBOX	TUGHRA	TULIPLIKE
TUBAIST	TUBFISH	TUCKERED	TUGHRAS	TULIPS
TUBAISTS	TUBFISHES	TUCKERING	TUGHRIK	TULIPWOOD
TUBAL	TUBFUL	TUCKERS	TUGHRIKS	TULLE

TULLES	TUMP	TUNEFUL	TUNNING	TURBIDLY
TULLIBEE	TUMPED	TUNEFULLY	TUNNINGS	TURBINAL
TULLIBEES	TUMPHIES	TUNELESS	TUNNY	TURBINALS
TULPA	TUMPHY	TUNER	TUNS	TURBINATE
TULPAS	TUMPIER	TUNERS	TUNY	TURBINE
TULSI	TUMPIEST	TUNES	TUP	TURBINED
TULSIS	TUMPING	TUNESMITH	TUPEK	TURBINES
TULWAR	TUMPLINE	TUNEUP	TUPEKS	TURBIT
TULWARS	TUMPLINES	TUNEUPS	TUPELO	TURBITH
TUM	TUMPS	TUNG	TUPELOS	TURBITHS
TUMBLE	TUMPY	TUNGS	TUPIK	TURBITS
TUMBLEBUG	TUMS	TUNGSTATE	TUPIKS	TURBO
TUMBLED	TUMSHIE	TUNGSTEN	TUPLE	TURBOCAR
TUMBLER	TUMSHIES	TUNGSTENS	TUPLES	TURBOCARS
TUMBLERS	TUMULAR	TUNGSTIC	TUPPED	TURBOFAN
TUMBLES	TUMULARY	TUNGSTITE	TUPPENCE	TURBOFANS
TUMBLESET	TUMULI	TUNGSTOUS	TUPPENCES	TURBOJET
TUMBLING	TUMULOSE	TUNIC	TUPPENNY	TURBOJETS
TUMBLINGS	TUMULOUS	TUNICA	TUPPING	TURBOND
TUMBREL	TUMULT	TUNICAE	TUPPINGS	TURBONDS
TUMBRELS	TUMULTED	TUNICATE	TUPS	TURBOPROP
TUMBRIL	TUMULTING	TUNICATED	TUPTOWING	TURBOS
TUMBRILS	TUMULTS	TUNICATES	TUPUNA	TURBOT
TUMEFIED	TUMULUS	TUNICIN	TUPUNAS	TURBOTS
TUMEFIES	TUMULUSES	TUNICINS	TUQUE	TURBULENT
TUMEFY	TUN	TUNICKED	TUQUES	TURCOPOLE
TUMEFYING	TUNA	TUNICLE	TURACIN	TURD
TUMESCE	TUNABLE	TUNICLES	TURACINS	TURDINE
TUMESCED	TUNABLY	TUNICS	TURACO	TURDION
TUMESCENT	TUNAS	TUNIER	TURACOS	TURDIONS
TUMESCES	TUNBELLY	TUNIEST	TURACOU	TURDOID
TUMESCING	TUND	TUNING	TURACOUS	TURDS
TUMID	TUNDED	TUNINGS	TURBAN	TURDUCKEN
TUMIDITY	TUNDING	TUNKET	TURBAND	TUREEN
TUMIDLY	TUNDISH	TUNKETS	TURBANDS	TUREENS
TUMIDNESS	TUNDISHES	TUNNAGE	TURBANED	TURF
TUMMIES	TUNDRA	TUNNAGES	TURBANNED	TURFED
TUMMLER	TUNDRAS	TUNNED	TURBANS	TURFEN
TUMMLERS	TUNDS	TUNNEL	TURBANT	TURFGRASS
TUMMY	TUNDUN	TUNNELED	TURBANTS	TURFIER
TUMOR	TUNDUNS	TUNNELER	TURBARIES	TURFIEST
TUMORAL	TUNE	TUNNELERS	TURBARY	TURFINESS
TUMORLIKE	TUNEABLE	TUNNELING	TURBETH	TURFING
TUMOROUS	TUNEABLY	TUNNELLED	TURBETHS	TURFINGS
TUMORS	TUNEAGE	TUNNELLER	TURBID	TURFITE
TUMOUR	TUNEAGES	TUNNELS	TURBIDITE	TURFITES
TUMOURS	TUNED	TUNNIES	TURBIDITY	TURFLESS

TURFLIKE	TURNAGAIN	TURNTABLE	TUSKIER	TUTELARY
TURFMAN	TURNBACK	TURNUP	TUSKIEST	TUTENAG
TURFMEN	TURNBACKS	TURNUPS	TUSKING	TUTENAGS
TURFS	TURNCOAT	TUROPHILE	TUSKINGS	TUTIORISM
TURFSKI	TURNCOATS	TURPETH	TUSKLESS	TUTIORIST
TURFSKIS	TURNCOCK	TURPETHS	TUSKLIKE	TUTMAN
TURFY	TURNCOCKS	TURPITUDE	TUSKS	TUTMEN
TURGENCY	TURNDOWN	TURPS	TUSKY	TUTOR
TURGENT	TURNDOWNS	TURPSES	TUSSAC	TUTORAGE
TURGENTLY	TURNDUN	TURQUOIS	TUSSAH	TUTORAGES
TURGID	TURNDUNS	TURQUOISE	TUSSAHS	TUTORED
TURGIDER	TURNED	TURR	TUSSAL	TUTORESS
TURGIDEST	TURNER	TURRET	TUSSAR	TUTORIAL
TURGIDITY	TURNERIES	TURRETED	TUSSARS	TUTORIALS
TURGIDLY	TURNERS	TURRETS	TUSSEH	TUTORING
TURGITE	TURNERY	TURRIBANT	TUSSEHS	TUTORINGS
TURGITES	TURNHALL	TURRICAL	TUSSER	TUTORISE
TURGOR	TURNHALLS	TURRS	TUSSERS	TUTORISED
TURGORS	TURNING	TURTLE	TUSSES	TUTORISES
TURION	TURNINGS	TURTLED	TUSSIS	TUTORISM
TURIONS	TURNIP	TURTLER	TUSSISES	TUTORISMS
TURISTA	TURNIPED	TURTLERS	TUSSIVE	TUTORIZE
TURISTAS	TURNIPING	TURTLES	TUSSLE	TUTORIZED
TURK	TURNIPS	TURTLING	TUSSLED	TUTORIZES
TURKEY	TURNIPY	TURTLINGS	TUSSLES	TUTORS
TURKEYS	TURNKEY	TURVES	TUSSLING	TUTORSHIP
TURKIES	TURNKEYS	TUSCHE	TUSSOCK	TUTOYED
TURKIESES	TURNOFF	TUSCHES	TUSSOCKED	TUTOYER
TURKIS	TURNOFFS	TUSH	TUSSOCKS	TUTOYERED
TURKISES	TURNON	TUSHED	TUSSOCKY	TUTOYERS
TURKOIS	TURNONS	TUSHERIES	TUSSOR	TUTRESS
TURKOISES	TURNOUT	TUSHERY	TUSSORE	TUTRESSES
TURKS	TURNOUTS	TUSHES	TUSSORES	TUTRICES
TURLOUGH	TURNOVER	TUSHIE	TUSSORS	TUTRIX
TURLOUGHS	TURNOVERS	TUSHIES	TUSSUCK	TUTRIXES
TURM	TURNPIKE	TUSHING	TUSSUCKS	TUTS
TURME	TURNPIKES	TUSHKAR	TUSSUR	TUTSAN
TURMERIC	TURNROUND	TUSHKARS	TUSSURS	TUTSANS
TURMERICS	TURNS	TUSHKER	TUT	TUTSED
TURMES	TURNSKIN	TUSHKERS	TUTANIA	TUTSES
TURMOIL	TURNSKINS	TUSHY	TUTANIAS	TUTSING
TURMOILED	TURNSOLE	TUSK	TUTEE	TUTTED
TURMOILS	TURNSOLES	TUSKAR	TUTEES	TUTTI
TURMS	TURNSPIT	TUSKARS	TUTELAGE	TUTTIES
TURN	TURNSPITS	TUSKED	TUTELAGES	TUTTING
TURNABLE	TURNSTILE	TUSKER	TUTELAR	TUTTINGS
TURNABOUT	TURNSTONE	TUSKERS	TUTELARS	TUTTIS

TUTTY	TWANGLED	TWEEDLERS	TWELVEMO	TWIGHT
TUTU	TWANGLER	TWEEDLES	TWELVEMOS	TWIGHTED
TUTUED	TWANGLERS	TWEEDLING	TWELVES	TWIGHTING
TUTUS	TWANGLES	TWEEDS	TWENTIES	TWIGHTS
TUTWORK	TWANGLING	TWEEDY	TWENTIETH	TWIGLESS
TUTWORKER	TWANGS	TWEEL	TWENTY	TWIGLET
TUTWORKS	TWANGY	TWEELED	TWENTYISH	TWIGLETS
TUX	TWANK	TWEELING	TWERK	TWIGLIKE
TUXEDO	TWANKAY	TWEELS	TWERKED	TWIGLOO
TUXEDOED	TWANKAYS	TWEELY	TWERKING	TWIGLOOS
TUXEDOES	TWANKIES	TWEEN	TWERKINGS	TWIGS
TUXEDOS	TWANKS	TWEENAGE	TWERKS	TWIGSOME
TUXES	TWANKY	TWEENAGER	TWERP	TWILIGHT
TUYER	TWAS	TWEENER	TWERPIER	TWILIGHTS
TUYERE	TWASOME	TWEENERS	TWERPIEST	TWILIT
TUYERES	TWASOMES	TWEENESS	TWERPS	TWILL
TUYERS	TWAT	TWEENIE	TWERPY	TWILLED
TUZZ	TWATS	TWEENIES	TWIBIL	TWILLIES
TUZZES	TWATTED	TWEENS	TWIBILL	TWILLING
TWA	TWATTING	TWEENY	TWIBILLS	TWILLINGS
TWADDLE	TWATTLE	TWEEP	TWIBILS	TWILLS
TWADDLED	TWATTLED	TWEEPLE	TWICE	TWILLY
TWADDLER	TWATTLER	TWEEPS	TWICER	TWILT
TWADDLERS	TWATTLERS	TWEER	TWICERS	TWILTED
TWADDLES	TWATTLES	TWEERED	TWICHILD	TWILTING
TWADDLIER	TWATTLING	TWEERING	TWIDDLE	TWILTS
TWADDLING	TWAY	TWEERS	TWIDDLED	TWIN
TWADDLY	TWAYBLADE	TWEEST	TWIDDLER	TWINBERRY
TWAE	TWAYS	TWEET	TWIDDLERS	TWINBORN
TWAES	TWEAK	TWEETABLE	TWIDDLES	TWINE
TWAFALD	TWEAKED	TWEETED	TWIDDLIER	TWINED
TWAIN	TWEAKER	TWEETER	TWIDDLING	TWINER
TWAINS	TWEAKERS	TWEETERS	TWIDDLY	TWINERS
TWAITE	TWEAKIER	TWEETING	TWIER	TWINES
TWAITES	TWEAKIEST	TWEETS	TWIERS	TWINGE
TWAL	TWEAKING	TWEETUP	TWIFOLD	TWINGED
TWALPENNY	TWEAKINGS	TWEETUPS	TWIFORKED	TWINGEING
TWALS	TWEAKS	TWEEZE	TWIFORMED	TWINGES
TWANG	TWEAKY	TWEEZED	TWIG	TWINGING
TWANGED	TWEE	TWEEZER	TWIGGED	TWINIER
TWANGER	TWEED	TWEEZERS	TWIGGEN	TWINIEST
TWANGERS	TWEEDIER	TWEEZES	TWIGGER	TWINIGHT
TWANGIER	TWEEDIEST	TWEEZING	TWIGGERS	TWINING
TWANGIEST	TWEEDILY	TWELFTH	TWIGGIER	TWININGLY
TWANGING	TWEEDLE	TWELFTHLY	TWIGGIEST	TWININGS
TWANGINGS	TWEEDLED	TWELFTHS	TWIGGING	TWINJET
TWANGLE	TWEEDLER	TWELVE	TWIGGY	TWINJETS

TWINK	TWISCARS	TWOCCINGS	TYGS	TYPEBARS
TWINKED	TWIST	TWOCKER	TYIN	TYPECASE
TWINKIE	TWISTABLE	TWOCKERS	TYING	TYPECASES
TWINKIES	TWISTED	TWOCKING	TYIYN	TYPECAST
TWINKING	TWISTER	TWOCKINGS	TYIYNS	TYPECASTS
TWINKLE	TWISTERS	TWOER	TYKE	TYPED
TWINKLED	TWISTIER	TWOERS	TYKES	TYPEFACE
TWINKLER	TWISTIEST	TWOFER	TYKISH	TYPEFACES
TWINKLERS	TWISTING	TWOFERS	TYLECTOMY	TYPES
TWINKLES	TWISTINGS	TWOFOLD	TYLER	TYPESET
TWINKLIER	TWISTOR	TWOFOLDS	TYLERS	TYPESETS
TWINKLING	TWISTORS	TWONESS	TYLOPOD	TYPESTYLE
TWINKLY	TWISTS	TWONESSES	TYLOPODS	TYPEWRITE
TWINKS	TWISTY	TWONIE	TYLOSES	TYPEWROTE
TWINKY	TWIT	TWONIES	TYLOSIN	TYPEY
TWINLING	TWITCH	TWOONIE	TYLOSINS	TYPHLITIC
TWINLINGS	TWITCHED	TWOONIES	TYLOSIS	TYPHLITIS
TWINNED	TWITCHER	TWOPENCE	TYLOTE	TYPHOID
TWINNING	TWITCHERS	TWOPENCES	TYLOTES	TYPHOIDAL
TWINNINGS	TWITCHES	TWOPENNY	TYMBAL	TYPHOIDIN
TWINS	TWITCHIER	TWOS	TYMBALS	TYPHOIDS
TWINSET	TWITCHILY	TWOSEATER	TYMP	TYPHON
TWINSETS	TWITCHING	TWOSOME	TYMPAN	TYPHONIAN
TWINSHIP	TWITCHY	TWOSOMES	TYMPANA	TYPHONIC
TWINSHIPS	TWITE	TWOSTROKE	TYMPANAL	TYPHONS
TWINTER	TWITES	TWP	TYMPANI	TYPHOON
TWINTERS	TWITS	TWYER	TYMPANIC	TYPHOONS
TWINY	TWITTED	TWYERE	TYMPANICS	TYPHOSE
TWIRE	TWITTEN	TWYERES	TYMPANIES	TYPHOUS
TWIRED	TWITTENS	TWYERS	TYMPANIST	TYPHUS
TWIRES	TWITTER	TWYFOLD	TYMPANO	TYPHUSES
TWIRING	TWITTERED	TYCHISM	TYMPANS	TYPIC
TWIRL	TWITTERER	TYCHISMS	TYMPANUM	TYPICAL
TWIRLED	TWITTERS	TYCOON	TYMPANUMS	TYPICALLY
TWIRLER	TWITTERY	TYCOONATE	TYMPANY	TYPIER
TWIRLERS	TWITTING	TYCOONERY	TYMPS	TYPIEST
TWIRLIER	TWITTINGS	TYCOONS	TYND	TYPIFIED
TWIRLIEST	TWITTISH	TYDE	TYNDE	TYPIFIER
TWIRLING	TWIXT	TYE	TYNE	TYPIFIERS
TWIRLS	TWIZZLE	TYED	TYNED	TYPIFIES
TWIRLY	TWIZZLED	TYEE	TYNES	TYPIFY
TWIRP	TWIZZLES	TYEES	TYNING	TYPIFYING
TWIRPIER	TWIZZLING	TYEING	TYPABLE	TYPING
TWIRPIEST	TWO	TYER	TYPAL	TYPINGS
TWIRPS	TWOCCER	TYERS	TYPE	TYPIST
TWIRPY	TWOCCERS	TYES	TYPEABLE	TYPISTS
TWISCAR	TWOCCING	TYG	TYPEBAR	TYPO

TYPOGRAPH	TYRANNESS	TYRO	TZADDIKIM	TZARITZAS
TYPOLOGIC	TYRANNIC	TYROCIDIN	TZADDIKS	TZARS
TYPOLOGY	TYRANNIES	TYROES	TZADDIQ	TZATZIKI
TYPOMANIA	TYRANNING	TYRONES	TZADDIQIM	TZATZIKIS
TYPOS	TYRANNIS	TYRONIC	TZADDIQS	TZEDAKAH
TYPP	TYRANNISE	TYROPITA	TZADDIS	TZEDAKAHS
TYPPS	TYRANNIZE	TYROPITAS	TZADIK	TZETSE
TYPTO	TYRANNOUS	TYROPITTA	TZADIKS	TZETSES
TYPTOED	TYRANNY	TYROS	TZAR	TZETZE
TYPTOING	TYRANS	TYROSINE	TZARDOM	TZETZES
TYPTOS	TYRANT	TYROSINES	TZARDOMS	TZIGANE
TYPY	TYRANTED	TYSTIE	TZAREVNA	TZIGANES
TYRAMINE	TYRANTING	TYSTIES	TZAREVNAS	TZIGANIES
TYRAMINES	TYRANTS	TYTE	TZARINA	TZIGANY
TYRAN	TYRE	TYTHE	TZARINAS	TZIMMES
TYRANED	TYRED	TYTHED	TZARISM	TZITZIS
TYRANING	TYRELESS	TYTHES	TZARISMS	TZITZIT
TYRANNE	TYREMAKER	TYTHING	TZARIST	TZITZITH
TYRANNED	TYRES	TZADDI	TZARISTS	TZURIS
TYRANNES	TYRING	TZADDIK	TZARITZA	TZURISES

U

UAKARI	UGGED	ULAMA	ULNAR	ULTRALEFT
UAKARIS	UGGING	ULAMAS	ULNARE	ULTRALOW
UBEROUS	UGH	ULAN	ULNARIA	ULTRAPOSH
UBERTIES	UGHS	ULANS	ULNAS	ULTRAPURE
UBERTY	UGLIED	ULCER	ULOSES	ULTRARARE
UBIETIES	UGLIER	ULCERATE	ULOSIS	ULTRARED
UBIETY	UGLIES	ULCERATED	ULOTRICHY	ULTRAREDS
UBIQUE	UGLIEST	ULCERATES	ULPAN	ULTRARICH
UBIQUITIN	UGLIFIED	ULCERED	ULPANIM	ULTRAS
UBIQUITY	UGLIFIER	ULCERING	ULSTER	ULTRASAFE
UBUNTU	UGLIFIERS	ULCEROUS	ULSTERED	ULTRASLOW
UBUNTUS	UGLIFIES	ULCERS	ULSTERS	ULTRASOFT
UCKERS	UGLIFY	ULE	ULTERIOR	ULTRATHIN
UDAL	UGLIFYING	ULEMA	ULTIMA	ULTRATINY
UDALLER	UGLILY	ULEMAS	ULTIMACY	ULTRAWIDE
UDALLERS	UGLINESS	ULES	ULTIMAS	ULU
UDALS	UGLY	ULEX	ULTIMATA	ULULANT
UDDER	UGLYING	ULEXES	ULTIMATE	ULULATE
UDDERED	UGS	ULEXITE	ULTIMATED	ULULATED
UDDERFUL	UGSOME	ULEXITES	ULTIMATES	ULULATES
UDDERLESS	UH	ULICES	ULTIMATUM	ULULATING
UDDERS	UHLAN	ULICON	ULTIMO	ULULATION
UDO	UHLANS	ULICONS	ULTION	ULUS
UDOMETER	UHURU	ULIGINOSE	ULTIONS	ULVA
UDOMETERS	UHURUS	ULIGINOUS	ULTISOL	ULVAS
UDOMETRIC	UILLEAN	ULIKON	ULTISOLS	ULYIE
UDOMETRY	UILLEANN	ULIKONS	ULTRA	ULYIES
UDON	UINTAHITE	ULITIS	ULTRACHIC	ULZIE
UDONS	UINTAITE	ULITISES	ULTRACOLD	ULZIES
UDOS	UINTAITES	ULLAGE	ULTRACOOL	UM
UDS	UITLANDER	ULLAGED	ULTRADRY	UMAMI
UEY	UJAMAA	ULLAGES	ULTRAFAST	UMAMIS
UEYS	UJAMAAS	ULLAGING	ULTRAFINE	UMANGITE
UFO	UKASE	ULLING	ULTRAHEAT	UMANGITES
UFOLOGIES	UKASES	ULLINGS	ULTRAHIGH	UMBEL
UFOLOGIST	UKE	ULMACEOUS	ULTRAHIP	UMBELED
UFOLOGY	UKELELE	ULMIN	ULTRAHOT	UMBELLAR
UFOS	UKELELES	ULMINS	ULTRAISM	UMBELLATE
UG	UKES	ULNA	ULTRAISMS	UMBELLED
UGALI	UKULELE	ULNAD	ULTRAIST	UMBELLET
UGALIS	UKULELES	ULNAE	ULTRAISTS	UMBELLETS

U

UMBELLULE
UMBELS
UMBELULE
UMBELULES
UMBER
UMBERED
UMBERING
UMBERS
UMBERY
UMBILICAL
UMBILICI
UMBILICUS
UMBLE
UMBLES
UMBO
UMBONAL
UMBONATE
UMBONES
UMBONIC
UMBOS
UMBRA
UMBRACULA
UMBRAE
UMBRAGE
UMBRAGED
UMBRAGES
UMBRAGING
UMBRAL
UMBRAS
UMBRATED
UMBRATIC
UMBRATILE
UMBRE
UMBREL
UMBRELLA
UMBRELLAS
UMBRELLO
UMBRELLOS
UMBRELS
UMBRERE
UMBRERES
UMBRES
UMBRETTE
UMBRETTES
UMBRIERE
UMBRIERES
UMBRIL

UMBRILS
UMBROSE
UMBROUS
UMFAZI
UMFAZIS
UMIAC
UMIACK
UMIACKS
UMIACS
UMIAK
UMIAKS
UMIAQ
UMIAQS
UMLAUT
UMLAUTED
UMLAUTING
UMLAUTS
UMLUNGU
UMLUNGUS
UMM
UMMA
UMMAH
UMMAHS
UMMAS
UMMED
UMMING
UMP
UMPED
UMPH
UMPHS
UMPIE
UMPIES
UMPING
UMPIRAGE
UMPIRAGES
UMPIRE
UMPIRED
UMPIRES
UMPIRING
UMPS
UMPTEEN
UMPTEENTH
UMPTIETH
UMPTY
UMPY
UMQUHILE
UMRA

UMRAH
UMRAHS
UMRAS
UMS
UMTEENTH
UMU
UMUS
UMWELT
UMWELTS
UMWHILE
UN
UNABASHED
UNABATED
UNABATING
UNABETTED
UNABIDING
UNABJURED
UNABLE
UNABORTED
UNABRADED
UNABUSED
UNABUSIVE
UNACCRUED
UNACCUSED
UNACERBIC
UNACHING
UNACIDIC
UNACTABLE
UNACTED
UNACTIVE
UNACTIVED
UNACTIVES
UNADAPTED
UNADDED
UNADEPT
UNADEPTLY
UNADEPTS
UNADMIRED
UNADOPTED
UNADORED
UNADORNED
UNADULT
UNADVISED
UNAFRAID
UNAGED
UNAGEING
UNAGILE

UNAGING
UNAGREED
UNAI
UNAIDABLE
UNAIDED
UNAIDEDLY
UNAIMED
UNAIRED
UNAIS
UNAKIN
UNAKING
UNAKITE
UNAKITES
UNALARMED
UNALERTED
UNALIGNED
UNALIKE
UNALIST
UNALISTS
UNALIVE
UNALLAYED
UNALLEGED
UNALLIED
UNALLOWED
UNALLOYED
UNALTERED
UNAMASSED
UNAMAZED
UNAMENDED
UNAMERCED
UNAMIABLE
UNAMUSED
UNAMUSING
UNANCHOR
UNANCHORS
UNANELED
UNANIMITY
UNANIMOUS
UNANNEXED
UNANNOYED
UNANXIOUS
UNAPPAREL
UNAPPLIED
UNAPT
UNAPTLY
UNAPTNESS
UNARCHED

UNARGUED
UNARISEN
UNARM
UNARMED
UNARMING
UNARMORED
UNARMS
UNAROUSED
UNARRAYED
UNARTFUL
UNARY
UNASHAMED
UNASKED
UNASSAYED
UNASSUMED
UNASSURED
UNATONED
UNATTIRED
UNATTUNED
UNAU
UNAUDITED
UNAUS
UNAVENGED
UNAVERAGE
UNAVERTED
UNAVOIDED
UNAVOWED
UNAWAKE
UNAWAKED
UNAWARDED
UNAWARE
UNAWARELY
UNAWARES
UNAWED
UNAWESOME
UNAXED
UNBACKED
UNBAFFLED
UNBAG
UNBAGGED
UNBAGGING
UNBAGS
UNBAITED
UNBAKED
UNBALANCE
UNBALE
UNBALED

U

UNBALES	UNBEING	UNBLENT	UNBOTTLE	UNBUILD
UNBALING	UNBEINGS	UNBLESS	UNBOTTLED	UNBUILDS
UNBAN	UNBEKNOWN	UNBLESSED	UNBOTTLES	UNBUILT
UNBANDAGE	UNBELIEF	UNBLESSES	UNBOUGHT	UNBULKIER
UNBANDED	UNBELIEFS	UNBLEST	UNBOUNCY	UNBULKY
UNBANKED	UNBELIEVE	UNBLIND	UNBOUND	UNBUNDLE
UNBANNED	UNBELOVED	UNBLINDED	UNBOUNDED	UNBUNDLED
UNBANNING	UNBELT	UNBLINDS	UNBOWED	UNBUNDLER
UNBANS	UNBELTED	UNBLOCK	UNBOWING	UNBUNDLES
UNBAPTISE	UNBELTING	UNBLOCKED	UNBOX	UNBURDEN
UNBAPTIZE	UNBELTS	UNBLOCKS	UNBOXED	UNBURDENS
UNBAR	UNBEMUSED	UNBLOODED	UNBOXES	UNBURIED
UNBARBED	UNBEND	UNBLOODY	UNBOXING	UNBURIES
UNBARE	UNBENDED	UNBLOTTED	UNBRACE	UNBURNED
UNBARED	UNBENDING	UNBLOWED	UNBRACED	UNBURNT
UNBARES	UNBENDS	UNBLOWN	UNBRACES	UNBURROW
UNBARING	UNBENIGN	UNBLUNTED	UNBRACING	UNBURROWS
UNBARK	UNBENT	UNBLURRED	UNBRAID	UNBURTHEN
UNBARKED	UNBEREFT	UNBOARDED	UNBRAIDED	UNBURY
UNBARKING	UNBERUFEN	UNBOBBED	UNBRAIDS	UNBURYING
UNBARKS	UNBESEEM	UNBODIED	UNBRAKE	UNBUSIED
UNBARRED	UNBESEEMS	UNBODING	UNBRAKED	UNBUSIER
UNBARRING	UNBESPEAK	UNBOILED	UNBRAKES	UNBUSIES
UNBARS	UNBESPOKE	UNBOLT	UNBRAKING	UNBUSIEST
UNBASED	UNBIAS	UNBOLTED	UNBRANDED	UNBUSTED
UNBASHFUL	UNBIASED	UNBOLTING	UNBRASTE	UNBUSY
UNBASTED	UNBIASES	UNBOLTS	UNBRED	UNBUSYING
UNBATED	UNBIASING	UNBONDED	UNBREECH	UNBUTTON
UNBATHED	UNBIASSED	UNBONE	UNBRIDGED	UNBUTTONS
UNBE	UNBIASSES	UNBONED	UNBRIDLE	UNCAGE
UNBEAR	UNBID	UNBONES	UNBRIDLED	UNCAGED
UNBEARDED	UNBIDDEN	UNBONING	UNBRIDLES	UNCAGES
UNBEARED	UNBIGOTED	UNBONNET	UNBRIEFED	UNCAGING
UNBEARING	UNBILLED	UNBONNETS	UNBRIGHT	UNCAKE
UNBEARS	UNBIND	UNBOOKED	UNBRIZZED	UNCAKED
UNBEATEN	UNBINDING	UNBOOKISH	UNBROILED	UNCAKES
UNBED	UNBINDS	UNBOOT	UNBROKE	UNCAKING
UNBEDDED	UNBISHOP	UNBOOTED	UNBROKEN	UNCALLED
UNBEDDING	UNBISHOPS	UNBOOTING	UNBROWNED	UNCANDID
UNBEDS	UNBITT	UNBOOTS	UNBRUISED	UNCANDLED
UNBEEN	UNBITTED	UNBORE	UNBRUSED	UNCANDOUR
UNBEGET	UNBITTEN	UNBORN	UNBRUSHED	UNCANNED
UNBEGETS	UNBITTER	UNBORNE	UNBUCKLE	UNCANNIER
UNBEGGED	UNBITTING	UNBOSOM	UNBUCKLED	UNCANNILY
UNBEGOT	UNBITTS	UNBOSOMED	UNBUCKLES	UNCANNY
UNBEGUILE	UNBLAMED	UNBOSOMER	UNBUDDED	UNCANONIC
UNBEGUN	UNBLENDED	UNBOSOMS	UNBUDGING	UNCAP

U

UNCAPABLE	UNCHARGED	UNCITED	UNCLOSE	UNCOMMON
UNCAPE	UNCHARGES	UNCIVIL	UNCLOSED	UNCONCERN
UNCAPED	UNCHARIER	UNCIVILLY	UNCLOSES	UNCONFINE
UNCAPES	UNCHARITY	UNCLAD	UNCLOSING	UNCONFORM
UNCAPING	UNCHARM	UNCLAIMED	UNCLOTHE	UNCONFUSE
UNCAPPED	UNCHARMED	UNCLAMP	UNCLOTHED	UNCONGEAL
UNCAPPING	UNCHARMS	UNCLAMPED	UNCLOTHES	UNCOOKED
UNCAPS	UNCHARNEL	UNCLAMPS	UNCLOUD	UNCOOL
UNCARDED	UNCHARRED	UNCLARITY	UNCLOUDED	UNCOOLED
UNCARED	UNCHARTED	UNCLASP	UNCLOUDS	UNCOPE
UNCAREFUL	UNCHARY	UNCLASPED	UNCLOUDY	UNCOPED
UNCARING	UNCHASTE	UNCLASPS	UNCLOVEN	UNCOPES
UNCART	UNCHASTER	UNCLASSED	UNCLOYED	UNCOPING
UNCARTED	UNCHECK	UNCLASSY	UNCLOYING	UNCORD
UNCARTING	UNCHECKED	UNCLAWED	UNCLUTCH	UNCORDED
UNCARTS	UNCHECKS	UNCLE	UNCLUTTER	UNCORDIAL
UNCARVED	UNCHEERED	UNCLEAN	UNCO	UNCORDING
UNCASE	UNCHEWED	UNCLEANED	UNCOATED	UNCORDS
UNCASED	UNCHIC	UNCLEANER	UNCOATING	UNCORK
UNCASES	UNCHICLY	UNCLEANLY	UNCOBBLED	UNCORKED
UNCASHED	UNCHILD	UNCLEAR	UNCOCK	UNCORKING
UNCASING	UNCHILDED	UNCLEARED	UNCOCKED	UNCORKS
UNCASKED	UNCHILDS	UNCLEARER	UNCOCKING	UNCORRUPT
UNCAST	UNCHILLED	UNCLEARLY	UNCOCKS	UNCOS
UNCASTED	UNCHOKE	UNCLED	UNCODED	UNCOSTLY
UNCASTING	UNCHOKED	UNCLEFT	UNCOER	UNCOUNTED
UNCASTS	UNCHOKES	UNCLENCH	UNCOERCED	UNCOUPLE
UNCATCHY	UNCHOKING	UNCLES	UNCOES	UNCOUPLED
UNCATE	UNCHOSEN	UNCLESHIP	UNCOEST	UNCOUPLER
UNCATERED	UNCHRISOM	UNCLEW	UNCOFFIN	UNCOUPLES
UNCAUGHT	UNCHURCH	UNCLEWED	UNCOFFINS	UNCOURTLY
UNCAUSED	UNCI	UNCLEWING	UNCOIL	UNCOUTH
UNCE	UNCIA	UNCLEWS	UNCOILED	UNCOUTHER
UNCEASING	UNCIAE	UNCLICHED	UNCOILING	UNCOUTHLY
UNCEDED	UNCIAL	UNCLIMBED	UNCOILS	UNCOVER
UNCERTAIN	UNCIALLY	UNCLINCH	UNCOINED	UNCOVERED
UNCES	UNCIALS	UNCLING	UNCOLORED	UNCOVERS
UNCESSANT	UNCIFORM	UNCLIP	UNCOLT	UNCOWL
UNCHAIN	UNCIFORMS	UNCLIPPED	UNCOLTED	UNCOWLED
UNCHAINED	UNCINAL	UNCLIPS	UNCOLTING	UNCOWLING
UNCHAINS	UNCINARIA	UNCLIPT	UNCOLTS	UNCOWLS
UNCHAIR	UNCINATE	UNCLOAK	UNCOMBED	UNCOY
UNCHAIRED	UNCINATED	UNCLOAKED	UNCOMBINE	UNCOYNED
UNCHAIRS	UNCINI	UNCLOAKS	UNCOMELY	UNCRACKED
UNCHANCY	UNCINUS	UNCLOG	UNCOMFIER	UNCRATE
UNCHANGED	UNCIPHER	UNCLOGGED	UNCOMFY	UNCRATED
UNCHARGE	UNCIPHERS	UNCLOGS	UNCOMIC	UNCRATES

UNCRATING	UNCUTE	UNDEIFIES	UNDERDECK	UNDERLAP
UNCRAZY	UNCYNICAL	UNDEIFY	UNDERDID	UNDERLAPS
UNCREATE	UNDAM	UNDELAYED	UNDERDO	UNDERLAY
UNCREATED	UNDAMAGED	UNDELETE	UNDERDOER	UNDERLAYS
UNCREATES	UNDAMMED	UNDELETED	UNDERDOES	UNDERLEAF
UNCREWED	UNDAMMING	UNDELETES	UNDERDOG	UNDERLET
UNCROPPED	UNDAMNED	UNDELIGHT	UNDERDOGS	UNDERLETS
UNCROSS	UNDAMPED	UNDELUDED	UNDERDONE	UNDERLIE
UNCROSSED	UNDAMS	UNDENIED	UNDERDOSE	UNDERLIER
UNCROSSES	UNDARING	UNDENTED	UNDERDRAW	UNDERLIES
UNCROWDED	UNDASHED	UNDER	UNDERDREW	UNDERLINE
UNCROWN	UNDATABLE	UNDERACT	UNDEREAT	UNDERLING
UNCROWNED	UNDATE	UNDERACTS	UNDEREATS	UNDERLIP
UNCROWNS	UNDATED	UNDERAGE	UNDERFED	UNDERLIPS
UNCRUDDED	UNDAUNTED	UNDERAGED	UNDERFEED	UNDERLIT
UNCRUMPLE	UNDAWNING	UNDERAGES	UNDERFELT	UNDERLOAD
UNCRUSHED	UNDAZZLE	UNDERARM	UNDERFIRE	UNDERMAN
UNCTION	UNDAZZLED	UNDERARMS	UNDERFISH	UNDERMANS
UNCTIONS	UNDAZZLES	UNDERATE	UNDERFLOW	UNDERMEN
UNCTUOUS	UNDE	UNDERBAKE	UNDERFONG	UNDERMINE
UNCUFF	UNDEAD	UNDERBEAR	UNDERFOOT	UNDERMOST
UNCUFFED	UNDEAF	UNDERBID	UNDERFUND	UNDERN
UNCUFFING	UNDEAFED	UNDERBIDS	UNDERFUR	UNDERNOTE
UNCUFFS	UNDEAFING	UNDERBIT	UNDERFURS	UNDERNS
UNCULLED	UNDEAFS	UNDERBITE	UNDERGIRD	UNDERPAD
UNCURABLE	UNDEALT	UNDERBODY	UNDERGIRT	UNDERPADS
UNCURABLY	UNDEAR	UNDERBORE	UNDERGO	UNDERPAID
UNCURB	UNDEBASED	UNDERBOSS	UNDERGOD	UNDERPART
UNCURBED	UNDEBATED	UNDERBRED	UNDERGODS	UNDERPASS
UNCURBING	UNDECAGON	UNDERBRIM	UNDERGOER	UNDERPAY
UNCURBS	UNDECAYED	UNDERBUD	UNDERGOES	UNDERPAYS
UNCURDLED	UNDECEIVE	UNDERBUDS	UNDERGONE	UNDERPEEP
UNCURED	UNDECENT	UNDERBUSH	UNDERGOWN	UNDERPIN
UNCURIOUS	UNDECIDED	UNDERBUY	UNDERGRAD	UNDERPINS
UNCURL	UNDECIMAL	UNDERBUYS	UNDERHAIR	UNDERPLAY
UNCURLED	UNDECK	UNDERCARD	UNDERHAND	UNDERPLOT
UNCURLING	UNDECKED	UNDERCART	UNDERHEAT	UNDERPROP
UNCURLS	UNDECKING	UNDERCAST	UNDERHUNG	UNDERRAN
UNCURRENT	UNDECKS	UNDERCLAD	UNDERIVED	UNDERRATE
UNCURSE	UNDEE	UNDERCLAY	UNDERJAW	UNDERRIPE
UNCURSED	UNDEEDED	UNDERCLUB	UNDERJAWS	UNDERRUN
UNCURSES	UNDEFACED	UNDERCOAT	UNDERKEEP	UNDERRUNS
UNCURSING	UNDEFIDE	UNDERCOOK	UNDERKEPT	UNDERSAID
UNCURTAIN	UNDEFIED	UNDERCOOL	UNDERKILL	UNDERSAY
UNCURVED	UNDEFILED	UNDERCUT	UNDERKING	UNDERSAYS
UNCUS	UNDEFINED	UNDERCUTS	UNDERLAID	UNDERSEA
UNCUT	UNDEIFIED	UNDERDAKS	UNDERLAIN	UNDERSEAL

U

UNDERSEAS	UNDIES	UNDRESSED	UNEATEN	UNEXPIRED
UNDERSELF	UNDIGHT	UNDRESSES	UNEATH	UNEXPOSED
UNDERSELL	UNDIGHTS	UNDREST	UNEATHES	UNEXTINCT
UNDERSET	UNDIGNIFY	UNDREW	UNEDGE	UNEXTREME
UNDERSETS	UNDILUTED	UNDRIED	UNEDGED	UNEYED
UNDERSHOT	UNDIMMED	UNDRILLED	UNEDGES	UNFABLED
UNDERSIDE	UNDINE	UNDRIVEN	UNEDGING	UNFACT
UNDERSIGN	UNDINES	UNDROSSY	UNEDIBLE	UNFACTS
UNDERSIZE	UNDINISM	UNDROWNED	UNEDITED	UNFADABLE
UNDERSKY	UNDINISMS	UNDRUNK	UNEFFACED	UNFADED
UNDERSOIL	UNDINTED	UNDUBBED	UNELATED	UNFADING
UNDERSOLD	UNDIPPED	UNDUE	UNELECTED	UNFAILING
UNDERSONG	UNDIVIDED	UNDUG	UNEMPTIED	UNFAIR
UNDERSOW	UNDIVINE	UNDULANCE	UNENDED	UNFAIRED
UNDERSOWN	UNDO	UNDULANCY	UNENDING	UNFAIRER
UNDERSOWS	UNDOABLE	UNDULANT	UNENDOWED	UNFAIREST
UNDERSPIN	UNDOCILE	UNDULAR	UNENGAGED	UNFAIRING
UNDERTAKE	UNDOCK	UNDULATE	UNENJOYED	UNFAIRLY
UNDERTANE	UNDOCKED	UNDULATED	UNENSURED	UNFAIRS
UNDERTAX	UNDOCKING	UNDULATES	UNENTERED	UNFAITH
UNDERTIME	UNDOCKS	UNDULATOR	UNENVIED	UNFAITHS
UNDERTINT	UNDOER	UNDULLED	UNENVIOUS	UNFAKED
UNDERTONE	UNDOERS	UNDULOSE	UNENVYING	UNFALLEN
UNDERTOOK	UNDOES	UNDULOUS	UNEQUABLE	UNFAMED
UNDERTOW	UNDOING	UNDULY	UNEQUAL	UNFAMOUS
UNDERTOWS	UNDOINGS	UNDUTEOUS	UNEQUALED	UNFANCIED
UNDERUSE	UNDONE	UNDUTIFUL	UNEQUALLY	UNFANCIER
UNDERUSED	UNDOOMED	UNDY	UNEQUALS	UNFANCY
UNDERUSES	UNDOS	UNDYED	UNERASED	UNFANNED
UNDERVEST	UNDOTTED	UNDYING	UNEROTIC	UNFASTEN
UNDERVOTE	UNDOUBLE	UNDYINGLY	UNERRING	UNFASTENS
UNDERWAY	UNDOUBLED	UNDYNAMIC	UNESPIED	UNFAULTY
UNDERWEAR	UNDOUBLES	UNEAGER	UNESSAYED	UNFAVORED
UNDERWENT	UNDOUBTED	UNEAGERLY	UNESSENCE	UNFAZED
UNDERWING	UNDRAINED	UNEARED	UNETH	UNFEARED
UNDERWIRE	UNDRAPE	UNEARNED	UNETHICAL	UNFEARFUL
UNDERWIT	UNDRAPED	UNEARTH	UNEVADED	UNFEARING
UNDERWITS	UNDRAPES	UNEARTHED	UNEVEN	UNFED
UNDERWOOD	UNDRAPING	UNEARTHLY	UNEVENER	UNFEED
UNDERWOOL	UNDRAW	UNEARTHS	UNEVENEST	UNFEELING
UNDERWORK	UNDRAWING	UNEASE	UNEVENLY	UNFEIGNED
UNDESERT	UNDRAWN	UNEASES	UNEVOLVED	UNFELLED
UNDESERTS	UNDRAWS	UNEASIER	UNEXALTED	UNFELT
UNDESERVE	UNDREADED	UNEASIEST	UNEXCITED	UNFELTED
UNDESIRED	UNDREAMED	UNEASILY	UNEXCUSED	UNFENCE
UNDEVOUT	UNDREAMT	UNEASY	UNEXOTIC	UNFENCED
UNDID	UNDRESS	UNEATABLE	UNEXPERT	UNFENCES

UNFENCING	UNFOLD	UNFROZEN	UNGILD	UNGRAZED
UNFERTILE	UNFOLDED	UNFUELLED	UNGILDED	UNGREASED
UNFETTER	UNFOLDER	UNFUMED	UNGILDING	UNGREEDY
UNFETTERS	UNFOLDERS	UNFUNDED	UNGILDS	UNGREEN
UNFEUDAL	UNFOLDING	UNFUNNIER	UNGILT	UNGREENER
UNFEUED	UNFOLDS	UNFUNNY	UNGIRD	UNGROOMED
UNFIGURED	UNFOLLOW	UNFURL	UNGIRDED	UNGROUND
UNFILDE	UNFOLLOWS	UNFURLED	UNGIRDING	UNGROUP
UNFILED	UNFOND	UNFURLING	UNGIRDS	UNGROUPED
UNFILIAL	UNFOOL	UNFURLS	UNGIRT	UNGROUPS
UNFILLED	UNFOOLED	UNFURNISH	UNGIRTH	UNGROWN
UNFILMED	UNFOOLING	UNFURRED	UNGIRTHED	UNGRUDGED
UNFINE	UNFOOLS	UNFUSED	UNGIRTHS	UNGUAL
UNFIRED	UNFOOTED	UNFUSSIER	UNGIVING	UNGUARD
UNFIRM	UNFORBID	UNFUSSILY	UNGLAD	UNGUARDED
UNFISHED	UNFORCED	UNFUSSY	UNGLAZED	UNGUARDS
UNFIT	UNFORGED	UNGAG	UNGLOSSED	UNGUENT
UNFITLY	UNFORGOT	UNGAGGED	UNGLOVE	UNGUENTA
UNFITNESS	UNFORKED	UNGAGGING	UNGLOVED	UNGUENTS
UNFITS	UNFORM	UNGAGS	UNGLOVES	UNGUENTUM
UNFITTED	UNFORMAL	UNGAIN	UNGLOVING	UNGUES
UNFITTER	UNFORMED	UNGAINFUL	UNGLUE	UNGUESSED
UNFITTEST	UNFORMING	UNGAINLY	UNGLUED	UNGUIDED
UNFITTING	UNFORMS	UNGALLANT	UNGLUES	UNGUIFORM
UNFIX	UNFORTUNE	UNGALLED	UNGLUING	UNGUILTY
UNFIXED	UNFOUGHT	UNGARBED	UNGOD	UNGUINOUS
UNFIXES	UNFOUND	UNGARBLED	UNGODDED	UNGUIS
UNFIXING	UNFOUNDED	UNGATED	UNGODDING	UNGULA
UNFIXITY	UNFRAMED	UNGAUGED	UNGODLIER	UNGULAE
UNFIXT	UNFRANKED	UNGAZED	UNGODLIKE	UNGULAR
UNFLAPPED	UNFRAUGHT	UNGAZING	UNGODLILY	UNGULATE
UNFLASHY	UNFREE	UNGEAR	UNGODLY	UNGULATES
UNFLAWED	UNFREED	UNGEARED	UNGODS	UNGULED
UNFLEDGED	UNFREEDOM	UNGEARING	UNGORD	UNGUM
UNFLESH	UNFREEING	UNGEARS	UNGORED	UNGUMMED
UNFLESHED	UNFREEMAN	UNGELDED	UNGORGED	UNGUMMING
UNFLESHES	UNFREEMEN	UNGENIAL	UNGOT	UNGUMS
UNFLESHLY	UNFREES	UNGENTEEL	UNGOTTEN	UNGYVE
UNFLEXED	UNFREEZE	UNGENTLE	UNGOWN	UNGYVED
UNFLOORED	UNFREEZES	UNGENTLY	UNGOWNED	UNGYVES
UNFLUSH	UNFRETTED	UNGENUINE	UNGOWNING	UNGYVING
UNFLUSHED	UNFRIEND	UNGERMANE	UNGOWNS	UNHABLE
UNFLUSHES	UNFRIENDS	UNGET	UNGRACED	UNHACKED
UNFLUTED	UNFROCK	UNGETS	UNGRADED	UNHAILED
UNFLYABLE	UNFROCKED	UNGETTING	UNGRASSED	UNHAIR
UNFOCUSED	UNFROCKS	UNGHOSTLY	UNGRAVELY	UNHAIRED
UNFOILED	UNFROZE	UNGIFTED	UNGRAVLY	UNHAIRER

UNHAIRERS	UNHEAD	UNHIPPEST	UNHUNG	UNIFYING
UNHAIRING	UNHEADED	UNHIRABLE	UNHUNTED	UNIFYINGS
UNHAIRS	UNHEADING	UNHIRED	UNHURRIED	UNIJUGATE
UNHALLOW	UNHEADS	UNHITCH	UNHURT	UNILINEAL
UNHALLOWS	UNHEAL	UNHITCHED	UNHURTFUL	UNILINEAR
UNHALSED	UNHEALED	UNHITCHES	UNHUSK	UNILLUMED
UNHALVED	UNHEALING	UNHIVE	UNHUSKED	UNILOBAR
UNHAND	UNHEALS	UNHIVED	UNHUSKING	UNILOBED
UNHANDED	UNHEALTH	UNHIVES	UNHUSKS	UNIMBUED
UNHANDIER	UNHEALTHS	UNHIVING	UNI	UNIMODAL
UNHANDILY	UNHEALTHY	UNHOARD	UNIALGAL	UNIMPEDED
UNHANDING	UNHEARD	UNHOARDED	UNIAXIAL	UNIMPOSED
UNHANDLED	UNHEARSE	UNHOARDS	UNIBODIES	UNINCITED
UNHANDS	UNHEARSED	UNHOLIER	UNIBODY	UNINDEXED
UNHANDY	UNHEARSES	UNHOLIEST	UNIBROW	UNINJURED
UNHANG	UNHEART	UNHOLILY	UNIBROWS	UNINSTAL
UNHANGED	UNHEARTED	UNHOLPEN	UNICA	UNINSTALL
UNHANGING	UNHEARTS	UNHOLY	UNICED	UNINSTALS
UNHANGS	UNHEATED	UNHOMELY	UNICITIES	UNINSURED
UNHAPPEN	UNHEDGED	UNHONEST	UNICITY	UNINURED
UNHAPPENS	UNHEEDED	UNHONORED	UNICOLOR	UNINVITED
UNHAPPIED	UNHEEDFUL	UNHOOD	UNICOLOUR	UNINVOKED
UNHAPPIER	UNHEEDIER	UNHOODED	UNICOM	UNION
UNHAPPIES	UNHEEDILY	UNHOODING	UNICOMS	UNIONISE
UNHAPPILY	UNHEEDING	UNHOODS	UNICORN	UNIONISED
UNHAPPY	UNHEEDY	UNHOOK	UNICORNS	UNIONISER
UNHARBOUR	UNHELE	UNHOOKED	UNICUM	UNIONISES
UNHARDIER	UNHELED	UNHOOKING	UNICYCLE	UNIONISM
UNHARDY	UNHELES	UNHOOKS	UNICYCLED	UNIONISMS
UNHARMED	UNHELING	UNHOOP	UNICYCLES	UNIONIST
UNHARMFUL	UNHELM	UNHOOPED	UNIDEAED	UNIONISTS
UNHARMING	UNHELMED	UNHOOPING	UNIDEAL	UNIONIZE
UNHARNESS	UNHELMING	UNHOOPS	UNIFACE	UNIONIZED
UNHARRIED	UNHELMS	UNHOPED	UNIFACES	UNIONIZER
UNHASP	UNHELPED	UNHOPEFUL	UNIFIABLE	UNIONIZES
UNHASPED	UNHELPFUL	UNHORSE	UNIFIC	UNIONS
UNHASPING	UNHEPPEN	UNHORSED	UNIFIED	UNIPAROUS
UNHASPS	UNHEROIC	UNHORSES	UNIFIER	UNIPED
UNHASTIER	UNHERST	UNHORSING	UNIFIERS	UNIPEDS
UNHASTING	UNHEWN	UNHOSTILE	UNIFIES	UNIPLANAR
UNHASTY	UNHIDDEN	UNHOUSE	UNIFILAR	UNIPOD
UNHAT	UNHINGE	UNHOUSED	UNIFORM	UNIPODS
UNHATCHED	UNHINGED	UNHOUSES	UNIFORMED	UNIPOLAR
UNHATS	UNHINGES	UNHOUSING	UNIFORMER	UNIPOTENT
UNHATTED	UNHINGING	UNHUMAN	UNIFORMLY	UNIQUE
UNHATTING	UNHIP	UNHUMANLY	UNIFORMS	UNIQUELY
UNHAUNTED	UNHIPPER	UNHUMBLED	UNIFY	UNIQUER

UNIQUES	UNITIZED	UNKIND	UNLASHING	UNLIKELY
UNIQUEST	UNITIZER	UNKINDER	UNLAST	UNLIKES
UNIRAMOSE	UNITIZERS	UNKINDEST	UNLASTE	UNLIMBER
UNIRAMOUS	UNITIZES	UNKINDLED	UNLATCH	UNLIMBERS
UNIRONED	UNITIZING	UNKINDLY	UNLATCHED	UNLIME
UNIRONIC	UNITRUST	UNKING	UNLATCHES	UNLIMED
UNIS	UNITRUSTS	UNKINGED	UNLAW	UNLIMES
UNISERIAL	UNITS	UNKINGING	UNLAWED	UNLIMING
UNISEX	UNITY	UNKINGLY	UNLAWFUL	UNLIMITED
UNISEXES	UNIVALENT	UNKINGS	UNLAWING	UNLINE
UNISEXUAL	UNIVALVE	UNKINK	UNLAWS	UNLINEAL
UNISIZE	UNIVALVED	UNKINKED	UNLAY	UNLINED
UNISON	UNIVALVES	UNKINKING	UNLAYING	UNLINES
UNISONAL	UNIVERSAL	UNKINKS	UNLAYS	UNLINING
UNISONANT	UNIVERSE	UNKISS	UNLEAD	UNLINK
UNISONOUS	UNIVERSES	UNKISSED	UNLEADED	UNLINKED
UNISONS	UNIVOCAL	UNKISSES	UNLEADEDS	UNLINKING
UNISSUED	UNIVOCALS	UNKISSING	UNLEADING	UNLINKS
UNIT	UNJADED	UNKNELLED	UNLEADS	UNLISTED
UNITAGE	UNJAM	UNKNIGHT	UNLEAL	UNLIT
UNITAGES	UNJAMMED	UNKNIGHTS	UNLEARN	UNLIVABLE
UNITAL	UNJAMMING	UNKNIT	UNLEARNED	UNLIVE
UNITARD	UNJAMS	UNKNITS	UNLEARNS	UNLIVED
UNITARDS	UNJEALOUS	UNKNITTED	UNLEARNT	UNLIVELY
UNITARIAN	UNJOINED	UNKNOT	UNLEASED	UNLIVES
UNITARILY	UNJOINT	UNKNOTS	UNLEASH	UNLIVING
UNITARY	UNJOINTED	UNKNOTTED	UNLEASHED	UNLOAD
UNITE	UNJOINTS	UNKNOWING	UNLEASHES	UNLOADED
UNITED	UNJOYFUL	UNKNOWN	UNLED	UNLOADER
UNITEDLY	UNJOYOUS	UNKNOWNS	UNLESS	UNLOADERS
UNITER	UNJUDGED	UNKOSHER	UNLET	UNLOADING
UNITERS	UNJUST	UNLABELED	UNLETHAL	UNLOADS
UNITES	UNJUSTER	UNLABORED	UNLETTED	UNLOBED
UNITIES	UNJUSTEST	UNLACE	UNLEVEL	UNLOCATED
UNITING	UNJUSTLY	UNLACED	UNLEVELED	UNLOCK
UNITINGS	UNKED	UNLACES	UNLEVELS	UNLOCKED
UNITION	UNKEELED	UNLACING	UNLEVIED	UNLOCKING
UNITIONS	UNKEMPT	UNLADE	UNLICH	UNLOCKS
UNITISE	UNKEMPTLY	UNLADED	UNLICKED	UNLOGICAL
UNITISED	UNKEND	UNLADEN	UNLID	UNLOOKED
UNITISER	UNKENNED	UNLADES	UNLIDDED	UNLOOSE
UNITISERS	UNKENNEL	UNLADING	UNLIDDING	UNLOOSED
UNITISES	UNKENNELS	UNLADINGS	UNLIDS	UNLOOSEN
UNITISING	UNKENT	UNLAID	UNLIGHTED	UNLOOSENS
UNITIVE	UNKEPT	UNLASH	UNLIKABLE	UNLOOSES
UNITIVELY	UNKET	UNLASHED	UNLIKE	UNLOOSING
UNITIZE	UNKID	UNLASHES	UNLIKED	UNLOPPED

UNLORD	UNMARRIED	UNMITER	UNMUSICAL	UNORDERED
UNLORDED	UNMARRIES	UNMITERED	UNMUZZLE	UNORDERLY
UNLORDING	UNMARRY	UNMITERS	UNMUZZLED	UNORDERS
UNLORDLY	UNMASK	UNMITRE	UNMUZZLES	UNORNATE
UNLORDS	UNMASKED	UNMITRED	UNNAIL	UNOWED
UNLOSABLE	UNMASKER	UNMITRES	UNNAILED	UNOWNED
UNLOST	UNMASKERS	UNMITRING	UNNAILING	UNPACED
UNLOVABLE	UNMASKING	UNMIX	UNNAILS	UNPACK
UNLOVE	UNMASKS	UNMIXABLE	UNNAMABLE	UNPACKED
UNLOVED	UNMATCHED	UNMIXED	UNNAMED	UNPACKER
UNLOVELY	UNMATED	UNMIXEDLY	UNNANELD	UNPACKERS
UNLOVES	UNMATTED	UNMIXES	UNNATIVE	UNPACKING
UNLOVING	UNMATURED	UNMIXING	UNNATIVED	UNPACKS
UNLUCKIER	UNMEANING	UNMIXT	UNNATIVES	UNPADDED
UNLUCKILY	UNMEANT	UNMOANED	UNNATURAL	UNPAGED
UNLUCKY	UNMEEK	UNMODISH	UNNEATH	UNPAID
UNLYRICAL	UNMEET	UNMOLD	UNNEEDED	UNPAINED
UNMACHO	UNMEETLY	UNMOLDED	UNNEEDFUL	UNPAINFUL
UNMADE	UNMELLOW	UNMOLDING	UNNERVE	UNPAINT
UNMAILED	UNMELTED	UNMOLDS	UNNERVED	UNPAINTED
UNMAIMED	UNMENDED	UNMOLTEN	UNNERVES	UNPAINTS
UNMAKABLE	UNMERITED	UNMONEYED	UNNERVING	UNPAIRED
UNMAKE	UNMERRIER	UNMONIED	UNNEST	UNPALSIED
UNMAKER	UNMERRY	UNMOOR	UNNESTED	UNPANEL
UNMAKERS	UNMESH	UNMOORED	UNNESTING	UNPANELS
UNMAKES	UNMESHED	UNMOORING	UNNESTS	UNPANGED
UNMAKING	UNMESHES	UNMOORS	UNNETHES	UNPANNEL
UNMAKINGS	UNMESHING	UNMORAL	UNNETTED	UNPANNELS
UNMAN	UNMET	UNMORALLY	UNNOBLE	UNPAPER
UNMANACLE	UNMETED	UNMORTISE	UNNOBLED	UNPAPERED
UNMANAGED	UNMETERED	UNMOTIVED	UNNOBLES	UNPAPERS
UNMANFUL	UNMEW	UNMOULD	UNNOBLING	UNPARED
UNMANLIER	UNMEWED	UNMOULDED	UNNOISIER	UNPARTED
UNMANLIKE	UNMEWING	UNMOULDS	UNNOISY	UNPARTIAL
UNMANLY	UNMEWS	UNMOUNT	UNNOTED	UNPATCHED
UNMANNED	UNMILKED	UNMOUNTED	UNNOTICED	UNPATHED
UNMANNING	UNMILLED	UNMOUNTS	UNNUANCED	UNPAVED
UNMANNISH	UNMINDED	UNMOURNED	UNOAKED	UNPAY
UNMANS	UNMINDFUL	UNMOVABLE	UNOBEYED	UNPAYABLE
UNMANTLE	UNMINED	UNMOVABLY	UNOBVIOUS	UNPAYING
UNMANTLED	UNMINGLE	UNMOVED	UNOFFERED	UNPAYS
UNMANTLES	UNMINGLED	UNMOVEDLY	UNOFTEN	UNPEELED
UNMANURED	UNMINGLES	UNMOVING	UNOILED	UNPEERED
UNMAPPED	UNMIRIER	UNMOWN	UNOPEN	UNPEG
UNMARD	UNMIRIEST	UNMUFFLE	UNOPENED	UNPEGGED
UNMARKED	UNMIRY	UNMUFFLED	UNOPPOSED	UNPEGGING
UNMARRED	UNMISSED	UNMUFFLES	UNORDER	UNPEGS

U

UNPEN	UNPLANNED	UNPREACH	UNQUIETER	UNREEL
UNPENNED	UNPLANTED	UNPRECISE	UNQUIETLY	UNREELED
UNPENNIED	UNPLAYED	UNPREDICT	UNQUIETS	UNREELER
UNPENNING	UNPLEASED	UNPREPARE	UNQUOTE	UNREELERS
UNPENS	UNPLEATED	UNPRESSED	UNQUOTED	UNREELING
UNPENT	UNPLEDGED	UNPRETTY	UNQUOTES	UNREELS
UNPEOPLE	UNPLIABLE	UNPRICED	UNQUOTING	UNREEVE
UNPEOPLED	UNPLIABLY	UNPRIEST	UNRACED	UNREEVED
UNPEOPLES	UNPLIANT	UNPRIESTS	UNRACKED	UNREEVES
UNPERCH	UNPLOWED	UNPRIMED	UNRAISED	UNREEVING
UNPERCHED	UNPLUCKED	UNPRINTED	UNRAKE	UNREFINED
UNPERCHES	UNPLUG	UNPRISON	UNRAKED	UNREFUTED
UNPERFECT	UNPLUGGED	UNPRISONS	UNRAKES	UNREIN
UNPERPLEX	UNPLUGS	UNPRIZED	UNRAKING	UNREINED
UNPERSON	UNPLUMB	UNPROBED	UNRANKED	UNREINING
UNPERSONS	UNPLUMBED	UNPROP	UNRATED	UNREINS
UNPERVERT	UNPLUMBS	UNPROPER	UNRAVAGED	UNRELATED
UNPICK	UNPLUME	UNPROPPED	UNRAVEL	UNRELAXED
UNPICKED	UNPLUMED	UNPROPS	UNRAVELED	UNREMOVED
UNPICKING	UNPLUMES	UNPROVED	UNRAVELS	UNRENEWED
UNPICKS	UNPLUMING	UNPROVEN	UNRAZED	UNRENT
UNPIERCED	UNPOETIC	UNPROVIDE	UNRAZORED	UNRENTED
UNPILE	UNPOINTED	UNPROVOKE	UNREACHED	UNREPAID
UNPILED	UNPOISED	UNPRUNED	UNREAD	UNREPAIR
UNPILES	UNPOISON	UNPUCKER	UNREADIER	UNREPAIRS
UNPILING	UNPOISONS	UNPUCKERS	UNREADILY	UNRESERVE
UNPILOTED	UNPOLICED	UNPULLED	UNREADY	UNREST
UNPIN	UNPOLISH	UNPURE	UNREAL	UNRESTED
UNPINKED	UNPOLITE	UNPURELY	UNREALISE	UNRESTFUL
UNPINKT	UNPOLITIC	UNPURGED	UNREALISM	UNRESTING
UNPINNED	UNPOLLED	UNPURSE	UNREALITY	UNRESTS
UNPINNING	UNPOPE	UNPURSED	UNREALIZE	UNRETIRE
UNPINS	UNPOPED	UNPURSES	UNREALLY	UNRETIRED
UNPITIED	UNPOPES	UNPURSING	UNREAPED	UNRETIRES
UNPITIFUL	UNPOPING	UNPURSUED	UNREASON	UNREVISED
UNPITTED	UNPOPULAR	UNPUZZLE	UNREASONS	UNREVOKED
UNPITYING	UNPOSED	UNPUZZLED	UNREAVE	UNRHYMED
UNPLACE	UNPOSTED	UNPUZZLES	UNREAVED	UNRIBBED
UNPLACED	UNPOTABLE	UNQUAKING	UNREAVES	UNRID
UNPLACES	UNPOTTED	UNQUALIFY	UNREAVING	UNRIDABLE
UNPLACING	UNPRAISE	UNQUEEN	UNREBATED	UNRIDDEN
UNPLAGUED	UNPRAISED	UNQUEENED	UNREBUKED	UNRIDDLE
UNPLAINED	UNPRAISES	UNQUEENLY	UNRECKED	UNRIDDLED
UNPLAIT	UNPRAY	UNQUEENS	UNRED	UNRIDDLER
UNPLAITED	UNPRAYED	UNQUELLED	UNREDREST	UNRIDDLES
UNPLAITS	UNPRAYING	UNQUIET	UNREDUCED	UNRIFLED
UNPLANKED	UNPRAYS	UNQUIETED	UNREDY	UNRIG

UNRIGGED

UNRIGGED	UNROPING	UNSALTED	UNSEATS	UNSEWS
UNRIGGING	UNROSINED	UNSALUTED	UNSECRET	UNSEX
UNRIGHT	UNROTTED	UNSAMPLED	UNSECRETS	UNSEXED
UNRIGHTED	UNROTTEN	UNSAPPED	UNSECULAR	UNSEXES
UNRIGHTS	UNROUGED	UNSASHED	UNSECURED	UNSEXIER
UNRIGS	UNROUGH	UNSATABLE	UNSEDUCED	UNSEXIEST
UNRIMED	UNROUND	UNSATED	UNSEEABLE	UNSEXING
UNRINGED	UNROUNDED	UNSATIATE	UNSEEDED	UNSEXIST
UNRINSED	UNROUNDS	UNSATING	UNSEEING	UNSEXUAL
UNRIP	UNROUSED	UNSAVED	UNSEEL	UNSEXY
UNRIPE	UNROVE	UNSAVORY	UNSEELED	UNSHACKLE
UNRIPELY	UNROVEN	UNSAVOURY	UNSEELIE	UNSHADED
UNRIPENED	UNROYAL	UNSAWED	UNSEELING	UNSHADOW
UNRIPER	UNROYALLY	UNSAWN	UNSEELS	UNSHADOWS
UNRIPEST	UNRUBBED	UNSAY	UNSEEMING	UNSHAKED
UNRIPPED	UNRUDE	UNSAYABLE	UNSEEMLY	UNSHAKEN
UNRIPPING	UNRUFFE	UNSAYING	UNSEEN	UNSHALE
UNRIPS	UNRUFFLE	UNSAYS	UNSEENS	UNSHALED
UNRISEN	UNRUFFLED	UNSCALE	UNSEIZED	UNSHALES
UNRIVALED	UNRUFFLES	UNSCALED	UNSELDOM	UNSHALING
UNRIVEN	UNRULE	UNSCALES	UNSELF	UNSHAMED
UNRIVET	UNRULED	UNSCALING	UNSELFED	UNSHAPE
UNRIVETED	UNRULES	UNSCANNED	UNSELFING	UNSHAPED
UNRIVETS	UNRULIER	UNSCARIER	UNSELFISH	UNSHAPELY
UNROASTED	UNRULIEST	UNSCARRED	UNSELFS	UNSHAPEN
UNROBE	UNRULY	UNSCARY	UNSELL	UNSHAPES
UNROBED	UNRUMPLED	UNSCATHED	UNSELLING	UNSHAPING
UNROBES	UNRUSHED	UNSCENTED	UNSELLS	UNSHARED
UNROBING	UNRUSTED	UNSCOURED	UNSELVES	UNSHARP
UNROLL	UNS	UNSCREW	UNSENSE	UNSHAVED
UNROLLED	UNSADDLE	UNSCREWED	UNSENSED	UNSHAVEN
UNROLLING	UNSADDLED	UNSCREWS	UNSENSES	UNSHEATHE
UNROLLS	UNSADDLES	UNSCYTHED	UNSENSING	UNSHED
UNROOF	UNSAFE	UNSEAL	UNSENT	UNSHELL
UNROOFED	UNSAFELY	UNSEALED	UNSERIOUS	UNSHELLED
UNROOFING	UNSAFER	UNSEALING	UNSERVED	UNSHELLS
UNROOFS	UNSAFEST	UNSEALS	UNSET	UNSHENT
UNROOST	UNSAFETY	UNSEAM	UNSETS	UNSHEWN
UNROOSTED	UNSAID	UNSEAMED	UNSETTING	UNSHIFT
UNROOSTS	UNSAILED	UNSEAMING	UNSETTLE	UNSHIFTED
UNROOT	UNSAINED	UNSEAMS	UNSETTLED	UNSHIFTS
UNROOTED	UNSAINT	UNSEARED	UNSETTLES	UNSHIP
UNROOTING	UNSAINTED	UNSEASON	UNSEVERED	UNSHIPPED
UNROOTS	UNSAINTLY	UNSEASONS	UNSEW	UNSHIPS
UNROPE	UNSAINTS	UNSEAT	UNSEWED	UNSHIRTED
UNROPED	UNSALABLE	UNSEATED	UNSEWING	UNSHOCKED
UNROPES	UNSALABLY	UNSEATING	UNSEWN	UNSHOD

UNSHOE	UNSKIMMED	UNSOLDER	UNSPOILT	UNSTOCKED
UNSHOED	UNSKINNED	UNSOLDERS	UNSPOKE	UNSTOCKS
UNSHOEING	UNSLAIN	UNSOLEMN	UNSPOKEN	UNSTONED
UNSHOES	UNSLAKED	UNSOLID	UNSPOOL	UNSTOP
UNSHOOT	UNSLICED	UNSOLIDLY	UNSPOOLED	UNSTOPPED
UNSHOOTED	UNSLICK	UNSOLVED	UNSPOOLS	UNSTOPPER
UNSHOOTS	UNSLING	UNSONCY	UNSPOTTED	UNSTOPS
UNSHORN	UNSLINGS	UNSONSIE	UNSPRAYED	UNSTOW
UNSHOT	UNSLUICE	UNSONSIER	UNSPRUNG	UNSTOWED
UNSHOTS	UNSLUICED	UNSONSY	UNSPUN	UNSTOWING
UNSHOTTED	UNSLUICES	UNSOOTE	UNSQUARED	UNSTOWS
UNSHOUT	UNSLUNG	UNSOOTHED	UNSTABLE	UNSTRAP
UNSHOUTED	UNSMART	UNSORTED	UNSTABLER	UNSTRAPS
UNSHOUTS	UNSMILING	UNSOUGHT	UNSTABLY	UNSTRESS
UNSHOWIER	UNSMITTEN	UNSOUL	UNSTACK	UNSTRING
UNSHOWN	UNSMOKED	UNSOULED	UNSTACKED	UNSTRINGS
UNSHOWY	UNSMOOTH	UNSOULING	UNSTACKS	UNSTRIP
UNSHRIVED	UNSMOOTHS	UNSOULS	UNSTAID	UNSTRIPED
UNSHRIVEN	UNSMOTE	UNSOUND	UNSTAINED	UNSTRIPS
UNSHROUD	UNSNAG	UNSOUNDED	UNSTALKED	UNSTRUCK
UNSHROUDS	UNSNAGGED	UNSOUNDER	UNSTAMPED	UNSTRUNG
UNSHRUBD	UNSNAGS	UNSOUNDLY	UNSTARCH	UNSTUCK
UNSHRUNK	UNSNAP	UNSOURCED	UNSTARRED	UNSTUDIED
UNSHUNNED	UNSNAPPED	UNSOURED	UNSTARRY	UNSTUFFED
UNSHUT	UNSNAPS	UNSOWED	UNSTATE	UNSTUFFY
UNSHUTS	UNSNARL	UNSOWN	UNSTATED	UNSTUFT
UNSHUTTER	UNSNARLED	UNSPAR	UNSTATES	UNSTUNG
UNSICKER	UNSNARLS	UNSPARED	UNSTATING	UNSTYLISH
UNSICKLED	UNSNECK	UNSPARING	UNSTAYED	UNSUBDUED
UNSIFTED	UNSNECKED	UNSPARRED	UNSTAYING	UNSUBJECT
UNSIGHING	UNSNECKS	UNSPARS	UNSTEADY	UNSUBTLE
UNSIGHT	UNSNUFFED	UNSPEAK	UNSTEEL	UNSUBTLY
UNSIGHTED	UNSOAKED	UNSPEAKS	UNSTEELED	UNSUCCESS
UNSIGHTLY	UNSOAPED	UNSPED	UNSTEELS	UNSUCKED
UNSIGHTS	UNSOBER	UNSPELL	UNSTEMMED	UNSUIT
UNSIGNED	UNSOBERED	UNSPELLED	UNSTEP	UNSUITED
UNSILENT	UNSOBERLY	UNSPELLS	UNSTEPPED	UNSUITING
UNSIMILAR	UNSOBERS	UNSPENT	UNSTEPS	UNSUITS
UNSINEW	UNSOCIAL	UNSPHERE	UNSTERILE	UNSULLIED
UNSINEWED	UNSOCKET	UNSPHERED	UNSTICK	UNSUMMED
UNSINEWS	UNSOCKETS	UNSPHERES	UNSTICKS	UNSUNG
UNSINFUL	UNSOD	UNSPIDE	UNSTIFLED	UNSUNK
UNSISTING	UNSODDEN	UNSPIED	UNSTILLED	UNSUNNED
UNSIZABLE	UNSOFT	UNSPILLED	UNSTINTED	UNSUNNIER
UNSIZED	UNSOILED	UNSPILT	UNSTIRRED	UNSUNNY
UNSKILFUL	UNSOLACED	UNSPLIT	UNSTITCH	UNSUPPLE
UNSKILLED	UNSOLD	UNSPOILED	UNSTOCK	UNSURE

UNSURED	UNTAXING	UNTIDILY	UNTRAPPED	UNTURFS
UNSURELY	UNTEACH	UNTIDY	UNTREAD	UNTURN
UNSURER	UNTEACHES	UNTIDYING	UNTREADED	UNTURNED
UNSUREST	UNTEAM	UNTIE	UNTREADS	UNTURNING
UNSUSPECT	UNTEAMED	UNTIED	UNTREATED	UNTURNS
UNSWADDLE	UNTEAMING	UNTIEING	UNTRENDY	UNTUTORED
UNSWATHE	UNTEAMS	UNTIES	UNTRESSED	UNTWILLED
UNSWATHED	UNTEMPER	UNTIL	UNTRIDE	UNTWINE
UNSWATHES	UNTEMPERS	UNTILE	UNTRIED	UNTWINED
UNSWAYED	UNTEMPTED	UNTILED	UNTRIM	UNTWINES
UNSWEAR	UNTENABLE	UNTILES	UNTRIMMED	UNTWINING
UNSWEARS	UNTENABLY	UNTILING	UNTRIMS	UNTWIST
UNSWEET	UNTENANT	UNTILLED	UNTROD	UNTWISTED
UNSWEPT	UNTENANTS	UNTILTED	UNTRODDEN	UNTWISTS
UNSWOLLEN	UNTENDED	UNTIMED	UNTRUE	UNTYING
UNSWORE	UNTENDER	UNTIMELY	UNTRUER	UNTYINGS
UNSWORN	UNTENT	UNTIMEOUS	UNTRUEST	UNTYPABLE
UNTACK	UNTENTED	UNTIN	UNTRUISM	UNTYPICAL
UNTACKED	UNTENTIER	UNTINGED	UNTRUISMS	UNUNBIUM
UNTACKING	UNTENTING	UNTINNED	UNTRULY	UNUNBIUMS
UNTACKLE	UNTENTS	UNTINNING	UNTRUSS	UNUNITED
UNTACKLED	UNTENTY	UNTINS	UNTRUSSED	UNUNUNIUM
UNTACKLES	UNTENURED	UNTIPPED	UNTRUSSER	UNURGED
UNTACKS	UNTESTED	UNTIRABLE	UNTRUSSES	UNUSABLE
UNTACTFUL	UNTETHER	UNTIRED	UNTRUST	UNUSABLY
UNTAGGED	UNTETHERS	UNTIRING	UNTRUSTED	UNUSED
UNTAILED	UNTHANKED	UNTITLED	UNTRUSTS	UNUSEFUL
UNTAINTED	UNTHATCH	UNTO	UNTRUSTY	UNUSHERED
UNTAKEN	UNTHAW	UNTOILING	UNTRUTH	UNUSUAL
UNTAMABLE	UNTHAWED	UNTOLD	UNTRUTHS	UNUSUALLY
UNTAMABLY	UNTHAWING	UNTOMB	UNTUCK	UNUTTERED
UNTAME	UNTHAWS	UNTOMBED	UNTUCKED	UNVAIL
UNTAMED	UNTHINK	UNTOMBING	UNTUCKING	UNVAILE
UNTAMES	UNTHINKS	UNTOMBS	UNTUCKS	UNVAILED
UNTAMING	UNTHOUGHT	UNTONED	UNTUFTED	UNVAILES
UNTANGLE	UNTHREAD	UNTORN	UNTUMBLED	UNVAILING
UNTANGLED	UNTHREADS	UNTOUCHED	UNTUNABLE	UNVAILS
UNTANGLES	UNTHRIFT	UNTOWARD	UNTUNABLY	UNVALUED
UNTANNED	UNTHRIFTS	UNTRACE	UNTUNE	UNVARIED
UNTAPPED	UNTHRIFTY	UNTRACED	UNTUNED	UNVARYING
UNTARRED	UNTHRONE	UNTRACES	UNTUNEFUL	UNVEIL
UNTASTED	UNTHRONED	UNTRACING	UNTUNES	UNVEILED
UNTAUGHT	UNTHRONES	UNTRACK	UNTUNING	UNVEILER
UNTAX	UNTIDIED	UNTRACKED	UNTURBID	UNVEILERS
UNTAXABLE	UNTIDIER	UNTRACKS	UNTURF	UNVEILING
UNTAXED	UNTIDIES	UNTRADED	UNTURFED	UNVEILS
UNTAXES	UNTIDIEST	UNTRAINED	UNTURFING	UNVEINED

UNVENTED	UNWATCHED	UNWIND	UNWORDED	UPASES
UNVERSED	UNWATER	UNWINDER	UNWORK	UPBEAR
UNVESTED	UNWATERED	UNWINDERS	UNWORKED	UPBEARER
UNVETTED	UNWATERS	UNWINDING	UNWORKING	UPBEARERS
UNVEXED	UNWATERY	UNWINDS	UNWORKS	UPBEARING
UNVEXT	UNWAXED	UNWINGED	UNWORLDLY	UPBEARS
UNVIABLE	UNWAYED	UNWINKING	UNWORMED	UPBEAT
UNVIEWED	UNWEAL	UNWIPED	UNWORN	UPBEATS
UNVIRTUE	UNWEALS	UNWIRE	UNWORRIED	UPBIND
UNVIRTUES	UNWEANED	UNWIRED	UNWORTH	UPBINDING
UNVISITED	UNWEAPON	UNWIRES	UNWORTHS	UPBINDS
UNVISOR	UNWEAPONS	UNWIRING	UNWORTHY	UPBLEW
UNVISORED	UNWEARIED	UNWISDOM	UNWOUND	UPBLOW
UNVISORS	UNWEARIER	UNWISDOMS	UNWOUNDED	UPBLOWING
UNVITAL	UNWEARIES	UNWISE	UNWOVE	UPBLOWN
UNVIZARD	UNWEARY	UNWISELY	UNWOVEN	UPBLOWS
UNVIZARDS	UNWEAVE	UNWISER	UNWRAP	UPBOIL
UNVOCAL	UNWEAVES	UNWISEST	UNWRAPPED	UPBOILED
UNVOICE	UNWEAVING	UNWISH	UNWRAPS	UPBOILING
UNVOICED	UNWEBBED	UNWISHED	UNWREAKED	UPBOILS
UNVOICES	UNWED	UNWISHES	UNWREATHE	UPBORE
UNVOICING	UNWEDDED	UNWISHFUL	UNWRINKLE	UPBORNE
UNVULGAR	UNWEEDED	UNWISHING	UNWRITE	UPBOUND
UNWAGED	UNWEENED	UNWIST	UNWRITES	UPBOUNDEN
UNWAKED	UNWEETING	UNWIT	UNWRITING	UPBOW
UNWAKENED	UNWEIGHED	UNWITCH	UNWRITTEN	UPBOWS
UNWALLED	UNWEIGHT	UNWITCHED	UNWROTE	UPBRAID
UNWANING	UNWEIGHTS	UNWITCHES	UNWROUGHT	UPBRAIDED
UNWANTED	UNWELCOME	UNWITS	UNWRUNG	UPBRAIDER
UNWARDED	UNWELDED	UNWITTED	UNYEANED	UPBRAIDS
UNWARE	UNWELDY	UNWITTIER	UNYOKE	UPBRAST
UNWARELY	UNWELL	UNWITTILY	UNYOKED	UPBRAY
UNWARES	UNWEPT	UNWITTING	UNYOKES	UPBRAYED
UNWARIE	UNWET	UNWITTY	UNYOKING	UPBRAYING
UNWARIER	UNWETTED	UNWIVE	UNYOUNG	UPBRAYS
UNWARIEST	UNWHIPPED	UNWIVED	UNZEALOUS	UPBREAK
UNWARILY	UNWHIPT	UNWIVES	UNZIP	UPBREAKS
UNWARLIKE	UNWHITE	UNWIVING	UNZIPPED	UPBRING
UNWARMED	UNWIELDLY	UNWOMAN	UNZIPPING	UPBRINGS
UNWARNED	UNWIELDY	UNWOMANED	UNZIPS	UPBROKE
UNWARPED	UNWIFELY	UNWOMANLY	UNZONED	UPBROKEN
UNWARY	UNWIGGED	UNWOMANS	UP	UPBROUGHT
UNWASHED	UNWILFUL	UNWON	UPADAISY	UPBUILD
UNWASHEDS	UNWILL	UNWONT	UPAITHRIC	UPBUILDER
UNWASHEN	UNWILLED	UNWONTED	UPALONG	UPBUILDS
UNWASTED	UNWILLING	UNWOODED	UPALONGS	UPBUILT
UNWASTING	UNWILLS	UNWOOED	UPAS	UPBURNING

U

UPBURST	UPDARTING	UPFLUNG	UPHAND	UPJET
UPBURSTS	UPDARTS	UPFOLD	UPHANG	UPJETS
UPBY	UPDATE	UPFOLDED	UPHANGING	UPJETTED
UPBYE	UPDATED	UPFOLDING	UPHANGS	UPJETTING
UPCAST	UPDATER	UPFOLDS	UPHAUD	UPKEEP
UPCASTING	UPDATERS	UPFOLLOW	UPHAUDING	UPKEEPS
UPCASTS	UPDATES	UPFOLLOWS	UPHAUDS	UPKNIT
UPCATCH	UPDATING	UPFRONT	UPHEAP	UPKNITS
UPCATCHES	UPDIVE	UPFURL	UPHEAPED	UPKNITTED
UPCAUGHT	UPDIVED	UPFURLED	UPHEAPING	UPLAID
UPCHEER	UPDIVES	UPFURLING	UPHEAPS	UPLAND
UPCHEERED	UPDIVING	UPFURLS	UPHEAVAL	UPLANDER
UPCHEERS	UPDO	UPGANG	UPHEAVALS	UPLANDERS
UPCHUCK	UPDOMING	UPGANGS	UPHEAVE	UPLANDISH
UPCHUCKED	UPDOMINGS	UPGATHER	UPHEAVED	UPLANDS
UPCHUCKS	UPDOS	UPGATHERS	UPHEAVER	UPLAY
UPCLIMB	UPDOVE	UPGAZE	UPHEAVERS	UPLAYING
UPCLIMBED	UPDRAFT	UPGAZED	UPHEAVES	UPLAYS
UPCLIMBS	UPDRAFTS	UPGAZES	UPHEAVING	UPLEAD
UPCLOSE	UPDRAG	UPGAZING	UPHELD	UPLEADING
UPCLOSED	UPDRAGGED	UPGIRD	UPHILD	UPLEADS
UPCLOSES	UPDRAGS	UPGIRDED	UPHILL	UPLEAN
UPCLOSING	UPDRAUGHT	UPGIRDING	UPHILLS	UPLEANED
UPCOAST	UPDRAW	UPGIRDS	UPHOARD	UPLEANING
UPCOIL	UPDRAWING	UPGIRT	UPHOARDED	UPLEANS
UPCOILED	UPDRAWN	UPGO	UPHOARDS	UPLEANT
UPCOILING	UPDRAWS	UPGOES	UPHOIST	UPLEAP
UPCOILS	UPDREW	UPGOING	UPHOISTED	UPLEAPED
UPCOME	UPDRIED	UPGOINGS	UPHOISTS	UPLEAPING
UPCOMES	UPDRIES	UPGONE	UPHOLD	UPLEAPS
UPCOMING	UPDRY	UPGRADE	UPHOLDER	UPLEAPT
UPCOUNTRY	UPDRYING	UPGRADED	UPHOLDERS	UPLED
UPCOURT	UPEND	UPGRADER	UPHOLDING	UPLIFT
UPCURL	UPENDED	UPGRADERS	UPHOLDS	UPLIFTED
UPCURLED	UPENDING	UPGRADES	UPHOLSTER	UPLIFTER
UPCURLING	UPENDS	UPGRADING	UPHOORD	UPLIFTERS
UPCURLS	UPFIELD	UPGREW	UPHOORDED	UPLIFTING
UPCURVE	UPFILL	UPGROW	UPHOORDS	UPLIFTS
UPCURVED	UPFILLED	UPGROWING	UPHOVE	UPLIGHT
UPCURVES	UPFILLING	UPGROWN	UPHROE	UPLIGHTED
UPCURVING	UPFILLS	UPGROWS	UPHROES	UPLIGHTER
UPCYCLE	UPFLING	UPGROWTH	UPHUDDEN	UPLIGHTS
UPCYCLED	UPFLINGS	UPGROWTHS	UPHUNG	UPLINK
UPCYCLES	UPFLOW	UPGUSH	UPHURL	UPLINKED
UPCYCLING	UPFLOWED	UPGUSHED	UPHURLED	UPLINKING
UPDART	UPFLOWING	UPGUSHES	UPHURLING	UPLINKS
UPDARTED	UPFLOWS	UPGUSHING	UPHURLS	UPLIT

UPLOAD
UPLOADED
UPLOADING
UPLOADS
UPLOCK
UPLOCKED
UPLOCKING
UPLOCKS
UPLOOK
UPLOOKED
UPLOOKING
UPLOOKS
UPLYING
UPMAKE
UPMAKER
UPMAKERS
UPMAKES
UPMAKING
UPMAKINGS
UPMANSHIP
UPMARKET
UPMARKETS
UPMOST
UPO
UPON
UPPED
UPPER
UPPERCASE
UPPERCUT
UPPERCUTS
UPPERMOST
UPPERPART
UPPERS
UPPILE
UPPILED
UPPILES
UPPILING
UPPING
UPPINGS
UPPISH
UPPISHLY
UPPITY
UPPROP
UPPROPPED
UPPROPS
UPRAISE
UPRAISED

UPRAISER
UPRAISERS
UPRAISES
UPRAISING
UPRAN
UPRATE
UPRATED
UPRATES
UPRATING
UPREACH
UPREACHED
UPREACHES
UPREAR
UPREARED
UPREARING
UPREARS
UPREST
UPRESTS
UPRIGHT
UPRIGHTED
UPRIGHTLY
UPRIGHTS
UPRISAL
UPRISALS
UPRISE
UPRISEN
UPRISER
UPRISERS
UPRISES
UPRISING
UPRISINGS
UPRIST
UPRISTS
UPRIVER
UPRIVERS
UPROAR
UPROARED
UPROARING
UPROARS
UPROLL
UPROLLED
UPROLLING
UPROLLS
UPROOT
UPROOTAL
UPROOTALS
UPROOTED

UPROOTER
UPROOTERS
UPROOTING
UPROOTS
UPROSE
UPROUSE
UPROUSED
UPROUSES
UPROUSING
UPRUN
UPRUNNING
UPRUNS
UPRUSH
UPRUSHED
UPRUSHES
UPRUSHING
UPRYST
UPS
UPSADAISY
UPSCALE
UPSCALED
UPSCALES
UPSCALING
UPSEE
UPSEES
UPSELL
UPSELLING
UPSELLS
UPSEND
UPSENDING
UPSENDS
UPSENT
UPSET
UPSETS
UPSETTER
UPSETTERS
UPSETTING
UPSEY
UPSEYS
UPSHIFT
UPSHIFTED
UPSHIFTS
UPSHOOT
UPSHOOTS
UPSHOT
UPSHOTS
UPSIDE

UPSIDES
UPSIES
UPSILON
UPSILONS
UPSITTING
UPSIZE
UPSIZED
UPSIZES
UPSIZING
UPSKILL
UPSKILLED
UPSKILLS
UPSKIRT
UPSLOPE
UPSLOPES
UPSOAR
UPSOARED
UPSOARING
UPSOARS
UPSOLD
UPSPAKE
UPSPEAK
UPSPEAKS
UPSPEAR
UPSPEARED
UPSPEARS
UPSPOKE
UPSPOKEN
UPSPRANG
UPSPRING
UPSPRINGS
UPSPRUNG
UPSTAGE
UPSTAGED
UPSTAGER
UPSTAGERS
UPSTAGES
UPSTAGING
UPSTAIR
UPSTAIRS
UPSTAND
UPSTANDS
UPSTARE
UPSTARED
UPSTARES
UPSTARING
UPSTART

UPSTARTED
UPSTARTS
UPSTATE
UPSTATER
UPSTATERS
UPSTATES
UPSTAY
UPSTAYED
UPSTAYING
UPSTAYS
UPSTEP
UPSTEPPED
UPSTEPS
UPSTIR
UPSTIRRED
UPSTIRS
UPSTOOD
UPSTREAM
UPSTREAMS
UPSTROKE
UPSTROKES
UPSURGE
UPSURGED
UPSURGES
UPSURGING
UPSWARM
UPSWARMED
UPSWARMS
UPSWAY
UPSWAYED
UPSWAYING
UPSWAYS
UPSWEEP
UPSWEEPS
UPSWELL
UPSWELLED
UPSWELLS
UPSWEPT
UPSWING
UPSWINGS
UPSWOLLEN
UPSWUNG
UPSY
UPTA
UPTAK
UPTAKE
UPTAKEN

U

UPTAKES	UPTRAINS	URALI	URBANISE	UREIDE
UPTAKING	UPTREND	URALIS	URBANISED	UREIDES
UPTAKS	UPTRENDS	URALITE	URBANISES	UREMIA
UPTALK	UPTRILLED	URALITES	URBANISM	UREMIAS
UPTALKED	UPTURN	URALITIC	URBANISMS	UREMIC
UPTALKING	UPTURNED	URALITISE	URBANIST	URENA
UPTALKS	UPTURNING	URALITIZE	URBANISTS	URENAS
UPTEAR	UPTURNS	URANIA	URBANITE	URENT
UPTEARING	UPTYING	URANIAN	URBANITES	UREOTELIC
UPTEARS	UPVALUE	URANIAS	URBANITY	URES
UPTEMPO	UPVALUED	URANIC	URBANIZE	URESES
UPTEMPOS	UPVALUES	URANIDE	URBANIZED	URESIS
UPTER	UPVALUING	URANIDES	URBANIZES	URETER
UPTHREW	UPWAFT	URANIN	URBEX	URETERAL
UPTHROW	UPWAFTED	URANINITE	URBEXES	URETERIC
UPTHROWN	UPWAFTING	URANINS	URBIA	URETERS
UPTHROWS	UPWAFTS	URANISCI	URBIAS	URETHAN
UPTHRUST	UPWARD	URANISCUS	URBS	URETHANE
UPTHRUSTS	UPWARDLY	URANISM	URCEOLATE	URETHANED
UPTHUNDER	UPWARDS	URANISMS	URCEOLI	URETHANES
UPTICK	UPWELL	URANITE	URCEOLUS	URETHANS
UPTICKS	UPWELLED	URANITES	URCHIN	URETHRA
UPTIE	UPWELLING	URANITIC	URCHINS	URETHRAE
UPTIED	UPWELLS	URANIUM	URD	URETHRAL
UPTIES	UPWENT	URANIUMS	URDE	URETHRAS
UPTIGHT	UPWHIRL	URANOLOGY	URDEE	URETIC
UPTIGHTER	UPWHIRLED	URANOUS	URDS	URGE
UPTILT	UPWHIRLS	URANYL	URDY	URGED
UPTILTED	UPWIND	URANYLIC	URE	URGENCE
UPTILTING	UPWINDING	URANYLS	UREA	URGENCES
UPTILTS	UPWINDS	URAO	UREAL	URGENCIES
UPTIME	UPWOUND	URAOS	UREAS	URGENCY
UPTIMES	UPWRAP	URARE	UREASE	URGENT
UPTITLING	UPWRAPS	URARES	UREASES	URGENTLY
UPTOOK	UPWROUGHT	URARI	UREDIA	URGER
UPTORE	UR	URARIS	UREDIAL	URGERS
UPTORN	URACHI	URASE	UREDINE	URGES
UPTOSS	URACHUS	URASES	UREDINES	URGING
UPTOSSED	URACHUSES	URATE	UREDINIA	URGINGLY
UPTOSSES	URACIL	URATES	UREDINIAL	URGINGS
UPTOSSING	URACILS	URATIC	UREDINIUM	URIAL
UPTOWN	URAEI	URB	UREDINOUS	URIALS
UPTOWNER	URAEMIA	URBAN	UREDIUM	URIC
UPTOWNERS	URAEMIAS	URBANE	UREDO	URICASE
UPTOWNS	URAEMIC	URBANELY	UREDOS	URICASES
UPTRAIN	URAEUS	URBANER	UREDOSORI	URIDINE
UPTRAINED	URAEUSES	URBANEST	UREIC	URIDINES

URIDYLIC	URODELANS	URSON	USHER	USURPERS
URINAL	URODELE	URSONS	USHERED	USURPING
URINALS	URODELES	URTEXT	USHERESS	USURPINGS
URINANT	URODELOUS	URTEXTE	USHERETTE	USURPS
URINARIES	UROGENOUS	URTEXTS	USHERING	USURY
URINARY	UROGRAM	URTICA	USHERINGS	USWARD
URINATE	UROGRAMS	URTICANT	USHERS	USWARDS
URINATED	UROGRAPHY	URTICANTS	USHERSHIP	UT
URINATES	UROKINASE	URTICARIA	USING	UTA
URINATING	UROLAGNIA	URTICAS	USNEA	UTAS
URINATION	UROLITH	URTICATE	USNEAS	UTASES
URINATIVE	UROLITHIC	URTICATED	USQUABAE	UTE
URINATOR	UROLITHS	URTICATES	USQUABAES	UTENSIL
URINATORS	UROLOGIC	URUBU	USQUE	UTENSILS
URINE	UROLOGIES	URUBUS	USQUEBAE	UTERI
URINED	UROLOGIST	URUS	USQUEBAES	UTERINE
URINEMIA	UROLOGY	URUSES	USQUES	UTERITIS
URINEMIAS	UROMERE	URUSHIOL	USTION	UTEROTOMY
URINEMIC	UROMERES	URUSHIOLS	USTIONS	UTERUS
URINES	UROPOD	URVA	USTULATE	UTERUSES
URINING	UROPODAL	URVAS	USTULATED	UTES
URINOLOGY	UROPODOUS	US	USTULATES	UTILE
URINOSE	UROPODS	USABILITY	USUAL	UTILES
URINOUS	UROPYGIA	USABLE	USUALLY	UTILIDOR
URITE	UROPYGIAL	USABLY	USUALNESS	UTILIDORS
URITES	UROPYGIUM	USAGE	USUALS	UTILISE
URMAN	UROSCOPIC	USAGER	USUCAPION	UTILISED
URMANS	UROSCOPY	USAGERS	USUCAPT	UTILISER
URN	UROSES	USAGES	USUCAPTED	UTILISERS
URNAL	UROSIS	USANCE	USUCAPTS	UTILISES
URNED	UROSOME	USANCES	USUFRUCT	UTILISING
URNFIELD	UROSOMES	USAUNCE	USUFRUCTS	UTILITIES
URNFIELDS	UROSTEGE	USAUNCES	USURE	UTILITY
URNFUL	UROSTEGES	USE	USURED	UTILIZE
URNFULS	UROSTOMY	USEABLE	USURER	UTILIZED
URNING	UROSTYLE	USEABLY	USURERS	UTILIZER
URNINGS	UROSTYLES	USED	USURES	UTILIZERS
URNLIKE	URP	USEFUL	USURESS	UTILIZES
URNS	URPED	USEFULLY	USURESSES	UTILIZING
UROBILIN	URPING	USEFULS	USURIES	UTIS
UROBILINS	URPS	USELESS	USURING	UTISES
UROBORIC	URSA	USELESSLY	USURIOUS	UTMOST
UROBOROS	URSAE	USER	USUROUS	UTMOSTS
UROCHORD	URSID	USERNAME	USURP	UTOPIA
UROCHORDS	URSIDS	USERNAMES	USURPED	UTOPIAN
UROCHROME	URSIFORM	USERS	USURPEDLY	UTOPIANS
URODELAN	URSINE	USES	USURPER	UTOPIAS

UTOPIAST

UTOPIAST	UTRICULUS	UTTERLESS	UVEA	UVULARS
UTOPIASTS	UTS	UTTERLY	UVEAL	UVULAS
UTOPISM	UTTER	UTTERMOST	UVEAS	UVULITIS
UTOPISMS	UTTERABLE	UTTERNESS	UVEITIC	UXORIAL
UTOPIST	UTTERANCE	UTTERS	UVEITIS	UXORIALLY
UTOPISTIC	UTTERED	UTU	UVEITISES	UXORICIDE
UTOPISTS	UTTERER	UTUS	UVEOUS	UXORIOUS
UTRICLE	UTTERERS	UVA	UVULA	
UTRICLES	UTTEREST	UVAE	UVULAE	
UTRICULAR	UTTERING	UVAROVITE	UVULAR	
UTRICULI	UTTERINGS	UVAS	UVULARLY	

V

VAC	VACUIST	VAGINATE	VAINESSES	VALES
VACANCE	VACUISTS	VAGINATED	VAINEST	VALET
VACANCES	VACUITIES	VAGINITIS	VAINGLORY	VALETA
VACANCIES	VACUITY	VAGINOSES	VAINLY	VALETAS
VACANCY	VACUOLAR	VAGINOSIS	VAINNESS	VALETE
VACANT	VACUOLATE	VAGINULA	VAIR	VALETED
VACANTLY	VACUOLE	VAGINULAE	VAIRE	VALETES
VACATABLE	VACUOLES	VAGINULE	VAIRIER	VALETING
VACATE	VACUOUS	VAGINULES	VAIRIEST	VALETINGS
VACATED	VACUOUSLY	VAGITUS	VAIRS	VALETS
VACATES	VACUUM	VAGITUSES	VAIRY	VALGOID
VACATING	VACUUMED	VAGOTOMY	VAIVODE	VALGOUS
VACATION	VACUUMING	VAGOTONIA	VAIVODES	VALGUS
VACATIONS	VACUUMS	VAGOTONIC	VAJAZZLE	VALGUSES
VACATUR	VADE	VAGRANCY	VAJAZZLED	VALI
VACATURS	VADED	VAGRANT	VAJAZZLES	VALIANCE
VACCINA	VADES	VAGRANTLY	VAKAS	VALIANCES
VACCINAL	VADING	VAGRANTS	VAKASES	VALIANCY
VACCINAS	VADOSE	VAGROM	VAKASS	VALIANT
VACCINATE	VAE	VAGS	VAKASSES	VALIANTLY
VACCINE	VAES	VAGUE	VAKEEL	VALIANTS
VACCINEE	VAG	VAGUED	VAKEELS	VALID
VACCINEES	VAGABOND	VAGUELY	VAKIL	VALIDATE
VACCINES	VAGABONDS	VAGUENESS	VAKILS	VALIDATED
VACCINIA	VAGAL	VAGUER	VALANCE	VALIDATES
VACCINIAL	VAGALLY	VAGUES	VALANCED	VALIDER
VACCINIAS	VAGARIES	VAGUEST	VALANCES	VALIDEST
VACCINIUM	VAGARIOUS	VAGUING	VALANCING	VALIDITY
VACHERIN	VAGARISH	VAGUISH	VALE	VALIDLY
VACHERINS	VAGARY	VAGUS	VALENCE	VALIDNESS
VACILLANT	VAGGED	VAHANA	VALENCES	VALINE
VACILLATE	VAGGING	VAHANAS	VALENCIA	VALINES
VACKED	VAGI	VAHINE	VALENCIAS	VALIS
VACKING	VAGILE	VAHINES	VALENCIES	VALISE
VACS	VAGILITY	VAIL	VALENCY	VALISES
VACUA	VAGINA	VAILED	VALENTINE	VALIUM
VACUATE	VAGINAE	VAILING	VALERATE	VALKYR
VACUATED	VAGINAL	VAILS	VALERATES	VALKYRIE
VACUATES	VAGINALLY	VAIN	VALERIAN	VALKYRIES
VACUATING	VAGINANT	VAINER	VALERIANS	VALKYRS
VACUATION	VAGINAS	VAINESSE	VALERIC	VALLAR

V

VALLARIES	VALUED	VAMPIRIC	VANILLAS	VAPIDLY
VALLARS	VALUELESS	VAMPIRING	VANILLIC	VAPIDNESS
VALLARY	VALUER	VAMPIRISE	VANILLIN	VAPING
VALLATE	VALUERS	VAMPIRISH	VANILLINS	VAPINGS
VALLATION	VALUES	VAMPIRISM	VANISH	VAPOR
VALLECULA	VALUING	VAMPIRIZE	VANISHED	VAPORABLE
VALLEY	VALUTA	VAMPISH	VANISHER	VAPORED
VALLEYED	VALUTAS	VAMPISHLY	VANISHERS	VAPORER
VALLEYS	VALVAL	VAMPLATE	VANISHES	VAPORERS
VALLHUND	VALVAR	VAMPLATES	VANISHING	VAPORETTI
VALLHUNDS	VALVASSOR	VAMPS	VANITAS	VAPORETTO
VALLONIA	VALVATE	VAMPY	VANITASES	VAPORIFIC
VALLONIAS	VALVE	VAN	VANITIED	VAPORING
VALLUM	VALVED	VANADATE	VANITIES	VAPORINGS
VALLUMS	VALVELESS	VANADATES	VANITORY	VAPORISE
VALONEA	VALVELET	VANADIATE	VANITY	VAPORISED
VALONEAS	VALVELETS	VANADIC	VANLOAD	VAPORISER
VALONIA	VALVELIKE	VANADIUM	VANLOADS	VAPORISES
VALONIAS	VALVES	VANADIUMS	VANMAN	VAPORISH
VALOR	VALVING	VANADOUS	VANMEN	VAPORIZE
VALORISE	VALVULA	VANASPATI	VANNED	VAPORIZED
VALORISED	VALVULAE	VANDA	VANNER	VAPORIZER
VALORISES	VALVULAR	VANDAL	VANNERS	VAPORIZES
VALORIZE	VALVULE	VANDALIC	VANNING	VAPORLESS
VALORIZED	VALVULES	VANDALISE	VANNINGS	VAPORLIKE
VALORIZES	VAMBRACE	VANDALISH	VANPOOL	VAPOROUS
VALOROUS	VAMBRACED	VANDALISM	VANPOOLS	VAPORS
VALORS	VAMBRACES	VANDALIZE	VANQUISH	VAPORWARE
VALOUR	VAMOOSE	VANDALS	VANS	VAPORY
VALOURS	VAMOOSED	VANDAS	VANT	VAPOUR
VALPROATE	VAMOOSES	VANDYKE	VANTAGE	VAPOURED
VALPROIC	VAMOOSING	VANDYKED	VANTAGED	VAPOURER
VALSE	VAMOSE	VANDYKES	VANTAGES	VAPOURERS
VALSED	VAMOSED	VANDYKING	VANTAGING	VAPOURING
VALSES	VAMOSES	VANE	VANTBRACE	VAPOURISH
VALSING	VAMOSING	VANED	VANTBRASS	VAPOURS
VALUABLE	VAMP	VANELESS	VANTS	VAPOURY
VALUABLES	VAMPED	VANES	VANWARD	VAPULATE
VALUABLY	VAMPER	VANESSA	VAPE	VAPULATED
VALUATE	VAMPERS	VANESSAS	VAPED	VAPULATES
VALUATED	VAMPIER	VANESSID	VAPER	VAQUERO
VALUATES	VAMPIEST	VANESSIDS	VAPERS	VAQUEROS
VALUATING	VAMPING	VANG	VAPES	VAR
VALUATION	VAMPINGS	VANGS	VAPID	VARA
VALUATOR	VAMPIRE	VANGUARD	VAPIDER	VARACTOR
VALUATORS	VAMPIRED	VANGUARDS	VAPIDEST	VARACTORS
VALUE	VAMPIRES	VANILLA	VAPIDITY	VARAN

VARANS	VARIETY	VARS	VASSALLED	VAULTERS
VARAS	VARIFOCAL	VARSAL	VASSALRY	VAULTIER
VARDIES	VARIFORM	VARSITIES	VASSALS	VAULTIEST
VARDY	VARIOLA	VARSITY	VAST	VAULTING
VARE	VARIOLAR	VARTABED	VASTER	VAULTINGS
VAREC	VARIOLAS	VARTABEDS	VASTEST	VAULTLIKE
VARECH	VARIOLATE	VARUS	VASTIDITY	VAULTS
VARECHS	VARIOLE	VARUSES	VASTIER	VAULTY
VARECS	VARIOLES	VARVE	VASTIEST	VAUNCE
VARENYKY	VARIOLITE	VARVED	VASTITIES	VAUNCED
VARES	VARIOLOID	VARVEL	VASTITUDE	VAUNCES
VAREUSE	VARIOLOUS	VARVELLED	VASTITY	VAUNCING
VAREUSES	VARIORUM	VARVELS	VASTLY	VAUNT
VARGUENO	VARIORUMS	VARVES	VASTNESS	VAUNTAGE
VARGUENOS	VARIOUS	VARY	VASTS	VAUNTAGES
VARIA	VARIOUSLY	VARYING	VASTY	VAUNTED
VARIABLE	VARISCITE	VARYINGLY	VAT	VAUNTER
VARIABLES	VARISIZED	VARYINGS	VATABLE	VAUNTERS
VARIABLY	VARISTOR	VAS	VATFUL	VAUNTERY
VARIANCE	VARISTORS	VASA	VATFULS	VAUNTFUL
VARIANCES	VARITYPE	VASAL	VATIC	VAUNTIE
VARIANT	VARITYPED	VASCULA	VATICAL	VAUNTIER
VARIANTS	VARITYPES	VASCULAR	VATICIDE	VAUNTIEST
VARIAS	VARIX	VASCULUM	VATICIDES	VAUNTING
VARIATE	VARLET	VASCULUMS	VATICINAL	VAUNTINGS
VARIATED	VARLETESS	VASE	VATMAN	VAUNTS
VARIATES	VARLETRY	VASECTOMY	VATMEN	VAUNTY
VARIATING	VARLETS	VASEFUL	VATS	VAURIEN
VARIATION	VARLETTO	VASEFULS	VATTED	VAURIENS
VARIATIVE	VARLETTOS	VASELIKE	VATTER	VAUS
VARICEAL	VARMENT	VASELINE	VATTERS	VAUT
VARICELLA	VARMENTS	VASELINED	VATTING	VAUTE
VARICES	VARMINT	VASELINES	VATU	VAUTED
VARICOID	VARMINTS	VASES	VATUS	VAUTES
VARICOSE	VARNA	VASIFORM	VAU	VAUTING
VARICOSED	VARNAS	VASOMOTOR	VAUCH	VAUTS
VARICOSES	VARNISH	VASOSPASM	VAUCHED	VAV
VARICOSIS	VARNISHED	VASOTOCIN	VAUCHES	VAVASOR
VARIED	VARNISHER	VASOTOMY	VAUCHING	VAVASORS
VARIEDLY	VARNISHES	VASOVAGAL	VAUDOO	VAVASORY
VARIEGATE	VARNISHY	VASSAIL	VAUDOOS	VAVASOUR
VARIER	VAROOM	VASSAILS	VAUDOUX	VAVASOURS
VARIERS	VAROOMED	VASSAL	VAULT	VAVASSOR
VARIES	VAROOMING	VASSALAGE	VAULTAGE	VAVASSORS
VARIETAL	VAROOMS	VASSALESS	VAULTAGES	VAVS
VARIETALS	VARROA	VASSALISE	VAULTED	VAW
VARIETIES	VARROAS	VASSALIZE	VAULTER	VAWARD

VAWARDS	VEERING	VEHICULAR	VELARISE	VELSKOENS
VAWNTIE	VEERINGLY	VEHM	VELARISED	VELUM
VAWNTIER	VEERINGS	VEHME	VELARISES	VELURE
VAWNTIEST	VEERS	VEHMIC	VELARIUM	VELURED
VAWS	VEERY	VEHMIQUE	VELARIZE	VELURES
VAWTE	VEES	VEIL	VELARIZED	VELURING
VAWTED	VEG	VEILED	VELARIZES	VELVERET
VAWTES	VEGA	VEILEDLY	VELARS	VELVERETS
VAWTING	VEGAN	VEILER	VELATE	VELVET
VEAL	VEGANIC	VEILERS	VELATED	VELVETED
VEALE	VEGANISM	VEILIER	VELATURA	VELVETEEN
VEALED	VEGANISMS	VEILIEST	VELATURAS	VELVETIER
VEALER	VEGANS	VEILING	VELCRO	VELVETING
VEALERS	VEGAS	VEILINGS	VELCROS	VELVETS
VEALES	VEGELATE	VEILLESS	VELD	VELVETY
VEALIER	VEGELATES	VEILLEUSE	VELDS	VENA
VEALIEST	VEGEMITE	VEILLIKE	VELDSKOEN	VENAE
VEALING	VEGEMITES	VEILS	VELDT	VENAL
VEALS	VEGES	VEILY	VELDTS	VENALITY
VEALY	VEGETABLE	VEIN	VELE	VENALLY
VECTOR	VEGETABLY	VEINAL	VELES	VENATIC
VECTORED	VEGETAL	VEINED	VELETA	VENATICAL
VECTORIAL	VEGETALLY	VEINER	VELETAS	VENATION
VECTORING	VEGETALS	VEINERS	VELIGER	VENATIONS
VECTORISE	VEGETANT	VEINIER	VELIGERS	VENATOR
VECTORIZE	VEGETATE	VEINIEST	VELITES	VENATORS
VECTORS	VEGETATED	VEINING	VELL	VEND
VEDALIA	VEGETATES	VEININGS	VELLEITY	VENDABLE
VEDALIAS	VEGETE	VEINLESS	VELLENAGE	VENDABLES
VEDETTE	VEGETIST	VEINLET	VELLET	VENDACE
VEDETTES	VEGETISTS	VEINLETS	VELLETS	VENDACES
VEDUTA	VEGETIVE	VEINLIKE	VELLICATE	VENDAGE
VEDUTE	VEGETIVES	VEINOUS	VELLON	VENDAGES
VEDUTISTA	VEGGED	VEINS	VELLONS	VENDANGE
VEDUTISTI	VEGGES	VEINSTONE	VELLS	VENDANGES
VEE	VEGGIE	VEINSTUFF	VELLUM	VENDED
VEEJAY	VEGGIES	VEINULE	VELLUMS	VENDEE
VEEJAYS	VEGGING	VEINULES	VELLUS	VENDEES
VEENA	VEGIE	VEINULET	VELOCE	VENDER
VEENAS	VEGIES	VEINULETS	VELOCITY	VENDERS
VEEP	VEGO	VEINY	VELODROME	VENDETTA
VEEPEE	VEGOS	VELA	VELOUR	VENDETTAS
VEEPEES	VEHEMENCE	VELAMEN	VELOURS	VENDEUSE
VEEPS	VEHEMENCY	VELAMINA	VELOUTE	VENDEUSES
VEER	VEHEMENT	VELAR	VELOUTES	VENDIBLE
VEERED	VEHICLE	VELARIA	VELOUTINE	VENDIBLES
VEERIES	VEHICLES	VELARIC	VELSKOEN	VENDIBLY

V

VENDING
VENDINGS
VENDIS
VENDISES
VENDISS
VENDISSES
VENDITION
VENDOR
VENDORS
VENDS
VENDU
VENDUE
VENDUES
VENDUS
VENEER
VENEERED
VENEERER
VENEERERS
VENEERING
VENEERS
VENEFIC
VENEFICAL
VENENATE
VENENATED
VENENATES
VENENE
VENENES
VENENOSE
VENERABLE
VENERABLY
VENERATE
VENERATED
VENERATES
VENERATOR
VENEREAL
VENEREAN
VENEREANS
VENEREOUS
VENERER
VENERERS
VENERIES
VENERY
VENETIAN
VENETIANS
VENEWE
VENEWES
VENEY

VENEYS
VENGE
VENGEABLE
VENGEABLY
VENGEANCE
VENGED
VENGEFUL
VENGEMENT
VENGER
VENGERS
VENGES
VENGING
VENIAL
VENIALITY
VENIALLY
VENIDIUM
VENIDIUMS
VENIN
VENINE
VENINES
VENINS
VENIRE
VENIREMAN
VENIREMEN
VENIRES
VENISON
VENISONS
VENITE
VENITES
VENNEL
VENNELS
VENOGRAM
VENOGRAMS
VENOLOGY
VENOM
VENOMED
VENOMER
VENOMERS
VENOMING
VENOMLESS
VENOMOUS
VENOMS
VENOSE
VENOSITY
VENOUS
VENOUSLY
VENT

VENTAGE
VENTAGES
VENTAIL
VENTAILE
VENTAILES
VENTAILS
VENTANA
VENTANAS
VENTAYLE
VENTAYLES
VENTED
VENTER
VENTERS
VENTIDUCT
VENTIFACT
VENTIGE
VENTIGES
VENTIL
VENTILATE
VENTILS
VENTING
VENTINGS
VENTLESS
VENTOSE
VENTOSES
VENTOSITY
VENTOUSE
VENTOUSES
VENTRAL
VENTRALLY
VENTRALS
VENTRE
VENTRED
VENTRES
VENTRICLE
VENTRING
VENTRINGS
VENTROUS
VENTS
VENTURE
VENTURED
VENTURER
VENTURERS
VENTURES
VENTURI
VENTURING
VENTURIS

VENTUROUS
VENUE
VENUES
VENULAR
VENULE
VENULES
VENULOSE
VENULOUS
VENUS
VENUSES
VENVILLE
VENVILLES
VERA
VERACIOUS
VERACITY
VERANDA
VERANDAED
VERANDAH
VERANDAHS
VERANDAS
VERAPAMIL
VERATRIA
VERATRIAS
VERATRIN
VERATRINE
VERATRINS
VERATRUM
VERATRUMS
VERB
VERBAL
VERBALISE
VERBALISM
VERBALIST
VERBALITY
VERBALIZE
VERBALLED
VERBALLY
VERBALS
VERBARIAN
VERBASCUM
VERBATIM
VERBENA
VERBENAS
VERBERATE
VERBIAGE
VERBIAGES
VERBICIDE

VERBID
VERBIDS
VERBIFIED
VERBIFIES
VERBIFY
VERBILE
VERBILES
VERBING
VERBINGS
VERBLESS
VERBOSE
VERBOSELY
VERBOSER
VERBOSEST
VERBOSITY
VERBOTEN
VERBS
VERD
VERDANCY
VERDANT
VERDANTLY
VERDELHO
VERDELHOS
VERDERER
VERDERERS
VERDEROR
VERDERORS
VERDET
VERDETS
VERDICT
VERDICTS
VERDIGRIS
VERDIN
VERDINS
VERDIT
VERDITE
VERDITER
VERDITERS
VERDITES
VERDITS
VERDOY
VERDOYS
VERDURE
VERDURED
VERDURES
VERDUROUS
VERECUND

V

VERGE	VERLIGTES	VERONAL	VERSIN	VERVAINS
VERGED	VERMAL	VERONALS	VERSINE	VERVE
VERGENCE	VERMEIL	VERONICA	VERSINES	VERVEL
VERGENCES	VERMEILED	VERONICAS	VERSING	VERVELLED
VERGENCY	VERMEILLE	VERONIQUE	VERSINGS	VERVELS
VERGER	VERMEILS	VERQUERE	VERSINS	VERVEN
VERGERS	VERMELL	VERQUERES	VERSION	VERVENS
VERGES	VERMELLS	VERQUIRE	VERSIONAL	VERVES
VERGING	VERMES	VERQUIRES	VERSIONED	VERVET
VERGLAS	VERMIAN	VERRA	VERSIONER	VERVETS
VERGLASES	VERMICIDE	VERREL	VERSIONS	VERY
VERIDIC	VERMICULE	VERRELS	VERSO	VESICA
VERIDICAL	VERMIFORM	VERREY	VERSOS	VESICAE
VERIER	VERMIFUGE	VERRINE	VERST	VESICAL
VERIEST	VERMIL	VERRINES	VERSTE	VESICANT
VERIFIED	VERMILIES	VERRUCA	VERSTES	VESICANTS
VERIFIER	VERMILION	VERRUCAE	VERSTS	VESICAS
VERIFIERS	VERMILLED	VERRUCAS	VERSUS	VESICATE
VERIFIES	VERMILS	VERRUCOSE	VERSUTE	VESICATED
VERIFY	VERMILY	VERRUCOUS	VERT	VESICATES
VERIFYING	VERMIN	VERRUGA	VERTEBRA	VESICLE
VERILY	VERMINATE	VERRUGAS	VERTEBRAE	VESICLES
VERISM	VERMINED	VERRY	VERTEBRAL	VESICULA
VERISMO	VERMINOUS	VERS	VERTEBRAS	VESICULAE
VERISMOS	VERMINS	VERSAL	VERTED	VESICULAR
VERISMS	VERMINY	VERSALS	VERTEX	VESPA
VERIST	VERMIS	VERSANT	VERTEXES	VESPAS
VERISTIC	VERMOULU	VERSANTS	VERTICAL	VESPER
VERISTS	VERMOUTH	VERSATILE	VERTICALS	VESPERAL
VERITABLE	VERMOUTHS	VERSE	VERTICES	VESPERALS
VERITABLY	VERMUTH	VERSED	VERTICIL	VESPERS
VERITAS	VERMUTHS	VERSELET	VERTICILS	VESPIARY
VERITATES	VERNACLE	VERSELETS	VERTICITY	VESPID
VERITE	VERNACLES	VERSEMAN	VERTIGO	VESPIDS
VERITES	VERNAL	VERSEMEN	VERTIGOES	VESPINE
VERITIES	VERNALISE	VERSER	VERTIGOS	VESPOID
VERITY	VERNALITY	VERSERS	VERTING	VESSAIL
VERJUICE	VERNALIZE	VERSES	VERTIPORT	VESSAILS
VERJUICED	VERNALLY	VERSET	VERTISOL	VESSEL
VERJUICES	VERNANT	VERSETS	VERTISOLS	VESSELED
VERJUS	VERNATION	VERSICLE	VERTS	VESSELS
VERJUSES	VERNICLE	VERSICLES	VERTU	VEST
VERKRAMP	VERNICLES	VERSIFIED	VERTUE	VESTA
VERLAN	VERNIER	VERSIFIER	VERTUES	VESTAL
VERLANS	VERNIERS	VERSIFIES	VERTUOUS	VESTALLY
VERLIG	VERNIX	VERSIFORM	VERTUS	VESTALS
VERLIGTE	VERNIXES	VERSIFY	VERVAIN	VESTAS

VESTED	VETKOEK	VIADUCT	VIBRATING	VICEROY
VESTEE	VETKOEKS	VIADUCTS	VIBRATION	VICEROYS
VESTEES	VETO	VIAE	VIBRATIVE	VICES
VESTIARY	VETOED	VIAL	VIBRATO	VICESIMAL
VESTIBULA	VETOER	VIALED	VIBRATOR	VICHIES
VESTIBULE	VETOERS	VIALFUL	VIBRATORS	VICHY
VESTIGE	VETOES	VIALFULS	VIBRATORY	VICIATE
VESTIGES	VETOING	VIALING	VIBRATOS	VICIATED
VESTIGIA	VETOLESS	VIALLED	VIBRIO	VICIATES
VESTIGIAL	VETS	VIALLING	VIBRIOID	VICIATING
VESTIGIUM	VETTED	VIALS	VIBRION	VICINAGE
VESTIMENT	VETTER	VIAMETER	VIBRIONIC	VICINAGES
VESTING	VETTERS	VIAMETERS	VIBRIONS	VICINAL
VESTINGS	VETTING	VIAND	VIBRIOS	VICING
VESTITURE	VETTINGS	VIANDS	VIBRIOSES	VICINITY
VESTLESS	VETTURA	VIAS	VIBRIOSIS	VICIOSITY
VESTLIKE	VETTURAS	VIATIC	VIBRISSA	VICIOUS
VESTMENT	VETTURINI	VIATICA	VIBRISSAE	VICIOUSLY
VESTMENTS	VETTURINO	VIATICAL	VIBRISSAL	VICOMTE
VESTRAL	VEX	VIATICALS	VIBRONIC	VICOMTES
VESTRIES	VEXATION	VIATICUM	VIBS	VICTIM
VESTRY	VEXATIONS	VIATICUMS	VIBURNUM	VICTIMISE
VESTRYMAN	VEXATIOUS	VIATOR	VIBURNUMS	VICTIMIZE
VESTRYMEN	VEXATORY	VIATORES	VICAR	VICTIMS
VESTS	VEXED	VIATORIAL	VICARAGE	VICTOR
VESTURAL	VEXEDLY	VIATORS	VICARAGES	VICTORESS
VESTURE	VEXEDNESS	VIBE	VICARATE	VICTORIA
VESTURED	VEXER	VIBES	VICARATES	VICTORIAS
VESTURER	VEXERS	VIBEX	VICARESS	VICTORIES
VESTURERS	VEXES	VIBEY	VICARIAL	VICTORINE
VESTURES	VEXIL	VIBICES	VICARIANT	VICTORS
VESTURING	VEXILLA	VIBIER	VICARIATE	VICTORY
VESUVIAN	VEXILLAR	VIBIEST	VICARIES	VICTRESS
VESUVIANS	VEXILLARY	VIBIST	VICARIOUS	VICTRIX
VET	VEXILLATE	VIBISTS	VICARLY	VICTRIXES
VETCH	VEXILLUM	VIBRACULA	VICARS	VICTROLA
VETCHES	VEXILS	VIBRAHARP	VICARSHIP	VICTROLAS
VETCHIER	VEXING	VIBRANCE	VICARY	VICTUAL
VETCHIEST	VEXINGLY	VIBRANCES	VICE	VICTUALED
VETCHLING	VEXINGS	VIBRANCY	VICED	VICTUALER
VETCHY	VEXT	VIBRANT	VICEGERAL	VICTUALS
VETERAN	VEZIR	VIBRANTLY	VICELESS	VICUGNA
VETERANS	VEZIRS	VIBRANTS	VICELIKE	VICUGNAS
VETIVER	VIA	VIBRATE	VICENARY	VICUNA
VETIVERS	VIABILITY	VIBRATED	VICENNIAL	VICUNAS
VETIVERT	VIABLE	VIBRATES	VICEREGAL	VID
VETIVERTS	VIABLY	VIBRATILE	VICEREINE	VIDALIA

VIDALIAS	VIEWBOOK	VIGORO	VILLAGERS	VINAS
VIDAME	VIEWBOOKS	VIGOROS	VILLAGERY	VINASSE
VIDAMES	VIEWDATA	VIGOROSO	VILLAGES	VINASSES
VIDE	VIEWDATAS	VIGOROUS	VILLAGEY	VINCA
VIDELICET	VIEWED	VIGORS	VILLAGIO	VINCAS
VIDENDA	VIEWER	VIGOUR	VILLAGIOS	VINCIBLE
VIDENDUM	VIEWERS	VIGOURS	VILLAGREE	VINCIBLY
VIDEO	VIEWIER	VIGS	VILLAIN	VINCULA
VIDEOCAM	VIEWIEST	VIHARA	VILLAINS	VINCULAR
VIDEOCAMS	VIEWINESS	VIHARAS	VILLAINY	VINCULUM
VIDEODISC	VIEWING	VIHUELA	VILLAN	VINCULUMS
VIDEODISK	VIEWINGS	VIHUELAS	VILLANAGE	VINDALOO
VIDEOED	VIEWLESS	VIKING	VILLANIES	VINDALOOS
VIDEOFIT	VIEWLY	VIKINGISM	VILLANOUS	VINDEMIAL
VIDEOFITS	VIEWPHONE	VIKINGS	VILLANS	VINDICATE
VIDEOGRAM	VIEWPOINT	VILAYET	VILLANY	VINE
VIDEOING	VIEWPORT	VILAYETS	VILLAR	VINEAL
VIDEOLAND	VIEWPORTS	VILD	VILLAS	VINED
VIDEOS	VIEWS	VILDE	VILLATIC	VINEGAR
VIDEOTAPE	VIEWSHED	VILDLY	VILLEIN	VINEGARED
VIDEOTEX	VIEWSHEDS	VILDNESS	VILLEINS	VINEGARS
VIDEOTEXT	VIEWY	VILE	VILLENAGE	VINEGARY
VIDETTE	VIFDA	VILELY	VILLI	VINELESS
VIDETTES	VIFDAS	VILENESS	VILLIACO	VINELIKE
VIDICON	VIFF	VILER	VILLIACOS	VINER
VIDICONS	VIFFED	VILEST	VILLIAGO	VINERIES
VIDIMUS	VIFFING	VILIACO	VILLIAGOS	VINERS
VIDIMUSES	VIFFS	VILIACOES	VILLIFORM	VINERY
VIDIOT	VIG	VILIACOS	VILLOSE	VINES
VIDIOTS	VIGA	VILIAGO	VILLOSITY	VINEW
VIDS	VIGAS	VILIAGOES	VILLOUS	VINEWED
VIDUAGE	VIGESIMAL	VILIAGOS	VILLOUSLY	VINEWING
VIDUAGES	VIGIA	VILIFIED	VILLS	VINEWS
VIDUAL	VIGIAS	VILIFIER	VILLUS	VINEYARD
VIDUITIES	VIGIL	VILIFIERS	VIM	VINEYARDS
VIDUITY	VIGILANCE	VILIFIES	VIMANA	VINIC
VIDUOUS	VIGILANT	VILIFY	VIMANAS	VINIER
VIE	VIGILANTE	VILIFYING	VIMEN	VINIEST
VIED	VIGILS	VILIPEND	VIMINA	VINIFERA
VIELLE	VIGNERON	VILIPENDS	VIMINAL	VINIFERAS
VIELLES	VIGNERONS	VILL	VIMINEOUS	VINIFIED
VIENNA	VIGNETTE	VILLA	VIMS	VINIFIES
VIER	VIGNETTED	VILLADOM	VIN	VINIFY
VIERS	VIGNETTER	VILLADOMS	VINA	VINIFYING
VIES	VIGNETTES	VILLAE	VINACEOUS	VINING
VIEW	VIGOR	VILLAGE	VINAL	VINO
VIEWABLE	VIGORISH	VILLAGER	VINALS	VINOLENT

VINOLOGY	VIOLERS	VIREO	VIRILIZE	VISA
VINOS	VIOLET	VIREONINE	VIRILIZED	VISAED
VINOSITY	VIOLETS	VIREOS	VIRILIZES	VISAGE
VINOUS	VIOLIN	VIRES	VIRILOCAL	VISAGED
VINOUSLY	VIOLINIST	VIRESCENT	VIRING	VISAGES
VINS	VIOLINS	VIRETOT	VIRINO	VISAGIST
VINT	VIOLIST	VIRETOTS	VIRINOS	VISAGISTE
VINTAGE	VIOLISTS	VIRGA	VIRION	VISAGISTS
VINTAGED	VIOLONE	VIRGAE	VIRIONS	VISAING
VINTAGER	VIOLONES	VIRGAS	VIRL	VISARD
VINTAGERS	VIOLS	VIRGATE	VIRLS	VISARDS
VINTAGES	VIOMYCIN	VIRGATES	VIROGENE	VISAS
VINTAGING	VIOMYCINS	VIRGE	VIROGENES	VISCACHA
VINTED	VIOSTEROL	VIRGER	VIROID	VISCACHAS
VINTING	VIPER	VIRGERS	VIROIDS	VISCARIA
VINTNER	VIPERFISH	VIRGES	VIROLOGIC	VISCARIAS
VINTNERS	VIPERINE	VIRGIN	VIROLOGY	VISCERA
VINTRIES	VIPERISH	VIRGINAL	VIROSE	VISCERAL
VINTRY	VIPEROUS	VIRGINALS	VIROSES	VISCERATE
VINTS	VIPERS	VIRGINED	VIROSIS	VISCID
VINY	VIRAEMIA	VIRGINIA	VIROUS	VISCIDITY
VINYL	VIRAEMIAS	VIRGINIAS	VIRTU	VISCIDLY
VINYLIC	VIRAEMIC	VIRGINING	VIRTUAL	VISCIN
VINYLS	VIRAGO	VIRGINITY	VIRTUALLY	VISCINS
VIOL	VIRAGOES	VIRGINIUM	VIRTUE	VISCOID
VIOLA	VIRAGOISH	VIRGINLY	VIRTUES	VISCOIDAL
VIOLABLE	VIRAGOS	VIRGINS	VIRTUOSA	VISCOSE
VIOLABLY	VIRAL	VIRGULATE	VIRTUOSAS	VISCOSES
VIOLAS	VIRALITY	VIRGULE	VIRTUOSE	VISCOSITY
VIOLATE	VIRALLY	VIRGULES	VIRTUOSI	VISCOUNT
VIOLATED	VIRALS	VIRICIDAL	VIRTUOSIC	VISCOUNTS
VIOLATER	VIRANDA	VIRICIDE	VIRTUOSO	VISCOUNTY
VIOLATERS	VIRANDAS	VIRICIDES	VIRTUOSOS	VISCOUS
VIOLATES	VIRANDO	VIRID	VIRTUOUS	VISCOUSLY
VIOLATING	VIRANDOS	VIRIDIAN	VIRTUS	VISCUM
VIOLATION	VIRE	VIRIDIANS	VIRUCIDAL	VISCUMS
VIOLATIVE	VIRED	VIRIDITE	VIRUCIDE	VISCUS
VIOLATOR	VIRELAI	VIRIDITES	VIRUCIDES	VISE
VIOLATORS	VIRELAIS	VIRIDITY	VIRULENCE	VISED
VIOLD	VIRELAY	VIRILE	VIRULENCY	VISEED
VIOLENCE	VIRELAYS	VIRILELY	VIRULENT	VISEING
VIOLENCES	VIREMENT	VIRILISE	VIRUS	VISELIKE
VIOLENT	VIREMENTS	VIRILISED	VIRUSES	VISES
VIOLENTED	VIREMIA	VIRILISES	VIRUSLIKE	VISHING
VIOLENTLY	VIREMIAS	VIRILISM	VIRUSOID	VISHINGS
VIOLENTS	VIREMIC	VIRILISMS	VIRUSOIDS	VISIBLE
VIOLER	VIRENT	VIRILITY	VIS	VISIBLES

V

VISIBLY
VISIE
VISIED
VISIEING
VISIER
VISIERS
VISIES
VISILE
VISILES
VISING
VISION
VISIONAL
VISIONARY
VISIONED
VISIONER
VISIONERS
VISIONING
VISIONIST
VISIONS
VISIT
VISITABLE
VISITANT
VISITANTS
VISITATOR
VISITE
VISITED
VISITEE
VISITEES
VISITER
VISITERS
VISITES
VISITING
VISITINGS
VISITOR
VISITORS
VISITRESS
VISITS
VISIVE
VISNE
VISNES
VISNOMIE
VISNOMIES
VISNOMY
VISON
VISONS
VISOR
VISORED

VISORING
VISORLESS
VISORS
VISTA
VISTAED
VISTAING
VISTAL
VISTALESS
VISTAS
VISTO
VISTOS
VISUAL
VISUALISE
VISUALIST
VISUALITY
VISUALIZE
VISUALLY
VISUALS
VITA
VITACEOUS
VITAE
VITAL
VITALISE
VITALISED
VITALISER
VITALISES
VITALISM
VITALISMS
VITALIST
VITALISTS
VITALITY
VITALIZE
VITALIZED
VITALIZER
VITALIZES
VITALLY
VITALNESS
VITALS
VITAMER
VITAMERS
VITAMIN
VITAMINE
VITAMINES
VITAMINIC
VITAMINS
VITAS
VITASCOPE

VITATIVE
VITE
VITELLARY
VITELLI
VITELLIN
VITELLINE
VITELLINS
VITELLUS
VITESSE
VITESSES
VITEX
VITEXES
VITIABLE
VITIATE
VITIATED
VITIATES
VITIATING
VITIATION
VITIATOR
VITIATORS
VITICETA
VITICETUM
VITICIDE
VITICIDES
VITILIGO
VITILIGOS
VITIOSITY
VITIOUS
VITRAGE
VITRAGES
VITRAIL
VITRAIN
VITRAINS
VITRAUX
VITREOUS
VITREUM
VITREUMS
VITRIC
VITRICS
VITRIFIED
VITRIFIES
VITRIFORM
VITRIFY
VITRINE
VITRINES
VITRIOL
VITRIOLED

VITRIOLIC
VITRIOLS
VITTA
VITTAE
VITTATE
VITTLE
VITTLED
VITTLES
VITTLING
VITULAR
VITULINE
VIVA
VIVACE
VIVACES
VIVACIOUS
VIVACITY
VIVAED
VIVAING
VIVAMENTE
VIVANDIER
VIVARIA
VIVARIES
VIVARIUM
VIVARIUMS
VIVARY
VIVAS
VIVAT
VIVATS
VIVDA
VIVDAS
VIVE
VIVELY
VIVENCIES
VIVENCY
VIVER
VIVERRA
VIVERRAS
VIVERRID
VIVERRIDS
VIVERRINE
VIVERS
VIVES
VIVIANITE
VIVID
VIVIDER
VIVIDEST
VIVIDITY

VIVIDLY
VIVIDNESS
VIVIFIC
VIVIFIED
VIVIFIER
VIVIFIERS
VIVIFIES
VIVIFY
VIVIFYING
VIVIPARA
VIVIPARY
VIVISECT
VIVISECTS
VIVO
VIVRES
VIXEN
VIXENISH
VIXENLY
VIXENS
VIZAMENT
VIZAMENTS
VIZARD
VIZARDED
VIZARDING
VIZARDS
VIZCACHA
VIZCACHAS
VIZIED
VIZIER
VIZIERATE
VIZIERIAL
VIZIERS
VIZIES
VIZIR
VIZIRATE
VIZIRATES
VIZIRIAL
VIZIRS
VIZIRSHIP
VIZOR
VIZORED
VIZORING
VIZORLESS
VIZORS
VIZSLA
VIZSLAS
VIZY

VIZYING	VOCATION	VOGUING	VOLAR	VOLPINO
VIZZIE	VOCATIONS	VOGUINGS	VOLARIES	VOLPINOS
VIZZIED	VOCATIVE	VOGUISH	VOLARY	VOLPLANE
VIZZIEING	VOCATIVES	VOGUISHLY	VOLATIC	VOLPLANED
VIZZIES	VOCES	VOICE	VOLATICS	VOLPLANES
VLEI	VOCODER	VOICED	VOLATILE	VOLS
VLEIS	VOCODERS	VOICEFUL	VOLATILES	VOLT
VLIES	VOCULAR	VOICELESS	VOLCANIAN	VOLTA
VLOG	VOCULE	VOICEMAIL	VOLCANIC	VOLTAGE
VLOGGED	VOCULES	VOICEOVER	VOLCANICS	VOLTAGES
VLOGGER	VODCAST	VOICER	VOLCANISE	VOLTAIC
VLOGGERS	VODCASTED	VOICERS	VOLCANISM	VOLTAISM
VLOGGING	VODCASTER	VOICES	VOLCANIST	VOLTAISMS
VLOGGINGS	VODCASTS	VOICING	VOLCANIZE	VOLTE
VLOGS	VODDIES	VOICINGS	VOLCANO	VOLTED
VLY	VODDY	VOID	VOLCANOES	VOLTES
VOAR	VODKA	VOIDABLE	VOLCANOS	VOLTI
VOARS	VODKAS	VOIDANCE	VOLE	VOLTIGEUR
VOCAB	VODOU	VOIDANCES	VOLED	VOLTING
VOCABLE	VODOUN	VOIDED	VOLENS	VOLTINISM
VOCABLES	VODOUNS	VOIDEE	VOLERIES	VOLTMETER
VOCABLY	VODOUS	VOIDEES	VOLERY	VOLTS
VOCABS	VODUN	VOIDER	VOLES	VOLUBIL
VOCABULAR	VODUNS	VOIDERS	VOLET	VOLUBLE
VOCAL	VOE	VOIDING	VOLETS	VOLUBLY
VOCALESE	VOEMA	VOIDINGS	VOLING	VOLUCRINE
VOCALESES	VOEMAS	VOIDNESS	VOLITANT	VOLUME
VOCALIC	VOERTSAK	VOIDS	VOLITATE	VOLUMED
VOCALICS	VOERTSEK	VOILA	VOLITATED	VOLUMES
VOCALION	VOES	VOILE	VOLITATES	VOLUMETER
VOCALIONS	VOETSAK	VOILES	VOLITIENT	VOLUMETRY
VOCALISE	VOETSEK	VOIP	VOLITION	VOLUMINAL
VOCALISED	VOG	VOIPS	VOLITIONS	VOLUMING
VOCALISER	VOGIE	VOISINAGE	VOLITIVE	VOLUMISE
VOCALISES	VOGIER	VOITURE	VOLITIVES	VOLUMISED
VOCALISM	VOGIEST	VOITURES	VOLK	VOLUMISER
VOCALISMS	VOGS	VOITURIER	VOLKS	VOLUMISES
VOCALIST	VOGUE	VOIVODE	VOLKSLIED	VOLUMIST
VOCALISTS	VOGUED	VOIVODES	VOLKSRAAD	VOLUMISTS
VOCALITY	VOGUEING	VOL	VOLLEY	VOLUMIZE
VOCALIZE	VOGUEINGS	VOLA	VOLLEYED	VOLUMIZED
VOCALIZED	VOGUER	VOLABLE	VOLLEYER	VOLUMIZER
VOCALIZER	VOGUERS	VOLAE	VOLLEYERS	VOLUMIZES
VOCALIZES	VOGUES	VOLAGE	VOLLEYING	VOLUNTARY
VOCALLY	VOGUEY	VOLANT	VOLLEYS	VOLUNTEER
VOCALNESS	VOGUIER	VOLANTE	VOLOST	VOLUSPA
VOCALS	VOGUIEST	VOLANTES	VOLOSTS	VOLUSPAS

VOLUTE	VONGOLE	VOTING	VOWELLED	VRYSTATER
VOLUTED	VOODOO	VOTINGS	VOWELLESS	VUG
VOLUTES	VOODOOED	VOTIVE	VOWELLING	VUGG
VOLUTIN	VOODOOING	VOTIVELY	VOWELLY	VUGGIER
VOLUTINS	VOODOOISM	VOTIVES	VOWELS	VUGGIEST
VOLUTION	VOODOOIST	VOTRESS	VOWER	VUGGS
VOLUTIONS	VOODOOS	VOTRESSES	VOWERS	VUGGY
VOLUTOID	VOORKAMER	VOUCH	VOWESS	VUGH
VOLVA	VOORSKOT	VOUCHED	VOWESSES	VUGHIER
VOLVAE	VOORSKOTS	VOUCHEE	VOWING	VUGHIEST
VOLVAS	VOR	VOUCHEES	VOWLESS	VUGHS
VOLVATE	VORACIOUS	VOUCHER	VOWS	VUGHY
VOLVE	VORACITY	VOUCHERED	VOX	VUGS
VOLVED	VORAGO	VOUCHERS	VOXEL	VUGULAR
VOLVES	VORAGOES	VOUCHES	VOXELS	VULCAN
VOLVING	VORAGOS	VOUCHING	VOYAGE	VULCANIAN
VOLVOX	VORANT	VOUCHSAFE	VOYAGED	VULCANIC
VOLVOXES	VORLAGE	VOUDON	VOYAGER	VULCANISE
VOLVULI	VORLAGES	VOUDONS	VOYAGERS	VULCANISM
VOLVULUS	VORPAL	VOUDOU	VOYAGES	VULCANIST
VOM	VORRED	VOUDOUED	VOYAGEUR	VULCANITE
VOMER	VORRING	VOUDOUING	VOYAGEURS	VULCANIZE
VOMERINE	VORS	VOUDOUN	VOYAGING	VULCANS
VOMERS	VORTEX	VOUDOUNS	VOYAGINGS	VULGAR
VOMICA	VORTEXES	VOUDOUS	VOYEUR	VULGARER
VOMICAE	VORTICAL	VOUGE	VOYEURISM	VULGAREST
VOMICAS	VORTICES	VOUGES	VOYEURS	VULGARIAN
VOMIT	VORTICISM	VOULGE	VOZHD	VULGARISE
VOMITED	VORTICIST	VOULGES	VOZHDS	VULGARISM
VOMITER	VORTICITY	VOULU	VRAIC	VULGARITY
VOMITERS	VORTICOSE	VOUSSOIR	VRAICKER	VULGARIZE
VOMITING	VOSTRO	VOUSSOIRS	VRAICKERS	VULGARLY
VOMITINGS	VOTABLE	VOUTSAFE	VRAICKING	VULGARS
VOMITIVE	VOTARESS	VOUTSAFED	VRAICS	VULGATE
VOMITIVES	VOTARIES	VOUTSAFES	VRIL	VULGATES
VOMITO	VOTARIST	VOUVRAY	VRILS	VULGO
VOMITORIA	VOTARISTS	VOUVRAYS	VROOM	VULGUS
VOMITORY	VOTARY	VOW	VROOMED	VULGUSES
VOMITOS	VOTE	VOWED	VROOMING	VULN
VOMITOUS	VOTEABLE	VOWEL	VROOMS	VULNED
VOMITS	VOTED	VOWELED	VROT	VULNERARY
VOMITUS	VOTEEN	VOWELISE	VROU	VULNERATE
VOMITUSES	VOTEENS	VOWELISED	VROUS	VULNING
VOMITY	VOTELESS	VOWELISES	VROUW	VULNS
VOMMED	VOTER	VOWELIZE	VROUWS	VULPICIDE
VOMMING	VOTERS	VOWELIZED	VROW	VULPINE
VOMS	VOTES	VOWELIZES	VROWS	VULPINISM

VULPINITE
VULSELLA
VULSELLAE
VULSELLUM
VULTURE
VULTURES
VULTURINE

VULTURISH
VULTURISM
VULTURN
VULTURNS
VULTUROUS
VULVA
VULVAE

VULVAL
VULVAR
VULVAS
VULVATE
VULVIFORM
VULVITIS
VUM

VUMMED
VUMMING
VUMS
VUTTIER
VUTTIEST
VUTTY
VUVUZELA

VUVUZELAS
VYING
VYINGLY
VYINGS

V

W

WAAC	WADD	WADMOLL	WAFFS	WAGGLIEST
WAACS	WADDED	WADMOLLS	WAFT	WAGGLING
WAAH	WADDER	WADMOLS	WAFTAGE	WAGGLY
WAB	WADDERS	WADS	WAFTAGES	WAGGON
WABAIN	WADDIE	WADSET	WAFTED	WAGGONED
WABAINS	WADDIED	WADSETS	WAFTER	WAGGONER
WABBIT	WADDIES	WADSETT	WAFTERS	WAGGONERS
WABBLE	WADDING	WADSETTED	WAFTING	WAGGONING
WABBLED	WADDINGS	WADSETTER	WAFTINGS	WAGGONS
WABBLER	WADDLE	WADSETTS	WAFTS	WAGHALTER
WABBLERS	WADDLED	WADT	WAFTURE	WAGING
WABBLES	WADDLER	WADTS	WAFTURES	WAGMOIRE
WABBLIER	WADDLERS	WADY	WAG	WAGMOIRES
WABBLIEST	WADDLES	WAE	WAGE	WAGON
WABBLING	WADDLIER	WAEFUL	WAGED	WAGONAGE
WABBLY	WADDLIEST	WAENESS	WAGELESS	WAGONAGES
WABOOM	WADDLING	WAENESSES	WAGENBOOM	WAGONED
WABOOMS	WADDLY	WAES	WAGER	WAGONER
WABS	WADDS	WAESOME	WAGERED	WAGONERS
WABSTER	WADDY	WAESUCK	WAGERER	WAGONETTE
WABSTERS	WADDYING	WAESUCKS	WAGERERS	WAGONFUL
WACK	WADE	WAFER	WAGERING	WAGONFULS
WACKE	WADEABLE	WAFERED	WAGERINGS	WAGONING
WACKED	WADED	WAFERING	WAGERS	WAGONLESS
WACKER	WADER	WAFERS	WAGES	WAGONLOAD
WACKERS	WADERS	WAFERY	WAGGA	WAGONS
WACKES	WADES	WAFF	WAGGAS	WAGS
WACKEST	WADGE	WAFFED	WAGGED	WAGSOME
WACKIER	WADGES	WAFFIE	WAGGER	WAGTAIL
WACKIEST	WADI	WAFFIES	WAGGERIES	WAGTAILS
WACKILY	WADIES	WAFFING	WAGGERS	WAGYU
WACKINESS	WADING	WAFFLE	WAGGERY	WAGYUS
WACKO	WADINGS	WAFFLED	WAGGING	WAHCONDA
WACKOES	WADIS	WAFFLER	WAGGISH	WAHCONDAS
WACKOS	WADMAAL	WAFFLERS	WAGGISHLY	WAHINE
WACKS	WADMAALS	WAFFLES	WAGGLE	WAHINES
WACKY	WADMAL	WAFFLIER	WAGGLED	WAHOO
WACONDA	WADMALS	WAFFLIEST	WAGGLER	WAHOOS
WACONDAS	WADMEL	WAFFLING	WAGGLERS	WAI
WAD	WADMELS	WAFFLINGS	WAGGLES	WAIATA
WADABLE	WADMOL	WAFFLY	WAGGLIER	WAIATAS

WAID	WAISTINGS	WAKEMAN	WALKAWAY	WALLIES
WAIDE	WAISTLESS	WAKEMEN	WALKAWAYS	WALLIEST
WAIF	WAISTLINE	WAKEN	WALKED	WALLING
WAIFED	WAISTS	WAKENED	WALKER	WALLINGS
WAIFING	WAIT	WAKENER	WALKERS	WALLOP
WAIFISH	WAITE	WAKENERS	WALKIES	WALLOPED
WAIFLIKE	WAITED	WAKENING	WALKING	WALLOPER
WAIFS	WAITER	WAKENINGS	WALKINGS	WALLOPERS
WAIFT	WAITERAGE	WAKENS	WALKMILL	WALLOPING
WAIFTS	WAITERED	WAKER	WALKMILLS	WALLOPS
WAIL	WAITERING	WAKERIFE	WALKOUT	WALLOW
WAILED	WAITERS	WAKERS	WALKOUTS	WALLOWED
WAILER	WAITES	WAKES	WALKOVER	WALLOWER
WAILERS	WAITING	WAKF	WALKOVERS	WALLOWERS
WAILFUL	WAITINGLY	WAKFS	WALKS	WALLOWING
WAILFULLY	WAITINGS	WAKIKI	WALKUP	WALLOWS
WAILING	WAITLIST	WAKIKIS	WALKUPS	WALLPAPER
WAILINGLY	WAITLISTS	WAKING	WALKWAY	WALLS
WAILINGS	WAITRESS	WAKINGS	WALKWAYS	WALLSEND
WAILS	WAITRON	WALD	WALKYRIE	WALLSENDS
WAILSOME	WAITRONS	WALDFLUTE	WALKYRIES	WALLWORT
WAIN	WAITS	WALDGRAVE	WALL	WALLWORTS
WAINAGE	WAITSTAFF	WALDHORN	WALLA	WALLY
WAINAGES	WAIVE	WALDHORNS	WALLABA	WALLYBALL
WAINED	WAIVED	WALDO	WALLABAS	WALLYDRAG
WAINING	WAIVER	WALDOES	WALLABIES	WALNUT
WAINS	WAIVERS	WALDOS	WALLABY	WALNUTS
WAINSCOT	WAIVES	WALDRAPP	WALLAH	WALRUS
WAINSCOTS	WAIVING	WALDRAPPS	WALLAHS	WALRUSES
WAIR	WAIVODE	WALDS	WALLAROO	WALTIER
WAIRED	WAIVODES	WALE	WALLAROOS	WALTIEST
WAIRING	WAIWODE	WALED	WALLAS	WALTY
WAIRS	WAIWODES	WALER	WALLBOARD	WALTZ
WAIRSH	WAKA	WALERS	WALLCHART	WALTZED
WAIRSHER	WAKAME	WALES	WALLED	WALTZER
WAIRSHEST	WAKAMES	WALI	WALLER	WALTZERS
WAIRUA	WAKANDA	WALIER	WALLERS	WALTZES
WAIRUAS	WAKANDAS	WALIES	WALLET	WALTZING
WAIS	WAKANE	WALIEST	WALLETS	WALTZINGS
WAIST	WAKANES	WALING	WALLEY	WALTZLIKE
WAISTBAND	WAKAS	WALIS	WALLEYE	WALY
WAISTBELT	WAKE	WALISE	WALLEYED	WAMBENGER
WAISTCOAT	WAKEBOARD	WALISES	WALLEYES	WAMBLE
WAISTED	WAKED	WALK	WALLEYS	WAMBLED
WAISTER	WAKEFUL	WALKABLE	WALLFISH	WAMBLES
WAISTERS	WAKEFULLY	WALKABOUT	WALLIE	WAMBLIER
WAISTING	WAKELESS	WALKATHON	WALLIER	WAMBLIEST

W

WAMBLING	WANEY	WANNESSES	WAPPED	WARDERED
WAMBLINGS	WANG	WANNEST	WAPPEND	WARDERING
WAMBLY	WANGAN	WANNIGAN	WAPPER	WARDERS
WAME	WANGANS	WANNIGANS	WAPPERED	WARDIAN
WAMED	WANGLE	WANNING	WAPPERING	WARDING
WAMEFOU	WANGLED	WANNION	WAPPERS	WARDINGS
WAMEFOUS	WANGLER	WANNIONS	WAPPING	WARDLESS
WAMEFUL	WANGLERS	WANNISH	WAPS	WARDMOTE
WAMEFULS	WANGLES	WANS	WAQF	WARDMOTES
WAMES	WANGLING	WANT	WAQFS	WARDOG
WAMMUL	WANGLINGS	WANTAGE	WAR	WARDOGS
WAMMULS	WANGS	WANTAGES	WARAGI	WARDRESS
WAMMUS	WANGUN	WANTAWAY	WARAGIS	WARDROBE
WAMMUSES	WANGUNS	WANTAWAYS	WARATAH	WARDROBED
WAMPEE	WANHOPE	WANTED	WARATAHS	WARDROBER
WAMPEES	WANHOPES	WANTER	WARB	WARDROBES
WAMPISH	WANIER	WANTERS	WARBIER	WARDROOM
WAMPISHED	WANIEST	WANTHILL	WARBIEST	WARDROOMS
WAMPISHES	WANIGAN	WANTHILLS	WARBIRD	WARDROP
WAMPUM	WANIGANS	WANTIES	WARBIRDS	WARDROPS
WAMPUMS	WANING	WANTING	WARBLE	WARDS
WAMPUS	WANINGS	WANTON	WARBLED	WARDSHIP
WAMPUSES	WANION	WANTONED	WARBLER	WARDSHIPS
WAMUS	WANIONS	WANTONER	WARBLERS	WARE
WAMUSES	WANK	WANTONERS	WARBLES	WARED
WAN	WANKED	WANTONEST	WARBLIER	WAREHOU
WANCHANCY	WANKER	WANTONING	WARBLIEST	WAREHOUS
WAND	WANKERS	WANTONISE	WARBLING	WAREHOUSE
WANDER	WANKIER	WANTONISE	WARBLINGS	WARELESS
WANDERED	WANKIEST	WANTONIZE	WARBLY	WAREROOM
WANDERER	WANKING	WANTONLY	WARBONNET	WAREROOMS
WANDERERS	WANKLE	WANTONS	WARBOT	WARES
WANDERING	WANKS	WANTS	WARBOTS	WAREZ
WANDEROO	WANKSTA	WANTY	WARBS	WARFARE
WANDEROOS	WANKSTAS	WANWORDY	WARBY	WARFARED
WANDERS	WANKY	WANWORTH	WARCRAFT	WARFARER
WANDLE	WANLE	WANWORTHS	WARCRAFTS	WARFARERS
WANDLED	WANLY	WANY	WARD	WARFARES
WANDLES	WANNA	WANZE	WARDCORN	WARFARIN
WANDLIKE	WANNABE	WANZED	WARDCORNS	WARFARING
WANDLING	WANNABEE	WANZES	WARDED	WARFARINS
WANDOO	WANNABEES	WANZING	WARDEN	WARGAME
WANDOOS	WANNABES	WAP	WARDENED	WARGAMED
WANDS	WANNED	WAPENSHAW	WARDENING	WARGAMER
WANE	WANNEL	WAPENTAKE	WARDENRY	WARGAMERS
WANED	WANNER	WAPINSHAW	WARDENS	WARGAMES
WANES	WANNESS	WAPITI	WARDER	WARGAMING
		WAPITIS		

WARHABLE	WARMOUTHS	WARRANTEE	WARTHOGS	WASHERED
WARHEAD	WARMS	WARRANTER	WARTIER	WASHERIES
WARHEADS	WARMTH	WARRANTOR	WARTIEST	WASHERING
WARHORSE	WARMTHS	WARRANTS	WARTIME	WASHERMAN
WARHORSES	WARMUP	WARRANTY	WARTIMES	WASHERMEN
WARIBASHI	WARMUPS	WARRAY	WARTLESS	WASHERS
WARIER	WARN	WARRAYED	WARTLIKE	WASHERY
WARIEST	WARNED	WARRAYING	WARTS	WASHES
WARILY	WARNER	WARRAYS	WARTWEED	WASHHAND
WARIMENT	WARNERS	WARRE	WARTWEEDS	WASHHOUSE
WARIMENTS	WARNING	WARRED	WARTWORT	WASHIER
WARINESS	WARNINGLY	WARREN	WARTWORTS	WASHIEST
WARING	WARNINGS	WARRENER	WARTY	WASHILY
WARISON	WARNS	WARRENERS	WARWOLF	WASHIN
WARISONS	WARP	WARRENS	WARWOLVES	WASHINESS
WARK	WARPAGE	WARREY	WARWORK	WASHING
WARKED	WARPAGES	WARREYED	WARWORKS	WASHINGS
WARKING	WARPAINT	WARREYING	WARWORN	WASHINS
WARKS	WARPAINTS	WARREYS	WARY	WASHLAND
WARLESS	WARPATH	WARRIGAL	WARZONE	WASHLANDS
WARLIKE	WARPATHS	WARRIGALS	WARZONES	WASHOUT
WARLING	WARPED	WARRING	WAS	WASHOUTS
WARLINGS	WARPER	WARRIOR	WASABI	WASHPOT
WARLOCK	WARPERS	WARRIORS	WASABIS	WASHPOTS
WARLOCKRY	WARPING	WARRISON	WASE	WASHRAG
WARLOCKS	WARPINGS	WARRISONS	WASES	WASHRAGS
WARLORD	WARPLANE	WARS	WASH	WASHROOM
WARLORDS	WARPLANES	WARSAW	WASHABLE	WASHROOMS
WARM	WARPOWER	WARSAWS	WASHABLES	WASHSTAND
WARMAKER	WARPOWERS	WARSHIP	WASHAWAY	WASHTUB
WARMAKERS	WARPS	WARSHIPS	WASHAWAYS	WASHTUBS
WARMAN	WARPWISE	WARSLE	WASHBAG	WASHUP
WARMBLOOD	WARRAGAL	WARSLED	WASHBAGS	WASHUPS
WARMED	WARRAGALS	WARSLER	WASHBALL	WASHWIPE
WARMEN	WARRAGLE	WARSLERS	WASHBALLS	WASHWIPES
WARMER	WARRAGLES	WARSLES	WASHBASIN	WASHWOMAN
WARMERS	WARRAGUL	WARSLING	WASHBOARD	WASHWOMEN
WARMEST	WARRAGULS	WARST	WASHBOWL	WASHY
WARMING	WARRAN	WARSTLE	WASHBOWLS	WASM
WARMINGS	WARRAND	WARSTLED	WASHCLOTH	WASMS
WARMISH	WARRANDED	WARSTLER	WASHDAY	WASP
WARMIST	WARRANDS	WARSTLERS	WASHDAYS	WASPIE
WARMISTS	WARRANED	WARSTLES	WASHDOWN	WASPIER
WARMLY	WARRANING	WARSTLING	WASHDOWNS	WASPIES
WARMNESS	WARRANS	WART	WASHED	WASPIEST
WARMONGER	WARRANT	WARTED	WASHEN	WASPILY
WARMOUTH	WARRANTED	WARTHOG	WASHER	WASPINESS

W

WASPISH	WASTREL	WATERDOG	WATTAPE	WAULKING
WASPISHLY	WASTRELS	WATERDOGS	WATTAPES	WAULKMILL
WASPLIKE	WASTRIE	WATERED	WATTER	WAULKS
WASPNEST	WASTRIES	WATERER	WATTEST	WAULS
WASPNESTS	WASTRIFE	WATERERS	WATTHOUR	WAUR
WASPS	WASTRIFES	WATERFALL	WATTHOURS	WAURED
WASPY	WASTRY	WATERFOWL	WATTLE	WAURING
WASSAIL	WASTS	WATERHEAD	WATTLED	WAURS
WASSAILED	WAT	WATERHEN	WATTLES	WAURST
WASSAILER	WATAP	WATERHENS	WATTLESS	WAVE
WASSAILRY	WATAPE	WATERIER	WATTLING	WAVEBAND
WASSAILS	WATAPES	WATERIEST	WATTLINGS	WAVEBANDS
WASSERMAN	WATAPS	WATERILY	WATTMETER	WAVED
WASSERMEN	WATCH	WATERING	WATTS	WAVEFORM
WASSUP	WATCHA	WATERINGS	WAUCHT	WAVEFORMS
WAST	WATCHABLE	WATERISH	WAUCHTED	WAVEFRONT
WASTABLE	WATCHBAND	WATERJET	WAUCHTING	WAVEGUIDE
WASTAGE	WATCHBOX	WATERJETS	WAUCHTS	WAVELESS
WASTAGES	WATCHCASE	WATERLEAF	WAUFF	WAVELET
WASTE	WATCHCRY	WATERLESS	WAUFFED	WAVELETS
WASTEBIN	WATCHDOG	WATERLILY	WAUFFING	WAVELIKE
WASTEBINS	WATCHDOGS	WATERLINE	WAUFFS	WAVELLITE
WASTED	WATCHED	WATERLOG	WAUGH	WAVEMETER
WASTEFUL	WATCHER	WATERLOGS	WAUGHED	WAVEOFF
WASTEL	WATCHERS	WATERLOO	WAUGHING	WAVEOFFS
WASTELAND	WATCHES	WATERLOOS	WAUGHS	WAVER
WASTELOT	WATCHET	WATERMAN	WAUGHT	WAVERED
WASTELOTS	WATCHETS	WATERMARK	WAUGHTED	WAVERER
WASTELS	WATCHEYE	WATERMEN	WAUGHTING	WAVERERS
WASTENESS	WATCHEYES	WATERMILL	WAUGHTS	WAVERIER
WASTER	WATCHFUL	WATERPOX	WAUK	WAVERIEST
WASTERED	WATCHING	WATERS	WAUKED	WAVERING
WASTERFUL	WATCHLIST	WATERSHED	WAUKER	WAVERINGS
WASTERIE	WATCHMAN	WATERSIDE	WAUKERS	WAVEROUS
WASTERIES	WATCHMEN	WATERSKI	WAUKING	WAVERS
WASTERING	WATCHOUT	WATERSKIS	WAUKMILL	WAVERY
WASTERS	WATCHOUTS	WATERWAY	WAUKMILLS	WAVES
WASTERY	WATCHWORD	WATERWAYS	WAUKRIFE	WAVESHAPE
WASTES	WATE	WATERWEED	WAUKS	WAVESON
WASTEWAY	WATER	WATERWORK	WAUL	WAVESONS
WASTEWAYS	WATERAGE	WATERWORN	WAULED	WAVETABLE
WASTEWEIR	WATERAGES	WATERY	WAULING	WAVEY
WASTFULL	WATERBED	WATERZOOI	WAULINGS	WAVEYS
WASTING	WATERBEDS	WATS	WAULK	WAVICLE
WASTINGLY	WATERBIRD	WATT	WAULKED	WAVICLES
WASTINGS	WATERBUCK	WATTAGE	WAULKER	WAVIER
WASTNESS	WATERBUS	WATTAGES	WAULKERS	WAVIES

WAVIEST	WAXWORK	WAYPOSTS	WEALD	WEARINGS
WAVILY	WAXWORKER	WAYS	WEALDS	WEARISH
WAVINESS	WAXWORKS	WAYSIDE	WEALS	WEARISOME
WAVING	WAXWORM	WAYSIDES	WEALSMAN	WEARPROOF
WAVINGS	WAXWORMS	WAYWARD	WEALSMEN	WEARS
WAVY	WAXY	WAYWARDLY	WEALTH	WEARY
WAW	WAY	WAYWISER	WEALTHIER	WEARYING
WAWA	WAYANG	WAYWISERS	WEALTHILY	WEASAND
WAWAED	WAYANGS	WAYWODE	WEALTHS	WEASANDS
WAWAING	WAYBILL	WAYWODES	WEALTHY	WEASEL
WAWAS	WAYBILLS	WAYWORN	WEAMB	WEASELED
WAWE	WAYBOARD	WAYZGOOSE	WEAMBS	WEASELER
WAWES	WAYBOARDS	WAZ	WEAN	WEASELERS
WAWL	WAYBREAD	WAZIR	WEANED	WEASELING
WAWLED	WAYBREADS	WAZIRS	WEANEL	WEASELLED
WAWLING	WAYED	WAZOO	WEANELS	WEASELLER
WAWLINGS	WAYFARE	WAZOOS	WEANER	WEASELLY
WAWLS	WAYFARED	WAZZ	WEANERS	WEASELS
WAWS	WAYFARER	WAZZED	WEANING	WEASELY
WAX	WAYFARERS	WAZZES	WEANINGS	WEASON
WAXABLE	WAYFARES	WAZZING	WEANLING	WEASONS
WAXBERRY	WAYFARING	WAZZOCK	WEANLINGS	WEATHER
WAXBILL	WAYGOING	WAZZOCKS	WEANS	WEATHERED
WAXBILLS	WAYGOINGS	WE	WEAPON	WEATHERER
WAXCLOTH	WAYGONE	WEAK	WEAPONED	WEATHERLY
WAXCLOTHS	WAYGOOSE	WEAKEN	WEAPONEER	WEATHERS
WAXED	WAYGOOSES	WEAKENED	WEAPONING	WEAVE
WAXEN	WAYING	WEAKENER	WEAPONISE	WEAVED
WAXER	WAYLAID	WEAKENERS	WEAPONIZE	WEAVER
WAXERS	WAYLAY	WEAKENING	WEAPONRY	WEAVERS
WAXES	WAYLAYER	WEAKENS	WEAPONS	WEAVES
WAXEYE	WAYLAYERS	WEAKER	WEAR	WEAVING
WAXEYES	WAYLAYING	WEAKEST	WEARABLE	WEAVINGS
WAXFLOWER	WAYLAYS	WEAKFISH	WEARABLES	WEAZAND
WAXIER	WAYLEAVE	WEAKISH	WEARED	WEAZANDS
WAXIEST	WAYLEAVES	WEAKISHLY	WEARER	WEAZEN
WAXILY	WAYLEGGO	WEAKLIER	WEARERS	WEAZENED
WAXINESS	WAYLESS	WEAKLIEST	WEARIED	WEAZENING
WAXING	WAYMARK	WEAKLING	WEARIER	WEAZENS
WAXINGS	WAYMARKED	WEAKLINGS	WEARIES	WEB
WAXLIKE	WAYMARKS	WEAKLY	WEARIEST	WEBAPP
WAXPLANT	WAYMENT	WEAKNESS	WEARIFUL	WEBAPPS
WAXPLANTS	WAYMENTED	WEAKON	WEARILESS	WEBBED
WAXWEED	WAYMENTS	WEAKONS	WEARILY	WEBBIE
WAXWEEDS	WAYPOINT	WEAKSIDE	WEARINESS	WEBBIER
WAXWING	WAYPOINTS	WEAKSIDES	WEARING	WEBBIES
WAXWINGS	WAYPOST	WEAL	WEARINGLY	WEBBIEST

W

WEBBING	WEBSTERS	WEEDBEDS	WEENING	WEFT
WEBBINGS	WEBWHEEL	WEEDED	WEENS	WEFTAGE
WEBBY	WEBWHEELS	WEEDER	WEENSIER	WEFTAGES
WEBCAM	WEBWORK	WEEDERIES	WEENSIEST	WEFTE
WEBCAMS	WEBWORKS	WEEDERS	WEENSY	WEFTED
WEBCAST	WEBWORM	WEEDERY	WEENY	WEFTES
WEBCASTED	WEBWORMS	WEEDHEAD	WEEP	WEFTING
WEBCASTER	WEBZINE	WEEDHEADS	WEEPER	WEFTS
WEBCASTS	WEBZINES	WEEDICIDE	WEEPERS	WEFTWISE
WEBCHAT	WECHT	WEEDIER	WEEPHOLE	WEID
WEBCHATS	WECHTED	WEEDIEST	WEEPHOLES	WEIDS
WEBER	WECHTING	WEEDILY	WEEPIE	WEIGELA
WEBERS	WECHTS	WEEDINESS	WEEPIER	WEIGELAS
WEBFED	WED	WEEDING	WEEPIES	WEIGELIA
WEBFEET	WEDDED	WEEDINGS	WEEPIEST	WEIGELIAS
WEBFOOT	WEDDER	WEEDLESS	WEEPILY	WEIGH
WEBFOOTED	WEDDERED	WEEDLIKE	WEEPINESS	WEIGHABLE
WEBHEAD	WEDDERING	WEEDLINE	WEEPING	WEIGHAGE
WEBHEADS	WEDDERS	WEEDLINES	WEEPINGLY	WEIGHAGES
WEBIFIED	WEDDING	WEEDS	WEEPINGS	WEIGHED
WEBIFIES	WEDDINGS	WEEDY	WEEPS	WEIGHER
WEBIFY	WEDEL	WEEING	WEEPY	WEIGHERS
WEBIFYING	WEDELED	WEEJUNS	WEER	WEIGHING
WEBINAR	WEDELING	WEEK	WEES	WEIGHINGS
WEBINARS	WEDELN	WEEKDAY	WEEST	WEIGHMAN
WEBISODE	WEDELNED	WEEKDAYS	WEET	WEIGHMEN
WEBISODES	WEDELNING	WEEKE	WEETE	WEIGHS
WEBLESS	WEDELNS	WEEKEND	WEETED	WEIGHT
WEBLIKE	WEDELS	WEEKENDED	WEETEN	WEIGHTAGE
WEBLISH	WEDGE	WEEKENDER	WEETER	WEIGHTED
WEBLISHES	WEDGED	WEEKENDS	WEETEST	WEIGHTER
WEBLOG	WEDGELIKE	WEEKES	WEETING	WEIGHTERS
WEBLOGGER	WEDGES	WEEKLIES	WEETINGLY	WEIGHTIER
WEBLOGS	WEDGEWISE	WEEKLONG	WEETLESS	WEIGHTILY
WEBMAIL	WEDGIE	WEEKLY	WEETS	WEIGHTING
WEBMAILS	WEDGIER	WEEKNIGHT	WEEVER	WEIGHTS
WEBMASTER	WEDGIES	WEEKS	WEEVERS	WEIGHTY
WEBPAGE	WEDGIEST	WEEL	WEEVIL	WEIL
WEBPAGES	WEDGING	WEELS	WEEVILED	WEILS
WEBRING	WEDGINGS	WEEM	WEEVILLED	WEINER
WEBRINGS	WEDGY	WEEMS	WEEVILLY	WEINERS
WEBS	WEDLOCK	WEEN	WEEVILS	WEIR
WEBSITE	WEDLOCKS	WEENED	WEEVILY	WEIRD
WEBSITES	WEDS	WEENIE	WEEWEE	WEIRDED
WEBSPACE	WEE	WEENIER	WEEWEED	WEIRDER
WEBSPACES	WEED	WEENIES	WEEWEEING	WEIRDEST
WEBSTER	WEEDBED	WEENIEST	WEEWEES	WEIRDIE

W

WEIRDIES	WELDOR	WELSHER	WERGELDS	WETBACK
WEIRDING	WELDORS	WELSHERS	WERGELT	WETBACKS
WEIRDLY	WELDS	WELSHES	WERGELTS	WETHER
WEIRDNESS	WELFARE	WELSHING	WERGILD	WETHERS
WEIRDO	WELFARES	WELT	WERGILDS	WETLAND
WEIRDOES	WELFARISM	WELTED	WERNERITE	WETLANDS
WEIRDOS	WELFARIST	WELTER	WERO	WETLY
WEIRDS	WELFARITE	WELTERED	WEROS	WETNESS
WEIRDY	WELK	WELTERING	WERRIS	WETNESSES
WEIRED	WELKE	WELTERS	WERRISES	WETPROOF
WEIRING	WELKED	WELTING	WERSH	WETS
WEIRS	WELKES	WELTINGS	WERSHER	WETSUIT
WEISE	WELKIN	WELTS	WERSHEST	WETSUITS
WEISED	WELKING	WEM	WERT	WETTABLE
WEISES	WELKINS	WEMB	WERWOLF	WETTED
WEISING	WELKS	WEMBS	WERWOLVES	WETTER
WEIZE	WELKT	WEMS	WESAND	WETTERS
WEIZED	WELL	WEN	WESANDS	WETTEST
WEIZES	WELLADAY	WENA	WESKIT	WETTIE
WEIZING	WELLADAYS	WENCH	WESKITS	WETTIES
WEKA	WELLANEAR	WENCHED	WESSAND	WETTING
WEKAS	WELLAWAY	WENCHER	WESSANDS	WETTINGS
WELAWAY	WELLAWAYS	WENCHERS	WEST	WETTISH
WELCH	WELLBEING	WENCHES	WESTABOUT	WETWARE
WELCHED	WELLBORN	WENCHING	WESTBOUND	WETWARES
WELCHER	WELLCURB	WEND	WESTED	WEX
WELCHERS	WELLCURBS	WENDED	WESTER	WEXE
WELCHES	WELLDOER	WENDIGO	WESTERED	WEXED
WELCHING	WELLDOERS	WENDIGOES	WESTERING	WEXES
WELCOME	WELLED	WENDIGOS	WESTERLY	WEXING
WELCOMED	WELLHEAD	WENDING	WESTERN	WEY
WELCOMELY	WELLHEADS	WENDS	WESTERNER	WEYARD
WELCOMER	WELLHOLE	WENGE	WESTERNS	WEYS
WELCOMERS	WELLHOLES	WENGES	WESTERS	WEYWARD
WELCOMES	WELLHOUSE	WENNIER	WESTIE	WEZAND
WELCOMING	WELLIE	WENNIEST	WESTIES	WEZANDS
WELD	WELLIES	WENNISH	WESTING	WHA
WELDABLE	WELLING	WENNY	WESTINGS	WHACK
WELDED	WELLINGS	WENS	WESTLIN	WHACKED
WELDER	WELLNESS	WENT	WESTLINS	WHACKER
WELDERS	WELLS	WENTS	WESTMOST	WHACKERS
WELDING	WELLSITE	WEPT	WESTS	WHACKIER
WELDINGS	WELLSITES	WERE	WESTWARD	WHACKIEST
WELDLESS	WELLY	WEREGILD	WESTWARDS	WHACKING
WELDMENT	WELS	WEREGILDS	WET	WHACKINGS
WELDMENTS	WELSH	WEREWOLF	WETA	WHACKO
WELDMESH	WELSHED	WERGELD	WETAS	WHACKOES

W

WHACKOS	WHANGED	WHAUR	WHEELSMEN	WHELKY
WHACKS	WHANGEE	WHAURS	WHEELSPIN	WHELM
WHACKY	WHANGEES	WHEAL	WHEELWORK	WHELMED
WHAE	WHANGING	WHEALS	WHEELY	WHELMING
WHAISLE	WHANGS	WHEAR	WHEEN	WHELMS
WHAISLED	WHAP	WHEARE	WHEENGE	WHELP
WHAISLES	WHAPPED	WHEAT	WHEENGED	WHELPED
WHAISLING	WHAPPER	WHEATEAR	WHEENGES	WHELPING
WHAIZLE	WHAPPERS	WHEATEARS	WHEENGING	WHELPLESS
WHAIZLED	WHAPPING	WHEATEN	WHEENS	WHELPS
WHAIZLES	WHAPS	WHEATENS	WHEEP	WHEMMLE
WHAIZLING	WHARE	WHEATGERM	WHEEPED	WHEMMLED
WHAKAIRO	WHARENUI	WHEATIER	WHEEPING	WHEMMLES
WHAKAIROS	WHARENUIS	WHEATIEST	WHEEPLE	WHEMMLING
WHAKAPAPA	WHAREPUNI	WHEATLAND	WHEEPLED	WHEN
WHALE	WHARES	WHEATLESS	WHEEPLES	WHENAS
WHALEBACK	WHARF	WHEATMEAL	WHEEPLING	WHENCE
WHALEBOAT	WHARFAGE	WHEATS	WHEEPS	WHENCES
WHALEBONE	WHARFAGES	WHEATWORM	WHEESH	WHENCEVER
WHALED	WHARFED	WHEATY	WHEESHED	WHENEVER
WHALELIKE	WHARFIE	WHEE	WHEESHES	WHENS
WHALEMAN	WHARFIES	WHEECH	WHEESHING	WHENUA
WHALEMEN	WHARFING	WHEECHED	WHEESHT	WHENUAS
WHALER	WHARFINGS	WHEECHING	WHEESHTED	WHENWE
WHALERIES	WHARFS	WHEECHS	WHEESHTS	WHENWES
WHALERS	WHARVE	WHEEDLE	WHEEZE	WHERE
WHALERY	WHARVES	WHEEDLED	WHEEZED	WHEREAS
WHALES	WHAT	WHEEDLER	WHEEZER	WHEREASES
WHALING	WHATA	WHEEDLERS	WHEEZERS	WHEREAT
WHALINGS	WHATAS	WHEEDLES	WHEEZES	WHEREBY
WHALLY	WHATCHA	WHEEDLING	WHEEZIER	WHEREFOR
WHAM	WHATEN	WHEEL	WHEEZIEST	WHEREFORE
WHAMMED	WHATEVER	WHEELBASE	WHEEZILY	WHEREFORS
WHAMMIES	WHATEVS	WHEELED	WHEEZING	WHEREFROM
WHAMMING	WHATNA	WHEELER	WHEEZINGS	WHEREIN
WHAMMO	WHATNESS	WHEELERS	WHEEZLE	WHEREINTO
WHAMMOS	WHATNOT	WHEELIE	WHEEZLED	WHERENESS
WHAMMY	WHATNOTS	WHEELIER	WHEEZLES	WHEREOF
WHAMO	WHATS	WHEELIES	WHEEZLING	WHEREON
WHAMPLE	WHATSIS	WHEELIEST	WHEEZY	WHEREOUT
WHAMPLES	WHATSISES	WHEELING	WHEFT	WHERES
WHAMS	WHATSIT	WHEELINGS	WHEFTS	WHERESO
WHANAU	WHATSITS	WHEELLESS	WHELK	WHERETO
WHANAUS	WHATSO	WHEELMAN	WHELKED	WHEREUNTO
WHANG	WHATTEN	WHEELMEN	WHELKIER	WHEREUPON
WHANGAM	WHAUP	WHEELS	WHELKIEST	WHEREVER
WHANGAMS	WHAUPS	WHEELSMAN	WHELKS	WHEREWITH

W

WHERRET
WHERRETED
WHERRETS
WHERRIED
WHERRIES
WHERRIT
WHERRITED
WHERRITS
WHERRY
WHERRYING
WHERRYMAN
WHERRYMEN
WHERVE
WHERVES
WHET
WHETHER
WHETS
WHETSTONE
WHETTED
WHETTER
WHETTERS
WHETTING
WHEUGH
WHEUGHED
WHEUGHING
WHEUGHS
WHEW
WHEWED
WHEWING
WHEWS
WHEY
WHEYEY
WHEYFACE
WHEYFACED
WHEYFACES
WHEYIER
WHEYIEST
WHEYISH
WHEYLIKE
WHEYS
WHICH
WHICHEVER
WHICKER
WHICKERED
WHICKERS
WHID
WHIDAH

WHIDAHS
WHIDDED
WHIDDER
WHIDDERED
WHIDDERS
WHIDDING
WHIDS
WHIFF
WHIFFED
WHIFFER
WHIFFERS
WHIFFET
WHIFFETS
WHIFFIER
WHIFFIEST
WHIFFING
WHIFFINGS
WHIFFLE
WHIFFLED
WHIFFLER
WHIFFLERS
WHIFFLERY
WHIFFLES
WHIFFLING
WHIFFS
WHIFFY
WHIFT
WHIFTS
WHIG
WHIGGED
WHIGGING
WHIGS
WHILE
WHILED
WHILERE
WHILES
WHILEVER
WHILING
WHILK
WHILLIED
WHILLIES
WHILLY
WHILLYING
WHILLYWHA
WHILOM
WHILST
WHIM

WHIMBERRY
WHIMBREL
WHIMBRELS
WHIMMED
WHIMMIER
WHIMMIEST
WHIMMING
WHIMMY
WHIMPER
WHIMPERED
WHIMPERER
WHIMPERS
WHIMPLE
WHIMPLED
WHIMPLES
WHIMPLING
WHIMS
WHIMSEY
WHIMSEYS
WHIMSICAL
WHIMSIED
WHIMSIER
WHIMSIES
WHIMSIEST
WHIMSILY
WHIMSY
WHIN
WHINBERRY
WHINCHAT
WHINCHATS
WHINE
WHINED
WHINER
WHINERS
WHINES
WHINEY
WHINGDING
WHINGE
WHINGED
WHINGEING
WHINGER
WHINGERS
WHINGES
WHINGIER
WHINGIEST
WHINGING
WHINGY

WHINIARD
WHINIARDS
WHINIER
WHINIEST
WHININESS
WHINING
WHININGLY
WHININGS
WHINNIED
WHINNIER
WHINNIES
WHINNIEST
WHINNY
WHINNYING
WHINS
WHINSTONE
WHINY
WHINYARD
WHINYARDS
WHIO
WHIOS
WHIP
WHIPBIRD
WHIPBIRDS
WHIPCAT
WHIPCATS
WHIPCORD
WHIPCORDS
WHIPCORDY
WHIPJACK
WHIPJACKS
WHIPLASH
WHIPLESS
WHIPLIKE
WHIPPED
WHIPPER
WHIPPERS
WHIPPET
WHIPPETS
WHIPPIER
WHIPPIEST
WHIPPING
WHIPPINGS
WHIPPIT
WHIPPITS
WHIPPY
WHIPRAY

WHIPRAYS
WHIPS
WHIPSAW
WHIPSAWED
WHIPSAWN
WHIPSAWS
WHIPSNAKE
WHIPSTAFF
WHIPSTALL
WHIPSTER
WHIPSTERS
WHIPSTOCK
WHIPT
WHIPTAIL
WHIPTAILS
WHIPWORM
WHIPWORMS
WHIR
WHIRL
WHIRLBAT
WHIRLBATS
WHIRLED
WHIRLER
WHIRLERS
WHIRLIER
WHIRLIES
WHIRLIEST
WHIRLIGIG
WHIRLING
WHIRLINGS
WHIRLPOOL
WHIRLS
WHIRLWIND
WHIRLY
WHIRR
WHIRRED
WHIRRET
WHIRRETED
WHIRRETS
WHIRRIED
WHIRRIER
WHIRRIES
WHIRRIEST
WHIRRING
WHIRRINGS
WHIRRS
WHIRRY

W

WHIRRYING	WHITEBAIT	WHITLINGS	WHOEVER	WHOOPER
WHIRS	WHITEBASS	WHITLOW	WHOLE	WHOOPERS
WHIRTLE	WHITEBEAM	WHITLOWS	WHOLEFOOD	WHOOPIE
WHIRTLES	WHITECAP	WHITRACK	WHOLEMEAL	WHOOPIES
WHISH	WHITECAPS	WHITRACKS	WHOLENESS	WHOOPING
WHISHED	WHITECOAT	WHITRET	WHOLES	WHOOPINGS
WHISHES	WHITECOMB	WHITRETS	WHOLESALE	WHOOPLA
WHISHING	WHITED	WHITRICK	WHOLESOME	WHOOPLAS
WHISHT	WHITEDAMP	WHITRICKS	WHOLISM	WHOOPS
WHISHTED	WHITEFACE	WHITS	WHOLISMS	WHOOPSIE
WHISHTING	WHITEFISH	WHITSTER	WHOLIST	WHOOPSIES
WHISHTS	WHITEFLY	WHITSTERS	WHOLISTIC	WHOOSH
WHISK	WHITEHEAD	WHITTAW	WHOLISTS	WHOOSHED
WHISKED	WHITELIST	WHITTAWER	WHOLLY	WHOOSHES
WHISKER	WHITELY	WHITTAWS	WHOLPHIN	WHOOSHING
WHISKERED	WHITEN	WHITTER	WHOLPHINS	WHOOSIS
WHISKERS	WHITENED	WHITTERED	WHOM	WHOOSISES
WHISKERY	WHITENER	WHITTERS	WHOMBLE	WHOOT
WHISKET	WHITENERS	WHITTLE	WHOMBLED	WHOOTED
WHISKETS	WHITENESS	WHITTLED	WHOMBLES	WHOOTING
WHISKEY	WHITENING	WHITTLER	WHOMBLING	WHOOTS
WHISKEYS	WHITENS	WHITTLERS	WHOMEVER	WHOP
WHISKIES	WHITEOUT	WHITTLES	WHOMMLE	WHOPPED
WHISKING	WHITEOUTS	WHITTLING	WHOMMLED	WHOPPER
WHISKS	WHITEPOT	WHITTRET	WHOMMLES	WHOPPERS
WHISKY	WHITEPOTS	WHITTRETS	WHOMMLING	WHOPPING
WHISPER	WHITER	WHITY	WHOMP	WHOPPINGS
WHISPERED	WHITES	WHIZ	WHOMPED	WHOPS
WHISPERER	WHITEST	WHIZBANG	WHOMPING	WHORE
WHISPERS	WHITETAIL	WHIZBANGS	WHOMPS	WHORED
WHISPERY	WHITEWALL	WHIZZ	WHOMSO	WHOREDOM
WHISS	WHITEWARE	WHIZZBANG	WHOOBUB	WHOREDOMS
WHISSED	WHITEWASH	WHIZZED	WHOOBUBS	WHORES
WHISSES	WHITEWING	WHIZZER	WHOOF	WHORESON
WHISSING	WHITEWOOD	WHIZZERS	WHOOFED	WHORESONS
WHIST	WHITEY	WHIZZES	WHOOFING	WHORING
WHISTED	WHITEYS	WHIZZIER	WHOOFS	WHORINGS
WHISTING	WHITHER	WHIZZIEST	WHOOMP	WHORISH
WHISTLE	WHITHERED	WHIZZING	WHOOMPH	WHORISHLY
WHISTLED	WHITHERS	WHIZZINGS	WHOOMPHS	WHORL
WHISTLER	WHITIER	WHIZZO	WHOOMPS	WHORLBAT
WHISTLERS	WHITIES	WHIZZY	WHOONGA	WHORLBATS
WHISTLES	WHITIEST	WHO	WHOONGAS	WHORLED
WHISTLING	WHITING	WHOA	WHOOP	WHORLING
WHISTS	WHITINGS	WHODUNIT	WHOOPED	WHORLS
WHIT	WHITISH	WHODUNITS	WHOOPEE	WHORT
WHITE	WHITLING	WHODUNNIT	WHOOPEES	WHORTLE

WHORTLES	WICCAS	WIDEN	WIELDY	WIGGLIER
WHORTS	WICE	WIDENED	WIELS	WIGGLIEST
WHOSE	WICH	WIDENER	WIENER	WIGGLING
WHOSESO	WICHES	WIDENERS	WIENERS	WIGGLY
WHOSEVER	WICK	WIDENESS	WIENIE	WIGGY
WHOSIS	WICKAPE	WIDENING	WIENIES	WIGHT
WHOSISES	WICKAPES	WIDENINGS	WIFE	WIGHTED
WHOSIT	WICKED	WIDENS	WIFED	WIGHTING
WHOSITS	WICKEDER	WIDEOUT	WIFEDOM	WIGHTLY
WHOSO	WICKEDEST	WIDEOUTS	WIFEDOMS	WIGHTS
WHOSOEVER	WICKEDLY	WIDER	WIFEHOOD	WIGLESS
WHOT	WICKEDS	WIDES	WIFEHOODS	WIGLET
WHOW	WICKEN	WIDEST	WIFELESS	WIGLETS
WHOWED	WICKENS	WIDGEON	WIFELIER	WIGLIKE
WHOWING	WICKER	WIDGEONS	WIFELIEST	WIGMAKER
WHOWS	WICKERED	WIDGET	WIFELIKE	WIGMAKERS
WHUMMLE	WICKERS	WIDGETS	WIFELY	WIGS
WHUMMLED	WICKET	WIDGIE	WIFES	WIGWAG
WHUMMLES	WICKETS	WIDGIES	WIFEY	WIGWAGGED
WHUMMLING	WICKIES	WIDISH	WIFEYS	WIGWAGGER
WHUMP	WICKING	WIDOW	WIFIE	WIGWAGS
WHUMPED	WICKINGS	WIDOWBIRD	WIFIES	WIGWAM
WHUMPING	WICKIUP	WIDOWED	WIFING	WIGWAMS
WHUMPS	WICKIUPS	WIDOWER	WIFTIER	WIKI
WHUNSTANE	WICKLESS	WIDOWERED	WIFTIEST	WIKIALITY
WHUP	WICKS	WIDOWERS	WIFTY	WIKIS
WHUPPED	WICKTHING	WIDOWHOOD	WIG	WIKIUP
WHUPPING	WICKY	WIDOWING	WIGAN	WIKIUPS
WHUPPINGS	WICKYUP	WIDOWMAN	WIGANS	WILCO
WHUPS	WICKYUPS	WIDOWMEN	WIGEON	WILD
WHY	WICOPIES	WIDOWS	WIGEONS	WILDCARD
WHYDA	WICOPY	WIDTH	WIGGA	WILDCARDS
WHYDAH	WIDDER	WIDTHS	WIGGAS	WILDCAT
WHYDAHS	WIDDERS	WIDTHWAY	WIGGED	WILDCATS
WHYDAS	WIDDIE	WIDTHWAYS	WIGGER	WILDED
WHYDUNIT	WIDDIES	WIDTHWISE	WIGGERIES	WILDER
WHYDUNITS	WIDDLE	WIEL	WIGGERS	WILDERED
WHYDUNNIT	WIDDLED	WIELD	WIGGERY	WILDERING
WHYEVER	WIDDLES	WIELDABLE	WIGGIER	WILDERS
WHYS	WIDDLING	WIELDED	WIGGIEST	WILDEST
WIBBLE	WIDDY	WIELDER	WIGGING	WILDFIRE
WIBBLED	WIDE	WIELDERS	WIGGINGS	WILDFIRES
WIBBLES	WIDEAWAKE	WIELDIER	WIGGLE	WILDFOWL
WIBBLING	WIDEBAND	WIELDIEST	WIGGLED	WILDFOWLS
WICCA	WIDEBANDS	WIELDING	WIGGLER	WILDGRAVE
WICCAN	WIDEBODY	WIELDLESS	WIGGLERS	WILDING
WICCANS	WIDELY	WIELDS	WIGGLES	WILDINGS

W

WILDISH	WILLIED	WIMPISHLY	WINDBREAK	WINDPACK
WILDLAND	WILLIES	WIMPLE	WINDBURN	WINDPACKS
WILDLANDS	WILLING	WIMPLED	WINDBURNS	WINDPIPE
WILDLIFE	WILLINGER	WIMPLES	WINDBURNT	WINDPIPES
WILDLIFES	WILLINGLY	WIMPLING	WINDCHILL	WINDPROOF
WILDLING	WILLIWAU	WIMPS	WINDED	WINDRING
WILDLINGS	WILLIWAUS	WIMPY	WINDER	WINDROW
WILDLY	WILLIWAW	WIN	WINDERS	WINDROWED
WILDNESS	WILLIWAWS	WINCE	WINDFALL	WINDROWER
WILDS	WILLOW	WINCED	WINDFALLS	WINDROWS
WILDWOOD	WILLOWED	WINCER	WINDFLAW	WINDS
WILDWOODS	WILLOWER	WINCERS	WINDFLAWS	WINDSAIL
WILE	WILLOWERS	WINCES	WINDGALL	WINDSAILS
WILED	WILLOWIER	WINCEY	WINDGALLS	WINDSES
WILEFUL	WILLOWING	WINCEYS	WINDGUN	WINDSHAKE
WILES	WILLOWISH	WINCH	WINDGUNS	WINDSHIP
WILFUL	WILLOWS	WINCHED	WINDHOVER	WINDSHIPS
WILFULLY	WILLOWY	WINCHER	WINDIER	WINDSLAB
WILGA	WILLPOWER	WINCHERS	WINDIEST	WINDSLABS
WILGAS	WILLS	WINCHES	WINDIGO	WINDSOCK
WILI	WILLY	WINCHING	WINDIGOES	WINDSOCKS
WILIER	WILLYARD	WINCHMAN	WINDIGOS	WINDSTORM
WILIEST	WILLYART	WINCHMEN	WINDILY	WINDSURF
WILILY	WILLYING	WINCING	WINDINESS	WINDSURFS
WILINESS	WILLYWAW	WINCINGLY	WINDING	WINDSWEPT
WILING	WILLYWAWS	WINCINGS	WINDINGLY	WINDTHROW
WILIS	WILT	WINCOPIPE	WINDINGS	WINDTIGHT
WILJA	WILTED	WIND	WINDLASS	WINDUP
WILJAS	WILTING	WINDABLE	WINDLE	WINDUPS
WILL	WILTJA	WINDAC	WINDLED	WINDWARD
WILLABLE	WILTJAS	WINDACS	WINDLES	WINDWARDS
WILLED	WILTS	WINDAGE	WINDLESS	WINDWAY
WILLEMITE	WILY	WINDAGES	WINDLING	WINDWAYS
WILLER	WIMBLE	WINDAS	WINDLINGS	WINDY
WILLERS	WIMBLED	WINDASES	WINDLOAD	WINE
WILLEST	WIMBLES	WINDBAG	WINDLOADS	WINEBERRY
WILLET	WIMBLING	WINDBAGS	WINDMILL	WINED
WILLETS	WIMBREL	WINDBELL	WINDMILLS	WINEGLASS
WILLEY	WIMBRELS	WINDBELLS	WINDOCK	WINELESS
WILLEYED	WIMMIN	WINDBILL	WINDOCKS	WINEMAKER
WILLEYING	WIMP	WINDBILLS	WINDORE	WINEPRESS
WILLEYS	WIMPED	WINDBLAST	WINDORES	WINERIES
WILLFUL	WIMPIER	WINDBLOW	WINDOW	WINERY
WILLFULLY	WIMPIEST	WINDBLOWN	WINDOWED	WINES
WILLIAM	WIMPINESS	WINDBLOWS	WINDOWING	WINESAP
WILLIAMS	WIMPING	WINDBORNE	WINDOWS	WINESAPS
WILLIE	WIMPISH	WINDBOUND	WINDOWY	WINESHOP

W

WINESHOPS	WINISH	WINSOMEST	WIREHAIRS	WISEGUYS
WINESKIN	WINK	WINTER	WIRELESS	WISELIER
WINESKINS	WINKED	WINTERED	WIRELIKE	WISELIEST
WINESOP	WINKER	WINTERER	WIRELINE	WISELING
WINESOPS	WINKERS	WINTERERS	WIRELINES	WISELINGS
WINEY	WINKING	WINTERFED	WIREMAN	WISELY
WING	WINKINGLY	WINTERIER	WIREMEN	WISENESS
WINGBACK	WINKINGS	WINTERING	WIREPHOTO	WISENT
WINGBACKS	WINKLE	WINTERISE	WIRER	WISENTS
WINGBEAT	WINKLED	WINTERISH	WIRERS	WISER
WINGBEATS	WINKLER	WINTERIZE	WIRES	WISES
WINGBOW	WINKLERS	WINTERLY	WIRETAP	WISEST
WINGBOWS	WINKLES	WINTERS	WIRETAPS	WISEWOMAN
WINGCHAIR	WINKLING	WINTERY	WIREWAY	WISEWOMEN
WINGDING	WINKS	WINTLE	WIREWAYS	WISH
WINGDINGS	WINLESS	WINTLED	WIREWORK	WISHA
WINGE	WINN	WINTLES	WIREWORKS	WISHBONE
WINGED	WINNA	WINTLING	WIREWORM	WISHBONES
WINGEDLY	WINNABLE	WINTRIER	WIREWORMS	WISHED
WINGEING	WINNARD	WINTRIEST	WIREWOVE	WISHER
WINGER	WINNARDS	WINTRILY	WIRIER	WISHERS
WINGERS	WINNED	WINTRY	WIRIEST	WISHES
WINGES	WINNER	WINY	WIRILDA	WISHFUL
WINGIER	WINNERS	WINZE	WIRILDAS	WISHFULLY
WINGIEST	WINNING	WINZES	WIRILY	WISHING
WINGING	WINNINGLY	WIPE	WIRINESS	WISHINGS
WINGLESS	WINNINGS	WIPEABLE	WIRING	WISHLESS
WINGLET	WINNLE	WIPED	WIRINGS	WISHT
WINGLETS	WINNLES	WIPEOUT	WIRRA	WISING
WINGLIKE	WINNOCK	WIPEOUTS	WIRRAH	WISKET
WINGMAN	WINNOCKS	WIPER	WIRRAHS	WISKETS
WINGMEN	WINNOW	WIPERS	WIRRICOW	WISP
WINGNUT	WINNOWED	WIPES	WIRRICOWS	WISPED
WINGNUTS	WINNOWER	WIPING	WIRY	WISPIER
WINGOVER	WINNOWERS	WIPINGS	WIS	WISPIEST
WINGOVERS	WINNOWING	WIPPEN	WISARD	WISPILY
WINGS	WINNOWS	WIPPENS	WISARDS	WISPINESS
WINGSPAN	WINNS	WIRABLE	WISDOM	WISPING
WINGSPANS	WINO	WIRE	WISDOMS	WISPISH
WINGSUIT	WINOES	WIRED	WISE	WISPLIKE
WINGSUITS	WINOS	WIREDRAW	WISEACRE	WISPS
WINGTIP	WINS	WIREDRAWN	WISEACRES	WISPY
WINGTIPS	WINSEY	WIREDRAWS	WISEASS	WISS
WINGY	WINSEYS	WIREDREW	WISEASSES	WISSED
WINIER	WINSOME	WIREFRAME	WISECRACK	WISSES
WINIEST	WINSOMELY	WIREGRASS	WISED	WISSING
WINING	WINSOMER	WIREHAIR	WISEGUY	WIST

W

WISTARIA	WITHERED	WITTERS	WOADWAXES	WOKEN
WISTARIAS	WITHERER	WITTICISM	WOAH	WOKKA
WISTED	WITHERERS	WITTIER	WOALD	WOKS
WISTERIA	WITHERING	WITTIEST	WOALDS	WOLD
WISTERIAS	WITHERITE	WITTILY	WOBBEGONG	WOLDS
WISTFUL	WITHEROD	WITTINESS	WOBBLE	WOLF
WISTFULLY	WITHERODS	WITTING	WOBBLED	WOLFBERRY
WISTING	WITHERS	WITTINGLY	WOBBLER	WOLFED
WISTITI	WITHES	WITTINGS	WOBBLERS	WOLFER
WISTITIS	WITHHAULT	WITTOL	WOBBLES	WOLFERS
WISTLY	WITHHELD	WITTOLLY	WOBBLIER	WOLFFISH
WISTS	WITHHOLD	WITTOLS	WOBBLIES	WOLFHOUND
WIT	WITHHOLDS	WITTY	WOBBLIEST	WOLFING
WITAN	WITHIER	WITWALL	WOBBLING	WOLFINGS
WITANS	WITHIES	WITWALLS	WOBBLINGS	WOLFISH
WITBLITS	WITHIEST	WITWANTON	WOBBLY	WOLFISHLY
WITCH	WITHIN	WIVE	WOBEGONE	WOLFKIN
WITCHED	WITHING	WIVED	WOCK	WOLFKINS
WITCHEN	WITHINS	WIVEHOOD	WOCKS	WOLFLIKE
WITCHENS	WITHOUT	WIVEHOODS	WODGE	WOLFLING
WITCHERY	WITHOUTEN	WIVER	WODGES	WOLFLINGS
WITCHES	WITHOUTS	WIVERN	WOE	WOLFRAM
WITCHETTY	WITHS	WIVERNS	WOEBEGONE	WOLFRAMS
WITCHHOOD	WITHSTAND	WIVERS	WOEFUL	WOLFS
WITCHIER	WITHSTOOD	WIVES	WOEFULLER	WOLFSBANE
WITCHIEST	WITHWIND	WIVING	WOEFULLY	WOLFSKIN
WITCHING	WITHWINDS	WIZ	WOENESS	WOLFSKINS
WITCHINGS	WITHY	WIZARD	WOENESSES	WOLLIES
WITCHKNOT	WITHYWIND	WIZARDLY	WOES	WOLLY
WITCHLIKE	WITING	WIZARDRY	WOESOME	WOLVE
WITCHWEED	WITLESS	WIZARDS	WOF	WOLVED
WITCHY	WITLESSLY	WIZEN	WOFS	WOLVER
WITE	WITLING	WIZENED	WOFUL	WOLVERENE
WITED	WITLINGS	WIZENING	WOFULLER	WOLVERINE
WITELESS	WITLOOF	WIZENS	WOFULLEST	WOLVERS
WITES	WITLOOFS	WIZES	WOFULLY	WOLVES
WITGAT	WITNESS	WIZIER	WOFULNESS	WOLVING
WITGATS	WITNESSED	WIZIERS	WOG	WOLVINGS
WITH	WITNESSER	WIZZEN	WOGGISH	WOLVISH
WITHAL	WITNESSES	WIZZENS	WOGGLE	WOLVISHLY
WITHDRAW	WITNEY	WIZZES	WOGGLES	WOMAN
WITHDRAWN	WITNEYS	WO	WOGS	WOMANED
WITHDRAWS	WITS	WOAD	WOIWODE	WOMANHOOD
WITHDREW	WITTED	WOADED	WOIWODES	WOMANING
WITHE	WITTER	WOADS	WOJUS	WOMANISE
WITHED	WITTERED	WOADWAX	WOK	WOMANISED
WITHER	WITTERING	WOADWAXEN	WOKE	WOMANISER

W

WOMANISES	WONDEROUS	WOODBORER	WOODLORES	WOODWASP
WOMANISH	WONDERS	WOODBOX	WOODLOT	WOODWASPS
WOMANISM	WONDRED	WOODBOXES	WOODLOTS	WOODWAX
WOMANISMS	WONDROUS	WOODCHAT	WOODLOUSE	WOODWAXEN
WOMANIST	WONGA	WOODCHATS	WOODMAN	WOODWAXES
WOMANISTS	WONGAS	WOODCHIP	WOODMEAL	WOODWIND
WOMANIZE	WONGI	WOODCHIPS	WOODMEALS	WOODWINDS
WOMANIZED	WONGIED	WOODCHOP	WOODMEN	WOODWORK
WOMANIZER	WONGIING	WOODCHOPS	WOODMICE	WOODWORKS
WOMANIZES	WONGIS	WOODCHUCK	WOODMOUSE	WOODWORM
WOMANKIND	WONING	WOODCOCK	WOODNESS	WOODWORMS
WOMANLESS	WONINGS	WOODCOCKS	WOODNOTE	WOODWOSE
WOMANLIER	WONK	WOODCRAFT	WOODNOTES	WOODWOSES
WOMANLIKE	WONKERIES	WOODCUT	WOODPILE	WOODY
WOMANLY	WONKERY	WOODCUTS	WOODPILES	WOODYARD
WOMANNED	WONKIER	WOODED	WOODPRINT	WOODYARDS
WOMANNESS	WONKIEST	WOODEN	WOODRAT	WOOED
WOMANNING	WONKILY	WOODENED	WOODRATS	WOOER
WOMANS	WONKISH	WOODENER	WOODREEVE	WOOERS
WOMB	WONKS	WOODENEST	WOODROOF	WOOF
WOMBAT	WONKY	WOODENING	WOODROOFS	WOOFED
WOMBATS	WONNED	WOODENLY	WOODRUFF	WOOFER
WOMBED	WONNER	WOODENS	WOODRUFFS	WOOFERS
WOMBIER	WONNERS	WOODENTOP	WOODRUSH	WOOFIER
WOMBIEST	WONNING	WOODFERN	WOODS	WOOFIEST
WOMBING	WONNINGS	WOODFERNS	WOODSCREW	WOOFING
WOMBLIKE	WONS	WOODFREE	WOODSHED	WOOFS
WOMBS	WONT	WOODGRAIN	WOODSHEDS	WOOFTAH
WOMBY	WONTED	WOODHEN	WOODSHOCK	WOOFTAHS
WOMEN	WONTEDLY	WOODHENS	WOODSIA	WOOFTER
WOMENFOLK	WONTING	WOODHOLE	WOODSIAS	WOOFTERS
WOMENKIND	WONTLESS	WOODHOLES	WOODSIER	WOOFY
WOMERA	WONTON	WOODHORSE	WOODSIEST	WOOHOO
WOMERAS	WONTONS	WOODHOUSE	WOODSKIN	WOOING
WOMMERA	WONTS	WOODIE	WOODSKINS	WOOINGLY
WOMMERAS	WOO	WOODIER	WOODSMAN	WOOINGS
WOMMIT	WOOABLE	WOODIES	WOODSMEN	WOOL
WOMMITS	WOOBUT	WOODIEST	WOODSPITE	WOOLD
WOMYN	WOOBUTS	WOODINESS	WOODSTONE	WOOLDED
WON	WOOD	WOODING	WOODSTOVE	WOOLDER
WONDER	WOODBIN	WOODLAND	WOODSY	WOOLDERS
WONDERED	WOODBIND	WOODLANDS	WOODTONE	WOOLDING
WONDERER	WOODBINDS	WOODLARK	WOODTONES	WOOLDINGS
WONDERERS	WOODBINE	WOODLARKS	WOODWALE	WOOLDS
WONDERFUL	WOODBINES	WOODLESS	WOODWALES	WOOLED
WONDERING	WOODBINS	WOODLICE	WOODWARD	WOOLEN
WONDERKID	WOODBLOCK	WOODLORE	WOODWARDS	WOOLENS

W

WOOLER	WOONS	WORDGAME	WORKFOLKS	WORKWEEKS
WOOLERS	WOOPIE	WORDGAMES	WORKFORCE	WORKWOMAN
WOOLFAT	WOOPIES	WORDIER	WORKFUL	WORKWOMEN
WOOLFATS	WOOPS	WORDIEST	WORKGIRL	WORLD
WOOLFELL	WOOPSED	WORDILY	WORKGIRLS	WORLDBEAT
WOOLFELLS	WOOPSES	WORDINESS	WORKGROUP	WORLDED
WOOLHAT	WOOPSING	WORDING	WORKHORSE	WORLDER
WOOLHATS	WOOPY	WORDINGS	WORKHOUR	WORLDERS
WOOLIE	WOORALI	WORDISH	WORKHOURS	WORLDIE
WOOLIER	WOORALIS	WORDLESS	WORKHOUSE	WORLDIES
WOOLIES	WOORARA	WORDLORE	WORKING	WORLDLIER
WOOLIEST	WOORARAS	WORDLORES	WORKINGS	WORLDLING
WOOLINESS	WOORARI	WORDPLAY	WORKLESS	WORLDLY
WOOLLED	WOORARIS	WORDPLAYS	WORKLOAD	WORLDS
WOOLLEN	WOOS	WORDS	WORKLOADS	WORLDVIEW
WOOLLENS	WOOSE	WORDSMITH	WORKMAN	WORLDWIDE
WOOLLIER	WOOSEL	WORDWRAP	WORKMANLY	WORM
WOOLLIES	WOOSELL	WORDWRAPS	WORKMATE	WORMCAST
WOOLLIEST	WOOSELLS	WORDY	WORKMATES	WORMCASTS
WOOLLIKE	WOOSELS	WORE	WORKMEN	WORMED
WOOLLILY	WOOSES	WORK	WORKOUT	WORMER
WOOLLY	WOOSH	WORKABLE	WORKOUTS	WORMERIES
WOOLMAN	WOOSHED	WORKABLY	WORKPIECE	WORMERS
WOOLMEN	WOOSHES	WORKADAY	WORKPLACE	WORMERY
WOOLPACK	WOOSHING	WORKADAYS	WORKPRINT	WORMFLIES
WOOLPACKS	WOOT	WORKBAG	WORKROOM	WORMFLY
WOOLS	WOOTZ	WORKBAGS	WORKROOMS	WORMGEAR
WOOLSACK	WOOTZES	WORKBENCH	WORKS	WORMGEARS
WOOLSACKS	WOOZIER	WORKBOAT	WORKSAFE	WORMHOLE
WOOLSEY	WOOZIEST	WORKBOATS	WORKSHEET	WORMHOLED
WOOLSEYS	WOOZILY	WORKBOOK	WORKSHOP	WORMHOLES
WOOLSHED	WOOZINESS	WORKBOOKS	WORKSHOPS	WORMIER
WOOLSHEDS	WOOZY	WORKBOOT	WORKSHY	WORMIEST
WOOLSKIN	WOP	WORKBOOTS	WORKSITE	WORMIL
WOOLSKINS	WOPPED	WORKBOX	WORKSITES	WORMILS
WOOLWARD	WOPPING	WORKBOXES	WORKSOME	WORMINESS
WOOLWORK	WOPS	WORKDAY	WORKSONG	WORMING
WOOLWORKS	WORCESTER	WORKDAYS	WORKSONGS	WORMISH
WOOLY	WORD	WORKED	WORKSPACE	WORMLIKE
WOOMERA	WORDAGE	WORKER ·	WORKTABLE	WORMROOT
WOOMERANG	WORDAGES	WORKERIST	WORKTOP	WORMROOTS
WOOMERAS	WORDBOOK	WORKERS	WORKTOPS	WORMS
WOON	WORDBOOKS	WORKFARE	WORKUP	WORMSEED
WOONED	WORDBOUND	WORKFARES	WORKUPS	WORMSEEDS
WOONERF	WORDBREAK	WORKFLOW	WORKWEAR	WORMWOOD
WOONERFS	WORDCOUNT	WORKFLOWS	WORKWEARS	WORMWOODS
WOONING	WORDED	WORKFOLK	WORKWEEK	WORMY

WORN	WORT	WOUNDS	WRAPPINGS	WREATHE
WORNNESS	WORTH	WOUNDWORT	WRAPROUND	WREATHED
WORRAL	WORTHED	WOUNDY	WRAPS	WREATHEN
WORRALS	WORTHFUL	WOURALI	WRAPT	WREATHER
WORREL	WORTHIED	WOURALIS	WRASSE	WREATHERS
WORRELS	WORTHIER	WOVE	WRASSES	WREATHES
WORRICOW	WORTHIES	WOVEN	WRASSLE	WREATHIER
WORRICOWS	WORTHIEST	WOVENS	WRASSLED	WREATHING
WORRIED	WORTHILY	WOW	WRASSLES	WREATHS
WORRIEDLY	WORTHING	WOWED	WRASSLING	WREATHY
WORRIER	WORTHLESS	WOWEE	WRAST	WRECK
WORRIERS	WORTHS	WOWF	WRASTED	WRECKAGE
WORRIES	WORTHY	WOWFER	WRASTING	WRECKAGES
WORRIMENT	WORTHYING	WOWFEST	WRASTLE	WRECKED
WORRISOME	WORTLE	WOWING	WRASTLED	WRECKER
WORRIT	WORTLES	WOWS	WRASTLES	WRECKERS
WORRITED	WORTS	WOWSER	WRASTLING	WRECKFISH
WORRITING	WOS	WOWSERS	WRASTS	WRECKFUL
WORRITS	WOSBIRD	WOX	WRATE	WRECKING
WORRY	WOSBIRDS	WOXEN	WRATH	WRECKINGS
WORRYCOW	WOST	WRACK	WRATHED	WRECKS
WORRYCOWS	WOT	WRACKED	WRATHFUL	WREN
WORRYGUTS	WOTCHA	WRACKFUL	WRATHIER	WRENCH
WORRYING	WOTCHER	WRACKING	WRATHIEST	WRENCHED
WORRYINGS	WOTS	WRACKS	WRATHILY	WRENCHER
WORRYWART	WOTTED	WRAITH	WRATHING	WRENCHERS
WORSE	WOTTEST	WRAITHS	WRATHLESS	WRENCHES
WORSED	WOTTETH	WRANG	WRATHS	WRENCHING
WORSEN	WOTTING	WRANGED	WRATHY	WRENS
WORSENED	WOUBIT	WRANGING	WRAWL	WRENTIT
WORSENESS	WOUBITS	WRANGLE	WRAWLED	WRENTITS
WORSENING	WOULD	WRANGLED	WRAWLING	WREST
WORSENS	WOULDEST	WRANGLER	WRAWLS	WRESTED
WORSER	WOULDS	WRANGLERS	WRAXLE	WRESTER
WORSES	WOULDST	WRANGLES	WRAXLED	WRESTERS
WORSET	WOUND	WRANGLING	WRAXLES	WRESTING
WORSETS	WOUNDABLE	WRANGS	WRAXLING	WRESTLE
WORSHIP	WOUNDED	WRAP	WRAXLINGS	WRESTLED
WORSHIPED	WOUNDEDLY	WRAPOVER	WREAK	WRESTLER
WORSHIPER	WOUNDER	WRAPOVERS	WREAKED	WRESTLERS
WORSHIPS	WOUNDERS	WRAPPAGE	WREAKER	WRESTLES
WORSING	WOUNDIER	WRAPPAGES	WREAKERS	WRESTLING
WORST	WOUNDIEST	WRAPPED	WREAKFUL	WRESTS
WORSTED	WOUNDILY	WRAPPER	WREAKING	WRETCH
WORSTEDS	WOUNDING	WRAPPERED	WREAKLESS	WRETCHED
WORSTING	WOUNDINGS	WRAPPERS	WREAKS	WRETCHES
WORSTS	WOUNDLESS	WRAPPING	WREATH	WRETHE

W

WRETHED	WRISTED	WROATH	WUD	WUTHERED
WRETHES	WRISTER	WROATHS	WUDDED	WUTHERING
WRETHING	WRISTERS	WROKE	WUDDING	WUTHERS
WRICK	WRISTIER	WROKEN	WUDJULA	WUXIA
WRICKED	WRISTIEST	WRONG	WUDJULAS	WUXIAS
WRICKING	WRISTING	WRONGDOER	WUDS	WUZ
WRICKS	WRISTLET	WRONGED	WUDU	WUZZLE
WRIED	WRISTLETS	WRONGER	WUDUS	WUZZLED
WRIER	WRISTLOCK	WRONGERS	WUKKAS	WUZZLES
WRIES	WRISTS	WRONGEST	WULFENITE	WUZZLING
WRIEST	WRISTY	WRONGFUL	WULL	WYANDOTTE
WRIGGLE	WRIT	WRONGING	WULLED	WYCH
WRIGGLED	WRITABLE	WRONGLY	WULLING	WYCHES
WRIGGLER	WRITATIVE	WRONGNESS	WULLS	WYE
WRIGGLERS	WRITE	WRONGOUS	WUNNER	WYES
WRIGGLES	WRITEABLE	WRONGS	WUNNERS	WYLE
WRIGGLIER	WRITEOFF	WROOT	WURLEY	WYLED
WRIGGLING	WRITEOFFS	WROOTED	WURLEYS	WYLES
WRIGGLY	WRITER	WROOTING	WURLIE	WYLIECOAT
WRIGHT	WRITERESS	WROOTS	WURLIES	WYLING
WRIGHTS	WRITERLY	WROTE	WURST	WYN
WRING	WRITERS	WROTH	WURSTS	WYND
WRINGED	WRITES	WROTHFUL	WURTZITE	WYNDS
WRINGER	WRITHE	WROUGHT	WURTZITES	WYNN
WRINGERS	WRITHED	WRUNG	WURZEL	WYNNS
WRINGING	WRITHEN	WRY	WURZELS	WYNS
WRINGS	WRITHER	WRYBILL	WUS	WYSIWYG
WRINKLE	WRITHERS	WRYBILLS	WUSES	WYTE
WRINKLED	WRITHES	WRYER	WUSHU	WYTED
WRINKLES	WRITHING	WRYEST	WUSHUS	WYTES
WRINKLIE	WRITHINGS	WRYING	WUSS	WYTING
WRINKLIER	WRITHLED	WRYLY	WUSSES	WYVERN
WRINKLIES	WRITING	WRYNECK	WUSSIER	WYVERNS
WRINKLING	WRITINGS	WRYNECKS	WUSSIES	
WRINKLY	WRITS	WRYNESS	WUSSIEST	
WRIST	WRITTEN	WRYNESSES	WUSSY	
WRISTBAND	WRIZLED	WRYTHEN	WUTHER	

W

X

XANTHAM	XENIUM	XERARCH	XIPHOID	XYLOID
XANTHAMS	XENOBLAST	XERASIA	XIPHOIDAL	XYLOIDIN
XANTHAN	XENOCRYST	XERASIAS	XIPHOIDS	XYLOIDINE
XANTHANS	XENOGAMY	XERIC	XIPHOPAGI	XYLOIDINS
XANTHATE	XENOGENIC	XERICALLY	XIS	XYLOL
XANTHATES	XENOGENY	XERISCAPE	XOANA	XYLOLOGY
XANTHEIN	XENOGRAFT	XEROCHASY	XOANON	XYLOLS
XANTHEINS	XENOLITH	XERODERMA	XRAY	XYLOMA
XANTHENE	XENOLITHS	XEROMA	XRAYS	XYLOMAS
XANTHENES	XENOMANIA	XEROMAS	XU	XYLOMATA
XANTHIC	XENOMENIA	XEROMATA	XYLAN	XYLOMETER
XANTHIN	XENON	XEROMORPH	XYLANS	XYLONIC
XANTHINE	XENONS	XEROPHAGY	XYLEM	XYLONITE
XANTHINES	XENOPHILE	XEROPHILE	XYLEMS	XYLONITES
XANTHINS	XENOPHOBE	XEROPHILY	XYLENE	XYLOPHAGE
XANTHISM	XENOPHOBY	XEROPHYTE	XYLENES	XYLOPHONE
XANTHISMS	XENOPHYA	XEROSERE	XYLENOL	XYLORIMBA
XANTHOMA	XENOPUS	XEROSERES	XYLENOLS	XYLOSE
XANTHOMAS	XENOPUSES	XEROSES	XYLIC	XYLOSES
XANTHONE	XENOTIME	XEROSIS	XYLIDIN	XYLOTOMY
XANTHONES	XENOTIMES	XEROSTOMA	XYLIDINE	XYLYL
XANTHOUS	XENURINE	XEROTES	XYLIDINES	XYLYLS
XANTHOXYL	XENURINES	XEROTIC	XYLIDINS	XYST
XEBEC	XERAFIN	XEROX	XYLITOL	XYSTER
XEBECS	XERAFINS	XEROXED	XYLITOLS	XYSTERS
XED	XERANSES	XEROXES	XYLOCARP	XYSTI
XENIA	XERANSIS	XEROXING	XYLOCARPS	XYSTOI
XENIAL	XERANTIC	XERUS	XYLOGEN	XYSTOS
XENIAS	XERAPHIN	XERUSES	XYLOGENS	XYSTS
XENIC	XERAPHINS	XI	XYLOGRAPH	XYSTUS

X

Y

YA	YAE	YAKOWS	YAOURTS	YARDER
YAAR	YAFF	YAKS	YAP	YARDERS
YAARS	YAFFED	YAKUZA	YAPOCK	YARDING
YABA	YAFFING	YALD	YAPOCKS	YARDINGS
YABAS	YAFFLE	YALE	YAPOK	YARDLAND
YABBA	YAFFLES	YALES	YAPOKS	YARDLANDS
YABBAS	YAFFS	YAM	YAPON	YARDMAN
YABBER	YAG	YAMALKA	YAPONS	YARDMEN
YABBERED	YAGE	YAMALKAS	YAPP	YARDS
YABBERING	YAGER	YAMEN	YAPPED	YARDSTICK
YABBERS	YAGERS	YAMENS	YAPPER	YARDWAND
YABBIE	YAGES	YAMMER	YAPPERS	YARDWANDS
YABBIED	YAGGER	YAMMERED	YAPPIE	YARDWORK
YABBIES	YAGGERS	YAMMERER	YAPPIER	YARDWORKS
YABBY	YAGI	YAMMERERS	YAPPIES	YARE
YABBYING	YAGIS	YAMMERING	YAPPIEST	YARELY
YACCA	YAGS	YAMMERS	YAPPING	YARER
YACCAS	YAH	YAMPIES	YAPPINGLY	YAREST
YACHT	YAHOO	YAMPY	YAPPINGS	YARFA
YACHTED	YAHOOISM	YAMS	YAPPS	YARFAS
YACHTER	YAHOOISMS	YAMULKA	YAPPY	YARK
YACHTERS	YAHOOS	YAMULKAS	YAPS	YARKED
YACHTIE	YAHRZEIT	YAMUN	YAPSTER	YARKING
YACHTIES	YAHRZEITS	YAMUNS	YAPSTERS	YARKS
YACHTING	YAHS	YANG	YAQONA	YARMELKE
YACHTINGS	YAIRD	YANGS	YAQONAS	YARMELKES
YACHTMAN	YAIRDS	YANK	YAR	YARMULKA
YACHTMEN	YAK	YANKED	YARAK	YARMULKAS
YACHTS	YAKHDAN	YANKEE	YARAKS	YARMULKE
YACHTSMAN	YAKHDANS	YANKEES	YARCO	YARMULKES
YACHTSMEN	YAKIMONO	YANKER	YARCOS	YARN
YACK	YAKIMONOS	YANKERS	YARD	YARNED
YACKA	YAKITORI	YANKIE	YARDAGE	YARNER
YACKAS	YAKITORIS	YANKIES	YARDAGES	YARNERS
YACKED	YAKKA	YANKING	YARDANG	YARNING
YACKER	YAKKAS	YANKS	YARDANGS	YARNS
YACKERS	YAKKED	YANQUI	YARDARM	YARPHA
YACKING	YAKKER	YANQUIS	YARDARMS	YARPHAS
YACKS	YAKKERS	YANTRA	YARDBIRD	YARR
YAD	YAKKING	YANTRAS	YARDBIRDS	YARRAMAN
YADS	YAKOW	YAOURT	YARDED	YARRAMANS

YARRAMEN	YAWING	YE	YEASTED	YELLOW
YARRAN	YAWL	YEA	YEASTIER	YELLOWED
YARRANS	YAWLED	YEAD	YEASTIEST	YELLOWER
YARRED	YAWLING	YEADING	YEASTILY	YELLOWEST
YARRING	YAWLS	YEADS	YEASTING	YELLOWFIN
YARROW	YAWMETER	YEAH	YEASTLESS	YELLOWIER
YARROWS	YAWMETERS	YEAHS	YEASTLIKE	YELLOWING
YARRS	YAWN	YEALDON	YEASTS	YELLOWISH
YARTA	YAWNED	YEALDONS	YEASTY	YELLOWLY
YARTAS	YAWNER	YEALING	YEBO	YELLOWS
YARTO	YAWNERS	YEALINGS	YECCH	YELLOWY
YARTOS	YAWNIER	YEALM	YECCHS	YELLS
YAS	YAWNIEST	YEALMED	YECH	YELM
YASHMAC	YAWNING	YEALMING	YECHIER	YELMED
YASHMACS	YAWNINGLY	YEALMS	YECHIEST	YELMING
YASHMAK	YAWNINGS	YEAN	YECHS	YELMS
YASHMAKS	YAWNS	YEANED	YECHY	YELP
YASMAK	YAWNSOME	YEANING	YEDE	YELPED
YASMAKS	YAWNY	YEANLING	YEDES	YELPER
YATAGAN	YAWP	YEANLINGS	YEDING	YELPERS
YATAGANS	YAWPED	YEANS	YEED	YELPING
YATAGHAN	YAWPER	YEAR	YEEDING	YELPINGS
YATAGHANS	YAWPERS	YEARBOOK	YEEDS	YELPS
YATE	YAWPING	YEARBOOKS	YEELIN	YELT
YATES	YAWPINGS	YEARD	YEELINS	YELTS
YATTER	YAWPS	YEARDED	YEESH	YEMMER
YATTERED	YAWS	YEARDING	YEGG	YEMMERS
YATTERING	YAWY	YEARDS	YEGGMAN	YEN
YATTERS	YAY	YEAREND	YEGGMEN	YENNED
YAUD	YAYS	YEARENDS	YEGGS	YENNING
YAUDS	YBET	YEARLIES	YEH	YENS
YAULD	YBLENT	YEARLING	YELD	YENTA
YAUP	YBORE	YEARLINGS	YELDRING	YENTAS
YAUPED	YBOUND	YEARLONG	YELDRINGS	YENTE
YAUPER	YBOUNDEN	YEARLY	YELDROCK	YENTES
YAUPERS	YBRENT	YEARN	YELDROCKS	YEOMAN
YAUPING	YCLAD	YEARNED	YELK	YEOMANLY
YAUPON	YCLED	YEARNER	YELKS	YEOMANRY
YAUPONS	YCLEEPE	YEARNERS	YELL	YEOMEN
YAUPS	YCLEEPED	YEARNING	YELLED	YEOW
YAUTIA	YCLEEPES	YEARNINGS	YELLER	YEP
YAUTIAS	YCLEEPING	YEARNS	YELLERS	YEPS
YAW	YCLEPED	YEARS	YELLING	YER
YAWED	YCLEPT	YEAS	YELLINGS	YERBA
YAWEY	YCOND	YEASAYER	YELLOCH	YERBAS
YAWIER	YDRAD	YEASAYERS	YELLOCHED	YERD
YAWIEST	YDRED	YEAST	YELLOCHS	YERDED

YERDING	YEUKING	YILLING	YMPE	YOGAS
YERDS	YEUKS	YILLS	YMPES	YOGEE
YERK	YEUKY	YIN	YMPING	YOGEES
YERKED	YEVE	YINCE	YMPT	YOGH
YERKING	YEVEN	YINDIE	YNAMBU	YOGHOURT
YERKS	YEVES	YINDIES	YNAMBUS	YOGHOURTS
YERSINIA	YEVING	YINGYANG	YO	YOGHS
YERSINIAE	YEW	YINGYANGS	YOB	YOGHURT
YERSINIAS	YEWEN	YINS	YOBBERIES	YOGHURTS
YES	YEWS	YIP	YOBBERY	YOGI
YESES	YEX	YIPE	YOBBIER	YOGIC
YESHIVA	YEXED	YIPES	YOBBIEST	YOGIN
YESHIVAH	YEXES	YIPPED	YOBBISH	YOGINI
YESHIVAHS	YEXING	YIPPEE	YOBBISHLY	YOGINIS
YESHIVAS	YEZ	YIPPER	YOBBISM	YOGINS
YESHIVOT	YFERE	YIPPERS	YOBBISMS	YOGIS
YESHIVOTH	YFERES	YIPPIE	YOBBO	YOGISM
YESK	YGLAUNST	YIPPIES	YOBBOES	YOGISMS
YESKED	YGO	YIPPING	YOBBOS	YOGOURT
YESKING	YGOE	YIPPY	YOBBY	YOGOURTS
YESKS	YIBBLES	YIPS	YOBS	YOGURT
YESSED	YICKER	YIRD	YOCK	YOGURTS
YESSES	YICKERED	YIRDED	YOCKED	YOHIMBE
YESSING	YICKERING	YIRDING	YOCKING	YOHIMBES
YESSIR	YICKERS	YIRDS	YOCKS	YOHIMBINE
YESSIREE	YID	YIRK	YOD	YOICK
YESSUM	YIDAKI	YIRKED	YODE	YOICKED
YEST	YIDAKIS	YIRKING	YODEL	YOICKING
YESTER	YIDS	YIRKS	YODELED	YOICKS
YESTERDAY	YIELD	YIRR	YODELER	YOICKSED
YESTEREVE	YIELDABLE	YIRRED	YODELERS	YOICKSES
YESTERN	YIELDED	YIRRING	YODELING	YOICKSING
YESTREEN	YIELDER	YIRRS	YODELLED	YOJAN
YESTREENS	YIELDERS	YIRTH	YODELLER	YOJANA
YESTS	YIELDING	YIRTHS	YODELLERS	YOJANAS
YESTY	YIELDINGS	YITE	YODELLING	YOJANS
YET	YIELDS	YITES	YODELS	YOK
YETI	YIKE	YITIE	YODH	YOKE
YETIS	YIKED	YITIES	YODHS	YOKED
YETT	YIKES	YITTEN	YODLE	YOKEL
YETTIE	YIKING	YLEM	YODLED	YOKELESS
YETTIES	YIKKER	YLEMS	YODLER	YOKELISH
YETTS	YIKKERED	YLIKE	YODLERS	YOKELS
YEUK	YIKKERING	YLKE	YODLES	YOKEMATE
YEUKED	YIKKERS	YLKES	YODLING	YOKEMATES
YEUKIER	YILL	YMOLT	YODS	YOKER
YEUKIEST	YILLED	YMOLTEN	YOGA	YOKERED

YOKERING	YORE	YOUTH	YSHENDING	YUKATAS
YOKERS	YORES	YOUTHEN	YSHENDS	YUKE
YOKES	YORK	YOUTHENED	YSHENT	YUKED
YOKING	YORKED	YOUTHENS	YSLAKED	YUKES
YOKINGS	YORKER	YOUTHFUL	YTOST	YUKIER
YOKKED	YORKERS	YOUTHHEAD	YTTERBIA	YUKIEST
YOKKING	YORKIE	YOUTHHOOD	YTTERBIAS	YUKING
YOKOZUNA	YORKIES	YOUTHIER	YTTERBIC	YUKKED
YOKOZUNAS	YORKING	YOUTHIEST	YTTERBITE	YUKKIER
YOKS	YORKS	YOUTHLESS	YTTERBIUM	YUKKIEST
YOKUL	YORLING	YOUTHLY	YTTERBOUS	YUKKING
YOLD	YORLINGS	YOUTHS	YTTRIA	YUKKY
YOLDRING	YORP	YOUTHSOME	YTTRIAS	YUKO
YOLDRINGS	YORPED	YOUTHY	YTTRIC	YUKOS
YOLK	YORPING	YOW	YTTRIOUS	YUKS
YOLKED	YORPS	YOWE	YTTRIUM	YUKY
YOLKIER	YOTTABYTE	YOWED	YTTRIUMS	YULAN
YOLKIEST	YOU	YOWES	YU	YULANS
YOLKLESS	YOUK	YOWIE	YUAN	YULE
YOLKS	YOUKED	YOWIES	YUANS	YULES
YOLKY	YOUKING	YOWING	YUCA	YULETIDE
YOM	YOUKS	YOWL	YUCAS	YULETIDES
YOMIM	YOUNG	YOWLED	YUCCA	YUM
YOMP	YOUNGER	YOWLER	YUCCAS	YUMBERRY
YOMPED	YOUNGERS	YOWLERS	YUCCH	YUMMIER
YOMPING	YOUNGEST	YOWLEY	YUCH	YUMMIES
YOMPS	YOUNGISH	YOWLEYS	YUCK	YUMMIEST
YON	YOUNGLING	YOWLING	YUCKED	YUMMINESS
YOND	YOUNGLY	YOWLINGS	YUCKER	YUMMO
YONDER	YOUNGNESS	YOWLS	YUCKERS	YUMMY
YONDERLY	YOUNGS	YOWS	YUCKIER	YUMP
YONDERS	YOUNGSTER	YPERITE	YUCKIEST	YUMPED
YONI	YOUNGTH	YPERITES	YUCKINESS	YUMPIE
YONIC	YOUNGTHLY	YPIGHT	YUCKING	YUMPIES
YONIS	YOUNGTHS	YPLAST	YUCKO	YUMPING
YONKER	YOUNKER	YPLIGHT	YUCKS	YUMPS
YONKERS	YOUNKERS	YPSILOID	YUCKY	YUNX
YONKS	YOUPON	YPSILON	YUFT	YUNXES
YONNIE	YOUPONS	YPSILONS	YUFTS	YUP
YONNIES	YOUR	YRAPT	YUG	YUPON
YONT	YOURN	YRAVISHED	YUGA	YUPONS
YOOF	YOURS	YRENT	YUGARIE	YUPPIE
YOOFS	YOURSELF	YRIVD	YUGARIES	YUPPIEDOM
YOOP	YOURT	YRNEH	YUGAS	YUPPIEISH
YOOPS	YOURTS	YRNEHS	YUGS	YUPPIES
YOPPER	YOUS	YSAME	YUK	YUPPIFIED
YOPPERS	YOUSE	YSHEND	YUKATA	YUPPIFIES

Y

YUPPIFY

YUPPIFY	YUPS	YURTA	YUTZ	YWIS
YUPPY	YUPSTER	YURTAS	YUTZES	YWROKE
YUPPYDOM	YUPSTERS	YURTS	YUZU	
YUPPYDOMS	YURT	YUS	YUZUS	

Z

ZA	ZAIKAIS	ZANAMIVIR	ZAPPING	ZEALANTS
ZABAIONE	ZAIRE	ZANANA	ZAPPY	ZEALFUL
ZABAIONES	ZAIRES	ZANANAS	ZAPS	ZEALLESS
ZABAJONE	ZAITECH	ZANDER	ZAPTIAH	ZEALOT
ZABAJONES	ZAITECHS	ZANDERS	ZAPTIAHS	ZEALOTISM
ZABETA	ZAKAT	ZANELLA	ZAPTIEH	ZEALOTRY
ZABETAS	ZAKATS	ZANELLAS	ZAPTIEHS	ZEALOTS
ZABRA	ZAKOUSKA	ZANIED	ZARAPE	ZEALOUS
ZABRAS	ZAKOUSKI	ZANIER	ZARAPES	ZEALOUSLY
ZABTIEH	ZAKUSKA	ZANIES	ZARATITE	ZEALS
ZABTIEHS	ZAKUSKI	ZANIEST	ZARATITES	ZEAS
ZACATON	ZAMAN	ZANILY	ZAREBA	ZEATIN
ZACATONS	ZAMANG	ZANINESS	ZAREBAS	ZEATINS
ZACK	ZAMANGS	ZANJA	ZAREEBA	ZEBEC
ZACKS	ZAMANS	ZANJAS	ZAREEBAS	ZEBECK
ZADDICK	ZAMARRA	ZANJERO	ZARF	ZEBECKS
ZADDICKS	ZAMARRAS	ZANJEROS	ZARFS	ZEBECS
ZADDIK	ZAMARRO	ZANTE	ZARI	ZEBRA
ZADDIKIM	ZAMARROS	ZANTES	ZARIBA	ZEBRAFISH
ZADDIKS	ZAMBO	ZANTEWOOD	ZARIBAS	ZEBRAIC
ZAFFAR	ZAMBOMBA	ZANTHOXYL	ZARIS	ZEBRANO
ZAFFARS	ZAMBOMBAS	ZANY	ZARNEC	ZEBRANOS
ZAFFER	ZAMBOORAK	ZANYING	ZARNECS	ZEBRAS
ZAFFERS	ZAMBOS	ZANYISH	ZARNICH	ZEBRASS
ZAFFIR	ZAMBUCK	ZANYISM	ZARNICHS	ZEBRASSES
ZAFFIRS	ZAMBUCKS	ZANYISMS	ZARZUELA	ZEBRAWOOD
ZAFFRE	ZAMBUK	ZANZA	ZARZUELAS	ZEBRINA
ZAFFRES	ZAMBUKS	ZANZAS	ZAS	ZEBRINAS
ZAFTIG	ZAMIA	ZANZE	ZASTRUGA	ZEBRINE
ZAG	ZAMIAS	ZANZES	ZASTRUGI	ZEBRINES
ZAGGED	ZAMINDAR	ZAP	ZATI	ZEBRINNY
ZAGGING	ZAMINDARI	ZAPATA	ZATIS	ZEBROID
ZAGS	ZAMINDARS	ZAPATEADO	ZAX	ZEBRULA
ZAIBATSU	ZAMINDARY	ZAPATEO	ZAXES	ZEBRULAS
ZAIDA	ZAMOUSE	ZAPATEOS	ZAYIN	ZEBRULE
ZAIDAS	ZAMOUSES	ZAPOTILLA	ZAYINS	ZEBRULES
ZAIDEH	ZAMPOGNA	ZAPPED	ZAZEN	ZEBU
ZAIDEHS	ZAMPOGNAS	ZAPPER	ZAZENS	ZEBUB
ZAIDIES	ZAMPONE	ZAPPERS	ZEA	ZEBUBS
ZAIDY	ZAMPONI	ZAPPIER	ZEAL	ZEBUS
ZAIKAI	ZAMZAWED	ZAPPIEST	ZEALANT	ZECCHIN

ZECCHINE	ZENDO	ZETA	ZIGZAGS	ZINCOID
ZECCHINES	ZENDOS	ZETAS	ZIKKURAT	ZINCOS
ZECCHINI	ZENITH	ZETETIC	ZIKKURATS	ZINCOUS
ZECCHINO	ZENITHAL	ZETETICS	ZIKURAT	ZINCS
ZECCHINOS	ZENITHS	ZETTABYTE	ZIKURATS	ZINCY
ZECCHINS	ZEOLITE	ZEUGMA	ZILA	ZINDABAD
ZECHIN	ZEOLITES	ZEUGMAS	ZILAS	ZINE
ZECHINS	ZEOLITIC	ZEUGMATIC	ZILCH	ZINEB
ZED	ZEP	ZEUXITE	ZILCHES	ZINEBS
ZEDA	ZEPHYR	ZEUXITES	ZILL	ZINES
ZEDAS	ZEPHYRS	ZEX	ZILLA	ZINFANDEL
ZEDOARIES	ZEPPELIN	ZEXES	ZILLAH	ZING
ZEDOARY	ZEPPELINS	ZEZE	ZILLAHS	ZINGANI
ZEDS	ZEPPOLE	ZEZES	ZILLAS	ZINGANO
ZEE	ZEPPOLES	ZHO	ZILLION	ZINGARA
ZEES	ZEPPOLI	ZHOMO	ZILLIONS	ZINGARE
ZEIN	ZEPS	ZHOMOS	ZILLIONTH	ZINGARI
ZEINS	ZERDA	ZHOOSH	ZILLS	ZINGARO
ZEITGEBER	ZERDAS	ZHOOSHED	ZIMB	ZINGED
ZEITGEIST	ZEREBA	ZHOOSHES	ZIMBI	ZINGEL
ZEK	ZEREBAS	ZHOOSHING	ZIMBIS	ZINGELS
ZEKS	ZERIBA	ZHOS	ZIMBS	ZINGER
ZEL	ZERIBAS	ZIBELINE	ZIMOCCA	ZINGERS
ZELANT	ZERK	ZIBELINES	ZIMOCCAS	ZINGIBER
ZELANTS	ZERKS	ZIBELLINE	ZIN	ZINGIBERS
ZELATOR	ZERO	ZIBET	ZINC	ZINGIER
ZELATORS	ZEROED	ZIBETH	ZINCATE	ZINGIEST
ZELATRICE	ZEROES	ZIBETHS	ZINCATES	ZINGING
ZELATRIX	ZEROING	ZIBETS	ZINCED	ZINGS
ZELKOVA	ZEROS	ZIFF	ZINCIC	ZINGY
ZELKOVAS	ZEROTH	ZIFFIUS	ZINCIER	ZINKE
ZELOSO	ZERUMBET	ZIFFIUSES	ZINCIEST	ZINKED
ZELOTYPIA	ZERUMBETS	ZIFFS	ZINCIFIED	ZINKENITE
ZELS	ZEST	ZIG	ZINCIFIES	ZINKES
ZEMINDAR	ZESTED	ZIGAN	ZINCIFY	ZINKIER
ZEMINDARI	ZESTER	ZIGANKA	ZINCING	ZINKIEST
ZEMINDARS	ZESTERS	ZIGANKAS	ZINCITE	ZINKIFIED
ZEMINDARY	ZESTFUL	ZIGANS	ZINCITES	ZINKIFIES
ZEMSTVA	ZESTFULLY	ZIGGED	ZINCKED	ZINKIFY
ZEMSTVO	ZESTIER	ZIGGING	ZINCKIER	ZINKING
ZEMSTVOS	ZESTIEST	ZIGGURAT	ZINCKIEST	ZINKY
ZENAIDA	ZESTILY	ZIGGURATS	ZINCKIFY	ZINNIA
ZENAIDAS	ZESTINESS	ZIGS	ZINCKING	ZINNIAS
ZENANA	ZESTING	ZIGZAG	ZINCKY	ZINS
ZENANAS	ZESTLESS	ZIGZAGGED	ZINCO	ZIP
ZENDIK	ZESTS	ZIGZAGGER	ZINCODE	ZIPLESS
ZENDIKS	ZESTY	ZIGZAGGY	ZINCODES	ZIPLINE

ZIPLINES	ZIZELS	ZOETROPE	ZONETIMES	ZOOGLOEA
ZIPLOCK	ZIZIT	ZOETROPES	ZONING	ZOOGLOEAE
ZIPLOCKED	ZIZITH	ZOETROPIC	ZONINGS	ZOOGLOEAL
ZIPLOCKS	ZIZYPHUS	ZOFTIG	ZONK	ZOOGLOEAS
ZIPOLA	ZIZZ	ZOIATRIA	ZONKED	ZOOGLOEIC
ZIPOLAS	ZIZZED	ZOIATRIAS	ZONKING	ZOOGONIES
ZIPPED	ZIZZES	ZOIATRICS	ZONKS	ZOOGONOUS
ZIPPER	ZIZZING	ZOIC	ZONOID	ZOOGONY
ZIPPERED	ZIZZLE	ZOISITE	ZONOIDS	ZOOGRAFT
ZIPPERING	ZIZZLED	ZOISITES	ZONULA	ZOOGRAFTS
ZIPPERS	ZIZZLES	ZOISM	ZONULAE	ZOOGRAPHY
ZIPPIER	ZIZZLING	ZOISMS	ZONULAR	ZOOID
ZIPPIEST	ZLOTE	ZOIST	ZONULAS	ZOOIDAL
ZIPPILY	ZLOTIES	ZOISTS	ZONULE	ZOOIDS
ZIPPING	ZLOTY	ZOL	ZONULES	ZOOIER
ZIPPO	ZLOTYCH	ZOLPIDEM	ZONULET	ZOOIEST
ZIPPOS	ZLOTYS	ZOLPIDEMS	ZONULETS	ZOOKEEPER
ZIPPY	ZO	ZOLS	ZONURE	ZOOKS
ZIPS	ZOA	ZOMBI	ZONURES	ZOOLATER
ZIPTOP	ZOAEA	ZOMBIE	ZOO	ZOOLATERS
ZIPWIRE	ZOAEAE	ZOMBIES	ZOOBIOTIC	ZOOLATRIA
ZIPWIRES	ZOAEAS	ZOMBIFIED	ZOOBLAST	ZOOLATRY
ZIRAM	ZOARIA	ZOMBIFIES	ZOOBLASTS	ZOOLITE
ZIRAMS	ZOARIAL	ZOMBIFY	ZOOCHORE	ZOOLITES
ZIRCALLOY	ZOARIUM	ZOMBIISM	ZOOCHORES	ZOOLITH
ZIRCALOY	ZOBO	ZOMBIISMS	ZOOCHORY	ZOOLITHIC
ZIRCALOYS	ZOBOS	ZOMBIS	ZOOCYTIA	ZOOLITHS
ZIRCON	ZOBU	ZOMBORUK	ZOOCYTIUM	ZOOLITIC
ZIRCONIA	ZOBUS	ZOMBORUKS	ZOOEA	ZOOLOGIC
ZIRCONIAS	ZOCALO	ZONA	ZOOEAE	ZOOLOGIES
ZIRCONIC	ZOCALOS	ZONAE	ZOOEAL	ZOOLOGIST
ZIRCONIUM	ZOCCO	ZONAL	ZOOEAS	ZOOLOGY
ZIRCONS	ZOCCOLO	ZONALLY	ZOOECIA	ZOOM
ZIT	ZOCCOLOS	ZONARY	ZOOECIUM	ZOOMABLE
ZITE	ZOCCOS	ZONATE	ZOOEY	ZOOMANCY
ZITHER	ZODIAC	ZONATED	ZOOGAMETE	ZOOMANIA
ZITHERIST	ZODIACAL	ZONATION	ZOOGAMIES	ZOOMANIAS
ZITHERN	ZODIACS	ZONATIONS	ZOOGAMOUS	ZOOMANTIC
ZITHERNS	ZOEA	ZONDA	ZOOGAMY	ZOOMED
ZITHERS	ZOEAE	ZONDAS	ZOOGENIC	ZOOMETRIC
ZITI	ZOEAL	ZONE	ZOOGENIES	ZOOMETRY
ZITIS	ZOEAS	ZONED	ZOOGENOUS	ZOOMING
ZITS	ZOECHROME	ZONELESS	ZOOGENY	ZOOMORPH
ZIZ	ZOECIA	ZONER	ZOOGLEA	ZOOMORPHS
ZIZANIA	ZOECIUM	ZONERS	ZOOGLEAE	ZOOMORPHY
ZIZANIAS	ZOEFORM	ZONES	ZOOGLEAL	ZOOMS
ZIZEL	ZOETIC	ZONETIME	ZOOGLEAS	ZOON

Z

ZOONAL	ZOOSPERM	ZORIL	ZUMBOORUK	ZYGOTIC
ZOONED	ZOOSPERMS	ZORILLA	ZUPA	ZYLONITE
ZOONIC	ZOOSPORE	ZORILLAS	ZUPAN	ZYLONITES
ZOONING	ZOOSPORES	ZORILLE	ZUPANS	ZYMASE
ZOONITE	ZOOSPORIC	ZORILLES	ZUPAS	ZYMASES
ZOONITES	ZOOSTEROL	ZORILLO	ZUPPA	ZYME
ZOONITIC	ZOOT	ZORILLOS	ZUPPAS	ZYMES
ZOONOMIA	ZOOTAXIES	ZORILS	ZURF	ZYMIC
ZOONOMIAS	ZOOTAXY	ZORINO	ZURFS	ZYMITE
ZOONOMIC	ZOOTECHNY	ZORINOS	ZUZ	ZYMITES
ZOONOMIES	ZOOTHECIA	ZORIS	ZUZIM	ZYMOGEN
ZOONOMIST	ZOOTHEISM	ZORRO	ZUZZIM	ZYMOGENE
ZOONOMY	ZOOTHOME	ZORROS	ZWANZIGER	ZYMOGENES
ZOONOSES	ZOOTHOMES	ZOS	ZWIEBACK	ZYMOGENIC
ZOONOSIS	ZOOTIER	ZOSTER	ZWIEBACKS	ZYMOGENS
ZOONOTIC	ZOOTIEST	ZOSTERS	ZYDECO	ZYMOGRAM
ZOONS	ZOOTOMIC	ZOUAVE	ZYDECOS	ZYMOGRAMS
ZOOPATHY	ZOOTOMIES	ZOUAVES	ZYGA	ZYMOID
ZOOPERAL	ZOOTOMIST	ZOUK	ZYGAENID	ZYMOLOGIC
ZOOPERIES	ZOOTOMY	ZOUKS	ZYGAENOID	ZYMOLOGY
ZOOPERIST	ZOOTOXIC	ZOUNDS	ZYGAL	ZYMOLYSES
ZOOPERY	ZOOTOXIN	ZOWEE	ZYGANTRA	ZYMOLYSIS
ZOOPHAGAN	ZOOTOXINS	ZOWIE	ZYGANTRUM	ZYMOLYTIC
ZOOPHAGY	ZOOTROPE	ZOYSIA	ZYGOCACTI	ZYMOME
ZOOPHILE	ZOOTROPES	ZOYSIAS	ZYGODONT	ZYMOMES
ZOOPHILES	ZOOTROPHY	ZUCCHETTI	ZYGOID	ZYMOMETER
ZOOPHILIA	ZOOTY	ZUCCHETTO	ZYGOMA	ZYMOSAN
ZOOPHILIC	ZOOTYPE	ZUCCHINI	ZYGOMAS	ZYMOSANS
ZOOPHILY	ZOOTYPES	ZUCCHINIS	ZYGOMATA	ZYMOSES
ZOOPHOBE	ZOOTYPIC	ZUCHETTA	ZYGOMATIC	ZYMOSIS
ZOOPHOBES	ZOOZOO	ZUCHETTAS	ZYGON	ZYMOTIC
ZOOPHOBIA	ZOOZOOS	ZUCHETTO	ZYGOPHYTE	ZYMOTICS
ZOOPHORI	ZOPILOTE	ZUCHETTOS	ZYGOSE	ZYMURGIES
ZOOPHORIC	ZOPILOTES	ZUFFOLI	ZYGOSES	ZYMURGY
ZOOPHORUS	ZOPPA	ZUFFOLO	ZYGOSIS	ZYTHUM
ZOOPHYTE	ZOPPO	ZUFOLI	ZYGOSITY	ZYTHUMS
ZOOPHYTES	ZORBING	ZUFOLO	ZYGOSPERM	ZYZZYVA
ZOOPHYTIC	ZORBINGS	ZUFOLOS	ZYGOSPORE	ZYZZYVAS
ZOOPLASTY	ZORBONAUT	ZUGZWANG	ZYGOTE	ZZZ
ZOOS	ZORGITE	ZUGZWANGS	ZYGOTENE	ZZZS
ZOOSCOPIC	ZORGITES	ZULU	ZYGOTENES	
ZOOSCOPY	ZORI	ZULUS	ZYGOTES	

Z

ten to fifteen
letter words

A

AARDWOLVES	ABERDEVINE	ABJOINTING	ABOMINATION	ABRIDGEMENT
ABACTERIAL	ABERDEVINES	ABJUNCTION	ABOMINATIONS	ABRIDGEMENTS
ABACTINALLY	ABERNETHIES	ABJUNCTIONS	ABOMINATOR	ABRIDGMENT
ABANDONEDLY	ABERRANCES	ABJURATION	ABOMINATORS	ABRIDGMENTS
ABANDONEES	ABERRANCIES	ABJURATIONS	ABONDANCES	ABROGATING
ABANDONERS	ABERRANTLY	ABLACTATION	ABONNEMENT	ABROGATION
ABANDONING	ABERRATING	ABLACTATIONS	ABONNEMENTS	ABROGATIONS
ABANDONMENT	ABERRATION	ABLATITIOUS	ABORIGINAL	ABROGATIVE
ABANDONMENTS	ABERRATIONAL	ABLATIVELY	ABORIGINALISM	ABROGATORS
ABANDONWARE	ABERRATIONS	ABLUTIONARY	ABORIGINALISMS	ABRUPTIONS
ABANDONWARES	ABEYANCIES	ABLUTOMANE	ABORIGINALITIES	ABRUPTNESS
ABASEMENTS	ABHOMINABLE	ABLUTOMANES	ABORIGINALITY	ABRUPTNESSES
ABASHMENTS	ABHORRENCE	ABNEGATING	ABORIGINALLY	ABSCESSING
ABATEMENTS	ABHORRENCES	ABNEGATION	ABORIGINALS	ABSCINDING
ABBOTSHIPS	ABHORRENCIES	ABNEGATIONS	ABORIGINES	ABSCISSINS
ABBREVIATE	ABHORRENCY	ABNEGATORS	ABORTICIDE	ABSCISSION
ABBREVIATED	ABHORRENTLY	ABNORMALISM	ABORTICIDES	ABSCISSIONS
ABBREVIATES	ABHORRINGS	ABNORMALISMS	ABORTIFACIENT	ABSCONDENCE
ABBREVIATING	ABIOGENESES	ABNORMALITIES	ABORTIFACIENTS	ABSCONDENCES
ABBREVIATION	ABIOGENESIS	ABNORMALITY	ABORTIONAL	ABSCONDERS
ABBREVIATIONS	ABIOGENETIC	ABNORMALLY	ABORTIONIST	ABSCONDING
ABBREVIATOR	ABIOGENETICALLY	ABNORMITIES	ABORTIONISTS	ABSCONDINGS
ABBREVIATORS	ABIOGENICALLY	ABODEMENTS	ABORTIVELY	ABSEILINGS
ABBREVIATORY	ABIOGENIST	ABOLISHABLE	ABORTIVENESS	ABSENTEEISM
ABBREVIATURE	ABIOGENISTS	ABOLISHERS	ABORTIVENESSES	ABSENTEEISMS
ABBREVIATURES	ABIOLOGICAL	ABOLISHING	ABORTUARIES	ABSENTMINDED
ABCOULOMBS	ABIOTICALLY	ABOLISHMENT	ABOVEBOARD	ABSENTMINDEDLY
ABDICATING	ABIOTROPHIC	ABOLISHMENTS	ABOVEGROUND	ABSINTHIATED
ABDICATION	ABIOTROPHIES	ABOLITIONAL	ABRACADABRA	ABSINTHISM
ABDICATIONS	ABIOTROPHY	ABOLITIONARY	ABRACADABRAS	ABSINTHISMS
ABDICATIVE	ABIRRITANT	ABOLITIONISM	ABRANCHIAL	ABSOLUTELY
ABDICATORS	ABIRRITANTS	ABOLITIONISMS	ABRANCHIATE	ABSOLUTENESS
ABDOMINALLY	ABIRRITATE	ABOLITIONIST	ABRASIVELY	ABSOLUTENESSES
ABDOMINALS	ABIRRITATED	ABOLITIONISTS	ABRASIVENESS	ABSOLUTEST
ABDOMINOPLASTY	ABIRRITATES	ABOLITIONS	ABRASIVENESSES	ABSOLUTION
ABDOMINOUS	ABIRRITATING	ABOMINABLE	ABREACTING	ABSOLUTIONS
ABDUCENTES	ABITURIENT	ABOMINABLENESS	ABREACTION	ABSOLUTISE
ABDUCTIONS	ABITURIENTS	ABOMINABLY	ABREACTIONS	ABSOLUTISED
ABDUCTORES	ABJECTIONS	ABOMINATED	ABREACTIVE	ABSOLUTISES
ABECEDARIAN	ABJECTNESS	ABOMINATES	ABRIDGABLE	ABSOLUTISING
ABECEDARIANS	ABJECTNESSES	ABOMINATING	ABRIDGEABLE	ABSOLUTISM

ABSOLUTISMS	ABSTEMIOUS	ABSTRICTION	ACAROPHILIES	ACCEPTABLENESS
ABSOLUTIST	ABSTEMIOUSLY	ABSTRICTIONS	ACAROPHILY	ACCEPTABLY
ABSOLUTISTIC	ABSTEMIOUSNESS	ABSTRUSELY	ACARPELLOUS	ACCEPTANCE
ABSOLUTISTS	ABSTENTION	ABSTRUSENESS	ACARPELOUS	ACCEPTANCES
ABSOLUTIVE	ABSTENTIONISM	ABSTRUSENESSES	ACATALECTIC	ACCEPTANCIES
ABSOLUTIVES	ABSTENTIONISMS	ABSTRUSEST	ACATALECTICS	ACCEPTANCY
ABSOLUTIZE	ABSTENTIONIST	ABSTRUSITIES	ACATALEPSIES	ACCEPTANTS
ABSOLUTIZED	ABSTENTIONISTS	ABSTRUSITY	ACATALEPSY	ACCEPTATION
ABSOLUTIZES	ABSTENTIONS	ABSURDISMS	ACATALEPTIC	ACCEPTATIONS
ABSOLUTIZING	ABSTENTIOUS	ABSURDISTS	ACATALEPTICS	ACCEPTEDLY
ABSOLUTORY	ABSTERGENT	ABSURDITIES	ACATAMATHESIA	ACCEPTILATION
ABSOLVABLE	ABSTERGENTS	ABSURDNESS	ACATAMATHESIAS	ACCEPTILATIONS
ABSOLVENTS	ABSTERGING	ABSURDNESSES	ACATHISIAS	ACCEPTINGLY
ABSOLVITOR	ABSTERSION	ABUNDANCES	ACAULESCENT	ACCEPTINGNESS
ABSOLVITORS	ABSTERSIONS	ABUNDANCIES	ACCEDENCES	ACCEPTINGNESSES
ABSORBABILITIES	ABSTERSIVE	ABUNDANTLY	ACCELERABLE	ACCEPTIVITIES
ABSORBABILITY	ABSTERSIVES	ABUSIVENESS	ACCELERANDO	ACCEPTIVITY
ABSORBABLE	ABSTINENCE	ABUSIVENESSES	ACCELERANDOS	ACCESSARIES
ABSORBANCE	ABSTINENCES	ABYSSOPELAGIC	ACCELERANT	ACCESSARILY
ABSORBANCES	ABSTINENCIES	ACADEMICAL	ACCELERANTS	ACCESSARINESS
ABSORBANCIES	ABSTINENCY	ACADEMICALISM	ACCELERATE	ACCESSARINESSES
ABSORBANCY	ABSTINENTLY	ACADEMICALISMS	ACCELERATED	ACCESSIBILITIES
ABSORBANTS	ABSTRACTABLE	ACADEMICALLY	ACCELERATES	ACCESSIBILITY
ABSORBATES	ABSTRACTED	ACADEMICALS	ACCELERATING	ACCESSIBLE
ABSORBEDLY	ABSTRACTEDLY	ACADEMICIAN	ACCELERATINGLY	ACCESSIBLENESS
ABSORBEFACIENT	ABSTRACTEDNESS	ACADEMICIANS	ACCELERATION	ACCESSIBLY
ABSORBEFACIENTS	ABSTRACTER	ACADEMICISM	ACCELERATIONS	ACCESSIONAL
ABSORBENCIES	ABSTRACTERS	ACADEMICISMS	ACCELERATIVE	ACCESSIONED
ABSORBENCY	ABSTRACTEST	ACADEMISMS	ACCELERATOR	ACCESSIONING
ABSORBENTS	ABSTRACTING	ACADEMISTS	ACCELERATORS	ACCESSIONS
ABSORBINGLY	ABSTRACTION	ACALCULIAS	ACCELERATORY	ACCESSORIAL
ABSORPTANCE	ABSTRACTIONAL	ACALEPHANS	ACCELEROMETER	ACCESSORIES
ABSORPTANCES	ABSTRACTIONISM	ACANACEOUS	ACCELEROMETERS	ACCESSORII
ABSORPTIOMETER	ABSTRACTIONISMS	ACANTHACEOUS	ACCENSIONS	ACCESSORILY
ABSORPTIOMETERS	ABSTRACTIONIST	ACANTHOCEPHALAN	ACCENTLESS	ACCESSORINESS
ABSORPTION	ABSTRACTIONISTS	ACANTHUSES	ACCENTUALITIES	ACCESSORINESSES
ABSORPTIONS	ABSTRACTIONS	ACARICIDAL	ACCENTUALITY	ACCESSORISE
ABSORPTIVE	ABSTRACTIVE	ACARICIDES	ACCENTUALLY	ACCESSORISED
ABSORPTIVENESS	ABSTRACTIVELY	ACARIDEANS	ACCENTUATE	ACCESSORISES
ABSORPTIVITIES	ABSTRACTIVES	ACARIDIANS	ACCENTUATED	ACCESSORISING
ABSORPTIVITY	ABSTRACTLY	ACARIDOMATIA	ACCENTUATES	ACCESSORIUS
ABSQUATULATE	ABSTRACTNESS	ACARIDOMATIUM	ACCENTUATING	ACCESSORIZE
ABSQUATULATED	ABSTRACTNESSES	ACARODOMATIA	ACCENTUATION	ACCESSORIZED
ABSQUATULATES	ABSTRACTOR	ACARODOMATIUM	ACCENTUATIONS	ACCESSORIZES
ABSQUATULATING	ABSTRACTORS	ACAROLOGIES	ACCEPTABILITIES	ACCESSORIZING
ABSTAINERS	ABSTRICTED	ACAROLOGIST	ACCEPTABILITY	ACCIACCATURA
ABSTAINING	ABSTRICTING	ACAROLOGISTS	ACCEPTABLE	ACCIACCATURAS

ACCIACCATURE
ACCIDENCES
ACCIDENTAL
ACCIDENTALISM
ACCIDENTALISMS
ACCIDENTALITIES
ACCIDENTALITY
ACCIDENTALLY
ACCIDENTALNESS
ACCIDENTALS
ACCIDENTED
ACCIDENTLY
ACCIDENTOLOGIES
ACCIDENTOLOGY
ACCIPITERS
ACCIPITRAL
ACCIPITRINE
ACCIPITRINES
ACCLAIMERS
ACCLAIMING
ACCLAMATION
ACCLAMATIONS
ACCLAMATORY
ACCLIMATABLE
ACCLIMATATION
ACCLIMATATIONS
ACCLIMATED
ACCLIMATES
ACCLIMATING
ACCLIMATION
ACCLIMATIONS
ACCLIMATISABLE
ACCLIMATISATION
ACCLIMATISE
ACCLIMATISED
ACCLIMATISER
ACCLIMATISERS
ACCLIMATISES
ACCLIMATISING
ACCLIMATIZABLE
ACCLIMATIZATION
ACCLIMATIZE
ACCLIMATIZED
ACCLIMATIZER
ACCLIMATIZERS
ACCLIMATIZES
ACCLIMATIZING

ACCLIVITIES
ACCLIVITOUS
ACCOASTING
ACCOLADING
ACCOMMODABLE
ACCOMMODATE
ACCOMMODATED
ACCOMMODATES
ACCOMMODATING
ACCOMMODATINGLY
ACCOMMODATION
ACCOMMODATIONAL
ACCOMMODATIONS
ACCOMMODATIVE
ACCOMMODATOR
ACCOMMODATORS
ACCOMPANIED
ACCOMPANIER
ACCOMPANIERS
ACCOMPANIES
ACCOMPANIMENT
ACCOMPANIMENTS
ACCOMPANIST
ACCOMPANISTS
ACCOMPANYING
ACCOMPANYIST
ACCOMPANYISTS
ACCOMPLICE
ACCOMPLICES
ACCOMPLISH
ACCOMPLISHABLE
ACCOMPLISHED
ACCOMPLISHER
ACCOMPLISHERS
ACCOMPLISHES
ACCOMPLISHING
ACCOMPLISHMENT
ACCOMPLISHMENTS
ACCOMPTABLE
ACCOMPTANT
ACCOMPTANTS
ACCOMPTING
ACCORAGING
ACCORDABLE
ACCORDANCE
ACCORDANCES
ACCORDANCIES

ACCORDANCY
ACCORDANTLY
ACCORDINGLY
ACCORDIONIST
ACCORDIONISTS
ACCORDIONS
ACCOSTABLE
ACCOUCHEMENT
ACCOUCHEMENTS
ACCOUCHEUR
ACCOUCHEURS
ACCOUCHEUSE
ACCOUCHEUSES
ACCOUNTABILITY
ACCOUNTABLE
ACCOUNTABLENESS
ACCOUNTABLY
ACCOUNTANCIES
ACCOUNTANCY
ACCOUNTANT
ACCOUNTANTS
ACCOUNTANTSHIP
ACCOUNTANTSHIPS
ACCOUNTING
ACCOUNTINGS
ACCOUPLEMENT
ACCOUPLEMENTS
ACCOURAGED
ACCOURAGES
ACCOURAGING
ACCOURTING
ACCOUSTREMENT
ACCOUSTREMENTS
ACCOUTERED
ACCOUTERING
ACCOUTERMENT
ACCOUTERMENTS
ACCOUTREMENT
ACCOUTREMENTS
ACCOUTRING
ACCREDITABLE
ACCREDITATION
ACCREDITATIONS
ACCREDITED
ACCREDITING
ACCRESCENCE
ACCRESCENCES

ACCRESCENT
ACCRETIONARY
ACCRETIONS
ACCRUEMENT
ACCRUEMENTS
ACCUBATION
ACCUBATIONS
ACCULTURAL
ACCULTURATE
ACCULTURATED
ACCULTURATES
ACCULTURATING
ACCULTURATION
ACCULTURATIONAL
ACCULTURATIONS
ACCULTURATIVE
ACCUMBENCIES
ACCUMBENCY
ACCUMULABLE
ACCUMULATE
ACCUMULATED
ACCUMULATES
ACCUMULATING
ACCUMULATION
ACCUMULATIONS
ACCUMULATIVE
ACCUMULATIVELY
ACCUMULATOR
ACCUMULATORS
ACCURACIES
ACCURATELY
ACCURATENESS
ACCURATENESSES
ACCURSEDLY
ACCURSEDNESS
ACCURSEDNESSES
ACCUSATION
ACCUSATIONS
ACCUSATIVAL
ACCUSATIVE
ACCUSATIVELY
ACCUSATIVES
ACCUSATORIAL
ACCUSATORY
ACCUSEMENT
ACCUSEMENTS
ACCUSINGLY

ACCUSTOMARY
ACCUSTOMATION
ACCUSTOMATIONS
ACCUSTOMED
ACCUSTOMEDNESS
ACCUSTOMING
ACCUSTREMENT
ACCUSTREMENTS
ACEPHALOUS
ACERACEOUS
ACERBATING
ACERBICALLY
ACERBITIES
ACERVATELY
ACERVATION
ACERVATIONS
ACESCENCES
ACESCENCIES
ACETABULAR
ACETABULUM
ACETABULUMS
ACETALDEHYDE
ACETALDEHYDES
ACETAMIDES
ACETAMINOPHEN
ACETAMINOPHENS
ACETANILID
ACETANILIDE
ACETANILIDES
ACETANILIDS
ACETAZOLAMIDE
ACETAZOLAMIDES
ACETIFICATION
ACETIFICATIONS
ACETIFIERS
ACETIFYING
ACETOMETER
ACETOMETERS
ACETONAEMIA
ACETONAEMIAS
ACETONEMIA
ACETONEMIAS
ACETONITRILE
ACETONITRILES
ACETONURIA
ACETONURIAS
ACETOPHENETIDIN

ACETYLATED
ACETYLATES
ACETYLATING
ACETYLATION
ACETYLATIONS
ACETYLATIVE
ACETYLCHOLINE
ACETYLCHOLINES
ACETYLENES
ACETYLENIC
ACETYLIDES
ACETYLSALICYLIC
ACHAENIUMS
ACHAENOCARP
ACHAENOCARPS
ACHALASIAS
ACHIEVABLE
ACHIEVEMENT
ACHIEVEMENTS
ACHINESSES
ACHLAMYDEOUS
ACHLORHYDRIA
ACHLORHYDRIAS
ACHLORHYDRIC
ACHONDRITE
ACHONDRITES
ACHONDRITIC
ACHONDROPLASIA
ACHONDROPLASIAS
ACHONDROPLASTIC
ACHROMATIC
ACHROMATICALLY
ACHROMATICITIES
ACHROMATICITY
ACHROMATIN
ACHROMATINS
ACHROMATISATION
ACHROMATISE
ACHROMATISED
ACHROMATISES
ACHROMATISING
ACHROMATISM
ACHROMATISMS
ACHROMATIZATION
ACHROMATIZE
ACHROMATIZED
ACHROMATIZES

ACHROMATIZING
ACHROMATOPSIA
ACHROMATOPSIAS
ACHROMATOUS
ACICLOVIRS
ACICULATED
ACIDANTHERA
ACIDANTHERAS
ACIDICALLY
ACIDIFIABLE
ACIDIFICATION
ACIDIFICATIONS
ACIDIFIERS
ACIDIFYING
ACIDIMETER
ACIDIMETERS
ACIDIMETRIC
ACIDIMETRICAL
ACIDIMETRICALLY
ACIDIMETRIES
ACIDIMETRY
ACIDNESSES
ACIDOMETER
ACIDOMETERS
ACIDOPHILE
ACIDOPHILES
ACIDOPHILIC
ACIDOPHILOUS
ACIDOPHILS
ACIDOPHILUS
ACIDOPHILUSES
ACIDULATED
ACIDULATES
ACIDULATING
ACIDULATION
ACIDULATIONS
ACIERATING
ACIERATION
ACIERATIONS
ACINACEOUS
ACINACIFORM
ACINETOBACTER
ACINETOBACTERS
ACKNOWLEDGE
ACKNOWLEDGEABLE
ACKNOWLEDGEABLY
ACKNOWLEDGED

ACKNOWLEDGEDLY
ACKNOWLEDGEMENT
ACKNOWLEDGER
ACKNOWLEDGERS
ACKNOWLEDGES
ACKNOWLEDGING
ACKNOWLEDGMENT
ACKNOWLEDGMENTS
ACOELOMATE
ACOELOMATES
ACOLOUTHIC
ACOLOUTHITE
ACOLOUTHITES
ACOLOUTHOS
ACOLOUTHOSES
ACONITINES
ACOTYLEDON
ACOTYLEDONOUS
ACOTYLEDONS
ACOUSTICAL
ACOUSTICALLY
ACOUSTICIAN
ACOUSTICIANS
ACQUAINTANCE
ACQUAINTANCES
ACQUAINTED
ACQUAINTING
ACQUIESCED
ACQUIESCENCE
ACQUIESCENCES
ACQUIESCENT
ACQUIESCENTLY
ACQUIESCENTS
ACQUIESCES
ACQUIESCING
ACQUIESCINGLY
ACQUIGHTING
ACQUIRABILITIES
ACQUIRABILITY
ACQUIRABLE
ACQUIREMENT
ACQUIREMENTS
ACQUISITION
ACQUISITIONAL
ACQUISITIONS
ACQUISITIVE
ACQUISITIVELY

ACQUISITIVENESS
ACQUISITOR
ACQUISITORS
ACQUITMENT
ACQUITMENTS
ACQUITTALS
ACQUITTANCE
ACQUITTANCED
ACQUITTANCES
ACQUITTANCING
ACQUITTERS
ACQUITTING
ACRIDITIES
ACRIDNESSES
ACRIFLAVIN
ACRIFLAVINE
ACRIFLAVINES
ACRIFLAVINS
ACRIMONIES
ACRIMONIOUS
ACRIMONIOUSLY
ACRIMONIOUSNESS
ACRITARCHS
ACROAMATIC
ACROAMATICAL
ACROBATICALLY
ACROBATICS
ACROBATISM
ACROBATISMS
ACROCARPOUS
ACROCENTRIC
ACROCENTRICS
ACROCYANOSES
ACROCYANOSIS
ACRODROMOUS
ACROGENOUS
ACROGENOUSLY
ACROLITHIC
ACROMEGALIC
ACROMEGALICS
ACROMEGALIES
ACROMEGALY
ACRONICALLY
ACRONYCALLY
ACRONYCHAL
ACRONYCHALLY
ACRONYMANIA

ACRONYMANIAS
ACRONYMICALLY
ACRONYMOUS
ACROPARESTHESIA
ACROPETALLY
ACROPHOBES
ACROPHOBIA
ACROPHOBIAS
ACROPHOBIC
ACROPHOBICS
ACROPHONETIC
ACROPHONIC
ACROPHONIES
ACROPOLISES
ACROSPIRES
ACROSTICAL
ACROSTICALLY
ACROTERIAL
ACROTERION
ACROTERIUM
ACROTERIUMS
ACRYLAMIDE
ACRYLAMIDES
ACRYLONITRILE
ACRYLONITRILES
ACTABILITIES
ACTABILITY
ACTINICALLY
ACTINIFORM
ACTINOBACILLI
ACTINOBACILLUS
ACTINOBIOLOGIES
ACTINOBIOLOGY
ACTINOCHEMISTRY
ACTINOLITE
ACTINOLITES
ACTINOMERE
ACTINOMERES
ACTINOMETER
ACTINOMETERS
ACTINOMETRIC
ACTINOMETRICAL
ACTINOMETRIES
ACTINOMETRY
ACTINOMORPHIC
ACTINOMORPHIES
ACTINOMORPHOUS

A

ACTINOMORPHY	ACUMINATED	ADDITAMENTS	ADHESIONAL	ADJUDICATOR
ACTINOMYCES	ACUMINATES	ADDITIONAL	ADHESIVELY	ADJUDICATORS
ACTINOMYCETE	ACUMINATING	ADDITIONALITIES	ADHESIVENESS	ADJUDICATORY
ACTINOMYCETES	ACUMINATION	ADDITIONALITY	ADHESIVENESSES	ADJUNCTION
ACTINOMYCETOUS	ACUMINATIONS	ADDITIONALLY	ADHIBITING	ADJUNCTIONS
ACTINOMYCIN	ACUPRESSURE	ADDITITIOUS	ADHIBITION	ADJUNCTIVE
ACTINOMYCINS	ACUPRESSURES	ADDITIVELY	ADHIBITIONS	ADJUNCTIVELY
ACTINOMYCOSES	ACUPUNCTURAL	ADDITIVITIES	ADHOCRACIES	ADJURATION
ACTINOMYCOSIS	ACUPUNCTURE	ADDITIVITY	ADIABATICALLY	ADJURATIONS
ACTINOMYCOTIC	ACUPUNCTURES	ADDLEMENTS	ADIABATICS	ADJURATORY
ACTINOPODS	ACUPUNCTURIST	ADDLEPATED	ADIACTINIC	ADJUSTABILITIES
ACTINOTHERAPIES	ACUPUNCTURISTS	ADDRESSABILITY	ADIAPHORISM	ADJUSTABILITY
ACTINOTHERAPY	ACUTENESSES	ADDRESSABLE	ADIAPHORISMS	ADJUSTABLE
ACTINOURANIUM	ACYCLOVIRS	ADDRESSEES	ADIAPHORIST	ADJUSTABLY
ACTINOURANIUMS	ACYLATIONS	ADDRESSERS	ADIAPHORISTIC	ADJUSTMENT
ACTINOZOAN	ADACTYLOUS	ADDRESSING	ADIAPHORISTS	ADJUSTMENTAL
ACTIONABLE	ADAMANCIES	ADDRESSINGS	ADIAPHORON	ADJUSTMENTS
ACTIONABLY	ADAMANTEAN	ADDRESSORS	ADIAPHOROUS	ADJUTANCIES
ACTIONISTS	ADAMANTINE	ADDUCEABLE	ADIATHERMANCIES	ADJUVANCIES
ACTIONLESS	ADAPTABILITIES	ADDUCTIONS	ADIATHERMANCY	ADMEASURED
ACTIVATING	ADAPTABILITY	ADELANTADO	ADIATHERMANOUS	ADMEASUREMENT
ACTIVATION	ADAPTABLENESS	ADELANTADOS	ADIATHERMIC	ADMEASUREMENTS
ACTIVATIONS	ADAPTABLENESSES	ADEMPTIONS	ADIPOCERES	ADMEASURES
ACTIVATORS	ADAPTATION	ADENECTOMIES	ADIPOCEROUS	ADMEASURING
ACTIVENESS	ADAPTATIONAL	ADENECTOMY	ADIPOCYTES	ADMINICLES
ACTIVENESSES	ADAPTATIONALLY	ADENITISES	ADIPOSITIES	ADMINICULAR
ACTIVISING	ADAPTATIONS	ADENOCARCINOMA	ADJACENCES	ADMINICULATE
ACTIVISTIC	ADAPTATIVE	ADENOCARCINOMAS	ADJACENCIES	ADMINICULATED
ACTIVITIES	ADAPTEDNESS	ADENOHYPOPHYSES	ADJACENTLY	ADMINICULATES
ACTIVIZING	ADAPTEDNESSES	ADENOHYPOPHYSIS	ADJECTIVAL	ADMINICULATING
ACTOMYOSIN	ADAPTIVELY	ADENOIDECTOMIES	ADJECTIVALLY	ADMINISTER
ACTOMYOSINS	ADAPTIVENESS	ADENOIDECTOMY	ADJECTIVELY	ADMINISTERED
ACTUALISATION	ADAPTIVENESSES	ADENOMATOUS	ADJECTIVES	ADMINISTERING
ACTUALISATIONS	ADAPTIVITIES	ADENOPATHIES	ADJOURNING	ADMINISTERS
ACTUALISED	ADAPTIVITY	ADENOPATHY	ADJOURNMENT	ADMINISTRABLE
ACTUALISES	ADAPTOGENIC	ADENOSINES	ADJOURNMENTS	ADMINISTRANT
ACTUALISING	ADAPTOGENS	ADENOVIRAL	ADJUDGEMENT	ADMINISTRANTS
ACTUALISTS	ADDERBEADS	ADENOVIRUS	ADJUDGEMENTS	ADMINISTRATE
ACTUALITES	ADDERSTONE	ADENOVIRUSES	ADJUDGMENT	ADMINISTRATED
ACTUALITIES	ADDERSTONES	ADEPTNESSES	ADJUDGMENTS	ADMINISTRATES
ACTUALIZATION	ADDERWORTS	ADEQUACIES	ADJUDICATE	ADMINISTRATING
ACTUALIZATIONS	ADDICTEDNESS	ADEQUATELY	ADJUDICATED	ADMINISTRATION
ACTUALIZED	ADDICTEDNESSES	ADEQUATENESS	ADJUDICATES	ADMINISTRATIONS
ACTUALIZES	ADDICTIONS	ADEQUATENESSES	ADJUDICATING	ADMINISTRATIVE
ACTUALIZING	ADDICTIVENESS	ADEQUATIVE	ADJUDICATION	ADMINISTRATOR
ACTUARIALLY	ADDICTIVENESSES	ADHERENCES	ADJUDICATIONS	ADMINISTRATORS
ACTUATIONS	ADDITAMENT	ADHERENTLY	ADJUDICATIVE	ADMINISTRATRIX

ADMIRABILITIES	ADOPTIANISMS	ADULTERANT	ADVANTAGING	ADVERSENESSES
ADMIRABILITY	ADOPTIANIST	ADULTERANTS	ADVECTIONS	ADVERSITIES
ADMIRABLENESS	ADOPTIANISTS	ADULTERATE	ADVENTITIA	ADVERTENCE
ADMIRABLENESSES	ADOPTIONISM	ADULTERATED	ADVENTITIAL	ADVERTENCES
ADMIRALSHIP	ADOPTIONISMS	ADULTERATES	ADVENTITIAS	ADVERTENCIES
ADMIRALSHIPS	ADOPTIONIST	ADULTERATING	ADVENTITIOUS	ADVERTENCY
ADMIRALTIES	ADOPTIONISTS	ADULTERATION	ADVENTITIOUSLY	ADVERTENTLY
ADMIRANCES	ADOPTIVELY	ADULTERATIONS	ADVENTIVES	ADVERTISED
ADMIRATION	ADORABILITIES	ADULTERATOR	ADVENTURED	ADVERTISEMENT
ADMIRATIONS	ADORABILITY	ADULTERATORS	ADVENTUREFUL	ADVERTISEMENTS
ADMIRATIVE	ADORABLENESS	ADULTERERS	ADVENTURER	ADVERTISER
ADMIRAUNCE	ADORABLENESSES	ADULTERESS	ADVENTURERS	ADVERTISERS
ADMIRAUNCES	ADORATIONS	ADULTERESSES	ADVENTURES	ADVERTISES
ADMIRINGLY	ADORNMENTS	ADULTERIES	ADVENTURESOME	ADVERTISING
ADMISSIBILITIES	ADPRESSING	ADULTERINE	ADVENTURESS	ADVERTISINGS
ADMISSIBILITY	ADRENALECTOMIES	ADULTERINES	ADVENTURESSES	ADVERTIZED
ADMISSIBLE	ADRENALECTOMY	ADULTERISE	ADVENTURING	ADVERTIZEMENT
ADMISSIBLENESS	ADRENALINE	ADULTERISED	ADVENTURINGS	ADVERTIZEMENTS
ADMISSIONS	ADRENALINES	ADULTERISES	ADVENTURISM	ADVERTIZER
ADMITTABLE	ADRENALINS	ADULTERISING	ADVENTURISMS	ADVERTIZERS
ADMITTANCE	ADRENALISED	ADULTERIZE	ADVENTURIST	ADVERTIZES
ADMITTANCES	ADRENALIZED	ADULTERIZED	ADVENTURISTIC	ADVERTIZING
ADMITTEDLY	ADRENERGIC	ADULTERIZES	ADVENTURISTS	ADVERTIZINGS
ADMIXTURES	ADRENERGICALLY	ADULTERIZING	ADVENTUROUS	ADVERTORIAL
ADMONISHED	ADRENOCHROME	ADULTEROUS	ADVENTUROUSLY	ADVERTORIALS
ADMONISHER	ADRENOCHROMES	ADULTEROUSLY	ADVENTUROUSNESS	ADVISABILITIES
ADMONISHERS	ADRENOCORTICAL	ADULTESCENT	ADVERBIALISE	ADVISABILITY
ADMONISHES	ADRIAMYCIN	ADULTESCENTS	ADVERBIALISED	ADVISABLENESS
ADMONISHING	ADRIAMYCINS	ADULTHOODS	ADVERBIALISES	ADVISABLENESSES
ADMONISHINGLY	ADROITNESS	ADULTNESSES	ADVERBIALISING	ADVISATORY
ADMONISHMENT	ADROITNESSES	ADULTRESSES	ADVERBIALIZE	ADVISEDNESS
ADMONISHMENTS	ADSCITITIOUS	ADUMBRATED	ADVERBIALIZED	ADVISEDNESSES
ADMONITION	ADSCITITIOUSLY	ADUMBRATES	ADVERBIALIZES	ADVISEMENT
ADMONITIONS	ADSCRIPTION	ADUMBRATING	ADVERBIALIZING	ADVISEMENTS
ADMONITIVE	ADSCRIPTIONS	ADUMBRATION	ADVERBIALLY	ADVISERSHIP
ADMONITORILY	ADSORBABILITIES	ADUMBRATIONS	ADVERBIALS	ADVISERSHIPS
ADMONITORS	ADSORBABILITY	ADUMBRATIVE	ADVERGAMING	ADVISORATE
ADMONITORY	ADSORBABLE	ADUMBRATIVELY	ADVERGAMINGS	ADVISORATES
ADNOMINALS	ADSORBATES	ADUNCITIES	ADVERSARIA	ADVISORIES
ADOLESCENCE	ADSORBENTS	ADVANCEMENT	ADVERSARIAL	ADVOCACIES
ADOLESCENCES	ADSORPTION	ADVANCEMENTS	ADVERSARIES	ADVOCATING
ADOLESCENT	ADSORPTIONS	ADVANCINGLY	ADVERSARINESS	ADVOCATION
ADOLESCENTLY	ADSORPTIVE	ADVANTAGEABLE	ADVERSARINESSES	ADVOCATIONS
ADOLESCENTS	ADULARESCENCE	ADVANTAGED	ADVERSATIVE	ADVOCATIVE
ADOPTABILITIES	ADULARESCENCES	ADVANTAGEOUS	ADVERSATIVELY	ADVOCATORS
ADOPTABILITY	ADULARESCENT	ADVANTAGEOUSLY	ADVERSATIVES	ADVOCATORY
ADOPTIANISM	ADULATIONS	ADVANTAGES	ADVERSENESS	ADVOUTRERS

ADVOUTRIES
AECIDIOSPORE
AECIDIOSPORES
AECIDOSPORE
AECIDOSPORES
AECIOSPORE
AECIOSPORES
AEDILESHIP
AEDILESHIPS
AEOLIPILES
AEOLIPYLES
AEOLOTROPIC
AEOLOTROPIES
AEOLOTROPY
AEPYORNISES
AERENCHYMA
AERENCHYMAS
AERENCHYMATOUS
AERIALISTS
AERIALITIES
AERIFICATION
AERIFICATIONS
AEROACOUSTICS
AEROBALLISTICS
AEROBATICS
AEROBICALLY
AEROBICISE
AEROBICISED
AEROBICISES
AEROBICISING
AEROBICIST
AEROBICISTS
AEROBICIZE
AEROBICIZED
AEROBICIZES
AEROBICIZING
AEROBIOLOGICAL
AEROBIOLOGIES
AEROBIOLOGIST
AEROBIOLOGISTS
AEROBIOLOGY
AEROBIONTS
AEROBIOSES
AEROBIOSIS
AEROBIOTIC
AEROBIOTICALLY
AEROBRAKED

AEROBRAKES
AEROBRAKING
AEROBRAKINGS
AEROBUSSES
AERODIGESTIVE
AERODONETICS
AERODROMES
AERODYNAMIC
AERODYNAMICAL
AERODYNAMICALLY
AERODYNAMICIST
AERODYNAMICISTS
AERODYNAMICS
AEROELASTIC
AEROELASTICIAN
AEROELASTICIANS
AEROELASTICITY
AEROEMBOLISM
AEROEMBOLISMS
AEROGENERATOR
AEROGENERATORS
AEROGRAMME
AEROGRAMMES
AEROGRAPHIES
AEROGRAPHS
AEROGRAPHY
AEROHYDROPLANE
AEROHYDROPLANES
AEROLITHOLOGIES
AEROLITHOLOGY
AEROLOGICAL
AEROLOGIES
AEROLOGIST
AEROLOGISTS
AEROMAGNETIC
AEROMANCIES
AEROMECHANIC
AEROMECHANICAL
AEROMECHANICS
AEROMEDICAL
AEROMEDICINE
AEROMEDICINES
AEROMETERS
AEROMETRIC
AEROMETRIES
AEROMODELLING
AEROMODELLINGS

AEROMOTORS
AERONAUTIC
AERONAUTICAL
AERONAUTICALLY
AERONAUTICS
AERONEUROSES
AERONEUROSIS
AERONOMERS
AERONOMICAL
AERONOMIES
AERONOMIST
AERONOMISTS
AEROPAUSES
AEROPHAGIA
AEROPHAGIAS
AEROPHAGIES
AEROPHOBES
AEROPHOBIA
AEROPHOBIAS
AEROPHOBIC
AEROPHONES
AEROPHORES
AEROPHYTES
AEROPLANES
AEROPLANKTON
AEROPLANKTONS
AEROPULSES
AEROSCOPES
AEROSHELLS
AEROSIDERITE
AEROSIDERITES
AEROSOLISATION
AEROSOLISATIONS
AEROSOLISE
AEROSOLISED
AEROSOLISES
AEROSOLISING
AEROSOLIZATION
AEROSOLIZATIONS
AEROSOLIZE
AEROSOLIZED
AEROSOLIZES
AEROSOLIZING
AEROSPACES
AEROSPHERE
AEROSPHERES
AEROSPIKES

AEROSTATIC
AEROSTATICAL
AEROSTATICS
AEROSTATION
AEROSTATIONS
AEROSTRUCTURE
AEROSTRUCTURES
AEROTACTIC
AEROTRAINS
AEROTROPIC
AEROTROPISM
AEROTROPISMS
AERUGINOUS
AESTHESIAS
AESTHESIOGEN
AESTHESIOGENIC
AESTHESIOGENS
AESTHETICAL
AESTHETICALLY
AESTHETICIAN
AESTHETICIANS
AESTHETICISE
AESTHETICISED
AESTHETICISES
AESTHETICISING
AESTHETICISM
AESTHETICISMS
AESTHETICIST
AESTHETICISTS
AESTHETICIZE
AESTHETICIZED
AESTHETICIZES
AESTHETICIZING
AESTHETICS
AESTIVATED
AESTIVATES
AESTIVATING
AESTIVATION
AESTIVATIONS
AESTIVATOR
AESTIVATORS
AETHEREALITIES
AETHEREALITY
AETHEREALLY
AETHRIOSCOPE
AETHRIOSCOPES
AETIOLOGICAL

AETIOLOGICALLY
AETIOLOGIES
AETIOLOGIST
AETIOLOGISTS
AFFABILITIES
AFFABILITY
AFFECTABILITIES
AFFECTABILITY
AFFECTABLE
AFFECTATION
AFFECTATIONS
AFFECTEDLY
AFFECTEDNESS
AFFECTEDNESSES
AFFECTINGLY
AFFECTIONAL
AFFECTIONALLY
AFFECTIONATE
AFFECTIONATELY
AFFECTIONED
AFFECTIONING
AFFECTIONLESS
AFFECTIONS
AFFECTIVELY
AFFECTIVENESS
AFFECTIVENESSES
AFFECTIVITIES
AFFECTIVITY
AFFECTLESS
AFFECTLESSNESS
AFFEERMENT
AFFEERMENTS
AFFENPINSCHER
AFFENPINSCHERS
AFFERENTLY
AFFETTUOSO
AFFIANCING
AFFICIONADO
AFFICIONADOS
AFFIDAVITS
AFFILIABLE
AFFILIATED
AFFILIATES
AFFILIATING
AFFILIATION
AFFILIATIONS
AFFINITIES

AFFINITIVE
AFFIRMABLE
AFFIRMANCE
AFFIRMANCES
AFFIRMANTS
AFFIRMATION
AFFIRMATIONS
AFFIRMATIVE
AFFIRMATIVELY
AFFIRMATIVES
AFFIRMATORY
AFFIRMINGLY
AFFIXATION
AFFIXATIONS
AFFIXMENTS
AFFIXTURES
AFFLATIONS
AFFLATUSES
AFFLICTERS
AFFLICTING
AFFLICTINGS
AFFLICTION
AFFLICTIONS
AFFLICTIVE
AFFLICTIVELY
AFFLUENCES
AFFLUENCIES
AFFLUENTIAL
AFFLUENTIALS
AFFLUENTLY
AFFLUENTNESS
AFFLUENTNESSES
AFFLUENZAS
AFFLUXIONS
AFFOORDING
AFFORCEMENT
AFFORCEMENTS
AFFORDABILITIES
AFFORDABILITY
AFFORDABLE
AFFORDABLY
AFFORESTABLE
AFFORESTATION
AFFORESTATIONS
AFFORESTED
AFFORESTING
AFFRANCHISE

AFFRANCHISED
AFFRANCHISEMENT
AFFRANCHISES
AFFRANCHISING
AFFRAPPING
AFFREIGHTMENT
AFFREIGHTMENTS
AFFRICATED
AFFRICATES
AFFRICATING
AFFRICATION
AFFRICATIONS
AFFRICATIVE
AFFRICATIVES
AFFRIGHTED
AFFRIGHTEDLY
AFFRIGHTEN
AFFRIGHTENED
AFFRIGHTENING
AFFRIGHTENS
AFFRIGHTFUL
AFFRIGHTING
AFFRIGHTMENT
AFFRIGHTMENTS
AFFRONTING
AFFRONTINGLY
AFFRONTINGS
AFFRONTIVE
AFICIONADA
AFICIONADAS
AFICIONADO
AFICIONADOS
AFLATOXINS
AFOREMENTIONED
AFORETHOUGHT
AFORETHOUGHTS
AFRORMOSIA
AFRORMOSIAS
AFTERBIRTH
AFTERBIRTHS
AFTERBODIES
AFTERBRAIN
AFTERBRAINS
AFTERBURNER
AFTERBURNERS
AFTERBURNING
AFTERBURNINGS

AFTERCARES
AFTERCLAPS
AFTERDAMPS
AFTERDECKS
AFTEREFFECT
AFTEREFFECTS
AFTEREYEING
AFTEREYING
AFTERGAMES
AFTERGLOWS
AFTERGRASS
AFTERGRASSES
AFTERGROWTH
AFTERGROWTHS
AFTERGUARD
AFTERGUARDS
AFTERHEATS
AFTERIMAGE
AFTERIMAGES
AFTERLIFES
AFTERLIVES
AFTERMARKET
AFTERMARKETS
AFTERMATHS
AFTERNOONS
AFTERPAINS
AFTERPARTIES
AFTERPARTY
AFTERPEAKS
AFTERPIECE
AFTERPIECES
AFTERSALES
AFTERSENSATION
AFTERSENSATIONS
AFTERSHAFT
AFTERSHAFTS
AFTERSHAVE
AFTERSHAVES
AFTERSHOCK
AFTERSHOCKS
AFTERSHOWS
AFTERSUPPER
AFTERSUPPERS
AFTERSWARM
AFTERSWARMS
AFTERTASTE
AFTERTASTES

AFTERTHOUGHT
AFTERTHOUGHTS
AFTERTIMES
AFTERTREATMENT
AFTERTREATMENTS
AFTERWARDS
AFTERWORDS
AFTERWORLD
AFTERWORLDS
AGALACTIAS
AGALMATOLITE
AGALMATOLITES
AGAMICALLY
AGAMOGENESES
AGAMOGENESIS
AGAMOGENETIC
AGAMOGONIES
AGAMOSPERMIES
AGAMOSPERMY
AGAPANTHUS
AGAPANTHUSES
AGARICACEOUS
AGATEWARES
AGATHODAIMON
AGATHODAIMONS
AGEDNESSES
AGELESSNESS
AGELESSNESSES
AGENDALESS
AGENTIVITIES
AGENTIVITY
AGFLATIONS
AGGIORNAMENTI
AGGIORNAMENTO
AGGIORNAMENTOS
AGGLOMERATE
AGGLOMERATED
AGGLOMERATES
AGGLOMERATING
AGGLOMERATION
AGGLOMERATIONS
AGGLOMERATIVE
AGGLUTINABILITY
AGGLUTINABLE
AGGLUTINANT
AGGLUTINANTS
AGGLUTINATE

AGGLUTINATED
AGGLUTINATES
AGGLUTINATING
AGGLUTINATION
AGGLUTINATIONS
AGGLUTINATIVE
AGGLUTININ
AGGLUTININS
AGGLUTINOGEN
AGGLUTINOGENIC
AGGLUTINOGENS
AGGRADATION
AGGRADATIONS
AGGRANDISE
AGGRANDISED
AGGRANDISEMENT
AGGRANDISEMENTS
AGGRANDISER
AGGRANDISERS
AGGRANDISES
AGGRANDISING
AGGRANDIZE
AGGRANDIZED
AGGRANDIZEMENT
AGGRANDIZEMENTS
AGGRANDIZER
AGGRANDIZERS
AGGRANDIZES
AGGRANDIZING
AGGRAVATED
AGGRAVATES
AGGRAVATING
AGGRAVATINGLY
AGGRAVATION
AGGRAVATIONS
AGGREGATED
AGGREGATELY
AGGREGATENESS
AGGREGATENESSES
AGGREGATES
AGGREGATING
AGGREGATION
AGGREGATIONAL
AGGREGATIONS
AGGREGATIVE
AGGREGATIVELY
AGGREGATOR

AGGREGATORS
AGGRESSING
AGGRESSION
AGGRESSIONS
AGGRESSIVE
AGGRESSIVELY
AGGRESSIVENESS
AGGRESSIVITIES
AGGRESSIVITY
AGGRESSORS
AGGRIEVEDLY
AGGRIEVEMENT
AGGRIEVEMENTS
AGGRIEVING
AGILENESSES
AGISTMENTS
AGITATEDLY
AGITATIONAL
AGITATIONS
AGNATICALLY
AGNOIOLOGIES
AGNOIOLOGY
AGNOLOTTIS
AGNOSTICISM
AGNOSTICISMS
AGONISEDLY
AGONISINGLY
AGONISTICAL
AGONISTICALLY
AGONISTICS
AGONIZEDLY
AGONIZINGLY
AGONOTHETES
AGORAPHOBE
AGORAPHOBES
AGORAPHOBIA
AGORAPHOBIAS
AGORAPHOBIC
AGORAPHOBICS
AGRAMMATICAL
AGRANULOCYTE
AGRANULOCYTES
AGRANULOCYTOSES
AGRANULOCYTOSIS
AGRANULOSES
AGRANULOSIS
AGRARIANISM

AGRARIANISMS
AGREEABILITIES
AGREEABILITY
AGREEABLENESS
AGREEABLENESSES
AGREEMENTS
AGREGATION
AGREGATIONS
AGRIBUSINESS
AGRIBUSINESSES
AGRIBUSINESSMAN
AGRIBUSINESSMEN
AGRICHEMICAL
AGRICHEMICALS
AGRICULTURAL
AGRICULTURALIST
AGRICULTURALLY
AGRICULTURE
AGRICULTURES
AGRICULTURIST
AGRICULTURISTS
AGRIFOODSTUFFS
AGRIMONIES
AGRIOLOGIES
AGRIPRODUCT
AGRIPRODUCTS
AGRITOURISM
AGRITOURISMS
AGRITOURIST
AGRITOURISTS
AGROBIOLOGICAL
AGROBIOLOGIES
AGROBIOLOGIST
AGROBIOLOGISTS
AGROBIOLOGY
AGROBUSINESS
AGROBUSINESSES
AGROCHEMICAL
AGROCHEMICALS
AGRODOLCES
AGROFORESTER
AGROFORESTERS
AGROFORESTRIES
AGROFORESTRY
AGROINDUSTRIAL
AGROINDUSTRIES
AGROINDUSTRY

AGROLOGICAL
AGROLOGIES
AGROLOGIST
AGROLOGISTS
AGRONOMIAL
AGRONOMICAL
AGRONOMICALLY
AGRONOMICS
AGRONOMIES
AGRONOMIST
AGRONOMISTS
AGROSTEMMA
AGROSTEMMAS
AGROSTEMMATA
AGROSTOLOGIC
AGROSTOLOGICAL
AGROSTOLOGIES
AGROSTOLOGIST
AGROSTOLOGISTS
AGROSTOLOGY
AGROTERRORISM
AGROTERRORISMS
AGROTOURISM
AGROTOURISMS
AGROTOURIST
AGROTOURISTS
AGRYPNOTIC
AGRYPNOTICS
AGTERSKOTS
AGUARDIENTE
AGUARDIENTES
AHISTORICAL
AHORSEBACK
AHURUHURUS
AICHMOPHOBIA
AICHMOPHOBIAS
AIGUILLETTE
AIGUILLETTES
AILANTHUSES
AILOUROPHILE
AILOUROPHILES
AILOUROPHILIA
AILOUROPHILIAS
AILOUROPHILIC
AILOUROPHOBE
AILOUROPHOBES
AILOUROPHOBIA

AILOUROPHOBIAS
AILOUROPHOBIC
AILUROPHILE
AILUROPHILES
AILUROPHILIA
AILUROPHILIAS
AILUROPHILIC
AILUROPHOBE
AILUROPHOBES
AILUROPHOBIA
AILUROPHOBIAS
AILUROPHOBIC
AIMLESSNESS
AIMLESSNESSES
AIRBOARDING
AIRBOARDINGS
AIRBRUSHED
AIRBRUSHES
AIRBRUSHING
AIRBURSTED
AIRBURSTING
AIRCOACHES
AIRCRAFTMAN
AIRCRAFTMEN
AIRCRAFTSMAN
AIRCRAFTSMEN
AIRCRAFTSWOMAN
AIRCRAFTSWOMEN
AIRCRAFTWOMAN
AIRCRAFTWOMEN
AIRDROPPED
AIRDROPPING
AIRFREIGHT
AIRFREIGHTED
AIRFREIGHTING
AIRFREIGHTS
AIRINESSES
AIRLESSNESS
AIRLESSNESSES
AIRLIFTING
AIRMAILING
AIRMANSHIP
AIRMANSHIPS
AIRPROOFED
AIRPROOFING
AIRSICKNESS
AIRSICKNESSES

AIRSTREAMS
AIRSTRIKES
AIRTIGHTNESS
AIRTIGHTNESSES
AIRWORTHIER
AIRWORTHIEST
AIRWORTHINESS
AIRWORTHINESSES
AITCHBONES
AKATHISIAS
AKOLOUTHOS
AKOLOUTHOSES
AKOLUTHOSES
ALABAMINES
ALABANDINE
ALABANDINES
ALABANDITE
ALABANDITES
ALABASTERS
ALABASTRINE
ALABLASTER
ALABLASTERS
ALACRITIES
ALACRITOUS
ALARMINGLY
ALBARELLOS
ALBATROSSES
ALBERTITES
ALBESCENCE
ALBESCENCES
ALBESPINES
ALBESPYNES
ALBINESSES
ALBINISTIC
ALBINOISMS
ALBITISING
ALBITIZING
ALBUGINEOUS
ALBUMBLATT
ALBUMBLATTER
ALBUMBLATTS
ALBUMENISE
ALBUMENISED
ALBUMENISES
ALBUMENISING
ALBUMENIZE
ALBUMENIZED

ALBUMENIZES	ALCOHOLISMS	ALEXANDERS	ALIENATIONS	ALKALINIZES
ALBUMENIZING	ALCOHOLIZATION	ALEXANDERSES	ALIENATORS	ALKALINIZING
ALBUMINATE	ALCOHOLIZATIONS	ALEXANDRINE	ALIENNESSES	ALKALISABLE
ALBUMINATES	ALCOHOLIZE	ALEXANDRINES	ALIGHTMENT	ALKALISERS
ALBUMINISE	ALCOHOLIZED	ALEXANDRITE	ALIGHTMENTS	ALKALISING
ALBUMINISED	ALCOHOLIZES	ALEXANDRITES	ALIGNMENTS	ALKALIZABLE
ALBUMINISES	ALCOHOLIZING	ALEXIPHARMAKON	ALIKENESSES	ALKALIZERS
ALBUMINISING	ALCOHOLOMETER	ALEXIPHARMAKONS	ALIMENTARY	ALKALIZING
ALBUMINIZE	ALCOHOLOMETERS	ALEXIPHARMIC	ALIMENTATION	ALKALOIDAL
ALBUMINIZED	ALCOHOLOMETRIES	ALEXIPHARMICS	ALIMENTATIONS	ALKYLATING
ALBUMINIZES	ALCOHOLOMETRY	ALEXITHYMIA	ALIMENTATIVE	ALKYLATION
ALBUMINIZING	ALCYONARIAN	ALEXITHYMIAS	ALIMENTING	ALKYLATIONS
ALBUMINOID	ALCYONARIANS	ALFILARIAS	ALIMENTIVENESS	ALLANTOIDAL
ALBUMINOIDS	ALDERFLIES	ALFILERIAS	ALINEATION	ALLANTOIDES
ALBUMINOUS	ALDERMANIC	ALGAECIDES	ALINEATIONS	ALLANTOIDS
ALBUMINURIA	ALDERMANITIES	ALGARROBAS	ALINEMENTS	ALLANTOINS
ALBUMINURIAS	ALDERMANITY	ALGARROBOS	ALISMACEOUS	ALLANTOISES
ALBUMINURIC	ALDERMANLIKE	ALGEBRAICAL	ALITERACIES	ALLARGANDO
ALBUTEROLS	ALDERMANLY	ALGEBRAICALLY	ALITERATES	ALLAYMENTS
ALCAICERIA	ALDERMANRIES	ALGEBRAIST	ALIVENESSES	ALLEGATION
ALCAICERIAS	ALDERMANRY	ALGEBRAISTS	ALIZARINES	ALLEGATIONS
ALCARRAZAS	ALDERMANSHIP	ALGIDITIES	ALKAHESTIC	ALLEGEANCE
ALCATRASES	ALDERMANSHIPS	ALGIDNESSES	ALKALESCENCE	ALLEGEANCES
ALCHEMICAL	ALDERWOMAN	ALGOLAGNIA	ALKALESCENCES	ALLEGIANCE
ALCHEMICALLY	ALDERWOMEN	ALGOLAGNIAC	ALKALESCENCIES	ALLEGIANCES
ALCHEMISED	ALDOHEXOSE	ALGOLAGNIACS	ALKALESCENCY	ALLEGIANTS
ALCHEMISES	ALDOHEXOSES	ALGOLAGNIAS	ALKALESCENT	ALLEGORICAL
ALCHEMISING	ALDOLISATION	ALGOLAGNIC	ALKALIFIED	ALLEGORICALLY
ALCHEMISTIC	ALDOLISATIONS	ALGOLAGNIST	ALKALIFIES	ALLEGORICALNESS
ALCHEMISTICAL	ALDOLIZATION	ALGOLAGNISTS	ALKALIFYING	ALLEGORIES
ALCHEMISTS	ALDOLIZATIONS	ALGOLOGICAL	ALKALIMETER	ALLEGORISATION
ALCHEMIZED	ALDOPENTOSE	ALGOLOGICALLY	ALKALIMETERS	ALLEGORISATIONS
ALCHEMIZES	ALDOPENTOSES	ALGOLOGIES	ALKALIMETRIC	ALLEGORISE
ALCHEMIZING	ALDOSTERONE	ALGOLOGIST	ALKALIMETRIES	ALLEGORISED
ALCHERINGA	ALDOSTERONES	ALGOLOGISTS	ALKALIMETRY	ALLEGORISER
ALCHERINGAS	ALDOSTERONISM	ALGOMETERS	ALKALINISATION	ALLEGORISERS
ALCOHOLICALLY	ALDOSTERONISMS	ALGOMETRIES	ALKALINISATIONS	ALLEGORISES
ALCOHOLICITIES	ALEATORIES	ALGOPHOBIA	ALKALINISE	ALLEGORISING
ALCOHOLICITY	ALEBENCHES	ALGOPHOBIAS	ALKALINISED	ALLEGORIST
ALCOHOLICS	ALECTRYONS	ALGORISMIC	ALKALINISES	ALLEGORISTS
ALCOHOLISATION	ALEGGEAUNCE	ALGORITHMIC	ALKALINISING	ALLEGORIZATION
ALCOHOLISATIONS	ALEGGEAUNCES	ALGORITHMICALLY	ALKALINITIES	ALLEGORIZATIONS
ALCOHOLISE	ALEMBICATED	ALGORITHMS	ALKALINITY	ALLEGORIZE
ALCOHOLISED	ALEMBICATION	ALIENABILITIES	ALKALINIZATION	ALLEGORIZED
ALCOHOLISES	ALEMBICATIONS	ALIENABILITY	ALKALINIZATIONS	ALLEGORIZER
ALCOHOLISING	ALEMBROTHS	ALIENATING	ALKALINIZE	ALLEGORIZERS
ALCOHOLISM	ALERTNESSES	ALIENATION	ALKALINIZED	ALLEGORIZES

ALLEGORIZING	ALLITERATIVE	ALLOPATRICALLY	ALLUSIVENESS	ALPHABETISES
ALLEGRETTO	ALLITERATIVELY	ALLOPATRIES	ALLUSIVENESSES	ALPHABETISING
ALLEGRETTOS	ALLNIGHTER	ALLOPHANES	ALLWEATHER	ALPHABETIZATION
ALLELOMORPH	ALLNIGHTERS	ALLOPHONES	ALLWEATHERS	ALPHABETIZE
ALLELOMORPHIC	ALLOANTIBODIES	ALLOPHONIC	ALLYCHOLLIES	ALPHABETIZED
ALLELOMORPHISM	ALLOANTIBODY	ALLOPLASMIC	ALLYCHOLLY	ALPHABETIZER
ALLELOMORPHISMS	ALLOANTIGEN	ALLOPLASMS	ALMACANTAR	ALPHABETIZERS
ALLELOMORPHS	ALLOANTIGENS	ALLOPLASTIC	ALMACANTARS	ALPHABETIZES
ALLELOPATHIC	ALLOCARPIES	ALLOPOLYPLOID	ALMANDINES	ALPHABETIZING
ALLELOPATHIES	ALLOCATABLE	ALLOPOLYPLOIDS	ALMANDITES	ALPHAMERIC
ALLELOPATHY	ALLOCATING	ALLOPOLYPLOIDY	ALMIGHTILY	ALPHAMERICAL
ALLELUIAHS	ALLOCATION	ALLOPURINOL	ALMIGHTINESS	ALPHAMERICALLY
ALLEMANDES	ALLOCATIONS	ALLOPURINOLS	ALMIGHTINESSES	ALPHAMETIC
ALLERGENIC	ALLOCATORS	ALLOSAURUS	ALMONDIEST	ALPHAMETICS
ALLERGENICITIES	ALLOCHEIRIA	ALLOSAURUSES	ALMONDITES	ALPHANUMERIC
ALLERGENICITY	ALLOCHEIRIAS	ALLOSTERIC	ALMSGIVERS	ALPHANUMERICAL
ALLERGISTS	ALLOCHIRIA	ALLOSTERICALLY	ALMSGIVING	ALPHANUMERICS
ALLETHRINS	ALLOCHIRIAS	ALLOSTERIES	ALMSGIVINGS	ALPHASORTED
ALLEVIANTS	ALLOCHTHONOUS	ALLOTETRAPLOID	ALMSHOUSES	ALPHASORTING
ALLEVIATED	ALLOCUTION	ALLOTETRAPLOIDS	ALMUCANTAR	ALPHASORTS
ALLEVIATES	ALLOCUTIONS	ALLOTETRAPLOIDY	ALMUCANTARS	ALPHATESTED
ALLEVIATING	ALLODYNIAS	ALLOTHEISM	ALOESWOODS	ALPHATESTING
ALLEVIATION	ALLOGAMIES	ALLOTHEISMS	ALOGICALLY	ALPHATESTS
ALLEVIATIONS	ALLOGAMOUS	ALLOTMENTS	ALONENESSES	ALPHOSISES
ALLEVIATIVE	ALLOGENEIC	ALLOTRIOMORPHIC	ALONGSHORE	ALSTROEMERIA
ALLEVIATOR	ALLOGRAFTED	ALLOTROPES	ALONGSHOREMAN	ALSTROEMERIAS
ALLEVIATORS	ALLOGRAFTING	ALLOTROPIC	ALONGSHOREMEN	ALTALTISSIMO
ALLEVIATORY	ALLOGRAFTS	ALLOTROPICALLY	ALOOFNESSES	ALTALTISSIMOS
ALLHALLOND	ALLOGRAPHIC	ALLOTROPIES	ALPARGATAS	ALTARPIECE
ALLHALLOWEN	ALLOGRAPHS	ALLOTROPISM	ALPENGLOWS	ALTARPIECES
ALLHALLOWN	ALLOIOSTROPHOS	ALLOTROPISMS	ALPENHORNS	ALTAZIMUTH
ALLHOLLOWN	ALLOMERISM	ALLOTROPOUS	ALPENSTOCK	ALTAZIMUTHS
ALLIACEOUS	ALLOMERISMS	ALLOTTERIES	ALPENSTOCKS	ALTERABILITIES
ALLICHOLIES	ALLOMEROUS	ALLOTYPICALLY	ALPESTRINE	ALTERABILITY
ALLIGARTAS	ALLOMETRIC	ALLOTYPIES	ALPHABETARIAN	ALTERATION
ALLIGATING	ALLOMETRIES	ALLOWABILITIES	ALPHABETARIANS	ALTERATIONS
ALLIGATION	ALLOMORPHIC	ALLOWABILITY	ALPHABETED	ALTERATIVE
ALLIGATIONS	ALLOMORPHISM	ALLOWABLENESS	ALPHABETIC	ALTERATIVES
ALLIGATORS	ALLOMORPHISMS	ALLOWABLENESSES	ALPHABETICAL	ALTERCATED
ALLINEATION	ALLOMORPHS	ALLOWABLES	ALPHABETICALLY	ALTERCATES
ALLINEATIONS	ALLONYMOUS	ALLOWANCED	ALPHABETIFORM	ALTERCATING
ALLITERATE	ALLOPATHIC	ALLOWANCES	ALPHABETING	ALTERCATION
ALLITERATED	ALLOPATHICALLY	ALLOWANCING	ALPHABETISATION	ALTERCATIONS
ALLITERATES	ALLOPATHIES	ALLUREMENT	ALPHABETISE	ALTERCATIVE
ALLITERATING	ALLOPATHIST	ALLUREMENTS	ALPHABETISED	ALTERITIES
ALLITERATION	ALLOPATHISTS	ALLURINGLY	ALPHABETISER	ALTERNANCE
ALLITERATIONS	ALLOPATRIC	ALLUSIVELY	ALPHABETISERS	ALTERNANCES

ALTERNANTS
ALTERNATED
ALTERNATELY
ALTERNATES
ALTERNATIM
ALTERNATING
ALTERNATION
ALTERNATIONS
ALTERNATIVE
ALTERNATIVELY
ALTERNATIVENESS
ALTERNATIVES
ALTERNATOR
ALTERNATORS
ALTIGRAPHS
ALTIMETERS
ALTIMETRICAL
ALTIMETRICALLY
ALTIMETRIES
ALTIPLANOS
ALTISONANT
ALTISSIMOS
ALTITONANT
ALTITUDINAL
ALTITUDINARIAN
ALTITUDINARIANS
ALTITUDINOUS
ALTOCUMULI
ALTOCUMULUS
ALTOGETHER
ALTOGETHERS
ALTORUFFLED
ALTOSTRATI
ALTOSTRATUS
ALTRICIALS
ALTRUISTIC
ALTRUISTICALLY
ALUMINATES
ALUMINIFEROUS
ALUMINISED
ALUMINISES
ALUMINISING
ALUMINIUMS
ALUMINIZED
ALUMINIZES
ALUMINIZING
ALUMINOSILICATE

ALUMINOSITIES
ALUMINOSITY
ALUMINOTHERMIES
ALUMINOTHERMY
ALUMSTONES
ALVEOLARLY
ALVEOLATION
ALVEOLATIONS
ALVEOLITIS
ALVEOLITISES
ALYCOMPAINE
ALYCOMPAINES
AMAKWEREKWERE
AMALGAMATE
AMALGAMATED
AMALGAMATES
AMALGAMATING
AMALGAMATION
AMALGAMATIONS
AMALGAMATIVE
AMALGAMATOR
AMALGAMATORS
AMANTADINE
AMANTADINES
AMANUENSES
AMANUENSIS
AMARACUSES
AMARANTACEOUS
AMARANTHACEOUS
AMARANTHINE
AMARANTINE
AMARYLLIDACEOUS
AMARYLLIDS
AMARYLLISES
AMASSMENTS
AMATEURISH
AMATEURISHLY
AMATEURISHNESS
AMATEURISM
AMATEURISMS
AMATEURSHIP
AMATEURSHIPS
AMATIVENESS
AMATIVENESSES
AMATORIALLY
AMATORIOUS
AMAZEBALLS

AMAZEDNESS
AMAZEDNESSES
AMAZEMENTS
AMAZONIANS
AMAZONITES
AMAZONSTONE
AMAZONSTONES
AMBAGITORY
AMBASSADOR
AMBASSADORIAL
AMBASSADORS
AMBASSADORSHIP
AMBASSADORSHIPS
AMBASSADRESS
AMBASSADRESSES
AMBASSAGES
AMBERGRISES
AMBERJACKS
AMBIDENTATE
AMBIDEXTER
AMBIDEXTERITIES
AMBIDEXTERITY
AMBIDEXTEROUS
AMBIDEXTERS
AMBIDEXTROUS
AMBIDEXTROUSLY
AMBIGUITIES
AMBIGUOUSLY
AMBIGUOUSNESS
AMBIGUOUSNESSES
AMBILATERAL
AMBIOPHONIES
AMBIOPHONY
AMBISEXUAL
AMBISEXUALITIES
AMBISEXUALITY
AMBISEXUALS
AMBISONICS
AMBITIONED
AMBITIONING
AMBITIONLESS
AMBITIOUSLY
AMBITIOUSNESS
AMBITIOUSNESSES
AMBIVALENCE
AMBIVALENCES
AMBIVALENCIES

AMBIVALENCY
AMBIVALENT
AMBIVALENTLY
AMBIVERSION
AMBIVERSIONS
AMBLYGONITE
AMBLYGONITES
AMBLYOPIAS
AMBOCEPTOR
AMBOCEPTORS
AMBOSEXUAL
AMBROSIALLY
AMBROTYPES
AMBULACRAL
AMBULACRUM
AMBULANCEMAN
AMBULANCEMEN
AMBULANCES
AMBULANCEWOMAN
AMBULANCEWOMEN
AMBULATING
AMBULATION
AMBULATIONS
AMBULATORIES
AMBULATORILY
AMBULATORS
AMBULATORY
AMBULETTES
AMBUSCADED
AMBUSCADER
AMBUSCADERS
AMBUSCADES
AMBUSCADING
AMBUSCADOES
AMBUSCADOS
AMBUSHMENT
AMBUSHMENTS
AMEBOCYTES
AMELIORABLE
AMELIORANT
AMELIORANTS
AMELIORATE
AMELIORATED
AMELIORATES
AMELIORATING
AMELIORATION
AMELIORATIONS

AMELIORATIVE
AMELIORATOR
AMELIORATORS
AMELIORATORY
AMELOBLAST
AMELOBLASTS
AMELOGENESES
AMELOGENESIS
AMENABILITIES
AMENABILITY
AMENABLENESS
AMENABLENESSES
AMENAUNCES
AMENDATORY
AMENDMENTS
AMENORRHEA
AMENORRHEAS
AMENORRHEIC
AMENORRHOEA
AMENORRHOEAS
AMENTACEOUS
AMENTIFEROUS
AMERCEABLE
AMERCEMENT
AMERCEMENTS
AMERCIABLE
AMERCIAMENT
AMERCIAMENTS
AMERICIUMS
AMETABOLIC
AMETABOLISM
AMETABOLISMS
AMETABOLOUS
AMETHYSTINE
AMETROPIAS
AMIABILITIES
AMIABILITY
AMIABLENESS
AMIABLENESSES
AMIANTHINE
AMIANTHOID
AMIANTHOIDAL
AMIANTHUSES
AMIANTUSES
AMICABILITIES
AMICABILITY
AMICABLENESS

AMICABLENESSES	AMNIOCENTESES	AMPHETAMINES	AMPHIMIXES	AMPLIATIONS
AMINOACIDURIA	AMNIOCENTESIS	AMPHIARTHROSES	AMPHIMIXIS	AMPLIATIVE
AMINOACIDURIAS	AMNIOTOMIES	AMPHIARTHROSIS	AMPHIOXUSES	AMPLIDYNES
AMINOBENZOIC	AMOBARBITAL	AMPHIASTER	AMPHIPATHIC	AMPLIFIABLE
AMINOBUTENE	AMOBARBITALS	AMPHIASTERS	AMPHIPHILE	AMPLIFICATION
AMINOBUTENES	AMOEBIASES	AMPHIBIANS	AMPHIPHILES	AMPLIFICATIONS
AMINOPEPTIDASE	AMOEBIASIS	AMPHIBIOTIC	AMPHIPHILIC	AMPLIFIERS
AMINOPEPTIDASES	AMOEBIFORM	AMPHIBIOUS	AMPHIPLOID	AMPLIFYING
AMINOPHENAZONE	AMOEBOCYTE	AMPHIBIOUSLY	AMPHIPLOIDIES	AMPLITUDES
AMINOPHENAZONES	AMOEBOCYTES	AMPHIBIOUSNESS	AMPHIPLOIDS	AMPLOSOMES
AMINOPHENOL	AMONTILLADO	AMPHIBLASTIC	AMPHIPLOIDY	AMPULLACEAL
AMINOPHENOLS	AMONTILLADOS	AMPHIBLASTULA	AMPHIPODOUS	AMPULLACEOUS
AMINOPHYLLINE	AMORALISMS	AMPHIBLASTULAE	AMPHIPROSTYLAR	AMPULLOSITIES
AMINOPHYLLINES	AMORALISTS	AMPHIBOLES	AMPHIPROSTYLE	AMPULLOSITY
AMINOPTERIN	AMORALITIES	AMPHIBOLIC	AMPHIPROSTYLES	AMPUTATING
AMINOPTERINS	AMOROSITIES	AMPHIBOLIES	AMPHIPROTIC	AMPUTATION
AMINOPYRINE	AMOROUSNESS	AMPHIBOLITE	AMPHISBAENA	AMPUTATIONS
AMINOPYRINES	AMOROUSNESSES	AMPHIBOLITES	AMPHISBAENAE	AMPUTATORS
AMISSIBILITIES	AMORPHISMS	AMPHIBOLOGICAL	AMPHISBAENAS	AMRITATTVA
AMISSIBILITY	AMORPHOUSLY	AMPHIBOLOGIES	AMPHISBAENIC	AMRITATTVAS
AMITOTICALLY	AMORPHOUSNESS	AMPHIBOLOGY	AMPHISCIAN	AMSINCKIAS
AMITRIPTYLINE	AMORPHOUSNESSES	AMPHIBOLOUS	AMPHISCIANS	AMUSEMENTS
AMITRIPTYLINES	AMORTISABLE	AMPHIBRACH	AMPHISTOMATAL	AMUSINGNESS
AMITRYPTYLINE	AMORTISATION	AMPHIBRACHIC	AMPHISTOMATIC	AMUSINGNESSES
AMITRYPTYLINES	AMORTISATIONS	AMPHIBRACHS	AMPHISTOMOUS	AMUSIVENESS
AMMOCOETES	AMORTISEMENT	AMPHICHROIC	AMPHISTYLAR	AMUSIVENESSES
AMMONIACAL	AMORTISEMENTS	AMPHICHROMATIC	AMPHISTYLARS	AMYGDALACEOUS
AMMONIACUM	AMORTISING	AMPHICOELOUS	AMPHITHEATER	AMYGDALATE
AMMONIACUMS	AMORTIZABLE	AMPHICTYON	AMPHITHEATERS	AMYGDALINE
AMMONIATED	AMORTIZATION	AMPHICTYONIC	AMPHITHEATRAL	AMYGDALINS
AMMONIATES	AMORTIZATIONS	AMPHICTYONIES	AMPHITHEATRE	AMYGDALOID
AMMONIATING	AMORTIZEMENT	AMPHICTYONS	AMPHITHEATRES	AMYGDALOIDAL
AMMONIATION	AMORTIZEMENTS	AMPHICTYONY	AMPHITHEATRIC	AMYGDALOIDS
AMMONIATIONS	AMORTIZING	AMPHIDENTATE	AMPHITHEATRICAL	AMYLACEOUS
AMMONIFICATION	AMOURETTES	AMPHIDIPLOID	AMPHITHECIA	AMYLOBARBITONE
AMMONIFICATIONS	AMOXICILLIN	AMPHIDIPLOIDIES	AMPHITHECIUM	AMYLOBARBITONES
AMMONIFIED	AMOXICILLINS	AMPHIDIPLOIDS	AMPHITRICHA	AMYLOIDOSES
AMMONIFIES	AMOXYCILLIN	AMPHIDIPLOIDY	AMPHITRICHOUS	AMYLOIDOSIS
AMMONIFYING	AMOXYCILLINS	AMPHIGASTRIA	AMPHITROPOUS	AMYLOLYSES
AMMONOLYSES	AMPELOGRAPHIES	AMPHIGASTRIUM	AMPHOLYTES	AMYLOLYSIS
AMMONOLYSIS	AMPELOGRAPHY	AMPHIGORIC	AMPHOTERIC	AMYLOLYTIC
AMMOPHILOUS	AMPELOPSES	AMPHIGORIES	AMPICILLIN	AMYLOPECTIN
AMMUNITION	AMPELOPSIS	AMPHIGOURI	AMPICILLINS	AMYLOPECTINS
AMMUNITIONED	AMPEROMETRIC	AMPHIGOURIS	AMPLENESSES	AMYLOPLAST
AMMUNITIONING	AMPERSANDS	AMPHIMACER	AMPLEXICAUL	AMYLOPLASTS
AMMUNITIONS	AMPERZANDS	AMPHIMACERS	AMPLEXUSES	AMYLOPSINS
AMNESTYING	AMPHETAMINE	AMPHIMICTIC	AMPLIATION	AMYOTONIAS

AMYOTROPHIC
AMYOTROPHIES
AMYOTROPHY
ANABANTIDS
ANABAPTISE
ANABAPTISED
ANABAPTISES
ANABAPTISING
ANABAPTISM
ANABAPTISMS
ANABAPTIST
ANABAPTISTIC
ANABAPTISTS
ANABAPTIZE
ANABAPTIZED
ANABAPTIZES
ANABAPTIZING
ANABLEPSES
ANABOLISMS
ANABOLITES
ANABOLITIC
ANABRANCHES
ANACARDIACEOUS
ANACARDIUM
ANACARDIUMS
ANACATHARSES
ANACATHARSIS
ANACATHARTIC
ANACATHARTICS
ANACHARISES
ANACHORISM
ANACHORISMS
ANACHRONIC
ANACHRONICAL
ANACHRONICALLY
ANACHRONISM
ANACHRONISMS
ANACHRONISTIC
ANACHRONOUS
ANACHRONOUSLY
ANACLASTIC
ANACOLUTHA
ANACOLUTHIA
ANACOLUTHIAS
ANACOLUTHIC
ANACOLUTHICALLY
ANACOLUTHON

ANACOLUTHONS
ANACOUSTIC
ANACREONTIC
ANACREONTICALLY
ANACREONTICS
ANACRUSTIC
ANADIPLOSES
ANADIPLOSIS
ANADROMOUS
ANADYOMENE
ANAEMICALLY
ANAEROBICALLY
ANAEROBIONT
ANAEROBIONTS
ANAEROBIOSES
ANAEROBIOSIS
ANAEROBIOTIC
ANAEROBIUM
ANAESTHESES
ANAESTHESIA
ANAESTHESIAS
ANAESTHESIOLOGY
ANAESTHESIS
ANAESTHETIC
ANAESTHETICALLY
ANAESTHETICS
ANAESTHETISE
ANAESTHETISED
ANAESTHETISES
ANAESTHETISING
ANAESTHETIST
ANAESTHETISTS
ANAESTHETIZE
ANAESTHETIZED
ANAESTHETIZES
ANAESTHETIZING
ANAGENESES
ANAGENESIS
ANAGLYPHIC
ANAGLYPHICAL
ANAGLYPHIES
ANAGLYPTIC
ANAGLYPTICAL
ANAGNORISES
ANAGNORISIS
ANAGOGICAL
ANAGOGICALLY

ANAGRAMMATIC
ANAGRAMMATICAL
ANAGRAMMATISE
ANAGRAMMATISED
ANAGRAMMATISES
ANAGRAMMATISING
ANAGRAMMATISM
ANAGRAMMATISMS
ANAGRAMMATIST
ANAGRAMMATISTS
ANAGRAMMATIZE
ANAGRAMMATIZED
ANAGRAMMATIZES
ANAGRAMMATIZING
ANAGRAMMED
ANAGRAMMER
ANAGRAMMERS
ANAGRAMMING
ANALEMMATA
ANALEMMATIC
ANALEPTICS
ANALGESIAS
ANALGESICS
ANALGETICS
ANALOGICAL
ANALOGICALLY
ANALOGISED
ANALOGISES
ANALOGISING
ANALOGISMS
ANALOGISTS
ANALOGIZED
ANALOGIZES
ANALOGIZING
ANALOGOUSLY
ANALOGOUSNESS
ANALOGOUSNESSES
ANALPHABET
ANALPHABETE
ANALPHABETES
ANALPHABETIC
ANALPHABETICS
ANALPHABETISM
ANALPHABETISMS
ANALPHABETS
ANALYSABILITIES
ANALYSABILITY

ANALYSABLE
ANALYSANDS
ANALYSATION
ANALYSATIONS
ANALYTICAL
ANALYTICALLY
ANALYTICITIES
ANALYTICITY
ANALYZABILITIES
ANALYZABILITY
ANALYZABLE
ANALYZATION
ANALYZATIONS
ANAMNESTIC
ANAMNESTICALLY
ANAMNIOTES
ANAMNIOTIC
ANAMORPHIC
ANAMORPHISM
ANAMORPHISMS
ANAMORPHOSCOPE
ANAMORPHOSCOPES
ANAMORPHOSES
ANAMORPHOSIS
ANAMORPHOUS
ANANDAMIDE
ANANDAMIDES
ANAPAESTIC
ANAPAESTICAL
ANAPESTICS
ANAPHORESES
ANAPHORESIS
ANAPHORICAL
ANAPHORICALLY
ANAPHRODISIA
ANAPHRODISIAC
ANAPHRODISIACS
ANAPHRODISIAS
ANAPHYLACTIC
ANAPHYLACTOID
ANAPHYLAXES
ANAPHYLAXIES
ANAPHYLAXIS
ANAPHYLAXY
ANAPLASIAS
ANAPLASMOSES
ANAPLASMOSIS

ANAPLASTIC
ANAPLASTIES
ANAPLEROSES
ANAPLEROSIS
ANAPLEROTIC
ANAPTYCTIC
ANAPTYCTICAL
ANARCHICAL
ANARCHICALLY
ANARCHISED
ANARCHISES
ANARCHISING
ANARCHISMS
ANARCHISTIC
ANARCHISTICALLY
ANARCHISTS
ANARCHIZED
ANARCHIZES
ANARCHIZING
ANARTHRIAS
ANARTHROUS
ANARTHROUSLY
ANARTHROUSNESS
ANASARCOUS
ANASTIGMAT
ANASTIGMATIC
ANASTIGMATISM
ANASTIGMATISMS
ANASTIGMATS
ANASTOMOSE
ANASTOMOSED
ANASTOMOSES
ANASTOMOSING
ANASTOMOSIS
ANASTOMOTIC
ANASTROPHE
ANASTROPHES
ANASTROZOLE
ANASTROZOLES
ANATHEMATA
ANATHEMATICAL
ANATHEMATICALS
ANATHEMATISE
ANATHEMATISED
ANATHEMATISES
ANATHEMATISING
ANATHEMATIZE

ANATHEMATIZED	ANCHOVETTA	ANDROMEDAS	ANEMOPHILY	ANGELOLOGIST
ANATHEMATIZES	ANCHOVETTAS	ANDROMEDOTOXIN	ANEMOPHOBIA	ANGELOLOGISTS
ANATHEMATIZING	ANCHYLOSED	ANDROMEDOTOXINS	ANEMOPHOBIAS	ANGELOLOGY
ANATOMICAL	ANCHYLOSES	ANDROMONOECIOUS	ANEMOSCOPE	ANGELOPHANIES
ANATOMICALLY	ANCHYLOSING	ANDROMONOECISM	ANEMOSCOPES	ANGELOPHANY
ANATOMISATION	ANCHYLOSIS	ANDROMONOECISMS	ANENCEPHALIA	ANGIOCARPOUS
ANATOMISATIONS	ANCHYLOTIC	ANDROPAUSE	ANENCEPHALIAS	ANGIOGENESES
ANATOMISED	ANCIENTEST	ANDROPAUSES	ANENCEPHALIC	ANGIOGENESIS
ANATOMISER	ANCIENTNESS	ANDROPHORE	ANENCEPHALIES	ANGIOGENIC
ANATOMISERS	ANCIENTNESSES	ANDROPHORES	ANENCEPHALY	ANGIOGRAMS
ANATOMISES	ANCIENTRIES	ANDROSPHINGES	ANESTHESIA	ANGIOGRAPHIC
ANATOMISING	ANCILLARIES	ANDROSPHINX	ANESTHESIAS	ANGIOGRAPHIES
ANATOMISTS	ANCIPITOUS	ANDROSPHINXES	ANESTHESIOLOGY	ANGIOGRAPHY
ANATOMIZATION	ANCYLOSTOMIASES	ANDROSTERONE	ANESTHETIC	ANGIOLOGIES
ANATOMIZATIONS	ANCYLOSTOMIASIS	ANDROSTERONES	ANESTHETICALLY	ANGIOMATOUS
ANATOMIZED	ANDALUSITE	ANECDOTAGE	ANESTHETICS	ANGIOPLASTIES
ANATOMIZER	ANDALUSITES	ANECDOTAGES	ANESTHETISATION	ANGIOPLASTY
ANATOMIZERS	ANDANTINOS	ANECDOTALISM	ANESTHETISE	ANGIOSARCOMA
ANATOMIZES	ANDOUILLES	ANECDOTALISMS	ANESTHETISED	ANGIOSARCOMAS
ANATOMIZING	ANDOUILLETTE	ANECDOTALIST	ANESTHETISES	ANGIOSARCOMATA
ANATROPIES	ANDOUILLETTES	ANECDOTALISTS	ANESTHETISING	ANGIOSPERM
ANATROPOUS	ANDRADITES	ANECDOTALLY	ANESTHETIST	ANGIOSPERMAL
ANCESTORED	ANDROCENTRIC	ANECDOTICAL	ANESTHETISTS	ANGIOSPERMOUS
ANCESTORIAL	ANDROCENTRISM	ANECDOTICALLY	ANESTHETIZATION	ANGIOSPERMS
ANCESTORING	ANDROCENTRISMS	ANECDOTIST	ANESTHETIZE	ANGIOSTOMATOUS
ANCESTRALLY	ANDROCEPHALOUS	ANECDOTISTS	ANESTHETIZED	ANGIOSTOMOUS
ANCESTRALS	ANDROCLINIA	ANELASTICITIES	ANESTHETIZES	ANGIOTENSIN
ANCESTRESS	ANDROCLINIUM	ANELASTICITY	ANESTHETIZING	ANGIOTENSINS
ANCESTRESSES	ANDRODIOECIOUS	ANEMICALLY	ANEUPLOIDIES	ANGLEBERRIES
ANCESTRIES	ANDRODIOECISM	ANEMOCHORE	ANEUPLOIDS	ANGLEBERRY
ANCHORAGES	ANDRODIOECISMS	ANEMOCHORES	ANEUPLOIDY	ANGLEDOZER
ANCHORESSES	ANDROECIAL	ANEMOCHOROUS	ANEURISMAL	ANGLEDOZERS
ANCHORETIC	ANDROECIUM	ANEMOGRAMS	ANEURISMALLY	ANGLERFISH
ANCHORETICAL	ANDROECIUMS	ANEMOGRAPH	ANEURISMATIC	ANGLERFISHES
ANCHORETTE	ANDROGENESES	ANEMOGRAPHIC	ANEURYSMAL	ANGLESITES
ANCHORETTES	ANDROGENESIS	ANEMOGRAPHIES	ANEURYSMALLY	ANGLETWITCH
ANCHORITES	ANDROGENETIC	ANEMOGRAPHS	ANEURYSMATIC	ANGLETWITCHES
ANCHORITIC	ANDROGENIC	ANEMOGRAPHY	ANFRACTUOSITIES	ANGLEWORMS
ANCHORITICAL	ANDROGENOUS	ANEMOLOGIES	ANFRACTUOSITY	ANGLICISATION
ANCHORITICALLY	ANDROGYNES	ANEMOMETER	ANFRACTUOUS	ANGLICISATIONS
ANCHORLESS	ANDROGYNIES	ANEMOMETERS	ANGASHORES	ANGLICISED
ANCHORPEOPLE	ANDROGYNOPHORE	ANEMOMETRIC	ANGELFISHES	ANGLICISES
ANCHORPERSON	ANDROGYNOPHORES	ANEMOMETRICAL	ANGELHOODS	ANGLICISING
ANCHORPERSONS	ANDROGYNOUS	ANEMOMETRIES	ANGELICALLY	ANGLICISMS
ANCHORWOMAN	ANDROLOGIES	ANEMOMETRY	ANGELOLATRIES	ANGLICISTS
ANCHORWOMEN	ANDROLOGIST	ANEMOPHILIES	ANGELOLATRY	ANGLICIZATION
ANCHOVETAS	ANDROLOGISTS	ANEMOPHILOUS	ANGELOLOGIES	ANGLICIZATIONS

ANGLICIZED	ANHELATION	ANIMALLIKE	ANNALISING	ANNULARITY
ANGLICIZES	ANHELATIONS	ANIMATEDLY	ANNALISTIC	ANNULATION
ANGLICIZING	ANHIDROSES	ANIMATENESS	ANNALIZING	ANNULATIONS
ANGLIFYING	ANHIDROSIS	ANIMATENESSES	ANNEALINGS	ANNULLABLE
ANGLISTICS	ANHIDROTIC	ANIMATINGLY	ANNELIDANS	ANNULMENTS
ANGLOMANIA	ANHIDROTICS	ANIMATIONS	ANNEXATION	ANNUNCIATE
ANGLOMANIAC	ANHUNGERED	ANIMATISMS	ANNEXATIONAL	ANNUNCIATED
ANGLOMANIACS	ANHYDRASES	ANIMATISTS	ANNEXATIONISM	ANNUNCIATES
ANGLOMANIAS	ANHYDRIDES	ANIMATRONIC	ANNEXATIONISMS	ANNUNCIATING
ANGLOPHILE	ANHYDRITES	ANIMATRONICALLY	ANNEXATIONIST	ANNUNCIATION
ANGLOPHILES	ANICONISMS	ANIMATRONICS	ANNEXATIONISTS	ANNUNCIATIONS
ANGLOPHILIA	ANICONISTS	ANIMOSITIES	ANNEXATIONS	ANNUNCIATIVE
ANGLOPHILIAS	ANILINCTUS	ANISEIKONIA	ANNEXMENTS	ANNUNCIATOR
ANGLOPHILIC	ANILINCTUSES	ANISEIKONIAS	ANNIHILABLE	ANNUNCIATORS
ANGLOPHILS	ANILINGUSES	ANISEIKONIC	ANNIHILATE	ANNUNCIATORY
ANGLOPHOBE	ANIMADVERSION	ANISOCERCAL	ANNIHILATED	ANNUNTIATE
ANGLOPHOBES	ANIMADVERSIONS	ANISODACTYL	ANNIHILATES	ANNUNTIATED
ANGLOPHOBIA	ANIMADVERT	ANISODACTYLOUS	ANNIHILATING	ANNUNTIATES
ANGLOPHOBIAC	ANIMADVERTED	ANISODACTYLS	ANNIHILATION	ANNUNTIATING
ANGLOPHOBIACS	ANIMADVERTER	ANISOGAMIES	ANNIHILATIONISM	ANODICALLY
ANGLOPHOBIAS	ANIMADVERTERS	ANISOGAMOUS	ANNIHILATIONS	ANODISATION
ANGLOPHOBIC	ANIMADVERTING	ANISOMERIC	ANNIHILATIVE	ANODISATIONS
ANGLOPHONE	ANIMADVERTS	ANISOMEROUS	ANNIHILATOR	ANODIZATION
ANGLOPHONES	ANIMALCULA	ANISOMETRIC	ANNIHILATORS	ANODIZATIONS
ANGLOPHONIC	ANIMALCULAR	ANISOMETROPIA	ANNIHILATORY	ANODONTIAS
ANGOPHORAS	ANIMALCULE	ANISOMETROPIAS	ANNIVERSARIES	ANOESTROUS
ANGOSTURAS	ANIMALCULES	ANISOMETROPIC	ANNIVERSARY	ANOINTINGS
ANGRINESSES	ANIMALCULISM	ANISOMORPHIC	ANNOTATABLE	ANOINTMENT
ANGUIFAUNA	ANIMALCULISMS	ANISOPHYLLIES	ANNOTATING	ANOINTMENTS
ANGUIFAUNAE	ANIMALCULIST	ANISOPHYLLOUS	ANNOTATION	ANOMALISTIC
ANGUIFAUNAS	ANIMALCULISTS	ANISOPHYLLY	ANNOTATIONS	ANOMALISTICAL
ANGUILLIFORM	ANIMALCULUM	ANISOTROPIC	ANNOTATIVE	ANOMALISTICALLY
ANGUIPEDES	ANIMALIERS	ANISOTROPICALLY	ANNOTATORS	ANOMALOUSLY
ANGUISHING	ANIMALISATION	ANISOTROPIES	ANNOUNCEMENT	ANOMALOUSNESS
ANGULARITIES	ANIMALISATIONS	ANISOTROPISM	ANNOUNCEMENTS	ANOMALOUSNESSES
ANGULARITY	ANIMALISED	ANISOTROPISMS	ANNOUNCERS	ANONACEOUS
ANGULARNESS	ANIMALISES	ANISOTROPY	ANNOUNCING	ANONYMISED
ANGULARNESSES	ANIMALISING	ANKLEBONES	ANNOYANCES	ANONYMISES
ANGULATING	ANIMALISMS	ANKYLOSAUR	ANNOYINGLY	ANONYMISING
ANGULATION	ANIMALISTIC	ANKYLOSAURS	ANNUALISED	ANONYMITIES
ANGULATIONS	ANIMALISTS	ANKYLOSAURUS	ANNUALISES	ANONYMIZED
ANGUSTIFOLIATE	ANIMALITIES	ANKYLOSAURUSES	ANNUALISING	ANONYMIZES
ANGUSTIROSTRATE	ANIMALIZATION	ANKYLOSING	ANNUALIZED	ANONYMIZING
ANGWANTIBO	ANIMALIZATIONS	ANKYLOSTOMIASES	ANNUALIZES	ANONYMOUSLY
ANGWANTIBOS	ANIMALIZED	ANKYLOSTOMIASIS	ANNUALIZING	ANONYMOUSNESS
ANHARMONIC	ANIMALIZES	ANNABERGITE	ANNUITANTS	ANONYMOUSNESSES
ANHEDONIAS	ANIMALIZING	ANNABERGITES	ANNULARITIES	ANOPHELINE

ANOPHELINES
ANORECTICS
ANOREXIGENIC
ANORTHITES
ANORTHITIC
ANORTHOSITE
ANORTHOSITES
ANORTHOSITIC
ANOTHERGUESS
ANOVULANTS
ANOVULATION
ANOVULATIONS
ANOVULATORY
ANOXAEMIAS
ANSAPHONES
ANSWERABILITIES
ANSWERABILITY
ANSWERABLE
ANSWERABLENESS
ANSWERABLY
ANSWERLESS
ANSWERPHONE
ANSWERPHONES
ANTAGONISABLE
ANTAGONISATION
ANTAGONISATIONS
ANTAGONISE
ANTAGONISED
ANTAGONISES
ANTAGONISING
ANTAGONISM
ANTAGONISMS
ANTAGONIST
ANTAGONISTIC
ANTAGONISTS
ANTAGONIZABLE
ANTAGONIZATION
ANTAGONIZATIONS
ANTAGONIZE
ANTAGONIZED
ANTAGONIZES
ANTAGONIZING
ANTALKALIES
ANTALKALINE
ANTALKALINES
ANTALKALIS
ANTAPHRODISIAC

ANTAPHRODISIACS
ANTARTHRITIC
ANTARTHRITICS
ANTASTHMATIC
ANTASTHMATICS
ANTEBELLUM
ANTECEDENCE
ANTECEDENCES
ANTECEDENT
ANTECEDENTLY
ANTECEDENTS
ANTECEDING
ANTECESSOR
ANTECESSORS
ANTECHAMBER
ANTECHAMBERS
ANTECHAPEL
ANTECHAPELS
ANTECHOIRS
ANTEDATING
ANTEDILUVIAL
ANTEDILUVIALLY
ANTEDILUVIAN
ANTEDILUVIANS
ANTEMERIDIAN
ANTEMORTEM
ANTEMUNDANE
ANTENATALLY
ANTENATALS
ANTENNIFEROUS
ANTENNIFORM
ANTENNULAR
ANTENNULES
ANTENUPTIAL
ANTENUPTIALS
ANTEORBITAL
ANTEPENDIA
ANTEPENDIUM
ANTEPENDIUMS
ANTEPENULT
ANTEPENULTIMA
ANTEPENULTIMAS
ANTEPENULTIMATE
ANTEPENULTS
ANTEPOSITION
ANTEPOSITIONS
ANTEPRANDIAL

ANTERIORITIES
ANTERIORITY
ANTERIORLY
ANTEROGRADE
ANTEVERSION
ANTEVERSIONS
ANTEVERTED
ANTEVERTING
ANTHELICES
ANTHELIONS
ANTHELIXES
ANTHELMINTHIC
ANTHELMINTHICS
ANTHELMINTIC
ANTHELMINTICS
ANTHEMISES
ANTHEMWISE
ANTHERIDIA
ANTHERIDIAL
ANTHERIDIUM
ANTHEROZOID
ANTHEROZOIDS
ANTHEROZOOID
ANTHEROZOOIDS
ANTHERSMUT
ANTHERSMUTS
ANTHOCARPOUS
ANTHOCARPS
ANTHOCHLORE
ANTHOCHLORES
ANTHOCYANIN
ANTHOCYANINS
ANTHOCYANS
ANTHOLOGICAL
ANTHOLOGIES
ANTHOLOGISE
ANTHOLOGISED
ANTHOLOGISER
ANTHOLOGISERS
ANTHOLOGISES
ANTHOLOGISING
ANTHOLOGIST
ANTHOLOGISTS
ANTHOLOGIZE
ANTHOLOGIZED
ANTHOLOGIZER
ANTHOLOGIZERS

ANTHOLOGIZES
ANTHOLOGIZING
ANTHOMANIA
ANTHOMANIAC
ANTHOMANIACS
ANTHOMANIAS
ANTHOPHILOUS
ANTHOPHORE
ANTHOPHORES
ANTHOPHYLLITE
ANTHOPHYLLITES
ANTHOTAXIES
ANTHOXANTHIN
ANTHOXANTHINS
ANTHOZOANS
ANTHRACENE
ANTHRACENES
ANTHRACITE
ANTHRACITES
ANTHRACITIC
ANTHRACNOSE
ANTHRACNOSES
ANTHRACOID
ANTHRACOSES
ANTHRACOSIS
ANTHRANILATE
ANTHRANILATES
ANTHRANILIC
ANTHRAQUINONE
ANTHRAQUINONES
ANTHROPICAL
ANTHROPOBIOLOGY
ANTHROPOCENTRIC
ANTHROPOGENESES
ANTHROPOGENESIS
ANTHROPOGENETIC
ANTHROPOGENIC
ANTHROPOGENIES
ANTHROPOGENY
ANTHROPOGONIES
ANTHROPOGONY
ANTHROPOGRAPHY
ANTHROPOID
ANTHROPOIDAL
ANTHROPOIDS
ANTHROPOLATRIES
ANTHROPOLATRY

ANTHROPOLOGICAL
ANTHROPOLOGIES
ANTHROPOLOGIST
ANTHROPOLOGISTS
ANTHROPOLOGY
ANTHROPOMETRIC
ANTHROPOMETRIES
ANTHROPOMETRIST
ANTHROPOMETRY
ANTHROPOMORPH
ANTHROPOMORPHIC
ANTHROPOMORPHS
ANTHROPOPATHIC
ANTHROPOPATHIES
ANTHROPOPATHISM
ANTHROPOPATHY
ANTHROPOPHAGI
ANTHROPOPHAGIC
ANTHROPOPHAGIES
ANTHROPOPHAGITE
ANTHROPOPHAGOUS
ANTHROPOPHAGUS
ANTHROPOPHAGY
ANTHROPOPHOBIA
ANTHROPOPHOBIAS
ANTHROPOPHOBIC
ANTHROPOPHOBICS
ANTHROPOPHUISM
ANTHROPOPHUISMS
ANTHROPOPHYTE
ANTHROPOPHYTES
ANTHROPOPSYCHIC
ANTHROPOSOPHIC
ANTHROPOSOPHIES
ANTHROPOSOPHIST
ANTHROPOSOPHY
ANTHROPOTOMIES
ANTHROPOTOMY
ANTHURIUMS
ANTIABORTION
ANTIABORTIONIST
ANTIACADEMIC
ANTIADITIS
ANTIADITISES
ANTIAGGRESSION
ANTIAIRCRAFT
ANTIAIRCRAFTS

ANTIALCOHOL
ANTIALCOHOLISM
ANTIALCOHOLISMS
ANTIALLERGENIC
ANTIANEMIA
ANTIANXIETY
ANTIAPARTHEID
ANTIAPHRODISIAC
ANTIARMOUR
ANTIARRHYTHMIC
ANTIARRHYTHMICS
ANTIARTHRITIC
ANTIARTHRITICS
ANTIARTHRITIS
ANTIASTHMA
ANTIASTHMATIC
ANTIASTHMATICS
ANTIAUTHORITY
ANTIAUXINS
ANTIBACCHII
ANTIBACCHIUS
ANTIBACKLASH
ANTIBACTERIAL
ANTIBACTERIALS
ANTIBALLISTIC
ANTIBARBARUS
ANTIBARBARUSES
ANTIBARYON
ANTIBARYONS
ANTIBILIOUS
ANTIBILLBOARD
ANTIBIOSES
ANTIBIOSIS
ANTIBIOTIC
ANTIBIOTICALLY
ANTIBIOTICS
ANTIBLACKISM
ANTIBLACKISMS
ANTIBODIES
ANTIBOURGEOIS
ANTIBOYCOTT
ANTIBURGLAR
ANTIBURGLARY
ANTIBUSERS
ANTIBUSINESS
ANTIBUSING
ANTICAKING

ANTICANCER
ANTICAPITALISM
ANTICAPITALISMS
ANTICAPITALIST
ANTICAPITALISTS
ANTICARCINOGEN
ANTICARCINOGENS
ANTICARIES
ANTICATALYST
ANTICATALYSTS
ANTICATHODE
ANTICATHODES
ANTICATHOLIC
ANTICELLULITE
ANTICENSORSHIP
ANTICHLORISTIC
ANTICHLORS
ANTICHOICE
ANTICHOICER
ANTICHOICERS
ANTICHOLESTEROL
ANTICHOLINERGIC
ANTICHRIST
ANTICHRISTIAN
ANTICHRISTIANLY
ANTICHRISTS
ANTICHTHONES
ANTICHURCH
ANTICIGARETTE
ANTICIPANT
ANTICIPANTS
ANTICIPATABLE
ANTICIPATE
ANTICIPATED
ANTICIPATES
ANTICIPATING
ANTICIPATION
ANTICIPATIONS
ANTICIPATIVE
ANTICIPATIVELY
ANTICIPATOR
ANTICIPATORILY
ANTICIPATORS
ANTICIPATORY
ANTICISING
ANTICIVISM
ANTICIVISMS

ANTICIZING
ANTICLASSICAL
ANTICLASTIC
ANTICLERICAL
ANTICLERICALISM
ANTICLERICALS
ANTICLIMACTIC
ANTICLIMACTICAL
ANTICLIMAX
ANTICLIMAXES
ANTICLINAL
ANTICLINALS
ANTICLINES
ANTICLINORIA
ANTICLINORIUM
ANTICLINORIUMS
ANTICLOCKWISE
ANTICLOTTING
ANTICOAGULANT
ANTICOAGULANTS
ANTICODONS
ANTICOINCIDENCE
ANTICOLLISION
ANTICOLONIAL
ANTICOLONIALISM
ANTICOLONIALIST
ANTICOMMERCIAL
ANTICOMMUNISM
ANTICOMMUNISMS
ANTICOMMUNIST
ANTICOMMUNISTS
ANTICOMPETITIVE
ANTICONSUMER
ANTICONVULSANT
ANTICONVULSANTS
ANTICONVULSIVE
ANTICONVULSIVES
ANTICORPORATE
ANTICORROSION
ANTICORROSIONS
ANTICORROSIVE
ANTICORROSIVES
ANTICORRUPTION
ANTICREATIVE
ANTICRUELTY
ANTICULTURAL
ANTICYCLONE

ANTICYCLONES
ANTICYCLONIC
ANTIDANDRUFF
ANTIDAZZLE
ANTIDEFAMATION
ANTIDEMOCRATIC
ANTIDEPRESSANT
ANTIDEPRESSANTS
ANTIDEPRESSION
ANTIDERIVATIVE
ANTIDERIVATIVES
ANTIDESICCANT
ANTIDESICCANTS
ANTIDEVELOPMENT
ANTIDIABETIC
ANTIDIABETICS
ANTIDIARRHEAL
ANTIDIARRHEALS
ANTIDIARRHOEAL
ANTIDIARRHOEALS
ANTIDILUTION
ANTIDIURETIC
ANTIDIURETICS
ANTIDOGMATIC
ANTIDOTALLY
ANTIDOTING
ANTIDROMIC
ANTIDROMICALLY
ANTIDUMPING
ANTIDUMPINGS
ANTIECONOMIC
ANTIEDUCATIONAL
ANTIEGALITARIAN
ANTIELECTRON
ANTIELECTRONS
ANTIELITES
ANTIELITISM
ANTIELITISMS
ANTIELITIST
ANTIELITISTS
ANTIEMETIC
ANTIEMETICS
ANTIENTROPIC
ANTIEPILEPSY
ANTIEPILEPTIC
ANTIEPILEPTICS
ANTIEROTIC

ANTIESTROGEN
ANTIESTROGENS
ANTIEVOLUTION
ANTIEVOLUTIONS
ANTIFAMILY
ANTIFASCISM
ANTIFASCISMS
ANTIFASCIST
ANTIFASCISTS
ANTIFASHION
ANTIFASHIONABLE
ANTIFASHIONS
ANTIFATIGUE
ANTIFEBRILE
ANTIFEBRILES
ANTIFEDERALIST
ANTIFEDERALISTS
ANTIFEMALE
ANTIFEMININE
ANTIFEMINISM
ANTIFEMINISMS
ANTIFEMINIST
ANTIFEMINISTS
ANTIFERROMAGNET
ANTIFERTILITY
ANTIFILIBUSTER
ANTIFILIBUSTERS
ANTIFOAMING
ANTIFOGGING
ANTIFORECLOSURE
ANTIFOREIGN
ANTIFOREIGNER
ANTIFORMALIST
ANTIFOULING
ANTIFOULINGS
ANTIFREEZE
ANTIFREEZES
ANTIFRICTION
ANTIFUNGAL
ANTIFUNGALS
ANTIGAMBLING
ANTIGENICALLY
ANTIGENICITIES
ANTIGENICITY
ANTIGLOBULIN
ANTIGLOBULINS
ANTIGOVERNMENT

ANTIGRAVITIES	ANTILIBERALISMS	ANTIMILITARISMS	ANTINEOPLASTIC	ANTIPATHIES
ANTIGRAVITY	ANTILIBERALS	ANTIMILITARIST	ANTINEOPLASTICS	ANTIPATHIST
ANTIGROPELOES	ANTILIBERTARIAN	ANTIMILITARISTS	ANTINEPHRITIC	ANTIPATHISTS
ANTIGROPELOS	ANTILIFERS	ANTIMILITARY	ANTINEPHRITICS	ANTIPERIODIC
ANTIGROWTH	ANTILITERATE	ANTIMISSILE	ANTINEPOTISM	ANTIPERIODICS
ANTIGUERRILLA	ANTILITTER	ANTIMISSILES	ANTINEUTRINO	ANTIPERISTALSES
ANTIHALATION	ANTILITTERING	ANTIMITOTIC	ANTINEUTRINOS	ANTIPERISTALSIS
ANTIHALATIONS	ANTILOGARITHM	ANTIMITOTICS	ANTINEUTRON	ANTIPERISTALTIC
ANTIHELICES	ANTILOGARITHMIC	ANTIMNEMONIC	ANTINEUTRONS	ANTIPERISTASES
ANTIHELIXES	ANTILOGARITHMS	ANTIMNEMONICS	ANTINOISES	ANTIPERISTASIS
ANTIHELMINTHIC	ANTILOGICAL	ANTIMODERN	ANTINOMIAN	ANTIPERSONNEL
ANTIHELMINTHICS	ANTILOGIES	ANTIMODERNIST	ANTINOMIANISM	ANTIPERSPIRANT
ANTIHEROES	ANTILOGOUS	ANTIMODERNISTS	ANTINOMIANISMS	ANTIPERSPIRANTS
ANTIHEROIC	ANTILOPINE	ANTIMONARCHICAL	ANTINOMIANS	ANTIPESTICIDE
ANTIHEROINE	ANTILYNCHING	ANTIMONARCHIST	ANTINOMICAL	ANTIPETALOUS
ANTIHEROINES	ANTIMACASSAR	ANTIMONARCHISTS	ANTINOMICALLY	ANTIPHLOGISTIC
ANTIHERPES	ANTIMACASSARS	ANTIMONATE	ANTINOMIES	ANTIPHLOGISTICS
ANTIHIJACK	ANTIMAGNETIC	ANTIMONATES	ANTINOVELIST	ANTIPHONAL
ANTIHISTAMINE	ANTIMALARIA	ANTIMONIAL	ANTINOVELISTS	ANTIPHONALLY
ANTIHISTAMINES	ANTIMALARIAL	ANTIMONIALS	ANTINOVELS	ANTIPHONALS
ANTIHISTAMINIC	ANTIMALARIALS	ANTIMONIATE	ANTINUCLEAR	ANTIPHONARIES
ANTIHISTAMINICS	ANTIMANAGEMENT	ANTIMONIATES	ANTINUCLEARIST	ANTIPHONARY
ANTIHISTORICAL	ANTIMARIJUANA	ANTIMONIDE	ANTINUCLEARISTS	ANTIPHONER
ANTIHOMOSEXUAL	ANTIMARKET	ANTIMONIDES	ANTINUCLEON	ANTIPHONERS
ANTIHUMANISM	ANTIMARKETEER	ANTIMONIES	ANTINUCLEONS	ANTIPHONIC
ANTIHUMANISMS	ANTIMARKETEERS	ANTIMONIOUS	ANTINUKERS	ANTIPHONICAL
ANTIHUMANISTIC	ANTIMASQUE	ANTIMONITE	ANTIOBESITY	ANTIPHONICALLY
ANTIHUNTER	ANTIMASQUES	ANTIMONITES	ANTIOBSCENITY	ANTIPHONIES
ANTIHUNTERS	ANTIMATERIALISM	ANTIMONOPOLIST	ANTIODONTALGIC	ANTIPHRASES
ANTIHUNTING	ANTIMATERIALIST	ANTIMONOPOLISTS	ANTIODONTALGICS	ANTIPHRASIS
ANTIHYDROGEN	ANTIMATTER	ANTIMONOPOLY	ANTIOESTROGEN	ANTIPHRASTIC
ANTIHYDROGENS	ANTIMATTERS	ANTIMONOUS	ANTIOESTROGENS	ANTIPHRASTICAL
ANTIHYSTERIC	ANTIMECHANIST	ANTIMONYLS	ANTIOXIDANT	ANTIPIRACY
ANTIHYSTERICS	ANTIMECHANISTS	ANTIMOSQUITO	ANTIOXIDANTS	ANTIPLAGUE
ANTIJACOBIN	ANTIMERGER	ANTIMUSICAL	ANTIOZONANT	ANTIPLAQUE
ANTIJACOBINS	ANTIMERISM	ANTIMUSICS	ANTIOZONANTS	ANTIPLEASURE
ANTIJAMMING	ANTIMERISMS	ANTIMUTAGEN	ANTIPARALLEL	ANTIPOACHING
ANTIJAMMINGS	ANTIMETABOLE	ANTIMUTAGENS	ANTIPARALLELS	ANTIPODALS
ANTIKICKBACK	ANTIMETABOLES	ANTIMYCINS	ANTIPARASITIC	ANTIPODEAN
ANTIKNOCKS	ANTIMETABOLIC	ANTIMYCOTIC	ANTIPARASITICS	ANTIPODEANS
ANTILEGOMENA	ANTIMETABOLITE	ANTINARRATIVE	ANTIPARTICLE	ANTIPOETIC
ANTILEPROSY	ANTIMETABOLITES	ANTINARRATIVES	ANTIPARTICLES	ANTIPOLICE
ANTILEPTON	ANTIMETATHESES	ANTINATIONAL	ANTIPARTIES	ANTIPOLITICAL
ANTILEPTONS	ANTIMETATHESIS	ANTINATIONALIST	ANTIPASTOS	ANTIPOLITICS
ANTILEUKEMIC	ANTIMICROBIAL	ANTINATURAL	ANTIPATHETIC	ANTIPOLLUTION
ANTILIBERAL	ANTIMICROBIALS	ANTINATURE	ANTIPATHETICAL	ANTIPOLLUTIONS
ANTILIBERALISM	ANTIMILITARISM	ANTINAUSEA	ANTIPATHIC	ANTIPOPULAR

ANTIPORNOGRAPHY	ANTIRATIONAL	ANTISEPSES	ANTISTATICS	ANTITRADES
ANTIPORTER	ANTIRATIONALISM	ANTISEPSIS	ANTISTORIES	ANTITRADITIONAL
ANTIPORTERS	ANTIRATIONALIST	ANTISEPTIC	ANTISTRESS	ANTITRAGUS
ANTIPOVERTY	ANTIRATIONALITY	ANTISEPTICALLY	ANTISTRIKE	ANTITRANSPIRANT
ANTIPREDATOR	ANTIREALISM	ANTISEPTICISE	ANTISTROPHE	ANTITRINITARIAN
ANTIPROGRESSIVE	ANTIREALISMS	ANTISEPTICISED	ANTISTROPHES	ANTITRUSTER
ANTIPROTON	ANTIREALIST	ANTISEPTICISES	ANTISTROPHIC	ANTITRUSTERS
ANTIPROTONS	ANTIREALISTS	ANTISEPTICISING	ANTISTROPHON	ANTITUBERCULAR
ANTIPRURITIC	ANTIRECESSION	ANTISEPTICISM	ANTISTROPHONS	ANTITUBERCULOUS
ANTIPRURITICS	ANTIREFLECTION	ANTISEPTICISMS	ANTISTUDENT	ANTITUMORAL
ANTIPSYCHIATRY	ANTIREFLECTIVE	ANTISEPTICIZE	ANTISTYLES	ANTITUMORS
ANTIPSYCHOTIC	ANTIREFORM	ANTISEPTICIZED	ANTISUBMARINE	ANTITUMOUR
ANTIPSYCHOTICS	ANTIREGULATORY	ANTISEPTICIZES	ANTISUBSIDY	ANTITUMOURAL
ANTIPYRESES	ANTIREJECTION	ANTISEPTICIZING	ANTISUBVERSION	ANTITUSSIVE
ANTIPYRESIS	ANTIRELIGION	ANTISEPTICS	ANTISUBVERSIVE	ANTITUSSIVES
ANTIPYRETIC	ANTIRELIGIONS	ANTISERUMS	ANTISUICIDE	ANTITYPHOID
ANTIPYRETICS	ANTIRELIGIOUS	ANTISEXIST	ANTISYMMETRIC	ANTITYPICAL
ANTIPYRINE	ANTIREPUBLICAN	ANTISEXISTS	ANTISYPHILITIC	ANTITYPICALLY
ANTIPYRINES	ANTIREPUBLICANS	ANTISEXUAL	ANTISYPHILITICS	ANTIUNIVERSITY
ANTIQUARIAN	ANTIRETROVIRAL	ANTISEXUALITIES	ANTISYZYGIES	ANTIVENENE
ANTIQUARIANISM	ANTIRETROVIRALS	ANTISEXUALITY	ANTISYZYGY	ANTIVENENES
ANTIQUARIANISMS	ANTIRHEUMATIC	ANTISEXUALS	ANTITAKEOVER	ANTIVENINS
ANTIQUARIANS	ANTIRHEUMATICS	ANTISHAKES	ANTITARNISH	ANTIVENOMS
ANTIQUARIES	ANTIRITUALISM	ANTISHOCKS	ANTITECHNOLOGY	ANTIVIOLENCE
ANTIQUARKS	ANTIRITUALISMS	ANTISHOPLIFTING	ANTITERRORISM	ANTIVIRALS
ANTIQUATED	ANTIROMANTIC	ANTISLAVERY	ANTITERRORISMS	ANTIVIRUSES
ANTIQUATEDNESS	ANTIROMANTICISM	ANTISMOKER	ANTITERRORIST	ANTIVITAMIN
ANTIQUATES	ANTIROMANTICS	ANTISMOKERS	ANTITERRORISTS	ANTIVITAMINS
ANTIQUATING	ANTIROYALIST	ANTISMOKING	ANTITHALIAN	ANTIVIVISECTION
ANTIQUATION	ANTIROYALISTS	ANTISMUGGLING	ANTITHEISM	ANTIWELFARE
ANTIQUATIONS	ANTIRRHINUM	ANTISOCIAL	ANTITHEISMS	ANTIWHALING
ANTIQUENESS	ANTIRRHINUMS	ANTISOCIALISM	ANTITHEIST	ANTIWORLDS
ANTIQUENESSES	ANTISATELLITE	ANTISOCIALISMS	ANTITHEISTIC	ANTIWRINKLE
ANTIQUITARIAN	ANTISCIANS	ANTISOCIALIST	ANTITHEISTS	ANTONINIANUS
ANTIQUITARIANS	ANTISCIENCE	ANTISOCIALISTS	ANTITHEORETICAL	ANTONINIANUSES
ANTIQUITIES	ANTISCIENCES	ANTISOCIALITIES	ANTITHESES	ANTONOMASIA
ANTIRABIES	ANTISCIENTIFIC	ANTISOCIALITY	ANTITHESIS	ANTONOMASIAS
ANTIRACHITIC	ANTISCORBUTIC	ANTISOCIALLY	ANTITHETIC	ANTONOMASTIC
ANTIRACHITICS	ANTISCORBUTICS	ANTISPASMODIC	ANTITHETICAL	ANTONYMIES
ANTIRACISM	ANTISCRIPTURAL	ANTISPASMODICS	ANTITHETICALLY	ANTONYMOUS
ANTIRACISMS	ANTISECRECY	ANTISPASTIC	ANTITHROMBIN	ANTRORSELY
ANTIRACIST	ANTISEGREGATION	ANTISPASTICS	ANTITHROMBINS	ANTSINESSES
ANTIRACISTS	ANTISEIZURE	ANTISPASTS	ANTITHROMBOTIC	ANUCLEATED
ANTIRADARS	ANTISENTIMENTAL	ANTISPECULATION	ANTITHROMBOTICS	ANXIOLYTIC
ANTIRADICAL	ANTISEPALOUS	ANTISPECULATIVE	ANTITHYROID	ANXIOLYTICS
ANTIRADICALISM	ANTISEPARATIST	ANTISPENDING	ANTITOBACCO	ANXIOUSNESS
ANTIRADICALISMS	ANTISEPARATISTS	ANTISTATIC	ANTITOXINS	ANXIOUSNESSES

ANYTHINGARIAN
ANYTHINGARIANS
ANYWHITHER
AORISTICALLY
AORTITISES
AORTOGRAPHIC
AORTOGRAPHIES
AORTOGRAPHY
APAGOGICAL
APAGOGICALLY
APARTHEIDS
APARTHOTEL
APARTHOTELS
APARTMENTAL
APARTMENTS
APARTNESSES
APATHATONS
APATHETICAL
APATHETICALLY
APATOSAURS
APATOSAURUS
APATOSAURUSES
APERIODICALLY
APERIODICITIES
APERIODICITY
APERITIVES
APERTNESSES
APFELSTRUDEL
APFELSTRUDELS
APHAERESES
APHAERESIS
APHAERETIC
APHANIPTEROUS
APHELANDRA
APHELANDRAS
APHELIOTROPIC
APHELIOTROPISM
APHELIOTROPISMS
APHETICALLY
APHETISING
APHETIZING
APHIDICIDE
APHIDICIDES
APHORISERS
APHORISING
APHORISTIC
APHORISTICALLY

APHORIZERS
APHORIZING
APHRODISIA
APHRODISIAC
APHRODISIACAL
APHRODISIACS
APHRODISIAS
APHRODITES
APICULTURAL
APICULTURE
APICULTURES
APICULTURIST
APICULTURISTS
APIOLOGIES
APISHNESSES
APITHERAPIES
APITHERAPY
APLACENTAL
APLANATICALLY
APLANATISM
APLANATISMS
APLANOGAMETE
APLANOGAMETES
APLANOSPORE
APLANOSPORES
APOAPSIDES
APOCALYPSE
APOCALYPSES
APOCALYPTIC
APOCALYPTICAL
APOCALYPTICALLY
APOCALYPTICISM
APOCALYPTICISMS
APOCALYPTISM
APOCALYPTISMS
APOCALYPTIST
APOCALYPTISTS
APOCARPIES
APOCARPOUS
APOCATASTASES
APOCATASTASIS
APOCHROMAT
APOCHROMATIC
APOCHROMATISM
APOCHROMATISMS
APOCHROMATS
APOCOPATED

APOCOPATES
APOCOPATING
APOCOPATION
APOCOPATIONS
APOCRYPHAL
APOCRYPHALLY
APOCRYPHALNESS
APOCRYPHON
APOCYNACEOUS
APOCYNTHION
APOCYNTHIONS
APODEICTIC
APODEICTICAL
APODEICTICALLY
APODICTICAL
APODICTICALLY
APODYTERIUM
APODYTERIUMS
APOENZYMES
APOGAMOUSLY
APOGEOTROPIC
APOGEOTROPISM
APOGEOTROPISMS
APOLAUSTIC
APOLAUSTICS
APOLIPOPROTEIN
APOLIPOPROTEINS
APOLITICAL
APOLITICALITIES
APOLITICALITY
APOLITICALLY
APOLITICISM
APOLITICISMS
APOLLONIAN
APOLLONICON
APOLLONICONS
APOLOGETIC
APOLOGETICAL
APOLOGETICALLY
APOLOGETICS
APOLOGISED
APOLOGISER
APOLOGISERS
APOLOGISES
APOLOGISING
APOLOGISTS
APOLOGIZED

APOLOGIZER
APOLOGIZERS
APOLOGIZES
APOLOGIZING
APOMICTICAL
APOMICTICALLY
APOMORPHIA
APOMORPHIAS
APOMORPHINE
APOMORPHINES
APONEUROSES
APONEUROSIS
APONEUROTIC
APOPEMPTIC
APOPEMPTICS
APOPHLEGMATIC
APOPHLEGMATICS
APOPHONIES
APOPHTHEGM
APOPHTHEGMATIC
APOPHTHEGMATISE
APOPHTHEGMATIST
APOPHTHEGMATIZE
APOPHTHEGMS
APOPHYLLITE
APOPHYLLITES
APOPHYSATE
APOPHYSEAL
APOPHYSIAL
APOPLECTIC
APOPLECTICAL
APOPLECTICALLY
APOPLECTICS
APOPLEXIES
APOPLEXING
APOPROTEIN
APOPROTEINS
APOSEMATIC
APOSEMATICALLY
APOSIOPESES
APOSIOPESIS
APOSIOPETIC
APOSPORIES
APOSPOROUS
APOSTACIES
APOSTASIES
APOSTATICAL

APOSTATISE
APOSTATISED
APOSTATISES
APOSTATISING
APOSTATIZE
APOSTATIZED
APOSTATIZES
APOSTATIZING
APOSTILLES
APOSTLESHIP
APOSTLESHIPS
APOSTOLATE
APOSTOLATES
APOSTOLICAL
APOSTOLICALLY
APOSTOLICISM
APOSTOLICISMS
APOSTOLICITIES
APOSTOLICITY
APOSTOLISE
APOSTOLISED
APOSTOLISES
APOSTOLISING
APOSTOLIZE
APOSTOLIZED
APOSTOLIZES
APOSTOLIZING
APOSTROPHE
APOSTROPHES
APOSTROPHIC
APOSTROPHISE
APOSTROPHISED
APOSTROPHISES
APOSTROPHISING
APOSTROPHIZE
APOSTROPHIZED
APOSTROPHIZES
APOSTROPHIZING
APOSTROPHUS
APOSTROPHUSES
APOTHECARIES
APOTHECARY
APOTHECIAL
APOTHECIUM
APOTHEGMATIC
APOTHEGMATICAL
APOTHEGMATISE

APOTHEGMATISED
APOTHEGMATISES
APOTHEGMATISING
APOTHEGMATIST
APOTHEGMATISTS
APOTHEGMATIZE
APOTHEGMATIZED
APOTHEGMATIZES
APOTHEGMATIZING
APOTHEOSES
APOTHEOSIS
APOTHEOSISE
APOTHEOSISED
APOTHEOSISES
APOTHEOSISING
APOTHEOSIZE
APOTHEOSIZED
APOTHEOSIZES
APOTHEOSIZING
APOTROPAIC
APOTROPAICALLY
APOTROPAISM
APOTROPAISMS
APOTROPOUS
APPALLINGLY
APPALOOSAS
APPARATCHIK
APPARATCHIKI
APPARATCHIKS
APPARATUSES
APPARELING
APPARELLED
APPARELLING
APPARELMENT
APPARELMENTS
APPARENCIES
APPARENTLY
APPARENTNESS
APPARENTNESSES
APPARITION
APPARITIONAL
APPARITIONS
APPARITORS
APPARTEMENT
APPARTEMENTS
APPASSIONATO
APPEACHING

APPEACHMENT
APPEACHMENTS
APPEALABILITIES
APPEALABILITY
APPEALABLE
APPEALINGLY
APPEALINGNESS
APPEALINGNESSES
APPEARANCE
APPEARANCES
APPEASABLE
APPEASEMENT
APPEASEMENTS
APPEASINGLY
APPELLANTS
APPELLATION
APPELLATIONAL
APPELLATIONS
APPELLATIVE
APPELLATIVELY
APPELLATIVES
APPENDAGES
APPENDANTS
APPENDECTOMIES
APPENDECTOMY
APPENDENTS
APPENDICECTOMY
APPENDICES
APPENDICITIS
APPENDICITISES
APPENDICLE
APPENDICLES
APPENDICULAR
APPENDICULARIAN
APPENDICULATE
APPENDIXES
APPERCEIVE
APPERCEIVED
APPERCEIVES
APPERCEIVING
APPERCEPTION
APPERCEPTIONS
APPERCEPTIVE
APPERCIPIENT
APPERTAINANCE
APPERTAINANCES
APPERTAINED

APPERTAINING
APPERTAINMENT
APPERTAINMENTS
APPERTAINS
APPERTINENT
APPERTINENTS
APPETEEZEMENT
APPETEEZEMENTS
APPETENCES
APPETENCIES
APPETISEMENT
APPETISEMENTS
APPETISERS
APPETISING
APPETISINGLY
APPETITION
APPETITIONS
APPETITIVE
APPETIZERS
APPETIZING
APPETIZINGLY
APPLAUDABLE
APPLAUDABLY
APPLAUDERS
APPLAUDING
APPLAUDINGLY
APPLAUSIVE
APPLAUSIVELY
APPLECARTS
APPLEDRAIN
APPLEDRAINS
APPLEJACKS
APPLERINGIE
APPLERINGIES
APPLESAUCE
APPLESAUCES
APPLETINIS
APPLIANCES
APPLICABILITIES
APPLICABILITY
APPLICABLE
APPLICABLENESS
APPLICABLY
APPLICANTS
APPLICATION
APPLICATIONS
APPLICATIVE

APPLICATIVELY
APPLICATOR
APPLICATORS
APPLICATORY
APPLIQUEING
APPOGGIATURA
APPOGGIATURAS
APPOGGIATURE
APPOINTEES
APPOINTERS
APPOINTING
APPOINTIVE
APPOINTMENT
APPOINTMENTS
APPOINTORS
APPORTIONABLE
APPORTIONED
APPORTIONER
APPORTIONERS
APPORTIONING
APPORTIONMENT
APPORTIONMENTS
APPORTIONS
APPOSITELY
APPOSITENESS
APPOSITENESSES
APPOSITION
APPOSITIONAL
APPOSITIONS
APPOSITIVE
APPOSITIVELY
APPOSITIVES
APPRAISABLE
APPRAISALS
APPRAISEES
APPRAISEMENT
APPRAISEMENTS
APPRAISERS
APPRAISING
APPRAISINGLY
APPRAISIVE
APPRAISIVELY
APPRECIABLE
APPRECIABLY
APPRECIATE
APPRECIATED
APPRECIATES

APPRECIATING
APPRECIATION
APPRECIATIONS
APPRECIATIVE
APPRECIATIVELY
APPRECIATOR
APPRECIATORILY
APPRECIATORS
APPRECIATORY
APPREHENDED
APPREHENDING
APPREHENDS
APPREHENSIBLE
APPREHENSIBLY
APPREHENSION
APPREHENSIONS
APPREHENSIVE
APPREHENSIVELY
APPRENTICE
APPRENTICED
APPRENTICEHOOD
APPRENTICEHOODS
APPRENTICEMENT
APPRENTICEMENTS
APPRENTICES
APPRENTICESHIP
APPRENTICESHIPS
APPRENTICING
APPRESSING
APPRESSORIA
APPRESSORIUM
APPRISINGS
APPRIZINGS
APPROACHABILITY
APPROACHABLE
APPROACHED
APPROACHES
APPROACHING
APPROBATED
APPROBATES
APPROBATING
APPROBATION
APPROBATIONS
APPROBATIVE
APPROBATORY
APPROPINQUATE
APPROPINQUATED

APPROPINQUATES	APRIORISMS	AQUAPORINS	ARACHNIDANS	ARBITRARINESSES
APPROPINQUATING	APRIORISTS	AQUARELLES	ARACHNOIDAL	ARBITRATED
APPROPINQUATION	APRIORITIES	AQUARELLIST	ARACHNOIDITIS	ARBITRATES
APPROPINQUE	APSIDIOLES	AQUARELLISTS	ARACHNOIDITISES	ARBITRATING
APPROPINQUED	APTERYGIAL	AQUARIISTS	ARACHNOIDS	ARBITRATION
APPROPINQUES	APTITUDINAL	AQUAROBICS	ARACHNOLOGICAL	ARBITRATIONAL
APPROPINQUING	APTITUDINALLY	AQUASCAPES	ARACHNOLOGIES	ARBITRATIONS
APPROPINQUITIES	AQUABATICS	AQUATICALLY	ARACHNOLOGIST	ARBITRATIVE
APPROPINQUITY	AQUABOARDS	AQUATINTAS	ARACHNOLOGISTS	ARBITRATOR
APPROPRIABLE	AQUACEUTICAL	AQUATINTED	ARACHNOLOGY	ARBITRATORS
APPROPRIACIES	AQUACEUTICALS	AQUATINTER	ARACHNOPHOBE	ARBITRATRICES
APPROPRIACY	AQUACULTURAL	AQUATINTERS	ARACHNOPHOBES	ARBITRATRIX
APPROPRIATE	AQUACULTURE	AQUATINTING	ARACHNOPHOBIA	ARBITRATRIXES
APPROPRIATED	AQUACULTURES	AQUATINTIST	ARACHNOPHOBIAS	ARBITREMENT
APPROPRIATELY	AQUACULTURIST	AQUATINTISTS	ARACHNOPHOBIC	ARBITREMENTS
APPROPRIATENESS	AQUACULTURISTS	AQUICULTURAL	ARACHNOPHOBICS	ARBITRESSES
APPROPRIATES	AQUADROMES	AQUICULTURE	ARAEOMETER	ARBITRIUMS
APPROPRIATING	AQUAEROBICS	AQUICULTURES	ARAEOMETERS	ARBLASTERS
APPROPRIATION	AQUAFARMED	AQUICULTURIST	ARAEOMETRIC	ARBORACEOUS
APPROPRIATIONS	AQUAFARMING	AQUICULTURISTS	ARAEOMETRICAL	ARBOREALLY
APPROPRIATIVE	AQUAFARMINGS	AQUIFEROUS	ARAEOMETRIES	ARBORESCENCE
APPROPRIATOR	AQUAFITNESS	AQUIFOLIACEOUS	ARAEOMETRY	ARBORESCENCES
APPROPRIATORS	AQUAFITNESSES	AQUILEGIAS	ARAEOSTYLE	ARBORESCENT
APPROVABLE	AQUAFORTIS	AQUILINITIES	ARAEOSTYLES	ARBORETUMS
APPROVABLY	AQUAFORTISES	AQUILINITY	ARAEOSYSTYLE	ARBORICULTURAL
APPROVANCE	AQUAFORTIST	ARABESQUED	ARAEOSYSTYLES	ARBORICULTURE
APPROVANCES	AQUAFORTISTS	ARABESQUES	ARAGONITES	ARBORICULTURES
APPROVINGLY	AQUALEATHER	ARABICISATION	ARAGONITIC	ARBORICULTURIST
APPROXIMAL	AQUALEATHERS	ARABICISATIONS	ARALIACEOUS	ARBORISATION
APPROXIMATE	AQUAMANALE	ARABICISED	ARAUCARIAN	ARBORISATIONS
APPROXIMATED	AQUAMANALES	ARABICISES	ARAUCARIAS	ARBORISING
APPROXIMATELY	AQUAMANILE	ARABICISING	ARBALESTER	ARBORIZATION
APPROXIMATES	AQUAMANILES	ARABICIZATION	ARBALESTERS	ARBORIZATIONS
APPROXIMATING	AQUAMARINE	ARABICIZATIONS	ARBALISTER	ARBORIZING
APPROXIMATION	AQUAMARINES	ARABICIZED	ARBALISTERS	ARBORVITAE
APPROXIMATIONS	AQUANAUTICS	ARABICIZES	ARBITRABLE	ARBORVITAES
APPROXIMATIVE	AQUAPHOBES	ARABICIZING	ARBITRAGED	ARBOVIRUSES
APPROXIMEETING	AQUAPHOBIA	ARABILITIES	ARBITRAGER	ARBUSCULAR
APPROXIMEETINGS	AQUAPHOBIAS	ARABINOSES	ARBITRAGERS	ARCANENESS
APPULSIVELY	AQUAPHOBIC	ARABINOSIDE	ARBITRAGES	ARCANENESSES
APPURTENANCE	AQUAPHOBICS	ARABINOSIDES	ARBITRAGEUR	ARCCOSINES
APPURTENANCES	AQUAPLANED	ARABISATION	ARBITRAGEURS	ARCHAEBACTERIA
APPURTENANT	AQUAPLANER	ARABISATIONS	ARBITRAGING	ARCHAEBACTERIUM
APPURTENANTS	AQUAPLANERS	ARABIZATION	ARBITRAMENT	ARCHAEOBOTANIES
APRICATING	AQUAPLANES	ARABIZATIONS	ARBITRAMENTS	ARCHAEOBOTANIST
APRICATION	AQUAPLANING	ARACHIDONIC	ARBITRARILY	ARCHAEOBOTANY
APRICATIONS	AQUAPLANINGS	ARACHNIDAN	ARBITRARINESS	ARCHAEOLOGICAL

ARCHAEOLOGIES	ARCHEGONIUM	ARCHIMAGES	ARCMINUTES	ARGILLITIC
ARCHAEOLOGIST	ARCHENEMIES	ARCHIMANDRITE	ARCOGRAPHS	ARGONAUTIC
ARCHAEOLOGISTS	ARCHENTERA	ARCHIMANDRITES	ARCOLOGIES	ARGUMENTATION
ARCHAEOLOGY	ARCHENTERIC	ARCHIPELAGIAN	ARCSECONDS	ARGUMENTATIONS
ARCHAEOMETRIC	ARCHENTERON	ARCHIPELAGIC	ARCTANGENT	ARGUMENTATIVE
ARCHAEOMETRIES	ARCHENTERONS	ARCHIPELAGO	ARCTANGENTS	ARGUMENTATIVELY
ARCHAEOMETRIST	ARCHEOASTRONOMY	ARCHIPELAGOES	ARCTICALLY	ARGUMENTIVE
ARCHAEOMETRISTS	ARCHEOBOTANIES	ARCHIPELAGOS	ARCTOPHILE	ARGUMENTUM
ARCHAEOMETRY	ARCHEOBOTANIST	ARCHIPHONEME	ARCTOPHILES	ARGUMENTUMS
ARCHAEOPTERYX	ARCHEOBOTANISTS	ARCHIPHONEMES	ARCTOPHILIA	ARGUTENESS
ARCHAEOPTERYXES	ARCHEOBOTANY	ARCHIPLASM	ARCTOPHILIAS	ARGUTENESSES
ARCHAEORNIS	ARCHEOLOGICAL	ARCHIPLASMIC	ARCTOPHILIES	ARGYRODITE
ARCHAEORNISES	ARCHEOLOGICALLY	ARCHIPLASMS	ARCTOPHILIST	ARGYRODITES
ARCHAEOZOOLOGY	ARCHEOLOGIES	ARCHITECTED	ARCTOPHILISTS	ARHATSHIPS
ARCHAEZOOLOGIES	ARCHEOLOGIST	ARCHITECTING	ARCTOPHILS	ARHYTHMIAS
ARCHAEZOOLOGY	ARCHEOLOGISTS	ARCHITECTONIC	ARCTOPHILY	ARIBOFLAVINOSES
ARCHAICALLY	ARCHEOLOGY	ARCHITECTONICS	ARCUATIONS	ARIBOFLAVINOSIS
ARCHAICISM	ARCHEOMAGNETISM	ARCHITECTS	ARCUBALIST	ARIDNESSES
ARCHAICISMS	ARCHEOMETRIES	ARCHITECTURAL	ARCUBALISTS	ARISTOCRACIES
ARCHAISERS	ARCHEOMETRY	ARCHITECTURALLY	ARDUOUSNESS	ARISTOCRACY
ARCHAISING	ARCHEOZOOLOGIES	ARCHITECTURE	ARDUOUSNESSES	ARISTOCRAT
ARCHAISTIC	ARCHEOZOOLOGIST	ARCHITECTURES	ARECOLINES	ARISTOCRATIC
ARCHAIZERS	ARCHEOZOOLOGY	ARCHITRAVE	AREFACTION	ARISTOCRATICAL
ARCHAIZING	ARCHERESSES	ARCHITRAVED	AREFACTIONS	ARISTOCRATISM
ARCHANGELIC	ARCHERFISH	ARCHITRAVES	ARENACEOUS	ARISTOCRATISMS
ARCHANGELS	ARCHERFISHES	ARCHITYPES	ARENATIONS	ARISTOCRATS
ARCHBISHOP	ARCHESPORE	ARCHIVISTS	ARENICOLOUS	ARISTOLOCHIA
ARCHBISHOPRIC	ARCHESPORES	ARCHIVOLTS	AREOCENTRIC	ARISTOLOCHIAS
ARCHBISHOPRICS	ARCHESPORIA	ARCHNESSES	AREOGRAPHIC	ARISTOLOGIES
ARCHBISHOPS	ARCHESPORIAL	ARCHOLOGIES	AREOGRAPHIES	ARISTOLOGY
ARCHDEACON	ARCHESPORIUM	ARCHONSHIP	AREOGRAPHY	ARISTOTLES
ARCHDEACONRIES	ARCHETYPAL	ARCHONSHIPS	AREOLATION	ARITHMETIC
ARCHDEACONRY	ARCHETYPALLY	ARCHONTATE	AREOLATIONS	ARITHMETICAL
ARCHDEACONS	ARCHETYPES	ARCHONTATES	AREOLOGIES	ARITHMETICALLY
ARCHDIOCESAN	ARCHETYPICAL	ARCHOPLASM	AREOMETERS	ARITHMETICIAN
ARCHDIOCESE	ARCHETYPICALLY	ARCHOPLASMIC	AREOMETRIES	ARITHMETICIANS
ARCHDIOCESES	ARCHFIENDS	ARCHOPLASMS	AREOSTYLES	ARITHMETICS
ARCHDRUIDS	ARCHGENETHLIAC	ARCHOSAURIAN	AREOSYSTILE	ARITHMOMANIA
ARCHDUCHESS	ARCHGENETHLIACS	ARCHOSAURS	AREOSYSTILES	ARITHMOMANIAS
ARCHDUCHESSES	ARCHICARPS	ARCHPRIEST	ARFVEDSONITE	ARITHMOMETER
ARCHDUCHIES	ARCHIDIACONAL	ARCHPRIESTHOOD	ARFVEDSONITES	ARITHMOMETERS
ARCHDUKEDOM	ARCHIDIACONATE	ARCHPRIESTHOODS	ARGENTIFEROUS	ARITHMOPHOBIA
ARCHDUKEDOMS	ARCHIDIACONATES	ARCHPRIESTS	ARGENTINES	ARITHMOPHOBIAS
ARCHEGONIA	ARCHIEPISCOPACY	ARCHPRIESTSHIP	ARGENTITES	ARMADILLOS
ARCHEGONIAL	ARCHIEPISCOPAL	ARCHPRIESTSHIPS	ARGILLACEOUS	ARMAMENTARIA
ARCHEGONIATE	ARCHIEPISCOPATE	ARCHRIVALS	ARGILLIFEROUS	ARMAMENTARIUM
ARCHEGONIATES	ARCHILOWES	ARCHSTONES	ARGILLITES	ARMAMENTARIUMS

ARMATURING	ARRAIGNERS	ARSMETRICK	ARTHROGRAPHY	ARTIFICIALIZED
ARMIGEROUS	ARRAIGNING	ARSMETRICKS	ARTHROMERE	ARTIFICIALIZES
ARMILLARIA	ARRAIGNINGS	ARSPHENAMINE	ARTHROMERES	ARTIFICIALIZING
ARMILLARIAS	ARRAIGNMENT	ARSPHENAMINES	ARTHROMERIC	ARTIFICIALLY
ARMIPOTENCE	ARRAIGNMENTS	ARTEFACTUAL	ARTHROPATHIES	ARTIFICIALNESS
ARMIPOTENCES	ARRANGEABLE	ARTEMISIAS	ARTHROPATHY	ARTILLERIES
ARMIPOTENT	ARRANGEMENT	ARTEMISININ	ARTHROPLASTIES	ARTILLERIST
ARMISTICES	ARRANGEMENTS	ARTEMISININS	ARTHROPLASTY	ARTILLERISTS
ARMLOCKING	ARRAYMENTS	ARTERIALISATION	ARTHROPODAL	ARTILLERYMAN
ARMORIALLY	ARREARAGES	ARTERIALISE	ARTHROPODAN	ARTILLERYMEN
ARMOURLESS	ARRESTABLE	ARTERIALISED	ARTHROPODOUS	ARTINESSES
AROMATASES	ARRESTANTS	ARTERIALISES	ARTHROPODS	ARTIODACTYL
AROMATHERAPIES	ARRESTATION	ARTERIALISING	ARTHROSCOPE	ARTIODACTYLOUS
AROMATHERAPIST	ARRESTATIONS	ARTERIALIZATION	ARTHROSCOPES	ARTIODACTYLS
AROMATHERAPISTS	ARRESTINGLY	ARTERIALIZE	ARTHROSCOPIC	ARTISANSHIP
AROMATHERAPY	ARRESTMENT	ARTERIALIZED	ARTHROSCOPIES	ARTISANSHIPS
AROMATICALLY	ARRESTMENTS	ARTERIALIZES	ARTHROSCOPY	ARTISTICAL
AROMATICITIES	ARRHENOTOKIES	ARTERIALIZING	ARTHROSPORE	ARTISTICALLY
AROMATICITY	ARRHENOTOKY	ARTERIALLY	ARTHROSPORES	ARTISTRIES
AROMATISATION	ARRHYTHMIA	ARTERIOGRAM	ARTHROSPORIC	ARTLESSNESS
AROMATISATIONS	ARRHYTHMIAS	ARTERIOGRAMS	ARTHROSPOROUS	ARTLESSNESSES
AROMATISED	ARRHYTHMIC	ARTERIOGRAPHIC	ARTICHOKES	ARTOCARPUS
AROMATISES	ARRIVANCES	ARTERIOGRAPHIES	ARTICULABLE	ARTOCARPUSES
AROMATISING	ARRIVANCIES	ARTERIOGRAPHY	ARTICULACIES	ARTSINESSES
AROMATIZATION	ARRIVEDERCI	ARTERIOLAR	ARTICULACY	ARUNDINACEOUS
AROMATIZATIONS	ARRIVISMES	ARTERIOLES	ARTICULATE	ARVICOLINE
AROMATIZED	ARRIVISTES	ARTERIOTOMIES	ARTICULATED	ARYBALLOID
AROMATIZES	ARROGANCES	ARTERIOTOMY	ARTICULATELY	ARYBALLOSES
AROMATIZING	ARROGANCIES	ARTERIOVENOUS	ARTICULATENESS	ARYTAENOID
ARPEGGIATE	ARROGANTLY	ARTERITIDES	ARTICULATES	ARYTAENOIDS
ARPEGGIATED	ARROGATING	ARTERITISES	ARTICULATING	ARYTENOIDAL
ARPEGGIATES	ARROGATION	ARTFULNESS	ARTICULATION	ARYTENOIDS
ARPEGGIATING	ARROGATIONS	ARTFULNESSES	ARTICULATIONS	ASAFETIDAS
ARPEGGIATION	ARROGATIVE	ARTHRALGIA	ARTICULATIVE	ASAFOETIDA
ARPEGGIATIONS	ARROGATORS	ARTHRALGIAS	ARTICULATOR	ASAFOETIDAS
ARPEGGIONE	ARRONDISSEMENT	ARTHRALGIC	ARTICULATORS	ASARABACCA
ARPEGGIONES	ARRONDISSEMENTS	ARTHRECTOMIES	ARTICULATORY	ASARABACCAS
ARPILLERAS	ARROWGRASS	ARTHRECTOMY	ARTIFACTUAL	ASBESTIFORM
ARQUEBUSADE	ARROWGRASSES	ARTHRITICALLY	ARTIFICERS	ASBESTOSES
ARQUEBUSADES	ARROWHEADS	ARTHRITICS	ARTIFICIAL	ASBESTOSIS
ARQUEBUSES	ARROWROOTS	ARTHRITIDES	ARTIFICIALISE	ASBESTUSES
ARQUEBUSIER	ARROWWOODS	ARTHRITISES	ARTIFICIALISED	ASCARIASES
ARQUEBUSIERS	ARROWWORMS	ARTHRODESES	ARTIFICIALISES	ASCARIASIS
ARRACACHAS	ARSENIATES	ARTHRODESIS	ARTIFICIALISING	ASCENDABLE
ARRAGONITE	ARSENICALS	ARTHRODIAE	ARTIFICIALITIES	ASCENDANCE
ARRAGONITES	ARSENOPYRITE	ARTHRODIAL	ARTIFICIALITY	ASCENDANCES
ARRAGONITIC	ARSENOPYRITES	ARTHROGRAPHIES	ARTIFICIALIZE	ASCENDANCIES

ASCENDANCY	ASEPTICIZE	ASPHETERISE	ASSASSINATING	ASSESSMENT
ASCENDANTLY	ASEPTICIZED	ASPHETERISED	ASSASSINATION	ASSESSMENTS
ASCENDANTS	ASEPTICIZES	ASPHETERISES	ASSASSINATIONS	ASSESSORIAL
ASCENDENCE	ASEPTICIZING	ASPHETERISING	ASSASSINATOR	ASSESSORSHIP
ASCENDENCES	ASEXUALITIES	ASPHETERISM	ASSASSINATORS	ASSESSORSHIPS
ASCENDENCIES	ASEXUALITY	ASPHETERISMS	ASSAULTERS	ASSEVERATE
ASCENDENCY	ASHAMEDNESS	ASPHETERIZE	ASSAULTING	ASSEVERATED
ASCENDENTS	ASHAMEDNESSES	ASPHETERIZED	ASSAULTIVE	ASSEVERATES
ASCENDEURS	ASHINESSES	ASPHETERIZES	ASSAULTIVELY	ASSEVERATING
ASCENDIBLE	ASHLARINGS	ASPHETERIZING	ASSAULTIVENESS	ASSEVERATINGLY
ASCENSIONAL	ASHLERINGS	ASPHYXIANT	ASSEGAAIED	ASSEVERATION
ASCENSIONIST	ASHRAMITES	ASPHYXIANTS	ASSEGAAIING	ASSEVERATIONS
ASCENSIONISTS	ASININITIES	ASPHYXIATE	ASSEGAIING	ASSEVERATIVE
ASCENSIONS	ASKEWNESSES	ASPHYXIATED	ASSEMBLAGE	ASSEVERING
ASCERTAINABLE	ASPARAGINASE	ASPHYXIATES	ASSEMBLAGES	ASSIBILATE
ASCERTAINABLY	ASPARAGINASES	ASPHYXIATING	ASSEMBLAGIST	ASSIBILATED
ASCERTAINED	ASPARAGINE	ASPHYXIATION	ASSEMBLAGISTS	ASSIBILATES
ASCERTAINING	ASPARAGINES	ASPHYXIATIONS	ASSEMBLANCE	ASSIBILATING
ASCERTAINMENT	ASPARAGUSES	ASPHYXIATOR	ASSEMBLANCES	ASSIBILATION
ASCERTAINMENTS	ASPARTAMES	ASPHYXIATORS	ASSEMBLAUNCE	ASSIBILATIONS
ASCERTAINS	ASPARTATES	ASPIDISTRA	ASSEMBLAUNCES	ASSIDUITIES
ASCETICALLY	ASPECTABLE	ASPIDISTRAS	ASSEMBLERS	ASSIDUOUSLY
ASCETICISM	ASPERATING	ASPIRATING	ASSEMBLIES	ASSIDUOUSNESS
ASCETICISMS	ASPERGATION	ASPIRATION	ASSEMBLING	ASSIDUOUSNESSES
ASCITITIOUS	ASPERGATIONS	ASPIRATIONAL	ASSEMBLYMAN	ASSIGNABILITIES
ASCLEPIADACEOUS	ASPERGILLA	ASPIRATIONS	ASSEMBLYMEN	ASSIGNABILITY
ASCLEPIADS	ASPERGILLI	ASPIRATORS	ASSEMBLYWOMAN	ASSIGNABLE
ASCLEPIASES	ASPERGILLOSES	ASPIRATORY	ASSEMBLYWOMEN	ASSIGNABLY
ASCOCARPIC	ASPERGILLOSIS	ASPIRINGLY	ASSENTANEOUS	ASSIGNATION
ASCOGONIUM	ASPERGILLS	ASPIRINGNESS	ASSENTATION	ASSIGNATIONS
ASCOMYCETE	ASPERGILLUM	ASPIRINGNESSES	ASSENTATIONS	ASSIGNMENT
ASCOMYCETES	ASPERGILLUMS	ASPLANCHNIC	ASSENTATOR	ASSIGNMENTS
ASCOMYCETOUS	ASPERGILLUS	ASPLENIUMS	ASSENTATORS	ASSIMILABILITY
ASCORBATES	ASPERITIES	ASPORTATION	ASSENTIENT	ASSIMILABLE
ASCOSPORES	ASPERSIONS	ASPORTATIONS	ASSENTIENTS	ASSIMILABLY
ASCOSPORIC	ASPERSIVELY	ASSAFETIDA	ASSENTINGLY	ASSIMILATE
ASCRIBABLE	ASPERSOIRS	ASSAFETIDAS	ASSENTIVENESS	ASSIMILATED
ASCRIPTION	ASPERSORIA	ASSAFOETIDA	ASSENTIVENESSES	ASSIMILATES
ASCRIPTIONS	ASPERSORIES	ASSAFOETIDAS	ASSERTABLE	ASSIMILATING
ASCRIPTIVE	ASPERSORIUM	ASSAGAIING	ASSERTEDLY	ASSIMILATION
ASEPTICALLY	ASPERSORIUMS	ASSAILABLE	ASSERTIBLE	ASSIMILATIONISM
ASEPTICISE	ASPHALTERS	ASSAILANTS	ASSERTIONS	ASSIMILATIONIST
ASEPTICISED	ASPHALTING	ASSAILMENT	ASSERTIVELY	ASSIMILATIONS
ASEPTICISES	ASPHALTITE	ASSAILMENTS	ASSERTIVENESS	ASSIMILATIVE
ASEPTICISING	ASPHALTITES	ASSASSINATE	ASSERTIVENESSES	ASSIMILATIVELY
ASEPTICISM	ASPHALTUMS	ASSASSINATED	ASSERTORIC	ASSIMILATOR
ASEPTICISMS	ASPHERICAL	ASSASSINATES	ASSESSABLE	ASSIMILATORS

ASSIMILATORY
ASSISTANCE
ASSISTANCES
ASSISTANTS
ASSISTANTSHIP
ASSISTANTSHIPS
ASSOCIABILITIES
ASSOCIABILITY
ASSOCIABLE
ASSOCIATED
ASSOCIATES
ASSOCIATESHIP
ASSOCIATESHIPS
ASSOCIATING
ASSOCIATION
ASSOCIATIONAL
ASSOCIATIONISM
ASSOCIATIONISMS
ASSOCIATIONIST
ASSOCIATIONISTS
ASSOCIATIONS
ASSOCIATIVE
ASSOCIATIVELY
ASSOCIATIVITIES
ASSOCIATIVITY
ASSOCIATOR
ASSOCIATORS
ASSOCIATORY
ASSOILMENT
ASSOILMENTS
ASSOILZIED
ASSOILZIEING
ASSOILZIES
ASSONANCES
ASSONANTAL
ASSONATING
ASSORTATIVE
ASSORTATIVELY
ASSORTEDNESS
ASSORTEDNESSES
ASSORTMENT
ASSORTMENTS
ASSUAGEMENT
ASSUAGEMENTS
ASSUAGINGS
ASSUBJUGATE
ASSUBJUGATED

ASSUBJUGATES
ASSUBJUGATING
ASSUEFACTION
ASSUEFACTIONS
ASSUETUDES
ASSUMABILITIES
ASSUMABILITY
ASSUMINGLY
ASSUMPSITS
ASSUMPTION
ASSUMPTIONS
ASSUMPTIVE
ASSUMPTIVELY
ASSURANCES
ASSUREDNESS
ASSUREDNESSES
ASSURGENCIES
ASSURGENCY
ASSYTHMENT
ASSYTHMENTS
ASTACOLOGICAL
ASTACOLOGIES
ASTACOLOGIST
ASTACOLOGISTS
ASTACOLOGY
ASTARBOARD
ASTATICALLY
ASTATICISM
ASTATICISMS
ASTEREOGNOSES
ASTEREOGNOSIS
ASTERIATED
ASTERIDIAN
ASTERIDIANS
ASTERISKED
ASTERISKING
ASTERISKLESS
ASTEROIDAL
ASTEROIDEAN
ASTEROIDEANS
ASTHENOPIA
ASTHENOPIAS
ASTHENOPIC
ASTHENOSPHERE
ASTHENOSPHERES
ASTHENOSPHERIC
ASTHMATICAL

ASTHMATICALLY
ASTHMATICS
ASTIGMATIC
ASTIGMATICALLY
ASTIGMATICS
ASTIGMATISM
ASTIGMATISMS
ASTOMATOUS
ASTONISHED
ASTONISHES
ASTONISHING
ASTONISHINGLY
ASTONISHMENT
ASTONISHMENTS
ASTOUNDING
ASTOUNDINGLY
ASTOUNDMENT
ASTOUNDMENTS
ASTRACHANS
ASTRAGALUS
ASTRAKHANS
ASTRANTIAS
ASTRAPHOBIA
ASTRAPHOBIAS
ASTRAPHOBIC
ASTRAPOPHOBIA
ASTRAPOPHOBIAS
ASTRICTING
ASTRICTION
ASTRICTIONS
ASTRICTIVE
ASTRICTIVELY
ASTRINGENCE
ASTRINGENCES
ASTRINGENCIES
ASTRINGENCY
ASTRINGENT
ASTRINGENTLY
ASTRINGENTS
ASTRINGERS
ASTRINGING
ASTROBIOLOGIES
ASTROBIOLOGIST
ASTROBIOLOGISTS
ASTROBIOLOGY
ASTROBLEME
ASTROBLEMES

ASTROBOTANIES
ASTROBOTANY
ASTROCHEMISTRY
ASTROCOMPASS
ASTROCOMPASSES
ASTROCYTES
ASTROCYTIC
ASTROCYTOMA
ASTROCYTOMAS
ASTROCYTOMATA
ASTRODOMES
ASTRODYNAMICIST
ASTRODYNAMICS
ASTROFELLS
ASTROGEOLOGIES
ASTROGEOLOGIST
ASTROGEOLOGISTS
ASTROGEOLOGY
ASTROHATCH
ASTROHATCHES
ASTROLABES
ASTROLATRIES
ASTROLATRY
ASTROLOGER
ASTROLOGERS
ASTROLOGIC
ASTROLOGICAL
ASTROLOGICALLY
ASTROLOGIES
ASTROLOGIST
ASTROLOGISTS
ASTROMETRIC
ASTROMETRICAL
ASTROMETRIES
ASTROMETRY
ASTRONAUTIC
ASTRONAUTICAL
ASTRONAUTICALLY
ASTRONAUTICS
ASTRONAUTS
ASTRONAVIGATION
ASTRONAVIGATOR
ASTRONAVIGATORS
ASTRONOMER
ASTRONOMERS
ASTRONOMIC
ASTRONOMICAL

ASTRONOMICALLY
ASTRONOMIES
ASTRONOMISE
ASTRONOMISED
ASTRONOMISES
ASTRONOMISING
ASTRONOMIZE
ASTRONOMIZED
ASTRONOMIZES
ASTRONOMIZING
ASTROPHELS
ASTROPHOBIA
ASTROPHOBIAS
ASTROPHOBIC
ASTROPHOTOGRAPH
ASTROPHYSICAL
ASTROPHYSICALLY
ASTROPHYSICIST
ASTROPHYSICISTS
ASTROPHYSICS
ASTROSPHERE
ASTROSPHERES
ASTROTOURISM
ASTROTOURISMS
ASTROTOURIST
ASTROTOURISTS
ASTROTURFER
ASTROTURFERS
ASTROTURFING
ASTROTURFINGS
ASTUCIOUSLY
ASTUCITIES
ASTUTENESS
ASTUTENESSES
ASYMMETRIC
ASYMMETRICAL
ASYMMETRICALLY
ASYMMETRIES
ASYMPTOMATIC
ASYMPTOTES
ASYMPTOTIC
ASYMPTOTICAL
ASYMPTOTICALLY
ASYNARTETE
ASYNARTETES
ASYNARTETIC
ASYNCHRONIES

ASYNCHRONISM	ATHROCYTOSIS	ATTAINABILITY	ATTESTATOR	ATTRACTION
ASYNCHRONISMS	ATHWARTSHIP	ATTAINABLE	ATTESTATORS	ATTRACTIONS
ASYNCHRONOUS	ATHWARTSHIPS	ATTAINABLENESS	ATTICISING	ATTRACTIVE
ASYNCHRONOUSLY	ATMOLOGIES	ATTAINDERS	ATTICIZING	ATTRACTIVELY
ASYNCHRONY	ATMOLOGIST	ATTAINMENT	ATTIREMENT	ATTRACTIVENESS
ASYNDETICALLY	ATMOLOGISTS	ATTAINMENTS	ATTIREMENTS	ATTRACTORS
ASYNDETONS	ATMOLYSING	ATTAINTING	ATTITUDINAL	ATTRAHENTS
ASYNERGIAS	ATMOLYZING	ATTAINTMENT	ATTITUDINALLY	ATTRAPPING
ASYNERGIES	ATMOMETERS	ATTAINTMENTS	ATTITUDINARIAN	ATTRIBUTABLE
ASYNTACTIC	ATMOMETRIES	ATTAINTURE	ATTITUDINARIANS	ATTRIBUTED
ASYSTOLISM	ATMOSPHERE	ATTAINTURES	ATTITUDINISE	ATTRIBUTER
ASYSTOLISMS	ATMOSPHERED	ATTEMPERED	ATTITUDINISED	ATTRIBUTERS
ATACAMITES	ATMOSPHERES	ATTEMPERING	ATTITUDINISER	ATTRIBUTES
ATARACTICS	ATMOSPHERIC	ATTEMPERMENT	ATTITUDINISERS	ATTRIBUTING
ATAVISTICALLY	ATMOSPHERICAL	ATTEMPERMENTS	ATTITUDINISES	ATTRIBUTION
ATCHIEVING	ATMOSPHERICALLY	ATTEMPTABILITY	ATTITUDINISING	ATTRIBUTIONAL
ATELECTASES	ATMOSPHERICS	ATTEMPTABLE	ATTITUDINISINGS	ATTRIBUTIONS
ATELECTASIS	ATOMICALLY	ATTEMPTERS	ATTITUDINIZE	ATTRIBUTIVE
ATELECTATIC	ATOMICITIES	ATTEMPTING	ATTITUDINIZED	ATTRIBUTIVELY
ATELEIOSES	ATOMISATION	ATTENDANCE	ATTITUDINIZER	ATTRIBUTIVENESS
ATELEIOSIS	ATOMISATIONS	ATTENDANCES	ATTITUDINIZERS	ATTRIBUTIVES
ATHANASIES	ATOMISTICAL	ATTENDANCIES	ATTITUDINIZES	ATTRIBUTOR
ATHEISTICAL	ATOMISTICALLY	ATTENDANCY	ATTITUDINIZING	ATTRIBUTORS
ATHEISTICALLY	ATOMIZATION	ATTENDANTS	ATTITUDINIZINGS	ATTRISTING
ATHEMATICALLY	ATOMIZATIONS	ATTENDEMENT	ATTOLASERS	ATTRITIONAL
ATHENAEUMS	ATONALISMS	ATTENDEMENTS	ATTOLLENTS	ATTRITIONS
ATHEOLOGICAL	ATONALISTS	ATTENDINGS	ATTOPHYSICS	ATTRITTING
ATHEOLOGIES	ATONALITIES	ATTENDMENT	ATTORNEYDOM	ATTUITIONAL
ATHEORETICAL	ATONEMENTS	ATTENDMENTS	ATTORNEYDOMS	ATTUITIONS
ATHERMANCIES	ATONICITIES	ATTENTIONAL	ATTORNEYED	ATTUITIVELY
ATHERMANCY	ATRABILIAR	ATTENTIONS	ATTORNEYING	ATTUNEMENT
ATHERMANOUS	ATRABILIOUS	ATTENTIVELY	ATTORNEYISM	ATTUNEMENTS
ATHEROGENESES	ATRABILIOUSNESS	ATTENTIVENESS	ATTORNEYISMS	ATYPICALITIES
ATHEROGENESIS	ATRACURIUM	ATTENTIVENESSES	ATTORNEYSHIP	ATYPICALITY
ATHEROGENIC	ATRACURIUMS	ATTENUANTS	ATTORNEYSHIPS	ATYPICALLY
ATHEROMATA	ATRAMENTAL	ATTENUATED	ATTORNMENT	AUBERGINES
ATHEROMATOUS	ATRAMENTOUS	ATTENUATES	ATTORNMENTS	AUBERGISTE
ATHEROSCLEROSES	ATROCIOUSLY	ATTENUATING	ATTRACTABLE	AUBERGISTES
ATHEROSCLEROSIS	ATROCIOUSNESS	ATTENUATION	ATTRACTANCE	AUBRIETIAS
ATHEROSCLEROTIC	ATROCIOUSNESSES	ATTENUATIONS	ATTRACTANCES	AUCTIONARY
ATHETISING	ATROCITIES	ATTENUATOR	ATTRACTANCIES	AUCTIONEER
ATHETIZING	ATROPHYING	ATTENUATORS	ATTRACTANCY	AUCTIONEERED
ATHLETICALLY	ATTACHABLE	ATTESTABLE	ATTRACTANT	AUCTIONEERING
ATHLETICISM	ATTACHMENT	ATTESTANTS	ATTRACTANTS	AUCTIONEERS
ATHLETICISMS	ATTACHMENTS	ATTESTATION	ATTRACTERS	AUCTIONING
ATHROCYTES	ATTACKABLE	ATTESTATIONS	ATTRACTING	AUDACIOUSLY
ATHROCYTOSES	ATTAINABILITIES	ATTESTATIVE	ATTRACTINGLY	AUDACIOUSNESS

AUDACIOUSNESSES
AUDACITIES
AUDIBILITIES
AUDIBILITY
AUDIBLENESS
AUDIBLENESSES
AUDIENCIAS
AUDIOBOOKS
AUDIOCASSETTE
AUDIOCASSETTES
AUDIOGENIC
AUDIOGRAMS
AUDIOGRAPH
AUDIOGRAPHS
AUDIOLOGIC
AUDIOLOGICAL
AUDIOLOGICALLY
AUDIOLOGIES
AUDIOLOGIST
AUDIOLOGISTS
AUDIOMETER
AUDIOMETERS
AUDIOMETRIC
AUDIOMETRICALLY
AUDIOMETRICIAN
AUDIOMETRICIANS
AUDIOMETRIES
AUDIOMETRIST
AUDIOMETRISTS
AUDIOMETRY
AUDIOPHILE
AUDIOPHILES
AUDIOPHILS
AUDIOTAPED
AUDIOTAPES
AUDIOTAPING
AUDIOTYPING
AUDIOTYPINGS
AUDIOTYPIST
AUDIOTYPISTS
AUDIOVISUAL
AUDIOVISUALLY
AUDIOVISUALS
AUDIPHONES
AUDITIONED
AUDITIONER
AUDITIONERS

AUDITIONING
AUDITORIAL
AUDITORIES
AUDITORILY
AUDITORIUM
AUDITORIUMS
AUDITORSHIP
AUDITORSHIPS
AUDITRESSES
AUGMENTABLE
AUGMENTATION
AUGMENTATIONS
AUGMENTATIVE
AUGMENTATIVELY
AUGMENTATIVES
AUGMENTERS
AUGMENTING
AUGMENTORS
AUGURSHIPS
AUGUSTNESS
AUGUSTNESSES
AURALITIES
AUREATENESS
AUREATENESSES
AURICULARLY
AURICULARS
AURICULATE
AURICULATED
AURICULATELY
AURIFEROUS
AURISCOPES
AURISCOPIC
AUSCULTATE
AUSCULTATED
AUSCULTATES
AUSCULTATING
AUSCULTATION
AUSCULTATIONS
AUSCULTATIVE
AUSCULTATOR
AUSCULTATORS
AUSCULTATORY
AUSFORMING
AUSFORMINGS
AUSLANDERS
AUSPICATED
AUSPICATES

AUSPICATING
AUSPICIOUS
AUSPICIOUSLY
AUSPICIOUSNESS
AUSTENITES
AUSTENITIC
AUSTERENESS
AUSTERENESSES
AUSTERITIES
AUSTRALITE
AUSTRALITES
AUSTRINGER
AUSTRINGERS
AUTARCHICAL
AUTARCHIES
AUTARCHIST
AUTARCHISTS
AUTARKICAL
AUTARKISTS
AUTECOLOGIC
AUTECOLOGICAL
AUTECOLOGIES
AUTECOLOGY
AUTEURISMS
AUTEURISTS
AUTHENTICAL
AUTHENTICALLY
AUTHENTICATE
AUTHENTICATED
AUTHENTICATES
AUTHENTICATING
AUTHENTICATION
AUTHENTICATIONS
AUTHENTICATOR
AUTHENTICATORS
AUTHENTICITIES
AUTHENTICITY
AUTHIGENIC
AUTHORCRAFT
AUTHORCRAFTS
AUTHORESSES
AUTHORINGS
AUTHORISABLE
AUTHORISATION
AUTHORISATIONS
AUTHORISED
AUTHORISER

AUTHORISERS
AUTHORISES
AUTHORISING
AUTHORISMS
AUTHORITARIAN
AUTHORITARIANS
AUTHORITATIVE
AUTHORITATIVELY
AUTHORITIES
AUTHORIZABLE
AUTHORIZATION
AUTHORIZATIONS
AUTHORIZED
AUTHORIZER
AUTHORIZERS
AUTHORIZES
AUTHORIZING
AUTHORLESS
AUTHORSHIP
AUTHORSHIPS
AUTISTICALLY
AUTOALLOGAMIES
AUTOALLOGAMY
AUTOANTIBODIES
AUTOANTIBODY
AUTOBAHNEN
AUTOBIOGRAPHER
AUTOBIOGRAPHERS
AUTOBIOGRAPHIC
AUTOBIOGRAPHIES
AUTOBIOGRAPHY
AUTOBODIES
AUTOBUSSES
AUTOCATALYSE
AUTOCATALYSED
AUTOCATALYSES
AUTOCATALYSING
AUTOCATALYSIS
AUTOCATALYTIC
AUTOCATALYZE
AUTOCATALYZED
AUTOCATALYZES
AUTOCATALYZING
AUTOCEPHALIC
AUTOCEPHALIES
AUTOCEPHALOUS
AUTOCEPHALY

AUTOCHANGER
AUTOCHANGERS
AUTOCHTHON
AUTOCHTHONAL
AUTOCHTHONES
AUTOCHTHONIC
AUTOCHTHONIES
AUTOCHTHONISM
AUTOCHTHONISMS
AUTOCHTHONOUS
AUTOCHTHONOUSLY
AUTOCHTHONS
AUTOCHTHONY
AUTOCLAVED
AUTOCLAVES
AUTOCLAVING
AUTOCOPROPHAGY
AUTOCORRELATION
AUTOCRACIES
AUTOCRATIC
AUTOCRATICAL
AUTOCRATICALLY
AUTOCRIMES
AUTOCRITIQUE
AUTOCRITIQUES
AUTOCROSSES
AUTOCUTIES
AUTOCYCLES
AUTODESTRUCT
AUTODESTRUCTED
AUTODESTRUCTING
AUTODESTRUCTIVE
AUTODESTRUCTS
AUTODIALED
AUTODIALING
AUTODIALLED
AUTODIALLING
AUTODIDACT
AUTODIDACTIC
AUTODIDACTICISM
AUTODIDACTS
AUTODROMES
AUTOECIOUS
AUTOECIOUSLY
AUTOECISMS
AUTOEROTIC
AUTOEROTICISM

AUTOEROTICISMS

AUTOEROTICISMS
AUTOEROTISM
AUTOEROTISMS
AUTOEXPOSURE
AUTOEXPOSURES
AUTOFLARES
AUTOFOCUSES
AUTOGAMIES
AUTOGAMOUS
AUTOGENESES
AUTOGENESIS
AUTOGENETIC
AUTOGENICS
AUTOGENIES
AUTOGENOUS
AUTOGENOUSLY
AUTOGRAFTED
AUTOGRAFTING
AUTOGRAFTS
AUTOGRAPHED
AUTOGRAPHIC
AUTOGRAPHICAL
AUTOGRAPHICALLY
AUTOGRAPHIES
AUTOGRAPHING
AUTOGRAPHS
AUTOGRAPHY
AUTOGRAVURE
AUTOGRAVURES
AUTOGUIDES
AUTOHYPNOSES
AUTOHYPNOSIS
AUTOHYPNOTIC
AUTOIMMUNE
AUTOIMMUNITIES
AUTOIMMUNITY
AUTOINFECTION
AUTOINFECTIONS
AUTOINOCULATION
AUTOIONISATION
AUTOIONISATIONS
AUTOIONIZATION
AUTOIONIZATIONS
AUTOJUMBLE
AUTOJUMBLES
AUTOKINESES
AUTOKINESIS

AUTOKINETIC
AUTOLATRIES
AUTOLOADED
AUTOLOADING
AUTOLOGIES
AUTOLOGOUS
AUTOLYSATE
AUTOLYSATES
AUTOLYSING
AUTOLYSINS
AUTOLYZATE
AUTOLYZATES
AUTOLYZING
AUTOMAGICALLY
AUTOMAKERS
AUTOMATABLE
AUTOMATICAL
AUTOMATICALLY
AUTOMATICITIES
AUTOMATICITY
AUTOMATICS
AUTOMATING
AUTOMATION
AUTOMATIONS
AUTOMATISATION
AUTOMATISATIONS
AUTOMATISE
AUTOMATISED
AUTOMATISES
AUTOMATISING
AUTOMATISM
AUTOMATISMS
AUTOMATIST
AUTOMATISTS
AUTOMATIZATION
AUTOMATIZATIONS
AUTOMATIZE
AUTOMATIZED
AUTOMATIZES
AUTOMATIZING
AUTOMATONS
AUTOMATOUS
AUTOMETERS
AUTOMOBILE
AUTOMOBILED
AUTOMOBILES
AUTOMOBILIA

AUTOMOBILING
AUTOMOBILISM
AUTOMOBILISMS
AUTOMOBILIST
AUTOMOBILISTS
AUTOMOBILITIES
AUTOMOBILITY
AUTOMORPHIC
AUTOMORPHICALLY
AUTOMORPHISM
AUTOMORPHISMS
AUTOMOTIVE
AUTONOMICAL
AUTONOMICALLY
AUTONOMICS
AUTONOMIES
AUTONOMIST
AUTONOMISTS
AUTONOMOUS
AUTONOMOUSLY
AUTONYMOUS
AUTOPHAGIA
AUTOPHAGIAS
AUTOPHAGIES
AUTOPHAGOUS
AUTOPHANOUS
AUTOPHOBIA
AUTOPHOBIAS
AUTOPHOBIES
AUTOPHONIES
AUTOPHYTES
AUTOPHYTIC
AUTOPHYTICALLY
AUTOPILOTS
AUTOPISTAS
AUTOPLASTIC
AUTOPLASTIES
AUTOPLASTY
AUTOPOINTS
AUTOPOLYPLOID
AUTOPOLYPLOIDS
AUTOPOLYPLOIDY
AUTOPSISTS
AUTOPSYING
AUTOPTICAL
AUTOPTICALLY
AUTORADIOGRAM

AUTORADIOGRAMS
AUTORADIOGRAPH
AUTORADIOGRAPHS
AUTORADIOGRAPHY
AUTOREPLIES
AUTOREVERSE
AUTOREVERSES
AUTORICKSHAW
AUTORICKSHAWS
AUTOROTATE
AUTOROTATED
AUTOROTATES
AUTOROTATING
AUTOROTATION
AUTOROTATIONS
AUTOROUTES
AUTOSAVING
AUTOSCHEDIASM
AUTOSCHEDIASMS
AUTOSCHEDIASTIC
AUTOSCHEDIAZE
AUTOSCHEDIAZED
AUTOSCHEDIAZES
AUTOSCHEDIAZING
AUTOSCOPIC
AUTOSCOPIES
AUTOSEXING
AUTOSEXINGS
AUTOSOMALLY
AUTOSPORES
AUTOSTABILITIES
AUTOSTABILITY
AUTOSTRADA
AUTOSTRADAS
AUTOSTRADE
AUTOSUGGEST
AUTOSUGGESTED
AUTOSUGGESTING
AUTOSUGGESTION
AUTOSUGGESTIONS
AUTOSUGGESTIVE
AUTOSUGGESTS
AUTOTELLER
AUTOTELLERS
AUTOTETRAPLOID
AUTOTETRAPLOIDS
AUTOTETRAPLOIDY

AUTOTHEISM
AUTOTHEISMS
AUTOTHEIST
AUTOTHEISTS
AUTOTIMERS
AUTOTOMIES
AUTOTOMISE
AUTOTOMISED
AUTOTOMISES
AUTOTOMISING
AUTOTOMIZE
AUTOTOMIZED
AUTOTOMIZES
AUTOTOMIZING
AUTOTOMOUS
AUTOTOXAEMIA
AUTOTOXAEMIAS
AUTOTOXEMIA
AUTOTOXEMIAS
AUTOTOXINS
AUTOTRANSFORMER
AUTOTRANSFUSION
AUTOTROPHIC
AUTOTROPHICALLY
AUTOTROPHIES
AUTOTROPHS
AUTOTROPHY
AUTOTYPIES
AUTOTYPING
AUTOTYPOGRAPHY
AUTOWINDER
AUTOWINDERS
AUTOWORKER
AUTOWORKERS
AUTOXIDATION
AUTOXIDATIONS
AUTUMNALLY
AUXANOMETER
AUXANOMETERS
AUXILIARIES
AUXOCHROME
AUXOCHROMES
AUXOMETERS
AUXOSPORES
AUXOTROPHIC
AUXOTROPHIES
AUXOTROPHS

AUXOTROPHY
AVAILABILITIES
AVAILABILITY
AVAILABLENESS
AVAILABLENESSES
AVAILINGLY
AVALANCHED
AVALANCHES
AVALANCHING
AVALEMENTS
AVANTURINE
AVANTURINES
AVARICIOUS
AVARICIOUSLY
AVARICIOUSNESS
AVASCULARITIES
AVASCULARITY
AVENACEOUS
AVENGEMENT
AVENGEMENTS
AVENGERESS
AVENGERESSES
AVENTAILES
AVENTURINE
AVENTURINES
AVENTURINS
AVERAGENESS
AVERAGENESSES
AVERAGINGS
AVERRUNCATE
AVERRUNCATED
AVERRUNCATES

AVERRUNCATING
AVERRUNCATION
AVERRUNCATIONS
AVERRUNCATOR
AVERRUNCATORS
AVERSENESS
AVERSENESSES
AVERSIVELY
AVERSIVENESS
AVERSIVENESSES
AVERTIMENT
AVERTIMENTS
AVGOLEMONO
AVGOLEMONOS
AVIANISING
AVIANIZING
AVIATRESSES
AVIATRICES
AVIATRIXES
AVICULTURE
AVICULTURES
AVICULTURIST
AVICULTURISTS
AVIDNESSES
AVISANDUMS
AVISEMENTS
AVITAMINOSES
AVITAMINOSIS
AVITAMINOTIC
AVIZANDUMS
AVOCATIONAL
AVOCATIONALLY

AVOCATIONS
AVOIDANCES
AVOIRDUPOIS
AVOIRDUPOISES
AVOPARCINS
AVOUCHABLE
AVOUCHMENT
AVOUCHMENTS
AVOUTERERS
AVOWABLENESS
AVOWABLENESSES
AVUNCULARITIES
AVUNCULARITY
AVUNCULARLY
AVUNCULATE
AVUNCULATES
AVVOGADORE
AVVOGADORES
AWAKENINGS
AWARENESSES
AWAYNESSES
AWELESSNESS
AWELESSNESSES
AWESOMENESS
AWESOMENESSES
AWESTRICKEN
AWESTRIKES
AWESTRIKING
AWFULNESSES
AWKWARDEST
AWKWARDISH
AWKWARDNESS

AWKWARDNESSES
AXENICALLY
AXEROPHTHOL
AXEROPHTHOLS
AXIALITIES
AXILLARIES
AXINOMANCIES
AXINOMANCY
AXIOLOGICAL
AXIOLOGICALLY
AXIOLOGIES
AXIOLOGIST
AXIOLOGISTS
AXIOMATICAL
AXIOMATICALLY
AXIOMATICS
AXIOMATISATION
AXIOMATISATIONS
AXIOMATISE
AXIOMATISED
AXIOMATISES
AXIOMATISING
AXIOMATIZATION
AXIOMATIZATIONS
AXIOMATIZE
AXIOMATIZED
AXIOMATIZES
AXIOMATIZING
AXISYMMETRIC
AXISYMMETRICAL
AXISYMMETRIES
AXISYMMETRY

AXOLEMMATA
AXONOMETRIC
AXONOMETRIES
AXONOMETRY
AXOPLASMIC
AYAHUASCAS
AYAHUASCOS
AYATOLLAHS
AYUNTAMIENTO
AYUNTAMIENTOS
AYURVEDICS
AZATHIOPRINE
AZATHIOPRINES
AZEDARACHS
AZEOTROPES
AZEOTROPIC
AZEOTROPIES
AZIDOTHYMIDINE
AZIDOTHYMIDINES
AZIMUTHALLY
AZOBENZENE
AZOBENZENES
AZOOSPERMIA
AZOOSPERMIAS
AZOOSPERMIC
AZOTAEMIAS
AZOTOBACTER
AZOTOBACTERS
AZYGOSPORE
AZYGOSPORES

A

B

BAALEBATIM	BACHELORHOODS	BACKCHECKS	BACKHANDEDLY	BACKSCATTERING
BABACOOTES	BACHELORISM	BACKCLOTHS	BACKHANDEDNESS	BACKSCATTERINGS
BABBITRIES	BACHELORISMS	BACKCOMBED	BACKHANDER	BACKSCATTERS
BABBITTING	BACHELORSHIP	BACKCOMBING	BACKHANDERS	BACKSCRATCH
BABBITTRIES	BACHELORSHIPS	BACKCOUNTRIES	BACKHANDING	BACKSCRATCHED
BABBLATIVE	BACILLAEMIA	BACKCOUNTRY	BACKHAULED	BACKSCRATCHER
BABBLEMENT	BACILLAEMIAS	BACKCOURTMAN	BACKHAULING	BACKSCRATCHERS
BABBLEMENTS	BACILLEMIA	BACKCOURTMEN	BACKHOEING	BACKSCRATCHES
BABELESQUE	BACILLEMIAS	BACKCOURTS	BACKHOUSES	BACKSCRATCHING
BABESIASES	BACILLICIDE	BACKCROSSED	BACKLASHED	BACKSCRATCHINGS
BABESIASIS	BACILLICIDES	BACKCROSSES	BACKLASHER	BACKSETTING
BABESIOSES	BACILLIFORM	BACKCROSSING	BACKLASHERS	BACKSHEESH
BABESIOSIS	BACILLURIA	BACKDATING	BACKLASHES	BACKSHEESHED
BABINGTONITE	BACILLURIAS	BACKDRAFTS	BACKLASHING	BACKSHEESHES
BABINGTONITES	BACITRACIN	BACKDRAUGHT	BACKLIGHTED	BACKSHEESHING
BABIROUSSA	BACITRACINS	BACKDRAUGHTS	BACKLIGHTING	BACKSHISHED
BABIROUSSAS	BACKACTERS	BACKDROPPED	BACKLIGHTS	BACKSHISHES
BABIRUSSAS	BACKBENCHER	BACKDROPPING	BACKLISTED	BACKSHISHING
BABOONERIES	BACKBENCHERS	BACKFIELDS	BACKLISTING	BACKSHORES
BABYCCINOS	BACKBENCHES	BACKFILLED	BACKLOADED	BACKSIGHTS
BABYPROOFED	BACKBITERS	BACKFILLING	BACKLOADING	BACKSLAPPED
BABYPROOFING	BACKBITING	BACKFILLINGS	BACKLOGGED	BACKSLAPPER
BABYPROOFS	BACKBITINGS	BACKFIRING	BACKLOGGING	BACKSLAPPERS
BABYSITTING	BACKBITTEN	BACKFISCHES	BACKMARKER	BACKSLAPPING
BACCALAUREAN	BACKBLOCKER	BACKFITTED	BACKMARKERS	BACKSLASHES
BACCALAUREATE	BACKBLOCKERS	BACKFITTING	BACKPACKED	BACKSLIDDEN
BACCALAUREATES	BACKBLOCKS	BACKFITTINGS	BACKPACKER	BACKSLIDER
BACCHANALIA	BACKBOARDS	BACKFLIPPED	BACKPACKERS	BACKSLIDERS
BACCHANALIAN	BACKBONELESS	BACKFLIPPING	BACKPACKING	BACKSLIDES
BACCHANALIANISM	BACKBREAKER	BACKFLIPPINGS	BACKPACKINGS	BACKSLIDING
BACCHANALIANS	BACKBREAKERS	BACKGAMMON	BACKPEDALED	BACKSLIDINGS
BACCHANALS	BACKBREAKING	BACKGAMMONED	BACKPEDALING	BACKSPACED
BACCHANTES	BACKBURNED	BACKGAMMONING	BACKPEDALLED	BACKSPACER
BACCIFEROUS	BACKBURNING	BACKGAMMONS	BACKPEDALLING	BACKSPACERS
BACCIVOROUS	BACKCASTING	BACKGROUND	BACKPEDALS	BACKSPACES
BACHARACHS	BACKCHANNEL	BACKGROUNDED	BACKPIECES	BACKSPACING
BACHELORDOM	BACKCHANNELS	BACKGROUNDER	BACKPLATES	BACKSPEERED
BACHELORDOMS	BACKCHATTED	BACKGROUNDERS	BACKRONYMS	BACKSPEERING
BACHELORETTE	BACKCHATTING	BACKGROUNDING	BACKRUSHES	BACKSPEERS
BACHELORETTES	BACKCHECKED	BACKGROUNDS	BACKSCATTER	BACKSPEIRED
BACHELORHOOD	BACKCHECKING	BACKHANDED	BACKSCATTERED	BACKSPEIRING

BACKSPEIRS	BACKWARDATION	BACTERIOPHAGOUS	BAGSWINGER	BALDERLOCKSES
BACKSPLASH	BACKWARDATIONS	BACTERIOPHAGY	BAGSWINGERS	BALDHEADED
BACKSPLASHES	BACKWARDLY	BACTERIOSES	BAHUVRIHIS	BALDICOOTS
BACKSTABBED	BACKWARDNESS	BACTERIOSIS	BAIGNOIRES	BALDMONEYS
BACKSTABBER	BACKWARDNESSES	BACTERIOSTASES	BAILIESHIP	BALDNESSES
BACKSTABBERS	BACKWASHED	BACTERIOSTASIS	BAILIESHIPS	BALECTIONS
BACKSTABBING	BACKWASHES	BACTERIOSTAT	BAILIFFSHIP	BALEFULNESS
BACKSTABBINGS	BACKWASHING	BACTERIOSTATIC	BAILIFFSHIPS	BALEFULNESSES
BACKSTAGES	BACKWATERS	BACTERIOSTATS	BAILIWICKS	BALIBUNTAL
BACKSTAIRS	BACKWINDED	BACTERIOTOXIN	BAILLIAGES	BALIBUNTALS
BACKSTALLED	BACKWINDING	BACTERIOTOXINS	BAILLIESHIP	BALKANISATION
BACKSTALLING	BACKWOODSMAN	BACTERISATION	BAILLIESHIPS	BALKANISATIONS
BACKSTALLS	BACKWOODSMEN	BACTERISATIONS	BAIRNLIEST	BALKANISED
BACKSTAMPED	BACKWOODSY	BACTERISED	BAISEMAINS	BALKANISES
BACKSTAMPING	BACKWORKER	BACTERISES	BAITFISHES	BALKANISING
BACKSTAMPS	BACKWORKERS	BACTERISING	BAJILLIONS	BALKANIZATION
BACKSTARTING	BACTERAEMIA	BACTERIURIA	BAKEAPPLES	BALKANIZATIONS
BACKSTARTINGS	BACTERAEMIAS	BACTERIURIAS	BAKEBOARDS	BALKANIZED
BACKSTITCH	BACTERAEMIC	BACTERIZATION	BAKEHOUSES	BALKANIZES
BACKSTITCHED	BACTEREMIA	BACTERIZATIONS	BAKESTONES	BALKANIZING
BACKSTITCHES	BACTEREMIAS	BACTERIZED	BAKHSHISHED	BALKINESSES
BACKSTITCHING	BACTEREMIC	BACTERIZES	BAKHSHISHES	BALLABILES
BACKSTOPPED	BACTERIALLY	BACTERIZING	BAKHSHISHING	BALLADEERED
BACKSTOPPING	BACTERIALS	BACTEROIDS	BAKSHEESHED	BALLADEERING
BACKSTORIES	BACTERICIDAL	BACTERURIA	BAKSHEESHES	BALLADEERS
BACKSTREET	BACTERICIDALLY	BACTERURIAS	BAKSHEESHING	BALLADINES
BACKSTREETS	BACTERICIDE	BACULIFORM	BAKSHISHED	BALLADISTS
BACKSTRETCH	BACTERICIDES	BACULOVIRUS	BAKSHISHES	BALLADMONGER
BACKSTRETCHES	BACTERIOCIN	BACULOVIRUSES	BAKSHISHING	BALLADMONGERS
BACKSTROKE	BACTERIOCINS	BADDELEYITE	BALACLAVAS	BALLADRIES
BACKSTROKED	BACTERIOID	BADDELEYITES	BALALAIKAS	BALLANTING
BACKSTROKES	BACTERIOIDS	BADDERLOCK	BALANCEABLE	BALLANWRASSE
BACKSTROKING	BACTERIOLOGIC	BADDERLOCKS	BALANCINGS	BALLANWRASSES
BACKSWIMMER	BACTERIOLOGICAL	BADINAGING	BALANITISES	BALLASTERS
BACKSWIMMERS	BACTERIOLOGIES	BADINERIES	BALAYAGING	BALLASTING
BACKSWINGS	BACTERIOLOGIST	BADMINTONS	BALBRIGGAN	BALLBREAKER
BACKSWORDMAN	BACTERIOLOGISTS	BADMOUTHED	BALBRIGGANS	BALLBREAKERS
BACKSWORDMEN	BACTERIOLOGY	BADMOUTHING	BALBUTIENT	BALLCARRIER
BACKSWORDS	BACTERIOLYSES	BAFFLEGABS	BALCONETTE	BALLCARRIERS
BACKSWORDSMAN	BACTERIOLYSIN	BAFFLEMENT	BALCONETTES	BALLERINAS
BACKSWORDSMEN	BACTERIOLYSINS	BAFFLEMENTS	BALDACHINO	BALLETICALLY
BACKTRACKED	BACTERIOLYSIS	BAFFLINGLY	BALDACHINOS	BALLETOMANE
BACKTRACKING	BACTERIOLYTIC	BAGASSOSES	BALDACHINS	BALLETOMANES
BACKTRACKINGS	BACTERIOPHAGE	BAGASSOSIS	BALDAQUINS	BALLETOMANIA
BACKTRACKS	BACTERIOPHAGES	BAGATELLES	BALDERDASH	BALLETOMANIAS
BACKVELDER	BACTERIOPHAGIC	BAGGINESSES	BALDERDASHES	BALLFLOWER
BACKVELDERS	BACTERIOPHAGIES	BAGPIPINGS	BALDERLOCKS	BALLFLOWERS

BALLHANDLING
BALLHANDLINGS
BALLHAWKED
BALLHAWKING
BALLICATTER
BALLICATTERS
BALLISTICALLY
BALLISTICS
BALLISTITE
BALLISTITES
BALLISTOSPORE
BALLISTOSPORES
BALLOCKSED
BALLOCKSES
BALLOCKSING
BALLOONING
BALLOONINGS
BALLOONIST
BALLOONISTS
BALLOTINGS
BALLOTTEMENT
BALLOTTEMENTS
BALLPLAYER
BALLPLAYERS
BALLPOINTS
BALLSINESS
BALLSINESSES
BALLYHOOED
BALLYHOOING
BALLYRAGGED
BALLYRAGGING
BALMACAANS
BALMINESSES
BALMORALITIES
BALMORALITY
BALNEARIES
BALNEATION
BALNEATIONS
BALNEOLOGICAL
BALNEOLOGIES
BALNEOLOGIST
BALNEOLOGISTS
BALNEOLOGY
BALNEOTHERAPIES
BALNEOTHERAPY
BALSAMIFEROUS
BALSAMINACEOUS

BALSAWOODS
BALTHASARS
BALTHAZARS
BALUSTERED
BALUSTRADE
BALUSTRADED
BALUSTRADES
BALZARINES
BAMBOOZLED
BAMBOOZLEMENT
BAMBOOZLEMENTS
BAMBOOZLER
BAMBOOZLERS
BAMBOOZLES
BAMBOOZLING
BANALISATION
BANALISATIONS
BANALISING
BANALITIES
BANALIZATION
BANALIZATIONS
BANALIZING
BANCASSURANCE
BANCASSURANCES
BANCASSURER
BANCASSURERS
BANDAGINGS
BANDALORES
BANDBRAKES
BANDEIRANTE
BANDEIRANTES
BANDELIERS
BANDERILLA
BANDERILLAS
BANDERILLERO
BANDERILLEROS
BANDEROLES
BANDERSNATCH
BANDERSNATCHES
BANDFISHES
BANDICOOTED
BANDICOOTING
BANDICOOTS
BANDINESSES
BANDITRIES
BANDLEADER
BANDLEADERS

BANDMASTER
BANDMASTERS
BANDOBASTS
BANDOBUSTS
BANDOLEERED
BANDOLEERS
BANDOLEONS
BANDOLEROS
BANDOLIERED
BANDOLIERS
BANDOLINED
BANDOLINES
BANDOLINING
BANDONEONS
BANDONIONS
BANDPASSES
BANDSHELLS
BANDSPREADING
BANDSPREADINGS
BANDSTANDS
BANDWAGONS
BANDWIDTHS
BANEBERRIES
BANEFULNESS
BANEFULNESSES
BANGSRINGS
BANISHMENT
BANISHMENTS
BANISTERED
BANJOLELES
BANJULELES
BANKABILITIES
BANKABILITY
BANKROLLED
BANKROLLER
BANKROLLERS
BANKROLLING
BANKRUPTCIES
BANKRUPTCY
BANKRUPTED
BANKRUPTING
BANNERALLS
BANNERETTE
BANNERETTES
BANNISTERS
BANQUETEER
BANQUETEERS

BANQUETERS
BANQUETING
BANQUETINGS
BANQUETTES
BANTAMWEIGHT
BANTAMWEIGHTS
BANTERINGLY
BANTERINGS
BANTINGISM
BANTINGISMS
BAPHOMETIC
BAPTISMALLY
BAPTISTERIES
BAPTISTERY
BAPTISTRIES
BARAESTHESIA
BARAESTHESIAS
BARAGOUINS
BARASINGAS
BARASINGHA
BARASINGHAS
BARATHRUMS
BARBARESQUE
BARBARIANISM
BARBARIANISMS
BARBARIANS
BARBARICALLY
BARBARISATION
BARBARISATIONS
BARBARISED
BARBARISES
BARBARISING
BARBARISMS
BARBARITIES
BARBARIZATION
BARBARIZATIONS
BARBARIZED
BARBARIZES
BARBARIZING
BARBAROUSLY
BARBAROUSNESS
BARBAROUSNESSES
BARBASCOES
BARBASTELLE
BARBASTELLES
BARBASTELS
BARBECUERS

BARBECUING
BARBELLATE
BARBEQUING
BARBERRIES
BARBERSHOP
BARBERSHOPS
BARBITONES
BARBITURATE
BARBITURATES
BARBITURIC
BARBOTINES
BARCAROLES
BARCAROLLE
BARCAROLLES
BARDOLATER
BARDOLATERS
BARDOLATRIES
BARDOLATROUS
BARDOLATRY
BAREBACKED
BAREBACKING
BAREBACKINGS
BAREFACEDLY
BAREFACEDNESS
BAREFACEDNESSES
BAREFOOTED
BAREHANDED
BAREHANDING
BAREHEADED
BARELEGGED
BARENESSES
BARESTHESIA
BARESTHESIAS
BARGAINERS
BARGAINING
BARGAININGS
BARGANDERS
BARGEBOARD
BARGEBOARDS
BARGEMASTER
BARGEMASTERS
BARGEPOLES
BARHOPPING
BARIATRICS
BARKANTINE
BARKANTINES
BARKEEPERS

BARKENTINE	BAROTITISES	BARRICADOES	BASIDIOMYCETE	BASTARDRIES
BARKENTINES	BAROTRAUMA	BARRICADOING	BASIDIOMYCETES	BASTINADED
BARLEYCORN	BAROTRAUMAS	BARRICADOS	BASIDIOMYCETOUS	BASTINADES
BARLEYCORNS	BAROTRAUMATA	BARRIERING	BASIDIOSPORE	BASTINADING
BARMBRACKS	BARPERSONS	BARRISTERIAL	BASIDIOSPORES	BASTINADOED
BARMINESSES	BARQUANTINE	BARRISTERS	BASIDIOSPOROUS	BASTINADOES
BARMITSVAH	BARQUANTINES	BARRISTERSHIP	BASIFICATION	BASTINADOING
BARMITSVAHS	BARQUENTINE	BARRISTERSHIPS	BASIFICATIONS	BASTNAESITE
BARMITZVAH	BARQUENTINES	BARROWFULS	BASILICONS	BASTNAESITES
BARMITZVAHS	BARQUETTES	BARTENDERS	BASIPETALLY	BASTNASITE
BARNBRACKS	BARRACKERS	BARTENDING	BASKETBALL	BASTNASITES
BARNSBREAKING	BARRACKING	BARTIZANED	BASKETBALLS	BATFOWLERS
BARNSBREAKINGS	BARRACKINGS	BARYCENTRE	BASKETFULS	BATFOWLING
BARNSTORMED	BARRACOONS	BARYCENTRES	BASKETLIKE	BATFOWLINGS
BARNSTORMER	BARRACOUTA	BARYCENTRIC	BASKETRIES	BATHETICALLY
BARNSTORMERS	BARRACOUTAS	BARYSPHERE	BASKETSFUL	BATHHOUSES
BARNSTORMING	BARRACUDAS	BARYSPHERES	BASKETWEAVE	BATHMITSVAH
BARNSTORMINGS	BARRAMUNDA	BASALTINES	BASKETWEAVER	BATHMITSVAHS
BARNSTORMS	BARRAMUNDAS	BASALTWARE	BASKETWEAVERS	BATHMITZVAH
BAROCEPTOR	BARRAMUNDI	BASALTWARES	BASKETWEAVES	BATHMITZVAHS
BAROCEPTORS	BARRAMUNDIES	BASEBALLER	BASKETWORK	BATHMIZVAH
BARODYNAMICS	BARRAMUNDIS	BASEBALLERS	BASKETWORKS	BATHMIZVAHS
BAROGNOSES	BARRATRIES	BASEBOARDS	BASMITZVAH	BATHOCHROME
BAROGNOSIS	BARRATROUS	BASEBURNER	BASMITZVAHS	BATHOCHROMES
BAROGRAPHIC	BARRATROUSLY	BASEBURNERS	BASOPHILES	BATHOCHROMIC
BAROGRAPHS	BARRELAGES	BASELESSLY	BASOPHILIA	BATHOLITES
BAROMETERS	BARRELFULS	BASELESSNESS	BASOPHILIAS	BATHOLITHIC
BAROMETRIC	BARRELHEAD	BASELESSNESSES	BASOPHILIC	BATHOLITHS
BAROMETRICAL	BARRELHEADS	BASELINERS	BASSETTING	BATHOLITIC
BAROMETRICALLY	BARRELHOUSE	BASEMENTLESS	BASSNESSES	BATHOMETER
BAROMETRIES	BARRELHOUSES	BASENESSES	BASSOONIST	BATHOMETERS
BAROMETZES	BARRELLING	BASEPLATES	BASSOONISTS	BATHOMETRIC
BARONESSES	BARRELSFUL	BASERUNNER	BASTARDIES	BATHOMETRICALLY
BARONETAGE	BARRENNESS	BASERUNNERS	BASTARDISATION	BATHOMETRIES
BARONETAGES	BARRENNESSES	BASERUNNING	BASTARDISATIONS	BATHOMETRY
BARONETCIES	BARRENWORT	BASERUNNINGS	BASTARDISE	BATHOPHILOUS
BARONETESS	BARRENWORTS	BASHAWISMS	BASTARDISED	BATHOPHOBIA
BARONETESSES	BARRETRIES	BASHAWSHIP	BASTARDISES	BATHOPHOBIAS
BARONETICAL	BARRETROUS	BASHAWSHIPS	BASTARDISING	BATHWATERS
BAROPHILES	BARRETROUSLY	BASHFULNESS	BASTARDISM	BATHYBIUSES
BAROPHILIC	BARRETTERS	BASHFULNESSES	BASTARDISMS	BATHYGRAPHIC
BAROPHORESES	BARRICADED	BASHIBAZOUK	BASTARDIZATION	BATHYGRAPHICAL
BAROPHORESIS	BARRICADER	BASHIBAZOUKS	BASTARDIZATIONS	BATHYLIMNETIC
BARORECEPTOR	BARRICADERS	BASICITIES	BASTARDIZE	BATHYLITES
BARORECEPTORS	BARRICADES	BASICRANIAL	BASTARDIZED	BATHYLITHIC
BAROSCOPES	BARRICADING	BASIDIOCARP	BASTARDIZES	BATHYLITHS
BAROSCOPIC	BARRICADOED	BASIDIOCARPS	BASTARDIZING	BATHYLITIC

BATHYMETER	BATTLEFIELD	BEACHGOERS	BEATBOXING	BECLAMOURED
BATHYMETERS	BATTLEFIELDS	BEACHHEADS	BEATBOXINGS	BECLAMOURING
BATHYMETRIC	BATTLEFRONT	BEACHWEARS	BEATIFICAL	BECLAMOURS
BATHYMETRICAL	BATTLEFRONTS	BEADBLASTED	BEATIFICALLY	BECLASPING
BATHYMETRICALLY	BATTLEGROUND	BEADBLASTER	BEATIFICATION	BECLOAKING
BATHYMETRIES	BATTLEGROUNDS	BEADBLASTERS	BEATIFICATIONS	BECLOGGING
BATHYMETRY	BATTLEMENT	BEADBLASTING	BEATIFYING	BECLOTHING
BATHYPELAGIC	BATTLEMENTED	BEADBLASTS	BEATITUDES	BECLOUDING
BATHYSCAPE	BATTLEMENTS	BEADHOUSES	BEAUJOLAIS	BECLOWNING
BATHYSCAPES	BATTLEPIECE	BEADINESSES	BEAUJOLAISES	BECOMINGLY
BATHYSCAPH	BATTLEPIECES	BEADLEDOMS	BEAUMONTAGE	BECOMINGNESS
BATHYSCAPHE	BATTLEPLANE	BEADLEHOOD	BEAUMONTAGES	BECOMINGNESSES
BATHYSCAPHES	BATTLEPLANES	BEADLEHOODS	BEAUMONTAGUE	BECOWARDED
BATHYSCAPHS	BATTLESHIP	BEADLESHIP	BEAUMONTAGUES	BECOWARDING
BATHYSPHERE	BATTLESHIPS	BEADLESHIPS	BEAUTEOUSLY	BECQUERELS
BATHYSPHERES	BATTLESPACE	BEADSWOMAN	BEAUTEOUSNESS	BECRAWLING
BATMITZVAH	BATTLESPACES	BEADSWOMEN	BEAUTEOUSNESSES	BECROWDING
BATMITZVAHS	BATTLEWAGON	BEAKERFULS	BEAUTICIAN	BECRUSTING
BATOLOGICAL	BATTLEWAGONS	BEAMINESSES	BEAUTICIANS	BECUDGELED
BATOLOGIES	BATTOLOGICAL	BEANFEASTS	BEAUTIFICATION	BECUDGELING
BATOLOGIST	BATTOLOGIES	BEANSPROUT	BEAUTIFICATIONS	BECUDGELLED
BATOLOGISTS	BAUDRICKES	BEANSPROUTS	BEAUTIFIED	BECUDGELLING
BATRACHIAN	BAUDRONSES	BEANSTALKS	BEAUTIFIER	BEDABBLING
BATRACHIANS	BAULKINESS	BEARABILITIES	BEAUTIFIERS	BEDAGGLING
BATRACHOPHOBIA	BAULKINESSES	BEARABILITY	BEAUTIFIES	BEDARKENED
BATRACHOPHOBIAS	BAULKINGLY	BEARABLENESS	BEAUTIFULLER	BEDARKENING
BATRACHOPHOBIC	BAULKLINES	BEARABLENESSES	BEAUTIFULLEST	BEDAZZLEMENT
BATSMANSHIP	BAVARDAGES	BEARBAITING	BEAUTIFULLY	BEDAZZLEMENTS
BATSMANSHIPS	BAVAROISES	BEARBAITINGS	BEAUTIFULNESS	BEDAZZLING
BATTAILOUS	BAWDINESSES	BEARBERRIES	BEAUTIFULNESSES	BEDCHAMBER
BATTALIONS	BAWDYHOUSE	BEARDEDNESS	BEAUTIFYING	BEDCHAMBERS
BATTEILANT	BAWDYHOUSES	BEARDEDNESSES	BEAVERBOARD	BEDCLOTHES
BATTELLING	BAYBERRIES	BEARDLESSNESS	BEAVERBOARDS	BEDCOVERING
BATTEMENTS	BAYNODDIES	BEARDLESSNESSES	BEBEERINES	BEDCOVERINGS
BATTENINGS	BAYONETING	BEARDTONGUE	BEBLOODING	BEDEAFENED
BATTERINGS	BAYONETTED	BEARDTONGUES	BEBLUBBERED	BEDEAFENING
BATTILLING	BAYONETTING	BEARGRASSES	BECARPETED	BEDEHOUSES
BATTINESSES	BAZILLIONS	BEARHUGGED	BECARPETING	BEDELLSHIP
BATTLEAXES	BEACHBALLS	BEARHUGGING	BECCACCIAS	BEDELLSHIPS
BATTLEBUSES	BEACHCOMBED	BEARISHNESS	BECCAFICOS	BEDELSHIPS
BATTLEBUSSES	BEACHCOMBER	BEARISHNESSES	BECHALKING	BEDEVILING
BATTLEDOOR	BEACHCOMBERS	BEARNAISES	BECHANCING	BEDEVILLED
BATTLEDOORS	BEACHCOMBING	BEASTHOODS	BECHARMING	BEDEVILLING
BATTLEDORE	BEACHCOMBINGS	BEASTLIEST	BECKONINGLY	BEDEVILMENT
BATTLEDORES	BEACHCOMBS	BEASTLINESS	BECKONINGS	BEDEVILMENTS
BATTLEDRESS	BEACHFRONT	BEASTLINESSES	BECLAMORED	BEDFELLOWS
BATTLEDRESSES	BEACHFRONTS	BEATBOXERS	BECLAMORING	BEDIAPERED

BEDIAPERING	BEETLEBRAINS	BEGLAMOURS	BEKNOTTING	BELLFOUNDRY
BEDIGHTING	BEETLEHEAD	BEGLERBEGS	BELABORING	BELLHANGER
BEDIMMINGS	BEETLEHEADED	BEGLOOMING	BELABOURED	BELLHANGERS
BEDIMPLING	BEETLEHEADS	BEGRIMMING	BELABOURING	BELLIBONES
BEDIRTYING	BEETMASTER	BEGROANING	BELAMOURES	BELLICOSELY
BEDIZENING	BEETMASTERS	BEGRUDGERIES	BELATEDNESS	BELLICOSITIES
BEDIZENMENT	BEETMISTER	BEGRUDGERS	BELATEDNESSES	BELLICOSITY
BEDIZENMENTS	BEETMISTERS	BEGRUDGERY	BELEAGUERED	BELLIGERATI
BEDLAMISMS	BEFINGERED	BEGRUDGING	BELEAGUERING	BELLIGERENCE
BEDLAMITES	BEFINGERING	BEGRUDGINGLY	BELEAGUERMENT	BELLIGERENCES
BEDPRESSER	BEFITTINGLY	BEGUILEMENT	BELEAGUERMENTS	BELLIGERENCIES
BEDPRESSERS	BEFLAGGING	BEGUILEMENTS	BELEAGUERS	BELLIGERENCY
BEDRAGGLED	BEFLECKING	BEGUILINGLY	BELEMNITES	BELLIGERENT
BEDRAGGLES	BEFLOWERED	BEGUINAGES	BELGICISMS	BELLIGERENTLY
BEDRAGGLING	BEFLOWERING	BEHAPPENED	BELIEFLESS	BELLIGERENTS
BEDRENCHED	BEFLUMMING	BEHAPPENING	BELIEVABILITIES	BELLOCKING
BEDRENCHES	BEFOREHAND	BEHAVIORAL	BELIEVABILITY	BELLOWINGS
BEDRENCHING	BEFORETIME	BEHAVIORALLY	BELIEVABLE	BELLWETHER
BEDRIVELED	BEFORTUNED	BEHAVIORISM	BELIEVABLY	BELLWETHERS
BEDRIVELING	BEFORTUNES	BEHAVIORISMS	BELIEVINGLY	BELLYACHED
BEDRIVELLED	BEFORTUNING	BEHAVIORIST	BELIEVINGS	BELLYACHER
BEDRIVELLING	BEFOULMENT	BEHAVIORISTIC	BELIQUORED	BELLYACHERS
BEDROPPING	BEFOULMENTS	BEHAVIORISTS	BELIQUORING	BELLYACHES
BEDRUGGING	BEFRETTING	BEHAVIOURAL	BELITTLEMENT	BELLYACHING
BEDSITTERS	BEFRIENDED	BEHAVIOURALLY	BELITTLEMENTS	BELLYACHINGS
BEDSITTING	BEFRIENDER	BEHAVIOURISM	BELITTLERS	BELLYBANDS
BEDSPREADS	BEFRIENDERS	BEHAVIOURISMS	BELITTLING	BELLYBUTTON
BEDSPRINGS	BEFRIENDING	BEHAVIOURIST	BELITTLINGLY	BELLYBUTTONS
BEDWARFING	BEFRINGING	BEHAVIOURISTIC	BELLADONNA	BELOMANCIES
BEDWARMERS	BEFUDDLEMENT	BEHAVIOURISTS	BELLADONNAS	BELONGINGNESS
BEDWETTERS	BEFUDDLEMENTS	BEHAVIOURS	BELLAMOURE	BELONGINGNESSES
BEECHDROPS	BEFUDDLING	BEHEADINGS	BELLAMOURES	BELONGINGS
BEECHMASTS	BEGGARDOMS	BEHIGHTING	BELLARMINE	BELOWDECKS
BEECHWOODS	BEGGARHOOD	BEHINDHAND	BELLARMINES	BELOWGROUND
BEEFBURGER	BEGGARHOODS	BEHOLDINGS	BELLETRISM	BELOWSTAIRS
BEEFBURGERS	BEGGARLINESS	BEINGNESSES	BELLETRISMS	BELSHAZZAR
BEEFEATERS	BEGGARLINESSES	BEINNESSES	BELLETRIST	BELSHAZZARS
BEEFINESSES	BEGGARWEED	BEJABERSES	BELLETRISTIC	BELTCOURSE
BEEFSTEAKS	BEGGARWEEDS	BEJEEZUSES	BELLETRISTICAL	BELTCOURSES
BEEKEEPERS	BEGINNINGLESS	BEJESUITED	BELLETRISTS	BELVEDERES
BEEKEEPING	BEGINNINGS	BEJESUITING	BELLETTRIST	BEMADAMING
BEEKEEPINGS	BEGIRDLING	BEJEWELING	BELLETTRISTS	BEMADDENED
BEERINESSES	BEGLADDING	BEJEWELLED	BELLFLOWER	BEMADDENING
BEESWAXING	BEGLAMORED	BEJEWELLING	BELLFLOWERS	BEMEDALLED
BEESWINGED	BEGLAMORING	BEJUMBLING	BELLFOUNDER	BEMEDALLING
BEETLEBRAIN	BEGLAMOURED	BEKNIGHTED	BELLFOUNDERS	BEMINGLING
BEETLEBRAINED	BEGLAMOURING	BEKNIGHTING	BELLFOUNDRIES	BEMOANINGS

B

BEMONSTERED
BEMONSTERING
BEMONSTERS
BEMOUTHING
BEMUDDLING
BEMUFFLING
BEMURMURED
BEMURMURING
BEMUSEMENT
BEMUSEMENTS
BEMUZZLING
BENCHERSHIP
BENCHERSHIPS
BENCHLANDS
BENCHMARKED
BENCHMARKING
BENCHMARKINGS
BENCHMARKS
BENCHWARMER
BENCHWARMERS
BENEDICITE
BENEDICITES
BENEDICTION
BENEDICTIONAL
BENEDICTIONALS
BENEDICTIONS
BENEDICTIVE
BENEDICTORY
BENEDICTUS
BENEDICTUSES
BENEFACTED
BENEFACTING
BENEFACTION
BENEFACTIONS
BENEFACTOR
BENEFACTORS
BENEFACTORY
BENEFACTRESS
BENEFACTRESSES
BENEFICENCE
BENEFICENCES
BENEFICENT
BENEFICENTIAL
BENEFICENTLY
BENEFICIAL
BENEFICIALLY
BENEFICIALNESS

BENEFICIALS
BENEFICIARIES
BENEFICIARY
BENEFICIATE
BENEFICIATED
BENEFICIATES
BENEFICIATING
BENEFICIATION
BENEFICIATIONS
BENEFICING
BENEFITERS
BENEFITING
BENEFITTED
BENEFITTING
BENEPLACITO
BENEVOLENCE
BENEVOLENCES
BENEVOLENT
BENEVOLENTLY
BENEVOLENTNESS
BENGALINES
BENIGHTEDLY
BENIGHTEDNESS
BENIGHTEDNESSES
BENIGHTENED
BENIGHTENING
BENIGHTENINGS
BENIGHTENS
BENIGHTERS
BENIGHTING
BENIGHTINGS
BENIGHTMENT
BENIGHTMENTS
BENIGNANCIES
BENIGNANCY
BENIGNANTLY
BENIGNITIES
BENTGRASSES
BENTHOPELAGIC
BENTHOSCOPE
BENTHOSCOPES
BENTONITES
BENTONITIC
BENUMBEDNESS
BENUMBEDNESSES
BENUMBINGLY
BENUMBMENT

BENUMBMENTS
BENZALDEHYDE
BENZALDEHYDES
BENZANTHRACENE
BENZANTHRACENES
BENZENECARBONYL
BENZENOIDS
BENZIDINES
BENZIMIDAZOLE
BENZIMIDAZOLES
BENZOAPYRENE
BENZOAPYRENES
BENZOCAINE
BENZOCAINES
BENZODIAZEPINE
BENZODIAZEPINES
BENZOFURAN
BENZOFURANS
BENZOLINES
BENZOPHENONE
BENZOPHENONES
BENZOQUINONE
BENZOQUINONES
BENZPYRENE
BENZPYRENES
BENZYLIDINE
BENZYLIDINES
BEPAINTING
BEPEARLING
BEPEPPERED
BEPEPPERING
BEPESTERED
BEPESTERING
BEPIMPLING
BEPLASTERED
BEPLASTERING
BEPLASTERS
BEPOMMELLED
BEPOMMELLING
BEPOWDERED
BEPOWDERING
BEPRAISING
BEQUEATHABLE
BEQUEATHAL
BEQUEATHALS
BEQUEATHED
BEQUEATHER

BEQUEATHERS
BEQUEATHING
BEQUEATHMENT
BEQUEATHMENTS
BERASCALED
BERASCALING
BERBERIDACEOUS
BERBERINES
BERBERISES
BEREAVEMENT
BEREAVEMENTS
BERGAMASKO
BERGAMASKOS
BERGAMASKS
BERGANDERS
BERGOMASKS
BERGSCHRUND
BERGSCHRUNDS
BERIBBONED
BERKELIUMS
BERRYFRUIT
BERRYFRUITS
BERSAGLIERE
BERSAGLIERI
BERSERKERS
BERTILLONAGE
BERTILLONAGES
BERYLLIOSES
BERYLLIOSIS
BERYLLIUMS
BESAINTING
BESCATTERED
BESCATTERING
BESCATTERS
BESCORCHED
BESCORCHES
BESCORCHING
BESCOURING
BESCRAWLED
BESCRAWLING
BESCREENED
BESCREENING
BESCRIBBLE
BESCRIBBLED
BESCRIBBLES
BESCRIBBLING
BESEECHERS

BESEECHING
BESEECHINGLY
BESEECHINGNESS
BESEECHINGS
BESEEMINGLY
BESEEMINGNESS
BESEEMINGNESSES
BESEEMINGS
BESEEMLIER
BESEEMLIEST
BESETMENTS
BESHADOWED
BESHADOWING
BESHIVERED
BESHIVERING
BESHOUTING
BESHREWING
BESHROUDED
BESHROUDING
BESIEGEMENT
BESIEGEMENTS
BESIEGINGLY
BESIEGINGS
BESLAVERED
BESLAVERING
BESLOBBERED
BESLOBBERING
BESLOBBERS
BESLUBBERED
BESLUBBERING
BESLUBBERS
BESMEARERS
BESMEARING
BESMIRCHED
BESMIRCHES
BESMIRCHING
BESMOOTHED
BESMOOTHING
BESMUDGING
BESMUTCHED
BESMUTCHES
BESMUTCHING
BESMUTTING
BESOOTHING
BESOTTEDLY
BESOTTEDNESS
BESOTTEDNESSES

BESPANGLED	BESTRADDLED	BETTERNESSES	BIBLIOGRAPHIC	BIBLIOPOLES
BESPANGLES	BESTRADDLES	BETULACEOUS	BIBLIOGRAPHICAL	BIBLIOPOLIC
BESPANGLING	BESTRADDLING	BETWEENBRAIN	BIBLIOGRAPHIES	BIBLIOPOLICAL
BESPATTERED	BESTRAUGHT	BETWEENBRAINS	BIBLIOGRAPHY	BIBLIOPOLIES
BESPATTERING	BESTREAKED	BETWEENITIES	BIBLIOLATER	BIBLIOPOLIST
BESPATTERS	BESTREAKING	BETWEENITY	BIBLIOLATERS	BIBLIOPOLISTS
BESPEAKING	BESTREWING	BETWEENNESS	BIBLIOLATRIES	BIBLIOPOLY
BESPECKLED	BESTRIDABLE	BETWEENNESSES	BIBLIOLATRIST	BIBLIOTHECA
BESPECKLES	BESTRIDDEN	BETWEENTIME	BIBLIOLATRISTS	BIBLIOTHECAE
BESPECKLING	BESTRIDING	BETWEENTIMES	BIBLIOLATROUS	BIBLIOTHECAL
BESPECTACLED	BESTROWING	BETWEENWHILES	BIBLIOLATRY	BIBLIOTHECARIES
BESPEEDING	BESTSELLER	BEVELLINGS	BIBLIOLOGICAL	BIBLIOTHECARY
BESPITTING	BESTSELLERDOM	BEVELMENTS	BIBLIOLOGIES	BIBLIOTHECAS
BESPORTING	BESTSELLERDOMS	BEVOMITING	BIBLIOLOGIST	BIBLIOTHERAPIES
BESPOTTEDNESS	BESTSELLERS	BEWAILINGLY	BIBLIOLOGISTS	BIBLIOTHERAPY
BESPOTTEDNESSES	BESTSELLING	BEWAILINGS	BIBLIOLOGY	BIBLIOTICS
BESPOTTING	BESTUDDING	BEWEARYING	BIBLIOMANCIES	BIBLIOTIST
BESPOUSING	BESWARMING	BEWELTERED	BIBLIOMANCY	BIBLIOTISTS
BESPOUTING	BETACAROTENE	BEWHISKERED	BIBLIOMANE	BIBULOUSLY
BESPREADING	BETACAROTENES	BEWILDERED	BIBLIOMANES	BIBULOUSNESS
BESPRINKLE	BETACYANIN	BEWILDEREDLY	BIBLIOMANIA	BIBULOUSNESSES
BESPRINKLED	BETACYANINS	BEWILDEREDNESS	BIBLIOMANIAC	BICAMERALISM
BESPRINKLES	BETATTERED	BEWILDERING	BIBLIOMANIACAL	BICAMERALISMS
BESPRINKLING	BETATTERING	BEWILDERINGLY	BIBLIOMANIACS	BICAMERALIST
BESTAINING	BETHANKING	BEWILDERMENT	BIBLIOMANIAS	BICAMERALISTS
BESTARRING	BETHANKITS	BEWILDERMENTS	BIBLIOPEGIC	BICAPSULAR
BESTEADING	BETHINKING	BEWITCHERIES	BIBLIOPEGIES	BICARBONATE
BESTIALISE	BETHORNING	BEWITCHERS	BIBLIOPEGIST	BICARBONATES
BESTIALISED	BETHRALLED	BEWITCHERY	BIBLIOPEGISTS	BICARPELLARY
BESTIALISES	BETHRALLING	BEWITCHING	BIBLIOPEGY	BICENTENARIES
BESTIALISING	BETHUMBING	BEWITCHINGLY	BIBLIOPHAGIST	BICENTENARY
BESTIALISM	BETHUMPING	BEWITCHMENT	BIBLIOPHAGISTS	BICENTENNIAL
BESTIALISMS	BETHWACKED	BEWITCHMENTS	BIBLIOPHIL	BICENTENNIALS
BESTIALITIES	BETHWACKING	BEWORRYING	BIBLIOPHILE	BICEPHALOUS
BESTIALITY	BETOKENING	BEWRAPPING	BIBLIOPHILES	BICHLORIDE
BESTIALIZE	BETREADING	BHIKKHUNIS	BIBLIOPHILIC	BICHLORIDES
BESTIALIZED	BETRIMMING	BIANNUALLY	BIBLIOPHILIES	BICHROMATE
BESTIALIZES	BETROTHALS	BIANNULATE	BIBLIOPHILISM	BICHROMATED
BESTIALIZING	BETROTHEDS	BIASNESSES	BIBLIOPHILISMS	BICHROMATES
BESTIARIES	BETROTHING	BIATHLETES	BIBLIOPHILIST	BICKERINGS
BESTICKING	BETROTHMENT	BIAURICULAR	BIBLIOPHILISTIC	BICOLLATERAL
BESTILLING	BETROTHMENTS	BIAURICULATE	BIBLIOPHILISTS	BICOLOURED
BESTIRRING	BETTERINGS	BIBLICALLY	BIBLIOPHILS	BICOMPONENT
BESTORMING	BETTERMENT	BIBLICISMS	BIBLIOPHILY	BICOMPONENTS
BESTOWMENT	BETTERMENTS	BIBLICISTS	BIBLIOPHOBIA	BICONCAVITIES
BESTOWMENTS	BETTERMOST	BIBLIOGRAPHER	BIBLIOPHOBIAS	BICONCAVITY
BESTRADDLE	BETTERNESS	BIBLIOGRAPHERS	BIBLIOPOLE	BICONDITIONAL

BICONDITIONALS
BICONVEXITIES
BICONVEXITY
BICORNUATE
BICORPORATE
BICULTURAL
BICULTURALISM
BICULTURALISMS
BICUSPIDATE
BICUSPIDATES
BICYCLICAL
BICYCLISTS
BIDDABILITIES
BIDDABILITY
BIDDABLENESS
BIDDABLENESSES
BIDENTATED
BIDIALECTAL
BIDIALECTALISM
BIDIALECTALISMS
BIDIRECTIONAL
BIDIRECTIONALLY
BIDONVILLE
BIDONVILLES
BIENNIALLY
BIENSEANCE
BIENSEANCES
BIERKELLER
BIERKELLERS
BIFACIALLY
BIFARIOUSLY
BIFIDITIES
BIFLAGELLATE
BIFOLIOLATE
BIFUNCTIONAL
BIFURCATED
BIFURCATES
BIFURCATING
BIFURCATION
BIFURCATIONS
BIGAMOUSLY
BIGARREAUS
BIGEMINIES
BIGFOOTING
BIGGITIEST
BIGHEADEDLY
BIGHEADEDNESS

BIGHEADEDNESSES
BIGHEARTED
BIGHEARTEDLY
BIGHEARTEDNESS
BIGMOUTHED
BIGNONIACEOUS
BIGUANIDES
BIJECTIONS
BIJOUTERIE
BIJOUTERIES
BILATERALISM
BILATERALISMS
BILATERALLY
BILBERRIES
BILDUNGSROMAN
BILDUNGSROMANS
BILECTIONS
BILESTONES
BILGEWATER
BILGEWATERS
BILHARZIAL
BILHARZIAS
BILHARZIASES
BILHARZIASIS
BILHARZIOSES
BILHARZIOSIS
BILIMBINGS
BILINGUALISM
BILINGUALISMS
BILINGUALLY
BILINGUALS
BILINGUIST
BILINGUISTS
BILIOUSNESS
BILIOUSNESSES
BILIRUBINS
BILIVERDIN
BILIVERDINS
BILLABONGS
BILLBOARDED
BILLBOARDING
BILLBOARDS
BILLETINGS
BILLFISHES
BILLINGSGATE
BILLINGSGATES
BILLIONAIRE

BILLIONAIRES
BILLIONTHS
BILLOWIEST
BILLOWINESS
BILLOWINESSES
BILLOWINGS
BILLPOSTER
BILLPOSTERS
BILLPOSTING
BILLPOSTINGS
BILLSTICKER
BILLSTICKERS
BILLSTICKING
BILLSTICKINGS
BILLYCOCKS
BILOCATION
BILOCATIONS
BILOCULATE
BIMANUALLY
BIMATERNAL
BIMESTRIAL
BIMESTRIALLY
BIMETALLIC
BIMETALLICS
BIMETALLISM
BIMETALLISMS
BIMETALLIST
BIMETALLISTIC
BIMETALLISTS
BIMILLENARIES
BIMILLENARY
BIMILLENNIA
BIMILLENNIAL
BIMILLENNIALS
BIMILLENNIUM
BIMILLENNIUMS
BIMODALITIES
BIMODALITY
BIMOLECULAR
BIMOLECULARLY
BIMONTHLIES
BIMORPHEMIC
BINATIONAL
BINAURALLY
BINDINGNESS
BINDINGNESSES
BINOCULARITIES

BINOCULARITY
BINOCULARLY
BINOCULARS
BINOMIALLY
BINOMINALS
BINTURONGS
BINUCLEATE
BINUCLEATED
BIOACCUMULATE
BIOACCUMULATED
BIOACCUMULATES
BIOACCUMULATING
BIOACCUMULATION
BIOACOUSTICS
BIOACTIVITIES
BIOACTIVITY
BIOAERATION
BIOAERATIONS
BIOAERONAUTICS
BIOARCHAEOLOGY
BIOASSAYED
BIOASSAYING
BIOASTRONAUTICS
BIOASTRONOMIES
BIOASTRONOMY
BIOAVAILABILITY
BIOAVAILABLE
BIOBANKING
BIOBANKINGS
BIOCATALYST
BIOCATALYSTS
BIOCATALYTIC
BIOCELLATE
BIOCENOLOGIES
BIOCENOLOGY
BIOCENOSES
BIOCENOSIS
BIOCENOTIC
BIOCHEMICAL
BIOCHEMICALLY
BIOCHEMICALS
BIOCHEMIST
BIOCHEMISTRIES
BIOCHEMISTRY
BIOCHEMISTS
BIOCLASTIC
BIOCLIMATIC

BIOCLIMATOLOGY
BIOCOENOLOGIES
BIOCOENOLOGY
BIOCOENOSES
BIOCOENOSIS
BIOCOENOTIC
BIOCOMPATIBLE
BIOCOMPUTING
BIOCOMPUTINGS
BIOCONTROL
BIOCONTROLS
BIOCONVERSION
BIOCONVERSIONS
BIODEGRADABLE
BIODEGRADATION
BIODEGRADATIONS
BIODEGRADE
BIODEGRADED
BIODEGRADES
BIODEGRADING
BIODESTRUCTIBLE
BIODIESELS
BIODIVERSE
BIODIVERSITIES
BIODIVERSITY
BIODYNAMIC
BIODYNAMICAL
BIODYNAMICS
BIOECOLOGICAL
BIOECOLOGICALLY
BIOECOLOGIES
BIOECOLOGIST
BIOECOLOGISTS
BIOECOLOGY
BIOELECTRIC
BIOELECTRICAL
BIOELECTRICITY
BIOENERGETIC
BIOENERGETICS
BIOENERGIES
BIOENGINEER
BIOENGINEERED
BIOENGINEERING
BIOENGINEERINGS
BIOENGINEERS
BIOETHANOL
BIOETHANOLS

BIOETHICAL	BIOINDUSTRY	BIOPHYSICIST	BIOSTATICALLY	BIPOLARISATION
BIOETHICIST	BIOINFORMATICS	BIOPHYSICISTS	BIOSTATICS	BIPOLARISATIONS
BIOETHICISTS	BIOLOGICAL	BIOPHYSICS	BIOSTATISTICAL	BIPOLARISE
BIOFEEDBACK	BIOLOGICALLY	BIOPIRACIES	BIOSTATISTICIAN	BIPOLARISED
BIOFEEDBACKS	BIOLOGICALS	BIOPIRATES	BIOSTATISTICS	BIPOLARISES
BIOFLAVONOID	BIOLOGISMS	BIOPLASMIC	BIOSTRATIGRAPHY	BIPOLARISING
BIOFLAVONOIDS	BIOLOGISTIC	BIOPOIESES	BIOSTROMES	BIPOLARITIES
BIOFOULERS	BIOLOGISTS	BIOPOIESIS	BIOSURGERIES	BIPOLARITY
BIOFOULING	BIOLUMINESCENCE	BIOPOLYMER	BIOSURGERY	BIPOLARIZATION
BIOFOULINGS	BIOLUMINESCENT	BIOPOLYMERS	BIOSYNTHESES	BIPOLARIZATIONS
BIOFUELLED	BIOMAGNETICS	BIOPRINTING	BIOSYNTHESIS	BIPOLARIZE
BIOGENESES	BIOMARKERS	BIOPRINTINGS	BIOSYNTHETIC	BIPOLARIZED
BIOGENESIS	BIOMATERIAL	BIOPRIVACIES	BIOSYSTEMATIC	BIPOLARIZES
BIOGENETIC	BIOMATERIALS	BIOPRIVACY	BIOSYSTEMATICS	BIPOLARIZING
BIOGENETICAL	BIOMATHEMATICAL	BIOPROSPECTING	BIOSYSTEMATIST	BIPROPELLANT
BIOGENETICALLY	BIOMATHEMATICS	BIOPROSPECTINGS	BIOSYSTEMATISTS	BIPROPELLANTS
BIOGENETICS	BIOMECHANICAL	BIOPSYCHOLOGIES	BIOTECHNICAL	BIPYRAMIDAL
BIOGEOCHEMICAL	BIOMECHANICALLY	BIOPSYCHOLOGY	BIOTECHNOLOGIES	BIPYRAMIDS
BIOGEOCHEMICALS	BIOMECHANICS	BIOREACTOR	BIOTECHNOLOGIST	BIQUADRATE
BIOGEOCHEMISTRY	BIOMEDICAL	BIOREACTORS	BIOTECHNOLOGY	BIQUADRATES
BIOGEOGRAPHER	BIOMEDICINE	BIOREAGENT	BIOTELEMETRIC	BIQUADRATIC
BIOGEOGRAPHERS	BIOMEDICINES	BIOREAGENTS	BIOTELEMETRIES	BIQUADRATICS
BIOGEOGRAPHIC	BIOMETEOROLOGY	BIOREGIONAL	BIOTELEMETRY	BIQUARTERLY
BIOGEOGRAPHICAL	BIOMETRICAL	BIOREGIONALISM	BIOTERRORS	BIQUINTILE
BIOGEOGRAPHIES	BIOMETRICALLY	BIOREGIONALISMS	BIOTICALLY	BIQUINTILES
BIOGEOGRAPHY	BIOMETRICIAN	BIOREGIONALIST	BIOTURBATION	BIRACIALISM
BIOGRAPHED	BIOMETRICIANS	BIOREGIONALISTS	BIOTURBATIONS	BIRACIALISMS
BIOGRAPHEE	BIOMETRICS	BIOREGIONS	BIOWEAPONS	BIRACIALLY
BIOGRAPHEES	BIOMETRIES	BIOREMEDIATION	BIPARENTAL	BIRADICALS
BIOGRAPHER	BIOMIMETIC	BIOREMEDIATIONS	BIPARENTALLY	BIRCHBARKS
BIOGRAPHERS	BIOMIMETICS	BIORHYTHMIC	BIPARIETAL	BIRDBRAINED
BIOGRAPHIC	BIOMIMICRIES	BIORHYTHMICALLY	BIPARTISAN	BIRDBRAINS
BIOGRAPHICAL	BIOMIMICRY	BIORHYTHMICS	BIPARTISANISM	BIRDDOGGED
BIOGRAPHICALLY	BIOMININGS	BIORHYTHMS	BIPARTISANISMS	BIRDDOGGING
BIOGRAPHIES	BIOMOLECULAR	BIOSAFETIES	BIPARTISANSHIP	BIRDDOGGINGS
BIOGRAPHING	BIOMOLECULE	BIOSATELLITE	BIPARTISANSHIPS	BIRDHOUSES
BIOGRAPHISE	BIOMOLECULES	BIOSATELLITES	BIPARTITELY	BIRDLIMING
BIOGRAPHISED	BIOMORPHIC	BIOSCIENCE	BIPARTITION	BIRDSFOOTS
BIOGRAPHISES	BIONOMICALLY	BIOSCIENCES	BIPARTITIONS	BIRDWATCHED
BIOGRAPHISING	BIONOMISTS	BIOSCIENTIFIC	BIPEDALISM	BIRDWATCHER
BIOGRAPHIZE	BIOPARENTS	BIOSCIENTIST	BIPEDALISMS	BIRDWATCHERS
BIOGRAPHIZED	BIOPESTICIDAL	BIOSCIENTISTS	BIPEDALITIES	BIRDWATCHES
BIOGRAPHIZES	BIOPESTICIDE	BIOSCOPIES	BIPEDALITY	BIRDWATCHING
BIOGRAPHIZING	BIOPESTICIDES	BIOSENSORS	BIPETALOUS	BIRDWATCHINGS
BIOHAZARDOUS	BIOPHILIAS	BIOSOCIALLY	BIPINNARIA	BIREFRINGENCE
BIOHAZARDS	BIOPHYSICAL	BIOSPHERES	BIPINNARIAS	BIREFRINGENCES
BIOINDUSTRIES	BIOPHYSICALLY	BIOSPHERIC	BIPINNATELY	BIREFRINGENT

B

B

BIROSTRATE	BISULPHATES	BITUMINISATION	BLACKBIRDS	BLACKLISTINGS
BIRTHDATES	BISULPHIDE	BITUMINISATIONS	BLACKBOARD	BLACKLISTS
BIRTHMARKS	BISULPHIDES	BITUMINISE	BLACKBOARDS	BLACKMAILED
BIRTHNAMES	BISULPHITE	BITUMINISED	BLACKBODIES	BLACKMAILER
BIRTHNIGHT	BISULPHITES	BITUMINISES	BLACKBUCKS	BLACKMAILERS
BIRTHNIGHTS	BISYMMETRIC	BITUMINISING	BLACKBUTTS	BLACKMAILING
BIRTHPLACE	BISYMMETRICAL	BITUMINIZATION	BLACKCOCKS	BLACKMAILS
BIRTHPLACES	BISYMMETRICALLY	BITUMINIZATIONS	BLACKCURRANT	BLACKNESSES
BIRTHRATES	BISYMMETRIES	BITUMINIZE	BLACKCURRANTS	BLACKPOLLS
BIRTHRIGHT	BISYMMETRY	BITUMINIZED	BLACKDAMPS	BLACKSMITH
BIRTHRIGHTS	BITARTRATE	BITUMINIZES	BLACKENERS	BLACKSMITHING
BIRTHROOTS	BITARTRATES	BITUMINIZING	BLACKENING	BLACKSMITHINGS
BIRTHSTONE	BITCHERIES	BITUMINOUS	BLACKENINGS	BLACKSMITHS
BIRTHSTONES	BITCHFESTS	BIUNIQUENESS	BLACKFACED	BLACKSNAKE
BIRTHWORTS	BITCHINESS	BIUNIQUENESSES	BLACKFACES	BLACKSNAKES
BISECTIONAL	BITCHINESSES	BIVALENCES	BLACKFELLA	BLACKSPOTS
BISECTIONALLY	BITEPLATES	BIVALENCIES	BLACKFELLAS	BLACKSTRAP
BISECTIONS	BITMAPPING	BIVALVULAR	BLACKFISHES	BLACKSTRAPS
BISECTRICES	BITONALITIES	BIVARIANTS	BLACKFLIES	BLACKTAILS
BISEXUALISM	BITONALITY	BIVARIATES	BLACKGAMES	BLACKTHORN
BISEXUALISMS	BITSTREAMS	BIVOUACKED	BLACKGUARD	BLACKTHORNS
BISEXUALITIES	BITTERBARK	BIVOUACKING	BLACKGUARDED	BLACKTOPPED
BISEXUALITY	BITTERBARKS	BIWEEKLIES	BLACKGUARDING	BLACKTOPPING
BISEXUALLY	BITTERBRUSH	BIZARRENESS	BLACKGUARDISM	BLACKWASHED
BISHOPBIRD	BITTERBRUSHES	BIZARRENESSES	BLACKGUARDISMS	BLACKWASHES
BISHOPBIRDS	BITTERCRESS	BIZARRERIE	BLACKGUARDLY	BLACKWASHING
BISHOPDOMS	BITTERCRESSES	BIZARRERIES	BLACKGUARDS	BLACKWATER
BISHOPESSES	BITTERLING	BLABBERING	BLACKHANDER	BLACKWATERS
BISHOPRICS	BITTERLINGS	BLABBERMOUTH	BLACKHANDERS	BLACKWOODS
BISHOPWEED	BITTERNESS	BLABBERMOUTHS	BLACKHEADED	BLADDERLIKE
BISHOPWEEDS	BITTERNESSES	BLACKAMOOR	BLACKHEADS	BLADDERNOSE
BISMUTHINITE	BITTERNUTS	BLACKAMOORS	BLACKHEART	BLADDERNOSES
BISMUTHINITES	BITTERROOT	BLACKBALLED	BLACKHEARTS	BLADDERNUT
BISMUTHOUS	BITTERROOTS	BLACKBALLING	BLACKISHLY	BLADDERNUTS
BISOCIATION	BITTERSWEET	BLACKBALLINGS	BLACKJACKED	BLADDERWORT
BISOCIATIONS	BITTERSWEETLY	BLACKBALLS	BLACKJACKING	BLADDERWORTS
BISOCIATIVE	BITTERSWEETNESS	BLACKBANDS	BLACKJACKS	BLADDERWRACK
BISPHENOLS	BITTERSWEETS	BLACKBERRIED	BLACKLANDS	BLADDERWRACKS
BISPHOSPHONATE	BITTERWEED	BLACKBERRIES	BLACKLEADED	BLADEWORKS
BISPHOSPHONATES	BITTERWEEDS	BLACKBERRY	BLACKLEADING	BLAEBERRIES
BISSEXTILE	BITTERWOOD	BLACKBERRYING	BLACKLEADS	BLAMABLENESS
BISSEXTILES	BITTERWOODS	BLACKBERRYINGS	BLACKLEGGED	BLAMABLENESSES
BISTOURIES	BITTINESSES	BLACKBIRDED	BLACKLEGGING	BLAMEABLENESS
BISULFATES	BITUMINATE	BLACKBIRDER	BLACKLISTED	BLAMEABLENESSES
BISULFIDES	BITUMINATED	BLACKBIRDERS	BLACKLISTER	BLAMEFULLY
BISULFITES	BITUMINATES	BLACKBIRDING	BLACKLISTERS	BLAMEFULNESS
BISULPHATE	BITUMINATING	BLACKBIRDINGS	BLACKLISTING	BLAMEFULNESSES

BLAMELESSLY
BLAMELESSNESS
BLAMELESSNESSES
BLAMESTORM
BLAMESTORMED
BLAMESTORMING
BLAMESTORMINGS
BLAMESTORMS
BLAMEWORTHINESS
BLAMEWORTHY
BLANCHISSEUSE
BLANCHISSEUSES
BLANCMANGE
BLANCMANGES
BLANDISHED
BLANDISHER
BLANDISHERS
BLANDISHES
BLANDISHING
BLANDISHMENT
BLANDISHMENTS
BLANDNESSES
BLANKETFLOWER
BLANKETFLOWERS
BLANKETIES
BLANKETING
BLANKETINGS
BLANKETLIKE
BLANKETWEED
BLANKETWEEDS
BLANKNESSES
BLANQUETTE
BLANQUETTES
BLARNEYING
BLASPHEMED
BLASPHEMER
BLASPHEMERS
BLASPHEMES
BLASPHEMIES
BLASPHEMING
BLASPHEMOUS
BLASPHEMOUSLY
BLASPHEMOUSNESS
BLASTEMATA
BLASTEMATIC
BLASTMENTS
BLASTOCHYLE

BLASTOCHYLES
BLASTOCOEL
BLASTOCOELE
BLASTOCOELES
BLASTOCOELIC
BLASTOCOELS
BLASTOCYST
BLASTOCYSTS
BLASTODERM
BLASTODERMIC
BLASTODERMS
BLASTODISC
BLASTODISCS
BLASTOGENESES
BLASTOGENESIS
BLASTOGENETIC
BLASTOGENIC
BLASTOMATA
BLASTOMERE
BLASTOMERES
BLASTOMERIC
BLASTOMYCOSES
BLASTOMYCOSIS
BLASTOPORAL
BLASTOPORE
BLASTOPORES
BLASTOPORIC
BLASTOPORS
BLASTOSPHERE
BLASTOSPHERES
BLASTOSPORE
BLASTOSPORES
BLASTULATION
BLASTULATIONS
BLATANCIES
BLATHERERS
BLATHERING
BLATHERSKITE
BLATHERSKITES
BLATTERING
BLAXPLOITATION
BLAXPLOITATIONS
BLAZONINGS
BLAZONRIES
BLEACHABLE
BLEACHERIES
BLEACHERITE

BLEACHERITES
BLEACHINGS
BLEAKNESSES
BLEARINESS
BLEARINESSES
BLEMISHERS
BLEMISHING
BLEMISHMENT
BLEMISHMENTS
BLENNIOIDS
BLENNORRHEA
BLENNORRHEAS
BLENNORRHOEA
BLENNORRHOEAS
BLEOMYCINS
BLEPHARISM
BLEPHARISMS
BLEPHARITIC
BLEPHARITIS
BLEPHARITISES
BLEPHAROPLAST
BLEPHAROPLASTS
BLEPHAROPLASTY
BLEPHAROSPASM
BLEPHAROSPASMS
BLESSEDEST
BLESSEDNESS
BLESSEDNESSES
BLETHERANSKATE
BLETHERANSKATES
BLETHERATION
BLETHERATIONS
BLETHERERS
BLETHERING
BLETHERINGS
BLETHERSKATE
BLETHERSKATES
BLIGHTINGLY
BLIGHTINGS
BLIMPERIES
BLIMPISHLY
BLIMPISHNESS
BLIMPISHNESSES
BLINDFISHES
BLINDFOLDED
BLINDFOLDING
BLINDFOLDS

BLINDINGLY
BLINDNESSES
BLINDSIDED
BLINDSIDES
BLINDSIDING
BLINDSIGHT
BLINDSIGHTS
BLINDSTOREY
BLINDSTOREYS
BLINDSTORIES
BLINDSTORY
BLINDWORMS
BLINGLISHES
BLINKERING
BLISSFULLY
BLISSFULNESS
BLISSFULNESSES
BLISTERIER
BLISTERIEST
BLISTERING
BLISTERINGLY
BLITHENESS
BLITHENESSES
BLITHERING
BLITHESOME
BLITHESOMELY
BLITHESOMENESS
BLITZKRIEG
BLITZKRIEGS
BLIZZARDED
BLIZZARDING
BLIZZARDLY
BLOATEDNESS
BLOATEDNESSES
BLOATWARES
BLOCKADERS
BLOCKADING
BLOCKBOARD
BLOCKBOARDS
BLOCKBUSTED
BLOCKBUSTER
BLOCKBUSTERS
BLOCKBUSTING
BLOCKBUSTINGS
BLOCKBUSTS
BLOCKHEADED
BLOCKHEADEDLY

BLOCKHEADEDNESS
BLOCKHEADS
BLOCKHOLES
BLOCKHOUSE
BLOCKHOUSES
BLOCKINESS
BLOCKINESSES
BLOCKISHLY
BLOCKISHNESS
BLOCKISHNESSES
BLOCKSHIPS
BLOCKWORKS
BLOGGERATI
BLOGJACKING
BLOGJACKINGS
BLOGOSPHERE
BLOGOSPHERES
BLOGSTREAM
BLOGSTREAMS
BLOKARTING
BLOKARTINGS
BLOKEISHNESS
BLOKEISHNESSES
BLOKISHNESS
BLOKISHNESSES
BLONDENESS
BLONDENESSES
BLONDINING
BLONDNESSES
BLOODBATHS
BLOODCURDLING
BLOODCURDLINGLY
BLOODGUILT
BLOODGUILTINESS
BLOODGUILTS
BLOODGUILTY
BLOODHOUND
BLOODHOUNDS
BLOODINESS
BLOODINESSES
BLOODLESSLY
BLOODLESSNESS
BLOODLESSNESSES
BLOODLETTER
BLOODLETTERS
BLOODLETTING
BLOODLETTINGS

BLOODLINES
BLOODLUSTS
BLOODMOBILE
BLOODMOBILES
BLOODROOTS
BLOODSHEDS
BLOODSPRENT
BLOODSTAIN
BLOODSTAINED
BLOODSTAINS
BLOODSTOCK
BLOODSTOCKS
BLOODSTONE
BLOODSTONES
BLOODSTREAM
BLOODSTREAMS
BLOODSUCKER
BLOODSUCKERS
BLOODSUCKING
BLOODTHIRSTIER
BLOODTHIRSTIEST
BLOODTHIRSTILY
BLOODTHIRSTY
BLOODWOODS
BLOODWORMS
BLOODWORTS
BLOOMERIES
BLOQUISTES
BLOSSOMING
BLOSSOMINGS
BLOSSOMLESS
BLOTCHIEST
BLOTCHINESS
BLOTCHINESSES
BLOTCHINGS
BLOTTESQUE
BLOTTESQUES
BLOVIATING
BLOVIATION
BLOVIATIONS
BLOWFISHES
BLOWINESSES
BLOWSINESS
BLOWSINESSES
BLOWTORCHED
BLOWTORCHES
BLOWTORCHING

BLOWZINESS
BLOWZINESSES
BLUBBERERS
BLUBBERIER
BLUBBERIEST
BLUBBERING
BLUDGEONED
BLUDGEONER
BLUDGEONERS
BLUDGEONING
BLUEBEARDS
BLUEBERRIES
BLUEBLOODS
BLUEBONNET
BLUEBONNETS
BLUEBOTTLE
BLUEBOTTLES
BLUEBREAST
BLUEBREASTS
BLUEBUSHES
BLUEFISHES
BLUEGRASSES
BLUEISHNESS
BLUEISHNESSES
BLUEJACKET
BLUEJACKETS
BLUEJACKING
BLUEJACKINGS
BLUELINERS
BLUEMOUTHS
BLUENESSES
BLUEPOINTS
BLUEPRINTED
BLUEPRINTING
BLUEPRINTS
BLUESHIFTED
BLUESHIFTS
BLUESNARFING
BLUESNARFINGS
BLUESTOCKING
BLUESTOCKINGS
BLUESTONES
BLUETHROAT
BLUETHROATS
BLUETONGUE
BLUETONGUES
BLUFFNESSES

BLUISHNESS
BLUISHNESSES
BLUNDERBUSS
BLUNDERBUSSES
BLUNDERERS
BLUNDERING
BLUNDERINGLY
BLUNDERINGS
BLUNTHEADS
BLUNTNESSES
BLURREDNESS
BLURREDNESSES
BLURRINESS
BLURRINESSES
BLURRINGLY
BLUSHINGLY
BLUSHLESSLY
BLUSTERERS
BLUSTERIER
BLUSTERIEST
BLUSTERING
BLUSTERINGLY
BLUSTERINGS
BLUSTEROUS
BLUSTEROUSLY
BLUTWURSTS
BOARDINGHOUSE
BOARDINGHOUSES
BOARDROOMS
BOARDSAILING
BOARDSAILINGS
BOARDSAILOR
BOARDSAILORS
BOARDWALKS
BOARFISHES
BOARHOUNDS
BOARISHNESS
BOARISHNESSES
BOASTFULLY
BOASTFULNESS
BOASTFULNESSES
BOASTINGLY
BOATBUILDER
BOATBUILDERS
BOATBUILDING
BOATBUILDINGS
BOATHOUSES

BOATLIFTED
BOATLIFTING
BOATSWAINS
BOBBEJAANS
BOBBITTING
BOBBLEHEAD
BOBBLEHEADS
BOBBYSOCKS
BOBBYSOXER
BOBBYSOXERS
BOBSLEDDED
BOBSLEDDER
BOBSLEDDERS
BOBSLEDDING
BOBSLEDDINGS
BOBSLEIGHED
BOBSLEIGHING
BOBSLEIGHS
BOBTAILING
BOBWEIGHTS
BOCCONCINI
BODACIOUSLY
BODDHISATTVA
BODDHISATTVAS
BODEGUEROS
BODHISATTVA
BODHISATTVAS
BODYBOARDED
BODYBOARDING
BODYBOARDINGS
BODYBOARDS
BODYBUILDER
BODYBUILDERS
BODYBUILDING
BODYBUILDINGS
BODYCHECKED
BODYCHECKING
BODYCHECKS
BODYGUARDED
BODYGUARDING
BODYGUARDS
BODYSHAPER
BODYSHAPERS
BODYSHELLS
BODYSURFED
BODYSURFER
BODYSURFERS

BODYSURFING
BODYSURFINGS
BODYWASHES
BODYWORKER
BODYWORKERS
BOEREMUSIEK
BOEREMUSIEKS
BOEREWORSES
BOGGINESSES
BOGTROTTER
BOGTROTTERS
BOGTROTTING
BOGTROTTINGS
BOGUSNESSES
BOHEMIANISM
BOHEMIANISMS
BOILERMAKER
BOILERMAKERS
BOILERMAKING
BOILERMAKINGS
BOILERPLATE
BOILERPLATED
BOILERPLATES
BOILERPLATING
BOILERSUIT
BOILERSUITS
BOISTEROUS
BOISTEROUSLY
BOISTEROUSNESS
BOKMAKIERIE
BOKMAKIERIES
BOLDFACING
BOLDNESSES
BOLECTIONS
BOLIVIANOS
BOLLETRIES
BOLLOCKING
BOLLOCKINGS
BOLLOCKSED
BOLLOCKSES
BOLLOCKSING
BOLOGNESES
BOLOGRAPHS
BOLOMETERS
BOLOMETRIC
BOLOMETRICALLY
BOLOMETRIES

BOLSHEVIKI
BOLSHEVIKS
BOLSHEVISE
BOLSHEVISED
BOLSHEVISES
BOLSHEVISING
BOLSHEVISM
BOLSHEVISMS
BOLSHEVIZE
BOLSHEVIZED
BOLSHEVIZES
BOLSHEVIZING
BOLSTERERS
BOLSTERING
BOLSTERINGS
BOMBACACEOUS
BOMBARDERS
BOMBARDIER
BOMBARDIERS
BOMBARDING
BOMBARDMENT
BOMBARDMENTS
BOMBARDONS
BOMBASINES
BOMBASTERS
BOMBASTICALLY
BOMBASTING
BOMBAZINES
BOMBILATED
BOMBILATES
BOMBILATING
BOMBILATION
BOMBILATIONS
BOMBINATED
BOMBINATES
BOMBINATING
BOMBINATION
BOMBINATIONS
BOMBPROOFED
BOMBPROOFING
BOMBPROOFS
BOMBSHELLS
BOMBSIGHTS
BONAMIASES
BONAMIASIS
BONASSUSES
BONBONNIERE

BONBONNIERES
BONDHOLDER
BONDHOLDERS
BONDMANSHIP
BONDMANSHIPS
BONDSERVANT
BONDSERVANTS
BONDSTONES
BONDSWOMAN
BONDSWOMEN
BONEBLACKS
BONEFISHES
BONEFISHING
BONEFISHINGS
BONEHEADED
BONEHEADEDNESS
BONESETTER
BONESETTERS
BONESHAKER
BONESHAKERS
BONHOMMIES
BONILASSES
BONINESSES
BONKBUSTER
BONKBUSTERS
BONNIBELLS
BONNILASSE
BONNILASSES
BONNINESSES
BONNYCLABBER
BONNYCLABBERS
BOOBIALLAS
BOOBOISIES
BOOGALOOED
BOOGALOOING
BOOKBINDER
BOOKBINDERIES
BOOKBINDERS
BOOKBINDERY
BOOKBINDING
BOOKBINDINGS
BOOKCROSSING
BOOKCROSSINGS
BOOKENDING
BOOKISHNESS
BOOKISHNESSES
BOOKKEEPER

BOOKKEEPERS
BOOKKEEPING
BOOKKEEPINGS
BOOKLIGHTS
BOOKMAKERS
BOOKMAKING
BOOKMAKINGS
BOOKMARKED
BOOKMARKER
BOOKMARKERS
BOOKMARKING
BOOKMOBILE
BOOKMOBILES
BOOKPLATES
BOOKSELLER
BOOKSELLERS
BOOKSELLING
BOOKSELLINGS
BOOKSHELVES
BOOKSTALLS
BOOKSTANDS
BOOKSTORES
BOOMERANGED
BOOMERANGING
BOOMERANGS
BOOMSLANGS
BOONDOGGLE
BOONDOGGLED
BOONDOGGLER
BOONDOGGLERS
BOONDOGGLES
BOONDOGGLING
BOONGARIES
BOORISHNESS
BOORISHNESSES
BOOSTERISH
BOOSTERISM
BOOSTERISMS
BOOTBLACKS
BOOTLEGGED
BOOTLEGGER
BOOTLEGGERS
BOOTLEGGING
BOOTLEGGINGS
BOOTLESSLY
BOOTLESSNESS
BOOTLESSNESSES

BOOTLICKED
BOOTLICKER
BOOTLICKERS
BOOTLICKING
BOOTLICKINGS
BOOTLOADER
BOOTLOADERS
BOOTMAKERS
BOOTMAKING
BOOTMAKINGS
BOOTSTRAPPED
BOOTSTRAPPING
BOOTSTRAPS
BOOTYLICIOUS
BOOZEHOUND
BOOZEHOUNDS
BOOZINESSES
BORAGINACEOUS
BORBORYGMAL
BORBORYGMI
BORBORYGMIC
BORBORYGMUS
BORDEREAUX
BORDERLAND
BORDERLANDS
BORDERLESS
BORDERLINE
BORDERLINES
BORDRAGING
BORDRAGINGS
BORESCOPES
BORGHETTOS
BORINGNESS
BORINGNESSES
BOROHYDRIDE
BOROHYDRIDES
BOROSILICATE
BOROSILICATES
BORROWINGS
BOSBERAADS
BOSCHVARKS
BOSCHVELDS
BOSKINESSES
BOSSINESSES
BOSSNAPPING
BOSSNAPPINGS
BOSSYBOOTS

BOTANICALLY
BOTANICALS
BOTANISERS
BOTANISING
BOTANIZERS
BOTANIZING
BOTANOMANCIES
BOTANOMANCY
BOTCHERIES
BOTCHINESS
BOTCHINESSES
BOTHERATION
BOTHERATIONS
BOTHERSOME
BOTRYOIDAL
BOTRYTISES
BOTTLEBRUSH
BOTTLEBRUSHES
BOTTLEFULS
BOTTLENECK
BOTTLENECKED
BOTTLENECKING
BOTTLENECKS
BOTTLENOSE
BOTTLENOSES
BOTTOMINGS
BOTTOMLAND
BOTTOMLANDS
BOTTOMLESS
BOTTOMLESSLY
BOTTOMLESSNESS
BOTTOMMOST
BOTTOMNESS
BOTTOMNESSES
BOTTOMRIES
BOTULINUMS
BOTULINUSES
BOUGAINVILIA
BOUGAINVILIAS
BOUGAINVILLAEA
BOUGAINVILLAEAS
BOUGAINVILLEA
BOUGAINVILLEAS
BOUILLABAISSE
BOUILLABAISSES
BOUILLOTTE
BOUILLOTTES

B

BOULDERERS
BOULDERING
BOULDERINGS
BOULEVARDIER
BOULEVARDIERS
BOULEVARDS
BOULEVERSEMENT
BOULEVERSEMENTS
BOULLEWORK
BOULLEWORKS
BOUNCEDOWN
BOUNCEDOWNS
BOUNCINESS
BOUNCINESSES
BOUNCINGLY
BOUNDARIES
BOUNDEDNESS
BOUNDEDNESSES
BOUNDERISH
BOUNDLESSLY
BOUNDLESSNESS
BOUNDLESSNESSES
BOUNDNESSES
BOUNTEOUSLY
BOUNTEOUSNESS
BOUNTEOUSNESSES
BOUNTIFULLY
BOUNTIFULNESS
BOUNTIFULNESSES
BOUNTYHEDS
BOUQUETIERE
BOUQUETIERES
BOURASQUES
BOURBONISM
BOURBONISMS
BOURGEOISE
BOURGEOISES
BOURGEOISIE
BOURGEOISIES
BOURGEOISIFIED
BOURGEOISIFIES
BOURGEOISIFY
BOURGEOISIFYING
BOURGEONED
BOURGEONING
BOURGUIGNON
BOURGUIGNONNE

BOURGUIGNONNES
BOURGUIGNONS
BOUSINGKEN
BOUSINGKENS
BOUSTROPHEDON
BOUSTROPHEDONIC
BOUSTROPHEDONS
BOUTONNIERE
BOUTONNIERES
BOUVARDIAS
BOVINITIES
BOWDLERISATION
BOWDLERISATIONS
BOWDLERISE
BOWDLERISED
BOWDLERISER
BOWDLERISERS
BOWDLERISES
BOWDLERISING
BOWDLERISM
BOWDLERISMS
BOWDLERIZATION
BOWDLERIZATIONS
BOWDLERIZE
BOWDLERIZED
BOWDLERIZER
BOWDLERIZERS
BOWDLERIZES
BOWDLERIZING
BOWERBIRDS
BOWERWOMAN
BOWERWOMEN
BOWHUNTERS
BOWHUNTING
BOWLINGUAL
BOWLINGUALS
BOWSTRINGED
BOWSTRINGING
BOWSTRINGS
BOXBERRIES
BOXERCISES
BOXHAULING
BOXINESSES
BOXKEEPERS
BOXWALLAHS
BOYCOTTERS
BOYCOTTING

BOYFRIENDS
BOYISHNESS
BOYISHNESSES
BOYSENBERRIES
BOYSENBERRY
BRAAIVLEIS
BRAAIVLEISES
BRABBLEMENT
BRABBLEMENTS
BRACHIATED
BRACHIATES
BRACHIATING
BRACHIATION
BRACHIATIONS
BRACHIATOR
BRACHIATORS
BRACHIOCEPHALIC
BRACHIOPOD
BRACHIOPODS
BRACHIOSAURUS
BRACHIOSAURUSES
BRACHISTOCHRONE
BRACHYAXES
BRACHYAXIS
BRACHYCEPHAL
BRACHYCEPHALIC
BRACHYCEPHALICS
BRACHYCEPHALIES
BRACHYCEPHALISM
BRACHYCEPHALOUS
BRACHYCEPHALS
BRACHYCEPHALY
BRACHYCEROUS
BRACHYDACTYL
BRACHYDACTYLIC
BRACHYDACTYLIES
BRACHYDACTYLISM
BRACHYDACTYLOUS
BRACHYDACTYLY
BRACHYDIAGONAL
BRACHYDIAGONALS
BRACHYDOME
BRACHYDOMES
BRACHYGRAPHIES
BRACHYGRAPHY
BRACHYLOGIES
BRACHYLOGOUS

BRACHYLOGY
BRACHYODONT
BRACHYPINAKOID
BRACHYPINAKOIDS
BRACHYPRISM
BRACHYPRISMS
BRACHYPTERISM
BRACHYPTERISMS
BRACHYPTEROUS
BRACHYTHERAPIES
BRACHYTHERAPY
BRACHYURAL
BRACHYURAN
BRACHYURANS
BRACHYUROUS
BRACKETING
BRACKETINGS
BRACKISHNESS
BRACKISHNESSES
BRACTEATES
BRACTEOLATE
BRACTEOLES
BRADYCARDIA
BRADYCARDIAC
BRADYCARDIAS
BRADYKINESIA
BRADYKINESIAS
BRADYKININ
BRADYKININS
BRADYPEPTIC
BRADYPEPTICS
BRADYSEISM
BRADYSEISMS
BRAGADISME
BRAGADISMES
BRAGGADOCIO
BRAGGADOCIOS
BRAGGADOCIOUS
BRAGGARTISM
BRAGGARTISMS
BRAGGARTLY
BRAGGINGLY
BRAHMANISM
BRAHMANISMS
BRAHMANIST
BRAHMANISTS
BRAHMINISM

BRAHMINISMS
BRAHMINIST
BRAHMINISTS
BRAILLEWRITER
BRAILLEWRITERS
BRAILLISTS
BRAINBOXES
BRAINCASES
BRAINCHILD
BRAINCHILDREN
BRAINFARTS
BRAINFOODS
BRAININESS
BRAININESSES
BRAINLESSLY
BRAINLESSNESS
BRAINLESSNESSES
BRAINPOWER
BRAINPOWERS
BRAINSICKLY
BRAINSICKNESS
BRAINSICKNESSES
BRAINSTEMS
BRAINSTORM
BRAINSTORMED
BRAINSTORMER
BRAINSTORMERS
BRAINSTORMING
BRAINSTORMINGS
BRAINSTORMS
BRAINTEASER
BRAINTEASERS
BRAINWASHED
BRAINWASHER
BRAINWASHERS
BRAINWASHES
BRAINWASHING
BRAINWASHINGS
BRAINWAVES
BRAINWORKS
BRAMBLIEST
BRAMBLINGS
BRANCHERIES
BRANCHIATE
BRANCHIEST
BRANCHINGS
BRANCHIOPOD

BRANCHIOPODS	BRATWURSTS	BREAKABLENESS	BREASTSUMMERS	BREEZEWAYS
BRANCHIOSTEGAL	BRAUNCHING	BREAKABLENESSES	BREASTWORK	BREEZINESS
BRANCHLESS	BRAUNSCHWEIGER	BREAKABLES	BREASTWORKS	BREEZINESSES
BRANCHLETS	BRAUNSCHWEIGERS	BREAKAWAYS	BREATHABILITIES	BREMSSTRAHLUNG
BRANCHLIKE	BRAVADOING	BREAKBEATS	BREATHABILITY	BREMSSTRAHLUNGS
BRANCHLINE	BRAVENESSES	BREAKDANCE	BREATHABLE	BRESSUMMER
BRANCHLINES	BRAVISSIMO	BREAKDANCED	BREATHALYSE	BRESSUMMERS
BRANDERING	BRAWNINESS	BREAKDANCER	BREATHALYSED	BRETASCHES
BRANDISHED	BRAWNINESSES	BREAKDANCERS	BREATHALYSER	BRETTICING
BRANDISHER	BRAZENNESS	BREAKDANCES	BREATHALYSERS	BREUNNERITE
BRANDISHERS	BRAZENNESSES	BREAKDANCING	BREATHALYSES	BREUNNERITES
BRANDISHES	BRAZENRIES	BREAKDANCINGS	BREATHALYSING	BREVETCIES
BRANDISHING	BRAZIERIES	BREAKDOWNS	BREATHALYZE	BREVETTING
BRANDLINGS	BRAZILEINS	BREAKEVENS	BREATHALYZED	BREVIARIES
BRANDRETHS	BRAZILWOOD	BREAKFASTED	BREATHALYZER	BREVIPENNATE
BRANFULNESS	BRAZILWOODS	BREAKFASTER	BREATHALYZERS	BREWHOUSES
BRANFULNESSES	BREADBASKET	BREAKFASTERS	BREATHALYZES	BREWMASTER
BRANGLINGS	BREADBASKETS	BREAKFASTING	BREATHALYZING	BREWMASTERS
BRANKURSINE	BREADBERRIES	BREAKFASTS	BREATHARIAN	BRIARROOTS
BRANKURSINES	BREADBERRY	BREAKFRONT	BREATHARIANISM	BRIARWOODS
BRANNIGANS	BREADBOARD	BREAKFRONTS	BREATHARIANISMS	BRICABRACS
BRASHINESS	BREADBOARDED	BREAKPOINT	BREATHARIANS	BRICKCLAYS
BRASHINESSES	BREADBOARDING	BREAKPOINTS	BREATHIEST	BRICKEARTH
BRASHNESSES	BREADBOARDS	BREAKTHROUGH	BREATHINESS	BRICKEARTHS
BRASILEINS	BREADBOXES	BREAKTHROUGHS	BREATHINESSES	BRICKFIELD
BRASSBOUND	BREADCRUMB	BREAKTIMES	BREATHINGS	BRICKFIELDER
BRASSERIES	BREADCRUMBED	BREAKWALLS	BREATHLESS	BRICKFIELDERS
BRASSFOUNDER	BREADCRUMBING	BREAKWATER	BREATHLESSLY	BRICKFIELDS
BRASSFOUNDERS	BREADCRUMBS	BREAKWATERS	BREATHLESSNESS	BRICKKILNS
BRASSFOUNDING	BREADFRUIT	BREASTBONE	BREATHTAKING	BRICKLAYER
BRASSFOUNDINGS	BREADFRUITS	BREASTBONES	BREATHTAKINGLY	BRICKLAYERS
BRASSICACEOUS	BREADHEADS	BREASTFEED	BRECCIATED	BRICKLAYING
BRASSIERES	BREADKNIFE	BREASTFEEDING	BRECCIATES	BRICKLAYINGS
BRASSINESS	BREADKNIVES	BREASTFEEDINGS	BRECCIATING	BRICKMAKER
BRASSINESSES	BREADLINES	BREASTFEEDS	BRECCIATION	BRICKMAKERS
BRASSWARES	BREADROOMS	BREASTPINS	BRECCIATIONS	BRICKMAKING
BRATPACKER	BREADROOTS	BREASTPLATE	BREECHBLOCK	BRICKMAKINGS
BRATPACKERS	BREADSTICK	BREASTPLATES	BREECHBLOCKS	BRICKSHAPED
BRATTICING	BREADSTICKS	BREASTPLOUGH	BREECHCLOTH	BRICKWALLS
BRATTICINGS	BREADSTUFF	BREASTPLOUGHS	BREECHCLOTHS	BRICKWORKS
BRATTINESS	BREADSTUFFS	BREASTRAIL	BREECHCLOUT	BRICKYARDS
BRATTINESSES	BREADTHWAYS	BREASTRAILS	BREECHCLOUTS	BRICOLAGES
BRATTISHED	BREADTHWISE	BREASTSTROKE	BREECHINGS	BRICOLEURS
BRATTISHES	BREADWINNER	BREASTSTROKER	BREECHLESS	BRIDECAKES
BRATTISHING	BREADWINNERS	BREASTSTROKERS	BREECHLOADER	BRIDEGROOM
BRATTISHINGS	BREADWINNING	BREASTSTROKES	BREECHLOADERS	BRIDEGROOMS
BRATTLINGS	BREADWINNINGS	BREASTSUMMER	BREEZELESS	BRIDEMAIDEN

BRIDEMAIDENS

BRIDEMAIDENS
BRIDEMAIDS
BRIDESMAID
BRIDESMAIDS
BRIDEWEALTH
BRIDEWEALTHS
BRIDEWELLS
BRIDEZILLA
BRIDEZILLAS
BRIDGEABLE
BRIDGEBOARD
BRIDGEBOARDS
BRIDGEHEAD
BRIDGEHEADS
BRIDGELESS
BRIDGEWORK
BRIDGEWORKS
BRIDLEWAYS
BRIDLEWISE
BRIEFCASES
BRIEFNESSES
BRIERROOTS
BRIERWOODS
BRIGADIERS
BRIGANDAGE
BRIGANDAGES
BRIGANDINE
BRIGANDINES
BRIGANDRIES
BRIGANTINE
BRIGANTINES
BRIGHTENED
BRIGHTENER
BRIGHTENERS
BRIGHTENING
BRIGHTNESS
BRIGHTNESSES
BRIGHTSOME
BRIGHTWORK
BRIGHTWORKS
BRILLIANCE
BRILLIANCES
BRILLIANCIES
BRILLIANCY
BRILLIANTE
BRILLIANTED
BRILLIANTINE

BRILLIANTINED
BRILLIANTINES
BRILLIANTING
BRILLIANTLY
BRILLIANTNESS
BRILLIANTNESSES
BRILLIANTS
BRIMFULLNESS
BRIMFULLNESSES
BRIMFULNESS
BRIMFULNESSES
BRIMSTONES
BRINELLING
BRINELLINGS
BRINGDOWNS
BRININESSES
BRINJARRIES
BRINKMANSHIP
BRINKMANSHIPS
BRINKSMANSHIP
BRINKSMANSHIPS
BRIOLETTES
BRIQUETTED
BRIQUETTES
BRIQUETTING
BRISKENING
BRISKNESSES
BRISTLECONE
BRISTLECONES
BRISTLELIKE
BRISTLETAIL
BRISTLETAILS
BRISTLIEST
BRISTLINESS
BRISTLINESSES
BRITANNIAS
BRITSCHKAS
BRITTANIAS
BRITTLENESS
BRITTLENESSES
BROADBANDS
BROADBEANS
BROADBILLS
BROADBRIMS
BROADBRUSH
BROADCASTED
BROADCASTER

BROADCASTERS
BROADCASTING
BROADCASTINGS
BROADCASTS
BROADCLOTH
BROADCLOTHS
BROADENERS
BROADENING
BROADLEAVED
BROADLEAVES
BROADLINES
BROADLOOMS
BROADNESSES
BROADPIECE
BROADPIECES
BROADSCALE
BROADSHEET
BROADSHEETS
BROADSIDED
BROADSIDES
BROADSIDING
BROADSWORD
BROADSWORDS
BROADTAILS
BROBDINGNAGIAN
BROCATELLE
BROCATELLES
BROCCOLINI
BROCCOLINIS
BROCHETTES
BROGUERIES
BROIDERERS
BROIDERIES
BROIDERING
BROIDERINGS
BROKENHEARTED
BROKENHEARTEDLY
BROKENNESS
BROKENNESSES
BROKERAGES
BROKERINGS
BROMEGRASS
BROMEGRASSES
BROMELAINS
BROMELIACEOUS
BROMELIADS
BROMEOSINS

BROMHIDROSES
BROMHIDROSIS
BROMIDROSES
BROMIDROSIS
BROMINATED
BROMINATES
BROMINATING
BROMINATION
BROMINATIONS
BROMINISMS
BROMOCRIPTINE
BROMOCRIPTINES
BROMOFORMS
BROMOURACIL
BROMOURACILS
BRONCHIALLY
BRONCHIECTASES
BRONCHIECTASIS
BRONCHIOLAR
BRONCHIOLE
BRONCHIOLES
BRONCHIOLITIS
BRONCHIOLITISES
BRONCHITIC
BRONCHITICS
BRONCHITIS
BRONCHITISES
BRONCHODILATOR
BRONCHODILATORS
BRONCHOGENIC
BRONCHOGRAPHIES
BRONCHOGRAPHY
BRONCHOSCOPE
BRONCHOSCOPES
BRONCHOSCOPIC
BRONCHOSCOPICAL
BRONCHOSCOPIES
BRONCHOSCOPIST
BRONCHOSCOPISTS
BRONCHOSCOPY
BRONCHOSPASM
BRONCHOSPASMS
BRONCHOSPASTIC
BRONCOBUSTER
BRONCOBUSTERS
BRONDYRONS
BRONTOBYTE

BRONTOBYTES
BRONTOSAUR
BRONTOSAURS
BRONTOSAURUS
BRONTOSAURUSES
BRONZIFIED
BRONZIFIES
BRONZIFYING
BROODINESS
BROODINESSES
BROODINGLY
BROODMARES
BROOKLIMES
BROOKWEEDS
BROOMBALLER
BROOMBALLERS
BROOMBALLS
BROOMCORNS
BROOMRAPES
BROOMSTAFF
BROOMSTAFFS
BROOMSTICK
BROOMSTICKS
BROTHERHOOD
BROTHERHOODS
BROTHERING
BROTHERLIKE
BROTHERLINESS
BROTHERLINESSES
BROUGHTASES
BROWALLIAS
BROWBEATEN
BROWBEATER
BROWBEATERS
BROWBEATING
BROWBEATINGS
BROWNFIELD
BROWNFIELDS
BROWNNESSES
BROWNNOSED
BROWNNOSER
BROWNNOSERS
BROWNNOSES
BROWNNOSING
BROWNSHIRT
BROWNSHIRTS
BROWNSTONE

B

BROWNSTONES	BRYOLOGISTS	BUDGERIGARS	BULLETWOODS	BUMBLEBEES
BROWRIDGES	BRYOPHYLLUM	BUDGETEERS	BULLFIGHTER	BUMBLEBERRIES
BROWSABLES	BRYOPHYLLUMS	BUDGETINGS	BULLFIGHTERS	BUMBLEBERRY
BRUCELLOSES	BRYOPHYTES	BUFFALOBERRIES	BULLFIGHTING	BUMBLEDOMS
BRUCELLOSIS	BRYOPHYTIC	BUFFALOBERRY	BULLFIGHTINGS	BUMBLINGLY
BRUGMANSIA	BUBBLEGUMS	BUFFALOFISH	BULLFIGHTS	BUMFREEZER
BRUGMANSIAS	BUBBLEHEAD	BUFFALOFISHES	BULLFINCHES	BUMFREEZERS
BRUMMAGEMS	BUBBLEHEADED	BUFFALOING	BULLHEADED	BUMFUZZLED
BRUSCHETTA	BUBBLEHEADS	BUFFERINGS	BULLHEADEDLY	BUMFUZZLES
BRUSCHETTAS	BUBONOCELE	BUFFETINGS	BULLHEADEDNESS	BUMFUZZLING
BRUSCHETTE	BUBONOCELES	BUFFLEHEAD	BULLIONIST	BUMMALOTIS
BRUSHABILITIES	BUCCANEERED	BUFFLEHEADS	BULLIONISTS	BUMPINESSES
BRUSHABILITY	BUCCANEERING	BUFFOONERIES	BULLISHNESS	BUMPKINISH
BRUSHBACKS	BUCCANEERINGS	BUFFOONERY	BULLISHNESSES	BUMPOLOGIES
BRUSHFIRES	BUCCANEERISH	BUFFOONISH	BULLMASTIFF	BUMPSADAISY
BRUSHLANDS	BUCCANEERS	BUFOTALINS	BULLMASTIFFS	BUMPTIOUSLY
BRUSHMARKS	BUCCANIERED	BUFOTENINE	BULLNECKED	BUMPTIOUSNESS
BRUSHSTROKE	BUCCANIERING	BUFOTENINES	BULLOCKIES	BUMPTIOUSNESSES
BRUSHSTROKES	BUCCANIERS	BUGGINESSES	BULLOCKING	BUMSUCKERS
BRUSHWHEEL	BUCCINATOR	BUGLEWEEDS	BULLROARER	BUMSUCKING
BRUSHWHEELS	BUCCINATORS	BUHRSTONES	BULLROARERS	BUMSUCKINGS
BRUSHWOODS	BUCCINATORY	BUILDDOWNS	BULLRUSHES	BUNBURYING
BRUSHWORKS	BUCELLASES	BUIRDLIEST	BULLSHITTED	BUNCHBERRIES
BRUSQUENESS	BUCENTAURS	BULBIFEROUS	BULLSHITTER	BUNCHBERRY
BRUSQUENESSES	BUCKBOARDS	BULBOSITIES	BULLSHITTERS	BUNCHGRASS
BRUSQUERIE	BUCKBRUSHES	BULBOUSNESS	BULLSHITTING	BUNCHGRASSES
BRUSQUERIES	BUCKETFULS	BULBOUSNESSES	BULLSHITTINGS	BUNCHINESS
BRUTALISATION	BUCKETINGS	BULGINESSES	BULLSNAKES	BUNCHINESSES
BRUTALISATIONS	BUCKETSFUL	BULKINESSES	BULLTERRIER	BUNDOBUSTS
BRUTALISED	BUCKHOUNDS	BULLBAITING	BULLTERRIERS	BUNGALOIDS
BRUTALISES	BUCKJUMPER	BULLBAITINGS	BULLWADDIE	BUNGLESOME
BRUTALISING	BUCKJUMPERS	BULLBRIERS	BULLWADDIES	BUNGLINGLY
BRUTALISMS	BUCKJUMPING	BULLDOGGED	BULLWHACKED	BUNKHOUSES
BRUTALISTS	BUCKJUMPINGS	BULLDOGGER	BULLWHACKING	BUOYANCIES
BRUTALITIES	BUCKLERING	BULLDOGGERS	BULLWHACKS	BUOYANTNESS
BRUTALIZATION	BUCKRAMING	BULLDOGGING	BULLWHIPPED	BUOYANTNESSES
BRUTALIZATIONS	BUCKSHISHED	BULLDOGGINGS	BULLWHIPPING	BUPIVACAINE
BRUTALIZED	BUCKSHISHES	BULLDOZERS	BULLYCIDES	BUPIVACAINES
BRUTALIZES	BUCKSHISHING	BULLDOZING	BULLYRAGGED	BUPRENORPHINE
BRUTALIZING	BUCKSKINNED	BULLETINED	BULLYRAGGING	BUPRENORPHINES
BRUTENESSES	BUCKTHORNS	BULLETINING	BULWADDEES	BUPRESTIDS
BRUTIFYING	BUCKTOOTHED	BULLETPROOF	BULWADDIES	BUPROPIONS
BRUTISHNESS	BUCKWHEATS	BULLETPROOFED	BULWARKING	BURDENSOME
BRUTISHNESSES	BUCKYBALLS	BULLETPROOFING	BUMBAILIFF	BUREAUCRACIES
BRYOLOGICAL	BUCKYTUBES	BULLETPROOFS	BUMBAILIFFS	BUREAUCRACY
BRYOLOGIES	BUCOLICALLY	BULLETRIES	BUMBERSHOOT	BUREAUCRAT
BRYOLOGIST	BUDGERIGAR	BULLETWOOD	BUMBERSHOOTS	BUREAUCRATESE

BUREAUCRATESES	BURNETTISES	BUSHMASTER	BUTCHNESSES	BUTTONBUSH
BUREAUCRATIC	BURNETTISING	BUSHMASTERS	BUTENEDIOIC	BUTTONBUSHES
BUREAUCRATISE	BURNETTIZE	BUSHRANGER	BUTEONINES	BUTTONHELD
BUREAUCRATISED	BURNETTIZED	BUSHRANGERS	BUTLERAGES	BUTTONHOLD
BUREAUCRATISES	BURNETTIZES	BUSHRANGING	BUTLERSHIP	BUTTONHOLDING
BUREAUCRATISING	BURNETTIZING	BUSHRANGINGS	BUTLERSHIPS	BUTTONHOLDS
BUREAUCRATISM	BURNISHABLE	BUSHWALKED	BUTTERBALL	BUTTONHOLE
BUREAUCRATISMS	BURNISHERS	BUSHWALKER	BUTTERBALLS	BUTTONHOLED
BUREAUCRATIST	BURNISHING	BUSHWALKERS	BUTTERBURS	BUTTONHOLER
BUREAUCRATISTS	BURNISHINGS	BUSHWALKING	BUTTERCUPS	BUTTONHOLERS
BUREAUCRATIZE	BURNISHMENT	BUSHWALKINGS	BUTTERDOCK	BUTTONHOLES
BUREAUCRATIZED	BURNISHMENTS	BUSHWHACKED	BUTTERDOCKS	BUTTONHOLING
BUREAUCRATIZES	BURRAMUNDI	BUSHWHACKER	BUTTERFATS	BUTTONHOOK
BUREAUCRATIZING	BURRAMUNDIS	BUSHWHACKERS	BUTTERFINGERED	BUTTONHOOKED
BUREAUCRATS	BURRAMYSES	BUSHWHACKING	BUTTERFINGERS	BUTTONHOOKING
BURGEONING	BURRAWANGS	BUSHWHACKINGS	BUTTERFISH	BUTTONHOOKS
BURGLARIES	BURRFISHES	BUSHWHACKS	BUTTERFISHES	BUTTONLESS
BURGLARING	BURROWSTOWN	BUSINESSES	BUTTERFLIED	BUTTONMOULD
BURGLARIOUS	BURROWSTOWNS	BUSINESSLIKE	BUTTERFLIES	BUTTONMOULDS
BURGLARIOUSLY	BURRSTONES	BUSINESSMAN	BUTTERFLYER	BUTTONWOOD
BURGLARISE	BURSARSHIP	BUSINESSMEN	BUTTERFLYERS	BUTTONWOODS
BURGLARISED	BURSARSHIPS	BUSINESSPEOPLE	BUTTERFLYFISH	BUTTRESSED
BURGLARISES	BURSERACEOUS	BUSINESSPERSON	BUTTERFLYFISHES	BUTTRESSES
BURGLARISING	BURSICULATE	BUSINESSPERSONS	BUTTERFLYING	BUTTRESSING
BURGLARIZE	BURSITISES	BUSINESSWOMAN	BUTTERIEST	BUTTSTOCKS
BURGLARIZED	BURTHENING	BUSINESSWOMEN	BUTTERINES	BUTYLATING
BURGLARIZES	BURTHENSOME	BUSTICATED	BUTTERINESS	BUTYLATION
BURGLARIZING	BUSHBABIES	BUSTICATES	BUTTERINESSES	BUTYLATIONS
BURGLARPROOF	BUSHBASHING	BUSTICATING	BUTTERLESS	BUTYRACEOUS
BURGOMASTER	BUSHBASHINGS	BUSTINESSES	BUTTERMILK	BUTYRALDEHYDE
BURGOMASTERS	BUSHCRAFTS	BUSTLINGLY	BUTTERMILKS	BUTYRALDEHYDES
BURGUNDIES	BUSHELLERS	BUSYBODIED	BUTTERNUTS	BUTYROPHENONE
BURLADEROS	BUSHELLING	BUSYBODIES	BUTTERSCOTCH	BUTYROPHENONES
BURLESQUED	BUSHELLINGS	BUSYBODYING	BUTTERSCOTCHES	BUXOMNESSES
BURLESQUELY	BUSHELWOMAN	BUSYBODYINGS	BUTTERWEED	BUZZKILLER
BURLESQUER	BUSHELWOMEN	BUSYNESSES	BUTTERWEEDS	BUZZKILLERS
BURLESQUERS	BUSHFIGHTING	BUTADIENES	BUTTERWORT	BYPRODUCTS
BURLESQUES	BUSHFIGHTINGS	BUTCHERBIRD	BUTTERWORTS	BYSSACEOUS
BURLESQUING	BUSHHAMMER	BUTCHERBIRDS	BUTTINSKIES	BYSSINOSES
BURLEYCUES	BUSHHAMMERS	BUTCHERERS	BUTTINSKIS	BYSSINOSIS
BURLINESSES	BUSHINESSES	BUTCHERIES	BUTTOCKING	BYSTANDERS
BURNETTISE	BUSHMANSHIP	BUTCHERING	BUTTONBALL	BYTOWNITES
BURNETTISED	BUSHMANSHIPS	BUTCHERINGS	BUTTONBALLS	

C

CABALETTAS
CABALISTIC
CABALISTICAL
CABALLEROS
CABBAGETOWN
CABBAGETOWNS
CABBAGEWORM
CABBAGEWORMS
CABBALISMS
CABBALISTIC
CABBALISTICAL
CABBALISTS
CABDRIVERS
CABINETMAKER
CABINETMAKERS
CABINETMAKING
CABINETMAKINGS
CABINETRIES
CABINETWORK
CABINETWORKS
CABINMATES
CABLECASTED
CABLECASTING
CABLECASTS
CABLEGRAMS
CABLEVISION
CABLEVISIONS
CABRIOLETS
CACAFUEGOS
CACCIATORA
CACCIATORE
CACHAEMIAS
CACHECTICAL
CACHINNATE
CACHINNATED
CACHINNATES
CACHINNATING
CACHINNATION
CACHINNATIONS
CACHINNATORY
CACHOLONGS

CACIQUISMS
CACKERMANDER
CACKERMANDERS
CACKLEBERRIES
CACKLEBERRY
CACODAEMON
CACODAEMONS
CACODEMONIC
CACODEMONS
CACODOXIES
CACOEPISTIC
CACOGASTRIC
CACOGENICS
CACOGRAPHER
CACOGRAPHERS
CACOGRAPHIC
CACOGRAPHICAL
CACOGRAPHIES
CACOGRAPHY
CACOLOGIES
CACOMISTLE
CACOMISTLES
CACOMIXLES
CACONYMIES
CACOPHONIC
CACOPHONICAL
CACOPHONICALLY
CACOPHONIES
CACOPHONIOUS
CACOPHONOUS
CACOPHONOUSLY
CACOTOPIAN
CACOTOPIAS
CACOTROPHIES
CACOTROPHY
CACTACEOUS
CACTOBLASTES
CACTOBLASTIS
CACUMINALS
CACUMINOUS
CADASTRALLY

CADAVERINE
CADAVERINES
CADAVEROUS
CADAVEROUSLY
CADAVEROUSNESS
CADDISFLIES
CADDISHNESS
CADDISHNESSES
CADDISWORM
CADDISWORMS
CADETSHIPS
CADUCITIES
CAECILIANS
CAECITISES
CAENOGENESES
CAENOGENESIS
CAENOGENETIC
CAESALPINOID
CAESAREANS
CAESARIANS
CAESARISMS
CAESAROPAPISM
CAESAROPAPISMS
CAESPITOSE
CAESPITOSELY
CAFETERIAS
CAFETIERES
CAFETORIUM
CAFETORIUMS
CAFFEINATED
CAFFEINISM
CAFFEINISMS
CAGEYNESSES
CAGINESSES
CAGMAGGING
CAGYNESSES
CAILLEACHS
CAILLIACHS
CAINOGENESES
CAINOGENESIS
CAINOGENETIC

CAIRNGORMS
CAJOLEMENT
CAJOLEMENTS
CAJOLERIES
CAJOLINGLY
CAKEWALKED
CAKEWALKER
CAKEWALKERS
CAKEWALKING
CAKINESSES
CALABASHES
CALABOGUSES
CALABOOSES
CALABRESES
CALAMANCOES
CALAMANCOS
CALAMANDER
CALAMANDERS
CALAMARIES
CALAMINING
CALAMITIES
CALAMITOUS
CALAMITOUSLY
CALAMITOUSNESS
CALAMONDIN
CALAMONDINS
CALANDRIAS
CALAVANCES
CALAVERITE
CALAVERITES
CALCAREOUS
CALCAREOUSLY
CALCARIFEROUS
CALCARIFORM
CALCEAMENTA
CALCEAMENTUM
CALCEATING
CALCEDONIES
CALCEDONIO
CALCEDONIOS
CALCEIFORM

CALCEOLARIA
CALCEOLARIAS
CALCEOLATE
CALCICOLES
CALCICOLOUS
CALCIFEROL
CALCIFEROLS
CALCIFEROUS
CALCIFICATION
CALCIFICATIONS
CALCIFUGAL
CALCIFUGES
CALCIFUGOUS
CALCIFYING
CALCIGEROUS
CALCIMINED
CALCIMINES
CALCIMINING
CALCINABLE
CALCINATION
CALCINATIONS
CALCINOSES
CALCINOSIS
CALCITONIN
CALCITONINS
CALCSINTER
CALCSINTERS
CALCULABILITIES
CALCULABILITY
CALCULABLE
CALCULABLY
CALCULATED
CALCULATEDLY
CALCULATEDNESS
CALCULATES
CALCULATING
CALCULATINGLY
CALCULATION
CALCULATIONAL
CALCULATIONS
CALCULATIVE

CALCULATOR	CALIBRATING	CALLOSITIES	CALVARIUMS	CAMORRISTS
CALCULATORS	CALIBRATION	CALLOUSING	CALYCANTHEMIES	CAMOUFLAGE
CALCULUSES	CALIBRATIONS	CALLOUSNESS	CALYCANTHEMY	CAMOUFLAGEABLE
CALEFACIENT	CALIBRATOR	CALLOUSNESSES	CALYCANTHUS	CAMOUFLAGED
CALEFACIENTS	CALIBRATORS	CALLOWNESS	CALYCANTHUSES	CAMOUFLAGES
CALEFACTION	CALIDITIES	CALLOWNESSES	CALYCIFORM	CAMOUFLAGIC
CALEFACTIONS	CALIFORNIUM	CALMATIVES	CALYCOIDEOUS	CAMOUFLAGING
CALEFACTIVE	CALIFORNIUMS	CALMNESSES	CALYCULATE	CAMOUFLETS
CALEFACTOR	CALIGINOSITIES	CALMODULIN	CALYPSONIAN	CAMOUFLEUR
CALEFACTORIES	CALIGINOSITY	CALMODULINS	CALYPSONIANS	CAMOUFLEURS
CALEFACTORS	CALIGINOUS	CALMSTANES	CALYPTERAS	CAMPAIGNED
CALEFACTORY	CALIMOCHOS	CALMSTONES	CALYPTRATE	CAMPAIGNER
CALEMBOURS	CALIOLOGIES	CALORESCENCE	CALYPTROGEN	CAMPAIGNERS
CALENDARED	CALIPASHES	CALORESCENCES	CALYPTROGENS	CAMPAIGNING
CALENDARER	CALIPERING	CALORESCENT	CAMANACHDS	CAMPANEROS
CALENDARERS	CALIPHATES	CALORICALLY	CAMARADERIE	CAMPANIFORM
CALENDARING	CALISTHENIC	CALORICITIES	CAMARADERIES	CAMPANILES
CALENDARISATION	CALISTHENICS	CALORICITY	CAMARILLAS	CAMPANISTS
CALENDARISE	CALLBOARDS	CALORIFICALLY	CAMBERINGS	CAMPANOLOGER
CALENDARISED	CALLIATURE	CALORIFICATION	CAMBISTRIES	CAMPANOLOGERS
CALENDARISES	CALLIATURES	CALORIFICATIONS	CAMCORDERS	CAMPANOLOGICAL
CALENDARISING	CALLIDITIES	CALORIFIER	CAMCORDING	CAMPANOLOGIES
CALENDARIST	CALLIGRAMME	CALORIFIERS	CAMELBACKS	CAMPANOLOGIST
CALENDARISTS	CALLIGRAMMES	CALORIMETER	CAMELEOPARD	CAMPANOLOGISTS
CALENDARIZATION	CALLIGRAMS	CALORIMETERS	CAMELEOPARDS	CAMPANOLOGY
CALENDARIZE	CALLIGRAPHER	CALORIMETRIC	CAMELHAIRS	CAMPANULACEOUS
CALENDARIZED	CALLIGRAPHERS	CALORIMETRICAL	CAMELOPARD	CAMPANULAR
CALENDARIZES	CALLIGRAPHIC	CALORIMETRIES	CAMELOPARDS	CAMPANULAS
CALENDARIZING	CALLIGRAPHICAL	CALORIMETRY	CAMERAPERSON	CAMPANULATE
CALENDERED	CALLIGRAPHIES	CALORISING	CAMERAPERSONS	CAMPCRAFTS
CALENDERER	CALLIGRAPHIST	CALORIZING	CAMERAPHONE	CAMPEADORS
CALENDERERS	CALLIGRAPHISTS	CALOTYPIST	CAMERAPHONES	CAMPESINOS
CALENDERING	CALLIGRAPHY	CALOTYPISTS	CAMERATION	CAMPESTRAL
CALENDERINGS	CALLIOPSIS	CALUMNIABLE	CAMERATIONS	CAMPESTRIAN
CALENDRERS	CALLIPASHES	CALUMNIATE	CAMERAWOMAN	CAMPGROUND
CALENDRICAL	CALLIPERED	CALUMNIATED	CAMERAWOMEN	CAMPGROUNDS
CALENDRIES	CALLIPERING	CALUMNIATES	CAMERAWORK	CAMPHORACEOUS
CALENDULAS	CALLIPYGEAN	CALUMNIATING	CAMERAWORKS	CAMPHORATE
CALENTURES	CALLIPYGIAN	CALUMNIATION	CAMERLENGO	CAMPHORATED
CALESCENCE	CALLIPYGOUS	CALUMNIATIONS	CAMERLENGOS	CAMPHORATES
CALESCENCES	CALLISTEMON	CALUMNIATOR	CAMERLINGO	CAMPHORATING
CALFDOZERS	CALLISTEMONS	CALUMNIATORS	CAMERLINGOS	CAMPIMETRIES
CALIATOURS	CALLISTHENIC	CALUMNIATORY	CAMIKNICKERS	CAMPIMETRY
CALIBRATED	CALLISTHENICS	CALUMNIOUS	CAMIKNICKS	CAMPINESSES
CALIBRATER	CALLITHUMP	CALUMNIOUSLY	CAMISADOES	CAMPNESSES
CALIBRATERS	CALLITHUMPIAN	CALUMNYING	CAMORRISTA	CAMPODEIDS
CALIBRATES	CALLITHUMPS	CALVADOSES	CAMORRISTI	CAMPODEIFORM

CAMPSHIRTS	CANCEROPHOBIAS	CANDLEWICK	CANNIBALISM	CANOPHILIST
CAMPSTOOLS	CANCEROUSLY	CANDLEWICKS	CANNIBALISMS	CANOPHILISTS
CAMPYLOBACTER	CANCERPHOBIA	CANDLEWOOD	CANNIBALISTIC	CANOPHOBIA
CAMPYLOBACTERS	CANCERPHOBIAS	CANDLEWOODS	CANNIBALIZATION	CANOPHOBIAS
CAMPYLOTROPOUS	CANCIONERO	CANDYFLOSS	CANNIBALIZE	CANOROUSLY
CAMSTEERIE	CANCIONEROS	CANDYFLOSSES	CANNIBALIZED	CANOROUSNESS
CAMWHORING	CANCRIFORM	CANDYGRAMS	CANNIBALIZES	CANOROUSNESSES
CANALBOATS	CANCRIZANS	CANDYTUFTS	CANNIBALIZING	CANTABANKS
CANALICULAR	CANDELABRA	CANEBRAKES	CANNIBALLY	CANTABILES
CANALICULATE	CANDELABRAS	CANEFRUITS	CANNINESSES	CANTALOUPE
CANALICULATED	CANDELABRUM	CANEPHORAS	CANNISTERS	CANTALOUPES
CANALICULI	CANDELABRUMS	CANEPHORES	CANNONADED	CANTALOUPS
CANALICULUS	CANDELILLA	CANEPHORUS	CANNONADES	CANTANKEROUS
CANALISATION	CANDELILLAS	CANEPHORUSES	CANNONADING	CANTANKEROUSLY
CANALISATIONS	CANDESCENCE	CANESCENCE	CANNONBALL	CANTATRICE
CANALISING	CANDESCENCES	CANESCENCES	CANNONBALLED	CANTATRICES
CANALIZATION	CANDESCENT	CANINITIES	CANNONBALLING	CANTATRICI
CANALIZATIONS	CANDESCENTLY	CANISTERED	CANNONBALLS	CANTERBURIES
CANALIZING	CANDIDACIES	CANISTERING	CANNONEERS	CANTERBURY
CANCELABLE	CANDIDATES	CANISTERISATION	CANNONIERS	CANTERBURYS
CANCELATION	CANDIDATESHIP	CANISTERISE	CANNONRIES	CANTHARIDAL
CANCELATIONS	CANDIDATESHIPS	CANISTERISED	CANNULATED	CANTHARIDES
CANCELBOTS	CANDIDATURE	CANISTERISES	CANNULATES	CANTHARIDIAN
CANCELEERED	CANDIDATURES	CANISTERISING	CANNULATING	CANTHARIDIC
CANCELEERING	CANDIDIASES	CANISTERIZATION	CANNULATION	CANTHARIDIN
CANCELEERS	CANDIDIASIS	CANISTERIZE	CANNULATIONS	CANTHARIDINS
CANCELIERED	CANDIDNESS	CANISTERIZED	CANOEWOODS	CANTHARIDS
CANCELIERING	CANDIDNESSES	CANISTERIZES	CANONESSES	CANTHAXANTHIN
CANCELIERS	CANDLEBERRIES	CANISTERIZING	CANONICALLY	CANTHAXANTHINE
CANCELLABLE	CANDLEBERRY	CANKEREDLY	CANONICALS	CANTHAXANTHINES
CANCELLARIAL	CANDLEFISH	CANKEREDNESS	CANONICATE	CANTHAXANTHINS
CANCELLARIAN	CANDLEFISHES	CANKEREDNESSES	CANONICATES	CANTHITISES
CANCELLARIATE	CANDLEHOLDER	CANKERWORM	CANONICITIES	CANTICOING
CANCELLARIATES	CANDLEHOLDERS	CANKERWORMS	CANONICITY	CANTICOYED
CANCELLATE	CANDLELIGHT	CANNABINOID	CANONISATION	CANTICOYING
CANCELLATED	CANDLELIGHTED	CANNABINOIDS	CANONISATIONS	CANTILENAS
CANCELLATION	CANDLELIGHTER	CANNABINOL	CANONISERS	CANTILEVER
CANCELLATIONS	CANDLELIGHTERS	CANNABINOLS	CANONISING	CANTILEVERED
CANCELLERS	CANDLELIGHTS	CANNABISES	CANONISTIC	CANTILEVERING
CANCELLING	CANDLENUTS	CANNELLINI	CANONIZATION	CANTILEVERS
CANCELLOUS	CANDLEPINS	CANNELLONI	CANONIZATIONS	CANTILLATE
CANCERATED	CANDLEPOWER	CANNELURES	CANONIZERS	CANTILLATED
CANCERATES	CANDLEPOWERS	CANNIBALISATION	CANONIZING	CANTILLATES
CANCERATING	CANDLESNUFFER	CANNIBALISE	CANOODLERS	CANTILLATING
CANCERATION	CANDLESNUFFERS	CANNIBALISED	CANOODLING	CANTILLATION
CANCERATIONS	CANDLESTICK	CANNIBALISES	CANOPHILIA	CANTILLATIONS
CANCEROPHOBIA	CANDLESTICKS	CANNIBALISING	CANOPHILIAS	CANTILLATORY

CANTINESSES	CAPACITORS	CAPITOLINE	CAPRYLATES	CARACOLING
CANTONISATION	CAPARISONED	CAPITULANT	CAPSAICINS	CARACOLLED
CANTONISATIONS	CAPARISONING	CAPITULANTS	CAPSIZABLE	CARACOLLING
CANTONISED	CAPARISONS	CAPITULARIES	CAPSOMERES	CARAGEENAN
CANTONISES	CAPELLINES	CAPITULARLY	CAPSULATED	CARAGEENANS
CANTONISING	CAPELLMEISTER	CAPITULARS	CAPSULATION	CARAMBOLAS
CANTONIZATION	CAPELLMEISTERS	CAPITULARY	CAPSULATIONS	CARAMBOLED
CANTONIZATIONS	CAPERCAILLIE	CAPITULATE	CAPSULISED	CARAMBOLES
CANTONIZED	CAPERCAILLIES	CAPITULATED	CAPSULISES	CARAMBOLING
CANTONIZES	CAPERCAILZIE	CAPITULATES	CAPSULISING	CARAMELISATION
CANTONIZING	CAPERCAILZIES	CAPITULATING	CAPSULIZED	CARAMELISATIONS
CANTONMENT	CAPERINGLY	CAPITULATION	CAPSULIZES	CARAMELISE
CANTONMENTS	CAPERNOITED	CAPITULATIONS	CAPSULIZING	CARAMELISED
CANULATING	CAPERNOITIE	CAPITULATOR	CAPTAINCIES	CARAMELISES
CANULATION	CAPERNOITIES	CAPITULATORS	CAPTAINING	CARAMELISING
CANULATIONS	CAPERNOITY	CAPITULATORY	CAPTAINRIES	CARAMELIZATION
CANVASBACK	CAPILLACEOUS	CAPNOMANCIES	CAPTAINSHIP	CARAMELIZATIONS
CANVASBACKS	CAPILLAIRE	CAPNOMANCY	CAPTAINSHIPS	CARAMELIZE
CANVASLIKE	CAPILLAIRES	CAPOCCHIAS	CAPTIONING	CARAMELIZED
CANVASSERS	CAPILLARIES	CAPODASTRO	CAPTIONLESS	CARAMELIZES
CANVASSINGS	CAPILLARITIES	CAPODASTROS	CAPTIOUSLY	CARAMELIZING
CANYONEERS	CAPILLARITY	CAPONIERES	CAPTIOUSNESS	CARAMELLED
CANYONINGS	CAPILLITIA	CAPONISING	CAPTIOUSNESSES	CARAMELLING
CANZONETTA	CAPILLITIUM	CAPONIZING	CAPTIVANCE	CARANGOIDS
CANZONETTAS	CAPILLITIUMS	CAPOTASTOS	CAPTIVANCES	CARAPACIAL
CANZONETTE	CAPITALISATION	CAPPARIDACEOUS	CAPTIVATED	CARAVANCES
CAOUTCHOUC	CAPITALISATIONS	CAPPELLETTI	CAPTIVATES	CARAVANEER
CAOUTCHOUCS	CAPITALISE	CAPPERNOITIES	CAPTIVATING	CARAVANEERS
CAPABILITIES	CAPITALISED	CAPPERNOITY	CAPTIVATINGLY	CARAVANERS
CAPABILITY	CAPITALISES	CAPPUCCINI	CAPTIVATION	CARAVANETTE
CAPABLENESS	CAPITALISING	CAPPUCCINO	CAPTIVATIONS	CARAVANETTES
CAPABLENESSES	CAPITALISM	CAPPUCCINOS	CAPTIVATOR	CARAVANING
CAPACIOUSLY	CAPITALISMS	CAPREOLATE	CAPTIVATORS	CARAVANINGS
CAPACIOUSNESS	CAPITALIST	CAPRICCIOS	CAPTIVAUNCE	CARAVANNED
CAPACIOUSNESSES	CAPITALISTIC	CAPRICCIOSO	CAPTIVAUNCES	CARAVANNER
CAPACITANCE	CAPITALISTS	CAPRICIOUS	CAPTIVITIES	CARAVANNERS
CAPACITANCES	CAPITALIZATION	CAPRICIOUSLY	CAPTOPRILS	CARAVANNING
CAPACITATE	CAPITALIZATIONS	CAPRICIOUSNESS	CARABINEER	CARAVANNINGS
CAPACITATED	CAPITALIZE	CAPRIFICATION	CARABINEERS	CARAVANSARAI
CAPACITATES	CAPITALIZED	CAPRIFICATIONS	CARABINERO	CARAVANSARAIS
CAPACITATING	CAPITALIZES	CAPRIFOILS	CARABINEROS	CARAVANSARIES
CAPACITATION	CAPITALIZING	CAPRIFOLES	CARABINERS	CARAVANSARY
CAPACITATIONS	CAPITATION	CAPRIFOLIACEOUS	CARABINIER	CARAVANSERAI
CAPACITIES	CAPITATIONS	CAPRIFYING	CARABINIERE	CARAVANSERAIS
CAPACITIVE	CAPITATIVE	CAPRIOLING	CARABINIERI	CARAVELLES
CAPACITIVELY	CAPITELLUM	CAPROLACTAM	CARABINIERS	CARBACHOLS
	CAPITOLIAN	CAPROLACTAMS	CARACOLERS	CARBAMATES

CARBAMAZEPINE	CARBONISING	CARBURETTER	CARDIALGIA	CARDOPHAGUS
CARBAMAZEPINES	CARBONIUMS	CARBURETTERS	CARDIALGIAS	CARDPHONES
CARBAMIDES	CARBONIZATION	CARBURETTING	CARDIALGIC	CARDPLAYER
CARBAMIDINE	CARBONIZATIONS	CARBURETTOR	CARDIALGIES	CARDPLAYERS
CARBAMIDINES	CARBONIZED	CARBURETTORS	CARDIGANED	CARDPUNCHES
CARBAMOYLS	CARBONIZER	CARBURISATION	CARDINALATE	CARDSHARPER
CARBANIONS	CARBONIZERS	CARBURISATIONS	CARDINALATES	CARDSHARPERS
CARBAZOLES	CARBONIZES	CARBURISED	CARDINALATIAL	CARDSHARPING
CARBIMAZOLE	CARBONIZING	CARBURISES	CARDINALITIAL	CARDSHARPINGS
CARBIMAZOLES	CARBONLESS	CARBURISING	CARDINALITIES	CARDSHARPS
CARBINEERS	CARBONNADE	CARBURIZATION	CARDINALITY	CARDUACEOUS
CARBINIERS	CARBONNADES	CARBURIZATIONS	CARDINALLY	CAREENAGES
CARBOCYCLIC	CARBONYLATE	CARBURIZED	CARDINALSHIP	CAREERISMS
CARBOHYDRASE	CARBONYLATED	CARBURIZES	CARDINALSHIPS	CAREERISTS
CARBOHYDRASES	CARBONYLATES	CARBURIZING	CARDIOCENTESES	CAREFREENESS
CARBOHYDRATE	CARBONYLATING	CARBYLAMINE	CARDIOCENTESIS	CAREFREENESSES
CARBOHYDRATES	CARBONYLATION	CARBYLAMINES	CARDIOGENIC	CAREFULLER
CARBOLATED	CARBONYLATIONS	CARCASSING	CARDIOGRAM	CAREFULLEST
CARBOLISED	CARBONYLIC	CARCINOGEN	CARDIOGRAMS	CAREFULNESS
CARBOLISES	CARBOREXIC	CARCINOGENESES	CARDIOGRAPH	CAREFULNESSES
CARBOLISING	CARBOREXICS	CARCINOGENESIS	CARDIOGRAPHER	CAREGIVERS
CARBOLIZED	CARBOXYLASE	CARCINOGENIC	CARDIOGRAPHERS	CAREGIVING
CARBOLIZES	CARBOXYLASES	CARCINOGENICITY	CARDIOGRAPHIC	CAREGIVINGS
CARBOLIZING	CARBOXYLATE	CARCINOGENS	CARDIOGRAPHICAL	CARELESSLY
CARBONACEOUS	CARBOXYLATED	CARCINOIDS	CARDIOGRAPHIES	CARELESSNESS
CARBONADES	CARBOXYLATES	CARCINOLOGICAL	CARDIOGRAPHS	CARELESSNESSES
CARBONADOED	CARBOXYLATING	CARCINOLOGIES	CARDIOGRAPHY	CARESSINGLY
CARBONADOES	CARBOXYLATION	CARCINOLOGIST	CARDIOLOGICAL	CARESSINGS
CARBONADOING	CARBOXYLATIONS	CARCINOLOGISTS	CARDIOLOGIES	CARESSIVELY
CARBONADOS	CARBOXYLIC	CARCINOLOGY	CARDIOLOGIST	CARETAKERS
CARBONARAS	CARBUNCLED	CARCINOMAS	CARDIOLOGISTS	CARETAKING
CARBONATED	CARBUNCLES	CARCINOMATA	CARDIOLOGY	CARETAKINGS
CARBONATES	CARBUNCULAR	CARCINOMATOID	CARDIOMEGALIES	CAREWORKER
CARBONATING	CARBURATED	CARCINOMATOSES	CARDIOMEGALY	CAREWORKERS
CARBONATION	CARBURATES	CARCINOMATOSIS	CARDIOMOTOR	CARFUFFLED
CARBONATIONS	CARBURATING	CARCINOMATOUS	CARDIOMYOPATHY	CARFUFFLES
CARBONATITE	CARBURATION	CARCINOSARCOMA	CARDIOPATHIES	CARFUFFLING
CARBONATITES	CARBURATIONS	CARCINOSARCOMAS	CARDIOPATHY	CARHOPPING
CARBONETTE	CARBURETED	CARCINOSES	CARDIOPLEGIA	CARHOPPINGS
CARBONETTES	CARBURETER	CARCINOSIS	CARDIOPLEGIAS	CARICATURA
CARBONIFEROUS	CARBURETERS	CARDAMINES	CARDIOPLEGIA	CARICATURAL
CARBONISATION	CARBURETING	CARDBOARDS	CARDIOPULMONARY	CARICATURAS
CARBONISATIONS	CARBURETION	CARDBOARDY	CARDIOTHORACIC	CARICATURE
CARBONISED	CARBURETIONS	CARDCASTLE	CARDIOTONIC	CARICATURED
CARBONISER	CARBURETOR	CARDCASTLES	CARDIOTONICS	CARICATURES
CARBONISERS	CARBURETORS	CARDHOLDER	CARDIOVASCULAR	CARICATURING
CARBONISES	CARBURETTED	CARDHOLDERS	CARDITISES	CARICATURIST

CARICATURISTS

CARICATURISTS
CARILLONED
CARILLONING
CARILLONIST
CARILLONISTS
CARILLONNED
CARILLONNEUR
CARILLONNEURS
CARILLONNING
CARIOGENIC
CARIOSITIES
CARIOUSNESS
CARIOUSNESSES
CARJACKERS
CARJACKING
CARJACKINGS
CARMAGNOLE
CARMAGNOLES
CARMELITES
CARMINATIVE
CARMINATIVES
CARNAHUBAS
CARNALISED
CARNALISES
CARNALISING
CARNALISMS
CARNALISTS
CARNALITIES
CARNALIZED
CARNALIZES
CARNALIZING
CARNALLING
CARNALLITE
CARNALLITES
CARNAPTIOUS
CARNAROLIS
CARNASSIAL
CARNASSIALS
CARNATIONED
CARNATIONS
CARNELIANS
CARNIFEXES
CARNIFICATION
CARNIFICATIONS
CARNIFICIAL
CARNIFYING
CARNITINES

CARNIVALESQUE
CARNIVORES
CARNIVORIES
CARNIVOROUS
CARNIVOROUSLY
CARNIVOROUSNESS
CARNOSAURS
CARNOSITIES
CARNOTITES
CAROLLINGS
CAROMELLED
CAROMELLING
CAROTENOID
CAROTENOIDS
CAROTINOID
CAROTINOIDS
CAROUSINGLY
CAROUSINGS
CARPACCIOS
CARPELLARY
CARPELLATE
CARPELLATES
CARPENTARIA
CARPENTARIAS
CARPENTERED
CARPENTERING
CARPENTERS
CARPENTRIES
CARPETBAGGED
CARPETBAGGER
CARPETBAGGERIES
CARPETBAGGERS
CARPETBAGGERY
CARPETBAGGING
CARPETBAGGINGS
CARPETBAGS
CARPETINGS
CARPETMONGER
CARPETMONGERS
CARPETWEED
CARPETWEEDS
CARPHOLOGIES
CARPHOLOGY
CARPOGONIA
CARPOGONIAL
CARPOGONIUM
CARPOLOGICAL

CARPOLOGIES
CARPOLOGIST
CARPOLOGISTS
CARPOMETACARPI
CARPOMETACARPUS
CARPOOLERS
CARPOOLING
CARPOOLINGS
CARPOPHAGOUS
CARPOPHORE
CARPOPHORES
CARPOSPORE
CARPOSPORES
CARRAGEENAN
CARRAGEENANS
CARRAGEENIN
CARRAGEENINS
CARRAGEENS
CARRAGHEEN
CARRAGHEENAN
CARRAGHEENANS
CARRAGHEENIN
CARRAGHEENINS
CARRAGHEENS
CARREFOURS
CARRIAGEABLE
CARRIAGEWAY
CARRIAGEWAYS
CARRITCHES
CARRIWITCHET
CARRIWITCHETS
CARRONADES
CARROTIEST
CARROTTOPPED
CARROTTOPS
CARROUSELS
CARRYBACKS
CARRYFORWARD
CARRYFORWARDS
CARRYOVERS
CARRYTALES
CARSHARING
CARSHARINGS
CARSICKNESS
CARSICKNESSES
CARTELISATION
CARTELISATIONS

CARTELISED
CARTELISES
CARTELISING
CARTELISMS
CARTELISTS
CARTELIZATION
CARTELIZATIONS
CARTELIZED
CARTELIZES
CARTELIZING
CARTHAMINE
CARTHAMINES
CARTHORSES
CARTILAGES
CARTILAGINOUS
CARTOGRAMS
CARTOGRAPHER
CARTOGRAPHERS
CARTOGRAPHIC
CARTOGRAPHICAL
CARTOGRAPHIES
CARTOGRAPHY
CARTOLOGICAL
CARTOLOGIES
CARTOMANCIES
CARTOMANCY
CARTONAGES
CARTONNAGE
CARTONNAGES
CARTOONIER
CARTOONIEST
CARTOONING
CARTOONINGS
CARTOONISH
CARTOONISHLY
CARTOONIST
CARTOONISTS
CARTOONLIKE
CARTOPHILE
CARTOPHILES
CARTOPHILIC
CARTOPHILIES
CARTOPHILIST
CARTOPHILISTS
CARTOPHILY
CARTOPPERS
CARTOUCHES

CARTRIDGES
CARTULARIES
CARTWHEELED
CARTWHEELER
CARTWHEELERS
CARTWHEELING
CARTWHEELS
CARTWRIGHT
CARTWRIGHTS
CARUNCULAR
CARUNCULATE
CARUNCULATED
CARUNCULOUS
CARVACROLS
CARYATIDAL
CARYATIDEAN
CARYATIDES
CARYATIDIC
CARYOPSIDES
CARYOPTERIS
CARYOPTERISES
CASCADURAS
CASCARILLA
CASCARILLAS
CASEATIONS
CASEBEARER
CASEBEARERS
CASEINATES
CASEINOGEN
CASEINOGENS
CASEMAKERS
CASEMENTED
CASEVACING
CASEWORKER
CASEWORKERS
CASHIERERS
CASHIERING
CASHIERINGS
CASHIERMENT
CASHIERMENTS
CASHMOBBING
CASHMOBBINGS
CASHPOINTS
CASINGHEAD
CASINGHEADS
CASKSTANDS
CASSAREEPS

CASSATIONS	CASUALISMS	CATAFALCOES	CATAMOUNTS	CATCALLERS
CASSEROLED	CASUALIZATION	CATAFALQUE	CATANANCHE	CATCALLING
CASSEROLES	CASUALIZATIONS	CATAFALQUES	CATANANCHES	CATCHCRIES
CASSEROLING	CASUALIZED	CATALECTIC	CATAPHONIC	CATCHFLIES
CASSIMERES	CASUALIZES	CATALECTICS	CATAPHONICS	CATCHINESS
CASSINGLES	CASUALIZING	CATALEPSIES	CATAPHORAS	CATCHINESSES
CASSIOPEIUM	CASUALNESS	CATALEPTIC	CATAPHORESES	CATCHLINES
CASSIOPEIUMS	CASUALNESSES	CATALEPTICALLY	CATAPHORESIS	CATCHMENTS
CASSITERITE	CASUALTIES	CATALEPTICS	CATAPHORETIC	CATCHPENNIES
CASSITERITES	CASUARINAS	CATALLACTIC	CATAPHORIC	CATCHPENNY
CASSOLETTE	CASUISTICAL	CATALLACTICALLY	CATAPHORICALLY	CATCHPHRASE
CASSOLETTES	CASUISTICALLY	CATALLACTICS	CATAPHRACT	CATCHPHRASES
CASSONADES	CASUISTRIES	CATALOGERS	CATAPHRACTIC	CATCHPOLES
CASSOULETS	CATABOLICALLY	CATALOGING	CATAPHRACTS	CATCHPOLLS
CASSOWARIES	CATABOLISE	CATALOGISE	CATAPHYLLARY	CATCHWATER
CASSUMUNAR	CATABOLISED	CATALOGISED	CATAPHYLLS	CATCHWATERS
CASSUMUNARS	CATABOLISES	CATALOGISES	CATAPHYSICAL	CATCHWEEDS
CASTABILITIES	CATABOLISING	CATALOGISING	CATAPLASIA	CATCHWEIGHT
CASTABILITY	CATABOLISM	CATALOGIZE	CATAPLASIAS	CATCHWORDS
CASTANOSPERMINE	CATABOLISMS	CATALOGIZED	CATAPLASMS	CATECHESES
CASTELLANS	CATABOLITE	CATALOGIZES	CATAPLASTIC	CATECHESIS
CASTELLATED	CATABOLITES	CATALOGIZING	CATAPLECTIC	CATECHETIC
CASTELLATION	CATABOLIZE	CATALOGUED	CATAPLEXIES	CATECHETICAL
CASTELLATIONS	CATABOLIZED	CATALOGUER	CATAPULTED	CATECHETICALLY
CASTELLUMS	CATABOLIZES	CATALOGUERS	CATAPULTIC	CATECHETICS
CASTIGATED	CATABOLIZING	CATALOGUES	CATAPULTIER	CATECHISATION
CASTIGATES	CATACAUSTIC	CATALOGUING	CATAPULTIERS	CATECHISATIONS
CASTIGATING	CATACAUSTICS	CATALOGUISE	CATAPULTING	CATECHISED
CASTIGATION	CATACHRESES	CATALOGUISED	CATARACTOUS	CATECHISER
CASTIGATIONS	CATACHRESIS	CATALOGUISES	CATARHINES	CATECHISERS
CASTIGATOR	CATACHRESTIC	CATALOGUISING	CATARRHALLY	CATECHISES
CASTIGATORS	CATACHRESTICAL	CATALOGUIST	CATARRHINE	CATECHISING
CASTIGATORY	CATACLASES	CATALOGUISTS	CATARRHINES	CATECHISINGS
CASTOREUMS	CATACLASIS	CATALOGUIZE	CATARRHOUS	CATECHISMAL
CASTRAMETATION	CATACLASMIC	CATALOGUIZED	CATASTASES	CATECHISMS
CASTRAMETATIONS	CATACLASMS	CATALOGUIZES	CATASTASIS	CATECHISTIC
CASTRATERS	CATACLASTIC	CATALOGUIZING	CATASTROPHE	CATECHISTICAL
CASTRATING	CATACLINAL	CATALYSERS	CATASTROPHES	CATECHISTICALLY
CASTRATION	CATACLYSMAL	CATALYSING	CATASTROPHIC	CATECHISTS
CASTRATIONS	CATACLYSMIC	CATALYTICAL	CATASTROPHISM	CATECHIZATION
CASTRATORS	CATACLYSMICALLY	CATALYTICALLY	CATASTROPHISMS	CATECHIZATIONS
CASTRATORY	CATACLYSMS	CATALYZERS	CATASTROPHIST	CATECHIZED
CASUALISATION	CATACOUSTICS	CATALYZING	CATASTROPHISTS	CATECHIZER
CASUALISATIONS	CATACUMBAL	CATAMARANS	CATATONIAS	CATECHIZERS
CASUALISED	CATADIOPTRIC	CATAMENIAL	CATATONICALLY	CATECHIZES
CASUALISES	CATADIOPTRICAL	CATAMOUNTAIN	CATATONICS	CATECHIZING
CASUALISING	CATADROMOUS	CATAMOUNTAINS	CATATONIES	CATECHIZINGS

CATECHOLAMINE
CATECHOLAMINES
CATECHUMEN
CATECHUMENAL
CATECHUMENATE
CATECHUMENATES
CATECHUMENICAL
CATECHUMENISM
CATECHUMENISMS
CATECHUMENS
CATECHUMENSHIP
CATECHUMENSHIPS
CATEGOREMATIC
CATEGORIAL
CATEGORIALLY
CATEGORICAL
CATEGORICALLY
CATEGORICALNESS
CATEGORIES
CATEGORISATION
CATEGORISATIONS
CATEGORISE
CATEGORISED
CATEGORISES
CATEGORISING
CATEGORIST
CATEGORISTS
CATEGORIZATION
CATEGORIZATIONS
CATEGORIZE
CATEGORIZED
CATEGORIZES
CATEGORIZING
CATENACCIO
CATENACCIOS
CATENARIAN
CATENARIES
CATENATING
CATENATION
CATENATIONS
CATENULATE
CATERCORNER
CATERCORNERED
CATERESSES
CATERPILLAR
CATERPILLARS
CATERWAULED

CATERWAULER
CATERWAULERS
CATERWAULING
CATERWAULINGS
CATERWAULS
CATFACINGS
CATHARISED
CATHARISES
CATHARISING
CATHARIZED
CATHARIZES
CATHARIZING
CATHARTICAL
CATHARTICALLY
CATHARTICS
CATHECTING
CATHEDRALS
CATHEDRATIC
CATHEPSINS
CATHETERISATION
CATHETERISE
CATHETERISED
CATHETERISES
CATHETERISING
CATHETERISM
CATHETERISMS
CATHETERIZATION
CATHETERIZE
CATHETERIZED
CATHETERIZES
CATHETERIZING
CATHETOMETER
CATHETOMETERS
CATHETUSES
CATHINONES
CATHIODERMIE
CATHIODERMIES
CATHODALLY
CATHODICAL
CATHODICALLY
CATHODOGRAPH
CATHODOGRAPHER
CATHODOGRAPHERS
CATHODOGRAPHIES
CATHODOGRAPHS
CATHODOGRAPHY
CATHOLICALLY

CATHOLICATE
CATHOLICATES
CATHOLICISATION
CATHOLICISE
CATHOLICISED
CATHOLICISES
CATHOLICISING
CATHOLICISM
CATHOLICISMS
CATHOLICITIES
CATHOLICITY
CATHOLICIZATION
CATHOLICIZE
CATHOLICIZED
CATHOLICIZES
CATHOLICIZING
CATHOLICLY
CATHOLICOI
CATHOLICON
CATHOLICONS
CATHOLICOS
CATHOLICOSES
CATHOLYTES
CATIONICALLY
CATNAPPERS
CATNAPPING
CATOPTRICAL
CATOPTRICS
CATTINESSES
CATTISHNESS
CATTISHNESSES
CAUCHEMARS
CAUCUSSING
CAUCUSSINGS
CAUDATIONS
CAUDILLISMO
CAUDILLISMOS
CAULESCENT
CAULICOLOUS
CAULICULATE
CAULICULUS
CAULICULUSES
CAULIFLORIES
CAULIFLOROUS
CAULIFLORY
CAULIFLOWER
CAULIFLOWERET

CAULIFLOWERETS
CAULIFLOWERS
CAULIGENOUS
CAUMSTANES
CAUMSTONES
CAUSABILITIES
CAUSABILITY
CAUSALGIAS
CAUSALITIES
CAUSATIONAL
CAUSATIONISM
CAUSATIONISMS
CAUSATIONIST
CAUSATIONISTS
CAUSATIONS
CAUSATIVELY
CAUSATIVENESS
CAUSATIVENESSES
CAUSATIVES
CAUSELESSLY
CAUSELESSNESS
CAUSELESSNESSES
CAUSEWAYED
CAUSEWAYING
CAUSTICALLY
CAUSTICITIES
CAUSTICITY
CAUSTICNESS
CAUSTICNESSES
CAUTERANTS
CAUTERISATION
CAUTERISATIONS
CAUTERISED
CAUTERISES
CAUTERISING
CAUTERISMS
CAUTERIZATION
CAUTERIZATIONS
CAUTERIZED
CAUTERIZES
CAUTERIZING
CAUTIONARY
CAUTIONERS
CAUTIONING
CAUTIONRIES
CAUTIOUSLY
CAUTIOUSNESS

CAUTIOUSNESSES
CAVALCADED
CAVALCADES
CAVALCADING
CAVALIERED
CAVALIERING
CAVALIERISH
CAVALIERISM
CAVALIERISMS
CAVALIERLY
CAVALLETTI
CAVALRYMAN
CAVALRYMEN
CAVEFISHES
CAVENDISHES
CAVERNICOLOUS
CAVERNOUSLY
CAVERNULOUS
CAVILLATION
CAVILLATIONS
CAVILLINGS
CAVITATING
CAVITATION
CAVITATIONS
CAVORTINGS
CEANOTHUSES
CEASEFIRES
CEASELESSLY
CEASELESSNESS
CEASELESSNESSES
CEBADILLAS
CECUTIENCIES
CECUTIENCY
CEDARBIRDS
CEDARWOODS
CEDRELACEOUS
CEILOMETER
CEILOMETERS
CELANDINES
CELEBRANTS
CELEBRATED
CELEBRATEDNESS
CELEBRATES
CELEBRATING
CELEBRATION
CELEBRATIONS
CELEBRATIVE

CELEBRATOR	CEMENTATION	CENTERINGS	CENTRALISMS	CENTRIFUGING
CELEBRATORS	CEMENTATIONS	CENTERLESS	CENTRALIST	CENTRIOLES
CELEBRATORY	CEMENTATORY	CENTERLINE	CENTRALISTIC	CENTRIPETAL
CELEBREALITIES	CEMENTITES	CENTERLINES	CENTRALISTS	CENTRIPETALISM
CELEBREALITY	CEMENTITIOUS	CENTERPIECE	CENTRALITIES	CENTRIPETALISMS
CELEBRITIES	CEMETERIES	CENTERPIECES	CENTRALITY	CENTRIPETALLY
CELEBUTANTE	CENESTHESES	CENTESIMAL	CENTRALIZATION	CENTROBARIC
CELEBUTANTES	CENESTHESIA	CENTESIMALLY	CENTRALIZATIONS	CENTROCLINAL
CELECOXIBS	CENESTHESIAS	CENTESIMALS	CENTRALIZE	CENTROIDAL
CELERITIES	CENESTHESIS	CENTESIMOS	CENTRALIZED	CENTROLECITHAL
CELESTIALLY	CENESTHETIC	CENTIGRADE	CENTRALIZER	CENTROMERE
CELESTIALS	CENOBITICAL	CENTIGRADES	CENTRALIZERS	CENTROMERES
CELESTINES	CENOGENESES	CENTIGRAMME	CENTRALIZES	CENTROMERIC
CELESTITES	CENOGENESIS	CENTIGRAMMES	CENTRALIZING	CENTROSOME
CELIBACIES	CENOGENETIC	CENTIGRAMS	CENTREBOARD	CENTROSOMES
CELIBATARIAN	CENOGENETICALLY	CENTILITER	CENTREBOARDS	CENTROSOMIC
CELIBATARIANS	CENOSPECIES	CENTILITERS	CENTREDNESS	CENTROSPHERE
CELLARAGES	CENOTAPHIC	CENTILITRE	CENTREDNESSES	CENTROSPHERES
CELLARETTE	CENSORABLE	CENTILITRES	CENTREFOLD	CENTROSYMMETRIC
CELLARETTES	CENSORIOUS	CENTILLION	CENTREFOLDS	CENTUMVIRATE
CELLARISTS	CENSORIOUSLY	CENTILLIONS	CENTREINGS	CENTUMVIRATES
CELLARWAYS	CENSORIOUSNESS	CENTILLIONTH	CENTRELESS	CENTUMVIRI
CELLBLOCKS	CENSORSHIP	CENTILLIONTHS	CENTRELINE	CENTUMVIRS
CELLENTANI	CENSORSHIPS	CENTIMETER	CENTRELINES	CENTUPLICATE
CELLENTANIS	CENSURABILITIES	CENTIMETERS	CENTREPIECE	CENTUPLICATED
CELLIFEROUS	CENSURABILITY	CENTIMETRE	CENTREPIECES	CENTUPLICATES
CELLOBIOSE	CENSURABLE	CENTIMETRES	CENTRICALLY	CENTUPLICATING
CELLOBIOSES	CENSURABLENESS	CENTIMETRIC	CENTRICALNESS	CENTUPLICATION
CELLOIDINS	CENSURABLY	CENTIMORGAN	CENTRICALNESSES	CENTUPLICATIONS
CELLOPHANE	CENTAUREAS	CENTIMORGANS	CENTRICITIES	CENTUPLING
CELLOPHANES	CENTAURIAN	CENTINELLS	CENTRICITY	CENTURIATION
CELLPHONES	CENTAURIES	CENTIPEDES	CENTRIFUGAL	CENTURIATIONS
CELLULARITIES	CENTENARIAN	CENTIPOISE	CENTRIFUGALISE	CENTURIATOR
CELLULARITY	CENTENARIANISM	CENTIPOISES	CENTRIFUGALISED	CENTURIATORS
CELLULASES	CENTENARIANISMS	CENTONATES	CENTRIFUGALISES	CENTURIONS
CELLULATED	CENTENARIANS	CENTONELLS	CENTRIFUGALIZE	CEPHALAGRA
CELLULIFEROUS	CENTENARIES	CENTONISTS	CENTRIFUGALIZED	CEPHALAGRAS
CELLULITES	CENTENIERS	CENTRALEST	CENTRIFUGALIZES	CEPHALALGIA
CELLULITIS	CENTENNIAL	CENTRALISATION	CENTRIFUGALLY	CEPHALALGIAS
CELLULITISES	CENTENNIALLY	CENTRALISATIONS	CENTRIFUGALS	CEPHALALGIC
CELLULOIDS	CENTENNIALS	CENTRALISE	CENTRIFUGATION	CEPHALALGICS
CELLULOLYTIC	CENTERBOARD	CENTRALISED	CENTRIFUGATIONS	CEPHALEXIN
CELLULOSES	CENTERBOARDS	CENTRALISER	CENTRIFUGE	CEPHALEXINS
CELLULOSIC	CENTEREDNESS	CENTRALISERS	CENTRIFUGED	CEPHALICALLY
CELLULOSICS	CENTEREDNESSES	CENTRALISES	CENTRIFUGENCE	CEPHALISATION
CELSITUDES	CENTERFOLD	CENTRALISING	CENTRIFUGENCES	CEPHALISATIONS
CEMBALISTS	CENTERFOLDS	CENTRALISM	CENTRIFUGES	CEPHALITIS

CEPHALITISES	CERCOPITHECOID	CEROGRAPHS	CETEOSAURUSES	CHAIRMANNING
CEPHALIZATION	CERCOPITHECOIDS	CEROGRAPHY	CETOLOGICAL	CHAIRMANSHIP
CEPHALIZATIONS	CEREALISTS	CEROMANCIES	CETOLOGIES	CHAIRMANSHIPS
CEPHALOCELE	CEREBELLAR	CEROPLASTIC	CETOLOGIST	CHAIRPERSON
CEPHALOCELES	CEREBELLIC	CEROPLASTICS	CETOLOGISTS	CHAIRPERSONS
CEPHALOCHORDATE	CEREBELLOUS	CERTAINEST	CETRIMIDES	CHAIRWARMER
CEPHALOMETER	CEREBELLUM	CERTAINTIES	CETUXIMABS	CHAIRWARMERS
CEPHALOMETERS	CEREBELLUMS	CERTIFIABLE	CEVADILLAS	CHAIRWOMAN
CEPHALOMETRIC	CEREBRALISM	CERTIFIABLY	CEYLANITES	CHAIRWOMEN
CEPHALOMETRIES	CEREBRALISMS	CERTIFICATE	CEYLONITES	CHAISELESS
CEPHALOMETRY	CEREBRALIST	CERTIFICATED	CHABAZITES	CHAKALAKAS
CEPHALOPOD	CEREBRALISTS	CERTIFICATES	CHACONINES	CHALANNING
CEPHALOPODAN	CEREBRALLY	CERTIFICATING	CHAENOMELES	CHALAZIONS
CEPHALOPODANS	CEREBRATED	CERTIFICATION	CHAENOMELESES	CHALAZOGAMIC
CEPHALOPODIC	CEREBRATES	CERTIFICATIONS	CHAETIFEROUS	CHALAZOGAMIES
CEPHALOPODOUS	CEREBRATING	CERTIFICATORIES	CHAETODONS	CHALAZOGAMY
CEPHALOPODS	CEREBRATION	CERTIFICATORY	CHAETOGNATH	CHALCANTHITE
CEPHALORIDINE	CEREBRATIONS	CERTIFIERS	CHAETOGNATHS	CHALCANTHITES
CEPHALORIDINES	CEREBRIFORM	CERTIFYING	CHAETOPODS	CHALCEDONIC
CEPHALOSPORIN	CEREBRITIS	CERTIORARI	CHAFFERERS	CHALCEDONIES
CEPHALOSPORINS	CEREBRITISES	CERTIORARIS	CHAFFERIES	CHALCEDONY
CEPHALOTHIN	CEREBROSIDE	CERTITUDES	CHAFFERING	CHALCEDONYX
CEPHALOTHINS	CEREBROSIDES	CERULOPLASMIN	CHAFFINCHES	CHALCEDONYXES
CEPHALOTHORACES	CEREBROSPINAL	CERULOPLASMINS	CHAFFINGLY	CHALCOCITE
CEPHALOTHORACIC	CEREBROTONIA	CERUMINOUS	CHAGRINING	CHALCOCITES
CEPHALOTHORAX	CEREBROTONIAS	CERUSSITES	CHAGRINNED	CHALCOGENIDE
CEPHALOTHORAXES	CEREBROTONIC	CERVELASES	CHAGRINNING	CHALCOGENIDES
CEPHALOTOMIES	CEREBROTONICS	CERVICITIS	CHAINBRAKE	CHALCOGENS
CEPHALOTOMY	CEREBROVASCULAR	CERVICITISES	CHAINBRAKES	CHALCOGRAPHER
CERAMICIST	CERECLOTHS	CERVICOGRAPHIES	CHAINFALLS	CHALCOGRAPHERS
CERAMICISTS	CEREMONIAL	CERVICOGRAPHY	CHAINPLATE	CHALCOGRAPHIC
CERAMOGRAPHIES	CEREMONIALISM	CESAREVICH	CHAINPLATES	CHALCOGRAPHICAL
CERAMOGRAPHY	CEREMONIALISMS	CESAREVICHES	CHAINSAWED	CHALCOGRAPHIES
CERARGYRITE	CEREMONIALIST	CESAREVITCH	CHAINSAWING	CHALCOGRAPHIST
CERARGYRITES	CEREMONIALISTS	CESAREVITCHES	CHAINSHOTS	CHALCOGRAPHISTS
CERASTIUMS	CEREMONIALLY	CESAREVNAS	CHAINSTITCH	CHALCOGRAPHY
CERATITISES	CEREMONIALS	CESAREWICH	CHAINSTITCHES	CHALCOLITHIC
CERATODUSES	CEREMONIES	CESAREWICHES	CHAINWHEEL	CHALCOPYRITE
CERATOPSIAN	CEREMONIOUS	CESAREWITCH	CHAINWHEELS	CHALCOPYRITES
CERATOPSIANS	CEREMONIOUSLY	CESAREWITCHES	CHAINWORKS	CHALICOTHERE
CERATOPSID	CEREMONIOUSNESS	CESPITOSELY	CHAIRBACKS	CHALICOTHERES
CERATOPSIDS	CERIFEROUS	CESSATIONS	CHAIRBORNE	CHALKBOARD
CERAUNOGRAPH	CEROGRAPHIC	CESSIONARIES	CHAIRBOUND	CHALKBOARDS
CERAUNOGRAPHS	CEROGRAPHICAL	CESSIONARY	CHAIRLIFTS	CHALKFACES
CERCARIANS	CEROGRAPHIES	CESTOIDEAN	CHAIRMANED	CHALKINESS
CERCOPITHECID	CEROGRAPHIST	CESTOIDEANS	CHAIRMANING	CHALKINESSES
CERCOPITHECIDS	CEROGRAPHISTS	CETEOSAURUS	CHAIRMANNED	CHALKMARKS

CHALKSTONE	CHAMPIGNONS	CHANGEOVER	CHAPERONAGE	CHARACTERISMS
CHALKSTONES	CHAMPIONED	CHANGEOVERS	CHAPERONAGES	CHARACTERISTIC
CHALKSTRIPE	CHAMPIONESS	CHANGEROUND	CHAPERONED	CHARACTERISTICS
CHALKSTRIPES	CHAMPIONESSES	CHANGEROUNDS	CHAPERONES	CHARACTERIZABLE
CHALLENGEABLE	CHAMPIONING	CHANNELERS	CHAPERONING	CHARACTERIZE
CHALLENGED	CHAMPIONSHIP	CHANNELING	CHAPFALLEN	CHARACTERIZED
CHALLENGER	CHAMPIONSHIPS	CHANNELISATION	CHAPLAINCIES	CHARACTERIZER
CHALLENGERS	CHAMPLEVES	CHANNELISATIONS	CHAPLAINCY	CHARACTERIZERS
CHALLENGES	CHANCELESS	CHANNELISE	CHAPLAINRIES	CHARACTERIZES
CHALLENGING	CHANCELLERIES	CHANNELISED	CHAPLAINRY	CHARACTERIZING
CHALLENGINGLY	CHANCELLERY	CHANNELISES	CHAPLAINSHIP	CHARACTERLESS
CHALUMEAUS	CHANCELLOR	CHANNELISING	CHAPLAINSHIPS	CHARACTEROLOGY
CHALUMEAUX	CHANCELLORIES	CHANNELIZATION	CHAPMANSHIP	CHARACTERS
CHALYBEATE	CHANCELLORS	CHANNELIZATIONS	CHAPMANSHIPS	CHARACTERY
CHALYBEATES	CHANCELLORSHIP	CHANNELIZE	CHAPPESSES	CHARBROILED
CHALYBITES	CHANCELLORSHIPS	CHANNELIZED	CHAPRASSIES	CHARBROILER
CHAMAELEON	CHANCELLORY	CHANNELIZES	CHAPRASSIS	CHARBROILERS
CHAMAELEONS	CHANCERIES	CHANNELIZING	CHAPSTICKS	CHARBROILING
CHAMAEPHYTE	CHANCINESS	CHANNELLED	CHAPTALISATION	CHARBROILS
CHAMAEPHYTES	CHANCINESSES	CHANNELLER	CHAPTALISATIONS	CHARCOALED
CHAMBERERS	CHANCROIDAL	CHANNELLERS	CHAPTALISE	CHARCOALING
CHAMBERHAND	CHANCROIDS	CHANNELLING	CHAPTALISED	CHARCUTERIE
CHAMBERHANDS	CHANDELIER	CHANSONETTE	CHAPTALISES	CHARCUTERIES
CHAMBERING	CHANDELIERED	CHANSONETTES	CHAPTALISING	CHARDONNAY
CHAMBERINGS	CHANDELIERS	CHANSONNIER	CHAPTALIZATION	CHARDONNAYS
CHAMBERLAIN	CHANDELLED	CHANSONNIERS	CHAPTALIZATIONS	CHARGEABILITIES
CHAMBERLAINS	CHANDELLES	CHANTARELLE	CHAPTALIZE	CHARGEABILITY
CHAMBERLAINSHIP	CHANDELLING	CHANTARELLES	CHAPTALIZED	CHARGEABLE
CHAMBERMAID	CHANDLERIES	CHANTECLER	CHAPTALIZES	CHARGEABLENESS
CHAMBERMAIDS	CHANDLERING	CHANTECLERS	CHAPTALIZING	CHARGEABLY
CHAMBERPOT	CHANDLERINGS	CHANTERELLE	CHAPTERHOUSE	CHARGEBACK
CHAMBERPOTS	CHANDLERLY	CHANTERELLES	CHAPTERHOUSES	CHARGEBACKS
CHAMBRANLE	CHANGEABILITIES	CHANTEUSES	CHAPTERING	CHARGEHAND
CHAMBRANLES	CHANGEABILITY	CHANTICLEER	CHARABANCS	CHARGEHANDS
CHAMELEONIC	CHANGEABLE	CHANTICLEERS	CHARACINOID	CHARGELESS
CHAMELEONLIKE	CHANGEABLENESS	CHANTINGLY	CHARACTERED	CHARGESHEET
CHAMELEONS	CHANGEABLY	CHANTRESSES	CHARACTERFUL	CHARGESHEETS
CHAMFERERS	CHANGEAROUND	CHANUKIAHS	CHARACTERIES	CHARGRILLED
CHAMFERING	CHANGEAROUNDS	CHAOLOGIES	CHARACTERING	CHARGRILLING
CHAMFRAINS	CHANGEFULLY	CHAOLOGIST	CHARACTERISABLE	CHARGRILLS
CHAMOISING	CHANGEFULNESS	CHAOLOGISTS	CHARACTERISE	CHARINESSES
CHAMOMILES	CHANGEFULNESSES	CHAOTICALLY	CHARACTERISED	CHARIOTEER
CHAMPAGNES	CHANGELESS	CHAPARAJOS	CHARACTERISER	CHARIOTEERED
CHAMPAIGNS	CHANGELESSLY	CHAPAREJOS	CHARACTERISERS	CHARIOTEERING
CHAMPERTIES	CHANGELESSNESS	CHAPARRALS	CHARACTERISES	CHARIOTEERS
CHAMPERTOUS	CHANGELING	CHAPATTIES	CHARACTERISING	CHARIOTING
CHAMPIGNON	CHANGELINGS	CHAPELRIES	CHARACTERISM	CHARISMATA

CHARISMATIC
CHARISMATICS
CHARITABLE
CHARITABLENESS
CHARITABLY
CHARIVARIED
CHARIVARIING
CHARIVARIS
CHARLADIES
CHARLATANIC
CHARLATANICAL
CHARLATANISM
CHARLATANISMS
CHARLATANISTIC
CHARLATANRIES
CHARLATANRY
CHARLATANS
CHARLESTON
CHARLESTONED
CHARLESTONING
CHARLESTONS
CHARLOTTES
CHARMEUSES
CHARMINGER
CHARMINGEST
CHARMINGLY
CHARMLESSLY
CHARMONIUM
CHAROSETHS
CHARREADAS
CHARTACEOUS
CHARTERERS
CHARTERING
CHARTERPARTIES
CHARTERPARTY
CHARTHOUSE
CHARTHOUSES
CHARTOGRAPHER
CHARTOGRAPHERS
CHARTOGRAPHIC
CHARTOGRAPHICAL
CHARTOGRAPHIES
CHARTOGRAPHY
CHARTREUSE
CHARTREUSES
CHARTULARIES
CHARTULARY

CHASEPORTS
CHASMOGAMIC
CHASMOGAMIES
CHASMOGAMOUS
CHASMOGAMY
CHASSEPOTS
CHASTENERS
CHASTENESS
CHASTENESSES
CHASTENING
CHASTENINGLY
CHASTENMENT
CHASTENMENTS
CHASTISABLE
CHASTISEMENT
CHASTISEMENTS
CHASTISERS
CHASTISING
CHASTITIES
CHATEAUBRIAND
CHATEAUBRIANDS
CHATELAINE
CHATELAINES
CHATELAINS
CHATOYANCE
CHATOYANCES
CHATOYANCIES
CHATOYANCY
CHATOYANTS
CHATTERATI
CHATTERBOX
CHATTERBOXES
CHATTERERS
CHATTERING
CHATTERINGS
CHATTINESS
CHATTINESSES
CHAUDFROID
CHAUDFROIDS
CHAUFFEURED
CHAUFFEURING
CHAUFFEURS
CHAUFFEUSE
CHAUFFEUSED
CHAUFFEUSES
CHAUFFEUSING
CHAULMOOGRA

CHAULMOOGRAS
CHAULMUGRA
CHAULMUGRAS
CHAUNTRESS
CHAUNTRESSES
CHAUNTRIES
CHAUSSURES
CHAUTAUQUA
CHAUTAUQUAS
CHAUVINISM
CHAUVINISMS
CHAUVINIST
CHAUVINISTIC
CHAUVINISTS
CHAVENDERS
CHAVTASTIC
CHAWBACONS
CHEAPENERS
CHEAPENING
CHEAPISHLY
CHEAPJACKS
CHEAPNESSES
CHEAPSHOTS
CHEAPSKATE
CHEAPSKATES
CHEATERIES
CHEATINGLY
CHECHAKOES
CHECHAQUOS
CHECKBOOKS
CHECKBOXES
CHECKCLERK
CHECKCLERKS
CHECKERBERRIES
CHECKERBERRY
CHECKERBLOOM
CHECKERBLOOMS
CHECKERBOARD
CHECKERBOARDS
CHECKERING
CHECKLATON
CHECKLATONS
CHECKLISTED
CHECKLISTING
CHECKLISTS
CHECKMARKED
CHECKMARKING

CHECKMARKS
CHECKMATED
CHECKMATES
CHECKMATING
CHECKPOINT
CHECKPOINTS
CHECKRAILS
CHECKREINS
CHECKROOMS
CHECKROWED
CHECKROWING
CHECKWEIGHER
CHECKWEIGHERS
CHEECHAKOES
CHEECHAKOS
CHEECHALKO
CHEECHALKOES
CHEECHALKOS
CHEEKBONES
CHEEKINESS
CHEEKINESSES
CHEEKPIECE
CHEEKPIECES
CHEEKPOUCH
CHEEKPOUCHES
CHEEKTEETH
CHEEKTOOTH
CHEERFULLER
CHEERFULLEST
CHEERFULLY
CHEERFULNESS
CHEERFULNESSES
CHEERINESS
CHEERINESSES
CHEERINGLY
CHEERISHNESS
CHEERISHNESSES
CHEERLEADER
CHEERLEADERS
CHEERLEADING
CHEERLEADS
CHEERLESSLY
CHEERLESSNESS
CHEERLESSNESSES
CHEESEBOARD
CHEESEBOARDS
CHEESEBURGER

CHEESEBURGERS
CHEESECAKE
CHEESECAKES
CHEESECLOTH
CHEESECLOTHS
CHEESECUTTER
CHEESECUTTERS
CHEESEHOPPER
CHEESEHOPPERS
CHEESEMITE
CHEESEMITES
CHEESEMONGER
CHEESEMONGERS
CHEESEPARER
CHEESEPARERS
CHEESEPARING
CHEESEPARINGS
CHEESEPRESS
CHEESEPRESSES
CHEESESTEAK
CHEESESTEAKS
CHEESETASTER
CHEESETASTERS
CHEESEVATS
CHEESEWIRE
CHEESEWIRES
CHEESEWOOD
CHEESEWOODS
CHEESEWRING
CHEESEWRINGS
CHEESINESS
CHEESINESSES
CHEILITISES
CHEIROMANCER
CHEIROMANCERS
CHEIROMANCIES
CHEIROMANCY
CHELASHIPS
CHELATABLE
CHELATIONS
CHELICERAE
CHELICERAL
CHELICERATE
CHELICERATES
CHELIFEROUS
CHELONIANS
CHELUVIATION

CHELUVIATIONS	CHEMOSORBS	CHERISHING	CHIAROSCURO	CHIHUAHUAS
CHEMAUTOTROPH	CHEMOSPHERE	CHERISHINGLY	CHIAROSCUROS	CHILBLAINED
CHEMAUTOTROPHIC	CHEMOSPHERES	CHERISHMENT	CHIASMATIC	CHILBLAINS
CHEMAUTOTROPHS	CHEMOSPHERIC	CHERISHMENTS	CHIASTOLITE	CHILDBEARING
CHEMIATRIC	CHEMOSTATS	CHERMOULAS	CHIASTOLITES	CHILDBEARINGS
CHEMICALLY	CHEMOSURGERIES	CHERNOZEMIC	CHIBOUQUES	CHILDBIRTH
CHEMICKING	CHEMOSURGERY	CHERNOZEMS	CHICALOTES	CHILDBIRTHS
CHEMICKINGS	CHEMOSURGICAL	CHERRYLIKE	CHICANERIES	CHILDCARES
CHEMIOSMOSES	CHEMOSYNTHESES	CHERRYSTONE	CHICANINGS	CHILDCROWING
CHEMIOSMOSIS	CHEMOSYNTHESIS	CHERRYSTONES	CHICCORIES	CHILDCROWINGS
CHEMIOSMOTIC	CHEMOSYNTHETIC	CHERSONESE	CHICKABIDDIES	CHILDERMAS
CHEMISETTE	CHEMOTACTIC	CHERSONESES	CHICKABIDDY	CHILDERMASES
CHEMISETTES	CHEMOTACTICALLY	CHERUBICAL	CHICKADEES	CHILDHOODS
CHEMISORBED	CHEMOTAXES	CHERUBICALLY	CHICKAREES	CHILDISHLY
CHEMISORBING	CHEMOTAXIS	CHERUBIMIC	CHICKENHEARTED	CHILDISHNESS
CHEMISORBS	CHEMOTAXONOMIC	CHERUBLIKE	CHICKENING	CHILDISHNESSES
CHEMISORPTION	CHEMOTAXONOMIES	CHERVONETS	CHICKENPOX	CHILDLESSNESS
CHEMISORPTIONS	CHEMOTAXONOMIST	CHESSBOARD	CHICKENPOXES	CHILDLESSNESSES
CHEMISTRIES	CHEMOTAXONOMY	CHESSBOARDS	CHICKENSHIT	CHILDLIEST
CHEMITYPES	CHEMOTHERAPIES	CHESSBOXING	CHICKENSHITS	CHILDLIKENESS
CHEMITYPIES	CHEMOTHERAPIST	CHESSBOXINGS	CHICKLINGS	CHILDLIKENESSES
CHEMOATTRACTANT	CHEMOTHERAPISTS	CHESSPIECE	CHICKORIES	CHILDMINDER
CHEMOAUTOTROPH	CHEMOTHERAPY	CHESSPIECES	CHICKWEEDS	CHILDMINDERS
CHEMOAUTOTROPHS	CHEMOTROPIC	CHESSPLAYER	CHICNESSES	CHILDMINDING
CHEMOAUTOTROPHY	CHEMOTROPICALLY	CHESSPLAYERS	CHIEFERIES	CHILDMINDINGS
CHEMOAUTROPH	CHEMOTROPISM	CHESSYLITE	CHIEFESSES	CHILDNESSES
CHEMOAUTROPHS	CHEMOTROPISMS	CHESSYLITES	CHIEFLINGS	CHILDPROOF
CHEMOCEPTOR	CHEMPADUKS	CHESTERFIELD	CHIEFSHIPS	CHILDRENSWEAR
CHEMOCEPTORS	CHEMTRAILS	CHESTERFIELDS	CHIEFTAINCIES	CHILDRENSWEARS
CHEMOKINES	CHEMURGICAL	CHESTINESS	CHIEFTAINCY	CHILIAGONS
CHEMOKINESES	CHEMURGIES	CHESTINESSES	CHIEFTAINESS	CHILIAHEDRA
CHEMOKINESIS	CHENOPODIACEOUS	CHEVALIERS	CHIEFTAINESSES	CHILIAHEDRON
CHEMOLITHOTROPH	CHEONGSAMS	CHEVELURES	CHIEFTAINRIES	CHILIAHEDRONS
CHEMONASTIES	CHEQUEBOOK	CHEVESAILE	CHIEFTAINRY	CHILIARCHIES
CHEMONASTY	CHEQUEBOOKS	CHEVESAILES	CHIEFTAINS	CHILIARCHS
CHEMOPREVENTION	CHEQUERBOARD	CHEVISANCE	CHIEFTAINSHIP	CHILIARCHY
CHEMOPSYCHIATRY	CHEQUERBOARDS	CHEVISANCES	CHIEFTAINSHIPS	CHILIASTIC
CHEMORECEPTION	CHEQUERING	CHEVRETTES	CHIFFCHAFF	CHILLAXING
CHEMORECEPTIONS	CHEQUERWISE	CHEVROTAIN	CHIFFCHAFFS	CHILLINESS
CHEMORECEPTIVE	CHEQUERWORK	CHEVROTAINS	CHIFFONADE	CHILLINESSES
CHEMORECEPTOR	CHEQUERWORKS	CHEWINESSES	CHIFFONADES	CHILLINGLY
CHEMORECEPTORS	CHERALITES	CHIACKINGS	CHIFFONIER	CHILLNESSES
CHEMOSMOSES	CHERIMOYAS	CHIAREZZAS	CHIFFONIERS	CHILOPODAN
CHEMOSMOSIS	CHERIMOYER	CHIAROSCURISM	CHIFFONNIER	CHILOPODANS
CHEMOSMOTIC	CHERIMOYERS	CHIAROSCURISMS	CHIFFONNIERS	CHILOPODOUS
CHEMOSORBED	CHERISHABLE	CHIAROSCURIST	CHIFFOROBE	CHILTEPINS
CHEMOSORBING	CHERISHERS	CHIAROSCURISTS	CHIFFOROBES	CHIMAERISM

CHIMAERISMS

CHIMAERISMS
CHIMERICAL
CHIMERICALLY
CHIMERICALNESS
CHIMERISMS
CHIMICHANGA
CHIMICHANGAS
CHIMNEYBOARD
CHIMNEYBOARDS
CHIMNEYBREAST
CHIMNEYBREASTS
CHIMNEYING
CHIMNEYLIKE
CHIMNEYPIECE
CHIMNEYPIECES
CHIMNEYPOT
CHIMNEYPOTS
CHIMPANZEE
CHIMPANZEES
CHINABERRIES
CHINABERRY
CHINACHINA
CHINACHINAS
CHINAROOTS
CHINAWARES
CHINCAPINS
CHINCHERINCHEE
CHINCHERINCHEES
CHINCHIEST
CHINCHILLA
CHINCHILLAS
CHINCOUGHS
CHINKAPINS
CHINKERINCHEE
CHINKERINCHEES
CHINOISERIE
CHINOISERIES
CHINOVNIKS
CHINQUAPIN
CHINQUAPINS
CHINSTRAPS
CHINTZIEST
CHINWAGGED
CHINWAGGING
CHIONODOXA
CHIONODOXAS
CHIPBOARDS

CHIPOCHIAS
CHIPOLATAS
CHIPPERING
CHIPPINESS
CHIPPINESSES
CHIQUICHIQUI
CHIQUICHIQUIS
CHIRAGRICAL
CHIRALITIES
CHIRIMOYAS
CHIROGNOMIES
CHIROGNOMIST
CHIROGNOMISTS
CHIROGNOMY
CHIROGRAPH
CHIROGRAPHER
CHIROGRAPHERS
CHIROGRAPHIC
CHIROGRAPHICAL
CHIROGRAPHIES
CHIROGRAPHIST
CHIROGRAPHISTS
CHIROGRAPHS
CHIROGRAPHY
CHIROLOGIES
CHIROLOGIST
CHIROLOGISTS
CHIROMANCER
CHIROMANCERS
CHIROMANCIES
CHIROMANCY
CHIROMANTIC
CHIROMANTICAL
CHIRONOMER
CHIRONOMERS
CHIRONOMIC
CHIRONOMID
CHIRONOMIDS
CHIRONOMIES
CHIROPODIAL
CHIROPODIES
CHIROPODIST
CHIROPODISTS
CHIROPRACTIC
CHIROPRACTICS
CHIROPRACTOR
CHIROPRACTORS

CHIROPTERAN
CHIROPTERANS
CHIROPTEROUS
CHIROPTERS
CHIRPINESS
CHIRPINESSES
CHIRRUPERS
CHIRRUPING
CHIRURGEON
CHIRURGEONLY
CHIRURGEONS
CHIRURGERIES
CHIRURGERY
CHIRURGICAL
CHISELLERS
CHISELLING
CHISELLINGS
CHITARRONE
CHITARRONI
CHITCHATTED
CHITCHATTING
CHITTAGONG
CHITTAGONGS
CHITTERING
CHITTERINGS
CHITTERLING
CHITTERLINGS
CHIVALRESQUE
CHIVALRIES
CHIVALROUS
CHIVALROUSLY
CHIVALROUSNESS
CHIVAREEING
CHIVARIING
CHIYOGAMIS
CHLAMYDATE
CHLAMYDEOUS
CHLAMYDIAE
CHLAMYDIAL
CHLAMYDIAS
CHLAMYDOMONADES
CHLAMYDOMONAS
CHLAMYDOSPORE
CHLAMYDOSPORES
CHLOANTHITE
CHLOANTHITES
CHLOASMATA

CHLORACETIC
CHLORACNES
CHLORALISM
CHLORALISMS
CHLORALOSE
CHLORALOSED
CHLORALOSES
CHLORAMBUCIL
CHLORAMBUCILS
CHLORAMINE
CHLORAMINES
CHLORAMPHENICOL
CHLORARGYRITE
CHLORARGYRITES
CHLORDANES
CHLORELLAS
CHLORENCHYMA
CHLORENCHYMAS
CHLORHEXIDINE
CHLORHEXIDINES
CHLORIDATE
CHLORIDATED
CHLORIDATES
CHLORIDATING
CHLORIDISE
CHLORIDISED
CHLORIDISES
CHLORIDISING
CHLORIDIZE
CHLORIDIZED
CHLORIDIZES
CHLORIDIZING
CHLORIMETER
CHLORIMETERS
CHLORIMETRIC
CHLORIMETRIES
CHLORIMETRY
CHLORINATE
CHLORINATED
CHLORINATES
CHLORINATING
CHLORINATION
CHLORINATIONS
CHLORINATOR
CHLORINATORS
CHLORINISE
CHLORINISED

CHLORINISES
CHLORINISING
CHLORINITIES
CHLORINITY
CHLORINIZE
CHLORINIZED
CHLORINIZES
CHLORINIZING
CHLORITISATION
CHLORITISATIONS
CHLORITIZATION
CHLORITIZATIONS
CHLOROACETIC
CHLOROARGYRITE
CHLOROBENZENE
CHLOROBENZENES
CHLOROBROMIDE
CHLOROBROMIDES
CHLOROCALCITE
CHLOROCALCITES
CHLOROCRUORIN
CHLOROCRUORINS
CHLORODYNE
CHLORODYNES
CHLOROFORM
CHLOROFORMED
CHLOROFORMER
CHLOROFORMERS
CHLOROFORMING
CHLOROFORMIST
CHLOROFORMISTS
CHLOROFORMS
CHLOROHYDRIN
CHLOROHYDRINS
CHLOROMETER
CHLOROMETERS
CHLOROMETHANE
CHLOROMETHANES
CHLOROMETRIC
CHLOROMETRIES
CHLOROMETRY
CHLOROPHYL
CHLOROPHYLL
CHLOROPHYLLOID
CHLOROPHYLLOUS
CHLOROPHYLLS
CHLOROPHYLS

C

CHLOROPHYTUM	CHOKEBERRIES	CHONDRICHTHYAN	CHORDOPHONE	CHOROGRAPHER
CHLOROPHYTUMS	CHOKEBERRY	CHONDRICHTHYANS	CHORDOPHONES	CHOROGRAPHERS
CHLOROPICRIN	CHOKEBORES	CHONDRIFICATION	CHORDOPHONIC	CHOROGRAPHIC
CHLOROPICRINS	CHOKECHERRIES	CHONDRIFIED	CHORDOTOMIES	CHOROGRAPHICAL
CHLOROPLAST	CHOKECHERRY	CHONDRIFIES	CHORDOTOMY	CHOROGRAPHIES
CHLOROPLASTAL	CHOKECOILS	CHONDRIFYING	CHOREGRAPH	CHOROGRAPHY
CHLOROPLASTIC	CHOKEDAMPS	CHONDRIOSOMAL	CHOREGRAPHED	CHOROIDITIS
CHLOROPLASTS	CHOKEHOLDS	CHONDRIOSOME	CHOREGRAPHER	CHOROIDITISES
CHLOROPRENE	CHOLAEMIAS	CHONDRIOSOMES	CHOREGRAPHERS	CHOROLOGICAL
CHLOROPRENES	CHOLAGOGIC	CHONDRITES	CHOREGRAPHIC	CHOROLOGIES
CHLOROQUIN	CHOLAGOGUE	CHONDRITIC	CHOREGRAPHIES	CHOROLOGIST
CHLOROQUINE	CHOLAGOGUES	CHONDRITIS	CHOREGRAPHING	CHOROLOGISTS
CHLOROQUINES	CHOLANGIOGRAM	CHONDRITISES	CHOREGRAPHS	CHOROPLETH
CHLOROQUINS	CHOLANGIOGRAMS	CHONDROBLAST	CHOREGRAPHY	CHOROPLETHS
CHLOROTHIAZIDE	CHOLANGIOGRAPHY	CHONDROBLASTS	CHOREGUSES	CHORUSMASTER
CHLOROTHIAZIDES	CHOLECALCIFEROL	CHONDROCRANIA	CHOREIFORM	CHORUSMASTERS
CHLORPICRIN	CHOLECYSTECTOMY	CHONDROCRANIUM	CHOREODRAMA	CHORUSSING
CHLORPICRINS	CHOLECYSTITIS	CHONDROCRANIUMS	CHOREODRAMAS	CHOUCROUTE
CHLORPROMAZINE	CHOLECYSTITISES	CHONDROGENESES	CHOREOGRAPH	CHOUCROUTES
CHLORPROMAZINES	CHOLECYSTOKININ	CHONDROGENESIS	CHOREOGRAPHED	CHOULTRIES
CHLORPROPAMIDE	CHOLECYSTOSTOMY	CHONDROITIN	CHOREOGRAPHER	CHOUNTERED
CHLORPROPAMIDES	CHOLECYSTOTOMY	CHONDROITINS	CHOREOGRAPHERS	CHOUNTERING
CHLORTHALIDONE	CHOLECYSTS	CHONDROMAS	CHOREOGRAPHIC	CHOWDERHEAD
CHLORTHALIDONES	CHOLELITHIASES	CHONDROMATA	CHOREOGRAPHIES	CHOWDERHEADED
CHOANOCYTE	CHOLELITHIASIS	CHONDROMATOSES	CHOREOGRAPHING	CHOWDERHEADS
CHOANOCYTES	CHOLELITHS	CHONDROMATOSIS	CHOREOGRAPHS	CHOWDERING
CHOCAHOLIC	CHOLERICALLY	CHONDROMATOUS	CHOREOGRAPHY	CHOWHOUNDS
CHOCAHOLICS	CHOLERICLY	CHONDROPHORE	CHOREOLOGIES	CHOWKIDARS
CHOCKABLOCK	CHOLESTASES	CHONDROPHORES	CHOREOLOGIST	CHREMATIST
CHOCKSTONE	CHOLESTASIS	CHONDROPHORINE	CHOREOLOGISTS	CHREMATISTIC
CHOCKSTONES	CHOLESTATIC	CHONDROPHORINES	CHOREOLOGY	CHREMATISTICS
CHOCOHOLIC	CHOLESTERIC	CHONDROSKELETON	CHOREPISCOPAL	CHREMATISTS
CHOCOHOLICS	CHOLESTERIN	CHONDROSTIAN	CHORIAMBIC	CHRESTOMATHIC
CHOCOLATES	CHOLESTERINS	CHONDROSTIANS	CHORIAMBICS	CHRESTOMATHICAL
CHOCOLATEY	CHOLESTEROL	CHONDRULES	CHORIAMBUS	CHRESTOMATHIES
CHOCOLATIER	CHOLESTEROLEMIA	CHOPFALLEN	CHORIAMBUSES	CHRESTOMATHY
CHOCOLATIERS	CHOLESTEROLS	CHOPHOUSES	CHORIOALLANTOIC	CHRISMATION
CHOCOLATIEST	CHOLESTYRAMINE	CHOPLOGICS	CHORIOALLANTOIS	CHRISMATIONS
CHOICENESS	CHOLESTYRAMINES	CHOPPERING	CHORIOCARCINOMA	CHRISMATORIES
CHOICENESSES	CHOLIAMBIC	CHOPPINESS	CHORISATION	CHRISMATORY
CHOIRGIRLS	CHOLIAMBICS	CHOPPINESSES	CHORISATIONS	CHRISTCROSS
CHOIRMASTER	CHOLINERGIC	CHOPSOCKIES	CHORISTERS	CHRISTCROSSES
CHOIRMASTERS	CHOLINERGICALLY	CHOPSTICKS	CHORIZATION	CHRISTENED
CHOIRSCREEN	CHOLINESTERASE	CHORAGUSES	CHORIZATIONS	CHRISTENER
CHOIRSCREENS	CHOLINESTERASES	CHORALISTS	CHORIZONTIST	CHRISTENERS
CHOIRSTALL	CHOMOPHYTE	CHORDAMESODERM	CHORIZONTISTS	CHRISTENING
CHOIRSTALLS	CHOMOPHYTES	CHORDAMESODERMS	CHORIZONTS	CHRISTENINGS

CHRISTIANIA
CHRISTIANIAS
CHRISTIANS
CHRISTOPHANIES
CHRISTOPHANY
CHROMAFFIN
CHROMAKEYS
CHROMATICALLY
CHROMATICISM
CHROMATICISMS
CHROMATICITIES
CHROMATICITY
CHROMATICNESS
CHROMATICNESSES
CHROMATICS
CHROMATIDS
CHROMATINIC
CHROMATINS
CHROMATIST
CHROMATISTS
CHROMATOGRAM
CHROMATOGRAMS
CHROMATOGRAPH
CHROMATOGRAPHED
CHROMATOGRAPHER
CHROMATOGRAPHIC
CHROMATOGRAPHS
CHROMATOGRAPHY
CHROMATOID
CHROMATOLOGIES
CHROMATOLOGIST
CHROMATOLOGISTS
CHROMATOLOGY
CHROMATOLYSES
CHROMATOLYSIS
CHROMATOLYTIC
CHROMATOPHORE
CHROMATOPHORES
CHROMATOPHORIC
CHROMATOPHOROUS
CHROMATOPSIA
CHROMATOPSIAS
CHROMATOSPHERE
CHROMATOSPHERES
CHROMATYPE
CHROMATYPES
CHROMIDIUM

CHROMINANCE
CHROMINANCES
CHROMISING
CHROMIZING
CHROMOCENTER
CHROMOCENTERS
CHROMOCENTRE
CHROMOCENTRES
CHROMODYNAMICS
CHROMOGENIC
CHROMOGENS
CHROMOGRAM
CHROMOGRAMS
CHROMOLIES
CHROMOMERE
CHROMOMERES
CHROMOMERIC
CHROMONEMA
CHROMONEMAL
CHROMONEMATA
CHROMONEMATIC
CHROMONEMIC
CHROMOPHIL
CHROMOPHILIC
CHROMOPHILS
CHROMOPHOBE
CHROMOPHOBES
CHROMOPHORE
CHROMOPHORES
CHROMOPHORIC
CHROMOPHOROUS
CHROMOPLAST
CHROMOPLASTS
CHROMOPROTEIN
CHROMOPROTEINS
CHROMOSCOPE
CHROMOSCOPES
CHROMOSOMAL
CHROMOSOMALLY
CHROMOSOME
CHROMOSOMES
CHROMOSPHERE
CHROMOSPHERES
CHROMOSPHERIC
CHROMOTHERAPIES
CHROMOTHERAPY
CHROMOTYPE

CHROMOTYPES
CHROMOXYLOGRAPH
CHRONAXIES
CHRONICALLY
CHRONICITIES
CHRONICITY
CHRONICLED
CHRONICLER
CHRONICLERS
CHRONICLES
CHRONICLING
CHRONOBIOLOGIC
CHRONOBIOLOGIES
CHRONOBIOLOGIST
CHRONOBIOLOGY
CHRONOGRAM
CHRONOGRAMMATIC
CHRONOGRAMS
CHRONOGRAPH
CHRONOGRAPHER
CHRONOGRAPHERS
CHRONOGRAPHIC
CHRONOGRAPHIES
CHRONOGRAPHS
CHRONOGRAPHY
CHRONOLOGER
CHRONOLOGERS
CHRONOLOGIC
CHRONOLOGICAL
CHRONOLOGICALLY
CHRONOLOGIES
CHRONOLOGISE
CHRONOLOGISED
CHRONOLOGISES
CHRONOLOGISING
CHRONOLOGIST
CHRONOLOGISTS
CHRONOLOGIZE
CHRONOLOGIZED
CHRONOLOGIZES
CHRONOLOGIZING
CHRONOLOGY
CHRONOMETER
CHRONOMETERS
CHRONOMETRIC
CHRONOMETRICAL
CHRONOMETRIES

CHRONOMETRY
CHRONOSCOPE
CHRONOSCOPES
CHRONOSCOPIC
CHRONOTHERAPIES
CHRONOTHERAPY
CHRONOTRON
CHRONOTRONS
CHRYSALIDAL
CHRYSALIDES
CHRYSALIDS
CHRYSALISES
CHRYSANTHEMUM
CHRYSANTHEMUMS
CHRYSANTHS
CHRYSAROBIN
CHRYSAROBINS
CHRYSOBERYL
CHRYSOBERYLS
CHRYSOCOLLA
CHRYSOCOLLAS
CHRYSOCRACIES
CHRYSOCRACY
CHRYSOLITE
CHRYSOLITES
CHRYSOLITIC
CHRYSOMELID
CHRYSOMELIDS
CHRYSOPHAN
CHRYSOPHANS
CHRYSOPHILITE
CHRYSOPHILITES
CHRYSOPHYTE
CHRYSOPHYTES
CHRYSOPRASE
CHRYSOPRASES
CHRYSOTILE
CHRYSOTILES
CHUBBINESS
CHUBBINESSES
CHUCKAWALLA
CHUCKAWALLAS
CHUCKHOLES
CHUCKLEHEAD
CHUCKLEHEADED
CHUCKLEHEADS
CHUCKLESOME

CHUCKLINGLY
CHUCKLINGS
CHUCKWALLA
CHUCKWALLAS
CHUFFINESS
CHUFFINESSES
CHUGALUGGED
CHUGALUGGING
CHUMMINESS
CHUMMINESSES
CHUNDERING
CHUNDEROUS
CHUNKINESS
CHUNKINESSES
CHUNNERING
CHUNTERING
CHUPATTIES
CHUPRASSIES
CHURCHGOER
CHURCHGOERS
CHURCHGOING
CHURCHGOINGS
CHURCHIANITIES
CHURCHIANITY
CHURCHIEST
CHURCHINGS
CHURCHISMS
CHURCHLESS
CHURCHLIER
CHURCHLIEST
CHURCHLINESS
CHURCHLINESSES
CHURCHMANLY
CHURCHMANSHIP
CHURCHMANSHIPS
CHURCHPEOPLE
CHURCHWARD
CHURCHWARDEN
CHURCHWARDENS
CHURCHWARDS
CHURCHWAYS
CHURCHWOMAN
CHURCHWOMEN
CHURCHYARD
CHURCHYARDS
CHURLISHLY
CHURLISHNESS

CHURLISHNESSES	CICATRIZER	CINEMATHEQUES	CIRCENSIAL	CIRCUMAMBIENCES
CHURNALISM	CICATRIZERS	CINEMATICALLY	CIRCENSIAN	CIRCUMAMBIENCY
CHURNALISMS	CICATRIZES	CINEMATISE	CIRCINATELY	CIRCUMAMBIENT
CHURNMILKS	CICATRIZING	CINEMATISED	CIRCUITEER	CIRCUMAMBIENTLY
CHURRIGUERESCO	CICERONEING	CINEMATISES	CIRCUITEERED	CIRCUMAMBULATE
CHURRIGUERESQUE	CICHORACEOUS	CINEMATISING	CIRCUITEERING	CIRCUMAMBULATED
CHYLACEOUS	CICINNUSES	CINEMATIZE	CIRCUITEERS	CIRCUMAMBULATES
CHYLIFEROUS	CICISBEISM	CINEMATIZED	CIRCUITIES	CIRCUMAMBULATOR
CHYLIFICATION	CICISBEISMS	CINEMATIZES	CIRCUITING	CIRCUMBENDIBUS
CHYLIFICATIONS	CICLATOUNS	CINEMATIZING	CIRCUITOUS	CIRCUMCENTER
CHYLIFYING	CICLOSPORIN	CINEMATOGRAPH	CIRCUITOUSLY	CIRCUMCENTERS
CHYLOMICRON	CICLOSPORINS	CINEMATOGRAPHED	CIRCUITOUSNESS	CIRCUMCENTRE
CHYLOMICRONS	CIGARETTES	CINEMATOGRAPHER	CIRCUITRIES	CIRCUMCENTRES
CHYMIFEROUS	CIGARILLOS	CINEMATOGRAPHS	CIRCULABLE	CIRCUMCIRCLE
CHYMIFICATION	CIGUATERAS	CINEMATOGRAPHIC	CIRCULARISATION	CIRCUMCIRCLES
CHYMIFICATIONS	CIGUATOXIN	CINEMATOGRAPHY	CIRCULARISE	CIRCUMCISE
CHYMIFYING	CIGUATOXINS	CINEMICROGRAPHY	CIRCULARISED	CIRCUMCISED
CHYMISTRIES	CILIATIONS	CINEPHILES	CIRCULARISER	CIRCUMCISER
CHYMOTRYPSIN	CIMETIDINE	CINEPLEXES	CIRCULARISERS	CIRCUMCISERS
CHYMOTRYPSINS	CIMETIDINES	CINERARIAS	CIRCULARISES	CIRCUMCISES
CHYMOTRYPTIC	CINCHONACEOUS	CINERARIUM	CIRCULARISING	CIRCUMCISING
CIBACHROME	CINCHONIDINE	CINERATION	CIRCULARITIES	CIRCUMCISION
CIBACHROMES	CINCHONIDINES	CINERATIONS	CIRCULARITY	CIRCUMCISIONS
CICADELLID	CINCHONINE	CINERATORS	CIRCULARIZATION	CIRCUMDUCE
CICADELLIDS	CINCHONINES	CINERITIOUS	CIRCULARIZE	CIRCUMDUCED
CICATRICES	CINCHONINIC	CINGULATED	CIRCULARIZED	CIRCUMDUCES
CICATRICHULE	CINCHONISATION	CINNABARIC	CIRCULARIZER	CIRCUMDUCING
CICATRICHULES	CINCHONISATIONS	CINNABARINE	CIRCULARIZERS	CIRCUMDUCT
CICATRICIAL	CINCHONISE	CINNAMONIC	CIRCULARIZES	CIRCUMDUCTED
CICATRICLE	CINCHONISED	CINNARIZINE	CIRCULARIZING	CIRCUMDUCTING
CICATRICLES	CINCHONISES	CINNARIZINES	CIRCULARLY	CIRCUMDUCTION
CICATRICOSE	CINCHONISING	CINQUECENTIST	CIRCULARNESS	CIRCUMDUCTIONS
CICATRICULA	CINCHONISM	CINQUECENTISTS	CIRCULARNESSES	CIRCUMDUCTORY
CICATRICULAS	CINCHONISMS	CINQUECENTO	CIRCULATABLE	CIRCUMDUCTS
CICATRISANT	CINCHONIZATION	CINQUECENTOS	CIRCULATED	CIRCUMFERENCE
CICATRISATION	CINCHONIZATIONS	CINQUEFOIL	CIRCULATES	CIRCUMFERENCES
CICATRISATIONS	CINCHONIZE	CINQUEFOILS	CIRCULATING	CIRCUMFERENTIAL
CICATRISED	CINCHONIZED	CIPHERINGS	CIRCULATINGS	CIRCUMFERENTOR
CICATRISER	CINCHONIZES	CIPHERTEXT	CIRCULATION	CIRCUMFERENTORS
CICATRISERS	CINCHONIZING	CIPHERTEXTS	CIRCULATIONS	CIRCUMFLECT
CICATRISES	CINCINNATE	CIPOLLINOS	CIRCULATIVE	CIRCUMFLECTED
CICATRISING	CINCINNUSES	CIPROFLOXACIN	CIRCULATOR	CIRCUMFLECTING
CICATRIXES	CINCTURING	CIPROFLOXACINS	CIRCULATORS	CIRCUMFLECTS
CICATRIZANT	CINEANGIOGRAPHY	CIRCASSIAN	CIRCULATORY	CIRCUMFLEX
CICATRIZATION	CINEMAGOER	CIRCASSIANS	CIRCUMAMBAGES	CIRCUMFLEXES
CICATRIZATIONS	CINEMAGOERS	CIRCASSIENNE	CIRCUMAMBAGIOUS	CIRCUMFLEXION
CICATRIZED	CINEMATHEQUE	CIRCASSIENNES	CIRCUMAMBIENCE	CIRCUMFLEXIONS

CIRCUMFLUENCE
CIRCUMFLUENCES
CIRCUMFLUENT
CIRCUMFLUOUS
CIRCUMFORANEAN
CIRCUMFORANEOUS
CIRCUMFUSE
CIRCUMFUSED
CIRCUMFUSES
CIRCUMFUSILE
CIRCUMFUSING
CIRCUMFUSION
CIRCUMFUSIONS
CIRCUMGYRATE
CIRCUMGYRATED
CIRCUMGYRATES
CIRCUMGYRATING
CIRCUMGYRATION
CIRCUMGYRATIONS
CIRCUMGYRATORY
CIRCUMINCESSION
CIRCUMINSESSION
CIRCUMJACENCIES
CIRCUMJACENCY
CIRCUMJACENT
CIRCUMLITTORAL
CIRCUMLOCUTE
CIRCUMLOCUTED
CIRCUMLOCUTES
CIRCUMLOCUTING
CIRCUMLOCUTION
CIRCUMLOCUTIONS
CIRCUMLOCUTORY
CIRCUMLUNAR
CIRCUMMURE
CIRCUMMURED
CIRCUMMURES
CIRCUMMURING
CIRCUMNAVIGABLE
CIRCUMNAVIGATE
CIRCUMNAVIGATED
CIRCUMNAVIGATES
CIRCUMNAVIGATOR
CIRCUMNUTATE
CIRCUMNUTATED
CIRCUMNUTATES
CIRCUMNUTATING

CIRCUMNUTATION
CIRCUMNUTATIONS
CIRCUMNUTATORY
CIRCUMPOLAR
CIRCUMPOSE
CIRCUMPOSED
CIRCUMPOSES
CIRCUMPOSING
CIRCUMPOSITION
CIRCUMPOSITIONS
CIRCUMSCISSILE
CIRCUMSCRIBABLE
CIRCUMSCRIBE
CIRCUMSCRIBED
CIRCUMSCRIBER
CIRCUMSCRIBERS
CIRCUMSCRIBES
CIRCUMSCRIBING
CIRCUMSCRIPTION
CIRCUMSCRIPTIVE
CIRCUMSOLAR
CIRCUMSPECT
CIRCUMSPECTION
CIRCUMSPECTIONS
CIRCUMSPECTIVE
CIRCUMSPECTLY
CIRCUMSPECTNESS
CIRCUMSTANCE
CIRCUMSTANCED
CIRCUMSTANCES
CIRCUMSTANCING
CIRCUMSTANTIAL
CIRCUMSTANTIALS
CIRCUMSTANTIATE
CIRCUMSTELLAR
CIRCUMVALLATE
CIRCUMVALLATED
CIRCUMVALLATES
CIRCUMVALLATING
CIRCUMVALLATION
CIRCUMVENT
CIRCUMVENTED
CIRCUMVENTER
CIRCUMVENTERS
CIRCUMVENTING
CIRCUMVENTION
CIRCUMVENTIONS

CIRCUMVENTIVE
CIRCUMVENTOR
CIRCUMVENTORS
CIRCUMVENTS
CIRCUMVOLUTION
CIRCUMVOLUTIONS
CIRCUMVOLUTORY
CIRCUMVOLVE
CIRCUMVOLVED
CIRCUMVOLVES
CIRCUMVOLVING
CIRRHIPEDE
CIRRHIPEDES
CIRRHOTICS
CIRRIGRADE
CIRRIPEDES
CIRROCUMULI
CIRROCUMULUS
CIRROSTRATI
CIRROSTRATIVE
CIRROSTRATUS
CISMONTANE
CISPLATINS
CISPONTINE
CISTACEOUS
CITATIONAL
CITHARISTIC
CITHARISTS
CITIFICATION
CITIFICATIONS
CITIZENESS
CITIZENESSES
CITIZENISE
CITIZENISED
CITIZENISES
CITIZENISING
CITIZENIZE
CITIZENIZED
CITIZENIZES
CITIZENIZING
CITIZENRIES
CITIZENSHIP
CITIZENSHIPS
CITRICULTURE
CITRICULTURES
CITRICULTURIST
CITRICULTURISTS

CITRONELLA
CITRONELLAL
CITRONELLALS
CITRONELLAS
CITRONELLOL
CITRONELLOLS
CITRULLINE
CITRULLINES
CITYFICATION
CITYFICATIONS
CITYSCAPES
CIVILIANISATION
CIVILIANISE
CIVILIANISED
CIVILIANISES
CIVILIANISING
CIVILIANIZATION
CIVILIANIZE
CIVILIANIZED
CIVILIANIZES
CIVILIANIZING
CIVILISABLE
CIVILISATION
CIVILISATIONAL
CIVILISATIONS
CIVILISERS
CIVILISING
CIVILITIES
CIVILIZABLE
CIVILIZATION
CIVILIZATIONAL
CIVILIZATIONS
CIVILIZERS
CIVILIZING
CIVILNESSES
CLABBERING
CLACKBOXES
CLACKDISHES
CLADISTICALLY
CLADISTICS
CLADOCERAN
CLADOCERANS
CLADOGENESES
CLADOGENESIS
CLADOGENETIC
CLADOGRAMS
CLADOPHYLL

CLADOPHYLLS
CLADOSPORIA
CLADOSPORIUM
CLADOSPORIUMS
CLAIRAUDIENCE
CLAIRAUDIENCES
CLAIRAUDIENT
CLAIRAUDIENTLY
CLAIRAUDIENTS
CLAIRCOLLE
CLAIRCOLLES
CLAIRSCHACH
CLAIRSCHACHS
CLAIRVOYANCE
CLAIRVOYANCES
CLAIRVOYANCIES
CLAIRVOYANCY
CLAIRVOYANT
CLAIRVOYANTLY
CLAIRVOYANTS
CLAMANCIES
CLAMATORIAL
CLAMBERERS
CLAMBERING
CLAMJAMFRIES
CLAMJAMFRY
CLAMJAMPHRIE
CLAMJAMPHRIES
CLAMMINESS
CLAMMINESSES
CLAMOROUSLY
CLAMOROUSNESS
CLAMOROUSNESSES
CLAMOURERS
CLAMOURING
CLAMPDOWNS
CLAMPERING
CLAMSHELLS
CLANDESTINE
CLANDESTINELY
CLANDESTINENESS
CLANDESTINITIES
CLANDESTINITY
CLANGBOXES
CLANGORING
CLANGOROUS
CLANGOROUSLY

C

CLANGOURED	CLARIONING	CLAUCHTING	CLEARANCES	CLERGYWOMAN
CLANGOURING	CLARTHEADS	CLAUDICATION	CLEARCOLED	CLERGYWOMEN
CLANJAMFRAY	CLASHINGLY	CLAUDICATIONS	CLEARCOLES	CLERICALISM
CLANJAMFRAYS	CLASSICALISM	CLAUGHTING	CLEARCOLING	CLERICALISMS
CLANKINGLY	CLASSICALISMS	CLAUSTRATION	CLEARCUTTING	CLERICALIST
CLANNISHLY	CLASSICALIST	CLAUSTRATIONS	CLEARCUTTINGS	CLERICALISTS
CLANNISHNESS	CLASSICALISTS	CLAUSTROPHILIA	CLEARHEADED	CLERICALLY
CLANNISHNESSES	CLASSICALITIES	CLAUSTROPHILIAS	CLEARHEADEDLY	CLERICATES
CLANSWOMAN	CLASSICALITY	CLAUSTROPHOBE	CLEARHEADEDNESS	CLERICITIES
CLANSWOMEN	CLASSICALLY	CLAUSTROPHOBES	CLEARINGHOUSE	CLERICITIES
CLAPBOARDED	CLASSICALNESS	CLAUSTROPHOBIA	CLEARINGHOUSES	CLERKESSES
CLAPBOARDING	CLASSICALNESSES	CLAUSTROPHOBIAS	CLEARNESSES	CLERKLIEST
CLAPBOARDS	CLASSICALS	CLAUSTROPHOBIC	CLEARSKINS	CLERKLINESS
CLAPBREADS	CLASSICISE	CLAVATIONS	CLEARSTORIED	CLERKLINESSES
CLAPDISHES	CLASSICISED	CLAVECINIST	CLEARSTORIES	CLERKLINGS
CLAPOMETER	CLASSICISES	CLAVECINISTS	CLEARSTORY	CLERKSHIPS
CLAPOMETERS	CLASSICISING	CLAVICEMBALO	CLEARWEEDS	CLEROMANCIES
CLAPPERBOARD	CLASSICISM	CLAVICEMBALOS	CLEARWINGS	CLEROMANCY
CLAPPERBOARDS	CLASSICISMS	CLAVICHORD	CLEAVABILITIES	CLERUCHIAL
CLAPPERBOY	CLASSICIST	CLAVICHORDIST	CLEAVABILITY	CLERUCHIAS
CLAPPERBOYS	CLASSICISTIC	CLAVICHORDISTS	CLEAVABLENESS	CLERUCHIES
CLAPPERCLAW	CLASSICISTS	CLAVICHORDS	CLEAVABLENESSES	CLEVERALITIES
CLAPPERCLAWED	CLASSICIZE	CLAVICORNS	CLEISTOGAMIC	CLEVERALITY
CLAPPERCLAWER	CLASSICIZED	CLAVICULAE	CLEISTOGAMIES	CLEVERDICK
CLAPPERCLAWERS	CLASSICIZES	CLAVICULAR	CLEISTOGAMOUS	CLEVERDICKS
CLAPPERCLAWING	CLASSICIZING	CLAVICULATE	CLEISTOGAMOUSLY	CLEVERNESS
CLAPPERCLAWS	CLASSIFIABLE	CLAVICYTHERIA	CLEISTOGAMY	CLEVERNESSES
CLAPPERING	CLASSIFICATION	CLAVICYTHERIUM	CLEMATISES	CLIANTHUSES
CLAPPERINGS	CLASSIFICATIONS	CLAVIERIST	CLEMENCIES	CLICKBAITS
CLAPTRAPPERIES	CLASSIFICATORY	CLAVIERISTIC	CLEMENTINE	CLICKETING
CLAPTRAPPERY	CLASSIFIED	CLAVIERISTS	CLEMENTINES	CLICKJACKING
CLARABELLA	CLASSIFIEDS	CLAVIGEROUS	CLENBUTEROL	CLICKJACKINGS
CLARABELLAS	CLASSIFIER	CLAWHAMMER	CLENBUTEROLS	CLICKSTREAM
CLARENDONS	CLASSIFIERS	CLAYMATION	CLEOPATRAS	CLICKSTREAMS
CLARIBELLA	CLASSIFIES	CLAYMATIONS	CLEPSYDRAE	CLICKTIVISM
CLARIBELLAS	CLASSIFYING	CLAYSTONES	CLEPSYDRAS	CLICKTIVISMS
CLARICHORD	CLASSINESS	CLAYTONIAS	CLEPTOCRACIES	CLICKWRAPS
CLARICHORDS	CLASSINESSES	CLEANABILITIES	CLEPTOCRACY	CLIENTAGES
CLARIFICATION	CLASSLESSNESS	CLEANABILITY	CLEPTOMANIA	CLIENTELES
CLARIFICATIONS	CLASSLESSNESSES	CLEANHANDED	CLEPTOMANIAC	CLIENTLESS
CLARIFIERS	CLASSMATES	CLEANLIEST	CLEPTOMANIACS	CLIENTSHIP
CLARIFYING	CLASSROOMS	CLEANLINESS	CLEPTOMANIAS	CLIENTSHIPS
CLARINETIST	CLASSWORKS	CLEANLINESSES	CLERESTORIED	CLIFFHANGER
CLARINETISTS	CLATHRATES	CLEANNESSES	CLERESTORIES	CLIFFHANGERS
CLARINETTIST	CLATTERERS	CLEANSABLE	CLERESTORY	CLIFFHANGING
CLARINETTISTS	CLATTERING	CLEANSINGS	CLERGIABLE	CLIFFHANGINGS
CLARIONETS	CLATTERINGLY	CLEANSKINS	CLERGYABLE	CLIFFHANGS
				CLIFFSIDES

CLIMACTERIC	CLINOCHLORE	CLITTERING	CLOTHBOUND	CLUBHAULED
CLIMACTERICAL	CLINOCHLORES	CLOACALINE	CLOTHESHORSE	CLUBHAULING
CLIMACTERICALLY	CLINODIAGONAL	CLOACITISES	CLOTHESHORSES	CLUBHOUSES
CLIMACTERICS	CLINODIAGONALS	CLOAKROOMS	CLOTHESLINE	CLUBMANSHIP
CLIMACTICAL	CLINOMETER	CLOBBERING	CLOTHESLINED	CLUBMANSHIPS
CLIMACTICALLY	CLINOMETERS	CLOCKMAKER	CLOTHESLINES	CLUBMASTER
CLIMATICAL	CLINOMETRIC	CLOCKMAKERS	CLOTHESLINING	CLUBMASTERS
CLIMATICALLY	CLINOMETRICAL	CLOCKWORKS	CLOTHESPIN	CLUBMOSSES
CLIMATISED	CLINOMETRIES	CLODDISHLY	CLOTHESPINS	CLUBRUSHES
CLIMATISES	CLINOMETRY	CLODDISHNESS	CLOTHESPRESS	CLUMPINESS
CLIMATISING	CLINOPINACOID	CLODDISHNESSES	CLOTHESPRESSES	CLUMPINESSES
CLIMATIZED	CLINOPINACOIDS	CLODHOPPER	CLOTTERING	CLUMSINESS
CLIMATIZES	CLINOPINAKOID	CLODHOPPERS	CLOTTINESS	CLUMSINESSES
CLIMATIZING	CLINOPINAKOIDS	CLODHOPPING	CLOTTINESSES	CLUSTERING
CLIMATOGRAPHIES	CLINOPYROXENE	CLOFIBRATE	CLOUDBERRIES	CLUSTERINGLY
CLIMATOGRAPHY	CLINOPYROXENES	CLOFIBRATES	CLOUDBERRY	CLUTCHIEST
CLIMATOLOGIC	CLINOSTATS	CLOGDANCES	CLOUDBURST	CLUTTERING
CLIMATOLOGICAL	CLINQUANTS	CLOGGINESS	CLOUDBURSTS	CLYPEIFORM
CLIMATOLOGIES	CLINTONIAS	CLOGGINESSES	CLOUDINESS	CNIDARIANS
CLIMATOLOGIST	CLIOMETRIC	CLOISONNAGE	CLOUDINESSES	CNIDOBLAST
CLIMATOLOGISTS	CLIOMETRICAL	CLOISONNAGES	CLOUDLANDS	CNIDOBLASTS
CLIMATOLOGY	CLIOMETRICIAN	CLOISONNES	CLOUDLESSLY	COACERVATE
CLIMATURES	CLIOMETRICIANS	CLOISTERED	CLOUDLESSNESS	COACERVATED
CLIMAXLESS	CLIOMETRICS	CLOISTERER	CLOUDLESSNESSES	COACERVATES
CLIMBDOWNS	CLIPBOARDS	CLOISTERERS	CLOUDSCAPE	COACERVATING
CLINANDRIA	CLIPSHEARS	CLOISTERING	CLOUDSCAPES	COACERVATION
CLINANDRIUM	CLIPSHEETS	CLOISTRESS	CLOUDTOWNS	COACERVATIONS
CLINCHINGLY	CLIQUINESS	CLOISTRESSES	CLOVERGRASS	COACHBUILDER
CLINDAMYCIN	CLIQUINESSES	CLOMIPHENE	CLOVERGRASSES	COACHBUILDERS
CLINDAMYCINS	CLIQUISHLY	CLOMIPHENES	CLOVERLEAF	COACHBUILDING
CLINGFILMS	CLIQUISHNESS	CLONAZEPAM	CLOVERLEAFS	COACHBUILDINGS
CLINGFISHES	CLIQUISHNESSES	CLONAZEPAMS	CLOVERLEAVES	COACHBUILT
CLINGINESS	CLISHMACLAVER	CLONICITIES	CLOWNERIES	COACHLINES
CLINGINESSES	CLISHMACLAVERS	CLONIDINES	CLOWNFISHES	COACHLOADS
CLINGINGLY	CLISTOGAMIES	CLOSEDOWNS	CLOWNISHLY	COACHWHIPS
CLINGINGNESS	CLISTOGAMY	CLOSEFISTED	CLOWNISHNESS	COACHWOODS
CLINGINGNESSES	CLITICISED	CLOSEHEADS	CLOWNISHNESSES	COACHWORKS
CLINGSTONE	CLITICISES	CLOSEMOUTHED	CLOXACILLIN	COACTIVELY
CLINGSTONES	CLITICISING	CLOSENESSES	CLOXACILLINS	COACTIVITIES
CLINGWRAPS	CLITICIZED	CLOSESTOOL	CLOZAPINES	COACTIVITY
CLINICALLY	CLITICIZES	CLOSESTOOLS	CLUBABILITIES	COADAPTATION
CLINICALNESS	CLITICIZING	CLOSETFULS	CLUBABILITY	COADAPTATIONS
CLINICALNESSES	CLITORECTOMIES	CLOSTRIDIA	CLUBBABILITIES	COADJACENCIES
CLINICIANS	CLITORECTOMY	CLOSTRIDIAL	CLUBBABILITY	COADJACENCY
CLINKERING	CLITORIDECTOMY	CLOSTRIDIAN	CLUBBINESS	COADJACENT
CLINKSTONE	CLITORIDES	CLOSTRIDIUM	CLUBBINESSES	COADJACENTS
CLINKSTONES	CLITORISES	CLOSTRIDIUMS	CLUBFOOTED	COADJUTANT

COADJUTANTS
COADJUTORS
COADJUTORSHIP
COADJUTORSHIPS
COADJUTRESS
COADJUTRESSES
COADJUTRICES
COADJUTRIX
COADJUTRIXES
COADMIRING
COADMITTED
COADMITTING
COADUNATED
COADUNATES
COADUNATING
COADUNATION
COADUNATIONS
COADUNATIVE
COAGENCIES
COAGULABILITIES
COAGULABILITY
COAGULABLE
COAGULANTS
COAGULASES
COAGULATED
COAGULATES
COAGULATING
COAGULATION
COAGULATIONS
COAGULATIVE
COAGULATOR
COAGULATORS
COAGULATORY
COALESCENCE
COALESCENCES
COALESCENT
COALESCING
COALFIELDS
COALFISHES
COALHOUSES
COALIFICATION
COALIFICATIONS
COALIFYING
COALITIONAL
COALITIONER
COALITIONERS
COALITIONISM

COALITIONISMS
COALITIONIST
COALITIONISTS
COALITIONS
COALMASTER
COALMASTERS
COALMINERS
COANCHORED
COANCHORING
COANNEXING
COAPPEARED
COAPPEARING
COAPTATION
COAPTATIONS
COARCTATED
COARCTATES
COARCTATING
COARCTATION
COARCTATIONS
COARSENESS
COARSENESSES
COARSENING
COASSISTED
COASSISTING
COASSUMING
COASTEERING
COASTEERINGS
COASTGUARD
COASTGUARDMAN
COASTGUARDMEN
COASTGUARDS
COASTGUARDSMAN
COASTGUARDSMEN
COASTLANDS
COASTLINES
COASTWARDS
COATDRESSES
COATIMUNDI
COATIMUNDIS
COATSTANDS
COATTENDED
COATTENDING
COATTESTED
COATTESTING
COAUTHORED
COAUTHORING
COAUTHORSHIP

COAUTHORSHIPS
COBALAMINS
COBALTIFEROUS
COBALTINES
COBALTITES
COBBLERIES
COBBLESTONE
COBBLESTONED
COBBLESTONES
COBBLESTONING
COBELLIGERENT
COBELLIGERENTS
COBWEBBERIES
COBWEBBERY
COBWEBBIER
COBWEBBIEST
COBWEBBING
COCAINISATION
COCAINISATIONS
COCAINISED
COCAINISES
COCAINISING
COCAINISMS
COCAINISTS
COCAINIZATION
COCAINIZATIONS
COCAINIZED
COCAINIZES
COCAINIZING
COCAPTAINED
COCAPTAINING
COCAPTAINS
COCARBOXYLASE
COCARBOXYLASES
COCARCINOGEN
COCARCINOGENIC
COCARCINOGENS
COCATALYST
COCATALYSTS
COCCIDIOSES
COCCIDIOSIS
COCCIDIOSTAT
COCCIDIOSTATS
COCCIFEROUS
COCCINEOUS
COCCOLITES
COCCOLITHS

COCHAIRING
COCHAIRMAN
COCHAIRMANSHIP
COCHAIRMANSHIPS
COCHAIRMEN
COCHAIRPERSON
COCHAIRPERSONS
COCHAIRWOMAN
COCHAIRWOMEN
COCHAMPION
COCHAMPIONS
COCHINEALS
COCHLEARES
COCHLEARIFORM
COCHLEATED
COCKABULLIES
COCKABULLY
COCKALEEKIE
COCKALEEKIES
COCKALORUM
COCKALORUMS
COCKAMAMIE
COCKATEELS
COCKATIELS
COCKATRICE
COCKATRICES
COCKBILLED
COCKBILLING
COCKCHAFER
COCKCHAFERS
COCKCROWING
COCKCROWINGS
COCKERNONIES
COCKERNONY
COCKEYEDLY
COCKEYEDNESS
COCKEYEDNESSES
COCKFIGHTING
COCKFIGHTINGS
COCKFIGHTS
COCKHORSES
COCKIELEEKIE
COCKIELEEKIES
COCKINESSES
COCKLEBOAT
COCKLEBOATS
COCKLEBURS

COCKLEERTS
COCKLESHELL
COCKLESHELLS
COCKMATCHES
COCKNEYDOM
COCKNEYDOMS
COCKNEYFICATION
COCKNEYFIED
COCKNEYFIES
COCKNEYFYING
COCKNEYISH
COCKNEYISM
COCKNEYISMS
COCKNIFICATION
COCKNIFICATIONS
COCKNIFIED
COCKNIFIES
COCKNIFYING
COCKROACHES
COCKSCOMBS
COCKSFOOTS
COCKSINESS
COCKSINESSES
COCKSUCKER
COCKSUCKERS
COCKSURELY
COCKSURENESS
COCKSURENESSES
COCKSWAINED
COCKSWAINING
COCKSWAINS
COCKTAILED
COCKTAILING
COCKTEASER
COCKTEASERS
COCKTHROWING
COCKTHROWINGS
COCKYLEEKIES
COCKYLEEKY
COCOMPOSER
COCOMPOSERS
COCONSCIOUS
COCONSCIOUSES
COCONSCIOUSNESS
COCONSPIRATOR
COCONSPIRATORS
COCOONERIES

COCOONINGS	CODIFICATION	COEMPLOYING	COERCIVENESSES	COFINANCED
COCOUNSELED	CODIFICATIONS	COEMPTIONS	COERCIVITIES	COFINANCES
COCOUNSELING	CODIRECTED	COENACTING	COERCIVITY	COFINANCING
COCOUNSELLED	CODIRECTING	COENAESTHESES	COERECTING	COFOUNDERS
COCOUNSELLING	CODIRECTION	COENAESTHESIA	COESSENTIAL	COFOUNDING
COCOUNSELS	CODIRECTIONS	COENAESTHESIAS	COESSENTIALITY	COFUNCTION
COCOZELLES	CODIRECTOR	COENAESTHESIS	COESSENTIALLY	COFUNCTIONS
COCREATING	CODIRECTORS	COENAMORED	COESSENTIALNESS	COGENERATION
COCREATORS	CODISCOVER	COENAMORING	COETANEOUS	COGENERATIONS
COCULTIVATE	CODISCOVERED	COENAMOURED	COETANEOUSLY	COGENERATOR
COCULTIVATED	CODISCOVERER	COENAMOURING	COETANEOUSNESS	COGENERATORS
COCULTIVATES	CODISCOVERERS	COENAMOURS	COETERNALLY	COGITATING
COCULTIVATING	CODISCOVERING	COENDURING	COETERNITIES	COGITATINGLY
COCULTIVATION	CODISCOVERS	COENENCHYMA	COETERNITY	COGITATION
COCULTIVATIONS	CODOLOGIES	COENENCHYMAS	COEVALITIES	COGITATIONS
COCULTURED	CODOMINANCE	COENENCHYMATA	COEVOLUTION	COGITATIVE
COCULTURES	CODOMINANCES	COENENCHYME	COEVOLUTIONARY	COGITATIVELY
COCULTURING	CODOMINANT	COENENCHYMES	COEVOLUTIONS	COGITATIVENESS
COCURATORS	CODOMINANTS	COENESTHESES	COEVOLVING	COGITATORS
COCURRICULAR	CODSWALLOP	COENESTHESIA	COEXECUTOR	COGNATENESS
COCUSWOODS	CODSWALLOPS	COENESTHESIAS	COEXECUTORS	COGNATENESSES
CODECLINATION	COEDUCATION	COENESTHESIS	COEXECUTRICES	COGNATIONS
CODECLINATIONS	COEDUCATIONAL	COENESTHETIC	COEXECUTRIX	COGNISABLE
CODEFENDANT	COEDUCATIONALLY	COENOBITES	COEXECUTRIXES	COGNISABLY
CODEFENDANTS	COEDUCATIONS	COENOBITIC	COEXERTING	COGNISANCE
CODEPENDENCE	COEFFICIENT	COENOBITICAL	COEXISTENCE	COGNISANCES
CODEPENDENCES	COEFFICIENTS	COENOBITISM	COEXISTENCES	COGNITIONAL
CODEPENDENCIES	COELACANTH	COENOBITISMS	COEXISTENT	COGNITIONS
CODEPENDENCY	COELACANTHIC	COENOCYTES	COEXISTING	COGNITIVELY
CODEPENDENT	COELACANTHS	COENOCYTIC	COEXTENDED	COGNITIVISM
CODEPENDENTS	COELANAGLYPHIC	COENOSARCS	COEXTENDING	COGNITIVISMS
CODERIVING	COELENTERA	COENOSPECIES	COEXTENSION	COGNITIVITIES
CODESIGNED	COELENTERATE	COENOSTEUM	COEXTENSIONS	COGNITIVITY
CODESIGNING	COELENTERATES	COENOSTEUMS	COEXTENSIVE	COGNIZABLE
CODETERMINATION	COELENTERIC	COENZYMATIC	COEXTENSIVELY	COGNIZABLY
CODEVELOPED	COELENTERON	COENZYMATICALLY	COFAVORITE	COGNIZANCE
CODEVELOPER	COELIOSCOPIES	COEQUALITIES	COFAVORITES	COGNIZANCES
CODEVELOPERS	COELIOSCOPY	COEQUALITY	COFEATURED	COGNOMINAL
CODEVELOPING	COELOMATES	COEQUALNESS	COFEATURES	COGNOMINALLY
CODEVELOPS	COELOMATIC	COEQUALNESSES	COFEATURING	COGNOMINATE
CODICILLARY	COELOSTATS	COEQUATING	COFFEEHOUSE	COGNOMINATED
CODICOLOGICAL	COELUROSAUR	COERCIMETER	COFFEEHOUSES	COGNOMINATES
CODICOLOGIES	COELUROSAURS	COERCIMETERS	COFFEEMAKER	COGNOMINATING
CODICOLOGY	COEMBODIED	COERCIONIST	COFFEEMAKERS	COGNOMINATION
CODIFIABILITIES	COEMBODIES	COERCIONISTS	COFFEEPOTS	COGNOMINATIONS
CODIFIABILITY	COEMBODYING	COERCIVELY	COFFERDAMS	COGNOSCENTE
CODIFIABLE	COEMPLOYED	COERCIVENESS	COFFINITES	COGNOSCENTI

COGNOSCIBLE	COINCIDENTLY	COLEMANITE	COLLAPSIBILITY	COLLECTIVISED
COGNOSCING	COINCIDING	COLEMANITES	COLLAPSIBLE	COLLECTIVISES
COHABITANT	COINFECTED	COLEOPTERA	COLLAPSING	COLLECTIVISING
COHABITANTS	COINFECTING	COLEOPTERAL	COLLARBONE	COLLECTIVISM
COHABITATION	COINFERRED	COLEOPTERAN	COLLARBONES	COLLECTIVISMS
COHABITATIONS	COINFERRING	COLEOPTERANS	COLLARETTE	COLLECTIVIST
COHABITEES	COINHERENCE	COLEOPTERIST	COLLARETTES	COLLECTIVISTIC
COHABITERS	COINHERENCES	COLEOPTERISTS	COLLARLESS	COLLECTIVISTS
COHABITING	COINHERING	COLEOPTERON	COLLARSTUD	COLLECTIVITIES
COHABITORS	COINHERITANCE	COLEOPTERONS	COLLARSTUDS	COLLECTIVITY
COHEIRESSES	COINHERITANCES	COLEOPTEROUS	COLLATABLE	COLLECTIVIZE
COHERENCES	COINHERITOR	COLEOPTERS	COLLATERAL	COLLECTIVIZED
COHERENCIES	COINHERITORS	COLEOPTILE	COLLATERALISE	COLLECTIVIZES
COHERENTLY	COINSTANTANEITY	COLEOPTILES	COLLATERALISED	COLLECTIVIZING
COHERITORS	COINSTANTANEOUS	COLEORHIZA	COLLATERALISES	COLLECTORATE
COHESIBILITIES	COINSURANCE	COLEORHIZAE	COLLATERALISING	COLLECTORATES
COHESIBILITY	COINSURANCES	COLEORHIZAS	COLLATERALITIES	COLLECTORS
COHESIONLESS	COINSURERS	COLEORRHIZA	COLLATERALITY	COLLECTORSHIP
COHESIVELY	COINSURING	COLEORRHIZAE	COLLATERALIZE	COLLECTORSHIPS
COHESIVENESS	COINTERRED	COLEORRHIZAS	COLLATERALIZED	COLLEGIALISM
COHESIVENESSES	COINTERRING	COLESTIPOL	COLLATERALIZES	COLLEGIALISMS
COHIBITING	COINTREAUS	COLESTIPOLS	COLLATERALIZING	COLLEGIALITIES
COHIBITION	COINVENTED	COLICKIEST	COLLATERALLY	COLLEGIALITY
COHIBITIONS	COINVENTING	COLICROOTS	COLLATERALS	COLLEGIALLY
COHIBITIVE	COINVENTOR	COLICWEEDS	COLLATIONS	COLLEGIANER
COHOBATING	COINVENTORS	COLINEARITIES	COLLEAGUED	COLLEGIANERS
COHOMOLOGICAL	COINVESTIGATOR	COLINEARITY	COLLEAGUES	COLLEGIANS
COHOMOLOGIES	COINVESTIGATORS	COLIPHAGES	COLLEAGUESHIP	COLLEGIATE
COHOMOLOGY	COINVESTOR	COLLABORATE	COLLEAGUESHIPS	COLLEGIATELY
COHORTATIVE	COKULORISES	COLLABORATED	COLLEAGUING	COLLEGIATES
COHORTATIVES	COLATITUDE	COLLABORATES	COLLECTABLE	COLLEGIUMS
COHOSTESSED	COLATITUDES	COLLABORATING	COLLECTABLES	COLLEMBOLAN
COHOSTESSES	COLCANNONS	COLLABORATION	COLLECTANEA	COLLEMBOLANS
COHOSTESSING	COLCHICINE	COLLABORATIONS	COLLECTEDLY	COLLEMBOLOUS
COHOUSINGS	COLCHICINES	COLLABORATIVE	COLLECTEDNESS	COLLENCHYMA
COHYPONYMS	COLCHICUMS	COLLABORATIVELY	COLLECTEDNESSES	COLLENCHYMAS
COIFFEUSES	COLCOTHARS	COLLABORATIVES	COLLECTIBLE	COLLENCHYMATA
COIFFURING	COLDBLOODS	COLLABORATOR	COLLECTIBLES	COLLENCHYMATOUS
COILABILITIES	COLDCOCKED	COLLABORATORS	COLLECTING	COLLETERIAL
COILABILITY	COLDCOCKING	COLLAGENASE	COLLECTINGS	COLLICULUS
COINCIDENCE	COLDHEARTED	COLLAGENASES	COLLECTION	COLLIERIES
COINCIDENCES	COLDHEARTEDLY	COLLAGENIC	COLLECTIONS	COLLIESHANGIE
COINCIDENCIES	COLDHEARTEDNESS	COLLAGENOUS	COLLECTIVE	COLLIESHANGIES
COINCIDENCY	COLDHOUSES	COLLAGISTS	COLLECTIVELY	COLLIGATED
COINCIDENT	COLDNESSES	COLLAPSABILITY	COLLECTIVENESS	COLLIGATES
COINCIDENTAL	COLECTOMIES	COLLAPSABLE	COLLECTIVES	COLLIGATING
COINCIDENTALLY		COLLAPSARS	COLLECTIVISE	COLLIGATION

COLLIGATIONS

C

COLLIGATIONS
COLLIGATIVE
COLLIMATED
COLLIMATES
COLLIMATING
COLLIMATION
COLLIMATIONS
COLLIMATOR
COLLIMATORS
COLLINEARITIES
COLLINEARITY
COLLINEARLY
COLLINSIAS
COLLIQUABLE
COLLIQUANT
COLLIQUATE
COLLIQUATED
COLLIQUATES
COLLIQUATING
COLLIQUATION
COLLIQUATIONS
COLLIQUATIVE
COLLIQUESCENCE
COLLIQUESCENCES
COLLISIONAL
COLLISIONALLY
COLLISIONS
COLLOCATED
COLLOCATES
COLLOCATING
COLLOCATION
COLLOCATIONAL
COLLOCATIONS
COLLOCUTOR
COLLOCUTORS
COLLOCUTORY
COLLODIONS
COLLODIUMS
COLLOGUING
COLLOIDALITIES
COLLOIDALITY
COLLOIDALLY
COLLOQUIAL
COLLOQUIALISM
COLLOQUIALISMS
COLLOQUIALIST
COLLOQUIALISTS

COLLOQUIALITIES
COLLOQUIALITY
COLLOQUIALLY
COLLOQUIALNESS
COLLOQUIALS
COLLOQUIED
COLLOQUIES
COLLOQUING
COLLOQUISE
COLLOQUISED
COLLOQUISES
COLLOQUISING
COLLOQUIST
COLLOQUISTS
COLLOQUIUM
COLLOQUIUMS
COLLOQUIZE
COLLOQUIZED
COLLOQUIZES
COLLOQUIZING
COLLOQUYING
COLLOTYPES
COLLOTYPIC
COLLOTYPIES
COLLUCTATION
COLLUCTATIONS
COLLUSIONS
COLLUSIVELY
COLLUVIUMS
COLLYRIUMS
COLLYWOBBLES
COLOBOMATA
COLOCATING
COLOCYNTHS
COLOGARITHM
COLOGARITHMS
COLOMBARDS
COLONELCIES
COLONELLING
COLONELLINGS
COLONELSHIP
COLONELSHIPS
COLONIALISE
COLONIALISED
COLONIALISES
COLONIALISING
COLONIALISM

COLONIALISMS
COLONIALIST
COLONIALISTIC
COLONIALISTS
COLONIALIZE
COLONIALIZED
COLONIALIZES
COLONIALIZING
COLONIALLY
COLONIALNESS
COLONIALNESSES
COLONISABLE
COLONISATION
COLONISATIONIST
COLONISATIONS
COLONISERS
COLONISING
COLONITISES
COLONIZABLE
COLONIZATION
COLONIZATIONIST
COLONIZATIONS
COLONIZERS
COLONIZING
COLONNADED
COLONNADES
COLONOSCOPE
COLONOSCOPES
COLONOSCOPIES
COLONOSCOPY
COLOPHONIES
COLOQUINTIDA
COLOQUINTIDAS
COLORABILITIES
COLORABILITY
COLORABLENESS
COLORABLENESSES
COLORATION
COLORATIONS
COLORATURA
COLORATURAS
COLORATURE
COLORATURES
COLORBREED
COLORBREEDING
COLORBREEDS
COLORCASTED

COLORCASTING
COLORCASTS
COLORECTAL
COLORFASTNESS
COLORFASTNESSES
COLORFULLY
COLORFULNESS
COLORFULNESSES
COLORIMETER
COLORIMETERS
COLORIMETRIC
COLORIMETRICAL
COLORIMETRIES
COLORIMETRY
COLORISATION
COLORISATIONS
COLORISERS
COLORISING
COLORISTIC
COLORISTICALLY
COLORIZATION
COLORIZATIONS
COLORIZERS
COLORIZING
COLORLESSLY
COLORLESSNESS
COLORLESSNESSES
COLORPOINT
COLORPOINTS
COLORWASHED
COLORWASHES
COLORWASHING
COLOSSALLY
COLOSSEUMS
COLOSSUSES
COLOSTOMIES
COLOSTROUS
COLOSTRUMS
COLOTOMIES
COLOURABILITIES
COLOURABILITY
COLOURABLE
COLOURABLENESS
COLOURABLY
COLOURANTS
COLOURATION
COLOURATIONS

COLOURBRED
COLOURBREED
COLOURBREEDING
COLOURBREEDS
COLOURCAST
COLOURCASTED
COLOURCASTING
COLOURCASTS
COLOURFAST
COLOURFASTNESS
COLOURFULLY
COLOURFULNESS
COLOURFULNESSES
COLOURINGS
COLOURISATION
COLOURISATIONS
COLOURISED
COLOURISER
COLOURISERS
COLOURISES
COLOURISING
COLOURISMS
COLOURISTIC
COLOURISTICALLY
COLOURISTS
COLOURIZATION
COLOURIZATIONS
COLOURIZED
COLOURIZER
COLOURIZERS
COLOURIZES
COLOURIZING
COLOURLESS
COLOURLESSLY
COLOURLESSNESS
COLOURPOINT
COLOURPOINTS
COLOURWASH
COLOURWASHED
COLOURWASHES
COLOURWASHING
COLOURWAYS
COLPITISES
COLPORTAGE
COLPORTAGES
COLPORTEUR
COLPORTEURS

COLPOSCOPE	COMBINATIONAL	COMFORTINGLY	COMMEMORATIVES	COMMENTORS
COLPOSCOPES	COMBINATIONS	COMFORTLESS	COMMEMORATOR	COMMERCIAL
COLPOSCOPICAL	COMBINATIVE	COMFORTLESSLY	COMMEMORATORS	COMMERCIALESE
COLPOSCOPICALLY	COMBINATORIAL	COMFORTLESSNESS	COMMEMORATORY	COMMERCIALESES
COLPOSCOPIES	COMBINATORIALLY	COMICALITIES	COMMENCEMENT	COMMERCIALISE
COLPOSCOPY	COMBINATORICS	COMICALITY	COMMENCEMENTS	COMMERCIALISED
COLPOTOMIES	COMBINATORY	COMICALNESS	COMMENCERS	COMMERCIALISES
COLTISHNESS	COMBININGS	COMICALNESSES	COMMENCING	COMMERCIALISING
COLTISHNESSES	COMBRETUMS	COMINGLING	COMMENDABLE	COMMERCIALISM
COLTSFOOTS	COMBURGESS	COMITADJIS	COMMENDABLENESS	COMMERCIALISMS
COLUBRIADS	COMBURGESSES	COMITATIVE	COMMENDABLY	COMMERCIALIST
COLUBRIFORM	COMBUSTIBILITY	COMITATIVES	COMMENDAMS	COMMERCIALISTIC
COLUMBARIA	COMBUSTIBLE	COMITATUSES	COMMENDATION	COMMERCIALISTS
COLUMBARIES	COMBUSTIBLENESS	COMMANDABLE	COMMENDATIONS	COMMERCIALITIES
COLUMBARIUM	COMBUSTIBLES	COMMANDANT	COMMENDATOR	COMMERCIALITY
COLUMBATES	COMBUSTIBLY	COMMANDANTS	COMMENDATORS	COMMERCIALIZE
COLUMBINES	COMBUSTING	COMMANDANTSHIP	COMMENDATORY	COMMERCIALIZED
COLUMBITES	COMBUSTION	COMMANDANTSHIPS	COMMENDERS	COMMERCIALIZES
COLUMBIUMS	COMBUSTIONS	COMMANDEER	COMMENDING	COMMERCIALIZING
COLUMELLAE	COMBUSTIOUS	COMMANDEERED	COMMENSALISM	COMMERCIALLY
COLUMELLAR	COMBUSTIVE	COMMANDEERING	COMMENSALISMS	COMMERCIALS
COLUMNARITIES	COMBUSTIVES	COMMANDEERS	COMMENSALITIES	COMMERCING
COLUMNARITY	COMBUSTORS	COMMANDERIES	COMMENSALITY	COMMERGING
COLUMNATED	COMEDDLING	COMMANDERS	COMMENSALLY	COMMINATED
COLUMNIATED	COMEDICALLY	COMMANDERSHIP	COMMENSALS	COMMINATES
COLUMNIATION	COMEDIENNE	COMMANDERSHIPS	COMMENSURABLE	COMMINATING
COLUMNIATIONS	COMEDIENNES	COMMANDERY	COMMENSURABLY	COMMINATION
COLUMNISTIC	COMEDIETTA	COMMANDING	COMMENSURATE	COMMINATIONS
COLUMNISTS	COMEDIETTAS	COMMANDINGLY	COMMENSURATELY	COMMINATIVE
COMANAGEMENT	COMEDOGENIC	COMMANDMENT	COMMENSURATION	COMMINATORY
COMANAGEMENTS	COMELINESS	COMMANDMENTS	COMMENSURATIONS	COMMINGLED
COMANAGERS	COMELINESSES	COMMANDOES	COMMENTARIAL	COMMINGLES
COMANAGING	COMESTIBLE	COMMEASURABLE	COMMENTARIAT	COMMINGLING
COMANCHERO	COMESTIBLES	COMMEASURE	COMMENTARIATS	COMMINUTED
COMANCHEROS	COMETOGRAPHIES	COMMEASURED	COMMENTARIES	COMMINUTES
COMATOSELY	COMETOGRAPHY	COMMEASURES	COMMENTARY	COMMINUTING
COMATULIDS	COMETOLOGIES	COMMEASURING	COMMENTATE	COMMINUTION
COMBATABLE	COMETOLOGY	COMMEMORABLE	COMMENTATED	COMMINUTIONS
COMBATANTS	COMEUPPANCE	COMMEMORATE	COMMENTATES	COMMISERABLE
COMBATIVELY	COMEUPPANCES	COMMEMORATED	COMMENTATING	COMMISERATE
COMBATIVENESS	COMFINESSES	COMMEMORATES	COMMENTATION	COMMISERATED
COMBATIVENESSES	COMFITURES	COMMEMORATING	COMMENTATIONS	COMMISERATES
COMBATTING	COMFORTABLE	COMMEMORATION	COMMENTATOR	COMMISERATING
COMBINABILITIES	COMFORTABLENESS	COMMEMORATIONAL	COMMENTATORIAL	COMMISERATINGLY
COMBINABILITY	COMFORTABLY	COMMEMORATIONS	COMMENTATORS	COMMISERATION
COMBINABLE	COMFORTERS	COMMEMORATIVE	COMMENTERS	COMMISERATIONS
COMBINATION	COMFORTING	COMMEMORATIVELY	COMMENTING	COMMISERATIVE

COMMISERATIVELY
COMMISERATOR
COMMISERATORS
COMMISSAIRE
COMMISSAIRES
COMMISSARIAL
COMMISSARIAT
COMMISSARIATS
COMMISSARIES
COMMISSARS
COMMISSARY
COMMISSARYSHIP
COMMISSARYSHIPS
COMMISSION
COMMISSIONAIRE
COMMISSIONAIRES
COMMISSIONAL
COMMISSIONARY
COMMISSIONED
COMMISSIONER
COMMISSIONERS
COMMISSIONING
COMMISSIONS
COMMISSURAL
COMMISSURE
COMMISSURES
COMMITMENT
COMMITMENTS
COMMITTABLE
COMMITTALS
COMMITTEEMAN
COMMITTEEMEN
COMMITTEES
COMMITTEESHIP
COMMITTEESHIPS
COMMITTEEWOMAN
COMMITTEEWOMEN
COMMITTERS
COMMITTING
COMMIXTION
COMMIXTIONS
COMMIXTURE
COMMIXTURES
COMMODIFICATION
COMMODIFIED
COMMODIFIES
COMMODIFYING

COMMODIOUS
COMMODIOUSLY
COMMODIOUSNESS
COMMODITIES
COMMODITISE
COMMODITISED
COMMODITISES
COMMODITISING
COMMODITIZE
COMMODITIZED
COMMODITIZES
COMMODITIZING
COMMODORES
COMMONABLE
COMMONAGES
COMMONALITIES
COMMONALITY
COMMONALTIES
COMMONALTY
COMMONHOLD
COMMONHOLDS
COMMONINGS
COMMONNESS
COMMONNESSES
COMMONPLACE
COMMONPLACED
COMMONPLACENESS
COMMONPLACES
COMMONPLACING
COMMONSENSE
COMMONSENSIBLE
COMMONSENSICAL
COMMONWEAL
COMMONWEALS
COMMONWEALTH
COMMONWEALTHS
COMMORANTS
COMMORIENTES
COMMOTIONAL
COMMOTIONS
COMMUNALISATION
COMMUNALISE
COMMUNALISED
COMMUNALISER
COMMUNALISERS
COMMUNALISES
COMMUNALISING

COMMUNALISM
COMMUNALISMS
COMMUNALIST
COMMUNALISTIC
COMMUNALISTS
COMMUNALITIES
COMMUNALITY
COMMUNALIZATION
COMMUNALIZE
COMMUNALIZED
COMMUNALIZER
COMMUNALIZERS
COMMUNALIZES
COMMUNALIZING
COMMUNALLY
COMMUNARDS
COMMUNAUTAIRE
COMMUNAUTAIRES
COMMUNICABILITY
COMMUNICABLE
COMMUNICABLY
COMMUNICANT
COMMUNICANTS
COMMUNICATE
COMMUNICATED
COMMUNICATEE
COMMUNICATEES
COMMUNICATES
COMMUNICATING
COMMUNICATION
COMMUNICATIONAL
COMMUNICATIONS
COMMUNICATIVE
COMMUNICATIVELY
COMMUNICATOR
COMMUNICATORS
COMMUNICATORY
COMMUNINGS
COMMUNIONAL
COMMUNIONALLY
COMMUNIONS
COMMUNIQUE
COMMUNIQUES
COMMUNISATION
COMMUNISATIONS
COMMUNISED
COMMUNISES

COMMUNISING
COMMUNISMS
COMMUNISTIC
COMMUNISTICALLY
COMMUNISTS
COMMUNITAIRE
COMMUNITAIRES
COMMUNITARIAN
COMMUNITARIANS
COMMUNITIES
COMMUNIZATION
COMMUNIZATIONS
COMMUNIZED
COMMUNIZES
COMMUNIZING
COMMUTABILITIES
COMMUTABILITY
COMMUTABLE
COMMUTABLENESS
COMMUTATED
COMMUTATES
COMMUTATING
COMMUTATION
COMMUTATIONS
COMMUTATIVE
COMMUTATIVELY
COMMUTATIVITIES
COMMUTATIVITY
COMMUTATOR
COMMUTATORS
COMMUTINGS
COMONOMERS
COMORBIDITIES
COMORBIDITY
COMPACTEDLY
COMPACTEDNESS
COMPACTEDNESSES
COMPACTERS
COMPACTEST
COMPACTIBLE
COMPACTIFIED
COMPACTIFIES
COMPACTIFY
COMPACTIFYING
COMPACTING
COMPACTION
COMPACTIONS

COMPACTNESS
COMPACTNESSES
COMPACTORS
COMPACTURE
COMPACTURES
COMPAGINATE
COMPAGINATED
COMPAGINATES
COMPAGINATING
COMPAGINATION
COMPAGINATIONS
COMPANDERS
COMPANDING
COMPANDORS
COMPANIABLE
COMPANIONABLE
COMPANIONABLY
COMPANIONATE
COMPANIONED
COMPANIONHOOD
COMPANIONHOODS
COMPANIONING
COMPANIONLESS
COMPANIONS
COMPANIONSHIP
COMPANIONSHIPS
COMPANIONWAY
COMPANIONWAYS
COMPANYING
COMPARABILITIES
COMPARABILITY
COMPARABLE
COMPARABLENESS
COMPARABLY
COMPARATIST
COMPARATISTS
COMPARATIVE
COMPARATIVELY
COMPARATIVENESS
COMPARATIVES
COMPARATIVIST
COMPARATIVISTS
COMPARATOR
COMPARATORS
COMPARISON
COMPARISONS
COMPARTING

COMPARTMENT	COMPENDIOUSLY	COMPLAINED	COMPLEXATION	COMPLICITOUS
COMPARTMENTAL	COMPENDIOUSNESS	COMPLAINER	COMPLEXATIONS	COMPLICITY
COMPARTMENTALLY	COMPENDIUM	COMPLAINERS	COMPLEXEDNESS	COMPLIMENT
COMPARTMENTED	COMPENDIUMS	COMPLAINING	COMPLEXEDNESSES	COMPLIMENTAL
COMPARTMENTING	COMPENSABILITY	COMPLAININGLY	COMPLEXEST	COMPLIMENTARILY
COMPARTMENTS	COMPENSABLE	COMPLAININGS	COMPLEXIFIED	COMPLIMENTARY
COMPASSABLE	COMPENSATE	COMPLAINTS	COMPLEXIFIES	COMPLIMENTED
COMPASSING	COMPENSATED	COMPLAISANCE	COMPLEXIFY	COMPLIMENTER
COMPASSINGS	COMPENSATES	COMPLAISANCES	COMPLEXIFYING	COMPLIMENTERS
COMPASSION	COMPENSATING	COMPLAISANT	COMPLEXING	COMPLIMENTING
COMPASSIONABLE	COMPENSATION	COMPLAISANTLY	COMPLEXION	COMPLIMENTS
COMPASSIONATE	COMPENSATIONAL	COMPLANATE	COMPLEXIONAL	COMPLISHED
COMPASSIONATED	COMPENSATIONS	COMPLANATION	COMPLEXIONED	COMPLISHES
COMPASSIONATELY	COMPENSATIVE	COMPLANATIONS	COMPLEXIONLESS	COMPLISHING
COMPASSIONATES	COMPENSATOR	COMPLEATED	COMPLEXIONS	COMPLOTTED
COMPASSIONATING	COMPENSATORS	COMPLEATING	COMPLEXITIES	COMPLOTTER
COMPASSIONED	COMPENSATORY	COMPLECTED	COMPLEXITY	COMPLOTTERS
COMPASSIONING	COMPESCING	COMPLECTING	COMPLEXNESS	COMPLOTTING
COMPASSIONLESS	COMPETENCE	COMPLEMENT	COMPLEXNESSES	COMPLUVIUM
COMPASSIONS	COMPETENCES	COMPLEMENTAL	COMPLEXOMETRIC	COMPLUVIUMS
COMPATIBILITIES	COMPETENCIES	COMPLEMENTALLY	COMPLEXONE	COMPONENCIES
COMPATIBILITY	COMPETENCY	COMPLEMENTARIES	COMPLEXONES	COMPONENCY
COMPATIBLE	COMPETENTLY	COMPLEMENTARILY	COMPLEXUSES	COMPONENTAL
COMPATIBLENESS	COMPETENTNESS	COMPLEMENTARITY	COMPLIABLE	COMPONENTIAL
COMPATIBLES	COMPETENTNESSES	COMPLEMENTARY	COMPLIABLENESS	COMPONENTS
COMPATIBLY	COMPETITION	COMPLEMENTATION	COMPLIABLY	COMPORTANCE
COMPATRIOT	COMPETITIONS	COMPLEMENTED	COMPLIANCE	COMPORTANCES
COMPATRIOTIC	COMPETITIVE	COMPLEMENTING	COMPLIANCES	COMPORTING
COMPATRIOTISM	COMPETITIVELY	COMPLEMENTISER	COMPLIANCIES	COMPORTMENT
COMPATRIOTISMS	COMPETITIVENESS	COMPLEMENTISERS	COMPLIANCY	COMPORTMENTS
COMPATRIOTS	COMPETITOR	COMPLEMENTIZER	COMPLIANTLY	COMPOSEDLY
COMPEARANCE	COMPETITORS	COMPLEMENTIZERS	COMPLIANTNESS	COMPOSEDNESS
COMPEARANCES	COMPILATION	COMPLEMENTS	COMPLIANTNESSES	COMPOSEDNESSES
COMPEARANT	COMPILATIONS	COMPLETABLE	COMPLICACIES	COMPOSITED
COMPEARANTS	COMPILATOR	COMPLETELY	COMPLICACY	COMPOSITELY
COMPEARING	COMPILATORS	COMPLETENESS	COMPLICANT	COMPOSITENESS
COMPEERING	COMPILATORY	COMPLETENESSES	COMPLICATE	COMPOSITENESSES
COMPELLABLE	COMPILEMENT	COMPLETERS	COMPLICATED	COMPOSITES
COMPELLABLY	COMPILEMENTS	COMPLETEST	COMPLICATEDLY	COMPOSITING
COMPELLATION	COMPLACENCE	COMPLETING	COMPLICATEDNESS	COMPOSITION
COMPELLATIONS	COMPLACENCES	COMPLETION	COMPLICATES	COMPOSITIONAL
COMPELLATIVE	COMPLACENCIES	COMPLETIONS	COMPLICATING	COMPOSITIONALLY
COMPELLATIVES	COMPLACENCY	COMPLETIST	COMPLICATION	COMPOSITIONS
COMPELLERS	COMPLACENT	COMPLETISTS	COMPLICATIONS	COMPOSITIVE
COMPELLING	COMPLACENTLY	COMPLETIVE	COMPLICATIVE	COMPOSITOR
COMPELLINGLY	COMPLAINANT	COMPLETORIES	COMPLICITIES	COMPOSITORIAL
COMPENDIOUS	COMPLAINANTS	COMPLETORY	COMPLICITLY	COMPOSITORS

C

COMPOSITOUS

COMPOSITOUS	COMPRESSIBLY	COMPULSIVITY	COMPUTERLESS	CONCEITFUL
COMPOSSIBILITY	COMPRESSING	COMPULSORIES	COMPUTERLIKE	CONCEITING
COMPOSSIBLE	COMPRESSION	COMPULSORILY	COMPUTERNIK	CONCEITLESS
COMPOSTABLE	COMPRESSIONAL	COMPULSORINESS	COMPUTERNIKS	CONCEIVABILITY
COMPOSTERS	COMPRESSIONS	COMPULSORY	COMPUTERPHOBE	CONCEIVABLE
COMPOSTING	COMPRESSIVE	COMPUNCTION	COMPUTERPHOBES	CONCEIVABLENESS
COMPOSTINGS	COMPRESSIVELY	COMPUNCTIONS	COMPUTERPHOBIA	CONCEIVABLY
COMPOSTURE	COMPRESSOR	COMPUNCTIOUS	COMPUTERPHOBIAS	CONCEIVERS
COMPOSTURED	COMPRESSORS	COMPUNCTIOUSLY	COMPUTERPHOBIC	CONCEIVING
COMPOSTURES	COMPRESSURE	COMPURGATION	COMPUTERPHOBICS	CONCELEBRANT
COMPOSTURING	COMPRESSURES	COMPURGATIONS	COMPUTINGS	CONCELEBRANTS
COMPOSURES	COMPRIMARIO	COMPURGATOR	COMPUTISTS	CONCELEBRATE
COMPOTATION	COMPRIMARIOS	COMPURGATORIAL	COMRADELINESS	CONCELEBRATED
COMPOTATIONS	COMPRINTED	COMPURGATORS	COMRADELINESSES	CONCELEBRATES
COMPOTATIONSHIP	COMPRINTING	COMPURGATORY	COMRADERIES	CONCELEBRATING
COMPOTATOR	COMPRISABLE	COMPURSION	COMRADESHIP	CONCELEBRATION
COMPOTATORS	COMPRISALS	COMPURSIONS	COMRADESHIPS	CONCELEBRATIONS
COMPOTATORY	COMPRISING	COMPUTABILITIES	COMSTOCKER	CONCENTERED
COMPOTIERS	COMPRIZING	COMPUTABILITY	COMSTOCKERIES	CONCENTERING
COMPOUNDABLE	COMPROMISE	COMPUTABLE	COMSTOCKERS	CONCENTERS
COMPOUNDED	COMPROMISED	COMPUTANTS	COMSTOCKERY	CONCENTRATE
COMPOUNDER	COMPROMISER	COMPUTATION	COMSTOCKISM	CONCENTRATED
COMPOUNDERS	COMPROMISERS	COMPUTATIONAL	COMSTOCKISMS	CONCENTRATEDLY
COMPOUNDING	COMPROMISES	COMPUTATIONALLY	CONACREISM	CONCENTRATES
COMPOUNDINGS	COMPROMISING	COMPUTATIONS	CONACREISMS	CONCENTRATING
COMPRADORE	COMPROMISINGLY	COMPUTATIVE	CONATIONAL	CONCENTRATION
COMPRADORES	COMPROVINCIAL	COMPUTATOR	CONCANAVALIN	CONCENTRATIONS
COMPRADORS	COMPTROLLED	COMPUTATORS	CONCANAVALINS	CONCENTRATIVE
COMPREHEND	COMPTROLLER	COMPUTERATE	CONCATENATE	CONCENTRATIVELY
COMPREHENDED	COMPTROLLERS	COMPUTERDOM	CONCATENATED	CONCENTRATOR
COMPREHENDIBLE	COMPTROLLERSHIP	COMPUTERDOMS	CONCATENATES	CONCENTRATORS
COMPREHENDING	COMPTROLLING	COMPUTERESE	CONCATENATING	CONCENTRED
COMPREHENDS	COMPTROLLS	COMPUTERESES	CONCATENATION	CONCENTRES
COMPREHENSIBLE	COMPULSATIVE	COMPUTERISABLE	CONCATENATIONS	CONCENTRIC
COMPREHENSIBLY	COMPULSATORY	COMPUTERISATION	CONCAVENESS	CONCENTRICAL
COMPREHENSION	COMPULSING	COMPUTERISE	CONCAVENESSES	CONCENTRICALLY
COMPREHENSIONS	COMPULSION	COMPUTERISED	CONCAVITIES	CONCENTRICITIES
COMPREHENSIVE	COMPULSIONIST	COMPUTERISES	CONCEALABLE	CONCENTRICITY
COMPREHENSIVELY	COMPULSIONISTS	COMPUTERISING	CONCEALERS	CONCENTRING
COMPREHENSIVES	COMPULSIONS	COMPUTERIST	CONCEALING	CONCEPTACLE
COMPREHENSIVISE	COMPULSITOR	COMPUTERISTS	CONCEALINGLY	CONCEPTACLES
COMPREHENSIVIZE	COMPULSITORS	COMPUTERIZABLE	CONCEALMENT	CONCEPTION
COMPRESSED	COMPULSIVE	COMPUTERIZATION	CONCEALMENTS	CONCEPTIONAL
COMPRESSEDLY	COMPULSIVELY	COMPUTERIZE	CONCEDEDLY	CONCEPTIONS
COMPRESSES	COMPULSIVENESS	COMPUTERIZED	CONCEITEDLY	CONCEPTIOUS
COMPRESSIBILITY	COMPULSIVES	COMPUTERIZES	CONCEITEDNESS	CONCEPTIVE
COMPRESSIBLE	COMPULSIVITIES	COMPUTERIZING	CONCEITEDNESSES	CONCEPTUAL

CONCEPTUALISE	CONCERTINO	CONCHOLOGISTS	CONCOLORATE	CONCRETIVELY
CONCEPTUALISED	CONCERTINOS	CONCHOLOGY	CONCOLOROUS	CONCRETIZATION
CONCEPTUALISER	CONCERTISE	CONCIERGES	CONCOMITANCE	CONCRETIZATIONS
CONCEPTUALISERS	CONCERTISED	CONCILIABLE	CONCOMITANCES	CONCRETIZE
CONCEPTUALISES	CONCERTISES	CONCILIARLY	CONCOMITANCIES	CONCRETIZED
CONCEPTUALISING	CONCERTISING	CONCILIARY	CONCOMITANCY	CONCRETIZES
CONCEPTUALISM	CONCERTIZE	CONCILIATE	CONCOMITANT	CONCRETIZING
CONCEPTUALISMS	CONCERTIZED	CONCILIATED	CONCOMITANTLY	CONCREWING
CONCEPTUALIST	CONCERTIZES	CONCILIATES	CONCOMITANTS	CONCUBINAGE
CONCEPTUALISTIC	CONCERTIZING	CONCILIATING	CONCORDANCE	CONCUBINAGES
CONCEPTUALISTS	CONCERTMASTER	CONCILIATION	CONCORDANCES	CONCUBINARIES
CONCEPTUALITIES	CONCERTMASTERS	CONCILIATIONS	CONCORDANT	CONCUBINARY
CONCEPTUALITY	CONCERTMEISTER	CONCILIATIVE	CONCORDANTLY	CONCUBINES
CONCEPTUALIZE	CONCERTMEISTERS	CONCILIATOR	CONCORDATS	CONCUBITANCIES
CONCEPTUALIZED	CONCERTMISTRESS	CONCILIATORILY	CONCORDIAL	CONCUBITANCY
CONCEPTUALIZER	CONCERTSTUCK	CONCILIATORS	CONCORDING	CONCUBITANT
CONCEPTUALIZERS	CONCERTSTUCKS	CONCILIATORY	CONCORPORATE	CONCUBITANTS
CONCEPTUALIZES	CONCESSIBLE	CONCINNITIES	CONCORPORATED	CONCUPISCENCE
CONCEPTUALIZING	CONCESSION	CONCINNITY	CONCORPORATES	CONCUPISCENCES
CONCEPTUALLY	CONCESSIONAIRE	CONCINNOUS	CONCORPORATING	CONCUPISCENT
CONCEPTUSES	CONCESSIONAIRES	CONCIPIENCIES	CONCOURSES	CONCUPISCIBLE
CONCERNANCIES	CONCESSIONAL	CONCIPIENCY	CONCREATED	CONCURRENCE
CONCERNANCY	CONCESSIONARIES	CONCIPIENT	CONCREATES	CONCURRENCES
CONCERNEDLY	CONCESSIONARY	CONCISENESS	CONCREATING	CONCURRENCIES
CONCERNEDNESS	CONCESSIONER	CONCISENESSES	CONCREMATION	CONCURRENCY
CONCERNEDNESSES	CONCESSIONERS	CONCISIONS	CONCREMATIONS	CONCURRENT
CONCERNING	CONCESSIONIST	CONCLAMATION	CONCRESCENCE	CONCURRENTLY
CONCERNMENT	CONCESSIONISTS	CONCLAMATIONS	CONCRESCENCES	CONCURRENTS
CONCERNMENTS	CONCESSIONNAIRE	CONCLAVISM	CONCRESCENT	CONCURRING
CONCERTANTE	CONCESSIONS	CONCLAVISMS	CONCRETELY	CONCURRINGLY
CONCERTANTES	CONCESSIVE	CONCLAVIST	CONCRETENESS	CONCUSSING
CONCERTANTI	CONCESSIVELY	CONCLAVISTS	CONCRETENESSES	CONCUSSION
CONCERTEDLY	CONCETTISM	CONCLUDERS	CONCRETING	CONCUSSIONS
CONCERTEDNESS	CONCETTISMS	CONCLUDING	CONCRETION	CONCUSSIVE
CONCERTEDNESSES	CONCETTIST	CONCLUSION	CONCRETIONARY	CONCYCLICALLY
CONCERTGOER	CONCETTISTS	CONCLUSIONARY	CONCRETIONS	CONDEMNABLE
CONCERTGOERS	CONCHIFEROUS	CONCLUSIONS	CONCRETISATION	CONDEMNABLY
CONCERTGOING	CONCHIFORM	CONCLUSIVE	CONCRETISATIONS	CONDEMNATION
CONCERTGOINGS	CONCHIGLIE	CONCLUSIVELY	CONCRETISE	CONDEMNATIONS
CONCERTINA	CONCHIOLIN	CONCLUSIVENESS	CONCRETISED	CONDEMNATORY
CONCERTINAED	CONCHIOLINS	CONCLUSORY	CONCRETISES	CONDEMNERS
CONCERTINAING	CONCHITISES	CONCOCTERS	CONCRETISING	CONDEMNING
CONCERTINAS	CONCHOIDAL	CONCOCTING	CONCRETISM	CONDEMNINGLY
CONCERTING	CONCHOIDALLY	CONCOCTION	CONCRETISMS	CONDEMNORS
CONCERTINI	CONCHOLOGICAL	CONCOCTIONS	CONCRETIST	CONDENSABILITY
CONCERTINIST	CONCHOLOGIES	CONCOCTIVE	CONCRETISTS	CONDENSABLE
CONCERTINISTS	CONCHOLOGIST	CONCOCTORS	CONCRETIVE	CONDENSATE

CONDENSATED
CONDENSATES
CONDENSATING
CONDENSATION
CONDENSATIONAL
CONDENSATIONS
CONDENSERIES
CONDENSERS
CONDENSERY
CONDENSIBILITY
CONDENSIBLE
CONDENSING
CONDESCEND
CONDESCENDED
CONDESCENDENCE
CONDESCENDENCES
CONDESCENDING
CONDESCENDINGLY
CONDESCENDS
CONDESCENSION
CONDESCENSIONS
CONDIDDLED
CONDIDDLES
CONDIDDLING
CONDIGNNESS
CONDIGNNESSES
CONDIMENTAL
CONDIMENTED
CONDIMENTING
CONDIMENTS
CONDISCIPLE
CONDISCIPLES
CONDITIONABLE
CONDITIONAL
CONDITIONALITY
CONDITIONALLY
CONDITIONALS
CONDITIONATE
CONDITIONATED
CONDITIONATES
CONDITIONATING
CONDITIONED
CONDITIONER
CONDITIONERS
CONDITIONING
CONDITIONINGS
CONDITIONS

CONDOLATORY
CONDOLEMENT
CONDOLEMENTS
CONDOLENCE
CONDOLENCES
CONDOLINGLY
CONDOMINIUM
CONDOMINIUMS
CONDONABLE
CONDONATION
CONDONATIONS
CONDOTTIERE
CONDOTTIERI
CONDUCEMENT
CONDUCEMENTS
CONDUCIBLE
CONDUCINGLY
CONDUCIVENESS
CONDUCIVENESSES
CONDUCTANCE
CONDUCTANCES
CONDUCTIBILITY
CONDUCTIBLE
CONDUCTIMETRIC
CONDUCTING
CONDUCTIOMETRIC
CONDUCTION
CONDUCTIONAL
CONDUCTIONS
CONDUCTIVE
CONDUCTIVELY
CONDUCTIVITIES
CONDUCTIVITY
CONDUCTOMETRIC
CONDUCTORIAL
CONDUCTORS
CONDUCTORSHIP
CONDUCTORSHIPS
CONDUCTRESS
CONDUCTRESSES
CONDUPLICATE
CONDUPLICATION
CONDUPLICATIONS
CONDYLOMAS
CONDYLOMATA
CONDYLOMATOUS
CONEFLOWER

CONEFLOWERS
CONFABBING
CONFABULAR
CONFABULATE
CONFABULATED
CONFABULATES
CONFABULATING
CONFABULATION
CONFABULATIONS
CONFABULATOR
CONFABULATORS
CONFABULATORY
CONFARREATE
CONFARREATION
CONFARREATIONS
CONFECTING
CONFECTION
CONFECTIONARIES
CONFECTIONARY
CONFECTIONER
CONFECTIONERIES
CONFECTIONERS
CONFECTIONERY
CONFECTIONS
CONFEDERACIES
CONFEDERACY
CONFEDERAL
CONFEDERATE
CONFEDERATED
CONFEDERATES
CONFEDERATING
CONFEDERATION
CONFEDERATIONS
CONFEDERATIVE
CONFERENCE
CONFERENCES
CONFERENCIER
CONFERENCIERS
CONFERENCING
CONFERENCINGS
CONFERENTIAL
CONFERMENT
CONFERMENTS
CONFERRABLE
CONFERRALS
CONFERREES
CONFERRENCE

CONFERRENCES
CONFERRERS
CONFERRING
CONFERVOID
CONFERVOIDS
CONFESSABLE
CONFESSANT
CONFESSANTS
CONFESSEDLY
CONFESSING
CONFESSION
CONFESSIONAL
CONFESSIONALISM
CONFESSIONALIST
CONFESSIONALLY
CONFESSIONALS
CONFESSIONARIES
CONFESSIONARY
CONFESSIONS
CONFESSORESS
CONFESSORESSES
CONFESSORS
CONFESSORSHIP
CONFESSORSHIPS
CONFIDANTE
CONFIDANTES
CONFIDANTS
CONFIDENCE
CONFIDENCES
CONFIDENCIES
CONFIDENCY
CONFIDENTIAL
CONFIDENTIALITY
CONFIDENTIALLY
CONFIDENTLY
CONFIDENTS
CONFIDINGLY
CONFIDINGNESS
CONFIDINGNESSES
CONFIGURATE
CONFIGURATED
CONFIGURATES
CONFIGURATING
CONFIGURATION
CONFIGURATIONAL
CONFIGURATIONS
CONFIGURATIVE

CONFIGURATOR
CONFIGURATORS
CONFIGURED
CONFIGURES
CONFIGURING
CONFINABLE
CONFINEABLE
CONFINEDLY
CONFINEDNESS
CONFINEDNESSES
CONFINELESS
CONFINEMENT
CONFINEMENTS
CONFIRMABILITY
CONFIRMABLE
CONFIRMAND
CONFIRMANDS
CONFIRMATION
CONFIRMATIONAL
CONFIRMATIONS
CONFIRMATIVE
CONFIRMATOR
CONFIRMATORS
CONFIRMATORY
CONFIRMEDLY
CONFIRMEDNESS
CONFIRMEDNESSES
CONFIRMEES
CONFIRMERS
CONFIRMING
CONFIRMINGS
CONFIRMORS
CONFISCABLE
CONFISCATABLE
CONFISCATE
CONFISCATED
CONFISCATES
CONFISCATING
CONFISCATION
CONFISCATIONS
CONFISCATOR
CONFISCATORS
CONFISCATORY
CONFISERIE
CONFISERIES
CONFISEURS
CONFITEORS

CONFITURES	CONFOUNDEDNESS	CONGENERICAL	CONGLUTINATING	CONGRUENCE
CONFLAGRANT	CONFOUNDER	CONGENERICS	CONGLUTINATION	CONGRUENCES
CONFLAGRATE	CONFOUNDERS	CONGENEROUS	CONGLUTINATIONS	CONGRUENCIES
CONFLAGRATED	CONFOUNDING	CONGENETIC	CONGLUTINATIVE	CONGRUENCY
CONFLAGRATES	CONFOUNDINGLY	CONGENIALITIES	CONGLUTINATOR	CONGRUENTLY
CONFLAGRATING	CONFRATERNAL	CONGENIALITY	CONGLUTINATORS	CONGRUITIES
CONFLAGRATION	CONFRATERNITIES	CONGENIALLY	CONGRATTERS	CONGRUOUSLY
CONFLAGRATIONS	CONFRATERNITY	CONGENIALNESS	CONGRATULABLE	CONGRUOUSNESS
CONFLAGRATIVE	CONFRERIES	CONGENIALNESSES	CONGRATULANT	CONGRUOUSNESSES
CONFLATING	CONFRONTAL	CONGENITAL	CONGRATULANTS	CONICITIES
CONFLATION	CONFRONTALS	CONGENITALLY	CONGRATULATE	CONIDIOPHORE
CONFLATIONS	CONFRONTATION	CONGENITALNESS	CONGRATULATED	CONIDIOPHORES
CONFLICTED	CONFRONTATIONAL	CONGESTIBLE	CONGRATULATES	CONIDIOPHOROUS
CONFLICTFUL	CONFRONTATIONS	CONGESTING	CONGRATULATING	CONIDIOSPORE
CONFLICTING	CONFRONTED	CONGESTION	CONGRATULATION	CONIDIOSPORES
CONFLICTINGLY	CONFRONTER	CONGESTIONS	CONGRATULATIONS	CONIFEROUS
CONFLICTION	CONFRONTERS	CONGESTIVE	CONGRATULATIVE	CONIOLOGIES
CONFLICTIONS	CONFRONTING	CONGIARIES	CONGRATULATOR	CONIROSTRAL
CONFLICTIVE	CONFRONTMENT	CONGLOBATE	CONGRATULATORS	CONJECTING
CONFLICTORY	CONFRONTMENTS	CONGLOBATED	CONGRATULATORY	CONJECTURABLE
CONFLICTUAL	CONFUSABILITIES	CONGLOBATES	CONGREEING	CONJECTURABLY
CONFLUENCE	CONFUSABILITY	CONGLOBATING	CONGREETED	CONJECTURAL
CONFLUENCES	CONFUSABLE	CONGLOBATION	CONGREETING	CONJECTURALLY
CONFLUENTLY	CONFUSABLES	CONGLOBATIONS	CONGREGANT	CONJECTURE
CONFLUENTS	CONFUSEDLY	CONGLOBING	CONGREGANTS	CONJECTURED
CONFOCALLY	CONFUSEDNESS	CONGLOBULATE	CONGREGATE	CONJECTURER
CONFORMABILITY	CONFUSEDNESSES	CONGLOBULATED	CONGREGATED	CONJECTURERS
CONFORMABLE	CONFUSIBLE	CONGLOBULATES	CONGREGATES	CONJECTURES
CONFORMABLENESS	CONFUSIBLES	CONGLOBULATING	CONGREGATING	CONJECTURING
CONFORMABLY	CONFUSINGLY	CONGLOBULATION	CONGREGATION	CONJOINERS
CONFORMANCE	CONFUSIONAL	CONGLOBULATIONS	CONGREGATIONAL	CONJOINING
CONFORMANCES	CONFUSIONS	CONGLOMERATE	CONGREGATIONS	CONJOINTLY
CONFORMATION	CONFUTABLE	CONGLOMERATED	CONGREGATIVE	CONJUGABLE
CONFORMATIONAL	CONFUTATION	CONGLOMERATES	CONGREGATOR	CONJUGALITIES
CONFORMATIONS	CONFUTATIONS	CONGLOMERATEUR	CONGREGATORS	CONJUGALITY
CONFORMERS	CONFUTATIVE	CONGLOMERATEURS	CONGRESSED	CONJUGALLY
CONFORMING	CONFUTEMENT	CONGLOMERATIC	CONGRESSES	CONJUGANTS
CONFORMINGLY	CONFUTEMENTS	CONGLOMERATING	CONGRESSING	CONJUGATED
CONFORMISM	CONGEALABLE	CONGLOMERATION	CONGRESSIONAL	CONJUGATELY
CONFORMISMS	CONGEALABLENESS	CONGLOMERATIONS	CONGRESSIONALLY	CONJUGATENESS
CONFORMIST	CONGEALERS	CONGLOMERATIVE	CONGRESSMAN	CONJUGATENESSES
CONFORMISTS	CONGEALING	CONGLOMERATOR	CONGRESSMEN	CONJUGATES
CONFORMITIES	CONGEALMENT	CONGLOMERATORS	CONGRESSPEOPLE	CONJUGATING
CONFORMITY	CONGEALMENTS	CONGLUTINANT	CONGRESSPERSON	CONJUGATINGS
CONFOUNDABLE	CONGELATION	CONGLUTINATE	CONGRESSPERSONS	CONJUGATION
CONFOUNDED	CONGELATIONS	CONGLUTINATED	CONGRESSWOMAN	CONJUGATIONAL
CONFOUNDEDLY	CONGENERIC	CONGLUTINATES	CONGRESSWOMEN	CONJUGATIONALLY

CONJUGATIONS	CONNATURALLY	CONNOTIVELY	CONSCIONABLE	CONSENTANEOUSLY
CONJUGATIVE	CONNATURALNESS	CONNUBIALISM	CONSCIONABLY	CONSENTERS
CONJUGATOR	CONNATURES	CONNUBIALISMS	CONSCIOUSES	CONSENTIENCE
CONJUGATORS	CONNECTABLE	CONNUBIALITIES	CONSCIOUSLY	CONSENTIENCES
CONJUNCTION	CONNECTEDLY	CONNUBIALITY	CONSCIOUSNESS	CONSENTIENT
CONJUNCTIONAL	CONNECTEDNESS	CONNUBIALLY	CONSCIOUSNESSES	CONSENTING
CONJUNCTIONALLY	CONNECTEDNESSES	CONNUMERATE	CONSCRIBED	CONSENTINGLY
CONJUNCTIONS	CONNECTERS	CONNUMERATED	CONSCRIBES	CONSEQUENCE
CONJUNCTIVA	CONNECTIBLE	CONNUMERATES	CONSCRIBING	CONSEQUENCED
CONJUNCTIVAE	CONNECTING	CONNUMERATING	CONSCRIPTED	CONSEQUENCES
CONJUNCTIVAL	CONNECTION	CONNUMERATION	CONSCRIPTING	CONSEQUENCING
CONJUNCTIVAS	CONNECTIONAL	CONNUMERATIONS	CONSCRIPTION	CONSEQUENT
CONJUNCTIVE	CONNECTIONISM	CONOIDALLY	CONSCRIPTIONAL	CONSEQUENTIAL
CONJUNCTIVELY	CONNECTIONISMS	CONOIDICAL	CONSCRIPTIONIST	CONSEQUENTIALLY
CONJUNCTIVENESS	CONNECTIONS	CONOMINEES	CONSCRIPTIONS	CONSEQUENTLY
CONJUNCTIVES	CONNECTIVE	CONOSCENTE	CONSCRIPTS	CONSEQUENTS
CONJUNCTIVITIS	CONNECTIVELY	CONOSCENTI	CONSECRATE	CONSERVABLE
CONJUNCTLY	CONNECTIVES	CONQUERABILITY	CONSECRATED	CONSERVANCIES
CONJUNCTURAL	CONNECTIVITIES	CONQUERABLE	CONSECRATEDNESS	CONSERVANCY
CONJUNCTURE	CONNECTIVITY	CONQUERABLENESS	CONSECRATES	CONSERVANT
CONJUNCTURES	CONNECTORS	CONQUERERS	CONSECRATING	CONSERVATION
CONJURATION	CONNEXIONAL	CONQUERESS	CONSECRATION	CONSERVATIONAL
CONJURATIONS	CONNEXIONS	CONQUERESSES	CONSECRATIONS	CONSERVATIONIST
CONJURATOR	CONNIPTION	CONQUERING	CONSECRATIVE	CONSERVATIONS
CONJURATORS	CONNIPTIONS	CONQUERINGLY	CONSECRATOR	CONSERVATISE
CONJUREMENT	CONNIVANCE	CONQUERORS	CONSECRATORS	CONSERVATISED
CONJUREMENTS	CONNIVANCES	CONQUISTADOR	CONSECRATORY	CONSERVATISES
CONJURINGS	CONNIVANCIES	CONQUISTADORES	CONSECTANEOUS	CONSERVATISING
CONNASCENCE	CONNIVANCY	CONQUISTADORS	CONSECTARIES	CONSERVATISM
CONNASCENCES	CONNIVENCE	CONSANGUINE	CONSECTARY	CONSERVATISMS
CONNASCENCIES	CONNIVENCES	CONSANGUINEOUS	CONSECUTION	CONSERVATIVE
CONNASCENCY	CONNIVENCIES	CONSANGUINITIES	CONSECUTIONS	CONSERVATIVELY
CONNASCENT	CONNIVENCY	CONSANGUINITY	CONSECUTIVE	CONSERVATIVES
CONNATENESS	CONNIVENTLY	CONSCIENCE	CONSECUTIVELY	CONSERVATIZE
CONNATENESSES	CONNIVERIES	CONSCIENCELESS	CONSECUTIVENESS	CONSERVATIZED
CONNATIONS	CONNIVINGLY	CONSCIENCES	CONSENESCENCE	CONSERVATIZES
CONNATURAL	CONNOISSEUR	CONSCIENTIOUS	CONSENESCENCES	CONSERVATIZING
CONNATURALISE	CONNOISSEURS	CONSCIENTIOUSLY	CONSENESCENCIES	CONSERVATOIRE
CONNATURALISED	CONNOISSEURSHIP	CONSCIENTISE	CONSENESCENCY	CONSERVATOIRES
CONNATURALISES	CONNOTATED	CONSCIENTISED	CONSENSION	CONSERVATOR
CONNATURALISING	CONNOTATES	CONSCIENTISES	CONSENSIONS	CONSERVATORIA
CONNATURALITIES	CONNOTATING	CONSCIENTISING	CONSENSUAL	CONSERVATORIAL
CONNATURALITY	CONNOTATION	CONSCIENTIZE	CONSENSUALLY	CONSERVATORIES
CONNATURALIZE	CONNOTATIONAL	CONSCIENTIZED	CONSENSUSES	CONSERVATORIUM
CONNATURALIZED	CONNOTATIONS	CONSCIENTIZES	CONSENTANEITIES	CONSERVATORIUMS
CONNATURALIZES	CONNOTATIVE	CONSCIENTIZING	CONSENTANEITY	CONSERVATORS
CONNATURALIZING	CONNOTATIVELY	CONSCIONABILITY	CONSENTANEOUS	CONSERVATORSHIP

CONSERVATORY	CONSIMILITIES	CONSONANCIES	CONSTABLEWICKS	CONSTITUTIONIST
CONSERVATRICES	CONSIMILITUDE	CONSONANCY	CONSTABULARIES	CONSTITUTIONS
CONSERVATRIX	CONSIMILITUDES	CONSONANTAL	CONSTABULARY	CONSTITUTIVE
CONSERVATRIXES	CONSIMILITY	CONSONANTALLY	CONSTANCIES	CONSTITUTIVELY
CONSERVERS	CONSISTENCE	CONSONANTLY	CONSTANTAN	CONSTITUTOR
CONSERVING	CONSISTENCES	CONSONANTS	CONSTANTANS	CONSTITUTORS
CONSIDERABLE	CONSISTENCIES	CONSORTABLE	CONSTANTLY	CONSTRAINABLE
CONSIDERABLES	CONSISTENCY	CONSORTERS	CONSTATATION	CONSTRAINED
CONSIDERABLY	CONSISTENT	CONSORTIAL	CONSTATATIONS	CONSTRAINEDLY
CONSIDERANCE	CONSISTENTLY	CONSORTING	CONSTATING	CONSTRAINER
CONSIDERANCES	CONSISTING	CONSORTISM	CONSTATIVE	CONSTRAINERS
CONSIDERATE	CONSISTORIAL	CONSORTISMS	CONSTATIVES	CONSTRAINING
CONSIDERATELY	CONSISTORIAN	CONSORTIUM	CONSTELLATE	CONSTRAINS
CONSIDERATENESS	CONSISTORIES	CONSORTIUMS	CONSTELLATED	CONSTRAINT
CONSIDERATION	CONSISTORY	CONSPECIFIC	CONSTELLATES	CONSTRAINTS
CONSIDERATIONS	CONSOCIATE	CONSPECIFICS	CONSTELLATING	CONSTRICTED
CONSIDERATIVE	CONSOCIATED	CONSPECTUITIES	CONSTELLATION	CONSTRICTING
CONSIDERATIVELY	CONSOCIATES	CONSPECTUITY	CONSTELLATIONAL	CONSTRICTION
CONSIDERED	CONSOCIATING	CONSPECTUS	CONSTELLATIONS	CONSTRICTIONS
CONSIDERER	CONSOCIATION	CONSPECTUSES	CONSTELLATORY	CONSTRICTIVE
CONSIDERERS	CONSOCIATIONAL	CONSPICUITIES	CONSTERING	CONSTRICTIVELY
CONSIDERING	CONSOCIATIONS	CONSPICUITY	CONSTERNATE	CONSTRICTOR
CONSIDERINGLY	CONSOLABLE	CONSPICUOUS	CONSTERNATED	CONSTRICTORS
CONSIGLIERE	CONSOLATED	CONSPICUOUSLY	CONSTERNATES	CONSTRICTS
CONSIGLIERES	CONSOLATES	CONSPICUOUSNESS	CONSTERNATING	CONSTRINGE
CONSIGLIERI	CONSOLATING	CONSPIRACIES	CONSTERNATION	CONSTRINGED
CONSIGNABLE	CONSOLATION	CONSPIRACY	CONSTERNATIONS	CONSTRINGENCE
CONSIGNATION	CONSOLATIONS	CONSPIRANT	CONSTIPATE	CONSTRINGENCES
CONSIGNATIONS	CONSOLATORIES	CONSPIRANTS	CONSTIPATED	CONSTRINGENCIES
CONSIGNATORIES	CONSOLATORY	CONSPIRATION	CONSTIPATES	CONSTRINGENCY
CONSIGNATORY	CONSOLATRICES	CONSPIRATIONAL	CONSTIPATING	CONSTRINGENT
CONSIGNEES	CONSOLATRIX	CONSPIRATIONS	CONSTIPATION	CONSTRINGES
CONSIGNERS	CONSOLATRIXES	CONSPIRATOR	CONSTIPATIONS	CONSTRINGING
CONSIGNIFIED	CONSOLEMENT	CONSPIRATORIAL	CONSTITUENCIES	CONSTRUABILITY
CONSIGNIFIES	CONSOLEMENTS	CONSPIRATORS	CONSTITUENCY	CONSTRUABLE
CONSIGNIFY	CONSOLIDATE	CONSPIRATORY	CONSTITUENT	CONSTRUALS
CONSIGNIFYING	CONSOLIDATED	CONSPIRATRESS	CONSTITUENTLY	CONSTRUCTABLE
CONSIGNING	CONSOLIDATES	CONSPIRATRESSES	CONSTITUENTS	CONSTRUCTED
CONSIGNMENT	CONSOLIDATING	CONSPIRERS	CONSTITUTE	CONSTRUCTER
CONSIGNMENTS	CONSOLIDATION	CONSPIRING	CONSTITUTED	CONSTRUCTERS
CONSIGNORS	CONSOLIDATIONS	CONSPIRINGLY	CONSTITUTER	CONSTRUCTIBLE
CONSILIENCE	CONSOLIDATIVE	CONSPURCATION	CONSTITUTERS	CONSTRUCTING
CONSILIENCES	CONSOLIDATOR	CONSPURCATIONS	CONSTITUTES	CONSTRUCTION
CONSILIENT	CONSOLIDATORS	CONSTABLES	CONSTITUTING	CONSTRUCTIONAL
CONSIMILAR	CONSOLINGLY	CONSTABLESHIP	CONSTITUTION	CONSTRUCTIONISM
CONSIMILARITIES	CONSONANCE	CONSTABLESHIPS	CONSTITUTIONAL	CONSTRUCTIONIST
CONSIMILARITY	CONSONANCES	CONSTABLEWICK	CONSTITUTIONALS	CONSTRUCTIONS

CONSTRUCTIVE	CONSULTIVE	CONTAGIONISTS	CONTEMPERATURE	CONTENEMENT
CONSTRUCTIVELY	CONSULTORS	CONTAGIONS	CONTEMPERATURES	CONTENEMENTS
CONSTRUCTIVISM	CONSULTORY	CONTAGIOUS	CONTEMPERED	CONTENTATION
CONSTRUCTIVISMS	CONSUMABLE	CONTAGIOUSLY	CONTEMPERING	CONTENTATIONS
CONSTRUCTIVIST	CONSUMABLES	CONTAGIOUSNESS	CONTEMPERS	CONTENTEDLY
CONSTRUCTIVISTS	CONSUMEDLY	CONTAINABLE	CONTEMPLABLE	CONTENTEDNESS
CONSTRUCTOR	CONSUMERISM	CONTAINERBOARD	CONTEMPLANT	CONTENTEDNESSES
CONSTRUCTORS	CONSUMERISMS	CONTAINERBOARDS	CONTEMPLANTS	CONTENTING
CONSTRUCTS	CONSUMERIST	CONTAINERISE	CONTEMPLATE	CONTENTION
CONSTRUCTURE	CONSUMERISTIC	CONTAINERISED	CONTEMPLATED	CONTENTIONS
CONSTRUCTURES	CONSUMERISTS	CONTAINERISES	CONTEMPLATES	CONTENTIOUS
CONSTRUERS	CONSUMERSHIP	CONTAINERISING	CONTEMPLATING	CONTENTIOUSLY
CONSTRUING	CONSUMERSHIPS	CONTAINERIZE	CONTEMPLATION	CONTENTIOUSNESS
CONSTUPRATE	CONSUMINGLY	CONTAINERIZED	CONTEMPLATIONS	CONTENTLESS
CONSTUPRATED	CONSUMINGS	CONTAINERIZES	CONTEMPLATIST	CONTENTMENT
CONSTUPRATES	CONSUMMATE	CONTAINERIZING	CONTEMPLATISTS	CONTENTMENTS
CONSTUPRATING	CONSUMMATED	CONTAINERLESS	CONTEMPLATIVE	CONTERMINAL
CONSTUPRATION	CONSUMMATELY	CONTAINERPORT	CONTEMPLATIVELY	CONTERMINALLY
CONSTUPRATIONS	CONSUMMATES	CONTAINERPORTS	CONTEMPLATIVES	CONTERMINANT
CONSUBSIST	CONSUMMATING	CONTAINERS	CONTEMPLATOR	CONTERMINATE
CONSUBSISTED	CONSUMMATION	CONTAINERSHIP	CONTEMPLATORS	CONTERMINOUS
CONSUBSISTING	CONSUMMATIONS	CONTAINERSHIPS	CONTEMPORANEAN	CONTERMINOUSLY
CONSUBSISTS	CONSUMMATIVE	CONTAINING	CONTEMPORANEANS	CONTESSERATION
CONSUBSTANTIAL	CONSUMMATOR	CONTAINMENT	CONTEMPORANEITY	CONTESSERATIONS
CONSUBSTANTIATE	CONSUMMATORS	CONTAINMENTS	CONTEMPORANEOUS	CONTESTABILITY
CONSUETUDE	CONSUMMATORY	CONTAMINABLE	CONTEMPORARIES	CONTESTABLE
CONSUETUDES	CONSUMPTION	CONTAMINANT	CONTEMPORARILY	CONTESTABLENESS
CONSUETUDINARY	CONSUMPTIONS	CONTAMINANTS	CONTEMPORARY	CONTESTABLY
CONSULAGES	CONSUMPTIVE	CONTAMINATE	CONTEMPORISE	CONTESTANT
CONSULATES	CONSUMPTIVELY	CONTAMINATED	CONTEMPORISED	CONTESTANTS
CONSULSHIP	CONSUMPTIVENESS	CONTAMINATES	CONTEMPORISES	CONTESTATION
CONSULSHIPS	CONSUMPTIVES	CONTAMINATING	CONTEMPORISING	CONTESTATIONS
CONSULTABLE	CONSUMPTIVITIES	CONTAMINATION	CONTEMPORIZE	CONTESTERS
CONSULTANCIES	CONSUMPTIVITY	CONTAMINATIONS	CONTEMPORIZED	CONTESTING
CONSULTANCY	CONTABESCENCE	CONTAMINATIVE	CONTEMPORIZES	CONTESTINGLY
CONSULTANT	CONTABESCENCES	CONTAMINATOR	CONTEMPORIZING	CONTEXTLESS
CONSULTANTS	CONTABESCENT	CONTAMINATORS	CONTEMPTIBILITY	CONTEXTUAL
CONSULTANTSHIP	CONTACTABLE	CONTANGOED	CONTEMPTIBLE	CONTEXTUALISE
CONSULTANTSHIPS	CONTACTEES	CONTANGOES	CONTEMPTIBLY	CONTEXTUALISED
CONSULTATION	CONTACTING	CONTANGOING	CONTEMPTUOUS	CONTEXTUALISES
CONSULTATIONS	CONTACTLESS	CONTEMNERS	CONTEMPTUOUSLY	CONTEXTUALISING
CONSULTATIVE	CONTACTORS	CONTEMNIBLE	CONTENDENT	CONTEXTUALIZE
CONSULTATIVELY	CONTACTUAL	CONTEMNIBLY	CONTENDENTS	CONTEXTUALIZED
CONSULTATORY	CONTACTUALLY	CONTEMNING	CONTENDERS	CONTEXTUALIZES
CONSULTEES	CONTADINAS	CONTEMNORS	CONTENDING	CONTEXTUALIZING
CONSULTERS	CONTADINOS	CONTEMPERATION	CONTENDINGLY	CONTEXTUALLY
CONSULTING	CONTAGIONIST	CONTEMPERATIONS	CONTENDINGS	CONTEXTURAL

CONTEXTURE
CONTEXTURES
CONTIGNATION
CONTIGNATIONS
CONTIGUITIES
CONTIGUITY
CONTIGUOUS
CONTIGUOUSLY
CONTIGUOUSNESS
CONTINENCE
CONTINENCES
CONTINENCIES
CONTINENCY
CONTINENTAL
CONTINENTALISM
CONTINENTALISMS
CONTINENTALIST
CONTINENTALISTS
CONTINENTALLY
CONTINENTALS
CONTINENTLY
CONTINENTS
CONTINGENCE
CONTINGENCES
CONTINGENCIES
CONTINGENCY
CONTINGENT
CONTINGENTLY
CONTINGENTS
CONTINUABLE
CONTINUALITIES
CONTINUALITY
CONTINUALLY
CONTINUALNESS
CONTINUALNESSES
CONTINUANCE
CONTINUANCES
CONTINUANT
CONTINUANTS
CONTINUATE
CONTINUATION
CONTINUATIONS
CONTINUATIVE
CONTINUATIVELY
CONTINUATIVES
CONTINUATOR
CONTINUATORS

CONTINUEDLY
CONTINUEDNESS
CONTINUEDNESSES
CONTINUERS
CONTINUING
CONTINUINGLY
CONTINUITIES
CONTINUITY
CONTINUOUS
CONTINUOUSLY
CONTINUOUSNESS
CONTINUUMS
CONTORNIATE
CONTORNIATES
CONTORTEDLY
CONTORTEDNESS
CONTORTEDNESSES
CONTORTING
CONTORTION
CONTORTIONAL
CONTORTIONATE
CONTORTIONED
CONTORTIONISM
CONTORTIONISMS
CONTORTIONIST
CONTORTIONISTIC
CONTORTIONISTS
CONTORTIONS
CONTORTIVE
CONTOURING
CONTRABAND
CONTRABANDISM
CONTRABANDISMS
CONTRABANDIST
CONTRABANDISTS
CONTRABANDS
CONTRABASS
CONTRABASSES
CONTRABASSI
CONTRABASSIST
CONTRABASSISTS
CONTRABASSO
CONTRABASSOON
CONTRABASSOONS
CONTRABASSOS
CONTRABBASSI
CONTRABBASSO

CONTRABBASSOS
CONTRACEPTION
CONTRACEPTIONS
CONTRACEPTIVE
CONTRACEPTIVES
CONTRACLOCKWISE
CONTRACTABILITY
CONTRACTABLE
CONTRACTABLY
CONTRACTED
CONTRACTEDLY
CONTRACTEDNESS
CONTRACTIBILITY
CONTRACTIBLE
CONTRACTIBLY
CONTRACTILE
CONTRACTILITIES
CONTRACTILITY
CONTRACTING
CONTRACTION
CONTRACTIONAL
CONTRACTIONARY
CONTRACTIONS
CONTRACTIVE
CONTRACTIVELY
CONTRACTIVENESS
CONTRACTOR
CONTRACTORS
CONTRACTUAL
CONTRACTUALLY
CONTRACTURAL
CONTRACTURE
CONTRACTURES
CONTRACYCLICAL
CONTRADANCE
CONTRADANCES
CONTRADICT
CONTRADICTABLE
CONTRADICTED
CONTRADICTER
CONTRADICTERS
CONTRADICTING
CONTRADICTION
CONTRADICTIONS
CONTRADICTIOUS
CONTRADICTIVE
CONTRADICTIVELY

CONTRADICTOR
CONTRADICTORIES
CONTRADICTORILY
CONTRADICTORS
CONTRADICTORY
CONTRADICTS
CONTRAFAGOTTI
CONTRAFAGOTTO
CONTRAFAGOTTOS
CONTRAFLOW
CONTRAFLOWS
CONTRAGESTION
CONTRAGESTIONS
CONTRAGESTIVE
CONTRAGESTIVES
CONTRAHENT
CONTRAHENTS
CONTRAINDICANT
CONTRAINDICANTS
CONTRAINDICATE
CONTRAINDICATED
CONTRAINDICATES
CONTRALATERAL
CONTRALTOS
CONTRANATANT
CONTRAOCTAVE
CONTRAOCTAVES
CONTRAPLEX
CONTRAPOSITION
CONTRAPOSITIONS
CONTRAPOSITIVE
CONTRAPOSITIVES
CONTRAPPOSTO
CONTRAPPOSTOS
CONTRAPROP
CONTRAPROPELLER
CONTRAPROPS
CONTRAPTION
CONTRAPTIONS
CONTRAPUNTAL
CONTRAPUNTALIST
CONTRAPUNTALLY
CONTRAPUNTIST
CONTRAPUNTISTS
CONTRARIAN
CONTRARIANS
CONTRARIED

CONTRARIES
CONTRARIETIES
CONTRARIETY
CONTRARILY
CONTRARINESS
CONTRARINESSES
CONTRARIOUS
CONTRARIOUSLY
CONTRARIOUSNESS
CONTRARIWISE
CONTRARYING
CONTRASEXUAL
CONTRASEXUALS
CONTRASTABLE
CONTRASTABLY
CONTRASTED
CONTRASTING
CONTRASTIVE
CONTRASTIVELY
CONTRATERRENE
CONTRAVALLATION
CONTRAVENE
CONTRAVENED
CONTRAVENER
CONTRAVENERS
CONTRAVENES
CONTRAVENING
CONTRAVENTION
CONTRAVENTIONS
CONTRAYERVA
CONTRAYERVAS
CONTRECOUP
CONTRECOUPS
CONTREDANCE
CONTREDANCES
CONTREDANSE
CONTREDANSES
CONTRETEMPS
CONTRIBUTABLE
CONTRIBUTARIES
CONTRIBUTARY
CONTRIBUTE
CONTRIBUTED
CONTRIBUTES
CONTRIBUTING
CONTRIBUTION
CONTRIBUTIONS

C

CONTRIBUTIVE
CONTRIBUTIVELY
CONTRIBUTOR
CONTRIBUTORIES
CONTRIBUTORS
CONTRIBUTORY
CONTRISTATION
CONTRISTATIONS
CONTRISTED
CONTRISTING
CONTRITELY
CONTRITENESS
CONTRITENESSES
CONTRITION
CONTRITIONS
CONTRITURATE
CONTRITURATED
CONTRITURATES
CONTRITURATING
CONTRIVABLE
CONTRIVANCE
CONTRIVANCES
CONTRIVEMENT
CONTRIVEMENTS
CONTRIVERS
CONTRIVING
CONTROLLABILITY
CONTROLLABLE
CONTROLLABLY
CONTROLLED
CONTROLLER
CONTROLLERS
CONTROLLERSHIP
CONTROLLERSHIPS
CONTROLLING
CONTROLMENT
CONTROLMENTS
CONTROULED
CONTROULING
CONTROVERSE
CONTROVERSES
CONTROVERSIAL
CONTROVERSIALLY
CONTROVERSIES
CONTROVERSY
CONTROVERT
CONTROVERTED

CONTROVERTER
CONTROVERTERS
CONTROVERTIBLE
CONTROVERTIBLY
CONTROVERTING
CONTROVERTIST
CONTROVERTISTS
CONTROVERTS
CONTUBERNAL
CONTUBERNYAL
CONTUMACIES
CONTUMACIOUS
CONTUMACIOUSLY
CONTUMACITIES
CONTUMACITY
CONTUMELIES
CONTUMELIOUS
CONTUMELIOUSLY
CONTUNDING
CONTUSIONED
CONTUSIONS
CONUNDRUMS
CONURBATION
CONURBATIONS
CONVALESCE
CONVALESCED
CONVALESCENCE
CONVALESCENCES
CONVALESCENCIES
CONVALESCENCY
CONVALESCENT
CONVALESCENTLY
CONVALESCENTS
CONVALESCES
CONVALESCING
CONVECTING
CONVECTION
CONVECTIONAL
CONVECTIONS
CONVECTIVE
CONVECTORS
CONVENABLE
CONVENANCE
CONVENANCES
CONVENERSHIP
CONVENERSHIPS
CONVENIENCE

CONVENIENCES
CONVENIENCIES
CONVENIENCY
CONVENIENT
CONVENIENTLY
CONVENINGS
CONVENORSHIP
CONVENORSHIPS
CONVENTICLE
CONVENTICLED
CONVENTICLER
CONVENTICLERS
CONVENTICLES
CONVENTICLING
CONVENTING
CONVENTION
CONVENTIONAL
CONVENTIONALISE
CONVENTIONALISM
CONVENTIONALIST
CONVENTIONALITY
CONVENTIONALIZE
CONVENTIONALLY
CONVENTIONALS
CONVENTIONARY
CONVENTIONEER
CONVENTIONEERS
CONVENTIONER
CONVENTIONERS
CONVENTIONIST
CONVENTIONISTS
CONVENTIONS
CONVENTUAL
CONVENTUALLY
CONVENTUALS
CONVERGENCE
CONVERGENCES
CONVERGENCIES
CONVERGENCY
CONVERGENT
CONVERGING
CONVERSABLE
CONVERSABLENESS
CONVERSABLY
CONVERSANCE
CONVERSANCES
CONVERSANCIES

CONVERSANCY
CONVERSANT
CONVERSANTLY
CONVERSATION
CONVERSATIONAL
CONVERSATIONISM
CONVERSATIONIST
CONVERSATIONS
CONVERSATIVE
CONVERSAZIONE
CONVERSAZIONES
CONVERSAZIONI
CONVERSELY
CONVERSERS
CONVERSING
CONVERSION
CONVERSIONAL
CONVERSIONARY
CONVERSIONS
CONVERTAPLANE
CONVERTAPLANES
CONVERTEND
CONVERTENDS
CONVERTERS
CONVERTIBILITY
CONVERTIBLE
CONVERTIBLENESS
CONVERTIBLES
CONVERTIBLY
CONVERTING
CONVERTIPLANE
CONVERTIPLANES
CONVERTITE
CONVERTITES
CONVERTIVE
CONVERTOPLANE
CONVERTOPLANES
CONVERTORS
CONVEXEDLY
CONVEXITIES
CONVEXNESS
CONVEXNESSES
CONVEYABLE
CONVEYANCE
CONVEYANCER
CONVEYANCERS
CONVEYANCES

CONVEYANCING
CONVEYANCINGS
CONVEYORISATION
CONVEYORISE
CONVEYORISED
CONVEYORISES
CONVEYORISING
CONVEYORIZATION
CONVEYORIZE
CONVEYORIZED
CONVEYORIZES
CONVEYORIZING
CONVICINITIES
CONVICINITY
CONVICTABLE
CONVICTIBLE
CONVICTING
CONVICTION
CONVICTIONAL
CONVICTIONS
CONVICTISM
CONVICTISMS
CONVICTIVE
CONVICTIVELY
CONVINCEMENT
CONVINCEMENTS
CONVINCERS
CONVINCIBLE
CONVINCING
CONVINCINGLY
CONVINCINGNESS
CONVIVIALIST
CONVIVIALISTS
CONVIVIALITIES
CONVIVIALITY
CONVIVIALLY
CONVOCATED
CONVOCATES
CONVOCATING
CONVOCATION
CONVOCATIONAL
CONVOCATIONIST
CONVOCATIONISTS
CONVOCATIONS
CONVOCATIVE
CONVOCATOR
CONVOCATORS

CONVOLUTED	COOPERATIVE	COPILOTING	COPROCESSINGS	COPULATION
CONVOLUTEDLY	COOPERATIVELY	COPINGSTONE	COPROCESSOR	COPULATIONS
CONVOLUTEDNESS	COOPERATIVENESS	COPINGSTONES	COPROCESSORS	COPULATIVE
CONVOLUTELY	COOPERATIVES	COPIOUSNESS	COPRODUCED	COPULATIVELY
CONVOLUTES	COOPERATIVITIES	COPIOUSNESSES	COPRODUCER	COPULATIVES
CONVOLUTING	COOPERATIVITY	COPLANARITIES	COPRODUCERS	COPULATORY
CONVOLUTION	COOPERATOR	COPLANARITY	COPRODUCES	COPURIFIED
CONVOLUTIONAL	COOPERATORS	COPLOTTING	COPRODUCING	COPURIFIES
CONVOLUTIONARY	COOPERINGS	COPLOTTINGS	COPRODUCTION	COPURIFYING
CONVOLUTIONS	COOPTATION	COPOLYMERIC	COPRODUCTIONS	COPYCATTED
CONVOLVING	COOPTATIONS	COPOLYMERISE	COPRODUCTS	COPYCATTING
CONVOLVULACEOUS	COOPTATIVE	COPOLYMERISED	COPROLALIA	COPYEDITED
CONVOLVULI	COORDINANCE	COPOLYMERISES	COPROLALIAC	COPYEDITING
CONVOLVULUS	COORDINANCES	COPOLYMERISING	COPROLALIAS	COPYFIGHTS
CONVOLVULUSES	COORDINATE	COPOLYMERIZE	COPROLITES	COPYGRAPHS
CONVULSANT	COORDINATED	COPOLYMERIZED	COPROLITHS	COPYHOLDER
CONVULSANTS	COORDINATELY	COPOLYMERIZES	COPROLITIC	COPYHOLDERS
CONVULSIBLE	COORDINATENESS	COPOLYMERIZING	COPROLOGIES	COPYLEFTED
CONVULSING	COORDINATES	COPOLYMERS	COPROMOTER	COPYLEFTING
CONVULSION	COORDINATING	COPPERASES	COPROMOTERS	COPYREADER
CONVULSIONAL	COORDINATION	COPPERHEAD	COPROPHAGAN	COPYREADERS
CONVULSIONARIES	COORDINATIONS	COPPERHEADS	COPROPHAGANS	COPYREADING
CONVULSIONARY	COORDINATIVE	COPPERINGS	COPROPHAGIC	COPYREADINGS
CONVULSIONIST	COORDINATOR	COPPERPLATE	COPROPHAGIES	COPYRIGHTABLE
CONVULSIONISTS	COORDINATORS	COPPERPLATES	COPROPHAGIST	COPYRIGHTED
CONVULSIONS	COPARCENARIES	COPPERSKIN	COPROPHAGISTS	COPYRIGHTER
CONVULSIVE	COPARCENARY	COPPERSKINS	COPROPHAGOUS	COPYRIGHTERS
CONVULSIVELY	COPARCENER	COPPERSMITH	COPROPHAGY	COPYRIGHTING
CONVULSIVENESS	COPARCENERIES	COPPERSMITHS	COPROPHILIA	COPYRIGHTS
COOKHOUSES	COPARCENERS	COPPERWORK	COPROPHILIAC	COPYTAKERS
COOKSHACKS	COPARCENERY	COPPERWORKS	COPROPHILIACS	COPYWRITER
COOKSTOVES	COPARCENIES	COPPERWORM	COPROPHILIAS	COPYWRITERS
COOLHEADED	COPARENTED	COPPERWORMS	COPROPHILIC	COPYWRITING
COOLHOUSES	COPARENTING	COPPICINGS	COPROPHILOUS	COPYWRITINGS
COOLINGNESS	COPARTNERED	COPRAEMIAS	COPROPRIETOR	COQUELICOT
COOLINGNESSES	COPARTNERIES	COPRESENCE	COPROPRIETORS	COQUELICOTS
COOLNESSES	COPARTNERING	COPRESENCES	COPROSPERITIES	COQUETRIES
COOMCEILED	COPARTNERS	COPRESENTED	COPROSPERITY	COQUETTING
COONHOUNDS	COPARTNERSHIP	COPRESENTING	COPROSTEROL	COQUETTISH
COOPERAGES	COPARTNERSHIPS	COPRESENTS	COPROSTEROLS	COQUETTISHLY
COOPERATED	COPARTNERY	COPRESIDENT	COPSEWOODS	COQUETTISHNESS
COOPERATES	COPATRIOTS	COPRESIDENTS	COPUBLISHED	COQUIMBITE
COOPERATING	COPAYMENTS	COPRINCIPAL	COPUBLISHER	COQUIMBITES
COOPERATION	COPERNICIUM	COPRINCIPALS	COPUBLISHERS	CORACIIFORM
COOPERATIONIST	COPERNICIUMS	COPRISONER	COPUBLISHES	CORADICATE
COOPERATIONISTS	COPESETTIC	COPRISONERS	COPUBLISHING	CORALBELLS
COOPERATIONS	COPESTONES	COPROCESSING	COPULATING	CORALBERRIES

CORALBERRY
CORALLACEOUS
CORALLIFEROUS
CORALLIFORM
CORALLIGENOUS
CORALLINES
CORALLITES
CORALLOIDAL
CORALROOTS
CORALWORTS
CORBEILLES
CORBELINGS
CORBELLING
CORBELLINGS
CORBICULAE
CORBICULATE
CORDECTOMIES
CORDECTOMY
CORDELLING
CORDGRASSES
CORDIALISE
CORDIALISED
CORDIALISES
CORDIALISING
CORDIALITIES
CORDIALITY
CORDIALIZE
CORDIALIZED
CORDIALIZES
CORDIALIZING
CORDIALNESS
CORDIALNESSES
CORDIERITE
CORDIERITES
CORDILLERA
CORDILLERAN
CORDILLERAS
CORDLESSES
CORDOCENTESES
CORDOCENTESIS
CORDONNETS
CORDOTOMIES
CORDUROYED
CORDUROYING
CORDWAINER
CORDWAINERIES
CORDWAINERS

CORDWAINERY
CORDYLINES
CORECIPIENT
CORECIPIENTS
COREDEEMED
COREDEEMING
COREFERENTIAL
COREGONINE
CORELATING
CORELATION
CORELATIONS
CORELATIVE
CORELATIVES
CORELIGIONIST
CORELIGIONISTS
COREOPSISES
COREPRESSOR
COREPRESSORS
COREQUISITE
COREQUISITES
CORESEARCHER
CORESEARCHERS
CORESIDENT
CORESIDENTIAL
CORESIDENTS
CORESPONDENT
CORESPONDENTS
CORFHOUSES
CORIACEOUS
CORIANDERS
CORINTHIANISE
CORINTHIANISED
CORINTHIANISES
CORINTHIANISING
CORINTHIANIZE
CORINTHIANIZED
CORINTHIANIZES
CORINTHIANIZING
CORIVALLED
CORIVALLING
CORIVALRIES
CORIVALSHIP
CORIVALSHIPS
CORKBOARDS
CORKBORERS
CORKINESSES
CORKSCREWED

CORKSCREWING
CORKSCREWS
CORMOPHYTE
CORMOPHYTES
CORMOPHYTIC
CORMORANTS
CORNACEOUS
CORNBORERS
CORNBRAIDED
CORNBRAIDING
CORNBRAIDS
CORNBRANDIES
CORNBRANDY
CORNBRASHES
CORNBREADS
CORNCOCKLE
CORNCOCKLES
CORNCRAKES
CORNEITISES
CORNELIANS
CORNEMUSES
CORNERBACK
CORNERBACKS
CORNERINGS
CORNERSTONE
CORNERSTONES
CORNERWAYS
CORNERWISE
CORNETCIES
CORNETISTS
CORNETTINI
CORNETTINO
CORNETTINOS
CORNETTIST
CORNETTISTS
CORNFIELDS
CORNFLAKES
CORNFLOURS
CORNFLOWER
CORNFLOWERS
CORNHUSKER
CORNHUSKERS
CORNHUSKING
CORNHUSKINGS
CORNICHONS
CORNICINGS
CORNICULATE

CORNICULUM
CORNICULUMS
CORNIFEROUS
CORNIFICATION
CORNIFICATIONS
CORNIFYING
CORNIGEROUS
CORNINESSES
CORNOPEANS
CORNROWING
CORNSTALKS
CORNSTARCH
CORNSTARCHES
CORNSTONES
CORNUCOPIA
CORNUCOPIAN
CORNUCOPIAS
COROLLACEOUS
COROLLARIES
COROLLIFLORAL
COROLLIFLOROUS
COROLLIFORM
COROMANDEL
COROMANDELS
CORONAGRAPH
CORONAGRAPHS
CORONARIES
CORONATING
CORONATION
CORONATIONS
CORONAVIRUS
CORONAVIRUSES
CORONERSHIP
CORONERSHIPS
CORONOGRAPH
CORONOGRAPHS
COROTATING
COROTATION
COROTATIONS
CORPORALES
CORPORALITIES
CORPORALITY
CORPORALLY
CORPORALSHIP
CORPORALSHIPS
CORPORASES
CORPORATELY

CORPORATENESS
CORPORATENESSES
CORPORATES
CORPORATION
CORPORATIONS
CORPORATISE
CORPORATISED
CORPORATISES
CORPORATISING
CORPORATISM
CORPORATISMS
CORPORATIST
CORPORATISTS
CORPORATIVE
CORPORATIVISM
CORPORATIVISMS
CORPORATIZE
CORPORATIZED
CORPORATIZES
CORPORATIZING
CORPORATOR
CORPORATORS
CORPOREALISE
CORPOREALISED
CORPOREALISES
CORPOREALISING
CORPOREALISM
CORPOREALISMS
CORPOREALIST
CORPOREALISTS
CORPOREALITIES
CORPOREALITY
CORPOREALIZE
CORPOREALIZED
CORPOREALIZES
CORPOREALIZING
CORPOREALLY
CORPOREALNESS
CORPOREALNESSES
CORPOREITIES
CORPOREITY
CORPORIFICATION
CORPORIFIED
CORPORIFIES
CORPORIFYING
CORPOSANTS
CORPULENCE

CORPULENCES	CORRELATORS	CORROBOREES	CORTICOIDS	COSMECEUTICAL
CORPULENCIES	CORRELIGIONIST	CORRODANTS	CORTICOLOUS	COSMECEUTICALS
CORPULENCY	CORRELIGIONISTS	CORRODENTS	CORTICOSTEROID	COSMETICAL
CORPULENTLY	CORREPTION	CORRODIBILITIES	CORTICOSTEROIDS	COSMETICALLY
CORPUSCLES	CORREPTIONS	CORRODIBILITY	CORTICOSTERONE	COSMETICIAN
CORPUSCULAR	CORRESPOND	CORRODIBLE	CORTICOSTERONES	COSMETICIANS
CORPUSCULARIAN	CORRESPONDED	CORROSIBILITIES	CORTICOTROPHIC	COSMETICISE
CORPUSCULARIANS	CORRESPONDENCE	CORROSIBILITY	CORTICOTROPHIN	COSMETICISED
CORPUSCULARITY	CORRESPONDENCES	CORROSIBLE	CORTICOTROPHINS	COSMETICISES
CORPUSCULE	CORRESPONDENCY	CORROSIONS	CORTICOTROPIC	COSMETICISING
CORPUSCULES	CORRESPONDENT	CORROSIVELY	CORTICOTROPIN	COSMETICISM
CORRALLING	CORRESPONDENTLY	CORROSIVENESS	CORTICOTROPINS	COSMETICISMS
CORRASIONS	CORRESPONDENTS	CORROSIVENESSES	CORTISONES	COSMETICIZE
CORRECTABLE	CORRESPONDING	CORROSIVES	CORUSCATED	COSMETICIZED
CORRECTEST	CORRESPONDINGLY	CORRUGATED	CORUSCATES	COSMETICIZES
CORRECTIBLE	CORRESPONDS	CORRUGATES	CORUSCATING	COSMETICIZING
CORRECTING	CORRESPONSIVE	CORRUGATING	CORUSCATION	COSMETICOLOGIES
CORRECTION	CORRIGENDA	CORRUGATION	CORUSCATIONS	COSMETICOLOGY
CORRECTIONAL	CORRIGENDUM	CORRUGATIONS	CORVETTING	COSMETOLOGIES
CORRECTIONER	CORRIGENTS	CORRUGATOR	CORYBANTES	COSMETOLOGIST
CORRECTIONERS	CORRIGIBILITIES	CORRUGATORS	CORYBANTIC	COSMETOLOGISTS
CORRECTIONS	CORRIGIBILITY	CORRUPTERS	CORYBANTISM	COSMETOLOGY
CORRECTITUDE	CORRIGIBLE	CORRUPTEST	CORYBANTISMS	COSMICALLY
CORRECTITUDES	CORRIGIBLY	CORRUPTIBILITY	CORYDALINE	COSMOCHEMICAL
CORRECTIVE	CORRIVALLED	CORRUPTIBLE	CORYDALINES	COSMOCHEMIST
CORRECTIVELY	CORRIVALLING	CORRUPTIBLENESS	CORYDALISES	COSMOCHEMISTRY
CORRECTIVES	CORRIVALRIES	CORRUPTIBLY	CORYLOPSES	COSMOCHEMISTS
CORRECTNESS	CORRIVALRY	CORRUPTING	CORYLOPSIS	COSMOCRATIC
CORRECTNESSES	CORRIVALSHIP	CORRUPTION	CORYMBOSELY	COSMOCRATS
CORRECTORS	CORRIVALSHIPS	CORRUPTIONIST	CORYNEBACTERIA	COSMODROME
CORRECTORY	CORROBORABLE	CORRUPTIONISTS	CORYNEBACTERIAL	COSMODROMES
CORREGIDOR	CORROBORANT	CORRUPTIONS	CORYNEBACTERIUM	COSMOGENIC
CORREGIDORS	CORROBORATE	CORRUPTIVE	CORYNEFORM	COSMOGENIES
CORRELATABLE	CORROBORATED	CORRUPTIVELY	CORYPHAEUS	COSMOGONAL
CORRELATED	CORROBORATES	CORRUPTNESS	CORYPHENES	COSMOGONIC
CORRELATES	CORROBORATING	CORRUPTNESSES	COSCINOMANCIES	COSMOGONICAL
CORRELATING	CORROBORATION	CORRUPTORS	COSCINOMANCY	COSMOGONIES
CORRELATION	CORROBORATIONS	CORSELETTE	COSCRIPTED	COSMOGONIST
CORRELATIONAL	CORROBORATIVE	CORSELETTES	COSCRIPTING	COSMOGONISTS
CORRELATIONS	CORROBORATIVELY	CORSETIERE	COSEISMALS	COSMOGRAPHER
CORRELATIVE	CORROBORATIVES	CORSETIERES	COSEISMICS	COSMOGRAPHERS
CORRELATIVELY	CORROBORATOR	CORSETIERS	COSENTIENT	COSMOGRAPHIC
CORRELATIVENESS	CORROBORATORS	CORSETRIES	COSHERINGS	COSMOGRAPHICAL
CORRELATIVES	CORROBORATORY	CORTICALLY	COSIGNATORIES	COSMOGRAPHIES
CORRELATIVITIES	CORROBOREE	CORTICATED	COSIGNATORY	COSMOGRAPHIST
CORRELATIVITY	CORROBOREED	CORTICATION	COSIGNIFICATIVE	COSMOGRAPHISTS
CORRELATOR	CORROBOREEING	CORTICATIONS	COSINESSES	COSMOGRAPHY

COSMOLATRIES
COSMOLATRY
COSMOLINED
COSMOLINES
COSMOLINING
COSMOLOGIC
COSMOLOGICAL
COSMOLOGICALLY
COSMOLOGIES
COSMOLOGIST
COSMOLOGISTS
COSMONAUTICS
COSMONAUTS
COSMOPLASTIC
COSMOPOLIS
COSMOPOLISES
COSMOPOLITAN
COSMOPOLITANISM
COSMOPOLITANS
COSMOPOLITE
COSMOPOLITES
COSMOPOLITIC
COSMOPOLITICAL
COSMOPOLITICS
COSMOPOLITISM
COSMOPOLITISMS
COSMORAMAS
COSMORAMIC
COSMOSPHERE
COSMOSPHERES
COSMOTHEISM
COSMOTHEISMS
COSMOTHETIC
COSMOTHETICAL
COSMOTRONS
COSPONSORED
COSPONSORING
COSPONSORS
COSPONSORSHIP
COSPONSORSHIPS
COSTALGIAS
COSTARDMONGER
COSTARDMONGERS
COSTARRING
COSTEANING
COSTEANINGS
COSTERMONGER

COSTERMONGERS
COSTIVENESS
COSTIVENESSES
COSTLESSLY
COSTLINESS
COSTLINESSES
COSTMARIES
COSTOTOMIES
COSTUMERIES
COSTUMIERS
COSURFACTANT
COSURFACTANTS
COTANGENTIAL
COTANGENTS
COTELETTES
COTEMPORANEOUS
COTEMPORARY
COTENANCIES
COTERMINOUS
COTERMINOUSLY
COTILLIONS
COTONEASTER
COTONEASTERS
COTRANSDUCE
COTRANSDUCED
COTRANSDUCES
COTRANSDUCING
COTRANSDUCTION
COTRANSDUCTIONS
COTRANSFER
COTRANSFERS
COTRANSPORT
COTRANSPORTED
COTRANSPORTING
COTRANSPORTS
COTRUSTEES
COTTABUSES
COTTAGINGS
COTTERLESS
COTTIERISM
COTTIERISMS
COTTONADES
COTTONMOUTH
COTTONMOUTHS
COTTONOCRACIES
COTTONOCRACY
COTTONSEED

COTTONSEEDS
COTTONTAIL
COTTONTAILS
COTTONWEED
COTTONWEEDS
COTTONWOOD
COTTONWOODS
COTYLEDONAL
COTYLEDONARY
COTYLEDONOID
COTYLEDONOUS
COTYLEDONS
COTYLIFORM
COTYLOIDAL
COTYLOIDALS
COTYLOSAUR
COTYLOSAURS
COUCHETTES
COUCHSURFING
COUCHSURFINGS
COULIBIACA
COULIBIACAS
COULIBIACS
COULOMBMETER
COULOMBMETERS
COULOMETER
COULOMETERS
COULOMETRIC
COULOMETRICALLY
COULOMETRIES
COULOMETRY
COUMARILIC
COUMARONES
COUNCILLOR
COUNCILLORS
COUNCILLORSHIP
COUNCILLORSHIPS
COUNCILMAN
COUNCILMANIC
COUNCILMEN
COUNCILORS
COUNCILORSHIP
COUNCILORSHIPS
COUNCILWOMAN
COUNCILWOMEN
COUNSELABLE

COUNSELEES
COUNSELING
COUNSELINGS
COUNSELLABLE
COUNSELLED
COUNSELLEE
COUNSELLEES
COUNSELLING
COUNSELLINGS
COUNSELLOR
COUNSELLORS
COUNSELLORSHIP
COUNSELLORSHIPS
COUNSELORS
COUNSELORSHIP
COUNSELORSHIPS
COUNTABILITIES
COUNTABILITY
COUNTBACKS
COUNTDOWNS
COUNTENANCE
COUNTENANCED
COUNTENANCER
COUNTENANCERS
COUNTENANCES
COUNTENANCING
COUNTERACT
COUNTERACTED
COUNTERACTING
COUNTERACTION
COUNTERACTIONS
COUNTERACTIVE
COUNTERACTIVELY
COUNTERACTS
COUNTERAGENT
COUNTERAGENTS
COUNTERARGUE
COUNTERARGUED
COUNTERARGUES
COUNTERARGUING
COUNTERARGUMENT
COUNTERASSAULT
COUNTERASSAULTS
COUNTERATTACK
COUNTERATTACKED
COUNTERATTACKER
COUNTERATTACKS

COUNTERBALANCE
COUNTERBALANCED
COUNTERBALANCES
COUNTERBASE
COUNTERBASES
COUNTERBID
COUNTERBIDDER
COUNTERBIDDERS
COUNTERBIDS
COUNTERBLAST
COUNTERBLASTS
COUNTERBLOCKADE
COUNTERBLOW
COUNTERBLOWS
COUNTERBLUFF
COUNTERBLUFFS
COUNTERBOND
COUNTERBONDS
COUNTERBORE
COUNTERBORED
COUNTERBORES
COUNTERBORING
COUNTERBRACE
COUNTERBRACED
COUNTERBRACES
COUNTERBRACING
COUNTERBUFF
COUNTERBUFFED
COUNTERBUFFING
COUNTERBUFFS
COUNTERCAMPAIGN
COUNTERCHANGE
COUNTERCHANGED
COUNTERCHANGES
COUNTERCHANGING
COUNTERCHARGE
COUNTERCHARGED
COUNTERCHARGES
COUNTERCHARGING
COUNTERCHARM
COUNTERCHARMED
COUNTERCHARMING
COUNTERCHARMS
COUNTERCHECK
COUNTERCHECKED
COUNTERCHECKING
COUNTERCHECKS

COUNTERCLAIM
COUNTERCLAIMANT
COUNTERCLAIMED
COUNTERCLAIMING
COUNTERCLAIMS
COUNTERCOUP
COUNTERCOUPS
COUNTERCRIES
COUNTERCRY
COUNTERCULTURAL
COUNTERCULTURE
COUNTERCULTURES
COUNTERCURRENT
COUNTERCURRENTS
COUNTERCYCLICAL
COUNTERDEMAND
COUNTERDEMANDS
COUNTERDRAW
COUNTERDRAWING
COUNTERDRAWN
COUNTERDRAWS
COUNTERDREW
COUNTEREFFORT
COUNTEREFFORTS
COUNTEREVIDENCE
COUNTEREXAMPLE
COUNTEREXAMPLES
COUNTERFACTUAL
COUNTERFACTUALS
COUNTERFECT
COUNTERFEISANCE
COUNTERFEIT
COUNTERFEITED
COUNTERFEITER
COUNTERFEITERS
COUNTERFEITING
COUNTERFEITINGS
COUNTERFEITLY
COUNTERFEITS
COUNTERFESAUNCE
COUNTERFIRE
COUNTERFIRES
COUNTERFLOW
COUNTERFLOWS
COUNTERFOIL
COUNTERFOILS
COUNTERFORCE

COUNTERFORCES
COUNTERFORT
COUNTERFORTS
COUNTERGLOW
COUNTERGLOWS
COUNTERGUERILLA
COUNTERIMAGE
COUNTERIMAGES
COUNTERING
COUNTERINSTANCE
COUNTERION
COUNTERIONS
COUNTERIRRITANT
COUNTERLIGHT
COUNTERLIGHTS
COUNTERMAN
COUNTERMAND
COUNTERMANDABLE
COUNTERMANDED
COUNTERMANDING
COUNTERMANDS
COUNTERMARCH
COUNTERMARCHED
COUNTERMARCHES
COUNTERMARCHING
COUNTERMARK
COUNTERMARKS
COUNTERMEASURE
COUNTERMEASURES
COUNTERMELODIES
COUNTERMELODY
COUNTERMEMO
COUNTERMEMOS
COUNTERMEN
COUNTERMINE
COUNTERMINED
COUNTERMINES
COUNTERMINING
COUNTERMOTION
COUNTERMOTIONS
COUNTERMOVE
COUNTERMOVED
COUNTERMOVEMENT
COUNTERMOVES
COUNTERMOVING
COUNTERMURE
COUNTERMURED

COUNTERMURES
COUNTERMURING
COUNTERMYTH
COUNTERMYTHS
COUNTEROFFER
COUNTEROFFERS
COUNTERORDER
COUNTERORDERED
COUNTERORDERING
COUNTERORDERS
COUNTERPACE
COUNTERPACES
COUNTERPANE
COUNTERPANES
COUNTERPART
COUNTERPARTIES
COUNTERPARTS
COUNTERPARTY
COUNTERPEISE
COUNTERPEISED
COUNTERPEISES
COUNTERPEISING
COUNTERPETITION
COUNTERPICKET
COUNTERPICKETED
COUNTERPICKETS
COUNTERPLAN
COUNTERPLANNED
COUNTERPLANNING
COUNTERPLANS
COUNTERPLAY
COUNTERPLAYED
COUNTERPLAYER
COUNTERPLAYERS
COUNTERPLAYING
COUNTERPLAYS
COUNTERPLEA
COUNTERPLEAD
COUNTERPLEADED
COUNTERPLEADING
COUNTERPLEADS
COUNTERPLEAS
COUNTERPLED
COUNTERPLOT
COUNTERPLOTS
COUNTERPLOTTED
COUNTERPLOTTING

COUNTERPLOY
COUNTERPLOYS
COUNTERPOINT
COUNTERPOINTED
COUNTERPOINTING
COUNTERPOINTS
COUNTERPOISE
COUNTERPOISED
COUNTERPOISES
COUNTERPOISING
COUNTERPOSE
COUNTERPOSED
COUNTERPOSES
COUNTERPOSING
COUNTERPOWER
COUNTERPOWERS
COUNTERPRESSURE
COUNTERPROJECT
COUNTERPROJECTS
COUNTERPROOF
COUNTERPROOFS
COUNTERPROPOSAL
COUNTERPROTEST
COUNTERPROTESTS
COUNTERPUNCH
COUNTERPUNCHED
COUNTERPUNCHER
COUNTERPUNCHERS
COUNTERPUNCHES
COUNTERPUNCHING
COUNTERQUESTION
COUNTERRAID
COUNTERRAIDED
COUNTERRAIDING
COUNTERRAIDS
COUNTERRALLIED
COUNTERRALLIES
COUNTERRALLY
COUNTERRALLYING
COUNTERREACTION
COUNTERREFORM
COUNTERREFORMED
COUNTERREFORMER
COUNTERREFORMS
COUNTERRESPONSE
COUNTERSANK
COUNTERSCARP

COUNTERSCARPS
COUNTERSEAL
COUNTERSEALED
COUNTERSEALING
COUNTERSEALS
COUNTERSHADING
COUNTERSHADINGS
COUNTERSHAFT
COUNTERSHAFTS
COUNTERSHOT
COUNTERSHOTS
COUNTERSIGN
COUNTERSIGNED
COUNTERSIGNING
COUNTERSIGNS
COUNTERSINK
COUNTERSINKING
COUNTERSINKS
COUNTERSNIPER
COUNTERSNIPERS
COUNTERSPELL
COUNTERSPELLS
COUNTERSPIES
COUNTERSPY
COUNTERSPYING
COUNTERSPYINGS
COUNTERSTAIN
COUNTERSTAINED
COUNTERSTAINING
COUNTERSTAINS
COUNTERSTATE
COUNTERSTATED
COUNTERSTATES
COUNTERSTATING
COUNTERSTEP
COUNTERSTEPS
COUNTERSTRATEGY
COUNTERSTREAM
COUNTERSTREAMS
COUNTERSTRICKEN
COUNTERSTRIKE
COUNTERSTRIKES
COUNTERSTRIKING
COUNTERSTROKE
COUNTERSTROKES
COUNTERSTRUCK
COUNTERSTYLE

C

COUNTERSTYLES	COUNTERWORDS	COURSEWORKS	COVELLITES	COXCOMBICALLY
COUNTERSUBJECT	COUNTERWORK	COURTCRAFT	COVENANTAL	COXCOMBRIES
COUNTERSUBJECTS	COUNTERWORKED	COURTCRAFTS	COVENANTALLY	COXCOMICAL
COUNTERSUE	COUNTERWORKER	COURTEOUSLY	COVENANTED	COXINESSES
COUNTERSUED	COUNTERWORKERS	COURTEOUSNESS	COVENANTEE	COXSWAINED
COUNTERSUES	COUNTERWORKING	COURTEOUSNESSES	COVENANTEES	COXSWAINING
COUNTERSUING	COUNTERWORKS	COURTESANS	COVENANTER	COYISHNESS
COUNTERSUIT	COUNTERWORLD	COURTESIED	COVENANTERS	COYISHNESSES
COUNTERSUITS	COUNTERWORLDS	COURTESIES	COVENANTING	COYOTILLOS
COUNTERSUNK	COUNTESSES	COURTESYING	COVENANTOR	COZINESSES
COUNTERTACTIC	COUNTINGHOUSE	COURTEZANS	COVENANTORS	CRABAPPLES
COUNTERTACTICS	COUNTINGHOUSES	COURTHOUSE	COVERALLED	CRABBEDNESS
COUNTERTENDENCY	COUNTLESSLY	COURTHOUSES	COVERMOUNT	CRABBEDNESSES
COUNTERTENOR	COUNTLINES	COURTIERISM	COVERMOUNTED	CRABBINESS
COUNTERTENORS	COUNTRIFIED	COURTIERISMS	COVERMOUNTING	CRABBINESSES
COUNTERTERROR	COUNTROLLED	COURTIERLIKE	COVERMOUNTS	CRABEATERS
COUNTERTERRORS	COUNTROLLING	COURTIERLY	COVERSINES	CRABGRASSES
COUNTERTHREAT	COUNTRYFIED	COURTLIEST	COVERSLIPS	CRABSTICKS
COUNTERTHREATS	COUNTRYISH	COURTLINESS	COVERTNESS	CRACKAJACK
COUNTERTHRUST	COUNTRYMAN	COURTLINESSES	COVERTNESSES	CRACKAJACKS
COUNTERTHRUSTS	COUNTRYMEN	COURTLINGS	COVERTURES	CRACKBACKS
COUNTERTOP	COUNTRYSEAT	COURTROOMS	COVETINGLY	CRACKBERRIES
COUNTERTOPS	COUNTRYSEATS	COURTSHIPS	COVETIVENESS	CRACKBERRY
COUNTERTRADE	COUNTRYSIDE	COURTSIDES	COVETIVENESSES	CRACKBRAIN
COUNTERTRADED	COUNTRYSIDES	COURTYARDS	COVETOUSLY	CRACKBRAINED
COUNTERTRADES	COUNTRYWIDE	COUSCOUSES	COVETOUSNESS	CRACKBRAINS
COUNTERTRADING	COUNTRYWOMAN	COUSCOUSOU	COVETOUSNESSES	CRACKDOWNS
COUNTERTREND	COUNTRYWOMEN	COUSCOUSOUS	COWARDICES	CRACKERJACK
COUNTERTRENDS	COUNTSHIPS	COUSINAGES	COWARDLINESS	CRACKERJACKS
COUNTERTYPE	COUPLEDOMS	COUSINHOOD	COWARDLINESSES	CRACKHEADS
COUNTERTYPES	COUPLEMENT	COUSINHOODS	COWARDRIES	CRACKLEWARE
COUNTERVAIL	COUPLEMENTS	COUSINRIES	COWARDSHIP	CRACKLEWARES
COUNTERVAILABLE	COUPONINGS	COUSINSHIP	COWARDSHIPS	CRACKLIEST
COUNTERVAILED	COURAGEFUL	COUSINSHIPS	COWBERRIES	CRACKLINGS
COUNTERVAILING	COURAGEOUS	COUTURIERE	COWCATCHER	CRACOVIENNE
COUNTERVAILS	COURAGEOUSLY	COUTURIERES	COWCATCHERS	CRACOVIENNES
COUNTERVIEW	COURAGEOUSNESS	COUTURIERS	COWERINGLY	CRADLESONG
COUNTERVIEWS	COURANTOES	COVALENCES	COWFEEDERS	CRADLESONGS
COUNTERVIOLENCE	COURBARILS	COVALENCIES	COWFETERIA	CRADLEWALK
COUNTERWEIGH	COURBETTES	COVALENTLY	COWFETERIAS	CRADLEWALKS
COUNTERWEIGHED	COURGETTES	COVARIANCE	COWGRASSES	CRAFTINESS
COUNTERWEIGHING	COURIERING	COVARIANCES	COWLSTAFFS	CRAFTINESSES
COUNTERWEIGHS	COURSEBOOK	COVARIANTS	COWLSTAVES	CRAFTMANSHIP
COUNTERWEIGHT	COURSEBOOKS	COVARIATES	COWPUNCHER	CRAFTMANSHIPS
COUNTERWEIGHTED	COURSEWARE	COVARIATION	COWPUNCHERS	CRAFTSMANLIKE
COUNTERWEIGHTS	COURSEWARES	COVARIATIONS	COXCOMBICAL	CRAFTSMANLY
COUNTERWORD	COURSEWORK	COVELLINES	COXCOMBICALITY	CRAFTSMANSHIP

CRAFTSMANSHIPS	CRANIOMETRY	CRATERINGS	CREATORSHIP	CREMATIONIST
CRAFTSPEOPLE	CRANIOPAGI	CRATERLESS	CREATORSHIPS	CREMATIONISTS
CRAFTSPERSON	CRANIOPAGUS	CRATERLETS	CREATRESSES	CREMATIONS
CRAFTSPERSONS	CRANIOSACRAL	CRATERLIKE	CREATRIXES	CREMATORIA
CRAFTSWOMAN	CRANIOSCOPIES	CRAUNCHABLE	CREATUREHOOD	CREMATORIAL
CRAFTSWOMEN	CRANIOSCOPIST	CRAUNCHIER	CREATUREHOODS	CREMATORIES
CRAFTWORKS	CRANIOSCOPISTS	CRAUNCHIEST	CREATURELINESS	CREMATORIUM
CRAGGEDNESS	CRANIOSCOPY	CRAUNCHINESS	CREATURELY	CREMATORIUMS
CRAGGEDNESSES	CRANIOTOMIES	CRAUNCHINESSES	CREATURESHIP	CREMOCARPS
CRAGGINESS	CRANIOTOMY	CRAUNCHING	CREATURESHIPS	CRENATIONS
CRAGGINESSES	CRANKCASES	CRAVATTING	CREDENTIAL	CRENATURES
CRAIGFLUKE	CRANKHANDLE	CRAVENNESS	CREDENTIALED	CRENELATED
CRAIGFLUKES	CRANKHANDLES	CRAVENNESSES	CREDENTIALING	CRENELATES
CRAKEBERRIES	CRANKINESS	CRAWDADDIES	CREDENTIALINGS	CRENELATING
CRAKEBERRY	CRANKINESSES	CRAWFISHED	CREDENTIALISM	CRENELATION
CRAMBOCLINK	CRANKNESSES	CRAWFISHES	CREDENTIALISMS	CRENELATIONS
CRAMBOCLINKS	CRANKSHAFT	CRAWFISHING	CREDENTIALLED	CRENELLATE
CRAMOISIES	CRANKSHAFTS	CRAWLINGLY	CREDENTIALLING	CRENELLATED
CRAMPBARKS	CRANREUCHS	CRAYFISHES	CREDENTIALLINGS	CRENELLATES
CRAMPFISHES	CRAPEHANGER	CRAYONISTS	CREDENTIALS	CRENELLATING
CRAMPONING	CRAPEHANGERS	CRAZINESSES	CREDIBILITIES	CRENELLATION
CRAMPONNING	CRAPEHANGING	CRAZYWEEDS	CREDIBILITY	CRENELLATIONS
CRAMPONNINGS	CRAPEHANGINGS	CREAKINESS	CREDIBLENESS	CRENELLING
CRANACHANS	CRAPSHOOTER	CREAKINESSES	CREDIBLENESSES	CRENULATED
CRANBERRIES	CRAPSHOOTERS	CREAKINGLY	CREDITABILITIES	CRENULATION
CRANEFLIES	CRAPSHOOTS	CREAMERIES	CREDITABILITY	CRENULATIONS
CRANESBILL	CRAPULENCE	CREAMINESS	CREDITABLE	CREOLISATION
CRANESBILLS	CRAPULENCES	CREAMINESSES	CREDITABLENESS	CREOLISATIONS
CRANIECTOMIES	CRAPULENTLY	CREAMPUFFS	CREDITABLY	CREOLISING
CRANIECTOMY	CRAPULOSITIES	CREAMWARES	CREDITLESS	CREOLIZATION
CRANIOCEREBRAL	CRAPULOSITY	CREASELESS	CREDITWORTHY	CREOLIZATIONS
CRANIOFACIAL	CRAPULOUSLY	CREASOTING	CREDULITIES	CREOLIZING
CRANIOGNOMIES	CRAPULOUSNESS	CREATIANISM	CREDULOUSLY	CREOPHAGIES
CRANIOGNOMY	CRAPULOUSNESSES	CREATIANISMS	CREDULOUSNESS	CREOPHAGOUS
CRANIOLOGICAL	CRAQUELURE	CREATININE	CREDULOUSNESSES	CREOSOTING
CRANIOLOGICALLY	CRAQUELURES	CREATININES	CREEKSIDES	CREPEHANGER
CRANIOLOGIES	CRASHINGLY	CREATIONAL	CREEPINESS	CREPEHANGERS
CRANIOLOGIST	CRASHWORTHINESS	CREATIONISM	CREEPINESSES	CREPEHANGING
CRANIOLOGISTS	CRASHWORTHY	CREATIONISMS	CREEPINGLY	CREPEHANGINGS
CRANIOLOGY	CRASSAMENTA	CREATIONIST	CREEPMOUSE	CREPINESSES
CRANIOMETER	CRASSAMENTUM	CREATIONISTIC	CREEPMOUSES	CREPITATED
CRANIOMETERS	CRASSITUDE	CREATIONISTS	CREESHIEST	CREPITATES
CRANIOMETRIC	CRASSITUDES	CREATIVELY	CREMAILLERE	CREPITATING
CRANIOMETRICAL	CRASSNESSES	CREATIVENESS	CREMAILLERES	CREPITATION
CRANIOMETRIES	CRASSULACEAN	CREATIVENESSES	CREMASTERS	CREPITATIONS
CRANIOMETRIST	CRASSULACEOUS	CREATIVITIES	CREMATIONISM	CREPITATIVE
CRANIOMETRISTS	CRATERIFORM	CREATIVITY	CREMATIONISMS	CREPITUSES

CREPOLINES	CRIMINALESES	CRINOIDEAN	CRITICISING	CROSSANDRAS
CREPUSCLES	CRIMINALISATION	CRINOIDEANS	CRITICISINGLY	CROSSBANDED
CREPUSCULAR	CRIMINALISE	CRINOLETTE	CRITICISMS	CROSSBANDING
CREPUSCULE	CRIMINALISED	CRINOLETTES	CRITICIZABLE	CROSSBANDINGS
CREPUSCULES	CRIMINALISES	CRINOLINED	CRITICIZED	CROSSBANDS
CREPUSCULOUS	CRIMINALISING	CRINOLINES	CRITICIZER	CROSSBARRED
CRESCENDOED	CRIMINALIST	CRIPPLEDOM	CRITICIZERS	CROSSBARRING
CRESCENDOES	CRIMINALISTICS	CRIPPLEDOMS	CRITICIZES	CROSSBARRINGS
CRESCENDOING	CRIMINALISTS	CRIPPLEWARE	CRITICIZING	CROSSBEAMS
CRESCENDOS	CRIMINALITIES	CRIPPLEWARES	CRITICIZINGLY	CROSSBEARER
CRESCENTADE	CRIMINALITY	CRIPPLINGLY	CRITIQUING	CROSSBEARERS
CRESCENTADES	CRIMINALIZATION	CRIPPLINGS	CROAKINESS	CROSSBENCH
CRESCENTED	CRIMINALIZE	CRISPATION	CROAKINESSES	CROSSBENCHER
CRESCENTIC	CRIMINALIZED	CRISPATIONS	CROCHETERS	CROSSBENCHERS
CRESCIVELY	CRIMINALIZES	CRISPATURE	CROCHETING	CROSSBENCHES
CRESCOGRAPH	CRIMINALIZING	CRISPATURES	CROCHETINGS	CROSSBILLS
CRESCOGRAPHS	CRIMINALLY	CRISPBREAD	CROCIDOLITE	CROSSBIRTH
CRESTFALLEN	CRIMINATED	CRISPBREADS	CROCIDOLITES	CROSSBIRTHS
CRESTFALLENLY	CRIMINATES	CRISPENING	CROCKERIES	CROSSBITES
CRESTFALLENNESS	CRIMINATING	CRISPHEADS	CROCODILES	CROSSBITING
CRETACEOUS	CRIMINATION	CRISPINESS	CROCODILIAN	CROSSBITTEN
CRETACEOUSES	CRIMINATIONS	CRISPINESSES	CROCODILIANS	CROSSBONES
CRETACEOUSLY	CRIMINATIVE	CRISPNESSES	CROCOISITE	CROSSBOWER
CRETINISED	CRIMINATOR	CRISSCROSS	CROCOISITES	CROSSBOWERS
CRETINISES	CRIMINATORS	CRISSCROSSED	CROCOSMIAS	CROSSBOWMAN
CRETINISING	CRIMINATORY	CRISSCROSSES	CROISSANTS	CROSSBOWMEN
CRETINISMS	CRIMINOGENIC	CRISSCROSSING	CROKINOLES	CROSSBREDS
CRETINIZED	CRIMINOLOGIC	CRISTIFORM	CROOKBACKED	CROSSBREED
CRETINIZES	CRIMINOLOGICAL	CRISTOBALITE	CROOKBACKS	CROSSBREEDING
CRETINIZING	CRIMINOLOGIES	CRISTOBALITES	CROOKEDEST	CROSSBREEDINGS
CRETINOIDS	CRIMINOLOGIST	CRITERIONS	CROOKEDNESS	CROSSBREEDS
CREVASSING	CRIMINOLOGISTS	CRITERIUMS	CROOKEDNESSES	CROSSBUCKS
CREWELISTS	CRIMINOLOGY	CRITHIDIAL	CROOKERIES	CROSSCHECK
CREWELLERIES	CRIMINOUSNESS	CRITHOMANCIES	CROOKNECKS	CROSSCHECKED
CREWELLERY	CRIMINOUSNESSES	CRITHOMANCY	CROPDUSTER	CROSSCHECKING
CREWELLING	CRIMSONING	CRITICALITIES	CROPDUSTERS	CROSSCHECKS
CREWELLINGS	CRIMSONNESS	CRITICALITY	CROPDUSTING	CROSSCLAIM
CREWELWORK	CRIMSONNESSES	CRITICALLY	CROPDUSTINGS	CROSSCLAIMS
CREWELWORKS	CRINGELING	CRITICALNESS	CROQUANTES	CROSSCOURT
CRIBRATION	CRINGELINGS	CRITICALNESSES	CROQUETING	CROSSCURRENT
CRIBRATIONS	CRINGEWORTHY	CRITICASTER	CROQUETTES	CROSSCURRENTS
CRIBRIFORM	CRINGINGLY	CRITICASTERS	CROQUIGNOLE	CROSSCUTTING
CRICKETERS	CRINICULTURAL	CRITICISABLE	CROQUIGNOLES	CROSSCUTTINGS
CRICKETING	CRINIGEROUS	CRITICISED	CROREPATIS	CROSSETTES
CRICKETINGS	CRINKLEROOT	CRITICISER	CROSSABILITIES	CROSSFALLS
CRIMEWAVES	CRINKLEROOTS	CRITICISERS	CROSSABILITY	CROSSFIELD
CRIMINALESE	CRINKLIEST	CRITICISES	CROSSANDRA	CROSSFIRES

CROSSFISHES	CROWDEDNESS	CRUMPLIEST	CRYOPRECIPITATE	CRYPTOGAMIC
CROSSHAIRS	CROWDEDNESSES	CRUMPLINGS	CRYOPRESERVE	CRYPTOGAMIES
CROSSHATCH	CROWDFUNDED	CRUNCHABLE	CRYOPRESERVED	CRYPTOGAMIST
CROSSHATCHED	CROWDFUNDING	CRUNCHIEST	CRYOPRESERVES	CRYPTOGAMISTS
CROSSHATCHES	CROWDFUNDINGS	CRUNCHINESS	CRYOPRESERVING	CRYPTOGAMOUS
CROSSHATCHING	CROWDFUNDS	CRUNCHINESSES	CRYOPROBES	CRYPTOGAMS
CROSSHATCHINGS	CROWDSOURCE	CRUNCHINGS	CRYOPROTECTANT	CRYPTOGAMY
CROSSHEADS	CROWDSOURCED	CRUSHABILITIES	CRYOPROTECTANTS	CRYPTOGENIC
CROSSJACKS	CROWDSOURCES	CRUSHABILITY	CRYOPROTECTIVE	CRYPTOGRAM
CROSSLIGHT	CROWDSOURCING	CRUSHINGLY	CRYOSCOPES	CRYPTOGRAMS
CROSSLIGHTS	CROWDSOURCINGS	CRUSHPROOF	CRYOSCOPIC	CRYPTOGRAPH
CROSSLINGUISTIC	CROWKEEPER	CRUSTACEAN	CRYOSCOPIES	CRYPTOGRAPHER
CROSSNESSES	CROWKEEPERS	CRUSTACEANS	CRYOSTATIC	CRYPTOGRAPHERS
CROSSOPTERYGIAN	CROWNLANDS	CRUSTACEOUS	CRYOSURGEON	CRYPTOGRAPHIC
CROSSOVERS	CROWNPIECE	CRUSTATION	CRYOSURGEONS	CRYPTOGRAPHICAL
CROSSPATCH	CROWNPIECES	CRUSTATIONS	CRYOSURGERIES	CRYPTOGRAPHIES
CROSSPATCHES	CROWNWORKS	CRUSTINESS	CRYOSURGERY	CRYPTOGRAPHIST
CROSSPIECE	CROWSTEPPED	CRUSTINESSES	CRYOSURGICAL	CRYPTOGRAPHISTS
CROSSPIECES	CRUCIATELY	CRUTCHINGS	CRYOTHERAPIES	CRYPTOGRAPHS
CROSSROADS	CRUCIFEROUS	CRYMOTHERAPIES	CRYOTHERAPY	CRYPTOGRAPHY
CROSSRUFFED	CRUCIFIERS	CRYMOTHERAPY	CRYPTAESTHESIA	CRYPTOLOGIC
CROSSRUFFING	CRUCIFIXES	CRYOBIOLOGICAL	CRYPTAESTHESIAS	CRYPTOLOGICAL
CROSSRUFFS	CRUCIFIXION	CRYOBIOLOGIES	CRYPTAESTHETIC	CRYPTOLOGIES
CROSSTALKS	CRUCIFIXIONS	CRYOBIOLOGIST	CRYPTANALYSES	CRYPTOLOGIST
CROSSTREES	CRUCIFORMLY	CRYOBIOLOGISTS	CRYPTANALYSIS	CRYPTOLOGISTS
CROSSWALKS	CRUCIFORMS	CRYOBIOLOGY	CRYPTANALYST	CRYPTOLOGY
CROSSWINDS	CRUCIFYING	CRYOCABLES	CRYPTANALYSTS	CRYPTOMERIA
CROSSWIRES	CRUCIVERBAL	CRYOCONITE	CRYPTANALYTIC	CRYPTOMERIAS
CROSSWORDS	CRUCIVERBALISM	CRYOCONITES	CRYPTANALYTICAL	CRYPTOMETER
CROSSWORTS	CRUCIVERBALISMS	CRYOGENICALLY	CRYPTARITHM	CRYPTOMETERS
CROTALARIA	CRUCIVERBALIST	CRYOGENICS	CRYPTARITHMS	CRYPTOMNESIA
CROTALARIAS	CRUCIVERBALISTS	CRYOGENIES	CRYPTESTHESIA	CRYPTOMNESIAS
CROTALISMS	CRUDENESSES	CRYOGLOBULIN	CRYPTESTHESIAS	CRYPTOMNESIC
CROTCHETED	CRUELNESSES	CRYOGLOBULINS	CRYPTESTHETIC	CRYPTONYMOUS
CROTCHETEER	CRUISERWEIGHT	CRYOHYDRATE	CRYPTICALLY	CRYPTONYMS
CROTCHETEERS	CRUISERWEIGHTS	CRYOHYDRATES	CRYPTOBIONT	CRYPTOPHYTE
CROTCHETIER	CRUISEWAYS	CRYOMETERS	CRYPTOBIONTS	CRYPTOPHYTES
CROTCHETIEST	CRUISEWEAR	CRYOMETRIC	CRYPTOBIOSES	CRYPTOPHYTIC
CROTCHETINESS	CRUISEWEARS	CRYOMETRIES	CRYPTOBIOSIS	CRYPTORCHID
CROTCHETINESSES	CRUMBCLOTH	CRYONICALLY	CRYPTOCLASTIC	CRYPTORCHIDISM
CROTONBUGS	CRUMBCLOTHS	CRYOPHILIC	CRYPTOCOCCAL	CRYPTORCHIDISMS
CROUPINESS	CRUMBLIEST	CRYOPHORUS	CRYPTOCOCCI	CRYPTORCHIDS
CROUPINESSES	CRUMBLINESS	CRYOPHORUSES	CRYPTOCOCCOSES	CRYPTORCHISM
CROUSTADES	CRUMBLINESSES	CRYOPHYSICS	CRYPTOCOCCOSIS	CRYPTORCHISMS
CROWBARRED	CRUMBLINGS	CRYOPHYTES	CRYPTOCOCCUS	CRYPTOSPORIDIA
CROWBARRING	CRUMMINESS	CRYOPLANKTON	CRYPTOCURRENCY	CRYPTOSPORIDIUM
CROWBERRIES	CRUMMINESSES	CRYOPLANKTONS	CRYPTOGAMIAN	CRYPTOZOIC

CRYPTOZOITE	CRYSTALLIZING	CUISINARTS	CUMBERSOMELY	CUPRAMMONIUM
CRYPTOZOITES	CRYSTALLOGRAPHY	CUISINIERS	CUMBERSOMENESS	CUPRAMMONIUMS
CRYPTOZOOLOGIES	CRYSTALLOID	CULICIFORM	CUMBRANCES	CUPRESSUSES
CRYPTOZOOLOGIST	CRYSTALLOIDAL	CULINARIAN	CUMBROUSLY	CUPRIFEROUS
CRYPTOZOOLOGY	CRYSTALLOIDS	CULINARIANS	CUMBROUSNESS	CUPRONICKEL
CRYSTALISABLE	CRYSTALLOMANCY	CULINARILY	CUMBROUSNESSES	CUPRONICKELS
CRYSTALISATION	CTENOPHORAN	CULLENDERS	CUMMERBUND	CUPULIFEROUS
CRYSTALISATIONS	CTENOPHORANS	CULMIFEROUS	CUMMERBUNDS	CURABILITIES
CRYSTALISE	CTENOPHORE	CULMINATED	CUMMINGTONITE	CURABILITY
CRYSTALISED	CTENOPHORES	CULMINATES	CUMMINGTONITES	CURABLENESS
CRYSTALISER	CUADRILLAS	CULMINATING	CUMULATELY	CURABLENESSES
CRYSTALISERS	CUBANELLES	CULMINATION	CUMULATING	CURANDERAS
CRYSTALISES	CUBBYHOLES	CULMINATIONS	CUMULATION	CURANDEROS
CRYSTALISING	CUBICALNESS	CULPABILITIES	CUMULATIONS	CURARISATION
CRYSTALIZABLE	CUBICALNESSES	CULPABILITY	CUMULATIVE	CURARISATIONS
CRYSTALIZATION	CUBICITIES	CULPABLENESS	CUMULATIVELY	CURARISING
CRYSTALIZATIONS	CUBISTICALLY	CULPABLENESSES	CUMULATIVENESS	CURARIZATION
CRYSTALIZE	CUCKOLDING	CULTISHNESS	CUMULIFORM	CURARIZATIONS
CRYSTALIZED	CUCKOLDISE	CULTISHNESSES	CUMULOCIRRI	CURARIZING
CRYSTALIZER	CUCKOLDISED	CULTIVABILITIES	CUMULOCIRRUS	CURATESHIP
CRYSTALIZERS	CUCKOLDISES	CULTIVABILITY	CUMULONIMBI	CURATESHIPS
CRYSTALIZES	CUCKOLDISING	CULTIVABLE	CUMULONIMBUS	CURATIVELY
CRYSTALIZING	CUCKOLDIZE	CULTIVATABLE	CUMULONIMBUSES	CURATIVENESS
CRYSTALLINE	CUCKOLDIZED	CULTIVATED	CUMULOSTRATI	CURATIVENESSES
CRYSTALLINES	CUCKOLDIZES	CULTIVATES	CUMULOSTRATUS	CURATORIAL
CRYSTALLINITIES	CUCKOLDIZING	CULTIVATING	CUNCTATION	CURATORSHIP
CRYSTALLINITY	CUCKOLDOMS	CULTIVATION	CUNCTATIONS	CURATORSHIPS
CRYSTALLISABLE	CUCKOLDRIES	CULTIVATIONS	CUNCTATIOUS	CURATRIXES
CRYSTALLISATION	CUCKOOFLOWER	CULTIVATOR	CUNCTATIVE	CURBSTONES
CRYSTALLISE	CUCKOOFLOWERS	CULTIVATORS	CUNCTATORS	CURCUMINES
CRYSTALLISED	CUCKOOPINT	CULTRIFORM	CUNCTATORY	CURDINESSES
CRYSTALLISER	CUCKOOPINTS	CULTURABLE	CUNEIFORMS	CURETTAGES
CRYSTALLISERS	CUCULIFORM	CULTURALLY	CUNNILINCTUS	CURETTEMENT
CRYSTALLISES	CUCULLATED	CULTURELESS	CUNNILINCTUSES	CURETTEMENTS
CRYSTALLISING	CUCULLATELY	CULTURISTS	CUNNILINGUS	CURFUFFLED
CRYSTALLITE	CUCUMIFORM	CULVERINEER	CUNNILINGUSES	CURFUFFLES
CRYSTALLITES	CUCURBITACEOUS	CULVERINEERS	CUNNINGEST	CURFUFFLING
CRYSTALLITIC	CUCURBITAL	CULVERTAGE	CUNNINGNESS	CURIALISMS
CRYSTALLITIS	CUDDLESOME	CULVERTAGES	CUNNINGNESSES	CURIALISTIC
CRYSTALLITISES	CUDGELINGS	CULVERTAILED	CUPBEARERS	CURIALISTS
CRYSTALLIZABLE	CUDGELLERS	CULVERTING	CUPBOARDED	CURIETHERAPIES
CRYSTALLIZATION	CUDGELLING	CUMBERBUND	CUPBOARDING	CURIETHERAPY
CRYSTALLIZE	CUDGELLINGS	CUMBERBUNDS	CUPELLATION	CURIOSITIES
CRYSTALLIZED	CUFFUFFLES	CUMBERLESS	CUPELLATIONS	CURIOUSEST
CRYSTALLIZER	CUIRASSIER	CUMBERMENT	CUPFERRONS	CURIOUSNESS
CRYSTALLIZERS	CUIRASSIERS	CUMBERMENTS	CUPIDINOUS	CURIOUSNESSES
CRYSTALLIZES	CUIRASSING	CUMBERSOME	CUPIDITIES	CURLICUING

CURLIEWURLIE	CURVACEOUSLY	CUSTOMISER	CYANOETHYLATING	CYBERNETICISTS
CURLIEWURLIES	CURVACEOUSNESS	CUSTOMISERS	CYANOETHYLATION	CYBERNETICS
CURLINESSES	CURVACIOUS	CUSTOMISES	CYANOGENAMIDE	CYBERPHOBIA
CURLPAPERS	CURVACIOUSLY	CUSTOMISING	CYANOGENAMIDES	CYBERPHOBIAS
CURMUDGEON	CURVACIOUSNESS	CUSTOMIZATION	CYANOGENESES	CYBERPHOBIC
CURMUDGEONLY	CURVATIONS	CUSTOMIZATIONS	CYANOGENESIS	CYBERPORNS
CURMUDGEONS	CURVATURES	CUSTOMIZED	CYANOGENETIC	CYBERPUNKS
CURMURRING	CURVEBALLED	CUSTOMIZER	CYANOGENIC	CYBERSECURITIES
CURMURRINGS	CURVEBALLING	CUSTOMIZERS	CYANOHYDRIN	CYBERSECURITY
CURNAPTIOUS	CURVEBALLS	CUSTOMIZES	CYANOHYDRINS	CYBERSEXES
CURRAJONGS	CURVEDNESS	CUSTOMIZING	CYANOMETER	CYBERSPACE
CURRANTIER	CURVEDNESSES	CUSTOMSHOUSE	CYANOMETERS	CYBERSPACES
CURRANTIEST	CURVETTING	CUSTOMSHOUSES	CYANOPHYTE	CYBERSQUATTER
CURRAWONGS	CURVICAUDATE	CUSTUMARIES	CYANOPHYTES	CYBERSQUATTERS
CURREJONGS	CURVICOSTATE	CUTABILITIES	CYANOTYPES	CYBERSQUATTING
CURRENCIES	CURVIFOLIATE	CUTABILITY	CYANURATES	CYBERSQUATTINGS
CURRENTNESS	CURVILINEAL	CUTANEOUSLY	CYATHIFORM	CYBERSTALKER
CURRENTNESSES	CURVILINEALLY	CUTCHERIES	CYBERATHLETE	CYBERSTALKERS
CURRICULAR	CURVILINEAR	CUTCHERRIES	CYBERATHLETES	CYBERSTALKING
CURRICULUM	CURVILINEARITY	CUTENESSES	CYBERATHLETICS	CYBERSTALKINGS
CURRICULUMS	CURVILINEARLY	CUTGRASSES	CYBERATTACK	CYBERTERRORISM
CURRIERIES	CURVINESSES	CUTINISATION	CYBERATTACKS	CYBERTERRORISMS
CURRIJONGS	CURVIROSTRAL	CUTINISATIONS	CYBERBULLIES	CYBERTERRORIST
CURRISHNESS	CUSHINESSES	CUTINISING	CYBERBULLY	CYBERTERRORISTS
CURRISHNESSES	CUSHIONETS	CUTINIZATION	CYBERBULLYING	CYBRARIANS
CURRYCOMBED	CUSHIONING	CUTINIZATIONS	CYBERBULLYINGS	CYCADACEOUS
CURRYCOMBING	CUSHIONINGS	CUTINIZING	CYBERCAFES	CYCADEOIDS
CURRYCOMBS	CUSHIONLESS	CUTTHROATS	CYBERCASTS	CYCADOPHYTE
CURSEDNESS	CUSPIDATED	CUTTLEBONE	CYBERCHONDRIA	CYCADOPHYTES
CURSEDNESSES	CUSPIDATION	CUTTLEBONES	CYBERCHONDRIAC	CYCLAMATES
CURSELARIE	CUSPIDATIONS	CUTTLEFISH	CYBERCHONDRIACS	CYCLANDELATE
CURSIVENESS	CUSPIDORES	CUTTLEFISHES	CYBERCHONDRIAS	CYCLANDELATES
CURSIVENESSES	CUSSEDNESS	CYANAMIDES	CYBERCRIME	CYCLANTHACEOUS
CURSORINESS	CUSSEDNESSES	CYANIDATION	CYBERCRIMES	CYCLAZOCINE
CURSORINESSES	CUSTODIANS	CYANIDATIONS	CYBERCRIMINAL	CYCLAZOCINES
CURSTNESSES	CUSTODIANSHIP	CYANIDINGS	CYBERCRIMINALS	CYCLEPATHS
CURTAILERS	CUSTODIANSHIPS	CYANOACETYLENE	CYBERNATED	CYCLICALITIES
CURTAILING	CUSTODIERS	CYANOACETYLENES	CYBERNATES	CYCLICALITY
CURTAILMENT	CUSTOMABLE	CYANOACRYLATE	CYBERNATING	CYCLICALLY
CURTAILMENTS	CUSTOMARIES	CYANOACRYLATES	CYBERNATION	CYCLICISMS
CURTAINING	CUSTOMARILY	CYANOBACTERIA	CYBERNATIONS	CYCLICITIES
CURTAINLESS	CUSTOMARINESS	CYANOBACTERIUM	CYBERNAUTS	CYCLISATION
CURTALAXES	CUSTOMARINESSES	CYANOCOBALAMIN	CYBERNETIC	CYCLISATIONS
CURTATIONS	CUSTOMHOUSE	CYANOCOBALAMINE	CYBERNETICAL	CYCLIZATION
CURTILAGES	CUSTOMHOUSES	CYANOCOBALAMINS	CYBERNETICALLY	CYCLIZATIONS
CURTNESSES	CUSTOMISATION	CYANOETHYLATE	CYBERNETICIAN	CYCLIZINES
CURTSEYING	CUSTOMISATIONS	CYANOETHYLATED	CYBERNETICIANS	CYCLOADDITION
CURVACEOUS	CUSTOMISED	CYANOETHYLATES	CYBERNETICIST	CYCLOADDITIONS

CYCLOALIPHATIC
CYCLOALKANE
CYCLOALKANES
CYCLOBARBITONE
CYCLOBARBITONES
CYCLODEXTRIN
CYCLODEXTRINS
CYCLODIALYSES
CYCLODIALYSIS
CYCLODIENE
CYCLODIENES
CYCLOGENESES
CYCLOGENESIS
CYCLOGIROS
CYCLOGRAPH
CYCLOGRAPHIC
CYCLOGRAPHS
CYCLOHEXANE
CYCLOHEXANES
CYCLOHEXANONE
CYCLOHEXANONES
CYCLOHEXIMIDE
CYCLOHEXIMIDES
CYCLOHEXYLAMINE
CYCLOIDALLY
CYCLOIDIAN
CYCLOIDIANS
CYCLOLITHS
CYCLOMETER
CYCLOMETERS
CYCLOMETRIES
CYCLOMETRY
CYCLONICAL
CYCLONICALLY
CYCLONITES
CYCLOOLEFIN
CYCLOOLEFINIC
CYCLOOLEFINS
CYCLOPAEDIA
CYCLOPAEDIAS
CYCLOPAEDIC
CYCLOPAEDIST
CYCLOPAEDISTS
CYCLOPARAFFIN
CYCLOPARAFFINS
CYCLOPEDIA
CYCLOPEDIAS
CYCLOPEDIC

CYCLOPEDIST
CYCLOPEDISTS
CYCLOPENTADIENE
CYCLOPENTANE
CYCLOPENTANES
CYCLOPENTOLATE
CYCLOPENTOLATES
CYCLOPLEGIA
CYCLOPLEGIAS
CYCLOPLEGIC
CYCLOPROPANE
CYCLOPROPANES
CYCLORAMAS
CYCLORAMIC
CYCLOSERINE
CYCLOSERINES
CYCLOSPERMOUS
CYCLOSPORIN
CYCLOSPORINE
CYCLOSPORINES
CYCLOSPORINS
CYCLOSTOMATE
CYCLOSTOMATOUS
CYCLOSTOME
CYCLOSTOMES
CYCLOSTOMOUS
CYCLOSTYLE
CYCLOSTYLED
CYCLOSTYLES
CYCLOSTYLING
CYCLOTHYME
CYCLOTHYMES
CYCLOTHYMIA
CYCLOTHYMIAC
CYCLOTHYMIACS
CYCLOTHYMIAS
CYCLOTHYMIC
CYCLOTHYMICS
CYCLOTOMIC
CYCLOTRONS
CYLINDERED
CYLINDERING
CYLINDRACEOUS
CYLINDRICAL
CYLINDRICALITY
CYLINDRICALLY
CYLINDRICALNESS
CYLINDRICITIES

CYLINDRICITY
CYLINDRIFORM
CYLINDRITE
CYLINDRITES
CYLINDROID
CYLINDROIDS
CYMAGRAPHS
CYMBALEERS
CYMBALISTS
CYMBIDIUMS
CYMIFEROUS
CYMOGRAPHIC
CYMOGRAPHS
CYMOPHANES
CYMOPHANOUS
CYMOTRICHIES
CYMOTRICHOUS
CYMOTRICHY
CYNGHANEDD
CYNGHANEDDS
CYNICALNESS
CYNICALNESSES
CYNOMOLGUS
CYNOMOLGUSES
CYNOPHILIA
CYNOPHILIAS
CYNOPHILIST
CYNOPHILISTS
CYNOPHOBIA
CYNOPHOBIAS
CYNOPODOUS
CYPERACEOUS
CYPRINODONT
CYPRINODONTS
CYPRINOIDS
CYPRIPEDIA
CYPRIPEDIUM
CYPRIPEDIUMS
CYPROHEPTADINE
CYPROHEPTADINES
CYPROTERONE
CYPROTERONES
CYSTEAMINE
CYSTEAMINES
CYSTECTOMIES
CYSTECTOMY
CYSTICERCI
CYSTICERCOID

CYSTICERCOIDS
CYSTICERCOSES
CYSTICERCOSIS
CYSTICERCUS
CYSTIDEANS
CYSTINOSES
CYSTINOSIS
CYSTINURIA
CYSTINURIAS
CYSTITIDES
CYSTITISES
CYSTOCARPIC
CYSTOCARPS
CYSTOCELES
CYSTOGENOUS
CYSTOGRAPHIES
CYSTOGRAPHY
CYSTOLITHIASES
CYSTOLITHIASIS
CYSTOLITHS
CYSTOSCOPE
CYSTOSCOPES
CYSTOSCOPIC
CYSTOSCOPIES
CYSTOSCOPY
CYSTOSTOMIES
CYSTOSTOMY
CYSTOTOMIES
CYSTOCHALASIN
CYTOCHALASIN
CYTOCHALASINS
CYTOCHEMICAL
CYTOCHEMISTRIES
CYTOCHEMISTRY
CYTOCHROME
CYTOCHROMES
CYTODIAGNOSES
CYTODIAGNOSIS
CYTOGENESES
CYTOGENESIS
CYTOGENETIC
CYTOGENETICAL
CYTOGENETICALLY
CYTOGENETICIST
CYTOGENETICISTS
CYTOGENETICS
CYTOGENIES
CYTOKINESES
CYTOKINESIS

CYTOKINETIC
CYTOKININS
CYTOLOGICAL
CYTOLOGICALLY
CYTOLOGIES
CYTOLOGIST
CYTOLOGISTS
CYTOLYSINS
CYTOMEGALIC
CYTOMEGALOVIRUS
CYTOMEMBRANE
CYTOMEMBRANES
CYTOMETERS
CYTOMETRIC
CYTOMETRIES
CYTOPATHIC
CYTOPATHIES
CYTOPATHOGENIC
CYTOPATHOLOGIES
CYTOPATHOLOGY
CYTOPENIAS
CYTOPHILIC
CYTOPHOTOMETRIC
CYTOPHOTOMETRY
CYTOPLASMIC
CYTOPLASMICALLY
CYTOPLASMS
CYTOPLASTIC
CYTOPLASTS
CYTOSKELETAL
CYTOSKELETON
CYTOSKELETONS
CYTOSTATIC
CYTOSTATICALLY
CYTOSTATICS
CYTOTAXONOMIC
CYTOTAXONOMIES
CYTOTAXONOMIST
CYTOTAXONOMISTS
CYTOTAXONOMY
CYTOTECHNOLOGY
CYTOTOXICITIES
CYTOTOXICITY
CYTOTOXINS
CZAREVICHES
CZAREVITCH
CZAREVITCHES

D

DABBLINGLY
DACHSHUNDS
DACOITAGES
DACQUOISES
DACTYLICALLY
DACTYLIOGRAPHY
DACTYLIOLOGIES
DACTYLIOLOGY
DACTYLIOMANCIES
DACTYLIOMANCY
DACTYLISTS
DACTYLOGRAM
DACTYLOGRAMS
DACTYLOGRAPHER
DACTYLOGRAPHERS
DACTYLOGRAPHIC
DACTYLOGRAPHIES
DACTYLOGRAPHY
DACTYLOLOGIES
DACTYLOLOGY
DACTYLOSCOPIES
DACTYLOSCOPY
DAFFADOWNDILLY
DAFFINESSES
DAFFODILLIES
DAFFODILLY
DAFTNESSES
DAGGERBOARD
DAGGERBOARDS
DAGGERLIKE
DAGUERREAN
DAGUERREOTYPE
DAGUERREOTYPED
DAGUERREOTYPER
DAGUERREOTYPERS
DAGUERREOTYPES
DAGUERREOTYPIES
DAGUERREOTYPING
DAGUERREOTYPIST
DAGUERREOTYPY
DAHABEEAHS

DAHABEEYAH
DAHABEEYAHS
DAHABIYAHS
DAHABIYEHS
DAILINESSES
DAILYNESSES
DAINTINESS
DAINTINESSES
DAIRYMAIDS
DAISYWHEEL
DAISYWHEELS
DALLIANCES
DALMATIANS
DALTONISMS
DAMAGEABILITIES
DAMAGEABILITY
DAMAGEABLE
DAMAGINGLY
DAMASCEENE
DAMASCEENED
DAMASCEENES
DAMASCEENING
DAMASCENED
DAMASCENES
DAMASCENING
DAMASCENINGS
DAMASKEENED
DAMASKEENING
DAMASKEENS
DAMASKINED
DAMASKINING
DAMASQUINED
DAMASQUINING
DAMASQUINS
DAMINOZIDE
DAMINOZIDES
DAMNABILITIES
DAMNABILITY
DAMNABLENESS
DAMNABLENESSES
DAMNATIONS

DAMNEDESTS
DAMNIFICATION
DAMNIFICATIONS
DAMNIFYING
DAMOISELLE
DAMOISELLES
DAMPCOURSE
DAMPCOURSES
DAMPISHNESS
DAMPISHNESSES
DAMPNESSES
DAMSELFISH
DAMSELFISHES
DAMSELFLIES
DANCEHALLS
DANDELIONS
DANDIFICATION
DANDIFICATIONS
DANDIFYING
DANDIPRATS
DANDYFUNKS
DANDYISHLY
DANDYPRATS
DANGERLESS
DANGEROUSLY
DANGEROUSNESS
DANGEROUSNESSES
DANGLINGLY
DANKNESSES
DANNEBROGS
DANTHONIAS
DAPPERLING
DAPPERLINGS
DAPPERNESS
DAPPERNESSES
DAREDEVILRIES
DAREDEVILRY
DAREDEVILS
DAREDEVILTRIES
DAREDEVILTRY
DARINGNESS

DARINGNESSES
DARKNESSES
DARLINGNESS
DARLINGNESSES
DARMSTADTIUM
DARMSTADTIUMS
DARNATIONS
DARNEDESTS
DARRAIGNED
DARRAIGNES
DARRAIGNING
DARRAIGNMENT
DARRAIGNMENTS
DARRAINING
DARRAYNING
DARTBOARDS
DARTITISES
DASHBOARDS
DASHLIGHTS
DASTARDIES
DASTARDLINESS
DASTARDLINESSES
DASTARDNESS
DASTARDNESSES
DASYMETERS
DASYPAEDAL
DASYPHYLLOUS
DATABASING
DATABUSSES
DATAGLOVES
DATAMATION
DATAMATIONS
DATAVEILLANCE
DATAVEILLANCES
DATEDNESSES
DATELINING
DAUGHTERBOARD
DAUGHTERBOARDS
DAUGHTERHOOD
DAUGHTERHOODS
DAUGHTERLESS

DAUGHTERLINESS
DAUGHTERLING
DAUGHTERLINGS
DAUGHTERLY
DAUNDERING
DAUNOMYCIN
DAUNOMYCINS
DAUNORUBICIN
DAUNORUBICINS
DAUNTINGLY
DAUNTLESSLY
DAUNTLESSNESS
DAUNTLESSNESSES
DAUNTONING
DAUPHINESS
DAUPHINESSES
DAVENPORTS
DAWDLINGLY
DAWSONITES
DAYCATIONS
DAYCENTRES
DAYDREAMED
DAYDREAMER
DAYDREAMERS
DAYDREAMING
DAYDREAMINGS
DAYDREAMLIKE
DAYFLOWERS
DAYLIGHTED
DAYLIGHTING
DAYLIGHTINGS
DAYSAILERS
DAYSAILING
DAYSAILORS
DAYSPRINGS
DAYWORKERS
DAZEDNESSES
DAZZLEMENT
DAZZLEMENTS
DAZZLINGLY
DEACIDIFICATION

DEACIDIFIED
DEACIDIFIES
DEACIDIFYING
DEACONESSES
DEACONHOOD
DEACONHOODS
DEACONRIES
DEACONSHIP
DEACONSHIPS
DEACTIVATE
DEACTIVATED
DEACTIVATES
DEACTIVATING
DEACTIVATION
DEACTIVATIONS
DEACTIVATOR
DEACTIVATORS
DEADENINGLY
DEADENINGS
DEADHEADED
DEADHEADING
DEADHOUSES
DEADLIFTED
DEADLIFTING
DEADLIGHTS
DEADLINESS
DEADLINESSES
DEADLINING
DEADLOCKED
DEADLOCKING
DEADNESSES
DEADPANNED
DEADPANNER
DEADPANNERS
DEADPANNING
DEADSTOCKS
DEADSTROKE
DEADWEIGHT
DEADWEIGHTS
DEAERATING
DEAERATION
DEAERATIONS
DEAERATORS
DEAFENINGLY
DEAFENINGS
DEAFNESSES
DEALATIONS

DEALBATION
DEALBATIONS
DEALBREAKER
DEALBREAKERS
DEALERSHIP
DEALERSHIPS
DEALFISHES
DEALIGNING
DEALMAKERS
DEAMBULATORIES
DEAMBULATORY
DEAMINASES
DEAMINATED
DEAMINATES
DEAMINATING
DEAMINATION
DEAMINATIONS
DEAMINISATION
DEAMINISATIONS
DEAMINISED
DEAMINISES
DEAMINISING
DEAMINIZATION
DEAMINIZATIONS
DEAMINIZED
DEAMINIZES
DEAMINIZING
DEARBOUGHT
DEARNESSES
DEARTICULATE
DEARTICULATED
DEARTICULATES
DEARTICULATING
DEASPIRATE
DEASPIRATED
DEASPIRATES
DEASPIRATING
DEASPIRATION
DEASPIRATIONS
DEATHBLOWS
DEATHLESSLY
DEATHLESSNESS
DEATHLESSNESSES
DEATHLIEST
DEATHLINESS
DEATHLINESSES
DEATHTRAPS

DEATHWARDS
DEATHWATCH
DEATHWATCHES
DEATTRIBUTE
DEATTRIBUTED
DEATTRIBUTES
DEATTRIBUTING
DEBAGGINGS
DEBARCATION
DEBARCATIONS
DEBARKATION
DEBARKATIONS
DEBARMENTS
DEBARRASSED
DEBARRASSES
DEBARRASSING
DEBASEDNESS
DEBASEDNESSES
DEBASEMENT
DEBASEMENTS
DEBASINGLY
DEBATEABLE
DEBATEMENT
DEBATEMENTS
DEBATINGLY
DEBAUCHEDLY
DEBAUCHEDNESS
DEBAUCHEDNESSES
DEBAUCHEES
DEBAUCHERIES
DEBAUCHERS
DEBAUCHERY
DEBAUCHING
DEBAUCHMENT
DEBAUCHMENTS
DEBEARDING
DEBENTURED
DEBENTURES
DEBILITATE
DEBILITATED
DEBILITATES
DEBILITATING
DEBILITATION
DEBILITATIONS
DEBILITATIVE
DEBILITIES
DEBONAIRLY

DEBONAIRNESS
DEBONAIRNESSES
DEBONNAIRE
DEBOUCHING
DEBOUCHMENT
DEBOUCHMENTS
DEBOUCHURE
DEBOUCHURES
DEBRIDEMENT
DEBRIDEMENTS
DEBRIEFERS
DEBRIEFING
DEBRIEFINGS
DEBRUISING
DEBUGGINGS
DEBUTANTES
DECACHORDS
DECADENCES
DECADENCIES
DECADENTLY
DECAFFEINATE
DECAFFEINATED
DECAFFEINATES
DECAFFEINATING
DECAGONALLY
DECAGRAMME
DECAGRAMMES
DECAGYNIAN
DECAGYNOUS
DECAHEDRAL
DECAHEDRON
DECAHEDRONS
DECALCIFICATION
DECALCIFIED
DECALCIFIER
DECALCIFIERS
DECALCIFIES
DECALCIFYING
DECALCOMANIA
DECALCOMANIAS
DECALESCENCE
DECALESCENCES
DECALESCENT
DECALITERS
DECALITRES
DECALOGIST
DECALOGISTS

DECALOGUES
DECAMERONIC
DECAMEROUS
DECAMETERS
DECAMETHONIUM
DECAMETHONIUMS
DECAMETRES
DECAMETRIC
DECAMPMENT
DECAMPMENTS
DECANDRIAN
DECANDROUS
DECANEDIOIC
DECANICALLY
DECANTATED
DECANTATES
DECANTATING
DECANTATION
DECANTATIONS
DECAPITALISE
DECAPITALISED
DECAPITALISES
DECAPITALISING
DECAPITALIZE
DECAPITALIZED
DECAPITALIZES
DECAPITALIZING
DECAPITATE
DECAPITATED
DECAPITATES
DECAPITATING
DECAPITATION
DECAPITATIONS
DECAPITATOR
DECAPITATORS
DECAPODANS
DECAPODOUS
DECAPSULATE
DECAPSULATED
DECAPSULATES
DECAPSULATING
DECAPSULATION
DECAPSULATIONS
DECARBONATE
DECARBONATED
DECARBONATES
DECARBONATING

DECARBONATION
DECARBONATIONS
DECARBONATOR
DECARBONATORS
DECARBONISATION
DECARBONISE
DECARBONISED
DECARBONISER
DECARBONISERS
DECARBONISES
DECARBONISING
DECARBONIZATION
DECARBONIZE
DECARBONIZED
DECARBONIZER
DECARBONIZERS
DECARBONIZES
DECARBONIZING
DECARBOXYLASE
DECARBOXYLASES
DECARBOXYLATE
DECARBOXYLATED
DECARBOXYLATES
DECARBOXYLATING
DECARBOXYLATION
DECARBURATION
DECARBURATIONS
DECARBURISATION
DECARBURISE
DECARBURISED
DECARBURISES
DECARBURISING
DECARBURIZATION
DECARBURIZE
DECARBURIZED
DECARBURIZES
DECARBURIZING
DECARTELISE
DECARTELISED
DECARTELISES
DECARTELISING
DECARTELIZE
DECARTELIZED
DECARTELIZES
DECARTELIZING
DECASTERES
DECASTICHS

DECASTYLES
DECASUALISATION
DECASUALISE
DECASUALISED
DECASUALISES
DECASUALISING
DECASUALIZATION
DECASUALIZE
DECASUALIZED
DECASUALIZES
DECASUALIZING
DECASYLLABIC
DECASYLLABICS
DECASYLLABLE
DECASYLLABLES
DECATHLETE
DECATHLETES
DECATHLONS
DECAUDATED
DECAUDATES
DECAUDATING
DECEITFULLY
DECEITFULNESS
DECEITFULNESSES
DECEIVABILITIES
DECEIVABILITY
DECEIVABLE
DECEIVABLENESS
DECEIVABLY
DECEIVINGLY
DECEIVINGS
DECELERATE
DECELERATED
DECELERATES
DECELERATING
DECELERATION
DECELERATIONS
DECELERATOR
DECELERATORS
DECELEROMETER
DECELEROMETERS
DECELERONS
DECEMVIRAL
DECEMVIRATE
DECEMVIRATES
DECENARIES
DECENNARIES

DECENNIALLY
DECENNIALS
DECENNIUMS
DECENNOVAL
DECENTERED
DECENTERING
DECENTNESS
DECENTNESSES
DECENTRALISE
DECENTRALISED
DECENTRALISES
DECENTRALISING
DECENTRALIST
DECENTRALISTS
DECENTRALIZE
DECENTRALIZED
DECENTRALIZES
DECENTRALIZING
DECENTRING
DECEPTIBILITIES
DECEPTIBILITY
DECEPTIBLE
DECEPTIONAL
DECEPTIONS
DECEPTIOUS
DECEPTIVELY
DECEPTIVENESS
DECEPTIVENESSES
DECEREBRATE
DECEREBRATED
DECEREBRATES
DECEREBRATING
DECEREBRATION
DECEREBRATIONS
DECEREBRISE
DECEREBRISED
DECEREBRISES
DECEREBRISING
DECEREBRIZE
DECEREBRIZED
DECEREBRIZES
DECEREBRIZING
DECERTIFICATION
DECERTIFIED
DECERTIFIES
DECERTIFYING
DECESSIONS

DECHEANCES
DECHLORINATE
DECHLORINATED
DECHLORINATES
DECHLORINATING
DECHLORINATION
DECHLORINATIONS
DECHRISTIANISE
DECHRISTIANISED
DECHRISTIANISES
DECHRISTIANIZE
DECHRISTIANIZED
DECHRISTIANIZES
DECIDABILITIES
DECIDABILITY
DECIDEDNESS
DECIDEDNESSES
DECIDUOUSLY
DECIDUOUSNESS
DECIDUOUSNESSES
DECIGRAMME
DECIGRAMMES
DECILITERS
DECILITRES
DECILLIONS
DECILLIONTH
DECILLIONTHS
DECIMALISATION
DECIMALISATIONS
DECIMALISE
DECIMALISED
DECIMALISES
DECIMALISING
DECIMALISM
DECIMALISMS
DECIMALIST
DECIMALISTS
DECIMALIZATION
DECIMALIZATIONS
DECIMALIZE
DECIMALIZED
DECIMALIZES
DECIMALIZING
DECIMATING
DECIMATION
DECIMATIONS
DECIMATORS

DECIMETERS
DECIMETRES
DECIMETRIC
DECINORMAL
DECIPHERABILITY
DECIPHERABLE
DECIPHERED
DECIPHERER
DECIPHERERS
DECIPHERING
DECIPHERMENT
DECIPHERMENTS
DECISIONAL
DECISIONED
DECISIONING
DECISIVELY
DECISIVENESS
DECISIVENESSES
DECISTERES
DECITIZENISE
DECITIZENISED
DECITIZENISES
DECITIZENISING
DECITIZENIZE
DECITIZENIZED
DECITIZENIZES
DECITIZENIZING
DECIVILISE
DECIVILISED
DECIVILISES
DECIVILISING
DECIVILIZE
DECIVILIZED
DECIVILIZES
DECIVILIZING
DECKCHAIRS
DECKHOUSES
DECLAIMANT
DECLAIMANTS
DECLAIMERS
DECLAIMING
DECLAIMINGS
DECLAMATION
DECLAMATIONS
DECLAMATORILY
DECLAMATORY
DECLARABLE

DECLARANTS

DECLARANTS
DECLARATION
DECLARATIONS
DECLARATIVE
DECLARATIVELY
DECLARATOR
DECLARATORILY
DECLARATORS
DECLARATORY
DECLAREDLY
DECLASSIFIABLE
DECLASSIFIED
DECLASSIFIES
DECLASSIFY
DECLASSIFYING
DECLASSING
DECLENSION
DECLENSIONAL
DECLENSIONALLY
DECLENSIONS
DECLINABLE
DECLINANTS
DECLINATION
DECLINATIONAL
DECLINATIONS
DECLINATOR
DECLINATORIES
DECLINATORS
DECLINATORY
DECLINATURE
DECLINATURES
DECLINISTS
DECLINOMETER
DECLINOMETERS
DECLIVITIES
DECLIVITOUS
DECLUTCHED
DECLUTCHES
DECLUTCHING
DECLUTTERED
DECLUTTERING
DECLUTTERS
DECOCTIBLE
DECOCTIONS
DECOCTURES
DECOHERENCE
DECOHERENCES

DECOHERERS
DECOLLATED
DECOLLATES
DECOLLATING
DECOLLATION
DECOLLATIONS
DECOLLATOR
DECOLLATORS
DECOLLETAGE
DECOLLETAGES
DECOLLETES
DECOLONISATION
DECOLONISATIONS
DECOLONISE
DECOLONISED
DECOLONISES
DECOLONISING
DECOLONIZATION
DECOLONIZATIONS
DECOLONIZE
DECOLONIZED
DECOLONIZES
DECOLONIZING
DECOLORANT
DECOLORANTS
DECOLORATE
DECOLORATED
DECOLORATES
DECOLORATING
DECOLORATION
DECOLORATIONS
DECOLORING
DECOLORISATION
DECOLORISATIONS
DECOLORISE
DECOLORISED
DECOLORISER
DECOLORISERS
DECOLORISES
DECOLORISING
DECOLORIZATION
DECOLORIZATIONS
DECOLORIZE
DECOLORIZED
DECOLORIZER
DECOLORIZERS
DECOLORIZES

DECOLORIZING
DECOLOURED
DECOLOURING
DECOLOURISATION
DECOLOURISE
DECOLOURISED
DECOLOURISES
DECOLOURISING
DECOLOURIZATION
DECOLOURIZE
DECOLOURIZED
DECOLOURIZES
DECOLOURIZING
DECOMMISSION
DECOMMISSIONED
DECOMMISSIONER
DECOMMISSIONERS
DECOMMISSIONING
DECOMMISSIONS
DECOMMITTED
DECOMMITTING
DECOMMUNISATION
DECOMMUNISE
DECOMMUNISED
DECOMMUNISES
DECOMMUNISING
DECOMMUNIZATION
DECOMMUNIZE
DECOMMUNIZED
DECOMMUNIZES
DECOMMUNIZING
DECOMPENSATE
DECOMPENSATED
DECOMPENSATES
DECOMPENSATING
DECOMPENSATION
DECOMPENSATIONS
DECOMPOSABILITY
DECOMPOSABLE
DECOMPOSED
DECOMPOSER
DECOMPOSERS
DECOMPOSES
DECOMPOSING
DECOMPOSITE
DECOMPOSITES
DECOMPOSITION

DECOMPOSITIONS
DECOMPOUND
DECOMPOUNDABLE
DECOMPOUNDED
DECOMPOUNDING
DECOMPOUNDS
DECOMPRESS
DECOMPRESSED
DECOMPRESSES
DECOMPRESSING
DECOMPRESSION
DECOMPRESSIONS
DECOMPRESSIVE
DECOMPRESSOR
DECOMPRESSORS
DECONCENTRATE
DECONCENTRATED
DECONCENTRATES
DECONCENTRATING
DECONCENTRATION
DECONDITION
DECONDITIONED
DECONDITIONING
DECONDITIONS
DECONGESTANT
DECONGESTANTS
DECONGESTED
DECONGESTING
DECONGESTION
DECONGESTIONS
DECONGESTIVE
DECONGESTS
DECONSECRATE
DECONSECRATED
DECONSECRATES
DECONSECRATING
DECONSECRATION
DECONSECRATIONS
DECONSTRUCT
DECONSTRUCTED
DECONSTRUCTING
DECONSTRUCTION
DECONSTRUCTIONS
DECONSTRUCTIVE
DECONSTRUCTOR
DECONSTRUCTORS
DECONSTRUCTS

DECONTAMINANT
DECONTAMINANTS
DECONTAMINATE
DECONTAMINATED
DECONTAMINATES
DECONTAMINATING
DECONTAMINATION
DECONTAMINATIVE
DECONTAMINATOR
DECONTAMINATORS
DECONTEXTUALISE
DECONTEXTUALIZE
DECONTROLLED
DECONTROLLING
DECONTROLS
DECORATING
DECORATINGS
DECORATION
DECORATIONS
DECORATIVE
DECORATIVELY
DECORATIVENESS
DECORATORS
DECOROUSLY
DECOROUSNESS
DECOROUSNESSES
DECORTICATE
DECORTICATED
DECORTICATES
DECORTICATING
DECORTICATION
DECORTICATIONS
DECORTICATOR
DECORTICATORS
DECOUPAGED
DECOUPAGES
DECOUPAGING
DECOUPLERS
DECOUPLING
DECOUPLINGS
DECRASSIFIED
DECRASSIFIES
DECRASSIFY
DECRASSIFYING
DECREASING
DECREASINGLY
DECREASINGS

DECREEABLE
DECREMENTAL
DECREMENTED
DECREMENTING
DECREMENTS
DECREPITATE
DECREPITATED
DECREPITATES
DECREPITATING
DECREPITATION
DECREPITATIONS
DECREPITLY
DECREPITNESS
DECREPITNESSES
DECREPITUDE
DECREPITUDES
DECRESCENCE
DECRESCENCES
DECRESCENDO
DECRESCENDOS
DECRESCENT
DECRETALIST
DECRETALISTS
DECRETISTS
DECRIMINALISE
DECRIMINALISED
DECRIMINALISES
DECRIMINALISING
DECRIMINALIZE
DECRIMINALIZED
DECRIMINALIZES
DECRIMINALIZING
DECROWNING
DECRUSTATION
DECRUSTATIONS
DECRYPTING
DECRYPTION
DECRYPTIONS
DECUMBENCE
DECUMBENCES
DECUMBENCIES
DECUMBENCY
DECUMBENTLY
DECUMBITURE
DECUMBITURES
DECUMULATION
DECUMULATIONS

DECURIONATE
DECURIONATES
DECURRENCIES
DECURRENCY
DECURRENTLY
DECURSIONS
DECURSIVELY
DECURVATION
DECURVATIONS
DECUSSATED
DECUSSATELY
DECUSSATES
DECUSSATING
DECUSSATION
DECUSSATIONS
DEDICATEDLY
DEDICATEES
DEDICATING
DEDICATION
DEDICATIONAL
DEDICATIONS
DEDICATIVE
DEDICATORIAL
DEDICATORS
DEDICATORY
DEDIFFERENTIATE
DEDRAMATISE
DEDRAMATISED
DEDRAMATISES
DEDRAMATISING
DEDRAMATIZE
DEDRAMATIZED
DEDRAMATIZES
DEDRAMATIZING
DEDUCEMENT
DEDUCEMENTS
DEDUCIBILITIES
DEDUCIBILITY
DEDUCIBLENESS
DEDUCIBLENESSES
DEDUCTIBILITIES
DEDUCTIBILITY
DEDUCTIBLE
DEDUCTIBLES
DEDUCTIONS
DEDUCTIVELY
DEDUPLICATE

DEDUPLICATED
DEDUPLICATES
DEDUPLICATING
DEDUPLICATION
DEDUPLICATIONS
DEEJAYINGS
DEEMSTERSHIP
DEEMSTERSHIPS
DEEPENINGS
DEEPFREEZE
DEEPFREEZES
DEEPFREEZING
DEEPFROZEN
DEEPNESSES
DEEPWATERMAN
DEEPWATERMEN
DEERBERRIES
DEERGRASSES
DEERHOUNDS
DEERSTALKER
DEERSTALKERS
DEERSTALKING
DEERSTALKINGS
DEFACEABLE
DEFACEMENT
DEFACEMENTS
DEFACINGLY
DEFAECATED
DEFAECATES
DEFAECATING
DEFAECATION
DEFAECATIONS
DEFAECATOR
DEFAECATORS
DEFALCATED
DEFALCATES
DEFALCATING
DEFALCATION
DEFALCATIONS
DEFALCATOR
DEFALCATORS
DEFAMATION
DEFAMATIONS
DEFAMATORILY
DEFAMATORY
DEFAULTERS
DEFAULTING

DEFEASANCE
DEFEASANCED
DEFEASANCES
DEFEASIBILITIES
DEFEASIBILITY
DEFEASIBLE
DEFEASIBLENESS
DEFEATISMS
DEFEATISTS
DEFEATURED
DEFEATURES
DEFEATURING
DEFECATING
DEFECATION
DEFECATIONS
DEFECATORS
DEFECTIBILITIES
DEFECTIBILITY
DEFECTIBLE
DEFECTIONIST
DEFECTIONISTS
DEFECTIONS
DEFECTIVELY
DEFECTIVENESS
DEFECTIVENESSES
DEFECTIVES
DEFEMINISATION
DEFEMINISATIONS
DEFEMINISE
DEFEMINISED
DEFEMINISES
DEFEMINISING
DEFEMINIZATION
DEFEMINIZATIONS
DEFEMINIZE
DEFEMINIZED
DEFEMINIZES
DEFEMINIZING
DEFENCELESS
DEFENCELESSLY
DEFENCELESSNESS
DEFENCEMAN
DEFENCEMEN
DEFENDABLE
DEFENDANTS
DEFENESTRATE
DEFENESTRATED

DEFENESTRATES
DEFENESTRATING
DEFENESTRATION
DEFENESTRATIONS
DEFENSATIVE
DEFENSATIVES
DEFENSELESS
DEFENSELESSLY
DEFENSELESSNESS
DEFENSEMAN
DEFENSEMEN
DEFENSIBILITIES
DEFENSIBILITY
DEFENSIBLE
DEFENSIBLENESS
DEFENSIBLY
DEFENSIVELY
DEFENSIVENESS
DEFENSIVENESSES
DEFENSIVES
DEFERENCES
DEFERENTIAL
DEFERENTIALLY
DEFERMENTS
DEFERRABLE
DEFERRABLES
DEFERVESCENCE
DEFERVESCENCES
DEFERVESCENCIES
DEFERVESCENCY
DEFEUDALISE
DEFEUDALISED
DEFEUDALISES
DEFEUDALISING
DEFEUDALIZE
DEFEUDALIZED
DEFEUDALIZES
DEFEUDALIZING
DEFIANTNESS
DEFIANTNESSES
DEFIBRILLATE
DEFIBRILLATED
DEFIBRILLATES
DEFIBRILLATING
DEFIBRILLATION
DEFIBRILLATIONS
DEFIBRILLATOR

D

D

DEFIBRILLATORS
DEFIBRINATE
DEFIBRINATED
DEFIBRINATES
DEFIBRINATING
DEFIBRINATION
DEFIBRINATIONS
DEFIBRINISE
DEFIBRINISED
DEFIBRINISES
DEFIBRINISING
DEFIBRINIZE
DEFIBRINIZED
DEFIBRINIZES
DEFIBRINIZING
DEFICIENCE
DEFICIENCES
DEFICIENCIES
DEFICIENCY
DEFICIENTLY
DEFICIENTNESS
DEFICIENTNESSES
DEFICIENTS
DEFILADING
DEFILEMENT
DEFILEMENTS
DEFILIATION
DEFILIATIONS
DEFINABILITIES
DEFINABILITY
DEFINEMENT
DEFINEMENTS
DEFINIENDA
DEFINIENDUM
DEFINIENTIA
DEFINITELY
DEFINITENESS
DEFINITENESSES
DEFINITION
DEFINITIONAL
DEFINITIONS
DEFINITISE
DEFINITISED
DEFINITISES
DEFINITISING
DEFINITIVE
DEFINITIVELY

DEFINITIVENESS
DEFINITIVES
DEFINITIZE
DEFINITIZED
DEFINITIZES
DEFINITIZING
DEFINITUDE
DEFINITUDES
DEFLAGRABILITY
DEFLAGRABLE
DEFLAGRATE
DEFLAGRATED
DEFLAGRATES
DEFLAGRATING
DEFLAGRATION
DEFLAGRATIONS
DEFLAGRATOR
DEFLAGRATORS
DEFLATIONARY
DEFLATIONIST
DEFLATIONISTS
DEFLATIONS
DEFLECTABLE
DEFLECTING
DEFLECTION
DEFLECTIONAL
DEFLECTIONS
DEFLECTIVE
DEFLECTORS
DEFLEXIONAL
DEFLEXIONS
DEFLEXURES
DEFLOCCULANT
DEFLOCCULANTS
DEFLOCCULATE
DEFLOCCULATED
DEFLOCCULATES
DEFLOCCULATING
DEFLOCCULATION
DEFLOCCULATIONS
DEFLORATED
DEFLORATES
DEFLORATING
DEFLORATION
DEFLORATIONS
DEFLOWERED
DEFLOWERER

DEFLOWERERS
DEFLOWERING
DEFLUXIONS
DEFOCUSING
DEFOCUSSED
DEFOCUSSES
DEFOCUSSING
DEFOLIANTS
DEFOLIATED
DEFOLIATES
DEFOLIATING
DEFOLIATION
DEFOLIATIONS
DEFOLIATOR
DEFOLIATORS
DEFORCEMENT
DEFORCEMENTS
DEFORCIANT
DEFORCIANTS
DEFORCIATION
DEFORCIATIONS
DEFORESTATION
DEFORESTATIONS
DEFORESTED
DEFORESTER
DEFORESTERS
DEFORESTING
DEFORMABILITIES
DEFORMABILITY
DEFORMABLE
DEFORMALISE
DEFORMALISED
DEFORMALISES
DEFORMALISING
DEFORMALIZE
DEFORMALIZED
DEFORMALIZES
DEFORMALIZING
DEFORMATION
DEFORMATIONAL
DEFORMATIONS
DEFORMATIVE
DEFORMEDLY
DEFORMEDNESS
DEFORMEDNESSES
DEFORMITIES
DEFRAGGERS

DEFRAGGING
DEFRAGGINGS
DEFRAGMENT
DEFRAGMENTED
DEFRAGMENTING
DEFRAGMENTS
DEFRAUDATION
DEFRAUDATIONS
DEFRAUDERS
DEFRAUDING
DEFRAUDMENT
DEFRAUDMENTS
DEFRAYABLE
DEFRAYMENT
DEFRAYMENTS
DEFREEZING
DEFRIENDED
DEFRIENDING
DEFROCKING
DEFROSTERS
DEFROSTING
DEFTNESSES
DEFUELLING
DEFUNCTION
DEFUNCTIONS
DEFUNCTIVE
DEFUNCTNESS
DEFUNCTNESSES
DEGARNISHED
DEGARNISHES
DEGARNISHING
DEGAUSSERS
DEGAUSSING
DEGEARINGS
DEGENDERED
DEGENDERING
DEGENERACIES
DEGENERACY
DEGENERATE
DEGENERATED
DEGENERATELY
DEGENERATENESS
DEGENERATES
DEGENERATING
DEGENERATION
DEGENERATIONIST
DEGENERATIONS

DEGENERATIVE
DEGENEROUS
DEGLACIATED
DEGLACIATION
DEGLACIATIONS
DEGLAMORISATION
DEGLAMORISE
DEGLAMORISED
DEGLAMORISES
DEGLAMORISING
DEGLAMORIZATION
DEGLAMORIZE
DEGLAMORIZED
DEGLAMORIZES
DEGLAMORIZING
DEGLUTINATE
DEGLUTINATED
DEGLUTINATES
DEGLUTINATING
DEGLUTINATION
DEGLUTINATIONS
DEGLUTITION
DEGLUTITIONS
DEGLUTITIVE
DEGLUTITORY
DEGRADABILITIES
DEGRADABILITY
DEGRADABLE
DEGRADATION
DEGRADATIONS
DEGRADATIVE
DEGRADEDLY
DEGRADINGLY
DEGRADINGNESS
DEGRADINGNESSES
DEGRANULATION
DEGRANULATIONS
DEGREASANT
DEGREASANTS
DEGREASERS
DEGREASING
DEGREELESS
DEGRESSION
DEGRESSIONS
DEGRESSIVE
DEGRESSIVELY
DEGRINGOLADE

DEGRINGOLADED	DEHYDROGENASES	DEIONIZATIONS	DELEGITIMISE	DELIGHTFULLY
DEGRINGOLADES	DEHYDROGENATE	DEIONIZERS	DELEGITIMISED	DELIGHTFULNESS
DEGRINGOLADING	DEHYDROGENATED	DEIONIZING	DELEGITIMISES	DELIGHTING
DEGRINGOLER	DEHYDROGENATES	DEIPNOSOPHIST	DELEGITIMISING	DELIGHTLESS
DEGRINGOLERED	DEHYDROGENATING	DEIPNOSOPHISTS	DELEGITIMIZE	DELIGHTSOME
DEGRINGOLERING	DEHYDROGENATION	DEISTICALLY	DELEGITIMIZED	DELIMITATE
DEGRINGOLERS	DEHYDROGENISE	DEJECTEDLY	DELEGITIMIZES	DELIMITATED
DEGUSTATED	DEHYDROGENISED	DEJECTEDNESS	DELEGITIMIZING	DELIMITATES
DEGUSTATES	DEHYDROGENISES	DEJECTEDNESSES	DELETERIOUS	DELIMITATING
DEGUSTATING	DEHYDROGENISING	DEJECTIONS	DELETERIOUSLY	DELIMITATION
DEGUSTATION	DEHYDROGENIZE	DEKALITERS	DELETERIOUSNESS	DELIMITATIONS
DEGUSTATIONS	DEHYDROGENIZED	DEKALITRES	DELEVERAGE	DELIMITATIVE
DEGUSTATORY	DEHYDROGENIZES	DEKALOGIES	DELEVERAGED	DELIMITERS
DEHISCENCE	DEHYDROGENIZING	DEKAMETERS	DELEVERAGES	DELIMITING
DEHISCENCES	DEHYDRORETINOL	DEKAMETRES	DELEVERAGING	DELINEABLE
DEHORTATION	DEHYDRORETINOLS	DEKAMETRIC	DELFTWARES	DELINEATED
DEHORTATIONS	DEHYPNOTISATION	DELAMINATE	DELIBATING	DELINEATES
DEHORTATIVE	DEHYPNOTISE	DELAMINATED	DELIBATION	DELINEATING
DEHORTATORY	DEHYPNOTISED	DELAMINATES	DELIBATIONS	DELINEATION
DEHUMANISATION	DEHYPNOTISES	DELAMINATING	DELIBERATE	DELINEATIONS
DEHUMANISATIONS	DEHYPNOTISING	DELAMINATION	DELIBERATED	DELINEATIVE
DEHUMANISE	DEHYPNOTIZATION	DELAMINATIONS	DELIBERATELY	DELINEATOR
DEHUMANISED	DEHYPNOTIZE	DELAPSIONS	DELIBERATENESS	DELINEATORS
DEHUMANISES	DEHYPNOTIZED	DELASSEMENT	DELIBERATES	DELINEAVIT
DEHUMANISING	DEHYPNOTIZES	DELASSEMENTS	DELIBERATING	DELINQUENCIES
DEHUMANIZATION	DEHYPNOTIZING	DELAYERING	DELIBERATION	DELINQUENCY
DEHUMANIZATIONS	DEICTICALLY	DELAYERINGS	DELIBERATIONS	DELINQUENT
DEHUMANIZE	DEIFICATION	DELAYINGLY	DELIBERATIVE	DELINQUENTLY
DEHUMANIZED	DEIFICATIONS	DELECTABILITIES	DELIBERATIVELY	DELINQUENTS
DEHUMANIZES	DEINDEXATION	DELECTABILITY	DELIBERATOR	DELIQUESCE
DEHUMANIZING	DEINDEXATIONS	DELECTABLE	DELIBERATORS	DELIQUESCED
DEHUMIDIFIED	DEINDEXING	DELECTABLENESS	DELICACIES	DELIQUESCENCE
DEHUMIDIFIER	DEINDIVIDUATION	DELECTABLES	DELICATELY	DELIQUESCENCES
DEHUMIDIFIERS	DEINDUSTRIALISE	DELECTABLY	DELICATENESS	DELIQUESCENT
DEHUMIDIFIES	DEINDUSTRIALIZE	DELECTATED	DELICATENESSES	DELIQUESCES
DEHUMIDIFY	DEINONYCHUS	DELECTATES	DELICATESSEN	DELIQUESCING
DEHUMIDIFYING	DEINONYCHUSES	DELECTATING	DELICATESSENS	DELIQUIUMS
DEHYDRATED	DEINOSAURS	DELECTATION	DELICIOUSLY	DELIRATION
DEHYDRATER	DEINOTHERE	DELECTATIONS	DELICIOUSNESS	DELIRATIONS
DEHYDRATERS	DEINOTHERES	DELEGACIES	DELICIOUSNESSES	DELIRIFACIENT
DEHYDRATES	DEINOTHERIUM	DELEGATEES	DELIGATION	DELIRIFACIENTS
DEHYDRATING	DEINOTHERIUMS	DELEGATING	DELIGATIONS	DELIRIOUSLY
DEHYDRATION	DEIONISATION	DELEGATION	DELIGHTEDLY	DELIRIOUSNESS
DEHYDRATIONS	DEIONISATIONS	DELEGATIONS	DELIGHTEDNESS	DELIRIOUSNESSES
DEHYDRATOR	DEIONISERS	DELEGATORS	DELIGHTEDNESSES	DELITESCENCE
DEHYDRATORS	DEIONISING	DELEGITIMATION	DELIGHTERS	DELITESCENCES
DEHYDROGENASE	DEIONIZATION	DELEGITIMATIONS	DELIGHTFUL	DELITESCENT

D

DELIVERABILITY	DEMAGNETISE	DEMATERIALISING	DEMINERALIZER	DEMOCRATIST
DELIVERABLE	DEMAGNETISED	DEMATERIALIZE	DEMINERALIZERS	DEMOCRATISTS
DELIVERABLES	DEMAGNETISER	DEMATERIALIZED	DEMINERALIZES	DEMOCRATIZATION
DELIVERANCE	DEMAGNETISERS	DEMATERIALIZES	DEMINERALIZING	DEMOCRATIZE
DELIVERANCES	DEMAGNETISES	DEMATERIALIZING	DEMIPIQUES	DEMOCRATIZED
DELIVERERS	DEMAGNETISING	DEMEANOURS	DEMIRELIEF	DEMOCRATIZER
DELIVERIES	DEMAGNETIZATION	DEMEASNURE	DEMIRELIEFS	DEMOCRATIZERS
DELIVERING	DEMAGNETIZE	DEMEASNURES	DEMIREPDOM	DEMOCRATIZES
DELIVERYMAN	DEMAGNETIZED	DEMENTATED	DEMIREPDOMS	DEMOCRATIZING
DELIVERYMEN	DEMAGNETIZER	DEMENTATES	DEMISEMIQUAVER	DEMODULATE
DELOCALISATION	DEMAGNETIZERS	DEMENTATING	DEMISEMIQUAVERS	DEMODULATED
DELOCALISATIONS	DEMAGNETIZES	DEMENTEDLY	DEMISSIONS	DEMODULATES
DELOCALISE	DEMAGNETIZING	DEMENTEDNESS	DEMITASSES	DEMODULATING
DELOCALISED	DEMAGOGICAL	DEMENTEDNESSES	DEMIURGEOUS	DEMODULATION
DELOCALISES	DEMAGOGICALLY	DEMERGERED	DEMIURGICAL	DEMODULATIONS
DELOCALISING	DEMAGOGIES	DEMERGERING	DEMIURGICALLY	DEMODULATOR
DELOCALIZATION	DEMAGOGING	DEMERITING	DEMIURGUSES	DEMODULATORS
DELOCALIZATIONS	DEMAGOGISM	DEMERITORIOUS	DEMIVEGGES	DEMOGRAPHER
DELOCALIZE	DEMAGOGISMS	DEMERITORIOUSLY	DEMIVIERGE	DEMOGRAPHERS
DELOCALIZED	DEMAGOGUED	DEMERSIONS	DEMIVIERGES	DEMOGRAPHIC
DELOCALIZES	DEMAGOGUERIES	DEMIBASTION	DEMIVOLTES	DEMOGRAPHICAL
DELOCALIZING	DEMAGOGUERY	DEMIBASTIONS	DEMIWORLDS	DEMOGRAPHICALLY
DELPHICALLY	DEMAGOGUES	DEMICANTON	DEMOBILISATION	DEMOGRAPHICS
DELPHINIUM	DEMAGOGUING	DEMICANTONS	DEMOBILISATIONS	DEMOGRAPHIES
DELPHINIUMS	DEMAGOGUISM	DEMIGODDESS	DEMOBILISE	DEMOGRAPHIST
DELPHINOID	DEMAGOGUISMS	DEMIGODDESSES	DEMOBILISED	DEMOGRAPHISTS
DELPHINOIDS	DEMANDABLE	DEMIGRATION	DEMOBILISES	DEMOGRAPHY
DELTIOLOGIES	DEMANDANTS	DEMIGRATIONS	DEMOBILISING	DEMOISELLE
DELTIOLOGIST	DEMANDINGLY	DEMILITARISE	DEMOBILIZATION	DEMOISELLES
DELTIOLOGISTS	DEMANDINGNESS	DEMILITARISED	DEMOBILIZATIONS	DEMOLISHED
DELTIOLOGY	DEMANDINGNESSES	DEMILITARISES	DEMOBILIZE	DEMOLISHER
DELTOIDEUS	DEMANNINGS	DEMILITARISING	DEMOBILIZED	DEMOLISHERS
DELUDINGLY	DEMANTOIDS	DEMILITARIZE	DEMOBILIZES	DEMOLISHES
DELUNDUNGS	DEMARCATED	DEMILITARIZED	DEMOBILIZING	DEMOLISHING
DELUSIONAL	DEMARCATES	DEMILITARIZES	DEMOCRACIES	DEMOLISHMENT
DELUSIONARY	DEMARCATING	DEMILITARIZING	DEMOCRATIC	DEMOLISHMENTS
DELUSIONIST	DEMARCATION	DEMIMONDAINE	DEMOCRATICAL	DEMOLITION
DELUSIONISTS	DEMARCATIONS	DEMIMONDAINES	DEMOCRATICALLY	DEMOLITIONIST
DELUSIVELY	DEMARCATOR	DEMIMONDES	DEMOCRATIES	DEMOLITIONISTS
DELUSIVENESS	DEMARCATORS	DEMINERALISE	DEMOCRATIFIABLE	DEMOLITIONS
DELUSIVENESSES	DEMARKATION	DEMINERALISED	DEMOCRATISATION	DEMOLOGIES
DELUSTERED	DEMARKATIONS	DEMINERALISER	DEMOCRATISE	DEMONESSES
DELUSTERING	DEMARKETED	DEMINERALISERS	DEMOCRATISED	DEMONETARISE
DELUSTRANT	DEMARKETING	DEMINERALISES	DEMOCRATISER	DEMONETARISED
DELUSTRANTS	DEMATERIALISE	DEMINERALISING	DEMOCRATISERS	DEMONETARISES
DELUSTRING	DEMATERIALISED	DEMINERALIZE	DEMOCRATISES	DEMONETARISING
DEMAGNETISATION	DEMATERIALISES	DEMINERALIZED	DEMOCRATISING	DEMONETARIZE

DEMONETARIZED
DEMONETARIZES
DEMONETARIZING
DEMONETISATION
DEMONETISATIONS
DEMONETISE
DEMONETISED
DEMONETISES
DEMONETISING
DEMONETIZATION
DEMONETIZATIONS
DEMONETIZE
DEMONETIZED
DEMONETIZES
DEMONETIZING
DEMONIACAL
DEMONIACALLY
DEMONIACISM
DEMONIACISMS
DEMONIANISM
DEMONIANISMS
DEMONICALLY
DEMONISATION
DEMONISATIONS
DEMONISING
DEMONIZATION
DEMONIZATIONS
DEMONIZING
DEMONOCRACIES
DEMONOCRACY
DEMONOLATER
DEMONOLATERS
DEMONOLATRIES
DEMONOLATRY
DEMONOLOGIC
DEMONOLOGICAL
DEMONOLOGIES
DEMONOLOGIST
DEMONOLOGISTS
DEMONOLOGY
DEMONOMANIA
DEMONOMANIAS
DEMONSTRABILITY
DEMONSTRABLE
DEMONSTRABLY
DEMONSTRATE
DEMONSTRATED

DEMONSTRATES
DEMONSTRATING
DEMONSTRATION
DEMONSTRATIONAL
DEMONSTRATIONS
DEMONSTRATIVE
DEMONSTRATIVELY
DEMONSTRATIVES
DEMONSTRATOR
DEMONSTRATORS
DEMONSTRATORY
DEMORALISATION
DEMORALISATIONS
DEMORALISE
DEMORALISED
DEMORALISER
DEMORALISERS
DEMORALISES
DEMORALISING
DEMORALISINGLY
DEMORALIZATION
DEMORALIZATIONS
DEMORALIZE
DEMORALIZED
DEMORALIZER
DEMORALIZERS
DEMORALIZES
DEMORALIZING
DEMORALIZINGLY
DEMOSCENES
DEMOTICIST
DEMOTICISTS
DEMOTIVATE
DEMOTIVATED
DEMOTIVATES
DEMOTIVATING
DEMOTIVATION
DEMOTIVATIONS
DEMOUNTABLE
DEMOUNTING
DEMULCENTS
DEMULSIFICATION
DEMULSIFIED
DEMULSIFIER
DEMULSIFIERS
DEMULSIFIES
DEMULSIFYING

DEMULTIPLEXER
DEMULTIPLEXERS
DEMURENESS
DEMURENESSES
DEMURRABLE
DEMURRAGES
DEMUTUALISATION
DEMUTUALISE
DEMUTUALISED
DEMUTUALISES
DEMUTUALISING
DEMUTUALIZATION
DEMUTUALIZE
DEMUTUALIZED
DEMUTUALIZES
DEMUTUALIZING
DEMYELINATE
DEMYELINATED
DEMYELINATES
DEMYELINATING
DEMYELINATION
DEMYELINATIONS
DEMYSTIFICATION
DEMYSTIFIED
DEMYSTIFIES
DEMYSTIFYING
DEMYTHIFICATION
DEMYTHIFIED
DEMYTHIFIES
DEMYTHIFYING
DEMYTHOLOGISE
DEMYTHOLOGISED
DEMYTHOLOGISER
DEMYTHOLOGISERS
DEMYTHOLOGISES
DEMYTHOLOGISING
DEMYTHOLOGIZE
DEMYTHOLOGIZED
DEMYTHOLOGIZER
DEMYTHOLOGIZERS
DEMYTHOLOGIZES
DEMYTHOLOGIZING
DENATIONALISE
DENATIONALISED
DENATIONALISES
DENATIONALISING
DENATIONALIZE

DENATIONALIZED
DENATIONALIZES
DENATIONALIZING
DENATURALISE
DENATURALISED
DENATURALISES
DENATURALISING
DENATURALIZE
DENATURALIZED
DENATURALIZES
DENATURALIZING
DENATURANT
DENATURANTS
DENATURATION
DENATURATIONS
DENATURING
DENATURISE
DENATURISED
DENATURISES
DENATURISING
DENATURIZE
DENATURIZED
DENATURIZES
DENATURIZING
DENAZIFICATION
DENAZIFICATIONS
DENAZIFIED
DENAZIFIES
DENAZIFYING
DENDRACHATE
DENDRACHATES
DENDRIFORM
DENDRIMERS
DENDRITICAL
DENDRITICALLY
DENDROBIUM
DENDROBIUMS
DENDROGLYPH
DENDROGLYPHS
DENDROGRAM
DENDROGRAMS
DENDROIDAL
DENDROLATRIES
DENDROLATRY
DENDROLOGIC
DENDROLOGICAL
DENDROLOGIES

DENDROLOGIST
DENDROLOGISTS
DENDROLOGOUS
DENDROLOGY
DENDROMETER
DENDROMETERS
DENDROPHIS
DENDROPHISES
DENEGATION
DENEGATIONS
DENERVATED
DENERVATES
DENERVATING
DENERVATION
DENERVATIONS
DENIABILITIES
DENIABILITY
DENIALISTS
DENIGRATED
DENIGRATES
DENIGRATING
DENIGRATION
DENIGRATIONS
DENIGRATIVE
DENIGRATOR
DENIGRATORS
DENIGRATORY
DENISATION
DENISATIONS
DENITRATED
DENITRATES
DENITRATING
DENITRATION
DENITRATIONS
DENITRIFICATION
DENITRIFICATOR
DENITRIFICATORS
DENITRIFIED
DENITRIFIER
DENITRIFIERS
DENITRIFIES
DENITRIFYING
DENIZATION
DENIZATIONS
DENIZENING
DENIZENSHIP
DENIZENSHIPS

D

DENOMINABLE
DENOMINATE
DENOMINATED
DENOMINATES
DENOMINATING
DENOMINATION
DENOMINATIONAL
DENOMINATIONS
DENOMINATIVE
DENOMINATIVELY
DENOMINATIVES
DENOMINATOR
DENOMINATORS
DENOTATING
DENOTATION
DENOTATIONS
DENOTATIVE
DENOTATIVELY
DENOTEMENT
DENOTEMENTS
DENOUEMENT
DENOUEMENTS
DENOUNCEMENT
DENOUNCEMENTS
DENOUNCERS
DENOUNCING
DENSENESSES
DENSIFICATION
DENSIFICATIONS
DENSIFIERS
DENSIFYING
DENSIMETER
DENSIMETERS
DENSIMETRIC
DENSIMETRIES
DENSIMETRY
DENSITOMETER
DENSITOMETERS
DENSITOMETRIC
DENSITOMETRIES
DENSITOMETRY
DENTALITIES
DENTALIUMS
DENTATIONS
DENTICULATE
DENTICULATED
DENTICULATELY

DENTICULATION
DENTICULATIONS
DENTIFRICE
DENTIFRICES
DENTIGEROUS
DENTILABIAL
DENTILINGUAL
DENTILINGUALS
DENTIROSTRAL
DENTISTRIES
DENTITIONS
DENTURISTS
DENUCLEARISE
DENUCLEARISED
DENUCLEARISES
DENUCLEARISING
DENUCLEARIZE
DENUCLEARIZED
DENUCLEARIZES
DENUCLEARIZING
DENUDATING
DENUDATION
DENUDATIONS
DENUDEMENT
DENUDEMENTS
DENUMERABILITY
DENUMERABLE
DENUMERABLY
DENUNCIATE
DENUNCIATED
DENUNCIATES
DENUNCIATING
DENUNCIATION
DENUNCIATIONS
DENUNCIATIVE
DENUNCIATOR
DENUNCIATORS
DENUNCIATORY
DEOBSTRUENT
DEOBSTRUENTS
DEODORANTS
DEODORISATION
DEODORISATIONS
DEODORISED
DEODORISER
DEODORISERS
DEODORISES

DEODORISING
DEODORIZATION
DEODORIZATIONS
DEODORIZED
DEODORIZER
DEODORIZERS
DEODORIZES
DEODORIZING
DEONTOLOGICAL
DEONTOLOGIES
DEONTOLOGIST
DEONTOLOGISTS
DEONTOLOGY
DEOPPILATE
DEOPPILATED
DEOPPILATES
DEOPPILATING
DEOPPILATION
DEOPPILATIONS
DEOPPILATIVE
DEOPPILATIVES
DEORBITING
DEOXIDATED
DEOXIDATES
DEOXIDATING
DEOXIDATION
DEOXIDATIONS
DEOXIDISATION
DEOXIDISATIONS
DEOXIDISED
DEOXIDISER
DEOXIDISERS
DEOXIDISES
DEOXIDISING
DEOXIDIZATION
DEOXIDIZATIONS
DEOXIDIZED
DEOXIDIZER
DEOXIDIZERS
DEOXIDIZES
DEOXIDIZING
DEOXYCORTONE
DEOXYCORTONES
DEOXYGENATE
DEOXYGENATED
DEOXYGENATES
DEOXYGENATING

DEOXYGENATION
DEOXYGENATIONS
DEOXYGENISE
DEOXYGENISED
DEOXYGENISES
DEOXYGENISING
DEOXYGENIZE
DEOXYGENIZED
DEOXYGENIZES
DEOXYGENIZING
DEOXYRIBOSE
DEOXYRIBOSES
DEPAINTING
DEPANNEURS
DEPARTEMENT
DEPARTEMENTS
DEPARTINGS
DEPARTMENT
DEPARTMENTAL
DEPARTMENTALISE
DEPARTMENTALISM
DEPARTMENTALIZE
DEPARTMENTALLY
DEPARTMENTS
DEPARTURES
DEPASTURED
DEPASTURES
DEPASTURING
DEPAUPERATE
DEPAUPERATED
DEPAUPERATES
DEPAUPERATING
DEPAUPERISE
DEPAUPERISED
DEPAUPERISES
DEPAUPERISING
DEPAUPERIZE
DEPAUPERIZED
DEPAUPERIZES
DEPAUPERIZING
DEPEINCTED
DEPEINCTING
DEPENDABILITIES
DEPENDABILITY
DEPENDABLE
DEPENDABLENESS
DEPENDABLY

DEPENDANCE
DEPENDANCES
DEPENDANCIES
DEPENDANCY
DEPENDANTS
DEPENDENCE
DEPENDENCES
DEPENDENCIES
DEPENDENCY
DEPENDENTLY
DEPENDENTS
DEPENDINGLY
DEPEOPLING
DEPERSONALISE
DEPERSONALISED
DEPERSONALISES
DEPERSONALISING
DEPERSONALIZE
DEPERSONALIZED
DEPERSONALIZES
DEPERSONALIZING
DEPHLEGMATE
DEPHLEGMATED
DEPHLEGMATES
DEPHLEGMATING
DEPHLEGMATION
DEPHLEGMATIONS
DEPHLEGMATOR
DEPHLEGMATORS
DEPHLOGISTICATE
DEPHOSPHORYLATE
DEPICTIONS
DEPICTURED
DEPICTURES
DEPICTURING
DEPIGMENTATION
DEPIGMENTATIONS
DEPIGMENTED
DEPIGMENTING
DEPIGMENTS
DEPILATING
DEPILATION
DEPILATIONS
DEPILATORIES
DEPILATORS
DEPILATORY
DEPLENISHED

D

DEPLENISHES
DEPLENISHING
DEPLETABLE
DEPLETIONS
DEPLORABILITIES
DEPLORABILITY
DEPLORABLE
DEPLORABLENESS
DEPLORABLY
DEPLORATION
DEPLORATIONS
DEPLORINGLY
DEPLOYABLE
DEPLOYMENT
DEPLOYMENTS
DEPLUMATION
DEPLUMATIONS
DEPOLARISATION
DEPOLARISATIONS
DEPOLARISE
DEPOLARISED
DEPOLARISER
DEPOLARISERS
DEPOLARISES
DEPOLARISING
DEPOLARIZATION
DEPOLARIZATIONS
DEPOLARIZE
DEPOLARIZED
DEPOLARIZER
DEPOLARIZERS
DEPOLARIZES
DEPOLARIZING
DEPOLISHED
DEPOLISHES
DEPOLISHING
DEPOLITICISE
DEPOLITICISED
DEPOLITICISES
DEPOLITICISING
DEPOLITICIZE
DEPOLITICIZED
DEPOLITICIZES
DEPOLITICIZING
DEPOLYMERISE
DEPOLYMERISED
DEPOLYMERISES

DEPOLYMERISING
DEPOLYMERIZE
DEPOLYMERIZED
DEPOLYMERIZES
DEPOLYMERIZING
DEPOPULATE
DEPOPULATED
DEPOPULATES
DEPOPULATING
DEPOPULATION
DEPOPULATIONS
DEPOPULATOR
DEPOPULATORS
DEPORTABLE
DEPORTATION
DEPORTATIONS
DEPORTMENT
DEPORTMENTS
DEPOSITARIES
DEPOSITARY
DEPOSITATION
DEPOSITATIONS
DEPOSITING
DEPOSITION
DEPOSITIONAL
DEPOSITIONS
DEPOSITIVE
DEPOSITORIES
DEPOSITORS
DEPOSITORY
DEPRAVATION
DEPRAVATIONS
DEPRAVEDLY
DEPRAVEDNESS
DEPRAVEDNESSES
DEPRAVEMENT
DEPRAVEMENTS
DEPRAVINGLY
DEPRAVITIES
DEPRECABLE
DEPRECATED
DEPRECATES
DEPRECATING
DEPRECATINGLY
DEPRECATION
DEPRECATIONS
DEPRECATIVE

DEPRECATIVELY
DEPRECATOR
DEPRECATORILY
DEPRECATORS
DEPRECATORY
DEPRECIABLE
DEPRECIATE
DEPRECIATED
DEPRECIATES
DEPRECIATING
DEPRECIATINGLY
DEPRECIATION
DEPRECIATIONS
DEPRECIATIVE
DEPRECIATOR
DEPRECIATORS
DEPRECIATORY
DEPREDATED
DEPREDATES
DEPREDATING
DEPREDATION
DEPREDATIONS
DEPREDATOR
DEPREDATORS
DEPREDATORY
DEPREHENDED
DEPREHENDING
DEPREHENDS
DEPRESSANT
DEPRESSANTS
DEPRESSIBLE
DEPRESSING
DEPRESSINGLY
DEPRESSION
DEPRESSIONS
DEPRESSIVE
DEPRESSIVELY
DEPRESSIVENESS
DEPRESSIVES
DEPRESSOMOTOR
DEPRESSOMOTORS
DEPRESSORS
DEPRESSURISE
DEPRESSURISED
DEPRESSURISES
DEPRESSURISING
DEPRESSURIZE

DEPRESSURIZED
DEPRESSURIZES
DEPRESSURIZING
DEPRIVABLE
DEPRIVATION
DEPRIVATIONS
DEPRIVATIVE
DEPRIVEMENT
DEPRIVEMENTS
DEPROGRAMED
DEPROGRAMING
DEPROGRAMME
DEPROGRAMMED
DEPROGRAMMER
DEPROGRAMMERS
DEPROGRAMMES
DEPROGRAMMING
DEPROGRAMS
DEPURATING
DEPURATION
DEPURATIONS
DEPURATIVE
DEPURATIVES
DEPURATORS
DEPURATORY
DEPUTATION
DEPUTATIONS
DEPUTISATION
DEPUTISATIONS
DEPUTISING
DEPUTIZATION
DEPUTIZATIONS
DEPUTIZING
DEQUEUEING
DERACIALISE
DERACIALISED
DERACIALISES
DERACIALISING
DERACIALIZE
DERACIALIZED
DERACIALIZES
DERACIALIZING
DERACINATE
DERACINATED
DERACINATES
DERACINATING
DERACINATION

DERACINATIONS
DERAIGNING
DERAIGNMENT
DERAIGNMENTS
DERAILLEUR
DERAILLEURS
DERAILMENT
DERAILMENTS
DERANGEMENT
DERANGEMENTS
DERATIONED
DERATIONING
DEREALISATION
DEREALISATIONS
DEREALIZATION
DEREALIZATIONS
DERECOGNISE
DERECOGNISED
DERECOGNISES
DERECOGNISING
DERECOGNITION
DERECOGNITIONS
DERECOGNIZE
DERECOGNIZED
DERECOGNIZES
DERECOGNIZING
DEREGISTER
DEREGISTERED
DEREGISTERING
DEREGISTERS
DEREGISTRATION
DEREGISTRATIONS
DEREGULATE
DEREGULATED
DEREGULATES
DEREGULATING
DEREGULATION
DEREGULATIONS
DEREGULATOR
DEREGULATORS
DEREGULATORY
DERELICTION
DERELICTIONS
DERELIGIONISE
DERELIGIONISED
DERELIGIONISES
DERELIGIONISING

D

DERELIGIONIZE	DERMAPLANINGS	DERRINGERS	DESCENDING	DESELECTION
DERELIGIONIZED	DERMAPTERAN	DESACRALISATION	DESCENDINGS	DESELECTIONS
DERELIGIONIZES	DERMAPTERANS	DESACRALISE	DESCENSION	DESENSITISATION
DERELIGIONIZING	DERMATITIS	DESACRALISED	DESCENSIONAL	DESENSITISE
DEREPRESSED	DERMATITISES	DESACRALISES	DESCENSIONS	DESENSITISED
DEREPRESSES	DERMATOGEN	DESACRALISING	DESCHOOLED	DESENSITISER
DEREPRESSING	DERMATOGENS	DESACRALIZATION	DESCHOOLER	DESENSITISERS
DEREPRESSION	DERMATOGLYPHIC	DESACRALIZE	DESCHOOLERS	DESENSITISES
DEREPRESSIONS	DERMATOGLYPHICS	DESACRALIZED	DESCHOOLING	DESENSITISING
DEREQUISITION	DERMATOGRAPHIA	DESACRALIZES	DESCHOOLINGS	DESENSITIZATION
DEREQUISITIONED	DERMATOGRAPHIAS	DESACRALIZING	DESCRAMBLE	DESENSITIZE
DEREQUISITIONS	DERMATOGRAPHIC	DESAGREMENT	DESCRAMBLED	DESENSITIZED
DERESTRICT	DERMATOGRAPHIES	DESAGREMENTS	DESCRAMBLER	DESENSITIZER
DERESTRICTED	DERMATOGRAPHY	DESALINATE	DESCRAMBLERS	DESENSITIZERS
DERESTRICTING	DERMATOLOGIC	DESALINATED	DESCRAMBLES	DESENSITIZES
DERESTRICTION	DERMATOLOGICAL	DESALINATES	DESCRAMBLING	DESENSITIZING
DERESTRICTIONS	DERMATOLOGIES	DESALINATING	DESCRIBABLE	DESERPIDINE
DERESTRICTS	DERMATOLOGIST	DESALINATION	DESCRIBERS	DESERPIDINES
DERIDINGLY	DERMATOLOGISTS	DESALINATIONS	DESCRIBING	DESERTIFICATION
DERISIVELY	DERMATOLOGY	DESALINATOR	DESCRIPTION	DESERTIFIED
DERISIVENESS	DERMATOMAL	DESALINATORS	DESCRIPTIONS	DESERTIFIES
DERISIVENESSES	DERMATOMES	DESALINISATION	DESCRIPTIVE	DESERTIFYING
DERIVATING	DERMATOMIC	DESALINISATIONS	DESCRIPTIVELY	DESERTIONS
DERIVATION	DERMATOMYOSITIS	DESALINISE	DESCRIPTIVENESS	DESERTISATION
DERIVATIONAL	DERMATOPHYTE	DESALINISED	DESCRIPTIVISM	DESERTISATIONS
DERIVATIONIST	DERMATOPHYTES	DESALINISES	DESCRIPTIVISMS	DESERTIZATION
DERIVATIONISTS	DERMATOPHYTIC	DESALINISING	DESCRIPTIVIST	DESERTIZATIONS
DERIVATIONS	DERMATOPHYTOSES	DESALINIZATION	DESCRIPTOR	DESERTLESS
DERIVATISATION	DERMATOPHYTOSIS	DESALINIZATIONS	DESCRIPTORS	DESERVEDLY
DERIVATISATIONS	DERMATOPLASTIC	DESALINIZE	DESCRIVING	DESERVEDNESS
DERIVATISE	DERMATOPLASTIES	DESALINIZED	DESECRATED	DESERVEDNESSES
DERIVATISED	DERMATOPLASTY	DESALINIZES	DESECRATER	DESERVINGLY
DERIVATISES	DERMATOSES	DESALINIZING	DESECRATERS	DESERVINGNESS
DERIVATISING	DERMATOSIS	DESALTINGS	DESECRATES	DESERVINGNESSES
DERIVATIVE	DERMESTIDS	DESATURATION	DESECRATING	DESERVINGS
DERIVATIVELY	DERMOGRAPHIES	DESATURATIONS	DESECRATION	DESEXUALISATION
DERIVATIVENESS	DERMOGRAPHY	DESCANTERS	DESECRATIONS	DESEXUALISE
DERIVATIVES	DEROGATELY	DESCANTING	DESECRATOR	DESEXUALISED
DERIVATIZATION	DEROGATING	DESCENDABLE	DESECRATORS	DESEXUALISES
DERIVATIZATIONS	DEROGATION	DESCENDANT	DESEGREGATE	DESEXUALISING
DERIVATIZE	DEROGATIONS	DESCENDANTS	DESEGREGATED	DESEXUALIZATION
DERIVATIZED	DEROGATIVE	DESCENDENT	DESEGREGATES	DESEXUALIZE
DERIVATIZES	DEROGATIVELY	DESCENDENTS	DESEGREGATING	DESEXUALIZED
DERIVATIZING	DEROGATORILY	DESCENDERS	DESEGREGATION	DESEXUALIZES
DERMABRASION	DEROGATORINESS	DESCENDEUR	DESEGREGATIONS	DESEXUALIZING
DERMABRASIONS	DEROGATORY	DESCENDEURS	DESELECTED	DESHABILLE
DERMAPLANING	DERRICKING	DESCENDIBLE	DESELECTING	DESHABILLES

DESICCANTS
DESICCATED
DESICCATES
DESICCATING
DESICCATION
DESICCATIONS
DESICCATIVE
DESICCATIVES
DESICCATOR
DESICCATORS
DESIDERATA
DESIDERATE
DESIDERATED
DESIDERATES
DESIDERATING
DESIDERATION
DESIDERATIONS
DESIDERATIVE
DESIDERATIVES
DESIDERATUM
DESIDERIUM
DESIDERIUMS
DESIGNABLE
DESIGNATED
DESIGNATES
DESIGNATING
DESIGNATION
DESIGNATIONS
DESIGNATIVE
DESIGNATOR
DESIGNATORS
DESIGNATORY
DESIGNEDLY
DESIGNINGLY
DESIGNINGS
DESIGNLESS
DESIGNMENT
DESIGNMENTS
DESILVERED
DESILVERING
DESILVERISATION
DESILVERISE
DESILVERISED
DESILVERISES
DESILVERISING
DESILVERIZATION
DESILVERIZE

DESILVERIZED
DESILVERIZES
DESILVERIZING
DESINENCES
DESINENTIAL
DESIPIENCE
DESIPIENCES
DESIPRAMINE
DESIPRAMINES
DESIRABILITIES
DESIRABILITY
DESIRABLENESS
DESIRABLENESSES
DESIRABLES
DESIRELESS
DESIROUSLY
DESIROUSNESS
DESIROUSNESSES
DESISTANCE
DESISTANCES
DESISTENCE
DESISTENCES
DESKILLING
DESKILLINGS
DESMODIUMS
DESMODROMIC
DESMOSOMAL
DESMOSOMES
DESNOODING
DESOBLIGEANTE
DESOBLIGEANTES
DESOLATELY
DESOLATENESS
DESOLATENESSES
DESOLATERS
DESOLATING
DESOLATINGLY
DESOLATION
DESOLATIONS
DESOLATORS
DESOLATORY
DESORIENTE
DESORPTION
DESORPTIONS
DESOXYRIBOSE
DESOXYRIBOSES
DESPAIRERS

DESPAIRFUL
DESPAIRING
DESPAIRINGLY
DESPATCHED
DESPATCHER
DESPATCHERS
DESPATCHES
DESPATCHING
DESPERADOES
DESPERADOS
DESPERATELY
DESPERATENESS
DESPERATENESSES
DESPERATION
DESPERATIONS
DESPICABILITIES
DESPICABILITY
DESPICABLE
DESPICABLENESS
DESPICABLY
DESPIRITUALISE
DESPIRITUALISED
DESPIRITUALISES
DESPIRITUALIZE
DESPIRITUALIZED
DESPIRITUALIZES
DESPISABLE
DESPISEDNESS
DESPISEDNESSES
DESPISEMENT
DESPISEMENTS
DESPISINGLY
DESPITEFUL
DESPITEFULLY
DESPITEFULNESS
DESPITEOUS
DESPITEOUSLY
DESPITEOUSNESS
DESPOILERS
DESPOILING
DESPOILINGS
DESPOILMENT
DESPOILMENTS
DESPOLIATION
DESPOLIATIONS
DESPONDENCE
DESPONDENCES

DESPONDENCIES
DESPONDENCY
DESPONDENT
DESPONDENTLY
DESPONDING
DESPONDINGLY
DESPONDINGS
DESPOTATES
DESPOTICAL
DESPOTICALLY
DESPOTICALNESS
DESPOTISMS
DESPOTOCRACIES
DESPOTOCRACY
DESPUMATED
DESPUMATES
DESPUMATING
DESPUMATION
DESPUMATIONS
DESQUAMATE
DESQUAMATED
DESQUAMATES
DESQUAMATING
DESQUAMATION
DESQUAMATIONS
DESQUAMATIVE
DESQUAMATORIES
DESQUAMATORY
DESSERTSPOON
DESSERTSPOONFUL
DESSERTSPOONS
DESSIATINE
DESSIATINES
DESSIGNMENT
DESSIGNMENTS
DESSYATINE
DESSYATINES
DESSYATINS
DESTABILISATION
DESTABILISE
DESTABILISED
DESTABILISER
DESTABILISERS
DESTABILISES
DESTABILISING
DESTABILIZATION
DESTABILIZE

DESTABILIZED
DESTABILIZER
DESTABILIZERS
DESTABILIZES
DESTABILIZING
DESTAINING
DESTEMPERED
DESTEMPERING
DESTEMPERS
DESTINATED
DESTINATES
DESTINATING
DESTINATION
DESTINATIONS
DESTITUTED
DESTITUTENESS
DESTITUTENESSES
DESTITUTES
DESTITUTING
DESTITUTION
DESTITUTIONS
DESTOCKING
DESTREAMED
DESTREAMING
DESTRESSED
DESTRESSES
DESTRESSING
DESTROYABLE
DESTROYERS
DESTROYING
DESTRUCTED
DESTRUCTIBILITY
DESTRUCTIBLE
DESTRUCTING
DESTRUCTION
DESTRUCTIONAL
DESTRUCTIONIST
DESTRUCTIONISTS
DESTRUCTIONS
DESTRUCTIVE
DESTRUCTIVELY
DESTRUCTIVENESS
DESTRUCTIVES
DESTRUCTIVISM
DESTRUCTIVISMS
DESTRUCTIVIST
DESTRUCTIVISTS

D

DESTRUCTIVITIES	DESULPHURIZES	DETERGENTS	DETERRABILITY	DETOXICATION
DESTRUCTIVITY	DESULPHURIZING	DETERIORATE	DETERRABLE	DETOXICATIONS
DESTRUCTOR	DESULPHURS	DETERIORATED	DETERRENCE	DETOXIFICATION
DESTRUCTORS	DESULTORILY	DETERIORATES	DETERRENCES	DETOXIFICATIONS
DESTRUCTOS	DESULTORINESS	DETERIORATING	DETERRENTLY	DETOXIFIED
DESUETUDES	DESULTORINESSES	DETERIORATION	DETERRENTS	DETOXIFIES
DESUGARING	DETACHABILITIES	DETERIORATIONS	DETERSIONS	DETOXIFYING
DESULFURATE	DETACHABILITY	DETERIORATIVE	DETERSIVES	DETRACTING
DESULFURATED	DETACHABLE	DETERIORISM	DETESTABILITIES	DETRACTINGLY
DESULFURATES	DETACHABLY	DETERIORISMS	DETESTABILITY	DETRACTINGS
DESULFURATING	DETACHEDLY	DETERIORITIES	DETESTABLE	DETRACTION
DESULFURATION	DETACHEDNESS	DETERIORITY	DETESTABLENESS	DETRACTIONS
DESULFURATIONS	DETACHEDNESSES	DETERMENTS	DETESTABLY	DETRACTIVE
DESULFURED	DETACHMENT	DETERMINABILITY	DETESTATION	DETRACTIVELY
DESULFURING	DETACHMENTS	DETERMINABLE	DETESTATIONS	DETRACTORS
DESULFURISATION	DETAILEDLY	DETERMINABLY	DETHATCHED	DETRACTORY
DESULFURISE	DETAILEDNESS	DETERMINACIES	DETHATCHES	DETRACTRESS
DESULFURISED	DETAILEDNESSES	DETERMINACY	DETHATCHING	DETRACTRESSES
DESULFURISER	DETAILINGS	DETERMINANT	DETHRONEMENT	DETRAINING
DESULFURISERS	DETAINABLE	DETERMINANTAL	DETHRONEMENTS	DETRAINMENT
DESULFURISES	DETAINMENT	DETERMINANTS	DETHRONERS	DETRAINMENTS
DESULFURISING	DETAINMENTS	DETERMINATE	DETHRONING	DETRAQUEES
DESULFURIZATION	DETANGLERS	DETERMINATED	DETHRONINGS	DETRIBALISATION
DESULFURIZE	DETANGLING	DETERMINATELY	DETHRONISE	DETRIBALISE
DESULFURIZED	DETASSELED	DETERMINATENESS	DETHRONISED	DETRIBALISED
DESULFURIZER	DETASSELING	DETERMINATES	DETHRONISES	DETRIBALISES
DESULFURIZERS	DETASSELLED	DETERMINATING	DETHRONISING	DETRIBALISING
DESULFURIZES	DETASSELLING	DETERMINATION	DETHRONIZE	DETRIBALIZATION
DESULFURIZING	DETECTABILITIES	DETERMINATIONS	DETHRONIZED	DETRIBALIZE
DESULPHURATE	DETECTABILITY	DETERMINATIVE	DETHRONIZES	DETRIBALIZED
DESULPHURATED	DETECTABLE	DETERMINATIVELY	DETHRONIZING	DETRIBALIZES
DESULPHURATES	DETECTIBLE	DETERMINATIVES	DETONABILITIES	DETRIBALIZING
DESULPHURATING	DETECTIONS	DETERMINATOR	DETONABILITY	DETRIMENTAL
DESULPHURATION	DETECTIVELIKE	DETERMINATORS	DETONATABLE	DETRIMENTALLY
DESULPHURATIONS	DETECTIVES	DETERMINED	DETONATING	DETRIMENTALS
DESULPHURED	DETECTIVIST	DETERMINEDLY	DETONATION	DETRIMENTS
DESULPHURING	DETECTIVISTS	DETERMINEDNESS	DETONATIONS	DETRITIONS
DESULPHURISE	DETECTOPHONE	DETERMINER	DETONATIVE	DETRITOVORE
DESULPHURISED	DETECTOPHONES	DETERMINERS	DETONATORS	DETRITOVORES
DESULPHURISER	DETECTORIST	DETERMINES	DETORSIONS	DETRUNCATE
DESULPHURISERS	DETECTORISTS	DETERMINING	DETORTIONS	DETRUNCATED
DESULPHURISES	DETENTIONS	DETERMINISM	DETOXICANT	DETRUNCATES
DESULPHURISING	DETENTISTS	DETERMINISMS	DETOXICANTS	DETRUNCATING
DESULPHURIZE	DETERGENCE	DETERMINIST	DETOXICATE	DETRUNCATION
DESULPHURIZED	DETERGENCES	DETERMINISTIC	DETOXICATED	DETRUNCATIONS
DESULPHURIZER	DETERGENCIES	DETERMINISTS	DETOXICATES	DETRUSIONS
DESULPHURIZERS	DETERGENCY	DETERRABILITIES	DETOXICATING	DETUMESCENCE

DETUMESCENCES	DEVALORIZING	DEVITALISATIONS	DEVOURMENT	DIABETOLOGIST
DETUMESCENT	DEVALUATED	DEVITALISE	DEVOURMENTS	DIABETOLOGISTS
DEUTERAGONIST	DEVALUATES	DEVITALISED	DEVOUTNESS	DIABLERIES
DEUTERAGONISTS	DEVALUATING	DEVITALISES	DEVOUTNESSES	DIABOLICAL
DEUTERANOMALIES	DEVALUATION	DEVITALISING	DEVVELLING	DIABOLICALLY
DEUTERANOMALOUS	DEVALUATIONS	DEVITALIZATION	DEWATERERS	DIABOLICALNESS
DEUTERANOMALY	DEVANAGARI	DEVITALIZATIONS	DEWATERING	DIABOLISED
DEUTERANOPE	DEVANAGARIS	DEVITALIZE	DEWATERINGS	DIABOLISES
DEUTERANOPES	DEVASTATED	DEVITALIZED	DEWBERRIES	DIABOLISING
DEUTERANOPIA	DEVASTATES	DEVITALIZES	DEWINESSES	DIABOLISMS
DEUTERANOPIAS	DEVASTATING	DEVITALIZING	DEXAMETHASONE	DIABOLISTS
DEUTERANOPIC	DEVASTATINGLY	DEVITRIFICATION	DEXAMETHASONES	DIABOLIZED
DEUTERATED	DEVASTATION	DEVITRIFIED	DEXAMPHETAMINE	DIABOLIZES
DEUTERATES	DEVASTATIONS	DEVITRIFIES	DEXAMPHETAMINES	DIABOLIZING
DEUTERATING	DEVASTATIVE	DEVITRIFYING	DEXIOTROPIC	DIABOLOGIES
DEUTERATION	DEVASTATOR	DEVOCALISE	DEXTERITIES	DIABOLOLOGIES
DEUTERATIONS	DEVASTATORS	DEVOCALISED	DEXTEROUSLY	DIABOLOLOGY
DEUTERIDES	DEVASTAVIT	DEVOCALISES	DEXTEROUSNESS	DIACATHOLICON
DEUTERIUMS	DEVASTAVITS	DEVOCALISING	DEXTEROUSNESSES	DIACATHOLICONS
DEUTEROGAMIES	DEVELOPABLE	DEVOCALIZE	DEXTERWISE	DIACAUSTIC
DEUTEROGAMIST	DEVELOPERS	DEVOCALIZED	DEXTRALITIES	DIACAUSTICS
DEUTEROGAMISTS	DEVELOPING	DEVOCALIZES	DEXTRALITY	DIACHRONIC
DEUTEROGAMY	DEVELOPMENT	DEVOCALIZING	DEXTRANASE	DIACHRONICALLY
DEUTEROPLASM	DEVELOPMENTAL	DEVOICINGS	DEXTRANASES	DIACHRONIES
DEUTEROPLASMS	DEVELOPMENTALLY	DEVOLUTION	DEXTROCARDIA	DIACHRONISM
DEUTEROSCOPIC	DEVELOPMENTS	DEVOLUTIONARY	DEXTROCARDIAC	DIACHRONISMS
DEUTEROSCOPIES	DEVELOPPES	DEVOLUTIONIST	DEXTROCARDIACS	DIACHRONISTIC
DEUTEROSCOPY	DEVERBATIVE	DEVOLUTIONISTS	DEXTROCARDIAS	DIACHRONOUS
DEUTEROSTOME	DEVERBATIVES	DEVOLUTIONS	DEXTROGLUCOSE	DIACHYLONS
DEUTEROSTOMES	DEVIANCIES	DEVOLVEMENT	DEXTROGLUCOSES	DIACHYLUMS
DEUTEROTOKIES	DEVIATIONISM	DEVOLVEMENTS	DEXTROGYRATE	DIACODIONS
DEUTEROTOKY	DEVIATIONISMS	DEVONPORTS	DEXTROGYRE	DIACODIUMS
DEUTOPLASM	DEVIATIONIST	DEVOTEDNESS	DEXTROROTARY	DIACONATES
DEUTOPLASMIC	DEVIATIONISTS	DEVOTEDNESSES	DEXTROROTATION	DIACONICON
DEUTOPLASMS	DEVIATIONS	DEVOTEMENT	DEXTROROTATIONS	DIACONICONS
DEUTOPLASTIC	DEVILESSES	DEVOTEMENTS	DEXTROROTATORY	DIACOUSTIC
DEVALORISATION	DEVILFISHES	DEVOTIONAL	DEXTRORSAL	DIACOUSTICS
DEVALORISATIONS	DEVILISHLY	DEVOTIONALIST	DEXTRORSELY	DIACRITICAL
DEVALORISE	DEVILISHNESS	DEVOTIONALISTS	DEXTROUSLY	DIACRITICALLY
DEVALORISED	DEVILISHNESSES	DEVOTIONALITIES	DEXTROUSNESS	DIACRITICS
DEVALORISES	DEVILMENTS	DEVOTIONALITY	DEXTROUSNESSES	DIACTINISM
DEVALORISING	DEVILSHIPS	DEVOTIONALLY	DEZINCKING	DIACTINISMS
DEVALORIZATION	DEVILTRIES	DEVOTIONALNESS	DHARMSALAS	DIADELPHOUS
DEVALORIZATIONS	DEVILWOODS	DEVOTIONALS	DHARMSHALA	DIADOCHIES
DEVALORIZE	DEVIOUSNESS	DEVOTIONIST	DHARMSHALAS	DIADROMOUS
DEVALORIZED	DEVIOUSNESSES	DEVOTIONISTS	DIABETICAL	DIAGENESES
DEVALORIZES	DEVITALISATION	DEVOURINGLY	DIABETOGENIC	DIAGENESIS

DIAGENETIC
DIAGENETICALLY
DIAGEOTROPIC
DIAGEOTROPISM
DIAGEOTROPISMS
DIAGNOSABILITY
DIAGNOSABLE
DIAGNOSEABLE
DIAGNOSING
DIAGNOSTIC
DIAGNOSTICAL
DIAGNOSTICALLY
DIAGNOSTICIAN
DIAGNOSTICIANS
DIAGNOSTICS
DIAGOMETER
DIAGOMETERS
DIAGONALISABLE
DIAGONALISATION
DIAGONALISE
DIAGONALISED
DIAGONALISES
DIAGONALISING
DIAGONALIZABLE
DIAGONALIZATION
DIAGONALIZE
DIAGONALIZED
DIAGONALIZES
DIAGONALIZING
DIAGONALLY
DIAGRAMING
DIAGRAMMABLE
DIAGRAMMATIC
DIAGRAMMATICAL
DIAGRAMMED
DIAGRAMMING
DIAGRAPHIC
DIAHELIOTROPIC
DIAHELIOTROPISM
DIAKINESES
DIAKINESIS
DIALECTALLY
DIALECTICAL
DIALECTICALLY
DIALECTICIAN
DIALECTICIANS
DIALECTICISM

DIALECTICISMS
DIALECTICS
DIALECTOLOGICAL
DIALECTOLOGIES
DIALECTOLOGIST
DIALECTOLOGISTS
DIALECTOLOGY
DIALLAGOID
DIALOGICAL
DIALOGICALLY
DIALOGISED
DIALOGISES
DIALOGISING
DIALOGISMS
DIALOGISTIC
DIALOGISTICAL
DIALOGISTS
DIALOGITES
DIALOGIZED
DIALOGIZES
DIALOGIZING
DIALOGUERS
DIALOGUING
DIALYPETALOUS
DIALYSABILITIES
DIALYSABILITY
DIALYSABLE
DIALYSATES
DIALYSATION
DIALYSATIONS
DIALYTICALLY
DIALYZABILITIES
DIALYZABILITY
DIALYZABLE
DIALYZATES
DIALYZATION
DIALYZATIONS
DIAMAGNETIC
DIAMAGNETICALLY
DIAMAGNETISM
DIAMAGNETISMS
DIAMAGNETS
DIAMANTIFEROUS
DIAMANTINE
DIAMETRALLY
DIAMETRICAL
DIAMETRICALLY

DIAMONDBACK
DIAMONDBACKS
DIAMONDIFEROUS
DIAMONDING
DIAMORPHINE
DIAMORPHINES
DIANTHUSES
DIAPASONAL
DIAPASONIC
DIAPAUSING
DIAPEDESES
DIAPEDESIS
DIAPEDETIC
DIAPERINGS
DIAPHANEITIES
DIAPHANEITY
DIAPHANOMETER
DIAPHANOMETERS
DIAPHANOUS
DIAPHANOUSLY
DIAPHANOUSNESS
DIAPHONIES
DIAPHORASE
DIAPHORASES
DIAPHORESES
DIAPHORESIS
DIAPHORETIC
DIAPHORETICS
DIAPHOTOTROPIC
DIAPHOTOTROPIES
DIAPHOTOTROPISM
DIAPHOTOTROPY
DIAPHRAGMAL
DIAPHRAGMATIC
DIAPHRAGMATITIS
DIAPHRAGMED
DIAPHRAGMING
DIAPHRAGMITIS
DIAPHRAGMS
DIAPHYSEAL
DIAPHYSIAL
DIAPIRISMS
DIAPOPHYSES
DIAPOPHYSIAL
DIAPOPHYSIS
DIAPOSITIVE
DIAPOSITIVES

DIAPYETICS
DIARCHICAL
DIARRHETIC
DIARRHOEAL
DIARRHOEAS
DIARRHOEIC
DIARTHRODIAL
DIARTHROSES
DIARTHROSIS
DIASCORDIUM
DIASCORDIUMS
DIASKEUAST
DIASKEUASTS
DIASTALSES
DIASTALSIS
DIASTALTIC
DIASTEMATA
DIASTEMATIC
DIASTEREOISOMER
DIASTEREOMER
DIASTEREOMERIC
DIASTEREOMERS
DIASTROPHIC
DIASTROPHICALLY
DIASTROPHISM
DIASTROPHISMS
DIATESSARON
DIATESSARONS
DIATHERMACIES
DIATHERMACY
DIATHERMAL
DIATHERMANCIES
DIATHERMANCY
DIATHERMANEITY
DIATHERMANOUS
DIATHERMIA
DIATHERMIAS
DIATHERMIC
DIATHERMIES
DIATHERMOUS
DIATOMACEOUS
DIATOMICITIES
DIATOMICITY
DIATOMISTS
DIATOMITES
DIATONICALLY
DIATONICISM

DIATONICISMS
DIATRETUMS
DIATRIBIST
DIATRIBISTS
DIATROPISM
DIATROPISMS
DIAZEUCTIC
DIAZOMETHANE
DIAZOMETHANES
DIAZONIUMS
DIAZOTISATION
DIAZOTISATIONS
DIAZOTISED
DIAZOTISES
DIAZOTISING
DIAZOTIZATION
DIAZOTIZATIONS
DIAZOTIZED
DIAZOTIZES
DIAZOTIZING
DIBASICITIES
DIBASICITY
DIBENZOFURAN
DIBENZOFURANS
DIBRANCHIATE
DIBRANCHIATES
DIBROMIDES
DICACITIES
DICACODYLS
DICARBOXYLIC
DICARPELLARY
DICASTERIES
DICENTRICS
DICEPHALISM
DICEPHALISMS
DICEPHALOUS
DICHASIALLY
DICHLAMYDEOUS
DICHLORACETIC
DICHLORIDE
DICHLORIDES
DICHLOROBENZENE
DICHLOROETHANE
DICHLOROETHANES
DICHLOROMETHANE
DICHLORVOS
DICHLORVOSES

DICHOGAMIC	DICKEYBIRD	DIDELPHINE	DIETICIANS	DIFFRANGIBILITY
DICHOGAMIES	DICKEYBIRDS	DIDELPHOUS	DIETITIANS	DIFFRANGIBLE
DICHOGAMOUS	DICKYBIRDS	DIDGERIDOO	DIFFARREATION	DIFFUSEDLY
DICHONDRAS	DICLINISMS	DIDGERIDOOS	DIFFARREATIONS	DIFFUSEDNESS
DICHOTICALLY	DICOTYLEDON	DIDJERIDOO	DIFFERENCE	DIFFUSEDNESSES
DICHOTOMIC	DICOTYLEDONOUS	DIDJERIDOOS	DIFFERENCED	DIFFUSENESS
DICHOTOMIES	DICOTYLEDONS	DIDJERIDUS	DIFFERENCES	DIFFUSENESSES
DICHOTOMISATION	DICOUMARIN	DIDRACHMAS	DIFFERENCIED	DIFFUSIBILITIES
DICHOTOMISE	DICOUMARINS	DIDYNAMIAN	DIFFERENCIES	DIFFUSIBILITY
DICHOTOMISED	DICOUMAROL	DIDYNAMIES	DIFFERENCING	DIFFUSIBLE
DICHOTOMISES	DICOUMAROLS	DIDYNAMOUS	DIFFERENCY	DIFFUSIBLENESS
DICHOTOMISING	DICROTISMS	DIECIOUSLY	DIFFERENCYING	DIFFUSIONAL
DICHOTOMIST	DICTATIONAL	DIECIOUSNESS	DIFFERENTIA	DIFFUSIONISM
DICHOTOMISTS	DICTATIONS	DIECIOUSNESSES	DIFFERENTIABLE	DIFFUSIONISMS
DICHOTOMIZATION	DICTATORIAL	DIEFFENBACHIA	DIFFERENTIAE	DIFFUSIONIST
DICHOTOMIZE	DICTATORIALLY	DIEFFENBACHIAS	DIFFERENTIAL	DIFFUSIONISTS
DICHOTOMIZED	DICTATORIALNESS	DIELECTRIC	DIFFERENTIALLY	DIFFUSIONS
DICHOTOMIZES	DICTATORSHIP	DIELECTRICALLY	DIFFERENTIALS	DIFFUSIVELY
DICHOTOMIZING	DICTATORSHIPS	DIELECTRICS	DIFFERENTIATE	DIFFUSIVENESS
DICHOTOMOUS	DICTATRESS	DIENCEPHALA	DIFFERENTIATED	DIFFUSIVENESSES
DICHOTOMOUSLY	DICTATRESSES	DIENCEPHALIC	DIFFERENTIATES	DIFFUSIVITIES
DICHOTOMOUSNESS	DICTATRICES	DIENCEPHALON	DIFFERENTIATING	DIFFUSIVITY
DICHROISCOPE	DICTATRIXES	DIENCEPHALONS	DIFFERENTIATION	DIFUNCTIONAL
DICHROISCOPES	DICTATURES	DIESELINGS	DIFFERENTIATOR	DIFUNCTIONALS
DICHROISCOPIC	DICTIONALLY	DIESELISATION	DIFFERENTIATORS	DIGASTRICS
DICHROISMS	DICTIONARIES	DIESELISATIONS	DIFFERENTLY	DIGESTANTS
DICHROITES	DICTIONARY	DIESELISED	DIFFERENTNESS	DIGESTEDLY
DICHROITIC	DICTYOGENS	DIESELISES	DIFFERENTNESSES	DIGESTIBILITIES
DICHROMATE	DICTYOPTERAN	DIESELISING	DIFFICULTIES	DIGESTIBILITY
DICHROMATES	DICTYOPTERANS	DIESELIZATION	DIFFICULTLY	DIGESTIBLE
DICHROMATIC	DICTYOSOME	DIESELIZATIONS	DIFFICULTY	DIGESTIBLENESS
DICHROMATICISM	DICTYOSOMES	DIESELIZED	DIFFIDENCE	DIGESTIBLY
DICHROMATICISMS	DICTYOSTELE	DIESELIZES	DIFFIDENCES	DIGESTIONAL
DICHROMATICS	DICTYOSTELES	DIESELIZING	DIFFIDENTLY	DIGESTIONS
DICHROMATISM	DICUMAROLS	DIESELLING	DIFFORMITIES	DIGESTIVELY
DICHROMATISMS	DICYNODONT	DIESELLINGS	DIFFORMITY	DIGESTIVES
DICHROMATS	DICYNODONTS	DIESINKERS	DIFFRACTED	DIGITALINS
DICHROMISM	DIDACTICAL	DIESTRUSES	DIFFRACTING	DIGITALISATION
DICHROMISMS	DIDACTICALLY	DIETARIANS	DIFFRACTION	DIGITALISATIONS
DICHROOSCOPE	DIDACTICISM	DIETETICAL	DIFFRACTIONS	DIGITALISE
DICHROOSCOPES	DIDACTICISMS	DIETETICALLY	DIFFRACTIVE	DIGITALISED
DICHROOSCOPIC	DIDACTYLISM	DIETHYLAMIDE	DIFFRACTIVELY	DIGITALISES
DICHROSCOPE	DIDACTYLISMS	DIETHYLAMIDES	DIFFRACTIVENESS	DIGITALISING
DICHROSCOPES	DIDACTYLOUS	DIETHYLAMINE	DIFFRACTOMETER	DIGITALISM
DICHROSCOPIC	DIDASCALIC	DIETHYLAMINES	DIFFRACTOMETERS	DIGITALISMS
DICKCISSEL	DIDELPHIAN	DIETHYLENE	DIFFRACTOMETRIC	DIGITALIZATION
DICKCISSELS	DIDELPHIDS	DIETHYLENES	DIFFRACTOMETRY	DIGITALIZATIONS

D

DIGITALIZE
DIGITALIZED
DIGITALIZES
DIGITALIZING
DIGITATELY
DIGITATION
DIGITATIONS
DIGITIFORM
DIGITIGRADE
DIGITIGRADES
DIGITISATION
DIGITISATIONS
DIGITISERS
DIGITISING
DIGITIZATION
DIGITIZATIONS
DIGITIZERS
DIGITIZING
DIGITONINS
DIGITORIUM
DIGITORIUMS
DIGITOXIGENIN
DIGITOXIGENINS
DIGITOXINS
DIGLADIATE
DIGLADIATED
DIGLADIATES
DIGLADIATING
DIGLADIATION
DIGLADIATIONS
DIGLADIATOR
DIGLADIATORS
DIGLOSSIAS
DIGLYCERIDE
DIGLYCERIDES
DIGNIFICATION
DIGNIFICATIONS
DIGNIFIEDLY
DIGNIFIEDNESS
DIGNIFIEDNESSES
DIGNIFYING
DIGNITARIES
DIGONEUTIC
DIGONEUTISM
DIGONEUTISMS
DIGRAPHICALLY
DIGRESSERS

DIGRESSING
DIGRESSION
DIGRESSIONAL
DIGRESSIONARY
DIGRESSIONS
DIGRESSIVE
DIGRESSIVELY
DIGRESSIVENESS
DIHYBRIDISM
DIHYBRIDISMS
DIHYDROCODEINE
DIHYDROCODEINES
DIHYDROGEN
DIJUDICATE
DIJUDICATED
DIJUDICATES
DIJUDICATING
DIJUDICATION
DIJUDICATIONS
DILACERATE
DILACERATED
DILACERATES
DILACERATING
DILACERATION
DILACERATIONS
DILAPIDATE
DILAPIDATED
DILAPIDATES
DILAPIDATING
DILAPIDATION
DILAPIDATIONS
DILAPIDATOR
DILAPIDATORS
DILATABILITIES
DILATABILITY
DILATABLENESS
DILATABLENESSES
DILATANCIES
DILATATION
DILATATIONAL
DILATATIONS
DILATATORS
DILATOMETER
DILATOMETERS
DILATOMETRIC
DILATOMETRIES
DILATOMETRY

DILATORILY
DILATORINESS
DILATORINESSES
DILEMMATIC
DILETTANTE
DILETTANTEISH
DILETTANTEISM
DILETTANTEISMS
DILETTANTES
DILETTANTI
DILETTANTISH
DILETTANTISM
DILETTANTISMS
DILIGENCES
DILIGENTLY
DILLYDALLIED
DILLYDALLIES
DILLYDALLY
DILLYDALLYING
DILTIAZEMS
DILUCIDATE
DILUCIDATED
DILUCIDATES
DILUCIDATING
DILUCIDATION
DILUCIDATIONS
DILUTABLES
DILUTENESS
DILUTENESSES
DILUTIONARY
DILUVIALISM
DILUVIALISMS
DILUVIALIST
DILUVIALISTS
DIMENHYDRINATE
DIMENHYDRINATES
DIMENSIONAL
DIMENSIONALITY
DIMENSIONALLY
DIMENSIONED
DIMENSIONING
DIMENSIONLESS
DIMENSIONS
DIMERCAPROL
DIMERCAPROLS
DIMERISATION
DIMERISATIONS

DIMERISING
DIMERIZATION
DIMERIZATIONS
DIMERIZING
DIMETHOATE
DIMETHOATES
DIMETHYLAMINE
DIMETHYLAMINES
DIMETHYLANILINE
DIMIDIATED
DIMIDIATES
DIMIDIATING
DIMIDIATION
DIMIDIATIONS
DIMINISHABLE
DIMINISHED
DIMINISHES
DIMINISHING
DIMINISHINGLY
DIMINISHINGS
DIMINISHMENT
DIMINISHMENTS
DIMINUENDO
DIMINUENDOES
DIMINUENDOS
DIMINUTION
DIMINUTIONS
DIMINUTIVAL
DIMINUTIVE
DIMINUTIVELY
DIMINUTIVENESS
DIMINUTIVES
DIMORPHISM
DIMORPHISMS
DIMORPHOUS
DIMPLEMENT
DIMPLEMENTS
DINANDERIE
DINANDERIES
DINARCHIES
DINGDONGED
DINGDONGING
DINGINESSES
DINGLEBERRIES
DINGLEBERRY
DINITROBENZENE
DINITROBENZENES

DINITROGEN
DINITROPHENOL
DINITROPHENOLS
DINNERLESS
DINNERTIME
DINNERTIMES
DINNERWARE
DINNERWARES
DINOCERASES
DINOFLAGELLATE
DINOFLAGELLATES
DINOMANIAS
DINOSAURIAN
DINOSAURIC
DINOTHERES
DINOTHERIA
DINOTHERIUM
DINOTHERIUMS
DINOTURBATION
DINOTURBATIONS
DINUCLEOTIDE
DINUCLEOTIDES
DIOECIOUSLY
DIOECIOUSNESS
DIOECIOUSNESSES
DIOESTRUSES
DIOICOUSLY
DIOICOUSNESS
DIOICOUSNESSES
DIOPHYSITE
DIOPHYSITES
DIOPTOMETER
DIOPTOMETERS
DIOPTOMETRIES
DIOPTOMETRY
DIOPTRICAL
DIOPTRICALLY
DIORISTICAL
DIORISTICALLY
DIORTHOSES
DIORTHOSIS
DIORTHOTIC
DIOSCOREACEOUS
DIOSGENINS
DIOTHELETE
DIOTHELETES
DIOTHELETIC

DIOTHELETICAL	DIPHYODONT	DIPLOSPEAK	DIRECTRICE	DISADORNING
DIOTHELISM	DIPHYODONTS	DIPLOSPEAKS	DIRECTRICES	DISADVANCE
DIOTHELISMS	DIPHYSITES	DIPLOSTEMONOUS	DIRECTRIXES	DISADVANCED
DIOTHELITE	DIPHYSITISM	DIPLOTENES	DIREFULNESS	DISADVANCES
DIOTHELITES	DIPHYSITISMS	DIPNETTING	DIREFULNESSES	DISADVANCING
DIOXONITRIC	DIPLEIDOSCOPE	DIPPERFULS	DIREMPTING	DISADVANTAGE
DIPEPTIDASE	DIPLEIDOSCOPES	DIPPINESSES	DIREMPTION	DISADVANTAGED
DIPEPTIDASES	DIPLOBIONT	DIPRIONIDIAN	DIREMPTIONS	DISADVANTAGEOUS
DIPEPTIDES	DIPLOBIONTIC	DIPROPELLANT	DIRENESSES	DISADVANTAGES
DIPETALOUS	DIPLOBIONTS	DIPROPELLANTS	DIRIGIBILITIES	DISADVANTAGING
DIPHENHYDRAMINE	DIPLOBLASTIC	DIPROTODON	DIRIGIBILITY	DISADVENTURE
DIPHENYLAMINE	DIPLOCARDIAC	DIPROTODONS	DIRIGIBLES	DISADVENTURES
DIPHENYLAMINES	DIPLOCOCCAL	DIPROTODONT	DIRIGISMES	DISADVENTUROUS
DIPHENYLENE	DIPLOCOCCI	DIPROTODONTID	DIRTINESSES	DISAFFECTED
DIPHENYLENIMINE	DIPLOCOCCIC	DIPROTODONTIDS	DISABILITIES	DISAFFECTEDLY
DIPHENYLKETONE	DIPLOCOCCUS	DIPROTODONTS	DISABILITY	DISAFFECTEDNESS
DIPHENYLKETONES	DIPLODOCUS	DIPSOMANIA	DISABLEMENT	DISAFFECTING
DIPHOSGENE	DIPLODOCUSES	DIPSOMANIAC	DISABLEMENTS	DISAFFECTION
DIPHOSGENES	DIPLOGENESES	DIPSOMANIACAL	DISABLISMS	DISAFFECTIONATE
DIPHOSPHATE	DIPLOGENESIS	DIPSOMANIACS	DISABLISTS	DISAFFECTIONS
DIPHOSPHATES	DIPLOIDIES	DIPSOMANIAS	DISABUSALS	DISAFFECTS
DIPHTHERIA	DIPLOMACIES	DIPSWITCHES	DISABUSING	DISAFFILIATE
DIPHTHERIAL	DIPLOMAING	DIPTERISTS	DISACCHARID	DISAFFILIATED
DIPHTHERIAS	DIPLOMATED	DIPTEROCARP	DISACCHARIDASE	DISAFFILIATES
DIPHTHERIC	DIPLOMATES	DIPTEROCARPOUS	DISACCHARIDASES	DISAFFILIATING
DIPHTHERITIC	DIPLOMATESE	DIPTEROCARPS	DISACCHARIDE	DISAFFILIATION
DIPHTHERITIS	DIPLOMATESES	DIPTEROSES	DISACCHARIDES	DISAFFILIATIONS
DIPHTHERITISES	DIPLOMATIC	DIRECTEDNESS	DISACCHARIDS	DISAFFIRMANCE
DIPHTHEROID	DIPLOMATICAL	DIRECTEDNESSES	DISACCOMMODATE	DISAFFIRMANCES
DIPHTHEROIDS	DIPLOMATICALLY	DIRECTIONAL	DISACCOMMODATED	DISAFFIRMATION
DIPHTHONGAL	DIPLOMATICS	DIRECTIONALITY	DISACCOMMODATES	DISAFFIRMATIONS
DIPHTHONGALLY	DIPLOMATING	DIRECTIONLESS	DISACCORDANT	DISAFFIRMED
DIPHTHONGED	DIPLOMATISE	DIRECTIONS	DISACCORDED	DISAFFIRMING
DIPHTHONGIC	DIPLOMATISED	DIRECTIVES	DISACCORDING	DISAFFIRMS
DIPHTHONGING	DIPLOMATISES	DIRECTIVITIES	DISACCORDS	DISAFFOREST
DIPHTHONGISE	DIPLOMATISING	DIRECTIVITY	DISACCREDIT	DISAFFORESTED
DIPHTHONGISED	DIPLOMATIST	DIRECTNESS	DISACCREDITED	DISAFFORESTING
DIPHTHONGISES	DIPLOMATISTS	DIRECTNESSES	DISACCREDITING	DISAFFORESTMENT
DIPHTHONGISING	DIPLOMATIZE	DIRECTORATE	DISACCREDITS	DISAFFORESTS
DIPHTHONGIZE	DIPLOMATIZED	DIRECTORATES	DISACCUSTOM	DISAGGREGATE
DIPHTHONGIZED	DIPLOMATIZES	DIRECTORIAL	DISACCUSTOMED	DISAGGREGATED
DIPHTHONGIZES	DIPLOMATIZING	DIRECTORIALLY	DISACCUSTOMING	DISAGGREGATES
DIPHTHONGIZING	DIPLOMATOLOGIES	DIRECTORIES	DISACCUSTOMS	DISAGGREGATING
DIPHTHONGS	DIPLOMATOLOGY	DIRECTORSHIP	DISACKNOWLEDGE	DISAGGREGATION
DIPHYCERCAL	DIPLONEMAS	DIRECTORSHIPS	DISACKNOWLEDGED	DISAGGREGATIONS
DIPHYLETIC	DIPLOPHASE	DIRECTRESS	DISACKNOWLEDGES	DISAGGREGATIVE
DIPHYLLOUS	DIPLOPHASES	DIRECTRESSES	DISADORNED	DISAGREEABILITY

DISAGREEABLE
DISAGREEABLES
DISAGREEABLY
DISAGREEING
DISAGREEMENT
DISAGREEMENTS
DISALLOWABLE
DISALLOWANCE
DISALLOWANCES
DISALLOWED
DISALLOWING
DISALLYING
DISAMBIGUATE
DISAMBIGUATED
DISAMBIGUATES
DISAMBIGUATING
DISAMBIGUATION
DISAMBIGUATIONS
DISAMENITIES
DISAMENITY
DISANALOGIES
DISANALOGOUS
DISANALOGY
DISANCHORED
DISANCHORING
DISANCHORS
DISANIMATE
DISANIMATED
DISANIMATES
DISANIMATING
DISANNEXED
DISANNEXES
DISANNEXING
DISANNULLED
DISANNULLER
DISANNULLERS
DISANNULLING
DISANNULLINGS
DISANNULMENT
DISANNULMENTS
DISANOINTED
DISANOINTING
DISANOINTS
DISAPPAREL
DISAPPARELLED
DISAPPARELLING
DISAPPARELS

DISAPPEARANCE
DISAPPEARANCES
DISAPPEARED
DISAPPEARING
DISAPPEARS
DISAPPLICATION
DISAPPLICATIONS
DISAPPLIED
DISAPPLIES
DISAPPLYING
DISAPPOINT
DISAPPOINTED
DISAPPOINTEDLY
DISAPPOINTING
DISAPPOINTINGLY
DISAPPOINTMENT
DISAPPOINTMENTS
DISAPPOINTS
DISAPPROBATION
DISAPPROBATIONS
DISAPPROBATIVE
DISAPPROBATORY
DISAPPROPRIATE
DISAPPROPRIATED
DISAPPROPRIATES
DISAPPROVAL
DISAPPROVALS
DISAPPROVE
DISAPPROVED
DISAPPROVER
DISAPPROVERS
DISAPPROVES
DISAPPROVING
DISAPPROVINGLY
DISARMAMENT
DISARMAMENTS
DISARMINGLY
DISARRANGE
DISARRANGED
DISARRANGEMENT
DISARRANGEMENTS
DISARRANGES
DISARRANGING
DISARRAYED
DISARRAYING
DISARTICULATE
DISARTICULATED

DISARTICULATES
DISARTICULATING
DISARTICULATION
DISARTICULATOR
DISARTICULATORS
DISASSEMBLE
DISASSEMBLED
DISASSEMBLER
DISASSEMBLERS
DISASSEMBLES
DISASSEMBLIES
DISASSEMBLING
DISASSEMBLY
DISASSIMILATE
DISASSIMILATED
DISASSIMILATES
DISASSIMILATING
DISASSIMILATION
DISASSIMILATIVE
DISASSOCIATE
DISASSOCIATED
DISASSOCIATES
DISASSOCIATING
DISASSOCIATION
DISASSOCIATIONS
DISASTROUS
DISASTROUSLY
DISATTIRED
DISATTIRES
DISATTIRING
DISATTRIBUTION
DISATTRIBUTIONS
DISATTUNED
DISATTUNES
DISATTUNING
DISAUTHORISE
DISAUTHORISED
DISAUTHORISES
DISAUTHORISING
DISAUTHORIZE
DISAUTHORIZED
DISAUTHORIZES
DISAUTHORIZING
DISAVAUNCE
DISAVAUNCED
DISAVAUNCES
DISAVAUNCING

DISAVENTROUS
DISAVENTURE
DISAVENTURES
DISAVOUCHED
DISAVOUCHES
DISAVOUCHING
DISAVOWABLE
DISAVOWALS
DISAVOWEDLY
DISAVOWERS
DISAVOWING
DISBANDING
DISBANDMENT
DISBANDMENTS
DISBARKING
DISBARMENT
DISBARMENTS
DISBARRING
DISBELIEFS
DISBELIEVE
DISBELIEVED
DISBELIEVER
DISBELIEVERS
DISBELIEVES
DISBELIEVING
DISBELIEVINGLY
DISBENCHED
DISBENCHES
DISBENCHING
DISBENEFIT
DISBENEFITS
DISBOSOMED
DISBOSOMING
DISBOWELED
DISBOWELING
DISBOWELLED
DISBOWELLING
DISBRANCHED
DISBRANCHES
DISBRANCHING
DISBUDDING
DISBURDENED
DISBURDENING
DISBURDENMENT
DISBURDENMENTS
DISBURDENS
DISBURSABLE

DISBURSALS
DISBURSEMENT
DISBURSEMENTS
DISBURSERS
DISBURSING
DISBURTHEN
DISBURTHENED
DISBURTHENING
DISBURTHENS
DISCALCEATE
DISCALCEATES
DISCANDERING
DISCANDERINGS
DISCANDIED
DISCANDIES
DISCANDYING
DISCANDYINGS
DISCANTERS
DISCANTING
DISCAPACITATE
DISCAPACITATED
DISCAPACITATES
DISCAPACITATING
DISCARDABLE
DISCARDERS
DISCARDING
DISCARDMENT
DISCARDMENTS
DISCARNATE
DISCEPTATION
DISCEPTATIONS
DISCEPTATIOUS
DISCEPTATOR
DISCEPTATORIAL
DISCEPTATORS
DISCEPTING
DISCERNABLE
DISCERNABLY
DISCERNERS
DISCERNIBLE
DISCERNIBLY
DISCERNING
DISCERNINGLY
DISCERNMENT
DISCERNMENTS
DISCERPIBILITY
DISCERPIBLE

DISCERPING	DISCLOSERS	DISCOMFORTING	DISCONFIRMED	DISCONTINUITY
DISCERPTIBLE	DISCLOSING	DISCOMFORTS	DISCONFIRMING	DISCONTINUOUS
DISCERPTION	DISCLOSURE	DISCOMMEND	DISCONFIRMS	DISCONTINUOUSLY
DISCERPTIONS	DISCLOSURES	DISCOMMENDABLE	DISCONFORMABLE	DISCOPHILE
DISCERPTIVE	DISCOBOLOS	DISCOMMENDATION	DISCONFORMITIES	DISCOPHILES
DISCHARGEABLE	DISCOBOLUS	DISCOMMENDED	DISCONFORMITY	DISCOPHORAN
DISCHARGED	DISCOBOLUSES	DISCOMMENDING	DISCONNECT	DISCOPHORANS
DISCHARGEE	DISCOGRAPHER	DISCOMMENDS	DISCONNECTED	DISCOPHOROUS
DISCHARGEES	DISCOGRAPHERS	DISCOMMISSION	DISCONNECTEDLY	DISCORDANCE
DISCHARGER	DISCOGRAPHIC	DISCOMMISSIONED	DISCONNECTER	DISCORDANCES
DISCHARGERS	DISCOGRAPHICAL	DISCOMMISSIONS	DISCONNECTERS	DISCORDANCIES
DISCHARGES	DISCOGRAPHIES	DISCOMMODE	DISCONNECTING	DISCORDANCY
DISCHARGING	DISCOGRAPHY	DISCOMMODED	DISCONNECTION	DISCORDANT
DISCHUFFED	DISCOLOGIES	DISCOMMODES	DISCONNECTIONS	DISCORDANTLY
DISCHURCHED	DISCOLOGIST	DISCOMMODING	DISCONNECTIVE	DISCORDFUL
DISCHURCHES	DISCOLOGISTS	DISCOMMODIOUS	DISCONNECTS	DISCORDING
DISCHURCHING	DISCOLORATION	DISCOMMODIOUSLY	DISCONNEXION	DISCORPORATE
DISCIPLESHIP	DISCOLORATIONS	DISCOMMODITIES	DISCONNEXIONS	DISCORPORATED
DISCIPLESHIPS	DISCOLORED	DISCOMMODITY	DISCONSENT	DISCORPORATES
DISCIPLINABLE	DISCOLORING	DISCOMMONED	DISCONSENTED	DISCORPORATING
DISCIPLINAL	DISCOLORMENT	DISCOMMONING	DISCONSENTING	DISCOTHEQUE
DISCIPLINANT	DISCOLORMENTS	DISCOMMONS	DISCONSENTS	DISCOTHEQUES
DISCIPLINANTS	DISCOLOURATION	DISCOMMUNITIES	DISCONSOLATE	DISCOUNSEL
DISCIPLINARIAN	DISCOLOURATIONS	DISCOMMUNITY	DISCONSOLATELY	DISCOUNSELLED
DISCIPLINARIANS	DISCOLOURED	DISCOMPOSE	DISCONSOLATION	DISCOUNSELLING
DISCIPLINARILY	DISCOLOURING	DISCOMPOSED	DISCONSOLATIONS	DISCOUNSELS
DISCIPLINARITY	DISCOLOURMENT	DISCOMPOSEDLY	DISCONTENT	DISCOUNTABLE
DISCIPLINARIUM	DISCOLOURMENTS	DISCOMPOSES	DISCONTENTED	DISCOUNTED
DISCIPLINARIUMS	DISCOLOURS	DISCOMPOSING	DISCONTENTEDLY	DISCOUNTENANCE
DISCIPLINARY	DISCOMBOBERATE	DISCOMPOSINGLY	DISCONTENTFUL	DISCOUNTENANCED
DISCIPLINE	DISCOMBOBERATED	DISCOMPOSURE	DISCONTENTING	DISCOUNTENANCES
DISCIPLINED	DISCOMBOBERATES	DISCOMPOSURES	DISCONTENTMENT	DISCOUNTER
DISCIPLINER	DISCOMBOBULATE	DISCOMYCETE	DISCONTENTMENTS	DISCOUNTERS
DISCIPLINERS	DISCOMBOBULATED	DISCOMYCETES	DISCONTENTS	DISCOUNTING
DISCIPLINES	DISCOMBOBULATES	DISCOMYCETOUS	DISCONTIGUITIES	DISCOURAGE
DISCIPLING	DISCOMEDUSAN	DISCONCERT	DISCONTIGUITY	DISCOURAGEABLE
DISCIPLINING	DISCOMEDUSANS	DISCONCERTED	DISCONTIGUOUS	DISCOURAGED
DISCIPULAR	DISCOMFITED	DISCONCERTEDLY	DISCONTINUANCE	DISCOURAGEMENT
DISCISSION	DISCOMFITER	DISCONCERTING	DISCONTINUANCES	DISCOURAGEMENTS
DISCISSIONS	DISCOMFITERS	DISCONCERTINGLY	DISCONTINUATION	DISCOURAGER
DISCLAIMED	DISCOMFITING	DISCONCERTION	DISCONTINUE	DISCOURAGERS
DISCLAIMER	DISCOMFITS	DISCONCERTIONS	DISCONTINUED	DISCOURAGES
DISCLAIMERS	DISCOMFITURE	DISCONCERTMENT	DISCONTINUER	DISCOURAGING
DISCLAIMING	DISCOMFITURES	DISCONCERTMENTS	DISCONTINUERS	DISCOURAGINGLY
DISCLAMATION	DISCOMFORT	DISCONCERTS	DISCONTINUES	DISCOURING
DISCLAMATIONS	DISCOMFORTABLE	DISCONFIRM	DISCONTINUING	DISCOURSAL
DISCLIMAXES	DISCOMFORTED	DISCONFIRMATION	DISCONTINUITIES	DISCOURSED

DISCOURSER	DISCRIMINABLE	DISDAINFULLY	DISEMBOWELMENT	DISENCHANTRESS
DISCOURSERS	DISCRIMINABLY	DISDAINFULNESS	DISEMBOWELMENTS	DISENCHANTS
DISCOURSES	DISCRIMINANT	DISDAINING	DISEMBOWELS	DISENCLOSE
DISCOURSING	DISCRIMINANTS	DISEASEDNESS	DISEMBRANGLE	DISENCLOSED
DISCOURSIVE	DISCRIMINATE	DISEASEDNESSES	DISEMBRANGLED	DISENCLOSES
DISCOURTEISE	DISCRIMINATED	DISEASEFUL	DISEMBRANGLES	DISENCLOSING
DISCOURTEOUS	DISCRIMINATELY	DISECONOMIES	DISEMBRANGLING	DISENCUMBER
DISCOURTEOUSLY	DISCRIMINATES	DISECONOMY	DISEMBROIL	DISENCUMBERED
DISCOURTESIES	DISCRIMINATING	DISEMBARKATION	DISEMBROILED	DISENCUMBERING
DISCOURTESY	DISCRIMINATION	DISEMBARKATIONS	DISEMBROILING	DISENCUMBERMENT
DISCOVERABLE	DISCRIMINATIONS	DISEMBARKED	DISEMBROILS	DISENCUMBERS
DISCOVERED	DISCRIMINATIVE	DISEMBARKING	DISEMBURDEN	DISENCUMBRANCE
DISCOVERER	DISCRIMINATOR	DISEMBARKMENT	DISEMBURDENED	DISENCUMBRANCES
DISCOVERERS	DISCRIMINATORS	DISEMBARKMENTS	DISEMBURDENING	DISENDOWED
DISCOVERIES	DISCRIMINATORY	DISEMBARKS	DISEMBURDENS	DISENDOWER
DISCOVERING	DISCROWNED	DISEMBARRASS	DISEMPLOYED	DISENDOWERS
DISCOVERTURE	DISCROWNING	DISEMBARRASSED	DISEMPLOYING	DISENDOWING
DISCOVERTURES	DISCULPATE	DISEMBARRASSES	DISEMPLOYMENT	DISENDOWMENT
DISCREDITABLE	DISCULPATED	DISEMBARRASSING	DISEMPLOYMENTS	DISENDOWMENTS
DISCREDITABLY	DISCULPATES	DISEMBELLISH	DISEMPLOYS	DISENFRANCHISE
DISCREDITED	DISCULPATING	DISEMBELLISHED	DISEMPOWER	DISENFRANCHISED
DISCREDITING	DISCUMBERED	DISEMBELLISHES	DISEMPOWERED	DISENFRANCHISES
DISCREDITS	DISCUMBERING	DISEMBELLISHING	DISEMPOWERING	DISENGAGED
DISCREETER	DISCUMBERS	DISEMBITTER	DISEMPOWERMENT	DISENGAGEDNESS
DISCREETEST	DISCURSION	DISEMBITTERED	DISEMPOWERMENTS	DISENGAGEMENT
DISCREETLY	DISCURSIONS	DISEMBITTERING	DISEMPOWERS	DISENGAGEMENTS
DISCREETNESS	DISCURSIST	DISEMBITTERS	DISEMVOWEL	DISENGAGES
DISCREETNESSES	DISCURSISTS	DISEMBODIED	DISEMVOWELLED	DISENGAGING
DISCREPANCE	DISCURSIVE	DISEMBODIES	DISEMVOWELLING	DISENNOBLE
DISCREPANCES	DISCURSIVELY	DISEMBODIMENT	DISEMVOWELS	DISENNOBLED
DISCREPANCIES	DISCURSIVENESS	DISEMBODIMENTS	DISENABLED	DISENNOBLES
DISCREPANCY	DISCURSORY	DISEMBODYING	DISENABLEMENT	DISENNOBLING
DISCREPANT	DISCURSUSES	DISEMBOGUE	DISENABLEMENTS	DISENROLLED
DISCREPANTLY	DISCUSSABLE	DISEMBOGUED	DISENABLES	DISENROLLING
DISCRETELY	DISCUSSANT	DISEMBOGUEMENT	DISENABLING	DISENROLLINGS
DISCRETENESS	DISCUSSANTS	DISEMBOGUEMENTS	DISENCHAIN	DISENSHROUD
DISCRETENESSES	DISCUSSERS	DISEMBOGUES	DISENCHAINED	DISENSHROUDED
DISCRETEST	DISCUSSIBLE	DISEMBOGUING	DISENCHAINING	DISENSHROUDING
DISCRETION	DISCUSSING	DISEMBOSOM	DISENCHAINS	DISENSHROUDS
DISCRETIONAL	DISCUSSION	DISEMBOSOMED	DISENCHANT	DISENSLAVE
DISCRETIONALLY	DISCUSSIONAL	DISEMBOSOMING	DISENCHANTED	DISENSLAVED
DISCRETIONARILY	DISCUSSIONS	DISEMBOSOMS	DISENCHANTER	DISENSLAVES
DISCRETIONARY	DISCUSSIVE	DISEMBOWEL	DISENCHANTERS	DISENSLAVING
DISCRETIONS	DISCUSSIVES	DISEMBOWELED	DISENCHANTING	DISENTAILED
DISCRETIVE	DISCUTIENT	DISEMBOWELING	DISENCHANTINGLY	DISENTAILING
DISCRETIVELY	DISCUTIENTS	DISEMBOWELLED	DISENCHANTMENT	DISENTAILMENT
DISCRETIVES	DISDAINFUL	DISEMBOWELLING	DISENCHANTMENTS	DISENTAILMENTS

DISENTAILS	DISENTWINES	DISFIGURATIONS	DISGLORIFIED	DISHABILITATED
DISENTANGLE	DISENTWINING	DISFIGURED	DISGLORIFIES	DISHABILITATES
DISENTANGLED	DISENVELOP	DISFIGUREMENT	DISGLORIFY	DISHABILITATING
DISENTANGLEMENT	DISENVELOPED	DISFIGUREMENTS	DISGLORIFYING	DISHABILITATION
DISENTANGLES	DISENVELOPING	DISFIGURER	DISGORGEMENT	DISHABILLE
DISENTANGLING	DISENVELOPS	DISFIGURERS	DISGORGEMENTS	DISHABILLES
DISENTHRAL	DISENVIRON	DISFIGURES	DISGORGERS	DISHABITED
DISENTHRALL	DISENVIRONED	DISFIGURING	DISGORGING	DISHABITING
DISENTHRALLED	DISENVIRONING	DISFLESHED	DISGOSPELLING	DISHABLING
DISENTHRALLING	DISENVIRONS	DISFLESHES	DISGOWNING	DISHALLOWED
DISENTHRALLMENT	DISEPALOUS	DISFLESHING	DISGRACEFUL	DISHALLOWING
DISENTHRALLS	DISEQUILIBRATE	DISFLUENCIES	DISGRACEFULLY	DISHALLOWS
DISENTHRALMENT	DISEQUILIBRATED	DISFLUENCY	DISGRACEFULNESS	DISHARMONIC
DISENTHRALMENTS	DISEQUILIBRATES	DISFORESTATION	DISGRACERS	DISHARMONIES
DISENTHRALS	DISEQUILIBRIA	DISFORESTATIONS	DISGRACING	DISHARMONIOUS
DISENTHRONE	DISEQUILIBRIUM	DISFORESTED	DISGRACIOUS	DISHARMONIOUSLY
DISENTHRONED	DISEQUILIBRIUMS	DISFORESTING	DISGRADATION	DISHARMONISE
DISENTHRONES	DISESPOUSE	DISFORESTS	DISGRADATIONS	DISHARMONISED
DISENTHRONING	DISESPOUSED	DISFORMING	DISGRADING	DISHARMONISES
DISENTITLE	DISESPOUSES	DISFRANCHISE	DISGREGATION	DISHARMONISING
DISENTITLED	DISESPOUSING	DISFRANCHISED	DISGREGATIONS	DISHARMONIZE
DISENTITLES	DISESTABLISH	DISFRANCHISES	DISGRUNTLE	DISHARMONIZED
DISENTITLING	DISESTABLISHED	DISFRANCHISING	DISGRUNTLED	DISHARMONIZES
DISENTOMBED	DISESTABLISHES	DISFROCKED	DISGRUNTLEMENT	DISHARMONIZING
DISENTOMBING	DISESTABLISHING	DISFROCKING	DISGRUNTLEMENTS	DISHARMONY
DISENTOMBS	DISESTEEMED	DISFUNCTION	DISGRUNTLES	DISHCLOTHS
DISENTRAIL	DISESTEEMING	DISFUNCTIONS	DISGRUNTLING	DISHCLOUTS
DISENTRAILED	DISESTEEMS	DISFURNISH	DISGUISABLE	DISHDASHAS
DISENTRAILING	DISESTIMATION	DISFURNISHED	DISGUISEDLY	DISHDASHES
DISENTRAILS	DISESTIMATIONS	DISFURNISHES	DISGUISEDNESS	DISHEARTEN
DISENTRAIN	DISFAVORED	DISFURNISHING	DISGUISEDNESSES	DISHEARTENED
DISENTRAINED	DISFAVORING	DISFURNISHMENT	DISGUISELESS	DISHEARTENING
DISENTRAINING	DISFAVOURED	DISFURNISHMENTS	DISGUISEMENT	DISHEARTENINGLY
DISENTRAINMENT	DISFAVOURER	DISGARNISH	DISGUISEMENTS	DISHEARTENMENT
DISENTRAINMENTS	DISFAVOURERS	DISGARNISHED	DISGUISERS	DISHEARTENMENTS
DISENTRAINS	DISFAVOURING	DISGARNISHES	DISGUISING	DISHEARTENS
DISENTRANCE	DISFAVOURS	DISGARNISHING	DISGUISINGS	DISHELMING
DISENTRANCED	DISFEATURE	DISGARRISON	DISGUSTEDLY	DISHERISON
DISENTRANCEMENT	DISFEATURED	DISGARRISONED	DISGUSTEDNESS	DISHERISONS
DISENTRANCES	DISFEATUREMENT	DISGARRISONING	DISGUSTEDNESSES	DISHERITED
DISENTRANCING	DISFEATUREMENTS	DISGARRISONS	DISGUSTFUL	DISHERITING
DISENTRAYLE	DISFEATURES	DISGAVELLED	DISGUSTFULLY	DISHERITOR
DISENTRAYLED	DISFEATURING	DISGAVELLING	DISGUSTFULNESS	DISHERITORS
DISENTRAYLES	DISFELLOWSHIP	DISGAVELLINGS	DISGUSTING	DISHEVELED
DISENTRAYLING	DISFELLOWSHIPED	DISGESTING	DISGUSTINGLY	DISHEVELING
DISENTWINE	DISFELLOWSHIPS	DISGESTION	DISGUSTINGNESS	DISHEVELLED
DISENTWINED	DISFIGURATION	DISGESTIONS	DISHABILITATE	DISHEVELLING

DISHEVELMENT	DISILLUSIONIZES	DISINFECTS	DISINTEGRATORS	DISJECTION
DISHEVELMENTS	DISILLUSIONMENT	DISINFESTANT	DISINTEREST	DISJECTIONS
DISHOARDED	DISILLUSIONS	DISINFESTANTS	DISINTERESTED	DISJOINABLE
DISHOARDING	DISILLUSIVE	DISINFESTATION	DISINTERESTEDLY	DISJOINING
DISHONESTIES	DISIMAGINE	DISINFESTATIONS	DISINTERESTING	DISJOINTED
DISHONESTLY	DISIMAGINED	DISINFESTED	DISINTERESTS	DISJOINTEDLY
DISHONESTY	DISIMAGINES	DISINFESTING	DISINTERMENT	DISJOINTEDNESS
DISHONORABLE	DISIMAGINING	DISINFESTS	DISINTERMENTS	DISJOINTING
DISHONORABLY	DISIMMURED	DISINFLATION	DISINTERRED	DISJUNCTION
DISHONORARY	DISIMMURES	DISINFLATIONARY	DISINTERRING	DISJUNCTIONS
DISHONORED	DISIMMURING	DISINFLATIONS	DISINTHRAL	DISJUNCTIVE
DISHONORER	DISIMPASSIONED	DISINFORMATION	DISINTHRALLED	DISJUNCTIVELY
DISHONORERS	DISIMPRISON	DISINFORMATIONS	DISINTHRALLING	DISJUNCTIVES
DISHONORING	DISIMPRISONED	DISINFORMED	DISINTHRALLINGS	DISJUNCTOR
DISHONOURABLE	DISIMPRISONING	DISINFORMING	DISINTHRALS	DISJUNCTORS
DISHONOURABLY	DISIMPRISONMENT	DISINFORMS	DISINTOXICATE	DISJUNCTURE
DISHONOURED	DISIMPRISONS	DISINGENUITIES	DISINTOXICATED	DISJUNCTURES
DISHONOURER	DISIMPROVE	DISINGENUITY	DISINTOXICATES	DISLEAFING
DISHONOURERS	DISIMPROVED	DISINGENUOUS	DISINTOXICATING	DISLEAVING
DISHONOURING	DISIMPROVES	DISINGENUOUSLY	DISINTOXICATION	DISLIKABLE
DISHONOURS	DISIMPROVING	DISINHERISON	DISINTRICATE	DISLIKEABLE
DISHORNING	DISINCARCERATE	DISINHERISONS	DISINTRICATED	DISLIKEFUL
DISHORSING	DISINCARCERATED	DISINHERIT	DISINTRICATES	DISLIKENED
DISHOUSING	DISINCARCERATES	DISINHERITANCE	DISINTRICATING	DISLIKENESS
DISHTOWELS	DISINCENTIVE	DISINHERITANCES	DISINURING	DISLIKENESSES
DISHUMOURED	DISINCENTIVES	DISINHERITED	DISINVENTED	DISLIKENING
DISHUMOURING	DISINCLINATION	DISINHERITING	DISINVENTING	DISLIMBING
DISHUMOURS	DISINCLINATIONS	DISINHERITS	DISINVENTS	DISLIMNING
DISHWASHER	DISINCLINE	DISINHIBIT	DISINVESTED	DISLINKING
DISHWASHERS	DISINCLINED	DISINHIBITED	DISINVESTING	DISLOADING
DISHWATERS	DISINCLINES	DISINHIBITING	DISINVESTITURE	DISLOCATED
DISILLUDED	DISINCLINING	DISINHIBITION	DISINVESTITURES	DISLOCATEDLY
DISILLUDES	DISINCLOSE	DISINHIBITIONS	DISINVESTMENT	DISLOCATES
DISILLUDING	DISINCLOSED	DISINHIBITORY	DISINVESTMENTS	DISLOCATING
DISILLUMINATE	DISINCLOSES	DISINHIBITS	DISINVESTS	DISLOCATION
DISILLUMINATED	DISINCLOSING	DISINHUMED	DISINVIGORATE	DISLOCATIONS
DISILLUMINATES	DISINCORPORATE	DISINHUMES	DISINVIGORATED	DISLODGEMENT
DISILLUMINATING	DISINCORPORATED	DISINHUMING	DISINVIGORATES	DISLODGEMENTS
DISILLUSION	DISINCORPORATES	DISINTEGRABLE	DISINVIGORATING	DISLODGING
DISILLUSIONARY	DISINFECTANT	DISINTEGRATE	DISINVITED	DISLODGMENT
DISILLUSIONED	DISINFECTANTS	DISINTEGRATED	DISINVITES	DISLODGMENTS
DISILLUSIONING	DISINFECTED	DISINTEGRATES	DISINVITING	DISLOIGNED
DISILLUSIONISE	DISINFECTING	DISINTEGRATING	DISINVOLVE	DISLOIGNING
DISILLUSIONISED	DISINFECTION	DISINTEGRATION	DISINVOLVED	DISLOYALLY
DISILLUSIONISES	DISINFECTIONS	DISINTEGRATIONS	DISINVOLVES	DISLOYALTIES
DISILLUSIONIZE	DISINFECTOR	DISINTEGRATIVE	DISINVOLVING	DISLOYALTY
DISILLUSIONIZED	DISINFECTORS	DISINTEGRATOR	DISJECTING	DISLUSTRED

DISLUSTRES
DISLUSTRING
DISMALITIES
DISMALLEST
DISMALNESS
DISMALNESSES
DISMANNING
DISMANTLED
DISMANTLEMENT
DISMANTLEMENTS
DISMANTLER
DISMANTLERS
DISMANTLES
DISMANTLING
DISMANTLINGS
DISMASKING
DISMASTING
DISMASTMENT
DISMASTMENTS
DISMAYEDNESS
DISMAYEDNESSES
DISMAYFULLY
DISMAYINGLY
DISMAYLING
DISMEMBERED
DISMEMBERER
DISMEMBERERS
DISMEMBERING
DISMEMBERMENT
DISMEMBERMENTS
DISMEMBERS
DISMISSALS
DISMISSIBLE
DISMISSING
DISMISSION
DISMISSIONS
DISMISSIVE
DISMISSIVELY
DISMISSORY
DISMOUNTABLE
DISMOUNTED
DISMOUNTING
DISMUTATION
DISMUTATIONS
DISNATURALISE
DISNATURALISED
DISNATURALISES

DISNATURALISING
DISNATURALIZE
DISNATURALIZED
DISNATURALIZES
DISNATURALIZING
DISNATURED
DISNATURES
DISNATURING
DISNESTING
DISOBEDIENCE
DISOBEDIENCES
DISOBEDIENT
DISOBEDIENTLY
DISOBEYERS
DISOBEYING
DISOBLIGATION
DISOBLIGATIONS
DISOBLIGATORY
DISOBLIGED
DISOBLIGEMENT
DISOBLIGEMENTS
DISOBLIGES
DISOBLIGING
DISOBLIGINGLY
DISOBLIGINGNESS
DISOPERATION
DISOPERATIONS
DISORDERED
DISORDEREDLY
DISORDEREDNESS
DISORDERING
DISORDERLIES
DISORDERLINESS
DISORDERLY
DISORDINATE
DISORDINATELY
DISORGANIC
DISORGANISATION
DISORGANISE
DISORGANISED
DISORGANISER
DISORGANISERS
DISORGANISES
DISORGANISING
DISORGANIZATION
DISORGANIZE
DISORGANIZED

DISORGANIZER
DISORGANIZERS
DISORGANIZES
DISORGANIZING
DISORIENTATE
DISORIENTATED
DISORIENTATES
DISORIENTATING
DISORIENTATION
DISORIENTATIONS
DISORIENTED
DISORIENTING
DISORIENTS
DISOWNMENT
DISOWNMENTS
DISPARAGED
DISPARAGEMENT
DISPARAGEMENTS
DISPARAGER
DISPARAGERS
DISPARAGES
DISPARAGING
DISPARAGINGLY
DISPARATELY
DISPARATENESS
DISPARATENESSES
DISPARATES
DISPARITIES
DISPARKING
DISPARTING
DISPASSION
DISPASSIONATE
DISPASSIONATELY
DISPASSIONS
DISPATCHED
DISPATCHER
DISPATCHERS
DISPATCHES
DISPATCHFUL
DISPATCHING
DISPATHIES
DISPAUPERED
DISPAUPERING
DISPAUPERISE
DISPAUPERISED
DISPAUPERISES
DISPAUPERISING

DISPAUPERIZE
DISPAUPERIZED
DISPAUPERIZES
DISPAUPERIZING
DISPAUPERS
DISPELLERS
DISPELLING
DISPENCING
DISPENDING
DISPENSABILITY
DISPENSABLE
DISPENSABLENESS
DISPENSABLY
DISPENSARIES
DISPENSARY
DISPENSATION
DISPENSATIONAL
DISPENSATIONS
DISPENSATIVE
DISPENSATIVELY
DISPENSATOR
DISPENSATORIES
DISPENSATORILY
DISPENSATORS
DISPENSATORY
DISPENSERS
DISPENSING
DISPEOPLED
DISPEOPLES
DISPEOPLING
DISPERMOUS
DISPERSALS
DISPERSANT
DISPERSANTS
DISPERSEDLY
DISPERSEDNESS
DISPERSEDNESSES
DISPERSERS
DISPERSIBLE
DISPERSING
DISPERSION
DISPERSIONS
DISPERSIVE
DISPERSIVELY
DISPERSIVENESS
DISPERSOID
DISPERSOIDS

DISPIRITED
DISPIRITEDLY
DISPIRITEDNESS
DISPIRITING
DISPIRITINGLY
DISPIRITMENT
DISPIRITMENTS
DISPITEOUS
DISPITEOUSLY
DISPITEOUSNESS
DISPLACEABLE
DISPLACEMENT
DISPLACEMENTS
DISPLACERS
DISPLACING
DISPLANTATION
DISPLANTATIONS
DISPLANTED
DISPLANTING
DISPLAYABLE
DISPLAYERS
DISPLAYING
DISPLEASANCE
DISPLEASANCES
DISPLEASANT
DISPLEASANTED
DISPLEASANTING
DISPLEASANTS
DISPLEASED
DISPLEASEDLY
DISPLEASEDNESS
DISPLEASES
DISPLEASING
DISPLEASINGLY
DISPLEASINGNESS
DISPLEASURE
DISPLEASURED
DISPLEASURES
DISPLEASURING
DISPLENISH
DISPLENISHED
DISPLENISHES
DISPLENISHING
DISPLENISHMENT
DISPLENISHMENTS
DISPLODING
DISPLOSION

D

DISPLOSIONS	DISPRISONS	DISPUTABLENESS	DISREGARDERS	DISSAVINGS
DISPLUMING	DISPRIVACIED	DISPUTABLY	DISREGARDFUL	DISSEATING
DISPONDAIC	DISPRIVILEGE	DISPUTANTS	DISREGARDFULLY	DISSECTIBLE
DISPONDEES	DISPRIVILEGED	DISPUTATION	DISREGARDING	DISSECTING
DISPONGING	DISPRIVILEGES	DISPUTATIONS	DISREGARDS	DISSECTINGS
DISPORTING	DISPRIVILEGING	DISPUTATIOUS	DISRELATED	DISSECTION
DISPORTMENT	DISPRIZING	DISPUTATIOUSLY	DISRELATION	DISSECTIONS
DISPORTMENTS	DISPROFESS	DISPUTATIVE	DISRELATIONS	DISSECTIVE
DISPOSABILITIES	DISPROFESSED	DISPUTATIVELY	DISRELISHED	DISSECTORS
DISPOSABILITY	DISPROFESSES	DISPUTATIVENESS	DISRELISHES	DISSEISEES
DISPOSABLE	DISPROFESSING	DISQUALIFIABLE	DISRELISHING	DISSEISING
DISPOSABLENESS	DISPROFITED	DISQUALIFIED	DISREMEMBER	DISSEISINS
DISPOSABLES	DISPROFITING	DISQUALIFIER	DISREMEMBERED	DISSEISORS
DISPOSEDLY	DISPROFITS	DISQUALIFIERS	DISREMEMBERING	DISSEIZEES
DISPOSINGLY	DISPROOVED	DISQUALIFIES	DISREMEMBERS	DISSEIZING
DISPOSINGS	DISPROOVES	DISQUALIFY	DISREPAIRS	DISSEIZINS
DISPOSITION	DISPROOVING	DISQUALIFYING	DISREPUTABILITY	DISSEIZORS
DISPOSITIONAL	DISPROPERTIED	DISQUANTITIED	DISREPUTABLE	DISSELBOOM
DISPOSITIONED	DISPROPERTIES	DISQUANTITIES	DISREPUTABLY	DISSELBOOMS
DISPOSITIONS	DISPROPERTY	DISQUANTITY	DISREPUTATION	DISSEMBLANCE
DISPOSITIVE	DISPROPERTYING	DISQUANTITYING	DISREPUTATIONS	DISSEMBLANCES
DISPOSITIVELY	DISPROPORTION	DISQUIETED	DISREPUTES	DISSEMBLED
DISPOSITOR	DISPROPORTIONAL	DISQUIETEDLY	DISRESPECT	DISSEMBLER
DISPOSITORS	DISPROPORTIONED	DISQUIETEDNESS	DISRESPECTABLE	DISSEMBLERS
DISPOSSESS	DISPROPORTIONS	DISQUIETEN	DISRESPECTED	DISSEMBLES
DISPOSSESSED	DISPROPRIATE	DISQUIETENED	DISRESPECTFUL	DISSEMBLIES
DISPOSSESSES	DISPROPRIATED	DISQUIETENING	DISRESPECTFULLY	DISSEMBLING
DISPOSSESSING	DISPROPRIATES	DISQUIETENS	DISRESPECTING	DISSEMBLINGLY
DISPOSSESSION	DISPROPRIATING	DISQUIETFUL	DISRESPECTS	DISSEMBLINGS
DISPOSSESSIONS	DISPROVABLE	DISQUIETING	DISROBEMENT	DISSEMINATE
DISPOSSESSOR	DISPROVALS	DISQUIETINGLY	DISROBEMENTS	DISSEMINATED
DISPOSSESSORS	DISPROVERS	DISQUIETIVE	DISROOTING	DISSEMINATES
DISPOSSESSORY	DISPROVIDE	DISQUIETLY	DISRUPTERS	DISSEMINATING
DISPOSTING	DISPROVIDED	DISQUIETNESS	DISRUPTING	DISSEMINATION
DISPOSURES	DISPROVIDES	DISQUIETNESSES	DISRUPTION	DISSEMINATIONS
DISPRAISED	DISPROVIDING	DISQUIETOUS	DISRUPTIONS	DISSEMINATIVE
DISPRAISER	DISPROVING	DISQUIETUDE	DISRUPTIVE	DISSEMINATOR
DISPRAISERS	DISPUNGING	DISQUIETUDES	DISRUPTIVELY	DISSEMINATORS
DISPRAISES	DISPURSING	DISQUISITION	DISRUPTIVENESS	DISSEMINULE
DISPRAISING	DISPURVEYANCE	DISQUISITIONAL	DISRUPTORS	DISSEMINULES
DISPRAISINGLY	DISPURVEYANCES	DISQUISITIONARY	DISSATISFACTION	DISSENSION
DISPREADING	DISPURVEYED	DISQUISITIONS	DISSATISFACTORY	DISSENSIONS
DISPREDDEN	DISPURVEYING	DISQUISITIVE	DISSATISFIED	DISSENSUSES
DISPREDDING	DISPURVEYS	DISQUISITORY	DISSATISFIEDLY	DISSENTERISH
DISPRINCED	DISPUTABILITIES	DISRANKING	DISSATISFIES	DISSENTERISM
DISPRISONED	DISPUTABILITY	DISREGARDED	DISSATISFY	DISSENTERISMS
DISPRISONING	DISPUTABLE	DISREGARDER	DISSATISFYING	DISSENTERS

DISSENTIENCE	DISSIDENCES	DISSOCIABLY	DISSUADERS	DISTENSILE
DISSENTIENCES	DISSIDENTLY	DISSOCIALISE	DISSUADING	DISTENSION
DISSENTIENCIES	DISSIDENTS	DISSOCIALISED	DISSUASION	DISTENSIONS
DISSENTIENCY	DISSILIENCE	DISSOCIALISES	DISSUASIONS	DISTENSIVE
DISSENTIENT	DISSILIENCES	DISSOCIALISING	DISSUASIVE	DISTENTION
DISSENTIENTLY	DISSILIENT	DISSOCIALITIES	DISSUASIVELY	DISTENTIONS
DISSENTIENTS	DISSIMILAR	DISSOCIALITY	DISSUASIVENESS	DISTHRONED
DISSENTING	DISSIMILARITIES	DISSOCIALIZE	DISSUASIVES	DISTHRONES
DISSENTINGLY	DISSIMILARITY	DISSOCIALIZED	DISSUASORIES	DISTHRONING
DISSENTION	DISSIMILARLY	DISSOCIALIZES	DISSUASORY	DISTHRONISE
DISSENTIONS	DISSIMILARS	DISSOCIALIZING	DISSUNDERED	DISTHRONISED
DISSENTIOUS	DISSIMILATE	DISSOCIATE	DISSUNDERING	DISTHRONISES
DISSEPIMENT	DISSIMILATED	DISSOCIATED	DISSUNDERS	DISTHRONISING
DISSEPIMENTAL	DISSIMILATES	DISSOCIATES	DISSYLLABIC	DISTHRONIZE
DISSEPIMENTS	DISSIMILATING	DISSOCIATING	DISSYLLABIFIED	DISTHRONIZED
DISSERTATE	DISSIMILATION	DISSOCIATION	DISSYLLABIFIES	DISTHRONIZES
DISSERTATED	DISSIMILATIONS	DISSOCIATIONS	DISSYLLABIFY	DISTHRONIZING
DISSERTATES	DISSIMILATIVE	DISSOCIATIVE	DISSYLLABIFYING	DISTICHOUS
DISSERTATING	DISSIMILATORY	DISSOLUBILITIES	DISSYLLABISM	DISTICHOUSLY
DISSERTATION	DISSIMILES	DISSOLUBILITY	DISSYLLABISMS	DISTILLABLE
DISSERTATIONAL	DISSIMILITUDE	DISSOLUBLE	DISSYLLABLE	DISTILLAND
DISSERTATIONIST	DISSIMILITUDES	DISSOLUBLENESS	DISSYLLABLES	DISTILLANDS
DISSERTATIONS	DISSIMULATE	DISSOLUTELY	DISSYMMETRIC	DISTILLATE
DISSERTATIVE	DISSIMULATED	DISSOLUTENESS	DISSYMMETRICAL	DISTILLATES
DISSERTATOR	DISSIMULATES	DISSOLUTENESSES	DISSYMMETRIES	DISTILLATION
DISSERTATORS	DISSIMULATING	DISSOLUTES	DISSYMMETRY	DISTILLATIONS
DISSERTING	DISSIMULATION	DISSOLUTION	DISTAINING	DISTILLATORY
DISSERVICE	DISSIMULATIONS	DISSOLUTIONISM	DISTANCELESS	DISTILLERIES
DISSERVICEABLE	DISSIMULATIVE	DISSOLUTIONISMS	DISTANCING	DISTILLERS
DISSERVICES	DISSIMULATOR	DISSOLUTIONIST	DISTANTNESS	DISTILLERY
DISSERVING	DISSIMULATORS	DISSOLUTIONISTS	DISTANTNESSES	DISTILLING
DISSEVERANCE	DISSIPABLE	DISSOLUTIONS	DISTASTEFUL	DISTILLINGS
DISSEVERANCES	DISSIPATED	DISSOLUTIVE	DISTASTEFULLY	DISTILMENT
DISSEVERATION	DISSIPATEDLY	DISSOLVABILITY	DISTASTEFULNESS	DISTILMENTS
DISSEVERATIONS	DISSIPATEDNESS	DISSOLVABLE	DISTASTING	DISTINCTER
DISSEVERED	DISSIPATER	DISSOLVABLENESS	DISTELFINK	DISTINCTEST
DISSEVERING	DISSIPATERS	DISSOLVENT	DISTELFINKS	DISTINCTION
DISSEVERMENT	DISSIPATES	DISSOLVENTS	DISTEMPERATE	DISTINCTIONS
DISSEVERMENTS	DISSIPATING	DISSOLVERS	DISTEMPERATURE	DISTINCTIVE
DISSHEATHE	DISSIPATION	DISSOLVING	DISTEMPERATURES	DISTINCTIVELY
DISSHEATHED	DISSIPATIONS	DISSOLVINGS	DISTEMPERED	DISTINCTIVENESS
DISSHEATHES	DISSIPATIVE	DISSONANCE	DISTEMPERING	DISTINCTIVES
DISSHEATHING	DISSIPATOR	DISSONANCES	DISTEMPERS	DISTINCTLY
DISSHIVERED	DISSIPATORS	DISSONANCIES	DISTENDERS	DISTINCTNESS
DISSHIVERING	DISSOCIABILITY	DISSONANCY	DISTENDING	DISTINCTNESSES
DISSHIVERS	DISSOCIABLE	DISSONANTLY	DISTENSIBILITY	DISTINCTURE
DISSIDENCE	DISSOCIABLENESS	DISSUADABLE	DISTENSIBLE	DISTINCTURES

D

DISTINGUEE	DISTRAUGHT	DISTRUSTFULLY	DISYLLABIFYING	DIURNALIST
DISTINGUISH	DISTRAUGHTLY	DISTRUSTFULNESS	DISYLLABISM	DIURNALISTS
DISTINGUISHABLE	DISTRESSED	DISTRUSTING	DISYLLABISMS	DIUTURNITIES
DISTINGUISHABLY	DISTRESSER	DISTRUSTLESS	DISYLLABLE	DIUTURNITY
DISTINGUISHED	DISTRESSERS	DISTURBANCE	DISYLLABLES	DIVAGATING
DISTINGUISHER	DISTRESSES	DISTURBANCES	DITCHDIGGER	DIVAGATION
DISTINGUISHERS	DISTRESSFUL	DISTURBANT	DITCHDIGGERS	DIVAGATIONS
DISTINGUISHES	DISTRESSFULLY	DISTURBANTS	DITCHWATER	DIVALENCES
DISTINGUISHING	DISTRESSFULNESS	DISTURBATIVE	DITCHWATERS	DIVALENCIES
DISTINGUISHMENT	DISTRESSING	DISTURBERS	DITHEISTIC	DIVARICATE
DISTORTEDLY	DISTRESSINGLY	DISTURBING	DITHEISTICAL	DIVARICATED
DISTORTEDNESS	DISTRESSINGS	DISTURBINGLY	DITHELETES	DIVARICATELY
DISTORTEDNESSES	DISTRIBUEND	DISUBSTITUTED	DITHELETIC	DIVARICATES
DISTORTERS	DISTRIBUENDS	DISULFATES	DITHELETICAL	DIVARICATING
DISTORTING	DISTRIBUTABLE	DISULFIDES	DITHELETISM	DIVARICATINGLY
DISTORTION	DISTRIBUTARIES	DISULFIRAM	DITHELETISMS	DIVARICATION
DISTORTIONAL	DISTRIBUTARY	DISULFIRAMS	DITHELISMS	DIVARICATIONS
DISTORTIONS	DISTRIBUTE	DISULFOTON	DITHELITISM	DIVARICATOR
DISTORTIVE	DISTRIBUTED	DISULFOTONS	DITHELITISMS	DIVARICATORS
DISTRACTABLE	DISTRIBUTEE	DISULPHATE	DITHERIEST	DIVEBOMBED
DISTRACTED	DISTRIBUTEES	DISULPHATES	DITHIOCARBAMATE	DIVEBOMBING
DISTRACTEDLY	DISTRIBUTER	DISULPHIDE	DITHIONATE	DIVELLICATE
DISTRACTEDNESS	DISTRIBUTERS	DISULPHIDES	DITHIONATES	DIVELLICATED
DISTRACTER	DISTRIBUTES	DISULPHURET	DITHIONITE	DIVELLICATES
DISTRACTERS	DISTRIBUTING	DISULPHURETS	DITHIONITES	DIVELLICATING
DISTRACTIBILITY	DISTRIBUTION	DISULPHURIC	DITHIONOUS	DIVERGEMENT
DISTRACTIBLE	DISTRIBUTIONAL	DISUNIONIST	DITHYRAMBIC	DIVERGEMENTS
DISTRACTING	DISTRIBUTIONS	DISUNIONISTS	DITHYRAMBICALLY	DIVERGENCE
DISTRACTINGLY	DISTRIBUTIVE	DISUNITERS	DITHYRAMBIST	DIVERGENCES
DISTRACTION	DISTRIBUTIVELY	DISUNITIES	DITHYRAMBISTS	DIVERGENCIES
DISTRACTIONS	DISTRIBUTIVES	DISUNITING	DITHYRAMBS	DIVERGENCY
DISTRACTIVE	DISTRIBUTIVITY	DISUTILITIES	DITRANSITIVE	DIVERGENTLY
DISTRACTIVELY	DISTRIBUTOR	DISUTILITY	DITRANSITIVES	DIVERGINGLY
DISTRACTOR	DISTRIBUTORS	DISVALUING	DITRIGLYPH	DIVERSENESS
DISTRACTORS	DISTRIBUTORSHIP	DISVOUCHED	DITRIGLYPHIC	DIVERSENESSES
DISTRAINABLE	DISTRICTED	DISVOUCHES	DITRIGLYPHS	DIVERSIFIABLE
DISTRAINED	DISTRICTING	DISVOUCHING	DITROCHEAN	DIVERSIFICATION
DISTRAINEE	DISTRINGAS	DISWORSHIP	DITROCHEES	DIVERSIFIED
DISTRAINEES	DISTRINGASES	DISWORSHIPED	DITSINESSES	DIVERSIFIER
DISTRAINER	DISTROUBLE	DISWORSHIPING	DITTANDERS	DIVERSIFIERS
DISTRAINERS	DISTROUBLED	DISWORSHIPPED	DITTOGRAPHIC	DIVERSIFIES
DISTRAINING	DISTROUBLES	DISWORSHIPPING	DITTOGRAPHIES	DIVERSIFORM
DISTRAINMENT	DISTROUBLING	DISWORSHIPS	DITTOGRAPHY	DIVERSIFYING
DISTRAINMENTS	DISTRUSTED	DISYLLABIC	DITTOLOGIES	DIVERSIONAL
DISTRAINOR	DISTRUSTER	DISYLLABIFIED	DITZINESSES	DIVERSIONARY
DISTRAINORS	DISTRUSTERS	DISYLLABIFIES	DIURETICALLY	DIVERSIONIST
DISTRAINTS	DISTRUSTFUL	DISYLLABIFY	DIURETICALNESS	DIVERSIONISTS

DIVERSIONS	DIVINIZATIONS	DOCIMASIES	DOCUMENTARIANS	DODGINESSES
DIVERSITIES	DIVINIZING	DOCIMASTIC	DOCUMENTARIES	DOGARESSAS
DIVERTIBILITIES	DIVISIBILITIES	DOCIMOLOGIES	DOCUMENTARILY	DOGBERRIES
DIVERTIBILITY	DIVISIBILITY	DOCIMOLOGY	DOCUMENTARISE	DOGBERRYISM
DIVERTIBLE	DIVISIBLENESS	DOCKISATION	DOCUMENTARISED	DOGBERRYISMS
DIVERTICULA	DIVISIBLENESSES	DOCKISATIONS	DOCUMENTARISES	DOGCATCHER
DIVERTICULAR	DIVISIONAL	DOCKIZATION	DOCUMENTARISING	DOGCATCHERS
DIVERTICULATE	DIVISIONALLY	DOCKIZATIONS	DOCUMENTARIST	DOGFIGHTING
DIVERTICULATED	DIVISIONARY	DOCKMASTER	DOCUMENTARISTS	DOGFIGHTINGS
DIVERTICULITIS	DIVISIONISM	DOCKMASTERS	DOCUMENTARIZE	DOGGEDNESS
DIVERTICULOSES	DIVISIONISMS	DOCKWALLOPER	DOCUMENTARIZED	DOGGEDNESSES
DIVERTICULOSIS	DIVISIONIST	DOCKWALLOPERS	DOCUMENTARIZES	DOGGINESSES
DIVERTICULUM	DIVISIONISTS	DOCKWORKER	DOCUMENTARIZING	DOGGISHNESS
DIVERTIMENTI	DIVISIVELY	DOCKWORKERS	DOCUMENTARY	DOGGISHNESSES
DIVERTIMENTO	DIVISIVENESS	DOCQUETING	DOCUMENTATION	DOGGONEDER
DIVERTIMENTOS	DIVISIVENESSES	DOCTORANDS	DOCUMENTATIONAL	DOGGONEDEST
DIVERTINGLY	DIVORCEABLE	DOCTORATED	DOCUMENTATIONS	DOGLEGGING
DIVERTISEMENT	DIVORCEMENT	DOCTORATES	DOCUMENTED	DOGMATICAL
DIVERTISEMENTS	DIVORCEMENTS	DOCTORATING	DOCUMENTER	DOGMATICALLY
DIVERTISSEMENT	DIVULGATED	DOCTORESSES	DOCUMENTERS	DOGMATICALNESS
DIVERTISSEMENTS	DIVULGATER	DOCTORINGS	DOCUMENTING	DOGMATISATION
DIVESTIBLE	DIVULGATERS	DOCTORLESS	DODDERIEST	DOGMATISATIONS
DIVESTITURE	DIVULGATES	DOCTORSHIP	DODDIPOLLS	DOGMATISED
DIVESTITURES	DIVULGATING	DOCTORSHIPS	DODDYPOLLS	DOGMATISER
DIVESTMENT	DIVULGATION	DOCTRESSES	DODECAGONAL	DOGMATISERS
DIVESTMENTS	DIVULGATIONS	DOCTRINAIRE	DODECAGONS	DOGMATISES
DIVESTURES	DIVULGATOR	DOCTRINAIRES	DODECAGYNIAN	DOGMATISING
DIVIDEDNESS	DIVULGATORS	DOCTRINAIRISM	DODECAGYNOUS	DOGMATISMS
DIVIDEDNESSES	DIVULGEMENT	DOCTRINAIRISMS	DODECAHEDRA	DOGMATISTS
DIVIDENDLESS	DIVULGEMENTS	DOCTRINALITIES	DODECAHEDRAL	DOGMATIZATION
DIVINATION	DIVULGENCE	DOCTRINALITY	DODECAHEDRON	DOGMATIZATIONS
DIVINATIONS	DIVULGENCES	DOCTRINALLY	DODECAHEDRONS	DOGMATIZED
DIVINATORIAL	DIVULSIONS	DOCTRINARIAN	DODECANDROUS	DOGMATIZER
DIVINATORS	DIZENMENTS	DOCTRINARIANISM	DODECANOIC	DOGMATIZERS
DIVINATORY	DIZZINESSES	DOCTRINARIANS	DODECAPHONIC	DOGMATIZES
DIVINENESS	DIZZYINGLY	DOCTRINARISM	DODECAPHONIES	DOGMATIZING
DIVINENESSES	DJELLABAHS	DOCTRINARISMS	DODECAPHONISM	DOGMATOLOGIES
DIVINERESS	DOBSONFLIES	DOCTRINISM	DODECAPHONISMS	DOGMATOLOGY
DIVINERESSES	DOCENTSHIP	DOCTRINISMS	DODECAPHONIST	DOGNAPINGS
DIVINIFIED	DOCENTSHIPS	DOCTRINIST	DODECAPHONISTS	DOGNAPPERS
DIVINIFIES	DOCHMIACAL	DOCTRINISTS	DODECAPHONY	DOGNAPPING
DIVINIFYING	DOCHMIUSES	DOCUDRAMAS	DODECASTYLE	DOGNAPPINGS
DIVINISATION	DOCIBILITIES	DOCUMENTABLE	DODECASTYLES	DOGROBBERS
DIVINISATIONS	DOCIBILITY	DOCUMENTAL	DODECASYLLABIC	DOGSBODIED
DIVINISING	DOCIBLENESS	DOCUMENTALIST	DODECASYLLABLE	DOGSBODIES
DIVINITIES	DOCIBLENESSES	DOCUMENTALISTS	DODECASYLLABLES	DOGSBODYING
DIVINIZATION	DOCILITIES	DOCUMENTARIAN	DODGEBALLS	DOGSLEDDED

DOGSLEDDER
DOGSLEDDERS
DOGSLEDDING
DOGTROTTED
DOGTROTTING
DOGWATCHES
DOLABRIFORM
DOLCELATTE
DOLCELATTES
DOLCEMENTE
DOLEFULLER
DOLEFULLEST
DOLEFULNESS
DOLEFULNESSES
DOLESOMELY
DOLICHOCEPHAL
DOLICHOCEPHALIC
DOLICHOCEPHALS
DOLICHOCEPHALY
DOLICHOSAURUS
DOLICHOSAURUSES
DOLICHOSES
DOLICHURUS
DOLICHURUSES
DOLLARBIRD
DOLLARBIRDS
DOLLARFISH
DOLLARFISHES
DOLLARISATION
DOLLARISATIONS
DOLLARISED
DOLLARISES
DOLLARISING
DOLLARIZATION
DOLLARIZATIONS
DOLLARIZED
DOLLARIZES
DOLLARIZING
DOLLARLESS
DOLLAROCRACIES
DOLLAROCRACY
DOLLARSHIP
DOLLARSHIPS
DOLLHOUSES
DOLLINESSES
DOLLISHNESS
DOLLISHNESSES

DOLLYBIRDS
DOLOMITISATION
DOLOMITISATIONS
DOLOMITISE
DOLOMITISED
DOLOMITISES
DOLOMITISING
DOLOMITIZATION
DOLOMITIZATIONS
DOLOMITIZE
DOLOMITIZED
DOLOMITIZES
DOLOMITIZING
DOLORIFEROUS
DOLORIMETRIES
DOLORIMETRY
DOLOROUSLY
DOLOROUSNESS
DOLOROUSNESSES
DOLOSTONES
DOLPHINARIA
DOLPHINARIUM
DOLPHINARIUMS
DOLPHINETS
DOLPHINFISH
DOLPHINFISHES
DOLTISHNESS
DOLTISHNESSES
DOMESTICABLE
DOMESTICAL
DOMESTICALLY
DOMESTICATE
DOMESTICATED
DOMESTICATES
DOMESTICATING
DOMESTICATION
DOMESTICATIONS
DOMESTICATIVE
DOMESTICATOR
DOMESTICATORS
DOMESTICISE
DOMESTICISED
DOMESTICISES
DOMESTICISING
DOMESTICITIES
DOMESTICITY
DOMESTICIZE

DOMESTICIZED
DOMESTICIZES
DOMESTICIZING
DOMESTIQUE
DOMESTIQUES
DOMICILIARY
DOMICILIATE
DOMICILIATED
DOMICILIATES
DOMICILIATING
DOMICILIATION
DOMICILIATIONS
DOMICILING
DOMINANCES
DOMINANCIES
DOMINANTLY
DOMINATING
DOMINATINGLY
DOMINATION
DOMINATIONS
DOMINATIVE
DOMINATORS
DOMINATRICES
DOMINATRIX
DOMINATRIXES
DOMINEERED
DOMINEERING
DOMINEERINGLY
DOMINEERINGNESS
DOMINICKER
DOMINICKERS
DOMINIQUES
DONATARIES
DONATISTIC
DONATISTICAL
DONATORIES
DONENESSES
DONEPEZILS
DONKEYWORK
DONKEYWORKS
DONNICKERS
DONNISHNESS
DONNISHNESSES
DONNYBROOK
DONNYBROOKS
DONORSHIPS
DOODLEBUGS

DOOHICKEYS
DOOHICKIES
DOOMSAYERS
DOOMSAYING
DOOMSAYINGS
DOOMSDAYER
DOOMSDAYERS
DOOMWATCHED
DOOMWATCHER
DOOMWATCHERS
DOOMWATCHES
DOOMWATCHING
DOOMWATCHINGS
DOORFRAMES
DOORKEEPER
DOORKEEPERS
DOORKNOCKED
DOORKNOCKER
DOORKNOCKERS
DOORKNOCKING
DOORKNOCKS
DOORNBOOMS
DOORPLATES
DOORSTEPPED
DOORSTEPPER
DOORSTEPPERS
DOORSTEPPING
DOORSTEPPINGS
DOORSTONES
DOPAMINERGIC
DOPESHEETS
DOPEYNESSES
DOPINESSES
DOPPELGANGER
DOPPELGANGERS
DOPPLERITE
DOPPLERITES
DORBEETLES
DORKINESSES
DORMANCIES
DORMITIONS
DORMITIVES
DORMITORIES
DORONICUMS
DORSIBRANCHIATE
DORSIFEROUS
DORSIFIXED

DORSIFLEXED
DORSIFLEXES
DORSIFLEXING
DORSIFLEXION
DORSIFLEXIONS
DORSIGRADE
DORSIVENTRAL
DORSIVENTRALITY
DORSIVENTRALLY
DORSOLATERAL
DORSOLUMBAR
DORSOVENTRAL
DORSOVENTRALITY
DORSOVENTRALLY
DORTINESSES
DOSEMETERS
DOSIMETERS
DOSIMETRIC
DOSIMETRICIAN
DOSIMETRICIANS
DOSIMETRIES
DOSIMETRIST
DOSIMETRISTS
DOSIOLOGIES
DOSOLOGIES
DOSSHOUSES
DOTCOMMERS
DOTTINESSES
DOUBLEHEADER
DOUBLEHEADERS
DOUBLENESS
DOUBLENESSES
DOUBLESPEAK
DOUBLESPEAKER
DOUBLESPEAKERS
DOUBLESPEAKS
DOUBLETHINK
DOUBLETHINKS
DOUBLETONS
DOUBLETREE
DOUBLETREES
DOUBTFULLY
DOUBTFULNESS
DOUBTFULNESSES
DOUBTINGLY
DOUBTLESSLY
DOUBTLESSNESS

D

DOUBTLESSNESSES	DOWNHILLER	DOWNTHROWS	DRAFTSWOMAN	DRAMATISING
DOUCENESSES	DOWNHILLERS	DOWNTOWNER	DRAFTSWOMEN	DRAMATISTS
DOUCEPERES	DOWNINESSES	DOWNTOWNERS	DRAGGINGLY	DRAMATIZABLE
DOUCHEBAGS	DOWNLIGHTER	DOWNTRENDED	DRAGGLETAILED	DRAMATIZATION
DOUGHBALLS	DOWNLIGHTERS	DOWNTRENDING	DRAGHOUNDS	DRAMATIZATIONS
DOUGHFACED	DOWNLIGHTS	DOWNTRENDS	DRAGONESSES	DRAMATIZED
DOUGHFACES	DOWNLINKED	DOWNTRODDEN	DRAGONFLIES	DRAMATIZER
DOUGHINESS	DOWNLINKING	DOWNTURNED	DRAGONHEAD	DRAMATIZERS
DOUGHINESSES	DOWNLOADABLE	DOWNWARDLY	DRAGONHEADS	DRAMATIZES
DOUGHNUTLIKE	DOWNLOADED	DOWNWARDNESS	DRAGONISED	DRAMATIZING
DOUGHNUTTED	DOWNLOADING	DOWNWARDNESSES	DRAGONISES	DRAMATURGE
DOUGHNUTTING	DOWNLOADINGS	DOWNWASHES	DRAGONISING	DRAMATURGES
DOUGHNUTTINGS	DOWNLOOKED	DOWNZONING	DRAGONISMS	DRAMATURGIC
DOUGHTIEST	DOWNPLAYED	DOXOGRAPHER	DRAGONIZED	DRAMATURGICAL
DOUGHTINESS	DOWNPLAYING	DOXOGRAPHERS	DRAGONIZES	DRAMATURGICALLY
DOUGHTINESSES	DOWNRATING	DOXOGRAPHIC	DRAGONIZING	DRAMATURGIES
DOULOCRACIES	DOWNREGULATION	DOXOGRAPHIES	DRAGONLIKE	DRAMATURGIST
DOULOCRACY	DOWNREGULATIONS	DOXOGRAPHY	DRAGONNADE	DRAMATURGISTS
DOUPPIONIS	DOWNRIGHTLY	DOXOLOGICAL	DRAGONNADED	DRAMATURGS
DOURNESSES	DOWNRIGHTNESS	DOXOLOGICALLY	DRAGONNADES	DRAMATURGY
DOUROUCOULI	DOWNRIGHTNESSES	DOXOLOGIES	DRAGONNADING	DRAPABILITIES
DOUROUCOULIS	DOWNRUSHES	DOXORUBICIN	DRAGONROOT	DRAPABILITY
DOVEISHNESS	DOWNSCALED	DOXORUBICINS	DRAGONROOTS	DRAPEABILITIES
DOVEISHNESSES	DOWNSCALES	DOXYCYCLINE	DRAGOONAGE	DRAPEABILITY
DOVETAILED	DOWNSCALING	DOXYCYCLINES	DRAGOONAGES	DRAPERYING
DOVETAILING	DOWNSHIFTED	DOZINESSES	DRAGOONING	DRASTICALLY
DOVETAILINGS	DOWNSHIFTER	DRABBINESS	DRAGSTRIPS	DRATCHELLS
DOVISHNESS	DOWNSHIFTERS	DRABBINESSES	DRAGSVILLE	DRAUGHTBOARD
DOVISHNESSES	DOWNSHIFTING	DRABBLINGS	DRAGSVILLES	DRAUGHTBOARDS
DOWDINESSES	DOWNSHIFTINGS	DRABNESSES	DRAINBOARD	DRAUGHTERS
DOWELLINGS	DOWNSHIFTS	DRACONIANISM	DRAINBOARDS	DRAUGHTIER
DOWFNESSES	DOWNSIZERS	DRACONIANISMS	DRAINLAYER	DRAUGHTIEST
DOWITCHERS	DOWNSIZING	DRACONICALLY	DRAINLAYERS	DRAUGHTILY
DOWNBURSTS	DOWNSIZINGS	DRACONISMS	DRAINPIPES	DRAUGHTINESS
DOWNCOMERS	DOWNSLIDES	DRACONITES	DRAKESTONE	DRAUGHTINESSES
DOWNCRYING	DOWNSLOPES	DRACONTIASES	DRAKESTONES	DRAUGHTING
DOWNDRAFTS	DOWNSPOUTS	DRACONTIASIS	DRAMATICAL	DRAUGHTMAN
DOWNDRAUGHT	DOWNSTAGES	DRACUNCULIASES	DRAMATICALLY	DRAUGHTMEN
DOWNDRAUGHTS	DOWNSTAIRS	DRACUNCULIASIS	DRAMATICISM	DRAUGHTPROOF
DOWNFALLEN	DOWNSTAIRSES	DRACUNCULUS	DRAMATICISMS	DRAUGHTPROOFED
DOWNFORCES	DOWNSTATER	DRACUNCULUSES	DRAMATISABLE	DRAUGHTPROOFING
DOWNGRADED	DOWNSTATERS	DRAFTINESS	DRAMATISATION	DRAUGHTPROOFS
DOWNGRADES	DOWNSTATES	DRAFTINESSES	DRAMATISATIONS	DRAUGHTSMAN
DOWNGRADING	DOWNSTREAM	DRAFTSMANSHIP	DRAMATISED	DRAUGHTSMANSHIP
DOWNHEARTED	DOWNSTROKE	DRAFTSMANSHIPS	DRAMATISER	DRAUGHTSMEN
DOWNHEARTEDLY	DOWNSTROKES	DRAFTSPERSON	DRAMATISERS	DRAUGHTSWOMAN
DOWNHEARTEDNESS	DOWNSWINGS	DRAFTSPERSONS	DRAMATISES	DRAUGHTSWOMEN

D

DRAWBRIDGE	DREARIMENT	DRIVELLING	DROUGHTIER	DUATHLETES
DRAWBRIDGES	DREARIMENTS	DRIVENNESS	DROUGHTIEST	DUBIOSITIES
DRAWERFULS	DREARINESS	DRIVENNESSES	DROUGHTINESS	DUBIOUSNESS
DRAWKNIVES	DREARINESSES	DRIVERLESS	DROUGHTINESSES	DUBIOUSNESSES
DRAWLINGLY	DREARISOME	DRIVESHAFT	DROUTHIEST	DUBITANCIES
DRAWLINGNESS	DRECKSILLS	DRIVESHAFTS	DROUTHINESS	DUBITATING
DRAWLINGNESSES	DREGGINESS	DRIVETHROUGH	DROUTHINESSES	DUBITATION
DRAWNWORKS	DREGGINESSES	DRIVETHROUGHS	DROWSIHEAD	DUBITATIONS
DRAWPLATES	DREIKANTER	DRIVETRAIN	DROWSIHEADS	DUBITATIVE
DRAWSHAVES	DREIKANTERS	DRIVETRAINS	DROWSIHEDS	DUBITATIVELY
DRAWSTRING	DRENCHINGS	DRIZZLIEST	DROWSINESS	DUCHESSING
DRAWSTRINGS	DREPANIUMS	DRIZZLINGLY	DROWSINESSES	DUCKBOARDS
DRAYHORSES	DRERIHEADS	DROICHIEST	DRUCKENNESS	DUCKSHOVED
DREADFULLY	DRESSGUARD	DROLLERIES	DRUCKENNESSES	DUCKSHOVER
DREADFULNESS	DRESSGUARDS	DROLLNESSES	DRUDGERIES	DUCKSHOVERS
DREADFULNESSES	DRESSINESS	DROMEDARES	DRUDGINGLY	DUCKSHOVES
DREADLESSLY	DRESSINESSES	DROMEDARIES	DRUGMAKERS	DUCKSHOVING
DREADLESSNESS	DRESSMAKER	DROMOPHOBIA	DRUGSTORES	DUCKWALKED
DREADLESSNESSES	DRESSMAKERS	DROMOPHOBIAS	DRUIDESSES	DUCKWALKING
DREADLOCKED	DRESSMAKES	DRONISHNESS	DRUMBEATER	DUCTILENESS
DREADLOCKS	DRESSMAKING	DRONISHNESSES	DRUMBEATERS	DUCTILENESSES
DREADNAUGHT	DRESSMAKINGS	DRONKVERDRIET	DRUMBEATING	DUCTILITIES
DREADNAUGHTS	DRIBBLIEST	DROOLWORTHY	DRUMBEATINGS	DUDENESSES
DREADNOUGHT	DRIBBLINGS	DROOPINESS	DRUMBLEDOR	DUENNASHIP
DREADNOUGHTS	DRICKSIEST	DROOPINESSES	DRUMBLEDORS	DUENNASHIPS
DREAMBOATS	DRIFTINGLY	DROOPINGLY	DRUMBLEDRANE	DUFFERDOMS
DREAMERIES	DRIFTWOODS	DROPCLOTHS	DRUMBLEDRANES	DUFFERISMS
DREAMFULLY	DRILLABILITIES	DROPFORGED	DRUMFISHES	DUIKERBOKS
DREAMFULNESS	DRILLABILITY	DROPFORGES	DRUMSTICKS	DUKKERIPEN
DREAMFULNESSES	DRILLHOLES	DROPFORGING	DRUNKALOGUE	DUKKERIPENS
DREAMHOLES	DRILLMASTER	DROPKICKER	DRUNKALOGUES	DULCAMARAS
DREAMINESS	DRILLMASTERS	DROPKICKERS	DRUNKATHON	DULCETNESS
DREAMINESSES	DRILLSHIPS	DROPLIGHTS	DRUNKATHONS	DULCETNESSES
DREAMINGLY	DRILLSTOCK	DROPPERFUL	DRUNKENNESS	DULCIFICATION
DREAMLANDS	DRILLSTOCKS	DROPPERFULS	DRUNKENNESSES	DULCIFICATIONS
DREAMLESSLY	DRINKABILITIES	DROPPERSFUL	DRUNKOMETER	DULCIFLUOUS
DREAMLESSNESS	DRINKABILITY	DROPSICALLY	DRUNKOMETERS	DULCIFYING
DREAMLESSNESSES	DRINKABLENESS	DROPSONDES	DRUPACEOUS	DULCILOQUIES
DREAMTIMES	DRINKABLENESSES	DROPSTONES	DRYASDUSTS	DULCILOQUY
DREAMWHILE	DRINKABLES	DROSERACEOUS	DRYBEATING	DULCIMORES
DREAMWHILES	DRIPSTONES	DROSOMETER	DRYOPITHECINE	DULCITUDES
DREAMWORLD	DRIVABILITIES	DROSOMETERS	DRYOPITHECINES	DULLNESSES
DREAMWORLDS	DRIVABILITY	DROSOPHILA	DRYSALTERIES	DULLSVILLE
DREARIHEAD	DRIVEABILITIES	DROSOPHILAE	DRYSALTERS	DULLSVILLES
DREARIHEADS	DRIVEABILITY	DROSOPHILAS	DRYSALTERY	DULOCRACIES
DREARIHOOD	DRIVELINES	DROSSINESS	DRYWALLING	DUMBFOUNDED
DREARIHOODS	DRIVELLERS	DROSSINESSES	DUALISTICALLY	DUMBFOUNDER

DUMBFOUNDERED	DUODECENNIAL	DUSKINESSES	DYNAMOMETERS	DYSGRAPHICS
DUMBFOUNDERING	DUODECILLION	DUSKISHNESS	DYNAMOMETRIC	DYSHARMONIC
DUMBFOUNDERS	DUODECILLIONS	DUSKISHNESSES	DYNAMOMETRICAL	DYSKINESIA
DUMBFOUNDING	DUODECIMAL	DUSKNESSES	DYNAMOMETRIES	DYSKINESIAS
DUMBFOUNDS	DUODECIMALLY	DUSTCLOTHS	DYNAMOMETRY	DYSKINETIC
DUMBLEDORE	DUODECIMALS	DUSTCOVERS	DYNAMOTORS	DYSLECTICS
DUMBLEDORES	DUODECIMOS	DUSTINESSES	DYNASTICAL	DYSLOGISTIC
DUMBNESSES	DUODENECTOMIES	DUSTSHEETS	DYNASTICALLY	DYSLOGISTICALLY
DUMBSIZING	DUODENECTOMY	DUSTSTORMS	DYNASTICISM	DYSMENORRHEA
DUMBSTRICKEN	DUODENITIS	DUTEOUSNESS	DYNASTICISMS	DYSMENORRHEAL
DUMBSTRUCK	DUODENITISES	DUTEOUSNESSES	DYNORPHINS	DYSMENORRHEAS
DUMBWAITER	DUOPOLISTIC	DUTIABILITIES	DYOPHYSITE	DYSMENORRHEIC
DUMBWAITERS	DUOPSONIES	DUTIABILITY	DYOPHYSITES	DYSMENORRHOEA
DUMFOUNDED	DUPABILITIES	DUTIFULNESS	DYOTHELETE	DYSMENORRHOEAL
DUMFOUNDER	DUPABILITY	DUTIFULNESSES	DYOTHELETES	DYSMENORRHOEAS
DUMFOUNDERED	DUPLEXITIES	DUUMVIRATE	DYOTHELETIC	DYSMENORRHOEIC
DUMFOUNDERING	DUPLICABILITIES	DUUMVIRATES	DYOTHELETICAL	DYSMORPHIC
DUMFOUNDERS	DUPLICABILITY	DWARFISHLY	DYOTHELETISM	DYSMORPHOPHOBIA
DUMFOUNDING	DUPLICABLE	DWARFISHNESS	DYOTHELETISMS	DYSMORPHOPHOBIC
DUMMELHEAD	DUPLICANDS	DWARFISHNESSES	DYOTHELISM	DYSPAREUNIA
DUMMELHEADS	DUPLICATED	DWARFNESSES	DYOTHELISMS	DYSPAREUNIAS
DUMMINESSES	DUPLICATELY	DWINDLEMENT	DYOTHELITE	DYSPATHETIC
DUMORTIERITE	DUPLICATES	DWINDLEMENTS	DYOTHELITES	DYSPATHIES
DUMORTIERITES	DUPLICATING	DYADICALLY	DYOTHELITIC	DYSPEPSIAS
DUMOSITIES	DUPLICATION	DYARCHICAL	DYOTHELITICAL	DYSPEPSIES
DUMPINESSES	DUPLICATIONS	DYEABILITIES	DYSAESTHESIA	DYSPEPTICAL
DUMPISHNESS	DUPLICATIVE	DYEABILITY	DYSAESTHESIAS	DYSPEPTICALLY
DUMPISHNESSES	DUPLICATOR	DYINGNESSES	DYSAESTHETIC	DYSPEPTICS
DUMPTRUCKS	DUPLICATORS	DYNAMETERS	DYSARTHRIA	DYSPHAGIAS
DUNDERFUNK	DUPLICATURE	DYNAMICALLY	DYSARTHRIAS	DYSPHAGIES
DUNDERFUNKS	DUPLICATURES	DYNAMICIST	DYSBINDINS	DYSPHASIAS
DUNDERHEAD	DUPLICIDENT	DYNAMICISTS	DYSCALCULIA	DYSPHASICS
DUNDERHEADED	DUPLICITIES	DYNAMISING	DYSCALCULIAS	DYSPHEMISM
DUNDERHEADISM	DUPLICITOUS	DYNAMISTIC	DYSCHROIAS	DYSPHEMISMS
DUNDERHEADISMS	DUPLICITOUSLY	DYNAMITARD	DYSCRASIAS	DYSPHEMISTIC
DUNDERHEADS	DURABILITIES	DYNAMITARDS	DYSCRASITE	DYSPHONIAS
DUNDERPATE	DURABILITY	DYNAMITERS	DYSCRASITES	DYSPHORIAS
DUNDERPATES	DURABLENESS	DYNAMITING	DYSENTERIC	DYSPLASIAS
DUNDREARIES	DURABLENESSES	DYNAMIZING	DYSENTERIES	DYSPLASTIC
DUNGEONERS	DURALUMINIUM	DYNAMOELECTRIC	DYSFUNCTION	DYSPRACTIC
DUNGEONING	DURALUMINIUMS	DYNAMOGENESES	DYSFUNCTIONAL	DYSPRAXIAS
DUNIEWASSAL	DURALUMINS	DYNAMOGENESIS	DYSFUNCTIONS	DYSPROSIUM
DUNIEWASSALS	DURATIONAL	DYNAMOGENIES	DYSGENESES	DYSPROSIUMS
DUNIWASSAL	DURCHKOMPONIERT	DYNAMOGENY	DYSGENESIS	DYSRHYTHMIA
DUNIWASSALS	DURCHKOMPONIRT	DYNAMOGRAPH	DYSGRAPHIA	DYSRHYTHMIAS
DUNNIEWASSAL	DURICRUSTS	DYNAMOGRAPHS	DYSGRAPHIAS	DYSRHYTHMIC
DUNNIEWASSALS	DUROMETERS	DYNAMOMETER	DYSGRAPHIC	DYSRHYTHMICS

DYSSYNERGIA

DYSSYNERGIA	DYSTELEOLOGICAL	DYSTHESIAS	DYSTOPIANS	DYSTROPHIN
DYSSYNERGIAS	DYSTELEOLOGIES	DYSTHYMIAC	DYSTROPHIA	DYSTROPHINS
DYSSYNERGIC	DYSTELEOLOGIST	DYSTHYMIACS	DYSTROPHIAS	DZIGGETAIS
DYSSYNERGIES	DYSTELEOLOGISTS	DYSTHYMIAS	DYSTROPHIC	
DYSSYNERGY	DYSTELEOLOGY	DYSTHYMICS	DYSTROPHIES	

D

E

EAGERNESSES	EARTHQUAKES	EAVESDROPPINGS	ECCENTRICALLY	ECHINODERMAL
EAGLEHAWKS	EARTHQUAKING	EAVESDROPS	ECCENTRICITIES	ECHINODERMATOUS
EAGLESTONE	EARTHRISES	EAVESTROUGH	ECCENTRICITY	ECHINODERMS
EAGLESTONES	EARTHSHAKER	EAVESTROUGHS	ECCENTRICS	ECHIUROIDS
EAGLEWOODS	EARTHSHAKERS	EBIONISING	ECCHYMOSED	ECHOCARDIOGRAM
EARBASHERS	EARTHSHAKING	EBIONITISM	ECCHYMOSES	ECHOCARDIOGRAMS
EARBASHING	EARTHSHAKINGLY	EBIONITISMS	ECCHYMOSIS	ECHOGRAPHIES
EARBASHINGS	EARTHSHATTERING	EBIONIZING	ECCHYMOTIC	ECHOGRAPHS
EARLIERISE	EARTHSHINE	EBOULEMENT	ECCLESIARCH	ECHOGRAPHY
EARLIERISED	EARTHSHINES	EBOULEMENTS	ECCLESIARCHS	ECHOICALLY
EARLIERISES	EARTHSTARS	EBRACTEATE	ECCLESIAST	ECHOLALIAS
EARLIERISING	EARTHWARDS	EBRACTEOLATE	ECCLESIASTIC	ECHOLOCATION
EARLIERIZE	EARTHWAXES	EBRILLADES	ECCLESIASTICAL	ECHOLOCATIONS
EARLIERIZED	EARTHWOLVES	EBRIOSITIES	ECCLESIASTICISM	ECHOPRAXES
EARLIERIZES	EARTHWOMAN	EBULLIENCE	ECCLESIASTICS	ECHOPRAXIA
EARLIERIZING	EARTHWOMEN	EBULLIENCES	ECCLESIASTS	ECHOPRAXIAS
EARLINESSES	EARTHWORKS	EBULLIENCIES	ECCLESIOLATER	ECHOPRAXIS
EARLYWOODS	EARTHWORMS	EBULLIENCY	ECCLESIOLATERS	ECHOVIRUSES
EARMARKING	EARWIGGING	EBULLIENTLY	ECCLESIOLATRIES	ECLAIRCISSEMENT
EARNESTNESS	EARWIGGINGS	EBULLIOMETER	ECCLESIOLATRY	ECLAMPSIAS
EARNESTNESSES	EARWITNESS	EBULLIOMETERS	ECCLESIOLOGICAL	ECLAMPSIES
EARSPLITTING	EARWITNESSES	EBULLIOMETRIES	ECCLESIOLOGIES	ECLECTICALLY
EARTHBOUND	EASEFULNESS	EBULLIOMETRY	ECCLESIOLOGIST	ECLECTICISM
EARTHENWARE	EASEFULNESSES	EBULLIOSCOPE	ECCLESIOLOGISTS	ECLECTICISMS
EARTHENWARES	EASINESSES	EBULLIOSCOPES	ECCLESIOLOGY	ECLIPSISES
EARTHFALLS	EASSELGATE	EBULLIOSCOPIC	ECCOPROTIC	ECLIPTICALLY
EARTHFLAXES	EASSELWARD	EBULLIOSCOPICAL	ECCOPROTICS	ECOCATASTROPHE
EARTHINESS	EASTERLIES	EBULLIOSCOPIES	ECCREMOCARPUS	ECOCATASTROPHES
EARTHINESSES	EASTERLING	EBULLIOSCOPY	ECCREMOCARPUSES	ECOCENTRIC
EARTHLIEST	EASTERLINGS	EBULLITION	ECCRINOLOGIES	ECOCLIMATE
EARTHLIGHT	EASTERMOST	EBULLITIONS	ECCRINOLOGY	ECOCLIMATES
EARTHLIGHTS	EASTERNERS	EBURNATION	ECDYSIASTS	ECOFEMINISM
EARTHLINESS	EASTERNMOST	EBURNATIONS	ECHELONING	ECOFEMINISMS
EARTHLINESSES	EASTWARDLY	EBURNIFICATION	ECHEVERIAS	ECOFEMINIST
EARTHLINGS	EASYGOINGNESS	EBURNIFICATIONS	ECHIDNINES	ECOFEMINISTS
EARTHMOVER	EASYGOINGNESSES	ECARDINATE	ECHINACEAS	ECOFRIENDLY
EARTHMOVERS	EAVESDRIPS	ECBLASTESES	ECHINOCOCCI	ECOLOGICAL
EARTHMOVING	EAVESDROPPED	ECBLASTESIS	ECHINOCOCCOSES	ECOLOGICALLY
EARTHMOVINGS	EAVESDROPPER	ECCALEOBION	ECHINOCOCCOSIS	ECOLOGISTS
EARTHQUAKE	EAVESDROPPERS	ECCALEOBIONS	ECHINOCOCCUS	ECOMMERCES
EARTHQUAKED	EAVESDROPPING	ECCENTRICAL	ECHINODERM	ECOMOVEMENT

ECOMOVEMENTS	ECOTERRORIST	ECTOPARASITES	EDITIONING	EDULCORATIVE
ECONOBOXES	ECOTERRORISTS	ECTOPARASITIC	EDITORIALISE	EDULCORATOR
ECONOMETER	ECOTOURING	ECTOPHYTES	EDITORIALISED	EDULCORATORS
ECONOMETERS	ECOTOURISM	ECTOPHYTIC	EDITORIALISER	EDUTAINMENT
ECONOMETRIC	ECOTOURISMS	ECTOPICALLY	EDITORIALISERS	EDUTAINMENTS
ECONOMETRICAL	ECOTOURIST	ECTOPLASMIC	EDITORIALISES	EELGRASSES
ECONOMETRICALLY	ECOTOURISTS	ECTOPLASMS	EDITORIALISING	EERINESSES
ECONOMETRICIAN	ECOTOXICOLOGIES	ECTOPLASTIC	EDITORIALIST	EFFACEABLE
ECONOMETRICIANS	ECOTOXICOLOGIST	ECTOPROCTS	EDITORIALISTS	EFFACEMENT
ECONOMETRICS	ECOTOXICOLOGY	ECTOSARCOUS	EDITORIALIZE	EFFACEMENTS
ECONOMETRIST	ECOTYPICALLY	ECTOTHERMIC	EDITORIALIZED	EFFECTIBLE
ECONOMETRISTS	ECPHONESES	ECTOTHERMS	EDITORIALIZER	EFFECTIVELY
ECONOMICAL	ECPHONESIS	ECTOTROPHIC	EDITORIALIZERS	EFFECTIVENESS
ECONOMICALLY	ECPHRACTIC	ECTROPIONS	EDITORIALIZES	EFFECTIVENESSES
ECONOMISATION	ECPHRACTICS	ECTROPIUMS	EDITORIALIZING	EFFECTIVES
ECONOMISATIONS	ECRITOIRES	ECTYPOGRAPHIES	EDITORIALLY	EFFECTIVITIES
ECONOMISED	ECSTASISED	ECTYPOGRAPHY	EDITORIALS	EFFECTIVITY
ECONOMISER	ECSTASISES	ECUMENICAL	EDITORSHIP	EFFECTLESS
ECONOMISERS	ECSTASISING	ECUMENICALISM	EDITORSHIPS	EFFECTUALITIES
ECONOMISES	ECSTASIZED	ECUMENICALISMS	EDITRESSES	EFFECTUALITY
ECONOMISING	ECSTASIZES	ECUMENICALLY	EDRIOPHTHALMIAN	EFFECTUALLY
ECONOMISMS	ECSTASIZING	ECUMENICISM	EDRIOPHTHALMIC	EFFECTUALNESS
ECONOMISTIC	ECSTASYING	ECUMENICISMS	EDRIOPHTHALMOUS	EFFECTUALNESSES
ECONOMISTS	ECSTATICALLY	ECUMENICIST	EDUCABILITIES	EFFECTUATE
ECONOMIZATION	ECTHLIPSES	ECUMENICISTS	EDUCABILITY	EFFECTUATED
ECONOMIZATIONS	ECTHLIPSIS	ECUMENICITIES	EDUCATABILITIES	EFFECTUATES
ECONOMIZED	ECTOBLASTIC	ECUMENICITY	EDUCATABILITY	EFFECTUATING
ECONOMIZER	ECTOBLASTS	ECUMENISMS	EDUCATABLE	EFFECTUATION
ECONOMIZERS	ECTOCRINES	ECUMENISTS	EDUCATEDNESS	EFFECTUATIONS
ECONOMIZES	ECTODERMAL	ECZEMATOUS	EDUCATEDNESSES	EFFEMINACIES
ECONOMIZING	ECTODERMIC	EDACIOUSLY	EDUCATIONAL	EFFEMINACY
ECOPHOBIAS	ECTOENZYME	EDACIOUSNESS	EDUCATIONALIST	EFFEMINATE
ECOPHYSIOLOGIES	ECTOENZYMES	EDACIOUSNESSES	EDUCATIONALISTS	EFFEMINATED
ECOPHYSIOLOGY	ECTOGENESES	EDAPHICALLY	EDUCATIONALLY	EFFEMINATELY
ECOREGIONS	ECTOGENESIS	EDAPHOLOGIES	EDUCATIONESE	EFFEMINATENESS
ECOSPECIES	ECTOGENETIC	EDAPHOLOGY	EDUCATIONESES	EFFEMINATES
ECOSPECIFIC	ECTOGENICALLY	EDELWEISSES	EDUCATIONIST	EFFEMINATING
ECOSPHERES	ECTOGENIES	EDENTULATE	EDUCATIONISTS	EFFEMINISE
ECOSSAISES	ECTOGENOUS	EDENTULOUS	EDUCATIONS	EFFEMINISED
ECOSYSTEMS	ECTOMORPHIC	EDGINESSES	EDUCEMENTS	EFFEMINISES
ECOTARIANISM	ECTOMORPHIES	EDIBILITIES	EDULCORANT	EFFEMINISING
ECOTARIANISMS	ECTOMORPHS	EDIBLENESS	EDULCORATE	EFFEMINIZE
ECOTARIANS	ECTOMORPHY	EDIBLENESSES	EDULCORATED	EFFEMINIZED
ECOTECTURE	ECTOMYCORRHIZA	EDIFICATION	EDULCORATES	EFFEMINIZES
ECOTECTURES	ECTOMYCORRHIZAE	EDIFICATIONS	EDULCORATING	EFFEMINIZING
ECOTERRORISM	ECTOMYCORRHIZAS	EDIFICATORY	EDULCORATION	EFFERENCES
ECOTERRORISMS	ECTOPARASITE	EDIFYINGLY	EDULCORATIONS	EFFERENTLY

EFFERVESCE
EFFERVESCED
EFFERVESCENCE
EFFERVESCENCES
EFFERVESCENCIES
EFFERVESCENCY
EFFERVESCENT
EFFERVESCENTLY
EFFERVESCES
EFFERVESCIBLE
EFFERVESCING
EFFERVESCINGLY
EFFETENESS
EFFETENESSES
EFFICACIES
EFFICACIOUS
EFFICACIOUSLY
EFFICACIOUSNESS
EFFICACITIES
EFFICACITY
EFFICIENCE
EFFICIENCES
EFFICIENCIES
EFFICIENCY
EFFICIENTLY
EFFICIENTS
EFFIERCING
EFFIGURATE
EFFIGURATION
EFFIGURATIONS
EFFLEURAGE
EFFLEURAGED
EFFLEURAGES
EFFLEURAGING
EFFLORESCE
EFFLORESCED
EFFLORESCENCE
EFFLORESCENCES
EFFLORESCENT
EFFLORESCES
EFFLORESCING
EFFLUENCES
EFFLUVIUMS
EFFLUXIONS
EFFORTFULLY
EFFORTFULNESS
EFFORTFULNESSES

EFFORTLESS
EFFORTLESSLY
EFFORTLESSNESS
EFFRONTERIES
EFFRONTERY
EFFULGENCE
EFFULGENCES
EFFULGENTLY
EFFUSIOMETER
EFFUSIOMETERS
EFFUSIVELY
EFFUSIVENESS
EFFUSIVENESSES
EGALITARIAN
EGALITARIANISM
EGALITARIANISMS
EGALITARIANS
EGAREMENTS
EGGBEATERS
EGGHEADEDNESS
EGGHEADEDNESSES
EGLANDULAR
EGLANDULOSE
EGLANTINES
EGOCENTRIC
EGOCENTRICAL
EGOCENTRICALLY
EGOCENTRICITIES
EGOCENTRICITY
EGOCENTRICS
EGOCENTRISM
EGOCENTRISMS
EGOISTICAL
EGOISTICALLY
EGOMANIACAL
EGOMANIACALLY
EGOMANIACS
EGOSURFING
EGOTHEISMS
EGOTISTICAL
EGOTISTICALLY
EGREGIOUSLY
EGREGIOUSNESS
EGREGIOUSNESSES
EGRESSIONS
EGRESSIVES
EGURGITATE

EGURGITATED
EGURGITATES
EGURGITATING
EICOSANOID
EICOSANOIDS
EIDERDOWNS
EIDETICALLY
EIDOGRAPHS
EIGENFREQUENCY
EIGENFUNCTION
EIGENFUNCTIONS
EIGENMODES
EIGENTONES
EIGENVALUE
EIGENVALUES
EIGENVECTOR
EIGENVECTORS
EIGHTBALLS
EIGHTEENMO
EIGHTEENMOS
EIGHTEENTH
EIGHTEENTHLY
EIGHTEENTHS
EIGHTFOILS
EIGHTIETHS
EIGHTPENCE
EIGHTPENCES
EIGHTPENNY
EIGHTSCORE
EIGHTSCORES
EIGHTSOMES
EINSTEINIUM
EINSTEINIUMS
EIRENICALLY
EIRENICONS
EISTEDDFOD
EISTEDDFODAU
EISTEDDFODIC
EISTEDDFODS
EJACULATED
EJACULATES
EJACULATING
EJACULATION
EJACULATIONS
EJACULATIVE
EJACULATOR
EJACULATORS

EJACULATORY
EJECTAMENTA
EJECTIVELY
EJECTMENTS
EKISTICIAN
EKISTICIANS
ELABORATED
ELABORATELY
ELABORATENESS
ELABORATENESSES
ELABORATES
ELABORATING
ELABORATION
ELABORATIONS
ELABORATIVE
ELABORATOR
ELABORATORIES
ELABORATORS
ELABORATORY
ELAEOLITES
ELAEOPTENE
ELAEOPTENES
ELAIOSOMES
ELASMOBRANCH
ELASMOBRANCHS
ELASMOSAUR
ELASMOSAURS
ELASTANCES
ELASTICALLY
ELASTICATE
ELASTICATED
ELASTICATES
ELASTICATING
ELASTICATION
ELASTICATIONS
ELASTICISE
ELASTICISED
ELASTICISES
ELASTICISING
ELASTICITIES
ELASTICITY
ELASTICIZE
ELASTICIZED
ELASTICIZES
ELASTICIZING
ELASTICNESS
ELASTICNESSES

ELASTOMERIC
ELASTOMERS
ELATEDNESS
ELATEDNESSES
ELATERITES
ELATERIUMS
ELBOWROOMS
ELDERBERRIES
ELDERBERRY
ELDERCARES
ELDERFLOWER
ELDERFLOWERS
ELDERLINESS
ELDERLINESSES
ELDERSHIPS
ELECAMPANE
ELECAMPANES
ELECTABILITIES
ELECTABILITY
ELECTIONEER
ELECTIONEERED
ELECTIONEERER
ELECTIONEERERS
ELECTIONEERING
ELECTIONEERINGS
ELECTIONEERS
ELECTIVELY
ELECTIVENESS
ELECTIVENESSES
ELECTIVITIES
ELECTIVITY
ELECTORALLY
ELECTORATE
ELECTORATES
ELECTORESS
ELECTORESSES
ELECTORIAL
ELECTORIALLY
ELECTORSHIP
ELECTORSHIPS
ELECTRESSES
ELECTRICAL
ELECTRICALLY
ELECTRICALS
ELECTRICIAN
ELECTRICIANS
ELECTRICITIES

E

ELECTRICITY
ELECTRIFIABLE
ELECTRIFICATION
ELECTRIFIED
ELECTRIFIER
ELECTRIFIERS
ELECTRIFIES
ELECTRIFYING
ELECTRIFYINGLY
ELECTRISATION
ELECTRISATIONS
ELECTRISED
ELECTRISES
ELECTRISING
ELECTRIZATION
ELECTRIZATIONS
ELECTRIZED
ELECTRIZES
ELECTRIZING
ELECTROACOUSTIC
ELECTROACTIVE
ELECTROACTIVITY
ELECTROANALYSES
ELECTROANALYSIS
ELECTROANALYTIC
ELECTROBIOLOGY
ELECTROCAUTERY
ELECTROCEMENT
ELECTROCEMENTS
ELECTROCHEMIC
ELECTROCHEMICAL
ELECTROCHEMIST
ELECTROCHEMISTS
ELECTROCLASH
ELECTROCLASHES
ELECTROCULTURE
ELECTROCULTURES
ELECTROCUTE
ELECTROCUTED
ELECTROCUTES
ELECTROCUTING
ELECTROCUTION
ELECTROCUTIONS
ELECTROCYTE
ELECTROCYTES
ELECTRODEPOSIT
ELECTRODEPOSITS

ELECTRODERMAL
ELECTRODES
ELECTRODIALYSES
ELECTRODIALYSIS
ELECTRODIALYTIC
ELECTRODYNAMIC
ELECTRODYNAMICS
ELECTROFISHING
ELECTROFISHINGS
ELECTROFLUOR
ELECTROFLUORS
ELECTROFORM
ELECTROFORMED
ELECTROFORMING
ELECTROFORMINGS
ELECTROFORMS
ELECTROGEN
ELECTROGENESES
ELECTROGENESIS
ELECTROGENIC
ELECTROGENS
ELECTROGILDING
ELECTROGILDINGS
ELECTROGRAM
ELECTROGRAMS
ELECTROGRAPH
ELECTROGRAPHIC
ELECTROGRAPHIES
ELECTROGRAPHS
ELECTROGRAPHY
ELECTROING
ELECTROJET
ELECTROJETS
ELECTROKINETIC
ELECTROKINETICS
ELECTROLESS
ELECTROLIER
ELECTROLIERS
ELECTROLOGIES
ELECTROLOGIST
ELECTROLOGISTS
ELECTROLOGY
ELECTROLYSATION
ELECTROLYSE
ELECTROLYSED
ELECTROLYSER
ELECTROLYSERS

ELECTROLYSES
ELECTROLYSING
ELECTROLYSIS
ELECTROLYTE
ELECTROLYTES
ELECTROLYTIC
ELECTROLYTICS
ELECTROLYZATION
ELECTROLYZE
ELECTROLYZED
ELECTROLYZER
ELECTROLYZERS
ELECTROLYZES
ELECTROLYZING
ELECTROMAGNET
ELECTROMAGNETIC
ELECTROMAGNETS
ELECTROMER
ELECTROMERIC
ELECTROMERISM
ELECTROMERISMS
ELECTROMERS
ELECTROMETER
ELECTROMETERS
ELECTROMETRIC
ELECTROMETRICAL
ELECTROMETRIES
ELECTROMETRY
ELECTROMOTANCE
ELECTROMOTANCES
ELECTROMOTIVE
ELECTROMOTOR
ELECTROMOTORS
ELECTROMYOGRAM
ELECTROMYOGRAMS
ELECTROMYOGRAPH
ELECTRONEGATIVE
ELECTRONIC
ELECTRONICA
ELECTRONICALLY
ELECTRONICAS
ELECTRONICS
ELECTRONVOLT
ELECTRONVOLTS
ELECTROOSMOSES
ELECTROOSMOSIS
ELECTROOSMOTIC

ELECTROPHILE
ELECTROPHILES
ELECTROPHILIC
ELECTROPHONE
ELECTROPHONES
ELECTROPHONIC
ELECTROPHORESE
ELECTROPHORESED
ELECTROPHORESES
ELECTROPHORESIS
ELECTROPHORETIC
ELECTROPHORI
ELECTROPHORUS
ELECTROPHORUSES
ELECTROPLATE
ELECTROPLATED
ELECTROPLATER
ELECTROPLATERS
ELECTROPLATES
ELECTROPLATING
ELECTROPLATINGS
ELECTROPOLAR
ELECTROPOSITIVE
ELECTROPUNCTURE
ELECTRORECEPTOR
ELECTRORHEOLOGY
ELECTROSCOPE
ELECTROSCOPES
ELECTROSCOPIC
ELECTROSHOCK
ELECTROSHOCKS
ELECTROSONDE
ELECTROSONDES
ELECTROSTATIC
ELECTROSTATICS
ELECTROSURGERY
ELECTROSURGICAL
ELECTROTECHNICS
ELECTROTHERAPY
ELECTROTHERMAL
ELECTROTHERMIC
ELECTROTHERMICS
ELECTROTHERMIES
ELECTROTHERMY
ELECTROTINT
ELECTROTINTS
ELECTROTONIC

ELECTROTONUS
ELECTROTONUSES
ELECTROTYPE
ELECTROTYPED
ELECTROTYPER
ELECTROTYPERS
ELECTROTYPES
ELECTROTYPIC
ELECTROTYPIES
ELECTROTYPING
ELECTROTYPIST
ELECTROTYPISTS
ELECTROTYPY
ELECTROVALENCE
ELECTROVALENCES
ELECTROVALENCY
ELECTROVALENT
ELECTROVALENTLY
ELECTROWEAK
ELECTROWINNING
ELECTROWINNINGS
ELECTUARIES
ELEDOISINS
ELEEMOSYNARY
ELEGANCIES
ELEGIACALLY
ELEMENTALISM
ELEMENTALISMS
ELEMENTALLY
ELEMENTALS
ELEMENTARILY
ELEMENTARINESS
ELEMENTARY
ELEOPTENES
ELEPHANTIASES
ELEPHANTIASIC
ELEPHANTIASIS
ELEPHANTINE
ELEPHANTOID
ELEUTHERARCH
ELEUTHERARCHS
ELEUTHERIAN
ELEUTHEROCOCCI
ELEUTHEROCOCCUS
ELEUTHERODACTYL
ELEUTHEROMANIA
ELEUTHEROMANIAS

ELEUTHEROPHOBIA	ELOPEMENTS	EMANCIPATING	EMBARRASSES	EMBLEMATICALLY
ELEUTHEROPHOBIC	ELOQUENCES	EMANCIPATION	EMBARRASSING	EMBLEMATISE
ELEVATIONAL	ELOQUENTLY	EMANCIPATIONIST	EMBARRASSINGLY	EMBLEMATISED
ELEVATIONS	ELSEWHITHER	EMANCIPATIONS	EMBARRASSMENT	EMBLEMATISES
ELEVENTHLY	ELUCIDATED	EMANCIPATIVE	EMBARRASSMENTS	EMBLEMATISING
ELFISHNESS	ELUCIDATES	EMANCIPATOR	EMBARRINGS	EMBLEMATIST
ELFISHNESSES	ELUCIDATING	EMANCIPATORS	EMBASEMENT	EMBLEMATISTS
ELICITABLE	ELUCIDATION	EMANCIPATORY	EMBASEMENTS	EMBLEMATIZE
ELICITATION	ELUCIDATIONS	EMANCIPIST	EMBASSADES	EMBLEMATIZED
ELICITATIONS	ELUCIDATIVE	EMANCIPISTS	EMBASSADOR	EMBLEMATIZES
ELIGIBILITIES	ELUCIDATOR	EMARGINATE	EMBASSADORS	EMBLEMATIZING
ELIGIBILITY	ELUCIDATORS	EMARGINATED	EMBASSAGES	EMBLEMENTS
ELIMINABILITIES	ELUCIDATORY	EMARGINATELY	EMBATTLEMENT	EMBLEMISED
ELIMINABILITY	ELUCUBRATE	EMARGINATES	EMBATTLEMENTS	EMBLEMISES
ELIMINABLE	ELUCUBRATED	EMARGINATING	EMBATTLING	EMBLEMISING
ELIMINANTS	ELUCUBRATES	EMARGINATION	EMBAYMENTS	EMBLEMIZED
ELIMINATED	ELUCUBRATING	EMARGINATIONS	EMBEDDINGS	EMBLEMIZES
ELIMINATES	ELUCUBRATION	EMASCULATE	EMBEDMENTS	EMBLEMIZING
ELIMINATING	ELUCUBRATIONS	EMASCULATED	EMBELLISHED	EMBLOOMING
ELIMINATION	ELUSIVENESS	EMASCULATES	EMBELLISHER	EMBLOSSOMED
ELIMINATIONS	ELUSIVENESSES	EMASCULATING	EMBELLISHERS	EMBLOSSOMING
ELIMINATIVE	ELUSORINESS	EMASCULATION	EMBELLISHES	EMBLOSSOMS
ELIMINATIVISM	ELUSORINESSES	EMASCULATIONS	EMBELLISHING	EMBODIMENT
ELIMINATIVISMS	ELUTRIATED	EMASCULATIVE	EMBELLISHINGLY	EMBODIMENTS
ELIMINATOR	ELUTRIATES	EMASCULATOR	EMBELLISHMENT	EMBOITEMENT
ELIMINATORS	ELUTRIATING	EMASCULATORS	EMBELLISHMENTS	EMBOITEMENTS
ELIMINATORY	ELUTRIATION	EMASCULATORY	EMBEZZLEMENT	EMBOLDENED
ELLIPSOGRAPH	ELUTRIATIONS	EMBALLINGS	EMBEZZLEMENTS	EMBOLDENER
ELLIPSOGRAPHS	ELUTRIATOR	EMBALMINGS	EMBEZZLERS	EMBOLDENERS
ELLIPSOIDAL	ELUTRIATORS	EMBALMMENT	EMBEZZLING	EMBOLDENING
ELLIPSOIDS	ELUVIATING	EMBALMMENTS	EMBITTERED	EMBOLECTOMIES
ELLIPTICAL	ELUVIATION	EMBANKMENT	EMBITTERER	EMBOLECTOMY
ELLIPTICALLY	ELUVIATIONS	EMBANKMENTS	EMBITTERERS	EMBOLISATION
ELLIPTICALNESS	ELVISHNESS	EMBARCADERO	EMBITTERING	EMBOLISATIONS
ELLIPTICALS	ELVISHNESSES	EMBARCADEROS	EMBITTERINGS	EMBOLISING
ELLIPTICITIES	ELYTRIFORM	EMBARCATION	EMBITTERMENT	EMBOLISMAL
ELLIPTICITY	ELYTRIGEROUS	EMBARCATIONS	EMBITTERMENTS	EMBOLISMIC
ELOCUTIONARY	EMACIATING	EMBARGOING	EMBLAZONED	EMBOLIZATION
ELOCUTIONIST	EMACIATION	EMBARKATION	EMBLAZONER	EMBOLIZATIONS
ELOCUTIONISTS	EMACIATIONS	EMBARKATIONS	EMBLAZONERS	EMBOLIZING
ELOCUTIONS	EMALANGENI	EMBARKMENT	EMBLAZONING	EMBONPOINT
ELOIGNMENT	EMANATIONAL	EMBARKMENTS	EMBLAZONMENT	EMBONPOINTS
ELOIGNMENTS	EMANATIONS	EMBARQUEMENT	EMBLAZONMENTS	EMBORDERED
ELOINMENTS	EMANATISTS	EMBARQUEMENTS	EMBLAZONRIES	EMBORDERING
ELONGATING	EMANCIPATE	EMBARRASSABLE	EMBLAZONRY	EMBOSCATAS
ELONGATION	EMANCIPATED	EMBARRASSED	EMBLEMATIC	EMBOSOMING
ELONGATIONS	EMANCIPATES	EMBARRASSEDLY	EMBLEMATICAL	EMBOSSABLE

EMBOSSMENT	EMBRITTLING	EMENDATION	EMOTIONABLE	EMPATHISED
EMBOSSMENTS	EMBROCATED	EMENDATIONS	EMOTIONALISE	EMPATHISES
EMBOTHRIUM	EMBROCATES	EMENDATORS	EMOTIONALISED	EMPATHISING
EMBOTHRIUMS	EMBROCATING	EMENDATORY	EMOTIONALISES	EMPATHISTS
EMBOUCHURE	EMBROCATION	EMERGENCES	EMOTIONALISING	EMPATHIZED
EMBOUCHURES	EMBROCATIONS	EMERGENCIES	EMOTIONALISM	EMPATHIZES
EMBOUNDING	EMBROGLIOS	EMERGENTLY	EMOTIONALISMS	EMPATHIZING
EMBOURGEOISE	EMBROIDERED	EMETICALLY	EMOTIONALIST	EMPATRONED
EMBOURGEOISED	EMBROIDERER	EMETOPHOBIA	EMOTIONALISTIC	EMPATRONING
EMBOURGEOISES	EMBROIDERERS	EMETOPHOBIAS	EMOTIONALISTS	EMPEACHING
EMBOURGEOISING	EMBROIDERIES	EMICATIONS	EMOTIONALITIES	EMPENNAGES
EMBOWELING	EMBROIDERING	EMIGRATING	EMOTIONALITY	EMPEOPLING
EMBOWELLED	EMBROIDERS	EMIGRATION	EMOTIONALIZE	EMPERISHED
EMBOWELLING	EMBROIDERY	EMIGRATIONAL	EMOTIONALIZED	EMPERISHES
EMBOWELMENT	EMBROILERS	EMIGRATIONIST	EMOTIONALIZES	EMPERISHING
EMBOWELMENTS	EMBROILING	EMIGRATIONISTS	EMOTIONALIZING	EMPERISING
EMBOWERING	EMBROILMENT	EMIGRATIONS	EMOTIONALLY	EMPERIZING
EMBOWERMENT	EMBROILMENTS	EMIGRATORY	EMOTIONLESS	EMPERORSHIP
EMBOWERMENTS	EMBROWNING	EMINENCIES	EMOTIONLESSLY	EMPERORSHIPS
EMBOWMENTS	EMBRUEMENT	EMINENTIAL	EMOTIONLESSNESS	EMPHASISED
EMBRACEABLE	EMBRUEMENTS	EMISSARIES	EMOTIVENESS	EMPHASISES
EMBRACEMENT	EMBRYECTOMIES	EMISSIVITIES	EMOTIVENESSES	EMPHASISING
EMBRACEMENTS	EMBRYECTOMY	EMISSIVITY	EMOTIVISMS	EMPHASIZED
EMBRACEORS	EMBRYOGENESES	EMITTANCES	EMOTIVITIES	EMPHASIZES
EMBRACERIES	EMBRYOGENESIS	EMMARBLING	EMPACKETED	EMPHASIZING
EMBRACINGLY	EMBRYOGENETIC	EMMENAGOGIC	EMPACKETING	EMPHATICAL
EMBRACINGNESS	EMBRYOGENIC	EMMENAGOGUE	EMPALEMENT	EMPHATICALLY
EMBRACINGNESSES	EMBRYOGENIES	EMMENAGOGUES	EMPALEMENTS	EMPHATICALNESS
EMBRAIDING	EMBRYOGENY	EMMENOLOGIES	EMPANELING	EMPHRACTIC
EMBRANCHMENT	EMBRYOLOGIC	EMMENOLOGY	EMPANELLED	EMPHRACTICS
EMBRANCHMENTS	EMBRYOLOGICAL	EMMETROPES	EMPANELLING	EMPHYSEMAS
EMBRANGLED	EMBRYOLOGICALLY	EMMETROPIA	EMPANELMENT	EMPHYSEMATOUS
EMBRANGLEMENT	EMBRYOLOGIES	EMMETROPIAS	EMPANELMENTS	EMPHYSEMIC
EMBRANGLEMENTS	EMBRYOLOGIST	EMMETROPIC	EMPANOPLIED	EMPHYSEMICS
EMBRANGLES	EMBRYOLOGISTS	EMOLLESCENCE	EMPANOPLIES	EMPHYTEUSES
EMBRANGLING	EMBRYOLOGY	EMOLLESCENCES	EMPANOPLYING	EMPHYTEUSIS
EMBRASURED	EMBRYONATE	EMOLLIATED	EMPARADISE	EMPHYTEUTIC
EMBRASURES	EMBRYONATED	EMOLLIATES	EMPARADISED	EMPIECEMENT
EMBRAZURES	EMBRYONICALLY	EMOLLIATING	EMPARADISES	EMPIECEMENTS
EMBREADING	EMBRYOPHYTE	EMOLLIENCE	EMPARADISING	EMPIERCING
EMBREATHED	EMBRYOPHYTES	EMOLLIENCES	EMPARLAUNCE	EMPIGHTING
EMBREATHES	EMBRYOTICALLY	EMOLLIENTS	EMPARLAUNCES	EMPIRICALLY
EMBREATHING	EMBRYOTOMIES	EMOLLITION	EMPASSIONATE	EMPIRICALNESS
EMBRITTLED	EMBRYOTOMY	EMOLLITIONS	EMPASSIONED	EMPIRICALNESSES
EMBRITTLEMENT	EMBRYULCIA	EMOLUMENTAL	EMPATHETIC	EMPIRICALS
EMBRITTLEMENTS	EMBRYULCIAS	EMOLUMENTARY	EMPATHETICALLY	EMPIRICISM
EMBRITTLES	EMENDATING	EMOLUMENTS	EMPATHICALLY	EMPIRICISMS

EMPIRICIST	EMPYREUMATIC	ENAMELWARE	ENCARNALISE	ENCHAINING
EMPIRICISTS	EMPYREUMATICAL	ENAMELWARES	ENCARNALISED	ENCHAINMENT
EMPIRICUTIC	EMPYREUMATISE	ENAMELWORK	ENCARNALISES	ENCHAINMENTS
EMPLACEMENT	EMPYREUMATISED	ENAMELWORKS	ENCARNALISING	ENCHANTERS
EMPLACEMENTS	EMPYREUMATISES	ENAMORADOS	ENCARNALIZE	ENCHANTING
EMPLASTERED	EMPYREUMATISING	ENAMOURING	ENCARNALIZED	ENCHANTINGLY
EMPLASTERING	EMPYREUMATIZE	ENANTHEMAS	ENCARNALIZES	ENCHANTMENT
EMPLASTERS	EMPYREUMATIZED	ENANTIODROMIA	ENCARNALIZING	ENCHANTMENTS
EMPLASTICS	EMPYREUMATIZES	ENANTIODROMIAS	ENCARPUSES	ENCHANTRESS
EMPLASTRON	EMPYREUMATIZING	ENANTIODROMIC	ENCASEMENT	ENCHANTRESSES
EMPLASTRONS	EMULATIONS	ENANTIOMER	ENCASEMENTS	ENCHARGING
EMPLASTRUM	EMULATIVELY	ENANTIOMERIC	ENCASHABLE	ENCHARMING
EMPLASTRUMS	EMULATRESS	ENANTIOMERS	ENCASHMENT	ENCHEASONS
EMPLEACHED	EMULATRESSES	ENANTIOMORPH	ENCASHMENTS	ENCHEERING
EMPLEACHES	EMULGENCES	ENANTIOMORPHIC	ENCAUSTICALLY	ENCHEIRIDIA
EMPLEACHING	EMULOUSNESS	ENANTIOMORPHIES	ENCAUSTICS	ENCHEIRIDION
EMPLECTONS	EMULOUSNESSES	ENANTIOMORPHISM	ENCEPHALALGIA	ENCHEIRIDIONS
EMPLECTUMS	EMULSIFIABLE	ENANTIOMORPHOUS	ENCEPHALALGIAS	ENCHILADAS
EMPLONGING	EMULSIFICATION	ENANTIOMORPHS	ENCEPHALIC	ENCHIRIDIA
EMPLOYABILITIES	EMULSIFICATIONS	ENANTIOMORPHY	ENCEPHALIN	ENCHIRIDION
EMPLOYABILITY	EMULSIFIED	ENANTIOPATHIES	ENCEPHALINE	ENCHIRIDIONS
EMPLOYABLE	EMULSIFIER	ENANTIOPATHY	ENCEPHALINES	ENCHONDROMA
EMPLOYABLES	EMULSIFIERS	ENANTIOSES	ENCEPHALINS	ENCHONDROMAS
EMPLOYMENT	EMULSIFIES	ENANTIOSIS	ENCEPHALITIC	ENCHONDROMATA
EMPLOYMENTS	EMULSIFYING	ENANTIOSTYLIES	ENCEPHALITIDES	ENCHONDROMATOUS
EMPOISONED	EMULSIONISE	ENANTIOSTYLOUS	ENCEPHALITIS	ENCINCTURE
EMPOISONING	EMULSIONISED	ENANTIOSTYLY	ENCEPHALITISES	ENCINCTURED
EMPOISONMENT	EMULSIONISES	ENANTIOTROPIC	ENCEPHALITOGEN	ENCINCTURES
EMPOISONMENTS	EMULSIONISING	ENANTIOTROPIES	ENCEPHALITOGENS	ENCINCTURING
EMPOLDERED	EMULSIONIZE	ENANTIOTROPY	ENCEPHALOCELE	ENCIPHERED
EMPOLDERING	EMULSIONIZED	ENARRATION	ENCEPHALOCELES	ENCIPHERER
EMPOVERISH	EMULSIONIZES	ENARRATIONS	ENCEPHALOGRAM	ENCIPHERERS
EMPOVERISHED	EMULSIONIZING	ENARTHRODIAL	ENCEPHALOGRAMS	ENCIPHERING
EMPOVERISHER	EMULSOIDAL	ENARTHROSES	ENCEPHALOGRAPH	ENCIPHERMENT
EMPOVERISHERS	EMUNCTIONS	ENARTHROSIS	ENCEPHALOGRAPHS	ENCIPHERMENTS
EMPOVERISHES	EMUNCTORIES	ENCAMPMENT	ENCEPHALOGRAPHY	ENCIRCLEMENT
EMPOVERISHING	ENABLEMENT	ENCAMPMENTS	ENCEPHALOID	ENCIRCLEMENTS
EMPOVERISHMENT	ENABLEMENTS	ENCANTHISES	ENCEPHALOMA	ENCIRCLING
EMPOVERISHMENTS	ENACTMENTS	ENCAPSULATE	ENCEPHALOMAS	ENCLASPING
EMPOWERING	ENALAPRILS	ENCAPSULATED	ENCEPHALOMATA	ENCLITICALLY
EMPOWERMENT	ENAMELINGS	ENCAPSULATES	ENCEPHALON	ENCLOISTER
EMPOWERMENTS	ENAMELISTS	ENCAPSULATING	ENCEPHALONS	ENCLOISTERED
EMPRESSEMENT	ENAMELLERS	ENCAPSULATION	ENCEPHALOPATHIC	ENCLOISTERING
EMPRESSEMENTS	ENAMELLING	ENCAPSULATIONS	ENCEPHALOPATHY	ENCLOISTERS
EMPTINESSES	ENAMELLINGS	ENCAPSULED	ENCEPHALOTOMIES	ENCLOSABLE
EMPURPLING	ENAMELLIST	ENCAPSULES	ENCEPHALOTOMY	ENCLOSURES
EMPYREUMATA	ENAMELLISTS	ENCAPSULING	ENCEPHALOUS	ENCLOTHING

ENCLOUDING
ENCODEMENT
ENCODEMENTS
ENCOIGNURE
ENCOIGNURES
ENCOLOURED
ENCOLOURING
ENCOLPIONS
ENCOLPIUMS
ENCOMENDERO
ENCOMENDEROS
ENCOMIASTIC
ENCOMIASTICAL
ENCOMIASTICALLY
ENCOMIASTS
ENCOMIENDA
ENCOMIENDAS
ENCOMPASSED
ENCOMPASSES
ENCOMPASSING
ENCOMPASSMENT
ENCOMPASSMENTS
ENCOPRESES
ENCOPRESIS
ENCOPRETIC
ENCOUNTERED
ENCOUNTERER
ENCOUNTERERS
ENCOUNTERING
ENCOUNTERS
ENCOURAGED
ENCOURAGEMENT
ENCOURAGEMENTS
ENCOURAGER
ENCOURAGERS
ENCOURAGES
ENCOURAGING
ENCOURAGINGLY
ENCOURAGINGS
ENCRADLING
ENCREASING
ENCRIMSONED
ENCRIMSONING
ENCRIMSONS
ENCRINITAL
ENCRINITES
ENCRINITIC

ENCROACHED
ENCROACHER
ENCROACHERS
ENCROACHES
ENCROACHING
ENCROACHINGLY
ENCROACHMENT
ENCROACHMENTS
ENCRUSTATION
ENCRUSTATIONS
ENCRUSTING
ENCRUSTMENT
ENCRUSTMENTS
ENCRYPTING
ENCRYPTION
ENCRYPTIONS
ENCULTURATE
ENCULTURATED
ENCULTURATES
ENCULTURATING
ENCULTURATION
ENCULTURATIONS
ENCULTURATIVE
ENCUMBERED
ENCUMBERING
ENCUMBERINGLY
ENCUMBERMENT
ENCUMBERMENTS
ENCUMBRANCE
ENCUMBRANCER
ENCUMBRANCERS
ENCUMBRANCES
ENCURTAINED
ENCURTAINING
ENCURTAINS
ENCYCLICAL
ENCYCLICALS
ENCYCLOPAEDIA
ENCYCLOPAEDIAS
ENCYCLOPAEDIC
ENCYCLOPAEDICAL
ENCYCLOPAEDISM
ENCYCLOPAEDISMS
ENCYCLOPAEDIST
ENCYCLOPAEDISTS
ENCYCLOPEDIA
ENCYCLOPEDIAN

ENCYCLOPEDIAS
ENCYCLOPEDIC
ENCYCLOPEDICAL
ENCYCLOPEDISM
ENCYCLOPEDISMS
ENCYCLOPEDIST
ENCYCLOPEDISTS
ENCYSTATION
ENCYSTATIONS
ENCYSTMENT
ENCYSTMENTS
ENDAMAGEMENT
ENDAMAGEMENTS
ENDAMAGING
ENDAMOEBAE
ENDAMOEBAS
ENDAMOEBIC
ENDANGERED
ENDANGERER
ENDANGERERS
ENDANGERING
ENDANGERMENT
ENDANGERMENTS
ENDARCHIES
ENDARTERECTOMY
ENDEARINGLY
ENDEARINGNESS
ENDEARINGNESSES
ENDEARMENT
ENDEARMENTS
ENDEAVORED
ENDEAVORER
ENDEAVORERS
ENDEAVORING
ENDEAVOURED
ENDEAVOURER
ENDEAVOURERS
ENDEAVOURING
ENDEAVOURMENT
ENDEAVOURMENTS
ENDEAVOURS
ENDECAGONS
ENDEIXISES
ENDEMICALLY
ENDEMICITIES
ENDEMICITY
ENDEMIOLOGIES

ENDEMIOLOGY
ENDENIZENED
ENDENIZENING
ENDENIZENS
ENDERGONIC
ENDERMATIC
ENDERMICAL
ENDLESSNESS
ENDLESSNESSES
ENDOBIOTIC
ENDOBLASTIC
ENDOBLASTS
ENDOCARDIA
ENDOCARDIAC
ENDOCARDIAL
ENDOCARDITIC
ENDOCARDITIS
ENDOCARDITISES
ENDOCARDIUM
ENDOCARPAL
ENDOCARPIC
ENDOCENTRIC
ENDOCHONDRAL
ENDOCHYLOUS
ENDOCRANIA
ENDOCRANIAL
ENDOCRANIUM
ENDOCRINAL
ENDOCRINES
ENDOCRINIC
ENDOCRINOLOGIC
ENDOCRINOLOGIES
ENDOCRINOLOGIST
ENDOCRINOLOGY
ENDOCRINOPATHIC
ENDOCRINOPATHY
ENDOCRINOUS
ENDOCRITIC
ENDOCUTICLE
ENDOCUTICLES
ENDOCYTOSES
ENDOCYTOSIS
ENDOCYTOTIC
ENDODERMAL
ENDODERMIC
ENDODERMIS
ENDODERMISES

ENDODONTAL
ENDODONTIC
ENDODONTICALLY
ENDODONTICS
ENDODONTIST
ENDODONTISTS
ENDOENZYME
ENDOENZYMES
ENDOGAMIES
ENDOGAMOUS
ENDOGENIES
ENDOGENOUS
ENDOGENOUSLY
ENDOLITHIC
ENDOLYMPHATIC
ENDOLYMPHS
ENDOMETRIA
ENDOMETRIAL
ENDOMETRIOSES
ENDOMETRIOSIS
ENDOMETRITIS
ENDOMETRITISES
ENDOMETRIUM
ENDOMITOSES
ENDOMITOSIS
ENDOMITOTIC
ENDOMIXISES
ENDOMORPHIC
ENDOMORPHIES
ENDOMORPHISM
ENDOMORPHISMS
ENDOMORPHS
ENDOMORPHY
ENDOMYCORRHIZA
ENDONEURIA
ENDONEURIUM
ENDONUCLEASE
ENDONUCLEASES
ENDONUCLEOLYTIC
ENDOPARASITE
ENDOPARASITES
ENDOPARASITIC
ENDOPARASITISM
ENDOPARASITISMS
ENDOPEPTIDASE
ENDOPEPTIDASES
ENDOPEROXIDE

ENDOPEROXIDES	ENDOSTEALLY	ENERGETICS	ENFRAMEMENTS	ENGRAFFING
ENDOPHAGIES	ENDOSTOSES	ENERGISATION	ENFRANCHISE	ENGRAFTATION
ENDOPHAGOUS	ENDOSTOSIS	ENERGISATIONS	ENFRANCHISED	ENGRAFTATIONS
ENDOPHITIC	ENDOSTYLES	ENERGISERS	ENFRANCHISEMENT	ENGRAFTING
ENDOPHYLLOUS	ENDOSULFAN	ENERGISING	ENFRANCHISER	ENGRAFTMENT
ENDOPHYTES	ENDOSULFANS	ENERGIZATION	ENFRANCHISERS	ENGRAFTMENTS
ENDOPHYTIC	ENDOSYMBIONT	ENERGIZATIONS	ENFRANCHISES	ENGRAILING
ENDOPHYTICALLY	ENDOSYMBIONTS	ENERGIZERS	ENFRANCHISING	ENGRAILMENT
ENDOPLASMIC	ENDOSYMBIOSES	ENERGIZING	ENFREEDOMED	ENGRAILMENTS
ENDOPLASMS	ENDOSYMBIOSIS	ENERGUMENS	ENFREEDOMING	ENGRAINEDLY
ENDOPLASTIC	ENDOSYMBIOTIC	ENERVATING	ENFREEDOMS	ENGRAINEDNESS
ENDOPLEURA	ENDOTHECIA	ENERVATION	ENFREEZING	ENGRAINEDNESSES
ENDOPLEURAS	ENDOTHECIAL	ENERVATIONS	ENGAGEMENT	ENGRAINERS
ENDOPODITE	ENDOTHECIUM	ENERVATIVE	ENGAGEMENTS	ENGRAINING
ENDOPODITES	ENDOTHELIA	ENERVATORS	ENGAGINGLY	ENGRAMMATIC
ENDOPOLYPLOID	ENDOTHELIAL	ENFACEMENT	ENGAGINGNESS	ENGRASPING
ENDOPOLYPLOIDY	ENDOTHELIOID	ENFACEMENTS	ENGAGINGNESSES	ENGRAVERIES
ENDOPROCTS	ENDOTHELIOMA	ENFEEBLEMENT	ENGARLANDED	ENGRAVINGS
ENDORADIOSONDE	ENDOTHELIOMAS	ENFEEBLEMENTS	ENGARLANDING	ENGRENAGES
ENDORADIOSONDES	ENDOTHELIOMATA	ENFEEBLERS	ENGARLANDS	ENGRIEVING
ENDORHIZAL	ENDOTHELIUM	ENFEEBLING	ENGARRISON	ENGROOVING
ENDORPHINS	ENDOTHERMAL	ENFELONING	ENGARRISONED	ENGROSSEDLY
ENDORSABLE	ENDOTHERMIC	ENFEOFFING	ENGARRISONING	ENGROSSERS
ENDORSATION	ENDOTHERMICALLY	ENFEOFFMENT	ENGARRISONS	ENGROSSING
ENDORSATIONS	ENDOTHERMIES	ENFEOFFMENTS	ENGENDERED	ENGROSSINGLY
ENDORSEMENT	ENDOTHERMISM	ENFESTERED	ENGENDERER	ENGROSSMENT
ENDORSEMENTS	ENDOTHERMISMS	ENFETTERED	ENGENDERERS	ENGROSSMENTS
ENDOSCOPES	ENDOTHERMS	ENFETTERING	ENGENDERING	ENGUARDING
ENDOSCOPIC	ENDOTHERMY	ENFEVERING	ENGENDERMENT	ENGULFMENT
ENDOSCOPICALLY	ENDOTOXINS	ENFIERCING	ENGENDERMENTS	ENGULFMENTS
ENDOSCOPIES	ENDOTRACHEAL	ENFILADING	ENGENDRURE	ENGULPHING
ENDOSCOPIST	ENDOTROPHIC	ENFLESHING	ENGENDRURES	ENGYSCOPES
ENDOSCOPISTS	ENDOWMENTS	ENFLEURAGE	ENGENDURES	ENHANCEMENT
ENDOSKELETAL	ENDPLAYING	ENFLEURAGES	ENGINEERED	ENHANCEMENTS
ENDOSKELETON	ENDUNGEONED	ENFLOWERED	ENGINEERING	ENHARMONIC
ENDOSKELETONS	ENDUNGEONING	ENFLOWERING	ENGINEERINGS	ENHARMONICAL
ENDOSMOMETER	ENDUNGEONS	ENFOLDMENT	ENGINERIES	ENHARMONICALLY
ENDOSMOMETERS	ENDURABILITIES	ENFOLDMENTS	ENGIRDLING	ENHEARSING
ENDOSMOMETRIC	ENDURABILITY	ENFORCEABILITY	ENGLACIALLY	ENHEARTENED
ENDOSMOSES	ENDURABLENESS	ENFORCEABLE	ENGLISHING	ENHEARTENING
ENDOSMOSIS	ENDURABLENESSES	ENFORCEDLY	ENGLOOMING	ENHEARTENS
ENDOSMOTIC	ENDURANCES	ENFORCEMENT	ENGLUTTING	ENHUNGERED
ENDOSMOTICALLY	ENDURINGLY	ENFORCEMENTS	ENGORGEMENT	ENHUNGERING
ENDOSPERMIC	ENDURINGNESS	ENFORESTED	ENGORGEMENTS	ENHYDRITES
ENDOSPERMS	ENDURINGNESSES	ENFORESTING	ENGOUEMENT	ENHYDRITIC
ENDOSPORES	ENERGETICAL	ENFOULDERED	ENGOUEMENTS	ENHYDROSES
ENDOSPOROUS	ENERGETICALLY	ENFRAMEMENT	ENGOUMENTS	ENHYPOSTASIA

ten to fifteen letter words | 853

ENHYPOSTASIAS	ENLARGEMENT	ENQUEUEING	ENSEPULCHRING	ENSWEEPING
ENHYPOSTATIC	ENLARGEMENTS	ENQUIRATION	ENSERFMENT	ENTABLATURE
ENHYPOSTATISE	ENLARGENED	ENQUIRATIONS	ENSERFMENTS	ENTABLATURES
ENHYPOSTATISED	ENLARGENING	ENRAGEMENT	ENSHEATHED	ENTABLEMENT
ENHYPOSTATISES	ENLEVEMENT	ENRAGEMENTS	ENSHEATHES	ENTABLEMENTS
ENHYPOSTATISING	ENLEVEMENTS	ENRANCKLED	ENSHEATHING	ENTAILMENT
ENHYPOSTATIZE	ENLIGHTENED	ENRANCKLES	ENSHELLING	ENTAILMENTS
ENHYPOSTATIZED	ENLIGHTENER	ENRANCKLING	ENSHELTERED	ENTAMOEBAE
ENHYPOSTATIZES	ENLIGHTENERS	ENRAPTURED	ENSHELTERING	ENTAMOEBAS
ENHYPOSTATIZING	ENLIGHTENING	ENRAPTURES	ENSHELTERS	ENTANGLEMENT
ENIGMATICAL	ENLIGHTENMENT	ENRAPTURING	ENSHIELDED	ENTANGLEMENTS
ENIGMATICALLY	ENLIGHTENMENTS	ENRAUNGING	ENSHIELDING	ENTANGLERS
ENIGMATISE	ENLIGHTENS	ENRAVISHED	ENSHRINEES	ENTANGLING
ENIGMATISED	ENLIGHTING	ENRAVISHES	ENSHRINEMENT	ENTELECHIES
ENIGMATISES	ENLISTMENT	ENRAVISHING	ENSHRINEMENTS	ENTELLUSES
ENIGMATISING	ENLISTMENTS	ENREGIMENT	ENSHRINING	ENTENDERED
ENIGMATIST	ENLIVENERS	ENREGIMENTED	ENSHROUDED	ENTENDERING
ENIGMATISTS	ENLIVENING	ENREGIMENTING	ENSHROUDING	ENTERCHAUNGE
ENIGMATIZE	ENLIVENMENT	ENREGIMENTS	ENSIGNCIES	ENTERCHAUNGED
ENIGMATIZED	ENLIVENMENTS	ENREGISTER	ENSIGNSHIP	ENTERCHAUNGES
ENIGMATIZES	ENLUMINING	ENREGISTERED	ENSIGNSHIPS	ENTERCHAUNGING
ENIGMATIZING	ENMESHMENT	ENREGISTERING	ENSILABILITIES	ENTERDEALE
ENIGMATOGRAPHY	ENMESHMENTS	ENREGISTERS	ENSILABILITY	ENTERDEALED
ENJAMBEMENT	ENNEAGONAL	ENRHEUMING	ENSILAGEING	ENTERDEALES
ENJAMBEMENTS	ENNEAGRAMS	ENRICHMENT	ENSILAGING	ENTERDEALING
ENJAMBMENT	ENNEAHEDRA	ENRICHMENTS	ENSLAVEMENT	ENTERECTOMIES
ENJAMBMENTS	ENNEAHEDRAL	ENROLLMENT	ENSLAVEMENTS	ENTERECTOMY
ENJOINDERS	ENNEAHEDRON	ENROLLMENTS	ENSNAREMENT	ENTERITIDES
ENJOINMENT	ENNEAHEDRONS	ENROLMENTS	ENSNAREMENTS	ENTERITISES
ENJOINMENTS	ENNEANDRIAN	ENROUGHING	ENSNARLING	ENTEROBACTERIA
ENJOYABLENESS	ENNEANDROUS	ENROUNDING	ENSORCELED	ENTEROBACTERIAL
ENJOYABLENESSES	ENNEASTYLE	ENSAMPLING	ENSORCELING	ENTEROBACTERIUM
ENJOYMENTS	ENNEATHLON	ENSANGUINATED	ENSORCELLED	ENTEROBIASES
ENKEPHALIN	ENNEATHLONS	ENSANGUINE	ENSORCELLING	ENTEROBIASIS
ENKEPHALINE	ENNOBLEMENT	ENSANGUINED	ENSORCELLMENT	ENTEROCELE
ENKEPHALINES	ENNOBLEMENTS	ENSANGUINES	ENSORCELLMENTS	ENTEROCELES
ENKEPHALINS	ENOKIDAKES	ENSANGUINING	ENSORCELLS	ENTEROCENTESES
ENKERNELLED	ENOKITAKES	ENSCHEDULE	ENSOULMENT	ENTEROCENTESIS
ENKERNELLING	ENOLOGICAL	ENSCHEDULED	ENSOULMENTS	ENTEROCOCCAL
ENKINDLERS	ENOLOGISTS	ENSCHEDULES	ENSPHERING	ENTEROCOCCI
ENKINDLING	ENORMITIES	ENSCHEDULING	ENSTAMPING	ENTEROCOCCUS
ENLACEMENT	ENORMOUSLY	ENSCONCING	ENSTATITES	ENTEROCOEL
ENLACEMENTS	ENORMOUSNESS	ENSCROLLED	ENSTEEPING	ENTEROCOELE
ENLARGEABLE	ENORMOUSNESSES	ENSCROLLING	ENSTRUCTURED	ENTEROCOELES
ENLARGEDLY	ENOUNCEMENT	ENSEPULCHRE	ENSWATHEMENT	ENTEROCOELIC
ENLARGEDNESS	ENOUNCEMENTS	ENSEPULCHRED	ENSWATHEMENTS	ENTEROCOELOUS
ENLARGEDNESSES	ENPHYTOTIC	ENSEPULCHRES	ENSWATHING	ENTEROCOELS

E

ENTEROCOLITIS	ENTHRALDOM	ENTOBLASTS	ENTRAINING	ENTROPIUMS
ENTEROCOLITISES	ENTHRALDOMS	ENTODERMAL	ENTRAINMENT	ENTRUSTING
ENTEROGASTRONE	ENTHRALLED	ENTODERMIC	ENTRAINMENTS	ENTRUSTMENT
ENTEROGASTRONES	ENTHRALLER	ENTOILMENT	ENTRAMMELED	ENTRUSTMENTS
ENTEROHEPATITIS	ENTHRALLERS	ENTOILMENTS	ENTRAMMELING	ENTWINEMENT
ENTEROKINASE	ENTHRALLING	ENTOMBMENT	ENTRAMMELLED	ENTWINEMENTS
ENTEROKINASES	ENTHRALLMENT	ENTOMBMENTS	ENTRAMMELLING	ENTWISTING
ENTEROLITH	ENTHRALLMENTS	ENTOMOFAUNA	ENTRAMMELS	ENUCLEATED
ENTEROLITHS	ENTHRALMENT	ENTOMOFAUNAE	ENTRANCEMENT	ENUCLEATES
ENTEROPATHIES	ENTHRALMENTS	ENTOMOFAUNAS	ENTRANCEMENTS	ENUCLEATING
ENTEROPATHY	ENTHRONEMENT	ENTOMOLOGIC	ENTRANCEWAY	ENUCLEATION
ENTEROPNEUST	ENTHRONEMENTS	ENTOMOLOGICAL	ENTRANCEWAYS	ENUCLEATIONS
ENTEROPNEUSTAL	ENTHRONING	ENTOMOLOGICALLY	ENTRANCING	ENUMERABILITIES
ENTEROPNEUSTS	ENTHRONISATION	ENTOMOLOGIES	ENTRANCINGLY	ENUMERABILITY
ENTEROPTOSES	ENTHRONISATIONS	ENTOMOLOGISE	ENTRAPMENT	ENUMERABLE
ENTEROPTOSIS	ENTHRONISE	ENTOMOLOGISED	ENTRAPMENTS	ENUMERATED
ENTEROSTOMAL	ENTHRONISED	ENTOMOLOGISES	ENTRAPPERS	ENUMERATES
ENTEROSTOMIES	ENTHRONISES	ENTOMOLOGISING	ENTRAPPING	ENUMERATING
ENTEROSTOMY	ENTHRONISING	ENTOMOLOGIST	ENTREASURE	ENUMERATION
ENTEROTOMIES	ENTHRONIZATION	ENTOMOLOGISTS	ENTREASURED	ENUMERATIONS
ENTEROTOMY	ENTHRONIZATIONS	ENTOMOLOGIZE	ENTREASURES	ENUMERATIVE
ENTEROTOXIN	ENTHRONIZE	ENTOMOLOGIZED	ENTREASURING	ENUMERATOR
ENTEROTOXINS	ENTHRONIZED	ENTOMOLOGIZES	ENTREATABLE	ENUMERATORS
ENTEROVIRAL	ENTHRONIZES	ENTOMOLOGIZING	ENTREATIES	ENUNCIABLE
ENTEROVIRUS	ENTHRONIZING	ENTOMOLOGY	ENTREATING	ENUNCIATED
ENTEROVIRUSES	ENTHUSIASM	ENTOMOPHAGIES	ENTREATINGLY	ENUNCIATES
ENTERPRISE	ENTHUSIASMS	ENTOMOPHAGOUS	ENTREATIVE	ENUNCIATING
ENTERPRISED	ENTHUSIAST	ENTOMOPHAGY	ENTREATMENT	ENUNCIATION
ENTERPRISER	ENTHUSIASTIC	ENTOMOPHILIES	ENTREATMENTS	ENUNCIATIONS
ENTERPRISERS	ENTHUSIASTICAL	ENTOMOPHILOUS	ENTRECHATS	ENUNCIATIVE
ENTERPRISES	ENTHUSIASTS	ENTOMOPHILY	ENTRECOTES	ENUNCIATIVELY
ENTERPRISING	ENTHYMEMATIC	ENTOMOSTRACAN	ENTREMESSE	ENUNCIATOR
ENTERPRISINGLY	ENTHYMEMATICAL	ENTOMOSTRACANS	ENTREMESSES	ENUNCIATORS
ENTERTAINED	ENTHYMEMES	ENTOMOSTRACOUS	ENTRENCHED	ENUNCIATORY
ENTERTAINER	ENTICEABLE	ENTOPHYTAL	ENTRENCHER	ENUREDNESS
ENTERTAINERS	ENTICEMENT	ENTOPHYTES	ENTRENCHERS	ENUREDNESSES
ENTERTAINING	ENTICEMENTS	ENTOPHYTIC	ENTRENCHES	ENUREMENTS
ENTERTAININGLY	ENTICINGLY	ENTOPHYTOUS	ENTRENCHING	ENURESISES
ENTERTAININGS	ENTICINGNESS	ENTOPLASTRA	ENTRENCHMENT	ENVASSALLED
ENTERTAINMENT	ENTICINGNESSES	ENTOPLASTRAL	ENTRENCHMENTS	ENVASSALLING
ENTERTAINMENTS	ENTIRENESS	ENTOPLASTRON	ENTREPRENEUR	ENVAULTING
ENTERTAINS	ENTIRENESSES	ENTOPROCTS	ENTREPRENEURIAL	ENVEIGLING
ENTERTAKEN	ENTIRETIES	ENTOURAGES	ENTREPRENEURS	ENVELOPERS
ENTERTAKES	ENTITATIVE	ENTRAILING	ENTREPRENEUSE	ENVELOPING
ENTERTAKING	ENTITLEMENT	ENTRAINEMENT	ENTREPRENEUSES	ENVELOPMENT
ENTERTISSUED	ENTITLEMENTS	ENTRAINEMENTS	ENTROPICALLY	ENVELOPMENTS
ENTHALPIES	ENTOBLASTIC	ENTRAINERS	ENTROPIONS	ENVENOMING

ENVENOMISATION
ENVENOMISATIONS
ENVENOMIZATION
ENVENOMIZATIONS
ENVERMEILED
ENVERMEILING
ENVERMEILS
ENVIABLENESS
ENVIABLENESSES
ENVIOUSNESS
ENVIOUSNESSES
ENVIRONICS
ENVIRONING
ENVIRONMENT
ENVIRONMENTAL
ENVIRONMENTALLY
ENVIRONMENTS
ENVISAGEMENT
ENVISAGEMENTS
ENVISAGING
ENVISIONED
ENVISIONING
ENVOYSHIPS
ENWALLOWED
ENWALLOWING
ENWHEELING
ENWRAPMENT
ENWRAPMENTS
ENWRAPPING
ENWRAPPINGS
ENWREATHED
ENWREATHES
ENWREATHING
ENZOOTICALLY
ENZYMATICALLY
ENZYMICALLY
ENZYMOLOGICAL
ENZYMOLOGIES
ENZYMOLOGIST
ENZYMOLOGISTS
ENZYMOLOGY
ENZYMOLYSES
ENZYMOLYSIS
ENZYMOLYTIC
EOHIPPUSES
EOSINOPHIL
EOSINOPHILE

EOSINOPHILES
EOSINOPHILIA
EOSINOPHILIAS
EOSINOPHILIC
EOSINOPHILOUS
EOSINOPHILS
EPAGOMENAL
EPANADIPLOSES
EPANADIPLOSIS
EPANALEPSES
EPANALEPSIS
EPANALEPTIC
EPANAPHORA
EPANAPHORAL
EPANAPHORAS
EPANODOSES
EPANORTHOSES
EPANORTHOSIS
EPANORTHOTIC
EPARCHATES
EPAULEMENT
EPAULEMENTS
EPAULETTED
EPAULETTES
EPEIROGENESES
EPEIROGENESIS
EPEIROGENETIC
EPEIROGENIC
EPEIROGENICALLY
EPEIROGENIES
EPEIROGENY
EPENCEPHALA
EPENCEPHALIC
EPENCEPHALON
EPENCEPHALONS
EPENTHESES
EPENTHESIS
EPENTHETIC
EPEOLATRIES
EPEXEGESES
EPEXEGESIS
EPEXEGETIC
EPEXEGETICAL
EPEXEGETICALLY
EPHEBOPHILE
EPHEBOPHILES
EPHEBOPHILIA

EPHEBOPHILIAS
EPHEDRINES
EPHEMERALITIES
EPHEMERALITY
EPHEMERALLY
EPHEMERALNESS
EPHEMERALNESSES
EPHEMERALS
EPHEMERIDES
EPHEMERIDIAN
EPHEMERIDS
EPHEMERIST
EPHEMERISTS
EPHEMERONS
EPHEMEROPTERAN
EPHEMEROPTERANS
EPHEMEROUS
EPHORALTIES
EPIBLASTIC
EPICALYCES
EPICALYXES
EPICANTHIC
EPICANTHUS
EPICARDIAC
EPICARDIAL
EPICARDIUM
EPICENISMS
EPICENTERS
EPICENTRAL
EPICENTRES
EPICENTRUM
EPICHEIREMA
EPICHEIREMAS
EPICHLOROHYDRIN
EPICONDYLE
EPICONDYLES
EPICONDYLITIS
EPICONDYLITISES
EPICONTINENTAL
EPICRANIUM
EPICRANIUMS
EPICUREANISM
EPICUREANISMS
EPICUREANS
EPICURISED
EPICURISES
EPICURISING

EPICURISMS
EPICURIZED
EPICURIZES
EPICURIZING
EPICUTICLE
EPICUTICLES
EPICUTICULAR
EPICYCLICAL
EPICYCLOID
EPICYCLOIDAL
EPICYCLOIDS
EPIDEICTIC
EPIDEICTICAL
EPIDEMICAL
EPIDEMICALLY
EPIDEMICITIES
EPIDEMICITY
EPIDEMIOLOGIC
EPIDEMIOLOGICAL
EPIDEMIOLOGIES
EPIDEMIOLOGIST
EPIDEMIOLOGISTS
EPIDEMIOLOGY
EPIDENDRONE
EPIDENDRONES
EPIDENDRUM
EPIDENDRUMS
EPIDERMISES
EPIDERMOID
EPIDERMOLYSES
EPIDERMOLYSIS
EPIDIASCOPE
EPIDIASCOPES
EPIDIDYMAL
EPIDIDYMIDES
EPIDIDYMIS
EPIDIDYMITIS
EPIDIDYMITISES
EPIDIORITE
EPIDIORITES
EPIDOSITES
EPIDOTISATION
EPIDOTISATIONS
EPIDOTISED
EPIDOTIZATION
EPIDOTIZATIONS
EPIDOTIZED

EPIGASTRIA
EPIGASTRIAL
EPIGASTRIC
EPIGASTRIUM
EPIGENESES
EPIGENESIS
EPIGENESIST
EPIGENESISTS
EPIGENETIC
EPIGENETICALLY
EPIGENETICIST
EPIGENETICISTS
EPIGENETICS
EPIGENISTS
EPIGLOTTAL
EPIGLOTTIC
EPIGLOTTIDES
EPIGLOTTIS
EPIGLOTTISES
EPIGNATHOUS
EPIGONISMS
EPIGRAMMATIC
EPIGRAMMATICAL
EPIGRAMMATISE
EPIGRAMMATISED
EPIGRAMMATISER
EPIGRAMMATISERS
EPIGRAMMATISES
EPIGRAMMATISING
EPIGRAMMATISM
EPIGRAMMATISMS
EPIGRAMMATIST
EPIGRAMMATISTS
EPIGRAMMATIZE
EPIGRAMMATIZED
EPIGRAMMATIZER
EPIGRAMMATIZERS
EPIGRAMMATIZES
EPIGRAMMATIZING
EPIGRAPHED
EPIGRAPHER
EPIGRAPHERS
EPIGRAPHIC
EPIGRAPHICAL
EPIGRAPHICALLY
EPIGRAPHIES
EPIGRAPHING

E

EPIGRAPHIST	EPINEPHRINS	EPISCOPANTS	EPISTOLISES	EPITHELIZE
EPIGRAPHISTS	EPINEURIAL	EPISCOPATE	EPISTOLISING	EPITHELIZED
EPILATIONS	EPINEURIUM	EPISCOPATED	EPISTOLIST	EPITHELIZES
EPILEPSIES	EPINEURIUMS	EPISCOPATES	EPISTOLISTS	EPITHELIZING
EPILEPTICAL	EPINICIONS	EPISCOPATING	EPISTOLIZE	EPITHEMATA
EPILEPTICALLY	EPINIKIANS	EPISCOPIES	EPISTOLIZED	EPITHERMAL
EPILEPTICS	EPINIKIONS	EPISCOPISE	EPISTOLIZES	EPITHETICAL
EPILEPTIFORM	EPIPELAGIC	EPISCOPISED	EPISTOLIZING	EPITHETICALLY
EPILEPTOGENIC	EPIPETALOUS	EPISCOPISES	EPISTOLOGRAPHY	EPITHETING
EPILEPTOID	EPIPHANIES	EPISCOPISING	EPISTROPHE	EPITHETONS
EPILIMNION	EPIPHANOUS	EPISCOPIZE	EPISTROPHES	EPITHYMETIC
EPILIMNIONS	EPIPHENOMENA	EPISCOPIZED	EPITAPHERS	EPITOMICAL
EPILOBIUMS	EPIPHENOMENAL	EPISCOPIZES	EPITAPHIAL	EPITOMISATION
EPILOGISED	EPIPHENOMENALLY	EPISCOPIZING	EPITAPHIAN	EPITOMISATIONS
EPILOGISES	EPIPHENOMENON	EPISEMATIC	EPITAPHING	EPITOMISED
EPILOGISING	EPIPHONEMA	EPISEPALOUS	EPITAPHIST	EPITOMISER
EPILOGISTIC	EPIPHONEMAS	EPISIOTOMIES	EPITAPHISTS	EPITOMISERS
EPILOGISTS	EPIPHRAGMS	EPISIOTOMY	EPITAXIALLY	EPITOMISES
EPILOGIZED	EPIPHYLLOUS	EPISODICAL	EPITHALAMIA	EPITOMISING
EPILOGIZES	EPIPHYSEAL	EPISODICALLY	EPITHALAMIC	EPITOMISTS
EPILOGIZING	EPIPHYSIAL	EPISOMALLY	EPITHALAMION	EPITOMIZATION
EPILOGUING	EPIPHYTICAL	EPISPASTIC	EPITHALAMIUM	EPITOMIZATIONS
EPILOGUISE	EPIPHYTICALLY	EPISPASTICS	EPITHALAMIUMS	EPITOMIZED
EPILOGUISED	EPIPHYTISM	EPISTASIES	EPITHELIAL	EPITOMIZER
EPILOGUISES	EPIPHYTISMS	EPISTAXISES	EPITHELIALISE	EPITOMIZERS
EPILOGUISING	EPIPHYTOLOGIES	EPISTEMICALLY	EPITHELIALISED	EPITOMIZES
EPILOGUIZE	EPIPHYTOLOGY	EPISTEMICS	EPITHELIALISES	EPITOMIZING
EPILOGUIZED	EPIPHYTOTIC	EPISTEMOLOGICAL	EPITHELIALISING	EPITRACHELION
EPILOGUIZES	EPIPHYTOTICS	EPISTEMOLOGIES	EPITHELIALIZE	EPITRACHELIONS
EPILOGUIZING	EPIPLASTRA	EPISTEMOLOGIST	EPITHELIALIZED	EPITROCHOID
EPIMELETIC	EPIPLASTRAL	EPISTEMOLOGISTS	EPITHELIALIZES	EPITROCHOIDS
EPIMERASES	EPIPLASTRON	EPISTEMOLOGY	EPITHELIALIZING	EPIZEUXISES
EPIMERISED	EPIPOLISMS	EPISTERNAL	EPITHELIOID	EPIZOOTICALLY
EPIMERISES	EPIROGENETIC	EPISTERNUM	EPITHELIOMA	EPIZOOTICS
EPIMERISING	EPIROGENIC	EPISTERNUMS	EPITHELIOMAS	EPIZOOTIES
EPIMERISMS	EPIROGENIES	EPISTILBITE	EPITHELIOMATA	EPIZOOTIOLOGIC
EPIMERIZED	EPIRRHEMAS	EPISTILBITES	EPITHELIOMATOUS	EPIZOOTIOLOGIES
EPIMERIZES	EPIRRHEMATIC	EPISTOLARIAN	EPITHELISATION	EPIZOOTIOLOGY
EPIMERIZING	EPISCOPACIES	EPISTOLARIANS	EPITHELISATIONS	EPONYCHIUM
EPIMORPHIC	EPISCOPACY	EPISTOLARIES	EPITHELISE	EPONYCHIUMS
EPIMORPHOSES	EPISCOPALIAN	EPISTOLARY	EPITHELISED	EPONYMOUSLY
EPIMORPHOSIS	EPISCOPALIANISM	EPISTOLATORY	EPITHELISES	EPOXIDATION
EPINASTICALLY	EPISCOPALIANS	EPISTOLERS	EPITHELISING	EPOXIDATIONS
EPINASTIES	EPISCOPALISM	EPISTOLETS	EPITHELIUM	EPOXIDISED
EPINEPHRIN	EPISCOPALISMS	EPISTOLICAL	EPITHELIUMS	EPOXIDISES
EPINEPHRINE	EPISCOPALLY	EPISTOLISE	EPITHELIZATION	EPOXIDISING
EPINEPHRINES	EPISCOPANT	EPISTOLISED	EPITHELIZATIONS	EPOXIDIZED

EPOXIDIZES
EPOXIDIZING
EPROUVETTE
EPROUVETTES
EPULATIONS
EPURATIONS
EQUABILITIES
EQUABILITY
EQUABLENESS
EQUABLENESSES
EQUALISATION
EQUALISATIONS
EQUALISERS
EQUALISING
EQUALITARIAN
EQUALITARIANISM
EQUALITARIANS
EQUALITIES
EQUALIZATION
EQUALIZATIONS
EQUALIZERS
EQUALIZING
EQUALNESSES
EQUANIMITIES
EQUANIMITY
EQUANIMOUS
EQUANIMOUSLY
EQUATABILITIES
EQUATABILITY
EQUATIONAL
EQUATIONALLY
EQUATORIAL
EQUATORIALLY
EQUATORIALS
EQUATORWARD
EQUESTRIAN
EQUESTRIANISM
EQUESTRIANISMS
EQUESTRIANS
EQUESTRIENNE
EQUESTRIENNES
EQUIANGULAR
EQUIANGULARITY
EQUIBALANCE
EQUIBALANCED
EQUIBALANCES
EQUIBALANCING

EQUICALORIC
EQUIDIFFERENT
EQUIDISTANCE
EQUIDISTANCES
EQUIDISTANT
EQUIDISTANTLY
EQUIFINALLY
EQUILATERAL
EQUILATERALLY
EQUILATERALS
EQUILIBRANT
EQUILIBRANTS
EQUILIBRATE
EQUILIBRATED
EQUILIBRATES
EQUILIBRATING
EQUILIBRATION
EQUILIBRATIONS
EQUILIBRATOR
EQUILIBRATORS
EQUILIBRATORY
EQUILIBRIA
EQUILIBRIST
EQUILIBRISTIC
EQUILIBRISTS
EQUILIBRITIES
EQUILIBRITY
EQUILIBRIUM
EQUILIBRIUMS
EQUIMOLECULAR
EQUIMULTIPLE
EQUIMULTIPLES
EQUINITIES
EQUINOCTIAL
EQUINOCTIALLY
EQUINOCTIALS
EQUINUMEROUS
EQUIPAGING
EQUIPARATE
EQUIPARATED
EQUIPARATES
EQUIPARATING
EQUIPARATION
EQUIPARATIONS
EQUIPARTITION
EQUIPARTITIONS
EQUIPMENTS

EQUIPOISED
EQUIPOISES
EQUIPOISING
EQUIPOLLENCE
EQUIPOLLENCES
EQUIPOLLENCIES
EQUIPOLLENCY
EQUIPOLLENT
EQUIPOLLENTLY
EQUIPOLLENTS
EQUIPONDERANCE
EQUIPONDERANCES
EQUIPONDERANCY
EQUIPONDERANT
EQUIPONDERATE
EQUIPONDERATED
EQUIPONDERATES
EQUIPONDERATING
EQUIPOTENT
EQUIPOTENTIAL
EQUIPOTENTIALS
EQUIPROBABILITY
EQUIPROBABLE
EQUISETACEOUS
EQUISETIFORM
EQUISETUMS
EQUITABILITIES
EQUITABILITY
EQUITABLENESS
EQUITABLENESSES
EQUITATION
EQUITATIONS
EQUIVALENCE
EQUIVALENCES
EQUIVALENCIES
EQUIVALENCY
EQUIVALENT
EQUIVALENTLY
EQUIVALENTS
EQUIVOCALITIES
EQUIVOCALITY
EQUIVOCALLY
EQUIVOCALNESS
EQUIVOCALNESSES
EQUIVOCATE
EQUIVOCATED
EQUIVOCATES

EQUIVOCATING
EQUIVOCATINGLY
EQUIVOCATION
EQUIVOCATIONS
EQUIVOCATOR
EQUIVOCATORS
EQUIVOCATORY
EQUIVOQUES
ERADIATING
ERADIATION
ERADIATIONS
ERADICABLE
ERADICABLY
ERADICANTS
ERADICATED
ERADICATES
ERADICATING
ERADICATION
ERADICATIONS
ERADICATIVE
ERADICATOR
ERADICATORS
ERASABILITIES
ERASABILITY
ERASEMENTS
ERECTILITIES
ERECTILITY
ERECTNESSES
EREMACAUSES
EREMACAUSIS
EREMITICAL
EREMITISMS
EREMURUSES
ERETHISMIC
ERETHISTIC
ERGASTOPLASM
ERGASTOPLASMIC
ERGASTOPLASMS
ERGATANDROMORPH
ERGATANERS
ERGATIVITIES
ERGATIVITY
ERGATOCRACIES
ERGATOCRACY
ERGATOGYNE
ERGATOGYNES
ERGATOMORPH

ERGATOMORPHIC
ERGATOMORPHS
ERGODICITIES
ERGODICITY
ERGOGRAPHS
ERGOMANIAC
ERGOMANIACS
ERGOMANIAS
ERGOMETERS
ERGOMETRIC
ERGOMETRIES
ERGONOMICALLY
ERGONOMICS
ERGONOMIST
ERGONOMISTS
ERGONOVINE
ERGONOVINES
ERGOPHOBIA
ERGOPHOBIAS
ERGOSTEROL
ERGOSTEROLS
ERGOTAMINE
ERGOTAMINES
ERGOTISING
ERGOTIZING
ERICACEOUS
ERINACEOUS
ERIOMETERS
ERIOPHOROUS
ERIOPHORUM
ERIOPHORUMS
ERIOPHYIDS
ERIOSTEMON
ERIOSTEMONS
ERISTICALLY
ERODIBILITIES
ERODIBILITY
EROGENEITIES
EROGENEITY
EROSIONALLY
EROSIVENESS
EROSIVENESSES
EROSIVITIES
EROTICALLY
EROTICISATION
EROTICISATIONS
EROTICISED

EROTICISES	ERUPTIVELY	ERYTHROPSIA	ESCHEATING	ESPIONAGES
EROTICISING	ERUPTIVENESS	ERYTHROPSIAS	ESCHEATMENT	ESPLANADES
EROTICISMS	ERUPTIVENESSES	ERYTHROSIN	ESCHEATMENTS	ESPRESSIVO
EROTICISTS	ERUPTIVITIES	ERYTHROSINE	ESCHEATORS	ESQUIRESSES
EROTICIZATION	ERUPTIVITY	ERYTHROSINES	ESCHSCHOLTZIA	ESSAYETTES
EROTICIZATIONS	ERVALENTAS	ERYTHROSINS	ESCHSCHOLTZIAS	ESSAYISTIC
EROTICIZED	ERYSIPELAS	ESCABECHES	ESCHSCHOLZIA	ESSENTIALISE
EROTICIZES	ERYSIPELASES	ESCADRILLE	ESCHSCHOLZIAS	ESSENTIALISED
EROTICIZING	ERYSIPELATOUS	ESCADRILLES	ESCLANDRES	ESSENTIALISES
EROTISATION	ERYSIPELOID	ESCALADERS	ESCOPETTES	ESSENTIALISING
EROTISATIONS	ERYSIPELOIDS	ESCALADING	ESCORTAGES	ESSENTIALISM
EROTIZATION	ERYTHEMATIC	ESCALADOES	ESCRIBANOS	ESSENTIALISMS
EROTIZATIONS	ERYTHEMATOUS	ESCALATING	ESCRITOIRE	ESSENTIALIST
EROTOGENIC	ERYTHORBATE	ESCALATION	ESCRITOIRES	ESSENTIALISTS
EROTOGENOUS	ERYTHORBATES	ESCALATIONS	ESCRITORIAL	ESSENTIALITIES
EROTOLOGICAL	ERYTHRAEMIA	ESCALATORS	ESCUTCHEON	ESSENTIALITY
EROTOLOGIES	ERYTHRAEMIAS	ESCALATORY	ESCUTCHEONED	ESSENTIALIZE
EROTOLOGIST	ERYTHREMIA	ESCALLONIA	ESCUTCHEONS	ESSENTIALIZED
EROTOLOGISTS	ERYTHREMIAS	ESCALLONIAS	ESEMPLASIES	ESSENTIALIZES
EROTOMANIA	ERYTHRINAS	ESCALLOPED	ESEMPLASTIC	ESSENTIALIZING
EROTOMANIAC	ERYTHRISMAL	ESCALLOPING	ESEMPLASTICALLY	ESSENTIALLY
EROTOMANIACS	ERYTHRISMS	ESCALOPING	ESOPHAGEAL	ESSENTIALNESS
EROTOMANIAS	ERYTHRISTIC	ESCAMOTAGE	ESOPHAGITIS	ESSENTIALNESSES
EROTOPHOBIA	ERYTHRITES	ESCAMOTAGES	ESOPHAGITISES	ESSENTIALS
EROTOPHOBIAS	ERYTHRITIC	ESCAPADOES	ESOPHAGOSCOPE	ESTABLISHABLE
ERRANTRIES	ERYTHRITOL	ESCAPELESS	ESOPHAGOSCOPES	ESTABLISHED
ERRATICALLY	ERYTHRITOLS	ESCAPEMENT	ESOPHAGOSCOPIES	ESTABLISHER
ERRATICISM	ERYTHROBLAST	ESCAPEMENTS	ESOPHAGOSCOPY	ESTABLISHERS
ERRATICISMS	ERYTHROBLASTIC	ESCAPOLOGIES	ESOPHAGUSES	ESTABLISHES
ERRONEOUSLY	ERYTHROBLASTS	ESCAPOLOGIST	ESOTERICALLY	ESTABLISHING
ERRONEOUSNESS	ERYTHROCYTE	ESCAPOLOGISTS	ESOTERICISM	ESTABLISHMENT
ERRONEOUSNESSES	ERYTHROCYTES	ESCAPOLOGY	ESOTERICISMS	ESTABLISHMENTS
ERUBESCENCE	ERYTHROCYTIC	ESCARMOUCHE	ESOTERICIST	ESTAFETTES
ERUBESCENCES	ERYTHROMELALGIA	ESCARMOUCHES	ESOTERICISTS	ESTAMINETS
ERUBESCENCIES	ERYTHROMYCIN	ESCARPMENT	ESOTERISMS	ESTANCIERO
ERUBESCENCY	ERYTHROMYCINS	ESCARPMENTS	ESOTROPIAS	ESTANCIEROS
ERUBESCENT	ERYTHRONIUM	ESCHAROTIC	ESPADRILLE	ESTATESMAN
ERUBESCITE	ERYTHRONIUMS	ESCHAROTICS	ESPADRILLES	ESTATESMEN
ERUBESCITES	ERYTHROPENIA	ESCHATOLOGIC	ESPAGNOLES	ESTERIFICATION
ERUCTATING	ERYTHROPENIAS	ESCHATOLOGICAL	ESPAGNOLETTE	ESTERIFICATIONS
ERUCTATION	ERYTHROPHOBIA	ESCHATOLOGIES	ESPAGNOLETTES	ESTERIFIED
ERUCTATIONS	ERYTHROPHOBIAS	ESCHATOLOGIST	ESPALIERED	ESTERIFIES
ERUCTATIVE	ERYTHROPOIESES	ESCHATOLOGISTS	ESPALIERING	ESTERIFYING
ERUDITENESS	ERYTHROPOIESIS	ESCHATOLOGY	ESPECIALLY	ESTHESIOGEN
ERUDITENESSES	ERYTHROPOIETIC	ESCHEATABLE	ESPERANCES	ESTHESIOGENS
ERUDITIONS	ERYTHROPOIETIN	ESCHEATAGE	ESPIEGLERIE	ESTHESISES
ERUPTIONAL	ERYTHROPOIETINS	ESCHEATAGES	ESPIEGLERIES	ESTHETICAL

ESTHETICALLY	ETERNALISED	ETHERIFICATIONS	ETHNOGRAPHIC	ETIQUETTES
ESTHETICIAN	ETERNALISES	ETHERIFIED	ETHNOGRAPHICA	ETONOGESTREL
ESTHETICIANS	ETERNALISING	ETHERIFIES	ETHNOGRAPHICAL	ETONOGESTRELS
ESTHETICISM	ETERNALIST	ETHERIFYING	ETHNOGRAPHIES	ETOURDERIE
ESTHETICISMS	ETERNALISTS	ETHERISATION	ETHNOGRAPHY	ETOURDERIES
ESTIMABLENESS	ETERNALITIES	ETHERISATIONS	ETHNOHISTORIAN	ETRANGERES
ESTIMABLENESSES	ETERNALITY	ETHERISERS	ETHNOHISTORIANS	ETYMOLOGICA
ESTIMATING	ETERNALIZATION	ETHERISING	ETHNOHISTORIC	ETYMOLOGICAL
ESTIMATION	ETERNALIZATIONS	ETHERIZATION	ETHNOHISTORICAL	ETYMOLOGICALLY
ESTIMATIONS	ETERNALIZE	ETHERIZATIONS	ETHNOHISTORIES	ETYMOLOGICON
ESTIMATIVE	ETERNALIZED	ETHERIZERS	ETHNOHISTORY	ETYMOLOGICUM
ESTIMATORS	ETERNALIZES	ETHERIZING	ETHNOLINGUIST	ETYMOLOGIES
ESTIPULATE	ETERNALIZING	ETHEROMANIA	ETHNOLINGUISTIC	ETYMOLOGISE
ESTIVATING	ETERNALNESS	ETHEROMANIAC	ETHNOLINGUISTS	ETYMOLOGISED
ESTIVATION	ETERNALNESSES	ETHEROMANIACS	ETHNOLOGIC	ETYMOLOGISES
ESTIVATIONS	ETERNISATION	ETHEROMANIAS	ETHNOLOGICAL	ETYMOLOGISING
ESTIVATORS	ETERNISATIONS	ETHICALITIES	ETHNOLOGICALLY	ETYMOLOGIST
ESTOPPAGES	ETERNISING	ETHICALITY	ETHNOLOGIES	ETYMOLOGISTS
ESTRADIOLS	ETERNITIES	ETHICALNESS	ETHNOLOGIST	ETYMOLOGIZE
ESTRAMAZONE	ETERNIZATION	ETHICALNESSES	ETHNOLOGISTS	ETYMOLOGIZED
ESTRAMAZONES	ETERNIZATIONS	ETHICISING	ETHNOMEDICINE	ETYMOLOGIZES
ESTRANGEDNESS	ETERNIZING	ETHICIZING	ETHNOMEDICINES	ETYMOLOGIZING
ESTRANGEDNESSES	ETHAMBUTOL	ETHIONAMIDE	ETHNOMUSICOLOGY	EUBACTERIA
ESTRANGELO	ETHAMBUTOLS	ETHIONAMIDES	ETHNOSCIENCE	EUBACTERIUM
ESTRANGELOS	ETHANEDIOIC	ETHIONINES	ETHNOSCIENCES	EUCALYPTOL
ESTRANGEMENT	ETHANEDIOL	ETHNARCHIES	ETHOLOGICAL	EUCALYPTOLE
ESTRANGEMENTS	ETHANEDIOLS	ETHNICALLY	ETHOLOGICALLY	EUCALYPTOLES
ESTRANGERS	ETHANOATES	ETHNICISMS	ETHOLOGIES	EUCALYPTOLS
ESTRANGHELO	ETHANOLAMINE	ETHNICITIES	ETHOLOGIST	EUCALYPTUS
ESTRANGHELOS	ETHANOLAMINES	ETHNOBIOLOGIES	ETHOLOGISTS	EUCALYPTUSES
ESTRANGING	ETHEOSTOMINE	ETHNOBIOLOGY	ETHOXYETHANE	EUCARYOTES
ESTRAPADES	ETHEREALISATION	ETHNOBOTANICAL	ETHOXYETHANES	EUCARYOTIC
ESTREATING	ETHEREALISE	ETHNOBOTANIES	ETHYLAMINE	EUCHARISES
ESTREPEMENT	ETHEREALISED	ETHNOBOTANIST	ETHYLAMINES	EUCHARISTIC
ESTREPEMENTS	ETHEREALISES	ETHNOBOTANISTS	ETHYLATING	EUCHLORINE
ESTRIBUTOR	ETHEREALISING	ETHNOBOTANY	ETHYLATION	EUCHLORINES
ESTRIBUTORS	ETHEREALITIES	ETHNOCENTRIC	ETHYLATIONS	EUCHLORINS
ESTRILDIDS	ETHEREALITY	ETHNOCENTRICITY	ETHYLBENZENE	EUCHOLOGIA
ESTROGENIC	ETHEREALIZATION	ETHNOCENTRISM	ETHYLBENZENES	EUCHOLOGIES
ESTROGENICALLY	ETHEREALIZE	ETHNOCENTRISMS	ETIOLATING	EUCHOLOGION
ESURIENCES	ETHEREALIZED	ETHNOCIDES	ETIOLATION	EUCHROMATIC
ESURIENCIES	ETHEREALIZES	ETHNOGENIC	ETIOLATIONS	EUCHROMATIN
ESURIENTLY	ETHEREALIZING	ETHNOGENIES	ETIOLOGICAL	EUCHROMATINS
ETEPIMELETIC	ETHEREALLY	ETHNOGENIST	ETIOLOGICALLY	EUCRYPHIAS
ETERNALISATION	ETHEREALNESS	ETHNOGENISTS	ETIOLOGIES	EUDAEMONIA
ETERNALISATIONS	ETHEREALNESSES	ETHNOGRAPHER	ETIOLOGIST	EUDAEMONIAS
ETERNALISE	ETHERIFICATION	ETHNOGRAPHERS	ETIOLOGISTS	EUDAEMONIC

EUDAEMONICS	EUHEMERISTIC	EUPHEMIZER	EURODEPOSITS	EUTHANATIZES
EUDAEMONIES	EUHEMERISTS	EUPHEMIZERS	EURODOLLAR	EUTHANATIZING
EUDAEMONISM	EUHEMERIZE	EUPHEMIZES	EURODOLLARS	EUTHANAZED
EUDAEMONISMS	EUHEMERIZED	EUPHEMIZING	EUROMARKET	EUTHANAZES
EUDAEMONIST	EUHEMERIZES	EUPHONICAL	EUROMARKETS	EUTHANAZING
EUDAEMONISTIC	EUHEMERIZING	EUPHONICALLY	EUROPHILES	EUTHANISED
EUDAEMONISTICAL	EUKARYOTES	EUPHONIOUS	EUROPHILIA	EUTHANISES
EUDAEMONISTS	EUKARYOTIC	EUPHONIOUSLY	EUROPHILIAS	EUTHANISING
EUDAIMONISM	EULOGISERS	EUPHONIOUSNESS	EUROPHOBIA	EUTHANIZED
EUDAIMONISMS	EULOGISING	EUPHONISED	EUROPHOBIAS	EUTHANIZES
EUDEMONIAS	EULOGISTIC	EUPHONISES	EUROPHOBIC	EUTHANIZING
EUDEMONICS	EULOGISTICAL	EUPHONISING	EUROTERMINAL	EUTHENISTS
EUDEMONISM	EULOGISTICALLY	EUPHONISMS	EUROTERMINALS	EUTHERIANS
EUDEMONISMS	EULOGIZERS	EUPHONIUMS	EURYBATHIC	EUTHYROIDS
EUDEMONIST	EULOGIZING	EUPHONIZED	EURYHALINE	EUTRAPELIA
EUDEMONISTIC	EUMELANINS	EUPHONIZES	EURYOECIOUS	EUTRAPELIAS
EUDEMONISTICAL	EUNUCHISED	EUPHONIZING	EURYPTERID	EUTRAPELIES
EUDEMONISTS	EUNUCHISES	EUPHORBIACEOUS	EURYPTERIDS	EUTROPHICATION
EUDIALYTES	EUNUCHISING	EUPHORBIAS	EURYPTEROID	EUTROPHICATIONS
EUDICOTYLEDON	EUNUCHISMS	EUPHORBIUM	EURYPTEROIDS	EUTROPHIES
EUDICOTYLEDONS	EUNUCHIZED	EUPHORBIUMS	EURYTHERMAL	EVACUATING
EUDIOMETER	EUNUCHIZES	EUPHORIANT	EURYTHERMIC	EVACUATION
EUDIOMETERS	EUNUCHIZING	EUPHORIANTS	EURYTHERMOUS	EVACUATIONS
EUDIOMETRIC	EUNUCHOIDISM	EUPHORICALLY	EURYTHERMS	EVACUATIVE
EUDIOMETRICAL	EUNUCHOIDISMS	EUPHRASIAS	EURYTHMICAL	EVACUATIVES
EUDIOMETRICALLY	EUNUCHOIDS	EUPHRASIES	EURYTHMICS	EVACUATORS
EUDIOMETRIES	EUONYMUSES	EUPHUISING	EURYTHMIES	EVAGATIONS
EUDIOMETRY	EUPATORIUM	EUPHUISTIC	EURYTHMIST	EVAGINATED
EUGENECIST	EUPATORIUMS	EUPHUISTICAL	EURYTHMISTS	EVAGINATES
EUGENECISTS	EUPATRIDAE	EUPHUISTICALLY	EUSPORANGIATE	EVAGINATING
EUGENICALLY	EUPEPTICITIES	EUPHUIZING	EUSTATICALLY	EVAGINATION
EUGENICIST	EUPEPTICITY	EUPLASTICS	EUTECTOIDS	EVAGINATIONS
EUGENICISTS	EUPHAUSIACEAN	EUPLOIDIES	EUTHANASED	EVALUATING
EUGEOSYNCLINAL	EUPHAUSIACEANS	EURHYTHMIC	EUTHANASES	EVALUATION
EUGEOSYNCLINE	EUPHAUSIDS	EURHYTHMICAL	EUTHANASIA	EVALUATIONS
EUGEOSYNCLINES	EUPHAUSIID	EURHYTHMICS	EUTHANASIAS	EVALUATIVE
EUGLENOIDS	EUPHAUSIIDS	EURHYTHMIES	EUTHANASIAST	EVALUATORS
EUGLOBULIN	EUPHEMISED	EURHYTHMIST	EUTHANASIASTS	EVANESCENCE
EUGLOBULINS	EUPHEMISER	EURHYTHMISTS	EUTHANASIC	EVANESCENCES
EUHARMONIC	EUPHEMISERS	EUROCHEQUE	EUTHANASIES	EVANESCENT
EUHEMERISE	EUPHEMISES	EUROCHEQUES	EUTHANASING	EVANESCENTLY
EUHEMERISED	EUPHEMISING	EUROCREDIT	EUTHANATISE	EVANESCING
EUHEMERISES	EUPHEMISMS	EUROCREDITS	EUTHANATISED	EVANGELARIUM
EUHEMERISING	EUPHEMISTIC	EUROCREEPS	EUTHANATISES	EVANGELARIUMS
EUHEMERISM	EUPHEMISTICALLY	EUROCURRENCIES	EUTHANATISING	EVANGELIAR
EUHEMERISMS	EUPHEMISTS	EUROCURRENCY	EUTHANATIZE	EVANGELIARIES
EUHEMERIST	EUPHEMIZED	EURODEPOSIT	EUTHANATIZED	EVANGELIARION

EVANGELIARIONS

EVANGELIARIONS EVAPORATING EVERDURING EVOLUTIONISTS EXAMINATIONAL
EVANGELIARIUM EVAPORATION EVERGLADES EVOLUTIONS EXAMINATIONS
EVANGELIARIUMS EVAPORATIONS EVERGREENS EVOLVEMENT EXAMINATOR
EVANGELIARS EVAPORATIVE EVERLASTING EVOLVEMENTS EXAMINATORS
EVANGELIARY EVAPORATOR EVERLASTINGLY EVONYMUSES EXAMINERSHIP
EVANGELICAL EVAPORATORS EVERLASTINGNESS EVULGATING EXAMINERSHIPS
EVANGELICALISM EVAPORIMETER EVERLASTINGS EXACERBATE EXANIMATION
EVANGELICALISMS EVAPORIMETERS EVERYDAYNESS EXACERBATED EXANIMATIONS
EVANGELICALLY EVAPORITES EVERYDAYNESSES EXACERBATES EXANTHEMAS
EVANGELICALNESS EVAPORITIC EVERYPLACE EXACERBATING EXANTHEMATA
EVANGELICALS EVAPOROGRAPH EVERYTHING EXACERBATION EXANTHEMATIC
EVANGELICISM EVAPOROGRAPHS EVERYWHENCE EXACERBATIONS EXANTHEMATOUS
EVANGELICISMS EVAPOROMETER EVERYWHERE EXACERBESCENCE EXARATIONS
EVANGELIES EVAPOROMETERS EVERYWHITHER EXACERBESCENCES EXARCHATES
EVANGELISATION EVASIVENESS EVERYWOMAN EXACTINGLY EXARCHISTS
EVANGELISATIONS EVASIVENESSES EVERYWOMEN EXACTINGNESS EXASPERATE
EVANGELISE EVECTIONAL EVIDENCING EXACTINGNESSES EXASPERATED
EVANGELISED EVENEMENTS EVIDENTIAL EXACTITUDE EXASPERATEDLY
EVANGELISER EVENHANDED EVIDENTIALLY EXACTITUDES EXASPERATER
EVANGELISERS EVENHANDEDLY EVIDENTIARY EXACTMENTS EXASPERATERS
EVANGELISES EVENHANDEDNESS EVILDOINGS EXACTNESSES EXASPERATES
EVANGELISING EVENNESSES EVILNESSES EXACTRESSES EXASPERATING
EVANGELISM EVENTFULLY EVINCEMENT EXAGGERATE EXASPERATINGLY
EVANGELISMS EVENTFULNESS EVINCEMENTS EXAGGERATED EXASPERATION
EVANGELIST EVENTFULNESSES EVISCERATE EXAGGERATEDLY EXASPERATIONS
EVANGELISTARIES EVENTRATED EVISCERATED EXAGGERATEDNESS EXASPERATIVE
EVANGELISTARION EVENTRATES EVISCERATES EXAGGERATES EXASPERATOR
EVANGELISTARY EVENTRATING EVISCERATING EXAGGERATING EXASPERATORS
EVANGELISTIC EVENTRATION EVISCERATION EXAGGERATINGLY EXCAMBIONS
EVANGELISTS EVENTRATIONS EVISCERATIONS EXAGGERATION EXCAMBIUMS
EVANGELIZATION EVENTUALISE EVISCERATOR EXAGGERATIONS EXCARNATED
EVANGELIZATIONS EVENTUALISED EVISCERATORS EXAGGERATIVE EXCARNATES
EVANGELIZE EVENTUALISES EVITATIONS EXAGGERATOR EXCARNATING
EVANGELIZED EVENTUALISING EVITERNALLY EXAGGERATORS EXCARNATION
EVANGELIZER EVENTUALITIES EVITERNITIES EXAGGERATORY EXCARNATIONS
EVANGELIZERS EVENTUALITY EVITERNITY EXAHERTZES EXCAVATING
EVANGELIZES EVENTUALIZE EVOCATIONS EXALBUMINOUS EXCAVATION
EVANGELIZING EVENTUALIZED EVOCATIVELY EXALTATION EXCAVATIONAL
EVANISHING EVENTUALIZES EVOCATIVENESS EXALTATIONS EXCAVATIONS
EVANISHMENT EVENTUALIZING EVOCATIVENESSES EXALTEDNESS EXCAVATORS
EVANISHMENTS EVENTUALLY EVOLUTIONAL EXALTEDNESSES EXCEEDABLE
EVANITIONS EVENTUATED EVOLUTIONARILY EXAMINABILITIES EXCEEDINGLY
EVAPORABILITIES EVENTUATES EVOLUTIONARY EXAMINABILITY EXCELLENCE
EVAPORABILITY EVENTUATING EVOLUTIONISM EXAMINABLE EXCELLENCES
EVAPORABLE EVENTUATION EVOLUTIONISMS EXAMINANTS EXCELLENCIES
EVAPORATED EVENTUATIONS EVOLUTIONIST EXAMINATES EXCELLENCY
EVAPORATES EVERBLOOMING EVOLUTIONISTIC EXAMINATION EXCELLENTLY

EXCELSIORS	EXCITEMENTS	EXCOMMUNICATES	EXCULPATIONS	EXECUTRICES
EXCENTRICS	EXCITINGLY	EXCOMMUNICATING	EXCULPATORY	EXECUTRIES
EXCEPTANTS	EXCLAIMERS	EXCOMMUNICATION	EXCURSIONED	EXECUTRIXES
EXCEPTIONABLE	EXCLAIMING	EXCOMMUNICATIVE	EXCURSIONING	EXEGETICAL
EXCEPTIONABLY	EXCLAMATION	EXCOMMUNICATOR	EXCURSIONISE	EXEGETICALLY
EXCEPTIONAL	EXCLAMATIONAL	EXCOMMUNICATORS	EXCURSIONISED	EXEGETISTS
EXCEPTIONALISM	EXCLAMATIONS	EXCOMMUNICATORY	EXCURSIONISES	EXEMPLARILY
EXCEPTIONALISMS	EXCLAMATIVE	EXCOMMUNION	EXCURSIONISING	EXEMPLARINESS
EXCEPTIONALITY	EXCLAMATIVES	EXCOMMUNIONS	EXCURSIONIST	EXEMPLARINESSES
EXCEPTIONALLY	EXCLAMATORILY	EXCORIATED	EXCURSIONISTS	EXEMPLARITIES
EXCEPTIONALNESS	EXCLAMATORY	EXCORIATES	EXCURSIONIZE	EXEMPLARITY
EXCEPTIONALS	EXCLAUSTRATION	EXCORIATING	EXCURSIONIZED	EXEMPLIFIABLE
EXCEPTIONS	EXCLAUSTRATIONS	EXCORIATION	EXCURSIONIZES	EXEMPLIFICATION
EXCEPTIOUS	EXCLOSURES	EXCORIATIONS	EXCURSIONIZING	EXEMPLIFICATIVE
EXCEPTLESS	EXCLUDABILITIES	EXCORTICATE	EXCURSIONS	EXEMPLIFIED
EXCERPTERS	EXCLUDABILITY	EXCORTICATED	EXCURSIVELY	EXEMPLIFIER
EXCERPTIBLE	EXCLUDABLE	EXCORTICATES	EXCURSIVENESS	EXEMPLIFIERS
EXCERPTING	EXCLUDIBLE	EXCORTICATING	EXCURSIVENESSES	EXEMPLIFIES
EXCERPTINGS	EXCLUSIONARY	EXCORTICATION	EXCURSUSES	EXEMPLIFYING
EXCERPTION	EXCLUSIONISM	EXCORTICATIONS	EXCUSABLENESS	EXEMPTIONS
EXCERPTIONS	EXCLUSIONISMS	EXCREMENTA	EXCUSABLENESSES	EXENTERATE
EXCERPTORS	EXCLUSIONIST	EXCREMENTAL	EXCUSATORY	EXENTERATED
EXCESSIVELY	EXCLUSIONISTS	EXCREMENTITIAL	EXECRABLENESS	EXENTERATES
EXCESSIVENESS	EXCLUSIONS	EXCREMENTITIOUS	EXECRABLENESSES	EXENTERATING
EXCESSIVENESSES	EXCLUSIVELY	EXCREMENTS	EXECRATING	EXENTERATION
EXCHANGEABILITY	EXCLUSIVENESS	EXCREMENTUM	EXECRATION	EXENTERATIONS
EXCHANGEABLE	EXCLUSIVENESSES	EXCRESCENCE	EXECRATIONS	EXEQUATURS
EXCHANGEABLY	EXCLUSIVES	EXCRESCENCES	EXECRATIVE	EXERCISABLE
EXCHANGERS	EXCLUSIVISM	EXCRESCENCIES	EXECRATIVELY	EXERCISERS
EXCHANGING	EXCLUSIVISMS	EXCRESCENCY	EXECRATORS	EXERCISING
EXCHEQUERED	EXCLUSIVIST	EXCRESCENT	EXECRATORY	EXERCITATION
EXCHEQUERING	EXCLUSIVISTS	EXCRESCENTIAL	EXECUTABLE	EXERCITATIONS
EXCHEQUERS	EXCLUSIVITIES	EXCRESCENTLY	EXECUTABLES	EXERCYCLES
EXCIPIENTS	EXCLUSIVITY	EXCRETIONS	EXECUTANCIES	EXERGAMING
EXCISIONAL	EXCOGITABLE	EXCRETORIES	EXECUTANCY	EXERGAMINGS
EXCITABILITIES	EXCOGITATE	EXCRUCIATE	EXECUTANTS	EXERTAINMENT
EXCITABILITY	EXCOGITATED	EXCRUCIATED	EXECUTARIES	EXERTAINMENTS
EXCITABLENESS	EXCOGITATES	EXCRUCIATES	EXECUTIONER	EXFILTRATE
EXCITABLENESSES	EXCOGITATING	EXCRUCIATING	EXECUTIONERS	EXFILTRATED
EXCITANCIES	EXCOGITATION	EXCRUCIATINGLY	EXECUTIONS	EXFILTRATES
EXCITATION	EXCOGITATIONS	EXCRUCIATION	EXECUTIVELY	EXFILTRATING
EXCITATIONS	EXCOGITATIVE	EXCRUCIATIONS	EXECUTIVES	EXFOLIANTS
EXCITATIVE	EXCOGITATOR	EXCULPABLE	EXECUTORIAL	EXFOLIATED
EXCITATORY	EXCOGITATORS	EXCULPATED	EXECUTORSHIP	EXFOLIATES
EXCITEDNESS	EXCOMMUNICABLE	EXCULPATES	EXECUTORSHIPS	EXFOLIATING
EXCITEDNESSES	EXCOMMUNICATE	EXCULPATING	EXECUTRESS	EXFOLIATION
EXCITEMENT	EXCOMMUNICATED	EXCULPATION	EXECUTRESSES	EXFOLIATIONS

EXFOLIATIVE	EXHILARATING	EXODONTISTS	EXORCISERS	EXPANSIONIST
EXFOLIATOR	EXHILARATINGLY	EXOENZYMES	EXORCISING	EXPANSIONISTIC
EXFOLIATORS	EXHILARATION	EXOERYTHROCYTIC	EXORCISTIC	EXPANSIONISTS
EXHALATION	EXHILARATIONS	EXOGENETIC	EXORCISTICAL	EXPANSIONS
EXHALATIONS	EXHILARATIVE	EXOGENISMS	EXORCIZERS	EXPANSIVELY
EXHAUSTEDLY	EXHILARATOR	EXOGENOUSLY	EXORCIZING	EXPANSIVENESS
EXHAUSTERS	EXHILARATORS	EXONERATED	EXOSKELETAL	EXPANSIVENESSES
EXHAUSTIBILITY	EXHILARATORY	EXONERATES	EXOSKELETON	EXPANSIVITIES
EXHAUSTIBLE	EXHORTATION	EXONERATING	EXOSKELETONS	EXPANSIVITY
EXHAUSTING	EXHORTATIONS	EXONERATION	EXOSPHERES	EXPATIATED
EXHAUSTINGLY	EXHORTATIVE	EXONERATIONS	EXOSPHERIC	EXPATIATES
EXHAUSTION	EXHORTATORY	EXONERATIVE	EXOSPHERICAL	EXPATIATING
EXHAUSTIONS	EXHUMATING	EXONERATOR	EXOSPORIUM	EXPATIATION
EXHAUSTIVE	EXHUMATION	EXONERATORS	EXOSPOROUS	EXPATIATIONS
EXHAUSTIVELY	EXHUMATIONS	EXONUCLEASE	EXOTERICAL	EXPATIATIVE
EXHAUSTIVENESS	EXIGENCIES	EXONUCLEASES	EXOTERICALLY	EXPATIATOR
EXHAUSTIVITIES	EXIGUITIES	EXONUMISTS	EXOTERICISM	EXPATIATORS
EXHAUSTIVITY	EXIGUOUSLY	EXOPARASITE	EXOTERICISMS	EXPATIATORY
EXHAUSTLESS	EXIGUOUSNESS	EXOPARASITES	EXOTHERMAL	EXPATRIATE
EXHAUSTLESSLY	EXIGUOUSNESSES	EXOPARASITIC	EXOTHERMALLY	EXPATRIATED
EXHAUSTLESSNESS	EXILEMENTS	EXOPEPTIDASE	EXOTHERMIC	EXPATRIATES
EXHEREDATE	EXIMIOUSLY	EXOPEPTIDASES	EXOTHERMICALLY	EXPATRIATING
EXHEREDATED	EXISTENCES	EXOPHAGIES	EXOTHERMICITIES	EXPATRIATION
EXHEREDATES	EXISTENTIAL	EXOPHAGOUS	EXOTHERMICITY	EXPATRIATIONS
EXHEREDATING	EXISTENTIALISM	EXOPHTHALMIA	EXOTICALLY	EXPATRIATISM
EXHEREDATION	EXISTENTIALISMS	EXOPHTHALMIAS	EXOTICISED	EXPATRIATISMS
EXHEREDATIONS	EXISTENTIALIST	EXOPHTHALMIC	EXOTICISES	EXPECTABLE
EXHIBITERS	EXISTENTIALISTS	EXOPHTHALMOS	EXOTICISING	EXPECTABLY
EXHIBITING	EXISTENTIALLY	EXOPHTHALMOSES	EXOTICISMS	EXPECTANCE
EXHIBITION	EXISTENTIALS	EXOPHTHALMUS	EXOTICISTS	EXPECTANCES
EXHIBITIONER	EXOBIOLOGICAL	EXOPHTHALMUSES	EXOTICIZED	EXPECTANCIES
EXHIBITIONERS	EXOBIOLOGIES	EXOPLANETS	EXOTICIZES	EXPECTANCY
EXHIBITIONISM	EXOBIOLOGIST	EXOPODITES	EXOTICIZING	EXPECTANTLY
EXHIBITIONISMS	EXOBIOLOGISTS	EXOPODITIC	EXOTICNESS	EXPECTANTS
EXHIBITIONIST	EXOBIOLOGY	EXORABILITIES	EXOTICNESSES	EXPECTATION
EXHIBITIONISTIC	EXOCENTRIC	EXORABILITY	EXOTROPIAS	EXPECTATIONAL
EXHIBITIONISTS	EXOCUTICLE	EXORATIONS	EXPANDABILITIES	EXPECTATIONS
EXHIBITIONS	EXOCUTICLES	EXORBITANCE	EXPANDABILITY	EXPECTATIVE
EXHIBITIVE	EXOCYTOSED	EXORBITANCES	EXPANDABLE	EXPECTATIVES
EXHIBITIVELY	EXOCYTOSES	EXORBITANCIES	EXPANSIBILITIES	EXPECTEDLY
EXHIBITORS	EXOCYTOSING	EXORBITANCY	EXPANSIBILITY	EXPECTEDNESS
EXHIBITORY	EXOCYTOSIS	EXORBITANT	EXPANSIBLE	EXPECTEDNESSES
EXHILARANT	EXOCYTOTIC	EXORBITANTLY	EXPANSIBLY	EXPECTINGLY
EXHILARANTS	EXODERMISES	EXORBITATE	EXPANSIONAL	EXPECTINGS
EXHILARATE	EXODONTIAS	EXORBITATED	EXPANSIONARY	EXPECTORANT
EXHILARATED	EXODONTICS	EXORBITATES	EXPANSIONISM	EXPECTORANTS
EXHILARATES	EXODONTIST	EXORBITATING	EXPANSIONISMS	EXPECTORATE

EXPECTORATED	EXPERIENCE	EXPLAINABLE	EXPLOSIBLE	EXPRESSING
EXPECTORATES	EXPERIENCEABLE	EXPLAINERS	EXPLOSIONS	EXPRESSION
EXPECTORATING	EXPERIENCED	EXPLAINING	EXPLOSIVELY	EXPRESSIONAL
EXPECTORATION	EXPERIENCELESS	EXPLANATION	EXPLOSIVENESS	EXPRESSIONISM
EXPECTORATIONS	EXPERIENCER	EXPLANATIONS	EXPLOSIVENESSES	EXPRESSIONISMS
EXPECTORATIVE	EXPERIENCERS	EXPLANATIVE	EXPLOSIVES	EXPRESSIONIST
EXPECTORATIVES	EXPERIENCES	EXPLANATIVELY	EXPONENTIAL	EXPRESSIONISTIC
EXPECTORATOR	EXPERIENCING	EXPLANATORILY	EXPONENTIALLY	EXPRESSIONISTS
EXPECTORATORS	EXPERIENTIAL	EXPLANATORY	EXPONENTIALS	EXPRESSIONLESS
EXPEDIENCE	EXPERIENTIALISM	EXPLANTATION	EXPONENTIATION	EXPRESSIONS
EXPEDIENCES	EXPERIENTIALIST	EXPLANTATIONS	EXPONENTIATIONS	EXPRESSIVE
EXPEDIENCIES	EXPERIENTIALLY	EXPLANTING	EXPORTABILITIES	EXPRESSIVELY
EXPEDIENCY	EXPERIMENT	EXPLETIVELY	EXPORTABILITY	EXPRESSIVENESS
EXPEDIENTIAL	EXPERIMENTAL	EXPLETIVES	EXPORTABLE	EXPRESSIVITIES
EXPEDIENTIALLY	EXPERIMENTALISE	EXPLICABLE	EXPORTATION	EXPRESSIVITY
EXPEDIENTLY	EXPERIMENTALISM	EXPLICABLY	EXPORTATIONS	EXPRESSMAN
EXPEDIENTS	EXPERIMENTALIST	EXPLICATED	EXPOSEDNESS	EXPRESSMEN
EXPEDITATE	EXPERIMENTALIZE	EXPLICATES	EXPOSEDNESSES	EXPRESSNESS
EXPEDITATED	EXPERIMENTALLY	EXPLICATING	EXPOSITING	EXPRESSNESSES
EXPEDITATES	EXPERIMENTATION	EXPLICATION	EXPOSITION	EXPRESSURE
EXPEDITATING	EXPERIMENTATIVE	EXPLICATIONS	EXPOSITIONAL	EXPRESSURES
EXPEDITATION	EXPERIMENTED	EXPLICATIVE	EXPOSITIONS	EXPRESSWAY
EXPEDITATIONS	EXPERIMENTER	EXPLICATIVELY	EXPOSITIVE	EXPRESSWAYS
EXPEDITELY	EXPERIMENTERS	EXPLICATOR	EXPOSITIVELY	EXPROBRATE
EXPEDITERS	EXPERIMENTING	EXPLICATORS	EXPOSITORILY	EXPROBRATED
EXPEDITING	EXPERIMENTIST	EXPLICATORY	EXPOSITORS	EXPROBRATES
EXPEDITION	EXPERIMENTISTS	EXPLICITLY	EXPOSITORY	EXPROBRATING
EXPEDITIONARY	EXPERIMENTS	EXPLICITNESS	EXPOSITRESS	EXPROBRATION
EXPEDITIONS	EXPERTISED	EXPLICITNESSES	EXPOSITRESSES	EXPROBRATIONS
EXPEDITIOUS	EXPERTISES	EXPLOITABLE	EXPOSTULATE	EXPROBRATIVE
EXPEDITIOUSLY	EXPERTISING	EXPLOITAGE	EXPOSTULATED	EXPROBRATORY
EXPEDITIOUSNESS	EXPERTISMS	EXPLOITAGES	EXPOSTULATES	EXPROMISSION
EXPEDITIVE	EXPERTIZED	EXPLOITATION	EXPOSTULATING	EXPROMISSIONS
EXPEDITORS	EXPERTIZES	EXPLOITATIONS	EXPOSTULATINGLY	EXPROMISSOR
EXPELLABLE	EXPERTIZING	EXPLOITATIVE	EXPOSTULATION	EXPROMISSORS
EXPELLANTS	EXPERTNESS	EXPLOITATIVELY	EXPOSTULATIONS	EXPROPRIABLE
EXPELLENTS	EXPERTNESSES	EXPLOITERS	EXPOSTULATIVE	EXPROPRIATE
EXPENDABILITIES	EXPIATIONS	EXPLOITING	EXPOSTULATOR	EXPROPRIATED
EXPENDABILITY	EXPIRATION	EXPLOITIVE	EXPOSTULATORS	EXPROPRIATES
EXPENDABLE	EXPIRATIONS	EXPLORATION	EXPOSTULATORY	EXPROPRIATING
EXPENDABLES	EXPIRATORY	EXPLORATIONAL	EXPOSTURES	EXPROPRIATION
EXPENDABLY	EXPISCATED	EXPLORATIONIST	EXPOUNDERS	EXPROPRIATIONS
EXPENDITURE	EXPISCATES	EXPLORATIONISTS	EXPOUNDING	EXPROPRIATOR
EXPENDITURES	EXPISCATING	EXPLORATIONS	EXPRESSAGE	EXPROPRIATORS
EXPENSIVELY	EXPISCATION	EXPLORATIVE	EXPRESSAGES	EXPUGNABLE
EXPENSIVENESS	EXPISCATIONS	EXPLORATIVELY	EXPRESSERS	EXPUGNATION
EXPENSIVENESSES	EXPISCATORY	EXPLORATORY	EXPRESSIBLE	EXPUGNATIONS

EXPULSIONS
EXPUNCTING
EXPUNCTION
EXPUNCTIONS
EXPURGATED
EXPURGATES
EXPURGATING
EXPURGATION
EXPURGATIONS
EXPURGATOR
EXPURGATORIAL
EXPURGATORS
EXPURGATORY
EXQUISITELY
EXQUISITENESS
EXQUISITENESSES
EXQUISITES
EXSANGUINATE
EXSANGUINATED
EXSANGUINATES
EXSANGUINATING
EXSANGUINATION
EXSANGUINATIONS
EXSANGUINE
EXSANGUINED
EXSANGUINEOUS
EXSANGUINITIES
EXSANGUINITY
EXSANGUINOUS
EXSCINDING
EXSECTIONS
EXSERTIONS
EXSICCANTS
EXSICCATED
EXSICCATES
EXSICCATING
EXSICCATION
EXSICCATIONS
EXSICCATIVE
EXSICCATOR
EXSICCATORS
EXSOLUTION
EXSOLUTIONS
EXSTIPULATE
EXSTROPHIES
EXSUFFLATE
EXSUFFLATED

EXSUFFLATES
EXSUFFLATING
EXSUFFLATION
EXSUFFLATIONS
EXSUFFLICATE
EXTEMPORAL
EXTEMPORALLY
EXTEMPORANEITY
EXTEMPORANEOUS
EXTEMPORARILY
EXTEMPORARINESS
EXTEMPORARY
EXTEMPORES
EXTEMPORISATION
EXTEMPORISE
EXTEMPORISED
EXTEMPORISER
EXTEMPORISERS
EXTEMPORISES
EXTEMPORISING
EXTEMPORIZATION
EXTEMPORIZE
EXTEMPORIZED
EXTEMPORIZER
EXTEMPORIZERS
EXTEMPORIZES
EXTEMPORIZING
EXTENDABILITIES
EXTENDABILITY
EXTENDABLE
EXTENDEDLY
EXTENDEDNESS
EXTENDEDNESSES
EXTENDIBILITIES
EXTENDIBILITY
EXTENDIBLE
EXTENSIBILITIES
EXTENSIBILITY
EXTENSIBLE
EXTENSIBLENESS
EXTENSIFICATION
EXTENSIMETER
EXTENSIMETERS
EXTENSIONAL
EXTENSIONALISM
EXTENSIONALISMS
EXTENSIONALITY

EXTENSIONALLY
EXTENSIONIST
EXTENSIONISTS
EXTENSIONS
EXTENSITIES
EXTENSIVELY
EXTENSIVENESS
EXTENSIVENESSES
EXTENSIVISATION
EXTENSIVIZATION
EXTENSOMETER
EXTENSOMETERS
EXTENUATED
EXTENUATES
EXTENUATING
EXTENUATINGLY
EXTENUATINGS
EXTENUATION
EXTENUATIONS
EXTENUATIVE
EXTENUATIVES
EXTENUATOR
EXTENUATORS
EXTENUATORY
EXTERIORISATION
EXTERIORISE
EXTERIORISED
EXTERIORISES
EXTERIORISING
EXTERIORITIES
EXTERIORITY
EXTERIORIZATION
EXTERIORIZE
EXTERIORIZED
EXTERIORIZES
EXTERIORIZING
EXTERIORLY
EXTERMINABLE
EXTERMINATE
EXTERMINATED
EXTERMINATES
EXTERMINATING
EXTERMINATION
EXTERMINATIONS
EXTERMINATIVE
EXTERMINATOR
EXTERMINATORS

EXTERMINATORY
EXTERMINED
EXTERMINES
EXTERMINING
EXTERNALISATION
EXTERNALISE
EXTERNALISED
EXTERNALISES
EXTERNALISING
EXTERNALISM
EXTERNALISMS
EXTERNALIST
EXTERNALISTS
EXTERNALITIES
EXTERNALITY
EXTERNALIZATION
EXTERNALIZE
EXTERNALIZED
EXTERNALIZES
EXTERNALIZING
EXTERNALLY
EXTERNSHIP
EXTERNSHIPS
EXTEROCEPTIVE
EXTEROCEPTOR
EXTEROCEPTORS
EXTERRITORIAL
EXTERRITORIALLY
EXTINCTING
EXTINCTION
EXTINCTIONS
EXTINCTIVE
EXTINCTURE
EXTINCTURES
EXTINGUISH
EXTINGUISHABLE
EXTINGUISHANT
EXTINGUISHANTS
EXTINGUISHED
EXTINGUISHER
EXTINGUISHERS
EXTINGUISHES
EXTINGUISHING
EXTINGUISHMENT
EXTINGUISHMENTS
EXTIRPABLE
EXTIRPATED

EXTIRPATES
EXTIRPATING
EXTIRPATION
EXTIRPATIONS
EXTIRPATIVE
EXTIRPATOR
EXTIRPATORS
EXTIRPATORY
EXTOLLINGLY
EXTOLMENTS
EXTORSIVELY
EXTORTIONARY
EXTORTIONATE
EXTORTIONATELY
EXTORTIONER
EXTORTIONERS
EXTORTIONIST
EXTORTIONISTS
EXTORTIONS
EXTRABOLDS
EXTRACANONICAL
EXTRACELLULAR
EXTRACELLULARLY
EXTRACORPOREAL
EXTRACRANIAL
EXTRACTABILITY
EXTRACTABLE
EXTRACTANT
EXTRACTANTS
EXTRACTIBLE
EXTRACTING
EXTRACTION
EXTRACTIONS
EXTRACTIVE
EXTRACTIVELY
EXTRACTIVES
EXTRACTORS
EXTRACURRICULAR
EXTRADITABLE
EXTRADITED
EXTRADITES
EXTRADITING
EXTRADITION
EXTRADITIONS
EXTRADOSES
EXTRADOTAL
EXTRADURAL

EXTRADURALS
EXTRAEMBRYONIC
EXTRAFLORAL
EXTRAFORANEOUS
EXTRAGALACTIC
EXTRAHEPATIC
EXTRAJUDICIAL
EXTRAJUDICIALLY
EXTRALEGAL
EXTRALEGALLY
EXTRALIMITAL
EXTRALIMITARY
EXTRALINGUISTIC
EXTRALITERARY
EXTRALITIES
EXTRALOGICAL
EXTRAMARITAL
EXTRAMARITALLY
EXTRAMETRICAL
EXTRAMUNDANE
EXTRAMURAL
EXTRAMURALLY
EXTRAMUSICAL
EXTRANEITIES
EXTRANEITY
EXTRANEOUS
EXTRANEOUSLY
EXTRANEOUSNESS
EXTRANUCLEAR
EXTRAORDINAIRE
EXTRAORDINARIES
EXTRAORDINARILY
EXTRAORDINARY

EXTRAPOLATE
EXTRAPOLATED
EXTRAPOLATES
EXTRAPOLATING
EXTRAPOLATION
EXTRAPOLATIONS
EXTRAPOLATIVE
EXTRAPOLATOR
EXTRAPOLATORS
EXTRAPOLATORY
EXTRAPOSED
EXTRAPOSES
EXTRAPOSING
EXTRAPOSITION
EXTRAPOSITIONS
EXTRAPYRAMIDAL
EXTRASENSORY
EXTRASOLAR
EXTRASYSTOLE
EXTRASYSTOLES
EXTRATEXTUAL
EXTRATROPICAL
EXTRAUTERINE
EXTRAVAGANCE
EXTRAVAGANCES
EXTRAVAGANCIES
EXTRAVAGANCY
EXTRAVAGANT
EXTRAVAGANTLY
EXTRAVAGANZA
EXTRAVAGANZAS
EXTRAVAGATE
EXTRAVAGATED

EXTRAVAGATES
EXTRAVAGATING
EXTRAVAGATION
EXTRAVAGATIONS
EXTRAVASATE
EXTRAVASATED
EXTRAVASATES
EXTRAVASATING
EXTRAVASATION
EXTRAVASATIONS
EXTRAVASCULAR
EXTRAVEHICULAR
EXTRAVERSION
EXTRAVERSIONS
EXTRAVERSIVE
EXTRAVERSIVELY
EXTRAVERTED
EXTRAVERTING
EXTRAVERTLY
EXTRAVERTS
EXTREATING
EXTREMENESS
EXTREMENESSES
EXTREMISMS
EXTREMISTS
EXTREMITIES
EXTREMOPHILE
EXTREMOPHILES
EXTRICABLE
EXTRICATED
EXTRICATES
EXTRICATING
EXTRICATION

EXTRICATIONS
EXTRINSICAL
EXTRINSICALITY
EXTRINSICALLY
EXTRINSICALS
EXTROVERSION
EXTROVERSIONS
EXTROVERSIVE
EXTROVERSIVELY
EXTROVERTED
EXTROVERTING
EXTROVERTLY
EXTROVERTS
EXTRUDABILITIES
EXTRUDABILITY
EXTRUDABLE
EXTRUSIBLE
EXTRUSIONS
EXTUBATING
EXUBERANCE
EXUBERANCES
EXUBERANCIES
EXUBERANCY
EXUBERANTLY
EXUBERATED
EXUBERATES
EXUBERATING
EXUDATIONS
EXULCERATE
EXULCERATED
EXULCERATES
EXULCERATING
EXULCERATION

EXULCERATIONS
EXULTANCES
EXULTANCIES
EXULTANTLY
EXULTATION
EXULTATIONS
EXULTINGLY
EXURBANITE
EXURBANITES
EXUVIATING
EXUVIATION
EXUVIATIONS
EYEBALLING
EYEBRIGHTS
EYEBROWING
EYEBROWLESS
EYEDNESSES
EYEDROPPER
EYEDROPPERS
EYEGLASSES
EYELETEERS
EYELETTING
EYEOPENERS
EYEPATCHES
EYEPOPPERS
EYESHADOWS
EYESTRAINS
EYESTRINGS
EYEWITNESS
EYEWITNESSES

F

FABRICANTS
FABRICATED
FABRICATES
FABRICATING
FABRICATION
FABRICATIONS
FABRICATIVE
FABRICATOR
FABRICATORS
FABRICKING
FABRICKINGS
FABULATING
FABULATORS
FABULISING
FABULISTIC
FABULIZING
FABULOSITIES
FABULOSITY
FABULOUSLY
FABULOUSNESS
FABULOUSNESSES
FACEBOOKED
FACEBOOKING
FACECLOTHS
FACELESSNESS
FACELESSNESSES
FACELIFTED
FACELIFTING
FACEPLATES
FACEPRINTS
FACETIMING
FACETIOUSLY
FACETIOUSNESS
FACETIOUSNESSES
FACEWORKER
FACEWORKERS
FACIALISTS
FACILENESS
FACILENESSES
FACILITATE
FACILITATED

FACILITATES
FACILITATING
FACILITATION
FACILITATIONS
FACILITATIVE
FACILITATOR
FACILITATORS
FACILITATORY
FACILITIES
FACINERIOUS
FACINOROUS
FACINOROUSNESS
FACSIMILED
FACSIMILEING
FACSIMILES
FACSIMILIST
FACSIMILISTS
FACTICITIES
FACTIONALISE
FACTIONALISED
FACTIONALISES
FACTIONALISING
FACTIONALISM
FACTIONALISMS
FACTIONALIST
FACTIONALISTS
FACTIONALIZE
FACTIONALIZED
FACTIONALIZES
FACTIONALIZING
FACTIONALLY
FACTIONARIES
FACTIONARY
FACTIONIST
FACTIONISTS
FACTIOUSLY
FACTIOUSNESS
FACTIOUSNESSES
FACTITIOUS
FACTITIOUSLY
FACTITIOUSNESS

FACTITIVELY
FACTORABILITIES
FACTORABILITY
FACTORABLE
FACTORAGES
FACTORIALLY
FACTORIALS
FACTORINGS
FACTORISATION
FACTORISATIONS
FACTORISED
FACTORISES
FACTORISING
FACTORIZATION
FACTORIZATIONS
FACTORIZED
FACTORIZES
FACTORIZING
FACTORSHIP
FACTORSHIPS
FACTORYLIKE
FACTSHEETS
FACTUALISM
FACTUALISMS
FACTUALIST
FACTUALISTIC
FACTUALISTS
FACTUALITIES
FACTUALITY
FACTUALNESS
FACTUALNESSES
FACULTATIVE
FACULTATIVELY
FACUNDITIES
FADDINESSES
FADDISHNESS
FADDISHNESSES
FADEDNESSES
FADELESSLY
FADOMETERS
FAGGOTINGS

FAGGOTRIES
FAGOTTISTS
FAINEANCES
FAINEANCIES
FAINEANTISE
FAINEANTISES
FAINNESSES
FAINTHEARTED
FAINTHEARTEDLY
FAINTINGLY
FAINTISHNESS
FAINTISHNESSES
FAINTNESSES
FAIRGROUND
FAIRGROUNDS
FAIRLEADER
FAIRLEADERS
FAIRNESSES
FAIRNITICKLE
FAIRNITICKLES
FAIRNITICLE
FAIRNITICLES
FAIRNYTICKLE
FAIRNYTICKLES
FAIRNYTICLE
FAIRNYTICLES
FAIRYFLOSS
FAIRYFLOSSES
FAIRYHOODS
FAIRYLANDS
FAITHCURES
FAITHFULLY
FAITHFULNESS
FAITHFULNESSES
FAITHLESSLY
FAITHLESSNESS
FAITHLESSNESSES
FAITHWORTHINESS
FAITHWORTHY
FALANGISMS
FALANGISTS

FALCATIONS
FALCONIFORM
FALCONOIDS
FALCONRIES
FALDERALED
FALDERALING
FALDISTORIES
FALDISTORY
FALDSTOOLS
FALLACIOUS
FALLACIOUSLY
FALLACIOUSNESS
FALLALERIES
FALLALISHLY
FALLBOARDS
FALLFISHES
FALLIBILISM
FALLIBILISMS
FALLIBILIST
FALLIBILISTS
FALLIBILITIES
FALLIBILITY
FALLIBLENESS
FALLIBLENESSES
FALLOWNESS
FALLOWNESSES
FALSEFACES
FALSEHOODS
FALSENESSES
FALSEWORKS
FALSIDICAL
FALSIFIABILITY
FALSIFIABLE
FALSIFICATION
FALSIFICATIONS
FALSIFIERS
FALSIFYING
FALTERINGLY
FALTERINGS
FAMILIARISATION
FAMILIARISE

FAMILIARISED	FANDANGOES	FARADIZATION	FARTHINGLANDS	FASTBALLER
FAMILIARISER	FANFARADES	FARADIZATIONS	FARTHINGLESS	FASTBALLERS
FAMILIARISERS	FANFARONADE	FARADIZERS	FARTHINGSWORTH	FASTENINGS
FAMILIARISES	FANFARONADED	FARADIZING	FARTHINGSWORTHS	FASTIDIOUS
FAMILIARISING	FANFARONADES	FARANDINES	FASCIATELY	FASTIDIOUSLY
FAMILIARITIES	FANFARONADING	FARANDOLES	FASCIATION	FASTIDIOUSNESS
FAMILIARITY	FANFARONAS	FARAWAYNESS	FASCIATIONS	FASTIGIATE
FAMILIARIZATION	FANFOLDING	FARAWAYNESSES	FASCICULAR	FASTIGIATED
FAMILIARIZE	FANTABULOUS	FARBOROUGH	FASCICULARLY	FASTIGIUMS
FAMILIARIZED	FANTASISED	FARBOROUGHS	FASCICULATE	FASTNESSES
FAMILIARIZER	FANTASISER	FARCEMEATS	FASCICULATED	FATALISTIC
FAMILIARIZERS	FANTASISERS	FARCICALITIES	FASCICULATELY	FATALISTICALLY
FAMILIARIZES	FANTASISES	FARCICALITY	FASCICULATION	FATALITIES
FAMILIARIZING	FANTASISING	FARCICALLY	FASCICULATIONS	FATALNESSES
FAMILIARLY	FANTASISTS	FARCICALNESS	FASCICULES	FATBRAINED
FAMILIARNESS	FANTASIZED	FARCICALNESSES	FASCICULUS	FATEFULNESS
FAMILIARNESSES	FANTASIZER	FARCIFYING	FASCIITISES	FATEFULNESSES
FAMILISTIC	FANTASIZERS	FAREWELLED	FASCINATED	FATHEADEDLY
FAMISHMENT	FANTASIZES	FAREWELLING	FASCINATEDLY	FATHEADEDNESS
FAMISHMENTS	FANTASIZING	FARFETCHEDNESS	FASCINATES	FATHEADEDNESSES
FAMOUSNESS	FANTASMALLY	FARINACEOUS	FASCINATING	FATHERHOOD
FAMOUSNESSES	FANTASMICALLY	FARINOSELY	FASCINATINGLY	FATHERHOODS
FANATICALLY	FANTASQUES	FARKLEBERRIES	FASCINATION	FATHERINGS
FANATICALNESS	FANTASTICAL	FARKLEBERRY	FASCINATIONS	FATHERLAND
FANATICALNESSES	FANTASTICALITY	FARMERESSES	FASCINATIVE	FATHERLANDS
FANATICISATION	FANTASTICALLY	FARMERETTE	FASCINATOR	FATHERLESS
FANATICISATIONS	FANTASTICALNESS	FARMERETTES	FASCINATORS	FATHERLESSNESS
FANATICISE	FANTASTICATE	FARMHOUSES	FASCIOLIASES	FATHERLIKE
FANATICISED	FANTASTICATED	FARMSTEADS	FASCIOLIASIS	FATHERLINESS
FANATICISES	FANTASTICATES	FARMWORKER	FASCISTICALLY	FATHERLINESSES
FANATICISING	FANTASTICATING	FARMWORKERS	FASCITISES	FATHERSHIP
FANATICISM	FANTASTICATION	FARNARKELED	FASHIONABILITY	FATHERSHIPS
FANATICISMS	FANTASTICATIONS	FARNARKELING	FASHIONABLE	FATHOMABLE
FANATICIZATION	FANTASTICISM	FARNARKELINGS	FASHIONABLENESS	FATHOMETER
FANATICIZATIONS	FANTASTICISMS	FARNARKELS	FASHIONABLES	FATHOMETERS
FANATICIZE	FANTASTICO	FARRAGINOUS	FASHIONABLY	FATHOMLESS
FANATICIZED	FANTASTICOES	FARRANDINE	FASHIONERS	FATHOMLESSLY
FANATICIZES	FANTASTICS	FARRANDINES	FASHIONING	FATHOMLESSNESS
FANATICIZING	FANTASTRIES	FARRIERIES	FASHIONIST	FATIDICALLY
FANCIFULLY	FANTASYING	FARSIGHTED	FASHIONISTA	FATIGABILITIES
FANCIFULNESS	FANTASYLAND	FARSIGHTEDLY	FASHIONISTAS	FATIGABILITY
FANCIFULNESSES	FANTASYLANDS	FARSIGHTEDNESS	FASHIONISTS	FATIGABLENESS
FANCIFYING	FANTOCCINI	FARTHERMORE	FASHIONMONGER	FATIGABLENESSES
FANCINESSES	FARADISATION	FARTHERMOST	FASHIONMONGERS	FATIGATING
FANCYWORKS	FARADISATIONS	FARTHINGALE	FASHIONMONGING	FATIGUABLE
FANDABIDOZI	FARADISERS	FARTHINGALES	FASHIOUSNESS	FATIGUABLENESS
FANDANGLES	FARADISING	FARTHINGLAND	FASHIOUSNESSES	FATIGUELESS

F

F

FATIGUINGLY	FEARFULLER	FEATHERSTITCHED	FEDERALIZATION	FELICITATORS
FATISCENCE	FEARFULLEST	FEATHERSTITCHES	FEDERALIZATIONS	FELICITIES
FATISCENCES	FEARFULNESS	FEATHERWEIGHT	FEDERALIZE	FELICITOUS
FATSHEDERA	FEARFULNESSES	FEATHERWEIGHTS	FEDERALIZED	FELICITOUSLY
FATSHEDERAS	FEARLESSLY	FEATLINESS	FEDERALIZES	FELICITOUSNESS
FATTENABLE	FEARLESSNESS	FEATLINESSES	FEDERALIZING	FELINENESS
FATTENINGS	FEARLESSNESSES	FEATURELESS	FEDERARIES	FELINENESSES
FATTINESSES	FEARMONGER	FEATURELESSNESS	FEDERATING	FELINITIES
FATUOUSNESS	FEARMONGERING	FEATURETTE	FEDERATION	FELLATIONS
FATUOUSNESSES	FEARMONGERINGS	FEATURETTES	FEDERATIONS	FELLATRICES
FAUCETRIES	FEARMONGERS	FEBRICITIES	FEDERATIVE	FELLATRIXES
FAULCHIONS	FEARNAUGHT	FEBRICULAS	FEDERATIVELY	FELLMONGER
FAULTFINDER	FEARNAUGHTS	FEBRICULES	FEDERATORS	FELLMONGERED
FAULTFINDERS	FEARNOUGHT	FEBRIFACIENT	FEEBLEMINDED	FELLMONGERIES
FAULTFINDING	FEARNOUGHTS	FEBRIFACIENTS	FEEBLEMINDEDLY	FELLMONGERING
FAULTFINDINGS	FEARSOMELY	FEBRIFEROUS	FEEBLENESS	FELLMONGERINGS
FAULTINESS	FEARSOMENESS	FEBRIFUGAL	FEEBLENESSES	FELLMONGERS
FAULTINESSES	FEARSOMENESSES	FEBRIFUGES	FEEDGRAINS	FELLMONGERY
FAULTLESSLY	FEASIBILITIES	FEBRILITIES	FEEDINGSTUFF	FELLNESSES
FAULTLESSNESS	FEASIBILITY	FECKLESSLY	FEEDINGSTUFFS	FELLOWSHIP
FAULTLESSNESSES	FEASIBLENESS	FECKLESSNESS	FEEDSTOCKS	FELLOWSHIPED
FAULTLINES	FEASIBLENESSES	FECKLESSNESSES	FEEDSTUFFS	FELLOWSHIPING
FAUNISTICALLY	FEATEOUSLY	FECULENCES	FEEDTHROUGH	FELLOWSHIPPED
FAUXBOURDON	FEATHERBED	FECULENCIES	FEEDTHROUGHS	FELLOWSHIPPING
FAUXBOURDONS	FEATHERBEDDED	FECUNDATED	FEEDWATERS	FELLOWSHIPS
FAUXMANCES	FEATHERBEDDING	FECUNDATES	FEELINGLESS	FELLWALKER
FAVORABLENESS	FEATHERBEDDINGS	FECUNDATING	FEELINGNESS	FELLWALKERS
FAVORABLENESSES	FEATHERBEDS	FECUNDATION	FEELINGNESSES	FELONIOUSLY
FAVOREDNESS	FEATHERBRAIN	FECUNDATIONS	FEIGNEDNESS	FELONIOUSNESS
FAVOREDNESSES	FEATHERBRAINED	FECUNDATOR	FEIGNEDNESSES	FELONIOUSNESSES
FAVORINGLY	FEATHERBRAINS	FECUNDATORS	FEIGNINGLY	FELSPATHIC
FAVORITISM	FEATHEREDGE	FECUNDATORY	FEISTINESS	FELSPATHOID
FAVORITISMS	FEATHEREDGED	FECUNDITIES	FEISTINESSES	FELSPATHOIDS
FAVOURABLE	FEATHEREDGES	FEDERACIES	FELDSCHARS	FELSPATHOSE
FAVOURABLENESS	FEATHEREDGING	FEDERALESE	FELDSCHERS	FEMALENESS
FAVOURABLY	FEATHERHEAD	FEDERALESES	FELDSPATHIC	FEMALENESSES
FAVOUREDNESS	FEATHERHEADED	FEDERALISATION	FELDSPATHOID	FEMALITIES
FAVOUREDNESSES	FEATHERHEADS	FEDERALISATIONS	FELDSPATHOIDS	FEMETARIES
FAVOURINGLY	FEATHERIER	FEDERALISE	FELDSPATHOSE	FEMINACIES
FAVOURITES	FEATHERIEST	FEDERALISED	FELDSPATHS	FEMINALITIES
FAVOURITISM	FEATHERINESS	FEDERALISES	FELICITATE	FEMINALITY
FAVOURITISMS	FEATHERINESSES	FEDERALISING	FELICITATED	FEMINEITIES
FAVOURLESS	FEATHERING	FEDERALISM	FELICITATES	FEMINILITIES
FAWNINGNESS	FEATHERINGS	FEDERALISMS	FELICITATING	FEMINILITY
FAWNINGNESSES	FEATHERLESS	FEDERALIST	FELICITATION	FEMININELY
FAZENDEIRO	FEATHERLIGHT	FEDERALISTIC	FELICITATIONS	FEMININENESS
FAZENDEIROS	FEATHERSTITCH	FEDERALISTS	FELICITATOR	FEMININENESSES

FEMININISM
FEMININISMS
FEMININITIES
FEMININITY
FEMINISATION
FEMINISATIONS
FEMINISING
FEMINISTIC
FEMINITIES
FEMINIZATION
FEMINIZATIONS
FEMINIZING
FEMTOSECOND
FEMTOSECONDS
FENCELESSNESS
FENCELESSNESSES
FENDERLESS
FENESTELLA
FENESTELLAE
FENESTELLAS
FENESTRALS
FENESTRATE
FENESTRATED
FENESTRATION
FENESTRATIONS
FENNELFLOWER
FENNELFLOWERS
FENUGREEKS
FEOFFMENTS
FERACITIES
FERETORIES
FERMENTABILITY
FERMENTABLE
FERMENTATION
FERMENTATIONS
FERMENTATIVE
FERMENTATIVELY
FERMENTERS
FERMENTESCIBLE
FERMENTING
FERMENTITIOUS
FERMENTIVE
FERMENTORS
FERNALLIES
FERNITICKLE
FERNITICKLES
FERNITICLE

FERNITICLES
FERNTICKLE
FERNTICKLED
FERNTICKLES
FERNTICLED
FERNTICLES
FERNYTICKLE
FERNYTICKLES
FERNYTICLE
FERNYTICLES
FEROCIOUSLY
FEROCIOUSNESS
FEROCIOUSNESSES
FEROCITIES
FERRANDINE
FERRANDINES
FERREDOXIN
FERREDOXINS
FERRELLING
FERRETINGS
FERRICYANIC
FERRICYANIDE
FERRICYANIDES
FERRICYANOGEN
FERRICYANOGENS
FERRIFEROUS
FERRIMAGNET
FERRIMAGNETIC
FERRIMAGNETISM
FERRIMAGNETISMS
FERRIMAGNETS
FERROCENES
FERROCHROME
FERROCHROMES
FERROCHROMIUM
FERROCHROMIUMS
FERROCONCRETE
FERROCONCRETES
FERROCYANIC
FERROCYANIDE
FERROCYANIDES
FERROCYANOGEN
FERROCYANOGENS
FERROELECTRIC
FERROELECTRICS
FERROGRAMS
FERROGRAPHIES

FERROGRAPHY
FERROMAGNESIAN
FERROMAGNET
FERROMAGNETIC
FERROMAGNETISM
FERROMAGNETISMS
FERROMAGNETS
FERROMANGANESE
FERROMANGANESES
FERROMOLYBDENUM
FERRONICKEL
FERRONICKELS
FERRONIERE
FERRONIERES
FERRONNIERE
FERRONNIERES
FERROPRUSSIATE
FERROPRUSSIATES
FERROSILICON
FERROSILICONS
FERROSOFERRIC
FERROTYPED
FERROTYPES
FERROTYPING
FERRUGINEOUS
FERRUGINOUS
FERRYBOATS
FERTIGATED
FERTIGATES
FERTIGATING
FERTIGATION
FERTIGATIONS
FERTILENESS
FERTILENESSES
FERTILISABLE
FERTILISATION
FERTILISATIONS
FERTILISED
FERTILISER
FERTILISERS
FERTILISES
FERTILISING
FERTILITIES
FERTILIZABLE
FERTILIZATION
FERTILIZATIONS
FERTILIZED

FERTILIZER
FERTILIZERS
FERTILIZES
FERTILIZING
FERULACEOUS
FERVENCIES
FERVENTEST
FERVENTNESS
FERVENTNESSES
FERVESCENT
FERVIDITIES
FERVIDNESS
FERVIDNESSES
FESCENNINE
FESTILOGIES
FESTINATED
FESTINATELY
FESTINATES
FESTINATING
FESTINATION
FESTINATIONS
FESTIVALGOER
FESTIVALGOERS
FESTIVENESS
FESTIVENESSES
FESTIVITIES
FESTOLOGIES
FESTOONERIES
FESTOONERY
FESTOONING
FESTSCHRIFT
FESTSCHRIFTEN
FESTSCHRIFTS
FETCHINGLY
FETICHISED
FETICHISES
FETICHISING
FETICHISMS
FETICHISTIC
FETICHISTS
FETICHIZED
FETICHIZES
FETICHIZING
FETIDITIES
FETIDNESSES
FETIPAROUS
FETISHISATION

FETISHISATIONS
FETISHISED
FETISHISES
FETISHISING
FETISHISMS
FETISHISTIC
FETISHISTICALLY
FETISHISTS
FETISHIZATION
FETISHIZATIONS
FETISHIZED
FETISHIZES
FETISHIZING
FETOLOGIES
FETOLOGIST
FETOLOGISTS
FETOPROTEIN
FETOPROTEINS
FETOSCOPES
FETOSCOPIES
FETTERLESS
FETTERLOCK
FETTERLOCKS
FETTUCCINE
FETTUCCINES
FETTUCCINI
FETTUCINES
FETTUCINIS
FEUDALISATION
FEUDALISATIONS
FEUDALISED
FEUDALISES
FEUDALISING
FEUDALISMS
FEUDALISTIC
FEUDALISTS
FEUDALITIES
FEUDALIZATION
FEUDALIZATIONS
FEUDALIZED
FEUDALIZES
FEUDALIZING
FEUDATORIES
FEUILLETES
FEUILLETON
FEUILLETONISM
FEUILLETONISMS

F

F

FEUILLETONIST	FIBRILLATIONS	FICTIONALITIES	FIDEICOMMISSUM	FIGURATIVENESS
FEUILLETONISTIC	FIBRILLIFORM	FICTIONALITY	FIDELISMOS	FIGUREHEAD
FEUILLETONISTS	FIBRILLINS	FICTIONALIZE	FIDELISTAS	FIGUREHEADS
FEUILLETONS	FIBRILLOSE	FICTIONALIZED	FIDELITIES	FIGURELESS
FEVERISHLY	FIBRILLOUS	FICTIONALIZES	FIDGETIEST	FIGUREWORK
FEVERISHNESS	FIBRINOGEN	FICTIONALIZING	FIDGETINESS	FIGUREWORKS
FEVERISHNESSES	FIBRINOGENIC	FICTIONALLY	FIDGETINESSES	FILAGGRINS
FEVEROUSLY	FIBRINOGENOUS	FICTIONEER	FIDGETINGLY	FILAGREEING
FEVERROOTS	FIBRINOGENS	FICTIONEERING	FIDUCIALLY	FILAMENTARY
FEVERWEEDS	FIBRINOIDS	FICTIONEERINGS	FIDUCIARIES	FILAMENTOUS
FEVERWORTS	FIBRINOLYSES	FICTIONEERS	FIDUCIARILY	FILARIASES
FIANCAILLES	FIBRINOLYSIN	FICTIONISATION	FIELDBOOTS	FILARIASIS
FIANCHETTI	FIBRINOLYSINS	FICTIONISATIONS	FIELDCRAFT	FILATORIES
FIANCHETTO	FIBRINOLYSIS	FICTIONISE	FIELDCRAFTS	FILCHINGLY
FIANCHETTOED	FIBRINOLYTIC	FICTIONISED	FIELDFARES	FILEFISHES
FIANCHETTOES	FIBRINOPEPTIDE	FICTIONISES	FIELDMOUSE	FILIALNESS
FIANCHETTOING	FIBRINOPEPTIDES	FICTIONISING	FIELDPIECE	FILIALNESSES
FIANCHETTOS	FIBROBLAST	FICTIONIST	FIELDPIECES	FILIATIONS
FIBERBOARD	FIBROBLASTIC	FICTIONISTS	FIELDSTONE	FILIBUSTER
FIBERBOARDS	FIBROBLASTS	FICTIONIZATION	FIELDSTONES	FILIBUSTERED
FIBERFILLS	FIBROCARTILAGE	FICTIONIZATIONS	FIELDSTRIP	FILIBUSTERER
FIBERGLASS	FIBROCARTILAGES	FICTIONIZE	FIELDSTRIPPED	FILIBUSTERERS
FIBERGLASSED	FIBROCEMENT	FICTIONIZED	FIELDSTRIPPING	FILIBUSTERING
FIBERGLASSES	FIBROCEMENTS	FICTIONIZES	FIELDSTRIPS	FILIBUSTERINGS
FIBERGLASSING	FIBROCYSTIC	FICTIONIZING	FIELDVOLES	FILIBUSTERISM
FIBERISATION	FIBROCYTES	FICTITIOUS	FIELDWARDS	FILIBUSTERISMS
FIBERISATIONS	FIBROLINES	FICTITIOUSLY	FIELDWORKER	FILIBUSTEROUS
FIBERISING	FIBROLITES	FICTITIOUSNESS	FIELDWORKERS	FILIBUSTERS
FIBERIZATION	FIBROMATOUS	FICTIVENESS	FIELDWORKS	FILICINEAN
FIBERIZATIONS	FIBROMYALGIA	FICTIVENESSES	FIENDISHLY	FILIGRAINS
FIBERIZING	FIBROMYALGIAS	FIDDIOUSED	FIENDISHNESS	FILIGRANES
FIBERSCOPE	FIBRONECTIN	FIDDIOUSES	FIENDISHNESSES	FILIGREEING
FIBERSCOPES	FIBRONECTINS	FIDDIOUSING	FIERCENESS	FILIOPIETISTIC
FIBREBOARD	FIBROSARCOMA	FIDDLEBACK	FIERCENESSES	FILIPENDULOUS
FIBREBOARDS	FIBROSARCOMAS	FIDDLEBACKS	FIERINESSES	FILLAGREED
FIBREFILLS	FIBROSARCOMATA	FIDDLEDEDEE	FIFTEENERS	FILLAGREEING
FIBREGLASS	FIBROSITIS	FIDDLEDEEDEE	FIFTEENTHLY	FILLAGREES
FIBREGLASSES	FIBROSITISES	FIDDLEHEAD	FIFTEENTHS	FILLESTERS
FIBREOPTIC	FIBROUSNESS	FIDDLEHEADS	FIGHTBACKS	FILLIPEENS
FIBRESCOPE	FIBROUSNESSES	FIDDLENECK	FIGURABILITIES	FILLISTERS
FIBRESCOPES	FIBROVASCULAR	FIDDLENECKS	FIGURABILITY	FILMGOINGS
FIBRILLARY	FICKLENESS	FIDDLESTICK	FIGURANTES	FILMICALLY
FIBRILLATE	FICKLENESSES	FIDDLESTICKS	FIGURATELY	FILMINESSES
FIBRILLATED	FICTIONALISE	FIDDLEWOOD	FIGURATION	FILMMAKERS
FIBRILLATES	FICTIONALISED	FIDDLEWOODS	FIGURATIONS	FILMMAKING
FIBRILLATING	FICTIONALISES	FIDEICOMMISSA	FIGURATIVE	FILMMAKINGS
FIBRILLATION	FICTIONALISING	FIDEICOMMISSARY	FIGURATIVELY	FILMOGRAPHIES

F

FILMOGRAPHY	FINANCIERS	FINICALITY	FIRELIGHTER	FISHTAILED
FILMSETTER	FINANCINGS	FINICALNESS	FIRELIGHTERS	FISHTAILING
FILMSETTERS	FINEABLENESS	FINICALNESSES	FIRELIGHTS	FISHWIFELY
FILMSETTING	FINEABLENESSES	FINICKETIER	FIREPLACED	FISHYBACKS
FILMSETTINGS	FINENESSES	FINICKETIEST	FIREPLACES	FISSICOSTATE
FILMSTRIPS	FINESSINGS	FINICKIEST	FIREPOWERS	FISSILINGUAL
FILOPLUMES	FINGERBOARD	FINICKINESS	FIREPROOFED	FISSILITIES
FILOPODIUM	FINGERBOARDS	FINICKINESSES	FIREPROOFING	FISSIONABILITY
FILOSELLES	FINGERBOWL	FINICKINGS	FIREPROOFINGS	FISSIONABLE
FILOVIRUSES	FINGERBOWLS	FINISHINGS	FIREPROOFS	FISSIONABLES
FILTERABILITIES	FINGERBREADTH	FINITENESS	FIRESCAPED	FISSIONING
FILTERABILITY	FINGERBREADTHS	FINITENESSES	FIRESCAPES	FISSIPALMATE
FILTERABLE	FINGERGLASS	FINNICKIER	FIRESCAPING	FISSIPARISM
FILTERABLENESS	FINGERGLASSES	FINNICKIEST	FIRESCAPINGS	FISSIPARISMS
FILTHINESS	FINGERGUARD	FINNOCHIOS	FIRESCREEN	FISSIPARITIES
FILTHINESSES	FINGERGUARDS	FINOCCHIOS	FIRESCREENS	FISSIPARITY
FILTRABILITIES	FINGERHOLD	FIORATURAE	FIRESTONES	FISSIPAROUS
FILTRABILITY	FINGERHOLDS	FIREBALLER	FIRESTORMS	FISSIPAROUSLY
FILTRATABLE	FINGERHOLE	FIREBALLERS	FIRETHORNS	FISSIPAROUSNESS
FILTRATING	FINGERHOLES	FIREBALLING	FIRETRUCKS	FISSIPEDAL
FILTRATION	FINGERINGS	FIREBOARDS	FIREWALLED	FISSIPEDES
FILTRATIONS	FINGERLESS	FIREBOMBED	FIREWALLING	FISSIROSTRAL
FIMBRIATED	FINGERLIKE	FIREBOMBER	FIREWARDEN	FISTFIGHTS
FIMBRIATES	FINGERLING	FIREBOMBERS	FIREWARDENS	FISTICUFFED
FIMBRIATING	FINGERLINGS	FIREBOMBING	FIREWATERS	FISTICUFFING
FIMBRIATION	FINGERMARK	FIREBOMBINGS	FIRMAMENTAL	FISTICUFFS
FIMBRIATIONS	FINGERMARKS	FIREBRANDS	FIRMAMENTS	FITFULNESS
FIMBRILLATE	FINGERNAIL	FIREBREAKS	FIRMNESSES	FITFULNESSES
FIMICOLOUS	FINGERNAILS	FIREBRICKS	FIRSTBORNS	FITTINGNESS
FINABLENESS	FINGERPICK	FIREBUSHES	FIRSTFRUITS	FITTINGNESSES
FINABLENESSES	FINGERPICKED	FIRECRACKER	FIRSTLINGS	FIVEFINGER
FINAGLINGS	FINGERPICKING	FIRECRACKERS	FIRSTNESSES	FIVEFINGERS
FINALISATION	FINGERPICKINGS	FIRECRESTS	FISCALISTS	FIVEPENCES
FINALISATIONS	FINGERPICKS	FIREDRAGON	FISHABILITIES	FIXEDNESSES
FINALISERS	FINGERPLATE	FIREDRAGONS	FISHABILITY	FIXTURELESS
FINALISING	FINGERPLATES	FIREDRAKES	FISHBURGER	FIZGIGGING
FINALISTIC	FINGERPOST	FIREFANGED	FISHBURGERS	FIZZENLESS
FINALITIES	FINGERPOSTS	FIREFANGING	FISHERFOLK	FIZZINESSES
FINALIZATION	FINGERPRINT	FIREFIGHTER	FISHERWOMAN	FLABBERGAST
FINALIZATIONS	FINGERPRINTED	FIREFIGHTERS	FISHERWOMEN	FLABBERGASTED
FINALIZERS	FINGERPRINTING	FIREFIGHTING	FISHFINGER	FLABBERGASTING
FINALIZING	FINGERPRINTINGS	FIREFIGHTINGS	FISHFINGERS	FLABBERGASTS
FINANCIALIST	FINGERPRINTS	FIREFIGHTS	FISHIFYING	FLABBINESS
FINANCIALISTS	FINGERSTALL	FIREFLOATS	FISHINESSES	FLABBINESSES
FINANCIALLY	FINGERSTALLS	FIREFLOODS	FISHMONGER	FLABELLATE
FINANCIERED	FINGERTIPS	FIREGUARDS	FISHMONGERS	FLABELLATION
FINANCIERING	FINICALITIES	FIREHOUSES	FISHPLATES	FLABELLATIONS

FLABELLIFORM	FLAGRANTNESS	FLANNELLED	FLATSHARES	FLAVOURISTS
FLABELLUMS	FLAGRANTNESSES	FLANNELLING	FLATTENERS	FLAVOURLESS
FLACCIDEST	FLAGSTAFFS	FLANNELMOUTHED	FLATTENING	FLAVOURSOME
FLACCIDITIES	FLAGSTAVES	FLAPDOODLE	FLATTERABLE	FLAWLESSLY
FLACCIDITY	FLAGSTICKS	FLAPDOODLES	FLATTERERS	FLAWLESSNESS
FLACCIDNESS	FLAGSTONES	FLAPPERHOOD	FLATTERIES	FLAWLESSNESSES
FLACCIDNESSES	FLAKINESSES	FLAPPERHOODS	FLATTERING	FLEAHOPPER
FLACKERIES	FLAMBEEING	FLAPPERISH	FLATTERINGLY	FLEAHOPPERS
FLACKERING	FLAMBOYANCE	FLAPTRACKS	FLATTEROUS	FLECHETTES
FLACKETING	FLAMBOYANCES	FLAREBACKS	FLATTEROUSLY	FLECKERING
FLAFFERING	FLAMBOYANCIES	FLASHBACKED	FLATULENCE	FLECTIONAL
FLAGELLANT	FLAMBOYANCY	FLASHBACKING	FLATULENCES	FLECTIONLESS
FLAGELLANTISM	FLAMBOYANT	FLASHBACKS	FLATULENCIES	FLEDGELING
FLAGELLANTISMS	FLAMBOYANTE	FLASHBANGS	FLATULENCY	FLEDGELINGS
FLAGELLANTS	FLAMBOYANTES	FLASHBOARD	FLATULENTLY	FLEDGLINGS
FLAGELLATE	FLAMBOYANTLY	FLASHBOARDS	FLATWASHES	FLEECELESS
FLAGELLATED	FLAMBOYANTS	FLASHBULBS	FLAUGHTERED	FLEECHINGS
FLAGELLATES	FLAMEPROOF	FLASHCARDS	FLAUGHTERING	FLEECHMENT
FLAGELLATING	FLAMEPROOFED	FLASHCUBES	FLAUGHTERS	FLEECHMENTS
FLAGELLATION	FLAMEPROOFER	FLASHFORWARD	FLAUGHTING	FLEECINESS
FLAGELLATIONS	FLAMEPROOFERS	FLASHFORWARDS	FLAUNCHING	FLEECINESSES
FLAGELLATOR	FLAMEPROOFING	FLASHINESS	FLAUNCHINGS	FLEERINGLY
FLAGELLATORS	FLAMEPROOFS	FLASHINESSES	FLAUNTIEST	FLEETINGLY
FLAGELLATORY	FLAMETHROWER	FLASHLAMPS	FLAUNTINESS	FLEETINGNESS
FLAGELLIFEROUS	FLAMETHROWERS	FLASHLIGHT	FLAUNTINESSES	FLEETINGNESSES
FLAGELLIFORM	FLAMINGOES	FLASHLIGHTS	FLAUNTINGLY	FLEETNESSES
FLAGELLINS	FLAMINICAL	FLASHMOBBING	FLAVANONES	FLEHMENING
FLAGELLOMANIA	FLAMMABILITIES	FLASHMOBBINGS	FLAVESCENT	FLEMISHING
FLAGELLOMANIAC	FLAMMABILITY	FLASHOVERS	FLAVIVIRUS	FLEROVIUMS
FLAGELLOMANIACS	FLAMMABLES	FLASHPACKER	FLAVIVIRUSES	FLESHHOODS
FLAGELLOMANIAS	FLAMMIFEROUS	FLASHPACKERS	FLAVONOIDS	FLESHINESS
FLAGELLUMS	FLAMMULATED	FLASHPOINT	FLAVOPROTEIN	FLESHINESSES
FLAGEOLETS	FLAMMULATION	FLASHPOINTS	FLAVOPROTEINS	FLESHLIEST
FLAGGINESS	FLAMMULATIONS	FLASHTUBES	FLAVOPURPURIN	FLESHLINESS
FLAGGINESSES	FLANCHINGS	FLATBREADS	FLAVOPURPURINS	FLESHLINESSES
FLAGGINGLY	FLANCONADE	FLATFISHES	FLAVORFULLY	FLESHLINGS
FLAGITATED	FLANCONADES	FLATFOOTED	FLAVORINGS	FLESHMENTS
FLAGITATES	FLANGELESS	FLATFOOTING	FLAVORISTS	FLESHMONGER
FLAGITATING	FLANKERING	FLATLANDER	FLAVORLESS	FLESHMONGERS
FLAGITATION	FLANNELBOARD	FLATLANDERS	FLAVORSOME	FLESHWORMS
FLAGITATIONS	FLANNELBOARDS	FLATLINERS	FLAVOURDYNAMICS	FLETCHINGS
FLAGITIOUS	FLANNELETS	FLATLINING	FLAVOURERS	FLEURETTES
FLAGITIOUSLY	FLANNELETTE	FLATNESSES	FLAVOURFUL	FLEXECUTIVE
FLAGITIOUSNESS	FLANNELETTES	FLATPICKED	FLAVOURFULLY	FLEXECUTIVES
FLAGRANCES	FLANNELGRAPH	FLATPICKING	FLAVOURING	FLEXIBILITIES
FLAGRANCIES	FLANNELGRAPHS	FLATSCREEN	FLAVOURINGS	FLEXIBILITY
FLAGRANTLY	FLANNELING	FLATSCREENS	FLAVOURIST	FLEXIBLENESS

FLEXIBLENESSES
FLEXICURITIES
FLEXICURITY
FLEXIHOURS
FLEXIONLESS
FLEXITARIAN
FLEXITARIANISM
FLEXITARIANISMS
FLEXITARIANS
FLEXITIMES
FLEXOGRAPHIC
FLEXOGRAPHIES
FLEXOGRAPHY
FLEXTIMERS
FLEXUOUSLY
FLIBBERTIGIBBET
FLICHTERED
FLICHTERING
FLICKERING
FLICKERINGLY
FLICKERTAIL
FLICKERTAILS
FLIGHTIEST
FLIGHTINESS
FLIGHTINESSES
FLIGHTLESS
FLIMFLAMMED
FLIMFLAMMER
FLIMFLAMMERIES
FLIMFLAMMERS
FLIMFLAMMERY
FLIMFLAMMING
FLIMSINESS
FLIMSINESSES
FLINCHINGLY
FLINCHINGS
FLINDERING
FLINDERSIA
FLINDERSIAS
FLINTHEADS
FLINTIFIED
FLINTIFIES
FLINTIFYING
FLINTINESS
FLINTINESSES
FLINTLOCKS
FLIPBOARDS

FLIPCHARTS
FLIPFLOPPED
FLIPFLOPPING
FLIPPANCIES
FLIPPANTLY
FLIPPANTNESS
FLIPPANTNESSES
FLIRTATION
FLIRTATIONS
FLIRTATIOUS
FLIRTATIOUSLY
FLIRTATIOUSNESS
FLIRTINGLY
FLITTERING
FLITTERMICE
FLITTERMOUSE
FLOATABILITIES
FLOATABILITY
FLOATATION
FLOATATIONS
FLOATINGLY
FLOATPLANE
FLOATPLANES
FLOCCILLATION
FLOCCILLATIONS
FLOCCULANT
FLOCCULANTS
FLOCCULATE
FLOCCULATED
FLOCCULATES
FLOCCULATING
FLOCCULATION
FLOCCULATIONS
FLOCCULATOR
FLOCCULATORS
FLOCCULENCE
FLOCCULENCES
FLOCCULENCIES
FLOCCULENCY
FLOCCULENT
FLOCCULENTLY
FLOODGATES
FLOODLIGHT
FLOODLIGHTED
FLOODLIGHTING
FLOODLIGHTINGS
FLOODLIGHTS

FLOODMARKS
FLOODPLAIN
FLOODPLAINS
FLOODTIDES
FLOODWALLS
FLOODWATER
FLOODWATERS
FLOORBOARD
FLOORBOARDS
FLOORCLOTH
FLOORCLOTHS
FLOORDROBE
FLOORDROBES
FLOORHEADS
FLOORSHOWS
FLOORWALKER
FLOORWALKERS
FLOPHOUSES
FLOPPINESS
FLOPPINESSES
FLOPTICALS
FLORENTINE
FLORENTINES
FLORESCENCE
FLORESCENCES
FLORESCENT
FLORIATION
FLORIATIONS
FLORIBUNDA
FLORIBUNDAS
FLORICANES
FLORICULTURAL
FLORICULTURE
FLORICULTURES
FLORICULTURIST
FLORICULTURISTS
FLORIDEANS
FLORIDEOUS
FLORIDITIES
FLORIDNESS
FLORIDNESSES
FLORIFEROUS
FLORIFEROUSNESS
FLORIGENIC
FLORILEGIA
FLORILEGIUM
FLORISTICALLY

FLORISTICS
FLORISTRIES
FLOSCULOUS
FLOTATIONS
FLOUNCIEST
FLOUNCINGS
FLOUNDERED
FLOUNDERING
FLOURISHED
FLOURISHER
FLOURISHERS
FLOURISHES
FLOURISHING
FLOURISHINGLY
FLOUTINGLY
FLOUTINGSTOCK
FLOUTINGSTOCKS
FLOWCHARTING
FLOWCHARTINGS
FLOWCHARTS
FLOWERAGES
FLOWERBEDS
FLOWERETTE
FLOWERETTES
FLOWERHORN
FLOWERIEST
FLOWERINESS
FLOWERINESSES
FLOWERINGS
FLOWERLESS
FLOWERLIKE
FLOWERPOTS
FLOWINGNESS
FLOWINGNESSES
FLOWMETERS
FLOWSTONES
FLUCTUATED
FLUCTUATES
FLUCTUATING
FLUCTUATION
FLUCTUATIONAL
FLUCTUATIONS
FLUEGELHORN
FLUEGELHORNS
FLUENTNESS
FLUENTNESSES
FLUFFINESS

FLUFFINESSES
FLUGELHORN
FLUGELHORNIST
FLUGELHORNISTS
FLUGELHORNS
FLUIDEXTRACT
FLUIDEXTRACTS
FLUIDIFIED
FLUIDIFIES
FLUIDIFYING
FLUIDISATION
FLUIDISATIONS
FLUIDISERS
FLUIDISING
FLUIDITIES
FLUIDIZATION
FLUIDIZATIONS
FLUIDIZERS
FLUIDIZING
FLUIDNESSES
FLUKINESSES
FLUMMERIES
FLUMMOXING
FLUNITRAZEPAM
FLUNITRAZEPAMS
FLUNKEYDOM
FLUNKEYDOMS
FLUNKEYISH
FLUNKEYISM
FLUNKEYISMS
FLUNKYISMS
FLUORAPATITE
FLUORAPATITES
FLUORESCED
FLUORESCEIN
FLUORESCEINE
FLUORESCEINES
FLUORESCEINS
FLUORESCENCE
FLUORESCENCES
FLUORESCENT
FLUORESCENTS
FLUORESCER
FLUORESCERS
FLUORESCES
FLUORESCING
FLUORIDATE

F

FLUORIDATED
FLUORIDATES
FLUORIDATING
FLUORIDATION
FLUORIDATIONS
FLUORIDISE
FLUORIDISED
FLUORIDISES
FLUORIDISING
FLUORIDIZE
FLUORIDIZED
FLUORIDIZES
FLUORIDIZING
FLUORIMETER
FLUORIMETERS
FLUORIMETRIC
FLUORIMETRIES
FLUORIMETRY
FLUORINATE
FLUORINATED
FLUORINATES
FLUORINATING
FLUORINATION
FLUORINATIONS
FLUOROACETATE
FLUOROACETATES
FLUOROCARBON
FLUOROCARBONS
FLUOROCHROME
FLUOROCHROMES
FLUOROGRAPHIC
FLUOROGRAPHIES
FLUOROGRAPHY
FLUOROMETER
FLUOROMETERS
FLUOROMETRIC
FLUOROMETRIES
FLUOROMETRY
FLUOROPHORE
FLUOROPHORES
FLUOROSCOPE
FLUOROSCOPED
FLUOROSCOPES
FLUOROSCOPIC
FLUOROSCOPIES
FLUOROSCOPING
FLUOROSCOPIST

FLUOROSCOPISTS
FLUOROSCOPY
FLUOROTYPE
FLUOROTYPES
FLUOROURACIL
FLUOROURACILS
FLUORSPARS
FLUOXETINE
FLUOXETINES
FLUPHENAZINE
FLUPHENAZINES
FLUSHNESSES
FLUSHWORKS
FLUSTEREDLY
FLUSTERING
FLUSTERMENT
FLUSTERMENTS
FLUSTRATED
FLUSTRATES
FLUSTRATING
FLUSTRATION
FLUSTRATIONS
FLUTEMOUTH
FLUTEMOUTHS
FLUTTERBOARD
FLUTTERBOARDS
FLUTTERERS
FLUTTERING
FLUTTERINGLY
FLUVIALIST
FLUVIALISTS
FLUVIATILE
FLUVIOMARINE
FLUVOXAMINE
FLUVOXAMINES
FLUXIONALLY
FLUXIONARY
FLUXIONIST
FLUXIONISTS
FLUXMETERS
FLYBLOWING
FLYBRIDGES
FLYCATCHER
FLYCATCHERS
FLYPITCHER
FLYPITCHERS
FLYPITCHES

FLYPOSTERS
FLYPOSTING
FLYPOSTINGS
FLYRODDERS
FLYSCREENS
FLYSPECKED
FLYSPECKING
FLYSTRIKES
FLYSWATTER
FLYSWATTERS
FLYWEIGHTS
FOAMFLOWER
FOAMFLOWERS
FOAMINESSES
FOCALISATION
FOCALISATIONS
FOCALISING
FOCALIZATION
FOCALIZATIONS
FOCALIZING
FOCIMETERS
FOCOMETERS
FODDERINGS
FOEDERATUS
FOETATIONS
FOETICIDAL
FOETICIDES
FOETIDNESS
FOETIDNESSES
FOETIPAROUS
FOETOSCOPIES
FOETOSCOPY
FOGGINESSES
FOGRAMITES
FOGRAMITIES
FOILSWOMAN
FOILSWOMEN
FOISONLESS
FOLIACEOUS
FOLIATIONS
FOLIATURES
FOLKISHNESS
FOLKISHNESSES
FOLKLORISH
FOLKLORIST
FOLKLORISTIC
FOLKLORISTS

FOLKSINESS
FOLKSINESSES
FOLKSINGER
FOLKSINGERS
FOLKSINGING
FOLKSINGINGS
FOLKSONOMIES
FOLKSONOMY
FOLKTRONICA
FOLKTRONICAS
FOLLICULAR
FOLLICULATE
FOLLICULATED
FOLLICULIN
FOLLICULINS
FOLLICULITIS
FOLLICULITISES
FOLLICULOSE
FOLLICULOUS
FOLLOWABLE
FOLLOWERSHIP
FOLLOWERSHIPS
FOLLOWINGS
FOLLOWSHIP
FOLLOWSHIPS
FOMENTATION
FOMENTATIONS
FONCTIONNAIRE
FONCTIONNAIRES
FONDLINGLY
FONDNESSES
FONTANELLE
FONTANELLES
FONTICULUS
FONTINALIS
FONTINALISES
FOODLESSNESS
FOODLESSNESSES
FOODSTUFFS
FOOLBEGGED
FOOLFISHES
FOOLHARDIER
FOOLHARDIEST
FOOLHARDILY
FOOLHARDINESS
FOOLHARDINESSES
FOOLHARDISE

FOOLHARDISES
FOOLHARDIZE
FOOLHARDIZES
FOOLISHEST
FOOLISHNESS
FOOLISHNESSES
FOOTBALLENE
FOOTBALLENES
FOOTBALLER
FOOTBALLERS
FOOTBALLING
FOOTBALLIST
FOOTBALLISTS
FOOTBOARDS
FOOTBRAKES
FOOTBREADTH
FOOTBREADTHS
FOOTBRIDGE
FOOTBRIDGES
FOOTCLOTHS
FOOTDRAGGER
FOOTDRAGGERS
FOOTDRAGGING
FOOTDRAGGINGS
FOOTFAULTED
FOOTFAULTING
FOOTFAULTS
FOOTGUARDS
FOOTLAMBERT
FOOTLAMBERTS
FOOTLESSLY
FOOTLESSNESS
FOOTLESSNESSES
FOOTLIGHTS
FOOTLOCKER
FOOTLOCKERS
FOOTNOTING
FOOTPLATEMAN
FOOTPLATEMEN
FOOTPLATES
FOOTPLATEWOMAN
FOOTPLATEWOMEN
FOOTPRINTS
FOOTSLOGGED
FOOTSLOGGER
FOOTSLOGGERS
FOOTSLOGGING

FOOTSLOGGINGS	FORCIPATION	FOREFATHER	FORELENDING	FORESEEINGLY
FOOTSORENESS	FORCIPATIONS	FOREFATHERLY	FORELIFTED	FORESHADOW
FOOTSORENESSES	FOREARMING	FOREFATHERS	FORELIFTING	FORESHADOWED
FOOTSTALKS	FOREBITTER	FOREFEELING	FORELOCKED	FORESHADOWER
FOOTSTALLS	FOREBITTERS	FOREFEELINGLY	FORELOCKING	FORESHADOWERS
FOOTSTOCKS	FOREBODEMENT	FOREFENDED	FOREMANSHIP	FORESHADOWING
FOOTSTONES	FOREBODEMENTS	FOREFENDING	FOREMANSHIPS	FORESHADOWINGS
FOOTSTOOLED	FOREBODERS	FOREFINGER	FOREMASTMAN	FORESHADOWS
FOOTSTOOLS	FOREBODIES	FOREFINGERS	FOREMASTMEN	FORESHANKS
FOPPISHNESS	FOREBODING	FOREFRONTS	FOREMEANING	FORESHEETS
FOPPISHNESSES	FOREBODINGLY	FOREGATHER	FOREMENTIONED	FORESHEWED
FORAMINATED	FOREBODINGNESS	FOREGATHERED	FOREMOTHER	FORESHEWING
FORAMINIFER	FOREBODINGS	FOREGATHERING	FOREMOTHERS	FORESHOCKS
FORAMINIFERA	FOREBRAINS	FOREGATHERS	FORENIGHTS	FORESHORES
FORAMINIFERAL	FORECABINS	FOREGLEAMS	FORENSICALITIES	FORESHORTEN
FORAMINIFERAN	FORECADDIE	FOREGOINGS	FORENSICALITY	FORESHORTENED
FORAMINIFERANS	FORECADDIES	FOREGONENESS	FORENSICALLY	FORESHORTENING
FORAMINIFEROUS	FORECARRIAGE	FOREGONENESSES	FOREORDAIN	FORESHORTENINGS
FORAMINIFERS	FORECARRIAGES	FOREGROUND	FOREORDAINED	FORESHORTENS
FORAMINOUS	FORECASTABLE	FOREGROUNDED	FOREORDAINING	FORESHOWED
FORBEARANCE	FORECASTED	FOREGROUNDING	FOREORDAINMENT	FORESHOWING
FORBEARANCES	FORECASTER	FOREGROUNDS	FOREORDAINMENTS	FORESIGHTED
FORBEARANT	FORECASTERS	FOREHANDED	FOREORDAINS	FORESIGHTEDLY
FORBEARERS	FORECASTING	FOREHANDEDLY	FOREORDINATION	FORESIGHTEDNESS
FORBEARING	FORECASTINGS	FOREHANDEDNESS	FOREORDINATIONS	FORESIGHTFUL
FORBEARINGLY	FORECASTLE	FOREHANDING	FOREPASSED	FORESIGHTLESS
FORBIDDALS	FORECASTLES	FOREHENTING	FOREPAYMENT	FORESIGHTS
FORBIDDANCE	FORECHECKED	FOREHOOVES	FOREPAYMENTS	FORESIGNIFIED
FORBIDDANCES	FORECHECKER	FOREIGNERS	FOREPLANNED	FORESIGNIFIES
FORBIDDENLY	FORECHECKERS	FOREIGNISM	FOREPLANNING	FORESIGNIFY
FORBIDDERS	FORECHECKING	FOREIGNISMS	FOREPOINTED	FORESIGNIFYING
FORBIDDING	FORECHECKS	FOREIGNNESS	FOREPOINTING	FORESKIRTS
FORBIDDINGLY	FORECHOSEN	FOREIGNNESSES	FOREPOINTS	FORESLACKED
FORBIDDINGNESS	FORECLOSABLE	FOREJUDGED	FOREQUARTER	FORESLACKING
FORBIDDINGS	FORECLOSED	FOREJUDGEMENT	FOREQUARTERS	FORESLACKS
FORCEDNESS	FORECLOSES	FOREJUDGEMENTS	FOREREACHED	FORESLOWED
FORCEDNESSES	FORECLOSING	FOREJUDGES	FOREREACHES	FORESLOWING
FORCEFULLY	FORECLOSURE	FOREJUDGING	FOREREACHING	FORESPEAKING
FORCEFULNESS	FORECLOSURES	FOREJUDGMENT	FOREREADING	FORESPEAKS
FORCEFULNESSES	FORECLOTHS	FOREJUDGMENTS	FOREREADINGS	FORESPENDING
FORCEMEATS	FORECOURSE	FOREKNOWABLE	FORERUNNER	FORESPENDS
FORCEPSLIKE	FORECOURSES	FOREKNOWING	FORERUNNERS	FORESPOKEN
FORCIBILITIES	FORECOURTS	FOREKNOWINGLY	FORERUNNING	FORESTAGES
FORCIBILITY	FOREDAMNED	FOREKNOWLEDGE	FORESAYING	FORESTAIRS
FORCIBLENESS	FOREDATING	FOREKNOWLEDGES	FORESEEABILITY	FORESTALLED
FORCIBLENESSES	FOREDOOMED	FORELADIES	FORESEEABLE	FORESTALLER
FORCIPATED	FOREDOOMING	FORELAYING	FORESEEING	FORESTALLERS

F

FORESTALLING
FORESTALLINGS
FORESTALLMENT
FORESTALLMENTS
FORESTALLS
FORESTALMENT
FORESTALMENTS
FORESTATION
FORESTATIONS
FORESTAYSAIL
FORESTAYSAILS
FORESTLAND
FORESTLANDS
FORESTLESS
FORESTRIES
FORESWEARING
FORESWEARS
FORETASTED
FORETASTES
FORETASTING
FORETAUGHT
FORETEACHES
FORETEACHING
FORETELLER
FORETELLERS
FORETELLING
FORETHINKER
FORETHINKERS
FORETHINKING
FORETHINKS
FORETHOUGHT
FORETHOUGHTFUL
FORETHOUGHTS
FORETOKENED
FORETOKENING
FORETOKENINGS
FORETOKENS
FORETOPMAN
FORETOPMAST
FORETOPMASTS
FORETOPMEN
FORETRIANGLE
FORETRIANGLES
FOREVERMORE
FOREVERNESS
FOREVERNESSES
FOREVOUCHED

FOREWARDED
FOREWARDING
FOREWARNED
FOREWARNER
FOREWARNERS
FOREWARNING
FOREWARNINGLY
FOREWARNINGS
FOREWEIGHED
FOREWEIGHING
FOREWEIGHS
FORFAIRING
FORFAITERS
FORFAITING
FORFAITINGS
FORFEITABLE
FORFEITERS
FORFEITING
FORFEITURE
FORFEITURES
FORFENDING
FORFEUCHEN
FORFICULATE
FORFOUGHEN
FORFOUGHTEN
FORGATHERED
FORGATHERING
FORGATHERS
FORGEABILITIES
FORGEABILITY
FORGETFULLY
FORGETFULNESS
FORGETFULNESSES
FORGETTABLE
FORGETTERIES
FORGETTERS
FORGETTERY
FORGETTING
FORGETTINGLY
FORGETTINGS
FORGIVABLE
FORGIVABLY
FORGIVENESS
FORGIVENESSES
FORGIVINGLY
FORGIVINGNESS
FORGIVINGNESSES

FORGOTTENNESS
FORGOTTENNESSES
FORHAILING
FORHENTING
FORHOOIEING
FORINSECAL
FORISFAMILIATE
FORISFAMILIATED
FORISFAMILIATES
FORJUDGING
FORJUDGMENT
FORJUDGMENTS
FORKEDNESS
FORKEDNESSES
FORKINESSES
FORKLIFTED
FORKLIFTING
FORLENDING
FORLORNEST
FORLORNNESS
FORLORNNESSES
FORMABILITIES
FORMABILITY
FORMALDEHYDE
FORMALDEHYDES
FORMALINES
FORMALISABLE
FORMALISATION
FORMALISATIONS
FORMALISED
FORMALISER
FORMALISERS
FORMALISES
FORMALISING
FORMALISMS
FORMALISTIC
FORMALISTICALLY
FORMALISTS
FORMALITER
FORMALITIES
FORMALIZABLE
FORMALIZATION
FORMALIZATIONS
FORMALIZED
FORMALIZER
FORMALIZERS
FORMALIZES

FORMALIZING
FORMALNESS
FORMALNESSES
FORMAMIDES
FORMATIONAL
FORMATIONS
FORMATIVELY
FORMATIVENESS
FORMATIVENESSES
FORMATIVES
FORMATTERS
FORMATTING
FORMATTINGS
FORMFITTING
FORMICARIA
FORMICARIES
FORMICARIUM
FORMICATED
FORMICATES
FORMICATING
FORMICATION
FORMICATIONS
FORMIDABILITIES
FORMIDABILITY
FORMIDABLE
FORMIDABLENESS
FORMIDABLY
FORMLESSLY
FORMLESSNESS
FORMLESSNESSES
FORMULAICALLY
FORMULARIES
FORMULARISATION
FORMULARISE
FORMULARISED
FORMULARISER
FORMULARISERS
FORMULARISES
FORMULARISING
FORMULARISTIC
FORMULARIZATION
FORMULARIZE
FORMULARIZED
FORMULARIZER
FORMULARIZERS
FORMULARIZES
FORMULARIZING

FORMULATED
FORMULATES
FORMULATING
FORMULATION
FORMULATIONS
FORMULATOR
FORMULATORS
FORMULISED
FORMULISES
FORMULISING
FORMULISMS
FORMULISTIC
FORMULISTS
FORMULIZED
FORMULIZES
FORMULIZING
FORNICATED
FORNICATES
FORNICATING
FORNICATION
FORNICATIONS
FORNICATOR
FORNICATORS
FORNICATRESS
FORNICATRESSES
FORSAKENLY
FORSAKENNESS
FORSAKENNESSES
FORSAKINGS
FORSLACKED
FORSLACKING
FORSLOEING
FORSLOWING
FORSPEAKING
FORSPENDING
FORSTERITE
FORSTERITES
FORSWEARER
FORSWEARERS
FORSWEARING
FORSWINKED
FORSWINKING
FORSWORNNESS
FORSWORNNESSES
FORSYTHIAS
FORTALICES
FORTEPIANIST

FORTEPIANISTS
FORTEPIANO
FORTEPIANOS
FORTHCOMES
FORTHCOMING
FORTHCOMINGNESS
FORTHGOING
FORTHGOINGS
FORTHINKING
FORTHOUGHT
FORTHRIGHT
FORTHRIGHTLY
FORTHRIGHTNESS
FORTHRIGHTS
FORTIFIABLE
FORTIFICATION
FORTIFICATIONS
FORTIFIERS
FORTIFYING
FORTIFYINGLY
FORTILAGES
FORTISSIMI
FORTISSIMO
FORTISSIMOS
FORTISSISSIMO
FORTITUDES
FORTITUDINOUS
FORTNIGHTLIES
FORTNIGHTLY
FORTNIGHTS
FORTRESSED
FORTRESSES
FORTRESSING
FORTRESSLIKE
FORTUITIES
FORTUITISM
FORTUITISMS
FORTUITIST
FORTUITISTS
FORTUITOUS
FORTUITOUSLY
FORTUITOUSNESS
FORTUNATELY
FORTUNATENESS
FORTUNATENESSES
FORTUNATES
FORTUNELESS

FORTUNISED
FORTUNISES
FORTUNISING
FORTUNIZED
FORTUNIZES
FORTUNIZING
FORWANDERED
FORWANDERING
FORWANDERS
FORWARDERS
FORWARDEST
FORWARDING
FORWARDINGS
FORWARDNESS
FORWARDNESSES
FORWARNING
FORWASTING
FORWEARIED
FORWEARIES
FORWEARYING
FOSCARNETS
FOSSICKERS
FOSSICKING
FOSSICKINGS
FOSSILIFEROUS
FOSSILISABLE
FOSSILISATION
FOSSILISATIONS
FOSSILISED
FOSSILISES
FOSSILISING
FOSSILIZABLE
FOSSILIZATION
FOSSILIZATIONS
FOSSILIZED
FOSSILIZES
FOSSILIZING
FOSTERAGES
FOSTERINGS
FOSTERLING
FOSTERLINGS
FOSTRESSES
FOTHERGILLA
FOTHERGILLAS
FOUDROYANT
FOUGHTIEST
FOULBROODS

FOULDERING
FOULMOUTHED
FOULNESSES
FOUNDATION
FOUNDATIONAL
FOUNDATIONALLY
FOUNDATIONARY
FOUNDATIONER
FOUNDATIONERS
FOUNDATIONLESS
FOUNDATIONS
FOUNDERING
FOUNDEROUS
FOUNDLINGS
FOUNDRESSES
FOUNTAINED
FOUNTAINHEAD
FOUNTAINHEADS
FOUNTAINING
FOUNTAINLESS
FOURCHETTE
FOURCHETTES
FOURDRINIER
FOURDRINIERS
FOURFOLDNESS
FOURFOLDNESSES
FOURPENCES
FOURPENNIES
FOURPLEXES
FOURRAGERE
FOURRAGERES
FOURSCORTH
FOURSQUARE
FOURSQUARELY
FOURSQUARENESS
FOURTEENER
FOURTEENERS
FOURTEENTH
FOURTEENTHLY
FOURTEENTHS
FOVEOLATED
FOXBERRIES
FOXHUNTERS
FOXHUNTING
FOXHUNTINGS
FOXINESSES
FOXTROTTED

FOXTROTTING
FOZINESSES
FRABJOUSLY
FRACTALITIES
FRACTALITY
FRACTIONAL
FRACTIONALISE
FRACTIONALISED
FRACTIONALISES
FRACTIONALISING
FRACTIONALISM
FRACTIONALISMS
FRACTIONALIST
FRACTIONALISTS
FRACTIONALIZE
FRACTIONALIZED
FRACTIONALIZES
FRACTIONALIZING
FRACTIONALLY
FRACTIONARY
FRACTIONATE
FRACTIONATED
FRACTIONATES
FRACTIONATING
FRACTIONATION
FRACTIONATIONS
FRACTIONATOR
FRACTIONATORS
FRACTIONED
FRACTIONING
FRACTIONISATION
FRACTIONISE
FRACTIONISED
FRACTIONISES
FRACTIONISING
FRACTIONIZATION
FRACTIONIZE
FRACTIONIZED
FRACTIONIZES
FRACTIONIZING
FRACTIONLET
FRACTIONLETS
FRACTIOUSLY
FRACTIOUSNESS
FRACTIOUSNESSES
FRACTOCUMULI
FRACTOCUMULUS

FRACTOGRAPHIES
FRACTOGRAPHY
FRACTOSTRATI
FRACTOSTRATUS
FRACTURABLE
FRACTURERS
FRACTURING
FRAGILENESS
FRAGILENESSES
FRAGILITIES
FRAGMENTAL
FRAGMENTALLY
FRAGMENTARILY
FRAGMENTARINESS
FRAGMENTARY
FRAGMENTATE
FRAGMENTATED
FRAGMENTATES
FRAGMENTATING
FRAGMENTATION
FRAGMENTATIONS
FRAGMENTED
FRAGMENTING
FRAGMENTISE
FRAGMENTISED
FRAGMENTISES
FRAGMENTISING
FRAGMENTIZE
FRAGMENTIZED
FRAGMENTIZES
FRAGMENTIZING
FRAGRANCED
FRAGRANCES
FRAGRANCIES
FRAGRANCING
FRAGRANTLY
FRAGRANTNESS
FRAGRANTNESSES
FRAICHEURS
FRAILNESSES
FRAMBESIAS
FRAMBOESIA
FRAMBOESIAS
FRAMBOISES
FRAMESHIFT
FRAMESHIFTS
FRAMEWORKS

F

FRANCHISED	FRANKLINITE	FRAXINELLA	FREELOADERS	FRENCHIFIES
FRANCHISEE	FRANKLINITES	FRAXINELLAS	FREELOADING	FRENCHIFYING
FRANCHISEES	FRANKNESSES	FREAKERIES	FREELOADINGS	FRENETICAL
FRANCHISEMENT	FRANKPLEDGE	FREAKINESS	FREEMARTIN	FRENETICALLY
FRANCHISEMENTS	FRANKPLEDGES	FREAKINESSES	FREEMARTINS	FRENETICISM
FRANCHISER	FRANSERIAS	FREAKISHLY	FREEMASONIC	FRENETICISMS
FRANCHISERS	FRANTICALLY	FREAKISHNESS	FREEMASONRIES	FRENETICNESS
FRANCHISES	FRANTICNESS	FREAKISHNESSES	FREEMASONRY	FRENETICNESSES
FRANCHISING	FRANTICNESSES	FRECKLIEST	FREEMASONS	FRENZIEDLY
FRANCHISOR	FRATCHIEST	FRECKLINGS	FREENESSES	FREQUENCES
FRANCHISORS	FRATERNALISM	FREEBASERS	FREEPHONES	FREQUENCIES
FRANCISATION	FRATERNALISMS	FREEBASING	FREESHEETS	FREQUENTABLE
FRANCISATIONS	FRATERNALLY	FREEBOARDS	FREESTANDING	FREQUENTATION
FRANCISING	FRATERNISATION	FREEBOOTED	FREESTONES	FREQUENTATIONS
FRANCIZATION	FRATERNISATIONS	FREEBOOTER	FREESTYLED	FREQUENTATIVE
FRANCIZATIONS	FRATERNISE	FREEBOOTERIES	FREESTYLER	FREQUENTATIVES
FRANCIZING	FRATERNISED	FREEBOOTERS	FREESTYLERS	FREQUENTED
FRANCOLINS	FRATERNISER	FREEBOOTERY	FREESTYLES	FREQUENTER
FRANCOMANIA	FRATERNISERS	FREEBOOTIES	FREESTYLING	FREQUENTERS
FRANCOMANIAS	FRATERNISES	FREEBOOTING	FREESTYLINGS	FREQUENTEST
FRANCOPHIL	FRATERNISING	FREEBOOTINGS	FREETHINKER	FREQUENTING
FRANCOPHILE	FRATERNITIES	FREECOOLING	FREETHINKERS	FREQUENTLY
FRANCOPHILES	FRATERNITY	FREECOOLINGS	FREETHINKING	FREQUENTNESS
FRANCOPHILS	FRATERNIZATION	FREECYCLED	FREETHINKINGS	FREQUENTNESSES
FRANCOPHOBE	FRATERNIZATIONS	FREECYCLES	FREEWHEELED	FRESCOINGS
FRANCOPHOBES	FRATERNIZE	FREECYCLING	FREEWHEELER	FRESCOISTS
FRANCOPHOBIA	FRATERNIZED	FREEDIVERS	FREEWHEELERS	FRESHENERS
FRANCOPHOBIAS	FRATERNIZER	FREEDIVING	FREEWHEELING	FRESHENING
FRANCOPHONE	FRATERNIZERS	FREEDIVINGS	FREEWHEELINGLY	FRESHERDOM
FRANCOPHONES	FRATERNIZES	FREEDWOMAN	FREEWHEELINGS	FRESHERDOMS
FRANGIBILITIES	FRATERNIZING	FREEDWOMEN	FREEWHEELS	FRESHMANSHIP
FRANGIBILITY	FRATRICIDAL	FREEGANISM	FREEWRITES	FRESHMANSHIPS
FRANGIBLENESS	FRATRICIDE	FREEGANISMS	FREEWRITING	FRESHNESSES
FRANGIBLENESSES	FRATRICIDES	FREEHANDED	FREEWRITINGS	FRESHWATER
FRANGIPANE	FRAUDFULLY	FREEHANDEDLY	FREEWRITTEN	FRESHWATERS
FRANGIPANES	FRAUDSTERS	FREEHANDEDNESS	FREEZINGLY	FRETBOARDS
FRANGIPANI	FRAUDULENCE	FREEHEARTED	FREIGHTAGE	FRETFULNESS
FRANGIPANIS	FRAUDULENCES	FREEHEARTEDLY	FREIGHTAGES	FRETFULNESSES
FRANGIPANNI	FRAUDULENCIES	FREEHOLDER	FREIGHTERS	FRIABILITIES
FRANKALMOIGN	FRAUDULENCY	FREEHOLDERS	FREIGHTING	FRIABILITY
FRANKALMOIGNS	FRAUDULENT	FREELANCED	FREIGHTLESS	FRIABLENESS
FRANKFORTS	FRAUDULENTLY	FREELANCER	FREMESCENCE	FRIABLENESSES
FRANKFURTER	FRAUDULENTNESS	FREELANCERS	FREMESCENCES	FRIARBIRDS
FRANKFURTERS	FRAUGHTAGE	FREELANCES	FREMESCENT	FRICANDEAU
FRANKFURTS	FRAUGHTAGES	FREELANCING	FREMITUSES	FRICANDEAUS
FRANKINCENSE	FRAUGHTEST	FREELOADED	FRENCHIFICATION	FRICANDEAUX
FRANKINCENSES	FRAUGHTING	FREELOADER	FRENCHIFIED	FRICANDOES

FRICASSEED	FRINGILLINE	FRONDESCENT	FROTHINESS	FRUITARIANISMS
FRICASSEEING	FRIPONNERIE	FRONDIFEROUS	FROTHINESSES	FRUITARIANS
FRICASSEES	FRIPONNERIES	FRONTAGERS	FROUGHIEST	FRUITCAKES
FRICATIVES	FRIPPERERS	FRONTALITIES	FROUZINESS	FRUITERERS
FRICTIONAL	FRIPPERIES	FRONTALITY	FROUZINESSES	FRUITERESS
FRICTIONALLY	FRISKINESS	FRONTBENCHER	FROWARDNESS	FRUITERESSES
FRICTIONLESS	FRISKINESSES	FRONTBENCHERS	FROWARDNESSES	FRUITERIES
FRICTIONLESSLY	FRISKINGLY	FRONTCOURT	FROWNINGLY	FRUITFULLER
FRIEDCAKES	FRITHBORHS	FRONTCOURTS	FROWSINESS	FRUITFULLEST
FRIENDINGS	FRITHSOKEN	FRONTENISES	FROWSINESSES	FRUITFULLY
FRIENDLESS	FRITHSOKENS	FRONTIERED	FROWSTIEST	FRUITFULNESS
FRIENDLESSNESS	FRITHSTOOL	FRONTIERING	FROWSTINESS	FRUITFULNESSES
FRIENDLIER	FRITHSTOOLS	FRONTIERSMAN	FROWSTINESSES	FRUITINESS
FRIENDLIES	FRITILLARIA	FRONTIERSMEN	FROWZINESS	FRUITINESSES
FRIENDLIEST	FRITILLARIAS	FRONTIERSWOMAN	FROWZINESSES	FRUITLESSLY
FRIENDLILY	FRITILLARIES	FRONTIERSWOMEN	FROZENNESS	FRUITLESSNESS
FRIENDLINESS	FRITILLARY	FRONTISPIECE	FROZENNESSES	FRUITLESSNESSES
FRIENDLINESSES	FRITTERERS	FRONTISPIECED	FRUCTIFEROUS	FRUITWOODS
FRIENDSHIP	FRITTERING	FRONTISPIECES	FRUCTIFEROUSLY	FRUMENTACEOUS
FRIENDSHIPS	FRIVOLITIES	FRONTISPIECING	FRUCTIFICATION	FRUMENTARIOUS
FRIEZELIKE	FRIVOLLERS	FRONTLESSLY	FRUCTIFICATIONS	FRUMENTATION
FRIGATOONS	FRIVOLLING	FRONTLINES	FRUCTIFIED	FRUMENTATIONS
FRIGHTENED	FRIVOLOUSLY	FRONTLISTS	FRUCTIFIER	FRUMENTIES
FRIGHTENER	FRIVOLOUSNESS	FRONTOGENESES	FRUCTIFIERS	FRUMPINESS
FRIGHTENERS	FRIVOLOUSNESSES	FRONTOGENESIS	FRUCTIFIES	FRUMPINESSES
FRIGHTENING	FRIZZINESS	FRONTOGENETIC	FRUCTIFYING	FRUMPISHLY
FRIGHTENINGLY	FRIZZINESSES	FRONTOLYSES	FRUCTIVOROUS	FRUMPISHNESS
FRIGHTFULLY	FRIZZLIEST	FRONTOLYSIS	FRUCTUARIES	FRUMPISHNESSES
FRIGHTFULNESS	FRIZZLINESS	FRONTPAGED	FRUCTUATED	FRUSEMIDES
FRIGHTFULNESSES	FRIZZLINESSES	FRONTPAGES	FRUCTUATES	FRUSTRATED
FRIGHTSOME	FROGFISHES	FRONTPAGING	FRUCTUATING	FRUSTRATER
FRIGIDARIA	FROGGERIES	FRONTRUNNER	FRUCTUATION	FRUSTRATERS
FRIGIDARIUM	FROGHOPPER	FRONTRUNNERS	FRUCTUATIONS	FRUSTRATES
FRIGIDITIES	FROGHOPPERS	FRONTRUNNING	FRUCTUOUSLY	FRUSTRATING
FRIGIDNESS	FROGMARCHED	FRONTRUNNINGS	FRUCTUOUSNESS	FRUSTRATINGLY
FRIGIDNESSES	FROGMARCHES	FRONTWARDS	FRUCTUOUSNESSES	FRUSTRATION
FRIGORIFIC	FROGMARCHING	FROSTBITES	FRUGALISTA	FRUSTRATIONS
FRIGORIFICO	FROGMOUTHS	FROSTBITING	FRUGALISTAS	FRUTESCENCE
FRIGORIFICOS	FROGSPAWNS	FROSTBITINGS	FRUGALISTS	FRUTESCENCES
FRIKKADELS	FROLICKERS	FROSTBITTEN	FRUGALITIES	FRUTESCENT
FRILLERIES	FROLICKING	FROSTBOUND	FRUGALNESS	FRUTIFYING
FRILLINESS	FROLICSOME	FROSTFISHES	FRUGALNESSES	FUCIVOROUS
FRILLINESSES	FROLICSOMELY	FROSTINESS	FRUGIFEROUS	FUCOXANTHIN
FRINGELESS	FROLICSOMENESS	FROSTINESSES	FRUGIVORES	FUCOXANTHINS
FRINGILLACEOUS	FROMENTIES	FROSTLINES	FRUGIVOROUS	FUGACIOUSLY
FRINGILLID	FRONDESCENCE	FROSTWORKS	FRUITARIAN	FUGACIOUSNESS
FRINGILLIFORM	FRONDESCENCES	FROTHERIES	FRUITARIANISM	FUGACIOUSNESSES

FUGACITIES

FUGACITIES	FUMATORIUM	FUNDAMENTALIST	FURCATIONS	FUSILLADES
FUGGINESSES	FUMATORIUMS	FUNDAMENTALISTS	FURCIFEROUS	FUSILLADING
FUGITATION	FUMBLINGLY	FUNDAMENTALITY	FURFURACEOUS	FUSILLATION
FUGITATIONS	FUMBLINGNESS	FUNDAMENTALLY	FURFURACEOUSLY	FUSILLATIONS
FUGITIVELY	FUMBLINGNESSES	FUNDAMENTALNESS	FURFURALDEHYDE	FUSIONISMS
FUGITIVENESS	FUMIGATING	FUNDAMENTALS	FURFURALDEHYDES	FUSIONISTS
FUGITIVENESSES	FUMIGATION	FUNDAMENTS	FURFUROLES	FUSIONLESS
FUGITOMETER	FUMIGATIONS	FUNDHOLDER	FURIOSITIES	FUSSBUDGET
FUGITOMETERS	FUMIGATORS	FUNDHOLDERS	FURIOUSNESS	FUSSBUDGETS
FULFILLERS	FUMIGATORY	FUNDHOLDING	FURIOUSNESSES	FUSSBUDGETY
FULFILLING	FUMITORIES	FUNDHOLDINGS	FURLOUGHED	FUSSINESSES
FULFILLINGS	FUMOSITIES	FUNDRAISED	FURLOUGHING	FUSTANELLA
FULFILLMENT	FUNAMBULATE	FUNDRAISER	FURMENTIES	FUSTANELLAS
FULFILLMENTS	FUNAMBULATED	FUNDRAISERS	FURNIMENTS	FUSTANELLE
FULFILMENT	FUNAMBULATES	FUNDRAISES	FURNISHERS	FUSTANELLES
FULFILMENTS	FUNAMBULATING	FUNDRAISING	FURNISHING	FUSTIANISE
FULGENCIES	FUNAMBULATION	FUNDRAISINGS	FURNISHINGS	FUSTIANISED
FULGURATED	FUNAMBULATIONS	FUNEREALLY	FURNISHMENT	FUSTIANISES
FULGURATES	FUNAMBULATOR	FUNGIBILITIES	FURNISHMENTS	FUSTIANISING
FULGURATING	FUNAMBULATORS	FUNGIBILITY	FURNITURES	FUSTIANIST
FULGURATION	FUNAMBULATORY	FUNGICIDAL	FUROSEMIDE	FUSTIANISTS
FULGURATIONS	FUNAMBULISM	FUNGICIDALLY	FUROSEMIDES	FUSTIANIZE
FULGURITES	FUNAMBULISMS	FUNGICIDES	FURRIERIES	FUSTIANIZED
FULIGINOSITIES	FUNAMBULIST	FUNGISTATIC	FURRINESSES	FUSTIANIZES
FULIGINOSITY	FUNAMBULISTS	FUNGISTATICALLY	FURROWLESS	FUSTIANIZING
FULIGINOUS	FUNCTIONAL	FUNGISTATS	FURSHLUGGINER	FUSTIGATED
FULIGINOUSLY	FUNCTIONALISM	FUNGOSITIES	FURTHCOMING	FUSTIGATES
FULIGINOUSNESS	FUNCTIONALISMS	FUNICULARS	FURTHCOMINGS	FUSTIGATING
FULLBLOODS	FUNCTIONALIST	FUNICULATE	FURTHERANCE	FUSTIGATION
FULLERENES	FUNCTIONALISTIC	FUNKINESSES	FURTHERANCES	FUSTIGATIONS
FULLERIDES	FUNCTIONALISTS	FUNNELFORM	FURTHERERS	FUSTIGATOR
FULLERITES	FUNCTIONALITIES	FUNNELLING	FURTHERING	FUSTIGATORS
FULLMOUTHED	FUNCTIONALITY	FUNNINESSES	FURTHERMORE	FUSTIGATORY
FULLNESSES	FUNCTIONALLY	FURACIOUSNESS	FURTHERMOST	FUSTILARIAN
FULMINANTS	FUNCTIONALS	FURACIOUSNESSES	FURTHERSOME	FUSTILARIANS
FULMINATED	FUNCTIONARIES	FURACITIES	FURTIVENESS	FUSTILIRIAN
FULMINATES	FUNCTIONARY	FURALDEHYDE	FURTIVENESSES	FUSTILIRIANS
FULMINATING	FUNCTIONATE	FURALDEHYDES	FURUNCULAR	FUSTILLIRIAN
FULMINATION	FUNCTIONATED	FURANOSIDE	FURUNCULOSES	FUSTILLIRIANS
FULMINATIONS	FUNCTIONATES	FURANOSIDES	FURUNCULOSIS	FUSTINESSES
FULMINATOR	FUNCTIONATING	FURAZOLIDONE	FURUNCULOUS	FUSULINIDS
FULMINATORS	FUNCTIONED	FURAZOLIDONES	FUSHIONLESS	FUTILENESS
FULMINATORY	FUNCTIONING	FURBEARERS	FUSIBILITIES	FUTILENESSES
FULMINEOUS	FUNCTIONLESS	FURBELOWED	FUSIBILITY	FUTILITARIAN
FULSOMENESS	FUNDAMENTAL	FURBELOWING	FUSIBLENESS	FUTILITARIANISM
FULSOMENESSES	FUNDAMENTALISM	FURBISHERS	FUSIBLENESSES	FUTILITARIANS
FUMATORIES	FUNDAMENTALISMS	FURBISHING	FUSILLADED	FUTILITIES

FUTURELESS
FUTURELESSNESS
FUTURISTIC

FUTURISTICALLY
FUTURISTICS
FUTURITIES

FUTURITION
FUTURITIONS
FUTUROLOGICAL

FUTUROLOGIES
FUTUROLOGIST
FUTUROLOGISTS

FUTUROLOGY
FUZZINESSES

G

GABAPENTIN
GABAPENTINS
GABARDINES
GABBINESSES
GABBLEMENT
GABBLEMENTS
GABBROITIC
GABERDINES
GABERLUNZIE
GABERLUNZIES
GABIONADES
GABIONAGES
GABIONNADE
GABIONNADES
GADGETEERS
GADGETRIES
GADOLINITE
GADOLINITES
GADOLINIUM
GADOLINIUMS
GADROONING
GADROONINGS
GADZOOKERIES
GADZOOKERY
GAELICISED
GAELICISES
GAELICISING
GAELICISMS
GAELICIZED
GAELICIZES
GAELICIZING
GAILLARDIA
GAILLARDIAS
GAINFULNESS
GAINFULNESSES
GAINGIVING
GAINGIVINGS
GAINLESSNESS
GAINLESSNESSES
GAINLINESS
GAINLINESSES

GAINSAYERS
GAINSAYING
GAINSAYINGS
GAINSHARING
GAINSHARINGS
GAINSTRIVE
GAINSTRIVED
GAINSTRIVEN
GAINSTRIVES
GAINSTRIVING
GAINSTROVE
GAITERLESS
GALABIYAHS
GALACTAGOGUE
GALACTAGOGUES
GALACTICOS
GALACTOMETER
GALACTOMETERS
GALACTOMETRIES
GALACTOMETRY
GALACTOPHOROUS
GALACTOPOIESES
GALACTOPOIESIS
GALACTOPOIETIC
GALACTOPOIETICS
GALACTORRHEA
GALACTORRHEAS
GALACTORRHOEA
GALACTORRHOEAS
GALACTOSAEMIA
GALACTOSAEMIAS
GALACTOSAEMIC
GALACTOSAMINE
GALACTOSAMINES
GALACTOSEMIA
GALACTOSEMIAS
GALACTOSEMIC
GALACTOSES
GALACTOSIDASE
GALACTOSIDASES
GALACTOSIDE

GALACTOSIDES
GALACTOSYL
GALACTOSYLS
GALANTAMINE
GALANTAMINES
GALANTINES
GALAVANTED
GALAVANTING
GALDRAGONS
GALENGALES
GALENICALS
GALEOPITHECINE
GALEOPITHECOID
GALIMATIAS
GALIMATIASES
GALINGALES
GALIONGEES
GALIVANTED
GALIVANTING
GALLABEAHS
GALLABIAHS
GALLABIEHS
GALLABIYAH
GALLABIYAHS
GALLABIYAS
GALLABIYEH
GALLABIYEHS
GALLAMINES
GALLANTEST
GALLANTING
GALLANTNESS
GALLANTNESSES
GALLANTRIES
GALLBLADDER
GALLBLADDERS
GALLEASSES
GALLERISTS
GALLERYGOER
GALLERYGOERS
GALLERYING
GALLERYITE

GALLERYITES
GALLIAMBIC
GALLIAMBICS
GALLIARDISE
GALLIARDISES
GALLIASSES
GALLICISATION
GALLICISATIONS
GALLICISED
GALLICISES
GALLICISING
GALLICISMS
GALLICIZATION
GALLICIZATIONS
GALLICIZED
GALLICIZES
GALLICIZING
GALLIGASKINS
GALLIMAUFRIES
GALLIMAUFRY
GALLINACEAN
GALLINACEANS
GALLINACEOUS
GALLINAZOS
GALLINIPPER
GALLINIPPERS
GALLINULES
GALLISISED
GALLISISES
GALLISISING
GALLISIZED
GALLISIZES
GALLISIZING
GALLIVANTED
GALLIVANTING
GALLIVANTS
GALLIWASPS
GALLOGLASS
GALLOGLASSES
GALLONAGES
GALLOPADED

GALLOPADES
GALLOPADING
GALLOWGLASS
GALLOWGLASSES
GALLOWSNESS
GALLOWSNESSES
GALLSICKNESS
GALLSICKNESSES
GALLSTONES
GALLUMPHED
GALLUMPHING
GALLYGASKINS
GALRAVAGED
GALRAVAGES
GALRAVAGING
GALRAVITCH
GALRAVITCHED
GALRAVITCHES
GALRAVITCHING
GALUMPHERS
GALUMPHING
GALVANICAL
GALVANICALLY
GALVANISATION
GALVANISATIONS
GALVANISED
GALVANISER
GALVANISERS
GALVANISES
GALVANISING
GALVANISMS
GALVANISTS
GALVANIZATION
GALVANIZATIONS
GALVANIZED
GALVANIZER
GALVANIZERS
GALVANIZES
GALVANIZING
GALVANOMETER
GALVANOMETERS

GALVANOMETRIC	GAMETOGENY	GANGPLANKS	GARLANDLESS	GASHLINESSES
GALVANOMETRICAL	GAMETOPHORE	GANGRENING	GARLANDRIES	GASHOLDERS
GALVANOMETRIES	GAMETOPHORES	GANGRENOUS	GARLICKIER	GASIFIABLE
GALVANOMETRY	GAMETOPHORIC	GANGSHAGGED	GARLICKIEST	GASIFICATION
GALVANOPLASTIC	GAMETOPHYTE	GANGSHAGGING	GARLICKING	GASIFICATIONS
GALVANOPLASTIES	GAMETOPHYTES	GANGSTERDOM	GARMENTING	GASOMETERS
GALVANOPLASTY	GAMETOPHYTIC	GANGSTERDOMS	GARMENTLESS	GASOMETRIC
GALVANOSCOPE	GAMEYNESSES	GANGSTERISH	GARMENTURE	GASOMETRICAL
GALVANOSCOPES	GAMIFICATION	GANGSTERISM	GARMENTURES	GASOMETRIES
GALVANOSCOPIC	GAMIFICATIONS	GANGSTERISMS	GARNETIFEROUS	GASPEREAUS
GALVANOSCOPIES	GAMINERIES	GANGSTERLAND	GARNIERITE	GASPEREAUX
GALVANOSCOPY	GAMINESQUE	GANGSTERLANDS	GARNIERITES	GASPINESSES
GALVANOTROPIC	GAMINESSES	GANNETRIES	GARNISHEED	GASSINESSES
GALVANOTROPISM	GAMMERSTANG	GANNISTERS	GARNISHEEING	GASTEROPOD
GALVANOTROPISMS	GAMMERSTANGS	GANTELOPES	GARNISHEEMENT	GASTEROPODOUS
GAMAHUCHED	GAMMOCKING	GANTLETING	GARNISHEEMENTS	GASTEROPODS
GAMAHUCHES	GAMMONINGS	GAOLBREAKING	GARNISHEES	GASTHAUSER
GAMAHUCHING	GAMOGENESES	GAOLBREAKS	GARNISHERS	GASTHAUSES
GAMARUCHED	GAMOGENESIS	GAOLBROKEN	GARNISHING	GASTIGHTNESS
GAMARUCHES	GAMOGENETIC	GAOLERESSES	GARNISHINGS	GASTIGHTNESSES
GAMARUCHING	GAMOGENETICAL	GARAGISTES	GARNISHMENT	GASTNESSES
GAMBADOING	GAMOGENETICALLY	GARBAGEMAN	GARNISHMENTS	GASTRAEUMS
GAMBOLLING	GAMOPETALOUS	GARBAGEMEN	GARNISHORS	GASTRALGIA
GAMEBREAKER	GAMOPHYLLOUS	GARBOLOGIES	GARNISHRIES	GASTRALGIAS
GAMEBREAKERS	GAMOSEPALOUS	GARBOLOGIST	GARNITURES	GASTRALGIC
GAMEFISHES	GAMOTROPIC	GARBOLOGISTS	GAROTTINGS	GASTRECTOMIES
GAMEKEEPER	GAMOTROPISM	GARDENFULS	GARRETEERS	GASTRECTOMY
GAMEKEEPERS	GAMOTROPISMS	GARDENINGS	GARRISONED	GASTRITIDES
GAMEKEEPING	GAMYNESSES	GARDENLESS	GARRISONING	GASTRITISES
GAMEKEEPINGS	GANDERISMS	GARDEROBES	GARROTTERS	GASTROCNEMII
GAMENESSES	GANGBANGED	GARGANTUAN	GARROTTING	GASTROCNEMIUS
GAMESMANSHIP	GANGBANGER	GARGANTUAS	GARROTTINGS	GASTROCOLIC
GAMESMANSHIPS	GANGBANGERS	GARGARISED	GARRULITIES	GASTRODUODENAL
GAMESOMELY	GANGBANGING	GARGARISES	GARRULOUSLY	GASTROENTERIC
GAMESOMENESS	GANGBOARDS	GARGARISING	GARRULOUSNESS	GASTROENTERITIC
GAMESOMENESSES	GANGBUSTER	GARGARISMS	GARRULOUSNESSES	GASTROENTERITIS
GAMETANGIA	GANGBUSTERS	GARGARIZED	GARRYOWENS	GASTROLITH
GAMETANGIAL	GANGBUSTING	GARGARIZES	GASBAGGING	GASTROLITHS
GAMETANGIUM	GANGBUSTINGS	GARGARIZING	GASCONADED	GASTROLOGER
GAMETICALLY	GANGLIATED	GARGOYLISM	GASCONADER	GASTROLOGERS
GAMETOCYTE	GANGLIFORM	GARGOYLISMS	GASCONADERS	GASTROLOGICAL
GAMETOCYTES	GANGLIONATED	GARIBALDIS	GASCONADES	GASTROLOGIES
GAMETOGENESES	GANGLIONIC	GARISHNESS	GASCONADING	GASTROLOGIST
GAMETOGENESIS	GANGLIOSIDE	GARISHNESSES	GASCONISMS	GASTROLOGISTS
GAMETOGENIC	GANGLIOSIDES	GARLANDAGE	GASEOUSNESS	GASTROLOGY
GAMETOGENIES	GANGMASTER	GARLANDAGES	GASEOUSNESSES	GASTROMANCIES
GAMETOGENOUS	GANGMASTERS	GARLANDING	GASHLINESS	GASTROMANCY

G

GASTRONOME	GATECRASHERS	GEANTICLINE	GELIGNITES	GENEALOGIES
GASTRONOMER	GATECRASHES	GEANTICLINES	GELLIFLOWRE	GENEALOGISE
GASTRONOMERS	GATECRASHING	GEARCHANGE	GELLIFLOWRES	GENEALOGISED
GASTRONOMES	GATEHOUSES	GEARCHANGES	GELSEMINES	GENEALOGISES
GASTRONOMIC	GATEKEEPER	GEARSHIFTS	GELSEMININE	GENEALOGISING
GASTRONOMICAL	GATEKEEPERS	GEARSTICKS	GELSEMININES	GENEALOGIST
GASTRONOMICALLY	GATEKEEPING	GEARWHEELS	GELSEMIUMS	GENEALOGISTS
GASTRONOMICS	GATEKEEPINGS	GEEKINESSES	GEMEINSCHAFT	GENEALOGIZE
GASTRONOMIES	GATHERABLE	GEEKSPEAKS	GEMEINSCHAFTEN	GENEALOGIZED
GASTRONOMIST	GATHERINGS	GEFUFFLING	GEMEINSCHAFTS	GENEALOGIZES
GASTRONOMISTS	GAUCHENESS	GEGENSCHEIN	GEMFIBROZIL	GENEALOGIZING
GASTRONOMY	GAUCHENESSES	GEGENSCHEINS	GEMFIBROZILS	GENECOLOGIES
GASTROPODAN	GAUCHERIES	GEHLENITES	GEMINATELY	GENECOLOGY
GASTROPODANS	GAUDEAMUSES	GEITONOGAMIES	GEMINATING	GENERALATE
GASTROPODOUS	GAUDINESSES	GEITONOGAMOUS	GEMINATION	GENERALATES
GASTROPODS	GAUFFERING	GEITONOGAMY	GEMINATIONS	GENERALCIES
GASTROPORN	GAUFFERINGS	GELANDESPRUNG	GEMMACEOUS	GENERALISABLE
GASTROPORNS	GAULEITERS	GELANDESPRUNGS	GEMMATIONS	GENERALISATION
GASTROPUBS	GAULTHERIA	GELATINATE	GEMMIFEROUS	GENERALISATIONS
GASTROSCOPE	GAULTHERIAS	GELATINATED	GEMMINESSES	GENERALISE
GASTROSCOPES	GAUNTLETED	GELATINATES	GEMMIPAROUS	GENERALISED
GASTROSCOPIC	GAUNTLETING	GELATINATING	GEMMIPAROUSLY	GENERALISER
GASTROSCOPIES	GAUNTNESSES	GELATINATION	GEMMOLOGICAL	GENERALISERS
GASTROSCOPIST	GAUSSMETER	GELATINATIONS	GEMMOLOGIES	GENERALISES
GASTROSCOPISTS	GAUSSMETERS	GELATINISATION	GEMMOLOGIST	GENERALISING
GASTROSCOPY	GAUZINESSES	GELATINISATIONS	GEMMOLOGISTS	GENERALISM
GASTROSOPH	GAVELKINDS	GELATINISE	GEMMULATION	GENERALISMS
GASTROSOPHER	GAWKIHOODS	GELATINISED	GEMMULATIONS	GENERALISSIMO
GASTROSOPHERS	GAWKINESSES	GELATINISER	GEMOLOGICAL	GENERALISSIMOS
GASTROSOPHIES	GAWKISHNESS	GELATINISERS	GEMOLOGIES	GENERALIST
GASTROSOPHS	GAWKISHNESSES	GELATINISES	GEMOLOGIST	GENERALISTS
GASTROSOPHY	GAYCATIONS	GELATINISING	GEMOLOGISTS	GENERALITIES
GASTROSTOMIES	GAZEHOUNDS	GELATINIZATION	GEMUTLICHKEIT	GENERALITY
GASTROSTOMY	GAZETTEERED	GELATINIZATIONS	GEMUTLICHKEITS	GENERALIZABLE
GASTROTOMIES	GAZETTEERING	GELATINIZE	GENDARMERIE	GENERALIZATION
GASTROTOMY	GAZETTEERISH	GELATINIZED	GENDARMERIES	GENERALIZATIONS
GASTROTRICH	GAZETTEERS	GELATINIZER	GENDARMERY	GENERALIZE
GASTROTRICHS	GAZILLIONAIRE	GELATINIZERS	GENDERISED	GENERALIZED
GASTROVASCULAR	GAZILLIONAIRES	GELATINIZES	GENDERISES	GENERALIZER
GASTRULATE	GAZILLIONS	GELATINIZING	GENDERISING	GENERALIZERS
GASTRULATED	GAZUMPINGS	GELATINOID	GENDERIZED	GENERALIZES
GASTRULATES	GAZUNDERED	GELATINOIDS	GENDERIZES	GENERALIZING
GASTRULATING	GAZUNDERER	GELATINOUS	GENDERIZING	GENERALLED
GASTRULATION	GAZUNDERERS	GELATINOUSLY	GENDERLESS	GENERALLING
GASTRULATIONS	GAZUNDERING	GELATINOUSNESS	GENEALOGIC	GENERALNESS
GATECRASHED	GEALOUSIES	GELIDITIES	GENEALOGICAL	GENERALNESSES
GATECRASHER	GEANTICLINAL	GELIDNESSES	GENEALOGICALLY	GENERALSHIP

GENERALSHIPS	GENICULATED	GENTILISED	GENUINENESS	GEOGRAPHICAL
GENERATING	GENICULATELY	GENTILISES	GENUINENESSES	GEOGRAPHICALLY
GENERATION	GENICULATES	GENTILISING	GEOBOTANIC	GEOGRAPHIES
GENERATIONAL	GENICULATING	GENTILISMS	GEOBOTANICAL	GEOHYDROLOGIC
GENERATIONALLY	GENICULATION	GENTILITIAL	GEOBOTANIES	GEOHYDROLOGIES
GENERATIONISM	GENICULATIONS	GENTILITIAN	GEOBOTANIST	GEOHYDROLOGIST
GENERATIONISMS	GENISTEINS	GENTILITIES	GEOBOTANISTS	GEOHYDROLOGISTS
GENERATIONS	GENITALIAL	GENTILITIOUS	GEOCACHERS	GEOHYDROLOGY
GENERATIVE	GENITIVALLY	GENTILIZED	GEOCACHING	GEOLATRIES
GENERATORS	GENITIVELY	GENTILIZES	GEOCACHINGS	GEOLINGUISTICS
GENERATRICES	GENITOURINARY	GENTILIZING	GEOCARPIES	GEOLOGIANS
GENERATRIX	GENITRICES	GENTILSHOMMES	GEOCENTRIC	GEOLOGICAL
GENERICALLY	GENITRIXES	GENTLEFOLK	GEOCENTRICAL	GEOLOGICALLY
GENERICNESS	GENLOCKING	GENTLEFOLKS	GEOCENTRICALLY	GEOLOGISED
GENERICNESSES	GENOCIDAIRE	GENTLEHOOD	GEOCENTRICISM	GEOLOGISES
GENEROSITIES	GENOCIDAIRES	GENTLEHOODS	GEOCENTRICISMS	GEOLOGISING
GENEROSITY	GENOPHOBIA	GENTLEMANHOOD	GEOCHEMICAL	GEOLOGISTS
GENEROUSLY	GENOPHOBIAS	GENTLEMANHOODS	GEOCHEMICALLY	GEOLOGIZED
GENEROUSNESS	GENOTYPICAL	GENTLEMANLIKE	GEOCHEMIST	GEOLOGIZES
GENEROUSNESSES	GENOTYPICALLY	GENTLEMANLINESS	GEOCHEMISTRIES	GEOLOGIZING
GENETHLIAC	GENOTYPICITIES	GENTLEMANLY	GEOCHEMISTRY	GEOMAGNETIC
GENETHLIACAL	GENOTYPICITY	GENTLEMANSHIP	GEOCHEMISTS	GEOMAGNETICALLY
GENETHLIACALLY	GENOUILLERE	GENTLEMANSHIPS	GEOCHRONOLOGIC	GEOMAGNETISM
GENETHLIACON	GENOUILLERES	GENTLENESS	GEOCHRONOLOGIES	GEOMAGNETISMS
GENETHLIACONS	GENSDARMES	GENTLENESSE	GEOCHRONOLOGIST	GEOMAGNETIST
GENETHLIACS	GENTAMICIN	GENTLENESSES	GEOCHRONOLOGY	GEOMAGNETISTS
GENETHLIALOGIC	GENTAMICINS	GENTLEPERSON	GEOCORONAE	GEOMANCERS
GENETHLIALOGIES	GENTEELEST	GENTLEPERSONS	GEOCORONAS	GEOMANCIES
GENETHLIALOGY	GENTEELISE	GENTLEWOMAN	GEODEMOGRAPHICS	GEOMECHANICS
GENETICALLY	GENTEELISED	GENTLEWOMANLY	GEODESICAL	GEOMEDICAL
GENETICIST	GENTEELISES	GENTLEWOMEN	GEODESISTS	GEOMEDICINE
GENETICISTS	GENTEELISH	GENTRIFICATION	GEODETICAL	GEOMEDICINES
GENETOTROPHIC	GENTEELISING	GENTRIFICATIONS	GEODETICALLY	GEOMETRICAL
GENETRICES	GENTEELISM	GENTRIFIED	GEODYNAMIC	GEOMETRICALLY
GENETRIXES	GENTEELISMS	GENTRIFIER	GEODYNAMICAL	GEOMETRICIAN
GENEVRETTE	GENTEELIZE	GENTRIFIERS	GEODYNAMICIST	GEOMETRICIANS
GENEVRETTES	GENTEELIZED	GENTRIFIES	GEODYNAMICISTS	GEOMETRICS
GENIALISED	GENTEELIZES	GENTRIFYING	GEODYNAMICS	GEOMETRIDS
GENIALISES	GENTEELIZING	GENUFLECTED	GEOENGINEERING	GEOMETRIES
GENIALISING	GENTEELNESS	GENUFLECTING	GEOENGINEERINGS	GEOMETRISATION
GENIALITIES	GENTEELNESSES	GENUFLECTION	GEOGNOSIES	GEOMETRISATIONS
GENIALIZED	GENTIANACEOUS	GENUFLECTIONS	GEOGNOSTIC	GEOMETRISE
GENIALIZES	GENTIANELLA	GENUFLECTOR	GEOGNOSTICAL	GEOMETRISED
GENIALIZING	GENTIANELLAS	GENUFLECTORS	GEOGNOSTICALLY	GEOMETRISES
GENIALNESS	GENTILESSE	GENUFLECTS	GEOGRAPHER	GEOMETRISING
GENIALNESSES	GENTILESSES	GENUFLEXION	GEOGRAPHERS	GEOMETRIST
GENICULATE	GENTILHOMME	GENUFLEXIONS	GEOGRAPHIC	GEOMETRISTS

G

GEOMETRIZATION
GEOMETRIZATIONS
GEOMETRIZE
GEOMETRIZED
GEOMETRIZES
GEOMETRIZING
GEOMORPHIC
GEOMORPHOGENIC
GEOMORPHOGENIES
GEOMORPHOGENIST
GEOMORPHOGENY
GEOMORPHOLOGIC
GEOMORPHOLOGIES
GEOMORPHOLOGIST
GEOMORPHOLOGY
GEOPHAGIAS
GEOPHAGIES
GEOPHAGISM
GEOPHAGISMS
GEOPHAGIST
GEOPHAGISTS
GEOPHAGOUS
GEOPHILOUS
GEOPHYSICAL
GEOPHYSICALLY
GEOPHYSICIST
GEOPHYSICISTS
GEOPHYSICS
GEOPOLITICAL
GEOPOLITICALLY
GEOPOLITICIAN
GEOPOLITICIANS
GEOPOLITICS
GEOPONICAL
GEOPRESSURED
GEORGETTES
GEOSCIENCE
GEOSCIENCES
GEOSCIENTIFIC
GEOSCIENTIST
GEOSCIENTISTS
GEOSPATIAL
GEOSPHERES
GEOSTATICS
GEOSTATIONARY
GEOSTRATEGIC
GEOSTRATEGICAL

GEOSTRATEGIES
GEOSTRATEGIST
GEOSTRATEGISTS
GEOSTRATEGY
GEOSTROPHIC
GEOSTROPHICALLY
GEOSYNCHRONOUS
GEOSYNCLINAL
GEOSYNCLINE
GEOSYNCLINES
GEOTACTICAL
GEOTACTICALLY
GEOTAGGING
GEOTECHNIC
GEOTECHNICAL
GEOTECHNICS
GEOTECHNOLOGIES
GEOTECHNOLOGY
GEOTECTONIC
GEOTECTONICALLY
GEOTECTONICS
GEOTEXTILE
GEOTEXTILES
GEOTHERMAL
GEOTHERMALLY
GEOTHERMIC
GEOTHERMOMETER
GEOTHERMOMETERS
GEOTROPICALLY
GEOTROPISM
GEOTROPISMS
GERANIACEOUS
GERATOLOGICAL
GERATOLOGIES
GERATOLOGIST
GERATOLOGISTS
GERATOLOGY
GERFALCONS
GERIATRICIAN
GERIATRICIANS
GERIATRICS
GERIATRIST
GERIATRISTS
GERMANDERS
GERMANENESS
GERMANENESSES
GERMANISATION

GERMANISATIONS
GERMANISED
GERMANISES
GERMANISING
GERMANITES
GERMANIUMS
GERMANIZATION
GERMANIZATIONS
GERMANIZED
GERMANIZES
GERMANIZING
GERMICIDAL
GERMICIDES
GERMINABILITIES
GERMINABILITY
GERMINABLE
GERMINALLY
GERMINATED
GERMINATES
GERMINATING
GERMINATION
GERMINATIONS
GERMINATIVE
GERMINATOR
GERMINATORS
GERMINESSES
GERMPLASMS
GERONTOCRACIES
GERONTOCRACY
GERONTOCRAT
GERONTOCRATIC
GERONTOCRATS
GERONTOLOGIC
GERONTOLOGICAL
GERONTOLOGIES
GERONTOLOGIST
GERONTOLOGISTS
GERONTOLOGY
GERONTOMORPHIC
GERONTOPHIL
GERONTOPHILE
GERONTOPHILES
GERONTOPHILIA
GERONTOPHILIAS
GERONTOPHILS
GERONTOPHOBE
GERONTOPHOBES

GERONTOPHOBIA
GERONTOPHOBIAS
GERRYMANDER
GERRYMANDERED
GERRYMANDERER
GERRYMANDERERS
GERRYMANDERING
GERRYMANDERINGS
GERRYMANDERS
GERUNDIVAL
GERUNDIVELY
GERUNDIVES
GESELLSCHAFT
GESELLSCHAFTEN
GESELLSCHAFTS
GESNERIADS
GESSAMINES
GESTALTISM
GESTALTISMS
GESTALTIST
GESTALTISTS
GESTATIONAL
GESTATIONS
GESTATORIAL
GESTICULANT
GESTICULATE
GESTICULATED
GESTICULATES
GESTICULATING
GESTICULATION
GESTICULATIONS
GESTICULATIVE
GESTICULATOR
GESTICULATORS
GESTICULATORY
GESTURALLY
GESUNDHEIT
GETTERINGS
GEWURZTRAMINER
GEWURZTRAMINERS
GEYSERITES
GHASTFULLY
GHASTLIEST
GHASTLINESS
GHASTLINESSES
GHASTNESSES
GHETTOISATION

GHETTOISATIONS
GHETTOISED
GHETTOISES
GHETTOISING
GHETTOIZATION
GHETTOIZATIONS
GHETTOIZED
GHETTOIZES
GHETTOIZING
GHOSTLIEST
GHOSTLINESS
GHOSTLINESSES
GHOSTWRITE
GHOSTWRITER
GHOSTWRITERS
GHOSTWRITES
GHOSTWRITING
GHOSTWRITTEN
GHOSTWROTE
GHOULISHLY
GHOULISHNESS
GHOULISHNESSES
GIANTESSES
GIANTHOODS
GIANTLIEST
GIANTSHIPS
GIARDIASES
GIARDIASIS
GIBBERELLIC
GIBBERELLIN
GIBBERELLINS
GIBBERISHES
GIBBETTING
GIBBOSITIES
GIBBOUSNESS
GIBBOUSNESSES
GIDDINESSES
GIFTEDNESS
GIFTEDNESSES
GIFTWRAPPED
GIFTWRAPPING
GIGACYCLES
GIGAHERTZES
GIGANTESQUE
GIGANTICALLY
GIGANTICIDE
GIGANTICIDES

G

GIGANTICNESS	GIMMICKRIES	GLACIOLOGICAL	GLAMOURING	GLASSPAPER
GIGANTICNESSES	GINGELLIES	GLACIOLOGIES	GLAMOURISE	GLASSPAPERED
GIGANTISMS	GINGERADES	GLACIOLOGIST	GLAMOURISED	GLASSPAPERING
GIGANTOLOGIES	GINGERBREAD	GLACIOLOGISTS	GLAMOURISES	GLASSPAPERS
GIGANTOLOGY	GINGERBREADED	GLACIOLOGY	GLAMOURISING	GLASSWARES
GIGANTOMACHIA	GINGERBREADS	GLADDENERS	GLAMOURIZE	GLASSWORKER
GIGANTOMACHIAS	GINGERBREADY	GLADDENING	GLAMOURIZED	GLASSWORKERS
GIGANTOMACHIES	GINGERLINESS	GLADFULNESS	GLAMOURIZES	GLASSWORKS
GIGANTOMACHY	GINGERLINESSES	GLADFULNESSES	GLAMOURIZING	GLASSWORMS
GIGGLESOME	GINGERROOT	GLADIATORIAL	GLAMOURLESS	GLASSWORTS
GIGGLINGLY	GINGERROOTS	GLADIATORIAN	GLAMOUROUS	GLASSYHEADED
GIGMANITIES	GINGERSNAP	GLADIATORS	GLAMOUROUSLY	GLAUBERITE
GILDSWOMAN	GINGERSNAPS	GLADIATORSHIP	GLAMOUROUSNESS	GLAUBERITES
GILDSWOMEN	GINGIVECTOMIES	GLADIATORSHIPS	GLAMOURPUSS	GLAUCESCENCE
GILLFLIRTS	GINGIVECTOMY	GLADIATORY	GLAMOURPUSSES	GLAUCESCENCES
GILLIFLOWER	GINGIVITIS	GLADIOLUSES	GLANCINGLY	GLAUCESCENT
GILLIFLOWERS	GINGIVITISES	GLADNESSES	GLANDEROUS	GLAUCOMATOUS
GILLNETTED	GINGLIMOID	GLADSOMELY	GLANDIFEROUS	GLAUCONITE
GILLNETTER	GIPSYHOODS	GLADSOMENESS	GLANDIFORM	GLAUCONITES
GILLNETTERS	GIPSYWORTS	GLADSOMENESSES	GLANDULARLY	GLAUCONITIC
GILLNETTING	GIRANDOLAS	GLADSOMEST	GLANDULIFEROUS	GLAUCOUSLY
GILLRAVAGE	GIRANDOLES	GLADSTONES	GLANDULOUS	GLAUCOUSNESS
GILLRAVAGED	GIRDLECAKE	GLADWRAPPED	GLANDULOUSLY	GLAUCOUSNESSES
GILLRAVAGES	GIRDLECAKES	GLADWRAPPING	GLARINESSES	GLAZIERIES
GILLRAVAGING	GIRDLESCONE	GLAIKETNESS	GLARINGNESS	GLAZINESSES
GILLRAVITCH	GIRDLESCONES	GLAIKETNESSES	GLARINGNESSES	GLEAMINGLY
GILLRAVITCHED	GIRDLESTEAD	GLAIKITNESS	GLASNOSTIAN	GLEEFULNESS
GILLRAVITCHES	GIRDLESTEADS	GLAIKITNESSES	GLASNOSTIC	GLEEFULNESSES
GILLRAVITCHING	GIRLFRIEND	GLAIRINESS	GLASSBLOWER	GLEEMAIDEN
GILLYFLOWER	GIRLFRIENDS	GLAIRINESSES	GLASSBLOWERS	GLEEMAIDENS
GILLYFLOWERS	GIRLISHNESS	GLAMORISATION	GLASSBLOWING	GLEGNESSES
GILRAVAGED	GIRLISHNESSES	GLAMORISATIONS	GLASSBLOWINGS	GLEISATION
GILRAVAGER	GIRTHLINES	GLAMORISED	GLASSCLOTH	GLEISATIONS
GILRAVAGERS	GISMOLOGIES	GLAMORISER	GLASSCLOTHS	GLEIZATION
GILRAVAGES	GITTARONES	GLAMORISERS	GLASSCUTTER	GLEIZATIONS
GILRAVAGING	GITTERNING	GLAMORISES	GLASSCUTTERS	GLENDOVEER
GILRAVITCH	GIVENNESSES	GLAMORISING	GLASSHOUSE	GLENDOVEERS
GILRAVITCHED	GIZMOLOGIES	GLAMORIZATION	GLASSHOUSES	GLENGARRIES
GILRAVITCHES	GLABRESCENT	GLAMORIZATIONS	GLASSIFIED	GLIBNESSES
GILRAVITCHING	GLABROUSNESS	GLAMORIZED	GLASSIFIES	GLIDEPATHS
GILSONITES	GLABROUSNESSES	GLAMORIZER	GLASSIFYING	GLIMMERING
GIMBALLING	GLACIALIST	GLAMORIZERS	GLASSINESS	GLIMMERINGLY
GIMCRACKERIES	GLACIALISTS	GLAMORIZES	GLASSINESSES	GLIMMERINGS
GIMCRACKERY	GLACIATING	GLAMORIZING	GLASSMAKER	GLIOBLASTOMA
GIMMICKIER	GLACIATION	GLAMOROUSLY	GLASSMAKERS	GLIOBLASTOMAS
GIMMICKIEST	GLACIATIONS	GLAMOROUSNESS	GLASSMAKING	GLIOBLASTOMATA
GIMMICKING	GLACIOLOGIC	GLAMOROUSNESSES	GLASSMAKINGS	GLIOMATOSES

GLIOMATOSIS
GLIOMATOUS
GLISSADERS
GLISSADING
GLISSANDOS
GLISTENING
GLISTENINGLY
GLISTERING
GLISTERINGLY
GLITCHIEST
GLITTERAND
GLITTERATI
GLITTERIER
GLITTERIEST
GLITTERING
GLITTERINGLY
GLITTERINGS
GLITZINESS
GLITZINESSES
GLOATINGLY
GLOBALISATION
GLOBALISATIONS
GLOBALISED
GLOBALISES
GLOBALISING
GLOBALISMS
GLOBALISTS
GLOBALIZATION
GLOBALIZATIONS
GLOBALIZED
GLOBALIZES
GLOBALIZING
GLOBEFISHES
GLOBEFLOWER
GLOBEFLOWERS
GLOBESITIES
GLOBETROTS
GLOBETROTTED
GLOBETROTTER
GLOBETROTTERS
GLOBETROTTING
GLOBETROTTINGS
GLOBIGERINA
GLOBIGERINAE
GLOBIGERINAS
GLOBOSENESS
GLOBOSENESSES

GLOBOSITIES
GLOBULARITIES
GLOBULARITY
GLOBULARLY
GLOBULARNESS
GLOBULARNESSES
GLOBULIFEROUS
GLOBULITES
GLOCHIDIATE
GLOCHIDIUM
GLOCKENSPIEL
GLOCKENSPIELS
GLOMERATED
GLOMERATES
GLOMERATING
GLOMERATION
GLOMERATIONS
GLOMERULAR
GLOMERULATE
GLOMERULES
GLOMERULUS
GLOOMFULLY
GLOOMINESS
GLOOMINESSES
GLORIFIABLE
GLORIFICATION
GLORIFICATIONS
GLORIFIERS
GLORIFYING
GLORIOUSLY
GLORIOUSNESS
GLORIOUSNESSES
GLOSSARIAL
GLOSSARIALLY
GLOSSARIES
GLOSSARIST
GLOSSARISTS
GLOSSATORS
GLOSSECTOMIES
GLOSSECTOMY
GLOSSEMATICS
GLOSSINESS
GLOSSINESSES
GLOSSINGLY
GLOSSITISES
GLOSSODYNIA
GLOSSODYNIAS

GLOSSOGRAPHER
GLOSSOGRAPHERS
GLOSSOGRAPHICAL
GLOSSOGRAPHIES
GLOSSOGRAPHY
GLOSSOLALIA
GLOSSOLALIAS
GLOSSOLALIST
GLOSSOLALISTS
GLOSSOLOGICAL
GLOSSOLOGIES
GLOSSOLOGIST
GLOSSOLOGISTS
GLOSSOLOGY
GLOTTIDEAN
GLOTTOGONIC
GLOTTOLOGIES
GLOTTOLOGY
GLOVEBOXES
GLOWERINGLY
GLOWSTICKS
GLUCINIUMS
GLUCOCORTICOID
GLUCOCORTICOIDS
GLUCOKINASE
GLUCOKINASES
GLUCONATES
GLUCONEOGENESES
GLUCONEOGENESIS
GLUCONEOGENIC
GLUCOPHORE
GLUCOPHORES
GLUCOPROTEIN
GLUCOPROTEINS
GLUCOSAMINE
GLUCOSAMINES
GLUCOSIDAL
GLUCOSIDASE
GLUCOSIDASES
GLUCOSIDES
GLUCOSIDIC
GLUCOSURIA
GLUCOSURIAS
GLUCOSURIC
GLUCURONIC
GLUCURONIDASE
GLUCURONIDASES

GLUCURONIDE
GLUCURONIDES
GLUEYNESSES
GLUINESSES
GLUMACEOUS
GLUMIFEROUS
GLUMNESSES
GLUTAMATES
GLUTAMINASE
GLUTAMINASES
GLUTAMINES
GLUTAMINIC
GLUTARALDEHYDE
GLUTARALDEHYDES
GLUTATHIONE
GLUTATHIONES
GLUTETHIMIDE
GLUTETHIMIDES
GLUTINOSITIES
GLUTINOSITY
GLUTINOUSLY
GLUTINOUSNESS
GLUTINOUSNESSES
GLUTTINGLY
GLUTTONIES
GLUTTONISE
GLUTTONISED
GLUTTONISES
GLUTTONISH
GLUTTONISING
GLUTTONIZE
GLUTTONIZED
GLUTTONIZES
GLUTTONIZING
GLUTTONOUS
GLUTTONOUSLY
GLUTTONOUSNESS
GLYCAEMIAS
GLYCATIONS
GLYCERALDEHYDE
GLYCERALDEHYDES
GLYCERIDES
GLYCERIDIC
GLYCERINATE
GLYCERINATED
GLYCERINATES
GLYCERINATING

GLYCERINES
GLYCOCOLLS
GLYCOGENESES
GLYCOGENESIS
GLYCOGENETIC
GLYCOGENIC
GLYCOGENOLYSES
GLYCOGENOLYSIS
GLYCOGENOLYTIC
GLYCOLIPID
GLYCOLIPIDS
GLYCOLYSES
GLYCOLYSIS
GLYCOLYTIC
GLYCONEOGENESES
GLYCONEOGENESIS
GLYCOPEPTIDE
GLYCOPEPTIDES
GLYCOPHYTE
GLYCOPHYTES
GLYCOPHYTIC
GLYCOPROTEIN
GLYCOPROTEINS
GLYCOSIDASE
GLYCOSIDASES
GLYCOSIDES
GLYCOSIDIC
GLYCOSIDICALLY
GLYCOSURIA
GLYCOSURIAS
GLYCOSURIC
GLYCOSYLATE
GLYCOSYLATED
GLYCOSYLATES
GLYCOSYLATING
GLYCOSYLATION
GLYCOSYLATIONS
GLYOXALINE
GLYOXALINES
GLYPHOGRAPH
GLYPHOGRAPHER
GLYPHOGRAPHERS
GLYPHOGRAPHIC
GLYPHOGRAPHICAL
GLYPHOGRAPHIES
GLYPHOGRAPHS
GLYPHOGRAPHY

GLYPTODONT
GLYPTODONTS
GLYPTOGRAPHER
GLYPTOGRAPHERS
GLYPTOGRAPHIC
GLYPTOGRAPHICAL
GLYPTOGRAPHIES
GLYPTOGRAPHY
GLYPTOTHECA
GLYPTOTHECAE
GMELINITES
GNAPHALIUM
GNAPHALIUMS
GNASHINGLY
GNATCATCHER
GNATCATCHERS
GNATHONICAL
GNATHONICALLY
GNATHOSTOMATOUS
GNATHOSTOME
GNATHOSTOMES
GNEISSITIC
GNETOPHYTE
GNETOPHYTES
GNOMICALLY
GNOMONICAL
GNOMONICALLY
GNOMONOLOGIES
GNOMONOLOGY
GNOSEOLOGIES
GNOSEOLOGY
GNOSIOLOGIES
GNOSIOLOGY
GNOSTICALLY
GNOSTICISM
GNOSTICISMS
GNOTOBIOLOGICAL
GNOTOBIOLOGIES
GNOTOBIOLOGY
GNOTOBIOSES
GNOTOBIOSIS
GNOTOBIOTE
GNOTOBIOTES
GNOTOBIOTIC
GNOTOBIOTICALLY
GNOTOBIOTICS
GOALKEEPER

GOALKEEPERS
GOALKEEPING
GOALKEEPINGS
GOALKICKER
GOALKICKERS
GOALKICKING
GOALKICKINGS
GOALMOUTHS
GOALTENDER
GOALTENDERS
GOALTENDING
GOALTENDINGS
GOATFISHES
GOATISHNESS
GOATISHNESSES
GOATSBEARD
GOATSBEARDS
GOATSUCKER
GOATSUCKERS
GOBBELINES
GOBBLEDEGOOK
GOBBLEDEGOOKS
GOBBLEDYGOOK
GOBBLEDYGOOKS
GOBSMACKED
GOBSTOPPER
GOBSTOPPERS
GODCHILDREN
GODDAMMING
GODDAMNDEST
GODDAMNEDEST
GODDAMNING
GODDAUGHTER
GODDAUGHTERS
GODDESSHOOD
GODDESSHOODS
GODFATHERED
GODFATHERING
GODFATHERS
GODFORSAKEN
GODLESSNESS
GODLESSNESSES
GODLIKENESS
GODLIKENESSES
GODLINESSES
GODMOTHERED
GODMOTHERING

GODMOTHERS
GODPARENTS
GODROONING
GODROONINGS
GOFFERINGS
GOGGLEBOXES
GOITROGENIC
GOITROGENICITY
GOITROGENS
GOLDARNING
GOLDBEATER
GOLDBEATERS
GOLDBRICKED
GOLDBRICKING
GOLDBRICKS
GOLDCRESTS
GOLDENBERRIES
GOLDENBERRY
GOLDENEYES
GOLDENNESS
GOLDENNESSES
GOLDENRODS
GOLDENSEAL
GOLDENSEALS
GOLDFIELDS
GOLDFINCHES
GOLDFINNIES
GOLDFISHES
GOLDILOCKS
GOLDILOCKSES
GOLDMINERS
GOLDSINNIES
GOLDSMITHERIES
GOLDSMITHERY
GOLDSMITHRIES
GOLDSMITHRY
GOLDSMITHS
GOLDSPINKS
GOLDSTICKS
GOLDSTONES
GOLDTHREAD
GOLDTHREADS
GOLIARDERIES
GOLIARDERY
GOLIARDIES
GOLIATHISE
GOLIATHISED

GOLIATHISES
GOLIATHISING
GOLIATHIZE
GOLIATHIZED
GOLIATHIZES
GOLIATHIZING
GOLLIWOGGS
GOLOMYNKAS
GOLOPTIOUS
GOLUPTIOUS
GOMBEENISM
GOMBEENISMS
GONADECTOMIES
GONADECTOMISED
GONADECTOMIZED
GONADECTOMY
GONADOTROPHIC
GONADOTROPHIN
GONADOTROPHINS
GONADOTROPIC
GONADOTROPIN
GONADOTROPINS
GONDOLIERS
GONENESSES
GONFALONIER
GONFALONIERS
GONGORISTIC
GONIATITES
GONIATITOID
GONIATITOIDS
GONIMOBLAST
GONIMOBLASTS
GONIOMETER
GONIOMETERS
GONIOMETRIC
GONIOMETRICAL
GONIOMETRICALLY
GONIOMETRIES
GONIOMETRY
GONIOSCOPE
GONIOSCOPES
GONOCOCCAL
GONOCOCCIC
GONOCOCCOID
GONOCOCCUS
GONOPHORES
GONOPHORIC

GONOPHOROUS
GONORRHEAL
GONORRHEAS
GONORRHEIC
GONORRHOEA
GONORRHOEAL
GONORRHOEAS
GONORRHOEIC
GOODFELLAS
GOODFELLOW
GOODFELLOWS
GOODFELLOWSHIP
GOODFELLOWSHIPS
GOODINESSES
GOODLIHEAD
GOODLIHEADS
GOODLINESS
GOODLINESSES
GOODLYHEAD
GOODLYHEADS
GOODNESSES
GOODNIGHTS
GOODWILLED
GOOEYNESSES
GOOFINESSES
GOOGLEWHACK
GOOGLEWHACKS
GOOGOLPLEX
GOOGOLPLEXES
GOOINESSES
GOONEYBIRD
GOONEYBIRDS
GOOPINESSES
GOOSANDERS
GOOSEBERRIES
GOOSEBERRY
GOOSEFISHES
GOOSEFLESH
GOOSEFLESHES
GOOSEFOOTS
GOOSEGRASS
GOOSEGRASSES
GOOSEHERDS
GOOSENECKED
GOOSENECKS
GOOSINESSES
GOPHERWOOD

G

GOPHERWOODS
GORBELLIES
GORBLIMEYS
GORBLIMIES
GOREHOUNDS
GORGEOUSLY
GORGEOUSNESS
GORGEOUSNESSES
GORGONEION
GORGONIANS
GORGONISED
GORGONISES
GORGONISING
GORGONIZED
GORGONIZES
GORGONIZING
GORILLAGRAM
GORILLAGRAMS
GORINESSES
GORMANDISE
GORMANDISED
GORMANDISER
GORMANDISERS
GORMANDISES
GORMANDISING
GORMANDISINGS
GORMANDISM
GORMANDISMS
GORMANDIZE
GORMANDIZED
GORMANDIZER
GORMANDIZERS
GORMANDIZES
GORMANDIZING
GORMANDIZINGS
GOSLARITES
GOSPELISED
GOSPELISES
GOSPELISING
GOSPELIZED
GOSPELIZES
GOSPELIZING
GOSPELLERS
GOSPELLING
GOSPELLINGS
GOSPELLISE
GOSPELLISED

GOSPELLISES
GOSPELLISING
GOSPELLIZE
GOSPELLIZED
GOSPELLIZES
GOSPELLIZING
GOSSIPINGLY
GOSSIPINGS
GOSSIPMONGER
GOSSIPMONGERS
GOSSIPPERS
GOSSIPPING
GOSSIPRIES
GOTHICALLY
GOTHICISED
GOTHICISES
GOTHICISING
GOTHICISMS
GOTHICIZED
GOTHICIZES
GOTHICIZING
GOURDINESS
GOURDINESSES
GOURMANDISE
GOURMANDISED
GOURMANDISES
GOURMANDISING
GOURMANDISM
GOURMANDISMS
GOURMANDIZE
GOURMANDIZED
GOURMANDIZES
GOURMANDIZING
GOUTINESSES
GOUVERNANTE
GOUVERNANTES
GOVERNABILITIES
GOVERNABILITY
GOVERNABLE
GOVERNABLENESS
GOVERNALLS
GOVERNANCE
GOVERNANCES
GOVERNANTE
GOVERNANTES
GOVERNESSED
GOVERNESSES

GOVERNESSING
GOVERNESSY
GOVERNMENT
GOVERNMENTAL
GOVERNMENTALISE
GOVERNMENTALISM
GOVERNMENTALIST
GOVERNMENTALIZE
GOVERNMENTALLY
GOVERNMENTESE
GOVERNMENTESES
GOVERNMENTS
GOVERNORATE
GOVERNORATES
GOVERNORSHIP
GOVERNORSHIPS
GOWDSPINKS
GOWPENFULS
GRACEFULLER
GRACEFULLEST
GRACEFULLY
GRACEFULNESS
GRACEFULNESSES
GRACELESSLY
GRACELESSNESS
GRACELESSNESSES
GRACILENESS
GRACILENESSES
GRACILITIES
GRACIOSITIES
GRACIOSITY
GRACIOUSLY
GRACIOUSNESS
GRACIOUSNESSES
GRADABILITIES
GRADABILITY
GRADABLENESS
GRADABLENESSES
GRADATIONAL
GRADATIONALLY
GRADATIONED
GRADATIONS
GRADATORIES
GRADDANING
GRADELIEST
GRADIENTER
GRADIENTERS

GRADIOMETER
GRADIOMETERS
GRADUALISM
GRADUALISMS
GRADUALIST
GRADUALISTIC
GRADUALISTS
GRADUALITIES
GRADUALITY
GRADUALNESS
GRADUALNESSES
GRADUATESHIP
GRADUATESHIPS
GRADUATING
GRADUATION
GRADUATIONS
GRADUATORS
GRAECISING
GRAECIZING
GRAFFITIED
GRAFFITIING
GRAFFITING
GRAFFITIST
GRAFFITISTS
GRAINFIELD
GRAINFIELDS
GRAININESS
GRAININESSES
GRALLATORIAL
GRALLOCHED
GRALLOCHING
GRAMERCIES
GRAMICIDIN
GRAMICIDINS
GRAMINACEOUS
GRAMINEOUS
GRAMINICOLOUS
GRAMINIVOROUS
GRAMINOLOGIES
GRAMINOLOGY
GRAMMALOGUE
GRAMMALOGUES
GRAMMARIAN
GRAMMARIANS
GRAMMARLESS
GRAMMATICAL
GRAMMATICALITY

GRAMMATICALLY
GRAMMATICALNESS
GRAMMATICASTER
GRAMMATICASTERS
GRAMMATICISE
GRAMMATICISED
GRAMMATICISES
GRAMMATICISING
GRAMMATICISM
GRAMMATICISMS
GRAMMATICIZE
GRAMMATICIZED
GRAMMATICIZES
GRAMMATICIZING
GRAMMATIST
GRAMMATISTS
GRAMMATOLOGIES
GRAMMATOLOGIST
GRAMMATOLOGISTS
GRAMMATOLOGY
GRAMOPHONE
GRAMOPHONES
GRAMOPHONIC
GRAMOPHONICALLY
GRAMOPHONIES
GRAMOPHONIST
GRAMOPHONISTS
GRAMOPHONY
GRANADILLA
GRANADILLAS
GRANDADDIES
GRANDAUNTS
GRANDBABIES
GRANDCHILD
GRANDCHILDREN
GRANDDADDIES
GRANDDADDY
GRANDDAUGHTER
GRANDDAUGHTERS
GRANDEESHIP
GRANDEESHIPS
GRANDFATHER
GRANDFATHERED
GRANDFATHERING
GRANDFATHERLY
GRANDFATHERS
GRANDIFLORA

GRANDIFLORAS	GRANGERISING	GRANULATES	GRAPHITIZATION	GRATEFULNESS
GRANDILOQUENCE	GRANGERISM	GRANULATING	GRAPHITIZATIONS	GRATEFULNESSES
GRANDILOQUENCES	GRANGERISMS	GRANULATION	GRAPHITIZE	GRATICULATION
GRANDILOQUENT	GRANGERIZATION	GRANULATIONS	GRAPHITIZED	GRATICULATIONS
GRANDILOQUENTLY	GRANGERIZATIONS	GRANULATIVE	GRAPHITIZES	GRATICULES
GRANDILOQUOUS	GRANGERIZE	GRANULATOR	GRAPHITIZING	GRATIFICATION
GRANDIOSELY	GRANGERIZED	GRANULATORS	GRAPHITOID	GRATIFICATIONS
GRANDIOSENESS	GRANGERIZER	GRANULIFEROUS	GRAPHOLECT	GRATIFIERS
GRANDIOSENESSES	GRANGERIZERS	GRANULIFORM	GRAPHOLECTS	GRATIFYING
GRANDIOSITIES	GRANGERIZES	GRANULITES	GRAPHOLOGIC	GRATIFYINGLY
GRANDIOSITY	GRANGERIZING	GRANULITIC	GRAPHOLOGICAL	GRATILLITIES
GRANDMAMAS	GRANITELIKE	GRANULITISATION	GRAPHOLOGIES	GRATILLITY
GRANDMAMMA	GRANITEWARE	GRANULITIZATION	GRAPHOLOGIST	GRATINATED
GRANDMAMMAS	GRANITEWARES	GRANULOCYTE	GRAPHOLOGISTS	GRATINATES
GRANDMASTER	GRANITIFICATION	GRANULOCYTES	GRAPHOLOGY	GRATINATING
GRANDMASTERS	GRANITIFORM	GRANULOCYTIC	GRAPHOMANIA	GRATINEEING
GRANDMOTHER	GRANITISATION	GRANULOMAS	GRAPHOMANIAS	GRATITUDES
GRANDMOTHERLY	GRANITISATIONS	GRANULOMATA	GRAPHOMOTOR	GRATUITIES
GRANDMOTHERS	GRANITISED	GRANULOMATOUS	GRAPHOPHOBIA	GRATUITOUS
GRANDNEPHEW	GRANITISES	GRANULOSES	GRAPHOPHOBIAS	GRATUITOUSLY
GRANDNEPHEWS	GRANITISING	GRANULOSIS	GRAPINESSES	GRATUITOUSNESS
GRANDNESSES	GRANITITES	GRAPEFRUIT	GRAPLEMENT	GRATULATED
GRANDNIECE	GRANITIZATION	GRAPEFRUITS	GRAPLEMENTS	GRATULATES
GRANDNIECES	GRANITIZATIONS	GRAPELOUSE	GRAPPLINGS	GRATULATING
GRANDPAPAS	GRANITIZED	GRAPESEEDS	GRAPTOLITE	GRATULATION
GRANDPARENT	GRANITIZES	GRAPESHOTS	GRAPTOLITES	GRATULATIONS
GRANDPARENTAL	GRANITIZING	GRAPESTONE	GRAPTOLITIC	GRATULATORY
GRANDPARENTHOOD	GRANIVORES	GRAPESTONES	GRASPINGLY	GRAUNCHERS
GRANDPARENTS	GRANIVOROUS	GRAPETREES	GRASPINGNESS	GRAUNCHING
GRANDSIRES	GRANNIEING	GRAPEVINES	GRASPINGNESSES	GRAVADLAXES
GRANDSTAND	GRANODIORITE	GRAPHEMICALLY	GRASSBIRDS	GRAVEDIGGER
GRANDSTANDED	GRANODIORITES	GRAPHEMICS	GRASSFINCH	GRAVEDIGGERS
GRANDSTANDER	GRANODIORITIC	GRAPHICACIES	GRASSFINCHES	GRAVELLING
GRANDSTANDERS	GRANOLITHIC	GRAPHICACY	GRASSHOOKS	GRAVENESSES
GRANDSTANDING	GRANOLITHICS	GRAPHICALLY	GRASSHOPPER	GRAVEOLENT
GRANDSTANDINGS	GRANOLITHS	GRAPHICALNESS	GRASSHOPPERS	GRAVEROBBER
GRANDSTANDS	GRANOPHYRE	GRAPHICALNESSES	GRASSINESS	GRAVEROBBERS
GRANDSTOOD	GRANOPHYRES	GRAPHICNESS	GRASSINESSES	GRAVESIDES
GRANDUNCLE	GRANOPHYRIC	GRAPHICNESSES	GRASSLANDS	GRAVESITES
GRANDUNCLES	GRANTSMANSHIP	GRAPHITISABLE	GRASSPLOTS	GRAVESTONE
GRANGERISATION	GRANTSMANSHIPS	GRAPHITISATION	GRASSQUITS	GRAVESTONES
GRANGERISATIONS	GRANULARITIES	GRAPHITISATIONS	GRASSROOTS	GRAVEYARDS
GRANGERISE	GRANULARITY	GRAPHITISE	GRASSWRACK	GRAVIDITIES
GRANGERISED	GRANULARLY	GRAPHITISED	GRASSWRACKS	GRAVIDNESS
GRANGERISER	GRANULATED	GRAPHITISES	GRATEFULLER	GRAVIDNESSES
GRANGERISERS	GRANULATER	GRAPHITISING	GRATEFULLEST	GRAVIMETER
GRANGERISES	GRANULATERS	GRAPHITIZABLE	GRATEFULLY	GRAVIMETERS

G

GRAVIMETRIC
GRAVIMETRICAL
GRAVIMETRICALLY
GRAVIMETRIES
GRAVIMETRY
GRAVIPERCEPTION
GRAVITASES
GRAVITATED
GRAVITATER
GRAVITATERS
GRAVITATES
GRAVITATING
GRAVITATION
GRAVITATIONAL
GRAVITATIONALLY
GRAVITATIONS
GRAVITATIVE
GRAVITINOS
GRAVITOMETER
GRAVITOMETERS
GRAYBEARDED
GRAYBEARDS
GRAYFISHES
GRAYHEADED
GRAYHOUNDS
GRAYLISTED
GRAYLISTING
GRAYNESSES
GRAYSTONES
GRAYWACKES
GRAYWATERS
GRAYWETHER
GRAYWETHERS
GREASEBALL
GREASEBALLS
GREASEBAND
GREASEBANDS
GREASEBUSH
GREASEBUSHES
GREASELESS
GREASEPAINT
GREASEPAINTS
GREASEPROOF
GREASEPROOFS
GREASEWOOD
GREASEWOODS
GREASINESS

GREASINESSES
GREATCOATED
GREATCOATS
GREATENING
GREATHEARTED
GREATHEARTEDLY
GREATNESSES
GRECIANISE
GRECIANISED
GRECIANISES
GRECIANISING
GRECIANIZE
GRECIANIZED
GRECIANIZES
GRECIANIZING
GREEDINESS
GREEDINESSES
GREENBACKER
GREENBACKERS
GREENBACKISM
GREENBACKISMS
GREENBACKS
GREENBELTS
GREENBONES
GREENBOTTLE
GREENBOTTLES
GREENBRIER
GREENBRIERS
GREENCLOTH
GREENCLOTHS
GREENERIES
GREENFIELD
GREENFIELDS
GREENFINCH
GREENFINCHES
GREENFLIES
GREENGAGES
GREENGROCER
GREENGROCERIES
GREENGROCERS
GREENGROCERY
GREENHANDS
GREENHEADS
GREENHEART
GREENHEARTS
GREENHORNS
GREENHOUSE

GREENHOUSES
GREENISHNESS
GREENISHNESSES
GREENKEEPER
GREENKEEPERS
GREENLIGHT
GREENLIGHTED
GREENLIGHTING
GREENLIGHTS
GREENLINGS
GREENMAILED
GREENMAILER
GREENMAILERS
GREENMAILING
GREENMAILS
GREENNESSES
GREENOCKITE
GREENOCKITES
GREENROOMS
GREENSANDS
GREENSHANK
GREENSHANKS
GREENSICKNESS
GREENSICKNESSES
GREENSKEEPER
GREENSKEEPERS
GREENSOMES
GREENSPEAK
GREENSPEAKS
GREENSTICK
GREENSTONE
GREENSTONES
GREENSTUFF
GREENSTUFFS
GREENSWARD
GREENSWARDS
GREENWASHED
GREENWASHES
GREENWASHING
GREENWEEDS
GREENWINGS
GREENWOODS
GREGARIANISM
GREGARIANISMS
GREGARINES
GREGARINIAN
GREGARIOUS

GREGARIOUSLY
GREGARIOUSNESS
GREISENISATION
GREISENISATIONS
GREISENISE
GREISENISED
GREISENISES
GREISENISING
GREISENIZATION
GREISENIZATIONS
GREISENIZE
GREISENIZED
GREISENIZES
GREISENIZING
GREMOLATAS
GRENADIERS
GRENADILLA
GRENADILLAS
GRENADINES
GRESSORIAL
GRESSORIOUS
GREVILLEAS
GREWHOUNDS
GREWSOMEST
GREYBEARDED
GREYBEARDS
GREYHEADED
GREYHOUNDS
GREYLISTED
GREYLISTING
GREYNESSES
GREYSCALES
GREYSTONES
GREYWACKES
GREYWETHER
GREYWETHERS
GRIDDLEBREAD
GRIDDLEBREADS
GRIDDLECAKE
GRIDDLECAKES
GRIDIRONED
GRIDIRONING
GRIDLOCKED
GRIDLOCKING
GRIEVANCES
GRIEVINGLY
GRIEVOUSLY

GRIEVOUSNESS
GRIEVOUSNESSES
GRIFFINISH
GRIFFINISM
GRIFFINISMS
GRILLERIES
GRILLROOMS
GRILLSTEAK
GRILLSTEAKS
GRILLWORKS
GRIMACINGLY
GRIMALKINS
GRIMINESSES
GRIMLOOKED
GRIMNESSES
GRINDELIAS
GRINDERIES
GRINDHOUSE
GRINDHOUSES
GRINDINGLY
GRINDSTONE
GRINDSTONES
GRINNINGLY
GRIPPINGLY
GRISAILLES
GRISEOFULVIN
GRISEOFULVINS
GRISLINESS
GRISLINESSES
GRISTLIEST
GRISTLINESS
GRISTLINESSES
GRISTMILLS
GRITSTONES
GRITTINESS
GRITTINESSES
GRIVATIONS
GRIZZLIEST
GROANINGLY
GROATSWORTH
GROATSWORTHS
GROCETERIA
GROCETERIAS
GROGGERIES
GROGGINESS
GROGGINESSES
GROMMETING

GROOVELESS
GROOVELIKE
GROOVINESS
GROOVINESSES
GROSGRAINS
GROSSIERETE
GROSSIERETES
GROSSNESSES
GROSSULARITE
GROSSULARITES
GROSSULARS
GROTESQUELY
GROTESQUENESS
GROTESQUENESSES
GROTESQUER
GROTESQUERIE
GROTESQUERIES
GROTESQUERY
GROTESQUES
GROTESQUEST
GROTTINESS
GROTTINESSES
GROUCHIEST
GROUCHINESS
GROUCHINESSES
GROUNDAGES
GROUNDBAIT
GROUNDBAITED
GROUNDBAITING
GROUNDBAITS
GROUNDBREAKER
GROUNDBREAKERS
GROUNDBREAKING
GROUNDBREAKINGS
GROUNDBURST
GROUNDBURSTS
GROUNDEDLY
GROUNDFISH
GROUNDFISHES
GROUNDHOGS
GROUNDINGS
GROUNDLESS
GROUNDLESSLY
GROUNDLESSNESS
GROUNDLING
GROUNDLINGS
GROUNDMASS

GROUNDMASSES
GROUNDNUTS
GROUNDOUTS
GROUNDPLOT
GROUNDPLOTS
GROUNDPROX
GROUNDPROXES
GROUNDSELL
GROUNDSELLS
GROUNDSELS
GROUNDSHARE
GROUNDSHARED
GROUNDSHARES
GROUNDSHARING
GROUNDSHEET
GROUNDSHEETS
GROUNDSILL
GROUNDSILLS
GROUNDSKEEPER
GROUNDSKEEPERS
GROUNDSMAN
GROUNDSMEN
GROUNDSPEED
GROUNDSPEEDS
GROUNDSWELL
GROUNDSWELLS
GROUNDWATER
GROUNDWATERS
GROUNDWOOD
GROUNDWOODS
GROUNDWORK
GROUNDWORKS
GROUPTHINK
GROUPTHINKS
GROUPUSCULE
GROUPUSCULES
GROUPWARES
GROUPWORKS
GROUSELIKE
GROVELINGLY
GROVELINGS
GROVELLERS
GROVELLING
GROVELLINGLY
GROVELLINGS
GROWLERIES
GROWLINESS

GROWLINESSES
GROWLINGLY
GROWTHIEST
GROWTHINESS
GROWTHINESSES
GROWTHISTS
GRUBBINESS
GRUBBINESSES
GRUBSTAKED
GRUBSTAKER
GRUBSTAKERS
GRUBSTAKES
GRUBSTAKING
GRUBSTREET
GRUDGELESS
GRUDGINGLY
GRUELINGLY
GRUELLINGLY
GRUELLINGS
GRUESOMELY
GRUESOMENESS
GRUESOMENESSES
GRUESOMEST
GRUFFNESSES
GRUMBLIEST
GRUMBLINGLY
GRUMBLINGS
GRUMMETING
GRUMNESSES
GRUMPINESS
GRUMPINESSES
GRUMPISHLY
GRUMPISHNESS
GRUMPISHNESSES
GRUNTINGLY
GUACAMOLES
GUACHAMOLE
GUACHAMOLES
GUACHAROES
GUANABANAS
GUANAZOLOS
GUANETHIDINE
GUANETHIDINES
GUANIDINES
GUANIFEROUS
GUANOSINES
GUARANTEED

GUARANTEEING
GUARANTEES
GUARANTIED
GUARANTIES
GUARANTORS
GUARANTYING
GUARDEDNESS
GUARDEDNESSES
GUARDHOUSE
GUARDHOUSES
GUARDIANSHIP
GUARDIANSHIPS
GUARDRAILS
GUARDROOMS
GUARDSHIPS
GUARISHING
GUAYABERAS
GUBERNACULA
GUBERNACULAR
GUBERNACULUM
GUBERNATION
GUBERNATIONS
GUBERNATOR
GUBERNATORIAL
GUBERNATORS
GUBERNIYAS
GUDGEONING
GUERDONERS
GUERDONING
GUERILLAISM
GUERILLAISMS
GUERRILLAISM
GUERRILLAISMS
GUERRILLAS
GUERRILLERO
GUERRILLEROS
GUESSINGLY
GUESSTIMATE
GUESSTIMATED
GUESSTIMATES
GUESSTIMATING
GUESSWORKS
GUESTBOOKS
GUESTENING
GUESTHOUSE
GUESTHOUSES
GUESTIMATE

GUESTIMATED
GUESTIMATES
GUESTIMATING
GUIDEBOOKS
GUIDELINES
GUIDEPOSTS
GUIDESHIPS
GUIDEWORDS
GUIDWILLIE
GUILDHALLS
GUILDSHIPS
GUILDSWOMAN
GUILDSWOMEN
GUILEFULLY
GUILEFULNESS
GUILEFULNESSES
GUILELESSLY
GUILELESSNESS
GUILELESSNESSES
GUILLEMETS
GUILLEMOTS
GUILLOCHED
GUILLOCHES
GUILLOCHING
GUILLOTINE
GUILLOTINED
GUILLOTINER
GUILLOTINERS
GUILLOTINES
GUILLOTINING
GUILTINESS
GUILTINESSES
GUILTLESSLY
GUILTLESSNESS
GUILTLESSNESSES
GUITARFISH
GUITARFISHES
GUITARISTS
GULLIBILITIES
GULLIBILITY
GULOSITIES
GUMMIFEROUS
GUMMINESSES
GUMMOSITIES
GUMSHIELDS
GUMSHOEING
GUMSUCKERS

G

GUNCOTTONS
GUNFIGHTER
GUNFIGHTERS
GUNFIGHTING
GUNFIGHTINGS
GUNKHOLING
GUNMANSHIP
GUNMANSHIPS
GUNNERSHIP
GUNNERSHIPS
GUNNYSACKS
GUNPOWDERS
GUNPOWDERY
GUNRUNNERS
GUNRUNNING
GUNRUNNINGS
GUNSLINGER
GUNSLINGERS
GUNSLINGING
GUNSLINGINGS
GUNSMITHING
GUNSMITHINGS
GURGITATION
GURGITATIONS
GUSHINESSES
GUSSETINGS
GUSTATIONS
GUSTATORILY
GUSTINESSES
GUTBUCKETS
GUTLESSNESS
GUTLESSNESSES
GUTSINESSES
GUTTATIONS

GUTTERBLOOD
GUTTERBLOODS
GUTTERINGS
GUTTERSNIPE
GUTTERSNIPES
GUTTERSNIPISH
GUTTIFEROUS
GUTTURALISATION
GUTTURALISE
GUTTURALISED
GUTTURALISES
GUTTURALISING
GUTTURALISM
GUTTURALISMS
GUTTURALITIES
GUTTURALITY
GUTTURALIZATION
GUTTURALIZE
GUTTURALIZED
GUTTURALIZES
GUTTURALIZING
GUTTURALLY
GUTTURALNESS
GUTTURALNESSES
GYMNASIARCH
GYMNASIARCHS
GYMNASIAST
GYMNASIASTS
GYMNASIUMS
GYMNASTICAL
GYMNASTICALLY
GYMNASTICS
GYMNORHINAL
GYMNOSOPHIES

GYMNOSOPHIST
GYMNOSOPHISTS
GYMNOSOPHS
GYMNOSOPHY
GYMNOSPERM
GYMNOSPERMIES
GYMNOSPERMOUS
GYMNOSPERMS
GYMNOSPERMY
GYNAECEUMS
GYNAECOCRACIES
GYNAECOCRACY
GYNAECOCRATIC
GYNAECOLOGIC
GYNAECOLOGICAL
GYNAECOLOGIES
GYNAECOLOGIST
GYNAECOLOGISTS
GYNAECOLOGY
GYNAECOMAST
GYNAECOMASTIA
GYNAECOMASTIAS
GYNAECOMASTIES
GYNAECOMASTS
GYNAECOMASTY
GYNANDRIES
GYNANDRISM
GYNANDRISMS
GYNANDROMORPH
GYNANDROMORPHIC
GYNANDROMORPHS
GYNANDROMORPHY
GYNANDROUS
GYNARCHIES

GYNECOCRACIES
GYNECOCRACY
GYNECOCRATIC
GYNECOLOGIC
GYNECOLOGICAL
GYNECOLOGIES
GYNECOLOGIST
GYNECOLOGISTS
GYNECOLOGY
GYNECOMASTIA
GYNECOMASTIAS
GYNIATRICS
GYNIATRIES
GYNIOLATRIES
GYNIOLATRY
GYNOCRACIES
GYNOCRATIC
GYNODIOECIOUS
GYNODIOECISM
GYNODIOECISMS
GYNOGENESES
GYNOGENESIS
GYNOGENETIC
GYNOMONOECIOUS
GYNOMONOECISM
GYNOMONOECISMS
GYNOPHOBES
GYNOPHOBIA
GYNOPHOBIAS
GYNOPHOBIC
GYNOPHOBICS
GYNOPHORES
GYNOPHORIC
GYNOSTEMIA

GYNOSTEMIUM
GYPSIFEROUS
GYPSOPHILA
GYPSOPHILAS
GYPSYHOODS
GYPSYWORTS
GYRATIONAL
GYRFALCONS
GYROCOMPASS
GYROCOMPASSES
GYROCOPTER
GYROCOPTERS
GYROFREQUENCIES
GYROFREQUENCY
GYROMAGNETIC
GYROMAGNETISM
GYROMAGNETISMS
GYROMANCIES
GYROPILOTS
GYROPLANES
GYROSCOPES
GYROSCOPIC
GYROSCOPICALLY
GYROSCOPICS
GYROSTABILISER
GYROSTABILISERS
GYROSTABILIZER
GYROSTABILIZERS
GYROSTATIC
GYROSTATICALLY
GYROSTATICS
GYROVAGUES

H

HAANEPOOTS	HACKBUTEER	HAEMATITIC	HAEMOCHROME	HAEMOPHILIACS
HABERDASHER	HACKBUTEERS	HAEMATOBLAST	HAEMOCHROMES	HAEMOPHILIAS
HABERDASHERIES	HACKBUTTER	HAEMATOBLASTIC	HAEMOCOELS	HAEMOPHILIC
HABERDASHERS	HACKBUTTERS	HAEMATOBLASTS	HAEMOCONIA	HAEMOPHILIOID
HABERDASHERY	HACKERAZZI	HAEMATOCELE	HAEMOCONIAS	HAEMOPOIESES
HABERDINES	HACKERAZZIS	HAEMATOCELES	HAEMOCYANIN	HAEMOPOIESIS
HABERGEONS	HACKMATACK	HAEMATOCRIT	HAEMOCYANINS	HAEMOPOIETIC
HABILATORY	HACKMATACKS	HAEMATOCRITS	HAEMOCYTES	HAEMOPROTEIN
HABILIMENT	HACKNEYING	HAEMATOCRYAL	HAEMOCYTOMETER	HAEMOPROTEINS
HABILIMENTS	HACKNEYISM	HAEMATOGENESES	HAEMOCYTOMETERS	HAEMOPTYSES
HABILITATE	HACKNEYISMS	HAEMATOGENESIS	HAEMODIALYSER	HAEMOPTYSIS
HABILITATED	HACKNEYMAN	HAEMATOGENETIC	HAEMODIALYSERS	HAEMORRHAGE
HABILITATES	HACKNEYMEN	HAEMATOGENIC	HAEMODIALYSES	HAEMORRHAGED
HABILITATING	HACKSAWING	HAEMATOGENOUS	HAEMODIALYSIS	HAEMORRHAGES
HABILITATION	HACKTIVISM	HAEMATOLOGIC	HAEMODIALYZER	HAEMORRHAGIC
HABILITATIONS	HACKTIVISMS	HAEMATOLOGICAL	HAEMODIALYZERS	HAEMORRHAGING
HABILITATOR	HACKTIVIST	HAEMATOLOGIES	HAEMODILUTION	HAEMORRHOID
HABILITATORS	HACKTIVISTS	HAEMATOLOGIST	HAEMODILUTIONS	HAEMORRHOIDAL
HABITABILITIES	HACQUETONS	HAEMATOLOGISTS	HAEMODYNAMIC	HAEMORRHOIDS
HABITABILITY	HADROSAURS	HAEMATOLOGY	HAEMODYNAMICS	HAEMOSIDERIN
HABITABLENESS	HADROSAURUS	HAEMATOLYSES	HAEMOFLAGELLATE	HAEMOSIDERINS
HABITABLENESSES	HADROSAURUSES	HAEMATOLYSIS	HAEMOGLOBIN	HAEMOSTASES
HABITATION	HAECCEITIES	HAEMATOMAS	HAEMOGLOBINS	HAEMOSTASIA
HABITATIONAL	HAEMACHROME	HAEMATOMATA	HAEMOGLOBINURIA	HAEMOSTASIAS
HABITATIONS	HAEMACHROMES	HAEMATOPHAGOUS	HAEMOGLOBINURIC	HAEMOSTASIS
HABITAUNCE	HAEMACYTOMETER	HAEMATOPOIESES	HAEMOLYMPH	HAEMOSTATIC
HABITAUNCES	HAEMACYTOMETERS	HAEMATOPOIESIS	HAEMOLYMPHS	HAEMOSTATICS
HABITUALLY	HAEMAGGLUTINATE	HAEMATOPOIETIC	HAEMOLYSED	HAEMOSTATS
HABITUALNESS	HAEMAGGLUTININ	HAEMATOSES	HAEMOLYSES	HAEMOTOXIC
HABITUALNESSES	HAEMAGGLUTININS	HAEMATOSIS	HAEMOLYSIN	HAEMOTOXIN
HABITUATED	HAEMAGOGUE	HAEMATOTHERMAL	HAEMOLYSING	HAEMOTOXINS
HABITUATES	HAEMAGOGUES	HAEMATOXYLIC	HAEMOLYSINS	HAGBERRIES
HABITUATING	HAEMANGIOMA	HAEMATOXYLIN	HAEMOLYSIS	HAGBUTEERS
HABITUATION	HAEMANGIOMAS	HAEMATOXYLINS	HAEMOLYTIC	HAGBUTTERS
HABITUATIONS	HAEMANGIOMATA	HAEMATOXYLON	HAEMOLYZED	HAGGADICAL
HABITUDINAL	HAEMATEINS	HAEMATOXYLONS	HAEMOLYZES	HAGGADISTIC
HACENDADOS	HAEMATEMESES	HAEMATOZOA	HAEMOLYZING	HAGGADISTS
HACIENDADO	HAEMATEMESIS	HAEMATOZOON	HAEMOPHILE	HAGGARDNESS
HACIENDADOS	HAEMATINIC	HAEMATURIA	HAEMOPHILES	HAGGARDNESSES
HACKAMORES	HAEMATINICS	HAEMATURIAS	HAEMOPHILIA	HAGGISHNESS
HACKBERRIES	HAEMATITES	HAEMATURIC	HAEMOPHILIAC	HAGGISHNESSES

HAGIARCHIES
HAGIOCRACIES
HAGIOCRACY
HAGIOGRAPHER
HAGIOGRAPHERS
HAGIOGRAPHIC
HAGIOGRAPHICAL
HAGIOGRAPHIES
HAGIOGRAPHIST
HAGIOGRAPHISTS
HAGIOGRAPHY
HAGIOLATER
HAGIOLATERS
HAGIOLATRIES
HAGIOLATROUS
HAGIOLATRY
HAGIOLOGIC
HAGIOLOGICAL
HAGIOLOGIES
HAGIOLOGIST
HAGIOLOGISTS
HAGIOSCOPE
HAGIOSCOPES
HAGIOSCOPIC
HAILSTONES
HAILSTORMS
HAIRBRAINED
HAIRBREADTH
HAIRBREADTHS
HAIRBRUSHES
HAIRCLOTHS
HAIRCUTTER
HAIRCUTTERS
HAIRCUTTING
HAIRCUTTINGS
HAIRDRESSER
HAIRDRESSERS
HAIRDRESSING
HAIRDRESSINGS
HAIRDRIERS
HAIRDRYERS
HAIRINESSES
HAIRLESSES
HAIRLESSNESS
HAIRLESSNESSES
HAIRPIECES
HAIRSBREADTH

HAIRSBREADTHS
HAIRSPLITTER
HAIRSPLITTERS
HAIRSPLITTING
HAIRSPLITTINGS
HAIRSPRAYS
HAIRSPRING
HAIRSPRINGS
HAIRSTREAK
HAIRSTREAKS
HAIRSTYLES
HAIRSTYLING
HAIRSTYLINGS
HAIRSTYLIST
HAIRSTYLISTS
HAIRWEAVING
HAIRWEAVINGS
HAIRYBACKS
HALACHISTS
HALAKHISTS
HALBERDIER
HALBERDIERS
HALCYONIAN
HALENESSES
HALFENDEALE
HALFENDEALES
HALFHEARTED
HALFHEARTEDLY
HALFHEARTEDNESS
HALFNESSES
HALFPENNIES
HALFPENNYWORTH
HALFPENNYWORTHS
HALFSERIOUSLY
HALFTRACKS
HALFWITTED
HALFWITTEDLY
HALFWITTEDNESS
HALIEUTICS
HALIOTISES
HALIPLANKTON
HALIPLANKTONS
HALLALLING
HALLEFLINTA
HALLEFLINTAS
HALLELUIAH
HALLELUIAHS

HALLELUJAH
HALLELUJAHS
HALLMARKED
HALLMARKING
HALLOWEDNESS
HALLOWEDNESSES
HALLOYSITE
HALLOYSITES
HALLSTANDS
HALLUCINANT
HALLUCINANTS
HALLUCINATE
HALLUCINATED
HALLUCINATES
HALLUCINATING
HALLUCINATION
HALLUCINATIONAL
HALLUCINATIONS
HALLUCINATIVE
HALLUCINATOR
HALLUCINATORS
HALLUCINATORY
HALLUCINOGEN
HALLUCINOGENIC
HALLUCINOGENICS
HALLUCINOGENS
HALLUCINOSES
HALLUCINOSIS
HALOBIONTIC
HALOBIONTS
HALOBIOTIC
HALOCARBON
HALOCARBONS
HALOCLINES
HALOGENATE
HALOGENATED
HALOGENATES
HALOGENATING
HALOGENATION
HALOGENATIONS
HALOGENOID
HALOGENOUS
HALOGETONS
HALOMORPHIC
HALOPERIDOL
HALOPERIDOLS
HALOPHILES

HALOPHILIC
HALOPHILIES
HALOPHILOUS
HALOPHOBES
HALOPHYTES
HALOPHYTIC
HALOPHYTISM
HALOPHYTISMS
HALOTHANES
HALTERBREAK
HALTERBREAKING
HALTERBREAKS
HALTERBROKE
HALTERBROKEN
HALTERNECK
HALTERNECKS
HALTINGNESS
HALTINGNESSES
HAMADRYADES
HAMADRYADS
HAMADRYASES
HAMAMELIDACEOUS
HAMAMELISES
HAMANTASCH
HAMANTASCHEN
HAMARTHRITIS
HAMARTHRITISES
HAMARTIOLOGIES
HAMARTIOLOGY
HAMBURGERS
HAMESUCKEN
HAMESUCKENS
HAMFATTERED
HAMFATTERING
HAMFATTERS
HAMMERCLOTH
HAMMERCLOTHS
HAMMERHEAD
HAMMERHEADED
HAMMERHEADS
HAMMERINGS
HAMMERKOPS
HAMMERLESS
HAMMERLOCK
HAMMERLOCKS
HAMMERSTONE
HAMMERSTONES

HAMMERTOES
HAMMINESSES
HAMPEREDNESS
HAMPEREDNESSES
HAMSHACKLE
HAMSHACKLED
HAMSHACKLES
HAMSHACKLING
HAMSTRINGED
HAMSTRINGING
HAMSTRINGS
HANDBAGGED
HANDBAGGING
HANDBAGGINGS
HANDBALLED
HANDBALLER
HANDBALLERS
HANDBALLING
HANDBARROW
HANDBARROWS
HANDBASKET
HANDBASKETS
HANDBRAKES
HANDBREADTH
HANDBREADTHS
HANDCLASPS
HANDCRAFTED
HANDCRAFTING
HANDCRAFTS
HANDCRAFTSMAN
HANDCRAFTSMEN
HANDCUFFED
HANDCUFFING
HANDEDNESS
HANDEDNESSES
HANDFASTED
HANDFASTING
HANDFASTINGS
HANDFEEDING
HANDICAPPED
HANDICAPPER
HANDICAPPERS
HANDICAPPING
HANDICRAFT
HANDICRAFTER
HANDICRAFTERS
HANDICRAFTS

HANDICRAFTSMAN	HANDSTROKES	HAPLOGRAPHY	HARDBOUNDS	HARMATTANS
HANDICRAFTSMEN	HANDSTURNS	HAPLOIDIES	HARDCOVERS	HARMDOINGS
HANDICUFFS	HANDTOWELS	HAPLOLOGIC	HARDENINGS	HARMFULNESS
HANDINESSES	HANDWHEELS	HAPLOLOGIES	HARDFISTED	HARMFULNESSES
HANDIWORKS	HANDWORKED	HAPLOSTEMONOUS	HARDGRASSES	HARMLESSLY
HANDKERCHER	HANDWORKER	HAPLOTYPES	HARDHANDED	HARMLESSNESS
HANDKERCHERS	HANDWORKERS	HAPPENCHANCE	HARDHANDEDNESS	HARMLESSNESSES
HANDKERCHIEF	HANDWRINGER	HAPPENCHANCES	HARDHEADED	HARMOLODIC
HANDKERCHIEFS	HANDWRINGERS	HAPPENINGS	HARDHEADEDLY	HARMOLODICS
HANDKERCHIEVES	HANDWRITES	HAPPENSTANCE	HARDHEADEDNESS	HARMONICAL
HANDLANGER	HANDWRITING	HAPPENSTANCES	HARDHEARTED	HARMONICALLY
HANDLANGERS	HANDWRITINGS	HAPPINESSES	HARDHEARTEDLY	HARMONICAS
HANDLEABLE	HANDWRITTEN	HAPTOGLOBIN	HARDHEARTEDNESS	HARMONICHORD
HANDLEBARS	HANDWROUGHT	HAPTOGLOBINS	HARDIHEADS	HARMONICHORDS
HANDLELESS	HANDYPERSON	HAPTOTROPIC	HARDIHOODS	HARMONICIST
HANDMAIDEN	HANDYPERSONS	HAPTOTROPISM	HARDIMENTS	HARMONICISTS
HANDMAIDENS	HANDYWORKS	HAPTOTROPISMS	HARDINESSES	HARMONICON
HANDPASSED	HANGABILITIES	HARAMZADAS	HARDINGGRASS	HARMONICONS
HANDPASSES	HANGABILITY	HARAMZADIS	HARDINGGRASSES	HARMONIOUS
HANDPASSING	HANKERINGS	HARANGUERS	HARDLINERS	HARMONIOUSLY
HANDPHONES	HANSARDISE	HARANGUING	HARDMOUTHED	HARMONIOUSNESS
HANDPICKED	HANSARDISED	HARASSEDLY	HARDNESSES	HARMONIPHON
HANDPICKING	HANSARDISES	HARASSINGLY	HARDSCAPES	HARMONIPHONE
HANDPRESSES	HANSARDISING	HARASSINGS	HARDSCRABBLE	HARMONIPHONES
HANDPRINTS	HANSARDIZE	HARASSMENT	HARDSCRABBLES	HARMONIPHONS
HANDSBREADTH	HANSARDIZED	HARASSMENTS	HARDSTANDING	HARMONISABLE
HANDSBREADTHS	HANSARDIZES	HARBINGERED	HARDSTANDINGS	HARMONISATION
HANDSELING	HANSARDIZING	HARBINGERING	HARDSTANDS	HARMONISATIONS
HANDSELLED	HANSELLING	HARBINGERS	HARDWAREMAN	HARMONISED
HANDSELLING	HANTAVIRUS	HARBORAGES	HARDWAREMEN	HARMONISER
HANDSHAKES	HANTAVIRUSES	HARBORFULS	HARDWIRING	HARMONISERS
HANDSHAKING	HAPAXANTHIC	HARBORLESS	HARDWORKING	HARMONISES
HANDSHAKINGS	HAPAXANTHOUS	HARBORMASTER	HAREBRAINED	HARMONISING
HANDSOMELY	HAPHAZARDLY	HARBORMASTERS	HARELIPPED	HARMONISTIC
HANDSOMENESS	HAPHAZARDNESS	HARBORSIDE	HARESTAILS	HARMONISTICALLY
HANDSOMENESSES	HAPHAZARDNESSES	HARBOURAGE	HARIOLATED	HARMONISTS
HANDSOMEST	HAPHAZARDRIES	HARBOURAGES	HARIOLATES	HARMONIUMIST
HANDSPIKES	HAPHAZARDRY	HARBOURERS	HARIOLATING	HARMONIUMISTS
HANDSPRING	HAPHAZARDS	HARBOURFUL	HARIOLATION	HARMONIUMS
HANDSPRINGS	HAPHTARAHS	HARBOURFULS	HARIOLATIONS	HARMONIZABLE
HANDSTAFFS	HAPHTAROTH	HARBOURING	HARLEQUINADE	HARMONIZATION
HANDSTAMPED	HAPLESSNESS	HARBOURLESS	HARLEQUINADES	HARMONIZATIONS
HANDSTAMPING	HAPLESSNESSES	HARBOURSIDE	HARLEQUINED	HARMONIZED
HANDSTAMPS	HAPLOBIONT	HARBOURSIDES	HARLEQUINING	HARMONIZER
HANDSTANDS	HAPLOBIONTIC	HARDBACKED	HARLEQUINS	HARMONIZERS
HANDSTAVES	HAPLOBIONTS	HARDBOARDS	HARLOTRIES	HARMONIZES
HANDSTROKE	HAPLOGRAPHIES	HARDBODIES	HARMALINES	HARMONIZING

H

HARMONOGRAM	HARUSPICIES	HAUSSMANNISING	HEADHUNTED	HEADSTRONG
HARMONOGRAMS	HARVESTABLE	HAUSSMANNIZE	HEADHUNTER	HEADSTRONGLY
HARMONOGRAPH	HARVESTERS	HAUSSMANNIZED	HEADHUNTERS	HEADSTRONGNESS
HARMONOGRAPHS	HARVESTING	HAUSSMANNIZES	HEADHUNTING	HEADWAITER
HARMONOMETER	HARVESTINGS	HAUSSMANNIZING	HEADHUNTINGS	HEADWAITERS
HARMONOMETERS	HARVESTLESS	HAUSTELLATE	HEADINESSES	HEADWATERS
HARMOSTIES	HARVESTMAN	HAUSTELLUM	HEADLEASES	HEADWORKER
HARMOTOMES	HARVESTMEN	HAUSTORIAL	HEADLESSNESS	HEADWORKERS
HARNESSERS	HARVESTTIME	HAUSTORIUM	HEADLESSNESSES	HEALTHCARE
HARNESSING	HARVESTTIMES	HAVERSACKS	HEADLIGHTS	HEALTHCARES
HARNESSLESS	HASENPFEFFER	HAVERSINES	HEADLINERS	HEALTHFULLY
HARPOONEER	HASENPFEFFERS	HAWFINCHES	HEADLINING	HEALTHFULNESS
HARPOONEERS	HASHEESHES	HAWKISHNESS	HEADMASTER	HEALTHFULNESSES
HARPOONERS	HASTEFULLY	HAWKISHNESSES	HEADMASTERLY	HEALTHIEST
HARPOONING	HASTINESSES	HAWKSBEARD	HEADMASTERS	HEALTHINESS
HARPSICHORD	HATBRUSHES	HAWKSBEARDS	HEADMASTERSHIP	HEALTHINESSES
HARPSICHORDIST	HATCHABILITIES	HAWKSBILLS	HEADMASTERSHIPS	HEALTHISMS
HARPSICHORDISTS	HATCHABILITY	HAWSEHOLES	HEADMISTRESS	HEALTHLESS
HARPSICHORDS	HATCHBACKS	HAWSEPIPES	HEADMISTRESSES	HEALTHLESSNESS
HARQUEBUSE	HATCHELING	HAYCATIONS	HEADMISTRESSY	HEALTHSOME
HARQUEBUSES	HATCHELLED	HAYMAKINGS	HEADPEACES	HEAPSTEADS
HARQUEBUSIER	HATCHELLER	HAZARDABLE	HEADPHONES	HEARKENERS
HARQUEBUSIERS	HATCHELLERS	HAZARDIZES	HEADPIECES	HEARKENING
HARQUEBUSS	HATCHELLING	HAZARDOUSLY	HEADQUARTER	HEARTACHES
HARQUEBUSSES	HATCHERIES	HAZARDOUSNESS	HEADQUARTERED	HEARTBEATS
HARROWINGLY	HATCHETTITE	HAZARDOUSNESSES	HEADQUARTERING	HEARTBREAK
HARROWINGS	HATCHETTITES	HAZARDRIES	HEADQUARTERS	HEARTBREAKER
HARROWMENT	HATCHLINGS	HAZELWOODS	HEADREACHED	HEARTBREAKERS
HARROWMENTS	HATCHMENTS	HAZINESSES	HEADREACHES	HEARTBREAKING
HARRUMPHED	HATEFULNESS	HEADACHIER	HEADREACHING	HEARTBREAKINGLY
HARRUMPHING	HATEFULNESSES	HEADACHIEST	HEADSCARVES	HEARTBREAKS
HARSHENING	HATELESSNESS	HEADBANGED	HEADSHAKES	HEARTBROKE
HARSHNESSES	HATELESSNESSES	HEADBANGING	HEADSHEETS	HEARTBROKEN
HARTBEESES	HATEWORTHY	HEADBANGINGS	HEADSHRINKER	HEARTBROKENLY
HARTBEESTS	HATINATORS	HEADBOARDS	HEADSHRINKERS	HEARTBROKENNESS
HARTEBEEST	HATLESSNESS	HEADBOROUGH	HEADSPACES	HEARTBURNING
HARTEBEESTS	HATLESSNESSES	HEADBOROUGHS	HEADSPRING	HEARTBURNINGS
HARTSHORNS	HAUBERGEON	HEADCHAIRS	HEADSPRINGS	HEARTBURNS
HARUMPHING	HAUBERGEONS	HEADCHEESE	HEADSQUARE	HEARTENERS
HARUSPICAL	HAUGHTIEST	HEADCHEESES	HEADSQUARES	HEARTENING
HARUSPICATE	HAUGHTINESS	HEADCLOTHS	HEADSTALLS	HEARTENINGLY
HARUSPICATED	HAUGHTINESSES	HEADCOUNTS	HEADSTANDS	HEARTHRUGS
HARUSPICATES	HAUNTINGLY	HEADDRESSES	HEADSTICKS	HEARTHSTONE
HARUSPICATING	HAUSFRAUEN	HEADFISHES	HEADSTOCKS	HEARTHSTONES
HARUSPICATION	HAUSSMANNISE	HEADFOREMOST	HEADSTONES	HEARTIKINS
HARUSPICATIONS	HAUSSMANNISED	HEADFRAMES	HEADSTREAM	HEARTINESS
HARUSPICES	HAUSSMANNISES	HEADGUARDS	HEADSTREAMS	HEARTINESSES

HEARTLANDS	HEATHENIZES	HEBRAIZING	HEEDLESSNESSES	HELILIFTING
HEARTLESSLY	HEATHENIZING	HECKELPHONE	HEELPIECES	HELIOCENTRIC
HEARTLESSNESS	HEATHENNESS	HECKELPHONES	HEELPLATES	HELIOCENTRICISM
HEARTLESSNESSES	HEATHENNESSES	HECOGENINS	HEFTINESSES	HELIOCENTRICITY
HEARTLINGS	HEATHENRIES	HECTICALLY	HEGEMONIAL	HELIOCHROME
HEARTRENDING	HEATHERIER	HECTOCOTYLI	HEGEMONICAL	HELIOCHROMES
HEARTRENDINGLY	HEATHERIEST	HECTOCOTYLUS	HEGEMONIES	HELIOCHROMIC
HEARTSEASE	HEATHFOWLS	HECTOGRAMME	HEGEMONISM	HELIOCHROMIES
HEARTSEASES	HEATHLANDS	HECTOGRAMMES	HEGEMONISMS	HELIOCHROMY
HEARTSEEDS	HEATSTROKE	HECTOGRAMS	HEGEMONIST	HELIOGRAMS
HEARTSICKNESS	HEATSTROKES	HECTOGRAPH	HEGEMONISTS	HELIOGRAPH
HEARTSICKNESSES	HEAVENLIER	HECTOGRAPHED	HEGUMENIES	HELIOGRAPHED
HEARTSINKS	HEAVENLIEST	HECTOGRAPHIC	HEGUMENOSES	HELIOGRAPHER
HEARTSOMELY	HEAVENLINESS	HECTOGRAPHIES	HEIGHTENED	HELIOGRAPHERS
HEARTSOMENESS	HEAVENLINESSES	HECTOGRAPHING	HEIGHTENER	HELIOGRAPHIC
HEARTSOMENESSES	HEAVENWARD	HECTOGRAPHS	HEIGHTENERS	HELIOGRAPHICAL
HEARTSORES	HEAVENWARDS	HECTOGRAPHY	HEIGHTENING	HELIOGRAPHIES
HEARTSTRING	HEAVINESSES	HECTOLITER	HEIGHTISMS	HELIOGRAPHING
HEARTSTRINGS	HEAVYHEARTED	HECTOLITERS	HEINOUSNESS	HELIOGRAPHS
HEARTTHROB	HEAVYHEARTEDLY	HECTOLITRE	HEINOUSNESSES	HELIOGRAPHY
HEARTTHROBS	HEAVYWEIGHT	HECTOLITRES	HEKTOGRAMS	HELIOGRAVURE
HEARTWARMING	HEAVYWEIGHTS	HECTOMETER	HELDENTENOR	HELIOGRAVURES
HEARTWATER	HEBDOMADAL	HECTOMETERS	HELDENTENORS	HELIOLATER
HEARTWATERS	HEBDOMADALLY	HECTOMETRE	HELIACALLY	HELIOLATERS
HEARTWOODS	HEBDOMADAR	HECTOMETRES	HELIANTHEMUM	HELIOLATRIES
HEARTWORMS	HEBDOMADARIES	HECTORINGLY	HELIANTHEMUMS	HELIOLATROUS
HEATEDNESS	HEBDOMADARS	HECTORINGS	HELIANTHUS	HELIOLATRY
HEATEDNESSES	HEBDOMADARY	HECTORISMS	HELIANTHUSES	HELIOLITHIC
HEATHBERRIES	HEBDOMADER	HECTORSHIP	HELIBUSSES	HELIOLOGIES
HEATHBERRY	HEBDOMADERS	HECTORSHIPS	HELICHRYSUM	HELIOMETER
HEATHBIRDS	HEBEPHRENIA	HECTOSTERE	HELICHRYSUMS	HELIOMETERS
HEATHCOCKS	HEBEPHRENIAC	HECTOSTERES	HELICITIES	HELIOMETRIC
HEATHENDOM	HEBEPHRENIACS	HEDGEBILLS	HELICLINES	HELIOMETRICAL
HEATHENDOMS	HEBEPHRENIAS	HEDGEHOPPED	HELICOGRAPH	HELIOMETRICALLY
HEATHENESSE	HEBEPHRENIC	HEDGEHOPPER	HELICOGRAPHS	HELIOMETRIES
HEATHENESSES	HEBEPHRENICS	HEDGEHOPPERS	HELICOIDAL	HELIOMETRY
HEATHENISE	HEBETATING	HEDGEHOPPING	HELICOIDALLY	HELIOPAUSE
HEATHENISED	HEBETATION	HEDGEHOPPINGS	HELICONIAS	HELIOPAUSES
HEATHENISES	HEBETATIONS	HEDONICALLY	HELICOPTED	HELIOPHILOUS
HEATHENISH	HEBETATIVE	HEDONISTIC	HELICOPTER	HELIOPHOBIC
HEATHENISHLY	HEBETUDINOSITY	HEDONISTICALLY	HELICOPTERED	HELIOPHYTE
HEATHENISHNESS	HEBETUDINOUS	HEDYPHANES	HELICOPTERING	HELIOPHYTES
HEATHENISING	HEBRAISATION	HEEDFULNESS	HELICOPTERS	HELIOSCIOPHYTE
HEATHENISM	HEBRAISATIONS	HEEDFULNESSES	HELICOPTING	HELIOSCIOPHYTES
HEATHENISMS	HEBRAISING	HEEDINESSES	HELICTITES	HELIOSCOPE
HEATHENIZE	HEBRAIZATION	HEEDLESSLY	HELIDROMES	HELIOSCOPES
HEATHENIZED	HEBRAIZATIONS	HEEDLESSNESS	HELILIFTED	HELIOSCOPIC

HELIOSPHERE
HELIOSPHERES
HELIOSTATIC
HELIOSTATS
HELIOTACTIC
HELIOTAXES
HELIOTAXIS
HELIOTHERAPIES
HELIOTHERAPY
HELIOTROPE
HELIOTROPES
HELIOTROPIC
HELIOTROPICAL
HELIOTROPICALLY
HELIOTROPIES
HELIOTROPIN
HELIOTROPINS
HELIOTROPISM
HELIOTROPISMS
HELIOTROPY
HELIOTYPED
HELIOTYPES
HELIOTYPIC
HELIOTYPIES
HELIOTYPING
HELIOZOANS
HELIPILOTS
HELISKIING
HELISPHERIC
HELISPHERICAL
HELLACIOUS
HELLACIOUSLY
HELLBENDER
HELLBENDERS
HELLBROTHS
HELLDIVERS
HELLEBORES
HELLEBORINE
HELLEBORINES
HELLENISATION
HELLENISATIONS
HELLENISED
HELLENISES
HELLENISING
HELLENIZATION
HELLENIZATIONS
HELLENIZED

HELLENIZES
HELLENIZING
HELLGRAMITE
HELLGRAMITES
HELLGRAMMITE
HELLGRAMMITES
HELLHOUNDS
HELLISHNESS
HELLISHNESSES
HELMETINGS
HELMETLIKE
HELMINTHIASES
HELMINTHIASIS
HELMINTHIC
HELMINTHICS
HELMINTHOID
HELMINTHOLOGIC
HELMINTHOLOGIES
HELMINTHOLOGIST
HELMINTHOLOGY
HELMINTHOUS
HELMSMANSHIP
HELMSMANSHIPS
HELOPHYTES
HELPFULNESS
HELPFULNESSES
HELPLESSLY
HELPLESSNESS
HELPLESSNESSES
HELVETIUMS
HEMACHROME
HEMACHROMES
HEMACYTOMETER
HEMACYTOMETERS
HEMAGGLUTINATE
HEMAGGLUTINATED
HEMAGGLUTINATES
HEMAGGLUTININ
HEMAGGLUTININS
HEMAGOGUES
HEMANGIOMA
HEMANGIOMAS
HEMANGIOMATA
HEMATEMESES
HEMATEMESIS
HEMATINICS
HEMATOBLAST

HEMATOBLASTIC
HEMATOBLASTS
HEMATOCELE
HEMATOCELES
HEMATOCRIT
HEMATOCRITS
HEMATOCRYAL
HEMATOGENESES
HEMATOGENESIS
HEMATOGENETIC
HEMATOGENIC
HEMATOGENOUS
HEMATOLOGIC
HEMATOLOGICAL
HEMATOLOGIES
HEMATOLOGIST
HEMATOLOGISTS
HEMATOLOGY
HEMATOLYSES
HEMATOLYSIS
HEMATOMATA
HEMATOPHAGOUS
HEMATOPOIESES
HEMATOPOIESIS
HEMATOPOIETIC
HEMATOPORPHYRIN
HEMATOTHERMAL
HEMATOXYLIN
HEMATOXYLINS
HEMATOZOON
HEMATURIAS
HEMELYTRAL
HEMELYTRON
HEMELYTRUM
HEMERALOPIA
HEMERALOPIAS
HEMERALOPIC
HEMEROCALLIS
HEMEROCALLISES
HEMERYTHRIN
HEMERYTHRINS
HEMIACETAL
HEMIACETALS
HEMIALGIAS
HEMIANOPIA
HEMIANOPIAS
HEMIANOPIC

HEMIANOPSIA
HEMIANOPSIAS
HEMIANOPTIC
HEMICELLULOSE
HEMICELLULOSES
HEMICHORDATE
HEMICHORDATES
HEMICRANIA
HEMICRANIAS
HEMICRYPTOPHYTE
HEMICRYSTALLINE
HEMICYCLES
HEMICYCLIC
HEMIELYTRA
HEMIELYTRAL
HEMIELYTRON
HEMIHEDRAL
HEMIHEDRIES
HEMIHEDRISM
HEMIHEDRISMS
HEMIHEDRON
HEMIHEDRONS
HEMIHYDRATE
HEMIHYDRATED
HEMIHYDRATES
HEMIMETABOLOUS
HEMIMORPHIC
HEMIMORPHIES
HEMIMORPHISM
HEMIMORPHISMS
HEMIMORPHITE
HEMIMORPHITES
HEMIMORPHY
HEMIONUSES
HEMIOPSIAS
HEMIPARASITE
HEMIPARASITES
HEMIPARASITIC
HEMIPLEGIA
HEMIPLEGIAS
HEMIPLEGIC
HEMIPLEGICS
HEMIPTERAL
HEMIPTERAN
HEMIPTERANS
HEMIPTERON
HEMIPTERONS

HEMIPTEROUS
HEMISPACES
HEMISPHERE
HEMISPHERES
HEMISPHERIC
HEMISPHERICAL
HEMISPHEROID
HEMISPHEROIDAL
HEMISPHEROIDS
HEMISTICHAL
HEMISTICHS
HEMITERPENE
HEMITERPENES
HEMITROPAL
HEMITROPES
HEMITROPIC
HEMITROPIES
HEMITROPISM
HEMITROPISMS
HEMITROPOUS
HEMIZYGOUS
HEMOCHROMATOSES
HEMOCHROMATOSIS
HEMOCHROME
HEMOCHROMES
HEMOCONIAS
HEMOCYANIN
HEMOCYANINS
HEMOCYTOMETER
HEMOCYTOMETERS
HEMODIALYSES
HEMODIALYSIS
HEMODIALYZER
HEMODIALYZERS
HEMODILUTION
HEMODILUTIONS
HEMODYNAMIC
HEMODYNAMICALLY
HEMODYNAMICS
HEMOFLAGELLATE
HEMOFLAGELLATES
HEMOGLOBIN
HEMOGLOBINS
HEMOGLOBINURIA
HEMOGLOBINURIAS
HEMOGLOBINURIC
HEMOLYMPHS

HEMOLYSING
HEMOLYSINS
HEMOLYZING
HEMOPHILES
HEMOPHILIA
HEMOPHILIAC
HEMOPHILIACS
HEMOPHILIAS
HEMOPHILIC
HEMOPHILICS
HEMOPHILIOID
HEMOPOIESES
HEMOPOIESIS
HEMOPOIETIC
HEMOPROTEIN
HEMOPROTEINS
HEMOPTYSES
HEMOPTYSIS
HEMORRHAGE
HEMORRHAGED
HEMORRHAGES
HEMORRHAGIC
HEMORRHAGING
HEMORRHOID
HEMORRHOIDAL
HEMORRHOIDALS
HEMORRHOIDS
HEMOSIDERIN
HEMOSIDERINS
HEMOSTASES
HEMOSTASIA
HEMOSTASIAS
HEMOSTASIS
HEMOSTATIC
HEMOSTATICS
HEMOTOXINS
HEMSTITCHED
HEMSTITCHER
HEMSTITCHERS
HEMSTITCHES
HEMSTITCHING
HENCEFORTH
HENCEFORWARD
HENCEFORWARDS
HENCHPERSON
HENCHPERSONS
HENCHWOMAN

HENCHWOMEN
HENDECAGON
HENDECAGONAL
HENDECAGONS
HENDECAHEDRA
HENDECAHEDRON
HENDECAHEDRONS
HENDECASYLLABIC
HENDECASYLLABLE
HENDIADYSES
HENOTHEISM
HENOTHEISMS
HENOTHEIST
HENOTHEISTIC
HENOTHEISTS
HENPECKERIES
HENPECKERY
HENPECKING
HEORTOLOGICAL
HEORTOLOGIES
HEORTOLOGIST
HEORTOLOGISTS
HEORTOLOGY
HEPARINISED
HEPARINIZED
HEPARINOID
HEPATECTOMIES
HEPATECTOMISED
HEPATECTOMIZED
HEPATECTOMY
HEPATICOLOGICAL
HEPATICOLOGIES
HEPATICOLOGIST
HEPATICOLOGISTS
HEPATICOLOGY
HEPATISATION
HEPATISATIONS
HEPATISING
HEPATITIDES
HEPATITISES
HEPATIZATION
HEPATIZATIONS
HEPATIZING
HEPATOCELLULAR
HEPATOCYTE
HEPATOCYTES
HEPATOGENOUS

HEPATOLOGIES
HEPATOLOGIST
HEPATOLOGISTS
HEPATOLOGY
HEPATOMATA
HEPATOMEGALIES
HEPATOMEGALY
HEPATOPANCREAS
HEPATOSCOPIES
HEPATOSCOPY
HEPATOTOXIC
HEPATOTOXICITY
HEPHTHEMIMER
HEPHTHEMIMERAL
HEPHTHEMIMERS
HEPTACHLOR
HEPTACHLORS
HEPTACHORD
HEPTACHORDS
HEPTADECANOIC
HEPTAGLOTS
HEPTAGONAL
HEPTAGYNOUS
HEPTAHEDRA
HEPTAHEDRAL
HEPTAHEDRON
HEPTAHEDRONS
HEPTAMEROUS
HEPTAMETER
HEPTAMETERS
HEPTAMETRICAL
HEPTANDROUS
HEPTANGULAR
HEPTAPODIC
HEPTAPODIES
HEPTARCHAL
HEPTARCHIC
HEPTARCHIES
HEPTARCHIST
HEPTARCHISTS
HEPTASTICH
HEPTASTICHS
HEPTASYLLABIC
HEPTATHLETE
HEPTATHLETES
HEPTATHLON
HEPTATHLONS

HEPTATONIC
HEPTAVALENT
HERALDICALLY
HERALDISTS
HERALDRIES
HERALDSHIP
HERALDSHIPS
HERBACEOUS
HERBACEOUSLY
HERBALISMS
HERBALISTS
HERBARIANS
HERBARIUMS
HERBICIDAL
HERBICIDALLY
HERBICIDES
HERBIVORES
HERBIVORIES
HERBIVOROUS
HERBIVOROUSLY
HERBIVOROUSNESS
HERBOLOGIES
HERBORISATION
HERBORISATIONS
HERBORISED
HERBORISES
HERBORISING
HERBORISTS
HERBORIZATION
HERBORIZATIONS
HERBORIZED
HERBORIZES
HERBORIZING
HERCOGAMIES
HERCOGAMOUS
HERCULESES
HERCYNITES
HEREABOUTS
HEREAFTERS
HEREDITABILITY
HEREDITABLE
HEREDITABLY
HEREDITAMENT
HEREDITAMENTS
HEREDITARIAN
HEREDITARIANISM
HEREDITARIANIST

HEREDITARIANS
HEREDITARILY
HEREDITARINESS
HEREDITARY
HEREDITIES
HEREDITIST
HEREDITISTS
HEREINABOVE
HEREINAFTER
HEREINBEFORE
HEREINBELOW
HERENESSES
HERESIARCH
HERESIARCHS
HERESIOGRAPHER
HERESIOGRAPHERS
HERESIOGRAPHIES
HERESIOGRAPHY
HERESIOLOGIES
HERESIOLOGIST
HERESIOLOGISTS
HERESIOLOGY
HERESTHETIC
HERESTHETICAL
HERESTHETICIAN
HERESTHETICIANS
HERESTHETICS
HERETICALLY
HERETICATE
HERETICATED
HERETICATES
HERETICATING
HERETOFORE
HERETOFORES
HERETRICES
HERETRIXES
HERIOTABLE
HERITABILITIES
HERITABILITY
HERITRESSES
HERITRICES
HERITRIXES
HERKOGAMIES
HERMANDADS
HERMAPHRODITE
HERMAPHRODITES
HERMAPHRODITIC

H

HERMAPHRODITISM	HERPETOFAUNAE	HETEROATOM	HETEROECISM	HETEROLOGY
HERMATYPIC	HERPETOFAUNAS	HETEROATOMS	HETEROECISMS	HETEROLYSES
HERMENEUTIC	HERPETOLOGIC	HETEROAUXIN	HETEROFLEXIBLE	HETEROLYSIS
HERMENEUTICAL	HERPETOLOGICAL	HETEROAUXINS	HETEROFLEXIBLES	HETEROLYTIC
HERMENEUTICALLY	HERPETOLOGIES	HETEROBLASTIC	HETEROGAMETE	HETEROMEROUS
HERMENEUTICS	HERPETOLOGIST	HETEROBLASTIES	HETEROGAMETES	HETEROMORPHIC
HERMENEUTIST	HERPETOLOGISTS	HETEROBLASTY	HETEROGAMETIC	HETEROMORPHIES
HERMENEUTISTS	HERPETOLOGY	HETEROCARPOUS	HETEROGAMETIES	HETEROMORPHISM
HERMETICAL	HERRENVOLK	HETEROCERCAL	HETEROGAMETY	HETEROMORPHISMS
HERMETICALLY	HERRENVOLKS	HETEROCERCALITY	HETEROGAMIES	HETEROMORPHOUS
HERMETICISM	HERRIMENTS	HETEROCERCIES	HETEROGAMOUS	HETEROMORPHY
HERMETICISMS	HERRINGBONE	HETEROCERCY	HETEROGAMY	HETERONOMIES
HERMETICITIES	HERRINGBONED	HETEROCHROMATIC	HETEROGENEITIES	HETERONOMOUS
HERMETICITY	HERRINGBONES	HETEROCHROMATIN	HETEROGENEITY	HETERONOMOUSLY
HERMETISMS	HERRINGBONING	HETEROCHROMOUS	HETEROGENEOUS	HETERONOMY
HERMETISTS	HERRINGERS	HETEROCHRONIC	HETEROGENEOUSLY	HETERONYMOUS
HERMITAGES	HERRYMENTS	HETEROCHRONIES	HETEROGENESES	HETERONYMOUSLY
HERMITESSES	HERSTORIES	HETEROCHRONISM	HETEROGENESIS	HETERONYMS
HERMITICAL	HESITANCES	HETEROCHRONISMS	HETEROGENETIC	HETEROOUSIAN
HERMITICALLY	HESITANCIES	HETEROCHRONOUS	HETEROGENIC	HETEROOUSIANS
HERMITISMS	HESITANTLY	HETEROCHRONY	HETEROGENIES	HETEROPHIL
HERMITRIES	HESITATERS	HETEROCLITE	HETEROGENOUS	HETEROPHILE
HERNIATING	HESITATING	HETEROCLITES	HETEROGENY	HETEROPHILES
HERNIATION	HESITATINGLY	HETEROCLITIC	HETEROGONIC	HETEROPHILS
HERNIATIONS	HESITATION	HETEROCLITOUS	HETEROGONIES	HETEROPHONIES
HERNIORRHAPHIES	HESITATIONS	HETEROCONT	HETEROGONOUS	HETEROPHONY
HERNIORRHAPHY	HESITATIVE	HETEROCONTS	HETEROGONOUSLY	HETEROPHYLLIES
HERNIOTOMIES	HESITATORS	HETEROCYCLE	HETEROGONY	HETEROPHYLLOUS
HERNIOTOMY	HESITATORY	HETEROCYCLES	HETEROGRAFT	HETEROPHYLLY
HEROICALLY	HESPERIDIA	HETEROCYCLIC	HETEROGRAFTS	HETEROPLASIA
HEROICALNESS	HESPERIDIN	HETEROCYCLICS	HETEROGRAPHIC	HETEROPLASIAS
HEROICALNESSES	HESPERIDINS	HETEROCYST	HETEROGRAPHICAL	HETEROPLASTIC
HEROICISED	HESPERIDIUM	HETEROCYSTOUS	HETEROGRAPHIES	HETEROPLASTIES
HEROICISES	HESPERIDIUMS	HETEROCYSTS	HETEROGRAPHY	HETEROPLASTY
HEROICISING	HESSONITES	HETERODACTYL	HETEROGYNOUS	HETEROPLOID
HEROICIZED	HETAERISMIC	HETERODACTYLOUS	HETEROKARYON	HETEROPLOIDIES
HEROICIZES	HETAERISMS	HETERODACTYLS	HETEROKARYONS	HETEROPLOIDS
HEROICIZING	HETAERISTIC	HETERODONT	HETEROKARYOSES	HETEROPLOIDY
HEROICNESS	HETAERISTS	HETERODOXIES	HETEROKARYOSIS	HETEROPODS
HEROICNESSES	HETAIRISMIC	HETERODOXY	HETEROKARYOTIC	HETEROPOLAR
HEROICOMIC	HETAIRISMS	HETERODUPLEX	HETEROKONT	HETEROPOLARITY
HEROICOMICAL	HETAIRISTIC	HETERODUPLEXES	HETEROKONTAN	HETEROPTERAN
HEROINISMS	HETAIRISTS	HETERODYNE	HETEROKONTS	HETEROPTERANS
HERONSHAWS	HETERARCHIES	HETERODYNED	HETEROLECITHAL	HETEROPTEROUS
HERPESVIRUS	HETERARCHY	HETERODYNES	HETEROLOGIES	HETEROSCEDASTIC
HERPESVIRUSES	HETERAUXESES	HETERODYNING	HETEROLOGOUS	HETEROSCIAN
HERPETOFAUNA	HETERAUXESIS	HETEROECIOUS	HETEROLOGOUSLY	HETEROSCIANS

HETEROSEXISM	HETEROTROPHIC	HEXAGYNIAN	HEXATHLONS	HIDALGOISMS
HETEROSEXISMS	HETEROTROPHIES	HEXAGYNOUS	HEXAVALENT	HIDDENITES
HETEROSEXIST	HETEROTROPHS	HEXAHEDRAL	HEXOBARBITAL	HIDDENMOST
HETEROSEXISTS	HETEROTROPHY	HEXAHEDRON	HEXOBARBITALS	HIDDENNESS
HETEROSEXUAL	HETEROTYPIC	HEXAHEDRONS	HEXOKINASE	HIDDENNESSES
HETEROSEXUALITY	HETEROTYPICAL	HEXAHEMERIC	HEXOKINASES	HIDEOSITIES
HETEROSEXUALLY	HETEROUSIAN	HEXAHEMERON	HEXOSAMINIDASE	HIDEOUSNESS
HETEROSEXUALS	HETEROUSIANS	HEXAHEMERONS	HEXOSAMINIDASES	HIDEOUSNESSES
HETEROSOCIAL	HETEROZYGOSES	HEXAHYDRATE	HEXYLRESORCINOL	HIERACIUMS
HETEROSOCIALITY	HETEROZYGOSIS	HEXAHYDRATED	HIBAKUSHAS	HIERACOSPHINGES
HETEROSOMATOUS	HETEROZYGOSITY	HEXAHYDRATES	HIBERNACLE	HIERACOSPHINX
HETEROSPECIFIC	HETEROZYGOTE	HEXAMERISM	HIBERNACLES	HIERACOSPHINXES
HETEROSPECIFICS	HETEROZYGOTES	HEXAMERISMS	HIBERNACULA	HIERARCHAL
HETEROSPORIES	HETEROZYGOUS	HEXAMEROUS	HIBERNACULUM	HIERARCHIC
HETEROSPOROUS	HETHERWARD	HEXAMETERS	HIBERNATED	HIERARCHICAL
HETEROSPORY	HETMANATES	HEXAMETHONIUM	HIBERNATES	HIERARCHICALLY
HETEROSTROPHIC	HETMANSHIP	HEXAMETHONIUMS	HIBERNATING	HIERARCHIES
HETEROSTROPHIES	HETMANSHIPS	HEXAMETRAL	HIBERNATION	HIERARCHISE
HETEROSTROPHY	HEULANDITE	HEXAMETRIC	HIBERNATIONS	HIERARCHISED
HETEROSTYLED	HEULANDITES	HEXAMETRICAL	HIBERNATOR	HIERARCHISES
HETEROSTYLIES	HEURISTICALLY	HEXAMETRISE	HIBERNATORS	HIERARCHISING
HETEROSTYLISM	HEURISTICS	HEXAMETRISED	HIBERNICISATION	HIERARCHISM
HETEROSTYLISMS	HEXACHLORETHANE	HEXAMETRISES	HIBERNICISE	HIERARCHISMS
HETEROSTYLOUS	HEXACHLORIDE	HEXAMETRISING	HIBERNICISED	HIERARCHIZE
HETEROSTYLY	HEXACHLORIDES	HEXAMETRIST	HIBERNICISES	HIERARCHIZED
HETEROTACTIC	HEXACHLOROPHANE	HEXAMETRISTS	HIBERNICISING	HIERARCHIZES
HETEROTACTOUS	HEXACHLOROPHENE	HEXAMETRIZE	HIBERNICIZATION	HIERARCHIZING
HETEROTAXES	HEXACHORDS	HEXAMETRIZED	HIBERNICIZE	HIERATICAL
HETEROTAXIA	HEXACOSANOIC	HEXAMETRIZES	HIBERNICIZED	HIERATICALLY
HETEROTAXIAS	HEXACTINAL	HEXAMETRIZING	HIBERNICIZES	HIERATICAS
HETEROTAXIC	HEXACTINELLID	HEXANDRIAN	HIBERNICIZING	HIEROCRACIES
HETEROTAXIES	HEXACTINELLIDS	HEXANDROUS	HIBERNISATION	HIEROCRACY
HETEROTAXIS	HEXADACTYLIC	HEXANGULAR	HIBERNISATIONS	HIEROCRATIC
HETEROTAXY	HEXADACTYLOUS	HEXAPLARIAN	HIBERNISED	HIEROCRATICAL
HETEROTHALLIC	HEXADECANE	HEXAPLARIC	HIBERNISES	HIEROCRATS
HETEROTHALLIES	HEXADECANES	HEXAPLOIDIES	HIBERNISING	HIERODULES
HETEROTHALLISM	HEXADECANOIC	HEXAPLOIDS	HIBERNIZATION	HIERODULIC
HETEROTHALLISMS	HEXADECIMAL	HEXAPLOIDY	HIBERNIZATIONS	HIEROGLYPH
HETEROTHALLY	HEXADECIMALS	HEXAPODIES	HIBERNIZED	HIEROGLYPHED
HETEROTHERMAL	HEXAEMERIC	HEXARCHIES	HIBERNIZES	HIEROGLYPHIC
HETEROTOPIA	HEXAEMERON	HEXASTICHAL	HIBERNIZING	HIEROGLYPHICAL
HETEROTOPIAS	HEXAEMERONS	HEXASTICHIC	HIBISCUSES	HIEROGLYPHICS
HETEROTOPIC	HEXAFLUORIDE	HEXASTICHON	HICCOUGHED	HIEROGLYPHING
HETEROTOPIES	HEXAFLUORIDES	HEXASTICHONS	HICCOUGHING	HIEROGLYPHIST
HETEROTOPOUS	HEXAGONALLY	HEXASTICHS	HICCUPPING	HIEROGLYPHISTS
HETEROTOPY	HEXAGRAMMOID	HEXASTYLES	HIDALGOISH	HIEROGLYPHS
HETEROTROPH	HEXAGRAMMOIDS	HEXATEUCHAL	HIDALGOISM	HIEROGRAMMAT

HIEROGRAMMATE	HIGHFALUTINGS	HINDERLINS	HIPPOPHAGOUS	HISPANISMS
HIEROGRAMMATES	HIGHFALUTINS	HINDERMOST	HIPPOPHAGY	HISPIDITIES
HIEROGRAMMATIC	HIGHFLIERS	HINDFOREMOST	HIPPOPHILE	HISTAMINASE
HIEROGRAMMATIST	HIGHFLYERS	HINDQUARTER	HIPPOPHILES	HISTAMINASES
HIEROGRAMMATS	HIGHJACKED	HINDQUARTERS	HIPPOPHOBE	HISTAMINERGIC
HIEROGRAMS	HIGHJACKER	HINDRANCES	HIPPOPHOBES	HISTAMINES
HIEROGRAPH	HIGHJACKERS	HINDSHANKS	HIPPOPOTAMI	HISTAMINIC
HIEROGRAPHER	HIGHJACKING	HINDSIGHTS	HIPPOPOTAMIAN	HISTIDINES
HIEROGRAPHERS	HIGHJACKINGS	HINTERLAND	HIPPOPOTAMIC	HISTIOCYTE
HIEROGRAPHIC	HIGHLANDER	HINTERLANDS	HIPPOPOTAMUS	HISTIOCYTES
HIEROGRAPHICAL	HIGHLANDERS	HIPPEASTRUM	HIPPOPOTAMUSES	HISTIOCYTIC
HIEROGRAPHIES	HIGHLIGHTED	HIPPEASTRUMS	HIPPURITES	HISTIOLOGIES
HIEROGRAPHS	HIGHLIGHTER	HIPPIATRIC	HIPPURITIC	HISTIOLOGY
HIEROGRAPHY	HIGHLIGHTERS	HIPPIATRICS	HIPSTERISM	HISTIOPHOROID
HIEROLATRIES	HIGHLIGHTING	HIPPIATRIES	HIPSTERISMS	HISTOBLAST
HIEROLATRY	HIGHLIGHTS	HIPPIATRIST	HIRCOCERVUS	HISTOBLASTS
HIEROLOGIC	HIGHNESSES	HIPPIATRISTS	HIRCOCERVUSES	HISTOCHEMICAL
HIEROLOGICAL	HIGHTAILED	HIPPIEDOMS	HIRCOSITIES	HISTOCHEMICALLY
HIEROLOGIES	HIGHTAILING	HIPPIENESS	HIRSELLING	HISTOCHEMIST
HIEROLOGIST	HIGHWAYMAN	HIPPIENESSES	HIRSELLINGS	HISTOCHEMISTRY
HIEROLOGISTS	HIGHWAYMEN	HIPPINESSES	HIRSUTENESS	HISTOCHEMISTS
HIEROMANCIES	HIGHWROUGHT	HIPPOCAMPAL	HIRSUTENESSES	HISTOCOMPATIBLE
HIEROMANCY	HIJACKINGS	HIPPOCAMPI	HIRSUTISMS	HISTOGENESES
HIEROPHANT	HILARIOUSLY	HIPPOCAMPUS	HIRUDINEAN	HISTOGENESIS
HIEROPHANTIC	HILARIOUSNESS	HIPPOCENTAUR	HIRUDINEANS	HISTOGENETIC
HIEROPHANTS	HILARIOUSNESSES	HIPPOCENTAURS	HIRUDINOID	HISTOGENIC
HIEROPHOBIA	HILARITIES	HIPPOCRASES	HIRUDINOUS	HISTOGENICALLY
HIEROPHOBIAS	HILLBILLIES	HIPPOCREPIAN	HISPANICISE	HISTOGENIES
HIEROPHOBIC	HILLCRESTS	HIPPOCREPIANS	HISPANICISED	HISTOGRAMS
HIEROPHOBICS	HILLINESSES	HIPPODAMES	HISPANICISES	HISTOLOGIC
HIEROSCOPIES	HILLSLOPES	HIPPODAMIST	HISPANICISING	HISTOLOGICAL
HIEROSCOPY	HILLWALKER	HIPPODAMISTS	HISPANICISM	HISTOLOGICALLY
HIERURGICAL	HILLWALKERS	HIPPODAMOUS	HISPANICISMS	HISTOLOGIES
HIERURGIES	HILLWALKING	HIPPODROME	HISPANICIZE	HISTOLOGIST
HIGHBALLED	HILLWALKINGS	HIPPODROMES	HISPANICIZED	HISTOLOGISTS
HIGHBALLING	HINDBERRIES	HIPPODROMIC	HISPANICIZES	HISTOLYSES
HIGHBINDER	HINDBRAINS	HIPPOGRIFF	HISPANICIZING	HISTOLYSIS
HIGHBINDERS	HINDCASTED	HIPPOGRIFFS	HISPANIDAD	HISTOLYTIC
HIGHBLOODED	HINDCASTING	HIPPOGRYPH	HISPANIDADS	HISTOLYTICALLY
HIGHBROWED	HINDERANCE	HIPPOGRYPHS	HISPANIOLISE	HISTOPATHOLOGIC
HIGHBROWISM	HINDERANCES	HIPPOLOGIES	HISPANIOLISED	HISTOPATHOLOGY
HIGHBROWISMS	HINDERINGLY	HIPPOLOGIST	HISPANIOLISES	HISTOPHYSIOLOGY
HIGHBUSHES	HINDERINGS	HIPPOLOGISTS	HISPANIOLISING	HISTOPLASMOSES
HIGHCHAIRS	HINDERLAND	HIPPOMANES	HISPANIOLIZE	HISTOPLASMOSIS
HIGHERMOST	HINDERLANDS	HIPPOPHAGIES	HISPANIOLIZED	HISTORIANS
HIGHFALUTIN	HINDERLANS	HIPPOPHAGIST	HISPANIOLIZES	HISTORIATED
HIGHFALUTING	HINDERLINGS	HIPPOPHAGISTS	HISPANIOLIZING	HISTORICAL

HISTORICALLY	HOACTZINES	HOIDENISHNESSES	HOLOGRAPHS	HOMEOBOXES
HISTORICALNESS	HOARFROSTS	HOJATOLESLAM	HOLOGRAPHY	HOMEOMERIC
HISTORICISE	HOARHOUNDS	HOJATOLESLAMS	HOLOGYNIES	HOMEOMERIES
HISTORICISED	HOARINESSES	HOJATOLISLAM	HOLOHEDRAL	HOMEOMEROUS
HISTORICISES	HOARSENESS	HOJATOLISLAMS	HOLOHEDRISM	HOMEOMORPH
HISTORICISING	HOARSENESSES	HOKEYNESSES	HOLOHEDRISMS	HOMEOMORPHIC
HISTORICISM	HOARSENING	HOKEYPOKEY	HOLOHEDRON	HOMEOMORPHIES
HISTORICISMS	HOBBITRIES	HOKEYPOKEYS	HOLOHEDRONS	HOMEOMORPHISM
HISTORICIST	HOBBLEBUSH	HOKINESSES	HOLOMETABOLIC	HOMEOMORPHISMS
HISTORICISTS	HOBBLEBUSHES	HOKYPOKIES	HOLOMETABOLISM	HOMEOMORPHOUS
HISTORICITIES	HOBBLEDEHOY	HOLARCHIES	HOLOMETABOLISMS	HOMEOMORPHS
HISTORICITY	HOBBLEDEHOYDOM	HOLDERBATS	HOLOMETABOLOUS	HOMEOMORPHY
HISTORICIZE	HOBBLEDEHOYDOMS	HOLDERSHIP	HOLOMORPHIC	HOMEOPATHIC
HISTORICIZED	HOBBLEDEHOYHOOD	HOLDERSHIPS	HOLOPHOTAL	HOMEOPATHICALLY
HISTORICIZES	HOBBLEDEHOYISH	HOLIDAYERS	HOLOPHOTES	HOMEOPATHIES
HISTORICIZING	HOBBLEDEHOYISM	HOLIDAYING	HOLOPHRASE	HOMEOPATHIST
HISTORIETTE	HOBBLEDEHOYISMS	HOLIDAYMAKER	HOLOPHRASES	HOMEOPATHISTS
HISTORIETTES	HOBBLEDEHOYS	HOLIDAYMAKERS	HOLOPHRASTIC	HOMEOPATHS
HISTORIFIED	HOBBLINGLY	HOLINESSES	HOLOPHYTES	HOMEOPATHY
HISTORIFIES	HOBBYHORSE	HOLISTICALLY	HOLOPHYTIC	HOMEOSTASES
HISTORIFYING	HOBBYHORSED	HOLLANDAISE	HOLOPHYTISM	HOMEOSTASIS
HISTORIOGRAPHER	HOBBYHORSES	HOLLANDAISES	HOLOPHYTISMS	HOMEOSTATIC
HISTORIOGRAPHIC	HOBBYHORSING	HOLLOWARES	HOLOPLANKTON	HOMEOTELEUTON
HISTORIOGRAPHY	HOBGOBLINISM	HOLLOWNESS	HOLOPLANKTONS	HOMEOTELEUTONS
HISTORIOLOGIES	HOBGOBLINISMS	HOLLOWNESSES	HOLOSTERIC	HOMEOTHERM
HISTORIOLOGY	HOBGOBLINRIES	HOLLOWWARE	HOLOTHURIAN	HOMEOTHERMAL
HISTORISMS	HOBGOBLINRY	HOLLOWWARES	HOLOTHURIANS	HOMEOTHERMIC
HISTORYING	HOBGOBLINS	HOLLYHOCKS	HOLSTERING	HOMEOTHERMIES
HISTRIONIC	HOBJOBBERS	HOLOBENTHIC	HOLYSTONED	HOMEOTHERMISM
HISTRIONICAL	HOBJOBBING	HOLOBLASTIC	HOLYSTONES	HOMEOTHERMISMS
HISTRIONICALLY	HOBJOBBINGS	HOLOBLASTICALLY	HOLYSTONING	HOMEOTHERMOUS
HISTRIONICISM	HOBNAILING	HOLOCAUSTAL	HOMALOGRAPHIC	HOMEOTHERMS
HISTRIONICISMS	HOBNOBBERS	HOLOCAUSTIC	HOMALOIDAL	HOMEOTHERMY
HISTRIONICS	HOBNOBBING	HOLOCAUSTS	HOMEBIRTHS	HOMEOTYPIC
HISTRIONISM	HOCHMAGANDIES	HOLOCRYSTALLINE	HOMEBODIES	HOMEOTYPICAL
HISTRIONISMS	HOCHMAGANDY	HOLODISCUS	HOMEBUYERS	HOMEOWNERS
HITCHHIKED	HODGEPODGE	HOLODISCUSES	HOMECOMERS	HOMEOWNERSHIP
HITCHHIKER	HODGEPODGES	HOLOENZYME	HOMECOMING	HOMEOWNERSHIPS
HITCHHIKERS	HODMANDODS	HOLOENZYMES	HOMECOMINGS	HOMEPLACES
HITCHHIKES	HODOGRAPHIC	HOLOGAMIES	HOMECRAFTS	HOMEPORTED
HITCHHIKING	HODOGRAPHS	HOLOGRAPHED	HOMELESSNESS	HOMEPORTING
HITCHHIKINGS	HODOMETERS	HOLOGRAPHER	HOMELESSNESSES	HOMESCHOOL
HITHERMOST	HODOMETRIES	HOLOGRAPHERS	HOMELINESS	HOMESCHOOLED
HITHERSIDE	HODOSCOPES	HOLOGRAPHIC	HOMELINESSES	HOMESCHOOLER
HITHERSIDES	HOGGISHNESS	HOLOGRAPHICALLY	HOMEMAKERS	HOMESCHOOLERS
HITHERWARD	HOGGISHNESSES	HOLOGRAPHIES	HOMEMAKING	HOMESCHOOLING
HITHERWARDS	HOIDENISHNESS	HOLOGRAPHING	HOMEMAKINGS	HOMESCHOOLS

HOMESCREETCH
HOMESCREETCHES
HOMESHORING
HOMESHORINGS
HOMESICKNESS
HOMESICKNESSES
HOMESOURCING
HOMESOURCINGS
HOMESTALLS
HOMESTANDS
HOMESTEADED
HOMESTEADER
HOMESTEADERS
HOMESTEADING
HOMESTEADINGS
HOMESTEADS
HOMESTRETCH
HOMESTRETCHES
HOMEWORKER
HOMEWORKERS
HOMEWORKING
HOMEWORKINGS
HOMEYNESSES
HOMICIDALLY
HOMILETICAL
HOMILETICALLY
HOMILETICS
HOMINESSES
HOMINISATION
HOMINISATIONS
HOMINISING
HOMINIZATION
HOMINIZATIONS
HOMINIZING
HOMOBLASTIC
HOMOBLASTIES
HOMOBLASTY
HOMOCENTRIC
HOMOCENTRICALLY
HOMOCERCAL
HOMOCERCIES
HOMOCHLAMYDEOUS
HOMOCHROMATIC
HOMOCHROMATISM
HOMOCHROMATISMS
HOMOCHROMIES
HOMOCHROMOUS

HOMOCHROMY
HOMOCYCLIC
HOMOCYSTEINE
HOMOCYSTEINES
HOMOEOMERIC
HOMOEOMERIES
HOMOEOMEROUS
HOMOEOMERY
HOMOEOMORPH
HOMOEOMORPHIC
HOMOEOMORPHIES
HOMOEOMORPHISM
HOMOEOMORPHISMS
HOMOEOMORPHOUS
HOMOEOMORPHS
HOMOEOMORPHY
HOMOEOPATH
HOMOEOPATHIC
HOMOEOPATHIES
HOMOEOPATHIST
HOMOEOPATHISTS
HOMOEOPATHS
HOMOEOPATHY
HOMOEOSTASES
HOMOEOSTASIS
HOMOEOSTATIC
HOMOEOTELEUTON
HOMOEOTELEUTONS
HOMOEOTHERM
HOMOEOTHERMAL
HOMOEOTHERMIC
HOMOEOTHERMOUS
HOMOEOTHERMS
HOMOEOTYPIC
HOMOEOTYPICAL
HOMOEROTIC
HOMOEROTICISM
HOMOEROTICISMS
HOMOEROTISM
HOMOEROTISMS
HOMOGAMETIC
HOMOGAMIES
HOMOGAMOUS
HOMOGENATE
HOMOGENATES
HOMOGENEITIES
HOMOGENEITY

HOMOGENEOUS
HOMOGENEOUSLY
HOMOGENEOUSNESS
HOMOGENESES
HOMOGENESIS
HOMOGENETIC
HOMOGENETICAL
HOMOGENIES
HOMOGENISATION
HOMOGENISATIONS
HOMOGENISE
HOMOGENISED
HOMOGENISER
HOMOGENISERS
HOMOGENISES
HOMOGENISING
HOMOGENIZATION
HOMOGENIZATIONS
HOMOGENIZE
HOMOGENIZED
HOMOGENIZER
HOMOGENIZERS
HOMOGENIZES
HOMOGENIZING
HOMOGENOUS
HOMOGONIES
HOMOGONOUS
HOMOGONOUSLY
HOMOGRAFTS
HOMOGRAPHIC
HOMOGRAPHIES
HOMOGRAPHS
HOMOGRAPHY
HOMOIOMEROUS
HOMOIOTHERM
HOMOIOTHERMAL
HOMOIOTHERMIC
HOMOIOTHERMIES
HOMOIOTHERMS
HOMOIOTHERMY
HOMOIOUSIAN
HOMOIOUSIANS
HOMOLOGATE
HOMOLOGATED
HOMOLOGATES
HOMOLOGATING
HOMOLOGATION

HOMOLOGATIONS
HOMOLOGICAL
HOMOLOGICALLY
HOMOLOGIES
HOMOLOGISE
HOMOLOGISED
HOMOLOGISER
HOMOLOGISERS
HOMOLOGISES
HOMOLOGISING
HOMOLOGIZE
HOMOLOGIZED
HOMOLOGIZER
HOMOLOGIZERS
HOMOLOGIZES
HOMOLOGIZING
HOMOLOGOUMENA
HOMOLOGOUS
HOMOLOGRAPHIC
HOMOLOGUES
HOMOLOGUMENA
HOMOLOSINE
HOMOMORPHIC
HOMOMORPHIES
HOMOMORPHISM
HOMOMORPHISMS
HOMOMORPHOSES
HOMOMORPHOSIS
HOMOMORPHOUS
HOMOMORPHS
HOMOMORPHY
HOMONUCLEAR
HOMONYMIES
HOMONYMITIES
HOMONYMITY
HOMONYMOUS
HOMONYMOUSLY
HOMOOUSIAN
HOMOOUSIANS
HOMOPHILES
HOMOPHOBES
HOMOPHOBIA
HOMOPHOBIAS
HOMOPHOBIC
HOMOPHONES
HOMOPHONIC
HOMOPHONICALLY

HOMOPHONIES
HOMOPHONOUS
HOMOPHYLIES
HOMOPHYLLIC
HOMOPLASIES
HOMOPLASMIES
HOMOPLASMY
HOMOPLASTIC
HOMOPLASTICALLY
HOMOPLASTIES
HOMOPLASTY
HOMOPOLARITIES
HOMOPOLARITY
HOMOPOLYMER
HOMOPOLYMERIC
HOMOPOLYMERS
HOMOPTERAN
HOMOPTERANS
HOMOPTEROUS
HOMORGANIC
HOMOSCEDASTIC
HOMOSEXUAL
HOMOSEXUALISM
HOMOSEXUALISMS
HOMOSEXUALIST
HOMOSEXUALISTS
HOMOSEXUALITIES
HOMOSEXUALITY
HOMOSEXUALLY
HOMOSEXUALS
HOMOSOCIAL
HOMOSOCIALITIES
HOMOSOCIALITY
HOMOSPORIES
HOMOSPOROUS
HOMOSTYLIES
HOMOTAXIAL
HOMOTAXIALLY
HOMOTHALLIC
HOMOTHALLIES
HOMOTHALLISM
HOMOTHALLISMS
HOMOTHALLY
HOMOTHERMAL
HOMOTHERMIC
HOMOTHERMIES
HOMOTHERMOUS

HOMOTHERMY	HONEYSUCKLES	HOPEFULNESSES	HOROLOGERS	HORSELAUGHS
HOMOTONIES	HONEYTRAPS	HOPELESSLY	HOROLOGICAL	HORSELEECH
HOMOTONOUS	HONORABILITIES	HOPELESSNESS	HOROLOGIES	HORSELEECHES
HOMOTRANSPLANT	HONORABILITY	HOPELESSNESSES	HOROLOGION	HORSEMANSHIP
HOMOTRANSPLANTS	HONORABLENESS	HOPLOLOGIES	HOROLOGIONS	HORSEMANSHIPS
HOMOTYPIES	HONORABLENESSES	HOPLOLOGIST	HOROLOGIST	HORSEMEATS
HOMOUSIANS	HONORARIES	HOPLOLOGISTS	HOROLOGISTS	HORSEMINTS
HOMOZYGOSES	HONORARILY	HOPPERCARS	HOROLOGIUM	HORSEPLAYER
HOMOZYGOSIS	HONORARIUM	HOPSACKING	HOROLOGIUMS	HORSEPLAYERS
HOMOZYGOSITIES	HONORARIUMS	HOPSACKINGS	HOROMETRICAL	HORSEPLAYS
HOMOZYGOSITY	HONORIFICAL	HOPSCOTCHED	HOROMETRIES	HORSEPONDS
HOMOZYGOTE	HONORIFICALLY	HOPSCOTCHES	HOROSCOPES	HORSEPOWER
HOMOZYGOTES	HONORIFICS	HOPSCOTCHING	HOROSCOPIC	HORSEPOWERS
HOMOZYGOTIC	HONOURABILITIES	HOREHOUNDS	HOROSCOPIES	HORSEPOXES
HOMOZYGOUS	HONOURABILITY	HORIATIKIS	HOROSCOPIST	HORSERACES
HOMOZYGOUSLY	HONOURABLE	HORIZONLESS	HOROSCOPISTS	HORSERADISH
HOMUNCULAR	HONOURABLENESS	HORIZONTAL	HORRENDOUS	HORSERADISHES
HOMUNCULES	HONOURABLY	HORIZONTALITIES	HORRENDOUSLY	HORSESHITS
HOMUNCULUS	HONOURLESS	HORIZONTALITY	HORRENDOUSNESS	HORSESHOED
HONESTNESS	HOODEDNESS	HORIZONTALLY	HORRIBLENESS	HORSESHOEING
HONESTNESSES	HOODEDNESSES	HORIZONTALNESS	HORRIBLENESSES	HORSESHOEINGS
HONEYBUNCH	HOODLUMISH	HORIZONTALS	HORRIDNESS	HORSESHOER
HONEYBUNCHES	HOODLUMISM	HORMOGONIA	HORRIDNESSES	HORSESHOERS
HONEYCOMBED	HOODLUMISMS	HORMOGONIUM	HORRIFICALLY	HORSESHOES
HONEYCOMBING	HOODOOISMS	HORMONALLY	HORRIFICATION	HORSETAILS
HONEYCOMBINGS	HOODWINKED	HORMONELIKE	HORRIFICATIONS	HORSEWEEDS
HONEYCOMBS	HOODWINKER	HORNBLENDE	HORRIFYING	HORSEWHIPPED
HONEYCREEPER	HOODWINKERS	HORNBLENDES	HORRIFYINGLY	HORSEWHIPPER
HONEYCREEPERS	HOODWINKING	HORNBLENDIC	HORRIPILANT	HORSEWHIPPERS
HONEYDEWED	HOOFPRINTS	HORNEDNESS	HORRIPILATE	HORSEWHIPPING
HONEYEATER	HOOKCHECKS	HORNEDNESSES	HORRIPILATED	HORSEWHIPS
HONEYEATERS	HOOKEDNESS	HORNFELSES	HORRIPILATES	HORSEWOMAN
HONEYGUIDE	HOOKEDNESSES	HORNINESSES	HORRIPILATING	HORSEWOMEN
HONEYGUIDES	HOOLACHANS	HORNLESSNESS	HORRIPILATION	HORSINESSES
HONEYMONTH	HOOLIGANISM	HORNLESSNESSES	HORRIPILATIONS	HORTATIONS
HONEYMONTHED	HOOLIGANISMS	HORNSTONES	HORRISONANT	HORTATIVELY
HONEYMONTHING	HOOPSKIRTS	HORNSWOGGLE	HORRISONOUS	HORTATORILY
HONEYMONTHS	HOOTANANNIE	HORNSWOGGLED	HORSEBACKS	HORTICULTURAL
HONEYMOONED	HOOTANANNIES	HORNSWOGGLES	HORSEBEANS	HORTICULTURALLY
HONEYMOONER	HOOTANANNY	HORNSWOGGLING	HORSEBOXES	HORTICULTURE
HONEYMOONERS	HOOTENANNIE	HORNWRACKS	HORSEFEATHERS	HORTICULTURES
HONEYMOONING	HOOTENANNIES	HORNYHEADS	HORSEFLESH	HORTICULTURIST
HONEYMOONS	HOOTENANNY	HORNYWINKS	HORSEFLESHES	HORTICULTURISTS
HONEYSUCKER	HOOTNANNIE	HOROGRAPHER	HORSEFLIES	HOSANNAING
HONEYSUCKERS	HOOTNANNIES	HOROGRAPHERS	HORSEHAIRS	HOSPITABLE
HONEYSUCKLE	HOOVERINGS	HOROGRAPHIES	HORSEHIDES	HOSPITABLENESS
HONEYSUCKLED	HOPEFULNESS	HOROGRAPHY	HORSELAUGH	HOSPITABLY

H

HOSPITAGES	HOUSEBOATER	HOUSELLING	HOWTOWDIES	HUMANITARIANIST
HOSPITALER	HOUSEBOATERS	HOUSELLINGS	HOYDENHOOD	HUMANITARIANS
HOSPITALERS	HOUSEBOATS	HOUSEMAIDS	HOYDENHOODS	HUMANITIES
HOSPITALES	HOUSEBOUND	HOUSEMASTER	HOYDENISHNESS	HUMANIZATION
HOSPITALISATION	HOUSEBREAK	HOUSEMASTERS	HOYDENISHNESSES	HUMANIZATIONS
HOSPITALISE	HOUSEBREAKER	HOUSEMATES	HOYDENISMS	HUMANIZERS
HOSPITALISED	HOUSEBREAKERS	HOUSEMISTRESS	HUBRISTICALLY	HUMANIZING
HOSPITALISES	HOUSEBREAKING	HOUSEMISTRESSES	HUCKABACKS	HUMANKINDS
HOSPITALISING	HOUSEBREAKINGS	HOUSEMOTHER	HUCKLEBERRIES	HUMANNESSES
HOSPITALIST	HOUSEBREAKS	HOUSEMOTHERS	HUCKLEBERRY	HUMBLEBEES
HOSPITALISTS	HOUSEBROKE	HOUSEPAINTER	HUCKLEBERRYING	HUMBLEBRAG
HOSPITALITIES	HOUSEBROKEN	HOUSEPAINTERS	HUCKLEBERRYINGS	HUMBLEBRAGS
HOSPITALITY	HOUSECARLS	HOUSEPARENT	HUCKLEBONE	HUMBLENESS
HOSPITALIZATION	HOUSECLEAN	HOUSEPARENTS	HUCKLEBONES	HUMBLENESSES
HOSPITALIZE	HOUSECLEANED	HOUSEPERSON	HUCKSTERAGE	HUMBLESSES
HOSPITALIZED	HOUSECLEANING	HOUSEPERSONS	HUCKSTERAGES	HUMBLINGLY
HOSPITALIZES	HOUSECLEANINGS	HOUSEPLANT	HUCKSTERED	HUMBUCKERS
HOSPITALIZING	HOUSECLEANS	HOUSEPLANTS	HUCKSTERESS	HUMBUGGABLE
HOSPITALLER	HOUSECOATS	HOUSEROOMS	HUCKSTERESSES	HUMBUGGERIES
HOSPITALLERS	HOUSECRAFT	HOUSESITTING	HUCKSTERIES	HUMBUGGERS
HOSTELINGS	HOUSECRAFTS	HOUSEWARES	HUCKSTERING	HUMBUGGERY
HOSTELLERS	HOUSEDRESS	HOUSEWARMING	HUCKSTERISM	HUMBUGGING
HOSTELLING	HOUSEDRESSES	HOUSEWARMINGS	HUCKSTERISMS	HUMDINGERS
HOSTELLINGS	HOUSEFATHER	HOUSEWIFELINESS	HUCKSTRESS	HUMDRUMNESS
HOSTELRIES	HOUSEFATHERS	HOUSEWIFELY	HUCKSTRESSES	HUMDRUMNESSES
HOSTESSING	HOUSEFLIES	HOUSEWIFERIES	HUDIBRASTIC	HUMDUDGEON
HOSTILITIES	HOUSEFRONT	HOUSEWIFERY	HUFFINESSES	HUMDUDGEONS
HOTCHPOTCH	HOUSEFRONTS	HOUSEWIFESHIP	HUFFISHNESS	HUMDURGEON
HOTCHPOTCHES	HOUSEGUEST	HOUSEWIFESHIPS	HUFFISHNESSES	HUMDURGEONS
HOTDOGGERS	HOUSEGUESTS	HOUSEWIFESKEP	HUGENESSES	HUMECTANTS
HOTDOGGING	HOUSEHOLDER	HOUSEWIFESKEPS	HUGEOUSNESS	HUMECTATED
HOTELLINGS	HOUSEHOLDERS	HOUSEWIFEY	HUGEOUSNESSES	HUMECTATES
HOTFOOTING	HOUSEHOLDERSHIP	HOUSEWIVES	HULLABALLOO	HUMECTATING
HOTHEADEDLY	HOUSEHOLDS	HOUSEWORKER	HULLABALLOOS	HUMECTATION
HOTHEADEDNESS	HOUSEHUSBAND	HOUSEWORKERS	HULLABALOO	HUMECTATIONS
HOTHEADEDNESSES	HOUSEHUSBANDS	HOUSEWORKS	HULLABALOOS	HUMECTIVES
HOTHOUSING	HOUSEKEEPER	HOUSTONIAS	HUMANENESS	HUMGRUFFIAN
HOTHOUSINGS	HOUSEKEEPERS	HOVERCRAFT	HUMANENESSES	HUMGRUFFIANS
HOTPRESSED	HOUSEKEEPING	HOVERCRAFTS	HUMANHOODS	HUMGRUFFIN
HOTPRESSES	HOUSEKEEPINGS	HOVERFLIES	HUMANISATION	HUMGRUFFINS
HOTPRESSING	HOUSEKEEPS	HOVERINGLY	HUMANISATIONS	HUMICOLOUS
HOTTENTOTS	HOUSELEEKS	HOVERPORTS	HUMANISERS	HUMIDIFICATION
HOUGHMAGANDIE	HOUSELESSNESS	HOVERTRAIN	HUMANISING	HUMIDIFICATIONS
HOUGHMAGANDIES	HOUSELESSNESSES	HOVERTRAINS	HUMANISTIC	HUMIDIFIED
HOUNDFISHES	HOUSELIGHTS	HOWLROUNDS	HUMANISTICALLY	HUMIDIFIER
HOURGLASSES	HOUSELINES	HOWSOMDEVER	HUMANITARIAN	HUMIDIFIERS
HOURPLATES	HOUSELINGS	HOWSOMEVER	HUMANITARIANISM	HUMIDIFIES

HUMIDIFYING	HUNCHBACKS	HYACINTHINE	HYDNOCARPATE	HYDROCEPHALICS
HUMIDISTAT	HUNDREDERS	HYALINISATION	HYDNOCARPATES	HYDROCEPHALIES
HUMIDISTATS	HUNDREDFOLD	HYALINISATIONS	HYDNOCARPIC	HYDROCEPHALOID
HUMIDITIES	HUNDREDFOLDS	HYALINISED	HYDRAEMIAS	HYDROCEPHALOUS
HUMIDNESSES	HUNDREDORS	HYALINISES	HYDRAGOGUE	HYDROCEPHALUS
HUMIFICATION	HUNDREDTHS	HYALINISING	HYDRAGOGUES	HYDROCEPHALUSES
HUMIFICATIONS	HUNDREDWEIGHT	HYALINIZATION	HYDRALAZINE	HYDROCEPHALY
HUMILIATED	HUNDREDWEIGHTS	HYALINIZATIONS	HYDRALAZINES	HYDROCHLORIC
HUMILIATES	HUNGERINGLY	HYALINIZED	HYDRANGEAS	HYDROCHLORIDE
HUMILIATING	HUNGRINESS	HYALINIZES	HYDRARGYRAL	HYDROCHLORIDES
HUMILIATINGLY	HUNGRINESSES	HYALINIZING	HYDRARGYRIA	HYDROCHORE
HUMILIATION	HUNTIEGOWK	HYALOMELAN	HYDRARGYRIAS	HYDROCHORES
HUMILIATIONS	HUNTIEGOWKED	HYALOMELANE	HYDRARGYRIC	HYDROCHORIC
HUMILIATIVE	HUNTIEGOWKING	HYALOMELANES	HYDRARGYRISM	HYDROCODONE
HUMILIATOR	HUNTIEGOWKS	HYALOMELANS	HYDRARGYRISMS	HYDROCODONES
HUMILIATORS	HUNTRESSES	HYALONEMAS	HYDRARGYRUM	HYDROCOLLOID
HUMILIATORY	HUNTSMANSHIP	HYALOPHANE	HYDRARGYRUMS	HYDROCOLLOIDAL
HUMILITIES	HUNTSMANSHIPS	HYALOPHANES	HYDRARTHROSES	HYDROCOLLOIDS
HUMMELLERS	HUPAITHRIC	HYALOPLASM	HYDRARTHROSIS	HYDROCORAL
HUMMELLING	HURLBARROW	HYALOPLASMIC	HYDRASTINE	HYDROCORALLINE
HUMMELLINGS	HURLBARROWS	HYALOPLASMS	HYDRASTINES	HYDROCORALLINES
HUMMINGBIRD	HURRICANES	HYALURONIC	HYDRASTININE	HYDROCORALS
HUMMINGBIRDS	HURRICANOES	HYALURONIDASE	HYDRASTININES	HYDROCORTISONE
HUMMOCKING	HURRIEDNESS	HYALURONIDASES	HYDRASTISES	HYDROCORTISONES
HUMORALISM	HURRIEDNESSES	HYBRIDISABLE	HYDRATIONS	HYDROCRACK
HUMORALISMS	HURRYINGLY	HYBRIDISATION	HYDRAULICALLY	HYDROCRACKED
HUMORALIST	HURTFULNESS	HYBRIDISATIONS	HYDRAULICKED	HYDROCRACKER
HUMORALISTS	HURTFULNESSES	HYBRIDISED	HYDRAULICKING	HYDROCRACKERS
HUMORESQUE	HURTLEBERRIES	HYBRIDISER	HYDRAULICKINGS	HYDROCRACKING
HUMORESQUES	HURTLEBERRY	HYBRIDISERS	HYDRAULICS	HYDROCRACKINGS
HUMORISTIC	HURTLESSLY	HYBRIDISES	HYDRAZIDES	HYDROCRACKS
HUMORLESSLY	HURTLESSNESS	HYBRIDISING	HYDRAZINES	HYDROCYANIC
HUMORLESSNESS	HURTLESSNESSES	HYBRIDISMS	HYDRICALLY	HYDRODYNAMIC
HUMORLESSNESSES	HUSBANDAGE	HYBRIDISTS	HYDROACOUSTICS	HYDRODYNAMICAL
HUMOROUSLY	HUSBANDAGES	HYBRIDITIES	HYDROBIOLOGICAL	HYDRODYNAMICIST
HUMOROUSNESS	HUSBANDERS	HYBRIDIZABLE	HYDROBIOLOGIES	HYDRODYNAMICS
HUMOROUSNESSES	HUSBANDING	HYBRIDIZATION	HYDROBIOLOGIST	HYDROELASTIC
HUMORSOMENESS	HUSBANDLAND	HYBRIDIZATIONS	HYDROBIOLOGISTS	HYDROELECTRIC
HUMORSOMENESSES	HUSBANDLANDS	HYBRIDIZED	HYDROBIOLOGY	HYDROEXTRACTOR
HUMOURLESS	HUSBANDLESS	HYBRIDIZER	HYDROBROMIC	HYDROEXTRACTORS
HUMOURLESSLY	HUSBANDLIKE	HYBRIDIZERS	HYDROCARBON	HYDROFLUORIC
HUMOURLESSNESS	HUSBANDMAN	HYBRIDIZES	HYDROCARBONS	HYDROFOILS
HUMOURSOME	HUSBANDMEN	HYBRIDIZING	HYDROCASTS	HYDROFORMING
HUMOURSOMENESS	HUSBANDRIES	HYBRIDOMAS	HYDROCELES	HYDROFORMINGS
HUMPBACKED	HUSHABYING	HYDANTOINS	HYDROCELLULOSE	HYDROGENASE
HUMPINESSES	HUSHPUPPIES	HYDATHODES	HYDROCELLULOSES	HYDROGENASES
HUNCHBACKED	HUSKINESSES	HYDATIDIFORM	HYDROCEPHALIC	HYDROGENATE

H

HYDROGENATED
HYDROGENATES
HYDROGENATING
HYDROGENATION
HYDROGENATIONS
HYDROGENATOR
HYDROGENATORS
HYDROGENISATION
HYDROGENISE
HYDROGENISED
HYDROGENISES
HYDROGENISING
HYDROGENIZATION
HYDROGENIZE
HYDROGENIZED
HYDROGENIZES
HYDROGENIZING
HYDROGENOLYSES
HYDROGENOLYSIS
HYDROGENOUS
HYDROGEOLOGICAL
HYDROGEOLOGIES
HYDROGEOLOGIST
HYDROGEOLOGISTS
HYDROGEOLOGY
HYDROGRAPH
HYDROGRAPHER
HYDROGRAPHERS
HYDROGRAPHIC
HYDROGRAPHICAL
HYDROGRAPHIES
HYDROGRAPHS
HYDROGRAPHY
HYDROKINETIC
HYDROKINETICAL
HYDROKINETICS
HYDROLASES
HYDROLOGIC
HYDROLOGICAL
HYDROLOGICALLY
HYDROLOGIES
HYDROLOGIST
HYDROLOGISTS
HYDROLYSABLE
HYDROLYSATE
HYDROLYSATES
HYDROLYSATION

HYDROLYSATIONS
HYDROLYSED
HYDROLYSER
HYDROLYSERS
HYDROLYSES
HYDROLYSING
HYDROLYSIS
HYDROLYTES
HYDROLYTIC
HYDROLYTICALLY
HYDROLYZABLE
HYDROLYZATE
HYDROLYZATES
HYDROLYZATION
HYDROLYZATIONS
HYDROLYZED
HYDROLYZER
HYDROLYZERS
HYDROLYZES
HYDROLYZING
HYDROMAGNETIC
HYDROMAGNETICS
HYDROMANCER
HYDROMANCERS
HYDROMANCIES
HYDROMANCY
HYDROMANIA
HYDROMANIAS
HYDROMANTIC
HYDROMECHANICAL
HYDROMECHANICS
HYDROMEDUSA
HYDROMEDUSAE
HYDROMEDUSAN
HYDROMEDUSANS
HYDROMEDUSAS
HYDROMEDUSOID
HYDROMEDUSOIDS
HYDROMETALLURGY
HYDROMETEOR
HYDROMETEORS
HYDROMETER
HYDROMETERS
HYDROMETRIC
HYDROMETRICAL
HYDROMETRICALLY
HYDROMETRIES

HYDROMETRY
HYDROMORPHIC
HYDRONAUTS
HYDRONEPHROSES
HYDRONEPHROSIS
HYDRONEPHROTIC
HYDRONICALLY
HYDRONIUMS
HYDROPATHIC
HYDROPATHICAL
HYDROPATHICALLY
HYDROPATHICS
HYDROPATHIES
HYDROPATHIST
HYDROPATHISTS
HYDROPATHS
HYDROPATHY
HYDROPEROXIDE
HYDROPEROXIDES
HYDROPHANE
HYDROPHANES
HYDROPHANOUS
HYDROPHILE
HYDROPHILES
HYDROPHILIC
HYDROPHILICITY
HYDROPHILIES
HYDROPHILITE
HYDROPHILITES
HYDROPHILOUS
HYDROPHILY
HYDROPHOBIA
HYDROPHOBIAS
HYDROPHOBIC
HYDROPHOBICITY
HYDROPHOBOUS
HYDROPHONE
HYDROPHONES
HYDROPHYTE
HYDROPHYTES
HYDROPHYTIC
HYDROPHYTON
HYDROPHYTONS
HYDROPHYTOUS
HYDROPLANE
HYDROPLANED
HYDROPLANES

HYDROPLANING
HYDROPNEUMATIC
HYDROPOLYP
HYDROPOLYPS
HYDROPONIC
HYDROPONICALLY
HYDROPONICS
HYDROPOWER
HYDROPOWERS
HYDROPSIES
HYDROPULTS
HYDROQUINOL
HYDROQUINOLS
HYDROQUINONE
HYDROQUINONES
HYDROSCOPE
HYDROSCOPES
HYDROSCOPIC
HYDROSCOPICAL
HYDROSERES
HYDROSOLIC
HYDROSOMAL
HYDROSOMATA
HYDROSOMATOUS
HYDROSOMES
HYDROSPACE
HYDROSPACES
HYDROSPHERE
HYDROSPHERES
HYDROSPHERIC
HYDROSTATIC
HYDROSTATICAL
HYDROSTATICALLY
HYDROSTATICS
HYDROSTATS
HYDROSULPHATE
HYDROSULPHATES
HYDROSULPHIDE
HYDROSULPHIDES
HYDROSULPHITE
HYDROSULPHITES
HYDROSULPHURIC
HYDROSULPHUROUS
HYDROTACTIC
HYDROTAXES
HYDROTAXIS
HYDROTHECA

HYDROTHECAE
HYDROTHERAPIC
HYDROTHERAPIES
HYDROTHERAPIST
HYDROTHERAPISTS
HYDROTHERAPY
HYDROTHERMAL
HYDROTHERMALLY
HYDROTHORACES
HYDROTHORACIC
HYDROTHORAX
HYDROTHORAXES
HYDROTROPIC
HYDROTROPICALLY
HYDROTROPISM
HYDROTROPISMS
HYDROVANES
HYDROXIDES
HYDROXIUMS
HYDROXONIUM
HYDROXONIUMS
HYDROXYAPATITE
HYDROXYAPATITES
HYDROXYBUTYRATE
HYDROXYCITRIC
HYDROXYLAMINE
HYDROXYLAMINES
HYDROXYLAPATITE
HYDROXYLASE
HYDROXYLASES
HYDROXYLATE
HYDROXYLATED
HYDROXYLATES
HYDROXYLATING
HYDROXYLATION
HYDROXYLATIONS
HYDROXYLIC
HYDROXYPROLINE
HYDROXYPROLINES
HYDROXYUREA
HYDROXYUREAS
HYDROXYZINE
HYDROXYZINES
HYDROZINCITE
HYDROZINCITES
HYDROZOANS
HYETOGRAPH

HYETOGRAPHIC	HYLOMORPHISMS	HYPABYSSAL	HYPERBARICALLY	HYPERCHARGING
HYETOGRAPHICAL	HYLOPATHISM	HYPABYSSALLY	HYPERBATIC	HYPERCIVILISED
HYETOGRAPHIES	HYLOPATHISMS	HYPAESTHESIA	HYPERBATICALLY	HYPERCIVILIZED
HYETOGRAPHS	HYLOPATHIST	HYPAESTHESIAS	HYPERBATON	HYPERCOAGULABLE
HYETOGRAPHY	HYLOPATHISTS	HYPAESTHESIC	HYPERBATONS	HYPERCOLOUR
HYETOLOGIES	HYLOPHAGOUS	HYPAETHRAL	HYPERBOLAE	HYPERCOLOURS
HYETOMETER	HYLOPHYTES	HYPAETHRON	HYPERBOLAS	HYPERCOMPLEX
HYETOMETERS	HYLOTHEISM	HYPAETHRONS	HYPERBOLES	HYPERCONSCIOUS
HYETOMETROGRAPH	HYLOTHEISMS	HYPALGESIA	HYPERBOLIC	HYPERCORRECT
HYGIENICALLY	HYLOTHEIST	HYPALGESIAS	HYPERBOLICAL	HYPERCORRECTION
HYGIENISTS	HYLOTHEISTS	HYPALGESIC	HYPERBOLICALLY	HYPERCORRECTLY
HYGRISTORS	HYLOTOMOUS	HYPALLACTIC	HYPERBOLISE	HYPERCRITIC
HYGROCHASIES	HYLOZOICAL	HYPALLAGES	HYPERBOLISED	HYPERCRITICAL
HYGROCHASTIC	HYLOZOISMS	HYPANTHIAL	HYPERBOLISES	HYPERCRITICALLY
HYGROCHASY	HYLOZOISTIC	HYPANTHIUM	HYPERBOLISING	HYPERCRITICISE
HYGRODEIKS	HYLOZOISTICALLY	HYPERACIDITIES	HYPERBOLISM	HYPERCRITICISED
HYGROGRAPH	HYLOZOISTS	HYPERACIDITY	HYPERBOLISMS	HYPERCRITICISES
HYGROGRAPHIC	HYMENAEANS	HYPERACTION	HYPERBOLIST	HYPERCRITICISM
HYGROGRAPHICAL	HYMENEALLY	HYPERACTIONS	HYPERBOLISTS	HYPERCRITICISMS
HYGROGRAPHS	HYMENOPHORE	HYPERACTIVE	HYPERBOLIZE	HYPERCRITICIZE
HYGROLOGIES	HYMENOPHORES	HYPERACTIVES	HYPERBOLIZED	HYPERCRITICIZED
HYGROMETER	HYMENOPLASTIES	HYPERACTIVITIES	HYPERBOLIZES	HYPERCRITICIZES
HYGROMETERS	HYMENOPLASTY	HYPERACTIVITY	HYPERBOLIZING	HYPERCRITICS
HYGROMETRIC	HYMENOPTERA	HYPERACUITIES	HYPERBOLOID	HYPERCUBES
HYGROMETRICAL	HYMENOPTERAN	HYPERACUITY	HYPERBOLOIDAL	HYPERDACTYL
HYGROMETRICALLY	HYMENOPTERANS	HYPERACUSES	HYPERBOLOIDS	HYPERDACTYLIES
HYGROMETRIES	HYMENOPTERON	HYPERACUSIS	HYPERBOREAN	HYPERDACTYLY
HYGROMETRY	HYMENOPTERONS	HYPERACUTE	HYPERBOREANS	HYPERDORIAN
HYGROPHILE	HYMENOPTEROUS	HYPERACUTENESS	HYPERCALCAEMIA	HYPERDULIA
HYGROPHILES	HYMNODICAL	HYPERADRENALISM	HYPERCALCAEMIAS	HYPERDULIAS
HYGROPHILOUS	HYMNODISTS	HYPERAEMIA	HYPERCALCAEMIC	HYPERDULIC
HYGROPHOBE	HYMNOGRAPHER	HYPERAEMIAS	HYPERCALCEMIA	HYPERDULICAL
HYGROPHOBES	HYMNOGRAPHERS	HYPERAEMIC	HYPERCALCEMIAS	HYPEREFFICIENT
HYGROPHYTE	HYMNOGRAPHIES	HYPERAESTHESIA	HYPERCALCEMIC	HYPEREMESES
HYGROPHYTES	HYMNOGRAPHY	HYPERAESTHESIAS	HYPERCAPNIA	HYPEREMESIS
HYGROPHYTIC	HYMNOLOGIC	HYPERAESTHESIC	HYPERCAPNIAS	HYPEREMETIC
HYGROSCOPE	HYMNOLOGICAL	HYPERAESTHETIC	HYPERCAPNIC	HYPEREMIAS
HYGROSCOPES	HYMNOLOGIES	HYPERAGGRESSIVE	HYPERCARBIA	HYPEREMOTIONAL
HYGROSCOPIC	HYMNOLOGIST	HYPERALERT	HYPERCARBIAS	HYPERENDEMIC
HYGROSCOPICAL	HYMNOLOGISTS	HYPERALGESIA	HYPERCATABOLISM	HYPERENERGETIC
HYGROSCOPICALLY	HYOPLASTRA	HYPERALGESIAS	HYPERCATALECTIC	HYPERESTHESIA
HYGROSCOPICITY	HYOPLASTRAL	HYPERALGESIC	HYPERCATALEXES	HYPERESTHESIAS
HYGROSTATS	HYOPLASTRON	HYPERAROUSAL	HYPERCATALEXIS	HYPERESTHETIC
HYLOGENESES	HYOSCYAMINE	HYPERAROUSALS	HYPERCAUTIOUS	HYPEREUTECTIC
HYLOGENESIS	HYOSCYAMINES	HYPERAWARE	HYPERCHARGE	HYPEREUTECTOID
HYLOMORPHIC	HYOSCYAMUS	HYPERAWARENESS	HYPERCHARGED	HYPEREXCITABLE
HYLOMORPHISM	HYOSCYAMUSES	HYPERBARIC	HYPERCHARGES	HYPEREXCITED

HYPEREXCITEMENT
HYPEREXCRETION
HYPEREXCRETIONS
HYPEREXTEND
HYPEREXTENDED
HYPEREXTENDING
HYPEREXTENDS
HYPEREXTENSION
HYPEREXTENSIONS
HYPERFASTIDIOUS
HYPERFOCAL
HYPERFUNCTION
HYPERFUNCTIONAL
HYPERFUNCTIONS
HYPERGAMIES
HYPERGAMOUS
HYPERGEOMETRIC
HYPERGLYCAEMIA
HYPERGLYCAEMIAS
HYPERGLYCAEMIC
HYPERGLYCEMIA
HYPERGLYCEMIAS
HYPERGLYCEMIC
HYPERGOLIC
HYPERGOLICALLY
HYPERHIDROSES
HYPERHIDROSIS
HYPERICINS
HYPERICUMS
HYPERIDROSES
HYPERIDROSIS
HYPERIMMUNE
HYPERIMMUNISE
HYPERIMMUNISED
HYPERIMMUNISES
HYPERIMMUNISING
HYPERIMMUNIZE
HYPERIMMUNIZED
HYPERIMMUNIZES
HYPERIMMUNIZING
HYPERINFLATED
HYPERINFLATION
HYPERINFLATIONS
HYPERINOSES
HYPERINOSIS
HYPERINOTIC
HYPERINSULINISM

HYPERINTENSE
HYPERINVOLUTION
HYPERIRRITABLE
HYPERKERATOSES
HYPERKERATOSIS
HYPERKERATOTIC
HYPERKINESES
HYPERKINESIA
HYPERKINESIAS
HYPERKINESIS
HYPERKINETIC
HYPERLINKED
HYPERLINKING
HYPERLINKS
HYPERLIPEMIA
HYPERLIPEMIAS
HYPERLIPEMIC
HYPERLIPIDAEMIA
HYPERLIPIDEMIA
HYPERLIPIDEMIAS
HYPERLYDIAN
HYPERMANIA
HYPERMANIAS
HYPERMANIC
HYPERMARKET
HYPERMARKETS
HYPERMARTS
HYPERMASCULINE
HYPERMEDIA
HYPERMEDIAS
HYPERMETABOLIC
HYPERMETABOLISM
HYPERMETER
HYPERMETERS
HYPERMETRIC
HYPERMETRICAL
HYPERMETROPIA
HYPERMETROPIAS
HYPERMETROPIC
HYPERMETROPICAL
HYPERMETROPIES
HYPERMETROPY
HYPERMILING
HYPERMILINGS
HYPERMNESIA
HYPERMNESIAS
HYPERMNESIC

HYPERMOBILITIES
HYPERMOBILITY
HYPERMODERN
HYPERMODERNISM
HYPERMODERNISMS
HYPERMODERNIST
HYPERMODERNISTS
HYPERMUTABILITY
HYPERMUTABLE
HYPERNATRAEMIA
HYPERNATRAEMIAS
HYPERNOVAE
HYPERNOVAS
HYPERNYMIES
HYPEROPIAS
HYPEROREXIA
HYPEROREXIAS
HYPEROSMIA
HYPEROSMIAS
HYPEROSTOSES
HYPEROSTOSIS
HYPEROSTOTIC
HYPERPARASITE
HYPERPARASITES
HYPERPARASITIC
HYPERPARASITISM
HYPERPHAGIA
HYPERPHAGIAS
HYPERPHAGIC
HYPERPHRYGIAN
HYPERPHYSICAL
HYPERPHYSICALLY
HYPERPIGMENTED
HYPERPITUITARY
HYPERPLANE
HYPERPLANES
HYPERPLASIA
HYPERPLASIAS
HYPERPLASTIC
HYPERPLOID
HYPERPLOIDIES
HYPERPLOIDS
HYPERPLOIDY
HYPERPNEAS
HYPERPNEIC
HYPERPNOEA
HYPERPNOEAS

HYPERPOLARISE
HYPERPOLARISED
HYPERPOLARISES
HYPERPOLARISING
HYPERPOLARIZE
HYPERPOLARIZED
HYPERPOLARIZES
HYPERPOLARIZING
HYPERPOWER
HYPERPOWERS
HYPERPRODUCER
HYPERPRODUCERS
HYPERPRODUCTION
HYPERPROSEXIA
HYPERPROSEXIAS
HYPERPYRETIC
HYPERPYREXIA
HYPERPYREXIAL
HYPERPYREXIAS
HYPERRATIONAL
HYPERREACTIVE
HYPERREACTIVITY
HYPERREACTOR
HYPERREACTORS
HYPERREALISM
HYPERREALISMS
HYPERREALIST
HYPERREALISTIC
HYPERREALISTS
HYPERREALITIES
HYPERREALITY
HYPERREALS
HYPERRESPONSIVE
HYPERROMANTIC
HYPERROMANTICS
HYPERSALINE
HYPERSALINITIES
HYPERSALINITY
HYPERSALIVATION
HYPERSARCOMA
HYPERSARCOMAS
HYPERSARCOMATA
HYPERSARCOSES
HYPERSARCOSIS
HYPERSECRETION
HYPERSECRETIONS
HYPERSENSITISE

HYPERSENSITISED
HYPERSENSITISES
HYPERSENSITIVE
HYPERSENSITIZE
HYPERSENSITIZED
HYPERSENSITIZES
HYPERSENSUAL
HYPERSEXUAL
HYPERSEXUALITY
HYPERSOMNIA
HYPERSOMNIAS
HYPERSOMNOLENCE
HYPERSONIC
HYPERSONICALLY
HYPERSONICS
HYPERSPACE
HYPERSPACES
HYPERSPATIAL
HYPERSTATIC
HYPERSTHENE
HYPERSTHENES
HYPERSTHENIA
HYPERSTHENIAS
HYPERSTHENIC
HYPERSTHENITE
HYPERSTHENITES
HYPERSTIMULATE
HYPERSTIMULATED
HYPERSTIMULATES
HYPERSTRESS
HYPERSTRESSES
HYPERSURFACE
HYPERSURFACES
HYPERTENSE
HYPERTENSION
HYPERTENSIONS
HYPERTENSIVE
HYPERTENSIVES
HYPERTEXTS
HYPERTHERMAL
HYPERTHERMIA
HYPERTHERMIAS
HYPERTHERMIC
HYPERTHERMIES
HYPERTHERMY
HYPERTHYMIA
HYPERTHYMIAS

H

HYPERTHYROID	HYPHENIZATIONS	HYPNOTISING	HYPOCORISMA	HYPOGYNOUS
HYPERTHYROIDISM	HYPHENIZED	HYPNOTISMS	HYPOCORISMAS	HYPOKALEMIA
HYPERTHYROIDS	HYPHENIZES	HYPNOTISTIC	HYPOCORISMS	HYPOKALEMIAS
HYPERTONIA	HYPHENIZING	HYPNOTISTS	HYPOCORISTIC	HYPOKALEMIC
HYPERTONIAS	HYPHENLESS	HYPNOTIZABILITY	HYPOCORISTICAL	HYPOLIMNIA
HYPERTONIC	HYPNAGOGIC	HYPNOTIZABLE	HYPOCOTYLOUS	HYPOLIMNION
HYPERTONICITIES	HYPNOANALYSES	HYPNOTIZATION	HYPOCOTYLS	HYPOLIMNIONS
HYPERTONICITY	HYPNOANALYSIS	HYPNOTIZATIONS	HYPOCRISIES	HYPOLYDIAN
HYPERTROPHIC	HYPNOANALYTIC	HYPNOTIZED	HYPOCRITES	HYPOMAGNESAEMIA
HYPERTROPHICAL	HYPNOBIRTHING	HYPNOTIZER	HYPOCRITIC	HYPOMAGNESEMIA
HYPERTROPHIED	HYPNOBIRTHINGS	HYPNOTIZERS	HYPOCRITICAL	HYPOMAGNESEMIAS
HYPERTROPHIES	HYPNOGENESES	HYPNOTIZES	HYPOCRITICALLY	HYPOMANIAS
HYPERTROPHOUS	HYPNOGENESIS	HYPNOTIZING	HYPOCRYSTALLINE	HYPOMANICS
HYPERTROPHY	HYPNOGENETIC	HYPOACIDITIES	HYPOCYCLOID	HYPOMENORRHEA
HYPERTROPHYING	HYPNOGENIC	HYPOACIDITY	HYPOCYCLOIDAL	HYPOMENORRHEAS
HYPERTYPICAL	HYPNOGENIES	HYPOAEOLIAN	HYPOCYCLOIDS	HYPOMENORRHOEA
HYPERURBANISM	HYPNOGENOUS	HYPOALLERGENIC	HYPODERMAL	HYPOMENORRHOEAS
HYPERURBANISMS	HYPNOGOGIC	HYPOBLASTIC	HYPODERMAS	HYPOMIXOLYDIAN
HYPERURICAEMIA	HYPNOIDISE	HYPOBLASTS	HYPODERMIC	HYPOMORPHIC
HYPERURICAEMIAS	HYPNOIDISED	HYPOCALCAEMIA	HYPODERMICALLY	HYPOMORPHS
HYPERURICEMIA	HYPNOIDISES	HYPOCALCAEMIAS	HYPODERMICS	HYPONASTIC
HYPERURICEMIAS	HYPNOIDISING	HYPOCALCAEMIC	HYPODERMIS	HYPONASTICALLY
HYPERVELOCITIES	HYPNOIDIZE	HYPOCALCEMIA	HYPODERMISES	HYPONASTIES
HYPERVELOCITY	HYPNOIDIZED	HYPOCALCEMIAS	HYPODIPLOID	HYPONATRAEMIA
HYPERVENTILATE	HYPNOIDIZES	HYPOCALCEMIC	HYPODIPLOIDIES	HYPONATRAEMIAS
HYPERVENTILATED	HYPNOIDIZING	HYPOCAUSTS	HYPODIPLOIDY	HYPONITRITE
HYPERVENTILATES	HYPNOLOGIC	HYPOCENTER	HYPODORIAN	HYPONITRITES
HYPERVIGILANCE	HYPNOLOGICAL	HYPOCENTERS	HYPOEUTECTIC	HYPONITROUS
HYPERVIGILANCES	HYPNOLOGIES	HYPOCENTRAL	HYPOEUTECTOID	HYPONYMIES
HYPERVIGILANT	HYPNOLOGIST	HYPOCENTRE	HYPOGAEOUS	HYPOPHARYNGES
HYPERVIRULENT	HYPNOLOGISTS	HYPOCENTRES	HYPOGASTRIA	HYPOPHARYNX
HYPERVISCOSITY	HYPNOPAEDIA	HYPOCHLORITE	HYPOGASTRIC	HYPOPHARYNXES
HYPESTHESIA	HYPNOPAEDIAS	HYPOCHLORITES	HYPOGASTRIUM	HYPOPHOSPHATE
HYPESTHESIAS	HYPNOPOMPIC	HYPOCHLOROUS	HYPOGENOUS	HYPOPHOSPHATES
HYPESTHESIC	HYPNOTHERAPIES	HYPOCHONDRIA	HYPOGLOSSAL	HYPOPHOSPHITE
HYPHENATED	HYPNOTHERAPIST	HYPOCHONDRIAC	HYPOGLOSSALS	HYPOPHOSPHITES
HYPHENATES	HYPNOTHERAPISTS	HYPOCHONDRIACAL	HYPOGLYCAEMIA	HYPOPHOSPHORIC
HYPHENATING	HYPNOTHERAPY	HYPOCHONDRIACS	HYPOGLYCAEMIAS	HYPOPHOSPHOROUS
HYPHENATION	HYPNOTICALLY	HYPOCHONDRIAS	HYPOGLYCAEMIC	HYPOPHRYGIAN
HYPHENATIONS	HYPNOTISABILITY	HYPOCHONDRIASES	HYPOGLYCEMIA	HYPOPHYGES
HYPHENISATION	HYPNOTISABLE	HYPOCHONDRIASIS	HYPOGLYCEMIAS	HYPOPHYSEAL
HYPHENISATIONS	HYPNOTISATION	HYPOCHONDRIASM	HYPOGLYCEMIC	HYPOPHYSECTOMY
HYPHENISED	HYPNOTISATIONS	HYPOCHONDRIASMS	HYPOGLYCEMICS	HYPOPHYSES
HYPHENISES	HYPNOTISED	HYPOCHONDRIAST	HYPOGNATHISM	HYPOPHYSIAL
HYPHENISING	HYPNOTISER	HYPOCHONDRIASTS	HYPOGNATHISMS	HYPOPHYSIS
HYPHENISMS	HYPNOTISERS	HYPOCHONDRIUM	HYPOGNATHOUS	HYPOPITUITARISM
HYPHENIZATION	HYPNOTISES	HYPOCORISM	HYPOGYNIES	HYPOPITUITARY

HYPOPLASIA	HYPOSTATISED	HYPOTHECATING	HYPOTHYMIA	HYPSOPHOBIA
HYPOPLASIAS	HYPOSTATISES	HYPOTHECATION	HYPOTHYMIAS	HYPSOPHOBIAS
HYPOPLASTIC	HYPOSTATISING	HYPOTHECATIONS	HYPOTHYROID	HYPSOPHYLL
HYPOPLASTIES	HYPOSTATIZATION	HYPOTHECATOR	HYPOTHYROIDISM	HYPSOPHYLLARY
HYPOPLASTRA	HYPOSTATIZE	HYPOTHECATORS	HYPOTHYROIDISMS	HYPSOPHYLLS
HYPOPLASTRON	HYPOSTATIZED	HYPOTHENUSE	HYPOTHYROIDS	HYRACOIDEAN
HYPOPLASTY	HYPOSTATIZES	HYPOTHENUSES	HYPOTONIAS	HYRACOIDEANS
HYPOPLOIDIES	HYPOSTATIZING	HYPOTHERMAL	HYPOTONICITIES	HYSTERANTHOUS
HYPOPLOIDS	HYPOSTHENIA	HYPOTHERMIA	HYPOTONICITY	HYSTERECTOMIES
HYPOPLOIDY	HYPOSTHENIAS	HYPOTHERMIAS	HYPOTROCHOID	HYSTERECTOMISE
HYPOPNOEAS	HYPOSTHENIC	HYPOTHERMIC	HYPOTROCHOIDS	HYSTERECTOMISED
HYPOSENSITISE	HYPOSTOMES	HYPOTHESES	HYPOTYPOSES	HYSTERECTOMISES
HYPOSENSITISED	HYPOSTRESS	HYPOTHESIS	HYPOTYPOSIS	HYSTERECTOMIZE
HYPOSENSITISES	HYPOSTRESSES	HYPOTHESISE	HYPOVENTILATION	HYSTERECTOMIZED
HYPOSENSITISING	HYPOSTROPHE	HYPOTHESISED	HYPOXAEMIA	HYSTERECTOMIZES
HYPOSENSITIZE	HYPOSTROPHES	HYPOTHESISER	HYPOXAEMIAS	HYSTERECTOMY
HYPOSENSITIZED	HYPOSTYLES	HYPOTHESISERS	HYPOXAEMIC	HYSTERESES
HYPOSENSITIZES	HYPOSULPHATE	HYPOTHESISES	HYPOXANTHINE	HYSTERESIAL
HYPOSENSITIZING	HYPOSULPHATES	HYPOTHESISING	HYPOXANTHINES	HYSTERESIS
HYPOSPADIAS	HYPOSULPHITE	HYPOTHESIST	HYPOXEMIAS	HYSTERETIC
HYPOSPADIASES	HYPOSULPHITES	HYPOTHESISTS	HYPSOCHROME	HYSTERETICALLY
HYPOSTASES	HYPOSULPHURIC	HYPOTHESIZE	HYPSOCHROMES	HYSTERICAL
HYPOSTASIS	HYPOSULPHUROUS	HYPOTHESIZED	HYPSOCHROMIC	HYSTERICALLY
HYPOSTASISATION	HYPOTACTIC	HYPOTHESIZER	HYPSOGRAPHIC	HYSTERICKY
HYPOSTASISE	HYPOTENSION	HYPOTHESIZERS	HYPSOGRAPHICAL	HYSTERITIS
HYPOSTASISED	HYPOTENSIONS	HYPOTHESIZES	HYPSOGRAPHIES	HYSTERITISES
HYPOSTASISES	HYPOTENSIVE	HYPOTHESIZING	HYPSOGRAPHY	HYSTEROGENIC
HYPOSTASISING	HYPOTENSIVES	HYPOTHETIC	HYPSOMETER	HYSTEROGENIES
HYPOSTASIZATION	HYPOTENUSE	HYPOTHETICAL	HYPSOMETERS	HYSTEROGENY
HYPOSTASIZE	HYPOTENUSES	HYPOTHETICALLY	HYPSOMETRIC	HYSTEROIDAL
HYPOSTASIZED	HYPOTHALAMI	HYPOTHETISE	HYPSOMETRICAL	HYSTEROMANIA
HYPOSTASIZES	HYPOTHALAMIC	HYPOTHETISED	HYPSOMETRICALLY	HYSTEROMANIAS
HYPOSTASIZING	HYPOTHALAMUS	HYPOTHETISES	HYPSOMETRIES	HYSTEROTOMIES
HYPOSTATIC	HYPOTHECAE	HYPOTHETISING	HYPSOMETRIST	HYSTEROTOMY
HYPOSTATICAL	HYPOTHECARY	HYPOTHETIZE	HYPSOMETRISTS	HYSTRICOMORPH
HYPOSTATICALLY	HYPOTHECATE	HYPOTHETIZED	HYPSOMETRY	HYSTRICOMORPHIC
HYPOSTATISATION	HYPOTHECATED	HYPOTHETIZES	HYPSOPHOBE	HYSTRICOMORPHS
HYPOSTATISE	HYPOTHECATES	HYPOTHETIZING	HYPSOPHOBES	

IAMBICALLY	ICHTHYOLATROUS	ICONOGRAPHER	ICTERICALS	IDEOGRAPHICALLY
IAMBOGRAPHER	ICHTHYOLATRY	ICONOGRAPHERS	ICTERITIOUS	IDEOGRAPHIES
IAMBOGRAPHERS	ICHTHYOLITE	ICONOGRAPHIC	IDEALISATION	IDEOGRAPHS
IATROCHEMICAL	ICHTHYOLITES	ICONOGRAPHICAL	IDEALISATIONS	IDEOGRAPHY
IATROCHEMIST	ICHTHYOLITIC	ICONOGRAPHIES	IDEALISERS	IDEOLOGICAL
IATROCHEMISTRY	ICHTHYOLOGIC	ICONOGRAPHY	IDEALISING	IDEOLOGICALLY
IATROCHEMISTS	ICHTHYOLOGICAL	ICONOLATER	IDEALISTIC	IDEOLOGIES
IATROGENIC	ICHTHYOLOGIES	ICONOLATERS	IDEALISTICALLY	IDEOLOGISE
IATROGENICALLY	ICHTHYOLOGIST	ICONOLATRIES	IDEALITIES	IDEOLOGISED
IATROGENICITIES	ICHTHYOLOGISTS	ICONOLATROUS	IDEALIZATION	IDEOLOGISES
IATROGENICITY	ICHTHYOLOGY	ICONOLATRY	IDEALIZATIONS	IDEOLOGISING
IATROGENIES	ICHTHYOPHAGIES	ICONOLOGICAL	IDEALIZERS	IDEOLOGIST
IBUPROFENS	ICHTHYOPHAGIST	ICONOLOGIES	IDEALIZING	IDEOLOGISTS
ICEBOATERS	ICHTHYOPHAGISTS	ICONOLOGIST	IDEALNESSES	IDEOLOGIZE
ICEBOATING	ICHTHYOPHAGOUS	ICONOLOGISTS	IDEALOGIES	IDEOLOGIZED
ICEBOATINGS	ICHTHYOPHAGY	ICONOMACHIES	IDEALOGUES	IDEOLOGIZES
ICEBREAKER	ICHTHYOPSID	ICONOMACHIST	IDEATIONAL	IDEOLOGIZING
ICEBREAKERS	ICHTHYOPSIDAN	ICONOMACHISTS	IDEATIONALLY	IDEOLOGUES
ICEBREAKING	ICHTHYOPSIDANS	ICONOMACHY	IDEMPOTENCIES	IDEOPHONES
ICEFISHING	ICHTHYOPSIDS	ICONOMATIC	IDEMPOTENCY	IDEOPOLISES
ICHNEUMONS	ICHTHYORNIS	ICONOMATICISM	IDEMPOTENT	IDEOPRAXIST
ICHNOFOSSIL	ICHTHYORNISES	ICONOMATICISMS	IDEMPOTENTS	IDEOPRAXISTS
ICHNOFOSSILS	ICHTHYOSAUR	ICONOMETER	IDENTICALLY	IDIOBLASTIC
ICHNOGRAPHIC	ICHTHYOSAURI	ICONOMETERS	IDENTICALNESS	IDIOBLASTS
ICHNOGRAPHICAL	ICHTHYOSAURIAN	ICONOMETRIES	IDENTICALNESSES	IDIOGLOSSIA
ICHNOGRAPHIES	ICHTHYOSAURIANS	ICONOMETRY	IDENTIFIABLE	IDIOGLOSSIAS
ICHNOGRAPHY	ICHTHYOSAURS	ICONOPHILISM	IDENTIFIABLY	IDIOGRAPHIC
ICHNOLITES	ICHTHYOSAURUS	ICONOPHILISMS	IDENTIFICATION	IDIOGRAPHS
ICHNOLOGICAL	ICHTHYOSAURUSES	ICONOPHILIST	IDENTIFICATIONS	IDIOLECTAL
ICHNOLOGIES	ICHTHYOSES	ICONOPHILISTS	IDENTIFIED	IDIOLECTIC
ICHTHYOCOLLA	ICHTHYOSIS	ICONOSCOPE	IDENTIFIER	IDIOMATICAL
ICHTHYOCOLLAS	ICHTHYOTIC	ICONOSCOPES	IDENTIFIERS	IDIOMATICALLY
ICHTHYODORULITE	ICKINESSES	ICONOSTASES	IDENTIFIES	IDIOMATICALNESS
ICHTHYODORYLITE	ICONICALLY	ICONOSTASIS	IDENTIFYING	IDIOMATICNESS
ICHTHYOFAUNA	ICONICITIES	ICOSAHEDRA	IDENTIKITS	IDIOMATICNESSES
ICHTHYOFAUNAE	ICONIFYING	ICOSAHEDRAL	IDENTITIES	IDIOMORPHIC
ICHTHYOFAUNAL	ICONOCLASM	ICOSAHEDRON	IDEOGRAMIC	IDIOMORPHICALLY
ICHTHYOFAUNAS	ICONOCLASMS	ICOSAHEDRONS	IDEOGRAMMATIC	IDIOMORPHISM
ICHTHYOIDAL	ICONOCLAST	ICOSANDRIAN	IDEOGRAMMIC	IDIOMORPHISMS
ICHTHYOIDS	ICONOCLASTIC	ICOSANDROUS	IDEOGRAPHIC	IDIOPATHIC
ICHTHYOLATRIES	ICONOCLASTS	ICOSITETRAHEDRA	IDEOGRAPHICAL	IDIOPATHICALLY

IDIOPATHIES

IDIOPATHIES
IDIOPHONES
IDIOPHONIC
IDIOPLASMATIC
IDIOPLASMIC
IDIOPLASMS
IDIORHYTHMIC
IDIORRHYTHMIC
IDIOSYNCRASIES
IDIOSYNCRASY
IDIOSYNCRATIC
IDIOSYNCRATICAL
IDIOTHERMOUS
IDIOTICALLY
IDIOTICALNESS
IDIOTICALNESSES
IDIOTICONS
IDLENESSES
IDOLATRESS
IDOLATRESSES
IDOLATRIES
IDOLATRISE
IDOLATRISED
IDOLATRISER
IDOLATRISERS
IDOLATRISES
IDOLATRISING
IDOLATRIZE
IDOLATRIZED
IDOLATRIZER
IDOLATRIZERS
IDOLATRIZES
IDOLATRIZING
IDOLATROUS
IDOLATROUSLY
IDOLATROUSNESS
IDOLISATION
IDOLISATIONS
IDOLIZATION
IDOLIZATIONS
IDOLOCLAST
IDOLOCLASTS
IDONEITIES
IDOXURIDINE
IDOXURIDINES
IDYLLICALLY
IFFINESSES

IGNESCENTS
IGNIMBRITE
IGNIMBRITES
IGNIPOTENT
IGNITABILITIES
IGNITABILITY
IGNITIBILITIES
IGNITIBILITY
IGNOBILITIES
IGNOBILITY
IGNOBLENESS
IGNOBLENESSES
IGNOMINIES
IGNOMINIOUS
IGNOMINIOUSLY
IGNOMINIOUSNESS
IGNORAMUSES
IGNORANCES
IGNORANTLY
IGNORANTNESS
IGNORANTNESSES
IGNORATION
IGNORATIONS
IGUANODONS
ILEOSTOMIES
ILLAQUEABLE
ILLAQUEATE
ILLAQUEATED
ILLAQUEATES
ILLAQUEATING
ILLAQUEATION
ILLAQUEATIONS
ILLATIVELY
ILLAUDABLE
ILLAUDABLY
ILLAWARRAS
ILLEGALISATION
ILLEGALISATIONS
ILLEGALISE
ILLEGALISED
ILLEGALISES
ILLEGALISING
ILLEGALITIES
ILLEGALITY
ILLEGALIZATION
ILLEGALIZATIONS
ILLEGALIZE

ILLEGALIZED
ILLEGALIZES
ILLEGALIZING
ILLEGIBILITIES
ILLEGIBILITY
ILLEGIBLENESS
ILLEGIBLENESSES
ILLEGITIMACIES
ILLEGITIMACY
ILLEGITIMATE
ILLEGITIMATED
ILLEGITIMATELY
ILLEGITIMATES
ILLEGITIMATING
ILLEGITIMATION
ILLEGITIMATIONS
ILLIBERALISE
ILLIBERALISED
ILLIBERALISES
ILLIBERALISING
ILLIBERALISM
ILLIBERALISMS
ILLIBERALITIES
ILLIBERALITY
ILLIBERALIZE
ILLIBERALIZED
ILLIBERALIZES
ILLIBERALIZING
ILLIBERALLY
ILLIBERALNESS
ILLIBERALNESSES
ILLICITNESS
ILLICITNESSES
ILLIMITABILITY
ILLIMITABLE
ILLIMITABLENESS
ILLIMITABLY
ILLIMITATION
ILLIMITATIONS
ILLIQUATION
ILLIQUATIONS
ILLIQUIDITIES
ILLIQUIDITY
ILLITERACIES
ILLITERACY
ILLITERATE
ILLITERATELY

ILLITERATENESS
ILLITERATES
ILLOCUTION
ILLOCUTIONARY
ILLOCUTIONS
ILLOGICALITIES
ILLOGICALITY
ILLOGICALLY
ILLOGICALNESS
ILLOGICALNESSES
ILLUMINABLE
ILLUMINANCE
ILLUMINANCES
ILLUMINANT
ILLUMINANTS
ILLUMINATE
ILLUMINATED
ILLUMINATES
ILLUMINATI
ILLUMINATING
ILLUMINATINGLY
ILLUMINATION
ILLUMINATIONAL
ILLUMINATIONS
ILLUMINATIVE
ILLUMINATO
ILLUMINATOR
ILLUMINATORS
ILLUMINERS
ILLUMINING
ILLUMINISM
ILLUMINISMS
ILLUMINIST
ILLUMINISTS
ILLUSIONAL
ILLUSIONARY
ILLUSIONED
ILLUSIONISM
ILLUSIONISMS
ILLUSIONIST
ILLUSIONISTIC
ILLUSIONISTS
ILLUSIVELY
ILLUSIVENESS
ILLUSIVENESSES
ILLUSORILY
ILLUSORINESS

ILLUSORINESSES
ILLUSTRATABLE
ILLUSTRATE
ILLUSTRATED
ILLUSTRATEDS
ILLUSTRATES
ILLUSTRATING
ILLUSTRATION
ILLUSTRATIONAL
ILLUSTRATIONS
ILLUSTRATIVE
ILLUSTRATIVELY
ILLUSTRATOR
ILLUSTRATORS
ILLUSTRATORY
ILLUSTRIOUS
ILLUSTRIOUSLY
ILLUSTRIOUSNESS
ILLUSTRISSIMO
ILLUVIATED
ILLUVIATES
ILLUVIATING
ILLUVIATION
ILLUVIATIONS
IMAGINABLE
IMAGINABLENESS
IMAGINABLY
IMAGINARIES
IMAGINARILY
IMAGINARINESS
IMAGINARINESSES
IMAGINATION
IMAGINATIONAL
IMAGINATIONS
IMAGINATIVE
IMAGINATIVELY
IMAGINATIVENESS
IMAGINEERED
IMAGINEERING
IMAGINEERS
IMAGININGS
IMAGINISTS
IMAGISTICALLY
IMBALANCED
IMBALANCES
IMBECILELY
IMBECILICALLY

IMBECILITIES	IMMACULATELY	IMMEDIATELY	IMMISCIBILITY	IMMODERATELY
IMBECILITY	IMMACULATENESS	IMMEDIATENESS	IMMISCIBLE	IMMODERATENESS
IMBIBITION	IMMANACLED	IMMEDIATENESSES	IMMISCIBLY	IMMODERATION
IMBIBITIONAL	IMMANACLES	IMMEDIATISM	IMMISERATION	IMMODERATIONS
IMBIBITIONS	IMMANACLING	IMMEDIATISMS	IMMISERATIONS	IMMODESTIES
IMBITTERED	IMMANATION	IMMEDICABLE	IMMISERISATION	IMMODESTLY
IMBITTERING	IMMANATIONS	IMMEDICABLENESS	IMMISERISATIONS	IMMOLATING
IMBOLDENED	IMMANENCES	IMMEDICABLY	IMMISERISE	IMMOLATION
IMBOLDENING	IMMANENCIES	IMMEMORIAL	IMMISERISED	IMMOLATIONS
IMBORDERED	IMMANENTAL	IMMEMORIALLY	IMMISERISES	IMMOLATORS
IMBORDERING	IMMANENTISM	IMMENSENESS	IMMISERISING	IMMOMENTOUS
IMBOSOMING	IMMANENTISMS	IMMENSENESSES	IMMISERIZATION	IMMORALISM
IMBOWERING	IMMANENTIST	IMMENSITIES	IMMISERIZATIONS	IMMORALISMS
IMBRANGLED	IMMANENTISTIC	IMMENSURABILITY	IMMISERIZE	IMMORALIST
IMBRANGLES	IMMANENTISTS	IMMENSURABLE	IMMISERIZED	IMMORALISTS
IMBRANGLING	IMMANENTLY	IMMERGENCE	IMMISERIZES	IMMORALITIES
IMBRICATED	IMMANITIES	IMMERGENCES	IMMISERIZING	IMMORALITY
IMBRICATELY	IMMANTLING	IMMERITOUS	IMMISSIONS	IMMORTALISATION
IMBRICATES	IMMARCESCIBLE	IMMERSIBLE	IMMITIGABILITY	IMMORTALISE
IMBRICATING	IMMARGINATE	IMMERSIONISM	IMMITIGABLE	IMMORTALISED
IMBRICATION	IMMATERIAL	IMMERSIONISMS	IMMITIGABLY	IMMORTALISER
IMBRICATIONS	IMMATERIALISE	IMMERSIONIST	IMMITTANCE	IMMORTALISERS
IMBROCCATA	IMMATERIALISED	IMMERSIONISTS	IMMITTANCES	IMMORTALISES
IMBROCCATAS	IMMATERIALISES	IMMERSIONS	IMMIXTURES	IMMORTALISING
IMBROGLIOS	IMMATERIALISING	IMMETHODICAL	IMMOBILISATION	IMMORTALITIES
IMBROWNING	IMMATERIALISM	IMMETHODICALLY	IMMOBILISATIONS	IMMORTALITY
IMBRUEMENT	IMMATERIALISMS	IMMIGRANCIES	IMMOBILISE	IMMORTALIZATION
IMBRUEMENTS	IMMATERIALIST	IMMIGRANCY	IMMOBILISED	IMMORTALIZE
IMBUEMENTS	IMMATERIALISTS	IMMIGRANTS	IMMOBILISER	IMMORTALIZED
IMIDAZOLES	IMMATERIALITIES	IMMIGRATED	IMMOBILISERS	IMMORTALIZER
IMINAZOLES	IMMATERIALITY	IMMIGRATES	IMMOBILISES	IMMORTALIZERS
IMINOUREAS	IMMATERIALIZE	IMMIGRATING	IMMOBILISING	IMMORTALIZES
IMIPRAMINE	IMMATERIALIZED	IMMIGRATION	IMMOBILISM	IMMORTALIZING
IMIPRAMINES	IMMATERIALIZES	IMMIGRATIONAL	IMMOBILISMS	IMMORTALLY
IMITABILITIES	IMMATERIALIZING	IMMIGRATIONS	IMMOBILITIES	IMMORTELLE
IMITABILITY	IMMATERIALLY	IMMIGRATOR	IMMOBILITY	IMMORTELLES
IMITABLENESS	IMMATERIALNESS	IMMIGRATORS	IMMOBILIZATION	IMMOTILITIES
IMITABLENESSES	IMMATURELY	IMMIGRATORY	IMMOBILIZATIONS	IMMOTILITY
IMITANCIES	IMMATURENESS	IMMINENCES	IMMOBILIZE	IMMOVABILITIES
IMITATIONAL	IMMATURENESSES	IMMINENCIES	IMMOBILIZED	IMMOVABILITY
IMITATIONS	IMMATURITIES	IMMINENTLY	IMMOBILIZER	IMMOVABLENESS
IMITATIVELY	IMMATURITY	IMMINENTNESS	IMMOBILIZERS	IMMOVABLENESSES
IMITATIVENESS	IMMEASURABILITY	IMMINENTNESSES	IMMOBILIZES	IMMOVABLES
IMITATIVENESSES	IMMEASURABLE	IMMINGLING	IMMOBILIZING	IMMOVEABILITIES
IMMACULACIES	IMMEASURABLY	IMMINUTION	IMMODERACIES	IMMOVEABILITY
IMMACULACY	IMMEASURED	IMMINUTIONS	IMMODERACY	IMMOVEABLE
IMMACULATE	IMMEDIACIES	IMMISCIBILITIES	IMMODERATE	IMMOVEABLENESS

IMMOVEABLES
IMMOVEABLY
IMMUNIFACIENT
IMMUNISATION
IMMUNISATIONS
IMMUNISERS
IMMUNISING
IMMUNITIES
IMMUNIZATION
IMMUNIZATIONS
IMMUNIZERS
IMMUNIZING
IMMUNOASSAY
IMMUNOASSAYABLE
IMMUNOASSAYIST
IMMUNOASSAYISTS
IMMUNOASSAYS
IMMUNOBLOT
IMMUNOBLOTS
IMMUNOBLOTTING
IMMUNOBLOTTINGS
IMMUNOCHEMICAL
IMMUNOCHEMIST
IMMUNOCHEMISTRY
IMMUNOCHEMISTS
IMMUNOCOMPETENT
IMMUNOCOMPLEX
IMMUNOCOMPLEXES
IMMUNODEFICIENT
IMMUNODIAGNOSES
IMMUNODIAGNOSIS
IMMUNODIFFUSION
IMMUNOGENESES
IMMUNOGENESIS
IMMUNOGENETIC
IMMUNOGENETICAL
IMMUNOGENETICS
IMMUNOGENIC
IMMUNOGENICALLY
IMMUNOGENICITY
IMMUNOGENS
IMMUNOGLOBULIN
IMMUNOGLOBULINS
IMMUNOLOGIC
IMMUNOLOGICAL
IMMUNOLOGICALLY
IMMUNOLOGIES

IMMUNOLOGIST
IMMUNOLOGISTS
IMMUNOLOGY
IMMUNOMODULATOR
IMMUNOPATHOLOGY
IMMUNOPHORESES
IMMUNOPHORESIS
IMMUNOREACTION
IMMUNOREACTIONS
IMMUNOREACTIVE
IMMUNOSORBENT
IMMUNOSORBENTS
IMMUNOSTIMULANT
IMMUNOSUPPRESS
IMMUNOTHERAPIES
IMMUNOTHERAPY
IMMUNOTOXIC
IMMUNOTOXIN
IMMUNOTOXINS
IMMUREMENT
IMMUREMENTS
IMMUTABILITIES
IMMUTABILITY
IMMUTABLENESS
IMMUTABLENESSES
IMPACTIONS
IMPACTITES
IMPAINTING
IMPAIRABLE
IMPAIRINGS
IMPAIRMENT
IMPAIRMENTS
IMPALEMENT
IMPALEMENTS
IMPALPABILITIES
IMPALPABILITY
IMPALPABLE
IMPALPABLY
IMPALUDISM
IMPALUDISMS
IMPANATION
IMPANATIONS
IMPANELING
IMPANELLED
IMPANELLING
IMPANELMENT
IMPANELMENTS

IMPANNELLED
IMPANNELLING
IMPARADISE
IMPARADISED
IMPARADISES
IMPARADISING
IMPARIDIGITATE
IMPARIPINNATE
IMPARISYLLABIC
IMPARITIES
IMPARKATION
IMPARKATIONS
IMPARLANCE
IMPARLANCES
IMPARTABLE
IMPARTATION
IMPARTATIONS
IMPARTIALITIES
IMPARTIALITY
IMPARTIALLY
IMPARTIALNESS
IMPARTIALNESSES
IMPARTIBILITIES
IMPARTIBILITY
IMPARTIBLE
IMPARTIBLY
IMPARTMENT
IMPARTMENTS
IMPASSABILITIES
IMPASSABILITY
IMPASSABLE
IMPASSABLENESS
IMPASSABLY
IMPASSIBILITIES
IMPASSIBILITY
IMPASSIBLE
IMPASSIBLENESS
IMPASSIBLY
IMPASSIONATE
IMPASSIONED
IMPASSIONEDLY
IMPASSIONEDNESS
IMPASSIONING
IMPASSIONS
IMPASSIVELY
IMPASSIVENESS
IMPASSIVENESSES

IMPASSIVITIES
IMPASSIVITY
IMPASTATION
IMPASTATIONS
IMPATIENCE
IMPATIENCES
IMPATIENTLY
IMPEACHABILITY
IMPEACHABLE
IMPEACHERS
IMPEACHING
IMPEACHMENT
IMPEACHMENTS
IMPEARLING
IMPECCABILITIES
IMPECCABILITY
IMPECCABLE
IMPECCABLY
IMPECCANCIES
IMPECCANCY
IMPECUNIOSITIES
IMPECUNIOSITY
IMPECUNIOUS
IMPECUNIOUSLY
IMPECUNIOUSNESS
IMPEDANCES
IMPEDIMENT
IMPEDIMENTA
IMPEDIMENTAL
IMPEDIMENTARY
IMPEDIMENTS
IMPEDINGLY
IMPEDITIVE
IMPELLENTS
IMPENDENCE
IMPENDENCES
IMPENDENCIES
IMPENDENCY
IMPENETRABILITY
IMPENETRABLE
IMPENETRABLY
IMPENETRATE
IMPENETRATED
IMPENETRATES
IMPENETRATING
IMPENETRATION
IMPENETRATIONS

IMPENITENCE
IMPENITENCES
IMPENITENCIES
IMPENITENCY
IMPENITENT
IMPENITENTLY
IMPENITENTNESS
IMPENITENTS
IMPERATIVAL
IMPERATIVE
IMPERATIVELY
IMPERATIVENESS
IMPERATIVES
IMPERATORIAL
IMPERATORIALLY
IMPERATORS
IMPERATORSHIP
IMPERATORSHIPS
IMPERCEABLE
IMPERCEIVABLE
IMPERCEPTIBLE
IMPERCEPTIBLY
IMPERCEPTION
IMPERCEPTIONS
IMPERCEPTIVE
IMPERCEPTIVELY
IMPERCEPTIVITY
IMPERCIPIENCE
IMPERCIPIENCES
IMPERCIPIENT
IMPERCIPIENTLY
IMPERFECTIBLE
IMPERFECTION
IMPERFECTIONS
IMPERFECTIVE
IMPERFECTIVELY
IMPERFECTIVES
IMPERFECTLY
IMPERFECTNESS
IMPERFECTNESSES
IMPERFECTS
IMPERFORABLE
IMPERFORATE
IMPERFORATED
IMPERFORATION
IMPERFORATIONS
IMPERIALISE

IMPERIALISED	IMPERSONALISES	IMPETUOSITIES	IMPLEMENTING	IMPONDERABILIA
IMPERIALISES	IMPERSONALISING	IMPETUOSITY	IMPLEMENTOR	IMPONDERABILITY
IMPERIALISING	IMPERSONALITIES	IMPETUOUSLY	IMPLEMENTORS	IMPONDERABLE
IMPERIALISM	IMPERSONALITY	IMPETUOUSNESS	IMPLEMENTS	IMPONDERABLES
IMPERIALISMS	IMPERSONALIZE	IMPETUOUSNESSES	IMPLETIONS	IMPONDERABLY
IMPERIALIST	IMPERSONALIZED	IMPICTURED	IMPLEXIONS	IMPONDEROUS
IMPERIALISTIC	IMPERSONALIZES	IMPIERCEABLE	IMPLEXUOUS	IMPORTABILITIES
IMPERIALISTS	IMPERSONALIZING	IMPIGNORATE	IMPLICATED	IMPORTABILITY
IMPERIALITIES	IMPERSONALLY	IMPIGNORATED	IMPLICATES	IMPORTABLE
IMPERIALITY	IMPERSONATE	IMPIGNORATES	IMPLICATING	IMPORTANCE
IMPERIALIZE	IMPERSONATED	IMPIGNORATING	IMPLICATION	IMPORTANCES
IMPERIALIZED	IMPERSONATES	IMPIGNORATION	IMPLICATIONAL	IMPORTANCIES
IMPERIALIZES	IMPERSONATING	IMPIGNORATIONS	IMPLICATIONS	IMPORTANCY
IMPERIALIZING	IMPERSONATION	IMPINGEMENT	IMPLICATIVE	IMPORTANTLY
IMPERIALLY	IMPERSONATIONS	IMPINGEMENTS	IMPLICATIVELY	IMPORTATION
IMPERIALNESS	IMPERSONATOR	IMPIOUSNESS	IMPLICATIVENESS	IMPORTATIONS
IMPERIALNESSES	IMPERSONATORS	IMPIOUSNESSES	IMPLICATURE	IMPORTINGS
IMPERILING	IMPERTINENCE	IMPISHNESS	IMPLICATURES	IMPORTUNACIES
IMPERILLED	IMPERTINENCES	IMPISHNESSES	IMPLICITIES	IMPORTUNACY
IMPERILLING	IMPERTINENCIES	IMPLACABILITIES	IMPLICITLY	IMPORTUNATE
IMPERILMENT	IMPERTINENCY	IMPLACABILITY	IMPLICITNESS	IMPORTUNATELY
IMPERILMENTS	IMPERTINENT	IMPLACABLE	IMPLICITNESSES	IMPORTUNATENESS
IMPERIOUSLY	IMPERTINENTLY	IMPLACABLENESS	IMPLODENTS	IMPORTUNED
IMPERIOUSNESS	IMPERTURBABLE	IMPLACABLY	IMPLORATION	IMPORTUNELY
IMPERIOUSNESSES	IMPERTURBABLY	IMPLACENTAL	IMPLORATIONS	IMPORTUNER
IMPERISHABILITY	IMPERTURBATION	IMPLANTABLE	IMPLORATOR	IMPORTUNERS
IMPERISHABLE	IMPERTURBATIONS	IMPLANTATION	IMPLORATORS	IMPORTUNES
IMPERISHABLES	IMPERVIABILITY	IMPLANTATIONS	IMPLORATORY	IMPORTUNING
IMPERISHABLY	IMPERVIABLE	IMPLANTERS	IMPLORINGLY	IMPORTUNINGS
IMPERMANENCE	IMPERVIABLENESS	IMPLANTING	IMPLOSIONS	IMPORTUNITIES
IMPERMANENCES	IMPERVIOUS	IMPLAUSIBILITY	IMPLOSIVELY	IMPORTUNITY
IMPERMANENCIES	IMPERVIOUSLY	IMPLAUSIBLE	IMPLOSIVES	IMPOSINGLY
IMPERMANENCY	IMPERVIOUSNESS	IMPLAUSIBLENESS	IMPLUNGING	IMPOSINGNESS
IMPERMANENT	IMPETICOSSED	IMPLAUSIBLY	IMPOCKETED	IMPOSINGNESSES
IMPERMANENTLY	IMPETICOSSES	IMPLEACHED	IMPOCKETING	IMPOSITION
IMPERMEABILITY	IMPETICOSSING	IMPLEACHES	IMPOLDERED	IMPOSITIONS
IMPERMEABLE	IMPETIGINES	IMPLEACHING	IMPOLDERING	IMPOSSIBILISM
IMPERMEABLENESS	IMPETIGINOUS	IMPLEADABLE	IMPOLICIES	IMPOSSIBILISMS
IMPERMEABLY	IMPETRATED	IMPLEADERS	IMPOLITELY	IMPOSSIBILIST
IMPERMISSIBLE	IMPETRATES	IMPLEADING	IMPOLITENESS	IMPOSSIBILISTS
IMPERMISSIBLY	IMPETRATING	IMPLEDGING	IMPOLITENESSES	IMPOSSIBILITIES
IMPERSCRIPTIBLE	IMPETRATION	IMPLEMENTAL	IMPOLITEST	IMPOSSIBILITY
IMPERSEVERANT	IMPETRATIONS	IMPLEMENTATION	IMPOLITICAL	IMPOSSIBLE
IMPERSISTENT	IMPETRATIVE	IMPLEMENTATIONS	IMPOLITICALLY	IMPOSSIBLENESS
IMPERSONAL	IMPETRATOR	IMPLEMENTED	IMPOLITICLY	IMPOSSIBLES
IMPERSONALISE	IMPETRATORS	IMPLEMENTER	IMPOLITICNESS	IMPOSSIBLY
IMPERSONALISED	IMPETRATORY	IMPLEMENTERS	IMPOLITICNESSES	IMPOSTHUMATE

IMPOSTHUMATED	IMPRECATED	IMPRESSIVELY	IMPROVIDENCE	IMPUGNMENTS
IMPOSTHUMATES	IMPRECATES	IMPRESSIVENESS	IMPROVIDENCES	IMPUISSANCE
IMPOSTHUMATING	IMPRECATING	IMPRESSMENT	IMPROVIDENT	IMPUISSANCES
IMPOSTHUMATION	IMPRECATION	IMPRESSMENTS	IMPROVIDENTLY	IMPUISSANT
IMPOSTHUMATIONS	IMPRECATIONS	IMPRESSURE	IMPROVINGLY	IMPULSIONS
IMPOSTHUME	IMPRECATORY	IMPRESSURES	IMPROVISATE	IMPULSIVELY
IMPOSTHUMED	IMPRECISELY	IMPRIMATUR	IMPROVISATED	IMPULSIVENESS
IMPOSTHUMES	IMPRECISENESS	IMPRIMATURS	IMPROVISATES	IMPULSIVENESSES
IMPOSTOROUS	IMPRECISENESSES	IMPRINTERS	IMPROVISATING	IMPULSIVITIES
IMPOSTROUS	IMPRECISION	IMPRINTING	IMPROVISATION	IMPULSIVITY
IMPOSTUMATE	IMPRECISIONS	IMPRINTINGS	IMPROVISATIONAL	IMPUNDULUS
IMPOSTUMATED	IMPREDICATIVE	IMPRISONABLE	IMPROVISATIONS	IMPUNITIES
IMPOSTUMATES	IMPREGNABILITY	IMPRISONED	IMPROVISATOR	IMPURENESS
IMPOSTUMATING	IMPREGNABLE	IMPRISONER	IMPROVISATORE	IMPURENESSES
IMPOSTUMATION	IMPREGNABLENESS	IMPRISONERS	IMPROVISATORES	IMPURITIES
IMPOSTUMATIONS	IMPREGNABLY	IMPRISONING	IMPROVISATORI	IMPURPLING
IMPOSTUMED	IMPREGNANT	IMPRISONMENT	IMPROVISATORIAL	IMPUTABILITIES
IMPOSTUMES	IMPREGNANTS	IMPRISONMENTS	IMPROVISATORS	IMPUTABILITY
IMPOSTURES	IMPREGNATABLE	IMPROBABILITIES	IMPROVISATORY	IMPUTABLENESS
IMPOSTUROUS	IMPREGNATE	IMPROBABILITY	IMPROVISATRICES	IMPUTABLENESSES
IMPOTENCES	IMPREGNATED	IMPROBABLE	IMPROVISATRIX	IMPUTATION
IMPOTENCIES	IMPREGNATES	IMPROBABLENESS	IMPROVISATRIXES	IMPUTATIONS
IMPOTENTLY	IMPREGNATING	IMPROBABLY	IMPROVISED	IMPUTATIVE
IMPOTENTNESS	IMPREGNATION	IMPROBATION	IMPROVISER	IMPUTATIVELY
IMPOTENTNESSES	IMPREGNATIONS	IMPROBATIONS	IMPROVISERS	INABILITIES
IMPOUNDABLE	IMPREGNATOR	IMPROBITIES	IMPROVISES	INABSTINENCE
IMPOUNDAGE	IMPREGNATORS	IMPROMPTUS	IMPROVISING	INABSTINENCES
IMPOUNDAGES	IMPREGNING	IMPROPERLY	IMPROVISOR	INACCESSIBILITY
IMPOUNDERS	IMPRESARIO	IMPROPERNESS	IMPROVISORS	INACCESSIBLE
IMPOUNDING	IMPRESARIOS	IMPROPERNESSES	IMPROVVISATORE	INACCESSIBLY
IMPOUNDMENT	IMPRESCRIPTIBLE	IMPROPRIATE	IMPROVVISATORES	INACCURACIES
IMPOUNDMENTS	IMPRESCRIPTIBLY	IMPROPRIATED	IMPROVVISATRICE	INACCURACY
IMPOVERISH	IMPRESSERS	IMPROPRIATES	IMPRUDENCE	INACCURATE
IMPOVERISHED	IMPRESSIBILITY	IMPROPRIATING	IMPRUDENCES	INACCURATELY
IMPOVERISHER	IMPRESSIBLE	IMPROPRIATION	IMPRUDENTLY	INACCURATENESS
IMPOVERISHERS	IMPRESSING	IMPROPRIATIONS	IMPSONITES	INACTIVATE
IMPOVERISHES	IMPRESSION	IMPROPRIATOR	IMPUDENCES	INACTIVATED
IMPOVERISHING	IMPRESSIONABLE	IMPROPRIATORS	IMPUDENCIES	INACTIVATES
IMPOVERISHMENT	IMPRESSIONAL	IMPROPRIETIES	IMPUDENTLY	INACTIVATING
IMPOVERISHMENTS	IMPRESSIONALLY	IMPROPRIETY	IMPUDENTNESS	INACTIVATION
IMPOWERING	IMPRESSIONISM	IMPROVABILITIES	IMPUDENTNESSES	INACTIVATIONS
IMPRACTICABLE	IMPRESSIONISMS	IMPROVABILITY	IMPUDICITIES	INACTIVELY
IMPRACTICABLY	IMPRESSIONIST	IMPROVABLE	IMPUDICITY	INACTIVENESS
IMPRACTICAL	IMPRESSIONISTIC	IMPROVABLENESS	IMPUGNABLE	INACTIVENESSES
IMPRACTICALITY	IMPRESSIONISTS	IMPROVABLY	IMPUGNATION	INACTIVITIES
IMPRACTICALLY	IMPRESSIONS	IMPROVEMENT	IMPUGNATIONS	INACTIVITY
IMPRACTICALNESS	IMPRESSIVE	IMPROVEMENTS	IMPUGNMENT	INADAPTABLE

INADAPTATION	INAPPETENT	INAUGURATED	INCAPABILITY	INCASEMENT
INADAPTATIONS	INAPPLICABILITY	INAUGURATES	INCAPABLENESS	INCASEMENTS
INADAPTIVE	INAPPLICABLE	INAUGURATING	INCAPABLENESSES	INCATENATE
INADEQUACIES	INAPPLICABLY	INAUGURATION	INCAPABLES	INCATENATED
INADEQUACY	INAPPOSITE	INAUGURATIONS	INCAPACIOUS	INCATENATES
INADEQUATE	INAPPOSITELY	INAUGURATOR	INCAPACIOUSNESS	INCATENATING
INADEQUATELY	INAPPOSITENESS	INAUGURATORS	INCAPACITANT	INCATENATION
INADEQUATENESS	INAPPRECIABLE	INAUGURATORY	INCAPACITANTS	INCATENATIONS
INADEQUATES	INAPPRECIABLY	INAURATING	INCAPACITATE	INCAUTIONS
INADMISSIBILITY	INAPPRECIATION	INAUSPICIOUS	INCAPACITATED	INCAUTIOUS
INADMISSIBLE	INAPPRECIATIONS	INAUSPICIOUSLY	INCAPACITATES	INCAUTIOUSLY
INADMISSIBLY	INAPPRECIATIVE	INAUTHENTIC	INCAPACITATING	INCAUTIOUSNESS
INADVERTENCE	INAPPREHENSIBLE	INAUTHENTICITY	INCAPACITATION	INCEDINGLY
INADVERTENCES	INAPPREHENSION	INBOUNDING	INCAPACITATIONS	INCENDIARIES
INADVERTENCIES	INAPPREHENSIONS	INBREATHED	INCAPACITIES	INCENDIARISM
INADVERTENCY	INAPPREHENSIVE	INBREATHES	INCAPACITY	INCENDIARISMS
INADVERTENT	INAPPROACHABLE	INBREATHING	INCAPSULATE	INCENDIARY
INADVERTENTLY	INAPPROACHABLY	INBREEDERS	INCAPSULATED	INCENDIVITIES
INADVISABILITY	INAPPROPRIATE	INBREEDING	INCAPSULATES	INCENDIVITY
INADVISABLE	INAPPROPRIATELY	INBREEDINGS	INCAPSULATING	INCENSATION
INADVISABLENESS	INAPTITUDE	INBRINGING	INCAPSULATION	INCENSATIONS
INADVISABLY	INAPTITUDES	INBRINGINGS	INCAPSULATIONS	INCENSEMENT
INALIENABILITY	INAPTNESSES	INBURSTING	INCARCERATE	INCENSEMENTS
INALIENABLE	INARGUABLE	INCALCULABILITY	INCARCERATED	INCENSORIES
INALIENABLENESS	INARGUABLY	INCALCULABLE	INCARCERATES	INCENTIVELY
INALIENABLY	INARTICULACIES	INCALCULABLY	INCARCERATING	INCENTIVES
INALTERABILITY	INARTICULACY	INCALESCENCE	INCARCERATION	INCENTIVISATION
INALTERABLE	INARTICULATE	INCALESCENCES	INCARCERATIONS	INCENTIVISE
INALTERABLENESS	INARTICULATELY	INCALESCENT	INCARCERATOR	INCENTIVISED
INALTERABLY	INARTICULATES	INCANDESCE	INCARCERATORS	INCENTIVISES
INAMORATAS	INARTICULATION	INCANDESCED	INCARDINATE	INCENTIVISING
INAMORATOS	INARTICULATIONS	INCANDESCENCE	INCARDINATED	INCENTIVIZATION
INANENESSES	INARTIFICIAL	INCANDESCENCES	INCARDINATES	INCENTIVIZE
INANIMATELY	INARTIFICIALLY	INCANDESCENCIES	INCARDINATING	INCENTIVIZED
INANIMATENESS	INARTISTIC	INCANDESCENCY	INCARDINATION	INCENTIVIZES
INANIMATENESSES	INARTISTICALLY	INCANDESCENT	INCARDINATIONS	INCENTIVIZING
INANIMATION	INATTENTION	INCANDESCENTLY	INCARNADINE	INCEPTIONS
INANIMATIONS	INATTENTIONS	INCANDESCENTS	INCARNADINED	INCEPTIVELY
INANITIONS	INATTENTIVE	INCANDESCES	INCARNADINES	INCEPTIVES
INAPPARENT	INATTENTIVELY	INCANDESCING	INCARNADINING	INCERTAINTIES
INAPPARENTLY	INATTENTIVENESS	INCANTATION	INCARNATED	INCERTAINTY
INAPPEASABLE	INAUDIBILITIES	INCANTATIONAL	INCARNATES	INCERTITUDE
INAPPELLABLE	INAUDIBILITY	INCANTATIONS	INCARNATING	INCERTITUDES
INAPPETENCE	INAUDIBLENESS	INCANTATOR	INCARNATION	INCESSANCIES
INAPPETENCES	INAUDIBLENESSES	INCANTATORS	INCARNATIONS	INCESSANCY
INAPPETENCIES	INAUGURALS	INCANTATORY	INCARVILLEA	INCESSANTLY
INAPPETENCY	INAUGURATE	INCAPABILITIES	INCARVILLEAS	INCESSANTNESS

INCESSANTNESSES
INCESTUOUS
INCESTUOUSLY
INCESTUOUSNESS
INCHARITABLE
INCHOATELY
INCHOATENESS
INCHOATENESSES
INCHOATING
INCHOATION
INCHOATIONS
INCHOATIVE
INCHOATIVELY
INCHOATIVES
INCIDENCES
INCIDENTAL
INCIDENTALLY
INCIDENTALNESS
INCIDENTALS
INCINERATE
INCINERATED
INCINERATES
INCINERATING
INCINERATION
INCINERATIONS
INCINERATOR
INCINERATORS
INCIPIENCE
INCIPIENCES
INCIPIENCIES
INCIPIENCY
INCIPIENTLY
INCISIFORM
INCISIVELY
INCISIVENESS
INCISIVENESSES
INCISORIAL
INCITATION
INCITATIONS
INCITATIVE
INCITATIVES
INCITEMENT
INCITEMENTS
INCITINGLY
INCIVILITIES
INCIVILITY
INCLASPING

INCLEMENCIES
INCLEMENCY
INCLEMENTLY
INCLEMENTNESS
INCLEMENTNESSES
INCLINABLE
INCLINABLENESS
INCLINATION
INCLINATIONAL
INCLINATIONS
INCLINATORIA
INCLINATORIUM
INCLINATORY
INCLININGS
INCLINOMETER
INCLINOMETERS
INCLIPPING
INCLOSABLE
INCLOSURES
INCLUDABLE
INCLUDEDNESS
INCLUDEDNESSES
INCLUDIBLE
INCLUSIONS
INCLUSIVELY
INCLUSIVENESS
INCLUSIVENESSES
INCLUSIVITIES
INCLUSIVITY
INCOAGULABLE
INCOERCIBLE
INCOGITABILITY
INCOGITABLE
INCOGITANCIES
INCOGITANCY
INCOGITANT
INCOGITATIVE
INCOGNISABLE
INCOGNISANCE
INCOGNISANCES
INCOGNISANT
INCOGNITAS
INCOGNITOS
INCOGNIZABLE
INCOGNIZANCE
INCOGNIZANCES
INCOGNIZANT

INCOHERENCE
INCOHERENCES
INCOHERENCIES
INCOHERENCY
INCOHERENT
INCOHERENTLY
INCOHERENTNESS
INCOHESIVE
INCOMBUSTIBLE
INCOMBUSTIBLES
INCOMBUSTIBLY
INCOMMENSURABLE
INCOMMENSURABLY
INCOMMENSURATE
INCOMMISCIBLE
INCOMMODED
INCOMMODES
INCOMMODING
INCOMMODIOUS
INCOMMODIOUSLY
INCOMMODITIES
INCOMMODITY
INCOMMUNICABLE
INCOMMUNICABLY
INCOMMUNICADO
INCOMMUNICATIVE
INCOMMUTABILITY
INCOMMUTABLE
INCOMMUTABLY
INCOMPARABILITY
INCOMPARABLE
INCOMPARABLY
INCOMPARED
INCOMPATIBILITY
INCOMPATIBLE
INCOMPATIBLES
INCOMPATIBLY
INCOMPETENCE
INCOMPETENCES
INCOMPETENCIES
INCOMPETENCY
INCOMPETENT
INCOMPETENTLY
INCOMPETENTS
INCOMPLETE
INCOMPLETELY
INCOMPLETENESS

INCOMPLETION
INCOMPLETIONS
INCOMPLIANCE
INCOMPLIANCES
INCOMPLIANCIES
INCOMPLIANCY
INCOMPLIANT
INCOMPLIANTLY
INCOMPOSED
INCOMPOSITE
INCOMPOSSIBLE
INCOMPREHENSION
INCOMPREHENSIVE
INCOMPRESSIBLE
INCOMPRESSIBLY
INCOMPUTABILITY
INCOMPUTABLE
INCOMPUTABLY
INCOMUNICADO
INCONCEIVABLE
INCONCEIVABLES
INCONCEIVABLY
INCONCINNITIES
INCONCINNITY
INCONCINNOUS
INCONCLUSION
INCONCLUSIONS
INCONCLUSIVE
INCONCLUSIVELY
INCONDENSABLE
INCONDENSIBLE
INCONDITELY
INCONFORMITIES
INCONFORMITY
INCONGRUENCE
INCONGRUENCES
INCONGRUENT
INCONGRUENTLY
INCONGRUITIES
INCONGRUITY
INCONGRUOUS
INCONGRUOUSLY
INCONGRUOUSNESS
INCONSCIENT
INCONSCIENTLY
INCONSCIONABLE
INCONSCIOUS

INCONSECUTIVE
INCONSECUTIVELY
INCONSEQUENCE
INCONSEQUENCES
INCONSEQUENT
INCONSEQUENTIAL
INCONSEQUENTLY
INCONSIDERABLE
INCONSIDERABLY
INCONSIDERATE
INCONSIDERATELY
INCONSIDERATION
INCONSISTENCE
INCONSISTENCES
INCONSISTENCIES
INCONSISTENCY
INCONSISTENT
INCONSISTENTLY
INCONSOLABILITY
INCONSOLABLE
INCONSOLABLY
INCONSONANCE
INCONSONANCES
INCONSONANT
INCONSONANTLY
INCONSPICUOUS
INCONSPICUOUSLY
INCONSTANCIES
INCONSTANCY
INCONSTANT
INCONSTANTLY
INCONSTRUABLE
INCONSUMABLE
INCONSUMABLY
INCONTESTABLE
INCONTESTABLY
INCONTIGUOUS
INCONTIGUOUSLY
INCONTINENCE
INCONTINENCES
INCONTINENCIES
INCONTINENCY
INCONTINENT
INCONTINENTLY
INCONTROLLABLE
INCONTROLLABLY
INCONVENIENCE

INCONVENIENCED	INCORRUPTED	INCREMENTALS	INCULPABLE	INCURVATURES
INCONVENIENCES	INCORRUPTIBLE	INCREMENTED	INCULPABLENESS	INCURVITIES
INCONVENIENCIES	INCORRUPTIBLES	INCREMENTING	INCULPABLY	INDAGATING
INCONVENIENCING	INCORRUPTIBLY	INCREMENTS	INCULPATED	INDAGATION
INCONVENIENCY	INCORRUPTION	INCRESCENT	INCULPATES	INDAGATIONS
INCONVENIENT	INCORRUPTIONS	INCRETIONARY	INCULPATING	INDAGATIVE
INCONVENIENTLY	INCORRUPTIVE	INCRETIONS	INCULPATION	INDAGATORS
INCONVERSABLE	INCORRUPTLY	INCRIMINATE	INCULPATIONS	INDAGATORY
INCONVERSANT	INCORRUPTNESS	INCRIMINATED	INCULPATIVE	INDAPAMIDE
INCONVERTIBLE	INCORRUPTNESSES	INCRIMINATES	INCULPATORY	INDAPAMIDES
INCONVERTIBLY	INCRASSATE	INCRIMINATING	INCUMBENCIES	INDEBTEDNESS
INCONVINCIBLE	INCRASSATED	INCRIMINATION	INCUMBENCY	INDEBTEDNESSES
INCONVINCIBLY	INCRASSATES	INCRIMINATIONS	INCUMBENTLY	INDECENCIES
INCOORDINATE	INCRASSATING	INCRIMINATOR	INCUMBENTS	INDECENTER
INCOORDINATION	INCRASSATION	INCRIMINATORS	INCUMBERED	INDECENTEST
INCOORDINATIONS	INCRASSATIONS	INCRIMINATORY	INCUMBERING	INDECENTLY
INCORONATE	INCRASSATIVE	INCROSSBRED	INCUMBERINGLY	INDECIDUATE
INCORONATED	INCRASSATIVES	INCROSSBREDS	INCUMBRANCE	INDECIDUOUS
INCORONATION	INCREASABLE	INCROSSBREED	INCUMBRANCER	INDECIPHERABLE
INCORONATIONS	INCREASEDLY	INCROSSBREEDING	INCUMBRANCERS	INDECIPHERABLY
INCORPORABLE	INCREASEFUL	INCROSSBREEDS	INCUMBRANCES	INDECISION
INCORPORAL	INCREASERS	INCROSSING	INCUNABLES	INDECISIONS
INCORPORALL	INCREASING	INCRUSTANT	INCUNABULA	INDECISIVE
INCORPORATE	INCREASINGLY	INCRUSTANTS	INCUNABULAR	INDECISIVELY
INCORPORATED	INCREASINGS	INCRUSTATION	INCUNABULIST	INDECISIVENESS
INCORPORATES	INCREATELY	INCRUSTATIONS	INCUNABULISTS	INDECLINABLE
INCORPORATING	INCREDIBILITIES	INCRUSTING	INCUNABULUM	INDECLINABLY
INCORPORATION	INCREDIBILITY	INCRUSTMENT	INCURABILITIES	INDECOMPOSABLE
INCORPORATIONS	INCREDIBLE	INCRUSTMENTS	INCURABILITY	INDECOROUS
INCORPORATIVE	INCREDIBLENESS	INCUBATING	INCURABLENESS	INDECOROUSLY
INCORPORATOR	INCREDIBLY	INCUBATION	INCURABLENESSES	INDECOROUSNESS
INCORPORATORS	INCREDULITIES	INCUBATIONAL	INCURABLES	INDECORUMS
INCORPOREAL	INCREDULITY	INCUBATIONS	INCURIOSITIES	INDEFATIGABLE
INCORPOREALITY	INCREDULOUS	INCUBATIVE	INCURIOSITY	INDEFATIGABLY
INCORPOREALLY	INCREDULOUSLY	INCUBATORS	INCURIOUSLY	INDEFEASIBILITY
INCORPOREITIES	INCREDULOUSNESS	INCUBATORY	INCURIOUSNESS	INDEFEASIBLE
INCORPOREITY	INCREMATED	INCULCATED	INCURIOUSNESSES	INDEFEASIBLY
INCORPSING	INCREMATES	INCULCATES	INCURRABLE	INDEFECTIBILITY
INCORRECTLY	INCREMATING	INCULCATING	INCURRENCE	INDEFECTIBLE
INCORRECTNESS	INCREMATION	INCULCATION	INCURRENCES	INDEFECTIBLY
INCORRECTNESSES	INCREMATIONS	INCULCATIONS	INCURSIONS	INDEFENSIBILITY
INCORRIGIBILITY	INCREMENTAL	INCULCATIVE	INCURVATED	INDEFENSIBLE
INCORRIGIBLE	INCREMENTALISM	INCULCATOR	INCURVATES	INDEFENSIBLY
INCORRIGIBLES	INCREMENTALISMS	INCULCATORS	INCURVATING	INDEFINABILITY
INCORRIGIBLY	INCREMENTALIST	INCULCATORY	INCURVATION	INDEFINABLE
INCORRODIBLE	INCREMENTALISTS	INCULPABILITIES	INCURVATIONS	INDEFINABLENESS
INCORROSIBLE	INCREMENTALLY	INCULPABILITY	INCURVATURE	INDEFINABLES

INDEFINABLY	INDETECTABLE	INDIFFERENTISTS	INDIRECTLY	INDISTINCTLY
INDEFINITE	INDETECTIBLE	INDIFFERENTLY	INDIRECTNESS	INDISTINCTNESS
INDEFINITELY	INDETERMINABLE	INDIFFERENTS	INDIRECTNESSES	INDISTRIBUTABLE
INDEFINITENESS	INDETERMINABLY	INDIGENCES	INDIRUBINS	INDITEMENT
INDEFINITES	INDETERMINACIES	INDIGENCIES	INDISCERNIBLE	INDITEMENTS
INDEHISCENCE	INDETERMINACY	INDIGENISATION	INDISCERNIBLY	INDIVERTIBLE
INDEHISCENCES	INDETERMINATE	INDIGENISATIONS	INDISCERPTIBLE	INDIVERTIBLY
INDEHISCENT	INDETERMINATELY	INDIGENISE	INDISCIPLINABLE	INDIVIDABLE
INDELIBILITIES	INDETERMINATION	INDIGENISED	INDISCIPLINE	INDIVIDUAL
INDELIBILITY	INDETERMINED	INDIGENISES	INDISCIPLINED	INDIVIDUALISE
INDELIBLENESS	INDETERMINISM	INDIGENISING	INDISCIPLINES	INDIVIDUALISED
INDELIBLENESSES	INDETERMINISMS	INDIGENITIES	INDISCOVERABLE	INDIVIDUALISER
INDELICACIES	INDETERMINIST	INDIGENITY	INDISCREET	INDIVIDUALISERS
INDELICACY	INDETERMINISTIC	INDIGENIZATION	INDISCREETLY	INDIVIDUALISES
INDELICATE	INDETERMINISTS	INDIGENIZATIONS	INDISCREETNESS	INDIVIDUALISING
INDELICATELY	INDEXATION	INDIGENIZE	INDISCRETE	INDIVIDUALISM
INDELICATENESS	INDEXATIONS	INDIGENIZED	INDISCRETELY	INDIVIDUALISMS
INDEMNIFICATION	INDEXICALS	INDIGENIZES	INDISCRETENESS	INDIVIDUALIST
INDEMNIFIED	INDEXTERITIES	INDIGENIZING	INDISCRETION	INDIVIDUALISTIC
INDEMNIFIER	INDEXTERITY	INDIGENOUS	INDISCRETIONARY	INDIVIDUALISTS
INDEMNIFIERS	INDEXTROUS	INDIGENOUSLY	INDISCRETIONS	INDIVIDUALITIES
INDEMNIFIES	INDICATABLE	INDIGENOUSNESS	INDISCRIMINATE	INDIVIDUALITY
INDEMNIFYING	INDICATING	INDIGENTLY	INDISPENSABLE	INDIVIDUALIZE
INDEMNITIES	INDICATION	INDIGESTED	INDISPENSABLES	INDIVIDUALIZED
INDEMONSTRABLE	INDICATIONAL	INDIGESTIBILITY	INDISPENSABLY	INDIVIDUALIZER
INDEMONSTRABLY	INDICATIONS	INDIGESTIBLE	INDISPOSED	INDIVIDUALIZERS
INDENTATION	INDICATIVE	INDIGESTIBLES	INDISPOSEDNESS	INDIVIDUALIZES
INDENTATIONS	INDICATIVELY	INDIGESTIBLY	INDISPOSES	INDIVIDUALIZING
INDENTIONS	INDICATIVES	INDIGESTING	INDISPOSING	INDIVIDUALLY
INDENTURED	INDICATORS	INDIGESTION	INDISPOSITION	INDIVIDUALS
INDENTURES	INDICATORY	INDIGESTIONS	INDISPOSITIONS	INDIVIDUATE
INDENTURESHIP	INDICOLITE	INDIGESTIVE	INDISPUTABILITY	INDIVIDUATED
INDENTURESHIPS	INDICOLITES	INDIGNANCE	INDISPUTABLE	INDIVIDUATES
INDENTURING	INDICTABLE	INDIGNANCES	INDISPUTABLY	INDIVIDUATING
INDEPENDENCE	INDICTABLY	INDIGNANTLY	INDISSOCIABLE	INDIVIDUATION
INDEPENDENCES	INDICTIONAL	INDIGNATION	INDISSOCIABLY	INDIVIDUATIONS
INDEPENDENCIES	INDICTIONS	INDIGNATIONS	INDISSOLUBILITY	INDIVIDUATOR
INDEPENDENCY	INDICTMENT	INDIGNIFIED	INDISSOLUBLE	INDIVIDUATORS
INDEPENDENT	INDICTMENTS	INDIGNIFIES	INDISSOLUBLY	INDIVIDUUM
INDEPENDENTLY	INDIFFERENCE	INDIGNIFYING	INDISSOLVABLE	INDIVISIBILITY
INDEPENDENTS	INDIFFERENCES	INDIGNITIES	INDISSUADABLE	INDIVISIBLE
INDESCRIBABLE	INDIFFERENCIES	INDIGOLITE	INDISSUADABLY	INDIVISIBLENESS
INDESCRIBABLES	INDIFFERENCY	INDIGOLITES	INDISTINCT	INDIVISIBLES
INDESCRIBABLY	INDIFFERENT	INDIGOTINS	INDISTINCTION	INDIVISIBLY
INDESIGNATE	INDIFFERENTISM	INDINAVIRS	INDISTINCTIONS	INDOCILITIES
INDESTRUCTIBLE	INDIFFERENTISMS	INDIRECTION	INDISTINCTIVE	INDOCILITY
INDESTRUCTIBLY	INDIFFERENTIST	INDIRECTIONS	INDISTINCTIVELY	INDOCTRINATE

INDOCTRINATED	INDUCTIVENESSES	INEBRIATES	INELEGANCIES	INERTIALLY
INDOCTRINATES	INDUCTIVITIES	INEBRIATING	INELEGANCY	INERTNESSES
INDOCTRINATING	INDUCTIVITY	INEBRIATION	INELEGANTLY	INESCAPABLE
INDOCTRINATION	INDULGENCE	INEBRIATIONS	INELIGIBILITIES	INESCAPABLY
INDOCTRINATIONS	INDULGENCED	INEBRIETIES	INELIGIBILITY	INESCULENT
INDOCTRINATOR	INDULGENCES	INEDIBILITIES	INELIGIBLE	INESCUTCHEON
INDOCTRINATORS	INDULGENCIES	INEDIBILITY	INELIGIBLENESS	INESCUTCHEONS
INDOLEACETIC	INDULGENCING	INEDUCABILITIES	INELIGIBLES	INESSENTIAL
INDOLEBUTYRIC	INDULGENCY	INEDUCABILITY	INELIGIBLY	INESSENTIALITY
INDOLENCES	INDULGENTLY	INEDUCABLE	INELOQUENCE	INESSENTIALS
INDOLENCIES	INDULGINGLY	INEFFABILITIES	INELOQUENCES	INESTIMABILITY
INDOLENTLY	INDUMENTUM	INEFFABILITY	INELOQUENT	INESTIMABLE
INDOMETACIN	INDUMENTUMS	INEFFABLENESS	INELOQUENTLY	INESTIMABLENESS
INDOMETACINS	INDUPLICATE	INEFFABLENESSES	INELUCTABILITY	INESTIMABLY
INDOMETHACIN	INDUPLICATED	INEFFACEABILITY	INELUCTABLE	INEVITABILITIES
INDOMETHACINS	INDUPLICATION	INEFFACEABLE	INELUCTABLY	INEVITABILITY
INDOMITABILITY	INDUPLICATIONS	INEFFACEABLY	INELUDIBILITIES	INEVITABLE
INDOMITABLE	INDURATING	INEFFECTIVE	INELUDIBILITY	INEVITABLENESS
INDOMITABLENESS	INDURATION	INEFFECTIVELY	INELUDIBLE	INEVITABLES
INDOMITABLY	INDURATIONS	INEFFECTIVENESS	INELUDIBLY	INEVITABLY
INDOPHENOL	INDURATIVE	INEFFECTUAL	INENARRABLE	INEXACTITUDE
INDOPHENOLS	INDUSTRIAL	INEFFECTUALITY	INEPTITUDE	INEXACTITUDES
INDORSABLE	INDUSTRIALISE	INEFFECTUALLY	INEPTITUDES	INEXACTNESS
INDORSATION	INDUSTRIALISED	INEFFECTUALNESS	INEPTNESSES	INEXACTNESSES
INDORSATIONS	INDUSTRIALISES	INEFFICACIES	INEQUALITIES	INEXCITABLE
INDORSEMENT	INDUSTRIALISING	INEFFICACIOUS	INEQUALITY	INEXCUSABILITY
INDORSEMENTS	INDUSTRIALISM	INEFFICACIOUSLY	INEQUATION	INEXCUSABLE
INDRAUGHTS	INDUSTRIALISMS	INEFFICACITIES	INEQUATIONS	INEXCUSABLENESS
INDRENCHED	INDUSTRIALIST	INEFFICACITY	INEQUIPOTENT	INEXCUSABLY
INDRENCHES	INDUSTRIALISTS	INEFFICACY	INEQUITABLE	INEXECRABLE
INDRENCHING	INDUSTRIALIZE	INEFFICIENCIES	INEQUITABLENESS	INEXECUTABLE
INDUBITABILITY	INDUSTRIALIZED	INEFFICIENCY	INEQUITABLY	INEXECUTION
INDUBITABLE	INDUSTRIALIZES	INEFFICIENT	INEQUITIES	INEXECUTIONS
INDUBITABLENESS	INDUSTRIALIZING	INEFFICIENTLY	INEQUIVALVE	INEXHAUSTED
INDUBITABLY	INDUSTRIALLY	INEFFICIENTS	INEQUIVALVED	INEXHAUSTIBLE
INDUCEMENT	INDUSTRIALS	INEGALITARIAN	INERADICABILITY	INEXHAUSTIBLY
INDUCEMENTS	INDUSTRIES	INEGALITARIANS	INERADICABLE	INEXHAUSTIVE
INDUCIBILITIES	INDUSTRIOUS	INELABORATE	INERADICABLY	INEXISTANT
INDUCIBILITY	INDUSTRIOUSLY	INELABORATED	INERASABLE	INEXISTENCE
INDUCTANCE	INDUSTRIOUSNESS	INELABORATELY	INERASABLY	INEXISTENCES
INDUCTANCES	INDUSTRYWIDE	INELABORATES	INERASIBLE	INEXISTENCIES
INDUCTILITIES	INDWELLERS	INELABORATING	INERASIBLY	INEXISTENCY
INDUCTILITY	INDWELLING	INELASTICALLY	INERRABILITIES	INEXISTENT
INDUCTIONAL	INDWELLINGS	INELASTICITIES	INERRABILITY	INEXORABILITIES
INDUCTIONS	INEARTHING	INELASTICITY	INERRABLENESS	INEXORABILITY
INDUCTIVELY	INEBRIANTS	INELEGANCE	INERRABLENESSES	INEXORABLE
INDUCTIVENESS	INEBRIATED	INELEGANCES	INERRANCIES	INEXORABLENESS

INEXORABLY	INEXTIRPABLE	INFANTILIZES	INFERRABLE	INFINITIVAL
INEXPANSIBLE	INEXTRICABILITY	INFANTILIZING	INFERRIBLE	INFINITIVALLY
INEXPECTANCIES	INEXTRICABLE	INFANTRIES	INFERTILELY	INFINITIVE
INEXPECTANCY	INEXTRICABLY	INFANTRYMAN	INFERTILITIES	INFINITIVELY
INEXPECTANT	INFALLIBILISM	INFANTRYMEN	INFERTILITY	INFINITIVES
INEXPECTATION	INFALLIBILISMS	INFARCTION	INFESTANTS	INFINITUDE
INEXPECTATIONS	INFALLIBILIST	INFARCTIONS	INFESTATION	INFINITUDES
INEXPEDIENCE	INFALLIBILISTS	INFATUATED	INFESTATIONS	INFIRMARER
INEXPEDIENCES	INFALLIBILITIES	INFATUATEDLY	INFEUDATION	INFIRMARERS
INEXPEDIENCIES	INFALLIBILITY	INFATUATES	INFEUDATIONS	INFIRMARIAN
INEXPEDIENCY	INFALLIBLE	INFATUATING	INFIBULATE	INFIRMARIANS
INEXPEDIENT	INFALLIBLENESS	INFATUATION	INFIBULATED	INFIRMARIES
INEXPEDIENTLY	INFALLIBLES	INFATUATIONS	INFIBULATES	INFIRMITIES
INEXPENSIVE	INFALLIBLY	INFEASIBILITIES	INFIBULATING	INFIRMNESS
INEXPENSIVELY	INFAMISING	INFEASIBILITY	INFIBULATION	INFIRMNESSES
INEXPENSIVENESS	INFAMIZING	INFEASIBLE	INFIBULATIONS	INFIXATION
INEXPERIENCE	INFAMONISE	INFEASIBLENESS	INFIDELITIES	INFIXATIONS
INEXPERIENCED	INFAMONISED	INFECTANTS	INFIDELITY	INFLAMABLE
INEXPERIENCES	INFAMONISES	INFECTIONS	INFIELDERS	INFLAMINGLY
INEXPERTLY	INFAMONISING	INFECTIOUS	INFIELDSMAN	INFLAMMABILITY
INEXPERTNESS	INFAMONIZE	INFECTIOUSLY	INFIELDSMEN	INFLAMMABLE
INEXPERTNESSES	INFAMONIZED	INFECTIOUSNESS	INFIGHTERS	INFLAMMABLENESS
INEXPIABLE	INFAMONIZES	INFECTIVELY	INFIGHTING	INFLAMMABLES
INEXPIABLENESS	INFAMONIZING	INFECTIVENESS	INFIGHTINGS	INFLAMMABLY
INEXPIABLY	INFAMOUSLY	INFECTIVENESSES	INFILLINGS	INFLAMMATION
INEXPLAINABLE	INFAMOUSNESS	INFECTIVITIES	INFILTRATE	INFLAMMATIONS
INEXPLAINABLY	INFAMOUSNESSES	INFECTIVITY	INFILTRATED	INFLAMMATORILY
INEXPLICABILITY	INFANGTHIEF	INFECUNDITIES	INFILTRATES	INFLAMMATORY
INEXPLICABLE	INFANGTHIEFS	INFECUNDITY	INFILTRATING	INFLATABLE
INEXPLICABLY	INFANTEERS	INFEFTMENT	INFILTRATION	INFLATABLES
INEXPLICIT	INFANTHOOD	INFEFTMENTS	INFILTRATIONS	INFLATEDLY
INEXPLICITLY	INFANTHOODS	INFELICITIES	INFILTRATIVE	INFLATEDNESS
INEXPLICITNESS	INFANTICIDAL	INFELICITOUS	INFILTRATOR	INFLATEDNESSES
INEXPRESSIBLE	INFANTICIDE	INFELICITOUSLY	INFILTRATORS	INFLATINGLY
INEXPRESSIBLES	INFANTICIDES	INFELICITY	INFINITANT	INFLATIONARY
INEXPRESSIBLY	INFANTILISATION	INFEOFFING	INFINITARY	INFLATIONISM
INEXPRESSIVE	INFANTILISE	INFERENCES	INFINITATE	INFLATIONISMS
INEXPRESSIVELY	INFANTILISED	INFERENCING	INFINITATED	INFLATIONIST
INEXPUGNABILITY	INFANTILISES	INFERENCINGS	INFINITATES	INFLATIONISTS
INEXPUGNABLE	INFANTILISING	INFERENTIAL	INFINITATING	INFLATIONS
INEXPUGNABLY	INFANTILISM	INFERENTIALLY	INFINITELY	INFLATUSES
INEXPUNGIBLE	INFANTILISMS	INFERIORITIES	INFINITENESS	INFLECTABLE
INEXTENDED	INFANTILITIES	INFERIORITY	INFINITENESSES	INFLECTEDNESS
INEXTENSIBILITY	INFANTILITY	INFERIORLY	INFINITESIMAL	INFLECTEDNESSES
INEXTENSIBLE	INFANTILIZATION	INFERNALITIES	INFINITESIMALLY	INFLECTING
INEXTENSION	INFANTILIZE	INFERNALITY	INFINITESIMALS	INFLECTION
INEXTENSIONS	INFANTILIZED	INFERNALLY	INFINITIES	INFLECTIONAL

INFLECTIONALLY	INFORMALITY	INFRANGIBLY	INFUSORIANS	INGRATIATING
INFLECTIONLESS	INFORMALLY	INFRAORBITAL	INFUSORIES	INGRATIATINGLY
INFLECTIONS	INFORMANTS	INFRAPOSED	INGATHERED	INGRATIATION
INFLECTIVE	INFORMATICIAN	INFRAPOSITION	INGATHERER	INGRATIATIONS
INFLECTORS	INFORMATICIANS	INFRAPOSITIONS	INGATHERERS	INGRATIATORY
INFLEXIBILITIES	INFORMATICS	INFRASONIC	INGATHERING	INGRATITUDE
INFLEXIBILITY	INFORMATION	INFRASOUND	INGATHERINGS	INGRATITUDES
INFLEXIBLE	INFORMATIONAL	INFRASOUNDS	INGEMINATE	INGRAVESCENCE
INFLEXIBLENESS	INFORMATIONALLY	INFRASPECIFIC	INGEMINATED	INGRAVESCENCES
INFLEXIBLY	INFORMATIONS	INFRASTRUCTURAL	INGEMINATES	INGRAVESCENT
INFLEXIONAL	INFORMATISATION	INFRASTRUCTURE	INGEMINATING	INGREDIENT
INFLEXIONALLY	INFORMATISE	INFRASTRUCTURES	INGEMINATION	INGREDIENTS
INFLEXIONLESS	INFORMATISED	INFREQUENCE	INGEMINATIONS	INGRESSION
INFLEXIONS	INFORMATISES	INFREQUENCES	INGENERATE	INGRESSIONS
INFLEXURES	INFORMATISING	INFREQUENCIES	INGENERATED	INGRESSIVE
INFLICTABLE	INFORMATIVE	INFREQUENCY	INGENERATES	INGRESSIVENESS
INFLICTERS	INFORMATIVELY	INFREQUENT	INGENERATING	INGRESSIVES
INFLICTING	INFORMATIVENESS	INFREQUENTLY	INGENERATION	INGROOVING
INFLICTION	INFORMATIZATION	INFRINGEMENT	INGENERATIONS	INGROSSING
INFLICTIONS	INFORMATIZE	INFRINGEMENTS	INGENIOUSLY	INGROUNDED
INFLICTIVE	INFORMATIZED	INFRINGERS	INGENIOUSNESS	INGROUNDING
INFLICTORS	INFORMATIZES	INFRINGING	INGENIOUSNESSES	INGROWNNESS
INFLORESCENCE	INFORMATIZING	INFRUCTUOUS	INGENUITIES	INGROWNNESSES
INFLORESCENCES	INFORMATORILY	INFRUCTUOUSLY	INGENUOUSLY	INGULFMENT
INFLORESCENT	INFORMATORY	INFUNDIBULA	INGENUOUSNESS	INGULFMENTS
INFLOWINGS	INFORMEDLY	INFUNDIBULAR	INGENUOUSNESSES	INGULPHING
INFLUENCEABLE	INFORMIDABLE	INFUNDIBULATE	INGESTIBLE	INGURGITATE
INFLUENCED	INFORMINGLY	INFUNDIBULIFORM	INGESTIONS	INGURGITATED
INFLUENCER	INFORTUNES	INFUNDIBULUM	INGLENEUKS	INGURGITATES
INFLUENCERS	INFOSPHERE	INFURIATED	INGLENOOKS	INGURGITATING
INFLUENCES	INFOSPHERES	INFURIATELY	INGLORIOUS	INGURGITATION
INFLUENCING	INFOTAINMENT	INFURIATES	INGLORIOUSLY	INGURGITATIONS
INFLUENTIAL	INFOTAINMENTS	INFURIATING	INGLORIOUSNESS	INHABITABILITY
INFLUENTIALLY	INFRACOSTAL	INFURIATINGLY	INGRAFTATION	INHABITABLE
INFLUENTIALS	INFRACTING	INFURIATION	INGRAFTATIONS	INHABITANCE
INFLUENZAL	INFRACTION	INFURIATIONS	INGRAFTING	INHABITANCES
INFLUENZAS	INFRACTIONS	INFUSCATED	INGRAFTMENT	INHABITANCIES
INFLUXIONS	INFRACTORS	INFUSIBILITIES	INGRAFTMENTS	INHABITANCY
INFOLDINGS	INFRAGRANT	INFUSIBILITY	INGRAINEDLY	INHABITANT
INFOLDMENT	INFRAHUMAN	INFUSIBLENESS	INGRAINEDNESS	INHABITANTS
INFOLDMENTS	INFRAHUMANS	INFUSIBLENESSES	INGRAINEDNESSES	INHABITATION
INFOMANIAS	INFRALAPSARIAN	INFUSIONISM	INGRAINERS	INHABITATIONS
INFOMERCIAL	INFRALAPSARIANS	INFUSIONISMS	INGRAINING	INHABITERS
INFOMERCIALS	INFRAMAXILLARY	INFUSIONIST	INGRATEFUL	INHABITING
INFOPRENEURIAL	INFRANGIBILITY	INFUSIONISTS	INGRATIATE	INHABITIVENESS
INFORMABLE	INFRANGIBLE	INFUSORIAL	INGRATIATED	INHABITORS
INFORMALITIES	INFRANGIBLENESS	INFUSORIAN	INGRATIATES	INHABITRESS

INHABITRESSES	INHOSPITALITIES	INITIATING	INNERSPRING	INNUTRITION
INHALATION	INHOSPITALITY	INITIATION	INNERVATED	INNUTRITIONS
INHALATIONAL	INHUMANELY	INITIATIONS	INNERVATES	INNUTRITIOUS
INHALATIONS	INHUMANITIES	INITIATIVE	INNERVATING	INOBEDIENCE
INHALATORIUM	INHUMANITY	INITIATIVELY	INNERVATION	INOBEDIENCES
INHALATORIUMS	INHUMANNESS	INITIATIVES	INNERVATIONS	INOBEDIENT
INHALATORS	INHUMANNESSES	INITIATORIES	INNERWEARS	INOBEDIENTLY
INHARMONIC	INHUMATING	INITIATORS	INNKEEPERS	INOBSERVABLE
INHARMONICAL	INHUMATION	INITIATORY	INNOCENCES	INOBSERVANCE
INHARMONICITIES	INHUMATIONS	INITIATRESS	INNOCENCIES	INOBSERVANCES
INHARMONICITY	INIMICALITIES	INITIATRESSES	INNOCENTER	INOBSERVANT
INHARMONIES	INIMICALITY	INITIATRICES	INNOCENTEST	INOBSERVANTLY
INHARMONIOUS	INIMICALLY	INITIATRIX	INNOCENTLY	INOBSERVATION
INHARMONIOUSLY	INIMICALNESS	INITIATRIXES	INNOCUITIES	INOBSERVATIONS
INHAUSTING	INIMICALNESSES	INJECTABLE	INNOCUOUSLY	INOBTRUSIVE
INHEARSING	INIMICITIOUS	INJECTABLES	INNOCUOUSNESS	INOBTRUSIVELY
INHERENCES	INIMITABILITIES	INJECTANTS	INNOCUOUSNESSES	INOBTRUSIVENESS
INHERENCIES	INIMITABILITY	INJECTIONS	INNOMINABLE	INOCCUPATION
INHERENTLY	INIMITABLE	INJELLYING	INNOMINABLES	INOCCUPATIONS
INHERITABILITY	INIMITABLENESS	INJOINTING	INNOMINATE	INOCULABILITIES
INHERITABLE	INIMITABLY	INJUDICIAL	INNOVATING	INOCULABILITY
INHERITABLENESS	INIQUITIES	INJUDICIALLY	INNOVATION	INOCULABLE
INHERITABLY	INIQUITOUS	INJUDICIOUS	INNOVATIONAL	INOCULANTS
INHERITANCE	INIQUITOUSLY	INJUDICIOUSLY	INNOVATIONIST	INOCULATED
INHERITANCES	INIQUITOUSNESS	INJUDICIOUSNESS	INNOVATIONISTS	INOCULATES
INHERITING	INITIALERS	INJUNCTING	INNOVATIONS	INOCULATING
INHERITORS	INITIALING	INJUNCTION	INNOVATIVE	INOCULATION
INHERITRESS	INITIALISATION	INJUNCTIONS	INNOVATIVELY	INOCULATIONS
INHERITRESSES	INITIALISATIONS	INJUNCTIVE	INNOVATIVENESS	INOCULATIVE
INHERITRICES	INITIALISE	INJUNCTIVELY	INNOVATORS	INOCULATOR
INHERITRIX	INITIALISED	INJURIOUSLY	INNOVATORY	INOCULATORS
INHERITRIXES	INITIALISES	INJURIOUSNESS	INNOXIOUSLY	INOCULATORY
INHIBITABLE	INITIALISING	INJURIOUSNESSES	INNOXIOUSNESS	INODOROUSLY
INHIBITEDLY	INITIALISM	INJUSTICES	INNOXIOUSNESSES	INODOROUSNESS
INHIBITERS	INITIALISMS	INKBERRIES	INNUENDOED	INODOROUSNESSES
INHIBITING	INITIALIZATION	INKHOLDERS	INNUENDOES	INOFFENSIVE
INHIBITION	INITIALIZATIONS	INKINESSES	INNUENDOING	INOFFENSIVELY
INHIBITIONS	INITIALIZE	INMARRIAGE	INNUMERABILITY	INOFFENSIVENESS
INHIBITIVE	INITIALIZED	INMARRIAGES	INNUMERABLE	INOFFICIOUS
INHIBITORS	INITIALIZES	INMIGRANTS	INNUMERABLENESS	INOFFICIOUSLY
INHIBITORY	INITIALIZING	INNATENESS	INNUMERABLY	INOFFICIOUSNESS
INHOLDINGS	INITIALLED	INNATENESSES	INNUMERACIES	INOPERABILITIES
INHOMOGENEITIES	INITIALLER	INNAVIGABLE	INNUMERACY	INOPERABILITY
INHOMOGENEITY	INITIALLERS	INNAVIGABLY	INNUMERATE	INOPERABLE
INHOMOGENEOUS	INITIALLING	INNERMOSTS	INNUMERATES	INOPERABLENESS
INHOSPITABLE	INITIALNESS	INNERNESSES	INNUMEROUS	INOPERABLY
INHOSPITABLY	INITIALNESSES	INNERSOLES	INNUTRIENT	INOPERATIVE

INOPERATIVENESS	INQUIRATION	INSATIETIES	INSELBERGE	INSHIPPING
INOPERCULATE	INQUIRATIONS	INSCIENCES	INSELBERGS	INSHRINEMENT
INOPERCULATES	INQUIRENDO	INSCONCING	INSEMINATE	INSHRINEMENTS
INOPPORTUNE	INQUIRENDOS	INSCRIBABLE	INSEMINATED	INSHRINING
INOPPORTUNELY	INQUIRINGLY	INSCRIBABLENESS	INSEMINATES	INSIDIOUSLY
INOPPORTUNENESS	INQUISITION	INSCRIBERS	INSEMINATING	INSIDIOUSNESS
INOPPORTUNITIES	INQUISITIONAL	INSCRIBING	INSEMINATION	INSIDIOUSNESSES
INOPPORTUNITY	INQUISITIONIST	INSCRIPTION	INSEMINATIONS	INSIGHTFUL
INORDINACIES	INQUISITIONISTS	INSCRIPTIONAL	INSEMINATOR	INSIGHTFULLY
INORDINACY	INQUISITIONS	INSCRIPTIONS	INSEMINATORS	INSIGNIFICANCE
INORDINATE	INQUISITIVE	INSCRIPTIVE	INSENSATELY	INSIGNIFICANCES
INORDINATELY	INQUISITIVELY	INSCRIPTIVELY	INSENSATENESS	INSIGNIFICANCY
INORDINATENESS	INQUISITIVENESS	INSCROLLED	INSENSATENESSES	INSIGNIFICANT
INORDINATION	INQUISITOR	INSCROLLING	INSENSIBILITIES	INSIGNIFICANTLY
INORDINATIONS	INQUISITORIAL	INSCRUTABILITY	INSENSIBILITY	INSIGNIFICATIVE
INORGANICALLY	INQUISITORIALLY	INSCRUTABLE	INSENSIBLE	INSINCERELY
INORGANISATION	INQUISITORS	INSCRUTABLENESS	INSENSIBLENESS	INSINCERITIES
INORGANISATIONS	INQUISITRESS	INSCRUTABLY	INSENSIBLY	INSINCERITY
INORGANISED	INQUISITRESSES	INSCULPING	INSENSITIVE	INSINEWING
INORGANIZATION	INQUISITURIENT	INSCULPTURE	INSENSITIVELY	INSINUATED
INORGANIZATIONS	INRUSHINGS	INSCULPTURED	INSENSITIVENESS	INSINUATES
INORGANIZED	INSALIVATE	INSCULPTURES	INSENSITIVITIES	INSINUATING
INOSCULATE	INSALIVATED	INSCULPTURING	INSENSITIVITY	INSINUATINGLY
INOSCULATED	INSALIVATES	INSECTARIA	INSENSUOUS	INSINUATION
INOSCULATES	INSALIVATING	INSECTARIES	INSENTIENCE	INSINUATIONS
INOSCULATING	INSALIVATION	INSECTARIUM	INSENTIENCES	INSINUATIVE
INOSCULATION	INSALIVATIONS	INSECTARIUMS	INSENTIENCIES	INSINUATOR
INOSCULATIONS	INSALUBRIOUS	INSECTICIDAL	INSENTIENCY	INSINUATORS
INPATIENTS	INSALUBRIOUSLY	INSECTICIDALLY	INSENTIENT	INSINUATORY
INPAYMENTS	INSALUBRITIES	INSECTICIDE	INSEPARABILITY	INSIPIDITIES
INPOURINGS	INSALUBRITY	INSECTICIDES	INSEPARABLE	INSIPIDITY
INQUIETING	INSALUTARY	INSECTIFORM	INSEPARABLENESS	INSIPIDNESS
INQUIETUDE	INSANENESS	INSECTIFUGE	INSEPARABLES	INSIPIDNESSES
INQUIETUDES	INSANENESSES	INSECTIFUGES	INSEPARABLY	INSIPIENCE
INQUILINES	INSANITARINESS	INSECTIONS	INSEPARATE	INSIPIENCES
INQUILINIC	INSANITARY	INSECTIVORE	INSERTABLE	INSIPIENTLY
INQUILINICS	INSANITATION	INSECTIVORES	INSERTIONAL	INSISTENCE
INQUILINISM	INSANITATIONS	INSECTIVOROUS	INSERTIONS	INSISTENCES
INQUILINISMS	INSANITIES	INSECTOLOGIES	INSESSORIAL	INSISTENCIES
INQUILINITIES	INSATIABILITIES	INSECTOLOGIST	INSEVERABLE	INSISTENCY
INQUILINITY	INSATIABILITY	INSECTOLOGISTS	INSHEATHED	INSISTENTLY
INQUILINOUS	INSATIABLE	INSECTOLOGY	INSHEATHES	INSISTINGLY
INQUINATED	INSATIABLENESS	INSECURELY	INSHEATHING	INSNAREMENT
INQUINATES	INSATIABLY	INSECURENESS	INSHELLING	INSNAREMENTS
INQUINATING	INSATIATELY	INSECURENESSES	INSHELTERED	INSOBRIETIES
INQUINATION	INSATIATENESS	INSECURITIES	INSHELTERING	INSOBRIETY
INQUINATIONS	INSATIATENESSES	INSECURITY	INSHELTERS	INSOCIABILITIES

INSOCIABILITY	INSPECTIONAL	INSTALLING	INSTINCTIVITY	INSTRUMENTATION
INSOCIABLE	INSPECTIONS	INSTALLMENT	INSTINCTUAL	INSTRUMENTED
INSOCIABLY	INSPECTIVE	INSTALLMENTS	INSTINCTUALLY	INSTRUMENTING
INSOLATING	INSPECTORAL	INSTALMENT	INSTITORIAL	INSTRUMENTS
INSOLATION	INSPECTORATE	INSTALMENTS	INSTITUTED	INSUBJECTION
INSOLATIONS	INSPECTORATES	INSTANCIES	INSTITUTER	INSUBJECTIONS
INSOLENCES	INSPECTORIAL	INSTANCING	INSTITUTERS	INSUBORDINATE
INSOLENTLY	INSPECTORS	INSTANTANEITIES	INSTITUTES	INSUBORDINATELY
INSOLIDITIES	INSPECTORSHIP	INSTANTANEITY	INSTITUTING	INSUBORDINATES
INSOLIDITY	INSPECTORSHIPS	INSTANTANEOUS	INSTITUTION	INSUBORDINATION
INSOLUBILISE	INSPHERING	INSTANTANEOUSLY	INSTITUTIONAL	INSUBSTANTIAL
INSOLUBILISED	INSPIRABLE	INSTANTIAL	INSTITUTIONALLY	INSUBSTANTIALLY
INSOLUBILISES	INSPIRATION	INSTANTIATE	INSTITUTIONARY	INSUFFERABLE
INSOLUBILISING	INSPIRATIONAL	INSTANTIATED	INSTITUTIONS	INSUFFERABLY
INSOLUBILITIES	INSPIRATIONALLY	INSTANTIATES	INSTITUTIST	INSUFFICIENCE
INSOLUBILITY	INSPIRATIONISM	INSTANTIATING	INSTITUTISTS	INSUFFICIENCES
INSOLUBILIZE	INSPIRATIONISMS	INSTANTIATION	INSTITUTIVE	INSUFFICIENCIES
INSOLUBILIZED	INSPIRATIONIST	INSTANTIATIONS	INSTITUTIVELY	INSUFFICIENCY
INSOLUBILIZES	INSPIRATIONISTS	INSTANTNESS	INSTITUTOR	INSUFFICIENT
INSOLUBILIZING	INSPIRATIONS	INSTANTNESSES	INSTITUTORS	INSUFFICIENTLY
INSOLUBLENESS	INSPIRATIVE	INSTARRING	INSTREAMING	INSUFFLATE
INSOLUBLENESSES	INSPIRATOR	INSTATEMENT	INSTREAMINGS	INSUFFLATED
INSOLUBLES	INSPIRATORS	INSTATEMENTS	INSTRESSED	INSUFFLATES
INSOLVABILITIES	INSPIRATORY	INSTAURATION	INSTRESSES	INSUFFLATING
INSOLVABILITY	INSPIRINGLY	INSTAURATIONS	INSTRESSING	INSUFFLATION
INSOLVABLE	INSPIRITED	INSTAURATOR	INSTRUCTED	INSUFFLATIONS
INSOLVABLY	INSPIRITER	INSTAURATORS	INSTRUCTIBLE	INSUFFLATOR
INSOLVENCIES	INSPIRITERS	INSTIGATED	INSTRUCTING	INSUFFLATORS
INSOLVENCY	INSPIRITING	INSTIGATES	INSTRUCTION	INSULARISM
INSOLVENTS	INSPIRITINGLY	INSTIGATING	INSTRUCTIONAL	INSULARISMS
INSOMNIACS	INSPIRITMENT	INSTIGATINGLY	INSTRUCTIONS	INSULARITIES
INSOMNIOUS	INSPIRITMENTS	INSTIGATION	INSTRUCTIVE	INSULARITY
INSOMNOLENCE	INSPISSATE	INSTIGATIONS	INSTRUCTIVELY	INSULATING
INSOMNOLENCES	INSPISSATED	INSTIGATIVE	INSTRUCTIVENESS	INSULATION
INSOUCIANCE	INSPISSATES	INSTIGATOR	INSTRUCTOR	INSULATIONS
INSOUCIANCES	INSPISSATING	INSTIGATORS	INSTRUCTORS	INSULATORS
INSOUCIANT	INSPISSATION	INSTILLATION	INSTRUCTORSHIP	INSULINASE
INSOUCIANTLY	INSPISSATIONS	INSTILLATIONS	INSTRUCTORSHIPS	INSULINASES
INSOULMENT	INSPISSATOR	INSTILLERS	INSTRUCTRESS	INSULSITIES
INSOULMENTS	INSPISSATORS	INSTILLING	INSTRUCTRESSES	INSULTABLE
INSOURCING	INSTABILITIES	INSTILLMENT	INSTRUMENT	INSULTINGLY
INSOURCINGS	INSTABILITY	INSTILLMENTS	INSTRUMENTAL	INSULTMENT
INSPANNING	INSTALLANT	INSTILMENT	INSTRUMENTALISM	INSULTMENTS
INSPECTABLE	INSTALLANTS	INSTILMENTS	INSTRUMENTALIST	INSUPERABILITY
INSPECTING	INSTALLATION	INSTINCTIVE	INSTRUMENTALITY	INSUPERABLE
INSPECTINGLY	INSTALLATIONS	INSTINCTIVELY	INSTRUMENTALLY	INSUPERABLENESS
INSPECTION	INSTALLERS	INSTINCTIVITIES	INSTRUMENTALS	INSUPERABLY

INSUPPORTABLE	INTEGRANDS	INTEMERATENESS	INTENSIVELY	INTERBEHAVIORS
INSUPPORTABLY	INTEGRANTS	INTEMPERANCE	INTENSIVENESS	INTERBEHAVIOUR
INSUPPRESSIBLE	INTEGRATED	INTEMPERANCES	INTENSIVENESSES	INTERBEHAVIOURS
INSUPPRESSIBLY	INTEGRATES	INTEMPERANT	INTENSIVES	INTERBLEND
INSURABILITIES	INTEGRATING	INTEMPERANTS	INTENTIONAL	INTERBLENDED
INSURABILITY	INTEGRATION	INTEMPERATE	INTENTIONALITY	INTERBLENDING
INSURANCER	INTEGRATIONIST	INTEMPERATELY	INTENTIONALLY	INTERBLENDS
INSURANCERS	INTEGRATIONISTS	INTEMPERATENESS	INTENTIONED	INTERBOROUGH
INSURANCES	INTEGRATIONS	INTEMPESTIVE	INTENTIONS	INTERBRAIN
INSURGENCE	INTEGRATIVE	INTEMPESTIVELY	INTENTNESS	INTERBRAINS
INSURGENCES	INTEGRATOR	INTEMPESTIVITY	INTENTNESSES	INTERBRANCH
INSURGENCIES	INTEGRATORS	INTENDANCE	INTERABANG	INTERBREED
INSURGENCY	INTEGRITIES	INTENDANCES	INTERABANGS	INTERBREEDING
INSURGENTLY	INTEGUMENT	INTENDANCIES	INTERACTANT	INTERBREEDINGS
INSURGENTS	INTEGUMENTAL	INTENDANCY	INTERACTANTS	INTERBREEDS
INSURMOUNTABLE	INTEGUMENTARY	INTENDANTS	INTERACTED	INTERBROKER
INSURMOUNTABLY	INTEGUMENTS	INTENDEDLY	INTERACTING	INTERCALAR
INSURRECTION	INTELLECTED	INTENDERED	INTERACTION	INTERCALARILY
INSURRECTIONAL	INTELLECTION	INTENDERING	INTERACTIONAL	INTERCALARY
INSURRECTIONARY	INTELLECTIONS	INTENDMENT	INTERACTIONISM	INTERCALATE
INSURRECTIONISM	INTELLECTIVE	INTENDMENTS	INTERACTIONISMS	INTERCALATED
INSURRECTIONIST	INTELLECTIVELY	INTENERATE	INTERACTIONIST	INTERCALATES
INSURRECTIONS	INTELLECTS	INTENERATED	INTERACTIONISTS	INTERCALATING
INSUSCEPTIBLE	INTELLECTUAL	INTENERATES	INTERACTIONS	INTERCALATION
INSUSCEPTIBLY	INTELLECTUALISE	INTENERATING	INTERACTIVE	INTERCALATIONS
INSUSCEPTIVE	INTELLECTUALISM	INTENERATION	INTERACTIVELY	INTERCALATIVE
INSUSCEPTIVELY	INTELLECTUALIST	INTENERATIONS	INTERACTIVITIES	INTERCAMPUS
INSWATHING	INTELLECTUALITY	INTENSATED	INTERACTIVITY	INTERCASTE
INSWINGERS	INTELLECTUALIZE	INTENSATES	INTERAGENCY	INTERCEDED
INTACTNESS	INTELLECTUALLY	INTENSATING	INTERALLELIC	INTERCEDENT
INTACTNESSES	INTELLECTUALS	INTENSATIVE	INTERALLIED	INTERCEDER
INTAGLIATED	INTELLIGENCE	INTENSATIVES	INTERAMBULACRA	INTERCEDERS
INTAGLIOED	INTELLIGENCER	INTENSENESS	INTERAMBULACRAL	INTERCEDES
INTAGLIOES	INTELLIGENCERS	INTENSENESSES	INTERAMBULACRUM	INTERCEDING
INTAGLIOING	INTELLIGENCES	INTENSIFICATION	INTERANIMATION	INTERCELLULAR
INTANGIBILITIES	INTELLIGENT	INTENSIFIED	INTERANIMATIONS	INTERCENSAL
INTANGIBILITY	INTELLIGENTIAL	INTENSIFIER	INTERANNUAL	INTERCEPTED
INTANGIBLE	INTELLIGENTLY	INTENSIFIERS	INTERARCHED	INTERCEPTER
INTANGIBLENESS	INTELLIGENTSIA	INTENSIFIES	INTERARCHES	INTERCEPTERS
INTANGIBLES	INTELLIGENTSIAS	INTENSIFYING	INTERARCHING	INTERCEPTING
INTANGIBLY	INTELLIGENTZIA	INTENSIONAL	INTERATOMIC	INTERCEPTION
INTEGRABILITIES	INTELLIGENTZIAS	INTENSIONALITY	INTERBASIN	INTERCEPTIONS
INTEGRABILITY	INTELLIGIBILITY	INTENSIONALLY	INTERBEDDED	INTERCEPTIVE
INTEGRABLE	INTELLIGIBLE	INTENSIONS	INTERBEDDING	INTERCEPTOR
INTEGRALITIES	INTELLIGIBLY	INTENSITIES	INTERBEDDINGS	INTERCEPTORS
INTEGRALITY	INTEMERATE	INTENSITIVE	INTERBEHAVIOR	INTERCEPTS
INTEGRALLY	INTEMERATELY	INTENSITIVES	INTERBEHAVIORAL	INTERCESSION

INTERCESSIONAL	INTERCOMMUNION	INTERCRURAL	INTERDIGITATES	INTERFEROMETERS
INTERCESSIONS	INTERCOMMUNIONS	INTERCULTURAL	INTERDIGITATING	INTERFEROMETRIC
INTERCESSOR	INTERCOMMUNITY	INTERCULTURALLY	INTERDIGITATION	INTERFEROMETRY
INTERCESSORIAL	INTERCOMPANY	INTERCULTURE	INTERDINED	INTERFERON
INTERCESSORS	INTERCOMPARE	INTERCULTURES	INTERDINES	INTERFERONS
INTERCESSORY	INTERCOMPARED	INTERCURRENCE	INTERDINING	INTERFERTILE
INTERCHAIN	INTERCOMPARES	INTERCURRENCES	INTERDISTRICT	INTERFERTILITY
INTERCHAINED	INTERCOMPARING	INTERCURRENT	INTERDIVISIONAL	INTERFIBER
INTERCHAINING	INTERCOMPARISON	INTERCURRENTLY	INTERDOMINION	INTERFIBRE
INTERCHAINS	INTERCONNECT	INTERCUTTING	INTERELECTRODE	INTERFILED
INTERCHANGE	INTERCONNECTED	INTERDASHED	INTERELECTRON	INTERFILES
INTERCHANGEABLE	INTERCONNECTING	INTERDASHES	INTERELECTRONIC	INTERFILING
INTERCHANGEABLY	INTERCONNECTION	INTERDASHING	INTEREPIDEMIC	INTERFLOWED
INTERCHANGED	INTERCONNECTOR	INTERDEALER	INTERESSED	INTERFLOWING
INTERCHANGEMENT	INTERCONNECTORS	INTERDEALERS	INTERESSES	INTERFLOWS
INTERCHANGER	INTERCONNECTS	INTERDEALING	INTERESSING	INTERFLUENCE
INTERCHANGERS	INTERCONNEXION	INTERDEALS	INTERESTED	INTERFLUENCES
INTERCHANGES	INTERCONNEXIONS	INTERDEALT	INTERESTEDLY	INTERFLUENT
INTERCHANGING	INTERCONVERSION	INTERDENTAL	INTERESTEDNESS	INTERFLUOUS
INTERCHANNEL	INTERCONVERT	INTERDENTALLY	INTERESTING	INTERFLUVE
INTERCHAPTER	INTERCONVERTED	INTERDEPEND	INTERESTINGLY	INTERFLUVES
INTERCHAPTERS	INTERCONVERTING	INTERDEPENDED	INTERESTINGNESS	INTERFLUVIAL
INTERCHURCH	INTERCONVERTS	INTERDEPENDENCE	INTERETHNIC	INTERFOLDED
INTERCIPIENT	INTERCOOLED	INTERDEPENDENCY	INTERFACED	INTERFOLDING
INTERCIPIENTS	INTERCOOLER	INTERDEPENDENT	INTERFACES	INTERFOLDS
INTERCLASS	INTERCOOLERS	INTERDEPENDING	INTERFACIAL	INTERFOLIATE
INTERCLAVICLE	INTERCORPORATE	INTERDEPENDS	INTERFACIALLY	INTERFOLIATED
INTERCLAVICLES	INTERCORRELATE	INTERDIALECTAL	INTERFACING	INTERFOLIATES
INTERCLAVICULAR	INTERCORRELATED	INTERDICTED	INTERFACINGS	INTERFOLIATING
INTERCLUDE	INTERCORRELATES	INTERDICTING	INTERFACULTY	INTERFRATERNITY
INTERCLUDED	INTERCORTICAL	INTERDICTION	INTERFAITH	INTERFRETTED
INTERCLUDES	INTERCOSTAL	INTERDICTIONS	INTERFAMILIAL	INTERFRONTAL
INTERCLUDING	INTERCOSTALLY	INTERDICTIVE	INTERFAMILY	INTERFUSED
INTERCLUSION	INTERCOSTALS	INTERDICTIVELY	INTERFASCICULAR	INTERFUSES
INTERCLUSIONS	INTERCOUNTRY	INTERDICTOR	INTERFEMORAL	INTERFUSING
INTERCLUSTER	INTERCOUNTY	INTERDICTORS	INTERFERED	INTERFUSION
INTERCOASTAL	INTERCOUPLE	INTERDICTORY	INTERFERENCE	INTERFUSIONS
INTERCOLLEGIATE	INTERCOURSE	INTERDICTS	INTERFERENCES	INTERGALACTIC
INTERCOLLINE	INTERCOURSES	INTERDIFFUSE	INTERFERENTIAL	INTERGENERATION
INTERCOLONIAL	INTERCRATER	INTERDIFFUSED	INTERFERER	INTERGENERIC
INTERCOLONIALLY	INTERCROPPED	INTERDIFFUSES	INTERFERERS	INTERGLACIAL
INTERCOLUMNAR	INTERCROPPING	INTERDIFFUSING	INTERFERES	INTERGLACIALS
INTERCOMMUNAL	INTERCROPS	INTERDIFFUSION	INTERFERING	INTERGRADATION
INTERCOMMUNE	INTERCROSS	INTERDIFFUSIONS	INTERFERINGLY	INTERGRADATIONS
INTERCOMMUNED	INTERCROSSED	INTERDIGITAL	INTERFEROGRAM	INTERGRADE
INTERCOMMUNES	INTERCROSSES	INTERDIGITATE	INTERFEROGRAMS	INTERGRADED
INTERCOMMUNING	INTERCROSSING	INTERDIGITATED	INTERFEROMETER	INTERGRADES

INTERGRADIENT	INTERJECTION	INTERLENDING	INTERLOCUTRICES	INTERMEDIATING
INTERGRADING	INTERJECTIONAL	INTERLENDS	INTERLOCUTRIX	INTERMEDIATION
INTERGRAFT	INTERJECTIONARY	INTERLEUKIN	INTERLOCUTRIXES	INTERMEDIATIONS
INTERGRAFTED	INTERJECTIONS	INTERLEUKINS	INTERLOOPED	INTERMEDIATOR
INTERGRAFTING	INTERJECTOR	INTERLIBRARY	INTERLOOPING	INTERMEDIATORS
INTERGRAFTS	INTERJECTORS	INTERLINEAL	INTERLOOPS	INTERMEDIATORY
INTERGRANULAR	INTERJECTORY	INTERLINEALLY	INTERLOPED	INTERMEDIN
INTERGROUP	INTERJECTS	INTERLINEAR	INTERLOPER	INTERMEDINS
INTERGROWING	INTERJECTURAL	INTERLINEARLY	INTERLOPERS	INTERMEDIUM
INTERGROWN	INTERJOINED	INTERLINEARS	INTERLOPES	INTERMEDIUMS
INTERGROWS	INTERJOINING	INTERLINEATE	INTERLOPING	INTERMEMBRANE
INTERGROWTH	INTERJOINS	INTERLINEATED	INTERLUDED	INTERMENSTRUAL
INTERGROWTHS	INTERKINESES	INTERLINEATES	INTERLUDES	INTERMENTS
INTERINDIVIDUAL	INTERKINESIS	INTERLINEATING	INTERLUDIAL	INTERMESHED
INTERINDUSTRY	INTERKNITS	INTERLINEATION	INTERLUDING	INTERMESHES
INTERINFLUENCE	INTERKNITTED	INTERLINEATIONS	INTERLUNAR	INTERMESHING
INTERINFLUENCED	INTERKNITTING	INTERLINED	INTERLUNARY	INTERMETALLIC
INTERINFLUENCES	INTERKNOTS	INTERLINER	INTERLUNATION	INTERMETALLICS
INTERINVOLVE	INTERKNOTTED	INTERLINERS	INTERLUNATIONS	INTERMEZZI
INTERINVOLVED	INTERKNOTTING	INTERLINES	INTERMARGINAL	INTERMEZZO
INTERINVOLVES	INTERLACED	INTERLINGUA	INTERMARRIAGE	INTERMEZZOS
INTERINVOLVING	INTERLACEDLY	INTERLINGUAL	INTERMARRIAGES	INTERMIGRATION
INTERIONIC	INTERLACEMENT	INTERLINGUALLY	INTERMARRIED	INTERMIGRATIONS
INTERIORISATION	INTERLACEMENTS	INTERLINGUAS	INTERMARRIES	INTERMINABILITY
INTERIORISE	INTERLACES	INTERLINING	INTERMARRY	INTERMINABLE
INTERIORISED	INTERLACING	INTERLININGS	INTERMARRYING	INTERMINABLY
INTERIORISES	INTERLACUSTRINE	INTERLINKED	INTERMATTED	INTERMINGLE
INTERIORISING	INTERLAMINAR	INTERLINKING	INTERMATTING	INTERMINGLED
INTERIORITIES	INTERLAMINATE	INTERLINKS	INTERMAXILLA	INTERMINGLES
INTERIORITY	INTERLAMINATED	INTERLOANS	INTERMAXILLAE	INTERMINGLING
INTERIORIZATION	INTERLAMINATES	INTERLOBULAR	INTERMAXILLARY	INTERMISSION
INTERIORIZE	INTERLAMINATING	INTERLOCAL	INTERMEDDLE	INTERMISSIONS
INTERIORIZED	INTERLAMINATION	INTERLOCATION	INTERMEDDLED	INTERMISSIVE
INTERIORIZES	INTERLAPPED	INTERLOCATIONS	INTERMEDDLER	INTERMITOTIC
INTERIORIZING	INTERLAPPING	INTERLOCKED	INTERMEDDLERS	INTERMITTED
INTERIORLY	INTERLARDED	INTERLOCKER	INTERMEDDLES	INTERMITTENCE
INTERISLAND	INTERLARDING	INTERLOCKERS	INTERMEDDLING	INTERMITTENCES
INTERJACENCIES	INTERLARDS	INTERLOCKING	INTERMEDIA	INTERMITTENCIES
INTERJACENCY	INTERLAYER	INTERLOCKS	INTERMEDIACIES	INTERMITTENCY
INTERJACENT	INTERLAYERED	INTERLOCUTION	INTERMEDIACY	INTERMITTENT
INTERJACULATE	INTERLAYERING	INTERLOCUTIONS	INTERMEDIAL	INTERMITTENTLY
INTERJACULATED	INTERLAYERS	INTERLOCUTOR	INTERMEDIARIES	INTERMITTER
INTERJACULATES	INTERLAYING	INTERLOCUTORILY	INTERMEDIARY	INTERMITTERS
INTERJACULATING	INTERLEAVE	INTERLOCUTORS	INTERMEDIATE	INTERMITTING
INTERJACULATORY	INTERLEAVED	INTERLOCUTORY	INTERMEDIATED	INTERMITTINGLY
INTERJECTED	INTERLEAVES	INTERLOCUTRESS	INTERMEDIATELY	INTERMITTOR
INTERJECTING	INTERLEAVING	INTERLOCUTRICE	INTERMEDIATES	INTERMITTORS

INTERMIXED	INTERNUCLEAR	INTERPELLATOR	INTERPOLATES	INTERPUNCTUATE
INTERMIXES	INTERNUCLEON	INTERPELLATORS	INTERPOLATING	INTERPUNCTUATED
INTERMIXING	INTERNUCLEONIC	INTERPENETRABLE	INTERPOLATION	INTERPUNCTUATES
INTERMIXTURE	INTERNUCLEOTIDE	INTERPENETRANT	INTERPOLATIONS	INTERPUPILLARY
INTERMIXTURES	INTERNUNCIAL	INTERPENETRATE	INTERPOLATIVE	INTERQUARTILE
INTERMODAL	INTERNUNCIO	INTERPENETRATED	INTERPOLATOR	INTERRACIAL
INTERMODULATION	INTERNUNCIOS	INTERPENETRATES	INTERPOLATORS	INTERRACIALLY
INTERMOLECULAR	INTEROBSERVER	INTERPERCEPTUAL	INTERPONED	INTERRADIAL
INTERMONTANE	INTEROCEAN	INTERPERMEATE	INTERPONES	INTERRADIALLY
INTERMOUNTAIN	INTEROCEANIC	INTERPERMEATED	INTERPONING	INTERRADII
INTERMUNDANE	INTEROCEPTION	INTERPERMEATES	INTERPOPULATION	INTERRADIUS
INTERMURED	INTEROCEPTIONS	INTERPERMEATING	INTERPOSABLE	INTERRADIUSES
INTERMURES	INTEROCEPTIVE	INTERPERSONAL	INTERPOSAL	INTERRAILED
INTERMURING	INTEROCEPTOR	INTERPERSONALLY	INTERPOSALS	INTERRAILER
INTERMUSCULAR	INTEROCEPTORS	INTERPETIOLAR	INTERPOSED	INTERRAILERS
INTERNALISATION	INTEROCULAR	INTERPHALANGEAL	INTERPOSER	INTERRAILING
INTERNALISE	INTEROFFICE	INTERPHASE	INTERPOSERS	INTERRAILS
INTERNALISED	INTEROPERABLE	INTERPHASES	INTERPOSES	INTERRAMAL
INTERNALISES	INTEROPERATIVE	INTERPHONE	INTERPOSING	INTERREGAL
INTERNALISING	INTERORBITAL	INTERPHONES	INTERPOSITION	INTERREGES
INTERNALITIES	INTERORGAN	INTERPILASTER	INTERPOSITIONS	INTERREGIONAL
INTERNALITY	INTEROSCULANT	INTERPILASTERS	INTERPRETABLE	INTERREGNA
INTERNALIZATION	INTEROSCULATE	INTERPLANETARY	INTERPRETABLY	INTERREGNAL
INTERNALIZE	INTEROSCULATED	INTERPLANT	INTERPRETATE	INTERREGNUM
INTERNALIZED	INTEROSCULATES	INTERPLANTED	INTERPRETATED	INTERREGNUMS
INTERNALIZES	INTEROSCULATING	INTERPLANTING	INTERPRETATES	INTERRELATE
INTERNALIZING	INTEROSCULATION	INTERPLANTS	INTERPRETATING	INTERRELATED
INTERNALLY	INTEROSSEAL	INTERPLAYED	INTERPRETATION	INTERRELATEDLY
INTERNALNESS	INTEROSSEOUS	INTERPLAYING	INTERPRETATIONS	INTERRELATES
INTERNALNESSES	INTERPAGED	INTERPLAYS	INTERPRETATIVE	INTERRELATING
INTERNATIONAL	INTERPAGES	INTERPLEAD	INTERPRETED	INTERRELATION
INTERNATIONALLY	INTERPAGING	INTERPLEADED	INTERPRETER	INTERRELATIONS
INTERNATIONALS	INTERPANDEMIC	INTERPLEADER	INTERPRETERS	INTERRELIGIOUS
INTERNECINE	INTERPARIETAL	INTERPLEADERS	INTERPRETERSHIP	INTERRENAL
INTERNECIVE	INTERPARISH	INTERPLEADING	INTERPRETESS	INTERROBANG
INTERNEURAL	INTERPAROCHIAL	INTERPLEADS	INTERPRETESSES	INTERROBANGS
INTERNEURON	INTERPAROXYSMAL	INTERPLEURAL	INTERPRETING	INTERROGABLE
INTERNEURONAL	INTERPARTICLE	INTERPLUVIAL	INTERPRETIVE	INTERROGANT
INTERNEURONS	INTERPARTY	INTERPLUVIALS	INTERPRETIVELY	INTERROGANTS
INTERNISTS	INTERPELLANT	INTERPOINT	INTERPRETRESS	INTERROGATE
INTERNMENT	INTERPELLANTS	INTERPOINTS	INTERPRETRESSES	INTERROGATED
INTERNMENTS	INTERPELLATE	INTERPOLABLE	INTERPRETS	INTERROGATEE
INTERNODAL	INTERPELLATED	INTERPOLAR	INTERPROVINCIAL	INTERROGATEES
INTERNODES	INTERPELLATES	INTERPOLATE	INTERPROXIMAL	INTERROGATES
INTERNODIAL	INTERPELLATING	INTERPOLATED	INTERPSYCHIC	INTERROGATING
INTERNSHIP	INTERPELLATION	INTERPOLATER	INTERPUNCTION	INTERROGATINGLY
INTERNSHIPS	INTERPELLATIONS	INTERPOLATERS	INTERPUNCTIONS	INTERROGATION

INTERROGATIONAL	INTERSERVICE	INTERSTRAIN	INTERTWISTED	INTERVOCALIC
INTERROGATIONS	INTERSESSION	INTERSTRAND	INTERTWISTING	INTERVOLVE
INTERROGATIVE	INTERSESSIONS	INTERSTRATIFIED	INTERTWISTINGLY	INTERVOLVED
INTERROGATIVELY	INTERSEXES	INTERSTRATIFIES	INTERTWISTS	INTERVOLVES
INTERROGATIVES	INTERSEXUAL	INTERSTRATIFY	INTERUNION	INTERVOLVING
INTERROGATOR	INTERSEXUALISM	INTERSUBJECTIVE	INTERUNIONS	INTERWEAVE
INTERROGATORIES	INTERSEXUALISMS	INTERSYSTEM	INTERUNIVERSITY	INTERWEAVED
INTERROGATORILY	INTERSEXUALITY	INTERTANGLE	INTERURBAN	INTERWEAVEMENT
INTERROGATORS	INTERSEXUALLY	INTERTANGLED	INTERVALES	INTERWEAVEMENTS
INTERROGATORY	INTERSIDEREAL	INTERTANGLEMENT	INTERVALLEY	INTERWEAVER
INTERROGEE	INTERSOCIETAL	INTERTANGLES	INTERVALLIC	INTERWEAVERS
INTERROGEES	INTERSOCIETY	INTERTANGLING	INTERVALLUM	INTERWEAVES
INTERRUPTED	INTERSPACE	INTERTARSAL	INTERVALLUMS	INTERWEAVING
INTERRUPTEDLY	INTERSPACED	INTERTENTACULAR	INTERVALOMETER	INTERWINDING
INTERRUPTER	INTERSPACES	INTERTERMINAL	INTERVALOMETERS	INTERWINDS
INTERRUPTERS	INTERSPACING	INTERTERMS	INTERVARSITY	INTERWORKED
INTERRUPTIBLE	INTERSPATIAL	INTERTEXTS	INTERVEINED	INTERWORKING
INTERRUPTING	INTERSPATIALLY	INTERTEXTUAL	INTERVEINING	INTERWORKINGS
INTERRUPTION	INTERSPECIES	INTERTEXTUALITY	INTERVEINS	INTERWORKS
INTERRUPTIONS	INTERSPECIFIC	INTERTEXTUALLY	INTERVENED	INTERWOUND
INTERRUPTIVE	INTERSPERSAL	INTERTEXTURE	INTERVENER	INTERWOVEN
INTERRUPTIVELY	INTERSPERSALS	INTERTEXTURES	INTERVENERS	INTERWREATHE
INTERRUPTOR	INTERSPERSE	INTERTIDAL	INTERVENES	INTERWREATHED
INTERRUPTORS	INTERSPERSED	INTERTIDALLY	INTERVENIENT	INTERWREATHES
INTERRUPTS	INTERSPERSEDLY	INTERTILLAGE	INTERVENING	INTERWREATHING
INTERSCAPULAR	INTERSPERSES	INTERTILLAGES	INTERVENOR	INTERWROUGHT
INTERSCHOLASTIC	INTERSPERSING	INTERTILLED	INTERVENORS	INTERZONAL
INTERSCHOOL	INTERSPERSION	INTERTILLING	INTERVENTION	INTERZONES
INTERSCRIBE	INTERSPERSIONS	INTERTILLS	INTERVENTIONAL	INTESTACIES
INTERSCRIBED	INTERSPINAL	INTERTISSUED	INTERVENTIONISM	INTESTATES
INTERSCRIBES	INTERSPINOUS	INTERTRAFFIC	INTERVENTIONIST	INTESTINAL
INTERSCRIBING	INTERSTADIAL	INTERTRAFFICS	INTERVENTIONS	INTESTINALLY
INTERSECTED	INTERSTADIALS	INTERTRIAL	INTERVENTOR	INTESTINES
INTERSECTING	INTERSTAGE	INTERTRIBAL	INTERVENTORS	INTHRALLED
INTERSECTION	INTERSTATE	INTERTRIGO	INTERVERTEBRAL	INTHRALLING
INTERSECTIONAL	INTERSTATES	INTERTRIGOS	INTERVIEWED	INTHRONING
INTERSECTIONS	INTERSTATION	INTERTROOP	INTERVIEWEE	INTIFADAHS
INTERSECTS	INTERSTELLAR	INTERTROPICAL	INTERVIEWEES	INTIFADEHS
INTERSEGMENT	INTERSTELLARY	INTERTWINE	INTERVIEWER	INTIMACIES
INTERSEGMENTAL	INTERSTERILE	INTERTWINED	INTERVIEWERS	INTIMATELY
INTERSEGMENTS	INTERSTERILITY	INTERTWINEMENT	INTERVIEWING	INTIMATENESS
INTERSENSORY	INTERSTICE	INTERTWINEMENTS	INTERVIEWS	INTIMATENESSES
INTERSEPTAL	INTERSTICES	INTERTWINES	INTERVILLAGE	INTIMATERS
INTERSERTAL	INTERSTIMULUS	INTERTWINING	INTERVISIBILITY	INTIMATING
INTERSERTED	INTERSTITIAL	INTERTWININGLY	INTERVISIBLE	INTIMATION
INTERSERTING	INTERSTITIALLY	INTERTWININGS	INTERVISITATION	INTIMATIONS
INTERSERTS	INTERSTITIALS	INTERTWIST	INTERVITAL	INTIMIDATE

INTIMIDATED	INTOXICATORS	INTRANSIGENCES	INTREATING	INTROFYING
INTIMIDATES	INTOXIMETER	INTRANSIGENCIES	INTREATINGLY	INTROGRESSANT
INTIMIDATING	INTOXIMETERS	INTRANSIGENCY	INTREATMENT	INTROGRESSANTS
INTIMIDATINGLY	INTRACAPSULAR	INTRANSIGENT	INTREATMENTS	INTROGRESSION
INTIMIDATION	INTRACARDIAC	INTRANSIGENTISM	INTRENCHANT	INTROGRESSIONS
INTIMIDATIONS	INTRACARDIAL	INTRANSIGENTIST	INTRENCHED	INTROGRESSIVE
INTIMIDATOR	INTRACARDIALLY	INTRANSIGENTLY	INTRENCHER	INTROITUSES
INTIMIDATORS	INTRACAVITARY	INTRANSIGENTS	INTRENCHERS	INTROJECTED
INTIMIDATORY	INTRACELLULAR	INTRANSITIVE	INTRENCHES	INTROJECTING
INTIMISTES	INTRACELLULARLY	INTRANSITIVELY	INTRENCHING	INTROJECTION
INTIMITIES	INTRACEREBRAL	INTRANSITIVITY	INTRENCHMENT	INTROJECTIONS
INTINCTION	INTRACEREBRALLY	INTRANSMISSIBLE	INTRENCHMENTS	INTROJECTIVE
INTINCTIONS	INTRACOMPANY	INTRANSMUTABLE	INTREPIDITIES	INTROJECTS
INTITULING	INTRACRANIAL	INTRANUCLEAR	INTREPIDITY	INTROMISSIBLE
INTOLERABILITY	INTRACRANIALLY	INTRAOCULAR	INTREPIDLY	INTROMISSION
INTOLERABLE	INTRACTABILITY	INTRAOCULARLY	INTREPIDNESS	INTROMISSIONS
INTOLERABLENESS	INTRACTABLE	INTRAPARIETAL	INTREPIDNESSES	INTROMISSIVE
INTOLERABLY	INTRACTABLENESS	INTRAPARTUM	INTRICACIES	INTROMITTED
INTOLERANCE	INTRACTABLY	INTRAPERITONEAL	INTRICATELY	INTROMITTENT
INTOLERANCES	INTRACUTANEOUS	INTRAPERSONAL	INTRICATENESS	INTROMITTER
INTOLERANT	INTRADERMAL	INTRAPETIOLAR	INTRICATENESSES	INTROMITTERS
INTOLERANTLY	INTRADERMALLY	INTRAPLATE	INTRIGANTE	INTROMITTING
INTOLERANTNESS	INTRADERMIC	INTRAPOPULATION	INTRIGANTES	INTRORSELY
INTOLERANTS	INTRADERMICALLY	INTRAPRENEUR	INTRIGANTS	INTROSPECT
INTOLERATION	INTRADOSES	INTRAPRENEURIAL	INTRIGUANT	INTROSPECTED
INTOLERATIONS	INTRAFALLOPIAN	INTRAPRENEURS	INTRIGUANTE	INTROSPECTING
INTONATING	INTRAFASCICULAR	INTRAPSYCHIC	INTRIGUANTES	INTROSPECTION
INTONATION	INTRAGALACTIC	INTRASEXUAL	INTRIGUANTS	INTROSPECTIONAL
INTONATIONAL	INTRAGENIC	INTRASPECIES	INTRIGUERS	INTROSPECTIONS
INTONATIONS	INTRAMEDULLARY	INTRASPECIFIC	INTRIGUING	INTROSPECTIVE
INTONATORS	INTRAMERCURIAL	INTRASTATE	INTRIGUINGLY	INTROSPECTIVELY
INTONINGLY	INTRAMOLECULAR	INTRATELLURIC	INTRINSICAL	INTROSPECTS
INTORSIONS	INTRAMUNDANE	INTRATHECAL	INTRINSICALITY	INTROSUSCEPTION
INTORTIONS	INTRAMURAL	INTRATHECALLY	INTRINSICALLY	INTROVERSIBLE
INTOXICABLE	INTRAMURALLY	INTRATHORACIC	INTRINSICALNESS	INTROVERSION
INTOXICANT	INTRAMURALS	INTRAUTERINE	INTRINSICATE	INTROVERSIONS
INTOXICANTS	INTRAMUSCULAR	INTRAVASATION	INTRODUCED	INTROVERSIVE
INTOXICATE	INTRAMUSCULARLY	INTRAVASATIONS	INTRODUCER	INTROVERSIVELY
INTOXICATED	INTRANASAL	INTRAVASCULAR	INTRODUCERS	INTROVERTED
INTOXICATEDLY	INTRANASALLY	INTRAVASCULARLY	INTRODUCES	INTROVERTING
INTOXICATES	INTRANATIONAL	INTRAVENOUS	INTRODUCIBLE	INTROVERTIVE
INTOXICATING	INTRANSIGEANCE	INTRAVENOUSLY	INTRODUCING	INTROVERTS
INTOXICATINGLY	INTRANSIGEANCES	INTRAVITAL	INTRODUCTION	INTRUDINGLY
INTOXICATION	INTRANSIGEANT	INTRAVITALLY	INTRODUCTIONS	INTRUSIONAL
INTOXICATIONS	INTRANSIGEANTLY	INTRAVITAM	INTRODUCTIVE	INTRUSIONIST
INTOXICATIVE	INTRANSIGEANTS	INTRAZONAL	INTRODUCTORILY	INTRUSIONISTS
INTOXICATOR	INTRANSIGENCE	INTREATFULL	INTRODUCTORY	INTRUSIONS

INTRUSIVELY	INTWISTING	INVALUABLENESS	INVERITIES	INVIGILATIONS
INTRUSIVENESS	INUMBRATED	INVALUABLY	INVERNESSES	INVIGILATOR
INTRUSIVENESSES	INUMBRATES	INVARIABILITIES	INVERSIONS	INVIGILATORS
INTRUSIVES	INUMBRATING	INVARIABILITY	INVERTASES	INVIGORANT
INTRUSTING	INUNCTIONS	INVARIABLE	INVERTEBRAL	INVIGORANTS
INTRUSTMENT	INUNDATING	INVARIABLENESS	INVERTEBRATE	INVIGORATE
INTRUSTMENTS	INUNDATION	INVARIABLES	INVERTEBRATES	INVIGORATED
INTUBATING	INUNDATIONS	INVARIABLY	INVERTEDLY	INVIGORATES
INTUBATION	INUNDATORS	INVARIANCE	INVERTIBILITIES	INVIGORATING
INTUBATIONS	INUNDATORY	INVARIANCES	INVERTIBILITY	INVIGORATINGLY
INTUITABLE	INURBANELY	INVARIANCIES	INVERTIBLE	INVIGORATION
INTUITIONAL	INURBANITIES	INVARIANCY	INVESTABLE	INVIGORATIONS
INTUITIONALISM	INURBANITY	INVARIANTS	INVESTIBLE	INVIGORATIVE
INTUITIONALISMS	INUREDNESS	INVASIVENESS	INVESTIGABLE	INVIGORATIVELY
INTUITIONALIST	INUREDNESSES	INVASIVENESSES	INVESTIGATE	INVIGORATOR
INTUITIONALISTS	INUREMENTS	INVEAGLING	INVESTIGATED	INVIGORATORS
INTUITIONALLY	INURNMENTS	INVECTIVELY	INVESTIGATES	INVINCIBILITIES
INTUITIONISM	INUSITATION	INVECTIVENESS	INVESTIGATING	INVINCIBILITY
INTUITIONISMS	INUSITATIONS	INVECTIVENESSES	INVESTIGATION	INVINCIBLE
INTUITIONIST	INUTILITIES	INVECTIVES	INVESTIGATIONAL	INVINCIBLENESS
INTUITIONISTS	INUTTERABLE	INVEIGHERS	INVESTIGATIONS	INVINCIBLY
INTUITIONS	INVAGINABLE	INVEIGHING	INVESTIGATIVE	INVIOLABILITIES
INTUITIVELY	INVAGINATE	INVEIGLEMENT	INVESTIGATOR	INVIOLABILITY
INTUITIVENESS	INVAGINATED	INVEIGLEMENTS	INVESTIGATORS	INVIOLABLE
INTUITIVENESSES	INVAGINATES	INVEIGLERS	INVESTIGATORY	INVIOLABLENESS
INTUITIVISM	INVAGINATING	INVEIGLING	INVESTITIVE	INVIOLABLY
INTUITIVISMS	INVAGINATION	INVENDIBILITIES	INVESTITURE	INVIOLACIES
INTUMESCED	INVAGINATIONS	INVENDIBILITY	INVESTITURES	INVIOLATED
INTUMESCENCE	INVALIDATE	INVENDIBLE	INVESTMENT	INVIOLATELY
INTUMESCENCES	INVALIDATED	INVENTABLE	INVESTMENTS	INVIOLATENESS
INTUMESCENCIES	INVALIDATES	INVENTIBLE	INVETERACIES	INVIOLATENESSES
INTUMESCENCY	INVALIDATING	INVENTIONAL	INVETERACY	INVISIBILITIES
INTUMESCENT	INVALIDATION	INVENTIONLESS	INVETERATE	INVISIBILITY
INTUMESCES	INVALIDATIONS	INVENTIONS	INVETERATELY	INVISIBLENESS
INTUMESCING	INVALIDATOR	INVENTIVELY	INVETERATENESS	INVISIBLENESSES
INTURBIDATE	INVALIDATORS	INVENTIVENESS	INVIABILITIES	INVISIBLES
INTURBIDATED	INVALIDHOOD	INVENTIVENESSES	INVIABILITY	INVITATION
INTURBIDATES	INVALIDHOODS	INVENTORIABLE	INVIABLENESS	INVITATIONAL
INTURBIDATING	INVALIDING	INVENTORIAL	INVIABLENESSES	INVITATIONALS
INTUSSUSCEPT	INVALIDINGS	INVENTORIALLY	INVIDIOUSLY	INVITATIONS
INTUSSUSCEPTED	INVALIDISM	INVENTORIED	INVIDIOUSNESS	INVITATORIES
INTUSSUSCEPTING	INVALIDISMS	INVENTORIES	INVIDIOUSNESSES	INVITATORY
INTUSSUSCEPTION	INVALIDITIES	INVENTORYING	INVIGILATE	INVITEMENT
INTUSSUSCEPTIVE	INVALIDITY	INVENTRESS	INVIGILATED	INVITEMENTS
INTUSSUSCEPTS	INVALIDNESS	INVENTRESSES	INVIGILATES	INVITINGLY
INTWINEMENT	INVALIDNESSES	INVERACITIES	INVIGILATING	INVITINGNESS
INTWINEMENTS	INVALUABLE	INVERACITY	INVIGILATION	INVITINGNESSES

INVOCATING	IODISATION	IRENICALLY	IRRADIATED	IRRECONCILABLE
INVOCATION	IODISATIONS	IRENICISMS	IRRADIATES	IRRECONCILABLES
INVOCATIONAL	IODIZATION	IRENOLOGIES	IRRADIATING	IRRECONCILABLY
INVOCATIONS	IODIZATIONS	IRIDACEOUS	IRRADIATION	IRRECONCILED
INVOCATIVE	IODOMETRIC	IRIDECTOMIES	IRRADIATIONS	IRRECONCILEMENT
INVOCATORS	IODOMETRICAL	IRIDECTOMY	IRRADIATIVE	IRRECOVERABLE
INVOCATORY	IODOMETRICALLY	IRIDESCENCE	IRRADIATOR	IRRECOVERABLY
INVOICINGS	IODOMETRIES	IRIDESCENCES	IRRADIATORS	IRRECUSABLE
INVOLUCELLA	IONICITIES	IRIDESCENT	IRRADICABLE	IRRECUSABLY
INVOLUCELLATE	IONISATION	IRIDESCENTLY	IRRADICABLY	IRREDEEMABILITY
INVOLUCELLATED	IONISATIONS	IRIDISATION	IRRADICATE	IRREDEEMABLE
INVOLUCELLUM	IONIZATION	IRIDISATIONS	IRRADICATED	IRREDEEMABLES
INVOLUCELS	IONIZATIONS	IRIDIZATION	IRRADICATES	IRREDEEMABLY
INVOLUCRAL	IONOPAUSES	IRIDIZATIONS	IRRADICATING	IRREDENTAS
INVOLUCRATE	IONOPHORES	IRIDOCYTES	IRRATIONAL	IRREDENTISM
INVOLUCRES	IONOPHORESES	IRIDOLOGIES	IRRATIONALISE	IRREDENTISMS
INVOLUCRUM	IONOPHORESIS	IRIDOLOGIST	IRRATIONALISED	IRREDENTIST
INVOLUNTARILY	IONOSONDES	IRIDOLOGISTS	IRRATIONALISES	IRREDENTISTS
INVOLUNTARINESS	IONOSPHERE	IRIDOSMINE	IRRATIONALISING	IRREDUCIBILITY
INVOLUNTARY	IONOSPHERES	IRIDOSMINES	IRRATIONALISM	IRREDUCIBLE
INVOLUTEDLY	IONOSPHERIC	IRIDOSMIUM	IRRATIONALISMS	IRREDUCIBLENESS
INVOLUTELY	IONOSPHERICALLY	IRIDOSMIUMS	IRRATIONALIST	IRREDUCIBLY
INVOLUTING	IONOTROPIC	IRIDOTOMIES	IRRATIONALISTIC	IRREDUCTIBILITY
INVOLUTION	IONOTROPIES	IRISATIONS	IRRATIONALISTS	IRREDUCTION
INVOLUTIONAL	IONTOPHORESES	IRKSOMENESS	IRRATIONALITIES	IRREDUCTIONS
INVOLUTIONS	IONTOPHORESIS	IRKSOMENESSES	IRRATIONALITY	IRREFLECTION
INVOLVEDLY	IONTOPHORETIC	IRONFISTED	IRRATIONALIZE	IRREFLECTIONS
INVOLVEMENT	IPECACUANHA	IRONHANDED	IRRATIONALIZED	IRREFLECTIVE
INVOLVEMENTS	IPECACUANHAS	IRONHEARTED	IRRATIONALIZES	IRREFLEXION
INVULNERABILITY	IPRATROPIUM	IRONICALLY	IRRATIONALIZING	IRREFLEXIONS
INVULNERABLE	IPRATROPIUMS	IRONICALNESS	IRRATIONALLY	IRREFLEXIVE
INVULNERABLY	IPRINDOLES	IRONICALNESSES	IRRATIONALNESS	IRREFORMABILITY
INVULTUATION	IPRONIAZID	IRONMASTER	IRRATIONALS	IRREFORMABLE
INVULTUATIONS	IPRONIAZIDS	IRONMASTERS	IRREALISABLE	IRREFORMABLY
INWARDNESS	IPSELATERAL	IRONMONGER	IRREALITIES	IRREFRAGABILITY
INWARDNESSES	IPSILATERAL	IRONMONGERIES	IRREALIZABLE	IRREFRAGABLE
INWORKINGS	IPSILATERALLY	IRONMONGERS	IRREBUTTABLE	IRREFRAGABLY
INWRAPMENT	IRACUNDITIES	IRONMONGERY	IRRECEPTIVE	IRREFRANGIBLE
INWRAPMENTS	IRACUNDITY	IRONNESSES	IRRECIPROCAL	IRREFRANGIBLY
INWRAPPING	IRACUNDULOUS	IRONSMITHS	IRRECIPROCITIES	IRREFUTABILITY
INWRAPPINGS	IRASCIBILITIES	IRONSTONES	IRRECIPROCITY	IRREFUTABLE
INWREATHED	IRASCIBILITY	IRONWORKER	IRRECLAIMABLE	IRREFUTABLENESS
INWREATHES	IRASCIBLENESS	IRONWORKERS	IRRECLAIMABLY	IRREFUTABLY
INWREATHING	IRASCIBLENESSES	IRRADIANCE	IRRECOGNISABLE	IRREGARDLESS
IODINATING	IRATENESSES	IRRADIANCES	IRRECOGNITION	IRREGULARITIES
IODINATION	IREFULNESS	IRRADIANCIES	IRRECOGNITIONS	IRREGULARITY
IODINATIONS	IREFULNESSES	IRRADIANCY	IRRECOGNIZABLE	IRREGULARLY

IRREGULARS	IRREPREHENSIBLE	IRREVERSIBILITY	ISOALLOXAZINE	ISOCRACIES
IRRELATION	IRREPREHENSIBLY	IRREVERSIBLE	ISOALLOXAZINES	ISOCRYMALS
IRRELATIONS	IRREPRESSIBLE	IRREVERSIBLY	ISOAMINILE	ISOCYANATE
IRRELATIVE	IRREPRESSIBLY	IRREVOCABILITY	ISOAMINILES	ISOCYANATES
IRRELATIVELY	IRREPROACHABLE	IRREVOCABLE	ISOANTIBODIES	ISOCYANIDE
IRRELATIVENESS	IRREPROACHABLY	IRREVOCABLENESS	ISOANTIBODY	ISOCYANIDES
IRRELEVANCE	IRREPRODUCIBLE	IRREVOCABLY	ISOANTIGEN	ISODIAMETRIC
IRRELEVANCES	IRREPROVABLE	IRRIDENTAS	ISOANTIGENIC	ISODIAMETRICAL
IRRELEVANCIES	IRREPROVABLY	IRRIGATING	ISOANTIGENS	ISODIAPHERE
IRRELEVANCY	IRRESISTANCE	IRRIGATION	ISOBARISMS	ISODIAPHERES
IRRELEVANT	IRRESISTANCES	IRRIGATIONAL	ISOBAROMETRIC	ISODIMORPHIC
IRRELEVANTLY	IRRESISTIBILITY	IRRIGATIONS	ISOBILATERAL	ISODIMORPHISM
IRRELIEVABLE	IRRESISTIBLE	IRRIGATIVE	ISOBUTANES	ISODIMORPHISMS
IRRELIGION	IRRESISTIBLY	IRRIGATORS	ISOBUTENES	ISODIMORPHOUS
IRRELIGIONIST	IRRESOLUBILITY	IRRITABILITIES	ISOBUTYLENE	ISODONTALS
IRRELIGIONISTS	IRRESOLUBLE	IRRITABILITY	ISOBUTYLENES	ISODYNAMIC
IRRELIGIONS	IRRESOLUBLY	IRRITABLENESS	ISOCALORIC	ISODYNAMICS
IRRELIGIOUS	IRRESOLUTE	IRRITABLENESSES	ISOCARBOXAZID	ISOELECTRIC
IRRELIGIOUSLY	IRRESOLUTELY	IRRITANCIES	ISOCARBOXAZIDS	ISOELECTRONIC
IRRELIGIOUSNESS	IRRESOLUTENESS	IRRITATEDLY	ISOCHASMIC	ISOENZYMATIC
IRREMEABLE	IRRESOLUTION	IRRITATING	ISOCHEIMAL	ISOENZYMES
IRREMEABLY	IRRESOLUTIONS	IRRITATINGLY	ISOCHEIMALS	ISOENZYMIC
IRREMEDIABLE	IRRESOLVABILITY	IRRITATION	ISOCHEIMENAL	ISOFLAVONE
IRREMEDIABLY	IRRESOLVABLE	IRRITATIONS	ISOCHEIMENALS	ISOFLAVONES
IRREMISSIBILITY	IRRESOLVABLY	IRRITATIVE	ISOCHEIMIC	ISOGAMETES
IRREMISSIBLE	IRRESPECTIVE	IRRITATORS	ISOCHIMALS	ISOGAMETIC
IRREMISSIBLY	IRRESPECTIVELY	IRROTATIONAL	ISOCHROMATIC	ISOGENETIC
IRREMISSION	IRRESPIRABLE	IRRUPTIONS	ISOCHROMOSOME	ISOGEOTHERM
IRREMISSIONS	IRRESPONSIBLE	IRRUPTIVELY	ISOCHROMOSOMES	ISOGEOTHERMAL
IRREMISSIVE	IRRESPONSIBLES	IRUKANDJIS	ISOCHRONAL	ISOGEOTHERMALS
IRREMOVABILITY	IRRESPONSIBLY	ISABELLINE	ISOCHRONALLY	ISOGEOTHERMIC
IRREMOVABLE	IRRESPONSIVE	ISABELLINES	ISOCHRONES	ISOGEOTHERMICS
IRREMOVABLENESS	IRRESPONSIVELY	ISALLOBARIC	ISOCHRONISE	ISOGEOTHERMS
IRREMOVABLY	IRRESTRAINABLE	ISALLOBARS	ISOCHRONISED	ISOGLOSSAL
IRRENOWNED	IRRESUSCITABLE	ISAPOSTOLIC	ISOCHRONISES	ISOGLOSSES
IRREPAIRABLE	IRRESUSCITABLY	ISCHAEMIAS	ISOCHRONISING	ISOGLOSSIC
IRREPARABILITY	IRRETENTION	ISCHURETIC	ISOCHRONISM	ISOGLOTTAL
IRREPARABLE	IRRETENTIONS	ISCHURETICS	ISOCHRONISMS	ISOGLOTTIC
IRREPARABLENESS	IRRETENTIVE	ISEIKONIAS	ISOCHRONIZE	ISOGRAFTED
IRREPARABLY	IRRETENTIVENESS	ISENTROPIC	ISOCHRONIZED	ISOGRAFTING
IRREPEALABILITY	IRRETRIEVABLE	ISENTROPICALLY	ISOCHRONIZES	ISOHYETALS
IRREPEALABLE	IRRETRIEVABLY	ISINGLASSES	ISOCHRONIZING	ISOIMMUNISATION
IRREPEALABLY	IRREVERENCE	ISLOMANIAS	ISOCHRONOUS	ISOIMMUNIZATION
IRREPLACEABLE	IRREVERENCES	ISMATICALNESS	ISOCHRONOUSLY	ISOKINETIC
IRREPLACEABLY	IRREVERENT	ISMATICALNESSES	ISOCHROOUS	ISOKONTANS
IRREPLEVIABLE	IRREVERENTIAL	ISOAGGLUTININ	ISOCLINALS	ISOLABILITIES
IRREPLEVISABLE	IRREVERENTLY	ISOAGGLUTININS	ISOCLINICS	ISOLABILITY

ISOLATABLE
ISOLATIONISM
ISOLATIONISMS
ISOLATIONIST
ISOLATIONISTS
ISOLATIONS
ISOLECITHAL
ISOLEUCINE
ISOLEUCINES
ISOMAGNETIC
ISOMAGNETICS
ISOMERASES
ISOMERISATION
ISOMERISATIONS
ISOMERISED
ISOMERISES
ISOMERISING
ISOMERISMS
ISOMERIZATION
ISOMERIZATIONS
ISOMERIZED
ISOMERIZES
ISOMERIZING
ISOMETRICAL
ISOMETRICALLY
ISOMETRICS
ISOMETRIES
ISOMETROPIA
ISOMETROPIAS
ISOMORPHIC
ISOMORPHICALLY
ISOMORPHISM

ISOMORPHISMS
ISOMORPHOUS
ISONIAZIDE
ISONIAZIDES
ISONIAZIDS
ISONITRILE
ISONITRILES
ISOOCTANES
ISOPACHYTE
ISOPACHYTES
ISOPERIMETER
ISOPERIMETERS
ISOPERIMETRICAL
ISOPERIMETRIES
ISOPERIMETRY
ISOPIESTIC
ISOPIESTICALLY
ISOPLETHIC
ISOPLUVIAL
ISOPLUVIALS
ISOPOLITIES
ISOPRENALINE
ISOPRENALINES
ISOPRENOID
ISOPRENOIDS
ISOPROPYLS
ISOPROTERENOL
ISOPROTERENOLS
ISOPTERANS
ISOPTEROUS
ISOPYCNALS
ISOPYCNICS

ISORHYTHMIC
ISOSEISMAL
ISOSEISMALS
ISOSEISMIC
ISOSEISMICS
ISOSMOTICALLY
ISOSPONDYLOUS
ISOSPORIES
ISOSPOROUS
ISOSTACIES
ISOSTASIES
ISOSTATICALLY
ISOSTEMONOUS
ISOSTHENURIA
ISOSTHENURIAS
ISOTENISCOPE
ISOTENISCOPES
ISOTHERALS
ISOTHERMAL
ISOTHERMALLY
ISOTHERMALS
ISOTONICALLY
ISOTONICITIES
ISOTONICITY
ISOTOPICALLY
ISOTRETINOIN
ISOTRETINOINS
ISOTROPICALLY
ISOTROPIES
ISOTROPISM
ISOTROPISMS
ISOTROPOUS

ISOXSUPRINE
ISOXSUPRINES
ISPAGHULAS
ITACOLUMITE
ITACOLUMITES
ITALIANATE
ITALIANATED
ITALIANATES
ITALIANATING
ITALIANISE
ITALIANISED
ITALIANISES
ITALIANISING
ITALIANIZE
ITALIANIZED
ITALIANIZES
ITALIANIZING
ITALICISATION
ITALICISATIONS
ITALICISED
ITALICISES
ITALICISING
ITALICIZATION
ITALICIZATIONS
ITALICIZED
ITALICIZES
ITALICIZING
ITCHINESSES
ITEMISATION
ITEMISATIONS
ITEMIZATION
ITEMIZATIONS

ITERATIONS
ITERATIVELY
ITERATIVENESS
ITERATIVENESSES
ITEROPARITIES
ITEROPARITY
ITEROPAROUS
ITHYPHALLI
ITHYPHALLIC
ITHYPHALLICS
ITHYPHALLUS
ITHYPHALLUSES
ITINERACIES
ITINERANCIES
ITINERANCY
ITINERANTLY
ITINERANTS
ITINERARIES
ITINERATED
ITINERATES
ITINERATING
ITINERATION
ITINERATIONS
IVERMECTIN
IVERMECTINS
IVORYBILLS
IVORYWOODS
IZVESTIYAS

J

JABBERINGLY	JACKROLLING	JAMBOKKING	JASPERIZING	JELLYGRAPH
JABBERINGS	JACKSCREWS	JAMBOLANAS	JASPERWARE	JELLYGRAPHED
JABBERWOCK	JACKSHAFTS	JANISARIES	JASPERWARES	JELLYGRAPHING
JABBERWOCKIES	JACKSMELTS	JANISSARIES	JASPIDEOUS	JELLYGRAPHS
JABBERWOCKS	JACKSMITHS	JANITORIAL	JASPILITES	JELLYROLLS
JABBERWOCKY	JACKSNIPES	JANITORSHIP	JAUNDICING	JEMMINESSES
JABORANDIS	JACKSTONES	JANITORSHIPS	JAUNTINESS	JENNETINGS
JABOTICABA	JACKSTRAWS	JANITRESSES	JAUNTINESSES	JEOPARDERS
JABOTICABAS	JACQUERIES	JANITRIXES	JAUNTINGLY	JEOPARDIED
JACARANDAS	JACTATIONS	JANIZARIAN	JAVELINING	JEOPARDIES
JACKALLING	JACTITATION	JANIZARIES	JAWBATIONS	JEOPARDING
JACKANAPES	JACTITATIONS	JAPANISING	JAWBONINGS	JEOPARDISE
JACKANAPESES	JACULATING	JAPANIZING	JAWBREAKER	JEOPARDISED
JACKAROOED	JACULATION	JAPONAISERIE	JAWBREAKERS	JEOPARDISES
JACKAROOING	JACULATIONS	JAPONAISERIES	JAWBREAKING	JEOPARDISING
JACKASSERIES	JACULATORS	JARDINIERE	JAWBREAKINGLY	JEOPARDIZE
JACKASSERY	JACULATORY	JARDINIERES	JAWCRUSHER	JEOPARDIZED
JACKBOOTED	JADEDNESSES	JARGONEERS	JAWCRUSHERS	JEOPARDIZES
JACKBOOTING	JADISHNESS	JARGONELLE	JAYHAWKERS	JEOPARDIZING
JACKEROOED	JADISHNESSES	JARGONELLES	JAYWALKERS	JEOPARDOUS
JACKEROOING	JAGGEDNESS	JARGONISATION	JAYWALKING	JEOPARDOUSLY
JACKETLESS	JAGGEDNESSES	JARGONISATIONS	JAYWALKINGS	JEOPARDYING
JACKFISHES	JAGGHERIES	JARGONISED	JAZZINESSES	JEQUERITIES
JACKFRUITS	JAGHIRDARS	JARGONISES	JEALOUSHOOD	JEQUIRITIES
JACKHAMMER	JAGUARONDI	JARGONISING	JEALOUSHOODS	JERFALCONS
JACKHAMMERED	JAGUARONDIS	JARGONISTIC	JEALOUSIES	JERKINESSES
JACKHAMMERING	JAGUARUNDI	JARGONISTS	JEALOUSING	JERKINHEAD
JACKHAMMERS	JAGUARUNDIS	JARGONIZATION	JEALOUSNESS	JERKINHEADS
JACKKNIFED	JAILBREAKER	JARGONIZATIONS	JEALOUSNESSES	JERKWATERS
JACKKNIFES	JAILBREAKERS	JARGONIZED	JEISTIECOR	JERRYMANDER
JACKKNIFING	JAILBREAKING	JARGONIZES	JEISTIECORS	JERRYMANDERED
JACKKNIVES	JAILBREAKS	JARGONIZING	JEJUNENESS	JERRYMANDERING
JACKLIGHTED	JAILBROKEN	JARLSBERGS	JEJUNENESSES	JERRYMANDERS
JACKLIGHTING	JAILERESSES	JAROVISING	JEJUNITIES	JESSAMINES
JACKLIGHTS	JAILHOUSES	JAROVIZING	JEJUNOSTOMIES	JESSERANTS
JACKPLANES	JAILORESSES	JASMONATES	JEJUNOSTOMY	JESUITICAL
JACKPOTTED	JALOALLOFANE	JASPERISED	JELLIFICATION	JESUITICALLY
JACKPOTTING	JALOALLOFANES	JASPERISES	JELLIFICATIONS	JESUITISMS
JACKRABBIT	JAMAHIRIYA	JASPERISING	JELLIFYING	JESUITRIES
JACKRABBITS	JAMAHIRIYAS	JASPERIZED	JELLYBEANS	JETSTREAMS
JACKROLLED	JAMBALAYAS	JASPERIZES	JELLYFISHES	JETTATURAS

JETTINESSES
JETTISONABLE
JETTISONED
JETTISONING
JEWELFISHES
JEWELLERIES
JEWELWEEDS
JICKAJOGGED
JICKAJOGGING
JICKAJOGGINGS
JIGAJIGGED
JIGAJIGGING
JIGAJOGGED
JIGAJOGGING
JIGAMAREES
JIGGERMAST
JIGGERMASTS
JIGGUMBOBS
JIGJIGGING
JILLFLIRTS
JIMPNESSES
JIMSONWEED
JIMSONWEEDS
JINGOISTIC
JINGOISTICALLY
JINRICKSHA
JINRICKSHAS
JINRICKSHAW
JINRICKSHAWS
JINRIKISHA
JINRIKISHAS
JINRIKSHAS
JITTERBUGGED
JITTERBUGGING
JITTERBUGS
JITTERIEST
JITTERINESS
JITTERINESSES
JOBCENTRES
JOBERNOWLS
JOBHOLDERS
JOBLESSNESS
JOBLESSNESSES
JOBSEEKERS
JOBSWORTHS
JOCKEYISMS
JOCKEYSHIP

JOCKEYSHIPS
JOCKSTRAPS
JOCKTELEGS
JOCOSENESS
JOCOSENESSES
JOCOSERIOUS
JOCOSITIES
JOCULARITIES
JOCULARITY
JOCULATORS
JOCUNDITIES
JOCUNDNESS
JOCUNDNESSES
JOGTROTTED
JOGTROTTING
JOHANNESES
JOHNNYCAKE
JOHNNYCAKES
JOHNSONGRASS
JOHNSONGRASSES
JOINTEDNESS
JOINTEDNESSES
JOINTNESSES
JOINTRESSES
JOINTURESS
JOINTURESSES
JOINTURING
JOINTWEEDS
JOINTWORMS
JOKESMITHS
JOKINESSES
JOLIOTIUMS
JOLLEYINGS
JOLLIFICATION
JOLLIFICATIONS
JOLLIFYING
JOLLIMENTS
JOLLINESSES
JOLLYBOATS
JOLLYHEADS
JOLTERHEAD
JOLTERHEADS
JONNYCAKES
JOSEPHINITE
JOSEPHINITES
JOSTLEMENT
JOSTLEMENTS

JOUISANCES
JOURNALESE
JOURNALESES
JOURNALING
JOURNALISATION
JOURNALISATIONS
JOURNALISE
JOURNALISED
JOURNALISER
JOURNALISERS
JOURNALISES
JOURNALISING
JOURNALISM
JOURNALISMS
JOURNALIST
JOURNALISTIC
JOURNALISTS
JOURNALIZATION
JOURNALIZATIONS
JOURNALIZE
JOURNALIZED
JOURNALIZER
JOURNALIZERS
JOURNALIZES
JOURNALIZING
JOURNALLED
JOURNALLING
JOURNEYERS
JOURNEYING
JOURNEYMAN
JOURNEYMEN
JOURNEYWORK
JOURNEYWORKS
JOUYSAUNCE
JOUYSAUNCES
JOVIALITIES
JOVIALNESS
JOVIALNESSES
JOVIALTIES
JOVYSAUNCE
JOVYSAUNCES
JOWLINESSES
JOYFULLEST
JOYFULNESS
JOYFULNESSES
JOYLESSNESS
JOYLESSNESSES

JOYOUSNESS
JOYOUSNESSES
JOYPOPPERS
JOYPOPPING
JOYRIDINGS
JUBILANCES
JUBILANCIES
JUBILANTLY
JUBILARIAN
JUBILARIANS
JUBILATING
JUBILATION
JUBILATIONS
JUDGEMENTAL
JUDGEMENTALLY
JUDGEMENTS
JUDGESHIPS
JUDGMATICAL
JUDGMATICALLY
JUDGMENTAL
JUDGMENTALLY
JUDICATION
JUDICATIONS
JUDICATIVE
JUDICATORIAL
JUDICATORIES
JUDICATORS
JUDICATORY
JUDICATURE
JUDICATURES
JUDICIALLY
JUDICIARIES
JUDICIARILY
JUDICIOUSLY
JUDICIOUSNESS
JUDICIOUSNESSES
JUGGERNAUT
JUGGERNAUTS
JUGGLERIES
JUGGLINGLY
JUGLANDACEOUS
JUGULATING
JUGULATION
JUGULATIONS
JUICEHEADS
JUICINESSES
JULIENNING

JUMBLINGLY
JUMBOISING
JUMBOIZING
JUMHOURIYA
JUMHOURIYAS
JUMPINESSES
JUNCACEOUS
JUNCTIONAL
JUNEATINGS
JUNGLEGYMS
JUNGLELIKE
JUNIORATES
JUNIORITIES
JUNKETEERED
JUNKETEERING
JUNKETEERS
JUNKETINGS
JUNKETTERS
JUNKETTING
JUNKINESSES
JURIDICALLY
JURISCONSULT
JURISCONSULTS
JURISDICTION
JURISDICTIONAL
JURISDICTIONS
JURISDICTIVE
JURISPRUDENCE
JURISPRUDENCES
JURISPRUDENT
JURISPRUDENTIAL
JURISPRUDENTS
JURISTICAL
JURISTICALLY
JUSTICESHIP
JUSTICESHIPS
JUSTICIABILITY
JUSTICIABLE
JUSTICIALISM
JUSTICIALISMS
JUSTICIARIES
JUSTICIARS
JUSTICIARSHIP
JUSTICIARSHIPS
JUSTICIARY
JUSTIFIABILITY
JUSTIFIABLE

J

JUSTIFIABLENESS
JUSTIFIABLY
JUSTIFICATION
JUSTIFICATIONS
JUSTIFICATIVE

JUSTIFICATOR
JUSTIFICATORS
JUSTIFICATORY
JUSTIFIERS
JUSTIFYING

JUSTNESSES
JUVENESCENCE
JUVENESCENCES
JUVENESCENT
JUVENILELY

JUVENILENESS
JUVENILENESSES
JUVENILITIES
JUVENILITY
JUXTAPOSED

JUXTAPOSES
JUXTAPOSING
JUXTAPOSITION
JUXTAPOSITIONAL
JUXTAPOSITIONS

J

K

KABALISTIC	KALLIKREINS	KARYOKINETIC	KAZATSKIES	KERATINIZES
KABARAGOYA	KALLITYPES	KARYOLOGIC	KAZILLIONS	KERATINIZING
KABARAGOYAS	KALSOMINED	KARYOLOGICAL	KEELHALING	KERATINOPHILIC
KABBALISMS	KALSOMINES	KARYOLOGIES	KEELHAULED	KERATINOUS
KABBALISTIC	KALSOMINING	KARYOLOGIST	KEELHAULING	KERATITIDES
KABBALISTS	KAMELAUKION	KARYOLOGISTS	KEELHAULINGS	KERATITISES
KABELJOUWS	KAMELAUKIONS	KARYOLYMPH	KEELIVINES	KERATOGENOUS
KACHUMBERS	KAMERADING	KARYOLYMPHS	KEELYVINES	KERATOMATA
KADAITCHAS	KANAMYCINS	KARYOLYSES	KEENNESSES	KERATOMETER
KAFFEEKLATSCH	KANGAROOED	KARYOLYSIS	KEEPERLESS	KERATOMETERS
KAFFEEKLATSCHES	KANGAROOING	KARYOLYTIC	KEEPERSHIP	KERATOPHYRE
KAFFIRBOOM	KANTIKOYED	KARYOMAPPING	KEEPERSHIPS	KERATOPHYRES
KAFFIRBOOMS	KANTIKOYING	KARYOMAPPINGS	KEESHONDEN	KERATOPLASTIC
KAHIKATEAS	KAOLINISED	KARYOPLASM	KEFUFFLING	KERATOPLASTIES
KAHIKATOAS	KAOLINISES	KARYOPLASMIC	KEKERENGUS	KERATOPLASTY
KAIKAWAKAS	KAOLINISING	KARYOPLASMS	KELPFISHES	KERATOTOMIES
KAIKOMAKOS	KAOLINITES	KARYOSOMES	KELYPHITIC	KERATOTOMY
KAILYAIRDS	KAOLINITIC	KARYOTYPED	KENNELLING	KERAUNOGRAPH
KAINOGENESES	KAOLINIZED	KARYOTYPES	KENNETTING	KERAUNOGRAPHS
KAINOGENESIS	KAOLINIZES	KARYOTYPIC	KENOGENESES	KERBSTONES
KAINOGENETIC	KAOLINIZING	KARYOTYPICAL	KENOGENESIS	KERCHIEFED
KAIROMONES	KAOLINOSES	KARYOTYPICALLY	KENOGENETIC	KERCHIEFING
KAISERDOMS	KAOLINOSIS	KARYOTYPING	KENOGENETICALLY	KERCHIEVES
KAISERISMS	KAPELLMEISTER	KATABOLICALLY	KENOPHOBIA	KERFUFFLED
KAISERSHIP	KAPELLMEISTERS	KATABOLISM	KENOPHOBIAS	KERFUFFLES
KAISERSHIPS	KARABINERS	KATABOLISMS	KENOTICIST	KERFUFFLING
KAKISTOCRACIES	KARANGAING	KATABOTHRON	KENOTICISTS	KERMESITES
KAKISTOCRACY	KARATEISTS	KATABOTHRONS	KENSPECKLE	KERNELLING
KALAMKARIS	KARMICALLY	KATADROMOUS	KENTLEDGES	KERNICTERUS
KALANCHOES	KARSTIFICATION	KATATHERMOMETER	KERATECTOMIES	KERNICTERUSES
KALASHNIKOV	KARSTIFICATIONS	KATAVOTHRON	KERATECTOMY	KERNMANTEL
KALASHNIKOVS	KARSTIFIED	KATAVOTHRONS	KERATINISATION	KERPLUNKED
KALEIDOPHONE	KARSTIFIES	KATHAKALIS	KERATINISATIONS	KERPLUNKING
KALEIDOPHONES	KARSTIFYING	KATHAREVOUSA	KERATINISE	KERSANTITE
KALEIDOSCOPE	KARUHIRUHI	KATHAREVOUSAS	KERATINISED	KERSANTITES
KALEIDOSCOPES	KARUHIRUHIS	KATHAROMETER	KERATINISES	KERSEYMERE
KALEIDOSCOPIC	KARYOGAMIC	KATHAROMETERS	KERATINISING	KERSEYMERES
KALENDARED	KARYOGAMIES	KATZENJAMMER	KERATINIZATION	KERYGMATIC
KALENDARING	KARYOGRAMS	KATZENJAMMERS	KERATINIZATIONS	KETOGENESES
KALIPHATES	KARYOKINESES	KAWANATANGA	KERATINIZE	KETOGENESIS
KALLIKREIN	KARYOKINESIS	KAWANATANGAS	KERATINIZED	KETONAEMIA

KETONAEMIAS	KIBBUTZNIK	KILOGRAMME	KINEMATOGRAPHS	KINGFISHERS
KETONEMIAS	KIBBUTZNIKS	KILOGRAMMES	KINEMATOGRAPHY	KINGFISHES
KETONURIAS	KICKABOUTS	KILOHERTZES	KINESCOPED	KINGLIHOOD
KETOSTEROID	KICKAROUND	KILOJOULES	KINESCOPES	KINGLIHOODS
KETOSTEROIDS	KICKAROUNDS	KILOLITERS	KINESCOPING	KINGLINESS
KETTLEDRUM	KICKBOARDS	KILOLITRES	KINESIATRIC	KINGLINESSES
KETTLEDRUMMER	KICKBOXERS	KILOMETERS	KINESIATRICS	KINGMAKERS
KETTLEDRUMMERS	KICKBOXING	KILOMETRES	KINESIOLOGIES	KINGSNAKES
KETTLEDRUMS	KICKBOXINGS	KILOMETRIC	KINESIOLOGIST	KINKINESSES
KETTLEFULS	KICKFLIPPED	KILOMETRICAL	KINESIOLOGISTS	KINNIKINIC
KETTLESTITCH	KICKFLIPPING	KILOPARSEC	KINESIOLOGY	KINNIKINICK
KETTLESTITCHES	KICKSHAWSES	KILOPARSECS	KINESIPATH	KINNIKINICKS
KEYBOARDED	KICKSORTER	KILOPASCAL	KINESIPATHIC	KINNIKINICS
KEYBOARDER	KICKSORTERS	KILOPASCALS	KINESIPATHIES	KINNIKINNICK
KEYBOARDERS	KICKSTANDS	KILOTONNES	KINESIPATHIST	KINNIKINNICKS
KEYBOARDING	KICKSTARTED	KIMBERLITE	KINESIPATHISTS	KINTLEDGES
KEYBOARDINGS	KICKSTARTING	KIMBERLITES	KINESIPATHS	KIRBIGRIPS
KEYBOARDIST	KICKSTARTS	KINAESTHESES	KINESIPATHY	KIRKYAIRDS
KEYBOARDISTS	KIDDIEWINK	KINAESTHESIA	KINESITHERAPIES	KIRSCHWASSER
KEYBUTTONS	KIDDIEWINKIE	KINAESTHESIAS	KINESITHERAPY	KIRSCHWASSERS
KEYLOGGERS	KIDDIEWINKIES	KINAESTHESIS	KINESTHESES	KISSAGRAMS
KEYLOGGING	KIDDIEWINKS	KINAESTHETIC	KINESTHESIA	KISSOGRAMS
KEYLOGGINGS	KIDDISHNESS	KINDERGARTEN	KINESTHESIAS	KISSPEPTIN
KEYPRESSES	KIDDISHNESSES	KINDERGARTENER	KINESTHESIS	KISSPEPTINS
KEYPUNCHED	KIDDYWINKS	KINDERGARTENERS	KINESTHETIC	KITCHENALIA
KEYPUNCHER	KIDNAPINGS	KINDERGARTENS	KINESTHETICALLY	KITCHENALIAS
KEYPUNCHERS	KIDNAPPEES	KINDERGARTNER	KINETHEODOLITE	KITCHENDOM
KEYPUNCHES	KIDNAPPERS	KINDERGARTNERS	KINETHEODOLITES	KITCHENDOMS
KEYPUNCHING	KIDNAPPING	KINDERSPIEL	KINETICALLY	KITCHENERS
KEYSTONING	KIDNAPPINGS	KINDERSPIELS	KINETICIST	KITCHENETS
KEYSTROKED	KIDNEYLIKE	KINDHEARTED	KINETICISTS	KITCHENETTE
KEYSTROKES	KIDOLOGIES	KINDHEARTEDLY	KINETOCHORE	KITCHENETTES
KEYSTROKING	KIDOLOGIST	KINDHEARTEDNESS	KINETOCHORES	KITCHENING
KEYSTROKINGS	KIDOLOGISTS	KINDLESSLY	KINETOGRAPH	KITCHENMAID
KEYWORKERS	KIESELGUHR	KINDLINESS	KINETOGRAPHS	KITCHENMAIDS
KHALIFATES	KIESELGUHRS	KINDLINESSES	KINETONUCLEI	KITCHENWARE
KHANSAMAHS	KIESELGURS	KINDNESSES	KINETONUCLEUS	KITCHENWARES
KHEDIVATES	KIESERITES	KINDREDNESS	KINETONUCLEUSES	KITEBOARDS
KHEDIVIATE	KILDERKINS	KINDREDNESSES	KINETOPLAST	KITESURFER
KHEDIVIATES	KILLIFISHES	KINDREDSHIP	KINETOPLASTS	KITESURFERS
KHIDMUTGAR	KILLIKINICK	KINDREDSHIPS	KINETOSCOPE	KITESURFING
KHIDMUTGARS	KILLIKINICKS	KINEMATICAL	KINETOSCOPES	KITESURFINGS
KHITMUTGAR	KILOCALORIE	KINEMATICALLY	KINETOSOME	KITSCHIEST
KHITMUTGARS	KILOCALORIES	KINEMATICS	KINETOSOMES	KITSCHIFIED
KHUSKHUSES	KILOCURIES	KINEMATOGRAPH	KINGCRAFTS	KITSCHIFIES
KIBBITZERS	KILOCYCLES	KINEMATOGRAPHER	KINGDOMLESS	KITSCHIFYING
KIBBITZING	KILOGAUSSES	KINEMATOGRAPHIC	KINGFISHER	KITSCHNESS

K

KITSCHNESSES
KITTENISHLY
KITTENISHNESS
KITTENISHNESSES
KITTIWAKES
KIWIFRUITS
KIWISPORTS
KLANGFARBE
KLANGFARBES
KLEBSIELLA
KLEBSIELLAS
KLEINHUISIE
KLEINHUISIES
KLENDUSITIES
KLENDUSITY
KLEPHTISMS
KLEPTOCRACIES
KLEPTOCRACY
KLEPTOCRATIC
KLEPTOMANIA
KLEPTOMANIAC
KLEPTOMANIACS
KLEPTOMANIAS
KLETTERSCHUH
KLETTERSCHUHE
KLINOSTATS
KLIPSPRINGER
KLIPSPRINGERS
KLONDIKERS
KLONDIKING
KLONDYKERS
KLONDYKING
KLOOCHMANS
KLOOTCHMAN
KLOOTCHMANS
KLOOTCHMEN
KLUTZINESS
KLUTZINESSES
KNACKERIES

KNACKERING
KNACKINESS
KNACKINESSES
KNACKWURST
KNACKWURSTS
KNAGGINESS
KNAGGINESSES
KNAPSACKED
KNAVESHIPS
KNAVISHNESS
KNAVISHNESSES
KNEECAPPED
KNEECAPPING
KNEECAPPINGS
KNEEPIECES
KNEVELLING
KNICKERBOCKER
KNICKERBOCKERS
KNICKKNACK
KNICKKNACKS
KNICKPOINT
KNICKPOINTS
KNIFEPOINT
KNIFEPOINTS
KNIFERESTS
KNIGHTAGES
KNIGHTHEAD
KNIGHTHEADS
KNIGHTHOOD
KNIGHTHOODS
KNIGHTLESS
KNIGHTLIER
KNIGHTLIEST
KNIGHTLINESS
KNIGHTLINESSES
KNIPHOFIAS
KNOBBINESS
KNOBBINESSES
KNOBBLIEST

KNOBKERRIE
KNOBKERRIES
KNOBSTICKS
KNOCKABOUT
KNOCKABOUTS
KNOCKBACKS
KNOCKDOWNS
KNOCKWURST
KNOCKWURSTS
KNOTGRASSES
KNOTTINESS
KNOTTINESSES
KNOWABLENESS
KNOWABLENESSES
KNOWINGEST
KNOWINGNESS
KNOWINGNESSES
KNOWLEDGABILITY
KNOWLEDGABLE
KNOWLEDGABLY
KNOWLEDGEABLE
KNOWLEDGEABLY
KNOWLEDGED
KNOWLEDGES
KNOWLEDGING
KNUBBLIEST
KNUCKLEBALL
KNUCKLEBALLER
KNUCKLEBALLERS
KNUCKLEBALLS
KNUCKLEBONE
KNUCKLEBONES
KNUCKLEDUSTER
KNUCKLEDUSTERS
KNUCKLEHEAD
KNUCKLEHEADED
KNUCKLEHEADS
KNUCKLIEST
KOEKSISTER

KOEKSISTERS
KOHLRABIES
KOHUTUHUTU
KOHUTUHUTUS
KOLINSKIES
KOLKHOZNIK
KOLKHOZNIKI
KOLKHOZNIKS
KOMONDOROCK
KOMONDOROK
KONIMETERS
KONIOLOGIES
KONISCOPES
KOOKABURRA
KOOKABURRAS
KOOKINESSES
KOTAHITANGA
KOTAHITANGAS
KOTTABOSES
KOTUKUTUKU
KOTUKUTUKUS
KOULIBIACA
KOULIBIACAS
KOURBASHED
KOURBASHES
KOURBASHING
KOUSKOUSES
KOWHAIWHAI
KOWHAIWHAIS
KRAKOWIAKS
KREASOTING
KREMLINOLOGIES
KREMLINOLOGIST
KREMLINOLOGISTS
KREMLINOLOGY
KREOSOTING
KRIEGSPIEL
KRIEGSPIELS
KRIEGSSPIEL

KRIEGSSPIELS
KROMESKIES
KRUGERRAND
KRUGERRANDS
KRUMMHORNS
KRYOMETERS
KRYPTONITE
KRYPTONITES
KUMARAHOUS
KUMMERBUND
KUMMERBUNDS
KUNDALINIS
KURBASHING
KURCHATOVIUM
KURCHATOVIUMS
KURDAITCHA
KURDAITCHAS
KURFUFFLED
KURFUFFLES
KURFUFFLING
KURRAJONGS
KURTOSISES
KVETCHIEST
KVETCHINESS
KVETCHINESSES
KWASHIORKOR
KWASHIORKORS
KYANISATION
KYANISATIONS
KYANIZATION
KYANIZATIONS
KYMOGRAPHIC
KYMOGRAPHIES
KYMOGRAPHS
KYMOGRAPHY

K

L

LABANOTATION	LABOUREDNESSES	LACHRYMARY	LACRYMATORY	LADYFINGERS
LABANOTATIONS	LABOURINGLY	LACHRYMATION	LACTALBUMIN	LADYFISHES
LABDACISMS	LABOURISMS	LACHRYMATIONS	LACTALBUMINS	LADYLIKENESS
LABEFACTATION	LABOURISTS	LACHRYMATOR	LACTARIANS	LADYLIKENESSES
LABEFACTATIONS	LABOURITES	LACHRYMATORIES	LACTATIONAL	LADYNESSES
LABEFACTION	LABOURSAVING	LACHRYMATORS	LACTATIONALLY	LAEOTROPIC
LABEFACTIONS	LABOURSOME	LACHRYMATORY	LACTATIONS	LAEVIGATED
LABELLABLE	LABRADOODLE	LACHRYMOSE	LACTESCENCE	LAEVIGATES
LABELLINGS	LABRADOODLES	LACHRYMOSELY	LACTESCENCES	LAEVIGATING
LABELLISTS	LABRADORESCENT	LACHRYMOSITIES	LACTESCENT	LAEVOGYRATE
LABELMATES	LABRADORITE	LACHRYMOSITY	LACTIFEROUS	LAEVOROTARY
LABIALISATION	LABRADORITES	LACINESSES	LACTIFEROUSNESS	LAEVOROTATION
LABIALISATIONS	LABYRINTHAL	LACINIATED	LACTIFLUOUS	LAEVOROTATIONS
LABIALISED	LABYRINTHIAN	LACINIATION	LACTIVISMS	LAEVOROTATORY
LABIALISES	LABYRINTHIC	LACINIATIONS	LACTIVISTS	LAEVULOSES
LABIALISING	LABYRINTHICAL	LACKADAISICAL	LACTOBACILLI	LAGENIFORM
LABIALISMS	LABYRINTHICALLY	LACKADAISICALLY	LACTOBACILLUS	LAGERPHONE
LABIALITIES	LABYRINTHINE	LACKADAISY	LACTOFLAVIN	LAGERPHONES
LABIALIZATION	LABYRINTHITIS	LACKLUSTER	LACTOFLAVINS	LAGGARDNESS
LABIALIZATIONS	LABYRINTHITISES	LACKLUSTERS	LACTOGENIC	LAGGARDNESSES
LABIALIZED	LABYRINTHODONT	LACKLUSTRE	LACTOGLOBULIN	LAGNIAPPES
LABIALIZES	LABYRINTHODONTS	LACKLUSTRES	LACTOGLOBULINS	LAGOMORPHIC
LABIALIZING	LABYRINTHS	LACONICALLY	LACTOMETER	LAGOMORPHOUS
LABILITIES	LACCOLITES	LACONICISM	LACTOMETERS	LAGOMORPHS
LABIODENTAL	LACCOLITHIC	LACONICISMS	LACTOPROTEIN	LAICISATION
LABIODENTALS	LACCOLITHS	LACQUERERS	LACTOPROTEINS	LAICISATIONS
LABIONASAL	LACCOLITIC	LACQUERING	LACTOSCOPE	LAICIZATION
LABIONASALS	LACEMAKERS	LACQUERINGS	LACTOSCOPES	LAICIZATIONS
LABIOVELAR	LACEMAKING	LACQUERWARE	LACTOSURIA	LAIRDLIEST
LABIOVELARS	LACEMAKINGS	LACQUERWARES	LACTOSURIAS	LAIRDSHIPS
LABORATORIES	LACERABILITIES	LACQUERWORK	LACTOVEGETARIAN	LAKEFRONTS
LABORATORY	LACERABILITY	LACQUERWORKS	LACUNOSITIES	LAKESHORES
LABOREDNESS	LACERATING	LACQUEYING	LACUNOSITY	LALAPALOOZA
LABOREDNESSES	LACERATION	LACRIMARIES	LACUSTRINE	LALAPALOOZAS
LABORINGLY	LACERATIONS	LACRIMATION	LADDERLIKE	LALLAPALOOZA
LABORIOUSLY	LACERATIVE	LACRIMATIONS	LADDERPROOF	LALLAPALOOZAS
LABORIOUSNESS	LACERTIANS	LACRIMATOR	LADDISHNESS	LALLATIONS
LABORIOUSNESSES	LACERTILIAN	LACRIMATORS	LADDISHNESSES	LALLYGAGGED
LABORSAVING	LACERTILIANS	LACRIMATORY	LADIESWEAR	LALLYGAGGING
LABOUREDLY	LACHRYMALS	LACRYMATOR	LADIESWEARS	LAMASERAIS
LABOUREDNESS	LACHRYMARIES	LACRYMATORS	LADYFINGER	LAMASERIES

LAMBASTING	LAMINARIZES	LANCINATED	LANDMASSES	LANGUISHES
LAMBDACISM	LAMINARIZING	LANCINATES	LANDMINING	LANGUISHING
LAMBDACISMS	LAMINATING	LANCINATING	LANDMININGS	LANGUISHINGLY
LAMBDOIDAL	LAMINATION	LANCINATION	LANDOWNERS	LANGUISHINGS
LAMBENCIES	LAMINATIONS	LANCINATIONS	LANDOWNERSHIP	LANGUISHMENT
LAMBITIVES	LAMINATORS	LANDAMMANN	LANDOWNERSHIPS	LANGUISHMENTS
LAMBREQUIN	LAMINECTOMIES	LANDAMMANNS	LANDOWNING	LANGUOROUS
LAMBREQUINS	LAMINECTOMY	LANDAMMANS	LANDOWNINGS	LANGUOROUSLY
LAMBRUSCOS	LAMINGTONS	LANDAULETS	LANDSCAPED	LANGUOROUSNESS
LAMBSWOOLS	LAMINITISES	LANDAULETTE	LANDSCAPER	LANIFEROUS
LAMEBRAINED	LAMMERGEIER	LANDAULETTES	LANDSCAPERS	LANIGEROUS
LAMEBRAINS	LAMMERGEIERS	LANDBOARDING	LANDSCAPES	LANKINESSES
LAMELLARLY	LAMMERGEYER	LANDBOARDINGS	LANDSCAPING	LANKNESSES
LAMELLATED	LAMMERGEYERS	LANDBOARDS	LANDSCAPINGS	LANOSITIES
LAMELLATELY	LAMPADARIES	LANDDAMNED	LANDSCAPIST	LANSQUENET
LAMELLATION	LAMPADEDROMIES	LANDDAMNES	LANDSCAPISTS	LANSQUENETS
LAMELLATIONS	LAMPADEDROMY	LANDDAMNING	LANDSHARKS	LANTERLOOS
LAMELLIBRANCH	LAMPADEPHORIA	LANDDROSES	LANDSKIPPED	LANTERNING
LAMELLIBRANCHS	LAMPADEPHORIAS	LANDDROSTS	LANDSKIPPING	LANTERNIST
LAMELLICORN	LAMPADISTS	LANDFILLED	LANDSKNECHT	LANTERNISTS
LAMELLICORNS	LAMPADOMANCIES	LANDFILLING	LANDSKNECHTS	LANTHANIDE
LAMELLIFORM	LAMPADOMANCY	LANDFILLINGS	LANDSLIDDEN	LANTHANIDES
LAMELLIROSTRAL	LAMPBLACKED	LANDFORCES	LANDSLIDES	LANTHANONS
LAMELLIROSTRATE	LAMPBLACKING	LANDGRAVATE	LANDSLIDING	LANTHANUMS
LAMELLOSITIES	LAMPBLACKS	LANDGRAVATES	LANDWAITER	LANUGINOSE
LAMELLOSITY	LAMPHOLDER	LANDGRAVES	LANDWAITERS	LANUGINOUS
LAMENESSES	LAMPHOLDERS	LANDGRAVIATE	LANDWASHES	LANUGINOUSNESS
LAMENTABLE	LAMPLIGHTER	LANDGRAVIATES	LANGBEINITE	LANZKNECHT
LAMENTABLENESS	LAMPLIGHTERS	LANDGRAVINE	LANGBEINITES	LANZKNECHTS
LAMENTABLY	LAMPLIGHTS	LANDGRAVINES	LANGLAUFER	LAODICEANS
LAMENTATION	LAMPOONERIES	LANDHOLDER	LANGLAUFERS	LAPAROSCOPE
LAMENTATIONS	LAMPOONERS	LANDHOLDERS	LANGOSTINO	LAPAROSCOPES
LAMENTEDLY	LAMPOONERY	LANDHOLDING	LANGOSTINOS	LAPAROSCOPIC
LAMENTINGLY	LAMPOONING	LANDHOLDINGS	LANGOUSTES	LAPAROSCOPIES
LAMENTINGS	LAMPOONIST	LANDLADIES	LANGOUSTINE	LAPAROSCOPIST
LAMESTREAM	LAMPOONISTS	LANDLESSNESS	LANGOUSTINES	LAPAROSCOPISTS
LAMESTREAMS	LAMPROPHYRE	LANDLESSNESSES	LANGRIDGES	LAPAROSCOPY
LAMINARIAN	LAMPROPHYRES	LANDLOCKED	LANGSPIELS	LAPAROTOMIES
LAMINARIANS	LAMPROPHYRIC	LANDLOPERS	LANGUAGELESS	LAPAROTOMY
LAMINARIAS	LAMPSHADES	LANDLORDISM	LANGUAGING	LAPIDARIAN
LAMINARINS	LAMPSHELLS	LANDLORDISMS	LANGUESCENT	LAPIDARIES
LAMINARISE	LAMPSTANDS	LANDLUBBER	LANGUETTES	LAPIDARIST
LAMINARISED	LANCEJACKS	LANDLUBBERLY	LANGUIDNESS	LAPIDARISTS
LAMINARISES	LANCEOLATE	LANDLUBBERS	LANGUIDNESSES	LAPIDATING
LAMINARISING	LANCEOLATED	LANDLUBBING	LANGUISHED	LAPIDATION
LAMINARIZE	LANCEOLATELY	LANDMARKED	LANGUISHER	LAPIDATIONS
LAMINARIZED	LANCEWOODS	LANDMARKING	LANGUISHERS	LAPIDESCENCE

LAPIDESCENCES	LARYNGOLOGISTS	LATERBORNS	LATTERMATH	LAURUSTINES
LAPIDESCENT	LARYNGOLOGY	LATERIGRADE	LATTERMATHS	LAURUSTINUS
LAPIDICOLOUS	LARYNGOPHONIES	LATERISATION	LATTERMOST	LAURUSTINUSES
LAPIDIFICATION	LARYNGOPHONY	LATERISATIONS	LATTICEWORK	LAURVIKITE
LAPIDIFICATIONS	LARYNGOSCOPE	LATERISING	LATTICEWORKS	LAURVIKITES
LAPIDIFIED	LARYNGOSCOPES	LATERITIOUS	LATTICINGS	LAVALIERES
LAPIDIFIES	LARYNGOSCOPIC	LATERIZATION	LATTICINIO	LAVALLIERE
LAPIDIFYING	LARYNGOSCOPIES	LATERIZATIONS	LAUDABILITIES	LAVALLIERES
LAPILLIFORM	LARYNGOSCOPIST	LATERIZING	LAUDABILITY	LAVATIONAL
LAPSTRAKES	LARYNGOSCOPISTS	LATEROVERSION	LAUDABLENESS	LAVATORIAL
LAPSTREAKS	LARYNGOSCOPY	LATEROVERSIONS	LAUDABLENESSES	LAVATORIES
LARCENISTS	LARYNGOSPASM	LATESCENCE	LAUDATIONS	LAVENDERED
LARCENOUSLY	LARYNGOSPASMS	LATESCENCES	LAUDATIVES	LAVENDERING
LARDACEOUS	LARYNGOTOMIES	LATHERIEST	LAUDATORIES	LAVERBREAD
LARDALITES	LARYNGOTOMY	LATHYRISMS	LAUGHABLENESS	LAVERBREADS
LARGEHEARTED	LASCIVIOUS	LATHYRITIC	LAUGHABLENESSES	LAVEROCKED
LARGEMOUTH	LASCIVIOUSLY	LATHYRUSES	LAUGHINGLY	LAVEROCKING
LARGEMOUTHS	LASCIVIOUSNESS	LATICIFEROUS	LAUGHINGSTOCK	LAVISHMENT
LARGENESSES	LASERDISCS	LATICIFERS	LAUGHINGSTOCKS	LAVISHMENTS
LARGHETTOS	LASERDISKS	LATICLAVES	LAUGHLINES	LAVISHNESS
LARGITIONS	LASERWORTS	LATIFUNDIA	LAUGHWORTHY	LAVISHNESSES
LARKINESSES	LASSITUDES	LATIFUNDIO	LAUNCEGAYE	LAVOLTAING
LARKISHNESS	LASTINGNESS	LATIFUNDIOS	LAUNCEGAYES	LAWBREAKER
LARKISHNESSES	LASTINGNESSES	LATIFUNDIUM	LAUNCHINGS	LAWBREAKERS
LARRIKINISM	LATCHSTRING	LATIMERIAS	LAUNCHPADS	LAWBREAKING
LARRIKINISMS	LATCHSTRINGS	LATINISATION	LAUNDERERS	LAWBREAKINGS
LARVICIDAL	LATECOMERS	LATINISATIONS	LAUNDERETTE	LAWFULNESS
LARVICIDES	LATEENRIGGED	LATINISING	LAUNDERETTES	LAWFULNESSES
LARVIKITES	LATENESSES	LATINITIES	LAUNDERING	LAWGIVINGS
LARVIPAROUS	LATENSIFICATION	LATINIZATION	LAUNDERINGS	LAWLESSNESS
LARYNGEALLY	LATERALING	LATINIZATIONS	LAUNDRESSES	LAWLESSNESSES
LARYNGEALS	LATERALISATION	LATINIZING	LAUNDRETTE	LAWMAKINGS
LARYNGECTOMEE	LATERALISATIONS	LATIROSTRAL	LAUNDRETTES	LAWMONGERS
LARYNGECTOMEES	LATERALISE	LATIROSTRATE	LAUNDRYMAN	LAWNMOWERS
LARYNGECTOMIES	LATERALISED	LATISEPTATE	LAUNDRYMEN	LAWRENCIUM
LARYNGECTOMISED	LATERALISES	LATITANCIES	LAUNDRYWOMAN	LAWRENCIUMS
LARYNGECTOMIZED	LATERALISING	LATITATION	LAUNDRYWOMEN	LAWYERINGS
LARYNGECTOMY	LATERALITIES	LATITATIONS	LAURACEOUS	LAWYERLIKE
LARYNGISMUS	LATERALITY	LATITUDINAL	LAURDALITE	LAXATIVENESS
LARYNGISMUSES	LATERALIZATION	LATITUDINALLY	LAURDALITES	LAXATIVENESSES
LARYNGITIC	LATERALIZATIONS	LATITUDINARIAN	LAUREATESHIP	LAYBACKING
LARYNGITIS	LATERALIZE	LATITUDINARIANS	LAUREATESHIPS	LAYMANISED
LARYNGITISES	LATERALIZED	LATITUDINOUS	LAUREATING	LAYMANISES
LARYNGOLOGIC	LATERALIZES	LATRATIONS	LAUREATION	LAYMANISING
LARYNGOLOGICAL	LATERALIZING	LATROCINIA	LAUREATIONS	LAYMANIZED
LARYNGOLOGIES	LATERALLED	LATROCINIES	LAURELLING	LAYMANIZES
LARYNGOLOGIST	LATERALLING	LATROCINIUM	LAURUSTINE	LAYMANIZING

LAYPERSONS
LAZARETTES
LAZARETTOS
LAZINESSES
LEACHABILITIES
LEACHABILITY
LEADENNESS
LEADENNESSES
LEADERBOARD
LEADERBOARDS
LEADERENES
LEADERETTE
LEADERETTES
LEADERLESS
LEADERSHIP
LEADERSHIPS
LEADPLANTS
LEADSCREWS
LEAFCUTTER
LEAFHOPPER
LEAFHOPPERS
LEAFINESSES
LEAFLESSNESS
LEAFLESSNESSES
LEAFLETEER
LEAFLETEERS
LEAFLETERS
LEAFLETING
LEAFLETTED
LEAFLETTING
LEAFSTALKS
LEAGUERING
LEAKINESSES
LEANNESSES
LEAPFROGGED
LEAPFROGGING
LEARINESSES
LEARNABILITIES
LEARNABILITY
LEARNEDNESS
LEARNEDNESSES
LEASEBACKS
LEASEHOLDER
LEASEHOLDERS
LEASEHOLDS
LEASTAWAYS
LEATHERBACK

LEATHERBACKS
LEATHERBOUND
LEATHERETTE
LEATHERETTES
LEATHERGOODS
LEATHERHEAD
LEATHERHEADS
LEATHERIER
LEATHERIEST
LEATHERINESS
LEATHERINESSES
LEATHERING
LEATHERINGS
LEATHERJACKET
LEATHERJACKETS
LEATHERLEAF
LEATHERLEAVES
LEATHERLIKE
LEATHERNECK
LEATHERNECKS
LEATHERWOOD
LEATHERWOODS
LEAVENINGS
LEBENSRAUM
LEBENSRAUMS
LECHEROUSLY
LECHEROUSNESS
LECHEROUSNESSES
LECITHINASE
LECITHINASES
LECTIONARIES
LECTIONARY
LECTISTERNIA
LECTISTERNIUM
LECTISTERNIUMS
LECTORATES
LECTORSHIP
LECTORSHIPS
LECTOTYPES
LECTRESSES
LECTURESHIP
LECTURESHIPS
LECYTHIDACEOUS
LEDERHOSEN
LEECHCRAFT
LEECHCRAFTS
LEERINESSES

LEETSPEAKS
LEFTWARDLY
LEGALISATION
LEGALISATIONS
LEGALISERS
LEGALISING
LEGALISTIC
LEGALISTICALLY
LEGALITIES
LEGALIZATION
LEGALIZATIONS
LEGALIZERS
LEGALIZING
LEGATARIES
LEGATESHIP
LEGATESHIPS
LEGATIONARY
LEGATISSIMO
LEGATORIAL
LEGENDARIES
LEGENDARILY
LEGENDISED
LEGENDISES
LEGENDISING
LEGENDISTS
LEGENDIZED
LEGENDIZES
LEGENDIZING
LEGENDRIES
LEGERDEMAIN
LEGERDEMAINIST
LEGERDEMAINISTS
LEGERDEMAINS
LEGERITIES
LEGGINESSES
LEGIBILITIES
LEGIBILITY
LEGIBLENESS
LEGIBLENESSES
LEGIONARIES
LEGIONELLA
LEGIONELLAE
LEGIONELLAS
LEGIONNAIRE
LEGIONNAIRES
LEGISLATED
LEGISLATES

LEGISLATING
LEGISLATION
LEGISLATIONS
LEGISLATIVE
LEGISLATIVELY
LEGISLATIVES
LEGISLATOR
LEGISLATORIAL
LEGISLATORS
LEGISLATORSHIP
LEGISLATORSHIPS
LEGISLATRESS
LEGISLATRESSES
LEGISLATURE
LEGISLATURES
LEGITIMACIES
LEGITIMACY
LEGITIMATE
LEGITIMATED
LEGITIMATELY
LEGITIMATENESS
LEGITIMATES
LEGITIMATING
LEGITIMATION
LEGITIMATIONS
LEGITIMATISE
LEGITIMATISED
LEGITIMATISES
LEGITIMATISING
LEGITIMATIZE
LEGITIMATIZED
LEGITIMATIZES
LEGITIMATIZING
LEGITIMATOR
LEGITIMATORS
LEGITIMISATION
LEGITIMISATIONS
LEGITIMISE
LEGITIMISED
LEGITIMISER
LEGITIMISERS
LEGITIMISES
LEGITIMISING
LEGITIMISM
LEGITIMISMS
LEGITIMIST
LEGITIMISTIC

LEGITIMISTS
LEGITIMIZATION
LEGITIMIZATIONS
LEGITIMIZE
LEGITIMIZED
LEGITIMIZER
LEGITIMIZERS
LEGITIMIZES
LEGITIMIZING
LEGLESSNESS
LEGLESSNESSES
LEGUMINOUS
LEGWARMERS
LEIOMYOMAS
LEIOMYOMATA
LEIOTRICHIES
LEIOTRICHOUS
LEIOTRICHY
LEISHMANIA
LEISHMANIAE
LEISHMANIAL
LEISHMANIAS
LEISHMANIASES
LEISHMANIASIS
LEISHMANIOSES
LEISHMANIOSIS
LEISTERING
LEISURABLE
LEISURABLY
LEISURELINESS
LEISURELINESSES
LEISUREWEAR
LEISUREWEARS
LEITMOTIFS
LEITMOTIVS
LEMMATISATION
LEMMATISATIONS
LEMMATISED
LEMMATISES
LEMMATISING
LEMMATIZATION
LEMMATIZATIONS
LEMMATIZED
LEMMATIZES
LEMMATIZING
LEMMINGLIKE
LEMNISCATE

LEMNISCATES
LEMONFISHES
LEMONGRASS
LEMONGRASSES
LEMONWOODS
LENGTHENED
LENGTHENER
LENGTHENERS
LENGTHENING
LENGTHIEST
LENGTHINESS
LENGTHINESSES
LENGTHSMAN
LENGTHSMEN
LENGTHWAYS
LENGTHWISE
LENIENCIES
LENITIVELY
LENOCINIUM
LENOCINIUMS
LENTAMENTE
LENTICELLATE
LENTICULAR
LENTICULARLY
LENTICULARS
LENTICULES
LENTIGINES
LENTIGINOSE
LENTIGINOUS
LENTISSIMO
LENTIVIRUS
LENTIVIRUSES
LEONTIASES
LEONTIASIS
LEONTOPODIUM
LEONTOPODIUMS
LEOPARDESS
LEOPARDESSES
LEOPARDSKIN
LEPIDODENDROID
LEPIDODENDROIDS
LEPIDOLITE
LEPIDOLITES
LEPIDOMELANE
LEPIDOMELANES
LEPIDOPTERA
LEPIDOPTERAN

LEPIDOPTERANS
LEPIDOPTERIST
LEPIDOPTERISTS
LEPIDOPTEROLOGY
LEPIDOPTERON
LEPIDOPTERONS
LEPIDOPTEROUS
LEPIDOSIREN
LEPIDOSIRENS
LEPRECHAUN
LEPRECHAUNISH
LEPRECHAUNS
LEPRECHAWN
LEPRECHAWNS
LEPROMATOUS
LEPROSARIA
LEPROSARIUM
LEPROSARIUMS
LEPROSERIE
LEPROSERIES
LEPROSITIES
LEPROUSNESS
LEPROUSNESSES
LEPTOCEPHALI
LEPTOCEPHALIC
LEPTOCEPHALOUS
LEPTOCEPHALUS
LEPTOCERCAL
LEPTODACTYL
LEPTODACTYLOUS
LEPTODACTYLS
LEPTOKURTIC
LEPTOPHOSES
LEPTOPHYLLOUS
LEPTORRHINE
LEPTOSOMATIC
LEPTOSOMES
LEPTOSOMIC
LEPTOSPIRAL
LEPTOSPIRE
LEPTOSPIRES
LEPTOSPIROSES
LEPTOSPIROSIS
LEPTOTENES
LESBIANISM
LESBIANISMS
LESPEDEZAS

LESSEESHIP
LESSEESHIPS
LESSENINGS
LESSONINGS
LETHALITIES
LETHARGICAL
LETHARGICALLY
LETHARGIED
LETHARGIES
LETHARGISE
LETHARGISED
LETHARGISES
LETHARGISING
LETHARGIZE
LETHARGIZED
LETHARGIZES
LETHARGIZING
LETHIFEROUS
LETROZOLES
LETTERBOXED
LETTERBOXES
LETTERBOXING
LETTERBOXINGS
LETTERFORM
LETTERFORMS
LETTERHEAD
LETTERHEADS
LETTERINGS
LETTERLESS
LETTERPRESS
LETTERPRESSES
LETTERSETS
LETTERSPACING
LETTERSPACINGS
LEUCAEMIAS
LEUCAEMOGEN
LEUCAEMOGENESES
LEUCAEMOGENESIS
LEUCAEMOGENIC
LEUCAEMOGENS
LEUCHAEMIA
LEUCHAEMIAS
LEUCITOHEDRA
LEUCITOHEDRON
LEUCITOHEDRONS
LEUCOBLAST
LEUCOBLASTS

LEUCOCIDIN
LEUCOCIDINS
LEUCOCRATIC
LEUCOCYTES
LEUCOCYTHAEMIA
LEUCOCYTHAEMIAS
LEUCOCYTIC
LEUCOCYTOLYSES
LEUCOCYTOLYSIS
LEUCOCYTOPENIA
LEUCOCYTOPENIAS
LEUCOCYTOSES
LEUCOCYTOSIS
LEUCOCYTOTIC
LEUCODEPLETED
LEUCODERMA
LEUCODERMAL
LEUCODERMAS
LEUCODERMIA
LEUCODERMIAS
LEUCODERMIC
LEUCOMAINE
LEUCOMAINES
LEUCOPENIA
LEUCOPENIAS
LEUCOPENIC
LEUCOPLAKIA
LEUCOPLAKIAS
LEUCOPLAKIC
LEUCOPLAST
LEUCOPLASTID
LEUCOPLASTIDS
LEUCOPLASTS
LEUCOPOIESES
LEUCOPOIESIS
LEUCOPOIETIC
LEUCORRHOEA
LEUCORRHOEAL
LEUCORRHOEAS
LEUCOTOMES
LEUCOTOMIES
LEUKAEMIAS
LEUKAEMOGEN
LEUKAEMOGENESES
LEUKAEMOGENESIS
LEUKAEMOGENIC
LEUKAEMOGENS

LEUKEMOGEN
LEUKEMOGENESES
LEUKEMOGENESIS
LEUKEMOGENIC
LEUKEMOGENS
LEUKOBLAST
LEUKOBLASTS
LEUKOCIDIN
LEUKOCIDINS
LEUKOCYTES
LEUKOCYTIC
LEUKOCYTOLYSES
LEUKOCYTOLYSIS
LEUKOCYTOPENIA
LEUKOCYTOPENIAS
LEUKOCYTOSES
LEUKOCYTOSIS
LEUKOCYTOTIC
LEUKODEPLETED
LEUKODERMA
LEUKODERMAL
LEUKODERMAS
LEUKODERMIC
LEUKODYSTROPHY
LEUKOPENIA
LEUKOPENIAS
LEUKOPENIC
LEUKOPLAKIA
LEUKOPLAKIAS
LEUKOPLAKIC
LEUKOPOIESES
LEUKOPOIESIS
LEUKOPOIETIC
LEUKORRHEA
LEUKORRHEAL
LEUKORRHEAS
LEUKOTOMES
LEUKOTOMIES
LEUKOTRIENE
LEUKOTRIENES
LEVANTINES
LEVELHEADED
LEVELHEADEDNESS
LEVELLINGS
LEVELNESSES
LEVERAGING
LEVIATHANS

L

LEVIGATING	LEXIGRAPHY	LIBERTARIAN	LICHTLYING	LIGAMENTARY
LEVIGATION	LEYLANDIIS	LIBERTARIANISM	LICITNESSES	LIGAMENTOUS
LEVIGATIONS	LHERZOLITE	LIBERTARIANISMS	LICKERISHLY	LIGATURING
LEVIGATORS	LHERZOLITES	LIBERTARIANS	LICKERISHNESS	LIGHTBULBS
LEVIRATICAL	LIABILITIES	LIBERTICIDAL	LICKERISHNESSES	LIGHTENERS
LEVIRATION	LIABLENESS	LIBERTICIDE	LICKPENNIES	LIGHTENING
LEVIRATIONS	LIABLENESSES	LIBERTICIDES	LICKSPITTLE	LIGHTENINGS
LEVITATING	LIBATIONAL	LIBERTINAGE	LICKSPITTLES	LIGHTERAGE
LEVITATION	LIBATIONARY	LIBERTINAGES	LIDOCAINES	LIGHTERAGES
LEVITATIONAL	LIBECCHIOS	LIBERTINES	LIEBFRAUMILCH	LIGHTERING
LEVITATIONS	LIBELLANTS	LIBERTINISM	LIEBFRAUMILCHS	LIGHTERMAN
LEVITATORS	LIBELLINGS	LIBERTINISMS	LIENHOLDER	LIGHTERMEN
LEVITICALLY	LIBELLOUSLY	LIBIDINALLY	LIENHOLDERS	LIGHTFACED
LEVOROTARY	LIBERALISATION	LIBIDINIST	LIENTERIES	LIGHTFACES
LEVOROTATORY	LIBERALISATIONS	LIBIDINISTS	LIEUTENANCIES	LIGHTFASTNESS
LEWDNESSES	LIBERALISE	LIBIDINOSITIES	LIEUTENANCY	LIGHTFASTNESSES
LEXICALISATION	LIBERALISED	LIBIDINOSITY	LIEUTENANT	LIGHTHEARTED
LEXICALISATIONS	LIBERALISER	LIBIDINOUS	LIEUTENANTRIES	LIGHTHEARTEDLY
LEXICALISE	LIBERALISERS	LIBIDINOUSLY	LIEUTENANTRY	LIGHTHOUSE
LEXICALISED	LIBERALISES	LIBIDINOUSNESS	LIEUTENANTS	LIGHTHOUSEMAN
LEXICALISES	LIBERALISING	LIBRAIRIES	LIEUTENANTSHIP	LIGHTHOUSEMEN
LEXICALISING	LIBERALISM	LIBRARIANS	LIEUTENANTSHIPS	LIGHTHOUSES
LEXICALITIES	LIBERALISMS	LIBRARIANSHIP	LIFEBLOODS	LIGHTLYING
LEXICALITY	LIBERALIST	LIBRARIANSHIPS	LIFEBOATMAN	LIGHTNESSES
LEXICALIZATION	LIBERALISTIC	LIBRATIONAL	LIFEBOATMEN	LIGHTNINGED
LEXICALIZATIONS	LIBERALISTS	LIBRATIONS	LIFEGUARDED	LIGHTNINGS
LEXICALIZE	LIBERALITIES	LIBRETTIST	LIFEGUARDING	LIGHTPLANE
LEXICALIZED	LIBERALITY	LIBRETTISTS	LIFEGUARDS	LIGHTPLANES
LEXICALIZES	LIBERALIZATION	LICENSABLE	LIFEHACKED	LIGHTPROOF
LEXICALIZING	LIBERALIZATIONS	LICENSURES	LIFEHACKER	LIGHTSHIPS
LEXICOGRAPHER	LIBERALIZE	LICENTIATE	LIFEHACKERS	LIGHTSOMELY
LEXICOGRAPHERS	LIBERALIZED	LICENTIATES	LIFEHACKING	LIGHTSOMENESS
LEXICOGRAPHIC	LIBERALIZER	LICENTIATESHIP	LIFELESSLY	LIGHTSOMENESSES
LEXICOGRAPHICAL	LIBERALIZERS	LICENTIATESHIPS	LIFELESSNESS	LIGHTTIGHT
LEXICOGRAPHIES	LIBERALIZES	LICENTIATION	LIFELESSNESSES	LIGHTWEIGHT
LEXICOGRAPHIST	LIBERALIZING	LICENTIATIONS	LIFELIKENESS	LIGHTWEIGHTS
LEXICOGRAPHISTS	LIBERALNESS	LICENTIOUS	LIFELIKENESSES	LIGHTWOODS
LEXICOGRAPHY	LIBERALNESSES	LICENTIOUSLY	LIFEMANSHIP	LIGNICOLOUS
LEXICOLOGICAL	LIBERATING	LICENTIOUSNESS	LIFEMANSHIPS	LIGNIFICATION
LEXICOLOGICALLY	LIBERATION	LICHANOSES	LIFESAVERS	LIGNIFICATIONS
LEXICOLOGIES	LIBERATIONISM	LICHENISMS	LIFESAVING	LIGNIFYING
LEXICOLOGIST	LIBERATIONISMS	LICHENISTS	LIFESAVINGS	LIGNIPERDOUS
LEXICOLOGISTS	LIBERATIONIST	LICHENOLOGICAL	LIFESTYLER	LIGNIVOROUS
LEXICOLOGY	LIBERATIONISTS	LICHENOLOGIES	LIFESTYLERS	LIGNOCAINE
LEXIGRAPHIC	LIBERATIONS	LICHENOLOGIST	LIFESTYLES	LIGNOCAINES
LEXIGRAPHICAL	LIBERATORS	LICHENOLOGISTS	LIFEWORLDS	LIGNOCELLULOSE
LEXIGRAPHIES	LIBERATORY	LICHENOLOGY	LIGAMENTAL	LIGNOCELLULOSES

LIGNOCELLULOSIC
LIGNOSULFONATE
LIGNOSULFONATES
LIGULIFLORAL
LIKABILITIES
LIKABILITY
LIKABLENESS
LIKABLENESSES
LIKEABILITIES
LIKEABILITY
LIKEABLENESS
LIKEABLENESSES
LIKELIHOOD
LIKELIHOODS
LIKELINESS
LIKELINESSES
LIKENESSES
LILIACEOUS
LILLIPUTIAN
LILLIPUTIANS
LILTINGNESS
LILTINGNESSES
LIMACIFORM
LIMACOLOGIES
LIMACOLOGIST
LIMACOLOGISTS
LIMACOLOGY
LIMBERNESS
LIMBERNESSES
LIMBURGITE
LIMBURGITES
LIMELIGHTED
LIMELIGHTER
LIMELIGHTERS
LIMELIGHTING
LIMELIGHTS
LIMERENCES
LIMESCALES
LIMESTONES
LIMEWASHES
LIMEWATERS
LIMICOLINE
LIMICOLOUS
LIMINESSES
LIMITABLENESS
LIMITABLENESSES
LIMITARIAN

LIMITARIANS
LIMITATION
LIMITATIONAL
LIMITATIONS
LIMITATIVE
LIMITEDNESS
LIMITEDNESSES
LIMITINGLY
LIMITLESSLY
LIMITLESSNESS
LIMITLESSNESSES
LIMITROPHE
LIMIVOROUS
LIMNOLOGIC
LIMNOLOGICAL
LIMNOLOGICALLY
LIMNOLOGIES
LIMNOLOGIST
LIMNOLOGISTS
LIMNOPHILOUS
LIMOUSINES
LIMPIDITIES
LIMPIDNESS
LIMPIDNESSES
LIMPNESSES
LINCOMYCIN
LINCOMYCINS
LINCRUSTAS
LINEALITIES
LINEAMENTAL
LINEAMENTS
LINEARISATION
LINEARISATIONS
LINEARISED
LINEARISES
LINEARISING
LINEARITIES
LINEARIZATION
LINEARIZATIONS
LINEARIZED
LINEARIZES
LINEARIZING
LINEATIONS
LINEBACKER
LINEBACKERS
LINEBACKING
LINEBACKINGS

LINEBREEDING
LINEBREEDINGS
LINECASTER
LINECASTERS
LINECASTING
LINECASTINGS
LINEOLATED
LINERBOARD
LINERBOARDS
LINGBERRIES
LINGERINGLY
LINGERINGS
LINGONBERRIES
LINGONBERRY
LINGUIFORM
LINGUISTER
LINGUISTERS
LINGUISTIC
LINGUISTICAL
LINGUISTICALLY
LINGUISTICIAN
LINGUISTICIANS
LINGUISTICS
LINGUISTRIES
LINGUISTRY
LINGULATED
LINISHINGS
LINKSLANDS
LINOLEATES
LINOTYPERS
LINOTYPING
LINTSTOCKS
LINTWHITES
LIONCELLES
LIONFISHES
LIONHEARTED
LIONHEARTEDNESS
LIONISATION
LIONISATIONS
LIONIZATION
LIONIZATIONS
LIPECTOMIES
LIPGLOSSES
LIPIDOPLAST
LIPIDOPLASTS
LIPOCHROME
LIPOCHROMES

LIPODYSTROPHIES
LIPODYSTROPHY
LIPOGENESES
LIPOGENESIS
LIPOGRAMMATIC
LIPOGRAMMATISM
LIPOGRAMMATISMS
LIPOGRAMMATIST
LIPOGRAMMATISTS
LIPOGRAPHIES
LIPOGRAPHY
LIPOMATOSES
LIPOMATOSIS
LIPOMATOUS
LIPOPHILIC
LIPOPLASTS
LIPOPROTEIN
LIPOPROTEINS
LIPOSCULPTURE
LIPOSCULPTURES
LIPOSUCKED
LIPOSUCKING
LIPOSUCTION
LIPOSUCTIONS
LIPOTROPIC
LIPOTROPIES
LIPOTROPIN
LIPOTROPINS
LIPPINESSES
LIPPITUDES
LIPREADERS
LIPREADING
LIPREADINGS
LIPSTICKED
LIPSTICKING
LIQUATIONS
LIQUEFACIENT
LIQUEFACIENTS
LIQUEFACTION
LIQUEFACTIONS
LIQUEFACTIVE
LIQUEFIABLE
LIQUEFIERS
LIQUEFYING
LIQUESCENCE
LIQUESCENCES
LIQUESCENCIES

LIQUESCENCY
LIQUESCENT
LIQUESCING
LIQUEURING
LIQUIDAMBAR
LIQUIDAMBARS
LIQUIDATED
LIQUIDATES
LIQUIDATING
LIQUIDATION
LIQUIDATIONISM
LIQUIDATIONISMS
LIQUIDATIONIST
LIQUIDATIONISTS
LIQUIDATIONS
LIQUIDATOR
LIQUIDATORS
LIQUIDISED
LIQUIDISER
LIQUIDISERS
LIQUIDISES
LIQUIDISING
LIQUIDITIES
LIQUIDIZED
LIQUIDIZER
LIQUIDIZERS
LIQUIDIZES
LIQUIDIZING
LIQUIDNESS
LIQUIDNESSES
LIQUIDUSES
LIQUIFACTION
LIQUIFACTIONS
LIQUIFACTIVE
LIQUIFIABLE
LIQUIFIERS
LIQUIFYING
LIQUORICES
LIQUORISHLY
LIQUORISHNESS
LIQUORISHNESSES
LIRIODENDRA
LIRIODENDRON
LIRIODENDRONS
LISSENCEPHALOUS
LISSOMENESS
LISSOMENESSES

L

LISSOMNESS
LISSOMNESSES
LISSOTRICHOUS
LISTENABILITIES
LISTENABILITY
LISTENABLE
LISTENERSHIP
LISTENERSHIPS
LISTENINGS
LISTERIOSES
LISTERIOSIS
LISTLESSLY
LISTLESSNESS
LISTLESSNESSES
LITENESSES
LITERACIES
LITERALISATION
LITERALISATIONS
LITERALISE
LITERALISED
LITERALISER
LITERALISERS
LITERALISES
LITERALISING
LITERALISM
LITERALISMS
LITERALIST
LITERALISTIC
LITERALISTS
LITERALITIES
LITERALITY
LITERALIZATION
LITERALIZATIONS
LITERALIZE
LITERALIZED
LITERALIZER
LITERALIZERS
LITERALIZES
LITERALIZING
LITERALNESS
LITERALNESSES
LITERARILY
LITERARINESS
LITERARINESSES
LITERARYISM
LITERARYISMS
LITERATELY

LITERATENESS
LITERATENESSES
LITERATION
LITERATIONS
LITERATORS
LITERATURE
LITERATURED
LITERATURES
LITEROSITIES
LITEROSITY
LITHENESSES
LITHESOMENESS
LITHESOMENESSES
LITHIFICATION
LITHIFICATIONS
LITHIFYING
LITHISTIDS
LITHOCHROMATIC
LITHOCHROMATICS
LITHOCHROMIES
LITHOCHROMY
LITHOCLAST
LITHOCLASTS
LITHOCYSTS
LITHODOMOUS
LITHOGENOUS
LITHOGLYPH
LITHOGLYPHS
LITHOGRAPH
LITHOGRAPHED
LITHOGRAPHER
LITHOGRAPHERS
LITHOGRAPHIC
LITHOGRAPHICAL
LITHOGRAPHIES
LITHOGRAPHING
LITHOGRAPHS
LITHOGRAPHY
LITHOLAPAXIES
LITHOLAPAXY
LITHOLATRIES
LITHOLATROUS
LITHOLATRY
LITHOLOGIC
LITHOLOGICAL
LITHOLOGICALLY
LITHOLOGIES

LITHOLOGIST
LITHOLOGISTS
LITHOMANCIES
LITHOMANCY
LITHOMARGE
LITHOMARGES
LITHOMETEOR
LITHOMETEORS
LITHONTHRYPTIC
LITHONTHRYPTICS
LITHONTRIPTIC
LITHONTRIPTICS
LITHONTRIPTIST
LITHONTRIPTISTS
LITHONTRIPTOR
LITHONTRIPTORS
LITHOPHAGOUS
LITHOPHANE
LITHOPHANES
LITHOPHILOUS
LITHOPHYSA
LITHOPHYSAE
LITHOPHYSE
LITHOPHYSES
LITHOPHYTE
LITHOPHYTES
LITHOPHYTIC
LITHOPONES
LITHOPRINT
LITHOPRINTS
LITHOSPERMUM
LITHOSPERMUMS
LITHOSPHERE
LITHOSPHERES
LITHOSPHERIC
LITHOSTATIC
LITHOTOMES
LITHOTOMIC
LITHOTOMICAL
LITHOTOMIES
LITHOTOMIST
LITHOTOMISTS
LITHOTOMOUS
LITHOTRIPSIES
LITHOTRIPSY
LITHOTRIPTER
LITHOTRIPTERS

LITHOTRIPTIC
LITHOTRIPTICS
LITHOTRIPTIST
LITHOTRIPTISTS
LITHOTRIPTOR
LITHOTRIPTORS
LITHOTRITE
LITHOTRITES
LITHOTRITIC
LITHOTRITICS
LITHOTRITIES
LITHOTRITISE
LITHOTRITISED
LITHOTRITISES
LITHOTRITISING
LITHOTRITIST
LITHOTRITISTS
LITHOTRITIZE
LITHOTRITIZED
LITHOTRITIZES
LITHOTRITIZING
LITHOTRITOR
LITHOTRITORS
LITHOTRITY
LITIGATING
LITIGATION
LITIGATIONS
LITIGATORS
LITIGIOUSLY
LITIGIOUSNESS
LITIGIOUSNESSES
LITTERATEUR
LITTERATEURS
LITTERBAGS
LITTERBUGS
LITTERMATE
LITTERMATES
LITTLENECK
LITTLENECKS
LITTLENESS
LITTLENESSES
LITTLEWORTH
LITURGICAL
LITURGICALLY
LITURGIOLOGIES
LITURGIOLOGIST
LITURGIOLOGISTS

LITURGIOLOGY
LITURGISMS
LITURGISTIC
LITURGISTS
LIVABILITIES
LIVABILITY
LIVABLENESS
LIVABLENESSES
LIVEABILITIES
LIVEABILITY
LIVEABLENESS
LIVEABLENESSES
LIVEBLOGGED
LIVEBLOGGER
LIVEBLOGGERS
LIVEBLOGGING
LIVEBLOGGINGS
LIVELIHEAD
LIVELIHEADS
LIVELIHOOD
LIVELIHOODS
LIVELINESS
LIVELINESSES
LIVENESSES
LIVERISHLY
LIVERISHNESS
LIVERISHNESSES
LIVERLEAVES
LIVERMORIUM
LIVERMORIUMS
LIVERWORTS
LIVERWURST
LIVERWURSTS
LIVESTOCKS
LIVESTREAM
LIVESTREAMED
LIVESTREAMING
LIVESTREAMS
LIVETRAPPED
LIVETRAPPING
LIVIDITIES
LIVIDNESSES
LIVINGNESS
LIVINGNESSES
LIVRAISONS
LIXIVIATED
LIXIVIATES

L

LIXIVIATING
LIXIVIATION
LIXIVIATIONS
LOADMASTER
LOADMASTERS
LOADSAMONEY
LOADSAMONEYS
LOADSAMONIES
LOADSPACES
LOADSTONES
LOAMINESSES
LOANSHIFTS
LOATHEDNESS
LOATHEDNESSES
LOATHFULNESS
LOATHFULNESSES
LOATHINGLY
LOATHLINESS
LOATHLINESSES
LOATHNESSES
LOATHSOMELY
LOATHSOMENESS
LOATHSOMENESSES
LOBECTOMIES
LOBLOLLIES
LOBOTOMIES
LOBOTOMISE
LOBOTOMISED
LOBOTOMISES
LOBOTOMISING
LOBOTOMIZE
LOBOTOMIZED
LOBOTOMIZES
LOBOTOMIZING
LOBSCOUSES
LOBSTERERS
LOBSTERING
LOBSTERINGS
LOBSTERLIKE
LOBSTERMAN
LOBSTERMEN
LOBTAILING
LOBULATION
LOBULATIONS
LOCALISABILITY
LOCALISABLE
LOCALISATION

LOCALISATIONS
LOCALISERS
LOCALISING
LOCALISTIC
LOCALITIES
LOCALIZABILITY
LOCALIZABLE
LOCALIZATION
LOCALIZATIONS
LOCALIZERS
LOCALIZING
LOCALNESSES
LOCATEABLE
LOCATIONAL
LOCATIONALLY
LOCKHOUSES
LOCKKEEPER
LOCKKEEPERS
LOCKMAKERS
LOCKSMITHERIES
LOCKSMITHERY
LOCKSMITHING
LOCKSMITHINGS
LOCKSMITHS
LOCKSTITCH
LOCKSTITCHED
LOCKSTITCHES
LOCKSTITCHING
LOCOMOBILE
LOCOMOBILES
LOCOMOBILITIES
LOCOMOBILITY
LOCOMOTING
LOCOMOTION
LOCOMOTIONS
LOCOMOTIVE
LOCOMOTIVELY
LOCOMOTIVENESS
LOCOMOTIVES
LOCOMOTIVITIES
LOCOMOTIVITY
LOCOMOTORS
LOCOMOTORY
LOCOPLANTS
LOCORESTIVE
LOCULAMENT
LOCULAMENTS

LOCULATION
LOCULATIONS
LOCULICIDAL
LOCUTIONARY
LOCUTORIES
LODESTONES
LODGEMENTS
LODGEPOLES
LOFTINESSES
LOGAGRAPHIA
LOGAGRAPHIAS
LOGANBERRIES
LOGANBERRY
LOGANIACEOUS
LOGAOEDICS
LOGARITHMIC
LOGARITHMICAL
LOGARITHMICALLY
LOGARITHMS
LOGGERHEAD
LOGGERHEADED
LOGGERHEADS
LOGICALITIES
LOGICALITY
LOGICALNESS
LOGICALNESSES
LOGICISING
LOGICIZING
LOGINESSES
LOGISTICAL
LOGISTICALLY
LOGISTICIAN
LOGISTICIANS
LOGJAMMING
LOGJAMMINGS
LOGNORMALITIES
LOGNORMALITY
LOGNORMALLY
LOGOCENTRISM
LOGOCENTRISMS
LOGODAEDALIC
LOGODAEDALIES
LOGODAEDALUS
LOGODAEDALUSES
LOGODAEDALY
LOGOGRAMMATIC
LOGOGRAPHER

LOGOGRAPHERS
LOGOGRAPHIC
LOGOGRAPHICAL
LOGOGRAPHICALLY
LOGOGRAPHIES
LOGOGRAPHS
LOGOGRAPHY
LOGOGRIPHIC
LOGOGRIPHS
LOGOMACHIES
LOGOMACHIST
LOGOMACHISTS
LOGOPAEDIC
LOGOPAEDICS
LOGOPEDICS
LOGOPHILES
LOGORRHEAS
LOGORRHEIC
LOGORRHOEA
LOGORRHOEAS
LOGOTHETES
LOGOTYPIES
LOGROLLERS
LOGROLLING
LOGROLLINGS
LOINCLOTHS
LOITERINGLY
LOITERINGS
LOLLAPALOOSA
LOLLAPALOOSAS
LOLLAPALOOZA
LOLLAPALOOZAS
LOLLYGAGGED
LOLLYGAGGING
LOMENTACEOUS
LONELINESS
LONELINESSES
LONENESSES
LONESOMELY
LONESOMENESS
LONESOMENESSES
LONGAEVOUS
LONGANIMITIES
LONGANIMITY
LONGANIMOUS
LONGBOARDS
LONGBOWMAN

LONGBOWMEN
LONGCLOTHS
LONGEVITIES
LONGHAIRED
LONGHEADED
LONGHEADEDNESS
LONGHOUSES
LONGICAUDATE
LONGICORNS
LONGINQUITIES
LONGINQUITY
LONGIPENNATE
LONGIROSTRAL
LONGITUDES
LONGITUDINAL
LONGITUDINALLY
LONGJUMPED
LONGJUMPING
LONGLEAVES
LONGLISTED
LONGLISTING
LONGNESSES
LONGPRIMER
LONGPRIMERS
LONGSHOREMAN
LONGSHOREMEN
LONGSHORING
LONGSHORINGS
LONGSIGHTED
LONGSIGHTEDNESS
LONGSOMELY
LONGSOMENESS
LONGSOMENESSES
LONGWEARING
LOOKALIKES
LOONINESSES
LOOPHOLING
LOOPINESSES
LOOSEBOXES
LOOSENESSES
LOOSENINGS
LOOSESTRIFE
LOOSESTRIFES
LOOYENWORK
LOOYENWORKS
LOPGRASSES
LOPHOBRANCH

L

LOPHOBRANCHIATE
LOPHOBRANCHS
LOPHOPHORATE
LOPHOPHORE
LOPHOPHORES
LOPSIDEDLY
LOPSIDEDNESS
LOPSIDEDNESSES
LOQUACIOUS
LOQUACIOUSLY
LOQUACIOUSNESS
LOQUACITIES
LORAZEPAMS
LORDLINESS
LORDLINESSES
LORDOLATRIES
LORDOLATRY
LORGNETTES
LORICATING
LORICATION
LORICATIONS
LORNNESSES
LOSABLENESS
LOSABLENESSES
LOSSMAKERS
LOSSMAKING
LOSTNESSES
LOTHNESSES
LOTUSLANDS
LOUDHAILER
LOUDHAILERS
LOUDMOUTHED
LOUDMOUTHS
LOUDNESSES
LOUDSPEAKER
LOUDSPEAKERS
LOUNDERING
LOUNDERINGS
LOUNGEWEAR
LOUNGEWEARS
LOUNGINGLY
LOUSEWORTS
LOUSINESSES
LOUTISHNESS
LOUTISHNESSES
LOVABILITIES
LOVABILITY

LOVABLENESS
LOVABLENESSES
LOVASTATIN
LOVASTATINS
LOVEABILITIES
LOVEABILITY
LOVEABLENESS
LOVEABLENESSES
LOVELESSLY
LOVELESSNESS
LOVELESSNESSES
LOVELIGHTS
LOVELIHEAD
LOVELIHEADS
LOVELINESS
LOVELINESSES
LOVELORNNESS
LOVELORNNESSES
LOVEMAKERS
LOVEMAKING
LOVEMAKINGS
LOVESICKNESS
LOVESICKNESSES
LOVESTRUCK
LOVEWORTHIES
LOVEWORTHY
LOVINGNESS
LOVINGNESSES
LOWBALLING
LOWBALLINGS
LOWBROWISM
LOWBROWISMS
LOWERCASED
LOWERCASES
LOWERCASING
LOWERCLASSMAN
LOWERCLASSMEN
LOWERINGLY
LOWLANDERS
LOWLIGHTED
LOWLIGHTING
LOWLIHEADS
LOWLINESSES
LOWSENINGS
LOXODROMES
LOXODROMIC
LOXODROMICAL

LOXODROMICALLY
LOXODROMICS
LOXODROMIES
LOYALNESSES
LUBBERLINESS
LUBBERLINESSES
LUBRICANTS
LUBRICATED
LUBRICATES
LUBRICATING
LUBRICATION
LUBRICATIONAL
LUBRICATIONS
LUBRICATIVE
LUBRICATOR
LUBRICATORS
LUBRICIOUS
LUBRICIOUSLY
LUBRICITIES
LUBRICOUSLY
LUBRITORIA
LUBRITORIUM
LUBRITORIUMS
LUCIDITIES
LUCIDNESSES
LUCIFERASE
LUCIFERASES
LUCIFERINS
LUCIFEROUS
LUCIFUGOUS
LUCKENBOOTH
LUCKENBOOTHS
LUCKENGOWAN
LUCKENGOWANS
LUCKINESSES
LUCKLESSLY
LUCKLESSNESS
LUCKLESSNESSES
LUCKPENNIES
LUCRATIVELY
LUCRATIVENESS
LUCRATIVENESSES
LUCTATIONS
LUCUBRATED
LUCUBRATES
LUCUBRATING
LUCUBRATION

LUCUBRATIONS
LUCUBRATOR
LUCUBRATORS
LUCULENTLY
LUDICROUSLY
LUDICROUSNESS
LUDICROUSNESSES
LUETICALLY
LUFTMENSCH
LUFTMENSCHEN
LUGUBRIOUS
LUGUBRIOUSLY
LUGUBRIOUSNESS
LUKEWARMISH
LUKEWARMLY
LUKEWARMNESS
LUKEWARMNESSES
LUKEWARMTH
LUKEWARMTHS
LULLABYING
LUMBAGINOUS
LUMBERINGLY
LUMBERINGNESS
LUMBERINGNESSES
LUMBERINGS
LUMBERJACK
LUMBERJACKET
LUMBERJACKETS
LUMBERJACKS
LUMBERSOME
LUMBERSOMENESS
LUMBERYARD
LUMBERYARDS
LUMBOSACRAL
LUMBRICALES
LUMBRICALIS
LUMBRICALISES
LUMBRICALS
LUMBRICIFORM
LUMBRICOID
LUMBRICUSES
LUMINAIRES
LUMINANCES
LUMINARIAS
LUMINARIES
LUMINARISM
LUMINARISMS

LUMINARIST
LUMINARISTS
LUMINATION
LUMINATIONS
LUMINESCED
LUMINESCENCE
LUMINESCENCES
LUMINESCENT
LUMINESCES
LUMINESCING
LUMINIFEROUS
LUMINOSITIES
LUMINOSITY
LUMINOUSLY
LUMINOUSNESS
LUMINOUSNESSES
LUMISTEROL
LUMISTEROLS
LUMPECTOMIES
LUMPECTOMY
LUMPFISHES
LUMPINESSES
LUMPISHNESS
LUMPISHNESSES
LUMPSUCKER
LUMPSUCKERS
LUNARNAUTS
LUNATICALLY
LUNCHBOXES
LUNCHBREAK
LUNCHBREAKS
LUNCHEONED
LUNCHEONETTE
LUNCHEONETTES
LUNCHEONING
LUNCHMEATS
LUNCHPAILS
LUNCHROOMS
LUNCHTIMES
LUNGFISHES
LUNINESSES
LUNKHEADED
LURIDNESSES
LUSCIOUSLY
LUSCIOUSNESS
LUSCIOUSNESSES
LUSHNESSES

LUSKISHNESS
LUSKISHNESSES
LUSTERLESS
LUSTERWARE
LUSTERWARES
LUSTFULNESS
LUSTFULNESSES
LUSTIHEADS
LUSTIHOODS
LUSTINESSES
LUSTRATING
LUSTRATION
LUSTRATIONS
LUSTRATIVE
LUSTRELESS
LUSTREWARE
LUSTREWARES
LUSTROUSLY
LUSTROUSNESS
LUSTROUSNESSES
LUTEINISATION
LUTEINISATIONS
LUTEINISED
LUTEINISES
LUTEINISING
LUTEINIZATION
LUTEINIZATIONS
LUTEINIZED
LUTEINIZES
LUTEINIZING
LUTEOTROPHIC
LUTEOTROPHIN
LUTEOTROPHINS

LUTEOTROPIC
LUTEOTROPIN
LUTEOTROPINS
LUTESTRING
LUTESTRINGS
LUVVIEDOMS
LUXULIANITE
LUXULIANITES
LUXULLIANITE
LUXULLIANITES
LUXULYANITE
LUXULYANITES
LUXURIANCE
LUXURIANCES
LUXURIANCIES
LUXURIANCY
LUXURIANTLY
LUXURIATED
LUXURIATES
LUXURIATING
LUXURIATION
LUXURIATIONS
LUXURIOUSLY
LUXURIOUSNESS
LUXURIOUSNESSES
LYCANTHROPE
LYCANTHROPES
LYCANTHROPIC
LYCANTHROPIES
LYCANTHROPIST
LYCANTHROPISTS
LYCANTHROPY
LYCHNOSCOPE

LYCHNOSCOPES
LYCOPODIUM
LYCOPODIUMS
LYMPHADENITIS
LYMPHADENITISES
LYMPHADENOPATHY
LYMPHANGIAL
LYMPHANGIOGRAM
LYMPHANGIOGRAMS
LYMPHANGITIC
LYMPHANGITIDES
LYMPHANGITIS
LYMPHANGITISES
LYMPHATICALLY
LYMPHATICS
LYMPHOADENOMA
LYMPHOADENOMAS
LYMPHOADENOMATA
LYMPHOBLAST
LYMPHOBLASTIC
LYMPHOBLASTS
LYMPHOCYTE
LYMPHOCYTES
LYMPHOCYTIC
LYMPHOCYTOPENIA
LYMPHOCYTOSES
LYMPHOCYTOSIS
LYMPHOCYTOTIC
LYMPHOGRAM
LYMPHOGRAMS
LYMPHOGRANULOMA
LYMPHOGRAPHIC
LYMPHOGRAPHIES

LYMPHOGRAPHY
LYMPHOKINE
LYMPHOKINES
LYMPHOMATA
LYMPHOMATOID
LYMPHOMATOSES
LYMPHOMATOSIS
LYMPHOMATOUS
LYMPHOPENIA
LYMPHOPENIAS
LYMPHOPOIESES
LYMPHOPOIESIS
LYMPHOPOIETIC
LYMPHOSARCOMA
LYMPHOSARCOMAS
LYMPHOSARCOMATA
LYMPHOTROPHIC
LYOPHILISATION
LYOPHILISATIONS
LYOPHILISE
LYOPHILISED
LYOPHILISER
LYOPHILISERS
LYOPHILISES
LYOPHILISING
LYOPHILIZATION
LYOPHILIZATIONS
LYOPHILIZE
LYOPHILIZED
LYOPHILIZER
LYOPHILIZERS
LYOPHILIZES
LYOPHILIZING

LYOSORPTION
LYOSORPTIONS
LYRICALNESS
LYRICALNESSES
LYRICISING
LYRICIZING
LYSERGIDES
LYSIGENETIC
LYSIGENOUS
LYSIMETERS
LYSIMETRIC
LYSOGENICITIES
LYSOGENICITY
LYSOGENIES
LYSOGENISATION
LYSOGENISATIONS
LYSOGENISE
LYSOGENISED
LYSOGENISES
LYSOGENISING
LYSOGENIZATION
LYSOGENIZATIONS
LYSOGENIZE
LYSOGENIZED
LYSOGENIZES
LYSOGENIZING
LYSOLECITHIN
LYSOLECITHINS
LYTHRACEOUS

L

M

MACABERESQUE
MACADAMIAS
MACADAMISATION
MACADAMISATIONS
MACADAMISE
MACADAMISED
MACADAMISER
MACADAMISERS
MACADAMISES
MACADAMISING
MACADAMIZATION
MACADAMIZATIONS
MACADAMIZE
MACADAMIZED
MACADAMIZER
MACADAMIZERS
MACADAMIZES
MACADAMIZING
MACARISING
MACARIZING
MACARONICALLY
MACARONICS
MACARONIES
MACCARONIES
MACCARONIS
MACCHERONCINI
MACCHERONCINIS
MACCHIATOS
MACEBEARER
MACEBEARERS
MACEDOINES
MACERANDUBA
MACERANDUBAS
MACERATERS
MACERATING
MACERATION
MACERATIONS
MACERATIVE
MACERATORS
MACHAIRODONT
MACHAIRODONTS

MACHIAVELIAN
MACHIAVELIANS
MACHIAVELLIAN
MACHIAVELLIANS
MACHICOLATE
MACHICOLATED
MACHICOLATES
MACHICOLATING
MACHICOLATION
MACHICOLATIONS
MACHINABILITIES
MACHINABILITY
MACHINABLE
MACHINATED
MACHINATES
MACHINATING
MACHINATION
MACHINATIONS
MACHINATOR
MACHINATORS
MACHINEABILITY
MACHINEABLE
MACHINEGUN
MACHINEGUNNED
MACHINEGUNNING
MACHINEGUNS
MACHINELESS
MACHINELIKE
MACHINEMAN
MACHINEMEN
MACHINERIES
MACHINIMAS
MACHININGS
MACHINISTS
MACHMETERS
MACHTPOLITIK
MACHTPOLITIKS
MACINTOSHES
MACKINTOSH
MACKINTOSHES
MACONOCHIE

MACONOCHIES
MACRENCEPHALIA
MACRENCEPHALIAS
MACRENCEPHALIES
MACRENCEPHALY
MACROAGGREGATE
MACROAGGREGATED
MACROAGGREGATES
MACROBIOTA
MACROBIOTE
MACROBIOTES
MACROBIOTIC
MACROBIOTICS
MACROCARPA
MACROCARPAS
MACROCEPHALIA
MACROCEPHALIAS
MACROCEPHALIC
MACROCEPHALIES
MACROCEPHALOUS
MACROCEPHALY
MACROCLIMATE
MACROCLIMATES
MACROCLIMATIC
MACROCODES
MACROCOPIES
MACROCOSMIC
MACROCOSMICALLY
MACROCOSMS
MACROCYCLE
MACROCYCLES
MACROCYCLIC
MACROCYSTS
MACROCYTES
MACROCYTIC
MACROCYTOSES
MACROCYTOSIS
MACRODACTYL
MACRODACTYLIC
MACRODACTYLIES
MACRODACTYLOUS

MACRODACTYLS
MACRODACTYLY
MACRODIAGONAL
MACRODIAGONALS
MACRODOMES
MACROECONOMIC
MACROECONOMICS
MACROEVOLUTION
MACROEVOLUTIONS
MACROFAUNA
MACROFAUNAE
MACROFAUNAS
MACROFLORA
MACROFLORAE
MACROFLORAS
MACROFOSSIL
MACROFOSSILS
MACROGAMETE
MACROGAMETES
MACROGLIAS
MACROGLOBULIN
MACROGLOBULINS
MACROGRAPH
MACROGRAPHIC
MACROGRAPHS
MACROLIDES
MACROLOGIES
MACROMARKETING
MACROMARKETINGS
MACROMERES
MACROMOLECULAR
MACROMOLECULE
MACROMOLECULES
MACROMOLES
MACROMUTATION
MACROMUTATIONS
MACRONUCLEAR
MACRONUCLEI
MACRONUCLEUS
MACRONUTRIENT
MACRONUTRIENTS

MACROPHAGE
MACROPHAGES
MACROPHAGIC
MACROPHAGOUS
MACROPHOTOGRAPH
MACROPHYLA
MACROPHYLUM
MACROPHYSICS
MACROPHYTE
MACROPHYTES
MACROPHYTIC
MACROPINACOID
MACROPINACOIDS
MACROPINAKOID
MACROPINAKOIDS
MACROPRISM
MACROPRISMS
MACROPSIAS
MACROPTEROUS
MACROSCALE
MACROSCALES
MACROSCOPIC
MACROSCOPICALLY
MACROSOCIOLOGY
MACROSPORANGIA
MACROSPORANGIUM
MACROSPORE
MACROSPORES
MACROSTRUCTURAL
MACROSTRUCTURE
MACROSTRUCTURES
MACROZAMIA
MACROZAMIAS
MACTATIONS
MACULATING
MACULATION
MACULATIONS
MACULATURE
MACULATURES
MADBRAINED
MADDENINGLY

MADDENINGNESS	MAGISTERIUM	MAGNETITIC	MAGNITUDES	MAINPERNOR
MADDENINGNESSES	MAGISTERIUMS	MAGNETIZABLE	MAGNITUDINOUS	MAINPERNORS
MADEFACTION	MAGISTRACIES	MAGNETIZATION	MAGNOLIACEOUS	MAINPRISED
MADEFACTIONS	MAGISTRACY	MAGNETIZATIONS	MAHARAJAHS	MAINPRISES
MADELEINES	MAGISTRALITIES	MAGNETIZED	MAHARANEES	MAINPRISING
MADEMOISELLE	MAGISTRALITY	MAGNETIZER	MAHARISHIS	MAINSHEETS
MADEMOISELLES	MAGISTRALLY	MAGNETIZERS	MAHATMAISM	MAINSPRING
MADERISATION	MAGISTRALS	MAGNETIZES	MAHATMAISMS	MAINSPRINGS
MADERISATIONS	MAGISTRAND	MAGNETIZING	MAHLSTICKS	MAINSTREAM
MADERISING	MAGISTRANDS	MAGNETOCHEMICAL	MAHOGANIES	MAINSTREAMED
MADERIZATION	MAGISTRATE	MAGNETOELECTRIC	MAIASAURAS	MAINSTREAMING
MADERIZATIONS	MAGISTRATES	MAGNETOGRAPH	MAIDENHAIR	MAINSTREAMINGS
MADERIZING	MAGISTRATESHIP	MAGNETOGRAPHS	MAIDENHAIRS	MAINSTREAMS
MADONNAISH	MAGISTRATESHIPS	MAGNETOMETER	MAIDENHEAD	MAINSTREETING
MADONNAWISE	MAGISTRATIC	MAGNETOMETERS	MAIDENHEADS	MAINSTREETINGS
MADRASSAHS	MAGISTRATICAL	MAGNETOMETRIC	MAIDENHOOD	MAINTAINABILITY
MADREPORAL	MAGISTRATICALLY	MAGNETOMETRIES	MAIDENHOODS	MAINTAINABLE
MADREPORES	MAGISTRATURE	MAGNETOMETRY	MAIDENLIKE	MAINTAINED
MADREPORIAN	MAGISTRATURES	MAGNETOMOTIVE	MAIDENLINESS	MAINTAINER
MADREPORIANS	MAGMATISMS	MAGNETOPAUSE	MAIDENLINESSES	MAINTAINERS
MADREPORIC	MAGNALIUMS	MAGNETOPAUSES	MAIDENWEED	MAINTAINING
MADREPORITE	MAGNANIMITIES	MAGNETOSPHERE	MAIDENWEEDS	MAINTENANCE
MADREPORITES	MAGNANIMITY	MAGNETOSPHERES	MAIDISHNESS	MAINTENANCED
MADREPORITIC	MAGNANIMOUS	MAGNETOSPHERIC	MAIDISHNESSES	MAINTENANCES
MADRIGALESQUE	MAGNANIMOUSLY	MAGNETOSTATIC	MAIDSERVANT	MAINTENANCING
MADRIGALIAN	MAGNANIMOUSNESS	MAGNETOSTATICS	MAIDSERVANTS	MAINTOPMAST
MADRIGALIST	MAGNATESHIP	MAGNETRONS	MAIEUTICAL	MAINTOPMASTS
MADRIGALISTS	MAGNATESHIPS	MAGNIFIABLE	MAILABILITIES	MAINTOPSAIL
MADRILENES	MAGNESITES	MAGNIFICAL	MAILABILITY	MAINTOPSAILS
MAELSTROMS	MAGNESIUMS	MAGNIFICALLY	MAILCOACHES	MAISONETTE
MAENADICALLY	MAGNESSTONE	MAGNIFICAT	MAILGRAMMED	MAISONETTES
MAENADISMS	MAGNESSTONES	MAGNIFICATION	MAILGRAMMING	MAISONNETTE
MAFFICKERS	MAGNETICAL	MAGNIFICATIONS	MAILMERGED	MAISONNETTES
MAFFICKING	MAGNETICALLY	MAGNIFICATS	MAILMERGES	MAISTERDOME
MAFFICKINGS	MAGNETICIAN	MAGNIFICENCE	MAILMERGING	MAISTERDOMES
MAGALOGUES	MAGNETICIANS	MAGNIFICENCES	MAILPOUCHES	MAISTERING
MAGAZINIST	MAGNETISABLE	MAGNIFICENT	MAILSHOTTED	MAISTRINGS
MAGAZINISTS	MAGNETISATION	MAGNIFICENTLY	MAILSHOTTING	MAJESTICAL
MAGDALENES	MAGNETISATIONS	MAGNIFICENTNESS	MAIMEDNESS	MAJESTICALLY
MAGGOTIEST	MAGNETISED	MAGNIFICOES	MAIMEDNESSES	MAJESTICALNESS
MAGGOTORIA	MAGNETISER	MAGNIFICOS	MAINBRACES	MAJESTICNESS
MAGGOTORIUM	MAGNETISERS	MAGNIFIERS	MAINFRAMES	MAJESTICNESSES
MAGIANISMS	MAGNETISES	MAGNIFYING	MAINLANDER	MAJOLICAWARE
MAGISTERIAL	MAGNETISING	MAGNILOQUENCE	MAINLANDERS	MAJOLICAWARES
MAGISTERIALLY	MAGNETISMS	MAGNILOQUENCES	MAINLINERS	MAJORDOMOS
MAGISTERIALNESS	MAGNETISTS	MAGNILOQUENT	MAINLINING	MAJORETTES
MAGISTERIES	MAGNETITES	MAGNILOQUENTLY	MAINLININGS	MAJORETTING

MAJORETTINGS

MAJORETTINGS
MAJORITAIRE
MAJORITAIRES
MAJORITARIAN
MAJORITARIANISM
MAJORITARIANS
MAJORITIES
MAJORSHIPS
MAJUSCULAR
MAJUSCULES
MAKEREADIES
MAKESHIFTS
MAKEWEIGHT
MAKEWEIGHTS
MAKUNOUCHI
MAKUNOUCHIS
MALABSORPTION
MALABSORPTIONS
MALACHITES
MALACOLOGICAL
MALACOLOGIES
MALACOLOGIST
MALACOLOGISTS
MALACOLOGY
MALACOPHILIES
MALACOPHILOUS
MALACOPHILY
MALACOPHYLLOUS
MALACOPTERYGIAN
MALACOSTRACAN
MALACOSTRACANS
MALACOSTRACOUS
MALADAPTATION
MALADAPTATIONS
MALADAPTED
MALADAPTIVE
MALADAPTIVELY
MALADDRESS
MALADDRESSES
MALADJUSTED
MALADJUSTIVE
MALADJUSTMENT
MALADJUSTMENTS
MALADMINISTER
MALADMINISTERED
MALADMINISTERS
MALADROITLY

MALADROITNESS
MALADROITNESSES
MALADROITS
MALAGUENAS
MALAGUETTA
MALAGUETTAS
MALAKATOONE
MALAKATOONES
MALAPERTLY
MALAPERTNESS
MALAPERTNESSES
MALAPPORTIONED
MALAPPROPRIATE
MALAPPROPRIATED
MALAPPROPRIATES
MALAPROPIAN
MALAPROPISM
MALAPROPISMS
MALAPROPIST
MALAPROPISTS
MALAPROPOS
MALARIOLOGIES
MALARIOLOGIST
MALARIOLOGISTS
MALARIOLOGY
MALASSIMILATION
MALATHIONS
MALAXATING
MALAXATION
MALAXATIONS
MALAXATORS
MALCONFORMATION
MALCONTENT
MALCONTENTED
MALCONTENTEDLY
MALCONTENTS
MALDEPLOYMENT
MALDEPLOYMENTS
MALDISTRIBUTION
MALEDICENT
MALEDICTED
MALEDICTING
MALEDICTION
MALEDICTIONS
MALEDICTIVE
MALEDICTORY
MALEFACTION

MALEFACTIONS
MALEFACTOR
MALEFACTORS
MALEFACTORY
MALEFACTRESS
MALEFACTRESSES
MALEFFECTS
MALEFICALLY
MALEFICENCE
MALEFICENCES
MALEFICENT
MALEFICIAL
MALENESSES
MALENGINES
MALENTENDU
MALENTENDUS
MALEVOLENCE
MALEVOLENCES
MALEVOLENT
MALEVOLENTLY
MALFEASANCE
MALFEASANCES
MALFEASANT
MALFEASANTS
MALFORMATION
MALFORMATIONS
MALFUNCTION
MALFUNCTIONED
MALFUNCTIONING
MALFUNCTIONINGS
MALFUNCTIONS
MALICIOUSLY
MALICIOUSNESS
MALICIOUSNESSES
MALIGNANCE
MALIGNANCES
MALIGNANCIES
MALIGNANCY
MALIGNANTLY
MALIGNANTS
MALIGNITIES
MALIGNMENT
MALIGNMENTS
MALIMPRINTED
MALIMPRINTING
MALIMPRINTINGS
MALINGERED

MALINGERER
MALINGERERS
MALINGERIES
MALINGERING
MALLANDERS
MALLEABILITIES
MALLEABILITY
MALLEABLENESS
MALLEABLENESSES
MALLEATING
MALLEATION
MALLEATIONS
MALLEIFORM
MALLEMAROKING
MALLEMAROKINGS
MALLEMUCKS
MALLENDERS
MALLEOLUSES
MALLOPHAGOUS
MALLOWPUFF
MALLOWPUFFS
MALMSTONES
MALNOURISHED
MALNUTRITION
MALNUTRITIONS
MALOCCLUDED
MALOCCLUSION
MALOCCLUSIONS
MALODOROUS
MALODOROUSLY
MALODOROUSNESS
MALOLACTIC
MALONYLUREA
MALONYLUREAS
MALPIGHIACEOUS
MALPIGHIAS
MALPOSITION
MALPOSITIONS
MALPRACTICE
MALPRACTICES
MALPRACTITIONER
MALPRESENTATION
MALTALENTS
MALTINESSES
MALTODEXTRIN
MALTODEXTRINS
MALTREATED

MALTREATER
MALTREATERS
MALTREATING
MALTREATMENT
MALTREATMENTS
MALVACEOUS
MALVERSATION
MALVERSATIONS
MALVOISIES
MAMAGUYING
MAMILLATED
MAMILLATION
MAMILLATIONS
MAMILLIFORM
MAMMALIANS
MAMMALIFEROUS
MAMMALITIES
MAMMALOGICAL
MAMMALOGIES
MAMMALOGIST
MAMMALOGISTS
MAMMAPLASTIES
MAMMAPLASTY
MAMMECTOMIES
MAMMECTOMY
MAMMETRIES
MAMMIFEROUS
MAMMILLARIA
MAMMILLARIAS
MAMMILLARY
MAMMILLATE
MAMMILLATED
MAMMILLATION
MAMMILLATIONS
MAMMILLIFORM
MAMMITIDES
MAMMOCKING
MAMMOGENIC
MAMMOGRAMS
MAMMOGRAPH
MAMMOGRAPHIC
MAMMOGRAPHIES
MAMMOGRAPHS
MAMMOGRAPHY
MAMMONISMS
MAMMONISTIC
MAMMONISTS

MAMMONITES MANDILIONS MANGULATING MANIPULATIVE MANSUETUDES
MAMMOPLASTIES MANDIOCCAS MANHANDLED MANIPULATIVELY MANTELLETTA
MAMMOPLASTY MANDOLINES MANHANDLES MANIPULATOR MANTELLETTAS
MANAGEABILITIES MANDOLINIST MANHANDLING MANIPULATORS MANTELPIECE
MANAGEABILITY MANDOLINISTS MANHATTANS MANIPULATORY MANTELPIECES
MANAGEABLE MANDRAGORA MANHUNTERS MANLINESSES MANTELSHELF
MANAGEABLENESS MANDRAGORAS MANIACALLY MANNEQUINS MANTELSHELVES
MANAGEABLY MANDUCABLE MANICOTTIS MANNERISMS MANTELTREE
MANAGEMENT MANDUCATED MANICURING MANNERISTIC MANTELTREES
MANAGEMENTAL MANDUCATES MANICURIST MANNERISTICAL MANTICALLY
MANAGEMENTS MANDUCATING MANICURISTS MANNERISTICALLY MANTICORAS
MANAGERESS MANDUCATION MANIFESTABLE MANNERISTS MANTICORES
MANAGERESSES MANDUCATIONS MANIFESTANT MANNERLESS MANTLETREE
MANAGERIAL MANDUCATORY MANIFESTANTS MANNERLESSNESS MANTLETREES
MANAGERIALISM MANDYLIONS MANIFESTATION MANNERLINESS MANTYHOSES
MANAGERIALISMS MANEUVERABILITY MANIFESTATIONAL MANNERLINESSES MANUBRIUMS
MANAGERIALIST MANEUVERABLE MANIFESTATIONS MANNIFEROUS MANUFACTORIES
MANAGERIALISTS MANEUVERED MANIFESTATIVE MANNISHNESS MANUFACTORY
MANAGERIALLY MANEUVERER MANIFESTED MANNISHNESSES MANUFACTURABLE
MANAGERSHIP MANEUVERERS MANIFESTER MANOEUVRABILITY MANUFACTURAL
MANAGERSHIPS MANEUVERING MANIFESTERS MANOEUVRABLE MANUFACTURE
MANCHESTER MANEUVERINGS MANIFESTIBLE MANOEUVRED MANUFACTURED
MANCHESTERS MANFULNESS MANIFESTING MANOEUVRER MANUFACTURER
MANCHINEEL MANFULNESSES MANIFESTLY MANOEUVRERS MANUFACTURERS
MANCHINEELS MANGABEIRA MANIFESTNESS MANOEUVRES MANUFACTURES
MANCIPATED MANGABEIRAS MANIFESTNESSES MANOEUVRING MANUFACTURING
MANCIPATES MANGALSUTRA MANIFESTOED MANOEUVRINGS MANUFACTURINGS
MANCIPATING MANGALSUTRAS MANIFESTOES MANOMETERS MANUMISSION
MANCIPATION MANGANATES MANIFESTOING MANOMETRIC MANUMISSIONS
MANCIPATIONS MANGANESES MANIFESTOS MANOMETRICAL MANUMITTED
MANCIPATORY MANGANESIAN MANIFOLDED MANOMETRICALLY MANUMITTER
MANDAMUSED MANGANIFEROUS MANIFOLDER MANOMETRIES MANUMITTERS
MANDAMUSES MANGANITES MANIFOLDERS MANORIALISM MANUMITTING
MANDAMUSING MANGELWURZEL MANIFOLDING MANORIALISMS MANURANCES
MANDARINATE MANGELWURZELS MANIFOLDLY MANOSCOPIES MANUSCRIPT
MANDARINATES MANGEMANGE MANIFOLDNESS MANRIKIGUSARI MANUSCRIPTS
MANDARINES MANGEMANGES MANIFOLDNESSES MANRIKIGUSARIS MANZANILLA
MANDARINIC MANGETOUTS MANIPULABILITY MANSCAPING MANZANILLAS
MANDARINISM MANGINESSES MANIPULABLE MANSCAPINGS MANZANITAS
MANDARINISMS MANGOLDWURZEL MANIPULARS MANSERVANT MAPMAKINGS
MANDATARIES MANGOLDWURZELS MANIPULATABLE MANSIONARIES MAPPEMONDS
MANDATORIES MANGOSTANS MANIPULATE MANSIONARY MAQUILADORA
MANDATORILY MANGOSTEEN MANIPULATED MANSLAUGHTER MAQUILADORAS
MANDIBULAR MANGOSTEENS MANIPULATES MANSLAUGHTERS MAQUILLAGE
MANDIBULATE MANGOUSTES MANIPULATING MANSLAYERS MAQUILLAGES
MANDIBULATED MANGULATED MANIPULATION MANSONRIES MAQUISARDS
MANDIBULATES MANGULATES MANIPULATIONS MANSUETUDE MARABUNTAS

M

MARANATHAS	MARESCHALS	MARICULTURISTS	MARLINESPIKES	MARROWFATS
MARASCHINO	MARGARINES	MARIGRAPHS	MARLINGSPIKE	MARROWLESS
MARASCHINOS	MARGARITAS	MARIHUANAS	MARLINGSPIKES	MARROWSKIED
MARASMUSES	MARGARITES	MARIJUANAS	MARLINSPIKE	MARROWSKIES
MARATHONER	MARGARITIC	MARIMBAPHONE	MARLINSPIKES	MARROWSKYING
MARATHONERS	MARGARITIFEROUS	MARIMBAPHONES	MARLSTONES	MARSEILLES
MARATHONING	MARGENTING	MARIMBISTS	MARMALADES	MARSHALCIES
MARATHONINGS	MARGHERITA	MARINADING	MARMALISED	MARSHALERS
MARAUDINGS	MARGHERITAS	MARINATING	MARMALISES	MARSHALING
MARBELISED	MARGINALIA	MARINATION	MARMALISING	MARSHALLED
MARBELISES	MARGINALISATION	MARINATIONS	MARMALIZED	MARSHALLER
MARBELISING	MARGINALISE	MARIONBERRIES	MARMALIZES	MARSHALLERS
MARBELIZED	MARGINALISED	MARIONBERRY	MARMALIZING	MARSHALLING
MARBELIZES	MARGINALISES	MARIONETTE	MARMARISED	MARSHALLINGS
MARBELIZING	MARGINALISING	MARIONETTES	MARMARISES	MARSHALSHIP
MARBLEISED	MARGINALISM	MARISCHALLED	MARMARISING	MARSHALSHIPS
MARBLEISES	MARGINALISMS	MARISCHALLING	MARMARIZED	MARSHBUCKS
MARBLEISING	MARGINALIST	MARISCHALS	MARMARIZES	MARSHELDER
MARBLEIZED	MARGINALISTS	MARIVAUDAGE	MARMARIZING	MARSHELDERS
MARBLEIZES	MARGINALITIES	MARIVAUDAGES	MARMAROSES	MARSHINESS
MARBLEIZING	MARGINALITY	MARKEDNESS	MARMAROSIS	MARSHINESSES
MARBLEWOOD	MARGINALIZATION	MARKEDNESSES	MARMELISED	MARSHLANDER
MARBLEWOODS	MARGINALIZE	MARKETABILITIES	MARMELISES	MARSHLANDERS
MARCANTANT	MARGINALIZED	MARKETABILITY	MARMELISING	MARSHLANDS
MARCANTANTS	MARGINALIZES	MARKETABLE	MARMELIZED	MARSHLOCKS
MARCASITES	MARGINALIZING	MARKETABLENESS	MARMELIZES	MARSHLOCKSES
MARCASITICAL	MARGINALLY	MARKETABLY	MARMELIZING	MARSHMALLOW
MARCATISSIMO	MARGINATED	MARKETEERS	MARMOREALLY	MARSHMALLOWS
MARCELLERS	MARGINATES	MARKETINGS	MAROONINGS	MARSHMALLOWY
MARCELLING	MARGINATING	MARKETISATION	MARPRELATE	MARSHWORTS
MARCESCENCE	MARGINATION	MARKETISATIONS	MARPRELATED	MARSIPOBRANCH
MARCESCENCES	MARGINATIONS	MARKETISED	MARPRELATES	MARSIPOBRANCHS
MARCESCENT	MARGRAVATE	MARKETISES	MARPRELATING	MARSQUAKES
MARCESCIBLE	MARGRAVATES	MARKETISING	MARQUESSATE	MARSUPIALIAN
MARCHANTIA	MARGRAVIAL	MARKETIZATION	MARQUESSATES	MARSUPIALIANS
MARCHANTIAS	MARGRAVIATE	MARKETIZATIONS	MARQUESSES	MARSUPIALS
MARCHIONESS	MARGRAVIATES	MARKETIZED	MARQUETERIE	MARSUPIANS
MARCHIONESSES	MARGRAVINE	MARKETIZES	MARQUETERIES	MARSUPIUMS
MARCHLANDS	MARGRAVINES	MARKETIZING	MARQUETRIES	MARTELLANDO
MARCHPANES	MARGUERITA	MARKETPLACE	MARQUISATE	MARTELLANDOS
MARCONIGRAM	MARGUERITAS	MARKETPLACES	MARQUISATES	MARTELLATO
MARCONIGRAMS	MARGUERITE	MARKSMANSHIP	MARQUISETTE	MARTELLATOS
MARCONIGRAPH	MARGUERITES	MARKSMANSHIPS	MARQUISETTES	MARTELLING
MARCONIGRAPHED	MARIALITES	MARKSWOMAN	MARRIAGEABILITY	MARTENSITE
MARCONIGRAPHING	MARICULTURE	MARKSWOMEN	MARRIAGEABLE	MARTENSITES
MARCONIGRAPHS	MARICULTURES	MARLACIOUS	MARROWBONE	MARTENSITIC
MARCONIING	MARICULTURIST	MARLINESPIKE	MARROWBONES	MARTENSITICALLY

MARTIALISM	MASCULINISED	MASSINESSES	MASTICATING	MATCHMAKERS
MARTIALISMS	MASCULINISES	MASSIVENESS	MASTICATION	MATCHMAKES
MARTIALIST	MASCULINISING	MASSIVENESSES	MASTICATIONS	MATCHMAKING
MARTIALISTS	MASCULINIST	MASSOTHERAPIES	MASTICATOR	MATCHMAKINGS
MARTIALNESS	MASCULINISTS	MASSOTHERAPIST	MASTICATORIES	MATCHMARKED
MARTIALNESSES	MASCULINITIES	MASSOTHERAPISTS	MASTICATORS	MATCHMARKING
MARTINETISH	MASCULINITY	MASSOTHERAPY	MASTICATORY	MATCHMARKS
MARTINETISM	MASCULINIZATION	MASSPRIEST	MASTIGOPHORAN	MATCHPLAYS
MARTINETISMS	MASCULINIZE	MASSPRIESTS	MASTIGOPHORANS	MATCHSTICK
MARTINGALE	MASCULINIZED	MASSYMORES	MASTIGOPHORE	MATCHSTICKS
MARTINGALES	MASCULINIZES	MASTECTOMIES	MASTIGOPHORES	MATCHWOODS
MARTINGALS	MASCULINIZING	MASTECTOMY	MASTIGOPHORIC	MATELASSES
MARTYRDOMS	MASCULISTS	MASTERATES	MASTIGOPHOROUS	MATELLASSE
MARTYRISATION	MASHGICHIM	MASTERCLASS	MASTITIDES	MATELLASSES
MARTYRISATIONS	MASKALLONGE	MASTERCLASSES	MASTITISES	MATELOTTES
MARTYRISED	MASKALLONGES	MASTERDOMS	MASTODONIC	MATERFAMILIAS
MARTYRISES	MASKALONGE	MASTERFULLY	MASTODONTIC	MATERFAMILIASES
MARTYRISING	MASKALONGES	MASTERFULNESS	MASTODONTS	MATERIALISATION
MARTYRIZATION	MASKANONGE	MASTERFULNESSES	MASTODYNIA	MATERIALISE
MARTYRIZATIONS	MASKANONGES	MASTERHOOD	MASTODYNIAS	MATERIALISED
MARTYRIZED	MASKINONGE	MASTERHOODS	MASTOIDECTOMIES	MATERIALISER
MARTYRIZES	MASKINONGES	MASTERINGS	MASTOIDECTOMY	MATERIALISERS
MARTYRIZING	MASKIROVKA	MASTERLESS	MASTOIDITIS	MATERIALISES
MARTYROLOGIC	MASKIROVKAS	MASTERLINESS	MASTOIDITISES	MATERIALISING
MARTYROLOGICAL	MASOCHISMS	MASTERLINESSES	MASTOPEXIES	MATERIALISM
MARTYROLOGIES	MASOCHISTIC	MASTERMIND	MASTURBATE	MATERIALISMS
MARTYROLOGIST	MASOCHISTICALLY	MASTERMINDED	MASTURBATED	MATERIALIST
MARTYROLOGISTS	MASOCHISTS	MASTERMINDING	MASTURBATES	MATERIALISTIC
MARTYROLOGY	MASONICALLY	MASTERMINDS	MASTURBATING	MATERIALISTICAL
MARVELLING	MASQUERADE	MASTERPIECE	MASTURBATION	MATERIALISTS
MARVELLOUS	MASQUERADED	MASTERPIECES	MASTURBATIONS	MATERIALITIES
MARVELLOUSLY	MASQUERADER	MASTERSHIP	MASTURBATOR	MATERIALITY
MARVELLOUSNESS	MASQUERADERS	MASTERSHIPS	MASTURBATORS	MATERIALIZATION
MARVELOUSLY	MASQUERADES	MASTERSINGER	MASTURBATORY	MATERIALIZE
MARVELOUSNESS	MASQUERADING	MASTERSINGERS	MATACHINAS	MATERIALIZED
MARVELOUSNESSES	MASSACRERS	MASTERSTROKE	MATAGOURIS	MATERIALIZER
MARZIPANNED	MASSACRING	MASTERSTROKES	MATCHBOARD	MATERIALIZERS
MARZIPANNING	MASSAGISTS	MASTERWORK	MATCHBOARDING	MATERIALIZES
MASCARAING	MASSARANDUBA	MASTERWORKS	MATCHBOARDINGS	MATERIALIZING
MASCARPONE	MASSARANDUBAS	MASTERWORT	MATCHBOARDS	MATERIALLY
MASCARPONES	MASSASAUGA	MASTERWORTS	MATCHBOOKS	MATERIALNESS
MASCULINELY	MASSASAUGAS	MASTHEADED	MATCHBOXES	MATERIALNESSES
MASCULINENESS	MASSERANDUBA	MASTHEADING	MATCHLESSLY	MATERNALISM
MASCULINENESSES	MASSERANDUBAS	MASTHOUSES	MATCHLESSNESS	MATERNALISMS
MASCULINES	MASSETERIC	MASTICABLE	MATCHLESSNESSES	MATERNALISTIC
MASCULINISATION	MASSIFICATION	MASTICATED	MATCHLOCKS	MATERNALLY
MASCULINISE	MASSIFICATIONS	MASTICATES	MATCHMAKER	MATERNITIES

M

MATEYNESSES
MATFELLONS
MATGRASSES
MATHEMATIC
MATHEMATICAL
MATHEMATICALLY
MATHEMATICIAN
MATHEMATICIANS
MATHEMATICISE
MATHEMATICISED
MATHEMATICISES
MATHEMATICISING
MATHEMATICISM
MATHEMATICISMS
MATHEMATICIZE
MATHEMATICIZED
MATHEMATICIZES
MATHEMATICIZING
MATHEMATICS
MATHEMATISATION
MATHEMATISE
MATHEMATISED
MATHEMATISES
MATHEMATISING
MATHEMATIZATION
MATHEMATIZE
MATHEMATIZED
MATHEMATIZES
MATHEMATIZING
MATINESSES
MATRESFAMILIAS
MATRIARCHAL
MATRIARCHALISM
MATRIARCHALISMS
MATRIARCHATE
MATRIARCHATES
MATRIARCHIC
MATRIARCHIES
MATRIARCHS
MATRIARCHY
MATRICIDAL
MATRICIDES
MATRICLINIC
MATRICLINOUS
MATRICULANT
MATRICULANTS
MATRICULAR

MATRICULAS
MATRICULATE
MATRICULATED
MATRICULATES
MATRICULATING
MATRICULATION
MATRICULATIONS
MATRICULATOR
MATRICULATORS
MATRICULATORY
MATRIFOCAL
MATRIFOCALITIES
MATRIFOCALITY
MATRILINEAL
MATRILINEALLY
MATRILINEAR
MATRILINIES
MATRILOCAL
MATRILOCALITIES
MATRILOCALITY
MATRILOCALLY
MATRIMONIAL
MATRIMONIALLY
MATRIMONIES
MATRIMONY
MATRIOSHKA
MATRIOSHKI
MATROCLINAL
MATROCLINIC
MATROCLINIES
MATROCLINOUS
MATROCLINY
MATRONAGES
MATRONHOOD
MATRONHOODS
MATRONISED
MATRONISES
MATRONISING
MATRONIZED
MATRONIZES
MATRONIZING
MATRONLINESS
MATRONLINESSES
MATRONSHIP
MATRONSHIPS
MATRONYMIC
MATRONYMICS
MATROYSHKA

MATROYSHKAS
MATRYOSHKA
MATRYOSHKI
MATSUTAKES
MATTAMORES
MATTERLESS
MATTIFYING
MATTRASSES
MATTRESSES
MATURATING
MATURATION
MATURATIONAL
MATURATIONS
MATURATIVE
MATURENESS
MATURENESSES
MATURITIES
MATUTINALLY
MAUDLINISM
MAUDLINISMS
MAUDLINNESS
MAUDLINNESSES
MAULSTICKS
MAUMETRIES
MAUNDERERS
MAUNDERING
MAUNDERINGS
MAUSOLEUMS
MAVERICKED
MAVERICKING
MAVOURNEEN
MAVOURNEENS
MAVOURNINS
MAWKISHNESS
MAWKISHNESSES
MAWMETRIES
MAXIDRESSES
MAXILLARIES
MAXILLIPED
MAXILLIPEDARY
MAXILLIPEDE
MAXILLIPEDES
MAXILLIPEDS
MAXILLOFACIAL
MAXILLULAE
MAXIMALIST
MAXIMALISTS

MAXIMAPHILIES
MAXIMAPHILY
MAXIMATION
MAXIMATIONS
MAXIMISATION
MAXIMISATIONS
MAXIMISERS
MAXIMISING
MAXIMIZATION
MAXIMIZATIONS
MAXIMIZERS
MAXIMIZING
MAYFLOWERS
MAYONNAISE
MAYONNAISES
MAYORALTIES
MAYORESSES
MAYORSHIPS
MAYSTERDOME
MAYSTERDOMES
MAZARINADE
MAZARINADES
MAZEDNESSES
MAZINESSES
MEADOWLAND
MEADOWLANDS
MEADOWLARK
MEADOWLARKS
MEADOWSWEET
MEADOWSWEETS
MEAGERNESS
MEAGERNESSES
MEAGRENESS
MEAGRENESSES
MEALINESSES
MEALYMOUTHED
MEANDERERS
MEANDERING
MEANDERINGLY
MEANINGFUL
MEANINGFULLY
MEANINGFULNESS
MEANINGLESS
MEANINGLESSLY
MEANINGLESSNESS
MEANNESSES
MEANWHILES

MEASLINESS
MEASLINESSES
MEASURABILITIES
MEASURABILITY
MEASURABLE
MEASURABLENESS
MEASURABLY
MEASUREDLY
MEASUREDNESS
MEASUREDNESSES
MEASURELESS
MEASURELESSLY
MEASURELESSNESS
MEASUREMENT
MEASUREMENTS
MEASURINGS
MEATINESSES
MEATLOAVES
MEATPACKER
MEATPACKERS
MEATPACKING
MEATPACKINGS
MEATSCREEN
MEATSCREENS
MEATSPACES
MECAMYLAMINE
MECAMYLAMINES
MECHANICAL
MECHANICALISM
MECHANICALISMS
MECHANICALLY
MECHANICALNESS
MECHANICALS
MECHANICIAN
MECHANICIANS
MECHANISABLE
MECHANISATION
MECHANISATIONS
MECHANISED
MECHANISER
MECHANISERS
MECHANISES
MECHANISING
MECHANISMS
MECHANISTIC
MECHANISTICALLY
MECHANISTS

M

MECHANIZABLE	MEDIATISED	MEDICOLEGAL	MEGADEATHS	MEGANEWTON
MECHANIZATION	MEDIATISES	MEDIEVALISM	MEGAFARADS	MEGANEWTONS
MECHANIZATIONS	MEDIATISING	MEDIEVALISMS	MEGAFAUNAE	MEGAPARSEC
MECHANIZED	MEDIATIZATION	MEDIEVALIST	MEGAFAUNAL	MEGAPARSECS
MECHANIZER	MEDIATIZATIONS	MEDIEVALISTIC	MEGAFAUNAS	MEGAPHONED
MECHANIZERS	MEDIATIZED	MEDIEVALISTS	MEGAFLORAE	MEGAPHONES
MECHANIZES	MEDIATIZES	MEDIEVALLY	MEGAFLORAS	MEGAPHONIC
MECHANIZING	MEDIATIZING	MEDIOCRACIES	MEGAGAMETE	MEGAPHONICALLY
MECHANOCHEMICAL	MEDIATORIAL	MEDIOCRACY	MEGAGAMETES	MEGAPHONING
MECHANOMORPHISM	MEDIATORIALLY	MEDIOCRITIES	MEGAGAMETOPHYTE	MEGAPHYLLS
MECHANORECEPTOR	MEDIATORSHIP	MEDIOCRITY	MEGAGAUSSES	MEGAPIXELS
MECHANOTHERAPY	MEDIATORSHIPS	MEDITATING	MEGAHERBIVORE	MEGAPLEXES
MECHATRONIC	MEDIATRESS	MEDITATION	MEGAHERBIVORES	MEGAPROJECT
MECHATRONICS	MEDIATRESSES	MEDITATIONS	MEGAHERTZES	MEGAPROJECTS
MECLIZINES	MEDIATRICES	MEDITATIVE	MEGAJOULES	MEGAQUAKES
MECONOPSES	MEDIATRIXES	MEDITATIVELY	MEGAKARYOCYTE	MEGASCOPES
MECONOPSIS	MEDICALISATION	MEDITATIVENESS	MEGAKARYOCYTES	MEGASCOPIC
MEDAILLONS	MEDICALISATIONS	MEDITATORS	MEGAKARYOCYTIC	MEGASCOPICALLY
MEDALLIONED	MEDICALISE	MEDITERRANEAN	MEGALITHIC	MEGASPORANGIA
MEDALLIONING	MEDICALISED	MEDIUMISTIC	MEGALITRES	MEGASPORANGIUM
MEDALLIONS	MEDICALISES	MEDIUMSHIP	MEGALOBLAST	MEGASPORES
MEDALLISTS	MEDICALISING	MEDIUMSHIPS	MEGALOBLASTIC	MEGASPORIC
MEDALPLAYS	MEDICALIZATION	MEDIVACING	MEGALOBLASTS	MEGASPOROPHYLL
MEDDLESOME	MEDICALIZATIONS	MEDIVACKED	MEGALOCARDIA	MEGASPOROPHYLLS
MEDDLESOMELY	MEDICALIZE	MEDIVACKING	MEGALOCARDIAS	MEGASTORES
MEDDLESOMENESS	MEDICALIZED	MEDRESSEHS	MEGALOCEPHALIC	MEGASTORMS
MEDDLINGLY	MEDICALIZES	MEDULLATED	MEGALOCEPHALIES	MEGASTRUCTURE
MEDEVACING	MEDICALIZING	MEDULLOBLASTOMA	MEGALOCEPHALOUS	MEGASTRUCTURES
MEDEVACKED	MEDICAMENT	MEDUSIFORM	MEGALOCEPHALY	MEGATECHNOLOGY
MEDEVACKING	MEDICAMENTAL	MEEKNESSES	MEGALODONS	MEGATHERES
MEDIAEVALISM	MEDICAMENTALLY	MEERSCHAUM	MEGALOMANIA	MEGATHERIAN
MEDIAEVALISMS	MEDICAMENTARY	MEERSCHAUMS	MEGALOMANIAC	MEGATHRUST
MEDIAEVALIST	MEDICAMENTED	MEETINGHOUSE	MEGALOMANIACAL	MEGATONNAGE
MEDIAEVALISTIC	MEDICAMENTING	MEETINGHOUSES	MEGALOMANIACS	MEGATONNAGES
MEDIAEVALISTS	MEDICAMENTOUS	MEETNESSES	MEGALOMANIAS	MEGAVERTEBRATE
MEDIAEVALLY	MEDICAMENTS	MEFLOQUINE	MEGALOMANIC	MEGAVERTEBRATES
MEDIAEVALS	MEDICASTER	MEFLOQUINES	MEGALOPOLIS	MEGAVITAMIN
MEDIAGENIC	MEDICASTERS	MEGACEPHALIC	MEGALOPOLISES	MEGAVITAMINS
MEDIASTINA	MEDICATING	MEGACEPHALIES	MEGALOPOLITAN	MEIOFAUNAE
MEDIASTINAL	MEDICATION	MEGACEPHALOUS	MEGALOPOLITANS	MEIOFAUNAL
MEDIASTINUM	MEDICATIONS	MEGACEPHALY	MEGALOPSES	MEIOFAUNAS
MEDIATENESS	MEDICATIVE	MEGACHURCH	MEGALOSAUR	MEIOSPORES
MEDIATENESSES	MEDICINABLE	MEGACHURCHES	MEGALOSAURI	MEIOTICALLY
MEDIATIONAL	MEDICINALLY	MEGACITIES	MEGALOSAURIAN	MEITNERIUM
MEDIATIONS	MEDICINALS	MEGACORPORATION	MEGALOSAURIANS	MEITNERIUMS
MEDIATISATION	MEDICINERS	MEGACURIES	MEGALOSAURS	MEKOMETERS
MEDIATISATIONS	MEDICINING	MEGACYCLES	MEGALOSAURUS	MELACONITE

M

MELACONITES	MELASTOMACEOUS	MELODIOUSNESSES	MEMORANDUMS	MENINGIOMAS
MELALEUCAS	MELASTOMES	MELODISERS	MEMORATIVE	MENINGIOMATA
MELAMPODES	MELATONINS	MELODISING	MEMORIALISATION	MENINGITIC
MELANAEMIA	MELIACEOUS	MELODIZERS	MEMORIALISE	MENINGITIDES
MELANAEMIAS	MELICOTTON	MELODIZING	MEMORIALISED	MENINGITIS
MELANCHOLIA	MELICOTTONS	MELODRAMAS	MEMORIALISER	MENINGITISES
MELANCHOLIAC	MELIORABLE	MELODRAMATIC	MEMORIALISERS	MENINGOCELE
MELANCHOLIACS	MELIORATED	MELODRAMATICS	MEMORIALISES	MENINGOCELES
MELANCHOLIAE	MELIORATES	MELODRAMATISE	MEMORIALISING	MENINGOCOCCAL
MELANCHOLIAS	MELIORATING	MELODRAMATISED	MEMORIALIST	MENINGOCOCCI
MELANCHOLIC	MELIORATION	MELODRAMATISES	MEMORIALISTS	MENINGOCOCCIC
MELANCHOLICALLY	MELIORATIONS	MELODRAMATISING	MEMORIALIZATION	MENINGOCOCCUS
MELANCHOLICS	MELIORATIVE	MELODRAMATIST	MEMORIALIZE	MENISCECTOMIES
MELANCHOLIES	MELIORATIVES	MELODRAMATISTS	MEMORIALIZED	MENISCECTOMY
MELANCHOLILY	MELIORATOR	MELODRAMATIZE	MEMORIALIZER	MENISCUSES
MELANCHOLINESS	MELIORATORS	MELODRAMATIZED	MEMORIALIZERS	MENISPERMACEOUS
MELANCHOLIOUS	MELIORISMS	MELODRAMATIZES	MEMORIALIZES	MENISPERMUM
MELANCHOLY	MELIORISTIC	MELODRAMATIZING	MEMORIALIZING	MENISPERMUMS
MELANISATION	MELIORISTS	MELODRAMES	MEMORIALLY	MENOLOGIES
MELANISATIONS	MELIORITIES	MELOMANIAC	MEMORISABLE	MENOMINEES
MELANISING	MELIPHAGOUS	MELOMANIACS	MEMORISATION	MENOPAUSAL
MELANISTIC	MELISMATIC	MELOMANIAS	MEMORISATIONS	MENOPAUSES
MELANIZATION	MELLIFEROUS	MELONGENES	MEMORISERS	MENOPAUSIC
MELANIZATIONS	MELLIFICATION	MELOXICAMS	MEMORISING	MENOPOLISES
MELANIZING	MELLIFICATIONS	MELPHALANS	MEMORIZABLE	MENORRHAGIA
MELANOBLAST	MELLIFLUENCE	MELTABILITIES	MEMORIZATION	MENORRHAGIAS
MELANOBLASTS	MELLIFLUENCES	MELTABILITY	MEMORIZATIONS	MENORRHAGIC
MELANOCHROI	MELLIFLUENT	MELTINGNESS	MEMORIZERS	MENORRHEAS
MELANOCHROIC	MELLIFLUENTLY	MELTINGNESSES	MEMORIZING	MENORRHOEA
MELANOCHROOUS	MELLIFLUOUS	MELTWATERS	MENACINGLY	MENORRHOEAS
MELANOCYTE	MELLIFLUOUSLY	MELUNGEONS	MENADIONES	MENSCHIEST
MELANOCYTES	MELLIFLUOUSNESS	MEMBERLESS	MENAGERIES	MENSERVANTS
MELANOGENESES	MELLIPHAGOUS	MEMBERSHIP	MENAQUINONE	MENSTRUALLY
MELANOGENESIS	MELLIVOROUS	MEMBERSHIPS	MENAQUINONES	MENSTRUATE
MELANOMATA	MELLOPHONE	MEMBRANACEOUS	MENARCHEAL	MENSTRUATED
MELANOPHORE	MELLOPHONES	MEMBRANEOUS	MENARCHIAL	MENSTRUATES
MELANOPHORES	MELLOTRONS	MEMBRANOUS	MENDACIOUS	MENSTRUATING
MELANOSITIES	MELLOWNESS	MEMBRANOUSLY	MENDACIOUSLY	MENSTRUATION
MELANOSITY	MELLOWNESSES	MEMOIRISMS	MENDACIOUSNESS	MENSTRUATIONS
MELANOSOME	MELLOWSPEAK	MEMOIRISTS	MENDACITIES	MENSTRUOUS
MELANOSOMES	MELLOWSPEAKS	MEMORABILE	MENDELEVIUM	MENSTRUUMS
MELANOTROPIN	MELOCOTONS	MEMORABILIA	MENDELEVIUMS	MENSURABILITIES
MELANOTROPINS	MELOCOTOON	MEMORABILITIES	MENDICANCIES	MENSURABILITY
MELANTERITE	MELOCOTOONS	MEMORABILITY	MENDICANCY	MENSURABLE
MELANTERITES	MELODICALLY	MEMORABLENESS	MENDICANTS	MENSURATION
MELANURIAS	MELODIOUSLY	MEMORABLENESSES	MENDICITIES	MENSURATIONAL
MELAPHYRES	MELODIOUSNESS	MEMORANDUM	MENINGIOMA	MENSURATIONS

MENSURATIVE	MERCERISATION	MERCURATES	MERITORIOUS	MESENCHYMES
MENTALESES	MERCERISATIONS	MERCURATING	MERITORIOUSLY	MESENTERIAL
MENTALISMS	MERCERISED	MERCURATION	MERITORIOUSNESS	MESENTERIC
MENTALISTIC	MERCERISER	MERCURATIONS	MERMAIDENS	MESENTERIES
MENTALISTICALLY	MERCERISERS	MERCURIALISE	MEROBLASTIC	MESENTERITIS
MENTALISTS	MERCERISES	MERCURIALISED	MEROBLASTICALLY	MESENTERITISES
MENTALITIES	MERCERISING	MERCURIALISES	MEROGENESES	MESENTERON
MENTATIONS	MERCERIZATION	MERCURIALISING	MEROGENESIS	MESENTERONIC
MENTHACEOUS	MERCERIZATIONS	MERCURIALISM	MEROGENETIC	MESHUGAASEN
MENTHOLATED	MERCERIZED	MERCURIALISMS	MEROGONIES	MESHUGASEN
MENTICIDES	MERCERIZER	MERCURIALIST	MEROMORPHIC	MESHUGGENAH
MENTIONABLE	MERCERIZERS	MERCURIALISTS	MEROMYOSIN	MESHUGGENAHS
MENTIONERS	MERCERIZES	MERCURIALITIES	MEROMYOSINS	MESHUGGENEH
MENTIONING	MERCERIZING	MERCURIALITY	MERONYMIES	MESHUGGENEHS
MENTONNIERE	MERCHANDISE	MERCURIALIZE	MEROPIDANS	MESHUGGENER
MENTONNIERES	MERCHANDISED	MERCURIALIZED	MEROPLANKTON	MESHUGGENERS
MENTORINGS	MERCHANDISER	MERCURIALIZES	MEROPLANKTONS	MESITYLENE
MENTORSHIP	MERCHANDISERS	MERCURIALIZING	MEROZOITES	MESITYLENES
MENTORSHIPS	MERCHANDISES	MERCURIALLY	MERPEOPLES	MESMERICAL
MENUISIERS	MERCHANDISING	MERCURIALNESS	MERRIMENTS	MESMERICALLY
MEPACRINES	MERCHANDISINGS	MERCURIALNESSES	MERRINESSES	MESMERISATION
MEPERIDINE	MERCHANDIZE	MERCURIALS	MERRYMAKER	MESMERISATIONS
MEPERIDINES	MERCHANDIZED	MERCURISED	MERRYMAKERS	MESMERISED
MEPHITICAL	MERCHANDIZER	MERCURISES	MERRYMAKING	MESMERISER
MEPHITICALLY	MERCHANDIZERS	MERCURISING	MERRYMAKINGS	MESMERISERS
MEPHITISES	MERCHANDIZES	MERCURIZED	MERRYTHOUGHT	MESMERISES
MEPHITISMS	MERCHANDIZING	MERCURIZES	MERRYTHOUGHTS	MESMERISING
MEPROBAMATE	MERCHANDIZINGS	MERCURIZING	MERVEILLEUSE	MESMERISMS
MEPROBAMATES	MERCHANTABILITY	MERDIVOROUS	MERVEILLEUSES	MESMERISTS
MERBROMINS	MERCHANTABLE	MEREOLOGICAL	MERVEILLEUX	MESMERIZATION
MERCANTILE	MERCHANTED	MEREOLOGIES	MERVEILLEUXES	MESMERIZATIONS
MERCANTILISM	MERCHANTING	MERESTONES	MESALLIANCE	MESMERIZED
MERCANTILISMS	MERCHANTINGS	MERETRICIOUS	MESALLIANCES	MESMERIZER
MERCANTILIST	MERCHANTLIKE	MERETRICIOUSLY	MESATICEPHALIC	MESMERIZERS
MERCANTILISTIC	MERCHANTMAN	MERGANSERS	MESATICEPHALIES	MESMERIZES
MERCANTILISTS	MERCHANTMEN	MERIDIONAL	MESATICEPHALOUS	MESMERIZING
MERCAPTANS	MERCHANTRIES	MERIDIONALITIES	MESATICEPHALY	MESNALTIES
MERCAPTIDE	MERCHANTRY	MERIDIONALITY	MESCALINES	MESOAMERICAN
MERCAPTIDES	MERCHILDREN	MERIDIONALLY	MESCALISMS	MESOBENTHOS
MERCAPTOPURINE	MERCIFULLY	MERIDIONALS	MESDEMOISELLES	MESOBENTHOSES
MERCAPTOPURINES	MERCIFULNESS	MERISTEMATIC	MESENCEPHALA	MESOBLASTIC
MERCENARIES	MERCIFULNESSES	MERISTICALLY	MESENCEPHALIC	MESOBLASTS
MERCENARILY	MERCIFYING	MERITOCRACIES	MESENCEPHALON	MESOCEPHALIC
MERCENARINESS	MERCILESSLY	MERITOCRACY	MESENCEPHALONS	MESOCEPHALICS
MERCENARINESSES	MERCILESSNESS	MERITOCRAT	MESENCHYMAL	MESOCEPHALIES
MERCENARISM	MERCILESSNESSES	MERITOCRATIC	MESENCHYMATOUS	MESOCEPHALISM
MERCENARISMS	MERCURATED	MERITOCRATS	MESENCHYME	MESOCEPHALISMS

MESOCEPHALOUS	MESOTHELIA	METABOLIZES	METAGENETICALLY	METALLISTS
MESOCEPHALY	MESOTHELIAL	METABOLIZING	METAGNATHISM	METALLIZATION
MESOCRANIES	MESOTHELIOMA	METABOLOME	METAGNATHISMS	METALLIZATIONS
MESOCRATIC	MESOTHELIOMAS	METABOLOMES	METAGNATHOUS	METALLIZED
MESOCYCLONE	MESOTHELIOMATA	METABOLOMICS	METAGRABOLISE	METALLIZES
MESOCYCLONES	MESOTHELIUM	METABOTROPIC	METAGRABOLISED	METALLIZING
MESODERMAL	MESOTHELIUMS	METACARPAL	METAGRABOLISES	METALLOCENE
MESODERMIC	MESOTHERAPIES	METACARPALS	METAGRABOLISING	METALLOCENES
MESOGASTRIA	MESOTHERAPY	METACARPUS	METAGRABOLIZE	METALLOGENETIC
MESOGASTRIC	MESOTHORACES	METACENTER	METAGRABOLIZED	METALLOGENIC
MESOGASTRIUM	MESOTHORACIC	METACENTERS	METAGRABOLIZES	METALLOGENIES
MESOGLOEAS	MESOTHORAX	METACENTRE	METAGRABOLIZING	METALLOGENY
MESOGNATHIES	MESOTHORAXES	METACENTRES	METAGROBOLISE	METALLOGRAPHER
MESOGNATHISM	MESOTHORIUM	METACENTRIC	METAGROBOLISED	METALLOGRAPHERS
MESOGNATHISMS	MESOTHORIUMS	METACENTRICS	METAGROBOLISES	METALLOGRAPHIC
MESOGNATHOUS	MESOTROPHIC	METACERCARIA	METAGROBOLISING	METALLOGRAPHIES
MESOGNATHY	MESQUINERIE	METACERCARIAE	METAGROBOLIZE	METALLOGRAPHIST
MESOHIPPUS	MESQUINERIES	METACERCARIAL	METAGROBOLIZED	METALLOGRAPHY
MESOHIPPUSES	MESSAGINGS	METACHROMATIC	METAGROBOLIZES	METALLOIDAL
MESOKURTIC	MESSALINES	METACHROMATISM	METAGROBOLIZING	METALLOIDS
MESOMERISM	MESSEIGNEURS	METACHROMATISMS	METALANGUAGE	METALLOPHONE
MESOMERISMS	MESSENGERED	METACHRONISM	METALANGUAGES	METALLOPHONES
MESOMORPHIC	MESSENGERING	METACHRONISMS	METALDEHYDE	METALLURGIC
MESOMORPHIES	MESSENGERS	METACHROSES	METALDEHYDES	METALLURGICAL
MESOMORPHISM	MESSIAHSHIP	METACHROSIS	METALEPSES	METALLURGICALLY
MESOMORPHISMS	MESSIAHSHIPS	METACINNABARITE	METALEPSIS	METALLURGIES
MESOMORPHOUS	MESSIANICALLY	METACOGNITION	METALEPTIC	METALLURGIST
MESOMORPHS	MESSIANISM	METACOGNITIONS	METALEPTICAL	METALLURGISTS
MESOMORPHY	MESSIANISMS	METACOMPUTER	METALHEADS	METALLURGY
MESONEPHRIC	MESSINESSES	METACOMPUTERS	METALINGUISTIC	METALMARKS
MESONEPHROI	MESTRANOLS	METACOMPUTING	METALINGUISTICS	METALSMITH
MESONEPHROS	METABISULPHITE	METACOMPUTINGS	METALISATION	METALSMITHS
MESONEPHROSES	METABISULPHITES	METAETHICAL	METALISATIONS	METALWARES
MESOPAUSES	METABOLICALLY	METAETHICS	METALISING	METALWORKER
MESOPELAGIC	METABOLIES	METAFEMALE	METALIZATION	METALWORKERS
MESOPHILES	METABOLISABLE	METAFEMALES	METALIZATIONS	METALWORKING
MESOPHILIC	METABOLISE	METAFICTION	METALIZING	METALWORKINGS
MESOPHYLLIC	METABOLISED	METAFICTIONAL	METALLICALLY	METALWORKS
MESOPHYLLOUS	METABOLISES	METAFICTIONIST	METALLIDING	METAMATERIAL
MESOPHYLLS	METABOLISING	METAFICTIONISTS	METALLIDINGS	METAMATERIALS
MESOPHYTES	METABOLISM	METAFICTIONS	METALLIFEROUS	METAMATHEMATICS
MESOPHYTIC	METABOLISMS	METAGALACTIC	METALLINGS	METAMERICALLY
MESOSCAPHE	METABOLITE	METAGALAXIES	METALLISATION	METAMERISM
MESOSCAPHES	METABOLITES	METAGALAXY	METALLISATIONS	METAMERISMS
MESOSPHERE	METABOLIZABLE	METAGENESES	METALLISED	METAMICTISATION
MESOSPHERES	METABOLIZE	METAGENESIS	METALLISES	METAMICTIZATION
MESOSPHERIC	METABOLIZED	METAGENETIC	METALLISING	METAMORPHIC

METAMORPHICALLY
METAMORPHISM
METAMORPHISMS
METAMORPHIST
METAMORPHISTS
METAMORPHOSE
METAMORPHOSED
METAMORPHOSES
METAMORPHOSING
METAMORPHOSIS
METAMORPHOUS
METANALYSES
METANALYSIS
METANARRATIVE
METANARRATIVES
METANEPHRIC
METANEPHROI
METANEPHROS
METAPERIODIC
METAPHASES
METAPHORIC
METAPHORICAL
METAPHORICALLY
METAPHORIST
METAPHORISTS
METAPHOSPHATE
METAPHOSPHATES
METAPHOSPHORIC
METAPHRASE
METAPHRASED
METAPHRASES
METAPHRASING
METAPHRASIS
METAPHRAST
METAPHRASTIC
METAPHRASTICAL
METAPHRASTS
METAPHYSIC
METAPHYSICAL
METAPHYSICALLY
METAPHYSICIAN
METAPHYSICIANS
METAPHYSICISE
METAPHYSICISED
METAPHYSICISES
METAPHYSICISING
METAPHYSICIST

METAPHYSICISTS
METAPHYSICIZE
METAPHYSICIZED
METAPHYSICIZES
METAPHYSICIZING
METAPHYSICS
METAPLASES
METAPLASIA
METAPLASIAS
METAPLASIS
METAPLASMIC
METAPLASMS
METAPLASTIC
METAPOLITICAL
METAPOLITICS
METAPSYCHIC
METAPSYCHICAL
METAPSYCHICS
METAPSYCHOLOGY
METARCHONS
METASEQUOIA
METASEQUOIAS
METASILICATE
METASILICATES
METASILICIC
METASOMATA
METASOMATIC
METASOMATISM
METASOMATISMS
METASOMATOSES
METASOMATOSIS
METASTABILITIES
METASTABILITY
METASTABLE
METASTABLES
METASTABLY
METASTASES
METASTASIS
METASTASISE
METASTASISED
METASTASISES
METASTASISING
METASTASIZE
METASTASIZED
METASTASIZES
METASTASIZING
METASTATIC

METASTATICALLY
METATARSAL
METATARSALS
METATARSUS
METATHEORETICAL
METATHEORIES
METATHEORY
METATHERIAN
METATHERIANS
METATHESES
METATHESIS
METATHESISE
METATHESISED
METATHESISES
METATHESISING
METATHESIZE
METATHESIZED
METATHESIZES
METATHESIZING
METATHETIC
METATHETICAL
METATHETICALLY
METATHORACES
METATHORACIC
METATHORAX
METATHORAXES
METATUNGSTIC
METAVANADIC
METAVERSES
METAXYLEMS
METECDYSES
METECDYSIS
METEMPIRIC
METEMPIRICAL
METEMPIRICALLY
METEMPIRICISM
METEMPIRICISMS
METEMPIRICIST
METEMPIRICISTS
METEMPIRICS
METEMPSYCHOSES
METEMPSYCHOSIS
METEMPSYCHOSIST
METENCEPHALA
METENCEPHALIC
METENCEPHALON
METENCEPHALONS

METEORICALLY
METEORISMS
METEORISTS
METEORITAL
METEORITES
METEORITIC
METEORITICAL
METEORITICIST
METEORITICISTS
METEORITICS
METEOROGRAM
METEOROGRAMS
METEOROGRAPH
METEOROGRAPHIC
METEOROGRAPHS
METEOROIDAL
METEOROIDS
METEOROLITE
METEOROLITES
METEOROLOGIC
METEOROLOGICAL
METEOROLOGIES
METEOROLOGIST
METEOROLOGISTS
METEOROLOGY
METERSTICK
METERSTICKS
METESTICKS
METESTROUS
METESTRUSES
METFORMINS
METHACRYLATE
METHACRYLATES
METHACRYLIC
METHADONES
METHAEMOGLOBIN
METHAEMOGLOBINS
METHAMPHETAMINE
METHANAMIDE
METHANAMIDES
METHANATION
METHANATIONS
METHANOMETER
METHANOMETERS
METHAQUALONE
METHAQUALONES
METHEDRINE

METHEDRINES
METHEGLINS
METHEMOGLOBIN
METHEMOGLOBINS
METHENAMINE
METHENAMINES
METHICILLIN
METHICILLINS
METHINKETH
METHIONINE
METHIONINES
METHODICAL
METHODICALLY
METHODICALNESS
METHODISATION
METHODISATIONS
METHODISED
METHODISER
METHODISERS
METHODISES
METHODISING
METHODISMS
METHODISTIC
METHODISTS
METHODIZATION
METHODIZATIONS
METHODIZED
METHODIZER
METHODIZERS
METHODIZES
METHODIZING
METHODOLOGICAL
METHODOLOGIES
METHODOLOGIST
METHODOLOGISTS
METHODOLOGY
METHOMANIA
METHOMANIAS
METHOTREXATE
METHOTREXATES
METHOXIDES
METHOXYBENZENE
METHOXYBENZENES
METHOXYCHLOR
METHOXYCHLORS
METHOXYFLURANE
METHOXYFLURANES

M

METHYLAMINE	METRICATES	METRORRHAGIAS	MICROBIOLOGISTS	MICROCLINES
METHYLAMINES	METRICATING	METROSEXUAL	MICROBIOLOGY	MICROCOCCAL
METHYLASES	METRICATION	METROSEXUALS	MICROBIOME	MICROCOCCI
METHYLATED	METRICATIONS	METROSTYLE	MICROBIOMES	MICROCOCCUS
METHYLATES	METRICIANS	METROSTYLES	MICROBIOTA	MICROCODES
METHYLATING	METRICISED	METTLESOME	MICROBLOGGER	MICROCOMPONENT
METHYLATION	METRICISES	METTLESOMENESS	MICROBLOGGERS	MICROCOMPONENTS
METHYLATIONS	METRICISING	MEZCALINES	MICROBLOGGING	MICROCOMPUTER
METHYLATOR	METRICISMS	MEZZALUNAS	MICROBLOGGINGS	MICROCOMPUTERS
METHYLATORS	METRICISTS	MEZZANINES	MICROBLOGS	MICROCOMPUTING
METHYLCELLULOSE	METRICIZED	MEZZOTINTED	MICROBREWER	MICROCOMPUTINGS
METHYLDOPA	METRICIZES	MEZZOTINTER	MICROBREWERIES	MICROCOPIED
METHYLDOPAS	METRICIZING	MEZZOTINTERS	MICROBREWERS	MICROCOPIES
METHYLENES	METRIFICATION	MEZZOTINTING	MICROBREWERY	MICROCOPYING
METHYLMERCURIES	METRIFICATIONS	MEZZOTINTO	MICROBREWING	MICROCOPYINGS
METHYLMERCURY	METRIFIERS	MEZZOTINTOS	MICROBREWINGS	MICROCOSMIC
METHYLPHENIDATE	METRIFONATE	MEZZOTINTS	MICROBREWS	MICROCOSMICAL
METHYLPHENOL	METRIFONATES	MIAROLITIC	MICROBUBBLES	MICROCOSMICALLY
METHYLPHENOLS	METRIFYING	MIASMATICAL	MICROBURST	MICROCOSMOS
METHYLTHIONINE	METRITISES	MIASMATOUS	MICROBURSTS	MICROCOSMOSES
METHYLTHIONINES	METROLOGIC	MIASMICALLY	MICROBUSES	MICROCOSMS
METHYLXANTHINE	METROLOGICAL	MICRIFYING	MICROBUSSES	MICROCRACK
METHYLXANTHINES	METROLOGICALLY	MICROAEROPHILE	MICROCAPSULE	MICROCRACKED
METHYSERGIDE	METROLOGIES	MICROAEROPHILES	MICROCAPSULES	MICROCRACKING
METHYSERGIDES	METROLOGIST	MICROAEROPHILIC	MICROCARDS	MICROCRACKINGS
METICULOSITIES	METROLOGISTS	MICROAMPERE	MICROCASSETTE	MICROCRACKS
METICULOSITY	METROMANIA	MICROAMPERES	MICROCASSETTES	MICROCRYSTAL
METICULOUS	METROMANIAS	MICROANALYSES	MICROCELEBRITY	MICROCRYSTALS
METICULOUSLY	METRONIDAZOLE	MICROANALYSIS	MICROCEPHAL	MICROCULTURAL
METICULOUSNESS	METRONIDAZOLES	MICROANALYST	MICROCEPHALIC	MICROCULTURE
METOESTROUS	METRONOMES	MICROANALYSTS	MICROCEPHALICS	MICROCULTURES
METOESTRUS	METRONOMIC	MICROANALYTIC	MICROCEPHALIES	MICROCURIE
METOESTRUSES	METRONOMICAL	MICROANALYTICAL	MICROCEPHALOUS	MICROCURIES
METONYMICAL	METRONOMICALLY	MICROANATOMICAL	MICROCEPHALS	MICROCYTES
METONYMICALLY	METRONYMIC	MICROANATOMIES	MICROCEPHALY	MICROCYTIC
METONYMIES	METRONYMICS	MICROANATOMY	MICROCHEMICAL	MICRODETECTION
METOPOSCOPIC	METROPLEXES	MICROARRAY	MICROCHEMISTRY	MICRODETECTIONS
METOPOSCOPICAL	METROPOLIS	MICROARRAYS	MICROCHIPPED	MICRODETECTOR
METOPOSCOPIES	METROPOLISES	MICROBALANCE	MICROCHIPPING	MICRODETECTORS
METOPOSCOPIST	METROPOLITAN	MICROBALANCES	MICROCHIPS	MICRODISSECTION
METOPOSCOPISTS	METROPOLITANATE	MICROBAROGRAPH	MICROCIRCUIT	MICRODONTOUS
METOPOSCOPY	METROPOLITANISE	MICROBAROGRAPHS	MICROCIRCUITRY	MICRODRIVE
METRALGIAS	METROPOLITANISM	MICROBEAMS	MICROCIRCUITS	MICRODRIVES
METRESTICK	METROPOLITANIZE	MICROBIOLOGIC	MICROCLIMATE	MICRODRONE
METRESTICKS	METROPOLITANS	MICROBIOLOGICAL	MICROCLIMATES	MICRODRONES
METRICALLY	METROPOLITICAL	MICROBIOLOGIES	MICROCLIMATIC	MICROEARTHQUAKE
METRICATED	METRORRHAGIA	MICROBIOLOGIST	MICROCLINE	MICROECONOMIC

MICROECONOMICS	MICROFOSSILS	MICROLITIC	MICRONATION	MICROPHYSICISTS
MICROELECTRODE	MICROFUNGI	MICROLITRE	MICRONATIONS	MICROPHYSICS
MICROELECTRODES	MICROFUNGUS	MICROLITRES	MICRONEEDLE	MICROPHYTE
MICROELECTRONIC	MICROGAMETE	MICROLOANS	MICRONEEDLES	MICROPHYTES
MICROELEMENT	MICROGAMETES	MICROLOGIC	MICRONISATION	MICROPHYTIC
MICROELEMENTS	MICROGAMETOCYTE	MICROLOGICAL	MICRONISATIONS	MICROPIPET
MICROEVOLUTION	MICROGENERATION	MICROLOGICALLY	MICRONISED	MICROPIPETS
MICROEVOLUTIONS	MICROGLIAS	MICROLOGIES	MICRONISES	MICROPIPETTE
MICROFARAD	MICROGRAMS	MICROLOGIST	MICRONISING	MICROPIPETTES
MICROFARADS	MICROGRANITE	MICROLOGISTS	MICRONIZATION	MICROPLANKTON
MICROFAUNA	MICROGRANITES	MICROLUCES	MICRONIZATIONS	MICROPLANKTONS
MICROFAUNAE	MICROGRANITIC	MICROLUXES	MICRONIZED	MICROPOLIS
MICROFAUNAL	MICROGRAPH	MICROMANAGE	MICRONIZES	MICROPOLISES
MICROFAUNAS	MICROGRAPHED	MICROMANAGED	MICRONIZING	MICROPORES
MICROFELSITIC	MICROGRAPHER	MICROMANAGEMENT	MICRONUCLEI	MICROPOROSITIES
MICROFIBER	MICROGRAPHERS	MICROMANAGER	MICRONUCLEUS	MICROPOROSITY
MICROFIBERS	MICROGRAPHIC	MICROMANAGERS	MICRONUCLEUSES	MICROPOROUS
MICROFIBRE	MICROGRAPHICS	MICROMANAGES	MICRONUTRIENT	MICROPOWER
MICROFIBRES	MICROGRAPHIES	MICROMANAGING	MICRONUTRIENTS	MICROPOWERS
MICROFIBRIL	MICROGRAPHING	MICROMARKETING	MICROORGANISM	MICROPRINT
MICROFIBRILLAR	MICROGRAPHS	MICROMARKETINGS	MICROORGANISMS	MICROPRINTED
MICROFIBRILS	MICROGRAPHY	MICROMERES	MICROPARASITE	MICROPRINTING
MICROFICHE	MICROGRAVITIES	MICROMESHES	MICROPARASITES	MICROPRINTINGS
MICROFICHES	MICROGRAVITY	MICROMETEORITE	MICROPARASITIC	MICROPRINTS
MICROFILAMENT	MICROGREENS	MICROMETEORITES	MICROPARTICLE	MICROPRISM
MICROFILAMENTS	MICROGROOVE	MICROMETEORITIC	MICROPARTICLES	MICROPRISMS
MICROFILARIA	MICROGROOVES	MICROMETEOROID	MICROPAYMENT	MICROPROBE
MICROFILARIAE	MICROHABITAT	MICROMETEOROIDS	MICROPAYMENTS	MICROPROBES
MICROFILARIAL	MICROHABITATS	MICROMETER	MICROPEGMATITE	MICROPROCESSING
MICROFILING	MICROIMAGE	MICROMETERS	MICROPEGMATITES	MICROPROCESSOR
MICROFILINGS	MICROIMAGES	MICROMETHOD	MICROPEGMATITIC	MICROPROCESSORS
MICROFILMABLE	MICROINCHES	MICROMETHODS	MICROPHAGE	MICROPROGRAM
MICROFILMED	MICROINJECT	MICROMETRE	MICROPHAGES	MICROPROGRAMS
MICROFILMER	MICROINJECTED	MICROMETRES	MICROPHAGOUS	MICROPROJECTION
MICROFILMERS	MICROINJECTING	MICROMETRIC	MICROPHONE	MICROPROJECTOR
MICROFILMING	MICROINJECTION	MICROMETRICAL	MICROPHONES	MICROPROJECTORS
MICROFILMS	MICROINJECTIONS	MICROMETRIES	MICROPHONIC	MICROPSIAS
MICROFILTER	MICROINJECTS	MICROMETRY	MICROPHONICS	MICROPTEROUS
MICROFILTERS	MICROLIGHT	MICROMICROCURIE	MICROPHOTOGRAPH	MICROPUBLISHER
MICROFLOPPIES	MICROLIGHTING	MICROMICROFARAD	MICROPHOTOMETER	MICROPUBLISHERS
MICROFLOPPY	MICROLIGHTINGS	MICROMILLIMETRE	MICROPHOTOMETRY	MICROPUBLISHING
MICROFLORA	MICROLIGHTS	MICROMINIATURE	MICROPHYLL	MICROPULSATION
MICROFLORAE	MICROLITER	MICROMINIS	MICROPHYLLOUS	MICROPULSATIONS
MICROFLORAL	MICROLITERS	MICROMOLAR	MICROPHYLLS	MICROPUMPS
MICROFLORAS	MICROLITES	MICROMOLES	MICROPHYSICAL	MICROPUNCTURE
MICROFORMS	MICROLITHIC	MICROMORPHOLOGY	MICROPHYSICALLY	MICROPUNCTURES
MICROFOSSIL	MICROLITHS	MICROMORTS	MICROPHYSICIST	MICROPYLAR

MICROPYLES	MICROSPOROPHYLL	MICROWAVING	MIDSHIPMATE	MILITARIZATIONS
MICROPYROMETER	MICROSPOROUS	MICROWIRES	MIDSHIPMATES	MILITARIZE
MICROPYROMETERS	MICROSTATE	MICROWORLD	MIDSHIPMEN	MILITARIZED
MICROQUAKE	MICROSTATES	MICROWORLDS	MIDSTORIES	MILITARIZES
MICROQUAKES	MICROSTOMATOUS	MICROWRITER	MIDSTREAMS	MILITARIZING
MICRORADIOGRAPH	MICROSTOMOUS	MICROWRITERS	MIDSUMMERS	MILITATING
MICROREADER	MICROSTRUCTURAL	MICRURGIES	MIDWATCHES	MILITATION
MICROREADERS	MICROSTRUCTURE	MICTURATED	MIDWIFERIES	MILITATIONS
MICROSATELLITE	MICROSTRUCTURES	MICTURATES	MIDWINTERS	MILITIAMAN
MICROSATELLITES	MICROSURGEON	MICTURATING	MIFEPRISTONE	MILITIAMEN
MICROSCALE	MICROSURGEONS	MICTURITION	MIFEPRISTONES	MILKFISHES
MICROSCALES	MICROSURGERIES	MICTURITIONS	MIFFINESSES	MILKINESSES
MICROSCOPE	MICROSURGERY	MIDDELMANNETJIE	MIGHTINESS	MILKSHAKES
MICROSCOPES	MICROSURGICAL	MIDDELSKOT	MIGHTINESSES	MILKSOPISM
MICROSCOPIC	MICROSWITCH	MIDDELSKOTS	MIGMATITES	MILKSOPISMS
MICROSCOPICAL	MICROSWITCHES	MIDDENSTEAD	MIGNONETTE	MILKSOPPING
MICROSCOPICALLY	MICROTECHNIC	MIDDENSTEADS	MIGNONETTES	MILKTOASTS
MICROSCOPIES	MICROTECHNICS	MIDDLEBREAKER	MIGRAINEUR	MILLBOARDS
MICROSCOPIST	MICROTECHNIQUE	MIDDLEBREAKERS	MIGRAINEURS	MILLEFEUILLE
MICROSCOPISTS	MICROTECHNIQUES	MIDDLEBROW	MIGRAINOUS	MILLEFEUILLES
MICROSCOPY	MICROTECHNOLOGY	MIDDLEBROWED	MIGRATIONAL	MILLEFIORI
MICROSECOND	MICROTOMES	MIDDLEBROWISM	MIGRATIONIST	MILLEFIORIS
MICROSECONDS	MICROTOMIC	MIDDLEBROWISMS	MIGRATIONISTS	MILLEFLEUR
MICROSEISM	MICROTOMICAL	MIDDLEBROWS	MIGRATIONS	MILLEFLEURS
MICROSEISMIC	MICROTOMIES	MIDDLEBUSTER	MILDNESSES	MILLENARIAN
MICROSEISMICAL	MICROTOMIST	MIDDLEBUSTERS	MILEOMETER	MILLENARIANISM
MICROSEISMICITY	MICROTOMISTS	MIDDLEMOST	MILEOMETERS	MILLENARIANISMS
MICROSEISMS	MICROTONAL	MIDDLEWARE	MILESTONES	MILLENARIANS
MICROSITES	MICROTONALITIES	MIDDLEWARES	MILITANCES	MILLENARIES
MICROSKIRT	MICROTONALITY	MIDDLEWEIGHT	MILITANCIES	MILLENARISM
MICROSKIRTS	MICROTONALLY	MIDDLEWEIGHTS	MILITANTLY	MILLENARISMS
MICROSLEEP	MICROTONES	MIDDLINGLY	MILITANTNESS	MILLENNIAL
MICROSLEEPS	MICROTUBULAR	MIDFIELDER	MILITANTNESSES	MILLENNIALISM
MICROSMATIC	MICROTUBULE	MIDFIELDERS	MILITARIES	MILLENNIALISMS
MICROSOMAL	MICROTUBULES	MIDINETTES	MILITARILY	MILLENNIALIST
MICROSOMES	MICROTUNNELLING	MIDISKIRTS	MILITARISATION	MILLENNIALISTS
MICROSPECIES	MICROVASCULAR	MIDLANDERS	MILITARISATIONS	MILLENNIALLY
MICROSPHERE	MICROVILLAR	MIDLATITUDE	MILITARISE	MILLENNIANISM
MICROSPHERES	MICROVILLI	MIDLATITUDES	MILITARISED	MILLENNIANISMS
MICROSPHERICAL	MICROVILLOUS	MIDLITTORAL	MILITARISES	MILLENNIARISM
MICROSPORANGIA	MICROVILLUS	MIDLITTORALS	MILITARISING	MILLENNIARISMS
MICROSPORANGIUM	MICROVOLTS	MIDNIGHTLY	MILITARISM	MILLENNIUM
MICROSPORE	MICROWATTS	MIDRASHOTH	MILITARISMS	MILLENNIUMS
MICROSPORES	MICROWAVABLE	MIDSAGITTAL	MILITARIST	MILLEPEDES
MICROSPORIC	MICROWAVEABLE	MIDSECTION	MILITARISTIC	MILLEPORES
MICROSPOROCYTE	MICROWAVED	MIDSECTIONS	MILITARISTS	MILLERITES
MICROSPOROCYTES	MICROWAVES	MIDSHIPMAN	MILITARIZATION	MILLESIMAL

MILLESIMALLY	MILLIPROBES	MINDBLOWERS	MINERALOGIZES	MINICOMPUTER
MILLESIMALS	MILLIRADIAN	MINDEDNESS	MINERALOGIZING	MINICOMPUTERS
MILLHOUSES	MILLIRADIANS	MINDEDNESSES	MINERALOGY	MINICOURSE
MILLIAMPERE	MILLIROENTGEN	MINDFULNESS	MINESHAFTS	MINICOURSES
MILLIAMPERES	MILLIROENTGENS	MINDFULNESSES	MINESTONES	MINIDISHES
MILLIARIES	MILLISECOND	MINDLESSLY	MINESTRONE	MINIDRESSES
MILLICURIE	MILLISECONDS	MINDLESSNESS	MINESTRONES	MINIFICATION
MILLICURIES	MILLISIEVERT	MINDLESSNESSES	MINESWEEPER	MINIFICATIONS
MILLIDEGREE	MILLISIEVERTS	MINDSHARES	MINESWEEPERS	MINIFLOPPIES
MILLIDEGREES	MILLIVOLTS	MINEFIELDS	MINESWEEPING	MINIFLOPPY
MILLIGRAMME	MILLIWATTS	MINEHUNTER	MINESWEEPINGS	MINIMALISM
MILLIGRAMMES	MILLOCRACIES	MINEHUNTERS	MINEWORKER	MINIMALISMS
MILLIGRAMS	MILLOCRACY	MINELAYERS	MINEWORKERS	MINIMALIST
MILLIHENRIES	MILLOCRATS	MINELAYING	MINGIMINGI	MINIMALISTIC
MILLIHENRY	MILLSCALES	MINELAYINGS	MINGIMINGIS	MINIMALISTS
MILLIHENRYS	MILLSTONES	MINERALISABLE	MINGINESSES	MINIMARKET
MILLILAMBERT	MILLSTREAM	MINERALISATION	MINGLEMENT	MINIMARKETS
MILLILAMBERTS	MILLSTREAMS	MINERALISATIONS	MINGLEMENTS	MINIMAXING
MILLILITER	MILLWHEELS	MINERALISE	MINGLINGLY	MINIMISATION
MILLILITERS	MILLWRIGHT	MINERALISED	MINIATIONS	MINIMISATIONS
MILLILITRE	MILLWRIGHTS	MINERALISER	MINIATURED	MINIMISERS
MILLILITRES	MILOMETERS	MINERALISERS	MINIATURES	MINIMISING
MILLILUCES	MILQUETOAST	MINERALISES	MINIATURING	MINIMIZATION
MILLILUXES	MILQUETOASTS	MINERALISING	MINIATURISATION	MINIMIZATIONS
MILLIMETER	MIMEOGRAPH	MINERALIST	MINIATURISE	MINIMIZERS
MILLIMETERS	MIMEOGRAPHED	MINERALISTS	MINIATURISED	MINIMIZING
MILLIMETRE	MIMEOGRAPHING	MINERALIZABLE	MINIATURISES	MINIRUGBIES
MILLIMETRES	MIMEOGRAPHS	MINERALIZATION	MINIATURISING	MINISCHOOL
MILLIMICRON	MIMETICALLY	MINERALIZATIONS	MINIATURIST	MINISCHOOLS
MILLIMICRONS	MIMIVIRUSES	MINERALIZE	MINIATURISTIC	MINISCULES
MILLIMOLAR	MIMMICKING	MINERALIZED	MINIATURISTS	MINISERIES
MILLIMOLES	MIMOGRAPHER	MINERALIZER	MINIATURIZATION	MINISKIRTED
MILLINERIES	MIMOGRAPHERS	MINERALIZERS	MINIATURIZE	MINISKIRTS
MILLIONAIRE	MIMOGRAPHIES	MINERALIZES	MINIATURIZED	MINISTATES
MILLIONAIRES	MIMOGRAPHY	MINERALIZING	MINIATURIZES	MINISTERED
MILLIONAIRESS	MIMOSACEOUS	MINERALOGIC	MINIATURIZING	MINISTERIA
MILLIONAIRESSES	MINACIOUSLY	MINERALOGICAL	MINIBIKERS	MINISTERIAL
MILLIONARY	MINACITIES	MINERALOGICALLY	MINIBREAKS	MINISTERIALIST
MILLIONFOLD	MINATORIAL	MINERALOGIES	MINIBUDGET	MINISTERIALISTS
MILLIONNAIRE	MINATORIALLY	MINERALOGISE	MINIBUDGETS	MINISTERIALLY
MILLIONNAIRES	MINATORILY	MINERALOGISED	MINIBUSSES	MINISTERING
MILLIONNAIRESS	MINAUDERIE	MINERALOGISES	MINICABBING	MINISTERIUM
MILLIONTHS	MINAUDERIES	MINERALOGISING	MINICABBINGS	MINISTERSHIP
MILLIOSMOL	MINAUDIERE	MINERALOGIST	MINICALCULATOR	MINISTERSHIPS
MILLIOSMOLS	MINAUDIERES	MINERALOGISTS	MINICALCULATORS	MINISTRANT
MILLIPEDES	MINCEMEATS	MINERALOGIZE	MINICASSETTE	MINISTRANTS
MILLIPROBE	MINDBLOWER	MINERALOGIZED	MINICASSETTES	MINISTRATION

M

MINISTRATIONS	MIRTHFULLY	MISALLOTMENTS	MISARRANGEMENTS	MISBEHAVIOURS
MINISTRATIVE	MIRTHFULNESS	MISALLOTTED	MISARRANGES	MISBELIEFS
MINISTRESS	MIRTHFULNESSES	MISALLOTTING	MISARRANGING	MISBELIEVE
MINISTRESSES	MIRTHLESSLY	MISALLYING	MISARTICULATE	MISBELIEVED
MINISTRIES	MIRTHLESSNESS	MISALTERED	MISARTICULATED	MISBELIEVER
MINISTROKE	MIRTHLESSNESSES	MISALTERING	MISARTICULATES	MISBELIEVERS
MINISTROKES	MISACCEPTATION	MISANALYSES	MISARTICULATING	MISBELIEVES
MINISYSTEM	MISACCEPTATIONS	MISANALYSIS	MISASSAYED	MISBELIEVING
MINISYSTEMS	MISADAPTED	MISANDRIES	MISASSAYING	MISBESEEMED
MINITOWERS	MISADAPTING	MISANDRIST	MISASSEMBLE	MISBESEEMING
MINITRACKS	MISADDRESS	MISANDRISTS	MISASSEMBLED	MISBESEEMS
MINIVOLLEY	MISADDRESSED	MISANDROUS	MISASSEMBLES	MISBESTOWAL
MINIVOLLEYS	MISADDRESSES	MISANTHROPE	MISASSEMBLING	MISBESTOWALS
MINNESINGER	MISADDRESSING	MISANTHROPES	MISASSIGNED	MISBESTOWED
MINNESINGERS	MISADJUSTED	MISANTHROPIC	MISASSIGNING	MISBESTOWING
MINNICKING	MISADJUSTING	MISANTHROPICAL	MISASSIGNS	MISBESTOWS
MINNOCKING	MISADJUSTS	MISANTHROPIES	MISASSUMPTION	MISBIASING
MINORITAIRE	MISADVENTURE	MISANTHROPIST	MISASSUMPTIONS	MISBIASSED
MINORITAIRES	MISADVENTURED	MISANTHROPISTS	MISATONING	MISBIASSES
MINORITIES	MISADVENTURER	MISANTHROPOS	MISATTRIBUTE	MISBIASSING
MINORSHIPS	MISADVENTURERS	MISANTHROPOSES	MISATTRIBUTED	MISBILLING
MINOXIDILS	MISADVENTURES	MISANTHROPY	MISATTRIBUTES	MISBINDING
MINSTRELSIES	MISADVENTUROUS	MISAPPLICATION	MISATTRIBUTING	MISBRANDED
MINSTRELSY	MISADVERTENCE	MISAPPLICATIONS	MISATTRIBUTION	MISBRANDING
MINUSCULAR	MISADVERTENCES	MISAPPLIED	MISATTRIBUTIONS	MISBUILDING
MINUSCULES	MISADVICES	MISAPPLIES	MISAUNTERS	MISBUTTONED
MINUTENESS	MISADVISED	MISAPPLYING	MISAVERRED	MISBUTTONING
MINUTENESSES	MISADVISEDLY	MISAPPRAISAL	MISAVERRING	MISBUTTONS
MIRABELLES	MISADVISEDNESS	MISAPPRAISALS	MISAWARDED	MISCALCULATE
MIRABILISES	MISADVISES	MISAPPRECIATE	MISAWARDING	MISCALCULATED
MIRACIDIAL	MISADVISING	MISAPPRECIATED	MISBALANCE	MISCALCULATES
MIRACIDIUM	MISALIGNED	MISAPPRECIATES	MISBALANCED	MISCALCULATING
MIRACULOUS	MISALIGNING	MISAPPRECIATING	MISBALANCES	MISCALCULATION
MIRACULOUSLY	MISALIGNMENT	MISAPPRECIATION	MISBALANCING	MISCALCULATIONS
MIRACULOUSNESS	MISALIGNMENTS	MISAPPRECIATIVE	MISBECOMES	MISCALCULATOR
MIRANDISED	MISALLEGED	MISAPPREHEND	MISBECOMING	MISCALCULATORS
MIRANDISES	MISALLEGES	MISAPPREHENDED	MISBECOMINGNESS	MISCALLERS
MIRANDISING	MISALLEGING	MISAPPREHENDING	MISBEGINNING	MISCALLING
MIRANDIZED	MISALLIANCE	MISAPPREHENDS	MISBEGOTTEN	MISCANTHUS
MIRANDIZES	MISALLIANCES	MISAPPREHENSION	MISBEHAVED	MISCANTHUSES
MIRANDIZING	MISALLOCATE	MISAPPREHENSIVE	MISBEHAVER	MISCAPTION
MIRIFICALLY	MISALLOCATED	MISAPPROPRIATE	MISBEHAVERS	MISCAPTIONED
MIRINESSES	MISALLOCATES	MISAPPROPRIATED	MISBEHAVES	MISCAPTIONING
MIRKINESSES	MISALLOCATING	MISAPPROPRIATES	MISBEHAVING	MISCAPTIONS
MIRRORINGS	MISALLOCATION	MISARRANGE	MISBEHAVIOR	MISCARRIAGE
MIRRORLIKE	MISALLOCATIONS	MISARRANGED	MISBEHAVIORS	MISCARRIAGES
MIRRORWISE	MISALLOTMENT	MISARRANGEMENT	MISBEHAVIOUR	MISCARRIED

MISCARRIES	MISCHARGES	MISCONCEIVERS	MISCORRELATIONS	MISDESCRIBING
MISCARRYING	MISCHARGING	MISCONCEIVES	MISCOUNSEL	MISDESCRIPTION
MISCASTING	MISCHIEFED	MISCONCEIVING	MISCOUNSELLED	MISDESCRIPTIONS
MISCATALOG	MISCHIEFING	MISCONCEPTION	MISCOUNSELLING	MISDESERTS
MISCATALOGED	MISCHIEVOUS	MISCONCEPTIONS	MISCOUNSELLINGS	MISDEVELOP
MISCATALOGING	MISCHIEVOUSLY	MISCONDUCT	MISCOUNSELS	MISDEVELOPED
MISCATALOGS	MISCHIEVOUSNESS	MISCONDUCTED	MISCOUNTED	MISDEVELOPING
MISCEGENATE	MISCHMETAL	MISCONDUCTING	MISCOUNTING	MISDEVELOPS
MISCEGENATED	MISCHMETALS	MISCONDUCTS	MISCREANCE	MISDEVOTION
MISCEGENATES	MISCHOICES	MISCONJECTURE	MISCREANCES	MISDEVOTIONS
MISCEGENATING	MISCHOOSES	MISCONJECTURED	MISCREANCIES	MISDIAGNOSE
MISCEGENATION	MISCHOOSING	MISCONJECTURES	MISCREANCY	MISDIAGNOSED
MISCEGENATIONAL	MISCIBILITIES	MISCONJECTURING	MISCREANTS	MISDIAGNOSES
MISCEGENATIONS	MISCIBILITY	MISCONNECT	MISCREATED	MISDIAGNOSING
MISCEGENATOR	MISCITATION	MISCONNECTED	MISCREATES	MISDIAGNOSIS
MISCEGENATORS	MISCITATIONS	MISCONNECTING	MISCREATING	MISDIALING
MISCEGENES	MISCLAIMED	MISCONNECTION	MISCREATION	MISDIALLED
MISCEGENETIC	MISCLAIMING	MISCONNECTIONS	MISCREATIONS	MISDIALLING
MISCEGENIST	MISCLASSED	MISCONNECTS	MISCREATIVE	MISDIETING
MISCEGENISTS	MISCLASSES	MISCONSTER	MISCREATOR	MISDIGHTED
MISCEGINES	MISCLASSIFIED	MISCONSTERED	MISCREATORS	MISDIGHTING
MISCELLANARIAN	MISCLASSIFIES	MISCONSTERING	MISCREAUNCE	MISDIRECTED
MISCELLANARIANS	MISCLASSIFY	MISCONSTERS	MISCREAUNCES	MISDIRECTING
MISCELLANEA	MISCLASSIFYING	MISCONSTRUCT	MISCREDITED	MISDIRECTION
MISCELLANEOUS	MISCLASSING	MISCONSTRUCTED	MISCREDITING	MISDIRECTIONS
MISCELLANEOUSLY	MISCOINING	MISCONSTRUCTING	MISCREDITS	MISDIRECTS
MISCELLANIES	MISCOLORED	MISCONSTRUCTION	MISCUTTING	MISDISTRIBUTION
MISCELLANIST	MISCOLORING	MISCONSTRUCTS	MISDEALERS	MISDIVIDED
MISCELLANISTS	MISCOLOURED	MISCONSTRUE	MISDEALING	MISDIVIDES
MISCELLANY	MISCOLOURING	MISCONSTRUED	MISDEEMFUL	MISDIVIDING
MISCHALLENGE	MISCOLOURS	MISCONSTRUES	MISDEEMING	MISDIVISION
MISCHALLENGES	MISCOMPREHEND	MISCONSTRUING	MISDEEMINGS	MISDIVISIONS
MISCHANCED	MISCOMPREHENDED	MISCONTENT	MISDEFINED	MISDOUBTED
MISCHANCEFUL	MISCOMPREHENDS	MISCONTENTED	MISDEFINES	MISDOUBTFUL
MISCHANCES	MISCOMPUTATION	MISCONTENTING	MISDEFINING	MISDOUBTING
MISCHANCING	MISCOMPUTATIONS	MISCONTENTMENT	MISDEMEANANT	MISDRAWING
MISCHANNEL	MISCOMPUTE	MISCONTENTMENTS	MISDEMEANANTS	MISDRAWINGS
MISCHANNELED	MISCOMPUTED	MISCONTENTS	MISDEMEANED	MISDREADED
MISCHANNELING	MISCOMPUTES	MISCOOKING	MISDEMEANING	MISDREADING
MISCHANNELLED	MISCOMPUTING	MISCOPYING	MISDEMEANOR	MISDRIVING
MISCHANNELLING	MISCONCEIT	MISCORRECT	MISDEMEANORS	MISEDITING
MISCHANNELS	MISCONCEITED	MISCORRECTED	MISDEMEANOUR	MISEDUCATE
MISCHANTER	MISCONCEITING	MISCORRECTING	MISDEMEANOURS	MISEDUCATED
MISCHANTERS	MISCONCEITS	MISCORRECTION	MISDEMEANS	MISEDUCATES
MISCHARACTERISE	MISCONCEIVE	MISCORRECTIONS	MISDESCRIBE	MISEDUCATING
MISCHARACTERIZE	MISCONCEIVED	MISCORRECTS	MISDESCRIBED	MISEDUCATION
MISCHARGED	MISCONCEIVER	MISCORRELATION	MISDESCRIBES	MISEDUCATIONS

MISEMPHASES
MISEMPHASIS
MISEMPHASISE
MISEMPHASISED
MISEMPHASISES
MISEMPHASISING
MISEMPHASIZE
MISEMPHASIZED
MISEMPHASIZES
MISEMPHASIZING
MISEMPLOYED
MISEMPLOYING
MISEMPLOYMENT
MISEMPLOYMENTS
MISEMPLOYS
MISENROLLED
MISENROLLING
MISENROLLS
MISENTERED
MISENTERING
MISENTREAT
MISENTREATED
MISENTREATING
MISENTREATS
MISENTRIES
MISERABILISM
MISERABILISMS
MISERABILIST
MISERABILISTS
MISERABLENESS
MISERABLENESSES
MISERABLES
MISERABLISM
MISERABLISMS
MISERABLIST
MISERABLISTS
MISERICORD
MISERICORDE
MISERICORDES
MISERICORDS
MISERLIEST
MISERLINESS
MISERLINESSES
MISESTEEMED
MISESTEEMING
MISESTEEMS
MISESTIMATE

MISESTIMATED
MISESTIMATES
MISESTIMATING
MISESTIMATION
MISESTIMATIONS
MISEVALUATE
MISEVALUATED
MISEVALUATES
MISEVALUATING
MISEVALUATION
MISEVALUATIONS
MISFALLING
MISFARINGS
MISFEASANCE
MISFEASANCES
MISFEASORS
MISFEATURE
MISFEATURED
MISFEATURES
MISFEATURING
MISFEEDING
MISFEIGNED
MISFEIGNING
MISFIELDED
MISFIELDING
MISFITTING
MISFOCUSED
MISFOCUSES
MISFOCUSING
MISFOCUSSED
MISFOCUSSES
MISFOCUSSING
MISFORMATION
MISFORMATIONS
MISFORMING
MISFORTUNE
MISFORTUNED
MISFORTUNES
MISFRAMING
MISFUNCTION
MISFUNCTIONED
MISFUNCTIONING
MISFUNCTIONS
MISGAUGING
MISGIVINGS
MISGOVERNANCE
MISGOVERNANCES

MISGOVERNAUNCE
MISGOVERNAUNCES
MISGOVERNED
MISGOVERNING
MISGOVERNMENT
MISGOVERNMENTS
MISGOVERNOR
MISGOVERNORS
MISGOVERNS
MISGRADING
MISGRAFTED
MISGRAFTING
MISGROWING
MISGROWTHS
MISGUESSED
MISGUESSES
MISGUESSING
MISGUGGLED
MISGUGGLES
MISGUGGLING
MISGUIDANCE
MISGUIDANCES
MISGUIDEDLY
MISGUIDEDNESS
MISGUIDEDNESSES
MISGUIDERS
MISGUIDING
MISHALLOWED
MISHANDLED
MISHANDLES
MISHANDLING
MISHANDLINGS
MISHANTERS
MISHAPPENED
MISHAPPENING
MISHAPPENS
MISHAPPING
MISHEARING
MISHEGAASEN
MISHGUGGLE
MISHGUGGLED
MISHGUGGLES
MISHGUGGLING
MISHITTING
MISHMASHES
MISHMOSHES
MISHUGASES

MISIDENTIFIED
MISIDENTIFIES
MISIDENTIFY
MISIDENTIFYING
MISIMPRESSION
MISIMPRESSIONS
MISIMPROVE
MISIMPROVED
MISIMPROVEMENT
MISIMPROVEMENTS
MISIMPROVES
MISIMPROVING
MISINFERRED
MISINFERRING
MISINFORMANT
MISINFORMANTS
MISINFORMATION
MISINFORMATIONS
MISINFORMED
MISINFORMER
MISINFORMERS
MISINFORMING
MISINFORMS
MISINSTRUCT
MISINSTRUCTED
MISINSTRUCTING
MISINSTRUCTION
MISINSTRUCTIONS
MISINSTRUCTS
MISINTELLIGENCE
MISINTENDED
MISINTENDING
MISINTENDS
MISINTERPRET
MISINTERPRETED
MISINTERPRETER
MISINTERPRETERS
MISINTERPRETING
MISINTERPRETS
MISINTERRED
MISINTERRING
MISJOINDER
MISJOINDERS
MISJOINING
MISJUDGEMENT
MISJUDGEMENTS
MISJUDGERS

MISJUDGING
MISJUDGMENT
MISJUDGMENTS
MISKEEPING
MISKENNING
MISKICKING
MISKNOWING
MISKNOWLEDGE
MISKNOWLEDGES
MISLABELED
MISLABELING
MISLABELLED
MISLABELLING
MISLABORED
MISLABORING
MISLABOURED
MISLABOURING
MISLABOURS
MISLEADERS
MISLEADING
MISLEADINGLY
MISLEARNED
MISLEARNING
MISLEEKING
MISLIGHTED
MISLIGHTING
MISLIKINGS
MISLIPPENED
MISLIPPENING
MISLIPPENS
MISLOCATED
MISLOCATES
MISLOCATING
MISLOCATION
MISLOCATIONS
MISLODGING
MISLUCKING
MISMANAGED
MISMANAGEMENT
MISMANAGEMENTS
MISMANAGER
MISMANAGERS
MISMANAGES
MISMANAGING
MISMANNERS
MISMARKING
MISMARRIAGE

MISMARRIAGES	MISORIENTATIONS	MISPOINTING	MISRECOLLECTION	MISSEEMINGS
MISMARRIED	MISORIENTED	MISPOISING	MISRECORDED	MISSELLING
MISMARRIES	MISORIENTING	MISPOSITION	MISRECORDING	MISSELLINGS
MISMARRYING	MISORIENTS	MISPOSITIONED	MISRECORDS	MISSENDING
MISMATCHED	MISPACKAGE	MISPOSITIONING	MISREFERENCE	MISSENSING
MISMATCHES	MISPACKAGED	MISPOSITIONS	MISREFERENCED	MISSETTING
MISMATCHING	MISPACKAGES	MISPRAISED	MISREFERENCES	MISSHAPENLY
MISMATCHMENT	MISPACKAGING	MISPRAISES	MISREFERENCING	MISSHAPENNESS
MISMATCHMENTS	MISPAINTED	MISPRAISING	MISREFERRED	MISSHAPENNESSES
MISMEASURE	MISPAINTING	MISPRICING	MISREFERRING	MISSHAPERS
MISMEASURED	MISPARSING	MISPRINTED	MISREGARDED	MISSHAPING
MISMEASUREMENT	MISPARTING	MISPRINTING	MISREGARDING	MISSHEATHED
MISMEASUREMENTS	MISPATCHED	MISPRISING	MISREGARDS	MISSILEERS
MISMEASURES	MISPATCHES	MISPRISION	MISREGISTER	MISSILEMAN
MISMEASURING	MISPATCHING	MISPRISIONS	MISREGISTERED	MISSILEMEN
MISMEETING	MISPENNING	MISPRIZERS	MISREGISTERING	MISSILERIES
MISMETRING	MISPERCEIVE	MISPRIZING	MISREGISTERS	MISSILRIES
MISNOMERED	MISPERCEIVED	MISPROGRAM	MISREGISTRATION	MISSIOLOGIES
MISNOMERING	MISPERCEIVES	MISPROGRAMED	MISRELATED	MISSIOLOGY
MISNUMBERED	MISPERCEIVING	MISPROGRAMING	MISRELATES	MISSIONARIES
MISNUMBERING	MISPERCEPTION	MISPROGRAMMED	MISRELATING	MISSIONARISE
MISNUMBERS	MISPERCEPTIONS	MISPROGRAMMING	MISRELATION	MISSIONARISED
MISOBSERVANCE	MISPERSUADE	MISPROGRAMS	MISRELATIONS	MISSIONARISES
MISOBSERVANCES	MISPERSUADED	MISPRONOUNCE	MISRELYING	MISSIONARISING
MISOBSERVE	MISPERSUADES	MISPRONOUNCED	MISREMEMBER	MISSIONARIZE
MISOBSERVED	MISPERSUADING	MISPRONOUNCES	MISREMEMBERED	MISSIONARIZED
MISOBSERVES	MISPERSUASION	MISPRONOUNCING	MISREMEMBERING	MISSIONARIZES
MISOBSERVING	MISPERSUASIONS	MISPROPORTION	MISREMEMBERS	MISSIONARIZING
MISOCAPNIC	MISPHRASED	MISPROPORTIONED	MISRENDERED	MISSIONARY
MISOGAMIES	MISPHRASES	MISPROPORTIONS	MISRENDERING	MISSIONERS
MISOGAMIST	MISPHRASING	MISPUNCTUATE	MISRENDERS	MISSIONING
MISOGAMISTS	MISPICKELS	MISPUNCTUATED	MISREPORTED	MISSIONISATION
MISOGYNIES	MISPLACEMENT	MISPUNCTUATES	MISREPORTER	MISSIONISATIONS
MISOGYNIST	MISPLACEMENTS	MISPUNCTUATING	MISREPORTERS	MISSIONISE
MISOGYNISTIC	MISPLACING	MISPUNCTUATION	MISREPORTING	MISSIONISED
MISOGYNISTICAL	MISPLANNED	MISPUNCTUATIONS	MISREPORTS	MISSIONISER
MISOGYNISTS	MISPLANNING	MISQUOTATION	MISREPRESENT	MISSIONISERS
MISOGYNOUS	MISPLANTED	MISQUOTATIONS	MISREPRESENTED	MISSIONISES
MISOLOGIES	MISPLANTING	MISQUOTERS	MISREPRESENTER	MISSIONISING
MISOLOGIST	MISPLAYING	MISQUOTING	MISREPRESENTERS	MISSIONIZATION
MISOLOGISTS	MISPLEADED	MISRAISING	MISREPRESENTING	MISSIONIZATIONS
MISONEISMS	MISPLEADING	MISREADING	MISREPRESENTS	MISSIONIZE
MISONEISTIC	MISPLEADINGS	MISREADINGS	MISROUTEING	MISSIONIZED
MISONEISTS	MISPLEASED	MISRECKONED	MISROUTING	MISSIONIZER
MISORDERED	MISPLEASES	MISRECKONING	MISSAYINGS	MISSIONIZERS
MISORDERING	MISPLEASING	MISRECKONINGS	MISSEATING	MISSIONIZES
MISORIENTATION	MISPOINTED	MISRECKONS	MISSEEMING	MISSIONIZING

M

MISSISHNESS	MISTENDING	MISTRUSTLESS	MITIGATIVE	MOBILITIES
MISSISHNESSES	MISTERMING	MISTRYSTED	MITIGATIVES	MOBILIZABLE
MISSORTING	MISTHINKING	MISTRYSTING	MITIGATORS	MOBILIZATION
MISSOUNDED	MISTHOUGHT	MISTUTORED	MITIGATORY	MOBILIZATIONS
MISSOUNDING	MISTHOUGHTS	MISTUTORING	MITOCHONDRIA	MOBILIZERS
MISSPACING	MISTHROWING	MISUNDERSTAND	MITOCHONDRIAL	MOBILIZING
MISSPEAKING	MISTIGRISES	MISUNDERSTANDS	MITOCHONDRION	MOBLOGGERS
MISSPELLED	MISTIMINGS	MISUNDERSTOOD	MITOGENETIC	MOBOCRACIES
MISSPELLING	MISTINESSES	MISUTILISATION	MITOGENICITIES	MOBOCRATIC
MISSPELLINGS	MISTITLING	MISUTILISATIONS	MITOGENICITY	MOBOCRATICAL
MISSPENDER	MISTLETOES	MISUTILIZATION	MITOMYCINS	MOCHINESSES
MISSPENDERS	MISTOUCHED	MISUTILIZATIONS	MITOTICALLY	MOCKERNUTS
MISSPENDING	MISTOUCHES	MISVALUING	MITRAILLES	MOCKINGBIRD
MISSTAMPED	MISTOUCHING	MISVENTURE	MITRAILLEUR	MOCKINGBIRDS
MISSTAMPING	MISTRACING	MISVENTURES	MITRAILLEURS	MOCKUMENTARIES
MISSTARTED	MISTRAINED	MISVENTUROUS	MITRAILLEUSE	MOCKUMENTARY
MISSTARTING	MISTRAINING	MISVOCALISATION	MITRAILLEUSES	MODAFINILS
MISSTATEMENT	MISTRANSCRIBE	MISVOCALIZATION	MITREWORTS	MODALISTIC
MISSTATEMENTS	MISTRANSCRIBED	MISWANDRED	MITTIMUSES	MODALITIES
MISSTATING	MISTRANSCRIBES	MISWEENING	MIXABILITIES	MODELLINGS
MISSTEERED	MISTRANSCRIBING	MISWENDING	MIXABILITY	MODELLISTS
MISSTEERING	MISTRANSLATE	MISWORDING	MIXEDNESSES	MODERATELY
MISSTEPPED	MISTRANSLATED	MISWORDINGS	MIXMASTERS	MODERATENESS
MISSTEPPING	MISTRANSLATES	MISWORSHIP	MIXOBARBARIC	MODERATENESSES
MISSTOPPED	MISTRANSLATING	MISWORSHIPPED	MIXOLOGIES	MODERATING
MISSTOPPING	MISTRANSLATION	MISWORSHIPPING	MIXOLOGIST	MODERATION
MISSTRICKEN	MISTRANSLATIONS	MISWORSHIPS	MIXOLOGISTS	MODERATIONS
MISSTRIKES	MISTRAYNED	MISWRITING	MIXOLYDIAN	MODERATISM
MISSTRIKING	MISTREADING	MISWRITTEN	MIXOTROPHIC	MODERATISMS
MISSTYLING	MISTREADINGS	MITERWORTS	MIZENMASTS	MODERATORS
MISSUITING	MISTREATED	MITHRADATIC	MIZZENMAST	MODERATORSHIP
MISSUMMATION	MISTREATING	MITHRIDATE	MIZZENMASTS	MODERATORSHIPS
MISSUMMATIONS	MISTREATMENT	MITHRIDATES	MIZZONITES	MODERATRICES
MISTAKABLE	MISTREATMENTS	MITHRIDATIC	MNEMONICAL	MODERATRIX
MISTAKABLY	MISTRESSED	MITHRIDATISE	MNEMONICALLY	MODERATRIXES
MISTAKEABLE	MISTRESSES	MITHRIDATISED	MNEMONISTS	MODERNISATION
MISTAKEABLY	MISTRESSING	MITHRIDATISES	MNEMOTECHNIC	MODERNISATIONS
MISTAKENLY	MISTRESSLESS	MITHRIDATISING	MNEMOTECHNICS	MODERNISED
MISTAKENNESS	MISTRESSLY	MITHRIDATISM	MNEMOTECHNIST	MODERNISER
MISTAKENNESSES	MISTRUSTED	MITHRIDATISMS	MNEMOTECHNISTS	MODERNISERS
MISTAKINGS	MISTRUSTER	MITHRIDATIZE	MOBCASTING	MODERNISES
MISTEACHES	MISTRUSTERS	MITHRIDATIZED	MOBCASTINGS	MODERNISING
MISTEACHING	MISTRUSTFUL	MITHRIDATIZES	MOBILISABLE	MODERNISMS
MISTELLING	MISTRUSTFULLY	MITHRIDATIZING	MOBILISATION	MODERNISTIC
MISTEMPERED	MISTRUSTFULNESS	MITIGATING	MOBILISATIONS	MODERNISTICALLY
MISTEMPERING	MISTRUSTING	MITIGATION	MOBILISERS	MODERNISTS
MISTEMPERS	MISTRUSTINGLY	MITIGATIONS	MOBILISING	MODERNITIES

MODERNIZATION	MOISTURIZER	MOLLYHAWKS	MONARCHISED	MONEYMAKERS
MODERNIZATIONS	MOISTURIZERS	MOLLYMAWKS	MONARCHISES	MONEYMAKING
MODERNIZED	MOISTURIZES	MOLOCHISED	MONARCHISING	MONEYMAKINGS
MODERNIZER	MOISTURIZING	MOLOCHISES	MONARCHISM	MONEYSPINNING
MODERNIZERS	MOITHERING	MOLOCHISING	MONARCHISMS	MONEYWORTS
MODERNIZES	MOLALITIES	MOLOCHIZED	MONARCHIST	MONGERINGS
MODERNIZING	MOLARITIES	MOLOCHIZES	MONARCHISTIC	MONGOLISMS
MODERNNESS	MOLASSESES	MOLOCHIZING	MONARCHISTS	MONGOLOIDS
MODERNNESSES	MOLDABILITIES	MOLYBDATES	MONARCHIZE	MONGRELISATION
MODIFIABILITIES	MOLDABILITY	MOLYBDENITE	MONARCHIZED	MONGRELISATIONS
MODIFIABILITY	MOLDAVITES	MOLYBDENITES	MONARCHIZES	MONGRELISE
MODIFIABLE	MOLDBOARDS	MOLYBDENOSES	MONARCHIZING	MONGRELISED
MODIFIABLENESS	MOLDINESSES	MOLYBDENOSIS	MONASTERIAL	MONGRELISER
MODIFICATION	MOLECATCHER	MOLYBDENOUS	MONASTERIES	MONGRELISERS
MODIFICATIONS	MOLECATCHERS	MOLYBDENUM	MONASTICAL	MONGRELISES
MODIFICATIVE	MOLECULARITIES	MOLYBDENUMS	MONASTICALLY	MONGRELISING
MODIFICATORY	MOLECULARITY	MOLYBDOSES	MONASTICISM	MONGRELISM
MODILLIONS	MOLECULARLY	MOLYBDOSIS	MONASTICISMS	MONGRELISMS
MODISHNESS	MOLENDINAR	MOMENTANEOUS	MONAURALLY	MONGRELIZATION
MODISHNESSES	MOLENDINARIES	MOMENTARILY	MONCHIQUITE	MONGRELIZATIONS
MODULABILITIES	MOLENDINARS	MOMENTARINESS	MONCHIQUITES	MONGRELIZE
MODULABILITY	MOLENDINARY	MOMENTARINESSES	MONDEGREEN	MONGRELIZED
MODULARISED	MOLESTATION	MOMENTOUSLY	MONDEGREENS	MONGRELIZER
MODULARITIES	MOLESTATIONS	MOMENTOUSNESS	MONECIOUSLY	MONGRELIZERS
MODULARITY	MOLIMINOUS	MOMENTOUSNESSES	MONERGISMS	MONGRELIZES
MODULARIZED	MOLLIFIABLE	MOMPRENEUR	MONESTROUS	MONGRELIZING
MODULATING	MOLLIFICATION	MOMPRENEURS	MONETARILY	MONILIASES
MODULATION	MOLLIFICATIONS	MONACHISMS	MONETARISM	MONILIASIS
MODULATIONS	MOLLIFIERS	MONACHISTS	MONETARISMS	MONILIFORM
MODULATIVE	MOLLIFYING	MONACTINAL	MONETARIST	MONISTICAL
MODULATORS	MOLLITIOUS	MONACTINES	MONETARISTS	MONISTICALLY
MODULATORY	MOLLUSCANS	MONADELPHOUS	MONETISATION	MONITORIAL
MOISTENERS	MOLLUSCICIDAL	MONADICALLY	MONETISATIONS	MONITORIALLY
MOISTENING	MOLLUSCICIDE	MONADIFORM	MONETISING	MONITORIES
MOISTIFIED	MOLLUSCICIDES	MONADISTIC	MONETIZATION	MONITORING
MOISTIFIES	MOLLUSCOID	MONADNOCKS	MONETIZATIONS	MONITORINGS
MOISTIFYING	MOLLUSCOIDAL	MONADOLOGIES	MONETIZING	MONITORSHIP
MOISTNESSES	MOLLUSCOIDS	MONADOLOGY	MONEYBOXES	MONITORSHIPS
MOISTURELESS	MOLLUSCOUS	MONANDRIES	MONEYCHANGER	MONITRESSES
MOISTURISE	MOLLUSKANS	MONANDROUS	MONEYCHANGERS	MONKEYGLAND
MOISTURISED	MOLLYCODDLE	MONANTHOUS	MONEYGRUBBING	MONKEYISMS
MOISTURISER	MOLLYCODDLED	MONARCHALLY	MONEYGRUBBINGS	MONKEYPODS
MOISTURISERS	MOLLYCODDLER	MONARCHIAL	MONEYLENDER	MONKEYPOTS
MOISTURISES	MOLLYCODDLERS	MONARCHICAL	MONEYLENDERS	MONKEYPOXES
MOISTURISING	MOLLYCODDLES	MONARCHICALLY	MONEYLENDING	MONKEYSHINE
MOISTURIZE	MOLLYCODDLING	MONARCHIES	MONEYLENDINGS	MONKEYSHINES
MOISTURIZED	MOLLYCODDLINGS	MONARCHISE	MONEYMAKER	MONKFISHES

M

MONKISHNESS
MONKISHNESSES
MONKSHOODS
MONOACIDIC
MONOAMINERGIC
MONOAMINES
MONOATOMIC
MONOBLEPSES
MONOBLEPSIS
MONOCARBOXYLIC
MONOCARDIAN
MONOCARDIANS
MONOCARPELLARY
MONOCARPIC
MONOCARPOUS
MONOCEROSES
MONOCEROUS
MONOCHASIA
MONOCHASIAL
MONOCHASIUM
MONOCHLAMYDEOUS
MONOCHLORIDE
MONOCHLORIDES
MONOCHORDS
MONOCHROIC
MONOCHROICS
MONOCHROMASIES
MONOCHROMASY
MONOCHROMAT
MONOCHROMATE
MONOCHROMATES
MONOCHROMATIC
MONOCHROMATICS
MONOCHROMATISM
MONOCHROMATISMS
MONOCHROMATOR
MONOCHROMATORS
MONOCHROMATS
MONOCHROME
MONOCHROMES
MONOCHROMIC
MONOCHROMICAL
MONOCHROMIES
MONOCHROMIST
MONOCHROMISTS
MONOCHROMY
MONOCLINAL

MONOCLINALLY
MONOCLINALS
MONOCLINES
MONOCLINIC
MONOCLINISM
MONOCLINISMS
MONOCLINOUS
MONOCLONAL
MONOCLONALS
MONOCOQUES
MONOCOTYLEDON
MONOCOTYLEDONS
MONOCOTYLS
MONOCRACIES
MONOCRATIC
MONOCROPPED
MONOCROPPING
MONOCRYSTAL
MONOCRYSTALLINE
MONOCRYSTALS
MONOCULARLY
MONOCULARS
MONOCULOUS
MONOCULTURAL
MONOCULTURE
MONOCULTURES
MONOCYCLES
MONOCYCLIC
MONOCYTOID
MONODACTYLOUS
MONODELPHIAN
MONODELPHIANS
MONODELPHIC
MONODELPHOUS
MONODICALLY
MONODISPERSE
MONODRAMAS
MONODRAMATIC
MONOECIOUS
MONOECIOUSLY
MONOECISMS
MONOESTERS
MONOFILAMENT
MONOFILAMENTS
MONOGAMIES
MONOGAMIST
MONOGAMISTIC

MONOGAMISTS
MONOGAMOUS
MONOGAMOUSLY
MONOGAMOUSNESS
MONOGASTRIC
MONOGENEAN
MONOGENEANS
MONOGENESES
MONOGENESIS
MONOGENETIC
MONOGENICALLY
MONOGENIES
MONOGENISM
MONOGENISMS
MONOGENIST
MONOGENISTIC
MONOGENISTS
MONOGENOUS
MONOGLYCERIDE
MONOGLYCERIDES
MONOGONIES
MONOGRAMED
MONOGRAMING
MONOGRAMMATIC
MONOGRAMMED
MONOGRAMMER
MONOGRAMMERS
MONOGRAMMING
MONOGRAPHED
MONOGRAPHER
MONOGRAPHERS
MONOGRAPHIC
MONOGRAPHICAL
MONOGRAPHICALLY
MONOGRAPHIES
MONOGRAPHING
MONOGRAPHIST
MONOGRAPHISTS
MONOGRAPHS
MONOGRAPHY
MONOGYNIAN
MONOGYNIES
MONOGYNIST
MONOGYNISTS
MONOGYNOUS
MONOHYBRID
MONOHYBRIDS

MONOHYDRATE
MONOHYDRATED
MONOHYDRATES
MONOHYDRIC
MONOHYDROGEN
MONOHYDROXY
MONOICOUSLY
MONOLATERS
MONOLATRIES
MONOLATRIST
MONOLATRISTS
MONOLATROUS
MONOLAYERS
MONOLINGUAL
MONOLINGUALISM
MONOLINGUALISMS
MONOLINGUALS
MONOLINGUIST
MONOLINGUISTS
MONOLITHIC
MONOLITHICALLY
MONOLOGGED
MONOLOGGING
MONOLOGICAL
MONOLOGIES
MONOLOGISE
MONOLOGISED
MONOLOGISES
MONOLOGISING
MONOLOGIST
MONOLOGISTS
MONOLOGIZE
MONOLOGIZED
MONOLOGIZES
MONOLOGIZING
MONOLOGUED
MONOLOGUES
MONOLOGUING
MONOLOGUISE
MONOLOGUISED
MONOLOGUISES
MONOLOGUISING
MONOLOGUIST
MONOLOGUISTS
MONOLOGUIZE
MONOLOGUIZED
MONOLOGUIZES

MONOLOGUIZING
MONOMACHIA
MONOMACHIAS
MONOMACHIES
MONOMANIAC
MONOMANIACAL
MONOMANIACALLY
MONOMANIACS
MONOMANIAS
MONOMEROUS
MONOMETALLIC
MONOMETALLISM
MONOMETALLISMS
MONOMETALLIST
MONOMETALLISTS
MONOMETERS
MONOMETRIC
MONOMETRICAL
MONOMOLECULAR
MONOMOLECULARLY
MONOMORPHEMIC
MONOMORPHIC
MONOMORPHISM
MONOMORPHISMS
MONOMORPHOUS
MONOMYARIAN
MONOMYARIANS
MONONUCLEAR
MONONUCLEARS
MONONUCLEATE
MONONUCLEATED
MONONUCLEOSES
MONONUCLEOSIS
MONONUCLEOTIDE
MONONUCLEOTIDES
MONOPETALOUS
MONOPHAGIES
MONOPHAGOUS
MONOPHASES
MONOPHASIC
MONOPHOBIA
MONOPHOBIAS
MONOPHOBIC
MONOPHOBICS
MONOPHONIC
MONOPHONICALLY
MONOPHONIES

MONOPHOSPHATE	MONOPOLIZATION	MONOSTABLE	MONOTHELETISMS	MONSTERING
MONOPHOSPHATES	MONOPOLIZATIONS	MONOSTELES	MONOTHELISM	MONSTERINGS
MONOPHTHONG	MONOPOLIZE	MONOSTELIC	MONOTHELISMS	MONSTRANCE
MONOPHTHONGAL	MONOPOLIZED	MONOSTELIES	MONOTHELITE	MONSTRANCES
MONOPHTHONGISE	MONOPOLIZER	MONOSTICHIC	MONOTHELITES	MONSTROSITIES
MONOPHTHONGISED	MONOPOLIZERS	MONOSTICHOUS	MONOTHELITISM	MONSTROSITY
MONOPHTHONGISES	MONOPOLIZES	MONOSTICHS	MONOTHELITISMS	MONSTROUSLY
MONOPHTHONGIZE	MONOPOLIZING	MONOSTOMOUS	MONOTHERAPIES	MONSTROUSNESS
MONOPHTHONGIZED	MONOPRIONIDIAN	MONOSTROPHE	MONOTHERAPY	MONSTROUSNESSES
MONOPHTHONGIZES	MONOPROPELLANT	MONOSTROPHES	MONOTOCOUS	MONSTRUOSITIES
MONOPHTHONGS	MONOPROPELLANTS	MONOSTROPHIC	MONOTONICALLY	MONSTRUOSITY
MONOPHYLETIC	MONOPSONIES	MONOSTROPHICS	MONOTONICITIES	MONSTRUOUS
MONOPHYLIES	MONOPSONIST	MONOSTYLAR	MONOTONICITY	MONTADALES
MONOPHYLLOUS	MONOPSONISTIC	MONOSTYLOUS	MONOTONIES	MONTAGNARD
MONOPHYODONT	MONOPSONISTS	MONOSYLLABIC	MONOTONING	MONTAGNARDS
MONOPHYODONTS	MONOPTERAL	MONOSYLLABICITY	MONOTONISE	MONTBRETIA
MONOPHYSITE	MONOPTEROI	MONOSYLLABISM	MONOTONISED	MONTBRETIAS
MONOPHYSITES	MONOPTERON	MONOSYLLABISMS	MONOTONISES	MONTELIMAR
MONOPHYSITIC	MONOPTEROS	MONOSYLLABLE	MONOTONISING	MONTELIMARS
MONOPHYSITISM	MONOPTEROSES	MONOSYLLABLES	MONOTONIZE	MONTGOLFIER
MONOPHYSITISMS	MONOPTOTES	MONOSYMMETRIC	MONOTONIZED	MONTGOLFIERS
MONOPITCHES	MONOPULSES	MONOSYMMETRICAL	MONOTONIZES	MONTHLINGS
MONOPLANES	MONORCHIDISM	MONOSYMMETRIES	MONOTONIZING	MONTICELLITE
MONOPLEGIA	MONORCHIDISMS	MONOSYMMETRY	MONOTONOUS	MONTICELLITES
MONOPLEGIAS	MONORCHIDS	MONOSYNAPTIC	MONOTONOUSLY	MONTICOLOUS
MONOPLEGIC	MONORCHISM	MONOTASKED	MONOTONOUSNESS	MONTICULATE
MONOPLEGICS	MONORCHISMS	MONOTASKING	MONOTREMATOUS	MONTICULES
MONOPLOIDS	MONORHINAL	MONOTASKINGS	MONOTREMES	MONTICULOUS
MONOPODIAL	MONORHINES	MONOTELEPHONE	MONOTRICHIC	MONTICULUS
MONOPODIALLY	MONORHYMED	MONOTELEPHONES	MONOTRICHOUS	MONTICULUSES
MONOPODIAS	MONORHYMES	MONOTERPENE	MONOTROCHS	MONTMORILLONITE
MONOPODIES	MONOSACCHARIDE	MONOTERPENES	MONOUNSATURATE	MONUMENTAL
MONOPODIUM	MONOSACCHARIDES	MONOTHALAMIC	MONOUNSATURATED	MONUMENTALISE
MONOPOLIES	MONOSATURATED	MONOTHALAMOUS	MONOUNSATURATES	MONUMENTALISED
MONOPOLISATION	MONOSEMIES	MONOTHECAL	MONOVALENCE	MONUMENTALISES
MONOPOLISATIONS	MONOSEPALOUS	MONOTHECOUS	MONOVALENCES	MONUMENTALISING
MONOPOLISE	MONOSKIERS	MONOTHEISM	MONOVALENCIES	MONUMENTALITIES
MONOPOLISED	MONOSKIING	MONOTHEISMS	MONOVALENCY	MONUMENTALITY
MONOPOLISER	MONOSKIINGS	MONOTHEIST	MONOVALENT	MONUMENTALIZE
MONOPOLISERS	MONOSODIUM	MONOTHEISTIC	MONOXYLONS	MONUMENTALIZED
MONOPOLISES	MONOSOMICS	MONOTHEISTICAL	MONOXYLOUS	MONUMENTALIZES
MONOPOLISING	MONOSOMIES	MONOTHEISTS	MONOZYGOTIC	MONUMENTALIZING
MONOPOLISM	MONOSPACED	MONOTHELETE	MONOZYGOUS	MONUMENTALLY
MONOPOLISMS	MONOSPECIFIC	MONOTHELETES	MONSEIGNEUR	MONUMENTED
MONOPOLIST	MONOSPECIFICITY	MONOTHELETIC	MONSIGNORI	MONUMENTING
MONOPOLISTIC	MONOSPERMAL	MONOTHELETICAL	MONSIGNORIAL	MONZONITES
MONOPOLISTS	MONOSPERMOUS	MONOTHELETISM	MONSIGNORS	MONZONITIC

M

MOODINESSES	MORALISATIONS	MORONITIES	MORPHOSYNTAX	MOSCHATELS
MOONCALVES	MORALISERS	MOROSENESS	MORPHOSYNTAXES	MOSCHIFEROUS
MOONCHILDREN	MORALISING	MOROSENESSES	MORPHOTROPIC	MOSKONFYTS
MOONCRAFTS	MORALISTIC	MOROSITIES	MORPHOTROPIES	MOSQUITOES
MOONFISHES	MORALISTICALLY	MORPHACTIN	MORPHOTROPY	MOSQUITOEY
MOONFLOWER	MORALITIES	MORPHACTINS	MORSELLING	MOSSBACKED
MOONFLOWERS	MORALIZATION	MORPHALLAXES	MORSELLINGS	MOSSBLUITER
MOONINESSES	MORALIZATIONS	MORPHALLAXIS	MORTADELLA	MOSSBLUITERS
MOONLIGHTED	MORALIZERS	MORPHEMICALLY	MORTADELLAS	MOSSBUNKER
MOONLIGHTER	MORALIZING	MORPHEMICS	MORTADELLE	MOSSBUNKERS
MOONLIGHTERS	MORATORIUM	MORPHINISM	MORTALISED	MOSSINESSES
MOONLIGHTING	MORATORIUMS	MORPHINISMS	MORTALISES	MOSSPLANTS
MOONLIGHTINGS	MORBIDEZZA	MORPHINOMANIA	MORTALISING	MOSSTROOPER
MOONLIGHTS	MORBIDEZZAS	MORPHINOMANIAC	MORTALITIES	MOSSTROOPERS
MOONPHASES	MORBIDITIES	MORPHINOMANIACS	MORTALIZED	MOTETTISTS
MOONQUAKES	MORBIDNESS	MORPHINOMANIAS	MORTALIZES	MOTHBALLED
MOONRAKERS	MORBIDNESSES	MORPHOGENESES	MORTALIZING	MOTHBALLING
MOONRAKING	MORBIFEROUS	MORPHOGENESIS	MORTARBOARD	MOTHERBOARD
MOONRAKINGS	MORBIFICALLY	MORPHOGENETIC	MORTARBOARDS	MOTHERBOARDS
MOONSCAPES	MORBILLIFORM	MORPHOGENIC	MORTARLESS	MOTHERCRAFT
MOONSHINED	MORBILLIVIRUS	MORPHOGENIES	MORTCLOTHS	MOTHERCRAFTS
MOONSHINER	MORBILLIVIRUSES	MORPHOGENS	MORTGAGEABLE	MOTHERESES
MOONSHINERS	MORBILLOUS	MORPHOGENY	MORTGAGEES	MOTHERFUCKER
MOONSHINES	MORDACIOUS	MORPHOGRAPHER	MORTGAGERS	MOTHERFUCKERS
MOONSHINIER	MORDACIOUSLY	MORPHOGRAPHERS	MORTGAGING	MOTHERFUCKING
MOONSHINIEST	MORDACIOUSNESS	MORPHOGRAPHIES	MORTGAGORS	MOTHERHOOD
MOONSHINING	MORDACITIES	MORPHOGRAPHY	MORTICIANS	MOTHERHOODS
MOONSHININGS	MORDANCIES	MORPHOLINE	MORTIFEROUS	MOTHERHOUSE
MOONSTONES	MORDANTING	MORPHOLINES	MORTIFEROUSNESS	MOTHERHOUSES
MOONSTRICKEN	MORENESSES	MORPHOLINO	MORTIFICATION	MOTHERINGS
MOONSTRIKE	MORGANATIC	MORPHOLINOS	MORTIFICATIONS	MOTHERLAND
MOONSTRIKES	MORGANATICALLY	MORPHOLOGIC	MORTIFIERS	MOTHERLANDS
MOONSTRUCK	MORGANITES	MORPHOLOGICAL	MORTIFYING	MOTHERLESS
MOONWALKED	MORGELLONS	MORPHOLOGICALLY	MORTIFYINGLY	MOTHERLESSNESS
MOONWALKER	MORGENSTERN	MORPHOLOGIES	MORTIFYINGS	MOTHERLINESS
MOONWALKERS	MORGENSTERNS	MORPHOLOGIST	MORTUARIES	MOTHERLINESSES
MOONWALKING	MORIBUNDITIES	MORPHOLOGISTS	MORULATION	MOTHERWORT
MOORBUZZARD	MORIBUNDITY	MORPHOLOGY	MORULATIONS	MOTHERWORTS
MOORBUZZARDS	MORIBUNDLY	MORPHOMETRIC	MOSAICALLY	MOTHPROOFED
MOOSEBIRDS	MORIGERATE	MORPHOMETRICS	MOSAICISMS	MOTHPROOFER
MOOSEWOODS	MORIGERATED	MORPHOMETRIES	MOSAICISTS	MOTHPROOFERS
MOOSEYARDS	MORIGERATES	MORPHOMETRY	MOSAICKING	MOTHPROOFING
MOOTNESSES	MORIGERATING	MORPHOPHONEME	MOSAICKINGS	MOTHPROOFS
MOPINESSES	MORIGERATION	MORPHOPHONEMES	MOSAICLIKE	MOTILITIES
MOPISHNESS	MORIGERATIONS	MORPHOPHONEMIC	MOSASAURUS	MOTIONISTS
MOPISHNESSES	MORIGEROUS	MORPHOPHONEMICS	MOSBOLLETJIE	MOTIONLESS
MORALISATION	MORONICALLY	MORPHOPHONOLOGY	MOSBOLLETJIES	MOTIONLESSLY

MOTIONLESSNESS	MOTORIZATIONS	MOUNTEBANKING	MOUTHWATERING	MUCKINESSES
MOTIVATING	MOTORIZING	MOUNTEBANKINGS	MOUTHWATERINGLY	MUCKRAKERS
MOTIVATION	MOTORMOUTH	MOUNTEBANKISM	MOUVEMENTE	MUCKRAKING
MOTIVATIONAL	MOTORMOUTHS	MOUNTEBANKISMS	MOVABILITIES	MUCKRAKINGS
MOTIVATIONALLY	MOTORSHIPS	MOUNTEBANKS	MOVABILITY	MUCKSPREAD
MOTIVATIONS	MOTORTRUCK	MOUNTENANCE	MOVABLENESS	MUCKSPREADER
MOTIVATIVE	MOTORTRUCKS	MOUNTENANCES	MOVABLENESSES	MUCKSPREADERS
MOTIVATORS	MOTOSCAFOS	MOUNTENAUNCE	MOVEABILITIES	MUCKSPREADING
MOTIVELESS	MOUCHARABIES	MOUNTENAUNCES	MOVEABILITY	MUCKSPREADS
MOTIVELESSLY	MOUCHARABY	MOURNFULLER	MOVEABLENESS	MUCKSWEATS
MOTIVELESSNESS	MOUDIEWART	MOURNFULLEST	MOVEABLENESSES	MUCKYMUCKS
MOTIVITIES	MOUDIEWARTS	MOURNFULLY	MOVELESSLY	MUCOCUTANEOUS
MOTOCROSSES	MOUDIEWORT	MOURNFULNESS	MOVELESSNESS	MUCOLYTICS
MOTONEURON	MOUDIEWORTS	MOURNFULNESSES	MOVELESSNESSES	MUCOMEMBRANOUS
MOTONEURONAL	MOUDIWARTS	MOURNINGLY	MOVIEGOERS	MUCOPEPTIDE
MOTONEURONS	MOUDIWORTS	MOURNIVALS	MOVIEGOING	MUCOPEPTIDES
MOTORBICYCLE	MOULDABILITIES	MOUSEBIRDS	MOVIEGOINGS	MUCOPROTEIN
MOTORBICYCLES	MOULDABILITY	MOUSEOVERS	MOVIELANDS	MUCOPROTEINS
MOTORBIKED	MOULDBOARD	MOUSEPIECE	MOVIEMAKER	MUCOPURULENT
MOTORBIKES	MOULDBOARDS	MOUSEPIECES	MOVIEMAKERS	MUCOSANGUINEOUS
MOTORBIKING	MOULDERING	MOUSETAILS	MOVIEMAKING	MUCOSITIES
MOTORBOATED	MOULDINESS	MOUSETRAPPED	MOVIEMAKINGS	MUCOVISCIDOSES
MOTORBOATER	MOULDINESSES	MOUSETRAPPING	MOWBURNING	MUCOVISCIDOSIS
MOTORBOATERS	MOULDWARPS	MOUSETRAPPINGS	MOWBURNINGS	MUCRONATED
MOTORBOATING	MOULDYWARP	MOUSETRAPS	MOWDIEWART	MUCRONATION
MOTORBOATINGS	MOULDYWARPS	MOUSINESSES	MOWDIEWARTS	MUCRONATIONS
MOTORBOATS	MOUNDBIRDS	MOUSQUETAIRE	MOWDIEWORT	MUDCAPPING
MOTORBUSES	MOUNTAINBOARD	MOUSQUETAIRES	MOWDIEWORTS	MUDCAPPINGS
MOTORBUSSES	MOUNTAINBOARDER	MOUSSELINE	MOXIBUSTION	MUDDINESSES
MOTORCADED	MOUNTAINBOARDS	MOUSSELINES	MOXIBUSTIONS	MUDDLEDNESS
MOTORCADES	MOUNTAINED	MOUSTACHED	MOYGASHELS	MUDDLEDNESSES
MOTORCADING	MOUNTAINEER	MOUSTACHES	MOZZARELLA	MUDDLEHEAD
MOTORCOACH	MOUNTAINEERED	MOUSTACHIAL	MOZZARELLAS	MUDDLEHEADED
MOTORCOACHES	MOUNTAINEERING	MOUSTACHIO	MRIDAMGAMS	MUDDLEHEADEDLY
MOTORCYCLE	MOUNTAINEERINGS	MOUSTACHIOED	MRIDANGAMS	MUDDLEHEADS
MOTORCYCLED	MOUNTAINEERS	MOUSTACHIOS	MUCEDINOUS	MUDDLEMENT
MOTORCYCLES	MOUNTAINOUS	MOUTHBREATHER	MUCHNESSES	MUDDLEMENTS
MOTORCYCLING	MOUNTAINOUSLY	MOUTHBREATHERS	MUCIDITIES	MUDDLINGLY
MOTORCYCLINGS	MOUNTAINOUSNESS	MOUTHBREEDER	MUCIDNESSES	MUDHOPPERS
MOTORCYCLIST	MOUNTAINSIDE	MOUTHBREEDERS	MUCIFEROUS	MUDLARKING
MOTORCYCLISTS	MOUNTAINSIDES	MOUTHBROODER	MUCILAGINOUS	MUDLOGGERS
MOTORHOMES	MOUNTAINTOP	MOUTHBROODERS	MUCILAGINOUSLY	MUDLOGGING
MOTORICALLY	MOUNTAINTOPS	MOUTHFEELS	MUCINOGENS	MUDLOGGINGS
MOTORISATION	MOUNTEBANK	MOUTHPARTS	MUCKAMUCKED	MUDPUPPIES
MOTORISATIONS	MOUNTEBANKED	MOUTHPIECE	MUCKAMUCKING	MUDSKIPPER
MOTORISING	MOUNTEBANKERIES	MOUTHPIECES	MUCKAMUCKS	MUDSKIPPERS
MOTORIZATION	MOUNTEBANKERY	MOUTHWASHES	MUCKENDERS	MUDSLINGER

M

MUDSLINGERS	MULTIBILLION	MULTICUSPIDS	MULTIGRADES	MULTIMEGATON
MUDSLINGING	MULTIBLADED	MULTICYCLE	MULTIGRAIN	MULTIMEGAWATT
MUDSLINGINGS	MULTIBRANCHED	MULTICYCLES	MULTIGRAVIDA	MULTIMEGAWATTS
MUFFETTEES	MULTIBUILDING	MULTIDENTATE	MULTIGRAVIDAE	MULTIMEMBER
MUFFINEERS	MULTICAMERATE	MULTIDIALECTAL	MULTIGRAVIDAS	MULTIMETALLIC
MUGEARITES	MULTICAMPUS	MULTIDIGITATE	MULTIGROUP	MULTIMETER
MUGGINESSES	MULTICAPITATE	MULTIDISCIPLINE	MULTIHEADED	MULTIMETERS
MUGWUMPERIES	MULTICARBON	MULTIDIVISIONAL	MULTIHOSPITAL	MULTIMILLENNIAL
MUGWUMPERY	MULTICASTS	MULTIDOMAIN	MULTIHULLS	MULTIMILLION
MUGWUMPISH	MULTICAULINE	MULTIELECTRODE	MULTIJUGATE	MULTIMODAL
MUGWUMPISM	MULTICAUSAL	MULTIELEMENT	MULTIJUGOUS	MULTIMOLECULAR
MUGWUMPISMS	MULTICELLED	MULTIEMPLOYER	MULTILANES	MULTINATION
MUJAHEDDIN	MULTICELLULAR	MULTIEMPLOYERS	MULTILATERAL	MULTINATIONAL
MUJAHEDEEN	MULTICENTER	MULTIENGINE	MULTILATERALISM	MULTINATIONALS
MUJAHIDEEN	MULTICENTRAL	MULTIENGINED	MULTILATERALIST	MULTINOMIAL
MUKHABARAT	MULTICENTRE	MULTIENZYME	MULTILATERALLY	MULTINOMIALS
MUKHABARATS	MULTICENTRIC	MULTIETHNIC	MULTILAYER	MULTINOMINAL
MULATRESSES	MULTICHAIN	MULTIETHNICS	MULTILAYERED	MULTINUCLEAR
MULATTRESS	MULTICHAMBERED	MULTIFACED	MULTILAYERS	MULTINUCLEATE
MULATTRESSES	MULTICHANNEL	MULTIFACETED	MULTILEVEL	MULTINUCLEATED
MULBERRIES	MULTICHARACTER	MULTIFACTOR	MULTILEVELED	MULTINUCLEOLAR
MULIEBRITIES	MULTICIDES	MULTIFACTORIAL	MULTILEVELLED	MULTINUCLEOLATE
MULIEBRITY	MULTICIPITAL	MULTIFAMILIES	MULTILINEAL	MULTIORGASMIC
MULISHNESS	MULTICLIENT	MULTIFAMILY	MULTILINEAR	MULTIPACKS
MULISHNESSES	MULTICOATED	MULTIFARIOUS	MULTILINES	MULTIPANED
MULLAHISMS	MULTICOLOR	MULTIFARIOUSLY	MULTILINGUAL	MULTIPARAE
MULLARKIES	MULTICOLORED	MULTIFIDLY	MULTILINGUALISM	MULTIPARAMETER
MULLIGATAWNIES	MULTICOLORS	MULTIFIDOUS	MULTILINGUALLY	MULTIPARAS
MULLIGATAWNY	MULTICOLOUR	MULTIFILAMENT	MULTILINGUIST	MULTIPARITIES
MULLIGRUBS	MULTICOLOURED	MULTIFILAMENTS	MULTILINGUISTS	MULTIPARITY
MULLIONING	MULTICOLOURS	MULTIFLASH	MULTILOBATE	MULTIPAROUS
MULTANGULAR	MULTICOLUMN	MULTIFLORA	MULTILOBED	MULTIPARTICLE
MULTANIMOUS	MULTICOMPONENT	MULTIFLORAS	MULTILOBES	MULTIPARTITE
MULTARTICULATE	MULTICONDUCTOR	MULTIFLOROUS	MULTILOBULAR	MULTIPARTY
MULTEITIES	MULTICOPIES	MULTIFOCAL	MULTILOBULATE	MULTIPARTYISM
MULTIACCESS	MULTICOSTATE	MULTIFOCALS	MULTILOCATIONAL	MULTIPARTYISMS
MULTIACCESSES	MULTICOUNTY	MULTIFOILS	MULTILOCULAR	MULTIPEDES
MULTIAGENCY	MULTICOURSE	MULTIFOLIATE	MULTILOCULATE	MULTIPHASE
MULTIANGULAR	MULTICULTI	MULTIFOLIOLATE	MULTILOQUENCE	MULTIPHASIC
MULTIARMED	MULTICULTIS	MULTIFORMITIES	MULTILOQUENCES	MULTIPHOTON
MULTIARTICULATE	MULTICULTURAL	MULTIFORMITY	MULTILOQUENT	MULTIPICTURE
MULTIAUTHOR	MULTICULTURALLY	MULTIFORMS	MULTILOQUIES	MULTIPIECE
MULTIAXIAL	MULTICURIE	MULTIFREQUENCY	MULTILOQUOUS	MULTIPISTON
MULTIBARREL	MULTICURRENCIES	MULTIFUNCTION	MULTILOQUY	MULTIPLANE
MULTIBARRELED	MULTICURRENCY	MULTIFUNCTIONAL	MULTIMANNED	MULTIPLANES
MULTIBARRELLED	MULTICUSPID	MULTIGENIC	MULTIMEDIA	MULTIPLANT
MULTIBARRELS	MULTICUSPIDATE	MULTIGRADE	MULTIMEDIAS	MULTIPLAYER

MULTIPLAYERS
MULTIPLETS
MULTIPLEXED
MULTIPLEXER
MULTIPLEXERS
MULTIPLEXES
MULTIPLEXING
MULTIPLEXINGS
MULTIPLEXOR
MULTIPLEXORS
MULTIPLIABLE
MULTIPLICABLE
MULTIPLICAND
MULTIPLICANDS
MULTIPLICATE
MULTIPLICATES
MULTIPLICATION
MULTIPLICATIONS
MULTIPLICATIVE
MULTIPLICATOR
MULTIPLICATORS
MULTIPLICITIES
MULTIPLICITY
MULTIPLIED
MULTIPLIER
MULTIPLIERS
MULTIPLIES
MULTIPLYING
MULTIPOLAR
MULTIPOLARITIES
MULTIPOLARITY
MULTIPOLES
MULTIPOTENT
MULTIPOTENTIAL
MULTIPOWER
MULTIPRESENCE
MULTIPRESENCES
MULTIPRESENT
MULTIPROBLEM
MULTIPROCESSING
MULTIPROCESSOR
MULTIPROCESSORS
MULTIPRODUCT
MULTIPRONGED
MULTIPURPOSE
MULTIRACIAL
MULTIRACIALISM

MULTIRACIALISMS
MULTIRACIALLY
MULTIRAMIFIED
MULTIRANGE
MULTIREGIONAL
MULTIRELIGIOUS
MULTIROOMED
MULTISCIENCE
MULTISCIENCES
MULTISCREEN
MULTISCREENS
MULTISENSE
MULTISENSORY
MULTISEPTATE
MULTISERIAL
MULTISERIATE
MULTISERVICE
MULTISIDED
MULTISKILL
MULTISKILLED
MULTISKILLING
MULTISKILLINGS
MULTISKILLS
MULTISONANT
MULTISOURCE
MULTISPECIES
MULTISPECTRAL
MULTISPEED
MULTISPIRAL
MULTISPORT
MULTISTAGE
MULTISTANDARD
MULTISTATE
MULTISTEMMED
MULTISTOREY
MULTISTOREYS
MULTISTORIED
MULTISTORIES
MULTISTORY
MULTISTRANDED
MULTISTRIKE
MULTISTRIKES
MULTISULCATE
MULTISYLLABIC
MULTISYSTEM
MULTITALENTED
MULTITASKED

MULTITASKING
MULTITASKINGS
MULTITASKS
MULTITERMINAL
MULTITHREADING
MULTITHREADINGS
MULTITIERED
MULTITONED
MULTITONES
MULTITOOLS
MULTITOWERED
MULTITRACK
MULTITRILLION
MULTITRILLIONS
MULTITUDES
MULTITUDINARY
MULTITUDINOUS
MULTITUDINOUSLY
MULTIUNION
MULTIUTILITIES
MULTIUTILITY
MULTIVALENCE
MULTIVALENCES
MULTIVALENCIES
MULTIVALENCY
MULTIVALENT
MULTIVALENTS
MULTIVARIABLE
MULTIVARIATE
MULTIVARIOUS
MULTIVERSE
MULTIVERSES
MULTIVERSITIES
MULTIVERSITY
MULTIVIBRATOR
MULTIVIBRATORS
MULTIVIOUS
MULTIVITAMIN
MULTIVITAMINS
MULTIVOCAL
MULTIVOCALS
MULTIVOLTINE
MULTIVOLUME
MULTIWARHEAD
MULTIWAVELENGTH
MULTIWINDOW
MULTIWINDOWS

MULTOCULAR
MULTUNGULATE
MULTUNGULATES
MUMBLEMENT
MUMBLEMENTS
MUMBLETYPEG
MUMBLETYPEGS
MUMBLINGLY
MUMCHANCES
MUMMERINGS
MUMMICHOGS
MUMMIFICATION
MUMMIFICATIONS
MUMMIFORMS
MUMMIFYING
MUMPISHNESS
MUMPISHNESSES
MUMPRENEUR
MUMPRENEURS
MUMPSIMUSES
MUMSINESSES
MUNCHABLES
MUNDANENESS
MUNDANENESSES
MUNDANITIES
MUNDIFICATION
MUNDIFICATIONS
MUNDIFICATIVE
MUNDIFICATIVES
MUNDIFYING
MUNDUNGUSES
MUNICIPALISE
MUNICIPALISED
MUNICIPALISES
MUNICIPALISING
MUNICIPALISM
MUNICIPALISMS
MUNICIPALIST
MUNICIPALISTS
MUNICIPALITIES
MUNICIPALITY
MUNICIPALIZE
MUNICIPALIZED
MUNICIPALIZES
MUNICIPALIZING
MUNICIPALLY
MUNICIPALS

MUNIFICENCE
MUNIFICENCES
MUNIFICENT
MUNIFICENTLY
MUNIFICENTNESS
MUNIFIENCE
MUNIFIENCES
MUNITIONED
MUNITIONEER
MUNITIONEERS
MUNITIONER
MUNITIONERS
MUNITIONETTE
MUNITIONETTES
MUNITIONING
MURDERABILIA
MURDERBALL
MURDERBALLS
MURDERESSES
MURDEROUSLY
MURDEROUSNESS
MURDEROUSNESSES
MURGEONING
MURKINESSES
MURMURATION
MURMURATIONS
MURMURINGLY
MURMURINGS
MURMUROUSLY
MURTHERERS
MURTHERING
MUSCADELLE
MUSCADELLES
MUSCADINES
MUSCARDINE
MUSCARDINES
MUSCARINES
MUSCARINIC
MUSCATORIA
MUSCATORIUM
MUSCAVADOS
MUSCOLOGIES
MUSCOVADOS
MUSCOVITES
MUSCULARITIES
MUSCULARITY
MUSCULARLY

M

MUSCULATION	MUSKETEERS	MUTILATION	MYCETOMATA	MYELENCEPHALON
MUSCULATIONS	MUSKETOONS	MUTILATIONS	MYCETOMATOUS	MYELENCEPHALONS
MUSCULATURE	MUSKETRIES	MUTILATIVE	MYCETOPHAGOUS	MYELINATED
MUSCULATURES	MUSKINESSES	MUTILATORS	MYCETOZOAN	MYELITIDES
MUSCULOSKELETAL	MUSKMELONS	MUTINEERED	MYCETOZOANS	MYELITISES
MUSEOLOGICAL	MUSQUASHES	MUTINEERING	MYCOBACTERIA	MYELOBLAST
MUSEOLOGIES	MUSQUETOON	MUTINOUSLY	MYCOBACTERIAL	MYELOBLASTIC
MUSEOLOGIST	MUSQUETOONS	MUTINOUSNESS	MYCOBACTERIUM	MYELOBLASTS
MUSEOLOGISTS	MUSSELCRACKER	MUTINOUSNESSES	MYCOBIONTS	MYELOCYTES
MUSHINESSES	MUSSELCRACKERS	MUTOSCOPES	MYCODOMATIA	MYELOCYTIC
MUSHMOUTHS	MUSSINESSES	MUTTERATION	MYCODOMATIUM	MYELOFIBROSES
MUSHROOMED	MUSSITATED	MUTTERATIONS	MYCOFLORAE	MYELOFIBROSIS
MUSHROOMER	MUSSITATES	MUTTERINGLY	MYCOFLORAS	MYELOFIBROTIC
MUSHROOMERS	MUSSITATING	MUTTERINGS	MYCOLOGICAL	MYELOGENOUS
MUSHROOMING	MUSSITATION	MUTTONBIRD	MYCOLOGICALLY	MYELOGRAMS
MUSHROOMINGS	MUSSITATIONS	MUTTONBIRDER	MYCOLOGIES	MYELOGRAPHIES
MUSICALISATION	MUSTACHIOED	MUTTONBIRDERS	MYCOLOGIST	MYELOGRAPHY
MUSICALISATIONS	MUSTACHIOS	MUTTONBIRDS	MYCOLOGISTS	MYELOMATOID
MUSICALISE	MUSTELINES	MUTTONCHOPS	MYCOPHAGIES	MYELOMATOUS
MUSICALISED	MUSTINESSES	MUTTONFISH	MYCOPHAGIST	MYELOPATHIC
MUSICALISES	MUTABILITIES	MUTTONFISHES	MYCOPHAGISTS	MYELOPATHIES
MUSICALISING	MUTABILITY	MUTTONHEAD	MYCOPHAGOUS	MYELOPATHY
MUSICALITIES	MUTABLENESS	MUTTONHEADED	MYCOPHILES	MYIOPHILIES
MUSICALITY	MUTABLENESSES	MUTTONHEADS	MYCOPLASMA	MYIOPHILOUS
MUSICALIZATION	MUTAGENESES	MUTUALISATION	MYCOPLASMAL	MYLOHYOIDS
MUSICALIZATIONS	MUTAGENESIS	MUTUALISATIONS	MYCOPLASMAS	MYLONITISATION
MUSICALIZE	MUTAGENICALLY	MUTUALISED	MYCOPLASMATA	MYLONITISATIONS
MUSICALIZED	MUTAGENICITIES	MUTUALISES	MYCOPLASMOSES	MYLONITISE
MUSICALIZES	MUTAGENICITY	MUTUALISING	MYCOPLASMOSIS	MYLONITISED
MUSICALIZING	MUTAGENISE	MUTUALISMS	MYCORHIZAE	MYLONITISES
MUSICALNESS	MUTAGENISED	MUTUALISTIC	MYCORHIZAL	MYLONITISING
MUSICALNESSES	MUTAGENISES	MUTUALISTS	MYCORHIZAS	MYLONITIZATION
MUSICIANER	MUTAGENISING	MUTUALITIES	MYCORRHIZA	MYLONITIZATIONS
MUSICIANERS	MUTAGENIZE	MUTUALIZATION	MYCORRHIZAE	MYLONITIZE
MUSICIANLY	MUTAGENIZED	MUTUALIZATIONS	MYCORRHIZAL	MYLONITIZED
MUSICIANSHIP	MUTAGENIZES	MUTUALIZED	MYCORRHIZAS	MYLONITIZES
MUSICIANSHIPS	MUTAGENIZING	MUTUALIZES	MYCOTOXICOLOGY	MYLONITIZING
MUSICOLOGICAL	MUTATIONAL	MUTUALIZING	MYCOTOXICOSES	MYOBLASTIC
MUSICOLOGICALLY	MUTATIONALLY	MUTUALNESS	MYCOTOXICOSIS	MYOCARDIAL
MUSICOLOGIES	MUTATIONIST	MUTUALNESSES	MYCOTOXINS	MYOCARDIOGRAPH
MUSICOLOGIST	MUTATIONISTS	MUZZINESSES	MYCOTOXOLOGIES	MYOCARDIOGRAPHS
MUSICOLOGISTS	MUTENESSES	MYASTHENIA	MYCOTOXOLOGY	MYOCARDIOPATHY
MUSICOLOGY	MUTESSARIF	MYASTHENIAS	MYCOTROPHIC	MYOCARDITIS
MUSICOTHERAPIES	MUTESSARIFAT	MYASTHENIC	MYCOVIRUSES	MYOCARDITISES
MUSICOTHERAPY	MUTESSARIFATS	MYASTHENICS	MYDRIATICS	MYOCARDIUM
MUSKELLUNGE	MUTESSARIFS	MYCETOLOGIES	MYELENCEPHALA	MYOCLONUSES
MUSKELLUNGES	MUTILATING	MYCETOLOGY	MYELENCEPHALIC	MYOELECTRIC

MYOELECTRICAL
MYOFIBRILLAR
MYOFIBRILS
MYOFILAMENT
MYOFILAMENTS
MYOGLOBINS
MYOGRAPHIC
MYOGRAPHICAL
MYOGRAPHICALLY
MYOGRAPHIES
MYOGRAPHIST
MYOGRAPHISTS
MYOINOSITOL
MYOINOSITOLS
MYOLOGICAL
MYOLOGISTS
MYOMANCIES
MYOMECTOMIES
MYOMECTOMY
MYOPATHIES
MYOPHILIES
MYOPHILOUS
MYOPICALLY
MYOSITISES
MYOSOTISES
MYOSTATINS
MYRIADFOLD
MYRIADFOLDS
MYRIAPODAN
MYRIAPODOUS
MYRINGITIS
MYRINGITISES
MYRINGOSCOPE

MYRINGOSCOPES
MYRINGOTOMIES
MYRINGOTOMY
MYRIORAMAS
MYRIOSCOPE
MYRIOSCOPES
MYRISTICIVOROUS
MYRMECOCHORIES
MYRMECOCHORY
MYRMECOLOGIC
MYRMECOLOGICAL
MYRMECOLOGIES
MYRMECOLOGIST
MYRMECOLOGISTS
MYRMECOLOGY
MYRMECOPHAGOUS
MYRMECOPHILE
MYRMECOPHILES
MYRMECOPHILIES
MYRMECOPHILOUS
MYRMECOPHILY
MYRMIDONES
MYRMIDONIAN
MYROBALANS
MYRTACEOUS
MYSOPHOBIA
MYSOPHOBIAS
MYSTAGOGIC
MYSTAGOGICAL
MYSTAGOGICALLY
MYSTAGOGIES
MYSTAGOGUE
MYSTAGOGUES

MYSTAGOGUS
MYSTAGOGUSES
MYSTERIOUS
MYSTERIOUSLY
MYSTERIOUSNESS
MYSTICALLY
MYSTICALNESS
MYSTICALNESSES
MYSTICETES
MYSTICISMS
MYSTIFICATION
MYSTIFICATIONS
MYSTIFIERS
MYSTIFYING
MYSTIFYINGLY
MYTHICALLY
MYTHICISATION
MYTHICISATIONS
MYTHICISED
MYTHICISER
MYTHICISERS
MYTHICISES
MYTHICISING
MYTHICISMS
MYTHICISTS
MYTHICIZATION
MYTHICIZATIONS
MYTHICIZED
MYTHICIZER
MYTHICIZERS
MYTHICIZES
MYTHICIZING
MYTHMAKERS

MYTHMAKING
MYTHMAKINGS
MYTHOGENESES
MYTHOGENESIS
MYTHOGRAPHER
MYTHOGRAPHERS
MYTHOGRAPHIES
MYTHOGRAPHY
MYTHOLOGER
MYTHOLOGERS
MYTHOLOGIAN
MYTHOLOGIANS
MYTHOLOGIC
MYTHOLOGICAL
MYTHOLOGICALLY
MYTHOLOGIES
MYTHOLOGISATION
MYTHOLOGISE
MYTHOLOGISED
MYTHOLOGISER
MYTHOLOGISERS
MYTHOLOGISES
MYTHOLOGISING
MYTHOLOGIST
MYTHOLOGISTS
MYTHOLOGIZATION
MYTHOLOGIZE
MYTHOLOGIZED
MYTHOLOGIZER
MYTHOLOGIZERS
MYTHOLOGIZES
MYTHOLOGIZING
MYTHOMANES

MYTHOMANIA
MYTHOMANIAC
MYTHOMANIACS
MYTHOMANIAS
MYTHOPOEIA
MYTHOPOEIAS
MYTHOPOEIC
MYTHOPOEISM
MYTHOPOEISMS
MYTHOPOEIST
MYTHOPOEISTS
MYTHOPOESES
MYTHOPOESIS
MYTHOPOETIC
MYTHOPOETICAL
MYTHOPOETS
MYTILIFORM
MYXAMOEBAE
MYXAMOEBAS
MYXEDEMATOUS
MYXOEDEMAS
MYXOEDEMATOUS
MYXOEDEMIC
MYXOMATOSES
MYXOMATOSIS
MYXOMATOUS
MYXOMYCETE
MYXOMYCETES
MYXOMYCETOUS
MYXOVIRUSES

M

N

NABOBERIES	NANOPARTICLES	NARCOANALYSES	NARRATOLOGISTS	NATIONALISER
NABOBESSES	NANOPHYSICS	NARCOANALYSIS	NARRATOLOGY	NATIONALISERS
NACHTMAALS	NANOPLANKTON	NARCOCATHARSES	NARROWBAND	NATIONALISES
NAFFNESSES	NANOPLANKTONS	NARCOCATHARSIS	NARROWBANDS	NATIONALISING
NAIFNESSES	NANOPUBLISHING	NARCOHYPNOSES	NARROWCAST	NATIONALISM
NAILBITERS	NANOPUBLISHINGS	NARCOHYPNOSIS	NARROWCASTED	NATIONALISMS
NAILBRUSHES	NANOSECOND	NARCOLEPSIES	NARROWCASTING	NATIONALIST
NAISSANCES	NANOSECONDS	NARCOLEPSY	NARROWCASTINGS	NATIONALISTIC
NAIVENESSES	NANOTECHNOLOGY	NARCOLEPTIC	NARROWCASTS	NATIONALISTS
NAKEDNESSES	NANOTESLAS	NARCOLEPTICS	NARROWINGS	NATIONALITIES
NALBUPHINE	NANOWORLDS	NARCOSYNTHESES	NARROWNESS	NATIONALITY
NALBUPHINES	NAPHTHALENE	NARCOSYNTHESIS	NARROWNESSES	NATIONALIZATION
NALORPHINE	NAPHTHALENES	NARCOTERRORISM	NASALISATION	NATIONALIZE
NALORPHINES	NAPHTHALIC	NARCOTERRORISMS	NASALISATIONS	NATIONALIZED
NALTREXONE	NAPHTHALIN	NARCOTERRORIST	NASALISING	NATIONALIZER
NALTREXONES	NAPHTHALINE	NARCOTERRORISTS	NASALITIES	NATIONALIZERS
NAMAYCUSHES	NAPHTHALINES	NARCOTICALLY	NASALIZATION	NATIONALIZES
NAMECHECKED	NAPHTHALINS	NARCOTINES	NASALIZATIONS	NATIONALIZING
NAMECHECKING	NAPHTHALISE	NARCOTISATION	NASALIZING	NATIONALLY
NAMECHECKS	NAPHTHALISED	NARCOTISATIONS	NASCENCIES	NATIONHOOD
NAMELESSLY	NAPHTHALISES	NARCOTISED	NASEBERRIES	NATIONHOODS
NAMELESSNESS	NAPHTHALISING	NARCOTISES	NASOFRONTAL	NATIONLESS
NAMELESSNESSES	NAPHTHALIZE	NARCOTISING	NASOGASTRIC	NATIONWIDE
NAMEPLATES	NAPHTHALIZED	NARCOTISMS	NASOLACRYMAL	NATIVENESS
NAMEWORTHY	NAPHTHALIZES	NARCOTISTS	NASOPHARYNGEAL	NATIVENESSES
NANDROLONE	NAPHTHALIZING	NARCOTIZATION	NASOPHARYNGES	NATIVISTIC
NANDROLONES	NAPHTHENES	NARCOTIZATIONS	NASOPHARYNX	NATIVITIES
NANISATION	NAPHTHENIC	NARCOTIZED	NASOPHARYNXES	NATRIURESES
NANISATIONS	NAPHTHYLAMINE	NARCOTIZES	NASTINESSES	NATRIURESIS
NANIZATION	NAPHTHYLAMINES	NARCOTIZING	NASTURTIUM	NATRIURETIC
NANIZATIONS	NAPOLEONITE	NARGHILIES	NASTURTIUMS	NATRIURETICS
NANNOPLANKTON	NAPOLEONITES	NARGHILLIES	NATALITIAL	NATROLITES
NANNOPLANKTONS	NAPPINESSES	NARGUILEHS	NATALITIES	NATTERJACK
NANOGRAMME	NAPRAPATHIES	NARRATABLE	NATATIONAL	NATTERJACKS
NANOGRAMMES	NAPRAPATHY	NARRATIONAL	NATATORIAL	NATTINESSES
NANOGRASSES	NARCISSISM	NARRATIONS	NATATORIUM	NATURALISATION
NANOMATERIAL	NARCISSISMS	NARRATIVELY	NATATORIUMS	NATURALISATIONS
NANOMATERIALS	NARCISSIST	NARRATIVES	NATHELESSE	NATURALISE
NANOMETERS	NARCISSISTIC	NARRATOLOGICAL	NATIONALISATION	NATURALISED
NANOMETRES	NARCISSISTS	NARRATOLOGIES	NATIONALISE	NATURALISES
NANOPARTICLE	NARCISSUSES	NARRATOLOGIST	NATIONALISED	NATURALISING

NATURALISM
NATURALISMS
NATURALIST
NATURALISTIC
NATURALISTS
NATURALIZATION
NATURALIZATIONS
NATURALIZE
NATURALIZED
NATURALIZES
NATURALIZING
NATURALNESS
NATURALNESSES
NATURISTIC
NATUROPATH
NATUROPATHIC
NATUROPATHIES
NATUROPATHS
NATUROPATHY
NAUGAHYDES
NAUGHTIEST
NAUGHTINESS
NAUGHTINESSES
NAUMACHIAE
NAUMACHIAS
NAUMACHIES
NAUPLIIFORM
NAUSEATING
NAUSEATINGLY
NAUSEATION
NAUSEATIONS
NAUSEATIVE
NAUSEOUSLY
NAUSEOUSNESS
NAUSEOUSNESSES
NAUTICALLY
NAUTILOIDS
NAUTILUSES
NAVARCHIES
NAVELWORTS
NAVICULARE
NAVICULARES
NAVICULARS
NAVIGABILITIES
NAVIGABILITY
NAVIGABLENESS
NAVIGABLENESSES

NAVIGATING
NAVIGATION
NAVIGATIONAL
NAVIGATIONALLY
NAVIGATIONS
NAVIGATORS
NAYSAYINGS
NAZIFICATION
NAZIFICATIONS
NEANDERTAL
NEANDERTALER
NEANDERTALERS
NEANDERTALS
NEANDERTHAL
NEANDERTHALER
NEANDERTHALERS
NEANDERTHALOID
NEANDERTHALS
NEAPOLITAN
NEAPOLITANS
NEARNESSES
NEARSHORED
NEARSHORES
NEARSHORING
NEARSIGHTED
NEARSIGHTEDLY
NEARSIGHTEDNESS
NEARTHROSES
NEARTHROSIS
NEATNESSES
NEBBISHERS
NEBENKERNS
NEBUCHADNEZZAR
NEBUCHADNEZZARS
NEBULISATION
NEBULISATIONS
NEBULISERS
NEBULISING
NEBULIZATION
NEBULIZATIONS
NEBULIZERS
NEBULIZING
NEBULOSITIES
NEBULOSITY
NEBULOUSLY
NEBULOUSNESS
NEBULOUSNESSES

NECESSAIRE
NECESSAIRES
NECESSARIAN
NECESSARIANISM
NECESSARIANISMS
NECESSARIANS
NECESSARIES
NECESSARILY
NECESSARINESS
NECESSARINESSES
NECESSITARIAN
NECESSITARIANS
NECESSITATE
NECESSITATED
NECESSITATES
NECESSITATING
NECESSITATION
NECESSITATIONS
NECESSITATIVE
NECESSITIED
NECESSITIES
NECESSITOUS
NECESSITOUSLY
NECESSITOUSNESS
NECKCLOTHS
NECKERCHIEF
NECKERCHIEFS
NECKERCHIEVES
NECKLACING
NECKLACINGS
NECKPIECES
NECKVERSES
NECROBIOSES
NECROBIOSIS
NECROBIOTIC
NECROGRAPHER
NECROGRAPHERS
NECROLATER
NECROLATERS
NECROLATRIES
NECROLATRY
NECROLOGIC
NECROLOGICAL
NECROLOGIES
NECROLOGIST
NECROLOGISTS
NECROMANCER

NECROMANCERS
NECROMANCIES
NECROMANCY
NECROMANIA
NECROMANIAC
NECROMANIACS
NECROMANIAS
NECROMANTIC
NECROMANTICAL
NECROMANTICALLY
NECROPHAGOUS
NECROPHILE
NECROPHILES
NECROPHILIA
NECROPHILIAC
NECROPHILIACS
NECROPHILIAS
NECROPHILIC
NECROPHILIES
NECROPHILISM
NECROPHILISMS
NECROPHILOUS
NECROPHILS
NECROPHILY
NECROPHOBE
NECROPHOBES
NECROPHOBIA
NECROPHOBIAS
NECROPHOBIC
NECROPHOROUS
NECROPOLEIS
NECROPOLES
NECROPOLIS
NECROPOLISES
NECROPSIED
NECROPSIES
NECROPSYING
NECROSCOPIC
NECROSCOPICAL
NECROSCOPIES
NECROSCOPY
NECROTISED
NECROTISES
NECROTISING
NECROTIZED
NECROTIZES
NECROTIZING

NECROTOMIES
NECROTROPH
NECROTROPHIC
NECROTROPHS
NECTAREOUS
NECTAREOUSNESS
NECTARIFEROUS
NECTARINES
NECTARIVOROUS
NECTOCALYCES
NECTOCALYX
NEEDCESSITIES
NEEDCESSITY
NEEDFULNESS
NEEDFULNESSES
NEEDINESSES
NEEDLECORD
NEEDLECORDS
NEEDLECRAFT
NEEDLECRAFTS
NEEDLEFISH
NEEDLEFISHES
NEEDLEFULS
NEEDLELIKE
NEEDLEPOINT
NEEDLEPOINTS
NEEDLESSLY
NEEDLESSNESS
NEEDLESSNESSES
NEEDLESTICK
NEEDLEWOMAN
NEEDLEWOMEN
NEEDLEWORK
NEEDLEWORKER
NEEDLEWORKERS
NEEDLEWORKS
NEESBERRIES
NEFARIOUSLY
NEFARIOUSNESS
NEFARIOUSNESSES
NEGATIONAL
NEGATIONIST
NEGATIONISTS
NEGATIVELY
NEGATIVENESS
NEGATIVENESSES
NEGATIVING

N

NEGATIVISM	NEGRITUDES	NEMATOLOGICAL	NEOLOGISED	NEOREALISMS
NEGATIVISMS	NEGROHEADS	NEMATOLOGIES	NEOLOGISES	NEOREALIST
NEGATIVIST	NEGROPHILE	NEMATOLOGIST	NEOLOGISING	NEOREALISTIC
NEGATIVISTIC	NEGROPHILES	NEMATOLOGISTS	NEOLOGISMS	NEOREALISTS
NEGATIVISTS	NEGROPHILISM	NEMATOLOGY	NEOLOGISTIC	NEOSTIGMINE
NEGATIVITIES	NEGROPHILISMS	NEMATOPHORE	NEOLOGISTICAL	NEOSTIGMINES
NEGATIVITY	NEGROPHILIST	NEMATOPHORES	NEOLOGISTICALLY	NEOTEINIAS
NEGLECTABLE	NEGROPHILISTS	NEMERTEANS	NEOLOGISTS	NEOTERICAL
NEGLECTEDNESS	NEGROPHILS	NEMERTIANS	NEOLOGIZED	NEOTERICALLY
NEGLECTEDNESSES	NEGROPHOBE	NEMERTINES	NEOLOGIZES	NEOTERICALS
NEGLECTERS	NEGROPHOBES	NEMOPHILAS	NEOLOGIZING	NEOTERISED
NEGLECTFUL	NEGROPHOBIA	NEOANTHROPIC	NEONATALLY	NEOTERISES
NEGLECTFULLY	NEGROPHOBIAS	NEOARSPHENAMINE	NEONATICIDE	NEOTERISING
NEGLECTFULNESS	NEIGHBORED	NEOCAPITALISM	NEONATICIDES	NEOTERISMS
NEGLECTING	NEIGHBORHOOD	NEOCAPITALISMS	NEONATOLOGIES	NEOTERISTS
NEGLECTINGLY	NEIGHBORHOODS	NEOCAPITALIST	NEONATOLOGIST	NEOTERIZED
NEGLECTION	NEIGHBORING	NEOCAPITALISTS	NEONATOLOGISTS	NEOTERIZES
NEGLECTIONS	NEIGHBORLESS	NEOCLASSIC	NEONATOLOGY	NEOTERIZING
NEGLECTIVE	NEIGHBORLINESS	NEOCLASSICAL	NEONOMIANISM	NEOTROPICS
NEGLECTORS	NEIGHBORLY	NEOCLASSICISM	NEONOMIANISMS	NEOVITALISM
NEGLIGEABLE	NEIGHBOURED	NEOCLASSICISMS	NEONOMIANS	NEOVITALISMS
NEGLIGENCE	NEIGHBOURHOOD	NEOCLASSICIST	NEOORTHODOX	NEOVITALIST
NEGLIGENCES	NEIGHBOURHOODS	NEOCLASSICISTS	NEOORTHODOXIES	NEOVITALISTS
NEGLIGENTLY	NEIGHBOURING	NEOCOLONIAL	NEOORTHODOXY	NEPENTHEAN
NEGLIGIBILITIES	NEIGHBOURLESS	NEOCOLONIALISM	NEOPAGANISE	NEPHALISMS
NEGLIGIBILITY	NEIGHBOURLINESS	NEOCOLONIALISMS	NEOPAGANISED	NEPHALISTS
NEGLIGIBLE	NEIGHBOURLY	NEOCOLONIALIST	NEOPAGANISES	NEPHELINES
NEGLIGIBLENESS	NEIGHBOURS	NEOCOLONIALISTS	NEOPAGANISING	NEPHELINIC
NEGLIGIBLY	NELUMBIUMS	NEOCONSERVATISM	NEOPAGANISM	NEPHELINITE
NEGOCIANTS	NEMATHELMINTH	NEOCONSERVATIVE	NEOPAGANISMS	NEPHELINITES
NEGOTIABILITIES	NEMATHELMINTHIC	NEOCORTEXES	NEOPAGANIZE	NEPHELINITIC
NEGOTIABILITY	NEMATHELMINTHS	NEOCORTICAL	NEOPAGANIZED	NEPHELITES
NEGOTIABLE	NEMATICIDAL	NEOCORTICES	NEOPAGANIZES	NEPHELOMETER
NEGOTIANTS	NEMATICIDE	NEODYMIUMS	NEOPAGANIZING	NEPHELOMETERS
NEGOTIATED	NEMATICIDES	NEOGENESES	NEOPHILIAC	NEPHELOMETRIC
NEGOTIATES	NEMATOBLAST	NEOGENESIS	NEOPHILIACS	NEPHELOMETRIES
NEGOTIATING	NEMATOBLASTS	NEOGENETIC	NEOPHILIAS	NEPHELOMETRY
NEGOTIATION	NEMATOCIDAL	NEOGOTHICS	NEOPHOBIAS	NEPHOGRAMS
NEGOTIATIONS	NEMATOCIDE	NEOGRAMMARIAN	NEOPILINAS	NEPHOGRAPH
NEGOTIATOR	NEMATOCIDES	NEOGRAMMARIANS	NEOPLASIAS	NEPHOGRAPHS
NEGOTIATORS	NEMATOCYST	NEOLIBERAL	NEOPLASTIC	NEPHOLOGIC
NEGOTIATORY	NEMATOCYSTIC	NEOLIBERALISM	NEOPLASTICISM	NEPHOLOGICAL
NEGOTIATRESS	NEMATOCYSTS	NEOLIBERALISMS	NEOPLASTICISMS	NEPHOLOGIES
NEGOTIATRESSES	NEMATODIRIASES	NEOLIBERALS	NEOPLASTICIST	NEPHOLOGIST
NEGOTIATRICES	NEMATODIRIASIS	NEOLOGIANS	NEOPLASTICISTS	NEPHOLOGISTS
NEGOTIATRIX	NEMATODIRUS	NEOLOGICAL	NEOPLASTIES	NEPHOSCOPE
NEGOTIATRIXES	NEMATODIRUSES	NEOLOGICALLY	NEOREALISM	NEPHOSCOPES

NEPHRALGIA
NEPHRALGIAS
NEPHRALGIC
NEPHRALGIES
NEPHRECTOMIES
NEPHRECTOMISE
NEPHRECTOMISED
NEPHRECTOMISES
NEPHRECTOMISING
NEPHRECTOMIZE
NEPHRECTOMIZED
NEPHRECTOMIZES
NEPHRECTOMIZING
NEPHRECTOMY
NEPHRIDIAL
NEPHRIDIUM
NEPHRITICAL
NEPHRITICS
NEPHRITIDES
NEPHRITISES
NEPHROBLASTOMA
NEPHROBLASTOMAS
NEPHROLEPIS
NEPHROLEPISES
NEPHROLOGICAL
NEPHROLOGIES
NEPHROLOGIST
NEPHROLOGISTS
NEPHROLOGY
NEPHROPATHIC
NEPHROPATHIES
NEPHROPATHY
NEPHROPEXIES
NEPHROPEXY
NEPHROPTOSES
NEPHROPTOSIS
NEPHROSCOPE
NEPHROSCOPES
NEPHROSCOPIES
NEPHROSCOPY
NEPHROSTOME
NEPHROSTOMES
NEPHROTICS
NEPHROTOMIES
NEPHROTOMY
NEPHROTOXIC
NEPHROTOXICITY

NEPOTISTIC
NEPTUNIUMS
NERDINESSES
NERVATIONS
NERVATURES
NERVELESSLY
NERVELESSNESS
NERVELESSNESSES
NERVINESSES
NERVOSITIES
NERVOUSNESS
NERVOUSNESSES
NERVURATION
NERVURATIONS
NESCIENCES
NESHNESSES
NESSELRODE
NESSELRODES
NETBALLERS
NETHERLINGS
NETHERMORE
NETHERMORES
NETHERMOST
NETHERSTOCK
NETHERSTOCKS
NETHERWARD
NETHERWARDS
NETHERWORLD
NETHERWORLDS
NETIQUETTE
NETIQUETTES
NETMINDERS
NETSURFERS
NETSURFING
NETSURFINGS
NETTLELIKE
NETTLESOME
NETWORKERS
NETWORKING
NETWORKINGS
NEURALGIAS
NEURAMINIDASE
NEURAMINIDASES
NEURASTHENIA
NEURASTHENIAC
NEURASTHENIACS
NEURASTHENIAS

NEURASTHENIC
NEURASTHENICS
NEURATIONS
NEURECTOMIES
NEURECTOMY
NEURILEMMA
NEURILEMMAL
NEURILEMMAS
NEURILITIES
NEURITIDES
NEURITISES
NEUROACTIVE
NEUROANATOMIC
NEUROANATOMICAL
NEUROANATOMIES
NEUROANATOMIST
NEUROANATOMISTS
NEUROANATOMY
NEUROBIOLOGICAL
NEUROBIOLOGIES
NEUROBIOLOGIST
NEUROBIOLOGISTS
NEUROBIOLOGY
NEUROBLAST
NEUROBLASTOMA
NEUROBLASTOMAS
NEUROBLASTOMATA
NEUROBLASTS
NEUROCHEMICAL
NEUROCHEMICALS
NEUROCHEMIST
NEUROCHEMISTRY
NEUROCHEMISTS
NEUROCHIPS
NEUROCOELE
NEUROCOELES
NEUROCOELS
NEUROCOGNITIVE
NEUROCOMPUTER
NEUROCOMPUTERS
NEUROCOMPUTING
NEUROCOMPUTINGS
NEUROECTODERMAL
NEUROENDOCRINE
NEUROETHOLOGIES
NEUROETHOLOGY
NEUROFEEDBACK

NEUROFEEDBACKS
NEUROFIBRIL
NEUROFIBRILAR
NEUROFIBRILLAR
NEUROFIBRILLARY
NEUROFIBRILS
NEUROFIBROMA
NEUROFIBROMAS
NEUROFIBROMATA
NEUROGENESES
NEUROGENESIS
NEUROGENIC
NEUROGENICALLY
NEUROGLIAL
NEUROGLIAS
NEUROGRAMS
NEUROHORMONAL
NEUROHORMONE
NEUROHORMONES
NEUROHUMOR
NEUROHUMORAL
NEUROHUMORS
NEUROHUMOUR
NEUROHUMOURS
NEUROHYPNOLOGY
NEUROHYPOPHYSES
NEUROHYPOPHYSIS
NEUROLEMMA
NEUROLEMMAS
NEUROLEPTIC
NEUROLEPTICS
NEUROLINGUIST
NEUROLINGUISTIC
NEUROLINGUISTS
NEUROLOGIC
NEUROLOGICAL
NEUROLOGICALLY
NEUROLOGIES
NEUROLOGIST
NEUROLOGISTS
NEUROLYSES
NEUROLYSIS
NEUROMARKETING
NEUROMARKETINGS
NEUROMASTS
NEUROMATOUS
NEUROMUSCULAR

NEUROPATHIC
NEUROPATHICAL
NEUROPATHICALLY
NEUROPATHIES
NEUROPATHIST
NEUROPATHISTS
NEUROPATHOLOGIC
NEUROPATHOLOGY
NEUROPATHS
NEUROPATHY
NEUROPEPTIDE
NEUROPEPTIDES
NEUROPHYSIOLOGY
NEUROPLASM
NEUROPLASMS
NEUROPSYCHIATRY
NEUROPSYCHOLOGY
NEUROPTERA
NEUROPTERAN
NEUROPTERANS
NEUROPTERIST
NEUROPTERISTS
NEUROPTERON
NEUROPTERONS
NEUROPTEROUS
NEURORADIOLOGY
NEUROSCIENCE
NEUROSCIENCES
NEUROSCIENTIFIC
NEUROSCIENTIST
NEUROSCIENTISTS
NEUROSECRETION
NEUROSECRETIONS
NEUROSECRETORY
NEUROSENSORY
NEUROSPORA
NEUROSPORAS
NEUROSURGEON
NEUROSURGEONS
NEUROSURGERIES
NEUROSURGERY
NEUROSURGICAL
NEUROSURGICALLY
NEUROSYPHILIS
NEUROSYPHILISES
NEUROTICALLY
NEUROTICISM

N

NEUROTICISMS	NEUTROPHIL	NEWSPAPERWOMAN	NICOTINISMS	NIGHTCLASS
NEUROTOMIES	NEUTROPHILE	NEWSPAPERWOMEN	NICROSILAL	NIGHTCLASSES
NEUROTOMIST	NEUTROPHILES	NEWSPEOPLE	NICROSILALS	NIGHTCLOTHES
NEUROTOMISTS	NEUTROPHILIC	NEWSPERSON	NICTATIONS	NIGHTCLUBBED
NEUROTOXIC	NEUTROPHILS	NEWSPERSONS	NICTITATED	NIGHTCLUBBER
NEUROTOXICITIES	NEVERMINDS	NEWSPRINTS	NICTITATES	NIGHTCLUBBERS
NEUROTOXICITY	NEVERTHELESS	NEWSREADER	NICTITATING	NIGHTCLUBBING
NEUROTOXIN	NEVERTHEMORE	NEWSREADERS	NICTITATION	NIGHTCLUBBINGS
NEUROTOXINS	NEWFANGLED	NEWSSHEETS	NICTITATIONS	NIGHTCLUBS
NEUROTROPHIC	NEWFANGLEDLY	NEWSSTANDS	NIDAMENTAL	NIGHTDRESS
NEUROTROPHIES	NEWFANGLEDNESS	NEWSTRADES	NIDAMENTUM	NIGHTDRESSES
NEUROTROPHY	NEWFANGLENESS	NEWSWEEKLIES	NIDDERINGS	NIGHTFALLS
NEUROTROPIC	NEWFANGLENESSES	NEWSWEEKLY	NIDDERLING	NIGHTFARING
NEUROVASCULAR	NEWFANGLES	NEWSWORTHINESS	NIDDERLINGS	NIGHTFIRES
NEURULATION	NEWISHNESS	NEWSWORTHY	NIDERLINGS	NIGHTGEARS
NEURULATIONS	NEWISHNESSES	NEWSWRITING	NIDICOLOUS	NIGHTGLOWS
NEURYPNOLOGIES	NEWMARKETS	NEWSWRITINGS	NIDIFICATE	NIGHTGOWNS
NEURYPNOLOGY	NEWSAGENCIES	NEXTNESSES	NIDIFICATED	NIGHTHAWKS
NEUTRALISATION	NEWSAGENCY	NIACINAMIDE	NIDIFICATES	NIGHTINGALE
NEUTRALISATIONS	NEWSAGENTS	NIACINAMIDES	NIDIFICATING	NIGHTINGALES
NEUTRALISE	NEWSBREAKS	NIAISERIES	NIDIFICATION	NIGHTLIFES
NEUTRALISED	NEWSCASTER	NIALAMIDES	NIDIFICATIONS	NIGHTLIVES
NEUTRALISER	NEWSCASTERS	NIBBLINGLY	NIDIFUGOUS	NIGHTMARES
NEUTRALISERS	NEWSCASTING	NICCOLITES	NIDULATION	NIGHTMARISH
NEUTRALISES	NEWSCASTINGS	NICENESSES	NIDULATIONS	NIGHTMARISHLY
NEUTRALISING	NEWSDEALER	NICKELIFEROUS	NIFEDIPINE	NIGHTMARISHNESS
NEUTRALISM	NEWSDEALERS	NICKELINES	NIFEDIPINES	NIGHTPIECE
NEUTRALISMS	NEWSFLASHES	NICKELISED	NIFFNAFFED	NIGHTPIECES
NEUTRALIST	NEWSGROUPS	NICKELISES	NIFFNAFFING	NIGHTRIDER
NEUTRALISTIC	NEWSHOUNDS	NICKELISING	NIFTINESSES	NIGHTRIDERS
NEUTRALISTS	NEWSINESSES	NICKELIZED	NIGGARDING	NIGHTRIDING
NEUTRALITIES	NEWSLETTER	NICKELIZES	NIGGARDISE	NIGHTRIDINGS
NEUTRALITY	NEWSLETTERS	NICKELIZING	NIGGARDISES	NIGHTSCOPE
NEUTRALIZATION	NEWSMAGAZINE	NICKELLING	NIGGARDIZE	NIGHTSCOPES
NEUTRALIZATIONS	NEWSMAGAZINES	NICKELODEON	NIGGARDIZES	NIGHTSHADE
NEUTRALIZE	NEWSMAKERS	NICKELODEONS	NIGGARDLINESS	NIGHTSHADES
NEUTRALIZED	NEWSMONGER	NICKNAMERS	NIGGARDLINESSES	NIGHTSHIRT
NEUTRALIZER	NEWSMONGERS	NICKNAMING	NIGGERDOMS	NIGHTSHIRTS
NEUTRALIZERS	NEWSPAPERDOM	NICKPOINTS	NIGGERHEAD	NIGHTSIDES
NEUTRALIZES	NEWSPAPERDOMS	NICKSTICKS	NIGGERHEADS	NIGHTSPOTS
NEUTRALIZING	NEWSPAPERED	NICKUMPOOP	NIGGERISMS	NIGHTSTAND
NEUTRALNESS	NEWSPAPERING	NICKUMPOOPS	NIGGERLING	NIGHTSTANDS
NEUTRALNESSES	NEWSPAPERISM	NICOMPOOPS	NIGGERLINGS	NIGHTSTICK
NEUTRETTOS	NEWSPAPERISMS	NICOTIANAS	NIGGLINGLY	NIGHTSTICKS
NEUTRINOLESS	NEWSPAPERMAN	NICOTINAMIDE	NIGHNESSES	NIGHTTIDES
NEUTROPENIA	NEWSPAPERMEN	NICOTINAMIDES	NIGHTBIRDS	NIGHTTIMES
NEUTROPENIAS	NEWSPAPERS	NICOTINISM	NIGHTBLIND	NIGHTWALKER

NIGHTWALKERS	NITPICKIEST	NITROMETER	NOCTILUCOUS	NOMENKLATURAS
NIGHTWATCHMAN	NITPICKING	NITROMETERS	NOCTIVAGANT	NOMINALISATION
NIGHTWATCHMEN	NITRAMINES	NITROMETHANE	NOCTIVAGANTS	NOMINALISATIONS
NIGHTWEARS	NITRANILINE	NITROMETHANES	NOCTIVAGATION	NOMINALISE
NIGRESCENCE	NITRANILINES	NITROMETRIC	NOCTIVAGATIONS	NOMINALISED
NIGRESCENCES	NITRATINES	NITROPARAFFIN	NOCTIVAGOUS	NOMINALISES
NIGRESCENT	NITRATIONS	NITROPARAFFINS	NOCTUARIES	NOMINALISING
NIGRIFYING	NITRAZEPAM	NITROPHILOUS	NOCTURNALITIES	NOMINALISM
NIGRITUDES	NITRAZEPAMS	NITROSAMINE	NOCTURNALITY	NOMINALISMS
NIGROMANCIES	NITRIDINGS	NITROSAMINES	NOCTURNALLY	NOMINALIST
NIGROMANCY	NITRIFIABLE	NITROSATION	NOCTURNALS	NOMINALISTIC
NIGROSINES	NITRIFICATION	NITROSATIONS	NOCUOUSNESS	NOMINALISTS
NIHILISTIC	NITRIFICATIONS	NITROTOLUENE	NOCUOUSNESSES	NOMINALIZATION
NIHILITIES	NITRIFIERS	NITROTOLUENES	NODALISING	NOMINALIZATIONS
NIKETHAMIDE	NITRIFYING	NITWITTEDNESS	NODALITIES	NOMINALIZE
NIKETHAMIDES	NITROBACTERIA	NITWITTEDNESSES	NODALIZING	NOMINALIZED
NILPOTENTS	NITROBACTERIUM	NITWITTERIES	NODOSITIES	NOMINALIZES
NIMBLENESS	NITROBENZENE	NITWITTERY	NODULATION	NOMINALIZING
NIMBLENESSES	NITROBENZENES	NOBBINESSES	NODULATIONS	NOMINATELY
NIMBLESSES	NITROCELLULOSE	NOBILESSES	NOEMATICAL	NOMINATING
NIMBLEWITS	NITROCELLULOSES	NOBILITATE	NOEMATICALLY	NOMINATION
NIMBLEWITTED	NITROCHLOROFORM	NOBILITATED	NOISELESSLY	NOMINATIONS
NIMBOSTRATI	NITROCOTTON	NOBILITATES	NOISELESSNESS	NOMINATIVAL
NIMBOSTRATUS	NITROCOTTONS	NOBILITATING	NOISELESSNESSES	NOMINATIVALLY
NIMBYNESSES	NITROFURAN	NOBILITATION	NOISEMAKER	NOMINATIVE
NINCOMPOOP	NITROFURANS	NOBILITATIONS	NOISEMAKERS	NOMINATIVELY
NINCOMPOOPERIES	NITROGELATIN	NOBILITIES	NOISEMAKING	NOMINATIVES
NINCOMPOOPERY	NITROGELATINE	NOBLENESSES	NOISEMAKINGS	NOMINATORS
NINCOMPOOPS	NITROGELATINES	NOBLEWOMAN	NOISINESSES	NOMOCRACIES
NINEPENCES	NITROGELATINS	NOBLEWOMEN	NOISOMENESS	NOMOGENIES
NINEPENNIES	NITROGENASE	NOCHELLING	NOISOMENESSES	NOMOGRAPHER
NINESCORES	NITROGENASES	NOCICEPTIVE	NOMADICALLY	NOMOGRAPHERS
NINETEENTH	NITROGENISATION	NOCICEPTOR	NOMADISATION	NOMOGRAPHIC
NINETEENTHLY	NITROGENISE	NOCICEPTORS	NOMADISATIONS	NOMOGRAPHICAL
NINETEENTHS	NITROGENISED	NOCIRECEPTOR	NOMADISING	NOMOGRAPHICALLY
NINETIETHS	NITROGENISES	NOCIRECEPTORS	NOMADIZATION	NOMOGRAPHIES
NINHYDRINS	NITROGENISING	NOCTAMBULATION	NOMADIZATIONS	NOMOGRAPHS
NINNYHAMMER	NITROGENIZATION	NOCTAMBULATIONS	NOMADIZING	NOMOGRAPHY
NINNYHAMMERS	NITROGENIZE	NOCTAMBULISM	NOMARCHIES	NOMOLOGICAL
NIPCHEESES	NITROGENIZED	NOCTAMBULISMS	NOMENCLATIVE	NOMOLOGICALLY
NIPPERKINS	NITROGENIZES	NOCTAMBULIST	NOMENCLATOR	NOMOLOGIES
NIPPINESSES	NITROGENIZING	NOCTAMBULISTS	NOMENCLATORIAL	NOMOLOGIST
NIPPLEWORT	NITROGENOUS	NOCTILUCAE	NOMENCLATORS	NOMOLOGISTS
NIPPLEWORTS	NITROGLYCERIN	NOCTILUCAS	NOMENCLATURAL	NOMOTHETES
NISBERRIES	NITROGLYCERINE	NOCTILUCENCE	NOMENCLATURE	NOMOTHETIC
NITPICKERS	NITROGLYCERINES	NOCTILUCENCES	NOMENCLATURES	NOMOTHETICAL
NITPICKIER	NITROGLYCERINS	NOCTILUCENT	NOMENKLATURA	NONABRASIVE

N

NONABSORBABLE
NONABSORBENT
NONABSORPTIVE
NONABSTRACT
NONACADEMIC
NONACADEMICS
NONACCEPTANCE
NONACCEPTANCES
NONACCIDENTAL
NONACCOUNTABLE
NONACCREDITED
NONACCRUAL
NONACHIEVEMENT
NONACHIEVEMENTS
NONACQUISITIVE
NONACTINGS
NONACTIONS
NONACTIVATED
NONADAPTIVE
NONADDICTIVE
NONADDICTS
NONADDITIVE
NONADDITIVITIES
NONADDITIVITY
NONADHESIVE
NONADIABATIC
NONADJACENT
NONADMIRER
NONADMIRERS
NONADMISSION
NONADMISSIONS
NONAESTHETIC
NONAFFILIATED
NONAFFLUENT
NONAGENARIAN
NONAGENARIANS
NONAGESIMAL
NONAGESIMALS
NONAGGRESSION
NONAGGRESSIONS
NONAGGRESSIVE
NONAGRICULTURAL
NONALCOHOLIC
NONALIGNED
NONALIGNMENT
NONALIGNMENTS
NONALLELIC

NONALLERGENIC
NONALLERGIC
NONALPHABETIC
NONALUMINUM
NONAMBIGUOUS
NONANALYTIC
NONANATOMIC
NONANSWERED
NONANSWERING
NONANSWERS
NONANTAGONISTIC
NONANTIBIOTIC
NONANTIBIOTICS
NONANTIGENIC
NONAPPEARANCE
NONAPPEARANCES
NONAQUATIC
NONAQUEOUS
NONARBITRARY
NONARCHITECT
NONARCHITECTS
NONARCHITECTURE
NONARGUMENT
NONARGUMENTS
NONARISTOCRATIC
NONAROMATIC
NONAROMATICS
NONARRIVAL
NONARRIVALS
NONARTISTIC
NONARTISTS
NONASCETIC
NONASCETICS
NONASPIRIN
NONASSERTIVE
NONASSOCIATED
NONASTRONOMICAL
NONATHLETE
NONATHLETES
NONATHLETIC
NONATTACHED
NONATTACHMENT
NONATTACHMENTS
NONATTENDANCE
NONATTENDANCES
NONATTENDER
NONATTENDERS

NONATTRIBUTABLE
NONAUDITORY
NONAUTHORS
NONAUTOMATED
NONAUTOMATIC
NONAUTOMOTIVE
NONAUTONOMOUS
NONAVAILABILITY
NONBACTERIAL
NONBANKING
NONBARBITURATE
NONBARBITURATES
NONBEARING
NONBEHAVIORAL
NONBEHAVIOURAL
NONBELIEFS
NONBELIEVER
NONBELIEVERS
NONBELLIGERENCY
NONBELLIGERENT
NONBELLIGERENTS
NONBETTING
NONBINDING
NONBIOGRAPHICAL
NONBIOLOGICAL
NONBIOLOGICALLY
NONBIOLOGIST
NONBIOLOGISTS
NONBONDING
NONBOTANIST
NONBOTANISTS
NONBREAKABLE
NONBREATHING
NONBREEDER
NONBREEDERS
NONBREEDING
NONBROADCAST
NONBUILDING
NONBURNABLE
NONBUSINESS
NONCABINET
NONCALLABLE
NONCALORIC
NONCANCELABLE
NONCANCELLABLE
NONCANCEROUS
NONCANDIDACIES

NONCANDIDACY
NONCANDIDATE
NONCANDIDATES
NONCAPITAL
NONCAPITALIST
NONCAPITALISTS
NONCARCINOGEN
NONCARCINOGENIC
NONCARCINOGENS
NONCARDIAC
NONCARRIER
NONCARRIERS
NONCELEBRATION
NONCELEBRATIONS
NONCELEBRITIES
NONCELEBRITY
NONCELLULAR
NONCELLULOSIC
NONCELLULOSICS
NONCENTRAL
NONCERTIFICATED
NONCERTIFIED
NONCHALANCE
NONCHALANCES
NONCHALANT
NONCHALANTLY
NONCHARACTER
NONCHARACTERS
NONCHARISMATIC
NONCHARISMATICS
NONCHAUVINIST
NONCHAUVINISTS
NONCHEMICAL
NONCHEMICALS
NONCHROMOSOMAL
NONCHURCHED
NONCHURCHES
NONCHURCHGOER
NONCHURCHGOERS
NONCHURCHING
NONCIRCULAR
NONCIRCULATING
NONCITIZEN
NONCITIZENS
NONCLANDESTINE
NONCLASSES
NONCLASSICAL

NONCLASSIFIED
NONCLASSROOM
NONCLERICAL
NONCLINICAL
NONCLOGGING
NONCOERCIVE
NONCOGNITIVE
NONCOGNITIVISM
NONCOGNITIVISMS
NONCOHERENT
NONCOINCIDENCE
NONCOINCIDENCES
NONCOLLECTOR
NONCOLLECTORS
NONCOLLEGE
NONCOLLEGIATE
NONCOLLINEAR
NONCOLORED
NONCOLORFAST
NONCOLOURED
NONCOLOURFAST
NONCOLOURS
NONCOMBATANT
NONCOMBATANTS
NONCOMBATIVE
NONCOMBUSTIBLE
NONCOMMERCIAL
NONCOMMISSIONED
NONCOMMITMENT
NONCOMMITMENTS
NONCOMMITTAL
NONCOMMITTALLY
NONCOMMITTED
NONCOMMUNICANT
NONCOMMUNICANTS
NONCOMMUNIST
NONCOMMUNISTS
NONCOMMUNITY
NONCOMMUTATIVE
NONCOMPARABLE
NONCOMPATIBLE
NONCOMPETITION
NONCOMPETITIVE
NONCOMPETITOR
NONCOMPETITORS
NONCOMPLETION
NONCOMPLETIONS

NONCOMPLEX
NONCOMPLIANCE
NONCOMPLIANCES
NONCOMPLICATED
NONCOMPLYING
NONCOMPLYINGS
NONCOMPOSER
NONCOMPOSERS
NONCOMPOUND
NONCOMPRESSIBLE
NONCOMPUTER
NONCOMPUTERISED
NONCOMPUTERIZED
NONCONCEPTUAL
NONCONCERN
NONCONCERNS
NONCONCLUSION
NONCONCLUSIONS
NONCONCURRED
NONCONCURRENCE
NONCONCURRENCES
NONCONCURRENT
NONCONCURRING
NONCONCURS
NONCONDENSABLE
NONCONDITIONED
NONCONDUCTING
NONCONDUCTION
NONCONDUCTIVE
NONCONDUCTOR
NONCONDUCTORS
NONCONFERENCE
NONCONFIDENCE
NONCONFIDENCES
NONCONFIDENTIAL
NONCONFLICTING
NONCONFORM
NONCONFORMANCE
NONCONFORMANCES
NONCONFORMED
NONCONFORMER
NONCONFORMERS
NONCONFORMING
NONCONFORMINGS
NONCONFORMISM
NONCONFORMISMS
NONCONFORMIST

NONCONFORMISTS
NONCONFORMITIES
NONCONFORMITY
NONCONFORMS
NONCONGRUENT
NONCONJUGATED
NONCONNECTION
NONCONNECTIONS
NONCONSCIOUS
NONCONSECUTIVE
NONCONSENSUAL
NONCONSERVATION
NONCONSERVATIVE
NONCONSOLIDATED
NONCONSTANT
NONCONSTRUCTION
NONCONSTRUCTIVE
NONCONSUMER
NONCONSUMERS
NONCONSUMING
NONCONSUMPTION
NONCONSUMPTIONS
NONCONSUMPTIVE
NONCONTACT
NONCONTACTS
NONCONTAGIOUS
NONCONTEMPORARY
NONCONTIGUOUS
NONCONTINGENT
NONCONTINUOUS
NONCONTRACT
NONCONTRACTUAL
NONCONTRIBUTORY
NONCONTROLLABLE
NONCONTROLLED
NONCONTROLLING
NONCONVENTIONAL
NONCONVERTIBLE
NONCOOPERATION
NONCOOPERATIONS
NONCOOPERATIVE
NONCOOPERATOR
NONCOOPERATORS
NONCOPLANAR
NONCORPORATE
NONCORRELATION
NONCORRELATIONS

NONCORRODIBLE
NONCORRODING
NONCORROSIVE
NONCOUNTRIES
NONCOUNTRY
NONCOVERAGE
NONCOVERAGES
NONCREATIVE
NONCREATIVITIES
NONCREATIVITY
NONCREDENTIALED
NONCRIMINAL
NONCRIMINALS
NONCRITICAL
NONCROSSOVER
NONCROSSOVERS
NONCRUSHABLE
NONCRYSTALLINE
NONCULINARY
NONCULTIVATED
NONCULTIVATION
NONCULTIVATIONS
NONCULTURAL
NONCUMULATIVE
NONCURRENT
NONCUSTODIAL
NONCUSTOMER
NONCUSTOMERS
NONCYCLICAL
NONDANCERS
NONDECEPTIVE
NONDECISION
NONDECISIONS
NONDECREASING
NONDEDUCTIBLE
NONDEDUCTIVE
NONDEFENCE
NONDEFENSE
NONDEFERRABLE
NONDEFORMING
NONDEGENERATE
NONDEGRADABLE
NONDELEGATE
NONDELEGATES
NONDELIBERATE
NONDELINQUENT
NONDELINQUENTS

NONDELIVERIES
NONDELIVERY
NONDEMANDING
NONDEMANDS
NONDEMOCRATIC
NONDEPARTMENTAL
NONDEPENDENT
NONDEPENDENTS
NONDEPLETABLE
NONDEPLETING
NONDEPOSITION
NONDEPOSITIONS
NONDEPRESSED
NONDERIVATIVE
NONDESCRIPT
NONDESCRIPTIVE
NONDESCRIPTLY
NONDESCRIPTNESS
NONDESCRIPTS
NONDESTRUCTIVE
NONDETACHABLE
NONDEVELOPMENT
NONDEVELOPMENTS
NONDEVIANT
NONDIABETIC
NONDIABETICS
NONDIALYSABLE
NONDIALYZABLE
NONDIAPAUSING
NONDIDACTIC
NONDIFFUSIBLE
NONDIMENSIONAL
NONDIPLOMATIC
NONDIRECTED
NONDIRECTIONAL
NONDIRECTIVE
NONDISABLED
NONDISCLOSURE
NONDISCLOSURES
NONDISCOUNT
NONDISCURSIVE
NONDISJUNCTION
NONDISJUNCTIONS
NONDISPERSIVE
NONDISRUPTIVE
NONDISTINCTIVE
NONDIVERSIFIED

NONDIVIDING
NONDOCTORS
NONDOCTRINAIRE
NONDOCUMENTARY
NONDOGMATIC
NONDOMESTIC
NONDOMICILED
NONDOMINANT
NONDORMANT
NONDRAMATIC
NONDRINKER
NONDRINKERS
NONDRINKING
NONDRIVERS
NONDURABLE
NONDURABLES
NONEARNING
NONECONOMIC
NONECONOMIST
NONECONOMISTS
NONEDIBLES
NONEDITORIAL
NONEDUCATION
NONEDUCATIONAL
NONEFFECTIVE
NONEFFECTIVES
NONELASTIC
NONELECTED
NONELECTION
NONELECTIONS
NONELECTIVE
NONELECTRIC
NONELECTRICAL
NONELECTRICS
NONELECTROLYTE
NONELECTROLYTES
NONELECTRONIC
NONELEMENTARY
NONEMERGENCIES
NONEMERGENCY
NONEMOTIONAL
NONEMPHATIC
NONEMPIRICAL
NONEMPLOYEE
NONEMPLOYEES
NONEMPLOYMENT
NONEMPLOYMENTS

N

NONENCAPSULATED	NONFACULTY	NONGRADUATE	NONIMPORTATIONS	NONINTERSECTING
NONENFORCEMENT	NONFAMILIAL	NONGRADUATES	NONINCLUSION	NONINTERVENTION
NONENFORCEMENTS	NONFAMILIES	NONGRAMMATICAL	NONINCLUSIONS	NONINTIMIDATING
NONENGAGEMENT	NONFARMERS	NONGRANULAR	NONINCREASING	NONINTOXICANT
NONENGAGEMENTS	NONFATTENING	NONGREGARIOUS	NONINCUMBENT	NONINTOXICANTS
NONENGINEERING	NONFEASANCE	NONGROWING	NONINCUMBENTS	NONINTOXICATING
NONENTITIES	NONFEASANCES	NONGROWTHS	NONINDEPENDENCE	NONINTRUSIVE
NONENTRIES	NONFEDERAL	NONHAEMOLYTIC	NONINDIGENOUS	NONINTUITIVE
NONENZYMATIC	NONFEDERATED	NONHALOGENATED	NONINDIVIDUAL	NONINVASIVE
NONENZYMIC	NONFEMINIST	NONHANDICAPPED	NONINDIVIDUALS	NONINVOLVED
NONEQUILIBRIA	NONFEMINISTS	NONHAPPENING	NONINDUCTIVE	NONINVOLVEMENT
NONEQUILIBRIUM	NONFERROUS	NONHAPPENINGS	NONINDUSTRIAL	NONINVOLVEMENTS
NONEQUILIBRIUMS	NONFICTION	NONHARMONIC	NONINDUSTRY	NONIONISING
NONEQUIVALENCE	NONFICTIONAL	NONHAZARDOUS	NONINFECTED	NONIONIZING
NONEQUIVALENCES	NONFICTIONALLY	NONHEMOLYTIC	NONINFECTIOUS	NONIRRADIATED
NONEQUIVALENT	NONFICTIONS	NONHEREDITARY	NONINFECTIVE	NONIRRIGATED
NONESSENTIAL	NONFIGURATIVE	NONHIERARCHICAL	NONINFESTED	NONIRRITANT
NONESSENTIALS	NONFILAMENTOUS	NONHISTONE	NONINFLAMMABLE	NONIRRITANTS
NONESTABLISHED	NONFILTERABLE	NONHISTORICAL	NONINFLAMMATORY	NONIRRITATING
NONESTERIFIED	NONFINANCIAL	NONHOMOGENEOUS	NONINFLATIONARY	NONJOINDER
NONESUCHES	NONFISSIONABLE	NONHOMOLOGOUS	NONINFLECTIONAL	NONJOINDERS
NONETHELESS	NONFLAMMABILITY	NONHOMOSEXUAL	NONINFLUENCE	NONJOINERS
NONETHICAL	NONFLAMMABLE	NONHOMOSEXUALS	NONINFLUENCES	NONJUDGEMENTAL
NONETHNICS	NONFLOWERING	NONHORMONAL	NONINFORMATION	NONJUDGMENTAL
NONEVALUATIVE	NONFLUENCIES	NONHOSPITAL	NONINFORMATIONS	NONJUDICIAL
NONEVIDENCE	NONFLUENCY	NONHOSPITALISED	NONINFRINGEMENT	NONJUSTICIABLE
NONEVIDENCES	NONFLUORESCENT	NONHOSPITALIZED	NONINITIAL	NONKOSHERS
NONEXCLUSIVE	NONFORFEITABLE	NONHOSTILE	NONINITIATE	NONLADDERING
NONEXECUTIVE	NONFORFEITURE	NONHOUSING	NONINITIATES	NONLANDOWNER
NONEXECUTIVES	NONFORFEITURES	NONHUNTERS	NONINSECTICIDAL	NONLANDOWNERS
NONEXEMPTS	NONFREEZING	NONHUNTING	NONINSECTS	NONLANGUAGE
NONEXISTENCE	NONFRIVOLOUS	NONHYGROSCOPIC	NONINSTALLMENT	NONLANGUAGES
NONEXISTENCES	NONFULFILLMENT	NONHYSTERICAL	NONINSTALLMENTS	NONLAWYERS
NONEXISTENT	NONFULFILLMENTS	NONIDENTICAL	NONINSTALMENT	NONLEGUMES
NONEXISTENTIAL	NONFULFILMENT	NONIDENTITIES	NONINSTRUMENTAL	NONLEGUMINOUS
NONEXPENDABLE	NONFULFILMENTS	NONIDENTITY	NONINSURANCE	NONLEXICAL
NONEXPERIMENTAL	NONFUNCTIONAL	NONIDEOLOGICAL	NONINSURANCES	NONLIBRARIAN
NONEXPERTS	NONFUNCTIONING	NONILLIONS	NONINSURED	NONLIBRARIANS
NONEXPLANATORY	NONGASEOUS	NONILLIONTH	NONINTEGRAL	NONLIBRARY
NONEXPLOITATION	NONGENETIC	NONILLIONTHS	NONINTEGRATED	NONLINEARITIES
NONEXPLOITATIVE	NONGENITAL	NONIMITATIVE	NONINTELLECTUAL	NONLINEARITY
NONEXPLOITIVE	NONGEOMETRICAL	NONIMMIGRANT	NONINTERACTING	NONLINGUISTIC
NONEXPLOSIVE	NONGLAMOROUS	NONIMMIGRANTS	NONINTERACTIVE	NONLIQUIDS
NONEXPOSED	NONGOLFERS	NONIMPACTS	NONINTERCOURSE	NONLITERAL
NONFACTORS	NONGONOCOCCAL	NONIMPLICATION	NONINTERCOURSES	NONLITERARY
NONFACTUAL	NONGOVERNMENT	NONIMPLICATIONS	NONINTEREST	NONLITERATE
NONFACULTIES	NONGOVERNMENTAL	NONIMPORTATION	NONINTERFERENCE	NONLITERATES

NONLIVINGS
NONLOGICAL
NONLUMINOUS
NONMAGNETIC
NONMAINSTREAM
NONMALIGNANT
NONMALLEABLE
NONMANAGEMENT
NONMANAGERIAL
NONMARITAL
NONMARKETS
NONMATERIAL
NONMATHEMATICAL
NONMATRICULATED
NONMEANINGFUL
NONMEASURABLE
NONMECHANICAL
NONMECHANISTIC
NONMEDICAL
NONMEETING
NONMEETINGS
NONMEMBERS
NONMEMBERSHIP
NONMEMBERSHIPS
NONMERCURIAL
NONMETALLIC
NONMETAMERIC
NONMETAPHORICAL
NONMETRICAL
NONMETROPOLITAN
NONMICROBIAL
NONMIGRANT
NONMIGRANTS
NONMIGRATORY
NONMILITANT
NONMILITANTS
NONMILITARY
NONMIMETIC
NONMINORITIES
NONMINORITY
NONMODERNS
NONMOLECULAR
NONMONETARIST
NONMONETARISTS
NONMONETARY
NONMONOGAMOUS
NONMORTALS

NONMOTILITIES
NONMOTILITY
NONMOTORISED
NONMOTORIZED
NONMUNICIPAL
NONMUSICAL
NONMUSICALS
NONMUSICIAN
NONMUSICIANS
NONMUTANTS
NONMYELINATED
NONMYSTICAL
NONNARRATIVE
NONNATIONAL
NONNATIONALS
NONNATIVES
NONNATURAL
NONNECESSITIES
NONNECESSITY
NONNEGATIVE
NONNEGLIGENT
NONNEGOTIABLE
NONNEGOTIABLES
NONNETWORK
NONNITROGENOUS
NONNORMATIVE
NONNUCLEAR
NONNUCLEATED
NONNUMERICAL
NONNUTRITIOUS
NONNUTRITIVE
NONOBJECTIVE
NONOBJECTIVISM
NONOBJECTIVISMS
NONOBJECTIVIST
NONOBJECTIVISTS
NONOBJECTIVITY
NONOBSCENE
NONOBSERVANCE
NONOBSERVANCES
NONOBSERVANT
NONOBVIOUS
NONOBVIOUSES
NONOCCUPATIONAL
NONOCCURRENCE
NONOCCURRENCES
NONOFFICIAL

NONOFFICIALS
NONOPERATIC
NONOPERATING
NONOPERATIONAL
NONOPERATIVE
NONOPTIMAL
NONORGANIC
NONORGASMIC
NONORTHODOX
NONOVERLAPPING
NONOXIDISING
NONOXIDIZING
NONPAPISTS
NONPARALLEL
NONPARAMETRIC
NONPARASITIC
NONPAREILS
NONPARENTS
NONPARITIES
NONPARTICIPANT
NONPARTICIPANTS
NONPARTIES
NONPARTISAN
NONPARTISANSHIP
NONPARTIZAN
NONPARTIZANSHIP
NONPASSERINE
NONPASSIVE
NONPATHOGENIC
NONPAYMENT
NONPAYMENTS
NONPERFORMANCE
NONPERFORMANCES
NONPERFORMER
NONPERFORMERS
NONPERFORMING
NONPERISHABLE
NONPERISHABLES
NONPERMANENT
NONPERMISSIVE
NONPERSISTENT
NONPERSONAL
NONPERSONS
NONPETROLEUM
NONPHILOSOPHER
NONPHILOSOPHERS
NONPHONEMIC

NONPHONETIC
NONPHOSPHATE
NONPHOTOGRAPHIC
NONPHYSICAL
NONPHYSICIAN
NONPHYSICIANS
NONPLASTIC
NONPLASTICS
NONPLAYERS
NONPLAYING
NONPLUSING
NONPLUSSED
NONPLUSSES
NONPLUSSING
NONPOISONOUS
NONPOLARISABLE
NONPOLARIZABLE
NONPOLITICAL
NONPOLITICALLY
NONPOLITICIAN
NONPOLITICIANS
NONPOLLUTING
NONPOSSESSION
NONPOSSESSIONS
NONPRACTICAL
NONPRACTICING
NONPRACTISING
NONPREGNANT
NONPRESCRIPTION
NONPROBLEM
NONPROBLEMS
NONPRODUCING
NONPRODUCTIVE
NONPRODUCTIVITY
NONPROFESSIONAL
NONPROFESSORIAL
NONPROFITS
NONPROGRAM
NONPROGRAMMER
NONPROGRAMMERS
NONPROGRESSIVE
NONPROPRIETARY
NONPROSSED
NONPROSSES
NONPROSSING
NONPROTEIN
NONPSYCHIATRIC

NONPSYCHIATRIST
NONPSYCHOTIC
NONPUNITIVE
NONPURPOSIVE
NONQUANTIFIABLE
NONQUANTITATIVE
NONRACIALLY
NONRADIOACTIVE
NONRAILROAD
NONRANDOMNESS
NONRANDOMNESSES
NONRATIONAL
NONREACTIVE
NONREACTOR
NONREACTORS
NONREADERS
NONREADING
NONREADINGS
NONREALISTIC
NONRECEIPT
NONRECEIPTS
NONRECIPROCAL
NONRECOGNITION
NONRECOGNITIONS
NONRECOMBINANT
NONRECOMBINANTS
NONRECOURSE
NONRECOVERABLE
NONRECURRENT
NONRECURRING
NONRECYCLABLE
NONRECYCLABLES
NONREDUCING
NONREDUNDANT
NONREFILLABLE
NONREFLECTING
NONREFLECTIVE
NONREFLEXIVE
NONREFUNDABLE
NONREGULATED
NONREGULATION
NONRELATIVE
NONRELATIVES
NONRELATIVISTIC
NONRELEVANT
NONRELIGIOUS
NONRENEWABLE

N

NONRENEWAL	NONSCIENTIST	NONSPECIALIST	NONSYNCHRONOUS	NONUNIVERSITY
NONRENEWALS	NONSCIENTISTS	NONSPECIALISTS	NONSYSTEMATIC	NONUTILITARIAN
NONREPAYABLE	NONSEASONAL	NONSPECIFIC	NONSYSTEMIC	NONUTILITIES
NONREPRODUCTIVE	NONSECRETOR	NONSPECIFICALLY	NONSYSTEMS	NONUTILITY
NONRESIDENCE	NONSECRETORS	NONSPECTACULAR	NONTALKERS	NONUTOPIAN
NONRESIDENCES	NONSECRETORY	NONSPECULAR	NONTAXABLE	NONVALIDITIES
NONRESIDENCIES	NONSECRETS	NONSPECULATIVE	NONTEACHING	NONVALIDITY
NONRESIDENCY	NONSECTARIAN	NONSPEECHES	NONTECHNICAL	NONVANISHING
NONRESIDENT	NONSEDIMENTABLE	NONSPHERICAL	NONTEMPORAL	NONVASCULAR
NONRESIDENTIAL	NONSEGREGATED	NONSPORTING	NONTENURED	NONVECTORS
NONRESIDENTS	NONSEGREGATION	NONSTANDARD	NONTERMINAL	NONVEGETARIAN
NONRESISTANCE	NONSEGREGATIONS	NONSTAPLES	NONTERMINALS	NONVEGETARIANS
NONRESISTANCES	NONSELECTED	NONSTARTER	NONTERMINATING	NONVENOMOUS
NONRESISTANT	NONSELECTIVE	NONSTARTERS	NONTHEATRICAL	NONVERBALLY
NONRESISTANTS	NONSENSATIONAL	NONSTATIONARY	NONTHEISTIC	NONVETERAN
NONRESONANT	NONSENSICAL	NONSTATISTICAL	NONTHEISTS	NONVETERANS
NONRESPONDENT	NONSENSICALITY	NONSTATIVE	NONTHEOLOGICAL	NONVIEWERS
NONRESPONDENTS	NONSENSICALLY	NONSTATIVES	NONTHEORETICAL	NONVINTAGE
NONRESPONDER	NONSENSICALNESS	NONSTEROID	NONTHERAPEUTIC	NONVIOLENCE
NONRESPONDERS	NONSENSITIVE	NONSTEROIDAL	NONTHERMAL	NONVIOLENCES
NONRESPONSE	NONSENSUOUS	NONSTEROIDS	NONTHINKING	NONVIOLENT
NONRESPONSES	NONSENTENCE	NONSTORIES	NONTHINKINGS	NONVIOLENTLY
NONRESPONSIVE	NONSENTENCES	NONSTRATEGIC	NONTHREATENING	NONVIRGINS
NONRESTRICTED	NONSEPTATE	NONSTRIATED	NONTOBACCO	NONVISCOUS
NONRESTRICTIVE	NONSEQUENTIAL	NONSTRUCTURAL	NONTOTALITARIAN	NONVOCATIONAL
NONRETRACTILE	NONSERIALS	NONSTRUCTURED	NONTRADITIONAL	NONVOLATILE
NONRETROACTIVE	NONSERIOUS	NONSTUDENT	NONTRANSFERABLE	NONVOLCANIC
NONRETURNABLE	NONSHRINKABLE	NONSTUDENTS	NONTRANSITIVE	NONVOLUNTARY
NONRETURNABLES	NONSIGNERS	NONSUBJECT	NONTREATMENT	NONWINNING
NONREUSABLE	NONSIGNIFICANT	NONSUBJECTIVE	NONTREATMENTS	NONWORKERS
NONREVERSIBLE	NONSIGNIFICANTS	NONSUBJECTS	NONTRIVIAL	NONWORKING
NONRHOTICITIES	NONSIMULTANEOUS	NONSUBSIDISED	NONTROPICAL	NONWRITERS
NONRHOTICITY	NONSINKABLE	NONSUBSIDIZED	NONTURBULENT	NONYELLOWING
NONRIOTERS	NONSKATERS	NONSUCCESS	NONTYPICAL	NOODLEDOMS
NONRIOTING	NONSKELETAL	NONSUCCESSES	NONUNANIMOUS	NOOGENESES
NONROTATING	NONSKILLED	NONSUITING	NONUNIFORM	NOOGENESIS
NONROUTINE	NONSMOKERS	NONSUPERVISORY	NONUNIFORMITIES	NOOMETRIES
NONRUMINANT	NONSMOKING	NONSUPPORT	NONUNIFORMITY	NOOSPHERES
NONRUMINANTS	NONSOCIALIST	NONSUPPORTS	NONUNIONISED	NOOTROPICS
NONRUNNERS	NONSOCIALISTS	NONSURGICAL	NONUNIONISM	NORADRENALIN
NONSALABLE	NONSOLUTION	NONSWIMMER	NONUNIONISMS	NORADRENALINE
NONSALEABLE	NONSOLUTIONS	NONSWIMMERS	NONUNIONIST	NORADRENALINES
NONSAPONIFIABLE	NONSOLVENT	NONSYLLABIC	NONUNIONISTS	NORADRENALINS
NONSCHEDULED	NONSPATIAL	NONSYLLABICS	NONUNIONIZED	NORADRENERGIC
NONSCIENCE	NONSPEAKER	NONSYMBOLIC	NONUNIQUENESS	NOREPINEPHRINE
NONSCIENCES	NONSPEAKERS	NONSYMMETRIC	NONUNIQUENESSES	NOREPINEPHRINES
NONSCIENTIFIC	NONSPEAKING	NONSYMMETRICAL	NONUNIVERSAL	NORETHINDRONE

NORETHINDRONES	NORTHEASTERS	NOSOGRAPHER	NOTCHELLED	NOTWORKINGS
NORETHISTERONE	NORTHEASTS	NOSOGRAPHERS	NOTCHELLING	NOUGATINES
NORETHISTERONES	NORTHEASTWARD	NOSOGRAPHIC	NOTEDNESSES	NOUMENALISM
NORMALCIES	NORTHEASTWARDLY	NOSOGRAPHIES	NOTEPAPERS	NOUMENALISMS
NORMALISABLE	NORTHEASTWARDS	NOSOGRAPHY	NOTEWORTHILY	NOUMENALIST
NORMALISATION	NORTHERING	NOSOLOGICAL	NOTEWORTHINESS	NOUMENALISTS
NORMALISATIONS	NORTHERLIES	NOSOLOGICALLY	NOTEWORTHY	NOUMENALITIES
NORMALISED	NORTHERLINESS	NOSOLOGIES	NOTHINGARIAN	NOUMENALITY
NORMALISER	NORTHERLINESSES	NOSOLOGIST	NOTHINGARIANISM	NOUMENALLY
NORMALISERS	NORTHERMOST	NOSOLOGISTS	NOTHINGARIANS	NOURISHABLE
NORMALISES	NORTHERNER	NOSOPHOBIA	NOTHINGISM	NOURISHERS
NORMALISING	NORTHERNERS	NOSOPHOBIAS	NOTHINGISMS	NOURISHING
NORMALITIES	NORTHERNISE	NOSTALGIAS	NOTHINGNESS	NOURISHINGLY
NORMALIZABLE	NORTHERNISED	NOSTALGICALLY	NOTHINGNESSES	NOURISHMENT
NORMALIZATION	NORTHERNISES	NOSTALGICS	NOTICEABILITIES	NOURISHMENTS
NORMALIZATIONS	NORTHERNISING	NOSTALGIST	NOTICEABILITY	NOURITURES
NORMALIZED	NORTHERNISM	NOSTALGISTS	NOTICEABLE	NOURRITURE
NORMALIZER	NORTHERNISMS	NOSTOLOGIC	NOTICEABLY	NOURRITURES
NORMALIZERS	NORTHERNIZE	NOSTOLOGICAL	NOTICEBOARD	NOUSELLING
NORMALIZES	NORTHERNIZED	NOSTOLOGIES	NOTICEBOARDS	NOVACULITE
NORMALIZING	NORTHERNIZES	NOSTOMANIA	NOTIFIABLE	NOVACULITES
NORMATIVELY	NORTHERNIZING	NOSTOMANIAS	NOTIFICATION	NOVELETTES
NORMATIVENESS	NORTHERNMOST	NOSTOPATHIES	NOTIFICATIONS	NOVELETTISH
NORMATIVENESSES	NORTHLANDS	NOSTOPATHY	NOTIONALIST	NOVELETTIST
NORMOGLYCAEMIA	NORTHWARDLY	NOSTRADAMIC	NOTIONALISTS	NOVELETTISTS
NORMOGLYCAEMIAS	NORTHWARDS	NOTABILITIES	NOTIONALITIES	NOVELISATION
NORMOGLYCAEMIC	NORTHWESTER	NOTABILITY	NOTIONALITY	NOVELISATIONS
NORMOGLYCEMIA	NORTHWESTERLIES	NOTABLENESS	NOTIONALLY	NOVELISERS
NORMOGLYCEMIAS	NORTHWESTERLY	NOTABLENESSES	NOTIONISTS	NOVELISING
NORMOGLYCEMIC	NORTHWESTERN	NOTAPHILIC	NOTOCHORDAL	NOVELISTIC
NORMOTENSION	NORTHWESTERS	NOTAPHILIES	NOTOCHORDS	NOVELISTICALLY
NORMOTENSIONS	NORTHWESTS	NOTAPHILISM	NOTODONTID	NOVELIZATION
NORMOTENSIVE	NORTHWESTWARD	NOTAPHILISMS	NOTODONTIDS	NOVELIZATIONS
NORMOTENSIVES	NORTHWESTWARDLY	NOTAPHILIST	NOTONECTAL	NOVELIZERS
NORMOTHERMIA	NORTHWESTWARDS	NOTAPHILISTS	NOTORIETIES	NOVELIZING
NORMOTHERMIAS	NORTRIPTYLINE	NOTARIALLY	NOTORIOUSLY	NOVEMDECILLION
NORMOTHERMIC	NORTRIPTYLINES	NOTARISATION	NOTORIOUSNESS	NOVEMDECILLIONS
NOROVIRUSES	NOSEBANDED	NOTARISATIONS	NOTORIOUSNESSES	NOVENARIES
NORSELLERS	NOSEBLEEDING	NOTARISING	NOTORNISES	NOVICEHOOD
NORSELLING	NOSEBLEEDINGS	NOTARIZATION	NOTOTHERIUM	NOVICEHOODS
NORTHBOUND	NOSEBLEEDS	NOTARIZATIONS	NOTOTHERIUMS	NOVICESHIP
NORTHCOUNTRYMAN	NOSEDIVING	NOTARIZING	NOTOUNGULATE	NOVICESHIPS
NORTHCOUNTRYMEN	NOSEGUARDS	NOTARYSHIP	NOTOUNGULATES	NOVICIATES
NORTHEASTER	NOSEPIECES	NOTARYSHIPS	NOTUNGULATE	NOVITIATES
NORTHEASTERLIES	NOSEWHEELS	NOTATIONAL	NOTUNGULATES	NOVOBIOCIN
NORTHEASTERLY	NOSINESSES	NOTCHBACKS	NOTWITHSTANDING	NOVOBIOCINS
NORTHEASTERN	NOSOCOMIAL	NOTCHELING	NOTWORKING	NOVOCAINES

N

NOVOCENTENARIES

NOVOCENTENARIES NUCLEOPROTEINS NUMBFISHES NUNCUPATED NUTRITIONARY
NOVOCENTENARY NUCLEOSIDE NUMBNESSES NUNCUPATES NUTRITIONIST
NOVODAMUSES NUCLEOSIDES NUMBNUTSES NUNCUPATING NUTRITIONISTS
NOWCASTING NUCLEOSOMAL NUMBSKULLED NUNCUPATION NUTRITIONS
NOWCASTINGS NUCLEOSOME NUMBSKULLS NUNCUPATIONS NUTRITIOUS
NOXIOUSNESS NUCLEOSOMES NUMERABILITIES NUNCUPATIVE NUTRITIOUSLY
NOXIOUSNESSES NUCLEOSYNTHESES NUMERABILITY NUNCUPATORY NUTRITIOUSNESS
NUBBINESSES NUCLEOSYNTHESIS NUMERACIES NUNNATIONS NUTRITIVELY
NUBIFEROUS NUCLEOSYNTHETIC NUMERAIRES NUNNISHNESS NUTRITIVES
NUBIGENOUS NUCLEOTIDASE NUMERATING NUNNISHNESSES NUTTINESSES
NUBILITIES NUCLEOTIDASES NUMERATION NUPTIALITIES NYCHTHEMERAL
NUCIFEROUS NUCLEOTIDE NUMERATIONS NUPTIALITY NYCHTHEMERON
NUCIVOROUS NUCLEOTIDES NUMERATIVE NURSEHOUND NYCHTHEMERONS
NUCLEARISATION NUDENESSES NUMERATORS NURSEHOUNDS NYCTAGINACEOUS
NUCLEARISATIONS NUDIBRANCH NUMERICALLY NURSELINGS NYCTALOPES
NUCLEARISE NUDIBRANCHIATE NUMEROLOGICAL NURSEMAIDED NYCTALOPIA
NUCLEARISED NUDIBRANCHIATES NUMEROLOGIES NURSEMAIDING NYCTALOPIAS
NUCLEARISES NUDIBRANCHS NUMEROLOGIST NURSEMAIDS NYCTALOPIC
NUCLEARISING NUDICAUDATE NUMEROLOGISTS NURSERYMAID NYCTANTHOUS
NUCLEARIZATION NUDICAULOUS NUMEROLOGY NURSERYMAIDS NYCTINASTIC
NUCLEARIZATIONS NUGATORINESS NUMEROSITIES NURSERYMAN NYCTINASTIES
NUCLEARIZE NUGATORINESSES NUMEROSITY NURSERYMEN NYCTINASTY
NUCLEARIZED NUGGETTING NUMEROUSLY NURTURABLE NYCTITROPIC
NUCLEARIZES NUISANCERS NUMEROUSNESS NURTURANCE NYCTITROPISM
NUCLEARIZING NULLIFICATION NUMEROUSNESSES NURTURANCES NYCTITROPISMS
NUCLEATING NULLIFICATIONS NUMINOUSES NUTATIONAL NYCTOPHOBIA
NUCLEATION NULLIFIDIAN NUMINOUSNESS NUTBUTTERS NYCTOPHOBIAS
NUCLEATIONS NULLIFIDIANS NUMINOUSNESSES NUTCRACKER NYCTOPHOBIC
NUCLEATORS NULLIFIERS NUMISMATIC NUTCRACKERS NYMPHAEACEOUS
NUCLEOCAPSID NULLIFYING NUMISMATICALLY NUTGRASSES NYMPHAEUMS
NUCLEOCAPSIDS NULLIPARAE NUMISMATICS NUTHATCHES NYMPHALIDS
NUCLEOLATE NULLIPARAS NUMISMATIST NUTJOBBERS NYMPHETTES
NUCLEOLATED NULLIPARITIES NUMISMATISTS NUTMEGGIER NYMPHOLEPSIES
NUCLEONICALLY NULLIPARITY NUMISMATOLOGIES NUTMEGGIEST NYMPHOLEPSY
NUCLEONICS NULLIPAROUS NUMISMATOLOGIST NUTMEGGING NYMPHOLEPT
NUCLEOPHILE NULLIPORES NUMISMATOLOGY NUTPECKERS NYMPHOLEPTIC
NUCLEOPHILES NULLNESSES NUMMULATED NUTRACEUTICAL NYMPHOLEPTS
NUCLEOPHILIC NUMBERABLE NUMMULATION NUTRACEUTICALS NYMPHOMANIA
NUCLEOPHILICITY NUMBERINGS NUMMULATIONS NUTRIGENETICS NYMPHOMANIAC
NUCLEOPLASM NUMBERLESS NUMMULITES NUTRIGENOMICS NYMPHOMANIACAL
NUCLEOPLASMATIC NUMBERLESSLY NUMMULITIC NUTRIMENTAL NYMPHOMANIACS
NUCLEOPLASMIC NUMBERLESSNESS NUMSKULLED NUTRIMENTS NYMPHOMANIAS
NUCLEOPLASMS NUMBERPLATE NUNCIATURE NUTRITIONAL NYSTAGMOID
NUCLEOPROTEIN NUMBERPLATES NUNCIATURES NUTRITIONALLY NYSTAGMUSES

O

OAFISHNESS	OBJECTIONABLY	OBLANCEOLATE	OBMUTESCENT	OBSERVABLY
OAFISHNESSES	OBJECTIONS	OBLATENESS	OBNOXIOUSLY	OBSERVANCE
OAKENSHAWS	OBJECTIVAL	OBLATENESSES	OBNOXIOUSNESS	OBSERVANCES
OAKINESSES	OBJECTIVATE	OBLATIONAL	OBNOXIOUSNESSES	OBSERVANCIES
OARSMANSHIP	OBJECTIVATED	OBLIGATELY	OBNUBILATE	OBSERVANCY
OARSMANSHIPS	OBJECTIVATES	OBLIGATING	OBNUBILATED	OBSERVANTLY
OASTHOUSES	OBJECTIVATING	OBLIGATION	OBNUBILATES	OBSERVANTS
OBBLIGATOS	OBJECTIVATION	OBLIGATIONAL	OBNUBILATING	OBSERVATION
OBCOMPRESSED	OBJECTIVATIONS	OBLIGATIONS	OBNUBILATION	OBSERVATIONAL
OBDURACIES	OBJECTIVELY	OBLIGATIVE	OBNUBILATIONS	OBSERVATIONALLY
OBDURATELY	OBJECTIVENESS	OBLIGATORILY	OBREPTIONS	OBSERVATIONS
OBDURATENESS	OBJECTIVENESSES	OBLIGATORINESS	OBREPTITIOUS	OBSERVATIVE
OBDURATENESSES	OBJECTIVES	OBLIGATORS	OBSCENENESS	OBSERVATOR
OBDURATING	OBJECTIVISE	OBLIGATORY	OBSCENENESSES	OBSERVATORIES
OBDURATION	OBJECTIVISED	OBLIGEMENT	OBSCENITIES	OBSERVATORS
OBDURATIONS	OBJECTIVISES	OBLIGEMENTS	OBSCURANTIC	OBSERVATORY
OBEDIENCES	OBJECTIVISING	OBLIGINGLY	OBSCURANTISM	OBSERVINGLY
OBEDIENTIAL	OBJECTIVISM	OBLIGINGNESS	OBSCURANTISMS	OBSESSIONAL
OBEDIENTIARIES	OBJECTIVISMS	OBLIGINGNESSES	OBSCURANTIST	OBSESSIONALLY
OBEDIENTIARY	OBJECTIVIST	OBLIQUATION	OBSCURANTISTS	OBSESSIONIST
OBEDIENTLY	OBJECTIVISTIC	OBLIQUATIONS	OBSCURANTS	OBSESSIONISTS
OBEISANCES	OBJECTIVISTS	OBLIQUENESS	OBSCURATION	OBSESSIONS
OBEISANTLY	OBJECTIVITIES	OBLIQUENESSES	OBSCURATIONS	OBSESSIVELY
OBELISCOID	OBJECTIVITY	OBLIQUITIES	OBSCUREMENT	OBSESSIVENESS
OBELISKOID	OBJECTIVIZE	OBLIQUITOUS	OBSCUREMENTS	OBSESSIVENESSES
OBESENESSES	OBJECTIVIZED	OBLITERATE	OBSCURENESS	OBSESSIVES
OBESOGENIC	OBJECTIVIZES	OBLITERATED	OBSCURENESSES	OBSIDIONAL
OBFUSCATED	OBJECTIVIZING	OBLITERATES	OBSCURITIES	OBSIDIONARY
OBFUSCATES	OBJECTLESS	OBLITERATING	OBSECRATED	OBSIGNATED
OBFUSCATING	OBJECTLESSNESS	OBLITERATION	OBSECRATES	OBSIGNATES
OBFUSCATION	OBJURATION	OBLITERATIONS	OBSECRATING	OBSIGNATING
OBFUSCATIONS	OBJURATIONS	OBLITERATIVE	OBSECRATION	OBSIGNATION
OBFUSCATORY	OBJURGATED	OBLITERATOR	OBSECRATIONS	OBSIGNATIONS
OBITUARIES	OBJURGATES	OBLITERATORS	OBSEQUIOUS	OBSIGNATORY
OBITUARIST	OBJURGATING	OBLIVIOUSLY	OBSEQUIOUSLY	OBSOLESCED
OBITUARISTS	OBJURGATION	OBLIVIOUSNESS	OBSEQUIOUSNESS	OBSOLESCENCE
OBJECTIFICATION	OBJURGATIONS	OBLIVIOUSNESSES	OBSERVABILITIES	OBSOLESCENCES
OBJECTIFIED	OBJURGATIVE	OBLIVISCENCE	OBSERVABILITY	OBSOLESCENT
OBJECTIFIES	OBJURGATOR	OBLIVISCENCES	OBSERVABLE	OBSOLESCENTLY
OBJECTIFYING	OBJURGATORS	OBMUTESCENCE	OBSERVABLENESS	OBSOLESCES
OBJECTIONABLE	OBJURGATORY	OBMUTESCENCES	OBSERVABLES	OBSOLESCING

OBSOLETELY	OBSTRUENTS	OCCASIONALISM	OCCURRENCE	OCTANDROUS
OBSOLETENESS	OBTAINABILITIES	OCCASIONALISMS	OCCURRENCES	OCTANEDIOIC
OBSOLETENESSES	OBTAINABILITY	OCCASIONALIST	OCCURRENTS	OCTANGULAR
OBSOLETING	OBTAINABLE	OCCASIONALISTS	OCEANARIUM	OCTAPEPTIDE
OBSOLETION	OBTAINMENT	OCCASIONALITIES	OCEANARIUMS	OCTAPEPTIDES
OBSOLETIONS	OBTAINMENTS	OCCASIONALITY	OCEANFRONT	OCTAPLOIDIES
OBSOLETISM	OBTEMPERATE	OCCASIONALLY	OCEANFRONTS	OCTAPLOIDS
OBSOLETISMS	OBTEMPERATED	OCCASIONED	OCEANGOING	OCTAPLOIDY
OBSTETRICAL	OBTEMPERATES	OCCASIONER	OCEANOGRAPHER	OCTAPODIES
OBSTETRICALLY	OBTEMPERATING	OCCASIONERS	OCEANOGRAPHERS	OCTARCHIES
OBSTETRICIAN	OBTEMPERED	OCCASIONING	OCEANOGRAPHIC	OCTASTICHON
OBSTETRICIANS	OBTEMPERING	OCCIDENTAL	OCEANOGRAPHICAL	OCTASTICHONS
OBSTETRICS	OBTENTIONS	OCCIDENTALISE	OCEANOGRAPHIES	OCTASTICHOUS
OBSTINACIES	OBTESTATION	OCCIDENTALISED	OCEANOGRAPHY	OCTASTICHS
OBSTINATELY	OBTESTATIONS	OCCIDENTALISES	OCEANOLOGICAL	OCTASTROPHIC
OBSTINATENESS	OBTRUDINGS	OCCIDENTALISING	OCEANOLOGIES	OCTASTYLES
OBSTINATENESSES	OBTRUNCATE	OCCIDENTALISM	OCEANOLOGIST	OCTAVALENT
OBSTIPATION	OBTRUNCATED	OCCIDENTALISMS	OCEANOLOGISTS	OCTENNIALLY
OBSTIPATIONS	OBTRUNCATES	OCCIDENTALIST	OCEANOLOGY	OCTILLIONS
OBSTREPERATE	OBTRUNCATING	OCCIDENTALISTS	OCELLATION	OCTILLIONTH
OBSTREPERATED	OBTRUSIONS	OCCIDENTALIZE	OCELLATIONS	OCTILLIONTHS
OBSTREPERATES	OBTRUSIVELY	OCCIDENTALIZED	OCHLOCRACIES	OCTINGENARIES
OBSTREPERATING	OBTRUSIVENESS	OCCIDENTALIZES	OCHLOCRACY	OCTINGENARY
OBSTREPEROUS	OBTRUSIVENESSES	OCCIDENTALIZING	OCHLOCRATIC	OCTINGENTENARY
OBSTREPEROUSLY	OBTUNDENTS	OCCIDENTALLY	OCHLOCRATICAL	OCTOCENTENARIES
OBSTRICTION	OBTUNDITIES	OCCIDENTALS	OCHLOCRATICALLY	OCTOCENTENARY
OBSTRICTIONS	OBTURATING	OCCIPITALLY	OCHLOCRATS	OCTODECILLION
OBSTROPALOUS	OBTURATION	OCCIPITALS	OCHLOPHOBIA	OCTODECILLIONS
OBSTROPULOUS	OBTURATIONS	OCCLUDENTS	OCHLOPHOBIAC	OCTODECIMO
OBSTRUCTED	OBTURATORS	OCCLUSIONS	OCHLOPHOBIACS	OCTODECIMOS
OBSTRUCTER	OBTUSENESS	OCCLUSIVENESS	OCHLOPHOBIAS	OCTOGENARIAN
OBSTRUCTERS	OBTUSENESSES	OCCLUSIVENESSES	OCHLOPHOBIC	OCTOGENARIANS
OBSTRUCTING	OBTUSITIES	OCCLUSIVES	OCHLOPHOBICS	OCTOGENARIES
OBSTRUCTION	OBUMBRATED	OCCULTATION	OCHRACEOUS	OCTOGENARY
OBSTRUCTIONAL	OBUMBRATES	OCCULTATIONS	OCHROLEUCOUS	OCTOGYNOUS
OBSTRUCTIONALLY	OBUMBRATING	OCCULTISMS	OCTACHORDAL	OCTOHEDRON
OBSTRUCTIONISM	OBUMBRATION	OCCULTISTS	OCTACHORDS	OCTOHEDRONS
OBSTRUCTIONISMS	OBUMBRATIONS	OCCULTNESS	OCTAGONALLY	OCTONARIAN
OBSTRUCTIONIST	OBVENTIONS	OCCULTNESSES	OCTAHEDRAL	OCTONARIANS
OBSTRUCTIONISTS	OBVERSIONS	OCCUPANCES	OCTAHEDRALLY	OCTONARIES
OBSTRUCTIONS	OBVIATIONS	OCCUPANCIES	OCTAHEDRITE	OCTONARIUS
OBSTRUCTIVE	OBVIOUSNESS	OCCUPATING	OCTAHEDRITES	OCTONOCULAR
OBSTRUCTIVELY	OBVIOUSNESSES	OCCUPATION	OCTAHEDRON	OCTOPETALOUS
OBSTRUCTIVENESS	OBVOLUTION	OCCUPATIONAL	OCTAHEDRONS	OCTOPLOIDS
OBSTRUCTIVES	OBVOLUTIONS	OCCUPATIONALLY	OCTAMEROUS	OCTOPODANS
OBSTRUCTOR	OBVOLUTIVE	OCCUPATIONS	OCTAMETERS	OCTOPODOUS
OBSTRUCTORS	OCCASIONAL	OCCUPATIVE	OCTANDRIAN	OCTOPUSHER

O

OCTOPUSHERS	ODONTOLOGIST	OESOPHAGEAL	OFFICIATOR	OLERACEOUS
OCTOPUSHES	ODONTOLOGISTS	OESOPHAGITIS	OFFICIATORS	OLFACTIBLE
OCTOSEPALOUS	ODONTOLOGY	OESOPHAGITISES	OFFICINALLY	OLFACTIONS
OCTOSTICHOUS	ODONTOMATA	OESOPHAGOSCOPE	OFFICINALS	OLFACTOLOGIES
OCTOSTYLES	ODONTOMATOUS	OESOPHAGOSCOPES	OFFICIOUSLY	OLFACTOLOGIST
OCTOSYLLABIC	ODONTOPHOBIA	OESOPHAGOSCOPY	OFFICIOUSNESS	OLFACTOLOGISTS
OCTOSYLLABICS	ODONTOPHOBIAS	OESOPHAGUS	OFFICIOUSNESSES	OLFACTOLOGY
OCTOSYLLABLE	ODONTOPHORAL	OESTRADIOL	OFFISHNESS	OLFACTOMETER
OCTOSYLLABLES	ODONTOPHORAN	OESTRADIOLS	OFFISHNESSES	OLFACTOMETERS
OCTOTHORPS	ODONTOPHORANS	OESTROGENIC	OFFLOADING	OLFACTOMETRIES
OCTUPLICATE	ODONTOPHORE	OESTROGENICALLY	OFFPRINTED	OLFACTOMETRY
OCTUPLICATES	ODONTOPHORES	OESTROGENS	OFFPRINTING	OLFACTORIES
OCULARISTS	ODONTOPHOROUS	OFFENCEFUL	OFFSADDLED	OLFACTRONICS
OCULOMOTOR	ODONTORHYNCHOUS	OFFENCELESS	OFFSADDLES	OLIGAEMIAS
ODALISQUES	ODONTORNITHES	OFFENDEDLY	OFFSADDLING	OLIGARCHAL
ODDSMAKERS	ODONTOSTOMATOUS	OFFENDRESS	OFFSCOURING	OLIGARCHIC
ODIOUSNESS	ODORIFEROUS	OFFENDRESSES	OFFSCOURINGS	OLIGARCHICAL
ODIOUSNESSES	ODORIFEROUSLY	OFFENSELESS	OFFSEASONS	OLIGARCHICALLY
ODOMETRIES	ODORIFEROUSNESS	OFFENSIVELY	OFFSETABLE	OLIGARCHIES
ODONATISTS	ODORIMETRIES	OFFENSIVENESS	OFFSETTING	OLIGOCHAETE
ODONATOLOGIES	ODORIMETRY	OFFENSIVENESSES	OFFSETTINGS	OLIGOCHAETES
ODONATOLOGIST	ODORIPHORE	OFFENSIVES	OFFSHORING	OLIGOCHROME
ODONATOLOGISTS	ODORIPHORES	OFFERTORIES	OFFSHORINGS	OLIGOCHROMES
ODONATOLOGY	ODOROUSNESS	OFFHANDEDLY	OFFSPRINGS	OLIGOCLASE
ODONTALGIA	ODOROUSNESSES	OFFHANDEDNESS	OFTENNESSES	OLIGOCLASES
ODONTALGIAS	OECOLOGICAL	OFFHANDEDNESSES	OFTENTIMES	OLIGOCYTHAEMIA
ODONTALGIC	OECOLOGICALLY	OFFICEHOLDER	OILINESSES	OLIGOCYTHAEMIAS
ODONTALGIES	OECOLOGIES	OFFICEHOLDERS	OINOLOGIES	OLIGODENDROCYTE
ODONTOBLAST	OECOLOGIST	OFFICERING	OLDFANGLED	OLIGODENDROGLIA
ODONTOBLASTIC	OECOLOGISTS	OFFICIALDOM	OLEAGINOUS	OLIGOGENES
ODONTOBLASTS	OECUMENICAL	OFFICIALDOMS	OLEAGINOUSLY	OLIGOMERIC
ODONTOCETE	OECUMENICALLY	OFFICIALESE	OLEAGINOUSNESS	OLIGOMERISATION
ODONTOCETES	OEDEMATOSE	OFFICIALESES	OLEANDOMYCIN	OLIGOMERIZATION
ODONTOGENIC	OEDEMATOUS	OFFICIALISM	OLEANDOMYCINS	OLIGOMEROUS
ODONTOGENIES	OEDOMETERS	OFFICIALISMS	OLECRANONS	OLIGONUCLEOTIDE
ODONTOGENY	OENOLOGICAL	OFFICIALITIES	OLEIFEROUS	OLIGOPEPTIDE
ODONTOGLOSSUM	OENOLOGIES	OFFICIALITY	OLEOGRAPHIC	OLIGOPEPTIDES
ODONTOGLOSSUMS	OENOLOGIST	OFFICIALLY	OLEOGRAPHIES	OLIGOPHAGIES
ODONTOGRAPH	OENOLOGISTS	OFFICIALTIES	OLEOGRAPHS	OLIGOPHAGOUS
ODONTOGRAPHIES	OENOMANCIES	OFFICIALTY	OLEOGRAPHY	OLIGOPHAGY
ODONTOGRAPHS	OENOMANIAS	OFFICIANTS	OLEOMARGARIN	OLIGOPOLIES
ODONTOGRAPHY	OENOMETERS	OFFICIARIES	OLEOMARGARINE	OLIGOPOLISTIC
ODONTOLITE	OENOPHILES	OFFICIATED	OLEOMARGARINES	OLIGOPSONIES
ODONTOLITES	OENOPHILIES	OFFICIATES	OLEOMARGARINS	OLIGOPSONISTIC
ODONTOLOGIC	OENOPHILIST	OFFICIATING	OLEOPHILIC	OLIGOPSONY
ODONTOLOGICAL	OENOPHILISTS	OFFICIATION	OLEORESINOUS	OLIGOSACCHARIDE
ODONTOLOGIES	OENOTHERAS	OFFICIATIONS	OLEORESINS	OLIGOSPERMIA

O

OLIGOSPERMIAS

OLIGOSPERMIAS
OLIGOTROPHIC
OLIGOTROPHIES
OLIGOTROPHY
OLIGURESES
OLIGURESIS
OLIGURETIC
OLINGUITOS
OLIVACEOUS
OLIVENITES
OLIVEWOODS
OLIVINITIC
OLOGOANING
OLOLIUQUIS
OMBROGENOUS
OMBROMETER
OMBROMETERS
OMBROPHILE
OMBROPHILES
OMBROPHILOUS
OMBROPHILS
OMBROPHOBE
OMBROPHOBES
OMBROPHOBOUS
OMBUDSMANSHIP
OMBUDSMANSHIPS
OMINOUSNESS
OMINOUSNESSES
OMISSIVENESS
OMISSIVENESSES
OMITTANCES
OMMATIDIAL
OMMATIDIUM
OMMATOPHORE
OMMATOPHORES
OMMATOPHOROUS
OMNIBENEVOLENCE
OMNIBENEVOLENT
OMNIBUSSES
OMNICOMPETENCE
OMNICOMPETENCES
OMNICOMPETENT
OMNIDIRECTIONAL
OMNIFARIOUS
OMNIFARIOUSLY
OMNIFARIOUSNESS
OMNIFEROUS

OMNIFICENCE
OMNIFICENCES
OMNIFICENT
OMNIFORMITIES
OMNIFORMITY
OMNIGENOUS
OMNIPARITIES
OMNIPARITY
OMNIPAROUS
OMNIPATIENT
OMNIPOTENCE
OMNIPOTENCES
OMNIPOTENCIES
OMNIPOTENCY
OMNIPOTENT
OMNIPOTENTLY
OMNIPOTENTS
OMNIPRESENCE
OMNIPRESENCES
OMNIPRESENT
OMNIRANGES
OMNISCIENCE
OMNISCIENCES
OMNISCIENT
OMNISCIENTLY
OMNIVORIES
OMNIVOROUS
OMNIVOROUSLY
OMNIVOROUSNESS
OMOPHAGIAS
OMOPHAGIES
OMOPHAGOUS
OMOPHORION
OMOPLATOSCOPIES
OMOPLATOSCOPY
OMPHACITES
OMPHALOMANCIES
OMPHALOMANCY
OMPHALOSKEPSES
OMPHALOSKEPSIS
ONAGRACEOUS
ONBOARDING
ONBOARDINGS
ONCHOCERCIASES
ONCHOCERCIASIS
ONCOGENESES
ONCOGENESIS

ONCOGENETICIST
ONCOGENETICISTS
ONCOGENICITIES
ONCOGENICITY
ONCOGENOUS
ONCOLOGICAL
ONCOLOGIES
ONCOLOGIST
ONCOLOGISTS
ONCOLYTICS
ONCOMETERS
ONCORNAVIRUS
ONCORNAVIRUSES
ONCOTOMIES
ONCOVIRUSES
ONDOGRAPHS
ONEIRICALLY
ONEIROCRITIC
ONEIROCRITICAL
ONEIROCRITICISM
ONEIROCRITICS
ONEIRODYNIA
ONEIRODYNIAS
ONEIROLOGIES
ONEIROLOGY
ONEIROMANCER
ONEIROMANCERS
ONEIROMANCIES
ONEIROMANCY
ONEIROSCOPIES
ONEIROSCOPIST
ONEIROSCOPISTS
ONEIROSCOPY
ONEROUSNESS
ONEROUSNESSES
ONGOINGNESS
ONGOINGNESSES
ONIONSKINS
ONOCENTAUR
ONOCENTAURS
ONOMASIOLOGIES
ONOMASIOLOGY
ONOMASTICALLY
ONOMASTICIAN
ONOMASTICIANS
ONOMASTICON
ONOMASTICONS

ONOMASTICS
ONOMATOLOGIES
ONOMATOLOGIST
ONOMATOLOGISTS
ONOMATOLOGY
ONOMATOPOEIA
ONOMATOPOEIAS
ONOMATOPOEIC
ONOMATOPOESES
ONOMATOPOESIS
ONOMATOPOETIC
ONOMATOPOIESES
ONOMATOPOIESIS
ONSETTINGS
ONSHORINGS
ONSLAUGHTS
ONTOGENESES
ONTOGENESIS
ONTOGENETIC
ONTOGENETICALLY
ONTOGENICALLY
ONTOGENIES
ONTOLOGICAL
ONTOLOGICALLY
ONTOLOGIES
ONTOLOGIST
ONTOLOGISTS
ONYCHITISES
ONYCHOCRYPTOSES
ONYCHOCRYPTOSIS
ONYCHOMANCIES
ONYCHOMANCY
ONYCHOPHAGIES
ONYCHOPHAGIST
ONYCHOPHAGISTS
ONYCHOPHAGY
ONYCHOPHORAN
ONYCHOPHORANS
OOGAMOUSLY
OOJAMAFLIP
OOJAMAFLIPS
OOPHORECTOMIES
OOPHORECTOMISE
OOPHORECTOMISED
OOPHORECTOMISES
OOPHORECTOMIZE
OOPHORECTOMIZED

OOPHORECTOMIZES
OOPHORECTOMY
OOPHORITIC
OOPHORITIS
OOPHORITISES
OOZINESSES
OPACIFIERS
OPACIFYING
OPALESCENCE
OPALESCENCES
OPALESCENT
OPALESCENTLY
OPALESCING
OPAQUENESS
OPAQUENESSES
OPEIDOSCOPE
OPEIDOSCOPES
OPENABILITIES
OPENABILITY
OPENHANDED
OPENHANDEDLY
OPENHANDEDNESS
OPENHEARTED
OPENHEARTEDLY
OPENHEARTEDNESS
OPENMOUTHED
OPENMOUTHEDLY
OPENMOUTHEDNESS
OPENNESSES
OPERABILITIES
OPERABILITY
OPERAGOERS
OPERAGOING
OPERAGOINGS
OPERATICALLY
OPERATIONAL
OPERATIONALISM
OPERATIONALISMS
OPERATIONALIST
OPERATIONALISTS
OPERATIONALLY
OPERATIONISM
OPERATIONISMS
OPERATIONIST
OPERATIONISTS
OPERATIONS
OPERATISED

O

OPERATISES	OPHIUROIDS	OPISTHOGRAPHY	OPPOSITIONLESS	OPTIMALIZATIONS
OPERATISING	OPHTHALMIA	OPISTHOSOMA	OPPOSITIONS	OPTIMALIZE
OPERATIVELY	OPHTHALMIAS	OPISTHOSOMATA	OPPOSITIVE	OPTIMALIZED
OPERATIVENESS	OPHTHALMIC	OPISTHOTONIC	OPPRESSING	OPTIMALIZES
OPERATIVENESSES	OPHTHALMIST	OPISTHOTONOS	OPPRESSINGLY	OPTIMALIZING
OPERATIVES	OPHTHALMISTS	OPISTHOTONOSES	OPPRESSION	OPTIMISATION
OPERATIVITIES	OPHTHALMITIS	OPOBALSAMS	OPPRESSIONS	OPTIMISATIONS
OPERATIVITY	OPHTHALMITISES	OPODELDOCS	OPPRESSIVE	OPTIMISERS
OPERATIZED	OPHTHALMOLOGIC	OPOPANAXES	OPPRESSIVELY	OPTIMISING
OPERATIZES	OPHTHALMOLOGIES	OPOTHERAPIES	OPPRESSIVENESS	OPTIMISTIC
OPERATIZING	OPHTHALMOLOGIST	OPOTHERAPY	OPPRESSORS	OPTIMISTICAL
OPERATORLESS	OPHTHALMOLOGY	OPPIGNERATE	OPPROBRIOUS	OPTIMISTICALLY
OPERCULARS	OPHTHALMOMETER	OPPIGNERATED	OPPROBRIOUSLY	OPTIMIZATION
OPERCULATE	OPHTHALMOMETERS	OPPIGNERATES	OPPROBRIOUSNESS	OPTIMIZATIONS
OPERCULATED	OPHTHALMOMETRY	OPPIGNERATING	OPPROBRIUM	OPTIMIZERS
OPERCULUMS	OPHTHALMOPHOBIA	OPPIGNORATE	OPPROBRIUMS	OPTIMIZING
OPERETTIST	OPHTHALMOPLEGIA	OPPIGNORATED	OPPUGNANCIES	OPTIONALITIES
OPERETTISTS	OPHTHALMOSCOPE	OPPIGNORATES	OPPUGNANCY	OPTIONALITY
OPEROSENESS	OPHTHALMOSCOPES	OPPIGNORATING	OPPUGNANTLY	OPTIONALLY
OPEROSENESSES	OPHTHALMOSCOPIC	OPPIGNORATION	OPPUGNANTS	OPTOACOUSTIC
OPEROSITIES	OPHTHALMOSCOPY	OPPIGNORATIONS	OPSIMATHIES	OPTOELECTRONIC
OPHICALCITE	OPINICUSES	OPPILATING	OPSIOMETER	OPTOELECTRONICS
OPHICALCITES	OPINIONATED	OPPILATION	OPSIOMETERS	OPTOKINETIC
OPHICLEIDE	OPINIONATEDLY	OPPILATIONS	OPSOMANIAC	OPTOLOGIES
OPHICLEIDES	OPINIONATEDNESS	OPPILATIVE	OPSOMANIACS	OPTOLOGIST
OPHIDIARIA	OPINIONATELY	OPPONENCIES	OPSOMANIAS	OPTOLOGISTS
OPHIDIARIUM	OPINIONATIVE	OPPORTUNELY	OPSONIFICATION	OPTOMETERS
OPHIDIARIUMS	OPINIONATIVELY	OPPORTUNENESS	OPSONIFICATIONS	OPTOMETRIC
OPHIOLATER	OPINIONATOR	OPPORTUNENESSES	OPSONIFIED	OPTOMETRICAL
OPHIOLATERS	OPINIONATORS	OPPORTUNISM	OPSONIFIES	OPTOMETRIES
OPHIOLATRIES	OPINIONIST	OPPORTUNISMS	OPSONIFYING	OPTOMETRIST
OPHIOLATROUS	OPINIONISTS	OPPORTUNIST	OPSONISATION	OPTOMETRISTS
OPHIOLATRY	OPISOMETER	OPPORTUNISTIC	OPSONISATIONS	OPTOPHONES
OPHIOLITES	OPISOMETERS	OPPORTUNISTS	OPSONISING	OPULENCIES
OPHIOLITIC	OPISTHOBRANCH	OPPORTUNITIES	OPSONIZATION	ORACULARITIES
OPHIOLOGIC	OPISTHOBRANCHS	OPPORTUNITY	OPSONIZATIONS	ORACULARITY
OPHIOLOGICAL	OPISTHOCOELIAN	OPPOSABILITIES	OPSONIZING	ORACULARLY
OPHIOLOGIES	OPISTHOCOELOUS	OPPOSABILITY	OPTATIVELY	ORACULARNESS
OPHIOLOGIST	OPISTHODOMOI	OPPOSELESS	OPTIMALISATION	ORACULARNESSES
OPHIOLOGISTS	OPISTHODOMOS	OPPOSINGLY	OPTIMALISATIONS	ORACULOUSLY
OPHIOMORPH	OPISTHOGLOSSAL	OPPOSITELY	OPTIMALISE	ORACULOUSNESS
OPHIOMORPHIC	OPISTHOGNATHISM	OPPOSITENESS	OPTIMALISED	ORACULOUSNESSES
OPHIOMORPHOUS	OPISTHOGNATHOUS	OPPOSITENESSES	OPTIMALISES	ORANGEADES
OPHIOMORPHS	OPISTHOGRAPH	OPPOSITION	OPTIMALISING	ORANGERIES
OPHIOPHAGOUS	OPISTHOGRAPHIC	OPPOSITIONAL	OPTIMALITIES	ORANGEWOOD
OPHIOPHILIST	OPISTHOGRAPHIES	OPPOSITIONIST	OPTIMALITY	ORANGEWOODS
OPHIOPHILISTS	OPISTHOGRAPHS	OPPOSITIONISTS	OPTIMALIZATION	ORANGUTANS

O

ORATORIANS
ORATORICAL
ORATORICALLY
ORATRESSES
ORBICULARES
ORBICULARIS
ORBICULARITIES
ORBICULARITY
ORBICULARLY
ORBICULATE
ORBICULATED
ORCHARDING
ORCHARDINGS
ORCHARDIST
ORCHARDISTS
ORCHARDMAN
ORCHARDMEN
ORCHESOGRAPHIES
ORCHESOGRAPHY
ORCHESTICS
ORCHESTRAL
ORCHESTRALIST
ORCHESTRALISTS
ORCHESTRALLY
ORCHESTRAS
ORCHESTRATE
ORCHESTRATED
ORCHESTRATER
ORCHESTRATERS
ORCHESTRATES
ORCHESTRATING
ORCHESTRATION
ORCHESTRATIONAL
ORCHESTRATIONS
ORCHESTRATOR
ORCHESTRATORS
ORCHESTRIC
ORCHESTRINA
ORCHESTRINAS
ORCHESTRION
ORCHESTRIONS
ORCHIDACEOUS
ORCHIDECTOMIES
ORCHIDECTOMY
ORCHIDEOUS
ORCHIDISTS
ORCHIDLIKE

ORCHIDOLOGIES
ORCHIDOLOGIST
ORCHIDOLOGISTS
ORCHIDOLOGY
ORCHIDOMANIA
ORCHIDOMANIAC
ORCHIDOMANIACS
ORCHIDOMANIAS
ORCHIECTOMIES
ORCHIECTOMY
ORCHITISES
ORDAINABLE
ORDAINMENT
ORDAINMENTS
ORDERLINESS
ORDERLINESSES
ORDINAIRES
ORDINANCES
ORDINARIER
ORDINARIES
ORDINARIEST
ORDINARILY
ORDINARINESS
ORDINARINESSES
ORDINATELY
ORDINATING
ORDINATION
ORDINATIONS
ORDONNANCE
ORDONNANCES
ORECCHIETTE
ORECCHIETTES
ORECCHIETTI
OREOGRAPHIC
OREOGRAPHICAL
OREOGRAPHICALLY
OREOGRAPHIES
OREOGRAPHY
OREOLOGICAL
OREOLOGIES
OREOLOGIST
OREOLOGISTS
OREPEARCHED
OREPEARCHES
OREPEARCHING
ORGANELLES
ORGANICALLY

ORGANICISM
ORGANICISMS
ORGANICIST
ORGANICISTIC
ORGANICISTS
ORGANICITIES
ORGANICITY
ORGANISABILITY
ORGANISABLE
ORGANISATION
ORGANISATIONAL
ORGANISATIONS
ORGANISERS
ORGANISING
ORGANISINGS
ORGANISMAL
ORGANISMALLY
ORGANISMIC
ORGANISMICALLY
ORGANISTRUM
ORGANISTRUMS
ORGANITIES
ORGANIZABILITY
ORGANIZABLE
ORGANIZATION
ORGANIZATIONAL
ORGANIZATIONS
ORGANIZERS
ORGANIZING
ORGANIZINGS
ORGANOCHLORINE
ORGANOCHLORINES
ORGANOGENESES
ORGANOGENESIS
ORGANOGENETIC
ORGANOGENIES
ORGANOGENY
ORGANOGRAM
ORGANOGRAMS
ORGANOGRAPHIC
ORGANOGRAPHICAL
ORGANOGRAPHIES
ORGANOGRAPHIST
ORGANOGRAPHISTS
ORGANOGRAPHY
ORGANOLEPTIC
ORGANOLOGICAL

ORGANOLOGIES
ORGANOLOGIST
ORGANOLOGISTS
ORGANOLOGY
ORGANOMERCURIAL
ORGANOMETALLIC
ORGANOMETALLICS
ORGANOPHOSPHATE
ORGANOSOLS
ORGANOTHERAPIES
ORGANOTHERAPY
ORGANZINES
ORGASMICALLY
ORGASTICALLY
ORGIASTICALLY
ORICALCHES
ORICHALCEOUS
ORIENTALISE
ORIENTALISED
ORIENTALISES
ORIENTALISING
ORIENTALISM
ORIENTALISMS
ORIENTALIST
ORIENTALISTS
ORIENTALITIES
ORIENTALITY
ORIENTALIZE
ORIENTALIZED
ORIENTALIZES
ORIENTALIZING
ORIENTALLY
ORIENTATED
ORIENTATES
ORIENTATING
ORIENTATION
ORIENTATIONAL
ORIENTATIONALLY
ORIENTATIONS
ORIENTATOR
ORIENTATORS
ORIENTEERED
ORIENTEERING
ORIENTEERINGS
ORIENTEERS
ORIFLAMMES
ORIGINALITIES

ORIGINALITY
ORIGINALLY
ORIGINATED
ORIGINATES
ORIGINATING
ORIGINATION
ORIGINATIONS
ORIGINATIVE
ORIGINATIVELY
ORIGINATOR
ORIGINATORS
ORINASALLY
ORISMOLOGICAL
ORISMOLOGIES
ORISMOLOGY
ORNAMENTAL
ORNAMENTALLY
ORNAMENTALS
ORNAMENTATION
ORNAMENTATIONS
ORNAMENTED
ORNAMENTER
ORNAMENTERS
ORNAMENTING
ORNAMENTIST
ORNAMENTISTS
ORNATENESS
ORNATENESSES
ORNERINESS
ORNERINESSES
ORNITHICHNITE
ORNITHICHNITES
ORNITHINES
ORNITHISCHIAN
ORNITHISCHIANS
ORNITHODELPHIAN
ORNITHODELPHIC
ORNITHODELPHOUS
ORNITHOGALUM
ORNITHOGALUMS
ORNITHOLOGIC
ORNITHOLOGICAL
ORNITHOLOGIES
ORNITHOLOGIST
ORNITHOLOGISTS
ORNITHOLOGY
ORNITHOMANCIES

O

ORNITHOMANCY	ORPHANISMS	ORTHOGENESIS	ORTHOPEDIA	ORTHOSCOPIC
ORNITHOMANTIC	ORPHARIONS	ORTHOGENETIC	ORTHOPEDIAS	ORTHOSILICATE
ORNITHOMORPH	ORPHEOREON	ORTHOGENIC	ORTHOPEDIC	ORTHOSILICATES
ORNITHOMORPHIC	ORPHEOREONS	ORTHOGENICALLY	ORTHOPEDICAL	ORTHOSTATIC
ORNITHOMORPHS	ORPHICALLY	ORTHOGENICS	ORTHOPEDICALLY	ORTHOSTICHIES
ORNITHOPHILIES	ORRISROOTS	ORTHOGNATHIC	ORTHOPEDICS	ORTHOSTICHOUS
ORNITHOPHILOUS	ORTANIQUES	ORTHOGNATHIES	ORTHOPEDIES	ORTHOSTICHY
ORNITHOPHILY	ORTHOBORATE	ORTHOGNATHISM	ORTHOPEDIST	ORTHOTISTS
ORNITHOPHOBIA	ORTHOBORATES	ORTHOGNATHISMS	ORTHOPEDISTS	ORTHOTONES
ORNITHOPHOBIAS	ORTHOBORIC	ORTHOGNATHOUS	ORTHOPHOSPHATE	ORTHOTONESES
ORNITHOPOD	ORTHOCAINE	ORTHOGNATHY	ORTHOPHOSPHATES	ORTHOTONESIS
ORNITHOPODS	ORTHOCAINES	ORTHOGONAL	ORTHOPHOSPHORIC	ORTHOTONIC
ORNITHOPTER	ORTHOCENTER	ORTHOGONALISE	ORTHOPHYRE	ORTHOTOPIC
ORNITHOPTERS	ORTHOCENTERS	ORTHOGONALISED	ORTHOPHYRES	ORTHOTROPIC
ORNITHORHYNCHUS	ORTHOCENTRE	ORTHOGONALISES	ORTHOPHYRIC	ORTHOTROPIES
ORNITHOSAUR	ORTHOCENTRES	ORTHOGONALISING	ORTHOPINAKOID	ORTHOTROPISM
ORNITHOSAURS	ORTHOCEPHALIC	ORTHOGONALITIES	ORTHOPINAKOIDS	ORTHOTROPISMS
ORNITHOSCOPIES	ORTHOCEPHALIES	ORTHOGONALITY	ORTHOPNOEA	ORTHOTROPOUS
ORNITHOSCOPY	ORTHOCEPHALOUS	ORTHOGONALIZE	ORTHOPNOEAS	ORTHOTROPY
ORNITHOSES	ORTHOCEPHALY	ORTHOGONALIZED	ORTHOPRAXES	ORTHOTUNGSTIC
ORNITHOSIS	ORTHOCHROMATIC	ORTHOGONALIZES	ORTHOPRAXIES	ORTHOVANADIC
OROBANCHACEOUS	ORTHOCHROMATISM	ORTHOGONALIZING	ORTHOPRAXIS	ORYCTOLOGIES
OROGENESES	ORTHOCLASE	ORTHOGONALLY	ORTHOPRAXY	ORYCTOLOGY
OROGENESIS	ORTHOCLASES	ORTHOGRADE	ORTHOPRISM	OSCILLATED
OROGENETIC	ORTHOCOUSINS	ORTHOGRAPH	ORTHOPRISMS	OSCILLATES
OROGENETICALLY	ORTHODIAGONAL	ORTHOGRAPHER	ORTHOPSYCHIATRY	OSCILLATING
OROGENICALLY	ORTHODIAGONALS	ORTHOGRAPHERS	ORTHOPTERA	OSCILLATION
OROGRAPHER	ORTHODONTIA	ORTHOGRAPHIC	ORTHOPTERAN	OSCILLATIONAL
OROGRAPHERS	ORTHODONTIAS	ORTHOGRAPHICAL	ORTHOPTERANS	OSCILLATIONS
OROGRAPHIC	ORTHODONTIC	ORTHOGRAPHIES	ORTHOPTERIST	OSCILLATIVE
OROGRAPHICAL	ORTHODONTICALLY	ORTHOGRAPHIST	ORTHOPTERISTS	OSCILLATOR
OROGRAPHICALLY	ORTHODONTICS	ORTHOGRAPHISTS	ORTHOPTEROID	OSCILLATORS
OROGRAPHIES	ORTHODONTIST	ORTHOGRAPHS	ORTHOPTEROIDS	OSCILLATORY
OROLOGICAL	ORTHODONTISTS	ORTHOGRAPHY	ORTHOPTEROLOGY	OSCILLOGRAM
OROLOGICALLY	ORTHODOXES	ORTHOHYDROGEN	ORTHOPTERON	OSCILLOGRAMS
OROLOGISTS	ORTHODOXIES	ORTHOHYDROGENS	ORTHOPTEROUS	OSCILLOGRAPH
OROPHARYNGEAL	ORTHODOXLY	ORTHOMOLECULAR	ORTHOPTERS	OSCILLOGRAPHIC
OROPHARYNGES	ORTHODROMIC	ORTHOMORPHIC	ORTHOPTICS	OSCILLOGRAPHIES
OROPHARYNX	ORTHODROMICS	ORTHONORMAL	ORTHOPTIST	OSCILLOGRAPHS
OROPHARYNXES	ORTHODROMIES	ORTHOPAEDIC	ORTHOPTISTS	OSCILLOGRAPHY
OROROTUNDITIES	ORTHODROMY	ORTHOPAEDICAL	ORTHOPYROXENE	OSCILLOSCOPE
OROROTUNDITY	ORTHOEPICAL	ORTHOPAEDICALLY	ORTHOPYROXENES	OSCILLOSCOPES
OROTUNDITIES	ORTHOEPICALLY	ORTHOPAEDICS	ORTHOREXIA	OSCILLOSCOPIC
OROTUNDITY	ORTHOEPIES	ORTHOPAEDIES	ORTHOREXIAS	OSCITANCES
ORPHANAGES	ORTHOEPIST	ORTHOPAEDIST	ORTHORHOMBIC	OSCITANCIES
ORPHANHOOD	ORTHOEPISTS	ORTHOPAEDISTS	ORTHOSCOPE	OSCITANTLY
ORPHANHOODS	ORTHOGENESES	ORTHOPAEDY	ORTHOSCOPES	OSCITATING

O

OSCITATION	OSTEOARTHRITIC	OSTEOPATHS	OSTREOPHAGOUS	OUTBARGAIN
OSCITATIONS	OSTEOARTHRITICS	OSTEOPATHY	OSTREOPHAGY	OUTBARGAINED
OSCULATING	OSTEOARTHRITIS	OSTEOPETROSES	OSTRICHISM	OUTBARGAINING
OSCULATION	OSTEOARTHROSES	OSTEOPETROSIS	OSTRICHISMS	OUTBARGAINS
OSCULATIONS	OSTEOARTHROSIS	OSTEOPHYTE	OSTRICHLIKE	OUTBARKING
OSCULATORIES	OSTEOBLAST	OSTEOPHYTES	OTHERGATES	OUTBARRING
OSCULATORY	OSTEOBLASTIC	OSTEOPHYTIC	OTHERGUESS	OUTBAWLING
OSMETERIUM	OSTEOBLASTS	OSTEOPLASTIC	OTHERNESSES	OUTBEAMING
OSMIDROSES	OSTEOCLASES	OSTEOPLASTIES	OTHERWHERE	OUTBEGGING
OSMIDROSIS	OSTEOCLASIS	OSTEOPLASTY	OTHERWHILE	OUTBIDDERS
OSMIRIDIUM	OSTEOCLAST	OSTEOPOROSES	OTHERWHILES	OUTBIDDING
OSMIRIDIUMS	OSTEOCLASTIC	OSTEOPOROSIS	OTHERWORLD	OUTBITCHED
OSMOLALITIES	OSTEOCLASTS	OSTEOPOROTIC	OTHERWORLDISH	OUTBITCHES
OSMOLALITY	OSTEOCOLLA	OSTEOSARCOMA	OTHERWORLDLY	OUTBITCHING
OSMOLARITIES	OSTEOCOLLAS	OSTEOSARCOMAS	OTHERWORLDS	OUTBLAZING
OSMOLARITY	OSTEOCYTES	OSTEOSARCOMATA	OTIOSENESS	OUTBLEATED
OSMOMETERS	OSTEODERMAL	OSTEOSISES	OTIOSENESSES	OUTBLEATING
OSMOMETRIC	OSTEODERMATOUS	OSTEOTOMES	OTIOSITIES	OUTBLESSED
OSMOMETRICALLY	OSTEODERMIC	OSTEOTOMIES	OTOLARYNGOLOGY	OUTBLESSES
OSMOMETRIES	OSTEODERMOUS	OSTLERESSES	OTOLOGICAL	OUTBLESSING
OSMOREGULATION	OSTEODERMS	OSTRACEANS	OTOLOGISTS	OUTBLOOMED
OSMOREGULATIONS	OSTEOFIBROSES	OSTRACEOUS	OTOPLASTIES	OUTBLOOMING
OSMOREGULATORY	OSTEOFIBROSIS	OSTRACISABLE	OTORRHOEAS	OUTBLUFFED
OSMOTICALLY	OSTEOGENESES	OSTRACISED	OTOSCLEROSES	OUTBLUFFING
OSMUNDINES	OSTEOGENESIS	OSTRACISER	OTOSCLEROSIS	OUTBLUSHED
OSSIFEROUS	OSTEOGENETIC	OSTRACISERS	OTOSCOPIES	OUTBLUSHES
OSSIFICATION	OSTEOGENIC	OSTRACISES	OTOTOXICITIES	OUTBLUSHING
OSSIFICATIONS	OSTEOGENIES	OSTRACISING	OTOTOXICITY	OUTBLUSTER
OSSIFRAGAS	OSTEOGENOUS	OSTRACISMS	OTTRELITES	OUTBLUSTERED
OSSIFRAGES	OSTEOGRAPHIES	OSTRACIZABLE	OUANANICHE	OUTBLUSTERING
OSSIVOROUS	OSTEOGRAPHY	OSTRACIZED	OUANANICHES	OUTBLUSTERS
OSTEICHTHYAN	OSTEOLOGICAL	OSTRACIZER	OUBLIETTES	OUTBOASTED
OSTEICHTHYANS	OSTEOLOGICALLY	OSTRACIZERS	OUGHTLINGS	OUTBOASTING
OSTEITIDES	OSTEOLOGIES	OSTRACIZES	OUGHTNESSES	OUTBRAGGED
OSTEITISES	OSTEOLOGIST	OSTRACIZING	OUROBOROSES	OUTBRAGGING
OSTENSIBILITIES	OSTEOLOGISTS	OSTRACODAN	OUROLOGIES	OUTBRAVING
OSTENSIBILITY	OSTEOMALACIA	OSTRACODERM	OUROSCOPIES	OUTBRAWLED
OSTENSIBLE	OSTEOMALACIAL	OSTRACODERMS	OUTACHIEVE	OUTBRAWLING
OSTENSIBLY	OSTEOMALACIAS	OSTRACODES	OUTACHIEVED	OUTBRAZENED
OSTENSIVELY	OSTEOMALACIC	OSTRACODOUS	OUTACHIEVES	OUTBRAZENING
OSTENSORIA	OSTEOMYELITIS	OSTREACEOUS	OUTACHIEVING	OUTBRAZENS
OSTENSORIES	OSTEOMYELITISES	OSTREICULTURE	OUTARGUING	OUTBREAKING
OSTENSORIUM	OSTEOPATHIC	OSTREICULTURES	OUTBACKERS	OUTBREATHE
OSTENTATION	OSTEOPATHICALLY	OSTREICULTURIST	OUTBALANCE	OUTBREATHED
OSTENTATIONS	OSTEOPATHIES	OSTREOPHAGE	OUTBALANCED	OUTBREATHES
OSTENTATIOUS	OSTEOPATHIST	OSTREOPHAGES	OUTBALANCES	OUTBREATHING
OSTENTATIOUSLY	OSTEOPATHISTS	OSTREOPHAGIES	OUTBALANCING	OUTBREEDING

O

OUTBREEDINGS	OUTCRAFTYING	OUTDRESSING	OUTFLUSHED	OUTGUIDING
OUTBRIBING	OUTCRAWLED	OUTDRINKING	OUTFLUSHES	OUTGUNNING
OUTBUILDING	OUTCRAWLING	OUTDRIVING	OUTFLUSHING	OUTGUSHING
OUTBUILDINGS	OUTCROPPED	OUTDROPPED	OUTFOOLING	OUTHANDLED
OUTBULGING	OUTCROPPING	OUTDROPPING	OUTFOOTING	OUTHANDLES
OUTBULKING	OUTCROPPINGS	OUTDUELING	OUTFROWNED	OUTHANDLING
OUTBULLIED	OUTCROSSED	OUTDUELLED	OUTFROWNING	OUTHAULERS
OUTBULLIES	OUTCROSSES	OUTDUELLING	OUTFUMBLED	OUTHEARING
OUTBULLYING	OUTCROSSING	OUTDWELLED	OUTFUMBLES	OUTHITTING
OUTBURNING	OUTCROSSINGS	OUTDWELLING	OUTFUMBLING	OUTHOMERED
OUTBURSTING	OUTCROWDED	OUTEARNING	OUTGAINING	OUTHOMERING
OUTCALLING	OUTCROWDING	OUTECHOING	OUTGALLOPED	OUTHOWLING
OUTCAPERED	OUTCROWING	OUTERCOATS	OUTGALLOPING	OUTHUMORED
OUTCAPERING	OUTCURSING	OUTERCOURSE	OUTGALLOPS	OUTHUMORING
OUTCASTING	OUTDACIOUS	OUTERCOURSES	OUTGAMBLED	OUTHUMOURED
OUTCATCHES	OUTDANCING	OUTERWEARS	OUTGAMBLES	OUTHUMOURING
OUTCATCHING	OUTDATEDLY	OUTFABLING	OUTGAMBLING	OUTHUMOURS
OUTCAVILED	OUTDATEDNESS	OUTFANGTHIEF	OUTGASSING	OUTHUNTING
OUTCAVILING	OUTDATEDNESSES	OUTFANGTHIEVES	OUTGASSINGS	OUTHUSTLED
OUTCAVILLED	OUTDAZZLED	OUTFASTING	OUTGENERAL	OUTHUSTLES
OUTCAVILLING	OUTDAZZLES	OUTFAWNING	OUTGENERALED	OUTHUSTLING
OUTCHARGED	OUTDAZZLING	OUTFEASTED	OUTGENERALING	OUTINTRIGUE
OUTCHARGES	OUTDEBATED	OUTFEASTING	OUTGENERALLED	OUTINTRIGUED
OUTCHARGING	OUTDEBATES	OUTFEELING	OUTGENERALLING	OUTINTRIGUES
OUTCHARMED	OUTDEBATING	OUTFENCING	OUTGENERALS	OUTINTRIGUING
OUTCHARMING	OUTDELIVER	OUTFIELDER	OUTGIVINGS	OUTJESTING
OUTCHEATED	OUTDELIVERED	OUTFIELDERS	OUTGLARING	OUTJETTING
OUTCHEATING	OUTDELIVERING	OUTFIGHTING	OUTGLEAMED	OUTJETTINGS
OUTCHIDDEN	OUTDELIVERS	OUTFIGHTINGS	OUTGLEAMING	OUTJINXING
OUTCHIDING	OUTDESIGNED	OUTFIGURED	OUTGLITTER	OUTJOCKEYED
OUTCLASSED	OUTDESIGNING	OUTFIGURES	OUTGLITTERED	OUTJOCKEYING
OUTCLASSES	OUTDESIGNS	OUTFIGURING	OUTGLITTERING	OUTJOCKEYS
OUTCLASSING	OUTDISTANCE	OUTFINDING	OUTGLITTERS	OUTJUGGLED
OUTCLIMBED	OUTDISTANCED	OUTFISHING	OUTGLOWING	OUTJUGGLES
OUTCLIMBING	OUTDISTANCES	OUTFITTERS	OUTGNAWING	OUTJUGGLING
OUTCOACHED	OUTDISTANCING	OUTFITTING	OUTGOINGNESS	OUTJUMPING
OUTCOACHES	OUTDODGING	OUTFITTINGS	OUTGOINGNESSES	OUTJUTTING
OUTCOACHING	OUTDOORSMAN	OUTFLANKED	OUTGRINNED	OUTJUTTINGS
OUTCOMPETE	OUTDOORSMANSHIP	OUTFLANKING	OUTGRINNING	OUTKEEPING
OUTCOMPETED	OUTDOORSMEN	OUTFLASHED	OUTGROSSED	OUTKICKING
OUTCOMPETES	OUTDRAGGED	OUTFLASHES	OUTGROSSES	OUTKILLING
OUTCOMPETING	OUTDRAGGING	OUTFLASHING	OUTGROSSING	OUTKISSING
OUTCOOKING	OUTDRAWING	OUTFLINGING	OUTGROWING	OUTLANDERS
OUTCOUNTED	OUTDREAMED	OUTFLOATED	OUTGROWTHS	OUTLANDISH
OUTCOUNTING	OUTDREAMING	OUTFLOATING	OUTGUESSED	OUTLANDISHLY
OUTCRAFTIED	OUTDRESSED	OUTFLOWING	OUTGUESSES	OUTLANDISHNESS
OUTCRAFTIES	OUTDRESSES	OUTFLOWINGS	OUTGUESSING	OUTLASHING

O

OUTLASTING	OUTMEASURE	OUTPLACEMENTS	OUTPSYCHING	OUTRIGGING
OUTLAUGHED	OUTMEASURED	OUTPLACERS	OUTPULLING	OUTRIGGINGS
OUTLAUGHING	OUTMEASURES	OUTPLACING	OUTPUNCHED	OUTRIGHTLY
OUTLAUNCED	OUTMEASURING	OUTPLANNED	OUTPUNCHES	OUTRINGING
OUTLAUNCES	OUTMODEDLY	OUTPLANNING	OUTPUNCHING	OUTRIVALED
OUTLAUNCHED	OUTMODEDNESS	OUTPLAYING	OUTPURSUED	OUTRIVALING
OUTLAUNCHES	OUTMODEDNESSES	OUTPLODDED	OUTPURSUES	OUTRIVALLED
OUTLAUNCHING	OUTMUSCLED	OUTPLODDING	OUTPURSUING	OUTRIVALLING
OUTLAUNCING	OUTMUSCLES	OUTPLOTTED	OUTPUSHING	OUTROARING
OUTLAWRIES	OUTMUSCLING	OUTPLOTTING	OUTPUTTING	OUTROCKING
OUTLEADING	OUTNIGHTED	OUTPOINTED	OUTQUARTERS	OUTROLLING
OUTLEAPING	OUTNIGHTING	OUTPOINTING	OUTQUOTING	OUTROOPERS
OUTLEARNED	OUTNUMBERED	OUTPOLITICK	OUTRAGEOUS	OUTROOTING
OUTLEARNING	OUTNUMBERING	OUTPOLITICKED	OUTRAGEOUSLY	OUTRUNNERS
OUTLODGING	OUTNUMBERS	OUTPOLITICKING	OUTRAGEOUSNESS	OUTRUNNING
OUTLODGINGS	OUTOFFICES	OUTPOLITICKS	OUTRAISING	OUTRUSHING
OUTLOOKING	OUTORGANISE	OUTPOLLING	OUTRANGING	OUTSAILING
OUTLUSTRED	OUTORGANISED	OUTPOPULATE	OUTRANKING	OUTSAVORED
OUTLUSTRES	OUTORGANISES	OUTPOPULATED	OUTREACHED	OUTSAVORING
OUTLUSTRING	OUTORGANISING	OUTPOPULATES	OUTREACHES	OUTSAVOURED
OUTMANEUVER	OUTORGANIZE	OUTPOPULATING	OUTREACHING	OUTSAVOURING
OUTMANEUVERED	OUTORGANIZED	OUTPORTERS	OUTREADING	OUTSAVOURS
OUTMANEUVERING	OUTORGANIZES	OUTPOURERS	OUTREASONED	OUTSCHEMED
OUTMANEUVERS	OUTORGANIZING	OUTPOURING	OUTREASONING	OUTSCHEMES
OUTMANIPULATE	OUTPAINTED	OUTPOURINGS	OUTREASONS	OUTSCHEMING
OUTMANIPULATED	OUTPAINTING	OUTPOWERED	OUTREBOUND	OUTSCOLDED
OUTMANIPULATES	OUTPASSING	OUTPOWERING	OUTREBOUNDED	OUTSCOLDING
OUTMANIPULATING	OUTPASSION	OUTPRAYING	OUTREBOUNDING	OUTSCOOPED
OUTMANNING	OUTPASSIONED	OUTPREACHED	OUTREBOUNDS	OUTSCOOPING
OUTMANOEUVRE	OUTPASSIONING	OUTPREACHES	OUTRECKONED	OUTSCORING
OUTMANOEUVRED	OUTPASSIONS	OUTPREACHING	OUTRECKONING	OUTSCORNED
OUTMANOEUVRES	OUTPATIENT	OUTPREENED	OUTRECKONS	OUTSCORNING
OUTMANOEUVRING	OUTPATIENTS	OUTPREENING	OUTRECUIDANCE	OUTSCREAMED
OUTMANTLED	OUTPEEPING	OUTPRESSED	OUTRECUIDANCES	OUTSCREAMING
OUTMANTLES	OUTPEERING	OUTPRESSES	OUTREDDENED	OUTSCREAMS
OUTMANTLING	OUTPEOPLED	OUTPRESSING	OUTREDDENING	OUTSELLING
OUTMARCHED	OUTPEOPLES	OUTPRICING	OUTREDDENS	OUTSERVING
OUTMARCHES	OUTPEOPLING	OUTPRIZING	OUTREDDING	OUTSETTING
OUTMARCHING	OUTPERFORM	OUTPRODUCE	OUTREDDINGS	OUTSETTINGS
OUTMARRIAGE	OUTPERFORMED	OUTPRODUCED	OUTREIGNED	OUTSETTLEMENT
OUTMARRIAGES	OUTPERFORMING	OUTPRODUCES	OUTREIGNING	OUTSETTLEMENTS
OUTMASTERED	OUTPERFORMS	OUTPRODUCING	OUTRELIEFS	OUTSHAMING
OUTMASTERING	OUTPITCHED	OUTPROMISE	OUTREPRODUCE	OUTSHINING
OUTMASTERS	OUTPITCHES	OUTPROMISED	OUTREPRODUCED	OUTSHOOTING
OUTMATCHED	OUTPITCHING	OUTPROMISES	OUTREPRODUCES	OUTSHOUTED
OUTMATCHES	OUTPITYING	OUTPROMISING	OUTREPRODUCING	OUTSHOUTING
OUTMATCHING	OUTPLACEMENT	OUTPSYCHED	OUTRIGGERS	OUTSIDERNESS

OUTSIDERNESSES	OUTSTANDINGLY	OUTSWINGERS	OUTWAITING	OVALNESSES
OUTSINGING	OUTSTARING	OUTSWINGING	OUTWALKING	OVARIECTOMIES
OUTSINNING	OUTSTARTED	OUTSWOLLEN	OUTWARDNESS	OVARIECTOMISED
OUTSITTING	OUTSTARTING	OUTTALKING	OUTWARDNESSES	OVARIECTOMIZED
OUTSKATING	OUTSTATING	OUTTASKING	OUTWARRING	OVARIECTOMY
OUTSLEEPING	OUTSTATION	OUTTELLING	OUTWASTING	OVARIOTOMIES
OUTSLICKED	OUTSTATIONS	OUTTHANKED	OUTWATCHED	OVARIOTOMIST
OUTSLICKING	OUTSTAYING	OUTTHANKING	OUTWATCHES	OVARIOTOMISTS
OUTSMARTED	OUTSTEERED	OUTTHIEVED	OUTWATCHING	OVARIOTOMY
OUTSMARTING	OUTSTEERING	OUTTHIEVES	OUTWEARIED	OVARITIDES
OUTSMELLED	OUTSTEPPED	OUTTHIEVING	OUTWEARIES	OVARITISES
OUTSMELLING	OUTSTEPPING	OUTTHINKING	OUTWEARING	OVERABOUND
OUTSMILING	OUTSTRAINED	OUTTHOUGHT	OUTWEARYING	OVERABOUNDED
OUTSMOKING	OUTSTRAINING	OUTTHROBBED	OUTWEEDING	OVERABOUNDING
OUTSNORING	OUTSTRAINS	OUTTHROBBING	OUTWEEPING	OVERABOUNDS
OUTSOARING	OUTSTRETCH	OUTTHROWING	OUTWEIGHED	OVERABSTRACT
OUTSOURCED	OUTSTRETCHED	OUTTHRUSTED	OUTWEIGHING	OVERABUNDANCE
OUTSOURCES	OUTSTRETCHES	OUTTHRUSTING	OUTWELLING	OVERABUNDANCES
OUTSOURCING	OUTSTRETCHING	OUTTHRUSTS	OUTWHIRLED	OVERABUNDANT
OUTSOURCINGS	OUTSTRIDDEN	OUTTONGUED	OUTWHIRLING	OVERACCENTUATE
OUTSPANNED	OUTSTRIDES	OUTTONGUES	OUTWICKING	OVERACCENTUATED
OUTSPANNING	OUTSTRIDING	OUTTONGUING	OUTWILLING	OVERACCENTUATES
OUTSPARKLE	OUTSTRIKES	OUTTOPPING	OUTWINDING	OVERACHIEVE
OUTSPARKLED	OUTSTRIKING	OUTTOWERED	OUTWINGING	OVERACHIEVED
OUTSPARKLES	OUTSTRIPPED	OUTTOWERING	OUTWINNING	OVERACHIEVEMENT
OUTSPARKLING	OUTSTRIPPING	OUTTRADING	OUTWISHING	OVERACHIEVER
OUTSPEAKING	OUTSTRIVEN	OUTTRAVELED	OUTWITTING	OVERACHIEVERS
OUTSPECKLE	OUTSTRIVES	OUTTRAVELING	OUTWORKERS	OVERACHIEVES
OUTSPECKLES	OUTSTRIVING	OUTTRAVELLED	OUTWORKING	OVERACHIEVING
OUTSPEEDED	OUTSTROKES	OUTTRAVELLING	OUTWORTHED	OVERACTING
OUTSPEEDING	OUTSTUDIED	OUTTRAVELS	OUTWORTHING	OVERACTION
OUTSPELLED	OUTSTUDIES	OUTTRICKED	OUTWRESTED	OVERACTIONS
OUTSPELLING	OUTSTUDYING	OUTTRICKING	OUTWRESTING	OVERACTIVE
OUTSPENDING	OUTSTUNTED	OUTTROTTED	OUTWRESTLE	OVERACTIVITIES
OUTSPOKENLY	OUTSTUNTING	OUTTROTTING	OUTWRESTLED	OVERACTIVITY
OUTSPOKENNESS	OUTSULKING	OUTTRUMPED	OUTWRESTLES	OVERADJUSTMENT
OUTSPOKENNESSES	OUTSUMMING	OUTTRUMPING	OUTWRESTLING	OVERADJUSTMENTS
OUTSPORTED	OUTSWEARING	OUTVALUING	OUTWRITING	OVERADVERTISE
OUTSPORTING	OUTSWEEPING	OUTVAUNTED	OUTWRITTEN	OVERADVERTISED
OUTSPREADING	OUTSWEETEN	OUTVAUNTING	OUTWROUGHT	OVERADVERTISES
OUTSPREADS	OUTSWEETENED	OUTVENOMED	OUTYELLING	OVERADVERTISING
OUTSPRINGING	OUTSWEETENING	OUTVENOMING	OUTYELPING	OVERADVERTIZE
OUTSPRINGS	OUTSWEETENS	OUTVILLAIN	OUTYIELDED	OVERADVERTIZED
OUTSPRINTED	OUTSWELLED	OUTVILLAINED	OUTYIELDING	OVERADVERTIZES
OUTSPRINTING	OUTSWELLING	OUTVILLAINING	OUVIRANDRA	OVERADVERTIZING
OUTSPRINTS	OUTSWIMMING	OUTVILLAINS	OUVIRANDRAS	OVERAGGRESSIVE
OUTSTANDING	OUTSWINGER	OUTVOICING	OVALBUMINS	OVERAMBITIOUS

O

OVERAMPLIFIED
OVERANALYSE
OVERANALYSED
OVERANALYSES
OVERANALYSING
OVERANALYSIS
OVERANALYTICAL
OVERANALYZE
OVERANALYZED
OVERANALYZES
OVERANALYZING
OVERANXIETIES
OVERANXIETY
OVERANXIOUS
OVERAPPLICATION
OVERARCHED
OVERARCHES
OVERARCHING
OVERARMING
OVERAROUSAL
OVERAROUSALS
OVERARRANGE
OVERARRANGED
OVERARRANGES
OVERARRANGING
OVERARTICULATE
OVERARTICULATED
OVERARTICULATES
OVERASSERT
OVERASSERTED
OVERASSERTING
OVERASSERTION
OVERASSERTIONS
OVERASSERTIVE
OVERASSERTS
OVERASSESSMENT
OVERASSESSMENTS
OVERATTENTION
OVERATTENTIONS
OVERATTENTIVE
OVERBAKING
OVERBALANCE
OVERBALANCED
OVERBALANCES
OVERBALANCING
OVERBEARING
OVERBEARINGLY

OVERBEARINGNESS
OVERBEATEN
OVERBEATING
OVERBEJEWELED
OVERBEJEWELLED
OVERBETTED
OVERBETTING
OVERBETTINGS
OVERBIDDEN
OVERBIDDER
OVERBIDDERS
OVERBIDDING
OVERBIDDINGS
OVERBILLED
OVERBILLING
OVERBLANKET
OVERBLANKETS
OVERBLEACH
OVERBLEACHED
OVERBLEACHES
OVERBLEACHING
OVERBLOUSE
OVERBLOUSES
OVERBLOWING
OVERBOILED
OVERBOILING
OVERBOLDLY
OVERBOOKED
OVERBOOKING
OVERBOOKINGS
OVERBORROW
OVERBORROWED
OVERBORROWING
OVERBORROWS
OVERBOUGHT
OVERBOUNDED
OVERBOUNDING
OVERBOUNDS
OVERBRAKED
OVERBRAKES
OVERBRAKING
OVERBREATHING
OVERBREATHINGS
OVERBREEDING
OVERBREEDS
OVERBRIDGE
OVERBRIDGED

OVERBRIDGES
OVERBRIDGING
OVERBRIEFED
OVERBRIEFING
OVERBRIEFS
OVERBRIGHT
OVERBRIMMED
OVERBRIMMING
OVERBROWED
OVERBROWING
OVERBROWSE
OVERBROWSED
OVERBROWSES
OVERBROWSING
OVERBRUTAL
OVERBUILDING
OVERBUILDS
OVERBULKED
OVERBULKING
OVERBURDEN
OVERBURDENED
OVERBURDENING
OVERBURDENS
OVERBURDENSOME
OVERBURNED
OVERBURNING
OVERBURTHEN
OVERBURTHENED
OVERBURTHENING
OVERBURTHENS
OVERBUSIED
OVERBUSIES
OVERBUSYING
OVERBUYING
OVERCALLED
OVERCALLING
OVERCANOPIED
OVERCANOPIES
OVERCANOPY
OVERCANOPYING
OVERCAPACITIES
OVERCAPACITY
OVERCAPITALISE
OVERCAPITALISED
OVERCAPITALISES
OVERCAPITALIZE
OVERCAPITALIZED

OVERCAPITALIZES
OVERCAREFUL
OVERCARRIED
OVERCARRIES
OVERCARRYING
OVERCASTED
OVERCASTING
OVERCASTINGS
OVERCATCHES
OVERCATCHING
OVERCAUGHT
OVERCAUTION
OVERCAUTIONS
OVERCAUTIOUS
OVERCAUTIOUSLY
OVERCENTRALISE
OVERCENTRALISED
OVERCENTRALISES
OVERCENTRALIZE
OVERCENTRALIZED
OVERCENTRALIZES
OVERCHARGE
OVERCHARGED
OVERCHARGES
OVERCHARGING
OVERCHARGINGS
OVERCHECKS
OVERCHILLED
OVERCHILLING
OVERCHILLS
OVERCIVILISED
OVERCIVILIZED
OVERCLAIMED
OVERCLAIMING
OVERCLAIMS
OVERCLASSES
OVERCLASSIFIED
OVERCLASSIFIES
OVERCLASSIFY
OVERCLASSIFYING
OVERCLEANED
OVERCLEANING
OVERCLEANS
OVERCLEARED
OVERCLEARING
OVERCLEARS
OVERCLOCKED

OVERCLOCKER
OVERCLOCKERS
OVERCLOCKING
OVERCLOCKINGS
OVERCLOCKS
OVERCLOUDED
OVERCLOUDING
OVERCLOUDS
OVERCLOYED
OVERCLOYING
OVERCLUBBED
OVERCLUBBING
OVERCOACHED
OVERCOACHES
OVERCOACHING
OVERCOATING
OVERCOATINGS
OVERCOLORED
OVERCOLORING
OVERCOLORS
OVERCOLOUR
OVERCOLOURED
OVERCOLOURING
OVERCOLOURS
OVERCOMERS
OVERCOMING
OVERCOMMIT
OVERCOMMITMENT
OVERCOMMITMENTS
OVERCOMMITS
OVERCOMMITTED
OVERCOMMITTING
OVERCOMMUNICATE
OVERCOMPENSATE
OVERCOMPENSATED
OVERCOMPENSATES
OVERCOMPLEX
OVERCOMPLIANCE
OVERCOMPLIANCES
OVERCOMPLICATE
OVERCOMPLICATED
OVERCOMPLICATES
OVERCOMPRESS
OVERCOMPRESSED
OVERCOMPRESSES
OVERCOMPRESSING
OVERCONCERN

OVERCONCERNED OVERCROWDED OVERDIVERSITIES OVEREDUCATE OVEREQUIPPED
OVERCONCERNING OVERCROWDING OVERDIVERSITY OVEREDUCATED OVEREQUIPPING
OVERCONCERNS OVERCROWDINGS OVERDOCUMENT OVEREDUCATES OVEREQUIPS
OVERCONFIDENCE OVERCROWDS OVERDOCUMENTED OVEREDUCATING OVERESTIMATE
OVERCONFIDENCES OVERCROWED OVERDOCUMENTING OVEREDUCATION OVERESTIMATED
OVERCONFIDENT OVERCROWING OVERDOCUMENTS OVEREDUCATIONS OVERESTIMATES
OVERCONFIDENTLY OVERCULTIVATION OVERDOMINANCE OVEREGGING OVERESTIMATING
OVERCONSCIOUS OVERCURING OVERDOMINANCES OVERELABORATE OVERESTIMATION
OVERCONSTRUCT OVERCUTTING OVERDOMINANT OVERELABORATED OVERESTIMATIONS
OVERCONSTRUCTED OVERCUTTINGS OVERDOSAGE OVERELABORATES OVEREVALUATION
OVERCONSTRUCTS OVERDARING OVERDOSAGES OVERELABORATING OVEREVALUATIONS
OVERCONSUME OVERDECKED OVERDOSING OVERELABORATION OVEREXAGGERATE
OVERCONSUMED OVERDECKING OVERDRAFTS OVEREMBELLISH OVEREXAGGERATED
OVERCONSUMES OVERDECORATE OVERDRAMATIC OVEREMBELLISHED OVEREXAGGERATES
OVERCONSUMING OVERDECORATED OVERDRAMATISE OVEREMBELLISHES OVEREXCITABLE
OVERCONSUMPTION OVERDECORATES OVERDRAMATISED OVEREMOTED OVEREXCITE
OVERCONTROL OVERDECORATING OVERDRAMATISES OVEREMOTES OVEREXCITED
OVERCONTROLLED OVERDECORATION OVERDRAMATISING OVEREMOTING OVEREXCITEMENT
OVERCONTROLLING OVERDECORATIONS OVERDRAMATIZE OVEREMOTIONAL OVEREXCITEMENTS
OVERCONTROLS OVERDEMANDING OVERDRAMATIZED OVEREMPHASES OVEREXCITES
OVERCOOKED OVERDEPENDENCE OVERDRAMATIZES OVEREMPHASIS OVEREXCITING
OVERCOOKING OVERDEPENDENCES OVERDRAMATIZING OVEREMPHASISE OVEREXERCISE
OVERCOOLED OVERDEPENDENT OVERDRAUGHT OVEREMPHASISED OVEREXERCISED
OVERCOOLING OVERDESIGN OVERDRAUGHTS OVEREMPHASISES OVEREXERCISES
OVERCORRECT OVERDESIGNED OVERDRAWING OVEREMPHASISING OVEREXERCISING
OVERCORRECTED OVERDESIGNING OVERDRESSED OVEREMPHASIZE OVEREXERTED
OVERCORRECTING OVERDESIGNS OVERDRESSES OVEREMPHASIZED OVEREXERTING
OVERCORRECTION OVERDETERMINED OVERDRESSING OVEREMPHASIZES OVEREXERTION
OVERCORRECTIONS OVERDEVELOP OVERDRINKING OVEREMPHASIZING OVEREXERTIONS
OVERCORRECTS OVERDEVELOPED OVERDRINKS OVEREMPHATIC OVEREXERTS
OVERCOUNTED OVERDEVELOPING OVERDRIVEN OVEREMPLOYMENT OVEREXPAND
OVERCOUNTING OVERDEVELOPMENT OVERDRIVES OVEREMPLOYMENTS OVEREXPANDED
OVERCOUNTS OVERDEVELOPS OVERDRIVING OVERENAMORED OVEREXPANDING
OVERCOVERED OVERDEVIATE OVERDRYING OVERENAMOURED OVEREXPANDS
OVERCOVERING OVERDEVIATED OVERDUBBED OVERENCOURAGE OVEREXPANSION
OVERCOVERS OVERDEVIATES OVERDUBBING OVERENCOURAGED OVEREXPANSIONS
OVERCRAMMED OVERDEVIATING OVERDUSTED OVERENCOURAGES OVEREXPECTATION
OVERCRAMMING OVERDIAGNOSES OVERDUSTING OVERENCOURAGING OVEREXPLAIN
OVERCRAMMINGS OVERDIAGNOSIS OVERDYEING OVERENERGETIC OVEREXPLAINED
OVERCRAWED OVERDIRECT OVEREAGERNESS OVERENGINEER OVEREXPLAINING
OVERCRAWING OVERDIRECTED OVEREAGERNESSES OVERENGINEERED OVEREXPLAINS
OVERCREDULITIES OVERDIRECTING OVEREARNEST OVERENGINEERING OVEREXPLICIT
OVERCREDULITY OVERDIRECTS OVEREATERS OVERENGINEERS OVEREXPLOIT
OVERCREDULOUS OVERDISCOUNT OVEREATING OVERENROLLED OVEREXPLOITED
OVERCRITICAL OVERDISCOUNTED OVEREATINGS OVERENTERTAINED OVEREXPLOITING
OVERCROPPED OVERDISCOUNTING OVEREDITED OVERENTHUSIASM OVEREXPLOITS
OVERCROPPING OVERDISCOUNTS OVEREDITING OVERENTHUSIASMS OVEREXPOSE

O

OVEREXPOSED
OVEREXPOSES
OVEREXPOSING
OVEREXPOSURE
OVEREXPOSURES
OVEREXTEND
OVEREXTENDED
OVEREXTENDING
OVEREXTENDS
OVEREXTENSION
OVEREXTENSIONS
OVEREXTRACTION
OVEREXTRACTIONS
OVEREXTRAVAGANT
OVEREXUBERANT
OVEREYEING
OVERFACILE
OVERFALLEN
OVERFALLING
OVERFAMILIAR
OVERFAMILIARITY
OVERFASTIDIOUS
OVERFATIGUE
OVERFATIGUED
OVERFATIGUES
OVERFATIGUING
OVERFAVORED
OVERFAVORING
OVERFAVORS
OVERFAVOUR
OVERFAVOURED
OVERFAVOURING
OVERFAVOURS
OVERFEARED
OVERFEARING
OVERFEEDING
OVERFEEDINGS
OVERFERTILISE
OVERFERTILISED
OVERFERTILISES
OVERFERTILISING
OVERFERTILIZE
OVERFERTILIZED
OVERFERTILIZES
OVERFERTILIZING
OVERFILLED
OVERFILLING

OVERFINENESS
OVERFINENESSES
OVERFINISHED
OVERFISHED
OVERFISHES
OVERFISHING
OVERFISHINGS
OVERFLIGHT
OVERFLIGHTS
OVERFLOODED
OVERFLOODING
OVERFLOODS
OVERFLOURISH
OVERFLOURISHED
OVERFLOURISHES
OVERFLOURISHING
OVERFLOWED
OVERFLOWING
OVERFLOWINGLY
OVERFLOWINGS
OVERFLUSHES
OVERFLYING
OVERFOCUSED
OVERFOCUSES
OVERFOCUSING
OVERFOCUSSED
OVERFOCUSSES
OVERFOCUSSING
OVERFOLDED
OVERFOLDING
OVERFONDLY
OVERFONDNESS
OVERFONDNESSES
OVERFORWARD
OVERFORWARDNESS
OVERFRAUGHT
OVERFREEDOM
OVERFREEDOMS
OVERFREELY
OVERFREIGHT
OVERFREIGHTING
OVERFREIGHTS
OVERFULFIL
OVERFULFILL
OVERFULFILLED
OVERFULFILLING
OVERFULFILLS

OVERFULFILS
OVERFULLNESS
OVERFULLNESSES
OVERFULNESS
OVERFULNESSES
OVERFUNDED
OVERFUNDING
OVERFUNDINGS
OVERFUSSIER
OVERFUSSIEST
OVERGALLED
OVERGALLING
OVERGANGING
OVERGARMENT
OVERGARMENTS
OVERGEARED
OVERGEARING
OVERGENERALISE
OVERGENERALISED
OVERGENERALISES
OVERGENERALIZE
OVERGENERALIZED
OVERGENERALIZES
OVERGENEROSITY
OVERGENEROUS
OVERGENEROUSLY
OVERGETTING
OVERGILDED
OVERGILDING
OVERGIRDED
OVERGIRDING
OVERGIVING
OVERGLAMORISE
OVERGLAMORISED
OVERGLAMORISES
OVERGLAMORISING
OVERGLAMORIZE
OVERGLAMORIZED
OVERGLAMORIZES
OVERGLAMORIZING
OVERGLANCE
OVERGLANCED
OVERGLANCES
OVERGLANCING
OVERGLAZED
OVERGLAZES
OVERGLAZING

OVERGLOOMED
OVERGLOOMING
OVERGLOOMS
OVERGOADED
OVERGOADING
OVERGOINGS
OVERGORGED
OVERGORGES
OVERGORGING
OVERGOVERN
OVERGOVERNED
OVERGOVERNING
OVERGOVERNS
OVERGRADED
OVERGRADES
OVERGRADING
OVERGRAINED
OVERGRAINER
OVERGRAINERS
OVERGRAINING
OVERGRAINS
OVERGRASSED
OVERGRASSES
OVERGRASSING
OVERGRAZED
OVERGRAZES
OVERGRAZING
OVERGRAZINGS
OVERGREEDY
OVERGREENED
OVERGREENING
OVERGREENS
OVERGROUND
OVERGROWING
OVERGROWTH
OVERGROWTHS
OVERHAILED
OVERHAILES
OVERHAILING
OVERHALING
OVERHANDED
OVERHANDING
OVERHANDLE
OVERHANDLED
OVERHANDLES
OVERHANDLING
OVERHANGING

OVERHARVEST
OVERHARVESTED
OVERHARVESTING
OVERHARVESTS
OVERHASTES
OVERHASTILY
OVERHASTINESS
OVERHASTINESSES
OVERHATING
OVERHAULED
OVERHAULING
OVERHEAPED
OVERHEAPING
OVERHEARING
OVERHEATED
OVERHEATING
OVERHEATINGS
OVERHENTING
OVERHITTING
OVERHOLDING
OVERHOMOGENISE
OVERHOMOGENISED
OVERHOMOGENISES
OVERHOMOGENIZE
OVERHOMOGENIZED
OVERHOMOGENIZES
OVERHONORED
OVERHONORING
OVERHONORS
OVERHONOUR
OVERHONOURED
OVERHONOURING
OVERHONOURS
OVERHOPING
OVERHUNTED
OVERHUNTING
OVERHUNTINGS
OVERHYPING
OVERIDEALISE
OVERIDEALISED
OVERIDEALISES
OVERIDEALISING
OVERIDEALIZE
OVERIDEALIZED
OVERIDEALIZES
OVERIDEALIZING
OVERIDENTIFIED

OVERIDENTIFIES
OVERIDENTIFY
OVERIDENTIFYING
OVERIMAGINATIVE
OVERIMPRESS
OVERIMPRESSED
OVERIMPRESSES
OVERIMPRESSING
OVERINCLINED
OVERINDULGE
OVERINDULGED
OVERINDULGENCE
OVERINDULGENCES
OVERINDULGENT
OVERINDULGES
OVERINDULGING
OVERINFLATE
OVERINFLATED
OVERINFLATES
OVERINFLATING
OVERINFLATION
OVERINFLATIONS
OVERINFORM
OVERINFORMED
OVERINFORMING
OVERINFORMS
OVERINGENIOUS
OVERINGENUITIES
OVERINGENUITY
OVERINSISTENT
OVERINSURANCE
OVERINSURANCES
OVERINSURE
OVERINSURED
OVERINSURES
OVERINSURING
OVERINTENSE
OVERINTENSITIES
OVERINTENSITY
OVERINVESTMENT
OVERINVESTMENTS
OVERISSUANCE
OVERISSUANCES
OVERISSUED
OVERISSUES
OVERISSUING
OVERJOYING

OVERJUMPED
OVERJUMPING
OVERKEEPING
OVERKILLED
OVERKILLING
OVERKINDNESS
OVERKINDNESSES
OVERLABORED
OVERLABORING
OVERLABORS
OVERLABOUR
OVERLABOURED
OVERLABOURING
OVERLABOURS
OVERLADING
OVERLANDED
OVERLANDER
OVERLANDERS
OVERLANDING
OVERLAPPED
OVERLAPPING
OVERLARDED
OVERLARDING
OVERLAUNCH
OVERLAUNCHED
OVERLAUNCHES
OVERLAUNCHING
OVERLAVISH
OVERLAYING
OVERLAYINGS
OVERLEAPED
OVERLEAPING
OVERLEARNED
OVERLEARNING
OVERLEARNS
OVERLEARNT
OVERLEATHER
OVERLEATHERS
OVERLEAVEN
OVERLEAVENED
OVERLEAVENING
OVERLEAVENS
OVERLENDING
OVERLENGTH
OVERLENGTHEN
OVERLENGTHENED
OVERLENGTHENING

OVERLENGTHENS
OVERLENGTHS
OVERLETTING
OVERLEVERAGED
OVERLIGHTED
OVERLIGHTING
OVERLIGHTS
OVERLITERAL
OVERLITERARY
OVERLIVING
OVERLOADED
OVERLOADING
OVERLOCKED
OVERLOCKER
OVERLOCKERS
OVERLOCKING
OVERLOCKINGS
OVERLOOKED
OVERLOOKER
OVERLOOKERS
OVERLOOKING
OVERLORDED
OVERLORDING
OVERLORDSHIP
OVERLORDSHIPS
OVERLOVING
OVERMANAGE
OVERMANAGED
OVERMANAGES
OVERMANAGING
OVERMANIES
OVERMANNED
OVERMANNERED
OVERMANNING
OVERMANNINGS
OVERMANTEL
OVERMANTELS
OVERMASTED
OVERMASTER
OVERMASTERED
OVERMASTERING
OVERMASTERS
OVERMASTING
OVERMATCHED
OVERMATCHES
OVERMATCHING
OVERMATTER

OVERMATTERS
OVERMATURE
OVERMATURITIES
OVERMATURITY
OVERMEASURE
OVERMEASURED
OVERMEASURES
OVERMEASURING
OVERMEDICATE
OVERMEDICATED
OVERMEDICATES
OVERMEDICATING
OVERMEDICATION
OVERMEDICATIONS
OVERMELTED
OVERMELTING
OVERMIGHTY
OVERMILKED
OVERMILKING
OVERMINING
OVERMIXING
OVERMODEST
OVERMODESTLY
OVERMOUNTED
OVERMOUNTING
OVERMOUNTS
OVERMUCHES
OVERMULTIPLIED
OVERMULTIPLIES
OVERMULTIPLY
OVERMULTIPLYING
OVERMULTITUDE
OVERMULTITUDED
OVERMULTITUDES
OVERMULTITUDING
OVERMUSCLED
OVERNAMING
OVERNETTED
OVERNETTING
OVERNICELY
OVERNICENESS
OVERNICENESSES
OVERNIGHTED
OVERNIGHTER
OVERNIGHTERS
OVERNIGHTING
OVERNIGHTS

OVERNOURISH
OVERNOURISHED
OVERNOURISHES
OVERNOURISHING
OVERNUTRITION
OVERNUTRITIONS
OVEROBVIOUS
OVEROFFICE
OVEROFFICED
OVEROFFICES
OVEROFFICING
OVEROPERATE
OVEROPERATED
OVEROPERATES
OVEROPERATING
OVEROPINIONATED
OVEROPTIMISM
OVEROPTIMISMS
OVEROPTIMIST
OVEROPTIMISTIC
OVEROPTIMISTS
OVERORCHESTRATE
OVERORGANISE
OVERORGANISED
OVERORGANISES
OVERORGANISING
OVERORGANIZE
OVERORGANIZED
OVERORGANIZES
OVERORGANIZING
OVERORNAMENT
OVERORNAMENTED
OVERORNAMENTING
OVERORNAMENTS
OVERPACKAGE
OVERPACKAGED
OVERPACKAGES
OVERPACKAGING
OVERPACKED
OVERPACKING
OVERPAINTED
OVERPAINTING
OVERPAINTS
OVERPARTED
OVERPARTICULAR
OVERPARTING
OVERPASSED

O

OVERPASSES	OVERPLOTTINGS	OVERPRIZES	OVERRATING	OVERRIPENESS
OVERPASSING	OVERPLUSES	OVERPRIZING	OVERRAUGHT	OVERRIPENESSES
OVERPAYING	OVERPLUSSES	OVERPROCESS	OVERREACHED	OVERRIPENING
OVERPAYMENT	OVERPLYING	OVERPROCESSED	OVERREACHER	OVERRIPENS
OVERPAYMENTS	OVERPOISED	OVERPROCESSES	OVERREACHERS	OVERROASTED
OVERPEDALED	OVERPOISES	OVERPROCESSING	OVERREACHES	OVERROASTING
OVERPEDALING	OVERPOISING	OVERPRODUCE	OVERREACHING	OVERROASTS
OVERPEDALLED	OVERPOPULATE	OVERPRODUCED	OVERREACTED	OVERRUFFED
OVERPEDALLING	OVERPOPULATED	OVERPRODUCES	OVERREACTING	OVERRUFFING
OVERPEDALLINGS	OVERPOPULATES	OVERPRODUCING	OVERREACTION	OVERRULERS
OVERPEDALS	OVERPOPULATING	OVERPRODUCTION	OVERREACTIONS	OVERRULING
OVERPEERED	OVERPOPULATION	OVERPRODUCTIONS	OVERREACTS	OVERRULINGS
OVERPEERING	OVERPOPULATIONS	OVERPROGRAM	OVERREADING	OVERRUNNER
OVERPEOPLE	OVERPOSTED	OVERPROGRAMED	OVERRECKON	OVERRUNNERS
OVERPEOPLED	OVERPOSTING	OVERPROGRAMING	OVERRECKONED	OVERRUNNING
OVERPEOPLES	OVERPOTENT	OVERPROGRAMMED	OVERRECKONING	OVERSAILED
OVERPEOPLING	OVERPOWERED	OVERPROGRAMMING	OVERRECKONS	OVERSAILING
OVERPERCHED	OVERPOWERING	OVERPROGRAMS	OVERREDDED	OVERSALTED
OVERPERCHES	OVERPOWERINGLY	OVERPROMISE	OVERREDDING	OVERSALTING
OVERPERCHING	OVERPOWERS	OVERPROMISED	OVERREFINE	OVERSANGUINE
OVERPERSUADE	OVERPRAISE	OVERPROMISES	OVERREFINED	OVERSATURATE
OVERPERSUADED	OVERPRAISED	OVERPROMISING	OVERREFINEMENT	OVERSATURATED
OVERPERSUADES	OVERPRAISES	OVERPROMOTE	OVERREFINEMENTS	OVERSATURATES
OVERPERSUADING	OVERPRAISING	OVERPROMOTED	OVERREFINES	OVERSATURATING
OVERPERSUASION	OVERPRECISE	OVERPROMOTES	OVERREFINING	OVERSATURATION
OVERPERSUASIONS	OVERPREPARATION	OVERPROMOTING	OVERREGULATE	OVERSATURATIONS
OVERPESSIMISTIC	OVERPREPARE	OVERPROOFS	OVERREGULATED	OVERSAUCED
OVERPICTURE	OVERPREPARED	OVERPROPORTION	OVERREGULATES	OVERSAUCES
OVERPICTURED	OVERPREPARES	OVERPROPORTIONS	OVERREGULATING	OVERSAUCING
OVERPICTURES	OVERPREPARING	OVERPROTECT	OVERREGULATION	OVERSAVING
OVERPICTURING	OVERPRESCRIBE	OVERPROTECTED	OVERREGULATIONS	OVERSCALED
OVERPITCHED	OVERPRESCRIBED	OVERPROTECTING	OVERRELIANCE	OVERSCHUTCHT
OVERPITCHES	OVERPRESCRIBES	OVERPROTECTION	OVERRELIANCES	OVERSCORED
OVERPITCHING	OVERPRESCRIBING	OVERPROTECTIONS	OVERRENNING	OVERSCORES
OVERPLACED	OVERPRESSED	OVERPROTECTIVE	OVERREPORT	OVERSCORING
OVERPLAIDED	OVERPRESSES	OVERPROTECTS	OVERREPORTED	OVERSCRUPULOUS
OVERPLAIDS	OVERPRESSING	OVERPUMPED	OVERREPORTING	OVERSCUTCHED
OVERPLANNED	OVERPRESSURE	OVERPUMPING	OVERREPORTS	OVERSECRETION
OVERPLANNING	OVERPRESSURES	OVERQUALIFIED	OVERREPRESENTED	OVERSECRETIONS
OVERPLANNINGS	OVERPRICED	OVERRACKED	OVERRESPOND	OVERSEEDED
OVERPLANTED	OVERPRICES	OVERRACKING	OVERRESPONDED	OVERSEEDING
OVERPLANTING	OVERPRICING	OVERRAKING	OVERRESPONDING	OVERSEEING
OVERPLANTS	OVERPRINTED	OVERRANKED	OVERRESPONDS	OVERSELLING
OVERPLAYED	OVERPRINTING	OVERRANKING	OVERRIDDEN	OVERSENSITIVE
OVERPLAYING	OVERPRINTS	OVERRASHLY	OVERRIDERS	OVERSENSITIVITY
OVERPLOTTED	OVERPRIVILEGED	OVERRASHNESS	OVERRIDING	OVERSERIOUS
OVERPLOTTING	OVERPRIZED	OVERRASHNESSES	OVERRIPENED	OVERSERIOUSLY

O

OVERSERVICE
OVERSERVICED
OVERSERVICES
OVERSERVICING
OVERSETTING
OVERSEWING
OVERSHADED
OVERSHADES
OVERSHADING
OVERSHADOW
OVERSHADOWED
OVERSHADOWING
OVERSHADOWS
OVERSHINES
OVERSHINING
OVERSHIRTS
OVERSHOOTING
OVERSHOOTS
OVERSHOWER
OVERSHOWERED
OVERSHOWERING
OVERSHOWERS
OVERSIGHTS
OVERSIMPLE
OVERSIMPLIFIED
OVERSIMPLIFIES
OVERSIMPLIFY
OVERSIMPLIFYING
OVERSIMPLISTIC
OVERSIMPLY
OVERSIZING
OVERSKIPPED
OVERSKIPPING
OVERSKIRTS
OVERSLAUGH
OVERSLAUGHED
OVERSLAUGHING
OVERSLAUGHS
OVERSLEEPING
OVERSLEEPS
OVERSLEEVE
OVERSLEEVES
OVERSLIPPED
OVERSLIPPING
OVERSMOKED
OVERSMOKES
OVERSMOKING

OVERSOAKED
OVERSOAKING
OVERSOLICITOUS
OVERSOWING
OVERSPECIALISE
OVERSPECIALISED
OVERSPECIALISES
OVERSPECIALIZE
OVERSPECIALIZED
OVERSPECIALIZES
OVERSPECULATE
OVERSPECULATED
OVERSPECULATES
OVERSPECULATING
OVERSPECULATION
OVERSPENDER
OVERSPENDERS
OVERSPENDING
OVERSPENDINGS
OVERSPENDS
OVERSPICED
OVERSPICES
OVERSPICING
OVERSPILLED
OVERSPILLING
OVERSPILLS
OVERSPREAD
OVERSPREADING
OVERSPREADS
OVERSTABILITIES
OVERSTABILITY
OVERSTAFFED
OVERSTAFFING
OVERSTAFFINGS
OVERSTAFFS
OVERSTAINED
OVERSTAINING
OVERSTAINS
OVERSTANDING
OVERSTANDS
OVERSTARED
OVERSTARES
OVERSTARING
OVERSTATED
OVERSTATEMENT
OVERSTATEMENTS
OVERSTATES

OVERSTATING
OVERSTAYED
OVERSTAYER
OVERSTAYERS
OVERSTAYING
OVERSTEERED
OVERSTEERING
OVERSTEERS
OVERSTEPPED
OVERSTEPPING
OVERSTIMULATE
OVERSTIMULATED
OVERSTIMULATES
OVERSTIMULATING
OVERSTIMULATION
OVERSTINKING
OVERSTINKS
OVERSTIRRED
OVERSTIRRING
OVERSTOCKED
OVERSTOCKING
OVERSTOCKS
OVERSTOREY
OVERSTOREYS
OVERSTORIES
OVERSTRAIN
OVERSTRAINED
OVERSTRAINING
OVERSTRAINS
OVERSTRESS
OVERSTRESSED
OVERSTRESSES
OVERSTRESSING
OVERSTRETCH
OVERSTRETCHED
OVERSTRETCHES
OVERSTRETCHING
OVERSTREWED
OVERSTREWING
OVERSTREWN
OVERSTREWS
OVERSTRIDDEN
OVERSTRIDE
OVERSTRIDES
OVERSTRIDING
OVERSTRIKE
OVERSTRIKES

OVERSTRIKING
OVERSTRODE
OVERSTRONG
OVERSTROOKE
OVERSTRUCK
OVERSTRUCTURED
OVERSTRUNG
OVERSTUDIED
OVERSTUDIES
OVERSTUDYING
OVERSTUFFED
OVERSTUFFING
OVERSTUFFS
OVERSUBSCRIBE
OVERSUBSCRIBED
OVERSUBSCRIBES
OVERSUBSCRIBING
OVERSUBTLE
OVERSUBTLETIES
OVERSUBTLETY
OVERSUDSED
OVERSUDSES
OVERSUDSING
OVERSUPPED
OVERSUPPING
OVERSUPPLIED
OVERSUPPLIES
OVERSUPPLY
OVERSUPPLYING
OVERSUSPICIOUS
OVERSWAYED
OVERSWAYING
OVERSWEARING
OVERSWEARS
OVERSWEETEN
OVERSWEETENED
OVERSWEETENING
OVERSWEETENS
OVERSWEETNESS
OVERSWEETNESSES
OVERSWELLED
OVERSWELLING
OVERSWELLS
OVERSWIMMING
OVERSWINGING
OVERSWINGS
OVERSWOLLEN

OVERTAKING
OVERTALKATIVE
OVERTALKED
OVERTALKING
OVERTASKED
OVERTASKING
OVERTAUGHT
OVERTAXATION
OVERTAXATIONS
OVERTAXING
OVERTEACHES
OVERTEACHING
OVERTEDIOUS
OVERTEEMED
OVERTEEMING
OVERTHINKING
OVERTHINKS
OVERTHOUGHT
OVERTHROWER
OVERTHROWERS
OVERTHROWING
OVERTHROWN
OVERTHROWS
OVERTHRUST
OVERTHRUSTS
OVERTHWART
OVERTHWARTED
OVERTHWARTING
OVERTHWARTS
OVERTIGHTEN
OVERTIGHTENED
OVERTIGHTENING
OVERTIGHTENS
OVERTIMELY
OVERTIMERS
OVERTIMING
OVERTIPPED
OVERTIPPING
OVERTIRING
OVERTNESSES
OVERTOILED
OVERTOILING
OVERTOPPED
OVERTOPPING
OVERTOPPINGS
OVERTOWERED
OVERTOWERING

O

OVERTOWERS	OVERVALUES	OVERWINDING	OVOVIVIPAROUS	OXYGENATOR
OVERTRADED	OVERVALUING	OVERWINGED	OVOVIVIPAROUSLY	OXYGENATORS
OVERTRADES	OVERVEILED	OVERWINGING	OVULATIONS	OXYGENISED
OVERTRADING	OVERVEILING	OVERWINTER	OVULIFEROUS	OXYGENISER
OVERTRADINGS	OVERVIOLENT	OVERWINTERED	OWERLOUPEN	OXYGENISERS
OVERTRAINED	OVERVOLTAGE	OVERWINTERING	OWERLOUPING	OXYGENISES
OVERTRAINING	OVERVOLTAGES	OVERWINTERS	OWERLOUPIT	OXYGENISING
OVERTRAINS	OVERVOTING	OVERWISELY	OWLISHNESS	OXYGENIZED
OVERTREATED	OVERWARMED	OVERWITHHELD	OWLISHNESSES	OXYGENIZER
OVERTREATING	OVERWARMING	OVERWITHHOLD	OWNERSHIPS	OXYGENIZERS
OVERTREATMENT	OVERWASHES	OVERWITHHOLDING	OWRECOMING	OXYGENIZES
OVERTREATMENTS	OVERWATCHED	OVERWITHHOLDS	OXACILLINS	OXYGENIZING
OVERTREATS	OVERWATCHES	OVERWORKED	OXALACETATE	OXYGENLESS
OVERTRICKS	OVERWATCHING	OVERWORKING	OXALACETATES	OXYHAEMOGLOBIN
OVERTRIMMED	OVERWATERED	OVERWRAPPED	OXALOACETATE	OXYHAEMOGLOBINS
OVERTRIMMING	OVERWATERING	OVERWRAPPING	OXALOACETATES	OXYHEMOGLOBIN
OVERTRIPPED	OVERWATERS	OVERWRESTED	OXIDATIONAL	OXYHEMOGLOBINS
OVERTRIPPING	OVERWEARIED	OVERWRESTING	OXIDATIONS	OXYHYDROGEN
OVERTRUMPED	OVERWEARIES	OVERWRESTLE	OXIDATIVELY	OXYHYDROGENS
OVERTRUMPING	OVERWEARING	OVERWRESTLED	OXIDIMETRIC	OXYMORONIC
OVERTRUMPS	OVERWEARYING	OVERWRESTLES	OXIDIMETRIES	OXYMORONICALLY
OVERTRUSTED	OVERWEATHER	OVERWRESTLING	OXIDIMETRY	OXYPHENBUTAZONE
OVERTRUSTING	OVERWEATHERED	OVERWRESTS	OXIDISABLE	OXYRHYNCHUS
OVERTRUSTS	OVERWEATHERING	OVERWRITES	OXIDISATION	OXYRHYNCHUSES
OVERTURING	OVERWEATHERS	OVERWRITING	OXIDISATIONS	OXYSULPHIDE
OVERTURNED	OVERWEENED	OVERWRITTEN	OXIDIZABLE	OXYSULPHIDES
OVERTURNER	OVERWEENING	OVERWROUGHT	OXIDIZATION	OXYTETRACYCLINE
OVERTURNERS	OVERWEENINGLY	OVERYEARED	OXIDIZATIONS	OXYURIASES
OVERTURNING	OVERWEENINGNESS	OVERYEARING	OXIDOREDUCTASE	OXYURIASIS
OVERTYPING	OVERWEENINGS	OVERZEALOUS	OXIDOREDUCTASES	OYSTERCATCHER
OVERURGING	OVERWEIGHED	OVERZEALOUSLY	OXIMETRIES	OYSTERCATCHERS
OVERUTILISATION	OVERWEIGHING	OVERZEALOUSNESS	OXYACETYLENE	OYSTERINGS
OVERUTILISE	OVERWEIGHS	OVIPARITIES	OXYACETYLENES	OZOCERITES
OVERUTILISED	OVERWEIGHT	OVIPAROUSLY	OXYCEPHALIC	OZOKERITES
OVERUTILISES	OVERWEIGHTED	OVIPOSITED	OXYCEPHALIES	OZONATIONS
OVERUTILISING	OVERWEIGHTING	OVIPOSITING	OXYCEPHALOUS	OZONIFEROUS
OVERUTILIZATION	OVERWEIGHTS	OVIPOSITION	OXYCEPHALY	OZONISATION
OVERUTILIZE	OVERWETTED	OVIPOSITIONAL	OXYCODONES	OZONISATIONS
OVERUTILIZED	OVERWETTING	OVIPOSITIONS	OXYGENASES	OZONIZATION
OVERUTILIZES	OVERWHELMED	OVIPOSITOR	OXYGENATED	OZONIZATIONS
OVERUTILIZING	OVERWHELMING	OVIPOSITORS	OXYGENATES	OZONOLYSES
OVERVALUATION	OVERWHELMINGLY	OVIRAPTORS	OXYGENATING	OZONOLYSIS
OVERVALUATIONS	OVERWHELMINGS	OVOVIVIPARITIES	OXYGENATION	OZONOSPHERE
OVERVALUED	OVERWHELMS	OVOVIVIPARITY	OXYGENATIONS	OZONOSPHERES

O

P

PACEMAKERS
PACEMAKING
PACEMAKINGS
PACESETTER
PACESETTERS
PACESETTING
PACESETTINGS
PACHYCARPOUS
PACHYDACTYL
PACHYDACTYLOUS
PACHYDERMAL
PACHYDERMATOUS
PACHYDERMIA
PACHYDERMIAS
PACHYDERMIC
PACHYDERMOUS
PACHYDERMS
PACHYMENINGITIS
PACHYMETER
PACHYMETERS
PACHYSANDRA
PACHYSANDRAS
PACHYTENES
PACIFIABLE
PACIFICALLY
PACIFICATE
PACIFICATED
PACIFICATES
PACIFICATING
PACIFICATION
PACIFICATIONS
PACIFICATOR
PACIFICATORS
PACIFICATORY
PACIFICISM
PACIFICISMS
PACIFICIST
PACIFICISTS
PACIFISTIC
PACIFISTICALLY
PACKABILITIES

PACKABILITY
PACKAGINGS
PACKBOARDS
PACKCLOTHS
PACKFRAMES
PACKHORSES
PACKINGHOUSE
PACKINGHOUSES
PACKNESSES
PACKSADDLE
PACKSADDLES
PACKSHEETS
PACKSTAFFS
PACKTHREAD
PACKTHREADS
PACLITAXEL
PACLITAXELS
PACTIONING
PADDLEBALL
PADDLEBALLS
PADDLEBOARD
PADDLEBOARDS
PADDLEBOAT
PADDLEBOATS
PADDLEFISH
PADDLEFISHES
PADDOCKING
PADDYMELON
PADDYMELONS
PADDYWACKED
PADDYWACKING
PADDYWACKS
PADDYWHACK
PADDYWHACKS
PADEMELONS
PADEREROES
PADLOCKING
PADRONISMS
PADYMELONS
PAEDAGOGIC
PAEDAGOGUE

PAEDAGOGUES
PAEDERASTIC
PAEDERASTIES
PAEDERASTS
PAEDERASTY
PAEDEUTICS
PAEDIATRIC
PAEDIATRICIAN
PAEDIATRICIANS
PAEDIATRICS
PAEDIATRIES
PAEDIATRIST
PAEDIATRISTS
PAEDOBAPTISM
PAEDOBAPTISMS
PAEDOBAPTIST
PAEDOBAPTISTS
PAEDODONTIC
PAEDODONTICS
PAEDOGENESES
PAEDOGENESIS
PAEDOGENETIC
PAEDOGENIC
PAEDOLOGICAL
PAEDOLOGIES
PAEDOLOGIST
PAEDOLOGISTS
PAEDOMORPHIC
PAEDOMORPHISM
PAEDOMORPHISMS
PAEDOMORPHOSES
PAEDOMORPHOSIS
PAEDOPHILE
PAEDOPHILES
PAEDOPHILIA
PAEDOPHILIAC
PAEDOPHILIACS
PAEDOPHILIAS
PAEDOPHILIC
PAEDOPHILICS
PAEDOTRIBE

PAEDOTRIBES
PAEDOTROPHIES
PAEDOTROPHY
PAGANISATION
PAGANISATIONS
PAGANISERS
PAGANISING
PAGANISTIC
PAGANISTICALLY
PAGANIZATION
PAGANIZATIONS
PAGANIZERS
PAGANIZING
PAGEANTRIES
PAGINATING
PAGINATION
PAGINATIONS
PAIDEUTICS
PAILLASSES
PAILLETTES
PAINFULLER
PAINFULLEST
PAINFULNESS
PAINFULNESSES
PAINKILLER
PAINKILLERS
PAINKILLING
PAINLESSLY
PAINLESSNESS
PAINLESSNESSES
PAINSTAKER
PAINSTAKERS
PAINSTAKING
PAINSTAKINGLY
PAINSTAKINGNESS
PAINSTAKINGS
PAINTBALLING
PAINTBALLINGS
PAINTBALLS
PAINTBOXES
PAINTBRUSH

PAINTBRUSHES
PAINTERLINESS
PAINTERLINESSES
PAINTINESS
PAINTINESSES
PAINTRESSES
PAINTWORKS
PAKIRIKIRI
PAKIRIKIRIS
PALAEANTHROPIC
PALAEBIOLOGIES
PALAEBIOLOGIST
PALAEBIOLOGISTS
PALAEBIOLOGY
PALAEETHNOLOGY
PALAEOANTHROPIC
PALAEOBIOLOGIC
PALAEOBIOLOGIES
PALAEOBIOLOGIST
PALAEOBIOLOGY
PALAEOBOTANIC
PALAEOBOTANICAL
PALAEOBOTANIES
PALAEOBOTANIST
PALAEOBOTANISTS
PALAEOBOTANY
PALAEOCLIMATE
PALAEOCLIMATES
PALAEOCLIMATIC
PALAEOCRYSTIC
PALAEOCURRENT
PALAEOCURRENTS
PALAEOECOLOGIC
PALAEOECOLOGIES
PALAEOECOLOGIST
PALAEOECOLOGY
PALAEOETHNOLOGY
PALAEOGAEA
PALAEOGAEAS
PALAEOGEOGRAPHY
PALAEOGRAPHER

P

PALAEOGRAPHERS

PALAEOGRAPHERS
PALAEOGRAPHIC
PALAEOGRAPHICAL
PALAEOGRAPHIES
PALAEOGRAPHIST
PALAEOGRAPHISTS
PALAEOGRAPHY
PALAEOLIMNOLOGY
PALAEOLITH
PALAEOLITHIC
PALAEOLITHS
PALAEOLOGIES
PALAEOLOGY
PALAEOMAGNETIC
PALAEOMAGNETISM
PALAEOMAGNETIST
PALAEONTOGRAPHY
PALAEONTOLOGIES
PALAEONTOLOGIST
PALAEONTOLOGY
PALAEOPATHOLOGY
PALAEOPEDOLOGY
PALAEOPHYTOLOGY
PALAEOSOLS
PALAEOTYPE
PALAEOTYPES
PALAEOTYPIC
PALAEOZOOLOGIES
PALAEOZOOLOGIST
PALAEOZOOLOGY
PALAESTRAE
PALAESTRAL
PALAESTRAS
PALAESTRIC
PALAESTRICAL
PALAFITTES
PALAGONITE
PALAGONITES
PALAMPORES
PALANKEENS
PALANQUINS
PALATABILITIES
PALATABILITY
PALATABLENESS
PALATABLENESSES
PALATALISATION
PALATALISATIONS

PALATALISE
PALATALISED
PALATALISES
PALATALISING
PALATALIZATION
PALATALIZATIONS
PALATALIZE
PALATALIZED
PALATALIZES
PALATALIZING
PALATIALLY
PALATIALNESS
PALATIALNESSES
PALATINATE
PALATINATES
PALAVERERS
PALAVERING
PALEACEOUS
PALEMPORES
PALENESSES
PALEOBIOLOGIC
PALEOBIOLOGICAL
PALEOBIOLOGIES
PALEOBIOLOGIST
PALEOBIOLOGISTS
PALEOBIOLOGY
PALEOBOTANIC
PALEOBOTANICAL
PALEOBOTANIES
PALEOBOTANIST
PALEOBOTANISTS
PALEOBOTANY
PALEOECOLOGIC
PALEOECOLOGICAL
PALEOECOLOGIES
PALEOECOLOGIST
PALEOECOLOGISTS
PALEOECOLOGY
PALEOGEOGRAPHIC
PALEOGEOGRAPHY
PALEOGRAPHER
PALEOGRAPHERS
PALEOGRAPHIC
PALEOGRAPHICAL
PALEOGRAPHIES
PALEOGRAPHY
PALEOLITHIC

PALEOLITHS
PALEOLOGIES
PALEOMAGNETIC
PALEOMAGNETISM
PALEOMAGNETISMS
PALEOMAGNETIST
PALEOMAGNETISTS
PALEONTOLOGIC
PALEONTOLOGICAL
PALEONTOLOGIES
PALEONTOLOGIST
PALEONTOLOGISTS
PALEONTOLOGY
PALEOPATHOLOGY
PALEOZOOLOGICAL
PALEOZOOLOGIES
PALEOZOOLOGIST
PALEOZOOLOGISTS
PALEOZOOLOGY
PALFRENIER
PALFRENIERS
PALIFICATION
PALIFICATIONS
PALILALIAS
PALILLOGIES
PALIMONIES
PALIMPSEST
PALIMPSESTS
PALINDROME
PALINDROMES
PALINDROMIC
PALINDROMICAL
PALINDROMIST
PALINDROMISTS
PALINGENESES
PALINGENESIA
PALINGENESIAS
PALINGENESIES
PALINGENESIS
PALINGENESIST
PALINGENESISTS
PALINGENESY
PALINGENETIC
PALINGENETICAL
PALINODIES
PALINOPIAS
PALINOPSIA

PALINOPSIAS
PALISADING
PALISADOED
PALISADOES
PALISADOING
PALISANDER
PALISANDERS
PALLADIOUS
PALLADIUMS
PALLBEARER
PALLBEARERS
PALLESCENCE
PALLESCENCES
PALLESCENT
PALLETISATION
PALLETISATIONS
PALLETISED
PALLETISER
PALLETISERS
PALLETISES
PALLETISING
PALLETIZATION
PALLETIZATIONS
PALLETIZED
PALLETIZER
PALLETIZERS
PALLETIZES
PALLETIZING
PALLIAMENT
PALLIAMENTS
PALLIASSES
PALLIATING
PALLIATION
PALLIATIONS
PALLIATIVE
PALLIATIVELY
PALLIATIVES
PALLIATORS
PALLIATORY
PALLIDITIES
PALLIDNESS
PALLIDNESSES
PALMACEOUS
PALMATIFID
PALMATIONS
PALMATIPARTITE
PALMATISECT

PALMCORDER
PALMCORDERS
PALMERWORM
PALMERWORMS
PALMETTOES
PALMHOUSES
PALMIFICATION
PALMIFICATIONS
PALMIPEDES
PALMISTERS
PALMISTRIES
PALMITATES
PALOVERDES
PALPABILITIES
PALPABILITY
PALPABLENESS
PALPABLENESSES
PALPATIONS
PALPEBRATE
PALPEBRATED
PALPEBRATES
PALPEBRATING
PALPITATED
PALPITATES
PALPITATING
PALPITATION
PALPITATIONS
PALSGRAVES
PALSGRAVINE
PALSGRAVINES
PALTRINESS
PALTRINESSES
PALUDAMENT
PALUDAMENTA
PALUDAMENTS
PALUDAMENTUM
PALUDAMENTUMS
PALUDICOLOUS
PALUDINOUS
PALUSTRIAN
PALUSTRINE
PALYNOLOGIC
PALYNOLOGICAL
PALYNOLOGICALLY
PALYNOLOGIES
PALYNOLOGIST
PALYNOLOGISTS

PALYNOLOGY
PAMPELMOOSE
PAMPELMOOSES
PAMPELMOUSE
PAMPELMOUSES
PAMPEREDNESS
PAMPEREDNESSES
PAMPHLETED
PAMPHLETEER
PAMPHLETEERED
PAMPHLETEERING
PAMPHLETEERINGS
PAMPHLETEERS
PAMPHLETING
PAMPOOTIES
PANACHAEAS
PANAESTHESIA
PANAESTHESIAS
PANAESTHETISM
PANAESTHETISMS
PANARITIUM
PANARITIUMS
PANARTHRITIS
PANARTHRITISES
PANATELLAS
PANBROILED
PANBROILING
PANCHAYATS
PANCHROMATIC
PANCHROMATISM
PANCHROMATISMS
PANCOSMISM
PANCOSMISMS
PANCRATIAN
PANCRATIAST
PANCRATIASTS
PANCRATIST
PANCRATISTS
PANCRATIUM
PANCRATIUMS
PANCREASES
PANCREATECTOMY
PANCREATIC
PANCREATIN
PANCREATINS
PANCREATITIDES
PANCREATITIS

PANCREATITISES
PANCREOZYMIN
PANCREOZYMINS
PANCYTOPENIA
PANCYTOPENIAS
PANDAEMONIUM
PANDAEMONIUMS
PANDANACEOUS
PANDANUSES
PANDATIONS
PANDECTIST
PANDECTISTS
PANDEMONIAC
PANDEMONIACAL
PANDEMONIAN
PANDEMONIANS
PANDEMONIC
PANDEMONIUM
PANDEMONIUMS
PANDERESSES
PANDERISMS
PANDERMITE
PANDERMITES
PANDICULATION
PANDICULATIONS
PANDOWDIES
PANDURATED
PANDURIFORM
PANEGOISMS
PANEGYRICA
PANEGYRICAL
PANEGYRICALLY
PANEGYRICON
PANEGYRICS
PANEGYRIES
PANEGYRISE
PANEGYRISED
PANEGYRISES
PANEGYRISING
PANEGYRIST
PANEGYRISTS
PANEGYRIZE
PANEGYRIZED
PANEGYRIZES
PANEGYRIZING
PANELLINGS
PANELLISED

PANELLISTS
PANELLIZED
PANENTHEISM
PANENTHEISMS
PANENTHEIST
PANENTHEISTS
PANESTHESIA
PANESTHESIAS
PANETELLAS
PANETTONES
PANFISHING
PANGENESES
PANGENESIS
PANGENETIC
PANGENETICALLY
PANGRAMMATIST
PANGRAMMATISTS
PANHANDLED
PANHANDLER
PANHANDLERS
PANHANDLES
PANHANDLING
PANHARMONICON
PANHARMONICONS
PANHELLENIC
PANHELLENION
PANHELLENIONS
PANHELLENIUM
PANHELLENIUMS
PANICKIEST
PANICMONGER
PANICMONGERS
PANICULATE
PANICULATED
PANICULATELY
PANIDIOMORPHIC
PANIFICATION
PANIFICATIONS
PANISLAMIST
PANJANDARUM
PANJANDARUMS
PANJANDRUM
PANJANDRUMS
PANLEUCOPENIA
PANLEUCOPENIAS
PANLEUKOPENIA
PANLEUKOPENIAS

PANLOGISMS
PANMIXISES
PANNICULUS
PANNICULUSES
PANNIKELLS
PANOMPHAEAN
PANOPHOBIA
PANOPHOBIAS
PANOPHTHALMIA
PANOPHTHALMIAS
PANOPHTHALMITIS
PANOPTICAL
PANOPTICALLY
PANOPTICON
PANOPTICONS
PANORAMICALLY
PANPHARMACON
PANPHARMACONS
PANPSYCHISM
PANPSYCHISMS
PANPSYCHIST
PANPSYCHISTIC
PANPSYCHISTS
PANRADIOMETER
PANRADIOMETERS
PANSEXUALISM
PANSEXUALISMS
PANSEXUALIST
PANSEXUALISTS
PANSEXUALITIES
PANSEXUALITY
PANSEXUALS
PANSOPHICAL
PANSOPHICALLY
PANSOPHIES
PANSOPHISM
PANSOPHISMS
PANSOPHIST
PANSOPHISTS
PANSPERMATIC
PANSPERMATISM
PANSPERMATISMS
PANSPERMATIST
PANSPERMATISTS
PANSPERMIA
PANSPERMIAS
PANSPERMIC

PANSPERMIES
PANSPERMISM
PANSPERMISMS
PANSPERMIST
PANSPERMISTS
PANTAGAMIES
PANTAGRAPH
PANTAGRAPHS
PANTALEONS
PANTALETTED
PANTALETTES
PANTALONES
PANTALOONED
PANTALOONERIES
PANTALOONERY
PANTALOONS
PANTDRESSES
PANTECHNICON
PANTECHNICONS
PANTHEISMS
PANTHEISTIC
PANTHEISTICAL
PANTHEISTICALLY
PANTHEISTS
PANTHENOLS
PANTHEOLOGIES
PANTHEOLOGIST
PANTHEOLOGISTS
PANTHEOLOGY
PANTHERESS
PANTHERESSES
PANTHERINE
PANTHERISH
PANTIHOSES
PANTILINGS
PANTISOCRACIES
PANTISOCRACY
PANTISOCRAT
PANTISOCRATIC
PANTISOCRATICAL
PANTISOCRATIST
PANTISOCRATISTS
PANTISOCRATS
PANTOFFLES
PANTOGRAPH
PANTOGRAPHER
PANTOGRAPHERS

P

PANTOGRAPHIC

PANTOGRAPHIC
PANTOGRAPHICAL
PANTOGRAPHIES
PANTOGRAPHS
PANTOGRAPHY
PANTOMIMED
PANTOMIMES
PANTOMIMIC
PANTOMIMICAL
PANTOMIMICALLY
PANTOMIMING
PANTOMIMIST
PANTOMIMISTS
PANTOPHAGIES
PANTOPHAGIST
PANTOPHAGISTS
PANTOPHAGOUS
PANTOPHAGY
PANTOPHOBIA
PANTOPHOBIAS
PANTOPRAGMATIC
PANTOPRAGMATICS
PANTOSCOPE
PANTOSCOPES
PANTOSCOPIC
PANTOTHENATE
PANTOTHENATES
PANTOTHENIC
PANTOUFLES
PANTROPICAL
PANTRYMAID
PANTRYMAIDS
PANTSUITED
PANTYHOSES
PANTYWAIST
PANTYWAISTS
PANZEROTTO
PANZEROTTOS
PANZOOTICS
PAPALISING
PAPALIZING
PAPAPRELATIST
PAPAPRELATISTS
PAPAVERACEOUS
PAPAVERINE
PAPAVERINES
PAPAVEROUS

PAPERBACKED
PAPERBACKER
PAPERBACKERS
PAPERBACKING
PAPERBACKS
PAPERBARKS
PAPERBOARD
PAPERBOARDS
PAPERBOUND
PAPERBOUNDS
PAPERCLIPS
PAPERGIRLS
PAPERHANGER
PAPERHANGERS
PAPERHANGING
PAPERHANGINGS
PAPERINESS
PAPERINESSES
PAPERKNIFE
PAPERKNIVES
PAPERMAKER
PAPERMAKERS
PAPERMAKING
PAPERMAKINGS
PAPERWARES
PAPERWEIGHT
PAPERWEIGHTS
PAPERWORKS
PAPETERIES
PAPILIONACEOUS
PAPILLATED
PAPILLIFEROUS
PAPILLIFORM
PAPILLITIS
PAPILLITISES
PAPILLOMAS
PAPILLOMATA
PAPILLOMATOSES
PAPILLOMATOSIS
PAPILLOMATOUS
PAPILLOMAVIRUS
PAPILLOTES
PAPILLULATE
PAPILLULES
PAPISTICAL
PAPISTICALLY
PAPISTRIES

PAPOVAVIRUS
PAPOVAVIRUSES
PAPPARDELLE
PAPPARDELLES
PAPULATION
PAPULATIONS
PAPULIFEROUS
PAPYRACEOUS
PAPYROLOGICAL
PAPYROLOGIES
PAPYROLOGIST
PAPYROLOGISTS
PAPYROLOGY
PARABAPTISM
PARABAPTISMS
PARABEMATA
PARABEMATIC
PARABIOSES
PARABIOSIS
PARABIOTIC
PARABIOTICALLY
PARABLASTIC
PARABLASTS
PARABLEPSES
PARABLEPSIES
PARABLEPSIS
PARABLEPSY
PARABLEPTIC
PARABOLANUS
PARABOLANUSES
PARABOLICAL
PARABOLICALLY
PARABOLISATION
PARABOLISATIONS
PARABOLISE
PARABOLISED
PARABOLISES
PARABOLISING
PARABOLIST
PARABOLISTS
PARABOLIZATION
PARABOLIZATIONS
PARABOLIZE
PARABOLIZED
PARABOLIZES
PARABOLIZING
PARABOLOID

PARABOLOIDAL
PARABOLOIDS
PARABRAKES
PARACASEIN
PARACASEINS
PARACENTESES
PARACENTESIS
PARACETAMOL
PARACETAMOLS
PARACHRONISM
PARACHRONISMS
PARACHUTED
PARACHUTES
PARACHUTIC
PARACHUTING
PARACHUTINGS
PARACHUTIST
PARACHUTISTS
PARACLETES
PARACROSTIC
PARACROSTICS
PARACYANOGEN
PARACYANOGENS
PARADIDDLE
PARADIDDLES
PARADIGMATIC
PARADIGMATICAL
PARADISAIC
PARADISAICAL
PARADISAICALLY
PARADISEAN
PARADISIAC
PARADISIACAL
PARADISIACALLY
PARADISIAL
PARADISIAN
PARADISICAL
PARADOCTOR
PARADOCTORS
PARADOXERS
PARADOXICAL
PARADOXICALITY
PARADOXICALLY
PARADOXICALNESS
PARADOXIDIAN
PARADOXIES
PARADOXIST

PARADOXISTS
PARADOXOLOGIES
PARADOXOLOGY
PARADOXURE
PARADOXURES
PARADOXURINE
PARADOXURINES
PARADROPPED
PARADROPPING
PARAENESES
PARAENESIS
PARAENETIC
PARAENETICAL
PARAESTHESIA
PARAESTHESIAS
PARAESTHETIC
PARAFFINED
PARAFFINES
PARAFFINIC
PARAFFINING
PARAFFINOID
PARAGENESES
PARAGENESIA
PARAGENESIAS
PARAGENESIS
PARAGENETIC
PARAGENETICALLY
PARAGLIDED
PARAGLIDER
PARAGLIDERS
PARAGLIDES
PARAGLIDING
PARAGLIDINGS
PARAGLOSSA
PARAGLOSSAE
PARAGLOSSAL
PARAGLOSSATE
PARAGNATHISM
PARAGNATHISMS
PARAGNATHOUS
PARAGNOSES
PARAGNOSIS
PARAGOGICAL
PARAGOGICALLY
PARAGOGUES
PARAGONING
PARAGONITE

PARAGONITES
PARAGRAMMATIST
PARAGRAMMATISTS
PARAGRAPHED
PARAGRAPHER
PARAGRAPHERS
PARAGRAPHIA
PARAGRAPHIAS
PARAGRAPHIC
PARAGRAPHICAL
PARAGRAPHICALLY
PARAGRAPHING
PARAGRAPHIST
PARAGRAPHISTS
PARAGRAPHS
PARAHELIOTROPIC
PARAHYDROGEN
PARAHYDROGENS
PARAINFLUENZA
PARAINFLUENZAS
PARAJOURNALISM
PARAJOURNALISMS
PARAKEELYA
PARAKEELYAS
PARAKELIAS
PARAKITING
PARAKITINGS
PARALALIAS
PARALANGUAGE
PARALANGUAGES
PARALDEHYDE
PARALDEHYDES
PARALEGALS
PARALEIPOMENA
PARALEIPOMENON
PARALEIPSES
PARALEIPSIS
PARALEXIAS
PARALIMNION
PARALIMNIONS
PARALINGUISTIC
PARALINGUISTICS
PARALIPOMENA
PARALIPOMENON
PARALIPSES
PARALIPSIS
PARALLACTIC

PARALLACTICAL
PARALLACTICALLY
PARALLAXES
PARALLELED
PARALLELEPIPED
PARALLELEPIPEDA
PARALLELEPIPEDS
PARALLELING
PARALLELINGS
PARALLELISE
PARALLELISED
PARALLELISES
PARALLELISING
PARALLELISM
PARALLELISMS
PARALLELIST
PARALLELISTIC
PARALLELISTS
PARALLELIZE
PARALLELIZED
PARALLELIZES
PARALLELIZING
PARALLELLED
PARALLELLING
PARALLELLY
PARALLELOGRAM
PARALLELOGRAMS
PARALLELOPIPED
PARALLELOPIPEDA
PARALLELOPIPEDS
PARALLELWISE
PARALOGIAS
PARALOGIES
PARALOGISE
PARALOGISED
PARALOGISES
PARALOGISING
PARALOGISM
PARALOGISMS
PARALOGIST
PARALOGISTIC
PARALOGISTS
PARALOGIZE
PARALOGIZED
PARALOGIZES
PARALOGIZING
PARALOGUES

PARALYMPIC
PARALYMPICS
PARALYSATION
PARALYSATIONS
PARALYSERS
PARALYSING
PARALYSINGLY
PARALYTICALLY
PARALYTICS
PARALYZATION
PARALYZATIONS
PARALYZERS
PARALYZING
PARALYZINGLY
PARAMAECIA
PARAMAECIUM
PARAMAGNET
PARAMAGNETIC
PARAMAGNETISM
PARAMAGNETISMS
PARAMAGNETS
PARAMASTOID
PARAMASTOIDS
PARAMATTAS
PARAMECIUM
PARAMECIUMS
PARAMEDICAL
PARAMEDICALS
PARAMEDICO
PARAMEDICOS
PARAMEDICS
PARAMENSTRUA
PARAMENSTRUUM
PARAMENSTRUUMS
PARAMETERISE
PARAMETERISED
PARAMETERISES
PARAMETERISING
PARAMETERIZE
PARAMETERIZED
PARAMETERIZES
PARAMETERIZING
PARAMETERS
PARAMETRAL
PARAMETRIC
PARAMETRICAL
PARAMETRICALLY

PARAMETRISATION
PARAMETRISE
PARAMETRISED
PARAMETRISES
PARAMETRISING
PARAMETRIZATION
PARAMETRIZE
PARAMETRIZED
PARAMETRIZES
PARAMETRIZING
PARAMILITARIES
PARAMILITARY
PARAMNESIA
PARAMNESIAS
PARAMOECIA
PARAMOECIUM
PARAMORPHIC
PARAMORPHINE
PARAMORPHINES
PARAMORPHISM
PARAMORPHISMS
PARAMORPHOUS
PARAMORPHS
PARAMOUNCIES
PARAMOUNCY
PARAMOUNTCIES
PARAMOUNTCY
PARAMOUNTLY
PARAMOUNTS
PARAMYLUMS
PARAMYXOVIRUS
PARAMYXOVIRUSES
PARANEPHRIC
PARANEPHROS
PARANEPHROSES
PARANOEICS
PARANOIACS
PARANOICALLY
PARANOIDAL
PARANORMAL
PARANORMALITIES
PARANORMALITY
PARANORMALLY
PARANORMALS
PARANTHELIA
PARANTHELION
PARANTHROPUS

PARANTHROPUSES
PARANYMPHS
PARAPARESES
PARAPARESIS
PARAPARETIC
PARAPENTES
PARAPENTING
PARAPENTINGS
PARAPERIODIC
PARAPHASIA
PARAPHASIAS
PARAPHASIC
PARAPHERNALIA
PARAPHILIA
PARAPHILIAC
PARAPHILIACS
PARAPHILIAS
PARAPHIMOSES
PARAPHIMOSIS
PARAPHONIA
PARAPHONIAS
PARAPHONIC
PARAPHRASABLE
PARAPHRASE
PARAPHRASED
PARAPHRASER
PARAPHRASERS
PARAPHRASES
PARAPHRASING
PARAPHRAST
PARAPHRASTIC
PARAPHRASTICAL
PARAPHRASTS
PARAPHRAXES
PARAPHRAXIA
PARAPHRAXIAS
PARAPHRAXIS
PARAPHRENIA
PARAPHRENIAS
PARAPHYSATE
PARAPHYSES
PARAPHYSIS
PARAPINEAL
PARAPLANNER
PARAPLANNERS
PARAPLEGIA
PARAPLEGIAS

P

PARAPLEGIC	PARASITICALNESS	PARASYNAPSES	PARCHMENTIZING	PARFOCALISE
PARAPLEGICS	PARASITICIDAL	PARASYNAPSIS	PARCHMENTS	PARFOCALISED
PARAPODIAL	PARASITICIDE	PARASYNAPTIC	PARCHMENTY	PARFOCALISES
PARAPODIUM	PARASITICIDES	PARASYNTHESES	PARCIMONIES	PARFOCALISING
PARAPOPHYSES	PARASITISATION	PARASYNTHESIS	PARDALISES	PARFOCALITIES
PARAPOPHYSIAL	PARASITISATIONS	PARASYNTHETA	PARDALOTES	PARFOCALITY
PARAPOPHYSIS	PARASITISE	PARASYNTHETIC	PARDONABLE	PARFOCALIZE
PARAPRAXES	PARASITISED	PARASYNTHETON	PARDONABLENESS	PARFOCALIZED
PARAPRAXIS	PARASITISES	PARATACTIC	PARDONABLY	PARFOCALIZES
PARAPSYCHIC	PARASITISING	PARATACTICAL	PARDONINGS	PARFOCALIZING
PARAPSYCHICAL	PARASITISM	PARATACTICALLY	PARDONLESS	PARGASITES
PARAPSYCHISM	PARASITISMS	PARATANIWHA	PAREGORICS	PARGETINGS
PARAPSYCHISMS	PARASITIZATION	PARATANIWHAS	PAREIDOLIA	PARGETTERS
PARAPSYCHOLOGY	PARASITIZATIONS	PARATHESES	PAREIDOLIAS	PARGETTING
PARAPSYCHOSES	PARASITIZE	PARATHESIS	PARENCEPHALA	PARGETTINGS
PARAPSYCHOSIS	PARASITIZED	PARATHIONS	PARENCEPHALON	PARGYLINES
PARAQUADRATE	PARASITIZES	PARATHORMONE	PARENCHYMA	PARHELIACAL
PARAQUADRATES	PARASITIZING	PARATHORMONES	PARENCHYMAL	PARHYPATES
PARAQUITOS	PARASITOID	PARATHYROID	PARENCHYMAS	PARIPINNATE
PARARHYMES	PARASITOIDS	PARATHYROIDS	PARENCHYMATA	PARISCHANE
PARAROSANILINE	PARASITOLOGIC	PARATROOPER	PARENCHYMATOUS	PARISCHANES
PARAROSANILINES	PARASITOLOGICAL	PARATROOPERS	PARENTAGES	PARISCHANS
PARARTHRIA	PARASITOLOGIES	PARATROOPS	PARENTALLY	PARISHIONER
PARARTHRIAS	PARASITOLOGIST	PARATUNGSTIC	PARENTERAL	PARISHIONERS
PARASAILED	PARASITOLOGISTS	PARATYPHOID	PARENTERALLY	PARISYLLABIC
PARASAILING	PARASITOLOGY	PARATYPHOIDS	PARENTHESES	PARKINSONIAN
PARASAILINGS	PARASITOSES	PARAWALKER	PARENTHESIS	PARKINSONIANS
PARASCENDER	PARASITOSIS	PARAWALKERS	PARENTHESISE	PARKINSONISM
PARASCENDERS	PARASKIING	PARBOILING	PARENTHESISED	PARKINSONISMS
PARASCENDING	PARASKIINGS	PARBREAKED	PARENTHESISES	PARKLEAVES
PARASCENDINGS	PARASOMNIA	PARBREAKING	PARENTHESISING	PARLEMENTS
PARASCENIA	PARASOMNIAS	PARBUCKLED	PARENTHESIZE	PARLEYVOOED
PARASCENIUM	PARASPHENOID	PARBUCKLES	PARENTHESIZED	PARLEYVOOING
PARASCEVES	PARASPHENOIDS	PARBUCKLING	PARENTHESIZES	PARLEYVOOS
PARASCIENCE	PARASTATAL	PARCELLING	PARENTHESIZING	PARLIAMENT
PARASCIENCES	PARASTATALS	PARCELWISE	PARENTHETIC	PARLIAMENTARIAN
PARASELENAE	PARASTICHIES	PARCENARIES	PARENTHETICAL	PARLIAMENTARILY
PARASELENE	PARASTICHOUS	PARCHEDNESS	PARENTHETICALLY	PARLIAMENTARISM
PARASELENIC	PARASTICHY	PARCHEDNESSES	PARENTHOOD	PARLIAMENTARY
PARASEXUAL	PARASUICIDE	PARCHEESIS	PARENTHOODS	PARLIAMENTING
PARASEXUALITIES	PARASUICIDES	PARCHMENTISE	PARENTINGS	PARLIAMENTINGS
PARASEXUALITY	PARASYMBIONT	PARCHMENTISED	PARENTLESS	PARLIAMENTS
PARASHIOTH	PARASYMBIONTS	PARCHMENTISES	PARESTHESIA	PARLOURMAID
PARASITAEMIA	PARASYMBIOSES	PARCHMENTISING	PARESTHESIAS	PARLOURMAIDS
PARASITAEMIAS	PARASYMBIOSIS	PARCHMENTIZE	PARESTHETIC	PARLOUSNESS
PARASITICAL	PARASYMBIOTIC	PARCHMENTIZED	PARFLECHES	PARLOUSNESSES
PARASITICALLY	PARASYMPATHETIC	PARCHMENTIZES	PARFLESHES	PARMACITIE

PARMACITIES	PAROXYSMALLY	PARTIALIZED	PARTICULARIZER	PASIGRAPHIC
PARMIGIANA	PAROXYSMIC	PARTIALIZES	PARTICULARIZERS	PASIGRAPHICAL
PARMIGIANO	PAROXYTONE	PARTIALIZING	PARTICULARIZES	PASIGRAPHIES
PAROCCIPITAL	PAROXYTONES	PARTIALLED	PARTICULARIZING	PASIGRAPHY
PAROCCIPITALS	PAROXYTONIC	PARTIALLING	PARTICULARLY	PASODOBLES
PAROCHIALISE	PARQUETING	PARTIALNESS	PARTICULARNESS	PASQUEFLOWER
PAROCHIALISED	PARQUETRIES	PARTIALNESSES	PARTICULARS	PASQUEFLOWERS
PAROCHIALISES	PARQUETTED	PARTIBILITIES	PARTICULATE	PASQUILANT
PAROCHIALISING	PARQUETTING	PARTIBILITY	PARTICULATES	PASQUILANTS
PAROCHIALISM	PARRAKEETS	PARTICIPABLE	PARTISANLY	PASQUILERS
PAROCHIALISMS	PARRAMATTA	PARTICIPANT	PARTISANSHIP	PASQUILLED
PAROCHIALITIES	PARRAMATTAS	PARTICIPANTLY	PARTISANSHIPS	PASQUILLING
PAROCHIALITY	PARRHESIAS	PARTICIPANTS	PARTITIONED	PASQUINADE
PAROCHIALIZE	PARRICIDAL	PARTICIPATE	PARTITIONER	PASQUINADED
PAROCHIALIZED	PARRICIDES	PARTICIPATED	PARTITIONERS	PASQUINADER
PAROCHIALIZES	PARRITCHES	PARTICIPATES	PARTITIONING	PASQUINADERS
PAROCHIALIZING	PARROCKING	PARTICIPATING	PARTITIONIST	PASQUINADES
PAROCHIALLY	PARROQUETS	PARTICIPATION	PARTITIONISTS	PASQUINADING
PAROCHINES	PARROTFISH	PARTICIPATIONAL	PARTITIONMENT	PASSABLENESS
PARODISTIC	PARROTFISHES	PARTICIPATIONS	PARTITIONMENTS	PASSABLENESSES
PAROECIOUS	PARROTRIES	PARTICIPATIVE	PARTITIONS	PASSACAGLIA
PAROECISMS	PARSIMONIES	PARTICIPATOR	PARTITIVELY	PASSACAGLIAS
PAROEMIACS	PARSIMONIOUS	PARTICIPATORS	PARTITIVES	PASSAGEWAY
PAROEMIOGRAPHER	PARSIMONIOUSLY	PARTICIPATORY	PARTITURAS	PASSAGEWAYS
PAROEMIOGRAPHY	PARSONAGES	PARTICIPIAL	PARTIZANSHIP	PASSAGEWORK
PAROEMIOLOGIES	PARSONICAL	PARTICIPIALLY	PARTIZANSHIPS	PASSAGEWORKS
PAROEMIOLOGY	PARTAKINGS	PARTICIPIALS	PARTNERING	PASSALONGS
PARONOMASIA	PARTHENOCARPIC	PARTICIPLE	PARTNERLESS	PASSAMENTED
PARONOMASIAS	PARTHENOCARPIES	PARTICIPLES	PARTNERSHIP	PASSAMENTING
PARONOMASIES	PARTHENOCARPOUS	PARTICLEBOARD	PARTNERSHIPS	PASSAMENTS
PARONOMASTIC	PARTHENOCARPY	PARTICLEBOARDS	PARTRIDGEBERRY	PASSAMEZZO
PARONOMASTICAL	PARTHENOGENESES	PARTICULAR	PARTRIDGES	PASSAMEZZOS
PARONOMASY	PARTHENOGENESIS	PARTICULARISE	PARTURIENCIES	PASSEMEASURE
PARONYCHIA	PARTHENOGENETIC	PARTICULARISED	PARTURIENCY	PASSEMEASURES
PARONYCHIAL	PARTHENOSPORE	PARTICULARISER	PARTURIENT	PASSEMENTED
PARONYCHIAS	PARTHENOSPORES	PARTICULARISERS	PARTURIENTS	PASSEMENTERIE
PARONYMIES	PARTIALISE	PARTICULARISES	PARTURIFACIENT	PASSEMENTERIES
PARONYMOUS	PARTIALISED	PARTICULARISING	PARTURIFACIENTS	PASSEMENTING
PARONYMOUSLY	PARTIALISES	PARTICULARISM	PARTURITION	PASSEMENTS
PAROTIDITIC	PARTIALISING	PARTICULARISMS	PARTURITIONS	PASSENGERS
PAROTIDITIS	PARTIALISM	PARTICULARIST	PARTYGOERS	PASSEPIEDS
PAROTIDITISES	PARTIALISMS	PARTICULARISTIC	PARVANIMITIES	PASSERINES
PAROTITIDES	PARTIALIST	PARTICULARISTS	PARVANIMITY	PASSIBILITIES
PAROTITISES	PARTIALISTS	PARTICULARITIES	PARVIFOLIATE	PASSIBILITY
PAROXETINE	PARTIALITIES	PARTICULARITY	PARVOLINES	PASSIBLENESS
PAROXETINES	PARTIALITY	PARTICULARIZE	PARVOVIRUS	PASSIBLENESSES
PAROXYSMAL	PARTIALIZE	PARTICULARIZED	PARVOVIRUSES	PASSIFLORA

P

PASSIFLORACEOUS	PASTEURISING	PATCHOULIES	PATHOGRAPHIES	PATRIARCHAL
PASSIFLORAS	PASTEURISM	PATCHOULIS	PATHOGRAPHY	PATRIARCHALISM
PASSIMETER	PASTEURISMS	PATCHWORKED	PATHOLOGIC	PATRIARCHALISMS
PASSIMETERS	PASTEURIZATION	PATCHWORKING	PATHOLOGICAL	PATRIARCHALLY
PASSIONALS	PASTEURIZATIONS	PATCHWORKS	PATHOLOGICALLY	PATRIARCHATE
PASSIONARIES	PASTEURIZE	PATELLECTOMIES	PATHOLOGIES	PATRIARCHATES
PASSIONARY	PASTEURIZED	PATELLECTOMY	PATHOLOGISE	PATRIARCHIES
PASSIONATE	PASTEURIZER	PATELLIFORM	PATHOLOGISED	PATRIARCHISM
PASSIONATED	PASTEURIZERS	PATENTABILITIES	PATHOLOGISES	PATRIARCHISMS
PASSIONATELY	PASTEURIZES	PATENTABILITY	PATHOLOGISING	PATRIARCHS
PASSIONATENESS	PASTEURIZING	PATENTABLE	PATHOLOGIST	PATRIARCHY
PASSIONATES	PASTICCIOS	PATERCOVES	PATHOLOGISTS	PATRIATING
PASSIONATING	PASTICHEUR	PATEREROES	PATHOLOGIZE	PATRIATION
PASSIONFLOWER	PASTICHEURS	PATERFAMILIAS	PATHOLOGIZED	PATRIATIONS
PASSIONFLOWERS	PASTINESSES	PATERFAMILIASES	PATHOLOGIZES	PATRICIANLY
PASSIONING	PASTITSIOS	PATERNALISM	PATHOLOGIZING	PATRICIANS
PASSIONLESS	PASTNESSES	PATERNALISMS	PATHOPHOBIA	PATRICIATE
PASSIONLESSLY	PASTORALES	PATERNALIST	PATHOPHOBIAS	PATRICIATES
PASSIONLESSNESS	PASTORALISM	PATERNALISTIC	PATHOPHYSIOLOGY	PATRICIDAL
PASSIVATED	PASTORALISMS	PATERNALISTS	PATIBULARY	PATRICIDES
PASSIVATES	PASTORALIST	PATERNALLY	PATIENTEST	PATRICLINIC
PASSIVATING	PASTORALISTS	PATERNITIES	PATIENTING	PATRICLINOUS
PASSIVATION	PASTORALLY	PATERNOSTER	PATINATING	PATRIFOCAL
PASSIVATIONS	PASTORALNESS	PATERNOSTERS	PATINATION	PATRIFOCALITIES
PASSIVENESS	PASTORALNESSES	PATHBREAKING	PATINATIONS	PATRIFOCALITY
PASSIVENESSES	PASTORATES	PATHETICAL	PATINISING	PATRILINEAGE
PASSIVISMS	PASTORIUMS	PATHETICALLY	PATINIZING	PATRILINEAGES
PASSIVISTS	PASTORSHIP	PATHFINDER	PATISSERIE	PATRILINEAL
PASSIVITIES	PASTORSHIPS	PATHFINDERS	PATISSERIES	PATRILINEALLY
PASSMENTED	PASTOURELLE	PATHFINDING	PATISSIERS	PATRILINEAR
PASSMENTING	PASTOURELLES	PATHFINDINGS	PATRESFAMILIAS	PATRILINEARLY
PASTEBOARD	PASTRYCOOK	PATHLESSNESS	PATRIALISATION	PATRILINIES
PASTEBOARDS	PASTRYCOOKS	PATHLESSNESSES	PATRIALISATIONS	PATRILOCAL
PASTEDOWNS	PASTURABLE	PATHOBIOLOGIES	PATRIALISE	PATRILOCALLY
PASTELISTS	PASTURAGES	PATHOBIOLOGY	PATRIALISED	PATRIMONIAL
PASTELLIST	PASTURELAND	PATHOGENES	PATRIALISES	PATRIMONIALLY
PASTELLISTS	PASTURELANDS	PATHOGENESES	PATRIALISING	PATRIMONIES
PASTEURELLA	PASTURELESS	PATHOGENESIS	PATRIALISM	PATRIOTICALLY
PASTEURELLAE	PATAPHYSICS	PATHOGENETIC	PATRIALISMS	PATRIOTISM
PASTEURELLAS	PATCHBOARD	PATHOGENIC	PATRIALITIES	PATRIOTISMS
PASTEURISATION	PATCHBOARDS	PATHOGENICITIES	PATRIALITY	PATRISTICAL
PASTEURISATIONS	PATCHCOCKE	PATHOGENICITY	PATRIALIZATION	PATRISTICALLY
PASTEURISE	PATCHCOCKES	PATHOGENIES	PATRIALIZATIONS	PATRISTICISM
PASTEURISED	PATCHERIES	PATHOGENOUS	PATRIALIZE	PATRISTICISMS
PASTEURISER	PATCHINESS	PATHOGNOMIES	PATRIALIZED	PATRISTICS
PASTEURISERS	PATCHINESSES	PATHOGNOMONIC	PATRIALIZES	PATROCLINAL
PASTEURISES	PATCHOCKES	PATHOGNOMY	PATRIALIZING	PATROCLINIC

PATROCLINIES	PAUNCHINESS	PEACELESSNESSES	PECKISHNESS	PEDAGOGUISHNESS
PATROCLINOUS	PAUNCHINESSES	PEACEMAKER	PECKISHNESSES	PEDAGOGUISM
PATROCLINY	PAUPERDOMS	PEACEMAKERS	PECTINACEOUS	PEDAGOGUISMS
PATROLLERS	PAUPERESSES	PEACEMAKING	PECTINATED	PEDALBOATS
PATROLLING	PAUPERISATION	PEACEMAKINGS	PECTINATELY	PEDALLINGS
PATROLOGICAL	PAUPERISATIONS	PEACETIMES	PECTINATION	PEDANTICAL
PATROLOGIES	PAUPERISED	PEACHBLOWS	PECTINATIONS	PEDANTICALLY
PATROLOGIST	PAUPERISES	PEACHERINO	PECTINESTERASE	PEDANTICISE
PATROLOGISTS	PAUPERISING	PEACHERINOS	PECTINESTERASES	PEDANTICISED
PATROLWOMAN	PAUPERISMS	PEACHINESS	PECTISABLE	PEDANTICISES
PATROLWOMEN	PAUPERIZATION	PEACHINESSES	PECTISATION	PEDANTICISING
PATRONAGED	PAUPERIZATIONS	PEACOCKERIES	PECTISATIONS	PEDANTICISM
PATRONAGES	PAUPERIZED	PEACOCKERY	PECTIZABLE	PEDANTICISMS
PATRONAGING	PAUPERIZES	PEACOCKIER	PECTIZATION	PEDANTICIZE
PATRONESSES	PAUPERIZING	PEACOCKIEST	PECTIZATIONS	PEDANTICIZED
PATRONISATION	PAUPIETTES	PEACOCKING	PECTOLITES	PEDANTICIZES
PATRONISATIONS	PAUSEFULLY	PEACOCKISH	PECTORALLY	PEDANTICIZING
PATRONISED	PAUSELESSLY	PEAKEDNESS	PECTORILOQUIES	PEDANTISED
PATRONISER	PAVEMENTED	PEAKEDNESSES	PECTORILOQUY	PEDANTISES
PATRONISERS	PAVEMENTING	PEARLASHES	PECULATING	PEDANTISING
PATRONISES	PAVILIONED	PEARLESCENCE	PECULATION	PEDANTISMS
PATRONISING	PAVILIONING	PEARLESCENCES	PECULATIONS	PEDANTIZED
PATRONISINGLY	PAVONAZZOS	PEARLESCENT	PECULATORS	PEDANTIZES
PATRONIZATION	PAWKINESSES	PEARLINESS	PECULIARISE	PEDANTIZING
PATRONIZATIONS	PAWNBROKER	PEARLINESSES	PECULIARISED	PEDANTOCRACIES
PATRONIZED	PAWNBROKERS	PEARLWORTS	PECULIARISES	PEDANTOCRACY
PATRONIZER	PAWNBROKING	PEARMONGER	PECULIARISING	PEDANTOCRAT
PATRONIZERS	PAWNBROKINGS	PEARMONGERS	PECULIARITIES	PEDANTOCRATIC
PATRONIZES	PAWNTICKET	PEARTNESSES	PECULIARITY	PEDANTOCRATS
PATRONIZING	PAWNTICKETS	PEASANTRIES	PECULIARIZE	PEDANTRIES
PATRONIZINGLY	PAYCHEQUES	PEASHOOTER	PECULIARIZED	PEDDLERIES
PATRONLESS	PAYMASTERS	PEASHOOTERS	PECULIARIZES	PEDERASTIC
PATRONYMIC	PAYNIMRIES	PEASOUPERS	PECULIARIZING	PEDERASTIES
PATRONYMICS	PAYSAGISTS	PEBBLEDASH	PECULIARLY	PEDEREROES
PATROONSHIP	PEABERRIES	PEBBLEDASHED	PECUNIARILY	PEDESTALED
PATROONSHIPS	PEACEABLENESS	PEBBLEDASHES	PEDAGOGICAL	PEDESTALING
PATTERNING	PEACEABLENESSES	PEBBLEDASHING	PEDAGOGICALLY	PEDESTALLED
PATTERNINGS	PEACEFULLER	PEBBLEWEAVE	PEDAGOGICS	PEDESTALLING
PATTERNLESS	PEACEFULLEST	PEBBLEWEAVES	PEDAGOGIES	PEDESTRIAN
PATTRESSES	PEACEFULLY	PECCABILITIES	PEDAGOGISM	PEDESTRIANISE
PATULOUSLY	PEACEFULNESS	PECCABILITY	PEDAGOGISMS	PEDESTRIANISED
PATULOUSNESS	PEACEFULNESSES	PECCADILLO	PEDAGOGUED	PEDESTRIANISES
PATULOUSNESSES	PEACEKEEPER	PECCADILLOES	PEDAGOGUERIES	PEDESTRIANISING
PAUCILOQUENT	PEACEKEEPERS	PECCADILLOS	PEDAGOGUERY	PEDESTRIANISM
PAUGHTIEST	PEACEKEEPING	PECCANCIES	PEDAGOGUES	PEDESTRIANISMS
PAULOWNIAS	PEACEKEEPINGS	PECKERWOOD	PEDAGOGUING	PEDESTRIANIZE
PAUNCHIEST	PEACELESSNESS	PECKERWOODS	PEDAGOGUISH	PEDESTRIANIZED

P

PEDESTRIANIZES	PEELGARLICS	PELOTHERAPIES	PENELOPIZED	PENICILLINS
PEDESTRIANIZING	PEERLESSLY	PELOTHERAPY	PENELOPIZES	PENICILLIUM
PEDESTRIANS	PEERLESSNESS	PELTATIONS	PENELOPIZING	PENICILLIUMS
PEDETENTOUS	PEERLESSNESSES	PELTMONGER	PENEPLAINS	PENICILLUS
PEDIATRICIAN	PEEVISHNESS	PELTMONGERS	PENEPLANATION	PENINSULAR
PEDIATRICIANS	PEEVISHNESSES	PELVIMETER	PENEPLANATIONS	PENINSULARITIES
PEDIATRICS	PEGMATITES	PELVIMETERS	PENEPLANES	PENINSULARITY
PEDIATRIST	PEGMATITIC	PELVIMETRIES	PENETRABILITIES	PENINSULAS
PEDIATRISTS	PEIRASTICALLY	PELVIMETRY	PENETRABILITY	PENINSULATE
PEDICELLARIA	PEJORATING	PELYCOSAUR	PENETRABLE	PENINSULATED
PEDICELLARIAE	PEJORATION	PELYCOSAURS	PENETRABLENESS	PENINSULATES
PEDICELLATE	PEJORATIONS	PEMPHIGOID	PENETRABLY	PENINSULATING
PEDICULATE	PEJORATIVE	PEMPHIGOIDS	PENETRALIA	PENISTONES
PEDICULATED	PEJORATIVELY	PEMPHIGOUS	PENETRALIAN	PENITENCES
PEDICULATES	PEJORATIVES	PEMPHIGUSES	PENETRANCE	PENITENCIES
PEDICULATION	PELARGONIC	PENALISATION	PENETRANCES	PENITENTIAL
PEDICULATIONS	PELARGONIUM	PENALISATIONS	PENETRANCIES	PENITENTIALLY
PEDICULOSES	PELARGONIUMS	PENALISING	PENETRANCY	PENITENTIALS
PEDICULOSIS	PELECYPODS	PENALITIES	PENETRANTS	PENITENTIARIES
PEDICULOUS	PELLAGRINS	PENALIZATION	PENETRATED	PENITENTIARY
PEDICURING	PELLAGROUS	PENALIZATIONS	PENETRATES	PENITENTLY
PEDICURIST	PELLETIFIED	PENALIZING	PENETRATING	PENMANSHIP
PEDICURISTS	PELLETIFIES	PENANNULAR	PENETRATINGLY	PENMANSHIPS
PEDIMENTAL	PELLETIFYING	PENCILINGS	PENETRATION	PENNACEOUS
PEDIMENTED	PELLETISATION	PENCILLERS	PENETRATIONS	PENNALISMS
PEDIPALPUS	PELLETISATIONS	PENCILLING	PENETRATIVE	PENNATULACEOUS
PEDOGENESES	PELLETISED	PENCILLINGS	PENETRATIVELY	PENNATULAE
PEDOGENESIS	PELLETISER	PENDENCIES	PENETRATIVENESS	PENNATULAS
PEDOGENETIC	PELLETISERS	PENDENTIVE	PENETRATOR	PENNILESSLY
PEDOLOGICAL	PELLETISES	PENDENTIVES	PENETRATORS	PENNILESSNESS
PEDOLOGIES	PELLETISING	PENDICLERS	PENETROMETER	PENNILESSNESSES
PEDOLOGIST	PELLETIZATION	PENDRAGONS	PENETROMETERS	PENNILLION
PEDOLOGISTS	PELLETIZATIONS	PENDRAGONSHIP	PENGUINERIES	PENNINITES
PEDOMETERS	PELLETIZED	PENDRAGONSHIPS	PENGUINERY	PENNONCELLE
PEDOPHILES	PELLETIZER	PENDULATED	PENGUINRIES	PENNONCELLES
PEDOPHILIA	PELLETIZERS	PENDULATES	PENHOLDERS	PENNONCELS
PEDOPHILIAC	PELLETIZES	PENDULATING	PENICILLAMINE	PENNYCRESS
PEDOPHILIACS	PELLETIZING	PENDULOSITIES	PENICILLAMINES	PENNYCRESSES
PEDOPHILIAS	PELLICULAR	PENDULOSITY	PENICILLATE	PENNYLANDS
PEDOPHILIC	PELLITORIES	PENDULOUSLY	PENICILLATELY	PENNYROYAL
PEDOPHILICS	PELLUCIDITIES	PENDULOUSNESS	PENICILLATION	PENNYROYALS
PEDUNCULAR	PELLUCIDITY	PENDULOUSNESSES	PENICILLATIONS	PENNYWEIGHT
PEDUNCULATE	PELLUCIDLY	PENELOPISE	PENICILLIA	PENNYWEIGHTS
PEDUNCULATED	PELLUCIDNESS	PENELOPISED	PENICILLIFORM	PENNYWHISTLE
PEDUNCULATION	PELLUCIDNESSES	PENELOPISES	PENICILLIN	PENNYWHISTLES
PEDUNCULATIONS	PELMANISMS	PENELOPISING	PENICILLINASE	PENNYWINKLE
PEELGARLIC	PELOLOGIES	PENELOPIZE	PENICILLINASES	PENNYWINKLES

PENNYWORTH
PENNYWORTHS
PENNYWORTS
PENOLOGICAL
PENOLOGICALLY
PENOLOGIES
PENOLOGIST
PENOLOGISTS
PENONCELLE
PENONCELLES
PENPUSHERS
PENPUSHING
PENPUSHINGS
PENSEROSOS
PENSIEROSO
PENSILENESS
PENSILENESSES
PENSILITIES
PENSIONABLE
PENSIONARIES
PENSIONARY
PENSIONEER
PENSIONERS
PENSIONING
PENSIONLESS
PENSIONNAT
PENSIONNATS
PENSIVENESS
PENSIVENESSES
PENSTEMONS
PENTABARBITAL
PENTABARBITALS
PENTACHORD
PENTACHORDS
PENTACRINOID
PENTACRINOIDS
PENTACTINAL
PENTACYCLIC
PENTADACTYL
PENTADACTYLE
PENTADACTYLES
PENTADACTYLIC
PENTADACTYLIES
PENTADACTYLISM
PENTADACTYLISMS
PENTADACTYLOUS
PENTADACTYLS

PENTADACTYLY
PENTADELPHOUS
PENTAGONAL
PENTAGONALLY
PENTAGONALS
PENTAGRAMS
PENTAGRAPH
PENTAGRAPHS
PENTAGYNIAN
PENTAGYNOUS
PENTAHEDRA
PENTAHEDRAL
PENTAHEDRON
PENTAHEDRONS
PENTALOGIES
PENTALPHAS
PENTAMERIES
PENTAMERISM
PENTAMERISMS
PENTAMEROUS
PENTAMETER
PENTAMETERS
PENTAMIDINE
PENTAMIDINES
PENTANDRIAN
PENTANDROUS
PENTANGLES
PENTANGULAR
PENTAPEPTIDE
PENTAPEPTIDES
PENTAPLOID
PENTAPLOIDIES
PENTAPLOIDS
PENTAPLOIDY
PENTAPODIC
PENTAPODIES
PENTAPOLIS
PENTAPOLISES
PENTAPOLITAN
PENTAPRISM
PENTAPRISMS
PENTAQUARK
PENTAQUARKS
PENTARCHICAL
PENTARCHIES
PENTASTICH
PENTASTICHOUS

PENTASTICHS
PENTASTYLE
PENTASTYLES
PENTASYLLABIC
PENTATEUCHAL
PENTATHLETE
PENTATHLETES
PENTATHLON
PENTATHLONS
PENTATHLUM
PENTATHLUMS
PENTATOMIC
PENTATONIC
PENTAVALENCE
PENTAVALENCES
PENTAVALENCIES
PENTAVALENCY
PENTAVALENT
PENTAZOCINE
PENTAZOCINES
PENTECONTER
PENTECONTERS
PENTETERIC
PENTHEMIMER
PENTHEMIMERAL
PENTHEMIMERS
PENTHOUSED
PENTHOUSES
PENTHOUSING
PENTIMENTI
PENTIMENTO
PENTLANDITE
PENTLANDITES
PENTOBARBITAL
PENTOBARBITALS
PENTOBARBITONE
PENTOBARBITONES
PENTOSANES
PENTOSIDES
PENTOXIDES
PENTSTEMON
PENTSTEMONS
PENTYLENES
PENULTIMAS
PENULTIMATE
PENULTIMATELY
PENULTIMATES

PENUMBROUS
PENURIOUSLY
PENURIOUSNESS
PENURIOUSNESSES
PEOPLEHOOD
PEOPLEHOODS
PEOPLELESS
PEPEROMIAS
PEPPERBOXES
PEPPERCORN
PEPPERCORNS
PEPPERCORNY
PEPPERGRASS
PEPPERGRASSES
PEPPERIDGE
PEPPERIDGES
PEPPERIEST
PEPPERINESS
PEPPERINESSES
PEPPERINGS
PEPPERMILL
PEPPERMILLS
PEPPERMINT
PEPPERMINTS
PEPPERMINTY
PEPPERONIS
PEPPERTREE
PEPPERTREES
PEPPERWORT
PEPPERWORTS
PEPPINESSES
PEPSINATED
PEPSINATES
PEPSINATING
PEPSINOGEN
PEPSINOGENS
PEPTALKING
PEPTICITIES
PEPTIDASES
PEPTIDOGLYCAN
PEPTIDOGLYCANS
PEPTISABLE
PEPTISATION
PEPTISATIONS
PEPTIZABLE
PEPTIZATION
PEPTIZATIONS

PEPTONISATION
PEPTONISATIONS
PEPTONISED
PEPTONISER
PEPTONISERS
PEPTONISES
PEPTONISING
PEPTONIZATION
PEPTONIZATIONS
PEPTONIZED
PEPTONIZER
PEPTONIZERS
PEPTONIZES
PEPTONIZING
PERACIDITIES
PERACIDITY
PERADVENTURE
PERADVENTURES
PERAEOPODS
PERAMBULATE
PERAMBULATED
PERAMBULATES
PERAMBULATING
PERAMBULATION
PERAMBULATIONS
PERAMBULATOR
PERAMBULATORS
PERAMBULATORY
PERBORATES
PERCALINES
PERCEIVABILITY
PERCEIVABLE
PERCEIVABLY
PERCEIVERS
PERCEIVING
PERCEIVINGS
PERCENTAGE
PERCENTAGES
PERCENTILE
PERCENTILES
PERCEPTIBILITY
PERCEPTIBLE
PERCEPTIBLY
PERCEPTION
PERCEPTIONAL
PERCEPTIONS
PERCEPTIVE

P

PERCEPTIVELY
PERCEPTIVENESS
PERCEPTIVITIES
PERCEPTIVITY
PERCEPTUAL
PERCEPTUALLY
PERCHERIES
PERCHERONS
PERCHLORATE
PERCHLORATES
PERCHLORIC
PERCHLORIDE
PERCHLORIDES
PERCHLOROETHENE
PERCIFORMS
PERCIPIENCE
PERCIPIENCES
PERCIPIENCIES
PERCIPIENCY
PERCIPIENT
PERCIPIENTLY
PERCIPIENTS
PERCOCTING
PERCOIDEAN
PERCOIDEANS
PERCOLABLE
PERCOLATED
PERCOLATES
PERCOLATING
PERCOLATION
PERCOLATIONS
PERCOLATIVE
PERCOLATOR
PERCOLATORS
PERCURRENT
PERCURSORY
PERCUSSANT
PERCUSSING
PERCUSSION
PERCUSSIONAL
PERCUSSIONIST
PERCUSSIONISTS
PERCUSSIONS
PERCUSSIVE
PERCUSSIVELY
PERCUSSIVENESS
PERCUSSORS

PERCUTANEOUS
PERCUTANEOUSLY
PERCUTIENT
PERCUTIENTS
PERDENDOSI
PERDITIONABLE
PERDITIONS
PERDUELLION
PERDUELLIONS
PERDURABILITIES
PERDURABILITY
PERDURABLE
PERDURABLY
PERDURANCE
PERDURANCES
PERDURATION
PERDURATIONS
PEREGRINATE
PEREGRINATED
PEREGRINATES
PEREGRINATING
PEREGRINATION
PEREGRINATIONS
PEREGRINATOR
PEREGRINATORS
PEREGRINATORY
PEREGRINES
PEREGRINITIES
PEREGRINITY
PEREIOPODS
PEREMPTORILY
PEREMPTORINESS
PEREMPTORY
PERENNATED
PERENNATES
PERENNATING
PERENNATION
PERENNATIONS
PERENNIALITIES
PERENNIALITY
PERENNIALLY
PERENNIALS
PERENNIBRANCH
PERENNIBRANCHS
PERENNITIES
PERESTROIKA
PERESTROIKAS

PERFECTATION
PERFECTATIONS
PERFECTERS
PERFECTEST
PERFECTIBILIAN
PERFECTIBILIANS
PERFECTIBILISM
PERFECTIBILISMS
PERFECTIBILIST
PERFECTIBILISTS
PERFECTIBILITY
PERFECTIBLE
PERFECTING
PERFECTION
PERFECTIONATE
PERFECTIONATED
PERFECTIONATES
PERFECTIONATING
PERFECTIONISM
PERFECTIONISMS
PERFECTIONIST
PERFECTIONISTIC
PERFECTIONISTS
PERFECTIONS
PERFECTIVE
PERFECTIVELY
PERFECTIVENESS
PERFECTIVES
PERFECTIVITIES
PERFECTIVITY
PERFECTNESS
PERFECTNESSES
PERFECTORS
PERFERVIDITIES
PERFERVIDITY
PERFERVIDLY
PERFERVIDNESS
PERFERVIDNESSES
PERFERVORS
PERFERVOUR
PERFERVOURS
PERFICIENT
PERFICIENTS
PERFIDIOUS
PERFIDIOUSLY
PERFIDIOUSNESS
PERFLUOROCARBON

PERFOLIATE
PERFOLIATION
PERFOLIATIONS
PERFORABLE
PERFORANSES
PERFORATED
PERFORATES
PERFORATING
PERFORATION
PERFORATIONS
PERFORATIVE
PERFORATOR
PERFORATORS
PERFORATORY
PERFORATUS
PERFORATUSES
PERFORMABILITY
PERFORMABLE
PERFORMANCE
PERFORMANCES
PERFORMATIVE
PERFORMATIVELY
PERFORMATIVES
PERFORMATORY
PERFORMERS
PERFORMING
PERFORMINGS
PERFUMELESS
PERFUMERIES
PERFUMIERS
PERFUNCTORILY
PERFUNCTORINESS
PERFUNCTORY
PERFUSATES
PERFUSIONIST
PERFUSIONISTS
PERFUSIONS
PERGAMENEOUS
PERGAMENTACEOUS
PERGUNNAHS
PERIASTRON
PERIASTRONS
PERIBLASTS
PERICARDIA
PERICARDIAC
PERICARDIAL
PERICARDIAN

PERICARDITIC
PERICARDITIS
PERICARDITISES
PERICARDIUM
PERICARDIUMS
PERICARPIAL
PERICARPIC
PERICENTER
PERICENTERS
PERICENTRAL
PERICENTRE
PERICENTRES
PERICENTRIC
PERICHAETIA
PERICHAETIAL
PERICHAETIUM
PERICHONDRAL
PERICHONDRIA
PERICHONDRIAL
PERICHONDRIUM
PERICHORESES
PERICHORESIS
PERICHYLOUS
PERICLASES
PERICLASTIC
PERICLINAL
PERICLINES
PERICLITATE
PERICLITATED
PERICLITATES
PERICLITATING
PERICRANIA
PERICRANIAL
PERICRANIUM
PERICRANIUMS
PERICULOUS
PERICYCLES
PERICYCLIC
PERICYNTHIA
PERICYNTHION
PERICYNTHIONS
PERIDERMAL
PERIDERMIC
PERIDESMIA
PERIDESMIUM
PERIDINIAN
PERIDINIANS

PERIDINIUM	PERINEPHRIA	PERIOSTITIC	PERISCOPIC	PERITONAEUM
PERIDINIUMS	PERINEPHRIC	PERIOSTITIS	PERISCOPICALLY	PERITONAEUMS
PERIDOTITE	PERINEPHRITIS	PERIOSTITISES	PERISELENIA	PERITONEAL
PERIDOTITES	PERINEPHRITISES	PERIOSTRACUM	PERISELENIUM	PERITONEALLY
PERIDOTITIC	PERINEPHRIUM	PERIOSTRACUMS	PERISHABILITIES	PERITONEOSCOPY
PERIDROMES	PERINEURAL	PERIPATETIC	PERISHABILITY	PERITONEUM
PERIEGESES	PERINEURIA	PERIPATETICAL	PERISHABLE	PERITONEUMS
PERIEGESIS	PERINEURIAL	PERIPATETICALLY	PERISHABLENESS	PERITONITIC
PERIGASTRIC	PERINEURITIC	PERIPATETICISM	PERISHABLES	PERITONITIS
PERIGASTRITIS	PERINEURITIS	PERIPATETICISMS	PERISHABLY	PERITONITISES
PERIGASTRITISES	PERINEURITISES	PERIPATETICS	PERISHINGLY	PERITRACKS
PERIGENESES	PERINEURIUM	PERIPATUSES	PERISPERMAL	PERITRICHA
PERIGENESIS	PERIODATES	PERIPETEIA	PERISPERMIC	PERITRICHOUS
PERIGLACIAL	PERIODICAL	PERIPETEIAN	PERISPERMS	PERITRICHOUSLY
PERIGONIAL	PERIODICALIST	PERIPETEIAS	PERISPOMENON	PERITRICHS
PERIGONIUM	PERIODICALISTS	PERIPETIAN	PERISPOMENONS	PERITYPHLITIS
PERIGYNIES	PERIODICALLY	PERIPETIAS	PERISSODACTYL	PERITYPHLITISES
PERIGYNOUS	PERIODICALS	PERIPETIES	PERISSODACTYLE	PERIVITELLINE
PERIHELIAL	PERIODICITIES	PERIPHERAL	PERISSODACTYLES	PERIWIGGED
PERIHELION	PERIODICITY	PERIPHERALITIES	PERISSODACTYLIC	PERIWIGGING
PERIHEPATIC	PERIODIDES	PERIPHERALITY	PERISSODACTYLS	PERIWINKLE
PERIHEPATITIS	PERIODISATION	PERIPHERALLY	PERISSOLOGIES	PERIWINKLES
PERIHEPATITISES	PERIODISATIONS	PERIPHERALS	PERISSOLOGY	PERJINKETY
PERIKARYAL	PERIODISED	PERIPHERIC	PERISSOSYLLABIC	PERJINKITIES
PERIKARYON	PERIODISES	PERIPHERICAL	PERISTALITH	PERJINKITY
PERILOUSLY	PERIODISING	PERIPHERIES	PERISTALITHS	PERJURIOUS
PERILOUSNESS	PERIODIZATION	PERIPHONIC	PERISTALSES	PERJURIOUSLY
PERILOUSNESSES	PERIODIZATIONS	PERIPHRASE	PERISTALSIS	PERKINESSES
PERILYMPHS	PERIODIZED	PERIPHRASED	PERISTALTIC	PERLEMOENS
PERIMENOPAUSAL	PERIODIZES	PERIPHRASES	PERISTALTICALLY	PERLOCUTION
PERIMENOPAUSE	PERIODIZING	PERIPHRASING	PERISTERITE	PERLOCUTIONARY
PERIMENOPAUSES	PERIODONTAL	PERIPHRASIS	PERISTERITES	PERLOCUTIONS
PERIMETERS	PERIODONTALLY	PERIPHRASTIC	PERISTERONIC	PERLUSTRATE
PERIMETRAL	PERIODONTIA	PERIPHRASTICAL	PERISTOMAL	PERLUSTRATED
PERIMETRIC	PERIODONTIAS	PERIPHYTIC	PERISTOMATIC	PERLUSTRATES
PERIMETRICAL	PERIODONTIC	PERIPHYTON	PERISTOMES	PERLUSTRATING
PERIMETRICALLY	PERIODONTICALLY	PERIPHYTONS	PERISTOMIAL	PERLUSTRATION
PERIMETRIES	PERIODONTICS	PERIPLASMS	PERISTOMIUM	PERLUSTRATIONS
PERIMORPHIC	PERIODONTIST	PERIPLASTS	PERISTREPHIC	PERMABEARS
PERIMORPHISM	PERIODONTISTS	PERIPLUSES	PERISTYLAR	PERMABULLS
PERIMORPHISMS	PERIODONTITIS	PERIPROCTS	PERISTYLES	PERMACULTURE
PERIMORPHOUS	PERIODONTITISES	PERIPTERAL	PERITECTIC	PERMACULTURES
PERIMORPHS	PERIODONTOLOGY	PERIPTERIES	PERITECTICS	PERMAFROST
PERIMYSIUM	PERIONYCHIA	PERISARCAL	PERITHECIA	PERMAFROSTS
PERIMYSIUMS	PERIONYCHIUM	PERISARCOUS	PERITHECIAL	PERMALINKS
PERINAEUMS	PERIOSTEAL	PERISCIANS	PERITHECIUM	PERMALLOYS
PERINATALLY	PERIOSTEUM	PERISCOPES	PERITONAEA	PERMANENCE

P

PERMANENCES

PERMANENCES	PERMUTATED	PERPENDING	PERRUQUIER	PERSISTENTS
PERMANENCIES	PERMUTATES	PERPETRABLE	PERRUQUIERS	PERSISTERS
PERMANENCY	PERMUTATING	PERPETRATE	PERSCRUTATION	PERSISTING
PERMANENTLY	PERMUTATION	PERPETRATED	PERSCRUTATIONS	PERSISTINGLY
PERMANENTNESS	PERMUTATIONAL	PERPETRATES	PERSECUTED	PERSISTIVE
PERMANENTNESSES	PERMUTATIONS	PERPETRATING	PERSECUTEE	PERSNICKETINESS
PERMANENTS	PERNANCIES	PERPETRATION	PERSECUTEES	PERSNICKETY
PERMANGANATE	PERNICIOUS	PERPETRATIONS	PERSECUTES	PERSONABLE
PERMANGANATES	PERNICIOUSLY	PERPETRATOR	PERSECUTING	PERSONABLENESS
PERMANGANIC	PERNICIOUSNESS	PERPETRATORS	PERSECUTION	PERSONABLY
PERMEABILITIES	PERNICKETINESS	PERPETUABLE	PERSECUTIONS	PERSONAGES
PERMEABILITY	PERNICKETY	PERPETUALISM	PERSECUTIVE	PERSONALIA
PERMEABLENESS	PERNOCTATE	PERPETUALISMS	PERSECUTOR	PERSONALISATION
PERMEABLENESSES	PERNOCTATED	PERPETUALIST	PERSECUTORS	PERSONALISE
PERMEAMETER	PERNOCTATES	PERPETUALISTS	PERSECUTORY	PERSONALISED
PERMEAMETERS	PERNOCTATING	PERPETUALITIES	PERSEITIES	PERSONALISES
PERMEANCES	PERNOCTATION	PERPETUALITY	PERSELINES	PERSONALISING
PERMEATING	PERNOCTATIONS	PERPETUALLY	PERSEVERANCE	PERSONALISM
PERMEATION	PERONEUSES	PERPETUALS	PERSEVERANCES	PERSONALISMS
PERMEATIONS	PERORATING	PERPETUANCE	PERSEVERANT	PERSONALIST
PERMEATIVE	PERORATION	PERPETUANCES	PERSEVERATE	PERSONALISTIC
PERMEATORS	PERORATIONAL	PERPETUATE	PERSEVERATED	PERSONALISTS
PERMETHRIN	PERORATIONS	PERPETUATED	PERSEVERATES	PERSONALITIES
PERMETHRINS	PERORATORS	PERPETUATES	PERSEVERATING	PERSONALITY
PERMILLAGE	PEROVSKIAS	PERPETUATING	PERSEVERATION	PERSONALIZATION
PERMILLAGES	PEROVSKITE	PERPETUATION	PERSEVERATIONS	PERSONALIZE
PERMISSIBILITY	PEROVSKITES	PERPETUATIONS	PERSEVERATIVE	PERSONALIZED
PERMISSIBLE	PEROXIDASE	PERPETUATOR	PERSEVERATOR	PERSONALIZES
PERMISSIBLENESS	PEROXIDASES	PERPETUATORS	PERSEVERATORS	PERSONALIZING
PERMISSIBLY	PEROXIDATION	PERPETUITIES	PERSEVERED	PERSONALLY
PERMISSION	PEROXIDATIONS	PERPETUITY	PERSEVERES	PERSONALTIES
PERMISSIONS	PEROXIDING	PERPHENAZINE	PERSEVERING	PERSONALTY
PERMISSIVE	PEROXIDISE	PERPHENAZINES	PERSEVERINGLY	PERSONATED
PERMISSIVELY	PEROXIDISED	PERPLEXEDLY	PERSICARIA	PERSONATES
PERMISSIVENESS	PEROXIDISES	PERPLEXEDNESS	PERSICARIAS	PERSONATING
PERMITTANCE	PEROXIDISING	PERPLEXEDNESSES	PERSIENNES	PERSONATINGS
PERMITTANCES	PEROXIDIZE	PERPLEXERS	PERSIFLAGE	PERSONATION
PERMITTEES	PEROXIDIZED	PERPLEXING	PERSIFLAGES	PERSONATIONS
PERMITTERS	PEROXIDIZES	PERPLEXINGLY	PERSIFLEUR	PERSONATIVE
PERMITTING	PEROXIDIZING	PERPLEXITIES	PERSIFLEURS	PERSONATOR
PERMITTIVITIES	PEROXISOMAL	PERPLEXITY	PERSIMMONS	PERSONATORS
PERMITTIVITY	PEROXISOME	PERQUISITE	PERSISTENCE	PERSONHOOD
PERMUTABILITIES	PEROXISOMES	PERQUISITES	PERSISTENCES	PERSONHOODS
PERMUTABILITY	PEROXYSULPHURIC	PERQUISITION	PERSISTENCIES	PERSONIFIABLE
PERMUTABLE	PERPENDICULAR	PERQUISITIONS	PERSISTENCY	PERSONIFICATION
PERMUTABLENESS	PERPENDICULARLY	PERQUISITOR	PERSISTENT	PERSONIFIED
PERMUTABLY	PERPENDICULARS	PERQUISITORS	PERSISTENTLY	PERSONIFIER

P

PERSONIFIERS	PERSUASIBILITY	PERTURBERS	PESTICIDES	PETRISSAGE
PERSONIFIES	PERSUASIBLE	PERTURBING	PESTIFEROUS	PETRISSAGES
PERSONIFYING	PERSUASION	PERTURBINGLY	PESTIFEROUSLY	PETROCHEMICAL
PERSONISED	PERSUASIONS	PERTUSIONS	PESTIFEROUSNESS	PETROCHEMICALLY
PERSONISES	PERSUASIVE	PERTUSSISES	PESTILENCE	PETROCHEMICALS
PERSONISING	PERSUASIVELY	PERVASIONS	PESTILENCES	PETROCHEMIST
PERSONIZED	PERSUASIVENESS	PERVASIVELY	PESTILENTIAL	PETROCHEMISTRY
PERSONIZES	PERSUASIVES	PERVASIVENESS	PESTILENTIALLY	PETROCHEMISTS
PERSONIZING	PERSUASORY	PERVASIVENESSES	PESTILENTLY	PETROCURRENCIES
PERSONNELS	PERSULFATE	PERVERSELY	PESTOLOGICAL	PETROCURRENCY
PERSONPOWER	PERSULFATES	PERVERSENESS	PESTOLOGIES	PETRODOLLAR
PERSONPOWERS	PERSULFURIC	PERVERSENESSES	PESTOLOGIST	PETRODOLLARS
PERSPECTIVAL	PERSULPHATE	PERVERSEST	PESTOLOGISTS	PETRODROME
PERSPECTIVE	PERSULPHATES	PERVERSION	PETAHERTZES	PETRODROMES
PERSPECTIVELY	PERSULPHURIC	PERVERSIONS	PETALIFEROUS	PETROGENESES
PERSPECTIVES	PERSWADING	PERVERSITIES	PETALODIES	PETROGENESIS
PERSPECTIVISM	PERTAINING	PERVERSITY	PETALOMANIA	PETROGENETIC
PERSPECTIVISMS	PERTINACIOUS	PERVERSIVE	PETALOMANIAS	PETROGENIES
PERSPECTIVIST	PERTINACIOUSLY	PERVERTEDLY	PETAURINES	PETROGLYPH
PERSPECTIVISTS	PERTINACITIES	PERVERTEDNESS	PETAURISTS	PETROGLYPHIC
PERSPICACIOUS	PERTINACITY	PERVERTEDNESSES	PETCHARIES	PETROGLYPHIES
PERSPICACIOUSLY	PERTINENCE	PERVERTERS	PETERSHAMS	PETROGLYPHS
PERSPICACITIES	PERTINENCES	PERVERTIBLE	PETHIDINES	PETROGLYPHY
PERSPICACITY	PERTINENCIES	PERVERTING	PETIOLATED	PETROGRAMS
PERSPICUITIES	PERTINENCY	PERVIATING	PETIOLULES	PETROGRAPHER
PERSPICUITY	PERTINENTLY	PERVICACIES	PETITENESS	PETROGRAPHERS
PERSPICUOUS	PERTINENTS	PERVICACIOUS	PETITENESSES	PETROGRAPHIC
PERSPICUOUSLY	PERTNESSES	PERVICACITIES	PETITIONARY	PETROGRAPHICAL
PERSPICUOUSNESS	PERTURBABLE	PERVICACITY	PETITIONED	PETROGRAPHIES
PERSPIRABLE	PERTURBABLY	PERVIOUSLY	PETITIONER	PETROGRAPHY
PERSPIRATE	PERTURBANCE	PERVIOUSNESS	PETITIONERS	PETROLAGES
PERSPIRATED	PERTURBANCES	PERVIOUSNESSES	PETITIONING	PETROLATUM
PERSPIRATES	PERTURBANT	PESCATARIAN	PETITIONINGS	PETROLATUMS
PERSPIRATING	PERTURBANTS	PESCATARIANS	PETITIONIST	PETROLEOUS
PERSPIRATION	PERTURBATE	PESCETARIAN	PETITIONISTS	PETROLEUMS
PERSPIRATIONS	PERTURBATED	PESCETARIANS	PETNAPINGS	PETROLEURS
PERSPIRATORY	PERTURBATES	PESKINESSES	PETNAPPERS	PETROLEUSE
PERSPIRING	PERTURBATING	PESSIMISMS	PETNAPPING	PETROLEUSES
PERSPIRINGLY	PERTURBATION	PESSIMISTIC	PETNAPPINGS	PETROLHEAD
PERSTRINGE	PERTURBATIONAL	PESSIMISTICAL	PETRICHORS	PETROLHEADS
PERSTRINGED	PERTURBATIONS	PESSIMISTICALLY	PETRIFACTION	PETROLIFEROUS
PERSTRINGES	PERTURBATIVE	PESSIMISTS	PETRIFACTIONS	PETROLLING
PERSTRINGING	PERTURBATOR	PESTERINGLY	PETRIFACTIVE	PETROLOGIC
PERSUADABILITY	PERTURBATORIES	PESTERMENT	PETRIFICATION	PETROLOGICAL
PERSUADABLE	PERTURBATORS	PESTERMENTS	PETRIFICATIONS	PETROLOGICALLY
PERSUADERS	PERTURBATORY	PESTHOUSES	PETRIFIERS	PETROLOGIES
PERSUADING	PERTURBEDLY	PESTICIDAL	PETRIFYING	PETROLOGIST

P

PETROLOGISTS	PHAENOTYPING	PHALAROPES	PHANTASYING	PHARMACOTHERAPY
PETROMONEY	PHAEOMELANIN	PHALLICALLY	PHANTOMATIC	PHARYNGALS
PETROMONEYS	PHAEOMELANINS	PHALLICISM	PHANTOMISH	PHARYNGEAL
PETROMONIES	PHAGEDAENA	PHALLICISMS	PHANTOMLIKE	PHARYNGEALS
PETRONELLA	PHAGEDAENAS	PHALLICIST	PHANTOSMES	PHARYNGITIC
PETRONELLAS	PHAGEDAENIC	PHALLICISTS	PHARISAICAL	PHARYNGITIDES
PETROPHYSICAL	PHAGEDENAS	PHALLOCENTRIC	PHARISAICALLY	PHARYNGITIS
PETROPHYSICIST	PHAGEDENIC	PHALLOCENTRISM	PHARISAICALNESS	PHARYNGITISES
PETROPHYSICISTS	PHAGOCYTES	PHALLOCENTRISMS	PHARISAISM	PHARYNGOLOGICAL
PETROPHYSICS	PHAGOCYTIC	PHALLOCRAT	PHARISAISMS	PHARYNGOLOGIES
PETROPOUNDS	PHAGOCYTICAL	PHALLOCRATIC	PHARISEEISM	PHARYNGOLOGIST
PETROSTATE	PHAGOCYTISE	PHALLOCRATS	PHARISEEISMS	PHARYNGOLOGISTS
PETROSTATES	PHAGOCYTISED	PHALLOIDIN	PHARMACEUTIC	PHARYNGOLOGY
PETTEDNESS	PHAGOCYTISES	PHALLOIDINS	PHARMACEUTICAL	PHARYNGOSCOPE
PETTEDNESSES	PHAGOCYTISING	PHANEROGAM	PHARMACEUTICALS	PHARYNGOSCOPES
PETTICHAPS	PHAGOCYTISM	PHANEROGAMIC	PHARMACEUTICS	PHARYNGOSCOPIC
PETTICHAPSES	PHAGOCYTISMS	PHANEROGAMOUS	PHARMACEUTIST	PHARYNGOSCOPIES
PETTICOATED	PHAGOCYTIZE	PHANEROGAMS	PHARMACEUTISTS	PHARYNGOSCOPY
PETTICOATS	PHAGOCYTIZED	PHANEROPHYTE	PHARMACIES	PHARYNGOTOMIES
PETTIFOGGED	PHAGOCYTIZES	PHANEROPHYTES	PHARMACIST	PHARYNGOTOMY
PETTIFOGGER	PHAGOCYTIZING	PHANSIGARS	PHARMACISTS	PHASCOGALE
PETTIFOGGERIES	PHAGOCYTOSE	PHANTASIAST	PHARMACODYNAMIC	PHASCOGALES
PETTIFOGGERS	PHAGOCYTOSED	PHANTASIASTS	PHARMACOGENOMIC	PHASEDOWNS
PETTIFOGGERY	PHAGOCYTOSES	PHANTASIED	PHARMACOGNOSIES	PHASEOLINS
PETTIFOGGING	PHAGOCYTOSING	PHANTASIES	PHARMACOGNOSIST	PHATICALLY
PETTIFOGGINGS	PHAGOCYTOSIS	PHANTASIME	PHARMACOGNOSTIC	PHEASANTRIES
PETTINESSES	PHAGOCYTOTIC	PHANTASIMES	PHARMACOGNOSY	PHEASANTRY
PETTISHNESS	PHAGOMANIA	PHANTASIMS	PHARMACOKINETIC	PHELLODERM
PETTISHNESSES	PHAGOMANIAC	PHANTASMAGORIA	PHARMACOLOGIC	PHELLODERMAL
PETULANCES	PHAGOMANIACS	PHANTASMAGORIAL	PHARMACOLOGICAL	PHELLODERMS
PETULANCIES	PHAGOMANIAS	PHANTASMAGORIAS	PHARMACOLOGIES	PHELLOGENETIC
PETULANTLY	PHAGOPHOBIA	PHANTASMAGORIC	PHARMACOLOGIST	PHELLOGENIC
PEWHOLDERS	PHAGOPHOBIAS	PHANTASMAGORIES	PHARMACOLOGISTS	PHELLOGENS
PHACOLITES	PHAGOSOMES	PHANTASMAGORY	PHARMACOLOGY	PHELLOPLASTIC
PHACOLITHS	PHALANGEAL	PHANTASMAL	PHARMACOPEIA	PHELLOPLASTICS
PHAELONION	PHALANGERS	PHANTASMALIAN	PHARMACOPEIAL	PHELONIONS
PHAELONIONS	PHALANGIDS	PHANTASMALITIES	PHARMACOPEIAS	PHENACAINE
PHAENOGAMIC	PHALANGIST	PHANTASMALITY	PHARMACOPOEIA	PHENACAINES
PHAENOGAMOUS	PHALANGISTS	PHANTASMALLY	PHARMACOPOEIAL	PHENACETIN
PHAENOGAMS	PHALANSTERIAN	PHANTASMATA	PHARMACOPOEIAN	PHENACETINS
PHAENOLOGIES	PHALANSTERIANS	PHANTASMIC	PHARMACOPOEIANS	PHENACITES
PHAENOLOGY	PHALANSTERIES	PHANTASMICAL	PHARMACOPOEIAS	PHENAKISMS
PHAENOMENA	PHALANSTERISM	PHANTASMICALLY	PHARMACOPOEIC	PHENAKISTOSCOPE
PHAENOMENON	PHALANSTERISMS	PHANTASTIC	PHARMACOPOEIST	PHENAKITES
PHAENOTYPE	PHALANSTERIST	PHANTASTICS	PHARMACOPOEISTS	PHENANTHRENE
PHAENOTYPED	PHALANSTERISTS	PHANTASTRIES	PHARMACOPOLIST	PHENANTHRENES
PHAENOTYPES	PHALANSTERY	PHANTASTRY	PHARMACOPOLISTS	PHENARSAZINE

PHENARSAZINES | PHENOMENALIZING | PHENYLTHIOUREAS | PHILISTINISM | PHILOSOPHIC
PHENAZINES | PHENOMENALLY | PHENYTOINS | PHILISTINISMS | PHILOSOPHICAL
PHENCYCLIDINE | PHENOMENAS | PHEROMONAL | PHILLABEGS | PHILOSOPHICALLY
PHENCYCLIDINES | PHENOMENISE | PHEROMONES | PHILLIBEGS | PHILOSOPHIES
PHENETICIST | PHENOMENISED | PHIALIFORM | PHILLIPSITE | PHILOSOPHISE
PHENETICISTS | PHENOMENISES | PHILADELPHUS | PHILLIPSITES | PHILOSOPHISED
PHENETIDINE | PHENOMENISING | PHILADELPHUSES | PHILLUMENIES | PHILOSOPHISER
PHENETIDINES | PHENOMENISM | PHILANDERED | PHILLUMENIST | PHILOSOPHISERS
PHENETOLES | PHENOMENISMS | PHILANDERER | PHILLUMENISTS | PHILOSOPHISES
PHENFORMIN | PHENOMENIST | PHILANDERERS | PHILLUMENY | PHILOSOPHISING
PHENFORMINS | PHENOMENISTS | PHILANDERING | PHILODENDRA | PHILOSOPHISINGS
PHENGOPHOBIA | PHENOMENIZE | PHILANDERINGS | PHILODENDRON | PHILOSOPHISM
PHENGOPHOBIAS | PHENOMENIZED | PHILANDERS | PHILODENDRONS | PHILOSOPHISMS
PHENMETRAZINE | PHENOMENIZES | PHILANTHROPE | PHILOGYNIES | PHILOSOPHIST
PHENMETRAZINES | PHENOMENIZING | PHILANTHROPES | PHILOGYNIST | PHILOSOPHISTIC
PHENOBARBITAL | PHENOMENOLOGIES | PHILANTHROPIC | PHILOGYNISTS | PHILOSOPHISTS
PHENOBARBITALS | PHENOMENOLOGIST | PHILANTHROPICAL | PHILOGYNOUS | PHILOSOPHIZE
PHENOBARBITONE | PHENOMENOLOGY | PHILANTHROPIES | PHILOLOGER | PHILOSOPHIZED
PHENOBARBITONES | PHENOMENON | PHILANTHROPIST | PHILOLOGERS | PHILOSOPHIZER
PHENOCOPIES | PHENOMENONS | PHILANTHROPISTS | PHILOLOGIAN | PHILOSOPHIZERS
PHENOCRYST | PHENOTHIAZINE | PHILANTHROPOID | PHILOLOGIANS | PHILOSOPHIZES
PHENOCRYSTIC | PHENOTHIAZINES | PHILANTHROPOIDS | PHILOLOGIC | PHILOSOPHIZING
PHENOCRYSTS | PHENOTYPED | PHILANTHROPY | PHILOLOGICAL | PHILOSOPHIZINGS
PHENOLATED | PHENOTYPES | PHILATELIC | PHILOLOGICALLY | PHILOSOPHY
PHENOLATES | PHENOTYPIC | PHILATELICALLY | PHILOLOGIES | PHILOXENIA
PHENOLATING | PHENOTYPICAL | PHILATELIES | PHILOLOGIST | PHILOXENIAS
PHENOLOGICAL | PHENOTYPICALLY | PHILATELIST | PHILOLOGISTS | PHILTERING
PHENOLOGICALLY | PHENOTYPING | PHILATELISTS | PHILOLOGUE | PHISNOMIES
PHENOLOGIES | PHENOXIDES | PHILAVERIES | PHILOLOGUES | PHLEBECTOMIES
PHENOLOGIST | PHENTOLAMINE | PHILHARMONIC | PHILOMATHIC | PHLEBECTOMY
PHENOLOGISTS | PHENTOLAMINES | PHILHARMONICS | PHILOMATHICAL | PHLEBITIDES
PHENOLPHTHALEIN | PHENYLALANIN | PHILHELLENE | PHILOMATHIES | PHLEBITISES
PHENOMENAL | PHENYLALANINE | PHILHELLENES | PHILOMATHS | PHLEBOGRAM
PHENOMENALISE | PHENYLALANINES | PHILHELLENIC | PHILOMATHY | PHLEBOGRAMS
PHENOMENALISED | PHENYLALANINS | PHILHELLENISM | PHILOMELAS | PHLEBOGRAPHIC
PHENOMENALISES | PHENYLAMINE | PHILHELLENISMS | PHILOPENAS | PHLEBOGRAPHIES
PHENOMENALISING | PHENYLAMINES | PHILHELLENIST | PHILOPOENA | PHLEBOGRAPHY
PHENOMENALISM | PHENYLBUTAZONE | PHILHELLENISTS | PHILOPOENAS | PHLEBOLITE
PHENOMENALISMS | PHENYLBUTAZONES | PHILHORSES | PHILOSOPHASTER | PHLEBOLITES
PHENOMENALIST | PHENYLENES | PHILIPPICS | PHILOSOPHASTERS | PHLEBOLOGIES
PHENOMENALISTIC | PHENYLEPHRINE | PHILIPPINA | PHILOSOPHE | PHLEBOLOGY
PHENOMENALISTS | PHENYLEPHRINES | PHILIPPINAS | PHILOSOPHER | PHLEBOSCLEROSES
PHENOMENALITIES | PHENYLKETONURIA | PHILIPPINE | PHILOSOPHERESS | PHLEBOSCLEROSIS
PHENOMENALITY | PHENYLKETONURIC | PHILIPPINES | PHILOSOPHERS | PHLEBOTOMIC
PHENOMENALIZE | PHENYLMETHYL | PHILISTIAS | PHILOSOPHES | PHLEBOTOMICAL
PHENOMENALIZED | PHENYLMETHYLS | PHILISTINE | PHILOSOPHESS | PHLEBOTOMIES
PHENOMENALIZES | PHENYLTHIOUREA | PHILISTINES | PHILOSOPHESSES | PHLEBOTOMISE

P

PHLEBOTOMISED	PHONASTHENIAS	PHONETISMS	PHONOPORES	PHOSPHOCREATINE
PHLEBOTOMISES	PHONATHONS	PHONETISTS	PHONOSCOPE	PHOSPHOCREATINS
PHLEBOTOMISING	PHONATIONS	PHONETIZATION	PHONOSCOPES	PHOSPHOKINASE
PHLEBOTOMIST	PHONAUTOGRAPH	PHONETIZATIONS	PHONOTACTIC	PHOSPHOKINASES
PHLEBOTOMISTS	PHONAUTOGRAPHIC	PHONETIZED	PHONOTACTICS	PHOSPHOLIPASE
PHLEBOTOMIZE	PHONAUTOGRAPHS	PHONETIZES	PHONOTYPED	PHOSPHOLIPASES
PHLEBOTOMIZED	PHONECARDS	PHONETIZING	PHONOTYPER	PHOSPHOLIPID
PHLEBOTOMIZES	PHONEMATIC	PHONEYNESS	PHONOTYPERS	PHOSPHOLIPIDS
PHLEBOTOMIZING	PHONEMATICALLY	PHONEYNESSES	PHONOTYPES	PHOSPHONIC
PHLEBOTOMY	PHONEMICALLY	PHONICALLY	PHONOTYPIC	PHOSPHONIUM
PHLEGMAGOGIC	PHONEMICISATION	PHONINESSES	PHONOTYPICAL	PHOSPHONIUMS
PHLEGMAGOGICS	PHONEMICISE	PHONMETERS	PHONOTYPIES	PHOSPHOPROTEIN
PHLEGMAGOGUE	PHONEMICISED	PHONOCAMPTIC	PHONOTYPING	PHOSPHOPROTEINS
PHLEGMAGOGUES	PHONEMICISES	PHONOCAMPTICS	PHONOTYPIST	PHOSPHORATE
PHLEGMASIA	PHONEMICISING	PHONOCARDIOGRAM	PHONOTYPISTS	PHOSPHORATED
PHLEGMASIAS	PHONEMICIST	PHONOCHEMISTRY	PHORMINGES	PHOSPHORATES
PHLEGMATIC	PHONEMICISTS	PHONOFIDDLE	PHOSGENITE	PHOSPHORATING
PHLEGMATICAL	PHONEMICIZATION	PHONOFIDDLES	PHOSGENITES	PHOSPHORES
PHLEGMATICALLY	PHONEMICIZE	PHONOGRAMIC	PHOSPHATASE	PHOSPHORESCE
PHLEGMATICNESS	PHONEMICIZED	PHONOGRAMICALLY	PHOSPHATASES	PHOSPHORESCED
PHLEGMIEST	PHONEMICIZES	PHONOGRAMMIC	PHOSPHATED	PHOSPHORESCENCE
PHLEGMONIC	PHONEMICIZING	PHONOGRAMS	PHOSPHATES	PHOSPHORESCENT
PHLEGMONOID	PHONENDOSCOPE	PHONOGRAPH	PHOSPHATIC	PHOSPHORESCES
PHLEGMONOUS	PHONENDOSCOPES	PHONOGRAPHER	PHOSPHATIDE	PHOSPHORESCING
PHLOGISTIC	PHONETICAL	PHONOGRAPHERS	PHOSPHATIDES	PHOSPHORET
PHLOGISTICATE	PHONETICALLY	PHONOGRAPHIC	PHOSPHATIDIC	PHOSPHORETS
PHLOGISTICATED	PHONETICIAN	PHONOGRAPHIES	PHOSPHATIDYL	PHOSPHORETTED
PHLOGISTICATES	PHONETICIANS	PHONOGRAPHIST	PHOSPHATIDYLS	PHOSPHORIC
PHLOGISTICATING	PHONETICISATION	PHONOGRAPHISTS	PHOSPHATING	PHOSPHORISE
PHLOGISTON	PHONETICISE	PHONOGRAPHS	PHOSPHATISATION	PHOSPHORISED
PHLOGISTONS	PHONETICISED	PHONOGRAPHY	PHOSPHATISE	PHOSPHORISES
PHLOGOPITE	PHONETICISES	PHONOLITES	PHOSPHATISED	PHOSPHORISING
PHLOGOPITES	PHONETICISING	PHONOLITIC	PHOSPHATISES	PHOSPHORISM
PHLORIZINS	PHONETICISM	PHONOLOGIC	PHOSPHATISING	PHOSPHORISMS
PHLYCTAENA	PHONETICISMS	PHONOLOGICAL	PHOSPHATIZATION	PHOSPHORITE
PHLYCTAENAE	PHONETICIST	PHONOLOGICALLY	PHOSPHATIZE	PHOSPHORITES
PHLYCTENAE	PHONETICISTS	PHONOLOGIES	PHOSPHATIZED	PHOSPHORITIC
PHOCOMELIA	PHONETICIZATION	PHONOLOGIST	PHOSPHATIZES	PHOSPHORIZE
PHOCOMELIAS	PHONETICIZE	PHONOLOGISTS	PHOSPHATIZING	PHOSPHORIZED
PHOCOMELIC	PHONETICIZED	PHONOMETER	PHOSPHATURIA	PHOSPHORIZES
PHOCOMELIES	PHONETICIZES	PHONOMETERS	PHOSPHATURIAS	PHOSPHORIZING
PHOENIXISM	PHONETICIZING	PHONOMETRIC	PHOSPHATURIC	PHOSPHOROLYSES
PHOENIXISMS	PHONETISATION	PHONOMETRICAL	PHOSPHENES	PHOSPHOROLYSIS
PHOENIXLIKE	PHONETISATIONS	PHONOPHOBIA	PHOSPHIDES	PHOSPHOROLYTIC
PHOLIDOSES	PHONETISED	PHONOPHOBIAS	PHOSPHINES	PHOSPHOROSCOPE
PHOLIDOSIS	PHONETISES	PHONOPHORE	PHOSPHITES	PHOSPHOROSCOPES
PHONASTHENIA	PHONETISING	PHONOPHORES	PHOSPHOCREATIN	PHOSPHOROUS

PHOSPHORUS
PHOSPHORUSES
PHOSPHORYL
PHOSPHORYLASE
PHOSPHORYLASES
PHOSPHORYLATE
PHOSPHORYLATED
PHOSPHORYLATES
PHOSPHORYLATING
PHOSPHORYLATION
PHOSPHORYLATIVE
PHOSPHORYLS
PHOSPHURET
PHOSPHURETS
PHOSPHURETTED
PHOTICALLY
PHOTOACTINIC
PHOTOACTIVE
PHOTOAUTOTROPH
PHOTOAUTOTROPHS
PHOTOBATHIC
PHOTOBIOLOGIC
PHOTOBIOLOGICAL
PHOTOBIOLOGIES
PHOTOBIOLOGIST
PHOTOBIOLOGISTS
PHOTOBIOLOGY
PHOTOBLOGGED
PHOTOBLOGGING
PHOTOBLOGS
PHOTOBOMBED
PHOTOBOMBING
PHOTOBOMBS
PHOTOCALLS
PHOTOCARDS
PHOTOCATALYSES
PHOTOCATALYSIS
PHOTOCATALYTIC
PHOTOCATHODE
PHOTOCATHODES
PHOTOCELLS
PHOTOCHEMICAL
PHOTOCHEMICALLY
PHOTOCHEMIST
PHOTOCHEMISTRY
PHOTOCHEMISTS
PHOTOCHROMIC

PHOTOCHROMICS
PHOTOCHROMIES
PHOTOCHROMISM
PHOTOCHROMISMS
PHOTOCHROMY
PHOTOCOMPOSE
PHOTOCOMPOSED
PHOTOCOMPOSER
PHOTOCOMPOSERS
PHOTOCOMPOSES
PHOTOCOMPOSING
PHOTOCONDUCTING
PHOTOCONDUCTION
PHOTOCONDUCTIVE
PHOTOCONDUCTOR
PHOTOCONDUCTORS
PHOTOCOPIABLE
PHOTOCOPIED
PHOTOCOPIER
PHOTOCOPIERS
PHOTOCOPIES
PHOTOCOPYING
PHOTOCOPYINGS
PHOTOCURRENT
PHOTOCURRENTS
PHOTODEGRADABLE
PHOTODETECTOR
PHOTODETECTORS
PHOTODIODE
PHOTODIODES
PHOTODISKS
PHOTODISSOCIATE
PHOTODUPLICATE
PHOTODUPLICATED
PHOTODUPLICATES
PHOTODYNAMIC
PHOTODYNAMICS
PHOTOELASTIC
PHOTOELASTICITY
PHOTOELECTRIC
PHOTOELECTRICAL
PHOTOELECTRODE
PHOTOELECTRODES
PHOTOELECTRON
PHOTOELECTRONIC
PHOTOELECTRONS
PHOTOEMISSION

PHOTOEMISSIONS
PHOTOEMISSIVE
PHOTOENGRAVE
PHOTOENGRAVED
PHOTOENGRAVER
PHOTOENGRAVERS
PHOTOENGRAVES
PHOTOENGRAVING
PHOTOENGRAVINGS
PHOTOEXCITATION
PHOTOEXCITED
PHOTOFINISHER
PHOTOFINISHERS
PHOTOFINISHING
PHOTOFINISHINGS
PHOTOFISSION
PHOTOFISSIONS
PHOTOFLASH
PHOTOFLASHES
PHOTOFLOOD
PHOTOFLOODS
PHOTOFLUOROGRAM
PHOTOGELATIN
PHOTOGELATINE
PHOTOGENES
PHOTOGENIC
PHOTOGENICALLY
PHOTOGENIES
PHOTOGEOLOGIC
PHOTOGEOLOGICAL
PHOTOGEOLOGIES
PHOTOGEOLOGIST
PHOTOGEOLOGISTS
PHOTOGEOLOGY
PHOTOGLYPH
PHOTOGLYPHIC
PHOTOGLYPHIES
PHOTOGLYPHS
PHOTOGLYPHY
PHOTOGRAMMETRIC
PHOTOGRAMMETRY
PHOTOGRAMS
PHOTOGRAPH
PHOTOGRAPHED
PHOTOGRAPHER
PHOTOGRAPHERS
PHOTOGRAPHIC

PHOTOGRAPHICAL
PHOTOGRAPHIES
PHOTOGRAPHING
PHOTOGRAPHIST
PHOTOGRAPHISTS
PHOTOGRAPHS
PHOTOGRAPHY
PHOTOGRAVURE
PHOTOGRAVURES
PHOTOINDUCED
PHOTOINDUCTION
PHOTOINDUCTIONS
PHOTOINDUCTIVE
PHOTOIONISATION
PHOTOIONISE
PHOTOIONISED
PHOTOIONISES
PHOTOIONISING
PHOTOIONIZATION
PHOTOIONIZE
PHOTOIONIZED
PHOTOIONIZES
PHOTOIONIZING
PHOTOJOURNALISM
PHOTOJOURNALIST
PHOTOKINESES
PHOTOKINESIS
PHOTOKINETIC
PHOTOLITHO
PHOTOLITHOGRAPH
PHOTOLITHOS
PHOTOLUMINESCE
PHOTOLUMINESCED
PHOTOLUMINESCES
PHOTOLYSABLE
PHOTOLYSED
PHOTOLYSES
PHOTOLYSING
PHOTOLYSIS
PHOTOLYTIC
PHOTOLYTICALLY
PHOTOLYZABLE
PHOTOLYZED
PHOTOLYZES
PHOTOLYZING
PHOTOMACHINE
PHOTOMACHINES

PHOTOMACROGRAPH
PHOTOMAPPED
PHOTOMAPPING
PHOTOMASKS
PHOTOMECHANICAL
PHOTOMETER
PHOTOMETERS
PHOTOMETRIC
PHOTOMETRICALLY
PHOTOMETRIES
PHOTOMETRIST
PHOTOMETRISTS
PHOTOMETRY
PHOTOMICROGRAPH
PHOTOMONTAGE
PHOTOMONTAGES
PHOTOMOSAIC
PHOTOMOSAICS
PHOTOMULTIPLIER
PHOTOMURAL
PHOTOMURALS
PHOTONASTIC
PHOTONASTIES
PHOTONASTY
PHOTONEGATIVE
PHOTONEUTRON
PHOTONEUTRONS
PHOTONOVEL
PHOTONOVELS
PHOTONUCLEAR
PHOTOOXIDATION
PHOTOOXIDATIONS
PHOTOOXIDATIVE
PHOTOOXIDISE
PHOTOOXIDISED
PHOTOOXIDISES
PHOTOOXIDISING
PHOTOOXIDIZE
PHOTOOXIDIZED
PHOTOOXIDIZES
PHOTOOXIDIZING
PHOTOPERIOD
PHOTOPERIODIC
PHOTOPERIODISM
PHOTOPERIODISMS
PHOTOPERIODS
PHOTOPHASE

P

PHOTOPHASES	PHOTOREFRACTIVE	PHOTOTAXIES	PHRAGMOPLASTS	PHRENOLOGIZING
PHOTOPHILIC	PHOTORESIST	PHOTOTAXIS	PHRASELESS	PHRENOLOGY
PHOTOPHILIES	PHOTORESISTS	PHOTOTELEGRAM	PHRASEMAKER	PHRENSICAL
PHOTOPHILOUS	PHOTOSCANNED	PHOTOTELEGRAMS	PHRASEMAKERS	PHRENSYING
PHOTOPHILS	PHOTOSCANNING	PHOTOTELEGRAPH	PHRASEMAKING	PHRONTISTERIES
PHOTOPHILY	PHOTOSCANS	PHOTOTELEGRAPHS	PHRASEMAKINGS	PHRONTISTERY
PHOTOPHOBE	PHOTOSENSITISE	PHOTOTELEGRAPHY	PHRASEMONGER	PHTHALATES
PHOTOPHOBES	PHOTOSENSITISED	PHOTOTHERAPIES	PHRASEMONGERING	PHTHALEINS
PHOTOPHOBIA	PHOTOSENSITISER	PHOTOTHERAPY	PHRASEMONGERS	PHTHALOCYANIN
PHOTOPHOBIAS	PHOTOSENSITISES	PHOTOTHERMAL	PHRASEOGRAM	PHTHALOCYANINE
PHOTOPHOBIC	PHOTOSENSITIVE	PHOTOTHERMALLY	PHRASEOGRAMS	PHTHALOCYANINES
PHOTOPHONE	PHOTOSENSITIZE	PHOTOTHERMIC	PHRASEOGRAPH	PHTHALOCYANINS
PHOTOPHONES	PHOTOSENSITIZED	PHOTOTONIC	PHRASEOGRAPHIC	PHTHIRIASES
PHOTOPHONIC	PHOTOSENSITIZER	PHOTOTONUS	PHRASEOGRAPHIES	PHTHIRIASIS
PHOTOPHONIES	PHOTOSENSITIZES	PHOTOTONUSES	PHRASEOGRAPHS	PHTHISICAL
PHOTOPHONY	PHOTOSENSOR	PHOTOTOPOGRAPHY	PHRASEOGRAPHY	PHTHISICKY
PHOTOPHORE	PHOTOSENSORS	PHOTOTOXIC	PHRASEOLOGIC	PHYCOBILIN
PHOTOPHORES	PHOTOSETTER	PHOTOTOXICITIES	PHRASEOLOGICAL	PHYCOBILINS
PHOTOPHORESES	PHOTOSETTERS	PHOTOTOXICITY	PHRASEOLOGIES	PHYCOBIONT
PHOTOPHORESIS	PHOTOSETTING	PHOTOTRANSISTOR	PHRASEOLOGIST	PHYCOBIONTS
PHOTOPLAYS	PHOTOSETTINGS	PHOTOTROPE	PHRASEOLOGISTS	PHYCOCYANIN
PHOTOPOLYMER	PHOTOSHOOT	PHOTOTROPES	PHRASEOLOGY	PHYCOCYANINS
PHOTOPOLYMERS	PHOTOSHOOTS	PHOTOTROPH	PHREAKINGS	PHYCOCYANS
PHOTOPOSITIVE	PHOTOSHOPPED	PHOTOTROPHIC	PHREATOPHYTE	PHYCOERYTHRIN
PHOTOPRODUCT	PHOTOSHOPPING	PHOTOTROPHS	PHREATOPHYTES	PHYCOERYTHRINS
PHOTOPRODUCTION	PHOTOSHOPS	PHOTOTROPIC	PHREATOPHYTIC	PHYCOLOGICAL
PHOTOPRODUCTS	PHOTOSPHERE	PHOTOTROPICALLY	PHRENESIAC	PHYCOLOGIES
PHOTOPSIAS	PHOTOSPHERES	PHOTOTROPIES	PHRENETICAL	PHYCOLOGIST
PHOTOPSIES	PHOTOSPHERIC	PHOTOTROPISM	PHRENETICALLY	PHYCOLOGISTS
PHOTOREACTION	PHOTOSTATED	PHOTOTROPISMS	PHRENETICNESS	PHYCOMYCETE
PHOTOREACTIONS	PHOTOSTATIC	PHOTOTROPY	PHRENETICNESSES	PHYCOMYCETES
PHOTOREALISM	PHOTOSTATING	PHOTOTUBES	PHRENETICS	PHYCOMYCETOUS
PHOTOREALISMS	PHOTOSTATS	PHOTOTYPED	PHRENITIDES	PHYCOPHAEIN
PHOTOREALIST	PHOTOSTATTED	PHOTOTYPES	PHRENITISES	PHYCOPHAEINS
PHOTOREALISTIC	PHOTOSTATTING	PHOTOTYPESET	PHRENOLOGIC	PHYCOXANTHIN
PHOTOREALISTS	PHOTOSYNTHATE	PHOTOTYPESETS	PHRENOLOGICAL	PHYCOXANTHINS
PHOTORECEPTION	PHOTOSYNTHATES	PHOTOTYPESETTER	PHRENOLOGICALLY	PHYLACTERIC
PHOTORECEPTIONS	PHOTOSYNTHESES	PHOTOTYPIC	PHRENOLOGIES	PHYLACTERICAL
PHOTORECEPTIVE	PHOTOSYNTHESIS	PHOTOTYPICALLY	PHRENOLOGISE	PHYLACTERIES
PHOTORECEPTOR	PHOTOSYNTHESISE	PHOTOTYPIES	PHRENOLOGISED	PHYLACTERY
PHOTORECEPTORS	PHOTOSYNTHESIZE	PHOTOTYPING	PHRENOLOGISES	PHYLARCHIES
PHOTOREDUCE	PHOTOSYNTHETIC	PHOTOTYPOGRAPHY	PHRENOLOGISING	PHYLAXISES
PHOTOREDUCED	PHOTOSYSTEM	PHOTOVOLTAIC	PHRENOLOGIST	PHYLESISES
PHOTOREDUCES	PHOTOSYSTEMS	PHOTOVOLTAICS	PHRENOLOGISTS	PHYLETICALLY
PHOTOREDUCING	PHOTOTACTIC	PHOTOXYLOGRAPHY	PHRENOLOGIZE	PHYLLARIES
PHOTOREDUCTION	PHOTOTACTICALLY	PHOTOZINCOGRAPH	PHRENOLOGIZED	PHYLLOCLAD
PHOTOREDUCTIONS	PHOTOTAXES	PHRAGMOPLAST	PHRENOLOGIZES	PHYLLOCLADE

PHYLLOCLADES	PHYSICALLY	PHYSIOTHERAPY	PHYTONADIONE	PICAYUNISHLY
PHYLLOCLADS	PHYSICALNESS	PHYSITHEISM	PHYTONADIONES	PICAYUNISHNESS
PHYLLODIAL	PHYSICALNESSES	PHYSITHEISMS	PHYTOPATHOGEN	PICCADILLIES
PHYLLODIES	PHYSICIANCIES	PHYSITHEISTIC	PHYTOPATHOGENIC	PICCADILLO
PHYLLODIUM	PHYSICIANCY	PHYSOCLISTOUS	PHYTOPATHOGENS	PICCADILLOES
PHYLLOMANIA	PHYSICIANER	PHYSOSTIGMIN	PHYTOPATHOLOGY	PICCADILLS
PHYLLOMANIAS	PHYSICIANERS	PHYSOSTIGMINE	PHYTOPHAGIC	PICCADILLY
PHYLLOPHAGOUS	PHYSICIANS	PHYSOSTIGMINES	PHYTOPHAGIES	PICCALILLI
PHYLLOPLANE	PHYSICIANSHIP	PHYSOSTIGMINS	PHYTOPHAGOUS	PICCALILLIS
PHYLLOPLANES	PHYSICIANSHIPS	PHYSOSTOMOUS	PHYTOPHAGY	PICCANINNIES
PHYLLOPODS	PHYSICISMS	PHYTOALEXIN	PHYTOPLANKTER	PICCANINNY
PHYLLOQUINONE	PHYSICISTS	PHYTOALEXINS	PHYTOPLANKTERS	PICCOLOIST
PHYLLOQUINONES	PHYSICKING	PHYTOBENTHOS	PHYTOPLANKTON	PICCOLOISTS
PHYLLOSILICATE	PHYSICOCHEMICAL	PHYTOBENTHOSES	PHYTOPLANKTONIC	PICHICIAGO
PHYLLOSILICATES	PHYSIOCRACIES	PHYTOCHEMICAL	PHYTOPLANKTONS	PICHICIAGOS
PHYLLOSPHERE	PHYSIOCRACY	PHYTOCHEMICALLY	PHYTOSANITARY	PICHICIEGO
PHYLLOSPHERES	PHYSIOCRAT	PHYTOCHEMICALS	PHYTOSOCIOLOGY	PICHICIEGOS
PHYLLOTACTIC	PHYSIOCRATIC	PHYTOCHEMIST	PHYTOSTEROL	PICHOLINES
PHYLLOTACTICAL	PHYSIOCRATS	PHYTOCHEMISTRY	PHYTOSTEROLS	PICKABACKED
PHYLLOTAXES	PHYSIOGNOMIC	PHYTOCHEMISTS	PHYTOTHERAPIES	PICKABACKING
PHYLLOTAXIES	PHYSIOGNOMICAL	PHYTOCHROME	PHYTOTHERAPY	PICKABACKS
PHYLLOTAXIS	PHYSIOGNOMIES	PHYTOCHROMES	PHYTOTOMIES	PICKADILLIES
PHYLLOTAXY	PHYSIOGNOMIST	PHYTOESTROGEN	PHYTOTOMIST	PICKADILLO
PHYLLOXERA	PHYSIOGNOMISTS	PHYTOESTROGENS	PHYTOTOMISTS	PICKADILLOES
PHYLLOXERAE	PHYSIOGNOMY	PHYTOFLAGELLATE	PHYTOTOXIC	PICKADILLS
PHYLLOXERAS	PHYSIOGRAPHER	PHYTOGENESES	PHYTOTOXICITIES	PICKADILLY
PHYLOGENESES	PHYSIOGRAPHERS	PHYTOGENESIS	PHYTOTOXICITY	PICKANINNIES
PHYLOGENESIS	PHYSIOGRAPHIC	PHYTOGENETIC	PHYTOTOXIN	PICKANINNY
PHYLOGENETIC	PHYSIOGRAPHICAL	PHYTOGENETICAL	PHYTOTOXINS	PICKAPACKED
PHYLOGENIC	PHYSIOGRAPHIES	PHYTOGENIC	PHYTOTRONS	PICKAPACKING
PHYLOGENIES	PHYSIOGRAPHY	PHYTOGENIES	PIACULARITIES	PICKAPACKS
PHYSALISES	PHYSIOLATER	PHYTOGEOGRAPHER	PIACULARITY	PICKAROONS
PHYSHARMONICA	PHYSIOLATERS	PHYTOGEOGRAPHIC	PIANISSIMI	PICKBACKED
PHYSHARMONICAS	PHYSIOLATRIES	PHYTOGEOGRAPHY	PIANISSIMO	PICKBACKING
PHYSIATRIC	PHYSIOLATRY	PHYTOGRAPHER	PIANISSIMOS	PICKEDNESS
PHYSIATRICAL	PHYSIOLOGIC	PHYTOGRAPHERS	PIANISSISSIMO	PICKEDNESSES
PHYSIATRICS	PHYSIOLOGICAL	PHYTOGRAPHIC	PIANISTICALLY	PICKEERERS
PHYSIATRIES	PHYSIOLOGICALLY	PHYTOGRAPHIES	PIANOFORTE	PICKEERING
PHYSIATRIST	PHYSIOLOGIES	PHYTOGRAPHY	PIANOFORTES	PICKELHAUBE
PHYSIATRISTS	PHYSIOLOGIST	PHYTOHORMONE	PIANOLISTS	PICKELHAUBES
PHYSICALISM	PHYSIOLOGISTS	PHYTOHORMONES	PICADILLOS	PICKERELWEED
PHYSICALISMS	PHYSIOLOGUS	PHYTOLITHS	PICANINNIES	PICKERELWEEDS
PHYSICALIST	PHYSIOLOGUSES	PHYTOLOGICAL	PICARESQUE	PICKETBOAT
PHYSICALISTIC	PHYSIOLOGY	PHYTOLOGICALLY	PICARESQUES	PICKETBOATS
PHYSICALISTS	PHYSIOPATHOLOGY	PHYTOLOGIES	PICAROONED	PICKETINGS
PHYSICALITIES	PHYSIOTHERAPIES	PHYTOLOGIST	PICAROONING	PICKINESSES
PHYSICALITY	PHYSIOTHERAPIST	PHYTOLOGISTS	PICAYUNISH	PICKPOCKET

P

PICKPOCKETS

PICKPOCKETS
PICKTHANKS
PICNICKERS
PICNICKING
PICOCURIES
PICOFARADS
PICOMETERS
PICOMETRES
PICORNAVIRUS
PICORNAVIRUSES
PICOSECOND
PICOSECONDS
PICOWAVING
PICQUETING
PICROCARMINE
PICROCARMINES
PICROTOXIN
PICROTOXINS
PICTARNIES
PICTOGRAMS
PICTOGRAPH
PICTOGRAPHIC
PICTOGRAPHIES
PICTOGRAPHS
PICTOGRAPHY
PICTORIALISE
PICTORIALISED
PICTORIALISES
PICTORIALISING
PICTORIALISM
PICTORIALISMS
PICTORIALIST
PICTORIALISTS
PICTORIALIZE
PICTORIALIZED
PICTORIALIZES
PICTORIALIZING
PICTORIALLY
PICTORIALNESS
PICTORIALNESSES
PICTORIALS
PICTORICAL
PICTORICALLY
PICTUREGOER
PICTUREGOERS
PICTUREPHONE
PICTUREPHONES

PICTURESQUE
PICTURESQUELY
PICTURESQUENESS
PICTURISATION
PICTURISATIONS
PICTURISED
PICTURISES
PICTURISING
PICTURIZATION
PICTURIZATIONS
PICTURIZED
PICTURIZES
PICTURIZING
PIDDLINGLY
PIDGINISATION
PIDGINISATIONS
PIDGINISED
PIDGINISES
PIDGINISING
PIDGINIZATION
PIDGINIZATIONS
PIDGINIZED
PIDGINIZES
PIDGINIZING
PIECEMEALED
PIECEMEALING
PIECEMEALS
PIECEWORKER
PIECEWORKERS
PIECEWORKS
PIEDMONTITE
PIEDMONTITES
PIEDNESSES
PIEMONTITE
PIEMONTITES
PIEPOWDERS
PIERCEABLE
PIERCINGLY
PIERCINGNESS
PIERCINGNESSES
PIERRETTES
PIETISTICAL
PIETISTICALLY
PIEZOCHEMISTRY
PIEZOELECTRIC
PIEZOMAGNETIC
PIEZOMAGNETISM

PIEZOMAGNETISMS
PIEZOMETER
PIEZOMETERS
PIEZOMETRIC
PIEZOMETRICALLY
PIEZOMETRIES
PIEZOMETRY
PIFFERAROS
PIGEONHOLE
PIGEONHOLED
PIGEONHOLER
PIGEONHOLERS
PIGEONHOLES
PIGEONHOLING
PIGEONITES
PIGEONRIES
PIGEONWING
PIGEONWINGS
PIGGINESSES
PIGGISHNESS
PIGGISHNESSES
PIGGYBACKED
PIGGYBACKING
PIGGYBACKS
PIGHEADEDLY
PIGHEADEDNESS
PIGHEADEDNESSES
PIGMENTARY
PIGMENTATION
PIGMENTATIONS
PIGMENTING
PIGMENTOSA
PIGMENTOSAS
PIGNERATED
PIGNERATES
PIGNERATING
PIGNERATION
PIGNERATIONS
PIGNORATED
PIGNORATES
PIGNORATING
PIGNORATION
PIGNORATIONS
PIGSCONCES
PIGSTICKED
PIGSTICKER
PIGSTICKERS

PIGSTICKING
PIGSTICKINGS
PIKEPERCHES
PIKESTAFFS
PIKESTAVES
PILASTERED
PILEORHIZA
PILEORHIZAS
PILFERABLE
PILFERAGES
PILFERINGLY
PILFERINGS
PILFERPROOF
PILGARLICK
PILGARLICKS
PILGARLICKY
PILGARLICS
PILGRIMAGE
PILGRIMAGED
PILGRIMAGER
PILGRIMAGERS
PILGRIMAGES
PILGRIMAGING
PILGRIMERS
PILGRIMING
PILGRIMISE
PILGRIMISED
PILGRIMISES
PILGRIMISING
PILGRIMIZE
PILGRIMIZED
PILGRIMIZES
PILGRIMIZING
PILIFEROUS
PILLAGINGS
PILLARISTS
PILLARLESS
PILLICOCKS
PILLIONING
PILLIONIST
PILLIONISTS
PILLIWINKS
PILLORISED
PILLORISES
PILLORISING
PILLORIZED
PILLORIZES

PILLORIZING
PILLORYING
PILLOWCASE
PILLOWCASES
PILLOWSLIP
PILLOWSLIPS
PILNIEWINKS
PILOCARPIN
PILOCARPINE
PILOCARPINES
PILOCARPINS
PILOSITIES
PILOTFISHES
PILOTHOUSE
PILOTHOUSES
PIMPERNELS
PIMPLINESS
PIMPLINESSES
PIMPMOBILE
PIMPMOBILES
PINACOIDAL
PINACOTHECA
PINACOTHECAE
PINAKOIDAL
PINAKOTHEK
PINAKOTHEKS
PINBALLING
PINCERLIKE
PINCHBECKS
PINCHCOCKS
PINCHCOMMONS
PINCHCOMMONSES
PINCHFISTS
PINCHINGLY
PINCHPENNIES
PINCHPENNY
PINCHPOINT
PINCHPOINTS
PINCUSHION
PINCUSHIONS
PINEALECTOMIES
PINEALECTOMISE
PINEALECTOMISED
PINEALECTOMISES
PINEALECTOMIZE
PINEALECTOMIZED
PINEALECTOMIZES

P

PINEALECTOMY	PINSPOTTERS	PIROUETTERS	PITCHPINES	PIXILLATING
PINEAPPLES	PINSPOTTING	PIROUETTES	PITCHPIPES	PIXILLATION
PINFEATHER	PINSTRIPED	PIROUETTING	PITCHPOLED	PIXILLATIONS
PINFEATHERS	PINSTRIPES	PISCATORIAL	PITCHPOLES	PIXINESSES
PINFOLDING	PINTADERAS	PISCATORIALLY	PITCHPOLING	PIZZICATOS
PINGRASSES	PINTUCKING	PISCATRIXES	PITCHSTONE	PLACABILITIES
PINGUEFIED	PINWHEELED	PISCICOLOUS	PITCHSTONES	PLACABILITY
PINGUEFIES	PINWHEELING	PISCICULTURAL	PITCHWOMAN	PLACABLENESS
PINGUEFYING	PINWRENCHES	PISCICULTURALLY	PITCHWOMEN	PLACABLENESSES
PINGUIDITIES	PIONEERING	PISCICULTURE	PITEOUSNESS	PLACARDING
PINGUIDITY	PIOUSNESSES	PISCICULTURES	PITEOUSNESSES	PLACATINGLY
PINGUITUDE	PIPECLAYED	PISCICULTURIST	PITHECANTHROPI	PLACATIONS
PINGUITUDES	PIPECLAYING	PISCICULTURISTS	PITHECANTHROPUS	PLACEHOLDER
PINHEADEDNESS	PIPEFISHES	PISCIFAUNA	PITHECOIDS	PLACEHOLDERS
PINHEADEDNESSES	PIPEFITTER	PISCIFAUNAE	PITHINESSES	PLACEKICKED
PINHOOKERS	PIPEFITTERS	PISCIFAUNAS	PITIABLENESS	PLACEKICKER
PINKERTONS	PIPEFITTING	PISCIVORES	PITIABLENESSES	PLACEKICKERS
PINKINESSES	PIPEFITTINGS	PISCIVOROUS	PITIFULLER	PLACEKICKING
PINKISHNESS	PIPELINING	PISSASPHALT	PITIFULLEST	PLACEKICKS
PINKISHNESSES	PIPELININGS	PISSASPHALTS	PITIFULNESS	PLACELESSLY
PINKNESSES	PIPERACEOUS	PISTACHIOS	PITIFULNESSES	PLACEMENTS
PINNACLING	PIPERAZINE	PISTAREENS	PITILESSLY	PLACENTALS
PINNATIFID	PIPERAZINES	PISTILLARY	PITILESSNESS	PLACENTATE
PINNATIFIDLY	PIPERIDINE	PISTILLATE	PITILESSNESSES	PLACENTATION
PINNATIONS	PIPERIDINES	PISTILLODE	PITTOSPORUM	PLACENTATIONS
PINNATIPARTITE	PIPERONALS	PISTILLODES	PITTOSPORUMS	PLACENTIFORM
PINNATIPED	PIPESTONES	PISTOLEERS	PITUITARIES	PLACENTOLOGIES
PINNATISECT	PIPINESSES	PISTOLEROS	PITUITRINS	PLACENTOLOGY
PINNIEWINKLE	PIPISTRELLE	PISTOLIERS	PITYRIASES	PLACIDITIES
PINNIEWINKLES	PIPISTRELLES	PISTOLLING	PITYRIASIS	PLACIDNESS
PINNIPEDES	PIPISTRELS	PITAPATTED	PITYROSPORUM	PLACIDNESSES
PINNIPEDIAN	PIPIWHARAUROA	PITAPATTING	PITYROSPORUMS	PLACODERMS
PINNIPEDIANS	PIPIWHARAUROAS	PITCHBENDS	PIWAKAWAKA	PLAGIARIES
PINNULATED	PIPSISSEWA	PITCHBLENDE	PIWAKAWAKAS	PLAGIARISE
PINNYWINKLE	PIPSISSEWAS	PITCHBLENDES	PIXELATING	PLAGIARISED
PINNYWINKLES	PIPSQUEAKS	PITCHERFUL	PIXELATION	PLAGIARISER
PINOCYTOSES	PIQUANCIES	PITCHERFULS	PIXELATIONS	PLAGIARISERS
PINOCYTOSIS	PIQUANTNESS	PITCHERSFUL	PIXELLATED	PLAGIARISES
PINOCYTOTIC	PIQUANTNESSES	PITCHFORKED	PIXELLATES	PLAGIARISING
PINOCYTOTICALLY	PIRACETAMS	PITCHFORKING	PIXELLATING	PLAGIARISM
PINPOINTED	PIRATICALLY	PITCHFORKS	PIXELLATION	PLAGIARISMS
PINPOINTING	PIRLICUING	PITCHINESS	PIXELLATIONS	PLAGIARIST
PINPRICKED	PIROPLASMA	PITCHINESSES	PIXILATING	PLAGIARISTIC
PINPRICKING	PIROPLASMATA	PITCHOMETER	PIXILATION	PLAGIARISTS
PINSETTERS	PIROPLASMS	PITCHOMETERS	PIXILATIONS	PLAGIARIZE
PINSPOTTED	PIROUETTED	PITCHPERSON	PIXILLATED	PLAGIARIZED
PINSPOTTER	PIROUETTER	PITCHPERSONS	PIXILLATES	PLAGIARIZER

P

PLAGIARIZERS

PLAGIARIZERS	PLANETARIA	PLANOMETER	PLASMOLYZED	PLASTINATION
PLAGIARIZES	PLANETARIES	PLANOMETERS	PLASMOLYZES	PLASTINATIONS
PLAGIARIZING	PLANETARIUM	PLANOMETRIC	PLASMOLYZING	PLASTIQUES
PLAGIOCEPHALIES	PLANETARIUMS	PLANOMETRICALLY	PLASMOSOMA	PLASTISOLS
PLAGIOCEPHALY	PLANETESIMAL	PLANOMETRIES	PLASMOSOMATA	PLASTOCYANIN
PLAGIOCLASE	PLANETESIMALS	PLANOMETRY	PLASMOSOME	PLASTOCYANINS
PLAGIOCLASES	PLANETICAL	PLANTAGINACEOUS	PLASMOSOMES	PLASTOGAMIES
PLAGIOCLASTIC	PLANETLIKE	PLANTATION	PLASTERBOARD	PLASTOGAMY
PLAGIOCLIMAX	PLANETOIDAL	PLANTATIONS	PLASTERBOARDS	PLASTOMETER
PLAGIOCLIMAXES	PLANETOIDS	PLANTIGRADE	PLASTERERS	PLASTOMETERS
PLAGIOSTOMATOUS	PLANETOLOGICAL	PLANTIGRADES	PLASTERINESS	PLASTOMETRIC
PLAGIOSTOME	PLANETOLOGIES	PLANTLINGS	PLASTERINESSES	PLASTOMETRIES
PLAGIOSTOMES	PLANETOLOGIST	PLANTOCRACIES	PLASTERING	PLASTOMETRY
PLAGIOSTOMOUS	PLANETOLOGISTS	PLANTOCRACY	PLASTERINGS	PLASTOQUINONE
PLAGIOTROPIC	PLANETOLOGY	PLANTSWOMAN	PLASTERSTONE	PLASTOQUINONES
PLAGIOTROPISM	PLANETWIDE	PLANTSWOMEN	PLASTERSTONES	PLATANACEOUS
PLAGIOTROPISMS	PLANGENCIES	PLANULIFORM	PLASTERWORK	PLATEAUING
PLAGIOTROPOUS	PLANGENTLY	PLAQUETTES	PLASTERWORKS	PLATEGLASS
PLAGUESOME	PLANIGRAMS	PLASMAGELS	PLASTICALLY	PLATELAYER
PLAINCHANT	PLANIGRAPH	PLASMAGENE	PLASTICATED	PLATELAYERS
PLAINCHANTS	PLANIGRAPHIES	PLASMAGENES	PLASTICENE	PLATEMAKER
PLAINCLOTHES	PLANIGRAPHS	PLASMAGENIC	PLASTICENES	PLATEMAKERS
PLAINCLOTHESMAN	PLANIGRAPHY	PLASMALEMMA	PLASTICINE	PLATEMAKING
PLAINCLOTHESMEN	PLANIMETER	PLASMALEMMAS	PLASTICINES	PLATEMAKINGS
PLAINNESSES	PLANIMETERS	PLASMAPHERESES	PLASTICISATION	PLATEMARKED
PLAINSONGS	PLANIMETRIC	PLASMAPHERESIS	PLASTICISATIONS	PLATEMARKING
PLAINSPOKEN	PLANIMETRICAL	PLASMASOLS	PLASTICISE	PLATEMARKS
PLAINSPOKENNESS	PLANIMETRICALLY	PLASMATICAL	PLASTICISED	PLATERESQUE
PLAINSTANES	PLANIMETRIES	PLASMINOGEN	PLASTICISER	PLATFORMED
PLAINSTONES	PLANIMETRY	PLASMINOGENS	PLASTICISERS	PLATFORMING
PLAINTEXTS	PLANISHERS	PLASMODESM	PLASTICISES	PLATFORMINGS
PLAINTIFFS	PLANISHING	PLASMODESMA	PLASTICISING	PLATINIFEROUS
PLAINTIVELY	PLANISPHERE	PLASMODESMAS	PLASTICITIES	PLATINIRIDIUM
PLAINTIVENESS	PLANISPHERES	PLASMODESMATA	PLASTICITY	PLATINIRIDIUMS
PLAINTIVENESSES	PLANISPHERIC	PLASMODESMS	PLASTICIZATION	PLATINISATION
PLAINTLESS	PLANKTONIC	PLASMODIAL	PLASTICIZATIONS	PLATINISATIONS
PLAINWORKS	PLANLESSLY	PLASMODIUM	PLASTICIZE	PLATINISED
PLAISTERED	PLANLESSNESS	PLASMOGAMIES	PLASTICIZED	PLATINISES
PLAISTERING	PLANLESSNESSES	PLASMOGAMY	PLASTICIZER	PLATINISING
PLANARIANS	PLANOBLAST	PLASMOLYSE	PLASTICIZERS	PLATINIZATION
PLANARITIES	PLANOBLASTS	PLASMOLYSED	PLASTICIZES	PLATINIZATIONS
PLANATIONS	PLANOGAMETE	PLASMOLYSES	PLASTICIZING	PLATINIZED
PLANCHETTE	PLANOGAMETES	PLASMOLYSING	PLASTIDIAL	PLATINIZES
PLANCHETTES	PLANOGRAMS	PLASMOLYSIS	PLASTIDULE	PLATINIZING
PLANELOADS	PLANOGRAPHIC	PLASMOLYTIC	PLASTIDULES	PLATINOCYANIC
PLANENESSES	PLANOGRAPHIES	PLASMOLYTICALLY	PLASTILINA	PLATINOCYANIDE
PLANESIDES	PLANOGRAPHY	PLASMOLYZE	PLASTILINAS	PLATINOCYANIDES

PLATINOIDS	PLAYACTING	PLEASUREFUL	PLENIPOTENCE	PLESIOSAURS
PLATINOTYPE	PLAYACTINGS	PLEASURELESS	PLENIPOTENCES	PLESSIMETER
PLATINOTYPES	PLAYACTORS	PLEASURERS	PLENIPOTENCIES	PLESSIMETERS
PLATITUDES	PLAYBUSSES	PLEASURING	PLENIPOTENCY	PLESSIMETRIC
PLATITUDINAL	PLAYDOUGHS	PLEBEIANISE	PLENIPOTENT	PLESSIMETRIES
PLATITUDINARIAN	PLAYFELLOW	PLEBEIANISED	PLENIPOTENTIAL	PLESSIMETRY
PLATITUDINISE	PLAYFELLOWS	PLEBEIANISES	PLENIPOTENTIARY	PLETHORICAL
PLATITUDINISED	PLAYFIELDS	PLEBEIANISING	PLENISHERS	PLETHORICALLY
PLATITUDINISER	PLAYFULNESS	PLEBEIANISM	PLENISHING	PLETHYSMOGRAM
PLATITUDINISERS	PLAYFULNESSES	PLEBEIANISMS	PLENISHINGS	PLETHYSMOGRAMS
PLATITUDINISES	PLAYGOINGS	PLEBEIANIZE	PLENISHMENT	PLETHYSMOGRAPH
PLATITUDINISING	PLAYGROUND	PLEBEIANIZED	PLENISHMENTS	PLETHYSMOGRAPHS
PLATITUDINIZE	PLAYGROUNDS	PLEBEIANIZES	PLENITUDES	PLETHYSMOGRAPHY
PLATITUDINIZED	PLAYGROUPS	PLEBEIANIZING	PLENITUDINOUS	PLEURAPOPHYSES
PLATITUDINIZER	PLAYHOUSES	PLEBEIANLY	PLENTEOUSLY	PLEURAPOPHYSIS
PLATITUDINIZERS	PLAYLEADER	PLEBIFICATION	PLENTEOUSNESS	PLEURISIES
PLATITUDINIZES	PLAYLEADERS	PLEBIFICATIONS	PLENTEOUSNESSES	PLEURITICAL
PLATITUDINIZING	PLAYLISTED	PLEBIFYING	PLENTIFULLY	PLEURITICS
PLATITUDINOUS	PLAYLISTING	PLEBISCITARY	PLENTIFULNESS	PLEURITISES
PLATITUDINOUSLY	PLAYMAKERS	PLEBISCITE	PLENTIFULNESSES	PLEUROCARPOUS
PLATONICALLY	PLAYMAKING	PLEBISCITES	PLENTITUDE	PLEUROCENTESES
PLATONISMS	PLAYMAKINGS	PLECOPTERAN	PLENTITUDES	PLEUROCENTESIS
PLATOONING	PLAYSCHOOL	PLECOPTERANS	PLEOCHROIC	PLEURODONT
PLATTELAND	PLAYSCHOOLS	PLECOPTEROUS	PLEOCHROISM	PLEURODONTS
PLATTELANDS	PLAYTHINGS	PLECTOGNATH	PLEOCHROISMS	PLEURODYNIA
PLATTERFUL	PLAYWRIGHT	PLECTOGNATHIC	PLEOMORPHIC	PLEURODYNIAS
PLATTERFULS	PLAYWRIGHTING	PLECTOGNATHOUS	PLEOMORPHIES	PLEURONIAS
PLATTERSFUL	PLAYWRIGHTINGS	PLECTOGNATHS	PLEOMORPHISM	PLEUROPNEUMONIA
PLATYCEPHALIC	PLAYWRIGHTS	PLECTOPTEROUS	PLEOMORPHISMS	PLEUROTOMIES
PLATYCEPHALOUS	PLAYWRITING	PLEDGEABLE	PLEOMORPHOUS	PLEUROTOMY
PLATYFISHES	PLAYWRITINGS	PLEINAIRISM	PLEOMORPHY	PLEUSTONIC
PLATYHELMINTH	PLEADINGLY	PLEINAIRISMS	PLEONASTES	PLEXIGLASS
PLATYHELMINTHIC	PLEASANCES	PLEINAIRIST	PLEONASTIC	PLEXIGLASSES
PLATYHELMINTHS	PLEASANTER	PLEINAIRISTS	PLEONASTICAL	PLEXIMETER
PLATYKURTIC	PLEASANTEST	PLEIOCHASIA	PLEONASTICALLY	PLEXIMETERS
PLATYPUSES	PLEASANTLY	PLEIOCHASIUM	PLEONECTIC	PLEXIMETRIC
PLATYRRHINE	PLEASANTNESS	PLEIOMERIES	PLEONEXIAS	PLEXIMETRIES
PLATYRRHINES	PLEASANTNESSES	PLEIOMEROUS	PLEROCERCOID	PLEXIMETRY
PLATYRRHINIAN	PLEASANTRIES	PLEIOTAXIES	PLEROCERCOIDS	PLIABILITIES
PLATYRRHINIANS	PLEASANTRY	PLEIOTROPIC	PLEROMATIC	PLIABILITY
PLAUDITORY	PLEASINGLY	PLEIOTROPIES	PLEROPHORIA	PLIABLENESS
PLAUSIBILITIES	PLEASINGNESS	PLEIOTROPISM	PLEROPHORIAS	PLIABLENESSES
PLAUSIBILITY	PLEASINGNESSES	PLEIOTROPISMS	PLEROPHORIES	PLIANTNESS
PLAUSIBLENESS	PLEASURABILITY	PLEIOTROPY	PLEROPHORY	PLIANTNESSES
PLAUSIBLENESSES	PLEASURABLE	PLENARTIES	PLESIOSAUR	PLICATENESS
PLAYABILITIES	PLEASURABLENESS	PLENILUNAR	PLESIOSAURIAN	PLICATENESSES
PLAYABILITY	PLEASURABLY	PLENILUNES	PLESIOSAURIANS	PLICATIONS

PLICATURES	PLUMBIFEROUS	PLURIPRESENCE	PNEUMATOMETERS	POCKETFULS
PLODDINGLY	PLUMBISOLVENCY	PLURIPRESENCES	PNEUMATOMETRIES	POCKETKNIFE
PLODDINGNESS	PLUMBISOLVENT	PLURISERIAL	PNEUMATOMETRY	POCKETKNIVES
PLODDINGNESSES	PLUMBNESSES	PLURISERIATE	PNEUMATOPHORE	POCKETLESS
PLOTLESSNESS	PLUMBOSOLVENCY	PLUSHINESS	PNEUMATOPHORES	POCKETPHONE
PLOTLESSNESSES	PLUMBOSOLVENT	PLUSHINESSES	PNEUMECTOMIES	POCKETPHONES
PLOTTERING	PLUMDAMASES	PLUSHNESSES	PNEUMECTOMY	POCKETSFUL
PLOTTINGLY	PLUMIGEROUS	PLUTOCRACIES	PNEUMOBACILLI	POCKMANKIES
PLOUGHABLE	PLUMMETING	PLUTOCRACY	PNEUMOBACILLUS	POCKMANTIE
PLOUGHBACK	PLUMOSITIES	PLUTOCRATIC	PNEUMOCOCCAL	POCKMANTIES
PLOUGHBACKS	PLUMPENING	PLUTOCRATICAL	PNEUMOCOCCI	POCKMARKED
PLOUGHBOYS	PLUMPNESSES	PLUTOCRATICALLY	PNEUMOCOCCUS	POCKMARKING
PLOUGHGATE	PLUMULACEOUS	PLUTOCRATS	PNEUMOCONIOSES	POCKPITTED
PLOUGHGATES	PLUMULARIAN	PLUTOLATRIES	PNEUMOCONIOSIS	POCOCURANTE
PLOUGHHEAD	PLUMULARIANS	PLUTOLATRY	PNEUMOCONIOTIC	POCOCURANTEISM
PLOUGHHEADS	PLUNDERABLE	PLUTOLOGIES	PNEUMOCONIOTICS	POCOCURANTEISMS
PLOUGHINGS	PLUNDERAGE	PLUTOLOGIST	PNEUMOCYSTIS	POCOCURANTES
PLOUGHLAND	PLUNDERAGES	PLUTOLOGISTS	PNEUMOCYSTISES	POCOCURANTISM
PLOUGHLANDS	PLUNDERERS	PLUTONISMS	PNEUMODYNAMICS	POCOCURANTISMS
PLOUGHMANSHIP	PLUNDERING	PLUTONIUMS	PNEUMOGASTRIC	POCOCURANTIST
PLOUGHMANSHIPS	PLUNDEROUS	PLUTONOMIES	PNEUMOGASTRICS	POCOCURANTISTS
PLOUGHSHARE	PLUPERFECT	PLUTONOMIST	PNEUMOGRAM	POCULIFORM
PLOUGHSHARES	PLUPERFECTS	PLUTONOMISTS	PNEUMOGRAMS	PODAGRICAL
PLOUGHSTAFF	PLURALISATION	PLUVIOMETER	PNEUMOGRAPH	PODARGUSES
PLOUGHSTAFFS	PLURALISATIONS	PLUVIOMETERS	PNEUMOGRAPHS	PODCASTERS
PLOUGHTAIL	PLURALISED	PLUVIOMETRIC	PNEUMOKONIOSES	PODCASTING
PLOUGHTAILS	PLURALISER	PLUVIOMETRICAL	PNEUMOKONIOSIS	PODCASTINGS
PLOUGHWISE	PLURALISERS	PLUVIOMETRIES	PNEUMONECTOMIES	PODGINESSES
PLOUGHWRIGHT	PLURALISES	PLUVIOMETRY	PNEUMONECTOMY	PODIATRIES
PLOUGHWRIGHTS	PLURALISING	PLYOMETRIC	PNEUMONIAS	PODIATRIST
PLOUTERING	PLURALISMS	PLYOMETRICS	PNEUMONICS	PODIATRISTS
PLOWMANSHIP	PLURALISTIC	PNEUMATHODE	PNEUMONITIS	PODOCONIOSES
PLOWMANSHIPS	PLURALISTICALLY	PNEUMATHODES	PNEUMONITISES	PODOCONIOSIS
PLOWSHARES	PLURALISTS	PNEUMATICAL	PNEUMONOLOGIES	PODOLOGIES
PLOWSTAFFS	PLURALITIES	PNEUMATICALLY	PNEUMONOLOGIST	PODOLOGIST
PLOWTERING	PLURALIZATION	PNEUMATICITIES	PNEUMONOLOGISTS	PODOLOGISTS
PLOWWRIGHT	PLURALIZATIONS	PNEUMATICITY	PNEUMONOLOGY	PODOPHTHALMOUS
PLOWWRIGHTS	PLURALIZED	PNEUMATICS	PNEUMOTHORACES	PODOPHYLIN
PLUCKINESS	PLURALIZER	PNEUMATOLOGICAL	PNEUMOTHORAX	PODOPHYLINS
PLUCKINESSES	PLURALIZERS	PNEUMATOLOGIES	PNEUMOTHORAXES	PODOPHYLLI
PLUGBOARDS	PLURALIZES	PNEUMATOLOGIST	POACHINESS	PODOPHYLLIN
PLUGUGLIES	PLURALIZING	PNEUMATOLOGISTS	POACHINESSES	PODOPHYLLINS
PLUMASSIER	PLURILITERAL	PNEUMATOLOGY	POCKETABLE	PODOPHYLLUM
PLUMASSIERS	PLURILOCULAR	PNEUMATOLYSES	POCKETBIKE	PODOPHYLLUMS
PLUMBAGINACEOUS	PLURIPARAE	PNEUMATOLYSIS	POCKETBIKES	PODOSPHERE
PLUMBAGINOUS	PLURIPARAS	PNEUMATOLYTIC	POCKETBOOK	PODOSPHERES
PLUMBERIES	PLURIPOTENT	PNEUMATOMETER	POCKETBOOKS	PODSOLISATION

P

PODSOLISATIONS	POIGNANCIES	POLARIMETRY	POLICYMAKERS	POLITIQUES
PODSOLISED	POIGNANTLY	POLARISABILITY	POLIOMYELITIDES	POLLARDING
PODSOLISES	POIKILITIC	POLARISABLE	POLIOMYELITIS	POLLENATED
PODSOLISING	POIKILOCYTE	POLARISATION	POLIOMYELITISES	POLLENATES
PODSOLIZATION	POIKILOCYTES	POLARISATIONS	POLIORCETIC	POLLENATING
PODSOLIZATIONS	POIKILOTHERM	POLARISCOPE	POLIORCETICS	POLLENIFEROUS
PODSOLIZED	POIKILOTHERMAL	POLARISCOPES	POLIOVIRUS	POLLENISER
PODSOLIZES	POIKILOTHERMIC	POLARISCOPIC	POLIOVIRUSES	POLLENISERS
PODSOLIZING	POIKILOTHERMIES	POLARISERS	POLISHABLE	POLLENIZER
PODZOLISATION	POIKILOTHERMISM	POLARISING	POLISHINGS	POLLENIZERS
PODZOLISATIONS	POIKILOTHERMS	POLARITIES	POLISHMENT	POLLENOSES
PODZOLISED	POIKILOTHERMY	POLARIZABILITY	POLISHMENTS	POLLENOSIS
PODZOLISES	POINCIANAS	POLARIZABLE	POLITBUROS	POLLICITATION
PODZOLISING	POINSETTIA	POLARIZATION	POLITENESS	POLLICITATIONS
PODZOLIZATION	POINSETTIAS	POLARIZATIONS	POLITENESSES	POLLINATED
PODZOLIZATIONS	POINTEDNESS	POLARIZERS	POLITESSES	POLLINATES
PODZOLIZED	POINTEDNESSES	POLARIZING	POLITICALISE	POLLINATING
PODZOLIZES	POINTELLES	POLAROGRAM	POLITICALISED	POLLINATION
PODZOLIZING	POINTILLES	POLAROGRAMS	POLITICALISES	POLLINATIONS
POENOLOGIES	POINTILLISM	POLAROGRAPH	POLITICALISING	POLLINATOR
POETASTERIES	POINTILLISME	POLAROGRAPHIC	POLITICALIZE	POLLINATORS
POETASTERING	POINTILLISMES	POLAROGRAPHIES	POLITICALIZED	POLLINIFEROUS
POETASTERINGS	POINTILLISMS	POLAROGRAPHS	POLITICALIZES	POLLINISED
POETASTERS	POINTILLIST	POLAROGRAPHY	POLITICALIZING	POLLINISER
POETASTERY	POINTILLISTE	POLEMARCHS	POLITICALLY	POLLINISERS
POETASTRIES	POINTILLISTES	POLEMICALLY	POLITICASTER	POLLINISES
POETICALLY	POINTILLISTIC	POLEMICISE	POLITICASTERS	POLLINISING
POETICALNESS	POINTILLISTS	POLEMICISED	POLITICIAN	POLLINIZED
POETICALNESSES	POINTLESSLY	POLEMICISES	POLITICIANS	POLLINIZER
POETICISED	POINTLESSNESS	POLEMICISING	POLITICISATION	POLLINIZERS
POETICISES	POINTLESSNESSES	POLEMICIST	POLITICISATIONS	POLLINIZES
POETICISING	POISONABLE	POLEMICISTS	POLITICISE	POLLINIZING
POETICISMS	POISONINGS	POLEMICIZE	POLITICISED	POLLINOSES
POETICIZED	POISONOUSLY	POLEMICIZED	POLITICISES	POLLINOSIS
POETICIZES	POISONOUSNESS	POLEMICIZES	POLITICISING	POLLTAKERS
POETICIZING	POISONOUSNESSES	POLEMICIZING	POLITICIZATION	POLLUCITES
POETICULES	POISONWOOD	POLEMISING	POLITICIZATIONS	POLLUSIONS
POETRESSES	POISONWOODS	POLEMIZING	POLITICIZE	POLLUTANTS
POGONOPHORAN	POKEBERRIES	POLEMONIACEOUS	POLITICIZED	POLLUTEDLY
POGONOPHORANS	POKELOGANS	POLEMONIUM	POLITICIZES	POLLUTEDNESS
POGONOTOMIES	POKERISHLY	POLEMONIUMS	POLITICIZING	POLLUTEDNESSES
POGONOTOMY	POKERWORKS	POLIANITES	POLITICKED	POLLUTIONS
POGROMISTS	POKINESSES	POLICEWOMAN	POLITICKER	POLLYANNAISH
POHUTUKAWA	POLARIMETER	POLICEWOMEN	POLITICKERS	POLLYANNAISM
POHUTUKAWAS	POLARIMETERS	POLICYHOLDER	POLITICKING	POLLYANNAISMS
POIGNADOES	POLARIMETRIC	POLICYHOLDERS	POLITICKINGS	POLLYANNAS
POIGNANCES	POLARIMETRIES	POLICYMAKER	POLITICOES	POLLYANNISH

POLONAISES	POLYCENTRICS	POLYCULTURES	POLYGAMIZING	POLYHEDRON
POLONISING	POLYCENTRISM	POLYCYCLIC	POLYGAMOUS	POLYHEDRONS
POLONIZING	POLYCENTRISMS	POLYCYCLICS	POLYGAMOUSLY	POLYHEDROSES
POLTERGEIST	POLYCHAETE	POLYCYSTIC	POLYGENESES	POLYHEDROSIS
POLTERGEISTS	POLYCHAETES	POLYCYTHAEMIA	POLYGENESIS	POLYHISTOR
POLTROONERIES	POLYCHAETOUS	POLYCYTHAEMIAS	POLYGENETIC	POLYHISTORIAN
POLTROONERY	POLYCHASIA	POLYCYTHEMIA	POLYGENETICALLY	POLYHISTORIANS
POLVERINES	POLYCHASIUM	POLYCYTHEMIAS	POLYGENIES	POLYHISTORIC
POLYACRYLAMIDE	POLYCHETES	POLYCYTHEMIC	POLYGENISM	POLYHISTORIES
POLYACRYLAMIDES	POLYCHETOUS	POLYDACTYL	POLYGENISMS	POLYHISTORS
POLYACTINAL	POLYCHLORINATED	POLYDACTYLIES	POLYGENIST	POLYHISTORY
POLYACTINE	POLYCHLOROPRENE	POLYDACTYLISM	POLYGENISTS	POLYHYBRID
POLYACTINES	POLYCHOTOMIES	POLYDACTYLISMS	POLYGENOUS	POLYHYBRIDS
POLYADELPHOUS	POLYCHOTOMOUS	POLYDACTYLOUS	POLYGLOTISM	POLYHYDRIC
POLYALCOHOL	POLYCHOTOMY	POLYDACTYLS	POLYGLOTISMS	POLYHYDROXY
POLYALCOHOLS	POLYCHREST	POLYDACTYLY	POLYGLOTTAL	POLYIMIDES
POLYAMIDES	POLYCHRESTS	POLYDAEMONISM	POLYGLOTTIC	POLYISOPRENE
POLYAMINES	POLYCHROIC	POLYDAEMONISMS	POLYGLOTTISM	POLYISOPRENES
POLYAMORIES	POLYCHROISM	POLYDEMONISM	POLYGLOTTISMS	POLYLEMMAS
POLYAMOROUS	POLYCHROISMS	POLYDEMONISMS	POLYGLOTTOUS	POLYLYSINE
POLYANDRIES	POLYCHROMATIC	POLYDIPSIA	POLYGLOTTS	POLYLYSINES
POLYANDROUS	POLYCHROMATISM	POLYDIPSIAS	POLYGONACEOUS	POLYMASTIA
POLYANTHAS	POLYCHROMATISMS	POLYDIPSIC	POLYGONALLY	POLYMASTIAS
POLYANTHUS	POLYCHROME	POLYDISPERSE	POLYGONATUM	POLYMASTIC
POLYANTHUSES	POLYCHROMED	POLYDISPERSITY	POLYGONATUMS	POLYMASTICS
POLYARCHIES	POLYCHROMES	POLYELECTROLYTE	POLYGONIES	POLYMASTIES
POLYARTHRITIDES	POLYCHROMIC	POLYEMBRYONATE	POLYGONUMS	POLYMASTISM
POLYARTHRITIS	POLYCHROMIES	POLYEMBRYONIC	POLYGRAPHED	POLYMASTISMS
POLYARTHRITISES	POLYCHROMING	POLYEMBRYONIES	POLYGRAPHER	POLYMATHIC
POLYATOMIC	POLYCHROMOUS	POLYEMBRYONY	POLYGRAPHERS	POLYMATHIES
POLYAXIALS	POLYCHROMY	POLYESTERS	POLYGRAPHIC	POLYMERASE
POLYAXONIC	POLYCISTRONIC	POLYESTROUS	POLYGRAPHICALLY	POLYMERASES
POLYBAGGED	POLYCLINIC	POLYETHENE	POLYGRAPHIES	POLYMERIDE
POLYBAGGING	POLYCLINICS	POLYETHENES	POLYGRAPHING	POLYMERIDES
POLYBASITE	POLYCLONAL	POLYETHYLENE	POLYGRAPHIST	POLYMERIES
POLYBASITES	POLYCLONALS	POLYETHYLENES	POLYGRAPHISTS	POLYMERISATION
POLYBUTADIENE	POLYCOTTON	POLYGALACEOUS	POLYGRAPHS	POLYMERISATIONS
POLYBUTADIENES	POLYCOTTONS	POLYGAMIES	POLYGRAPHY	POLYMERISE
POLYCARBONATE	POLYCOTYLEDON	POLYGAMISE	POLYGYNIAN	POLYMERISED
POLYCARBONATES	POLYCOTYLEDONS	POLYGAMISED	POLYGYNIES	POLYMERISES
POLYCARBOXYLATE	POLYCROTIC	POLYGAMISES	POLYGYNIST	POLYMERISING
POLYCARBOXYLIC	POLYCROTISM	POLYGAMISING	POLYGYNISTS	POLYMERISM
POLYCARPELLARY	POLYCROTISMS	POLYGAMIST	POLYGYNOUS	POLYMERISMS
POLYCARPIC	POLYCRYSTAL	POLYGAMISTS	POLYHALITE	POLYMERIZATION
POLYCARPIES	POLYCRYSTALLINE	POLYGAMIZE	POLYHALITES	POLYMERIZATIONS
POLYCARPOUS	POLYCRYSTALS	POLYGAMIZED	POLYHEDRAL	POLYMERIZE
POLYCENTRIC	POLYCULTURE	POLYGAMIZES	POLYHEDRIC	POLYMERIZED

POLYMERIZES	POLYPHONES	POLYSORBATES	POLYTONALITIES	POMPELMOUSE
POLYMERIZING	POLYPHONIC	POLYSTICHOUS	POLYTONALITY	POMPELMOUSES
POLYMEROUS	POLYPHONICALLY	POLYSTYLAR	POLYTONALLY	POMPHOLYGOUS
POLYMORPHIC	POLYPHONIES	POLYSTYLES	POLYTROPHIC	POMPHOLYXES
POLYMORPHICALLY	POLYPHONIST	POLYSTYRENE	POLYTUNNEL	POMPOSITIES
POLYMORPHISM	POLYPHONISTS	POLYSTYRENES	POLYTUNNELS	POMPOUSNESS
POLYMORPHISMS	POLYPHONOUS	POLYSULFIDE	POLYTYPICAL	POMPOUSNESSES
POLYMORPHOUS	POLYPHONOUSLY	POLYSULFIDES	POLYTYPING	PONDERABILITIES
POLYMORPHOUSLY	POLYPHOSPHORIC	POLYSULPHIDE	POLYUNSATURATE	PONDERABILITY
POLYMORPHS	POLYPHYLETIC	POLYSULPHIDES	POLYUNSATURATED	PONDERABLE
POLYMYOSITIS	POLYPHYLLOUS	POLYSYLLABIC	POLYUNSATURATES	PONDERABLES
POLYMYOSITISES	POLYPHYODONT	POLYSYLLABICAL	POLYURETHAN	PONDERABLY
POLYMYXINS	POLYPIDOMS	POLYSYLLABICISM	POLYURETHANE	PONDERANCE
POLYNEURITIS	POLYPLOIDAL	POLYSYLLABISM	POLYURETHANES	PONDERANCES
POLYNEURITISES	POLYPLOIDIC	POLYSYLLABISMS	POLYURETHANS	PONDERANCIES
POLYNOMIAL	POLYPLOIDIES	POLYSYLLABLE	POLYVALENCE	PONDERANCY
POLYNOMIALISM	POLYPLOIDS	POLYSYLLABLES	POLYVALENCES	PONDERATED
POLYNOMIALISMS	POLYPLOIDY	POLYSYLLOGISM	POLYVALENCIES	PONDERATES
POLYNOMIALS	POLYPODIES	POLYSYLLOGISMS	POLYVALENCY	PONDERATING
POLYNUCLEAR	POLYPODOUS	POLYSYNAPTIC	POLYVALENT	PONDERATION
POLYNUCLEATE	POLYPROPENE	POLYSYNDETON	POLYVINYLIDENE	PONDERATIONS
POLYNUCLEOTIDE	POLYPROPENES	POLYSYNDETONS	POLYVINYLIDENES	PONDERINGLY
POLYNUCLEOTIDES	POLYPROPYLENE	POLYSYNTHESES	POLYVINYLS	PONDERMENT
POLYOLEFIN	POLYPROPYLENES	POLYSYNTHESIS	POLYWATERS	PONDERMENTS
POLYOLEFINS	POLYPROTODONT	POLYSYNTHESISM	POLYZOARIA	PONDEROSAS
POLYOMINOS	POLYPROTODONTS	POLYSYNTHESISMS	POLYZOARIAL	PONDEROSITIES
POLYONYMIC	POLYPTYCHS	POLYSYNTHETIC	POLYZOARIES	PONDEROSITY
POLYONYMIES	POLYRHYTHM	POLYSYNTHETICAL	POLYZOARIUM	PONDEROUSLY
POLYONYMOUS	POLYRHYTHMIC	POLYSYNTHETISM	POMEGRANATE	PONDEROUSNESS
POLYPARIES	POLYRHYTHMS	POLYSYNTHETISMS	POMEGRANATES	PONDEROUSNESSES
POLYPARIUM	POLYRIBOSOMAL	POLYTECHNIC	POMICULTURE	PONDOKKIES
POLYPEPTIDE	POLYRIBOSOME	POLYTECHNICAL	POMICULTURES	PONEROLOGIES
POLYPEPTIDES	POLYRIBOSOMES	POLYTECHNICS	POMIFEROUS	PONEROLOGY
POLYPEPTIDIC	POLYSACCHARIDE	POLYTENIES	POMMELLING	PONIARDING
POLYPETALOUS	POLYSACCHARIDES	POLYTHALAMOUS	POMOERIUMS	PONTIANACS
POLYPHAGIA	POLYSACCHAROSE	POLYTHEISM	POMOLOGICAL	PONTIANAKS
POLYPHAGIAS	POLYSACCHAROSES	POLYTHEISMS	POMOLOGICALLY	PONTICELLO
POLYPHAGIES	POLYSEMANT	POLYTHEIST	POMOLOGIES	PONTICELLOS
POLYPHAGOUS	POLYSEMANTS	POLYTHEISTIC	POMOLOGIST	PONTIFICAL
POLYPHARMACIES	POLYSEMIES	POLYTHEISTICAL	POMOLOGISTS	PONTIFICALITIES
POLYPHARMACY	POLYSEMOUS	POLYTHEISTS	POMOSEXUAL	PONTIFICALITY
POLYPHASIC	POLYSEPALOUS	POLYTHENES	POMOSEXUALS	PONTIFICALLY
POLYPHENOL	POLYSILOXANE	POLYTOCOUS	POMPADOURED	PONTIFICALS
POLYPHENOLIC	POLYSILOXANES	POLYTONALISM	POMPADOURS	PONTIFICATE
POLYPHENOLS	POLYSOMICS	POLYTONALISMS	POMPELMOOSE	PONTIFICATED
POLYPHLOESBOEAN	POLYSOMIES	POLYTONALIST	POMPELMOOSES	PONTIFICATES
POLYPHLOISBIC	POLYSORBATE	POLYTONALISTS	POMPELMOUS	PONTIFICATING

P

PONTIFICATION
PONTIFICATIONS
PONTIFICATOR
PONTIFICATORS
PONTIFICES
PONTIFYING
PONTLEVISES
PONTONEERS
PONTONIERS
PONTONNIER
PONTONNIERS
PONTOONERS
PONTOONING
PONYTAILED
POORHOUSES
POORMOUTHED
POORMOUTHING
POORMOUTHS
POORNESSES
POPLINETTE
POPLINETTES
POPMOBILITIES
POPMOBILITY
POPPERINGS
POPPYCOCKS
POPPYHEADS
POPULARISATION
POPULARISATIONS
POPULARISE
POPULARISED
POPULARISER
POPULARISERS
POPULARISES
POPULARISING
POPULARIST
POPULARITIES
POPULARITY
POPULARIZATION
POPULARIZATIONS
POPULARIZE
POPULARIZED
POPULARIZER
POPULARIZERS
POPULARIZES
POPULARIZING
POPULATING
POPULATION

POPULATIONAL
POPULATIONS
POPULISTIC
POPULOUSLY
POPULOUSNESS
POPULOUSNESSES
PORBEAGLES
PORCELAINEOUS
PORCELAINISE
PORCELAINISED
PORCELAINISES
PORCELAINISING
PORCELAINIZE
PORCELAINIZED
PORCELAINIZES
PORCELAINIZING
PORCELAINLIKE
PORCELAINOUS
PORCELAINS
PORCELANEOUS
PORCELLANEOUS
PORCELLANISE
PORCELLANISED
PORCELLANISES
PORCELLANISING
PORCELLANITE
PORCELLANITES
PORCELLANIZE
PORCELLANIZED
PORCELLANIZES
PORCELLANIZING
PORCELLANOUS
PORCHETTAS
PORCUPINES
PORCUPINISH
PORIFERANS
PORIFEROUS
PORINESSES
PORISMATIC
PORISMATICAL
PORISTICAL
PORKINESSES
PORLOCKING
PORNIFICATION
PORNIFICATIONS
PORNOCRACIES
PORNOCRACY

PORNOGRAPHER
PORNOGRAPHERS
PORNOGRAPHIC
PORNOGRAPHIES
PORNOGRAPHY
PORNOTOPIA
PORNOTOPIAN
PORNOTOPIAS
POROGAMIES
POROMERICS
POROSCOPES
POROSCOPIC
POROSCOPIES
POROSITIES
POROUSNESS
POROUSNESSES
PORPENTINE
PORPENTINES
PORPHYRIAS
PORPHYRIES
PORPHYRINS
PORPHYRIOS
PORPHYRITE
PORPHYRITES
PORPHYRITIC
PORPHYROGENITE
PORPHYROGENITES
PORPHYROID
PORPHYROIDS
PORPHYROPSIN
PORPHYROPSINS
PORPHYROUS
PORPOISING
PORRACEOUS
PORRECTING
PORRECTION
PORRECTIONS
PORRENGERS
PORRIGINOUS
PORRINGERS
PORTABELLA
PORTABELLAS
PORTABELLO
PORTABELLOS
PORTABILITIES
PORTABILITY
PORTAMENTI

PORTAMENTO
PORTAPACKS
PORTATIVES
PORTCULLIS
PORTCULLISED
PORTCULLISES
PORTCULLISING
PORTENDING
PORTENTOUS
PORTENTOUSLY
PORTENTOUSNESS
PORTEOUSES
PORTERAGES
PORTERESSES
PORTERHOUSE
PORTERHOUSES
PORTFOLIOS
PORTHORSES
PORTHOUSES
PORTIONERS
PORTIONING
PORTIONIST
PORTIONISTS
PORTIONLESS
PORTLINESS
PORTLINESSES
PORTMANTEAU
PORTMANTEAUS
PORTMANTEAUX
PORTMANTLE
PORTMANTLES
PORTMANTUA
PORTMANTUAS
PORTOBELLO
PORTOBELLOS
PORTOLANOS
PORTRAITED
PORTRAITING
PORTRAITIST
PORTRAITISTS
PORTRAITURE
PORTRAITURES
PORTRAYABLE
PORTRAYALS
PORTRAYERS
PORTRAYING
PORTREEVES

PORTRESSES
PORTULACACEOUS
PORTULACAS
PORWIGGLES
POSHNESSES
POSITIONAL
POSITIONALLY
POSITIONED
POSITIONING
POSITIONINGS
POSITIVELY
POSITIVENESS
POSITIVENESSES
POSITIVEST
POSITIVISM
POSITIVISMS
POSITIVIST
POSITIVISTIC
POSITIVISTS
POSITIVITIES
POSITIVITY
POSITRONIUM
POSITRONIUMS
POSOLOGICAL
POSOLOGIES
POSSESSABLE
POSSESSEDLY
POSSESSEDNESS
POSSESSEDNESSES
POSSESSING
POSSESSION
POSSESSIONAL
POSSESSIONARY
POSSESSIONATE
POSSESSIONATES
POSSESSIONED
POSSESSIONLESS
POSSESSIONS
POSSESSIVE
POSSESSIVELY
POSSESSIVENESS
POSSESSIVES
POSSESSORS
POSSESSORSHIP
POSSESSORSHIPS
POSSESSORY
POSSIBILISM

POSSIBILISMS
POSSIBILIST
POSSIBILISTS
POSSIBILITIES
POSSIBILITY
POSSIBLEST
POSTABORTION
POSTACCIDENT
POSTADOLESCENT
POSTADOLESCENTS
POSTAMPUTATION
POSTAPOCALYPTIC
POSTARREST
POSTATOMIC
POSTATTACK
POSTBELLUM
POSTBIBLICAL
POSTBOURGEOIS
POSTBUSSES
POSTCAPITALIST
POSTCARDED
POSTCARDING
POSTCARDLIKE
POSTCLASSIC
POSTCLASSICAL
POSTCODING
POSTCOITAL
POSTCOLLEGE
POSTCOLLEGIATE
POSTCOLONIAL
POSTCONCEPTION
POSTCONCERT
POSTCONQUEST
POSTCONSONANTAL
POSTCONVENTION
POSTCOPULATORY
POSTCORONARY
POSTCRANIAL
POSTCRANIALLY
POSTCRISIS
POSTDATING
POSTDEADLINE
POSTDEBATE
POSTDEBUTANTE
POSTDELIVERY
POSTDEPRESSION
POSTDEVALUATION

POSTDILUVIAL
POSTDILUVIAN
POSTDILUVIANS
POSTDIVESTITURE
POSTDIVORCE
POSTDOCTORAL
POSTDOCTORATE
POSTEDITING
POSTEDITINGS
POSTELECTION
POSTEMBRYONAL
POSTEMBRYONIC
POSTEMERGENCE
POSTEMERGENCY
POSTEPILEPTIC
POSTERIORITIES
POSTERIORITY
POSTERIORLY
POSTERIORS
POSTERISATION
POSTERISATIONS
POSTERISED
POSTERISES
POSTERISING
POSTERITIES
POSTERIZATION
POSTERIZATIONS
POSTERIZED
POSTERIZES
POSTERIZING
POSTEROLATERAL
POSTERUPTIVE
POSTEXERCISE
POSTEXILIAN
POSTEXILIC
POSTEXPERIENCE
POSTEXPOSURE
POSTFEMINISM
POSTFEMINISMS
POSTFEMINIST
POSTFEMINISTS
POSTFIXING
POSTFLIGHT
POSTFORMED
POSTFORMING
POSTFRACTURE
POSTFREEZE

POSTGANGLIONIC
POSTGLACIAL
POSTGRADUATE
POSTGRADUATES
POSTGRADUATION
POSTGRADUATIONS
POSTHARVEST
POSTHASTES
POSTHEATED
POSTHEATING
POSTHEMORRHAGIC
POSTHOLDER
POSTHOLDERS
POSTHOLIDAY
POSTHOLOCAUST
POSTHORSES
POSTHOSPITAL
POSTHOUSES
POSTHUMOUS
POSTHUMOUSLY
POSTHUMOUSNESS
POSTHYPNOTIC
POSTILIONS
POSTILLATE
POSTILLATED
POSTILLATES
POSTILLATING
POSTILLATION
POSTILLATIONS
POSTILLATOR
POSTILLATORS
POSTILLERS
POSTILLING
POSTILLION
POSTILLIONS
POSTIMPACT
POSTIMPERIAL
POSTINAUGURAL
POSTINDUSTRIAL
POSTINFECTION
POSTINJECTION
POSTINOCULATION
POSTIRRADIATION
POSTISCHEMIC
POSTISOLATION
POSTLANDING
POSTLAPSARIAN

POSTLAUNCH
POSTLIBERATION
POSTLIMINARY
POSTLIMINIA
POSTLIMINIARY
POSTLIMINIES
POSTLIMINIOUS
POSTLIMINIUM
POSTLIMINOUS
POSTLIMINY
POSTLITERATE
POSTMARITAL
POSTMARKED
POSTMARKING
POSTMASTECTOMY
POSTMASTER
POSTMASTERS
POSTMASTERSHIP
POSTMASTERSHIPS
POSTMATING
POSTMEDIEVAL
POSTMENOPAUSAL
POSTMENSTRUAL
POSTMERIDIAN
POSTMIDNIGHT
POSTMILLENARIAN
POSTMILLENNIAL
POSTMISTRESS
POSTMISTRESSES
POSTMODERN
POSTMODERNISM
POSTMODERNISMS
POSTMODERNIST
POSTMODERNISTS
POSTMORTEM
POSTMORTEMS
POSTNATALLY
POSTNEONATAL
POSTNUPTIAL
POSTOCULAR
POSTOCULARS
POSTOPERATIVE
POSTOPERATIVELY
POSTORBITAL
POSTORGASMIC
POSTPARTUM
POSTPERSON

POSTPERSONS
POSTPOLLINATION
POSTPONABLE
POSTPONEMENT
POSTPONEMENTS
POSTPONENCE
POSTPONENCES
POSTPONERS
POSTPONING
POSTPOSING
POSTPOSITION
POSTPOSITIONAL
POSTPOSITIONS
POSTPOSITIVE
POSTPOSITIVELY
POSTPOSITIVES
POSTPRANDIAL
POSTPRIMARY
POSTPRISON
POSTPRODUCTION
POSTPRODUCTIONS
POSTPUBERTIES
POSTPUBERTY
POSTPUBESCENT
POSTRECESSION
POSTRETIREMENT
POSTRIDERS
POSTROMANTIC
POSTROMANTICS
POSTSCENIUM
POSTSCENIUMS
POSTSCRIPT
POSTSCRIPTS
POSTSEASON
POSTSEASONS
POSTSECONDARY
POSTSTIMULATION
POSTSTIMULATORY
POSTSTIMULUS
POSTSTRIKE
POSTSURGICAL
POSTSYNAPTIC
POSTSYNCED
POSTSYNCHRONISE
POSTSYNCHRONIZE
POSTSYNCING
POSTTENSION

P

POSTTENSIONED	POTAMOLOGISTS	POTICHOMANIAS	POWELLIZED	PRACTICKING
POSTTENSIONING	POTAMOLOGY	POTLATCHED	POWELLIZES	PRACTICUMS
POSTTENSIONS	POTASSIUMS	POTLATCHES	POWELLIZING	PRACTIQUES
POSTTRANSFUSION	POTATOBUGS	POTLATCHING	POWERBOATING	PRACTISANT
POSTTRAUMATIC	POTBELLIED	POTOMETERS	POWERBOATINGS	PRACTISANTS
POSTTREATMENT	POTBELLIES	POTPOURRIS	POWERBOATS	PRACTISERS
POSTTREATMENTS	POTBOILERS	POTSHOTTING	POWERFULLY	PRACTISING
POSTULANCIES	POTBOILING	POTSHOTTINGS	POWERFULNESS	PRACTITIONER
POSTULANCY	POTBOILINGS	POTTERINGLY	POWERFULNESSES	PRACTITIONERS
POSTULANTS	POTENTATES	POTTERINGS	POWERHOUSE	PRACTOLOLS
POSTULANTSHIP	POTENTIALITIES	POTTINESSES	POWERHOUSES	PRAEAMBLES
POSTULANTSHIPS	POTENTIALITY	POTTINGARS	POWERLESSLY	PRAECOCIAL
POSTULATED	POTENTIALLY	POTTINGERS	POWERLESSNESS	PRAECORDIAL
POSTULATES	POTENTIALS	POTTYMOUTH	POWERLESSNESSES	PRAEDIALITIES
POSTULATING	POTENTIARIES	POTTYMOUTHS	POWERLIFTER	PRAEDIALITY
POSTULATION	POTENTIARY	POTWALLERS	POWERLIFTERS	PRAEFECTORIAL
POSTULATIONAL	POTENTIATE	POULTERERS	POWERLIFTING	PRAELECTED
POSTULATIONALLY	POTENTIATED	POULTICING	POWERLIFTINGS	PRAELECTING
POSTULATIONS	POTENTIATES	POULTROONE	POWERPLAYS	PRAELUDIUM
POSTULATOR	POTENTIATING	POULTROONES	POWERTRAIN	PRAEMUNIRE
POSTULATORS	POTENTIATION	POULTRYMAN	POWERTRAINS	PRAEMUNIRES
POSTULATORY	POTENTIATIONS	POULTRYMEN	POWSOWDIES	PRAENOMENS
POSTULATUM	POTENTIATOR	POUNDCAKES	POXVIRUSES	PRAENOMINA
POSTURINGS	POTENTIATORS	POURBOIRES	POZZOLANAS	PRAENOMINAL
POSTURISED	POTENTILLA	POURPARLER	POZZOLANIC	PRAENOMINALLY
POSTURISES	POTENTILLAS	POURPARLERS	POZZUOLANA	PRAEPOSTOR
POSTURISING	POTENTIOMETER	POURPOINTS	POZZUOLANAS	PRAEPOSTORS
POSTURISTS	POTENTIOMETERS	POURSEWING	PRACHARAKS	PRAESIDIUM
POSTURIZED	POTENTIOMETRIC	POURTRAHED	PRACTICABILITY	PRAESIDIUMS
POSTURIZES	POTENTIOMETRIES	POURTRAICT	PRACTICABLE	PRAETORIAL
POSTURIZING	POTENTIOMETRY	POURTRAICTS	PRACTICABLENESS	PRAETORIAN
POSTVACCINAL	POTENTISED	POURTRAYED	PRACTICABLY	PRAETORIANS
POSTVACCINATION	POTENTISES	POURTRAYING	PRACTICALISM	PRAETORIUM
POSTVAGOTOMY	POTENTISING	POUSOWDIES	PRACTICALISMS	PRAETORIUMS
POSTVASECTOMY	POTENTIZED	POUSSETTED	PRACTICALIST	PRAETORSHIP
POSTVOCALIC	POTENTIZES	POUSSETTES	PRACTICALISTS	PRAETORSHIPS
POSTWEANING	POTENTIZING	POUSSETTING	PRACTICALITIES	PRAGMATICAL
POSTWORKSHOP	POTENTNESS	POUTASSOUS	PRACTICALITY	PRAGMATICALITY
POTABILITIES	POTENTNESSES	POUTHERING	PRACTICALLY	PRAGMATICALLY
POTABILITY	POTHECARIES	POWDERIEST	PRACTICALNESS	PRAGMATICALNESS
POTABLENESS	POTHOLDERS	POWDERINGS	PRACTICALNESSES	PRAGMATICISM
POTABLENESSES	POTHOLINGS	POWDERLESS	PRACTICALS	PRAGMATICISMS
POTAMOGETON	POTHUNTERS	POWDERLIKE	PRACTICERS	PRAGMATICIST
POTAMOGETONS	POTHUNTING	POWELLISED	PRACTICIAN	PRAGMATICISTS
POTAMOLOGICAL	POTHUNTINGS	POWELLISES	PRACTICIANS	PRAGMATICS
POTAMOLOGIES	POTICARIES	POWELLISING	PRACTICING	PRAGMATISATION
POTAMOLOGIST	POTICHOMANIA	POWELLITES	PRACTICKED	PRAGMATISATIONS

PRAGMATISE	PRAXEOLOGY	PREADMITTED	PREARRANGED	PRECANCELING
PRAGMATISED	PRAXINOSCOPE	PREADMITTING	PREARRANGEMENT	PRECANCELLATION
PRAGMATISER	PRAXINOSCOPES	PREADMONISH	PREARRANGEMENTS	PRECANCELLED
PRAGMATISERS	PRAYERFULLY	PREADMONISHED	PREARRANGES	PRECANCELLING
PRAGMATISES	PRAYERFULNESS	PREADMONISHES	PREARRANGING	PRECANCELS
PRAGMATISING	PRAYERFULNESSES	PREADMONISHING	PREASSEMBLED	PRECANCEROUS
PRAGMATISM	PRAYERLESS	PREADMONITION	PREASSIGNED	PRECANCERS
PRAGMATISMS	PRAYERLESSLY	PREADMONITIONS	PREASSIGNING	PRECAPITALIST
PRAGMATIST	PRAYERLESSNESS	PREADOLESCENCE	PREASSIGNS	PRECARIOUS
PRAGMATISTIC	PREABSORBED	PREADOLESCENCES	PREASSURANCE	PRECARIOUSLY
PRAGMATISTS	PREABSORBING	PREADOLESCENT	PREASSURANCES	PRECARIOUSNESS
PRAGMATIZATION	PREABSORBS	PREADOLESCENTS	PREASSURED	PRECASTING
PRAGMATIZATIONS	PREACCUSED	PREADOPTED	PREASSURES	PRECAUTION
PRAGMATIZE	PREACCUSES	PREADOPTING	PREASSURING	PRECAUTIONAL
PRAGMATIZED	PREACCUSING	PREAGRICULTURAL	PREATTUNED	PRECAUTIONARY
PRAGMATIZER	PREACHABLE	PREALLOTTED	PREATTUNES	PRECAUTIONED
PRAGMATIZERS	PREACHERSHIP	PREALLOTTING	PREATTUNING	PRECAUTIONING
PRAGMATIZES	PREACHERSHIPS	PREALTERED	PREAUDIENCE	PRECAUTIONS
PRAGMATIZING	PREACHIEST	PREALTERING	PREAUDIENCES	PRECAUTIOUS
PRAISEACHS	PREACHIFIED	PREAMBLING	PREAVERRED	PRECEDENCE
PRAISELESS	PREACHIFIES	PREAMBULARY	PREAVERRING	PRECEDENCES
PRAISEWORTHILY	PREACHIFYING	PREAMBULATE	PREAXIALLY	PRECEDENCIES
PRAISEWORTHY	PREACHIFYINGS	PREAMBULATED	PREBENDARIES	PRECEDENCY
PRAISINGLY	PREACHINESS	PREAMBULATES	PREBENDARY	PRECEDENTED
PRALLTRILLER	PREACHINESSES	PREAMBULATING	PREBIBLICAL	PRECEDENTIAL
PRALLTRILLERS	PREACHINGLY	PREAMBULATORY	PREBIDDING	PRECEDENTIALLY
PRANAYAMAS	PREACHINGS	PREAMPLIFIER	PREBIDDINGS	PRECEDENTLY
PRANCINGLY	PREACHMENT	PREAMPLIFIERS	PREBILLING	PRECEDENTS
PRANDIALLY	PREACHMENTS	PREANAESTHETIC	PREBINDING	PRECENSORED
PRANKINGLY	PREACQUAINT	PREANAESTHETICS	PREBIOLOGIC	PRECENSORING
PRANKISHLY	PREACQUAINTANCE	PREANESTHETIC	PREBIOLOGICAL	PRECENSORS
PRANKISHNESS	PREACQUAINTED	PREANNOUNCE	PREBIOTICS	PRECENTING
PRANKISHNESSES	PREACQUAINTING	PREANNOUNCED	PREBLESSED	PRECENTORIAL
PRANKSTERS	PREACQUAINTS	PREANNOUNCES	PREBLESSES	PRECENTORS
PRASEODYMIUM	PREACQUISITION	PREANNOUNCING	PREBLESSING	PRECENTORSHIP
PRASEODYMIUMS	PREADAMITE	PREAPPLIED	PREBOARDED	PRECENTORSHIPS
PRATFALLEN	PREADAMITES	PREAPPLIES	PREBOARDING	PRECENTRESS
PRATFALLING	PREADAPTATION	PREAPPLYING	PREBOILING	PRECENTRESSES
PRATINCOLE	PREADAPTATIONS	PREAPPOINT	PREBOOKING	PRECENTRICES
PRATINCOLES	PREADAPTED	PREAPPOINTED	PREBREAKFAST	PRECENTRIX
PRATTLEBOX	PREADAPTING	PREAPPOINTING	PREBUDGETS	PRECENTRIXES
PRATTLEBOXES	PREADAPTIVE	PREAPPOINTS	PREBUILDING	PRECEPTIAL
PRATTLEMENT	PREADJUSTED	PREAPPROVE	PREBUTTALS	PRECEPTIVE
PRATTLEMENTS	PREADJUSTING	PREAPPROVED	PRECALCULI	PRECEPTIVELY
PRATTLINGLY	PREADJUSTS	PREAPPROVES	PRECALCULUS	PRECEPTORAL
PRAXEOLOGICAL	PREADMISSION	PREAPPROVING	PRECALCULUSES	PRECEPTORATE
PRAXEOLOGIES	PREADMISSIONS	PREARRANGE	PRECANCELED	PRECEPTORATES

P

PRECEPTORIAL PRECIPITATES PRECOGNISE PRECONCERTS PRECORDIAL
PRECEPTORIALS PRECIPITATING PRECOGNISED PRECONCILIAR PRECREASED
PRECEPTORIES PRECIPITATION PRECOGNISES PRECONDEMN PRECREASES
PRECEPTORS PRECIPITATIONS PRECOGNISING PRECONDEMNED PRECREASING
PRECEPTORSHIP PRECIPITATIVE PRECOGNITION PRECONDEMNING PRECRITICAL
PRECEPTORSHIPS PRECIPITATOR PRECOGNITIONS PRECONDEMNS PRECURRERS
PRECEPTORY PRECIPITATORS PRECOGNITIVE PRECONDITION PRECURSING
PRECEPTRESS PRECIPITIN PRECOGNIZANT PRECONDITIONED PRECURSIVE
PRECEPTRESSES PRECIPITINOGEN PRECOGNIZE PRECONDITIONING PRECURSORS
PRECESSING PRECIPITINOGENS PRECOGNIZED PRECONDITIONS PRECURSORY
PRECESSION PRECIPITINS PRECOGNIZES PRECONISATION PRECUTTING
PRECESSIONAL PRECIPITOUS PRECOGNIZING PRECONISATIONS PRECYCLING
PRECESSIONALLY PRECIPITOUSLY PRECOGNOSCE PRECONISED PREDACEOUS
PRECESSIONS PRECIPITOUSNESS PRECOGNOSCED PRECONISES PREDACEOUSNESS
PRECHARGED PRECISENESS PRECOGNOSCES PRECONISING PREDACIOUS
PRECHARGES PRECISENESSES PRECOGNOSCING PRECONIZATION PREDACIOUSNESS
PRECHARGING PRECISIANISM PRECOLLEGE PRECONIZATIONS PREDACITIES
PRECHECKED PRECISIANISMS PRECOLLEGIATE PRECONIZED PREDATIONS
PRECHECKING PRECISIANIST PRECOLONIAL PRECONIZES PREDATISMS
PRECHILLED PRECISIANISTS PRECOMBUSTION PRECONIZING PREDATORILY
PRECHILLING PRECISIANS PRECOMBUSTIONS PRECONQUEST PREDATORINESS
PRECHOOSES PRECISIONISM PRECOMMITMENT PRECONSCIOUS PREDATORINESSES
PRECHOOSING PRECISIONISMS PRECOMMITMENTS PRECONSCIOUSES PREDECEASE
PRECHRISTIAN PRECISIONIST PRECOMPETITIVE PRECONSCIOUSLY PREDECEASED
PRECIEUSES PRECISIONISTS PRECOMPOSE PRECONSONANTAL PREDECEASES
PRECIOSITIES PRECISIONS PRECOMPOSED PRECONSTRUCT PREDECEASING
PRECIOSITY PRECLASSICAL PRECOMPOSES PRECONSTRUCTED PREDECESSOR
PRECIOUSES PRECLEANED PRECOMPOSING PRECONSTRUCTING PREDECESSORS
PRECIOUSLY PRECLEANING PRECOMPUTE PRECONSTRUCTION PREDEDUCTED
PRECIOUSNESS PRECLEARANCE PRECOMPUTED PRECONSTRUCTS PREDEDUCTING
PRECIOUSNESSES PRECLEARANCES PRECOMPUTER PRECONSUME PREDEDUCTS
PRECIPICED PRECLEARED PRECOMPUTES PRECONSUMED PREDEFINED
PRECIPICES PRECLEARING PRECOMPUTING PRECONSUMES PREDEFINES
PRECIPITABILITY PRECLINICAL PRECONCEIT PRECONSUMING PREDEFINING
PRECIPITABLE PRECLINICALLY PRECONCEITED PRECONTACT PREDEFINITION
PRECIPITANCE PRECLUDABLE PRECONCEITING PRECONTACTS PREDEFINITIONS
PRECIPITANCES PRECLUDING PRECONCEITS PRECONTRACT PREDELIVERIES
PRECIPITANCIES PRECLUSION PRECONCEIVE PRECONTRACTED PREDELIVERY
PRECIPITANCY PRECLUSIONS PRECONCEIVED PRECONTRACTING PREDENTATE
PRECIPITANT PRECLUSIVE PRECONCEIVES PRECONTRACTS PREDEPARTURE
PRECIPITANTLY PRECLUSIVELY PRECONCEIVING PRECONVENTION PREDEPOSIT
PRECIPITANTNESS PRECOCIALS PRECONCEPTION PRECONVICTION PREDEPOSITED
PRECIPITANTS PRECOCIOUS PRECONCEPTIONS PRECONVICTIONS PREDEPOSITING
PRECIPITATE PRECOCIOUSLY PRECONCERT PRECOOKERS PREDEPOSITS
PRECIPITATED PRECOCIOUSNESS PRECONCERTED PRECOOKING PREDESIGNATE
PRECIPITATELY PRECOCITIES PRECONCERTEDLY PRECOOLING PREDESIGNATED
PRECIPITATENESS PRECOGNISANT PRECONCERTING PRECOPULATORY PREDESIGNATES

PREDESIGNATING	PREDIABETIC	PREDISPOSAL	PREEMPLOYMENT	PREFECTSHIPS
PREDESIGNATION	PREDIABETICS	PREDISPOSALS	PREEMPTING	PREFECTURAL
PREDESIGNATIONS	PREDIALITIES	PREDISPOSE	PREEMPTION	PREFECTURE
PREDESIGNATORY	PREDIALITY	PREDISPOSED	PREEMPTIONS	PREFECTURES
PREDESIGNED	PREDICABILITIES	PREDISPOSES	PREEMPTIVE	PREFERABILITIES
PREDESIGNING	PREDICABILITY	PREDISPOSING	PREEMPTIVELY	PREFERABILITY
PREDESIGNS	PREDICABLE	PREDISPOSITION	PREEMPTORS	PREFERABLE
PREDESTINABLE	PREDICABLENESS	PREDISPOSITIONS	PREENACTED	PREFERABLENESS
PREDESTINARIAN	PREDICABLES	PREDNISOLONE	PREENACTING	PREFERABLY
PREDESTINARIANS	PREDICAMENT	PREDNISOLONES	PREENROLLMENT	PREFERENCE
PREDESTINATE	PREDICAMENTAL	PREDNISONE	PREERECTED	PREFERENCES
PREDESTINATED	PREDICAMENTS	PREDNISONES	PREERECTING	PREFERENTIAL
PREDESTINATES	PREDICANTS	PREDOCTORAL	PREESTABLISH	PREFERENTIALISM
PREDESTINATING	PREDICATED	PREDOMINANCE	PREESTABLISHED	PREFERENTIALIST
PREDESTINATION	PREDICATES	PREDOMINANCES	PREESTABLISHES	PREFERENTIALITY
PREDESTINATIONS	PREDICATING	PREDOMINANCIES	PREESTABLISHING	PREFERENTIALLY
PREDESTINATIVE	PREDICATION	PREDOMINANCY	PREETHICAL	PREFERMENT
PREDESTINATOR	PREDICATIONS	PREDOMINANT	PREEXCITED	PREFERMENTS
PREDESTINATORS	PREDICATIVE	PREDOMINANTLY	PREEXCITES	PREFERRABLE
PREDESTINE	PREDICATIVELY	PREDOMINATE	PREEXCITING	PREFERRERS
PREDESTINED	PREDICATOR	PREDOMINATED	PREEXEMPTED	PREFERRING
PREDESTINES	PREDICATORS	PREDOMINATELY	PREEXEMPTING	PREFIGURATE
PREDESTINIES	PREDICATORY	PREDOMINATES	PREEXEMPTS	PREFIGURATED
PREDESTINING	PREDICTABILITY	PREDOMINATING	PREEXISTED	PREFIGURATES
PREDESTINY	PREDICTABLE	PREDOMINATION	PREEXISTENCE	PREFIGURATING
PREDETERMINABLE	PREDICTABLENESS	PREDOMINATIONS	PREEXISTENCES	PREFIGURATION
PREDETERMINATE	PREDICTABLY	PREDOMINATOR	PREEXISTENT	PREFIGURATIONS
PREDETERMINE	PREDICTERS	PREDOMINATORS	PREEXISTING	PREFIGURATIVE
PREDETERMINED	PREDICTING	PREDOOMING	PREEXPERIMENT	PREFIGURATIVELY
PREDETERMINER	PREDICTION	PREDRILLED	PREEXPOSED	PREFIGURED
PREDETERMINERS	PREDICTIONS	PREDRILLING	PREEXPOSES	PREFIGUREMENT
PREDETERMINES	PREDICTIVE	PREDYNASTIC	PREEXPOSING	PREFIGUREMENTS
PREDETERMINING	PREDICTIVELY	PREECLAMPSIA	PREFABBING	PREFIGURES
PREDETERMINISM	PREDICTORS	PREECLAMPSIAS	PREFABRICATE	PREFIGURING
PREDETERMINISMS	PREDIGESTED	PREECLAMPTIC	PREFABRICATED	PREFINANCE
PREDEVALUATION	PREDIGESTING	PREEDITING	PREFABRICATES	PREFINANCED
PREDEVELOP	PREDIGESTION	PREELECTED	PREFABRICATING	PREFINANCES
PREDEVELOPED	PREDIGESTIONS	PREELECTING	PREFABRICATION	PREFINANCING
PREDEVELOPING	PREDIGESTS	PREELECTION	PREFABRICATIONS	PREFINANCINGS
PREDEVELOPMENT	PREDIKANTS	PREELECTRIC	PREFABRICATOR	PREFIXALLY
PREDEVELOPMENTS	PREDILECTED	PREEMBARGO	PREFABRICATORS	PREFIXIONS
PREDEVELOPS	PREDILECTION	PREEMERGENCE	PREFASCIST	PREFIXTURE
PREDEVOTED	PREDILECTIONS	PREEMERGENT	PREFATORIAL	PREFIXTURES
PREDEVOTES	PREDINNERS	PREEMINENCE	PREFATORIALLY	PREFLIGHTED
PREDEVOTING	PREDISCHARGE	PREEMINENCES	PREFATORILY	PREFLIGHTING
PREDIABETES	PREDISCOVERIES	PREEMINENT	PREFECTORIAL	PREFLIGHTS
PREDIABETESES	PREDISCOVERY	PREEMINENTLY	PREFECTSHIP	PREFLORATION

P

PREFLORATIONS

PREFLORATIONS
PREFOCUSED
PREFOCUSES
PREFOCUSING
PREFOCUSSED
PREFOCUSSES
PREFOCUSSING
PREFOLIATION
PREFOLIATIONS
PREFORMATION
PREFORMATIONISM
PREFORMATIONIST
PREFORMATIONS
PREFORMATIVE
PREFORMATIVES
PREFORMATS
PREFORMATTED
PREFORMATTING
PREFORMING
PREFORMULATE
PREFORMULATED
PREFORMULATES
PREFORMULATING
PREFRANKED
PREFRANKING
PREFREEZES
PREFREEZING
PREFRESHMAN
PREFRONTAL
PREFRONTALS
PREFULGENT
PREFUNDING
PREGANGLIONIC
PREGENITAL
PREGLACIAL
PREGNABILITIES
PREGNABILITY
PREGNANCES
PREGNANCIES
PREGNANTLY
PREGNENOLONE
PREGNENOLONES
PREGROWTHS
PREGUIDING
PREGUSTATION
PREGUSTATIONS
PREHALLUCES

PREHANDLED
PREHANDLES
PREHANDLING
PREHARDENED
PREHARDENING
PREHARDENS
PREHARVEST
PREHARVESTS
PREHEADACHE
PREHEATERS
PREHEATING
PREHEMINENCE
PREHEMINENCES
PREHENDING
PREHENSIBLE
PREHENSILE
PREHENSILITIES
PREHENSILITY
PREHENSION
PREHENSIONS
PREHENSIVE
PREHENSORIAL
PREHENSORS
PREHENSORY
PREHISTORIAN
PREHISTORIANS
PREHISTORIC
PREHISTORICAL
PREHISTORICALLY
PREHISTORIES
PREHISTORY
PREHOLIDAY
PREHOMINID
PREHOMINIDS
PREIGNITION
PREIGNITIONS
PREIMPLANTATION
PREIMPOSED
PREIMPOSES
PREIMPOSING
PREINAUGURAL
PREINDUCTION
PREINDUSTRIAL
PREINFORMED
PREINFORMING
PREINFORMS
PREINSERTED

PREINSERTING
PREINSERTS
PREINTERVIEW
PREINTERVIEWED
PREINTERVIEWING
PREINTERVIEWS
PREINVASION
PREINVITED
PREINVITES
PREINVITING
PREJUDGEMENT
PREJUDGEMENTS
PREJUDGERS
PREJUDGING
PREJUDGMENT
PREJUDGMENTS
PREJUDICANT
PREJUDICATE
PREJUDICATED
PREJUDICATES
PREJUDICATING
PREJUDICATION
PREJUDICATIONS
PREJUDICATIVE
PREJUDICED
PREJUDICES
PREJUDICIAL
PREJUDICIALLY
PREJUDICIALNESS
PREJUDICING
PREJUDIZES
PREKINDERGARTEN
PRELAPSARIAN
PRELATESHIP
PRELATESHIPS
PRELATESSES
PRELATICAL
PRELATICALLY
PRELATIONS
PRELATISED
PRELATISES
PRELATISING
PRELATISMS
PRELATISTS
PRELATIZED
PRELATIZES
PRELATIZING

PRELATURES
PRELAUNCHED
PRELAUNCHES
PRELAUNCHING
PRELECTING
PRELECTION
PRELECTIONS
PRELECTORS
PRELEXICAL
PRELIBATION
PRELIBATIONS
PRELIMINARIES
PRELIMINARILY
PRELIMINARY
PRELIMITED
PRELIMITING
PRELINGUAL
PRELINGUALLY
PRELITERACIES
PRELITERACY
PRELITERARY
PRELITERATE
PRELITERATES
PRELOADING
PRELOCATED
PRELOCATES
PRELOCATING
PRELOGICAL
PRELUDIOUS
PRELUNCHEON
PRELUNCHEONS
PRELUSIONS
PRELUSIVELY
PRELUSORILY
PREMALIGNANT
PREMANDIBULAR
PREMANDIBULARS
PREMANUFACTURE
PREMANUFACTURED
PREMANUFACTURES
PREMARITAL
PREMARITALLY
PREMARKETED
PREMARKETING
PREMARKETS
PREMARRIAGE
PREMATURELY

PREMATURENESS
PREMATURENESSES
PREMATURES
PREMATURITIES
PREMATURITY
PREMAXILLA
PREMAXILLAE
PREMAXILLARIES
PREMAXILLARY
PREMAXILLAS
PREMEASURE
PREMEASURED
PREMEASURES
PREMEASURING
PREMEDICAL
PREMEDICALLY
PREMEDICATE
PREMEDICATED
PREMEDICATES
PREMEDICATING
PREMEDICATION
PREMEDICATIONS
PREMEDIEVAL
PREMEDITATE
PREMEDITATED
PREMEDITATEDLY
PREMEDITATES
PREMEDITATING
PREMEDITATION
PREMEDITATIONS
PREMEDITATIVE
PREMEDITATOR
PREMEDITATORS
PREMEIOTIC
PREMENOPAUSAL
PREMENSTRUAL
PREMENSTRUALLY
PREMIERING
PREMIERSHIP
PREMIERSHIPS
PREMIGRATION
PREMILLENARIAN
PREMILLENARIANS
PREMILLENNIAL
PREMILLENNIALLY
PREMISSING
PREMODIFICATION

PREMODIFIED	PRENOTIONS	PREPARATION	PREPORTIONS	PREPROGRAMING
PREMODIFIES	PRENTICESHIP	PREPARATIONS	PREPOSITION	PREPROGRAMMED
PREMODIFYING	PRENTICESHIPS	PREPARATIVE	PREPOSITIONAL	PREPROGRAMMING
PREMOISTEN	PRENTICING	PREPARATIVELY	PREPOSITIONALLY	PREPROGRAMMINGS
PREMOISTENED	PRENUMBERED	PREPARATIVES	PREPOSITIONS	PREPROGRAMS
PREMOISTENING	PRENUMBERING	PREPARATOR	PREPOSITIVE	PREPSYCHEDELIC
PREMOISTENS	PRENUMBERS	PREPARATORILY	PREPOSITIVELY	PREPUBERAL
PREMOLDING	PRENUPTIAL	PREPARATORS	PREPOSITIVES	PREPUBERTAL
PREMONISHED	PREOBTAINED	PREPARATORY	PREPOSITOR	PREPUBERTIES
PREMONISHES	PREOBTAINING	PREPAREDLY	PREPOSITORS	PREPUBERTY
PREMONISHING	PREOBTAINS	PREPAREDNESS	PREPOSSESS	PREPUBESCENCE
PREMONISHMENT	PREOCCUPANCIES	PREPAREDNESSES	PREPOSSESSED	PREPUBESCENCES
PREMONISHMENTS	PREOCCUPANCY	PREPASTING	PREPOSSESSES	PREPUBESCENT
PREMONITION	PREOCCUPANT	PREPATELLAR	PREPOSSESSING	PREPUBESCENTS
PREMONITIONS	PREOCCUPANTS	PREPAYABLE	PREPOSSESSINGLY	PREPUBLICATION
PREMONITIVE	PREOCCUPATE	PREPAYMENT	PREPOSSESSION	PREPUBLICATIONS
PREMONITOR	PREOCCUPATED	PREPAYMENTS	PREPOSSESSIONS	PREPUNCHED
PREMONITORILY	PREOCCUPATES	PREPENSELY	PREPOSTEROUS	PREPUNCHES
PREMONITORS	PREOCCUPATING	PREPENSING	PREPOSTEROUSLY	PREPUNCHING
PREMONITORY	PREOCCUPATION	PREPENSIVE	PREPOSTORS	PREPUNCTUAL
PREMOTIONS	PREOCCUPATIONS	PREPERFORMANCE	PREPOTENCE	PREPURCHASE
PREMOULDED	PREOCCUPIED	PREPLACING	PREPOTENCES	PREPURCHASED
PREMOULDING	PREOCCUPIES	PREPLANNED	PREPOTENCIES	PREPURCHASES
PREMOVEMENT	PREOCCUPYING	PREPLANNING	PREPOTENCY	PREPURCHASING
PREMOVEMENTS	PREOCULARS	PREPLANTING	PREPOTENTLY	PREQUALIFIED
PREMUNITION	PREOPENING	PREPOLLENCE	PREPPINESS	PREQUALIFIES
PREMUNITIONS	PREOPERATIONAL	PREPOLLENCES	PREPPINESSES	PREQUALIFY
PREMYCOTIC	PREOPERATIVE	PREPOLLENCIES	PREPRANDIAL	PREQUALIFYING
PRENATALLY	PREOPERATIVELY	PREPOLLENCY	PREPREPARED	PREREADING
PRENEGOTIATE	PREOPTIONS	PREPOLLENT	PREPRESIDENTIAL	PRERECESSION
PRENEGOTIATED	PREORDAINED	PREPOLLICES	PREPRESSES	PRERECORDED
PRENEGOTIATES	PREORDAINING	PREPONDERANCE	PREPRICING	PRERECORDING
PRENEGOTIATING	PREORDAINMENT	PREPONDERANCES	PREPRIMARIES	PRERECORDS
PRENEGOTIATION	PREORDAINMENTS	PREPONDERANCIES	PREPRIMARY	PREREGISTER
PRENEGOTIATIONS	PREORDAINS	PREPONDERANCY	PREPRINTED	PREREGISTERED
PRENOMINAL	PREORDERED	PREPONDERANT	PREPRINTING	PREREGISTERING
PRENOMINALLY	PREORDERING	PREPONDERANTLY	PREPROCESS	PREREGISTERS
PRENOMINATE	PREORDINANCE	PREPONDERATE	PREPROCESSED	PREREGISTRATION
PRENOMINATED	PREORDINANCES	PREPONDERATED	PREPROCESSES	PREREHEARSAL
PRENOMINATES	PREORDINATION	PREPONDERATELY	PREPROCESSING	PRERELEASE
PRENOMINATING	PREORDINATIONS	PREPONDERATES	PREPROCESSOR	PRERELEASED
PRENOMINATION	PREOVULATORY	PREPONDERATING	PREPROCESSORS	PRERELEASES
PRENOMINATIONS	PREPACKAGE	PREPONDERATION	PREPRODUCTION	PRERELEASING
PRENOTIFICATION	PREPACKAGED	PREPONDERATIONS	PREPRODUCTIONS	PREREQUIRE
PRENOTIFIED	PREPACKAGES	PREPORTION	PREPROFESSIONAL	PREREQUIRED
PRENOTIFIES	PREPACKAGING	PREPORTIONED	PREPROGRAM	PREREQUIRES
PRENOTIFYING	PREPACKING	PREPORTIONING	PREPROGRAMED	PREREQUIRING

P

PREREQUISITE
PREREQUISITES
PRERETIREMENT
PREREVISIONIST
PREREVOLUTION
PRERINSING
PREROGATIVE
PREROGATIVED
PREROGATIVELY
PREROGATIVES
PREROMANTIC
PREROMANTICS
PRESAGEFUL
PRESAGEFULLY
PRESAGEMENT
PRESAGEMENTS
PRESANCTIFIED
PRESANCTIFIES
PRESANCTIFY
PRESANCTIFYING
PRESBYACOUSES
PRESBYACOUSIS
PRESBYACUSES
PRESBYACUSIS
PRESBYCOUSES
PRESBYCOUSIS
PRESBYCUSES
PRESBYCUSIS
PRESBYOPES
PRESBYOPIA
PRESBYOPIAS
PRESBYOPIC
PRESBYOPICS
PRESBYOPIES
PRESBYTERAL
PRESBYTERATE
PRESBYTERATES
PRESBYTERIAL
PRESBYTERIALLY
PRESBYTERIALS
PRESBYTERIAN
PRESBYTERIANISE
PRESBYTERIANISM
PRESBYTERIANIZE
PRESBYTERIANS
PRESBYTERIES
PRESBYTERS

PRESBYTERSHIP
PRESBYTERSHIPS
PRESBYTERY
PRESBYTISM
PRESBYTISMS
PRESCHEDULE
PRESCHEDULED
PRESCHEDULES
PRESCHEDULING
PRESCHOOLER
PRESCHOOLERS
PRESCHOOLS
PRESCIENCE
PRESCIENCES
PRESCIENTIFIC
PRESCIENTLY
PRESCINDED
PRESCINDENT
PRESCINDING
PRESCISSION
PRESCISSIONS
PRESCORING
PRESCREENED
PRESCREENING
PRESCREENS
PRESCRIBED
PRESCRIBER
PRESCRIBERS
PRESCRIBES
PRESCRIBING
PRESCRIBINGS
PRESCRIPTIBLE
PRESCRIPTION
PRESCRIPTIONS
PRESCRIPTIVE
PRESCRIPTIVELY
PRESCRIPTIVISM
PRESCRIPTIVISMS
PRESCRIPTIVIST
PRESCRIPTIVISTS
PRESCRIPTS
PRESEASONS
PRESELECTED
PRESELECTING
PRESELECTION
PRESELECTIONS
PRESELECTOR

PRESELECTORS
PRESELECTS
PRESELLING
PRESENSION
PRESENSIONS
PRESENTABILITY
PRESENTABLE
PRESENTABLENESS
PRESENTABLY
PRESENTATION
PRESENTATIONAL
PRESENTATIONISM
PRESENTATIONIST
PRESENTATIONS
PRESENTATIVE
PRESENTEEISM
PRESENTEEISMS
PRESENTEES
PRESENTENCE
PRESENTENCED
PRESENTENCES
PRESENTENCING
PRESENTERS
PRESENTIAL
PRESENTIALITIES
PRESENTIALITY
PRESENTIALLY
PRESENTIENT
PRESENTIMENT
PRESENTIMENTAL
PRESENTIMENTS
PRESENTING
PRESENTISM
PRESENTISMS
PRESENTIST
PRESENTISTS
PRESENTIVE
PRESENTIVENESS
PRESENTIVES
PRESENTMENT
PRESENTMENTS
PRESENTNESS
PRESENTNESSES
PRESERVABILITY
PRESERVABLE
PRESERVABLY
PRESERVATION

PRESERVATIONIST
PRESERVATIONS
PRESERVATIVE
PRESERVATIVES
PRESERVATORIES
PRESERVATORY
PRESERVERS
PRESERVICE
PRESERVING
PRESETTING
PRESETTLED
PRESETTLEMENT
PRESETTLES
PRESETTLING
PRESHAPING
PRESHIPPED
PRESHIPPING
PRESHOWING
PRESHRINKING
PRESHRINKS
PRESHRUNKEN
PRESIDENCIES
PRESIDENCY
PRESIDENTESS
PRESIDENTESSES
PRESIDENTIAL
PRESIDENTIALLY
PRESIDENTS
PRESIDENTSHIP
PRESIDENTSHIPS
PRESIDIARY
PRESIDIUMS
PRESIFTING
PRESIGNALED
PRESIGNALING
PRESIGNALLED
PRESIGNALLING
PRESIGNALS
PRESIGNIFIED
PRESIGNIFIES
PRESIGNIFY
PRESIGNIFYING
PRESLAUGHTER
PRESLICING
PRESOAKING
PRESOLVING
PRESORTING

PRESPECIFIED
PRESPECIFIES
PRESPECIFY
PRESPECIFYING
PRESSBOARD
PRESSBOARDS
PRESSGANGS
PRESSINGLY
PRESSINGNESS
PRESSINGNESSES
PRESSMARKS
PRESSROOMS
PRESSURELESS
PRESSURING
PRESSURISATION
PRESSURISATIONS
PRESSURISE
PRESSURISED
PRESSURISER
PRESSURISERS
PRESSURISES
PRESSURISING
PRESSURIZATION
PRESSURIZATIONS
PRESSURIZE
PRESSURIZED
PRESSURIZER
PRESSURIZERS
PRESSURIZES
PRESSURIZING
PRESSWOMAN
PRESSWOMEN
PRESSWORKS
PRESTAMPED
PRESTAMPING
PRESTATION
PRESTATIONS
PRESTERILISE
PRESTERILISED
PRESTERILISES
PRESTERILISING
PRESTERILIZE
PRESTERILIZED
PRESTERILIZES
PRESTERILIZING
PRESTERNUM
PRESTERNUMS

PRESTIDIGITATOR | PRESWEETENS | PRETERPERFECT | PREVALUING | PREWARNING
PRESTIGEFUL | PRESYMPTOMATIC | PRETERPERFECTS | PREVARICATE | PREWASHING
PRESTIGIATOR | PRESYNAPTIC | PRETESTING | PREVARICATED | PREWEANING
PRESTIGIATORS | PRESYNAPTICALLY | PRETEXTING | PREVARICATES | PREWEIGHED
PRESTIGIOUS | PRETASTING | PRETEXTINGS | PREVARICATING | PREWEIGHING
PRESTIGIOUSLY | PRETELEVISION | PRETHEATER | PREVARICATION | PREWORKING
PRESTIGIOUSNESS | PRETELLING | PRETHEATRE | PREVARICATIONS | PREWRAPPED
PRESTISSIMO | PRETENCELESS | PRETORIANS | PREVARICATOR | PREWRAPPING
PRESTISSIMOS | PRETENDANT | PRETORSHIP | PREVARICATORS | PREWRITING
PRESTORAGE | PRETENDANTS | PRETORSHIPS | PREVENANCIES | PREWRITINGS
PRESTORING | PRETENDEDLY | PRETOURNAMENT | PREVENANCY | PRICELESSLY
PRESTRESSED | PRETENDENT | PRETRAINED | PREVENIENCE | PRICELESSNESS
PRESTRESSES | PRETENDENTS | PRETRAINING | PREVENIENCES | PRICELESSNESSES
PRESTRESSING | PRETENDERS | PRETREATED | PREVENIENT | PRICINESSES
PRESTRICTION | PRETENDERSHIP | PRETREATING | PREVENIENTLY | PRICKLIEST
PRESTRICTIONS | PRETENDERSHIPS | PRETREATMENT | PREVENTABILITY | PRICKLINESS
PRESTRUCTURE | PRETENDING | PRETREATMENTS | PREVENTABLE | PRICKLINESSES
PRESTRUCTURED | PRETENDINGLY | PRETRIMMED | PREVENTABLY | PRICKLINGS
PRESTRUCTURES | PRETENSION | PRETRIMMING | PREVENTATIVE | PRICKWOODS
PRESTRUCTURING | PRETENSIONED | PRETTIFICATION | PREVENTATIVES | PRIDEFULLY
PRESUMABLE | PRETENSIONING | PRETTIFICATIONS | PREVENTERS | PRIDEFULNESS
PRESUMABLY | PRETENSIONLESS | PRETTIFIED | PREVENTIBILITY | PRIDEFULNESSES
PRESUMEDLY | PRETENSIONS | PRETTIFIER | PREVENTIBLE | PRIESTCRAFT
PRESUMINGLY | PRETENSIVE | PRETTIFIERS | PREVENTIBLY | PRIESTCRAFTS
PRESUMMITS | PRETENTIOUS | PRETTIFIES | PREVENTING | PRIESTESSES
PRESUMPTION | PRETENTIOUSLY | PRETTIFYING | PREVENTION | PRIESTHOOD
PRESUMPTIONS | PRETENTIOUSNESS | PRETTINESS | PREVENTIONS | PRIESTHOODS
PRESUMPTIVE | PRETERHUMAN | PRETTINESSES | PREVENTIVE | PRIESTLIER
PRESUMPTIVELY | PRETERISTS | PRETTYISMS | PREVENTIVELY | PRIESTLIEST
PRESUMPTIVENESS | PRETERITENESS | PRETZELLED | PREVENTIVENESS | PRIESTLIKE
PRESUMPTUOUS | PRETERITENESSES | PRETZELLING | PREVENTIVES | PRIESTLINESS
PRESUMPTUOUSLY | PRETERITES | PREUNIFICATION | PREVIEWERS | PRIESTLINESSES
PRESUPPOSE | PRETERITION | PREUNITING | PREVIEWING | PRIESTLING
PRESUPPOSED | PRETERITIONS | PREUNIVERSITY | PREVIOUSLY | PRIESTLINGS
PRESUPPOSES | PRETERITIVE | PREVAILERS | PREVIOUSNESS | PRIESTSHIP
PRESUPPOSING | PRETERMINAL | PREVAILING | PREVIOUSNESSES | PRIESTSHIPS
PRESUPPOSITION | PRETERMINATION | PREVAILINGLY | PREVISIONAL | PRIGGERIES
PRESUPPOSITIONS | PRETERMINATIONS | PREVAILMENT | PREVISIONARY | PRIGGISHLY
PRESURGERY | PRETERMISSION | PREVAILMENTS | PREVISIONED | PRIGGISHNESS
PRESURMISE | PRETERMISSIONS | PREVALENCE | PREVISIONING | PRIGGISHNESSES
PRESURMISES | PRETERMITS | PREVALENCES | PREVISIONS | PRIMAEVALLY
PRESURVEYED | PRETERMITTED | PREVALENCIES | PREVISITED | PRIMALITIES
PRESURVEYING | PRETERMITTER | PREVALENCY | PREVISITING | PRIMAQUINE
PRESURVEYS | PRETERMITTERS | PREVALENTLY | PREVOCALIC | PRIMAQUINES
PRESWEETEN | PRETERMITTING | PREVALENTNESS | PREVOCALICALLY | PRIMARINESS
PRESWEETENED | PRETERNATURAL | PREVALENTNESSES | PREVOCATIONAL | PRIMARINESSES
PRESWEETENING | PRETERNATURALLY | PREVALENTS | PREWARMING | PRIMATESHIP

P

PRIMATESHIPS
PRIMATIALS
PRIMATICAL
PRIMATOLOGICAL
PRIMATOLOGIES
PRIMATOLOGIST
PRIMATOLOGISTS
PRIMATOLOGY
PRIMAVERAS
PRIMENESSES
PRIMEVALLY
PRIMIGENIAL
PRIMIGRAVIDA
PRIMIGRAVIDAE
PRIMIGRAVIDAS
PRIMIPARAE
PRIMIPARAS
PRIMIPARITIES
PRIMIPARITY
PRIMIPAROUS
PRIMITIVELY
PRIMITIVENESS
PRIMITIVENESSES
PRIMITIVES
PRIMITIVISM
PRIMITIVISMS
PRIMITIVIST
PRIMITIVISTIC
PRIMITIVISTS
PRIMITIVITIES
PRIMITIVITY
PRIMNESSES
PRIMOGENIAL
PRIMOGENIT
PRIMOGENITAL
PRIMOGENITARY
PRIMOGENITIVE
PRIMOGENITIVES
PRIMOGENITOR
PRIMOGENITORS
PRIMOGENITRICES
PRIMOGENITRIX
PRIMOGENITRIXES
PRIMOGENITS
PRIMOGENITURE
PRIMOGENITURES
PRIMORDIAL

PRIMORDIALISM
PRIMORDIALISMS
PRIMORDIALITIES
PRIMORDIALITY
PRIMORDIALLY
PRIMORDIALS
PRIMORDIUM
PRIMROSING
PRIMULACEOUS
PRIMULINES
PRINCEDOMS
PRINCEHOOD
PRINCEHOODS
PRINCEKINS
PRINCELETS
PRINCELIER
PRINCELIEST
PRINCELIKE
PRINCELINESS
PRINCELINESSES
PRINCELING
PRINCELINGS
PRINCESHIP
PRINCESHIPS
PRINCESSES
PRINCESSLY
PRINCIFIED
PRINCIPALITIES
PRINCIPALITY
PRINCIPALLY
PRINCIPALNESS
PRINCIPALNESSES
PRINCIPALS
PRINCIPALSHIP
PRINCIPALSHIPS
PRINCIPATE
PRINCIPATES
PRINCIPIAL
PRINCIPIUM
PRINCIPLED
PRINCIPLES
PRINCIPLING
PRINTABILITIES
PRINTABILITY
PRINTABLENESS
PRINTABLENESSES
PRINTERIES

PRINTHEADS
PRINTMAKER
PRINTMAKERS
PRINTMAKING
PRINTMAKINGS
PRINTWHEEL
PRINTWHEELS
PRINTWORKS
PRIORESSES
PRIORITIES
PRIORITISATION
PRIORITISATIONS
PRIORITISE
PRIORITISED
PRIORITISES
PRIORITISING
PRIORITIZATION
PRIORITIZATIONS
PRIORITIZE
PRIORITIZED
PRIORITIZES
PRIORITIZING
PRIORSHIPS
PRISMATICAL
PRISMATICALLY
PRISMATOID
PRISMATOIDAL
PRISMATOIDS
PRISMOIDAL
PRISONMENT
PRISONMENTS
PRISSINESS
PRISSINESSES
PRISTINELY
PRIVATDOCENT
PRIVATDOCENTS
PRIVATDOZENT
PRIVATDOZENTS
PRIVATEERED
PRIVATEERING
PRIVATEERINGS
PRIVATEERS
PRIVATEERSMAN
PRIVATEERSMEN
PRIVATENESS
PRIVATENESSES
PRIVATIONS

PRIVATISATION
PRIVATISATIONS
PRIVATISED
PRIVATISER
PRIVATISERS
PRIVATISES
PRIVATISING
PRIVATISMS
PRIVATISTS
PRIVATIVELY
PRIVATIVES
PRIVATIZATION
PRIVATIZATIONS
PRIVATIZED
PRIVATIZER
PRIVATIZERS
PRIVATIZES
PRIVATIZING
PRIVILEGED
PRIVILEGES
PRIVILEGING
PRIZEFIGHT
PRIZEFIGHTER
PRIZEFIGHTERS
PRIZEFIGHTING
PRIZEFIGHTINGS
PRIZEFIGHTS
PRIZEWINNER
PRIZEWINNERS
PRIZEWINNING
PRIZEWOMAN
PRIZEWOMEN
PROABORTION
PROACTIONS
PROAIRESES
PROAIRESIS
PROBABILIORISM
PROBABILIORISMS
PROBABILIORIST
PROBABILIORISTS
PROBABILISM
PROBABILISMS
PROBABILIST
PROBABILISTIC
PROBABILISTS
PROBABILITIES
PROBABILITY

PROBATIONAL
PROBATIONALLY
PROBATIONARIES
PROBATIONARY
PROBATIONER
PROBATIONERS
PROBATIONERSHIP
PROBATIONS
PROBATIVELY
PROBENECID
PROBENECIDS
PROBIOTICS
PROBLEMATIC
PROBLEMATICAL
PROBLEMATICALLY
PROBLEMATICS
PROBLEMIST
PROBLEMISTS
PROBOSCIDEAN
PROBOSCIDEANS
PROBOSCIDES
PROBOSCIDIAN
PROBOSCIDIANS
PROBOSCISES
PROBOULEUTIC
PROBUSINESS
PROCACIOUS
PROCACITIES
PROCAMBIAL
PROCAMBIUM
PROCAMBIUMS
PROCAPITALIST
PROCARBAZINE
PROCARBAZINES
PROCARYONS
PROCARYOTE
PROCARYOTES
PROCARYOTIC
PROCATHEDRAL
PROCATHEDRALS
PROCEDURAL
PROCEDURALLY
PROCEDURALS
PROCEDURES
PROCEEDERS
PROCEEDING
PROCEEDINGS

P

PROCELEUSMATIC	PROCLITICS	PROCTOLOGICAL	PRODIGALISES	PROFESSIONAL
PROCELEUSMATICS	PROCLIVITIES	PROCTOLOGIES	PRODIGALISING	PROFESSIONALISE
PROCELLARIAN	PROCLIVITY	PROCTOLOGIST	PRODIGALITIES	PROFESSIONALISM
PROCELLARIANS	PROCOELOUS	PROCTOLOGISTS	PRODIGALITY	PROFESSIONALIST
PROCEPHALIC	PROCONSULAR	PROCTOLOGY	PRODIGALIZE	PROFESSIONALIZE
PROCERCOID	PROCONSULATE	PROCTORAGE	PRODIGALIZED	PROFESSIONALLY
PROCERCOIDS	PROCONSULATES	PROCTORAGES	PRODIGALIZES	PROFESSIONALS
PROCEREBRA	PROCONSULS	PROCTORIAL	PRODIGALIZING	PROFESSIONS
PROCEREBRAL	PROCONSULSHIP	PROCTORIALLY	PRODIGALLY	PROFESSORATE
PROCEREBRUM	PROCONSULSHIPS	PROCTORING	PRODIGIOSITIES	PROFESSORATES
PROCEREBRUMS	PROCRASTINATE	PROCTORISE	PRODIGIOSITY	PROFESSORESS
PROCERITIES	PROCRASTINATED	PROCTORISED	PRODIGIOUS	PROFESSORESSES
PROCESSABILITY	PROCRASTINATES	PROCTORISES	PRODIGIOUSLY	PROFESSORIAL
PROCESSABLE	PROCRASTINATING	PROCTORISING	PRODIGIOUSNESS	PROFESSORIALLY
PROCESSERS	PROCRASTINATION	PROCTORIZE	PRODITORIOUS	PROFESSORIAT
PROCESSIBILITY	PROCRASTINATIVE	PROCTORIZED	PRODNOSING	PROFESSORIATE
PROCESSIBLE	PROCRASTINATOR	PROCTORIZES	PRODROMATA	PROFESSORIATES
PROCESSING	PROCRASTINATORS	PROCTORIZING	PRODUCEMENT	PROFESSORIATS
PROCESSINGS	PROCRASTINATORY	PROCTORSHIP	PRODUCEMENTS	PROFESSORS
PROCESSION	PROCREANTS	PROCTORSHIPS	PRODUCIBILITIES	PROFESSORSHIP
PROCESSIONAL	PROCREATED	PROCTOSCOPE	PRODUCIBILITY	PROFESSORSHIPS
PROCESSIONALIST	PROCREATES	PROCTOSCOPES	PRODUCIBLE	PROFFERERS
PROCESSIONALLY	PROCREATING	PROCTOSCOPIC	PRODUCTIBILITY	PROFFERING
PROCESSIONALS	PROCREATION	PROCTOSCOPIES	PRODUCTILE	PROFICIENCE
PROCESSIONARIES	PROCREATIONAL	PROCTOSCOPY	PRODUCTION	PROFICIENCES
PROCESSIONARY	PROCREATIONS	PROCUMBENT	PRODUCTIONAL	PROFICIENCIES
PROCESSIONED	PROCREATIVE	PROCURABLE	PRODUCTIONS	PROFICIENCY
PROCESSIONER	PROCREATIVENESS	PROCURACIES	PRODUCTIVE	PROFICIENT
PROCESSIONERS	PROCREATOR	PROCURANCE	PRODUCTIVELY	PROFICIENTLY
PROCESSIONING	PROCREATORS	PROCURANCES	PRODUCTIVENESS	PROFICIENTS
PROCESSIONINGS	PROCRUSTEAN	PROCURATION	PRODUCTIVITIES	PROFILINGS
PROCESSIONS	PROCRYPSES	PROCURATIONS	PRODUCTIVITY	PROFILISTS
PROCESSORS	PROCRYPSIS	PROCURATOR	PROEMBRYOS	PROFITABILITIES
PROCESSUAL	PROCRYPTIC	PROCURATORIAL	PROENZYMES	PROFITABILITY
PROCHRONISM	PROCRYPTICALLY	PROCURATORIES	PROESTRUSES	PROFITABLE
PROCHRONISMS	PROCTALGIA	PROCURATORS	PROFANATION	PROFITABLENESS
PROCIDENCE	PROCTALGIAS	PROCURATORSHIP	PROFANATIONS	PROFITABLY
PROCIDENCES	PROCTITIDES	PROCURATORSHIPS	PROFANATORY	PROFITEERED
PROCLAIMANT	PROCTITISES	PROCURATORY	PROFANENESS	PROFITEERING
PROCLAIMANTS	PROCTODAEA	PROCUREMENT	PROFANENESSES	PROFITEERINGS
PROCLAIMED	PROCTODAEAL	PROCUREMENTS	PROFANITIES	PROFITEERS
PROCLAIMER	PROCTODAEUM	PROCURESSES	PROFASCIST	PROFITEROLE
PROCLAIMERS	PROCTODAEUMS	PROCUREURS	PROFECTITIOUS	PROFITEROLES
PROCLAIMING	PROCTODEAL	PROCURINGS	PROFEMINIST	PROFITINGS
PROCLAMATION	PROCTODEUM	PROCYONIDS	PROFESSEDLY	PROFITLESS
PROCLAMATIONS	PROCTODEUMS	PRODIGALISE	PROFESSING	PROFITLESSLY
PROCLAMATORY	PROCTOLOGIC	PRODIGALISED	PROFESSION	PROFITWISE

P

PROFLIGACIES	PROGNATHISM	PROGRESSIVE	PROJECTIVITIES	PROLIFERATED
PROFLIGACY	PROGNATHISMS	PROGRESSIVELY	PROJECTIVITY	PROLIFERATES
PROFLIGATE	PROGNATHOUS	PROGRESSIVENESS	PROJECTIZATION	PROLIFERATING
PROFLIGATELY	PROGNOSING	PROGRESSIVES	PROJECTIZATIONS	PROLIFERATION
PROFLIGATES	PROGNOSTIC	PROGRESSIVISM	PROJECTMENT	PROLIFERATIONS
PROFLUENCE	PROGNOSTICATE	PROGRESSIVISMS	PROJECTMENTS	PROLIFERATIVE
PROFLUENCES	PROGNOSTICATED	PROGRESSIVIST	PROJECTORS	PROLIFEROUS
PROFOUNDER	PROGNOSTICATES	PROGRESSIVISTIC	PROJECTURE	PROLIFEROUSLY
PROFOUNDEST	PROGNOSTICATING	PROGRESSIVISTS	PROJECTURES	PROLIFICACIES
PROFOUNDLY	PROGNOSTICATION	PROGRESSIVITIES	PROKARYONS	PROLIFICACY
PROFOUNDNESS	PROGNOSTICATIVE	PROGRESSIVITY	PROKARYOTE	PROLIFICAL
PROFOUNDNESSES	PROGNOSTICATOR	PROGYMNASIA	PROKARYOTES	PROLIFICALLY
PROFULGENT	PROGNOSTICATORS	PROGYMNASIUM	PROKARYOTIC	PROLIFICATION
PROFUNDITIES	PROGNOSTICS	PROGYMNASIUMS	PROKARYOTS	PROLIFICATIONS
PROFUNDITY	PROGRADATION	PROHIBITED	PROLACTINS	PROLIFICITIES
PROFUSENESS	PROGRADATIONS	PROHIBITER	PROLAMINES	PROLIFICITY
PROFUSENESSES	PROGRADING	PROHIBITERS	PROLAPSING	PROLIFICNESS
PROFUSIONS	PROGRAMABLE	PROHIBITING	PROLAPSUSES	PROLIFICNESSES
PROGENITIVE	PROGRAMERS	PROHIBITION	PROLATENESS	PROLIXIOUS
PROGENITIVENESS	PROGRAMING	PROHIBITIONARY	PROLATENESSES	PROLIXITIES
PROGENITOR	PROGRAMINGS	PROHIBITIONISM	PROLATIONS	PROLIXNESS
PROGENITORIAL	PROGRAMMABILITY	PROHIBITIONISMS	PROLEGOMENA	PROLIXNESSES
PROGENITORS	PROGRAMMABLE	PROHIBITIONIST	PROLEGOMENAL	PROLOCUTION
PROGENITORSHIP	PROGRAMMABLES	PROHIBITIONISTS	PROLEGOMENARY	PROLOCUTIONS
PROGENITORSHIPS	PROGRAMMATIC	PROHIBITIONS	PROLEGOMENON	PROLOCUTOR
PROGENITRESS	PROGRAMMED	PROHIBITIVE	PROLEGOMENOUS	PROLOCUTORS
PROGENITRESSES	PROGRAMMER	PROHIBITIVELY	PROLEPTICAL	PROLOCUTORSHIP
PROGENITRICES	PROGRAMMERS	PROHIBITIVENESS	PROLEPTICALLY	PROLOCUTORSHIPS
PROGENITRIX	PROGRAMMES	PROHIBITOR	PROLETARIAN	PROLOCUTRICES
PROGENITRIXES	PROGRAMMING	PROHIBITORS	PROLETARIANISE	PROLOCUTRIX
PROGENITURE	PROGRAMMINGS	PROHIBITORY	PROLETARIANISED	PROLOCUTRIXES
PROGENITURES	PROGRESSED	PROINSULIN	PROLETARIANISES	PROLOGISED
PROGESTATIONAL	PROGRESSES	PROINSULINS	PROLETARIANISM	PROLOGISES
PROGESTERONE	PROGRESSING	PROJECTABLE	PROLETARIANISMS	PROLOGISING
PROGESTERONES	PROGRESSION	PROJECTILE	PROLETARIANIZE	PROLOGISTS
PROGESTINS	PROGRESSIONAL	PROJECTILES	PROLETARIANIZED	PROLOGIZED
PROGESTOGEN	PROGRESSIONALLY	PROJECTING	PROLETARIANIZES	PROLOGIZES
PROGESTOGENIC	PROGRESSIONARY	PROJECTINGS	PROLETARIANNESS	PROLOGIZING
PROGESTOGENS	PROGRESSIONISM	PROJECTION	PROLETARIANS	PROLOGUING
PROGGINSES	PROGRESSIONISMS	PROJECTIONAL	PROLETARIAT	PROLOGUISE
PROGLOTTIC	PROGRESSIONIST	PROJECTIONIST	PROLETARIATE	PROLOGUISED
PROGLOTTID	PROGRESSIONISTS	PROJECTIONISTS	PROLETARIATES	PROLOGUISES
PROGLOTTIDEAN	PROGRESSIONS	PROJECTIONS	PROLETARIATS	PROLOGUISING
PROGLOTTIDES	PROGRESSISM	PROJECTISATION	PROLETARIES	PROLOGUIZE
PROGLOTTIDS	PROGRESSISMS	PROJECTISATIONS	PROLICIDAL	PROLOGUIZED
PROGLOTTIS	PROGRESSIST	PROJECTIVE	PROLICIDES	PROLOGUIZES
PROGNATHIC	PROGRESSISTS	PROJECTIVELY	PROLIFERATE	PROLOGUIZING

PROLONGABLE
PROLONGATE
PROLONGATED
PROLONGATES
PROLONGATING
PROLONGATION
PROLONGATIONS
PROLONGERS
PROLONGING
PROLONGMENT
PROLONGMENTS
PROLUSIONS
PROMACHOSES
PROMENADED
PROMENADER
PROMENADERS
PROMENADES
PROMENADING
PROMETHAZINE
PROMETHAZINES
PROMETHEUM
PROMETHEUMS
PROMETHIUM
PROMETHIUMS
PROMILITARY
PROMINENCE
PROMINENCES
PROMINENCIES
PROMINENCY
PROMINENTLY
PROMINENTNESS
PROMINENTNESSES
PROMISCUITIES
PROMISCUITY
PROMISCUOUS
PROMISCUOUSLY
PROMISCUOUSNESS
PROMISEFUL
PROMISELESS
PROMISINGLY
PROMISSIVE
PROMISSORILY
PROMISSORS
PROMISSORY
PROMONARCHIST
PROMONTORIES
PROMONTORY

PROMOTABILITIES
PROMOTABILITY
PROMOTABLE
PROMOTIONAL
PROMOTIONS
PROMOTIVENESS
PROMOTIVENESSES
PROMPTBOOK
PROMPTBOOKS
PROMPTINGS
PROMPTITUDE
PROMPTITUDES
PROMPTNESS
PROMPTNESSES
PROMPTUARIES
PROMPTUARY
PROMPTURES
PROMULGATE
PROMULGATED
PROMULGATES
PROMULGATING
PROMULGATION
PROMULGATIONS
PROMULGATOR
PROMULGATORS
PROMULGING
PROMUSCIDATE
PROMUSCIDES
PROMYCELIA
PROMYCELIAL
PROMYCELIUM
PRONATIONS
PRONATORES
PRONENESSES
PRONEPHRIC
PRONEPHROI
PRONEPHROS
PRONEPHROSES
PRONGBUCKS
PRONGHORNS
PRONOMINAL
PRONOMINALISE
PRONOMINALISED
PRONOMINALISES
PRONOMINALISING
PRONOMINALIZE
PRONOMINALIZED

PRONOMINALIZES
PRONOMINALIZING
PRONOMINALLY
PRONOUNCEABLE
PRONOUNCED
PRONOUNCEDLY
PRONOUNCEMENT
PRONOUNCEMENTS
PRONOUNCER
PRONOUNCERS
PRONOUNCES
PRONOUNCING
PRONOUNCINGS
PRONUCLEAR
PRONUCLEARIST
PRONUCLEARISTS
PRONUCLEUS
PRONUCLEUSES
PRONUNCIAMENTO
PRONUNCIAMENTOS
PRONUNCIATION
PRONUNCIATIONAL
PRONUNCIATIONS
PRONUNCIOS
PROOEMIONS
PROOEMIUMS
PROOFREADER
PROOFREADERS
PROOFREADING
PROOFREADINGS
PROOFREADS
PROOFROOMS
PROPAEDEUTIC
PROPAEDEUTICAL
PROPAEDEUTICS
PROPAGABILITIES
PROPAGABILITY
PROPAGABLE
PROPAGABLENESS
PROPAGANDA
PROPAGANDAS
PROPAGANDISE
PROPAGANDISED
PROPAGANDISER
PROPAGANDISERS
PROPAGANDISES
PROPAGANDISING

PROPAGANDISM
PROPAGANDISMS
PROPAGANDIST
PROPAGANDISTIC
PROPAGANDISTS
PROPAGANDIZE
PROPAGANDIZED
PROPAGANDIZER
PROPAGANDIZERS
PROPAGANDIZES
PROPAGANDIZING
PROPAGATED
PROPAGATES
PROPAGATING
PROPAGATION
PROPAGATIONAL
PROPAGATIONS
PROPAGATIVE
PROPAGATOR
PROPAGATORS
PROPAGULES
PROPAGULUM
PROPANEDIOIC
PROPANONES
PROPAROXYTONE
PROPAROXYTONES
PROPELLANT
PROPELLANTS
PROPELLENT
PROPELLENTS
PROPELLERS
PROPELLING
PROPELLINGS
PROPELLORS
PROPELMENT
PROPELMENTS
PROPENDENT
PROPENDING
PROPENSELY
PROPENSENESS
PROPENSENESSES
PROPENSION
PROPENSIONS
PROPENSITIES
PROPENSITY
PROPENSIVE
PROPERDINS

PROPERISPOMENA
PROPERISPOMENON
PROPERNESS
PROPERNESSES
PROPERTIED
PROPERTIES
PROPERTYING
PROPERTYLESS
PROPHECIES
PROPHESIABLE
PROPHESIED
PROPHESIER
PROPHESIERS
PROPHESIES
PROPHESYING
PROPHESYINGS
PROPHETESS
PROPHETESSES
PROPHETHOOD
PROPHETHOODS
PROPHETICAL
PROPHETICALLY
PROPHETICISM
PROPHETICISMS
PROPHETISM
PROPHETISMS
PROPHETSHIP
PROPHETSHIPS
PROPHYLACTIC
PROPHYLACTICS
PROPHYLAXES
PROPHYLAXIS
PROPINQUITIES
PROPINQUITY
PROPIONATE
PROPIONATES
PROPITIABLE
PROPITIATE
PROPITIATED
PROPITIATES
PROPITIATING
PROPITIATION
PROPITIATIONS
PROPITIATIOUS
PROPITIATIVE
PROPITIATOR
PROPITIATORIES

P

PROPITIATORILY	PROPRAETORIAL	PROPYLITIZED	PROSECUTIONS	PROSODIANS
PROPITIATORS	PROPRAETORIAN	PROPYLITIZES	PROSECUTOR	PROSODICAL
PROPITIATORY	PROPRAETORS	PROPYLITIZING	PROSECUTORIAL	PROSODICALLY
PROPITIOUS	PROPRANOLOL	PRORATABLE	PROSECUTORS	PROSODISTS
PROPITIOUSLY	PROPRANOLOLS	PRORATIONS	PROSECUTRICES	PROSOPAGNOSIA
PROPITIOUSNESS	PROPRETORS	PRORECTORS	PROSECUTRIX	PROSOPAGNOSIAS
PROPLASTID	PROPRIETARIES	PROROGATED	PROSECUTRIXES	PROSOPOGRAPHER
PROPLASTIDS	PROPRIETARILY	PROROGATES	PROSELYTED	PROSOPOGRAPHERS
PROPODEONS	PROPRIETARY	PROROGATING	PROSELYTES	PROSOPOGRAPHIES
PROPODEUMS	PROPRIETIES	PROROGATION	PROSELYTIC	PROSOPOGRAPHY
PROPOLISES	PROPRIETOR	PROROGATIONS	PROSELYTING	PROSOPOPEIA
PROPONENTS	PROPRIETORIAL	PROROGUING	PROSELYTISATION	PROSOPOPEIAL
PROPORTION	PROPRIETORIALLY	PROSAICALLY	PROSELYTISE	PROSOPOPEIAS
PROPORTIONABLE	PROPRIETORS	PROSAICALNESS	PROSELYTISED	PROSOPOPOEIA
PROPORTIONABLY	PROPRIETORSHIP	PROSAICALNESSES	PROSELYTISER	PROSOPOPOEIAL
PROPORTIONAL	PROPRIETORSHIPS	PROSAICISM	PROSELYTISERS	PROSOPOPOEIAS
PROPORTIONALITY	PROPRIETRESS	PROSAICISMS	PROSELYTISES	PROSPECTED
PROPORTIONALLY	PROPRIETRESSES	PROSAICNESS	PROSELYTISING	PROSPECTING
PROPORTIONALS	PROPRIETRICES	PROSAICNESSES	PROSELYTISM	PROSPECTINGS
PROPORTIONATE	PROPRIETRIX	PROSATEURS	PROSELYTISMS	PROSPECTION
PROPORTIONATED	PROPRIETRIXES	PROSAUROPOD	PROSELYTIZATION	PROSPECTIONS
PROPORTIONATELY	PROPRIOCEPTION	PROSAUROPODS	PROSELYTIZE	PROSPECTIVE
PROPORTIONATES	PROPRIOCEPTIONS	PROSCENIUM	PROSELYTIZED	PROSPECTIVELY
PROPORTIONATING	PROPRIOCEPTIVE	PROSCENIUMS	PROSELYTIZER	PROSPECTIVENESS
PROPORTIONED	PROPRIOCEPTOR	PROSCIUTTI	PROSELYTIZERS	PROSPECTIVES
PROPORTIONING	PROPRIOCEPTORS	PROSCIUTTO	PROSELYTIZES	PROSPECTLESS
PROPORTIONINGS	PROPROCTOR	PROSCIUTTOS	PROSELYTIZING	PROSPECTOR
PROPORTIONLESS	PROPROCTORS	PROSCRIBED	PROSEMINAR	PROSPECTORS
PROPORTIONMENT	PROPUGNATION	PROSCRIBER	PROSEMINARS	PROSPECTUS
PROPORTIONMENTS	PROPUGNATIONS	PROSCRIBERS	PROSENCEPHALA	PROSPECTUSES
PROPORTIONS	PROPULSION	PROSCRIBES	PROSENCEPHALIC	PROSPERING
PROPOSABLE	PROPULSIONS	PROSCRIBING	PROSENCEPHALON	PROSPERITIES
PROPOSITAE	PROPULSIVE	PROSCRIPTION	PROSENCHYMA	PROSPERITY
PROPOSITION	PROPULSORS	PROSCRIPTIONS	PROSENCHYMAS	PROSPEROUS
PROPOSITIONAL	PROPULSORY	PROSCRIPTIVE	PROSENCHYMATA	PROSPEROUSLY
PROPOSITIONALLY	PROPYLAEUM	PROSCRIPTIVELY	PROSENCHYMATOUS	PROSPEROUSNESS
PROPOSITIONED	PROPYLAMINE	PROSCRIPTS	PROSEUCHAE	PROSTACYCLIN
PROPOSITIONING	PROPYLAMINES	PROSECTING	PROSIFYING	PROSTACYCLINS
PROPOSITIONS	PROPYLENES	PROSECTORIAL	PROSILIENCIES	PROSTAGLANDIN
PROPOSITUS	PROPYLITES	PROSECTORS	PROSILIENCY	PROSTAGLANDINS
PROPOUNDED	PROPYLITISATION	PROSECTORSHIP	PROSILIENT	PROSTANTHERA
PROPOUNDER	PROPYLITISE	PROSECTORSHIPS	PROSIMIANS	PROSTANTHERAS
PROPOUNDERS	PROPYLITISED	PROSECUTABLE	PROSINESSES	PROSTATECTOMIES
PROPOUNDING	PROPYLITISES	PROSECUTED	PROSLAMBANOMENE	PROSTATECTOMY
PROPOXYPHENE	PROPYLITISING	PROSECUTES	PROSLAVERY	PROSTATISM
PROPOXYPHENES	PROPYLITIZATION	PROSECUTING	PROSOBRANCH	PROSTATISMS
PROPRAETOR	PROPYLITIZE	PROSECUTION	PROSOBRANCHS	PROSTATITIS

PROSTATITISES	PROTANOPIAS	PROTEOCLASTIC	PROTHROMBINS	PROTOMARTYRS
PROSTERNUM	PROTANOPIC	PROTEOGLYCAN	PROTISTANS	PROTOMORPHIC
PROSTERNUMS	PROTEACEOUS	PROTEOGLYCANS	PROTISTOLOGIES	PROTONATED
PROSTHESES	PROTECTANT	PROTEOLYSE	PROTISTOLOGIST	PROTONATES
PROSTHESIS	PROTECTANTS	PROTEOLYSED	PROTISTOLOGISTS	PROTONATING
PROSTHETIC	PROTECTERS	PROTEOLYSES	PROTISTOLOGY	PROTONATION
PROSTHETICALLY	PROTECTING	PROTEOLYSING	PROTOACTINIUM	PROTONATIONS
PROSTHETICS	PROTECTINGLY	PROTEOLYSIS	PROTOACTINIUMS	PROTONEMAL
PROSTHETIST	PROTECTION	PROTEOLYTIC	PROTOAVISES	PROTONEMATA
PROSTHETISTS	PROTECTIONISM	PROTEOLYTICALLY	PROTOCHORDATE	PROTONEMATAL
PROSTHODONTIA	PROTECTIONISMS	PROTEOMICS	PROTOCHORDATES	PROTONOTARIAL
PROSTHODONTIAS	PROTECTIONIST	PROTERANDRIES	PROTOCOCCAL	PROTONOTARIAT
PROSTHODONTICS	PROTECTIONISTS	PROTERANDROUS	PROTOCOLED	PROTONOTARIATS
PROSTHODONTIST	PROTECTIONS	PROTERANDRY	PROTOCOLIC	PROTONOTARIES
PROSTHODONTISTS	PROTECTIVE	PROTEROGYNIES	PROTOCOLING	PROTONOTARY
PROSTITUTE	PROTECTIVELY	PROTEROGYNOUS	PROTOCOLISE	PROTOPATHIC
PROSTITUTED	PROTECTIVENESS	PROTEROGYNY	PROTOCOLISED	PROTOPATHIES
PROSTITUTES	PROTECTIVES	PROTERVITIES	PROTOCOLISES	PROTOPATHY
PROSTITUTING	PROTECTORAL	PROTERVITY	PROTOCOLISING	PROTOPHILIC
PROSTITUTION	PROTECTORATE	PROTESTANT	PROTOCOLIST	PROTOPHLOEM
PROSTITUTIONS	PROTECTORATES	PROTESTANTS	PROTOCOLISTS	PROTOPHLOEMS
PROSTITUTOR	PROTECTORIAL	PROTESTATION	PROTOCOLIZE	PROTOPHYTE
PROSTITUTORS	PROTECTORIES	PROTESTATIONS	PROTOCOLIZED	PROTOPHYTES
PROSTOMIAL	PROTECTORLESS	PROTESTERS	PROTOCOLIZES	PROTOPHYTIC
PROSTOMIUM	PROTECTORS	PROTESTING	PROTOCOLIZING	PROTOPLANET
PROSTOMIUMS	PROTECTORSHIP	PROTESTINGLY	PROTOCOLLED	PROTOPLANETARY
PROSTRATED	PROTECTORSHIPS	PROTESTORS	PROTOCOLLING	PROTOPLANETS
PROSTRATES	PROTECTORY	PROTHALAMIA	PROTOCTIST	PROTOPLASM
PROSTRATING	PROTECTRESS	PROTHALAMION	PROTOCTISTS	PROTOPLASMAL
PROSTRATION	PROTECTRESSES	PROTHALAMIUM	PROTODERMS	PROTOPLASMATIC
PROSTRATIONS	PROTECTRICES	PROTHALLIA	PROTOGALAXIES	PROTOPLASMIC
PROSYLLOGISM	PROTECTRIX	PROTHALLIAL	PROTOGALAXY	PROTOPLASMS
PROSYLLOGISMS	PROTECTRIXES	PROTHALLIC	PROTOGENIC	PROTOPLAST
PROTACTINIUM	PROTEIFORM	PROTHALLIUM	PROTOGINES	PROTOPLASTIC
PROTACTINIUMS	PROTEINACEOUS	PROTHALLOID	PROTOGYNIES	PROTOPLASTS
PROTAGONISM	PROTEINASE	PROTHALLUS	PROTOGYNOUS	PROTOPORPHYRIN
PROTAGONISMS	PROTEINASES	PROTHALLUSES	PROTOHISTORIAN	PROTOPORPHYRINS
PROTAGONIST	PROTEINOUS	PROTHETICALLY	PROTOHISTORIANS	PROTOSPATAIRE
PROTAGONISTS	PROTEINURIA	PROTHONOTARIAL	PROTOHISTORIC	PROTOSPATAIRES
PROTAMINES	PROTEINURIAS	PROTHONOTARIAT	PROTOHISTORIES	PROTOSPATHAIRE
PROTANDRIES	PROTENDING	PROTHONOTARIATS	PROTOHISTORY	PROTOSPATHAIRES
PROTANDROUS	PROTENSION	PROTHONOTARIES	PROTOHUMAN	PROTOSPATHARIUS
PROTANOMALIES	PROTENSIONS	PROTHONOTARY	PROTOHUMANS	PROTOSTARS
PROTANOMALOUS	PROTENSITIES	PROTHORACES	PROTOLANGUAGE	PROTOSTELE
PROTANOMALY	PROTENSITY	PROTHORACIC	PROTOLANGUAGES	PROTOSTELES
PROTANOPES	PROTENSIVE	PROTHORAXES	PROTOLITHIC	PROTOSTELIC
PROTANOPIA	PROTENSIVELY	PROTHROMBIN	PROTOMARTYR	PROTOSTOME

P

PROTOSTOMES	PROTRUSIVELY	PROVERBIALISM	PROVITAMINS	PRUSSIANISATION
PROTOTHERIAN	PROTRUSIVENESS	PROVERBIALISMS	PROVOCABLE	PRUSSIANISE
PROTOTHERIANS	PROTUBERANCE	PROVERBIALIST	PROVOCANTS	PRUSSIANISED
PROTOTROPH	PROTUBERANCES	PROVERBIALISTS	PROVOCATEUR	PRUSSIANISES
PROTOTROPHIC	PROTUBERANCIES	PROVERBIALIZE	PROVOCATEURS	PRUSSIANISING
PROTOTROPHIES	PROTUBERANCY	PROVERBIALIZED	PROVOCATION	PRUSSIANIZATION
PROTOTROPHS	PROTUBERANT	PROVERBIALIZES	PROVOCATIONS	PRUSSIANIZE
PROTOTROPHY	PROTUBERANTLY	PROVERBIALIZING	PROVOCATIVE	PRUSSIANIZED
PROTOTYPAL	PROTUBERATE	PROVERBIALLY	PROVOCATIVELY	PRUSSIANIZES
PROTOTYPED	PROTUBERATED	PROVERBING	PROVOCATIVENESS	PRUSSIANIZING
PROTOTYPES	PROTUBERATES	PROVIDABLE	PROVOCATIVES	PRUSSIATES
PROTOTYPIC	PROTUBERATING	PROVIDENCE	PROVOCATOR	PSALIGRAPHIES
PROTOTYPICAL	PROTUBERATION	PROVIDENCES	PROVOCATORS	PSALIGRAPHY
PROTOTYPICALLY	PROTUBERATIONS	PROVIDENTIAL	PROVOCATORY	PSALMBOOKS
PROTOTYPING	PROUDHEARTED	PROVIDENTIALLY	PROVOKABLE	PSALMODICAL
PROTOXIDES	PROUDNESSES	PROVIDENTLY	PROVOKEMENT	PSALMODIES
PROTOXYLEM	PROUSTITES	PROVINCEWIDE	PROVOKEMENTS	PSALMODISE
PROTOXYLEMS	PROVABILITIES	PROVINCIAL	PROVOKINGLY	PSALMODISED
PROTOZOANS	PROVABILITY	PROVINCIALISE	PROVOLONES	PSALMODISES
PROTOZOOLOGICAL	PROVABLENESS	PROVINCIALISED	PROVOSTRIES	PSALMODISING
PROTOZOOLOGIES	PROVABLENESSES	PROVINCIALISES	PROVOSTSHIP	PSALMODIST
PROTOZOOLOGIST	PROVANTING	PROVINCIALISING	PROVOSTSHIPS	PSALMODISTS
PROTOZOOLOGISTS	PROVASCULAR	PROVINCIALISM	PROWLINGLY	PSALMODIZE
PROTOZOOLOGY	PROVEABILITIES	PROVINCIALISMS	PROXIMALLY	PSALMODIZED
PROTOZOONS	PROVEABILITY	PROVINCIALIST	PROXIMATELY	PSALMODIZES
PROTRACTED	PROVECTION	PROVINCIALISTS	PROXIMATENESS	PSALMODIZING
PROTRACTEDLY	PROVECTIONS	PROVINCIALITIES	PROXIMATENESSES	PSALTERIAN
PROTRACTEDNESS	PROVEDITOR	PROVINCIALITY	PROXIMATION	PSALTERIES
PROTRACTIBLE	PROVEDITORE	PROVINCIALIZE	PROXIMATIONS	PSALTERIUM
PROTRACTILE	PROVEDITORES	PROVINCIALIZED	PROXIMITIES	PSALTRESSES
PROTRACTING	PROVEDITORS	PROVINCIALIZES	PROZYMITES	PSAMMOPHIL
PROTRACTION	PROVEDORES	PROVINCIALIZING	PRUDENTIAL	PSAMMOPHILE
PROTRACTIONS	PROVENANCE	PROVINCIALLY	PRUDENTIALISM	PSAMMOPHILES
PROTRACTIVE	PROVENANCES	PROVINCIALS	PRUDENTIALISMS	PSAMMOPHILOUS
PROTRACTOR	PROVENDERED	PROVIRUSES	PRUDENTIALIST	PSAMMOPHILS
PROTRACTORS	PROVENDERING	PROVISIONAL	PRUDENTIALISTS	PSAMMOPHYTE
PROTREPTIC	PROVENDERS	PROVISIONALLY	PRUDENTIALITIES	PSAMMOPHYTES
PROTREPTICAL	PROVENIENCE	PROVISIONALS	PRUDENTIALITY	PSAMMOPHYTIC
PROTREPTICS	PROVENIENCES	PROVISIONARIES	PRUDENTIALLY	PSELLISMUS
PROTRUDABLE	PROVENTRICULAR	PROVISIONARY	PRUDENTIALS	PSELLISMUSES
PROTRUDENT	PROVENTRICULI	PROVISIONED	PRUDISHNESS	PSEPHOANALYSES
PROTRUDING	PROVENTRICULUS	PROVISIONER	PRUDISHNESSES	PSEPHOANALYSIS
PROTRUSIBLE	PROVERBIAL	PROVISIONERS	PRURIENCES	PSEPHOLOGICAL
PROTRUSILE	PROVERBIALISE	PROVISIONING	PRURIENCIES	PSEPHOLOGICALLY
PROTRUSION	PROVERBIALISED	PROVISIONS	PRURIENTLY	PSEPHOLOGIES
PROTRUSIONS	PROVERBIALISES	PROVISORILY	PRURIGINOUS	PSEPHOLOGIST
PROTRUSIVE	PROVERBIALISING	PROVITAMIN	PRURITUSES	PSEPHOLOGISTS

PSEPHOLOGY
PSEUDAESTHESIA
PSEUDAESTHESIAS
PSEUDARTHROSES
PSEUDARTHROSIS
PSEUDEPIGRAPH
PSEUDEPIGRAPHA
PSEUDEPIGRAPHIC
PSEUDEPIGRAPHON
PSEUDEPIGRAPHS
PSEUDEPIGRAPHY
PSEUDERIES
PSEUDIMAGINES
PSEUDIMAGO
PSEUDIMAGOS
PSEUDOACID
PSEUDOACIDS
PSEUDOALLELE
PSEUDOALLELES
PSEUDOARTHROSES
PSEUDOARTHROSIS
PSEUDOBULB
PSEUDOBULBS
PSEUDOCARP
PSEUDOCARPOUS
PSEUDOCARPS
PSEUDOCIDE
PSEUDOCIDES
PSEUDOCLASSIC
PSEUDOCLASSICS
PSEUDOCODE
PSEUDOCODES
PSEUDOCOEL
PSEUDOCOELOMATE
PSEUDOCOELS
PSEUDOCYESES
PSEUDOCYESIS
PSEUDOEPHEDRINE
PSEUDOGRAPH
PSEUDOGRAPHIES
PSEUDOGRAPHS
PSEUDOGRAPHY
PSEUDOLOGIA
PSEUDOLOGIAS
PSEUDOLOGIES
PSEUDOLOGUE
PSEUDOLOGUES

PSEUDOLOGY
PSEUDOMARTYR
PSEUDOMARTYRS
PSEUDOMEMBRANE
PSEUDOMEMBRANES
PSEUDOMONAD
PSEUDOMONADES
PSEUDOMONADS
PSEUDOMONAS
PSEUDOMORPH
PSEUDOMORPHIC
PSEUDOMORPHISM
PSEUDOMORPHISMS
PSEUDOMORPHOUS
PSEUDOMORPHS
PSEUDOMUTUALITY
PSEUDONYMITIES
PSEUDONYMITY
PSEUDONYMOUS
PSEUDONYMOUSLY
PSEUDONYMS
PSEUDOPODAL
PSEUDOPODIA
PSEUDOPODIAL
PSEUDOPODIUM
PSEUDOPODS
PSEUDOPREGNANCY
PSEUDOPREGNANT
PSEUDORANDOM
PSEUDOSCALAR
PSEUDOSCALARS
PSEUDOSCIENCE
PSEUDOSCIENCES
PSEUDOSCIENTIST
PSEUDOSCOPE
PSEUDOSCOPES
PSEUDOSCORPION
PSEUDOSCORPIONS
PSEUDOSOLUTION
PSEUDOSOLUTIONS
PSEUDOSYMMETRY
PSEUDOVECTOR
PSEUDOVECTORS
PSILANTHROPIC
PSILANTHROPIES
PSILANTHROPISM
PSILANTHROPISMS

PSILANTHROPIST
PSILANTHROPISTS
PSILANTHROPY
PSILOCYBIN
PSILOCYBINS
PSILOMELANE
PSILOMELANES
PSILOPHYTE
PSILOPHYTES
PSILOPHYTIC
PSITTACINE
PSITTACINES
PSITTACOSES
PSITTACOSIS
PSITTACOTIC
PSORIATICS
PSYCHAGOGUE
PSYCHAGOGUES
PSYCHASTHENIA
PSYCHASTHENIAS
PSYCHASTHENIC
PSYCHASTHENICS
PSYCHEDELIA
PSYCHEDELIAS
PSYCHEDELIC
PSYCHEDELICALLY
PSYCHEDELICS
PSYCHIATER
PSYCHIATERS
PSYCHIATRIC
PSYCHIATRICAL
PSYCHIATRICALLY
PSYCHIATRIES
PSYCHIATRIST
PSYCHIATRISTS
PSYCHIATRY
PSYCHICALLY
PSYCHICISM
PSYCHICISMS
PSYCHICIST
PSYCHICISTS
PSYCHOACOUSTIC
PSYCHOACOUSTICS
PSYCHOACTIVE
PSYCHOANALYSE
PSYCHOANALYSED
PSYCHOANALYSER

PSYCHOANALYSERS
PSYCHOANALYSES
PSYCHOANALYSING
PSYCHOANALYSIS
PSYCHOANALYST
PSYCHOANALYSTS
PSYCHOANALYTIC
PSYCHOANALYZE
PSYCHOANALYZED
PSYCHOANALYZER
PSYCHOANALYZERS
PSYCHOANALYZES
PSYCHOANALYZING
PSYCHOBABBLE
PSYCHOBABBLER
PSYCHOBABBLERS
PSYCHOBABBLES
PSYCHOBILLIES
PSYCHOBILLY
PSYCHOBIOGRAPHY
PSYCHOBIOLOGIC
PSYCHOBIOLOGIES
PSYCHOBIOLOGIST
PSYCHOBIOLOGY
PSYCHOCHEMICAL
PSYCHOCHEMICALS
PSYCHOCHEMISTRY
PSYCHODELIA
PSYCHODELIAS
PSYCHODELIC
PSYCHODELICALLY
PSYCHODRAMA
PSYCHODRAMAS
PSYCHODRAMATIC
PSYCHODYNAMIC
PSYCHODYNAMICS
PSYCHOGALVANIC
PSYCHOGASES
PSYCHOGENESES
PSYCHOGENESIS
PSYCHOGENETIC
PSYCHOGENETICAL
PSYCHOGENETICS
PSYCHOGENIC
PSYCHOGENICALLY
PSYCHOGERIATRIC
PSYCHOGNOSES

PSYCHOGNOSIS
PSYCHOGNOSTIC
PSYCHOGONIES
PSYCHOGONY
PSYCHOGRAM
PSYCHOGRAMS
PSYCHOGRAPH
PSYCHOGRAPHIC
PSYCHOGRAPHICAL
PSYCHOGRAPHICS
PSYCHOGRAPHIES
PSYCHOGRAPHS
PSYCHOGRAPHY
PSYCHOHISTORIAN
PSYCHOHISTORIES
PSYCHOHISTORY
PSYCHOKINESES
PSYCHOKINESIS
PSYCHOKINETIC
PSYCHOLINGUIST
PSYCHOLINGUISTS
PSYCHOLOGIC
PSYCHOLOGICAL
PSYCHOLOGICALLY
PSYCHOLOGIES
PSYCHOLOGISE
PSYCHOLOGISED
PSYCHOLOGISES
PSYCHOLOGISING
PSYCHOLOGISM
PSYCHOLOGISMS
PSYCHOLOGIST
PSYCHOLOGISTIC
PSYCHOLOGISTS
PSYCHOLOGIZE
PSYCHOLOGIZED
PSYCHOLOGIZES
PSYCHOLOGIZING
PSYCHOLOGY
PSYCHOMACHIA
PSYCHOMACHIAS
PSYCHOMACHIES
PSYCHOMACHY
PSYCHOMETER
PSYCHOMETERS
PSYCHOMETRIC
PSYCHOMETRICAL

P

PSYCHOMETRICIAN	PSYCHOTHERAPIST	PTERYLOGRAPHIES	PUERILITIES	PULSATILITY
PSYCHOMETRICS	PSYCHOTHERAPY	PTERYLOGRAPHY	PUERPERALLY	PULSATILLA
PSYCHOMETRIES	PSYCHOTICALLY	PTERYLOSES	PUERPERIUM	PULSATILLAS
PSYCHOMETRIST	PSYCHOTICISM	PTERYLOSIS	PUERPERIUMS	PULSATIONS
PSYCHOMETRISTS	PSYCHOTICISMS	PTOCHOCRACIES	PUFFINESSES	PULSATIVELY
PSYCHOMETRY	PSYCHOTICS	PTOCHOCRACY	PUFFTALOONAS	PULSEBEATS
PSYCHOMOTOR	PSYCHOTOMIMETIC	PTYALAGOGIC	PUFTALOONIES	PULSELESSNESS
PSYCHONEUROSES	PSYCHOTOXIC	PTYALAGOGUE	PUFTALOONS	PULSELESSNESSES
PSYCHONEUROSIS	PSYCHOTROPIC	PTYALAGOGUES	PUGGINESSES	PULSIMETER
PSYCHONEUROTIC	PSYCHOTROPICS	PTYALISING	PUGILISTIC	PULSIMETERS
PSYCHONEUROTICS	PSYCHROMETER	PTYALIZING	PUGILISTICAL	PULSOMETER
PSYCHONOMIC	PSYCHROMETERS	PUBCRAWLER	PUGILISTICALLY	PULSOMETERS
PSYCHONOMICS	PSYCHROMETRIC	PUBCRAWLERS	PUGNACIOUS	PULTACEOUS
PSYCHOPATH	PSYCHROMETRICAL	PUBERULENT	PUGNACIOUSLY	PULTRUDING
PSYCHOPATHIC	PSYCHROMETRIES	PUBERULOUS	PUGNACIOUSNESS	PULTRUSION
PSYCHOPATHICS	PSYCHROMETRY	PUBESCENCE	PUGNACITIES	PULTRUSIONS
PSYCHOPATHIES	PSYCHROPHILIC	PUBESCENCES	PUISSANCES	PULVERABLE
PSYCHOPATHIST	PTARMIGANS	PUBLICALLY	PUISSANTLY	PULVERATION
PSYCHOPATHISTS	PTERANODON	PUBLICATION	PUISSAUNCE	PULVERATIONS
PSYCHOPATHOLOGY	PTERANODONS	PUBLICATIONS	PUISSAUNCES	PULVERINES
PSYCHOPATHS	PTERIDINES	PUBLICISED	PULCHRITUDE	PULVERISABLE
PSYCHOPATHY	PTERIDOLOGICAL	PUBLICISES	PULCHRITUDES	PULVERISATION
PSYCHOPHILIES	PTERIDOLOGIES	PUBLICISING	PULCHRITUDINOUS	PULVERISATIONS
PSYCHOPHILY	PTERIDOLOGIST	PUBLICISTS	PULLULATED	PULVERISED
PSYCHOPHYSICAL	PTERIDOLOGISTS	PUBLICITIES	PULLULATES	PULVERISER
PSYCHOPHYSICIST	PTERIDOLOGY	PUBLICIZED	PULLULATING	PULVERISERS
PSYCHOPHYSICS	PTERIDOMANIA	PUBLICIZES	PULLULATION	PULVERISES
PSYCHOPOMP	PTERIDOMANIAS	PUBLICIZING	PULLULATIONS	PULVERISING
PSYCHOPOMPS	PTERIDOPHILIST	PUBLICNESS	PULMOBRANCH	PULVERIZABLE
PSYCHOSEXUAL	PTERIDOPHILISTS	PUBLICNESSES	PULMOBRANCHIATE	PULVERIZATION
PSYCHOSEXUALITY	PTERIDOPHYTE	PUBLISHABLE	PULMOBRANCHS	PULVERIZATIONS
PSYCHOSEXUALLY	PTERIDOPHYTES	PUBLISHERS	PULMONATES	PULVERIZED
PSYCHOSOCIAL	PTERIDOPHYTIC	PUBLISHING	PULMONOLOGIES	PULVERIZER
PSYCHOSOCIALLY	PTERIDOPHYTOUS	PUBLISHINGS	PULMONOLOGIST	PULVERIZERS
PSYCHOSOCIOLOGY	PTERIDOSPERM	PUBLISHMENT	PULMONOLOGISTS	PULVERIZES
PSYCHOSOMATIC	PTERIDOSPERMS	PUBLISHMENTS	PULMONOLOGY	PULVERIZING
PSYCHOSOMATICS	PTERODACTYL	PUCCINIACEOUS	PULPBOARDS	PULVERULENCE
PSYCHOSOMIMETIC	PTERODACTYLE	PUCKERIEST	PULPIFYING	PULVERULENCES
PSYCHOSURGEON	PTERODACTYLES	PUCKEROOED	PULPINESSES	PULVERULENT
PSYCHOSURGEONS	PTERODACTYLS	PUCKISHNESS	PULPITEERED	PULVILISED
PSYCHOSURGERIES	PTEROSAURIAN	PUCKISHNESSES	PULPITEERING	PULVILIZED
PSYCHOSURGERY	PTEROSAURIANS	PUDDENINGS	PULPITEERS	PULVILLIFORM
PSYCHOSURGICAL	PTEROSAURS	PUDGINESSES	PULPITRIES	PULVILLING
PSYCHOSYNTHESES	PTERYGIALS	PUDIBUNDITIES	PULPSTONES	PULVILLIOS
PSYCHOSYNTHESIS	PTERYGIUMS	PUDIBUNDITY	PULSATANCE	PULVINATED
PSYCHOTECHNICS	PTERYGOIDS	PUDICITIES	PULSATANCES	PULVINULES
PSYCHOTHERAPIES	PTERYLOGRAPHIC	PUERILISMS	PULSATILITIES	PUMICATING

PUMMELLING	PUNCTURERS	PUREBLOODS	PURPOSELESSNESS	PUTATIVELY
PUMMELLINGS	PUNCTURING	PURENESSES	PURPOSIVELY	PUTONGHUAS
PUMPERNICKEL	PUNDIGRION	PURGATIONS	PURPOSIVENESS	PUTREFACIENT
PUMPERNICKELS	PUNDIGRIONS	PURGATIVELY	PURPOSIVENESSES	PUTREFACTION
PUMPKINSEED	PUNDITRIES	PURGATIVES	PURPRESTURE	PUTREFACTIONS
PUMPKINSEEDS	PUNDONORES	PURGATORIAL	PURPRESTURES	PUTREFACTIVE
PUNCHBALLS	PUNGENCIES	PURGATORIALLY	PURSERSHIP	PUTREFIABLE
PUNCHBOARD	PUNICACEOUS	PURGATORIAN	PURSERSHIPS	PUTREFIERS
PUNCHBOARDS	PUNINESSES	PURGATORIANS	PURSINESSES	PUTREFYING
PUNCHBOWLS	PUNISHABILITIES	PURGATORIES	PURSUANCES	PUTRESCENCE
PUNCHINELLO	PUNISHABILITY	PURIFICATION	PURSUANTLY	PUTRESCENCES
PUNCHINELLOES	PUNISHABLE	PURIFICATIONS	PURSUINGLY	PUTRESCENT
PUNCHINELLOS	PUNISHINGLY	PURIFICATIVE	PURSUIVANT	PUTRESCIBILITY
PUNCHINESS	PUNISHMENT	PURIFICATOR	PURSUIVANTS	PUTRESCIBLE
PUNCHINESSES	PUNISHMENTS	PURIFICATORS	PURTENANCE	PUTRESCIBLES
PUNCHLINES	PUNITIVELY	PURIFICATORY	PURTENANCES	PUTRESCINE
PUNCTATION	PUNITIVENESS	PURISTICAL	PURULENCES	PUTRESCINES
PUNCTATIONS	PUNITIVENESSES	PURISTICALLY	PURULENCIES	PUTRIDITIES
PUNCTATORS	PUNKINESSES	PURITANICAL	PURULENTLY	PUTRIDNESS
PUNCTILIOS	PUPIGEROUS	PURITANICALLY	PURVEYANCE	PUTRIDNESSES
PUNCTILIOUS	PUPILABILITIES	PURITANICALNESS	PURVEYANCES	PUTSCHISTS
PUNCTILIOUSLY	PUPILABILITY	PURITANISE	PUSCHKINIA	PUTTYROOTS
PUNCTILIOUSNESS	PUPILARITIES	PURITANISED	PUSCHKINIAS	PUZZLEDOMS
PUNCTUALIST	PUPILARITY	PURITANISES	PUSHCHAIRS	PUZZLEHEADED
PUNCTUALISTS	PUPILLAGES	PURITANISING	PUSHFULNESS	PUZZLEMENT
PUNCTUALITIES	PUPILLARITIES	PURITANISM	PUSHFULNESSES	PUZZLEMENTS
PUNCTUALITY	PUPILLARITY	PURITANISMS	PUSHINESSES	PUZZLINGLY
PUNCTUALLY	PUPILLATED	PURITANIZE	PUSHINGNESS	PUZZOLANAS
PUNCTUATED	PUPILLATES	PURITANIZED	PUSHINGNESSES	PYCNIDIOSPORE
PUNCTUATES	PUPILLATING	PURITANIZES	PUSILLANIMITIES	PYCNIDIOSPORES
PUNCTUATING	PUPILSHIPS	PURITANIZING	PUSILLANIMITY	PYCNOCONIDIA
PUNCTUATION	PUPIPAROUS	PURLICUING	PUSILLANIMOUS	PYCNOCONIDIUM
PUNCTUATIONIST	PUPPETEERED	PURLOINERS	PUSILLANIMOUSLY	PYCNODYSOSTOSES
PUNCTUATIONISTS	PUPPETEERING	PURLOINING	PUSSYFOOTED	PYCNODYSOSTOSIS
PUNCTUATIONS	PUPPETEERS	PUROMYCINS	PUSSYFOOTER	PYCNOGONID
PUNCTUATIVE	PUPPETLIKE	PURPLEHEART	PUSSYFOOTERS	PYCNOGONIDS
PUNCTUATOR	PUPPETRIES	PURPLEHEARTS	PUSSYFOOTING	PYCNOGONOID
PUNCTUATORS	PUPPYHOODS	PURPLENESS	PUSSYFOOTINGS	PYCNOMETER
PUNCTULATE	PURBLINDLY	PURPLENESSES	PUSSYFOOTS	PYCNOMETERS
PUNCTULATED	PURBLINDNESS	PURPORTEDLY	PUSTULANTS	PYCNOMETRIC
PUNCTULATES	PURBLINDNESSES	PURPORTING	PUSTULATED	PYCNOSOMES
PUNCTULATING	PURCHASABILITY	PURPORTLESS	PUSTULATES	PYCNOSPORE
PUNCTULATION	PURCHASABLE	PURPOSEFUL	PUSTULATING	PYCNOSPORES
PUNCTULATIONS	PURCHASERS	PURPOSEFULLY	PUSTULATION	PYCNOSTYLE
PUNCTURABLE	PURCHASING	PURPOSEFULNESS	PUSTULATIONS	PYCNOSTYLES
PUNCTURATION	PURCHASINGS	PURPOSELESS	PUTANGITANGI	PYELITISES
PUNCTURATIONS	PURDONIUMS	PURPOSELESSLY	PUTANGITANGIS	PYELOGRAMS

P

PYELOGRAPHIC
PYELOGRAPHIES
PYELOGRAPHY
PYELONEPHRITIC
PYELONEPHRITIS
PYGARGUSES
PYGOSTYLES
PYKNODYSOSTOSES
PYKNODYSOSTOSIS
PYKNOMETER
PYKNOMETERS
PYKNOSOMES
PYLORECTOMIES
PYLORECTOMY
PYOGENESES
PYOGENESIS
PYORRHOEAL
PYORRHOEAS
PYORRHOEIC
PYRACANTHA
PYRACANTHAS
PYRACANTHS
PYRALIDIDS
PYRAMIDALLY
PYRAMIDICAL
PYRAMIDICALLY
PYRAMIDING
PYRAMIDION
PYRAMIDIONS
PYRAMIDIST
PYRAMIDISTS
PYRAMIDOLOGIES
PYRAMIDOLOGIST
PYRAMIDOLOGISTS
PYRAMIDOLOGY
PYRAMIDONS
PYRANOMETER
PYRANOMETERS
PYRANOSIDE
PYRANOSIDES
PYRARGYRITE
PYRARGYRITES
PYRENEITES

PYRENOCARP
PYRENOCARPS
PYRENOMYCETOUS
PYRETHRINS
PYRETHROID
PYRETHROIDS
PYRETHRUMS
PYRETOLOGIES
PYRETOLOGY
PYRETOTHERAPIES
PYRETOTHERAPY
PYRGEOMETER
PYRGEOMETERS
PYRHELIOMETER
PYRHELIOMETERS
PYRHELIOMETRIC
PYRIDOXALS
PYRIDOXAMINE
PYRIDOXAMINES
PYRIDOXINE
PYRIDOXINES
PYRIDOXINS
PYRIMETHAMINE
PYRIMETHAMINES
PYRIMIDINE
PYRIMIDINES
PYRITHIAMINE
PYRITHIAMINES
PYRITIFEROUS
PYRITISING
PYRITIZING
PYRITOHEDRA
PYRITOHEDRAL
PYRITOHEDRON
PYROBALLOGIES
PYROBALLOGY
PYROCATECHIN
PYROCATECHINS
PYROCATECHOL
PYROCATECHOLS
PYROCERAMS
PYROCHEMICAL
PYROCHEMICALLY

PYROCLASTIC
PYROCLASTICS
PYROCLASTS
PYROELECTRIC
PYROELECTRICITY
PYROELECTRICS
PYROGALLATE
PYROGALLATES
PYROGALLIC
PYROGALLOL
PYROGALLOLS
PYROGENETIC
PYROGENICITIES
PYROGENICITY
PYROGENOUS
PYROGNOSTIC
PYROGNOSTICS
PYROGRAPHER
PYROGRAPHERS
PYROGRAPHIC
PYROGRAPHIES
PYROGRAPHY
PYROGRAVURE
PYROGRAVURES
PYROKINESES
PYROKINESIS
PYROLATERS
PYROLATRIES
PYROLIGNEOUS
PYROLIGNIC
PYROLISING
PYROLIZING
PYROLOGIES
PYROLUSITE
PYROLUSITES
PYROLYSABLE
PYROLYSATE
PYROLYSATES
PYROLYSERS
PYROLYSING
PYROLYTICALLY
PYROLYZABLE
PYROLYZATE

PYROLYZATES
PYROLYZERS
PYROLYZING
PYROMAGNETIC
PYROMANCER
PYROMANCERS
PYROMANCIES
PYROMANIAC
PYROMANIACAL
PYROMANIACS
PYROMANIAS
PYROMANTIC
PYROMERIDE
PYROMERIDES
PYROMETALLURGY
PYROMETERS
PYROMETRIC
PYROMETRICAL
PYROMETRICALLY
PYROMETRIES
PYROMORPHITE
PYROMORPHITES
PYRONINOPHILIC
PYROPHOBIA
PYROPHOBIAS
PYROPHOBIC
PYROPHOBICS
PYROPHONES
PYROPHORIC
PYROPHOROUS
PYROPHORUS
PYROPHORUSES
PYROPHOSPHATE
PYROPHOSPHATES
PYROPHOSPHORIC
PYROPHOTOGRAPH
PYROPHOTOGRAPHS
PYROPHOTOGRAPHY
PYROPHOTOMETER
PYROPHOTOMETERS
PYROPHOTOMETRY
PYROPHYLLITE
PYROPHYLLITES

PYROSCOPES
PYROSTATIC
PYROSULFITE
PYROSULFITES
PYROSULPHATE
PYROSULPHATES
PYROSULPHURIC
PYROTARTRATE
PYROTARTRATES
PYROTECHNIC
PYROTECHNICAL
PYROTECHNICALLY
PYROTECHNICIAN
PYROTECHNICIANS
PYROTECHNICS
PYROTECHNIES
PYROTECHNIST
PYROTECHNISTS
PYROTECHNY
PYROVANADIC
PYROXENITE
PYROXENITES
PYROXENITIC
PYROXENOID
PYROXENOIDS
PYROXYLINE
PYROXYLINES
PYROXYLINS
PYRRHICIST
PYRRHICISTS
PYRRHOTINE
PYRRHOTINES
PYRRHOTITE
PYRRHOTITES
PYRRHULOXIA
PYRRHULOXIAS
PYRROLIDINE
PYRROLIDINES
PYTHOGENIC
PYTHONESSES
PYTHONOMORPH
PYTHONOMORPHS

P

Q

QABALISTIC
QINGHAOSUS
QUACKERIES
QUACKSALVER
QUACKSALVERS
QUACKSALVING
QUADPLEXES
QUADRAGENARIAN
QUADRAGENARIANS
QUADRAGESIMAL
QUADRANGLE
QUADRANGLES
QUADRANGULAR
QUADRANGULARLY
QUADRANTAL
QUADRANTES
QUADRAPHONIC
QUADRAPHONICS
QUADRAPHONIES
QUADRAPHONY
QUADRAPLEGIA
QUADRAPLEGIAS
QUADRAPLEGIC
QUADRAPLEGICS
QUADRASONIC
QUADRASONICS
QUADRATICAL
QUADRATICALLY
QUADRATICS
QUADRATING
QUADRATRICES
QUADRATRIX
QUADRATRIXES
QUADRATURA
QUADRATURE
QUADRATURES
QUADRATUSES
QUADRELLAS
QUADRENNIA
QUADRENNIAL
QUADRENNIALLY

QUADRENNIALS
QUADRENNIUM
QUADRENNIUMS
QUADRICEPS
QUADRICEPSES
QUADRICIPITAL
QUADRICONE
QUADRICONES
QUADRIENNIA
QUADRIENNIAL
QUADRIENNIUM
QUADRIENNIUMS
QUADRIFARIOUS
QUADRIFOLIATE
QUADRIFORM
QUADRIGEMINAL
QUADRIGEMINATE
QUADRIGEMINOUS
QUADRILATERAL
QUADRILATERALS
QUADRILINGUAL
QUADRILITERAL
QUADRILITERALS
QUADRILLED
QUADRILLER
QUADRILLERS
QUADRILLES
QUADRILLING
QUADRILLION
QUADRILLIONS
QUADRILLIONTH
QUADRILLIONTHS
QUADRILOCULAR
QUADRINGENARIES
QUADRINGENARY
QUADRINOMIAL
QUADRINOMIALS
QUADRIPARTITE
QUADRIPARTITION
QUADRIPHONIC
QUADRIPHONICS

QUADRIPLEGIA
QUADRIPLEGIAS
QUADRIPLEGIC
QUADRIPLEGICS
QUADRIPOLE
QUADRIPOLES
QUADRIREME
QUADRIREMES
QUADRISECT
QUADRISECTED
QUADRISECTING
QUADRISECTION
QUADRISECTIONS
QUADRISECTS
QUADRISYLLABIC
QUADRISYLLABICS
QUADRISYLLABLE
QUADRISYLLABLES
QUADRIVALENCE
QUADRIVALENCES
QUADRIVALENCIES
QUADRIVALENCY
QUADRIVALENT
QUADRIVALENTS
QUADRIVIAL
QUADRIVIUM
QUADRIVIUMS
QUADROPHONIC
QUADROPHONICS
QUADROPHONIES
QUADROPHONY
QUADRUMANE
QUADRUMANES
QUADRUMANOUS
QUADRUMANS
QUADRUMVIR
QUADRUMVIRATE
QUADRUMVIRATES
QUADRUMVIRS
QUADRUPEDAL
QUADRUPEDS

QUADRUPLED
QUADRUPLES
QUADRUPLET
QUADRUPLETS
QUADRUPLEX
QUADRUPLEXED
QUADRUPLEXES
QUADRUPLEXING
QUADRUPLICATE
QUADRUPLICATED
QUADRUPLICATES
QUADRUPLICATING
QUADRUPLICATION
QUADRUPLICITIES
QUADRUPLICITY
QUADRUPLIES
QUADRUPLING
QUADRUPOLE
QUADRUPOLES
QUAESITUMS
QUAESTIONARIES
QUAESTIONARY
QUAESTORIAL
QUAESTORSHIP
QUAESTORSHIPS
QUAESTUARIES
QUAESTUARY
QUAGGINESS
QUAGGINESSES
QUAGMIRIER
QUAGMIRIEST
QUAGMIRING
QUAINTNESS
QUAINTNESSES
QUAKINESSES
QUALIFIABLE
QUALIFICATION
QUALIFICATIONS
QUALIFICATIVE
QUALIFICATIVES
QUALIFICATOR

QUALIFICATORS
QUALIFICATORY
QUALIFIEDLY
QUALIFIERS
QUALIFYING
QUALIFYINGS
QUALITATIVE
QUALITATIVELY
QUALMISHLY
QUALMISHNESS
QUALMISHNESSES
QUANDARIES
QUANGOCRACIES
QUANGOCRACY
QUANTIFIABLE
QUANTIFICATION
QUANTIFICATIONS
QUANTIFIED
QUANTIFIER
QUANTIFIERS
QUANTIFIES
QUANTIFYING
QUANTISATION
QUANTISATIONS
QUANTISERS
QUANTISING
QUANTITATE
QUANTITATED
QUANTITATES
QUANTITATING
QUANTITATION
QUANTITATIONS
QUANTITATIVE
QUANTITATIVELY
QUANTITIES
QUANTITIVE
QUANTITIVELY
QUANTIVALENCE
QUANTIVALENCES
QUANTIVALENT
QUANTIZATION

QUANTIZATIONS	QUARTERFINAL	QUATREFEUILLES	QUERSPRUNGS	QUICKSTEPPED
QUANTIZERS	QUARTERFINALIST	QUATREFOIL	QUERULOUSLY	QUICKSTEPPING
QUANTIZING	QUARTERFINALS	QUATREFOILS	QUERULOUSNESS	QUICKSTEPS
QUANTOMETER	QUARTERING	QUATTROCENTISM	QUERULOUSNESSES	QUICKTHORN
QUANTOMETERS	QUARTERINGS	QUATTROCENTISMS	QUERYINGLY	QUICKTHORNS
QUAQUAVERSAL	QUARTERLIES	QUATTROCENTIST	QUESADILLA	QUIDDANIED
QUAQUAVERSALLY	QUARTERLIFE	QUATTROCENTISTS	QUESADILLAS	QUIDDANIES
QUARANTINE	QUARTERLIGHT	QUATTROCENTO	QUESTINGLY	QUIDDANYING
QUARANTINED	QUARTERLIGHTS	QUATTROCENTOS	QUESTIONABILITY	QUIDDITATIVE
QUARANTINES	QUARTERMASTER	QUAVERIEST	QUESTIONABLE	QUIDDITCHES
QUARANTINING	QUARTERMASTERS	QUAVERINGLY	QUESTIONABLY	QUIDDITIES
QUARENDENS	QUARTERMISTRESS	QUAVERINGS	QUESTIONARIES	QUIESCENCE
QUARENDERS	QUARTEROON	QUEACHIEST	QUESTIONARY	QUIESCENCES
QUARRELERS	QUARTEROONS	QUEASINESS	QUESTIONED	QUIESCENCIES
QUARRELING	QUARTERSAW	QUEASINESSES	QUESTIONEE	QUIESCENCY
QUARRELINGS	QUARTERSAWED	QUEBRACHOS	QUESTIONEES	QUIESCENTLY
QUARRELLED	QUARTERSAWING	QUEECHIEST	QUESTIONER	QUIETENERS
QUARRELLER	QUARTERSAWN	QUEENCAKES	QUESTIONERS	QUIETENING
QUARRELLERS	QUARTERSAWS	QUEENCRAFT	QUESTIONING	QUIETENINGS
QUARRELLING	QUARTERSTAFF	QUEENCRAFTS	QUESTIONINGLY	QUIETISTIC
QUARRELLINGS	QUARTERSTAFFS	QUEENFISHES	QUESTIONINGS	QUIETNESSES
QUARRELLOUS	QUARTERSTAVES	QUEENHOODS	QUESTIONIST	QUILLBACKS
QUARRELSOME	QUARTETTES	QUEENLIEST	QUESTIONISTS	QUILLWORKS
QUARRELSOMELY	QUARTODECIMAN	QUEENLINESS	QUESTIONLESS	QUILLWORTS
QUARRELSOMENESS	QUARTODECIMANS	QUEENLINESSES	QUESTIONLESSLY	QUINACRINE
QUARRENDER	QUARTZIEST	QUEENSHIPS	QUESTIONNAIRE	QUINACRINES
QUARRENDERS	QUARTZIFEROUS	QUEENSIDES	QUESTIONNAIRES	QUINALBARBITONE
QUARRIABLE	QUARTZITES	QUEERCORES	QUESTORIAL	QUINAQUINA
QUARRINGTON	QUARTZITIC	QUEERITIES	QUESTORSHIP	QUINAQUINAS
QUARRINGTONS	QUASICRYSTAL	QUEERNESSES	QUESTORSHIPS	QUINCENTENARIES
QUARRYINGS	QUASICRYSTALS	QUELQUECHOSE	QUESTRISTS	QUINCENTENARY
QUARRYMASTER	QUASIPARTICLE	QUELQUECHOSES	QUIBBLINGLY	QUINCENTENNIAL
QUARRYMASTERS	QUASIPARTICLES	QUENCHABLE	QUIBBLINGS	QUINCENTENNIALS
QUARTATION	QUASIPERIODIC	QUENCHINGS	QUICKBEAMS	QUINCUNCIAL
QUARTATIONS	QUATERCENTENARY	QUENCHLESS	QUICKENERS	QUINCUNCIALLY
QUARTERAGE	QUATERNARIES	QUENCHLESSLY	QUICKENING	QUINCUNXES
QUARTERAGES	QUATERNARY	QUERCETINS	QUICKENINGS	QUINCUNXIAL
QUARTERBACK	QUATERNATE	QUERCETUMS	QUICKLIMES	QUINDECAGON
QUARTERBACKED	QUATERNION	QUERCITINS	QUICKNESSES	QUINDECAGONS
QUARTERBACKING	QUATERNIONIST	QUERCITRON	QUICKSANDS	QUINDECAPLET
QUARTERBACKINGS	QUATERNIONISTS	QUERCITRONS	QUICKSILVER	QUINDECAPLETS
QUARTERBACKS	QUATERNIONS	QUERIMONIES	QUICKSILVERED	QUINDECENNIAL
QUARTERDECK	QUATERNITIES	QUERIMONIOUS	QUICKSILVERING	QUINDECENNIALS
QUARTERDECKER	QUATERNITY	QUERIMONIOUSLY	QUICKSILVERINGS	QUINDECILLION
QUARTERDECKERS	QUATORZAIN	QUERNSTONE	QUICKSILVERISH	QUINDECILLIONS
QUARTERDECKS	QUATORZAINS	QUERNSTONES	QUICKSILVERS	QUINGENTENARIES
QUARTERERS	QUATREFEUILLE	QUERSPRUNG	QUICKSILVERY	QUINGENTENARY

QUINIDINES
QUINOLINES
QUINOLONES
QUINQUAGENARIAN
QUINQUAGESIMAL
QUINQUECOSTATE
QUINQUEFARIOUS
QUINQUEFOLIATE
QUINQUENNIA
QUINQUENNIAD
QUINQUENNIADS
QUINQUENNIAL
QUINQUENNIALLY
QUINQUENNIALS
QUINQUENNIUM
QUINQUENNIUMS
QUINQUEPARTITE
QUINQUEREME
QUINQUEREMES

QUINQUEVALENCE
QUINQUEVALENCES
QUINQUEVALENCY
QUINQUEVALENT
QUINQUINAS
QUINQUIVALENCE
QUINQUIVALENCES
QUINQUIVALENCY
QUINQUIVALENT
QUINTESSENCE
QUINTESSENCES
QUINTESSENTIAL
QUINTETTES
QUINTILLION
QUINTILLIONS
QUINTILLIONTH
QUINTILLIONTHS
QUINTROONS
QUINTUPLED

QUINTUPLES
QUINTUPLET
QUINTUPLETS
QUINTUPLICATE
QUINTUPLICATED
QUINTUPLICATES
QUINTUPLICATING
QUINTUPLICATION
QUINTUPLING
QUIRISTERS
QUIRKINESS
QUIRKINESSES
QUISLINGISM
QUISLINGISMS
QUITCLAIMED
QUITCLAIMING
QUITCLAIMS
QUITTANCED
QUITTANCES

QUITTANCING
QUIVERFULS
QUIVERIEST
QUIVERINGLY
QUIVERINGS
QUIXOTICAL
QUIXOTICALLY
QUIXOTISMS
QUIXOTRIES
QUIZMASTER
QUIZMASTERS
QUIZZERIES
QUIZZICALITIES
QUIZZICALITY
QUIZZICALLY
QUIZZIFICATION
QUIZZIFICATIONS
QUIZZIFIED
QUIZZIFIES

QUIZZIFYING
QUIZZINESS
QUIZZINESSES
QUODLIBETARIAN
QUODLIBETARIANS
QUODLIBETIC
QUODLIBETICAL
QUODLIBETICALLY
QUODLIBETS
QUOTABILITIES
QUOTABILITY
QUOTABLENESS
QUOTABLENESSES
QUOTATIONS
QUOTATIOUS
QUOTATIVES
QUOTEWORTHY
QUOTIDIANS
QUOTITIONS

Q

R

RABATMENTS	RACEWALKERS	RADIALISING	RADIESTHESIST	RADIOGRAPHIC
RABATTEMENT	RACEWALKING	RADIALITIES	RADIESTHESISTS	RADIOGRAPHIES
RABATTEMENTS	RACEWALKINGS	RADIALIZATION	RADIESTHETIC	RADIOGRAPHING
RABATTINGS	RACHIOTOMIES	RADIALIZATIONS	RADIOACTIVATE	RADIOGRAPHS
RABBINATES	RACHIOTOMY	RADIALIZED	RADIOACTIVATED	RADIOGRAPHY
RABBINICAL	RACHISCHISES	RADIALIZES	RADIOACTIVATES	RADIOIODINE
RABBINICALLY	RACHISCHISIS	RADIALIZING	RADIOACTIVATING	RADIOIODINES
RABBINISMS	RACHITIDES	RADIANCIES	RADIOACTIVATION	RADIOISOTOPE
RABBINISTIC	RACHITISES	RADIATIONAL	RADIOACTIVE	RADIOISOTOPES
RABBINISTS	RACIALISED	RADIATIONLESS	RADIOACTIVELY	RADIOISOTOPIC
RABBINITES	RACIALISES	RADIATIONS	RADIOACTIVITIES	RADIOLABEL
RABBITBRUSH	RACIALISING	RADICALISATION	RADIOACTIVITY	RADIOLABELED
RABBITBRUSHES	RACIALISMS	RADICALISATIONS	RADIOAUTOGRAPH	RADIOLABELING
RABBITFISH	RACIALISTIC	RADICALISE	RADIOAUTOGRAPHS	RADIOLABELLED
RABBITFISHES	RACIALISTS	RADICALISED	RADIOAUTOGRAPHY	RADIOLABELLING
RABBITINGS	RACIALIZED	RADICALISES	RADIOBIOLOGIC	RADIOLABELS
RABBITRIES	RACIALIZES	RADICALISING	RADIOBIOLOGICAL	RADIOLARIAN
RABBLEMENT	RACIALIZING	RADICALISM	RADIOBIOLOGIES	RADIOLARIANS
RABBLEMENTS	RACIATIONS	RADICALISMS	RADIOBIOLOGIST	RADIOLOCATION
RABIDITIES	RACINESSES	RADICALISTIC	RADIOBIOLOGISTS	RADIOLOCATIONAL
RABIDNESSES	RACKABONES	RADICALITIES	RADIOBIOLOGY	RADIOLOCATIONS
RACCAHOUTS	RACKETEERED	RADICALITY	RADIOCARBON	RADIOLOGIC
RACECOURSE	RACKETEERING	RADICALIZATION	RADIOCARBONS	RADIOLOGICAL
RACECOURSES	RACKETEERINGS	RADICALIZATIONS	RADIOCHEMICAL	RADIOLOGICALLY
RACEGOINGS	RACKETEERS	RADICALIZE	RADIOCHEMICALLY	RADIOLOGIES
RACEHORSES	RACKETIEST	RADICALIZED	RADIOCHEMIST	RADIOLOGIST
RACEMATION	RACKETRIES	RADICALIZES	RADIOCHEMISTRY	RADIOLOGISTS
RACEMATIONS	RACONTEURING	RADICALIZING	RADIOCHEMISTS	RADIOLUCENCIES
RACEMISATION	RACONTEURINGS	RADICALNESS	RADIOECOLOGIES	RADIOLUCENCY
RACEMISATIONS	RACONTEURS	RADICALNESSES	RADIOECOLOGY	RADIOLUCENT
RACEMISING	RACONTEUSE	RADICATING	RADIOELEMENT	RADIOLYSES
RACEMIZATION	RACONTEUSES	RADICATION	RADIOELEMENTS	RADIOLYSIS
RACEMIZATIONS	RACQUETBALL	RADICATIONS	RADIOGENIC	RADIOLYTIC
RACEMIZING	RACQUETBALLS	RADICCHIOS	RADIOGOLDS	RADIOMETER
RACEMOSELY	RACQUETING	RADICELLOSE	RADIOGONIOMETER	RADIOMETERS
RACEMOUSLY	RADARSCOPE	RADICICOLOUS	RADIOGONIOMETRY	RADIOMETRIC
RACETRACKER	RADARSCOPES	RADICIFORM	RADIOGRAMS	RADIOMETRICALLY
RACETRACKERS	RADIALISATION	RADICIVOROUS	RADIOGRAPH	RADIOMETRIES
RACETRACKS	RADIALISATIONS	RADICULOSE	RADIOGRAPHED	RADIOMETRY
RACEWALKED	RADIALISED	RADIESTHESIA	RADIOGRAPHER	RADIOMICROMETER
RACEWALKER	RADIALISES	RADIESTHESIAS	RADIOGRAPHERS	RADIOMIMETIC

RADIONUCLIDE	RADIOTELEMETERS	RAILWORKER	RAMIFICATION	RANGEFINDERS
RADIONUCLIDES	RADIOTELEMETRIC	RAILWORKERS	RAMIFICATIONS	RANGEFINDING
RADIOPACITIES	RADIOTELEMETRY	RAINBOWLIKE	RAMMISHNESS	RANGEFINDINGS
RADIOPACITY	RADIOTELEPHONE	RAINCHECKS	RAMMISHNESSES	RANGELANDS
RADIOPAGER	RADIOTELEPHONED	RAINFOREST	RAMOSITIES	RANGERSHIP
RADIOPAGERS	RADIOTELEPHONES	RAINFORESTS	RAMPACIOUS	RANGERSHIPS
RADIOPAGING	RADIOTELEPHONIC	RAININESSES	RAMPAGEOUS	RANGINESSES
RADIOPAGINGS	RADIOTELEPHONY	RAINMAKERS	RAMPAGEOUSLY	RANIVOROUS
RADIOPAQUE	RADIOTELETYPE	RAINMAKING	RAMPAGEOUSNESS	RANKNESSES
RADIOPHONE	RADIOTELETYPES	RAINMAKINGS	RAMPAGINGS	RANKSHIFTED
RADIOPHONES	RADIOTHERAPIES	RAINPROOFED	RAMPALLIAN	RANKSHIFTING
RADIOPHONIC	RADIOTHERAPIST	RAINPROOFING	RAMPALLIANS	RANKSHIFTS
RADIOPHONICALLY	RADIOTHERAPISTS	RAINPROOFS	RAMPANCIES	RANSACKERS
RADIOPHONICS	RADIOTHERAPY	RAINSPOUTS	RAMPARTING	RANSACKING
RADIOPHONIES	RADIOTHERMIES	RAINSQUALL	RAMPAUGING	RANSACKINGS
RADIOPHONIST	RADIOTHERMY	RAINSQUALLS	RAMRODDING	RANSHACKLE
RADIOPHONISTS	RADIOTHONS	RAINSTICKS	RAMSHACKLE	RANSHACKLED
RADIOPHONY	RADIOTHORIUM	RAINSTORMS	RANCHERIAS	RANSHACKLES
RADIOPHOSPHORUS	RADIOTHORIUMS	RAINWASHED	RANCHERIES	RANSHACKLING
RADIOPHOTO	RADIOTOXIC	RAINWASHES	RANCIDITIES	RANSHAKLED
RADIOPHOTOS	RADIOTRACER	RAINWASHING	RANCIDNESS	RANSHAKLES
RADIOPROTECTION	RADIOTRACERS	RAINWATERS	RANCIDNESSES	RANSHAKLING
RADIOPROTECTIVE	RADULIFORM	RAISONNEUR	RANCOROUSLY	RANSOMABLE
RADIORESISTANT	RAFFINATES	RAISONNEURS	RANCOROUSNESS	RANSOMLESS
RADIOSCOPE	RAFFINOSES	RAIYATWARI	RANCOROUSNESSES	RANSOMWARE
RADIOSCOPES	RAFFISHNESS	RAIYATWARIS	RANDINESSES	RANSOMWARES
RADIOSCOPIC	RAFFISHNESSES	RAJAHSHIPS	RANDOMISATION	RANTERISMS
RADIOSCOPICALLY	RAFFLESIAS	RAJPRAMUKH	RANDOMISATIONS	RANTIPOLED
RADIOSCOPIES	RAFTERINGS	RAJPRAMUKHS	RANDOMISED	RANTIPOLES
RADIOSCOPY	RAGAMUFFIN	RAKESHAMES	RANDOMISER	RANTIPOLING
RADIOSENSITISE	RAGAMUFFINS	RAKISHNESS	RANDOMISERS	RANUNCULACEOUS
RADIOSENSITISED	RAGGAMUFFIN	RAKISHNESSES	RANDOMISES	RANUNCULUS
RADIOSENSITISES	RAGGAMUFFINS	RALLENTANDI	RANDOMISING	RANUNCULUSES
RADIOSENSITIVE	RAGGEDIEST	RALLENTANDO	RANDOMIZATION	RAPACIOUSLY
RADIOSENSITIZE	RAGGEDNESS	RALLENTANDOS	RANDOMIZATIONS	RAPACIOUSNESS
RADIOSENSITIZED	RAGGEDNESSES	RALLYCROSS	RANDOMIZED	RAPACIOUSNESSES
RADIOSENSITIZES	RAGMATICAL	RALLYCROSSES	RANDOMIZER	RAPACITIES
RADIOSONDE	RAGPICKERS	RALLYINGLY	RANDOMIZERS	RAPIDITIES
RADIOSONDES	RAILBUSSES	RAMAPITHECINE	RANDOMIZES	RAPIDNESSES
RADIOSTRONTIUM	RAILLERIES	RAMAPITHECINES	RANDOMIZING	RAPIERLIKE
RADIOSTRONTIUMS	RAILROADED	RAMBLINGLY	RANDOMNESS	RAPPELLING
RADIOTELEGRAM	RAILROADER	RAMBOUILLET	RANDOMNESSES	RAPPELLINGS
RADIOTELEGRAMS	RAILROADERS	RAMBOUILLETS	RANDOMWISE	RAPPORTAGE
RADIOTELEGRAPH	RAILROADING	RAMBUNCTIOUS	RANGATIRAS	RAPPORTAGES
RADIOTELEGRAPHS	RAILROADINGS	RAMBUNCTIOUSLY	RANGATIRATANGA	RAPPORTEUR
RADIOTELEGRAPHY	RAILWAYMAN	RAMENTACEOUS	RANGATIRATANGAS	RAPPORTEURS
RADIOTELEMETER	RAILWAYMEN	RAMGUNSHOCH	RANGEFINDER	RAPPROCHEMENT

R

RAPPROCHEMENTS

RAPPROCHEMENTS	RATABLENESS	RATIONALIZABLE	RAYGRASSES	REACCUSTOMING
RAPSCALLION	RATABLENESSES	RATIONALIZATION	RAYLESSNESS	REACCUSTOMS
RAPSCALLIONS	RATAPLANNED	RATIONALIZE	RAYLESSNESSES	REACQUAINT
RAPTATORIAL	RATAPLANNING	RATIONALIZED	RAZMATAZES	REACQUAINTANCE
RAPTNESSES	RATATOUILLE	RATIONALIZER	RAZORBACKS	REACQUAINTANCES
RAPTURELESS	RATATOUILLES	RATIONALIZERS	RAZORBILLS	REACQUAINTED
RAPTURISED	RATBAGGERIES	RATIONALIZES	RAZORCLAMS	REACQUAINTING
RAPTURISES	RATBAGGERY	RATIONALIZING	RAZORFISHES	REACQUAINTS
RAPTURISING	RATCHETING	RATIONALLY	RAZZAMATAZZ	REACQUIRED
RAPTURISTS	RATEABILITIES	RATIONALNESS	RAZZAMATAZZES	REACQUIRES
RAPTURIZED	RATEABILITY	RATIONALNESSES	RAZZBERRIES	REACQUIRING
RAPTURIZES	RATEABLENESS	RATIONINGS	RAZZMATAZZ	REACQUISITION
RAPTURIZING	RATEABLENESSES	RATTENINGS	RAZZMATAZZES	REACQUISITIONS
RAPTUROUSLY	RATEMETERS	RATTINESSES	REABSORBED	REACTANCES
RAPTUROUSNESS	RATEPAYERS	RATTLEBAGS	REABSORBING	REACTIONAL
RAPTUROUSNESSES	RATHERIPES	RATTLEBOXES	REABSORPTION	REACTIONARIES
RAREFACTION	RATHSKELLER	RATTLEBRAIN	REABSORPTIONS	REACTIONARISM
RAREFACTIONAL	RATHSKELLERS	RATTLEBRAINED	REACCEDING	REACTIONARISMS
RAREFACTIONS	RATIFIABLE	RATTLEBRAINS	REACCELERATE	REACTIONARIST
RAREFACTIVE	RATIFICATION	RATTLEPODS	REACCELERATED	REACTIONARISTS
RAREFIABLE	RATIFICATIONS	RATTLESNAKE	REACCELERATES	REACTIONARY
RAREFICATION	RATIOCINATE	RATTLESNAKES	REACCELERATING	REACTIONARYISM
RAREFICATIONAL	RATIOCINATED	RATTLETRAP	REACCENTED	REACTIONARYISMS
RAREFICATIONS	RATIOCINATES	RATTLETRAPS	REACCENTING	REACTIONISM
RARENESSES	RATIOCINATING	RATTLINGLY	REACCEPTED	REACTIONISMS
RASCAILLES	RATIOCINATION	RATTOONING	REACCEPTING	REACTIONIST
RASCALDOMS	RATIOCINATIONS	RAUCOUSNESS	REACCESSION	REACTIONISTS
RASCALISMS	RATIOCINATIVE	RAUCOUSNESSES	REACCESSIONS	REACTIVATE
RASCALITIES	RATIOCINATOR	RAUNCHIEST	REACCLAIMED	REACTIVATED
RASCALLIEST	RATIOCINATORS	RAUNCHINESS	REACCLAIMING	REACTIVATES
RASCALLION	RATIOCINATORY	RAUNCHINESSES	REACCLAIMS	REACTIVATING
RASCALLIONS	RATIONALES	RAUWOLFIAS	REACCLIMATISE	REACTIVATION
RASHNESSES	RATIONALISABLE	RAVAGEMENT	REACCLIMATISED	REACTIVATIONS
RASPATORIES	RATIONALISATION	RAVAGEMENTS	REACCLIMATISES	REACTIVELY
RASPBERRIES	RATIONALISE	RAVELLINGS	REACCLIMATISING	REACTIVENESS
RASPINESSES	RATIONALISED	RAVELMENTS	REACCLIMATIZE	REACTIVENESSES
RASTAFARIAN	RATIONALISER	RAVENINGLY	REACCLIMATIZED	REACTIVITIES
RASTAFARIANS	RATIONALISERS	RAVENOUSLY	REACCLIMATIZES	REACTIVITY
RASTAFARIS	RATIONALISES	RAVENOUSNESS	REACCLIMATIZING	REACTUATED
RASTERISED	RATIONALISING	RAVENOUSNESSES	REACCREDIT	REACTUATES
RASTERISES	RATIONALISM	RAVIGOTTES	REACCREDITATION	REACTUATING
RASTERISING	RATIONALISMS	RAVISHINGLY	REACCREDITED	READABILITIES
RASTERIZED	RATIONALIST	RAVISHMENT	REACCREDITING	READABILITY
RASTERIZES	RATIONALISTIC	RAVISHMENTS	REACCREDITS	READABLENESS
RASTERIZING	RATIONALISTS	RAWINSONDE	REACCUSING	READABLENESSES
RATABILITIES	RATIONALITIES	RAWINSONDES	REACCUSTOM	READAPTATION
RATABILITY	RATIONALITY	RAWMAISHES	REACCUSTOMED	READAPTATIONS

EADAPTING	REAFFIRMATIONS	REALTERING	REAPPRAISEMENT	REASSAILED
EADDICTED	REAFFIRMED	REAMENDING	REAPPRAISEMENTS	REASSAILING
EADDICTING	REAFFIRMING	REAMENDMENT	REAPPRAISER	REASSEMBLAGE
EADDRESSED	REAFFIXING	REAMENDMENTS	REAPPRAISERS	REASSEMBLAGES
EADDRESSES	REAFFOREST	REANALYSED	REAPPRAISES	REASSEMBLE
EADDRESSING	REAFFORESTATION	REANALYSES	REAPPRAISING	REASSEMBLED
EADERSHIP	REAFFORESTED	REANALYSING	REAPPROPRIATE	REASSEMBLES
EADERSHIPS	REAFFORESTING	REANALYSIS	REAPPROPRIATED	REASSEMBLIES
EADINESSES	REAFFORESTS	REANALYZED	REAPPROPRIATES	REASSEMBLING
EADJUSTABLE	REAGENCIES	REANALYZES	REAPPROPRIATING	REASSEMBLY
EADJUSTED	REAGGREGATE	REANALYZING	REAPPROVED	REASSERTED
EADJUSTER	REAGGREGATED	REANIMATED	REAPPROVES	REASSERTING
EADJUSTERS	REAGGREGATES	REANIMATES	REAPPROVING	REASSERTION
EADJUSTING	REAGGREGATING	REANIMATING	REARGUARDS	REASSERTIONS
EADJUSTMENT	REAGGREGATION	REANIMATION	REARGUMENT	REASSESSED
EADJUSTMENTS	REAGGREGATIONS	REANIMATIONS	REARGUMENTS	REASSESSES
EADMISSION	REALIGNING	REANNEXATION	REARHORSES	REASSESSING
EADMISSIONS	REALIGNMENT	REANNEXATIONS	REARMAMENT	REASSESSMENT
EADMITTANCE	REALIGNMENTS	REANNEXING	REARMAMENTS	REASSESSMENTS
EADMITTANCES	REALISABILITIES	REANOINTED	REAROUSALS	REASSIGNED
EADMITTED	REALISABILITY	REANOINTING	REAROUSING	REASSIGNING
EADMITTING	REALISABLE	REANSWERED	REARRANGED	REASSIGNMENT
EADOPTING	REALISABLY	REANSWERING	REARRANGEMENT	REASSIGNMENTS
EADOPTION	REALISATION	REAPPARELLED	REARRANGEMENTS	REASSORTED
EADOPTIONS	REALISATIONS	REAPPARELLING	REARRANGER	REASSORTING
EADORNING	REALISTICALLY	REAPPARELS	REARRANGERS	REASSORTMENT
EADVANCED	REALIZABILITIES	REAPPEARANCE	REARRANGES	REASSORTMENTS
EADVANCES	REALIZABILITY	REAPPEARANCES	REARRANGING	REASSUMING
EADVANCING	REALIZABLE	REAPPEARED	REARRESTED	REASSUMPTION
EADVERTISE	REALIZABLY	REAPPEARING	REARRESTING	REASSUMPTIONS
EADVERTISED	REALIZATION	REAPPLICATION	REARTICULATE	REASSURANCE
EADVERTISEMENT	REALIZATIONS	REAPPLICATIONS	REARTICULATED	REASSURANCES
EADVERTISES	REALLOCATE	REAPPLYING	REARTICULATES	REASSURERS
EADVERTISING	REALLOCATED	REAPPOINTED	REARTICULATING	REASSURING
EADVERTIZE	REALLOCATES	REAPPOINTING	REASCENDED	REASSURINGLY
EADVERTIZED	REALLOCATING	REAPPOINTMENT	REASCENDING	REASTINESS
EADVERTIZEMENT	REALLOCATION	REAPPOINTMENTS	REASCENSION	REASTINESSES
EADVERTIZES	REALLOCATIONS	REAPPOINTS	REASCENSIONS	REATTACHED
EADVERTIZING	REALLOTMENT	REAPPORTION	REASONABILITIES	REATTACHES
EADVISING	REALLOTMENTS	REAPPORTIONED	REASONABILITY	REATTACHING
EADYMADES	REALLOTTED	REAPPORTIONING	REASONABLE	REATTACHMENT
EAEDIFIED	REALLOTTING	REAPPORTIONMENT	REASONABLENESS	REATTACHMENTS
EAEDIFIES	REALNESSES	REAPPORTIONS	REASONABLY	REATTACKED
EAEDIFYED	REALPOLITIK	REAPPRAISAL	REASONEDLY	REATTACKING
EAEDIFYES	REALPOLITIKER	REAPPRAISALS	REASONINGS	REATTAINED
EAEDIFYING	REALPOLITIKERS	REAPPRAISE	REASONLESS	REATTAINING
EAFFIRMATION	REALPOLITIKS	REAPPRAISED	REASONLESSLY	REATTEMPTED

R

REATTEMPTING
REATTEMPTS
REATTRIBUTE
REATTRIBUTED
REATTRIBUTES
REATTRIBUTING
REATTRIBUTION
REATTRIBUTIONS
REAUTHORISATION
REAUTHORISE
REAUTHORISED
REAUTHORISES
REAUTHORISING
REAUTHORIZATION
REAUTHORIZE
REAUTHORIZED
REAUTHORIZES
REAUTHORIZING
REAVAILING
REAWAKENED
REAWAKENING
REAWAKENINGS
REBALANCED
REBALANCES
REBALANCING
REBAPTISED
REBAPTISES
REBAPTISING
REBAPTISMS
REBAPTIZED
REBAPTIZES
REBAPTIZING
REBARBATIVE
REBARBATIVELY
REBATEABLE
REBATEMENT
REBATEMENTS
REBBETZINS
REBEGINNING
REBELLIONS
REBELLIOUS
REBELLIOUSLY
REBELLIOUSNESS
REBELLOWED
REBELLOWING
REBIRTHERS
REBIRTHING

REBIRTHINGS
REBLENDING
REBLOCHONS
REBLOOMING
REBLOSSOMED
REBLOSSOMING
REBLOSSOMS
REBOARDING
REBOATIONS
REBORROWED
REBORROWING
REBOTTLING
REBOUNDERS
REBOUNDING
REBRANCHED
REBRANCHES
REBRANCHING
REBRANDING
REBRANDINGS
REBREEDING
REBROADCAST
REBROADCASTED
REBROADCASTING
REBROADCASTS
REBUILDING
REBUILDINGS
REBUKEFULLY
REBUKINGLY
REBUTMENTS
REBUTTABLE
REBUTTONED
REBUTTONING
RECALCITRANCE
RECALCITRANCES
RECALCITRANCIES
RECALCITRANCY
RECALCITRANT
RECALCITRANTS
RECALCITRATE
RECALCITRATED
RECALCITRATES
RECALCITRATING
RECALCITRATION
RECALCITRATIONS
RECALCULATE
RECALCULATED
RECALCULATES

RECALCULATING
RECALCULATION
RECALCULATIONS
RECALESCED
RECALESCENCE
RECALESCENCES
RECALESCENT
RECALESCES
RECALESCING
RECALIBRATE
RECALIBRATED
RECALIBRATES
RECALIBRATING
RECALIBRATION
RECALIBRATIONS
RECALLABILITIES
RECALLABILITY
RECALLABLE
RECALLMENT
RECALLMENTS
RECALMENTS
RECANALISATION
RECANALISATIONS
RECANALISE
RECANALISED
RECANALISES
RECANALISING
RECANALIZATION
RECANALIZATIONS
RECANALIZE
RECANALIZED
RECANALIZES
RECANALIZING
RECANTATION
RECANTATIONS
RECAPITALISE
RECAPITALISED
RECAPITALISES
RECAPITALISING
RECAPITALIZE
RECAPITALIZED
RECAPITALIZES
RECAPITALIZING
RECAPITULATE
RECAPITULATED
RECAPITULATES
RECAPITULATING

RECAPITULATION
RECAPITULATIONS
RECAPITULATIVE
RECAPITULATORY
RECAPPABLE
RECAPTIONS
RECAPTURED
RECAPTURER
RECAPTURERS
RECAPTURES
RECAPTURING
RECARPETED
RECARPETING
RECARRYING
RECATALOGED
RECATALOGING
RECATALOGS
RECATALOGUE
RECATALOGUED
RECATALOGUES
RECATALOGUING
RECATCHING
RECAUTIONED
RECAUTIONING
RECAUTIONS
RECEIPTING
RECEIPTORS
RECEIVABILITIES
RECEIVABILITY
RECEIVABLE
RECEIVABLENESS
RECEIVABLES
RECEIVERSHIP
RECEIVERSHIPS
RECEIVINGS
RECEMENTED
RECEMENTING
RECENSIONS
RECENSORED
RECENSORING
RECENTNESS
RECENTNESSES
RECENTRIFUGE
RECENTRIFUGED
RECENTRIFUGES
RECENTRIFUGING
RECENTRING

RECEPTACLE
RECEPTACLES
RECEPTACULA
RECEPTACULAR
RECEPTACULUM
RECEPTIBILITIES
RECEPTIBILITY
RECEPTIBLE
RECEPTIONIST
RECEPTIONISTS
RECEPTIONS
RECEPTIVELY
RECEPTIVENESS
RECEPTIVENESSES
RECEPTIVITIES
RECEPTIVITY
RECERTIFICATION
RECERTIFIED
RECERTIFIES
RECERTIFYING
RECESSIONAL
RECESSIONALS
RECESSIONARY
RECESSIONISTA
RECESSIONISTAS
RECESSIONS
RECESSIVELY
RECESSIVENESS
RECESSIVENESSES
RECESSIVES
RECHALLENGE
RECHALLENGED
RECHALLENGES
RECHALLENGING
RECHANGING
RECHANNELED
RECHANNELING
RECHANNELLED
RECHANNELLING
RECHANNELS
RECHARGEABLE
RECHARGERS
RECHARGING
RECHARTERED
RECHARTERING
RECHARTERS
RECHARTING

RECHAUFFES	RECIRCULATES	RECODIFICATION	RECOLLECTIVE	RECOMMENDS
RECHEATING	RECIRCULATING	RECODIFICATIONS	RECOLLECTIVELY	RECOMMISSION
RECHECKING	RECIRCULATION	RECODIFIED	RECOLLECTS	RECOMMISSIONED
RECHIPPING	RECIRCULATIONS	RECODIFIES	RECOLONISATION	RECOMMISSIONING
RECHIPPINGS	RECITALIST	RECODIFYING	RECOLONISATIONS	RECOMMISSIONS
RECHOOSING	RECITALISTS	RECOGNISABILITY	RECOLONISE	RECOMMITMENT
RECHOREOGRAPH	RECITATION	RECOGNISABLE	RECOLONISED	RECOMMITMENTS
RECHOREOGRAPHED	RECITATIONIST	RECOGNISABLY	RECOLONISES	RECOMMITTAL
RECHOREOGRAPHS	RECITATIONISTS	RECOGNISANCE	RECOLONISING	RECOMMITTALS
RECHRISTEN	RECITATIONS	RECOGNISANCES	RECOLONIZATION	RECOMMITTED
RECHRISTENED	RECITATIVE	RECOGNISANT	RECOLONIZATIONS	RECOMMITTING
RECHRISTENING	RECITATIVES	RECOGNISED	RECOLONIZE	RECOMPACTED
RECHRISTENS	RECITATIVI	RECOGNISEE	RECOLONIZED	RECOMPACTING
RECHROMATOGRAPH	RECITATIVO	RECOGNISEES	RECOLONIZES	RECOMPACTS
RECIDIVISM	RECITATIVOS	RECOGNISER	RECOLONIZING	RECOMPENCE
RECIDIVISMS	RECKLESSLY	RECOGNISERS	RECOLORING	RECOMPENCES
RECIDIVIST	RECKLESSNESS	RECOGNISES	RECOLOURED	RECOMPENSABLE
RECIDIVISTIC	RECKLESSNESSES	RECOGNISING	RECOLOURING	RECOMPENSE
RECIDIVISTS	RECKONINGS	RECOGNISOR	RECOMBINANT	RECOMPENSED
RECIDIVOUS	RECLADDING	RECOGNISORS	RECOMBINANTS	RECOMPENSER
RECIPIENCE	RECLAIMABLE	RECOGNITION	RECOMBINATION	RECOMPENSERS
RECIPIENCES	RECLAIMABLY	RECOGNITIONS	RECOMBINATIONAL	RECOMPENSES
RECIPIENCIES	RECLAIMANT	RECOGNITIVE	RECOMBINATIONS	RECOMPENSING
RECIPIENCY	RECLAIMANTS	RECOGNITORY	RECOMBINED	RECOMPILATION
RECIPIENTS	RECLAIMERS	RECOGNIZABILITY	RECOMBINES	RECOMPILATIONS
RECIPROCAL	RECLAIMING	RECOGNIZABLE	RECOMBINING	RECOMPILED
RECIPROCALITIES	RECLAMATION	RECOGNIZABLY	RECOMFORTED	RECOMPILES
RECIPROCALITY	RECLAMATIONS	RECOGNIZANCE	RECOMFORTING	RECOMPILING
RECIPROCALLY	RECLASPING	RECOGNIZANCES	RECOMFORTLESS	RECOMPOSED
RECIPROCALS	RECLASSIFIED	RECOGNIZANT	RECOMFORTS	RECOMPOSES
RECIPROCANT	RECLASSIFIES	RECOGNIZED	RECOMFORTURE	RECOMPOSING
RECIPROCANTS	RECLASSIFY	RECOGNIZEE	RECOMFORTURES	RECOMPOSITION
RECIPROCATE	RECLASSIFYING	RECOGNIZEES	RECOMMENCE	RECOMPOSITIONS
RECIPROCATED	RECLEANING	RECOGNIZER	RECOMMENCED	RECOMPRESS
RECIPROCATES	RECLIMBING	RECOGNIZERS	RECOMMENCEMENT	RECOMPRESSED
RECIPROCATING	RECLINABLE	RECOGNIZES	RECOMMENCEMENTS	RECOMPRESSES
RECIPROCATION	RECLINATION	RECOGNIZING	RECOMMENCES	RECOMPRESSING
RECIPROCATIONS	RECLINATIONS	RECOGNIZOR	RECOMMENCING	RECOMPRESSION
RECIPROCATIVE	RECLOSABLE	RECOGNIZORS	RECOMMENDABLE	RECOMPRESSIONS
RECIPROCATOR	RECLOTHING	RECOILLESS	RECOMMENDABLY	RECOMPUTATION
RECIPROCATORS	RECLUSENESS	RECOINAGES	RECOMMENDATION	RECOMPUTATIONS
RECIPROCATORY	RECLUSENESSES	RECOLLECTED	RECOMMENDATIONS	RECOMPUTED
RECIPROCITIES	RECLUSIONS	RECOLLECTEDLY	RECOMMENDATORY	RECOMPUTES
RECIPROCITY	RECLUSIVELY	RECOLLECTEDNESS	RECOMMENDED	RECOMPUTING
RECIRCLING	RECLUSIVENESS	RECOLLECTING	RECOMMENDER	RECONCEIVE
RECIRCULATE	RECLUSIVENESSES	RECOLLECTION	RECOMMENDERS	RECONCEIVED
RECIRCULATED	RECLUSORIES	RECOLLECTIONS	RECOMMENDING	RECONCEIVES

R

RECONCEIVING	RECONFINES	RECONSIGNS	RECONTOURS	RECOVERABLENESS
RECONCENTRATE	RECONFINING	RECONSOLED	RECONVALESCE	RECOVEREES
RECONCENTRATED	RECONFIRMATION	RECONSOLES	RECONVALESCED	RECOVERERS
RECONCENTRATES	RECONFIRMATIONS	RECONSOLIDATE	RECONVALESCENCE	RECOVERIES
RECONCENTRATING	RECONFIRMED	RECONSOLIDATED	RECONVALESCENT	RECOVERING
RECONCENTRATION	RECONFIRMING	RECONSOLIDATES	RECONVALESCES	RECOVERORS
RECONCEPTION	RECONFIRMS	RECONSOLIDATING	RECONVALESCING	RECOWERING
RECONCEPTIONS	RECONNAISSANCE	RECONSOLIDATION	RECONVENED	RECREANCES
RECONCEPTUALISE	RECONNAISSANCES	RECONSOLING	RECONVENES	RECREANCIES
RECONCEPTUALIZE	RECONNECTED	RECONSTITUENT	RECONVENING	RECREANTLY
RECONCILABILITY	RECONNECTING	RECONSTITUENTS	RECONVERSION	RECREATING
RECONCILABLE	RECONNECTION	RECONSTITUTABLE	RECONVERSIONS	RECREATION
RECONCILABLY	RECONNECTIONS	RECONSTITUTE	RECONVERTED	RECREATIONAL
RECONCILED	RECONNECTS	RECONSTITUTED	RECONVERTING	RECREATIONIST
RECONCILEMENT	RECONNOISSANCE	RECONSTITUTES	RECONVERTS	RECREATIONISTS
RECONCILEMENTS	RECONNOISSANCES	RECONSTITUTING	RECONVEYANCE	RECREATIONS
RECONCILER	RECONNOITER	RECONSTITUTION	RECONVEYANCES	RECREATIVE
RECONCILERS	RECONNOITERED	RECONSTITUTIONS	RECONVEYED	RECREATIVELY
RECONCILES	RECONNOITERER	RECONSTRUCT	RECONVEYING	RECREATORS
RECONCILIATION	RECONNOITERERS	RECONSTRUCTED	RECONVICTED	RECREMENTAL
RECONCILIATIONS	RECONNOITERING	RECONSTRUCTIBLE	RECONVICTING	RECREMENTITIAL
RECONCILIATORY	RECONNOITERS	RECONSTRUCTING	RECONVICTION	RECREMENTITIOUS
RECONCILING	RECONNOITRE	RECONSTRUCTION	RECONVICTIONS	RECREMENTS
RECONDENSATION	RECONNOITRED	RECONSTRUCTIONS	RECONVICTS	RECRIMINATE
RECONDENSATIONS	RECONNOITRER	RECONSTRUCTIVE	RECONVINCE	RECRIMINATED
RECONDENSE	RECONNOITRERS	RECONSTRUCTOR	RECONVINCED	RECRIMINATES
RECONDENSED	RECONNOITRES	RECONSTRUCTORS	RECONVINCES	RECRIMINATING
RECONDENSES	RECONNOITRING	RECONSTRUCTS	RECONVINCING	RECRIMINATION
RECONDENSING	RECONNOITRINGS	RECONSULTED	RECORDABLE	RECRIMINATIONS
RECONDITELY	RECONQUERED	RECONSULTING	RECORDATION	RECRIMINATIVE
RECONDITENESS	RECONQUERING	RECONSULTS	RECORDATIONS	RECRIMINATOR
RECONDITENESSES	RECONQUERS	RECONTACTED	RECORDERSHIP	RECRIMINATORS
RECONDITION	RECONQUEST	RECONTACTING	RECORDERSHIPS	RECRIMINATORY
RECONDITIONED	RECONQUESTS	RECONTACTS	RECORDINGS	RECROSSING
RECONDITIONING	RECONSECRATE	RECONTAMINATE	RECORDISTS	RECROWNING
RECONDITIONS	RECONSECRATED	RECONTAMINATED	RECOUNTALS	RECRUDESCE
RECONDUCTED	RECONSECRATES	RECONTAMINATES	RECOUNTERS	RECRUDESCED
RECONDUCTING	RECONSECRATING	RECONTAMINATING	RECOUNTING	RECRUDESCENCE
RECONDUCTS	RECONSECRATION	RECONTAMINATION	RECOUNTMENT	RECRUDESCENCES
RECONFERRED	RECONSECRATIONS	RECONTEXTUALISE	RECOUNTMENTS	RECRUDESCENCIES
RECONFERRING	RECONSIDER	RECONTEXTUALIZE	RECOUPABLE	RECRUDESCENCY
RECONFIGURATION	RECONSIDERATION	RECONTINUE	RECOUPLING	RECRUDESCENT
RECONFIGURE	RECONSIDERED	RECONTINUED	RECOUPMENT	RECRUDESCES
RECONFIGURED	RECONSIDERING	RECONTINUES	RECOUPMENTS	RECRUDESCING
RECONFIGURES	RECONSIDERS	RECONTINUING	RECOURSING	RECRUITABLE
RECONFIGURING	RECONSIGNED	RECONTOURED	RECOVERABILITY	RECRUITALS
RECONFINED	RECONSIGNING	RECONTOURING	RECOVERABLE	RECRUITERS

RECRUITING	RECULTIVATES	REDBAITING	REDEMPTIBLE	REDIGRESSED
RECRUITINGS	RECULTIVATING	REDBELLIES	REDEMPTION	REDIGRESSES
RECRUITMENT	RECUMBENCE	REDBREASTS	REDEMPTIONAL	REDIGRESSING
RECRUITMENTS	RECUMBENCES	REDCURRANT	REDEMPTIONER	REDINGOTES
RECRYSTALLISE	RECUMBENCIES	REDCURRANTS	REDEMPTIONERS	REDINTEGRATE
RECRYSTALLISED	RECUMBENCY	REDDISHNESS	REDEMPTIONS	REDINTEGRATED
RECRYSTALLISES	RECUMBENTLY	REDDISHNESSES	REDEMPTIVE	REDINTEGRATES
RECRYSTALLISING	RECUPERABLE	REDECIDING	REDEMPTIVELY	REDINTEGRATING
RECRYSTALLIZE	RECUPERATE	REDECORATE	REDEMPTORY	REDINTEGRATION
RECRYSTALLIZED	RECUPERATED	REDECORATED	REDEPLOYED	REDINTEGRATIONS
RECRYSTALLIZES	RECUPERATES	REDECORATES	REDEPLOYING	REDINTEGRATIVE
RECRYSTALLIZING	RECUPERATING	REDECORATING	REDEPLOYMENT	REDIRECTED
RECTANGLED	RECUPERATION	REDECORATION	REDEPLOYMENTS	REDIRECTING
RECTANGLES	RECUPERATIONS	REDECORATIONS	REDEPOSITED	REDIRECTION
RECTANGULAR	RECUPERATIVE	REDECORATOR	REDEPOSITING	REDIRECTIONS
RECTANGULARITY	RECUPERATOR	REDECORATORS	REDEPOSITS	REDISBURSE
RECTANGULARLY	RECUPERATORS	REDECRAFTS	REDESCENDED	REDISBURSED
RECTIFIABILITY	RECUPERATORY	REDEDICATE	REDESCENDING	REDISBURSES
RECTIFIABLE	RECURELESS	REDEDICATED	REDESCENDS	REDISBURSING
RECTIFICATION	RECURRENCE	REDEDICATES	REDESCRIBE	REDISCOUNT
RECTIFICATIONS	RECURRENCES	REDEDICATING	REDESCRIBED	REDISCOUNTABLE
RECTIFIERS	RECURRENCIES	REDEDICATION	REDESCRIBES	REDISCOUNTED
RECTIFYING	RECURRENCY	REDEDICATIONS	REDESCRIBING	REDISCOUNTING
RECTILINEAL	RECURRENTLY	REDEEMABILITIES	REDESCRIPTION	REDISCOUNTS
RECTILINEALLY	RECURRINGLY	REDEEMABILITY	REDESCRIPTIONS	REDISCOVER
RECTILINEAR	RECURSIONS	REDEEMABLE	REDESIGNED	REDISCOVERED
RECTILINEARITY	RECURSIVELY	REDEEMABLENESS	REDESIGNING	REDISCOVERER
RECTILINEARLY	RECURSIVENESS	REDEEMABLY	REDETERMINATION	REDISCOVERERS
RECTIPETALIES	RECURSIVENESSES	REDEEMLESS	REDETERMINE	REDISCOVERIES
RECTIPETALITIES	RECURVIROSTRAL	REDEFEATED	REDETERMINED	REDISCOVERING
RECTIPETALITY	RECUSANCES	REDEFEATING	REDETERMINES	REDISCOVERS
RECTIPETALY	RECUSANCIES	REDEFECTED	REDETERMINING	REDISCOVERY
RECTIROSTRAL	RECUSATION	REDEFECTING	REDEVELOPED	REDISCUSSED
RECTISERIAL	RECUSATIONS	REDEFINING	REDEVELOPER	REDISCUSSES
RECTITISES	RECYCLABLE	REDEFINITION	REDEVELOPERS	REDISCUSSING
RECTITUDES	RECYCLABLES	REDEFINITIONS	REDEVELOPING	REDISPLAYED
RECTITUDINOUS	RECYCLATES	REDELIVERANCE	REDEVELOPMENT	REDISPLAYING
RECTOCELES	RECYCLEABLE	REDELIVERANCES	REDEVELOPMENTS	REDISPLAYS
RECTORATES	RECYCLEABLES	REDELIVERED	REDEVELOPS	REDISPOSED
RECTORESSES	RECYCLINGS	REDELIVERER	REDIALLING	REDISPOSES
RECTORIALS	RECYCLISTS	REDELIVERERS	REDICTATED	REDISPOSING
RECTORSHIP	REDACTIONAL	REDELIVERIES	REDICTATES	REDISPOSITION
RECTORSHIPS	REDACTIONS	REDELIVERING	REDICTATING	REDISPOSITIONS
RECTRESSES	REDACTORIAL	REDELIVERS	REDIGESTED	REDISSOLUTION
RECTRICIAL	REDAMAGING	REDELIVERY	REDIGESTING	REDISSOLUTIONS
RECULTIVATE	REDARGUING	REDEMANDED	REDIGESTION	REDISSOLVE
RECULTIVATED	REDBAITERS	REDEMANDING	REDIGESTIONS	REDISSOLVED

R

REDISSOLVES	REDRILLING	REELECTING	REENCOUNTERING	REEQUIPPED
REDISSOLVING	REDRUTHITE	REELECTION	REENCOUNTERS	REEQUIPPING
REDISTILLATION	REDRUTHITES	REELECTIONS	REENDOWING	REERECTING
REDISTILLATIONS	REDSHIFTED	REELEVATED	REENERGISE	REESCALATE
REDISTILLED	REDSHIRTED	REELEVATES	REENERGISED	REESCALATED
REDISTILLING	REDSHIRTING	REELEVATING	REENERGISES	REESCALATES
REDISTILLS	REDSTREAKS	REELIGIBILITIES	REENERGISING	REESCALATING
REDISTRIBUTE	REDUCIBILITIES	REELIGIBILITY	REENERGIZE	REESCALATION
REDISTRIBUTED	REDUCIBILITY	REELIGIBLE	REENERGIZED	REESCALATIONS
REDISTRIBUTES	REDUCIBLENESS	REEMBARKED	REENERGIZES	REESTABLISH
REDISTRIBUTING	REDUCIBLENESSES	REEMBARKING	REENERGIZING	REESTABLISHED
REDISTRIBUTION	REDUCTANTS	REEMBODIED	REENFORCED	REESTABLISHES
REDISTRIBUTIONS	REDUCTASES	REEMBODIES	REENFORCES	REESTABLISHING
REDISTRIBUTIVE	REDUCTIONAL	REEMBODYING	REENFORCING	REESTABLISHMENT
REDISTRICT	REDUCTIONISM	REEMBRACED	REENGAGEMENT	REESTIMATE
REDISTRICTED	REDUCTIONISMS	REEMBRACES	REENGAGEMENTS	REESTIMATED
REDISTRICTING	REDUCTIONIST	REEMBRACING	REENGAGING	REESTIMATES
REDISTRICTS	REDUCTIONISTIC	REEMBROIDER	REENGINEER	REESTIMATING
REDIVIDING	REDUCTIONISTS	REEMBROIDERED	REENGINEERED	REEVALUATE
REDIVISION	REDUCTIONS	REEMBROIDERING	REENGINEERING	REEVALUATED
REDIVISIONS	REDUCTIVELY	REEMBROIDERS	REENGINEERS	REEVALUATES
REDIVORCED	REDUCTIVENESS	REEMERGENCE	REENGRAVED	REEVALUATING
REDIVORCES	REDUCTIVENESSES	REEMERGENCES	REENGRAVES	REEVALUATION
REDIVORCING	REDUCTIVES	REEMERGING	REENGRAVING	REEVALUATIONS
REDLININGS	REDUNDANCE	REEMISSION	REENJOYING	REEXAMINATION
REDOLENCES	REDUNDANCES	REEMISSIONS	REENLARGED	REEXAMINATIONS
REDOLENCIES	REDUNDANCIES	REEMITTING	REENLARGES	REEXAMINED
REDOLENTLY	REDUNDANCY	REEMPHASES	REENLARGING	REEXAMINES
REDOUBLEMENT	REDUNDANTLY	REEMPHASIS	REENLISTED	REEXAMINING
REDOUBLEMENTS	REDUPLICATE	REEMPHASISE	REENLISTING	REEXECUTED
REDOUBLERS	REDUPLICATED	REEMPHASISED	REENLISTMENT	REEXECUTES
REDOUBLING	REDUPLICATES	REEMPHASISES	REENLISTMENTS	REEXECUTING
REDOUBTABLE	REDUPLICATING	REEMPHASISING	REENROLLED	REEXHIBITED
REDOUBTABLENESS	REDUPLICATION	REEMPHASIZE	REENROLLING	REEXHIBITING
REDOUBTABLY	REDUPLICATIONS	REEMPHASIZED	REENSLAVED	REEXHIBITS
REDOUBTING	REDUPLICATIVE	REEMPHASIZES	REENSLAVES	REEXPELLED
REDOUNDING	REDUPLICATIVELY	REEMPHASIZING	REENSLAVING	REEXPELLING
REDOUNDINGS	REEDIFYING	REEMPLOYED	REENTERING	REEXPERIENCE
REDRAFTING	REEDINESSES	REEMPLOYING	REENTHRONE	REEXPERIENCED
REDREAMING	REEDITIONS	REEMPLOYMENT	REENTHRONED	REEXPERIENCES
REDRESSABLE	REEDUCATED	REEMPLOYMENTS	REENTHRONES	REEXPERIENCING
REDRESSALS	REEDUCATES	REENACTING	REENTHRONING	REEXPLAINED
REDRESSERS	REEDUCATING	REENACTMENT	REENTRANCE	REEXPLAINING
REDRESSIBLE	REEDUCATION	REENACTMENTS	REENTRANCES	REEXPLAINS
REDRESSING	REEDUCATIONS	REENACTORS	REENTRANTS	REEXPLORED
REDRESSIVE	REEDUCATIVE	REENCOUNTER	REEQUIPMENT	REEXPLORES
REDRESSORS	REEJECTING	REENCOUNTERED	REEQUIPMENTS	REEXPLORING

EEXPORTATION	REFINANCINGS	REFLECTORS	REFORMATIONIST	REFRACTURE
EEXPORTATIONS	REFINEDNESS	REFLEXIBILITIES	REFORMATIONISTS	REFRACTURED
EEXPORTED	REFINEDNESSES	REFLEXIBILITY	REFORMATIONS	REFRACTURES
EEXPORTING	REFINEMENT	REFLEXIBLE	REFORMATIVE	REFRACTURING
EEXPOSING	REFINEMENTS	REFLEXIONAL	REFORMATORIES	REFRAINERS
EEXPOSURE	REFINERIES	REFLEXIONS	REFORMATORY	REFRAINING
EEXPOSURES	REFINISHED	REFLEXIVELY	REFORMATTED	REFRAINMENT
EEXPRESSED	REFINISHER	REFLEXIVENESS	REFORMATTING	REFRAINMENTS
EEXPRESSES	REFINISHERS	REFLEXIVENESSES	REFORMINGS	REFRANGIBILITY
EEXPRESSING	REFINISHES	REFLEXIVES	REFORMISMS	REFRANGIBLE
EFASHIONED	REFINISHING	REFLEXIVITIES	REFORMISTS	REFRANGIBLENESS
EFASHIONING	REFITMENTS	REFLEXIVITY	REFORMULATE	REFREEZING
EFASHIONMENT	REFITTINGS	REFLEXOLOGICAL	REFORMULATED	REFRESHENED
EFASHIONMENTS	REFLAGGING	REFLEXOLOGIES	REFORMULATES	REFRESHENER
EFASHIONS	REFLATIONARY	REFLEXOLOGIST	REFORMULATING	REFRESHENERS
EFASTENED	REFLATIONS	REFLEXOLOGISTS	REFORMULATION	REFRESHENING
EFASTENING	REFLECTANCE	REFLEXOLOGY	REFORMULATIONS	REFRESHENS
EFECTIONER	REFLECTANCES	REFLOATING	REFORTIFICATION	REFRESHERS
EFECTIONERS	REFLECTERS	REFLOODING	REFORTIFIED	REFRESHFUL
EFECTIONS	REFLECTING	REFLOWERED	REFORTIFIES	REFRESHFULLY
EFECTORIAN	REFLECTINGLY	REFLOWERING	REFORTIFYING	REFRESHING
EFECTORIANS	REFLECTION	REFLOWERINGS	REFOUNDATION	REFRESHINGLY
EFECTORIES	REFLECTIONAL	REFLOWINGS	REFOUNDATIONS	REFRESHMENT
EFEREEING	REFLECTIONLESS	REFLUENCES	REFOUNDERS	REFRESHMENTS
EFERENCED	REFLECTIONS	REFOCILLATE	REFOUNDING	REFRIGERANT
EFERENCER	REFLECTIVE	REFOCILLATED	REFRACTABLE	REFRIGERANTS
EFERENCERS	REFLECTIVELY	REFOCILLATES	REFRACTARIES	REFRIGERATE
EFERENCES	REFLECTIVENESS	REFOCILLATING	REFRACTARY	REFRIGERATED
EFERENCING	REFLECTIVITIES	REFOCILLATION	REFRACTILE	REFRIGERATES
EFERENCINGS	REFLECTIVITY	REFOCILLATIONS	REFRACTING	REFRIGERATING
EFERENDARIES	REFLECTOGRAM	REFOCUSING	REFRACTION	REFRIGERATION
PEFERENDARY	REFLECTOGRAMS	REFOCUSSED	REFRACTIONS	REFRIGERATIONS
EFERENDUM	REFLECTOGRAPH	REFOCUSSES	REFRACTIVE	REFRIGERATIVE
EFERENDUMS	REFLECTOGRAPHS	REFOCUSSING	REFRACTIVELY	REFRIGERATOR
EFERENTIAL	REFLECTOGRAPHY	REFORESTATION	REFRACTIVENESS	REFRIGERATORIES
PEFERENTIALITY	REFLECTOMETER	REFORESTATIONS	REFRACTIVITIES	REFRIGERATORS
EFERENTIALLY	REFLECTOMETERS	REFORESTED	REFRACTIVITY	REFRIGERATORY
EFERRABLE	REFLECTOMETRIES	REFORESTING	REFRACTOMETER	REFRINGENCE
EFERRIBLE	REFLECTOMETRY	REFORMABILITIES	REFRACTOMETERS	REFRINGENCES
EFIGHTING	REFLECTORISE	REFORMABILITY	REFRACTOMETRIC	REFRINGENCIES
EFIGURING	REFLECTORISED	REFORMABLE	REFRACTOMETRIES	REFRINGENCY
EFILLABLE	REFLECTORISES	REFORMADES	REFRACTOMETRY	REFRINGENT
EFILTERED	REFLECTORISING	REFORMADOES	REFRACTORIES	REFRINGING
EFILTERING	REFLECTORIZE	REFORMADOS	REFRACTORILY	REFRONTING
EFINANCED	REFLECTORIZED	REFORMATES	REFRACTORINESS	REFUELABLE
EFINANCES	REFLECTORIZES	REFORMATION	REFRACTORS	REFUELINGS
EFINANCING	REFLECTORIZING	REFORMATIONAL	REFRACTORY	REFUELLABLE

REFUELLING	REGELATION	REGISTERER	REGROUPINGS	REHAMMERING
REFUELLINGS	REGELATIONS	REGISTERERS	REGUERDONED	REHANDLING
REFUGEEISM	REGENERABLE	REGISTERING	REGUERDONING	REHANDLINGS
REFUGEEISMS	REGENERACIES	REGISTRABLE	REGUERDONS	REHARDENED
REFULGENCE	REGENERACY	REGISTRANT	REGULARISATION	REHARDENING
REFULGENCES	REGENERATE	REGISTRANTS	REGULARISATIONS	REHEARINGS
REFULGENCIES	REGENERATED	REGISTRARIES	REGULARISE	REHEARSALS
REFULGENCY	REGENERATELY	REGISTRARS	REGULARISED	REHEARSERS
REFULGENTLY	REGENERATENESS	REGISTRARSHIP	REGULARISES	REHEARSING
REFUNDABILITIES	REGENERATES	REGISTRARSHIPS	REGULARISING	REHEARSINGS
REFUNDABILITY	REGENERATING	REGISTRARY	REGULARITIES	REHEATINGS
REFUNDABLE	REGENERATION	REGISTRATION	REGULARITY	REHOSPITALISE
REFUNDMENT	REGENERATIONS	REGISTRATIONAL	REGULARIZATION	REHOSPITALISED
REFUNDMENTS	REGENERATIVE	REGISTRATIONS	REGULARIZATIONS	REHOSPITALISES
REFURBISHED	REGENERATIVELY	REGISTRIES	REGULARIZE	REHOSPITALISING
REFURBISHER	REGENERATOR	REGLORIFIED	REGULARIZED	REHOSPITALIZE
REFURBISHERS	REGENERATORS	REGLORIFIES	REGULARIZES	REHOSPITALIZED
REFURBISHES	REGENERATORY	REGLORIFYING	REGULARIZING	REHOSPITALIZES
REFURBISHING	REGENTSHIP	REGLOSSING	REGULATING	REHOSPITALIZING
REFURBISHINGS	REGENTSHIPS	REGNANCIES	REGULATION	REHOUSINGS
REFURBISHMENT	REGGAETONS	REGRAFTING	REGULATIONS	REHUMANISE
REFURBISHMENTS	REGIMENTAL	REGRANTING	REGULATIVE	REHUMANISED
REFURNISHED	REGIMENTALLY	REGRATINGS	REGULATIVELY	REHUMANISES
REFURNISHES	REGIMENTALS	REGREDIENCE	REGULATORS	REHUMANISING
REFURNISHING	REGIMENTATION	REGREDIENCES	REGULATORY	REHUMANIZE
REFUSENIKS	REGIMENTATIONS	REGREENING	REGULISING	REHUMANIZED
REFUTABILITIES	REGIMENTED	REGREETING	REGULIZING	REHUMANIZES
REFUTABILITY	REGIMENTING	REGRESSING	REGURGITANT	REHUMANIZING
REFUTATION	REGIONALISATION	REGRESSION	REGURGITANTS	REHYDRATABLE
REFUTATIONS	REGIONALISE	REGRESSIONS	REGURGITATE	REHYDRATED
REGAINABLE	REGIONALISED	REGRESSIVE	REGURGITATED	REHYDRATES
REGAINMENT	REGIONALISES	REGRESSIVELY	REGURGITATES	REHYDRATING
REGAINMENTS	REGIONALISING	REGRESSIVENESS	REGURGITATING	REHYDRATION
REGALEMENT	REGIONALISM	REGRESSIVITIES	REGURGITATION	REHYDRATIONS
REGALEMENTS	REGIONALISMS	REGRESSIVITY	REGURGITATIONS	REHYPNOTISE
REGALITIES	REGIONALIST	REGRESSORS	REHABILITANT	REHYPNOTISED
REGALNESSES	REGIONALISTIC	REGRETFULLY	REHABILITANTS	REHYPNOTISES
REGARDABLE	REGIONALISTS	REGRETFULNESS	REHABILITATE	REHYPNOTISING
REGARDFULLY	REGIONALIZATION	REGRETFULNESSES	REHABILITATED	REHYPNOTIZE
REGARDFULNESS	REGIONALIZE	REGRETTABLE	REHABILITATES	REHYPNOTIZED
REGARDFULNESSES	REGIONALIZED	REGRETTABLY	REHABILITATING	REHYPNOTIZES
REGARDLESS	REGIONALIZES	REGRETTERS	REHABILITATION	REHYPNOTIZING
REGARDLESSLY	REGIONALIZING	REGRETTING	REHABILITATIONS	REICHSMARK
REGARDLESSNESS	REGIONALLY	REGRINDING	REHABILITATIVE	REICHSMARKS
REGATHERED	REGISSEURS	REGROOMING	REHABILITATOR	REIDENTIFIED
REGATHERING	REGISTERABLE	REGROOVING	REHABILITATORS	REIDENTIFIES
REGELATING	REGISTERED	REGROUPING	REHAMMERED	REIDENTIFY

REIDENTIFYING	REINCARNATIONS	REINFUNDED	REINSTALLING	REINTRODUCE
REIFICATION	REINCITING	REINFUNDING	REINSTALLS	REINTRODUCED
REIFICATIONS	REINCORPORATE	REINFUSING	REINSTALMENT	REINTRODUCES
REIFICATORY	REINCORPORATED	REINHABITED	REINSTALMENTS	REINTRODUCING
REIGNITING	REINCORPORATES	REINHABITING	REINSTATED	REINTRODUCTION
REIGNITION	REINCORPORATING	REINHABITS	REINSTATEMENT	REINTRODUCTIONS
REIGNITIONS	REINCORPORATION	REINITIATE	REINSTATEMENTS	REINVADING
REILLUMINE	REINCREASE	REINITIATED	REINSTATES	REINVASION
REILLUMINED	REINCREASED	REINITIATES	REINSTATING	REINVASIONS
REILLUMINES	REINCREASES	REINITIATING	REINSTATION	REINVENTED
REILLUMING	REINCREASING	REINJECTED	REINSTATIONS	REINVENTING
REILLUMINING	REINCURRED	REINJECTING	REINSTATOR	REINVENTION
REIMAGINED	REINCURRING	REINJECTION	REINSTATORS	REINVENTIONS
REIMAGINES	REINDEXING	REINJECTIONS	REINSTITUTE	REINVESTED
REIMAGINING	REINDICTED	REINJURIES	REINSTITUTED	REINVESTIGATE
REIMBURSABLE	REINDICTING	REINJURING	REINSTITUTES	REINVESTIGATED
REIMBURSED	REINDICTMENT	REINNERVATE	REINSTITUTING	REINVESTIGATES
REIMBURSEMENT	REINDICTMENTS	REINNERVATED	REINSTITUTION	REINVESTIGATING
REIMBURSEMENTS	REINDUCING	REINNERVATES	REINSTITUTIONS	REINVESTIGATION
REIMBURSER	REINDUCTED	REINNERVATING	REINSURANCE	REINVESTING
REIMBURSERS	REINDUCTING	REINNERVATION	REINSURANCES	REINVESTMENT
REIMBURSES	REINDUSTRIALISE	REINNERVATIONS	REINSURERS	REINVESTMENTS
REIMBURSING	REINDUSTRIALIZE	REINOCULATE	REINSURING	REINVIGORATE
REIMMERSED	REINFECTED	REINOCULATED	REINTEGRATE	REINVIGORATED
REIMMERSES	REINFECTING	REINOCULATES	REINTEGRATED	REINVIGORATES
REIMMERSING	REINFECTION	REINOCULATING	REINTEGRATES	REINVIGORATING
REIMPLANTATION	REINFECTIONS	REINOCULATION	REINTEGRATING	REINVIGORATION
REIMPLANTATIONS	REINFESTATION	REINOCULATIONS	REINTEGRATION	REINVIGORATIONS
REIMPLANTED	REINFESTATIONS	REINSERTED	REINTEGRATIONS	REINVIGORATOR
REIMPLANTING	REINFLAMED	REINSERTING	REINTEGRATIVE	REINVIGORATORS
REIMPLANTS	REINFLAMES	REINSERTION	REINTERMENT	REINVITING
REIMPORTATION	REINFLAMING	REINSERTIONS	REINTERMENTS	REINVOKING
REIMPORTATIONS	REINFLATED	REINSPECTED	REINTERPRET	REINVOLVED
REIMPORTED	REINFLATES	REINSPECTING	REINTERPRETED	REINVOLVES
REIMPORTER	REINFLATING	REINSPECTION	REINTERPRETING	REINVOLVING
REIMPORTERS	REINFLATION	REINSPECTIONS	REINTERPRETS	REIOYNDURE
REIMPORTING	REINFLATIONS	REINSPECTS	REINTERRED	REIOYNDURES
REIMPOSING	REINFORCEABLE	REINSPIRED	REINTERRING	REISSUABLE
REIMPOSITION	REINFORCED	REINSPIRES	REINTERROGATE	REISTAFELS
REIMPOSITIONS	REINFORCEMENT	REINSPIRING	REINTERROGATED	REITERANCE
REIMPRESSION	REINFORCEMENTS	REINSPIRIT	REINTERROGATES	REITERANCES
REIMPRESSIONS	REINFORCER	REINSPIRITED	REINTERROGATING	REITERATED
REINCARNATE	REINFORCERS	REINSPIRITING	REINTERROGATION	REITERATEDLY
REINCARNATED	REINFORCES	REINSPIRITS	REINTERVIEW	REITERATES
REINCARNATES	REINFORCING	REINSTALLATION	REINTERVIEWED	REITERATING
REINCARNATING	REINFORMED	REINSTALLATIONS	REINTERVIEWING	REITERATION
REINCARNATION	REINFORMING	REINSTALLED	REINTERVIEWS	REITERATIONS

R

REITERATIVE
REITERATIVELY
REITERATIVES
REJACKETED
REJACKETING
REJECTABLE
REJECTAMENTA
REJECTIBLE
REJECTINGLY
REJECTIONIST
REJECTIONISTS
REJECTIONS
REJIGGERED
REJIGGERING
REJOICEFUL
REJOICEMENT
REJOICEMENTS
REJOICINGLY
REJOICINGS
REJOINDERS
REJOINDURE
REJOINDURES
REJONEADOR
REJONEADORA
REJONEADORAS
REJONEADORES
REJOURNING
REJUGGLING
REJUSTIFIED
REJUSTIFIES
REJUSTIFYING
REJUVENATE
REJUVENATED
REJUVENATES
REJUVENATING
REJUVENATION
REJUVENATIONS
REJUVENATOR
REJUVENATORS
REJUVENESCE
REJUVENESCED
REJUVENESCENCE
REJUVENESCENCES
REJUVENESCENT
REJUVENESCES
REJUVENESCING
REJUVENISE

REJUVENISED
REJUVENISES
REJUVENISING
REJUVENIZE
REJUVENIZED
REJUVENIZES
REJUVENIZING
REKEYBOARD
REKEYBOARDED
REKEYBOARDING
REKEYBOARDS
REKINDLING
REKNITTING
REKNITTINGS
REKNOTTING
REKNOTTINGS
RELABELING
RELABELLED
RELABELLING
RELACQUERED
RELACQUERING
RELACQUERS
RELANDSCAPE
RELANDSCAPED
RELANDSCAPES
RELANDSCAPING
RELATEDNESS
RELATEDNESSES
RELATIONAL
RELATIONALLY
RELATIONISM
RELATIONISMS
RELATIONIST
RELATIONISTS
RELATIONLESS
RELATIONSHIP
RELATIONSHIPS
RELATIVELY
RELATIVENESS
RELATIVENESSES
RELATIVISATION
RELATIVISATIONS
RELATIVISE
RELATIVISED
RELATIVISES
RELATIVISING
RELATIVISM

RELATIVISMS
RELATIVIST
RELATIVISTIC
RELATIVISTS
RELATIVITIES
RELATIVITIST
RELATIVITISTS
RELATIVITY
RELATIVIZATION
RELATIVIZATIONS
RELATIVIZE
RELATIVIZED
RELATIVIZES
RELATIVIZING
RELAUNCHED
RELAUNCHES
RELAUNCHING
RELAUNDERED
RELAUNDERING
RELAUNDERS
RELAXATION
RELAXATIONS
RELAXATIVE
RELAXATIVES
RELAXEDNESS
RELAXEDNESSES
RELEARNING
RELEASABLE
RELEASEMENT
RELEASEMENTS
RELEGATABLE
RELEGATING
RELEGATION
RELEGATIONS
RELENTINGS
RELENTLESS
RELENTLESSLY
RELENTLESSNESS
RELENTMENT
RELENTMENTS
RELETTERED
RELETTERING
RELEVANCES
RELEVANCIES
RELEVANTLY
RELIABILITIES
RELIABILITY

RELIABLENESS
RELIABLENESSES
RELICENSED
RELICENSES
RELICENSING
RELICENSURE
RELICENSURES
RELICTIONS
RELIEFLESS
RELIEVABLE
RELIEVEDLY
RELIGHTING
RELIGIEUSE
RELIGIEUSES
RELIGIONARIES
RELIGIONARY
RELIGIONER
RELIGIONERS
RELIGIONISE
RELIGIONISED
RELIGIONISES
RELIGIONISING
RELIGIONISM
RELIGIONISMS
RELIGIONIST
RELIGIONISTS
RELIGIONIZE
RELIGIONIZED
RELIGIONIZES
RELIGIONIZING
RELIGIONLESS
RELIGIOSELY
RELIGIOSITIES
RELIGIOSITY
RELIGIOSOS
RELIGIOUSES
RELIGIOUSLY
RELIGIOUSNESS
RELIGIOUSNESSES
RELINQUISH
RELINQUISHED
RELINQUISHER
RELINQUISHERS
RELINQUISHES
RELINQUISHING
RELINQUISHMENT
RELINQUISHMENTS

RELIQUAIRE
RELIQUAIRES
RELIQUARIES
RELIQUEFIED
RELIQUEFIES
RELIQUEFYING
RELISHABLE
RELIVERING
RELLISHING
RELOCATABLE
RELOCATEES
RELOCATING
RELOCATION
RELOCATIONS
RELOCATORS
RELUBRICATE
RELUBRICATED
RELUBRICATES
RELUBRICATING
RELUBRICATION
RELUBRICATIONS
RELUCTANCE
RELUCTANCES
RELUCTANCIES
RELUCTANCY
RELUCTANTLY
RELUCTATED
RELUCTATES
RELUCTATING
RELUCTATION
RELUCTATIONS
RELUCTIVITIES
RELUCTIVITY
RELUMINING
REMAINDERED
REMAINDERING
REMAINDERMAN
REMAINDERMEN
REMAINDERS
REMANDMENT
REMANDMENTS
REMANENCES
REMANENCIES
REMANUFACTURE
REMANUFACTURED
REMANUFACTURER
REMANUFACTURERS

REMANUFACTURES
REMANUFACTURING
REMARKABILITIES
REMARKABILITY
REMARKABLE
REMARKABLENESS
REMARKABLES
REMARKABLY
REMARKETED
REMARKETING
REMARRIAGE
REMARRIAGES
REMARRYING
REMASTERED
REMASTERING
REMATCHING
REMATERIALISE
REMATERIALISED
REMATERIALISES
REMATERIALISING
REMATERIALIZE
REMATERIALIZED
REMATERIALIZES
REMATERIALIZING
REMEASURED
REMEASUREMENT
REMEASUREMENTS
REMEASURES
REMEASURING
REMEDIABILITIES
REMEDIABILITY
REMEDIABLE
REMEDIABLY
REMEDIALLY
REMEDIATED
REMEDIATES
REMEDIATING
REMEDIATION
REMEDIATIONS
REMEDILESS
REMEDILESSLY
REMEDILESSNESS
REMEMBERABILITY
REMEMBERABLE
REMEMBERABLY
REMEMBERED
REMEMBERER

REMEMBERERS
REMEMBERING
REMEMBRANCE
REMEMBRANCER
REMEMBRANCERS
REMEMBRANCES
REMERCYING
REMIGATING
REMIGATION
REMIGATIONS
REMIGRATED
REMIGRATES
REMIGRATING
REMIGRATION
REMIGRATIONS
REMILITARISE
REMILITARISED
REMILITARISES
REMILITARISING
REMILITARIZE
REMILITARIZED
REMILITARIZES
REMILITARIZING
REMINERALISE
REMINERALISED
REMINERALISES
REMINERALISING
REMINERALIZE
REMINERALIZED
REMINERALIZES
REMINERALIZING
REMINISCED
REMINISCENCE
REMINISCENCES
REMINISCENT
REMINISCENTIAL
REMINISCENTLY
REMINISCENTS
REMINISCER
REMINISCERS
REMINISCES
REMINISCING
REMISSIBILITIES
REMISSIBILITY
REMISSIBLE
REMISSIBLENESS
REMISSIBLY

REMISSIONS
REMISSIVELY
REMISSNESS
REMISSNESSES
REMITMENTS
REMITTABLE
REMITTANCE
REMITTANCES
REMITTENCE
REMITTENCES
REMITTENCIES
REMITTENCY
REMITTENTLY
REMIXTURES
REMOBILISATION
REMOBILISATIONS
REMOBILISE
REMOBILISED
REMOBILISES
REMOBILISING
REMOBILIZATION
REMOBILIZATIONS
REMOBILIZE
REMOBILIZED
REMOBILIZES
REMOBILIZING
REMODELERS
REMODELING
REMODELINGS
REMODELLED
REMODELLER
REMODELLERS
REMODELLING
REMODELLINGS
REMODIFIED
REMODIFIES
REMODIFYING
REMOISTENED
REMOISTENING
REMOISTENS
REMONETISATION
REMONETISATIONS
REMONETISE
REMONETISED
REMONETISES
REMONETISING
REMONETIZATION

REMONETIZATIONS
REMONETIZE
REMONETIZED
REMONETIZES
REMONETIZING
REMONSTRANCE
REMONSTRANCES
REMONSTRANT
REMONSTRANTLY
REMONSTRANTS
REMONSTRATE
REMONSTRATED
REMONSTRATES
REMONSTRATING
REMONSTRATINGLY
REMONSTRATION
REMONSTRATIONS
REMONSTRATIVE
REMONSTRATIVELY
REMONSTRATOR
REMONSTRATORS
REMONSTRATORY
REMONTANTS
REMONTOIRE
REMONTOIRES
REMONTOIRS
REMORALISATION
REMORALISATIONS
REMORALISE
REMORALISED
REMORALISES
REMORALISING
REMORALIZATION
REMORALIZATIONS
REMORALIZE
REMORALIZED
REMORALIZES
REMORALIZING
REMORSEFUL
REMORSEFULLY
REMORSEFULNESS
REMORSELESS
REMORSELESSLY
REMORSELESSNESS
REMORTGAGE
REMORTGAGED
REMORTGAGES

REMORTGAGING
REMOTENESS
REMOTENESSES
REMOTIVATE
REMOTIVATED
REMOTIVATES
REMOTIVATING
REMOTIVATION
REMOTIVATIONS
REMOULADES
REMOULDING
REMOUNTING
REMOVABILITIES
REMOVABILITY
REMOVABLENESS
REMOVABLENESSES
REMOVALIST
REMOVALISTS
REMOVEABLE
REMOVEDNESS
REMOVEDNESSES
REMUNERABILITY
REMUNERABLE
REMUNERATE
REMUNERATED
REMUNERATES
REMUNERATING
REMUNERATION
REMUNERATIONS
REMUNERATIVE
REMUNERATIVELY
REMUNERATOR
REMUNERATORS
REMUNERATORY
REMURMURED
REMURMURING
REMYTHOLOGISE
REMYTHOLOGISED
REMYTHOLOGISES
REMYTHOLOGISING
REMYTHOLOGIZE
REMYTHOLOGIZED
REMYTHOLOGIZES
REMYTHOLOGIZING
RENAISSANCE
RENAISSANCES
RENASCENCE

R

RENASCENCES
RENATIONALISE
RENATIONALISED
RENATIONALISES
RENATIONALISING
RENATIONALIZE
RENATIONALIZED
RENATIONALIZES
RENATIONALIZING
RENATURATION
RENATURATIONS
RENATURING
RENCONTRED
RENCONTRES
RENCONTRING
RENCOUNTER
RENCOUNTERED
RENCOUNTERING
RENCOUNTERS
RENDERABLE
RENDERINGS
RENDEZVOUS
RENDEZVOUSED
RENDEZVOUSES
RENDEZVOUSING
RENDITIONED
RENDITIONING
RENDITIONS
RENEAGUING
RENEGADING
RENEGADOES
RENEGATION
RENEGATIONS
RENEGOTIABLE
RENEGOTIATE
RENEGOTIATED
RENEGOTIATES
RENEGOTIATING
RENEGOTIATION
RENEGOTIATIONS
RENEWABILITIES
RENEWABILITY
RENEWABLES
RENEWEDNESS
RENEWEDNESSES
RENFORCING
RENITENCES

RENITENCIES
RENOGRAPHIC
RENOGRAPHIES
RENOGRAPHY
RENOMINATE
RENOMINATED
RENOMINATES
RENOMINATING
RENOMINATION
RENOMINATIONS
RENORMALISATION
RENORMALISE
RENORMALISED
RENORMALISES
RENORMALISING
RENORMALIZATION
RENORMALIZE
RENORMALIZED
RENORMALIZES
RENORMALIZING
RENOSTERVELD
RENOSTERVELDS
RENOTIFIED
RENOTIFIES
RENOTIFYING
RENOUNCEABLE
RENOUNCEMENT
RENOUNCEMENTS
RENOUNCERS
RENOUNCING
RENOVASCULAR
RENOVATING
RENOVATION
RENOVATIONS
RENOVATIVE
RENOVATORS
RENSSELAERITE
RENSSELAERITES
RENTABILITIES
RENTABILITY
RENTALLERS
RENUMBERED
RENUMBERING
RENUNCIATE
RENUNCIATES
RENUNCIATION
RENUNCIATIONS

RENUNCIATIVE
RENUNCIATORY
RENVERSEMENT
RENVERSEMENTS
RENVERSING
REOBJECTED
REOBJECTING
REOBSERVED
REOBSERVES
REOBSERVING
REOBTAINED
REOBTAINING
REOCCUPATION
REOCCUPATIONS
REOCCUPIED
REOCCUPIES
REOCCUPYING
REOCCURRED
REOCCURRENCE
REOCCURRENCES
REOCCURRING
REOFFENDED
REOFFENDER
REOFFENDERS
REOFFENDING
REOFFERING
REOPENINGS
REOPERATED
REOPERATES
REOPERATING
REOPERATION
REOPERATIONS
REOPPOSING
REORCHESTRATE
REORCHESTRATED
REORCHESTRATES
REORCHESTRATING
REORCHESTRATION
REORDAINED
REORDAINING
REORDERING
REORDINATION
REORDINATIONS
REORGANISATION
REORGANISATIONS
REORGANISE
REORGANISED

REORGANISER
REORGANISERS
REORGANISES
REORGANISING
REORGANIZATION
REORGANIZATIONS
REORGANIZE
REORGANIZED
REORGANIZER
REORGANIZERS
REORGANIZES
REORGANIZING
REORIENTATE
REORIENTATED
REORIENTATES
REORIENTATING
REORIENTATION
REORIENTATIONS
REORIENTED
REORIENTING
REOUTFITTED
REOUTFITTING
REOVIRUSES
REOXIDATION
REOXIDATIONS
REOXIDISED
REOXIDISES
REOXIDISING
REOXIDIZED
REOXIDIZES
REOXIDIZING
REPACIFIED
REPACIFIES
REPACIFYING
REPACKAGED
REPACKAGER
REPACKAGERS
REPACKAGES
REPACKAGING
REPAGINATE
REPAGINATED
REPAGINATES
REPAGINATING
REPAGINATION
REPAGINATIONS
REPAINTING
REPAINTINGS

REPAIRABILITIES
REPAIRABILITY
REPAIRABLE
REPANELING
REPANELLED
REPANELLING
REPAPERING
REPARABILITIES
REPARABILITY
REPARATION
REPARATIONS
REPARATIVE
REPARATORY
REPARTEEING
REPARTITION
REPARTITIONED
REPARTITIONING
REPARTITIONS
REPASSAGES
REPASTURES
REPATCHING
REPATRIATE
REPATRIATED
REPATRIATES
REPATRIATING
REPATRIATION
REPATRIATIONS
REPATRIATOR
REPATRIATORS
REPATTERNED
REPATTERNING
REPATTERNS
REPAYMENTS
REPEALABLE
REPEATABILITIES
REPEATABILITY
REPEATABLE
REPEATEDLY
REPEATINGS
REPECHAGES
REPELLANCE
REPELLANCES
REPELLANCIES
REPELLANCY
REPELLANTLY
REPELLANTS
REPELLENCE

R

REPELLENCES	REPINEMENTS	REPLOUGHING	REPOSITION	REPRESENTERS
REPELLENCIES	REPININGLY	REPLUMBING	REPOSITIONED	REPRESENTING
REPELLENCY	REPLACEABILITY	REPLUNGING	REPOSITIONING	REPRESENTMENT
REPELLENTLY	REPLACEABLE	REPOINTING	REPOSITIONS	REPRESENTMENTS
REPELLENTS	REPLACEMENT	REPOINTINGS	REPOSITORIES	REPRESENTOR
REPELLINGLY	REPLACEMENTS	REPOLARISATION	REPOSITORS	REPRESENTORS
REPENTANCE	REPLANNING	REPOLARISATIONS	REPOSITORY	REPRESENTS
REPENTANCES	REPLANTATION	REPOLARISE	REPOSSESSED	REPRESSERS
REPENTANTLY	REPLANTATIONS	REPOLARISED	REPOSSESSES	REPRESSIBILITY
REPENTANTS	REPLANTING	REPOLARISES	REPOSSESSING	REPRESSIBLE
REPENTINGLY	REPLASTERED	REPOLARISING	REPOSSESSION	REPRESSIBLY
REPEOPLING	REPLASTERING	REPOLARIZATION	REPOSSESSIONS	REPRESSING
REPERCUSSED	REPLASTERS	REPOLARIZATIONS	REPOSSESSOR	REPRESSION
REPERCUSSES	REPLEADERS	REPOLARIZE	REPOSSESSORS	REPRESSIONIST
REPERCUSSING	REPLEADING	REPOLARIZED	REPOTTINGS	REPRESSIONISTS
REPERCUSSION	REPLEDGING	REPOLARIZES	REPOUSSAGE	REPRESSIONS
REPERCUSSIONS	REPLENISHABLE	REPOLARIZING	REPOUSSAGES	REPRESSIVE
REPERCUSSIVE	REPLENISHED	REPOLISHED	REPOUSSOIR	REPRESSIVELY
REPERTOIRE	REPLENISHER	REPOLISHES	REPOUSSOIRS	REPRESSIVENESS
REPERTOIRES	REPLENISHERS	REPOLISHING	REPOWERING	REPRESSORS
REPERTORIAL	REPLENISHES	REPOPULARISE	REPREEVING	REPRESSURISE
REPERTORIES	REPLENISHING	REPOPULARISED	REPREHENDABLE	REPRESSURISED
REPERUSALS	REPLENISHMENT	REPOPULARISES	REPREHENDED	REPRESSURISES
REPERUSING	REPLENISHMENTS	REPOPULARISING	REPREHENDER	REPRESSURISING
REPETITEUR	REPLETENESS	REPOPULARIZE	REPREHENDERS	REPRESSURIZE
REPETITEURS	REPLETENESSES	REPOPULARIZED	REPREHENDING	REPRESSURIZED
REPETITEUSE	REPLETIONS	REPOPULARIZES	REPREHENDS	REPRESSURIZES
REPETITEUSES	REPLEVIABLE	REPOPULARIZING	REPREHENSIBLE	REPRESSURIZING
REPETITION	REPLEVINED	REPOPULATE	REPREHENSIBLY	REPRIEVABLE
REPETITIONAL	REPLEVINING	REPOPULATED	REPREHENSION	REPRIEVALS
REPETITIONARY	REPLEVISABLE	REPOPULATES	REPREHENSIONS	REPRIEVERS
REPETITIONS	REPLEVYING	REPOPULATING	REPREHENSIVE	REPRIEVING
REPETITIOUS	REPLICABILITIES	REPOPULATION	REPREHENSIVELY	REPRIMANDED
REPETITIOUSLY	REPLICABILITY	REPOPULATIONS	REPREHENSORY	REPRIMANDING
REPETITIOUSNESS	REPLICABLE	REPORTABLE	REPRESENTABLE	REPRIMANDS
REPETITIVE	REPLICANTS	REPORTAGES	REPRESENTAMEN	REPRINTERS
REPETITIVELY	REPLICASES	REPORTEDLY	REPRESENTAMENS	REPRINTING
REPETITIVENESS	REPLICATED	REPORTINGLY	REPRESENTANT	REPRISTINATE
REPHOTOGRAPH	REPLICATES	REPORTINGS	REPRESENTANTS	REPRISTINATED
REPHOTOGRAPHED	REPLICATING	REPORTORIAL	REPRESENTATION	REPRISTINATES
REPHOTOGRAPHING	REPLICATION	REPORTORIALLY	REPRESENTATIONS	REPRISTINATING
REPHOTOGRAPHS	REPLICATIONS	REPOSEDNESS	REPRESENTATIVE	REPRISTINATION
REPHRASING	REPLICATIVE	REPOSEDNESSES	REPRESENTATIVES	REPRISTINATIONS
REPIGMENTED	REPLICATOR	REPOSEFULLY	REPRESENTED	REPRIVATISATION
REPIGMENTING	REPLICATORS	REPOSEFULNESS	REPRESENTEE	REPRIVATISE
REPIGMENTS	REPLOTTING	REPOSEFULNESSES	REPRESENTEES	REPRIVATISED
REPINEMENT	REPLOUGHED	REPOSITING	REPRESENTER	REPRIVATISES

R

REPRIVATISING	REPRODUCTION	REPUBLICATIONS	REPUTELESS	REREBRACES
REPRIVATIZATION	REPRODUCTIONS	REPUBLISHED	REQUALIFIED	RERECORDED
REPRIVATIZE	REPRODUCTIVE	REPUBLISHER	REQUALIFIES	RERECORDING
REPRIVATIZED	REPRODUCTIVELY	REPUBLISHERS	REQUALIFYING	REREDORTER
REPRIVATIZES	REPRODUCTIVES	REPUBLISHES	REQUESTERS	REREDORTERS
REPRIVATIZING	REPRODUCTIVITY	REPUBLISHING	REQUESTING	REREDOSSES
REPROACHABLE	REPROGRAMED	REPUDIABLE	REQUESTORS	REREGISTER
REPROACHABLY	REPROGRAMING	REPUDIATED	REQUICKENED	REREGISTERED
REPROACHED	REPROGRAMMABLE	REPUDIATES	REQUICKENING	REREGISTERING
REPROACHER	REPROGRAMME	REPUDIATING	REQUICKENS	REREGISTERS
REPROACHERS	REPROGRAMMED	REPUDIATION	REQUIESCAT	REREGISTRATION
REPROACHES	REPROGRAMMES	REPUDIATIONIST	REQUIESCATS	REREGISTRATIONS
REPROACHFUL	REPROGRAMMING	REPUDIATIONISTS	REQUIGHTED	REREGULATE
REPROACHFULLY	REPROGRAMS	REPUDIATIONS	REQUIGHTING	REREGULATED
REPROACHFULNESS	REPROGRAPHER	REPUDIATIVE	REQUIRABLE	REREGULATES
REPROACHING	REPROGRAPHERS	REPUDIATOR	REQUIREMENT	REREGULATING
REPROACHINGLY	REPROGRAPHIC	REPUDIATORS	REQUIREMENTS	REREGULATION
REPROACHLESS	REPROGRAPHICS	REPUGNANCE	REQUIRINGS	REREGULATIONS
REPROBACIES	REPROGRAPHIES	REPUGNANCES	REQUISITELY	RERELEASED
REPROBANCE	REPROGRAPHY	REPUGNANCIES	REQUISITENESS	RERELEASES
REPROBANCES	REPROOFING	REPUGNANCY	REQUISITENESSES	RERELEASING
REPROBATED	REPROVABLE	REPUGNANTLY	REQUISITES	REREMINDED
REPROBATER	REPROVINGLY	REPULSIONS	REQUISITION	REREMINDING
REPROBATERS	REPROVISION	REPULSIVELY	REQUISITIONARY	REREPEATED
REPROBATES	REPROVISIONED	REPULSIVENESS	REQUISITIONED	REREPEATING
REPROBATING	REPROVISIONING	REPULSIVENESSES	REQUISITIONING	REREVIEWED
REPROBATION	REPROVISIONS	REPUNCTUATION	REQUISITIONIST	REREVIEWING
REPROBATIONARY	REPTATIONS	REPUNCTUATIONS	REQUISITIONISTS	REREVISING
REPROBATIONS	REPTILIANLY	REPURCHASE	REQUISITIONS	REROUTEING
REPROBATIVE	REPTILIANS	REPURCHASED	REQUISITOR	RESADDLING
REPROBATIVELY	REPTILIFEROUS	REPURCHASES	REQUISITORIES	RESALEABLE
REPROBATOR	REPTILIFORM	REPURCHASING	REQUISITORS	RESALUTING
REPROBATORS	REPTILIOUS	REPURIFIED	REQUISITORY	RESAMPLING
REPROBATORY	REPTILOIDS	REPURIFIES	REQUITABLE	RESCHEDULE
REPROCESSED	REPUBLICAN	REPURIFYING	REQUITEFUL	RESCHEDULED
REPROCESSES	REPUBLICANISE	REPURPOSED	REQUITELESS	RESCHEDULES
REPROCESSING	REPUBLICANISED	REPURPOSES	REQUITEMENT	RESCHEDULING
REPROCESSINGS	REPUBLICANISES	REPURPOSING	REQUITEMENTS	RESCHEDULINGS
REPRODUCED	REPUBLICANISING	REPURSUING	REQUITTING	RESCHOOLED
REPRODUCER	REPUBLICANISM	REPUTABILITIES	REQUOYLING	RESCHOOLING
REPRODUCERS	REPUBLICANISMS	REPUTABILITY	RERADIATED	RESCINDABLE
REPRODUCES	REPUBLICANIZE	REPUTATION	RERADIATES	RESCINDERS
REPRODUCIBILITY	REPUBLICANIZED	REPUTATIONAL	RERADIATING	RESCINDING
REPRODUCIBLE	REPUBLICANIZES	REPUTATIONLESS	RERADIATION	RESCINDMENT
REPRODUCIBLES	REPUBLICANIZING	REPUTATIONS	RERADIATIONS	RESCINDMENTS
REPRODUCIBLY	REPUBLICANS	REPUTATIVE	RERAILINGS	RESCISSIBLE
REPRODUCING	REPUBLICATION	REPUTATIVELY	REREADINGS	RESCISSION

RESCISSIONS
RESCISSORY
RESCREENED
RESCREENING
RESCRIPTED
RESCRIPTING
RESCRIPTION
RESCRIPTIONS
RESCULPTED
RESCULPTING
RESEALABLE
RESEARCHABLE
RESEARCHED
RESEARCHER
RESEARCHERS
RESEARCHES
RESEARCHFUL
RESEARCHING
RESEARCHIST
RESEARCHISTS
RESEASONED
RESEASONING
RESECTABILITIES
RESECTABILITY
RESECTABLE
RESECTIONAL
RESECTIONS
RESECURING
RESEGREGATE
RESEGREGATED
RESEGREGATES
RESEGREGATING
RESEGREGATION
RESEGREGATIONS
RESEIZURES
RESELECTED
RESELECTING
RESELECTION
RESELECTIONS
RESEMBLANCE
RESEMBLANCES
RESEMBLANT
RESEMBLERS
RESEMBLING
RESENSITISE
RESENSITISED
RESENSITISES

RESENSITISING
RESENSITIZE
RESENSITIZED
RESENSITIZES
RESENSITIZING
RESENTENCE
RESENTENCED
RESENTENCES
RESENTENCING
RESENTFULLY
RESENTFULNESS
RESENTFULNESSES
RESENTINGLY
RESENTMENT
RESENTMENTS
RESERPINES
RESERVABLE
RESERVATION
RESERVATIONIST
RESERVATIONISTS
RESERVATIONS
RESERVATORIES
RESERVATORY
RESERVEDLY
RESERVEDNESS
RESERVEDNESSES
RESERVICED
RESERVICES
RESERVICING
RESERVISTS
RESERVOIRED
RESERVOIRING
RESERVOIRS
RESETTABLE
RESETTLEMENT
RESETTLEMENTS
RESETTLING
RESHAPINGS
RESHARPENED
RESHARPENING
RESHARPENS
RESHINGLED
RESHINGLES
RESHINGLING
RESHIPMENT
RESHIPMENTS
RESHIPPERS

RESHIPPING
RESHOOTING
RESHOWERED
RESHOWERING
RESHUFFLED
RESHUFFLES
RESHUFFLING
RESIDENCES
RESIDENCIES
RESIDENTER
RESIDENTERS
RESIDENTIAL
RESIDENTIALLY
RESIDENTIARIES
RESIDENTIARY
RESIDENTSHIP
RESIDENTSHIPS
RESIDUALLY
RESIGHTING
RESIGNATION
RESIGNATIONS
RESIGNEDLY
RESIGNEDNESS
RESIGNEDNESSES
RESIGNMENT
RESIGNMENTS
RESILEMENT
RESILEMENTS
RESILIENCE
RESILIENCES
RESILIENCIES
RESILIENCY
RESILIENTLY
RESILVERED
RESILVERING
RESINATING
RESINIFEROUS
RESINIFICATION
RESINIFICATIONS
RESINIFIED
RESINIFIES
RESINIFYING
RESINISING
RESINIZING
RESINOUSLY
RESINOUSNESS
RESINOUSNESSES

RESIPISCENCE
RESIPISCENCES
RESIPISCENCIES
RESIPISCENCY
RESIPISCENT
RESISTANCE
RESISTANCES
RESISTANTS
RESISTENTS
RESISTIBILITIES
RESISTIBILITY
RESISTIBLE
RESISTIBLY
RESISTINGLY
RESISTIVELY
RESISTIVENESS
RESISTIVENESSES
RESISTIVITIES
RESISTIVITY
RESISTLESS
RESISTLESSLY
RESISTLESSNESS
RESITTINGS
RESITUATED
RESITUATES
RESITUATING
RESKETCHED
RESKETCHES
RESKETCHING
RESKILLING
RESKILLINGS
RESKINNING
RESMELTING
RESMOOTHED
RESMOOTHING
RESNATRONS
RESOCIALISATION
RESOCIALISE
RESOCIALISED
RESOCIALISES
RESOCIALISING
RESOCIALIZATION
RESOCIALIZE
RESOCIALIZED
RESOCIALIZES
RESOCIALIZING
RESOFTENED

RESOFTENING
RESOLDERED
RESOLDERING
RESOLIDIFIED
RESOLIDIFIES
RESOLIDIFY
RESOLIDIFYING
RESOLUBILITIES
RESOLUBILITY
RESOLUBLENESS
RESOLUBLENESSES
RESOLUTELY
RESOLUTENESS
RESOLUTENESSES
RESOLUTEST
RESOLUTION
RESOLUTIONER
RESOLUTIONERS
RESOLUTIONIST
RESOLUTIONISTS
RESOLUTIONS
RESOLUTIVE
RESOLVABILITIES
RESOLVABILITY
RESOLVABLE
RESOLVABLENESS
RESOLVEDLY
RESOLVEDNESS
RESOLVEDNESSES
RESOLVENTS
RESONANCES
RESONANTLY
RESONATING
RESONATION
RESONATIONS
RESONATORS
RESORBENCE
RESORBENCES
RESORCINAL
RESORCINOL
RESORCINOLS
RESORPTION
RESORPTIONS
RESORPTIVE
RESOUNDING
RESOUNDINGLY
RESOURCEFUL

R

RESOURCEFULLY
RESOURCEFULNESS
RESOURCELESS
RESOURCING
RESOURCINGS
RESPEAKING
RESPECIFIED
RESPECIFIES
RESPECIFYING
RESPECTABILISE
RESPECTABILISED
RESPECTABILISES
RESPECTABILITY
RESPECTABILIZE
RESPECTABILIZED
RESPECTABILIZES
RESPECTABLE
RESPECTABLENESS
RESPECTABLES
RESPECTABLY
RESPECTANT
RESPECTERS
RESPECTFUL
RESPECTFULLY
RESPECTFULNESS
RESPECTING
RESPECTIVE
RESPECTIVELY
RESPECTIVENESS
RESPECTLESS
RESPELLING
RESPELLINGS
RESPIRABILITIES
RESPIRABILITY
RESPIRABLE
RESPIRATION
RESPIRATIONAL
RESPIRATIONS
RESPIRATOR
RESPIRATORS
RESPIRATORY
RESPIRITUALISE
RESPIRITUALISED
RESPIRITUALISES
RESPIRITUALIZE
RESPIRITUALIZED
RESPIRITUALIZES

RESPIROLOGIES
RESPIROLOGIST
RESPIROLOGISTS
RESPIROLOGY
RESPIROMETER
RESPIROMETERS
RESPIROMETRIC
RESPIROMETRIES
RESPIROMETRY
RESPITELESS
RESPLENDED
RESPLENDENCE
RESPLENDENCES
RESPLENDENCIES
RESPLENDENCY
RESPLENDENT
RESPLENDENTLY
RESPLENDING
RESPLICING
RESPLITTING
RESPONDENCE
RESPONDENCES
RESPONDENCIES
RESPONDENCY
RESPONDENT
RESPONDENTIA
RESPONDENTIAS
RESPONDENTS
RESPONDERS
RESPONDING
RESPONSELESS
RESPONSERS
RESPONSIBILITY
RESPONSIBLE
RESPONSIBLENESS
RESPONSIBLY
RESPONSIONS
RESPONSIVE
RESPONSIVELY
RESPONSIVENESS
RESPONSORIAL
RESPONSORIALS
RESPONSORIES
RESPONSORS
RESPONSORY
RESPONSUMS
RESPOOLING

RESPOTTING
RESPRAYING
RESPREADING
RESPRINGING
RESPROUTED
RESPROUTING
RESSALDARS
RESSENTIMENT
RESSENTIMENTS
RESTABILISE
RESTABILISED
RESTABILISES
RESTABILISING
RESTABILIZE
RESTABILIZED
RESTABILIZES
RESTABILIZING
RESTABLING
RESTACKING
RESTAFFING
RESTAMPING
RESTARTABLE
RESTARTERS
RESTARTING
RESTATEMENT
RESTATEMENTS
RESTATIONED
RESTATIONING
RESTATIONS
RESTAURANT
RESTAURANTEUR
RESTAURANTEURS
RESTAURANTS
RESTAURATEUR
RESTAURATEURS
RESTAURATION
RESTAURATIONS
RESTEMMING
RESTFULLER
RESTFULLEST
RESTFULNESS
RESTFULNESSES
RESTHARROW
RESTHARROWS
RESTIMULATE
RESTIMULATED
RESTIMULATES

RESTIMULATING
RESTIMULATION
RESTIMULATIONS
RESTITCHED
RESTITCHES
RESTITCHING
RESTITUTED
RESTITUTES
RESTITUTING
RESTITUTION
RESTITUTIONISM
RESTITUTIONISMS
RESTITUTIONIST
RESTITUTIONISTS
RESTITUTIONS
RESTITUTIVE
RESTITUTOR
RESTITUTORS
RESTITUTORY
RESTIVENESS
RESTIVENESSES
RESTLESSLY
RESTLESSNESS
RESTLESSNESSES
RESTOCKING
RESTORABLE
RESTORABLENESS
RESTORATION
RESTORATIONISM
RESTORATIONISMS
RESTORATIONIST
RESTORATIONISTS
RESTORATIONS
RESTORATIVE
RESTORATIVELY
RESTORATIVES
RESTRAINABLE
RESTRAINED
RESTRAINEDLY
RESTRAINEDNESS
RESTRAINER
RESTRAINERS
RESTRAINING
RESTRAININGS
RESTRAINTS
RESTRENGTHEN
RESTRENGTHENED

RESTRENGTHENING
RESTRENGTHENS
RESTRESSED
RESTRESSES
RESTRESSING
RESTRETCHED
RESTRETCHES
RESTRETCHING
RESTRICKEN
RESTRICTED
RESTRICTEDLY
RESTRICTEDNESS
RESTRICTING
RESTRICTION
RESTRICTIONISM
RESTRICTIONISMS
RESTRICTIONIST
RESTRICTIONISTS
RESTRICTIONS
RESTRICTIVE
RESTRICTIVELY
RESTRICTIVENESS
RESTRICTIVES
RESTRIKING
RESTRINGED
RESTRINGEING
RESTRINGENT
RESTRINGENTS
RESTRINGES
RESTRINGING
RESTRIVING
RESTRUCTURE
RESTRUCTURED
RESTRUCTURES
RESTRUCTURING
RESTRUCTURINGS
RESTUDYING
RESTUFFING
RESTUMPING
RESUBJECTED
RESUBJECTING
RESUBJECTS
RESUBMISSION
RESUBMISSIONS
RESUBMITTED
RESUBMITTING
RESULTANTLY

R

RESULTANTS	RESUSCITATION	RETAINERSHIPS	RETHREADING	RETIREMENTS
RESULTATIVE	RESUSCITATIONS	RETAINMENT	RETICELLAS	RETIRINGLY
RESULTATIVES	RESUSCITATIVE	RETAINMENTS	RETICENCES	RETIRINGNESS
RESULTLESS	RESUSCITATOR	RETALIATED	RETICENCIES	RETIRINGNESSES
RESULTLESSNESS	RESUSCITATORS	RETALIATES	RETICENTLY	RETORSIONS
RESUMMONED	RESUSPENDED	RETALIATING	RETICULARLY	RETORTIONS
RESUMMONING	RESUSPENDING	RETALIATION	RETICULARY	RETOTALING
RESUMPTION	RESUSPENDS	RETALIATIONIST	RETICULATE	RETOTALLED
RESUMPTIONS	RESVERATROL	RETALIATIONISTS	RETICULATED	RETOTALLING
RESUMPTIVE	RESVERATROLS	RETALIATIONS	RETICULATELY	RETOUCHABLE
RESUMPTIVELY	RESWALLOWED	RETALIATIVE	RETICULATES	RETOUCHERS
RESUPINATE	RESWALLOWING	RETALIATOR	RETICULATING	RETOUCHING
RESUPINATION	RESWALLOWS	RETALIATORS	RETICULATION	RETRACEABLE
RESUPINATIONS	RESYNCHRONISE	RETALIATORY	RETICULATIONS	RETRACEMENT
RESUPPLIED	RESYNCHRONISED	RETALLYING	RETICULOCYTE	RETRACEMENTS
RESUPPLIES	RESYNCHRONISES	RETARDANTS	RETICULOCYTES	RETRACKING
RESUPPLYING	RESYNCHRONISING	RETARDATES	RETICULUMS	RETRACTABILITY
RESURFACED	RESYNCHRONIZE	RETARDATION	RETIGHTENED	RETRACTABLE
RESURFACER	RESYNCHRONIZED	RETARDATIONS	RETIGHTENING	RETRACTATION
RESURFACERS	RESYNCHRONIZES	RETARDATIVE	RETIGHTENS	RETRACTATIONS
RESURFACES	RESYNCHRONIZING	RETARDATORY	RETINACULA	RETRACTIBILITY
RESURFACING	RESYNTHESES	RETARDMENT	RETINACULAR	RETRACTIBLE
RESURGENCE	RESYNTHESIS	RETARDMENTS	RETINACULUM	RETRACTILE
RESURGENCES	RESYNTHESISE	RETARGETED	RETINALITE	RETRACTILITIES
RESURRECTED	RESYNTHESISED	RETARGETING	RETINALITES	RETRACTILITY
RESURRECTING	RESYNTHESISES	RETEACHING	RETINISPORA	RETRACTING
RESURRECTION	RESYNTHESISING	RETELLINGS	RETINISPORAS	RETRACTION
RESURRECTIONAL	RESYNTHESIZE	RETEMPERED	RETINITIDES	RETRACTIONS
RESURRECTIONARY	RESYNTHESIZED	RETEMPERING	RETINITISES	RETRACTIVE
RESURRECTIONISE	RESYNTHESIZES	RETENTIONIST	RETINOBLASTOMA	RETRACTIVELY
RESURRECTIONISM	RESYNTHESIZING	RETENTIONISTS	RETINOBLASTOMAS	RETRACTORS
RESURRECTIONIST	RESYSTEMATISE	RETENTIONS	RETINOPATHIES	RETRAINABLE
RESURRECTIONIZE	RESYSTEMATISED	RETENTIVELY	RETINOPATHY	RETRAINEES
RESURRECTIONS	RESYSTEMATISES	RETENTIVENESS	RETINOSCOPE	RETRAINING
RESURRECTIVE	RESYSTEMATISING	RETENTIVENESSES	RETINOSCOPES	RETRAININGS
RESURRECTOR	RESYSTEMATIZE	RETENTIVES	RETINOSCOPIC	RETRANSFER
RESURRECTORS	RESYSTEMATIZED	RETENTIVITIES	RETINOSCOPIES	RETRANSFERRED
RESURRECTS	RESYSTEMATIZES	RETENTIVITY	RETINOSCOPIST	RETRANSFERRING
RESURVEYED	RESYSTEMATIZING	RETESTIFIED	RETINOSCOPISTS	RETRANSFERS
RESURVEYING	RETACKLING	RETESTIFIES	RETINOSCOPY	RETRANSFORM
RESUSCITABLE	RETAILINGS	RETESTIFYING	RETINOSPORA	RETRANSFORMED
RESUSCITANT	RETAILMENT	RETEXTURED	RETINOSPORAS	RETRANSFORMING
RESUSCITANTS	RETAILMENTS	RETEXTURES	RETINOTECTAL	RETRANSFORMS
RESUSCITATE	RETAILORED	RETEXTURING	RETIRACIES	RETRANSLATE
RESUSCITATED	RETAILORING	RETHINKERS	RETIREDNESS	RETRANSLATED
RESUSCITATES	RETAINABLE	RETHINKING	RETIREDNESSES	RETRANSLATES
RESUSCITATING	RETAINERSHIP	RETHREADED	RETIREMENT	RETRANSLATING

R

RETRANSLATION
RETRANSLATIONS
RETRANSMISSION
RETRANSMISSIONS
RETRANSMIT
RETRANSMITS
RETRANSMITTED
RETRANSMITTING
RETREADING
RETREATANT
RETREATANTS
RETREATERS
RETREATING
RETRENCHABLE
RETRENCHED
RETRENCHES
RETRENCHING
RETRENCHMENT
RETRENCHMENTS
RETRIBUTED
RETRIBUTES
RETRIBUTING
RETRIBUTION
RETRIBUTIONS
RETRIBUTIVE
RETRIBUTIVELY
RETRIBUTOR
RETRIBUTORS
RETRIBUTORY
RETRIEVABILITY
RETRIEVABLE
RETRIEVABLENESS
RETRIEVABLY
RETRIEVALS
RETRIEVEMENT
RETRIEVEMENTS
RETRIEVERS
RETRIEVING
RETRIEVINGS
RETRIMMING
RETROACTED
RETROACTING
RETROACTION
RETROACTIONS
RETROACTIVE
RETROACTIVELY
RETROACTIVENESS

RETROACTIVITIES
RETROACTIVITY
RETROBULBAR
RETROCEDED
RETROCEDENCE
RETROCEDENCES
RETROCEDENT
RETROCEDES
RETROCEDING
RETROCESSION
RETROCESSIONS
RETROCESSIVE
RETROCHOIR
RETROCHOIRS
RETROCOGNITION
RETROCOGNITIONS
RETRODICTED
RETRODICTING
RETRODICTION
RETRODICTIONS
RETRODICTIVE
RETRODICTS
RETROENGINE
RETROENGINES
RETROFIRED
RETROFIRES
RETROFIRING
RETROFITTED
RETROFITTING
RETROFITTINGS
RETROFLECTED
RETROFLECTION
RETROFLECTIONS
RETROFLEXED
RETROFLEXES
RETROFLEXING
RETROFLEXION
RETROFLEXIONS
RETROGRADATION
RETROGRADATIONS
RETROGRADE
RETROGRADED
RETROGRADELY
RETROGRADES
RETROGRADING
RETROGRESS
RETROGRESSED

RETROGRESSES
RETROGRESSING
RETROGRESSION
RETROGRESSIONAL
RETROGRESSIONS
RETROGRESSIVE
RETROGRESSIVELY
RETROJECTED
RETROJECTING
RETROJECTION
RETROJECTIONS
RETROJECTS
RETROLENTAL
RETROMINGENCIES
RETROMINGENCY
RETROMINGENT
RETROMINGENTS
RETROPACKS
RETROPERITONEAL
RETROPHILIA
RETROPHILIAC
RETROPHILIACS
RETROPHILIAS
RETROPULSION
RETROPULSIONS
RETROPULSIVE
RETROREFLECTION
RETROREFLECTIVE
RETROREFLECTOR
RETROREFLECTORS
RETROROCKET
RETROROCKETS
RETRORSELY
RETROSEXUAL
RETROSEXUALS
RETROSPECT
RETROSPECTED
RETROSPECTING
RETROSPECTION
RETROSPECTIONS
RETROSPECTIVE
RETROSPECTIVELY
RETROSPECTIVES
RETROSPECTS
RETROUSSAGE
RETROUSSAGES
RETROVERSE

RETROVERSION
RETROVERSIONS
RETROVERTED
RETROVERTING
RETROVERTS
RETROVIRAL
RETROVIRUS
RETROVIRUSES
RETURNABILITIES
RETURNABILITY
RETURNABLE
RETURNABLES
RETURNLESS
RETWEETING
RETWISTING
REUNIFICATION
REUNIFICATIONS
REUNIFYING
REUNIONISM
REUNIONISMS
REUNIONIST
REUNIONISTIC
REUNIONISTS
REUNITABLE
REUPHOLSTER
REUPHOLSTERED
REUPHOLSTERING
REUPHOLSTERS
REUPTAKING
REUSABILITIES
REUSABILITY
REUTILISATION
REUTILISATIONS
REUTILISED
REUTILISES
REUTILISING
REUTILIZATION
REUTILIZATIONS
REUTILIZED
REUTILIZES
REUTILIZING
REUTTERING
REVACCINATE
REVACCINATED
REVACCINATES
REVACCINATING
REVACCINATION

REVACCINATIONS
REVALENTAS
REVALIDATE
REVALIDATED
REVALIDATES
REVALIDATING
REVALIDATION
REVALIDATIONS
REVALORISATION
REVALORISATIONS
REVALORISE
REVALORISED
REVALORISES
REVALORISING
REVALORIZATION
REVALORIZATIONS
REVALORIZE
REVALORIZED
REVALORIZES
REVALORIZING
REVALUATED
REVALUATES
REVALUATING
REVALUATION
REVALUATIONS
REVAMPINGS
REVANCHISM
REVANCHISMS
REVANCHIST
REVANCHISTS
REVARNISHED
REVARNISHES
REVARNISHING
REVEALABILITIES
REVEALABILITY
REVEALABLE
REVEALINGLY
REVEALINGNESS
REVEALINGNESSES
REVEALINGS
REVEALMENT
REVEALMENTS
REVEGETATE
REVEGETATED
REVEGETATES
REVEGETATING
REVEGETATION

REVEGETATIONS	REVERENTNESSES	REVISIONAL	REVIVISCENCIES	REVULSIVELY
REVELATION	REVERIFIED	REVISIONARY	REVIVISCENCY	REVULSIVES
REVELATIONAL	REVERIFIES	REVISIONISM	REVIVISCENT	REWAKENING
REVELATIONIST	REVERIFYING	REVISIONISMS	REVOCABILITIES	REWARDABLE
REVELATIONISTS	REVERSEDLY	REVISIONIST	REVOCABILITY	REWARDABLENESS
REVELATIONS	REVERSELESS	REVISIONISTS	REVOCABLENESS	REWARDINGLY
REVELATIVE	REVERSIBILITIES	REVISITANT	REVOCABLENESSES	REWARDLESS
REVELATORS	REVERSIBILITY	REVISITANTS	REVOCATION	REWATERING
REVELATORY	REVERSIBLE	REVISITATION	REVOCATIONS	REWEIGHING
REVELLINGS	REVERSIBLES	REVISITATIONS	REVOCATORY	REWIDENING
REVELMENTS	REVERSIBLY	REVISITING	REVOKABILITIES	REWILDINGS
REVENDICATE	REVERSINGS	REVISUALISATION	REVOKABILITY	REWINDINGS
REVENDICATED	REVERSIONAL	REVISUALIZATION	REVOKEMENT	REWORDINGS
REVENDICATES	REVERSIONALLY	REVITALISATION	REVOKEMENTS	REWORKINGS
REVENDICATING	REVERSIONARIES	REVITALISATIONS	REVOLTINGLY	REWRAPPING
REVENDICATION	REVERSIONARY	REVITALISE	REVOLUTION	REWRITABLE
REVENDICATIONS	REVERSIONER	REVITALISED	REVOLUTIONAL	REWRITEABLE
REVENGEFUL	REVERSIONERS	REVITALISES	REVOLUTIONARIES	RHABDOCOELE
REVENGEFULLY	REVERSIONS	REVITALISING	REVOLUTIONARILY	RHABDOCOELES
REVENGEFULNESS	REVERSISES	REVITALIZATION	REVOLUTIONARY	RHABDOLITH
REVENGELESS	REVERTANTS	REVITALIZATIONS	REVOLUTIONER	RHABDOLITHS
REVENGEMENT	REVERTIBLE	REVITALIZE	REVOLUTIONERS	RHABDOMANCER
REVENGEMENTS	REVESTIARIES	REVITALIZED	REVOLUTIONISE	RHABDOMANCERS
REVENGINGLY	REVESTIARY	REVITALIZES	REVOLUTIONISED	RHABDOMANCIES
REVENGINGS	REVESTRIES	REVITALIZING	REVOLUTIONISER	RHABDOMANCY
REVERBERANT	REVETMENTS	REVIVABILITIES	REVOLUTIONISERS	RHABDOMANTIST
REVERBERANTLY	REVIBRATED	REVIVABILITY	REVOLUTIONISES	RHABDOMANTISTS
REVERBERATE	REVIBRATES	REVIVALISM	REVOLUTIONISING	RHABDOMERE
REVERBERATED	REVIBRATING	REVIVALISMS	REVOLUTIONISM	RHABDOMERES
REVERBERATES	REVICTUALED	REVIVALIST	REVOLUTIONISMS	RHABDOMYOMA
REVERBERATING	REVICTUALING	REVIVALISTIC	REVOLUTIONIST	RHABDOMYOMAS
REVERBERATION	REVICTUALLED	REVIVALISTS	REVOLUTIONISTS	RHABDOMYOMATA
REVERBERATIONS	REVICTUALLING	REVIVEMENT	REVOLUTIONIZE	RHABDOSPHERE
REVERBERATIVE	REVICTUALS	REVIVEMENTS	REVOLUTIONIZED	RHABDOSPHERES
REVERBERATOR	REVIEWABLE	REVIVESCENCE	REVOLUTIONIZER	RHABDOVIRUS
REVERBERATORIES	REVILEMENT	REVIVESCENCES	REVOLUTIONIZERS	RHABDOVIRUSES
REVERBERATORS	REVILEMENTS	REVIVESCENCIES	REVOLUTIONIZES	RHACHIDIAL
REVERBERATORY	REVILINGLY	REVIVESCENCY	REVOLUTIONIZING	RHACHILLAS
REVERENCED	REVINDICATE	REVIVESCENT	REVOLUTIONS	RHACHITISES
REVERENCER	REVINDICATED	REVIVIFICATION	REVOLVABLE	RHADAMANTHINE
REVERENCERS	REVINDICATES	REVIVIFICATIONS	REVOLVABLY	RHAGADIFORM
REVERENCES	REVINDICATING	REVIVIFIED	REVOLVENCIES	RHAMNACEOUS
REVERENCING	REVINDICATION	REVIVIFIES	REVOLVENCY	RHAMPHOTHECA
REVERENTIAL	REVINDICATIONS	REVIVIFYING	REVOLVINGLY	RHAMPHOTHECAE
REVERENTIALLY	REVIOLATED	REVIVINGLY	REVOLVINGS	RHAPONTICS
REVERENTLY	REVIOLATES	REVIVISCENCE	REVULSIONARY	RHAPSODICAL
REVERENTNESS	REVIOLATING	REVIVISCENCES	REVULSIONS	RHAPSODICALLY

R

RHAPSODIES

RHAPSODIES	RHEUMATICALLY	RHINOPLASTY	RHIZOSPHERE	RHOPALOCEROUS
RHAPSODISE	RHEUMATICKY	RHINORRHAGIA	RHIZOSPHERES	RHOTACISED
RHAPSODISED	RHEUMATICS	RHINORRHAGIAS	RHIZOTOMIES	RHOTACISES
RHAPSODISES	RHEUMATISE	RHINORRHOEA	RHODAMINES	RHOTACISING
RHAPSODISING	RHEUMATISES	RHINORRHOEAL	RHODANATES	RHOTACISMS
RHAPSODIST	RHEUMATISM	RHINORRHOEAS	RHODANISED	RHOTACISTIC
RHAPSODISTIC	RHEUMATISMAL	RHINOSCLEROMA	RHODANISES	RHOTACISTS
RHAPSODISTS	RHEUMATISMS	RHINOSCLEROMAS	RHODANISING	RHOTACIZED
RHAPSODIZE	RHEUMATIZE	RHINOSCLEROMATA	RHODANIZED	RHOTACIZES
RHAPSODIZED	RHEUMATIZES	RHINOSCOPE	RHODANIZES	RHOTACIZING
RHAPSODIZES	RHEUMATOID	RHINOSCOPES	RHODANIZING	RHOTICITIES
RHAPSODIZING	RHEUMATOIDALLY	RHINOSCOPIC	RHODOCHROSITE	RHUBARBING
RHEOCHORDS	RHEUMATOLOGICAL	RHINOSCOPIES	RHODOCHROSITES	RHUBARBINGS
RHEOLOGICAL	RHEUMATOLOGIES	RHINOSCOPY	RHODODAPHNE	RHUMBATRON
RHEOLOGICALLY	RHEUMATOLOGIST	RHINOTHECA	RHODODAPHNES	RHUMBATRONS
RHEOLOGIES	RHEUMATOLOGISTS	RHINOTHECAE	RHODODENDRA	RHYMESTERS
RHEOLOGIST	RHEUMATOLOGY	RHINOVIRUS	RHODODENDRON	RHYNCHOCOEL
RHEOLOGISTS	RHIGOLENES	RHINOVIRUSES	RHODODENDRONS	RHYNCHOCOELS
RHEOMETERS	RHINENCEPHALA	RHIPIDIONS	RHODOLITES	RHYNCHODONT
RHEOMETRIC	RHINENCEPHALIC	RHIPIDIUMS	RHODOMONTADE	RHYNCHOPHORE
RHEOMETRICAL	RHINENCEPHALON	RHIZANTHOUS	RHODOMONTADED	RHYNCHOPHORES
RHEOMETRIES	RHINENCEPHALONS	RHIZOCARPIC	RHODOMONTADES	RHYNCHOPHOROUS
RHEOMORPHIC	RHINESTONE	RHIZOCARPOUS	RHODOMONTADING	RHYPAROGRAPHER
RHEOMORPHISM	RHINESTONED	RHIZOCARPS	RHODONITES	RHYPAROGRAPHERS
RHEOMORPHISMS	RHINESTONES	RHIZOCAULS	RHODOPHANE	RHYPAROGRAPHIC
RHEOPHILES	RHINITIDES	RHIZOCEPHALAN	RHODOPHANES	RHYPAROGRAPHIES
RHEORECEPTOR	RHINITISES	RHIZOCEPHALANS	RHODOPSINS	RHYPAROGRAPHY
RHEORECEPTORS	RHINOCERICAL	RHIZOCEPHALOUS	RHOEADINES	RHYTHMICAL
RHEOSTATIC	RHINOCEROS	RHIZOCTONIA	RHOICISSUS	RHYTHMICALLY
RHEOTACTIC	RHINOCEROSES	RHIZOCTONIAS	RHOICISSUSES	RHYTHMICITIES
RHEOTROPES	RHINOCEROT	RHIZOGENETIC	RHOMBENCEPHALA	RHYTHMICITY
RHEOTROPIC	RHINOCEROTE	RHIZOGENIC	RHOMBENCEPHALON	RHYTHMISATION
RHEOTROPISM	RHINOCEROTES	RHIZOGENOUS	RHOMBENPORPHYR	RHYTHMISATIONS
RHEOTROPISMS	RHINOCEROTIC	RHIZOMATOUS	RHOMBENPORPHYRS	RHYTHMISED
RHETORICAL	RHINOLALIA	RHIZOMORPH	RHOMBENPORPHYRY	RHYTHMISES
RHETORICALLY	RHINOLALIAS	RHIZOMORPHOUS	RHOMBOHEDRA	RHYTHMISING
RHETORICIAN	RHINOLITHS	RHIZOMORPHS	RHOMBOHEDRAL	RHYTHMISTS
RHETORICIANS	RHINOLOGICAL	RHIZOPHAGOUS	RHOMBOHEDRON	RHYTHMIZATION
RHETORISED	RHINOLOGIES	RHIZOPHILOUS	RHOMBOHEDRONS	RHYTHMIZATIONS
RHETORISES	RHINOLOGIST	RHIZOPHORE	RHOMBOIDAL	RHYTHMIZED
RHETORISING	RHINOLOGISTS	RHIZOPHORES	RHOMBOIDEI	RHYTHMIZES
RHETORIZED	RHINOPHONIA	RHIZOPLANE	RHOMBOIDES	RHYTHMIZING
RHETORIZES	RHINOPHONIAS	RHIZOPLANES	RHOMBOIDEUS	RHYTHMLESS
RHETORIZING	RHINOPHYMA	RHIZOPODAN	RHOMBPORPHYRIES	RHYTHMOMETER
RHEUMATEESE	RHINOPHYMAS	RHIZOPODANS	RHOMBPORPHYRY	RHYTHMOMETERS
RHEUMATEESES	RHINOPLASTIC	RHIZOPODOUS	RHOPALISMS	RHYTHMOPOEIA
RHEUMATICAL	RHINOPLASTIES	RHIZOPUSES	RHOPALOCERAL	RHYTHMOPOEIAS

RHYTHMUSES
RHYTIDECTOMIES
RHYTIDECTOMY
RHYTIDOMES
RIBALDRIES
RIBATTUTAS
RIBAUDRIES
RIBAVIRINS
RIBBONFISH
RIBBONFISHES
RIBBONLIKE
RIBBONRIES
RIBBONWOOD
RIBBONWOODS
RIBGRASSES
RIBOFLAVIN
RIBOFLAVINE
RIBOFLAVINES
RIBOFLAVINS
RIBONUCLEASE
RIBONUCLEASES
RIBONUCLEIC
RIBONUCLEOSIDE
RIBONUCLEOSIDES
RIBONUCLEOTIDE
RIBONUCLEOTIDES
RICEFIELDS
RICERCARES
RICERCATAS
RICHNESSES
RICINOLEIC
RICKBURNER
RICKBURNERS
RICKETIEST
RICKETINESS
RICKETINESSES
RICKETTIER
RICKETTIEST
RICKETTSIA
RICKETTSIAE
RICKETTSIAL
RICKETTSIAS
RICKSTANDS
RICKSTICKS
RICOCHETED
RICOCHETING
RICOCHETTED

RICOCHETTING
RIDABILITIES
RIDABILITY
RIDDLINGLY
RIDERSHIPS
RIDESHARING
RIDESHARINGS
RIDGEBACKS
RIDGELINES
RIDGELINGS
RIDGEPOLES
RIDGETREES
RIDICULERS
RIDICULING
RIDICULOUS
RIDICULOUSLY
RIDICULOUSNESS
RIEBECKITE
RIEBECKITES
RIFACIMENTI
RIFACIMENTO
RIFAMPICIN
RIFAMPICINS
RIFAMYCINS
RIFENESSES
RIFLEBIRDS
RIGAMAROLE
RIGAMAROLES
RIGHTABLENESS
RIGHTABLENESSES
RIGHTENING
RIGHTEOUSLY
RIGHTEOUSNESS
RIGHTEOUSNESSES
RIGHTFULLY
RIGHTFULNESS
RIGHTFULNESSES
RIGHTNESSES
RIGHTSIZED
RIGHTSIZES
RIGHTSIZING
RIGHTSIZINGS
RIGHTWARDLY
RIGHTWARDS
RIGIDIFICATION
RIGIDIFICATIONS
RIGIDIFIED

RIGIDIFIES
RIGIDIFYING
RIGIDISING
RIGIDITIES
RIGIDIZING
RIGIDNESSES
RIGMAROLES
RIGORISTIC
RIGOROUSLY
RIGOROUSNESS
RIGOROUSNESSES
RIGSDALERS
RIGWIDDIES
RIGWOODIES
RIJKSDAALER
RIJKSDAALERS
RIJSTAFELS
RIJSTTAFEL
RIJSTTAFELS
RIMINESSES
RIMOSITIES
RINDERPEST
RINDERPESTS
RINFORZANDO
RINGBARKED
RINGBARKING
RINGHALSES
RINGLEADER
RINGLEADERS
RINGMASTER
RINGMASTERS
RINGSIDERS
RINGSTANDS
RINGSTRAKED
RINGTOSSES
RINKHALSES
RINSABILITIES
RINSABILITY
RINSIBILITIES
RINSIBILITY
RINTHEREOUT
RINTHEREOUTS
RIOTOUSNESS
RIOTOUSNESSES
RIPENESSES
RIPIDOLITE
RIPIDOLITES

RIPIENISTS
RIPPLINGLY
RIPRAPPING
RIPSNORTER
RIPSNORTERS
RIPSNORTING
RIPSNORTINGLY
RISIBILITIES
RISIBILITY
RISKINESSES
RISORGIMENTO
RISORGIMENTOS
RITARDANDO
RITARDANDOS
RITONAVIRS
RITORNELLE
RITORNELLES
RITORNELLI
RITORNELLO
RITORNELLOS
RITORNELLS
RITOURNELLE
RITOURNELLES
RITUALISATION
RITUALISATIONS
RITUALISED
RITUALISES
RITUALISING
RITUALISMS
RITUALISTIC
RITUALISTICALLY
RITUALISTS
RITUALIZATION
RITUALIZATIONS
RITUALIZED
RITUALIZES
RITUALIZING
RITUXIMABS
RITZINESSES
RIVALESSES
RIVALISING
RIVALITIES
RIVALIZING
RIVALSHIPS
RIVERBANKS
RIVERBOATS
RIVERCRAFT

RIVERCRAFTS
RIVERFRONT
RIVERFRONTS
RIVERHEADS
RIVERSCAPE
RIVERSCAPES
RIVERSIDES
RIVERWALKS
RIVERWARDS
RIVERWEEDS
RIVERWORTHINESS
RIVERWORTHY
RIVETINGLY
ROADABILITIES
ROADABILITY
ROADBLOCKED
ROADBLOCKING
ROADBLOCKS
ROADCRAFTS
ROADHEADER
ROADHEADERS
ROADHOLDING
ROADHOLDINGS
ROADHOUSES
ROADMAKING
ROADMAKINGS
ROADMENDER
ROADMENDERS
ROADROLLER
ROADROLLERS
ROADRUNNER
ROADRUNNERS
ROADSTEADS
ROADWORTHIES
ROADWORTHINESS
ROADWORTHY
ROBERDSMAN
ROBERDSMEN
ROBERTSMAN
ROBERTSMEN
ROBORATING
ROBOTICALLY
ROBOTISATION
ROBOTISATIONS
ROBOTISING
ROBOTIZATION
ROBOTIZATIONS

R

ROBOTIZING	ROENTGENIZING	ROMANICITES	RONTGENOLOGICAL	ROSINESSES
ROBUSTIOUS	ROENTGENOGRAM	ROMANISATION	RONTGENOLOGIES	ROSINWEEDS
ROBUSTIOUSLY	ROENTGENOGRAMS	ROMANISATIONS	RONTGENOLOGIST	ROSMARINES
ROBUSTIOUSNESS	ROENTGENOGRAPH	ROMANISING	RONTGENOLOGISTS	ROSTELLATE
ROBUSTNESS	ROENTGENOGRAPHS	ROMANIZATION	RONTGENOLOGY	ROSTELLUMS
ROBUSTNESSES	ROENTGENOGRAPHY	ROMANIZATIONS	RONTGENOPAQUE	ROSTERINGS
ROCAMBOLES	ROENTGENOLOGIC	ROMANIZING	RONTGENOSCOPE	ROSTROCARINATE
ROCKABILLIES	ROENTGENOLOGIES	ROMANTICAL	RONTGENOSCOPES	ROSTROCARINATES
ROCKABILLY	ROENTGENOLOGIST	ROMANTICALITIES	RONTGENOSCOPIC	ROTACHUTES
ROCKCRESSES	ROENTGENOLOGY	ROMANTICALITY	RONTGENOSCOPIES	ROTAMETERS
ROCKETEERS	ROENTGENOPAQUE	ROMANTICALLY	RONTGENOSCOPY	ROTAPLANES
ROCKETRIES	ROENTGENOSCOPE	ROMANTICISATION	RONTGENOTHERAPY	ROTATIONAL
ROCKFISHES	ROENTGENOSCOPES	ROMANTICISE	ROOFLESSNESS	ROTATIVELY
ROCKHOPPER	ROENTGENOSCOPIC	ROMANTICISED	ROOFLESSNESSES	ROTAVATING
ROCKHOPPERS	ROENTGENOSCOPY	ROMANTICISES	ROOFSCAPES	ROTAVATORS
ROCKHOUNDING	ROGUESHIPS	ROMANTICISING	ROOMINESSES	ROTAVIRUSES
ROCKHOUNDINGS	ROGUISHNESS	ROMANTICISM	ROOTEDNESS	ROTGRASSES
ROCKHOUNDS	ROGUISHNESSES	ROMANTICISMS	ROOTEDNESSES	ROTIFERANS
ROCKINESSES	ROISTERERS	ROMANTICIST	ROOTINESSES	ROTIFEROUS
ROCKSHAFTS	ROISTERING	ROMANTICISTS	ROOTLESSNESS	ROTISSERIE
ROCKSLIDES	ROISTERINGS	ROMANTICIZATION	ROOTLESSNESSES	ROTISSERIES
ROCKSTEADIES	ROISTEROUS	ROMANTICIZE	ROOTSERVER	ROTOGRAPHED
ROCKSTEADY	ROISTEROUSLY	ROMANTICIZED	ROOTSERVERS	ROTOGRAPHING
ROCKWATERS	ROLLCOLLAR	ROMANTICIZES	ROOTSINESS	ROTOGRAPHS
RODENTICIDE	ROLLCOLLARS	ROMANTICIZING	ROOTSINESSES	ROTOGRAVURE
RODENTICIDES	ROLLERBALL	ROMELDALES	ROOTSTALKS	ROTOGRAVURES
RODFISHERS	ROLLERBALLS	ROMPISHNESS	ROOTSTOCKS	ROTORCRAFT
RODFISHING	ROLLERBLADE	ROMPISHNESSES	ROPEDANCER	ROTORCRAFTS
RODFISHINGS	ROLLERBLADED	RONDOLETTO	ROPEDANCERS	ROTOSCOPED
RODGERSIAS	ROLLERBLADER	RONDOLETTOS	ROPEDANCING	ROTOSCOPES
RODOMONTADE	ROLLERBLADERS	RONTGENISATION	ROPEDANCINGS	ROTOSCOPING
RODOMONTADED	ROLLERBLADES	RONTGENISATIONS	ROPEWALKER	ROTOTILLED
RODOMONTADER	ROLLERBLADING	RONTGENISE	ROPEWALKERS	ROTOTILLER
RODOMONTADERS	ROLLERBLADINGS	RONTGENISED	ROPINESSES	ROTOTILLERS
RODOMONTADES	ROLLERCOASTER	RONTGENISES	ROQUELAURE	ROTOTILLING
RODOMONTADING	ROLLERCOASTERED	RONTGENISING	ROQUELAURES	ROTOVATING
ROENTGENISATION	ROLLERCOASTERS	RONTGENIZATION	ROSANILINE	ROTOVATORS
ROENTGENISE	ROLLERDROME	RONTGENIZATIONS	ROSANILINES	ROTTENNESS
ROENTGENISED	ROLLERDROMES	RONTGENIZE	ROSANILINS	ROTTENNESSES
ROENTGENISES	ROLLICKING	RONTGENIZED	ROSEBUSHES	ROTTENSTONE
ROENTGENISING	ROLLICKINGS	RONTGENIZES	ROSEFINCHES	ROTTENSTONED
ROENTGENIUM	ROLLOCKING	RONTGENIZING	ROSEFISHES	ROTTENSTONES
ROENTGENIUMS	ROLLOCKINGS	RONTGENOGRAM	ROSEMALING	ROTTENSTONING
ROENTGENIZATION	ROMANCICAL	RONTGENOGRAMS	ROSEMALINGS	ROTTWEILER
ROENTGENIZE	ROMANCINGS	RONTGENOGRAPH	ROSEMARIES	ROTTWEILERS
ROENTGENIZED	ROMANESCOS	RONTGENOGRAPHS	ROSETTINGS	ROTUNDITIES
ROENTGENIZES	ROMANICITE	RONTGENOGRAPHY	ROSEWATERS	ROTUNDNESS

R

ROTUNDNESSES	ROUNDTABLE	RUBBERISING	RUDDERPOSTS	RUMELGUMPTION
ROUGHBACKS	ROUNDTABLES	RUBBERIZED	RUDDERSTOCK	RUMELGUMPTIONS
ROUGHCASTED	ROUNDTRIPPING	RUBBERIZES	RUDDERSTOCKS	RUMFUSTIAN
ROUGHCASTER	ROUNDTRIPPINGS	RUBBERIZING	RUDDINESSES	RUMFUSTIANS
ROUGHCASTERS	ROUNDTRIPS	RUBBERLIKE	RUDENESSES	RUMGUMPTION
ROUGHCASTING	ROUNDWOODS	RUBBERNECK	RUDIMENTAL	RUMGUMPTIONS
ROUGHCASTS	ROUNDWORMS	RUBBERNECKED	RUDIMENTALLY	RUMINANTLY
ROUGHDRIED	ROUSEABOUT	RUBBERNECKER	RUDIMENTARILY	RUMINATING
ROUGHDRIES	ROUSEABOUTS	RUBBERNECKERS	RUDIMENTARINESS	RUMINATINGLY
ROUGHDRYING	ROUSEDNESS	RUBBERNECKING	RUDIMENTARY	RUMINATION
ROUGHENING	ROUSEDNESSES	RUBBERNECKS	RUEFULNESS	RUMINATIONS
ROUGHHEWED	ROUSEMENTS	RUBBERWEAR	RUEFULNESSES	RUMINATIVE
ROUGHHEWING	ROUSSETTES	RUBBERWEARS	RUFESCENCE	RUMINATIVELY
ROUGHHOUSE	ROUSTABOUT	RUBBISHING	RUFESCENCES	RUMINATORS
ROUGHHOUSED	ROUSTABOUTS	RUBBLEWORK	RUFFIANING	RUMLEGUMPTION
ROUGHHOUSES	ROUTEMARCH	RUBBLEWORKS	RUFFIANISH	RUMLEGUMPTIONS
ROUGHHOUSING	ROUTEMARCHED	RUBEFACIENT	RUFFIANISM	RUMMELGUMPTION
ROUGHHOUSINGS	ROUTEMARCHES	RUBEFACIENTS	RUFFIANISMS	RUMMELGUMPTIONS
ROUGHNECKED	ROUTEMARCHING	RUBEFACTION	RUGGEDISATION	RUMMINESSES
ROUGHNECKING	ROUTINEERS	RUBEFACTIONS	RUGGEDISATIONS	RUMMISHING
ROUGHNECKS	ROUTINISATION	RUBELLITES	RUGGEDISED	RUMMLEGUMPTION
ROUGHNESSES	ROUTINISATIONS	RUBESCENCE	RUGGEDISES	RUMMLEGUMPTIONS
ROUGHRIDER	ROUTINISED	RUBESCENCES	RUGGEDISING	RUMORMONGER
ROUGHRIDERS	ROUTINISES	RUBIACEOUS	RUGGEDIZATION	RUMORMONGERING
ROULETTING	ROUTINISING	RUBICELLES	RUGGEDIZATIONS	RUMORMONGERINGS
ROUNCEVALS	ROUTINISMS	RUBICONING	RUGGEDIZED	RUMORMONGERS
ROUNDABOUT	ROUTINISTS	RUBICUNDITIES	RUGGEDIZES	RUMRUNNERS
ROUNDABOUTATION	ROUTINIZATION	RUBICUNDITY	RUGGEDIZING	RUNAROUNDS
ROUNDABOUTED	ROUTINIZATIONS	RUBIGINOSE	RUGGEDNESS	RUNECRAFTS
ROUNDABOUTEDLY	ROUTINIZED	RUBIGINOUS	RUGGEDNESSES	RUNNINESSES
ROUNDABOUTILITY	ROUTINIZES	RUBRICALLY	RUGOSITIES	RUNTINESSES
ROUNDABOUTING	ROUTINIZING	RUBRICATED	RUINATIONS	RUPESTRIAN
ROUNDABOUTLY	ROWANBERRIES	RUBRICATES	RUINOUSNESS	RUPICOLINE
ROUNDABOUTNESS	ROWANBERRY	RUBRICATING	RUINOUSNESSES	RUPICOLOUS
ROUNDABOUTS	ROWDINESSES	RUBRICATION	RULERSHIPS	RUPTURABLE
ROUNDARCHED	ROWDYDOWED	RUBRICATIONS	RUMBLEDETHUMP	RUPTUREWORT
ROUNDBALLS	ROWDYDOWING	RUBRICATOR	RUMBLEDETHUMPS	RUPTUREWORTS
ROUNDEDNESS	ROYALISING	RUBRICATORS	RUMBLEGUMPTION	RURALISATION
ROUNDEDNESSES	ROYALISTIC	RUBRICIANS	RUMBLEGUMPTIONS	RURALISATIONS
ROUNDELAYS	ROYALIZING	RUBYTHROAT	RUMBLINGLY	RURALISING
ROUNDHANDS	ROYALMASTS	RUBYTHROATS	RUMBULLION	RURALITIES
ROUNDHEADED	ROYSTERERS	RUCTATIONS	RUMBULLIONS	RURALIZATION
ROUNDHEADEDNESS	ROYSTERING	RUDBECKIAS	RUMBUNCTIOUS	RURALIZATIONS
ROUNDHEELS	ROYSTEROUS	RUDDERHEAD	RUMBUSTICAL	RURALIZING
ROUNDHOUSE	RUBBERIEST	RUDDERHEADS	RUMBUSTIOUS	RURALNESSES
ROUNDHOUSES	RUBBERISED	RUDDERLESS	RUMBUSTIOUSLY	RURIDECANAL
ROUNDNESSES	RUBBERISES	RUDDERPOST	RUMBUSTIOUSNESS	RUSHINESSES

R

RUSHLIGHTS

RUSHLIGHTS
RUSSETINGS
RUSSETTING
RUSSETTINGS
RUSSIFYING
RUSTBUCKET
RUSTICALLY
RUSTICATED
RUSTICATES
RUSTICATING

RUSTICATINGS
RUSTICATION
RUSTICATIONS
RUSTICATOR
RUSTICATORS
RUSTICISED
RUSTICISES
RUSTICISING
RUSTICISMS
RUSTICITIES

RUSTICIZED
RUSTICIZES
RUSTICIZING
RUSTICWORK
RUSTICWORKS
RUSTINESSES
RUSTLINGLY
RUSTPROOFED
RUSTPROOFING
RUSTPROOFINGS

RUSTPROOFS
RUTHENIOUS
RUTHENIUMS
RUTHERFORD
RUTHERFORDIUM
RUTHERFORDIUMS
RUTHERFORDS
RUTHFULNESS
RUTHFULNESSES
RUTHLESSLY

RUTHLESSNESS
RUTHLESSNESSES
RUTTINESSES
RUTTISHNESS
RUTTISHNESSES
RYBAUDRYES
RYEGRASSES

S

SABADILLAS	SACCHARIMETERS	SACERDOTALISING	SACRAMENTS	SADDLECLOTHS
SABBATARIAN	SACCHARIMETRIES	SACERDOTALISM	SACRARIUMS	SADDLELESS
SABBATICAL	SACCHARIMETRY	SACERDOTALISMS	SACREDNESS	SADDLERIES
SABBATICALS	SACCHARINE	SACERDOTALIST	SACREDNESSES	SADDLEROOM
SABBATISED	SACCHARINELY	SACERDOTALISTS	SACRIFICEABLE	SADDLEROOMS
SABBATISES	SACCHARINES	SACERDOTALIZE	SACRIFICED	SADDLETREE
SABBATISING	SACCHARINITIES	SACERDOTALIZED	SACRIFICER	SADDLETREES
SABBATISMS	SACCHARINITY	SACERDOTALIZES	SACRIFICERS	SADISTICALLY
SABBATIZED	SACCHARINS	SACERDOTALIZING	SACRIFICES	SADOMASOCHISM
SABBATIZES	SACCHARISATION	SACERDOTALLY	SACRIFICIAL	SADOMASOCHISMS
SABBATIZING	SACCHARISATIONS	SACHEMDOMS	SACRIFICIALLY	SADOMASOCHIST
SABERMETRICIAN	SACCHARISE	SACHEMSHIP	SACRIFICING	SADOMASOCHISTIC
SABERMETRICIANS	SACCHARISED	SACHEMSHIPS	SACRIFYING	SADOMASOCHISTS
SABERMETRICS	SACCHARISES	SACKCLOTHS	SACRILEGES	SAFECRACKER
SABLEFISHES	SACCHARISING	SACRALGIAS	SACRILEGIOUS	SAFECRACKERS
SABOTAGING	SACCHARIZATION	SACRALISATION	SACRILEGIOUSLY	SAFECRACKING
SABRETACHE	SACCHARIZATIONS	SACRALISATIONS	SACRILEGIST	SAFECRACKINGS
SABRETACHES	SACCHARIZE	SACRALISED	SACRILEGISTS	SAFEGUARDED
SABREWINGS	SACCHARIZED	SACRALISES	SACRISTANS	SAFEGUARDING
SABULOSITIES	SACCHARIZES	SACRALISING	SACRISTIES	SAFEGUARDS
SABULOSITY	SACCHARIZING	SACRALITIES	SACROCOCCYGEAL	SAFEKEEPING
SABURRATION	SACCHAROID	SACRALIZATION	SACROCOSTAL	SAFEKEEPINGS
SABURRATIONS	SACCHAROIDAL	SACRALIZATIONS	SACROCOSTALS	SAFELIGHTS
SACAHUISTA	SACCHAROIDS	SACRALIZED	SACROILIAC	SAFENESSES
SACAHUISTAS	SACCHAROMETER	SACRALIZES	SACROILIACS	SAFFLOWERS
SACAHUISTE	SACCHAROMETERS	SACRALIZING	SACROILIITIS	SAFRANINES
SACAHUISTES	SACCHAROMETRIES	SACRAMENTAL	SACROILIITISES	SAGACIOUSLY
SACCADICALLY	SACCHAROMETRY	SACRAMENTALISM	SACROSANCT	SAGACIOUSNESS
SACCHARASE	SACCHAROMYCES	SACRAMENTALISMS	SACROSANCTITIES	SAGACIOUSNESSES
SACCHARASES	SACCHAROMYCETES	SACRAMENTALIST	SACROSANCTITY	SAGACITIES
SACCHARATE	SACCHAROSE	SACRAMENTALISTS	SACROSANCTNESS	SAGANASHES
SACCHARATED	SACCHAROSES	SACRAMENTALITY	SADDLEBACK	SAGAPENUMS
SACCHARATES	SACCHARUMS	SACRAMENTALLY	SADDLEBACKED	SAGEBRUSHES
SACCHARIDE	SACCULATED	SACRAMENTALNESS	SADDLEBACKS	SAGENESSES
SACCHARIDES	SACCULATION	SACRAMENTALS	SADDLEBAGS	SAGINATING
SACCHARIFEROUS	SACCULATIONS	SACRAMENTARIAN	SADDLEBILL	SAGINATION
SACCHARIFIED	SACCULIFORM	SACRAMENTARIANS	SADDLEBILLS	SAGINATIONS
SACCHARIFIES	SACERDOTAL	SACRAMENTARIES	SADDLEBOWS	SAGITTALLY
SACCHARIFY	SACERDOTALISE	SACRAMENTARY	SADDLEBRED	SAGITTARIES
SACCHARIFYING	SACERDOTALISED	SACRAMENTED	SADDLEBREDS	SAGITTIFORM
SACCHARIMETER	SACERDOTALISES	SACRAMENTING	SADDLECLOTH	SAILBOARDED

S

SAILBOARDER	SALAMANDROIDS	SALINISATIONS	SALSUGINOUS	SALUTATORIANS
SAILBOARDERS	SALANGANES	SALINISING	SALTARELLI	SALUTATORIES
SAILBOARDING	SALBUTAMOL	SALINITIES	SALTARELLO	SALUTATORILY
SAILBOARDINGS	SALBUTAMOLS	SALINIZATION	SALTARELLOS	SALUTATORY
SAILBOARDS	SALEABILITIES	SALINIZATIONS	SALTATIONISM	SALUTIFEROUS
SAILBOATER	SALEABILITY	SALINIZING	SALTATIONISMS	SALVABILITIES
SAILBOATERS	SALEABLENESS	SALINOMETER	SALTATIONIST	SALVABILITY
SAILBOATING	SALEABLENESSES	SALINOMETERS	SALTATIONISTS	SALVABLENESS
SAILBOATINGS	SALERATUSES	SALINOMETRIC	SALTATIONS	SALVABLENESSES
SAILCLOTHS	SALESCLERK	SALINOMETRIES	SALTATORIAL	SALVAGEABILITY
SAILFISHES	SALESCLERKS	SALINOMETRY	SALTATORIOUS	SALVAGEABLE
SAILMAKERS	SALESGIRLS	SALIVATING	SALTBUSHES	SALVARSANS
SAILMAKING	SALESLADIES	SALIVATION	SALTCELLAR	SALVATIONAL
SAILMAKINGS	SALESMANSHIP	SALIVATIONS	SALTCELLARS	SALVATIONISM
SAILORINGS	SALESMANSHIPS	SALIVATORS	SALTCHUCKER	SALVATIONISMS
SAILORLESS	SALESPEOPLE	SALLENDERS	SALTCHUCKERS	SALVATIONIST
SAILORLIKE	SALESPERSON	SALLOWNESS	SALTCHUCKS	SALVATIONISTS
SAILPLANED	SALESPERSONS	SALLOWNESSES	SALTFISHES	SALVATIONS
SAILPLANER	SALESROOMS	SALLYPORTS	SALTIGRADE	SALVATORIES
SAILPLANERS	SALESWOMAN	SALMAGUNDI	SALTIGRADES	SALVERFORM
SAILPLANES	SALESWOMEN	SALMAGUNDIES	SALTIMBANCO	SALVIFICAL
SAILPLANING	SALIAUNCES	SALMAGUNDIS	SALTIMBANCOS	SALVIFICALLY
SAILPLANINGS	SALICACEOUS	SALMAGUNDY	SALTIMBOCCA	SALVINIACEOUS
SAINTESSES	SALICETUMS	SALMANASER	SALTIMBOCCAS	SAMARIFORM
SAINTFOINS	SALICIONAL	SALMANASERS	SALTINESSES	SAMARITANS
SAINTHOODS	SALICIONALS	SALMANAZAR	SALTIREWISE	SAMARSKITE
SAINTLIEST	SALICORNIA	SALMANAZARS	SALTISHNESS	SAMARSKITES
SAINTLINESS	SALICORNIAS	SALMONBERRIES	SALTISHNESSES	SAMENESSES
SAINTLINESSES	SALICYLAMIDE	SALMONBERRY	SALTNESSES	SAMEYNESSES
SAINTLINGS	SALICYLAMIDES	SALMONELLA	SALTPETERS	SAMNITISES
SAINTPAULIA	SALICYLATE	SALMONELLAE	SALTPETREMAN	SAMPLERIES
SAINTPAULIAS	SALICYLATED	SALMONELLAS	SALTPETREMEN	SANATORIUM
SAINTSHIPS	SALICYLATES	SALMONELLOSES	SALTPETRES	SANATORIUMS
SALABILITIES	SALICYLATING	SALMONELLOSIS	SALTSHAKER	SANBENITOS
SALABILITY	SALICYLISM	SALMONOIDS	SALTSHAKERS	SANCTIFIABLE
SALABLENESS	SALICYLISMS	SALOMETERS	SALUBRIOUS	SANCTIFICATION
SALABLENESSES	SALIENCIES	SALOPETTES	SALUBRIOUSLY	SANCTIFICATIONS
SALACIOUSLY	SALIENTIAN	SALPIGLOSSES	SALUBRIOUSNESS	SANCTIFIED
SALACIOUSNESS	SALIENTIANS	SALPIGLOSSIS	SALUBRITIES	SANCTIFIEDLY
SALACIOUSNESSES	SALIFEROUS	SALPIGLOSSISES	SALURETICS	SANCTIFIER
SALACITIES	SALIFIABLE	SALPINGECTOMIES	SALUTARILY	SANCTIFIERS
SALAMANDER	SALIFICATION	SALPINGECTOMY	SALUTARINESS	SANCTIFIES
SALAMANDERS	SALIFICATIONS	SALPINGIAN	SALUTARINESSES	SANCTIFYING
SALAMANDRIAN	SALIMETERS	SALPINGITIC	SALUTATION	SANCTIFYINGLY
SALAMANDRIANS	SALIMETRIC	SALPINGITIS	SALUTATIONAL	SANCTIFYINGS
SALAMANDRINE	SALIMETRIES	SALPINGITISES	SALUTATIONS	SANCTIMONIES
SALAMANDROID	SALINISATION	SALSOLACEOUS	SALUTATORIAN	SANCTIMONIOUS

SANCTIMONIOUSLY	SANDGROUSE	SANITARIAN	SAPIENCIES	SAPROPHYTISMS
SANCTIMONY	SANDGROUSES	SANITARIANISM	SAPIENTIAL	SAPROTROPH
SANCTIONABLE	SANDINESSES	SANITARIANISMS	SAPIENTIALLY	SAPROTROPHIC
SANCTIONED	SANDLOTTER	SANITARIANS	SAPINDACEOUS	SAPROTROPHS
SANCTIONEER	SANDLOTTERS	SANITARIES	SAPLESSNESS	SAPSUCKERS
SANCTIONEERS	SANDPAINTING	SANITARILY	SAPLESSNESSES	SARABANDES
SANCTIONER	SANDPAINTINGS	SANITARINESS	SAPODILLAS	SARBACANES
SANCTIONERS	SANDPAPERED	SANITARINESSES	SAPOGENINS	SARCASTICALLY
SANCTIONING	SANDPAPERING	SANITARIST	SAPONACEOUS	SARCENCHYMATOUS
SANCTIONLESS	SANDPAPERINGS	SANITARISTS	SAPONACEOUSNESS	SARCENCHYME
SANCTITIES	SANDPAPERS	SANITARIUM	SAPONARIAS	SARCENCHYMES
SANCTITUDE	SANDPAPERY	SANITARIUMS	SAPONIFIABLE	SARCOCARPS
SANCTITUDES	SANDPIPERS	SANITATING	SAPONIFICATION	SARCOCOLLA
SANCTUARIES	SANDSPOUTS	SANITATION	SAPONIFICATIONS	SARCOCOLLAS
SANCTUARISE	SANDSTONES	SANITATIONIST	SAPONIFIED	SARCOCYSTIS
SANCTUARISED	SANDSTORMS	SANITATIONISTS	SAPONIFIER	SARCOCYSTISES
SANCTUARISES	SANDSUCKER	SANITATIONS	SAPONIFIERS	SARCOIDOSES
SANCTUARISING	SANDSUCKERS	SANITISATION	SAPONIFIES	SARCOIDOSIS
SANCTUARIZE	SANDWICHED	SANITISATIONS	SAPONIFYING	SARCOLEMMA
SANCTUARIZED	SANDWICHES	SANITISERS	SAPOTACEOUS	SARCOLEMMAL
SANCTUARIZES	SANDWICHING	SANITISING	SAPPANWOOD	SARCOLEMMAS
SANCTUARIZING	SANENESSES	SANITIZATION	SAPPANWOODS	SARCOLEMMATA
SANDALLING	SANGFROIDS	SANITIZATIONS	SAPPERMENT	SARCOLOGIES
SANDALWOOD	SANGUIFEROUS	SANITIZERS	SAPPHIRINE	SARCOMATOID
SANDALWOODS	SANGUIFICATION	SANITIZING	SAPPHIRINES	SARCOMATOSES
SANDARACHS	SANGUIFICATIONS	SANITORIUM	SAPPINESSES	SARCOMATOSIS
SANDBAGGED	SANGUIFIED	SANITORIUMS	SAPRAEMIAS	SARCOMATOUS
SANDBAGGER	SANGUIFIES	SANNYASINS	SAPROBIONT	SARCOMERES
SANDBAGGERS	SANGUIFYING	SANSCULOTTE	SAPROBIONTS	SARCOPHAGAL
SANDBAGGING	SANGUINARIA	SANSCULOTTERIE	SAPROBIOTIC	SARCOPHAGI
SANDBLASTED	SANGUINARIAS	SANSCULOTTERIES	SAPROGENIC	SARCOPHAGOUS
SANDBLASTER	SANGUINARILY	SANSCULOTTES	SAPROGENICITIES	SARCOPHAGUS
SANDBLASTERS	SANGUINARINESS	SANSCULOTTIC	SAPROGENICITY	SARCOPHAGUSES
SANDBLASTING	SANGUINARY	SANSCULOTTIDES	SAPROGENOUS	SARCOPLASM
SANDBLASTINGS	SANGUINELY	SANSCULOTTISH	SAPROLEGNIA	SARCOPLASMIC
SANDBLASTS	SANGUINENESS	SANSCULOTTISM	SAPROLEGNIAS	SARCOPLASMS
SANDCASTLE	SANGUINENESSES	SANSCULOTTISMS	SAPROLITES	SARCOSOMAL
SANDCASTLES	SANGUINEOUS	SANSCULOTTIST	SAPROLITIC	SARCOSOMES
SANDCRACKS	SANGUINEOUSNESS	SANSCULOTTISTS	SAPROPELIC	SARDONIANS
SANDERLING	SANGUINING	SANSEVIERIA	SAPROPELITE	SARDONICAL
SANDERLINGS	SANGUINITIES	SANSEVIERIAS	SAPROPELITES	SARDONICALLY
SANDERSWOOD	SANGUINITY	SANTALACEOUS	SAPROPHAGOUS	SARDONICISM
SANDERSWOODS	SANGUINIVOROUS	SANTOLINAS	SAPROPHYTE	SARDONICISMS
SANDFISHES	SANGUINOLENCIES	SANTONICAS	SAPROPHYTES	SARDONYXES
SANDGLASSES	SANGUINOLENCY	SAPANWOODS	SAPROPHYTIC	SARGASSOES
SANDGROPER	SANGUINOLENT	SAPIDITIES	SAPROPHYTICALLY	SARGASSUMS
SANDGROPERS	SANGUIVOROUS	SAPIDNESSES	SAPROPHYTISM	SARKINESSES

S

SARMENTACEOUS
SARMENTOSE
SARMENTOUS
SARPANCHES
SARRACENIA
SARRACENIACEOUS
SARRACENIAS
SARRUSOPHONE
SARRUSOPHONES
SARSAPARILLA
SARSAPARILLAS
SARTORIALLY
SARTORIUSES
SASKATOONS
SASQUATCHES
SASSAFRASES
SASSARARAS
SASSINESSES
SASSOLITES
SASSYWOODS
SATANICALLY
SATANICALNESS
SATANICALNESSES
SATANITIES
SATANOLOGIES
SATANOLOGY
SATANOPHANIES
SATANOPHANY
SATANOPHOBIA
SATANOPHOBIAS
SATCHELFUL
SATCHELFULS
SATCHELLED
SATCHELSFUL
SATEDNESSES
SATELLITED
SATELLITES
SATELLITIC
SATELLITING
SATELLITISE
SATELLITISED
SATELLITISES
SATELLITISING
SATELLITIUM
SATELLITIUMS
SATELLITIZE
SATELLITIZED

SATELLITIZES
SATELLITIZING
SATIABILITIES
SATIABILITY
SATIATIONS
SATINETTAS
SATINETTES
SATINFLOWER
SATINFLOWERS
SATINWOODS
SATIRICALLY
SATIRICALNESS
SATIRICALNESSES
SATIRISABLE
SATIRISATION
SATIRISATIONS
SATIRISERS
SATIRISING
SATIRIZABLE
SATIRIZATION
SATIRIZATIONS
SATIRIZERS
SATIRIZING
SATISFACTION
SATISFACTIONS
SATISFACTORILY
SATISFACTORY
SATISFIABLE
SATISFICED
SATISFICER
SATISFICERS
SATISFICES
SATISFICING
SATISFICINGS
SATISFIERS
SATISFYING
SATISFYINGLY
SATURABILITIES
SATURABILITY
SATURATERS
SATURATING
SATURATION
SATURATIONS
SATURATORS
SATURNALIA
SATURNALIAN
SATURNALIANLY

SATURNALIAS
SATURNIIDS
SATURNINELY
SATURNINITIES
SATURNINITY
SATURNISMS
SATURNISTS
SATYAGRAHA
SATYAGRAHAS
SATYAGRAHI
SATYAGRAHIS
SATYRESQUE
SATYRESSES
SATYRIASES
SATYRIASIS
SAUCEBOATS
SAUCEBOXES
SAUCERFULS
SAUCERLESS
SAUCERLIKE
SAUCINESSES
SAUCISSONS
SAUERBRATEN
SAUERBRATENS
SAUERKRAUT
SAUERKRAUTS
SAUNTERERS
SAUNTERING
SAUNTERINGLY
SAUNTERINGS
SAURISCHIAN
SAURISCHIANS
SAUROGNATHOUS
SAUROPODOUS
SAUROPSIDAN
SAUROPSIDANS
SAUROPTERYGIAN
SAUROPTERYGIANS
SAUSSURITE
SAUSSURITES
SAUSSURITIC
SAVABLENESS
SAVABLENESSES
SAVAGEDOMS
SAVAGENESS
SAVAGENESSES
SAVAGERIES

SAVEABLENESS
SAVEABLENESSES
SAVEGARDED
SAVEGARDING
SAVINGNESS
SAVINGNESSES
SAVORINESS
SAVORINESSES
SAVOURIEST
SAVOURINESS
SAVOURINESSES
SAVOURLESS
SAVVINESSES
SAWBONESES
SAWDUSTING
SAWGRASSES
SAWTIMBERS
SAXICAVOUS
SAXICOLINE
SAXICOLOUS
SAXIFRAGACEOUS
SAXIFRAGES
SAXITOXINS
SAXOPHONES
SAXOPHONIC
SAXOPHONIST
SAXOPHONISTS
SCABBARDED
SCABBARDING
SCABBARDLESS
SCABBEDNESS
SCABBEDNESSES
SCABBINESS
SCABBINESSES
SCABERULOUS
SCABIOUSES
SCABRIDITIES
SCABRIDITY
SCABROUSLY
SCABROUSNESS
SCABROUSNESSES
SCAFFOLAGE
SCAFFOLAGES
SCAFFOLDAGE
SCAFFOLDAGES
SCAFFOLDED
SCAFFOLDER

SCAFFOLDERS
SCAFFOLDING
SCAFFOLDINGS
SCAGLIOLAS
SCAITHLESS
SCALABILITIES
SCALABILITY
SCALABLENESS
SCALABLENESSES
SCALARIFORM
SCALARIFORMLY
SCALATIONS
SCALDBERRIES
SCALDBERRY
SCALDFISHES
SCALDHEADS
SCALDSHIPS
SCALEBOARD
SCALEBOARDS
SCALENOHEDRA
SCALENOHEDRON
SCALENOHEDRONS
SCALETAILS
SCALEWORKS
SCALINESSES
SCALLAWAGS
SCALLOPERS
SCALLOPING
SCALLOPINGS
SCALLOPINI
SCALLOPINIS
SCALLYWAGS
SCALOGRAMS
SCALOPPINE
SCALOPPINES
SCALOPPINI
SCALPELLIC
SCALPELLIFORM
SCALPRIFORM
SCAMBAITING
SCAMBAITINGS
SCAMBLINGLY
SCAMBLINGS
SCAMMONIATE
SCAMMONIES
SCAMPERERS
SCAMPERING

S

SCAMPISHLY	SCAPHOCEPHALIC	SCARFSKINS	SCATTEROMETER	SCEUOPHYLAX
SCAMPISHNESS	SCAPHOCEPHALICS	SCARIFICATION	SCATTEROMETERS	SCEUOPHYLAXES
SCAMPISHNESSES	SCAPHOCEPHALIES	SCARIFICATIONS	SCATTERSHOT	SCHADENFREUDE
SCANDALING	SCAPHOCEPHALISM	SCARIFICATOR	SCATTINESS	SCHADENFREUDES
SCANDALISATION	SCAPHOCEPHALOUS	SCARIFICATORS	SCATTINESSES	SCHALSTEIN
SCANDALISATIONS	SCAPHOCEPHALUS	SCARIFIERS	SCATURIENT	SCHALSTEINS
SCANDALISE	SCAPHOCEPHALY	SCARIFYING	SCAVENGERED	SCHAPPEING
SCANDALISED	SCAPHOPODS	SCARIFYINGLY	SCAVENGERIES	SCHATCHENS
SCANDALISER	SCAPIGEROUS	SCARINESSES	SCAVENGERING	SCHECHITAH
SCANDALISERS	SCAPOLITES	SCARLATINA	SCAVENGERINGS	SCHECHITAHS
SCANDALISES	SCAPULARIES	SCARLATINAL	SCAVENGERS	SCHECHITAS
SCANDALISING	SCAPULATED	SCARLATINAS	SCAVENGERY	SCHECKLATON
SCANDALIZATION	SCAPULIMANCIES	SCARLETING	SCAVENGING	SCHECKLATONS
SCANDALIZATIONS	SCAPULIMANCY	SCARPERING	SCAVENGINGS	SCHEDULERS
SCANDALIZE	SCAPULIMANTIC	SCATHEFULNESS	SCAZONTICS	SCHEDULING
SCANDALIZED	SCAPULOMANCIES	SCATHEFULNESSES	SCELERATES	SCHEELITES
SCANDALIZER	SCAPULOMANCY	SCATHELESS	SCENARISATION	SCHEFFLERA
SCANDALIZERS	SCAPULOMANTIC	SCATHINGLY	SCENARISATIONS	SCHEFFLERAS
SCANDALIZES	SCARABAEAN	SCATOLOGIC	SCENARISED	SCHEMATICAL
SCANDALIZING	SCARABAEANS	SCATOLOGICAL	SCENARISES	SCHEMATICALLY
SCANDALLED	SCARABAEID	SCATOLOGIES	SCENARISING	SCHEMATICS
SCANDALLING	SCARABAEIDS	SCATOLOGIST	SCENARISTS	SCHEMATISATION
SCANDALMONGER	SCARABAEIST	SCATOLOGISTS	SCENARIZATION	SCHEMATISATIONS
SCANDALMONGERS	SCARABAEISTS	SCATOPHAGIES	SCENARIZATIONS	SCHEMATISE
SCANDALOUS	SCARABAEOID	SCATOPHAGOUS	SCENARIZED	SCHEMATISED
SCANDALOUSLY	SCARABAEOIDS	SCATOPHAGY	SCENARIZES	SCHEMATISES
SCANDALOUSNESS	SCARABAEUS	SCATTERABLE	SCENARIZING	SCHEMATISING
SCANSORIAL	SCARABAEUSES	SCATTERATION	SCENESHIFTER	SCHEMATISM
SCANTINESS	SCARABOIDS	SCATTERATIONS	SCENESHIFTERS	SCHEMATISMS
SCANTINESSES	SCARAMOUCH	SCATTERBRAIN	SCENESTERS	SCHEMATIST
SCANTITIES	SCARAMOUCHE	SCATTERBRAINED	SCENICALLY	SCHEMATISTS
SCANTLINGS	SCARAMOUCHED	SCATTERBRAINS	SCENOGRAPHER	SCHEMATIZATION
SCANTNESSES	SCARAMOUCHES	SCATTEREDLY	SCENOGRAPHERS	SCHEMATIZATIONS
SCAPEGALLOWS	SCARAMOUCHING	SCATTERERS	SCENOGRAPHIC	SCHEMATIZE
SCAPEGALLOWSES	SCARCEMENT	SCATTERGOOD	SCENOGRAPHICAL	SCHEMATIZED
SCAPEGOATED	SCARCEMENTS	SCATTERGOODS	SCENOGRAPHIES	SCHEMATIZES
SCAPEGOATING	SCARCENESS	SCATTERGRAM	SCENOGRAPHY	SCHEMATIZING
SCAPEGOATINGS	SCARCENESSES	SCATTERGRAMS	SCENTLESSNESS	SCHEMINGLY
SCAPEGOATISM	SCARCITIES	SCATTERGUN	SCENTLESSNESSES	SCHEMOZZLE
SCAPEGOATISMS	SCARECROWS	SCATTERGUNS	SCEPTERING	SCHEMOZZLED
SCAPEGOATS	SCAREHEADS	SCATTERING	SCEPTERLESS	SCHEMOZZLES
SCAPEGRACE	SCAREMONGER	SCATTERINGLY	SCEPTICALLY	SCHEMOZZLING
SCAPEGRACES	SCAREMONGERING	SCATTERINGS	SCEPTICISM	SCHERZANDI
SCAPEMENTS	SCAREMONGERINGS	SCATTERLING	SCEPTICISMS	SCHERZANDO
SCAPEWHEEL	SCAREMONGERS	SCATTERLINGS	SCEPTRELESS	SCHERZANDOS
SCAPEWHEELS	SCAREWARES	SCATTERMOUCH	SCEUOPHYLACIA	SCHIAVONES
SCAPHOCEPHALI	SCARFISHES	SCATTERMOUCHES	SCEUOPHYLACIUM	SCHILLERISATION

S

SCHILLERISE
SCHILLERISED
SCHILLERISES
SCHILLERISING
SCHILLERIZATION
SCHILLERIZE
SCHILLERIZED
SCHILLERIZES
SCHILLERIZING
SCHILLINGS
SCHINDYLESES
SCHINDYLESIS
SCHINDYLETIC
SCHIPPERKE
SCHIPPERKES
SCHISMATIC
SCHISMATICAL
SCHISMATICALLY
SCHISMATICALS
SCHISMATICS
SCHISMATISE
SCHISMATISED
SCHISMATISES
SCHISMATISING
SCHISMATIZE
SCHISMATIZED
SCHISMATIZES
SCHISMATIZING
SCHISTOSITIES
SCHISTOSITY
SCHISTOSOMAL
SCHISTOSOME
SCHISTOSOMES
SCHISTOSOMIASES
SCHISTOSOMIASIS
SCHIZAEACEOUS
SCHIZANTHUS
SCHIZANTHUSES
SCHIZOCARP
SCHIZOCARPIC
SCHIZOCARPOUS
SCHIZOCARPS
SCHIZOGENESES
SCHIZOGENESIS
SCHIZOGENETIC
SCHIZOGENIC
SCHIZOGNATHOUS

SCHIZOGONIC
SCHIZOGONIES
SCHIZOGONOUS
SCHIZOGONY
SCHIZOIDAL
SCHIZOMYCETE
SCHIZOMYCETES
SCHIZOMYCETIC
SCHIZOMYCETOUS
SCHIZOPHRENE
SCHIZOPHRENES
SCHIZOPHRENETIC
SCHIZOPHRENIA
SCHIZOPHRENIAS
SCHIZOPHRENIC
SCHIZOPHRENICS
SCHIZOPHYCEOUS
SCHIZOPHYTE
SCHIZOPHYTES
SCHIZOPHYTIC
SCHIZOPODAL
SCHIZOPODOUS
SCHIZOPODS
SCHIZOTHYMIA
SCHIZOTHYMIAS
SCHIZOTHYMIC
SCHIZZIEST
SCHLEMIELS
SCHLEMIHLS
SCHLEPPERS
SCHLEPPIER
SCHLEPPIEST
SCHLEPPING
SCHLIERENS
SCHLIMAZEL
SCHLIMAZELS
SCHLOCKERS
SCHLOCKIER
SCHLOCKIEST
SCHLUMBERGERA
SCHLUMBERGERAS
SCHLUMPIER
SCHLUMPIEST
SCHLUMPING
SCHMALTZES
SCHMALTZIER
SCHMALTZIEST

SCHMALZIER
SCHMALZIEST
SCHMEARING
SCHMECKERS
SCHMECKING
SCHMEERING
SCHMICKEST
SCHMOOSING
SCHMOOZERS
SCHMOOZIER
SCHMOOZIEST
SCHMOOZING
SCHMUCKIER
SCHMUCKIEST
SCHMUCKING
SCHMUTTERS
SCHNAPPERS
SCHNAPPSES
SCHNAUZERS
SCHNITZELS
SCHNORKELED
SCHNORKELING
SCHNORKELLED
SCHNORKELLING
SCHNORKELS
SCHNORRERS
SCHNORRING
SCHNOZZLES
SCHOLARCHS
SCHOLARLIER
SCHOLARLIEST
SCHOLARLINESS
SCHOLARLINESSES
SCHOLARSHIP
SCHOLARSHIPS
SCHOLASTIC
SCHOLASTICAL
SCHOLASTICALLY
SCHOLASTICATE
SCHOLASTICATES
SCHOLASTICISM
SCHOLASTICISMS
SCHOLASTICS
SCHOLIASTIC
SCHOLIASTS
SCHOOLBAGS
SCHOOLBOOK

SCHOOLBOOKS
SCHOOLBOYISH
SCHOOLBOYS
SCHOOLCHILD
SCHOOLCHILDREN
SCHOOLCRAFT
SCHOOLCRAFTS
SCHOOLDAYS
SCHOOLERIES
SCHOOLFELLOW
SCHOOLFELLOWS
SCHOOLGIRL
SCHOOLGIRLISH
SCHOOLGIRLS
SCHOOLGOING
SCHOOLGOINGS
SCHOOLHOUSE
SCHOOLHOUSES
SCHOOLINGS
SCHOOLKIDS
SCHOOLMAID
SCHOOLMAIDS
SCHOOLMARM
SCHOOLMARMISH
SCHOOLMARMS
SCHOOLMASTER
SCHOOLMASTERED
SCHOOLMASTERING
SCHOOLMASTERISH
SCHOOLMASTERLY
SCHOOLMASTERS
SCHOOLMATE
SCHOOLMATES
SCHOOLMISTRESS
SCHOOLMISTRESSY
SCHOOLROOM
SCHOOLROOMS
SCHOOLTEACHER
SCHOOLTEACHERS
SCHOOLTEACHING
SCHOOLTEACHINGS
SCHOOLTIDE
SCHOOLTIDES
SCHOOLTIME
SCHOOLTIMES
SCHOOLWARD
SCHOOLWARDS

SCHOOLWORK
SCHOOLWORKS
SCHOOLYARD
SCHOOLYARDS
SCHORLACEOUS
SCHORLOMITE
SCHORLOMITES
SCHOTTISCHE
SCHOTTISCHES
SCHRECKLICH
SCHTUPPING
SCHUSSBOOMER
SCHUSSBOOMERS
SCHVARTZES
SCHVITZING
SCHWARMEREI
SCHWARMEREIS
SCHWARMERISCH
SCHWARTZES
SCHWARZLOT
SCHWARZLOTS
SCIAENOIDS
SCIAMACHIES
SCIENTIFIC
SCIENTIFICAL
SCIENTIFICALLY
SCIENTIFICITIES
SCIENTIFICITY
SCIENTISED
SCIENTISES
SCIENTISING
SCIENTISMS
SCIENTISTIC
SCIENTISTS
SCIENTIZED
SCIENTIZES
SCIENTIZING
SCINCOIDIAN
SCINCOIDIANS
SCINDAPSUS
SCINDAPSUSES
SCINTIGRAM
SCINTIGRAMS
SCINTIGRAPHIC
SCINTIGRAPHIES
SCINTIGRAPHY
SCINTILLAE

S

SCINTILLANT
SCINTILLANTLY
SCINTILLAS
SCINTILLASCOPE
SCINTILLASCOPES
SCINTILLATE
SCINTILLATED
SCINTILLATES
SCINTILLATING
SCINTILLATINGLY
SCINTILLATION
SCINTILLATIONS
SCINTILLATOR
SCINTILLATORS
SCINTILLISCAN
SCINTILLISCANS
SCINTILLOMETER
SCINTILLOMETERS
SCINTILLON
SCINTILLONS
SCINTILLOSCOPE
SCINTILLOSCOPES
SCINTISCAN
SCINTISCANNER
SCINTISCANNERS
SCINTISCANS
SCIOLISTIC
SCIOMACHIES
SCIOMANCER
SCIOMANCERS
SCIOMANCIES
SCIOMANTIC
SCIOPHYTES
SCIOPHYTIC
SCIOSOPHIES
SCIRRHOSITIES
SCIRRHOSITY
SCIRRHUSES
SCISSIPARITIES
SCISSIPARITY
SCISSORERS
SCISSORING
SCISSORTAIL
SCISSORTAILS
SCISSORWISE
SCITAMINEOUS
SCLAUNDERS

SCLEREIDES
SCLERENCHYMA
SCLERENCHYMAS
SCLERENCHYMATA
SCLERIASES
SCLERIASIS
SCLERITISES
SCLEROCAULIES
SCLEROCAULOUS
SCLEROCAULY
SCLERODERM
SCLERODERMA
SCLERODERMAS
SCLERODERMATA
SCLERODERMATOUS
SCLERODERMIA
SCLERODERMIAS
SCLERODERMIC
SCLERODERMITE
SCLERODERMITES
SCLERODERMOUS
SCLERODERMS
SCLEROMALACIA
SCLEROMALACIAS
SCLEROMATA
SCLEROMETER
SCLEROMETERS
SCLEROMETRIC
SCLEROPHYLL
SCLEROPHYLLIES
SCLEROPHYLLOUS
SCLEROPHYLLS
SCLEROPHYLLY
SCLEROPROTEIN
SCLEROPROTEINS
SCLEROSING
SCLEROTALS
SCLEROTIAL
SCLEROTICS
SCLEROTINS
SCLEROTIOID
SCLEROTISATION
SCLEROTISATIONS
SCLEROTISE
SCLEROTISED
SCLEROTISES
SCLEROTISING

SCLEROTITIS
SCLEROTITISES
SCLEROTIUM
SCLEROTIZATION
SCLEROTIZATIONS
SCLEROTIZE
SCLEROTIZED
SCLEROTIZES
SCLEROTIZING
SCLEROTOMIES
SCLEROTOMY
SCOFFINGLY
SCOLDINGLY
SCOLECIFORM
SCOLECITES
SCOLLOPING
SCOLOPACEOUS
SCOLOPENDRA
SCOLOPENDRAS
SCOLOPENDRID
SCOLOPENDRIDS
SCOLOPENDRIFORM
SCOLOPENDRINE
SCOLOPENDRIUM
SCOLOPENDRIUMS
SCOLYTOIDS
SCOMBROIDS
SCOMFISHED
SCOMFISHES
SCOMFISHING
SCONCHEONS
SCOOTCHING
SCOOTERING
SCOOTERIST
SCOOTERISTS
SCOPELOIDS
SCOPOLAMINE
SCOPOLAMINES
SCOPOLINES
SCOPOPHILIA
SCOPOPHILIAC
SCOPOPHILIACS
SCOPOPHILIAS
SCOPOPHILIC
SCOPOPHOBIA
SCOPOPHOBIAS
SCOPTOPHILIA

SCOPTOPHILIAS
SCOPTOPHOBIA
SCOPTOPHOBIAS
SCORBUTICALLY
SCORCHINGLY
SCORCHINGNESS
SCORCHINGNESSES
SCORCHINGS
SCORDATURA
SCORDATURAS
SCOREBOARD
SCOREBOARDS
SCORECARDS
SCOREKEEPER
SCOREKEEPERS
SCORELINES
SCORESHEET
SCORESHEETS
SCORIACEOUS
SCORIFICATION
SCORIFICATIONS
SCORIFIERS
SCORIFYING
SCORNFULLY
SCORNFULNESS
SCORNFULNESSES
SCORODITES
SCORPAENID
SCORPAENIDS
SCORPAENOID
SCORPAENOIDS
SCORPIOIDS
SCORPIONIC
SCORZONERA
SCORZONERAS
SCOTODINIA
SCOTODINIAS
SCOTOMATOUS
SCOTOMETER
SCOTOMETERS
SCOUNDRELLY
SCOUNDRELS
SCOURGINGS
SCOUTCRAFT
SCOUTCRAFTS
SCOUTHERED
SCOUTHERING

SCOUTHERINGS
SCOUTMASTER
SCOUTMASTERS
SCOWDERING
SCOWDERINGS
SCOWLINGLY
SCOWTHERED
SCOWTHERING
SCRABBLERS
SCRABBLIER
SCRABBLIEST
SCRABBLING
SCRAGGEDNESS
SCRAGGEDNESSES
SCRAGGIEST
SCRAGGINESS
SCRAGGINESSES
SCRAGGLIER
SCRAGGLIEST
SCRAGGLING
SCRAICHING
SCRAIGHING
SCRAMBLERS
SCRAMBLING
SCRAMBLINGLY
SCRAMBLINGS
SCRANCHING
SCRANNIEST
SCRAPBOOKED
SCRAPBOOKING
SCRAPBOOKINGS
SCRAPBOOKS
SCRAPEGOOD
SCRAPEGOODS
SCRAPEGUTS
SCRAPEPENNIES
SCRAPEPENNY
SCRAPERBOARD
SCRAPERBOARDS
SCRAPHEAPS
SCRAPPAGES
SCRAPPIEST
SCRAPPINESS
SCRAPPINESSES
SCRAPPINGS
SCRAPYARDS
SCRATCHBACK

S

SCRATCHBACKS
SCRATCHBOARD
SCRATCHBOARDS
SCRATCHBUILD
SCRATCHBUILDER
SCRATCHBUILDERS
SCRATCHBUILDING
SCRATCHBUILDS
SCRATCHBUILT
SCRATCHCARD
SCRATCHCARDS
SCRATCHERS
SCRATCHIER
SCRATCHIES
SCRATCHIEST
SCRATCHILY
SCRATCHINESS
SCRATCHINESSES
SCRATCHING
SCRATCHINGLY
SCRATCHINGS
SCRATCHLESS
SCRATCHPLATE
SCRATCHPLATES
SCRATTLING
SCRAUCHING
SCRAUGHING
SCRAVELING
SCRAVELLED
SCRAVELLING
SCRAWLIEST
SCRAWLINGLY
SCRAWLINGS
SCRAWNIEST
SCRAWNINESS
SCRAWNINESSES
SCREAKIEST
SCREAMINGLY
SCREAMINGS
SCREECHERS
SCREECHIER
SCREECHIEST
SCREECHING
SCREEDINGS
SCREENABLE
SCREENAGER
SCREENAGERS

SCREENCRAFT
SCREENCRAFTS
SCREENFULS
SCREENINGS
SCREENLAND
SCREENLANDS
SCREENLIKE
SCREENPLAY
SCREENPLAYS
SCREENSAVER
SCREENSAVERS
SCREENSHOT
SCREENSHOTS
SCREENWRITER
SCREENWRITERS
SCREENWRITING
SCREENWRITINGS
SCREEVINGS
SCREICHING
SCREIGHING
SCREWBALLS
SCREWBEANS
SCREWDRIVER
SCREWDRIVERS
SCREWINESS
SCREWINESSES
SCREWWORMS
SCRIBACIOUS
SCRIBACIOUSNESS
SCRIBBLEMENT
SCRIBBLEMENTS
SCRIBBLERS
SCRIBBLIER
SCRIBBLIEST
SCRIBBLING
SCRIBBLINGLY
SCRIBBLINGS
SCRIECHING
SCRIEVEBOARD
SCRIEVEBOARDS
SCRIGGLIER
SCRIGGLIEST
SCRIGGLING
SCRIMMAGED
SCRIMMAGER
SCRIMMAGERS
SCRIMMAGES

SCRIMMAGING
SCRIMPIEST
SCRIMPINESS
SCRIMPINESSES
SCRIMPINGS
SCRIMPNESS
SCRIMPNESSES
SCRIMSHANDER
SCRIMSHANDERED
SCRIMSHANDERING
SCRIMSHANDERS
SCRIMSHANDIED
SCRIMSHANDIES
SCRIMSHANDY
SCRIMSHANDYING
SCRIMSHANK
SCRIMSHANKED
SCRIMSHANKER
SCRIMSHANKERS
SCRIMSHANKING
SCRIMSHANKS
SCRIMSHAWED
SCRIMSHAWING
SCRIMSHAWS
SCRIMSHONER
SCRIMSHONERS
SCRIPHOLDER
SCRIPHOLDERS
SCRIPOPHILE
SCRIPOPHILES
SCRIPOPHILIES
SCRIPOPHILIST
SCRIPOPHILISTS
SCRIPOPHILY
SCRIPPAGES
SCRIPTORIA
SCRIPTORIAL
SCRIPTORIUM
SCRIPTORIUMS
SCRIPTURAL
SCRIPTURALISM
SCRIPTURALISMS
SCRIPTURALIST
SCRIPTURALISTS
SCRIPTURALLY
SCRIPTURES
SCRIPTURISM

SCRIPTURISMS
SCRIPTURIST
SCRIPTURISTS
SCRIPTWRITER
SCRIPTWRITERS
SCRIPTWRITING
SCRIPTWRITINGS
SCRITCHING
SCRIVEBOARD
SCRIVEBOARDS
SCRIVENERS
SCRIVENERSHIP
SCRIVENERSHIPS
SCRIVENING
SCRIVENINGS
SCROBBLING
SCROBICULAR
SCROBICULATE
SCROBICULATED
SCROBICULE
SCROBICULES
SCROFULOUS
SCROFULOUSLY
SCROFULOUSNESS
SCROGGIEST
SCROLLABLE
SCROLLINGS
SCROLLWISE
SCROLLWORK
SCROLLWORKS
SCROOCHING
SCROOTCHED
SCROOTCHES
SCROOTCHING
SCROPHULARIA
SCROPHULARIAS
SCROUNGERS
SCROUNGIER
SCROUNGIEST
SCROUNGING
SCROUNGINGS
SCROWDGING
SCRUBBABLE
SCRUBBIEST
SCRUBBINESS
SCRUBBINESSES
SCRUBBINGS

SCRUBLANDS
SCRUBWOMAN
SCRUBWOMEN
SCRUFFIEST
SCRUFFINESS
SCRUFFINESSES
SCRUMDOWNS
SCRUMMAGED
SCRUMMAGER
SCRUMMAGERS
SCRUMMAGES
SCRUMMAGING
SCRUMMIEST
SCRUMPLING
SCRUMPOXES
SCRUMPTIOUS
SCRUMPTIOUSLY
SCRUMPTIOUSNESS
SCRUNCHEON
SCRUNCHEONS
SCRUNCHIER
SCRUNCHIES
SCRUNCHIEST
SCRUNCHING
SCRUNCHION
SCRUNCHIONS
SCRUNTIEST
SCRUPLELESS
SCRUPULOSITIES
SCRUPULOSITY
SCRUPULOUS
SCRUPULOUSLY
SCRUPULOUSNESS
SCRUTABILITIES
SCRUTABILITY
SCRUTATORS
SCRUTINEER
SCRUTINEERS
SCRUTINIES
SCRUTINISE
SCRUTINISED
SCRUTINISER
SCRUTINISERS
SCRUTINISES
SCRUTINISING
SCRUTINISINGLY
SCRUTINIZE

SCRUTINIZED	SCURVINESS	SEANNACHIE	SECESSIONISM	SECTARIANISE
SCRUTINIZER	SCURVINESSES	SEANNACHIES	SECESSIONISMS	SECTARIANISED
SCRUTINIZERS	SCUTATIONS	SEAQUARIUM	SECESSIONIST	SECTARIANISES
SCRUTINIZES	SCUTCHEONLESS	SEAQUARIUMS	SECESSIONISTS	SECTARIANISING
SCRUTINIZING	SCUTCHEONS	SEARCHABLE	SECESSIONS	SECTARIANISM
SCRUTINIZINGLY	SCUTCHINGS	SEARCHINGLY	SECLUDEDLY	SECTARIANISMS
SCRUTINOUS	SCUTELLATE	SEARCHINGNESS	SECLUDEDNESS	SECTARIANIZE
SCRUTINOUSLY	SCUTELLATED	SEARCHINGNESSES	SECLUDEDNESSES	SECTARIANIZED
SCRUTOIRES	SCUTELLATION	SEARCHINGS	SECLUSIONIST	SECTARIANIZES
SCUDDALERS	SCUTELLATIONS	SEARCHLESS	SECLUSIONISTS	SECTARIANIZING
SCUFFLINGS	SCUTTERING	SEARCHLIGHT	SECLUSIONS	SECTARIANS
SCULDUDDERIES	SCUTTLEBUTT	SEARCHLIGHTS	SECLUSIVELY	SECTILITIES
SCULDUDDERY	SCUTTLEBUTTS	SEAREDNESS	SECLUSIVENESS	SECTIONALISE
SCULDUDDRIES	SCUTTLEFUL	SEAREDNESSES	SECLUSIVENESSES	SECTIONALISED
SCULDUDDRY	SCUTTLEFULS	SEARNESSES	SECOBARBITAL	SECTIONALISES
SCULDUGGERIES	SCUTTLINGS	SEASICKEST	SECOBARBITALS	SECTIONALISING
SCULDUGGERY	SCUZZBALLS	SEASICKNESS	SECONDARIES	SECTIONALISM
SCULLERIES	SCYPHIFORM	SEASICKNESSES	SECONDARILY	SECTIONALISMS
SCULPTRESS	SCYPHISTOMA	SEASONABILITIES	SECONDARINESS	SECTIONALIST
SCULPTRESSES	SCYPHISTOMAE	SEASONABILITY	SECONDARINESSES	SECTIONALISTS
SCULPTURAL	SCYPHISTOMAS	SEASONABLE	SECONDHAND	SECTIONALIZE
SCULPTURALLY	SCYPHOZOAN	SEASONABLENESS	SECONDINGS	SECTIONALIZED
SCULPTURED	SCYPHOZOANS	SEASONABLY	SECONDMENT	SECTIONALIZES
SCULPTURES	SCYTHELIKE	SEASONALITIES	SECONDMENTS	SECTIONALIZING
SCULPTURESQUE	SDEIGNFULL	SEASONALITY	SECRETAGES	SECTIONALLY
SCULPTURESQUELY	SDEIGNFULLY	SEASONALLY	SECRETAGOGIC	SECTIONALS
SCULPTURING	SDRUCCIOLA	SEASONALNESS	SECRETAGOGUE	SECTIONING
SCULPTURINGS	SEABEACHES	SEASONALNESSES	SECRETAGOGUES	SECTIONISATION
SCUMBERING	SEABORGIUM	SEASONINGS	SECRETAIRE	SECTIONISATIONS
SCUMBLINGS	SEABORGIUMS	SEASONLESS	SECRETAIRES	SECTIONISE
SCUMFISHED	SEABOTTLES	SEASTRANDS	SECRETARIAL	SECTIONISED
SCUMFISHES	SEACUNNIES	SEAWORTHIER	SECRETARIAT	SECTIONISES
SCUMFISHING	SEAFARINGS	SEAWORTHIEST	SECRETARIATE	SECTIONISING
SCUNCHEONS	SEAGRASSES	SEAWORTHINESS	SECRETARIATES	SECTIONIZATION
SCUNGILLIS	SEALIFTING	SEAWORTHINESSES	SECRETARIATS	SECTIONIZATIONS
SCUNNERING	SEALPOINTS	SEBIFEROUS	SECRETARIES	SECTIONIZE
SCUPPERING	SEAMANLIKE	SEBORRHEAL	SECRETARYSHIP	SECTIONIZED
SCUPPERNONG	SEAMANSHIP	SEBORRHEAS	SECRETARYSHIPS	SECTIONIZES
SCUPPERNONGS	SEAMANSHIPS	SEBORRHEIC	SECRETIONAL	SECTIONIZING
SCURFINESS	SEAMINESSES	SEBORRHOEA	SECRETIONARY	SECTORIALS
SCURFINESSES	SEAMLESSLY	SEBORRHOEAL	SECRETIONS	SECTORISATION
SCURRILITIES	SEAMLESSNESS	SEBORRHOEAS	SECRETIVELY	SECTORISATIONS
SCURRILITY	SEAMLESSNESSES	SEBORRHOEIC	SECRETIVENESS	SECTORISED
SCURRILOUS	SEAMSTRESS	SECERNENTS	SECRETIVENESSES	SECTORISES
SCURRILOUSLY	SEAMSTRESSES	SECERNMENT	SECRETNESS	SECTORISING
SCURRILOUSNESS	SEAMSTRESSIES	SECERNMENTS	SECRETNESSES	SECTORIZATION
SCURRIOURS	SEAMSTRESSY	SECESSIONAL	SECRETORIES	SECTORIZATIONS

S

SECTORIZED

SECTORIZED	SECURITIZING	SEEMINGNESS	SEIGNORIES	SELECTNESS
SECTORIZES	SECUROCRAT	SEEMINGNESSES	SEISMICALLY	SELECTNESSES
SECTORIZING	SECUROCRATS	SEEMLIHEAD	SEISMICITIES	SELECTORATE
SECULARISATION	SEDATENESS	SEEMLIHEADS	SEISMICITY	SELECTORATES
SECULARISATIONS	SEDATENESSES	SEEMLIHEDS	SEISMOGRAM	SELECTORIAL
SECULARISE	SEDENTARILY	SEEMLINESS	SEISMOGRAMS	SELEGILINE
SECULARISED	SEDENTARINESS	SEEMLINESSES	SEISMOGRAPH	SELEGILINES
SECULARISER	SEDENTARINESSES	SEEMLYHEDS	SEISMOGRAPHER	SELENIFEROUS
SECULARISERS	SEDGELANDS	SEERSUCKER	SEISMOGRAPHERS	SELENOCENTRIC
SECULARISES	SEDIGITATED	SEERSUCKERS	SEISMOGRAPHIC	SELENODONT
SECULARISING	SEDIMENTABLE	SEETHINGLY	SEISMOGRAPHICAL	SELENODONTS
SECULARISM	SEDIMENTARILY	SEGHOLATES	SEISMOGRAPHIES	SELENOGRAPH
SECULARISMS	SEDIMENTARY	SEGMENTALLY	SEISMOGRAPHS	SELENOGRAPHER
SECULARIST	SEDIMENTATION	SEGMENTARY	SEISMOGRAPHY	SELENOGRAPHERS
SECULARISTIC	SEDIMENTATIONS	SEGMENTATE	SEISMOLOGIC	SELENOGRAPHIC
SECULARISTS	SEDIMENTED	SEGMENTATION	SEISMOLOGICAL	SELENOGRAPHICAL
SECULARITIES	SEDIMENTING	SEGMENTATIONS	SEISMOLOGICALLY	SELENOGRAPHIES
SECULARITY	SEDIMENTOLOGIC	SEGMENTING	SEISMOLOGIES	SELENOGRAPHIST
SECULARIZATION	SEDIMENTOLOGIES	SEGREGABLE	SEISMOLOGIST	SELENOGRAPHISTS
SECULARIZATIONS	SEDIMENTOLOGIST	SEGREGANTS	SEISMOLOGISTS	SELENOGRAPHS
SECULARIZE	SEDIMENTOLOGY	SEGREGATED	SEISMOLOGY	SELENOGRAPHY
SECULARIZED	SEDIMENTOUS	SEGREGATES	SEISMOMETER	SELENOLOGICAL
SECULARIZER	SEDITIONARIES	SEGREGATING	SEISMOMETERS	SELENOLOGIES
SECULARIZERS	SEDITIONARY	SEGREGATION	SEISMOMETRIC	SELENOLOGIST
SECULARIZES	SEDITIOUSLY	SEGREGATIONAL	SEISMOMETRICAL	SELENOLOGISTS
SECULARIZING	SEDITIOUSNESS	SEGREGATIONIST	SEISMOMETRIES	SELENOLOGY
SECUNDINES	SEDITIOUSNESSES	SEGREGATIONISTS	SEISMOMETRY	SELFISHNESS
SECUNDOGENITURE	SEDUCEABLE	SEGREGATIONS	SEISMONASTIC	SELFISHNESSES
SECURANCES	SEDUCEMENT	SEGREGATIVE	SEISMONASTIES	SELFLESSLY
SECUREMENT	SEDUCEMENTS	SEGREGATOR	SEISMONASTY	SELFLESSNESS
SECUREMENTS	SEDUCINGLY	SEGREGATORS	SEISMOSCOPE	SELFLESSNESSES
SECURENESS	SEDUCTIONS	SEGUIDILLA	SEISMOSCOPES	SELFNESSES
SECURENESSES	SEDUCTIVELY	SEGUIDILLAS	SEISMOSCOPIC	SELFSAMENESS
SECURIFORM	SEDUCTIVENESS	SEIGNEURIAL	SELACHIANS	SELFSAMENESSES
SECURITANS	SEDUCTIVENESSES	SEIGNEURIE	SELAGINELLA	SELLOTAPED
SECURITIES	SEDUCTRESS	SEIGNEURIES	SELAGINELLAS	SELLOTAPES
SECURITISATION	SEDUCTRESSES	SEIGNIORAGE	SELDOMNESS	SELLOTAPING
SECURITISATIONS	SEDULITIES	SEIGNIORAGES	SELDOMNESSES	SELTZOGENE
SECURITISE	SEDULOUSLY	SEIGNIORALTIES	SELECTABLE	SELTZOGENES
SECURITISED	SEDULOUSNESS	SEIGNIORALTY	SELECTIONIST	SELVEDGING
SECURITISES	SEDULOUSNESSES	SEIGNIORIAL	SELECTIONISTS	SEMAINIERS
SECURITISING	SEECATCHIE	SEIGNIORIES	SELECTIONS	SEMANTEMES
SECURITIZATION	SEEDEATERS	SEIGNIORSHIP	SELECTIVELY	SEMANTICAL
SECURITIZATIONS	SEEDINESSES	SEIGNIORSHIPS	SELECTIVENESS	SEMANTICALLY
SECURITIZE	SEEDNESSES	SEIGNORAGE	SELECTIVENESSES	SEMANTICIST
SECURITIZED	SEEDSTOCKS	SEIGNORAGES	SELECTIVITIES	SEMANTICISTS
SECURITIZES	SEEMELESSE	SEIGNORIAL	SELECTIVITY	SEMANTIDES

S

SEMAPHORED
SEMAPHORES
SEMAPHORIC
SEMAPHORICAL
SEMAPHORICALLY
SEMAPHORING
SEMASIOLOGICAL
SEMASIOLOGIES
SEMASIOLOGIST
SEMASIOLOGISTS
SEMASIOLOGY
SEMATOLOGIES
SEMATOLOGY
SEMBLABLES
SEMBLANCES
SEMBLATIVE
SEMEIOLOGIC
SEMEIOLOGICAL
SEMEIOLOGIES
SEMEIOLOGIST
SEMEIOLOGISTS
SEMEIOLOGY
SEMEIOTICALLY
SEMEIOTICIAN
SEMEIOTICIANS
SEMEIOTICS
SEMELPARITIES
SEMELPARITY
SEMELPAROUS
SEMESTRIAL
SEMIABSTRACT
SEMIABSTRACTION
SEMIANGLES
SEMIANNUAL
SEMIANNUALLY
SEMIAQUATIC
SEMIARBOREAL
SEMIARIDITIES
SEMIARIDITY
SEMIAUTOMATED
SEMIAUTOMATIC
SEMIAUTOMATICS
SEMIAUTONOMOUS
SEMIBASEMENT
SEMIBASEMENTS
SEMIBREVES
SEMICARBAZIDE

SEMICARBAZIDES
SEMICARBAZONE
SEMICARBAZONES
SEMICENTENNIAL
SEMICENTENNIALS
SEMICHORUS
SEMICHORUSES
SEMICIRCLE
SEMICIRCLED
SEMICIRCLES
SEMICIRCULAR
SEMICIRCULARLY
SEMICIRQUE
SEMICIRQUES
SEMICIVILISED
SEMICIVILIZED
SEMICLASSIC
SEMICLASSICAL
SEMICLASSICS
SEMICOLONIAL
SEMICOLONIALISM
SEMICOLONIES
SEMICOLONS
SEMICOLONY
SEMICOMATOSE
SEMICOMMERCIAL
SEMICONDUCTING
SEMICONDUCTION
SEMICONDUCTIONS
SEMICONDUCTOR
SEMICONDUCTORS
SEMICONSCIOUS
SEMICONSCIOUSLY
SEMICONSONANT
SEMICONSONANTS
SEMICRYSTALLIC
SEMICRYSTALLINE
SEMICYLINDER
SEMICYLINDERS
SEMICYLINDRICAL
SEMIDARKNESS
SEMIDARKNESSES
SEMIDEIFIED
SEMIDEIFIES
SEMIDEIFYING
SEMIDEPONENT
SEMIDEPONENTS

SEMIDESERT
SEMIDESERTS
SEMIDETACHED
SEMIDIAMETER
SEMIDIAMETERS
SEMIDIURNAL
SEMIDIVINE
SEMIDOCUMENTARY
SEMIDOMINANT
SEMIDRIEST
SEMIDRYING
SEMIDWARFS
SEMIDWARVES
SEMIELLIPTICAL
SEMIEMPIRICAL
SEMIEVERGREEN
SEMIFEUDAL
SEMIFINALIST
SEMIFINALISTS
SEMIFINALS
SEMIFINISHED
SEMIFITTED
SEMIFLEXIBLE
SEMIFLUIDIC
SEMIFLUIDITIES
SEMIFLUIDITY
SEMIFLUIDS
SEMIFORMAL
SEMIFREDDI
SEMIFREDDO
SEMIFREDDOS
SEMIGLOBES
SEMIGLOBULAR
SEMIGLOSSES
SEMIGROUPS
SEMIHOBOES
SEMILEGENDARY
SEMILETHAL
SEMILETHALS
SEMILIQUID
SEMILIQUIDS
SEMILITERATE
SEMILITERATES
SEMILOGARITHMIC
SEMILUCENT
SEMILUNATE
SEMILUSTROUS

SEMIMANUFACTURE
SEMIMENSTRUAL
SEMIMETALLIC
SEMIMETALS
SEMIMONASTIC
SEMIMONTHLIES
SEMIMONTHLY
SEMIMYSTICAL
SEMINALITIES
SEMINALITY
SEMINARIAL
SEMINARIAN
SEMINARIANS
SEMINARIES
SEMINARIST
SEMINARISTS
SEMINATING
SEMINATION
SEMINATIONS
SEMINATURAL
SEMINIFEROUS
SEMINOMADIC
SEMINOMADS
SEMINOMATA
SEMINUDITIES
SEMINUDITY
SEMIOCHEMICAL
SEMIOCHEMICALS
SEMIOFFICIAL
SEMIOFFICIALLY
SEMIOLOGIC
SEMIOLOGICAL
SEMIOLOGICALLY
SEMIOLOGIES
SEMIOLOGIST
SEMIOLOGISTS
SEMIOPAQUE
SEMIOTICALLY
SEMIOTICIAN
SEMIOTICIANS
SEMIOTICIST
SEMIOTICISTS
SEMIOVIPAROUS
SEMIPALMATE
SEMIPALMATED
SEMIPALMATION
SEMIPALMATIONS

SEMIPARASITE
SEMIPARASITES
SEMIPARASITIC
SEMIPARASITISM
SEMIPARASITISMS
SEMIPELLUCID
SEMIPERIMETER
SEMIPERIMETERS
SEMIPERMANENT
SEMIPERMEABLE
SEMIPLUMES
SEMIPOLITICAL
SEMIPOPULAR
SEMIPORCELAIN
SEMIPORCELAINS
SEMIPORNOGRAPHY
SEMIPOSTAL
SEMIPOSTALS
SEMIPRECIOUS
SEMIPRIVATE
SEMIPUBLIC
SEMIQUAVER
SEMIQUAVERS
SEMIRELIGIOUS
SEMIRETIRED
SEMIRETIREMENT
SEMIRETIREMENTS
SEMIROUNDS
SEMISACRED
SEMISECRET
SEMISEDENTARY
SEMISHRUBBY
SEMISKILLED
SEMISOLIDS
SEMISOLUSES
SEMISUBMERSIBLE
SEMISYNTHETIC
SEMITERETE
SEMITERRESTRIAL
SEMITONALLY
SEMITONICALLY
SEMITRAILER
SEMITRAILERS
SEMITRANSLUCENT
SEMITRANSPARENT
SEMITROPIC
SEMITROPICAL

S

SEMITROPICS
SEMITRUCKS
SEMIVITREOUS
SEMIVOCALIC
SEMIVOWELS
SEMIWEEKLIES
SEMIWEEKLY
SEMIYEARLY
SEMPERVIVUM
SEMPERVIVUMS
SEMPITERNAL
SEMPITERNALLY
SEMPITERNITIES
SEMPITERNITY
SEMPITERNUM
SEMPITERNUMS
SEMPSTERING
SEMPSTERINGS
SEMPSTRESS
SEMPSTRESSES
SEMPSTRESSING
SEMPSTRESSINGS
SENARMONTITE
SENARMONTITES
SENATORIAL
SENATORIALLY
SENATORIAN
SENATORSHIP
SENATORSHIPS
SENECTITUDE
SENECTITUDES
SENESCENCE
SENESCENCES
SENESCHALS
SENESCHALSHIP
SENESCHALSHIPS
SENHORITAS
SENILITIES
SENIORITIES
SENNACHIES
SENSATIONAL
SENSATIONALISE
SENSATIONALISED
SENSATIONALISES
SENSATIONALISM
SENSATIONALISMS
SENSATIONALIST

SENSATIONALISTS
SENSATIONALIZE
SENSATIONALIZED
SENSATIONALIZES
SENSATIONALLY
SENSATIONISM
SENSATIONISMS
SENSATIONIST
SENSATIONISTS
SENSATIONLESS
SENSATIONS
SENSELESSLY
SENSELESSNESS
SENSELESSNESSES
SENSIBILIA
SENSIBILITIES
SENSIBILITY
SENSIBLENESS
SENSIBLENESSES
SENSIBLEST
SENSITISATION
SENSITISATIONS
SENSITISED
SENSITISER
SENSITISERS
SENSITISES
SENSITISING
SENSITIVELY
SENSITIVENESS
SENSITIVENESSES
SENSITIVES
SENSITIVITIES
SENSITIVITY
SENSITIZATION
SENSITIZATIONS
SENSITIZED
SENSITIZER
SENSITIZERS
SENSITIZES
SENSITIZING
SENSITOMETER
SENSITOMETERS
SENSITOMETRIC
SENSITOMETRIES
SENSITOMETRY
SENSOMOTOR
SENSORIALLY

SENSORIMOTOR
SENSORINEURAL
SENSORIUMS
SENSUALISATION
SENSUALISATIONS
SENSUALISE
SENSUALISED
SENSUALISES
SENSUALISING
SENSUALISM
SENSUALISMS
SENSUALIST
SENSUALISTIC
SENSUALISTS
SENSUALITIES
SENSUALITY
SENSUALIZATION
SENSUALIZATIONS
SENSUALIZE
SENSUALIZED
SENSUALIZES
SENSUALIZING
SENSUALNESS
SENSUALNESSES
SENSUOSITIES
SENSUOSITY
SENSUOUSLY
SENSUOUSNESS
SENSUOUSNESSES
SENTENCERS
SENTENCING
SENTENTIAE
SENTENTIAL
SENTENTIALLY
SENTENTIOUS
SENTENTIOUSLY
SENTENTIOUSNESS
SENTIENCES
SENTIENCIES
SENTIENTLY
SENTIMENTAL
SENTIMENTALISE
SENTIMENTALISED
SENTIMENTALISES
SENTIMENTALISM
SENTIMENTALISMS
SENTIMENTALIST

SENTIMENTALISTS
SENTIMENTALITY
SENTIMENTALIZE
SENTIMENTALIZED
SENTIMENTALIZES
SENTIMENTALLY
SENTIMENTS
SENTINELED
SENTINELING
SENTINELLED
SENTINELLING
SEPALODIES
SEPARABILITIES
SEPARABILITY
SEPARABLENESS
SEPARABLENESSES
SEPARATELY
SEPARATENESS
SEPARATENESSES
SEPARATING
SEPARATION
SEPARATIONISM
SEPARATIONISMS
SEPARATIONIST
SEPARATIONISTS
SEPARATIONS
SEPARATISM
SEPARATISMS
SEPARATIST
SEPARATISTIC
SEPARATISTS
SEPARATIVE
SEPARATIVELY
SEPARATIVENESS
SEPARATORIES
SEPARATORS
SEPARATORY
SEPARATRICES
SEPARATRIX
SEPARATUMS
SEPIOLITES
SEPIOSTAIRE
SEPIOSTAIRES
SEPTATIONS
SEPTAVALENT
SEPTEMVIRATE
SEPTEMVIRATES

SEPTEMVIRI
SEPTEMVIRS
SEPTENARIES
SEPTENARII
SEPTENARIUS
SEPTENDECILLION
SEPTENNATE
SEPTENNATES
SEPTENNIAL
SEPTENNIALLY
SEPTENNIUM
SEPTENNIUMS
SEPTENTRIAL
SEPTENTRION
SEPTENTRIONAL
SEPTENTRIONALLY
SEPTENTRIONES
SEPTENTRIONS
SEPTICAEMIA
SEPTICAEMIAS
SEPTICAEMIC
SEPTICALLY
SEPTICEMIA
SEPTICEMIAS
SEPTICEMIC
SEPTICIDAL
SEPTICIDALLY
SEPTICITIES
SEPTIFEROUS
SEPTIFRAGAL
SEPTILATERAL
SEPTILLION
SEPTILLIONS
SEPTILLIONTH
SEPTILLIONTHS
SEPTIMOLES
SEPTIVALENT
SEPTUAGENARIAN
SEPTUAGENARIANS
SEPTUAGENARIES
SEPTUAGENARY
SEPTUPLETS
SEPTUPLICATE
SEPTUPLICATES
SEPTUPLING
SEPULCHERED
SEPULCHERING

S

SEPULCHERS
SEPULCHRAL
SEPULCHRALLY
SEPULCHRED
SEPULCHRES
SEPULCHRING
SEPULCHROUS
SEPULTURAL
SEPULTURED
SEPULTURES
SEPULTURING
SEQUACIOUS
SEQUACIOUSLY
SEQUACIOUSNESS
SEQUACITIES
SEQUELISED
SEQUELISES
SEQUELISING
SEQUELIZED
SEQUELIZES
SEQUELIZING
SEQUENCERS
SEQUENCIES
SEQUENCING
SEQUENCINGS
SEQUENTIAL
SEQUENTIALITIES
SEQUENTIALITY
SEQUENTIALLY
SEQUESTERED
SEQUESTERING
SEQUESTERS
SEQUESTRABLE
SEQUESTRAL
SEQUESTRANT
SEQUESTRANTS
SEQUESTRATE
SEQUESTRATED
SEQUESTRATES
SEQUESTRATING
SEQUESTRATION
SEQUESTRATIONS
SEQUESTRATOR
SEQUESTRATORS
SEQUESTRUM
SEQUESTRUMS
SERAPHICAL

SERAPHICALLY
SERAPHINES
SERASKIERATE
SERASKIERATES
SERASKIERS
SERENADERS
SERENADING
SERENATING
SERENDIPITIES
SERENDIPITIST
SERENDIPITISTS
SERENDIPITOUS
SERENDIPITOUSLY
SERENDIPITY
SERENENESS
SERENENESSES
SERENITIES
SERGEANCIES
SERGEANTIES
SERGEANTSHIP
SERGEANTSHIPS
SERIALISATION
SERIALISATIONS
SERIALISED
SERIALISES
SERIALISING
SERIALISMS
SERIALISTS
SERIALITIES
SERIALIZATION
SERIALIZATIONS
SERIALIZED
SERIALIZES
SERIALIZING
SERIATIONS
SERICICULTURE
SERICICULTURES
SERICICULTURIST
SERICITISATION
SERICITISATIONS
SERICITIZATION
SERICITIZATIONS
SERICTERIA
SERICTERIUM
SERICULTURAL
SERICULTURE
SERICULTURES

SERICULTURIST
SERICULTURISTS
SERIGRAPHER
SERIGRAPHERS
SERIGRAPHIC
SERIGRAPHIES
SERIGRAPHS
SERIGRAPHY
SERINETTES
SERIOCOMIC
SERIOCOMICAL
SERIOCOMICALLY
SERIOUSNESS
SERIOUSNESSES
SERJEANCIES
SERJEANTIES
SERJEANTRIES
SERJEANTRY
SERJEANTSHIP
SERJEANTSHIPS
SERMONEERS
SERMONETTE
SERMONETTES
SERMONICAL
SERMONINGS
SERMONISED
SERMONISER
SERMONISERS
SERMONISES
SERMONISING
SERMONISINGS
SERMONIZED
SERMONIZER
SERMONIZERS
SERMONIZES
SERMONIZING
SERMONIZINGS
SEROCONVERSION
SEROCONVERSIONS
SEROCONVERT
SEROCONVERTED
SEROCONVERTING
SEROCONVERTS
SERODIAGNOSES
SERODIAGNOSIS
SERODIAGNOSTIC
SEROGROUPS

SEROLOGICAL
SEROLOGICALLY
SEROLOGIES
SEROLOGIST
SEROLOGISTS
SERONEGATIVE
SERONEGATIVITY
SEROPOSITIVE
SEROPOSITIVITY
SEROPURULENT
SEROSITIES
SEROTAXONOMIES
SEROTAXONOMY
SEROTHERAPIES
SEROTHERAPY
SEROTINIES
SEROTINOUS
SEROTONERGIC
SEROTONINERGIC
SEROTONINS
SEROTYPING
SEROTYPINGS
SEROUSNESS
SEROUSNESSES
SERPENTIFORM
SERPENTINE
SERPENTINED
SERPENTINELY
SERPENTINES
SERPENTINIC
SERPENTINING
SERPENTININGLY
SERPENTININGS
SERPENTINISE
SERPENTINISED
SERPENTINISES
SERPENTINISING
SERPENTINITE
SERPENTINITES
SERPENTINIZE
SERPENTINIZED
SERPENTINIZES
SERPENTINIZING
SERPENTINOUS
SERPENTISE
SERPENTISED
SERPENTISES

SERPENTISING
SERPENTIZE
SERPENTIZED
SERPENTIZES
SERPENTIZING
SERPENTLIKE
SERPENTRIES
SERPIGINES
SERPIGINOUS
SERPIGINOUSLY
SERPULITES
SERRADELLA
SERRADELLAS
SERRADILLA
SERRADILLAS
SERRANOIDS
SERRASALMO
SERRASALMOS
SERRATIONS
SERRATIROSTRAL
SERRATULATE
SERRATURES
SERRATUSES
SERREFILES
SERRICORNS
SERRIEDNESS
SERRIEDNESSES
SERRULATED
SERRULATION
SERRULATIONS
SERTULARIAN
SERTULARIANS
SERVANTHOOD
SERVANTHOODS
SERVANTING
SERVANTLESS
SERVANTRIES
SERVANTSHIP
SERVANTSHIPS
SERVICEABILITY
SERVICEABLE
SERVICEABLENESS
SERVICEABLY
SERVICEBERRIES
SERVICEBERRY
SERVICELESS
SERVICEMAN

S

SERVICEMEN
SERVICEWOMAN
SERVICEWOMEN
SERVICINGS
SERVIETTES
SERVILENESS
SERVILENESSES
SERVILISMS
SERVILITIES
SERVITORIAL
SERVITORSHIP
SERVITORSHIPS
SERVITRESS
SERVITRESSES
SERVITUDES
SERVOCONTROL
SERVOCONTROLS
SERVOMECHANICAL
SERVOMECHANISM
SERVOMECHANISMS
SERVOMOTOR
SERVOMOTORS
SESQUIALTER
SESQUIALTERA
SESQUIALTERAS
SESQUIALTERS
SESQUICARBONATE
SESQUICENTENARY
SESQUIOXIDE
SESQUIOXIDES
SESQUIPEDAL
SESQUIPEDALIAN
SESQUIPEDALIANS
SESQUIPEDALITY
SESQUIPEDALS
SESQUIPLICATE
SESQUISULPHIDE
SESQUISULPHIDES
SESQUITERPENE
SESQUITERPENES
SESQUITERTIA
SESQUITERTIAS
SESSILITIES
SESSIONALLY
SESTERTIUM
SESTERTIUS
SETACEOUSLY

SETIFEROUS
SETIGEROUS
SETTERWORT
SETTERWORTS
SETTLEABLE
SETTLEDNESS
SETTLEDNESSES
SETTLEMENT
SETTLEMENTS
SEVENPENCE
SEVENPENCES
SEVENPENNIES
SEVENPENNY
SEVENTEENS
SEVENTEENTH
SEVENTEENTHLY
SEVENTEENTHS
SEVENTIETH
SEVENTIETHS
SEVERABILITIES
SEVERABILITY
SEVERALFOLD
SEVERALTIES
SEVERANCES
SEVERENESS
SEVERENESSES
SEVERITIES
SEWABILITIES
SEWABILITY
SEXAGENARIAN
SEXAGENARIANS
SEXAGENARIES
SEXAGENARY
SEXAGESIMAL
SEXAGESIMALLY
SEXAGESIMALS
SEXAHOLICS
SEXANGULAR
SEXANGULARLY
SEXAVALENT
SEXCENTENARIES
SEXCENTENARY
SEXDECILLION
SEXDECILLIONS
SEXENNIALLY
SEXENNIALS
SEXERCISES

SEXINESSES
SEXIVALENT
SEXLESSNESS
SEXLESSNESSES
SEXLOCULAR
SEXOLOGICAL
SEXOLOGIES
SEXOLOGIST
SEXOLOGISTS
SEXPARTITE
SEXPLOITATION
SEXPLOITATIONS
SEXTARIUSES
SEXTILLION
SEXTILLIONS
SEXTILLIONTH
SEXTILLIONTHS
SEXTODECIMO
SEXTODECIMOS
SEXTONESSES
SEXTONSHIP
SEXTONSHIPS
SEXTUPLETS
SEXTUPLICATE
SEXTUPLICATED
SEXTUPLICATES
SEXTUPLICATING
SEXTUPLIED
SEXTUPLIES
SEXTUPLING
SEXTUPLYING
SEXUALISATION
SEXUALISATIONS
SEXUALISED
SEXUALISES
SEXUALISING
SEXUALISMS
SEXUALISTS
SEXUALITIES
SEXUALIZATION
SEXUALIZATIONS
SEXUALIZED
SEXUALIZES
SEXUALIZING
SFORZANDOS
SHABBINESS
SHABBINESSES

SHABRACQUE
SHABRACQUES
SHACKLEBONE
SHACKLEBONES
SHADBERRIES
SHADBUSHES
SHADCHANIM
SHADINESSES
SHADKHANIM
SHADOWBOXED
SHADOWBOXES
SHADOWBOXING
SHADOWCAST
SHADOWCASTING
SHADOWCASTINGS
SHADOWCASTS
SHADOWGRAPH
SHADOWGRAPHIES
SHADOWGRAPHS
SHADOWGRAPHY
SHADOWIEST
SHADOWINESS
SHADOWINESSES
SHADOWINGS
SHADOWLESS
SHADOWLIKE
SHAGGEDNESS
SHAGGEDNESSES
SHAGGINESS
SHAGGINESSES
SHAGGYMANE
SHAGGYMANES
SHAGREENED
SHAGTASTIC
SHAHTOOSHES
SHAKEDOWNS
SHAKINESSES
SHAKUHACHI
SHAKUHACHIS
SHALLOWEST
SHALLOWING
SHALLOWINGS
SHALLOWNESS
SHALLOWNESSES
SHAMANISMS
SHAMANISTIC
SHAMANISTS

SHAMATEURISM
SHAMATEURISMS
SHAMATEURS
SHAMBLIEST
SHAMBLINGS
SHAMBOLICALLY
SHAMEFACED
SHAMEFACEDLY
SHAMEFACEDNESS
SHAMEFASTNESS
SHAMEFASTNESSES
SHAMEFULLY
SHAMEFULNESS
SHAMEFULNESSES
SHAMELESSLY
SHAMELESSNESS
SHAMELESSNESSES
SHAMEWORTHY
SHAMIANAHS
SHAMIYANAH
SHAMIYANAHS
SHAMMASHIM
SHAMOISING
SHAMPOOERS
SHAMPOOING
SHANACHIES
SHANDRYDAN
SHANDRYDANS
SHANDYGAFF
SHANDYGAFFS
SHANGHAIED
SHANGHAIER
SHANGHAIERS
SHANGHAIING
SHANKBONES
SHANKPIECE
SHANKPIECES
SHANTYTOWN
SHANTYTOWNS
SHAPELESSLY
SHAPELESSNESS
SHAPELESSNESSES
SHAPELIEST
SHAPELINESS
SHAPELINESSES
SHAPEWEARS
SHARAWADGI

S

SHARAWADGIS	SHEATFISHES	SHELFTALKERS	SHERARDISE	SHILLALAHS
SHARAWAGGI	SHEATHBILL	SHELLACKED	SHERARDISED	SHILLELAGH
SHARAWAGGIS	SHEATHBILLS	SHELLACKER	SHERARDISES	SHILLELAGHS
SHAREABILITIES	SHEATHFISH	SHELLACKERS	SHERARDISING	SHILLELAHS
SHAREABILITY	SHEATHFISHES	SHELLACKING	SHERARDIZATION	SHILLINGLESS
SHARECROPPED	SHEATHIEST	SHELLACKINGS	SHERARDIZATIONS	SHILLINGSWORTH
SHARECROPPER	SHEATHINGS	SHELLBACKS	SHERARDIZE	SHILLINGSWORTHS
SHARECROPPERS	SHEATHLESS	SHELLBARKS	SHERARDIZED	SHILLYSHALLIED
SHARECROPPING	SHEBEENERS	SHELLBOUND	SHERARDIZES	SHILLYSHALLIER
SHARECROPPINGS	SHEBEENING	SHELLCRACKER	SHERARDIZING	SHILLYSHALLIERS
SHARECROPS	SHEBEENINGS	SHELLCRACKERS	SHEREEFIAN	SHILLYSHALLIES
SHAREFARMER	SHECHITAHS	SHELLDRAKE	SHERGOTTITE	SHILLYSHALLY
SHAREFARMERS	SHECKLATON	SHELLDRAKES	SHERGOTTITES	SHILLYSHALLYING
SHAREHOLDER	SHECKLATONS	SHELLDUCKS	SHERIFFALTIES	SHIMMERIER
SHAREHOLDERS	SHEEPBERRIES	SHELLFIRES	SHERIFFALTY	SHIMMERIEST
SHAREHOLDING	SHEEPBERRY	SHELLFISHERIES	SHERIFFDOM	SHIMMERING
SHAREHOLDINGS	SHEEPCOTES	SHELLFISHERY	SHERIFFDOMS	SHIMMERINGLY
SHAREMILKER	SHEEPFOLDS	SHELLFISHES	SHERIFFSHIP	SHIMMERINGS
SHAREMILKERS	SHEEPHEADS	SHELLINESS	SHERIFFSHIPS	SHIMOZZLES
SHAREWARES	SHEEPHERDER	SHELLINESSES	SHERLOCKED	SHINGLIEST
SHARKSKINS	SHEEPHERDERS	SHELLPROOF	SHERLOCKING	SHINGLINGS
SHARKSUCKER	SHEEPHERDING	SHELLSHOCK	SHEWBREADS	SHINGUARDS
SHARKSUCKERS	SHEEPHERDINGS	SHELLSHOCKED	SHIBBOLETH	SHININESSES
SHARPBENDER	SHEEPISHLY	SHELLSHOCKS	SHIBBOLETHS	SHININGNESS
SHARPBENDERS	SHEEPISHNESS	SHELLWORKS	SHIBUICHIS	SHININGNESSES
SHARPENERS	SHEEPISHNESSES	SHELLYCOAT	SHIDDUCHIM	SHINLEAVES
SHARPENING	SHEEPSHANK	SHELLYCOATS	SHIELDINGS	SHINNERIES
SHARPENINGS	SHEEPSHANKS	SHELTERBELT	SHIELDLESS	SHINNEYING
SHARPNESSES	SHEEPSHEAD	SHELTERBELTS	SHIELDLIKE	SHINPLASTER
SHARPSHOOTER	SHEEPSHEADS	SHELTERERS	SHIELDLING	SHINPLASTERS
SHARPSHOOTERS	SHEEPSHEARER	SHELTERING	SHIELDLINGS	SHINSPLINTS
SHARPSHOOTING	SHEEPSHEARERS	SHELTERINGS	SHIELDRAKE	SHIPBOARDS
SHARPSHOOTINGS	SHEEPSHEARING	SHELTERLESS	SHIELDRAKES	SHIPBROKER
SHASHLICKS	SHEEPSHEARINGS	SHEMOZZLED	SHIELDWALL	SHIPBROKERS
SHATOOSHES	SHEEPSKINS	SHEMOZZLES	SHIELDWALLS	SHIPBUILDER
SHATTERERS	SHEEPTRACK	SHEMOZZLING	SHIFTINESS	SHIPBUILDERS
SHATTERING	SHEEPTRACKS	SHENANIGAN	SHIFTINESSES	SHIPBUILDING
SHATTERINGLY	SHEEPWALKS	SHENANIGANS	SHIFTLESSLY	SHIPBUILDINGS
SHATTERPROOF	SHEERNESSES	SHEPHERDED	SHIFTLESSNESS	SHIPFITTER
SHAUCHLIER	SHEETROCKED	SHEPHERDESS	SHIFTLESSNESSES	SHIPFITTERS
SHAUCHLIEST	SHEETROCKING	SHEPHERDESSES	SHIFTSTICK	SHIPLAPPED
SHAUCHLING	SHEETROCKS	SHEPHERDING	SHIFTSTICKS	SHIPLAPPING
SHAVELINGS	SHEIKHDOMS	SHEPHERDLESS	SHIFTWORKS	SHIPLAPPINGS
SHAVETAILS	SHELDDUCKS	SHEPHERDLING	SHIGELLOSES	SHIPMASTER
SHEARLINGS	SHELDRAKES	SHEPHERDLINGS	SHIGELLOSIS	SHIPMASTERS
SHEARWATER	SHELFROOMS	SHERARDISATION	SHIKARRING	SHIPOWNERS
SHEARWATERS	SHELFTALKER	SHERARDISATIONS	SHILLABERS	SHIPPOUNDS

S

SHIPWRECKED	SHLUMPIEST	SHOPBREAKING	SHORTHAIRED	SHOWBIZZES
SHIPWRECKING	SHMALTZIER	SHOPBREAKINGS	SHORTHAIRS	SHOWBOATED
SHIPWRECKS	SHMALTZIEST	SHOPFITTER	SHORTHANDED	SHOWBOATER
SHIPWRIGHT	SHMOOZIEST	SHOPFITTERS	SHORTHANDS	SHOWBOATERS
SHIPWRIGHTS	SHMUCKIEST	SHOPFRONTS	SHORTHEADS	SHOWBOATING
SHIRRALEES	SHOALINESS	SHOPKEEPER	SHORTHORNS	SHOWBREADS
SHIRTBANDS	SHOALINESSES	SHOPKEEPERS	SHORTLISTED	SHOWCASING
SHIRTDRESS	SHOALNESSES	SHOPKEEPING	SHORTLISTING	SHOWERHEAD
SHIRTDRESSES	SHOCKABILITIES	SHOPKEEPINGS	SHORTLISTS	SHOWERHEADS
SHIRTFRONT	SHOCKABILITY	SHOPLIFTED	SHORTNESSES	SHOWERIEST
SHIRTFRONTS	SHOCKHEADED	SHOPLIFTER	SHORTSHEET	SHOWERINESS
SHIRTINESS	SHOCKINGLY	SHOPLIFTERS	SHORTSHEETED	SHOWERINESSES
SHIRTINESSES	SHOCKINGNESS	SHOPLIFTING	SHORTSHEETING	SHOWERINGS
SHIRTLIFTER	SHOCKINGNESSES	SHOPLIFTINGS	SHORTSHEETS	SHOWERLESS
SHIRTLIFTERS	SHOCKPROOF	SHOPSOILED	SHORTSIGHTED	SHOWERPROOF
SHIRTMAKER	SHOCKSTALL	SHOPWALKER	SHORTSIGHTEDLY	SHOWERPROOFED
SHIRTMAKERS	SHOCKSTALLS	SHOPWALKERS	SHORTSTOPS	SHOWERPROOFING
SHIRTSLEEVE	SHOCKUMENTARIES	SHOPWINDOW	SHORTSWORD	SHOWERPROOFINGS
SHIRTSLEEVED	SHOCKUMENTARY	SHOPWINDOWS	SHORTSWORDS	SHOWERPROOFS
SHIRTSLEEVES	SHODDINESS	SHOREBIRDS	SHORTWAVED	SHOWGROUND
SHIRTTAILED	SHODDINESSES	SHOREFRONT	SHORTWAVES	SHOWGROUNDS
SHIRTTAILING	SHOEBLACKS	SHOREFRONTS	SHORTWAVING	SHOWINESSES
SHIRTTAILS	SHOEBRUSHES	SHORELINES	SHOTFIRERS	SHOWJUMPED
SHIRTWAIST	SHOEHORNED	SHORESIDES	SHOTGUNNED	SHOWJUMPER
SHIRTWAISTED	SHOEHORNING	SHOREWARDS	SHOTGUNNER	SHOWJUMPERS
SHIRTWAISTER	SHOEMAKERS	SHOREWEEDS	SHOTGUNNERS	SHOWJUMPING
SHIRTWAISTERS	SHOEMAKING	SHORTARSES	SHOTGUNNING	SHOWJUMPINGS
SHIRTWAISTS	SHOEMAKINGS	SHORTBOARD	SHOTMAKERS	SHOWMANCES
SHITCANNED	SHOESHINES	SHORTBOARDS	SHOTMAKING	SHOWMANSHIP
SHITCANNING	SHOESTRING	SHORTBREAD	SHOTMAKINGS	SHOWMANSHIPS
SHITHOUSES	SHOESTRINGS	SHORTBREADS	SHOULDERED	SHOWPIECES
SHITTIMWOOD	SHOGGLIEST	SHORTCAKES	SHOULDERING	SHOWPLACES
SHITTIMWOODS	SHOGUNATES	SHORTCHANGE	SHOULDERINGS	SHOWROOMING
SHITTINESS	SHONGOLOLO	SHORTCHANGED	SHOUTHERED	SHOWROOMINGS
SHITTINESSES	SHONGOLOLOS	SHORTCHANGER	SHOUTHERING	SHOWSTOPPER
SHIVAREEING	SHOOGIEING	SHORTCHANGERS	SHOUTINGLY	SHOWSTOPPERS
SHIVERIEST	SHOOGLIEST	SHORTCHANGES	SHOUTLINES	SHOWSTOPPING
SHIVERINGLY	SHOOTAROUND	SHORTCHANGING	SHOVELBOARD	SHREDDIEST
SHIVERINGS	SHOOTAROUNDS	SHORTCOMING	SHOVELBOARDS	SHREDDINGS
SHLEMIEHLS	SHOOTDOWNS	SHORTCOMINGS	SHOVELFULS	SHREWDNESS
SHLEMOZZLE	SHOPAHOLIC	SHORTCRUST	SHOVELHEAD	SHREWDNESSES
SHLEMOZZLED	SHOPAHOLICS	SHORTCUTTING	SHOVELHEADS	SHREWISHLY
SHLEMOZZLES	SHOPAHOLISM	SHORTENERS	SHOVELLERS	SHREWISHNESS
SHLEMOZZLING	SHOPAHOLISMS	SHORTENING	SHOVELLING	SHREWISHNESSES
SHLEPPIEST	SHOPBOARDS	SHORTENINGS	SHOVELNOSE	SHREWMOUSE
SHLIMAZELS	SHOPBREAKER	SHORTFALLS	SHOVELNOSES	SHRIECHING
SHLOCKIEST	SHOPBREAKERS	SHORTGOWNS	SHOVELSFUL	SHRIEKIEST

S

SHRIEKINGLY	SHUTTERBUG	SICKLINESSES	SIDESTROKE	SIGMOIDOSCOPIC
SHRIEKINGS	SHUTTERBUGS	SICKNESSES	SIDESTROKES	SIGMOIDOSCOPIES
SHRIEVALTIES	SHUTTERING	SICKNURSED	SIDESWIPED	SIGMOIDOSCOPY
SHRIEVALTY	SHUTTERINGS	SICKNURSES	SIDESWIPER	SIGNALINGS
SHRILLIEST	SHUTTERLESS	SICKNURSING	SIDESWIPERS	SIGNALISATION
SHRILLINGS	SHUTTLECOCK	SICKNURSINGS	SIDESWIPES	SIGNALISATIONS
SHRILLNESS	SHUTTLECOCKED	SIDDHUISMS	SIDESWIPING	SIGNALISED
SHRILLNESSES	SHUTTLECOCKING	SIDEARMING	SIDETABLES	SIGNALISES
SHRIMPIEST	SHUTTLECOCKS	SIDEBOARDS	SIDETRACKED	SIGNALISING
SHRIMPINGS	SHUTTLELESS	SIDEBURNED	SIDETRACKING	SIGNALIZATION
SHRIMPLIKE	SHUTTLEWISE	SIDECHECKS	SIDETRACKS	SIGNALIZATIONS
SHRINELIKE	SHYLOCKING	SIDEDNESSES	SIDEWHEELER	SIGNALIZED
SHRINKABLE	SIALAGOGIC	SIDEDRESSES	SIDEWHEELERS	SIGNALIZES
SHRINKAGES	SIALAGOGUE	SIDELEVERS	SIDEWHEELS	SIGNALIZING
SHRINKINGLY	SIALAGOGUES	SIDELIGHTS	SIDEWINDER	SIGNALLERS
SHRINKPACK	SIALOGOGIC	SIDELINERS	SIDEWINDERS	SIGNALLING
SHRINKPACKS	SIALOGOGUE	SIDELINING	SIEGECRAFT	SIGNALLINGS
SHRITCHING	SIALOGOGUES	SIDEPIECES	SIEGECRAFTS	SIGNALMENT
SHRIVELING	SIALOGRAMS	SIDERATING	SIEGEWORKS	SIGNALMENTS
SHRIVELLED	SIALOGRAPHIES	SIDERATION	SIFFLEUSES	SIGNATORIES
SHRIVELLING	SIALOGRAPHY	SIDERATIONS	SIGHTLESSLY	SIGNATURES
SHROFFAGES	SIALOLITHS	SIDEREALLY	SIGHTLESSNESS	SIGNBOARDS
SHROUDIEST	SIALORRHOEA	SIDEROLITE	SIGHTLESSNESSES	SIGNEURIES
SHROUDINGS	SIALORRHOEAS	SIDEROLITES	SIGHTLIEST	SIGNIFIABLE
SHROUDLESS	SIBILANCES	SIDEROPENIA	SIGHTLINES	SIGNIFICANCE
SHRUBBERIED	SIBILANCIES	SIDEROPENIAS	SIGHTLINESS	SIGNIFICANCES
SHRUBBERIES	SIBILANTLY	SIDEROPHILE	SIGHTLINESSES	SIGNIFICANCIES
SHRUBBIEST	SIBILATING	SIDEROPHILES	SIGHTSCREEN	SIGNIFICANCY
SHRUBBINESS	SIBILATION	SIDEROPHILIC	SIGHTSCREENS	SIGNIFICANT
SHRUBBINESSES	SIBILATIONS	SIDEROPHILIN	SIGHTSEEING	SIGNIFICANTLY
SHRUBLANDS	SIBILATORS	SIDEROPHILINS	SIGHTSEEINGS	SIGNIFICANTS
SHTETELACH	SIBILATORY	SIDEROSTAT	SIGHTSEERS	SIGNIFICATE
SHTICKIEST	SICCATIVES	SIDEROSTATIC	SIGHTWORTHY	SIGNIFICATES
SHUBUNKINS	SICILIANAS	SIDEROSTATS	SIGILLARIAN	SIGNIFICATION
SHUDDERING	SICILIANOS	SIDESADDLE	SIGILLARIANS	SIGNIFICATIONS
SHUDDERINGLY	SICILIENNE	SIDESADDLES	SIGILLARID	SIGNIFICATIVE
SHUDDERINGS	SICILIENNES	SIDESHOOTS	SIGILLARIDS	SIGNIFICATIVELY
SHUDDERSOME	SICKENINGLY	SIDESLIPPED	SIGILLATION	SIGNIFICATOR
SHUFFLEBOARD	SICKENINGS	SIDESLIPPING	SIGILLATIONS	SIGNIFICATORS
SHUFFLEBOARDS	SICKERNESS	SIDESPLITTING	SIGMATIONS	SIGNIFICATORY
SHUFFLINGLY	SICKERNESSES	SIDESPLITTINGLY	SIGMATISMS	SIGNIFIEDS
SHUFFLINGS	SICKISHNESS	SIDESTEPPED	SIGMATRONS	SIGNIFIERS
SHUNAMITISM	SICKISHNESSES	SIDESTEPPER	SIGMOIDALLY	SIGNIFYING
SHUNAMITISMS	SICKLEBILL	SIDESTEPPERS	SIGMOIDECTOMIES	SIGNIFYINGS
SHUNPIKERS	SICKLEBILLS	SIDESTEPPING	SIGMOIDECTOMY	SIGNIORIES
SHUNPIKING	SICKLEMIAS	SIDESTEPPINGS	SIGMOIDOSCOPE	SIGNORINAS
SHUNPIKINGS	SICKLINESS	SIDESTREAM	SIGMOIDOSCOPES	SIGNPOSTED

S

SIGNPOSTING
SIGNPOSTINGS
SIKORSKIES
SILENTIARIES
SILENTIARY
SILENTNESS
SILENTNESSES
SILHOUETTE
SILHOUETTED
SILHOUETTES
SILHOUETTING
SILHOUETTIST
SILHOUETTISTS
SILICATING
SILICICOLOUS
SILICIFEROUS
SILICIFICATION
SILICIFICATIONS
SILICIFIED
SILICIFIES
SILICIFYING
SILICONISED
SILICONIZED
SILICOTICS
SILICULOSE
SILIQUACEOUS
SILKALENES
SILKALINES
SILKGROWER
SILKGROWERS
SILKINESSES
SILKOLINES
SILKSCREEN
SILKSCREENED
SILKSCREENING
SILKSCREENS
SILLIMANITE
SILLIMANITES
SILLINESSES
SILTATIONS
SILTSTONES
SILVERBACK
SILVERBACKS
SILVERBERRIES
SILVERBERRY
SILVERBILL
SILVERBILLS

SILVEREYES
SILVERFISH
SILVERFISHES
SILVERHORN
SILVERHORNS
SILVERIEST
SILVERINESS
SILVERINESSES
SILVERINGS
SILVERISED
SILVERISES
SILVERISING
SILVERIZED
SILVERIZES
SILVERIZING
SILVERLING
SILVERLINGS
SILVERPOINT
SILVERPOINTS
SILVERSIDE
SILVERSIDES
SILVERSIDESES
SILVERSKIN
SILVERSKINS
SILVERSMITH
SILVERSMITHING
SILVERSMITHINGS
SILVERSMITHS
SILVERTAIL
SILVERTAILS
SILVERTIPS
SILVERWARE
SILVERWARES
SILVERWEED
SILVERWEEDS
SILVESTRIAN
SILVICULTURAL
SILVICULTURALLY
SILVICULTURE
SILVICULTURES
SILVICULTURIST
SILVICULTURISTS
SILYMARINS
SIMAROUBACEOUS
SIMAROUBAS
SIMARUBACEOUS
SIMILARITIES

SIMILARITY
SIMILATIVE
SIMILISING
SIMILITUDE
SIMILITUDES
SIMILIZING
SIMILLIMUM
SIMILLIMUMS
SIMONIACAL
SIMONIACALLY
SIMONISING
SIMONIZING
SIMPERINGLY
SIMPERINGS
SIMPLEMINDED
SIMPLEMINDEDLY
SIMPLENESS
SIMPLENESSES
SIMPLESSES
SIMPLETONS
SIMPLICIAL
SIMPLICIALLY
SIMPLICIDENTATE
SIMPLICITER
SIMPLICITIES
SIMPLICITY
SIMPLIFIABLE
SIMPLIFICATION
SIMPLIFICATIONS
SIMPLIFICATIVE
SIMPLIFICATOR
SIMPLIFICATORS
SIMPLIFIED
SIMPLIFIER
SIMPLIFIERS
SIMPLIFIES
SIMPLIFYING
SIMPLISTES
SIMPLISTIC
SIMPLISTICALLY
SIMULACRES
SIMULACRUM
SIMULACRUMS
SIMULATING
SIMULATION
SIMULATIONS
SIMULATIVE

SIMULATIVELY
SIMULATORS
SIMULATORY
SIMULCASTED
SIMULCASTING
SIMULCASTS
SIMULTANEITIES
SIMULTANEITY
SIMULTANEOUS
SIMULTANEOUSES
SIMULTANEOUSLY
SINANTHROPUS
SINANTHROPUSES
SINARCHISM
SINARCHISMS
SINARCHIST
SINARCHISTS
SINARQUISM
SINARQUISMS
SINARQUIST
SINARQUISTS
SINCERENESS
SINCERENESSES
SINCERITIES
SINCIPITAL
SINDONOLOGIES
SINDONOLOGIST
SINDONOLOGISTS
SINDONOLOGY
SINDONOPHANIES
SINDONOPHANY
SINECURISM
SINECURISMS
SINECURIST
SINECURISTS
SINEWINESS
SINEWINESSES
SINFONIETTA
SINFONIETTAS
SINFULNESS
SINFULNESSES
SINGABLENESS
SINGABLENESSES
SINGALONGS
SINGLEDOMS
SINGLEHOOD
SINGLEHOODS

SINGLENESS
SINGLENESSES
SINGLESTICK
SINGLESTICKS
SINGLETONS
SINGLETRACK
SINGLETRACKS
SINGLETREE
SINGLETREES
SINGSONGED
SINGSONGING
SINGSPIELS
SINGULARISATION
SINGULARISE
SINGULARISED
SINGULARISES
SINGULARISING
SINGULARISM
SINGULARISMS
SINGULARIST
SINGULARISTS
SINGULARITIES
SINGULARITY
SINGULARIZATION
SINGULARIZE
SINGULARIZED
SINGULARIZES
SINGULARIZING
SINGULARLY
SINGULARNESS
SINGULARNESSES
SINGULTUSES
SINICISING
SINICIZING
SINISTERITIES
SINISTERITY
SINISTERLY
SINISTERNESS
SINISTERNESSES
SINISTERWISE
SINISTRALITIES
SINISTRALITY
SINISTRALLY
SINISTRALS
SINISTRODEXTRAL
SINISTRORSAL
SINISTRORSALLY

S

SINISTRORSE	SISERARIES	SKATEBOARDERS	SKEUOMORPHS	SKINNINESSES
SINISTRORSELY	SISSINESSES	SKATEBOARDING	SKEWBACKED	SKINTIGHTS
SINISTROUS	SISSYNESSES	SKATEBOARDINGS	SKEWNESSES	SKIPPERING
SINISTROUSLY	SISTERHOOD	SKATEBOARDS	SKIAGRAPHS	SKIPPERINGS
SINLESSNESS	SISTERHOODS	SKATEPARKS	SKIAMACHIES	SKIPPINGLY
SINLESSNESSES	SISTERLESS	SKEDADDLED	SKIASCOPES	SKIRMISHED
SINNINGIAS	SISTERLIKE	SKEDADDLER	SKIASCOPIES	SKIRMISHER
SINOATRIAL	SISTERLINESS	SKEDADDLERS	SKIBOBBERS	SKIRMISHERS
SINOLOGICAL	SISTERLINESSES	SKEDADDLES	SKIBOBBING	SKIRMISHES
SINOLOGIES	SITATUNGAS	SKEDADDLING	SKIBOBBINGS	SKIRMISHING
SINOLOGIST	SITIOLOGIES	SKELDERING	SKIDDOOING	SKIRMISHINGS
SINOLOGISTS	SITIOPHOBIA	SKELETALLY	SKIJORINGS	SKITTERIER
SINOLOGUES	SITIOPHOBIAS	SKELETOGENOUS	SKIJUMPERS	SKITTERIEST
SINSEMILLA	SITOLOGIES	SKELETONIC	SKIKJORERS	SKITTERING
SINSEMILLAS	SITOPHOBIA	SKELETONISE	SKIKJORING	SKITTISHLY
SINTERABILITIES	SITOPHOBIAS	SKELETONISED	SKIKJORINGS	SKITTISHNESS
SINTERABILITY	SITOSTEROL	SKELETONISER	SKILFULNESS	SKITTISHNESSES
SINUATIONS	SITOSTEROLS	SKELETONISERS	SKILFULNESSES	SKREEGHING
SINUITISES	SITUATIONAL	SKELETONISES	SKILLCENTRE	SKREIGHING
SINUOSITIES	SITUATIONALLY	SKELETONISING	SKILLCENTRES	SKRIECHING
SINUOUSNESS	SITUATIONISM	SKELETONIZE	SKILLESSNESS	SKRIEGHING
SINUOUSNESSES	SITUATIONISMS	SKELETONIZED	SKILLESSNESSES	SKRIMMAGED
SINUPALLIAL	SITUATIONS	SKELETONIZER	SKILLFULLY	SKRIMMAGES
SINUPALLIATE	SITUTUNGAS	SKELETONIZERS	SKILLFULNESS	SKRIMMAGING
SINUSITISES	SITZKRIEGS	SKELETONIZES	SKILLFULNESSES	SKRIMSHANK
SINUSOIDAL	SIXPENNIES	SKELETONIZING	SKILLIGALEE	SKRIMSHANKED
SINUSOIDALLY	SIXTEENERS	SKELLOCHED	SKILLIGALEES	SKRIMSHANKER
SIPHONAGES	SIXTEENMOS	SKELLOCHING	SKILLIGOLEE	SKRIMSHANKERS
SIPHONOGAM	SIXTEENTHLY	SKELTERING	SKILLIGOLEES	SKRIMSHANKING
SIPHONOGAMIES	SIXTEENTHS	SKEPTICALLY	SKIMBOARDED	SKRIMSHANKS
SIPHONOGAMS	SIZABLENESS	SKEPTICALNESS	SKIMBOARDER	SKULDUDDERIES
SIPHONOGAMY	SIZABLENESSES	SKEPTICALNESSES	SKIMBOARDERS	SKULDUDDERY
SIPHONOPHORE	SIZARSHIPS	SKEPTICISM	SKIMBOARDING	SKULDUGGERIES
SIPHONOPHORES	SIZEABLENESS	SKEPTICISMS	SKIMBOARDS	SKULDUGGERY
SIPHONOPHOROUS	SIZEABLENESSES	SKETCHABILITIES	SKIMMINGLY	SKULKINGLY
SIPHONOSTELE	SIZINESSES	SKETCHABILITY	SKIMMINGTON	SKULLDUGGERIES
SIPHONOSTELES	SIZZLINGLY	SKETCHABLE	SKIMMINGTONS	SKULLDUGGERY
SIPHONOSTELIC	SJAMBOKING	SKETCHBOOK	SKIMOBILED	SKUMMERING
SIPHUNCLES	SJAMBOKKED	SKETCHBOOKS	SKIMOBILES	SKUNKBIRDS
SIPUNCULID	SJAMBOKKING	SKETCHIEST	SKIMOBILING	SKUNKWEEDS
SIPUNCULIDS	SKAITHLESS	SKETCHINESS	SKIMPINESS	SKUTTERUDITE
SIPUNCULOID	SKALDSHIPS	SKETCHINESSES	SKIMPINESSES	SKUTTERUDITES
SIPUNCULOIDS	SKANKINESS	SKETCHPADS	SKIMPINGLY	SKYBRIDGES
SIRENISING	SKANKINESSES	SKEUOMORPH	SKINFLICKS	SKYDIVINGS
SIRENIZING	SKATEBOARD	SKEUOMORPHIC	SKINFLINTS	SKYJACKERS
SIRONISING	SKATEBOARDED	SKEUOMORPHISM	SKINFLINTY	SKYJACKING
SIRONIZING	SKATEBOARDER	SKEUOMORPHISMS	SKINNINESS	SKYJACKINGS

S

SKYLARKERS
SKYLARKING
SKYLARKINGS
SKYLIGHTED
SKYROCKETED
SKYROCKETING
SKYROCKETS
SKYSCRAPER
SKYSCRAPERS
SKYSURFERS
SKYSURFING
SKYSURFINGS
SKYWATCHED
SKYWATCHES
SKYWATCHING
SKYWRITERS
SKYWRITING
SKYWRITINGS
SKYWRITTEN
SLABBERERS
SLABBERIER
SLABBERIEST
SLABBERING
SLABBINESS
SLABBINESSES
SLABSTONES
SLACKENERS
SLACKENING
SLACKENINGS
SLACKLINING
SLACKLININGS
SLACKNESSES
SLACKTIVISM
SLACKTIVISMS
SLACKTIVIST
SLACKTIVISTS
SLACTIVISM
SLACTIVISMS
SLACTIVIST
SLACTIVISTS
SLAISTERED
SLAISTERIES
SLAISTERING
SLALOMISTS
SLAMDANCED
SLAMDANCES
SLAMDANCING

SLAMMAKINS
SLAMMERKIN
SLAMMERKINS
SLANDERERS
SLANDERING
SLANDEROUS
SLANDEROUSLY
SLANDEROUSNESS
SLANGINESS
SLANGINESSES
SLANGINGLY
SLANGUAGES
SLANTENDICULAR
SLANTINDICULAR
SLANTINGLY
SLANTINGWAYS
SLAPDASHED
SLAPDASHES
SLAPDASHING
SLAPHAPPIER
SLAPHAPPIEST
SLAPSTICKS
SLASHFESTS
SLASHINGLY
SLATHERING
SLATINESSES
SLATTERING
SLATTERNLINESS
SLATTERNLY
SLAUGHTERABLE
SLAUGHTERED
SLAUGHTERER
SLAUGHTERERS
SLAUGHTERHOUSE
SLAUGHTERHOUSES
SLAUGHTERIES
SLAUGHTERING
SLAUGHTERMAN
SLAUGHTERMEN
SLAUGHTEROUS
SLAUGHTEROUSLY
SLAUGHTERS
SLAUGHTERY
SLAVEHOLDER
SLAVEHOLDERS
SLAVEHOLDING
SLAVEHOLDINGS

SLAVERINGLY
SLAVERINGS
SLAVISHNESS
SLAVISHNESSES
SLAVOCRACIES
SLAVOCRACY
SLAVOCRATS
SLAVOPHILE
SLAVOPHILES
SLAVOPHILS
SLEAZEBAGS
SLEAZEBALL
SLEAZEBALLS
SLEAZINESS
SLEAZINESSES
SLEDGEHAMMER
SLEDGEHAMMERED
SLEDGEHAMMERING
SLEDGEHAMMERS
SLEECHIEST
SLEEKENING
SLEEKNESSES
SLEEKSTONE
SLEEKSTONES
SLEEPINESS
SLEEPINESSES
SLEEPLESSLY
SLEEPLESSNESS
SLEEPLESSNESSES
SLEEPOVERS
SLEEPSUITS
SLEEPWALKED
SLEEPWALKER
SLEEPWALKERS
SLEEPWALKING
SLEEPWALKINGS
SLEEPWALKS
SLEEPWEARS
SLEEPYHEAD
SLEEPYHEADED
SLEEPYHEADS
SLEETINESS
SLEETINESSES
SLEEVEHAND
SLEEVEHANDS
SLEEVELESS
SLEEVELETS

SLEEVELIKE
SLEIGHINGS
SLENDEREST
SLENDERISE
SLENDERISED
SLENDERISES
SLENDERISING
SLENDERIZE
SLENDERIZED
SLENDERIZES
SLENDERIZING
SLENDERNESS
SLENDERNESSES
SLEUTHHOUND
SLEUTHHOUNDS
SLEUTHINGS
SLICKENERS
SLICKENING
SLICKENSIDE
SLICKENSIDED
SLICKENSIDES
SLICKNESSES
SLICKROCKS
SLICKSTERS
SLICKSTONE
SLICKSTONES
SLIDDERING
SLIGHTINGLY
SLIGHTNESS
SLIGHTNESSES
SLIMEBALLS
SLIMINESSES
SLIMNASTICS
SLIMNESSES
SLIMPSIEST
SLINGBACKS
SLINGSHOTS
SLINGSTONE
SLINGSTONES
SLINKINESS
SLINKINESSES
SLINKSKINS
SLINKWEEDS
SLIPCOVERED
SLIPCOVERING
SLIPCOVERS
SLIPDRESSES

SLIPFORMED
SLIPFORMING
SLIPNOOSES
SLIPPERIER
SLIPPERIEST
SLIPPERILY
SLIPPERINESS
SLIPPERINESSES
SLIPPERING
SLIPPERWORT
SLIPPERWORTS
SLIPPINESS
SLIPPINESSES
SLIPSHEETED
SLIPSHEETING
SLIPSHEETS
SLIPSHODDINESS
SLIPSHODNESS
SLIPSHODNESSES
SLIPSLOPPIER
SLIPSLOPPIEST
SLIPSLOPPY
SLIPSTREAM
SLIPSTREAMED
SLIPSTREAMING
SLIPSTREAMS
SLITHERIER
SLITHERIEST
SLITHERING
SLIVOVICAS
SLIVOVICES
SLIVOVITZES
SLIVOWITZES
SLOBBERERS
SLOBBERIER
SLOBBERIEST
SLOBBERING
SLOBBISHNESS
SLOBBISHNESSES
SLOCKDOLAGER
SLOCKDOLAGERS
SLOCKDOLIGER
SLOCKDOLIGERS
SLOCKDOLOGER
SLOCKDOLOGERS
SLOCKENING
SLOEBUSHES

S

SLOETHORNS	SLUGGARDIZES	SMACKHEADS	SMICKERINGS	SMOOTHNESSES
SLOGANEERED	SLUGGARDIZING	SMALLCLOTHES	SMIERCASES	SMOOTHPATE
SLOGANEERING	SLUGGARDLINESS	SMALLHOLDER	SMIFLIGATE	SMOOTHPATES
SLOGANEERINGS	SLUGGARDLY	SMALLHOLDERS	SMIFLIGATED	SMORGASBORD
SLOGANEERS	SLUGGARDNESS	SMALLHOLDING	SMIFLIGATES	SMORGASBORDS
SLOGANISED	SLUGGARDNESSES	SMALLHOLDINGS	SMIFLIGATING	SMORREBROD
SLOGANISES	SLUGGISHLY	SMALLMOUTH	SMILACACEOUS	SMORREBRODS
SLOGANISING	SLUGGISHNESS	SMALLMOUTHS	SMILINGNESS	SMOTHERERS
SLOGANISINGS	SLUGGISHNESSES	SMALLNESSES	SMILINGNESSES	SMOTHERINESS
SLOGANIZED	SLUGHORNES	SMALLPOXES	SMIRKINGLY	SMOTHERINESSES
SLOGANIZES	SLUICEGATE	SMALLSWORD	SMITHCRAFT	SMOTHERING
SLOGANIZING	SLUICEGATES	SMALLSWORDS	SMITHCRAFTS	SMOTHERINGLY
SLOGANIZINGS	SLUICELIKE	SMALMINESS	SMITHEREEN	SMOTHERINGS
SLOMMOCKED	SLUICEWAYS	SMALMINESSES	SMITHEREENED	SMOULDERED
SLOMMOCKING	SLUMBERERS	SMARAGDINE	SMITHEREENING	SMOULDERING
SLOPINGNESS	SLUMBERFUL	SMARAGDITE	SMITHEREENS	SMOULDERINGLY
SLOPINGNESSES	SLUMBERING	SMARAGDITES	SMITHERIES	SMOULDERINGS
SLOPPINESS	SLUMBERINGLY	SMARMINESS	SMITHSONITE	SMOULDRIER
SLOPPINESSES	SLUMBERINGS	SMARMINESSES	SMITHSONITES	SMOULDRIEST
SLOPWORKER	SLUMBERLAND	SMARTARSED	SMOKEBOARD	SMUDGELESS
SLOPWORKERS	SLUMBERLANDS	SMARTARSES	SMOKEBOARDS	SMUDGINESS
SLOTHFULLY	SLUMBERLESS	SMARTASSES	SMOKEBOXES	SMUDGINESSES
SLOTHFULNESS	SLUMBEROUS	SMARTENING	SMOKEBUSHES	SMUGGERIES
SLOTHFULNESSES	SLUMBEROUSLY	SMARTINGLY	SMOKEHOODS	SMUGGLINGS
SLOUCHIEST	SLUMBEROUSNESS	SMARTMOUTH	SMOKEHOUSE	SMUGNESSES
SLOUCHINESS	SLUMBERSOME	SMARTMOUTHS	SMOKEHOUSES	SMUTCHIEST
SLOUCHINESSES	SLUMBROUSLY	SMARTNESSES	SMOKEJACKS	SMUTTINESS
SLOUCHINGLY	SLUMBROUSNESS	SMARTPHONE	SMOKELESSLY	SMUTTINESSES
SLOUGHIEST	SLUMBROUSNESSES	SMARTPHONES	SMOKELESSNESS	SNACKETTES
SLOVENLIER	SLUMGULLION	SMARTWATCH	SMOKELESSNESSES	SNAGGLETEETH
SLOVENLIEST	SLUMGULLIONS	SMARTWATCHES	SMOKEPROOF	SNAGGLETOOTH
SLOVENLIKE	SLUMMOCKED	SMARTWEEDS	SMOKESCREEN	SNAGGLETOOTHED
SLOVENLINESS	SLUMMOCKING	SMARTYPANTS	SMOKESCREENS	SNAILERIES
SLOVENLINESSES	SLUMPFLATION	SMASHEROOS	SMOKESTACK	SNAILFISHES
SLOVENRIES	SLUMPFLATIONARY	SMASHINGLY	SMOKESTACKS	SNAKEBIRDS
SLOWCOACHES	SLUMPFLATIONS	SMASHMOUTH	SMOKETIGHT	SNAKEBITES
SLOWNESSES	SLUNGSHOTS	SMATTERERS	SMOKINESSES	SNAKEBITTEN
SLUBBERING	SLUSHINESS	SMATTERING	SMOLDERING	SNAKEFISHES
SLUBBERINGLY	SLUSHINESSES	SMATTERINGLY	SMOOCHIEST	SNAKEHEADS
SLUBBERINGS	SLUTCHIEST	SMATTERINGS	SMOOTHABLE	SNAKEMOUTH
SLUGGABEDS	SLUTTERIES	SMEARCASES	SMOOTHBORE	SNAKEMOUTHS
SLUGGARDISE	SLUTTINESS	SMEARINESS	SMOOTHBORED	SNAKEROOTS
SLUGGARDISED	SLUTTINESSES	SMEARINESSES	SMOOTHBORES	SNAKESKINS
SLUGGARDISES	SLUTTISHLY	SMELLINESS	SMOOTHENED	SNAKESTONE
SLUGGARDISING	SLUTTISHNESS	SMELLINESSES	SMOOTHENING	SNAKESTONES
SLUGGARDIZE	SLUTTISHNESSES	SMELTERIES	SMOOTHINGS	SNAKEWEEDS
SLUGGARDIZED	SMACKDOWNS	SMICKERING	SMOOTHNESS	SNAKEWOODS

S

SNAKINESSES	SNEEZEWORTS	SNOBOGRAPHY	SNOWFLICKS	SOAPFLAKES
SNAKISHNESS	SNICKERERS	SNOCOACHES	SNOWGLOBES	SOAPINESSES
SNAKISHNESSES	SNICKERING	SNOLLYGOSTER	SNOWINESSES	SOAPOLALLIE
SNAPDRAGON	SNICKERSNEE	SNOLLYGOSTERS	SNOWMAKERS	SOAPOLALLIES
SNAPDRAGONS	SNICKERSNEED	SNOOKERING	SNOWMAKING	SOAPSTONES
SNAPHANCES	SNICKERSNEEING	SNOOPERSCOPE	SNOWMOBILE	SOBERINGLY
SNAPHAUNCE	SNICKERSNEES	SNOOPERSCOPES	SNOWMOBILED	SOBERISING
SNAPHAUNCES	SNIDENESSES	SNOOTINESS	SNOWMOBILER	SOBERIZING
SNAPHAUNCH	SNIFFINESS	SNOOTINESSES	SNOWMOBILERS	SOBERNESSES
SNAPHAUNCHES	SNIFFINESSES	SNORKELERS	SNOWMOBILES	SOBERSIDED
SNAPPERING	SNIFFINGLY	SNORKELING	SNOWMOBILING	SOBERSIDEDNESS
SNAPPINESS	SNIFFISHLY	SNORKELINGS	SNOWMOBILINGS	SOBERSIDES
SNAPPINESSES	SNIFFISHNESS	SNORKELLED	SNOWMOBILIST	SOBOLIFEROUS
SNAPPINGLY	SNIFFISHNESSES	SNORKELLER	SNOWMOBILISTS	SOBRIETIES
SNAPPISHLY	SNIFFLIEST	SNORKELLERS	SNOWMOULDS	SOBRIQUETS
SNAPPISHNESS	SNIFTERING	SNORKELLING	SNOWPLOUGH	SOCDOLAGER
SNAPPISHNESSES	SNIGGERERS	SNORKELLINGS	SNOWPLOUGHED	SOCDOLAGERS
SNAPSHOOTER	SNIGGERING	SNORTINGLY	SNOWPLOUGHING	SOCDOLIGER
SNAPSHOOTERS	SNIGGERINGLY	SNOTTERIES	SNOWPLOUGHS	SOCDOLIGERS
SNAPSHOOTING	SNIGGERINGS	SNOTTERING	SNOWPLOWED	SOCDOLOGER
SNAPSHOOTINGS	SNIGGLINGS	SNOTTINESS	SNOWPLOWING	SOCDOLOGERS
SNAPSHOTTED	SNIPEFISHES	SNOTTINESSES	SNOWSCAPES	SOCIABILITIES
SNAPSHOTTING	SNIPERSCOPE	SNOWBALLED	SNOWSHOEING	SOCIABILITY
SNARLINGLY	SNIPERSCOPES	SNOWBALLING	SNOWSHOEINGS	SOCIABLENESS
SNATCHIEST	SNIPPERSNAPPER	SNOWBERRIES	SNOWSHOERS	SOCIABLENESSES
SNATCHINGLY	SNIPPERSNAPPERS	SNOWBLADER	SNOWSLIDES	SOCIALISABLE
SNATCHINGS	SNIPPETIER	SNOWBLADERS	SNOWSTORMS	SOCIALISATION
SNAZZINESS	SNIPPETIEST	SNOWBLADES	SNOWSURFING	SOCIALISATIONS
SNAZZINESSES	SNIPPETINESS	SNOWBLADING	SNOWSURFINGS	SOCIALISED
SNEAKBOXES	SNIPPETINESSES	SNOWBLADINGS	SNOWTUBING	SOCIALISER
SNEAKINESS	SNIPPINESS	SNOWBLINKS	SNOWTUBINGS	SOCIALISERS
SNEAKINESSES	SNIPPINESSES	SNOWBLOWER	SNUBBINESS	SOCIALISES
SNEAKINGLY	SNITCHIEST	SNOWBLOWERS	SNUBBINESSES	SOCIALISING
SNEAKINGNESS	SNIVELLERS	SNOWBOARDED	SNUBBINGLY	SOCIALISINGS
SNEAKINGNESSES	SNIVELLING	SNOWBOARDER	SNUBNESSES	SOCIALISMS
SNEAKISHLY	SNIVELLINGS	SNOWBOARDERS	SNUFFBOXES	SOCIALISTIC
SNEAKISHNESS	SNOBBERIES	SNOWBOARDING	SNUFFINESS	SOCIALISTICALLY
SNEAKISHNESSES	SNOBBISHLY	SNOWBOARDINGS	SNUFFINESSES	SOCIALISTS
SNEAKSBIES	SNOBBISHNESS	SNOWBOARDS	SNUFFLIEST	SOCIALITES
SNEERINGLY	SNOBBISHNESSES	SNOWBRUSHES	SNUFFLINGS	SOCIALITIES
SNEESHINGS	SNOBBOCRACIES	SNOWBUSHES	SNUGGERIES	SOCIALIZABLE
SNEEZELESS	SNOBBOCRACY	SNOWCAPPED	SNUGGLIEST	SOCIALIZATION
SNEEZEWEED	SNOBOCRACIES	SNOWCLONES	SNUGNESSES	SOCIALIZATIONS
SNEEZEWEEDS	SNOBOCRACY	SNOWDRIFTS	SOAPBERRIES	SOCIALIZED
SNEEZEWOOD	SNOBOGRAPHER	SNOWFIELDS	SOAPBOXING	SOCIALIZER
SNEEZEWOODS	SNOBOGRAPHERS	SNOWFLAKES	SOAPDISHES	SOCIALIZERS
SNEEZEWORT	SNOBOGRAPHIES	SNOWFLECKS	SOAPFISHES	SOCIALIZES

SOCIALIZING
SOCIALIZINGS
SOCIALNESS
SOCIALNESSES
SOCIATIONS
SOCIETALLY
SOCIOBIOLOGICAL
SOCIOBIOLOGIES
SOCIOBIOLOGIST
SOCIOBIOLOGISTS
SOCIOBIOLOGY
SOCIOCULTURAL
SOCIOCULTURALLY
SOCIOECONOMIC
SOCIOGRAMS
SOCIOHISTORICAL
SOCIOLECTS
SOCIOLINGUIST
SOCIOLINGUISTIC
SOCIOLINGUISTS
SOCIOLOGESE
SOCIOLOGESES
SOCIOLOGIC
SOCIOLOGICAL
SOCIOLOGICALLY
SOCIOLOGIES
SOCIOLOGISM
SOCIOLOGISMS
SOCIOLOGIST
SOCIOLOGISTIC
SOCIOLOGISTS
SOCIOMETRIC
SOCIOMETRIES
SOCIOMETRIST
SOCIOMETRISTS
SOCIOMETRY
SOCIOPATHIC
SOCIOPATHIES
SOCIOPATHS
SOCIOPATHY
SOCIOPOLITICAL
SOCIORELIGIOUS
SOCIOSEXUAL
SOCKDOLAGER
SOCKDOLAGERS
SOCKDOLIGER
SOCKDOLIGERS

SOCKDOLOGER
SOCKDOLOGERS
SODALITIES
SODBUSTERS
SODDENNESS
SODDENNESSES
SODICITIES
SODOMISING
SODOMITICAL
SODOMITICALLY
SODOMIZING
SOFTBALLER
SOFTBALLERS
SOFTBOUNDS
SOFTCOVERS
SOFTENINGS
SOFTHEADED
SOFTHEADEDLY
SOFTHEADEDNESS
SOFTHEARTED
SOFTHEARTEDLY
SOFTHEARTEDNESS
SOFTNESSES
SOFTSCAPES
SOFTSHELLS
SOGDOLAGER
SOGDOLAGERS
SOGDOLIGER
SOGDOLIGERS
SOGDOLOGER
SOGDOLOGERS
SOGGINESSES
SOILINESSES
SOJOURNERS
SOJOURNING
SOJOURNINGS
SOJOURNMENT
SOJOURNMENTS
SOKEMANRIES
SOLACEMENT
SOLACEMENTS
SOLANACEOUS
SOLARIMETER
SOLARIMETERS
SOLARISATION
SOLARISATIONS
SOLARISING

SOLARIZATION
SOLARIZATIONS
SOLARIZING
SOLDATESQUE
SOLDERABILITIES
SOLDERABILITY
SOLDERABLE
SOLDERINGS
SOLDIERIES
SOLDIERING
SOLDIERINGS
SOLDIERLIKE
SOLDIERLINESS
SOLDIERLINESSES
SOLDIERSHIP
SOLDIERSHIPS
SOLECISING
SOLECISTIC
SOLECISTICAL
SOLECISTICALLY
SOLECIZING
SOLEMNESSES
SOLEMNIFICATION
SOLEMNIFIED
SOLEMNIFIES
SOLEMNIFYING
SOLEMNISATION
SOLEMNISATIONS
SOLEMNISED
SOLEMNISER
SOLEMNISERS
SOLEMNISES
SOLEMNISING
SOLEMNITIES
SOLEMNIZATION
SOLEMNIZATIONS
SOLEMNIZED
SOLEMNIZER
SOLEMNIZERS
SOLEMNIZES
SOLEMNIZING
SOLEMNNESS
SOLEMNNESSES
SOLENESSES
SOLENETTES
SOLENODONS
SOLENOIDAL

SOLENOIDALLY
SOLEPLATES
SOLEPRINTS
SOLFATARAS
SOLFATARIC
SOLFEGGIOS
SOLFERINOS
SOLICITANT
SOLICITANTS
SOLICITATION
SOLICITATIONS
SOLICITIES
SOLICITING
SOLICITINGS
SOLICITORS
SOLICITORSHIP
SOLICITORSHIPS
SOLICITOUS
SOLICITOUSLY
SOLICITOUSNESS
SOLICITUDE
SOLICITUDES
SOLIDARISM
SOLIDARISMS
SOLIDARIST
SOLIDARISTIC
SOLIDARISTS
SOLIDARITIES
SOLIDARITY
SOLIDATING
SOLIDIFIABLE
SOLIDIFICATION
SOLIDIFICATIONS
SOLIDIFIED
SOLIDIFIER
SOLIDIFIERS
SOLIDIFIES
SOLIDIFYING
SOLIDITIES
SOLIDNESSES
SOLIDUNGULATE
SOLIDUNGULATES
SOLIDUNGULOUS
SOLIFIDIAN
SOLIFIDIANISM
SOLIFIDIANISMS
SOLIFIDIANS

SOLIFLUCTION
SOLIFLUCTIONS
SOLIFLUXION
SOLIFLUXIONS
SOLILOQUIES
SOLILOQUISE
SOLILOQUISED
SOLILOQUISER
SOLILOQUISERS
SOLILOQUISES
SOLILOQUISING
SOLILOQUIST
SOLILOQUISTS
SOLILOQUIZE
SOLILOQUIZED
SOLILOQUIZER
SOLILOQUIZERS
SOLILOQUIZES
SOLILOQUIZING
SOLIPEDOUS
SOLIPSISMS
SOLIPSISTIC
SOLIPSISTICALLY
SOLIPSISTS
SOLITAIRES
SOLITARIAN
SOLITARIANS
SOLITARIES
SOLITARILY
SOLITARINESS
SOLITARINESSES
SOLITUDINARIAN
SOLITUDINARIANS
SOLITUDINOUS
SOLIVAGANT
SOLIVAGANTS
SOLLICKERS
SOLMISATION
SOLMISATIONS
SOLMIZATION
SOLMIZATIONS
SOLONCHAKS
SOLONETSES
SOLONETZES
SOLONETZIC
SOLONISATION
SOLONISATIONS

S

SOLONIZATION	SOMATOLOGIST	SOMERSETTING	SOMNILOQUISING	SONOGRAPHERS
SOLONIZATIONS	SOMATOLOGISTS	SOMESTHESIA	SOMNILOQUISM	SONOGRAPHIES
SOLSTITIAL	SOMATOLOGY	SOMESTHESIAS	SOMNILOQUISMS	SONOGRAPHS
SOLSTITIALLY	SOMATOMEDIN	SOMESTHESIS	SOMNILOQUIST	SONOGRAPHY
SOLUBILISATION	SOMATOMEDINS	SOMESTHESISES	SOMNILOQUISTS	SONOMETERS
SOLUBILISATIONS	SOMATOPLASM	SOMESTHETIC	SOMNILOQUIZE	SONORITIES
SOLUBILISE	SOMATOPLASMS	SOMETHINGS	SOMNILOQUIZED	SONOROUSLY
SOLUBILISED	SOMATOPLASTIC	SOMEWHENCE	SOMNILOQUIZES	SONOROUSNESS
SOLUBILISES	SOMATOPLEURAL	SOMEWHERES	SOMNILOQUIZING	SONOROUSNESSES
SOLUBILISING	SOMATOPLEURE	SOMEWHILES	SOMNILOQUOUS	SOOTERKINS
SOLUBILITIES	SOMATOPLEURES	SOMEWHITHER	SOMNILOQUY	SOOTFLAKES
SOLUBILITY	SOMATOPLEURIC	SOMMELIERS	SOMNOLENCE	SOOTHERING
SOLUBILIZATION	SOMATOSENSORY	SOMNAMBULANCE	SOMNOLENCES	SOOTHFASTLY
SOLUBILIZATIONS	SOMATOSTATIN	SOMNAMBULANCES	SOMNOLENCIES	SOOTHFASTNESS
SOLUBILIZE	SOMATOSTATINS	SOMNAMBULANT	SOMNOLENCY	SOOTHFASTNESSES
SOLUBILIZED	SOMATOTENSIC	SOMNAMBULANTS	SOMNOLENTLY	SOOTHINGLY
SOLUBILIZES	SOMATOTONIA	SOMNAMBULAR	SOMNOLESCENT	SOOTHINGNESS
SOLUBILIZING	SOMATOTONIAS	SOMNAMBULARY	SONGCRAFTS	SOOTHINGNESSES
SOLUBLENESS	SOMATOTONIC	SOMNAMBULATE	SONGFULNESS	SOOTHSAYER
SOLUBLENESSES	SOMATOTONICS	SOMNAMBULATED	SONGFULNESSES	SOOTHSAYERS
SOLUTIONAL	SOMATOTROPHIC	SOMNAMBULATES	SONGLESSLY	SOOTHSAYING
SOLUTIONED	SOMATOTROPHIN	SOMNAMBULATING	SONGOLOLOS	SOOTHSAYINGS
SOLUTIONING	SOMATOTROPHINS	SOMNAMBULATION	SONGSHEETS	SOOTINESSES
SOLUTIONIST	SOMATOTROPIC	SOMNAMBULATIONS	SONGSMITHS	SOPAIPILLA
SOLUTIONISTS	SOMATOTROPIN	SOMNAMBULATOR	SONGSTRESS	SOPAIPILLAS
SOLVABILITIES	SOMATOTROPINE	SOMNAMBULATORS	SONGSTRESSES	SOPAPILLAS
SOLVABILITY	SOMATOTROPINES	SOMNAMBULE	SONGWRITER	SOPHISTERS
SOLVABLENESS	SOMATOTROPINS	SOMNAMBULES	SONGWRITERS	SOPHISTICAL
SOLVABLENESSES	SOMATOTYPE	SOMNAMBULIC	SONGWRITING	SOPHISTICALLY
SOLVATIONS	SOMATOTYPED	SOMNAMBULISM	SONGWRITINGS	SOPHISTICATE
SOLVENCIES	SOMATOTYPES	SOMNAMBULISMS	SONICATING	SOPHISTICATED
SOLVENTLESS	SOMATOTYPING	SOMNAMBULIST	SONICATION	SOPHISTICATEDLY
SOLVOLYSES	SOMBERNESS	SOMNAMBULISTIC	SONICATIONS	SOPHISTICATES
SOLVOLYSIS	SOMBERNESSES	SOMNAMBULISTS	SONICATORS	SOPHISTICATING
SOLVOLYTIC	SOMBRENESS	SOMNIATING	SONIFEROUS	SOPHISTICATION
SOMAESTHESIA	SOMBRENESSES	SOMNIATIVE	SONNETEERING	SOPHISTICATIONS
SOMAESTHESIAS	SOMBRERITE	SOMNIATORY	SONNETEERINGS	SOPHISTICATOR
SOMAESTHESIS	SOMBRERITES	SOMNIFACIENT	SONNETEERS	SOPHISTICATORS
SOMAESTHESISES	SOMEBODIES	SOMNIFACIENTS	SONNETISED	SOPHISTRIES
SOMAESTHETIC	SOMEPLACES	SOMNIFEROUS	SONNETISES	SOPHOMORES
SOMASCOPES	SOMERSAULT	SOMNIFEROUSLY	SONNETISING	SOPHOMORIC
SOMATICALLY	SOMERSAULTED	SOMNILOQUENCE	SONNETIZED	SOPHOMORICAL
SOMATOGENIC	SOMERSAULTING	SOMNILOQUENCES	SONNETIZES	SOPORIFEROUS
SOMATOLOGIC	SOMERSAULTS	SOMNILOQUIES	SONNETIZING	SOPORIFEROUSLY
SOMATOLOGICAL	SOMERSETED	SOMNILOQUISE	SONNETTING	SOPORIFICALLY
SOMATOLOGICALLY	SOMERSETING	SOMNILOQUISED	SONOFABITCH	SOPORIFICS
SOMATOLOGIES	SOMERSETTED	SOMNILOQUISES	SONOGRAPHER	SOPPINESSES

SOPRANINOS
SOPRANISTS
SORBABILITIES
SORBABILITY
SORBEFACIENT
SORBEFACIENTS
SORBITISATION
SORBITISATIONS
SORBITISED
SORBITISES
SORBITISING
SORBITIZATION
SORBITIZATIONS
SORBITIZED
SORBITIZES
SORBITIZING
SORCERESSES
SORDAMENTE
SORDIDNESS
SORDIDNESSES
SOREHEADED
SOREHEADEDLY
SOREHEADEDNESS
SORENESSES
SORICIDENT
SORORIALLY
SORORICIDAL
SORORICIDE
SORORICIDES
SORORISING
SORORITIES
SORORIZING
SORRINESSES
SORROWFULLY
SORROWFULNESS
SORROWFULNESSES
SORROWINGS
SORROWLESS
SORTATIONS
SORTILEGER
SORTILEGERS
SORTILEGES
SORTILEGIES
SORTITIONS
SOSTENUTOS
SOTERIOLOGIC
SOTERIOLOGICAL

SOTERIOLOGIES
SOTERIOLOGY
SOTTISHNESS
SOTTISHNESSES
SOTTISIERS
SOUBRETTES
SOUBRETTISH
SOUBRIQUET
SOUBRIQUETS
SOULDIERED
SOULDIERING
SOULFULNESS
SOULFULNESSES
SOULLESSLY
SOULLESSNESS
SOULLESSNESSES
SOUNDALIKE
SOUNDALIKES
SOUNDBITES
SOUNDBOARD
SOUNDBOARDS
SOUNDBOXES
SOUNDCARDS
SOUNDINGLY
SOUNDLESSLY
SOUNDLESSNESS
SOUNDLESSNESSES
SOUNDNESSES
SOUNDPOSTS
SOUNDPROOF
SOUNDPROOFED
SOUNDPROOFING
SOUNDPROOFINGS
SOUNDPROOFS
SOUNDSCAPE
SOUNDSCAPES
SOUNDSTAGE
SOUNDSTAGES
SOUNDTRACK
SOUNDTRACKED
SOUNDTRACKING
SOUNDTRACKS
SOUPSPOONS
SOURCEBOOK
SOURCEBOOKS
SOURCELESS
SOURDELINE

SOURDELINES
SOURDOUGHS
SOURNESSES
SOURPUSSES
SOUSAPHONE
SOUSAPHONES
SOUSAPHONIST
SOUSAPHONISTS
SOUTENEURS
SOUTERRAIN
SOUTERRAINS
SOUTHBOUND
SOUTHEASTER
SOUTHEASTERLIES
SOUTHEASTERLY
SOUTHEASTERN
SOUTHEASTERS
SOUTHEASTS
SOUTHEASTWARD
SOUTHEASTWARDS
SOUTHERING
SOUTHERLIES
SOUTHERLINESS
SOUTHERLINESSES
SOUTHERMOST
SOUTHERNER
SOUTHERNERS
SOUTHERNISE
SOUTHERNISED
SOUTHERNISES
SOUTHERNISING
SOUTHERNISM
SOUTHERNISMS
SOUTHERNIZE
SOUTHERNIZED
SOUTHERNIZES
SOUTHERNIZING
SOUTHERNLY
SOUTHERNMOST
SOUTHERNNESS
SOUTHERNNESSES
SOUTHERNWOOD
SOUTHERNWOODS
SOUTHLANDER
SOUTHLANDERS
SOUTHLANDS
SOUTHSAYING

SOUTHWARDLY
SOUTHWARDS
SOUTHWESTER
SOUTHWESTERLIES
SOUTHWESTERLY
SOUTHWESTERN
SOUTHWESTERS
SOUTHWESTS
SOUTHWESTWARD
SOUTHWESTWARDLY
SOUTHWESTWARDS
SOUVENIRED
SOUVENIRING
SOUVLAKIAS
SOVENANCES
SOVEREIGNLY
SOVEREIGNS
SOVEREIGNTIES
SOVEREIGNTIST
SOVEREIGNTISTS
SOVEREIGNTY
SOVIETISATION
SOVIETISATIONS
SOVIETISED
SOVIETISES
SOVIETISING
SOVIETISMS
SOVIETISTIC
SOVIETISTS
SOVIETIZATION
SOVIETIZATIONS
SOVIETIZED
SOVIETIZES
SOVIETIZING
SOVIETOLOGICAL
SOVIETOLOGIST
SOVIETOLOGISTS
SOVRANTIES
SOWBELLIES
SPACEBANDS
SPACEBORNE
SPACECRAFT
SPACECRAFTS
SPACEFARING
SPACEFARINGS
SPACEFLIGHT
SPACEFLIGHTS

SPACEPLANE
SPACEPLANES
SPACEPORTS
SPACESHIPS
SPACESUITS
SPACEWALKED
SPACEWALKER
SPACEWALKERS
SPACEWALKING
SPACEWALKS
SPACEWOMAN
SPACEWOMEN
SPACINESSES
SPACIOUSLY
SPACIOUSNESS
SPACIOUSNESSES
SPADASSINS
SPADEFISHES
SPADEWORKS
SPADICEOUS
SPADICIFLORAL
SPADILLIOS
SPAGHETTIFIED
SPAGHETTIFIES
SPAGHETTIFY
SPAGHETTIFYING
SPAGHETTILIKE
SPAGHETTINI
SPAGHETTINIS
SPAGHETTIS
SPAGIRISTS
SPAGYRICAL
SPAGYRICALLY
SPAGYRISTS
SPALLATION
SPALLATIONS
SPANAEMIAS
SPANAKOPITA
SPANAKOPITAS
SPANCELING
SPANCELLED
SPANCELLING
SPANGHEWED
SPANGHEWING
SPANGLIEST
SPANGLINGS
SPANIELLED

S

SPANIELLING	SPARTICLES	SPEARFISHING	SPECIFICALLY	SPECTRALNESSES
SPANIOLATE	SPASMATICAL	SPEARHEADED	SPECIFICATE	SPECTROGRAM
SPANIOLATED	SPASMODICAL	SPEARHEADING	SPECIFICATED	SPECTROGRAMS
SPANIOLATES	SPASMODICALLY	SPEARHEADS	SPECIFICATES	SPECTROGRAPH
SPANIOLATING	SPASMODIST	SPEARMINTS	SPECIFICATING	SPECTROGRAPHIC
SPANIOLISE	SPASMODISTS	SPEARWORTS	SPECIFICATION	SPECTROGRAPHIES
SPANIOLISED	SPASMOLYTIC	SPECIALEST	SPECIFICATIONS	SPECTROGRAPHS
SPANIOLISES	SPASMOLYTICS	SPECIALISATION	SPECIFICATIVE	SPECTROGRAPHY
SPANIOLISING	SPASTICALLY	SPECIALISATIONS	SPECIFICITIES	SPECTROLOGICAL
SPANIOLIZE	SPASTICITIES	SPECIALISE	SPECIFICITY	SPECTROLOGIES
SPANIOLIZED	SPASTICITY	SPECIALISED	SPECIFIERS	SPECTROLOGY
SPANIOLIZES	SPATANGOID	SPECIALISER	SPECIFYING	SPECTROMETER
SPANIOLIZING	SPATANGOIDS	SPECIALISERS	SPECIOCIDE	SPECTROMETERS
SPANKINGLY	SPATCHCOCK	SPECIALISES	SPECIOCIDES	SPECTROMETRIC
SPANOKOPITA	SPATCHCOCKED	SPECIALISING	SPECIOSITIES	SPECTROMETRIES
SPANOKOPITAS	SPATCHCOCKING	SPECIALISM	SPECIOSITY	SPECTROMETRY
SPARAGMATIC	SPATCHCOCKS	SPECIALISMS	SPECIOUSLY	SPECTROSCOPE
SPARAGRASS	SPATHACEOUS	SPECIALIST	SPECIOUSNESS	SPECTROSCOPES
SPARAGRASSES	SPATHIPHYLLUM	SPECIALISTIC	SPECIOUSNESSES	SPECTROSCOPIC
SPARAXISES	SPATHIPHYLLUMS	SPECIALISTS	SPECKLEDNESS	SPECTROSCOPICAL
SPARENESSES	SPATHULATE	SPECIALITIES	SPECKLEDNESSES	SPECTROSCOPIES
SPARGANIUM	SPATIALISATION	SPECIALITY	SPECKSIONEER	SPECTROSCOPIST
SPARGANIUMS	SPATIALISATIONS	SPECIALIZATION	SPECKSIONEERS	SPECTROSCOPISTS
SPARINGNESS	SPATIALITIES	SPECIALIZATIONS	SPECKTIONEER	SPECTROSCOPY
SPARINGNESSES	SPATIALITY	SPECIALIZE	SPECKTIONEERS	SPECULARITIES
SPARKISHLY	SPATIALIZATION	SPECIALIZED	SPECTACLED	SPECULARITY
SPARKLEBERRIES	SPATIALIZATIONS	SPECIALIZER	SPECTACLES	SPECULARLY
SPARKLEBERRY	SPATIOTEMPORAL	SPECIALIZERS	SPECTACULAR	SPECULATED
SPARKLESSLY	SPATTERDASH	SPECIALIZES	SPECTACULARITY	SPECULATES
SPARKLIEST	SPATTERDASHES	SPECIALIZING	SPECTACULARLY	SPECULATING
SPARKLINGLY	SPATTERDOCK	SPECIALLED	SPECTACULARS	SPECULATION
SPARKLINGS	SPATTERDOCKS	SPECIALLING	SPECTATING	SPECULATIONS
SPARKPLUGGED	SPATTERING	SPECIALNESS	SPECTATORIAL	SPECULATIST
SPARKPLUGGING	SPATTERWORK	SPECIALNESSES	SPECTATORS	SPECULATISTS
SPARKPLUGS	SPATTERWORKS	SPECIALOGUE	SPECTATORSHIP	SPECULATIVE
SPARROWFART	SPEAKEASIES	SPECIALOGUES	SPECTATORSHIPS	SPECULATIVELY
SPARROWFARTS	SPEAKERINE	SPECIALTIES	SPECTATRESS	SPECULATIVENESS
SPARROWGRASS	SPEAKERINES	SPECIATING	SPECTATRESSES	SPECULATOR
SPARROWGRASSES	SPEAKERPHONE	SPECIATION	SPECTATRICES	SPECULATORS
SPARROWHAWK	SPEAKERPHONES	SPECIATIONAL	SPECTATRIX	SPECULATORY
SPARROWHAWKS	SPEAKERSHIP	SPECIATIONS	SPECTATRIXES	SPECULATRICE
SPARROWLIKE	SPEAKERSHIPS	SPECIESISM	SPECTINOMYCIN	SPECULATRICES
SPARSENESS	SPEAKINGLY	SPECIESISMS	SPECTINOMYCINS	SPECULATRIX
SPARSENESSES	SPEARCARRIER	SPECIESIST	SPECTRALITIES	SPECULATRIXES
SPARSITIES	SPEARCARRIERS	SPECIESISTS	SPECTRALITY	SPEECHCRAFT
SPARTEINES	SPEARFISHED	SPECIFIABLE	SPECTRALLY	SPEECHCRAFTS
SPARTERIES	SPEARFISHES	SPECIFICAL	SPECTRALNESS	SPEECHFULNESS

S

SPEECHFULNESSES	SPELEOLOGICAL	SPERMATICS	SPERMIDUCT	SPHENODONT
SPEECHIFICATION	SPELEOLOGIES	SPERMATIDS	SPERMIDUCTS	SPHENODONTS
SPEECHIFIED	SPELEOLOGIST	SPERMATIUM	SPERMIOGENESES	SPHENOGRAM
SPEECHIFIER	SPELEOLOGISTS	SPERMATOBLAST	SPERMIOGENESIS	SPHENOGRAMS
SPEECHIFIERS	SPELEOLOGY	SPERMATOBLASTIC	SPERMIOGENETIC	SPHENOIDAL
SPEECHIFIES	SPELEOTHEM	SPERMATOBLASTS	SPERMOGONE	SPHENOPSID
SPEECHIFYING	SPELEOTHEMS	SPERMATOCELE	SPERMOGONES	SPHENOPSIDS
SPEECHIFYINGS	SPELEOTHERAPIES	SPERMATOCELES	SPERMOGONIA	SPHERELESS
SPEECHLESS	SPELEOTHERAPY	SPERMATOCIDAL	SPERMOGONIUM	SPHERELIKE
SPEECHLESSLY	SPELLBINDER	SPERMATOCIDE	SPERMOPHILE	SPHERICALITIES
SPEECHLESSNESS	SPELLBINDERS	SPERMATOCIDES	SPERMOPHILES	SPHERICALITY
SPEECHMAKER	SPELLBINDING	SPERMATOCYTE	SPERMOPHYTE	SPHERICALLY
SPEECHMAKERS	SPELLBINDINGLY	SPERMATOCYTES	SPERMOPHYTES	SPHERICALNESS
SPEECHMAKING	SPELLBINDS	SPERMATOGENESES	SPERMOPHYTIC	SPHERICALNESSES
SPEECHMAKINGS	SPELLBOUND	SPERMATOGENESIS	SPERRYLITE	SPHERICITIES
SPEECHWRITER	SPELLCHECK	SPERMATOGENETIC	SPERRYLITES	SPHERICITY
SPEECHWRITERS	SPELLCHECKED	SPERMATOGENIC	SPESSARTINE	SPHERISTERION
SPEEDBALLED	SPELLCHECKER	SPERMATOGENIES	SPESSARTINES	SPHERISTERIONS
SPEEDBALLING	SPELLCHECKERS	SPERMATOGENOUS	SPESSARTITE	SPHEROCYTE
SPEEDBALLINGS	SPELLCHECKING	SPERMATOGENY	SPESSARTITES	SPHEROCYTES
SPEEDBALLS	SPELLCHECKS	SPERMATOGONIA	SPETSNAZES	SPHEROCYTOSES
SPEEDBOATING	SPELLDOWNS	SPERMATOGONIAL	SPETZNAZES	SPHEROCYTOSIS
SPEEDBOATINGS	SPELLICANS	SPERMATOGONIUM	SPEWINESSES	SPHEROIDAL
SPEEDBOATS	SPELLINGLY	SPERMATOPHORAL	SPHACELATE	SPHEROIDALLY
SPEEDFREAK	SPELLSTOPT	SPERMATOPHORE	SPHACELATED	SPHEROIDICALLY
SPEEDFREAKS	SPELUNKERS	SPERMATOPHORES	SPHACELATES	SPHEROIDICITIES
SPEEDFULLY	SPELUNKING	SPERMATOPHYTE	SPHACELATING	SPHEROIDICITY
SPEEDINESS	SPELUNKINGS	SPERMATOPHYTES	SPHACELATION	SPHEROIDISATION
SPEEDINESSES	SPENDTHRIFT	SPERMATOPHYTIC	SPHACELATIONS	SPHEROIDISE
SPEEDOMETER	SPENDTHRIFTS	SPERMATORRHEA	SPHACELUSES	SPHEROIDISED
SPEEDOMETERS	SPERMACETI	SPERMATORRHEAS	SPHAERIDIA	SPHEROIDISES
SPEEDREADING	SPERMACETIS	SPERMATORRHOEA	SPHAERIDIUM	SPHEROIDISING
SPEEDREADS	SPERMADUCT	SPERMATORRHOEAS	SPHAERITES	SPHEROIDIZATION
SPEEDSKATING	SPERMADUCTS	SPERMATOTHECA	SPHAEROCRYSTAL	SPHEROIDIZE
SPEEDSKATINGS	SPERMAGONIA	SPERMATOTHECAE	SPHAEROCRYSTALS	SPHEROIDIZED
SPEEDSTERS	SPERMAGONIUM	SPERMATOTHECAS	SPHAEROSIDERITE	SPHEROIDIZES
SPEEDWALKS	SPERMAPHYTE	SPERMATOZOA	SPHAGNICOLOUS	SPHEROIDIZING
SPEEDWELLS	SPERMAPHYTES	SPERMATOZOAL	SPHAGNOLOGIES	SPHEROMETER
SPELAEOLOGICAL	SPERMAPHYTIC	SPERMATOZOAN	SPHAGNOLOGIST	SPHEROMETERS
SPELAEOLOGIES	SPERMARIES	SPERMATOZOANS	SPHAGNOLOGISTS	SPHEROPLAST
SPELAEOLOGIST	SPERMARIUM	SPERMATOZOIC	SPHAGNOLOGY	SPHEROPLASTS
SPELAEOLOGISTS	SPERMATHECA	SPERMATOZOID	SPHAIRISTIKE	SPHERULITE
SPELAEOLOGY	SPERMATHECAE	SPERMATOZOIDS	SPHAIRISTIKES	SPHERULITES
SPELAEOTHEM	SPERMATHECAL	SPERMATOZOON	SPHALERITE	SPHERULITIC
SPELAEOTHEMS	SPERMATIAL	SPERMICIDAL	SPHALERITES	SPHINCTERAL
SPELDERING	SPERMATICAL	SPERMICIDE	SPHENDONES	SPHINCTERIAL
SPELDRINGS	SPERMATICALLY	SPERMICIDES	SPHENODONS	SPHINCTERIC

S

SPHINCTERS
SPHINGOMYELIN
SPHINGOMYELINS
SPHINGOSINE
SPHINGOSINES
SPHINXLIKE
SPHRAGISTIC
SPHRAGISTICS
SPHYGMOGRAM
SPHYGMOGRAMS
SPHYGMOGRAPH
SPHYGMOGRAPHIC
SPHYGMOGRAPHIES
SPHYGMOGRAPHS
SPHYGMOGRAPHY
SPHYGMOLOGIES
SPHYGMOLOGY
SPHYGMOMETER
SPHYGMOMETERS
SPHYGMOPHONE
SPHYGMOPHONES
SPHYGMOSCOPE
SPHYGMOSCOPES
SPHYGMUSES
SPICEBERRIES
SPICEBERRY
SPICEBUSHES
SPICILEGES
SPICINESSES
SPICULATED
SPICULATION
SPICULATIONS
SPIDERIEST
SPIDERLIKE
SPIDERWEBS
SPIDERWOOD
SPIDERWOODS
SPIDERWORK
SPIDERWORKS
SPIDERWORT
SPIDERWORTS
SPIEGELEISEN
SPIEGELEISENS
SPIFFINESS
SPIFFINESSES
SPIFFLICATE
SPIFFLICATED

SPIFFLICATES
SPIFFLICATING
SPIFFLICATION
SPIFFLICATIONS
SPIFLICATE
SPIFLICATED
SPIFLICATES
SPIFLICATING
SPIFLICATION
SPIFLICATIONS
SPIKEFISHES
SPIKENARDS
SPIKINESSES
SPILLIKINS
SPILLOVERS
SPILOSITES
SPINACENES
SPINACEOUS
SPINACHLIKE
SPINDLELEGS
SPINDLESHANKS
SPINDLIEST
SPINDLINGS
SPINDRIFTS
SPINELESSLY
SPINELESSNESS
SPINELESSNESSES
SPINESCENCE
SPINESCENCES
SPINESCENT
SPINIFEROUS
SPINIFEXES
SPINIGEROUS
SPINIGRADE
SPINIGRADES
SPININESSES
SPINMEISTER
SPINMEISTERS
SPINNAKERS
SPINNERETS
SPINNERETTE
SPINNERETTES
SPINNERIES
SPINNERULE
SPINNERULES
SPINOSITIES
SPINSTERDOM

SPINSTERDOMS
SPINSTERHOOD
SPINSTERHOODS
SPINSTERIAL
SPINSTERIAN
SPINSTERISH
SPINSTERLY
SPINSTERSHIP
SPINSTERSHIPS
SPINSTRESS
SPINSTRESSES
SPINTHARISCOPE
SPINTHARISCOPES
SPINULESCENT
SPINULIFEROUS
SPIRACULAR
SPIRACULATE
SPIRACULUM
SPIRALIFORM
SPIRALISMS
SPIRALISTS
SPIRALITIES
SPIRALLING
SPIRASTERS
SPIRATIONS
SPIRIFEROUS
SPIRILLOSES
SPIRILLOSIS
SPIRITEDLY
SPIRITEDNESS
SPIRITEDNESSES
SPIRITINGS
SPIRITISMS
SPIRITISTIC
SPIRITISTS
SPIRITLESS
SPIRITLESSLY
SPIRITLESSNESS
SPIRITOUSNESS
SPIRITOUSNESSES
SPIRITUALISE
SPIRITUALISED
SPIRITUALISER
SPIRITUALISERS
SPIRITUALISES
SPIRITUALISING
SPIRITUALISM

SPIRITUALISMS
SPIRITUALIST
SPIRITUALISTIC
SPIRITUALISTS
SPIRITUALITIES
SPIRITUALITY
SPIRITUALIZE
SPIRITUALIZED
SPIRITUALIZER
SPIRITUALIZERS
SPIRITUALIZES
SPIRITUALIZING
SPIRITUALLY
SPIRITUALNESS
SPIRITUALNESSES
SPIRITUALS
SPIRITUALTIES
SPIRITUALTY
SPIRITUELLE
SPIRITUOSITIES
SPIRITUOSITY
SPIRITUOUS
SPIRITUOUSNESS
SPIRITUSES
SPIRKETTING
SPIRKETTINGS
SPIROCHAETAEMIA
SPIROCHAETAL
SPIROCHAETE
SPIROCHAETES
SPIROCHAETOSES
SPIROCHAETOSIS
SPIROCHETAL
SPIROCHETE
SPIROCHETES
SPIROCHETOSES
SPIROCHETOSIS
SPIROGRAMS
SPIROGRAPH
SPIROGRAPHIC
SPIROGRAPHIES
SPIROGRAPHS
SPIROGRAPHY
SPIROGYRAS
SPIROMETER
SPIROMETERS
SPIROMETRIC

SPIROMETRIES
SPIROMETRY
SPIRONOLACTONE
SPIRONOLACTONES
SPIROPHORE
SPIROPHORES
SPIRULINAE
SPIRULINAS
SPISSITUDE
SPISSITUDES
SPITBALLED
SPITBALLING
SPITCHCOCK
SPITCHCOCKED
SPITCHCOCKING
SPITCHCOCKS
SPITCHERED
SPITCHERING
SPITEFULLER
SPITEFULLEST
SPITEFULLY
SPITEFULNESS
SPITEFULNESSES
SPITSTICKER
SPITSTICKERS
SPITTLEBUG
SPITTLEBUGS
SPITTLIEST
SPIVVERIES
SPLANCHNIC
SPLANCHNOCELE
SPLANCHNOCELES
SPLANCHNOLOGIES
SPLANCHNOLOGY
SPLASHBACK
SPLASHBACKS
SPLASHBOARD
SPLASHBOARDS
SPLASHDOWN
SPLASHDOWNS
SPLASHIEST
SPLASHINESS
SPLASHINESSES
SPLASHINGS
SPLASHPROOF
SPLATCHING
SPLATTERED

S

SPLATTERING	SPLEUCHANS	SPOLIATIONS	SPOOKINESS	SPOROPHYTE
SPLATTERPUNK	SPLINTERED	SPOLIATIVE	SPOOKINESSES	SPOROPHYTES
SPLATTERPUNKS	SPLINTERIER	SPOLIATORS	SPOONBAITS	SPOROPHYTIC
SPLATTINGS	SPLINTERIEST	SPOLIATORY	SPOONBILLS	SPOROPOLLENIN
SPLAYFOOTED	SPLINTERING	SPONDAICAL	SPOONDRIFT	SPOROPOLLENINS
SPLAYFOOTEDLY	SPLINTLIKE	SPONDOOLICKS	SPOONDRIFTS	SPOROTRICHOSES
SPLEENFULLY	SPLINTWOOD	SPONDULICKS	SPOONERISM	SPOROTRICHOSIS
SPLEENIEST	SPLINTWOODS	SPONDYLITIC	SPOONERISMS	SPOROZOANS
SPLEENLESS	SPLITTINGS	SPONDYLITICS	SPOONHOOKS	SPOROZOITE
SPLEENSTONE	SPLITTISMS	SPONDYLITIS	SPOONWORMS	SPOROZOITES
SPLEENSTONES	SPLITTISTS	SPONDYLITISES	SPORADICAL	SPORTABILITIES
SPLEENWORT	SPLODGIEST	SPONDYLOLYSES	SPORADICALLY	SPORTABILITY
SPLEENWORTS	SPLODGINESS	SPONDYLOLYSIS	SPORADICALNESS	SPORTANCES
SPLENATIVE	SPLODGINESSES	SPONDYLOSES	SPORANGIAL	SPORTBIKES
SPLENDIDER	SPLOOSHING	SPONDYLOSIS	SPORANGIOLA	SPORTCASTER
SPLENDIDEST	SPLOTCHIER	SPONDYLOSISES	SPORANGIOLE	SPORTCASTERS
SPLENDIDIOUS	SPLOTCHIEST	SPONDYLOUS	SPORANGIOLES	SPORTFISHERMAN
SPLENDIDLY	SPLOTCHILY	SPONGEABLE	SPORANGIOLUM	SPORTFISHERMEN
SPLENDIDNESS	SPLOTCHINESS	SPONGEBAGS	SPORANGIOPHORE	SPORTFISHING
SPLENDIDNESSES	SPLOTCHINESSES	SPONGELIKE	SPORANGIOPHORES	SPORTFISHINGS
SPLENDIDOUS	SPLOTCHING	SPONGEWARE	SPORANGIOSPORE	SPORTFULLY
SPLENDIFEROUS	SPLURGIEST	SPONGEWARES	SPORANGIOSPORES	SPORTFULNESS
SPLENDIFEROUSLY	SPLUTTERED	SPONGEWOOD	SPORANGIUM	SPORTFULNESSES
SPLENDOROUS	SPLUTTERER	SPONGEWOODS	SPORICIDAL	SPORTINESS
SPLENDOURS	SPLUTTERERS	SPONGICOLOUS	SPORICIDES	SPORTINESSES
SPLENDROUS	SPLUTTERING	SPONGIFORM	SPORIDESMS	SPORTINGLY
SPLENECTOMIES	SPLUTTERINGLY	SPONGINESS	SPOROCARPS	SPORTIVELY
SPLENECTOMISE	SPLUTTERINGS	SPONGINESSES	SPOROCYSTIC	SPORTIVENESS
SPLENECTOMISED	SPODOGRAMS	SPONGIOBLAST	SPOROCYSTS	SPORTIVENESSES
SPLENECTOMISES	SPODOMANCIES	SPONGIOBLASTIC	SPOROCYTES	SPORTSCAST
SPLENECTOMISING	SPODOMANCY	SPONGIOBLASTS	SPOROGENESES	SPORTSCASTER
SPLENECTOMIZE	SPODOMANTIC	SPONGOLOGIES	SPOROGENESIS	SPORTSCASTERS
SPLENECTOMIZED	SPODUMENES	SPONGOLOGIST	SPOROGENIC	SPORTSCASTS
SPLENECTOMIZES	SPOILFIVES	SPONGOLOGISTS	SPOROGENIES	SPORTSMANLIKE
SPLENECTOMIZING	SPOILSPORT	SPONGOLOGY	SPOROGENOUS	SPORTSMANLY
SPLENECTOMY	SPOILSPORTS	SPONSIONAL	SPOROGONIA	SPORTSMANSHIP
SPLENETICAL	SPOKESHAVE	SPONSORIAL	SPOROGONIAL	SPORTSMANSHIPS
SPLENETICALLY	SPOKESHAVES	SPONSORING	SPOROGONIC	SPORTSPEOPLE
SPLENETICS	SPOKESMANSHIP	SPONSORSHIP	SPOROGONIES	SPORTSPERSON
SPLENISATION	SPOKESMANSHIPS	SPONSORSHIPS	SPOROGONIUM	SPORTSPERSONS
SPLENISATIONS	SPOKESPEOPLE	SPONTANEITIES	SPOROPHORE	SPORTSWEAR
SPLENITISES	SPOKESPERSON	SPONTANEITY	SPOROPHORES	SPORTSWEARS
SPLENIUSES	SPOKESPERSONS	SPONTANEOUS	SPOROPHORIC	SPORTSWOMAN
SPLENIZATION	SPOKESWOMAN	SPONTANEOUSLY	SPOROPHOROUS	SPORTSWOMEN
SPLENIZATIONS	SPOKESWOMEN	SPONTANEOUSNESS	SPOROPHYLL	SPORTSWRITER
SPLENOMEGALIES	SPOLIATING	SPOOFERIES	SPOROPHYLLS	SPORTSWRITERS
SPLENOMEGALY	SPOLIATION	SPOOKERIES	SPOROPHYLS	SPORTSWRITING

S

SPORTSWRITINGS	SPREETHING	SPRINGWORT	SQUABASHERS	SQUARISHLY
SPORULATED	SPREKELIAS	SPRINGWORTS	SQUABASHES	SQUARISHNESS
SPORULATES	SPRIGGIEST	SPRINKLERED	SQUABASHING	SQUARISHNESSES
SPORULATING	SPRIGHTFUL	SPRINKLERING	SQUABBIEST	SQUARSONAGE
SPORULATION	SPRIGHTFULLY	SPRINKLERS	SQUABBLERS	SQUARSONAGES
SPORULATIONS	SPRIGHTFULNESS	SPRINKLING	SQUABBLING	SQUASHABLE
SPORULATIVE	SPRIGHTING	SPRINKLINGS	SQUABBLINGS	SQUASHIEST
SPOTLESSLY	SPRIGHTLESS	SPRINTINGS	SQUADOOSHES	SQUASHINESS
SPOTLESSNESS	SPRIGHTLIER	SPRITEFULLY	SQUADRONAL	SQUASHINESSES
SPOTLESSNESSES	SPRIGHTLIEST	SPRITEFULNESS	SQUADRONED	SQUATNESSES
SPOTLIGHTED	SPRIGHTLINESS	SPRITEFULNESSES	SQUADRONES	SQUATTERED
SPOTLIGHTING	SPRIGHTLINESSES	SPRITELIER	SQUADRONING	SQUATTERING
SPOTLIGHTS	SPRIGTAILS	SPRITELIEST	SQUAILINGS	SQUATTIEST
SPOTTEDNESS	SPRINGALDS	SPRITSAILS	SQUALIDEST	SQUATTINESS
SPOTTEDNESSES	SPRINGBOARD	SPRITZIEST	SQUALIDITIES	SQUATTINESSES
SPOTTINESS	SPRINGBOARDS	SPROUTINGS	SQUALIDITY	SQUATTINGS
SPOTTINESSES	SPRINGBOKS	SPRUCENESS	SQUALIDNESS	SQUATTLING
SPOUSELESS	SPRINGBUCK	SPRUCENESSES	SQUALIDNESSES	SQUATTOCRACIES
SPOYLEFULL	SPRINGBUCKS	SPRYNESSES	SQUALLIEST	SQUATTOCRACY
SPRACHGEFUHL	SPRINGEING	SPUILZIEING	SQUALLINGS	SQUAWBUSHES
SPRACHGEFUHLS	SPRINGHAAS	SPULEBLADE	SQUAMATION	SQUAWFISHES
SPRACKLING	SPRINGHALT	SPULEBLADES	SQUAMATIONS	SQUAWKIEST
SPRADDLING	SPRINGHALTS	SPULYIEING	SQUAMELLAS	SQUAWKINGS
SPRANGLING	SPRINGHASE	SPULZIEING	SQUAMIFORM	SQUAWROOTS
SPRATTLING	SPRINGHEAD	SPUMESCENCE	SQUAMOSALS	SQUEAKERIES
SPRAUCHLED	SPRINGHEADS	SPUMESCENCES	SQUAMOSELY	SQUEAKIEST
SPRAUCHLES	SPRINGHOUSE	SPUMESCENT	SQUAMOSENESS	SQUEAKINESS
SPRAUCHLING	SPRINGHOUSES	SPUNBONDED	SQUAMOSENESSES	SQUEAKINESSES
SPRAUNCIER	SPRINGIEST	SPUNKINESS	SQUAMOSITIES	SQUEAKINGLY
SPRAUNCIEST	SPRINGINESS	SPUNKINESSES	SQUAMOSITY	SQUEAKINGS
SPRAWLIEST	SPRINGINESSES	SPURGALLED	SQUAMOUSLY	SQUEALINGS
SPREADABILITIES	SPRINGINGS	SPURGALLING	SQUAMOUSNESS	SQUEAMISHLY
SPREADABILITY	SPRINGKEEPER	SPURIOSITIES	SQUAMOUSNESSES	SQUEAMISHNESS
SPREADABLE	SPRINGKEEPERS	SPURIOSITY	SQUAMULOSE	SQUEAMISHNESSES
SPREADEAGLED	SPRINGLESS	SPURIOUSLY	SQUANDERED	SQUEEGEEING
SPREADINGLY	SPRINGLETS	SPURIOUSNESS	SQUANDERER	SQUEEZABILITIES
SPREADINGS	SPRINGLIKE	SPURIOUSNESSES	SQUANDERERS	SQUEEZABILITY
SPREADSHEET	SPRINGTAIL	SPUTTERERS	SQUANDERING	SQUEEZABLE
SPREADSHEETS	SPRINGTAILS	SPUTTERING	SQUANDERINGLY	SQUEEZIEST
SPREAGHERIES	SPRINGTIDE	SPUTTERINGLY	SQUANDERINGS	SQUEEZINGS
SPREAGHERY	SPRINGTIDES	SPUTTERINGS	SQUANDERMANIA	SQUEGGINGS
SPREATHING	SPRINGTIME	SPYCATCHER	SQUANDERMANIAS	SQUELCHERS
SPRECHERIES	SPRINGTIMES	SPYCATCHERS	SQUAREHEAD	SQUELCHIER
SPRECHGESANG	SPRINGWATER	SPYGLASSES	SQUAREHEADS	SQUELCHIEST
SPRECHGESANGS	SPRINGWATERS	SPYMASTERS	SQUARENESS	SQUELCHING
SPRECHSTIMME	SPRINGWOOD	SQUABASHED	SQUARENESSES	SQUELCHINGS
SPRECHSTIMMES	SPRINGWOODS	SQUABASHER	SQUAREWISE	SQUETEAGUE

SQUETEAGUES	SQUIRRELLED	STADDLESTONE	STAINABILITY	STALEMATES
SQUIBBINGS	SQUIRRELLING	STADDLESTONES	STAINLESSES	STALEMATING
SQUIDGIEST	SQUIRRELLY	STADHOLDER	STAINLESSLY	STALENESSES
SQUIFFIEST	SQUIRTINGS	STADHOLDERATE	STAINLESSNESS	STALKINESS
SQUIGGLERS	SQUISHIEST	STADHOLDERATES	STAINLESSNESSES	STALKINESSES
SQUIGGLIER	SQUISHINESS	STADHOLDERS	STAINPROOF	STALLENGER
SQUIGGLIEST	SQUISHINESSES	STADHOLDERSHIP	STAIRCASED	STALLENGERS
SQUIGGLING	SQUOOSHIER	STADHOLDERSHIPS	STAIRCASES	STALLHOLDER
SQUILGEEING	SQUOOSHIEST	STADIOMETER	STAIRCASING	STALLHOLDERS
SQUILLIONS	SQUOOSHING	STADIOMETERS	STAIRCASINGS	STALLINGER
SQUINANCIES	STABBINGLY	STADTHOLDER	STAIRFOOTS	STALLINGERS
SQUINCHING	STABILATES	STADTHOLDERATE	STAIRHEADS	STALLMASTER
SQUINNIEST	STABILISATION	STADTHOLDERATES	STAIRLIFTS	STALLMASTERS
SQUINNYING	STABILISATIONS	STADTHOLDERS	STAIRSTEPPED	STALWARTLY
SQUINTIEST	STABILISATOR	STADTHOLDERSHIP	STAIRSTEPPING	STALWARTNESS
SQUINTINGLY	STABILISATORS	STAFFRIDER	STAIRSTEPS	STALWARTNESSES
SQUINTINGS	STABILISED	STAFFRIDERS	STAIRWELLS	STALWORTHS
SQUIRALITIES	STABILISER	STAFFROOMS	STAIRWORKS	STAMINEOUS
SQUIRALITY	STABILISERS	STAGECOACH	STAKEHOLDER	STAMINIFEROUS
SQUIRALTIES	STABILISES	STAGECOACHES	STAKEHOLDERS	STAMINODES
SQUIRARCHAL	STABILISING	STAGECOACHING	STAKHANOVISM	STAMINODIA
SQUIRARCHICAL	STABILITIES	STAGECOACHINGS	STAKHANOVISMS	STAMINODIES
SQUIRARCHIES	STABILIZATION	STAGECOACHMAN	STAKHANOVITE	STAMINODIUM
SQUIRARCHS	STABILIZATIONS	STAGECOACHMEN	STAKHANOVITES	STAMMERERS
SQUIRARCHY	STABILIZATOR	STAGECRAFT	STAKTOMETER	STAMMERING
SQUIREAGES	STABILIZATORS	STAGECRAFTS	STAKTOMETERS	STAMMERINGLY
SQUIREARCH	STABILIZED	STAGEHANDS	STALACTICAL	STAMMERINGS
SQUIREARCHAL	STABILIZER	STAGESTRUCK	STALACTIFORM	STAMPEDERS
SQUIREARCHICAL	STABILIZERS	STAGFLATION	STALACTITAL	STAMPEDING
SQUIREARCHIES	STABILIZES	STAGFLATIONARY	STALACTITE	STAMPEDOED
SQUIREARCHS	STABILIZING	STAGFLATIONS	STALACTITED	STAMPEDOING
SQUIREARCHY	STABLEBOYS	STAGGERBUSH	STALACTITES	STANCHABLE
SQUIREDOMS	STABLEMATE	STAGGERBUSHES	STALACTITIC	STANCHELLED
SQUIREHOOD	STABLEMATES	STAGGERERS	STALACTITICAL	STANCHELLING
SQUIREHOODS	STABLENESS	STAGGERING	STALACTITICALLY	STANCHERED
SQUIRELIKE	STABLENESSES	STAGGERINGLY	STALACTITIFORM	STANCHERING
SQUIRELING	STABLISHED	STAGGERINGS	STALACTITIOUS	STANCHINGS
SQUIRELINGS	STABLISHES	STAGHOUNDS	STALAGMITE	STANCHIONED
SQUIRESHIP	STABLISHING	STAGINESSES	STALAGMITES	STANCHIONING
SQUIRESHIPS	STABLISHMENT	STAGNANCES	STALAGMITIC	STANCHIONS
SQUIRESSES	STABLISHMENTS	STAGNANCIES	STALAGMITICAL	STANCHLESS
SQUIRMIEST	STACATIONS	STAGNANTLY	STALAGMITICALLY	STANCHNESS
SQUIRMINGLY	STACCATISSIMO	STAGNATING	STALAGMOMETER	STANCHNESSES
SQUIRRELED	STACKROOMS	STAGNATION	STALAGMOMETERS	STANDARDBRED
SQUIRRELFISH	STACKYARDS	STAGNATIONS	STALAGMOMETRIES	STANDARDBREDS
SQUIRRELFISHES	STACTOMETER	STAIDNESSES	STALAGMOMETRY	STANDARDISATION
SQUIRRELING	STACTOMETERS	STAINABILITIES	STALEMATED	STANDARDISE

S

STANDARDISED	STAPHYLOCOCCI	STARTLEMENTS	STATISTICIANS	STEALTHFUL
STANDARDISER	STAPHYLOCOCCIC	STARTLINGLY	STATISTICS	STEALTHIER
STANDARDISERS	STAPHYLOCOCCUS	STARTLINGS	STATOBLAST	STEALTHIEST
STANDARDISES	STAPHYLOMA	STARVATION	STATOBLASTS	STEALTHILY
STANDARDISING	STAPHYLOMAS	STARVATIONS	STATOCYSTS	STEALTHINESS
STANDARDIZATION	STAPHYLOMATA	STARVELING	STATOLATRIES	STEALTHINESSES
STANDARDIZE	STAPHYLOPLASTIC	STARVELINGS	STATOLATRY	STEALTHING
STANDARDIZED	STAPHYLOPLASTY	STASIDIONS	STATOLITHIC	STEALTHINGS
STANDARDIZER	STAPHYLORRHAPHY	STASIMORPHIES	STATOLITHS	STEAMBOATS
STANDARDIZERS	STARBOARDED	STASIMORPHY	STATOSCOPE	STEAMERING
STANDARDIZES	STARBOARDING	STATECRAFT	STATOSCOPES	STEAMFITTER
STANDARDIZING	STARBOARDS	STATECRAFTS	STATUARIES	STEAMFITTERS
STANDARDLESS	STARBURSTS	STATEHOODS	STATUESQUE	STEAMINESS
STANDARDLY	STARCHEDLY	STATEHOUSE	STATUESQUELY	STEAMINESSES
STANDDOWNS	STARCHEDNESS	STATEHOUSES	STATUESQUENESS	STEAMPUNKS
STANDFASTS	STARCHEDNESSES	STATELESSNESS	STATUETTES	STEAMROLLED
STANDFIRST	STARCHIEST	STATELESSNESSES	STATUTABLE	STEAMROLLER
STANDFIRSTS	STARCHINESS	STATELIEST	STATUTABLY	STEAMROLLERED
STANDGALES	STARCHINESSES	STATELINESS	STATUTORILY	STEAMROLLERING
STANDISHES	STARCHLIKE	STATELINESSES	STAUNCHABLE	STEAMROLLERS
STANDOFFISH	STARDRIFTS	STATEMENTED	STAUNCHERS	STEAMROLLING
STANDOFFISHLY	STARFISHED	STATEMENTING	STAUNCHEST	STEAMROLLS
STANDOFFISHNESS	STARFISHES	STATEMENTINGS	STAUNCHING	STEAMSHIPS
STANDOVERS	STARFLOWER	STATEMENTS	STAUNCHINGS	STEAMTIGHT
STANDPATTER	STARFLOWERS	STATEROOMS	STAUNCHLESS	STEAMTIGHTNESS
STANDPATTERS	STARFRUITS	STATESMANLIKE	STAUNCHNESS	STEAROPTENE
STANDPATTISM	STARFUCKER	STATESMANLY	STAUNCHNESSES	STEAROPTENES
STANDPATTISMS	STARFUCKERS	STATESMANSHIP	STAUROLITE	STEARSMATE
STANDPIPES	STARFUCKING	STATESMANSHIPS	STAUROLITES	STEARSMATES
STANDPOINT	STARFUCKINGS	STATESPERSON	STAUROLITIC	STEATOCELE
STANDPOINTS	STARGAZERS	STATESPERSONS	STAUROSCOPE	STEATOCELES
STANDSTILL	STARGAZING	STATESWOMAN	STAUROSCOPES	STEATOLYSES
STANDSTILLS	STARGAZINGS	STATESWOMEN	STAUROSCOPIC	STEATOLYSIS
STANNARIES	STARKENING	STATICALLY	STAVESACRE	STEATOMATOUS
STANNATORS	STARKNESSES	STATIONARIES	STAVESACRES	STEATOPYGA
STANNIFEROUS	STARLIGHTED	STATIONARILY	STAVUDINES	STEATOPYGAS
STANNOTYPE	STARLIGHTS	STATIONARINESS	STAYCATION	STEATOPYGIA
STANNOTYPES	STARMONGER	STATIONARY	STAYCATIONS	STEATOPYGIAS
STAPEDECTOMIES	STARMONGERS	STATIONERIES	STAYMAKERS	STEATOPYGIC
STAPEDECTOMY	STAROSTIES	STATIONERS	STEADFASTLY	STEATOPYGOUS
STAPEDIUSES	STARRINESS	STATIONERY	STEADFASTNESS	STEATORRHEA
STAPHYLINE	STARRINESSES	STATIONING	STEADFASTNESSES	STEATORRHEAS
STAPHYLINID	STARSHINES	STATIONMASTER	STEADINESS	STEATORRHOEA
STAPHYLINIDS	STARSTONES	STATIONMASTERS	STEADINESSES	STEATORRHOEAS
STAPHYLITIS	STARSTRUCK	STATISTICAL	STEAKHOUSE	STEDFASTLY
STAPHYLITISES	STARTINGLY	STATISTICALLY	STEAKHOUSES	STEDFASTNESS
STAPHYLOCOCCAL	STARTLEMENT	STATISTICIAN	STEALINGLY	STEDFASTNESSES

S

STEELHEADS	STEGANOGRAPHS	STENCILLING	STEPCHILDREN	STEREOBATIC
STEELINESS	STEGANOGRAPHY	STENCILLINGS	STEPDANCER	STEREOBLIND
STEELINESSES	STEGANOPOD	STENOBATHIC	STEPDANCERS	STEREOCARD
STEELMAKER	STEGANOPODOUS	STENOBATHS	STEPDANCING	STEREOCARDS
STEELMAKERS	STEGANOPODS	STENOCARDIA	STEPDANCINGS	STEREOCHEMICAL
STEELMAKING	STEGNOTICS	STENOCARDIAS	STEPDAUGHTER	STEREOCHEMISTRY
STEELMAKINGS	STEGOCARPOUS	STENOCHROME	STEPDAUGHTERS	STEREOCHROME
STEELWARES	STEGOCEPHALIAN	STENOCHROMES	STEPFAMILIES	STEREOCHROMED
STEELWORKER	STEGOCEPHALIANS	STENOCHROMIES	STEPFAMILY	STEREOCHROMES
STEELWORKERS	STEGOCEPHALOUS	STENOCHROMY	STEPFATHER	STEREOCHROMIES
STEELWORKING	STEGODONTS	STENOGRAPH	STEPFATHERS	STEREOCHROMING
STEELWORKINGS	STEGOMYIAS	STENOGRAPHED	STEPHANITE	STEREOCHROMY
STEELWORKS	STEGOPHILIST	STENOGRAPHER	STEPHANITES	STEREOGNOSES
STEELYARDS	STEGOPHILISTS	STENOGRAPHERS	STEPHANOTIS	STEREOGNOSIS
STEENBRASES	STEGOSAURIAN	STENOGRAPHIC	STEPHANOTISES	STEREOGRAM
STEENBUCKS	STEGOSAURIANS	STENOGRAPHICAL	STEPLADDER	STEREOGRAMS
STEENKIRKS	STEGOSAURS	STENOGRAPHIES	STEPLADDERS	STEREOGRAPH
STEEPDOWNE	STEGOSAURUS	STENOGRAPHING	STEPMOTHER	STEREOGRAPHED
STEEPEDOWNE	STEGOSAURUSES	STENOGRAPHIST	STEPMOTHERLY	STEREOGRAPHIC
STEEPENING	STEINBOCKS	STENOGRAPHISTS	STEPMOTHERS	STEREOGRAPHICAL
STEEPINESS	STEINKIRKS	STENOGRAPHS	STEPPARENT	STEREOGRAPHIES
STEEPINESSES	STELLARATOR	STENOGRAPHY	STEPPARENTING	STEREOGRAPHING
STEEPLEBUSH	STELLARATORS	STENOHALINE	STEPPARENTINGS	STEREOGRAPHS
STEEPLEBUSHES	STELLATELY	STENOPAEIC	STEPPARENTS	STEREOGRAPHY
STEEPLECHASE	STELLERIDAN	STENOPETALOUS	STEPSISTER	STEREOISOMER
STEEPLECHASED	STELLERIDANS	STENOPHAGOUS	STEPSISTERS	STEREOISOMERIC
STEEPLECHASER	STELLERIDS	STENOPHYLLOUS	STEPSTOOLS	STEREOISOMERISM
STEEPLECHASERS	STELLIFEROUS	STENOTHERM	STERADIANS	STEREOISOMERS
STEEPLECHASES	STELLIFIED	STENOTHERMAL	STERCORACEOUS	STEREOISOMETRIC
STEEPLECHASING	STELLIFIES	STENOTHERMS	STERCORANISM	STEREOLOGICAL
STEEPLECHASINGS	STELLIFORM	STENOTOPIC	STERCORANISMS	STEREOLOGICALLY
STEEPLEJACK	STELLIFYING	STENOTROPIC	STERCORANIST	STEREOLOGIES
STEEPLEJACKS	STELLIFYINGS	STENOTYPED	STERCORANISTS	STEREOLOGY
STEEPNESSES	STELLIONATE	STENOTYPER	STERCORARIES	STEREOMETER
STEERAGEWAY	STELLIONATES	STENOTYPERS	STERCORARIOUS	STEREOMETERS
STEERAGEWAYS	STELLULARLY	STENOTYPES	STERCORARY	STEREOMETRIC
STEERLINGS	STELLULATE	STENOTYPIC	STERCORATE	STEREOMETRICAL
STEERSMATE	STEMMATOUS	STENOTYPIES	STERCORATED	STEREOMETRIES
STEERSMATES	STEMMERIES	STENOTYPING	STERCORATES	STEREOMETRY
STEGANOGRAM	STEMWINDER	STENOTYPIST	STERCORATING	STEREOPHONIC
STEGANOGRAMS	STEMWINDERS	STENOTYPISTS	STERCORICOLOUS	STEREOPHONIES
STEGANOGRAPH	STENCHIEST	STENTMASTER	STERCULIACEOUS	STEREOPHONY
STEGANOGRAPHER	STENCILERS	STENTMASTERS	STERCULIAS	STEREOPSES
STEGANOGRAPHERS	STENCILING	STENTORIAN	STEREOACUITIES	STEREOPSIS
STEGANOGRAPHIC	STENCILLED	STEPBAIRNS	STEREOACUITY	STEREOPTICON
STEGANOGRAPHIES	STENCILLER	STEPBROTHER	STEREOBATE	STEREOPTICONS
STEGANOGRAPHIST	STENCILLERS	STEPBROTHERS	STEREOBATES	STEREOPTICS

S

STEREOREGULAR
STEREOSCOPE
STEREOSCOPES
STEREOSCOPIC
STEREOSCOPICAL
STEREOSCOPIES
STEREOSCOPIST
STEREOSCOPISTS
STEREOSCOPY
STEREOSONIC
STEREOSPECIFIC
STEREOTACTIC
STEREOTACTICAL
STEREOTAXES
STEREOTAXIA
STEREOTAXIAS
STEREOTAXIC
STEREOTAXICALLY
STEREOTAXIS
STEREOTOMIES
STEREOTOMY
STEREOTROPIC
STEREOTROPISM
STEREOTROPISMS
STEREOTYPE
STEREOTYPED
STEREOTYPER
STEREOTYPERS
STEREOTYPES
STEREOTYPIC
STEREOTYPICAL
STEREOTYPICALLY
STEREOTYPIES
STEREOTYPING
STEREOTYPINGS
STEREOTYPIST
STEREOTYPISTS
STEREOTYPY
STEREOVISION
STEREOVISIONS
STERICALLY
STERIGMATA
STERILANTS
STERILISABLE
STERILISATION
STERILISATIONS
STERILISED

STERILISER
STERILISERS
STERILISES
STERILISING
STERILITIES
STERILIZABLE
STERILIZATION
STERILIZATIONS
STERILIZED
STERILIZER
STERILIZERS
STERILIZES
STERILIZING
STERLINGLY
STERLINGNESS
STERLINGNESSES
STERNALGIA
STERNALGIAS
STERNALGIC
STERNBOARD
STERNBOARDS
STERNEBRAE
STERNFASTS
STERNFOREMOST
STERNNESSES
STERNOCOSTAL
STERNOTRIBE
STERNPORTS
STERNPOSTS
STERNSHEET
STERNSHEETS
STERNUTATION
STERNUTATIONS
STERNUTATIVE
STERNUTATIVES
STERNUTATOR
STERNUTATORIES
STERNUTATORS
STERNUTATORY
STERNWARDS
STERNWORKS
STEROIDOGENESES
STEROIDOGENESIS
STEROIDOGENIC
STERTOROUS
STERTOROUSLY
STERTOROUSNESS

STETHOSCOPE
STETHOSCOPES
STETHOSCOPIC
STETHOSCOPIES
STETHOSCOPIST
STETHOSCOPISTS
STETHOSCOPY
STEVEDORED
STEVEDORES
STEVEDORING
STEVEDORINGS
STEVENGRAPH
STEVENGRAPHS
STEWARDESS
STEWARDESSES
STEWARDING
STEWARDRIES
STEWARDSHIP
STEWARDSHIPS
STEWARTRIES
STIACCIATO
STIACCIATOS
STIBIALISM
STIBIALISMS
STICCADOES
STICCATOES
STICHARION
STICHARIONS
STICHICALLY
STICHIDIUM
STICHOLOGIES
STICHOLOGY
STICHOMETRIC
STICHOMETRICAL
STICHOMETRIES
STICHOMETRY
STICHOMYTHIA
STICHOMYTHIAS
STICHOMYTHIC
STICHOMYTHIES
STICHOMYTHY
STICKABILITIES
STICKABILITY
STICKBALLS
STICKERING
STICKHANDLE
STICKHANDLED

STICKHANDLER
STICKHANDLERS
STICKHANDLES
STICKHANDLING
STICKHANDLINGS
STICKINESS
STICKINESSES
STICKLEADER
STICKLEADERS
STICKLEBACK
STICKLEBACKS
STICKLINGS
STICKSEEDS
STICKTIGHT
STICKTIGHTS
STICKWEEDS
STICKWORKS
STICKYBEAK
STICKYBEAKED
STICKYBEAKING
STICKYBEAKS
STIDDIEING
STIFFENERS
STIFFENING
STIFFENINGS
STIFFNESSES
STIFFWARES
STIFLINGLY
STIGMARIAN
STIGMARIANS
STIGMASTEROL
STIGMASTEROLS
STIGMATICAL
STIGMATICALLY
STIGMATICS
STIGMATIFEROUS
STIGMATISATION
STIGMATISATIONS
STIGMATISE
STIGMATISED
STIGMATISER
STIGMATISERS
STIGMATISES
STIGMATISING
STIGMATISM
STIGMATISMS
STIGMATIST

STIGMATISTS
STIGMATIZATION
STIGMATIZATIONS
STIGMATIZE
STIGMATIZED
STIGMATIZER
STIGMATIZERS
STIGMATIZES
STIGMATIZING
STIGMATOPHILIA
STIGMATOPHILIAS
STIGMATOPHILIST
STIGMATOSE
STILBESTROL
STILBESTROLS
STILBOESTROL
STILBOESTROLS
STILETTOED
STILETTOES
STILETTOING
STILLATORIES
STILLATORY
STILLBIRTH
STILLBIRTHS
STILLBORNS
STILLHOUSE
STILLHOUSES
STILLICIDE
STILLICIDES
STILLIFORM
STILLNESSES
STILLROOMS
STILPNOSIDERITE
STILTBIRDS
STILTEDNESS
STILTEDNESSES
STILTINESS
STILTINESSES
STIMPMETER
STIMPMETERS
STIMULABLE
STIMULANCIES
STIMULANCY
STIMULANTS
STIMULATED
STIMULATER
STIMULATERS

S

STIMULATES
STIMULATING
STIMULATINGLY
STIMULATION
STIMULATIONS
STIMULATIVE
STIMULATIVES
STIMULATOR
STIMULATORS
STIMULATORY
STINGAREES
STINGBULLS
STINGFISHES
STINGINESS
STINGINESSES
STINGINGLY
STINGINGNESS
STINGINGNESSES
STINKBIRDS
STINKEROOS
STINKHORNS
STINKINGLY
STINKINGNESS
STINKINGNESSES
STINKSTONE
STINKSTONES
STINKWEEDS
STINKWOODS
STINTEDNESS
STINTEDNESSES
STINTINGLY
STIPELLATE
STIPENDIARIES
STIPENDIARY
STIPENDIATE
STIPENDIATED
STIPENDIATES
STIPENDIATING
STIPITIFORM
STIPPLINGS
STIPULABLE
STIPULACEOUS
STIPULATED
STIPULATES
STIPULATING
STIPULATION
STIPULATIONS

STIPULATOR
STIPULATORS
STIPULATORY
STIRABOUTS
STIRPICULTURE
STIRPICULTURES
STIRRINGLY
STITCHCRAFT
STITCHCRAFTS
STITCHERIES
STITCHINGS
STITCHWORK
STITCHWORKS
STITCHWORT
STITCHWORTS
STOCCADOES
STOCHASTIC
STOCHASTICALLY
STOCKADING
STOCKBREEDER
STOCKBREEDERS
STOCKBREEDING
STOCKBREEDINGS
STOCKBROKER
STOCKBROKERAGE
STOCKBROKERAGES
STOCKBROKERS
STOCKBROKING
STOCKBROKINGS
STOCKFISHES
STOCKHOLDER
STOCKHOLDERS
STOCKHOLDING
STOCKHOLDINGS
STOCKHORNS
STOCKHORSE
STOCKHORSES
STOCKINESS
STOCKINESSES
STOCKINETS
STOCKINETTE
STOCKINETTES
STOCKINGED
STOCKINGER
STOCKINGERS
STOCKINGLESS
STOCKISHLY

STOCKISHNESS
STOCKISHNESSES
STOCKJOBBER
STOCKJOBBERIES
STOCKJOBBERS
STOCKJOBBERY
STOCKJOBBING
STOCKJOBBINGS
STOCKKEEPER
STOCKKEEPERS
STOCKLISTS
STOCKLOCKS
STOCKPILED
STOCKPILER
STOCKPILERS
STOCKPILES
STOCKPILING
STOCKPILINGS
STOCKPUNISHT
STOCKROOMS
STOCKROUTE
STOCKROUTES
STOCKTAKEN
STOCKTAKES
STOCKTAKING
STOCKTAKINGS
STOCKWORKS
STOCKYARDS
STODGINESS
STODGINESSES
STOECHIOLOGICAL
STOECHIOLOGIES
STOECHIOLOGY
STOECHIOMETRIC
STOECHIOMETRIES
STOECHIOMETRY
STOICALNESS
STOICALNESSES
STOICHEIOLOGIES
STOICHEIOLOGY
STOICHEIOMETRIC
STOICHEIOMETRY
STOICHIOLOGICAL
STOICHIOLOGIES
STOICHIOLOGY
STOICHIOMETRIC
STOICHIOMETRIES

STOICHIOMETRY
STOITERING
STOKEHOLDS
STOKEHOLES
STOLENWISE
STOLIDITIES
STOLIDNESS
STOLIDNESSES
STOLONIFEROUS
STOMACHACHE
STOMACHACHES
STOMACHERS
STOMACHFUL
STOMACHFULNESS
STOMACHFULS
STOMACHICAL
STOMACHICS
STOMACHING
STOMACHLESS
STOMACHOUS
STOMATITIC
STOMATITIDES
STOMATITIS
STOMATITISES
STOMATODAEA
STOMATODAEUM
STOMATOGASTRIC
STOMATOLOGICAL
STOMATOLOGIES
STOMATOLOGIST
STOMATOLOGISTS
STOMATOLOGY
STOMATOPLASTIES
STOMATOPLASTY
STOMATOPOD
STOMATOPODS
STOMODAEAL
STOMODAEUM
STOMODAEUMS
STOMODEUMS
STONEBOATS
STONEBORER
STONEBORERS
STONEBRASH
STONEBRASHES
STONEBREAK
STONEBREAKER

STONEBREAKERS
STONEBREAKS
STONECASTS
STONECHATS
STONECROPS
STONECUTTER
STONECUTTERS
STONECUTTING
STONECUTTINGS
STONEFISHES
STONEFLIES
STONEGROUND
STONEHANDS
STONEHORSE
STONEHORSES
STONELESSNESS
STONELESSNESSES
STONEMASON
STONEMASONRIES
STONEMASONRY
STONEMASONS
STONESHOTS
STONEWALLED
STONEWALLER
STONEWALLERS
STONEWALLING
STONEWALLINGS
STONEWALLS
STONEWARES
STONEWASHED
STONEWASHES
STONEWASHING
STONEWORKER
STONEWORKERS
STONEWORKS
STONEWORTS
STONINESSES
STONISHING
STONKERING
STONYHEARTED
STOOLBALLS
STOOPBALLS
STOOPINGLY
STOPLIGHTS
STOPPERING
STOPWATCHES
STORECARDS

S

STOREFRONT	STOVEPIPES	STRAIGHTLACED	STRANGULATE	STRATIFICATIONS
STOREFRONTS	STRABISMAL	STRAIGHTLY	STRANGULATED	STRATIFIED
STOREHOUSE	STRABISMIC	STRAIGHTNESS	STRANGULATES	STRATIFIES
STOREHOUSES	STRABISMICAL	STRAIGHTNESSES	STRANGULATING	STRATIFORM
STOREKEEPER	STRABISMOMETER	STRAIGHTWAY	STRANGULATION	STRATIFYING
STOREKEEPERS	STRABISMOMETERS	STRAIGHTWAYS	STRANGULATIONS	STRATIGRAPHER
STOREKEEPING	STRABISMUS	STRAINEDLY	STRANGURIES	STRATIGRAPHERS
STOREKEEPINGS	STRABISMUSES	STRAININGS	STRAPHANGED	STRATIGRAPHIC
STOREROOMS	STRABOMETER	STRAITENED	STRAPHANGER	STRATIGRAPHICAL
STORESHIPS	STRABOMETERS	STRAITENING	STRAPHANGERS	STRATIGRAPHIES
STORIETTES	STRABOTOMIES	STRAITJACKET	STRAPHANGING	STRATIGRAPHIST
STORIOLOGIES	STRABOTOMY	STRAITJACKETED	STRAPHANGINGS	STRATIGRAPHISTS
STORIOLOGIST	STRACCHINI	STRAITJACKETING	STRAPHANGS	STRATIGRAPHY
STORIOLOGISTS	STRACCHINO	STRAITJACKETS	STRAPLESSES	STRATOCRACIES
STORIOLOGY	STRADDLEBACK	STRAITLACED	STRAPLINES	STRATOCRACY
STORKSBILL	STRADDLERS	STRAITLACEDLY	STRAPONTIN	STRATOCRAT
STORKSBILLS	STRADDLING	STRAITLACEDNESS	STRAPONTINS	STRATOCRATIC
STORMBIRDS	STRAGGLERS	STRAITNESS	STRAPPADOED	STRATOCRATS
STORMBOUND	STRAGGLIER	STRAITNESSES	STRAPPADOES	STRATOCUMULI
STORMCOCKS	STRAGGLIEST	STRAITWAISTCOAT	STRAPPADOING	STRATOCUMULUS
STORMFULLY	STRAGGLING	STRAMACONS	STRAPPADOS	STRATOPAUSE
STORMFULNESS	STRAGGLINGLY	STRAMASHED	STRAPPIEST	STRATOPAUSES
STORMFULNESSES	STRAGGLINGS	STRAMASHES	STRAPPINGS	STRATOSPHERE
STORMINESS	STRAICHTER	STRAMASHING	STRAPWORTS	STRATOSPHERES
STORMINESSES	STRAICHTEST	STRAMAZONS	STRATAGEMS	STRATOSPHERIC
STORMPROOF	STRAIGHTAWAY	STRAMINEOUS	STRATEGETIC	STRATOSPHERICAL
STORMSTAYED	STRAIGHTAWAYS	STRAMONIES	STRATEGETICAL	STRATOTANKER
STORYBOARD	STRAIGHTBRED	STRAMONIUM	STRATEGICAL	STRATOTANKERS
STORYBOARDED	STRAIGHTBREDS	STRAMONIUMS	STRATEGICALLY	STRATOVOLCANO
STORYBOARDING	STRAIGHTED	STRANDEDNESS	STRATEGICS	STRATOVOLCANOES
STORYBOARDS	STRAIGHTEDGE	STRANDEDNESSES	STRATEGIES	STRATOVOLCANOS
STORYBOOKS	STRAIGHTEDGED	STRANDFLAT	STRATEGISE	STRAUCHTED
STORYETTES	STRAIGHTEDGES	STRANDFLATS	STRATEGISED	STRAUCHTER
STORYLINES	STRAIGHTEN	STRANDLINE	STRATEGISES	STRAUCHTEST
STORYTELLER	STRAIGHTENED	STRANDLINES	STRATEGISING	STRAUCHTING
STORYTELLERS	STRAIGHTENER	STRANDWOLF	STRATEGIST	STRAUGHTED
STORYTELLING	STRAIGHTENERS	STRANDWOLVES	STRATEGISTS	STRAUGHTER
STORYTELLINGS	STRAIGHTENING	STRANGENESS	STRATEGIZE	STRAUGHTEST
STOTTERING	STRAIGHTENS	STRANGENESSES	STRATEGIZED	STRAUGHTING
STOUTENING	STRAIGHTER	STRANGERED	STRATEGIZES	STRAVAGING
STOUTHEARTED	STRAIGHTEST	STRANGERING	STRATEGIZING	STRAVAIGED
STOUTHEARTEDLY	STRAIGHTFORTH	STRANGLEHOLD	STRATHSPEY	STRAVAIGER
STOUTHERIE	STRAIGHTFORWARD	STRANGLEHOLDS	STRATHSPEYS	STRAVAIGERS
STOUTHERIES	STRAIGHTING	STRANGLEMENT	STRATICULATE	STRAVAIGING
STOUTHRIEF	STRAIGHTISH	STRANGLEMENTS	STRATICULATION	STRAWBERRIES
STOUTHRIEFS	STRAIGHTJACKET	STRANGLERS	STRATICULATIONS	STRAWBERRY
STOUTNESSES	STRAIGHTJACKETS	STRANGLING	STRATIFICATION	STRAWBOARD

S

STRAWBOARDS	STREETSCAPES	STREPTOKINASES	STRIDENCES	STRINGIEST
STRAWFLOWER	STREETSMART	STREPTOLYSIN	STRIDENCIES	STRINGINESS
STRAWFLOWERS	STREETWALKER	STREPTOLYSINS	STRIDENTLY	STRINGINESSES
STRAWWEIGHT	STREETWALKERS	STREPTOMYCES	STRIDEWAYS	STRINGINGS
STRAWWEIGHTS	STREETWALKING	STREPTOMYCETE	STRIDULANCE	STRINGLESS
STRAWWORMS	STREETWALKINGS	STREPTOMYCETES	STRIDULANCES	STRINGLIKE
STRAYLINGS	STREETWARD	STREPTOMYCIN	STRIDULANT	STRINGPIECE
STREAKIEST	STREETWARDS	STREPTOMYCINS	STRIDULANTLY	STRINGPIECES
STREAKINESS	STREETWEAR	STREPTOSOLEN	STRIDULATE	STRINGYBARK
STREAKINESSES	STREETWEARS	STREPTOSOLENS	STRIDULATED	STRINGYBARKS
STREAKINGS	STREETWISE	STREPTOTHRICIN	STRIDULATES	STRINKLING
STREAKLIKE	STREIGNING	STREPTOTHRICINS	STRIDULATING	STRINKLINGS
STREAMBEDS	STRELITZES	STRESSBUSTER	STRIDULATION	STRIPAGRAM
STREAMERED	STRELITZIA	STRESSBUSTERS	STRIDULATIONS	STRIPAGRAMS
STREAMIEST	STRELITZIAS	STRESSBUSTING	STRIDULATOR	STRIPELESS
STREAMINESS	STRENGTHEN	STRESSFULLY	STRIDULATORS	STRIPINESS
STREAMINESSES	STRENGTHENED	STRESSFULNESS	STRIDULATORY	STRIPINESSES
STREAMINGLY	STRENGTHENER	STRESSFULNESSES	STRIDULOUS	STRIPLINGS
STREAMINGS	STRENGTHENERS	STRESSIEST	STRIDULOUSLY	STRIPOGRAM
STREAMLESS	STRENGTHENING	STRESSLESS	STRIDULOUSNESS	STRIPOGRAMS
STREAMLETS	STRENGTHENINGS	STRESSLESSNESS	STRIFELESS	STRIPPABLE
STREAMLIKE	STRENGTHENS	STRETCHABILITY	STRIGIFORM	STRIPPAGRAM
STREAMLINE	STRENGTHFUL	STRETCHABLE	STRIKEBOUND	STRIPPAGRAMS
STREAMLINED	STRENGTHLESS	STRETCHERED	STRIKEBREAKER	STRIPPERGRAM
STREAMLINER	STRENUITIES	STRETCHERING	STRIKEBREAKERS	STRIPPERGRAMS
STREAMLINERS	STRENUOSITIES	STRETCHERS	STRIKEBREAKING	STRIPPINGS
STREAMLINES	STRENUOSITY	STRETCHIER	STRIKEBREAKINGS	STRIPTEASE
STREAMLING	STRENUOUSLY	STRETCHIEST	STRIKELESS	STRIPTEASER
STREAMLINGS	STRENUOUSNESS	STRETCHINESS	STRIKEOUTS	STRIPTEASERS
STREAMLINING	STRENUOUSNESSES	STRETCHINESSES	STRIKEOVER	STRIPTEASES
STREAMLININGS	STREPEROUS	STRETCHING	STRIKEOVERS	STRIVINGLY
STREAMSIDE	STREPHOSYMBOLIA	STRETCHINGS	STRIKINGLY	STROBILACEOUS
STREAMSIDES	STREPITANT	STRETCHLESS	STRIKINGNESS	STROBILATE
STREETAGES	STREPITATION	STRETCHMARKS	STRIKINGNESSES	STROBILATED
STREETBOYS	STREPITATIONS	STREWMENTS	STRINGBOARD	STROBILATES
STREETCARS	STREPITOSO	STRIATIONS	STRINGBOARDS	STROBILATING
STREETFULS	STREPITOUS	STRIATURES	STRINGCOURSE	STROBILATION
STREETIEST	STREPSIPTEROUS	STRICKENLY	STRINGCOURSES	STROBILATIONS
STREETKEEPER	STREPTOBACILLI	STRICKLING	STRINGENCIES	STROBILIFORM
STREETKEEPERS	STREPTOBACILLUS	STRICTIONS	STRINGENCY	STROBILINE
STREETLAMP	STREPTOCARPUS	STRICTNESS	STRINGENDO	STROBILISATION
STREETLAMPS	STREPTOCARPUSES	STRICTNESSES	STRINGENTLY	STROBILISATIONS
STREETLIGHT	STREPTOCOCCAL	STRICTURED	STRINGENTNESS	STROBILIZATION
STREETLIGHTS	STREPTOCOCCI	STRICTURES	STRINGENTNESSES	STROBILIZATIONS
STREETROOM	STREPTOCOCCIC	STRIDDLING	STRINGHALT	STROBILOID
STREETROOMS	STREPTOCOCCUS	STRIDELEGGED	STRINGHALTED	STROBILUSES
STREETSCAPE	STREPTOKINASE	STRIDELEGS	STRINGHALTS	STROBOSCOPE

S

STROBOSCOPES
STROBOSCOPIC
STROBOSCOPICAL
STROBOTRON
STROBOTRONS
STRODDLING
STROGANOFF
STROGANOFFS
STROKEPLAY
STROLLINGS
STROMATOLITE
STROMATOLITES
STROMATOLITIC
STROMATOUS
STROMBULIFEROUS
STROMBULIFORM
STROMBUSES
STRONGARMED
STRONGARMING
STRONGARMS
STRONGBOXES
STRONGHOLD
STRONGHOLDS
STRONGNESS
STRONGNESSES
STRONGPOINT
STRONGPOINTS
STRONGROOM
STRONGROOMS
STRONGYLES
STRONGYLOID
STRONGYLOIDOSES
STRONGYLOIDOSIS
STRONGYLOIDS
STRONGYLOSES
STRONGYLOSIS
STRONTIANITE
STRONTIANITES
STRONTIANS
STRONTIUMS
STROPHANTHIN
STROPHANTHINS
STROPHANTHUS
STROPHANTHUSES
STROPHICAL
STROPHIOLATE
STROPHIOLATED

STROPHIOLE
STROPHIOLES
STROPHOIDS
STROPHULUS
STROPPIEST
STROPPINESS
STROPPINESSES
STROUDINGS
STROUPACHS
STRUCTURAL
STRUCTURALISE
STRUCTURALISED
STRUCTURALISES
STRUCTURALISING
STRUCTURALISM
STRUCTURALISMS
STRUCTURALIST
STRUCTURALISTS
STRUCTURALIZE
STRUCTURALIZED
STRUCTURALIZES
STRUCTURALIZING
STRUCTURALLY
STRUCTURATION
STRUCTURATIONS
STRUCTURED
STRUCTURELESS
STRUCTURES
STRUCTURING
STRUGGLERS
STRUGGLING
STRUGGLINGLY
STRUGGLINGS
STRUMITISES
STRUMPETED
STRUMPETING
STRUTHIOID
STRUTHIOIDS
STRUTHIOUS
STRUTTINGLY
STRUTTINGS
STRYCHNIAS
STRYCHNINE
STRYCHNINED
STRYCHNINES
STRYCHNINING
STRYCHNINISM

STRYCHNINISMS
STRYCHNISM
STRYCHNISMS
STUBBINESS
STUBBINESSES
STUBBLIEST
STUBBORNED
STUBBORNER
STUBBORNEST
STUBBORNING
STUBBORNLY
STUBBORNNESS
STUBBORNNESSES
STUCCOWORK
STUCCOWORKS
STUDDINGSAIL
STUDDINGSAILS
STUDENTRIES
STUDENTSHIP
STUDENTSHIPS
STUDFISHES
STUDHORSES
STUDIEDNESS
STUDIEDNESSES
STUDIOUSLY
STUDIOUSNESS
STUDIOUSNESSES
STUFFINESS
STUFFINESSES
STULTIFICATION
STULTIFICATIONS
STULTIFIED
STULTIFIER
STULTIFIERS
STULTIFIES
STULTIFYING
STUMBLEBUM
STUMBLEBUMS
STUMBLIEST
STUMBLINGLY
STUMPINESS
STUMPINESSES
STUMPWORKS
STUNNINGLY
STUNTEDNESS
STUNTEDNESSES
STUNTWOMAN

STUNTWOMEN
STUPEFACIENT
STUPEFACIENTS
STUPEFACTION
STUPEFACTIONS
STUPEFACTIVE
STUPEFIERS
STUPEFYING
STUPEFYINGLY
STUPENDIOUS
STUPENDOUS
STUPENDOUSLY
STUPENDOUSNESS
STUPIDITIES
STUPIDNESS
STUPIDNESSES
STUPRATING
STUPRATION
STUPRATIONS
STURDINESS
STURDINESSES
STUTTERERS
STUTTERING
STUTTERINGLY
STUTTERINGS
STYLEBOOKS
STYLELESSNESS
STYLELESSNESSES
STYLIFEROUS
STYLISATION
STYLISATIONS
STYLISHNESS
STYLISHNESSES
STYLISTICALLY
STYLISTICS
STYLITISMS
STYLIZATION
STYLIZATIONS
STYLOBATES
STYLOGRAPH
STYLOGRAPHIC
STYLOGRAPHICAL
STYLOGRAPHIES
STYLOGRAPHS
STYLOGRAPHY
STYLOLITES
STYLOLITIC

STYLOMETRIES
STYLOMETRY
STYLOPHONE
STYLOPHONES
STYLOPISED
STYLOPISES
STYLOPISING
STYLOPIZED
STYLOPIZES
STYLOPIZING
STYLOPODIA
STYLOPODIUM
STYLOSTIXES
STYLOSTIXIS
STYPTICITIES
STYPTICITY
STYRACACEOUS
STYROFOAMS
SUABILITIES
SUASIVENESS
SUASIVENESSES
SUAVENESSES
SUAVEOLENT
SUBABDOMINAL
SUBACETATE
SUBACETATES
SUBACIDITIES
SUBACIDITY
SUBACIDNESS
SUBACIDNESSES
SUBACTIONS
SUBACUTELY
SUBADOLESCENT
SUBADOLESCENTS
SUBAERIALLY
SUBAFFLUENT
SUBAGENCIES
SUBAGGREGATE
SUBAGGREGATES
SUBAGGREGATION
SUBAGGREGATIONS
SUBAHDARIES
SUBAHSHIPS
SUBALLIANCE
SUBALLIANCES
SUBALLOCATION
SUBALLOCATIONS

S

SUBALTERNANT	SUBBASEMENTS	SUBCHELATE	SUBCONSCIOUSES	SUBDEALERS
SUBALTERNANTS	SUBBITUMINOUS	SUBCHLORIDE	SUBCONSCIOUSLY	SUBDEANERIES
SUBALTERNATE	SUBBRANCHES	SUBCHLORIDES	SUBCONSULS	SUBDEANERY
SUBALTERNATES	SUBBUREAUS	SUBCIRCUIT	SUBCONTIGUOUS	SUBDEBUTANTE
SUBALTERNATION	SUBBUREAUX	SUBCIRCUITS	SUBCONTINENT	SUBDEBUTANTES
SUBALTERNATIONS	SUBCABINET	SUBCIVILISATION	SUBCONTINENTAL	SUBDECANAL
SUBALTERNITIES	SUBCABINETS	SUBCIVILISED	SUBCONTINENTS	SUBDECISION
SUBALTERNITY	SUBCALIBER	SUBCIVILIZATION	SUBCONTINUOUS	SUBDECISIONS
SUBALTERNS	SUBCALIBRE	SUBCIVILIZED	SUBCONTRACT	SUBDELIRIA
SUBANGULAR	SUBCANTORS	SUBCLASSED	SUBCONTRACTED	SUBDELIRIOUS
SUBANTARCTIC	SUBCAPSULAR	SUBCLASSES	SUBCONTRACTING	SUBDELIRIUM
SUBAPOSTOLIC	SUBCARDINAL	SUBCLASSIFIED	SUBCONTRACTINGS	SUBDELIRIUMS
SUBAPPEARANCE	SUBCARDINALS	SUBCLASSIFIES	SUBCONTRACTOR	SUBDEPARTMENT
SUBAPPEARANCES	SUBCARRIER	SUBCLASSIFY	SUBCONTRACTORS	SUBDEPARTMENTS
SUBAQUATIC	SUBCARRIERS	SUBCLASSIFYING	SUBCONTRACTS	SUBDEPUTIES
SUBAQUEOUS	SUBCATEGORIES	SUBCLASSING	SUBCONTRAOCTAVE	SUBDERMALLY
SUBARACHNOID	SUBCATEGORISE	SUBCLAUSES	SUBCONTRARIES	SUBDEVELOPMENT
SUBARACHNOIDAL	SUBCATEGORISED	SUBCLAVIAN	SUBCONTRARIETY	SUBDEVELOPMENTS
SUBARBOREAL	SUBCATEGORISES	SUBCLAVIANS	SUBCONTRARY	SUBDIACONAL
SUBARBORESCENT	SUBCATEGORISING	SUBCLAVICULAR	SUBCOOLING	SUBDIACONATE
SUBARCTICS	SUBCATEGORIZE	SUBCLIMACTIC	SUBCORDATE	SUBDIACONATES
SUBARCUATE	SUBCATEGORIZED	SUBCLIMAXES	SUBCORIACEOUS	SUBDIALECT
SUBARCUATION	SUBCATEGORIZES	SUBCLINICAL	SUBCORTEXES	SUBDIALECTS
SUBARCUATIONS	SUBCATEGORIZING	SUBCLINICALLY	SUBCORTICAL	SUBDIRECTOR
SUBARRATION	SUBCATEGORY	SUBCLUSTER	SUBCORTICES	SUBDIRECTORS
SUBARRATIONS	SUBCAVITIES	SUBCLUSTERED	SUBCOSTALS	SUBDISCIPLINE
SUBARRHATION	SUBCEILING	SUBCLUSTERING	SUBCOUNTIES	SUBDISCIPLINES
SUBARRHATIONS	SUBCEILINGS	SUBCLUSTERS	SUBCRANIAL	SUBDISTRICT
SUBARTICLE	SUBCELESTIAL	SUBCOLLECTION	SUBCRITICAL	SUBDISTRICTS
SUBARTICLES	SUBCELESTIALS	SUBCOLLECTIONS	SUBCRUSTAL	SUBDIVIDABLE
SUBASSEMBLE	SUBCELLARS	SUBCOLLEGE	SUBCULTURAL	SUBDIVIDED
SUBASSEMBLED	SUBCELLULAR	SUBCOLLEGES	SUBCULTURALLY	SUBDIVIDER
SUBASSEMBLES	SUBCENTERS	SUBCOLLEGIATE	SUBCULTURE	SUBDIVIDERS
SUBASSEMBLIES	SUBCENTRAL	SUBCOLONIES	SUBCULTURED	SUBDIVIDES
SUBASSEMBLING	SUBCENTRALLY	SUBCOMMISSION	SUBCULTURES	SUBDIVIDING
SUBASSEMBLY	SUBCENTRES	SUBCOMMISSIONED	SUBCULTURING	SUBDIVISIBLE
SUBASSOCIATION	SUBCEPTION	SUBCOMMISSIONER	SUBCURATIVE	SUBDIVISION
SUBASSOCIATIONS	SUBCEPTIONS	SUBCOMMISSIONS	SUBCUTANEOUS	SUBDIVISIONAL
SUBATMOSPHERIC	SUBCHANTER	SUBCOMMITTEE	SUBCUTANEOUSLY	SUBDIVISIONS
SUBATOMICS	SUBCHANTERS	SUBCOMMITTEES	SUBCUTISES	SUBDIVISIVE
SUBAUDIBLE	SUBCHAPTER	SUBCOMMUNITIES	SUBDEACONATE	SUBDOMINANT
SUBAUDITION	SUBCHAPTERS	SUBCOMMUNITY	SUBDEACONATES	SUBDOMINANTS
SUBAUDITIONS	SUBCHARTER	SUBCOMPACT	SUBDEACONRIES	SUBDUCTING
SUBAURICULAR	SUBCHARTERED	SUBCOMPACTS	SUBDEACONRY	SUBDUCTION
SUBAVERAGE	SUBCHARTERING	SUBCOMPONENT	SUBDEACONS	SUBDUCTIONS
SUBAXILLARY	SUBCHARTERS	SUBCOMPONENTS	SUBDEACONSHIP	SUBDUEDNESS
SUBBASEMENT	SUBCHASERS	SUBCONSCIOUS	SUBDEACONSHIPS	SUBDUEDNESSES

S

SUBDUEMENT	SUBGROUPING	SUBINTRODUCE	SUBJECTSHIP	SUBLIMATION
SUBDUEMENTS	SUBHARMONIC	SUBINTRODUCED	SUBJECTSHIPS	SUBLIMATIONS
SUBDUPLICATE	SUBHARMONICS	SUBINTRODUCES	SUBJOINDER	SUBLIMENESS
SUBECONOMIC	SUBHASTATION	SUBINTRODUCING	SUBJOINDERS	SUBLIMENESSES
SUBECONOMIES	SUBHASTATIONS	SUBINVOLUTION	SUBJOINING	SUBLIMINAL
SUBECONOMY	SUBHEADING	SUBINVOLUTIONS	SUBJUGABLE	SUBLIMINALLY
SUBEDITING	SUBHEADINGS	SUBIRRIGATE	SUBJUGATED	SUBLIMINALS
SUBEDITORIAL	SUBIMAGINAL	SUBIRRIGATED	SUBJUGATES	SUBLIMINGS
SUBEDITORS	SUBIMAGINES	SUBIRRIGATES	SUBJUGATING	SUBLIMISED
SUBEDITORSHIP	SUBIMAGOES	SUBIRRIGATING	SUBJUGATION	SUBLIMISES
SUBEDITORSHIPS	SUBINCISED	SUBIRRIGATION	SUBJUGATIONS	SUBLIMISING
SUBEMPLOYED	SUBINCISES	SUBIRRIGATIONS	SUBJUGATOR	SUBLIMITIES
SUBEMPLOYMENT	SUBINCISING	SUBITANEOUS	SUBJUGATORS	SUBLIMIZED
SUBEMPLOYMENTS	SUBINCISION	SUBITISING	SUBJUNCTION	SUBLIMIZES
SUBENTRIES	SUBINCISIONS	SUBITIZING	SUBJUNCTIONS	SUBLIMIZING
SUBEPIDERMAL	SUBINDEXES	SUBJACENCIES	SUBJUNCTIVE	SUBLINEATION
SUBEQUATORIAL	SUBINDICATE	SUBJACENCY	SUBJUNCTIVELY	SUBLINEATIONS
SUBERISATION	SUBINDICATED	SUBJACENTLY	SUBJUNCTIVES	SUBLINGUAL
SUBERISATIONS	SUBINDICATES	SUBJECTABILITY	SUBKINGDOM	SUBLITERACIES
SUBERISING	SUBINDICATING	SUBJECTABLE	SUBKINGDOMS	SUBLITERACY
SUBERIZATION	SUBINDICATION	SUBJECTIFIED	SUBLANCEOLATE	SUBLITERARY
SUBERIZATIONS	SUBINDICATIONS	SUBJECTIFIES	SUBLANGUAGE	SUBLITERATE
SUBERIZING	SUBINDICATIVE	SUBJECTIFY	SUBLANGUAGES	SUBLITERATES
SUBFACTORIAL	SUBINDICES	SUBJECTIFYING	SUBLAPSARIAN	SUBLITERATURE
SUBFACTORIALS	SUBINDUSTRIES	SUBJECTING	SUBLAPSARIANISM	SUBLITERATURES
SUBFAMILIES	SUBINDUSTRY	SUBJECTION	SUBLAPSARIANS	SUBLITTORAL
SUBFERTILE	SUBINFEUDATE	SUBJECTIONS	SUBLATIONS	SUBLITTORALS
SUBFERTILITIES	SUBINFEUDATED	SUBJECTIVE	SUBLEASING	SUBLUXATED
SUBFERTILITY	SUBINFEUDATES	SUBJECTIVELY	SUBLESSEES	SUBLUXATES
SUBFEUDATION	SUBINFEUDATING	SUBJECTIVENESS	SUBLESSORS	SUBLUXATING
SUBFEUDATIONS	SUBINFEUDATION	SUBJECTIVES	SUBLETHALLY	SUBLUXATION
SUBFEUDATORY	SUBINFEUDATIONS	SUBJECTIVISE	SUBLETTERS	SUBLUXATIONS
SUBFOSSILS	SUBINFEUDATORY	SUBJECTIVISED	SUBLETTING	SUBMANAGER
SUBFREEZING	SUBINFEUDED	SUBJECTIVISES	SUBLETTINGS	SUBMANAGERS
SUBFUSCOUS	SUBINFEUDING	SUBJECTIVISING	SUBLIBRARIAN	SUBMANDIBULAR
SUBGENERATION	SUBINFEUDS	SUBJECTIVISM	SUBLIBRARIANS	SUBMANDIBULARS
SUBGENERATIONS	SUBINHIBITORY	SUBJECTIVISMS	SUBLICENSE	SUBMARGINAL
SUBGENERIC	SUBINSINUATION	SUBJECTIVIST	SUBLICENSED	SUBMARGINALLY
SUBGENERICALLY	SUBINSINUATIONS	SUBJECTIVISTIC	SUBLICENSES	SUBMARINED
SUBGENUSES	SUBINSPECTOR	SUBJECTIVISTS	SUBLICENSING	SUBMARINER
SUBGLACIAL	SUBINSPECTORS	SUBJECTIVITIES	SUBLIEUTENANCY	SUBMARINERS
SUBGLACIALLY	SUBINTELLECTION	SUBJECTIVITY	SUBLIEUTENANT	SUBMARINES
SUBGLOBOSE	SUBINTELLIGENCE	SUBJECTIVIZE	SUBLIEUTENANTS	SUBMARINING
SUBGLOBULAR	SUBINTELLIGITUR	SUBJECTIVIZED	SUBLIMABLE	SUBMARKETS
SUBGOVERNMENT	SUBINTERVAL	SUBJECTIVIZES	SUBLIMATED	SUBMATRICES
SUBGOVERNMENTS	SUBINTERVALS	SUBJECTIVIZING	SUBLIMATES	SUBMATRIXES
SUBGROUPED	SUBINTRANT	SUBJECTLESS	SUBLIMATING	SUBMAXILLARIES

S

SUBMAXILLARY	SUBMISSNESSES	SUBOPTIMISING	SUBPREFECTS	SUBSATURATIONS
SUBMAXIMAL	SUBMITTABLE	SUBOPTIMIZATION	SUBPREFECTURE	SUBSCAPULAR
SUBMEDIANT	SUBMITTALS	SUBOPTIMIZE	SUBPREFECTURES	SUBSCAPULARS
SUBMEDIANTS	SUBMITTERS	SUBOPTIMIZED	SUBPRIMATE	SUBSCHEMATA
SUBMERGEMENT	SUBMITTING	SUBOPTIMIZES	SUBPRIMATES	SUBSCIENCE
SUBMERGEMENTS	SUBMITTINGS	SUBOPTIMIZING	SUBPRINCIPAL	SUBSCIENCES
SUBMERGENCE	SUBMOLECULE	SUBOPTIMUM	SUBPRINCIPALS	SUBSCRIBABLE
SUBMERGENCES	SUBMOLECULES	SUBORBICULAR	SUBPRIORESS	SUBSCRIBED
SUBMERGIBILITY	SUBMONTANE	SUBORBITAL	SUBPRIORESSES	SUBSCRIBER
SUBMERGIBLE	SUBMONTANELY	SUBORDINAL	SUBPROBLEM	SUBSCRIBERS
SUBMERGIBLES	SUBMUCOSAE	SUBORDINANCIES	SUBPROBLEMS	SUBSCRIBES
SUBMERGING	SUBMUCOSAL	SUBORDINANCY	SUBPROCESS	SUBSCRIBING
SUBMERSIBILITY	SUBMUCOSAS	SUBORDINARIES	SUBPROCESSES	SUBSCRIBINGS
SUBMERSIBLE	SUBMULTIPLE	SUBORDINARY	SUBPRODUCT	SUBSCRIPTION
SUBMERSIBLES	SUBMULTIPLES	SUBORDINATE	SUBPRODUCTS	SUBSCRIPTIONS
SUBMERSING	SUBMUNITION	SUBORDINATED	SUBPROFESSIONAL	SUBSCRIPTIVE
SUBMERSION	SUBMUNITIONS	SUBORDINATELY	SUBPROGRAM	SUBSCRIPTS
SUBMERSIONS	SUBNASCENT	SUBORDINATENESS	SUBPROGRAMS	SUBSECRETARIES
SUBMETACENTRIC	SUBNATIONAL	SUBORDINATES	SUBPROJECT	SUBSECRETARY
SUBMETACENTRICS	SUBNATURAL	SUBORDINATING	SUBPROJECTS	SUBSECTION
SUBMICROGRAM	SUBNETWORK	SUBORDINATION	SUBPROLETARIAT	SUBSECTIONS
SUBMICRONS	SUBNETWORKED	SUBORDINATIONS	SUBPROLETARIATS	SUBSECTORS
SUBMICROSCOPIC	SUBNETWORKING	SUBORDINATIVE	SUBRATIONAL	SUBSEGMENT
SUBMILLIMETER	SUBNETWORKS	SUBORDINATOR	SUBREFERENCE	SUBSEGMENTS
SUBMILLIMETERS	SUBNORMALITIES	SUBORDINATORS	SUBREFERENCES	SUBSEIZURE
SUBMILLIMETRE	SUBNORMALITY	SUBORGANISATION	SUBREGIONAL	SUBSEIZURES
SUBMILLIMETRES	SUBNORMALLY	SUBORGANIZATION	SUBREGIONS	SUBSELLIUM
SUBMINIATURE	SUBNORMALS	SUBORNATION	SUBRENTING	SUBSENSIBLE
SUBMINIATURES	SUBNUCLEAR	SUBORNATIONS	SUBREPTION	SUBSENTENCE
SUBMINIATURISE	SUBNUCLEUS	SUBORNATIVE	SUBREPTIONS	SUBSENTENCES
SUBMINIATURISED	SUBNUCLEUSES	SUBOSCINES	SUBREPTITIOUS	SUBSEQUENCE
SUBMINIATURISES	SUBOCCIPITAL	SUBPANATION	SUBREPTITIOUSLY	SUBSEQUENCES
SUBMINIATURIZE	SUBOCEANIC	SUBPANATIONS	SUBREPTIVE	SUBSEQUENT
SUBMINIATURIZED	SUBOCTAVES	SUBPARAGRAPH	SUBROGATED	SUBSEQUENTIAL
SUBMINIATURIZES	SUBOCTUPLE	SUBPARAGRAPHS	SUBROGATES	SUBSEQUENTLY
SUBMINIMAL	SUBOFFICER	SUBPARALLEL	SUBROGATING	SUBSEQUENTNESS
SUBMINISTER	SUBOFFICERS	SUBPENAING	SUBROGATION	SUBSEQUENTS
SUBMINISTERED	SUBOFFICES	SUBPERIODS	SUBROGATIONS	SUBSERVIENCE
SUBMINISTERING	SUBOPERCULA	SUBPHRENIC	SUBROUTINE	SUBSERVIENCES
SUBMINISTERS	SUBOPERCULAR	SUBPHYLUMS	SUBROUTINES	SUBSERVIENCIES
SUBMISSIBLE	SUBOPERCULUM	SUBPOENAED	SUBSAMPLED	SUBSERVIENCY
SUBMISSION	SUBOPERCULUMS	SUBPOENAING	SUBSAMPLES	SUBSERVIENT
SUBMISSIONS	SUBOPTIMAL	SUBPOPULATION	SUBSAMPLING	SUBSERVIENTLY
SUBMISSIVE	SUBOPTIMISATION	SUBPOPULATIONS	SUBSATELLITE	SUBSERVIENTS
SUBMISSIVELY	SUBOPTIMISE	SUBPOTENCIES	SUBSATELLITES	SUBSERVING
SUBMISSIVENESS	SUBOPTIMISED	SUBPOTENCY	SUBSATURATED	SUBSESSILE
SUBMISSNESS	SUBOPTIMISES	SUBPREFECT	SUBSATURATION	SUBSHRUBBY

S

SUBSIDENCE
SUBSIDENCES
SUBSIDENCIES
SUBSIDENCY
SUBSIDIARIAT
SUBSIDIARIATS
SUBSIDIARIES
SUBSIDIARILY
SUBSIDIARINESS
SUBSIDIARITIES
SUBSIDIARITY
SUBSIDIARY
SUBSIDISABLE
SUBSIDISATION
SUBSIDISATIONS
SUBSIDISED
SUBSIDISER
SUBSIDISERS
SUBSIDISES
SUBSIDISING
SUBSIDIZABLE
SUBSIDIZATION
SUBSIDIZATIONS
SUBSIDIZED
SUBSIDIZER
SUBSIDIZERS
SUBSIDIZES
SUBSIDIZING
SUBSISTENCE
SUBSISTENCES
SUBSISTENT
SUBSISTENTIAL
SUBSISTERS
SUBSISTING
SUBSOCIALLY
SUBSOCIETIES
SUBSOCIETY
SUBSOILERS
SUBSOILING
SUBSOILINGS
SUBSONICALLY
SUBSPECIALISE
SUBSPECIALISED
SUBSPECIALISES
SUBSPECIALISING
SUBSPECIALIST
SUBSPECIALISTS

SUBSPECIALITIES
SUBSPECIALITY
SUBSPECIALIZE
SUBSPECIALIZED
SUBSPECIALIZES
SUBSPECIALIZING
SUBSPECIALTIES
SUBSPECIALTY
SUBSPECIES
SUBSPECIFIC
SUBSPECIFICALLY
SUBSPINOUS
SUBSPONTANEOUS
SUBSTANCELESS
SUBSTANCES
SUBSTANDARD
SUBSTANTIAL
SUBSTANTIALISE
SUBSTANTIALISED
SUBSTANTIALISES
SUBSTANTIALISM
SUBSTANTIALISMS
SUBSTANTIALIST
SUBSTANTIALISTS
SUBSTANTIALITY
SUBSTANTIALIZE
SUBSTANTIALIZED
SUBSTANTIALIZES
SUBSTANTIALLY
SUBSTANTIALNESS
SUBSTANTIALS
SUBSTANTIATE
SUBSTANTIATED
SUBSTANTIATES
SUBSTANTIATING
SUBSTANTIATION
SUBSTANTIATIONS
SUBSTANTIATIVE
SUBSTANTIATOR
SUBSTANTIATORS
SUBSTANTIVAL
SUBSTANTIVALLY
SUBSTANTIVE
SUBSTANTIVELY
SUBSTANTIVENESS
SUBSTANTIVES
SUBSTANTIVISE

SUBSTANTIVISED
SUBSTANTIVISES
SUBSTANTIVISING
SUBSTANTIVITIES
SUBSTANTIVITY
SUBSTANTIVIZE
SUBSTANTIVIZED
SUBSTANTIVIZES
SUBSTANTIVIZING
SUBSTATION
SUBSTATIONS
SUBSTELLAR
SUBSTERNAL
SUBSTITUENT
SUBSTITUENTS
SUBSTITUTABLE
SUBSTITUTE
SUBSTITUTED
SUBSTITUTES
SUBSTITUTING
SUBSTITUTION
SUBSTITUTIONAL
SUBSTITUTIONARY
SUBSTITUTIONS
SUBSTITUTIVE
SUBSTITUTIVELY
SUBSTITUTIVITY
SUBSTRACTED
SUBSTRACTING
SUBSTRACTION
SUBSTRACTIONS
SUBSTRACTOR
SUBSTRACTORS
SUBSTRACTS
SUBSTRATAL
SUBSTRATES
SUBSTRATIVE
SUBSTRATOSPHERE
SUBSTRATUM
SUBSTRATUMS
SUBSTRUCTED
SUBSTRUCTING
SUBSTRUCTION
SUBSTRUCTIONS
SUBSTRUCTS
SUBSTRUCTURAL
SUBSTRUCTURE

SUBSTRUCTURES
SUBSULTIVE
SUBSULTORILY
SUBSULTORY
SUBSULTUSES
SUBSUMABLE
SUBSUMPTION
SUBSUMPTIONS
SUBSUMPTIVE
SUBSURFACE
SUBSURFACES
SUBSYSTEMS
SUBTACKSMAN
SUBTACKSMEN
SUBTANGENT
SUBTANGENTS
SUBTEMPERATE
SUBTENANCIES
SUBTENANCY
SUBTENANTS
SUBTENDING
SUBTENURES
SUBTERFUGE
SUBTERFUGES
SUBTERMINAL
SUBTERNATURAL
SUBTERRAIN
SUBTERRAINS
SUBTERRANE
SUBTERRANEAN
SUBTERRANEANLY
SUBTERRANEANS
SUBTERRANEOUS
SUBTERRANEOUSLY
SUBTERRANES
SUBTERRENE
SUBTERRENES
SUBTERRESTRIAL
SUBTERRESTRIALS
SUBTEXTUAL
SUBTHERAPEUTIC
SUBTHRESHOLD
SUBTILENESS
SUBTILENESSES
SUBTILISATION
SUBTILISATIONS
SUBTILISED

SUBTILISER
SUBTILISERS
SUBTILISES
SUBTILISIN
SUBTILISING
SUBTILISINS
SUBTILITIES
SUBTILIZATION
SUBTILIZATIONS
SUBTILIZED
SUBTILIZER
SUBTILIZERS
SUBTILIZES
SUBTILIZING
SUBTILTIES
SUBTITLING
SUBTITLINGS
SUBTITULAR
SUBTLENESS
SUBTLENESSES
SUBTLETIES
SUBTOTALED
SUBTOTALING
SUBTOTALLED
SUBTOTALLING
SUBTOTALLY
SUBTRACTED
SUBTRACTER
SUBTRACTERS
SUBTRACTING
SUBTRACTION
SUBTRACTIONS
SUBTRACTIVE
SUBTRACTOR
SUBTRACTORS
SUBTRAHEND
SUBTRAHENDS
SUBTREASURER
SUBTREASURERS
SUBTREASURIES
SUBTREASURY
SUBTRIANGULAR
SUBTRIPLICATE
SUBTROPICAL
SUBTROPICALLY
SUBTROPICS
SUBTRUDING

S

SUBTYPICAL	SUBVOCALISE	SUCCINCTER	SUDATORIES	SUFFRAGANSHIPS
SUBUMBRELLA	SUBVOCALISED	SUCCINCTEST	SUDATORIUM	SUFFRAGETTE
SUBUMBRELLAR	SUBVOCALISES	SUCCINCTLY	SUDATORIUMS	SUFFRAGETTES
SUBUMBRELLAS	SUBVOCALISING	SUCCINCTNESS	SUDDENNESS	SUFFRAGETTISM
SUBUNGULATE	SUBVOCALIZATION	SUCCINCTNESSES	SUDDENNESSES	SUFFRAGETTISMS
SUBUNGULATES	SUBVOCALIZE	SUCCINCTORIA	SUDDENTIES	SUFFRAGISM
SUBURBANISATION	SUBVOCALIZED	SUCCINCTORIES	SUDORIFEROUS	SUFFRAGISMS
SUBURBANISE	SUBVOCALIZES	SUCCINCTORIUM	SUDORIFICS	SUFFRAGIST
SUBURBANISED	SUBVOCALIZING	SUCCINCTORIUMS	SUDORIPAROUS	SUFFRAGISTS
SUBURBANISES	SUBVOCALLY	SUCCINCTORY	SUEABILITIES	SUFFRUTESCENT
SUBURBANISING	SUBWARDENS	SUCCINITES	SUEABILITY	SUFFRUTICOSE
SUBURBANISM	SUBWOOFERS	SUCCINYLCHOLINE	SUFFERABLE	SUFFUMIGATE
SUBURBANISMS	SUBWRITERS	SUCCORABLE	SUFFERABLENESS	SUFFUMIGATED
SUBURBANITE	SUCCEDANEA	SUCCORLESS	SUFFERABLY	SUFFUMIGATES
SUBURBANITES	SUCCEDANEOUS	SUCCOTASHES	SUFFERANCE	SUFFUMIGATING
SUBURBANITIES	SUCCEDANEUM	SUCCOURABLE	SUFFERANCES	SUFFUMIGATION
SUBURBANITY	SUCCEDANEUMS	SUCCOURERS	SUFFERINGLY	SUFFUMIGATIONS
SUBURBANIZATION	SUCCEDENTS	SUCCOURING	SUFFERINGS	SUFFUSIONS
SUBURBANIZE	SUCCEEDABLE	SUCCOURLESS	SUFFICIENCE	SUGARALLIE
SUBURBANIZED	SUCCEEDERS	SUCCUBUSES	SUFFICIENCES	SUGARALLIES
SUBURBANIZES	SUCCEEDING	SUCCULENCE	SUFFICIENCIES	SUGARBERRIES
SUBURBANIZING	SUCCEEDINGLY	SUCCULENCES	SUFFICIENCY	SUGARBERRY
SUBURBICARIAN	SUCCENTORS	SUCCULENCIES	SUFFICIENT	SUGARBUSHES
SUBVARIETIES	SUCCENTORSHIP	SUCCULENCY	SUFFICIENTLY	SUGARCANES
SUBVARIETY	SUCCENTORSHIPS	SUCCULENTLY	SUFFICIENTS	SUGARCOATED
SUBVASSALS	SUCCESSANTLY	SUCCULENTS	SUFFICINGNESS	SUGARCOATING
SUBVENTION	SUCCESSFUL	SUCCUMBERS	SUFFICINGNESSES	SUGARCOATS
SUBVENTIONARY	SUCCESSFULLY	SUCCUMBING	SUFFIGANCE	SUGARHOUSE
SUBVENTIONS	SUCCESSFULNESS	SUCCURSALE	SUFFIGANCES	SUGARHOUSES
SUBVERSALS	SUCCESSION	SUCCURSALES	SUFFISANCE	SUGARINESS
SUBVERSING	SUCCESSIONAL	SUCCURSALS	SUFFISANCES	SUGARINESSES
SUBVERSION	SUCCESSIONALLY	SUCCUSSATION	SUFFIXATION	SUGARLOAVES
SUBVERSIONARIES	SUCCESSIONIST	SUCCUSSATIONS	SUFFIXATIONS	SUGARPLUMS
SUBVERSIONARY	SUCCESSIONISTS	SUCCUSSING	SUFFIXIONS	SUGGESTERS
SUBVERSIONS	SUCCESSIONLESS	SUCCUSSION	SUFFLATING	SUGGESTIBILITY
SUBVERSIVE	SUCCESSIONS	SUCCUSSIONS	SUFFLATION	SUGGESTIBLE
SUBVERSIVELY	SUCCESSIVE	SUCCUSSIVE	SUFFLATIONS	SUGGESTIBLENESS
SUBVERSIVENESS	SUCCESSIVELY	SUCHNESSES	SUFFOCATED	SUGGESTIBLY
SUBVERSIVES	SUCCESSIVENESS	SUCKERFISH	SUFFOCATES	SUGGESTING
SUBVERTEBRAL	SUCCESSLESS	SUCKERFISHES	SUFFOCATING	SUGGESTION
SUBVERTERS	SUCCESSLESSLY	SUCKFISHES	SUFFOCATINGLY	SUGGESTIONISE
SUBVERTICAL	SUCCESSLESSNESS	SUCKHOLING	SUFFOCATINGS	SUGGESTIONISED
SUBVERTING	SUCCESSORAL	SUCRALFATE	SUFFOCATION	SUGGESTIONISES
SUBVIRUSES	SUCCESSORS	SUCRALFATES	SUFFOCATIONS	SUGGESTIONISING
SUBVISIBLE	SUCCESSORSHIP	SUCRALOSES	SUFFOCATIVE	SUGGESTIONISM
SUBVITREOUS	SUCCESSORSHIPS	SUCTIONING	SUFFRAGANS	SUGGESTIONISMS
SUBVOCALISATION	SUCCINATES	SUCTORIANS	SUFFRAGANSHIP	SUGGESTIONIST

S

SUGGESTIONISTS	SULFONAMIDES	SULPHATASES	SULPHURISED	SUMMERIEST
SUGGESTIONIZE	SULFONATED	SULPHATHIAZOLE	SULPHURISES	SUMMERINESS
SUGGESTIONIZED	SULFONATES	SULPHATHIAZOLES	SULPHURISING	SUMMERINESSES
SUGGESTIONIZES	SULFONATING	SULPHATING	SULPHURIZATION	SUMMERINGS
SUGGESTIONIZING	SULFONATION	SULPHATION	SULPHURIZATIONS	SUMMERLESS
SUGGESTIONS	SULFONATIONS	SULPHATIONS	SULPHURIZE	SUMMERLIKE
SUGGESTIVE	SULFONIUMS	SULPHHYDRYL	SULPHURIZED	SUMMERLONG
SUGGESTIVELY	SULFONMETHANE	SULPHHYDRYLS	SULPHURIZES	SUMMERSAULT
SUGGESTIVENESS	SULFONMETHANES	SULPHINPYRAZONE	SULPHURIZING	SUMMERSAULTED
SUICIDALLY	SULFONYLUREA	SULPHINYLS	SULPHUROUS	SUMMERSAULTING
SUICIDOLOGIES	SULFONYLUREAS	SULPHONAMIDE	SULPHUROUSLY	SUMMERSAULTS
SUICIDOLOGIST	SULFOXIDES	SULPHONAMIDES	SULPHUROUSNESS	SUMMERSETS
SUICIDOLOGISTS	SULFURATED	SULPHONATE	SULPHURWORT	SUMMERSETTED
SUICIDOLOGY	SULFURATES	SULPHONATED	SULPHURWORTS	SUMMERSETTING
SUITABILITIES	SULFURATING	SULPHONATES	SULPHURYLS	SUMMERTIDE
SUITABILITY	SULFURATION	SULPHONATING	SULTANATES	SUMMERTIDES
SUITABLENESS	SULFURATIONS	SULPHONATION	SULTANESSES	SUMMERTIME
SUITABLENESSES	SULFUREOUS	SULPHONATIONS	SULTANSHIP	SUMMERTIMES
SUITRESSES	SULFURETED	SULPHONIUM	SULTANSHIPS	SUMMERWEIGHT
SULCALISED	SULFURETING	SULPHONIUMS	SULTRINESS	SUMMERWOOD
SULCALISES	SULFURETTED	SULPHONMETHANE	SULTRINESSES	SUMMERWOODS
SULCALISING	SULFURETTING	SULPHONMETHANES	SUMBITCHES	SUMMITEERS
SULCALIZED	SULFURISATION	SULPHONYLS	SUMMABILITIES	SUMMITLESS
SULCALIZES	SULFURISATIONS	SULPHONYLUREA	SUMMABILITY	SUMMITRIES
SULCALIZING	SULFURISED	SULPHONYLUREAS	SUMMARINESS	SUMMONABLE
SULCATIONS	SULFURISES	SULPHOXIDE	SUMMARINESSES	SUMMONSING
SULFACETAMIDE	SULFURISING	SULPHOXIDES	SUMMARISABLE	SUMPHISHNESS
SULFACETAMIDES	SULFURIZATION	SULPHURATE	SUMMARISATION	SUMPHISHNESSES
SULFADIAZINE	SULFURIZATIONS	SULPHURATED	SUMMARISATIONS	SUMPSIMUSES
SULFADIAZINES	SULFURIZED	SULPHURATES	SUMMARISED	SUMPTUOSITIES
SULFADIMIDINE	SULFURIZES	SULPHURATING	SUMMARISER	SUMPTUOSITY
SULFADIMIDINES	SULFURIZING	SULPHURATION	SUMMARISERS	SUMPTUOUSLY
SULFADOXINE	SULFUROUSLY	SULPHURATIONS	SUMMARISES	SUMPTUOUSNESS
SULFADOXINES	SULFUROUSNESS	SULPHURATOR	SUMMARISING	SUMPTUOUSNESSES
SULFAMETHAZINE	SULFUROUSNESSES	SULPHURATORS	SUMMARISTS	SUNBATHERS
SULFAMETHAZINES	SULKINESSES	SULPHUREOUS	SUMMARIZABLE	SUNBATHING
SULFANILAMIDE	SULLENNESS	SULPHUREOUSLY	SUMMARIZATION	SUNBATHINGS
SULFANILAMIDES	SULLENNESSES	SULPHUREOUSNESS	SUMMARIZATIONS	SUNBERRIES
SULFATASES	SULPHACETAMIDE	SULPHURETED	SUMMARIZED	SUNBONNETED
SULFATHIAZOLE	SULPHACETAMIDES	SULPHURETING	SUMMARIZER	SUNBONNETS
SULFATHIAZOLES	SULPHADIAZINE	SULPHURETS	SUMMARIZERS	SUNBURNING
SULFATIONS	SULPHADIAZINES	SULPHURETTED	SUMMARIZES	SUNDERABLE
SULFHYDRYL	SULPHADOXINE	SULPHURETTING	SUMMARIZING	SUNDERANCE
SULFHYDRYLS	SULPHADOXINES	SULPHURING	SUMMATIONAL	SUNDERANCES
SULFINPYRAZONE	SULPHANILAMIDE	SULPHURISATION	SUMMATIONS	SUNDERINGS
SULFINPYRAZONES	SULPHANILAMIDES	SULPHURISATIONS	SUMMERHOUSE	SUNDERMENT
SULFONAMIDE	SULPHATASE	SULPHURISE	SUMMERHOUSES	SUNDERMENTS

S

SUNDOWNERS
SUNDOWNING
SUNDRENCHED
SUNDRESSES
SUNFLOWERS
SUNGAZINGS
SUNGLASSES
SUNLESSNESS
SUNLESSNESSES
SUNLOUNGER
SUNLOUNGERS
SUNNINESSES
SUNPORCHES
SUNRISINGS
SUNSCREENING
SUNSCREENINGS
SUNSCREENS
SUNSEEKERS
SUNSETTING
SUNSETTINGS
SUNSPOTTED
SUNSTROKES
SUNTANNING
SUNTANNINGS
SUNWORSHIPPER
SUNWORSHIPPERS
SUOVETAURILIA
SUOVETAURILIAS
SUPERABILITIES
SUPERABILITY
SUPERABLENESS
SUPERABLENESSES
SUPERABOUND
SUPERABOUNDED
SUPERABOUNDING
SUPERABOUNDS
SUPERABSORBENT
SUPERABSORBENTS
SUPERABUNDANCE
SUPERABUNDANCES
SUPERABUNDANT
SUPERABUNDANTLY
SUPERACHIEVER
SUPERACHIEVERS
SUPERACTIVE
SUPERACTIVITIES
SUPERACTIVITY

SUPERACUTE
SUPERADDED
SUPERADDING
SUPERADDITION
SUPERADDITIONAL
SUPERADDITIONS
SUPERAGENCIES
SUPERAGENCY
SUPERAGENT
SUPERAGENTS
SUPERALLOY
SUPERALLOYS
SUPERALTAR
SUPERALTARS
SUPERALTERN
SUPERALTERNS
SUPERAMBITIOUS
SUPERANNUABLE
SUPERANNUATE
SUPERANNUATED
SUPERANNUATES
SUPERANNUATING
SUPERANNUATION
SUPERANNUATIONS
SUPERATHLETE
SUPERATHLETES
SUPERATING
SUPERATION
SUPERATIONS
SUPERATOMS
SUPERBANKS
SUPERBAZAAR
SUPERBAZAARS
SUPERBAZAR
SUPERBAZARS
SUPERBIKES
SUPERBITCH
SUPERBITCHES
SUPERBITIES
SUPERBLOCK
SUPERBLOCKS
SUPERBNESS
SUPERBNESSES
SUPERBOARD
SUPERBOARDS
SUPERBOMBER
SUPERBOMBERS

SUPERBOMBS
SUPERBRAIN
SUPERBRAINS
SUPERBRATS
SUPERBRIGHT
SUPERBUREAUCRAT
SUPERCABINET
SUPERCABINETS
SUPERCALENDER
SUPERCALENDERED
SUPERCALENDERS
SUPERCARGO
SUPERCARGOES
SUPERCARGOS
SUPERCARGOSHIP
SUPERCARGOSHIPS
SUPERCARRIER
SUPERCARRIERS
SUPERCAUTIOUS
SUPERCEDED
SUPERCEDES
SUPERCEDING
SUPERCELESTIAL
SUPERCELLS
SUPERCENTER
SUPERCENTERS
SUPERCHARGE
SUPERCHARGED
SUPERCHARGER
SUPERCHARGERS
SUPERCHARGES
SUPERCHARGING
SUPERCHERIE
SUPERCHERIES
SUPERCHURCH
SUPERCHURCHES
SUPERCILIARIES
SUPERCILIARY
SUPERCILIOUS
SUPERCILIOUSLY
SUPERCITIES
SUPERCIVILISED
SUPERCIVILIZED
SUPERCLASS
SUPERCLASSES
SUPERCLEAN
SUPERCLUBS

SUPERCLUSTER
SUPERCLUSTERS
SUPERCOILED
SUPERCOILING
SUPERCOILS
SUPERCOLLIDER
SUPERCOLLIDERS
SUPERCOLOSSAL
SUPERCOLUMNAR
SUPERCOMPUTER
SUPERCOMPUTERS
SUPERCOMPUTING
SUPERCOMPUTINGS
SUPERCONDUCT
SUPERCONDUCTED
SUPERCONDUCTING
SUPERCONDUCTION
SUPERCONDUCTIVE
SUPERCONDUCTOR
SUPERCONDUCTORS
SUPERCONDUCTS
SUPERCONFIDENCE
SUPERCONFIDENT
SUPERCONTINENT
SUPERCONTINENTS
SUPERCONVENIENT
SUPERCOOLED
SUPERCOOLING
SUPERCOOLS
SUPERCOVER
SUPERCOVERS
SUPERCRIMINAL
SUPERCRIMINALS
SUPERCRITICAL
SUPERCURRENT
SUPERCURRENTS
SUPERDAINTIER
SUPERDAINTIEST
SUPERDAINTY
SUPERDELEGATE
SUPERDELEGATES
SUPERDELUXE
SUPERDENSE
SUPERDIPLOMAT
SUPERDIPLOMATS
SUPERDOMINANT
SUPERDOMINANTS

SUPEREFFECTIVE
SUPEREFFICIENCY
SUPEREFFICIENT
SUPEREGOIST
SUPEREGOISTS
SUPERELASTIC
SUPERELEVATE
SUPERELEVATED
SUPERELEVATES
SUPERELEVATING
SUPERELEVATION
SUPERELEVATIONS
SUPERELITE
SUPEREMINENCE
SUPEREMINENCES
SUPEREMINENT
SUPEREMINENTLY
SUPEREROGANT
SUPEREROGATE
SUPEREROGATED
SUPEREROGATES
SUPEREROGATING
SUPEREROGATION
SUPEREROGATIONS
SUPEREROGATIVE
SUPEREROGATOR
SUPEREROGATORS
SUPEREROGATORY
SUPERESSENTIAL
SUPERETTES
SUPEREVIDENT
SUPEREXALT
SUPEREXALTATION
SUPEREXALTED
SUPEREXALTING
SUPEREXALTS
SUPEREXCELLENCE
SUPEREXCELLENT
SUPEREXPENSIVE
SUPEREXPRESS
SUPEREXPRESSES
SUPERFAMILIES
SUPERFAMILY
SUPERFARMS
SUPERFATTED
SUPERFECTA
SUPERFECTAS

S

SUPERFEMALE	SUPERGENES	SUPERHUMANIZE	SUPERIORITIES	SUPERMILITANT
SUPERFEMALES	SUPERGIANT	SUPERHUMANIZED	SUPERIORITY	SUPERMILITANTS
SUPERFETATE	SUPERGIANTS	SUPERHUMANIZES	SUPERIORLY	SUPERMINDS
SUPERFETATED	SUPERGLACIAL	SUPERHUMANIZING	SUPERIORSHIP	SUPERMINIS
SUPERFETATES	SUPERGLUED	SUPERHUMANLY	SUPERIORSHIPS	SUPERMINISTER
SUPERFETATING	SUPERGLUEING	SUPERHUMANNESS	SUPERJACENT	SUPERMINISTERS
SUPERFETATION	SUPERGLUES	SUPERHUMERAL	SUPERJOCKS	SUPERMODEL
SUPERFETATIONS	SUPERGLUING	SUPERHUMERALS	SUPERJUMBO	SUPERMODELS
SUPERFICIAL	SUPERGOVERNMENT	SUPERHYPED	SUPERJUMBOS	SUPERMODERN
SUPERFICIALISE	SUPERGRAPHICS	SUPERHYPES	SUPERKINGDOM	SUPERMOTOS
SUPERFICIALISED	SUPERGRASS	SUPERHYPING	SUPERKINGDOMS	SUPERMUNDANE
SUPERFICIALISES	SUPERGRASSES	SUPERIMPORTANT	SUPERLARGE	SUPERNACULA
SUPERFICIALITY	SUPERGRAVITIES	SUPERIMPOSABLE	SUPERLATIVE	SUPERNACULAR
SUPERFICIALIZE	SUPERGRAVITY	SUPERIMPOSE	SUPERLATIVELY	SUPERNACULUM
SUPERFICIALIZED	SUPERGROUP	SUPERIMPOSED	SUPERLATIVENESS	SUPERNALLY
SUPERFICIALIZES	SUPERGROUPS	SUPERIMPOSES	SUPERLATIVES	SUPERNANNIES
SUPERFICIALLY	SUPERGROWTH	SUPERIMPOSING	SUPERLAWYER	SUPERNANNY
SUPERFICIALNESS	SUPERGROWTHS	SUPERIMPOSITION	SUPERLAWYERS	SUPERNATANT
SUPERFICIALS	SUPERHARDEN	SUPERINCUMBENCE	SUPERLIGHT	SUPERNATANTS
SUPERFICIES	SUPERHARDENED	SUPERINCUMBENCY	SUPERLINER	SUPERNATATION
SUPERFINENESS	SUPERHARDENING	SUPERINCUMBENT	SUPERLINERS	SUPERNATATIONS
SUPERFINENESSES	SUPERHARDENS	SUPERINDIVIDUAL	SUPERLOADS	SUPERNATED
SUPERFIRMS	SUPERHEATED	SUPERINDUCE	SUPERLOBBYIST	SUPERNATES
SUPERFIXES	SUPERHEATER	SUPERINDUCED	SUPERLOBBYISTS	SUPERNATING
SUPERFLACK	SUPERHEATERS	SUPERINDUCEMENT	SUPERLOYALIST	SUPERNATION
SUPERFLACKS	SUPERHEATING	SUPERINDUCES	SUPERLOYALISTS	SUPERNATIONAL
SUPERFLUID	SUPERHEATS	SUPERINDUCING	SUPERLUMINAL	SUPERNATIONALLY
SUPERFLUIDITIES	SUPERHEAVIES	SUPERINDUCTION	SUPERLUNAR	SUPERNATIONS
SUPERFLUIDITY	SUPERHEAVY	SUPERINDUCTIONS	SUPERLUNARY	SUPERNATURAL
SUPERFLUIDS	SUPERHELICAL	SUPERINFECT	SUPERLUXURIES	SUPERNATURALISE
SUPERFLUITIES	SUPERHELICES	SUPERINFECTED	SUPERLUXURIOUS	SUPERNATURALISM
SUPERFLUITY	SUPERHELIX	SUPERINFECTING	SUPERLUXURY	SUPERNATURALIST
SUPERFLUOUS	SUPERHELIXES	SUPERINFECTION	SUPERLYING	SUPERNATURALIZE
SUPERFLUOUSLY	SUPERHEROES	SUPERINFECTIONS	SUPERMACHO	SUPERNATURALLY
SUPERFLUOUSNESS	SUPERHEROINE	SUPERINFECTS	SUPERMAJORITIES	SUPERNATURALS
SUPERFLUXES	SUPERHEROINES	SUPERINSULATED	SUPERMAJORITY	SUPERNATURE
SUPERFOETATION	SUPERHETERODYNE	SUPERINTEND	SUPERMALES	SUPERNATURES
SUPERFOETATIONS	SUPERHIGHWAY	SUPERINTENDED	SUPERMARKET	SUPERNORMAL
SUPERFOODS	SUPERHIGHWAYS	SUPERINTENDENCE	SUPERMARKETS	SUPERNORMALITY
SUPERFRONTAL	SUPERHIVES	SUPERINTENDENCY	SUPERMARTS	SUPERNORMALLY
SUPERFRONTALS	SUPERHUMAN	SUPERINTENDENT	SUPERMASCULINE	SUPERNOVAE
SUPERFUNDS	SUPERHUMANISE	SUPERINTENDENTS	SUPERMASSIVE	SUPERNOVAS
SUPERFUSED	SUPERHUMANISED	SUPERINTENDING	SUPERMAXES	SUPERNUMERARIES
SUPERFUSES	SUPERHUMANISES	SUPERINTENDS	SUPERMEMBRANE	SUPERNUMERARY
SUPERFUSING	SUPERHUMANISING	SUPERINTENSITY	SUPERMEMBRANES	SUPERNURSE
SUPERFUSION	SUPERHUMANITIES	SUPERIORESS	SUPERMICRO	SUPERNURSES
SUPERFUSIONS	SUPERHUMANITY	SUPERIORESSES	SUPERMICROS	SUPERNUTRIENT

SUPERNUTRIENTS	SUPERPHYSICAL	SUPERSAFETIES	SUPERSEDURES	SUPERSTIMULATE
SUPERNUTRITION	SUPERPIMPS	SUPERSAFETY	SUPERSELLER	SUPERSTIMULATED
SUPERNUTRITIONS	SUPERPLANE	SUPERSALES	SUPERSELLERS	SUPERSTIMULATES
SUPEROCTAVE	SUPERPLANES	SUPERSALESMAN	SUPERSELLING	SUPERSTITION
SUPEROCTAVES	SUPERPLASTIC	SUPERSALESMEN	SUPERSELLS	SUPERSTITIONS
SUPERORDER	SUPERPLASTICITY	SUPERSALTS	SUPERSENSIBLE	SUPERSTITIOUS
SUPERORDERS	SUPERPLASTICS	SUPERSATURATE	SUPERSENSIBLY	SUPERSTITIOUSLY
SUPERORDINAL	SUPERPLAYER	SUPERSATURATED	SUPERSENSITIVE	SUPERSTOCK
SUPERORDINARY	SUPERPLAYERS	SUPERSATURATES	SUPERSENSORY	SUPERSTOCKS
SUPERORDINATE	SUPERPLUSES	SUPERSATURATING	SUPERSENSUAL	SUPERSTORE
SUPERORDINATED	SUPERPOLITE	SUPERSATURATION	SUPERSESSION	SUPERSTORES
SUPERORDINATES	SUPERPOLYMER	SUPERSAURS	SUPERSESSIONS	SUPERSTORM
SUPERORDINATING	SUPERPOLYMERS	SUPERSAVER	SUPERSEXES	SUPERSTORMS
SUPERORDINATION	SUPERPORTS	SUPERSAVERS	SUPERSEXUALITY	SUPERSTRATA
SUPERORGANIC	SUPERPOSABLE	SUPERSCALAR	SUPERSHARP	SUPERSTRATUM
SUPERORGANICISM	SUPERPOSED	SUPERSCALE	SUPERSHOWS	SUPERSTRATUMS
SUPERORGANICIST	SUPERPOSES	SUPERSCHOOL	SUPERSINGER	SUPERSTRENGTH
SUPERORGANISM	SUPERPOSING	SUPERSCHOOLS	SUPERSINGERS	SUPERSTRENGTHS
SUPERORGANISMS	SUPERPOSITION	SUPERSCOUT	SUPERSIZED	SUPERSTRIKE
SUPERORGASM	SUPERPOSITIONS	SUPERSCOUTS	SUPERSIZES	SUPERSTRIKES
SUPERORGASMS	SUPERPOWER	SUPERSCREEN	SUPERSIZING	SUPERSTRING
SUPEROVULATE	SUPERPOWERED	SUPERSCREENS	SUPERSLEUTH	SUPERSTRINGS
SUPEROVULATED	SUPERPOWERFUL	SUPERSCRIBE	SUPERSLEUTHS	SUPERSTRONG
SUPEROVULATES	SUPERPOWERS	SUPERSCRIBED	SUPERSLICK	SUPERSTRUCT
SUPEROVULATING	SUPERPRAISE	SUPERSCRIBES	SUPERSMART	SUPERSTRUCTED
SUPEROVULATION	SUPERPRAISED	SUPERSCRIBING	SUPERSMOOTH	SUPERSTRUCTING
SUPEROVULATIONS	SUPERPRAISES	SUPERSCRIPT	SUPERSONIC	SUPERSTRUCTION
SUPEROXIDE	SUPERPRAISING	SUPERSCRIPTION	SUPERSONICALLY	SUPERSTRUCTIONS
SUPEROXIDES	SUPERPREMIUM	SUPERSCRIPTIONS	SUPERSONICS	SUPERSTRUCTIVE
SUPERPARASITISM	SUPERPREMIUMS	SUPERSCRIPTS	SUPERSOUND	SUPERSTRUCTS
SUPERPARTICLE	SUPERPROFIT	SUPERSECRECIES	SUPERSOUNDS	SUPERSTRUCTURAL
SUPERPARTICLES	SUPERPROFITS	SUPERSECRECY	SUPERSPECIAL	SUPERSTRUCTURE
SUPERPATRIOT	SUPERQUALITIES	SUPERSECRET	SUPERSPECIALIST	SUPERSTRUCTURES
SUPERPATRIOTIC	SUPERQUALITY	SUPERSECRETS	SUPERSPECIALS	SUPERSTUDS
SUPERPATRIOTISM	SUPERRACES	SUPERSEDABLE	SUPERSPECIES	SUPERSUBTILE
SUPERPATRIOTS	SUPERREALISM	SUPERSEDEAS	SUPERSPECTACLE	SUPERSUBTLE
SUPERPERSON	SUPERREALISMS	SUPERSEDEASES	SUPERSPECTACLES	SUPERSUBTLETIES
SUPERPERSONAL	SUPERREALIST	SUPERSEDED	SUPERSPEED	SUPERSUBTLETY
SUPERPERSONS	SUPERREALISTS	SUPERSEDENCE	SUPERSPEEDS	SUPERSURGEON
SUPERPHENOMENA	SUPERREFINE	SUPERSEDENCES	SUPERSPIES	SUPERSURGEONS
SUPERPHENOMENON	SUPERREFINED	SUPERSEDER	SUPERSTARDOM	SUPERSWEET
SUPERPHONE	SUPERREFINES	SUPERSEDERE	SUPERSTARDOMS	SUPERSYMMETRIC
SUPERPHONES	SUPERREFINING	SUPERSEDERES	SUPERSTARS	SUPERSYMMETRIES
SUPERPHOSPHATE	SUPERREGIONAL	SUPERSEDERS	SUPERSTATE	SUPERSYMMETRY
SUPERPHOSPHATES	SUPERREGIONALS	SUPERSEDES	SUPERSTATES	SUPERSYSTEM
SUPERPHYLA	SUPERROADS	SUPERSEDING	SUPERSTATION	SUPERSYSTEMS
SUPERPHYLUM	SUPERROMANTIC	SUPERSEDURE	SUPERSTATIONS	SUPERTANKER

S

SUPERTANKERS	SUPERVOLUTE	SUPPLETIVE	SUPPOSITION	SUPRAMAXILLARY
SUPERTAXES	SUPERWAIFS	SUPPLETIVES	SUPPOSITIONAL	SUPRAMOLECULAR
SUPERTEACHER	SUPERWAVES	SUPPLETORILY	SUPPOSITIONALLY	SUPRAMOLECULE
SUPERTEACHERS	SUPERWEAPON	SUPPLETORY	SUPPOSITIONARY	SUPRAMOLECULES
SUPERTERRANEAN	SUPERWEAPONS	SUPPLIABLE	SUPPOSITIONLESS	SUPRAMUNDANE
SUPERTERRIFIC	SUPERWEEDS	SUPPLIANCE	SUPPOSITIONS	SUPRANATIONAL
SUPERTHICK	SUPERWIDES	SUPPLIANCES	SUPPOSITIOUS	SUPRANATIONALLY
SUPERTHRILLER	SUPERWIVES	SUPPLIANTLY	SUPPOSITIOUSLY	SUPRAOPTIC
SUPERTHRILLERS	SUPERWOMAN	SUPPLIANTS	SUPPOSITITIOUS	SUPRAORBITAL
SUPERTIGHT	SUPERWOMEN	SUPPLICANT	SUPPOSITIVE	SUPRAPUBIC
SUPERTITLE	SUPINATING	SUPPLICANTS	SUPPOSITIVELY	SUPRARATIONAL
SUPERTITLES	SUPINATION	SUPPLICATE	SUPPOSITIVES	SUPRARENAL
SUPERTONIC	SUPINATIONS	SUPPLICATED	SUPPOSITORIES	SUPRARENALS
SUPERTONICS	SUPINATORS	SUPPLICATES	SUPPOSITORY	SUPRASEGMENTAL
SUPERTRAMS	SUPINENESS	SUPPLICATING	SUPPRESSANT	SUPRASENSIBLE
SUPERTRUCK	SUPINENESSES	SUPPLICATINGLY	SUPPRESSANTS	SUPRATEMPORAL
SUPERTRUCKS	SUPPEAGOES	SUPPLICATION	SUPPRESSED	SUPRAVITAL
SUPERTWIST	SUPPEDANEA	SUPPLICATIONS	SUPPRESSEDLY	SUPRAVITALLY
SUPERTWISTS	SUPPEDANEUM	SUPPLICATORY	SUPPRESSER	SUPREMACIES
SUPERUSERS	SUPPERLESS	SUPPLICATS	SUPPRESSERS	SUPREMACISM
SUPERVENED	SUPPERTIME	SUPPLICAVIT	SUPPRESSES	SUPREMACISMS
SUPERVENES	SUPPERTIMES	SUPPLICAVITS	SUPPRESSIBILITY	SUPREMACIST
SUPERVENIENCE	SUPPLANTATION	SUPPLYMENT	SUPPRESSIBLE	SUPREMACISTS
SUPERVENIENCES	SUPPLANTATIONS	SUPPLYMENTS	SUPPRESSING	SUPREMATISM
SUPERVENIENT	SUPPLANTED	SUPPORTABILITY	SUPPRESSION	SUPREMATISMS
SUPERVENING	SUPPLANTER	SUPPORTABLE	SUPPRESSIONS	SUPREMATIST
SUPERVENTION	SUPPLANTERS	SUPPORTABLENESS	SUPPRESSIVE	SUPREMATISTS
SUPERVENTIONS	SUPPLANTING	SUPPORTABLY	SUPPRESSIVENESS	SUPREMENESS
SUPERVIRILE	SUPPLEJACK	SUPPORTANCE	SUPPRESSOR	SUPREMENESSES
SUPERVIRTUOSI	SUPPLEJACKS	SUPPORTANCES	SUPPRESSORS	SUPREMITIES
SUPERVIRTUOSO	SUPPLEMENT	SUPPORTERS	SUPPURATED	SURADDITION
SUPERVIRTUOSOS	SUPPLEMENTAL	SUPPORTING	SUPPURATES	SURADDITIONS
SUPERVIRULENT	SUPPLEMENTALLY	SUPPORTINGS	SUPPURATING	SURBASEMENT
SUPERVISAL	SUPPLEMENTALS	SUPPORTIVE	SUPPURATION	SURBASEMENTS
SUPERVISALS	SUPPLEMENTARIES	SUPPORTIVELY	SUPPURATIONS	SURBEDDING
SUPERVISED	SUPPLEMENTARILY	SUPPORTIVENESS	SUPPURATIVE	SURCEASING
SUPERVISEE	SUPPLEMENTARY	SUPPORTLESS	SUPPURATIVES	SURCHARGED
SUPERVISEES	SUPPLEMENTATION	SUPPORTMENT	SUPRACHIASMIC	SURCHARGEMENT
SUPERVISES	SUPPLEMENTED	SUPPORTMENTS	SUPRACILIARY	SURCHARGEMENTS
SUPERVISING	SUPPLEMENTER	SUPPORTRESS	SUPRACOSTAL	SURCHARGER
SUPERVISION	SUPPLEMENTERS	SUPPORTRESSES	SUPRACRUSTAL	SURCHARGERS
SUPERVISIONS	SUPPLEMENTING	SUPPORTURE	SUPRAGLOTTAL	SURCHARGES
SUPERVISOR	SUPPLEMENTS	SUPPORTURES	SUPRALAPSARIAN	SURCHARGING
SUPERVISORS	SUPPLENESS	SUPPOSABLE	SUPRALAPSARIANS	SURCINGLED
SUPERVISORSHIP	SUPPLENESSES	SUPPOSABLY	SUPRALIMINAL	SURCINGLES
SUPERVISORSHIPS	SUPPLETION	SUPPOSEDLY	SUPRALIMINALLY	SURCINGLING
SUPERVISORY	SUPPLETIONS	SUPPOSINGS	SUPRALUNAR	SURCULUSES

S

SUREFOOTED	SURMOUNTED	SURRENDEREE	SURVIVALISMS	SUSPENSIVE
SUREFOOTEDLY	SURMOUNTER	SURRENDEREES	SURVIVALIST	SUSPENSIVELY
SUREFOOTEDNESS	SURMOUNTERS	SURRENDERER	SURVIVALISTS	SUSPENSIVENESS
SURENESSES	SURMOUNTING	SURRENDERERS	SURVIVANCE	SUSPENSOID
SURETYSHIP	SURMOUNTINGS	SURRENDERING	SURVIVANCES	SUSPENSOIDS
SURETYSHIPS	SURMULLETS	SURRENDEROR	SURVIVORSHIP	SUSPENSORIA
SURFACELESS	SURNOMINAL	SURRENDERORS	SURVIVORSHIPS	SUSPENSORIAL
SURFACEMAN	SURPASSABLE	SURRENDERS	SUSCEPTANCE	SUSPENSORIES
SURFACEMEN	SURPASSERS	SURRENDRIES	SUSCEPTANCES	SUSPENSORIUM
SURFACINGS	SURPASSING	SURREPTITIOUS	SUSCEPTIBILITY	SUSPENSORS
SURFACTANT	SURPASSINGLY	SURREPTITIOUSLY	SUSCEPTIBLE	SUSPENSORY
SURFACTANTS	SURPASSINGNESS	SURROGACIES	SUSCEPTIBLENESS	SUSPERCOLLATE
SURFBOARDED	SURPLUSAGE	SURROGATED	SUSCEPTIBLY	SUSPERCOLLATED
SURFBOARDER	SURPLUSAGES	SURROGATES	SUSCEPTIVE	SUSPERCOLLATES
SURFBOARDERS	SURPLUSING	SURROGATESHIP	SUSCEPTIVENESS	SUSPERCOLLATING
SURFBOARDING	SURPLUSSED	SURROGATESHIPS	SUSCEPTIVITIES	SUSPICIONAL
SURFBOARDINGS	SURPLUSSES	SURROGATING	SUSCEPTIVITY	SUSPICIONED
SURFBOARDS	SURPLUSSING	SURROGATION	SUSCEPTORS	SUSPICIONING
SURFCASTER	SURPRINTED	SURROGATIONS	SUSCIPIENT	SUSPICIONLESS
SURFCASTERS	SURPRINTING	SURROGATUM	SUSCIPIENTS	SUSPICIONS
SURFCASTING	SURPRISALS	SURROGATUMS	SUSCITATED	SUSPICIOUS
SURFCASTINGS	SURPRISEDLY	SURROUNDED	SUSCITATES	SUSPICIOUSLY
SURFEITERS	SURPRISERS	SURROUNDING	SUSCITATING	SUSPICIOUSNESS
SURFEITING	SURPRISING	SURROUNDINGS	SUSCITATION	SUSPIRATION
SURFEITINGS	SURPRISINGLY	SURTARBRAND	SUSCITATIONS	SUSPIRATIONS
SURFFISHES	SURPRISINGNESS	SURTARBRANDS	SUSPECTABLE	SUSPIRIOUS
SURFPERCHES	SURPRISINGS	SURTURBRAND	SUSPECTEDLY	SUSTAINABILITY
SURFRIDDEN	SURPRIZING	SURTURBRANDS	SUSPECTEDNESS	SUSTAINABLE
SURFRIDERS	SURQUEDIES	SURVEILING	SUSPECTEDNESSES	SUSTAINABLY
SURFRIDING	SURQUEDRIES	SURVEILLANCE	SUSPECTERS	SUSTAINEDLY
SURFRIDINGS	SURREALISM	SURVEILLANCES	SUSPECTFUL	SUSTAINERS
SURGEONCIES	SURREALISMS	SURVEILLANT	SUSPECTING	SUSTAINING
SURGEONFISH	SURREALIST	SURVEILLANTS	SUSPECTLESS	SUSTAININGLY
SURGEONFISHES	SURREALISTIC	SURVEILLED	SUSPENDERED	SUSTAININGS
SURGEONSHIP	SURREALISTS	SURVEILLES	SUSPENDERS	SUSTAINMENT
SURGEONSHIPS	SURREBUTTAL	SURVEILLING	SUSPENDIBILITY	SUSTAINMENTS
SURGICALLY	SURREBUTTALS	SURVEYABLE	SUSPENDIBLE	SUSTENANCE
SURJECTION	SURREBUTTED	SURVEYANCE	SUSPENDING	SUSTENANCES
SURJECTIONS	SURREBUTTER	SURVEYANCES	SUSPENSEFUL	SUSTENTACULA
SURJECTIVE	SURREBUTTERS	SURVEYINGS	SUSPENSEFULLY	SUSTENTACULAR
SURLINESSES	SURREBUTTING	SURVEYORSHIP	SUSPENSEFULNESS	SUSTENTACULUM
SURMASTERS	SURREJOINDER	SURVEYORSHIPS	SUSPENSELESS	SUSTENTATE
SURMISABLE	SURREJOINDERS	SURVIEWING	SUSPENSERS	SUSTENTATED
SURMISINGS	SURREJOINED	SURVIVABILITIES	SUSPENSIBILITY	SUSTENTATES
SURMISTRESS	SURREJOINING	SURVIVABILITY	SUSPENSIBLE	SUSTENTATING
SURMISTRESSES	SURREJOINS	SURVIVABLE	SUSPENSION	SUSTENTATION
SURMOUNTABLE	SURRENDERED	SURVIVALISM	SUSPENSIONS	SUSTENTATIONS

S

SUSTENTATIVE
SUSTENTATOR
SUSTENTATORS
SUSTENTION
SUSTENTIONS
SUSTENTIVE
SUSURRATED
SUSURRATES
SUSURRATING
SUSURRATION
SUSURRATIONS
SUSURRUSES
SUTLERSHIP
SUTLERSHIPS
SUTTEEISMS
SUTTLETIES
SUTURATION
SUTURATIONS
SUZERAINTIES
SUZERAINTY
SVARABHAKTI
SVARABHAKTIS
SVELTENESS
SVELTENESSES
SWAGGERERS
SWAGGERING
SWAGGERINGLY
SWAGGERINGS
SWAINISHNESS
SWAINISHNESSES
SWALLOWABLE
SWALLOWERS
SWALLOWING
SWALLOWTAIL
SWALLOWTAILS
SWALLOWWORT
SWALLOWWORTS
SWAMPINESS
SWAMPINESSES
SWAMPLANDS
SWANKINESS
SWANKINESSES
SWANNERIES
SWANSDOWNS
SWARAJISMS
SWARAJISTS
SWARTHIEST

SWARTHINESS
SWARTHINESSES
SWARTHNESS
SWARTHNESSES
SWARTNESSES
SWASHBUCKLE
SWASHBUCKLED
SWASHBUCKLER
SWASHBUCKLERS
SWASHBUCKLES
SWASHBUCKLING
SWASHWORKS
SWATCHBOOK
SWATCHBOOKS
SWATHEABLE
SWATTERING
SWAYBACKED
SWEARWORDS
SWEATBANDS
SWEATBOXES
SWEATERDRESS
SWEATERDRESSES
SWEATINESS
SWEATINESSES
SWEATPANTS
SWEATSHIRT
SWEATSHIRTS
SWEATSHOPS
SWEATSUITS
SWEEPBACKS
SWEEPINGLY
SWEEPINGNESS
SWEEPINGNESSES
SWEEPSTAKE
SWEEPSTAKES
SWEETBREAD
SWEETBREADS
SWEETBRIAR
SWEETBRIARS
SWEETBRIER
SWEETBRIERS
SWEETCORNS
SWEETENERS
SWEETENING
SWEETENINGS
SWEETFISHES
SWEETHEART

SWEETHEARTED
SWEETHEARTING
SWEETHEARTINGS
SWEETHEARTS
SWEETIEWIFE
SWEETIEWIVES
SWEETISHLY
SWEETISHNESS
SWEETISHNESSES
SWEETMEATS
SWEETNESSES
SWEETSHOPS
SWEETVELDS
SWEETWATER
SWEETWATERS
SWEETWOODS
SWEIRNESSES
SWELLFISHES
SWELLHEADED
SWELLHEADEDNESS
SWELLHEADS
SWELLINGLY
SWELTERING
SWELTERINGLY
SWELTERINGS
SWELTRIEST
SWEPTWINGS
SWERVELESS
SWIFTNESSES
SWIMFEEDER
SWIMFEEDERS
SWIMMERETS
SWIMMINGLY
SWIMMINGNESS
SWIMMINGNESSES
SWINDLINGS
SWINEHERDS
SWINEHOODS
SWINEPOXES
SWINESTONE
SWINESTONES
SWINGBEATS
SWINGBOATS
SWINGEINGLY
SWINGINGEST
SWINGINGLY
SWINGLETREE

SWINGLETREES
SWINGLINGS
SWINGOMETER
SWINGOMETERS
SWINGTREES
SWINISHNESS
SWINISHNESSES
SWIRLINGLY
SWISHINGLY
SWITCHABLE
SWITCHBACK
SWITCHBACKED
SWITCHBACKING
SWITCHBACKS
SWITCHBLADE
SWITCHBLADES
SWITCHBOARD
SWITCHBOARDS
SWITCHEROO
SWITCHEROOS
SWITCHGEAR
SWITCHGEARS
SWITCHGIRL
SWITCHGIRLS
SWITCHGRASS
SWITCHGRASSES
SWITCHIEST
SWITCHINGS
SWITCHLIKE
SWITCHOVER
SWITCHOVERS
SWITCHYARD
SWITCHYARDS
SWITHERING
SWIVELBLOCK
SWIVELBLOCKS
SWIVELLING
SWOLLENNESS
SWOLLENNESSES
SWOONINGLY
SWOOPSTAKE
SWORDBEARER
SWORDBEARERS
SWORDBILLS
SWORDCRAFT
SWORDCRAFTS
SWORDFISHES

SWORDPLAYER
SWORDPLAYERS
SWORDPLAYS
SWORDPROOF
SWORDSMANSHIP
SWORDSMANSHIPS
SWORDSTICK
SWORDSTICKS
SWORDSWOMAN
SWORDSWOMEN
SWORDTAILS
SYBARITICAL
SYBARITICALLY
SYBARITISH
SYBARITISM
SYBARITISMS
SYCOPHANCIES
SYCOPHANCY
SYCOPHANTIC
SYCOPHANTICAL
SYCOPHANTICALLY
SYCOPHANTISE
SYCOPHANTISED
SYCOPHANTISES
SYCOPHANTISH
SYCOPHANTISHLY
SYCOPHANTISING
SYCOPHANTISM
SYCOPHANTISMS
SYCOPHANTIZE
SYCOPHANTIZED
SYCOPHANTIZES
SYCOPHANTIZING
SYCOPHANTLY
SYCOPHANTRIES
SYCOPHANTRY
SYCOPHANTS
SYLLABARIA
SYLLABARIES
SYLLABARIUM
SYLLABICAL
SYLLABICALLY
SYLLABICATE
SYLLABICATED
SYLLABICATES
SYLLABICATING
SYLLABICATION

S

SYLLABICATIONS	SYLVICULTURE	SYMMETRICAL	SYMPHILISM	SYNADELPHITES
SYLLABICITIES	SYLVICULTURES	SYMMETRICALLY	SYMPHILISMS	SYNAERESES
SYLLABICITY	SYLVINITES	SYMMETRICALNESS	SYMPHILOUS	SYNAERESIS
SYLLABIFICATION	SYMBIONTIC	SYMMETRIES	SYMPHONICALLY	SYNAESTHESES
SYLLABIFIED	SYMBIONTICALLY	SYMMETRISATION	SYMPHONIES	SYNAESTHESIA
SYLLABIFIES	SYMBIOTICAL	SYMMETRISATIONS	SYMPHONION	SYNAESTHESIAS
SYLLABIFYING	SYMBIOTICALLY	SYMMETRISE	SYMPHONIONS	SYNAESTHESIS
SYLLABISED	SYMBOLICAL	SYMMETRISED	SYMPHONIOUS	SYNAESTHETIC
SYLLABISES	SYMBOLICALLY	SYMMETRISES	SYMPHONIOUSLY	SYNAGOGICAL
SYLLABISING	SYMBOLICALNESS	SYMMETRISING	SYMPHONIST	SYNAGOGUES
SYLLABISMS	SYMBOLISATION	SYMMETRIZATION	SYMPHONISTS	SYNALEPHAS
SYLLABIZED	SYMBOLISATIONS	SYMMETRIZATIONS	SYMPHYLOUS	SYNALLAGMATIC
SYLLABIZES	SYMBOLISED	SYMMETRIZE	SYMPHYSEAL	SYNALOEPHA
SYLLABIZING	SYMBOLISER	SYMMETRIZED	SYMPHYSEOTOMIES	SYNALOEPHAS
SYLLABLING	SYMBOLISERS	SYMMETRIZES	SYMPHYSEOTOMY	SYNANDRIUM
SYLLABOGRAM	SYMBOLISES	SYMMETRIZING	SYMPHYSIAL	SYNANDROUS
SYLLABOGRAMS	SYMBOLISING	SYMMETROPHOBIA	SYMPHYSIOTOMIES	SYNANTHEROUS
SYLLABOGRAPHIES	SYMBOLISMS	SYMMETROPHOBIAS	SYMPHYSIOTOMY	SYNANTHESES
SYLLABOGRAPHY	SYMBOLISTIC	SYMPATHECTOMIES	SYMPHYSTIC	SYNANTHESIS
SYLLABUSES	SYMBOLISTICAL	SYMPATHECTOMY	SYMPIESOMETER	SYNANTHETIC
SYLLEPTICAL	SYMBOLISTICALLY	SYMPATHETIC	SYMPIESOMETERS	SYNANTHIES
SYLLEPTICALLY	SYMBOLISTS	SYMPATHETICAL	SYMPLASTIC	SYNANTHOUS
SYLLOGISATION	SYMBOLIZATION	SYMPATHETICALLY	SYMPODIALLY	SYNAPHEIAS
SYLLOGISATIONS	SYMBOLIZATIONS	SYMPATHETICS	SYMPOSIACS	SYNAPOSEMATIC
SYLLOGISED	SYMBOLIZED	SYMPATHIES	SYMPOSIARCH	SYNAPOSEMATISM
SYLLOGISER	SYMBOLIZER	SYMPATHINS	SYMPOSIARCHS	SYNAPOSEMATISMS
SYLLOGISERS	SYMBOLIZERS	SYMPATHIQUE	SYMPOSIAST	SYNAPTASES
SYLLOGISES	SYMBOLIZES	SYMPATHISE	SYMPOSIASTS	SYNAPTICAL
SYLLOGISING	SYMBOLIZING	SYMPATHISED	SYMPOSIUMS	SYNAPTICALLY
SYLLOGISMS	SYMBOLLING	SYMPATHISER	SYMPTOMATIC	SYNAPTOSOMAL
SYLLOGISTIC	SYMBOLOGICAL	SYMPATHISERS	SYMPTOMATICAL	SYNAPTOSOME
SYLLOGISTICAL	SYMBOLOGIES	SYMPATHISES	SYMPTOMATICALLY	SYNAPTOSOMES
SYLLOGISTICALLY	SYMBOLOGIST	SYMPATHISING	SYMPTOMATISE	SYNARCHIES
SYLLOGISTICS	SYMBOLOGISTS	SYMPATHIZE	SYMPTOMATISED	SYNARTHRODIAL
SYLLOGISTS	SYMBOLOGRAPHIES	SYMPATHIZED	SYMPTOMATISES	SYNARTHRODIALLY
SYLLOGIZATION	SYMBOLOGRAPHY	SYMPATHIZER	SYMPTOMATISING	SYNARTHROSES
SYLLOGIZATIONS	SYMBOLOLATRIES	SYMPATHIZERS	SYMPTOMATIZE	SYNARTHROSIS
SYLLOGIZED	SYMBOLOLATRY	SYMPATHIZES	SYMPTOMATIZED	SYNASTRIES
SYLLOGIZER	SYMBOLOLOGIES	SYMPATHIZING	SYMPTOMATIZES	SYNAXARION
SYLLOGIZERS	SYMBOLOLOGY	SYMPATHOLYTIC	SYMPTOMATIZING	SYNBIOTICS
SYLLOGIZES	SYMMETALISM	SYMPATHOLYTICS	SYMPTOMATOLOGIC	SYNCARPIES
SYLLOGIZING	SYMMETALISMS	SYMPATHOMIMETIC	SYMPTOMATOLOGY	SYNCARPOUS
SYLPHIDINE	SYMMETALLIC	SYMPATRICALLY	SYMPTOMLESS	SYNCHONDROSES
SYLVANITES	SYMMETALLISM	SYMPATRIES	SYMPTOMOLOGICAL	SYNCHONDROSIS
SYLVESTRAL	SYMMETALLISMS	SYMPETALIES	SYMPTOMOLOGIES	SYNCHORESES
SYLVESTRIAN	SYMMETRIAN	SYMPETALOUS	SYMPTOMOLOGY	SYNCHORESIS
SYLVICULTURAL	SYMMETRIANS	SYMPHILIES	SYNADELPHITE	SYNCHROFLASH

S

SYNCHROFLASHES
SYNCHROMESH
SYNCHROMESHES
SYNCHRONAL
SYNCHRONEITIES
SYNCHRONEITY
SYNCHRONIC
SYNCHRONICAL
SYNCHRONICALLY
SYNCHRONICITIES
SYNCHRONICITY
SYNCHRONIES
SYNCHRONISATION
SYNCHRONISE
SYNCHRONISED
SYNCHRONISER
SYNCHRONISERS
SYNCHRONISES
SYNCHRONISING
SYNCHRONISM
SYNCHRONISMS
SYNCHRONISTIC
SYNCHRONISTICAL
SYNCHRONIZATION
SYNCHRONIZE
SYNCHRONIZED
SYNCHRONIZER
SYNCHRONIZERS
SYNCHRONIZES
SYNCHRONIZING
SYNCHRONOLOGIES
SYNCHRONOLOGY
SYNCHRONOSCOPE
SYNCHRONOSCOPES
SYNCHRONOUS
SYNCHRONOUSLY
SYNCHRONOUSNESS
SYNCHROSCOPE
SYNCHROSCOPES
SYNCHROTRON
SYNCHROTRONS
SYNCLASTIC
SYNCLINALS
SYNCLINORIA
SYNCLINORIUM
SYNCOPATED
SYNCOPATES

SYNCOPATING
SYNCOPATION
SYNCOPATIONS
SYNCOPATIVE
SYNCOPATOR
SYNCOPATORS
SYNCRETISATION
SYNCRETISATIONS
SYNCRETISE
SYNCRETISED
SYNCRETISES
SYNCRETISING
SYNCRETISM
SYNCRETISMS
SYNCRETIST
SYNCRETISTIC
SYNCRETISTS
SYNCRETIZATION
SYNCRETIZATIONS
SYNCRETIZE
SYNCRETIZED
SYNCRETIZES
SYNCRETIZING
SYNDACTYLIES
SYNDACTYLISM
SYNDACTYLISMS
SYNDACTYLOUS
SYNDACTYLS
SYNDACTYLY
SYNDERESES
SYNDERESIS
SYNDESISES
SYNDESMOSES
SYNDESMOSIS
SYNDESMOTIC
SYNDETICAL
SYNDETICALLY
SYNDICALISM
SYNDICALISMS
SYNDICALIST
SYNDICALISTIC
SYNDICALISTS
SYNDICATED
SYNDICATES
SYNDICATING
SYNDICATION
SYNDICATIONS

SYNDICATOR
SYNDICATORS
SYNDICSHIP
SYNDICSHIPS
SYNDIOTACTIC
SYNDYASMIAN
SYNECDOCHE
SYNECDOCHES
SYNECDOCHIC
SYNECDOCHICAL
SYNECDOCHICALLY
SYNECDOCHISM
SYNECDOCHISMS
SYNECOLOGIC
SYNECOLOGICAL
SYNECOLOGICALLY
SYNECOLOGIES
SYNECOLOGIST
SYNECOLOGISTS
SYNECOLOGY
SYNECPHONESES
SYNECPHONESIS
SYNECTICALLY
SYNEIDESES
SYNEIDESIS
SYNERGETIC
SYNERGETICALLY
SYNERGICALLY
SYNERGISED
SYNERGISES
SYNERGISING
SYNERGISMS
SYNERGISTIC
SYNERGISTICALLY
SYNERGISTS
SYNERGIZED
SYNERGIZES
SYNERGIZING
SYNESTHESIA
SYNESTHESIAS
SYNESTHETIC
SYNGENESES
SYNGENESIOUS
SYNGENESIS
SYNGENETIC
SYNGNATHOUS
SYNKARYONIC

SYNKARYONS
SYNODICALLY
SYNOECETES
SYNOECIOSES
SYNOECIOSIS
SYNOECIOUS
SYNOECISED
SYNOECISES
SYNOECISING
SYNOECISMS
SYNOECIZED
SYNOECIZES
SYNOECIZING
SYNOECOLOGIES
SYNOECOLOGY
SYNOEKETES
SYNONYMATIC
SYNONYMICAL
SYNONYMICON
SYNONYMICONS
SYNONYMIES
SYNONYMISE
SYNONYMISED
SYNONYMISES
SYNONYMISING
SYNONYMIST
SYNONYMISTS
SYNONYMITIES
SYNONYMITY
SYNONYMIZE
SYNONYMIZED
SYNONYMIZES
SYNONYMIZING
SYNONYMOUS
SYNONYMOUSLY
SYNONYMOUSNESS
SYNOPSISED
SYNOPSISES
SYNOPSISING
SYNOPSIZED
SYNOPSIZES
SYNOPSIZING
SYNOPTICAL
SYNOPTICALLY
SYNOPTISTIC
SYNOPTISTS
SYNOSTOSES

SYNOSTOSIS
SYNOVIALLY
SYNOVITISES
SYNSEPALOUS
SYNTACTICAL
SYNTACTICALLY
SYNTACTICS
SYNTAGMATA
SYNTAGMATIC
SYNTAGMATITE
SYNTAGMATITES
SYNTECTICAL
SYNTENOSES
SYNTENOSIS
SYNTERESES
SYNTERESIS
SYNTEXISES
SYNTHESISATION
SYNTHESISATIONS
SYNTHESISE
SYNTHESISED
SYNTHESISER
SYNTHESISERS
SYNTHESISES
SYNTHESISING
SYNTHESIST
SYNTHESISTS
SYNTHESIZATION
SYNTHESIZATIONS
SYNTHESIZE
SYNTHESIZED
SYNTHESIZER
SYNTHESIZERS
SYNTHESIZES
SYNTHESIZING
SYNTHESPIAN
SYNTHESPIANS
SYNTHETASE
SYNTHETASES
SYNTHETICAL
SYNTHETICALLY
SYNTHETICISM
SYNTHETICISMS
SYNTHETICS
SYNTHETISATION
SYNTHETISATIONS
SYNTHETISE

SYNTHETISED
SYNTHETISER
SYNTHETISERS
SYNTHETISES
SYNTHETISING
SYNTHETISM
SYNTHETISMS
SYNTHETIST
SYNTHETISTS
SYNTHETIZATION
SYNTHETIZATIONS
SYNTHETIZE
SYNTHETIZED
SYNTHETIZER
SYNTHETIZERS
SYNTHETIZES
SYNTHETIZING
SYNTHRONUS
SYNTONICALLY
SYNTONISED
SYNTONISES

SYNTONISING
SYNTONIZED
SYNTONIZES
SYNTONIZING
SYPHERINGS
SYPHILISATION
SYPHILISATIONS
SYPHILISED
SYPHILISES
SYPHILISING
SYPHILITIC
SYPHILITICALLY
SYPHILITICS
SYPHILIZATION
SYPHILIZATIONS
SYPHILIZED
SYPHILIZES
SYPHILIZING
SYPHILOLOGIES
SYPHILOLOGIST
SYPHILOLOGISTS

SYPHILOLOGY
SYPHILOMAS
SYPHILOMATA
SYPHILOPHOBIA
SYPHILOPHOBIAS
SYRINGITIS
SYRINGITISES
SYRINGOMYELIA
SYRINGOMYELIAS
SYRINGOMYELIC
SYRINGOTOMIES
SYRINGOTOMY
SYSSARCOSES
SYSSARCOSIS
SYSSARCOTIC
SYSTEMATIC
SYSTEMATICAL
SYSTEMATICALLY
SYSTEMATICIAN
SYSTEMATICIANS
SYSTEMATICNESS

SYSTEMATICS
SYSTEMATISATION
SYSTEMATISE
SYSTEMATISED
SYSTEMATISER
SYSTEMATISERS
SYSTEMATISES
SYSTEMATISING
SYSTEMATISM
SYSTEMATISMS
SYSTEMATIST
SYSTEMATISTS
SYSTEMATIZATION
SYSTEMATIZE
SYSTEMATIZED
SYSTEMATIZER
SYSTEMATIZERS
SYSTEMATIZES
SYSTEMATIZING
SYSTEMATOLOGIES
SYSTEMATOLOGY

SYSTEMICALLY
SYSTEMISATION
SYSTEMISATIONS
SYSTEMISED
SYSTEMISER
SYSTEMISERS
SYSTEMISES
SYSTEMISING
SYSTEMIZATION
SYSTEMIZATIONS
SYSTEMIZED
SYSTEMIZER
SYSTEMIZERS
SYSTEMIZES
SYSTEMIZING
SYSTEMLESS
SYZYGETICALLY

S

T

TABASHEERS
TABBOULEHS
TABBYHOODS
TABEFACTION
TABEFACTIONS
TABELLIONS
TABERNACLE
TABERNACLED
TABERNACLES
TABERNACLING
TABERNACULAR
TABESCENCE
TABESCENCES
TABLANETTE
TABLANETTES
TABLATURES
TABLECLOTH
TABLECLOTHS
TABLELANDS
TABLEMATES
TABLESPOON
TABLESPOONFUL
TABLESPOONFULS
TABLESPOONS
TABLESPOONSFUL
TABLETOPPED
TABLETTING
TABLEWARES
TABOGGANED
TABOGGANING
TABOPARESES
TABOPARESIS
TABULARISATION
TABULARISATIONS
TABULARISE
TABULARISED
TABULARISES
TABULARISING
TABULARIZATION
TABULARIZATIONS
TABULARIZE

TABULARIZED
TABULARIZES
TABULARIZING
TABULATING
TABULATION
TABULATIONS
TABULATORS
TABULATORY
TACAMAHACS
TACHEOMETER
TACHEOMETERS
TACHEOMETRIC
TACHEOMETRICAL
TACHEOMETRIES
TACHEOMETRY
TACHISTOSCOPE
TACHISTOSCOPES
TACHISTOSCOPIC
TACHOGRAMS
TACHOGRAPH
TACHOGRAPHS
TACHOMETER
TACHOMETERS
TACHOMETRIC
TACHOMETRICAL
TACHOMETRICALLY
TACHOMETRIES
TACHOMETRY
TACHYARRHYTHMIA
TACHYCARDIA
TACHYCARDIAC
TACHYCARDIAS
TACHYGRAPH
TACHYGRAPHER
TACHYGRAPHERS
TACHYGRAPHIC
TACHYGRAPHICAL
TACHYGRAPHIES
TACHYGRAPHIST
TACHYGRAPHISTS
TACHYGRAPHS

TACHYGRAPHY
TACHYLITES
TACHYLITIC
TACHYLYTES
TACHYLYTIC
TACHYMETER
TACHYMETERS
TACHYMETRIC
TACHYMETRICAL
TACHYMETRICALLY
TACHYMETRIES
TACHYMETRY
TACHYPHASIA
TACHYPHASIAS
TACHYPHRASIA
TACHYPHRASIAS
TACHYPHYLAXES
TACHYPHYLAXIS
TACHYPNEAS
TACHYPNOEA
TACHYPNOEAS
TACITNESSES
TACITURNITIES
TACITURNITY
TACITURNLY
TACKBOARDS
TACKIFIERS
TACKIFYING
TACKINESSES
TACMAHACKS
TACTFULNESS
TACTFULNESSES
TACTICALLY
TACTICIANS
TACTICITIES
TACTILISTS
TACTILITIES
TACTLESSLY
TACTLESSNESS
TACTLESSNESSES
TACTUALITIES

TACTUALITY
TAEKWONDOS
TAENIACIDE
TAENIACIDES
TAENIAFUGE
TAENIAFUGES
TAFFETASES
TAFFETISED
TAFFETIZED
TAGLIARINI
TAGLIARINIS
TAGLIATELLE
TAGLIATELLES
TAHSILDARS
TAIKONAUTS
TAILBOARDS
TAILCOATED
TAILENDERS
TAILGATERS
TAILGATING
TAILGATINGS
TAILHOPPING
TAILHOPPINGS
TAILLESSLY
TAILLESSNESS
TAILLESSNESSES
TAILLIGHTS
TAILORBIRD
TAILORBIRDS
TAILORESSES
TAILORINGS
TAILORMADE
TAILORMAKE
TAILORMAKES
TAILORMAKING
TAILPIECES
TAILPIPING
TAILPLANES
TAILSLIDES
TAILSPINNED
TAILSPINNING

TAILSTOCKS
TAILWATERS
TAILWHEELS
TAINTLESSLY
TAKINGNESS
TAKINGNESSES
TALBOTYPES
TALEBEARER
TALEBEARERS
TALEBEARING
TALEBEARINGS
TALEGALLAS
TALENTLESS
TALETELLER
TALETELLERS
TALETELLING
TALETELLINGS
TALISMANIC
TALISMANICAL
TALISMANICALLY
TALKABILITIES
TALKABILITY
TALKATHONS
TALKATIVELY
TALKATIVENESS
TALKATIVENESSES
TALKINESSES
TALLGRASSES
TALLIATING
TALLNESSES
TALLYHOING
TALLYSHOPS
TALLYWOMAN
TALLYWOMEN
TALMUDISMS
TAMABILITIES
TAMABILITY
TAMABLENESS
TAMABLENESSES
TAMARILLOS
TAMBOURERS

TAMBOURINE	TANTALISATION	TAPSALTEERIE	TARNATIONS	TASTELESSLY
TAMBOURINES	TANTALISATIONS	TAPSALTEERIES	TARNISHABLE	TASTELESSNESS
TAMBOURING	TANTALISED	TAPSIETEERIE	TARNISHERS	TASTELESSNESSES
TAMBOURINIST	TANTALISER	TAPSIETEERIES	TARNISHING	TASTEMAKER
TAMBOURINISTS	TANTALISERS	TAPSTRESSES	TARPAULING	TASTEMAKERS
TAMBOURINS	TANTALISES	TARABISHES	TARPAULINGS	TASTINESSES
TAMEABILITIES	TANTALISING	TARADIDDLE	TARPAULINS	TATAHASHES
TAMEABILITY	TANTALISINGLY	TARADIDDLES	TARRADIDDLE	TATPURUSHA
TAMEABLENESS	TANTALISINGS	TARAMASALATA	TARRADIDDLES	TATPURUSHAS
TAMEABLENESSES	TANTALISMS	TARAMASALATAS	TARRIANCES	TATTERDEMALION
TAMELESSNESS	TANTALITES	TARANTARAED	TARRINESSES	TATTERDEMALIONS
TAMELESSNESSES	TANTALIZATION	TARANTARAING	TARSALGIAS	TATTERDEMALLION
TAMENESSES	TANTALIZATIONS	TARANTARAS	TARSOMETATARSAL	TATTERSALL
TAMOXIFENS	TANTALIZED	TARANTASES	TARSOMETATARSI	TATTERSALLS
TAMPERINGS	TANTALIZER	TARANTASSES	TARSOMETATARSUS	TATTINESSES
TAMPERPROOF	TANTALIZERS	TARANTELLA	TARTANALIA	TATTLETALE
TAMPONADES	TANTALIZES	TARANTELLAS	TARTANALIAS	TATTLETALED
TAMPONAGES	TANTALIZING	TARANTISMS	TARTANRIES	TATTLETALES
TANDEMWISE	TANTALIZINGLY	TARANTISTS	TARTAREOUS	TATTLETALING
TANGENCIES	TANTALIZINGS	TARANTULAE	TARTARISATION	TATTLINGLY
TANGENTALLY	TANTALUSES	TARANTULAS	TARTARISATIONS	TATTOOISTS
TANGENTIAL	TANTAMOUNT	TARATANTARA	TARTARISED	TAUNTINGLY
TANGENTIALITIES	TANTARARAS	TARATANTARAED	TARTARISES	TAUROBOLIA
TANGENTIALITY	TANZANITES	TARATANTARAING	TARTARISING	TAUROBOLIUM
TANGENTIALLY	TAPERINGLY	TARATANTARAS	TARTARIZATION	TAUROMACHIAN
TANGERINES	TAPERNESSES	TARAXACUMS	TARTARIZATIONS	TAUROMACHIES
TANGHININS	TAPERSTICK	TARBOGGINED	TARTARIZED	TAUROMACHY
TANGIBILITIES	TAPERSTICKS	TARBOGGINING	TARTARIZES	TAUROMORPHOUS
TANGIBILITY	TAPESCRIPT	TARBOGGINS	TARTARIZING	TAUTNESSES
TANGIBLENESS	TAPESCRIPTS	TARBOOSHES	TARTINESSES	TAUTOCHRONE
TANGIBLENESSES	TAPESTRIED	TARBOUCHES	TARTNESSES	TAUTOCHRONES
TANGINESSES	TAPESTRIES	TARBOUSHES	TARTRAZINE	TAUTOCHRONISM
TANGLEFOOT	TAPESTRYING	TARDIGRADE	TARTRAZINES	TAUTOCHRONISMS
TANGLEFOOTS	TAPHEPHOBIA	TARDIGRADES	TASEOMETER	TAUTOCHRONOUS
TANGLEMENT	TAPHEPHOBIAS	TARDINESSES	TASEOMETERS	TAUTOLOGIC
TANGLEMENTS	TAPHEPHOBIC	TARGETABLE	TASIMETERS	TAUTOLOGICAL
TANGLESOME	TAPHONOMIC	TARGETEERS	TASIMETRIC	TAUTOLOGICALLY
TANGLEWEED	TAPHONOMICAL	TARGETINGS	TASIMETRIES	TAUTOLOGIES
TANGLEWEEDS	TAPHONOMIES	TARGETITIS	TASKMASTER	TAUTOLOGISE
TANGLINGLY	TAPHONOMIST	TARGETITISES	TASKMASTERS	TAUTOLOGISED
TANISTRIES	TAPHONOMISTS	TARGETLESS	TASKMISTRESS	TAUTOLOGISES
TANKBUSTER	TAPHOPHOBIA	TARIFFICATION	TASKMISTRESSES	TAUTOLOGISING
TANKBUSTERS	TAPHOPHOBIAS	TARIFFICATIONS	TASSELLING	TAUTOLOGISM
TANKBUSTING	TAPHROGENESES	TARIFFLESS	TASSELLINGS	TAUTOLOGISMS
TANKBUSTINGS	TAPHROGENESIS	TARMACADAM	TASTEFULLY	TAUTOLOGIST
TANOREXICS	TAPOTEMENT	TARMACADAMS	TASTEFULNESS	TAUTOLOGISTS
TANTALATES	TAPOTEMENTS	TARMACKING	TASTEFULNESSES	TAUTOLOGIZE

T

TAUTOLOGIZED
TAUTOLOGIZES
TAUTOLOGIZING
TAUTOLOGOUS
TAUTOLOGOUSLY
TAUTOMERIC
TAUTOMERISM
TAUTOMERISMS
TAUTOMETRIC
TAUTOMETRICAL
TAUTONYMIC
TAUTONYMIES
TAUTONYMOUS
TAUTOPHONIC
TAUTOPHONICAL
TAUTOPHONIES
TAUTOPHONY
TAWDRINESS
TAWDRINESSES
TAWHEOWHEO
TAWHEOWHEOS
TAWNINESSES
TAXABILITIES
TAXABILITY
TAXABLENESS
TAXABLENESSES
TAXAMETERS
TAXATIONAL
TAXIDERMAL
TAXIDERMIC
TAXIDERMIES
TAXIDERMISE
TAXIDERMISED
TAXIDERMISES
TAXIDERMISING
TAXIDERMIST
TAXIDERMISTS
TAXIDERMIZE
TAXIDERMIZED
TAXIDERMIZES
TAXIDERMIZING
TAXIMETERS
TAXIPLANES
TAXONOMERS
TAXONOMICAL
TAXONOMICALLY
TAXONOMIES

TAXONOMIST
TAXONOMISTS
TAXPAYINGS
TAYASSUIDS
TAYBERRIES
TCHOTCHKES
TCHOUKBALL
TCHOUKBALLS
TEABERRIES
TEACHABILITIES
TEACHABILITY
TEACHABLENESS
TEACHABLENESSES
TEACHERLESS
TEACHERSHIP
TEACHERSHIPS
TEACUPFULS
TEACUPSFUL
TEAKETTLES
TEARFULNESS
TEARFULNESSES
TEARGASSED
TEARGASSES
TEARGASSING
TEARINESSES
TEARJERKER
TEARJERKERS
TEARLESSLY
TEARSHEETS
TEARSTAINED
TEARSTAINS
TEARSTRIPS
TEASELINGS
TEASELLERS
TEASELLING
TEASELLINGS
TEASPOONFUL
TEASPOONFULS
TEASPOONSFUL
TEATASTERS
TEAZELLING
TECHINESSES
TECHNETIUM
TECHNETIUMS
TECHNETRONIC
TECHNICALISE
TECHNICALISED

TECHNICALISES
TECHNICALISING
TECHNICALITIES
TECHNICALITY
TECHNICALIZE
TECHNICALIZED
TECHNICALIZES
TECHNICALIZING
TECHNICALLY
TECHNICALNESS
TECHNICALNESSES
TECHNICALS
TECHNICIAN
TECHNICIANS
TECHNICISE
TECHNICISED
TECHNICISES
TECHNICISING
TECHNICISM
TECHNICISMS
TECHNICIST
TECHNICISTS
TECHNICIZE
TECHNICIZED
TECHNICIZES
TECHNICIZING
TECHNICOLOUR
TECHNICOLOURED
TECHNIKONS
TECHNIQUES
TECHNOBABBLE
TECHNOBABBLES
TECHNOCRACIES
TECHNOCRACY
TECHNOCRAT
TECHNOCRATIC
TECHNOCRATS
TECHNOFEAR
TECHNOFEARS
TECHNOGRAPHIES
TECHNOGRAPHY
TECHNOJUNKIE
TECHNOJUNKIES
TECHNOLOGIC
TECHNOLOGICAL
TECHNOLOGICALLY
TECHNOLOGIES

TECHNOLOGISE
TECHNOLOGISED
TECHNOLOGISES
TECHNOLOGISING
TECHNOLOGIST
TECHNOLOGISTS
TECHNOLOGIZE
TECHNOLOGIZED
TECHNOLOGIZES
TECHNOLOGIZING
TECHNOLOGY
TECHNOMANIA
TECHNOMANIAC
TECHNOMANIACS
TECHNOMANIAS
TECHNOMUSIC
TECHNOMUSICS
TECHNOPHILE
TECHNOPHILES
TECHNOPHILIA
TECHNOPHILIAS
TECHNOPHOBE
TECHNOPHOBES
TECHNOPHOBIA
TECHNOPHOBIAS
TECHNOPHOBIC
TECHNOPHOBICS
TECHNOPOLE
TECHNOPOLES
TECHNOPOLIS
TECHNOPOLISES
TECHNOPOLITAN
TECHNOPOLITANS
TECHNOPOPS
TECHNOSPEAK
TECHNOSPEAKS
TECHNOSTRESS
TECHNOSTRESSES
TECHNOSTRUCTURE
TECTIBRANCH
TECTIBRANCHIATE
TECTIBRANCHS
TECTONICALLY
TECTONISMS
TECTRICIAL
TEDIOSITIES
TEDIOUSNESS

TEDIOUSNESSES
TEDIOUSOME
TEEMINGNESS
TEEMINGNESSES
TEENTSIEST
TEENYBOPPER
TEENYBOPPERS
TEETERBOARD
TEETERBOARDS
TEETHRIDGE
TEETHRIDGES
TEETOTALED
TEETOTALER
TEETOTALERS
TEETOTALING
TEETOTALISM
TEETOTALISMS
TEETOTALIST
TEETOTALISTS
TEETOTALLED
TEETOTALLER
TEETOTALLERS
TEETOTALLING
TEETOTALLY
TEGUMENTAL
TEGUMENTARY
TEHSILDARS
TEICHOPSIA
TEICHOPSIAS
TEINOSCOPE
TEINOSCOPES
TEKNONYMIES
TEKNONYMOUS
TELAESTHESIA
TELAESTHESIAS
TELAESTHETIC
TELANGIECTASES
TELANGIECTASIA
TELANGIECTASIAS
TELANGIECTASIS
TELANGIECTATIC
TELAUTOGRAPHIC
TELAUTOGRAPHIES
TELAUTOGRAPHY
TELEARCHICS
TELEBANKING
TELEBANKINGS

TELEBRIDGE	TELEGRAMMIC	TELEOLOGIC	TELEPHOTOGRAPHS	TELESOFTWARES
TELEBRIDGES	TELEGRAMMING	TELEOLOGICAL	TELEPHOTOGRAPHY	TELESTEREOSCOPE
TELECAMERA	TELEGRAPHED	TELEOLOGICALLY	TELEPHOTOS	TELESTHESIA
TELECAMERAS	TELEGRAPHER	TELEOLOGIES	TELEPOINTS	TELESTHESIAS
TELECASTED	TELEGRAPHERS	TELEOLOGISM	TELEPORTATION	TELESTHETIC
TELECASTER	TELEGRAPHESE	TELEOLOGISMS	TELEPORTATIONS	TELESTICHS
TELECASTERS	TELEGRAPHESES	TELEOLOGIST	TELEPORTED	TELESURGERIES
TELECASTING	TELEGRAPHIC	TELEOLOGISTS	TELEPORTING	TELESURGERY
TELECHIRIC	TELEGRAPHICALLY	TELEONOMIC	TELEPRESENCE	TELETYPESETTING
TELECOMMAND	TELEGRAPHIES	TELEONOMIES	TELEPRESENCES	TELETYPEWRITER
TELECOMMANDS	TELEGRAPHING	TELEOSAURIAN	TELEPRINTED	TELETYPEWRITERS
TELECOMMUTE	TELEGRAPHIST	TELEOSAURIANS	TELEPRINTER	TELETYPING
TELECOMMUTED	TELEGRAPHISTS	TELEOSAURS	TELEPRINTERS	TELEUTOSPORE
TELECOMMUTER	TELEGRAPHS	TELEOSTEAN	TELEPRINTING	TELEUTOSPORES
TELECOMMUTERS	TELEGRAPHY	TELEOSTEANS	TELEPRINTS	TELEUTOSPORIC
TELECOMMUTES	TELEHEALTH	TELEOSTOME	TELEPROCESSING	TELEVANGELICAL
TELECOMMUTING	TELEHEALTHS	TELEOSTOMES	TELEPROCESSINGS	TELEVANGELISM
TELECOMMUTINGS	TELEJOURNALISM	TELEOSTOMOUS	TELERECORD	TELEVANGELISMS
TELECONFERENCE	TELEJOURNALISMS	TELEPATHED	TELERECORDED	TELEVANGELIST
TELECONFERENCES	TELEJOURNALIST	TELEPATHIC	TELERECORDING	TELEVANGELISTS
TELECONNECTION	TELEJOURNALISTS	TELEPATHICALLY	TELERECORDINGS	TELEVERITE
TELECONNECTIONS	TELEKINESES	TELEPATHIES	TELERECORDS	TELEVERITES
TELECONTROL	TELEKINESIS	TELEPATHING	TELERGICALLY	TELEVIEWED
TELECONTROLS	TELEKINETIC	TELEPATHISE	TELESCIENCE	TELEVIEWER
TELECONVERTER	TELEKINETICALLY	TELEPATHISED	TELESCIENCES	TELEVIEWERS
TELECONVERTERS	TELEMARKED	TELEPATHISES	TELESCOPED	TELEVIEWING
TELECOPIES	TELEMARKETER	TELEPATHISING	TELESCOPES	TELEVIEWINGS
TELECOTTAGE	TELEMARKETERS	TELEPATHIST	TELESCOPIC	TELEVISERS
TELECOTTAGES	TELEMARKETING	TELEPATHISTS	TELESCOPICAL	TELEVISING
TELECOTTAGING	TELEMARKETINGS	TELEPATHIZE	TELESCOPICALLY	TELEVISION
TELECOTTAGINGS	TELEMARKING	TELEPATHIZED	TELESCOPIES	TELEVISIONAL
TELECOURSE	TELEMATICS	TELEPATHIZES	TELESCOPIFORM	TELEVISIONALLY
TELECOURSES	TELEMEDICINE	TELEPATHIZING	TELESCOPING	TELEVISIONARY
TELEDILDONICS	TELEMEDICINES	TELEPHEMES	TELESCOPIST	TELEVISIONS
TELEFACSIMILE	TELEMEETING	TELEPHERIQUE	TELESCOPISTS	TELEVISORS
TELEFACSIMILES	TELEMEETINGS	TELEPHERIQUES	TELESCREEN	TELEVISUAL
TELEFAXING	TELEMETERED	TELEPHONED	TELESCREENS	TELEVISUALLY
TELEFERIQUE	TELEMETERING	TELEPHONER	TELESELLING	TELEWORKED
TELEFERIQUES	TELEMETERS	TELEPHONERS	TELESELLINGS	TELEWORKER
TELEGENICALLY	TELEMETRIC	TELEPHONES	TELESERVICES	TELEWORKERS
TELEGNOSES	TELEMETRICAL	TELEPHONIC	TELESHOPPED	TELEWORKING
TELEGNOSIS	TELEMETRICALLY	TELEPHONICALLY	TELESHOPPING	TELEWORKINGS
TELEGNOSTIC	TELEMETRIES	TELEPHONIES	TELESHOPPINGS	TELEWRITER
TELEGONIES	TELENCEPHALA	TELEPHONING	TELESMATIC	TELEWRITERS
TELEGONOUS	TELENCEPHALIC	TELEPHONIST	TELESMATICAL	TELFERAGES
TELEGRAMMATIC	TELENCEPHALON	TELEPHONISTS	TELESMATICALLY	TELICITIES
TELEGRAMMED	TELENCEPHALONS	TELEPHOTOGRAPH	TELESOFTWARE	TELIOSPORE

T

TELIOSPORES	TEMPERALITIE	TEMPORISED	TENDENCIOUS	TENEBRIFIC
TELLERSHIP	TEMPERALITIES	TEMPORISER	TENDENCIOUSLY	TENEBRIONID
TELLERSHIPS	TEMPERAMENT	TEMPORISERS	TENDENCIOUSNESS	TENEBRIONIDS
TELLURATES	TEMPERAMENTAL	TEMPORISES	TENDENTIAL	TENEBRIOUS
TELLURETTED	TEMPERAMENTALLY	TEMPORISING	TENDENTIALLY	TENEBRIOUSNESS
TELLURIANS	TEMPERAMENTFUL	TEMPORISINGLY	TENDENTIOUS	TENEBRISMS
TELLURIDES	TEMPERAMENTS	TEMPORISINGS	TENDENTIOUSLY	TENEBRISTS
TELLURIONS	TEMPERANCE	TEMPORIZATION	TENDENTIOUSNESS	TENEBRITIES
TELLURISED	TEMPERANCES	TEMPORIZATIONS	TENDERABLE	TENEBROSITIES
TELLURISES	TEMPERATED	TEMPORIZED	TENDERFEET	TENEBROSITY
TELLURISING	TEMPERATELY	TEMPORIZER	TENDERFOOT	TENEBROUSNESS
TELLURITES	TEMPERATENESS	TEMPORIZERS	TENDERFOOTS	TENEBROUSNESSES
TELLURIUMS	TEMPERATENESSES	TEMPORIZES	TENDERHEARTED	TENEMENTAL
TELLURIZED	TEMPERATES	TEMPORIZING	TENDERHEARTEDLY	TENEMENTARY
TELLURIZES	TEMPERATING	TEMPORIZINGLY	TENDERINGS	TENEMENTED
TELLURIZING	TEMPERATIVE	TEMPORIZINGS	TENDERISATION	TENESMUSES
TELLUROMETER	TEMPERATURE	TEMPTABILITIES	TENDERISATIONS	TENIACIDES
TELLUROMETERS	TEMPERATURES	TEMPTABILITY	TENDERISED	TENIAFUGES
TELNETTING	TEMPERINGS	TEMPTABLENESS	TENDERISER	TENNANTITE
TELOCENTRIC	TEMPESTING	TEMPTABLENESSES	TENDERISERS	TENNANTITES
TELOCENTRICS	TEMPESTIVE	TEMPTATION	TENDERISES	TENORRHAPHIES
TELOMERASE	TEMPESTUOUS	TEMPTATIONS	TENDERISING	TENORRHAPHY
TELOMERASES	TEMPESTUOUSLY	TEMPTATIOUS	TENDERIZATION	TENOSYNOVITIS
TELOMERISATION	TEMPESTUOUSNESS	TEMPTINGLY	TENDERIZATIONS	TENOSYNOVITISES
TELOMERISATIONS	TEMPOLABILE	TEMPTINGNESS	TENDERIZED	TENOTOMIES
TELOMERIZATION	TEMPORALISE	TEMPTINGNESSES	TENDERIZER	TENOTOMIST
TELOMERIZATIONS	TEMPORALISED	TEMPTRESSES	TENDERIZERS	TENOTOMISTS
TELOPHASES	TEMPORALISES	TEMULENCES	TENDERIZES	TENOVAGINITIS
TELOPHASIC	TEMPORALISING	TEMULENCIES	TENDERIZING	TENOVAGINITISES
TELPHERAGE	TEMPORALITIES	TEMULENTLY	TENDERLING	TENPOUNDER
TELPHERAGES	TEMPORALITY	TENABILITIES	TENDERLINGS	TENPOUNDERS
TELPHERING	TEMPORALIZE	TENABILITY	TENDERLOIN	TENSENESSES
TELPHERLINE	TEMPORALIZED	TENABLENESS	TENDERLOINS	TENSIBILITIES
TELPHERLINES	TEMPORALIZES	TENABLENESSES	TENDERNESS	TENSIBILITY
TELPHERMAN	TEMPORALIZING	TENACIOUSLY	TENDERNESSES	TENSIBLENESS
TELPHERMEN	TEMPORALLY	TENACIOUSNESS	TENDEROMETER	TENSIBLENESSES
TELPHERWAY	TEMPORALNESS	TENACIOUSNESSES	TENDEROMETERS	TENSILENESS
TELPHERWAYS	TEMPORALNESSES	TENACITIES	TENDINITIS	TENSILENESSES
TEMAZEPAMS	TEMPORALTIES	TENACULUMS	TENDINITISES	TENSILITIES
TEMERARIOUS	TEMPORALTY	TENAILLONS	TENDONITIS	TENSIMETER
TEMERARIOUSLY	TEMPORANEOUS	TENANTABLE	TENDONITISES	TENSIMETERS
TEMERARIOUSNESS	TEMPORARIES	TENANTLESS	TENDOVAGINITIS	TENSIOMETER
TEMERITIES	TEMPORARILY	TENANTRIES	TENDRESSES	TENSIOMETERS
TEMEROUSLY	TEMPORARINESS	TENANTSHIP	TENDRILLAR	TENSIOMETRIC
TEMPERABILITIES	TEMPORARINESSES	TENANTSHIPS	TENDRILLED	TENSIOMETRIES
TEMPERABILITY	TEMPORISATION	TENDENCIALLY	TENDRILLOUS	TENSIOMETRY
TEMPERABLE	TEMPORISATIONS	TENDENCIES	TENDRILOUS	TENSIONALLY

TENSIONERS	TERATOLOGIST	TERMINATES	TERREPLEINS	TERRORIZES
TENSIONING	TERATOLOGISTS	TERMINATING	TERRESTRIAL	TERRORIZING
TENSIONLESS	TERATOLOGY	TERMINATION	TERRESTRIALLY	TERRORLESS
TENTACULAR	TERATOMATA	TERMINATIONAL	TERRESTRIALNESS	TERSANCTUS
TENTACULATE	TERATOMATOUS	TERMINATIONS	TERRESTRIALS	TERSANCTUSES
TENTACULIFEROUS	TERATOPHOBIA	TERMINATIVE	TERRIBILITIES	TERSENESSES
TENTACULITE	TERATOPHOBIAS	TERMINATIVELY	TERRIBILITY	TERTIARIES
TENTACULITES	TERCENTENARIES	TERMINATOR	TERRIBLENESS	TERVALENCIES
TENTACULOID	TERCENTENARY	TERMINATORS	TERRIBLENESSES	TERVALENCY
TENTACULUM	TERCENTENNIAL	TERMINATORY	TERRICOLES	TESCHENITE
TENTATIONS	TERCENTENNIALS	TERMINISMS	TERRICOLOUS	TESCHENITES
TENTATIVELY	TEREBINTHINE	TERMINISTS	TERRIFICALLY	TESSARAGLOT
TENTATIVENESS	TEREBINTHS	TERMINOLOGICAL	TERRIFIERS	TESSELATED
TENTATIVENESSES	TEREBRANTS	TERMINOLOGIES	TERRIFYING	TESSELATES
TENTATIVES	TEREBRATED	TERMINOLOGIST	TERRIFYINGLY	TESSELATING
TENTERHOOK	TEREBRATES	TERMINOLOGISTS	TERRIGENOUS	TESSELLATE
TENTERHOOKS	TEREBRATING	TERMINOLOGY	TERRITORIAL	TESSELLATED
TENTIGINOUS	TEREBRATION	TERMINUSES	TERRITORIALISE	TESSELLATES
TENTMAKERS	TEREBRATIONS	TERMITARIA	TERRITORIALISED	TESSELLATING
TENTORIUMS	TEREBRATULA	TERMITARIES	TERRITORIALISES	TESSELLATION
TENUIROSTRAL	TEREBRATULAE	TERMITARIUM	TERRITORIALISM	TESSELLATIONS
TENUOUSNESS	TEREBRATULAS	TERMITARIUMS	TERRITORIALISMS	TESSERACTS
TENUOUSNESSES	TEREPHTHALATE	TERNEPLATE	TERRITORIALIST	TESSITURAS
TENURIALLY	TEREPHTHALATES	TERNEPLATES	TERRITORIALISTS	TESTABILITIES
TEPEFACTION	TEREPHTHALIC	TEROTECHNOLOGY	TERRITORIALITY	TESTABILITY
TEPEFACTIONS	TERGIVERSANT	TERPENELESS	TERRITORIALIZE	TESTACEANS
TEPHIGRAMS	TERGIVERSANTS	TERPENOIDS	TERRITORIALIZED	TESTACEOUS
TEPHROITES	TERGIVERSATE	TERPINEOLS	TERRITORIALIZES	TESTAMENTAL
TEPHROMANCIES	TERGIVERSATED	TERPOLYMER	TERRITORIALLY	TESTAMENTAR
TEPHROMANCY	TERGIVERSATES	TERPOLYMERS	TERRITORIALS	TESTAMENTARILY
TEPIDARIUM	TERGIVERSATING	TERPSICHOREAL	TERRITORIED	TESTAMENTARY
TEPIDITIES	TERGIVERSATION	TERPSICHOREAN	TERRITORIES	TESTAMENTS
TEPIDNESSES	TERGIVERSATIONS	TERRACELESS	TERRORISATION	TESTATIONS
TERAHERTZES	TERGIVERSATOR	TERRACETTE	TERRORISATIONS	TESTATRICES
TERATOCARCINOMA	TERGIVERSATORS	TERRACETTES	TERRORISED	TESTATRIXES
TERATOGENESES	TERGIVERSATORY	TERRACINGS	TERRORISER	TESTCROSSED
TERATOGENESIS	TERMAGANCIES	TERRACOTTA	TERRORISERS	TESTCROSSES
TERATOGENIC	TERMAGANCY	TERRACOTTAS	TERRORISES	TESTCROSSING
TERATOGENICIST	TERMAGANTLY	TERRAFORMED	TERRORISING	TESTERNING
TERATOGENICISTS	TERMAGANTS	TERRAFORMING	TERRORISMS	TESTICULAR
TERATOGENICITY	TERMINABILITIES	TERRAFORMINGS	TERRORISTIC	TESTICULATE
TERATOGENIES	TERMINABILITY	TERRAFORMS	TERRORISTS	TESTICULATED
TERATOGENS	TERMINABLE	TERRAMARES	TERRORIZATION	TESTIFICATE
TERATOGENY	TERMINABLENESS	TERRAQUEOUS	TERRORIZATIONS	TESTIFICATES
TERATOLOGIC	TERMINABLY	TERRARIUMS	TERRORIZED	TESTIFICATION
TERATOLOGICAL	TERMINALLY	TERREMOTIVE	TERRORIZER	TESTIFICATIONS
TERATOLOGIES	TERMINATED	TERREPLEIN	TERRORIZERS	TESTIFICATOR

TESTIFICATORS
TESTIFICATORY
TESTIFIERS
TESTIFYING
TESTIMONIAL
TESTIMONIALISE
TESTIMONIALISED
TESTIMONIALISES
TESTIMONIALIZE
TESTIMONIALIZED
TESTIMONIALIZES
TESTIMONIALS
TESTIMONIED
TESTIMONIES
TESTIMONYING
TESTINESSES
TESTOSTERONE
TESTOSTERONES
TESTUDINAL
TESTUDINARY
TESTUDINEOUS
TESTUDINES
TETANICALLY
TETANISATION
TETANISATIONS
TETANISING
TETANIZATION
TETANIZATIONS
TETANIZING
TETARTOHEDRAL
TETARTOHEDRALLY
TETARTOHEDRISM
TETARTOHEDRISMS
TETCHINESS
TETCHINESSES
TETHERBALL
TETHERBALLS
TETRABASIC
TETRABASICITIES
TETRABASICITY
TETRABRACH
TETRABRACHS
TETRABRANCHIATE
TETRACAINE
TETRACAINES
TETRACHLORIDE
TETRACHLORIDES

TETRACHORD
TETRACHORDAL
TETRACHORDS
TETRACHOTOMIES
TETRACHOTOMOUS
TETRACHOTOMY
TETRACTINAL
TETRACTINE
TETRACYCLIC
TETRACYCLINE
TETRACYCLINES
TETRADACTYL
TETRADACTYLIES
TETRADACTYLOUS
TETRADACTYLS
TETRADACTYLY
TETRADITES
TETRADRACHM
TETRADRACHMS
TETRADYMITE
TETRADYMITES
TETRADYNAMOUS
TETRAETHYL
TETRAETHYLLEAD
TETRAETHYLLEADS
TETRAETHYLS
TETRAFLUORIDE
TETRAFLUORIDES
TETRAGONAL
TETRAGONALLY
TETRAGONALNESS
TETRAGONOUS
TETRAGRAMMATON
TETRAGRAMMATONS
TETRAGRAMS
TETRAGYNIAN
TETRAGYNOUS
TETRAHEDRA
TETRAHEDRAL
TETRAHEDRALLY
TETRAHEDRITE
TETRAHEDRITES
TETRAHEDRON
TETRAHEDRONS
TETRAHYDROFURAN
TETRAHYMENA
TETRAHYMENAS

TETRALOGIES
TETRAMERAL
TETRAMERIC
TETRAMERISM
TETRAMERISMS
TETRAMEROUS
TETRAMETER
TETRAMETERS
TETRAMETHYL
TETRAMETHYLLEAD
TETRAMORPHIC
TETRANDRIAN
TETRANDROUS
TETRAPLEGIA
TETRAPLEGIAS
TETRAPLEGIC
TETRAPLOID
TETRAPLOIDIES
TETRAPLOIDS
TETRAPLOIDY
TETRAPODIC
TETRAPODIES
TETRAPODOUS
TETRAPOLIS
TETRAPOLISES
TETRAPOLITAN
TETRAPTERAN
TETRAPTEROUS
TETRAPTOTE
TETRAPTOTES
TETRAPYRROLE
TETRAPYRROLES
TETRARCHATE
TETRARCHATES
TETRARCHIC
TETRARCHICAL
TETRARCHIES
TETRASEMIC
TETRASPORANGIA
TETRASPORANGIUM
TETRASPORE
TETRASPORES
TETRASPORIC
TETRASPOROUS
TETRASTICH
TETRASTICHAL
TETRASTICHIC

TETRASTICHOUS
TETRASTICHS
TETRASTYLE
TETRASTYLES
TETRASYLLABIC
TETRASYLLABICAL
TETRASYLLABLE
TETRASYLLABLES
TETRATHEISM
TETRATHEISMS
TETRATHLON
TETRATHLONS
TETRATOMIC
TETRAVALENCE
TETRAVALENCES
TETRAVALENCIES
TETRAVALENCY
TETRAVALENT
TETRAVALENTS
TETRAZOLIUM
TETRAZOLIUMS
TETRAZZINI
TETRODOTOXIN
TETRODOTOXINS
TETROTOXIN
TETROTOXINS
TETROXIDES
TEUTONISED
TEUTONISES
TEUTONISING
TEUTONIZED
TEUTONIZES
TEUTONIZING
TEXTBOOKISH
TEXTPHONES
TEXTSPEAKS
TEXTUALISM
TEXTUALISMS
TEXTUALIST
TEXTUALISTS
TEXTUARIES
TEXTURALLY
TEXTURELESS
TEXTURISED
TEXTURISES
TEXTURISING
TEXTURIZED

TEXTURIZES
TEXTURIZING
THALAMENCEPHALA
THALAMICALLY
THALAMIFLORAL
THALASSAEMIA
THALASSAEMIAS
THALASSAEMIC
THALASSEMIA
THALASSEMIAS
THALASSEMIC
THALASSEMICS
THALASSIAN
THALASSIANS
THALASSOCRACIES
THALASSOCRACY
THALASSOCRAT
THALASSOCRATS
THALASSOGRAPHER
THALASSOGRAPHIC
THALASSOGRAPHY
THALASSOTHERAPY
THALATTOCRACIES
THALATTOCRACY
THALICTRUM
THALICTRUMS
THALIDOMIDE
THALIDOMIDES
THALLIFORM
THALLOPHYTE
THALLOPHYTES
THALLOPHYTIC
THANATISMS
THANATISTS
THANATOGNOMONIC
THANATOGRAPHIES
THANATOGRAPHY
THANATOLOGICAL
THANATOLOGIES
THANATOLOGIST
THANATOLOGISTS
THANATOLOGY
THANATOPHOBIA
THANATOPHOBIAS
THANATOPSES
THANATOPSIS
THANATOSES

THANATOSIS	THAUMATURGUS	THEATRICIZES	THEOGONIES	THEOPATHETIC
THANEHOODS	THAUMATURGUSES	THEATRICIZING	THEOGONIST	THEOPATHIC
THANESHIPS	THAUMATURGY	THEATROMANIA	THEOGONISTS	THEOPATHIES
THANKFULLER	THEANTHROPIC	THEATROMANIAS	THEOLOGASTER	THEOPHAGIES
THANKFULLEST	THEANTHROPIES	THEATROPHONE	THEOLOGASTERS	THEOPHAGOUS
THANKFULLY	THEANTHROPISM	THEATROPHONES	THEOLOGATE	THEOPHANIC
THANKFULNESS	THEANTHROPISMS	THECODONTS	THEOLOGATES	THEOPHANIES
THANKFULNESSES	THEANTHROPIST	THEFTUOUSLY	THEOLOGERS	THEOPHANOUS
THANKLESSLY	THEANTHROPISTS	THEIRSELVES	THEOLOGIAN	THEOPHOBIA
THANKLESSNESS	THEANTHROPY	THEISTICAL	THEOLOGIANS	THEOPHOBIAC
THANKLESSNESSES	THEARCHIES	THEISTICALLY	THEOLOGICAL	THEOPHOBIACS
THANKSGIVER	THEATERGOER	THELEMENTS	THEOLOGICALLY	THEOPHOBIAS
THANKSGIVERS	THEATERGOERS	THELITISES	THEOLOGIES	THEOPHOBIST
THANKSGIVING	THEATERGOING	THELYTOKIES	THEOLOGISATION	THEOPHOBISTS
THANKSGIVINGS	THEATERGOINGS	THELYTOKOUS	THEOLOGISATIONS	THEOPHORIC
THANKWORTHILY	THEATERLAND	THEMATICALLY	THEOLOGISE	THEOPHYLLINE
THANKWORTHINESS	THEATERLANDS	THEMATISATION	THEOLOGISED	THEOPHYLLINES
THANKWORTHY	THEATREGOER	THEMATISATIONS	THEOLOGISER	THEOPNEUST
THARBOROUGH	THEATREGOERS	THEMATIZATION	THEOLOGISERS	THEOPNEUSTIC
THARBOROUGHS	THEATREGOING	THEMATIZATIONS	THEOLOGISES	THEOPNEUSTIES
THATCHIEST	THEATREGOINGS	THEMSELVES	THEOLOGISING	THEOPNEUSTY
THATCHINGS	THEATRELAND	THENABOUTS	THEOLOGIST	THEORBISTS
THATCHLESS	THEATRELANDS	THENARDITE	THEOLOGISTS	THEOREMATIC
THATNESSES	THEATRICAL	THENARDITES	THEOLOGIZATION	THEOREMATICAL
THAUMASITE	THEATRICALISE	THENCEFORTH	THEOLOGIZATIONS	THEOREMATICALLY
THAUMASITES	THEATRICALISED	THENCEFORWARD	THEOLOGIZE	THEOREMATIST
THAUMATINS	THEATRICALISES	THENCEFORWARDS	THEOLOGIZED	THEOREMATISTS
THAUMATOGENIES	THEATRICALISING	THEOBROMINE	THEOLOGIZER	THEORETICAL
THAUMATOGENY	THEATRICALISM	THEOBROMINES	THEOLOGIZERS	THEORETICALLY
THAUMATOGRAPHY	THEATRICALISMS	THEOCENTRIC	THEOLOGIZES	THEORETICIAN
THAUMATOLATRIES	THEATRICALITIES	THEOCENTRICISM	THEOLOGIZING	THEORETICIANS
THAUMATOLATRY	THEATRICALITY	THEOCENTRICISMS	THEOLOGOUMENA	THEORETICS
THAUMATOLOGIES	THEATRICALIZE	THEOCENTRICITY	THEOLOGOUMENON	THEORIQUES
THAUMATOLOGY	THEATRICALIZED	THEOCENTRISM	THEOLOGUES	THEORISATION
THAUMATROPE	THEATRICALIZES	THEOCENTRISMS	THEOMACHIES	THEORISATIONS
THAUMATROPES	THEATRICALIZING	THEOCRACIES	THEOMACHIST	THEORISERS
THAUMATROPICAL	THEATRICALLY	THEOCRASIES	THEOMACHISTS	THEORISING
THAUMATURGE	THEATRICALNESS	THEOCRATIC	THEOMANCIES	THEORIZATION
THAUMATURGES	THEATRICALS	THEOCRATICAL	THEOMANIAC	THEORIZATIONS
THAUMATURGIC	THEATRICISE	THEOCRATICALLY	THEOMANIACS	THEORIZERS
THAUMATURGICAL	THEATRICISED	THEODICEAN	THEOMANIAS	THEORIZING
THAUMATURGICS	THEATRICISES	THEODICEANS	THEOMANTIC	THEOSOPHER
THAUMATURGIES	THEATRICISING	THEODICIES	THEOMORPHIC	THEOSOPHERS
THAUMATURGISM	THEATRICISM	THEODOLITE	THEOMORPHISM	THEOSOPHIC
THAUMATURGISMS	THEATRICISMS	THEODOLITES	THEOMORPHISMS	THEOSOPHICAL
THAUMATURGIST	THEATRICIZE	THEODOLITIC	THEONOMIES	THEOSOPHICALLY
THAUMATURGISTS	THEATRICIZED	THEOGONICAL	THEONOMOUS	THEOSOPHIES

T

THEOSOPHISE	THERIOMORPHIC	THERMOCOUPLES	THERMOMOTORS	THERMOTAXES
THEOSOPHISED	THERIOMORPHISM	THERMODURIC	THERMONASTIES	THERMOTAXIC
THEOSOPHISES	THERIOMORPHISMS	THERMODYNAMIC	THERMONASTY	THERMOTAXIS
THEOSOPHISING	THERIOMORPHOSES	THERMODYNAMICAL	THERMONUCLEAR	THERMOTENSILE
THEOSOPHISM	THERIOMORPHOSIS	THERMODYNAMICS	THERMOPERIODIC	THERMOTHERAPIES
THEOSOPHISMS	THERIOMORPHOUS	THERMOELECTRIC	THERMOPERIODISM	THERMOTHERAPY
THEOSOPHIST	THERIOMORPHS	THERMOELECTRON	THERMOPHIL	THERMOTICAL
THEOSOPHISTICAL	THERMAESTHESIA	THERMOELECTRONS	THERMOPHILE	THERMOTICS
THEOSOPHISTS	THERMAESTHESIAS	THERMOELEMENT	THERMOPHILES	THERMOTOLERANT
THEOSOPHIZE	THERMALISATION	THERMOELEMENTS	THERMOPHILIC	THERMOTROPIC
THEOSOPHIZED	THERMALISATIONS	THERMOFORM	THERMOPHILOUS	THERMOTROPICS
THEOSOPHIZES	THERMALISE	THERMOFORMABLE	THERMOPHILS	THERMOTROPISM
THEOSOPHIZING	THERMALISED	THERMOFORMED	THERMOPHYLLOUS	THERMOTROPISMS
THEOTECHNIC	THERMALISES	THERMOFORMING	THERMOPILE	THEROLOGIES
THEOTECHNIES	THERMALISING	THERMOFORMS	THERMOPILES	THEROPHYTE
THEOTECHNY	THERMALIZATION	THERMOGENESES	THERMOPLASTIC	THEROPHYTES
THERALITES	THERMALIZATIONS	THERMOGENESIS	THERMOPLASTICS	THEROPODAN
THERAPEUSES	THERMALIZE	THERMOGENETIC	THERMORECEPTOR	THEROPODANS
THERAPEUSIS	THERMALIZED	THERMOGENIC	THERMORECEPTORS	THERSITICAL
THERAPEUTIC	THERMALIZES	THERMOGENOUS	THERMOREGULATE	THESAURUSES
THERAPEUTICAL	THERMALIZING	THERMOGRAM	THERMOREGULATED	THESMOTHETE
THERAPEUTICALLY	THERMESTHESIA	THERMOGRAMS	THERMOREGULATES	THESMOTHETES
THERAPEUTICS	THERMESTHESIAS	THERMOGRAPH	THERMOREGULATOR	THETICALLY
THERAPEUTIST	THERMETTES	THERMOGRAPHER	THERMOREMANENCE	THEURGICAL
THERAPEUTISTS	THERMICALLY	THERMOGRAPHERS	THERMOREMANENT	THEURGICALLY
THERAPISTS	THERMIDORS	THERMOGRAPHIC	THERMOSCOPE	THEURGISTS
THERAPSIDS	THERMIONIC	THERMOGRAPHIES	THERMOSCOPES	THIABENDAZOLE
THEREABOUT	THERMIONICS	THERMOGRAPHS	THERMOSCOPIC	THIABENDAZOLES
THEREABOUTS	THERMISTOR	THERMOGRAPHY	THERMOSCOPICAL	THIAMINASE
THEREAFTER	THERMISTORS	THERMOHALINE	THERMOSETS	THIAMINASES
THEREAGAINST	THERMOBALANCE	THERMOJUNCTION	THERMOSETTING	THICKENERS
THEREAMONG	THERMOBALANCES	THERMOJUNCTIONS	THERMOSIPHON	THICKENING
THEREANENT	THERMOBARIC	THERMOLABILE	THERMOSIPHONS	THICKENINGS
THEREBESIDE	THERMOBAROGRAPH	THERMOLABILITY	THERMOSPHERE	THICKHEADED
THEREINAFTER	THERMOBAROMETER	THERMOLOGIES	THERMOSPHERES	THICKHEADEDNESS
THEREINBEFORE	THERMOCHEMICAL	THERMOLOGY	THERMOSPHERIC	THICKHEADS
THERENESSES	THERMOCHEMIST	THERMOLYSES	THERMOSTABILITY	THICKLEAVES
THERETHROUGH	THERMOCHEMISTRY	THERMOLYSIS	THERMOSTABLE	THICKNESSES
THERETOFORE	THERMOCHEMISTS	THERMOLYTIC	THERMOSTAT	THICKSKINS
THEREUNDER	THERMOCHROMIC	THERMOMAGNETIC	THERMOSTATED	THIEVERIES
THEREWITHAL	THERMOCHROMIES	THERMOMETER	THERMOSTATIC	THIEVISHLY
THEREWITHIN	THERMOCHROMISM	THERMOMETERS	THERMOSTATICS	THIEVISHNESS
THERIANTHROPIC	THERMOCHROMISMS	THERMOMETRIC	THERMOSTATING	THIEVISHNESSES
THERIANTHROPISM	THERMOCHROMY	THERMOMETRICAL	THERMOSTATS	THIGHBONES
THERIOLATRIES	THERMOCLINE	THERMOMETRIES	THERMOSTATTED	THIGMOTACTIC
THERIOLATRY	THERMOCLINES	THERMOMETRY	THERMOSTATTING	THIGMOTAXES
THERIOMORPH	THERMOCOUPLE	THERMOMOTOR	THERMOTACTIC	THIGMOTAXIS

THIGMOTROPIC	THINGUMMYJIGS	THIRTEENTH	THOROUGHBASSES	THREADINESS
THIGMOTROPISM	THINKABLENESS	THIRTEENTHLY	THOROUGHBRACE	THREADINESSES
THIGMOTROPISMS	THINKABLENESSES	THIRTEENTHS	THOROUGHBRACED	THREADLESS
THIMBLEBERRIES	THINKINGLY	THIRTIETHS	THOROUGHBRACES	THREADLIKE
THIMBLEBERRY	THINKINGNESS	THIRTYFOLD	THOROUGHBRED	THREADMAKER
THIMBLEFUL	THINKINGNESSES	THIRTYSOMETHING	THOROUGHBREDS	THREADMAKERS
THIMBLEFULS	THINKPIECE	THISNESSES	THOROUGHER	THREADWORM
THIMBLERIG	THINKPIECES	THISTLEDOWN	THOROUGHEST	THREADWORMS
THIMBLERIGGED	THINNESSES	THISTLEDOWNS	THOROUGHFARE	THREATENED
THIMBLERIGGER	THIOALCOHOL	THISTLIEST	THOROUGHFARES	THREATENER
THIMBLERIGGERS	THIOALCOHOLS	THITHERWARD	THOROUGHGOING	THREATENERS
THIMBLERIGGING	THIOBACILLI	THITHERWARDS	THOROUGHGOINGLY	THREATENING
THIMBLERIGGINGS	THIOBACILLUS	THIXOTROPE	THOROUGHLY	THREATENINGLY
THIMBLERIGS	THIOBARBITURATE	THIXOTROPES	THOROUGHNESS	THREATENINGS
THIMBLESFUL	THIOCARBAMIDE	THIXOTROPIC	THOROUGHNESSES	THREEFOLDNESS
THIMBLEWEED	THIOCARBAMIDES	THIXOTROPIES	THOROUGHPACED	THREEFOLDNESSES
THIMBLEWEEDS	THIOCYANATE	THIXOTROPY	THOROUGHPIN	THREENESSES
THIMBLEWIT	THIOCYANATES	THOLEIITES	THOROUGHPINS	THREEPEATED
THIMBLEWITS	THIOCYANIC	THOLEIITIC	THOROUGHWAX	THREEPEATING
THIMBLEWITTED	THIODIGLYCOL	THOLOBATES	THOROUGHWAXES	THREEPEATS
THIMEROSAL	THIODIGLYCOLS	THORACENTESES	THOROUGHWORT	THREEPENCE
THIMEROSALS	THIOFURANS	THORACENTESIS	THOROUGHWORTS	THREEPENCES
THINGAMABOB	THIOPENTAL	THORACICALLY	THOUGHTCAST	THREEPENCEWORTH
THINGAMABOBS	THIOPENTALS	THORACOCENTESES	THOUGHTCASTS	THREEPENNIES
THINGAMAJIG	THIOPENTONE	THORACOCENTESIS	THOUGHTFUL	THREEPENNY
THINGAMAJIGS	THIOPENTONES	THORACOPLASTIES	THOUGHTFULLY	THREEPENNYWORTH
THINGAMIES	THIOPHENES	THORACOPLASTY	THOUGHTFULNESS	THREEQUELS
THINGAMYBOB	THIORIDAZINE	THORACOSCOPE	THOUGHTLESS	THREESCORE
THINGAMYBOBS	THIORIDAZINES	THORACOSCOPES	THOUGHTLESSLY	THREESCORES
THINGAMYJIG	THIOSINAMINE	THORACOSTOMIES	THOUGHTLESSNESS	THREESOMES
THINGAMYJIGS	THIOSINAMINES	THORACOSTOMY	THOUGHTWAY	THREMMATOLOGIES
THINGHOODS	THIOSULFATE	THORACOTOMIES	THOUGHTWAYS	THREMMATOLOGY
THINGINESS	THIOSULFATES	THORACOTOMY	THOUSANDFOLD	THRENETICAL
THINGINESSES	THIOSULFURIC	THORIANITE	THOUSANDFOLDS	THRENODIAL
THINGLINESS	THIOSULPHATE	THORIANITES	THOUSANDTH	THRENODIES
THINGLINESSES	THIOSULPHATES	THORNBACKS	THOUSANDTHS	THRENODIST
THINGNESSES	THIOSULPHURIC	THORNBILLS	THRAIPINGS	THRENODISTS
THINGUMABOB	THIOURACIL	THORNBIRDS	THRALLDOMS	THREONINES
THINGUMABOBS	THIOURACILS	THORNBUSHES	THRAPPLING	THRESHINGS
THINGUMAJIG	THIRDBOROUGH	THORNHEDGE	THRASHIEST	THRESHOLDS
THINGUMAJIGS	THIRDBOROUGHS	THORNHEDGES	THRASHINGS	THRIFTIEST
THINGUMBOB	THIRDSTREAM	THORNINESS	THRASONICAL	THRIFTINESS
THINGUMBOBS	THIRDSTREAMS	THORNINESSES	THRASONICALLY	THRIFTINESSES
THINGUMMIES	THIRSTIEST	THORNPROOF	THREADBARE	THRIFTLESS
THINGUMMYBOB	THIRSTINESS	THORNPROOFS	THREADBARENESS	THRIFTLESSLY
THINGUMMYBOBS	THIRSTINESSES	THORNTREES	THREADFINS	THRIFTLESSNESS
THINGUMMYJIG	THIRSTLESS	THOROUGHBASS	THREADIEST	THRILLIEST

THRILLINGLY
THRILLINGNESS
THRILLINGNESSES
THRIVELESS
THRIVINGLY
THRIVINGNESS
THRIVINGNESSES
THROATIEST
THROATINESS
THROATINESSES
THROATLASH
THROATLASHES
THROATLATCH
THROATLATCHES
THROATWORT
THROATWORTS
THROBBINGLY
THROBBINGS
THROMBOCYTE
THROMBOCYTES
THROMBOCYTIC
THROMBOEMBOLIC
THROMBOEMBOLISM
THROMBOGEN
THROMBOGENS
THROMBOKINASE
THROMBOKINASES
THROMBOLYSES
THROMBOLYSIS
THROMBOLYTIC
THROMBOLYTICS
THROMBOPHILIA
THROMBOPHILIAS
THROMBOPLASTIC
THROMBOPLASTIN
THROMBOPLASTINS
THROMBOSED
THROMBOSES
THROMBOSING
THROMBOSIS
THROMBOTIC
THROMBOXANE
THROMBOXANES
THRONELESS
THRONGINGS
THROPPLING
THROTTLEABLE

THROTTLEHOLD
THROTTLEHOLDS
THROTTLERS
THROTTLING
THROTTLINGS
THROUGHFARE
THROUGHFARES
THROUGHGAUN
THROUGHGAUNS
THROUGHITHER
THROUGHOTHER
THROUGHOUT
THROUGHPUT
THROUGHPUTS
THROUGHWAY
THROUGHWAYS
THROWAWAYS
THROWBACKS
THROWDOWNS
THROWOVERS
THROWSTERS
THRUMMIEST
THRUMMINGLY
THRUMMINGS
THRUPENNIES
THRUPPENCE
THRUPPENCES
THRUPPENNIES
THRUPPENNY
THRUSTINGS
THRUTCHING
THUDDINGLY
THUGGERIES
THUMBHOLES
THUMBIKINS
THUMBLINGS
THUMBNAILS
THUMBPIECE
THUMBPIECES
THUMBPRINT
THUMBPRINTS
THUMBSCREW
THUMBSCREWS
THUMBSTALL
THUMBSTALLS
THUMBTACKED
THUMBTACKING

THUMBTACKS
THUMBWHEEL
THUMBWHEELS
THUMPINGLY
THUNBERGIA
THUNBERGIAS
THUNDERBIRD
THUNDERBIRDS
THUNDERBOLT
THUNDERBOLTS
THUNDERBOX
THUNDERBOXES
THUNDERCLAP
THUNDERCLAPS
THUNDERCLOUD
THUNDERCLOUDS
THUNDERERS
THUNDERFLASH
THUNDERFLASHES
THUNDERHEAD
THUNDERHEADS
THUNDERIER
THUNDERIEST
THUNDERING
THUNDERINGLY
THUNDERINGS
THUNDERLESS
THUNDEROUS
THUNDEROUSLY
THUNDEROUSNESS
THUNDERSHOWER
THUNDERSHOWERS
THUNDERSTONE
THUNDERSTONES
THUNDERSTORM
THUNDERSTORMS
THUNDERSTRICKEN
THUNDERSTRIKE
THUNDERSTRIKES
THUNDERSTRIKING
THUNDERSTROKE
THUNDERSTROKES
THUNDERSTRUCK
THURIFEROUS
THURIFICATION
THURIFICATIONS
THURIFYING

THUSNESSES
THWACKINGS
THWARTEDLY
THWARTINGLY
THWARTINGS
THWARTSHIP
THWARTSHIPS
THWARTWAYS
THWARTWISE
THYLACINES
THYLAKOIDS
THYMECTOMIES
THYMECTOMISE
THYMECTOMISED
THYMECTOMISES
THYMECTOMISING
THYMECTOMIZE
THYMECTOMIZED
THYMECTOMIZES
THYMECTOMIZING
THYMECTOMY
THYMELAEACEOUS
THYMIDINES
THYMIDYLIC
THYMOCYTES
THYRATRONS
THYRISTORS
THYROCALCITONIN
THYROGLOBULIN
THYROGLOBULINS
THYROIDECTOMIES
THYROIDECTOMY
THYROIDITIS
THYROIDITISES
THYROTOXICOSES
THYROTOXICOSIS
THYROTROPHIC
THYROTROPHIN
THYROTROPHINS
THYROTROPIC
THYROTROPIN
THYROTROPINS
THYROXINES
THYRSOIDAL
THYSANOPTEROUS
THYSANURAN
THYSANURANS

THYSANUROUS
TIBIOFIBULA
TIBIOFIBULAE
TIBIOFIBULAS
TIBIOTARSI
TIBIOTARSUS
TIBOUCHINA
TIBOUCHINAS
TICHORRHINE
TICHORRHINES
TICKETINGS
TICKETLESS
TICKETTYBOO
TICKLISHLY
TICKLISHNESS
TICKLISHNESSES
TICKTACKED
TICKTACKING
TICKTACKTOE
TICKTACKTOES
TICKTOCKED
TICKTOCKING
TICTACKING
TICTOCKING
TIDDLEDYWINK
TIDDLEDYWINKS
TIDDLEYWINK
TIDDLEYWINKS
TIDDLYWINK
TIDDLYWINKS
TIDEWAITER
TIDEWAITERS
TIDEWATERS
TIDINESSES
TIDIVATING
TIDIVATION
TIDIVATIONS
TIEBREAKER
TIEBREAKERS
TIEMANNITE
TIEMANNITES
TIERCELETS
TIERCERONS
TIGERISHLY
TIGERISHNESS
TIGERISHNESSES
TIGERWOODS

TIGGYWINKLE	TIMBROPHILIST	TINCTORIALLY	TITANIFEROUS	TITULARITY
TIGGYWINKLES	TIMBROPHILISTS	TINCTURING	TITANOSAUR	TOADEATERS
TIGHTASSED	TIMBROPHILY	TINDERBOXES	TITANOSAURS	TOADFISHES
TIGHTASSES	TIMEFRAMES	TINGLINGLY	TITANOTHERE	TOADFLAXES
TIGHTENERS	TIMEKEEPER	TINGUAITES	TITANOTHERES	TOADGRASSES
TIGHTENING	TIMEKEEPERS	TININESSES	TITARAKURA	TOADRUSHES
TIGHTENINGS	TIMEKEEPING	TINKERINGS	TITARAKURAS	TOADSTONES
TIGHTFISTED	TIMEKEEPINGS	TINKERTOYS	TITHINGMAN	TOADSTOOLS
TIGHTFISTEDNESS	TIMELESSLY	TINKLINGLY	TITHINGMEN	TOASTMASTER
TIGHTISHLY	TIMELESSNESS	TINNINESSES	TITILLATED	TOASTMASTERS
TIGHTNESSES	TIMELESSNESSES	TINNITUSES	TITILLATES	TOASTMISTRESS
TIGHTROPES	TIMELINESS	TINPLATING	TITILLATING	TOASTMISTRESSES
TIGHTWIRES	TIMELINESSES	TINSELLING	TITILLATINGLY	TOBACCANALIAN
TIGRISHNESS	TIMENOGUYS	TINSELRIES	TITILLATION	TOBACCANALIANS
TIGRISHNESSES	TIMEPASSED	TINSMITHING	TITILLATIONS	TOBACCOLESS
TIKOLOSHES	TIMEPASSES	TINSMITHINGS	TITILLATIVE	TOBACCONIST
TIKTAALIKS	TIMEPASSING	TINTINESSES	TITILLATOR	TOBACCONISTS
TILEFISHES	TIMEPIECES	TINTINNABULA	TITILLATORS	TOBOGGANED
TILIACEOUS	TIMEPLEASER	TINTINNABULANT	TITIPOUNAMU	TOBOGGANER
TILLANDSIA	TIMEPLEASERS	TINTINNABULAR	TITIPOUNAMUS	TOBOGGANERS
TILLANDSIAS	TIMESAVERS	TINTINNABULARY	TITIVATING	TOBOGGANING
TILLERLESS	TIMESAVING	TINTINNABULATE	TITIVATION	TOBOGGANINGS
TILTMETERS	TIMESCALES	TINTINNABULATED	TITIVATIONS	TOBOGGANIST
TILTROTORS	TIMESERVER	TINTINNABULATES	TITIVATORS	TOBOGGANISTS
TIMBERDOODLE	TIMESERVERS	TINTINNABULOUS	TITLEHOLDER	TOBOGGINED
TIMBERDOODLES	TIMESERVING	TINTINNABULUM	TITLEHOLDERS	TOBOGGINING
TIMBERHEAD	TIMESERVINGS	TINTOMETER	TITLEHOLDING	TOCCATELLA
TIMBERHEADS	TIMESHARES	TINTOMETERS	TITRATABLE	TOCCATELLAS
TIMBERINGS	TIMESTAMPED	TINTOOKIES	TITRATIONS	TOCCATINAS
TIMBERLAND	TIMESTAMPING	TIPPYTOEING	TITRIMETRIC	TOCHERLESS
TIMBERLANDS	TIMESTAMPS	TIPSIFYING	TITTERINGLY	TOCOLOGIES
TIMBERLINE	TIMETABLED	TIPSINESSES	TITTERINGS	TOCOPHEROL
TIMBERLINES	TIMETABLES	TIPTRONICS	TITTIVATED	TOCOPHEROLS
TIMBERWORK	TIMETABLING	TIRAILLEUR	TITTIVATES	TOCOPHOBIA
TIMBERWORKS	TIMETABLINGS	TIRAILLEURS	TITTIVATING	TOCOPHOBIAS
TIMBERYARD	TIMEWORKER	TIREDNESSES	TITTIVATION	TODDLERHOOD
TIMBERYARDS	TIMEWORKERS	TIRELESSLY	TITTIVATIONS	TODDLERHOODS
TIMBRELLED	TIMIDITIES	TIRELESSNESS	TITTIVATOR	TOENAILING
TIMBROLOGIES	TIMIDNESSES	TIRELESSNESSES	TITTIVATORS	TOERAGGERS
TIMBROLOGIST	TIMOCRACIES	TIREMAKERS	TITTLEBATS	TOFFISHNESS
TIMBROLOGISTS	TIMOCRATIC	TIRESOMELY	TITTUPPING	TOFFISHNESSES
TIMBROLOGY	TIMOCRATICAL	TIRESOMENESS	TITUBANCIES	TOGAVIRUSES
TIMBROMANIA	TIMOROUSLY	TIRESOMENESSES	TITUBATING	TOGETHERNESS
TIMBROMANIAC	TIMOROUSNESS	TIROCINIUM	TITUBATION	TOGETHERNESSES
TIMBROMANIACS	TIMOROUSNESSES	TIROCINIUMS	TITUBATIONS	TOILETINGS
TIMBROMANIAS	TIMPANISTS	TITANESSES	TITULARIES	TOILETRIES
TIMBROPHILIES	TINCTORIAL	TITANICALLY	TITULARITIES	TOILFULNESS

TOILFULNESSES	TOMBSTONES	TOOLHOUSES	TOPLOFTIER	TORCHIERES
TOILINETTE	TOMBSTONING	TOOLMAKERS	TOPLOFTIEST	TORCHLIGHT
TOILINETTES	TOMBSTONINGS	TOOLMAKING	TOPLOFTILY	TORCHLIGHTS
TOILSOMELY	TOMCATTING	TOOLMAKINGS	TOPLOFTINESS	TORCHWOODS
TOILSOMENESS	TOMCATTINGS	TOOLPUSHER	TOPLOFTINESSES	TORMENTEDLY
TOILSOMENESSES	TOMFOOLERIES	TOOLPUSHERS	TOPMAKINGS	TORMENTERS
TOKENISTIC	TOMFOOLERY	TOOLPUSHES	TOPMINNOWS	TORMENTILS
TOKOLOGIES	TOMFOOLING	TOOTHACHES	TOPNOTCHER	TORMENTING
TOKOLOSHES	TOMFOOLISH	TOOTHBRUSH	TOPNOTCHERS	TORMENTINGLY
TOKOLOSHIS	TOMFOOLISHNESS	TOOTHBRUSHES	TOPOCENTRIC	TORMENTINGS
TOKOPHOBIA	TOMOGRAPHIC	TOOTHBRUSHING	TOPOCHEMISTRIES	TORMENTORS
TOKOPHOBIAS	TOMOGRAPHIES	TOOTHBRUSHINGS	TOPOCHEMISTRY	TORMENTUMS
TOKTOKKIES	TOMOGRAPHS	TOOTHCOMBS	TOPOGRAPHER	TOROIDALLY
TOLBUTAMIDE	TOMOGRAPHY	TOOTHFISHES	TOPOGRAPHERS	TOROSITIES
TOLBUTAMIDES	TONALITIES	TOOTHINESS	TOPOGRAPHIC	TORPEDINOUS
TOLERABILITIES	TONALITIVE	TOOTHINESSES	TOPOGRAPHICAL	TORPEDOERS
TOLERABILITY	TONELESSLY	TOOTHPASTE	TOPOGRAPHICALLY	TORPEDOING
TOLERABLENESS	TONELESSNESS	TOOTHPASTES	TOPOGRAPHIES	TORPEDOIST
TOLERABLENESSES	TONELESSNESSES	TOOTHPICKS	TOPOGRAPHS	TORPEDOISTS
TOLERANCES	TONETICALLY	TOOTHSHELL	TOPOGRAPHY	TORPEFYING
TOLERANTLY	TONGUELESS	TOOTHSHELLS	TOPOISOMERASE	TORPESCENCE
TOLERATING	TONGUELETS	TOOTHSOMELY	TOPOISOMERASES	TORPESCENCES
TOLERATION	TONGUELIKE	TOOTHSOMENESS	TOPOLOGICAL	TORPESCENT
TOLERATIONISM	TONGUESTER	TOOTHSOMENESSES	TOPOLOGICALLY	TORPIDITIES
TOLERATIONISMS	TONGUESTERS	TOOTHWASHES	TOPOLOGIES	TORPIDNESS
TOLERATIONIST	TONICITIES	TOOTHWORTS	TOPOLOGIST	TORPIDNESSES
TOLERATIONISTS	TONISHNESS	TOPAGNOSES	TOPOLOGISTS	TORPITUDES
TOLERATIONS	TONISHNESSES	TOPAGNOSIA	TOPOMETRIES	TORPORIFIC
TOLERATIVE	TONNISHNESS	TOPAGNOSIAS	TOPONYMICAL	TORREFACTION
TOLERATORS	TONNISHNESSES	TOPAGNOSIS	TOPONYMICS	TORREFACTIONS
TOLLBOOTHS	TONOMETERS	TOPARCHIES	TOPONYMIES	TORREFYING
TOLLBRIDGE	TONOMETRIC	TOPAZOLITE	TOPONYMIST	TORRENTIAL
TOLLBRIDGES	TONOMETRIES	TOPAZOLITES	TOPONYMISTS	TORRENTIALITIES
TOLLDISHES	TONOPLASTS	TOPCROSSES	TOPOPHILIA	TORRENTIALITY
TOLLGATING	TONSILITIS	TOPDRESSING	TOPOPHILIAS	TORRENTIALLY
TOLLHOUSES	TONSILITISES	TOPDRESSINGS	TOPSCORING	TORRENTUOUS
TOLLKEEPER	TONSILLARY	TOPECTOMIES	TOPSOILING	TORRIDITIES
TOLLKEEPERS	TONSILLECTOMIES	TOPGALLANT	TOPSOILINGS	TORRIDNESS
TOLUIDIDES	TONSILLECTOMY	TOPGALLANTS	TOPSTITCHED	TORRIDNESSES
TOLUIDINES	TONSILLITIC	TOPHACEOUS	TOPSTITCHES	TORRIFYING
TOMAHAWKED	TONSILLITIS	TOPIARISTS	TOPSTITCHING	TORSIBILITIES
TOMAHAWKING	TONSILLITISES	TOPICALITIES	TOPWORKING	TORSIBILITY
TOMATILLOES	TONSILLOTOMIES	TOPICALITY	TORBANITES	TORSIOGRAPH
TOMATILLOS	TONSILLOTOMY	TOPKNOTTED	TORBERNITE	TORSIOGRAPHS
TOMBOYISHLY	TOOLCHESTS	TOPLESSNESS	TORBERNITES	TORSIONALLY
TOMBOYISHNESS	TOOLHOLDER	TOPLESSNESSES	TORCHBEARER	TORTELLINI
TOMBOYISHNESSES	TOOLHOLDERS	TOPLOFTICAL	TORCHBEARERS	TORTELLINIS

TORTFEASOR	TOTIPALMATE	TOVARISHES	TOXOPHILIES	TRACHOMATOUS
TORTFEASORS	TOTIPALMATION	TOWARDLINESS	TOXOPHILITE	TRACHYPTERUS
TORTICOLLAR	TOTIPALMATIONS	TOWARDLINESSES	TOXOPHILITES	TRACHYPTERUSES
TORTICOLLIS	TOTIPOTENCIES	TOWARDNESS	TOXOPHILITIC	TRACHYTOID
TORTICOLLISES	TOTIPOTENCY	TOWARDNESSES	TOXOPLASMA	TRACKBALLS
TORTILITIES	TOTIPOTENT	TOWELETTES	TOXOPLASMAS	TRACKERBALL
TORTILLONS	TOTTERINGLY	TOWELHEADS	TOXOPLASMIC	TRACKERBALLS
TORTIOUSLY	TOTTERINGS	TOWELLINGS	TOXOPLASMOSES	TRACKLAYER
TORTOISESHELL	TOUCHABLENESS	TOWERINGLY	TOXOPLASMOSIS	TRACKLAYERS
TORTOISESHELLS	TOUCHABLENESSES	TOWNHOUSES	TOYISHNESS	TRACKLAYING
TORTRICIDS	TOUCHBACKS	TOWNSCAPED	TOYISHNESSES	TRACKLAYINGS
TORTUOSITIES	TOUCHDOWNS	TOWNSCAPES	TRABEATION	TRACKLEMENT
TORTUOSITY	TOUCHHOLES	TOWNSCAPING	TRABEATIONS	TRACKLEMENTS
TORTUOUSLY	TOUCHINESS	TOWNSCAPINGS	TRABECULAE	TRACKLESSLY
TORTUOUSNESS	TOUCHINESSES	TOWNSFOLKS	TRABECULAR	TRACKLESSNESS
TORTUOUSNESSES	TOUCHINGLY	TOWNSPEOPLE	TRABECULAS	TRACKLESSNESSES
TORTUREDLY	TOUCHINGNESS	TOWNSPEOPLES	TRABECULATE	TRACKROADS
TORTURESOME	TOUCHINGNESSES	TOWNSWOMAN	TRABECULATED	TRACKSIDES
TORTURINGLY	TOUCHLINES	TOWNSWOMEN	TRACASSERIE	TRACKSUITS
TORTURINGS	TOUCHMARKS	TOXALBUMIN	TRACASSERIES	TRACKWALKER
TORTUROUSLY	TOUCHPAPER	TOXALBUMINS	TRACEABILITIES	TRACKWALKERS
TOSSICATED	TOUCHPAPERS	TOXAPHENES	TRACEABILITY	TRACTABILITIES
TOSTICATED	TOUCHSTONE	TOXICATION	TRACEABLENESS	TRACTABILITY
TOSTICATION	TOUCHSTONES	TOXICATIONS	TRACEABLENESSES	TRACTABLENESS
TOSTICATIONS	TOUCHTONES	TOXICITIES	TRACELESSLY	TRACTABLENESSES
TOTALISATION	TOUCHWOODS	TOXICOGENIC	TRACHEARIAN	TRACTARIAN
TOTALISATIONS	TOUGHENERS	TOXICOLOGIC	TRACHEARIANS	TRACTARIANS
TOTALISATOR	TOUGHENING	TOXICOLOGICAL	TRACHEARIES	TRACTATORS
TOTALISATORS	TOUGHENINGS	TOXICOLOGICALLY	TRACHEATED	TRACTILITIES
TOTALISERS	TOUGHNESSES	TOXICOLOGIES	TRACHEATES	TRACTILITY
TOTALISING	TOURBILLION	TOXICOLOGIST	TRACHEIDAL	TRACTIONAL
TOTALISTIC	TOURBILLIONS	TOXICOLOGISTS	TRACHEIDES	TRACTORATION
TOTALITARIAN	TOURBILLON	TOXICOLOGY	TRACHEITIS	TRACTORATIONS
TOTALITARIANISE	TOURBILLONS	TOXICOMANIA	TRACHEITISES	TRACTORFEED
TOTALITARIANISM	TOURISTICALLY	TOXICOMANIAS	TRACHELATE	TRACTORFEEDS
TOTALITARIANIZE	TOURMALINE	TOXICOPHAGOUS	TRACHEOLAR	TRACTRICES
TOTALITARIANS	TOURMALINES	TOXICOPHOBIA	TRACHEOLES	TRADECRAFT
TOTALITIES	TOURMALINIC	TOXICOPHOBIAS	TRACHEOPHYTE	TRADECRAFTS
TOTALIZATION	TOURNAMENT	TOXIGENICITIES	TRACHEOPHYTES	TRADEMARKED
TOTALIZATIONS	TOURNAMENTS	TOXIGENICITY	TRACHEOSCOPIES	TRADEMARKING
TOTALIZATOR	TOURNEYERS	TOXIPHAGOUS	TRACHEOSCOPY	TRADEMARKS
TOTALIZATORS	TOURNEYING	TOXIPHOBIA	TRACHEOSTOMIES	TRADENAMES
TOTALIZERS	TOURNIQUET	TOXIPHOBIAC	TRACHEOSTOMY	TRADERSHIP
TOTALIZING	TOURNIQUETS	TOXIPHOBIACS	TRACHEOTOMIES	TRADERSHIPS
TOTAQUINES	TOURTIERES	TOXIPHOBIAS	TRACHEOTOMY	TRADESCANTIA
TOTEMICALLY	TOVARICHES	TOXOCARIASES	TRACHINUSES	TRADESCANTIAS
TOTEMISTIC	TOVARISCHES	TOXOCARIASIS	TRACHITISES	TRADESFOLK

TRADESFOLKS	TRAFFICKED	TRAINSPOTTERISH	TRANQUILER	TRANSACTOR
TRADESMANLIKE	TRAFFICKER	TRAINSPOTTERS	TRANQUILEST	TRANSACTORS
TRADESPEOPLE	TRAFFICKERS	TRAIPSINGS	TRANQUILISATION	TRANSALPINE
TRADESPEOPLES	TRAFFICKING	TRAITORESS	TRANQUILISE	TRANSALPINES
TRADESPERSON	TRAFFICKINGS	TRAITORESSES	TRANQUILISED	TRANSAMINASE
TRADESWOMAN	TRAFFICLESS	TRAITORHOOD	TRANQUILISER	TRANSAMINASES
TRADESWOMEN	TRAGACANTH	TRAITORHOODS	TRANQUILISERS	TRANSAMINATION
TRADITIONAL	TRAGACANTHS	TRAITORISM	TRANQUILISES	TRANSAMINATIONS
TRADITIONALISE	TRAGEDIANS	TRAITORISMS	TRANQUILISING	TRANSANDEAN
TRADITIONALISED	TRAGEDIENNE	TRAITOROUS	TRANQUILISINGLY	TRANSANDINE
TRADITIONALISES	TRAGEDIENNES	TRAITOROUSLY	TRANQUILITIES	TRANSATLANTIC
TRADITIONALISM	TRAGELAPHINE	TRAITOROUSNESS	TRANQUILITY	TRANSAXLES
TRADITIONALISMS	TRAGELAPHS	TRAITORSHIP	TRANQUILIZATION	TRANSCALENCIES
TRADITIONALIST	TRAGICALLY	TRAITORSHIPS	TRANQUILIZE	TRANSCALENCY
TRADITIONALISTS	TRAGICALNESS	TRAITRESSES	TRANQUILIZED	TRANSCALENT
TRADITIONALITY	TRAGICALNESSES	TRAJECTILE	TRANQUILIZER	TRANSCAUCASIAN
TRADITIONALIZE	TRAGICOMEDIES	TRAJECTING	TRANQUILIZERS	TRANSCEIVER
TRADITIONALIZED	TRAGICOMEDY	TRAJECTION	TRANQUILIZES	TRANSCEIVERS
TRADITIONALIZES	TRAGICOMIC	TRAJECTIONS	TRANQUILIZING	TRANSCENDED
TRADITIONALLY	TRAGICOMICAL	TRAJECTORIES	TRANQUILIZINGLY	TRANSCENDENCE
TRADITIONARILY	TRAGICOMICALLY	TRAJECTORY	TRANQUILLER	TRANSCENDENCES
TRADITIONARY	TRAILBASTON	TRALATICIOUS	TRANQUILLEST	TRANSCENDENCIES
TRADITIONER	TRAILBASTONS	TRALATITIOUS	TRANQUILLISE	TRANSCENDENCY
TRADITIONERS	TRAILBLAZER	TRAMELLING	TRANQUILLISED	TRANSCENDENT
TRADITIONIST	TRAILBLAZERS	TRAMMELERS	TRANQUILLISER	TRANSCENDENTAL
TRADITIONISTS	TRAILBLAZING	TRAMMELING	TRANQUILLISERS	TRANSCENDENTALS
TRADITIONLESS	TRAILBLAZINGS	TRAMMELLED	TRANQUILLISES	TRANSCENDENTLY
TRADITIONS	TRAILBREAKER	TRAMMELLER	TRANQUILLISING	TRANSCENDENTS
TRADITORES	TRAILBREAKERS	TRAMMELLERS	TRANQUILLITIES	TRANSCENDING
TRADUCEMENT	TRAILERABLE	TRAMMELLING	TRANQUILLITY	TRANSCENDINGLY
TRADUCEMENTS	TRAILERING	TRAMONTANA	TRANQUILLIZE	TRANSCENDS
TRADUCIANISM	TRAILERINGS	TRAMONTANAS	TRANQUILLIZED	TRANSCODED
TRADUCIANISMS	TRAILERIST	TRAMONTANE	TRANQUILLIZER	TRANSCODER
TRADUCIANIST	TRAILERISTS	TRAMONTANES	TRANQUILLIZERS	TRANSCODERS
TRADUCIANISTIC	TRAILERITE	TRAMPETTES	TRANQUILLIZES	TRANSCODES
TRADUCIANISTS	TRAILERITES	TRAMPLINGS	TRANQUILLIZING	TRANSCODING
TRADUCIANS	TRAILHEADS	TRAMPOLINE	TRANQUILLY	TRANSCRANIAL
TRADUCIBLE	TRAILINGLY	TRAMPOLINED	TRANQUILNESS	TRANSCRIBABLE
TRADUCINGLY	TRAINABILITIES	TRAMPOLINER	TRANQUILNESSES	TRANSCRIBE
TRADUCINGS	TRAINABILITY	TRAMPOLINERS	TRANSACTED	TRANSCRIBED
TRADUCTION	TRAINBANDS	TRAMPOLINES	TRANSACTING	TRANSCRIBER
TRADUCTIONS	TRAINBEARER	TRAMPOLINING	TRANSACTINIDE	TRANSCRIBERS
TRADUCTIVE	TRAINBEARERS	TRAMPOLININGS	TRANSACTINIDES	TRANSCRIBES
TRAFFICABILITY	TRAINEESHIP	TRAMPOLINIST	TRANSACTION	TRANSCRIBING
TRAFFICABLE	TRAINEESHIPS	TRAMPOLINISTS	TRANSACTIONAL	TRANSCRIPT
TRAFFICATOR	TRAINLOADS	TRAMPOLINS	TRANSACTIONALLY	TRANSCRIPTASE
TRAFFICATORS	TRAINSPOTTER	TRANCELIKE	TRANSACTIONS	TRANSCRIPTASES

TRANSCRIPTION	TRANSFERASES	TRANSFUSER	TRANSIENCES	TRANSLATING
TRANSCRIPTIONAL	TRANSFEREE	TRANSFUSERS	TRANSIENCIES	TRANSLATION
TRANSCRIPTIONS	TRANSFEREES	TRANSFUSES	TRANSIENCY	TRANSLATIONAL
TRANSCRIPTIVE	TRANSFERENCE	TRANSFUSIBLE	TRANSIENTLY	TRANSLATIONALLY
TRANSCRIPTIVELY	TRANSFERENCES	TRANSFUSING	TRANSIENTNESS	TRANSLATIONS
TRANSCRIPTOME	TRANSFERENTIAL	TRANSFUSION	TRANSIENTNESSES	TRANSLATIVE
TRANSCRIPTOMES	TRANSFEROR	TRANSFUSIONAL	TRANSIENTS	TRANSLATIVES
TRANSCRIPTS	TRANSFERORS	TRANSFUSIONIST	TRANSILIENCE	TRANSLATOR
TRANSCULTURAL	TRANSFERRABLE	TRANSFUSIONISTS	TRANSILIENCES	TRANSLATORIAL
TRANSCURRENT	TRANSFERRAL	TRANSFUSIONS	TRANSILIENCIES	TRANSLATORS
TRANSCUTANEOUS	TRANSFERRALS	TRANSFUSIVE	TRANSILIENCY	TRANSLATORY
TRANSDERMAL	TRANSFERRED	TRANSFUSIVELY	TRANSILIENT	TRANSLEITHAN
TRANSDUCED	TRANSFERRER	TRANSGENDER	TRANSILLUMINATE	TRANSLITERATE
TRANSDUCER	TRANSFERRERS	TRANSGENDERED	TRANSISTHMIAN	TRANSLITERATED
TRANSDUCERS	TRANSFERRIBLE	TRANSGENDERS	TRANSISTOR	TRANSLITERATES
TRANSDUCES	TRANSFERRIN	TRANSGENES	TRANSISTORISE	TRANSLITERATING
TRANSDUCING	TRANSFERRING	TRANSGENESES	TRANSISTORISED	TRANSLITERATION
TRANSDUCTANT	TRANSFERRINS	TRANSGENESIS	TRANSISTORISES	TRANSLITERATOR
TRANSDUCTANTS	TRANSFIGURATION	TRANSGENIC	TRANSISTORISING	TRANSLITERATORS
TRANSDUCTION	TRANSFIGURE	TRANSGENICS	TRANSISTORIZE	TRANSLOCATE
TRANSDUCTIONAL	TRANSFIGURED	TRANSGRESS	TRANSISTORIZED	TRANSLOCATED
TRANSDUCTIONS	TRANSFIGUREMENT	TRANSGRESSED	TRANSISTORIZES	TRANSLOCATES
TRANSDUCTOR	TRANSFIGURES	TRANSGRESSES	TRANSISTORIZING	TRANSLOCATING
TRANSDUCTORS	TRANSFIGURING	TRANSGRESSING	TRANSISTORS	TRANSLOCATION
TRANSECTED	TRANSFINITE	TRANSGRESSION	TRANSITABLE	TRANSLOCATIONS
TRANSECTING	TRANSFIXED	TRANSGRESSIONAL	TRANSITING	TRANSLUCENCE
TRANSECTION	TRANSFIXES	TRANSGRESSIONS	TRANSITION	TRANSLUCENCES
TRANSECTIONS	TRANSFIXING	TRANSGRESSIVE	TRANSITIONAL	TRANSLUCENCIES
TRANSENNAS	TRANSFIXION	TRANSGRESSIVELY	TRANSITIONALLY	TRANSLUCENCY
TRANSEPTAL	TRANSFIXIONS	TRANSGRESSOR	TRANSITIONALS	TRANSLUCENT
TRANSEPTATE	TRANSFORMABLE	TRANSGRESSORS	TRANSITIONARY	TRANSLUCENTLY
TRANSEXUAL	TRANSFORMATION	TRANSHIPMENT	TRANSITIONED	TRANSLUCID
TRANSEXUALISM	TRANSFORMATIONS	TRANSHIPMENTS	TRANSITIONING	TRANSLUCIDITIES
TRANSEXUALISMS	TRANSFORMATIVE	TRANSHIPPED	TRANSITIONS	TRANSLUCIDITY
TRANSEXUALITIES	TRANSFORMED	TRANSHIPPER	TRANSITIVE	TRANSLUMENAL
TRANSEXUALITY	TRANSFORMER	TRANSHIPPERS	TRANSITIVELY	TRANSLUMINAL
TRANSEXUALS	TRANSFORMERS	TRANSHIPPING	TRANSITIVENESS	TRANSLUNAR
TRANSFECTED	TRANSFORMING	TRANSHIPPINGS	TRANSITIVES	TRANSLUNARY
TRANSFECTING	TRANSFORMINGS	TRANSHISTORICAL	TRANSITIVITIES	TRANSMANCHE
TRANSFECTION	TRANSFORMISM	TRANSHUMANCE	TRANSITIVITY	TRANSMARINE
TRANSFECTIONS	TRANSFORMISMS	TRANSHUMANCES	TRANSITORILY	TRANSMEMBRANE
TRANSFECTS	TRANSFORMIST	TRANSHUMANT	TRANSITORINESS	TRANSMEWED
TRANSFERABILITY	TRANSFORMISTIC	TRANSHUMANTS	TRANSITORY	TRANSMEWING
TRANSFERABLE	TRANSFORMISTS	TRANSHUMED	TRANSLATABILITY	TRANSMIGRANT
TRANSFERAL	TRANSFORMS	TRANSHUMES	TRANSLATABLE	TRANSMIGRANTS
TRANSFERALS	TRANSFUSABLE	TRANSHUMING	TRANSLATED	TRANSMIGRATE
TRANSFERASE	TRANSFUSED	TRANSIENCE	TRANSLATES	TRANSMIGRATED

TRANSMIGRATES	TRANSMUTED	TRANSPLANTINGS	TRANSSEXUALS	TRANSVERSALS
TRANSMIGRATING	TRANSMUTER	TRANSPLANTS	TRANSSHAPE	TRANSVERSE
TRANSMIGRATION	TRANSMUTERS	TRANSPOLAR	TRANSSHAPED	TRANSVERSED
TRANSMIGRATIONS	TRANSMUTES	TRANSPONDER	TRANSSHAPES	TRANSVERSELY
TRANSMIGRATIVE	TRANSMUTING	TRANSPONDERS	TRANSSHAPING	TRANSVERSENESS
TRANSMIGRATOR	TRANSNATIONAL	TRANSPONDOR	TRANSSHIPMENT	TRANSVERSES
TRANSMIGRATORS	TRANSNATURAL	TRANSPONDORS	TRANSSHIPMENTS	TRANSVERSING
TRANSMIGRATORY	TRANSOCEANIC	TRANSPONTINE	TRANSSHIPPED	TRANSVERSION
TRANSMISSIBLE	TRANSONICS	TRANSPORTABLE	TRANSSHIPPER	TRANSVERSIONS
TRANSMISSION	TRANSPACIFIC	TRANSPORTAL	TRANSSHIPPERS	TRANSVERTER
TRANSMISSIONAL	TRANSPADANE	TRANSPORTALS	TRANSSHIPPING	TRANSVERTERS
TRANSMISSIONS	TRANSPARENCE	TRANSPORTANCE	TRANSSHIPPINGS	TRANSVESTED
TRANSMISSIVE	TRANSPARENCES	TRANSPORTANCES	TRANSSHIPS	TRANSVESTIC
TRANSMISSIVELY	TRANSPARENCIES	TRANSPORTATION	TRANSSONIC	TRANSVESTING
TRANSMISSIVITY	TRANSPARENCY	TRANSPORTATIONS	TRANSTHORACIC	TRANSVESTISM
TRANSMISSOMETER	TRANSPARENT	TRANSPORTED	TRANSUBSTANTIAL	TRANSVESTISMS
TRANSMITTABLE	TRANSPARENTISE	TRANSPORTEDLY	TRANSUDATE	TRANSVESTIST
TRANSMITTAL	TRANSPARENTISED	TRANSPORTEDNESS	TRANSUDATES	TRANSVESTISTS
TRANSMITTALS	TRANSPARENTISES	TRANSPORTER	TRANSUDATION	TRANSVESTITE
TRANSMITTANCE	TRANSPARENTIZE	TRANSPORTERS	TRANSUDATIONS	TRANSVESTITES
TRANSMITTANCES	TRANSPARENTIZED	TRANSPORTING	TRANSUDATORY	TRANSVESTITISM
TRANSMITTANCIES	TRANSPARENTIZES	TRANSPORTINGLY	TRANSUDING	TRANSVESTITISMS
TRANSMITTANCY	TRANSPARENTLY	TRANSPORTINGS	TRANSUMING	TRANSVESTS
TRANSMITTED	TRANSPARENTNESS	TRANSPORTIVE	TRANSUMPTION	TRAPANNERS
TRANSMITTER	TRANSPERSONAL	TRANSPORTS	TRANSUMPTIONS	TRAPANNING
TRANSMITTERS	TRANSPICUOUS	TRANSPOSABILITY	TRANSUMPTIVE	TRAPESINGS
TRANSMITTIBLE	TRANSPICUOUSLY	TRANSPOSABLE	TRANSUMPTS	TRAPEZIFORM
TRANSMITTING	TRANSPIERCE	TRANSPOSAL	TRANSURANIAN	TRAPEZISTS
TRANSMITTIVITY	TRANSPIERCED	TRANSPOSALS	TRANSURANIC	TRAPEZIUMS
TRANSMOGRIFIED	TRANSPIERCES	TRANSPOSED	TRANSURANICS	TRAPEZIUSES
TRANSMOGRIFIES	TRANSPIERCING	TRANSPOSER	TRANSURANIUM	TRAPEZOHEDRA
TRANSMOGRIFY	TRANSPIRABLE	TRANSPOSERS	TRANSVAGINAL	TRAPEZOHEDRAL
TRANSMOGRIFYING	TRANSPIRATION	TRANSPOSES	TRANSVALUATE	TRAPEZOHEDRON
TRANSMONTANE	TRANSPIRATIONAL	TRANSPOSING	TRANSVALUATED	TRAPEZOHEDRONS
TRANSMONTANES	TRANSPIRATIONS	TRANSPOSINGS	TRANSVALUATES	TRAPEZOIDAL
TRANSMOUNTAIN	TRANSPIRATORY	TRANSPOSITION	TRANSVALUATING	TRAPEZOIDS
TRANSMOVED	TRANSPIRED	TRANSPOSITIONAL	TRANSVALUATION	TRAPNESTED
TRANSMOVES	TRANSPIRES	TRANSPOSITIONS	TRANSVALUATIONS	TRAPNESTING
TRANSMOVING	TRANSPIRING	TRANSPOSITIVE	TRANSVALUE	TRAPPINESS
TRANSMUNDANE	TRANSPLACENTAL	TRANSPOSON	TRANSVALUED	TRAPPINESSES
TRANSMUTABILITY	TRANSPLANT	TRANSPOSONS	TRANSVALUER	TRAPSHOOTER
TRANSMUTABLE	TRANSPLANTABLE	TRANSPUTER	TRANSVALUERS	TRAPSHOOTERS
TRANSMUTABLY	TRANSPLANTATION	TRANSPUTERS	TRANSVALUES	TRAPSHOOTING
TRANSMUTATION	TRANSPLANTED	TRANSSEXUAL	TRANSVALUING	TRAPSHOOTINGS
TRANSMUTATIONAL	TRANSPLANTER	TRANSSEXUALISM	TRANSVERSAL	TRASHERIES
TRANSMUTATIONS	TRANSPLANTERS	TRANSSEXUALISMS	TRANSVERSALITY	TRASHINESS
TRANSMUTATIVE	TRANSPLANTING	TRANSSEXUALITY	TRANSVERSALLY	TRASHINESSES

TRASHTRIES	TRAYCLOTHS	TREEHOUSES	TRENDINESSES	TRIALLINGS
TRATTORIAS	TRAYMOBILE	TREELESSNESS	TRENDSETTER	TRIALLISTS
TRAUCHLING	TRAYMOBILES	TREELESSNESSES	TRENDSETTERS	TRIALOGUES
TRAUMATICALLY	TRAZODONES	TREENWARES	TRENDSETTING	TRIALWARES
TRAUMATISATION	TREACHERER	TREGETOURS	TRENDSETTINGS	TRIAMCINOLONE
TRAUMATISATIONS	TREACHERERS	TREHALOSES	TRENDYISMS	TRIAMCINOLONES
TRAUMATISE	TREACHERIES	TREILLAGED	TREPANATION	TRIANDRIAN
TRAUMATISED	TREACHEROUS	TREILLAGES	TREPANATIONS	TRIANDROUS
TRAUMATISES	TREACHEROUSLY	TREKSCHUIT	TREPANNERS	TRIANGULAR
TRAUMATISING	TREACHEROUSNESS	TREKSCHUITS	TREPANNING	TRIANGULARITIES
TRAUMATISM	TREACHETOUR	TRELLISING	TREPANNINGS	TRIANGULARITY
TRAUMATISMS	TREACHETOURS	TRELLISWORK	TREPHINATION	TRIANGULARLY
TRAUMATIZATION	TREACHOURS	TRELLISWORKS	TREPHINATIONS	TRIANGULATE
TRAUMATIZATIONS	TREACLIEST	TREMATODES	TREPHINERS	TRIANGULATED
TRAUMATIZE	TREACLINESS	TREMATOIDS	TREPHINING	TRIANGULATELY
TRAUMATIZED	TREACLINESSES	TREMBLEMENT	TREPHININGS	TRIANGULATES
TRAUMATIZES	TREADLINGS	TREMBLEMENTS	TREPIDATION	TRIANGULATING
TRAUMATIZING	TREADMILLS	TREMBLIEST	TREPIDATIONS	TRIANGULATION
TRAUMATOLOGICAL	TREADWHEEL	TREMBLINGLY	TREPIDATORY	TRIANGULATIONS
TRAUMATOLOGIES	TREADWHEELS	TREMBLINGS	TREPONEMAL	TRIAPSIDAL
TRAUMATOLOGY	TREASONABLE	TREMENDOUS	TREPONEMAS	TRIARCHIES
TRAUMATONASTIES	TREASONABLENESS	TREMENDOUSLY	TREPONEMATA	TRIATHLETE
TRAUMATONASTY	TREASONABLY	TREMENDOUSNESS	TREPONEMATOSES	TRIATHLETES
TRAVAILING	TREASONOUS	TREMOLANDI	TREPONEMATOSIS	TRIATHLONS
TRAVELATOR	TREASURABLE	TREMOLANDO	TREPONEMATOUS	TRIATOMICALLY
TRAVELATORS	TREASURELESS	TREMOLANDOS	TREPONEMES	TRIAXIALITIES
TRAVELINGS	TREASURERS	TREMOLANTS	TRESPASSED	TRIAXIALITY
TRAVELLERS	TREASURERSHIP	TREMOLITES	TRESPASSER	TRIBADISMS
TRAVELLING	TREASURERSHIPS	TREMOLITIC	TRESPASSERS	TRIBALISMS
TRAVELLINGS	TREASURIES	TREMORLESS	TRESPASSES	TRIBALISTIC
TRAVELOGUE	TREASURING	TREMULANTS	TRESPASSING	TRIBALISTS
TRAVELOGUES	TREATABILITIES	TREMULATED	TRESTLETREE	TRIBESPEOPLE
TRAVERSABLE	TREATABILITY	TREMULATES	TRESTLETREES	TRIBESWOMAN
TRAVERSALS	TREATMENTS	TREMULATING	TRESTLEWORK	TRIBESWOMEN
TRAVERSERS	TREATYLESS	TREMULOUSLY	TRESTLEWORKS	TRIBOELECTRIC
TRAVERSING	TREBBIANOS	TREMULOUSNESS	TRETINOINS	TRIBOLOGICAL
TRAVERSINGS	TREBLENESS	TREMULOUSNESSES	TREVALLIES	TRIBOLOGIES
TRAVERTINE	TREBLENESSES	TRENCHANCIES	TRIABLENESS	TRIBOLOGIST
TRAVERTINES	TREBUCHETS	TRENCHANCY	TRIABLENESSES	TRIBOLOGISTS
TRAVERTINS	TREBUCKETS	TRENCHANTLY	TRIACETATE	TRIBOMETER
TRAVESTIED	TRECENTIST	TRENCHARDS	TRIACETATES	TRIBOMETERS
TRAVESTIES	TRECENTISTS	TRENCHERMAN	TRIACONTER	TRIBRACHIAL
TRAVESTYING	TREDECILLION	TRENCHERMEN	TRIACONTERS	TRIBRACHIC
TRAVOLATOR	TREDECILLIONS	TRENDIFIED	TRIACTINAL	TRIBROMOETHANOL
TRAVOLATORS	TREDRILLES	TRENDIFIES	TRIADELPHOUS	TRIBROMOMETHANE
TRAWLERMAN	TREEHOPPER	TRENDIFYING	TRIADICALLY	TRIBULATED
TRAWLERMEN	TREEHOPPERS	TRENDINESS	TRIALITIES	TRIBULATES

T

TRIBULATING	TRICHINOSING	TRICHOTOMIES	TRICOLOURS	TRIFLURALINS
TRIBULATION	TRICHINOSIS	TRICHOTOMISE	TRICONSONANTAL	TRIFOLIATE
TRIBULATIONS	TRICHINOTIC	TRICHOTOMISED	TRICONSONANTIC	TRIFOLIATED
TRIBUNATES	TRICHINOUS	TRICHOTOMISES	TRICORNERED	TRIFOLIOLATE
TRIBUNESHIP	TRICHLORACETIC	TRICHOTOMISING	TRICORPORATE	TRIFOLIUMS
TRIBUNESHIPS	TRICHLORFON	TRICHOTOMIZE	TRICORPORATED	TRIFURCATE
TRIBUNICIAL	TRICHLORFONS	TRICHOTOMIZED	TRICOSTATE	TRIFURCATED
TRIBUNICIAN	TRICHLORIDE	TRICHOTOMIZES	TRICOTEUSE	TRIFURCATES
TRIBUNITIAL	TRICHLORIDES	TRICHOTOMIZING	TRICOTEUSES	TRIFURCATING
TRIBUNITIAN	TRICHLOROACETIC	TRICHOTOMOUS	TRICOTINES	TRIFURCATION
TRIBUTARIES	TRICHLOROETHANE	TRICHOTOMOUSLY	TRICROTISM	TRIFURCATIONS
TRIBUTARILY	TRICHLORPHON	TRICHOTOMY	TRICROTISMS	TRIGAMISTS
TRIBUTARINESS	TRICHLORPHONS	TRICHROISM	TRICROTOUS	TRIGEMINAL
TRIBUTARINESSES	TRICHOBACTERIA	TRICHROISMS	TRICUSPIDAL	TRIGEMINALS
TRICAMERAL	TRICHOCYST	TRICHROMAT	TRICUSPIDATE	TRIGEMINUS
TRICARBOXYLIC	TRICHOCYSTIC	TRICHROMATIC	TRICUSPIDS	TRIGGERFISH
TRICARPELLARY	TRICHOCYSTS	TRICHROMATISM	TRICYCLERS	TRIGGERFISHES
TRICENTENARIES	TRICHOGYNE	TRICHROMATISMS	TRICYCLICS	TRIGGERING
TRICENTENARY	TRICHOGYNES	TRICHROMATS	TRICYCLING	TRIGGERLESS
TRICENTENNIAL	TRICHOGYNIAL	TRICHROMIC	TRICYCLINGS	TRIGGERMAN
TRICENTENNIALS	TRICHOGYNIC	TRICHROMICS	TRICYCLIST	TRIGGERMEN
TRICEPHALOUS	TRICHOLOGICAL	TRICHRONOUS	TRICYCLISTS	TRIGLYCERIDE
TRICERATOPS	TRICHOLOGIES	TRICHURIASES	TRIDACTYLOUS	TRIGLYCERIDES
TRICERATOPSES	TRICHOLOGIST	TRICHURIASIS	TRIDENTATE	TRIGLYPHIC
TRICERIONS	TRICHOLOGISTS	TRICKERIES	TRIDIMENSIONAL	TRIGLYPHICAL
TRICHIASES	TRICHOLOGY	TRICKINESS	TRIDOMINIA	TRIGNESSES
TRICHIASIS	TRICHOMONACIDAL	TRICKINESSES	TRIDOMINIUM	TRIGONALLY
TRICHINELLA	TRICHOMONACIDE	TRICKISHLY	TRIDYMITES	TRIGONOMETER
TRICHINELLAE	TRICHOMONACIDES	TRICKISHNESS	TRIENNIALLY	TRIGONOMETERS
TRICHINELLAS	TRICHOMONAD	TRICKISHNESSES	TRIENNIALS	TRIGONOMETRIC
TRICHINIASES	TRICHOMONADAL	TRICKLIEST	TRIENNIUMS	TRIGONOMETRICAL
TRICHINIASIS	TRICHOMONADS	TRICKLINGLY	TRIERARCHAL	TRIGONOMETRIES
TRICHINISATION	TRICHOMONAL	TRICKLINGS	TRIERARCHIES	TRIGONOMETRY
TRICHINISATIONS	TRICHOMONIASES	TRICKSIEST	TRIERARCHS	TRIGRAMMATIC
TRICHINISE	TRICHOMONIASIS	TRICKSINESS	TRIERARCHY	TRIGRAMMIC
TRICHINISED	TRICHOPHYTON	TRICKSINESSES	TRIETHIODIDE	TRIGRAPHIC
TRICHINISES	TRICHOPHYTONS	TRICKSTERING	TRIETHIODIDES	TRIHALOMETHANE
TRICHINISING	TRICHOPHYTOSES	TRICKSTERINGS	TRIETHYLAMINE	TRIHALOMETHANES
TRICHINIZATION	TRICHOPHYTOSIS	TRICKSTERS	TRIETHYLAMINES	TRIHEDRALS
TRICHINIZATIONS	TRICHOPTERAN	TRICKTRACK	TRIFACIALS	TRIHEDRONS
TRICHINIZE	TRICHOPTERANS	TRICKTRACKS	TRIFARIOUS	TRIHYBRIDS
TRICHINIZED	TRICHOPTERIST	TRICLINIUM	TRIFFIDIAN	TRIHYDRATE
TRICHINIZES	TRICHOPTERISTS	TRICLOSANS	TRIFLINGLY	TRIHYDRATED
TRICHINIZING	TRICHOPTEROUS	TRICOLETTE	TRIFLINGNESS	TRIHYDRATES
TRICHINOSE	TRICHOTHECENE	TRICOLETTES	TRIFLINGNESSES	TRIHYDROXY
TRICHINOSED	TRICHOTHECENES	TRICOLORED	TRIFLUOPERAZINE	TRIIODOMETHANE
TRICHINOSES	TRICHOTOMIC	TRICOLOURED	TRIFLURALIN	TRIIODOMETHANES

TRILATERAL
TRILATERALISM
TRILATERALISMS
TRILATERALIST
TRILATERALISTS
TRILATERALLY
TRILATERALS
TRILATERATION
TRILATERATIONS
TRILINEATE
TRILINGUAL
TRILINGUALISM
TRILINGUALISMS
TRILINGUALLY
TRILITERAL
TRILITERALISM
TRILITERALISMS
TRILITERALS
TRILITHONS
TRILLIONAIRE
TRILLIONAIRES
TRILLIONTH
TRILLIONTHS
TRILOBATED
TRILOBITES
TRILOBITIC
TRILOCULAR
TRIMERISMS
TRIMESTERS
TRIMESTRAL
TRIMESTRIAL
TRIMETHADIONE
TRIMETHADIONES
TRIMETHOPRIM
TRIMETHOPRIMS
TRIMETHYLAMINE
TRIMETHYLAMINES
TRIMETHYLENE
TRIMETHYLENES
TRIMETRICAL
TRIMETROGON
TRIMETROGONS
TRIMMINGLY
TRIMNESSES
TRIMOLECULAR
TRIMONTHLY
TRIMORPHIC

TRIMORPHISM
TRIMORPHISMS
TRIMORPHOUS
TRIMPHONES
TRINACRIAN
TRINACRIFORM
TRINISCOPE
TRINISCOPES
TRINITARIAN
TRINITRATE
TRINITRATES
TRINITRINS
TRINITROBENZENE
TRINITROCRESOL
TRINITROCRESOLS
TRINITROPHENOL
TRINITROPHENOLS
TRINITROTOLUENE
TRINITROTOLUOL
TRINITROTOLUOLS
TRINKETERS
TRINKETING
TRINKETINGS
TRINKETRIES
TRINOCULAR
TRINOMIALISM
TRINOMIALISMS
TRINOMIALIST
TRINOMIALISTS
TRINOMIALLY
TRINOMIALS
TRINUCLEOTIDE
TRINUCLEOTIDES
TRIOECIOUS
TRIOXOBORIC
TRIOXYGENS
TRIPALMITIN
TRIPALMITINS
TRIPARTISM
TRIPARTISMS
TRIPARTITE
TRIPARTITELY
TRIPARTITION
TRIPARTITIONS
TRIPEHOUND
TRIPEHOUNDS
TRIPERSONAL

TRIPERSONALISM
TRIPERSONALISMS
TRIPERSONALIST
TRIPERSONALISTS
TRIPERSONALITY
TRIPETALOUS
TRIPHAMMER
TRIPHAMMERS
TRIPHENYLAMINE
TRIPHENYLAMINES
TRIPHIBIOUS
TRIPHOSPHATE
TRIPHOSPHATES
TRIPHTHONG
TRIPHTHONGAL
TRIPHTHONGS
TRIPHYLITE
TRIPHYLITES
TRIPHYLLOUS
TRIPINNATE
TRIPINNATELY
TRIPITAKAS
TRIPLENESS
TRIPLENESSES
TRIPLETAIL
TRIPLETAILS
TRIPLEXING
TRIPLICATE
TRIPLICATED
TRIPLICATES
TRIPLICATING
TRIPLICATION
TRIPLICATIONS
TRIPLICITIES
TRIPLICITY
TRIPLOBLASTIC
TRIPLOIDIES
TRIPPERISH
TRIPPINGLY
TRIPTEROUS
TRIPTYQUES
TRIPUDIARY
TRIPUDIATE
TRIPUDIATED
TRIPUDIATES
TRIPUDIATING
TRIPUDIATION

TRIPUDIATIONS
TRIPUDIUMS
TRIQUETRAE
TRIQUETRAL
TRIQUETROUS
TRIQUETROUSLY
TRIQUETRUM
TRIRADIATE
TRIRADIATELY
TRISACCHARIDE
TRISACCHARIDES
TRISAGIONS
TRISECTING
TRISECTION
TRISECTIONS
TRISECTORS
TRISECTRICES
TRISECTRIX
TRISKELION
TRISKELIONS
TRISOCTAHEDRA
TRISOCTAHEDRAL
TRISOCTAHEDRON
TRISOCTAHEDRONS
TRISTEARIN
TRISTEARINS
TRISTESSES
TRISTFULLY
TRISTFULNESS
TRISTFULNESSES
TRISTICHIC
TRISTICHOUS
TRISTIMULUS
TRISUBSTITUTED
TRISULCATE
TRISULFIDE
TRISULFIDES
TRISULPHIDE
TRISULPHIDES
TRISYLLABIC
TRISYLLABICAL
TRISYLLABICALLY
TRISYLLABLE
TRISYLLABLES
TRITAGONIST
TRITAGONISTS
TRITANOPES

TRITANOPIA
TRITANOPIAS
TRITANOPIC
TRITENESSES
TRITERNATE
TRITHEISMS
TRITHEISTIC
TRITHEISTICAL
TRITHEISTS
TRITHIONATE
TRITHIONATES
TRITHIONIC
TRITIATING
TRITIATION
TRITIATIONS
TRITICALES
TRITICALLY
TRITICALNESS
TRITICALNESSES
TRITICEOUS
TRITICISMS
TRITUBERCULAR
TRITUBERCULATE
TRITUBERCULIES
TRITUBERCULISM
TRITUBERCULISMS
TRITUBERCULY
TRITURABLE
TRITURATED
TRITURATES
TRITURATING
TRITURATION
TRITURATIONS
TRITURATOR
TRITURATORS
TRIUMPHALISM
TRIUMPHALISMS
TRIUMPHALIST
TRIUMPHALISTS
TRIUMPHALS
TRIUMPHANT
TRIUMPHANTLY
TRIUMPHERIES
TRIUMPHERS
TRIUMPHERY
TRIUMPHING
TRIUMPHINGS

T

TRIUMVIRAL	TROCHOMETERS	TROPHOBIOTIC	TROPOPHYTIC	TROWELLING
TRIUMVIRATE	TROCHOPHORE	TROPHOBLAST	TROPOSCATTER	TRUANTRIES
TRIUMVIRATES	TROCHOPHORES	TROPHOBLASTIC	TROPOSCATTERS	TRUANTSHIP
TRIUMVIRIES	TROCHOSPHERE	TROPHOBLASTS	TROPOSPHERE	TRUANTSHIPS
TRIUNITIES	TROCHOSPHERES	TROPHOLOGIES	TROPOSPHERES	TRUCKLINES
TRIVALENCE	TROCHOTRON	TROPHOLOGY	TROPOSPHERIC	TRUCKLINGS
TRIVALENCES	TROCHOTRONS	TROPHONEUROSES	TROPOTAXES	TRUCKLOADS
TRIVALENCIES	TROCTOLITE	TROPHONEUROSIS	TROPOTAXIS	TRUCKMASTER
TRIVALENCY	TROCTOLITES	TROPHOPLASM	TROTHPLIGHT	TRUCKMASTERS
TRIVALVULAR	TROGLODYTE	TROPHOPLASMS	TROTHPLIGHTED	TRUCKSTOPS
TRIVIALISATION	TROGLODYTES	TROPHOTACTIC	TROTHPLIGHTING	TRUCULENCE
TRIVIALISATIONS	TROGLODYTIC	TROPHOTAXES	TROTHPLIGHTS	TRUCULENCES
TRIVIALISE	TROGLODYTICAL	TROPHOTAXIS	TROUBADOUR	TRUCULENCIES
TRIVIALISED	TROGLODYTISM	TROPHOTROPIC	TROUBADOURS	TRUCULENCY
TRIVIALISES	TROGLODYTISMS	TROPHOTROPISM	TROUBLEDLY	TRUCULENTLY
TRIVIALISING	TROLLEYBUS	TROPHOTROPISMS	TROUBLEFREE	TRUEHEARTED
TRIVIALISM	TROLLEYBUSES	TROPHOZOITE	TROUBLEMAKER	TRUEHEARTEDNESS
TRIVIALISMS	TROLLEYBUSSES	TROPHOZOITES	TROUBLEMAKERS	TRUENESSES
TRIVIALIST	TROLLEYING	TROPICALISATION	TROUBLEMAKING	TRUEPENNIES
TRIVIALISTS	TROLLIUSES	TROPICALISE	TROUBLEMAKINGS	TRUFFLINGS
TRIVIALITIES	TROLLOPEES	TROPICALISED	TROUBLESHOOT	TRUMPERIES
TRIVIALITY	TROLLOPING	TROPICALISES	TROUBLESHOOTER	TRUMPETERS
TRIVIALIZATION	TROLLOPISH	TROPICALISING	TROUBLESHOOTERS	TRUMPETING
TRIVIALIZATIONS	TROMBICULID	TROPICALITIES	TROUBLESHOOTING	TRUMPETINGS
TRIVIALIZE	TROMBICULIDS	TROPICALITY	TROUBLESHOOTS	TRUMPETLIKE
TRIVIALIZED	TROMBIDIASES	TROPICALIZATION	TROUBLESHOT	TRUMPETWEED
TRIVIALIZES	TROMBIDIASIS	TROPICALIZE	TROUBLESOME	TRUMPETWEEDS
TRIVIALIZING	TROMBONIST	TROPICALIZED	TROUBLESOMELY	TRUNCATELY
TRIVIALNESS	TROMBONISTS	TROPICALIZES	TROUBLESOMENESS	TRUNCATING
TRIVIALNESSES	TROMOMETER	TROPICALIZING	TROUBLINGS	TRUNCATINGS
TRIWEEKLIES	TROMOMETERS	TROPICALLY	TROUBLOUSLY	TRUNCATION
TROCHAICALLY	TROMOMETRIC	TROPICBIRD	TROUBLOUSNESS	TRUNCATIONS
TROCHANTER	TROOPSHIPS	TROPICBIRDS	TROUBLOUSNESSES	TRUNCHEONED
TROCHANTERAL	TROOSTITES	TROPISMATIC	TROUGHINGS	TRUNCHEONER
TROCHANTERIC	TROPAEOLIN	TROPOCOLLAGEN	TROUGHLIKE	TRUNCHEONERS
TROCHANTERS	TROPAEOLINS	TROPOCOLLAGENS	TROUNCINGS	TRUNCHEONING
TROCHEAMETER	TROPAEOLUM	TROPOLOGIC	TROUSERING	TRUNCHEONS
TROCHEAMETERS	TROPAEOLUMS	TROPOLOGICAL	TROUSERINGS	TRUNKFISHES
TROCHELMINTH	TROPEOLINS	TROPOLOGICALLY	TROUSERLESS	TRUNKSLEEVE
TROCHELMINTHS	TROPHALLACTIC	TROPOLOGIES	TROUSSEAUS	TRUNKSLEEVES
TROCHILUSES	TROPHALLAXES	TROPOMYOSIN	TROUSSEAUX	TRUNKWORKS
TROCHISCUS	TROPHALLAXIS	TROPOMYOSINS	TROUTLINGS	TRUNNIONED
TROCHISCUSES	TROPHESIAL	TROPOPAUSE	TROUTSTONE	TRUSTABILITIES
TROCHLEARS	TROPHESIES	TROPOPAUSES	TROUTSTONES	TRUSTABILITY
TROCHOIDAL	TROPHICALLY	TROPOPHILOUS	TROUVAILLE	TRUSTAFARIAN
TROCHOIDALLY	TROPHOBIOSES	TROPOPHYTE	TROUVAILLES	TRUSTAFARIANS
TROCHOMETER	TROPHOBIOSIS	TROPOPHYTES	TROWELLERS	TRUSTBUSTER

TRUSTBUSTERS	TRYPTOPHANE	TUBERCULOID	TUILYIEING	TUMULTUOUSLY
TRUSTBUSTING	TRYPTOPHANES	TUBERCULOMA	TUILZIEING	TUMULTUOUSNESS
TRUSTBUSTINGS	TRYPTOPHANS	TUBERCULOMAS	TUITIONARY	TUNABILITIES
TRUSTEEING	TSAREVICHES	TUBERCULOMATA	TULARAEMIA	TUNABILITY
TRUSTEESHIP	TSAREVITCH	TUBERCULOSE	TULARAEMIAS	TUNABLENESS
TRUSTEESHIPS	TSAREVITCHES	TUBERCULOSED	TULARAEMIC	TUNABLENESSES
TRUSTFULLY	TSCHERNOSEM	TUBERCULOSES	TULAREMIAS	TUNBELLIED
TRUSTFULNESS	TSCHERNOSEMS	TUBERCULOSIS	TULIPOMANIA	TUNBELLIES
TRUSTFULNESSES	TSESAREVICH	TUBERCULOUS	TULIPOMANIAS	TUNEFULNESS
TRUSTINESS	TSESAREVICHES	TUBERCULOUSLY	TULIPWOODS	TUNEFULNESSES
TRUSTINESSES	TSESAREVITCH	TUBERCULUM	TUMATAKURU	TUNELESSLY
TRUSTINGLY	TSESAREVITCHES	TUBERIFEROUS	TUMATAKURUS	TUNELESSNESS
TRUSTINGNESS	TSESAREVNA	TUBERIFORM	TUMBLEBUGS	TUNELESSNESSES
TRUSTINGNESSES	TSESAREVNAS	TUBEROSITIES	TUMBLEDOWN	TUNESMITHS
TRUSTLESSLY	TSESAREWICH	TUBEROSITY	TUMBLEHOME	TUNGSTATES
TRUSTLESSNESS	TSESAREWICHES	TUBICOLOUS	TUMBLEHOMES	TUNGSTITES
TRUSTLESSNESSES	TSESAREWITCH	TUBIFICIDS	TUMBLERFUL	TUNNELINGS
TRUSTWORTHILY	TSESAREWITCHES	TUBIFLOROUS	TUMBLERFULS	TUNNELLERS
TRUSTWORTHINESS	TSOTSITAAL	TUBOCURARINE	TUMBLERSFUL	TUNNELLIKE
TRUSTWORTHY	TSOTSITAALS	TUBOCURARINES	TUMBLESETS	TUNNELLING
TRUTHFULLY	TSUNAMIGENIC	TUBOPLASTIES	TUMBLEWEED	TUNNELLINGS
TRUTHFULNESS	TSUTSUGAMUSHI	TUBOPLASTY	TUMBLEWEEDS	TUPPENNIES
TRUTHFULNESSES	TSUTSUGAMUSHIS	TUBULARIAN	TUMEFACIENT	TUPTOWINGS
TRUTHINESS	TUBBINESSES	TUBULARIANS	TUMEFACTION	TURACOVERDIN
TRUTHINESSES	TUBECTOMIES	TUBULARITIES	TUMEFACTIONS	TURACOVERDINS
TRUTHLESSNESS	TUBERACEOUS	TUBULARITY	TUMESCENCE	TURANGAWAEWAE
TRUTHLESSNESSES	TUBERCULAR	TUBULATING	TUMESCENCES	TURANGAWAEWAES
TRYINGNESS	TUBERCULARLY	TUBULATION	TUMESCENTLY	TURBELLARIAN
TRYINGNESSES	TUBERCULARS	TUBULATIONS	TUMIDITIES	TURBELLARIANS
TRYPAFLAVINE	TUBERCULATE	TUBULATORS	TUMIDNESSES	TURBIDIMETER
TRYPAFLAVINES	TUBERCULATED	TUBULATURE	TUMORGENIC	TURBIDIMETERS
TRYPANOCIDAL	TUBERCULATELY	TUBULATURES	TUMORGENICITIES	TURBIDIMETRIC
TRYPANOCIDE	TUBERCULATION	TUBULIFLORAL	TUMORGENICITY	TURBIDIMETRIES
TRYPANOCIDES	TUBERCULATIONS	TUBULIFLOROUS	TUMORIGENESES	TURBIDIMETRY
TRYPANOSOMAL	TUBERCULES	TUBULOUSLY	TUMORIGENESIS	TURBIDITES
TRYPANOSOME	TUBERCULIN	TUCKERBAGS	TUMORIGENIC	TURBIDITIES
TRYPANOSOMES	TUBERCULINS	TUCKERBOXES	TUMORIGENICITY	TURBIDNESS
TRYPANOSOMIASES	TUBERCULISATION	TUFFACEOUS	TUMULOSITIES	TURBIDNESSES
TRYPANOSOMIASIS	TUBERCULISE	TUFFTAFFETA	TUMULOSITY	TURBINACIOUS
TRYPANOSOMIC	TUBERCULISED	TUFFTAFFETAS	TUMULTUARY	TURBINATED
TRYPARSAMIDE	TUBERCULISES	TUFFTAFFETIES	TUMULTUATE	TURBINATES
TRYPARSAMIDES	TUBERCULISING	TUFFTAFFETY	TUMULTUATED	TURBINATION
TRYPSINOGEN	TUBERCULIZATION	TUFTAFFETA	TUMULTUATES	TURBINATIONS
TRYPSINOGENS	TUBERCULIZE	TUFTAFFETAS	TUMULTUATING	TURBOCHARGED
TRYPTAMINE	TUBERCULIZED	TUFTAFFETIES	TUMULTUATION	TURBOCHARGER
TRYPTAMINES	TUBERCULIZES	TUFTAFFETY	TUMULTUATIONS	TURBOCHARGERS
TRYPTOPHAN	TUBERCULIZING	TUILLETTES	TUMULTUOUS	TURBOCHARGING

T

TURBOCHARGINGS	TURNVEREIN	TWEEDLEDEES	TYPECASTER	TYPOGRAPHISTS
TURBOELECTRIC	TURNVEREINS	TWEENAGERS	TYPECASTERS	TYPOGRAPHS
TURBOGENERATOR	TUROPHILES	TWEENESSES	TYPECASTING	TYPOGRAPHY
TURBOGENERATORS	TURPENTINE	TWELVEFOLD	TYPECASTINGS	TYPOLOGICAL
TURBOMACHINERY	TURPENTINED	TWELVEMONTH	TYPEFOUNDER	TYPOLOGICALLY
TURBOPROPS	TURPENTINES	TWELVEMONTHS	TYPEFOUNDERS	TYPOLOGIES
TURBOSHAFT	TURPENTINING	TWENTIETHS	TYPEFOUNDING	TYPOLOGIST
TURBOSHAFTS	TURPENTINY	TWENTYFOLD	TYPEFOUNDINGS	TYPOLOGISTS
TURBULATOR	TURPITUDES	TWENTYFOLDS	TYPEFOUNDRIES	TYPOMANIAS
TURBULATORS	TURQUOISES	TWICHILDREN	TYPEFOUNDRY	TYPOTHETAE
TURBULENCE	TURRIBANTS	TWIDDLIEST	TYPESCRIPT	TYRANNESSES
TURBULENCES	TURRICULATE	TWIDDLINGS	TYPESCRIPTS	TYRANNICAL
TURBULENCIES	TURRICULATED	TWILIGHTED	TYPESETTER	TYRANNICALLY
TURBULENCY	TURTLEBACK	TWILIGHTING	TYPESETTERS	TYRANNICALNESS
TURBULENTLY	TURTLEBACKS	TWINBERRIES	TYPESETTING	TYRANNICIDAL
TURCOPOLES	TURTLEDOVE	TWINFLOWER	TYPESETTINGS	TYRANNICIDE
TURCOPOLIER	TURTLEDOVES	TWINFLOWERS	TYPESTYLES	TYRANNICIDES
TURCOPOLIERS	TURTLEHEAD	TWINKLIEST	TYPEWRITER	TYRANNISED
TURDUCKENS	TURTLEHEADS	TWINKLINGS	TYPEWRITERS	TYRANNISER
TURFGRASSES	TURTLENECK	TWISTABILITIES	TYPEWRITES	TYRANNISERS
TURFINESSES	TURTLENECKED	TWISTABILITY	TYPEWRITING	TYRANNISES
TURFSKIING	TURTLENECKS	TWITCHIEST	TYPEWRITINGS	TYRANNISING
TURFSKIINGS	TUTELARIES	TWITCHINGS	TYPEWRITTEN	TYRANNIZED
TURGENCIES	TUTIORISMS	TWITTERATI	TYPHACEOUS	TYRANNIZER
TURGESCENCE	TUTIORISTS	TWITTERERS	TYPHLITISES	TYRANNIZERS
TURGESCENCES	TUTORESSES	TWITTERING	TYPHLOLOGIES	TYRANNIZES
TURGESCENCIES	TUTORIALLY	TWITTERINGLY	TYPHLOLOGY	TYRANNIZING
TURGESCENCY	TUTORISING	TWITTERINGS	TYPHLOSOLE	TYRANNOSAUR
TURGESCENT	TUTORIZING	TWITTINGLY	TYPHLOSOLES	TYRANNOSAURS
TURGIDITIES	TUTORSHIPS	TWOFOLDNESS	TYPHOGENIC	TYRANNOSAURUS
TURGIDNESS	TUTOYERING	TWOFOLDNESSES	TYPHOIDINS	TYRANNOSAURUSES
TURGIDNESSES	TUTWORKERS	TWOPENCEWORTH	TYPICALITIES	TYRANNOUSLY
TURMOILING	TUTWORKMAN	TWOPENCEWORTHS	TYPICALITY	TYRANNOUSNESS
TURNABOUTS	TUTWORKMEN	TWOPENNIES	TYPICALNESS	TYRANNOUSNESSES
TURNAGAINS	TWADDLIEST	TWOSEATERS	TYPICALNESSES	TYREMAKERS
TURNAROUND	TWADDLINGS	TYCOONATES	TYPIFICATION	TYROCIDINE
TURNAROUNDS	TWALPENNIES	TYCOONERIES	TYPIFICATIONS	TYROCIDINES
TURNBROACH	TWANGINGLY	TYLECTOMIES	TYPOGRAPHED	TYROCIDINS
TURNBROACHES	TWANGLINGLY	TYMPANIFORM	TYPOGRAPHER	TYROGLYPHID
TURNBUCKLE	TWANGLINGS	TYMPANISTS	TYPOGRAPHERS	TYROGLYPHIDS
TURNBUCKLES	TWATTLINGS	TYMPANITES	TYPOGRAPHIA	TYROPITTAS
TURNROUNDS	TWAYBLADES	TYMPANITESES	TYPOGRAPHIC	TYROSINASE
TURNSTILES	TWEEDINESS	TYMPANITIC	TYPOGRAPHICAL	TYROSINASES
TURNSTONES	TWEEDINESSES	TYMPANITIS	TYPOGRAPHICALLY	TYROTHRICIN
TURNTABLES	TWEEDLEDEE	TYMPANITISES	TYPOGRAPHIES	TYROTHRICINS
TURNTABLIST	TWEEDLEDEED	TYNDALLIMETRIES	TYPOGRAPHING	
TURNTABLISTS	TWEEDLEDEEING	TYNDALLIMETRY	TYPOGRAPHIST	

U

UBERSEXUAL	ULTIMACIES	ULTRAFILTRATE	ULTRAMODERNIST	ULTRASENSITIVE
UBERSEXUALS	ULTIMATELY	ULTRAFILTRATES	ULTRAMODERNISTS	ULTRASENSUAL
UBIQUARIAN	ULTIMATENESS	ULTRAFILTRATION	ULTRAMONTANE	ULTRASERIOUS
UBIQUINONE	ULTIMATENESSES	ULTRAGLAMOROUS	ULTRAMONTANES	ULTRASHARP
UBIQUINONES	ULTIMATING	ULTRAHAZARDOUS	ULTRAMONTANISM	ULTRASHORT
UBIQUITARIAN	ULTIMATUMS	ULTRAHEATED	ULTRAMONTANISMS	ULTRASIMPLE
UBIQUITARIANISM	ULTIMOGENITURE	ULTRAHEATING	ULTRAMONTANIST	ULTRASLICK
UBIQUITARIANS	ULTIMOGENITURES	ULTRAHEATS	ULTRAMONTANISTS	ULTRASMALL
UBIQUITARY	ULTRABASIC	ULTRAHEAVY	ULTRAMUNDANE	ULTRASMART
UBIQUITIES	ULTRABASICS	ULTRAHUMAN	ULTRANATIONAL	ULTRASMOOTH
UBIQUITINATION	ULTRACAREFUL	ULTRAISTIC	ULTRAORTHODOX	ULTRASONIC
UBIQUITINATIONS	ULTRACASUAL	ULTRALARGE	ULTRAPATRIOTIC	ULTRASONICALLY
UBIQUITINS	ULTRACAUTIOUS	ULTRALEFTISM	ULTRAPHYSICAL	ULTRASONICS
UBIQUITOUS	ULTRACENTRIFUGE	ULTRALEFTISMS	ULTRAPOWERFUL	ULTRASONOGRAPHY
UBIQUITOUSLY	ULTRACIVILISED	ULTRALEFTIST	ULTRAPRACTICAL	ULTRASOUND
UBIQUITOUSNESS	ULTRACIVILIZED	ULTRALEFTISTS	ULTRAPRECISE	ULTRASOUNDS
UDOMETRIES	ULTRACLEAN	ULTRALIBERAL	ULTRAPRECISION	ULTRASTRUCTURAL
UFOLOGICAL	ULTRACOMMERCIAL	ULTRALIBERALISM	ULTRAPRECISIONS	ULTRASTRUCTURE
UFOLOGISTS	ULTRACOMPACT	ULTRALIBERALS	ULTRAQUIET	ULTRASTRUCTURES
UGLIFICATION	ULTRACOMPETENT	ULTRALIGHT	ULTRARADICAL	ULTRAVACUA
UGLIFICATIONS	ULTRACONVENIENT	ULTRALIGHTS	ULTRARADICALS	ULTRAVACUUM
UGLINESSES	ULTRACREPIDATE	ULTRAMAFIC	ULTRARAPID	ULTRAVACUUMS
UGSOMENESS	ULTRACREPIDATED	ULTRAMARATHON	ULTRAREFIED	ULTRAVIOLENCE
UGSOMENESSES	ULTRACREPIDATES	ULTRAMARATHONER	ULTRARATIONAL	ULTRAVIOLENCES
UINTAHITES	ULTRACRITICAL	ULTRAMARATHONS	ULTRAREALISM	ULTRAVIOLENT
UINTATHERE	ULTRADEMOCRATIC	ULTRAMARINE	ULTRAREALISMS	ULTRAVIOLET
UINTATHERES	ULTRADENSE	ULTRAMARINES	ULTRAREALIST	ULTRAVIOLETS
UITLANDERS	ULTRADISTANCE	ULTRAMASCULINE	ULTRAREALISTIC	ULTRAVIRILE
ULCERATING	ULTRADISTANT	ULTRAMICRO	ULTRAREALISTS	ULTRAVIRILITIES
ULCERATION	ULTRAEFFICIENT	ULTRAMICROMETER	ULTRAREFINED	ULTRAVIRILITY
ULCERATIONS	ULTRAENERGETIC	ULTRAMICROSCOPE	ULTRARELIABLE	ULTRAVIRUS
ULCERATIVE	ULTRAEXCLUSIVE	ULTRAMICROSCOPY	ULTRARIGHT	ULTRAVIRUSES
ULCEROGENIC	ULTRAFAMILIAR	ULTRAMICROTOME	ULTRARIGHTISM	ULTRAWIDEBAND
ULCEROUSLY	ULTRAFASTIDIOUS	ULTRAMICROTOMES	ULTRARIGHTISMS	ULTRAWIDEBANDS
ULCEROUSNESS	ULTRAFEMININE	ULTRAMICROTOMY	ULTRARIGHTIST	ULTRONEOUS
ULCEROUSNESSES	ULTRAFICHE	ULTRAMILITANT	ULTRARIGHTISTS	ULTRONEOUSLY
ULOTRICHIES	ULTRAFICHES	ULTRAMILITANTS	ULTRARIGHTS	ULTRONEOUSNESS
ULOTRICHOUS	ULTRAFILTER	ULTRAMINIATURE	ULTRAROMANTIC	ULULATIONS
ULSTERETTE	ULTRAFILTERED	ULTRAMODERN	ULTRAROYALIST	UMBELLATED
ULSTERETTES	ULTRAFILTERING	ULTRAMODERNISM	ULTRAROYALISTS	UMBELLATELY
ULTERIORLY	ULTRAFILTERS	ULTRAMODERNISMS	ULTRASECRET	UMBELLIFER

U

UMBELLIFEROUS	UNACCEPTANCES	UNADVISABLY	UNANALYSABLE	UNAPPLICABLE
UMBELLIFERS	UNACCEPTED	UNADVISEDLY	UNANALYSED	UNAPPOINTED
UMBELLULATE	UNACCLIMATED	UNADVISEDNESS	UNANALYTIC	UNAPPRECIATED
UMBELLULES	UNACCLIMATISED	UNADVISEDNESSES	UNANALYTICAL	UNAPPRECIATION
UMBILICALLY	UNACCLIMATIZED	UNAESTHETIC	UNANALYZABLE	UNAPPRECIATIONS
UMBILICALS	UNACCOMMODATED	UNAFFECTED	UNANALYZED	UNAPPRECIATIVE
UMBILICATE	UNACCOMMODATING	UNAFFECTEDLY	UNANCHORED	UNAPPREHENDED
UMBILICATED	UNACCOMPANIED	UNAFFECTEDNESS	UNANCHORING	UNAPPREHENSIBLE
UMBILICATION	UNACCOMPLISHED	UNAFFECTING	UNANESTHETISED	UNAPPREHENSIVE
UMBILICATIONS	UNACCOUNTABLE	UNAFFECTIONATE	UNANESTHETIZED	UNAPPRISED
UMBILICUSES	UNACCOUNTABLY	UNAFFILIATED	UNANIMATED	UNAPPROACHABLE
UMBILIFORM	UNACCOUNTED	UNAFFLUENT	UNANIMITIES	UNAPPROACHABLY
UMBONATION	UNACCREDITED	UNAFFORDABLE	UNANIMOUSLY	UNAPPROACHED
UMBONATIONS	UNACCULTURATED	UNAGGRESSIVE	UNANIMOUSNESS	UNAPPROPRIATE
UMBRACULATE	UNACCUSABLE	UNAGREEABLE	UNANIMOUSNESSES	UNAPPROPRIATED
UMBRACULIFORM	UNACCUSABLY	UNALIENABLE	UNANNEALED	UNAPPROPRIATES
UMBRACULUM	UNACCUSTOMED	UNALIENABLY	UNANNOTATED	UNAPPROPRIATING
UMBRAGEOUS	UNACCUSTOMEDLY	UNALIENATED	UNANNOUNCED	UNAPPROVED
UMBRAGEOUSLY	UNACHIEVABLE	UNALLEVIATED	UNANSWERABILITY	UNAPPROVING
UMBRAGEOUSNESS	UNACHIEVED	UNALLOCATED	UNANSWERABLE	UNAPPROVINGLY
UMBRATICAL	UNACKNOWLEDGED	UNALLOTTED	UNANSWERABLY	UNAPTNESSES
UMBRATILES	UNACQUAINT	UNALLOWABLE	UNANSWERED	UNARGUABLE
UMBRATILOUS	UNACQUAINTANCE	UNALLURING	UNANTICIPATED	UNARGUABLY
UMBRELLAED	UNACQUAINTANCES	UNALTERABILITY	UNANTICIPATEDLY	UNARMOURED
UMBRELLAING	UNACQUAINTED	UNALTERABLE	UNAPOLOGETIC	UNARRANGED
UMBRELLOES	UNACQUAINTING	UNALTERABLENESS	UNAPOLOGISING	UNARROGANT
UMBRIFEROUS	UNACQUAINTS	UNALTERABLY	UNAPOLOGIZING	UNARTFULLY
UMPIRESHIP	UNACTIVING	UNALTERING	UNAPOSTOLIC	UNARTICULATE
UMPIRESHIPS	UNACTORISH	UNAMBIGUOUS	UNAPOSTOLICAL	UNARTICULATED
UMPTEENTHS	UNACTUATED	UNAMBIGUOUSLY	UNAPOSTOLICALLY	UNARTIFICIAL
UNABASHEDLY	UNADAPTABLE	UNAMBITIOUS	UNAPPALLED	UNARTIFICIALLY
UNABATEDLY	UNADDRESSED	UNAMBITIOUSLY	UNAPPARELLED	UNARTISTIC
UNABBREVIATED	UNADJUDICATED	UNAMBIVALENT	UNAPPARELLING	UNARTISTLIKE
UNABOLISHED	UNADJUSTED	UNAMBIVALENTLY	UNAPPARELS	UNASCENDABLE
UNABRIDGED	UNADMIRING	UNAMENABLE	UNAPPARENT	UNASCENDED
UNABROGATED	UNADMITTED	UNAMENDABLE	UNAPPEALABLE	UNASCENDIBLE
UNABSOLVED	UNADMONISHED	UNAMIABILITIES	UNAPPEALABLY	UNASCERTAINABLE
UNABSORBED	UNADOPTABLE	UNAMIABILITY	UNAPPEALING	UNASCERTAINED
UNABSORBENT	UNADULTERATE	UNAMIABLENESS	UNAPPEALINGLY	UNASHAMEDLY
UNACADEMIC	UNADULTERATED	UNAMIABLENESSES	UNAPPEASABLE	UNASHAMEDNESS
UNACADEMICALLY	UNADULTERATEDLY	UNAMORTISED	UNAPPEASABLY	UNASHAMEDNESSES
UNACCENTED	UNADVENTROUS	UNAMORTIZED	UNAPPEASED	UNASPIRATED
UNACCENTUATED	UNADVENTUROUS	UNAMPLIFIED	UNAPPETISING	UNASPIRING
UNACCEPTABILITY	UNADVENTUROUSLY	UNAMUSABLE	UNAPPETISINGLY	UNASPIRINGLY
UNACCEPTABLE	UNADVERTISED	UNAMUSINGLY	UNAPPETIZING	UNASPIRINGNESS
UNACCEPTABLY	UNADVISABLE	UNANAESTHETISED	UNAPPETIZINGLY	UNASSAILABILITY
UNACCEPTANCE	UNADVISABLENESS	UNANAESTHETIZED	UNAPPLAUSIVE	UNASSAILABLE

UNASSAILABLY
UNASSAILED
UNASSEMBLED
UNASSERTIVE
UNASSERTIVELY
UNASSIGNABLE
UNASSIGNED
UNASSIMILABLE
UNASSIMILATED
UNASSISTED
UNASSISTEDLY
UNASSISTING
UNASSOCIATED
UNASSUAGEABLE
UNASSUAGED
UNASSUMING
UNASSUMINGLY
UNASSUMINGNESS
UNATHLETIC
UNATONABLE
UNATTACHED
UNATTAINABLE
UNATTAINABLY
UNATTAINTED
UNATTEMPTED
UNATTENDED
UNATTENDING
UNATTENTIVE
UNATTENUATED
UNATTESTED
UNATTRACTIVE
UNATTRACTIVELY
UNATTRIBUTABLE
UNATTRIBUTED
UNAUGMENTED
UNAUSPICIOUS
UNAUTHENTIC
UNAUTHENTICATED
UNAUTHENTICITY
UNAUTHORISED
UNAUTHORITATIVE
UNAUTHORIZED
UNAUTOMATED
UNAVAILABILITY
UNAVAILABLE
UNAVAILABLENESS
UNAVAILABLY

UNAVAILING
UNAVAILINGLY
UNAVAILINGNESS
UNAVERTABLE
UNAVERTIBLE
UNAVOIDABILITY
UNAVOIDABLE
UNAVOIDABLENESS
UNAVOIDABLY
UNAVOWEDLY
UNAWAKENED
UNAWAKENING
UNAWARENESS
UNAWARENESSES
UNBAILABLE
UNBALANCED
UNBALANCES
UNBALANCING
UNBALLASTED
UNBANDAGED
UNBANDAGES
UNBANDAGING
UNBAPTISED
UNBAPTISES
UNBAPTISING
UNBAPTIZED
UNBAPTIZES
UNBAPTIZING
UNBARBERED
UNBARRICADE
UNBARRICADED
UNBARRICADES
UNBARRICADING
UNBATTERED
UNBEARABLE
UNBEARABLENESS
UNBEARABLY
UNBEATABLE
UNBEATABLY
UNBEAUTIFUL
UNBEAUTIFULLY
UNBEAVERED
UNBECOMING
UNBECOMINGLY
UNBECOMINGNESS
UNBECOMINGS
UNBEDIMMED

UNBEDINNED
UNBEFITTING
UNBEFRIENDED
UNBEGETTING
UNBEGINNING
UNBEGOTTEN
UNBEGUILED
UNBEGUILES
UNBEGUILING
UNBEHOLDEN
UNBEKNOWNST
UNBELIEVABILITY
UNBELIEVABLE
UNBELIEVABLY
UNBELIEVED
UNBELIEVER
UNBELIEVERS
UNBELIEVES
UNBELIEVING
UNBELIEVINGLY
UNBELIEVINGNESS
UNBELLIGERENT
UNBENDABLE
UNBENDINGLY
UNBENDINGNESS
UNBENDINGNESSES
UNBENDINGS
UNBENEFICED
UNBENEFICIAL
UNBENEFITED
UNBENEFITTED
UNBENIGHTED
UNBENIGNANT
UNBENIGNLY
UNBESEEMED
UNBESEEMING
UNBESEEMINGLY
UNBESOUGHT
UNBESPEAKING
UNBESPEAKS
UNBESPOKEN
UNBESTOWED
UNBETRAYED
UNBETTERABLE
UNBETTERED
UNBEWAILED
UNBIASEDLY

UNBIASEDNESS
UNBIASEDNESSES
UNBIASSEDLY
UNBIASSEDNESS
UNBIASSEDNESSES
UNBIASSING
UNBIASSINGS
UNBIBLICAL
UNBINDINGS
UNBIRTHDAY
UNBIRTHDAYS
UNBISHOPED
UNBISHOPING
UNBLAMABLE
UNBLAMABLY
UNBLAMEABLE
UNBLAMEABLY
UNBLEACHED
UNBLEMISHED
UNBLENCHED
UNBLENCHING
UNBLESSEDNESS
UNBLESSEDNESSES
UNBLESSING
UNBLINDFOLD
UNBLINDFOLDED
UNBLINDFOLDING
UNBLINDFOLDS
UNBLINDING
UNBLINKING
UNBLINKINGLY
UNBLISSFUL
UNBLOCKING
UNBLOODIED
UNBLOODIER
UNBLOODIEST
UNBLUSHING
UNBLUSHINGLY
UNBLUSHINGNESS
UNBOASTFUL
UNBONNETED
UNBONNETING
UNBORROWED
UNBOSOMERS
UNBOSOMING
UNBOTTLING
UNBOTTOMED

UNBOUNCIER
UNBOUNCIEST
UNBOUNDEDLY
UNBOUNDEDNESS
UNBOUNDEDNESSES
UNBOWDLERISED
UNBOWDLERIZED
UNBRACKETED
UNBRAIDING
UNBRANCHED
UNBREACHABLE
UNBREACHED
UNBREAKABLE
UNBREATHABLE
UNBREATHED
UNBREATHING
UNBREECHED
UNBREECHES
UNBREECHING
UNBRIBABLE
UNBRIDGEABLE
UNBRIDLEDLY
UNBRIDLEDNESS
UNBRIDLEDNESSES
UNBRIDLING
UNBRILLIANT
UNBROKENLY
UNBROKENNESS
UNBROKENNESSES
UNBROTHERLIKE
UNBROTHERLY
UNBUCKLING
UNBUDGEABLE
UNBUDGEABLY
UNBUDGETED
UNBUDGINGLY
UNBUFFERED
UNBUILDABLE
UNBUILDING
UNBULKIEST
UNBUNDLERS
UNBUNDLING
UNBUNDLINGS
UNBURDENED
UNBURDENING
UNBUREAUCRATIC
UNBURNABLE

U

ten to fifteen letter words | 1179

UNBURNISHED	UNCATEGORISABLE	UNCHASTELY	UNCINARIAS	UNCLIMBABLENESS
UNBURROWED	UNCATEGORIZABLE	UNCHASTENED	UNCINARIASES	UNCLINCHED
UNBURROWING	UNCEASINGLY	UNCHASTENESS	UNCINARIASIS	UNCLINCHES
UNBURTHENED	UNCEASINGNESS	UNCHASTENESSES	UNCINEMATIC	UNCLINCHING
UNBURTHENING	UNCEASINGNESSES	UNCHASTEST	UNCIPHERED	UNCLIPPING
UNBURTHENS	UNCELEBRATED	UNCHASTISABLE	UNCIPHERING	UNCLOAKING
UNBUSINESSLIKE	UNCENSORED	UNCHASTISED	UNCIRCULATED	UNCLOGGING
UNBUTTERED	UNCENSORIOUS	UNCHASTITIES	UNCIRCUMCISED	UNCLOISTER
UNBUTTONED	UNCENSURED	UNCHASTITY	UNCIRCUMCISION	UNCLOISTERED
UNBUTTONING	UNCEREBRAL	UNCHASTIZABLE	UNCIRCUMCISIONS	UNCLOISTERING
UNCALCIFIED	UNCEREMONIOUS	UNCHASTIZED	UNCIRCUMSCRIBED	UNCLOISTERS
UNCALCINED	UNCEREMONIOUSLY	UNCHAUVINISTIC	UNCIVILISED	UNCLOTHING
UNCALCULATED	UNCERTAINLY	UNCHECKABLE	UNCIVILISEDLY	UNCLOUDEDLY
UNCALCULATING	UNCERTAINNESS	UNCHECKING	UNCIVILISEDNESS	UNCLOUDEDNESS
UNCALIBRATED	UNCERTAINNESSES	UNCHEERFUL	UNCIVILITIES	UNCLOUDEDNESSES
UNCALLOUSED	UNCERTAINTIES	UNCHEERFULLY	UNCIVILITY	UNCLOUDIER
UNCANCELED	UNCERTAINTY	UNCHEERFULNESS	UNCIVILIZED	UNCLOUDIEST
UNCANCELLED	UNCERTIFICATED	UNCHEWABLE	UNCIVILIZEDLY	UNCLOUDING
UNCANDIDLY	UNCERTIFIED	UNCHILDING	UNCIVILIZEDNESS	UNCLUBABLE
UNCANDIDNESS	UNCHAINING	UNCHILDLIKE	UNCIVILNESS	UNCLUBBABLE
UNCANDIDNESSES	UNCHAIRING	UNCHIVALROUS	UNCIVILNESSES	UNCLUTCHED
UNCANDOURS	UNCHALLENGEABLE	UNCHIVALROUSLY	UNCLAMPING	UNCLUTCHES
UNCANNIEST	UNCHALLENGEABLY	UNCHLORINATED	UNCLARIFIED	UNCLUTCHING
UNCANNINESS	UNCHALLENGED	UNCHOREOGRAPHED	UNCLARITIES	UNCLUTTERED
UNCANNINESSES	UNCHALLENGING	UNCHRISTEN	UNCLASPING	UNCLUTTERING
UNCANONICAL	UNCHANCIER	UNCHRISTENED	UNCLASSICAL	UNCLUTTERS
UNCANONICALNESS	UNCHANCIEST	UNCHRISTENING	UNCLASSIER	UNCOALESCE
UNCANONISE	UNCHANGEABILITY	UNCHRISTENS	UNCLASSIEST	UNCOALESCED
UNCANONISED	UNCHANGEABLE	UNCHRISTIAN	UNCLASSIFIABLE	UNCOALESCES
UNCANONISES	UNCHANGEABLY	UNCHRISTIANED	UNCLASSIFIED	UNCOALESCING
UNCANONISING	UNCHANGING	UNCHRISTIANING	UNCLEANEST	UNCOATINGS
UNCANONIZE	UNCHANGINGLY	UNCHRISTIANISE	UNCLEANLIER	UNCODIFIED
UNCANONIZED	UNCHANGINGNESS	UNCHRISTIANISED	UNCLEANLIEST	UNCOERCIVE
UNCANONIZES	UNCHANNELED	UNCHRISTIANISES	UNCLEANLINESS	UNCOERCIVELY
UNCANONIZING	UNCHANNELLED	UNCHRISTIANIZE	UNCLEANLINESSES	UNCOFFINED
UNCAPITALISED	UNCHAPERONED	UNCHRISTIANIZED	UNCLEANNESS	UNCOFFINING
UNCAPITALIZED	UNCHARGING	UNCHRISTIANIZES	UNCLEANNESSES	UNCOLLECTABLE
UNCAPSIZABLE	UNCHARIEST	UNCHRISTIANLIKE	UNCLEANSED	UNCOLLECTABLES
UNCAPTIONED	UNCHARISMATIC	UNCHRISTIANLY	UNCLEAREST	UNCOLLECTED
UNCAPTURABLE	UNCHARITABLE	UNCHRISTIANS	UNCLEARNESS	UNCOLLECTIBLE
UNCARPETED	UNCHARITABLY	UNCHRONICLED	UNCLEARNESSES	UNCOLLECTIBLES
UNCASTRATED	UNCHARITIES	UNCHRONOLOGICAL	UNCLENCHED	UNCOLOURED
UNCATALOGED	UNCHARMING	UNCHURCHED	UNCLENCHES	UNCOMATABLE
UNCATALOGUED	UNCHARNELLED	UNCHURCHES	UNCLENCHING	UNCOMBATIVE
UNCATCHABLE	UNCHARNELLING	UNCHURCHING	UNCLERICAL	UNCOMBINED
UNCATCHIER	UNCHARNELS	UNCHURCHLY	UNCLESHIPS	UNCOMBINES
UNCATCHIEST	UNCHARTERED	UNCILIATED	UNCLIMBABLE	UNCOMBINING

UNCOMEATABLE	UNCOMPROMISABLE	UNCONJECTURED	UNCONTRACTED	UNCREATEDNESS
UNCOMELIER	UNCOMPROMISING	UNCONJUGAL	UNCONTRADICTED	UNCREATEDNESSES
UNCOMELIEST	UNCOMPUTERISED	UNCONJUGATED	UNCONTRIVED	UNCREATING
UNCOMELINESS	UNCOMPUTERIZED	UNCONJUNCTIVE	UNCONTROLLABLE	UNCREATIVE
UNCOMELINESSES	UNCONCEALABLE	UNCONNECTED	UNCONTROLLABLY	UNCREDENTIALED
UNCOMFIEST	UNCONCEALED	UNCONNECTEDLY	UNCONTROLLED	UNCREDIBLE
UNCOMFORTABLE	UNCONCEALING	UNCONNECTEDNESS	UNCONTROLLEDLY	UNCREDITABLE
UNCOMFORTABLY	UNCONCEIVABLE	UNCONNIVING	UNCONTROVERSIAL	UNCREDITED
UNCOMFORTED	UNCONCEIVABLY	UNCONQUERABLE	UNCONTROVERTED	UNCRIPPLED
UNCOMMENDABLE	UNCONCEIVED	UNCONQUERABLY	UNCONVENTIONAL	UNCRITICAL
UNCOMMENDABLY	UNCONCERNED	UNCONQUERED	UNCONVERSABLE	UNCRITICALLY
UNCOMMENDED	UNCONCERNEDLY	UNCONSCIENTIOUS	UNCONVERSANT	UNCROSSABLE
UNCOMMERCIAL	UNCONCERNEDNESS	UNCONSCIONABLE	UNCONVERTED	UNCROSSING
UNCOMMITTED	UNCONCERNING	UNCONSCIONABLY	UNCONVERTIBLE	UNCROWNING
UNCOMMONER	UNCONCERNMENT	UNCONSCIOUS	UNCONVICTED	UNCRUMPLED
UNCOMMONEST	UNCONCERNMENTS	UNCONSCIOUSES	UNCONVINCED	UNCRUMPLES
UNCOMMONLY	UNCONCERNS	UNCONSCIOUSLY	UNCONVINCING	UNCRUMPLING
UNCOMMONNESS	UNCONCERTED	UNCONSCIOUSNESS	UNCONVINCINGLY	UNCRUSHABLE
UNCOMMONNESSES	UNCONCILIATORY	UNCONSECRATE	UNCONVOYED	UNCRYSTALLISED
UNCOMMUNICABLE	UNCONCLUSIVE	UNCONSECRATED	UNCOOPERATIVE	UNCRYSTALLIZED
UNCOMMUNICATED	UNCONCOCTED	UNCONSECRATES	UNCOOPERATIVELY	UNCTIONLESS
UNCOMMUNICATIVE	UNCONDITIONAL	UNCONSECRATING	UNCOORDINATED	UNCTUOSITIES
UNCOMMUTED	UNCONDITIONALLY	UNCONSENTANEOUS	UNCOPYRIGHTABLE	UNCTUOSITY
UNCOMPACTED	UNCONDITIONED	UNCONSENTING	UNCOQUETTISH	UNCTUOUSLY
UNCOMPANIED	UNCONFEDERATED	UNCONSIDERED	UNCORRECTABLE	UNCTUOUSNESS
UNCOMPANIONABLE	UNCONFESSED	UNCONSIDERING	UNCORRECTED	UNCTUOUSNESSES
UNCOMPANIONED	UNCONFINABLE	UNCONSOLED	UNCORRELATED	UNCUCKOLDED
UNCOMPASSIONATE	UNCONFINED	UNCONSOLIDATED	UNCORROBORATED	UNCULTIVABLE
UNCOMPELLED	UNCONFINEDLY	UNCONSTANT	UNCORRUPTED	UNCULTIVATABLE
UNCOMPELLING	UNCONFINES	UNCONSTRAINABLE	UNCORSETED	UNCULTIVATED
UNCOMPENSATED	UNCONFINING	UNCONSTRAINED	UNCOSTLIER	UNCULTURED
UNCOMPETITIVE	UNCONFIRMED	UNCONSTRAINEDLY	UNCOSTLIEST	UNCUMBERED
UNCOMPLACENT	UNCONFORMABLE	UNCONSTRAINT	UNCOUNSELLED	UNCURBABLE
UNCOMPLAINING	UNCONFORMABLY	UNCONSTRAINTS	UNCOUNTABLE	UNCURTAILED
UNCOMPLAININGLY	UNCONFORMING	UNCONSTRICTED	UNCOUPLERS	UNCURTAINED
UNCOMPLAISANT	UNCONFORMITIES	UNCONSTRUCTED	UNCOUPLING	UNCURTAINING
UNCOMPLAISANTLY	UNCONFORMITY	UNCONSTRUCTIVE	UNCOURAGEOUS	UNCURTAINS
UNCOMPLETED	UNCONFOUNDED	UNCONSUMED	UNCOURTEOUS	UNCUSTOMARILY
UNCOMPLIANT	UNCONFUSED	UNCONSUMMATED	UNCOURTLIER	UNCUSTOMARY
UNCOMPLICATED	UNCONFUSEDLY	UNCONTAINABLE	UNCOURTLIEST	UNCUSTOMED
UNCOMPLIMENTARY	UNCONFUSES	UNCONTAMINATED	UNCOURTLINESS	UNCYNICALLY
UNCOMPLYING	UNCONFUSING	UNCONTEMNED	UNCOURTLINESSES	UNDANCEABLE
UNCOMPOSABLE	UNCONGEALED	UNCONTEMPLATED	UNCOUTHEST	UNDAUNTABLE
UNCOMPOUNDED	UNCONGEALING	UNCONTEMPORARY	UNCOUTHNESS	UNDAUNTEDLY
UNCOMPREHENDED	UNCONGEALS	UNCONTENTIOUS	UNCOUTHNESSES	UNDAUNTEDNESS
UNCOMPREHENDING	UNCONGENIAL	UNCONTESTABLE	UNCOVENANTED	UNDAUNTEDNESSES
UNCOMPREHENSIVE	UNCONGENIALITY	UNCONTESTED	UNCOVERING	UNDAZZLING

U

UNDEBARRED
UNDEBATABLE
UNDEBATABLY
UNDEBAUCHED
UNDECADENT
UNDECAGONS
UNDECEIVABLE
UNDECEIVED
UNDECEIVER
UNDECEIVERS
UNDECEIVES
UNDECEIVING
UNDECIDABILITY
UNDECIDABLE
UNDECIDEDLY
UNDECIDEDNESS
UNDECIDEDNESSES
UNDECIDEDS
UNDECILLION
UNDECILLIONS
UNDECIMOLE
UNDECIMOLES
UNDECIPHERABLE
UNDECIPHERED
UNDECISIVE
UNDECLARED
UNDECLINING
UNDECOMPOSABLE
UNDECOMPOSED
UNDECORATED
UNDEDICATED
UNDEFEATED
UNDEFENDED
UNDEFINABLE
UNDEFOLIATED
UNDEFORMED
UNDEIFYING
UNDELAYING
UNDELECTABLE
UNDELEGATED
UNDELETING
UNDELIBERATE
UNDELIGHTED
UNDELIGHTFUL
UNDELIGHTS
UNDELIVERABLE
UNDELIVERED

UNDEMANDING
UNDEMOCRATIC
UNDEMONSTRABLE
UNDEMONSTRATIVE
UNDENIABLE
UNDENIABLENESS
UNDENIABLY
UNDEPENDABLE
UNDEPENDING
UNDEPLORED
UNDEPRAVED
UNDEPRECIATED
UNDEPRESSED
UNDEPRIVED
UNDERACHIEVE
UNDERACHIEVED
UNDERACHIEVER
UNDERACHIEVERS
UNDERACHIEVES
UNDERACHIEVING
UNDERACTED
UNDERACTING
UNDERACTION
UNDERACTIONS
UNDERACTIVE
UNDERACTIVITIES
UNDERACTIVITY
UNDERACTOR
UNDERACTORS
UNDERAGENT
UNDERAGENTS
UNDERBAKED
UNDERBAKES
UNDERBAKING
UNDERBEARER
UNDERBEARERS
UNDERBEARING
UNDERBEARINGS
UNDERBEARS
UNDERBELLIES
UNDERBELLY
UNDERBIDDER
UNDERBIDDERS
UNDERBIDDING
UNDERBITES
UNDERBITING
UNDERBITTEN

UNDERBLANKET
UNDERBLANKETS
UNDERBODIES
UNDERBORNE
UNDERBOSSES
UNDERBOUGH
UNDERBOUGHS
UNDERBOUGHT
UNDERBREATH
UNDERBREATHS
UNDERBREEDING
UNDERBREEDINGS
UNDERBRIDGE
UNDERBRIDGES
UNDERBRIMS
UNDERBRUSH
UNDERBRUSHED
UNDERBRUSHES
UNDERBRUSHING
UNDERBUDDED
UNDERBUDDING
UNDERBUDGET
UNDERBUDGETED
UNDERBUDGETING
UNDERBUDGETS
UNDERBUILD
UNDERBUILDER
UNDERBUILDERS
UNDERBUILDING
UNDERBUILDS
UNDERBUILT
UNDERBURNT
UNDERBUSHED
UNDERBUSHES
UNDERBUSHING
UNDERBUYING
UNDERCAPITALISE
UNDERCAPITALIZE
UNDERCARDS
UNDERCARRIAGE
UNDERCARRIAGES
UNDERCARTS
UNDERCASTS
UNDERCHARGE
UNDERCHARGED
UNDERCHARGES
UNDERCHARGING

UNDERCLASS
UNDERCLASSES
UNDERCLASSMAN
UNDERCLASSMEN
UNDERCLAYS
UNDERCLIFF
UNDERCLIFFS
UNDERCLOTHE
UNDERCLOTHED
UNDERCLOTHES
UNDERCLOTHING
UNDERCLOTHINGS
UNDERCLUBBED
UNDERCLUBBING
UNDERCLUBS
UNDERCOATED
UNDERCOATING
UNDERCOATINGS
UNDERCOATS
UNDERCOOKED
UNDERCOOKING
UNDERCOOKS
UNDERCOOLED
UNDERCOOLING
UNDERCOOLS
UNDERCOUNT
UNDERCOUNTED
UNDERCOUNTING
UNDERCOUNTS
UNDERCOVER
UNDERCOVERT
UNDERCOVERTS
UNDERCRACKERS
UNDERCREST
UNDERCRESTED
UNDERCRESTING
UNDERCRESTS
UNDERCROFT
UNDERCROFTS
UNDERCURRENT
UNDERCURRENTS
UNDERCUTTING
UNDERDAMPER
UNDERDAMPERS
UNDERDECKS
UNDERDEVELOP
UNDERDEVELOPED

UNDERDEVELOPING
UNDERDEVELOPS
UNDERDOERS
UNDERDOING
UNDERDOSED
UNDERDOSES
UNDERDOSING
UNDERDRAIN
UNDERDRAINAGE
UNDERDRAINAGES
UNDERDRAINED
UNDERDRAINING
UNDERDRAINS
UNDERDRAWERS
UNDERDRAWING
UNDERDRAWINGS
UNDERDRAWN
UNDERDRAWS
UNDERDRESS
UNDERDRESSED
UNDERDRESSES
UNDERDRESSING
UNDERDRIVE
UNDERDRIVES
UNDEREARTH
UNDEREARTHS
UNDEREATEN
UNDEREATING
UNDEREDUCATED
UNDEREMPHASES
UNDEREMPHASIS
UNDEREMPHASISE
UNDEREMPHASISED
UNDEREMPHASISES
UNDEREMPHASIZE
UNDEREMPHASIZED
UNDEREMPHASIZES
UNDEREMPLOYED
UNDEREMPLOYMENT
UNDERESTIMATE
UNDERESTIMATED
UNDERESTIMATES
UNDERESTIMATING
UNDERESTIMATION
UNDEREXPLOIT
UNDEREXPLOITED
UNDEREXPLOITING

UNDEREXPLOITS
UNDEREXPOSE
UNDEREXPOSED
UNDEREXPOSES
UNDEREXPOSING
UNDEREXPOSURE
UNDEREXPOSURES
UNDERFEEDING
UNDERFEEDS
UNDERFELTS
UNDERFINANCED
UNDERFINISHED
UNDERFIRED
UNDERFIRES
UNDERFIRING
UNDERFISHED
UNDERFISHES
UNDERFISHING
UNDERFLOOR
UNDERFLOWS
UNDERFONGED
UNDERFONGING
UNDERFONGS
UNDERFOOTED
UNDERFOOTING
UNDERFOOTS
UNDERFULFIL
UNDERFULFILL
UNDERFULFILLED
UNDERFULFILLING
UNDERFULFILLS
UNDERFULFILS
UNDERFUNDED
UNDERFUNDING
UNDERFUNDINGS
UNDERFUNDS
UNDERGARMENT
UNDERGARMENTS
UNDERGIRDED
UNDERGIRDING
UNDERGIRDS
UNDERGLAZE
UNDERGLAZES
UNDERGOERS
UNDERGOING
UNDERGOWNS
UNDERGRADS

UNDERGRADUATE
UNDERGRADUATES
UNDERGRADUETTE
UNDERGRADUETTES
UNDERGROUND
UNDERGROUNDER
UNDERGROUNDERS
UNDERGROUNDS
UNDERGROVE
UNDERGROVES
UNDERGROWN
UNDERGROWTH
UNDERGROWTHS
UNDERHAIRS
UNDERHANDED
UNDERHANDEDLY
UNDERHANDEDNESS
UNDERHANDS
UNDERHEATED
UNDERHEATING
UNDERHEATS
UNDERHONEST
UNDERINFLATED
UNDERINFLATION
UNDERINFLATIONS
UNDERINSURE
UNDERINSURED
UNDERINSURES
UNDERINSURING
UNDERINVEST
UNDERINVESTED
UNDERINVESTING
UNDERINVESTMENT
UNDERINVESTS
UNDERJAWED
UNDERKEEPER
UNDERKEEPERS
UNDERKEEPING
UNDERKEEPS
UNDERKILLS
UNDERKINGDOM
UNDERKINGDOMS
UNDERKINGS
UNDERLAPPED
UNDERLAPPING
UNDERLAYER
UNDERLAYERS

UNDERLAYING
UNDERLAYMENT
UNDERLAYMENTS
UNDERLEASE
UNDERLEASED
UNDERLEASES
UNDERLEASING
UNDERLEAVES
UNDERLETTER
UNDERLETTERS
UNDERLETTING
UNDERLETTINGS
UNDERLEVERAGED
UNDERLIERS
UNDERLINED
UNDERLINEN
UNDERLINENS
UNDERLINES
UNDERLINGS
UNDERLINING
UNDERLININGS
UNDERLOADED
UNDERLOADING
UNDERLOADS
UNDERLOOKER
UNDERLOOKERS
UNDERLYING
UNDERLYINGLY
UNDERMANNED
UNDERMANNING
UNDERMANNINGS
UNDERMASTED
UNDERMEANING
UNDERMEANINGS
UNDERMENTIONED
UNDERMINDE
UNDERMINDED
UNDERMINDES
UNDERMINDING
UNDERMINED
UNDERMINER
UNDERMINERS
UNDERMINES
UNDERMINING
UNDERMININGS
UNDERNAMED
UNDERNEATH

UNDERNEATHS
UNDERNICENESS
UNDERNICENESSES
UNDERNOTED
UNDERNOTES
UNDERNOTING
UNDERNOURISH
UNDERNOURISHED
UNDERNOURISHES
UNDERNOURISHING
UNDERNTIME
UNDERNTIMES
UNDERNUTRITION
UNDERNUTRITIONS
UNDEROCCUPIED
UNDERPAINTING
UNDERPAINTINGS
UNDERPANTS
UNDERPARTS
UNDERPASSES
UNDERPASSION
UNDERPASSIONS
UNDERPAYING
UNDERPAYMENT
UNDERPAYMENTS
UNDERPEEPED
UNDERPEEPING
UNDERPEEPS
UNDERPEOPLED
UNDERPERFORM
UNDERPERFORMED
UNDERPERFORMING
UNDERPERFORMS
UNDERPINNED
UNDERPINNING
UNDERPINNINGS
UNDERPITCH
UNDERPLANT
UNDERPLANTED
UNDERPLANTING
UNDERPLANTS
UNDERPLAYED
UNDERPLAYING
UNDERPLAYS
UNDERPLOTS
UNDERPOPULATED
UNDERPOWERED

UNDERPRAISE
UNDERPRAISED
UNDERPRAISES
UNDERPRAISING
UNDERPREPARED
UNDERPRICE
UNDERPRICED
UNDERPRICES
UNDERPRICING
UNDERPRICINGS
UNDERPRISE
UNDERPRISED
UNDERPRISES
UNDERPRISING
UNDERPRIVILEGED
UNDERPRIZE
UNDERPRIZED
UNDERPRIZES
UNDERPRIZING
UNDERPRODUCE
UNDERPRODUCED
UNDERPRODUCES
UNDERPRODUCING
UNDERPRODUCTION
UNDERPROOF
UNDERPROPPED
UNDERPROPPER
UNDERPROPPERS
UNDERPROPPING
UNDERPROPS
UNDERPUBLICISED
UNDERPUBLICIZED
UNDERQUALIFIED
UNDERQUOTE
UNDERQUOTED
UNDERQUOTES
UNDERQUOTING
UNDERRATED
UNDERRATES
UNDERRATING
UNDERREACT
UNDERREACTED
UNDERREACTING
UNDERREACTION
UNDERREACTIONS
UNDERREACTS
UNDERREPORT

U

UNDERREPORTED
UNDERREPORTING
UNDERREPORTS
UNDERRUNNING
UNDERRUNNINGS
UNDERSATURATED
UNDERSAYING
UNDERSCORE
UNDERSCORED
UNDERSCORES
UNDERSCORING
UNDERSCORINGS
UNDERSCRUB
UNDERSCRUBS
UNDERSEALED
UNDERSEALING
UNDERSEALINGS
UNDERSEALS
UNDERSECRETARY
UNDERSELLER
UNDERSELLERS
UNDERSELLING
UNDERSELLS
UNDERSELVES
UNDERSENSE
UNDERSENSES
UNDERSERVED
UNDERSETTING
UNDERSEXED
UNDERSHAPEN
UNDERSHERIFF
UNDERSHERIFFS
UNDERSHIRT
UNDERSHIRTED
UNDERSHIRTS
UNDERSHOOT
UNDERSHOOTING
UNDERSHOOTS
UNDERSHORTS
UNDERSHRUB
UNDERSHRUBS
UNDERSIDES
UNDERSIGNED
UNDERSIGNING
UNDERSIGNS
UNDERSIZED
UNDERSKIES

UNDERSKINKER
UNDERSKINKERS
UNDERSKIRT
UNDERSKIRTS
UNDERSLEEVE
UNDERSLEEVES
UNDERSLUNG
UNDERSOILS
UNDERSONGS
UNDERSOWED
UNDERSOWING
UNDERSPEND
UNDERSPENDING
UNDERSPENDINGS
UNDERSPENDS
UNDERSPENT
UNDERSPINS
UNDERSTAFFED
UNDERSTAFFING
UNDERSTAFFINGS
UNDERSTAND
UNDERSTANDABLE
UNDERSTANDABLY
UNDERSTANDED
UNDERSTANDER
UNDERSTANDERS
UNDERSTANDING
UNDERSTANDINGLY
UNDERSTANDINGS
UNDERSTANDS
UNDERSTATE
UNDERSTATED
UNDERSTATEDLY
UNDERSTATEMENT
UNDERSTATEMENTS
UNDERSTATES
UNDERSTATING
UNDERSTEER
UNDERSTEERED
UNDERSTEERING
UNDERSTEERS
UNDERSTOCK
UNDERSTOCKED
UNDERSTOCKING
UNDERSTOCKS
UNDERSTOOD
UNDERSTOREY

UNDERSTOREYS
UNDERSTORIES
UNDERSTORY
UNDERSTRAPPER
UNDERSTRAPPERS
UNDERSTRAPPING
UNDERSTRATA
UNDERSTRATUM
UNDERSTRENGTH
UNDERSTUDIED
UNDERSTUDIES
UNDERSTUDY
UNDERSTUDYING
UNDERSUBSCRIBED
UNDERSUPPLIED
UNDERSUPPLIES
UNDERSUPPLY
UNDERSUPPLYING
UNDERSURFACE
UNDERSURFACES
UNDERTAKABLE
UNDERTAKEN
UNDERTAKER
UNDERTAKERS
UNDERTAKES
UNDERTAKING
UNDERTAKINGS
UNDERTAXED
UNDERTAXES
UNDERTAXING
UNDERTENANCIES
UNDERTENANCY
UNDERTENANT
UNDERTENANTS
UNDERTHINGS
UNDERTHIRST
UNDERTHIRSTS
UNDERTHRUST
UNDERTHRUSTING
UNDERTHRUSTS
UNDERTIMED
UNDERTIMES
UNDERTINTS
UNDERTONED
UNDERTONES
UNDERTRICK
UNDERTRICKS

UNDERTRUMP
UNDERTRUMPED
UNDERTRUMPING
UNDERTRUMPS
UNDERUSING
UNDERUTILISE
UNDERUTILISED
UNDERUTILISES
UNDERUTILISING
UNDERUTILIZE
UNDERUTILIZED
UNDERUTILIZES
UNDERUTILIZING
UNDERVALUATION
UNDERVALUATIONS
UNDERVALUE
UNDERVALUED
UNDERVALUER
UNDERVALUERS
UNDERVALUES
UNDERVALUING
UNDERVESTS
UNDERVIEWER
UNDERVIEWERS
UNDERVOICE
UNDERVOICES
UNDERVOTES
UNDERWATER
UNDERWATERS
UNDERWEARS
UNDERWEIGHT
UNDERWEIGHTS
UNDERWHELM
UNDERWHELMED
UNDERWHELMING
UNDERWHELMS
UNDERWINGS
UNDERWIRED
UNDERWIRES
UNDERWIRING
UNDERWIRINGS
UNDERWOODS
UNDERWOOLS
UNDERWORKED
UNDERWORKER
UNDERWORKERS
UNDERWORKING

UNDERWORKS
UNDERWORLD
UNDERWORLDS
UNDERWRITE
UNDERWRITER
UNDERWRITERS
UNDERWRITES
UNDERWRITING
UNDERWRITINGS
UNDERWRITTEN
UNDERWROTE
UNDERWROUGHT
UNDESCENDABLE
UNDESCENDED
UNDESCENDIBLE
UNDESCRIBABLE
UNDESCRIBED
UNDESCRIED
UNDESERVED
UNDESERVEDLY
UNDESERVEDNESS
UNDESERVER
UNDESERVERS
UNDESERVES
UNDESERVING
UNDESERVINGLY
UNDESIGNATED
UNDESIGNED
UNDESIGNEDLY
UNDESIGNEDNESS
UNDESIGNING
UNDESIRABILITY
UNDESIRABLE
UNDESIRABLENESS
UNDESIRABLES
UNDESIRABLY
UNDESIRING
UNDESIROUS
UNDESPAIRING
UNDESPAIRINGLY
UNDESPATCHED
UNDESPOILED
UNDESTROYED
UNDETECTABLE
UNDETECTED
UNDETERMINABLE
UNDETERMINATE

UNDETERMINATION	UNDISHONOURED	UNDOMESTICATING	UNEATABLENESSES	UNENLARGED
UNDETERMINED	UNDISMANTLED	UNDOUBLING	UNECCENTRIC	UNENLIGHTENED
UNDETERRED	UNDISMAYED	UNDOUBTABLE	UNECLIPSED	UNENLIGHTENING
UNDEVELOPED	UNDISORDERED	UNDOUBTEDLY	UNECOLOGICAL	UNENQUIRING
UNDEVIATING	UNDISPATCHED	UNDOUBTFUL	UNECONOMIC	UNENRICHED
UNDEVIATINGLY	UNDISPENSED	UNDOUBTING	UNECONOMICAL	UNENSLAVED
UNDIAGNOSABLE	UNDISPOSED	UNDOUBTINGLY	UNEDIFYING	UNENTAILED
UNDIAGNOSED	UNDISPUTABLE	UNDRAINABLE	UNEDUCABLE	UNENTERPRISING
UNDIALECTICAL	UNDISPUTED	UNDRAMATIC	UNEDUCATED	UNENTERTAINED
UNDIDACTIC	UNDISPUTEDLY	UNDRAMATICALLY	UNEFFECTED	UNENTERTAINING
UNDIFFERENCED	UNDISSEMBLED	UNDRAMATISED	UNELABORATE	UNENTHRALLED
UNDIGESTED	UNDISSOCIATED	UNDRAMATIZED	UNELABORATED	UNENTHUSIASTIC
UNDIGESTIBLE	UNDISSOLVED	UNDREADING	UNELECTABLE	UNENTITLED
UNDIGHTING	UNDISSOLVING	UNDREAMING	UNELECTRIFIED	UNENVIABLE
UNDIGNIFIED	UNDISTEMPERED	UNDRESSING	UNEMBARRASSED	UNENVIABLY
UNDIGNIFIES	UNDISTILLED	UNDRESSINGS	UNEMBELLISHED	UNEQUALLED
UNDIGNIFYING	UNDISTINCTIVE	UNDRINKABLE	UNEMBITTERED	UNEQUIPPED
UNDIMINISHABLE	UNDISTINGUISHED	UNDRIVEABLE	UNEMBODIED	UNEQUITABLE
UNDIMINISHED	UNDISTORTED	UNDROOPING	UNEMOTIONAL	UNEQUIVOCABLE
UNDIPLOMATIC	UNDISTRACTED	UNDROSSIER	UNEMOTIONALLY	UNEQUIVOCABLY
UNDIRECTED	UNDISTRACTEDLY	UNDROSSIEST	UNEMOTIONED	UNEQUIVOCAL
UNDISAPPOINTING	UNDISTRACTING	UNDULANCES	UNEMPHATIC	UNEQUIVOCALLY
UNDISCERNED	UNDISTRIBUTED	UNDULANCIES	UNEMPHATICALLY	UNEQUIVOCALNESS
UNDISCERNEDLY	UNDISTURBED	UNDULATELY	UNEMPIRICAL	UNERASABLE
UNDISCERNIBLE	UNDISTURBEDLY	UNDULATING	UNEMPLOYABILITY	UNERRINGLY
UNDISCERNIBLY	UNDISTURBING	UNDULATINGLY	UNEMPLOYABLE	UNERRINGNESS
UNDISCERNING	UNDIVERSIFIED	UNDULATION	UNEMPLOYABLES	UNERRINGNESSES
UNDISCERNINGS	UNDIVERTED	UNDULATIONIST	UNEMPLOYED	UNESCAPABLE
UNDISCHARGED	UNDIVERTING	UNDULATIONISTS	UNEMPLOYEDS	UNESCORTED
UNDISCIPLINABLE	UNDIVESTED	UNDULATIONS	UNEMPLOYMENT	UNESSENCED
UNDISCIPLINE	UNDIVESTEDLY	UNDULATORS	UNEMPLOYMENTS	UNESSENCES
UNDISCIPLINED	UNDIVIDABLE	UNDULATORY	UNENCHANTED	UNESSENCING
UNDISCIPLINES	UNDIVIDEDLY	UNDUPLICATED	UNENCLOSED	UNESSENTIAL
UNDISCLOSED	UNDIVIDEDNESS	UNDUTIFULLY	UNENCOURAGING	UNESSENTIALLY
UNDISCOMFITED	UNDIVIDEDNESSES	UNDUTIFULNESS	UNENCUMBERED	UNESSENTIALS
UNDISCORDANT	UNDIVORCED	UNDUTIFULNESSES	UNENDANGERED	UNESTABLISHED
UNDISCORDING	UNDIVULGED	UNDYINGNESS	UNENDEARED	UNESTHETIC
UNDISCOURAGED	UNDOCTORED	UNDYINGNESSES	UNENDEARING	UNETHICALLY
UNDISCOVERABLE	UNDOCTRINAIRE	UNEARMARKED	UNENDINGLY	UNEVALUATED
UNDISCOVERABLY	UNDOCTRINAIRES	UNEARTHING	UNENDINGNESS	UNEVANGELICAL
UNDISCOVERED	UNDOCUMENTED	UNEARTHLIER	UNENDINGNESSES	UNEVENNESS
UNDISCUSSABLE	UNDOGMATIC	UNEARTHLIEST	UNENDURABLE	UNEVENNESSES
UNDISCUSSED	UNDOGMATICALLY	UNEARTHLINESS	UNENDURABLENESS	UNEVENTFUL
UNDISCUSSIBLE	UNDOMESTIC	UNEARTHLINESSES	UNENDURABLY	UNEVENTFULLY
UNDISGUISABLE	UNDOMESTICATE	UNEASINESS	UNENFORCEABLE	UNEVENTFULNESS
UNDISGUISED	UNDOMESTICATED	UNEASINESSES	UNENFORCED	UNEVIDENCED
UNDISGUISEDLY	UNDOMESTICATES	UNEATABLENESS	UNENJOYABLE	UNEXACTING

U

UNEXAGGERATED
UNEXAMINED
UNEXAMPLED
UNEXCAVATED
UNEXCELLED
UNEXCEPTIONABLE
UNEXCEPTIONABLY
UNEXCEPTIONAL
UNEXCEPTIONALLY
UNEXCITABLE
UNEXCITING
UNEXCLUDED
UNEXCLUSIVE
UNEXCLUSIVELY
UNEXECUTED
UNEXEMPLIFIED
UNEXERCISED
UNEXHAUSTED
UNEXPANDED
UNEXPECTANT
UNEXPECTED
UNEXPECTEDLY
UNEXPECTEDNESS
UNEXPENDED
UNEXPENSIVE
UNEXPENSIVELY
UNEXPERIENCED
UNEXPERIENT
UNEXPIATED
UNEXPLAINABLE
UNEXPLAINED
UNEXPLODED
UNEXPLOITED
UNEXPLORED
UNEXPRESSED
UNEXPRESSIBLE
UNEXPRESSIVE
UNEXPUGNABLE
UNEXPURGATED
UNEXTENDED
UNEXTENUATED
UNEXTINGUISHED
UNEXTRAORDINARY
UNFADINGLY
UNFADINGNESS
UNFADINGNESSES
UNFAILINGLY

UNFAILINGNESS
UNFAILINGNESSES
UNFAIRNESS
UNFAIRNESSES
UNFAITHFUL
UNFAITHFULLY
UNFAITHFULNESS
UNFALLIBLE
UNFALSIFIABLE
UNFALTERING
UNFALTERINGLY
UNFAMILIAR
UNFAMILIARITIES
UNFAMILIARITY
UNFAMILIARLY
UNFANCIEST
UNFASHIONABLE
UNFASHIONABLY
UNFASHIONED
UNFASTENED
UNFASTENING
UNFASTIDIOUS
UNFATHERED
UNFATHERLY
UNFATHOMABLE
UNFATHOMABLY
UNFATHOMED
UNFAULTIER
UNFAULTIEST
UNFAVORABLE
UNFAVORABLENESS
UNFAVORABLY
UNFAVORITE
UNFAVOURABLE
UNFAVOURABLY
UNFAVOURED
UNFAVOURITE
UNFEARFULLY
UNFEASIBLE
UNFEATHERED
UNFEATURED
UNFEELINGLY
UNFEELINGNESS
UNFEELINGNESSES
UNFEIGNEDLY
UNFEIGNEDNESS
UNFEIGNEDNESSES

UNFEIGNING
UNFELLOWED
UNFEMININE
UNFERMENTED
UNFERTILISED
UNFERTILIZED
UNFETTERED
UNFETTERING
UNFEUDALISE
UNFEUDALISED
UNFEUDALISES
UNFEUDALISING
UNFEUDALIZE
UNFEUDALIZED
UNFEUDALIZES
UNFEUDALIZING
UNFILIALLY
UNFILLABLE
UNFILLETED
UNFILTERABLE
UNFILTERED
UNFILTRABLE
UNFINDABLE
UNFINISHED
UNFINISHING
UNFINISHINGS
UNFITNESSES
UNFITTEDNESS
UNFITTEDNESSES
UNFITTINGLY
UNFIXEDNESS
UNFIXEDNESSES
UNFIXITIES
UNFLAGGING
UNFLAGGINGLY
UNFLAMBOYANT
UNFLAPPABILITY
UNFLAPPABLE
UNFLAPPABLENESS
UNFLAPPABLY
UNFLASHIER
UNFLASHIEST
UNFLATTERING
UNFLATTERINGLY
UNFLAVOURED
UNFLESHING
UNFLESHLIER

UNFLESHLIEST
UNFLINCHING
UNFLINCHINGLY
UNFLUSHING
UNFLUSTERED
UNFOCUSSED
UNFOLDINGS
UNFOLDMENT
UNFOLDMENTS
UNFOLLOWED
UNFOLLOWING
UNFORBIDDEN
UNFORCEDLY
UNFORCIBLE
UNFORDABLE
UNFOREBODING
UNFOREKNOWABLE
UNFOREKNOWN
UNFORESEEABLE
UNFORESEEING
UNFORESEEN
UNFORESKINNED
UNFORESTED
UNFORETOLD
UNFOREWARNED
UNFORFEITED
UNFORGETTABLE
UNFORGETTABLY
UNFORGIVABLE
UNFORGIVABLY
UNFORGIVEN
UNFORGIVENESS
UNFORGIVENESSES
UNFORGIVING
UNFORGIVINGNESS
UNFORGOTTEN
UNFORMALISED
UNFORMALIZED
UNFORMATTED
UNFORMIDABLE
UNFORMULATED
UNFORSAKEN
UNFORTHCOMING
UNFORTIFIED
UNFORTUNATE
UNFORTUNATELY
UNFORTUNATENESS

UNFORTUNATES
UNFORTUNED
UNFORTUNES
UNFOSSILIFEROUS
UNFOSSILISED
UNFOSSILIZED
UNFOSTERED
UNFOUGHTEN
UNFOUNDEDLY
UNFOUNDEDNESS
UNFOUNDEDNESSES
UNFRANCHISED
UNFRAUGHTED
UNFRAUGHTING
UNFRAUGHTS
UNFREEDOMS
UNFREEZING
UNFREEZINGS
UNFREQUENT
UNFREQUENTED
UNFREQUENTING
UNFREQUENTLY
UNFREQUENTS
UNFRIENDED
UNFRIENDEDNESS
UNFRIENDING
UNFRIENDLIER
UNFRIENDLIEST
UNFRIENDLILY
UNFRIENDLINESS
UNFRIENDLY
UNFRIENDSHIP
UNFRIENDSHIPS
UNFRIGHTED
UNFRIGHTENED
UNFRIVOLOUS
UNFROCKING
UNFRUCTUOUS
UNFRUITFUL
UNFRUITFULLY
UNFRUITFULNESS
UNFULFILLABLE
UNFULFILLED
UNFULFILLING
UNFUNNIEST
UNFURNISHED
UNFURNISHES

UNFURNISHING	UNGRACEFULNESS	UNHANDSOME	UNHESITATING	UNICAMERALIST
UNFURROWED	UNGRACIOUS	UNHANDSOMELY	UNHESITATINGLY	UNICAMERALISTS
UNFUSSIEST	UNGRACIOUSLY	UNHANDSOMENESS	UNHIDEBOUND	UNICAMERALLY
UNGAINLIER	UNGRACIOUSNESS	UNHAPPENED	UNHINDERED	UNICELLULAR
UNGAINLIEST	UNGRAMMATIC	UNHAPPENING	UNHINGEMENT	UNICELLULARITY
UNGAINLINESS	UNGRAMMATICAL	UNHAPPIEST	UNHINGEMENTS	UNICENTRAL
UNGAINLINESSES	UNGRAMMATICALLY	UNHAPPINESS	UNHISTORIC	UNICOLORATE
UNGAINSAID	UNGRASPABLE	UNHAPPINESSES	UNHISTORICAL	UNICOLORED
UNGAINSAYABLE	UNGRATEFUL	UNHAPPYING	UNHITCHING	UNICOLOROUS
UNGALLANTLY	UNGRATEFULLY	UNHARBOURED	UNHOARDING	UNICOLOURED
UNGARMENTED	UNGRATEFULNESS	UNHARBOURING	UNHOLINESS	UNICOSTATE
UNGARNERED	UNGRATIFIED	UNHARBOURS	UNHOLINESSES	UNICYCLING
UNGARNISHED	UNGREEDIER	UNHARDENED	UNHOMELIER	UNICYCLIST
UNGARTERED	UNGREEDIEST	UNHARDIEST	UNHOMELIEST	UNICYCLISTS
UNGATHERED	UNGREENEST	UNHARMFULLY	UNHOMELIKE	UNIDEALISM
UNGENEROSITIES	UNGROUNDED	UNHARMONIOUS	UNHOMOGENISED	UNIDEALISMS
UNGENEROSITY	UNGROUNDEDLY	UNHARNESSED	UNHOMOGENIZED	UNIDEALISTIC
UNGENEROUS	UNGROUNDEDNESS	UNHARNESSES	UNHONOURED	UNIDENTIFIABLE
UNGENEROUSLY	UNGROUPING	UNHARNESSING	UNHOPEFULLY	UNIDENTIFIED
UNGENITURED	UNGRUDGING	UNHARVESTED	UNHOSPITABLE	UNIDEOLOGICAL
UNGENTEELLY	UNGRUDGINGLY	UNHASTIEST	UNHOUSELED	UNIDIMENSIONAL
UNGENTILITIES	UNGUARDEDLY	UNHATTINGS	UNHOUZZLED	UNIDIOMATIC
UNGENTILITY	UNGUARDEDNESS	UNHAZARDED	UNHUMANISE	UNIDIOMATICALLY
UNGENTLEMANLIKE	UNGUARDEDNESSES	UNHAZARDOUS	UNHUMANISED	UNIDIRECTIONAL
UNGENTLEMANLY	UNGUARDING	UNHEALABLE	UNHUMANISES	UNIFICATION
UNGENTLENESS	UNGUENTARIA	UNHEALTHFUL	UNHUMANISING	UNIFICATIONS
UNGENTLENESSES	UNGUENTARIES	UNHEALTHFULLY	UNHUMANIZE	UNIFLOROUS
UNGENTRIFIED	UNGUENTARIUM	UNHEALTHFULNESS	UNHUMANIZED	UNIFOLIATE
UNGENUINENESS	UNGUENTARY	UNHEALTHIER	UNHUMANIZES	UNIFOLIOLATE
UNGENUINENESSES	UNGUERDONED	UNHEALTHIEST	UNHUMANIZING	UNIFORMEST
UNGERMINATED	UNGUESSABLE	UNHEALTHILY	UNHUMOROUS	UNIFORMING
UNGETATABLE	UNGUICULATE	UNHEALTHINESS	UNHURRIEDLY	UNIFORMITARIAN
UNGHOSTLIER	UNGUICULATED	UNHEALTHINESSES	UNHURRYING	UNIFORMITARIANS
UNGHOSTLIEST	UNGUICULATES	UNHEARSING	UNHURTFULLY	UNIFORMITIES
UNGIMMICKY	UNGUILTIER	UNHEARTING	UNHURTFULNESS	UNIFORMITY
UNGIRTHING	UNGUILTIEST	UNHEEDEDLY	UNHURTFULNESSES	UNIFORMNESS
UNGLAMORISED	UNGULIGRADE	UNHEEDFULLY	UNHUSBANDED	UNIFORMNESSES
UNGLAMORIZED	UNHABITABLE	UNHEEDIEST	UNHYDROLYSED	UNIGENITURE
UNGLAMOROUS	UNHABITUATED	UNHEEDINGLY	UNHYDROLYZED	UNIGENITURES
UNGODLIEST	UNHACKNEYED	UNHELMETED	UNHYGIENIC	UNIGNORABLE
UNGODLINESS	UNHALLOWED	UNHELPABLE	UNHYPHENATED	UNILABIATE
UNGODLINESSES	UNHALLOWING	UNHELPFULLY	UNHYSTERICAL	UNILATERAL
UNGOVERNABLE	UNHAMPERED	UNHELPFULNESS	UNHYSTERICALLY	UNILATERALISM
UNGOVERNABLY	UNHANDIEST	UNHELPFULNESSES	UNIAXIALLY	UNILATERALISMS
UNGOVERNED	UNHANDINESS	UNHERALDED	UNICAMERAL	UNILATERALIST
UNGRACEFUL	UNHANDINESSES	UNHEROICAL	UNICAMERALISM	UNILATERALISTS
UNGRACEFULLY	UNHANDSELLED	UNHEROICALLY	UNICAMERALISMS	UNILATERALITIES

U

UNILATERALITY

UNILATERALITY UNINCLOSED UNINTELLIGENTLY UNIRRADIATED UNIVERSALNESS
UNILATERALLY UNINCORPORATED UNINTELLIGIBLE UNIRRIGATED UNIVERSALNESSES
UNILINGUAL UNINCUMBERED UNINTELLIGIBLY UNISEPTATE UNIVERSALS
UNILINGUALISM UNINDEARED UNINTENDED UNISERIALLY UNIVERSITARIAN
UNILINGUALISMS UNINDICTED UNINTENTIONAL UNISERIATE UNIVERSITIES
UNILINGUALIST UNINFECTED UNINTENTIONALLY UNISERIATELY UNIVERSITY
UNILINGUALISTS UNINFLAMED UNINTEREST UNISEXUALITIES UNIVOCALLY
UNILINGUALS UNINFLAMMABLE UNINTERESTED UNISEXUALITY UNIVOLTINE
UNILITERAL UNINFLATED UNINTERESTEDLY UNISEXUALLY UNJAUNDICED
UNILLUMINATED UNINFLECTED UNINTERESTING UNISONALLY UNJOINTING
UNILLUMINATING UNINFLUENCED UNINTERESTINGLY UNISONANCE UNJUSTIFIABLE
UNILLUMINED UNINFLUENTIAL UNINTERESTS UNISONANCES UNJUSTIFIABLY
UNILLUSIONED UNINFORCEABLE UNINTERMITTED UNITARIANISM UNJUSTIFIED
UNILLUSTRATED UNINFORCED UNINTERMITTEDLY UNITARIANISMS UNJUSTNESS
UNILOBULAR UNINFORMATIVE UNINTERMITTING UNITARIANS UNJUSTNESSES
UNILOCULAR UNINFORMATIVELY UNINTERPRETABLE UNITEDNESS UNKEMPTNESS
UNIMAGINABLE UNINFORMED UNINTERRUPTED UNITEDNESSES UNKEMPTNESSES
UNIMAGINABLY UNINFORMING UNINTERRUPTEDLY UNITHOLDER UNKENNELED
UNIMAGINATIVE UNINGRATIATING UNINTIMIDATED UNITHOLDERS UNKENNELING
UNIMAGINATIVELY UNINHABITABLE UNINTOXICATING UNITISATION UNKENNELLED
UNIMAGINED UNINHABITED UNINTRODUCED UNITISATIONS UNKENNELLING
UNIMMORTAL UNINHIBITED UNINUCLEAR UNITIZATION UNKINDLIER
UNIMMUNISED UNINHIBITEDLY UNINUCLEATE UNITIZATIONS UNKINDLIEST
UNIMMUNIZED UNINHIBITEDNESS UNINVENTIVE UNIVALENCE UNKINDLINESS
UNIMOLECULAR UNINITIATE UNINVESTED UNIVALENCES UNKINDLINESSES
UNIMPAIRED UNINITIATED UNINVIDIOUS UNIVALENCIES UNKINDNESS
UNIMPARTED UNINITIATES UNINVITING UNIVALENCY UNKINDNESSES
UNIMPASSIONED UNINOCULATED UNINVOLVED UNIVALENTS UNKINGLIER
UNIMPEACHABLE UNINQUIRING UNIONISATION UNIVALVULAR UNKINGLIEST
UNIMPEACHABLY UNINQUISITIVE UNIONISATIONS UNIVARIANT UNKINGLIKE
UNIMPEACHED UNINSCRIBED UNIONISERS UNIVARIATE UNKNIGHTED
UNIMPEDEDLY UNINSPECTED UNIONISING UNIVERSALISE UNKNIGHTING
UNIMPLORED UNINSPIRED UNIONISTIC UNIVERSALISED UNKNIGHTLIER
UNIMPORTANCE UNINSPIRING UNIONIZATION UNIVERSALISES UNKNIGHTLIEST
UNIMPORTANCES UNINSTALLED UNIONIZATIONS UNIVERSALISING UNKNIGHTLINESS
UNIMPORTANT UNINSTALLING UNIONIZERS UNIVERSALISM UNKNIGHTLY
UNIMPORTUNED UNINSTALLS UNIONIZING UNIVERSALISMS UNKNITTING
UNIMPOSING UNINSTRUCTED UNIPARENTAL UNIVERSALIST UNKNOTTING
UNIMPREGNATED UNINSTRUCTIVE UNIPARENTALLY UNIVERSALISTIC UNKNOWABILITIES
UNIMPRESSED UNINSULATED UNIPARTITE UNIVERSALISTS UNKNOWABILITY
UNIMPRESSIBLE UNINSURABLE UNIPERSONAL UNIVERSALITIES UNKNOWABLE
UNIMPRESSIVE UNINSUREDS UNIPERSONALITY UNIVERSALITY UNKNOWABLENESS
UNIMPRISONED UNINTEGRATED UNIPOLARITIES UNIVERSALIZE UNKNOWABLES
UNIMPROVED UNINTELLECTUAL UNIPOLARITY UNIVERSALIZED UNKNOWABLY
UNIMPUGNABLE UNINTELLIGENCE UNIQUENESS UNIVERSALIZES UNKNOWINGLY
UNINAUGURATED UNINTELLIGENCES UNIQUENESSES UNIVERSALIZING UNKNOWINGNESS
UNINCHANTED UNINTELLIGENT UNIRONICALLY UNIVERSALLY UNKNOWINGNESSES

U

UNKNOWINGS	UNLIMBERING	UNMALLEABILITY	UNMECHANIZED	UNMISTAKEABLY
UNKNOWLEDGEABLE	UNLIMITEDLY	UNMALLEABLE	UNMECHANIZES	UNMISTRUSTFUL
UNKNOWNNESS	UNLIMITEDNESS	UNMANACLED	UNMECHANIZING	UNMITERING
UNKNOWNNESSES	UNLIMITEDNESSES	UNMANACLES	UNMEDIATED	UNMITIGABLE
UNLABELLED	UNLIQUEFIED	UNMANACLING	UNMEDICATED	UNMITIGABLY
UNLABORING	UNLIQUIDATED	UNMANAGEABLE	UNMEDICINABLE	UNMITIGATED
UNLABORIOUS	UNLIQUORED	UNMANAGEABLY	UNMEDITATED	UNMITIGATEDLY
UNLABOURED	UNLISTENABLE	UNMANFULLY	UNMEETNESS	UNMITIGATEDNESS
UNLABOURING	UNLISTENED	UNMANIPULATED	UNMEETNESSES	UNMODERATED
UNLADYLIKE	UNLISTENING	UNMANLIEST	UNMELLOWED	UNMODERNISED
UNLAMENTED	UNLITERARY	UNMANLINESS	UNMELODIOUS	UNMODERNIZED
UNLATCHING	UNLIVEABLE	UNMANLINESSES	UNMELODIOUSNESS	UNMODIFIABLE
UNLAUNDERED	UNLIVELIER	UNMANNERED	UNMEMORABLE	UNMODIFIED
UNLAWFULLY	UNLIVELIEST	UNMANNEREDLY	UNMEMORABLY	UNMODULATED
UNLAWFULNESS	UNLIVELINESS	UNMANNERLINESS	UNMENTIONABLE	UNMOISTENED
UNLAWFULNESSES	UNLIVELINESSES	UNMANNERLY	UNMENTIONABLES	UNMOLESTED
UNLEARNABLE	UNLOADINGS	UNMANTLING	UNMENTIONABLY	UNMONITORED
UNLEARNEDLY	UNLOCALISED	UNMANUFACTURED	UNMENTIONED	UNMORALISED
UNLEARNEDNESS	UNLOCALIZED	UNMARKETABLE	UNMERCENARY	UNMORALISING
UNLEARNEDNESSES	UNLOCKABLE	UNMARRIABLE	UNMERCHANTABLE	UNMORALITIES
UNLEARNING	UNLOOSENED	UNMARRIAGEABLE	UNMERCIFUL	UNMORALITY
UNLEASHING	UNLOOSENING	UNMARRIEDS	UNMERCIFULLY	UNMORALIZED
UNLEAVENED	UNLORDLIER	UNMARRYING	UNMERCIFULNESS	UNMORALIZING
UNLEISURED	UNLORDLIEST	UNMASCULINE	UNMERITABLE	UNMORTGAGED
UNLEISURELY	UNLOVEABLE	UNMASKINGS	UNMERITEDLY	UNMORTIFIED
UNLESSONED	UNLOVELIER	UNMASTERED	UNMERITING	UNMORTISED
UNLETTABLE	UNLOVELIEST	UNMATCHABLE	UNMERRIEST	UNMORTISES
UNLETTERED	UNLOVELINESS	UNMATERIAL	UNMETABOLISED	UNMORTISING
UNLEVELING	UNLOVELINESSES	UNMATERIALISED	UNMETABOLIZED	UNMOTHERLY
UNLEVELLED	UNLOVERLIKE	UNMATERIALIZED	UNMETALLED	UNMOTIVATED
UNLEVELLING	UNLOVINGLY	UNMATERNAL	UNMETAPHORICAL	UNMOULDING
UNLIBERATED	UNLOVINGNESS	UNMATHEMATICAL	UNMETAPHYSICAL	UNMOUNTING
UNLIBIDINOUS	UNLOVINGNESSES	UNMATRICULATED	UNMETHODICAL	UNMOVEABLE
UNLICENSED	UNLUCKIEST	UNMEANINGLY	UNMETHODISED	UNMOVEABLY
UNLIFELIKE	UNLUCKINESS	UNMEANINGNESS	UNMETHODIZED	UNMUFFLING
UNLIGHTENED	UNLUCKINESSES	UNMEANINGNESSES	UNMETRICAL	UNMUNITIONED
UNLIGHTSOME	UNLUXURIANT	UNMEASURABLE	UNMILITARY	UNMURMURING
UNLIKEABLE	UNLUXURIOUS	UNMEASURABLY	UNMINDFULLY	UNMURMURINGLY
UNLIKELIER	UNMACADAMISED	UNMEASURED	UNMINDFULNESS	UNMUSICALLY
UNLIKELIEST	UNMACADAMIZED	UNMEASUREDLY	UNMINDFULNESSES	UNMUSICALNESS
UNLIKELIHOOD	UNMAGNIFIED	UNMECHANIC	UNMINGLING	UNMUSICALNESSES
UNLIKELIHOODS	UNMAIDENLY	UNMECHANICAL	UNMINISTERIAL	UNMUTILATED
UNLIKELINESS	UNMAILABLE	UNMECHANISE	UNMIRACULOUS	UNMUZZLING
UNLIKELINESSES	UNMAINTAINABLE	UNMECHANISED	UNMISSABLE	UNMUZZLINGS
UNLIKENESS	UNMAINTAINED	UNMECHANISES	UNMISTAKABLE	UNMYELINATED
UNLIKENESSES	UNMALICIOUS	UNMECHANISING	UNMISTAKABLY	UNNAMEABLE
UNLIMBERED	UNMALICIOUSLY	UNMECHANIZE	UNMISTAKEABLE	UNNATIVING

U

UNNATURALISE	UNOBSERVABLES	UNOXYGENATED	UNPAVILIONED	UNPHILOSOPHIC
UNNATURALISED	UNOBSERVANCE	UNPACIFIED	UNPEACEABLE	UNPHILOSOPHICAL
UNNATURALISES	UNOBSERVANCES	UNPACKINGS	UNPEACEABLENESS	UNPHONETIC
UNNATURALISING	UNOBSERVANT	UNPAINTABLE	UNPEACEFUL	UNPICKABLE
UNNATURALIZE	UNOBSERVED	UNPAINTING	UNPEACEFULLY	UNPICTURESQUE
UNNATURALIZED	UNOBSERVEDLY	UNPALATABILITY	UNPEDANTIC	UNPILLARED
UNNATURALIZES	UNOBSERVING	UNPALATABLE	UNPEDIGREED	UNPILLOWED
UNNATURALIZING	UNOBSTRUCTED	UNPALATABLY	UNPEERABLE	UNPITIFULLY
UNNATURALLY	UNOBSTRUCTIVE	UNPAMPERED	UNPENSIONED	UNPITIFULNESS
UNNATURALNESS	UNOBTAINABLE	UNPANELLED	UNPEOPLING	UNPITIFULNESSES
UNNATURALNESSES	UNOBTAINED	UNPANELLING	UNPEPPERED	UNPITYINGLY
UNNAVIGABLE	UNOBTRUSIVE	UNPANNELLED	UNPERCEIVABLE	UNPLAITING
UNNAVIGATED	UNOBTRUSIVELY	UNPANNELLING	UNPERCEIVABLY	UNPLASTERED
UNNECESSARILY	UNOBTRUSIVENESS	UNPAPERING	UNPERCEIVED	UNPLASTICISED
UNNECESSARINESS	UNOCCUPIED	UNPARADISE	UNPERCEIVEDLY	UNPLASTICIZED
UNNECESSARY	UNOFFENDED	UNPARADISED	UNPERCEPTIVE	UNPLAUSIBLE
UNNEEDFULLY	UNOFFENDING	UNPARADISES	UNPERCHING	UNPLAUSIBLY
UNNEGOTIABLE	UNOFFENSIVE	UNPARADISING	UNPERFECTED	UNPLAUSIVE
UNNEIGHBORLY	UNOFFICERED	UNPARAGONED	UNPERFECTION	UNPLAYABLE
UNNEIGHBOURED	UNOFFICIAL	UNPARALLEL	UNPERFECTIONS	UNPLEASANT
UNNEIGHBOURLY	UNOFFICIALLY	UNPARALLELED	UNPERFECTLY	UNPLEASANTLY
UNNERVINGLY	UNOFFICIOUS	UNPARASITISED	UNPERFECTNESS	UNPLEASANTNESS
UNNEUROTIC	UNOPENABLE	UNPARASITIZED	UNPERFECTNESSES	UNPLEASANTRIES
UNNEWSWORTHY	UNOPERATIVE	UNPARDONABLE	UNPERFORATED	UNPLEASANTRY
UNNILHEXIUM	UNOPPRESSIVE	UNPARDONABLY	UNPERFORMABLE	UNPLEASING
UNNILHEXIUMS	UNORDAINED	UNPARDONED	UNPERFORMED	UNPLEASINGLY
UNNILPENTIUM	UNORDERING	UNPARDONING	UNPERFORMING	UNPLEASURABLE
UNNILPENTIUMS	UNORDINARY	UNPARENTAL	UNPERFUMED	UNPLEASURABLY
UNNILQUADIUM	UNORGANISED	UNPARENTED	UNPERILOUS	UNPLOUGHED
UNNILQUADIUMS	UNORGANIZED	UNPARLIAMENTARY	UNPERISHABLE	UNPLUGGING
UNNILSEPTIUM	UNORIGINAL	UNPASSABLE	UNPERISHED	UNPLUMBING
UNNILSEPTIUMS	UNORIGINALITIES	UNPASSABLENESS	UNPERISHING	UNPOETICAL
UNNOISIEST	UNORIGINALITY	UNPASSIONATE	UNPERJURED	UNPOETICALLY
UNNOTICEABLE	UNORIGINATE	UNPASSIONED	UNPERPETRATED	UNPOETICALNESS
UNNOTICEABLY	UNORIGINATED	UNPASTEURISED	UNPERPLEXED	UNPOISONED
UNNOTICING	UNORNAMENTAL	UNPASTEURIZED	UNPERPLEXES	UNPOISONING
UNNOURISHED	UNORNAMENTED	UNPASTORAL	UNPERPLEXING	UNPOLARISABLE
UNNOURISHING	UNORTHODOX	UNPASTURED	UNPERSECUTED	UNPOLARISED
UNNUMBERED	UNORTHODOXIES	UNPATENTABLE	UNPERSONED	UNPOLARIZABLE
UNNURTURED	UNORTHODOXLY	UNPATENTED	UNPERSONING	UNPOLARIZED
UNOBEDIENT	UNORTHODOXY	UNPATHETIC	UNPERSUADABLE	UNPOLICIED
UNOBJECTIONABLE	UNOSSIFIED	UNPATHWAYED	UNPERSUADED	UNPOLISHABLE
UNOBJECTIONABLY	UNOSTENTATIOUS	UNPATRIOTIC	UNPERSUASIVE	UNPOLISHED
UNOBLIGING	UNOVERCOME	UNPATRIOTICALLY	UNPERTURBED	UNPOLISHES
UNOBNOXIOUS	UNOVERTHROWN	UNPATRONISED	UNPERVERTED	UNPOLISHING
UNOBSCURED	UNOXIDISED	UNPATRONIZED	UNPERVERTING	UNPOLITELY
UNOBSERVABLE	UNOXIDIZED	UNPATTERNED	UNPERVERTS	UNPOLITENESS

UNPOLITENESSES	UNPREPARING	UNPROFANED	UNPROVISIONED	UNQUENCHED
UNPOLITICAL	UNPREPOSSESSED	UNPROFESSED	UNPROVOCATIVE	UNQUESTIONABLE
UNPOLLUTED	UNPREPOSSESSING	UNPROFESSIONAL	UNPROVOKED	UNQUESTIONABLY
UNPOPULARITIES	UNPRESCRIBED	UNPROFESSIONALS	UNPROVOKEDLY	UNQUESTIONED
UNPOPULARITY	UNPRESENTABLE	UNPROFITABILITY	UNPROVOKES	UNQUESTIONING
UNPOPULARLY	UNPRESSURED	UNPROFITABLE	UNPROVOKING	UNQUESTIONINGLY
UNPOPULATED	UNPRESSURISED	UNPROFITABLY	UNPUBLICISED	UNQUICKENED
UNPOPULOUS	UNPRESSURIZED	UNPROFITED	UNPUBLICIZED	UNQUIETEST
UNPORTIONED	UNPRESUMING	UNPROFITING	UNPUBLISHABLE	UNQUIETING
UNPOSSESSED	UNPRESUMPTUOUS	UNPROFITINGS	UNPUBLISHED	UNQUIETNESS
UNPOSSESSING	UNPRETENDING	UNPROGRAMMABLE	UNPUCKERED	UNQUIETNESSES
UNPOSSIBLE	UNPRETENDINGLY	UNPROGRAMMED	UNPUCKERING	UNQUOTABLE
UNPOWDERED	UNPRETENTIOUS	UNPROGRESSIVE	UNPUNCTUAL	UNRANSOMED
UNPRACTICABLE	UNPRETENTIOUSLY	UNPROGRESSIVELY	UNPUNCTUALITIES	UNRATIFIED
UNPRACTICAL	UNPRETTIER	UNPROHIBITED	UNPUNCTUALITY	UNRAVELING
UNPRACTICALITY	UNPRETTIEST	UNPROJECTED	UNPUNCTUATED	UNRAVELLED
UNPRACTICALLY	UNPRETTINESS	UNPROLIFIC	UNPUNISHABLE	UNRAVELLER
UNPRACTICALNESS	UNPRETTINESSES	UNPROMISED	UNPUNISHABLY	UNRAVELLERS
UNPRACTICED	UNPREVAILING	UNPROMISING	UNPUNISHED	UNRAVELLING
UNPRACTISED	UNPREVENTABLE	UNPROMISINGLY	UNPURCHASABLE	UNRAVELLINGS
UNPRACTISEDNESS	UNPREVENTED	UNPROMPTED	UNPURCHASEABLE	UNRAVELMENT
UNPRAISEWORTHY	UNPRIESTED	UNPRONOUNCEABLE	UNPURCHASED	UNRAVELMENTS
UNPRAISING	UNPRIESTING	UNPRONOUNCED	UNPURIFIED	UNRAVISHED
UNPREACHED	UNPRIESTLIER	UNPROPERLY	UNPURPOSED	UNREACHABLE
UNPREACHES	UNPRIESTLIEST	UNPROPERTIED	UNPURVAIDE	UNREACTIVE
UNPREACHING	UNPRIESTLY	UNPROPHETIC	UNPURVEYED	UNREADABILITIES
UNPRECEDENTED	UNPRINCELIER	UNPROPHETICAL	UNPUTDOWNABLE	UNREADABILITY
UNPRECEDENTEDLY	UNPRINCELIEST	UNPROPITIOUS	UNPUZZLING	UNREADABLE
UNPREDICTABLE	UNPRINCELY	UNPROPITIOUSLY	UNQUALIFIABLE	UNREADABLENESS
UNPREDICTABLES	UNPRINCIPLED	UNPROPORTIONATE	UNQUALIFIED	UNREADABLY
UNPREDICTABLY	UNPRINTABLE	UNPROPORTIONED	UNQUALIFIEDLY	UNREADIEST
UNPREDICTED	UNPRINTABLENESS	UNPROPOSED	UNQUALIFIEDNESS	UNREADINESS
UNPREDICTING	UNPRINTABLY	UNPROPPING	UNQUALIFIES	UNREADINESSES
UNPREDICTS	UNPRISABLE	UNPROSPEROUS	UNQUALIFYING	UNREALISABLE
UNPREFERRED	UNPRISONED	UNPROSPEROUSLY	UNQUALITED	UNREALISED
UNPREGNANT	UNPRISONING	UNPROTECTED	UNQUALITIED	UNREALISES
UNPREJUDICED	UNPRIVILEGED	UNPROTECTEDNESS	UNQUANTIFIABLE	UNREALISING
UNPREJUDICEDLY	UNPRIZABLE	UNPROTESTANTISE	UNQUANTIFIED	UNREALISMS
UNPRELATICAL	UNPROBLEMATIC	UNPROTESTANTIZE	UNQUANTISED	UNREALISTIC
UNPREMEDITABLE	UNPROCEDURAL	UNPROTESTED	UNQUANTIZED	UNREALISTICALLY
UNPREMEDITATED	UNPROCESSED	UNPROTESTING	UNQUARRIED	UNREALITIES
UNPREMEDITATION	UNPROCLAIMED	UNPROVABLE	UNQUEENING	UNREALIZABLE
UNPREOCCUPIED	UNPROCURABLE	UNPROVIDED	UNQUEENLIER	UNREALIZED
UNPREPARED	UNPRODUCED	UNPROVIDEDLY	UNQUEENLIEST	UNREALIZES
UNPREPAREDLY	UNPRODUCTIVE	UNPROVIDENT	UNQUEENLIKE	UNREALIZING
UNPREPAREDNESS	UNPRODUCTIVELY	UNPROVIDES	UNQUENCHABLE	UNREASONABLE
UNPREPARES	UNPRODUCTIVITY	UNPROVIDING	UNQUENCHABLY	UNREASONABLY

U

UNREASONED	UNREFLECTINGLY	UNREMEDIED	UNREPRODUCIBLE	UNRETIRING
UNREASONING	UNREFLECTIVE	UNREMEMBERED	UNREPROVABLE	UNRETOUCHED
UNREASONINGLY	UNREFLECTIVELY	UNREMEMBERING	UNREPROVED	UNRETURNABLE
UNRECALLABLE	UNREFORMABLE	UNREMINISCENT	UNREPROVING	UNRETURNED
UNRECALLED	UNREFORMED	UNREMITTED	UNREPUGNANT	UNRETURNING
UNRECALLING	UNREFRACTED	UNREMITTEDLY	UNREPULSABLE	UNRETURNINGLY
UNRECAPTURABLE	UNREFRESHED	UNREMITTENT	UNREQUIRED	UNREVEALABLE
UNRECEIPTED	UNREFRESHING	UNREMITTENTLY	UNREQUISITE	UNREVEALED
UNRECEIVED	UNREFRIGERATED	UNREMITTING	UNREQUITED	UNREVEALING
UNRECEPTIVE	UNREGARDED	UNREMITTINGLY	UNREQUITEDLY	UNREVENGED
UNRECIPROCATED	UNREGARDING	UNREMITTINGNESS	UNRESCINDED	UNREVENGEFUL
UNRECKONABLE	UNREGENERACIES	UNREMORSEFUL	UNRESENTED	UNREVEREND
UNRECKONED	UNREGENERACY	UNREMORSEFULLY	UNRESENTFUL	UNREVERENT
UNRECLAIMABLE	UNREGENERATE	UNREMORSELESS	UNRESENTING	UNREVERSED
UNRECLAIMABLY	UNREGENERATED	UNREMOVABLE	UNRESERVED	UNREVERTED
UNRECLAIMED	UNREGENERATELY	UNREMUNERATIVE	UNRESERVEDLY	UNREVIEWABLE
UNRECOGNISABLE	UNREGENERATES	UNRENDERED	UNRESERVEDNESS	UNREVIEWED
UNRECOGNISABLY	UNREGIMENTED	UNREPAIRABLE	UNRESERVES	UNREVOLUTIONARY
UNRECOGNISED	UNREGISTERED	UNREPAIRED	UNRESISTANT	UNREWARDED
UNRECOGNISING	UNREGRETTED	UNREPEALABLE	UNRESISTED	UNREWARDEDLY
UNRECOGNIZABLE	UNREGULATED	UNREPEALED	UNRESISTIBLE	UNREWARDING
UNRECOGNIZABLY	UNREHEARSED	UNREPEATABLE	UNRESISTING	UNRHETORICAL
UNRECOGNIZED	UNREINFORCED	UNREPEATED	UNRESISTINGLY	UNRHYTHMIC
UNRECOGNIZING	UNREJOICED	UNREPELLED	UNRESOLVABLE	UNRHYTHMICAL
UNRECOLLECTED	UNREJOICING	UNREPENTANCE	UNRESOLVED	UNRHYTHMICALLY
UNRECOMMENDABLE	UNRELATIVE	UNREPENTANCES	UNRESOLVEDNESS	UNRIDDLEABLE
UNRECOMMENDED	UNRELENTING	UNREPENTANT	UNRESPECTABLE	UNRIDDLERS
UNRECOMPENSED	UNRELENTINGLY	UNREPENTANTLY	UNRESPECTED	UNRIDDLING
UNRECONCILABLE	UNRELENTINGNESS	UNREPENTED	UNRESPECTIVE	UNRIDEABLE
UNRECONCILABLY	UNRELENTOR	UNREPENTING	UNRESPITED	UNRIGHTEOUS
UNRECONCILED	UNRELENTORS	UNREPENTINGLY	UNRESPONSIVE	UNRIGHTEOUSLY
UNRECONCILIABLE	UNRELIABILITIES	UNREPINING	UNRESPONSIVELY	UNRIGHTEOUSNESS
UNRECONSTRUCTED	UNRELIABILITY	UNREPININGLY	UNRESTFULNESS	UNRIGHTFUL
UNRECORDED	UNRELIABLE	UNREPLACEABLE	UNRESTFULNESSES	UNRIGHTFULLY
UNRECOUNTED	UNRELIABLENESS	UNREPLENISHED	UNRESTINGLY	UNRIGHTFULNESS
UNRECOVERABLE	UNRELIABLY	UNREPORTABLE	UNRESTINGNESS	UNRIGHTING
UNRECOVERABLY	UNRELIEVABLE	UNREPORTED	UNRESTINGNESSES	UNRIPENESS
UNRECOVERED	UNRELIEVED	UNREPOSEFUL	UNRESTORED	UNRIPENESSES
UNRECTIFIED	UNRELIEVEDLY	UNREPOSING	UNRESTRAINABLE	UNRIPPINGS
UNRECURING	UNRELIGIOUS	UNREPRESENTED	UNRESTRAINED	UNRIVALLED
UNRECYCLABLE	UNRELIGIOUSLY	UNREPRESSED	UNRESTRAINEDLY	UNRIVETING
UNREDEEMABLE	UNRELISHED	UNREPRIEVABLE	UNRESTRAINT	UNRIVETTED
UNREDEEMED	UNRELUCTANT	UNREPRIEVED	UNRESTRAINTS	UNRIVETTING
UNREDRESSED	UNREMAINING	UNREPRIMANDED	UNRESTRICTED	UNROADWORTHY
UNREDUCIBLE	UNREMARKABLE	UNREPROACHED	UNRESTRICTEDLY	UNROMANISED
UNREFLECTED	UNREMARKABLY	UNREPROACHFUL	UNRETARDED	UNROMANIZED
UNREFLECTING	UNREMARKED	UNREPROACHING	UNRETENTIVE	UNROMANTIC

UNROMANTICAL	UNSATISFIED	UNSCRUTINISED	UNSENSUALISED	UNSHIPPING
UNROMANTICALLY	UNSATISFIEDNESS	UNSCRUTINIZED	UNSENSUALISES	UNSHOCKABLE
UNROMANTICISED	UNSATISFYING	UNSCULPTURED	UNSENSUALISING	UNSHOOTING
UNROMANTICIZED	UNSATURATE	UNSEALABLE	UNSENSUALIZE	UNSHOTTING
UNROOSTING	UNSATURATED	UNSEARCHABLE	UNSENSUALIZED	UNSHOUTING
UNROUNDING	UNSATURATES	UNSEARCHABLES	UNSENSUALIZES	UNSHOWERED
UNRUFFABLE	UNSATURATION	UNSEARCHABLY	UNSENSUALIZING	UNSHOWIEST
UNRUFFLEDNESS	UNSATURATIONS	UNSEARCHED	UNSENTENCED	UNSHRINKABLE
UNRUFFLEDNESSES	UNSAVORILY	UNSEASONABLE	UNSENTIMENTAL	UNSHRINKING
UNRUFFLING	UNSAVORINESS	UNSEASONABLY	UNSEPARABLE	UNSHRINKINGLY
UNRULIMENT	UNSAVORINESSES	UNSEASONED	UNSEPARATED	UNSHROUDED
UNRULIMENTS	UNSAVOURILY	UNSEASONEDNESS	UNSEPULCHRED	UNSHROUDING
UNRULINESS	UNSAVOURINESS	UNSEASONING	UNSERIOUSNESS	UNSHRUBBED
UNRULINESSES	UNSAVOURINESSES	UNSEAWORTHINESS	UNSERIOUSNESSES	UNSHUNNABLE
UNSADDLING	UNSAYABLES	UNSEAWORTHY	UNSERVICEABLE	UNSHUTTERED
UNSAFENESS	UNSCABBARD	UNSECONDED	UNSETTLEDLY	UNSHUTTERING
UNSAFENESSES	UNSCABBARDED	UNSECRETED	UNSETTLEDNESS	UNSHUTTERS
UNSAFETIES	UNSCABBARDING	UNSECRETING	UNSETTLEDNESSES	UNSHUTTING
UNSAILORLIKE	UNSCABBARDS	UNSECTARIAN	UNSETTLEMENT	UNSIGHTEDLY
UNSAINTING	UNSCALABLE	UNSECTARIANISM	UNSETTLEMENTS	UNSIGHTING
UNSAINTLIER	UNSCARIEST	UNSECTARIANISMS	UNSETTLING	UNSIGHTLIER
UNSAINTLIEST	UNSCAVENGERED	UNSECTARIANS	UNSETTLINGLY	UNSIGHTLIEST
UNSAINTLINESS	UNSCEPTRED	UNSEEMINGS	UNSETTLINGS	UNSIGHTLINESS
UNSAINTLINESSES	UNSCHEDULED	UNSEEMLIER	UNSHACKLED	UNSIGHTLINESSES
UNSALABILITIES	UNSCHOLARLIKE	UNSEEMLIEST	UNSHACKLES	UNSINEWING
UNSALABILITY	UNSCHOLARLY	UNSEEMLINESS	UNSHACKLING	UNSINKABLE
UNSALARIED	UNSCHOOLED	UNSEEMLINESSES	UNSHADOWABLE	UNSINNOWED
UNSALEABILITIES	UNSCIENTIFIC	UNSEGMENTED	UNSHADOWED	UNSISTERED
UNSALEABILITY	UNSCISSORED	UNSEGREGATED	UNSHADOWING	UNSISTERLINESS
UNSALEABLE	UNSCORCHED	UNSEISABLE	UNSHAKABLE	UNSISTERLY
UNSALEABLY	UNSCOTTIFIED	UNSEIZABLE	UNSHAKABLENESS	UNSIZEABLE
UNSALVAGEABLE	UNSCRAMBLE	UNSELECTED	UNSHAKABLY	UNSKILFULLY
UNSANCTIFIED	UNSCRAMBLED	UNSELECTIVE	UNSHAKEABLE	UNSKILFULNESS
UNSANCTIFIES	UNSCRAMBLER	UNSELECTIVELY	UNSHAKEABLENESS	UNSKILFULNESSES
UNSANCTIFY	UNSCRAMBLERS	UNSELFCONSCIOUS	UNSHAKEABLY	UNSKILLFUL
UNSANCTIFYING	UNSCRAMBLES	UNSELFISHLY	UNSHAKENLY	UNSKILLFULLY
UNSANCTIONED	UNSCRAMBLING	UNSELFISHNESS	UNSHAPELIER	UNSKILLFULNESS
UNSANDALLED	UNSCRATCHED	UNSELFISHNESSES	UNSHAPELIEST	UNSLAKABLE
UNSANITARY	UNSCREENED	UNSELLABLE	UNSHARPENED	UNSLEEPING
UNSATIABLE	UNSCREWING	UNSEMINARIED	UNSHEATHED	UNSLEEPINGS
UNSATIATED	UNSCRIPTED	UNSENSATIONAL	UNSHEATHES	UNSLINGING
UNSATIATING	UNSCRIPTURAL	UNSENSIBLE	UNSHEATHING	UNSLIPPING
UNSATIRICAL	UNSCRIPTURALLY	UNSENSIBLY	UNSHELLING	UNSLUICING
UNSATISFACTION	UNSCRUPLED	UNSENSITISED	UNSHELTERED	UNSLUMBERING
UNSATISFACTIONS	UNSCRUPULOSITY	UNSENSITIVE	UNSHIELDED	UNSLUMBROUS
UNSATISFACTORY	UNSCRUPULOUS	UNSENSITIZED	UNSHIFTING	UNSMILINGLY
UNSATISFIABLE	UNSCRUPULOUSLY	UNSENSUALISE	UNSHINGLED	UNSMIRCHED

U

UNSMOKABLE
UNSMOOTHED
UNSMOOTHING
UNSMOTHERABLE
UNSNAGGING
UNSNAPPING
UNSNARLING
UNSNECKING
UNSOBERING
UNSOCIABILITIES
UNSOCIABILITY
UNSOCIABLE
UNSOCIABLENESS
UNSOCIABLY
UNSOCIALISED
UNSOCIALISM
UNSOCIALISMS
UNSOCIALITIES
UNSOCIALITY
UNSOCIALIZED
UNSOCIALLY
UNSOCKETED
UNSOCKETING
UNSOFTENED
UNSOFTENING
UNSOLDERED
UNSOLDERING
UNSOLDIERLIKE
UNSOLDIERLY
UNSOLICITED
UNSOLICITOUS
UNSOLIDITIES
UNSOLIDITY
UNSOLVABLE
UNSONSIEST
UNSOPHISTICATE
UNSOPHISTICATED
UNSOUNDABLE
UNSOUNDEST
UNSOUNDNESS
UNSOUNDNESSES
UNSPARINGLY
UNSPARINGNESS
UNSPARINGNESSES
UNSPARRING
UNSPEAKABLE
UNSPEAKABLENESS

UNSPEAKABLY
UNSPEAKING
UNSPECIALISED
UNSPECIALIZED
UNSPECIFIABLE
UNSPECIFIC
UNSPECIFICALLY
UNSPECIFIED
UNSPECTACLED
UNSPECTACULAR
UNSPECULATIVE
UNSPELLING
UNSPHERING
UNSPIRITED
UNSPIRITUAL
UNSPIRITUALISE
UNSPIRITUALISED
UNSPIRITUALISES
UNSPIRITUALIZE
UNSPIRITUALIZED
UNSPIRITUALIZES
UNSPIRITUALLY
UNSPLINTERABLE
UNSPOOLING
UNSPORTING
UNSPORTSMANLIKE
UNSPOTTEDNESS
UNSPOTTEDNESSES
UNSPRINKLED
UNSTABLENESS
UNSTABLENESSES
UNSTABLEST
UNSTACKING
UNSTAIDNESS
UNSTAIDNESSES
UNSTAINABLE
UNSTANCHABLE
UNSTANCHED
UNSTANDARDISED
UNSTANDARDIZED
UNSTARCHED
UNSTARCHES
UNSTARCHING
UNSTARTLING
UNSTATESMANLIKE
UNSTATUTABLE
UNSTATUTABLY

UNSTAUNCHABLE
UNSTAUNCHED
UNSTEADFAST
UNSTEADFASTLY
UNSTEADFASTNESS
UNSTEADIED
UNSTEADIER
UNSTEADIES
UNSTEADIEST
UNSTEADILY
UNSTEADINESS
UNSTEADINESSES
UNSTEADYING
UNSTEELING
UNSTEPPING
UNSTERCORATED
UNSTERILISED
UNSTERILIZED
UNSTICKING
UNSTIGMATISED
UNSTIGMATIZED
UNSTIMULATED
UNSTINTING
UNSTINTINGLY
UNSTITCHED
UNSTITCHES
UNSTITCHING
UNSTOCKING
UNSTOCKINGED
UNSTOOPING
UNSTOPPABLE
UNSTOPPABLY
UNSTOPPERED
UNSTOPPERING
UNSTOPPERS
UNSTOPPING
UNSTRAINED
UNSTRAPPED
UNSTRAPPING
UNSTRATIFIED
UNSTREAMED
UNSTRENGTHENED
UNSTRESSED
UNSTRESSES
UNSTRESSING
UNSTRIATED
UNSTRINGED

UNSTRINGING
UNSTRIPPED
UNSTRIPPING
UNSTRUCTURED
UNSTUFFIER
UNSTUFFIEST
UNSUBDUABLE
UNSUBJECTED
UNSUBJECTING
UNSUBJECTS
UNSUBLIMATED
UNSUBLIMED
UNSUBMERGED
UNSUBMISSIVE
UNSUBMITTING
UNSUBSCRIBE
UNSUBSCRIBED
UNSUBSCRIBER
UNSUBSCRIBERS
UNSUBSCRIBES
UNSUBSCRIBING
UNSUBSIDISED
UNSUBSIDIZED
UNSUBSTANTIAL
UNSUBSTANTIALLY
UNSUBSTANTIATED
UNSUCCEEDED
UNSUCCESSES
UNSUCCESSFUL
UNSUCCESSFULLY
UNSUCCESSIVE
UNSUCCOURED
UNSUFFERABLE
UNSUFFICIENT
UNSUITABILITIES
UNSUITABILITY
UNSUITABLE
UNSUITABLENESS
UNSUITABLY
UNSUMMERED
UNSUMMONED
UNSUNNIEST
UNSUPERFLUOUS
UNSUPERVISED
UNSUPPLENESS
UNSUPPLENESSES
UNSUPPLIED

UNSUPPORTABLE
UNSUPPORTED
UNSUPPORTEDLY
UNSUPPOSABLE
UNSUPPRESSED
UNSURFACED
UNSURMISED
UNSURMOUNTABLE
UNSURPASSABLE
UNSURPASSABLY
UNSURPASSED
UNSURPRISED
UNSURPRISING
UNSURPRISINGLY
UNSURVEYED
UNSUSCEPTIBLE
UNSUSPECTED
UNSUSPECTEDLY
UNSUSPECTEDNESS
UNSUSPECTING
UNSUSPECTINGLY
UNSUSPENDED
UNSUSPICION
UNSUSPICIONS
UNSUSPICIOUS
UNSUSPICIOUSLY
UNSUSTAINABLE
UNSUSTAINED
UNSUSTAINING
UNSWADDLED
UNSWADDLES
UNSWADDLING
UNSWALLOWED
UNSWATHING
UNSWAYABLE
UNSWEARING
UNSWEARINGS
UNSWEETENED
UNSWERVING
UNSWERVINGLY
UNSYLLABLED
UNSYMMETRICAL
UNSYMMETRICALLY
UNSYMMETRIES
UNSYMMETRISED
UNSYMMETRIZED
UNSYMMETRY

U

UNSYMPATHETIC	UNTERMINATED	UNTIMELIEST	UNTREASURING	UNUSUALNESS
UNSYMPATHIES	UNTERRESTRIAL	UNTIMELINESS	UNTREATABLE	UNUSUALNESSES
UNSYMPATHISING	UNTERRIFIED	UNTIMELINESSES	UNTREMBLING	UNUTILISED
UNSYMPATHIZING	UNTERRIFYING	UNTIMEOUSLY	UNTREMBLINGLY	UNUTILIZED
UNSYMPATHY	UNTESTABLE	UNTINCTURED	UNTREMENDOUS	UNUTTERABLE
UNSYNCHRONISED	UNTETHERED	UNTIRINGLY	UNTREMULOUS	UNUTTERABLENESS
UNSYNCHRONIZED	UNTETHERING	UNTOCHERED	UNTRENCHED	UNUTTERABLES
UNSYSTEMATIC	UNTHANKFUL	UNTOGETHER	UNTRENDIER	UNUTTERABLY
UNSYSTEMATICAL	UNTHANKFULLY	UNTORMENTED	UNTRENDIEST	UNVACCINATED
UNSYSTEMATISED	UNTHANKFULNESS	UNTORTURED	UNTRESPASSING	UNVALUABLE
UNSYSTEMATIZED	UNTHATCHED	UNTOUCHABILITY	UNTRIMMING	UNVANQUISHABLE
UNSYSTEMIC	UNTHATCHES	UNTOUCHABLE	UNTROUBLED	UNVANQUISHED
UNTACKLING	UNTHATCHING	UNTOUCHABLES	UNTROUBLEDLY	UNVARIABLE
UNTAINTEDLY	UNTHEOLOGICAL	UNTOWARDLINESS	UNTRUENESS	UNVARIEGATED
UNTAINTEDNESS	UNTHEORETICAL	UNTOWARDLY	UNTRUENESSES	UNVARNISHED
UNTAINTEDNESSES	UNTHICKENED	UNTOWARDNESS	UNTRUSSERS	UNVARYINGLY
UNTAINTING	UNTHINKABILITY	UNTOWARDNESSES	UNTRUSSING	UNVEILINGS
UNTALENTED	UNTHINKABLE	UNTRACEABLE	UNTRUSSINGS	UNVENDIBLE
UNTAMABLENESS	UNTHINKABLENESS	UNTRACKING	UNTRUSTFUL	UNVENERABLE
UNTAMABLENESSES	UNTHINKABLY	UNTRACTABLE	UNTRUSTIER	UNVENTILATED
UNTAMEABLE	UNTHINKING	UNTRACTABLENESS	UNTRUSTIEST	UNVERACIOUS
UNTAMEABLENESS	UNTHINKINGLY	UNTRADITIONAL	UNTRUSTINESS	UNVERACITIES
UNTAMEABLY	UNTHINKINGNESS	UNTRADITIONALLY	UNTRUSTINESSES	UNVERACITY
UNTAMEDNESS	UNTHOROUGH	UNTRAMMELED	UNTRUSTING	UNVERBALISED
UNTAMEDNESSES	UNTHOUGHTFUL	UNTRAMMELLED	UNTRUSTWORTHILY	UNVERBALIZED
UNTANGIBLE	UNTHOUGHTFULLY	UNTRAMPLED	UNTRUSTWORTHY	UNVERIFIABILITY
UNTANGLING	UNTHREADED	UNTRANQUIL	UNTRUTHFUL	UNVERIFIABLE
UNTARNISHED	UNTHREADING	UNTRANSFERABLE	UNTRUTHFULLY	UNVERIFIED
UNTASTEFUL	UNTHREATENED	UNTRANSFERRABLE	UNTRUTHFULNESS	UNVIOLATED
UNTEACHABLE	UNTHREATENING	UNTRANSFORMED	UNTUCKERED	UNVIRTUOUS
UNTEACHABLENESS	UNTHRIFTIER	UNTRANSLATABLE	UNTUMULTUOUS	UNVIRTUOUSLY
UNTEACHING	UNTHRIFTIEST	UNTRANSLATABLY	UNTUNABLENESS	UNVISITABLE
UNTEARABLE	UNTHRIFTIHEAD	UNTRANSLATED	UNTUNABLENESSES	UNVISORING
UNTECHNICAL	UNTHRIFTIHEADS	UNTRANSMIGRATED	UNTUNEABLE	UNVITIATED
UNTELLABLE	UNTHRIFTILY	UNTRANSMISSIBLE	UNTUNEFULLY	UNVITRIFIABLE
UNTEMPERED	UNTHRIFTINESS	UNTRANSMITTED	UNTUNEFULNESS	UNVITRIFIED
UNTEMPERING	UNTHRIFTINESSES	UNTRANSMUTABLE	UNTUNEFULNESSES	UNVIZARDED
UNTENABILITIES	UNTHRIFTYHEAD	UNTRANSMUTED	UNTURNABLE	UNVIZARDING
UNTENABILITY	UNTHRIFTYHEADS	UNTRANSPARENT	UNTWISTING	UNVOCALISED
UNTENABLENESS	UNTHRIFTYHED	UNTRAVELED	UNTWISTINGS	UNVOCALIZED
UNTENABLENESSES	UNTHRIFTYHEDS	UNTRAVELLED	UNTYPICALLY	UNVOICINGS
UNTENANTABLE	UNTHRONING	UNTRAVERSABLE	UNTYREABLE	UNVOYAGEABLE
UNTENANTED	UNTIDINESS	UNTRAVERSED	UNUNUNIUMS	UNVULGARISE
UNTENANTING	UNTIDINESSES	UNTREADING	UNUPLIFTED	UNVULGARISED
UNTENDERED	UNTILLABLE	UNTREASURE	UNUSEFULLY	UNVULGARISES
UNTENDERLY	UNTIMBERED	UNTREASURED	UNUSEFULNESS	UNVULGARISING
UNTENTIEST	UNTIMELIER	UNTREASURES	UNUSEFULNESSES	UNVULGARIZE

U

UNVULGARIZED	UNWELLNESS	UNWONTEDNESSES	UPDRAGGING	UPPERCUTTING
UNVULGARIZES	UNWELLNESSES	UNWORKABILITIES	UPDRAGGINGS	UPPERPARTS
UNVULGARIZING	UNWHISTLEABLE	UNWORKABILITY	UPDRAUGHTS	UPPERWORKS
UNVULNERABLE	UNWHOLESOME	UNWORKABLE	UPFILLINGS	UPPISHNESS
UNWANDERING	UNWHOLESOMELY	UNWORKMANLIKE	UPFLASHING	UPPISHNESSES
UNWARENESS	UNWHOLESOMENESS	UNWORLDLIER	UPFLINGING	UPPITINESS
UNWARENESSES	UNWIELDIER	UNWORLDLIEST	UPFOLLOWED	UPPITINESSES
UNWARINESS	UNWIELDIEST	UNWORLDLINESS	UPFOLLOWING	UPPITYNESS
UNWARINESSES	UNWIELDILY	UNWORLDLINESSES	UPGATHERED	UPPITYNESSES
UNWARRANTABLE	UNWIELDINESS	UNWORSHIPFUL	UPGATHERING	UPPROPPING
UNWARRANTABLY	UNWIELDINESSES	UNWORSHIPPED	UPGRADABILITIES	UPREACHING
UNWARRANTED	UNWIELDLILY	UNWORTHIER	UPGRADABILITY	UPRIGHTEOUSLY
UNWARRANTEDLY	UNWIELDLINESS	UNWORTHIES	UPGRADABLE	UPRIGHTING
UNWASHEDNESS	UNWIELDLINESSES	UNWORTHIEST	UPGRADATION	UPRIGHTNESS
UNWASHEDNESSES	UNWIFELIER	UNWORTHILY	UPGRADATIONS	UPRIGHTNESSES
UNWATCHABLE	UNWIFELIEST	UNWORTHINESS	UPGRADEABILITY	UPROARIOUS
UNWATCHFUL	UNWIFELIKE	UNWORTHINESSES	UPGRADEABLE	UPROARIOUSLY
UNWATCHFULLY	UNWILLINGLY	UNWOUNDABLE	UPGROWINGS	UPROARIOUSNESS
UNWATCHFULNESS	UNWILLINGNESS	UNWRAPPING	UPHEAPINGS	UPROOTEDNESS
UNWATERING	UNWILLINGNESSES	UNWREATHED	UPHILLWARD	UPROOTEDNESSES
UNWAVERING	UNWINDABLE	UNWREATHES	UPHOARDING	UPROOTINGS
UNWAVERINGLY	UNWINDINGS	UNWREATHING	UPHOISTING	UPSETTABLE
UNWEAKENED	UNWINKINGLY	UNWRINKLED	UPHOLDINGS	UPSETTINGLY
UNWEAPONED	UNWINNABLE	UNWRINKLES	UPHOLSTERED	UPSETTINGS
UNWEAPONING	UNWINNOWED	UNWRINKLING	UPHOLSTERER	UPSHIFTING
UNWEARABLE	UNWISENESS	UNYIELDING	UPHOLSTERERS	UPSHOOTING
UNWEARIABLE	UNWISENESSES	UNYIELDINGLY	UPHOLSTERIES	UPSIDEOWNE
UNWEARIABLY	UNWITCHING	UNYIELDINGNESS	UPHOLSTERING	UPSITTINGS
UNWEARIEDLY	UNWITHDRAWING	UPBRAIDERS	UPHOLSTERS	UPSKILLING
UNWEARIEDNESS	UNWITHERED	UPBRAIDING	UPHOLSTERY	UPSPEAKING
UNWEARIEDNESSES	UNWITHERING	UPBRAIDINGLY	UPHOLSTRESS	UPSPEARING
UNWEARIEST	UNWITHHELD	UPBRAIDINGS	UPHOLSTRESSES	UPSPRINGING
UNWEARYING	UNWITHHOLDEN	UPBREAKING	UPHOORDING	UPSTANDING
UNWEARYINGLY	UNWITHHOLDING	UPBRINGING	UPKNITTING	UPSTANDINGNESS
UNWEATHERED	UNWITHSTOOD	UPBRINGINGS	UPLIFTINGLY	UPSTARTING
UNWEDGABLE	UNWITNESSED	UPBUILDERS	UPLIFTINGS	UPSTEPPING
UNWEDGEABLE	UNWITTIEST	UPBUILDING	UPLIGHTERS	UPSTEPPINGS
UNWEETINGLY	UNWITTINGLY	UPBUILDINGS	UPLIGHTING	UPSTIRRING
UNWEIGHING	UNWITTINGNESS	UPBUOYANCE	UPLINKINGS	UPSTREAMED
UNWEIGHTED	UNWITTINGNESSES	UPBUOYANCES	UPMANSHIPS	UPSTREAMING
UNWEIGHTING	UNWOMANING	UPBURSTING	UPMARKETED	UPSTRETCHED
UNWEIGHTINGS	UNWOMANLIER	UPCATCHING	UPMARKETING	UPSURGENCE
UNWELCOMED	UNWOMANLIEST	UPCHEERING	UPPERCASED	UPSURGENCES
UNWELCOMELY	UNWOMANLINESS	UPCHUCKING	UPPERCASES	UPSWARMING
UNWELCOMENESS	UNWOMANLINESSES	UPCLIMBING	UPPERCASING	UPSWEEPING
UNWELCOMENESSES	UNWONTEDLY	UPCOUNTRIES	UPPERCLASSMAN	UPSWELLING
UNWELCOMING	UNWONTEDNESS	UPDATEABLE	UPPERCLASSMEN	UPSWINGING

U

UPTALKINGS
UPTHROWING
UPTHRUSTED
UPTHRUSTING
UPTHUNDERED
UPTHUNDERING
UPTHUNDERS
UPTIGHTEST
UPTIGHTNESS
UPTIGHTNESSES
UPTITLINGS
UPTRAINING
UPTURNINGS
UPVALUATION
UPVALUATIONS
UPWARDNESS
UPWARDNESSES
UPWELLINGS
UPWHIRLING
URALITISATION
URALITISATIONS
URALITISED
URALITISES
URALITISING
URALITIZATION
URALITIZATIONS
URALITIZED
URALITIZES
URALITIZING
URANALYSES
URANALYSIS
URANINITES
URANOGRAPHER
URANOGRAPHERS
URANOGRAPHIC
URANOGRAPHICAL
URANOGRAPHIES
URANOGRAPHIST
URANOGRAPHISTS
URANOGRAPHY
URANOLOGIES
URANOMETRIES
URANOMETRY
URANOPLASTIES
URANOPLASTY
URBANENESS

URBANENESSES
URBANISATION
URBANISATIONS
URBANISING
URBANISTIC
URBANISTICALLY
URBANITIES
URBANIZATION
URBANIZATIONS
URBANIZING
URBANOLOGIES
URBANOLOGIST
URBANOLOGISTS
URBANOLOGY
URCEOLUSES
UREDINIOSPORE
UREDINIOSPORES
UREDINIUMS
UREDIOSPORE
UREDIOSPORES
UREDOSORUS
UREDOSPORE
UREDOSPORES
UREOTELISM
UREOTELISMS
URETERITIS
URETERITISES
URETHANING
URETHRITIC
URETHRITIS
URETHRITISES
URETHROSCOPE
URETHROSCOPES
URETHROSCOPIC
URETHROSCOPIES
URETHROSCOPY
URICOSURIC
URICOTELIC
URICOTELISM
URICOTELISMS
URINALYSES
URINALYSIS
URINATIONS
URINIFEROUS
URINIPAROUS
URINOGENITAL

URINOLOGIES
URINOMETER
URINOMETERS
URINOSCOPIES
URINOSCOPY
UROBILINOGEN
UROBILINOGENS
UROBOROSES
UROCHORDAL
UROCHORDATE
UROCHORDATES
UROCHROMES
URODYNAMICS
UROGENITAL
UROGRAPHIC
UROGRAPHIES
UROKINASES
UROLAGNIAS
UROLITHIASES
UROLITHIASIS
UROLOGICAL
UROLOGISTS
UROPOIESES
UROPOIESIS
UROPYGIUMS
UROSCOPIES
UROSCOPIST
UROSCOPISTS
UROSTEGITE
UROSTEGITES
UROSTHENIC
UROSTOMIES
URTICACEOUS
URTICARIAL
URTICARIAS
URTICARIOUS
URTICATING
URTICATION
URTICATIONS
USABILITIES
USABLENESS
USABLENESSES
USEABILITIES
USEABILITY
USEABLENESS
USEABLENESSES

USEFULNESS
USEFULNESSES
USELESSNESS
USELESSNESSES
USHERESSES
USHERETTES
USHERSHIPS
USQUEBAUGH
USQUEBAUGHS
USTILAGINEOUS
USTILAGINOUS
USTULATING
USTULATION
USTULATIONS
USUALNESSES
USUCAPIENT
USUCAPIENTS
USUCAPIONS
USUCAPTIBLE
USUCAPTING
USUCAPTION
USUCAPTIONS
USUFRUCTED
USUFRUCTING
USUFRUCTUARIES
USUFRUCTUARY
USURIOUSLY
USURIOUSNESS
USURIOUSNESSES
USURPATION
USURPATIONS
USURPATIVE
USURPATORY
USURPATURE
USURPATURES
USURPINGLY
UTERECTOMIES
UTERECTOMY
UTERITISES
UTEROGESTATION
UTEROGESTATIONS
UTEROTOMIES
UTILISABLE
UTILISATION
UTILISATIONS
UTILITARIAN

UTILITARIANISE
UTILITARIANISED
UTILITARIANISES
UTILITARIANISM
UTILITARIANISMS
UTILITARIANIZE
UTILITARIANIZED
UTILITARIANIZES
UTILITARIANS
UTILIZABLE
UTILIZATION
UTILIZATIONS
UTOPIANISE
UTOPIANISED
UTOPIANISER
UTOPIANISERS
UTOPIANISES
UTOPIANISING
UTOPIANISM
UTOPIANISMS
UTOPIANIZE
UTOPIANIZED
UTOPIANIZER
UTOPIANIZERS
UTOPIANIZES
UTOPIANIZING
UTRICULARIA
UTRICULARIAS
UTRICULATE
UTRICULITIS
UTRICULITISES
UTTERABLENESS
UTTERABLENESSES
UTTERANCES
UTTERMOSTS
UTTERNESSES
UVAROVITES
UVULITISES
UXORICIDAL
UXORICIDES
UXORILOCAL
UXORIOUSLY
UXORIOUSNESS
UXORIOUSNESSES

U

V

VACANTNESS	VAGABONDED	VALEDICTIONS	VALUELESSNESSES	VANQUISHED
VACANTNESSES	VAGABONDING	VALEDICTORIAN	VALVASSORS	VANQUISHER
VACATIONED	VAGABONDISE	VALEDICTORIANS	VALVULITIS	VANQUISHERS
VACATIONER	VAGABONDISED	VALEDICTORIES	VALVULITISES	VANQUISHES
VACATIONERS	VAGABONDISES	VALEDICTORY	VAMPIRISED	VANQUISHING
VACATIONING	VAGABONDISH	VALENTINES	VAMPIRISES	VANQUISHMENT
VACATIONIST	VAGABONDISING	VALERIANACEOUS	VAMPIRISING	VANQUISHMENTS
VACATIONISTS	VAGABONDISM	VALETUDINARIAN	VAMPIRISMS	VANTAGELESS
VACATIONLAND	VAGABONDISMS	VALETUDINARIANS	VAMPIRIZED	VANTBRACES
VACATIONLANDS	VAGABONDIZE	VALETUDINARIES	VAMPIRIZES	VANTBRASSES
VACATIONLESS	VAGABONDIZED	VALETUDINARY	VAMPIRIZING	VAPIDITIES
VACCINATED	VAGABONDIZES	VALIANCIES	VANADIATES	VAPIDNESSES
VACCINATES	VAGABONDIZING	VALIANTNESS	VANADINITE	VAPORABILITIES
VACCINATING	VAGARIOUSLY	VALIANTNESSES	VANADINITES	VAPORABILITY
VACCINATION	VAGILITIES	VALIDATING	VANASPATIS	VAPORESCENCE
VACCINATIONS	VAGINECTOMIES	VALIDATION	VANCOMYCIN	VAPORESCENCES
VACCINATOR	VAGINECTOMY	VALIDATIONS	VANCOMYCINS	VAPORESCENT
VACCINATORS	VAGINICOLINE	VALIDATORY	VANDALISATION	VAPORETTOS
VACCINATORY	VAGINICOLOUS	VALIDITIES	VANDALISATIONS	VAPORIFORM
VACCINIUMS	VAGINISMUS	VALIDNESSES	VANDALISED	VAPORIMETER
VACILLATED	VAGINISMUSES	VALLATIONS	VANDALISES	VAPORIMETERS
VACILLATES	VAGINITIDES	VALLECULAE	VANDALISING	VAPORISABLE
VACILLATING	VAGINITISES	VALLECULAR	VANDALISMS	VAPORISATION
VACILLATINGLY	VAGOTOMIES	VALLECULAS	VANDALISTIC	VAPORISATIONS
VACILLATION	VAGOTONIAS	VALLECULATE	VANDALIZATION	VAPORISERS
VACILLATIONS	VAGOTROPIC	VALORISATION	VANDALIZATIONS	VAPORISHNESS
VACILLATOR	VAGRANCIES	VALORISATIONS	VANDALIZED	VAPORISHNESSES
VACILLATORS	VAGRANTNESS	VALORISING	VANDALIZES	VAPORISING
VACILLATORY	VAGRANTNESSES	VALORIZATION	VANDALIZING	VAPORIZABLE
VACUATIONS	VAGUENESSES	VALORIZATIONS	VANGUARDISM	VAPORIZATION
VACUOLATED	VAINGLORIED	VALORIZING	VANGUARDISMS	VAPORIZATIONS
VACUOLATION	VAINGLORIES	VALOROUSLY	VANGUARDIST	VAPORIZERS
VACUOLATIONS	VAINGLORIOUS	VALPOLICELLA	VANGUARDISTS	VAPORIZING
VACUOLISATION	VAINGLORIOUSLY	VALPOLICELLAS	VANISHINGLY	VAPOROSITIES
VACUOLISATIONS	VAINGLORYING	VALPROATES	VANISHINGS	VAPOROSITY
VACUOLIZATION	VAINNESSES	VALUABLENESS	VANISHMENT	VAPOROUSLY
VACUOLIZATIONS	VAIVODESHIP	VALUABLENESSES	VANISHMENTS	VAPOROUSNESS
VACUOUSNESS	VAIVODESHIPS	VALUATIONAL	VANITORIES	VAPOROUSNESSES
VACUOUSNESSES	VAJAZZLING	VALUATIONALLY	VANPOOLING	VAPORWARES
VAGABONDAGE	VAJAZZLINGS	VALUATIONS	VANPOOLINGS	VAPOURABILITIES
VAGABONDAGES	VALEDICTION	VALUELESSNESS	VANQUISHABLE	VAPOURABILITY

VAPOURABLE	VARIOLATING	VASECTOMISED	VATICINATING	VEGETATIVE
VAPOURINGLY	VARIOLATION	VASECTOMISES	VATICINATION	VEGETATIVELY
VAPOURINGS	VARIOLATIONS	VASECTOMISING	VATICINATIONS	VEGETATIVENESS
VAPOURISHNESS	VARIOLATOR	VASECTOMIZE	VATICINATOR	VEGGIEBURGER
VAPOURISHNESSES	VARIOLATORS	VASECTOMIZED	VATICINATORS	VEGGIEBURGERS
VAPOURLESS	VARIOLISATION	VASECTOMIZES	VATICINATORY	VEHEMENCES
VAPOURWARE	VARIOLISATIONS	VASECTOMIZING	VAUDEVILLE	VEHEMENCIES
VAPOURWARES	VARIOLITES	VASELINING	VAUDEVILLEAN	VEHEMENTLY
VAPULATING	VARIOLITIC	VASOACTIVE	VAUDEVILLEANS	VEILLEUSES
VAPULATION	VARIOLIZATION	VASOACTIVITIES	VAUDEVILLES	VEINSTONES
VAPULATIONS	VARIOLIZATIONS	VASOACTIVITY	VAUDEVILLIAN	VEINSTUFFS
VARIABILITIES	VARIOLOIDS	VASOCONSTRICTOR	VAUDEVILLIANS	VELARISATION
VARIABILITY	VARIOMETER	VASODILATATION	VAUDEVILLIST	VELARISATIONS
VARIABLENESS	VARIOMETERS	VASODILATATIONS	VAUDEVILLISTS	VELARISING
VARIABLENESSES	VARIOUSNESS	VASODILATATORY	VAULTINGLY	VELARIZATION
VARIATIONAL	VARIOUSNESSES	VASODILATION	VAUNTERIES	VELARIZATIONS
VARIATIONALLY	VARISCITES	VASODILATIONS	VAUNTINGLY	VELARIZING
VARIATIONIST	VARITYPING	VASODILATOR	VAVASORIES	VELDSCHOEN
VARIATIONISTS	VARITYPIST	VASODILATORS	VECTOGRAPH	VELDSCHOENS
VARIATIONS	VARITYPISTS	VASODILATORY	VECTOGRAPHS	VELDSKOENS
VARICELLAR	VARLETESSES	VASOINHIBITOR	VECTORIALLY	VELITATION
VARICELLAS	VARLETRIES	VASOINHIBITORS	VECTORINGS	VELITATIONS
VARICELLATE	VARNISHERS	VASOINHIBITORY	VECTORISATION	VELLEITIES
VARICELLOID	VARNISHING	VASOPRESSIN	VECTORISATIONS	VELLENAGES
VARICELLOUS	VARNISHINGS	VASOPRESSINS	VECTORISED	VELLICATED
VARICOCELE	VARSOVIENNE	VASOPRESSOR	VECTORISES	VELLICATES
VARICOCELES	VARSOVIENNES	VASOPRESSORS	VECTORISING	VELLICATING
VARICOLORED	VASCULARISATION	VASOSPASMS	VECTORIZATION	VELLICATION
VARICOLOURED	VASCULARISE	VASOSPASTIC	VECTORIZATIONS	VELLICATIONS
VARICOSITIES	VASCULARISED	VASOTOCINS	VECTORIZED	VELLICATIVE
VARICOSITY	VASCULARISES	VASOTOMIES	VECTORIZES	VELOCIMETER
VARICOTOMIES	VASCULARISING	VASSALAGES	VECTORIZING	VELOCIMETERS
VARICOTOMY	VASCULARITIES	VASSALESSES	VECTORSCOPE	VELOCIMETRIES
VARIEDNESS	VASCULARITY	VASSALISED	VECTORSCOPES	VELOCIMETRY
VARIEDNESSES	VASCULARIZATION	VASSALISES	VEGEBURGER	VELOCIPEDE
VARIEGATED	VASCULARIZE	VASSALISING	VEGEBURGERS	VELOCIPEDEAN
VARIEGATES	VASCULARIZED	VASSALIZED	VEGETABLES	VELOCIPEDEANS
VARIEGATING	VASCULARIZES	VASSALIZES	VEGETARIAN	VELOCIPEDED
VARIEGATION	VASCULARIZING	VASSALIZING	VEGETARIANISM	VELOCIPEDER
VARIEGATIONS	VASCULARLY	VASSALLING	VEGETARIANISMS	VELOCIPEDERS
VARIEGATOR	VASCULATURE	VASSALRIES	VEGETARIANS	VELOCIPEDES
VARIEGATORS	VASCULATURES	VASTIDITIES	VEGETATING	VELOCIPEDIAN
VARIETALLY	VASCULIFORM	VASTITUDES	VEGETATINGS	VELOCIPEDIANS
VARIFOCALS	VASCULITIDES	VASTNESSES	VEGETATION	VELOCIPEDING
VARIFORMLY	VASCULITIS	VATICINATE	VEGETATIONAL	VELOCIPEDIST
VARIOLATED	VASECTOMIES	VATICINATED	VEGETATIONS	VELOCIPEDISTS
VARIOLATES	VASECTOMISE	VATICINATES	VEGETATIOUS	VELOCIRAPTOR

V

VELOCIRAPTORS

VELOCIRAPTORS	VENEREOLOGICAL	VENTRICOSITIES	VERBALISATION	VERGENCIES
VELOCITIES	VENEREOLOGIES	VENTRICOSITY	VERBALISATIONS	VERGERSHIP
VELODROMES	VENEREOLOGIST	VENTRICOUS	VERBALISED	VERGERSHIPS
VELOUTINES	VENEREOLOGISTS	VENTRICULAR	VERBALISER	VERIDICALITIES
VELUTINOUS	VENEREOLOGY	VENTRICULE	VERBALISERS	VERIDICALITY
VELVETEENED	VENESECTION	VENTRICULES	VERBALISES	VERIDICALLY
VELVETEENS	VENESECTIONS	VENTRICULI	VERBALISING	VERIDICOUS
VELVETIEST	VENGEANCES	VENTRICULUS	VERBALISMS	VERIFIABILITIES
VELVETINESS	VENGEFULLY	VENTRILOQUAL	VERBALISTIC	VERIFIABILITY
VELVETINESSES	VENGEFULNESS	VENTRILOQUIAL	VERBALISTS	VERIFIABLE
VELVETINGS	VENGEFULNESSES	VENTRILOQUIALLY	VERBALITIES	VERIFIABLENESS
VELVETLIKE	VENGEMENTS	VENTRILOQUIES	VERBALIZATION	VERIFIABLY
VENALITIES	VENIALITIES	VENTRILOQUISE	VERBALIZATIONS	VERIFICATION
VENATICALLY	VENIALNESS	VENTRILOQUISED	VERBALIZED	VERIFICATIONS
VENATIONAL	VENIALNESSES	VENTRILOQUISES	VERBALIZER	VERIFICATIVE
VENATORIAL	VENIPUNCTURE	VENTRILOQUISING	VERBALIZERS	VERIFICATORY
VENDETTIST	VENIPUNCTURES	VENTRILOQUISM	VERBALIZES	VERISIMILAR
VENDETTISTS	VENISECTION	VENTRILOQUISMS	VERBALIZING	VERISIMILARLY
VENDIBILITIES	VENISECTIONS	VENTRILOQUIST	VERBALLING	VERISIMILITIES
VENDIBILITY	VENOGRAPHIC	VENTRILOQUISTIC	VERBARIANS	VERISIMILITUDE
VENDIBLENESS	VENOGRAPHICAL	VENTRILOQUISTS	VERBASCUMS	VERISIMILITUDES
VENDIBLENESSES	VENOGRAPHIES	VENTRILOQUIZE	VERBENACEOUS	VERISIMILITY
VENDITATION	VENOGRAPHY	VENTRILOQUIZED	VERBERATED	VERISIMILOUS
VENDITATIONS	VENOLOGIES	VENTRILOQUIZES	VERBERATES	VERITABLENESS
VENDITIONS	VENOMOUSLY	VENTRILOQUIZING	VERBERATING	VERITABLENESSES
VENEERINGS	VENOMOUSNESS	VENTRILOQUOUS	VERBERATION	VERJUICING
VENEFICALLY	VENOMOUSNESSES	VENTRILOQUY	VERBERATIONS	VERKRAMPTE
VENEFICIOUS	VENOSCLEROSES	VENTRIPOTENT	VERBICIDES	VERKRAMPTES
VENEFICIOUSLY	VENOSCLEROSIS	VENTROLATERAL	VERBIFICATION	VERMEILING
VENEFICOUS	VENOSITIES	VENTROMEDIAL	VERBIFICATIONS	VERMEILLED
VENEFICOUSLY	VENOUSNESS	VENTURESOME	VERBIFYING	VERMEILLES
VENENATING	VENOUSNESSES	VENTURESOMELY	VERBIGERATE	VERMEILLING
VENEPUNCTURE	VENTIDUCTS	VENTURESOMENESS	VERBIGERATED	VERMICELLI
VENEPUNCTURES	VENTIFACTS	VENTURINGLY	VERBIGERATES	VERMICELLIS
VENERABILITIES	VENTILABLE	VENTURINGS	VERBIGERATING	VERMICIDAL
VENERABILITY	VENTILATED	VENTUROUSLY	VERBIGERATION	VERMICIDES
VENERABLENESS	VENTILATES	VENTUROUSNESS	VERBIGERATIONS	VERMICULAR
VENERABLENESSES	VENTILATING	VENTUROUSNESSES	VERBOSENESS	VERMICULARLY
VENERABLES	VENTILATION	VERACIOUSLY	VERBOSENESSES	VERMICULATE
VENERATING	VENTILATIONS	VERACIOUSNESS	VERBOSITIES	VERMICULATED
VENERATION	VENTILATIVE	VERACIOUSNESSES	VERDANCIES	VERMICULATES
VENERATIONAL	VENTILATOR	VERACITIES	VERDIGRISED	VERMICULATING
VENERATIONS	VENTILATORS	VERANDAHED	VERDIGRISES	VERMICULATION
VENERATIVE	VENTILATORY	VERAPAMILS	VERDIGRISING	VERMICULATIONS
VENERATIVENESS	VENTOSITIES	VERATRIDINE	VERDURELESS	VERMICULES
VENERATORS	VENTRICLES	VERATRIDINES	VERGEBOARD	VERMICULITE
VENEREALLY	VENTRICOSE	VERATRINES	VERGEBOARDS	VERMICULITES

VERMICULOUS	VERNALIZING	VERTICILLATE	VESTIMENTAL	VIBRATIONLESS
VERMICULTURE	VERNATIONS	VERTICILLATED	VESTIMENTARY	VIBRATIONS
VERMICULTURES	VERNISSAGE	VERTICILLATELY	VESTIMENTS	VIBRATIUNCLE
VERMIFUGAL	VERNISSAGES	VERTICILLATION	VESTITURES	VIBRATIUNCLES
VERMIFUGES	VERRUCIFORM	VERTICILLATIONS	VESTMENTAL	VIBRATOLESS
VERMILIONED	VERRUCOSITIES	VERTICILLIUM	VESTMENTED	VIBROFLOTATION
VERMILIONING	VERRUCOSITY	VERTICILLIUMS	VESUVIANITE	VIBROFLOTATIONS
VERMILIONS	VERSABILITIES	VERTICITIES	VESUVIANITES	VIBROGRAPH
VERMILLING	VERSABILITY	VERTIGINES	VETCHLINGS	VIBROGRAPHS
VERMILLION	VERSATILELY	VERTIGINOUS	VETERINARIAN	VIBROMETER
VERMILLIONS	VERSATILENESS	VERTIGINOUSLY	VETERINARIANS	VIBROMETERS
VERMINATED	VERSATILENESSES	VERTIGINOUSNESS	VETERINARIES	VICARESSES
VERMINATES	VERSATILITIES	VERTIPORTS	VETERINARY	VICARIANCE
VERMINATING	VERSATILITY	VERUMONTANA	VETTURINOS	VICARIANCES
VERMINATION	VERSICOLOR	VERUMONTANUM	VEXATIOUSLY	VICARIANTS
VERMINATIONS	VERSICOLORED	VERUMONTANUMS	VEXATIOUSNESS	VICARIATES
VERMINOUSLY	VERSICOLOUR	VESICATING	VEXATIOUSNESSES	VICARIOUSLY
VERMINOUSNESS	VERSICOLOURED	VESICATION	VEXEDNESSES	VICARIOUSNESS
VERMINOUSNESSES	VERSICULAR	VESICATIONS	VEXILLARIES	VICARIOUSNESSES
VERMIVOROUS	VERSIFICATION	VESICATORIES	VEXILLATION	VICARSHIPS
VERNACULAR	VERSIFICATIONS	VESICATORY	VEXILLATIONS	VICEGERENCIES
VERNACULARISE	VERSIFICATOR	VESICULARITIES	VEXILLOLOGIC	VICEGERENCY
VERNACULARISED	VERSIFICATORS	VESICULARITY	VEXILLOLOGICAL	VICEGERENT
VERNACULARISES	VERSIFIERS	VESICULARLY	VEXILLOLOGIES	VICEGERENTS
VERNACULARISING	VERSIFYING	VESICULATE	VEXILLOLOGIST	VICEREGALLY
VERNACULARISM	VERSIONERS	VESICULATED	VEXILLOLOGISTS	VICEREGENT
VERNACULARISMS	VERSIONING	VESICULATES	VEXILLOLOGY	VICEREGENTS
VERNACULARIST	VERSIONINGS	VESICULATING	VEXINGNESS	VICEREINES
VERNACULARISTS	VERSIONIST	VESICULATION	VEXINGNESSES	VICEROYALTIES
VERNACULARITIES	VERSIONISTS	VESICULATIONS	VIABILITIES	VICEROYALTY
VERNACULARITY	VERSLIBRIST	VESICULOSE	VIBRACULAR	VICEROYSHIP
VERNACULARIZE	VERSLIBRISTE	VESPERTILIAN	VIBRACULARIA	VICEROYSHIPS
VERNACULARIZED	VERSLIBRISTES	VESPERTILIONID	VIBRACULARIUM	VICHYSSOIS
VERNACULARIZES	VERSLIBRISTS	VESPERTILIONIDS	VIBRACULOID	VICHYSSOISE
VERNACULARIZING	VERTEBRALLY	VESPERTILIONINE	VIBRACULUM	VICHYSSOISES
VERNACULARLY	VERTEBRATE	VESPERTINAL	VIBRAHARPIST	VICINITIES
VERNACULARS	VERTEBRATED	VESPERTINE	VIBRAHARPISTS	VICIOSITIES
VERNALISATION	VERTEBRATES	VESPIARIES	VIBRAHARPS	VICIOUSNESS
VERNALISATIONS	VERTEBRATION	VESTIARIES	VIBRANCIES	VICIOUSNESSES
VERNALISED	VERTEBRATIONS	VESTIBULAR	VIBRAPHONE	VICISSITUDE
VERNALISES	VERTICALITIES	VESTIBULED	VIBRAPHONES	VICISSITUDES
VERNALISING	VERTICALITY	VESTIBULES	VIBRAPHONIST	VICISSITUDINARY
VERNALITIES	VERTICALLY	VESTIBULING	VIBRAPHONISTS	VICISSITUDINOUS
VERNALIZATION	VERTICALNESS	VESTIBULITIS	VIBRATILITIES	VICOMTESSE
VERNALIZATIONS	VERTICALNESSES	VESTIBULITISES	VIBRATILITY	VICOMTESSES
VERNALIZED	VERTICILLASTER	VESTIBULUM	VIBRATINGLY	VICTIMHOOD
VERNALIZES	VERTICILLASTERS	VESTIGIALLY	VIBRATIONAL	VICTIMHOODS

V

VICTIMISATION	VIDEOGRAPHY	VILIPENDED	VINDEMIATES	VINTAGINGS
VICTIMISATIONS	VIDEOLANDS	VILIPENDER	VINDEMIATING	VINYLCYANIDE
VICTIMISED	VIDEOPHILE	VILIPENDERS	VINDICABILITIES	VINYLCYANIDES
VICTIMISER	VIDEOPHILES	VILIPENDING	VINDICABILITY	VINYLIDENE
VICTIMISERS	VIDEOPHONE	VILLAGERIES	VINDICABLE	VINYLIDENES
VICTIMISES	VIDEOPHONES	VILLAGIOES	VINDICATED	VIOLABILITIES
VICTIMISING	VIDEOPHONIC	VILLAGISATION	VINDICATES	VIOLABILITY
VICTIMIZATION	VIDEOTAPED	VILLAGISATIONS	VINDICATING	VIOLABLENESS
VICTIMIZATIONS	VIDEOTAPES	VILLAGIZATION	VINDICATION	VIOLABLENESSES
VICTIMIZED	VIDEOTAPING	VILLAGIZATIONS	VINDICATIONS	VIOLACEOUS
VICTIMIZER	VIDEOTELEPHONE	VILLAGREES	VINDICATIVE	VIOLATIONS
VICTIMIZERS	VIDEOTELEPHONES	VILLAINAGE	VINDICATIVENESS	VIOLENTING
VICTIMIZES	VIDEOTEXES	VILLAINAGES	VINDICATOR	VIOLINISTIC
VICTIMIZING	VIDEOTEXTS	VILLAINESS	VINDICATORILY	VIOLINISTICALLY
VICTIMLESS	VIDEOTHEQUE	VILLAINESSES	VINDICATORS	VIOLINISTS
VICTIMOLOGIES	VIDEOTHEQUES	VILLAINIES	VINDICATORY	VIOLONCELLI
VICTIMOLOGIST	VIEWERSHIP	VILLAINOUS	VINDICATRESS	VIOLONCELLIST
VICTIMOLOGISTS	VIEWERSHIPS	VILLAINOUSLY	VINDICATRESSES	VIOLONCELLISTS
VICTIMOLOGY	VIEWFINDER	VILLAINOUSNESS	VINDICTIVE	VIOLONCELLO
VICTORESSES	VIEWFINDERS	VILLANAGES	VINDICTIVELY	VIOLONCELLOS
VICTORIANA	VIEWINESSES	VILLANELLA	VINDICTIVENESS	VIOSTEROLS
VICTORINES	VIEWLESSLY	VILLANELLAS	VINEDRESSER	VIPERFISHES
VICTORIOUS	VIEWPHONES	VILLANELLE	VINEDRESSERS	VIPERIFORM
VICTORIOUSLY	VIEWPOINTS	VILLANELLES	VINEGARETTE	VIPERISHLY
VICTORIOUSNESS	VIGILANCES	VILLANOUSLY	VINEGARETTES	VIPEROUSLY
VICTORYLESS	VIGILANTES	VILLEGGIATURA	VINEGARING	VIRAGINIAN
VICTRESSES	VIGILANTISM	VILLEGGIATURAS	VINEGARISH	VIRAGINOUS
VICTUALAGE	VIGILANTISMS	VILLEINAGE	VINEGARRETTE	VIRALITIES
VICTUALAGES	VIGILANTLY	VILLEINAGES	VINEGARRETTES	VIREONINES
VICTUALERS	VIGILANTNESS	VILLENAGES	VINEGARROON	VIRESCENCE
VICTUALING	VIGILANTNESSES	VILLIACOES	VINEGARROONS	VIRESCENCES
VICTUALLAGE	VIGINTILLION	VILLIAGOES	VINEYARDIST	VIRGINALIST
VICTUALLAGES	VIGINTILLIONS	VILLICATION	VINEYARDISTS	VIRGINALISTS
VICTUALLED	VIGNETTERS	VILLICATIONS	VINICULTURAL	VIRGINALLED
VICTUALLER	VIGNETTING	VILLOSITIES	VINICULTURE	VIRGINALLING
VICTUALLERS	VIGNETTINGS	VINAIGRETTE	VINICULTURES	VIRGINALLY
VICTUALLESS	VIGNETTIST	VINAIGRETTES	VINICULTURIST	VIRGINHOOD
VICTUALLING	VIGNETTISTS	VINBLASTINE	VINICULTURISTS	VIRGINHOODS
VIDEOCASSETTE	VIGORISHES	VINBLASTINES	VINIFEROUS	VIRGINITIES
VIDEOCASSETTES	VIGOROUSLY	VINCIBILITIES	VINIFICATION	VIRGINIUMS
VIDEOCONFERENCE	VIGOROUSNESS	VINCIBILITY	VINIFICATIONS	VIRIDESCENCE
VIDEODISCS	VIGOROUSNESSES	VINCIBLENESS	VINIFICATOR	VIRIDESCENCES
VIDEODISKS	VIKINGISMS	VINCIBLENESSES	VINIFICATORS	VIRIDESCENT
VIDEOGRAMS	VILDNESSES	VINCRISTINE	VINOLOGIES	VIRIDITIES
VIDEOGRAPHER	VILENESSES	VINCRISTINES	VINOLOGIST	VIRILESCENCE
VIDEOGRAPHERS	VILIFICATION	VINDEMIATE	VINOLOGISTS	VIRILESCENCES
VIDEOGRAPHIES	VILIFICATIONS	VINDEMIATED	VINOSITIES	VIRILESCENT

V

VIRILISATION	VISCEROPTOSIS	VISITATIONS	VITELLICLES	VITRIFIABILITY
VIRILISATIONS	VISCEROTONIA	VISITATIVE	VITELLIGENOUS	VITRIFIABLE
VIRILISING	VISCEROTONIAS	VISITATORIAL	VITELLINES	VITRIFICATION
VIRILITIES	VISCEROTONIC	VISITATORS	VITELLOGENESES	VITRIFICATIONS
VIRILIZATION	VISCIDITIES	VISITORIAL	VITELLOGENESIS	VITRIFYING
VIRILIZATIONS	VISCIDNESS	VISITRESSES	VITELLOGENIC	VITRIOLATE
VIRILIZING	VISCIDNESSES	VISUALISATION	VITELLUSES	VITRIOLATED
VIROLOGICAL	VISCOELASTIC	VISUALISATIONS	VITIATIONS	VITRIOLATES
VIROLOGICALLY	VISCOELASTICITY	VISUALISED	VITICETUMS	VITRIOLATING
VIROLOGIES	VISCOMETER	VISUALISER	VITICOLOUS	VITRIOLATION
VIROLOGIST	VISCOMETERS	VISUALISERS	VITICULTURAL	VITRIOLATIONS
VIROLOGISTS	VISCOMETRIC	VISUALISES	VITICULTURALLY	VITRIOLING
VIRTUALISE	VISCOMETRICAL	VISUALISING	VITICULTURE	VITRIOLISATION
VIRTUALISED	VISCOMETRIES	VISUALISTS	VITICULTURER	VITRIOLISATIONS
VIRTUALISES	VISCOMETRY	VISUALITIES	VITICULTURERS	VITRIOLISE
VIRTUALISING	VISCOSIMETER	VISUALIZATION	VITICULTURES	VITRIOLISED
VIRTUALISM	VISCOSIMETERS	VISUALIZATIONS	VITICULTURIST	VITRIOLISES
VIRTUALISMS	VISCOSIMETRIC	VISUALIZED	VITICULTURISTS	VITRIOLISING
VIRTUALIST	VISCOSIMETRICAL	VISUALIZER	VITIFEROUS	VITRIOLIZATION
VIRTUALISTS	VISCOSIMETRIES	VISUALIZERS	VITILITIGATE	VITRIOLIZATIONS
VIRTUALITIES	VISCOSIMETRY	VISUALIZES	VITILITIGATED	VITRIOLIZE
VIRTUALITY	VISCOSITIES	VISUALIZING	VITILITIGATES	VITRIOLIZED
VIRTUALIZE	VISCOUNTCIES	VITALISATION	VITILITIGATING	VITRIOLIZES
VIRTUALIZED	VISCOUNTCY	VITALISATIONS	VITILITIGATION	VITRIOLIZING
VIRTUALIZES	VISCOUNTESS	VITALISERS	VITILITIGATIONS	VITRIOLLED
VIRTUALIZING	VISCOUNTESSES	VITALISING	VITIOSITIES	VITRIOLLING
VIRTUELESS	VISCOUNTIES	VITALISTIC	VITRAILLED	VITUPERABLE
VIRTUOSITIES	VISCOUNTSHIP	VITALISTICALLY	VITRAILLIST	VITUPERATE
VIRTUOSITY	VISCOUNTSHIPS	VITALITIES	VITRAILLISTS	VITUPERATED
VIRTUOSOSHIP	VISCOUSNESS	VITALIZATION	VITRECTOMIES	VITUPERATES
VIRTUOSOSHIPS	VISCOUSNESSES	VITALIZATIONS	VITRECTOMY	VITUPERATING
VIRTUOUSLY	VISIBILITIES	VITALIZERS	VITREORETINAL	VITUPERATION
VIRTUOUSNESS	VISIBILITY	VITALIZING	VITREOSITIES	VITUPERATIONS
VIRTUOUSNESSES	VISIBLENESS	VITALNESSES	VITREOSITY	VITUPERATIVE
VIRULENCES	VISIBLENESSES	VITAMINISE	VITREOUSES	VITUPERATIVELY
VIRULENCIES	VISIOGENIC	VITAMINISED	VITREOUSLY	VITUPERATOR
VIRULENTLY	VISIONALLY	VITAMINISES	VITREOUSNESS	VITUPERATORS
VIRULIFEROUS	VISIONARIES	VITAMINISING	VITREOUSNESSES	VITUPERATORY
VISAGISTES	VISIONARINESS	VITAMINIZE	VITRESCENCE	VIVACIOUSLY
VISCACHERA	VISIONARINESSES	VITAMINIZED	VITRESCENCES	VIVACIOUSNESS
VISCACHERAS	VISIONINGS	VITAMINIZES	VITRESCENT	VIVACIOUSNESSES
VISCERALLY	VISIONISTS	VITAMINIZING	VITRESCIBILITY	VIVACISSIMO
VISCERATED	VISIONLESS	VITASCOPES	VITRESCIBLE	VIVACITIES
VISCERATES	VISIOPHONE	VITATIVENESS	VITRIFACTION	VIVANDIERE
VISCERATING	VISIOPHONES	VITATIVENESSES	VITRIFACTIONS	VIVANDIERES
VISCEROMOTOR	VISITATION	VITELLARIES	VITRIFACTURE	VIVANDIERS
VISCEROPTOSES	VISITATIONAL	VITELLICLE	VITRIFACTURES	VIVERRINES

V

VIVIANITES	VOCALISING	VOICEOVERS	VOLCANOLOGISTS	VOLUNTARILY
VIVIDITIES	VOCALITIES	VOICEPRINT	VOLCANOLOGY	VOLUNTARINESS
VIVIDNESSES	VOCALIZATION	VOICEPRINTS	VOLITATING	VOLUNTARINESSES
VIVIFICATION	VOCALIZATIONS	VOIDABLENESS	VOLITATION	VOLUNTARISM
VIVIFICATIONS	VOCALIZERS	VOIDABLENESSES	VOLITATIONAL	VOLUNTARISMS
VIVIPARIES	VOCALIZING	VOIDNESSES	VOLITATIONS	VOLUNTARIST
VIVIPARISM	VOCALNESSES	VOISINAGES	VOLITIONAL	VOLUNTARISTIC
VIVIPARISMS	VOCATIONAL	VOITURIERS	VOLITIONALLY	VOLUNTARISTS
VIVIPARITIES	VOCATIONALISM	VOIVODESHIP	VOLITIONARY	VOLUNTARYISM
VIVIPARITY	VOCATIONALISMS	VOIVODESHIPS	VOLITIONLESS	VOLUNTARYISMS
VIVIPAROUS	VOCATIONALIST	VOLATILENESS	VOLITORIAL	VOLUNTARYIST
VIVIPAROUSLY	VOCATIONALISTS	VOLATILENESSES	VOLKSLIEDER	VOLUNTARYISTS
VIVIPAROUSNESS	VOCATIONALLY	VOLATILISABLE	VOLKSRAADS	VOLUNTATIVE
VIVISECTED	VOCATIVELY	VOLATILISATION	VOLLEYBALL	VOLUNTATIVES
VIVISECTING	VOCICULTURAL	VOLATILISATIONS	VOLLEYBALLS	VOLUNTEERED
VIVISECTION	VOCIFERANCE	VOLATILISE	VOLPLANING	VOLUNTEERING
VIVISECTIONAL	VOCIFERANCES	VOLATILISED	VOLTAMETER	VOLUNTEERISM
VIVISECTIONALLY	VOCIFERANT	VOLATILISES	VOLTAMETERS	VOLUNTEERISMS
VIVISECTIONIST	VOCIFERANTS	VOLATILISING	VOLTAMETRIC	VOLUNTEERS
VIVISECTIONISTS	VOCIFERATE	VOLATILITIES	VOLTAMMETER	VOLUNTOURISM
VIVISECTIONS	VOCIFERATED	VOLATILITY	VOLTAMMETERS	VOLUNTOURISMS
VIVISECTIVE	VOCIFERATES	VOLATILIZABLE	VOLTIGEURS	VOLUPTUARIES
VIVISECTOR	VOCIFERATING	VOLATILIZATION	VOLTINISMS	VOLUPTUARY
VIVISECTORIA	VOCIFERATION	VOLATILIZATIONS	VOLTMETERS	VOLUPTUOSITIES
VIVISECTORIUM	VOCIFERATIONS	VOLATILIZE	VOLUBILITIES	VOLUPTUOSITY
VIVISECTORIUMS	VOCIFERATOR	VOLATILIZED	VOLUBILITY	VOLUPTUOUS
VIVISECTORS	VOCIFERATORS	VOLATILIZES	VOLUBLENESS	VOLUPTUOUSLY
VIVISEPULTURE	VOCIFEROSITIES	VOLATILIZING	VOLUBLENESSES	VOLUPTUOUSNESS
VIVISEPULTURES	VOCIFEROSITY	VOLCANICALLY	VOLUMENOMETER	VOLUTATION
VIXENISHLY	VOCIFEROUS	VOLCANICITIES	VOLUMENOMETERS	VOLUTATIONS
VIXENISHNESS	VOCIFEROUSLY	VOLCANICITY	VOLUMETERS	VOLVULUSES
VIXENISHNESSES	VOCIFEROUSNESS	VOLCANISATION	VOLUMETRIC	VOMERONASAL
VIZIERATES	VODCASTERS	VOLCANISATIONS	VOLUMETRICAL	VOMITORIES
VIZIERSHIP	VODCASTING	VOLCANISED	VOLUMETRICALLY	VOMITORIUM
VIZIERSHIPS	VODCASTINGS	VOLCANISES	VOLUMETRIES	VOMITURITION
VIZIRSHIPS	VOETGANGER	VOLCANISING	VOLUMINOSITIES	VOMITURITIONS
VOCABULARIAN	VOETGANGERS	VOLCANISMS	VOLUMINOSITY	VOODOOISMS
VOCABULARIANS	VOETSTOETS	VOLCANISTS	VOLUMINOUS	VOODOOISTIC
VOCABULARIED	VOETSTOOTS	VOLCANIZATION	VOLUMINOUSLY	VOODOOISTS
VOCABULARIES	VOGUISHNESS	VOLCANIZATIONS	VOLUMINOUSNESS	VOORKAMERS
VOCABULARY	VOGUISHNESSES	VOLCANIZED	VOLUMISERS	VOORTREKKER
VOCABULIST	VOICEFULNESS	VOLCANIZES	VOLUMISING	VOORTREKKERS
VOCABULISTS	VOICEFULNESSES	VOLCANIZING	VOLUMIZERS	VORACIOUSLY
VOCALICALLY	VOICELESSLY	VOLCANOLOGIC	VOLUMIZING	VORACIOUSNESS
VOCALISATION	VOICELESSNESS	VOLCANOLOGICAL	VOLUMOMETER	VORACIOUSNESSES
VOCALISATIONS	VOICELESSNESSES	VOLCANOLOGIES	VOLUMOMETERS	VORACITIES
VOCALISERS	VOICEMAILS	VOLCANOLOGIST	VOLUNTARIES	VORAGINOUS

VORTICALLY
VORTICELLA
VORTICELLAE
VORTICELLAS
VORTICISMS
VORTICISTS
VORTICITIES
VORTICULAR
VORTIGINOUS
VOTARESSES
VOTIVENESS
VOTIVENESSES
VOUCHERING
VOUCHSAFED
VOUCHSAFEMENT
VOUCHSAFEMENTS
VOUCHSAFES
VOUCHSAFING
VOUCHSAFINGS
VOUSSOIRED
VOUSSOIRING

VOUTSAFING
VOWELISATION
VOWELISATIONS
VOWELISING
VOWELIZATION
VOWELIZATIONS
VOWELIZING
VOYAGEABLE
VOYEURISMS
VOYEURISTIC
VOYEURISTICALLY
VRAICKINGS
VRAISEMBLANCE
VRAISEMBLANCES
VRYSTATERS
VULCANICITIES
VULCANICITY
VULCANISABLE
VULCANISATE
VULCANISATES
VULCANISATION

VULCANISATIONS
VULCANISED
VULCANISER
VULCANISERS
VULCANISES
VULCANISING
VULCANISMS
VULCANISTS
VULCANITES
VULCANIZABLE
VULCANIZATE
VULCANIZATES
VULCANIZATION
VULCANIZATIONS
VULCANIZED
VULCANIZER
VULCANIZERS
VULCANIZES
VULCANIZING
VULCANOLOGICAL
VULCANOLOGIES

VULCANOLOGIST
VULCANOLOGISTS
VULCANOLOGY
VULGARIANS
VULGARISATION
VULGARISATIONS
VULGARISED
VULGARISER
VULGARISERS
VULGARISES
VULGARISING
VULGARISMS
VULGARITIES
VULGARIZATION
VULGARIZATIONS
VULGARIZED
VULGARIZER
VULGARIZERS
VULGARIZES
VULGARIZING
VULNERABILITIES

VULNERABILITY
VULNERABLE
VULNERABLENESS
VULNERABLY
VULNERARIES
VULNERATED
VULNERATES
VULNERATING
VULNERATION
VULNERATIONS
VULPECULAR
VULPICIDES
VULPINISMS
VULPINITES
VULTURISMS
VULVITISES
VULVOVAGINAL
VULVOVAGINITIS

W

WACKINESSES	WAISTLINES	WALLFLOWERS	WAPENSCHAWS	WARLIKENESSES
WADSETTERS	WAITERAGES	WALLOPINGS	WAPENSHAWS	WARLOCKRIES
WADSETTING	WAITERHOOD	WALLOWINGS	WAPENTAKES	WARLORDISM
WAFFLESTOMPER	WAITERHOODS	WALLPAPERED	WAPINSCHAW	WARLORDISMS
WAFFLESTOMPERS	WAITERINGS	WALLPAPERING	WAPINSCHAWS	WARMBLOODS
WAGELESSNESS	WAITLISTED	WALLPAPERS	WAPINSHAWS	WARMHEARTED
WAGELESSNESSES	WAITLISTING	WALLPEPPER	WAPPENSCHAW	WARMHEARTEDNESS
WAGENBOOMS	WAITPERSON	WALLPEPPERS	WAPPENSCHAWING	WARMNESSES
WAGEWORKER	WAITPERSONS	WALLPOSTER	WAPPENSCHAWINGS	WARMONGERING
WAGEWORKERS	WAITRESSED	WALLPOSTERS	WAPPENSCHAWS	WARMONGERINGS
WAGGISHNESS	WAITRESSES	WALLYBALLS	WAPPENSHAW	WARMONGERS
WAGGISHNESSES	WAITRESSING	WALLYDRAGS	WAPPENSHAWING	WARRANDICE
WAGGLINGLY	WAITRESSINGS	WALLYDRAIGLE	WAPPENSHAWINGS	WARRANDICES
WAGGONETTE	WAITSTAFFS	WALLYDRAIGLES	WAPPENSHAWS	WARRANDING
WAGGONETTES	WAKEBOARDED	WALNUTWOOD	WARBLINGLY	WARRANTABILITY
WAGGONLESS	WAKEBOARDER	WALNUTWOODS	WARBONNETS	WARRANTABLE
WAGGONLOAD	WAKEBOARDERS	WAMBENGERS	WARCHALKER	WARRANTABLENESS
WAGGONLOADS	WAKEBOARDING	WAMBLINESS	WARCHALKERS	WARRANTABLY
WAGHALTERS	WAKEBOARDINGS	WAMBLINESSES	WARCHALKING	WARRANTEES
WAGONETTES	WAKEBOARDS	WAMBLINGLY	WARCHALKINGS	WARRANTERS
WAGONLOADS	WAKEFULNESS	WAMPISHING	WARDENRIES	WARRANTIED
WAGONWRIGHT	WAKEFULNESSES	WAMPUMPEAG	WARDENSHIP	WARRANTIES
WAGONWRIGHTS	WALDFLUTES	WAMPUMPEAGS	WARDENSHIPS	WARRANTING
WAINSCOTED	WALDGRAVES	WANCHANCIE	WARDERSHIP	WARRANTINGS
WAINSCOTING	WALDGRAVINE	WANDERINGLY	WARDERSHIPS	WARRANTISE
WAINSCOTINGS	WALDGRAVINES	WANDERINGS	WARDRESSES	WARRANTISED
WAINSCOTTED	WALDSTERBEN	WANDERLUST	WARDROBERS	WARRANTISES
WAINSCOTTING	WALDSTERBENS	WANDERLUSTS	WARDROBING	WARRANTISING
WAINSCOTTINGS	WALKABOUTS	WANRESTFUL	WAREHOUSED	WARRANTIZE
WAINWRIGHT	WALKATHONS	WANTHRIVEN	WAREHOUSEMAN	WARRANTIZED
WAINWRIGHTS	WALKINGSTICK	WANTONISED	WAREHOUSEMEN	WARRANTIZES
WAISTBANDS	WALKINGSTICKS	WANTONISES	WAREHOUSER	WARRANTIZING
WAISTBELTS	WALKSHORTS	WANTONISING	WAREHOUSERS	WARRANTLESS
WAISTCLOTH	WALLBOARDS	WANTONIZED	WAREHOUSES	WARRANTORS
WAISTCLOTHS	WALLCHARTS	WANTONIZES	WAREHOUSING	WARRANTYING
WAISTCOATED	WALLCLIMBER	WANTONIZING	WAREHOUSINGS	WARRIORESS
WAISTCOATEER	WALLCLIMBERS	WANTONNESS	WARFARINGS	WARRIORESSES
WAISTCOATEERS	WALLCOVERING	WANTONNESSES	WARGAMINGS	WASHABILITIES
WAISTCOATING	WALLCOVERINGS	WANWORDIER	WARIBASHIS	WASHABILITY
WAISTCOATINGS	WALLFISHES	WANWORDIEST	WARINESSES	WASHATERIA
WAISTCOATS	WALLFLOWER	WAPENSCHAW	WARLIKENESS	WASHATERIAS

W

WASHBASINS	WATCHGLASSES	WATERFLOODING	WATERSCAPES	WAYMENTING
WASHBOARDS	WATCHGUARD	WATERFLOODINGS	WATERSHEDS	WAYWARDNESS
WASHCLOTHS	WATCHGUARDS	WATERFLOODS	WATERSIDER	WAYWARDNESSES
WASHERWOMAN	WATCHLISTS	WATERFOWLER	WATERSIDERS	WAYZGOOSES
WASHERWOMEN	WATCHMAKER	WATERFOWLERS	WATERSIDES	WEAKENINGS
WASHETERIA	WATCHMAKERS	WATERFOWLING	WATERSKIING	WEAKFISHES
WASHETERIAS	WATCHMAKING	WATERFOWLINGS	WATERSKIINGS	WEAKHEARTED
WASHHOUSES	WATCHMAKINGS	WATERFOWLS	WATERSMEET	WEAKISHNESS
WASHINESSES	WATCHSPRING	WATERFRONT	WATERSMEETS	WEAKISHNESSES
WASHINGTONIA	WATCHSPRINGS	WATERFRONTS	WATERSPOUT	WEAKLINESS
WASHINGTONIAS	WATCHSTRAP	WATERGLASS	WATERSPOUTS	WEAKLINESSES
WASHSTANDS	WATCHSTRAPS	WATERGLASSES	WATERTHRUSH	WEAKNESSES
WASPINESSES	WATCHTOWER	WATERHEADS	WATERTHRUSHES	WEALTHIEST
WASPISHNESS	WATCHTOWERS	WATERINESS	WATERTIGHT	WEALTHINESS
WASPISHNESSES	WATCHWORDS	WATERINESSES	WATERTIGHTNESS	WEALTHINESSES
WASSAILERS	WATERBIRDS	WATERISHNESS	WATERWEEDS	WEALTHLESS
WASSAILING	WATERBOARDING	WATERISHNESSES	WATERWHEEL	WEAPONEERED
WASSAILINGS	WATERBOARDINGS	WATERLEAFS	WATERWHEELS	WEAPONEERING
WASSAILRIES	WATERBORNE	WATERLESSNESS	WATERWORKS	WEAPONEERINGS
WASTEBASKET	WATERBRAIN	WATERLESSNESSES	WATERZOOIS	WEAPONEERS
WASTEBASKETS	WATERBRAINS	WATERLILIES	WATTLEBARK	WEAPONISED
WASTEFULLY	WATERBUCKS	WATERLINES	WATTLEBARKS	WEAPONISES
WASTEFULNESS	WATERBUSES	WATERLOGGED	WATTLEBIRD	WEAPONISING
WASTEFULNESSES	WATERBUSSES	WATERLOGGING	WATTLEBIRDS	WEAPONIZED
WASTELANDS	WATERCOLOR	WATERLOGGINGS	WATTLEWORK	WEAPONIZES
WASTENESSES	WATERCOLORIST	WATERMANSHIP	WATTLEWORKS	WEAPONIZING
WASTEPAPER	WATERCOLORISTS	WATERMANSHIPS	WATTMETERS	WEAPONLESS
WASTEPAPERS	WATERCOLORS	WATERMARKED	WAULKMILLS	WEAPONRIES
WASTERFULLY	WATERCOLOUR	WATERMARKING	WAVEFRONTS	WEARABILITIES
WASTERFULNESS	WATERCOLOURIST	WATERMARKS	WAVEGUIDES	WEARABILITY
WASTERFULNESSES	WATERCOLOURISTS	WATERMELON	WAVELENGTH	WEARIFULLY
WASTEWATER	WATERCOLOURS	WATERMELONS	WAVELENGTHS	WEARIFULNESS
WASTEWATERS	WATERCOOLER	WATERMILLS	WAVELESSLY	WEARIFULNESSES
WASTEWEIRS	WATERCOOLERS	WATERPOWER	WAVELLITES	WEARILESSLY
WASTNESSES	WATERCOURSE	WATERPOWERS	WAVEMETERS	WEARINESSES
WATCHABLES	WATERCOURSES	WATERPOXES	WAVERINGLY	WEARISOMELY
WATCHBANDS	WATERCRAFT	WATERPROOF	WAVERINGNESS	WEARISOMENESS
WATCHBOXES	WATERCRAFTS	WATERPROOFED	WAVERINGNESSES	WEARISOMENESSES
WATCHCASES	WATERCRESS	WATERPROOFER	WAVESHAPES	WEARYINGLY
WATCHCRIES	WATERCRESSES	WATERPROOFERS	WAVETABLES	WEASELLERS
WATCHDOGGED	WATERDRIVE	WATERPROOFING	WAVINESSES	WEASELLING
WATCHDOGGING	WATERDRIVES	WATERPROOFINGS	WAXBERRIES	WEATHERABILITY
WATCHDOGGINGS	WATERFALLS	WATERPROOFNESS	WAXFLOWERS	WEATHERABLE
WATCHFULLY	WATERFINDER	WATERPROOFS	WAXINESSES	WEATHERBOARD
WATCHFULNESS	WATERFINDERS	WATERQUAKE	WAXWORKERS	WEATHERBOARDED
WATCHFULNESSES	WATERFLOOD	WATERQUAKES	WAYFARINGS	WEATHERBOARDING
WATCHGLASS	WATERFLOODED	WATERSCAPE	WAYMARKING	WEATHERBOARDS

W

WEATHERCAST
WEATHERCASTER
WEATHERCASTERS
WEATHERCASTS
WEATHERCLOTH
WEATHERCLOTHS
WEATHERCOCK
WEATHERCOCKED
WEATHERCOCKING
WEATHERCOCKS
WEATHERERS
WEATHERGIRL
WEATHERGIRLS
WEATHERGLASS
WEATHERGLASSES
WEATHERING
WEATHERINGS
WEATHERISATION
WEATHERISATIONS
WEATHERISE
WEATHERISED
WEATHERISES
WEATHERISING
WEATHERIZATION
WEATHERIZATIONS
WEATHERIZE
WEATHERIZED
WEATHERIZES
WEATHERIZING
WEATHERLINESS
WEATHERLINESSES
WEATHERMAN
WEATHERMEN
WEATHERMOST
WEATHEROMETER
WEATHEROMETERS
WEATHERPERSON
WEATHERPERSONS
WEATHERPROOF
WEATHERPROOFED
WEATHERPROOFING
WEATHERPROOFS
WEATHERWOMAN
WEATHERWOMEN
WEATHERWORN
WEAVERBIRD
WEAVERBIRDS

WEBCASTERS
WEBCASTING
WEBLIOGRAPHIES
WEBLIOGRAPHY
WEBLOGGERS
WEBLOGGING
WEBLOGGINGS
WEBMASTERS
WEEDICIDES
WEEDINESSES
WEEDKILLER
WEEDKILLERS
WEEKENDERS
WEEKENDING
WEEKENDINGS
WEEKNIGHTS
WEELDLESSE
WEEPINESSES
WEIGHBOARD
WEIGHBOARDS
WEIGHBRIDGE
WEIGHBRIDGES
WEIGHTAGES
WEIGHTIEST
WEIGHTINESS
WEIGHTINESSES
WEIGHTINGS
WEIGHTLESS
WEIGHTLESSLY
WEIGHTLESSNESS
WEIGHTLIFTER
WEIGHTLIFTERS
WEIGHTLIFTING
WEIGHTLIFTINGS
WEIMARANER
WEIMARANERS
WEIRDNESSES
WEISENHEIMER
WEISENHEIMERS
WELCOMENESS
WELCOMENESSES
WELCOMINGLY
WELDABILITIES
WELDABILITY
WELDMESHES
WELFARISMS
WELFARISTIC

WELFARISTS
WELFARITES
WELLBEINGS
WELLHOUSES
WELLINGTON
WELLINGTONIA
WELLINGTONIAS
WELLINGTONS
WELLNESSES
WELLSPRING
WELLSPRINGS
WELTANSCHAUUNG
WELTANSCHAUUNGS
WELTERWEIGHT
WELTERWEIGHTS
WELTSCHMERZ
WELTSCHMERZES
WELWITSCHIA
WELWITSCHIAS
WENSLEYDALE
WENSLEYDALES
WENTLETRAP
WENTLETRAPS
WEREWOLFERIES
WEREWOLFERY
WEREWOLFISH
WEREWOLFISM
WEREWOLFISMS
WEREWOLVES
WERNERITES
WERWOLFISH
WESTERINGS
WESTERLIES
WESTERLINESS
WESTERLINESSES
WESTERNERS
WESTERNISATION
WESTERNISATIONS
WESTERNISE
WESTERNISED
WESTERNISES
WESTERNISING
WESTERNISM
WESTERNISMS
WESTERNIZATION
WESTERNIZATIONS
WESTERNIZE

WESTERNIZED
WESTERNIZES
WESTERNIZING
WESTERNMOST
WESTWARDLY
WETTABILITIES
WETTABILITY
WHAIKORERO
WHAIKOREROS
WHAKAPAPAS
WHALEBACKS
WHALEBOATS
WHALEBONES
WHAREPUNIS
WHARFINGER
WHARFINGERS
WHARFMASTER
WHARFMASTERS
WHATABOUTERIES
WHATABOUTERY
WHATABOUTS
WHATCHAMACALLIT
WHATNESSES
WHATSERNAME
WHATSERNAMES
WHATSHERNAME
WHATSHERNAMES
WHATSHISNAME
WHATSHISNAMES
WHATSISNAME
WHATSISNAMES
WHATSITSNAME
WHATSITSNAMES
WHATSOEVER
WHATSOMEVER
WHEATFIELD
WHEATFIELDS
WHEATGERMS
WHEATGRASS
WHEATGRASSES
WHEATLANDS
WHEATMEALS
WHEATWORMS
WHEEDLESOME
WHEEDLINGLY
WHEEDLINGS
WHEELBARROW

WHEELBARROWED
WHEELBARROWING
WHEELBARROWS
WHEELBASES
WHEELCHAIR
WHEELCHAIRS
WHEELHORSE
WHEELHORSES
WHEELHOUSE
WHEELHOUSES
WHEELSPINS
WHEELWORKS
WHEELWRIGHT
WHEELWRIGHTS
WHEESHTING
WHEEZINESS
WHEEZINESSES
WHEEZINGLY
WHENCEFORTH
WHENCESOEVER
WHENSOEVER
WHEREABOUT
WHEREABOUTS
WHEREAFTER
WHEREAGAINST
WHEREFORES
WHEREINSOEVER
WHERENESSES
WHERESOEVER
WHERETHROUGH
WHEREUNDER
WHEREUNTIL
WHEREWITHAL
WHEREWITHALS
WHEREWITHS
WHERRETING
WHERRITING
WHETSTONES
WHEWELLITE
WHEWELLITES
WHEYISHNESS
WHEYISHNESSES
WHICHSOEVER
WHICKERING
WHIDDERING
WHIFFLERIES
WHIFFLETREE

W

WHIFFLETREES	WHIPSTAFFS	WHITECOATS	WHODUNITRIES	WICKEDNESS
WHIFFLINGS	WHIPSTALLED	WHITECOMBS	WHODUNITRY	WICKEDNESSES
WHIGGAMORE	WHIPSTALLING	WHITEDAMPS	WHODUNNITRIES	WICKERWORK
WHIGGAMORES	WHIPSTALLS	WHITEFACES	WHODUNNITRY	WICKERWORKS
WHIGMALEERIE	WHIPSTITCH	WHITEFISHES	WHODUNNITS	WICKETKEEPER
WHIGMALEERIES	WHIPSTITCHED	WHITEFLIES	WHOLEFOODS	WICKETKEEPERS
WHIGMALEERY	WHIPSTITCHES	WHITEHEADS	WHOLEGRAIN	WICKTHINGS
WHILLYWHAED	WHIPSTITCHING	WHITELISTED	WHOLEGRAINS	WIDDERSHINS
WHILLYWHAING	WHIPSTOCKS	WHITELISTING	WHOLEHEARTED	WIDEAWAKES
WHILLYWHAS	WHIPTAILED	WHITELISTS	WHOLEHEARTEDLY	WIDEBODIES
WHILLYWHAW	WHIRLABOUT	WHITENESSES	WHOLEMEALS	WIDECHAPPED
WHILLYWHAWED	WHIRLABOUTS	WHITENINGS	WHOLENESSES	WIDEMOUTHED
WHILLYWHAWING	WHIRLBLAST	WHITESMITH	WHOLESALED	WIDENESSES
WHILLYWHAWS	WHIRLBLASTS	WHITESMITHS	WHOLESALER	WIDERSHINS
WHIMBERRIES	WHIRLIGIGS	WHITETAILS	WHOLESALERS	WIDESCREEN
WHIMPERERS	WHIRLINGLY	WHITETHORN	WHOLESALES	WIDESPREAD
WHIMPERING	WHIRLPOOLS	WHITETHORNS	WHOLESALING	WIDOWBIRDS
WHIMPERINGLY	WHIRLWINDS	WHITETHROAT	WHOLESALINGS	WIDOWERHOOD
WHIMPERINGS	WHIRLYBIRD	WHITETHROATS	WHOLESOMELY	WIDOWERHOODS
WHIMSICALITIES	WHIRLYBIRDS	WHITEWALLS	WHOLESOMENESS	WIDOWHOODS
WHIMSICALITY	WHIRRETING	WHITEWARES	WHOLESOMENESSES	WIELDINESS
WHIMSICALLY	WHISKERANDO	WHITEWASHED	WHOLESOMER	WIELDINESSES
WHIMSICALNESS	WHISKERANDOED	WHITEWASHER	WHOLESOMEST	WIENERWURST
WHIMSICALNESSES	WHISKERANDOS	WHITEWASHERS	WHOLESTITCH	WIENERWURSTS
WHIMSINESS	WHISKERIER	WHITEWASHES	WHOLESTITCHES	WIFELINESS
WHIMSINESSES	WHISKERIEST	WHITEWASHING	WHOLEWHEAT	WIFELINESSES
WHINBERRIES	WHISKEYFIED	WHITEWASHINGS	WHOMSOEVER	WIGWAGGERS
WHINGDINGS	WHISKIFIED	WHITEWATER	WHOREHOUSE	WIGWAGGING
WHINGEINGLY	WHISPERERS	WHITEWINGS	WHOREHOUSES	WIKIALITIES
WHINGEINGS	WHISPERING	WHITEWOODS	WHOREMASTER	WIKITORIAL
WHININESSES	WHISPERINGLY	WHITEYWOOD	WHOREMASTERIES	WIKITORIALS
WHINSTONES	WHISPERINGS	WHITEYWOODS	WHOREMASTERLY	WILDCATTED
WHIPLASHED	WHISPEROUSLY	WHITHERING	WHOREMASTERS	WILDCATTER
WHIPLASHES	WHISTLEABLE	WHITHERSOEVER	WHOREMASTERY	WILDCATTERS
WHIPLASHING	WHISTLEBLOWING	WHITHERWARD	WHOREMISTRESS	WILDCATTING
WHIPPERSNAPPER	WHISTLEBLOWINGS	WHITHERWARDS	WHOREMISTRESSES	WILDCATTINGS
WHIPPERSNAPPERS	WHISTLINGLY	WHITISHNESS	WHOREMONGER	WILDEBEEST
WHIPPETING	WHISTLINGS	WHITISHNESSES	WHOREMONGERIES	WILDEBEESTS
WHIPPETINGS	WHITEBAITS	WHITLEATHER	WHOREMONGERS	WILDERMENT
WHIPPINESS	WHITEBASSES	WHITLEATHERS	WHOREMONGERY	WILDERMENTS
WHIPPINESSES	WHITEBEAMS	WHITTAWERS	WHORISHNESS	WILDERNESS
WHIPPLETREE	WHITEBEARD	WHITTERICK	WHORISHNESSES	WILDERNESSES
WHIPPLETREES	WHITEBEARDS	WHITTERICKS	WHORTLEBERRIES	WILDFLOWER
WHIPPOORWILL	WHITEBOARD	WHITTERING	WHORTLEBERRY	WILDFLOWERS
WHIPPOORWILLS	WHITEBOARDS	WHITTLINGS	WHOSESOEVER	WILDFOWLER
WHIPSAWING	WHITEBOYISM	WHIZZBANGS	WHUNSTANES	WILDFOWLERS
WHIPSNAKES	WHITEBOYISMS	WHIZZINGLY	WHYDUNNITS	WILDFOWLING

W

WILDFOWLINGS

WILDFOWLINGS
WILDGRAVES
WILDNESSES
WILFULNESS
WILFULNESSES
WILINESSES
WILLEMITES
WILLFULNESS
WILLFULNESSES
WILLIEWAUGHT
WILLIEWAUGHTS
WILLINGEST
WILLINGNESS
WILLINGNESSES
WILLOWHERB
WILLOWHERBS
WILLOWIEST
WILLOWLIKE
WILLOWWARE
WILLOWWARES
WILLPOWERS
WIMPINESSES
WIMPISHNESS
WIMPISHNESSES
WINCEYETTE
WINCEYETTES
WINCHESTER
WINCHESTERS
WINCOPIPES
WINDBAGGERIES
WINDBAGGERY
WINDBLASTS
WINDBREAKER
WINDBREAKERS
WINDBREAKS
WINDBURNED
WINDBURNING
WINDCHEATER
WINDCHEATERS
WINDCHILLS
WINDFALLEN
WINDFLOWER
WINDFLOWERS
WINDGALLED
WINDHOVERS
WINDINESSES
WINDJAMMER

WINDJAMMERS
WINDJAMMING
WINDJAMMINGS
WINDLASSED
WINDLASSES
WINDLASSING
WINDLESSLY
WINDLESSNESS
WINDLESSNESSES
WINDLESTRAE
WINDLESTRAES
WINDLESTRAW
WINDLESTRAWS
WINDMILLED
WINDMILLING .
WINDOWINGS
WINDOWLESS
WINDOWPANE
WINDOWPANES
WINDOWSILL
WINDOWSILLS
WINDPROOFED
WINDPROOFING
WINDPROOFS
WINDROWERS
WINDROWING
WINDSCREEN
WINDSCREENS
WINDSHAKES
WINDSHIELD
WINDSHIELDS
WINDSTORMS
WINDSUCKER
WINDSUCKERS
WINDSURFED
WINDSURFER
WINDSURFERS
WINDSURFING
WINDSURFINGS
WINDTHROWS
WINEBERRIES
WINEBIBBER
WINEBIBBERS
WINEBIBBING
WINEBIBBINGS
WINEGLASSES
WINEGLASSFUL

WINEGLASSFULS
WINEGROWER
WINEGROWERS
WINEGROWING
WINEGROWINGS
WINEMAKERS
WINEMAKING
WINEMAKINGS
WINEPRESSES
WINGCHAIRS
WINGLESSNESS
WINGLESSNESSES
WINGSPREAD
WINGSPREADS
WINNABILITIES
WINNABILITY
WINNINGEST
WINNINGNESS
WINNINGNESSES
WINNOWINGS
WINSOMENESS
WINSOMENESSES
WINTERBERRIES
WINTERBERRY
WINTERBOURNE
WINTERBOURNES
WINTERCRESS
WINTERCRESSES
WINTERFEED
WINTERFEEDING
WINTERFEEDS
WINTERGREEN
WINTERGREENS
WINTERIEST
WINTERINESS
WINTERINESSES
WINTERISATION
WINTERISATIONS
WINTERISED
WINTERISES
WINTERISING
WINTERIZATION
WINTERIZATIONS
WINTERIZED
WINTERIZES
WINTERIZING
WINTERKILL

WINTERKILLED
WINTERKILLING
WINTERKILLINGS
WINTERKILLS
WINTERLESS
WINTERLINESS
WINTERLINESSES
WINTERTIDE
WINTERTIDES
WINTERTIME
WINTERTIMES
WINTERWEIGHT
WINTRINESS
WINTRINESSES
WIREDRAWER
WIREDRAWERS
WIREDRAWING
WIREDRAWINGS
WIREFRAMES
WIREGRASSES
WIREHAIRED
WIRELESSED
WIRELESSES
WIRELESSING
WIRELESSLY
WIREPHOTOS
WIREPULLER
WIREPULLERS
WIREPULLING
WIREPULLINGS
WIRETAPPED
WIRETAPPER
WIRETAPPERS
WIRETAPPING
WIRETAPPINGS
WIREWALKER
WIREWALKERS
WIREWORKER
WIREWORKERS
WIREWORKING
WIREWORKINGS
WIRINESSES
WISECRACKED
WISECRACKER
WISECRACKERS
WISECRACKING
WISECRACKS

WISENESSES
WISENHEIMER
WISENHEIMERS
WISHFULNESS
WISHFULNESSES
WISHTONWISH
WISHTONWISHES
WISPINESSES
WISTFULNESS
WISTFULNESSES
WITBLITSES
WITCHBROOM
WITCHBROOMS
WITCHCRAFT
WITCHCRAFTS
WITCHERIES
WITCHETTIES
WITCHGRASS
WITCHGRASSES
WITCHHOODS
WITCHINGLY
WITCHKNOTS
WITCHWEEDS
WITENAGEMOT
WITENAGEMOTE
WITENAGEMOTES
WITENAGEMOTS
WITGATBOOM
WITGATBOOMS
WITHDRAWABLE
WITHDRAWAL
WITHDRAWALS
WITHDRAWER
WITHDRAWERS
WITHDRAWING
WITHDRAWMENT
WITHDRAWMENTS
WITHDRAWNNESS
WITHDRAWNNESSES
WITHEREDNESS
WITHEREDNESSES
WITHERINGLY
WITHERINGS
WITHERITES
WITHERSHINS
WITHHOLDEN
WITHHOLDER

W

WITHHOLDERS	WOMANISHLY	WOODCARVING	WOODSWALLOWS	WORKABILITY
WITHHOLDING	WOMANISHNESS	WOODCARVINGS	WOODTHRUSH	WORKABLENESS
WITHHOLDMENT	WOMANISHNESSES	WOODCHOPPER	WOODTHRUSHES	WORKABLENESSES
WITHHOLDMENTS	WOMANISING	WOODCHOPPERS	WOODWAXENS	WORKAHOLIC
WITHINDOORS	WOMANISINGS	WOODCHUCKS	WOODWORKER	WORKAHOLICS
WITHOUTDOORS	WOMANIZERS	WOODCRAFTS	WOODWORKERS	WORKAHOLISM
WITHSTANDER	WOMANIZING	WOODCRAFTSMAN	WOODWORKING	WORKAHOLISMS
WITHSTANDERS	WOMANIZINGS	WOODCRAFTSMEN	WOODWORKINGS	WORKAROUND
WITHSTANDING	WOMANKINDS	WOODCUTTER	WOOLGATHERER	WORKAROUNDS
WITHSTANDS	WOMANLIEST	WOODCUTTERS	WOOLGATHERERS	WORKBASKET
WITHYWINDS	WOMANLINESS	WOODCUTTING	WOOLGATHERING	WORKBASKETS
WITLESSNESS	WOMANLINESSES	WOODCUTTINGS	WOOLGATHERINGS	WORKBENCHES
WITLESSNESSES	WOMANNESSES	WOODENHEAD	WOOLGROWER	WORKERISTS
WITNESSABLE	WOMANPOWER	WOODENHEADED	WOOLGROWERS	WORKERLESS
WITNESSERS	WOMANPOWERS	WOODENHEADS	WOOLGROWING	WORKFELLOW
WITNESSING	WOMENFOLKS	WOODENNESS	WOOLGROWINGS	WORKFELLOWS
WITTICISMS	WOMENKINDS	WOODENNESSES	WOOLINESSES	WORKFORCES
WITTINESSES	WOMENSWEAR	WOODENTOPS	WOOLLINESS	WORKGROUPS
WITWANTONED	WOMENSWEARS	WOODENWARE	WOOLLINESSES	WORKHORSES
WITWANTONING	WONDERFULLY	WOODENWARES	WOOLLYBACK	WORKHOUSES
WITWANTONS	WONDERFULNESS	WOODGRAINS	WOOLLYBACKS	WORKINGMAN
WIZARDRIES	WONDERFULNESSES	WOODGROUSE	WOOLLYBUTT	WORKINGMEN
WOADWAXENS	WONDERINGLY	WOODGROUSES	WOOLLYBUTTS	WORKINGWOMAN
WOBBEGONGS	WONDERINGS	WOODHORSES	WOOLLYFOOT	WORKINGWOMEN
WOBBLINESS	WONDERKIDS	WOODHOUSES	WOOLLYFOOTS	WORKLESSNESS
WOBBLINESSES	WONDERLAND	WOODINESSES	WOOLSORTER	WORKLESSNESSES
WOEBEGONENESS	WONDERLANDS	WOODLANDER	WOOLSORTERS	WORKMANLIKE
WOEBEGONENESSES	WONDERLESS	WOODLANDERS	WOOMERANGS	WORKMANSHIP
WOEFULLEST	WONDERMENT	WOODLESSNESS	WOOZINESSES	WORKMANSHIPS
WOEFULNESS	WONDERMENTS	WOODLESSNESSES	WORCESTERBERRY	WORKMASTER
WOEFULNESSES	WONDERMONGER	WOODNESSES	WORCESTERS	WORKMASTERS
WOFULNESSES	WONDERMONGERING	WOODPECKER	WORDBREAKS	WORKMISTRESS
WOLFBERRIES	WONDERMONGERS	WOODPECKERS	WORDCOUNTS	WORKMISTRESSES
WOLFFISHES	WONDERSTRUCK	WOODPRINTS	WORDINESSES	WORKPEOPLE
WOLFHOUNDS	WONDERWORK	WOODREEVES	WORDISHNESS	WORKPIECES
WOLFISHNESS	WONDERWORKS	WOODRUSHES	WORDISHNESSES	WORKPLACES
WOLFISHNESSES	WONDROUSLY	WOODSCREWS	WORDLESSLY	WORKPRINTS
WOLFRAMITE	WONDROUSNESS	WOODSHEDDED	WORDLESSNESS	WORKSHEETS
WOLFRAMITES	WONDROUSNESSES	WOODSHEDDING	WORDLESSNESSES	WORKSHOPPED
WOLFSBANES	WONTEDNESS	WOODSHEDDINGS	WORDMONGER	WORKSHOPPING
WOLLASTONITE	WONTEDNESSES	WOODSHOCKS	WORDMONGERS	WORKSPACES
WOLLASTONITES	WOODBLOCKS	WOODSHRIKE	WORDSEARCH	WORKSTATION
WOLVERENES	WOODBORERS	WOODSHRIKES	WORDSEARCHES	WORKSTATIONS
WOLVERINES	WOODBURYTYPE	WOODSPITES	WORDSMITHERIES	WORKSTREAM
WOMANFULLY	WOODBURYTYPES	WOODSTONES	WORDSMITHERY	WORKSTREAMS
WOMANHOODS	WOODCARVER	WOODSTOVES	WORDSMITHS	WORKTABLES
WOMANISERS	WOODCARVERS	WOODSWALLOW	WORKABILITIES	WORKWATCHER

W

WORKWATCHERS

WORKWATCHERS
WORLDBEATS
WORLDLIEST
WORLDLINESS
WORLDLINESSES
WORLDLINGS
WORLDSCALE
WORLDSCALES
WORLDVIEWS
WORMINESSES
WORNNESSES
WORRIMENTS
WORRISOMELY
WORRISOMENESS
WORRISOMENESSES
WORRYINGLY
WORRYWARTS
WORSENESSES
WORSENINGS
WORSHIPABLE

WORSHIPERS
WORSHIPFUL
WORSHIPFULLY
WORSHIPFULNESS
WORSHIPING
WORSHIPLESS
WORSHIPPED
WORSHIPPER
WORSHIPPERS
WORSHIPPING
WORTHINESS
WORTHINESSES
WORTHLESSLY
WORTHLESSNESS
WORTHLESSNESSES
WORTHWHILE
WORTHWHILENESS
WOUNDINGLY
WOUNDWORTS
WRAITHLIKE

WRANGLERSHIP
WRANGLERSHIPS
WRANGLESOME
WRANGLINGS
WRAPAROUND
WRAPAROUNDS
WRAPPERING
WRAPROUNDS
WRATHFULLY
WRATHFULNESS
WRATHFULNESSES
WRATHINESS
WRATHINESSES
WREATHIEST
WREATHLESS
WREATHLIKE
WRECKFISHES
WRECKMASTER
WRECKMASTERS
WRENCHINGLY

WRENCHINGS
WRESTLINGS
WRETCHEDER
WRETCHEDEST
WRETCHEDLY
WRETCHEDNESS
WRETCHEDNESSES
WRIGGLIEST
WRIGGLINGS
WRINKLELESS
WRINKLIEST
WRISTBANDS
WRISTLOCKS
WRISTWATCH
WRISTWATCHES
WRITERESSES
WRITERSHIP
WRITERSHIPS
WRITHINGLY
WRONGDOERS

WRONGDOING
WRONGDOINGS
WRONGFULLY
WRONGFULNESS
WRONGFULNESSES
WRONGHEADED
WRONGHEADEDLY
WRONGHEADEDNESS
WRONGNESSES
WRONGOUSLY
WULFENITES
WUNDERKIND
WUNDERKINDER
WUNDERKINDS
WYANDOTTES
WYLIECOATS

W

X

XANTHATION
XANTHATIONS
XANTHOCHROIA
XANTHOCHROIAS
XANTHOCHROIC
XANTHOCHROID
XANTHOCHROIDS
XANTHOCHROISM
XANTHOCHROISMS
XANTHOCHROMIA
XANTHOCHROMIAS
XANTHOCHROOUS
XANTHOMATA
XANTHOMATOUS
XANTHOMELANOUS
XANTHOPHYL
XANTHOPHYLL
XANTHOPHYLLOUS
XANTHOPHYLLS
XANTHOPHYLS
XANTHOPSIA
XANTHOPSIAS
XANTHOPTERIN
XANTHOPTERINE
XANTHOPTERINES
XANTHOPTERINS
XANTHOXYLS
XENARTHRAL
XENOBIOTIC
XENOBIOTICS
XENOBLASTS
XENOCRYSTS

XENODIAGNOSES
XENODIAGNOSIS
XENODIAGNOSTIC
XENODOCHIUM
XENODOCHIUMS
XENOGAMIES
XENOGAMOUS
XENOGENEIC
XENOGENESES
XENOGENESIS
XENOGENETIC
XENOGENIES
XENOGENOUS
XENOGLOSSIA
XENOGLOSSIAS
XENOGLOSSIES
XENOGLOSSY
XENOGRAFTS
XENOLITHIC
XENOMANIAS
XENOMENIAS
XENOMORPHIC
XENOMORPHICALLY
XENOPHILES
XENOPHOBES
XENOPHOBIA
XENOPHOBIAS
XENOPHOBIC
XENOPHOBICALLY
XENOPHOBIES
XENOPLASTIC
XENOTRANSPLANT

XENOTRANSPLANTS
XENOTROPIC
XERANTHEMUM
XERANTHEMUMS
XERISCAPED
XERISCAPES
XERISCAPING
XEROCHASIES
XERODERMAE
XERODERMAS
XERODERMATIC
XERODERMATOUS
XERODERMIA
XERODERMIAS
XERODERMIC
XEROGRAPHER
XEROGRAPHERS
XEROGRAPHIC
XEROGRAPHICALLY
XEROGRAPHIES
XEROGRAPHY
XEROMORPHIC
XEROMORPHOUS
XEROMORPHS
XEROPHAGIES
XEROPHILES
XEROPHILIES
XEROPHILOUS
XEROPHTHALMIA
XEROPHTHALMIAS
XEROPHTHALMIC
XEROPHYTES

XEROPHYTIC
XEROPHYTICALLY
XEROPHYTISM
XEROPHYTISMS
XERORADIOGRAPHY
XEROSTOMAS
XEROSTOMATA
XEROSTOMIA
XEROSTOMIAS
XEROTHERMIC
XEROTRIPSES
XEROTRIPSIS
XIPHIHUMERALIS
XIPHIPLASTRA
XIPHIPLASTRAL
XIPHIPLASTRALS
XIPHIPLASTRON
XIPHISTERNA
XIPHISTERNUM
XIPHISTERNUMS
XIPHOPAGIC
XIPHOPAGOUS
XIPHOPAGUS
XIPHOPAGUSES
XIPHOPHYLLOUS
XIPHOSURAN
XIPHOSURANS
XYLOBALSAMUM
XYLOBALSAMUMS
XYLOCARPOUS
XYLOCHROME
XYLOCHROMES

XYLOGENOUS
XYLOGRAPHED
XYLOGRAPHER
XYLOGRAPHERS
XYLOGRAPHIC
XYLOGRAPHICAL
XYLOGRAPHIES
XYLOGRAPHING
XYLOGRAPHS
XYLOGRAPHY
XYLOIDINES
XYLOLOGIES
XYLOMETERS
XYLOPHAGAN
XYLOPHAGANS
XYLOPHAGES
XYLOPHAGOUS
XYLOPHILOUS
XYLOPHONES
XYLOPHONIC
XYLOPHONIST
XYLOPHONISTS
XYLOPYROGRAPHY
XYLORIMBAS
XYLOTOMIES
XYLOTOMIST
XYLOTOMISTS
XYLOTOMOUS
XYLOTYPOGRAPHIC
XYLOTYPOGRAPHY
XYRIDACEOUS

X

Y

YACHTSMANSHIP
YACHTSMANSHIPS
YACHTSWOMAN
YACHTSWOMEN
YAFFINGALE
YAFFINGALES
YAMMERINGS
YARBOROUGH
YARBOROUGHS
YARDMASTER
YARDMASTERS
YARDSTICKS
YATTERINGLY
YATTERINGS
YEARNINGLY
YEASTINESS
YEASTINESSES
YELLOCHING
YELLOWBACK
YELLOWBACKS
YELLOWBARK

YELLOWBARKS
YELLOWBIRD
YELLOWBIRDS
YELLOWCAKE
YELLOWCAKES
YELLOWFINS
YELLOWHAMMER
YELLOWHAMMERS
YELLOWHEAD
YELLOWHEADS
YELLOWIEST
YELLOWISHNESS
YELLOWISHNESSES
YELLOWLEGS
YELLOWNESS
YELLOWNESSES
YELLOWTAIL
YELLOWTAILS
YELLOWTHROAT
YELLOWTHROATS
YELLOWWARE

YELLOWWARES
YELLOWWEED
YELLOWWEEDS
YELLOWWOOD
YELLOWWOODS
YELLOWWORT
YELLOWWORTS
YEOMANRIES
YERSINIOSES
YERSINIOSIS
YESTERDAYS
YESTEREVEN
YESTEREVENING
YESTEREVENINGS
YESTEREVENS
YESTEREVES
YESTERMORN
YESTERMORNING
YESTERMORNINGS
YESTERMORNS
YESTERNIGHT

YESTERNIGHTS
YESTERYEAR
YESTERYEARS
YIELDABLENESS
YIELDABLENESSES
YIELDINGLY
YIELDINGNESS
YIELDINGNESSES
YOCTOSECOND
YOCTOSECONDS
YOHIMBINES
YOKEFELLOW
YOKEFELLOWS
YOTTABYTES
YOUNGBERRIES
YOUNGBERRY
YOUNGLINGS
YOUNGNESSES
YOUNGSTERS
YOURSELVES
YOUTHENING

YOUTHFULLY
YOUTHFULNESS
YOUTHFULNESSES
YOUTHHEADS
YOUTHHOODS
YOUTHQUAKE
YOUTHQUAKES
YPSILIFORM
YTHUNDERED
YTTERBITES
YTTERBIUMS
YTTRIFEROUS
YUCKINESSES
YUMBERRIES
YUMMINESSES
YUPPIEDOMS
YUPPIFICATION
YUPPIFICATIONS
YUPPIFYING